Exploring PSYCHOLOGY IN MODULES

tenth edition

DAVID G. MYERS

HOPE COLLEGE
HOLLAND, MICHIGAN

C. NATHAN DEWALL

UNIVERSITY OF KENTUCKY
LEXINGTON, KENTUCKY

worth publishers
Macmillan Learning

New York

Publisher, Psychology and Sociology: Rachel Losh
Development Editors: Christine Brune, Nancy Fleming, Trish Morgan, Danielle Slevens
Editorial Assistant: Katie Pachnos
Executive Marketing Manager: Katherine Nurre
Marketing Assistant: Morgan Ratner
Executive Media Editor: Rachel Comerford
Media Editor: Laura Burden
Supplements Editor: Betty Probert
Director, Content Management Enhancement: Tracey Kuehn
Managing Editor, Sciences and Social Sciences: Lisa Kinne
Project Editor: Robert Errera
Media Producer: Eve Conte
Senior Production Manager: Sarah Segal
Photo Editor: Robin Fadool
Photo Researcher: Candice Cheesman
Director of Design, Content Management Enhancement: Diana Blume
Cover Design: Blake Logan
Interior Design: Charles Yuen
Layout Designer: Lee Ann McKevitt
Art Manager: Matthew McAdams
Illustration Coordinator: Janice Donnola
Illustrations: Evelyn Pence
Composition: MPS Ltd.
Printing and Binding: LSC Communications
Cover Photo: Josef F. Steufer/Getty Images

Library of Congress Control Number: 2015957828

ISBN-13: 978-1-4641-5438-6

ISBN-10: 1-4641-5438-4

Copyright © 2016, 2014, 2011, 2008 by Worth Publishers

Printed in the United States of America

Fifth printing 2018

David Myers' royalties from the sale of this book are assigned to the David and Carol
Myers Foundation, which exists to receive and distribute funds to other charitable
organizations.

Worth Publishers
One New York Plaza
New York, NY 10004-1562
www.MacmillanHigherEd.com

[DM] For my kindred spirits, Malcolm and Ruth Jeeves, with gratitude for your hospitality and friendship.

[ND] To Alice DeWall —
    love of my life

About the Authors

David Myers received his B.A. in chemistry from Whitworth University, and his psychology Ph.D. from the University of Iowa. He has spent his career at Hope College in Michigan, where he has taught dozens of introductory psychology sections. Hope College students have invited him to be their commencement speaker and voted him "outstanding professor."

His research and writings have been recognized by the Gordon Allport Intergroup Relations Prize, by a 2010 Honored Scientist award from the Federation of Associations in Behavioral & Brain Sciences, by a 2010 Award for Service on Behalf of Personality and Social Psychology, by a 2013 Presidential Citation from APA Division 2, and by three honorary doctorates.

With support from National Science Foundation grants, Myers' scientific articles have appeared in three dozen scientific periodicals, including *Science, American Scientist, Psychological Science*, and the *American Psychologist*. In addition to his scholarly writing and his textbooks for introductory and social psychology, he also digests psychological science for the general public. His writings have appeared in four dozen magazines, from *Today's Education* to *Scientific American*. He also has authored five general audience books, including *The Pursuit of Happiness* and *Intuition: Its Powers and Perils*.

David Myers has chaired his city's Human Relations Commission, helped found a thriving assistance center for families in poverty, and spoken to hundreds of college, community, and professional groups worldwide.

Drawing on his experience, he also has written articles and a book *(A Quiet World)* about hearing loss, and he is advocating a transformation in American assistive listening technology (see www.HearingLoop.org). For his leadership, he received an American Academy of Audiology Presidential Award in 2011, and the Hearing Loss Association of America Walter T. Ridder Award in 2012.

He bikes to work year-round and plays regular pickup basketball. David and Carol Myers have raised two sons and a daughter, and have one granddaughter.

Nathan DeWall is professor of psychology and director of the Social Psychology Lab at the University of Kentucky. He received his bachelor's degree from St. Olaf College, a master's degree in social science from the University of Chicago, and a master's degree and Ph.D. in social psychology from Florida State University. DeWall received the 2011 College of Arts and Sciences Outstanding Teaching Award, which recognizes excellence in undergraduate and graduate teaching. In 2011, the Association for Psychological Science identified DeWall as a "Rising Star" for "making significant contributions to the field of psychological science."

DeWall conducts research on close relationships, self-control, and aggression. With funding from the National Institutes of Health and the National Science Foundation, he has published over 170 scientific articles and chapters. DeWall's research awards include the SAGE Young Scholars Award from the Foundation for Personality and Social Psychology, the Young Investigator Award from the International Society for Research on Aggression, and the Early Career Award from the International Society for Self and Identity. His research has been covered by numerous media outlets, including *Good Morning America, Wall Street Journal, Newsweek, Atlantic Monthly, New York Times, Los Angeles Times, Harvard Business Review, USA Today*, and *National Public Radio*. DeWall blogs for *Psychology Today*. He has lectured nationally and internationally, including in Hong Kong, China, the Netherlands, England, Greece, Hungary, Sweden, and Australia.

Nathan is happily married to Alice DeWall and is the proud father of Beverly "Bevy" DeWall. He enjoys playing with his two golden retrievers, Finnegan and Atticus. In his spare time, he writes novels, watches sports, and runs and runs and runs. He has braved all climates—from freezing to ferocious heat—to complete hundreds of miles' worth of ultramarathons.

Brief Contents

Contents

Consciousness and the Two-Track Mind 79

Developing Through the Life Span 119

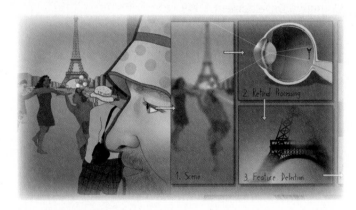

Stress, Health, and Human Flourishing 405

Social Psychology 441

Personality 491

Psychological Disorders 527

Therapy 569

Preface

In the 27 years since Worth Publishers invited me (David Myers) to write this book, so much has changed in the world, in psychology, and within these course resources, across ten editions. With this edition, I continue as lead author while beginning a gradual, decade-long process of welcoming a successor author, the award-winning teacher-scholar-writer Nathan DeWall.

Yet across nearly three decades of *Exploring Psychology* there has also been a stability of purpose: *to merge rigorous science with a broad human perspective that engages both mind and heart.* We aim to offer a state-of-the-art introduction to psychological science that speaks to students' needs and interests. We aspire to help students understand and appreciate the wonders of their everyday lives. And we seek to convey the inquisitive spirit with which psychologists *do* psychology.

We are enthusiastic about psychology and its applicability to our lives. Psychological science has the potential to expand our minds and enlarge our hearts. By studying and applying its tools, ideas, and insights, we can supplement our intuition with critical thinking, restrain our judgmentalism with compassion, and replace our illusions with understanding. By the time students complete this guided tour of psychology, they will also, we hope, have a deeper understanding of our moods and memories, about the reach of our unconscious, about how we flourish and struggle,

⌄ TABLE 1

Evolutionary Psychology and Behavior Genetics

In addition to the coverage found in Module 6, the evolutionary perspective is covered on the following pages:

Aging, pp. 161–162

Anger, pp. 416–417

Anxiety-related disorders, pp. 542–544

Biological predispositions:

    in learning, pp. 267–269

    in operant conditioning, p. 269

Brainstem, pp. 52–53

Classical conditioning, p. 250

Consciousness, p. 80

Darwin, Charles, pp. 6, 8

Depression and light exposure therapy, p. 588

Emotion, effects of facial expressions and, p. 401

Emotional expression, p. 400

Evolutionary perspective, defined, p. 11

Fear, pp. 326–327

Feature detection, p. 215

Fight or flight, p. 409

Gene-environment interaction, p. 514

Hearing, p. 226

Hunger and taste preference, p. 381

Instincts, p. 366

Intelligence, pp. 360–365

Language, pp. 335, 341

Love, pp. 163–165

Math and spatial ability, p. 363

Mating preferences, pp. 175, 193–194

Menopause, p. 158

Need to belong, p. 370

Obesity, p. 382

Overconfidence, pp. 327–328

Perceptual adaptation, pp. 223–224

Sensation, p. 201

Sensory adaptation, pp. 204–205

Sexual orientation, pp. 189–190

Sexuality, pp. 181, 189–190, 192–195

Sleep, pp. 87, 92–93

Smell, p. 237

Taste, p. 236

In addition to the coverage found in Module 6, behavior genetics is covered on the following pages:

Abuse, intergenerational transmission of, p. 276

Adaptability, p. 5

Aggression, pp. 468–473

    intergenerational transmission of, p. 276

Autism spectrum disorder, pp. 135–137

Behavior genetics perspective, pp. 8, 11

Biological perspective, p. 38

Brain plasticity, pp. 62–63

Continuity and stages, pp. 120–121

Deprivation of attachment, pp. 142–144

Depth perception, p. 218

Development, p. 120

Drives and incentives, p. 367

Drug use, pp. 113–116

Eating disorders, pp. 565–566

Epigenetics, pp. 124, 146, 530, 543, 550, 560

Happiness, pp. 435–436

Hunger and taste preference, p. 382

Intelligence:

    Down syndrome, pp. 357–358

    genetic and environmental influences, pp. 360–365

Learning, pp. 267–272

Motor development, pp. 128–129

Nature-nurture, p. 8

    twins, p. 8

Obesity and weight control, pp. 382–385

Optimism, p. 423

Pain, pp. 231–233

Parenting styles, pp. 144–145

Perception, pp. 223–224

Personality traits, p. 496

Psychological disorders and:

    ADHD, p. 532

    anxiety-related disorders, pp. 541–544

    biopsychosocial approach, pp. 529–530

    bipolar disorder and major depressive disorder, pp. 549–552

    depressed thinking, p. 552

    obsessive-compulsive disorder, pp. 541–544

    personality disorders, pp. 563–564

    posttraumatic stress disorder, pp. 541–544

    schizophrenia, pp. 557–560

    suicide, p. 553

    violent behavior, pp. 563–564

Reward deficiency syndrome, p. 56

Romantic love, pp. 163–165

Sexual dysfunctions, pp. 183–184

Sexual orientation, pp. 189–192

Sexuality, pp. 189–191

Sleep patterns, pp. 91–92

Smell, p. 238

Stress, personality, and illness, pp. 413–417

    benefits of exercise, pp. 426–427

Traits, pp. 357–358, 360–361

    gay-straight trait differences, pp. 191, 192

about how we perceive our physical and social worlds, and about how our biology and culture in turn shape us. (See **TABLES** 1 and 2.)

Believing with Thoreau that "anything living is easily and naturally expressed in popular language," we seek to communicate psychology's scholarship with crisp narrative and vivid storytelling. We hope to tell psychology's story in a way that is warmly personal as well as rigorously scientific. We love to reflect on

connections between psychology and other realms, such as literature, philosophy, history, sports, religion, politics, and popular culture. And we love to provoke thought, to play with words, and to laugh. For his pioneering 1890 *Principles of Psychology,* William James sought "humor and pathos." And so do we.

We are grateful for the privilege of assisting with the teaching of this mind-expanding discipline to so many students, in so many countries, through so many different languages. To be entrusted with discerning and communicating psychology's insights is both an exciting honor and a great responsibility.

Creating this book is a team sport. Like so many human achievements, it reflects a collective intelligence. Woodrow Wilson spoke for us: "I not only use all the brains I have, but all I can borrow." The thousands of instructors and millions of students across the globe who have taught or studied (or both!) with our books have contributed immensely to their development. Much of this contribution has occurred spontaneously, through correspondence and conversations. For this edition, we also formally involved dozens of researchers, teaching psychologists, and students in our efforts to gather accurate and up-to-date information about psychology and instructor and student needs. And we look forward to continuing feedback as we strive, over future editions, to create an ever better set of resources for this course.

New Co-Author

For this edition I [DM] welcome my new co-author, University of Kentucky professor Nathan DeWall. (For more information and videos that introduce Nathan and our collaboration, see www.MacmillanHigherEd.com/ DeWallVideos.) Nathan is not only one of psychology's "rising stars" (as the Association for Psychological Science rightly said in 2011), he also is an award-winning teacher and someone who shares my passion for writing—and for communicating psychological science through writing. Although I continue as lead author, Nathan's fresh insights and contributions are already enriching this book, especially for this tenth edition, through his leading the revision of The Biology of Behavior (Modules 3–6); Developing Through the Life Span (Modules 10–13); Stress, Health, and Human Flourishing (Modules 33–34); and Personality (Modules 38–39). But my fingerprints are also on those module revisions, even as his are on the other modules. With support from our wonderful editors, this is a team project. In addition to our work together on the textbook, Nathan and I enjoy contributing to the monthly Teaching Current Directions in Psychological Science column in the *APS Observer* (tinyurl.com/MyersDeWall). We also blog at www.TalkPsych.com, where we share exciting new findings, everyday applications, and observations on all things psychology.

MYERS & DEWALL
TALK PSYCH

Why a Modular Book?

This 45-module text has been a wish come true for me [DM]. It breaks out of the box by restructuring the material into a buffet of (a) short, digestible chapters (called modules) that (b) can be selected and assigned in any order.

- Have we not all heard the familiar student complaint: "The chapters are too long!" A text's typical 30- to 50-page chapter cannot be read in a single sitting before the eyes grow weary and the mind wanders. So, why not parse the material into readable units? Ask your students whether they would prefer a 600-page book to be organized as fifteen 40-page chapters or as forty 15-page chapters. You may be surprised at their overwhelming support for shorter chapters. Indeed, students digest material better when they process it in smaller chunks—as spaced rather than massed practice.

- I have equally often heard from instructors bemoaning the fact that they "just can't get to everything" in the book. Sometimes instructors want to cover certain sections in a traditional, long chapter but not others. For example, in the typical Consciousness chapter, someone may want to cover Sleep and Dreams but not Drugs. In *Exploring Psychology, Tenth Edition in Modules*, instructors could easily choose to cover Module 8, Sleep and Dreams, but not Module 9, Drugs and Consciousness.

How Is This Different From *Exploring Psychology, Tenth Edition?*

The primary differences between this book and *Exploring Psychology,* tenth edition, are organization and module independence.

Organization

The book really IS *Exploring Psychology,* tenth edition—just in a different format. So, this modular version contains all the updated research and innovative new coverage from *Exploring Psychology,* tenth edition. This version offers the same content from *Exploring Psychology,* tenth edition's 15 chapters parsed instead into 45 modules.

The Modules Are Independent

Each module in this book is self-standing rather than dependent upon the others for understanding. Cross-references to other parts of the book are accompanied by brief explanations. In some cases, illustrations or key terms are repeated to avoid possible confusion. No assumptions are made about what students have read prior to each module. This independence gives instructors ultimate flexibility in deciding which modules to use, and in what order. Connections among psychology's subfields and findings are still made—they are just made in a way that does not assume knowledge of other parts of the book.

What Else Is New Since *Exploring Psychology, Ninth Edition in Modules?*

This tenth edition is the most carefully reworked and extensively updated of all the revisions to date. This new edition features improvements to the organization and presentation, especially to our system of supporting student learning and remembering. And we offer the exciting new ***Immersive Learning: How Would You Know?*** feature in LaunchPad, engaging students in the scientific process.

"Immersive Learning: How Would You Know?" Research Activities

We [ND and DM] created these online activities to engage students in the scientific process, showing them how psychological research begins with a question, and how key decision points can alter the meaning and value of a psychological study. In a fun, interactive environment, students learn about important aspects

of research design and interpretation, and develop *scientific literacy* and *critical thinking* skills in the process. I [ND] have enjoyed taking the lead on this project and sharing my research experience and enthusiasm with students. Topics include: "How Would You Know If a Cup of Coffee Can Warm Up Relationships?," "How Would You Know If People Can Learn to Reduce Anxiety?," and "How Would You Know If Schizophrenia Is Inherited?"

New Visual Scaffolding Module Group Openers

We were aware that students often skip over a text's typical two-page module group opener—under the assumption it serves little purpose in learning the material to come. So, for this new edition, we worked with a talented artist to make more pedagogically effective use of this space. This new feature provides an enticing and helpful way for students to SURVEY the content in each group of modules, before they QUESTION, READ, RETRIEVE, and REVIEW it (SQ3R). We've provided *visual scaffolding* at the beginning of each group of modules, offering students a *basic cognitive structure for the content to come*. Flip to the beginning of any group of modules to see a sample.

Hundreds of New Research Citations

Our ongoing scrutiny of dozens of scientific periodicals and science news sources, enhanced by commissioned reviews and countless e-mails from instructors and students, enables integrating our field's most important, thought-provoking, and student-relevant new discoveries. Part of the pleasure that sustains this work is learning something new every day! See p. xxxvii for a list of significant **Content Changes** to this edition.

Reorganized Modules

In addition to the new research activities, visual scaffolding openers, and updated coverage, we've introduced the following organizational changes:

- **Module 1,** The History and Scope of Psychology, now has a clearer organization and greater emphasis on modern approaches, including Cross-Cultural and Gender Psychology, and new coverage of Positive Psychology (see also TABLE 3).

- **Module 2,** Research Strategies, now offers greater emphasis on designing psychological studies, and on psychology's research ethics.

- Hypnosis is now covered in the Pain discussion in **Module 18**, The Nonvisual Senses (moved from the ninth edition's **Module 7**).

- The Social Psychology modules now precede the Personality modules.

LaunchPad for *Exploring Psychology, Tenth Edition in Modules*

Built to solve key challenges in this course, LaunchPad gives students everything they need to prepare for class and exams, while giving instructors everything *they* need to quickly set up a course, shape the content to their syllabus, craft presentations and lectures, assign and assess homework, and guide the progress of individual students and the class as a whole. LaunchPad for *Exploring Psychology, Tenth Edition in Modules* includes **LearningCurve** formative assessment, and NEW **Immersive Learning: How Would You Know?** activities, **PsychSim 6** tutorials, and **Assess Your Strengths** projects. (For details, see p. xxviii and www.MacmillanHigherEd.com/LaunchPad/Exploring10eInModules.)

For this new edition, you will see that we've offered callouts from the text pages to especially pertinent, helpful resources from LaunchPad. (See **FIGURE 1** for a sample.)

What Continues?
Eight Guiding Principles

Despite all the exciting changes, this new edition retains its predecessors' voice, as well as much of the content and organization. It also retains the goals—the guiding principles—that have animated the previous nine editions:

Facilitating the Learning Experience

1. **To teach critical thinking** By presenting research as intellectual detective work, we illustrate an inquiring, analytical mind-set. Whether students are studying development, cognition, or social behavior, they will become involved in, and see the rewards of, critical reasoning. Moreover, they will discover how an empirical approach can help them evaluate competing ideas and claims for highly publicized phenomena—ranging from ESP and alternative therapies to group differences in intelligence and repressed and recovered memories.

2. **To integrate principles and applications** Throughout—by means of anecdotes, case histories, and the posing of hypothetical situations—we relate the findings of basic research to their applications and implications. Where psychology can illuminate pressing human issues—be they racism and sexism, health and happiness, or violence and war—we have not hesitated to shine its light.

3. **To reinforce learning at every step** Everyday examples and rhetorical questions encourage students to process the material actively. Concepts presented earlier are frequently applied, and reinforced. For instance, in **Module 2**, students learn that much of our information processing occurs outside of our conscious awareness. Ensuing modules drive home this concept. Numbered Learning Objective Questions and Retrieve It self-tests throughout each module, a Review and *Experience the Testing Effect* self-test at the end of each module, and a marginal glossary help students learn and retain important concepts and terminology.

Demonstrating the Science of Psychology

4. **To exemplify the process of inquiry** We strive to show students not just the outcome of research, but how the research process works. Throughout, we try to excite the reader's curiosity. We invite readers to imagine themselves as participants in classic experiments. Several modules introduce research stories as mysteries that progressively unravel as one clue after another falls into place. Our new "Immersive Learning: How Would You Know?" activities in LaunchPad encourage students to think about research questions and how they may be studied effectively.

5. **To be as up-to-date as possible** Few things dampen students' interest as quickly as the sense that they are reading stale news. While retaining psychology's classic studies and concepts, we also present the discipline's most important recent developments. In this edition, 701 references are dated 2013–2015. Likewise, new photos and everyday examples are drawn from today's world.

∨ TABLE 3

Positive Psychology

Coverage of positive psychology topics can be found in the following modules:	
Topic	**Module**
Altruism/compassion	12, 25, 37, 38, 45
Coping	34
Courage	37
Creativity	22, 25, 29, 38
Emotional Intelligence	27, 37
Empathy	11, 21, 32, 35, 44
Flow	Appendix B
Gratitude	34
Happiness/Life Satisfaction	13, 29, 34, 44, 45
Humility	1
Humor	34, 35
Justice	35
Leadership	35, 39, Appendix B
Love	13, 15, 29, 37, 39, 44
Morality	12
Optimism	34, 38
Personal control	34
Resilience	11, 33, 45
Self-discipline	12, 29, 39
Self-efficacy	39
Self-esteem	29, 38, 39
Spirituality	34, 35
Toughness (grit)	27, 29
Wisdom	1, 25, 34, 35, 39

🔵 **LaunchPad** To review the classic conformity studies and experience a simulated experiment, visit LaunchPad's *PsychSim 6: Everybody's Doing It!*

∧ FIGURE 1

Sample LaunchPad callout from Module 35.

6. **To put facts in the service of concepts** Our intention is not to fill students' intellectual file drawers with facts, but to reveal psychology's major concepts—to teach students how to think, and to offer psychological ideas worth thinking about. In each module, we place emphasis on those concepts we hope students will carry with them long after they complete the course. Always, we try to follow Albert Einstein's purported dictum that "everything should be made as simple as possible, but not simpler." Learning Objective Questions, Retrieve It questions, and *Experience the Testing Effect* questions in each module help students learn and retain the key concepts.

Promoting Big Ideas and Broadened Horizons

7. **To enhance comprehension by providing continuity** We often present concepts with a significant issue or theme that links subtopics, forming a thread that ties ideas together. The Learning modules convey the idea that bold thinkers can serve as intellectual pioneers. The Thinking, Language, and Intelligence modules raise the issue of human rationality and irrationality. The Psychological Disorders modules convey empathy for, and understanding of, troubled lives. Other threads, such as cognitive neuroscience, dual processing, and cultural and gender diversity, weave throughout the whole book, and students hear a consistent voice.

8. **To convey respect for human unity and diversity** Throughout the book, readers will see evidence of our human kinship—our shared biological heritage, our common mechanisms of seeing and learning, hungering and feeling, loving and hating. They will also better understand the dimensions of our diversity—our individual diversity in development and aptitudes, temperament and personality, and disorder and health; and our cultural diversity in attitudes and expressive styles, child raising and care for the elderly, and life priorities.

Study System Follows Best Practices From Learning and Memory Research

Exploring Psychology, Tenth Edition in Modules' learning system harnesses the *testing effect*, which documents the benefits of actively retrieving information through self-testing (**FIGURE 2**). Thus, each module offers Retrieve It questions interspersed throughout, with *Experience the Testing Effect* self-test questions at the end of each module. Creating these *desirable difficulties* for students along the way optimizes the testing effect, as does *immediate feedback* (via an inverted answer beneath Retrieve It questions and in a text appendix for the self-test questions).

In addition, text sections begin with numbered questions that establish learning objectives and direct student reading. A Review section follows each module, providing students an opportunity to practice rehearsing what they've just learned. The Review offers self-testing by repeating the Learning Objective Questions (with answers for checking in the Complete Module Reviews Appendix), along with a page-referenced list of key terms.

Continually Improving Cultural and Gender Diversity Coverage

Discussion of the relevance of cultural and gender diversity begins on the first page and continues throughout the text.

This edition presents an even more thoroughly cross-cultural perspective on psychology (**TABLE 4**)—reflected in research findings, and text and photo examples. Cross-cultural and gender psychology are now given greater visibility with enhanced coverage moved to **Module 1**. There is focused coverage of the psychology of women and men in the Sex, Gender, and Sexuality modules, with

Make Things Memorable!
How to study and LEARN more effectively.
With David G. Myers, author

^ FIGURE 2

How to learn and remember For a 5-minute animated guide to more effective studying, visit www.tinyurl.com/HowToRemember.

∨ TABLE 4

Culture and Multicultural Experience

Coverage of culture and multicultural experience can be found on the following pages:

Adolescence, p. 147

Adulthood, emerging, pp. 156–157

Aggression, pp. 173, 470–473
   and video games, pp. 277, 472–473

AIDS, pp. 412–413

Anger, pp. 416–417

Animal research ethics, pp. 28–29

Attraction: matchmaking, pp. 476–477

Attractiveness, pp. 475–479

Attribution: political effects of, pp. 442–443

Behavioral effects of culture, pp. 9, 448

Body ideal, pp. 539–540

Body image, pp. 539–540

Categorization, p. 322

Conformity, pp. 450–451

Corporal punishment practices, p. 262

Cultural neuroscience, p. 523

Cultural norms, pp. 175, 448

Culture:
   context effects, p. 207
   definition, p. 454
   experiencing other, p. 332
   variation over time, p. 448

Culture and the self, pp. 521–523

Culture shock, p. 407

Deaf culture, pp. 63, 66, 336–337, 339

Development:
   adolescence, p. 147
   attachment, p. 141
   child raising, pp. 145–146
   cognitive development, p. 135
   moral development, p. 150

parenting styles, pp. 144–145
   social development, pp. 153–154

Drug use, pp. 116–117

Emotion:
   emotion-detecting ability, p. 397
   expressing, pp. 398–401

Enemy perceptions, p. 485

Fear, pp. 325–327

Flow, p. B–1

Fundamental attribution error, p. 442

Gender:
   cultural norms, pp. 172, 178
   equality, pp. 194–195
   roles, pp. 177–178
   social power, p. 173

Grief, expressing, p. 168

Happiness, pp. 431–432, 434, 435–436

Hindsight bias, pp. 15–16

History of psychology, pp. 4–7

Homosexuality, views on, p. 187

Human diversity/kinship, pp. 9, 76–77, 447–448, 488

Identity: forming social, p. 153

Individualism/collectivism, pp. 521–523

Intelligence, pp. 347, 363–365
   and nutrition, pp. 362, 365
   bias, pp. 366–368
   Down syndrome, pp. 357–358

Language, pp. 337–339, 342–344, 448
   critical periods, pp. 338–339
   bilingualism, pp. 343–344
   universal grammar, p. 336

Leaving the nest, pp. 156–157

Life satisfaction, pp. 433–434

Life span and well-being, pp. 166–167

Management styles, pp. B–11–B–13

Marriage, pp. 163–165, 480

Memory, encoding, p. 290

Menopause, p. 158

Mental illness rate, pp. 534–535

Morality, development of, pp. 150–152

Motivating achievement, pp. 376, B–11

Motivation: hierarchy of needs, pp. 374–375

Need to belong, pp. 375–378

Neurotransmitters: curare, p. 44

Normality, perceptions of, pp. 529–530

Obedience, pp. 452–453

Obesity, p. 388

Observational learning: television and aggression, pp. 276–277

Organ donation, p. 329

Pace of life, p. 20

Pain: perception of, pp. 233, 372

Parent and peer relationships, pp. 154–156

Participative management, p. B–13

Peacemaking:
   conciliation, pp. 487–488
   contact, p. 486
   cooperation, pp. 486–487

Personality, pp. 508–510

Power of individuals, p. 460

Prejudice, pp. 10, 30, 462, 464, 467–468
   "missing women," p. 464

Prejudice prototypes, p. 322

Psychological disorders:
   amok, p. 530

cultural norms, pp. 528–529
   dissociative identity disorder, p. 562
   eating disorders, pp. 530, 566
   schizophrenia, pp. 530, 559
   suicide, p. 553
   susto, p. 530
   taijin-kyofusho, p. 530

Psychotherapy:
   culture and values in, pp. 590–591
   EMDR training, p. 588

Puberty and adult independence, pp. 156–157

Self-esteem, p. 368

Self-serving bias, pp. 518–520

Sex drive, p. 193

Sexual activity: middle and late adulthood, p. 158

Sexual orientation, p. 187

Similarities, pp. 76–77

Sleep patterns, p. 92

Social clock, p. 163

Social-cultural perspective, pp. 10–11

Social loafing, pp. 456–457

Social networking, p. 373

Spirituality, p. 429

Stress:
   adjusting to a new culture, p. 407
   health consequences, pp. 407, 412–413, 415–417
   racism and, p. 409
   social support and, p. 423

Taste preferences, p. 381

Teen pregnancy, pp. 173, 448

Testing bias, pp. 366–368

See also Modules 35, 36, and 37.

thoroughly integrated coverage throughout the text (see **TABLE 5**, on the next page). In addition, we are working to offer a world-based psychology for our worldwide student readership. We continually search the world for research findings and text and photo examples, conscious that readers may be in Sydney, Seattle, or Singapore. Although we reside in the United States, we travel abroad regularly and maintain contact with colleagues in Canada, Britain, South Africa, China, and many

▼ TABLE 5

The Psychology of Men and Women

Coverage of the psychology of men and women can be found on the following pages:

other places; and subscribe to European periodicals. Thus, each new edition offers a broad, world-based perspective, and includes research from around the world. We are all citizens of a shrinking world, so American students, too, benefit from information and examples that internationalize their world-consciousness. And if psychology seeks to explain *human* behavior (not just American or Canadian or Australian behavior), the broader the scope of studies presented, the more accurate is our picture of this world's people. Our aim is to expose all students to the world beyond their own culture, and we continue to welcome input and suggestions from all readers.

Strong Critical Thinking Coverage

We love to write in a way that gets students thinking and keeps them active as they read, and we aim to introduce students to critical thinking throughout the book. Revised and more plentiful Learning Objective Questions at the beginning of text sections, and even more regular Retrieve It questions encourage critical reading to glean an understanding of important concepts. This tenth edition also includes the following opportunities for students to learn or practice their critical thinking skills.

- The *Thinking Critically With Psychological Science* modules introduce students to psychology's research methods, emphasizing the fallacies of our everyday intuition and common sense and, thus, the need for psychological science. Critical thinking is introduced as a key term on page 3. Appendix A, Statistical Reasoning in Everyday Life, encourages students to "focus on thinking smarter by applying simple statistical principles to everyday reasoning."

- *"Thinking Critically About . . ." boxes* are found throughout the book, modeling for students a critical approach to some key issues in psychology. For example, see "Thinking Critically About: Why We Fear the Wrong Things" (**Module 25**), or "Thinking Critically About: The Stigma of Introversion" (**Module 39**).

- *Detective-style stories* throughout the narrative get students thinking critically about psychology's key research questions. For example, in **Module 43**, we present the causes of schizophrenia piece by piece, showing students how researchers put the puzzle together.

- *"Apply this" and "Think about it"* style discussions keep students active in their study. In **Module 35**, for example, students take the perspective of participants in a Solomon Asch conformity experiment, and later in one of Stanley Milgram's obedience experiments. We've also asked students to join the fun by taking part in activities they can try along the way. For example, in **Module 16**, they try out a quick sensory adaptation activity. In **Module 32**, they try matching expressions to faces and test the effects of different facial expressions on themselves.

- *Critical examinations of pop psychology* spark interest and provide important lessons in thinking critically about everyday topics. For example, **Module 18** offers an examination of ESP claims, and **Module 24** examines claims of the repression of painful memories.

See **TABLE 6** (on the next page) for a complete list of this text's coverage of critical thinking topics and Thinking Critically About boxes.

APA Assessment Tools

In 2011, the American Psychological Association (APA) approved the **Principles for Quality Undergraduate Education in Psychology.** These broad-based principles and their associated recommendations were designed to "produce psychologically literate citizens who apply the principles of psychological science at work and at home." (See www.APA.org/Education/Undergrad/Principles.aspx.)

APA's more specific **2013 Learning Goals and Outcomes,** from their *Guidelines for the Undergraduate Psychology Major,* Version 2.0, were designed to gauge progress in students graduating with psychology majors. (See www.APA.org/Ed/Precollege/About/PsyMajor-Guidelines.pdf.) Many psychology departments use these goals and outcomes to help establish their own benchmarks for departmental assessment purposes.

Some instructors are eager to know whether a given text for the introductory course helps students get a good start at achieving these APA benchmarks. TABLE 7 (on the next page) outlines the way *Exploring Psychology, Tenth Edition in Modules,* could help you to address the 2013 APA Learning Goals and Outcomes in your department.

▼ TABLE 6

Critical Thinking and Research Emphasis Critical thinking coverage, and in-depth stories of psychology's **scientific research** process, can be found on the following pages:

Thinking Critically About . . . boxes:

Research Design: How Would You Know?, p. 26	ESP—Perception Without Sensation?, p. 241	Lie Detection, p. 394
Addiction, p. 105	Does Viewing Media Violence Trigger Violent Behavior?, p. 277	Anger Management, pp. 416–417
How Much Credit or Blame Do Parents Deserve?, p. 155	Repressed or Constructed Memories of Abuse?, p. 311	The Stigma of Introversion, p. 507
Subliminal Persuasion, p. 203		ADHD—Normal High Energy or Disordered Behavior?, p. 532
Hypnosis and Pain Relief, p. 235	The Fear Factor—Why We Fear the Wrong Things, pp. 326–327	Are People With Psychological Disorders Dangerous?, p. 533

Critical Examinations of Pop Psychology:

Perceiving order in random events, p. 15	Critiquing the evolutionary perspective, pp. 194–195	How valid is the Rorschach test?, pp. 497–498
The need for psychological science, pp. 15–17	Sensory restriction, p. 223	Is Freud credible?, pp. 498–500
Do we use only 10 percent of our brains?, p. 61	Can hypnosis alleviate pain?, p. 235	Is repression a myth?, pp. 499–500
Has the concept of "addiction" been stretched too far?, p. 105	Is there extrasensory perception?, p. 241	Is psychotherapy effective?, pp. 584–586
Near-death experiences, p. 112	Do other species have language?, pp. 341–342	Evaluating alternative therapies, pp. 587–589
How much credit or blame do parents deserve?, p. 155	Do violent video games teach social scripts for violence?, pp. 472–473	

Thinking Critically With Psychological Science:

The scientific attitude, pp. 2–3	Exploring cause and effect, pp. 23–25	Statistical reasoning, pp. A-1–A-10
"Critical thinking" introduced as a key term, p. 3	Random assignment, p. 24	Describing data, pp. A-1–A-6
The limits of intuition and common sense, pp. 15–17	Independent and dependent variables, pp. 25–26	Regression toward the mean, A-6
The scientific method, pp. 17–27	Choosing the right research design, p. 26	Making inferences, pp. A-6–A-9
Correlation and causation, pp. 22–23	The evolutionary perspective on human sexuality, pp. 192–195	

Scientific Detective Stories:

Is breast milk better than formula?, pp. 23–24	How are memories constructed?, pp. 306–310, 311	The pursuit of happiness: Who is happy, and why?, pp. 431–438
Our divided brains, pp. 63–66	How do we store memories in our brain?, pp. 292–296	Why do people fail to help in emergencies?, pp. 481–483
Twin and adoption studies, pp. 69–73	Do other species exhibit language?, pp. 341–342	Self-esteem versus self-serving bias, pp. 518–520
Why do we sleep?, pp. 92–93	Aging and intelligence, p. 355–356	
Why we dream, pp. 99–102	Why do we feel hunger?, pp. 378–380	What causes major depressive disorder and bipolar disorder?, pp. 547–555
How a child's mind develops, p. 130	Why—and in whom—does stress contribute to heart disease?, pp. 414–417	Do prenatal viral infections increase the risk of schizophrenia?, pp. 558–559
What determines sexual orientation?, pp. 189–191		
How do we see in color?, pp. 213–214	How and why is social support linked with health?, pp. 423–425	Is psychotherapy effective?, pp. 584–586
Parallel processing, p. 216		
How can hypnosis provide pain relief?, p. 235		

In addition, an APA working group in 2013 drafted guidelines for **Strengthening the Common Core of the Introductory Psychology Course** (http://tinyurl.com/14dsdx5). Their goals are to "strike a nuanced balance providing flexibility yet guidance." The group noted that "a mature science should be able to agree upon and communicate its unifying core while embracing diversity."

MCAT Now Includes Psychology

Since 2015, the Medical College Admission Test (MCAT) has devoted 25 percent of its questions to the "Psychological, Social, and Biological Foundations of

TABLE 7

Exploring Psychology, Tenth Edition in Modules Corresponds to 2013 APA Learning Goals

Relevant Feature from *Exploring Psychology, Tenth Edition in Modules*	APA Learning Goals				
	Knowledge Base in Psychology	Scientific Inquiry and Critical Thinking	Ethical and Social Responsibility in a Diverse World	Communication	Professional Development
Text content	•	•	•	•	•
Thinking Critically boxes	•	•	•		•
Learning Objective Questions previewing text sections	•	•		•	
Retrieve It self-tests throughout text	•	•		•	
Module Reviews	•	•		•	
"Try this"-style activities integrated throughout	•	•		•	•
Experience the Testing Effect self-tests	•	•		•	
Psychology at Work appendix	•	•	•		•
Subfields of Psychology appendix, with Careers in Psychology in LaunchPad	•		•		•
LaunchPad with LearningCurve formative quizzing	•	•	•		•
"Immersive Learning: How Would You Know?" activities in LaunchPad	•	•	•	•	
Assess Your Strengths feature in LaunchPad	•	•	•	•	•

Behavior," with most of those questions coming from the psychological science taught in introductory psychology courses. From 1977 to 2014, the MCAT focused on biology, chemistry, and physics. Hereafter, reported the *Preview Guide for MCAT 2015*, the exam will also recognize "the importance of sociocultural and behavioral determinants of health and health outcomes." The exam's new psychology section includes the breadth of topics in this text. For example, see **TABLE 8** (on the next page), which outlines the precise correlation between the topics in this text's Sensation and Perception modules and the corresponding portion of the MCAT exam. To improve their MCAT preparation, I [ND] have taught premedical students an intensive course covering the topics that appear in this text. For a complete pairing of the new MCAT psychology topics with this book's contents, see www.MacmillanHigherEd.com/Catalog/Product/ExploringPsychologyInModules-TenthEdition-Myers.

Multimedia for *Exploring Psychology, Tenth Edition in Modules*

Exploring Psychology, Tenth Edition in Modules, boasts impressive multimedia options. For more information about any of these choices, visit Worth Publishers' online catalog at www.MacmillanHigherEd.com/Catalog/Product/ExploringPsychologyInModules-TenthEdition-Myers.

⌄ TABLE 8

Sample MCAT Correlation With *Exploring Psychology, Tenth Edition in Modules*

MCAT 2015	*Exploring Psychology, Tenth Edition in Modules* Correlations	
Sample Content Category 6A: Sensing the environment		Page Number
Sensory Processing	**Sensation and Perception**	**198–243**
Sensation	Basic Concepts of Sensation and Perception	200–209
Thresholds	Thresholds	201–203
	Difference Thresholds	202–203
Weber's Law	*Weber's law* (key term)	202–203
Signal detection theory	*Signal detection theory* (key term)	201
Sensory adaptation	Sensory Adaptation	204–205
Sensory receptors	Transduction	200
Sensory pathways	Vision: Sensory and Perceptual Processing	209–225
	Hearing	226–230
	Pain	231–235
	Taste	236
	Smell	236–238
	Body Position and Movement	238–239
Types of sensory receptors	The Eye	209–211
	Color Processing	213–214
	Hearing	226–230
	Understanding Pain	231–233
	Taste	236
	Smell	236–238
	Body Position and Movement	238–239
	Table 18.2, Summarizing the Senses	240
Vision	Vision: Sensory and Perceptual Processing	209–225
Structure and function of the eye	The Eye	209–211
Visual processing	Information Processing in the Eye and Brain	211–216
Visual pathways in the brain	*Figure 17.6, Pathway from the eyes to the visual cortex*	212
Parallel processing	*Parallel Processing*	216
Feature detection	*Feature Detection*	214–215
Hearing	Hearing	226–230
Auditory processing	Hearing	226–230
Auditory pathways in the brain	The Ear	227–229
	Pitch (key term)	226
	Figure 18.1, The physical properties of waves	227
	Locating Sounds	230
Sensory reception by hair cells	*The Ear*	227–229
	Table 18.2, Summarizing the Senses	240

TABLE 8

Sample MCAT Correlation With *Exploring Psychology, Tenth Edition in Modules* (continued)

MCAT 2015	*Exploring Psychology, Tenth Edition in Modules* Correlations	
Sample Content Category 6A: Sensing the environment		Page Number
Other Senses	Touch, Taste, Smell, Body Position and Movement	230–239
Somatosensation	Touch	230–231
	Sensory Functions (of the cortex)	58
	Somatosensory cortex (key term)	58
	Table 18.2, Summarizing the Senses	240
Pain perception	Pain	231–235
	Understanding Pain	231–233
	Controlling Pain	234–235
	Hypnosis and Pain Relief	235
Taste	Taste	236
Taste buds/chemoreceptors that detect specific chemicals	Taste	236
	Table 18.2, Summarizing the Senses	240
	Figure 18.10, Taste, smell, and memory	238
Smell	Smell	236–238
Olfactory cells/chemoreceptors that detect specific chemicals	Smell	236–238
	Table 18.2, Summarizing the Senses	240
Pheromones	*Smell of sex-related hormones*	190–192
Olfactory pathways in the brain	*Figure 18.10, Taste, smell, and memory*	238
	Sensory Interaction	239–243
Kinesthetic sense	Body Position and Movement	238–239
Vestibular sense	Body Position and Movement	238–239
Perception	Sensation and Perception	198–243
Perception	Basic Concepts of Sensation and Perception	200–209
Bottom-up/Top-down processing	Basic Concepts of Sensation and Perception: *bottom-up* and *top-down* processing (key terms)	200
Perceptual organization (e.g., depth, form, motion, constancy)	Perceptual Organization: Form Perception, Depth Perception, and Perceptual Constancy (also includes relative motion)	217–222
	Figure 17.11, Parallel processing (of motion, form, depth, color)	216
Gestalt principles	Perceptual Organization: Form Perception—*gestalt* (key term)	217

LaunchPad With LearningCurve Quizzing and "Immersive Learning: How Would You Know?" Activities

Built to solve key challenges in the course, LaunchPad (www.MacmillanHigherEd.com/LaunchPad/Exploring10eInModules) (see **FIGURE 3** on the next page) gives students everything they need to prepare for class and exams, while giving instructors everything they need to quickly set up a course, shape the content

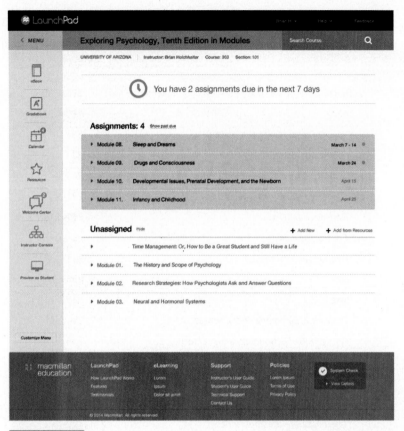

∧ FIGURE 3

Sample from LaunchPad

to their syllabus, craft presentations and lectures, assign and assess homework, and guide the progress of individual students and the class as a whole.

- **An interactive e-Book** integrates the text and all student media, including the new ***Immersive Learning: How Would You Know?*** activities, ***PsychSim 6*** tutorials, and ***Assess Your Strengths*** activities.

- **LearningCurve adaptive quizzing** gives individualized question sets and feedback based on each student's correct and incorrect responses. All the questions are tied back to the e-Book to encourage students to read the book in preparation for class time and exams.

- **PsychSim 6 has arrived!** Tom Ludwig's (Hope College) fabulous new tutorials further strengthen LaunchPad's abundance of helpful student activity resources.

- The new **Video Assignment Tool** makes it easy to assign and assess video-based activities and projects, and provides a convenient way for students to submit video coursework.

- **LaunchPad Gradebook** gives a clear window on performance for the whole class, for individual students, and for individual assignments.

- A **streamlined interface** helps students manage their schedule of assignments, while ***social commenting tools*** let them connect with classmates, and learn from one another. 24/7 help is a click away, accessible from a link in the upper right-hand corner.

- We [DM and ND] curated **optional pre-built module units,** which can be used as is or customized. Or choose not to use them and build your course from scratch.

- **Book-specific instructor resources** include PowerPoint sets, textbook graphics, lecture and activity suggestions, test banks, and more.

- LaunchPad offers **easy LMS integration** into your school's learning management system.

Faculty Support and Student Resources

- **Instructor's Resources** available in LaunchPad

- **Lecture Guides** available in LaunchPad

- **Macmillan Community** Created *by* instructors *for* instructors, this is an ideal forum for interacting with fellow educators—including Macmillan authors—in your discipline (FIGURE 4). Join ongoing conversations about everything from course prep and presentations to assignments and assessments to teaching with media, keeping pace with—and influencing—new directions in your field. Includes exclusive access to classroom resources, blogs, webinars, professional development opportunities, and more.

- Enhanced course management solutions (including course cartridges)

- e-Book in various available formats

Video and Presentation

- The **Video Collection** is now the single resource for all videos for introductory psychology from Worth Publishers. Available on flash drive and in LaunchPad, this includes over 130 clips.

- **Interactive Presentation Slides for Introductory Psychology** is an extraordinary series of PowerPoint® lectures. This is a dynamic, yet easy-to-use way to engage students during classroom presentations of core psychology topics. This collection provides opportunities for discussion and interaction, and includes an unprecedented number of embedded video clips and animations.

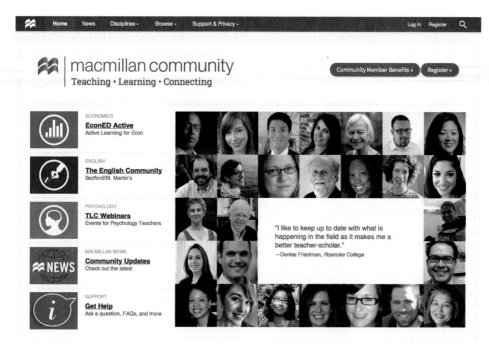

∧ FIGURE 4

Sample from Macmillan Community (http://Community. Macmillan.com)

Assessment

- **LearningCurve** quizzing in LaunchPad
- Diploma Test Banks, downloadable from LaunchPad and our online catalog
- Module Quizzes in LaunchPad
- Clicker Question Presentation Slides now in PowerPoint®

Print

- Study Guide
- *Pursuing Human Strengths: A Positive Psychology Guide,* Second Edition
- *Critical Thinking Companion,* Third Edition
- *Psychology and the Real World: Essays Illustrating Fundamental Contributions to Society,* Second Edition. This project of the FABBS Foundation brought together a virtual "Who's Who" of contemporary psychological scientists to describe—in clear, captivating ways—the research they have passionately pursued and what it means to the "real world." Each contribution is an original essay written for this project.
- *The Horse That Won't Go Away* Tom Heinzen, Scott Lilienfeld, and Susan Nolan explore the confounding story of Clever Hans and how we continue to be deceived by beliefs with no supporting logic or evidence. This supplemental book shows just how important it is to rely on the scientific method as we navigate our way through everyday life.

In Appreciation

If it is true that "whoever walks with the wise becomes wise" then we are wiser for all the wisdom and advice received from colleagues. Aided by thousands of consultants and reviewers over the last three decades, this has become a better, more effective, more accurate book than two authors alone (these two authors, at least) could write. All of us together are smarter than any one of us.

Our indebtedness continues to each of the teacher-scholars whose influence was acknowledged in the nine previous editions, to the innumerable researchers who have been so willing to share their time and talent to help us accurately report their

research, and to the hundreds of instructors who have taken the time to offer feedback over the phone, in a survey or review, or at one of our face-to-face focus groups.

Our gratitude extends to the colleagues who contributed criticism, corrections, and creative ideas related to the content, pedagogy, and format of this new edition and its teaching package. For their expertise and encouragement, and the gifts of their time to the teaching of psychology, we thank the reviewers and consultants listed here.

Steven Alessandri
Rosemont College

Alison Allen-Hall
Becker College, Worcester Campus

Michael Amlung
University of Missouri

Robin Anderson
St. Ambrose University

Kerri Augusto
Becker College

Renee Babcock
Central Michigan University

Debra Bacon
Bristol Community College

Christi Bamford
Jacksonville University

Darin Baskin
Houston Community College

Kristi Bitz
University of Mary

Kristin Bonnie
Beloit College

Jennifer Breneiser
Valdosta State University

Eurnestine Brown
Winthrop University

Stephen Burgess
Southwestern Oklahoma State University

Verne Cox
University of Texas, Arlington

Gregory Cutler
Bay de Noc Community College

Jennifer Dale
Community College of Aurora

Patrick Devine
Kennesaw State University

David Devonis
Graceland College

Virginia Diehl
Western Illinois University

Joshua Feinberg
Saint Peter's University

Jessica Fortune
Louisiana Delta Community College

Debra Frame
University of Cincinnati, Blue Ash

Kristel Gallagher
Keystone College

Bilal Ghandour
Queens University of Charlotte

Nicholas Greco
Columbia College of Missouri, Lake County

Michael Green
Lone Star College, Montgomery

Jill Haasch
Elizabeth City State University

Matthew Hand
Texas Wesleyan University

Vivian Hsu
Rutgers University, Livingston

Cameron John
Utah Valley University

Barry Johnson
Davidson County Community College

Jerwen Jou
University of Texas, Pan American

Michelle LaBrie
College of the Canyons

Kay Lesh
Pima Community College

Angelina MacKewn
University of Tennessee, Martin

Crystal March
University of Tennessee, Martin

Kathy McGuire
Western Illinois University

Kathleen Mentink
Chippewa Valley Technical College

Joanna Schnelker Merrill
Kalamazoo College

Nicholas Palmieri
Palm Beach Atlantic University

W. Gerrod Parrott
Georgetown University

Stephanie Payne
Texas A&M University, College Station

Jennifer Perillo
Winston-Salem State University

Virginia Pitts
Shippensburg University of Pennsylvania

Michael Rader
Johnson County Community College

Chris Roddenberry
Wake Technical Community College

John Roop
Columbus State University

Nancy Ross
Eastern Nazarene College

Conni Rush
Pittsburg State University

Seth Sebold
The City College of New York (CUNY)

Kezia Shirkey
North Park University

Aisha Siddiqui
Midwestern State University

Megan St. Peters
Ferrum College

Elena Stepanova
The University of Southern Mississippi

Michael Stroud
Merrimack College

Helen Sullivan
Rider University

Rachel Sumrall
Grayson College

Lawrence Voight
Washtenaw Community College

Kerri Williams
Lourdes University

Manda Williamson
University of Nebraska, Lincoln

Joseph Wister
Chatham University

Dana Wohl
Thomas College

Jennifer Yanowitz
Utica College

We were pleased to be supported by a 2012/2013 Content Advisory Board, which helped guide the development of this new edition of *Exploring Psychology, Tenth Edition in Modules,* as well as our other introductory psychology titles. For their helpful input and support, we thank

Barbara Angleberger, *Frederick Community College*

Chip (Charles) Barker, *Olympic College*

Mimi Dumville, *Raritan Valley Community College*

Paula Frioli-Peters, *Truckee Meadows Community College*

Deborah Garfin, *Georgia State University*

Karla Gingerich, *Colorado State University*

Toni Henderson, *Langara College*

Bernadette Jacobs, *Santa Fe Community College*

Mary Livingston, *Louisiana Tech University*

Molly Lynch, *Northern Virginia Community College*

Shelly Metz, *Central New Mexico Community College*

Jake Musgrove, *Broward College - Central Campus*

Robin Musselman, *Lehigh Carbon Community College*

Dana Narter, *The University of Arizona*

Lee Osterhout, *University of Washington*

Nicholas Schmitt, *Heartland Community College*

Christine Shea-Hunt, *Kirkwood Community College*

Brenda Shook, *National University*

Starlette Sinclair, *Columbus State University*

David Williams, *Spartanburg Community College*

Melissa (Liz) Wright, *Northwest Vista College*

We appreciate the guidance offered by the following teaching psychologists, who reviewed and offered helpful feedback on the development of our new "Immersive Learning: How Would You Know?" feature in LaunchPad. (See www.Macmillan-HigherEd.com/LaunchPad/Exploring10eInModules for details.)

Pamela Ansburg, *Metropolitan State University of Denver*

Makenzie Bayles, *Jacksonville State University*

Lisamarie Bensman, *University of Hawaii at Manoa*

Jeffrey Blum, *Los Angeles City College*

Pamela Costa, *Tacoma Community College*

Jennifer Dale, *Community College of Aurora*

Michael Devoley, *Lone Star College, Montgomery*

Rock Doddridge, *Asheville-Buncombe Technical Community College*

Kristen Doran, *Delaware County Community College*

Nathaniel Douda, *Colorado State University*

Celeste Favela, *El Paso Community College*

Nicholas Fernandez, *El Paso Community College*

Nathalie Franco, *Broward College*

Sara Garvey, *Colorado State University*

Nichelle Gause, *Clayton State University*

Michael Green, *Lone Star College, Montgomery*

Christine Grela, *McHenry County College*

Rodney Joseph Grisham, *Indian River State College*

Toni Henderson, *Langara College*

Jessica Irons, *James Madison University*

Darren Iwamoto, *Chaminade University of Honolulu*

Jerwen Jou, *University of Texas, Pan American*

Rosalyn King, *Northern Virginia Community College, Loudoun Campus*

Claudia Lampman, *University of Alaska Anchorage*

Mary Livingston, *Louisiana Tech University*

Christine Lofgren, *University of California, Irvine*

Thomas Ludwig, *Hope College*

Theresa Luhrs, *DePaul University*

Megan McIlreavy, *Coastal Carolina University*

Elizabeth Mosser, *Harford Community College*

Robin Musselman, *Lehigh Carbon Community College*

Kelly O'Dell, *Community College of Aurora*

William Keith Pannell, *El Paso Community College*

Eirini Papafratzeskakou, *Mercer County Community College*

Jennifer Poole, *Langara College*

James Rodgers, *Hawkeye Community College*

Regina Roof-Ray, *Harford Community College*

Lisa Routh, *Pikes Peak Community College*

Conni Rush, *Pittsburg State University*

Randi Smith, *Metropolitan State University of Denver*

Laura Talcott, *Indiana University, South Bend*

Cynthia Turk, *Washburn University*

Parita Vithlani, *Harford Community College*

David Williams, *Spartanburg Community College*

And we are grateful for the dozens of instructors in our Macmillan Community (http://Community.Macmillan.com) who so graciously offered input on our new *visual scaffolding* module group openers, and for students from the following schools who helpfully reviewed samples:

Creighton University

Lake Superior College

Iowa State University

University of Illinois

University of Minnesota

University of Nebraska Omaha

University of St. Thomas

At Worth Publishers a host of people played key roles in creating this tenth edition.

Although the information gathering is never ending, the formal planning began as the author-publisher team gathered for a two-day retreat. This happy and creative gathering included John Brink, Thomas Ludwig, Richard Straub, Nathan, and Dave from the author team, along with assistants Kathryn Brownson and Sara Neevel. We were joined by Worth Publishers executives Tom Scotty, Joan Feinberg, Craig Bleyer, Doug Bolton, Catherine Woods, Kevin Feyen, and Elizabeth Widdicombe; editors Christine Brune, Nancy Fleming, Tracey Kuehn, Betty Probert, Trish Morgan, and Dora Figueiredo; sales and marketing colleagues Kate Nurre, Carlise Stembridge, Tom Kling, Lindsay Johnson, Mike Krotine, Kelli Goldenberg, Jen Cawsey, and Janie Pierce-Bratcher; media specialists Rachel Comerford, Gayle Yamazaki, Andrea Messineo, and Pepper Williams; and special guest Jennifer Peluso (Florida Atlantic University). The input and brainstorming during this meeting of minds gave birth, among other things, to LaunchPad's new "Immersive Learning: How Would You Know?" activities and the text's improved and expanded system of study aids.

Publisher Rachel Losh has been a valued team leader, thanks to her dedication, creativity, and sensitivity. Rachel has overseen, encouraged, and guided our author-editor team. Media Editor Lauren Samuelson helped envision our new "Immersive Learning: How Would You Know?" activities and directed all the details of their production. Executive Media Editor Rachel Comerford and Media Editor Laura Burden expertly coordinated production of the huge collection of media resources for this edition. Betty Probert efficiently edited and produced the Instructors' Resources, Lecture Guides, Test Bank, and Study Guide and, in the process, also helped fine-tune the whole book. Editorial Assistant Katie Pachnos provided invaluable support in commissioning and organizing the multitude of reviews, sending information to instructors, and handling numerous other daily tasks related to the book's development and production. Lee McKevitt did a splendid job of laying out each page. Robin Fadool and Candice Cheesman worked together to locate the myriad photos. Art Manager Matthew McAdams coordinated our working with artist Evelyn Pence to create the lovely new module group openers.

Tracey Kuehn, Director of Content Management Enhancement, displayed tireless tenacity, commitment, and impressive organization in leading Worth's gifted artistic production team and coordinating editorial input throughout the production process. Project Editor Robert Errera and Senior Production Manager Sarah Segal masterfully kept the book to its tight schedule, and Director of Design, Content Management Enhancement Diana Blume skillfully directed creation of the beautiful new design and art program. Production Manager Stacey Alexander, along with Supplements Project Editor Julio Espin, did their usual excellent work of producing the print supplements.

Christine Brune, chief editor for all ten editions, is a wonder worker. She offers just the right mix of encouragement, gentle admonition, attention to detail, and passion for excellence. An author could not ask for more. Development Editor Nancy Fleming is one of those rare editors who is gifted both at "thinking big" about a module—and with a kindred spirit to our own—while also applying her sensitive, graceful, line-by-line touches. Development Editors Trish Morgan and Danielle Slevens amazed us with their meticulous focus, impressive knowledge, and deft editing. And Deborah Heimann did an excellent job with the copyediting.

To achieve our goal of supporting the teaching of psychology, this teaching package not only must be authored, reviewed, edited, and produced, but also made available to teachers of psychology. For their exceptional success in doing that, our author team is grateful to Worth Publishers' professional sales and marketing team. We are especially grateful to Executive Marketing Manager Kate Nurre and Senior Marketing Manager Lindsay Johnson, both for their tireless efforts to inform our teaching colleagues of our efforts to assist their teaching, and for the joy of working with them.

At Hope College, the supporting team members for this edition included Kathryn Brownson, who researched countless bits of information and proofed hundreds of pages. Kathryn is a knowledgeable and sensitive adviser on many matters, and Sara Neevel is our high-tech manuscript developer, par excellence. At the University of Kentucky, Lorie Hailey has showcased a variety of indispensable qualities, including a sharp eye and a strong work ethic.

Again, I [DM] gratefully acknowledge the editing assistance and mentoring of my writing coach, poet Jack Ridl, whose influence resides in the voice you will be hearing in the pages that follow. He, more than anyone, cultivated my delight in dancing with the language, and taught me to approach writing as a craft that shades into art. Likewise, I [ND] am grateful to my intellectual hero and mentor, Roy Baumeister, who taught me how to hone my writing and embrace the writing life.

After hearing countless dozens of people say that this book's resource package has taken their teaching to a new level, we reflect on how fortunate we are to be a part of a team in which everyone has produced on-time work marked by the highest professional standards. For their remarkable talents, their long-term dedication, and their friendship, we thank John Brink, Thomas Ludwig, and Richard Straub. With this new edition, we also welcome and thank Sue Frantz for her gift of instructors' resources.

Finally, our gratitude extends to the many students and instructors who have written to offer suggestions, or just an encouraging word. It is for them, and those about to begin their study of psychology, that we have done our best to introduce the field we love.

*   *   *

The day this book went to press was the day we started gathering information and ideas for the next edition. Your input will influence how this book continues to evolve. So, please, do share your thoughts.

David Myers

Hope College
Holland, Michigan 49422-9000 USA
www.DavidMyers.org

Nathan DeWall

University of Kentucky
Lexington, Kentucky 40506-0044 USA
www.NathanDeWall.com

Content Changes

Exploring Psychology, Tenth Edition in Modules includes hundreds of new research citations, new "Immersive Learning: How Would You Know?" research activities in LaunchPad, exciting new "visual scaffolding" two-page module group openers, a lightly revised organization, a fresh new design, and many fun new photos and cartoons. In addition, you will find the following significant content changes in this new tenth edition.

Thinking Critically With Psychological Science

MODULE 1 The History and Scope of Psychology

- The Scientific Attitude and Critical Thinking now appear in this module (moved here from the ninth edition's Module 2), establishing these foundational principles at the discussion's outset.
- Improved organization and expanded coverage of psychology's historical and contemporary development.
- New discussion of cross-cultural and gender psychology, with new illustrations.
- New introduction of positive psychology.
- New photos provide examples of famous psychology majors.
- *Evolutionary psychology* and *behavior genetics* are now key terms.
- New material on *community psychology*, which is now a key term.
- New illustration introduces the biopsychosocial approach more effectively.
- Updated table of current perspectives.

MODULE 2 Research Strategies: How Psychologists Ask and Answer Questions

- Updated discussion of critical thinking in public policy.
- New research support for hindsight bias in people of all ages from across the world.
- Importance of research replication given increased emphasis.
- New research with figure on Twitter message moods, and on the relationship between negative emotions on Twitter and heart disease rates in more than a thousand U.S. counties, illustrates discussion of "big data" methods in naturalistic observation.
- Updated research examples reinforce correlational studies' not being cause-effect.

- New research updates breast-feeding versus bottle-feeding example.
- New research examples update discussion of the placebo effect, and indicate that the effect persists even upon learning that one has received a placebo.
- New Thinking Critically About Research Design: How Would You Know? feature explores research design in psychological science and introduces the new "Immersive Learning: How Would You Know?" LaunchPad activities.

The Biology of Behavior

- New co-author Nathan DeWall led the revision of these modules for the tenth edition.

MODULE 3 Neural and Hormonal Systems

- New research explores our inaccurate tendency to consider biological and psychological influences on behavior separately.
- Research updates discussion of neural network pruning throughout life.
- New photo illustrates complex network of human cortical neurons.
- Expanded discussion of how neurons generate electricity from chemical events, with new figure.
- Improved figure more effectively demonstrates action potential.
- New discussion, with *refractory period* as new key term.
- *All-or-none response* and *reuptake* are now key terms.
- New coverage of *agonists* and *antagonists*, which are now key terms.
- Sensory neurons are now identified as afferent (inward), and motor neurons as efferent (outward).
- Expanded illustration of the functional divisions of the nervous system.
- Updated research on the effect of oxytocin on social trust.

MODULE
4 Tools of Discovery and Older Brain Structures

- The Tools of Discovery boxed essay has been expanded, updated, and transformed into text discussion.
- New photo shows living human brain.
- New research on use of neuroimaging in the media and advertising.
- Updated information on massive Human Connectome Project.
- Hippocampus now a key term here as well as in the **Module 23**, with new research example.
- New research examples demonstrate the amygdala's role in fear and rage.
- Updated discussion of the hypothalamus with new research on *hedonic hotspots,* desire, and substance use disorders.

MODULE
5 The Cerebral Cortex and Our Divided Brain

- New research example of robotic limbs controlled by a device implanted in the motor cortex.
- *Coverage of the somatosensory cortex* (previously referred to as the "sensory cortex") has been fully updated.
- New research notes the effects of simple versus complex tasks on brain activity.
- New research updates discussion of Phineas Gage, with new art.
- New photo example of brain injury, crime, and punishment.
- New diffusion spectrum image shows neural networks connecting hemispheres.
- Includes new research on brain plasticity in those who cannot hear.

MODULE
6 Genetics, Evolutionary Psychology, and Behavior

- New photo explains the nature–nurture interaction.
- *Heredity* and *genome* are new key terms.
- Updated discussion of twin and adoption studies, includes autism spectrum disorder diagnoses, and personality and behavioral similarities.
- New photo examples of identical twins and unrelated lookalikes.
- New photo examples of celebrities who were adopted.
- Gene-Environment Interaction includes new research on identical twins creating shared experiences.
- New photo example of space study with astronauts Scott and Mark Kelly.

- Distinction between genetics and epigenetics clarified.
- Additional examples demonstrate effects of environmental factors on epigenetic molecules.
- New research examples illustrate the mismatch of our prehistoric genetic legacy with modern life.
- Updated discussion of evolution and faith.

Consciousness and the Two-Track Mind

MODULE
7 Consciousness: Some Basic Concepts

- Expanded coverage of conscious awareness, with new research examples.
- New art illustrates inattentional blindness.
- New research example illustrates the effects of driver distraction on traffic accidents.
- Includes new Eric Kandel estimate that 80 to 90 percent of what we do is unconscious.
- *Parallel processing* is now a key term in this module, as well as in **Module 17**.

MODULE
8 Sleep and Dreams

- New research updates discussion of night "owls" and morning "larks."
- New research examples illustrate sleep pattern variations.
- Suprachiasmatic nucleus figure is improved.
- Updated research on sleep's functions and benefits, sleep deprivation, and the function of dreams.
- Updated table on natural sleep aids.
- New photo illustrates CPAP machine for sleep apnea.
- New research example explores "The Great Sleep Recession."
- New research suggests sleep-deprived brains find fatty foods more enticing.
- Updated research on sleep-deprived students experiencing more relationship conflicts.
- What We Dream section updated with new research, including cases of those unable to see or walk from birth having these abilities in their dreams.
- Lightly updated table compares dream theories.
- New figure illustrates sleep's consolidation of learning into long-term memory.
- New research suggests we can learn to associate sounds with odors while asleep.
- New figure and photo illustrate sleep patterns across the life span.

MODULE
9 Drugs and Consciousness

- Coverage of hypnosis now appears in a Thinking Critically box on pain control in **Module 18**, The Nonvisual Senses.
- *Cocaine* is now a key term.
- New table outlines When Is Drug Use a Disorder?
- New research on alcohol "intervention studies" that have lowered college students' positive expectations and also reduced consumption.
- Powerful new photo shows firefighters reenacting an alcohol-related car accident.
- Expanded explanation of the opiates and their effects.
- Updates on lethal effects of smoking, including life expectancy 10+ years shorter.
- New research on smokers' relapse under stress.
- New coverage of synthetic marijuana, or "spice," and its effects.
- New research suggests drop in IQ scores among persistent teen marijuana users.
- Discussion of biological influences on drug use updated with new research.
- Table showing selected psychoactive drugs has been expanded and updated.
- New photo shows media models of smoking that influence teens.
- Updated graph of high school trends in drug use.

Developing Through the Life Span

- New co-author Nathan DeWall led the revision of these modules for the tenth edition.

MODULE
10 Developmental Issues, Prenatal Development, and the Newborn

- New research expands Stability and Change discussion.
- Conception discussion expanded and clarified.
- New research demonstrates newborns' preference for hearing their mother's language.
- New research shows effects of smoking and extreme stress during pregnancy.

MODULE
11 Infancy and Childhood

- New research explores relationship between rapid increase in infant brain size and early development.
- New research in Brain Development shows that premature babies given skin-to-skin contact are better off even 10 years later.
- New research notes that mice and monkeys, like human children, forget their early life.

- New photo shows egocentrism in action.
- New same-sex marriage example illustrates accommodation.
- New research demonstrates the ways preschoolers think like scientists.
- New real-life example illustrates the *curse of knowledge*.
- New research suggests social benefits for children with advanced ability to take another's perspective.
- New research suggests benefits of positive self-talk are not limited to children.
- "Autism Spectrum Disorder and Mind-Blindness" boxed essay has been updated and improved and has become its own text section, "Autism Spectrum Disorder."
- New photo of twins with ASD.
- Expanded perspective on the Harry Harlow experiments includes quotes from Harlow and his biographer.
- New research demonstrates relationship between heredity, temperament, and attachment style.
- Attachment Styles and Later Relationships updated with new research examples demonstrating the later effects of secure and insecure attachments.
- New table outlines dual-parenting facts.
- New research illuminates the effects of deprivation of attachment and growing up under adversity.
- New research shows effects of abuse and conflict on children's brains, and epigenetic marks left by child abuse.
- New research discussion of Western parents' assertions that their children are more special than other children.
- New Gallup survey illustrates joy and stress of raising children.

MODULE
12 Adolescence

- New research and new figure explores adolescent decision making and risk taking, and effects of frontal lobe immaturity in juvenile offenders and drug users.
- Developing Morality section updated with new research demonstrating development of moral judgment, benefits of moral action, effects of delayed gratification on human flourishing, and connections to the two-track mind.
- New photo illustrates moral reasoning during Superstorm Sandy.
- Includes new research on American teens' contentment with their lives and the importance of emotional intimacy to adolescent identity formation.
- New research illustrates increased brain activation in adolescents when in one another's company, and the effects of this activation.

- Updated research notes the different types of teen-parent bickering that typically occur with adolescent boys versus adolescent girls.
- Thinking Critically About: How Much Credit or Blame Do Parents Deserve? feature updated with new research on cultural differences in parenting.
- New research notes teens' tendency to discount the future and focus on immediate rewards when in the presence of their peers.
- New research notes prevalence of online social networking and its effects on peer relationships.
- Emerging Adulthood discussion includes updated figure on the lengthening transition to adulthood.

MODULE 13 Adulthood

- New research on baseball players demonstrating that humans peak physically in their mid-twenties.
- New research explains effects of aging on the brain, and the brain's plasticity.
- New research supports benefits of exercising on aging.
- New research on "reminiscence bump," and older adults' greater tendency for tip-of-the-tongue memories.
- New section on Sustaining Mental Abilities includes concept of "brain fitness."
- New research indicates human tendency to prefer social connection over learning when facing death.
- Personal examples from authors demonstrate importance of chance events in our development.
- New research shows lowering divorce rates.
- Adulthood's Commitments section expanded and updated.
- New figure illustrates increased online meeting of relationship partners.
- New photo illustrates connection between job satisfaction and life satisfaction.
- New figure shows importance of social connecting throughout life.
- New research explores older adults' experience of complex emotions, tendency to attend more to positive information, and reduced number and increased stability of friendships.
- New research with grieving parents explores factors that may prolong the grieving process.

Sex, Gender, and Sexuality

- Title changed from "Gender and Sexuality" in previous edition, reflecting new discussion of the distinction between gender and biological sex.
- Updated introduction includes new research on women's and men's evolving gender roles and women in business, as well as new personal stories from the authors.

MODULE 14 Gender Development

- *Sex*, now a key term, is included in an updated, expanded discussion of differentiating sex and gender.
- New photo example illustrates tragic effects of *relational aggression*, which is now a key term.
- Thoroughly updated discussion of male-female differences in aggression, social power, and social connectedness, with new research examples throughout.
- Expanded and updated discussion of biological sex, including differences in sexual development, with new research examples throughout.
- *Spermarche* is now a key term.
- *Disorder of sexual development* is now a key term.
- The Nurture of Gender section revised and updated with new research throughout, including preferential hiring of female professors to teach STEM classes.
- New coverage of gender cognition in transgender children.
- How Do We Learn Gender? section updated with new photos of Caitlyn Jenner's transition.
- *Androgyny* is now a key term.

MODULE 15 Human Sexuality

- New research indicates that people's brains crave their partner's presence.
- New research updates discussion of effects of women's hormonal surges at ovulation.
- New research considers whether women's mate preferences change across the menstrual cycle.
- Statistics updated on the worldwide prevalence of sexually transmitted infections.
- New data on the proportion of women with HIV and number of worldwide HIV deaths.
- New research explores relationship of fantasy to orgasms in women.
- Teen Pregnancy updated with new research.
- New photo illustrates the hypersexualization of female characters in video games.
- New research indicates the cross-cultural differences in attitudes toward same-sex unions.
- New research updates the numbers of people who identify with particular sexual orientations, and explores accuracy of self-identification.
- New research explores effects of a lack of social support on nonheterosexual teens.
- Updated research on the relative fluidity of women's sexual orientation.
- Discussion of genetic influences on sexuality updated with new research examples.

- New hands-on activity asks students to predict research answers to questions about male-female sexuality differences.
- Male-Female Differences in Sexuality updated with new research on sex drives and sexual habits of heterosexual and homosexual men and women.
- Reworked and updated Natural Selection and Mating Preferences section includes new research on what men and women seek in potential mates.
- New research examples question evolutionary psychology's explanation of mating preferences.
- Critiquing the Evolutionary Perspective includes new counter-argument noting the smaller behavioral differences between men and women in cultures with greater gender equality, and the influence of social scripts.
- New Sex and Human Values section includes new research on benefits of sex in committed relationships and the interplay between sexual desire and love.

Sensation and Perception

MODULE 16 Basic Concepts of Sensation and Perception

- New neuroscience research on the ability of priming to evoke brain activity without conscious awareness.
- New coverage of the adaptation of emotion perception, with photo example for students to try.
- New figure illustrates perceptual set.
- New photo asks students to identify an emotion removed from its context.
- New research example notes the effect of holding a firearm on one's perceptions of others as gun-toting, and the tragic consequences of this phenomenon.
- Updated research on music's effect on perception.
- New research on how emotions and motives color our social and environmental perceptions.

MODULE 17 Vision: Sensory and Perceptual Processing

- New research details the effects of light intensity—including even imagined light intensity—and our cognitive and emotional states on the pupil and iris.
- Color Processing section shifted up to follow discussion of Retinal Processing.
- Updated art more effectively demonstrates the figure-ground relationship.
- New research example explores the role of learning in infants' depth perception.
- New research supports performing cataract surgery in children at as young an age as possible.

MODULE 18 The Nonvisual Senses

- New coverage of the speed of audition.
- Updated coverage of hearing loss, including global statistics and cochlear implants, with new art.
- Includes new research on the influence of cognition on response to touch, including the effect of familiar touch on experience of pain.
- New research shows women's greater sensitivity to pain.
- New photo example illustrates powerful effect of distraction on experience of pain.
- New research shows women's tendency to recall pain of childbirth in terms of average of peak and end pain.
- New research shows how the ending of an experience affects perception of pain and also pleasure.
- New research supports maximizing pain relief with placebos, distraction, and hypnosis.
- Hypnosis moved here from ninth edition Module 7; now covered in a new Thinking Critically About: Hypnosis and Pain Relief box.
- Includes new research example of learning to like what we eat.
- New research notes that each taste receptor has a matching partner cell in the brain.
- New cognitive neuroscience research helps explain smell-cognition connection.
- New research illustrates blending of tactile and social judgments.
- New photo example demonstrates value of sensory interaction for hard-of-hearing people.
- Updated Summarizing the Senses table includes new column noting the key brain areas in which events take place.
- ESP discussion includes new research on psychic predictions about missing-person cases, and on multiple unsuccessful attempts to replicate experiments demonstrating psychic abilities.

Learning

- Compelling new introduction.

MODULE 19 Basic Learning Concepts and Classical Conditioning

- New figure illustrates Pavlov's device for recording salivation.
- New research shows how we tend to fall back on old habits when our willpower is low.
- Research update supports finding that we generalize our like or dislike based on learned facial features.
- New information on what happened to "Little Albert."

MODULE 20 Operant Conditioning

- New research supports idea that children's compliance increases after "time out" punishment.
- Discussion of physical punishment and increased aggressiveness updated with new research, as well as global figures on legal protections for children.
- New research supports idea that punishment should focus on prohibitions rather than positive obligations.
- Updated research on how adaptive learning software supports individualized learning.
- Updated summary of how best to reinforce desired behaviors.

MODULE 21 Biology, Cognition, and Learning

- New photo illustrates research on the association of the color red with sexual attractiveness.
- New research suggests that a focus on intrinsic rewards in schooling and career may lead to extrinsic rewards as well.
- New research supports children's and infants' natural propensity for imitation.
- New research supports vicarious reinforcement, with even learned fears being extinguished when we observe others safely navigating the feared situation.
- New discussion of current debate regarding importance of mirror neurons.
- Updated research on the prevalence of imitation in other species.
- Expanded coverage, with new photos, of social learning among other animals.
- Includes new research on the effects of a vicarious prompt on empathy and imitation.
- New research notes how prosocial media boosts helping behaviors.
- Thinking Critically About: Does Viewing Media Violence Trigger Violent Behavior? feature updated with new research examples.

Memory

MODULE 22 Studying and Encoding Memories

- Includes new music and face recognition research examples, and new photo of face recognition in sheep research.
- New research shows those with large working memory capacity retain more after sleep and tend to be creative problem solvers.
- New research details the spacing effect's influence on motor skills and online game performance, and the benefits of distributed practice.

- New research supports testing effect and notes ineffectiveness of other common study habits.

MODULE 23 Storing and Retrieving Memories

- New research shows memory components' distribution across a network, with some of those brain cells activating again upon memory retrieval.
- *Episodic memory* and *semantic memory* are now key terms.
- New research notes activity of the hippocampus and nearby brain networks as people form explicit memories, with new image of the hippocampus.
- *Memory consolidation* is now a key term.
- Updated discussion of infantile amnesia includes new research on increased retention in the maturing hippocampus.
- New research on flashbulb memory and tunnel vision memory.
- Research update on how experience and learning increase synaptic number as well as efficiency.
- *Hippocampus* is now a key term.
- New personal story from author illustrates effect of having insufficient time for memory consolidation.
- Discussion of synaptic changes in memory processing includes new research on memory-blocking drugs.
- Updated research explores how priming can influence behaviors.
- New examples illustrate context-dependent memory.

MODULE 24 Forgetting, Memory Construction, and Improving Memory

- New research updates discussion of those with superior autobiographical memories.
- Discussion of Henry Molaison updated with new research on the effects of his hippocampus removal, and his nondeclarative memory abilities.
- Includes new research on wide belief in repression of traumatic memories.
- *Reconsolidation* is now a key term.
- Memory construction now demonstrated with author's personal experience at Loftus presentation.
- New research updates discussion of memory reconsolidation of negative or traumatic events.
- Updated research on false memories examines mistakenly convicted people who were victims of faulty eyewitness identification.
- New photo illustrates research on false memories.
- Discussion of memories of abuse includes new research and has become a Thinking Critically About feature.
- New research offers more tips for effective study habits.
- New research updates discussion of encoding failure.

Thinking, Language, and Intelligence

MODULE 25 Thinking

- New narrative and photo examples of *prototype*.
- New figure demonstrates how categorizing faces influences recollection.
- New research shows how insight improves when electrical stimulation disrupts assumptions created by past experiences.
- Updated research supports effectiveness of intuitive judgments.
- Discussion of availability heuristic enhanced with climate change example.
- Includes new research about cigarette package warnings.
- Updated discussion of why we fear the wrong things, with new research examples throughout.
- New research example demonstrates how overconfidence can feed extreme political views.
- New research explains the planning fallacy.
- Includes new research on value and perils of using intuition for complex decisions; new examples relate to attitudes and decision making.
- Research updates discussion of unconsciously learned associations.
- Includes new research on importance of intelligence and working memory for aptitude.
- Includes new research and photo example on the development of creative traits in girls.
- New research expands discussion of fostering creativity.
- Discussion of animals' cognitive skills updated with new research.

MODULE 26 Language and Thought

- Updated research shows humans, regardless of language, prefer some syllables over others.
- New research updates discussion of babies' language comprehension and productive language development.
- New research supports diversity of human language.
- Discussion of the brain and language updated with new research on distributed processing of language in the brain.
- Includes new research on animal cognition, as well as neuroscience research on a gene unique to humans that helps enable speech.
- Improved figure illustrates brain activity when speaking and hearing words.
- New research updates discussion of language's ability to influence our thinking, emotions, and cultural associations.
- Additional research example demonstrates language's impact on perceived differences.
- Includes new research on the advantages of bilingualism.

MODULE 27 Intelligence and Its Assessment

- Discussion of the g factor includes new research exploring how distinct brain networks enable distinct abilities.
- Now includes Gardner's ninth possible intelligence, existential intelligence.
- Includes new photo example of savant syndrome.
- New photo demonstrates spatial intelligence genius.
- New research with professional musicians demonstrates importance of both natural talent and self-disciplined grit in achieving success.
- Updated table comparing theories of intelligence includes new category, *emotional intelligence*.
- Expanded discussion of history of intelligence tests includes more on Alfred Binet's research and Lewis Terman's support of the eugenics movement.
- Discussion of intelligence's stability over the life span includes new data from the Scottish intelligence survey of 1932, with new figure.
- Updated discussion of intelligence extremes includes new research on adult achievements of those who scored high on SAT in their youth.

MODULE 28 Genetic and Environmental Influences on Intelligence

- New research updates and clarifies discussion of the heritability of intelligence.
- New research supports quality preschool programs and experiences, nutritional supplements for newborns and mothers, and interactive reading programs.
- New research notes the increased variability of males' intelligence.
- New photo example of Shakuntala Devi, "the human computer."
- New cross-cultural research supports impact of cultural and other expectations on academic flourishing.
- New research updates discussion of intelligence variation due to racial, ethnic, and socioeconomic differences.
- New research discusses influence of stereotype threat on gender gap in high-level math achievements.
- Includes updated discussion of stereotype threat, importance of a growth mind-set and self-discipline, belief in the power of effort, and intellectual curiosity for real-world achievements.
- New research notes the limitations of general intelligence tests in reflecting competence.

Motivation and Emotion

- Powerful new introduction.

MODULE 29 Basic Motivational Concepts, Affiliation, and Achievement

- New research on risk-taking behavior, and on uncertainty amplifying motivation.
- New research examples illustrate the search for arousal in the absence of stimulation and the effects of overstimulation.
- New research suggests decreasing arousal can decrease stress.
- *Hunger Games* example now illustrates Maslow's hierarchy.
- New table compares Classic Motivation Theories.
- *Affiliation need* is now a key term.
- Includes new research on attachment bonds, whom we befriend, and the benefits of close friendship.
- Updated research on the relationship between marriage and life satisfaction.
- New research example notes increased doctor visits in lonely older adults.
- Includes new research on need to belong driving formation of social connections, and benefits of these connections.
- The Pain of Being Shut Out updated with new research, with *ostracism* a new key term.
- Connecting and Social Networking section fully updated, with *narcissism* now a key term.
- New research in Achievement Motivation demonstrates importance of *grit,* now a key term.

MODULE 30 Hunger

- New *Unbroken* photo example illustrates how hunger can drive an obsession with food.
- New research illustrates power of motivational "hot" states from hunger, fatigue, or sexual arousal.
- New research on the body's weight regulation.
- New research updates discussion of biological and cultural influences on taste preferences and situational influences on eating.
- New research offers ways to encourage healthier eating in children.
- Obesity and Weight Control updated with cross-cultural comparisons and global statistics; new research on physiology of obesity; negative social, health, and memory effects of obesity; and genetic basis for weight.
- Waist Management boxed essay is now a table of evidence-based tips for weight loss.

MODULE 31 Theories and Physiology of Emotion

- New research shows subjectivity of emotional experience.
- New research illustrates brain activity underlying emotions and emotion-fed actions.
- Includes new research on reappraisal and its effects.

MODULE 32 Expressing and Experiencing Emotion

- New research updates discussion of gender differences in emotional experience.
- New research on humans' ability to detect nonverbal threats and status signs.
- New research updates discussion of effects of facial expressions, including findings on Botox, depression, and the facial feedback effect.
- *Behavior feedback effect* now a key term.

Stress, Health, and Human Flourishing

- New co-author Nathan DeWall led the revision of these modules for the tenth edition.
- Compelling new introduction.

MODULE 33 Stress and Illness

- New figure demonstrates how researchers study stress.
- New research shows effects of stress on workers and pregnant women.
- Includes new research on stress effects of traumatic events.
- Now introduces concept of *acculturative stress.*
- New research shows younger adults reporting higher daily stress.
- New research updates discussion of daily hassles and social stress.
- Includes new research on lasting effects of childhood stress.
- New research shows effects of stress on vaccine effectiveness.
- Discussion of stress and AIDS updated with new research and current data.
- Updated research on the stress-cancer link.
- New research and data updates discussion of stress and heart disease.
- The ninth edition boxed essay on Handling Anger has been revised and updated to become Thinking Critically About: Anger Management.
- Includes new discussion of the Type D personality.
- New research updates the discussion of the health effects of pessimism and depression.

MODULE 34 Health and Happiness

- Coping With Stress updated with new research.
- Includes expanded explanation of learned helplessness.
- New research updates Depleting and Strengthening Self-Control.
- Includes new research on the traits of optimists and pessimists, and the potential for learning optimism.
- New research demonstrates importance of social support to psychological and physical well-being, with information on cultural differences in seeking support.
- New research illustrates effect of aerobic exercise on longevity, depression, and relationships, and the recent decline of Americans' physical activity.
- Relaxation and Meditation section revised and updated, including research showing link between meditation and decreased depression and anxiety, and improved decision making.
- *Mindfulness meditation* is now a key term.
- New research suggests happiest 20-year-olds were later more likely to marry and less likely to divorce.
- New research illustrates do-good, feel-good phenomenon.
- New research suggests mood rebounds after bad events, and happiness levels can return to near-normal after significant trauma.
- New research updates list of tips for being happier.
- New research explores connection between wealth and well-being, including well-being effects of income inequality.

Social Psychology

- Social Psychology modules now precede Personality modules.

MODULE 35 Social Thinking and Social Influence

- New research updates discussion of the effect of attribution on our judgment of others.
- New photo example of Charleston Bible study murders demonstrates dispositional versus situational attributions.
- Discussion of effect of attitudes on actions updated with climate-change debate example.
- Role Playing updated with new research on reliability of Zimbardo study and effects of military training.
- New research illuminates brain activity associated with cognitive dissonance.
- Discussion of automatic mimicry updated with new research.

- Milgram discussion includes updated coverage of replications of his research with different groups, and new discoveries about his data.
- New research example considers how the circumstances of the Rwandan genocide promoted obedience.
- Includes updates on the Internet as social amplifier, demonstrating group polarization online.
- New table compares social facilitation, social loafing, and deindividuation.

MODULE 36 Antisocial Relations

- New research demonstrates accuracies and inaccuracies of stereotypes.
- Updated research on sexual orientation prejudice.
- New research explores unfounded prejudice toward Muslims, with new photo example.
- New photo example of Trayvon Martin illustrates the updated discussion of race-influenced perceptions.
- New research explores effects of networking and mutual support on ingroup bias.
- New research offers additional contributors to aggression, and updates the biopsychosocial understanding of aggression figure.
- New research updates discussion of media models for aggression.

MODULE 37 Prosocial Relations

- New research updates discussion of modern matchmaking, including meeting online, with new graph.
- New photo example of Angela Merkel illustrates the mere exposure effect.
- Includes new research clarifying the *reward theory of attraction*.
- New research suggests charitable donations increase the giver's happiness levels.
- New research shows people who are generously treated tend later to be generous themselves.
- New research illustrates mirror-image perceptions feeding global hostilities.
- *Self-fulfilling prophecy* is a new key term.
- New research updates discussion of promoting peace.

Personality

- New co-author Nathan DeWall led the revision of these modules for the tenth edition.
- Personality modules now follow Social Psychology modules.
- Compelling new introduction.

MODULE
38 Classic Perspectives on Personality

- Updated coverage of Freud's ideas and their significance.

- Now includes brief explanation of Thematic Apperception Test (TAT).

- New research updates critique of Rorschach test.

- New research expands discussion of the modern unconscious mind.

- New research supports value of humanistic psychology's positive regard and empathic listening.

MODULE
39 Contemporary Perspectives on Personality

- New Thinking Critically About: The Stigma of Introversion feature.

- Big Five discussion updated with new research on cultural changes over time and brain structure/function, with new figure.

- New research examples, and new personal example from author, explore stability and endurance of personality traits.

- New research explores maladaptive personality traits.

- New research suggests music preferences, personal and online spaces, and written communications relate to personality traits.

- Social-Cognitive Theories revised and updated; now includes gene-environment interaction.

- New photo example from the TV show *Chopped* demonstrates the value of assessing behavior in situations.

- Table comparing major personality theories lightly updated.

- Exploring the Self section updated with new research.

- New research outlines importance of positive goal-setting in considering possible selves.

- Benefits of Self-Esteem updated with new research, including on the damaging effects of undeserved praise, and on effects of threats to self-esteem.

- Revised and updated discussion of self-serving bias and its effects.

- Discussion of narcissism updated with new research.

- Expanded, revised, and updated discussion of individualism and collectivism, with new cross-cultural research examples.

- New discussion explores effects of social history and biology on cultural differences, and introduces subfield of cultural neuroscience.

Psychological Disorders

- New organization groups the disorders into four manageable modules and better reflects the DSM-5 updates:

Basic Concepts of Psychological Disorders; Anxiety Disorders, OCD, and PTSD; Major Depressive Disorder and Bipolar Disorder; and Schizophrenia and Other Disorders.

MODULE
40 Basic Concepts of Psychological Disorders

- New table demonstrates how care providers use the DSM-5.

- New photos illustrate different cultures' perceptions of normality.

- New photo of Stone Age trephination demonstrates brutal "therapies" of the past.

- Updated research on prevalence of mental health problems on college campuses.

- Discussion of biopsychosocial approach enriched with coverage of epigenetics, with associated updates throughout these modules; *epigenetics* is a new key term.

- New research updates discussion of ADHD, including controversies related to higher diagnoses.

- Thinking Critically About: Insanity feature significantly revised, with new focus and title—Are People With Psychological Disorders Dangerous? Includes new photo example of Newtown shootings.

- New *Iron Man 3* photo example of improved media portrayals of psychological disorders.

MODULE
41 Anxiety Disorders, OCD, and PTSD

- New research updates discussion of stimuli perception for those with anxiety disorders.

- New research shows greater panic symptoms in smokers.

- New pro golfer photo example illustrates successful coping with panic disorder.

- Updated statistics on OCD prevalence.

- Discussion of PTSD updated with new research and prevalence information, with new photo example.

- New research and examples update discussion of learning and neural, hormonal, and genetic influences on anxiety disorders, OCD, and PTSD.

- New research supports genetic basis for anxiety disorders and the interaction between genes and experience.

- New research discusses brain activity of those with PTSD when viewing traumatic images.

- New research shows infants attending more to sounds of ancient than modern-day threats.

MODULE
42 Major Depressive Disorder and Bipolar Disorder

- New art offers insight into the experience of bipolar disorder.

- Updated research on relationship of low self-esteem to depressed mood.

- New research shows mild sadness improves recall of faces.
- Discussion of major depressive disorder and bipolar disorder updated with new research, including current statistics and data on gender and age differences and cultural influences.
- Explanation of heritability expanded and clarified.
- Includes new research on factors that put women at greater risk for depression.
- Discussion of bipolar disorder updated with new data on prevalence, including among those in creative professions.
- Understanding Major Depressive Disorder and Bipolar Disorder updated with new research exploring genetic, biochemical, cognitive, and behavioral predictors, with new photo example.
- *Rumination* is a new key term.
- Discussion of suicide rates and nonsuicidal self-injury updated.
- Includes new suicide-prevention guidelines and resources.

MODULE 43 Schizophrenia and Other Disorders

- *Chronic* and *acute schizophrenia* are new key terms.
- New information on schizophrenia recovery rates.
- New research updates discussion of schizophrenia's symptoms, onset, and development.
- Includes new research on brain abnormalities (and their genetic basis) in people with schizophrenia.
- Updated discussion of prenatal environment contributing to risk of schizophrenia.
- Includes new international study of genome locations linked with schizophrenia.
- Updated research on the debates surrounding dissociative identity disorder, including abnormal brain anatomy that may accompany DID, and new photo example of Shirley Mason.
- New research on emotional intelligence and impulsivity in antisocial personality disorder.
- Understanding Antisocial Personality Disorder updated and improved with new genetics research and discussion of adaptive aspects of some symptoms of psychopathy, such as fearlessness and dominance.
- Eating Disorders updated with new examples and new research (including genetic), with new photo.

Therapy

MODULE 44 Introduction to Therapy and the Psychological Therapies

- Discussion now distinguishes psychotherapy and biomedical therapy more clearly.

- Psychoanalysis and Psychodynamic Therapy revised and updated with new research examples.
- New photos illustrate virtual reality exposure therapy.
- New research on positive reinforcement in children with ASD.
- Cognitive Therapies discussion updated with new research and examples.
- New paragraph discusses techniques and goals of dialectical behavior therapy.
- Updated discussion of self-help groups notes importance of redemptive narrative for maintaining sobriety.
- New research updates discussion of psychotherapy's effectiveness.
- New research and new photo support importance of *therapeutic alliance,* now a key term.
- New research suggests "culture of honor" may prompt reluctance to seek mental health care.

MODULE 45 The Biomedical Therapies and Preventing Psychological Disorders

- Includes updated explanation of who now prescribes psychiatric drugs.
- New research suggests exposure to advertising about a drug's effectiveness can increase its effect.
- Includes new research on newer-generation antipsychotics for those with severe symptoms.
- Revised explanation more explicitly differentiates today's gentler ECT from its earlier forms.
- New research introduces possibility of quicker-acting antidepressants.
- Includes new neuroscience research on how ECT may work.
- New research updates discussion of neurostimulation, including rTMS, for depression.
- New image from Human Connectome Project shows possible "depression switch" in the brain.
- Therapeutic Lifestyle Change updated with new research supporting value of healthy choices, including time spent outdoors.
- Updated research suggests importance of envisioning new possibilities to foster *posttraumatic growth,* now a key term.

APPENDIX A: Statistical Reasoning in Everyday Life

- New research and real-life examples demonstrate that we find precise numbers more credible.
- Now explains and distinguishes descriptive and inferential statistics.
- New research demonstrates the dangers of statistical illiteracy.

APPENDIX B: Psychology at Work

- New research suggests intrinsic motivation predicts performance.
- Includes new research on training programs' positive effect on job seeking.
- New research demonstrates stability of people's interests, and shows interests predicting academic and career success.
- Revised, expanded Discovering Your Interests and Strengths section includes links to several resources helping students to discover their personal strengths and vocational interests.
- New research suggests those who are conscientious and agreeable will flourish in many work settings.
- New research suggests interviewers judge people relative to those interviewed just before and after them.
- Includes new photo example of positive coaching.
- New research shows social leadership and team building increase morale and productivity.
- New research suggests workers in family-friendly organizations with flexible-time hours report greater job satisfaction and loyalty to their employers.

APPENDIX C: Subfields of Psychology

- This appendix focuses on educational requirements, type of work, and likely places to work for each of psychology's main subfields. LaunchPad offers a related, regularly updated Careers in Psychology unit.
- New photo examples illustrate community psychology and forensic psychology.

APPENDIX D: Complete Module Reviews

- In an effort to encourage students to self-test, the Reviews at the end of each module include only a list of the Learning Objective Questions—repeated from within that module. Answers to those questions form these Complete Module Reviews, which students may use to check their answers or review the material.

APPENDIX E: Answers to *Experience the Testing Effect* Questions

- Students may check their answers here for the multiple-format questions found in a self-test at the end of each module.

Time Management

Or, How to Be a Great Student and Still Have a Life

—Richard O. Straub, University of Michigan, Dearborn

© Desislava Draganova/Alamy

WE all face challenges in our schedules. If you are making the transition from high school to college, you may be delighting in new freedoms, but also struggling to balance your many new responsibilities. Or you may be a student returning to school after spending a few years at work. You may be balancing work and family along with your classes.

How can you balance all of your life's demands and be successful? Time management. Manage the time you have so that you can find the time you need.

In this section, I will outline a simple, four-step process for improving the way you make use of your time.

1. Keep a time-use diary to understand how you are using your time. You may be surprised at how much time you're wasting.

2. Design a new schedule for using your time more effectively.

3. Make the most of your study time so that your new schedule will work for you.

4. If necessary, refine your new schedule, based on what you've learned.

How Are You Using Your Time Now?

Although everyone gets 24 hours in the day and seven days in the week, we fill those hours and days with different obligations and interests. If you are like most people, you probably use your time wisely in some ways, and not so wisely in others. Answering the questions in **TABLE 1** can help you find trouble spots—and hopefully more time for the things that matter most to you.

The next thing you need to know is how you actually spend your time. To find out, record your activities in a time-use diary for one week. Be realistic. Take notes on how much time you spend attending class, studying, working, commuting, meeting personal and family needs, fixing and eating meals, socializing (don't forget texting, gaming, and social networking), exercising, and anything else that occupies your time, including life's small practical tasks, which can take up plenty of your 24/7. As you record your activities, take notes on how you are feeling at various times of the day. When does your energy slump, and when do you feel most energetic?

⟫ How Are You Using Your Time Now?

⟫ Design a Better Schedule

Plan the Term

Plan Your Week

⟫ Make Every Minute of Your Study Time Count

Take Useful Class Notes

Create a Study Space That Helps You Learn

Set Specific, Realistic Daily Goals

Use SQ3R to Help You Master This Text

Don't Forget About Rewards!

⟫ Do You Need to Revise Your New Schedule?

Are You Doing Well in Some Courses But Not in Others?

Have You Received a Poor Grade on a Test?

Are You Trying to Study Regularly for the First Time and Feeling Overwhelmed?

⌄ TABLE 1

Study Habits Survey

Answer the following questions, writing *Yes* or *No* for each line.

1. Do you usually set up a schedule to budget your time for studying, work, recreation, and other activities?

    _____

2. Do you often put off studying until time pressures force you to cram?

    _____

3. Do other students seem to study less than you do, but get better grades?

    _____

4. Do you usually spend hours at a time studying one subject, rather than dividing that time among several subjects?

    _____

5. Do you often have trouble remembering what you have just read in your course work? _____

6. Before reading a module, do you skim through it and read the section headings?

    _____

7. Do you try to predict test questions from your class notes and reading?

    _____

8. Do you usually try to summarize in your own words what you have just finished reading? _____

9. Do you find it difficult to concentrate for very long when you study?

    _____

10. Do you often feel that you studied the wrong material for a test?

    _____

Thousands of students have participated in similar surveys. Students who are fully realizing their academic potential usually respond as follows: (1) yes, (2) no, (3) no, (4) no, (5) no, (6) yes, (7) yes, (8) yes, (9) no, (10) no.

Do your responses fit that pattern? If not, you could benefit from improving your time management and study habits.

Design a Better Schedule

Take a good look at your time-use diary. Where do you think you may be wasting time? Do you spend a lot of time commuting, for example? If so, could you use that time more productively? If you take public transportation, commuting is a great time to read and test yourself for review.

Did you remember to include time for meals, personal care, work schedules, family commitments, and other fixed activities?

How much do you sleep? In the battle to meet all of life's daily commitments and interests, we tend to treat sleep as optional. Do your best to manage your life so that you can get enough sleep to feel rested. You will feel better and be healthier, and you will also do better academically and in relationships with your family and friends. (You will read more about this in **Module 8**.)

Are you dedicating enough time for focused study? Take a last look at your notes to see if any other patterns pop out. Now it's time to create a new and more efficient schedule.

Plan the Term

Before you draw up your new schedule, think ahead. Use your phone's calendar feature, or buy a portable calendar that covers the entire school term, with a writing space for each day. Using the course outlines provided by your instructors, enter the dates of all exams, term-paper deadlines, and other important assignments. Also be sure to enter your own long-range personal plans (work and family commitments, etc.). Keep your calendar up-to-date, refer to it often, and change it as needed. Through this process, you will develop a regular schedule that will help you achieve success.

Plan Your Week

To pass those exams, meet those deadlines, and keep up with your life outside of class, you will need to convert your long-term goals into a daily schedule. Be realistic—you will be living with this routine for the entire school term. Here are some more things to add to your calendar.

1. Enter your class times, work hours, and any other fixed obligations. Be thorough. Allow plenty of time for such things as commuting, meals, and laundry.

MGP/Photodisc/Getty Images

2. Set up a study schedule for each course. Remember what you learned about yourself in the study habits survey (TABLE 1) and your time-use diary. TABLE 2, More Tips for Effective Scheduling, offers some detailed guidance drawn from psychology's research.

3. After you have budgeted time for studying, fill in slots for other obligations, exercise, fun, and relaxation.

Make Every Minute of Your Study Time Count

How do you study from a textbook? Many students simply read and reread in a passive manner. As a result, they remember the wrong things—the catchy stories but not the main points that show up later in test questions. To make things worse, many students take poor notes during class. Here are some tips that will help you get the most from your class and your text.

Take Useful Class Notes

Good notes will boost your understanding and retention. Are yours thorough? Do they form a sensible outline of each lecture? If not, you may need to make some changes.

Keep Each Course's Notes Separate and Organized

Keeping all your notes for a course in one location will allow you to flip back and forth easily to find answers to questions. Three options are (1) separate notebooks for each course, (2) clearly marked sections in a shared ring binder, or (3) carefully organized folders if you opt to take notes electronically. For the print options, removable pages will allow you to add new information and weed out past mistakes. Choosing notebook pages with lots of space, or using mark-up options in electronic files, will allow you to add comments when you review and revise your notes after class.

Use an Outline Format

Use Roman numerals for major points, letters for supporting arguments, and so on. (See FIGURE 1 for a sample.) In some courses, taking notes will be easy, but some instructors may be less organized, and you will have to work harder to form your outline.

Clean Up Your Notes After Class

Try to reorganize your notes soon after class. Expand or clarify your comments and clean up any hard-to-read scribbles while the material is fresh in your mind. Write important questions in the margin, or by using an electronic markup feature, next to notes that answer them. (For example: "What are the sleep stages?") This will help you when you review your notes before a test.

Create a Study Space That Helps You Learn

It's easier to study effectively if your work area is well designed.

© Hero Images/Corbis

▼ TABLE 2

More Tips for Effective Scheduling

There are a few other things you will want to keep in mind when you set up your schedule.

Spaced study is more effective than massed study. If you need 3 hours to study one subject, for example, it's best to divide that into shorter periods spaced over several days.

Alternate subjects, but avoid interference. Alternating the subjects you study in any given session will keep you fresh and will, surprisingly, increase your ability to remember what you're learning in each different area. Studying similar topics back-to-back, however, such as two different foreign languages, could lead to interference in your learning. (You will hear more about this in **Module 24**).

Be smart about your Smartphone. Texting, snapchatting, browsing, and e-mail can be real distractions. When your concentration is interrupted, it takes extra time and energy to regain the focus you need to make study time count. Consider scheduling a time for checking the phone—perhaps once per hour on the hour—and ignore it during the rest of your study time. (**Module 29** has more tips for maintaining balance and focus in your social networking.)

Determine the amount of study time you need to do well in each course. The time you need depends on the difficulty of your courses and the effectiveness of your study methods. Ideally, you would spend at least 1 to 2 hours studying for each hour spent in class. Increase your study time slowly by setting weekly goals that will gradually bring you up to the desired level.

Create a schedule that makes sense. Tailor your schedule to meet the demands of each course. For the course that emphasizes lecture notes, plan a daily review of your notes soon after each class. If you are evaluated for class participation (for example, in a language course), allow time for a review just before the class meets. Schedule study time for your most difficult (or least motivating) courses during hours when you are the most alert and distractions are fewest.

Schedule open study time. Life can be unpredictable. Emergencies and new obligations can throw off your schedule. Or you may simply need some extra time for a project or for review in one of your courses. Try to allow for some flexibility in your schedule each week.

Following these guidelines will help you find a schedule that works for you!

When is my daily peak in circadian arousal? Study hardest subject then!

Sleep (Module 8)

I. Biological Rhythms

    A. Circadian Rhythm (circa-about; diem-day)—24-hour cycle.

        1. Ups and downs throughout day/night.

           Dip in afternoon (siesta time).

        2. Melatonin—hormone that makes us sleepy. Produced by pineal gland in brain. Bright light shuts down production of melatonin. (Dim the lights at night to get sleepy.)

    B. FOUR Sleep Stages, cycle through every 90 minutes all night! Aserinsky discovered—his son—REM sleep (dreams, rapid eye movement, muscles paralyzed but brain super active). EEG measurements showed sleep stages.

        1. NREM-1 (non-Rapid Eye Movement sleep; brief, images like hallucinations; hypnagogic jerks)

        2. NREM-2 (harder to waken, sleep spindles)

        3. NREM-3 (DEEP sleep—hard to wake up! Long slow waves on EEG; bedwetting, night terrors, sleepwalking occurs here; asleep but not dead—can still hear, smell, etc. Will wake up for baby.)

        4. REM Sleep (Dreams…)

⌃ FIGURE 1

Sample class notes in outline form Here is a sample from a student's notes taken in outline form from a lecture on sleep.

Organize Your Space

Work at a desk or table, not on your bed or in a comfy chair that will tempt you to nap.

Minimize Distractions

Turn the TV off, put away your phone, and close distracting windows on your computer. If you must listen to music to mask outside noise, play soft instrumentals, not vocal selections that will draw your mind to the lyrics.

Ask Others to Honor Your Quiet Time

Tell roommates, family, and friends about your new schedule. Try to find a study place where you are least likely to be disturbed.

Set Specific, Realistic Daily Goals

The simple note "7–8 P.M.: Study Psychology" is too broad to be useful. Instead, break your studying into manageable tasks. For example, you will want to subdivide large reading assignments. If you aren't used to studying for long periods, start with relatively short periods of concentrated study, with breaks in between. In this text, for example, you might decide to read one major section before each break. Limit your breaks to 5 or 10 minutes to stretch or move around a bit.

Your attention span is a good indicator of whether you are pacing yourself successfully. At this early stage, it's important to remember that you're in training.

If your attention begins to wander, get up immediately and take a short break. It is better to study effectively for 15 minutes and then take a break than to fritter away 45 minutes out of your study hour. As your endurance develops, you can increase the length of study periods.

Use SQ3R to Help You Master This Text

David Myers and Nathan DeWall organized this text by using a system called SQ3R (Survey, Question, Read, Retrieve, Review). Using SQ3R can help you to understand what you read, and to retain that information longer.

You will hear more about SQ3R in Module 2.

Applying SQ3R may feel at first as though it's taking more time and effort to "read" a module, but with practice, these steps will become automatic.

Survey

Before you read a module, survey its key parts. Study the two-page opener at the beginning of each group of modules, which provides a sort of visual scaffolding for the key content to come. Note that text sections have numbered Learning Objective Questions to help you focus. Pay attention to headings, which indicate important subtopics, and to words set in bold type.

Surveying gives you the big picture of a module's content and organization. Understanding the module's logical sections will help you break your work into manageable pieces in your study sessions.

Question

As you survey, don't limit yourself to the numbered Learning Objective Questions that appear throughout the module. Jotting down additional questions of your own will cause you to look at the material in a new way. (You might, for example, scan this section's headings and ask "What does 'SQ3R' mean?") Information becomes easier to remember when you make it personally meaningful. Trying to answer your questions while reading will keep you in an active learning mode.

Read

As you read, keep your questions in mind and actively search for the answers. If you come to material that seems to answer an important question that you haven't jotted down, stop and write down that new question.

Be sure to read everything. Don't skip photo or art captions, graphs, boxes, tables, or quotes. An idea that seems vague when you read about it may become clear when you see it in a graph or table. Keep in mind that instructors sometimes base their test questions on figures and tables.

Retrieve

When you have found the answer to one of your questions, close your eyes and mentally recite the question and its answer. Then write the answer next to the question in your own words. Trying to explain something in your own words will help you figure out where there are gaps in your understanding. These kinds of opportunities to practice *retrieving* develop the skills you will need when you are taking exams. If you study without ever putting your book and notes aside, you may develop false confidence about what you know. With the material available, you may be able to recognize the correct answer to your questions. But will you be able to recall it later, when you take an exam without having your mental props in sight?

Test your understanding as often as you can. Testing yourself is part of successful learning, because the act of testing forces your brain to work at remembering, thus establishing the memory more permanently (so you can find it later for the

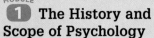

MODULE

1 The History and Scope of Psychology

1890

Critical Thinkers!

skeptical

humble

curious

Sample of Psychologists

Researcher

Clinical Psychologist

Instructor

MODULE

2 Research Strategies: How Psychologists Ask and Answer Questions

Experiment

Survey

Naturalistic Observation

Case Study

1 = Experimental group   2 = Control group

Are You Trying to Study Regularly for the First Time and Feeling Overwhelmed?

Perhaps you've set your initial goals too high. Remember, the point of time management is to identify a regular schedule that will help you achieve success. Like any skill, time management takes practice. Accept your limitations and revise your schedule to work slowly up to where you know you need to be—perhaps adding 15 minutes of study time per day.

* * *

I hope that these suggestions help make you more successful academically, and that they enhance the quality of your life in general. Having the necessary skills makes any job a lot easier and more pleasant. Let me repeat my warning not to attempt to make too drastic a change in your lifestyle immediately. Good habits require time and self-discipline to develop. Once established, they can last a lifetime.

→ REVIEW   Time Management: Or, How to Be a Great Student and Still Have a Life

1. **How Are You Using Your Time Now?**
   - Identify your areas of weakness.
   - Keep a time-use diary.
   - Record the time you actually spend on activities.
   - Record your energy levels to find your most productive times.

2. **Design a Better Schedule**
   - Decide on your goals for the term and for each week.
   - Enter class times, work times, social times (for family and friends), and time needed for other obligations and for practical activities.
   - Tailor study times to avoid interference and to meet each course's needs.

3. **Make Every Minute of Your Study Time Count**
   - Take careful class notes (in outline form) that will help you recall and rehearse material covered in lectures.
   - Try to eliminate distractions to your study time, and ask friends and family to help you focus on your work.
   - Set specific, realistic daily goals to help you focus on each day's tasks.
   - Use the SQ3R system (survey, question, read, retrieve, review) to master material covered in your text.
   - When you achieve your daily goals, reward yourself with something that you value.

4. **Do You Need to Revise Your New Schedule?**
   - Allocate extra study time for courses that are more difficult, and a little less time for courses that are easy for you.
   - Study your test results to help determine a more effective balance in your schedule.
   - Make sure your schedule is not too ambitious. Gradually establish a schedule that will be effective for the long term.

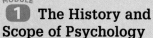

1890

Critical Thinkers!

skeptical
humble
curious

Sample of Psychologists

INTRODUCTORY
PSYCHOLOGY

Researcher

Clinical Psychologist

Instructor

MODULE
2 Research Strategies:
How Psychologists Ask
and Answer Questions

Experiment

Survey

Naturalistic Observation

1

2

Case
Study

1= Experimental group   2= Control group

If your attention begins to wander, get up immediately and take a short break. It is better to study effectively for 15 minutes and then take a break than to fritter away 45 minutes out of your study hour. As your endurance develops, you can increase the length of study periods.

Use SQ3R to Help You Master This Text

David Myers and Nathan DeWall organized this text by using a system called SQ3R (Survey, Question, Read, Retrieve, Review). Using SQ3R can help you to understand what you read, and to retain that information longer.

You will hear more about SQ3R in Module 2.

Applying SQ3R may feel at first as though it's taking more time and effort to "read" a module, but with practice, these steps will become automatic.

Survey

Before you read a module, survey its key parts. Study the two-page opener at the beginning of each group of modules, which provides a sort of visual scaffolding for the key content to come. Note that text sections have numbered Learning Objective Questions to help you focus. Pay attention to headings, which indicate important subtopics, and to words set in bold type.

Surveying gives you the big picture of a module's content and organization. Understanding the module's logical sections will help you break your work into manageable pieces in your study sessions.

Question

As you survey, don't limit yourself to the numbered Learning Objective Questions that appear throughout the module. Jotting down additional questions of your own will cause you to look at the material in a new way. (You might, for example, scan this section's headings and ask "What does 'SQ3R' mean?") Information becomes easier to remember when you make it personally meaningful. Trying to answer your questions while reading will keep you in an active learning mode.

Read

As you read, keep your questions in mind and actively search for the answers. If you come to material that seems to answer an important question that you haven't jotted down, stop and write down that new question.

Be sure to read everything. Don't skip photo or art captions, graphs, boxes, tables, or quotes. An idea that seems vague when you read about it may become clear when you see it in a graph or table. Keep in mind that instructors sometimes base their test questions on figures and tables.

Retrieve

When you have found the answer to one of your questions, close your eyes and mentally recite the question and its answer. Then write the answer next to the question in your own words. Trying to explain something in your own words will help you figure out where there are gaps in your understanding. These kinds of opportunities to practice *retrieving* develop the skills you will need when you are taking exams. If you study without ever putting your book and notes aside, you may develop false confidence about what you know. With the material available, you may be able to recognize the correct answer to your questions. But will you be able to recall it later, when you take an exam without having your mental props in sight?

Test your understanding as often as you can. Testing yourself is part of successful learning, because the act of testing forces your brain to work at remembering, thus establishing the memory more permanently (so you can find it later for the

exam!). Use the self-testing opportunities throughout each module, including the periodic Retrieve It items. Also take advantage of the self-testing that is available through LearningCurve and other quizzes in LaunchPad.

Review

After working your way through the module, read over your questions and your written answers. Take an extra few minutes to create a brief written summary covering all of your questions and answers. At the end of each module, you should take advantage of the important opportunities for self-testing and review—a list of that module's Learning Objective Questions for you to try answering before checking **Appendix D** (Complete Module Reviews), a list of that module's key terms for you to try to define before checking the referenced page, and the *Experience the Testing Effect* self-test questions (with answers in Appendix E).

Don't Forget About Rewards!

If you have trouble studying regularly, giving yourself a reward may help. What kind of reward works best? That depends on what you enjoy. You might start by making a list of 5 or 10 things that put a smile on your face. Spending time with a loved one, taking a walk or going for a bike ride, relaxing with a magazine or novel, or watching a favorite show can provide immediate rewards for achieving short-term study goals.

To motivate yourself when you're having trouble sticking to your schedule, allow yourself an immediate reward for completing a specific task. If running makes you smile, change your shoes, grab a friend, and head out the door! You deserve a reward for a job well done.

Do You Need to Revise Your New Schedule?

What if you've lived with your schedule for a few weeks, but you aren't making progress toward your academic and personal goals? What if your studying hasn't paid off in better grades? Don't despair and abandon your program, but do take a little time to figure out what's gone wrong.

Are You Doing Well in Some Courses But Not in Others?

Perhaps you need to shift your priorities a bit. You may need to allow more study time for chemistry, for example, and less time for some other course.

Have You Received a Poor Grade on a Test?

Did your grade fail to reflect the effort you spent preparing for the test? This can happen to even the hardest-working student, often on a first test with a new instructor. This common experience can be upsetting. "What do I have to do to get an A?" "The test was unfair!" "I studied the wrong material!"

Try to figure out what went wrong. Analyze the questions you missed, dividing them into two categories: class-based questions and text-based questions. How many questions did you miss in each category? If you find far more errors in one category than in the other, you'll have some clues to help you revise your schedule. Depending on the pattern you've found, you can add extra study time to review of class notes, or to studying the text.

Businessperson

Correlation

Length of marriage is **CORRELATED** with baldness. Does this mean length of marriage CAUSES baldness?

No!

2018

Thinking Critically With Psychological Science

HOPING to satisfy their curiosity about people and to relieve their own woes, millions turn to "psychology." They watch television shows aimed at helping people cope with their problems, overcome their addictions, and save their marriages. They read articles on psychic powers. They attend stop-smoking hypnosis seminars. They play online games hoping to strengthen their brain. They immerse themselves in self-help websites and books on the meaning of dreams, the path to true love, and the road to personal happiness.

Others, intrigued by claims of psychological truth, wonder: How—and how much—does parenting shape children's personalities and abilities? What factors affect our drive to achieve? Do dreams have deep meaning? Do we remember events that never happened? Does psychotherapy heal?

In working with such questions, how can we separate uninformed opinions from examined conclusions? *How can we best use psychology to understand why people think, feel, and act as they do?* In Module 1, we focus on the importance of scientific and critical thinking, trace psychology's roots, and survey the scope of this field. In Module 2, we consider how psychology's researchers put the scientific method into action to learn more about this fascinating field. ■

A smile is a smile the world around Throughout this book, you will see examples not only of our cultural and gender diversity but also of the similarities that define our shared human nature. People in different cultures vary in when and how often they smile, but a naturally happy smile *means* the same thing anywhere in the world.

To assist your active learning of psychology, numbered Learning Objectives, framed as questions, appear at the beginning of major sections. You can test your understanding by trying to answer the question before, and then again after, you read the section.

critical thinking thinking that does not blindly accept arguments and conclusions. Rather, it examines assumptions, appraises the source, discerns hidden biases, evaluates evidence, and assesses conclusions.

MODULE 1 The History and Scope of Psychology

According to portrayals in the news and popular media, psychologists seem to analyze personality, offer counseling, dispense child-raising advice, and testify in court. Do psychologists actually do these things? *Yes*—and much more. Consider some of psychology's questions, which may have also been yours:

- Have you ever found yourself reacting to something as one of your biological parents would—perhaps in a way you vowed you never would—and then wondered how much of your personality you inherited? *To what extent do genes predispose our individual personality differences? To what extent do home and community environments shape us?*

- Have you ever worried about how to act among people of a different culture, race, gender, or sexual orientation? *In what ways are we alike as members of the human family? How do we differ?*

- Have you ever awakened from a nightmare and, with a wave of relief, wondered why you had such a crazy dream? *How often, and why, do we dream?*

- Have you ever played peekaboo with a 6-month-old and wondered why the baby finds the game so delightful? *What do babies actually perceive and think?*

- Have you ever wondered what fosters school and work success? Are some people just born smarter? *Does sheer intelligence explain why some people get richer, think more creatively, or relate more sensitively?*

- Have you ever become depressed or anxious and wondered whether you'll ever feel "normal"? *What triggers our bad moods—and our good ones? What's the line between a normal mood swing and a psychological disorder?*

Psychology is a science that seeks to answer such questions.

The Scientific Attitude: Curious, Skeptical, and Humble

1-1 How do the scientific attitude's three main components relate to critical thinking?

Underlying all science is, first, a hard-headed curiosity, a passion to explore and understand without misleading or being misled. Some questions *(Is there life after death?)* are beyond science. Answering them in any way requires a leap of faith. With many other ideas *(Can some people demonstrate ESP?)*, the proof is in the pudding. Let the facts speak for themselves.

Magician and paranormal investigator James Randi has used this *empirical approach* when testing those claiming to see glowing auras around people's bodies:

Randi: *Do you see an aura around my head?*

Aura seer: *Yes, indeed.*

Randi: *Can you still see the aura if I put this magazine in front of my face?*

Aura seer: *Of course.*

Randi: *Then if I were to step behind a wall barely taller than I am, you could determine my location from the aura visible above my head, right?*

Randi once told me [DM] that no aura seer had yet agreed to take this simple test.

No matter how sensible-seeming or wild an idea, the smart thinker asks: *Does it work?* When put to the test, can its predictions be confirmed? Subjected to

such scrutiny, crazy-sounding ideas sometimes find support. More often, science becomes society's garbage disposal, sending crazy-sounding ideas to the waste heap, atop previous claims of perpetual motion machines, miracle cancer cures, and out-of-body travels into centuries past. To sift reality from fantasy, sense from nonsense, requires a scientific attitude: being skeptical but not cynical, open but not gullible.

"To believe with certainty," says a Polish proverb, "we must begin by doubting." As scientists, psychologists approach the world of behavior with a *curious skepticism*, persistently asking two questions: *What do you mean? How do you know?*

Putting a scientific attitude into practice requires not only curiosity and skepticism but also *humility*—awareness of our own vulnerability to error and openness to surprises and new perspectives. In the last analysis, what matters are the truths nature reveals in response to our questioning. If people or other animals don't behave as our ideas predict, then so much the worse for our ideas. This humble attitude was expressed in one of psychology's early mottos: "The rat is always right."

Historians of science tell us that these three attitudes—curiosity, skepticism, and humility—helped make modern science possible. Some deeply religious people may view science, including psychological science, as a threat. Yet many of the leaders of the scientific revolution, including Copernicus and Newton, were deeply religious people acting on the idea that "in order to love and honor God, it is necessary to fully appreciate the wonders of his handiwork" (Stark, 2003a,b).

Of course, scientists, like anyone else, can have big egos and may cling to their preconceptions. It's easy to get defensive when others challenge our cherished ideas. Nevertheless, the ideal of curious, skeptical, humble scrutiny of competing ideas unifies psychologists as a community as they check and recheck one another's findings and conclusions.

The Amazing Randi The magician James Randi exemplifies skepticism. He has tested and debunked supposed psychic phenomena.

"My deeply held belief is that if a god anything like the traditional sort exists, our curiosity and intelligence are provided by such a god. We would be unappreciative of those gifts . . . if we suppressed our passion to explore the universe and ourselves."

Carl Sagan, Broca's Brain, *1979*

THE IRRESISTIBLE FORCE MEETS THE IMMOVABLE OBJECT

THE FACTS AS THEY ARE

THE TRUTH AS I SEE IT

WILEY 5-16

Reprinted by permission of Universal Press Syndicate.
© 1997 Wiley.

Critical Thinking

The scientific attitude prepares us to think smarter. **Critical thinking** examines assumptions, appraises the source, discerns hidden biases, evaluates evidence, and assesses conclusions. Whether reading online commentary or listening to a conversation, critical thinkers ask questions: *How do they know that? What is this person's agenda? Is the conclusion based on a personal story and gut feelings, or on evidence? Does the evidence justify a cause-effect conclusion? What alternative explanations are possible?*

Critical inquiry can lead us to surprising findings. Other modules illustrate some examples from psychological science: Massive losses of brain tissue early in life may have minimal long-term effects. Within days, newborns can recognize their mother's odor. After brain damage, a person may be able to learn new skills yet be unaware of such learning. Diverse groups—men and women, old and young, rich and middle class, those with disabilities and without—report roughly comparable levels of personal happiness.

Throughout the text, important concepts are **boldfaced**. As you study, you can find these terms with their definitions in a nearby margin and in the Glossary at the end of the book.

From a Twitter feed:
"The problem with quotes on the Internet is that you never know if they're true."

Abraham Lincoln

Life after studying psychology
The study of psychology, and its critical thinking strategies, have helped prepare people for varied occupations, as illustrated by Facebook founder Mark Zuckerberg (who studied psychology and computer science at Harvard) and satirist Jon Stewart (a psych major at William and Mary).

Critical inquiry sometimes also debunks popular presumptions, as we may also see in other modules: Evidence indicates that sleepwalkers are *not* acting out their dreams. Our past experiences are *not* all recorded verbatim in our brains; with brain stimulation or hypnosis, one *cannot* simply "hit the replay button" and relive long-buried or repressed memories. Most people do *not* suffer from unrealistically low self-esteem, and high self-esteem is *not* all good. Opposites do *not* generally attract. In each of these instances and many others, what scientists have learned is not what is widely believed.

Paul Sakuma, File/AP Photo

Brad Barket/AP Photo

Psychology's critical inquiry can also identify effective policies. To deter crime, should we invest money in lengthening prison sentences or increase the likelihood of arrest? To help people recover from a trauma, should counselors help them relive it, or not? To increase voting, should we tell people about the low turnout problem, or emphasize that their peers are voting? When put to critical thinking's test—and contrary to common practice—the second option in each case wins (Shafir, 2013).

Throughout the book, information sources are cited in parentheses, with researchers' names and the date the research was published. Every citation can be found in the end-of-book References section, with complete documentation that follows American Psychological Association (APA) style.

Study Tip: Memory research reveals a *testing effect:* We retain information much better if we actively retrieve it by self-testing and rehearsing. To bolster your learning and memory, take advantage of the Retrieve It opportunities you'll find throughout this text.

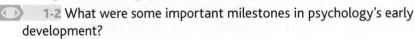

RETRIEVE IT   [✱]

● "For a lot of bad ideas, science is society's garbage disposal." Describe what this tells us about the scientific attitude and what's involved in critical thinking.

ANSWER: Many ideas and questions may be scrutinized scientifically, and the bad ones end up discarded as a result. Scientific thinking combines (1) *curiosity* about the world around us, (2) *skepticism* about unproven claims and ideas, and (3) *humility* about one's own understanding. This process leads us to evaluate evidence, assess conclusions, and examine our own assumptions, which are essential parts of critical thinking.

Psychology's Roots

1-2 What were some important milestones in psychology's early development?

To be human is to be curious about ourselves and the world around us. Before 300 B.C.E., the Greek philosopher Aristotle theorized about learning and memory, motivation and emotion, perception and personality. Today we chuckle at some of his guesses, like his suggestion that the source of our personality is the heart. But credit Aristotle with asking the right questions.

Psychological Science Is Born

PSYCHOLOGY'S FIRST LABORATORY Philosophers' thinking about thinking continued until the birth of psychology on a December day in 1879, in a small,

third-floor room at Germany's University of Leipzig. There, two young men were helping an austere, middle-aged professor, Wilhelm Wundt, create an experimental apparatus. Their machine measured the time it took for people to press a telegraph key after hearing a ball hit a platform (Hunt, 1993). Curiously, people responded in about one-tenth of a second when asked to press the key as soon as the sound occurred—and in about two-tenths of a second when asked to press the key as soon as they were consciously aware of perceiving the sound. (To be aware of one's awareness takes a little longer.) Wundt was seeking to measure "atoms of the mind"—the fastest and simplest mental processes. So began the first psychological laboratory, staffed by Wundt and by psychology's first graduate students.

PSYCHOLOGY'S FIRST SCHOOLS OF THOUGHT Before long, this new science of psychology became organized into different branches, or schools of thought, each promoted by pioneering thinkers. Two early schools were **structuralism** and **functionalism**. As physicists and chemists discerned the structure of matter, so psychologist Edward Bradford Titchener aimed to discover the mind's structure. He engaged people in self-reflective *introspection* (looking inward), training them to report elements of their experience as they looked at a rose, listened to a metronome, smelled a scent, or tasted a substance. What were their immediate sensations, their images, their feelings? And how did these relate to one another? Alas, introspection proved somewhat unreliable. It required smart, verbal people, and its results varied from person to person and experience to experience. As introspection waned, so did structuralism. Hoping to assemble the mind's structure from simple elements was rather like trying to understand a car by examining its disconnected parts.

Wilhelm Wundt Wundt established the first psychology laboratory at the University of Leipzig, Germany.

Philosopher-psychologist William James thought it would be more fruitful to consider the evolved *functions* of our thoughts and feelings. Smelling is what the nose does; thinking is what the brain does. But *why* do the nose and brain do these things? Under the influence of evolutionary theorist Charles Darwin, James assumed that thinking, like smelling, developed because it was *adaptive*—it contributed to our ancestors' survival. Consciousness serves a function. It enables us to consider our past, adjust to our present, and plan our future. To explore the mind's adaptive functions, James studied down-to-earth emotions, memories, willpower, habits, and moment-to-moment streams of consciousness.

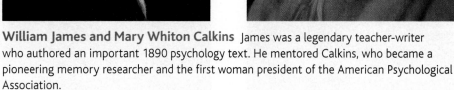

William James and Mary Whiton Calkins James was a legendary teacher-writer who authored an important 1890 psychology text. He mentored Calkins, who became a pioneering memory researcher and the first woman president of the American Psychological Association.

PSYCHOLOGY'S FIRST WOMEN As these names illustrate, the early pioneers of most fields, including psychology, were predominantly men. In 1890—thirty years before American women had the right to vote—James admitted Mary Whiton Calkins into his graduate seminar over the objections of Harvard's president (Scarborough & Furumoto, 1987). When Calkins joined, the other students (all men) dropped out. So James tutored her alone. Later, she finished all of Harvard's Ph.D. requirements, outscoring all the male students on the qualifying exams. Alas, Harvard denied her the degree she had earned, offering her instead a degree from Radcliffe College, its undergraduate "sister" school for women. Calkins resisted the unequal treatment and refused the degree. She nevertheless

structuralism early school of thought promoted by Wundt and Titchener; used introspection to reveal the structure of the human mind.

functionalism early school of thought promoted by James and influenced by Darwin; explored how mental and behavioral processes function—how they enable the organism to adapt, survive, and flourish.

Margaret Floy Washburn The first woman to receive a psychology Ph.D., Washburn synthesized animal behavior research in *The Animal Mind* (1908).

went on to become a distinguished memory researcher and the American Psychological Association's (APA's) first female president in 1905.

The honor of being the first official female psychology Ph.D. later fell to Margaret Floy Washburn, who also wrote an influential book, *The Animal Mind,* and became the APA's second female president in 1921. But Washburn's gender barred doors for her, too. Although her thesis was the first foreign study Wundt published in his psychology journal, she could not join the all-male organization of experimental psychologists founded by Titchener, her own graduate adviser (Johnson, 1997).

RETRIEVE IT [✖]

• What event defined the start of scientific psychology?

ANSWER: Scientific psychology began in Germany in 1879 when Wilhelm Wundt opened the first psychology laboratory.

• Why did introspection fail as a method for understanding how the mind works?

ANSWER: People's self-reports varied, depending on the experience and the person's intelligence and verbal ability.

• The school of _____ used introspection to define the mind's makeup; _____ focused on how mental processes enable us to adapt, survive, and flourish.

ANSWER: structuralism; functionalism

Psychological Science Develops

1-3 How did psychology continue to develop from the 1920s through today?

In psychology's early days, many psychologists shared with English essayist C. S. Lewis the view that "there is one thing, and only one in the whole universe which we know more about than we could learn from external observation." That one thing, Lewis said, is ourselves: "We have, so to speak, inside information" (1960, pp. 18–19). Wundt and Titchener focused on inner sensations, images, and feelings. James also engaged in introspective examination of the stream of consciousness and emotion. For these and other early pioneers, *psychology* was defined as "the science of mental life."

That definition endured until the 1920s, when the first of two provocative American psychologists appeared on the scene.

BEHAVIORISM John B. Watson, and later B. F. Skinner, dismissed introspection and redefined *psychology* as "the scientific study of observable behavior." You cannot observe a sensation, a feeling, or a thought, they said. But you can observe and record people's *behavior* as they are *conditioned*—responding to and learning in different situations. Many agreed, and **behaviorism** became one of psychology's two major forces well into the 1960s.

FREUDIAN PSYCHOLOGY The second major force was *Freudian psychology,* which emphasized the ways our unconscious thought processes and emotional responses to childhood experiences affect our behavior. (In other modules, we'll look more closely at Sigmund Freud's ideas.)

John B. Watson and Rosalie Rayner Working with Rayner, Watson championed psychology as the scientific study of behavior. In a controversial study, he and Rayner showed that fear could be learned, in experiments on a baby who became famous as "Little Albert."

HUMANISTIC PSYCHOLOGY As the behaviorists had rejected the early-twentieth-century definition of *psychology,* other groups rejected the behaviorists' definition in the 1960s. The **humanistic psychologists,** led by Carl Rogers and Abraham Maslow, found both Freudian psychology and behaviorism too limiting. Rather than focusing on the meaning of early childhood memories or the learning of conditioned responses, the humanistic psychologists drew attention to ways that current environmental influences can nurture or limit our growth potential, and to the importance of having our needs for love and acceptance satisfied.

MODERN DEFINITION OF PSYCHOLOGY Today's psychology builds upon the work of these earlier scientists and their schools of thought. To encompass psychology's concern with observable behavior and with inner thoughts and feelings, today we define **psychology** as the *science of behavior and mental processes.* Let's unpack this definition. *Behavior* is anything an organism *does*—any action we can observe and record. Yelling, smiling, blinking, sweating, talking, and questionnaire marking are all observable behaviors. *Mental processes* are the internal, subjective experiences we infer from behavior—sensations, perceptions, dreams, thoughts, beliefs, and feelings.

The key word in psychology's definition is *science.* Psychology is less a set of findings than a way of asking and answering questions. Our aim, then, is not merely to report results but also to show you how psychologists play their game. You will see how researchers evaluate conflicting opinions and ideas. And you will learn how all of us, whether scientists or simply curious people, can think smarter when experiencing and explaining the events of our lives.

B. F. Skinner This leading behaviorist rejected introspection and studied how consequences shape behavior.

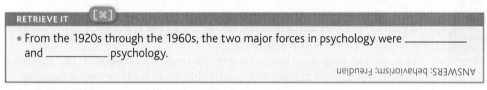

RETRIEVE IT [✱]

- From the 1920s through the 1960s, the two major forces in psychology were _____ and _____ psychology.

ANSWERS: behaviorism; Freudian

Contemporary Psychology

👁 **1-4** How has our understanding of biology and experience, culture and gender, and human flourishing shaped contemporary psychology?

Psychology's roots lie in many disciplines and countries. The young science of psychology developed from the more established fields of philosophy and biology. Wundt was both a philosopher and a physiologist. Ivan Pavlov, who pioneered the study of learning, was a Russian physiologist. Freud was an Austrian physician. Jean Piaget, the last century's most influential observer of children, was a Swiss biologist. James was an American philosopher. This list of pioneering psychologists—"Magellans of the mind," as science writer Morton Hunt (1993) has called them—illustrates the diversity of psychology's origins.

Like the pioneers, today's psychologists are citizens of many lands. The International Union of Psychological Science has 82 member nations, from Albania to Zimbabwe. Psychology is *growing* and it is *globalizing.* The story of psychology is being written in many places, with interests ranging from nerve cell activity to international conflicts.

The Cognitive Revolution

Psychologists in the 1960s pioneered a *"cognitive revolution,"* leading the field back to its early interest in mental processes. *Cognitive psychology* today continues its scientific exploration of how we perceive, process, and remember information, and the cognitive roots of anxiety, depression, and other psychological

Sigmund Freud The controversial ideas of this famed personality theorist and therapist have influenced humanity's self-understanding.

behaviorism the view that psychology (1) should be an objective science that (2) studies behavior without reference to mental processes. Most psychologists today agree with (1) but not with (2).

humanistic psychology historically significant perspective that emphasized human growth potential.

psychology the science of behavior and mental processes.

A nature-made nature–nurture experiment Because identical twins have the same genes, they are ideal participants in studies designed to shed light on hereditary and environmental influences on intelligence, personality, and other traits. Studies of identical and fraternal twins provide a rich array of findings—described in other modules— that underscore the importance of both nature and nurture.

disorders. **Cognitive neuroscience** was birthed by the marriage of cognitive psychology (the science of mind) and neuroscience (the science of brain). This interdisciplinary field studies the brain activity underlying mental activity.

Evolutionary Psychology and Behavior Genetics

Are our human traits present at birth, or do they develop through experience? The debate over this huge **nature–nurture issue** is ancient. Greek philosopher Plato (428–348 B.C.E.) assumed that we inherit character and intelligence and that certain ideas are inborn. Aristotle (384–322 B.C.E.) countered that there is nothing in the mind that does not first come in from the external world through the senses.

More insight into nature's influence on behavior arose after a 22-year-old seafaring voyager, Charles Darwin, pondered the incredible species variation he encountered, including tortoises on one island that differed from those on nearby islands. His 1859 *On the Origin of Species* explained this diversity by proposing the evolutionary process of **natural selection:** From among chance variations, nature selects traits that best enable an organism to survive and reproduce in a particular environment. Darwin's principle of natural selection is still with us 150+ years later as biology's organizing principle, and now an important principle for twenty-first-century psychology. This would surely have pleased Darwin, who believed his theory explained not only animal structures (such as a polar bear's white coat) but also animal behaviors (such as the emotional expressions associated with human lust and rage).

The nature–nurture issue recurs throughout this text as today's psychologists explore the relative contributions of biology and experience. They ask, for example, how are we humans alike because of our common biology and evolutionary history? That's the focus of **evolutionary psychology.** And how are we diverse because of our differing genes and environments? That's the focus of **behavior genetics.** Are gender differences biologically predisposed or socially constructed? Is children's grammar mostly innate or formed by experience? How are intelligence and personality differences influenced by heredity, and by environment? Are sexual behaviors more "pushed" by inner biology or "pulled" by external incentives? Should we treat psychological disorders—depression, for example—as disorders of the brain, disorders of thought, or both?

Over and over again we will see that in contemporary science, the nature–nurture tension dissolves: *Nurture works on what nature endows.* Our species is biologically endowed with an enormous capacity to learn and adapt. Moreover, every psychological event (every thought, every emotion) is simultaneously a biological event. Thus, depression can be both a brain disorder and a thought disorder.

cognitive neuroscience the interdisciplinary study of the brain activity linked with cognition (including perception, thinking, memory, and language).

nature–nurture issue the longstanding controversy over the relative contributions that genes and experience make to the development of psychological traits and behaviors. Today's science sees traits and behaviors arising from the interaction of nature and nurture.

RETRIEVE IT   [✴]

• How did the cognitive revolution affect the field of psychology?

ANSWER: It recaptured the field's early interest in mental processes and made them legitimate topics for scientific study.

• What is natural selection?

ANSWER: This is the process by which nature selects from chance variations the traits that best enable an organism to survive and reproduce in a particular environment.

• What is contemporary psychology's position on the nature–nurture issue?

ANSWER: Psychological events often stem from the interaction of nature and nurture, rather than from either of them acting alone.

Cross-Cultural and Gender Psychology

What can we learn about people in general from psychological studies done in one time and place—often with participants from what some psychologists (Henrich et al., 2010) call the WEIRD cultures (*W*estern, *E*ducated, *I*ndustrialized, *R*ich, and *D*emocratic)? As we will see time and again, **culture**—shared ideas and behaviors that one generation passes on to the next—matters. Our culture shapes our standards of promptness and frankness, our attitudes toward premarital sex and varying body shapes, our tendency to be casual or formal, our willingness to make eye contact, our conversational distance, and much, much more. Being aware of such differences, we can restrain our assumptions that others will think and act as we do.

It is also true, however, that our shared biological heritage unites us as a universal human family. The same underlying processes guide people everywhere. Some examples:

- People with specific learning disorder (formerly called dyslexia) exhibit the same brain malfunction whether they are Italian, French, or British (Paulesu et al., 2001).

- Variation in languages may impede communication across cultures. Yet all languages share deep principles of grammar, and people from opposite hemispheres can communicate with a smile or a frown.

- People in different cultures vary in feelings of loneliness (Lykes & Kemmelmeier, 2014). But across cultures, loneliness is magnified by shyness, low self-esteem, and being unmarried (Jones et al., 1985; Rokach et al., 2002).

We are each in certain respects like all others, like some others, and like no other. Studying people of all races and cultures helps us discern our similarities and our differences, our human kinship and our diversity.

You will see throughout this book that *gender* matters, too. Researchers report gender differences in what we dream, in how we express and detect emotions, and in our risk for alcohol use disorder, depression, and eating disorders. Gender differences fascinate us, and studying them is potentially beneficial. For example, many researchers have observed that women carry on conversations more readily to build relationships, while men talk more to give information and advice (Tannen, 2001). Knowing this difference can help us prevent conflicts and misunderstandings in everyday interactions.

But again, psychologically as well as biologically, women and men are overwhelmingly similar. Whether female or male, we learn to walk at about the same age. We experience the same sensations of light and sound. We remember vivid emotional events and forget mundane details. We feel the same pangs of hunger, desire, and fear. We exhibit similar overall intelligence and well-being.

The point to remember: Even when specific attitudes

natural selection the principle that those chance inherited traits that better enable an organism to survive and reproduce in a particular environment will most likely be passed on to succeeding generations.

evolutionary psychology the study of the evolution of behavior and the mind, using principles of natural selection.

behavior genetics the study of the relative power and limits of genetic and environmental influences on behavior.

culture the enduring behaviors, ideas, attitudes, values, and traditions shared by a group of people and transmitted from one generation to the next.

"All people are the same; only their habits differ."

Confucius, 551–479 B.C.E.

Culture and kissing Kissing crosses cultures. Yet how we do it varies. Imagine yourself kissing someone on the lips. Do you tilt your head right or left? In Western cultures, in which people read from left to right, about two-thirds of couples kiss right, as in William and Kate's famous kiss, and in Auguste Rodin's sculpture, *The Kiss*. In one study, 77 percent of Hebrew- and Arabic-language right-to-left readers kissed tilting left (Shaki, 2013).

© Hemis/Alamy

Mark Cuthbert/UK Press Getty Images

and behaviors vary by gender or across cultures, as they often do, the underlying processes are much the same.

Positive Psychology

Psychology's first hundred years focused on understanding and treating troubles, such as abuse and anxiety, depression and disease, prejudice and poverty. Much of today's psychology continues the exploration of such challenges. Without slighting the need to repair damage and cure disease, Martin Seligman and others (2002, 2005, 2011) have called for more research on *human flourishing.* These psychologists call their approach **positive psychology.** They believe that happiness is a by-product of a pleasant, engaged, and meaningful life. Thus, positive psychology uses scientific methods to explore the building of a "good life" that engages our skills, and a "meaningful life" that points beyond ourselves.

Psychology's Three Main Levels of Analysis

◉   **1-5** What are psychology's levels of analysis and related perspectives?

Each of us is a complex system that is part of a larger social system. But each of us is also composed of smaller systems, such as our nervous system and body organs, which are composed of still smaller systems—cells, molecules, and atoms.

These tiered systems suggest different **levels of analysis,** which offer complementary outlooks. It's like explaining horrific school shootings. Is it because the shooters have brain disorders or genetic tendencies that cause them to be violent? Because they have been rewarded for violent behavior? Because they live in a gun-promoting society that accepts violence? Such perspectives are complementary because "everything is related to everything else" (Brewer, 1996). Together, different levels of analysis form a **biopsychosocial approach,** which integrates biological, psychological, and social-cultural factors (**FIGURE 1.1**).

Each level provides a valuable playing card in psychology's explanatory deck. It's a vantage point for viewing a behavior or mental process, yet each by itself is incomplete. Like different academic disciplines, psychology's varied perspectives ask different questions and have their own limits. The different perspectives

⌄ FIGURE 1.1

Biopsychosocial approach This integrated viewpoint incorporates various levels of analysis and offers a more complete picture of any given behavior or mental process.

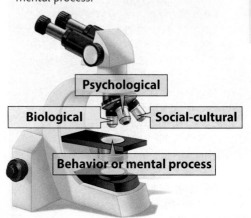

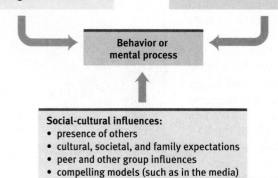

Biological influences:
• genetic predispositions (genetically influenced traits)
• genetic mutations
• natural selection of adaptive traits and behaviors passed down through generations
• genes responding to the environment

Psychological influences:
• learned fears and other learned expectations
• emotional responses
• cognitive processing and perceptual interpretations

Behavior or mental process

Social-cultural influences:
• presence of others
• cultural, societal, and family expectations
• peer and other group influences
• compelling models (such as in the media)

∨ TABLE 1.1

Psychology's Current Perspectives

Perspective	Focus	Sample Questions	Examples of Subfields Using This Perspective
Neuroscience	How the body and brain enable emotions, memories, and sensory experiences	How do pain messages travel from the hand to the brain? How is blood chemistry linked with moods and motives?	Biological; cognitive; clinical
Evolutionary	How the natural selection of traits has promoted the survival of genes	How does evolution influence behavior tendencies?	Biological; developmental; social
Behavior genetics	How our genes and our environment influence our individual differences	To what extent are psychological traits such as intelligence, personality, sexual orientation, and vulnerability to depression products of our genes? Of our environment?	Personality; developmental; legal/forensic
Psychodynamic	How behavior springs from unconscious drives and conflicts	How can someone's personality traits and disorders be explained by unfulfilled wishes and childhood traumas?	Clinical; counseling; personality
Behavioral	How we learn observable responses	How do we learn to fear particular objects or situations? What is the most effective way to alter our behavior, say, to lose weight or stop smoking?	Clinical; counseling; industrial-organizational
Cognitive	How we encode, process, store, and retrieve information	How do we use information in remembering? Reasoning? Solving problems?	Cognitive neuroscience; clinical; counseling; industrial-organizational
Social-cultural	How behavior and thinking vary across situations and cultures	How are we alike as members of one human family? How do we differ as products of our environment?	Developmental; social; clinical; counseling

described in **TABLE 1.1** complement one another. Consider, for example, how they shed light on anger:

JUERGEN SCHWARZ/AFP/Getty Images

- Someone working from the *neuroscience perspective* might study brain circuits that cause us to be red in the face and "hot under the collar."

- Someone working from the *evolutionary perspective* might analyze how anger facilitated the survival of our ancestors' genes.

- Someone working from a *behavior genetics perspective* might study how heredity and experience influence our individual differences in temperament.

- Someone working from the *psychodynamic perspective* might view an outburst as an outlet for unconscious hostility.

- Someone working from the *behavioral perspective* might attempt to determine what triggers angry responses or aggressive acts.

- Someone working from the *cognitive perspective* might study how our interpretation of a situation affects our anger and how our anger affects our thinking.

- Someone working from the *social-cultural perspective* might explore how expressions of anger vary across cultural contexts.

The point to remember: Like two-dimensional views of a three-dimensional object, each of psychology's perspectives is helpful. But each by itself fails to reveal the whole picture.

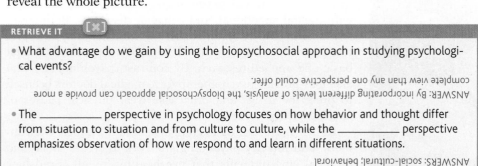

RETRIEVE IT [✱]

- What advantage do we gain by using the biopsychosocial approach in studying psychological events?

ANSWER: By incorporating different levels of analysis, the biopsychosocial approach can provide a more complete view than any one perspective could offer.

- The _____ perspective in psychology focuses on how behavior and thought differ from situation to situation and from culture to culture, while the _____ perspective emphasizes observation of how we respond to and learn in different situations.

ANSWERS: social-cultural; behavioral

positive psychology the scientific study of human functioning, with the goals of discovering and promoting strengths and virtues that help individuals and communities to thrive.

levels of analysis the differing complementary views, from biological to psychological to social-cultural, for analyzing any given phenomenon.

biopsychosocial approach an integrated approach that incorporates biological, psychological, and social-cultural levels of analysis.

"I'm a social scientist, Michael. That means I can't explain electricity or anything like that, but if you ever want to know about people I'm your man."

basic research pure science that aims to increase the scientific knowledge base.

applied research scientific study that aims to solve practical problems.

counseling psychology a branch of psychology that assists people with problems in living (often related to school, work, or marriage) and in achieving greater well-being.

clinical psychology a branch of psychology that studies, assesses, and treats people with psychological disorders.

Psychology in court Forensic psychologists apply psychology's principles and methods in the criminal justice system. They may assess witness credibility, or testify in court on a defendant's state of mind and future risk.

Psychology's Subfields

1-6 What are psychology's main subfields?

Picturing a chemist at work, you probably envision a scientist in a laboratory, surrounded by test tubes and high-tech equipment. Picture a psychologist at work and you would be right to envision

- a white-coated scientist probing a rat's brain.
- an intelligence researcher measuring how quickly an infant shows boredom by looking away from a familiar picture.
- an executive evaluating a new "healthy lifestyles" training program for employees.
- a researcher at a computer analyzing "big data" from Twitter or Facebook status updates.
- a therapist listening carefully to a depressed client's thoughts.
- a traveler visiting another culture and collecting data on variations in human values and behaviors.
- a teacher or writer sharing the joy of psychology with others.

The cluster of subfields we call psychology is a meeting ground for different disciplines. Thus, it's a perfect home for those with wide-ranging interests. In its diverse activities, from biological experimentation to cultural comparisons, psychology is united by a common quest: *describing and explaining behavior and the mind underlying it.*

Some psychologists conduct **basic research** that builds psychology's knowledge base. We will meet a wide variety of such researchers, including *biological psychologists* exploring the links between brain and mind; *developmental psychologists* studying our changing abilities from womb to tomb; *cognitive psychologists* experimenting with how we perceive, think, and solve problems; *personality psychologists* investigating our persistent traits; and *social psychologists* exploring how we view and affect one another.

These and other psychologists also may conduct **applied research,** tackling practical problems. *Industrial-organizational psychologists*, for example, use psychology's concepts and methods in the workplace to help organizations and companies select and train employees, boost morale and productivity, design products, and implement systems.

Although most psychology textbooks focus on psychological science, psychology is also a helping profession devoted to such practical issues as how to have a happy marriage, how to overcome anxiety or depression, and how to raise thriving children. As a science, psychology at its best bases such interventions on *evidence of effectiveness.* **Counseling psychologists** help people to cope with challenges and crises (including academic, vocational, and marital issues) and to improve their personal and social functioning. **Clinical psychologists** assess and treat people with mental, emotional, and behavior disorders. Both counseling and clinical psychologists administer and interpret tests, provide counseling and therapy, and sometimes conduct basic and applied research. By contrast, **psychiatrists,** who also may provide psychotherapy, are medical doctors licensed to prescribe drugs and otherwise treat physical causes of psychological disorders.

Rather than seeking to change people to fit their environment, **community psychologists** work to create social and physical environments that are healthy for all (Bradshaw

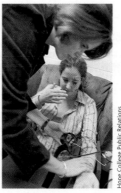

Psychology: A science and a profession Psychologists experiment with, observe, test, and modify behavior. Here we see psychologists doing face-to-face therapy, measuring emotion-related physiology, and testing a child.

et al., 2009; Trickett, 2009). To prevent bullying, for example, they might study how the school and neighborhood foster bullying and how to increase bystander intervention (Polanin et al., 2012).

With perspectives ranging from the biological to the social, and with settings ranging from the laboratory to the clinic to the office, psychology relates to many fields. Psychologists teach not only in psychology departments, but also in medical schools, business schools, law schools, and theological seminaries, and they work in hospitals, factories, and corporate offices. They engage in interdisciplinary studies, such as psychohistory (the study of people's historical motivations), psycholinguistics (the study of language and thinking), and psychoceramics (the study of crackpots).[1]

Psychology also influences culture. And psychology deepens our appreciation for how we humans perceive, think, feel, and act. By so doing it can indeed enrich our lives and enlarge our vision. Through this book we hope to help guide you toward that end. As educator Charles Eliot said a century ago: "Books are the quietest and most constant of friends, and the most patient of teachers."

LaunchPad Want to learn more? See Appendix C, Subfields of Psychology, at the end of this book, and go to LaunchPad's regularly updated **CAREERS IN PSYCHOLOGY** resource to learn about the many interesting options available to those with bachelor's, master's, and doctoral degrees in psychology.

psychiatry a branch of medicine dealing with psychological disorders; practiced by physicians who sometimes provide medical (for example, drug) treatments as well as psychological therapy.

community psychology a branch of psychology that studies how people interact with their social environments and how social institutions affect individuals and groups.

RETRIEVE IT [✱]

• Match the specialty on the left with the description on the right.

1. Clinical psychology | a. Helps people cope with life challenges, such as issues at school, at work, or in relationships.
2. Psychiatry | b. Studies, assesses, and treats people with psychological disorders but usually does not provide medical therapy.
3. Counseling psychology | c. Branch of medicine dealing with psychological disorders.

ANSWERS: 1. b, 2. c, 3. a

MODULE 1 REVIEW The History and Scope of Psychology

Learning Objectives

Test Yourself by taking a moment to answer each of these Learning Objective Questions (repeated here from within the module). Then turn to Appendix D, Complete Module Reviews, to check your answers. Research suggests that trying to answer these questions on your own will improve your long-term memory of the concepts (McDaniel et al., 2009).

1-1 How do the scientific attitude's three main components relate to critical thinking?

1-2 What were some important milestones in psychology's early development?

1-3 How did psychology continue to develop from the 1920s through today?

1-4 How has our understanding of biology and experience, culture and gender, and human flourishing shaped contemporary psychology?

1-5 What are psychology's levels of analysis and related perspectives?

1-6 What are psychology's main subfields?

1. Confession: I [DM] wrote the last part of this sentence on April Fool's Day.

■·[··] Terms and Concepts to Remember

Test yourself on these terms by trying to write down the definition in your own words before flipping back to the referenced page to check your answers.

critical thinking, p. 3
structuralism, p. 5
functionalism, p. 5
behaviorism, p. 6
humanistic psychology, p. 7

psychology, p. 7
cognitive neuroscience, p. 8
nature–nurture issue, p. 8
natural selection, p. 8
evolutionary psychology, p. 8
behavior genetics, p. 8
culture, p. 9
positive psychology, p. 10

levels of analysis, p. 10
biopsychosocial approach, p. 10
basic research, p. 12
applied research, p. 12
counseling psychology, p. 12
clinical psychology, p. 12
psychiatry, p. 12
community psychology, p. 12

[×] Experience the Testing Effect

Test yourself repeatedly throughout your studies. This will not only help you figure out what you know and don't know; the testing itself will help you learn and remember the information more effectively thanks to the *testing effect*.

1. In 1879, in psychology's first experiment, _____ and his students measured the time lag between hearing a ball hit a platform and pressing a key.

2. William James would be considered a(n) _____. Wilhelm Wundt and Edward Titchener would be considered _____.
   a. functionalist; structuralists
   b. structuralist; functionalists
   c. evolutionary theorist; structuralists
   d. functionalist; evolutionary theorists

3. In the early twentieth century, _____ redefined psychology as "the science of observable behavior."
   a. John B. Watson   c. William James
   b. Abraham Maslow   d. Sigmund Freud

4. Nature is to nurture as
   a. personality is to intelligence.
   b. biology is to experience.

c. intelligence is to biology.
d. psychological traits are to behaviors.

5. "Nurture works on what nature endows." Describe what this means, using your own words.

6. A psychologist treating emotionally troubled adolescents at a local mental health agency is most likely to be a(n)
   a. research psychologist.
   b. psychiatrist.
   c. industrial-organizational psychologist.
   d. clinical psychologist.

7. A mental health professional with a medical degree who can prescribe medication is a _____.

8. A psychologist conducting basic research to expand psychology's knowledge base would be most likely to
   a. design a computer screen with limited glare and assess the effect on computer operators' eyes after a day's work.
   b. treat older people who are overcome by depression.
   c. observe 3- and 6-year-olds solving puzzles and analyze differences in their abilities.
   d. interview children with behavioral problems and suggest treatments.

Find answers to these questions in Appendix E, in the back of the book.

Use ♨ LearningCurve to create your personalized study plan, which will direct you to the resources that will help you most in ♨ LaunchPad.

---

^{MODULE}
2 Research Strategies: How Psychologists Ask and Answer Questions

Although in some ways we outsmart the smartest computers, our intuition often goes awry. To err is human. Enter psychological science. With its procedures for gathering and sifting evidence, science restrains error. As we familiarize ourselves

with psychology's strategies and incorporate its underlying principles into our daily thinking, we can think smarter. *Psychologists use the science of behavior and mental processes to better understand why people think, feel, and act as they do.*

The Need for Psychological Science

What About Intuition and Common Sense?

👁 **2-1** How does our everyday thinking sometimes lead us to a wrong conclusion?

Some people suppose that psychology merely documents and dresses in jargon what people already know: "You get paid for using fancy methods to prove what my grandmother knows?" Others place their faith in human **intuition**: "Buried deep within each and every one of us, there is an instinctive, heart-felt awareness that provides—if we allow it to—the most reliable guide," offered Prince Charles (2000). Today's psychological science does document a vast intuitive mind. As we will see, our thinking, memory, and attitudes operate on two levels—conscious and unconscious—with the larger part operating off-screen, automatically. Like jumbo jets, we fly mostly on autopilot.

So, are we smart to listen to the whispers of our inner wisdom, to simply trust "the force within"? Or should we more often be subjecting our intuitive hunches to skeptical scrutiny?

This much seems certain: We often underestimate intuition's perils. My [DM's] geographical intuition tells me that Reno is east of Los Angeles, that Rome is south of New York, that Atlanta is east of Detroit. But I am wrong, wrong, and wrong. As novelist Madeleine L'Engle observed, "The naked intellect is an extraordinarily inaccurate instrument" (1973). Three phenomena—*hindsight bias, overconfidence,* and our *tendency to perceive patterns in random events*—illustrate why we cannot rely solely on intuition and common sense.

DID WE KNOW IT ALL ALONG? HINDSIGHT BIAS Consider how easy it is to draw the bull's-eye *after* the arrow strikes. As we often say, "Hindsight is 20/20." After the stock market drops, people say it was "due for a correction." After the football game, we credit the coach if a "gutsy play" wins the game, and fault the coach for the "stupid play" if it doesn't. After a war or an election, its outcome usually seems obvious. Although history may therefore seem like a series of inevitable events, the actual future is seldom foreseen. No one's diary recorded, "Today the Hundred Years War began."

This **hindsight bias** (also known as the *I-knew-it-all-along phenomenon*) is easy to demonstrate: Give half the members of a group some purported psychological finding, and give the other half an opposite result. Tell the first group, "Psychologists have found that separation weakens romantic attraction. As the saying goes, 'Out of sight, out of mind.'" Ask them to imagine why this might be true. Most people can, and nearly all will then view this true finding as unsurprising.

Tell the second group the opposite: "Psychologists have found that separation strengthens romantic attraction. As the saying goes, 'Absence makes the heart grow fonder.'" People given this untrue result can also easily imagine it, and most will also see it as unsurprising. When opposite findings both seem like common sense, there is a problem.

Such errors in our recollections and explanations show why we need psychological research. Just asking people how and why they felt or acted as they did can sometimes be misleading—not because common sense is usually wrong, but because common sense better describes what *has* happened than what *will* happen.

More than 800 scholarly papers have shown hindsight bias in people young and old from across the world (Roese & Vohs, 2012). Nevertheless, Grandma's intuition is often right. As Yogi Berra once said, "You can observe a

The limits of intuition Personnel interviewers tend to be overconfident of their gut feelings about job applicants. Their confidence stems partly from their recalling cases where their favorable impression proved right, and partly from their ignorance about rejected applicants who succeeded elsewhere.

"Those who trust in their own wits are fools."

Proverbs 28:26

"Life is lived forwards, but understood backwards."

Philosopher Søren Kierkegaard, 1813–1855

"Anything seems commonplace, once explained."

Dr. Watson to Sherlock Holmes

intuition an effortless, immediate, automatic feeling or thought, as contrasted with explicit, conscious reasoning.

hindsight bias the tendency to believe, after learning an outcome, that one would have foreseen it. (Also known as the *I-knew-it-all-along phenomenon*.)

REUTERS/U.S. Coast Guard/Handout

Hindsight bias When drilling its Deepwater Horizon oil well in 2010, BP employees took shortcuts and ignored warning signs, without intending to harm any people, the environment, or their company's reputation. *After* the resulting Gulf oil spill, with the benefit of 20/20 hindsight, the foolishness of those judgments became obvious.

Overconfidence in history:

"We don't like their sound. Groups of guitars are on their way out."

Decca Records, in turning down a recording contract with the Beatles in 1962

"Computers in the future may weigh no more than 1.5 tons."

Popular Mechanics, *1949*

"They couldn't hit an elephant at this distance."

General John Sedgwick just before being killed during a U.S. Civil War battle, 1864

"The telephone may be appropriate for our American cousins, but not here, because we have an adequate supply of messenger boys."

British expert group evaluating the invention of the telephone

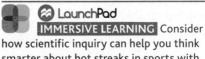

LaunchPad

IMMERSIVE LEARNING Consider how scientific inquiry can help you think smarter about hot streaks in sports with LaunchPad's *How Would You Know If There Is a Hot Hand in Basketball?*

lot by watching." (We have Berra to thank for other gems, such as "Nobody ever comes here—it's too crowded," and "If the people don't want to come out to the ballpark, nobody's gonna stop 'em.") Because we're all behavior watchers, it would be surprising if many of psychology's findings had *not* been foreseen. Many people believe that love breeds happiness, for example, and they are right (we have what researchers identify as a deep "need to belong").

OVERCONFIDENCE We humans tend to think we know more than we do. Asked how sure we are of our answers to factual questions *(Is Boston north or south of Paris?)*, we tend to be more confident than correct.[2] Or consider these three anagrams, which Richard Goranson (1978) asked people to unscramble:

WREAT   ···>   WATER
ETRYN   ···>   ENTRY
GRABE   ···>   BARGE

About how many seconds do you think it would have taken you to unscramble each of these? Knowing the answers tends to make us overconfident. (Surely the solution would take only 10 seconds or so.) In reality, the average problem solver spends 3 minutes, as you also might, given a similar anagram without the solution: OCHSA.[3]

Are we any better at predicting social behavior? Psychologist Philip Tetlock (1998, 2005) collected more than 27,000 expert predictions of world events, such as the future of South Africa or whether Quebec would separate from Canada. His repeated finding: These predictions, which experts made with 80 percent confidence on average, were right less than 40 percent of the time. Nevertheless, even those who erred maintained their confidence by noting they were "almost right": "The Québécois separatists *almost* won the secessionist referendum."

RETRIEVE IT [✴]

• Why, after friends start dating, do we often feel that we *knew* they were meant to be together?

ANSWER: We often suffer from hindsight bias—after we've learned a situation's outcome, that outcome seems familiar and therefore obvious.

PERCEIVING ORDER IN RANDOM EVENTS We have a built-in eagerness to make sense of our world. People see a face on the Moon, hear Satanic messages in music, or perceive the Virgin Mary's image on a grilled cheese sandwich. Even in random data, we often find patterns, because—here's a curious fact of life—*random sequences often don't look random* (Falk, R. et al., 2009; Nickerson, 2002, 2005). Flip a coin 50 times and you may be surprised at the streaks of heads and tails. In actual random sequences, patterns and streaks (such as repeating digits) occur more often than people expect (Oskarsson et al., 2009).

BIZARRE SEQUENCE OF COMPUTER-GENERATED RANDOM NUMBERS

© 1990 by Sidney Harris/American Scientist magazine.

Bizarre-looking, perhaps. But actually no more unlikely than any other number sequence.

---

2. Boston is south of Paris.

3. The anagram solution: CHAOS.

Some happenings, such as winning the lottery twice, seem so extraordinary that we find it difficult to conceive an ordinary, chance-related explanation. "But with a large enough sample, any outrageous thing is likely to happen," note statisticians Persi Diaconis and Frederick Mosteller (1989). An event that happens to but 1 in 1 billion people every day occurs about 7 times a day, more than 2500 times a year.

The point to remember: Hindsight bias, overconfidence, and our tendency to perceive patterns in random events often lead us to overestimate our intuition. But scientific inquiry can help us sift reality from illusion.

The Scientific Method

Psychologists arm their scientific attitude with the *scientific method*—a self-correcting process for evaluating ideas with observation and analysis. In its attempt to describe and explain human nature, psychological science welcomes hunches and plausible-sounding theories. And it puts them to the test. If a theory works—if the data support its predictions—so much the better for that theory. If the predictions fail, the theory will be revised or rejected.

Constructing Theories

2-2 How do theories advance psychological science?

In everyday conversation, we often use *theory* to mean "mere hunch." Someone might, for example, discount evolution as "only a theory"—as if it were mere speculation. In science, a **theory** *explains* behaviors or events by offering ideas that *organize* what we have observed. By organizing isolated facts, a theory simplifies. By linking facts with deeper principles, a theory offers a useful summary. As we connect the observed dots, a coherent picture emerges.

A theory about sleep effects on memory, for example, helps us organize countless sleep-related observations into a short list of principles. Imagine that we observe over and over that people with good sleep habits tend to answer questions accurately in class and do well at test time. We might therefore theorize that sleep improves memory. So far so good: Our principle neatly summarizes a list of facts about the effects of a good night's sleep on memory.

Yet no matter how reasonable a theory may sound—and it does seem reasonable to suggest that sleep could improve memory—we must put it to the test. A good theory produces testable *predictions*, called **hypotheses.** Such predictions specify what results (what behaviors or events) would support the theory and what results would oppose it. To test our theory about the effects of sleep on memory, our hypothesis might be that when sleep deprived, people will remember less from the day before. To test that hypothesis, we might assess how well people remember course materials they studied before a good night's sleep, or before a shortened night's sleep (**FIGURE 2.1** on the next page). The results will either support our theory or lead us to revise or reject it.

Our theories can bias our observations. Having theorized that better memory springs from more sleep, we may see what we expect: We may perceive sleepy people's comments as less insightful. The urge to see what we expect is ever-present, both inside and outside the laboratory, as when people's views of climate change influence their interpretation of local weather events.

As a check on their biases, psychologists report their research with precise **operational definitions** of procedures and concepts. *Sleep deprived,* for example, might be defined as "X hours less" than one's natural sleep. Using these carefully worded statements, others can **replicate** (repeat) the original observations with

Roland Weihrauch/dpa/picture-alliance/Newscom

Given enough random events, some weird-seeming streaks will occur During the 2010 World Cup, a German octopus—Paul, "the oracle of Oberhausen"— was offered two boxes, each with mussels and with a national flag on one side. Paul selected the correct box eight out of eight times in predicting the outcome of Germany's seven matches and Spain's triumph in the final.

theory an explanation using an integrated set of principles that organizes observations and predicts behaviors or events.

hypothesis a testable prediction, often implied by a theory.

operational definition a carefully worded statement of the exact procedures (operations) used in a research study. For example, *human intelligence* may be operationally defined as what an intelligence test measures.

replication repeating the essence of a research study, usually with different participants in different situations, to see whether the basic finding can be reproduced.

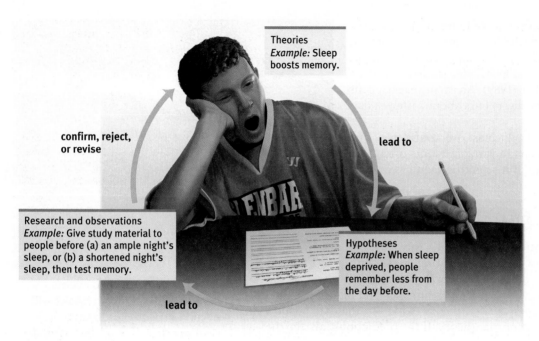

Theories
Example: Sleep boosts memory.

confirm, reject, or revise

lead to

Research and observations
Example: Give study material to people before (a) an ample night's sleep, or (b) a shortened night's sleep, then test memory.

Hypotheses
Example: When sleep deprived, people remember less from the day before.

lead to

^ FIGURE 2.1

The scientific method A self-correcting process for asking questions and observing nature's answers.

For more information about statistical methods that psychological scientists use in their work, see Appendix A, Statistical Reasoning in Everyday Life.

different participants, materials, and circumstances. If they get similar results, confidence in the finding's reliability grows. The first study of hindsight bias aroused psychologists' curiosity. Now, after many successful replications with different people and questions, we feel sure of the phenomenon's power. Although "mere replications" of others' research are unglamorous—they seldom make headline news—today's science is placing greater value on replication studies. International research teams are repeating high-profile studies. In one project, which attempted replications of 13 studies, researchers convincingly replicated 10 findings with similar or greater effects. They replicated one with a weaker effect. And they failed to replicate two studies (Klein et al., 2014). Such replication forms an essential part of good science. Replication = confirmation.

In the end, our theory will be useful if it (1) *organizes* observations and (2) implies *predictions* that anyone can use to check the theory or to derive practical applications. (Does people's sleep predict their retention?) Eventually, our research may (3) stimulate further research that leads to a revised theory that better organizes and predicts.

As we will see next, we can test our hypotheses and refine our theories using *descriptive* methods (which describe behaviors, often through case studies, naturalistic observations, or surveys), *correlational* methods (which associate different factors), and *experimental* methods (which manipulate factors to discover their effects). To think critically about popular psychology claims, we need to understand these methods and know what conclusions they allow.

RETRIEVE IT [✖]

• What does a good theory do?

ANSWER: 1. It *organizes* observed facts. 2. It implies hypotheses that offer testable *predictions* and, sometimes, practical applications. 3. It often stimulates further research.

• Why is replication important?

ANSWER: When other investigators are able to replicate an experiment with the same (or better) results, scientists can confirm the result and become more confident of its reliability.

Description

2-3 How do psychologists use case studies, naturalistic observations, and surveys to observe and describe behavior, and why is random sampling important?

The starting point of any science is description. In everyday life, we all observe and describe people, often drawing conclusions about why they act as they do. Professional psychologists do much the same, though more objectively and systematically, through

• *case studies* (in-depth analyses of individuals or groups).

- *naturalistic observations* (recording individuals' behavior in their natural setting).
- *surveys* and interviews (self-reports in which people answer questions about their behavior or attitudes).

THE CASE STUDY Among the oldest research methods, the **case study** examines one individual or group in depth in the hope of revealing things true of us all. Some examples: Much of our early knowledge about the brain came from case studies of individuals who suffered a particular impairment after damage to a certain brain region. Jean Piaget taught us about children's thinking after carefully observing and questioning only a few children. Studies of only a few chimpanzees revealed their capacity for understanding and language. Intensive case studies are sometimes very revealing, and they often suggest directions for further study.

But atypical individual cases may mislead us. Both in our everyday lives and in science, unrepresentative information can lead to mistaken conclusions. Indeed, anytime a researcher mentions a finding *(Smokers die younger: 95 percent of men over 85 are nonsmokers)* someone is sure to offer a contradictory anecdote *(Well, I have an uncle who smoked two packs a day and lived to be 89)*. Dramatic stories and personal experiences (even psychological case examples) command our attention and are easily remembered. Journalists understand that, and often begin their articles with personal stories. Stories move us. But stories can mislead. Which of the following do you find more memorable? (1) "In one study of 1300 dream reports concerning a kidnapped child, only 5 percent correctly envisioned the child as dead" (Murray & Wheeler, 1937). (2) "I know a man who dreamed his sister was in a car accident, and two days later she died in a head-on collision!" Numbers can be numbing, but *the plural of anecdote is not evidence*. A psychologist's single case of someone who reportedly changed from gay to straight is not evidence that sexual orientation is a choice. As psychologist Gordon Allport (1954, p. 9) said, "Given a thimbleful of [dramatic] facts we rush to make generalizations as large as a tub."

The point to remember: Individual cases can suggest fruitful ideas. What's true of all of us can be glimpsed in any one of us. But to discern the general truths that cover individual cases, we must employ other research methods.

RETRIEVE IT [✳]

- We cannot assume that case studies always reveal general principles that apply to all of us. Why not?

ANSWER: Case studies involve only one individual or group, so we can't know for sure whether the principles observed would apply to a larger population.

NATURALISTIC OBSERVATION A second descriptive method records behavior in natural environments. These **naturalistic observations** range from watching chimpanzee societies in the jungle, to videotaping and analyzing parent-child interactions in different cultures, to recording racial differences in students' self-seating patterns in a school lunchroom.

Naturalistic observation has mostly been "small science"—science that can be done with pen and paper rather than fancy equipment and a big budget (Provine, 2012). But new technologies, such as smart-phone apps, body-worn sensors, and social media, are enabling "big data" naturalistic observation. Using such tools, researchers can track people's location, activities, and opinions—without interference. The billions of people on Facebook, Twitter, and Google have also created a huge but sometimes controversial new opportunity for big-data naturalistic observation. Meanwhile, the data pour in. One research team studied the ups and downs

🌀 **LaunchPad** See LaunchPad's *Video: Case Studies* for a helpful tutorial animation.

"'Well my dear,' said Miss Marple, 'human nature is very much the same everywhere, and of course, one has opportunities of observing it at closer quarters in a village'."
Agatha Christie, The Tuesday Club Murders, *1933*

Skye Hohmann/Alamy

Freud and Little Hans Sigmund Freud's case study of 5-year-old Hans' extreme fear of horses led Freud to his theory of childhood sexuality. He conjectured that Hans felt unconscious desire for his mother, feared castration by his rival father, and then transferred this fear into his phobia about being bitten by a horse. Today's psychological science discounts Freud's theory of childhood sexuality but acknowledges that much of the human mind operates outside our conscious awareness.

case study a descriptive technique in which one individual or group is studied in depth in the hope of revealing universal principles.

naturalistic observation a descriptive technique of observing and recording behavior in naturally occurring situations without trying to manipulate and control the situation.

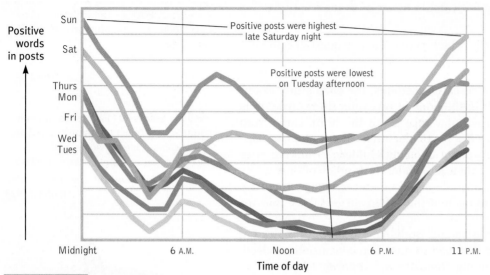

^ FIGURE 2.2

Twitter message moods, by time and by day This illustrates how, without knowing anyone's identity, big data enable researchers to study human behavior on a massive scale. It now is also possible to associate people's moods with, for example, their locations or with the weather, and to study the spread of ideas through social networks. (Data from Golder & Macy, 2011.)

of human moods by counting positive and negative words in 504 million Twitter messages from 84 countries (Golder & Macy, 2011). As **FIGURE 2.2** shows, people seem happier on weekends, shortly after arising, and in the evenings. (Are late Saturday evenings often a happy time for you, too?) Another study found that the proportion of negative emotion (especially anger-related) words in 148 million tweets from 1347 U.S. counties predicted the counties' heart disease rates, and did so even better than other predictors such as smoking and obesity (Eichstaedt et al., 2015).

Like the case study, naturalistic observation does not *explain* behavior. It *describes* it. Nevertheless, descriptions can be revealing. We once thought, for example, that only humans use tools. Then naturalistic observation revealed that chimpanzees sometimes insert a stick in a termite mound and withdraw it, eating the stick's load of termites. Such unobtrusive naturalistic observations paved the way for later studies of animal thinking, language, and emotion, which further expanded our understanding of our fellow animals. Thanks to researchers' observations, we know that chimpanzees and baboons use deception: Psychologists repeatedly saw one young baboon pretending to have been attacked by another as a tactic to get its mother to drive the other baboon away from its food (Byrne & Whiten, 1988; Whiten & Byrne, 1988). "Observations, made in the natural habitat, helped to show that the societies and behavior of animals are far more complex than previously supposed," chimpanzee observer Jane Goodall noted (1998).

Naturalistic observations also illuminate human behavior. Here are three findings you might enjoy:

- *A funny finding.* We humans laugh 30 times more often in social situations than in solitary situations (Provine, 2001). (Have you noticed how seldom you laugh when alone?)

- *Sounding out students.* What, really, are introductory psychology students saying and doing during their everyday lives? To find out, Matthias Mehl and James Pennebaker (2003) equipped 52 such students from the University of Texas with electronic recorders, which enabled the researchers to eavesdrop on more than 10,000 half-minute life slices of students' waking hours. On what percentage of the slices do you suppose they found the students talking with someone? The answer: 28 percent.

- *Culture, climate, and the pace of life.* Naturalistic observation also enabled Robert Levine and Ara Norenzayan (1999) to compare the pace of life—the walking speed, speed of postal clerks, and so forth—in 31 countries. Their conclusion: Life is fastest paced in Japan and Western Europe and slower paced in economically less-developed countries.

Naturalistic observation offers interesting snapshots of everyday life, but it does so without controlling for all the factors that may influence behavior. It's one thing to observe the pace of life in various places, but another to understand what makes some people walk faster than others. Even so, the observation of natural everyday behavior is an important part of psychological science.

LaunchPad See LaunchPad's *Video: Naturalistic Observation* for a helpful tutorial animation.

THE SURVEY A **survey** looks at many cases in less depth by asking people to report their behavior or opinions. Questions about everything from sexual practices to political opinions are put to the public. In recent surveys:

- Saturdays and Sundays have been the week's happiest days (confirming what the Twitter researchers found) (Stone et al., 2012).

- 1 in 5 people across 22 countries report believing that alien beings have come to Earth and now walk among us disguised as humans (Ipsos, 2010b).

- 68 percent of all humans—some 4.6 billion people—say that religion is important in their daily lives (from Gallup World Poll data analyzed by Diener et al., 2011).

But asking questions is tricky, and the answers often depend on question wording and respondent selection.

WORDING EFFECTS Even subtle changes in the order or wording of questions can have major effects. People are much more approving of "aid to the needy" than of "welfare," of "affirmative action" than of "preferential treatment," of "not allowing" televised cigarette ads and pornography than of "censoring" them, and of "revenue enhancers" than of "taxes." Because wording is such a delicate matter, critical thinkers will reflect on how the phrasing of a question might affect people's expressed opinions.

RANDOM SAMPLING In everyday thinking, we tend to generalize from cases we observe, especially vivid cases. Given (a) a statistical summary of a professor's student evaluations and (b) the vivid comments of a biased sample (two irate students), an administrator's impression of the professor may be influenced as much by the two unhappy students as by the many favorable evaluations in the statistical summary. The temptation to ignore the *sampling bias* and to generalize from a few vivid but unrepresentative cases is nearly irresistible.

So how do you obtain a *representative sample* of, say, the students at your college or university? It's not always possible to survey the whole group you want to study and describe. How could you choose a group that would represent the total student **population?** Typically, you would seek a **random sample,** in which every person in the total group has an equal chance of being included in the sample group. You might number the names in the general student listing and then use a random number generator to pick your survey participants. (Sending each student a questionnaire wouldn't work because the conscientious people who returned it would not be a random sample.) Large representative samples are better than small ones, but a small representative sample of 100 is better than an unrepresentative sample of 500.

Political pollsters sample voters in national election surveys just this way. Using some 1500 randomly sampled people, drawn from all areas of a country, they can provide a remarkably accurate snapshot of the nation's opinions. Without random sampling (also called *random selection*), large samples—including unrepresentative call-in phone samples and TV or website polls—often give misleading results.

The point to remember: Before accepting survey findings, think critically. Consider the sample. The best basis for generalizing is from a representative sample. You cannot compensate for an unrepresentative sample by simply adding more people.

An EAR for naturalistic observation
Psychologists Matthias Mehl and James Pennebaker have used electronically activated recorders (EARs) to sample naturally occurring slices of daily life.

Courtesy of Matthias Mehl

- What are the advantages and disadvantages of naturalistic observation, such as Mehl and Pennebaker used in this study?

ANSWER: The researchers were able to carefully observe and record naturally occurring behaviors outside the artificiality of the lab. However, they were not able to control for all the factors that may have influenced the everyday interactions they were recording.

With very large samples, estimates become quite reliable. *E* is estimated to represent 12.7 percent of the letters in written English. *E*, in fact, is 12.3 percent of the 925,141 letters in Melville's *Moby-Dick*, 12.4 percent of the 586,747 letters in Dickens' *A Tale of Two Cities*, and 12.1 percent of the 3,901,021 letters in 12 of Mark Twain's works (*Chance News*, 1997).

survey a descriptive technique for obtaining the self-reported attitudes or behaviors of a particular group, usually by questioning a representative, *random sample* of the group.

population all those in a group being studied, from which samples may be drawn. (*Note:* Except for national studies, this does *not* refer to a country's whole population.)

random sample a sample that fairly represents a population because each member has an equal chance of inclusion.

- What is an unrepresentative sample, and how do researchers avoid it?

ANSWER: An unrepresentative sample is a group that does not represent the population being studied. *Random sampling* helps researchers form a representative sample, because each member of the population has an equal chance of being included.

correlation a measure of the extent to which two factors vary together, and thus of how well either factor predicts the other.

correlation coefficient a statistical index of the relationship between two things (from −1.00 to +1.00).

Correlation

2-4 What are positive and negative correlations, and why do they enable prediction but not cause-effect explanation?

Describing behavior is a first step toward predicting it. Naturalistic observations and surveys often show us that one trait or behavior relates to another. In such cases, we say the two **correlate.** A statistical measure (the **correlation coefficient**) indicates how closely two things vary together, and thus how well either one *predicts* the other. Knowing how much aptitude test scores *correlate* with school success tells us how well the scores *predict* school success.

A *positive correlation* (above 0 to +1.00) indicates a *direct* relationship, meaning that two things increase together or decrease together. For example, height and weight are positively correlated.

A *negative correlation* (below 0 to −1.00) indicates an *inverse* relationship: As one thing increases, the other decreases. The weekly number of hours spent in TV watching and video gaming correlates negatively with grades. Negative correlations could go as low as −1.00, which means that, like people on opposite ends of a teeter-totter, one set of scores goes down precisely as the other goes up.

Though informative, psychology's correlations usually explain only part of the variation among individuals. As we will see, there is a positive correlation between parents' abusiveness and their children's later abusiveness when they become parents. But this does not mean that most abused children become abusive. The correlation simply indicates a statistical relationship: Most abused children do not grow into abusers, but nonabused children are even less likely to become abusive. Correlations point us toward predictions, but usually imperfect ones.

The point to remember: A correlation coefficient helps us see the world more clearly by revealing the extent to which two things relate.

🅜 **LaunchPad** See LaunchPad's *Video: Correlational Studies* for a helpful tutorial animation.

RETRIEVE IT [✖]

- Indicate whether each association is a positive correlation or a negative correlation.

1. The more children and youth used various media, the less happy they were with their lives (Rideout et al., 2010). _____

2. The less sexual content teens saw on TV, the less likely they were to have sex (Collins et al., 2004). _____

3. The longer children were breast-fed, the greater their later academic achievement (Horwood & Ferguson, 1998). _____

4. The more income rose among a sample of poor families, the fewer psychiatric symptoms their children experienced (Costello et al., 2003). _____

ANSWERS: 1. negative, 2. positive, 3. positive, 4. negative

🅜 **LaunchPad** For an animated tutorial on correlations, visit LaunchPad's *Concept Practice: Positive and Negative Correlations.*

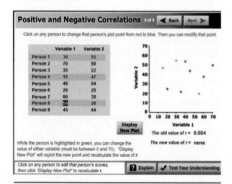

CORRELATION AND CAUSATION Consider some recent newsworthy correlations:

- "Study finds that increased parental support for college results in lower grades" (Jaschik, 2013).

- "People with mental illness more likely to be smokers, study finds" (Belluck, 2013).

- "Teens who play mature-rated, risk-glorifying video games [tend] to become reckless drivers" (Bowen, 2012).

What shall we make of these correlations? Do they indicate that students would achieve more if their parents supported them less? That stopping smoking would improve mental health? That abstaining from video games would make reckless teen drivers more responsible?

No, because such correlations do not come with built-in cause-effect arrows. But correlations do help us *predict.* An example: Self-esteem correlates negatively with (and therefore predicts) depression. (The lower people's self-esteem, the more they are at risk for depression.) So, does low self-esteem *cause* depression?

If, based on the correlational evidence, you assume that it does, you have much company. A nearly irresistible thinking error is assuming that an association, sometimes presented as a correlation coefficient, proves causation. But no matter how strong the relationship, it does not. As **FIGURE 2.3** indicates, we'd get the same negative correlation between self-esteem and depression if depression caused people to be down on themselves, or if some third factor—such as heredity or distressing events—caused both low self-esteem and depression.

This point is so important—so fundamental to thinking smarter with psychology—that it merits another example. A survey of over 12,000 adolescents found that the more teens feel loved by their parents, the less likely they are to behave in unhealthy ways—having early sex, smoking, abusing alcohol and drugs, exhibiting violence (Resnick et al., 1997). "Adults have a powerful effect on their children's behavior right through the high school years," gushed an Associated Press (AP) story reporting the finding. But again, correlations come with no built-in cause-effect arrow. The AP could as well have reported, "Well-behaved teens feel their parents' love and approval; out-of-bounds teens more often think their parents are disapproving."

The point to remember (turn the volume up here): *Correlation does not prove causation. Correlation indicates the* possibility *of a cause-effect relationship but does not prove such.* Remember this principle and you will be wiser as you read and hear news of scientific studies.

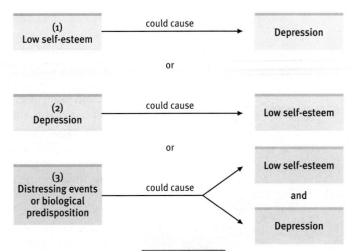

^ FIGURE 2.3

Three possible cause-effect relationships People low in self-esteem are more likely to report depression than are those high in self-esteem. One possible explanation of this negative correlation is that a bad self-image causes depressed feelings. But, as the diagram indicates, other cause-effect relationships are possible.

RETRIEVE IT [✱]

Correlation need not mean causation.

- In two recent studies, sexual hook-ups positively correlated with college women's experiencing depression; delaying sexual intimacy correlated with positive outcomes such as greater relationship satisfaction and stability (Fielder et al., 2014; Willoughby et al., 2014). Do these findings mean that sexual restraint causes better outcomes?

ANSWER: It might. But in this case, as in many others, causation might work the other way around (more depressed people are more likely to hook up), or some third factor, such as lower impulsivity, might underlie both sexual restraint and psychological well-being.

Experimentation

 2-5 What are the characteristics of experimentation that make it possible to isolate cause and effect?

Happy are they, remarked the Roman poet Virgil, "who have been able to perceive the causes of things." How might psychologists perceive causes in correlational studies, such as the correlation between breast feeding and intelligence? Is breast really best?

Intelligence scores of children who were breast-fed as infants are somewhat higher than the scores of children who were bottle-fed (Angelsen et al., 2001; Mortensen et al., 2002; Quinn et al., 2001). Moreover, the longer they breast-feed, the higher their later IQ scores (Jedrychowski et al., 2012).

What do such findings mean? Do the nutrients of mother's milk, as some researchers believe, contribute to brain development? Or do smarter mothers have smarter children? (Breast-fed children tend to be healthier and higher achieving than other children. But their bottle-fed siblings, born and raised in the same families, tend to be similarly healthy and high achieving [Colen & Ramey, 2014].) To find answers to such questions—to isolate cause and effect—researchers can **experiment.** Experiments enable researchers to isolate the effects of one or more factors by (1) *manipulating the factors of interest* and (2) *holding constant (controlling) other factors.* To do so, they often create an **experimental group,** in which people receive the treatment, and a contrasting **control group** whose members do not receive the treatment. To minimize any preexisting differences between the two groups,

Recall that in a well-done survey, *random sampling* is important. In an experiment, *random assignment* is equally important.

experiment a research method in which an investigator manipulates one or more factors (independent variables) to observe the effect on some behavior or mental process (the dependent variable). By *random assignment* of participants, the experimenter aims to control other relevant factors.

experimental group in an experiment, the group exposed to the treatment, that is, to one version of the independent variable.

control group in an experiment, the group *not* exposed to the treatment; contrasts with the experimental group and serves as a comparison for evaluating the effect of the treatment.

Lane Oatey/Getty Images

⊛ **LaunchPad** See LaunchPad's *Video: Random Assignment* for a helpful tutorial animation.

random assignment assigning participants to experimental and control groups by chance, thus minimizing preexisting differences between the different groups.

double-blind procedure an experimental procedure in which both the research participants and the research staff are ignorant (blind) about whether the research participants have received the treatment or a placebo. Commonly used in drug-evaluation studies.

placebo [pluh-SEE-bo; Latin for "I shall please"] **effect** experimental results caused by expectations alone; any effect on behavior caused by the administration of an inert substance or condition, which the recipient assumes is an active agent.

researchers **randomly assign** people to the two conditions. Random assignment—whether with a random numbers table or flip of the coin—effectively equalizes the two groups. If one-third of the volunteers for an experiment can wiggle their ears, then about one-third of the people in each group will be ear wigglers. So, too, with ages, attitudes, and other characteristics, which will be similar in the experimental and control groups. Thus, if the groups differ at the experiment's end, we can surmise that the treatment had an effect.

To experiment with breast feeding, one research team randomly assigned some 17,000 Belarus newborns and their mothers either to a control group given normal pediatric care, or to an experimental group that promoted breast feeding, thus increasing expectant mothers' breast-feeding intentions (Kramer et al., 2008). At 3 months of age, 43 percent of the experimental group infants were being exclusively breast-fed, as were 6 percent in the control group. At age 6, when nearly 14,000 of the children were restudied, those who had been in the breast-feeding-promotion group had intelligence test scores averaging six points higher than their control group counterparts.

With parental permission, one British research team directly experimented with breast milk. They randomly assigned 424 hospitalized premature infants either to formula feedings or to breast-milk feedings (Lucas et al., 1992). Their finding: For premature infants' developing intelligence, breast was best. On intelligence tests taken at age 8, those nourished with breast milk scored significantly higher than those who were formula-fed.

No single experiment is conclusive, of course. But randomly assigning participants to one feeding group or the other effectively eliminated all factors except nutrition. This supported the conclusion that for developing intelligence, breast is indeed best. If test performance changes when we vary infant nutrition, then we infer that nutrition matters.

The point to remember: Unlike correlational studies, which uncover naturally occurring relationships, an experiment manipulates a factor to determine its effect.

Consider, then, how we might assess therapeutic interventions. Our tendency to seek new remedies when we are ill or emotionally down can produce misleading testimonies. If three days into a cold we start taking vitamin C tablets and find our cold symptoms lessening, we may credit the pills rather than the cold naturally subsiding. In the 1700s, bloodletting *seemed* effective. People sometimes improved after the treatment; when they didn't, the practitioner inferred the disease was too advanced to be reversed. So, whether or not a remedy is truly effective, enthusiastic users will probably endorse it. To determine its effect, we must control for other factors.

And that is precisely how investigators evaluate new drug treatments and new methods of psychological therapy. They randomly assign participants either to the group receiving a treatment (such as a medication), or to a group receiving a pseudotreatment—an inert *placebo* (perhaps a pill with no drug in it). The participants are often *blind* (uninformed) about what treatment, if any, they are receiving. If the study is using a **double-blind procedure,** neither the participants nor those who administer the drug or placebo and collect the data will know which group is receiving the treatment.

In double-blind studies, researchers check a treatment's actual effects apart from the participants' and the staff's belief in its healing powers. Just *thinking* you are getting a treatment can boost your spirits, relax your body, and relieve your symptoms. This **placebo effect** is well documented in reducing pain, depression, and anxiety (Kirsch, 2010). Athletes have run faster when given a supposed performance-enhancing drug (McClung & Collins, 2007). Drinking decaf coffee has boosted vigor and alertness—for those who thought it had caffeine in it (Dawkins et al., 2011). People have felt better after receiving a phony mood-enhancing drug (Michael et al., 2012). And the more expensive the placebo, the more "real" it seems to us—a fake pill that costs $2.50 works better than one

costing 10 cents (Waber et al., 2008). A pain-reducing placebo effect, if repeatedly experienced, can persist. Even when people learn they received a placebo, they continue to report reduced pain (Schafer et al., 2015). To know how effective a therapy really is, researchers must control for a possible placebo effect.

RETRIEVE IT ⬚✕

• What measures do researchers use to prevent the *placebo effect* from confusing their results?

ANSWER: Research designed to prevent the placebo effect randomly assigns participants to an *experimental group* (receives the real treatment) or to a *control group* (receives a placebo), using a *double-blind procedure* (neither those who receive nor those who administer the treatment know who gets the placebo versus the actual treatment). A comparison of the results will demonstrate whether the real treatment produces better results than *belief* in that treatment.

INDEPENDENT AND DEPENDENT VARIABLES Here is an even more potent example: The drug Viagra was approved for use after 21 clinical trials. One trial was an experiment in which researchers randomly assigned 329 men with erectile disorder to either an experimental group (Viagra takers) or a control group (placebo takers given an identical-looking pill). The procedure was double-blind—neither the men nor the person giving them the pills knew what they were receiving. The result: At peak doses, 69 percent of Viagra-assisted attempts at intercourse were successful, compared with 22 percent for men receiving the placebo (Goldstein et al., 1998). Viagra performed.

This simple experiment manipulated just one factor: the drug dosage (none versus peak dose). We call this experimental factor the **independent variable** because we can vary it *independently* of other factors, such as the men's age, weight, and personality. Other factors which could influence a study's results are called **confounding variables.** Random assignment controls for possible confounding variables.

Experiments examine the effect of one or more independent variables on some measurable behavior, called the **dependent variable** because it can vary *depending* on what takes place during the experiment. Both variables are given precise *operational definitions,* which specify the procedures that manipulate the independent variable (in this study, the exact drug dosage and timing) or measure the dependent variable (the questions that assessed the men's responses). These definitions answer the "What do you mean?" question with a level of precision that enables others to *replicate* the study. (See **FIGURE 2.4** for the British breast milk experiment's design.)

Let's pause to check your understanding using a simple psychology experiment: To test the effect of perceived ethnicity on the availability of rental housing, Adrian Carpusor and William Loges (2006) sent identically worded e-mail inquiries to 1115 Los Angeles-area landlords. The researchers varied the ethnic connotation of the sender's name and tracked the percentage of positive replies (invitations to view the apartment in person). "Patrick McDougall," "Said Al-Rahman," and "Tyrell Jackson" received, respectively, 89 percent, 66 percent, and 56 percent invitations.

Experiments can also help us evaluate social programs. Do early childhood education programs boost impoverished children's chances for success? What are the effects of different antismoking campaigns? Do school sex-education programs reduce teen pregnancies? To answer such questions, we can experiment: If an intervention is welcomed but resources are scarce, we could use a lottery to randomly assign some people (or regions) to experience the new program and others to a control condition. If later the two groups differ, the intervention's effect will be supported (Passell, 1993).

---

independent variable in an experiment, the factor that is manipulated; the variable whose effect is being studied.

confounding variable a factor other than the factor being studied that might produce an effect.

dependent variable in an experiment, the outcome that is measured; the variable that may change when the independent variable is manipulated.

"If I don't think it's going to work, will it still work?"

Random assignment (controlling for other variables such as parental intelligence and environment)

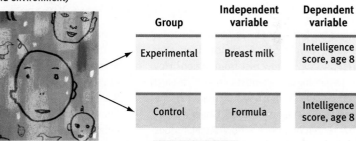

Group	Independent variable	Dependent variable
Experimental	Breast milk	Intelligence score, age 8
Control	Formula	Intelligence score, age 8

▲ FIGURE 2.4

Experimentation To discern causation, psychologists may randomly assign some participants to an experimental group, others to a control group. Measuring the dependent variable (intelligence score in later childhood) will determine the effect of the independent variable (type of milk).

⌄ TABLE 2.1

Comparing Research Methods

Research Method	Basic Purpose	How Conducted	What Is Manipulated	Weaknesses
Descriptive	To observe and record behavior	Do case studies, naturalistic observations, or surveys	Nothing	No control of variables; single cases may be misleading
Correlational	To detect naturally occurring relationships; to assess how well one variable predicts another	Collect data on two or more variables; no manipulation	Nothing	Cannot specify cause and effect
Experimental	To explore cause and effect	Manipulate one or more factors; use random assignment	The independent variable(s)	Sometimes not feasible; results may not generalize to other contexts; not ethical to manipulate certain variables

Let's recap. A *variable* is anything that can vary (infant nutrition, intelligence, TV exposure—anything within the bounds of what is feasible and ethical). Experiments aim to *manipulate* an *independent* variable, *measure* a *dependent variable,* and control *confounding* variables. An experiment has at least two different conditions: an *experimental condition* and a *comparison* or *control condition. Random assignment* works to minimize preexisting differences between the groups before any treatment effects occur. In this way, an experiment tests the effect of at least one independent variable (what we manipulate) on at least one dependent variable (the outcome we measure).

🔵 **LaunchPad** See LaunchPad's *Videos: Experiments* and *Confounding Variables* for helpful tutorial animations.

TABLE 2.1 compares the features of psychology's main research methods. Other modules explain additional research designs, including *cross-sectional* and *longitudinal research,* and *twin studies.* To help you understand how researchers design their studies, we have created activities that invite you to play the role of researcher (see Thinking Critically About Research Design: How Would You Know?)

THINKING CRITICALLY ABOUT

Research Design: How Would You Know?

Throughout this book, you will read about amazing psychological science discoveries. But *how do we know* fact from fiction? How do psychological scientists choose research methods and design their studies in ways that provide meaningful results? Understanding how research is done—how testable questions are developed and studied—is key to appreciating all of psychology.

In psychological research, no questions are off limits, except untestable ones. Does free will exist? Are people born evil? Is there an afterlife? Psychologists can't test those questions, but they *can* test whether free will beliefs, aggressive personalities, and a belief in life after death influence how people think, feel, and act (Dechesne et al., 2003; Shariff et al., 2014; Webster et al., 2014).

To help you build your understanding, and your *scientific literacy skills,* we created IMMERSIVE LEARNING research activities in LaunchPad. In these *How Would You*

Know? activities, you get to play the role of the researcher, making choices about the best ways to test interesting questions, such as How Would You Know If Having Children Relates to Being Happier?, How Would You Know If a Cup of Coffee Can Warm Up Relationships?, and How Would You Know If People Can Learn to Reduce Anxiety?

Having chosen their question, psychologists then select the most appropriate research design—*experimental, correlational, case study, naturalistic observation, twin study, longitudinal,* or *cross-sectional*—and determine how to set it up most effectively. They consider how much money and time are available, ethical issues, and other limitations. For example, it wouldn't be ethical for a researcher studying child development to use the experimental method and *randomly assign* children to loving versus punishing homes.

Next, psychological scientists decide how to measure the behavior or mental

process being studied. For example, consider the researchers mentioned earlier in this box, who tested whether aggressive personalities affect how people act. They measured aggression by determining participants' willingness to blast a stranger with intense noise.

Researchers want to have confidence in their findings, so they carefully consider *confounding variables*—factors other than those being studied that may affect their interpretation of results.

Psychological research is a fun and creative adventure. The new ***Immersive Learning: How Would You Know?*** activities invite you to join the scientific journey to uncover new knowledge. We will both [DM and ND] encourage you via videos as you DESIGN each of your studies, MEASURE target behaviors, INTERPRET your results, and learn more about the fascinating process of scientific discovery along the way!

 LaunchPad To review and test your understanding of experimental methods and concepts, visit LaunchPad's *Concept Practice: The Language of Experiments,* and the interactive *PsychSim 6: Understanding Psychological Research.* For a 9.5-minute video synopsis of psychology's scientific research strategies, visit LaunchPad's *Video: Research Methods.*

RETRIEVE IT [✖]

- In the experiment on the effects of perceived ethnicity on availability of rental housing, what was the independent variable? The dependent variable?

ANSWER: The independent variable, which the researchers manipulated, was the set of ethnically distinct names. The dependent variable, which they measured, was the positive response rate.

- By using *random assignment,* researchers are able to control for _____ _____, which are other factors besides the independent variable(s) that may influence research results.

ANSWER: confounding variables

- Match the term on the left with the description on the right.

  1. double-blind procedure   a. helps researchers generalize from a small set of survey responses to a larger population

  2. random sampling   b. helps minimize preexisting differences between experimental and control groups

  3. random assignment   c. controls for the placebo effect; neither researchers nor participants know who receives the real treatment

ANSWERS: 1. c, 2. a, 3. b

- Why, when testing a new drug to control blood pressure, would we learn more about its effectiveness from giving it to half of the participants in a group of 1000 than to all 1000 participants?

ANSWER: We learn more about the drug's effectiveness when we can compare the results of those who took the drug (the experimental group) with the results of those who did not (the control group). If we gave the drug to all 1000 participants, we would have no way of knowing whether the drug is serving as a placebo or is actually medically effective.

Predicting Real Behavior

 2-6 Can laboratory experiments illuminate everyday life?

When you see or hear about psychological research, do you ever wonder whether people's behavior in the lab will predict their behavior in real life? Does detecting the blink of a faint red light in a dark room say anything useful about flying a plane at night? After viewing a violent, sexually explicit film, does an aroused man's increased willingness to push buttons that he thinks will electrically shock a woman really say anything about whether violent pornography makes a man more likely to abuse a woman?

Before you answer, consider: The experimenter *intends* the laboratory environment to be a simplified reality—one that simulates and controls important features of everyday life. Just as a wind tunnel lets airplane designers re-create airflow forces under controlled conditions, a laboratory experiment lets psychologists re-create psychological forces under controlled conditions.

An experiment's purpose is not to re-create the exact behaviors of everyday life, but to test *theoretical principles* (Mook, 1983). In aggression studies, deciding whether to push a button that delivers a noise blast may not be the same as slapping someone in the face, but the principle is the same. It is the *resulting principles—not the specific findings—that help explain everyday behaviors.*

When psychologists apply laboratory research on aggression to actual violence, they are applying theoretical principles of aggressive behavior, principles refined through many experiments. Similarly, it is the principles of the visual system, developed from experiments in artificial settings (such as looking at red lights in the dark), that researchers apply to more complex behaviors such as night flying. And many investigations have demonstrated that principles derived in the laboratory do typically generalize to the everyday world (Anderson et al., 1999).

The point to remember: Psychological science focuses less on particular behaviors than on seeking general principles that help explain many behaviors.

Psychology's Research Ethics

👁 **2-7** Why do psychologists study animals, and what ethical guidelines safeguard human and animal research participants? How do human values influence psychology?

We have reflected on how a scientific approach can restrain biases. We have seen how case studies, naturalistic observations, and surveys help us describe behavior. We have established how correlational studies assess the association between two factors, which indicates how well one thing predicts another. We have examined the logic that underlies experiments, which use control conditions and random assignment of participants to isolate the effects of an independent variable on a dependent variable.

Yet, even knowing this much, you may still be approaching psychology with a mixture of curiosity and apprehension. So before we plunge in, let's entertain some common questions about psychology's ethics and values.

Protecting Research Participants

STUDYING AND PROTECTING ANIMALS Many psychologists study nonhuman animals because they find them fascinating. They want to understand how different species learn, think, and behave. Psychologists also study animals to learn about people. We humans are not *like* animals; we *are* animals, sharing a common biology. Animal experiments have therefore led to treatments for human diseases—insulin for diabetes, vaccines to prevent polio and rabies, transplants to replace defective organs.

Humans are more complex, but the same processes by which we learn are present in rats, monkeys, and even sea slugs. The simplicity of the sea slug's nervous system is precisely what makes it so revealing of the neural mechanisms of learning. Sharing such similarities, should we respect rather than experiment on our animal relatives? The animal protection movement protests the use of animals in psychological, biological, and medical research.

Out of this heated debate, two issues emerge. The basic one is whether it is right to place the well-being of humans above that of other animals. In experiments on stress and cancer, is it right that mice get tumors in the hope that people might not? Should some monkeys be exposed to an HIV-like virus in the search for an AIDS vaccine? Is our use and consumption of other animals as natural as the behavior of carnivorous hawks, cats, and whales? (Humans raise and slaughter 56 billion animals a year [Worldwatch Institute, 2013].) Or not?

Second, if we do give human life first priority, what safeguards should protect the well-being of animals in research? In one survey of animal researchers, 98 percent supported government regulations protecting primates, dogs, and cats, and 74 percent supported regulations providing for the humane care of rats and mice (Plous & Herzog, 2000). Many professional associations and funding agencies already have such guidelines. Most universities screen research proposals, often through an animal care ethics committee, and laboratories are regulated and inspected. British Psychological Society (BPS) guidelines call for housing animals under reasonably natural living conditions, with companions for social animals (Lea, 2000). American Psychological Association (APA) guidelines state that researchers must ensure the "comfort, health, and humane treatment" of animals and minimize "infection, illness, and pain" (APA, 2002).

Animals have themselves benefited from animal research. One Ohio team of research psychologists measured stress hormone levels in samples of millions of dogs brought each year to animal shelters. They devised handling and stroking methods to reduce stress and ease the dogs' transition to adoptive homes (Tuber et al., 1999). Other studies have helped improve care and management in animals' natural habitats. By revealing our behavioral kinship with animals and the

---

📱 **LaunchPad** See LaunchPad's *Video: Research Ethics* for a helpful tutorial animation.

"Rats are very similar to humans except that they are not stupid enough to purchase lottery tickets."

Dave Barry, July 2, 2002

Animal research benefiting animals Psychologists have helped zoos enrich animal environments (Weir, 2013). Thanks partly to research on the benefits of novelty, control, and stimulation, these gorillas are enjoying an improved quality of life in New York's Bronx Zoo.

Mary Altaffer/AP Photo

remarkable intelligence of chimpanzees, gorillas, and other animals, experiments have also led to increased empathy and protection for them. At its best, a psychology concerned for humans and sensitive to animals serves the welfare of both.

STUDYING AND PROTECTING HUMANS What about human participants? Does the image of white-coated scientists seeming to deliver electric shocks trouble you? Actually, most psychological studies are free of such stress. With people, blinking lights, flashing words, and pleasant social interactions are more common. Moreover, psychology's experiments are mild compared with the stress and humiliation often inflicted in the modern "experiments" of reality television. In one episode of *The Bachelor,* a man dumped his new fiancée—on camera, at the producers' request—for the woman who earlier had finished second (Collins, 2009).

Occasionally, researchers do temporarily stress or deceive people, but only when they believe it is essential to a justifiable end, such as understanding and controlling violent behavior or studying mood swings. Some experiments won't work if participants know everything beforehand. (Wanting to be helpful, the participants might try to confirm the researcher's predictions.)

The ethics codes of the APA and the BPS urge researchers to (1) obtain human participants' **informed consent** before the experiment, (2) protect participants from greater-than-usual harm and discomfort, (3) keep information about individual participants confidential, and (4) fully **debrief** people (explain the research afterward). Moreover, university ethics committees screen research proposals and safeguard participants' well-being.

Values in Research

Values affect what we study, how we study it, and how we interpret results. Researchers' values influence their choice of topics. Should we study worker productivity or worker morale? Sex discrimination or gender differences? Conformity or independence? Values can also color "the facts." As we noted earlier, our preconceptions can bias our observations and interpretations; sometimes we see what we want or expect to see (**FIGURE 2.5**).

In psychology and in everyday speech, labels describe and labels evaluate: One person's *rigidity* is another's *consistency.* One person's *faith* is another's *fanaticism.* One country's *enhanced interrogation techniques* become *torture* when practiced by its enemies. Our labeling someone as *firm* or *stubborn, careful* or *picky, discreet* or *secretive* reveals our own attitudes.

Popular applications of psychology also contain hidden values. If you defer to "professional" guidance about how to live—how to raise children, how to achieve self-fulfillment, how to respond to sexual feelings, how to get ahead at work—you are accepting value-laden advice. A science of behavior and mental processes can help us reach our goals. But it cannot decide what those goals should be.

Knowledge transforms us. Learning about the solar system and the germ theory of disease alters the way people think and act. Learning about psychology's findings also changes people: They less often judge psychological disorders as moral failings, treatable by punishment and ostracism. They less often regard and treat women as men's mental inferiors. They less often view and raise children as ignorant, willful beasts in need of taming. "In each case," noted Morton Hunt (1990, p. 206), "knowledge has modified attitudes, and, through them, behavior." Once aware of psychology's well-researched ideas—about how body and mind connect, how a child's mind grows, how we construct our perceptions, how we remember (and misremember) our experiences, how people across the world differ (and are alike)—your mind may never again be quite the same.

But bear in mind psychology's limits. Don't expect it to answer the ultimate questions, such as those posed by Russian novelist Leo Tolstoy (1904): "Why should I live? Why should I do anything? Is there in life any purpose which the inevitable death that awaits me does not undo and destroy?"

"Please do not forget those of us who suffer from incurable diseases or disabilities who hope for a cure through research that requires the use of animals."

Psychologist Dennis Feeney (1987)

"The greatness of a nation can be judged by the way its animals are treated."

Mahatma Gandhi, 1869–1948

⌃ FIGURE 2.5

What do you see? Our expectations influence what we perceive. Did you see a duck or a rabbit? Show some friends this image with the rabbit photo covered up and see if they are more likely to perceive a duck instead. (Inspired by Shepard, 1990.)

informed consent giving potential participants enough information about a study to enable them to choose whether they wish to participate.

debriefing the postexperimental explanation of a study, including its purpose and any deceptions, to its participants.

Psychology speaks In making its historic 1954 school desegregation decision, the U.S. Supreme Court cited the expert testimony and research of psychologists Kenneth Clark and Mamie Phipps Clark (1947). The Clarks reported that, when given a choice between Black and White dolls, most African-American children chose the White doll, which seemingly indicated internalized anti-Black prejudice.

"If you read a piece of text through twenty times, you will not learn it by heart so easily as if you read it ten times while attempting to recite it from time to time and consulting the text when your memory fails."

Francis Bacon, Novum Organum, *1620*

Although many of life's significant questions are beyond psychology, some very important ones are illuminated by even a first psychology course. Through painstaking research, psychologists have gained insights into brain and mind, dreams and memories, depression and joy. Even the unanswered questions can renew our sense of mystery about "things too wonderful" for us yet to understand. Moreover, your study of psychology can help teach you how to ask and answer important questions—how to think critically as you evaluate competing ideas and claims.

If some people see psychology as merely common sense, others have a different concern—that it is becoming dangerously powerful. Is it an accident that astronomy is the oldest science and psychology the youngest? To some, exploring the external universe seems far safer than exploring our own inner universe. Might psychology, they ask, be used to manipulate people?

Knowledge, like all power, can be used for good or evil. Nuclear power has been used to light up cities—and to demolish them. Persuasive power has been used to educate people—and to deceive them. Although psychology does have the power to deceive, its purpose is to enlighten. Every day, psychologists explore ways to enhance learning, creativity, and compassion. Psychology speaks to many of our world's great problems—war, overpopulation, prejudice, family crises, crime—all of which involve attitudes and behaviors. Psychology also speaks to our deepest longings—for nourishment, for love, for happiness. Psychology cannot address all of life's great questions, but it speaks to some mighty important ones.

RETRIEVE IT

• How are animal and human research participants protected?

ANSWER: Animal protection legislation, laboratory regulation and inspection, and local ethics committees serve to protect animal and human welfare. At universities, ethics committees screen research proposals. Ethical principles developed by international psychological organizations urge researchers using human participants to obtain *informed consent*, to protect them from harm and discomfort, to treat their personal information confidentially, and to fully *debrief* all participants.

Improve Your Retention—and Your Grades

2-8 How can psychological principles help you learn and remember?

Do you, like most students, assume that the way to cement your new learning is to reread? What helps even more—and what this book therefore encourages—is repeated self-testing and rehearsal of previously studied material. Memory researchers Henry Roediger and Jeffrey Karpicke (2006) call this phenomenon the **testing effect.** (It is also sometimes called the *retrieval practice effect* or *test-enhanced learning.*) They note that "testing is a powerful means of improving learning, not just assessing it." In one of their studies, students recalled the meaning of 40 previously learned Swahili words much better if tested repeatedly than if they spent the same time restudying the words (Karpicke & Roediger, 2008). Across many other studies, including in college classrooms, frequent quizzing and self-testing has boosted students' retention (Pennebaker et al., 2013; Rowland, 2014).

As you will see in the Memory modules, to master information you must *actively process it*. Your mind is not like your stomach, something to be filled passively; it is more like a muscle that grows stronger with exercise. Countless experiments reveal that people learn and remember best when they put material in their own words, rehearse it, and then retrieve and review it again.

The **SQ3R** study method incorporates these principles (McDaniel et al., 2009; Robinson, 1970). SQ3R is an acronym for its five steps: Survey, Question, Read, Retrieve,[4] Review.

---
4. Also sometimes called "Recite."

To study a module, first *survey.* Use the colorful, two-page opening for each group of modules to visually survey the contents to come. Scan each module's headings, and notice how the module is organized.

Before you read each main section, try to answer its numbered Learning Objective *Question* (for this section: "How can psychological principles help you learn and remember?"). Roediger and Bridgid Finn (2009) have found that "trying and failing to retrieve the answer is actually helpful to learning." Those who test their understanding *before* reading, and discover what they don't yet know, will learn and remember better.

Then *read,* actively searching for the answer to the question. At each sitting, read only as much of the module (usually a single main section) as you can absorb without tiring. Read actively and critically. Ask questions. Take notes. Make the ideas your own: How does what you've read relate to your own life? Does it support or challenge your assumptions? How convincing is the evidence?

Having read a section, *retrieve* its main ideas. "Active retrieval promotes meaningful learning," says Karpicke (2012). So *test yourself.* This will help you figure out what you know. Moreover, the testing itself will help you learn and retain the information more effectively. Even better, test yourself repeatedly. To facilitate this, we offer periodic Retrieve It opportunities throughout each module (see, for example, the questions in this module). After trying to answer these questions yourself, you can check the inverted answers, and reread as needed.

Finally, *review:* Read over any notes you have taken, again with an eye on the module's organization, and quickly review the whole module. Write or say what a concept is before rereading to check your understanding.

Survey, question, read, retrieve, review. We have organized this book's modules to facilitate your use of the SQ3R study system. Each group of modules begins with an illustrated *survey* of the content to come. Headings and Learning Objective *Questions* suggest issues and concepts you should consider as you *read.* The material is organized into sections of readable length. The Retrieve It questions will challenge you to *retrieve* what you have learned, and thus better remember it. The end-of-module *Review* includes the collected Learning Objective Questions and key terms for self-testing. Complete Module Reviews can be found in Appendix D. Additional self-test questions in a variety of formats appear together, organized by section, at the end of each module, with answers appearing in Appendix E.

Four additional study tips may further boost your learning:

Distribute your study time. One of psychology's oldest findings is that *spaced practice* promotes better retention than does *massed practice.* You'll remember material better if you space your practice time over several study periods—perhaps one hour a day, six days a week—rather than cram it into one week-long (or all night) study blitz. For example, rather than trying to read an entire module in a single sitting, read just one main section and then turn to something else. *Interleaving* your study of psychology with your study of other subjects will boost your long-term retention and will protect against overconfidence (Kornell & Bjork, 2008; Taylor & Rohrer, 2010).

Spacing your study sessions requires a disciplined approach to managing your time. Richard O. Straub explains time management in a helpful preface at the beginning of this text.

Learn to think critically. Whether you are reading or in class, note people's assumptions and values. What perspective or bias underlies an argument? Evaluate evidence. Is it anecdotal? Or is it based on informative experiments? Assess conclusions. Are there alternative explanations?

Process class information actively. Listen for a lecture's main ideas and sub-ideas. *Write them down.* Ask questions during and after class. In class, as in your private study, process the information actively and you will understand and retain it better. As psychologist William James urged a century ago, *"No reception without reaction, no impression without . . . expression."* Make the information your own. Take notes in

testing effect enhanced memory after retrieving, rather than simply rereading, information. Also referred to as a *retrieval practice effect* or *test-enhanced learning.*

SQ3R a study method incorporating five steps: *Survey, Question, Read, Retrieve, Review.*

"It pays better to wait and recollect by an effort from within, than to look at the book again."

William James, Principles of Psychology, *1890*

More learning tips To learn more about the testing effect and the SQ3R method, view the 5-minute animation, Make Things Memorable, at tinyurl.com/HowToRemember.

your own words. Relate what you read to what you already know. Tell someone else about it. (As any teacher will confirm, to teach is to remember.)

Overlearn. Psychology tells us that overlearning improves retention. We are prone to overestimating how much we know. You may understand a module as you read it, but that feeling of familiarity can be deceptively comforting. Using the Retrieve It opportunities, carve out study time for testing your knowledge.

Memory experts Elizabeth Bjork and Robert Bjork (2011, p. 63) offer the bottom line for how to improve your retention and your grades:

> Spend less time on the input side and more time on the output side, such as summarizing what you have read from memory or getting together with friends and asking each other questions. Any activities that involve testing yourself—that is, activities that require you to retrieve or generate information, rather than just representing information to yourself—will make your learning both more durable and flexible.

RETRIEVE IT [✖]

• The _____ _____ describes the enhanced memory that results from repeated retrieval (as in self-testing) rather than from simple rereading of new information.

ANSWER: testing effect

• What does the acronym SQ3R stand for?

ANSWER: Survey, Question, Read, Retrieve, and Review

MODULE
2 REVIEW Research Strategies: How Psychologists Ask and Answer Questions

◯ Learning Objectives

Test Yourself by taking a moment to answer each of these Learning Objective Questions (repeated here from within the module). Then turn to Appendix D, Complete Module Reviews, to check your answers. Research suggests that trying to answer these questions on your own will improve your long-term memory of the concepts (McDaniel et al., 2009).

2-1 How does our everyday thinking sometimes lead us to a wrong conclusion?

2-2 How do theories advance psychological science?

2-3 How do psychologists use case studies, naturalistic observations, and surveys to observe and describe behavior, and why is random sampling important?

2-4 What are positive and negative correlations, and why do they enable prediction but not cause-effect explanation?

2-5 What are the characteristics of experimentation that make it possible to isolate cause and effect?

2-6 Can laboratory experiments illuminate everyday life?

2-7 Why do psychologists study animals, and what ethical guidelines safeguard human and animal research participants? How do human values influence psychology?

2-8 How can psychological principles help you learn and remember?

■·[·] Terms and Concepts to Remember

Test yourself on these terms by trying to write down the definition in your own words before flipping back to the referenced page to check your answers.

intuition, p. 15

hindsight bias, p. 15

theory, p. 17

hypothesis, p. 17

operational definition, p. 17

replication, p. 17

case study, p. 19

naturalistic observation, p. 19

survey, p. 21

population, p. 21

random sample, p. 21

correlation, p. 22

correlation coefficient, p. 22

experiment, p. 23

experimental group, p. 23

control group, p. 23

random assignment, p. 24

double-blind procedure, p. 24

placebo [pluh-SEE-bo] effect, p. 24

independent variable, p. 25

confounding variable, p. 25

dependent variable, p. 25

informed consent, p. 29

debriefing, p. 29

testing effect, p. 30

SQ3R, p. 30

[✱] Experience the Testing Effect

Test yourself repeatedly throughout your studies. This will not only help you figure out what you know and don't know; the testing itself will help you learn and remember the information more effectively thanks to the *testing effect*.

1. _____ _____ refers to our tendency to perceive events as obvious or inevitable after the fact.

2. As scientists, psychologists
   a. do not disclose their methods, so as to avoid other scientists' replicating their research.
   b. assume the truth of articles published in leading scientific journals.
   c. discount evidence that competes with established assumptions.
   d. are willing to ask questions and to reject claims that cannot be verified by research.

3. How can critical thinking help you evaluate claims in the media, even if you're not a scientific expert on the issue?

4. Theory-based predictions are called _____.

5. Which of the following is NOT one of the descriptive methods psychologists use to observe and describe behavior?
   a. A case study   c. Correlational research
   b. Naturalistic observation   d. A phone survey

6. You wish to survey a group of people who truly represent the country's adult population. The best way to ensure this is to question a _____ sample of the population, in which each member has an equal chance of inclusion.

7. A study finds that the more childbirth training classes women attend, the less pain medication they require during childbirth. This finding can be stated as a _____ (positive/negative) correlation.

8. Knowing that two events are correlated provides
   a. a basis for prediction.
   b. an explanation of why the events are related.
   c. proof that as one increases, the other also increases.
   d. an indication that an underlying third factor is at work.

9. Here are some recently reported correlations, with interpretations drawn by journalists. Knowing just these correlations, can you come up with other possible explanations for each of these?
   a. Alcohol use is associated with violence. (One interpretation: Drinking triggers or unleashes aggressive behavior.)
   b. Educated people live longer, on average, than less-educated people. (One interpretation: Education lengthens life and enhances health.)
   c. Teens engaged in team sports are less likely to use drugs, smoke, have sex, carry weapons, and eat junk food than are teens who do not engage in team sports. (One interpretation: Team sports encourage healthy living.)
   d. Adolescents who frequently see smoking in movies are more likely to smoke. (One interpretation: Movie stars' behavior influences impressionable teens.)

10. To explain behaviors and clarify cause and effect, psychologists use _____.

11. To test the effect of a new drug on depression, we randomly assign people to control and experimental groups. Those in the control group take a pill that contains no medication. This is a _____.

12. In a double-blind procedure,
   a. only the participants know whether they are in the control group or the experimental group.
   b. experimental and control group members will be carefully matched for age, sex, income, and education level.
   c. neither the participants nor the researchers know who is in the experimental group or control group.
   d. someone separate from the researcher will ask people to volunteer for the experimental group or the control group.

13. A researcher wants to determine whether noise level affects workers' blood pressure. In one group, she varies the level of noise in the environment and records participants' blood pressure. In this experiment, the level of noise is the _____ _____.

14. The laboratory environment is designed to
   a. exactly re-create the events of everyday life.
   b. re-create psychological forces under controlled conditions.
   c. provide a safe place.
   d. minimize the use of animals and humans in psychological research.

15. In defending their experimental research with animals, psychologists have noted that
   a. animal research is subject to codes of ethics that ensure the animals' health, safety, and comfort.
   b. animal experimentation sometimes helps animals as well as humans.
   c. advancing the well-being of humans justifies animal experimentation.
   d. all of these statements are correct.

Find answers to these questions in Appendix E, in the back of the book.

Use 🅰 LearningCurve to create your personalized study plan, which will direct you to the resources that will help you most in 🅰 LaunchPad.

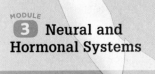

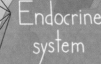

Nervous system

Endocrine system

Her communicating nervous and endocrine systems keep bodily processes functioning, enabling enjoyment of sights, sounds, and scores of the day.

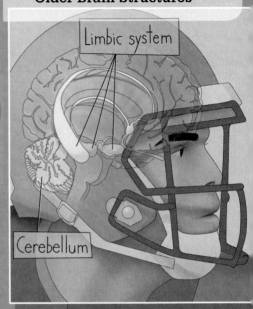

Limbic system

Cerebellum

The cerebellum offers the player agility, and the limbic system enables his emotions and drive.

His cerebral cortex enables higher level functions — body positioning, vision, hearing, touch sensations, movement, cognitive abilities.

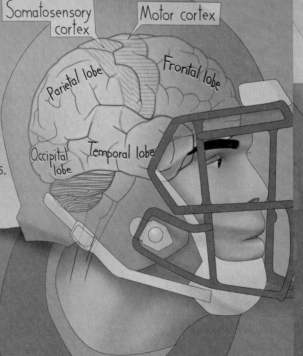

Somatosensory cortex

Motor cortex

Parietal lobe

Frontal lobe

Occipital lobe

Temporal lobe

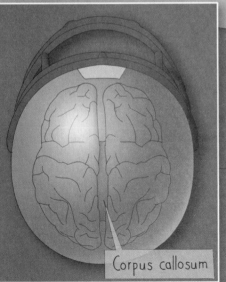

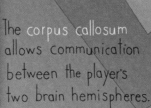

Corpus callosum

The corpus callosum allows communication between the player's two brain hemispheres.

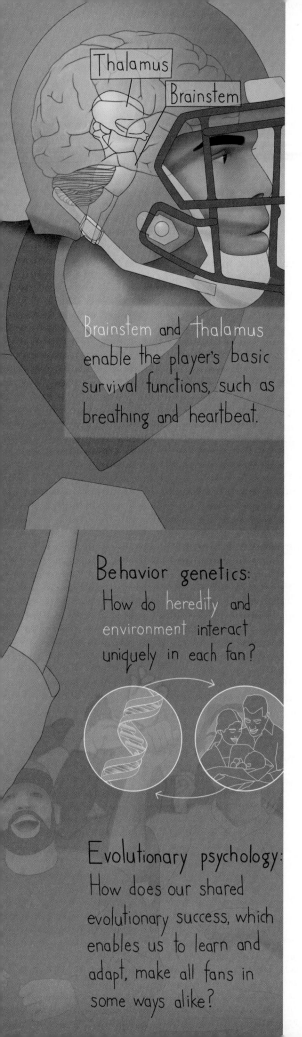

Brainstem and thalamus enable the player's basic survival functions, such as breathing and heartbeat.

Behavior genetics: How do heredity and environment interact uniquely in each fan?

Evolutionary psychology: How does our shared evolutionary success, which enables us to learn and adapt, make all fans in some ways alike?

The Biology of Behavior

IN 2000, a Virginia teacher began collecting sex magazines, visiting child pornography websites, and then making subtle advances on his young stepdaughter. When his wife called the police, he was arrested and later convicted of child molestation. Though put into a sexual addiction rehabilitation program, he still felt overwhelmed by his sexual urges. The day before being sentenced to prison, he went to his local emergency room complaining of a headache and thoughts of suicide. He was also distraught over his uncontrollable impulses, which led him to proposition nurses.

A brain scan located the problem—in his mind's biology. Behind his right temple there was an egg-sized brain tumor. After surgeons removed the tumor, his lewd impulses faded and he returned home to his wife and stepdaughter. All was well until a year later, when the tumor partially grew back, and with it the sexual urges. A second tumor removal again lessened the urges (Burns & Swerdlow, 2003).

This case illustrates what you likely believe: that you reside in your head. If surgeons transplanted all your organs below your neck, and even your skin and limbs, you would *(Yes?)* still be you. An acquaintance of mine [DM's] received a new heart from a woman who, in a rare operation, had received a matched heart-lung transplant. When the two chanced to meet in their hospital ward, she introduced herself: "I think you have my heart." But only her heart. Her self, she assumed, still resided in her head. We rightly presume that our brain enables our mind.

Indeed, no principle is more central to today's psychology than this: *Everything psychological is simultaneously biological.* Throughout this book, you will find examples of this interplay.

In Modules 3 through 5, we start small and build from the bottom up—from nerve cells up to the brain. In Module 6, we consider how our genetic histories predispose our shared human nature, and, in combination with our environments, our individual differences. ■

35

MODULE 3 Neural and Hormonal Systems

◀◉▶ **3-1** Why are psychologists concerned with human biology?

Your every idea, every mood, every urge is a biological happening. You love, laugh, and cry with your body. Without your body—your genes, your brain, your appearance—you would, indeed, be nobody. **Biological psychologists** study the links between our biology and behavior. We find it convenient and intuitive to talk separately of biological and psychological influences on behavior (Forstmann & Burgmer, 2015). But we need to remember that to think, feel, or act without a body would be like running without legs.

Neural Communication

For scientists, it is a happy fact of nature that the information systems of humans and other animals operate similarly—so much so that you could not distinguish between small samples of brain tissue from a human and a monkey. This similarity allows researchers to study relatively simple animals to discover how our neural systems operate. Cars differ, but all have engines, accelerators, steering wheels, and brakes. A space alien could study any one of them and grasp the operating principles. Likewise, animals differ, yet their nervous systems operate similarly. Though the human brain is more complex than a rat's, both follow the same principles.

Neurons

◀◉▶ **3-2** What are neurons, and how do they transmit information?

Our body's neural information system is complexity built from simplicity. Its building blocks are **neurons,** or nerve cells. Throughout life, new neurons are born and unused neurons wither away (Shors, 2014). To fathom our thoughts and actions, our memories and moods, we must first understand how neurons work and communicate.

Neurons differ, but all are variations on the same theme (**FIGURE 3.1**). Each consists of a *cell body* and its branching fibers. The often bushy **dendrite** fibers receive information and conduct it toward the cell body. From there, the cell's single lengthy **axon** fiber passes the message through its terminal branches to other neurons or to muscles or glands. (See **FIGURE 3.2**.) Dendrites listen. Axons speak.

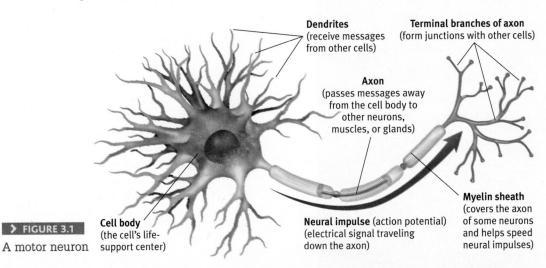

Dendrites
(receive messages from other cells)

Terminal branches of axon
(form junctions with other cells)

Axon
(passes messages away from the cell body to other neurons, muscles, or glands)

Myelin sheath
(covers the axon of some neurons and helps speed neural impulses)

Cell body
(the cell's life-support center)

Neural impulse (action potential)
(electrical signal traveling down the axon)

❯ **FIGURE 3.1**
A motor neuron

Unlike the short dendrites, axons may be very long, projecting several feet through the body. A human neuron carrying orders to a leg muscle, for example, has a cell body and axon roughly on the scale of a basketball attached to a 4-mile-long rope. Much as home electrical wire is insulated, some axons are encased in a **myelin sheath,** a layer of fatty tissue that insulates them and speeds their impulses. As myelin is laid down up to about age 25, neural efficiency, judgment, and self-control grow (Fields, 2008). If the myelin sheath degenerates, *multiple sclerosis* results: Communication to muscles slows, with eventual loss of muscle control.

Supporting our billions of nerve cells are spidery **glial cells** ("glue cells"). Neurons are like queen bees; on their own they cannot feed or sheathe themselves. Glial cells are worker bees. They provide nutrients and insulating myelin, guide neural connections, and clean up after neurons send messages to one another. Glia also play a role in learning and thinking. By "chatting" with neurons they participate in information transmission and memory (Fields, 2011, 2013; Miller, 2005).

In more complex animal brains, the proportion of glia to neurons increases. A postmortem analysis of Albert Einstein's brain did not find more or larger-than-usual neurons, but it did reveal a much greater concentration of glial cells than found in an average Albert's head (Fields, 2004).

The Neural Impulse

Neurons transmit messages when stimulated by signals from our senses or when triggered by chemical signals from neighboring neurons. A neuron sends a message by firing an impulse, called the **action potential**—a brief electrical charge that travels down its axon.

Depending on the type of fiber, a neural impulse travels at speeds ranging from a sluggish 2 miles per hour to more than 200 miles per hour. But even its top speed is 3 million times slower than that of electricity through a wire. We measure brain activity in milliseconds (thousandths of a second) and computer activity in nanoseconds (billionths of a second). Thus, unlike the nearly instantaneous reactions of a computer, your reaction to a sudden event, such as a child darting in front of your car, may take a quarter-second or more. Your brain is vastly more complex than a computer but slower at executing simple responses. And if you were an elephant—whose round-trip message travel time from a yank on the tail to the brain and back to the tail is 100 times longer than that of a tiny shrew—your reflexes would be slower yet (More et al., 2010).

Like batteries, neurons generate electricity from chemical events. In the neuron's chemistry-to-electricity process, *ions* (electrically charged atoms) are exchanged. The fluid outside an axon's membrane has mostly positively charged sodium ions. A resting axon's fluid interior (which includes both large, negatively charged protein ions and smaller, positively charged potassium ions) has a mostly negative charge. Like a tightly guarded facility, the axon's surface is selective about what it allows through its doors. We say the axon's surface is *selectively permeable.* This positive-outside/negative-inside state is called the *resting potential* (measured at about –70 mV [millivolts]; see **FIGURE 3.3** on the next page).

When a neuron fires, the first section of the axon opens its gates, rather like a sewer cover flipping open, and positively charged sodium ions (attracted to the negative interior) flood in through the now-open channels (Figure 3.3 on the next page). The loss of the inside/outside charge difference, called *depolarization,* causes the next section of axon channels to open, and then the next, like a line of falling dominos. This temporary inflow of positive ions is the neural impulse—the action potential (measured at about +40 mV). Each neuron is itself a miniature decision-making device performing complex calculations as it receives signals from hundreds, even thousands, of other neurons. The mind boggles when

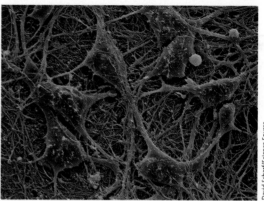

^ FIGURE 3.2

Neurons communicating When we learn about neurons, we often see them one at a time to learn their parts. But our billions of neurons exist in a vast and dense interconnected web. One neuron's terminal branches send messages to neighboring dendrites. Read on to learn more about this complex and fascinating electrochemical communication process.

biological psychology the scientific study of the links between biological (genetic, neural, hormonal) and psychological processes. (Some biological psychologists call themselves *behavioral neuroscientists, neuropsychologists, behavior geneticists, physiological psychologists,* or *biopsychologists.*)

neuron a nerve cell; the basic building block of the nervous system.

dendrites a neuron's often bushy, branching extensions that receive messages and conduct impulses toward the cell body.

axon the neuron extension that passes messages through its branches to other neurons or to muscles or glands.

myelin [MY-uh-lin] sheath a fatty tissue layer segmentally encasing the axons of some neurons; enables vastly greater transmission speed as neural impulses hop from one node to the next.

glial cells (glia) cells in the nervous system that support, nourish, and protect neurons; they may also play a role in learning, thinking, and memory.

action potential a neural impulse; a brief electrical charge that travels down an axon.

> FIGURE 3.3

Action potential Bodily sensations and actions—detecting a hug or kicking a soccer ball—happen when our neurons are stimulated enough that their membrane's electrical charge reaches a threshold (–55 mV in this example—see graph at right). This prompts each of those neurons to "fire" an impulse—an action potential—which travels down its axon (see numbered drawings below) and transmits a message to other neurons, muscles, or glands.

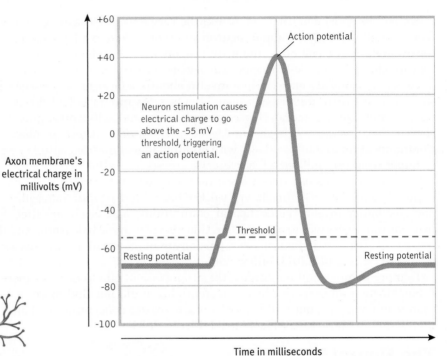

Axon membrane's electrical charge in millivolts (mV)

Action potential

Neuron stimulation causes electrical charge to go above the -55 mV threshold, triggering an action potential.

Threshold

Resting potential   Resting potential

Time in milliseconds

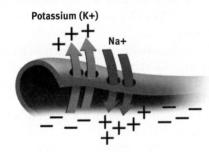

Sodium ions (Na+)

Cell body end of axon

1. Neuron stimulation causes a brief change in electrical charge. If strong enough, this opens gates to allow positively-charged sodium ions to flood in, producing a momentary depolarization called the action potential.

2. This initial depolarization influences the electrical charge of the next portion of the axon. Gates in this neighboring area now open, allowing positively-charged sodium ions to flow in and depolarize that area. Meanwhile, other gates open in the first part of the axon, allowing potassium ions to flow out, repolarizing this section.

Potassium (K+)

Na+

3. As the action potential moves speedily down the axon, sodium/potassium pumps in the cell membrane finish restoring the first section of the axon to its resting potential.

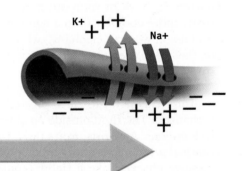

K+   Na+

Direction of action potential: toward axon terminals

imagining this electrochemical process repeating up to 100 or even 1000 times a second. But this is just the first of many astonishments.

Most neural signals are *excitatory*, somewhat like pushing a neuron's accelerator. Some are *inhibitory*, more like pushing its brake. If excitatory signals exceed the inhibitory signals by a minimum intensity, or **threshold** (about –55 mV; see Figure 3.3), the combined signals trigger an action potential. (Think of it this way: If the excitatory party animals outvote the inhibitory party poopers, the party's on.) The action potential then travels down the axon, which branches into junctions with hundreds or thousands of other neurons or with the body's muscles and glands.

Neurons need tiny breaks between action potentials. During a resting pause called the **refractory period,** subsequent action potentials cannot occur until the axon returns to its resting state. Then the neuron can fire again.

Increasing the level of stimulation above the threshold will not increase the neural impulse's intensity. The neuron's reaction is an **all-or-none response:** Like guns, neurons either fire or they don't. How, then, do we detect the intensity of a stimulus? How do we distinguish a gentle touch from a big hug? A strong stimulus can trigger *more* neurons to fire, and to fire more often. But it does not affect the action potential's strength or speed. Squeezing a trigger harder won't make a bullet go faster.

 LaunchPad For an animated explanation of this process, visit LaunchPad's *Concept Practice: Action Potentials.*

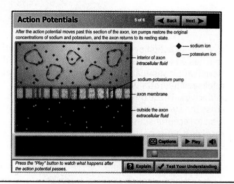

RETRIEVE IT   [✖]

- When a neuron fires an action potential, the information travels through the axon, the dendrites, and the cell body, but not in that order. Place these three structures in the correct order.

ANSWER: dendrites, cell body, axon

- How does our nervous system allow us to experience the difference between a slap and a tap on the back?

ANSWER: Stronger stimuli (the slap) cause more neurons to fire and to fire more frequently than happens with weaker stimuli (the tap).

How Neurons Communicate

3-3 How do nerve cells communicate with other nerve cells?

Neurons interweave so intricately that even with a microscope you would have trouble seeing where one neuron ends and another begins. Scientists once believed that the axon of one cell fused with the dendrites of another in an uninterrupted fabric. Then British physiologist Sir Charles Sherrington (1857–1952) noticed that neural impulses were taking an unexpectedly long time to travel a neural pathway. Inferring that there must be a brief interruption in the transmission, Sherrington called the meeting point between neurons a **synapse.**

We now know that the axon terminal of one neuron is in fact separated from the receiving neuron by a *synaptic gap (or synaptic cleft)* less than a millionth of an inch wide. Spanish anatomist Santiago Ramón y Cajal (1852–1934) marveled at these near-unions of neurons, calling them "protoplasmic kisses." "Like elegant ladies air-kissing so as not to muss their makeup, dendrites and axons don't quite touch," noted poet Diane Ackerman (2004, p. 37). How do the neurons execute this protoplasmic kiss, sending information across the tiny synaptic gap? The answer is one of the important scientific discoveries of our age.

threshold the level of stimulation required to trigger a neural impulse.

refractory period a brief resting pause that occurs after a neuron has fired; subsequent action potentials cannot occur until the axon returns to its resting state.

all-or-none response a neuron's reaction of either firing (with a full-strength response) or not firing.

synapse [SIN-aps] the junction between the axon tip of the sending neuron and the dendrite or cell body of the receiving neuron. The tiny gap at this junction is called the *synaptic gap* or *synaptic cleft*.

"All information processing in the brain involves neurons 'talking to' each other at synapses."

Neuroscientist Solomon H. Snyder (1984)

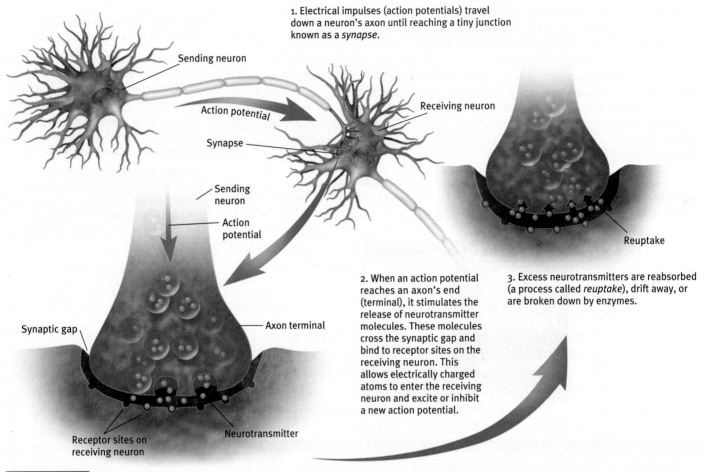

1. Electrical impulses (action potentials) travel down a neuron's axon until reaching a tiny junction known as a *synapse*.

Sending neuron

Action potential

Receiving neuron

Synapse

Sending neuron

Action potential

Reuptake

Synaptic gap

Axon terminal

2. When an action potential reaches an axon's end (terminal), it stimulates the release of neurotransmitter molecules. These molecules cross the synaptic gap and bind to receptor sites on the receiving neuron. This allows electrically charged atoms to enter the receiving neuron and excite or inhibit a new action potential.

3. Excess neurotransmitters are reabsorbed (a process called *reuptake*), drift away, or are broken down by enzymes.

Receptor sites on receiving neuron

Neurotransmitter

∧ FIGURE 3.4

How neurons communicate

When an action potential reaches the knob-like terminals at an axon's end, it triggers the release of chemical messengers, called **neurotransmitters** (**FIGURE 3.4**). Within 1/10,000th of a second, the neurotransmitter molecules cross the synaptic gap and bind to receptor sites on the receiving neuron—as precisely as a key fits a lock. For an instant, the neurotransmitter unlocks tiny channels at the receiving site, and electrically charged atoms flow in, exciting or inhibiting the receiving neuron's readiness to fire. The excess neurotransmitters then drift away, are broken down by enzymes, or are reabsorbed by the sending neuron—a process called **reuptake.**

neurotransmitters chemical messengers that cross the synaptic gaps between neurons. When released by the sending neuron, neurotransmitters travel across the synapse and bind to receptor sites on the receiving neuron, thereby influencing whether that neuron will generate a neural impulse.

reuptake a neurotransmitter's reabsorption by the sending neuron.

endorphins [en-DOR-fins] "morphine within"—natural, opiate-like neurotransmitters linked to pain control and to pleasure.

RETRIEVE IT [✖]

• What happens in the *synaptic gap?*

ANSWER: Neurons send neurotransmitters (chemical messengers) across this tiny space between one neuron's terminal branch and the next neuron's dendrite or cell body.

• What is *reuptake?* What two other things can happen to excess neurotransmitters after a neuron reacts?

ANSWER: Reuptake occurs when excess neurotransmitters are reabsorbed by the sending neuron. They can also drift away or be broken down by enzymes.

How Neurotransmitters Influence Us

◀●▶ 3-4 How do neurotransmitters influence behavior, and how do drugs and other chemicals affect neurotransmission?

In their quest to understand neural communication, researchers have discovered several dozen neurotransmitters and almost as many new questions: Are certain neurotransmitters found only in specific places? How do neurotransmitters

affect our moods, memories, and mental abilities? Can we boost or diminish these effects through drugs or diet?

Other modules explore neurotransmitter influences on hunger and thinking, depression and euphoria, addictions and therapy. For now, let's glimpse how neurotransmitters influence our motions and emotions. Particular neurotransmitters affect specific behaviors and emotions (**TABLE 3.1**).

One of the best-understood neurotransmitters, *acetylcholine (ACh)*, plays a role in learning and memory. In addition, it is the messenger at every junction between motor neurons (which carry information from the brain and spinal cord to the body's tissues) and skeletal muscles. When ACh is released to our muscle cell receptors, the muscle contracts. If ACh transmission is blocked, as happens during some kinds of anesthesia and with some poisons, the muscles cannot contract and we are paralyzed.

Candace Pert and Solomon Snyder (1973) made an exciting discovery about neurotransmitters when they attached a radioactive tracer to morphine, showing where it was taken up in an animal's brain. The morphine, an opiate drug that elevates mood and eases pain, bound to receptors in areas linked with mood and pain sensations. But why would the brain have these "opiate receptors"? Why would it have a chemical lock, unless it also had a natural key to open it?

Researchers soon confirmed that the brain does indeed produce its own naturally occurring opiates. Our body releases several types of neurotransmitter molecules similar to morphine in response to pain and vigorous exercise. These **endorphins** (short for *endogenous* [produced within] *morphine*) help explain good feelings such as the "runner's high" (Boecker et al., 2008), the painkilling effects of acupuncture, and the indifference to pain in some severely injured people. But once again, new knowledge led to new questions.

> "When it comes to the brain, if you want to see the action, follow the neurotransmitters."
>
> *Neuroscientist Floyd Bloom (1993)*

> Physician Lewis Thomas, on the endorphins: "There it is, a biologically universal act of mercy. I cannot explain it, except to say that I would have put it in had I been around at the very beginning, sitting as a member of a planning committee."
>
> The Youngest Science, *1983*

⌄ TABLE 3.1

Some Neurotransmitters and Their Functions

Neurotransmitter	Function	Examples of Malfunctions
Acetylcholine (ACh)	Enables muscle action, learning, and memory	With Alzheimer's disease, ACh-producing neurons deteriorate.
Dopamine	Influences movement, learning, attention, and emotion	Oversupply linked to schizophrenia. Undersupply linked to tremors and decreased mobility in Parkinson's disease.
Serotonin	Affects mood, hunger, sleep, and arousal	Undersupply linked to depression. Some drugs that raise serotonin levels are used to treat depression.
Norepinephrine	Helps control alertness and arousal	Undersupply can depress mood.
GABA (gamma-aminobutyric acid)	A major inhibitory neurotransmitter	Undersupply linked to seizures, tremors, and insomnia.
Glutamate	A major excitatory neurotransmitter; involved in memory	Oversupply can overstimulate brain, producing migraines or seizures (which is why some people avoid MSG, monosodium glutamate, in food).
Endorphins	Neurotransmitters that influence the perception of pain or pleasure	Oversupply with opiate drugs can suppress the body's natural endorphin supply.

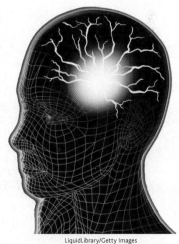

LiquidLibrary/Getty Images

HOW DRUGS AND OTHER CHEMICALS ALTER NEUROTRANSMISSION If indeed the endorphins lessen pain and boost mood, why not flood the brain with artificial opiates, thereby intensifying the brain's own "feel-good" chemistry? But there is a problem: When flooded with opiate drugs such as heroin and morphine, the brain, to maintain its chemical balance, may stop producing its own natural

agonist a molecule that increases a neurotransmitter's action.

antagonist a molecule that inhibits or blocks a neurotransmitter's action.

nervous system the body's speedy, electrochemical communication network, consisting of all the nerve cells of the peripheral and central nervous systems.

central nervous system (CNS) the brain and spinal cord.

peripheral nervous system (PNS) the sensory and motor neurons that connect the central nervous system (CNS) to the rest of the body.

nerves bundled axons that form neural cables connecting the central nervous system with muscles, glands, and sense organs.

sensory (afferent) neurons neurons that carry incoming information from the sensory receptors to the brain and spinal cord.

LaunchPad For an illustrated review of neural communication, visit Launch-Pad's *PsychSim 6: Neural Messages*.

opiates. When the drug is withdrawn, the brain may then be deprived of any form of opiate, causing intense discomfort. For suppressing the body's own neurotransmitter production, nature charges a price.

Drugs and other chemicals affect brain chemistry, often by either exciting or inhibiting neurons' firing. **Agonist** molecules increase a neurotransmitter's action. Agonists may increase the production or release of neurotransmitters, or block reuptake in the synapse. Other agonists may be similar enough to a neurotransmitter to bind to its receptor and mimic its excitatory or inhibitory effects. Some opiate drugs are agonists and produce a temporary "high" by amplifying normal sensations of arousal or pleasure.

Antagonists decrease a neurotransmitter's action by blocking production or release. Botulin, a poison that can form in improperly canned food, causes paralysis by blocking ACh release. (Small injections of botulin—Botox—smooth wrinkles by paralyzing the underlying facial muscles.) These antagonists are enough like the natural neurotransmitter to occupy its receptor site and block its effect, but are not similar enough to stimulate the receptor (rather like foreign coins that fit into, but won't operate, a candy machine). Curare, a poison some South American Indians have applied to hunting-dart tips, occupies and blocks ACh receptor sites on muscles, producing paralysis in their prey.

RETRIEVE IT [✳]

• Serotonin, dopamine, and endorphins are all chemical messengers called _____.

ANSWER: neurotransmitters

• Curare poisoning paralyzes its victims by blocking ACh receptors involved in muscle movements. Morphine mimics endorphin actions. Which is an agonist, and which is an antagonist?

ANSWER: Morphine is an agonist; curare is an antagonist.

The Nervous System

◔ **3-5** What are the functions of the nervous system's main divisions, and what are the three main types of neurons?

All those neurons communicating with neurotransmitters make up our body's **nervous system** (**FIGURE 3.5**). This communication network allows us to take in information from the world and the body's tissues, to make decisions, and to send back information and orders to the body's tissues. A quick overview: The brain and spinal cord form the **central nervous system (CNS),** the body's decision maker. The **peripheral nervous system (PNS)** is responsible for gathering information and for transmitting CNS decisions to other body parts. **Nerves,** electrical cables formed of bundles of axons, link the CNS with the body's sensory receptors, muscles, and glands. The optic nerve, for example, bundles a million axons into a single cable carrying the messages each eye sends to the brain (Mason & Kandel, 1991).

Information travels in the nervous system through three types of neurons. **Sensory neurons** carry messages from the body's tissues and sensory receptors inward (thus, they are *afferent*) to

❤ FIGURE 3.5

The functional divisions of the human nervous system

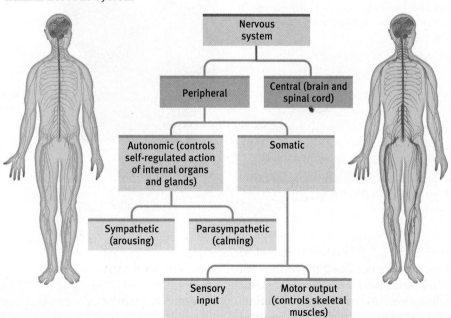

the brain and spinal cord for processing. **Motor neurons** (which are *efferent*) carry instructions from the central nervous system out to the body's muscles and glands. Between the sensory input and motor output, information is processed via the **interneurons.** Our complexity resides mostly in these interneurons. Our nervous system has a few million sensory neurons, a few million motor neurons, and billions and billions of interneurons.

The Peripheral Nervous System

Our peripheral nervous system has two components—somatic and autonomic. Our **somatic nervous system** enables voluntary control of our skeletal muscles. As you reach the end of this page, your somatic nervous system will report to your brain the current state of your skeletal muscles and carry instructions back, triggering a response from your hand so you can read on.

Our **autonomic nervous system (ANS)** controls our glands and our internal organ muscles. The ANS influences functions such as glandular activity, heartbeat, and digestion. (*Autonomic* means "self-regulating.") Like an automatic pilot, this system may be consciously overridden, but usually it operates on its own (autonomously).

The autonomic nervous system serves two important functions (**FIGURE 3.6**). The **sympathetic nervous system** arouses and expends energy. If something alarms or challenges you (such as a longed-for job interview), your sympathetic

motor (efferent) neurons neurons that carry outgoing information from the brain and spinal cord to the muscles and glands.

interneurons neurons within the brain and spinal cord; communicate internally and process information between the sensory inputs and motor outputs.

somatic nervous system the division of the peripheral nervous system that controls the body's skeletal muscles. Also called the *skeletal nervous system.*

autonomic [aw-tuh-NAHM-ik] nervous system (ANS) the part of the peripheral nervous system that controls the glands and the muscles of the internal organs (such as the heart). Its sympathetic division arouses; its parasympathetic division calms.

sympathetic nervous system the division of the autonomic nervous system that arouses the body, mobilizing its energy.

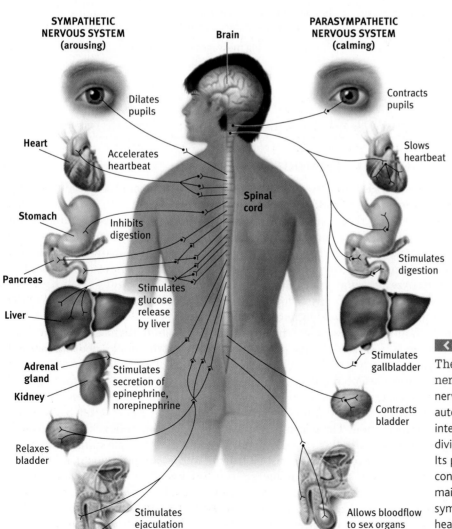

SYMPATHETIC NERVOUS SYSTEM (arousing)

Brain

PARASYMPATHETIC NERVOUS SYSTEM (calming)

Dilates pupils

Contracts pupils

Heart

Accelerates heartbeat

Slows heartbeat

Spinal cord

Stomach

Inhibits digestion

Stimulates digestion

Pancreas

Stimulates glucose release by liver

Liver

Adrenal gland

Stimulates secretion of epinephrine, norepinephrine

Stimulates gallbladder

Kidney

Contracts bladder

Relaxes bladder

Stimulates ejaculation in male

Allows bloodflow to sex organs

‹ FIGURE 3.6

The dual functions of the autonomic nervous system The autonomic nervous system controls the more autonomous (or self-regulating) internal functions. Its sympathetic division arouses and expends energy. Its parasympathetic division calms and conserves energy, allowing routine maintenance activity. For example, sympathetic stimulation accelerates heartbeat, whereas parasympathetic stimulation slows it.

parasympathetic nervous system the division of the autonomic nervous system that calms the body, conserving its energy.

reflex a simple, automatic response to a sensory stimulus, such as the knee-jerk response.

endocrine [EN-duh-krin] system the body's "slow" chemical communication system; a set of glands that secrete hormones into the bloodstream.

hormones chemical messengers that are manufactured by the endocrine glands, travel through the bloodstream, and affect other tissues.

nervous system will accelerate your heartbeat, raise your blood pressure, slow your digestion, raise your blood sugar, and cool you with perspiration, making you alert and ready for action. When the stress subsides (the interview is over), your **parasympathetic nervous system** will produce the opposite effects, conserving energy as it calms you. The sympathetic and parasympathetic nervous systems work together to keep us in a steady internal state called *homeostasis*.

I [DM] recently experienced my ANS in action. Before sending me into an MRI machine for a shoulder scan, the technician asked if I had issues with claustrophobia. "No, I'm fine," I assured her, with perhaps a hint of macho swagger. Moments later, as I found myself on my back, stuck deep inside a coffin-sized box and unable to move, my sympathetic nervous system had a different idea. Claustrophobia overtook me. My heart began pounding, and I felt a desperate urge to escape. Just as I was about to cry out for release, I felt my calming parasympathetic nervous system kick in. My heart rate slowed and my body relaxed, though my arousal surged again before the 20-minute confinement ended. "You did well!" the technician said, unaware of my ANS roller-coaster ride.

RETRIEVE IT [✖]

- Match the type of neuron to its description.

Type	Description
1. Motor neurons	a. carry incoming messages from sensory receptors to the CNS.
2. Sensory neurons	b. communicate within the CNS and process information between incoming and outgoing messages.
3. Interneurons	c. carry outgoing messages from the CNS to muscles and glands.

ANSWERS: 1. c, 2. a, 3. b

- What bodily changes does your ANS direct before and after you give an important speech?

ANSWER: Responding to this challenge, your ANS *sympathetic* division will arouse you. It accelerates your heartbeat, raises your blood pressure and blood sugar, slows your digestion, and cools you with perspiration. After you give the speech, your ANS *parasympathetic* division will reverse these effects.

The Central Nervous System

From neurons "talking" to other neurons arises the complexity of the central nervous system's brain and spinal cord.

It is the brain that enables our humanity—our thinking, feeling, and acting. Tens of billions of neurons, each communicating with thousands of other neurons, yield an ever-changing wiring diagram. By one estimate—projecting from neuron counts in small brain samples—our brains have some 86 billion neurons (Azevedo et al. 2009; Herculano-Houzel, 2012).

The brain's neurons cluster into work groups called *neural networks*. To understand why, Stephen Kosslyn and Olivier Koenig (1992, p. 12) have invited us to "think about why cities exist; why don't people distribute themselves more evenly across the countryside?" Like people networking with people, neurons network with nearby neurons with which they can have short, fast connections.

The other part of the CNS, the *spinal cord,* is a two-way information highway connecting the peripheral nervous system and the brain. Ascending neural fibers send up sensory information, and descending fibers send back motor-control information. The neural pathways governing our **reflexes,** our automatic responses to stimuli, illustrate the spinal cord's work. A simple spinal reflex pathway is composed of a single sensory neuron and a single motor neuron. These often communicate through an interneuron. The knee-jerk response, for example, involves one such simple pathway. A headless warm body could do it.

Another neural circuit enables the pain reflex (**FIGURE 3.7**). When your finger touches a flame, neural activity (excited by the heat) travels via sensory neurons

"The body is made up of millions and millions of crumbs."

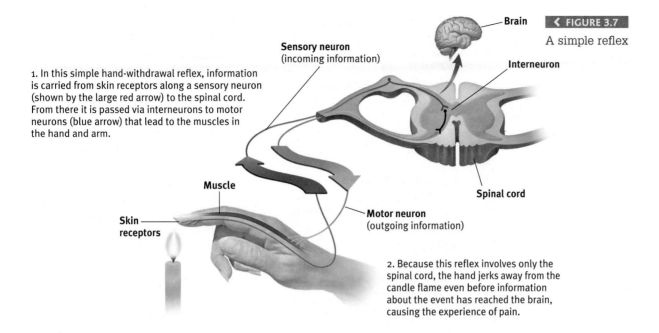

❮ FIGURE 3.7

A simple reflex

1. In this simple hand-withdrawal reflex, information is carried from skin receptors along a sensory neuron (shown by the large red arrow) to the spinal cord. From there it is passed via interneurons to motor neurons (blue arrow) that lead to the muscles in the hand and arm.

Brain

Sensory neuron (incoming information)

Interneuron

Muscle

Skin receptors

Spinal cord

Motor neuron (outgoing information)

2. Because this reflex involves only the spinal cord, the hand jerks away from the candle flame even before information about the event has reached the brain, causing the experience of pain.

to interneurons in your spinal cord. These interneurons respond by activating motor neurons leading to the muscles in your arm. Because the simple pain-reflex pathway runs through the spinal cord and right back out, your hand jerks away from the candle's flame *before* your brain receives and responds to the information that causes you to feel pain. That's why it feels as if your hand jerks away not by your choice, but on its own.

Information travels to and from the brain by way of the spinal cord. Were the top of your spinal cord severed, you would not feel pain from your paralyzed body below. Nor would you feel pleasure. With your brain literally out of touch with your body, you would lose all sensation and voluntary movement in body regions with sensory and motor connections to the spinal cord below its point of injury. You would exhibit the knee-jerk response without feeling the tap. Men paralyzed below the waist may be capable of an erection (a simple reflex) if their genitals are stimulated (Goldstein, 2000). Women similarly paralyzed may respond with vaginal lubrication. But, depending on where and how completely the spinal cord is severed, they may be genitally unresponsive to erotic images and have no genital feeling (Kennedy & Over, 1990; Sipski & Alexander, 1999). To produce bodily pain or pleasure, the sensory information must reach the brain.

The Endocrine System

◐ 3-6 How does the endocrine system transmit information and interact with the nervous system?

So far, we have focused on the body's speedy electrochemical information system. Interconnected with your nervous system is a second communication system, the **endocrine system** (**FIGURE 3.8** on the next page). The endocrine system's glands secrete another form of chemical messengers, **hormones,** which travel through the bloodstream and affect other tissues, including the brain. When hormones act on the brain, they influence our interest in sex, food, and aggression.

Some hormones are chemically identical to neurotransmitters (the chemical messengers that diffuse across a synapse and excite or inhibit an adjacent neuron). The endocrine system and nervous system are therefore close relatives: Both produce molecules that act on receptors elsewhere. Like many relatives,

"If the nervous system be cut off between the brain and other parts, the experiences of those other parts are nonexistent for the mind. The eye is blind, the ear deaf, the hand insensible and motionless."

William James,
Principles of Psychology, *1890*

> FIGURE 3.8

The endocrine system

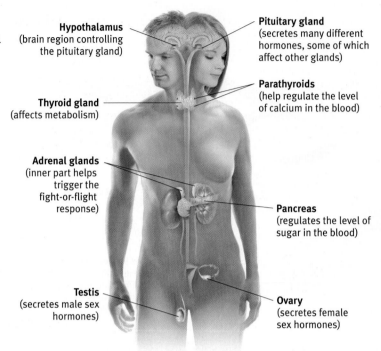

Hypothalamus
(brain region controlling
the pituitary gland)

Pituitary gland
(secretes many different
hormones, some of which
affect other glands)

Parathyroids
(help regulate the level
of calcium in the blood)

Thyroid gland
(affects metabolism)

Adrenal glands
(inner part helps
trigger the
fight-or-flight
response)

Pancreas
(regulates the level of
sugar in the blood)

Testis
(secretes male sex
hormones)

Ovary
(secretes female
sex hormones)

they also differ. The speedy nervous system zips messages from eyes to brain to hand in a fraction of a second. Endocrine messages trudge along in the bloodstream, taking several seconds or more to travel from the gland to the target tissue. If the nervous system transmits information with text-message speed, the endocrine system delivers an old-fashioned letter.

Endocrine messages tend to outlast the effects of neural messages. That helps explain why upset feelings may linger beyond our awareness of what upset us. When this happens, it takes time for us to "simmer down."

In a moment of danger, for example, the ANS orders the **adrenal glands** on top of the kidneys to release *epinephrine* and *norepinephrine* (also called *adrenaline* and *noradrenaline*). These hormones increase heart rate, blood pressure, and blood sugar, providing a surge of energy. When the emergency passes, the hormones—and the feelings—linger a while.

The most influential endocrine gland is the **pituitary gland,** a pea-sized structure located in the core of the brain, where it is controlled by an adjacent brain area, the *hypothalamus*. Among the hormones released by the pituitary is a growth hormone that stimulates physical development. Another is *oxytocin,* which enables contractions associated with birthing, milk flow during nursing, and orgasm. Oxytocin also promotes pair bonding, group cohesion, and social trust (De Dreu et al., 2010; Zak, 2012). During a laboratory game, those given a nasal squirt of oxytocin rather than a placebo were more likely to trust strangers with their money and with confidential information (Kosfeld et al., 2005; Mikolajczak et al., 2010).

Pituitary secretions also direct other endocrine glands to release their hormones. The pituitary, then, is a master gland (whose own master is the hypothalamus). For example, under the brain's influence, the pituitary triggers your sex glands to release sex hormones. These in turn influence your brain and behavior (Goetz et al., 2014).

This feedback system (brain → pituitary → other glands → hormones → body and brain) reveals the intimate connection of the nervous and endocrine systems. The nervous system directs endocrine secretions, which then affect the nervous system. Conducting and coordinating this whole electrochemical orchestra is that maestro we call the brain.

adrenal [ah-DREEN-el] glands a pair of endocrine glands that sit just above the kidneys and secrete hormones (epinephrine and norepinephrine) that help arouse the body in times of stress.

pituitary gland the endocrine system's most influential gland. Under the influence of the hypothalamus, the pituitary regulates growth and controls other endocrine glands.

RETRIEVE IT

● Why is the pituitary gland called the "master gland"?

ANSWER: Responding to signals from the hypothalamus, the pituitary releases hormones that trigger other endocrine glands to secrete hormones, which in turn influence brain and behavior.

● How are the nervous and endocrine systems alike, and how do they differ?

ANSWER: Both of these communication systems produce chemical molecules that act on the body's receptors to influence our behavior and emotions. The endocrine system, which secretes hormones into the bloodstream, delivers its messages much more slowly than the speedy nervous system, and the effects of the endocrine system's messages tend to linger much longer than those of the nervous system.

Learning Objectives

Test Yourself by taking a moment to answer each of these Learning Objective Questions (repeated here from within the module). Then turn to Appendix D, Complete Module Reviews, to check your answers. Research suggests that trying to answer these questions on your own will improve your long-term memory of the concepts (McDaniel et al., 2009).

3-1 Why are psychologists concerned with human biology?

3-2 What are neurons, and how do they transmit information?

3-3 How do nerve cells communicate with other nerve cells?

3-4 How do neurotransmitters influence behavior, and how do drugs and other chemicals affect neurotransmission?

3-5 What are the functions of the nervous system's main divisions, and what are the three main types of neurons?

3-6 How does the endocrine system transmit information and interact with the nervous system?

Terms and Concepts to Remember

Test yourself on these terms by trying to write down the definition in your own words before flipping back to the referenced page to check your answers.

biological psychology, p. 36

neuron, p. 36

dendrites, p. 36

axon, p. 36

myelin [MY-uh-lin] sheath, p. 37

glial cells (glia), p. 37

action potential, p. 37

threshold, p. 38

refractory period, p. 39

all-or-none response, p. 39

synapse [SIN-aps], p. 39

neurotransmitters, p. 40

reuptake, p. 40

endorphins [en-DOR-fins], p. 41

agonist, p. 42

antagonist, p. 42

nervous system, p. 42

central nervous system (CNS), p. 42

peripheral nervous system (PNS), p. 42

nerves, p. 42

sensory (afferent) neurons, p. 42

motor (efferent) neurons, p. 43

interneurons, p. 43

somatic nervous system, p. 43

autonomic [aw-tuh-NAHM-ik] nervous system (ANS), p. 43

sympathetic nervous system, p. 43

parasympathetic nervous system, p. 44

reflex, p. 44

endocrine [EN-duh-krin] system, p. 45

hormones, p. 45

adrenal [ah-DREEN-el] glands, p. 46

pituitary gland, p. 46

Experience the Testing Effect

Test yourself repeatedly throughout your studies. This will not only help you figure out what you know and don't know; the testing itself will help you learn and remember the information more effectively thanks to the *testing effect*.

1. The neuron fiber that passes messages through its branches to other neurons or to muscles and glands is the _____.

2. The tiny space between the axon of one neuron and the dendrite or cell body of another is called the
   a. axon terminal.
   b. branching fiber.
   c. synaptic gap.
   d. threshold.

3. Regarding a neuron's response to stimulation, the intensity of the stimulus determines
   a. whether or not an impulse is generated.
   b. how fast an impulse is transmitted.
   c. how intense an impulse will be.
   d. whether reuptake will occur.

4. In a sending neuron, when an action potential reaches an axon terminal, the impulse triggers the release of chemical messengers called _____.

5. Endorphins are released in the brain in response to
   a. morphine or heroin.
   b. pain or vigorous exercise.

   c. the all-or-none response.
   d. all of the above.

6. The autonomic nervous system controls internal functions, such as heart rate and glandular activity. The word *autonomic* means
   a. calming.   c. self-regulating.
   b. voluntary.   d. arousing.

7. The sympathetic nervous system arouses us for action and the parasympathetic nervous system calms us down. Together, the two systems make up the _____ nervous system.

8. The neurons of the spinal cord are part of the _____ nervous system.

9. The most influential endocrine gland, known as the master gland, is the
   a. pituitary.   c. thyroid.
   b. hypothalamus.   d. pancreas.

10. The _____ _____ secrete(s) epinephrine and norepinephrine, helping to arouse the body during times of stress.

Find answers to these questions in Appendix E, in the back of the book.

Use ◎ LearningCurve to create your personalized study plan, which will direct you to the resources that will help you most in ◎ LaunchPad.

"You're certainly a lot less fun since the operation."

"I am a brain, Watson. The rest of me is a mere appendix."

Sherlock Holmes, in Arthur Conan Doyle's "The Adventure of the Mazarin Stone"

MODULE 4 Tools of Discovery and Older Brain Structures

The mind seeking to understand the brain—that is among the ultimate scientific challenges. And so it will always be. To paraphrase cosmologist John Barrow, a brain simple enough to be fully understood is too simple to produce a mind able to understand it.

When you think *about* your brain, you're thinking *with* your brain—by firing across millions of synapses and releasing billions of neurotransmitter molecules. Indeed, say neuroscientists, *the mind is what the brain does.*

The Tools of Discovery: Having Our Head Examined

👁 **4-1** How do neuroscientists study the brain's connections to behavior and mind?

A century ago, scientists had no tools high powered yet gentle enough to explore the living human brain. Early case studies helped localize some brain functions. Damage to one side of the brain often caused numbness or paralysis on the opposite side, suggesting that the body's right side is wired to the brain's left side, and vice versa. Damage to the back of the brain disrupted vision, and damage to the left-front part of the brain produced speech difficulties. Gradually, these early explorers were mapping the brain.

A living human brain exposed Today's neuroscience tools enable us to "look under the hood" and glimpse the brain at work, enabling the mind.

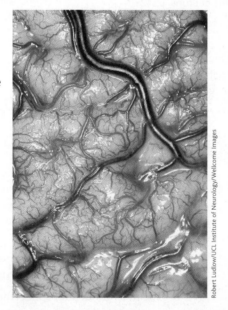

Now, within a lifetime, a new generation of neural mapmakers is charting the known universe's most amazing organ. Whether in the interests of science or medicine, they can selectively **lesion** (destroy) tiny clusters of normal or defective brain cells, leaving the surrounding tissue unharmed. Today's scientists can snoop on the messages of individual neurons, using modern microelectrodes with tips small enough to detect the electrical pulse in a single neuron. For example, they can now detect exactly where the information goes in a cat's brain when someone strokes its whisker. They can also stimulate various brain parts and note the effect, eavesdrop on the chatter of billions of neurons, and see color representations of the brain's energy-consuming activity. These techniques for peering into the thinking, feeling brain are doing for psychology what the microscope did for biology and the telescope did for astronomy.

Right now, your mental activity is emitting telltale electrical, metabolic, and magnetic signals that would enable neuroscientists to observe your brain at work. Electrical activity in your brain's billions of neurons sweeps in regular waves across its surface. An **electroencephalogram (EEG)** is an amplified readout of such waves (**FIGURE 4.1**). Researchers record the brain waves through a shower-cap-like hat that is filled with electrodes covered with a conductive gel.

"You must look into people, as well as at them," advised Lord Chesterfield in a 1746 letter to his son. Unlike EEGs, newer neuroimaging techniques give us that Superman-like ability to see inside the living brain. One such tool, the **PET (positron emission tomography) scan** (**FIGURE 4.2**), depicts brain activity by

lesion [LEE-zhuhn] tissue destruction. A brain lesion is a naturally or experimentally caused destruction of brain tissue.

electroencephalogram (EEG) an amplified recording of the waves of electrical activity sweeping across the brain's surface. These waves are measured by electrodes placed on the scalp.

PET (positron emission tomography) scan a visual display of brain activity that detects where a radioactive form of glucose goes while the brain performs a given task.

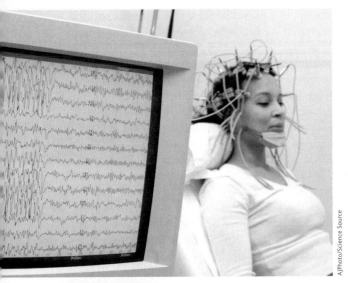

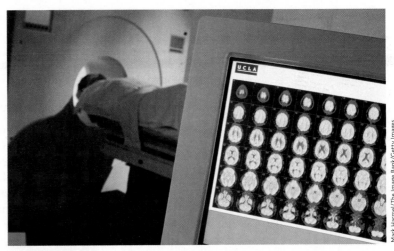

^ FIGURE 4.2

^ FIGURE 4.1

Brain hacking An electroencephalograph provides amplified tracings of waves of electrical activity in the brain.

The PET scan To obtain a PET scan, researchers inject volunteers with a low and harmless dose of a short-lived radioactive sugar. Detectors around the person's head pick up the release of gamma rays from the sugar, which has concentrated in active brain areas. A computer then processes and translates these signals into a map of the brain at work.

showing each brain area's consumption of its chemical fuel, the sugar glucose. Active neurons are glucose hogs. Our brain, though only about 2 percent of our body weight, consumes 20 percent of our calorie intake. After a person receives temporarily radioactive glucose, the PET scan can track the gamma rays released by this "food for thought" as a task is performed. Rather like weather radar showing rain activity, PET-scan "hot spots" show the most active brain areas as the person does mathematical calculations, looks at images of faces, or daydreams.

In **MRI (magnetic resonance imaging)** brain scans, the person's head is put in a strong magnetic field, which aligns the spinning atoms of brain molecules. Then, a radio-wave pulse momentarily disorients the atoms. When the atoms return to their normal spin, they emit signals that provide a detailed picture of soft tissues, including the brain. MRI scans have revealed a larger-than-average neural area in the left hemisphere of musicians who display perfect pitch (Schlaug et al., 1995). They have also revealed enlarged *ventricles*—fluid-filled brain areas (marked by the red arrows in **FIGURE 4.3**)—in some patients who have schizophrenia, a disabling psychological disorder.

A special application of MRI—**fMRI (functional MRI)**—can reveal the brain's functioning as well as its structure. Where the brain is especially active, blood goes. By comparing successive MRI scans, researchers can watch as specific brain areas activate, showing increased oxygen-laden bloodflow. As a person looks at a scene, for example, the fMRI machine detects blood rushing to the back of the brain, which processes visual information (see Figure 5.3). When the brain is unoccupied, blood continues to flow via a web of brain regions called the *default network* (Mason et al., 2007).

Such snapshots of the brain's activity provide new insights into how the brain divides its labor. A mountain of recent fMRI studies suggests which brain areas are most active when people feel pain or rejection, listen to angry voices, think about scary things, feel happy, or become sexually excited. The technology enables a very crude sort of mind reading. One neuroscience team scanned 129 people's brains as they did eight different mental tasks (such as reading, gambling, or rhyming). Later, they were able, with 80 percent accuracy, to predict which of these mental activities their participants had been doing (Poldrack et al., 2009).

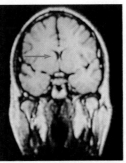
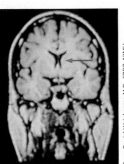

^ FIGURE 4.3

MRI scan of a healthy individual (left) and a person with schizophrenia (right) Note the enlarged ventricle, the fluid-filled brain region at the tip of the arrow in the image on the right.

MRI (magnetic resonance imaging) a technique that uses magnetic fields and radio waves to produce computer-generated images of soft tissue. MRI scans show brain anatomy.

fMRI (functional MRI) a technique for revealing bloodflow and, therefore, brain activity by comparing successive MRI scans. fMRI scans show brain function as well as structure.

You've seen the pictures—of colorful brains with accompanying headlines, such as "your brain on music." Hot brains make hot news (Fine, 2010). But "neuro-skeptics" caution against overblown claims (Satel & Lilienfeld, 2013; Vul et al., 2009a,b). Neuromarketing, neuropolitics, and neurotheology are often neuro-hype. Imaging techniques illuminate brain structure and activity, and sometimes help us test different theories of behavior (Mather et al., 2013). But given that all human experience is brain-based, it's no surprise that different brain areas become active when one listens to a lecture or lusts for a lover.

Nevertheless, to learn about the neurosciences now is like studying world geography when Magellan explored the seas. The $40 million Human Connectome Project (2013; Gorman, 2014), for example, seeks "neural pathways [that] will reveal much about what makes us uniquely human and what makes every person different from all others." It harnesses the power of *diffusion spectrum imaging*, a type of MRI technology that maps long-distance brain fiber connections (Jarbo & Verstynen, 2015). Today's whole-brain mapping effort has been likened to last century's Apollo program, which landed humans on the Moon. This truly is the golden age of brain science.

RETRIEVE IT [✱]

• Match the scanning technique with the correct description.

Technique:	Description:
1. fMRI scan	a. tracks radioactive glucose to reveal brain activity.
2. PET scan	b. tracks successive images of brain tissue to show brain function.
3. MRI scan	c. uses magnetic fields and radio waves to show brain anatomy.

ANSWERS: 1. b, 2. a, 3. c

Older Brain Structures

4-2 What structures make up the brainstem, and what are the functions of the brainstem, thalamus, reticular formation, and cerebellum?

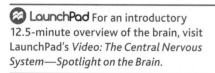

An animal's capacities come from its brain structures. In primitive animals, such as sharks, a not-so-complex brain primarily regulates basic survival functions: breathing, resting, and feeding. In lower mammals, such as rodents, a more complex brain enables emotion and greater memory. In advanced mammals, such as humans, a brain that processes more information enables increased foresight as well.

This increasing complexity arises from new brain systems built on top of the old, much as Earth's landscape covers the old with the new. Digging down, one discovers the fossil remnants of the past—brainstem components performing for us much as they did for our distant ancestors. Let's start with the brain's base and work up to the newer systems.

Stefan Klein/imagebroker/Alamy

The Brainstem

The brain's oldest and innermost region is the **brainstem.** It begins where the spinal cord swells slightly after entering the skull. This slight swelling is the **medulla (FIGURE 4.4)**. Here lie the controls for your heartbeat and breathing. As brain-damaged patients in a vegetative state illustrate, we need no higher brain or conscious mind to orchestrate our heart's pumping and lungs' breathing. The brainstem handles those tasks. Just above the medulla sits the *pons,* which helps coordinate movements and control sleep.

LaunchPad For an introductory 12.5-minute overview of the brain, visit LaunchPad's *Video: The Central Nervous System—Spotlight on the Brain.*

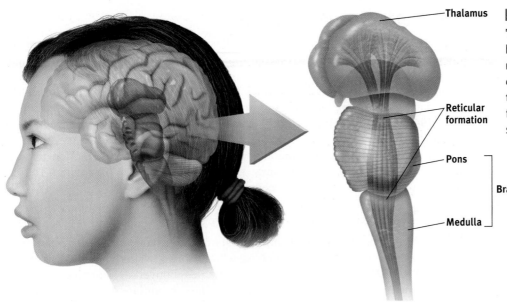

Thalamus

Reticular formation

Pons

Brainstem

Medulla

< FIGURE 4.4

The brainstem and thalamus The brainstem, including the pons and medulla, is an extension of the spinal cord. The thalamus is attached to the top of the brainstem. The reticular formation passes through both structures.

If a cat's brainstem is severed from the rest of the brain above it, the animal will still breathe and live—and even run, climb, and groom (Klemm, 1990). But cut off from the brain's higher regions, it won't *purposefully* run or climb to get food.

The brainstem is a crossover point, where most nerves to and from each side of the brain connect with the body's opposite side (**FIGURE 4.5**). This peculiar cross-wiring is but one of the brain's many surprises.

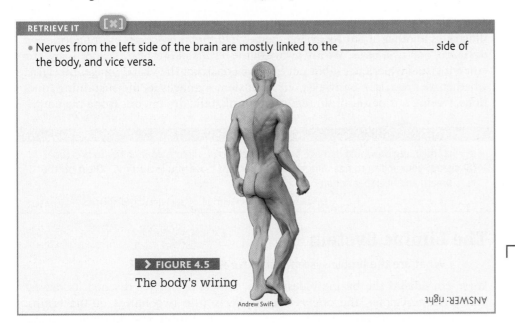

RETRIEVE IT   [✱]

• Nerves from the left side of the brain are mostly linked to the _____ side of the body, and vice versa.

> FIGURE 4.5

The body's wiring

Andrew Swift

ANSWER: right

The Thalamus

Sitting atop the brainstem is the **thalamus,** a pair of egg-shaped structures that act as the brain's sensory control center (Figure 4.4). The thalamus receives information from all the senses except smell, and routes that information to higher brain regions that deal with seeing, hearing, tasting, and touching. The thalamus also receives some of the higher brain's replies, which it then directs to the medulla and to the cerebellum. Think of the thalamus as being to sensory information what London is to England's trains: a hub through which traffic passes en route to various destinations.

brainstem the oldest part and central core of the brain, beginning where the spinal cord swells as it enters the skull; the brainstem is responsible for automatic survival functions.

medulla [muh-DUL-uh] the base of the brainstem; controls heartbeat and breathing.

thalamus [THAL-uh-muss] the brain's sensory control center, located on top of the brainstem; it directs messages to the sensory receiving areas in the cortex and transmits replies to the cerebellum and medulla.

Cerebellum

Spinal cord

The brain's organ of agility Hanging at the back of the brain, the cerebellum coordinates our voluntary movements.

Sergio Torres/AP Photo

reticular formation a nerve network that travels through the brainstem into the thalamus and plays an important role in controlling arousal.

cerebellum [sehr-uh-BELL-um] the "little brain" at the rear of the brainstem; functions include processing sensory input, coordinating movement output and balance, and enabling nonverbal learning and memory.

limbic system neural system (including the *amygdala, hypothalamus,* and *hippocampus*) located below the cerebral hemispheres; associated with emotions and drives.

amygdala [uh-MIG-duh-la] two lima-bean-sized neural clusters in the limbic system; linked to emotion.

hypothalamus [hi-po-THAL-uh-muss] a neural structure lying below *(hypo)* the thalamus; it directs several maintenance activities (eating, drinking, body temperature), helps govern the endocrine system via the pituitary gland, and is linked to emotion and reward.

The Reticular Formation

Inside the brainstem, between your ears, lies the **reticular** ("netlike") **formation,** a neuron network extending from the spinal cord right up through the thalamus. As the spinal cord's sensory input flows up to the thalamus, some of it travels through the reticular formation, which filters incoming stimuli, relays important information to other brain areas, and controls arousal.

In 1949, Giuseppe Moruzzi and Horace Magoun discovered that electrically stimulating a sleeping cat's reticular formation almost instantly produced an awake, alert animal. When Magoun *severed* a cat's reticular formation without damaging nearby sensory pathways, the effect was equally dramatic: The cat lapsed into a coma from which it never awakened.

The Cerebellum

Extending from the rear of the brainstem is the baseball-sized **cerebellum,** meaning "little brain," which is what its two wrinkled halves resemble (**FIGURE 4.6**). The cerebellum enables nonverbal learning and skill memory. It also helps us judge time, modulate our emotions, and discriminate sounds and textures (Bower & Parsons, 2003). And (with assistance from the pons) it coordinates voluntary movement. When a soccer player executes a perfect bicycle kick, give the player's cerebellum some credit. Under alcohol's influence, coordination suffers. And if you injured your cerebellum, you would have difficulty walking, keeping your balance, or shaking hands. Your movements would be jerky and exaggerated. Gone would be any dreams of being a dancer or guitarist.

* * *

Note: These older brain functions all occur without any conscious effort. This illustrates another of our recurring themes: *Our brain processes most information outside of our awareness.* We are aware of the *results* of our brain's labor—say, our current visual experience—but not *how* we construct the visual image. Likewise, whether we are asleep or awake, our brainstem manages its life-sustaining functions, freeing our newer brain regions to think, talk, dream, or savor a memory.

RETRIEVE IT   [✕]

• In what brain region would damage be most likely to (1) disrupt your ability to skip rope? (2) disrupt your ability to hear and taste? (3) perhaps leave you in a coma? (4) cut off the very breath and heartbeat of life?

ANSWERS: 1. cerebellum, 2. thalamus, 3. reticular formation, 4. medulla

The Limbic System

4-3 What are the limbic system's structures and functions?

We've considered the brain's oldest parts, but we've not yet reached its newest and highest regions, the *cerebral hemispheres* (the two halves of the brain). Between the oldest and newest brain areas lies the **limbic system** (*limbus* means "border"). This system contains the *amygdala,* the *hypothalamus,* and the *hippocampus* (**FIGURE 4.7**).

THE AMYGDALA Research has linked the **amygdala,** two lima-bean-sized neural clusters, to aggression and fear. In 1939, psychologist Heinrich Klüver and neurosurgeon Paul Bucy surgically removed a rhesus monkey's amygdala, turning the normally ill-tempered animal into the most mellow of creatures. So, too, with human patients. Those with amygdala lesions often display reduced arousal to fear- and anger-arousing stimuli (Berntson et al., 2011). One such woman, patient S. M., has been called "the woman with no fear," even of being threatened with a gun (Feinstein et al., 2013).

What then might happen if we electrically stimulated the amygdala of a normally placid domestic animal, such as a cat? Do so in one spot and the cat prepares to attack, hissing with its back arched, its pupils dilated, its hair on end. Move the electrode only slightly within the amygdala, cage the cat with a small mouse, and now it cowers in terror.

GK Hart/Vikki Hart/Gettyimages

These and other experiments have confirmed the amygdala's role in fear and rage. One study found math anxiety associated with hyperactivity in the right amygdala (Young et al., 2012). Other studies link criminal behavior with amygdala dysfunction (Boccardi et al., 2011; Ermer et al., 2012). But we must be careful. The brain is not neatly organized into structures that correspond to our behavior categories. When we feel or act in aggressive or fearful ways, there is neural activity in many areas of our brain—not just the amygdala. If you destroy a car's dead battery, you can't start the engine. Yet the battery is merely one link in an integrated system.

RETRIEVE IT [✖]

- Electrical stimulation of a cat's amygdala provokes angry reactions. Which *autonomic nervous system* division is activated by such stimulation?

ANSWER: The sympathetic nervous system

THE HYPOTHALAMUS Just below *(hypo)* the thalamus is the **hypothalamus** (**FIGURE 4.8**), an important link in the command chain governing bodily maintenance. Some neural clusters in the hypothalamus influence hunger; others regulate thirst, body temperature, and sexual behavior. Together, they help maintain a steady *(homeostatic)* internal state.

As the hypothalamus monitors the state of your body, it tunes into your blood chemistry and any incoming orders from other brain parts. For example, picking up signals from your brain's cerebral cortex that you are thinking about sex, your hypothalamus will secrete hormones. These hormones will in turn trigger the adjacent "master gland" of the endocrine system, your pituitary (see Figure 4.7), to influence your sex glands to release their hormones. These will intensify the thoughts of sex in your cerebral cortex. (Once again, we see the interplay between the nervous and endocrine systems: The brain influences the endocrine system, which in turn influences the brain.)

A remarkable discovery about the hypothalamus illustrates how progress in science often occurs—when curious, open-minded investigators make an unexpected observation. Two young McGill University neuropsychologists, James Olds and Peter Milner (1954), were trying to implant an electrode in a rat's reticular formation when they made a magnificent mistake: They placed the electrode incorrectly (Olds, 1975). Curiously, as if seeking more stimulation, the rat kept returning to the location where it had been stimulated by this misplaced electrode. On discovering that they had actually placed the device in a region of the hypothalamus, Olds and Milner realized they had stumbled upon a brain center that provides pleasurable rewards (Olds, 1975).

Later experiments located other "pleasure centers" (Olds, 1958). (What the rats actually experience only they know, and they aren't telling. Rather than attribute human feelings to rats, today's scientists refer to *reward centers*, not "pleasure centers.") Just how rewarding are these reward centers? Enough to cause rats to self-stimulate these brain regions more than 1000 times per hour. In other species, including dolphins and monkeys, researchers later discovered other limbic system reward centers, such as the *nucleus accumbens* in front of the hypothalamus. Animal research has also revealed both a general dopamine-related reward system and specific centers associated with the

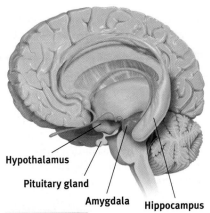

▲ FIGURE 4.7

The limbic system This neural system sits between the brain's older parts and its cerebral hemispheres. The limbic system's hypothalamus controls the nearby pituitary gland.

Hypothalamus

Pituitary gland

Amygdala   Hippocampus

▼ FIGURE 4.8

The hypothalamus This small but important structure, colored yellow/orange in this MRI-scan photograph, helps keep the body's internal environment in a steady state.

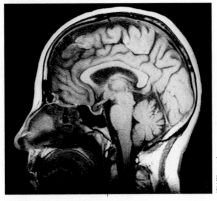

ISM/Phototake

hippocampus a neural center located in the limbic system; helps process explicit memories for storage.

"If you were designing a robot vehicle to walk into the future and survive, . . . you'd wire it up so that behavior that ensured the survival of the self or the species— like sex and eating—would be naturally reinforcing."

Candace Pert (1986)

pleasures of eating, drinking, and sex. Animals, it seems, come equipped with built-in systems that reward activities essential to survival.

Do humans have limbic centers for pleasure? To calm violent patients, one neurosurgeon implanted electrodes in such areas. Stimulated patients reported mild pleasure; unlike Olds' rats, however, they were not driven to a frenzy (Deutsch, 1972; Hooper & Teresi, 1986). Moreover, newer research reveals that stimulating the brain's "hedonic hotspots" (its reward circuits) produces more *desire* than pure enjoyment (Kringelbach & Berridge, 2012).

Some researchers believe that substance use disorders may stem from malfunctions in natural brain systems for pleasure and well-being (Balodis & Potenza, 2015). People genetically predisposed to this *reward deficiency syndrome* may crave whatever provides that missing pleasure or relieves negative feelings (Blum et al., 1996).

THE HIPPOCAMPUS The **hippocampus** processes conscious, explicit memories and decreases in size and function as we grow older. Animals or humans who lose their hippocampus to surgery or injury lose their ability to form new memories of facts and events. Those who survive a hippocampal brain tumor in childhood struggle to remember new information in adulthood (Jayakar et al., 2015). Other modules discuss how hippocampus size and function decrease as we grow older, and how our two-track mind uses the hippocampus to process our memories.

* * *

FIGURE 4.9 locates the brain areas we've discussed, as well as the *cerebral cortex*.

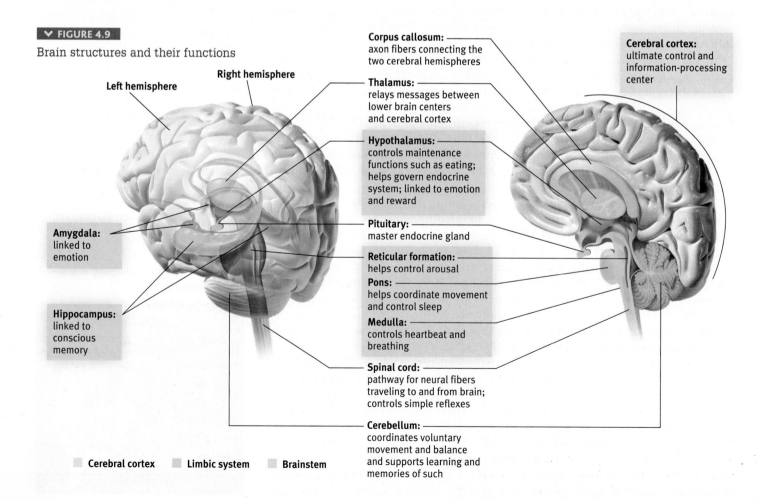

⌄ FIGURE 4.9

Brain structures and their functions

Left hemisphere

Right hemisphere

Corpus callosum: axon fibers connecting the two cerebral hemispheres

Thalamus: relays messages between lower brain centers and cerebral cortex

Hypothalamus: controls maintenance functions such as eating; helps govern endocrine system; linked to emotion and reward

Pituitary: master endocrine gland

Reticular formation: helps control arousal

Pons: helps coordinate movement and control sleep

Medulla: controls heartbeat and breathing

Spinal cord: pathway for neural fibers traveling to and from brain; controls simple reflexes

Cerebellum: coordinates voluntary movement and balance and supports learning and memories of such

Cerebral cortex: ultimate control and information-processing center

Amygdala: linked to emotion

Hippocampus: linked to conscious memory

▪ Cerebral cortex   ▪ Limbic system   ▪ Brainstem

RETRIEVE IT [✱]

• What are the three key structures of the limbic system, and what functions do they serve?

ANSWER: (1) The *amygdala* is involved in aggression and fear responses. (2) The *hypothalamus* is involved in bodily maintenance, pleasurable rewards, and control of the hormonal systems. (3) The *hippocampus* processes conscious memory.

LaunchPad To review and assess your understanding, visit LaunchPad's *Concept Practice: The Limbic System.*

MODULE 4 REVIEW Tools of Discovery and Older Brain Structures

◉ Learning Objectives

Test Yourself by taking a moment to answer each of these Learning Objective Questions (repeated here from within the module). Then turn to Appendix D, Complete Module Reviews, to check your answers. Research suggests that trying to answer these questions on your own will improve your long-term memory of the concepts (McDaniel et al., 2009).

4-1 How do neuroscientists study the brain's connections to behavior and mind?

4-2 What structures make up the brainstem, and what are the functions of the brainstem, thalamus, reticular formation, and cerebellum?

4-3 What are the limbic system's structures and functions?

■·[-] Terms and Concepts to Remember

Test yourself on these terms by trying to write down the definition in your own words before flipping back to the referenced page to check your answers.

lesion [LEE-zhuhn], p. 48

electroencephalogram (EEG), p. 48

PET (positron emission tomography) scan, p. 48

MRI (magnetic resonance imaging), p. 49

fMRI (functional MRI), p. 49

brainstem, p. 50

medulla [muh-DUL-uh], p. 50

thalamus [THAL-uh-muss], p. 51

reticular formation, p. 52

cerebellum [sehr-uh-BELL-um], p. 52

limbic system, p. 52

amygdala [uh-MIG-duh-la], p. 52

hypothalamus [hi-po-THAL-uh-muss], p. 53

hippocampus, p. 54

[✱] Experience the Testing Effect

Test yourself repeatedly throughout your studies. This will not only help you figure out what you know and don't know; the testing itself will help you learn and remember the information more effectively thanks to the *testing effect.*

1. The part of the brainstem that controls heartbeat and breathing is the
   a. cerebellum.
   b. medulla.
   c. cortex.
   d. thalamus.

2. The thalamus functions as a
   a. memory bank.
   b. balance center.
   c. breathing regulator.
   d. sensory control center.

3. The lower brain structure that governs arousal is the
   a. spinal cord.
   b. cerebellum.
   c. reticular formation.
   d. medulla.

4. The part of the brain that coordinates voluntary movement and enables nonverbal learning and memory is the _____.

5. Two parts of the limbic system are the amygdala and the
   a. cerebral hemispheres.
   b. hippocampus.
   c. thalamus.
   d. pituitary.

6. A cat's ferocious response to electrical brain stimulation would lead you to suppose the electrode had touched the _____.

7. The neural structure that most directly regulates eating, drinking, and body temperature is the
   a. endocrine system.
   b. hypothalamus.
   c. hippocampus.
   d. amygdala.

8. The initial reward center discovered by Olds and Milner was located in the _____.

Find answers to these questions in Appendix E, in the back of the book.

Use **LearningCurve** to create your personalized study plan, which will direct you to the resources that will help you most in **LaunchPad**.

cerebral [seh-REE-bruhl] cortex the intricate fabric of interconnected neural cells covering the cerebral hemispheres; the body's ultimate control and information-processing center.

frontal lobes portion of the cerebral cortex lying just behind the forehead; involved in speaking and muscle movements and in making plans and judgments.

parietal [puh-RYE-uh-tuhl] lobes portion of the cerebral cortex lying at the top of the head and toward the rear; receives sensory input for touch and body position.

occipital [ahk-SIP-uh-tuhl] lobes portion of the cerebral cortex lying at the back of the head; includes areas that receive information from the visual fields.

temporal lobes portion of the cerebral cortex lying roughly above the ears; includes the auditory areas, each receiving information primarily from the opposite ear.

The people who first dissected and labeled the brain used the language of scholars—Latin and Greek. Their words are actually attempts at graphic description: For example, *cortex* means "bark," *cerebellum* is "little brain," and *thalamus* is "inner chamber."

MODULE 5 The Cerebral Cortex and Our Divided Brain

The Cerebral Cortex

5-1 What are the functions of the various cerebral cortex regions?

Older brain networks sustain basic life functions and enable memory, emotions, and basic drives. Newer neural networks within the *cerebrum*—the two cerebral hemispheres contributing 85 percent of the brain's weight—form specialized work teams that enable our perceiving, thinking, and speaking. Like other structures above the brainstem (including the thalamus, hippocampus, and amygdala), the cerebral hemispheres come as a pair. Covering those hemispheres, like bark on a tree, is the **cerebral cortex,** a thin surface layer of interconnected neural cells. It is your brain's thinking crown, your body's ultimate control and information-processing center.

As we move up the ladder of animal life, the cerebral cortex expands, tight genetic controls relax, and the organism's adaptability increases. Frogs and other small-cortex amphibians operate extensively on preprogrammed genetic instructions. The larger cortex of mammals offers increased capacities for learning and thinking, enabling them to be more adaptable. What makes us distinctively human mostly arises from the complex functions of our cerebral cortex.

RETRIEVE IT [✖]

• Which area of the human brain is most similar to that of less complex animals? Which part of the human brain distinguishes us most from less complex animals?

ANSWERS: The brainstem; the cerebral cortex

Structure of the Cortex

If you opened a human skull, exposing the brain, you would see a wrinkled organ, shaped somewhat like an oversized walnut. Without these wrinkles, a flattened cerebral cortex would require triple the area—roughly that of a large pizza. The brain's left and right hemispheres are filled mainly with axons connecting the cortex to the brain's other regions. The cerebral cortex—that thin surface layer—contains some 20 to 23 billion of the brain's nerve cells and 300 trillion synaptic connections (de Courten-Myers, 2005). Being human takes a lot of nerve.

Each hemisphere's cortex is subdivided into four *lobes,* separated by prominent *fissures,* or folds (**FIGURE 5.1**). Starting at the front of your brain and moving over the top, there are the **frontal lobes** (behind your forehead), the **parietal lobes** (at the top and to the rear), and the **occipital lobes** (at the back of your head). Reversing direction and moving forward, just above your ears, you find the **temporal lobes.** Each of the four lobes carries out many functions, and many functions require the interplay of several lobes.

✓ FIGURE 5.1

The cortex and its basic subdivisions

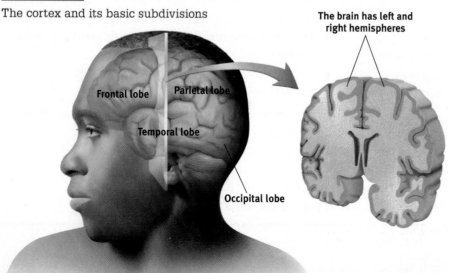

The brain has left and right hemispheres

Frontal lobe   Parietal lobe

Temporal lobe

Occipital lobe

Functions of the Cortex

More than a century ago, surgeons found damaged cortical areas during autopsies of people who had been partially paralyzed or speechless. This rather crude evidence did not prove that specific parts of the cortex control complex functions like movement or speech. After all, if the entire cortex controlled speech and movement, damage to almost any area might produce the same effect. A TV with its power cord cut would go dead, but we would be fooling ourselves if we thought we had "localized" the picture in the cord.

MOTOR FUNCTIONS Scientists had better luck in localizing simpler brain functions. For example, in 1870, German physicians Gustav Fritsch and Eduard Hitzig made an important discovery: Mild electrical stimulation to parts of an animal's cortex made parts of its body move. The effects were selective: Stimulation caused movement only when applied to an arch-shaped region at the back of the frontal lobe, running roughly ear-to-ear across the top of the brain. Moreover, stimulating parts of this region in the left or right hemisphere caused movements of specific body parts on the *opposite* side of the body. Fritsch and Hitzig had discovered what is now called the **motor cortex.**

MAPPING THE MOTOR CORTEX Lucky for brain surgeons and their patients, the brain has no sensory receptors. Knowing this, in the 1930s, Otfrid Foerster and Wilder Penfield were able to map the motor cortex in hundreds of wide-awake patients by stimulating different cortical areas and observing the body's responses. They discovered that body areas requiring precise control, such as the fingers and mouth, occupy the greatest amount of cortical space (**FIGURE 5.2**). In one of his many demonstrations of motor behavior mechanics, Spanish neuroscientist José Delgado stimulated a spot on a patient's left motor cortex, triggering the right hand to make a fist. Asked to keep the fingers open during the next stimulation, the patient, whose fingers closed despite his best efforts, remarked, "I guess, Doctor, that your electricity is stronger than my will" (Delgado, 1969, p. 114).

> **motor cortex** an area at the rear of the frontal lobes that controls voluntary movements.

∨ FIGURE 5.2

Left hemisphere tissue devoted to each body part in the motor cortex and the somatosensory cortex As you can see from this classic though inexact representation, the amount of cortex devoted to a body part in the motor cortex (in the frontal lobes) or in the somatosensory cortex (in the parietal lobes) is not proportional to that body part's size. Rather, the brain devotes more tissue to sensitive areas and to areas requiring precise control. Thus, the fingers have a greater representation in the cortex than does the upper arm.

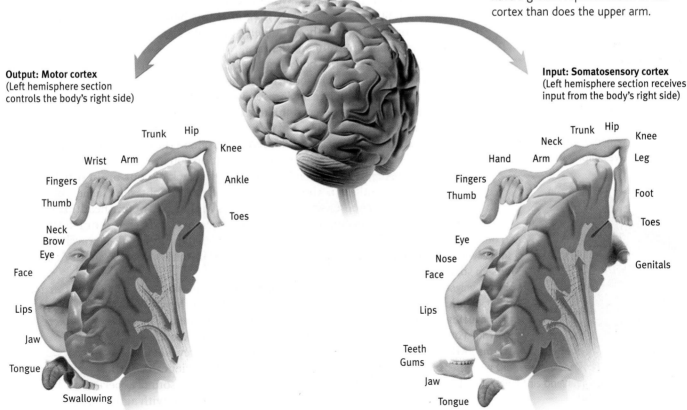

Output: Motor cortex
(Left hemisphere section controls the body's right side)

Trunk · Hip · Knee · Wrist · Arm · Ankle · Fingers · Thumb · Toes · Neck · Brow · Eye · Face · Lips · Jaw · Tongue · Swallowing

Input: Somatosensory cortex
(Left hemisphere section receives input from the body's right side)

Trunk · Hip · Neck · Knee · Hand · Arm · Leg · Fingers · Thumb · Foot · Toes · Eye · Nose · Face · Genitals · Lips · Teeth · Gums · Jaw · Tongue

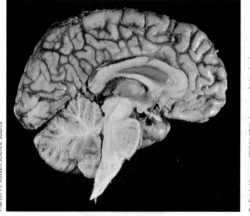
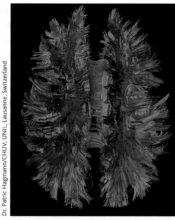

Martin M. Rotker/Science Source

Dr. Patric Hagmann/CHUV, UNIL, Lausanne, Switzerland

∧ FIGURE 5.8

The corpus callosum This large band of neural fibers connects the two brain hemispheres. To photograph the half brain above left, a surgeon separated the hemispheres by cutting through the corpus callosum (see blue arrow) and lower brain regions. The high-resolution diffusion spectrum image above right, showing a top-facing brain from above, reveals brain neural networks within the two hemispheres, and the corpus callosum neural bridge between them.

❯ FIGURE 5.9

The information highway from eye to brain

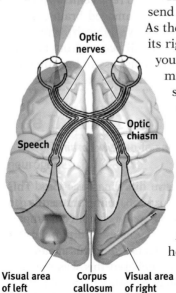

Left visual field

Right visual field

Optic nerves

Speech

Optic chiasm

Visual area of left hemisphere

Corpus callosum

Visual area of right hemisphere

corpus callosum [KOR-pus kah-LOW-sum] the large band of neural fibers connecting the two brain hemispheres and carrying messages between them.

split brain a condition resulting from surgery that isolates the brain's two hemispheres by cutting the fibers (mainly those of the corpus callosum) connecting them.

Splitting the Brain

In 1961, Los Angeles neurosurgeons Philip Vogel and Joseph Bogen speculated that major epileptic seizures were caused by an amplification of abnormal brain activity bouncing back and forth between the two cerebral hemispheres, which work together as a whole system. If so, they wondered, could they end this biological tennis match by severing the **corpus callosum,** the wide band of axon fibers connecting the two hemispheres and carrying messages between them (**FIGURE 5.8**)? Vogel and Bogen knew that psychologists Roger Sperry, Ronald Myers, and Michael Gazzaniga had divided cats' and monkeys' brains in this manner, with no serious ill effects.

So the surgeons operated. The result? The seizures all but disappeared. The patients with these **split brains** were surprisingly normal, their personality and intellect hardly affected. Waking from surgery, one even joked that he had a "splitting headache" (Gazzaniga, 1967). By sharing their experiences, these patients have greatly expanded our understanding of interactions between the intact brain's two hemispheres.

To appreciate these findings, we need to focus for a minute on the peculiar nature of our visual wiring, illustrated in **FIGURE 5.9**. Note that each eye receives sensory information from the entire visual field. But in each eye, information from the left half of your field of vision goes to your right hemisphere, and information from the right half of your visual field goes to your left hemisphere, which usually controls speech. Information received by either hemisphere is quickly transmitted to the other across the corpus callosum. In a person with a severed corpus callosum, this information-sharing does not take place.

Knowing these facts, Sperry and Gazzaniga could send information to a patient's left or right hemisphere. As the person stared at a spot, they flashed a stimulus to its right or left. They could do this with you, too, but in your intact brain, the hemisphere receiving the information would instantly pass the news to the other side. Because the split-brain surgery had cut the communication lines between the hemispheres, the researchers could, with these patients, quiz each hemisphere separately.

In an early experiment, Gazzaniga (1967) asked split-brain patients to stare at a dot as he flashed HE·ART on a screen (**FIGURE 5.10**). Thus, HE appeared in their left visual field (which transmits to the right hemisphere) and ART in the right field (which transmits to the left hemisphere). When he then asked them to *say* what they had seen, the patients reported that they had seen ART. But when asked to *point* to the word they had seen, they were startled when

Functions of the Cortex

More than a century ago, surgeons found damaged cortical areas during autopsies of people who had been partially paralyzed or speechless. This rather crude evidence did not prove that specific parts of the cortex control complex functions like movement or speech. After all, if the entire cortex controlled speech and movement, damage to almost any area might produce the same effect. A TV with its power cord cut would go dead, but we would be fooling ourselves if we thought we had "localized" the picture in the cord.

MOTOR FUNCTIONS Scientists had better luck in localizing simpler brain functions. For example, in 1870, German physicians Gustav Fritsch and Eduard Hitzig made an important discovery: Mild electrical stimulation to parts of an animal's cortex made parts of its body move. The effects were selective: Stimulation caused movement only when applied to an arch-shaped region at the back of the frontal lobe, running roughly ear-to-ear across the top of the brain. Moreover, stimulating parts of this region in the left or right hemisphere caused movements of specific body parts on the *opposite* side of the body. Fritsch and Hitzig had discovered what is now called the **motor cortex.**

MAPPING THE MOTOR CORTEX Lucky for brain surgeons and their patients, the brain has no sensory receptors. Knowing this, in the 1930s, Otfrid Foerster and Wilder Penfield were able to map the motor cortex in hundreds of wide-awake patients by stimulating different cortical areas and observing the body's responses. They discovered that body areas requiring precise control, such as the fingers and mouth, occupy the greatest amount of cortical space (**FIGURE 5.2**). In one of his many demonstrations of motor behavior mechanics, Spanish neuroscientist José Delgado stimulated a spot on a patient's left motor cortex, triggering the right hand to make a fist. Asked to keep the fingers open during the next stimulation, the patient, whose fingers closed despite his best efforts, remarked, "I guess, Doctor, that your electricity is stronger than my will" (Delgado, 1969, p. 114).

motor cortex an area at the rear of the frontal lobes that controls voluntary movements.

⌄ FIGURE 5.2

Left hemisphere tissue devoted to each body part in the motor cortex and the somatosensory cortex As you can see from this classic though inexact representation, the amount of cortex devoted to a body part in the motor cortex (in the frontal lobes) or in the somatosensory cortex (in the parietal lobes) is not proportional to that body part's size. Rather, the brain devotes more tissue to sensitive areas and to areas requiring precise control. Thus, the fingers have a greater representation in the cortex than does the upper arm.

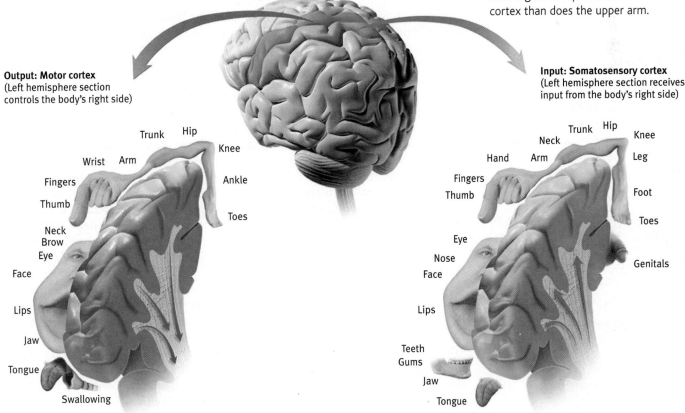

Output: Motor cortex
(Left hemisphere section controls the body's right side)

Trunk Hip
Wrist Arm
Fingers
Thumb
Knee
Ankle
Toes
Neck
Brow
Eye
Face
Lips
Jaw
Tongue
Swallowing

Input: Somatosensory cortex
(Left hemisphere section receives input from the body's right side)

Trunk Hip
Neck
Hand Arm
Fingers
Thumb
Knee
Leg
Foot
Toes
Eye
Nose
Face
Genitals
Lips
Teeth
Gums
Jaw
Tongue

somatosensory cortex area at the front of the parietal lobes that registers and processes body touch and movement sensations.

RETRIEVE IT [✗]

• Try moving your right hand in a circular motion, as if cleaning a table. Then start your right foot doing the same motion, synchronized with your hand. Now reverse the right foot's motion, but not the hand's. Finally, try moving the *left* foot opposite to the right hand.

1. Why is reversing the right foot's motion so hard?

2. Why is it easier to move the left foot opposite to the right hand?

ANSWERS: 1. The right limbs' opposed activities interfere with each other because both are controlled by the same (left) side of your brain. 2. Opposite sides of your brain control your left and right limbs, so the reversed motion causes less interference.

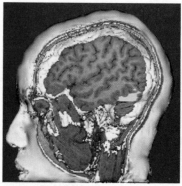

⌃ FIGURE 5.3

The brain in action This fMRI (functional MRI) scan shows the visual cortex in the occipital lobes activated (color represents increased bloodflow) as a research participant looks at a photo. When the person stops looking, the region instantly calms down.

Neurolmage, Vol. 4, V.P. Clark, K. Keill, J. Ma, Maisog, S. Courtney, L. G. Ungerleider, and J. V. Haxby, Functional Magnetic Resonance Imaging of Human Visual Cortex during Face Matching: A Comparison with Positron Emission Tomography, August 1996, with permission from Elsevier.

⌄ FIGURE 5.4

The visual cortex and auditory cortex The visual cortex in the occipital lobes at the rear of your brain receives input from your eyes. The auditory cortex, in your temporal lobes—above your ears—receives information from your ears.

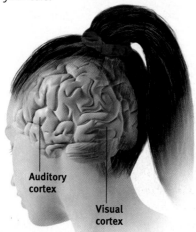

Auditory cortex

Visual cortex

More recently, scientists were able to predict a monkey's arm motion a tenth of a second *before* it moved—by repeatedly measuring motor cortex activity preceding specific arm movements (Gibbs, 1996). Such findings have opened the door to research on brain-controlled computers.

What might happen, some researchers are asking, if we implant a device to detect motor cortex activity in humans? Could such devices help severely paralyzed people learn to command a cursor to write e-mail or work online? Clinical trials are now under way with people who have suffered paralysis or amputation (Andersen et al., 2010; Nurmikko et al., 2010). The first patient, a paralyzed 25-year-old man, was able to mentally control a TV, draw shapes on a computer screen, and play video games—all thanks to an aspirin-sized chip with 100 microelectrodes recording activity in his motor cortex (Hochberg et al., 2006). Since then, others with paralysis who have been given implants have learned to direct robotic arms with their thoughts (Collinger et al., 2013; Hochberg et al., 2012).

SENSORY FUNCTIONS If the motor cortex sends messages out to the body, where does the cortex receive incoming messages? Penfield identified a cortical area—at the front of the parietal lobes, parallel to and just behind the motor cortex—that specializes in receiving information from the skin senses and from the movement of body parts. We now call this area the **somatosensory cortex** (Figure 5.2). Stimulate a point on the top of this band of tissue and a person may report being touched on the shoulder; stimulate some point on the side and the person may feel something on the face.

The more sensitive the body region, the larger the somatosensory cortex area devoted to it (Figure 5.2). Your supersensitive lips project to a larger brain area than do your toes, which is one reason we kiss rather than touch toes. Rats have a large area of the brain devoted to their whisker sensations, and owls to their hearing sensations.

Scientists have identified additional areas where the cortex receives input from senses other than touch. Any visual information you are receiving now is going to the visual cortex in your occipital lobes, at the back of your brain (**FIGURES 5.3 and 5.4**). Stimulated in the occipital lobes, you might see flashes of light or dashes of color. (In a sense, we *do* have eyes in the back of our head!) Having lost much of his right occipital lobe to a tumor removal, a friend of mine [DM's] was blind to the left half of his field of vision. Visual information travels from the occipital lobes to other areas that specialize in tasks such as identifying words, detecting emotions, and recognizing faces.

Any sound you now hear is processed by your auditory cortex in your temporal lobes (just above your ears; see Figure 5.4). Most of this auditory information travels a circuitous route from one ear to the auditory receiving area above your opposite ear. If stimulated in your auditory cortex, you might hear a sound. MRI scans of people with schizophrenia have revealed active auditory areas in the temporal lobes during the false sensory experience of auditory *hallucinations* (Lennox et al., 1999). Even the phantom ringing sound experienced by people with hearing loss is—if heard in one ear—associated with activity in the temporal lobe on the brain's opposite side (Muhlnickel, 1998).

ASSOCIATION AREAS So far, we have pointed out small cortical areas that either receive sensory input or direct muscular output. Together, these occupy about one-fourth of the human brain's thin, wrinkled cover. What, then, goes on in the remaining vast regions of the cortex? In these **association areas** (the peach-colored areas in **FIGURE 5.5**), neurons are busy with higher mental functions—many of the tasks that make us human.

Electrically probing an association area won't trigger any observable response. So, unlike the somatosensory and motor areas, association area functions cannot be neatly mapped. Their silence has led to what Donald McBurney (1996, p. 44) called "one of the hardiest weeds in the garden of psychology": the claim that we ordinarily use only 10 percent of our brain. (If true, wouldn't this imply a 90 percent chance that a bullet to your brain would land in an unused area?) Surgically lesioned animals and brain-damaged humans bear witness that association areas are not dormant. Rather, these areas interpret, integrate, and act on sensory information and link it with stored memories—a very important part of thinking. Simple tasks often increase activity in small brain patches, involving far less than 10 percent of the brain. Yet complex tasks integrate many islands of brain activity, some performing automatic tasks and others requiring conscious control (Chein & Schneider, 2012). The brain is a whole system, with no dead spot for a stray bullet.

Association areas are found in all four lobes. The *prefrontal cortex* in the forward part of the frontal lobes enables judgment, planning, and processing of new memories. People with damaged frontal lobes may have intact memories, high scores on intelligence tests, and great cake-baking skills. Yet they would not be able to plan ahead to *begin* baking a cake for a birthday party (Huey et al., 2006).

Frontal lobe damage also can alter personality and remove a person's inhibitions. Consider the classic *case study* of railroad worker Phineas Gage. One afternoon in 1848, Gage, then 25 years old, was using a tamping iron to pack gunpowder into a rock. A spark ignited the gunpowder, shooting the rod up through his left cheek and out the top of his skull, leaving his frontal lobes damaged (**FIGURE 5.6**).

> **association areas** areas of the cerebral cortex that are not involved in primary motor or sensory functions; rather, they are involved in higher mental functions such as learning, remembering, thinking, and speaking

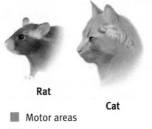  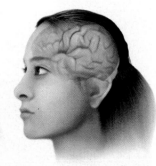

Rat

Cat

■ Motor areas
■ Somatosensory areas
■ Association areas

Chimpanzee

Human

⌃ **FIGURE 5.5**

Areas of the cortex in four mammals More intelligent animals have increased "uncommitted" or association areas of the cortex. These vast areas of the brain are responsible for interpreting, integrating, and acting on sensory information and linking it with stored memories.

LaunchPad See LaunchPad's *Video: Case Studies* for a helpful tutorial animation.

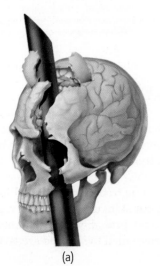

(a)

Collection of Jack and Beverly Wilgus

(b)

‹ **FIGURE 5.6**

A blast from the past (a) Phineas Gage's skull was kept as a medical record. Using measurements and modern neuroimaging techniques, researchers have reconstructed the probable path of the rod through Gage's brain (Van Horn et al., 2012). (b) This photo shows Gage after his accident. (The image has been reversed to show the features correctly. Early photos, including this one, were actually mirror images.)

To everyone's amazement, Gage was immediately able to sit up and speak, and after the wound healed he returned to work. But having lost some of the neural tracts that enabled his frontal lobes to control his emotions (Van Horn et al., 2012), the affable, soft-spoken man was now irritable, profane, and dishonest. This person, said his friends, was "no longer Gage." His mental abilities and memories were intact, but his personality was not. (Although Gage lost his rail-road job, he did, over time, adapt to his injury and find work as a stage coach driver [Macmillan & Lena, 2010].)

Studies of others with damaged frontal lobes have revealed similar impairments. Not only may they become less inhibited (without the frontal lobe brakes on their impulses), but their moral judgments may seem unrestrained. Cecil Clayton lost 20 percent of his left frontal lobe in a 1972 sawmill accident. Thereafter, his intelligence test score dropped to an elementary school level and he displayed increased impulsivity. In 1996, he fatally shot a deputy sheriff. In 2015, when he was 74, the State of Missouri executed him (Williams, 2015).

Would you advocate pushing one person in front of a runaway trolley to save five others? Most people would not, but those with damage to a brain area behind the eyes are often untroubled by such ethical dilemmas (Koenigs et al., 2007). The frontal lobes help steer us away from violent actions (Molenberghs et al., 2015; Yang & Raine, 2009).

Association areas also perform other mental functions. The parietal lobes, parts of which were large and unusually shaped in Einstein's normal-weight brain, enable mathematical and spatial reasoning (Ibos & Freedman, 2014; Witelson et al., 1999). On the underside of the right temporal lobe, another association area enables us to recognize faces. If a stroke or head injury destroyed this area of your brain, you would still be able to describe facial features and to recognize someone's gender and approximate age, yet be strangely unable to identify the person as, say, Taylor Swift, or even your grandmother.

Nevertheless, complex mental functions don't reside in any one place. There is no one spot in a rat's small association cortex that, when damaged, will obliterate its ability to learn or remember a maze. Your memory, language, and attention result from synchronized activity among distinct brain areas and neural networks (Knight, 2007). Ditto for religious experience. More than 40 distinct brain regions become active in different religious states, such as prayer and meditation, indicating that there is no simple "God spot" (Fingelkurts & Fingelkurts, 2009). *The point to remember:* Our mental experiences arise from coordinated brain activity.

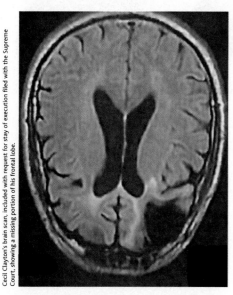

Cecil Clayton's brain scan, included with request for stay of execution filed with the Supreme Court, showing a missing portion of his frontal lobe.

Missing frontal lobe brakes With part of his left frontal lobe (in this downward-facing brain scan) lost to injury, Cecil Clayton became more impulsive and killed a deputy sheriff, for which, nine years later, his state executed him.

RETRIEVE IT

• Why are association areas important?

ANSWER: Association areas are involved in higher mental functions—interpreting, integrating, and acting on information processed in other areas.

The Brain's Plasticity

5-2 To what extent can a damaged brain reorganize itself, and what is neurogenesis?

Our brains are sculpted not only by our genes but also by our experiences. In other modules, we'll focus more on how experience molds the brain. For now, let's turn to another aspect of the brain's **plasticity:** its ability to modify itself after damage.

Some brain-damage effects described earlier can be traced to two hard facts: (1) Severed brain and spinal cord neurons, unlike cut skin, usually do not regenerate. (If your spinal cord were severed, you would probably be permanently paralyzed.) And (2) some brain functions seem preassigned to specific areas. One

plasticity the brain's ability to change, especially during childhood, by reorganizing after damage or by building new pathways based on experience.

neurogenesis the formation of new neurons.

newborn who suffered damage to temporal lobe facial recognition areas later remained unable to recognize faces (Farah et al., 2000). But there is good news: Some neural tissue can *reorganize* in response to damage. Under the surface of our awareness, the brain is constantly changing, building new pathways as it adjusts to little mishaps and new experiences.

Plasticity may also occur after serious damage, especially in young children (Kolb, 1989; see also **FIGURE 5.7**). The brain's plasticity is good news for those with vision or hearing loss. Blindness or deafness makes unused brain areas available for other uses (Amedi et al., 2005). If a blind person uses one finger to read Braille, the brain area dedicated to that finger expands as the sense of touch invades the visual cortex that normally helps people see (Barinaga, 1992; Sadato et al., 1996).

Plasticity also helps explain why some studies have found that deaf people have enhanced peripheral and motion-detection vision (Bosworth & Dobkins, 1999; Shiell et al., 2014). In deaf people whose native language is sign, the temporal lobe area normally dedicated to hearing waits in vain for stimulation. Finally, it looks for other signals to process, such as those from the visual system.

Similar reassignment may occur when disease or damage frees up other brain areas normally dedicated to specific functions. If a slow-growing left hemisphere tumor disrupts language (which resides mostly in the left hemisphere), the right hemisphere may compensate (Thiel et al., 2006). If a finger is amputated, the somatosensory cortex that received its input will begin to receive input from the adjacent fingers, which then become more sensitive (Fox, 1984). So what do you suppose was the sexual intercourse experience of one patient whose lower leg had been amputated? "I actually experience my orgasm in my [phantom] foot. [Note that in Figure 5.2, the toes region is adjacent to the genitals.] And there it's much bigger than it used to be because it's no longer just confined to my genitals" (Ramachandran & Blakeslee, 1998, p. 36).

Although the brain often attempts self-repair by reorganizing existing tissue, it sometimes attempts to mend itself by producing new brain cells. This process, known as **neurogenesis,** has been found in adult mice, birds, monkeys, and humans (Jessberger et al., 2008). These baby neurons originate deep in the brain and may then migrate elsewhere and form connections with neighboring neurons (Aimone et al., 2010; Gould, 2007).

Master stem cells that can develop into any type of brain cell have also been discovered in the human embryo. If mass-produced in a lab and injected into a damaged brain, might neural stem cells turn themselves into replacements for lost brain cells? Might surgeons someday be able to rebuild damaged brains, much as landscapers reseed damaged lawns? Stay tuned. Today's biotech companies are exploring such possibilities. In the meantime, we can all benefit from natural promoters of neurogenesis, such as exercise, sleep, and nonstressful but stimulating environments (Iso et al., 2007; Pereira et al., 2007; Stranahan et al., 2006).

Our Divided Brain

 5-3 What do split brains reveal about the functions of our two brain hemispheres?

Our brain's look-alike left and right hemispheres serve differing functions. This *lateralization* is apparent after brain damage. Research spanning more than a century has shown that left hemisphere accidents, strokes, and tumors can impair reading, writing, speaking, arithmetic reasoning, and understanding. Similar right hemisphere damage has less visibly dramatic effects. Does this mean that the right hemisphere is just along for the ride? Many believed this was the case until the 1960s, when a fascinating chapter in psychology's history began to unfold: Researchers found that the "minor" right hemisphere was not so limited after all.

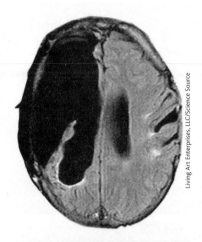

^ FIGURE 5.7

Brain plasticity This 6-year-old had surgery to end her life-threatening seizures. Although most of an entire hemisphere was removed (see MRI of hemispherectomy above), her remaining hemisphere compensated by putting other areas to work. One Johns Hopkins medical team reflected on the child hemispherectomies they had performed. Although use of the opposite arm was compromised, the team reported being "awed" by how well the children had retained their memory, personality, and humor (Vining et al., 1997). The younger the child, the greater the chance that the remaining hemisphere can take over the functions of the one that was surgically removed (Choi, 2008; Danelli et al., 2013).

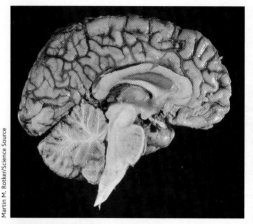
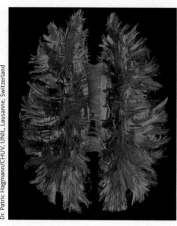

⌃ FIGURE 5.8

The corpus callosum This large band of neural fibers connects the two brain hemispheres. To photograph the half brain above left, a surgeon separated the hemispheres by cutting through the corpus callosum (see blue arrow) and lower brain regions. The high-resolution diffusion spectrum image above right, showing a top-facing brain from above, reveals brain neural networks within the two hemispheres, and the corpus callosum neural bridge between them.

⟩ FIGURE 5.9

The information highway from eye to brain

Left visual field

Right visual field

Optic nerves

Optic chiasm

Speech

Visual area of left hemisphere

Corpus callosum

Visual area of right hemisphere

corpus callosum [KOR-pus kah-LOW-sum] the large band of neural fibers connecting the two brain hemispheres and carrying messages between them.

split brain a condition resulting from surgery that isolates the brain's two hemispheres by cutting the fibers (mainly those of the corpus callosum) connecting them.

Splitting the Brain

In 1961, Los Angeles neurosurgeons Philip Vogel and Joseph Bogen speculated that major epileptic seizures were caused by an amplification of abnormal brain activity bouncing back and forth between the two cerebral hemispheres, which work together as a whole system. If so, they wondered, could they end this biological tennis match by severing the **corpus callosum,** the wide band of axon fibers connecting the two hemispheres and carrying messages between them (**FIGURE 5.8**)? Vogel and Bogen knew that psychologists Roger Sperry, Ronald Myers, and Michael Gazzaniga had divided cats' and monkeys' brains in this manner, with no serious ill effects.

So the surgeons operated. The result? The seizures all but disappeared. The patients with these **split brains** were surprisingly normal, their personality and intellect hardly affected. Waking from surgery, one even joked that he had a "splitting headache" (Gazzaniga, 1967). By sharing their experiences, these patients have greatly expanded our understanding of interactions between the intact brain's two hemispheres.

To appreciate these findings, we need to focus for a minute on the peculiar nature of our visual wiring, illustrated in **FIGURE 5.9**. Note that each eye receives sensory information from the entire visual field. But in each eye, information from the left half of your field of vision goes to your right hemisphere, and information from the right half of your visual field goes to your left hemisphere, which usually controls speech. Information received by either hemisphere is quickly transmitted to the other across the corpus callosum. In a person with a severed corpus callosum, this information-sharing does not take place.

Knowing these facts, Sperry and Gazzaniga could send information to a patient's left or right hemisphere. As the person stared at a spot, they flashed a stimulus to its right or left. They could do this with you, too, but in your intact brain, the hemisphere receiving the information would instantly pass the news to the other side. Because the split-brain surgery had cut the communication lines between the hemispheres, the researchers could, with these patients, quiz each hemisphere separately.

In an early experiment, Gazzaniga (1967) asked split-brain patients to stare at a dot as he flashed HE·ART on a screen (**FIGURE 5.10**). Thus, HE appeared in their left visual field (which transmits to the right hemisphere) and ART in the right field (which transmits to the left hemisphere). When he then asked them to *say* what they had seen, the patients reported that they had seen ART. But when asked to *point* to the word they had seen, they were startled when

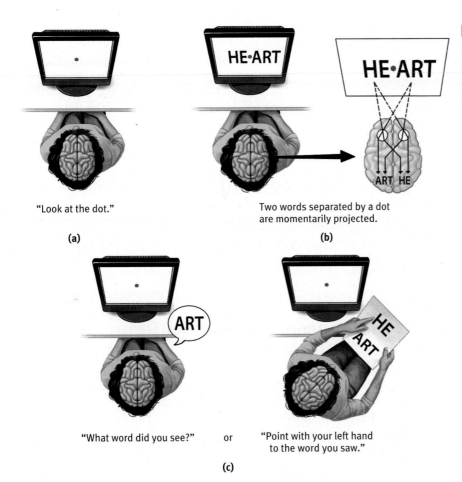

"Look at the dot."

(a)

Two words separated by a dot
are momentarily projected.

(b)

"What word did you see?"   or   "Point with your left hand
to the word you saw."

(c)

< FIGURE 5.10

One skull, two minds When an experimenter flashes the word HEART across the visual field, a woman with a split brain verbally reports seeing the portion of the word transmitted to her left hemisphere. However, if asked to indicate with her left hand what she saw, she points to the portion of the word transmitted to her right hemisphere. (From Gazzaniga, 1983.)

their left hand (controlled by the right hemisphere) pointed to HE. Given an opportunity to express itself, each hemisphere indicated what it had seen. The right hemisphere (controlling the left hand) intuitively knew what it could not verbally report.

When a picture of a spoon was flashed to their right hemisphere, the patients could not *say* what they had viewed. But when asked to *identify* what they had viewed by feeling an assortment of hidden objects with their left hand, they readily selected the spoon. If the experimenter said, "Correct!" the patient might reply, "What? Correct? How could I possibly pick out the correct object when I don't know what I saw?" It is, of course, the left hemisphere doing the talking here, bewildered by what the nonverbal right hemisphere knows.

A few people who have had split-brain surgery have been for a time bothered by the unruly independence of their left hand, which might unbutton a shirt while the right hand buttoned it, or put grocery store items back on the shelf after the right hand put them in the cart. It was as if each hemisphere was thinking "I've half a mind to wear my green (blue) shirt today." Indeed, said Sperry (1964), split-brain surgery leaves people "with two separate minds." With a split brain, both hemispheres can comprehend and follow an instruction to copy—*simultaneously*—different figures with the left and right hands (Franz et al., 2000; see also **FIGURE 5.11**).

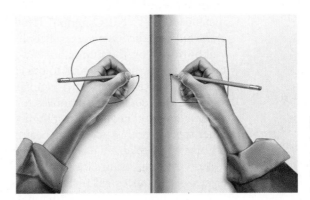

< FIGURE 5.11

Try this! People who have had split-brain surgery can simultaneously draw two different shapes.

"Do not let your left hand know what your right hand is doing."

Matthew 6:3

 **IMMERSIVE LEARNING** Have you ever been asked if you are "left-brained" or "right-brained"? Consider this popular misconception with LaunchPad's *How Would You Know If People Can Be "Left-Brained" or "Right-Brained"?*

(Reading these reports, one can fantasize a patient enjoying a solitary game of "rock, paper, scissors"—left versus right hand.)

When the "two minds" are at odds, the left hemisphere does mental gymnastics to rationalize reactions it does not understand. If a patient follows an order ("Walk") sent to the right hemisphere, a strange thing happens. The left hemisphere, unaware of the order, doesn't know why the patient begins walking. If asked why, the patient doesn't reply, "I don't know." Instead, the left hemisphere improvises—"I'm going into the house to get a Coke." Gazzaniga (2006), who described these patients as "the most fascinating people on earth," realized that the conscious left hemisphere is an "interpreter" that instantly constructs explanations. The brain, he concluded, often runs on autopilot; it acts first and then explains itself.

RETRIEVE IT

- (1) If we flash a red light to the right hemisphere of a person with a split brain, and flash a green light to the left hemisphere, will each observe its own color? (2) Will the person be aware that the colors differ? (3) What will the person verbally report seeing?

ANSWERS: 1. yes, 2. no, 3. green

Right-Left Differences in the Intact Brain

So, what about the 99.99+ percent of us with undivided brains? Does each of *our* hemispheres also perform distinct functions? Several different types of studies indicate they do. When a person performs a *perceptual* task, for example, brain waves, bloodflow, and glucose consumption reveal increased activity in the *right* hemisphere. When the person speaks or calculates, activity usually increases in the *left* hemisphere.

A dramatic demonstration of hemispheric specialization happens before some types of brain surgery. To locate the patient's language centers, the surgeon injects a sedative into the neck artery feeding blood to the left hemisphere, which usually controls speech. Before the injection, the patient is lying down, arms in the air, chatting with the doctor. Can you predict what probably happens when the drug puts the left hemisphere to sleep? Within seconds, the person's right arm falls limp. If the left hemisphere is controlling language, the patient will be speechless until the drug wears off. If the drug is injected into the artery to the right hemisphere, the *left* arm will fall limp, but the person will still be able to speak.

To the brain, language is language, whether spoken or signed. Just as hearing people usually use the left hemisphere to process spoken language, deaf people use the left hemisphere to process sign language (Corina et al., 1992; Hickok et al., 2001). Thus, a left hemisphere stroke disrupts a deaf person's signing, much as it would disrupt a hearing person's speaking (Corina, 1998).

Although the left hemisphere is skilled at making quick, literal interpretations of language, the right hemisphere excels at *making inferences* (Beeman & Chiarello, 1998; Bowden & Beeman, 1998; Mason & Just, 2004). It also *helps us modulate our speech* to make meaning clear—as when we say "Let's eat, Grandpa" instead of "Let's eat Grandpa" (Heller, 1990). The right hemisphere also *helps orchestrate our self-awareness.* People who suffer partial paralysis will sometimes stubbornly deny their impairment—strangely claiming they can move a paralyzed limb—if the damage is to the right hemisphere (Berti et al., 2005).

Simply looking at the two hemispheres, so alike to the naked eye, who would suppose they contribute uniquely to the harmony of the whole? Yet a variety of observations—of people with split brains, of people with normal brains, and even of other species' brains—converge beautifully, leaving little doubt that we have unified brains with specialized parts (Hopkins & Cantalupo, 2008; MacNeilage et al., 2009).

How does the brain's intricate networking emerge? How does our *heredity*—the legacy of our ancestral history—conspire with our experiences to organize and "wire" the brain? To that we turn next.

LaunchPad For a helpful animated review of split-brain research, see LaunchPad's *PsychSim 6: Hemispheric Specialization.*

5 REVIEW The Cerebral Cortex and Our Divided Brain

◉ Learning Objectives

Test Yourself by taking a moment to answer each of these Learning Objective Questions (repeated here from within the module). Then turn to Appendix D, Complete Module Reviews, to check your answers. Research suggests that trying to answer these questions on your own will improve your long-term memory of the concepts (McDaniel et al., 2009).

5-1 What are the functions of the various cerebral cortex regions?

5-2 To what extent can a damaged brain reorganize itself, and what is neurogenesis?

5-3 What do split brains reveal about the functions of our two brain hemispheres?

▣ Terms and Concepts to Remember

Test yourself on these terms by trying to write down the definition in your own words before flipping back to the referenced page to check your answers.

cerebral [seh-REE-bruhl] cortex, p. 56
frontal lobes, p. 56
parietal [puh-RYE-uh-tuhl] lobes, p. 56
occipital [ahk-SIP-uh-tuhl] lobes, p. 56
temporal lobes, p. 56
motor cortex, p. 57
somatosensory cortex, p. 58
association areas, p. 59
plasticity, p. 60
neurogenesis, p. 61
corpus callosum [KOR-pus kah-LOW-sum], p. 62
split brain, p. 62

▣ Experience the Testing Effect

Test yourself repeatedly throughout your studies. This will not only help you figure out what you know and don't know; the testing itself will help you learn and remember the information more effectively thanks to the *testing effect*.

1. If a neurosurgeon stimulated your right motor cortex, you would most likely
   a. see light.
   b. hear a sound.
   c. feel a touch on the right arm.
   d. move your left leg.

2. How do different neural networks communicate with one another to let you respond when a friend greets you at a party?

3. Which of the following body regions has the greatest representation in the somatosensory cortex?
   a. Upper arm
   b. Toes
   c. Lips
   d. All regions are equally represented.

4. Judging and planning are enabled by the _____ lobes.

5. What would it be like to talk on the phone if you didn't have temporal lobe association areas? What would you hear? What would you understand?

6. The "uncommitted" areas that make up about three-fourths of the cerebral cortex are called _____ _____.

7. Plasticity is especially evident in the brains of
   a. split-brain patients.
   b. young adults.
   c. young children.
   d. right-handed people.

8. An experimenter flashes the word HERON across the visual field of a man whose corpus callosum has been severed. HER is transmitted to his right hemisphere and ON to his left hemisphere. When asked to indicate what he saw, the man says he saw _____ but points to _____.

9. Studies of people with split brains and brain scans of those with undivided brains indicate that the left hemisphere excels in
   a. processing language.
   b. visual perceptions.
   c. making inferences.
   d. neurogenesis.

10. Damage to the brain's right hemisphere is most likely to reduce a person's ability to
    a. recite the alphabet rapidly.
    b. make inferences.
    c. understand verbal instructions.
    d. solve arithmetic problems.

Find answers to these questions in Appendix E, in the back of the book.

Use ❷ LearningCurve to create your personalized study plan, which will direct you to the resources that will help you most in ❷ LaunchPad.

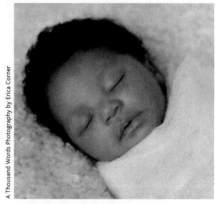

The nurture of nature Parents everywhere wonder: Will my baby grow up to be peaceful or aggressive? Homely or attractive? Successful or struggling at every step? What comes built in, and what is nurtured—and how? Research reveals that nature and nurture together shape our development—every step of the way.

✔ FIGURE 6.1

The life code The nucleus of every human cell contains chromosomes, each of which is made up of two strands of DNA connected in a double helix. Genes are DNA segments that, when expressed (turned on), direct the development of proteins that influence a person's individual development.

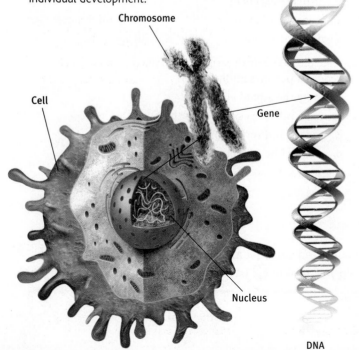

Chromosome

Cell

Gene

Nucleus

DNA

MODULE 6 Genetics, Evolutionary Psychology, and Behavior

Behavior Genetics: Predicting Individual Differences

6-1 What are *chromosomes, DNA, genes,* and the human *genome?* How do behavior geneticists explain our individual differences?

Our shared brain architecture predisposes some common behavioral tendencies. Whether we live in the Arctic or the tropics, we sense the world, develop language, and feel hunger through identical mechanisms. We prefer sweet tastes to sour. We divide the color spectrum into similar colors. And we feel drawn to behaviors that produce and protect offspring.

Our human family shares not only a common biological heritage—cut us and we bleed—but also common social behaviors. Whether named Gonzales, Nkomo, Smith, or Wong, we start fearing strangers at about eight months, and as adults we prefer the company of those with attitudes and attributes similar to our own. As members of one species, we affiliate, conform, return favors, punish offenses, organize hierarchies of status, and grieve a child's death. A visitor from outer space could drop in anywhere and find humans dancing and feasting, singing and worshiping, playing sports and games, laughing and crying, living in families and forming groups. We are the leaves of one tree.

But in important ways, we also are each unique. We look different. We sound different. We have varying personalities, interests, and cultural and family backgrounds. What causes our striking diversity? How much of it is shaped by our differing genes, and how much by our **environment**—by every external influence, from maternal nutrition while in the womb to social support while nearing the tomb? How does our **heredity** interact with our experiences to create both our universal human nature and our individual and social diversity? Such questions intrigue **behavior geneticists.**

Genes: Our Codes for Life

Barely more than a century ago, few would have guessed that every cell nucleus in your body contains the genetic master code for your entire body. It's as if every room in Dubai's Burj Khalifa (the world's tallest building) contained a book detailing the architect's plans for the entire structure. The plans for your own book of life run to 46 chapters—23 donated by your mother's egg and 23 by your father's sperm. Each of these 46 chapters, called a **chromosome,** is composed of a coiled chain of the molecule **DNA** (*deoxyribonucleic acid*). **Genes,** small segments of the giant DNA molecules, form the words of those chapters (**FIGURE 6.1**). Altogether, you have 20,000 to 25,000 genes, which can be either active (*expressed*) or inactive. Environmental events "turn on" genes, rather like hot water enabling a tea bag to express its flavor. When turned on, genes provide the code for creating *protein molecules,* our body's building blocks.

Genetically speaking, every other human is nearly your identical twin. Human **genome** researchers have discovered the common sequence within human DNA. This shared genetic profile makes us humans, rather than tulips, bananas, or chimpanzees.

The occasional variations found at particular gene sites in human DNA fascinate geneticists and psychologists. Slight person-to-person variations from the common pattern give clues to our uniqueness—why one person has a disease that another does not, why one person is tall and another short, why one is anxious and another calm.

Most of our traits have complex genetic roots. How tall you are, for example, reflects the size of your face, vertebrae, leg bones, and so forth—each of which may be influenced by different genes interacting with your specific environment. Traits such as intelligence, happiness, and aggressiveness are similarly influenced by groups of genes. Thus, our genes help explain both our shared human nature and our human diversity. But knowing our heredity tells only part of our story. To form us, environmental influences interact with our genetic predispositions.

RETRIEVE IT [✱]

- Put the following cell structures in order from smallest to largest: nucleus, gene, chromosome

  ANSWER: gene, chromosome, nucleus

- When the mother's egg and the father's sperm unite, each contributes 23 _____.

  ANSWER: chromosomes

Twin and Adoption Studies

6-2 How do twin and adoption studies help us understand the effects and interactions of nature and nurture?

To scientifically tease apart the influences of environment and heredity, behavior geneticists could wish for two types of experiments. The first would control heredity while varying the home environment. The second would control the home environment while varying heredity. Although such experiments with human infants would be unethical, nature has done this work for us.

IDENTICAL VERSUS FRATERNAL TWINS Identical *(monozygotic)* **twins** develop from a single fertilized egg that splits in two. Thus they are *genetically* identical—nature's own human clones (**FIGURE 6.2**). Indeed, they are clones who share not only the same genes but the same conception and uterus, and usually the same birth date and cultural history.

Identical twins   **Fraternal twins**

Same sex only   **Same or opposite sex**

< **FIGURE 6.2**

Same fertilized egg, same genes; different eggs, different genes Identical twins develop from a single fertilized egg, fraternal twins from two.

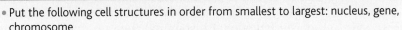
"Thanks for almost everything, Dad."

"We share half our genes with the banana."
Evolutionary biologist Robert May, president of Britain's Royal Society, 2001

"Your DNA and mine are 99.9 percent the same. . . . At the DNA level, we are clearly all part of one big worldwide family."
Francis Collins, Human Genome Project director, 2007

LaunchPad See LaunchPad's *Video: Twin Studies* for a helpful tutorial animation.

environment every nongenetic influence, from prenatal nutrition to the people and things around us.

heredity the genetic transfer of characteristics from parents to offspring.

behavior genetics the study of the relative power and limits of genetic and environmental influences on behavior.

chromosomes threadlike structures made of DNA molecules that contain the genes.

DNA (deoxyribonucleic acid) a complex molecule containing the genetic information that makes up the chromosomes.

genes the biochemical units of heredity that make up the chromosomes; segments of DNA capable of synthesizing proteins.

genome the complete instructions for making an organism, consisting of all the genetic material in that organism's chromosomes.

identical (monozygotic) twins develop from a single fertilized egg that splits in two, creating two genetically identical organisms.

Skin deep Do identical twins have similar personalities because people respond to their similar looks? These women look like identical twins, but they aren't genetically related. Such "twins" do not report similar personalities (Segal, 2013).

Twins Lorraine and Levinia Christmas, driving to deliver Christmas presents to each other near Flitcham, England, collided (Shepherd, 1997).

┌   ┐
fraternal (dizygotic) twins develop from separate fertilized eggs. They are genetically no closer than ordinary brothers and sisters, but they share a prenatal environment.
└   ┘

Fraternal *(dizygotic)* **twins** develop from two separate fertilized eggs. As womb-mates, they share a prenatal environment, but they are genetically no more similar than ordinary brothers and sisters.

Shared genes can translate into shared experiences. A person whose identical twin has autism spectrum disorder, for example, has about a 3 in 4 risk of being similarly diagnosed. If the affected twin is fraternal, the co-twin has about a 1 in 3 risk (Ronald & Hoekstra, 2011). To study the effects of genes and environments, hundreds of researchers have studied some 800,000 identical and fraternal twin pairs (Johnson et al., 2009).

Are genetically identical twins also *behaviorally* more similar than fraternal twins? Studies of thousands of twin pairs have found that identical twins are much more alike in *extraversion* (outgoingness) and *neuroticism* (emotional instability) than are fraternal twins (Kandler et al., 2011; Laceulle et al., 2011; Loehlin, 2012).

Identical twins, more than fraternal twins, look alike. So, do people's responses to their looks account for their similarities? *No.* In one clever study, a researcher compared personality similarity between identical twins and unrelated look-alike pairs (Segal, 2013). Only the identical twins reported similar personalities. Other studies have shown that identical twins whose parents treated them alike (for example, dressing them identically) were not psychologically more alike than identical twins who were treated less similarly (Kendler et al., 1994; Loehlin & Nichols, 1976). In explaining individual differences, genes matter.

SEPARATED TWINS Imagine the following science fiction experiment: A mad scientist decides to separate identical twins at birth, then raise them in differing environments. Better yet, consider a *true* story:

On a chilly February morning in 1979, some time after divorcing his first wife, Linda, Jim Lewis awoke in his modest home next to his second wife, Betty. Determined to make this marriage work, Jim made a habit of leaving love notes to Betty around the house. As he lay in bed he thought about others he had loved, including his son, James Alan, and his faithful dog, Toy.

Jim looked forward to spending part of the day in his basement woodworking shop, where he enjoyed building furniture, picture frames, and other items, including a white bench now circling a tree in his front yard. Jim also liked to spend free time driving his Chevy, watching stock car racing, and drinking Miller Lite beer.

Jim was basically healthy, except for occasional half-day migraine headaches and blood pressure that was a little high, perhaps related to his chain-smoking habit. He had become overweight a while back but had shed some of the pounds. Having undergone a vasectomy, he was done having children.

What was extraordinary about Jim Lewis, however, was that at that same moment (we are not making this up) there existed another man—also named Jim—for whom all these things (right down to the dog's name) were also true.[1] This other Jim—Jim Springer—just happened, 38 years earlier, to have been his fetal partner. Thirty-seven days after their birth, these genetically identical twins were separated, adopted by blue-collar families, and raised with no contact or knowledge of each other's whereabouts until the day Jim Lewis received a call from his genetic clone (who, having been told he had a twin, set out to find him).

One month later, the brothers became the first of many separated twin pairs tested by University of Minnesota psychologist Thomas Bouchard and his

---

1. Actually, this description of the two Jims errs in one respect: Jim Lewis named his son James Alan. Jim Springer named his James Allan.

colleagues (Miller, 2012). The brothers' voice intonations and inflections were so similar that, hearing a playback of an earlier interview, Jim Springer guessed "That's me." Wrong—it was Jim Lewis. Given tests measuring their personality, intelligence, heart rate, and brain waves, the Jim twins—despite 38 years of separation—were virtually as alike as the same person tested twice. Both married women named Dorothy Jane Scheckelburger. Okay, the last item is a joke. But as Judith Rich Harris (2006) has noted, it would hardly be weirder than some other reported similarities.

Aided by media publicity, Bouchard (2009) and his colleagues located and studied 74 pairs of identical twins raised apart. They continued to find similarities not only of tastes and physical attributes but also of personality (characteristic patterns of thinking, feeling, and acting), abilities, attitudes, interests, and even fears.

In Sweden, researchers identified 99 separated identical twin pairs and more than 200 separated fraternal twin pairs (Pedersen et al., 1988). Compared with equivalent samples of identical twins raised together, the separated identical twins had somewhat less identical personalities. Still, separated twins were more alike if genetically identical than if fraternal. And separation shortly after birth (rather than, say, at age 8) did not amplify their personality differences.

Stories of startling twin similarities have not impressed critics, who remind us that "The plural of *anecdote* is not *data.*" They note that if any two strangers were to spend hours comparing their behaviors and life histories, they would probably discover many coincidental similarities. If researchers created a control group of biologically unrelated pairs of the same age, sex, and ethnicity, who had not grown up together but who were as similar to one another in economic and cultural background as are many of the separated twin pairs, wouldn't these pairs also exhibit striking similarities (Joseph, 2001)? Twin researchers have replied that separated fraternal twins do not exhibit similarities comparable with those of separated identical twins.

The impressive data from personality assessments are clouded by the reunion of many of the separated twins some years before they were tested. And adoption agencies also tend to place separated twins in similar homes. Despite these criticisms, the striking twin-study results helped shift scientific thinking toward a greater appreciation of genetic influences.

If genetic influences help explain individual differences, can the same be said of trait differences *between* groups? Not necessarily. Individual differences in height and weight, for example, are highly *heritable;* yet nutrition (an environmental factor) rather than genetic influences explains why, as a group, today's adults are taller and heavier than those of a century ago. The two groups differ, but not because human genes have changed in a mere century's eyeblink of time. Ditto aggressiveness, a genetically influenced trait. Today's peaceful Scandinavians differ from their more aggressive Viking ancestors, despite carrying many of the same genes.

BIOLOGICAL VERSUS ADOPTIVE RELATIVES For behavior geneticists, nature's second real-life experiment—adoption—creates two groups: *genetic relatives* (biological parents and siblings) and *environmental relatives* (adoptive parents and siblings). For personality or any other given trait, we can therefore ask whether adopted children are more like their biological parents, who contributed their genes, or their adoptive parents, who contribute a home environment. While sharing that home environment, do adopted siblings also come to share traits?

The stunning finding from studies of hundreds of adoptive families is that, with the exception of identical twins, people who grow up together do not much

In 2009, thieves broke into a Berlin store and stole jewelry worth $6.8 million. One thief left a drop of sweat—a link to his genetic signature. Police analyzed the DNA and encountered two matches: The DNA belonged to identical twin brothers. The court ruled that "at least one of the brothers took part in the crime, but it has not been possible to determine which one." Birds of a feather can rob together.

Coincidences are not unique to twins. Patricia Kern of Colorado was born March 13, 1941, and named Patricia Ann Campbell. Patricia DiBiasi of Oregon also was born March 13, 1941, and named Patricia Ann Campbell. Both had fathers named Robert, worked as bookkeepers, and at the time of this comparison had children ages 21 and 19. Both studied cosmetology, enjoyed oil painting as a hobby, and married military men, within 11 days of each other. They are not genetically related. (From an AP report, May 2, 1983.)

Mona Friis Bertheussen/Moment Film

Identical twins are people two
Identical twin sisters Mia (left) and Alexandra (right), featured in the film *Twin Sisters* (2013), are nearly always worlds apart. Adopted to different families as infants, Mia lives in suburban California and Alexandra lives in a Norwegian village. Mia plays the piano and enjoys golf, whereas Alexandra roams the countryside and plays with her pet mouse. Despite these differences, they share striking similarities. Both girls dislike tomatoes, olives, and messy rooms but are wild about chocolate.

Nature or nurture or both? When talent runs in families, as with Wynton Marsalis, Branford Marsalis, and Delfeayo Marsalis, how do heredity and environment together do their work?

"Do you, Ashley, take Nesbitt and his genome to be your husband?"

resemble one another in personality (McGue & Bouchard, 1998; Plomin, 2011; Rowe, 1990). In personality traits such as extraversion and agreeableness, people who have been adopted are more similar to their biological parents than to their caregiving adoptive parents.

The finding is important enough to bear repeating: *The environment shared by a family's children has virtually no discernible impact on their personalities.* Two adopted children raised in the same home are no more likely to share personality traits with each other than with the child down the block. Heredity shapes other primates' personalities, too. Macaque monkeys raised by foster mothers exhibited social behaviors that resembled their biological, rather than foster, mothers (Maestripieri, 2003). Add in the similarity of identical twins, whether they grow up together or apart, and the effect of a shared environment seems shockingly modest.

The genetic leash may limit the family environment's influence on personality, but it does not mean that adoptive parenting is a fruitless venture. As a new adoptive parent, I [ND] especially find it heartening to know that parents do influence their children's attitudes, values, manners, politics, and faith (Reifman & Cleveland, 2007). Religious involvement is genetically influenced (Steger et al., 2011). But a pair of adopted children or identical twins *will*, especially during adolescence, have more similar religious beliefs if raised together (Koenig et al., 2005). Parenting matters!

Moreover, child neglect and abuse and even parental divorce are rare in adoptive homes. (Adoptive parents are carefully screened; biological parents are not.) So it is not surprising that studies have shown that, despite a slightly greater risk of psychological disorder, most adopted children thrive, especially when adopted as infants (Loehlin et al., 2007; van IJzendoorn & Juffer, 2006; Wierzbicki, 1993). Seven in eight adopted children have reported feeling strongly attached to one or both adoptive parents. As children of self-giving parents, they have grown up to be more self-giving and altruistic than average (Sharma et al., 1998). Many scored higher than their biological parents and raised-apart biological siblings on intelligence tests, and most grew into happier and more stable adults (Kendler et al.,

Adoption matters As country music singer Faith Hill and late Apple founder Steve Jobs experienced, children benefit from one of the biggest gifts of love: adoption.

2015; van IJzendoorn et al., 2005). In one Swedish study, children adopted as infants grew up with fewer problems than were experienced by children whose biological mothers initially registered them for adoption but then decided to raise the children themselves (Bohman & Sigvardsson, 1990). Regardless of personality differences between adoptive family members, most adopted children benefit from adoption.

> **interaction** the interplay that occurs when the effect of one factor (such as environment) depends on another factor (such as heredity).

RETRIEVE IT

- How do researchers use twin and adoption studies to learn about psychological principles?

ANSWER: Researchers use twin and adoption studies to understand how much variation among individuals is due to genetic makeup and how much to environmental factors. Some studies compare the traits and behaviors of identical twins (same genes) and fraternal twins (different genes), as in any two siblings). They also compare adopted children with their adoptive and biological parents. Some studies compare traits and behaviors of twins raised together or separately.

Gene-Environment Interaction

 6-3 How do heredity and environment work together?

Among our similarities, the most important—the behavioral hallmark of our species—is our enormous adaptive capacity. Some human traits, such as having two eyes, develop the same in virtually every environment. But other traits are expressed only in particular environments. Go barefoot for a summer and you will develop toughened, callused feet—a biological adaptation to friction. Meanwhile, your shod neighbor will remain a tenderfoot. The difference between the two of you is an effect of environment. But it is also the product of a biological mechanism—adaptation.

Genes and environment—nature and nurture—work together, like two hands clapping. Genes are *self-regulating*. Rather than acting as blueprints that lead to the same result no matter the context, genes react. An African butterfly that is green in summer turns brown in fall, thanks to a temperature-controlled genetic switch. The same genes that produced green in one situation produce brown in another.

To say that genes and experience are *both* important is true. But more precisely, they **interact.** Imagine two babies, one genetically predisposed to be attractive, sociable, and easygoing, the other less so. Assume further that the first baby attracts more affectionate and stimulating care and so develops into a warmer and more outgoing person. As the two children grow older, the more naturally outgoing child may seek more activities and friends that encourage further social confidence.

"Men's natures are alike; it is their habits that carry them far apart."

Confucius, Analects, *500 B.C.E.*

Genetic space exploration In 2015, Scott (left) and Mark (right) Kelly embarked on a twin study that is literally out of this world. Scott will spend a year orbiting the planet in the International Space Station. His identical twin, Mark, will stay on Earth. Both twins will undergo the same physical and psychological testing. The study results will help scientists understand how genes and environment—in outer space and on Earth—interact.

Robert Markowitz/N.A.S.A/SIPA/Newscom

epigenetics the study of environmental influences on gene expression that occur without a DNA change.

evolutionary psychology the study of the evolution of behavior and the mind, using principles of natural selection.

natural selection the principle that those chance inherited traits that better enable an organism to survive and reproduce in a particular environment will most likely be passed on to succeeding generations.

What has caused their resulting personality differences? Neither heredity nor experience act alone. Environments trigger gene activity. And our genetically influenced traits *evoke* significant responses in others. Thus, a child's impulsivity and aggression may evoke an angry response from a parent or teacher, who reacts warmly to well-behaved children in the family or classroom. In such cases, the child's nature and the adult's nurture interact. Gene and scene dance together.

Identical twins not only share the same genetic predispositions, they also seek and create similar experiences that express their shared genes (Kandler et al., 2012). Evocative interactions may help explain why identical twins raised in different families have recalled their parents' warmth as remarkably similar—almost as similar as if they had been raised by the same parents (Plomin et al., 1988, 1991, 1994). Fraternal twins have more differing recollections of their early family life—even if raised in the same family! "Children experience us as different parents, depending on their own qualities," noted Sandra Scarr (1990).

Recall that genes can be either active (expressed, as the hot water activates the tea bag) or inactive. **Epigenetics** (meaning "in addition to" or "above and beyond" genetics), studies the molecular mechanisms by which environments can trigger or block genetic expression. Our experiences create *epigenetic marks,* which are often organic methyl molecules attached to part of a DNA strand (**FIGURE 6.3**). If a mark instructs the cell to ignore any gene present in that DNA segment, those genes will be "turned off"—they will prevent the DNA from producing the proteins coded by that gene. As one geneticist said, "Things written in pen you can't change. That's DNA. But things written in pencil you can. That's epigenetics" (Reed, 2011).

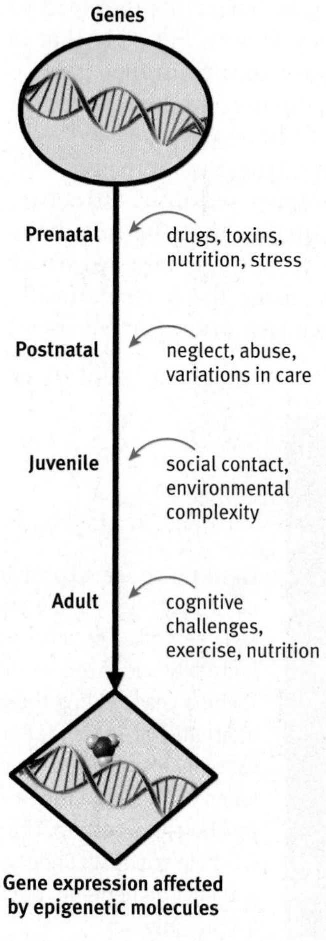

Environmental factors such as diet, drugs, and stress can affect the epigenetic molecules that regulate gene expression. Mother rats normally lick their infants. Deprived of this licking in experiments, infant rats had more epigenetic molecules blocking access to their brain's "on" switch for developing stress hormone receptors. When stressed, those animals had above-average levels of free-floating stress hormones and were more stressed (Champagne et al., 2003; Champagne & Mashoodh, 2009). Epigenetics research may solve some scientific mysteries, such as why only one member of an identical twin pair may develop a genetically influenced mental disorder, and how childhood abuse leaves its fingerprints in a person's brain (Spector, 2012).

Epigenetics can also help explain why identical twins may look slightly different. Researchers studying mice have found that in utero exposure to certain chemicals can cause genetically identical twins to have different-colored fur (Dolinoy et al., 2007). Such discoveries will be made easier by efforts such as the National Institutes of Health–funded Roadmap Epigenetics Project, a massive undertaking aimed at making epigenetic data publicly available.

So, if Beyoncé and Jay Z's daughter, Blue Ivy, grows up to be a popular recording artist, should we attribute her musical talent to her "superstar genes"? To her growing up in a musically rich environment? To high expectations? The best answer

Genes

Prenatal — drugs, toxins, nutrition, stress

Postnatal — neglect, abuse, variations in care

Juvenile — social contact, environmental complexity

Adult — cognitive challenges, exercise, nutrition

Gene expression affected by epigenetic molecules

> FIGURE 6.3

Epigenetics influences gene expression Life experiences beginning in the womb lay down epigenetic marks—often organic methyl molecules—that can affect the expression of any gene in the associated DNA segment. (Research from Champagne, 2010.)

seems to be "All of the above." From conception onward, we are the product of a cascade of interactions between our genetic predispositions and our surrounding environments (McGue, 2010). Our genes affect how people react to and influence us. Forget nature *versus* nurture; think nature *via* nurture.

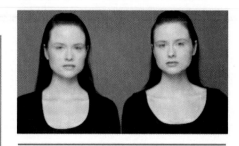

LaunchPad For a 7-minute explanation of genes and environment, visit LaunchPad's *Video: Behavior Genetics.*

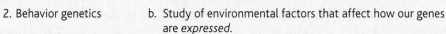

RETRIEVE IT [✖]

● Match the following terms to the correct explanation.

1. Epigenetics

2. Behavior genetics

a. Study of the relative effects of our genes and our environment on our behavior.

b. Study of environmental factors that affect how our genes are *expressed*.

ANSWERS: 1. b, 2. a

Evolutionary Psychology: Understanding Human Nature

<>> 6-4 How do evolutionary psychologists use natural selection to explain behavior tendencies?

Behavior geneticists explore the genetic and environmental roots of human differences. **Evolutionary psychologists** instead focus mostly on what makes us so much alike as humans. They use Charles Darwin's principle of **natural selection** to understand the roots of behavior and mental processes. The idea, simplified, is this:

• Organisms' varied offspring compete for survival.

• Certain biological and behavioral variations increase organisms' reproductive and survival chances in their particular environment.

• Offspring that survive are more likely to pass their genes to ensuing generations.

• Thus, over time, population characteristics may change.

To see these principles at work, let's consider a straightforward example in foxes.

Natural Selection and Adaptation

A fox is a wild and wary animal. If you capture a fox and try to befriend it, be careful. Stick your hand in the cage and, if the timid fox cannot flee, it may snack on your fingers. Russian scientist Dmitry Belyaev wondered how our human ancestors had domesticated dogs from their equally wild wolf forebears. Might he, within a comparatively short stretch of time, accomplish a similar feat by transforming the fearful fox into a friendly fox?

To find out, Belyaev set to work with 30 male and 100 female foxes. From their offspring he selected and mated the tamest 5 percent of males and 20 percent of females. (He measured tameness by the foxes' responses to attempts to feed, handle, and stroke them.) Over more than 30 generations of foxes, Belyaev and his successor, Lyudmila Trut, repeated that simple procedure. Forty years and 45,000 foxes later, they had a new breed of foxes that, in Trut's (1999) words, were "docile, eager to please, and unmistakably domesticated. . . . Before our eyes, 'the Beast' has turned into 'beauty,' as the aggressive behavior of our herd's wild [ancestors] entirely disappeared." So friendly and eager for human contact

Eric Isselée/Shutterstock

mutation a random error in gene replication that leads to a change.

were these animals, so inclined to whimper to attract attention and to lick people like affectionate dogs, that the cash-strapped institute seized on a way to raise funds—marketing its foxes as house pets.

Over time, traits that give an individual or species a reproductive advantage are *selected* and will prevail. Animal-breeding experiments manipulate genetic selection. Dog breeders have given us sheepdogs that herd, retrievers that retrieve, trackers that track, and pointers that point (Plomin et al., 1997). Psychologists, too, have bred animals to be serene or reactive, quick learners or slow ones.

Does the same process work with naturally occurring selection? Does natural selection explain our human tendencies? Nature has indeed selected advantageous variations from the new gene combinations produced at each human conception plus the **mutations** (random errors in gene replication) that sometimes result. But the tight genetic leash that predisposes a dog's retrieving, a cat's pouncing, or a bird's nesting is looser on humans. The genes selected during our ancestral history provide more than a long leash; they give us a great capacity to learn and therefore to *adapt* to life in varied environments, from the tundra to the jungle. Genes and experience together wire the brain. Our adaptive flexibility in responding to different environments contributes to our *fitness*—our ability to survive and reproduce.

RETRIEVE IT [✱]

• How are Belyaev and Trut's breeding practices similar to, and how do they differ from, the way natural selection normally occurs?

ANSWER: Over multiple generations, Belyaev and Trut selected and bred foxes that exhibited a trait they desired: tameness. This process is similar to naturally occurring selection, but it differs in that natural selection is much slower, and normally favors traits (including those arising from mutations) that contribute to reproduction and survival.

Evolutionary Success Helps Explain Similarities

Our behavioral and biological similarities arise from our shared human genome, our common genetic profile. How did we develop our genetic kinship?

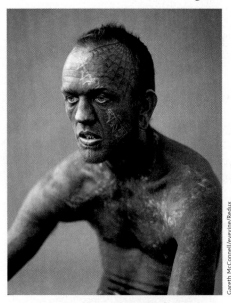

Differences grab attention, but our similarities run deep Lucky Diamond Rich, born Gregory Paul McLaren, is a New Zealand performance artist. He has held the world record for the most tattoos. But he also shares a common human concern for disadvantaged children.

Gareth McConnell/eyevine/Redux

OUR GENETIC LEGACY At the dawn of human history, our ancestors faced certain questions: Who is my ally, who is my foe? With whom should I mate? What food should I eat? Some individuals answered those questions more successfully than others. For example, women who experienced nausea in the critical first three months of pregnancy were genetically predisposed to avoid certain bitter, strongly flavored, and novel foods. Avoiding such foods has survival value, since they are the very foods most often toxic to prenatal development (Profet, 1992; Schmitt & Pilcher, 2004). Early humans disposed to eat nourishing rather than poisonous foods survived to contribute their genes to later generations. Those who deemed leopards "nice to pet" often did not.

Similarly successful were those whose mating helped them produce and nurture offspring. Over generations, the genes of individuals not so disposed tended to be lost from the human gene pool. As success-enhancing genes continued to be selected, behavioral tendencies and thinking and learning capacities emerged that prepared our Stone Age ancestors to survive, reproduce, and send their genes into the future, and into you.

As inheritors of this prehistoric legacy, we are genetically predisposed to behave in ways that promoted our ancestors' surviving and reproducing.

But in some ways, we are biologically prepared for a world that no longer exists. We face problems our ancestors could not imagine, such as how to create the perfect online dating profile or how to overcome the urge to constantly check our smart phones (Parkinson & Wheatley, 2015). We love the taste of sweets and fats, nutrients that prepared our physically active ancestors to survive food shortages. But few of us now hunt and gather our food. Too often, we search for sweets and fats in fast-food outlets and vending machines. Our natural dispositions, rooted deep in history, are mismatched with today's junk-food and often inactive lifestyle.

EVOLUTIONARY PSYCHOLOGY TODAY Darwin's theory of evolution has become one of biology's organizing principles. "Virtually no contemporary scientists believe that Darwin was basically wrong," noted Jared Diamond (2001). Today, Darwin's theory lives on in the *second Darwinian revolution,* the application of evolutionary principles to psychology. In concluding *On the Origin of Species,* Darwin (1859, p. 346) anticipated this, foreseeing "open fields for far more important researches. Psychology will be based on a new foundation."

Elsewhere in this text, we address questions that intrigue evolutionary psychologists: Why do infants start to fear strangers about the time they become mobile? Why are biological fathers so much less likely than unrelated boyfriends to abuse and murder the children with whom they share a home? Why do so many more people have phobias about spiders, snakes, and heights than about more dangerous threats, such as guns and electricity? And why do we fear air travel so much more than driving?

Jacob Hamblin/Shutterstock

* * *

We know from our correspondence and from surveys that some readers are troubled by the naturalism and evolutionism of contemporary science. (A note to readers from other nations: In the United States there is a wide gulf between scientific and lay thinking about evolution.) "The idea that human minds are the product of evolution is . . . unassailable fact," declared a 2007 editorial in *Nature,* a leading science journal. In *The Language of God,* Human Genome Project director Francis Collins (2006, pp. 141, 146), a self-described evangelical Christian, compiled the "utterly compelling" evidence that led him to conclude that Darwin's big idea is "unquestionably correct." Yet Gallup pollsters report that 42 percent of U.S. adults believe that humans were created "pretty much in their present form" within the last 10,000 years (Newport, 2014). Many people who dispute the scientific story worry that a science of behavior (and evolutionary science in particular) will destroy our sense of the beauty, mystery, and spiritual significance of the human creature. For those concerned, we offer some reassuring thoughts.

When Isaac Newton explained the rainbow in terms of light of differing wavelengths, the British poet John Keats feared that Newton had destroyed the rainbow's mysterious beauty. Yet, as evolutionary biologist Richard Dawkins (1998) noted in *Unweaving the Rainbow,* Newton's analysis led to an even deeper mystery—Einstein's theory of special relativity. Nothing about Newton's optics need diminish our appreciation for the dramatic elegance of a rainbow arching across a brightening sky.

When Galileo assembled evidence that Earth revolved around the Sun, not vice versa, he did not offer irrefutable proof for his theory. Rather, he offered a coherent explanation for a variety of observations, such as the changing shadows cast by the Moon's mountains. His explanation eventually won the day because it described and explained things in a way that made sense, that hung together.

Despite high infant mortality and rampant disease in past millennia, not one of your countless ancestors died childless.

Those who are troubled by an apparent conflict between scientific and religious accounts of human origins may find it helpful to consider that different perspectives of life can be complementary. For example, the scientific account attempts to tell us *when* and *how;* religious creation stories usually aim to tell about an ultimate *who* and *why.* As Galileo explained to the Grand Duchess Christina, "The Bible teaches how to go to heaven, not how the heavens go."

Darwin's theory of evolution likewise is a coherent view of natural history. It offers an organizing principle that unifies various observations.

Many people of faith find the scientific idea of human origins congenial with their spirituality. In the fifth century, St. Augustine (quoted by Wilford, 1999) wrote, "The universe was brought into being in a less than fully formed state, but was gifted with the capacity to transform itself from unformed matter into a truly marvelous array of structures and life forms." Some 1600 years later, Pope Francis in 2014 welcomed a science-religion dialogue, saying, "Evolution in nature is not inconsistent with the notion of creation, because evolution requires the creation of beings that evolve."

Meanwhile, many people of science are awestruck at the emerging understanding of the universe and the human creature. It boggles the mind—the entire universe popping out of a point some 14 billion years ago, and instantly inflating to cosmological size. Had the energy of this Big Bang been the tiniest bit less, the universe would have collapsed back on itself. Had it been the tiniest bit more, the result would have been a soup too thin to support life. Astronomer Sir Martin Rees has described *Just Six Numbers* (1999), any one of which, if changed ever so slightly, would produce a cosmos in which life could not exist. Had gravity been a tad stronger or weaker, or had the weight of a carbon proton been a wee bit different, our universe just wouldn't have worked.

What caused this almost-too-good-to-be-true, finely tuned universe? Why is there something rather than nothing? How did it come to be, in the words of Harvard-Smithsonian astrophysicist Owen Gingerich (1999), "so extraordinarily right, that it seemed the universe had been expressly designed to produce intelligent, sentient beings"? On such matters, a humble, awed, scientific silence is appropriate, suggested philosopher Ludwig Wittgenstein: "Whereof one cannot speak, thereof one must be silent" (1922, p. 189).

Rather than fearing science, we can welcome its enlarging our understanding and awakening our sense of awe. In *The Fragile Species*, Lewis Thomas (1992) described his utter amazement that Earth in time gave rise to bacteria and eventually to Bach's Mass in B Minor. In a short 4 billion years, life on Earth has come from nothing to structures as complex as a 6-billion-unit strand of DNA and the incomprehensible intricacy of the human brain. Atoms no different from those in a rock somehow formed dynamic entities that produce extraordinary, self-replicating, information-processing systems—us (Davies, 2007). Although we appear to have been created from dust, over eons of time, the end result is a priceless creature, one rich with potential beyond our imagining.

MODULE 6 REVIEW Genetics, Evolutionary Psychology, and Behavior

👁 Learning Objectives

Test Yourself by taking a moment to answer each of these Learning Objective Questions (repeated here from within the module). Then turn to Appendix D, Complete Module Reviews, to check your answers. Research suggests that trying to answer these questions on your own will improve your long-term memory of the concepts (McDaniel et al., 2009).

6-1 What are *chromosomes, DNA, genes,* and the human *genome?* How do behavior geneticists explain our individual differences?

6-2 How do twin and adoption studies help us understand the effects and interactions of nature and nurture?

6-3 How do heredity and environment work together?

6-4 How do evolutionary psychologists use natural selection to explain behavior tendencies?

▪·[·] Terms and Concepts to Remember

Test yourself on these terms by trying to write down the definition in your own words before flipping back to the referenced page to check your answers.

environment, p. 66
heredity, p. 66

behavior genetics, p. 66
chromosomes, p. 66
DNA (deoxyribonucleic acid), p. 66
genes, p. 66
genome, p. 66
identical (monozygotic) twins, p. 67

fraternal (dizygotic) twins, p. 68
interaction, p. 71
epigenetics, p. 72
evolutionary psychology, p. 73
natural selection, p. 73
mutation, p. 74

[*] Experience the Testing Effect

Test yourself repeatedly throughout your studies. This will not only help you figure out what you know and don't know; the testing itself will help you learn and remember the information more effectively thanks to the *testing effect*.

1. The threadlike structures made largely of DNA molecules are called _____.

2. A small segment of DNA that codes for particular proteins is referred to as a _____.

3. When the mother's egg and the father's sperm unite, each contributes
   a. one chromosome pair.
   b. 23 chromosomes.
   c. 23 chromosome pairs.
   d. 25,000 chromosomes.

4. Fraternal twins result when
   a. a single egg is fertilized by a single sperm and then splits.
   b. a single egg is fertilized by two sperm and then splits.
   c. two eggs are fertilized by two sperm.
   d. two eggs are fertilized by a single sperm.

5. _____ twins share the same DNA.

6. Adoption studies seek to understand genetic influences on personality. They do this mainly by
   a. comparing adopted children with nonadopted children.
   b. evaluating whether adopted children's personalities more closely resemble those of their adoptive parents or their biological parents.
   c. studying the effect of prior neglect on adopted children.
   d. studying the effect of children's age at adoption.

7. Epigenetics is the study of the molecular mechanisms by which _____ trigger or block genetic expression.

8. Behavior geneticists are most interested in exploring _____ (commonalities/differences) in our behaviors. Evolutionary psychologists are most interested in exploring _____ (commonalities/differences).

9. Evolutionary psychologists are most likely to focus on
   a. how individuals differ from one another.
   b. ancestral hunting and gathering behaviors.
   c. natural selection of the fittest adaptations.
   d. twin and adoption studies.

Find answers to these questions in Appendix E, in the back of the book.

Use 🐢 LearningCurve to create your personalized study plan, which will direct you to the resources that will help you most in 🐢 LaunchPad.

States
of
Consciousness

Cognitive

Neuroscience

← Selective
attention

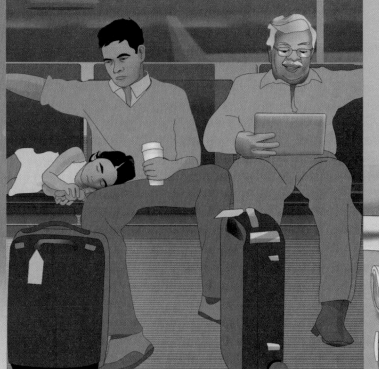

How and why do we sleep?

What are sleep disorders?

How and why do we dream?

How can we sleep better?
Why should we?

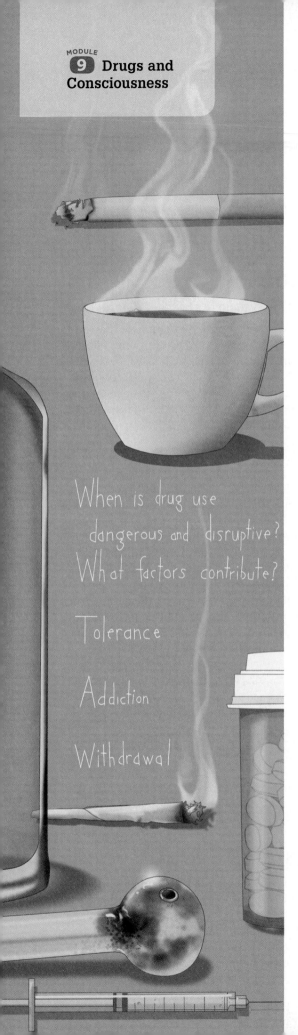

When is drug use dangerous and disruptive?

What factors contribute?

Tolerance

Addiction

Withdrawal

Consciousness and the Two-Track Mind

CONSCIOUSNESS can be a funny thing. It offers us weird experiences, as when entering sleep or leaving a dream, and sometimes it leaves us wondering who is really in control. After zoning me [DM] out with nitrous oxide, my dentist tells me to turn my head to the left. My conscious mind resists: "No way," I silently say. "You can't boss me around!" Whereupon my robotic head, ignoring my conscious mind, turns obligingly under the dentist's control.

Then there are those times when consciousness seems to split. Reading *Green Eggs and Ham* to one of my preschoolers for the umpteenth time, my obliging mouth could say the words while my mind wandered elsewhere. Sometimes, my mind wanders while giving a well-practiced speech. And if someone drops by my office while I'm typing a sentence, it's not a problem. My fingers continue their keyboard dance as I strike up a conversation.

What do such experiences reveal? Was my drug-induced dental experience akin to people's experiences with other *psychoactive drugs* (mood- and perception-altering substances)? Does the mind's wandering while reading, speaking, or typing reveal a split in consciousness? And during sleep, when do those weird dream experiences occur, and why? Before considering these questions and more, we will ask a fundamental question: What is *consciousness*?

In Module 7, we consider the mind's two tracks (one conscious and controlled, the other beneath our awareness and automatic). Module 8 explores the fascinating world of our sleep and dreams. In Module 9, we take a close look at the influence of psychoactive drugs. ◼

consciousness our awareness of ourselves and our environment.

cognitive neuroscience the interdisciplinary study of the brain activity linked with cognition (including perception, thinking, memory, and language).

selective attention the focusing of conscious awareness on a particular stimulus.

"Psychology must discard all reference to consciousness."

Behaviorist John B. Watson (1913)

MODULE 7 Consciousness: Some Basic Concepts

Every science has concepts so fundamental they are nearly impossible to define. Biologists agree on what is alive but not on precisely what life is. In physics, *matter* and *energy* elude simple definition. To psychologists, consciousness is similarly a fundamental yet slippery concept.

Defining Consciousness

7-1 What is the place of consciousness in psychology's history?

At its beginning, *psychology* was "the description and explanation of states of consciousness" (Ladd, 1887). But during the first half of the twentieth century, the difficulty of scientifically studying consciousness led many psychologists—including those in the emerging school of *behaviorism*—to turn to direct observations of behavior. By the 1960s, psychology had nearly lost consciousness and was defining itself as "the science of behavior." Consciousness was likened to a car's speedometer: "It doesn't make the car go, it just reflects what's happening" (Seligman, 1991, p. 24).

After 1960, psychology began regaining consciousness. Neuroscience advances linked brain activity to sleeping, dreaming, and other mental states. Researchers began studying consciousness altered by drugs, hypnosis, and meditation. (More on hypnosis in Module 18 and meditation in Module 34.) Psychologists of all persuasions were affirming the importance of *cognition*, or mental processes.

Most psychologists now define **consciousness** as our awareness of ourselves and our environment (Paller & Suzuki, 2014). This awareness allows us to assemble information from many sources as we reflect on our past, adapt to our present, and plan for our future. And it focuses our attention when we learn a complex concept or behavior. When learning to drive, we focus on the car and the traffic. With practice, driving becomes semi-automatic, freeing us to focus our attention elsewhere. Over time, we flit between different *states of consciousness,* including normal waking awareness and various altered states (**FIGURE 7.1**).

Some states occur spontaneously	Daydreaming	Drowsiness	Dreaming
Some are physiologically induced	Hallucinations	Orgasm	Food or oxygen starvation
Some are psychologically induced	Sensory deprivation	Hypnosis	Meditation

∧ FIGURE 7.1

Altered states of consciousness In addition to normal, waking awareness, consciousness comes to us in altered states, including daydreaming, drug-induced hallucinating, and meditating.

Studying Consciousness

Today's science explores the biology of consciousness. Scientists now assume, in the words of neuroscientist Marvin Minsky (1986, p. 287), that "the mind is what the brain does."

Evolutionary psychologists presume that consciousness offers a reproductive advantage (Barash, 2006; Murdik et al., 2011). By considering consequences and reading others' intentions, consciousness helps us to cope with novel situations and act in our long-term interests. Even so, that leaves us with what

researchers call the "hard problem": How do brain cells jabbering to one another create our awareness of the taste of a taco, the idea of infinity, the feeling of fright? The question of how consciousness arises from the material brain is one of life's deepest mysteries. Such questions are at the heart of **cognitive neuroscience**—the interdisciplinary study of the brain activity linked with our mental processes.

A stunning demonstration of consciousness appeared in brain scans of a noncommunicative patient—a 23-year-old woman who had been in a car accident and showed no outward signs of conscious awareness (Owen, 2014; Owen et al., 2006). When researchers asked her to *imagine* playing tennis, fMRI scans revealed activity in a brain area that normally controls arm and leg movements (**FIGURE 7.2**). Even in a motionless body, the researchers concluded, the brain—and the mind—may still be active. A follow-up analysis of 42 behaviorally unresponsive patients revealed 13 more who also showed meaningful, though diminished, brain responses to questions (Stender et al., 2014).

Some neuroscientists believe that conscious experience arises from synchronized activity across the brain (Gaillard et al., 2009; Koch & Greenfield, 2007; Schurger et al., 2010). If a stimulus activates enough brain-wide coordinated neural activity—as strong signals in one brain area trigger activity elsewhere—it crosses a threshold for consciousness. A weaker stimulus—perhaps a word flashed too briefly to consciously perceive—may trigger localized visual cortex activity that quickly fades. A stronger stimulus will engage other brain areas, such as those involved with language, attention, and memory. Such reverberating activity (detected by brain scans) is a telltale sign of conscious awareness (Boly et al., 2011). For example, awareness of your body involves communication between several brain areas (Blanke, 2012; Olivé et al., 2015). How the synchronized activity produces awareness—how matter makes mind—remains a mystery.

^ FIGURE 7.2

Evidence of awareness? When asked to imagine playing tennis or navigating her home, a noncommunicative patient's brain (top) exhibited activity similar to a healthy person's brain (bottom). Researchers wonder if such fMRI scans might enable a "conversation" with some unresponsive patients, by instructing them, for example, to answer *yes* to a question by imagining playing tennis (top and bottom left), and *no* by imagining walking around their home (top and bottom right).

Courtesy of Adrian M. Owen, the Brain and Mind Institute, Western University

---

RETRIEVE IT [✱]

• Those working in the interdisciplinary field called _____ _____ study the brain activity associated with the mental processes of perception, thinking, memory, and language.

ANSWER: cognitive neuroscience

Selective Attention

<> 7-2 How does selective attention direct our perceptions?

Through **selective attention,** our awareness focuses, like a flashlight beam, on a minute aspect of all that we experience. We may think we can fully attend to a conversation or a class lecture while checking and returning text messages. Actually, our consciousness focuses on but one thing at a time.

By one estimate, our five senses take in 11,000,000 bits of information per second, of which we consciously process about 40 (Wilson, 2002). Yet our mind's unconscious track intuitively makes great use of the other 10,999,960 bits. Until reading this sentence, for example, you have been unaware of the chair pressing against your bottom or that your nose is in your line of vision. Now, suddenly, your attentional spotlight shifts. You feel the chair, your nose stubbornly intrudes on the words before you. While focusing on these words, you've also been blocking other parts of your environment from awareness, though your peripheral vision would let you see them easily. You can change that. As you stare at the X below, notice what surrounds these sentences (the edges of the page, the desktop, the floor).

X

"Has a generation of texters, surfers, and twitterers evolved the enviable ability to process multiple streams of novel information in parallel? Most cognitive psychologists doubt it."

Steven Pinker, "Not at All," 2011

"I wasn't texting, I was building this ship in a bottle."

 LaunchPad Visit LaunchPad to watch the thought-provoking *Video—Automatic Skills: Disrupting a Pilot's Performance.*

When phone partners use a video phone that enables them to see the road and pause their conversation, accident rates in driving simulations are no greater than when drivers talk to an in-car passenger (Gaspar et al., 2014).

A classic example of selective attention is the *cocktail party effect*—your ability to attend to only one voice among many. But what happens when another voice speaks your name? Your cognitive radar, operating on your mind's other track, instantly brings that unattended voice into consciousness. This effect might have prevented an embarrassing and dangerous situation in 2009, when two Northwest Airlines pilots "lost track of time." Focused on their laptops and in conversation, they ignored alarmed air traffic controllers' attempts to reach them and overflew their Minneapolis destination by 150 miles. If only the controllers had known and spoken the pilots' names.

Selective Attention and Accidents

Talk, text, route plan, or attend to music selections while driving, and your selective attention will shift back and forth between the road and its electronic competition. Indeed, it shifts more often than we realize. One study left people in a room free to surf the Internet and to control and watch a TV. On average, participants guessed their attention switched 15 times during the 28-minute session. But they were not even close. Eye-tracking revealed eight times that many attentional switches—120 in all (Brasel & Gips, 2011). Such "rapid toggling" between activities is today's great enemy of sustained, focused attention.

We pay a toll for switching attentional gears, especially when we shift to complex tasks, like noticing and avoiding cars around us. The toll is a slight and sometimes fatal delay in coping (Rubenstein et al., 2001). About 28 percent of traffic accidents occur when people are chatting or texting on cell phones—something one in four drivers admits to doing (National Safety Council, 2010; Pew, 2011). In brain areas vital to driving, fMRI scans indicate that activity decreases an average 37 percent when a driver is attending to conversation (Just et al., 2008). One study, which tracked long-haul truck drivers for 18 months, showed they were at 23 times greater risk of a collision while texting (Olson et al., 2009). Another study, which focused vehicle video cams on teen drivers, found that 58 percent of crashes followed driver distraction from other passengers or phones (AAA, 2015). Mindful of such findings, most U.S. states now ban drivers from texting while driving.

Even hands-free cell-phone talking is more distracting than chatting with passengers, who can see the driving demands, pause the conversation, and alert the driver to risks.

- University of Sydney researchers analyzed phone records for the moments before a car crash. Cell-phone users (even those with hands-free sets) were, like the average drunk driver, four times more at risk (McEvoy et al., 2005, 2007). Having a passenger increased risk only 1.6 times.

- Teen drivers' crashes and near-crashes have increased sevenfold when dialing or reaching for a phone, and fourfold when sending or receiving a text message (Klauer et al., 2014).

- This risk difference also appeared when drivers were asked to pull off at a freeway rest stop 8 miles ahead. Of drivers conversing with a passenger, 88 percent did so. Of those talking on a cell phone, 50 percent drove on by (Strayer & Drews, 2007). And the increased risks are equal for handheld and hands-free phones, indicating that the distraction effect is mostly cognitive rather than visual (Strayer & Watson, 2012).

Selective Inattention

At the level of conscious awareness, we are "blind" to all but a tiny sliver of visual stimuli. To demonstrate this **inattentional blindness,** researchers showed people a one-minute video in which images of three black-shirted men tossing

‹ FIGURE 7.3

Selective inattention Viewers who were attending to basketball tosses among the black-shirted players usually failed to notice the umbrella-toting woman sauntering across the screen (Neisser, 1979).

a basketball were superimposed over the images of three white-shirted players (Becklen & Cervone, 1983; Neisser, 1979). The viewers' supposed task was to press a key every time a black-shirted player passed the ball. Most viewers focused their attention so completely on the game that they failed to notice a young woman carrying an umbrella saunter across the screen midway through the video (**FIGURE 7.3**). Seeing a replay of the video, viewers were astonished to see her (Mack & Rock, 2000). This inattentional blindness is a by-product of what we are really good at: focusing attention on some part of our environment.

In a repeat of the experiment, smart-aleck researchers sent a gorilla-suited assistant through a swirl of players (Simons & Chabris, 1999). During its 5- to 9-second cameo appearance, the gorilla paused and thumped its chest. The chest-thumping gorilla did not steal the show: Half the conscientious pass-counting viewers failed to see it. Psychologists like to have fun, and they have continued to do so with the help of invisible gorillas. When 24 radiologists were looking for cancer nodules in lung scans, 20 of them missed the gorilla superimposed in the upper right (**FIGURE 7.4**)—though, to their credit, their focus enabled them to discover the much tinier cancer tissue (Drew et al., 2013). The serious point to this psychological mischief: Attention is powerfully selective. Your conscious mind is in one place at a time.

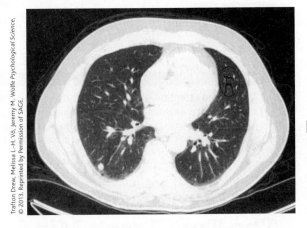

Trafton Drew, Melissa L.-H. Võ, Jeremy M. Wolfe *Psychological Science*, © 2013. Reprinted by Permission of SAGE.

‹ FIGURE 7.4

The invisible gorilla strikes again When repeatedly exposed to the gorilla in the upper right while searching for much tinier cancer nodules, radiologists usually failed to see it (Drew et al., 2013).

Given that most people miss someone in a gorilla suit while their attention is riveted elsewhere, imagine the fun that magicians can have by manipulating our selective attention. Misdirect people's attention and they will miss the hand slipping into the pocket. "Every time you perform a magic trick, you're engaging in experimental psychology," says magician Teller (2009), a master of mind-messing methods. One Swedish psychologist was surprised on a Stockholm street by a woman exposing herself; only later did he realize that he had been pick-pocketed, outwitted by thieves who understood the power of selective inattention (Gallace, 2012).

Magicians also exploit our **change blindness.** Participants in laboratory experiments on change blindness have failed to notice that, after a brief visual interruption, a big Coke bottle had disappeared, a railing had risen, or clothing color

inattentional blindness failing to see visible objects when our attention is directed elsewhere.

change blindness failing to notice changes in the environment.

> FIGURE 7.5

Change blindness
While a man (in red)
provides directions to a
construction worker, two
experimenters rudely pass
between them carrying
a door. During this
interruption, the original
worker switches places
with another person
wearing different-colored clothing. Most
people, focused on their direction giving,
do not notice the switch (Simons &
Levin, 1998).

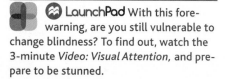

LaunchPad With this fore-
warning, are you still vulnerable to
change blindness? To find out, watch the
3-minute *Video: Visual Attention,* and prepare to be stunned.

^ FIGURE 7.6

The pop-out phenomenon

had changed (Chabris & Simons, 2010; Resnick et al., 1997). Two-thirds of those who were focused on giving directions to a construction worker failed to notice when he was replaced by another worker during a staged interruption (**FIGURE 7.5**). Out of sight, out of mind.

Some stimuli, however, are so powerful, so strikingly distinct, that we experience *popout,* as with the only smiling face in **FIGURE 7.6**. We don't choose to attend to these stimuli; they draw our eye and demand our attention.

The dual-track mind is active even during sleep, as we see next.

RETRIEVE IT [✖]

• Explain three attentional principles that magicians may use to fool us.

ANSWER: Our *selective attention* allows us to focus on only a limited portion of our surroundings. *Inattentional blindness* explains why we don't perceive some things when we are distracted. And *change blindness* happens when we fail to notice a relatively unimportant change in our environment. All these principles help magicians fool us, as they direct our attention elsewhere to perform their tricks.

Dual Processing: The Two-Track Mind

7-3 What is the *dual processing* being revealed by today's cognitive neuroscience?

Discovering which brain region becomes active with a particular conscious experience strikes many people as interesting, but not mind blowing. (If everything psychological is simultaneously biological, then our ideas, emotions, and spirituality must all, somehow, be embodied.) What *is* mind blowing to many of us is the growing evidence that we have, so to speak, two minds, each supported by its own neural equipment.

At any moment, we are aware of little more than what's on the screen of our consciousness. But beneath the surface, unconscious information processing occurs simultaneously on many parallel tracks. When we look at a bird flying, we are consciously aware of the result of our cognitive processing ("It's a hummingbird!") but not of our subprocessing of the bird's color, form, movement, and distance. One of the grand ideas of recent cognitive neuroscience is that much

of our brain work occurs off stage, out of sight. Perception, memory, thinking, language, and attitudes all operate on two levels—a conscious, deliberate "high road," and an unconscious, automatic "low road." The high road is reflective, the low road intuitive (Evans & Stanovich, 2013; Kahneman, 2011). Today's researchers call this **dual processing.** We know more than we know we know.

If you are a driver, consider how you move into a right lane. Drivers know this unconsciously but cannot accurately explain it (Eagleman, 2011). Most say they would bank to the right, then straighten out—a procedure that would actually steer them off the road. In reality, an experienced driver, after moving right, automatically reverses the steering wheel just as far to the left of center, and only then returns to the center position. The lesson: The human brain is a device for converting conscious into unconscious knowledge.

Or consider this story, which illustrates how science can be stranger than science fiction. During my sojourns at Scotland's University of St Andrews, I [DM] came to know cognitive neuroscientists David Milner and Melvyn Goodale (2008). A local woman, whom they called D. F., suffered brain damage when overcome by carbon monoxide, leaving her unable to recognize and discriminate objects visually. Consciously, D. F. could see nothing. Yet she exhibited **blindsight**—she acted *as though* she could see. Asked to slip a postcard into a vertical or horizontal mail slot, she could do so without error. Asked the width of a block in front of her, she was at a loss, but she could grasp it with just the right finger-thumb distance.

How could this be? Don't we have one visual system? Goodale and Milner knew from animal research that the eye sends information simultaneously to different brain areas, which support different tasks (Weiskrantz, 2009, 2010). Sure enough, a scan of D. F.'s brain activity revealed normal activity in the area concerned with reaching for, grasping, and navigating objects, but damage in the area concerned with consciously recognizing objects. (See another example in **FIGURE 7.7.**)

How strangely intricate is this thing we call vision, conclude Goodale and Milner in their aptly titled book, *Sight Unseen* (2004). We may think of our vision as a single system that controls our visually guided actions. Actually, it is a dual-processing system. A *visual perception track* enables us "to think about the world"—to recognize things and to plan future actions. A *visual action track* guides our moment-to-moment movements.

The dual-track mind also appeared in a patient who lost all of his left visual cortex, leaving him blind to objects and faces presented on the right side of his field of vision. He nevertheless could sense the emotion expressed in faces, which he did not consciously perceive (de Gelder, 2010). The same is true of normally sighted people whose visual cortex has been disabled with magnetic stimulation. Such findings suggest that brain areas below the cortex are processing emotion-related information.

People often have trouble accepting that much of our everyday thinking, feeling, and acting operates outside our conscious awareness (Bargh &

dual processing the principle that information is often simultaneously processed on separate conscious and unconscious tracks.

blindsight a condition in which a person can respond to a visual stimulus without consciously experiencing it.

❮ FIGURE 7.7

When the blind can "see" In this compelling demonstration of blindsight and the two-track mind, researcher Lawrence Weiskrantz trailed a blindsight patient down a cluttered hallway. Although told the hallway was empty, the patient meandered around all the obstacles without any awareness of them.

parallel processing the processing of many aspects of a problem simultaneously; the brain's natural mode of information processing for many functions.

LaunchPad To think further about conscious awareness and decision making, visit LaunchPad's *PsychSim 6: Who's in Charge?*

Chartrand, 1999). Some "80 to 90 percent of what we do is unconscious," says Nobel Laureate and memory expert Eric Kandel (2008). We are understandably inclined to believe that our intentions and deliberate choices rule our lives. But consciousness, though enabling us to exert voluntary control and to communicate our mental states to others, is but the tip of the information-processing iceberg. Being intensely focused on an activity (such as reading this module, we'd love to think) increases your total brain activity no more than 5 percent above its baseline rate. And even when you rest, activity whirls inside your head (Raichle, 2010).

Parallel processing enables your mind to take care of routine business. Unconscious parallel processing is faster than conscious sequential processing, but both are essential. Sequential processing is best for solving new problems, which requires your focused attention. Try this: If you are right-handed, move your right foot in a smooth counterclockwise circle and write the number 3 repeatedly with your right hand—at the same time. Try something equally difficult: Tap a steady beat three times with your left hand while tapping four times with your right hand. Both tasks require conscious attention, which can be in only one place at a time. If time is nature's way of keeping everything from happening at once, then consciousness is nature's way of keeping us from thinking and doing everything at once.

RETRIEVE IT [✖]

• What are the mind's two tracks, and what is *dual processing*?

ANSWER: Our mind simultaneously processes information on a conscious track *and* an unconscious track (dual processing) as we organize and interpret information.

MODULE
7 REVIEW **Consciousness: Some Basic Concepts**

Learning Objectives

Test Yourself by taking a moment to answer each of these Learning Objective Questions (repeated here from within the module). Then turn to Appendix D, Complete Module Reviews, to check your answers. Research suggests that trying to answer these questions on your own will improve your long-term memory of the concepts (McDaniel et al., 2009).

7-1 What is the place of consciousness in psychology's history?

7-2 How does selective attention direct our perceptions?

7-3 What is the *dual processing* being revealed by today's cognitive neuroscience?

Terms and Concepts to Remember

Test yourself on these terms by trying to write down the definition in your own words before flipping back to the referenced page to check your answers.

consciousness, p. 80

cognitive neuroscience, p. 81

selective attention, p. 81

inattentional blindness, p. 82

change blindness, p. 83

dual processing, p. 85

blindsight, p. 85

parallel processing, p. 86

Experience the Testing Effect

Test yourself repeatedly throughout your studies. This will not only help you figure out what you know and don't know; the testing itself will help you learn and remember the information more effectively thanks to the *testing effect*.

1. Failure to see visible objects because our attention is occupied elsewhere is called _____.

2. We register and react to stimuli outside of our awareness by means of _____ processing. When we devote deliberate attention to stimuli, we use _____ processing.

3. _____ blindness and change blindness are forms of selective attention.

Find answers to these questions in Appendix E, in the back of the book.

Use **LearningCurve** to create your personalized study plan, which will direct you to the resources that will help you most in **LaunchPad**.

8 Sleep and Dreams

8-1 What is sleep?

Sleep—the irresistible tempter to whom we inevitably succumb. Sleep—the equalizer of presidents and peasants. Sleep—sweet, renewing, mysterious sleep. While sleeping, you may feel "dead to the world," but you are not. Even when you are deeply asleep, your perceptual window is open a crack. You move around on your bed, but you manage not to fall out. The roar of my [ND] neighborhood garbage truck leaves my sleep undisturbed, but my baby's cry interrupts it. The sound of your name can also cause your unconscious body to perk up. EEG recordings confirm that the brain's auditory cortex responds to sound stimuli even during sleep (Kutas, 1990). And when you sleep, as when awake, you process most information outside your conscious awareness.

Now, by recording the brain waves and muscle movements of sleeping participants, and by observing and occasionally waking them, researchers are solving some of sleep's deepest mysteries. Perhaps you can anticipate some of their discoveries. Are the following statements true or false?

1. When people dream of performing some activity, their limbs often move in concert with the dream.

2. Older adults sleep more than young adults.

3. Sleepwalkers are acting out their dreams.

4. Sleep experts recommend treating insomnia with an occasional sleeping pill.

5. Some people dream every night; others seldom dream.

All these statements (adapted from Palladino & Carducci, 1983) are *false*. To see why, read on.

Biological Rhythms and Sleep

Like the ocean, life has its rhythmic tides. Over varying time periods, our bodies fluctuate, and with them, our minds. Let's look more closely at two of those biological rhythms—our 24-hour biological clock and our 90-minute sleep cycle.

Circadian Rhythm

8-2 How do our biological rhythms influence our daily functioning?

Eric Isselée/Shutterstock

The rhythm of the day parallels the rhythm of life—from our waking at a new day's birth to our nightly return to what Shakespeare called "death's counterfeit." Our bodies roughly synchronize with the 24-hour cycle of day and night thanks to an internal biological clock called the **circadian rhythm** (from the Latin *circa*, "about," and *diem*, "day"). As morning approaches, body temperature rises; it then peaks during the day, dips for a time in early afternoon (when many in Mediterranean and Central American regions take siestas), and begins to drop again in the evening. Thinking is sharpest and memory most accurate when we are at our daily peak in circadian arousal. Try pulling an all-nighter or working an occasional night shift. You'll feel groggiest in the middle of the night but may gain new energy when your normal wake-up time arrives.

Age and experience can alter our circadian rhythm. Most 20-year-olds are evening-energized "owls," with performance improving across the day (May & Hasher, 1998). Most older adults are morning-loving "larks," with performance

---

sleep periodic, natural loss of consciousness—as distinct from unconsciousness resulting from a coma, general anesthesia, or hibernation. (Adapted from Dement, 1999.)

circadian [ser-KAY-dee-an] rhythm the biological clock; regular bodily rhythms (for example, of temperature and wakefulness) that occur on a 24-hour cycle.

"I love to sleep. Do you? Isn't it great? It really is the best of both worlds. You get to be alive and unconscious."

Comedian Rita Rudner, 1993

Some students sleep like the fellow who stayed up all night to see where the Sun went. (Then it dawned on him.)

Peter Chadwick/Science Source

REM sleep rapid eye movement sleep; a recurring sleep stage during which vivid dreams commonly occur. Also known as *paradoxical sleep,* because the muscles are relaxed (except for minor twitches) but other body systems are active.

alpha waves the relatively slow brain waves of a relaxed, awake state.

hallucinations false sensory experiences, such as seeing something in the absence of an external visual stimulus.

delta waves the large, slow brain waves associated with deep sleep.

declining as the day wears on. By mid-evening, when the night has hardly begun for many young adults, retirement homes are typically quiet. After about age 20 (slightly earlier for women), we begin to shift from being owls to being larks (Roenneberg et al., 2004). Women become more morning oriented as they have children and also as they transition to menopause (Leonhard & Randler, 2009; Randler & Bausback, 2010). Night owls tend to be smart and creative (Giampietro & Cavallera, 2007). Morning types tend to do better in school, arrive at their appointments on time, take more initiative, and to be less vulnerable to depression (Preckel et al., 2013; Randler, 2008, 2009; Werner et al., 2015).

Sleep Stages

8-3 What is the biological rhythm of our sleeping and dreaming stages?

Sooner or later, sleep overtakes us and consciousness fades as different parts of our brain's cortex stop communicating (Massimini et al., 2005). Yet the sleeping brain remains active and has its own biological rhythm.

About every 90 minutes, you cycle through four distinct sleep stages. This fact came to light after 8-year-old Armond Aserinsky went to bed one night in 1952. His father, Eugene, a University of Chicago graduate student, needed to test an electroencephalograph he had repaired that day (Aserinsky, 1988; Seligman & Yellen, 1987). Placing electrodes near Armond's eyes to record the rolling eye movements then believed to occur during sleep, Aserinsky watched the machine go wild, tracing deep zigzags on the graph paper. Could the machine still be broken? As the night proceeded and the activity recurred, Aserinsky realized that the periods of fast, jerky eye movements were accompanied by energetic brain activity. Awakened during one such episode, Armond reported having a dream. Aserinsky had discovered what we now know as **REM sleep** (*r*apid *e*ye *m*ovement sleep).

Similar procedures used with thousands of volunteers showed the cycles were a normal part of sleep (Kleitman, 1960). To appreciate these studies, imagine yourself as a participant. As the hour grows late, you feel sleepy and yawn in response to reduced brain metabolism. (Yawning, which is also socially contagious, stretches your neck muscles and increases your heart rate, which increases your alertness [Moorcroft, 2003].) When you are ready for bed, a researcher comes in and tapes electrodes to your scalp (to detect your brain waves), on your chin (to detect muscle tension), and just outside the corners of your eyes (to detect eye movements) (**FIGURE 8.1**). Other devices will record your heart rate, respiration rate, and genital arousal.

> **FIGURE 8.1**

Measuring sleep activity Sleep researchers measure brain-wave activity, eye movements, and muscle tension with electrodes that pick up weak electrical signals from the brain, eyes, and facial muscles. (From Dement, 1978.)

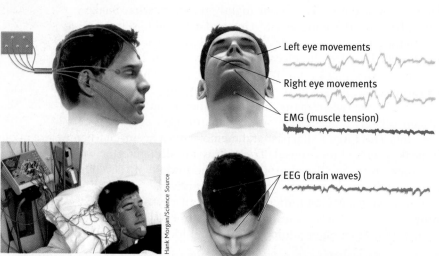

Left eye movements

Right eye movements

EMG (muscle tension)

EEG (brain waves)

Hank Morgan/Science Source

When you are in bed with your eyes closed, the researcher in the next room sees on the EEG the relatively slow **alpha waves** of your awake but relaxed state (**FIGURE 8.2**). As you adapt to all this equipment, you grow tired and, in an unremembered moment, slip into sleep (**FIGURE 8.3**). The transition is marked by the slowed breathing and the irregular brain waves of non-REM stage 1 sleep. Using the American Academy of Sleep Medicine classification of sleep stages, this is called *NREM-1* sleep (Silber et al., 2008).

In one of his 15,000 research participants, William Dement (1999) observed the moment the brain's perceptual window to the outside world slammed shut. Dement asked this sleep-deprived young man with eyelids taped open to press a button every time a strobe light flashed in his eyes (about every 6 seconds). After a few minutes the young man missed one. Asked why, he said, "Because there was no flash." But there was a flash. He missed it because (as his brain activity revealed) he had fallen asleep for 2 seconds, missing not only the flash 6 inches from his nose but also the awareness of the abrupt moment of entry into sleep.

During this brief NREM-1 sleep you may experience fantastic images resembling **hallucinations**—sensory experiences that occur without a sensory stimulus. You may have a sensation of falling (at which moment your body may suddenly jerk) or of floating weightlessly. These *hypnagogic* sensations may later be incorporated into your memories. People who claim to have been abducted by aliens—often shortly after getting into bed—commonly recall being floated off (or pinned down on) their beds (Clancy, 2005; McNally, 2012).

You then relax more deeply and begin about 20 minutes of *NREM-2* sleep, with its periodic *sleep spindles*—bursts of rapid, rhythmic brain-wave activity. Although you could still be awakened without too much difficulty, you are now clearly asleep.

Then you transition to the deep sleep of *NREM-3*. During this slow-wave sleep, which lasts for about 30 minutes, your brain emits large, slow **delta waves** and you are hard to awaken. (It is at the end of the deep, slow-wave NREM-3 sleep that children may wet the bed.)

Dolphins, porpoises, and whales sleep with one side of their brain at a time (Miller et al., 2008).

"My problem has always been an overabundance of alpha waves."

To catch your own hypnagogic experiences, you might use your alarm's snooze function.

LaunchPad To better understand EEG readings and their relationship to consciousness, sleep, and dreams, experience the tutorial and simulation at LaunchPad's *PsychSim 6: EEG and Sleep Stages.*

> **< FIGURE 8.2**

Brain waves and sleep stages The beta waves of an alert, waking state and the regular alpha waves of an awake, relaxed state differ from the slower, larger delta waves of deep NREM-3 sleep. Although the rapid REM sleep waves resemble the near-waking NREM-1 sleep waves, the body is more aroused during REM sleep than during NREM sleep.

Waking Beta

Waking Alpha

NREM-1

100 nV

NREM-2

NREM-3

REM

6 sec

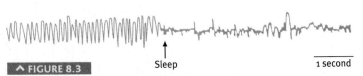

> **^ FIGURE 8.3**

Sleep

1 second

The moment of sleep We seem unaware of the moment we fall into sleep, but someone watching our brain waves could tell (Dement, 1999).

REM Sleep

About an hour after you first fall asleep, a strange thing happens. Rather than continuing in deep slumber, you ascend from your initial sleep dive. Returning through NREM-2 (where you spend about half your night), you enter the most intriguing sleep phase—REM sleep (**FIGURE 8.4**). For about 10 minutes, your brain waves become rapid and saw-toothed, more like those of the nearly awake NREM-1 sleep. But unlike NREM-1, during REM sleep your heart rate rises, your breathing becomes rapid and irregular, and every half-minute or so your eyes dart around in momentary bursts of activity behind closed lids. These eye movements announce the beginning of a dream—often emotional, usually story-like, and richly hallucinatory. Because anyone watching a sleeper's eyes can notice these REM bursts, it is amazing that science was ignorant of REM sleep until 1952.

Except during very scary dreams, your genitals become aroused during REM sleep. You have an erection or increased vaginal lubrication and clitoral engorgement, regardless of whether the dream's content is sexual (Karacan et al., 1966). Men's common "morning erection" stems from the night's last REM period, often just before waking. In young men, sleep-related erections outlast REM periods, lasting 30 to 45 minutes on average (Karacan et al., 1983; Schiavi & Schreiner-Engel, 1988). A typical 25-year-old man therefore has an erection during nearly half his night's sleep, a 65-year-old man for one-quarter. Many men troubled by *erectile disorder* (impotence) have sleep-related erections, suggesting the problem is not between their legs.

Your brain's motor cortex is active during REM sleep, but your brainstem blocks its messages. This leaves your muscles relaxed, so much so that, except for an occasional finger, toe, or facial twitch, you are essentially paralyzed. Moreover, you cannot easily be awakened. REM sleep is thus sometimes called *paradoxical sleep:* The body is internally aroused, with waking-like brain activity, yet asleep and externally calm.

People rarely snore during dreams. When REM starts, snoring stops.

Horses, which spend 92 percent of each day standing and can sleep standing, must lie down for REM sleep (Morrison, 2003).

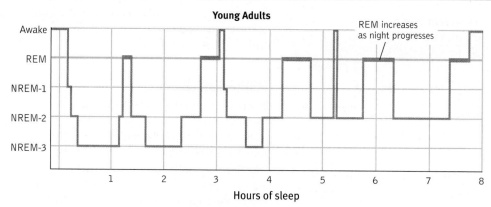

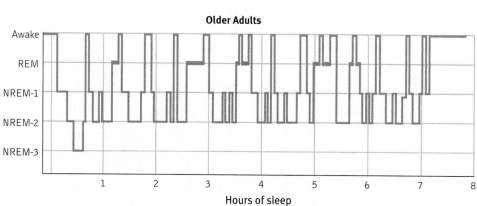

> **> FIGURE 8.4**

The stages in a typical night's sleep People pass through a multistage sleep cycle several times each night, with the periods of deep sleep diminishing and REM sleep periods increasing in duration. As people age, sleep becomes more fragile, with awakenings common among older adults (Kamel & Gammack, 2006; Neubauer, 1999).

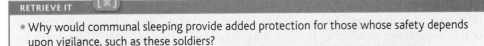

RETRIEVE IT [✖]

• Why would communal sleeping provide added protection for those whose safety depends upon vigilance, such as these soldiers?

Uriel Sinai/Getty Images

ANSWER: With each soldier cycling through the sleep stages independently, it is very likely that at any given time at least one of them will be awake or easily wakened in the event of a threat.

The sleep cycle repeats itself about every 90 minutes for younger adults (somewhat more frequently for older adults). As the night wears on, deep NREM-3 sleep grows shorter and disappears. The REM and NREM-2 sleep periods get longer (see Figure 8.4). By morning, we have spent 20 to 25 percent of an average night's sleep—some 100 minutes—in REM sleep. Thirty-seven percent of people report rarely or never having dreams "that you can remember the next morning" (Moore, 2004). Yet even they will, more than 80 percent of the time, recall a dream after being awakened during REM sleep. We spend about 600 hours a year experiencing some 1500 dreams, or more than 100,000 dreams over a typical lifetime—dreams swallowed by the night but not acted out, thanks to REM's protective paralysis.

RETRIEVE IT [✖]

• What are the four sleep stages, and in what order do we normally travel through those stages?

ANSWER: REM, NREM-1, NREM-2, NREM-3; normally we move through NREM-1, then NREM-2, then NREM-3, then back up through NREM-2 before we experience REM sleep.

• Can you match the cognitive experience with the sleep stage?

1. NREM-1   a. story-like dreams

2. NREM-3   b. fleeting images

3. REM   c. minimal awareness

ANSWERS: 1. b, 2. c, 3. a

What Affects Our Sleep Patterns?

 8-4 How do biology and environment interact in our sleep patterns?

The idea that "everyone needs 8 hours of sleep" is untrue. To know how much sleep people need, the first clue is their age. Newborns often sleep two-thirds of their day, most adults no more than one-third (with some thriving on fewer than 6 hours nightly, others racking up 9 or more). But there is more to our sleep differences

suprachiasmatic nucleus (SCN) a pair of cell clusters in the hypothalamus that controls circadian rhythm. In response to light, the SCN causes the pineal gland to adjust melatonin production, thus modifying our feelings of sleepiness.

than age. Some are awake between nightly sleep periods—sometimes called "first sleep" and "second sleep" (Randall, 2012). And some find that a 15-minute midday nap is as effective as another hour of nighttime sleep (Horne, 2011). Sleep patterns are genetically influenced, and researchers are discovering the genes that regulate sleep in humans and animals (Donlea et al., 2009; He et al., 2009; Hor & Tafti, 2009).

Canadian, American, British, German, and Japanese adults average 6½ to 7 hours of sleep on workdays and 7 to 8 hours on other days (National Sleep Foundation, 2013). Thanks to modern lighting, shift work, and social media diversions, many who would have gone to bed at 9:00 P.M. a century ago are now up until 11:00 P.M. or later. With sleep, as with waking behavior, biology and environment interact.

Being bathed in (or deprived of) light disrupts our 24-hour biological clock (Czeisler et al., 1999; Dement, 1999). Bright light affects our sleepiness by activating light-sensitive retinal proteins. This signals the brain's **suprachiasmatic nucleus (SCN)** to decrease production of *melatonin*, a sleep-inducing hormone (Gandhi et al., 2015; and **FIGURE 8.5**). Our ancestors' body clocks were attuned to the rising and setting Sun of the 24-hour day. Many of today's young adults adopt something closer to a 25-hour day, by staying up too late to get 8 hours of sleep. Most animals, too, when placed under unnatural constant illumination will exceed a 24-hour day.

Sleep often eludes those who stay up late and sleep in on weekends, and then go to bed earlier on Sunday to prepare for the week ahead (Oren & Terman, 1998). For North Americans who fly to Europe and need to be up when their circadian rhythm cries *"SLEEP,"* bright light (spending the next day outdoors) helps reset the biological clock (Czeisler et al., 1986, 1989; Eastman et al., 1995).

A circadian disadvantage: One study of a decade's 24,121 Major League Baseball games found that teams who had crossed three time zones before playing a multiday series had nearly a 60 percent chance of losing their first game (Winter et al., 2009).

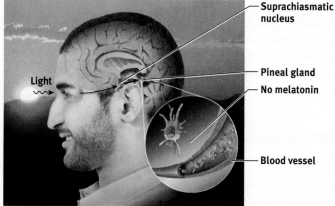

Melatonin production suppressed

— Suprachiasmatic nucleus

— Pineal gland
— No melatonin

Light

— Blood vessel

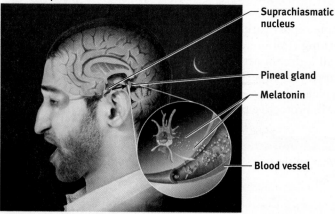

Melatonin produced

— Suprachiasmatic nucleus

— Pineal gland
— Melatonin

— Blood vessel

▲ FIGURE 8.5

The biological clock Light striking the retina signals the suprachiasmatic nucleus (SCN) to suppress the pineal gland's production of the sleep hormone melatonin. At night, the SCN quiets down, allowing the pineal gland to release melatonin into the bloodstream.

RETRIEVE IT   [✳]

• The _____ nucleus helps monitor the brain's release of melatonin, which affects our _____ rhythm.

ANSWERS: suprachiasmatic; circadian

Why Do We Sleep?

◀◉▶ 8-5 What are sleep's functions?

So, our sleep patterns differ from person to person. But why do we have this need for sleep? Psychologists offer five possible reasons.

1. ***Sleep protects.*** When darkness shut down the day's hunting, food gathering, and travel, our distant ancestors were better off asleep in a cave, out of harm's way. Those who didn't try to navigate around dark cliffs were more

likely to leave descendants. This fits a broader principle: A species' sleep pattern tends to suit its ecological niche (Siegel, 2009). Animals with the greatest need to graze and the least ability to hide tend to sleep less. Animals also sleep less, with no ill effects, during times of mating and migration (Siegel, 2012). (For a sampling of animal sleep times, see **FIGURE 8.6**.)

2. ***Sleep helps us recuperate.*** Sleep helps restore the immune system and repair brain tissue. Bats and other animals with high waking metabolism burn a lot of calories, producing a lot of *free radicals*, molecules that are toxic to neurons. Sleeping a lot gives resting neurons time to repair themselves, while pruning or weakening unused connections (Gilestro et al., 2009; Tononi & Cirelli, 2013). Sleep also enables house cleaning. Studies of mice show that sleep sweeps the brain of toxic metabolic waste products (Xie et al., 2013). Think of it this way: When consciousness leaves your house, workers come in for a makeover, saying "Good night. Sleep tidy."

3. ***Sleep helps restore and rebuild our fading memories of the day's experiences.*** Sleep consolidates our memories. It replays or "reactivates" recent learning and strengthens its neural connections (Yang et al., 2014). Sleep also shifts experiences stored in the hippocampus to permanent storage elsewhere in the cortex (Diekelmann & Born, 2010; Racsmány et al., 2010). Adults and children trained to perform tasks therefore recall them better after a night's sleep, or even after a short nap, than after several hours awake (Friedrich et al., 2015; Kurdziel et al., 2013; Stickgold & Ellenbogen, 2008). After sleeping well, older people remember more of recently learned material (Drummond, 2010). Sleep, it seems, strengthens memories in a way that being awake does not.

4. ***Sleep feeds creative thinking.*** Dreams can inspire noteworthy artistic and scientific achievements, such as the dreams that clued chemist August Kekulé to the structure of benzene (Ross, 2006) and inspired medical researcher Carl Alving (2011) to invent the vaccine patch. More commonplace is the boost that a complete night's sleep gives to our thinking and learning. After working on a task, then sleeping on it, people solve difficult problems more insightfully than do those who stay awake (Barrett, 2011; Sio et al., 2013). They also are better at spotting connections among novel pieces of information (Ellenbogen et al., 2007). To think smart and see connections, it often pays to ponder a problem just before bed and then sleep on it.

5. ***Sleep supports growth.*** During deep sleep, the pituitary gland releases a growth hormone that is necessary for muscle development. A regular full night's sleep can also "*dramatically* improve your athletic ability," report James Maas and Rebecca Robbins (2010). Well-rested athletes have faster reaction times, more energy, and greater endurance. Teams that build 8 to 10 hours of daily sleep into their training show improved performance.

Given all the benefits of sleep, it's no wonder that sleep loss hits us so hard.

> "Sleep faster, we need the pillows."
> *Yiddish proverb*

> "Corduroy pillows make headlines."
> *Anonymous*

⌄ FIGURE 8.6

Animal sleep time Would you rather be a brown bat and sleep 20 hours a day or a giraffe and sleep 2 hours a day? (Data from NIH, 2010.)

20 hours

16 hours

12 hours

10 hours

8 hours

4 hours

2 hours

Kruglov_Orda/Shutterstock
Courtesy of Andrew D. Myers
Utekhina Anna/Shutterstock
Steffen Foerster Photography/Shutterstock
Rubberball/Vetta/Getty Images
Eric Isselée/Shutterstock
pandapaw/Shutterstock

RETRIEVE IT [✱]

• What are five proposed reasons for our need for sleep?

ANSWER: (1) Sleep has survival value. (2) Sleep helps restore and repair brain tissue. (3) During sleep we consolidate memories. (4) Sleep fuels creativity. (5) Sleep plays a role in the growth process.

Sleep Deprivation and Sleep Disorders

8-6 How does sleep loss affect us, and what are the major sleep disorders?

When our body yearns for sleep but does not get it, we begin to feel terrible. Trying to stay awake, we will eventually lose. In the tiredness battle, sleep always wins.

Effects of Sleep Loss

Today, more than ever, our sleep patterns leave us not only sleepy but drained of energy and feelings of well-being. After a succession of 5-hour nights, we accumulate a sleep debt that need not be entirely repaid but cannot be satisfied by one long sleep. "The brain keeps an accurate count of sleep debt for at least two weeks," reported sleep researcher William Dement (1999, p. 64).

Obviously, then, we need sleep. Sleep commands roughly one-third of our lives—some 25 years, on average. Allowed to sleep unhindered, most adults will sleep at least 9 hours a night (Coren, 1996). With that much sleep, we awaken refreshed, sustain better moods, and perform more efficiently and accurately. The U.S. Navy and the National Institutes of Health have demonstrated the benefits of unrestricted sleep in experiments in which volunteers spent 14 hours daily in bed for at least a week. For the first few days, the volunteers averaged 12 hours of sleep or more per day, apparently paying off a sleep debt that averaged 25 to 30 hours. That accomplished, they then settled back to 7.5 to 9 hours nightly and felt energized and happier (Dement, 1999). In one Gallup survey (Mason, 2005), 63 percent of adults who reported getting the sleep they needed also reported being "very satisfied" with their personal life (as did only 36 percent of those needing more sleep).

College and university students are especially sleep deprived; 69 percent in one national survey reported "feeling tired" or "having little energy" on at least several days during the last two weeks (AP, 2009). This trend toward tiredness has increased in recent years, causing some researchers to label current times as the "Great Sleep Recession" (Keyes et al., 2015). For students, less sleep also predicts more conflicts in friendships and romantic relationships (Gordon & Chen, 2014; Tavernier & Willoughby, 2014). Tired triggers crabbiness. In another survey, 28 percent of high school students acknowledged falling asleep in class at least once a week (National Sleep Foundation, 2006). The going needn't get boring before students start snoring.

Sleep loss is also a predictor of depression. Researchers who studied 15,500 12- to 18-year-olds found that those who slept 5 or fewer hours a night had a 71 percent higher risk of depression than their peers who slept 8 hours or more (Gangwisch et al., 2010). This link does not appear to reflect an effect of depression on sleep. When children and youth are followed through time, sleep loss predicts depression rather than vice versa (Gregory et al., 2009). Moreover, REM sleep's processing of emotional experiences helps protect against depression (Walker & van der Helm, 2009). After a good night's sleep, we often do feel better the next day. And that may help to explain why parentally enforced bedtimes predict less depression, and why pushing back school start time leads to improved

"Maybe 'Bring Your Pillow To Work Day' wasn't such a good idea."

© 2011 Marty Bucella

In 1989, Michael Doucette was named America's Safest Driving Teen. In 1990, while driving home from college, he fell asleep at the wheel and collided with an oncoming car, killing both himself and the other driver. Michael's driving instructor later acknowledged never having mentioned sleep deprivation and drowsy driving (Dement, 1999).

LaunchPad To see whether you are one of the many sleep-deprived students, try LaunchPad's self-assessment activity—*Assess Your Strengths: Sleep Deprivation.*

adolescent sleep, alertness, and mood (Gregory et al., 2009; Owens et al., 2010; Perkinson-Gloor et al., 2013). Thus, the American Academy of Pediatrics (2014) advocates delaying adolescents' school start times to "allow students the opportunity to achieve optimal levels of sleep (8 ½–9 ½ hours)."

Sleep-deprived students often function below their peak. And they know it: Four in five teens and three in five 18- to 29-year-olds wish they could get more sleep on weekdays (Mason, 2003, 2005). "Sleep deprivation has consequences—difficulty studying, diminished productivity, tendency to make mistakes, irritability, fatigue," noted Dement (1999, p. 231). A large sleep debt "makes you stupid." Yet that teen who staggers glumly out of bed in response to an unwelcome alarm, yawns through morning classes, and feels half-depressed much of the day may be energized at 11:00 P.M. and mindless of the next day's looming sleepiness (Carskadon, 2002).

Lack of sleep can also make you gain weight. Sleep deprivation

- increases *ghrelin*, a hunger-arousing hormone, and decreases its hunger-suppressing partner, *leptin* (Shilsky et al., 2012).

- decreases metabolic rate, a gauge of energy use (Buxton et al., 2012).

- increases *cortisol*, a stress hormone that stimulates the body to make fat.

- enhances limbic brain responses to the mere sight of food and decreases cortical inhibition (Benedict et al., 2012; Greer et al., 2013; St-Onge et al., 2012).

Thus, children and adults who sleep less are fatter than average, and in recent decades people have been sleeping less and weighing more (Shiromani et al., 2012). Moreover, experimental sleep deprivation increases appetite and eating; our tired brains find fatty foods more enticing (Fang et al., 2015; Nixon et al., 2008; Patel et al., 2006; Spiegel et al., 2004; Van Cauter et al., 2007). So, sleep loss helps explain the weight gain common among sleep-deprived students (Hull et al., 2007).

Sleep also affects our physical health. When infections do set in, we typically sleep more, boosting our immune cells. Sleep deprivation can suppress the immune cells that battle viral infections and cancer (Möller-Levet et al., 2013; Motivala & Irwin, 2007). In one experiment, when researchers exposed volunteers to a cold virus, those who had been averaging less than 7 hours sleep a night were three times more likely to develop the cold than were those sleeping 8 or more hours a night (Cohen et al., 2009). Sleep's protective effect may help explain why people who sleep 7 to 8 hours a night tend to outlive those who are chronically sleep deprived, and why older adults who have no difficulty falling or staying asleep tend to live longer than their sleep-deprived agemates (Dew et al., 2003; Parthasarathy et al., 2015).

Sleep deprivation slows reactions and increases errors on visual attention tasks similar to those involved in screening airport baggage, performing surgery, and reading X-rays (Caldwell, 2012; Lim & Dinges, 2010). Slow responses can also spell disaster for those operating equipment, piloting, or driving. Driver fatigue has contributed to an estimated 20 percent of American traffic accidents (Brody, 2002) and to some 30 percent of Australian highway deaths (Maas, 1999). One 2-year study examined the driving accidents of more than 20,000 Virginia 16- to 18-year-olds in two major cities. In one city, the high schools started 75 to 80 minutes later than in the other. The late starters had about 25 percent fewer crashes (Vorona et al., 2011). When sleepy frontal lobes confront an unexpected situation, misfortune often results.

Stanley Coren capitalized on what is, for many North Americans, a semi-annual sleep-manipulation experiment—the "spring forward" to daylight saving time and "fall backward" to standard time. Searching millions of records, Coren found that in both Canada and the United States, accidents increased immediately after the time change that shortens sleep (**FIGURE 8.7** on the next page). Less sleep = more accidents.

In a 2013 Gallup poll, 40 percent of Americans reported getting 6 hours or less sleep a night (Jones, 2013).

"You wake up in the middle of the night and grab your smartphone to check the time—it's 3 A.M.—and see an alert. Before you know it, you fall down a rabbit hole of email and Twitter. Sleep? Forget it."

Nick Bilton, "Disruptions: For a Restful Night, Make Your Smartphone Sleep on the Couch," 2014

"Remember to sleep because you have to sleep to remember."

James B. Maas and Rebecca S. Robbins, Sleep for Success, *2010*

"So shut your eyes
Kiss me goodbye
And sleep
Just sleep."

Sleep *by My Chemical Romance*

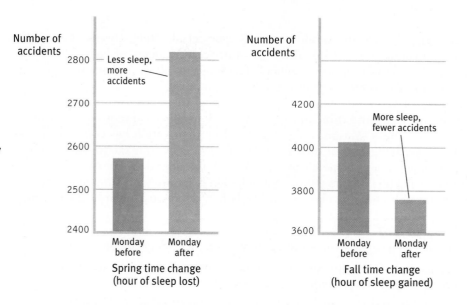

> FIGURE 8.7

Canadian traffic accidents On the Monday after the spring time change, when people lose one hour of sleep, accidents increased, as compared with the Monday before. In the fall, traffic accidents normally increase because of greater snow, ice, and darkness, but they diminished after the time change. (Data from Coren, 1996.)

IMMERSIVE LEARNING Consider how researchers have addressed these issues in LaunchPad's *How Would You Know If Sleep Deprivation Affects Academic Performance?*

FIGURE 8.8 summarizes the effects of sleep deprivation. But there is good news! Psychologists have discovered a treatment that strengthens memory, increases concentration, boosts mood, moderates hunger, reduces obesity, fortifies the immune system, and lessens the risk of fatal accidents. Even better news: The treatment feels good, it can be self-administered, the supplies are limitless, and it's free! If you are a typical university-age student, often going to bed near 2:00 A.M. and dragged out of bed 6 hours later by the dreaded alarm, the treatment is simple: Each night, just add 15 minutes to your sleep. Repeat until you feel more like a rested and energized student than a zombie.

> FIGURE 8.8

How sleep deprivation affects us

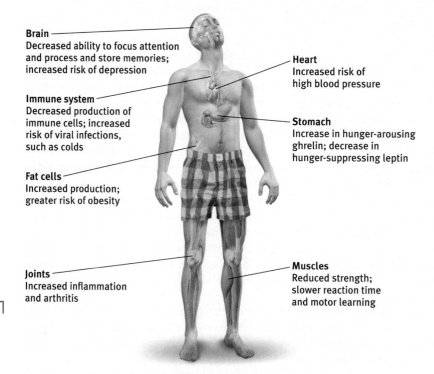

insomnia recurring problems in falling or staying asleep.

narcolepsy a sleep disorder characterized by uncontrollable sleep attacks. The sufferer may lapse directly into REM sleep, often at inopportune times.

sleep apnea a sleep disorder characterized by temporary cessations of breathing during sleep and repeated momentary awakenings.

Major Sleep Disorders

No matter what their normal need for sleep, 1 in 10 adults, and 1 in 4 older adults, complain of **insomnia**—persistent problems in either falling or staying asleep (Irwin et al., 2006). The result is tiredness and increased risk of depression (Baglioni et al., 2011). All of us, when anxious or excited, may have trouble sleeping.

(And smart phones under the pillow and used as alarm clocks increase the likelihood of disrupted sleep.) From middle age on, awakening occasionally during the night becomes the norm, not something to fret over or treat with medication (Vitiello, 2009). Ironically, insomnia is worsened by fretting about it. In laboratory studies, people who think they have insomnia do sleep less than others. But they typically overestimate how long it takes them to fall asleep and underestimate how long they actually have slept (Harvey & Tang, 2012). Even if we have been awake only an hour or two, we may *think* we have had very little sleep because it's the waking part we remember.

The most common quick fixes for true insomnia—sleeping pills and alcohol—can aggravate the problem, reducing REM sleep and leaving the person with next-day blahs. Such aids can also lead to *tolerance*—a state in which increasing doses are needed to produce an effect. An ideal sleep aid would mimic the natural chemicals abundant during sleep, reliably producing sound sleep without side effects. Until scientists can supply this magic pill, sleep experts have offered some tips for getting better quality sleep (**TABLE 8.1**).

Falling asleep is not the problem for people with **narcolepsy** (from the Greek *narke*, "numbness," and *lepsis*, "seizure"), who have sudden attacks of overwhelming sleepiness, usually lasting less than 5 minutes. Narcolepsy attacks can occur at the most inopportune times, often triggered by strong emotions—perhaps just after taking a terrific swing at a softball or when laughing loudly, shouting angrily, or having sex (Dement, 1978, 1999). In severe cases, the person collapses directly into a brief period of REM sleep, with loss of muscular tension. People with narcolepsy—1 in 2000 of us, estimated the Stanford University Center for Narcolepsy (2002)—must therefore live with extra caution. As a traffic menace, "snoozing is second only to boozing," says the American Sleep Disorders Association, and those with narcolepsy are especially at risk (Aldrich, 1989).

Although 1 in 20 of us have **sleep apnea,** it was unknown before modern sleep research. *Apnea* means "with no breath," and people with this condition intermittently stop breathing during sleep. After an airless minute or so, decreased blood oxygen arouses them enough to snort in air for a few seconds, in a process that repeats hundreds of times each night, depriving them of slow-wave sleep. Apnea sufferers don't recall these episodes the next day. So, despite feeling fatigued and depressed—and hearing their mate's complaints about their loud "snoring"—many are unaware of their disorder (Peppard et al., 2006).

Sleep apnea is associated with obesity, and as the number of obese Americans has increased, so has sleep apnea, particularly among overweight men (Keller, 2007). Apnea-related sleep loss also contributes to obesity. In addition to loud snoring, other warning signs are daytime sleepiness, irritability, and (possibly)

"The lion and the lamb shall lie down together, but the lamb will not be very sleepy."

Woody Allen, in the movie Love and Death, *1975*

"Sleep is like love or happiness. If you pursue it too ardently it will elude you."

Wilse Webb, Sleep: The Gentle Tyrant, *1992*

Did Brahms need his own lullabies? Cranky, overweight, and nap-prone, classical composer Johannes Brahms exhibited common symptoms of sleep apnea (Margolis, 2000).

⌄ **TABLE 8.1**

Some Natural Sleep Aids

- Exercise regularly but not in the late evening. (Late afternoon is best.)

- Avoid caffeine after early afternoon, and avoid food and drink near bedtime. The exception would be a glass of milk, which provides raw materials for the manufacture of serotonin, a neurotransmitter that facilitates sleep.

- Relax before bedtime, using dimmer light.

- Sleep on a regular schedule (rise at the same time even after a restless night) and avoid long naps.

- Hide the time so you aren't tempted to check repeatedly.

- Reassure yourself that temporary sleep loss causes no great harm.

- Focus your mind on nonarousing, engaging thoughts, such as song lyrics, TV programs, or vacation travel (Gellis et al., 2013).

- If all else fails, settle for less sleep, either going to bed later or getting up earlier.

Now I lay me down to sleep For many with sleep apnea, a continuous positive airway pressure (CPAP) machine makes for sounder sleeping and better quality of life.

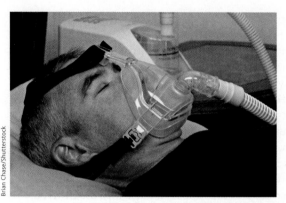

Brian Chase/Shutterstock

high blood pressure, which increases the risk of a stroke or heart attack (Dement, 1999). If one doesn't mind looking a little goofy in the dark, the treatment—a masklike device with an air pump that keeps the sleeper's airway open (imagine a snorkeler at a slumber party)—can effectively relieve apnea symptoms. By so doing, it can also alleviate the depression symptoms that often accompany sleep apnea (Levine, 2012; Wheaton et al., 2012).

Unlike sleep apnea, **night terrors** target mostly children, who may sit up or walk around, talk incoherently, experience doubled heart and breathing rates, and appear terrified while asleep (Hartmann, 1981). They seldom wake up fully during an episode and recall little or nothing the next morning—at most, a fleeting, frightening image. Unlike nightmares—which, like other dreams, typically occur during early morning REM sleep—night terrors usually occur during the first few hours of NREM-3.

Sleepwalking—another NREM-3 sleep disorder—and *sleeptalking* are usually childhood disorders and, like narcolepsy, they run in families. (Sleeptalking—usually garbled or nonsensical—can occur during any sleep stage [Mahowald & Ettinger, 1990].) Occasional childhood sleepwalking occurs for about one-third of those with a sleepwalking fraternal twin and half of those with a sleepwalking identical twin. The same is true for sleeptalking (Hublin et al., 1997, 1998). Sleepwalking is usually harmless. After returning to bed on their own or with the help of a family member, few sleepwalkers recall their trip the next morning. About 20 percent of 3- to 12-year-olds have at least one episode of sleepwalking, usually lasting 2 to 10 minutes; some 5 percent have repeated episodes (Giles et al., 1994). Young children, who have the deepest and lengthiest NREM-3 sleep, are the most likely to experience both night terrors and sleepwalking. As we grow older and deep NREM-3 sleep diminishes, so do night terrors and sleepwalking.

RETRIEVE IT [✱]

• A well-rested person would be more likely to have _____ (trouble concentrating/quick reaction times) and a sleep-deprived person would be more likely to _____ (gain weight/fight off a cold).

ANSWERS: quick reaction times; gain weight

Dreams

Now playing at an inner theater near you: the premiere showing of a sleeping person's vivid dream. This never-before-seen mental movie features captivating characters wrapped in a plot so original and unlikely, yet so intricate and so seemingly real, that the viewer later marvels at its creativity.

Waking from a troubling dream (you were late to something and your legs weren't working), who among us has not wondered about this weird state of consciousness? How can our brain so creatively, colorfully, and completely construct this alternative world? In the shadowland between our dreaming and waking consciousness, we may even wonder for a moment which is real.

Discovering the link between REM sleep and dreaming ushered in a new era in dream research. Instead of relying on someone's hazy recall hours or days after having a dream, researchers could catch dreams as they happened. They could awaken people during or within 3 minutes after a REM sleep period and hear a vivid account.

night terrors a sleep disorder characterized by high arousal and an appearance of being terrified; unlike nightmares, night terrors occur during NREM-3 sleep, within two or three hours of falling asleep, and are seldom remembered.

dream a sequence of images, emotions, and thoughts passing through a sleeping person's mind.

What We Dream

8-7 What do we dream?

Daydreams tend to involve the familiar details of our life—perhaps picturing ourselves explaining to an instructor why a paper will be late, or replaying in our minds personal encounters we relish or regret. REM **dreams** are vivid, emotional, and often bizarre—so vivid we may confuse them with reality. Awakening from a nightmare, a 4-year-old may be sure there is a bear in the house.

We spend 6 years of our life in dreams, many of which are anything but sweet. For both women and men, 8 in 10 dreams are marked by at least one negative event or emotion (Domhoff, 2007). Common themes include repeatedly failing in an attempt to do something; being attacked, pursued, or rejected; or experiencing misfortune (Hall et al., 1982). Dreams with sexual imagery occur less often than you might think. In one study, only 1 in 10 dreams among young men and 1 in 30 among young women had sexual content (Domhoff, 1996).

More commonly, a dream's story line incorporates traces of previous days' nonsexual experiences and preoccupations (De Koninck, 2000):

- After suffering a trauma, people commonly report nightmares, which help extinguish daytime fears (Levin & Nielsen, 2007, 2009). One sample of Americans recording their dreams during September, 2001 reported an increase in threatening dreams following the 9/11 terrorist attacks (Propper et al., 2007).

- Compared with city dwellers, people in hunter-gatherer societies more often dream of animals (Mestel, 1997). Compared with nonmusicians, musicians report twice as many dreams of music (Uga et al., 2006).

- Studies in four countries have found blind people mostly dreaming of using their nonvisual senses (Buquet, 1988; Taha, 1972; Vekassy, 1977). But even natively blind people sometimes "see" in their dreams (Bértolo, 2005). Likewise, people born paralyzed below the waist sometimes dream of walking, standing, running, or cycling (Saurat et al., 2011; Voss et al., 2011).

Our two-track mind continues to monitor our environment while we sleep. Sensory stimuli—a particular odor or a phone's ringing—may be instantly and ingeniously woven into the dream story. In a classic experiment, researchers lightly sprayed cold water on dreamers' faces (Dement & Wolpert, 1958). Compared with sleepers who did not get the cold-water treatment, these people were more likely to dream about a waterfall, a leaky roof, or even about being sprayed by someone.

So, could we learn a foreign language by hearing it played while we sleep? If only. While sleeping, we can learn to associate a sound with a mild electric shock (and to react to the sound accordingly). We can also learn to associate a particular sound with a pleasant or unpleasant odor (Arzi et al., 2012). But we do not remember recorded information played while we are soundly asleep (Eich, 1990; Wyatt & Bootzin, 1994). In fact, anything that happens during the 5 minutes just before we fall asleep is typically lost from memory (Roth et al., 1988). This explains why sleep apnea patients, who repeatedly awaken with a gasp and then immediately fall back to sleep, do not recall the episodes. Ditto someone who awakens momentarily, sends a text message, and the next day can't remember doing so. It also explains why dreams that momentarily awaken us are mostly forgotten by morning. To remember a dream, get up and stay awake for a few minutes.

Why We Dream

8-8 What functions have theorists proposed for dreams?

Dream theorists have proposed several explanations of why we dream, including these five:

To satisfy our own wishes. In 1900, in his landmark book *The Interpretation of Dreams*, Sigmund Freud offered what he thought was "the most valuable

"I do not believe that I am now dreaming, but I cannot prove that I am not."
Philosopher Bertrand Russell (1872–1970)

"For what one has dwelt on by day, these things are seen in visions of the night."
Menander of Athens (342–292 B.C.E.), Fragments

A popular sleep myth: If you dream you are falling and hit the ground (or if you dream of dying), you die. Unfortunately, those who could confirm these ideas are not around to do so. Many people, however, have had such dreams and are alive to report them.

"Follow your dreams, except for that one where you're naked at work."
Attributed to comedian Henny Youngman

manifest content according to Freud, the remembered story line of a dream (as distinct from its latent, or hidden, content).

latent content according to Freud, the underlying meaning of a dream (as distinct from its manifest content).

"When people interpret [a dream] as if it were meaningful and then sell those interpretations, it's quackery."

Sleep researcher J. Allan Hobson (1995)

Rapid eye movements also stir the liquid behind the cornea; this delivers fresh oxygen to corneal cells, preventing their suffocation.

of all the discoveries it has been my good fortune to make." He proposed that dreams provide a psychic safety valve that discharges otherwise unacceptable feelings. He viewed a dream's **manifest content** (the apparent and remembered story line) as a censored, symbolic version of its **latent content,** the unconscious drives and wishes that would be threatening if expressed directly. Although most dreams have no overt sexual imagery, Freud nevertheless believed that most adult dreams could be "traced back by analysis to erotic wishes." Thus, a gun might be a disguised representation of a penis.

Freud considered dreams the key to understanding our inner conflicts. However, his critics say it is time to wake up from Freud's dream theory, which they regard as a scientific nightmare. Based on the accumulated science, "there is no reason to believe any of Freud's specific claims about dreams and their purposes," observed dream researcher William Domhoff (2003). Some contend that even if dreams are symbolic, they could be interpreted any way one wished. Others maintain that dreams hide nothing. A dream about a gun is a dream about a gun. Legend has it that even Freud, who loved to smoke cigars, acknowledged that "sometimes, a cigar is just a cigar." Freud's wish-fulfillment theory of dreams has in large part given way to other theories.

To file away memories. The *information-processing* perspective proposes that dreams may help sift, sort, and fix the day's experiences in our memory. Some studies support this view. When tested the day after learning a task, those who had been deprived of both slow-wave and REM sleep did not do as well as those who had slept undisturbed (Stickgold, 2012). In other studies, people who heard unusual phrases or learned to find hidden visual images before bedtime remembered less the next morning if they had been awakened every time they began REM sleep than if awakened during other sleep stages (Empson & Clarke, 1970; Karni & Sagi, 1994).

Brain scans confirm the link between REM sleep and memory. The brain regions that buzzed as rats learned to navigate a maze, or as people learned to perform a visual-discrimination task, buzzed again later during REM sleep (Louie & Wilson, 2001; Maquet, 2001). So precise were these activity patterns that scientists could tell where in the maze the rat would be if awake. Some researchers dispute the dreaming-strengthens-memory idea, noting that REM sleep may support memory for reasons unrelated to dreaming and that memory consolidation may also occur during non-REM sleep (Diekelmann & Born, 2010). This much seems true: A night of solid sleep (and dreaming) has an important place in our lives. To sleep, perchance to remember.

This is important news for students, many of whom, observed researcher Robert Stickgold (2000), suffer from a kind of sleep bulimia—binge sleeping on the weekend and "purging" during the week. "If you don't get good sleep and enough sleep after you learn new stuff, you won't integrate it effectively into your memories," he warned. That helps explain why high school students with high grades have averaged 25 minutes more sleep a night than their lower-achieving classmates (Wolfson & Carskadon, 1998; see **FIGURE 8.9**). Sacrificing sleep time to study actually *worsens* academic performance, by making it harder the next day to understand class material or do well on a test (Gillen-O'Neel et al., 2012).

To develop and preserve neural pathways. Perhaps dreams, or the brain activity associated with REM sleep, serve a *physiological* function, providing the sleeping brain with periodic stimulation. This theory makes developmental sense. Stimulating experiences preserve and expand the brain's neural pathways. Infants, whose neural networks are fast developing, spend much of their abundant sleep time in REM sleep (**FIGURE 8.10**).

To make sense of neural static. Other theories propose that dreams erupt from *neural activation* spreading upward from the brainstem (Antrobus, 1991; Hobson, 2003, 2004, 2009). According to "activation-synthesis theory," dreams

(a) Learning

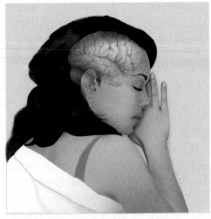

(b) Sleep consolidates our learning into long-term memory.

(c) Learning is retained.

^ FIGURE 8.9

A sleeping brain is a working brain

are the brain's attempt to synthesize random neural activity. Much as a neurosurgeon can produce hallucinations by stimulating different parts of a patient's cortex, so can stimulation originating within the brain. These internal stimuli activate brain areas that process visual images, but not the visual cortex area, which receives raw input from the eyes. As Freud might have expected, PET scans of sleeping people also reveal increased activity in the emotion-related limbic system (in the amygdala) during emotional dreams (Schwartz, 2012). In contrast, frontal lobe regions responsible for inhibition and logical thinking seem to idle, which may explain why our dreams are less inhibited than we are when awake (Maquet et al., 1996). Add the limbic system's emotional tone to the brain's visual bursts and—Voila!—we dream. Damage either the limbic system or the visual centers active during dreaming, and dreaming itself may be impaired (Domhoff, 2003).

To reflect cognitive development. Some dream researchers dispute both the Freudian and neural activation theories, preferring instead to see dreams as part of brain maturation and cognitive development (Domhoff, 2010, 2011; Foulkes, 1999). For example, prior to age 9, children's dreams seem more like a slide show and less like an active story in which the dreamer is an actor. Dreams overlap with waking cognition and feature coherent speech. They *simulate reality* by drawing on our concepts and knowledge. They engage brain networks that also are active during daydreaming—and so may be viewed as intensified

Question: Does eating spicy foods cause us to dream more?
Answer: Any food that causes you to awaken more increases your chance of recalling a dream (Moorcroft, 2003).

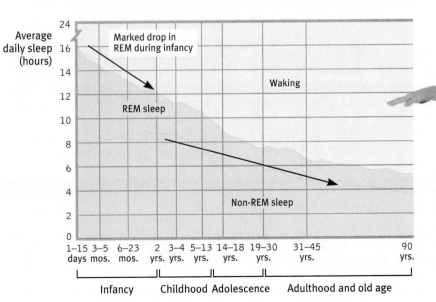

swissmacky/Shutterstock

< FIGURE 8.10

Sleep across the life span As we age, our sleep patterns change. During our first few months, we spend progressively less time in REM sleep. During our first 20 years, we spend progressively less time asleep. (Data from Snyder & Scott, 1972.)

REM rebound the tendency for REM sleep to increase following REM sleep deprivation.

mind wandering, enhanced by visual imagery (Fox et al., 2013). Unlike the idea that dreams arise from bottom-up brain activation, the cognitive perspective emphasizes our mind's top-down control of our dream content (Nir & Tononi, 2010).

TABLE 8.2 compares these major dream theories. Although today's sleep researchers debate dreams' functions—and some are skeptical that dreams serve any function—there is one thing they agree on: We need REM sleep. Deprived of it by repeatedly being awakened, people return more and more quickly to the REM stage after falling back to sleep. When finally allowed to sleep undisturbed, they literally sleep like babies—with increased REM sleep, a phenomenon called **REM rebound.** Withdrawing REM-suppressing sleeping medications also increases REM sleep, but with accompanying nightmares. Most other mammals also experience REM rebound, suggesting that the causes and functions of REM sleep are deeply biological. (That REM sleep occurs in mammals—and not in animals such as fish, whose behavior is less influenced by learning—fits the information-processing theory of dreams.)

⌄ TABLE 8.2

Dream Theories

Theory	Explanation	Critical Considerations
Freud's wish-fulfillment	Dreams preserve sleep and provide a "psychic safety valve"—expressing otherwise unacceptable feelings; contain manifest (remembered) content and a deeper layer of latent content (a hidden meaning).	Lacks any scientific support; dreams may be interpreted in many different ways.
Information-processing	Dreams help us sort out the day's events and consolidate our memories.	But why do we sometimes dream about things we have not experienced and about past events?
Physiological function	Regular brain stimulation from REM sleep may help develop and preserve neural pathways.	This does not explain why we experience meaningful dreams.
Neural activation	REM sleep triggers neural activity that evokes random visual memories, which our sleeping brain weaves into stories.	The individual's brain is weaving the stories, which still tells us something about the dreamer.
Cognitive development	Dream content reflects dreamers' level of cognitive development—their knowledge and understanding. Dreams simulate our lives, including worst-case scenarios.	Does not propose an adaptive function of dreams.

So does this mean that because dreams serve physiological functions and extend normal cognition, they are psychologically meaningless? Not necessarily. Every psychologically meaningful experience involves an active brain. We are once again reminded of a basic principle: *Biological and psychological explanations of behavior are partners, not competitors.*

Dreams are a fascinating altered state of consciousness. But they are not the only altered state. As we will see next, drugs also alter conscious awareness.

RETRIEVE IT [✖]

• What five theories propose explanations for why we dream?

ANSWERS: (1) Freud's wish-fulfillment (dreams as a psychic safety valve), (2) information-processing (dreams sort the day's events and form memories), (3) physiological function (dreams pave neural pathways), (4) neural activation (REM sleep triggers random neural activity that the mind weaves into stories), and (5) cognitive development (dreams reflect the dreamer's developmental stage).

MODULE 8 REVIEW   Sleep and Dreams

◖◗ Learning Objectives

Test Yourself by taking a moment to answer each of these Learning Objective Questions (repeated here from within the module). Then turn to Appendix D, Complete Module Reviews, to check your answers. Research suggests that trying to answer these questions on your own will improve your long-term memory of the concepts (McDaniel et al., 2009).

8-1 What is sleep?

8-2 How do our biological rhythms influence our daily functioning?

8-3 What is the biological rhythm of our sleeping and dreaming stages?

8-4 How do biology and environment interact in our sleep patterns?

8-5 What are sleep's functions?

8-6 How does sleep loss affect us, and what are the major sleep disorders?

8-7 What do we dream?

8-8 What functions have theorists proposed for dreams?

▣·◖◗ Terms and Concepts to Remember

Test yourself on these terms by trying to write down the definition in your own words before flipping back to the referenced page to check your answers.

sleep, p. 87

circadian [ser-KAY-dee-an] rhythm, p. 87

REM sleep, p. 88

alpha waves, p. 89

hallucinations, p. 89

delta waves, p. 89

suprachiasmatic nucleus (SCN), p. 92

insomnia, p. 96

narcolepsy, p. 97

sleep apnea, p. 97

night terrors, p. 98

dream, p. 99

manifest content, p. 100

latent content, p. 100

REM rebound, p. 102

[✗] Experience the Testing Effect

Test yourself repeatedly throughout your studies. This will not only help you figure out what you know and don't know; the testing itself will help you learn and remember the information more effectively thanks to the *testing effect*.

1. Our body temperature tends to rise and fall in sync with a biological clock, which is referred to as _____ _____.

2. During the NREM-1 sleep stage, a person is most likely to experience
   a. sleep spindles.
   b. hallucinations.
   c. night terrors or nightmares.
   d. rapid eye movements.

3. The brain emits large, slow delta waves during _____ sleep.

4. As the night progresses, what happens to the REM stage of sleep?

5. Which of the following is NOT one of the reasons that have been proposed to explain why we need sleep?
   a. Sleep has survival value.
   b. Sleep helps us recuperate.
   c. Sleep rests the eyes.
   d. Sleep plays a role in the growth process.

6. What is the difference between narcolepsy and sleep apnea?

7. In interpreting dreams, Freud was most interested in their
   a. information-processing function.
   b. physiological function.
   c. manifest content, or story line.
   d. latent content, or hidden meaning.

8. How has *neural activation* been used to explain why we dream?

9. "For what one has dwelt on by day, these things are seen in visions of the night" (Menander of Athens, *Fragments*). How might the information-processing perspective on dreaming interpret this ancient Greek quote?

10. The tendency for REM sleep to increase following REM sleep deprivation is referred to as _____ _____.

Find answers to these questions in Appendix E, in the back of the book.

Use ⊛ LearningCurve to create your personalized study plan, which will direct you to the resources that will help you most in ⊛ LaunchPad.

9 MODULE Drugs and Consciousness

Let's imagine a day in the life of a legal-drug user. It begins with a wake-up energy drink. By midday, several cigarettes have calmed frazzled nerves before an appointment at the plastic surgeon's office for wrinkle-smoothing Botox injections. A diet pill before dinner helps stem the appetite, and its stimulating effects can later be partially offset with a beer or two Advil PMs. And if performance needs enhancing, there are beta blockers for onstage performers, Viagra for middle-aged men, hormone-delivering "libido patches" for middle-aged women, and Adderall for students hoping to focus their concentration.

Tolerance and Addiction

👁 **9-1** What are substance use disorders, and what roles do tolerance, withdrawal, and addiction play in these disorders?

Chemical substances that change our perceptions and moods are termed **psychoactive drugs,** and most of us manage to use such substances, which include caffeine and alcohol, in moderation and without disrupting our lives. But some of us develop a self-harming **substance use disorder (TABLE 9.1).** A drug's overall effect depends not only on its biological effects but also on the user's expectations, which vary with social and cultural contexts (Gu et al., 2015; Ward, 1994). If one culture assumes that a particular drug produces euphoria (or

The odds of getting hooked after using various drugs:

Tobacco	32%
Heroin	23%
Alcohol	15%
Marijuana	9%

Source: National Academy of Science, Institute of Medicine (Brody, 2003).

⌄ TABLE 9.1

When Is Drug Use a Disorder? According to the American Psychiatric Association, a person may be diagnosed with *substance use disorder* when drug use continues despite significant life disruption. Resulting brain changes may persist after quitting use of the substance (thus leading to strong cravings when exposed to people and situations that trigger memories of drug use). The severity of substance use disorder varies from *mild* (two to three of these indicators) to *moderate* (four to five indicators) to *severe* (six or more indicators). (*Source:* American Psychiatric Association, 2013.)

Diminished Control

1. Uses more substance, or for longer, than intended.
2. Tries unsuccessfully to regulate use of substance.
3. Spends much time acquiring, using, or recovering from effects of substance.
4. Craves the substance.

Diminished Social Functioning

5. Use disrupts commitments at work, school, or home.
6. Continues use despite social problems.
7. Causes reduced social, recreational, and work activities.

Hazardous Use

8. Continues use despite hazards.
9. Continues use despite worsening physical or psychological problems.

Drug Action

10. Experiences tolerance (needing more substance for the desired effect).
11. Experiences withdrawal when attempting to end use.

psychoactive drug a chemical substance that alters perceptions and moods.

substance use disorder continued substance craving and use despite significant life disruption and/or physical risk.

tolerance the diminishing effect with regular use of the same dose of a drug, requiring the user to take larger and larger doses before experiencing the drug's effect.

addiction compulsive craving of drugs or certain behaviors (such as gambling) despite known adverse consequences.

withdrawal the discomfort and distress that follow discontinuing an addictive drug or behavior.

aggression or sexual arousal) and another does not, each culture may find its expectations fulfilled. We'll take a closer look at these interacting forces in the use and potential abuse of particular psychoactive drugs. But first, let's consider how our bodies react to the ongoing use of psychoactive drugs.

Why might a person who rarely drinks alcohol get buzzed on one can of beer while a long-term drinker shows few effects until the second six-pack? The answer is **tolerance.** With continued use of alcohol and some other drugs (but not marijuana), the user's brain chemistry adapts to offset the drug effect (a process called *neuroadaptation*). To experience the same effect, the user requires larger and larger doses (**FIGURE 9.1**). Ever-increasing doses of most psycho-active drugs may lead to **addiction:** The person craves and uses the substance despite its adverse consequences. (See Thinking Critically About: Addiction.) The World Health Organization (WHO, 2008b) has reported that, worldwide, 90 million people suffer from such problems related to alcohol and other drugs. Regular users often try to fight their addiction, but abruptly stopping the drug may lead to the undesirable side effects of **withdrawal.**

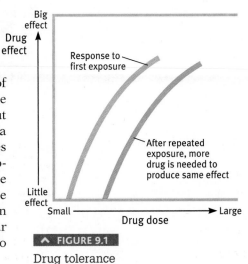

∧ FIGURE 9.1

Drug tolerance

THINKING CRITICALLY ABOUT

Addiction

9-2 How has the concept of addiction changed?

In recent years, the concept of addiction has been extended to cover many behaviors formerly considered bad habits or even sins. Psychologists debate whether the concept has been stretched too far, and whether addictions are really as irresistible as commonly believed. For example, "even for a very addictive drug like cocaine, only 15 to 16 percent of people become addicted within 10 years of first use," observed Terry Robinson and Kent Berridge (2003).

Addictions can be powerful, and many addicts do benefit from therapy or group support. Alcoholics Anonymous has supported millions in overcoming their alcohol addiction. But viewing addiction as an uncontrollable disease can undermine people's self-confidence and their belief that they can change. And that, critics say, would be unfortunate, for many people do voluntarily stop using addictive drugs, without any treatment. Most ex-smokers, for example, have kicked the habit on their own (Newport, 2013).

The addiction-as-disease-needing-treatment idea has been offered for a host of driven, excessive behaviors—eating, gambling, work, sex, and accumulating wealth. However, critics suggest that "addiction" can become an all-purpose excuse when used not as a metaphor ("I'm a science fiction addict") but as reality.

A social-networking addiction?

Moreover, they note that labeling a behavior doesn't explain it. Attributing serial adultery to a "sex addiction" does not *explain* the sexual impulsiveness (Radford, 2010).

Sometimes, though, behaviors such as gambling, video gaming, or online surfing do become compulsive and dysfunctional, much like abusive drug-taking (Gentile, 2009; Griffiths, 2001; Hoeft et al., 2008). Thus, psychiatry's manual of disorders now includes behavior addictions such as "gambling disorders," and proposes Internet gaming disorder for further study

(American Psychiatric Association, 2013). Studies in Asia, Europe, and North America estimate gaming addiction rates of from 3 to 12 percent of players (Anderson & Warburton, 2012; Ferguson et al., 2011). Some Internet users display an apparent inability to resist logging on and staying on, even when this excessive use impairs their work and relationships (Ko et al., 2005). But there is hope. One research review found both psychological and drug therapies for Internet addiction "highly effective" (Winkler et al., 2013).

Types of Psychoactive Drugs

The three major categories of psychoactive drugs are *depressants, stimulants,* and *hallucinogens.* All do their work at the brain's synapses, stimulating, inhibiting, or mimicking the activity of the brain's own chemical messengers, the neurotransmitters.

Depressants

9-3 What are depressants, and what are their effects?

Depressants are drugs such as alcohol, barbiturates (tranquilizers), and opiates that calm neural activity and slow body functions.

ALCOHOL True or false? In small amounts, alcohol is a stimulant. *False.* Low doses of alcohol may, indeed, enliven a drinker, but they do so by acting as a *disinhibitor*—they slow brain activity that controls judgment and inhibitions. Alcohol is an equal-opportunity drug: It increases (disinhibits) helpful tendencies, as when tipsy restaurant patrons leave extravagant tips and social drinkers bond in groups (Hirsh et al., 2011; Lynn, 1988; Sayette et al., 2012). And it increases harmful tendencies, as when sexually aroused men become more disposed to sexual aggression. When drinking, both men and women are more disposed to casual sex (Garcia et al., 2012; Rehm et al., 2012). *The bottom line*: The urges you would feel if sober are the ones you will more likely act upon when intoxicated.

> **FIGURE 9.2**

Disordered drinking shrinks the brain   MRI scans show brain shrinkage in women with alcohol use disorder (left) compared with women in a control group (right).

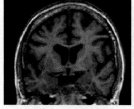
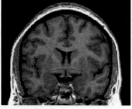

Scan of woman with alcohol use disorder

Scan of woman without alcohol use disorder

Daniel Hommer, NIAAA, NIH, HHS

The prolonged and excessive drinking that characterizes **alcohol use disorder** can shrink the brain (**FIGURE 9.2**). Girls and young women (who have less of a stomach enzyme that digests alcohol) can become addicted to alcohol more quickly than boys and young men, and they are at risk for lung, brain, and liver damage at lower consumption levels (CASA, 2003).

SLOWED NEURAL PROCESSING Low doses of alcohol relax the drinker by slowing sympathetic nervous system activity. Larger doses cause reactions to slow, speech to slur, and skilled performance to deteriorate. Paired with sleep deprivation, alcohol is a potent sedative. Add these physical effects to lowered inhibitions, and the result can be deadly. Worldwide, several hundred thousand lives are lost each year in alcohol-related accidents and violent crime. As blood-alcohol levels rise and judgment falters, people's qualms about drinking and driving lessen. In experiments, virtually all drinkers who had insisted when sober that they would not drive under the influence later decided to drive home from a bar, even when given a breathalyzer test and told they were intoxicated (Denton & Krebs, 1990; MacDonald et al., 1995). Alcohol can also be life threatening when heavy drinking follows an earlier period of moderate drinking, which depresses the vomiting response. People may poison themselves with an overdose that their bodies would normally throw up.

MEMORY DISRUPTION Alcohol can disrupt memory formation, and heavy drinking can have long-term effects on the brain and cognition. In rats, at a developmental period corresponding to human adolescence, binge drinking contributes to nerve cell death and reduces the birth of new nerve cells. It also impairs the growth of synaptic connections (Crews et al., 2006, 2007). In humans, heavy drinking may lead to blackouts, in which drinkers are unable to recall people they met the night before or what they said or did while intoxicated. These blackouts result partly from the way alcohol suppresses REM sleep, which helps fix the day's experiences into permanent memories.

REDUCED SELF-AWARENESS AND SELF-CONTROL In one experiment, those who consumed alcohol (rather than a placebo beverage) were doubly likely to be caught mind-wandering during a reading task, yet were *less* likely to notice that they zoned out (Sayette et al., 2009). Alcohol not only reduces self-awareness, it also produces a sort of "myopia" by focusing attention on an arousing situation (say, a provocation) and distracting it from normal inhibitions and future consequences (Giancola et al., 2010; Hull et al., 1986; Steele & Josephs, 1990).

Reduced self-awareness may help explain why people who want to suppress their awareness of failures or shortcomings are more likely to drink than are those who feel good about themselves. Losing a business deal, a game, or a romantic partner sometimes elicits a drinking binge.

EXPECTANCY EFFECTS As with other drugs, expectations influence behavior. When people *believe* that alcohol affects social behavior in certain ways, and *believe* that they have been drinking alcohol, they will behave accordingly (Moss & Albery, 2009). In a classic experiment, researchers gave Rutgers University men (who had volunteered for a study on "alcohol and sexual stimulation") either an alcoholic or a nonalcoholic drink (Abrams & Wilson, 1983). (Both had strong tastes that masked any alcohol.) After watching an erotic movie clip, the men who *thought* they had consumed alcohol were more likely to report having strong sexual fantasies and feeling guilt free. Being able to *attribute* their sexual responses to alcohol released their inhibitions—whether or not they had actually consumed any alcohol.

So, alcohol's effect lies partly in that powerful sex organ, the mind. Fourteen "intervention studies" have educated college drinkers about that very point (Scott-Sheldon et al., 2014). Most participants came away with lower positive expectations of alcohol and reduced their drinking the ensuing month.

BARBITURATES Like alcohol, the **barbiturate** drugs, or *tranquilizers*, depress nervous system activity. Barbiturates such as Nembutal, Seconal, and Amytal are sometimes prescribed to induce sleep or reduce anxiety. In larger doses, they can impair memory and judgment. If combined with alcohol—as sometimes happens when people take a sleeping pill after an evening of heavy drinking—the total depressive effect on body functions can be lethal.

OPIATES The **opiates**—opium and its derivatives—also depress neural functioning. When using opiates, which include *heroin*, pupils constrict, breathing slows, and lethargy sets in as blissful pleasure replaces pain and anxiety. For this short-term pleasure, opiate users may pay a long-term price: a gnawing craving for another fix, a need for progressively larger doses (as tolerance develops), and the extreme discomfort of withdrawal. When repeatedly flooded with an artificial opiate, the brain eventually stops producing *endorphins*, its own opiates. If the artificial opiate is then withdrawn, the brain lacks the normal level of these

Drinking disaster demo Firefighters reenacted the trauma of an alcohol-related car accident, providing a memorable demonstration for these high school students. Alcohol consumption leads to feelings of invincibility, which become especially dangerous behind the wheel of a car.

depressants drugs (such as alcohol, barbiturates, and opiates) that reduce neural activity and slow body functions.

alcohol use disorder (popularly known as *alcoholism*) alcohol use marked by tolerance, withdrawal, and a drive to continue problematic use.

barbiturates drugs that depress central nervous system activity, reducing anxiety but impairing memory and judgment.

opiates opium and its derivatives, such as morphine and heroin; depress neural activity, temporarily lessening pain and anxiety.

stimulants drugs (such as caffeine, nicotine, and the more powerful amphetamines, cocaine, Ecstasy, and methamphetamine) that excite neural activity and speed up body functions.

amphetamines drugs that stimulate neural activity, causing accelerated body functions and associated energy and mood changes.

nicotine a stimulating and highly addictive psychoactive drug in tobacco.

painkilling neurotransmitters. Those who cannot or choose not to tolerate this state may, as their dosage increases, pay an ultimate price—death by overdose. Opiates include the *narcotics,* such as codeine and morphine (and the synthetic *methadone,* a heroin substitute), which physicians may prescribe for pain relief and which can also lead to addiction.

RETRIEVE IT

• How is a "shopping addiction" different from the psychological definition of addiction?

ANSWER: Being strongly interested in something in a way that is not compulsive and dysfunctional is not an addiction. It does not involve obsessive craving in spite of known negative consequences.

• Alcohol, barbiturates, and opiates are all in a class of drugs called _____.

ANSWER: depressants

Stimulants

 9-4 What are stimulants, and what are their effects?

A **stimulant** excites neural activity and speeds up bodily functions. Pupils dilate, heart and breathing rates increase, and blood sugar levels rise, causing a drop in appetite. Energy and self-confidence also rise.

Stimulants include caffeine, nicotine, cocaine, Ecstasy, the **amphetamines,** and *methamphetamine.* People use stimulants to feel alert, lose weight, or boost mood or athletic performance. Unfortunately, stimulants can be addictive, as you may know if you are one of the many who use caffeine daily in your coffee, tea, soda, or energy drinks. Cut off from your usual dose, you may crash into fatigue, headaches, irritability, and depression (Silverman et al., 1992). A mild dose of caffeine typically lasts three or four hours, which—if taken in the evening—may be long enough to impair sleep.

NICOTINE Cigarettes, e-cigarettes, and other tobacco products deliver highly addictive **nicotine.** Imagine that cigarettes were harmless—except, once in every 25,000 packs, an occasional innocent-looking one is filled with dynamite instead of tobacco. Not such a bad risk of having your head blown off. But with 250 million packs a day consumed worldwide, we could expect more than 10,000 gruesome daily deaths (more than three times the 9/11 terrorist fatalities each and every day)—surely enough to have cigarettes banned everywhere.[1]

Vasca / Shutterstock

The lost lives from these dynamite-loaded cigarettes approximate those from today's actual cigarettes. A teen-to-the-grave smoker has a 50 percent chance of dying from the habit, and each year, tobacco kills nearly 5.4 million of its 1.3 billion customers worldwide. (Imagine the outrage if terrorists took down an equivalent of 25 loaded jumbo jets today, let alone tomorrow and every day thereafter.) By 2030, annual deaths are expected to increase to 8 million. That means that *1 billion* twenty-first-century people may be killed by tobacco (WHO, 2012).

Smoke a cigarette and nature will charge you 12 minutes—ironically, just about the length of time you spend smoking it (Discover, 1996). Smokers die, on average, at least a decade before nonsmokers (Jha et al., 2013). Eliminating smoking would increase life expectancy more than any other preventive measure.

Tobacco products are as powerfully and quickly addictive as heroin and cocaine. Attempts to quit even within the first weeks of smoking often fail (DiFranza, 2008). As with other addictions, smokers develop *tolerance,* and

"Smoking cures weight problems . . . eventually."

Comedian-writer Steven Wright

For HIV patients who smoke, the virus is now much less lethal than the smoking (Helleberg et al., 2013).

---

1. This analogy, adapted here with world-based numbers, was suggested by mathematician Sam Saunders, as reported by K. C. Cole (1998).

quitting causes withdrawal symptoms, including craving, insomnia, anxiety, irritability, and distractibility. Nicotine-deprived smokers trying to focus on a task experience a tripled rate of mind wandering (Sayette et al., 2010). When not craving a cigarette, they tend to underestimate the power of such cravings (Sayette et al., 2008).

All it takes to relieve this aversive state is a single puff on a cigarette. Within 7 seconds, a rush of nicotine signals the central nervous system to release a flood of neurotransmitters (**FIGURE 9.3**). Epinephrine and norepinephrine diminish appetite and boost alertness and mental efficiency. Dopamine and opioids temporarily calm anxiety and reduce sensitivity to pain (Ditre et al., 2011; Gavin, 2004). Thus, ex-smokers will sometimes, under stress, return to smoking—as did some 1 million Americans after the 9/11 terrorist attacks (Pesko, 2014).

These rewards keep people smoking, even among the 3 in 4 smokers who wish they could stop (Newport, 2013). Each year, fewer than 1 in 7 smokers who want to quit will be able to resist. Even those who know they are committing slow-motion suicide may be unable to stop (Saad, 2002). Asked "If you had to do it all over again, would you start smoking?" more than 85 percent of adult smokers have answered *No* (Slovic et al., 2002).

Nevertheless, repeated attempts seem to pay off. Half of all Americans who have ever smoked have quit, sometimes aided by a nicotine replacement drug and with encouragement from a counselor or support group. Success is equally likely whether smokers quit abruptly or gradually (Fiore et al., 2008; Lichtenstein et al., 2010; Lindson et al., 2010). For those who endure, the acute craving and withdrawal symptoms gradually dissipate over the ensuing 6 months (Ward et al., 1997). After a year's abstinence, only 10 percent will relapse in the next year (Hughes, 2010). These nonsmokers may live not only healthier but also happier lives. Smoking correlates with higher rates of depression, chronic disabilities, and divorce (Doherty & Doherty, 1998; Edwards & Kendler, 2012; Vita et al., 1998). Healthy living seems to add both years to life and life to years.

Humorist Dave Barry (1995) recalling why he smoked his first cigarette the summer he turned 15: "Arguments against smoking: 'It's a repulsive addiction that slowly but surely turns you into a gasping, gray-skinned, tumor-ridden invalid, hacking up brownish gobs of toxic waste from your one remaining lung.' Arguments for smoking: 'Other teenagers are doing it.' Case closed! Let's light up!"

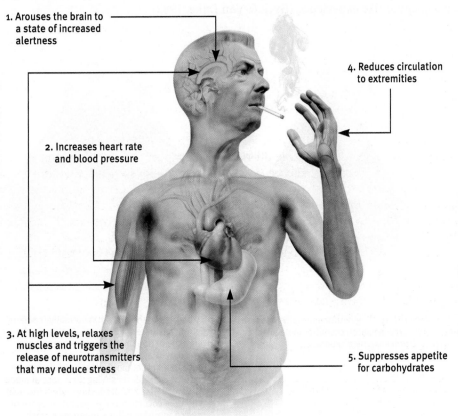

1. Arouses the brain to a state of increased alertness

4. Reduces circulation to extremities

2. Increases heart rate and blood pressure

3. At high levels, relaxes muscles and triggers the release of neurotransmitters that may reduce stress

5. Suppresses appetite for carbohydrates

< FIGURE 9.3

Where there's smoke . . . : The physiological effects of nicotine Nicotine reaches the brain within 7 seconds, twice as fast as intravenous heroin. Within minutes, the amount in the blood soars.

cocaine a powerful and addictive stimulant derived from the coca plant; produces temporarily increased alertness and euphoria.

"Cocaine makes you a new man. And the first thing that new man wants is more cocaine."

*Comedian George Carlin
(1937–2008)*

COCAINE The recipe for Coca-Cola originally included an extract of the coca plant, creating a cocaine tonic for tired elderly people. Between 1896 and 1905, Coke was indeed "the real thing." But no longer. **Cocaine** is now snorted, injected, or smoked. It enters the bloodstream quickly, producing a rush of euphoria that depletes the brain's supply of the neurotransmitters dopamine, serotonin, and norepinephrine (**FIGURE 9.4**). Within the hour, a crash of agitated depression follows as the drug's effect wears off.

In situations that trigger aggression, ingesting cocaine may heighten reactions. Caged rats fight when given foot shocks, and they fight even more when given cocaine *and* foot shocks. Likewise, humans who voluntarily ingest high doses of cocaine in laboratory experiments impose higher shock levels on a presumed opponent than do those receiving a placebo (Licata et al., 1993). Cocaine use may also lead to emotional disturbances, suspiciousness, convulsions, cardiac arrest, or respiratory failure.

In national surveys, 3 percent of U.S. high school seniors and 6 percent of British 18- to 24-year-olds reported having tried cocaine during the past year (ACMD, 2009; Johnston et al., 2015). Of those, nearly half had smoked *crack*, a faster-working crystallized form of cocaine that produces a briefer but more intense high, followed by a more intense crash. After several hours, the craving for more wanes, only to return several days later (Gawin, 1991).

Cocaine's psychological effects depend in part on the dosage and form consumed, but the situation and the user's expectations and personality also play a role. Given a placebo, cocaine users who *thought* they were taking cocaine often had a cocaine-like experience (Byck & Van Dyke, 1982).

∨ FIGURE 9.4

Cocaine euphoria and crash

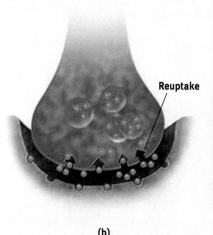

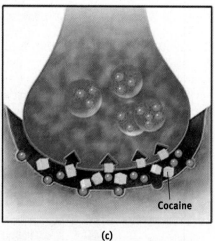

(a) Neurotransmitters carry a message from a sending neuron across a synapse to receptor sites on a receiving neuron.

(b) The sending neuron normally reabsorbs excess neurotransmitter molecules, a process called *reuptake*.

(c) By binding to the sites that normally reabsorb neurotransmitter molecules, cocaine blocks reuptake of dopamine, norepinephrine, and serotonin (Ray & Ksir, 1990). The extra neurotransmitter molecules therefore remain in the synapse, intensifying their normal mood-altering effects and producing a euphoric rush. When the cocaine level drops, the absence of these neurotransmitters produces a crash.

METHAMPHETAMINE **Methamphetamine** is chemically related to its parent drug, *amphetamine* (NIDA, 2002, 2005), but has greater effects. Methamphetamine triggers the release of the neurotransmitter dopamine, which stimulates brain cells that enhance energy and mood, leading to 8 hours or so of heightened energy and euphoria. Its aftereffects may include irritability, insomnia, hypertension, seizures, social isolation, depression, and occasional violent outbursts (Homer et al., 2008). Over time, methamphetamine may reduce baseline dopamine levels, leaving the user with depressed functioning.

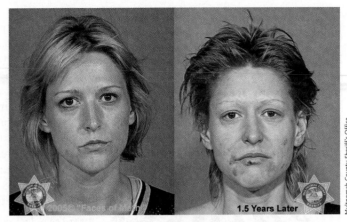

Dramatic drug-induced decline
In the 18 months between these two mug shots, this woman's methamphetamine addiction led to obvious physical changes.

ECSTASY **Ecstasy,** a street name for **MDMA** (methylenedioxy-methamphetamine, also known in its powder form as "Molly"), is both a stimulant and a mild hallucinogen. As an amphetamine derivative, Ecstasy triggers dopamine release, but its major effect is releasing stored serotonin and blocking its reuptake, thus prolonging serotonin's feel-good flood (Braun, 2001). Users feel the effect about a half-hour after taking an Ecstasy pill. For 3 or 4 hours, they experience high energy, emotional elevation, and (given a social context) connectedness with those around them ("I love everyone").

During the 1990s, Ecstasy's popularity soared as a "club drug" taken at nightclubs and all-night dance parties (Landry, 2002). The drug's popularity crosses national borders, with an estimated 60 million tablets consumed annually in Britain (ACMD, 2009). There are, however, reasons not to be ecstatic about Ecstasy. One is its dehydrating effect, which—when combined with prolonged dancing—can lead to severe overheating, increased blood pressure, and death. Another is that long-term, repeated leaching of brain serotonin can damage serotonin-producing neurons, leading to decreased output and increased risk of permanently depressed mood (Croft et al., 2001; McCann et al., 2000; Roiser et al., 2005). Ecstasy also suppresses the disease-fighting immune system, impairs memory, slows thought, and disrupts sleep by interfering with serotonin's control of the circadian clock (Laws & Kokkalis, 2007; Schilt et al., 2007; Wagner et al., 2012). Ecstasy delights for the night but dispirits the morrow.

The hug drug
MDMA, known as Ecstasy, produces a euphoric high and feelings of intimacy. But repeated use can destroy serotonin-producing neurons, impair memory, and permanently deflate mood.

Hallucinogens

9-5 What are hallucinogens, and what are their effects?

Hallucinogens distort perceptions and evoke sensory images in the absence of sensory input (which is why these drugs are also called *psychedelics*, meaning "mind-manifesting"). Some, such as LSD and MDMA (Ecstasy), are synthetic. Others, including the mild hallucinogen marijuana, are natural substances.

Whether provoked to hallucinate by drugs, loss of oxygen, or extreme sensory deprivation, the brain hallucinates in basically the same way (Siegel, 1982). The experience typically begins with simple geometric forms, such as a lattice, cobweb, or spiral. The next phase consists of more meaningful images; some may be superimposed on a tunnel or funnel, others may be replays of past emotional experiences. As the hallucination peaks, people frequently feel separated from their body and experience dreamlike scenes so real that they may become panic-stricken or harm themselves.

methamphetamine a powerfully addictive drug that stimulates the central nervous system, with accelerated body functions and associated energy and mood changes; over time, appears to reduce baseline dopamine levels.

Ecstasy (MDMA) a synthetic stimulant and mild hallucinogen. Produces euphoria and social intimacy, but with short-term health risks and longer-term harm to serotonin-producing neurons and to mood and cognition.

hallucinogens psychedelic ("mind-manifesting") drugs, such as LSD, that distort perceptions and evoke sensory images in the absence of sensory input.

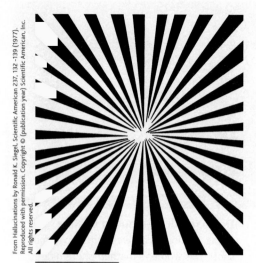

⌃ FIGURE 9.5

Near-death vision or hallucination? Psychologist Ronald Siegel (1977) reported that people under the influence of hallucinogenic drugs often see "a bright light in the center of the field of vision. . . . The location of this point of light create[s] a tunnel-like perspective." This is very similar to others' near-death experiences.

near-death experience an altered state of consciousness reported after a close brush with death (such as cardiac arrest); often similar to drug-induced hallucinations.

LSD a powerful hallucinogenic drug; also known as acid (lysergic acid diethylamide).

THC the major active ingredient in marijuana; triggers a variety of effects, including mild hallucinations.

These sensations are strikingly similar to the **near-death experience,** an altered state of consciousness reported by about 10 to 15 percent of patients revived from cardiac arrest (Agrillo, 2011; Greyson, 2010; Parnia et al., 2014). Many describe visions of tunnels (**FIGURE 9.5**), bright lights or beings of light, a replay of old memories, and out-of-body sensations (Siegel, 1980). Given that oxygen deprivation and other insults to the brain are known to produce hallucinations, it is difficult to resist wondering whether a brain under stress manufactures the near-death experience. During epileptic seizures and migraines, patients may experience similar hallucinations of geometric patterns (Billock & Tsou, 2012). So have solitary sailors and polar explorers while enduring monotony, isolation, and cold (Suedfeld & Mocellin, 1987). Such experiences represent "neural funny business," surmises philosopher-neuroscientist Patricia Churchland (2013, p. 70).

LSD Chemist Albert Hofmann created—and on one Friday afternoon in April 1943 accidentally ingested—**LSD** (lysergic acid diethylamide). The result—"an uninterrupted stream of fantastic pictures, extraordinary shapes with intense, kaleidoscopic play of colors"—reminded him of a childhood mystical experience that had left him longing for another glimpse of "a miraculous, powerful, unfathomable reality" (Siegel, 1984; Smith, 2006).

The emotions of an LSD trip range from euphoria to detachment to panic. Users' current mood and expectations (their "high hopes") color the emotional experience, but the perceptual distortions and hallucinations have some commonalities.

MARIJUANA Marijuana leaves and flowers contain **THC** (delta-9-tetrahydrocannabinol). Whether smoked (getting to the brain in about 7 seconds) or eaten (causing its peak concentration to be reached at a slower, unpredictable rate), THC produces a mix of effects. Synthetic marijuana ("K2," also called "Spice") mimics THC. Its harmful side effects, which can include agitation, seizures, hallucinations, and suicidal or aggressive thoughts and actions, have led to continuing efforts to make it illegal, including the U.S. Synthetic Drug Abuse Prevention Act of 2012.

The straight dope on marijuana: It is a mild hallucinogen, amplifying sensitivity to colors, sounds, tastes, and smells. But like alcohol, marijuana relaxes, disinhibits, and may produce a euphoric high. Both alcohol and marijuana impair the motor coordination, perceptual skills, and reaction time necessary for safely operating an automobile or other machine. "THC causes animals to misjudge events," reported Ronald Siegel (1990, p. 163). "Pigeons wait too long to respond to buzzers or lights that tell them food is available for brief periods; and rats turn the wrong way in mazes."

Marijuana and alcohol also differ. The body eliminates alcohol within hours. THC and its by-products linger in the body for more than a week, which means that regular users experience less abrupt withdrawal and may achieve a high with smaller-than-usual drug amounts. This is unlike typical tolerance, in which repeat users need to take larger doses to feel the same effect.

A marijuana user's experience can vary with the situation. If the person feels anxious or depressed, marijuana may intensify the feelings. The more often the person uses marijuana, especially during adolescence, the greater the risk of anxiety, depression, or addiction (Bambico et al., 2010; Hurd et al., 2013; Murray et al., 2007).

Researchers are studying and debating marijuana's effect on the brain and cognition. Some evidence indicates that marijuana disrupts memory formation (Bossong et al., 2012). Such cognitive effects outlast the period of smoking (Messinis et al., 2006). Heavy adult use for over 20 years has been associated with a shrinkage of brain areas that process memories and emotions (Filbey et al., 2014; Yücel et al., 2008). One study, which has tracked more than 1000 New Zealanders from birth, found that the IQ scores of persistent marijuana users before age 18 predicted lower adult intelligence (Meier et al., 2012). Other researchers are unconvinced that marijuana smoking harms the brain (Rogeberg, 2013; Weiland et al., 2015).

In some cases, legal *medical marijuana* use has been granted to relieve the pain and nausea associated with diseases such as AIDS and cancer (Munsey, 2010; Watson et al., 2000). In such cases, the Institute of Medicine recommends delivering the THC with medical inhalers. Marijuana smoke, like cigarette smoke, is toxic and can cause cancer, lung damage, and pregnancy complications (BLF, 2012).

* * *

Despite their differences, the psychoactive drugs summarized in **TABLE 9.2** share a common feature: They trigger negative aftereffects that offset their immediate positive effects and grow stronger with repetition. And that helps explain both tolerance and withdrawal. As the opposing, negative aftereffects grow stronger, it takes larger and larger doses to produce the desired high *(tolerance),* causing the aftereffects to worsen in the drug's absence *(withdrawal).* This in turn creates a need to switch off the withdrawal symptoms by taking yet more of the drug.

∨ TABLE 9.2

A Guide to Selected Psychoactive Drugs

Drug	Type	Pleasurable Effects	Negative Aftereffects
Alcohol	Depressant	Initial high followed by relaxation and disinhibition	Depression, memory loss, organ damage, impaired reactions
Heroin	Depressant	Rush of euphoria, relief from pain	Depressed physiology, agonizing withdrawal
Caffeine	Stimulant	Increased alertness and wakefulness	Anxiety, restlessness, and insomnia in high doses; uncomfortable withdrawal
Nicotine	Stimulant	Arousal and relaxation, sense of well-being	Heart disease, cancer
Cocaine	Stimulant	Rush of euphoria, confidence, energy	Cardiovascular stress, suspiciousness, depressive crash
Methamphetamine	Stimulant	Euphoria, alertness, energy	Irritability, insomnia, hypertension, seizures
Ecstasy (MDMA)	Stimulant; mild hallucinogen	Emotional elevation, disinhibition	Dehydration, overheating, depressed mood, impaired cognitive and immune functioning
LSD	Hallucinogen	Visual "trip"	Risk of panic
Marijuana (THC)	Mild hallucinogen	Enhanced sensation, relief of pain, distortion of time, relaxation	Impaired learning and memory, increased risk of psychological disorders, lung damage from smoke

RETRIEVE IT

"How strange would appear to be this thing that men call pleasure! And how curiously it is related to what is thought to be its opposite, pain! . . . Wherever the one is found, the other follows up behind."

Plato, *Phaedo,* fourth century B.C.E.

• How does this pleasure-pain description apply to the repeated use of psychoactive drugs?

ANSWER: Psychoactive drugs create pleasure by altering brain chemistry. With repeated use of the drug, the brain develops tolerance and needs more of the drug to achieve the desired effect. (Marijuana is an exception.) Discontinuing use of the substance then produces painful or psychologically unpleasant withdrawal symptoms.

Influences on Drug Use

 9-6 Why do some people become regular users of consciousness-altering drugs?

Drug use by North American youth increased during the 1970s. Then, with increased drug education and a more realistic and deglamorized media depiction of taking drugs, drug use declined sharply (except for a small rise in the mid-1980s). After the early 1990s, the cultural antidrug voice softened, and some

LaunchPad To review the basic psychoactive drugs and their actions, and to play the role of experimenter as you administer drugs and observe their effects, visit LaunchPad's *PsychSim 6: Your Mind on Drugs.*

Trends in drug use The percentage of U.S. high school seniors who report having used alcohol, marijuana, or cocaine during the past 30 days largely declined from the late 1970s to 1992, when it partially rebounded for a few years. (Data from Johnston et al., 2015.)

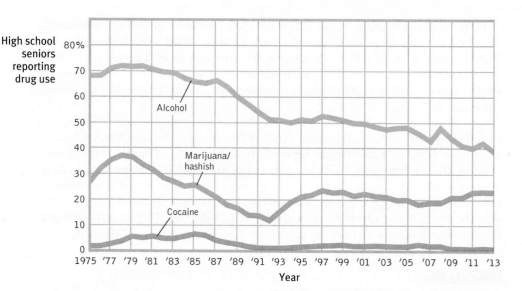

drugs for a time were again glamorized in music and films. Consider, for example, historical trends in the use of marijuana:

- In the University of Michigan's annual survey of 15,000 U.S. high school seniors, the proportion who said there is "great risk" in regular marijuana use rose from 35 percent in 1978 to 79 percent in 1991, then retreated to 36 percent in 2014 (Johnston et al., 2015).

- After peaking in 1978, marijuana use by U.S. high school seniors declined through 1992, then rose, but has recently been holding steady (see **FIGURE 9.6**). Among Canadian 15- to 24-year-olds, 23 percent report using marijuana monthly, weekly, or daily (Health Canada, 2012).

For some adolescents, occasional drug use represents thrill seeking. Why, though, do others become regular drug users? In search of answers, researchers have engaged biological, psychological, and social-cultural levels of analysis.

Biological Influences

Some people may be biologically vulnerable to particular drugs. For example, heredity influences some aspects of substance use problems, especially those appearing by early adulthood (Crabbe, 2002):

- Having an identical rather than fraternal twin with alcohol use disorder puts one at increased risk for alcohol problems. In marijuana use, too, identical twins more closely resemble each other than do fraternal twins (Kendler et al., 2002).

- Boys who at age 6 are excitable, impulsive, and fearless (genetically influenced traits) are more likely as teens to smoke, drink, and use other drugs (Masse & Tremblay, 1997).

- Researchers have identified genes that are more common among people and animals predisposed to alcohol use disorder, and they are seeking genes that contribute to tobacco addiction (Stacey et al., 2012). These culprit genes seemingly produce deficiencies in the brain's natural dopamine reward system: While triggering temporary dopamine-produced pleasure, the addictive drugs disrupt normal dopamine balance. Studies of how drugs reprogram the brain's reward systems raise hopes for anti-addiction drugs that might block or blunt the effects of alcohol and other drugs (Miller, 2008; Wilson & Kuhn, 2005).

- Biological influences on drug use extend to other drugs as well. One study tracked 18,115 Swedish adoptees. Those with drug-abusing biological parents

Warning signs of alcohol use disorder

- Drinking binges
- Craving alcohol
- Use results in unfulfilled work, school, or home tasks
- Failing to honor a resolve to drink less
- Continued use despite health risk
- Avoiding family or friends when drinking

were at doubled risk of drug abuse, indicating a genetic influence. But then those with drug-abusing adoptive siblings also had a doubled risk of drug abuse, indicating an environmental influence (Kendler et al., 2012). So, what might those environmental influences be?

Psychological and Social-Cultural Influences

Throughout this text, we see that biological, psychological, and social-cultural factors interact to produce behavior. So, too, with disordered drug use (**FIGURE 9.7**). One psychological factor that has appeared in studies of youth and young adults is the feeling that life is meaningless and directionless (Newcomb & Harlow, 1986). This feeling is common among school dropouts who subsist without job skills, without privilege, and with little hope.

Sometimes the psychological influence is obvious. Many heavy users of alcohol, marijuana, and cocaine have experienced significant stress or failure and are depressed. Girls with a history of depression, eating disorders, or sexual or physical abuse are at increased risk for substance addiction. So are youth undergoing school or neighborhood transitions (CASA, 2003; Logan et al., 2002). Collegians who have not yet achieved a clear identity are also at greater risk (Bishop et al., 2005). By temporarily dulling the pain of self-awareness, psychoactive drugs may offer a way to avoid coping with depression, anger, anxiety, or insomnia. The relief may be temporary, but behavior is often controlled more by its immediate consequences than by its later ones.

Smoking usually begins during early adolescence. (If you are in college or university, and the cigarette manufacturers haven't yet made you their devoted customer, they almost surely never will.) Adolescents, self-conscious and often thinking the world is watching their every move, are vulnerable to smoking's allure. They may first light up to imitate glamorous celebrities, to project a mature image, to handle stress, or to get the social reward of acceptance by other smokers (Cin et al., 2007; DeWall & Pond, 2011; Tickle et al., 2006). Mindful of these tendencies, cigarette companies have effectively modeled smoking with themes that appeal to youths: attractiveness, independence, adventure-seeking, social approval (Surgeon General, 2012). Typically, teens who start smoking also have friends who smoke, who suggest its pleasures and offer them cigarettes (Rose et al., 1999). Among teens whose parents and best friends are nonsmokers, the smoking rate is close to zero (Moss et al., 1992; also see **FIGURE 9.8**).

Rates of drug use also vary across cultural and ethnic groups. One survey of 100,000 teens in 35 European countries found that marijuana use in the prior 30 days ranged from zero to 1 percent in Romania and Sweden to 20 to 22 percent in Britain, Switzerland, and France (ESPAD, 2003). Independent U.S. government studies of drug use in households and among high schoolers nationwide reveal that African-American teens have sharply lower rates of drinking, smoking, and cocaine use (Johnston et al., 2007). Alcohol and other drug addiction rates have also been low among actively religious people, with extremely low rates among Orthodox Jews, Mormons, Mennonites, and the Amish (Salas-Wright et al., 2012; Vaughn et al., 2011; Yeung et al., 2009).

Whether in cities or rural areas, peers influence attitudes about drugs. They also throw the parties and provide (or don't provide) the drugs. If an adolescent's friends use drugs, the odds are that he or she will, too. If the friends do not, the opportunity may not even arise. Teens who come from happy families, who do not begin drinking before age 15, and who do well in school tend not to use drugs, largely because they rarely associate with those who do (Bachman et al., 2007; Hingson et al., 2006; Odgers et al., 2008).

Peer influence is more than what friends do or say. Adolescents' expectations—what they *believe* friends are doing and favoring—influence their behavior

Biological influences:
• genetic predispositions
• variations in neurotransmitter systems

Psychological influences:
• lacking sense of purpose
• significant stress
• psychological disorders, such as depression

Disordered drug use

Social-cultural influences:
• difficult environment
• cultural acceptance of drug use
• negative peer influences

∧ FIGURE 9.7

Levels of analysis for disordered drug use The biopsychosocial approach enables researchers to investigate disordered drug use from complementary perspectives.

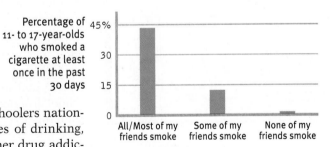

Percentage of 11- to 17-year-olds who smoked a cigarette at least once in the past 30 days

∧ FIGURE 9.8

Peer influence Kids don't smoke if their friends don't (Philip Morris, 2003). A correlation-causation question: Does the close link between teen smoking and friends' smoking reflect peer influence? Teens seeking similar friends? Or both?

Nic-A-Teen Virtually nobody starts smoking past the vulnerable teen years. Eager to hook customers whose addiction will give them business for years to come, cigarette companies target teens. Portrayals of smoking by popular actors, such as Emma Stone in *Gangster Squad*, entice teens to imitate.

Once upon a time, peer pressure caused Bob to start smoking.

RESTAURANT

Twenty years later, it forces him to quit.

▼ TABLE 9.3

Facts About "Higher" Education

- College and university students drink more alcohol than their nonstudent peers and exhibit 2.5 times the general population's rate of substance abuse.

- Fraternity and sorority members report nearly twice the binge-drinking rate of nonmembers.

- Since 1993, campus smoking rates have declined, alcohol use has been steady, and abuse of prescription opioids, stimulants, tranquilizers, and sedatives has increased, as has marijuana use.

Source: NCASA, 2007.

(Vitória et al., 2009). One study surveyed sixth graders in 22 U.S. states. How many believed their friends had smoked marijuana? About 14 percent. How many of those friends acknowledged doing so? Only 4 percent (Wren, 1999). University students are not immune to such misperceptions: Drinking dominates social occasions partly because students overestimate their peers' enthusiasm for alcohol and underestimate their views of its risks (Prentice & Miller, 1993; Self, 1994) (**TABLE 9.3**). When students' overestimates of peer drinking are corrected, alcohol use often subsides (Moreira et al., 2009).

People whose beginning use of drugs was influenced by their peers are more likely to stop using when friends stop or their social network changes (Kandel & Raveis, 1989). One study that followed 12,000 adults over 32 years found that smokers tend to quit in clusters (Christakis & Fowler, 2008). Within a social network, the odds of a person quitting increased when a spouse, friend, or co-worker stopped smoking. Similarly, most soldiers who became drug addicted while in Vietnam ceased their drug use after returning home (Robins et al., 1974).

As always with correlations, the traffic between friends' drug use and our own may be two-way: Our friends influence us. Social networks matter. But we also select as friends those who share our likes and dislikes.

What do the findings on drug use suggest for drug prevention and treatment programs? Three channels of influence seem possible:

- Educate young people about the long-term costs of a drug's temporary pleasures.

- Help young people find other ways to boost their self-esteem and discover their purpose in life.

- Attempt to modify peer associations or to "inoculate" youths against peer pressures by training them in refusal skills.

People rarely abuse drugs if they understand the physical and psychological costs, feel good about themselves and the direction their lives are taking, and are in a peer group that disapproves of using drugs. These educational, psychological, and social-cultural factors may help explain why 26 percent of U.S. high school dropouts, but only 6 percent of those with a postgraduate education, report smoking (CDC, 2011).

RETRIEVE IT

- Why do tobacco companies try so hard to get customers hooked as teens?

ANSWER: Nicotine is powerfully addictive, and those who start paving the neural pathways when young may find it very hard to stop using nicotine. As a result, tobacco companies may have lifelong customers. Moreover, evidence suggests that if cigarette manufacturers haven't hooked customers by early adulthood, they most likely won't.

- Studies have found that people who begin drinking in their early teens are much more likely to develop alcohol use disorder than those who begin at age 21 or after. What possible explanations might there be for this correlation?

ANSWER: Possible explanations include (a) a biological predisposition to both early use and later abuse; (b) brain changes triggered by early use; and (c) enduring habits, attitudes, activities, or peer relationships that foster alcohol misuse.

MODULE 9 REVIEW Drugs and Consciousness

Learning Objectives

Test Yourself by taking a moment to answer each of these Learning Objective Questions (repeated here from within the module). Then turn to Appendix D, Complete Module Reviews, to check your answers. Research suggests that trying to answer these questions on your own will improve your long-term memory of the concepts (McDaniel et al., 2009).

9-1 What are substance use disorders, and what roles do tolerance, withdrawal, and addiction play in these disorders?

9-2 How has the concept of addiction changed?

9-3 What are depressants, and what are their effects?

9-4 What are stimulants, and what are their effects?

9-5 What are hallucinogens, and what are their effects?

9-6 Why do some people become regular users of consciousness-altering drugs?

Terms and Concepts to Remember

Test yourself on these terms by trying to write down the definition in your own words before flipping back to the referenced page to check your answers.

psychoactive drug, p. 104
substance use disorder, p. 104
tolerance, p. 105
addiction, p. 105

withdrawal, p. 105
depressants, p. 106
alcohol use disorder, p. 106
barbiturates, p. 107
opiates, p. 107
stimulants, p. 108
amphetamines, p. 108
nicotine, p. 108

cocaine, p. 110
methamphetamine, p. 111
Ecstasy (MDMA), p. 111
hallucinogens, p. 111
near-death experience, p. 112
LSD, p. 112
THC, p. 112

Experience the Testing Effect

Test yourself repeatedly throughout your studies. This will not only help you figure out what you know and don't know; the testing itself will help you learn and remember the information more effectively thanks to the *testing effect*.

1. After continued use of a psychoactive drug, the drug user needs to take larger doses to get the desired effect. This is referred to as _____.

2. The depressants include alcohol, barbiturates,
   a. and opiates.
   b. cocaine, and morphine.
   c. caffeine, nicotine, and marijuana.
   d. and amphetamines.

3. Why might alcohol make a person more helpful *or* more aggressive?

4. Long-term use of Ecstasy can
   a. depress sympathetic nervous system activity.
   b. deplete the brain's supply of epinephrine.
   c. deplete the brain's supply of dopamine.
   d. damage serotonin-producing neurons.

5. Near-death experiences are strikingly similar to the experiences evoked by _____ drugs.

6. Use of marijuana
   a. impairs motor coordination, perception, reaction time, and memory.
   b. inhibits people's emotions.
   c. leads to dehydration and overheating.
   d. stimulates brain cell development.

7. An important psychological contributor to drug use is
   a. inflated self-esteem.
   b. the feeling that life is meaningless and directionless.
   c. genetic predispositions.
   d. overprotective parents.

Find answers to these questions in Appendix E, in the back of the book.

Use **LearningCurve** to create your personalized study plan, which will direct you to the resources that will help you most in **LaunchPad**.

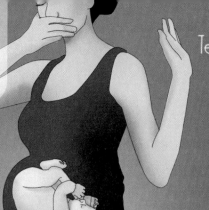

MODULE
10 Developmental Issues, Prenatal Development, and the Newborn

Prenatal development

Teratogen

MODULE
11 Infancy and Childhood

MODULE
12 Adolescence

Physical Development

- Experience affects *brain development.*
- Predictable *motor development* sequence

Puberty; teenage brain not fully developed

Cognitive Development

Piaget's stages and Vygotsky's *scaffolding*

Developing reasoning power

Social Development

Attachment,
effects of *parenting styles,*
and cultural differences

Erikson's stage of *identity vs. role confusion;*
changing parent/peer relationships

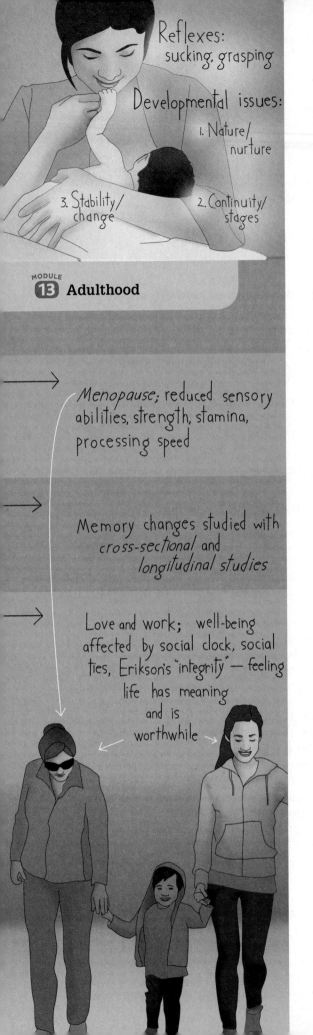

Reflexes:
sucking, grasping

Developmental issues:

1. Nature/nurture

3. Stability/change

2. Continuity/stages

Menopause; reduced sensory abilities, strength, stamina, processing speed

Memory changes studied with *cross-sectional* and *longitudinal studies*

Love and work; well-being affected by social clock, social ties, Erikson's "integrity" — feeling life has meaning and is worthwhile

Developing Through the Life Span

LIFE is a journey, from womb to tomb. So it is for me [DM], and so it will be for you. My story, and yours, began when a man and a woman together contributed 20,000+ genes to an egg that became a unique person. Those genes coded the protein building blocks that, with astonishing precision, formed our bodies and predisposed our traits. My grandmother handed down to my mother a rare hearing-loss pattern, which she, in turn, gave to me (the least of her gifts). My father was an amiable extravert, and sometimes I forget to stop talking. As a child, my talking was impeded by painful stuttering, for which Seattle Public Schools provided speech therapy.

Along with my parents' nature, I also received their nurture. Like you, I was born into a particular family and culture, with its own way of viewing the world. My values have been shaped by a family culture filled with talking and laughter, by a religious culture that speaks of love and justice, and by an academic culture that encourages critical thinking (asking, *What do you mean? How do you know?*).

We are formed by our genes, and by our contexts, so our stories will differ. But in many ways we are each like nearly everyone else on Earth. Being human, you and I have a need to belong. My mental video library, which began after age 4, is filled with scenes of social attachment. Over time, my attachments to parents loosened as peer friendships grew. After lacking confidence to date in high school, I fell in love with a college classmate and married at age 20. Natural selection predisposes us to survive and perpetuate our genes. Sure enough, two years later a child entered our lives and I experienced a new form of love that surprised me with its intensity.

But life is marked by change. That child and his brother now live 2000 miles away, and their sister has found her calling in South Africa. The tight rubber bands linking parent and child have loosened, as yours likely have as well.

Change also marks most vocational lives, which for me transitioned from a teen working in the family insurance agency, to a premed chemistry major and hospital aide, to (after discarding my half-completed medical school applications) a psychology professor and author. I predict that in 10 years you, too, will be doing things you do not currently anticipate.

Stability also marks our development. When I look in the mirror I do not see the person I once was, but I feel like the person I have always been. I am the same person who, as a late teen, played basketball and discovered love. A half-century later, I still play basketball and still love (with less passion but more security) the life partner with whom I have shared life's griefs and joys.

We experience a continuous self, but that self morphs through stages—growing up, raising children, enjoying a career, and, eventually, life's final stage, which will demand my presence. As I wend my way through this cycle of life and death, I am mindful that life's journey is a continuing process of development, seeded by nature and shaped by nurture, animated by love and focused by work, begun with wide-eyed curiosity and completed, for those blessed to live to a good old age, with peace and never-ending hope.

Across the life span, we grow from newborn to toddler, from toddler to teenager, and from teen to mature adult. At each stage of life there are physical, cognitive, and social milestones. We begin with prenatal development and the newborn (Module 10). Then we'll turn our attention to infancy and childhood (Module 11), adolescence (Module 12), and adulthood (Module 13). ■

developmental psychology a branch of psychology that studies physical, cognitive, and social change throughout the life span.

MODULE
❿ Developmental Issues, Prenatal Development, and the Newborn

Developmental Psychology's Major Issues

◀◆▶ **10-1** What three issues have engaged developmental psychologists?

Researchers find human development interesting for the same reasons most of the rest of us do—they are eager to understand more about how we've become our current selves, and how we may change in the years ahead. **Developmental psychology** examines our physical, cognitive, and social development across the life span, with a focus on three major issues:

1. *Nature and nurture:* How does our genetic inheritance (our *nature*) interact with our experiences (our *nurture*) to influence our development? How have your nature and your nurture influenced *your* life story?

2. *Continuity and stages:* What parts of development are gradual and continuous, like riding an escalator? What parts change abruptly in separate stages, like climbing rungs on a ladder?

3. *Stability and change:* Which of our traits persist through life? How do we change as we age?

"Nature is all that a man brings with him into the world; nurture is every influence that affects him after his birth."

Francis Galton,
English Men of Science, 1874

Nature and Nurture

The unique gene combination created when our mother's egg engulfed our father's sperm helped form us, as individuals. Genes predispose both our shared humanity and our individual differences.

But our experiences also shape us. Our families and peer relationships teach us how to think and act. Even differences initiated by our nature may be amplified by our nurture. We are not formed by either nature or nurture, but by the interaction between them. Biological, psychological, and social-cultural forces interact.

Mindful of how others differ from us, however, we often fail to notice the similarities stemming from our shared biology. Regardless of our culture, we humans share the same life cycle. We speak to our infants in similar ways and respond similarly to their coos and cries (Bornstein et al., 1992a,b). All over the world, the children of warm and supportive parents feel better about themselves and are less hostile than are the children of punishing and rejecting parents (Rohner, 1986; Scott et al., 1991). Although ethnic groups have differed in some ways, including average school achievement, the differences are "no more than skin deep." To the extent that family structure, peer influences, and parental education predict behavior in one of these ethnic groups, they do so for the others as well. Compared with the person-to-person differences within groups, between-group differences are small.

Continuity and Stages

Do adults differ from infants as a giant redwood differs from its seedling—a difference created by gradual, cumulative growth? Or do they differ as a butterfly differs from a caterpillar—a difference of distinct stages?

Researchers who emphasize experience and learning typically see development as a slow, continuous shaping process. Those who emphasize biological maturation tend to see development as a sequence of genetically predisposed stages or

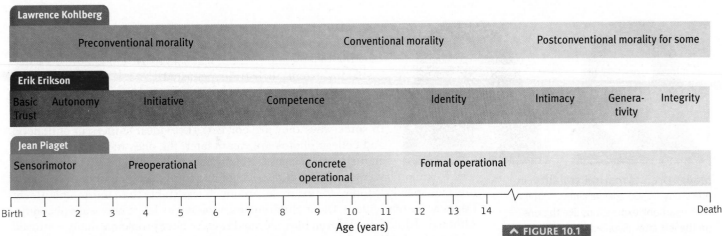

Lawrence Kohlberg															
Preconventional morality					Conventional morality							Postconventional morality for some			

Erik Erikson															
Basic Trust	Autonomy	Initiative			Competence				Identity			Intimacy		Genera-tivity	Integrity

Jean Piaget															
Sensorimotor		Preoperational				Concrete operational			Formal operational						

Birth 1   2   3   4   5   6   7   8   9   10   11   12   13   14   Death

Age (years)

△ FIGURE 10.1

Comparing the stage theories (With thanks to Dr. Sandra Gibbs, Muskegon Community College, for inspiring this illustration.)

steps: Although progress through the various stages may be quick or slow, everyone passes through the stages in the same order.

Are there clear-cut stages of psychological development, as there are physical stages such as walking before running? The stage theories we will consider—of Jean Piaget on cognitive development, Lawrence Kohlberg on moral development, and Erik Erikson on psychosocial development—propose developmental stages (summarized in **FIGURE 10.1**). But as we will also see, some research casts doubt on the idea that life proceeds through neatly defined age-linked stages. Young children have some abilities Piaget attributed to later stages. Kohlberg's work reflected an individualist worldview and emphasized thinking over acting. And adult life does not progress through a fixed, predictable series of steps. Chance events can influence us in ways we would never have predicted.

Although many modern developmental psychologists do not identify as stage theorists, the stage concept remains useful. The human brain does experience growth spurts during childhood and puberty that correspond roughly to Piaget's stages (Thatcher et al., 1987). And stage theories contribute a developmental perspective on the whole life span, by suggesting how people of one age think and act differently when they arrive at a later age.

Stability and Change

As we follow lives through time, do we find more evidence for stability or change? If reunited with a long-lost grade-school friend, do we instantly realize that "it's the same old Andy"? Or do people we befriend during one period of life seem like strangers at a later period? (At least one acquaintance of mine [DM's] would choose the second option. He failed to recognize a former classmate at his 40-year college reunion. The aghast classmate was his long-ago first wife.)

Research reveals that we experience both stability and change. Some of our characteristics, such as *temperament,* are very stable:

- One research team that studied 1000 people from ages 3 to 38 was struck by the consistency of temperament and emotionality across time (Moffitt et al., 2013; Slutske et al., 2012). Out-of-control 3-year-olds were the most likely to become teen smokers or adult criminals or out-of-control gamblers.

- Other studies have found that hyperactive, inattentive 5-year-olds required more teacher effort at age 12 (Houts et al., 2010); that 6-year-old Canadian boys with conduct problems were four times more likely than other boys to be convicted of a violent crime by age 24 (Hodgins et al., 2013); and that extraversion among British 16-year-olds predicted their future happiness as 60-year-olds (Gale et al., 2013).

Stages of the life cycle

"At 70, I would say the advantage is that you take life more calmly. You know that 'this, too, shall pass'!"

Eleanor Roosevelt, 1954

Smiles predict marital stability In one study of 306 college alums, 1 in 4 with yearbook expressions like the one on the left later divorced, as did only 1 in 20 with smiles like the one on the right (Hertenstein et al., 2009).

As adults grow older, there is continuity of self.

- Another research team interviewed adults who, 40 years earlier, had their talkativeness, impulsiveness, and humility rated by their elementary school teachers (Nave et al., 2010). To a striking extent, their traits persisted.

"As at 7, so at 70," says a Jewish proverb. People predict that they will not change much in the future (Quoidbach et al., 2013). In some ways they are correct. The widest smilers in childhood and college photos are, years later, the ones most likely to enjoy enduring marriages (Hertenstein et al., 2009).

We cannot, however, predict all aspects of our future selves based on our early life. Our social attitudes, for example, are much less stable than our temperament (Moss & Susman, 1980). Older children and adolescents learn new ways of coping. Although delinquent children have elevated rates of later problems, many confused and troubled children blossom into mature, successful adults (Moffitt et al., 2002; Roberts et al., 2013; Thomas & Chess, 1986). The struggles of the present may be laying a foundation for a happier tomorrow. Life is a process of becoming.

In some ways, we *all* change with age. Most shy, fearful toddlers begin opening up by age 4, and most people become more conscientious, stable, agreeable, and self-confident in the years after adolescence (Lucas & Donnellan, 2009; Roberts & Mroczek, 2008; Shaw et al., 2010). Many irresponsible 18-year-olds have matured into 40-year-old business or cultural leaders. (If you are the former, you aren't done yet.) Openness, self-esteem, and agreeableness often peak in midlife (Lucas & Donnellan, 2011; Orth et al., 2012, 2015; Specht et al., 2011). Such changes can occur without changing a person's position *relative to others* of the same age. The hard-driving young adult may mellow by later life, yet still be a relatively driven senior citizen.

Life requires *both* stability and change. Stability provides our identity. It enables us to depend on others and be concerned about children's healthy development. Our potential for change gives us our hope for a brighter future. It motivates our concerns about present influences and lets us adapt and grow with experience.

RETRIEVE IT [✱]

- Developmental researchers who consider how biological, psychological, and social-cultural forces interact are focusing on _____ and _____.

  ANSWERS: nature; nurture

- Developmental researchers who emphasize learning and experience are supporting _____; those who emphasize biological maturation are supporting _____.

  ANSWERS: continuity; stages

- What findings in psychology support (1) the stage theory of development and (2) the idea of stability in personality across the life span? What findings challenge these ideas?

  ANSWER: (1) Stage theory is supported by the work of Piaget (cognitive development), Kohlberg (moral development), and Erikson (psychosocial development), but it is challenged by findings that change is more gradual and less culturally universal than these theorists supposed. (2) Some traits, such as temperament, do exhibit remarkable stability across many years. But we do change in other ways, such as in our social attitudes.

Prenatal Development and the Newborn

◆◆ 10-2 What is the course of prenatal development, and how do teratogens affect that development?

Conception

Nothing is more natural than a species reproducing itself. And nothing is more wondrous. For you, the process started inside your *grandmother*—as an egg formed inside a developing female inside of her. (Your mother was born with all

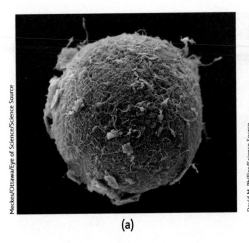

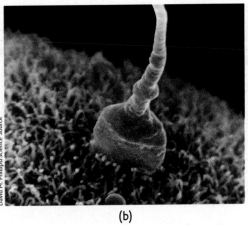

(a)   (b)

◀ FIGURE 10.2

Life is sexually transmitted
(a) Sperm cells surround an egg. (b) As one sperm penetrates the egg's jellylike outer coating, a series of chemical events begins that will cause sperm and egg to fuse into a single cell. If all goes well, that cell will subdivide again and again to emerge 9 months later as a 100-trillion-cell human being.

the immature eggs she would ever have.) Your father, in contrast, began producing sperm cells nonstop at *puberty*—in the beginning at a rate of more than 1000 sperm during the second it takes to read this phrase.

Some time after puberty, your mother's ovary released a mature egg—a cell roughly the size of the period at the end of this sentence. Like space voyagers approaching a huge planet, some 250 million deposited sperm began their race upstream, approaching a cell 85,000 times their own size. Those reaching the egg released digestive enzymes that ate away its protective coating (**FIGURE 10.2a**). As soon as one sperm penetrated the coating and was welcomed in (Figure 10.2b), the egg's surface blocked out the others. Before half a day elapsed, the egg nucleus and the sperm nucleus fused: The two became one.

Consider it your most fortunate of moments. Among 250 million sperm, the one needed to make you, in combination with that one particular egg, won the race. And so it was for innumerable generations before us. If any one of our ancestors had been conceived with a different sperm or egg, or died before conceiving, or not chanced to meet their partner or. . . . The mind boggles at the improbable, unbroken chain of events that produced us.

Prenatal Development

How many fertilized eggs, called **zygotes,** survive beyond the first 2 weeks? Fewer than half (Grobstein, 1979; Hall, 2004). But for us, good fortune prevailed. One cell became 2, then 4—each just like the first—until this cell division had produced some 100 identical cells within the first week. Then the cells began to differentiate—to specialize in structure and function. ("I'll become a brain, you become intestines!")

About 10 days after conception, the zygote attaches to the mother's uterine wall, beginning approximately 37 weeks of the closest human relationship. The zygote's inner cells become the **embryo** (**FIGURE 10.3a** on the next page). Many of its outer cells become the *placenta*, the life-link that transfers nutrients and oxygen from mother to embryo. Over the next 6 weeks, the embryo's organs begin to form and function. The heart begins to beat.

By 9 weeks after conception, an embryo looks unmistakably human (Figure 10.3b). It is now a **fetus** (Latin for "offspring" or "young one"). During the sixth month, organs such as the stomach have developed enough to give the fetus a good chance of survival if born prematurely.

At each prenatal stage, genetic and environmental factors affect our development. By the sixth month, microphone readings taken inside the uterus reveal that the fetus is responsive to sound and is exposed to the sound of its mother's muffled voice (Ecklund-Flores, 1992; Hepper, 2005). Immediately after emerging from their underwater world, newborns prefer their mother's voice to another woman's, or to their father's (Busnel et al., 1992; DeCasper et al., 1984, 1986, 1994).

Care to guess your body's total number of cells?

ANSWER: By one careful estimate, the average human has 37.2 trillion cells (Bianconi et al., 2013).

zygote the fertilized egg; it enters a 2-week period of rapid cell division and develops into an embryo.

embryo the developing human organism from about 2 weeks after fertilization through the second month.

fetus the developing human organism from 9 weeks after conception to birth.

> FIGURE 10.3

Prenatal development (a) The embryo grows and develops rapidly. At 40 days, the spine is visible and the arms and legs are beginning to grow. (b) By the end of the second month, when the fetal period begins, facial features, hands, and feet have formed. (c) As the fetus enters the fourth month, its 3 ounces could fit in the palm of your hand.

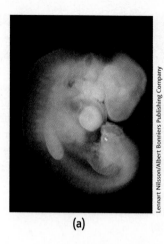

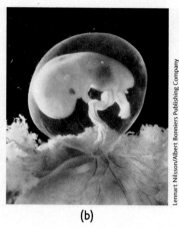

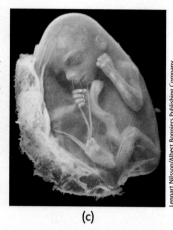

(a)   (b)   (c)

Prenatal development
Zygote: Conception to 2 weeks
Embryo: 2 to 9 weeks
Fetus: 9 weeks to birth

"You shall conceive and bear a son. So then drink no wine or strong drink."

Judges 13:7

teratogens (literally, "monster maker") agents, such as chemicals and viruses, that can reach the embryo or fetus during prenatal development and cause harm.

fetal alcohol syndrome (FAS) physical and cognitive abnormalities in children caused by a pregnant woman's heavy drinking. In severe cases, signs include a small, out-of-proportion head and abnormal facial features.

habituation decreasing responsiveness with repeated stimulation. As infants gain familiarity with repeated exposure to a stimulus, their interest wanes and they look away sooner.

They also prefer hearing their mother's language. At about 30 hours old, American and Swedish newborns pause more in their pacifier sucking when listening to familiar vowels from their mother's language (Moon et al., 2013). After repeatedly hearing a fake word *(tatata)* in the womb, Finnish newborns' brain waves display recognition when hearing the word after birth (Partanen et al., 2014). If their mother spoke two languages during pregnancy, they display interest in both (Byers-Heinlein et al., 2010). And just after birth, babies born to French-speaking mothers tend to cry with the rising intonation of French; babies born to German-speaking mothers cry with the falling tones of German (Mampe et al., 2009). Would you have guessed? The learning of language begins in the womb.

In the two months before birth, fetuses demonstrate learning in other ways, as when they adapt to a vibrating, honking device placed on their mother's abdomen (Dirix et al., 2009). Like people who adapt to the sound of trains in their neighborhood, fetuses get used to the honking. Moreover, four weeks later, they recall the sound (as evidenced by their blasé response, compared with the reactions of those not previously exposed).

Sounds are not the only stimuli fetuses are exposed to in the womb. In addition to transferring nutrients and oxygen from mother to fetus, the placenta screens out many harmful substances. But some slip by. **Teratogens,** agents such as viruses and drugs, can damage an embryo or fetus. This is one reason pregnant women are advised not to drink alcoholic beverages or smoke cigarettes. A pregnant woman never drinks or smokes alone. When alcohol enters her bloodstream and that of her fetus, it reduces activity in both their central nervous systems. Alcohol use during pregnancy may prime the woman's offspring to like alcohol and may put them at risk for heavy drinking and alcohol use disorder during their teen years. In experiments, when pregnant rats drank alcohol, their young offspring later displayed a liking for alcohol's taste and odor (Youngentob et al., 2007, 2009).

Even light drinking or occasional binge drinking can affect the fetal brain (Braun, 1996; Ikonomidou et al., 2000; Marjonen et al., 2015; Sayal et al., 2009). Persistent heavy drinking puts the fetus at risk for a dangerously low birth weight, birth defects, and for future behavior problems, hyperactivity, and lower intelligence. For 1 in about 700 children, the effects are visible as **fetal alcohol syndrome (FAS),** marked by lifelong physical and mental abnormalities (May et al., 2014). The fetal damage may occur because alcohol has an *epigenetic effect:* It leaves chemical marks on DNA that switch genes abnormally on or off (Liu et al., 2009). Smoking during pregnancy also leaves epigenetic scars that weaken infants' ability to handle stress (Stroud et al., 2014).

moodboard/JupiterImages

If a pregnant woman experiences extreme stress, the stress hormones flooding her body may indicate a survival threat to the fetus and produce an earlier delivery (Glynn & Sandman, 2011). Some stress in early life prepares us to cope with later adversity in life. But substantial prenatal stress exposure puts a child at increased risk for health problems such as hypertension, heart disease, obesity, and psychiatric disorders.

LaunchPad For an interactive review of prenatal development, see LaunchPad's *PsychSim 6: Conception to Birth*. LaunchPad also offers the 8-minute *Video: Prenatal Development*.

RETRIEVE IT [✘]

• The first two weeks of prenatal development is the period of the _____. The period of the _____ lasts from 9 weeks after conception until birth. The time between those two prenatal periods is considered the period of the _____.

ANSWERS: zygote; fetus; embryo

The Competent Newborn

10-3 What are some newborn abilities, and how do researchers explore infants' mental abilities?

Babies come with software preloaded on their neural hard drives. Having survived prenatal hazards, we as newborns came equipped with automatic reflex responses ideally suited for our survival. We withdrew our limbs to escape pain. If a cloth over our face interfered with our breathing, we turned our head from side to side and swiped at it.

New parents are often in awe of the coordinated sequence of reflexes by which their baby gets food. When something touches their cheek, babies turn toward that touch, open their mouth, and vigorously *root* for a nipple. Finding one, they automatically close on it and begin *sucking*—which itself requires a coordinated sequence of reflexive *tonguing, swallowing,* and *breathing.* Failing to find satisfaction, the hungry baby may *cry*—a behavior parents find highly unpleasant and very rewarding to relieve.

The pioneering American psychologist William James presumed that newborns experience a "blooming, buzzing confusion," an assumption few people challenged until the 1960s. Then scientists discovered that babies can tell you a lot—if you know how to ask. To ask, you must capitalize on what babies can do—gaze, suck, turn their heads. So, equipped with eye-tracking machines and pacifiers wired to electronic gear, researchers set out to answer parents' age-old questions: What can my baby see, hear, smell, and think?

Consider how researchers exploit **habituation**—decreased responding with repeated stimulation. We saw this earlier when fetuses adapted to a vibrating, honking device placed on their mother's abdomen. The novel stimulus gets attention when first presented. With repetition, the response weakens. This seeming boredom with familiar stimuli gives us a way to ask infants what they see and remember.

Even as newborns, we prefer sights and sounds that facilitate social responsiveness. We turn our heads in the direction of human voices. We gaze longer at a drawing of a face-like image (**FIGURE 10.4**). We prefer to look at objects 8 to 12 inches away, which—wonder of wonders—just happens to be the approximate distance between a nursing infant's eyes and its mother's (Maurer & Maurer, 1988). Our brain's default settings help us connect socially.

Within days after birth, our brain's neural networks were stamped with the smell of our mother's body. Week-old nursing babies, placed between a gauze pad from their mother's bra and one from another nursing mother, have usually turned toward the smell of their own mother's pad (MacFarlane, 1978). What's more, that smell preference lasts. One experiment capitalized on the fact that some nursing mothers in a French maternity ward used a chamomile-scented balm to prevent nipple soreness

"I felt like a man trapped in a woman's body. Then I was born."

Comedian Chris Bliss

⌄ FIGURE 10.4

Newborns' preference for faces When shown these two stimuli with the same elements, Italian newborns spent nearly twice as many seconds looking at the face-like image (Johnson & Morton, 1991). Canadian newborns—average age 53 minutes in one study—displayed the same apparently inborn preference to look toward faces (Mondloch et al., 1999).

(Delaunay-El Allam, 2010). Twenty-one months later, their toddlers preferred playing with chamomile-scented toys! Their peers who had not sniffed the scent while breast feeding showed no such preference. (Hmm. Will adults, who as babies associated chamomile scent with their mother's breast, become devoted chamomile tea drinkers?) Such studies reveal the remarkable abilities with which we enter our world.

Prepared to feed and eat Animals are predisposed to respond to their offsprings' cries for nourishment.

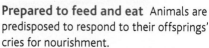

RETRIEVE IT [✗]

• Developmental psychologists use repeated stimulation to test an infant's _____ to a stimulus.

ANSWER: habituation

MODULE 10 REVIEW   Developmental Issues, Prenatal Development, and the Newborn

◉ Learning Objectives

Test Yourself by taking a moment to answer each of these Learning Objective Questions (repeated here from within the module). Then turn to Appendix D, Complete Module Reviews, to check your answers. Research suggests that trying to answer these questions on your own will improve your long-term memory of the concepts (McDaniel et al., 2009).

10-1 What three issues have engaged developmental psychologists?

10-2 What is the course of prenatal development, and how do teratogens affect that development?

10-3 What are some newborn abilities, and how do researchers explore infants' mental abilities?

▪▫ Terms and Concepts to Remember

Test yourself on these terms by trying to write down the definition in your own words before flipping back to the referenced page to check your answers.

developmental psychology, p. 120

zygote, p. 123

embryo, p. 123

fetus, p. 123

teratogens, p. 124

fetal alcohol syndrome (FAS), p. 124

habituation, p. 125

[✗] Experience the Testing Effect

Test yourself repeatedly throughout your studies. This will not only help you figure out what you know and don't know; the testing itself will help you learn and remember the information more effectively thanks to the *testing effect*.

1. The three major issues that interest developmental psychologists are nature/nurture, stability/change, and _____ / _____.

2. Although development is lifelong, there is stability of personality over time. For example,
   a. most personality traits emerge in infancy and persist throughout life.
   b. temperament tends to remain stable throughout life.
   c. few people change significantly after adolescence.
   d. people tend to undergo greater personality changes as they age.

3. From the very first weeks of life, infants differ in their characteristic emotional reactions, with some infants being intense and anxious, while others are easygoing and relaxed. These differences are usually explained as differences in _____.

4. Body organs first begin to form and function during the period of the _____; within 6 months, during the period of the _____, the organs are sufficiently functional to allow a good chance of survival.
   a. zygote; embryo
   b. zygote; fetus
   c. embryo; fetus
   d. placenta; fetus

5. Chemicals that pass through the placenta's screen and may harm an embryo or fetus are called _____.

Find answers to these questions in Appendix E, in the back of the book.

Use 🔁 LearningCurve to create your personalized study plan, which will direct you to the resources that will help you most in 🔁 LaunchPad.

⑪ Infancy and Childhood

As a flower unfolds in accord with its genetic instructions, so do we. **Maturation**—the orderly sequence of biological growth—decrees many of our commonalities. We stand before walking. We use nouns before adjectives. Severe deprivation or abuse can slow development, yet genetic growth patterns are inborn. Maturation (nature) sets the basic course of development; experience (nurture) adjusts it. Genes and scenes interact.

> **maturation** biological growth processes that enable orderly changes in behavior, relatively uninfluenced by experience.

> "It is a rare privilege to watch the birth, growth, and first feeble struggles of a living human mind."
>
> *Annie Sullivan, in Helen Keller's* The Story of My Life, *1903*

Physical Development

11-1 During infancy and childhood, how do the brain and motor skills develop?

Brain Development

Our formative nurture began at conception, with the prenatal environment in the womb. Nurture continued outside the womb, where our early experiences fostered brain development.

In your mother's womb, your developing brain formed nerve cells at the explosive rate of nearly one-quarter million per minute. On the day you were born, you had most of the brain cells you would ever have. However, the wiring among these cells—your nervous system—was immature: After birth, these neural networks had a wild growth spurt branching and linking in patterns that would eventually enable you to walk, talk, and remember (**FIGURE 11.1**). This rapid development helps explain why infant brain size increases rapidly in the early days after birth (Holland et al., 2014).

From ages 3 to 6, the most rapid brain growth was in your frontal lobes, which enable rational planning. During those years, your brain required vast amounts of energy (Kuzawa et al., 2014). This energy-intensive process caused rapid progress in your ability to control your attention and behavior (Garon et al., 2008; Thompson-Schill et al., 2009). Frontal lobe development continues into adolescence and beyond.

The last cortical areas to develop are the association areas—those linked with thinking, memory, and language. As they develop, mental abilities surge (Chugani & Phelps, 1986; Thatcher et al., 1987). The neural pathways supporting agility, language, and self-control proliferate into puberty. Under the influence of adrenal hormones, tens of billions of synapses form and organize, while a use-it-or-lose-it *pruning* process shuts down unused links (Paus et al., 1999; Thompson et al., 2000).

Your genes dictate your overall brain architecture, rather like the lines of a coloring book, but experience fills in the details (Kenrick et al., 2009). So how do early experiences leave their "fingerprints" in the brain? Mark Rosenzweig, David Krech, and their colleagues (1962) opened a window on that process when they raised some young rats in solitary confinement, and others in a communal playground that simulated a natural environment. When the researchers later analyzed the rats' brains, those living in the enriched environment had usually developed a heavier and thicker brain cortex (**FIGURE 11.2** on the next page). So great are the effects that, shown brief video clips, you could tell from the rats' activity and curiosity whether their environment had been impoverished or enriched (Renner & Renner, 1993). After 60 days in the enriched environment, the rats' brain weights increased 7 to 10 percent and the number of synapses mushroomed by about 20 percent (Kolb & Whishaw, 1998).

Such results have motivated improvements in environments for laboratory, farm, and zoo animals—and for children in institutions. Stimulation by touch or massage also benefits infant rats and premature babies (Field et al., 2007; Sarro

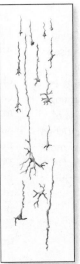  

Newborn   3 months   15 months

∧ FIGURE 11.1

Drawings of human cerebral cortex sections In humans, the brain is immature at birth. As the child matures, the neural networks grow increasingly more complex.

Courtesy of C. Brune

Stringing the circuits young String musicians who started playing before age 12 have larger and more complex neural circuits controlling the note-making left-hand fingers than do string musicians whose training started later (Elbert et al., 1995).

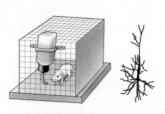 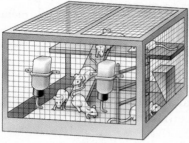 

Impoverished   Impoverished
environment   rat brain cell

Enriched
environment

Enriched
rat brain cell

^ FIGURE 11.2

Experience affects brain development Mark Rosenzweig, David Krech, and their colleagues (1962) raised rats either alone in an environment without playthings, or with other rats in an environment enriched with playthings changed daily. In 14 of 16 repetitions of this basic experiment, rats in the enriched environment developed significantly more cerebral cortex (relative to the rest of the brain's tissue) than did those in the impoverished environment.

"Genes and experiences are just two ways of doing the same thing—wiring synapses."

Joseph LeDoux,
The Synaptic Self, 2002

> FIGURE 11.3

A trained brain A well-learned finger-tapping task activates more motor cortex neurons (orange area, right) than were active in this monkey's brain before training (left). (From Karni et al., 1998.)

et al., 2014). "Handled" infants of both species develop faster neurologically and gain weight more rapidly. Preemies who have had skin-to-skin contact with their mothers sleep better, experience less stress, and show better cognitive development 10 years later (Feldman et al., 2014).

Nature and nurture interact to sculpt our synapses. Brain maturation provides us with an abundance of neural connections. Experiences—sights and smells, touches and tastes, music and movement—activate and strengthen some neural pathways while others weaken from disuse. Like forest pathways, popular tracks are broadened and less-traveled ones gradually disappear. The result by puberty is a massive loss of unemployed connections.

Here at the juncture of nurture and nature is the biological reality of early childhood learning. During early childhood—while excess connections are still on call—youngsters can most easily master such skills as the grammar and accent of another language. We seem to have a **critical period** for some skills. Lacking any exposure to spoken, written, or signed language before adolescence, a person will never master any language. Likewise, lacking visual experience during the early years, a person whose vision is restored by cataract removal will never achieve normal perceptions (Gregory, 1978; Wiesel, 1982). Without that early visual stimulation, the brain cells normally assigned to vision will die during the pruning process or be diverted to other uses. The maturing brain's rule: Use it or lose it.

Although normal stimulation during the early years is critical, the brain's development does not end with childhood. Thanks to the brain's amazing *plasticity*, our neural tissue is ever changing and reorganizing in response to new experiences. New neurons also are born. If a monkey pushes a lever with the same finger many times a day, brain tissue controlling that finger changes to reflect the experience (**FIGURE 11.3**). Human brains work similarly. Whether learning to keyboard, skateboard, or navigate London's streets, we perform with increasing skill as our brain incorporates the learning (Ambrose, 2010; Maguire et al., 2000).

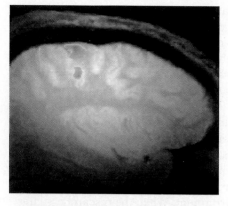 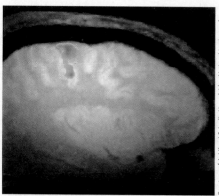

Courtesy of Avi Karni & Leslie Ungerleider, National Institute of Mental Health

Motor Development

The developing brain enables physical coordination. As an infant exercises its maturing muscles and nervous system, skills emerge. With occasional exceptions, the sequence of physical (motor) development is universal. Babies roll over before they sit unsupported, and they usually crawl on all fours before they walk. These behaviors reflect not imitation but a maturing nervous system; blind children, too, crawl before they walk.

In the United States, 25 percent of all babies walk by 11 months of age, 50 percent within a week after their first birthday, and 90 percent by age 15 months

critical period an optimal period early in the life of an organism when exposure to certain stimuli or experiences produces normal development.

(Frankenburg et al., 1992). In some regions of Africa, the Caribbean, and India, caregivers frequently massage and exercise babies, which can accelerate the process of learning to walk (Karasik et al., 2010). The recommended infant *back to sleep position* (putting babies to sleep on their backs to reduce the risk of a smothering crib death) has been associated with somewhat later crawling but not with later walking (Davis et al., 1998; Lipsitt, 2003).

Genes guide motor development. Identical twins typically begin walking on nearly the same day (Wilson, 1979). Maturation—including the rapid development of the cerebellum at the back of the brain—creates our readiness to learn walking at about age 1. The same is true for other physical skills, including bowel and bladder control. Before necessary muscular and neural maturation, neither pleading nor punishment will produce successful toilet training.

Physical development Sit, crawl, walk, run—the sequence of these motor development milestones is the same the world around, though babies reach them at varying ages.

Juice Images/JupiterImages

In the eight years following the 1994 launch of a U.S. Back to Sleep educational campaign, the number of infants sleeping on their stomach dropped from 70 to 11 percent—and sudden unexpected infant deaths fell significantly (Braiker, 2005).

RETRIEVE IT [✳]

- The biological growth process, called _____, explains why most children begin walking by about 12 to 15 months.

ANSWER: maturation

Brain Maturation and Infant Memory

Can you recall your first day of preschool or your third birthday party? Studies have confirmed that our average age of earliest conscious memory is 3.5 years (Bauer, 2002, 2007). But as children mature, by age 7 or so, *infantile amnesia* wanes, and they become increasingly capable of remembering experiences, even for a year or more (Bauer & Larkina, 2014; Morris et al., 2010). Mice and monkeys also forget their early life, as rapid neuron growth disrupts the circuits that stored old memories (Akers et al., 2014). The brain areas underlying memory, such as the hippocampus and frontal lobes, continue to mature into adolescence (Bauer, 2007).

Apart from constructed memories based on photos and family stories, we *consciously* recall little from our early years, yet our brain was processing and storing information. While finishing her doctoral work in psychology, Carolyn Rovee-Collier observed nonverbal infant memory in action. Her colicky 2-month-old, Benjamin, could be calmed by moving a crib mobile. Weary of hitting the mobile, she strung a cloth ribbon connecting the mobile to Benjamin's foot. Soon, he was kicking his foot to move the mobile. Thinking about her unintended home experiment, Rovee-Collier realized that, contrary to popular opinion in the 1960s, babies can learn. To know for sure that her son wasn't just a whiz kid, she repeated the experiment with other infants (Rovee-Collier, 1989, 1999). Sure enough, they, too, soon kicked more when hitched to a mobile, both on the day of the experiment and the day after. If, however, she hitched them to a different mobile the next day, the infants showed no learning, indicating that they remembered the original mobile and recognized the difference. Moreover, when tethered to the familiar mobile a month later, they remembered the association and again began kicking (**FIGURE 11.4**).

Traces of forgotten childhood languages may also persist. One study tested English-speaking British adults who had no conscious memory of the Hindi or Zulu they had spoken as children. Yet, up to age 40, they could relearn subtle sound contrasts in these languages that other people could *not* learn (Bowers et al., 2009). What the conscious mind does not know and cannot express in words, the nervous system and our two-track mind somehow remember.

"Someday we'll look back at this time in our lives and be unable to remember it."

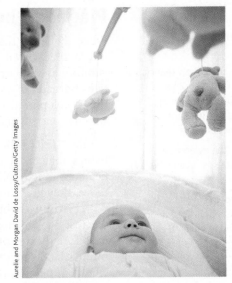

Aurelie and Morgan David de Lossy/Cultura/Getty Images

‹ FIGURE 11.4

Infant at work Babies only 3 months old can learn that kicking moves a mobile, and they can retain that learning for a month (Rovee-Collier, 1989, 1997).

Cognitive Development

11-2 From the perspectives of Piaget, Vygotsky, and today's researchers, how does a child's mind develop?

Somewhere on your life journey, you became conscious. When was that? Jean Piaget [pee-ah-ZHAY] was a pioneering developmental psychologist who spent his life searching for the answers to such questions. He studied children's **cognitive** development—all the mental activities associated with thinking, knowing, remembering, and communicating. His interest began in 1920, when he was in Paris developing questions for children's intelligence tests. While administering the tests, Piaget became intrigued by children's wrong answers, which were often strikingly similar among same-age children. Where others saw childish mistakes, Piaget saw intelligence at work. Such accidental discoveries are among the fruits of psychological science.

A half-century spent with children convinced Piaget that a child's mind is not a miniature model of an adult's. Thanks partly to his careful observations, we now understand that children reason *differently* than adults, in "wildly illogical ways about problems whose solutions are self-evident to adults" (Brainerd, 1996).

Piaget's studies led him to believe that a child's mind develops through a series of stages, in an upward march from the newborn's simple reflexes to the adult's abstract reasoning power. Thus, an 8-year-old can comprehend things a toddler cannot, such as the analogy that "getting an idea is like having a light turn on in your head," or that a miniature slide is too small for sliding, and a miniature car is much too small to get into.

Piaget's core idea was that our intellectual progression reflects an unceasing struggle to make sense of our experiences. To this end, the maturing brain builds **schemas,** concepts or mental molds into which we pour our experiences. By adulthood we have built countless schemas, ranging from *cats* and *dogs* to our concept of *love.*

To explain how we use and adjust our schemas, Piaget proposed two more concepts. First, we **assimilate** new experiences—we interpret them in terms of our current understandings (schemas). Having a simple schema for *dog,* for example, a toddler may call all four-legged animals *dogs.* But as we interact with the world, we also adjust, or **accommodate,** our schemas to incorporate information provided by new experiences. Thus, the child soon learns that the original *dog* schema is too broad and accommodates by refining the category. Many people whose schema of *marriage* was a union between a man and a woman have now accommodated same-sex marriage, with a broadened marriage concept.

Piaget's Theory and Current Thinking

Piaget believed that children construct their understanding of the world while interacting with it. Their minds experience spurts of change, followed by greater stability as they move from one cognitive plateau to the next, each with distinctive characteristics that permit specific kinds of thinking. In Piaget's view, cognitive development consisted of four major stages—*sensorimotor, preoperational, concrete operational,* and *formal operational.*

SENSORIMOTOR STAGE In the **sensorimotor stage,** from birth to nearly age 2, babies take in the world through their senses and actions—through looking, hearing, touching, mouthing, and grasping. As their hands and limbs begin to move, they learn to make things happen.

Very young babies seem to live in the present: Out of sight is out of mind. In one test, Piaget showed an infant an appealing toy and then flopped his beret over it. Before the age of 6 months, the infant acted as if the toy ceased to exist. Young infants lack **object permanence**—the awareness that objects continue to exist when not perceived. By 8 months, infants begin exhibiting memory for things no longer seen. If you hide a toy, the infant will momentarily look for it (**FIGURE 11.5**).

Jean Piaget (1896–1980) "If we examine the intellectual development of the individual or of the whole of humanity, we shall find that the human spirit goes through a certain number of stages, each different from the other" (1930).

cognition all the mental activities associated with thinking, knowing, remembering, and communicating.

schema a concept or framework that organizes and interprets information.

assimilation interpreting our new experiences in terms of our existing schemas.

accommodation adapting our current understandings (schemas) to incorporate new information.

sensorimotor stage in Piaget's theory, the stage (from birth to nearly 2 years of age) during which infants know the world mostly in terms of their sensory impressions and motor activities.

object permanence the awareness that things continue to exist even when not perceived.

preoperational stage in Piaget's theory, the stage (from about 2 to about 6 or 7 years of age) during which a child learns to use language but does not yet comprehend the mental operations of concrete logic.

▲ FIGURE 11.5

Object permanence Infants younger than 6 months seldom understand that things continue to exist when they are out of sight. But for this older infant, out of sight is definitely not out of mind.

Within another month or two, the infant will look for it even after being restrained for several seconds.

So does object permanence in fact blossom suddenly at 8 months, much as tulips blossom in spring? Today's researchers believe object permanence unfolds gradually, and they see development as more continuous than Piaget did. Even young infants will at least momentarily look for a toy where they saw it hidden a second before (Wang et al., 2004).

Researchers also believe Piaget and his followers underestimated young children's competence. Preschoolers think like little scientists. They test ideas, make causal inferences, and learn from statistical patterns (Gopnik et al., 2015). Consider these simple experiments:

- *Baby physics:* Like adults staring in disbelief at a magic trick (the *"Whoa!"* look), infants look longer at and explore an unexpected, impossible, or unfamiliar scene—a car seeming to pass through a solid object, a ball stopping in midair, or an object violating object permanence by magically disappearing (Baillargeon, 1995, 2008; Shuwairi & Johnson, 2013; Stahl & Feigenson, 2015).

- *Baby math:* Karen Wynn (1992, 2000, 2008) showed 5-month-olds one or two objects (**FIGURE 11.6a**). Then she hid the objects behind a screen, and visibly removed or added one (Figure 11.6d). When she lifted the screen, the infants sometimes did a double take, staring longer when shown a wrong number of objects (Figure 11.6f). But were they just responding to a greater or smaller *mass* of objects, rather than a change in *number* (Feigenson et al., 2002)? Later experiments showed that babies' number sense extends to larger numbers, to ratios, and to such things as drumbeats and motions (Libertus & Brannon, 2009; McCrink & Wynn, 2004; Spelke et al., 2013). If accustomed to a Daffy Duck puppet jumping three times on stage, they showed surprise if it jumped only twice.

Clearly, infants are smarter than Piaget appreciated. Even as babies, we had a lot on our minds.

▼ FIGURE 11.6

Baby math Shown a numerically impossible outcome, 5-month-old infants stare longer (Wynn, 1992).

Then either: possible outcome
(e) Screen drops revealing 1 object

or: impossible outcome
(f) Screen drops revealing 2 objects

(a) Objects placed in case (b) Screen comes up (c) Empty hand enters (d) One object removed

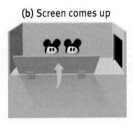 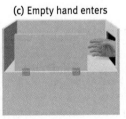 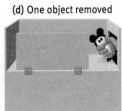

PREOPERATIONAL STAGE Piaget believed that until about age 6 or 7, children are in a **preoperational stage**—able to represent things with words and images but too young to perform *mental operations* (such as imagining an action and mentally reversing it). For a 5-year-old, the milk that seems "too much" in a tall,

^ FIGURE 11.7

Piaget's test of conservation This visually focused preoperational child does not yet understand the principle of conservation. When the milk is poured into a tall, narrow glass, it suddenly seems like "more" than when it was in the shorter, wider glass. In another year or so, she will understand that the amount stays the same.

LaunchPad For quick video examples of children being tested for conservation, visit LaunchPad's *Concept Practice: Piaget and Conservation.*

narrow glass may become an acceptable amount if poured into a short, wide glass. Focusing only on the height dimension, this child cannot perform the operation of mentally pouring the milk back. Before about age 6, said Piaget, children lack the concept of **conservation**—the principle that quantity remains the same despite changes in shape (**FIGURE 11.7**).

PRETEND PLAY A child who can perform mental operations can think in symbols and enjoy *pretend play.* Researchers have found that symbolic thinking appears at an earlier age than Piaget supposed. Judy DeLoache (1987) showed children a model of a room and hid a miniature stuffed dog behind its miniature couch. The 2½-year-olds easily remembered where to find the miniature toy, but they could not use the model to locate an actual stuffed dog behind a couch in a real room. Three-year-olds—only 6 months older—usually went right to the actual stuffed animal in the real room, showing they *could* think of the model as a symbol for the room. Although Piaget did not view the stage transitions as abrupt, he probably would have been surprised to see symbolic thinking at such an early age.

Egocentrism in action "Look, Granddaddy, a match!" So said my [DM's] granddaughter, Allie, at age 4 when showing me two memory game cards with matching pictures—that face her.

EGOCENTRISM Piaget contended that preschool children are **egocentric:** They have difficulty perceiving things from another's point of view. They are like the person who, when asked by someone across a river, "How do I get to the other side?" answered "You are *on* the other side." Asked to "show Mommy your picture," 2-year-old Gabriella holds the picture up facing her own eyes. Three-year-old Gray makes himself "invisible" by putting his hands over his eyes, assuming that if he can't see his grandparents, they can't see him. Children's conversations also reveal their egocentrism, as one young boy demonstrated (Phillips, 1969, p. 61):

> *"Do you have a brother?"*
> *"Yes."*
> *"What's his name?"*
> *"Jim."*
> *"Does Jim have a brother?"*
> *"No."*

Like Gabriella, TV-watching preschoolers who block your view of the TV assume that you see what they see. They simply have not yet developed the ability to take another's viewpoint. Even we adults may overestimate the extent to which others share our opinions and perspectives, a trait known as the *curse of knowledge.* We assume that something will be clear to others if it is clear to us, or that e-mail recipients will "hear" our "just kidding" intent (Epley et al., 2004;

Kruger et al., 2005). Perhaps you can recall asking someone to guess a simple tune such as "Happy Birthday" as you clapped or tapped it out. With the tune in your head, it seemed so obvious! But you suffered the egocentric curse of knowledge, by assuming that what was in your head was also in someone else's.

THEORY OF MIND When Little Red Riding Hood realized her "grandmother" was really a wolf, she swiftly revised her ideas about the creature's intentions and raced away. Preschoolers, although still egocentric, develop this ability to infer others' mental states when they begin forming a **theory of mind** (Premack & Woodruff, 1978). The theory of mind concept was first used to describe chimpanzees' seeming ability to read others' intentions. Later, psychologists aimed to identify when humans develop a theory of mind.

As the ability to take another's perspective gradually develops, preschoolers come to understand what made a playmate angry, when a sibling will share, and what might make a parent buy a toy. And they begin to tease, empathize, and persuade. Being able to take another's perspective enables relationships. Children who have an advanced ability to understand others' minds tend to be more popular (Slaughter et al., 2015).

Between about ages 3 and 4½, children worldwide come to realize that others may hold false beliefs (Callaghan et al., 2005; Rubio-Fernández & Geurtz, 2013; Sabbagh et al., 2006). Jennifer Jenkins and Janet Astington (1996) showed Toronto children a Band-Aid box and asked them what was inside. Expecting Band-Aids, the children were surprised to discover that the box actually contained pencils. Asked what a child who had never seen the box would think was inside, 3-year-olds typically answered "pencils." By age 4 to 5, the children's theory of mind had leapt forward, and they anticipated their friends' false belief that the box would hold Band-Aids. Children with *autism spectrum disorder* have difficulty understanding that another's state of mind differs from their own.

CONCRETE OPERATIONAL STAGE By about age 7, said Piaget, children enter the **concrete operational stage.** Given concrete (physical) materials, they begin to grasp conservation. Understanding that change in form does not mean change in quantity, they can mentally pour milk back and forth between glasses of different shapes. They also enjoy jokes that use this new understanding:

> Mr. Jones went into a restaurant and ordered a whole pizza for his dinner. When the waiter asked if he wanted it cut into 6 or 8 pieces, Mr. Jones said, "Oh, you'd better make it 6, I could never eat 8 pieces!" (McGhee, 1976)

Piaget believed that during the concrete operational stage, children become able to comprehend mathematical transformations and conservation. When my [DM's] daughter, Laura, was 6, I was astonished at her inability to reverse simple arithmetic. Asked, "What is 8 plus 4?" she required 5 seconds to compute "12," and another 5 seconds to then compute 12 minus 4. By age 8, she could answer a reversed question instantly.

FORMAL OPERATIONAL STAGE By about age 12, our reasoning expands from the purely concrete (involving actual experience) to encompass abstract thinking (involving imagined realities and symbols). As children approach adolescence, said Piaget, they can ponder hypothetical propositions and deduce consequences: *If* this, *then* that. Systematic reasoning, what Piaget called **formal operational** thinking, is now within their grasp.

Although full-blown logic and reasoning await adolescence, the rudiments of formal operational thinking begin earlier than Piaget realized. Consider this simple problem:

> If John is in school, then Mary is in school. John is in school. What can you say about Mary?

Formal operational thinkers have no trouble answering correctly. But neither do most 7-year-olds (Suppes, 1982). **TABLE 11.1** on the next page summarizes the four stages in Piaget's theory.

"The curse of knowledge is the single best explanation I know of why good people write bad prose. It simply doesn't occur to the writer that her readers don't know what she knows."

Psychologist Steven Pinker,
The Sense of Style, *2014*

conservation the principle (which Piaget believed to be a part of concrete operational reasoning) that properties such as mass, volume, and number remain the same despite changes in the forms of objects.

egocentrism in Piaget's theory, the preoperational child's difficulty taking another's point of view.

theory of mind people's ideas about their own and others' mental states—about their feelings, perceptions, and thoughts, and the behaviors these might predict.

concrete operational stage in Piaget's theory, the stage of cognitive development (from about 7 to 11 years of age) during which children gain the mental operations that enable them to think logically about concrete events.

formal operational stage in Piaget's theory, the stage of cognitive development (normally beginning about age 12) during which people begin to think logically about abstract concepts.

Pretend play

TABLE 11.1

Piaget's Stages of Cognitive Development

Typical Age Range	Description of Stage	Developmental Phenomena
Birth to nearly 2 years	*Sensorimotor* Experiencing the world through senses and actions (looking, hearing, touching, mouthing, and grasping)	• Object permanence • Stranger anxiety
About 2 to about 6 or 7 years	*Preoperational* Representing things with words and images; using intuitive rather than logical reasoning	• Pretend play • Egocentrism
About 7 to 11 years	*Concrete operational* Thinking logically about concrete events; grasping concrete analogies and performing arithmetical operations	• Conservation • Mathematical transformations
About 12 through adulthood	*Formal operational* Abstract reasoning	• Abstract logic • Potential for mature moral reasoning

An Alternative Viewpoint: Lev Vygotsky and the Social Child

As Piaget was forming his theory of cognitive development, Russian psychologist Lev Vygotsky was also studying how children think and learn. He noted that by age 7, they increasingly think in words and use words to solve problems. They do this, he said, by internalizing their culture's language and relying on inner speech (Fernyhough, 2008). Parents who say *"No, no!"* when pulling a child's hand away from a cake are giving the child a self-control tool. When the child later needs to resist temptation, he may likewise say *"No, no!"* Second graders who muttered to themselves while doing math problems grasped third-grade math better the following year (Berk, 1994). Whether out loud or inaudibly, talking to themselves helps children control their behavior and emotions and master new skills. The self-talk advantage is not limited to children. Adults who motivate themselves using self-talk ("You can do it!") also experience better performance (Kross et al., 2014).

Lev Vygotsky (1896–1934) Vygotsky, pictured here with his daughter, was a Russian developmental psychologist. He studied how a child's mind feeds on the language of social interaction.

Where Piaget emphasized how the child's mind grows through interaction with the physical environment, Vygotsky emphasized how the child's mind grows through interaction with the *social* environment. If Piaget's child was a young scientist, Vygotsky's was a young apprentice. By mentoring children and giving them new words, parents and others provide a temporary *scaffold* from which children can step to higher levels of thinking (Renninger & Granott, 2005). Language, an important ingredient of social mentoring, provides the building blocks for thinking, noted Vygotsky (who was born the same year as Piaget, but died prematurely of tuberculosis).

- Object permanence, pretend play, conservation, and abstract logic are developmental milestones for which of Piaget's stages, respectively?

ANSWER: Object permanence for the sensorimotor stage, pretend play for the preoperational stage, conservation for the concrete operational stage, and abstract logic for the formal operational stage.

- Match the correct cognitive developmental stage (a–d) to each developmental phenomenon (1–6).

  a. Sensorimotor   b. Preoperational   c. Concrete operational   d. Formal operational

  1. Thinking about abstract concepts, such as "freedom."

  2. Enjoying imaginary play (such as dress-up).

  3. Understanding that physical properties stay the same even when objects change form.

  4. Having the ability to reverse math operations.

  5. Understanding that something is not gone for good when it disappears from sight, as when Mom "disappears" behind the shower curtain.

  6. Having difficulty taking another's point of view (as when blocking someone's view of the TV).

ANSWERS: 1. d, 2. b, 3. c, 4. c, 5. a, 6. b

"It's too late, Roger—they've seen us."
Roger has not outgrown his early childhood egocentrism.

Reflecting on Piaget's Theory

What remains of Piaget's ideas about the child's mind? Plenty—enough to merit his being singled out by *Time* magazine as one of the twentieth century's 20 most influential scientists and thinkers and his being rated in a survey of British psychologists as the last century's greatest psychologist (*Psychologist*, 2003). Piaget identified significant cognitive milestones and stimulated worldwide interest in how the mind develops. His emphasis was less on the ages at which children typically reach specific milestones than on their sequence. Studies around the globe, from aboriginal Australia to Algeria to North America, have confirmed that human cognition unfolds basically in the sequence Piaget described (Lourenco & Machado, 1996; Segall et al., 1990).

However, today's researchers see development as more continuous than did Piaget. By detecting the beginnings of each type of thinking at earlier ages, they have revealed conceptual abilities Piaget missed. Moreover, they see formal logic as a smaller part of cognition than he did. Piaget would not be surprised that today, as part of our own cognitive development, we are adapting his ideas to accommodate new findings.

IMPLICATIONS FOR PARENTS AND TEACHERS Future parents and teachers, remember this: Young children are incapable of adult logic. Preschoolers who block one's view of the TV simply have not learned to take another's viewpoint. What seems simple and obvious to us—getting off a teeter-totter will cause a friend on the other end to crash—may be incomprehensible to a 3-year-old. Also remember that children are not passive receptacles waiting to be filled with knowledge. Better to build on what they already know, engaging them in concrete demonstrations and stimulating them to think for themselves. Finally, accept children's cognitive immaturity as adaptive. It is nature's strategy for keeping children close to protective adults and providing time for learning and socialization (Bjorklund & Green, 1992).

Autism Spectrum Disorder

 11-3 What is autism spectrum disorder?

Diagnoses of **autism spectrum disorder (ASD),** a disorder marked by social deficiencies and repetitive behaviors, have been increasing. Once believed to affect 1 in 2500 children (and referred to simply as *autism*), ASD now gets diagnosed in 1 in 68 American children by age 8. But the reported rates vary by place, with New Jersey

"Assessing the impact of Piaget on developmental psychology is like assessing the impact of Shakespeare on English literature."

Developmental psychologist Harry Beilin (1992)

"Childhood has its own way of seeing, thinking, and feeling, and there is nothing more foolish than the attempt to put ours in its place."

Philosopher Jean-Jacques Rousseau, 1798

🔁 **LaunchPad** For a 7-minute synopsis of Piaget's concepts, see LaunchPad's *Video: Cognitive Development*.

autism spectrum disorder (ASD) a disorder that appears in childhood and is marked by significant deficiencies in communication and social interaction, and by rigidly fixated interests and repetitive behaviors.

Autism spectrum disorder This speech-language pathologist is helping a boy with ASD learn to form sounds and words. ASD is marked by deficient social communication and difficulty grasping others' states of mind.

"Autism" case number 1 In 1943, Donald Gray Triplett, an "odd" child with unusual gifts and social deficits, was the first person to receive the diagnosis of "autism." (After a 2013 change in the diagnosis manual, his condition is now called autism spectrum disorder.) In 2010, at age 77, Triplett was still living in his native home and Mississippi town, where he often played golf (Donvan & Zucker, 2010).

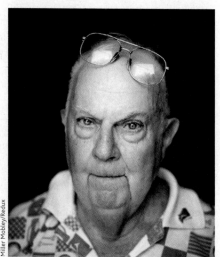

having four times the reported prevalence of Alabama, while Britain's children have a 1 in 100 rate, and South Korea's 1 in 38 (CDC, 2014; Kim et al., 2011; NAS, 2011). The increase in ASD diagnoses has been offset by a decrease in the number of children with a "cognitive disability" or "learning disability," which suggests a relabeling of children's disorders (Gernsbacher et al., 2005; Grinker, 2007; Shattuck, 2006).

The underlying source of ASD's symptoms seems to be poor communication among brain regions that normally work together to let us take another's viewpoint. From age 2 months on, as other children spend more and more time looking into others' eyes, those who later develop ASD do so less and less (Jones & Klin, 2013). People with ASD are said to have an *impaired theory of mind* (Rajendran & Mitchell, 2007; Senju et al., 2009). Mind reading that most of us find intuitive *(Is that face conveying a smirk or a sneer?)* is difficult for those with ASD. They have difficulty inferring and remembering others' thoughts and feelings, learning that twinkling eyes mean happiness or mischief, and appreciating that playmates and parents might view things differently (Boucher et al., 2012; Frith & Frith, 2001). Partly for such reasons, a national survey of parents and school staff reported that 46 percent of adolescents with ASD had suffered the taunts and torments of bullying—about four times the 11 percent rate for other children (Sterzing et al., 2012). In hopes of a cure, desperate parents have sometimes subjected children to dubious therapies (Lilienfeld et al. 2014; Shute, 2010).

ASD has differing levels of severity. Some (those diagnosed with what used to be called *Asperger syndrome)* generally function at a high level. They have normal intelligence, often accompanied by exceptional skill or talent in a specific area, but deficient social and communication skills and a tendency to become distracted by irrelevant stimuli (Remington et al., 2009). Those at the spectrum's lower end struggle to use language at all.

Biological factors, including genetic influences and abnormal brain development, contribute to ASD (State & Šestan, 2012). Studies suggest that the prenatal environment matters, especially when altered by maternal infection and inflammation, psychiatric drug use, or stress hormones (NIH, 2013; Wang, 2014). Childhood MMR vaccinations do not contribute to ASD (Demicheli et al., 2012; DeStefano et al., 2013). Based on a fraudulent 1998 study—"the most damaging medical hoax of the last 100 years" (Flaherty, 2011)—some parents were misled into thinking that the childhood MMR vaccine increased risk of ASD. The unfortunate result was a drop in vaccination rates and an increase in cases of measles and mumps. Some unvaccinated children suffered long-term harm or even death.

Both boys and girls can have ASD, but there are large gender differences. ASD afflicts about four boys for every girl. Children for whom amniotic fluid analyses indicated high prenatal testosterone develop more masculine and ASD-related traits (Auyeung et al., 2009). Psychologist Simon Baron-Cohen (2008, 2009) argues that ASD represents an "extreme male brain." Girls are naturally predisposed to be "empathizers," he contends. They tend to be better at reading facial expressions and gestures, though less so if given testosterone (van Honk et al., 2011). And, although the sexes overlap, he believes boys are more often "systemizers"—better at understanding things according to rules or laws, as in mathematical and mechanical systems.

Numerous studies verify biology's influence. If one identical twin is diagnosed with ASD, the chances are 50 to 70 percent that the co-twin will be as well (Lichtenstein et al., 2010; Sebat et al., 2007). A younger sibling of a child with ASD also is at a heightened risk (Sutcliffe, 2008). No one "autism gene" accounts for the disorder. Rather, many genes—with more than 200 identified so far—appear to contribute (Gaugler et al., 2014; Heil & Schaaf, 2013). Random genetic mutations in sperm-producing cells may also play a role. As men age, these mutations become more frequent, which may help explain why an over-40 man has a much higher risk of fathering a child with ASD than does a man under 30 (Reichenberg et al., 2007).

Researchers are also sleuthing ASD's telltale signs in the brain's structure. Several studies have revealed *underconnectivity*—fewer-than-normal fiber tracts connecting the front of the brain to the back (Ecker et al., 2012; Just et al., 2012; Wolff et al., 2012). With underconnectivity, there is less of the whole-brain synchrony that, for example, integrates visual and emotional information.

Biology's role in ASD also appears in the brain's functioning. People without ASD often yawn after seeing others yawn. And as they view and imitate another's smiling or frowning, they feel something of what the other is feeling. Not so among those with ASD, who are less imitative and show much less activity in brain areas involved in mirroring others' actions (Dapretto et al., 2006; Perra et al., 2008; Senju et al., 2007). When people with ASD watch another person's hand movements, for example, their brain displays less-than-normal mirroring activity (Oberman & Ramachandran, 2007; Théoret et al., 2005). Scientists are exploring and debating this idea that the brains of people with ASD have "broken mirrors" (Gallese et al., 2011). And they are exploring whether treatment with oxytocin, the hormone that promotes social bonding, might improve social behavior in those with ASD (Gordon et al., 2013; Lange & McDougle, 2013).

Seeking to "systemize empathy," Baron-Cohen and his Cambridge University colleagues (2007; Golan et al., 2010) collaborated with Britain's National Autistic Society and a film production company. Knowing that television shows with vehicles have been popular among kids with ASD, they created animations with toy vehicle characters in a pretend boy's bedroom, grafting emotion-conveying faces onto toy trams, trains, and tractors (**FIGURE 11.8**). After the boy leaves for school, the characters come to life and have experiences that lead them to display various emotions (see www.thetransporters.com). The children were surprisingly able to generalize what they had learned to a new, real context. By the intervention's end, their previously deficient ability to recognize emotions on real faces now equaled that of children without ASD.

Sharing more than appearance
Twins Johanna and Eva share a genetically influenced mild ASD.

(a) Emotion-conveying faces were grafted onto toy trains.

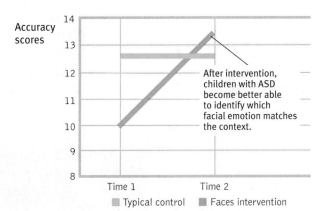

Accuracy scores

After intervention, children with ASD become better able to identify which facial emotion matches the context.

■ Typical control   ■ Faces intervention

❮ FIGURE 11.8

The neighbor's dog has bitten people before. He is barking at Louise. Point to the face that shows how Louise is feeling.

(b) Children matched the correct face with the story.

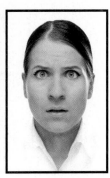

Transported into a world of emotion (a) A research team at Cambridge University's Autism Research Centre introduced children with ASD to emotions experienced and displayed by toy vehicles. (b) After four weeks of viewing animations, the children displayed a markedly increased ability to recognize emotions not only in the toy faces but also in humans. (The graph above shows data for two trials.)

Social Development

11-4 How do parent-infant attachment bonds form?

From birth, babies are normally very social creatures, developing an intense bond with their caregivers. Infants come to prefer familiar faces and voices, then to coo and gurgle when given a parent's attention. After about 8 months, soon after object permanence emerges and children become mobile, a curious thing happens: They develop **stranger anxiety.** They may greet strangers by crying and reaching for familiar caregivers. "No! Don't leave me!" their distress seems to say. Children this age have schemas for familiar faces; when they cannot assimilate the new face into these remembered schemas, they become distressed (Kagan, 1984). Once again, we see an important principle: *The brain, mind, and social-emotional behavior develop together.*

Human Bonding

One-year-olds typically cling tightly to a parent when they are frightened or expect separation. Reunited after being apart, they shower the parent with smiles and hugs. This **attachment** bond is a powerful survival impulse that keeps infants close to their caregivers. Infants become attached to those—typically their parents—who are comfortable and familiar. For many years, psychologists reasoned that infants became attached to those who satisfied their need for nourishment. But an accidental finding overturned this explanation.

Stranger anxiety A newly emerging ability to evaluate people as unfamiliar and possibly threatening helps protect babies 8 months and older.

BODY CONTACT During the 1950s, University of Wisconsin psychologists Harry Harlow and Margaret Harlow bred monkeys for their learning studies. To equalize experiences and to isolate any disease, they separated the infant monkeys from their mothers shortly after birth and raised them in sanitary individual cages, which included a cheesecloth baby blanket (Harlow et al., 1971). Then came a surprise: When their soft blankets were taken to be laundered, the monkeys became distressed.

The Harlows recognized that this intense attachment to the blanket contradicted the idea that attachment derives from an association with nourishment. But how could they show this more convincingly? To pit the drawing power of a food source against the contact comfort of the blanket, they created two artificial mothers. One was a bare wire cylinder with a wooden head and an attached feeding bottle, the other a cylinder wrapped with terry cloth.

▸ FIGURE 11.9

The Harlows' monkey mothers Psychologists Harry Harlow and Margaret Harlow raised monkeys with two artificial mothers—one a bare wire cylinder with a wooden head and an attached feeding bottle, the other a cylinder with no bottle but covered with foam rubber and wrapped with terry cloth. The Harlows' discovery surprised many psychologists: The infants much preferred contact with the comfortable cloth mother, even while feeding from the nourishing mother.

When raised with both, the monkeys overwhelmingly preferred the comfy cloth mother (**FIGURE 11.9**). Like other infants clinging to their live mothers, the monkey babies would cling to their cloth mothers when anxious. When exploring their environment, they used her as a *secure base,* as if attached to her by an invisible elastic band that stretched only so far

before pulling them back. Researchers soon learned that other qualities—rocking, warmth, and feeding—made the cloth mother even more appealing.

Human infants, too, become attached to parents who are soft and warm and who rock, feed, and pat. Much parent-infant emotional communication occurs via touch (Hertenstein et al., 2006), which can be either soothing (snuggles) or arousing (tickles). Human attachment also consists of one person providing another with a secure base from which to explore and a safe haven when distressed. As we mature, our secure base and safe haven shift—from parents to peers and partners (Cassidy & Shaver, 1999). But at all ages we are social creatures. We gain strength when someone offers, by words and actions, a safe haven: "I will be here. I am interested in you. Come what may, I will support you" (Crowell & Waters, 1994).

FAMILIARITY Contact is one key to attachment. Another is familiarity. In many animals, attachments based on familiarity form during a *critical period*—an optimal period when certain events must take place to facilitate proper development (Bornstein, 1989). Humans seem to have a critical period for language. Goslings, ducklings, and chicks have a critical period for attachment, called **imprinting,** which falls in the hours shortly after hatching, when the first moving object they see is normally their mother. From then on, the young fowl follow her, and her alone.

Konrad Lorenz (1937) explored this rigid attachment process. He wondered: What would ducklings do if he was the first moving creature they observed? What they did was follow him around: Everywhere that Konrad went, the ducks were sure to go. Although baby birds imprint best to their own species, they also will imprint on a variety of moving objects—an animal of another species, a box on wheels, a bouncing ball (Colombo, 1982; Johnson, 1992). Once formed, this attachment is difficult to reverse.

For some people, a perceived relationship with God functions as do other attachments, by providing a secure base for exploration and a safe haven when threatened (Granqvist et al., 2010; Kirkpatrick, 1999).

Mark Peterson/Redux

Imprinting Whooping cranes normally learn to migrate by following their parents. These cranes, hand-raised from eggs, have imprinted on a crane-costumed ultralight pilot, who then guided them to winter nesting grounds (Mooallem, 2009).

Children—unlike ducklings—do not imprint. However, they do become attached to what they've known. *Mere exposure* to people and things fosters fondness. Children like to reread the same books, rewatch the same movies, reenact family traditions. They prefer to eat familiar foods, live in the same familiar neighborhood, attend school with the same old friends. Familiarity is a safety signal. Familiarity breeds content.

stranger anxiety the fear of strangers that infants commonly display, beginning by about 8 months of age.

attachment an emotional tie with another person; shown in young children by their seeking closeness to the caregiver and showing distress on separation.

imprinting the process by which certain animals form strong attachments during early life.

RETRIEVE IT [✱]

• What distinguishes imprinting from attachment?

ANSWER: Attachment is the normal process by which we form emotional ties with important others. Imprinting occurs only in certain animals that have a critical period very early in their development during which they must form their attachments, and they do so in an inflexible manner.

Attachment Differences

11-5 How have psychologists studied attachment differences, and what have they learned?

What accounts for children's attachment differences? To answer this question, Mary Ainsworth (1979) designed the *strange situation* experiment. She observed mother-infant pairs at home during their first six months. Later she observed the 1-year-old infants in a strange situation (usually a laboratory playroom). Such research has shown that about 60 percent of infants display *secure attachment*. In their mother's presence they play comfortably, happily exploring their new environment. When she leaves, they become distressed; when she returns, they seek contact with her.

Other infants avoid attachment or show *insecure attachment*, marked either by *anxiety* or *avoidance* of trusting relationships. They are less likely to explore their surroundings; they may even cling to their mother. When she leaves, they either cry loudly and remain upset or seem indifferent to her departure and return (Ainsworth, 1973, 1989; Kagan, 1995; van IJzendoorn & Kroonenberg, 1988).

Ainsworth and others found that sensitive, responsive mothers—those who noticed what their babies were doing and responded appropriately—had infants who exhibited secure attachment (De Wolff & van IJzendoorn, 1997). Insensitive, unresponsive mothers—mothers who attended to their babies when they felt like doing so but ignored them at other times—often had infants who were insecurely attached. The Harlows' monkey studies, with unresponsive artificial mothers, produced even more striking effects. When put in strange situations without their artificial mothers, the deprived infants were terrified (**FIGURE 11.10**).

Although remembered by some as the researcher who tortured helpless monkeys, Harry Harlow defended his methods: "Remember, for every mistreated monkey there exist a million mistreated children," he said, expressing the hope that his research would sensitize people to child abuse and neglect. "No one who knows Harry's work could ever argue that babies do fine without companionship, that a caring mother doesn't matter," noted Harlow biographer Deborah Blum (2002, p. 307). "And since we . . . didn't fully believe that before Harry Harlow came along, then perhaps we needed—just once—to be smacked really hard with that truth so that we could never again doubt."

So, caring parents matter. But is attachment style the *result* of parenting? Or are other factors also at work?

TEMPERAMENT AND ATTACHMENT How does **temperament**—a person's characteristic emotional reactivity and intensity—affect attachment style? Twin and developmental studies reveal that heredity affects temperament, and temperament affects attachment style (Picardi et al., 2011; Raby et al., 2012).

Shortly after birth, some babies are noticeably difficult—irritable, intense, and unpredictable. Others are easy—cheerful, relaxed, and feeding and sleeping on predictable schedules (Chess & Thomas, 1987). The genetic effect appears in physiological differences. Anxious, inhibited infants have high and variable heart rates and a reactive nervous system. When facing new or strange situations, they become more physiologically aroused (Kagan & Snidman, 2004; Roque et al., 2012). One form of a gene that regulates the neurotransmitter serotonin predisposes a fearful temperament and, in combination with unsupportive caregiving, an emotionally reactive child (Raby et al., 2012).

Temperament differences typically persist. Consider:

- The most emotionally reactive newborns tended also to be the most reactive 9-month-olds (Wilson & Matheny, 1986; Worobey & Blajda, 1989).

- Exceptionally shy 6-month-olds often were still shy as 13-year-olds; over 4 in 10 children rated as consistently shy developed anxiety problems in adolescence (Prior et al., 2000).

Harlow Primate Laboratroy

⌃ FIGURE 11.10

Social deprivation and fear In the Harlows' experiments, monkeys raised with inanimate surrogate mothers were overwhelmed when placed in strange situations without that source of emotional security. (Today there is greater oversight and concern for animal welfare, which would regulate this type of study.)

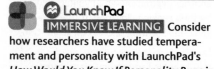

LaunchPad

IMMERSIVE LEARNING Consider how researchers have studied temperament and personality with LaunchPad's *How Would You Know If Personality Runs in the Genes?*

- Emotionally intense preschoolers have tended to be relatively intense young adults (Larsen & Diener, 1987). In one long-term study of more than 900 New Zealanders, emotionally reactive and impulsive 3-year-olds developed into somewhat more impulsive, aggressive, and conflict-prone 21-year-olds (Caspi, 2000).

- Identical twins, more than fraternal twins, often have similar temperaments (Fraley & Tancredy, 2012; Kandler et al., 2013).

> **temperament** a person's characteristic emotional reactivity and intensity.

Parenting studies that neglect such inborn differences, noted Judith Harris (1998), do the equivalent of "comparing foxhounds reared in kennels with poodles reared in apartments." To separate the effects of nature and nurture on attachment, we would need to vary parenting while controlling temperament. (Pause and think: If you were the researcher, how might you have done this?)

Dutch researcher Dymphna van den Boom's solution was to randomly assign 100 temperamentally difficult 6- to 9-month-olds to either an experimental group, in which mothers received personal training in sensitive responding, or to a control group, in which they did not. At 12 months of age, 68 percent of the experimental group were rated securely attached, as were only 28 percent of the control group infants. Other studies have confirmed that intervention programs can increase parental sensitivity and, to a lesser extent, infant attachment security (Bakermans-Kranenburg et al., 2003; Van Zeijl et al., 2006).

As many of these examples indicate, researchers have more often studied mother care than father care, but fathers are more than just mobile sperm banks. Despite the widespread attitude that "fathering a child" means impregnating, and "mothering" means nurturing, nearly 100 studies worldwide have shown that a father's love and acceptance are comparable with a mother's love in predicting an offspring's health and well-being (Rohner & Veneziano, 2001; see also **TABLE 11.2**). In one mammoth British study following 7259 children from birth to adulthood, those whose fathers were most involved in parenting (through outings, reading to them, and taking an interest in their education) tended to achieve more in school, even after controlling for other factors such as parental education and family wealth (Flouri & Buchanan, 2004). Fathers matter.

∨ TABLE 11.2

Dual Parenting Facts

Some hard facts about declining father care:	Some encouraging findings:
• *Increased father separation.* From 1960 to 2010, the number of children in the United States living apart from their fathers more than doubled (Livingston & Parker, 2011).	• *Active dads are caregiving more.* Today's co-parenting fathers are more engaged, with a doubling in the weekly hours spent with their children, compared with fathers in 1965 (Livingston & Parker, 2011).
• *Increased father absence.* Only one in five absent fathers say they visit their children more than once a week, and 27 percent say they have not seen their children in the last year (Livingston & Parker, 2011).	• *Couples that share housework and child care are happier in their relationships and less divorce prone* (Wilcox & Marquardt, 2011).
• *Nonmarital births predict father separation.* Increased father absence accompanies increased nonmarital births. Even among couples cohabiting when a first child is born, the 39 percent odds of their relationship ending during the child's first years are triple the 13 percent odds of parental breakup among those who are married when their first baby is born (Hymowitz et al., 2013).	• *Dual parenting supports children, regardless of parent gender.* After controlling for other factors, children average better life outcomes "if raised by both parents" (Taylor, 2014). The American Academy of Pediatrics (2013) reports that what matters is competent, secure, nurturing parents, regardless of their gender and sexual orientation. The American Sociological Association (2013) concurs: Decades of research confirm that parental stability and resources matter. "Whether a child is raised by same-sex or opposite-sex parents has no bearing on a child's well-being."

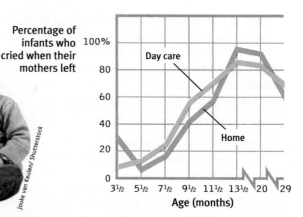

> FIGURE 11.11

Infants' distress over separation from parents
In an experiment, infants were left by their mothers in an unfamiliar room. Regardless of whether the infant had experienced day care, the percentage who cried when the mother left peaked at about 13 months of age (Kagan, 1976).

Percentage of infants who cried when their mothers left

"Out of the conflict between trust and mistrust, the infant develops hope, which is the earliest form of what gradually becomes faith in adults."

Erik Erikson (1983)

Children's anxiety over separation from parents peaks at around 13 months, then gradually declines (**FIGURE 11.11**). This happens whether they live with one parent or two, are cared for at home or in a day-care center, live in North America, Guatemala, or the Kalahari Desert. Does this mean our need for and love of others also fades away? Hardly. Our capacity for love grows, and our pleasure in touching and holding those we love never ceases.

ATTACHMENT STYLES AND LATER RELATIONSHIPS Developmental theorist Erik Erikson (1902–1994), working with his wife, Joan Erikson (1902–1997), believed that securely attached children approach life with a sense of **basic trust**—a sense that the world is predictable and reliable. He attributed basic trust not to environment or inborn temperament, but to early parenting. He theorized that infants blessed with sensitive, loving caregivers form a lifelong attitude of trust rather than fear.

Many researchers now believe that our early attachments form the foundation for our adult relationships (Birnbaum et al., 2006; Fraley et al., 2013). People who report secure relationships with their parents tend to enjoy secure friendships (Gorrese & Ruggieri, 2012). When leaving home to attend college—another kind of "strange situation"—those securely attached to parents tend to adjust well (Mattanah et al., 2011). Secure, responsive mothers tend to have children who flourish socially and academically (Raby et al., 2014).

Feeling *in*securely attached to others may take either of two main forms (Fraley et al., 2011). With *insecure-anxious attachment,* people constantly crave acceptance but remain alert to signs of rejection. With *insecure-avoidant attachment,* people experience discomfort when getting close to others and use avoidant strategies to maintain distance from others. In one study of over 90,000 adults in 81 countries, anxious attachment peaked in young adulthood, whereas avoidant attachment was highest among older adults (Chopik & Edelstein, 2014). As we journey through life and gather many relationship experiences, we tend to become less alert to signs of rejection and prefer independence.

Adult attachment styles affect relationships with romantic partners and one's own children (Hadden et al., 2014; Jones et al., 2015). An anxious attachment style hinders social connections. An avoidant style decreases commitment and increases conflict (DeWall et al., 2011; Li & Chan, 2012). But say this for those (nearly half of all people) who exhibit wary, insecure attachments: Anxious or avoidant tendencies have helped our groups detect or escape dangers (Ein-Dor et al., 2010).

Deprivation of Attachment

11-6 How does childhood neglect or abuse affect children's attachments?

If secure attachment fosters social trust, what happens when circumstances prevent a child from forming attachments? In all of psychology, there is no sadder research literature. Babies locked away at home under conditions of abuse

or extreme neglect are often withdrawn, frightened, even speechless. The same is true of those raised in institutions without the stimulation and attention of a regular caregiver, as was tragically illustrated during the 1970s and 1980s in Romania. Having decided that economic growth for his impoverished country required more human capital, Nicolae Ceauşescu, Romania's Communist dictator, outlawed contraception, forbade abortion, and taxed families with fewer than five children. The birthrate skyrocketed. But unable to afford the children they had been coerced into having, many families abandoned them to government-run orphanages with untrained and overworked staff. Child-to-caregiver ratios often were 15 to 1, so the children were deprived of healthy attachments with at least one adult. When tested after Ceauşescu's 1989 execution, these socially deprived children had lower intelligence scores, reduced brain development, abnormal stress responses, and double the 20 percent rate of anxiety symptoms found in children assigned to quality foster care settings (Bick et al., 2015; McLaughlin et al., 2015; Nelson et al., 2009, 2014). Dozens of other studies across 19 countries have confirmed that orphaned children tend to fare better on later intelligence tests if raised in family homes. This is especially so for those placed at an early age (van IJzendoorn et al., 2008).

Most children growing up under adversity (as did the surviving children of the Holocaust) are *resilient;* they withstand the trauma and become well-adjusted adults (Helmreich, 1992; Masten, 2001). So do most victims of childhood sexual abuse, noted Harvard researcher Susan Clancy (2010), while emphasizing that using children for sex is revolting and never the victim's fault. Indeed, hardship short of trauma often boosts mental toughness (Seery, 2011). And though growing up poor puts children at risk for some social pathologies, growing up rich puts them at risk for other pathologies. Affluent children are at elevated risk for substance abuse, eating disorders, anxiety, and depression (Lund & Dearing, 2012; Luthar et al., 2013). So when you face adversity, consider the possible silver lining.

But those who experience enduring abuse don't bounce back so readily. The Harlows' monkeys raised in total isolation, without even an artificial mother, bore lifelong scars. As adults, when placed with other monkeys their age, they either cowered in fright or lashed out in aggression. When they reached sexual maturity, most were incapable of mating. If artificially impregnated, females often were neglectful, abusive, even murderous toward their first-born. Another primate experiment confirmed the abuse-breeds-abuse phenomenon in rhesus monkeys: 9 of 16 females who had been abused by their mothers became abusive parents, as did *no* female raised by a nonabusive mother (Maestripieri, 2005).

In humans, too, the unloved may become the unloving. Most abusive parents—and many condemned murderers—have reported being neglected or battered as children (Kempe & Kempe, 1978; Lewis et al., 1988). Some 30 percent of people who have been abused later abuse their children—a rate lower than that found in the primate study, but four times the U.S. national rate of child abuse (Dumont et al., 2007; Kaufman & Zigler, 1987).

Although most abused children do *not* later become violent criminals or abusive parents, extreme early trauma may nevertheless leave footprints on the brain. Like battle-stressed soldiers, abused children's brains respond to angry faces with heightened activity in threat-detecting areas (McCrory et al., 2011). In conflict-plagued homes, even sleeping infants' brains show heightened reactivity to hearing angry speech (Graham et al., 2013). As adults, these children exhibit stronger startle responses (Jovanovic et al., 2009). If repeatedly threatened and attacked while

basic trust according to Erik Erikson, a sense that the world is predictable and trustworthy; said to be formed during infancy by appropriate experiences with responsive caregivers.

"What is learned in the cradle, lasts to the grave."

French proverb

The deprivation of attachment In this Romanian orphanage, the 250 children between ages one and five outnumbered caregivers 15 to 1.

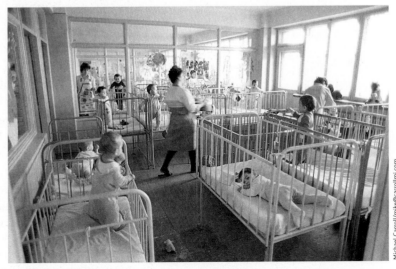

Michael Carroll/mike@carrollimj.com

young, normally placid golden hamsters grow up to be cowards when caged with same-sized hamsters, or bullies when caged with weaker ones (Ferris, 1996). Such animals show changes in the brain chemical serotonin, which calms aggressive impulses. A similarly sluggish serotonin response has been found in abused children who become aggressive teens and adults. By sensitizing the stress response system, early stress can permanently heighten reactions to later stress and increase stress-related disease (Fagundes & Way, 2014; van Zuiden et al., 2012; Wei et al., 2012). Child abuse also leaves epigenetic marks—chemical tags—that can alter the normal gene expression (McGowan et al., 2009; Romens et al., 2015).

Such findings help explain why young children who have survived severe or prolonged physical abuse, childhood sexual abuse, bullying, or wartime atrocities are at increased risk for health problems, psychological disorders, substance abuse, and criminality (Lereya et al., 2015; Nanni et al., 2012; Trickett et al., 2011; Whitelock et al., 2013; Wolke et al., 2013). In one national study of 43,093 adults, 8 percent reported experiencing physical abuse at least fairly often before age 18 (Sugaya et al., 2012). Among these, 84 percent had experienced at least one psychiatric disorder. Moreover, the greater the abuse, the greater the odds of anxiety, depression, and substance use disorder, and of attempted suicide. Abuse victims are at considerable risk for depression *if* they carry a gene variation that spurs stress-hormone production (Bradley et al., 2008). As we will see again and again, behavior and emotion arise from a particular environment interacting with particular genes. Nature *and* nurture matter.

We adults also suffer when our attachment bonds are severed. Whether through death or separation, a break produces a predictable sequence. Agitated preoccupation with the lost partner is followed by deep sadness and, eventually, the beginnings of emotional detachment and a return to normal living (Hazan & Shaver, 1994). Newly separated couples who have long ago ceased feeling affection are sometimes surprised at their desire to be near the former partner. Detaching is a process, not an event.

> "Stress can set off a ripple of hormonal changes that permanently wire a child's brain to cope with a malevolent world."
> *Abuse researcher Martin Teicher (2002)*

Parenting Styles

11-7 What are three parenting styles, and how do children's traits relate to them?

Some parents spank, some reason. Some are strict, some are lax. Some show little affection, some liberally hug and kiss. Do such differences in parenting styles affect children?

The most heavily researched aspect of parenting has been how, and to what extent, parents seek to control their children. Investigators have identified three parenting styles:

1. **Authoritarian** parents are *coercive*. They impose rules and expect obedience: "Don't interrupt." "Keep your room clean." "Don't stay out late or you'll be grounded." "Why? Because I said so."

2. **Permissive** parents are *unrestraining*. They make few demands and use little punishment. They may be indifferent, unresponsive, or unwilling to set limits.

3. **Authoritative** parents are *confrontive*. They are both demanding and responsive. They exert control by setting rules, but, especially with older children, they encourage open discussion and allow exceptions.

Too hard, too soft, and just right, these styles have been called, especially by pioneering researcher Diana Baumrind and her followers. Research indicates that children with the highest self-esteem, self-reliance, and social competence usually have warm, concerned, *authoritative* parents (Baumrind, 1996, 2013; Buri et al., 1988; Coopersmith, 1967). Those with authoritarian parents tend to have less social skill and self-esteem, and those with permissive parents tend to be more aggressive and immature. The participants in most studies have been

middle-class White families, and some critics suggest that effective parenting may vary by culture. Yet studies with families in more than 200 cultures worldwide have confirmed the social and academic correlates of loving and authoritative parenting (Rohner & Veneziano, 2001; Sorkhabi, 2005; Steinberg & Morris, 2001). For example, two studies of thousands living in Germany found that those whose parents had maintained a curfew exhibited better adjustment and greater achievements in young adulthood than did those with permissive parents (Haase et al., 2008).

A word of caution: The association between certain parenting styles (being firm but open) and certain childhood outcomes (social competence) is correlational. *Correlation is not causation.* Perhaps you can imagine possible explanations for this parenting-competence link.

Parents who struggle with conflicting advice should also remember that *all advice reflects the advice-giver's values.* For parents who prize unquestioning obedience or whose children live in dangerous environments, an authoritarian style may have the desired effect. For those who value children's sociability and self-reliance, authoritative firm-but-open parenting is advisable.

CULTURE AND CHILD RAISING   Child-raising practices reflect not only individual values, but also cultural values, which vary across time and place. Should children be independent or obedient? If you live in a Westernized culture, you likely prefer independence. "You are responsible for yourself," Western families and schools tell their children. "Follow your conscience. Be true to yourself. Discover your gifts. Think through your personal needs."

In recent years, some Western parents have gone further, telling their children, "You are more special than other children" (Brummelman et al., 2015). (Not surprisingly, these puffed-up children tend to have inflated self-views years later.) A half-century ago and more, however, Western cultural values placed greater priority on obedience, respect, and sensitivity to others (Alwin, 1990; Remley, 1988). "Be true to your traditions," parents then taught their children. "Be loyal to your heritage and country. Show respect toward your parents and other superiors." Cultures can change.

Children across time and place have thrived under various child-raising systems. Many Americans now give children their own bedrooms and entrust them to day care. Upper-class British parents traditionally handed off routine caregiving to nannies, then sent their 10-year-olds away to boarding school. These children generally grew up to be pillars of British society.

Many Asian and African cultures place less value on independence and more on a strong sense of *family self*—a feeling that what shames the child shames the family, and what brings honor to the family brings honor to the self. These cultures also value emotional closeness, and infants and toddlers may sleep with their mothers and spend their days close to a family member (Morelli et al., 1992; Whiting & Edwards, 1988). In the African Gusii society, babies have nursed freely but spent most of the day on their mother's back—with lots of body contact but little face-to-face and language interaction. When the mother becomes pregnant again, the toddler is weaned and handed over to someone else, often an older sibling. Westerners may wonder about the negative effects of this lack of verbal interaction, but then the African Gusii may in turn wonder about Western mothers pushing their babies around in strollers and leaving them in playpens (Small, 1997).

Such diversity in child raising cautions us against presuming that our culture's way is the only way to raise children successfully. One thing is certain, however: Whatever our culture, the investment in raising a child buys many years not only of joy and love but also of worry and irritation. In a national Gallup survey, adults with children under 18 at home were more likely than other adults to report smiling and laughing "a lot yesterday"— but also to have experienced stress "a lot of the day yesterday" (Witters,

Stephen H. Reehl

Cultures vary   Parents everywhere care about their children, but raise and protect them differently depending on the surrounding culture. Parents raising children in New York City keep them close. In Scotland's Orkney Islands' town of Stromness, social trust has enabled parents to park their toddlers outside shops.

⬤ **LaunchPad**   See LaunchPad's *Video: Correlational Studies* for a helpful tutorial animation about correlational research design.

Parental involvement promotes development   Parents in every culture facilitate their children's discovery of their world, but cultures differ in what they deem important. Asian cultures place more emphasis on school and hard work than do North American cultures. This may help explain why Japanese and Taiwanese children get higher scores on mathematics achievement tests.

Indeed/Getty Images

"You are the bows from which your children as living arrows are sent forth."

Kahlil Gibran, The Prophet, 1923

2014). Yet for most people who become parents, a child is one's biological and social legacy—one's personal investment in the human future. To paraphrase psychiatrist Carl Jung, we reach backward into our parents and forward into our children, and through their children into a future we will never see, but about which we must therefore care.

RETRIEVE IT

- The three parenting styles have been called "too hard, too soft, and just right." Which one is "too hard," which one "too soft," and which one "just right," and why?

ANSWER: The authoritarian style would be too hard, the permissive style too soft, and the authoritative style just right. Parents using the authoritative style tend to have children with high self-esteem, self-reliance, and social competence.

MODULE 11 REVIEW Infancy and Childhood

◉ Learning Objectives

Test Yourself by taking a moment to answer each of these Learning Objective Questions (repeated here from within the module). Then turn to Appendix D, Complete Module Reviews, to check your answers. Research suggests that trying to answer these questions on your own will improve your long-term memory of the concepts (McDaniel et al., 2009).

11-1 During infancy and childhood, how do the brain and motor skills develop?

11-2 From the perspectives of Piaget, Vygotsky, and today's researchers, how does a child's mind develop?

11-3 What is autism spectrum disorder?

11-4 How do parent-infant attachment bonds form?

11-5 How have psychologists studied attachment differences, and what have they learned?

11-6 How does childhood neglect or abuse affect children's attachments?

11-7 What are three parenting styles, and how do children's traits relate to them?

▣ Terms and Concepts to Remember

Test yourself on these terms by trying to write down the definition in your own words before flipping back to the referenced page to check your answers.

maturation, p. 127
critical period, p. 128
cognition, p. 130
schema, p. 130

assimilation, p. 130
accommodation, p. 130
sensorimotor stage, p. 130
object permanence, p. 130
preoperational stage, p. 131
conservation, p. 132
egocentrism, p. 132
theory of mind, p. 133

concrete operational stage, p. 133
formal operational stage, p. 133
autism spectrum disorder (ASD), p. 135
stranger anxiety, p. 138
attachment, p. 138
imprinting, p. 139
temperament, p. 140
basic trust, p. 142

[✶] Experience the Testing Effect

Test yourself repeatedly throughout your studies. This will not only help you figure out what you know and don't know; the testing itself will help you learn and remember the information more effectively thanks to the *testing effect*.

1. Stroke a newborn's cheek and the infant will root for a nipple. This illustrates
   a. a reflex.
   b. nurture.
   c. differentiation.
   d. continuity.

2. Between ages 3 and 6, the human brain experiences the greatest growth in the _____ lobes, which enable rational planning and aid memory.

3. Which of the following is true of motor-skill development?
   a. It is determined solely by genetic factors.
   b. The sequence, but not the timing, is universal.
   c. The timing, but not the sequence, is universal.
   d. It is determined solely by environmental factors.

4. Why can't we consciously recall how we learned to walk when we were infants?

5. Use Piaget's first three stages of cognitive development to explain why young children are not just miniature adults in the way they think.

6. Although Piaget's stage theory continues to inform our understanding of children's thinking, many researchers believe that

   a. Piaget's stages begin earlier and development is more continuous than he realized.

   b. children do not progress as rapidly as Piaget predicted.

   c. few children progress to the concrete operational stage.

   d. there is no way of testing much of Piaget's theoretical work.

7. An 8-month-old infant who reacts to a new babysitter by crying and clinging to his father's shoulder is showing _____ _____.

8. In a series of experiments, the Harlows found that monkeys raised with artificial mothers tended, when afraid, to cling to their cloth mother, rather than to a wire mother holding the feeding bottle. Why was this finding important?

Find answers to these questions in Appendix E, in the back of the book.

Use 🅜 LearningCurve to create your personalized study plan, which will direct you to the resources that will help you most in 🅜 LaunchPad.

MODULE 12 Adolescence

12-1 How is adolescence defined, and how do physical changes affect developing teens?

Many psychologists once believed that childhood sets our traits. Today's developmental psychologists see development as lifelong. As this *life-span perspective* emerged, psychologists began to look at how maturation and experience shape us not only in infancy and childhood, but also in adolescence and beyond. **Adolescence**—the years spent morphing from child to adult—starts with the physical beginnings of sexual maturity and ends with the social achievement of independent adult status. In some cultures, where teens are self-supporting, this means that adolescence hardly exists.

G. Stanley Hall (1904), one of the first psychologists to describe adolescence, believed that the tension between biological maturity and social dependence creates a period of "storm and stress." Indeed, after age 30, many who grow up in independence-fostering Western cultures look back on their teenage years as a time they would not want to relive, a time when their peers' social approval was imperative, their sense of direction in life was in flux, and their feeling of alienation from their parents was deepest (Arnett, 1999; Macfarlane, 1964).

But for many, adolescence is a time of vitality without the cares of adulthood, a time of rewarding friendships, heightened idealism, and a growing sense of life's exciting possibilities.

Physical Development

Adolescence begins with **puberty,** the time when we mature sexually. Puberty follows a surge of hormones, which may intensify moods and which trigger a series of bodily changes outlined in the Sex, Gender, and Sexuality modules.

Early versus late maturing. Just as in the earlier life stages, the *sequence* of physical changes in puberty (for example, breast buds and visible pubic hair before *menarche*—the first menstrual period) is far more predictable than their *timing.* Some girls start their growth spurt at 9, some boys as late as age 16. Though such variations have little effect on height at maturity, they may have psychological consequences: It is not only when we mature that counts, but how people react to our physical development.

adolescence the transition period from childhood to adulthood, extending from puberty to independence.

puberty the period of sexual maturation, during which a person becomes capable of reproducing.

How will you look back on your life 10 years from now? Are you making choices that someday you will recollect with satisfaction?

At a five-year high school reunion, former best friends may be surprised at their divergence; a decade later, they may have trouble sustaining a conversation.

For boys, early maturation has mixed effects. Boys who are stronger and more athletic during their early teen years tend to be more popular, self-assured, and independent, though also more at risk for alcohol use, delinquency, and premature sexual activity (Conley & Rudolph, 2009; Copeland et al., 2010; Lynne et al., 2007). For girls, early maturation can be a challenge (Mendle et al., 2007). If a young girl's body and hormone-fed feelings are out of sync with her emotional maturity and her friends' physical development and experiences, she may begin associating with older adolescents or may suffer teasing or sexual harassment (Ge & Natsuaki, 2009). She may also be somewhat more vulnerable to an anxiety disorder (Weingarden & Renshaw, 2012).

The teenage brain. An adolescent's brain is also a work in progress. Until puberty, brain cells increase their connections, like trees growing more roots and branches. Then, during adolescence, comes a selective *pruning* of unused neurons and connections (Blakemore, 2008). What we don't use, we lose.

As teens mature, their frontal lobes also continue to develop. The growth of *myelin*, the fatty tissue that forms around axons and speeds neurotransmission, enables better communication with other brain regions (Kuhn, 2006; Silveri et al., 2006). These developments bring improved judgment, impulse control, and long-term planning.

Maturation of the frontal lobes nevertheless lags behind that of the emotional limbic system. Puberty's hormonal surge and limbic system development help explain teens' occasional impulsiveness, risky behaviors, and emotional storms—slamming doors and turning up the music (Casey et al., 2008, 2013). No wonder younger teens (whose unfinished frontal lobes aren't yet fully equipped for making long-term plans and curbing impulses) may succumb to the tobacco corporations, which most adult smokers could tell them they will later regret. Teens actually don't underestimate the risks of smoking—or fast driving or unprotected sex. They just, when reasoning from their gut, weigh the immediate benefits more heavily (Reyna & Farley, 2006; Steinberg, 2007, 2010). Teens find rewards more exciting than adults do. So they seek thrills and rewards, without a fully developed brake pedal controlling their impulses (**FIGURE 12.1**).

So, when Junior drives recklessly and struggles academically, should his parents reassure themselves that "he can't help it; his frontal cortex isn't yet fully grown"? They can take hope: Brain changes underlie teens' new self-consciousness about what others are thinking and their valuing of risky rewards (Barkley-Levenson & Galván, 2014; Somerville et al., 2013). And the brain with which Junior begins his teens differs from the brain with which he will end his teens. Unless he slows his brain development with heavy drinking—leaving him prone to impulsivity and addiction—his frontal lobes will continue maturing until about age 25 (Crews et al., 2007; Giedd, 2015). They will also become better connected with the limbic system, enabling better emotion regulation (Steinberg, 2012).

In 2004, the American Psychological Association (APA) joined seven other medical and mental health associations in filing U.S. Supreme Court briefs arguing against the death penalty for 16- and 17-year-olds. The briefs documented the teen

Compared with adults, teens listen more to music and prefer more intense music (Bonneville-Roussy et al., 2013).

"*Young man, go to your room and stay there until your cerebral cortex matures.*"

> FIGURE 12.1

Impulse control lags reward seeking National surveys of more than 7000 American 12- to 24-year-olds reveal that sensation seeking peaks in the mid-teens, with impulse control developing more slowly as frontal lobes mature. (National Longitudinal Study of Youth and Children and Young Adults survey data presented by Steinberg, 2013.)

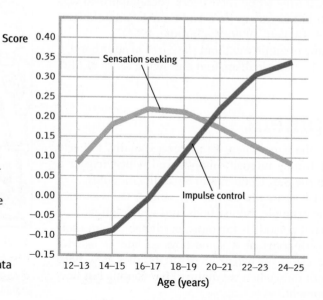

brain's immaturity "in areas that bear upon adolescent decision making." Brain scans of young teens reveal that frontal lobe immaturity is most evident among juvenile offenders and drug users (Shannon et al., 2011; Whelan et al., 2012). Thus, teens are "less guilty by reason of adolescence," suggested psychologist Laurence Steinberg and law professor Elizabeth Scott (2003; Steinberg et al., 2009). In 2005, by a 5-to-4 margin, the Court concurred, declaring juvenile death penalties

"Be afraid to try new things!"

unconstitutional. In 2012, the APA offered similar arguments against sentencing juveniles to life without parole (Banville, 2012; Steinberg, 2013). Once again, the Court, by a narrow 5-to-4 vote, concurred.

Cognitive Development

12-2 How did Piaget, Kohlberg, and later researchers describe adolescent cognitive and moral development?

During the early teen years, reasoning is often self-focused. Adolescents may think their private experiences are unique, something parents just could not understand: "But, Mom, *you* don't really know how it feels to be in love" (Elkind, 1978). Capable of thinking about their own thinking, and about other people's thinking, they also begin imagining what others are thinking about *them*. (They might worry less if they understood their peers' similar self-absorption.) Gradually, though, most begin to reason more abstractly.

Developing Reasoning Power

When adolescents achieve the intellectual summit that Jean Piaget called *formal operations,* they apply their new abstract reasoning tools to the world around them. They may think about what is ideally possible and compare that with the imperfect reality of their society, their parents, and themselves. They may debate human nature, good and evil, truth and justice. Their sense of what's fair changes from simple equality to equity—to what's proportional to merit (Almås et al., 2010). Having left behind the concrete images of early childhood, they may now seek a deeper conception of God and existence (Boyatzis, 2012; Elkind, 1970). Reasoning hypothetically and deducing consequences also enables adolescents to detect inconsistencies and spot hypocrisy in others' reasoning, sometimes leading to heated debates with parents and silent vows never to lose sight of their own ideals (Peterson et al., 1986).

"I helped a so-called friend commit armed robbery and murder. . . . I was just 17 years old. . . . Been in prison for over 20 years . . . longer than I was ever free. . . . I am among the 300 plus "Juvenile Lifers" . . . in Michigan prisons. I learned and matured a lot since my time incarcerated. I experience great remorse and regret over the tragedy that I ashamedly participated in. But I salvage this experience by learning and growing from it."

M. H., Michigan prison inmate, personal correspondence, 2015

"When the pilot told us to brace and grab our ankles, the first thing that went through my mind was that we must all look pretty stupid."

Jeremiah Rawlings, age 12, after a 1989 DC-10 crash in Sioux City, Iowa

Demonstrating their reasoning ability Although on opposite sides of the immigration policy debate, these teens are all demonstrating their ability to think logically about abstract topics. According to Piaget, they are in the final cognitive stage, formal operations.

⌄ TABLE 12.1

Kohlberg's Levels of Moral Thinking

Level (approximate age)	Focus	Example
Preconventional morality (before age 9)	Self-interest; obey rules to avoid punishment or gain concrete rewards.	"If you save your dying wife, you'll be a hero."
Conventional morality (early adolescence)	Uphold laws and rules to gain social approval or maintain social order.	"If you steal the drug for her, everyone will think you're a criminal."
Postconventional morality (adolescence and beyond)	Actions reflect belief in basic rights and self-defined ethical principles.	"People have a right to live."

Developing Morality

Two crucial tasks of childhood and adolescence are discerning right from wrong and developing character—the psychological muscles for controlling impulses. To be a moral person is to *think* morally and *act* accordingly. Jean Piaget and Lawrence Kohlberg proposed that moral reasoning guides moral actions. A more recent view builds on psychology's game-changing new recognition that much of our functioning occurs not on the "high road" of deliberate, conscious thinking but on the "low road," unconscious and automatic. Our morality provides another demonstration of our two-track mind.

MORAL REASONING Piaget (1932) believed that children's moral judgments build on their cognitive development. Agreeing with Piaget, Lawrence Kohlberg (1981, 1984) sought to describe the development of *moral reasoning*, the thinking that occurs as we consider right and wrong. Kohlberg posed moral dilemmas (for example, whether a person should steal medicine to save a loved one's life) and asked children, adolescents, and adults whether the action was right or wrong. His analysis of their answers led him to propose three basic levels of moral thinking: preconventional, conventional, and postconventional (**TABLE 12.1**). Kohlberg claimed these levels form a moral ladder. As with all stage theories, the sequence is unvarying. We begin on the bottom rung and later ascend to varying heights, where we may place others' comfort above our own (Crockett et al., 2014). Preschoolers, typically identifying with their cultural group, conform to and enforce its moral norms (Haun et al., 2014; Schmidt & Tomasello, 2012). When those norms reward kind actions, preschoolers help others (Carragan & Dweck, 2014). Kohlberg's critics have noted that his postconventional stage is culturally limited, appearing mostly among people who prize individualism (Eckensberger, 1994; Miller & Bersoff, 1995).

MORAL INTUITION Psychologist Jonathan Haidt [HITE] (2003, 2012) believes that much of our morality is rooted in *moral intuitions*—"quick gut feelings, or affectively laden intuitions." In this intuitionist view, the mind makes moral judgments as it makes aesthetic judgments—quickly and automatically. We feel disgust when seeing people engaged in degrading or subhuman acts (Olatunji & Puncochar, 2014). Even a disgusting taste in the mouth heightens people's disgust over various moral digressions (Eskine et al., 2011). We feel elevation—a tingly, warm, glowing feeling in the chest—when seeing people display exceptional generosity, compassion, or courage. Such feelings in turn trigger moral reasoning, says Haidt.

One woman recalled driving through her snowy neighborhood with three young men as they passed "an elderly woman with a shovel in her driveway. I did not think much of it, when one of the guys in the back asked the driver to let him off there. . . . When I saw him jump out of the back seat and approach the lady, my mouth dropped in shock as I realized that he was offering to shovel her walk for her." Witnessing this unexpected goodness triggered elevation: "I felt like jumping out of the car and hugging this guy. I felt like singing and running, or skipping and laughing. I felt like saying nice things about people" (Haidt, 2000).

"Could human morality really be run by the moral emotions," Haidt wonders, "while moral reasoning struts about pretending to be in control?" Consider the desire to punish. Laboratory games reveal

Moral reasoning Some Staten Island, New York, residents faced a moral dilemma in 2012 when Superstorm Sandy caused disastrous flooding. Should they risk their lives to try to rescue family, friends, and neighbors in dangerously flooded areas? Their reasoning likely reflected different levels of moral thinking, even if they behaved similarly.

Adam Hunger/Reuters

that the desire to punish wrongdoings is mostly driven not by reason (such as an objective calculation that punishment deters crime) but rather by emotional reactions, such as moral outrage (Darley, 2009). After the emotional fact, moral reasoning—our mind's press secretary—aims to convince us and others of the logic of what we have intuitively felt.

This intuitionist perspective on morality finds support in a study of moral paradoxes. Imagine seeing a runaway trolley headed for five people. All will certainly be killed unless you throw a switch that diverts the trolley onto another track, where it will kill one person. Should you throw the switch? Most say *Yes*. Kill one, save five.

Now imagine the same dilemma, except that your opportunity to save the five requires you to push a large stranger onto the tracks, where he will die as his body stops the trolley. The logic is the same—kill one, save five?—but most say *No*. Seeking to understand why, a Princeton research team led by Joshua Greene (2001) used brain imaging to spy on people's neural responses as they contemplated such dilemmas. Only when given the body-pushing type of moral dilemma did their brain's emotion areas activate. Thus, our moral judgments provide another example of the two-track mind—of dual processing (Feinberg et al., 2012). Moral reasoning, centered in one brain area, says throw the switch. Our intuitive moral emotions, rooted in other brain areas, override reason when saying *don't* push the man.

While the new research illustrates the many ways moral intuitions trump moral reasoning, other research reaffirms the importance of moral reasoning (Johnson, 2014). The religious and moral reasoning of the Amish, for example, shapes their practices of forgiveness, communal life, and modesty (Narvaez, 2010). Joshua Greene (2010) likens our moral cognition to our phone's camera. Usually, we rely on the automatic point-and-shoot mode. But sometimes we use reason to manually override the camera's automatic impulse.

MORAL ACTION Our moral thinking and feeling surely affect our moral talk. But sometimes talk is cheap and emotions are fleeting. Morality involves *doing* the right thing, and what we do also depends on social influences. As political theorist Hannah Arendt (1963) observed, many Nazi concentration camp guards during World War II were ordinary "moral" people who were corrupted by a powerfully evil situation.

Today's character education programs tend to focus on the whole moral package—thinking, feeling, and *doing* the right thing. In service-learning programs, where teens have tutored, cleaned up their neighborhoods, and assisted older adults, their sense of competence and desire to serve has increased, and their school absenteeism and drop-out rates have diminished (Andersen, 1998; Piliavin, 2003). Moral action feeds moral attitudes.

A big part of moral development is the self-discipline needed to restrain one's own impulses—to delay small gratifications now to enable bigger rewards later. One of psychology's best-known experiments was inspired by Walter Mischel (1988, 1989, 2014) observing his three preschool daughters' "remarkable progression" in self-control. To explore this phenomenon, Mischel gave Stanford nursery school 4-year-olds a choice between one marshmallow now, or two marshmallows when he returned a few minutes later. The children who had the willpower to delay gratification went on to have higher college completion rates and incomes, and less often suffered addiction problems. Moreover, when a sample of Mischel's marshmallow alums were retested on a new willpower test 40 years later, their differences persisted (Casey et al., 2011).

Our capacity to *delay gratification*—to decline small rewards now for bigger rewards later—is basic to our future academic, vocational, and social success. Teachers and parents rate children who delay gratification on a marshmallow-like test as more self-controlled (Duckworth et al., 2013). A preference for large-later rather than small-now rewards minimizes one's risk of problem gambling,

"This might not be ethical. Is that a problem for anybody?"

"It is a delightful harmony when doing and saying go together."

Michel Eyquem de Montaigne (1533–1592)

identity our sense of self; according to Erikson, the adolescent's task is to solidify a sense of self by testing and integrating various roles.

social identity the "we" aspect of our self-concept; the part of our answer to "Who am I?" that comes from our group memberships.

intimacy in Erikson's theory, the ability to form close, loving relationships; a primary developmental task in young adulthood.

"Somewhere between the ages of 10 and 13 (depending on how hormone-enhanced their beef was), children entered adolescence, a.k.a. 'the de-cutening.'"

Jon Stewart et al.,
Earth (The Book), 2010

smoking, and delinquency (Callan et al., 2011; Ert et al., 2013; van Gelder et al., 2013). The moral of the story: Delaying gratification—living with one eye on the future—fosters flourishing.

RETRIEVE IT [✖]

• According to Kohlberg, _____ morality focuses on self-interest, _____ morality focuses on self-defined ethical principles, and _____ morality focuses on upholding laws and social rules.

ANSWERS: preconventional; postconventional; conventional

Social Development

👁 **12-3** What are the social tasks and challenges of adolescence?

Theorist Erik Erikson (1963) contended that each stage of life has its own *psychosocial* task, a crisis that needs resolution. Young children wrestle with issues of *trust,* then *autonomy* (independence), then *initiative.* School-age children strive for *competence,* feeling able and productive. The adolescent's task is to synthesize past, present, and future possibilities into a clearer sense of self (**TABLE 12.2**). Adolescents wonder, "Who am I as an individual? What do I want to do with my life? What values should I live by? What do I believe in?" Erikson called this quest the adolescent's *search for identity.*

∨ TABLE 12.2

Erikson's Stages of Psychosocial Development

Stage (approximate age)	Issue	Description of Task
Infancy (to 1 year)	Trust vs. mistrust	If needs are dependably met, infants develop a sense of basic trust.
Toddlerhood (1 to 3 years)	Autonomy vs. shame and doubt	Toddlers learn to exercise their will and do things for themselves, or they doubt their abilities.
Preschool (3 to 6 years)	Initiative vs. guilt	Preschoolers learn to initiate tasks and carry out plans, or they feel guilty about their efforts to be independent.
Elementary school (6 years to puberty)	Competence vs. inferiority	Children learn the pleasure of applying themselves to tasks, or they feel inferior.
Adolescence (teen years into 20s)	Identity vs. role confusion	Teenagers work at refining a sense of self by testing roles and then integrating them to form a single identity, or they become confused about who they are.
Young adulthood (20s to early 40s)	Intimacy vs. isolation	Young adults struggle to form close relationships and to gain the capacity for intimate love, or they feel socially isolated.
Middle adulthood (40s to 60s)	Generativity vs. stagnation	In middle age, people discover a sense of contributing to the world, usually through family and work, or they may feel a lack of purpose.
Late adulthood (late 60s and up)	Integrity vs. despair	Reflecting on their lives, older adults may feel a sense of satisfaction or failure.

© Ron Chapple/Corbis

Competence vs. inferiority

© Oliver Rossi/Corbis

Intimacy vs. isolation

Forming an Identity

To refine their sense of identity, adolescents in individualist cultures usually try out different "selves" in different situations. They may act out one self at home, another with friends, and still another at school or online. If two situations overlap—as when a teenager brings new friends home—the discomfort can be considerable (Klimstra et al., 2015). The teen asks, "Which self should I be? Which is the real me?" The resolution is a self-definition that unifies the various selves into a consistent and comfortable sense of who one is—an **identity.**

For both adolescents and adults, group identities are often formed by how we differ from those around us. When living in Britain, I [DM] become conscious of my Americanness. When spending time with collaborators in Hong Kong, I [ND] become conscious of my minority White race. When surrounded by women, we are both mindful of our male gender identity. For international students, for those of a minority ethnic group, for gay and transgender people, or for people with a disability, a **social identity** often forms around their distinctiveness.

Erikson noticed that some adolescents forge their identity early, simply by adopting their parents' values and expectations. (Traditional, less individualist cultures teach adolescents who they are, rather than encouraging them to decide on their own.) Other adolescents may adopt the identity of a particular peer group—jocks, preps, geeks, band kids, debaters.

Most young people do develop a sense of contentment with their lives. A question: Which statement best describes you? "I would choose my life the way it is right now" or, "I wish I were somebody else"? When American teens answered, 81 percent picked the first, and 19 percent the second (Lyons, 2004). Reflecting on their existence, 75 percent of American collegians say they "discuss religion/spirituality" with friends, "pray," and agree that "we are all spiritual beings" and "search for meaning/purpose in life" (Astin et al., 2004; Bryant & Astin, 2008). This would not surprise Stanford psychologist William Damon and his colleagues (2003), who have contended that a key task of adolescence is to achieve a purpose—a desire to accomplish something personally meaningful that makes a difference to the world beyond oneself.

Several nationwide studies indicate that young Americans' self-esteem falls during the early to mid-teen years, and, for girls, depression scores often increase. But then self-image rebounds during the late teens and twenties (Chung et al., 2014; Orth et al., 2015; Wagner et al., 2013). Late adolescence is also a time when agreeableness and emotional stability scores increase (Klimstra et al., 2009).

These are the years when many people in industrialized countries begin exploring new opportunities by attending college or working full time. Many college seniors have achieved a clearer identity and a more positive self-concept than they had as first-year students (Waterman, 1988). Collegians who have achieved a clear sense of identity are less prone to alcohol misuse (Bishop et al., 2005).

Erikson contended that adolescent identity formation (which continues into adulthood) is followed in young adulthood by a developing capacity for **intimacy,** the ability to form emotionally close relationships. When Mihaly Csikszentmihalyi [chick-SENT-me-hi] and Jeremy Hunter (2003) used a beeper to sample the daily experiences of American teens, they found them unhappiest when alone and happiest when with friends. Romantic relationships, which tend to be emotionally intense, are reported by some two in three North American 17-year-olds, but fewer among those in collectivist countries such as China (Collins et al., 2009; Li et al., 2010). Those who enjoy high-quality (intimate, supportive) relationships

Nine times out of ten, it's all about peer pressure.

"Self-consciousness, the recognition of a creature by itself as a 'self,' [cannot] exist except in contrast with an 'other,' a something which is not the self."

C. S. Lewis,
The Problem of Pain, 1940

Who shall I be today? By varying the way they look, adolescents try out different "selves." Although we eventually form a consistent and stable sense of identity, the self we present may change with the situation.

Ⓡ LaunchPad For an interactive self-assessment of your own identity, see LaunchPad's *PsychSim 6: Who Am I?*

"She says she's someone from your past who gave birth to you, and raised you, and sacrificed everything so you could have whatever you wanted."

"Men resemble the times more than they resemble their fathers."
Ancient Arab proverb

"I love u guys."
Emily Keyes' final text message to her parents before dying in a Colorado school shooting, 2006

with family and friends tend also to enjoy similarly high-quality romantic relationships in adolescence, which set the stage for healthy adult relationships. Such relationships are, for most of us, a source of great pleasure.

Parent and Peer Relationships

◀▶ **12-4** How do parents and peers influence adolescents?

As adolescents in Western cultures seek to form their own identities, they begin to pull away from their parents (Shanahan et al., 2007). The preschooler who can't be close enough to her mother, who loves to touch and cling to her, becomes the 14-year-old who wouldn't be caught dead holding hands with Mom. The transition occurs gradually, but this period is typically a time of diminishing parental influence and growing peer influence.

As Aristotle long ago recognized, we humans are "the social animal." At all ages, but especially during childhood and adolescence, we seek to fit in with our groups (Harris, 1998, 2002). Teens who start smoking typically have friends who model smoking, suggest its pleasures, and offer cigarettes (J. S. Rose et al., 1999; R. J. Rose et al., 2003). Part of this peer similarity may result from a *selection effect*, as kids seek out peers with similar attitudes and interests. Those who smoke (or don't) may select as friends those who also smoke (or don't). Put two teens together and their brains become hypersensitive to reward (Albert et al., 2013). This increased activation helps explain why teens take more driving risks when with friends than they do alone (Chein et al., 2011).

By adolescence, parent-child arguments occur more often, usually over mundane things—household chores, bedtime, homework (Tesser et al., 1989). Conflict during the transition to adolescence tends to be greater with first-born than with second-born children, and greater with mothers than with fathers (Burk et al., 2009; Shanahan et al., 2007).

For a minority of parents and their adolescents, differences lead to real splits and great stress (Steinberg & Morris, 2001). But most disagreements are at the level of harmless bickering. With sons, the issues often are behavior problems, such as acting out or hygiene; for daughters, the issues commonly involve relationships, such as dating and friendships (Schlomer et al., 2011). Most adolescents—6000 of them in 10 countries, from Australia to Bangladesh to Turkey—have said they like their parents (Offer et al., 1988). "We usually get along but . . . ," adolescents often reported (Galambos, 1992; Steinberg, 1987).

Positive parent-teen relations and positive peer relations often go hand in hand. High school girls who had the most affectionate relationships with their mothers tended also to enjoy the most intimate friendships with girlfriends (Gold & Yanof, 1985). And teens who felt close to their parents have tended to be healthy and happy and to do well in school (Resnick et al., 1997). Of course, we can state this correlation the other way: Misbehaving teens are more likely to have tense relationships with parents and other adults.

Although heredity does much of the heavy lifting in forming individual temperament and personality differences, parents and peers influence teen's behaviors and attitudes (See Thinking Critically About: How Much Credit or Blame Do Parents Deserve?)

"It's you who don't understand me—I've been fifteen, but you have never been forty-eight."

When with peers, teens discount the future and focus more on immediate rewards (O'Brien et al., 2011). Most teens are herd animals, talking, dressing, and acting more like their peers than their parents. What their friends are, they often become, and what "everybody's doing," they often do.

Part of what everybody's doing is networking—a lot. Teens rapidly adopt social media. U.S. teens typically send 30 text messages daily and average 145 Facebook friends (Lenhart, 2015). They tweet, post videos to Snapchat, and share pictures on Instagram. Online communication stimulates intimate self-disclosure—both for better (support groups) and for worse (online predators and extremist groups) (Subrahmanyam & Greenfield, 2008; Valkenburg & Peter, 2009). Facebook, from a study of all its English-language users, reports this: Among parents and children, 371 days elapse, on average, before they include each other in their circle of self-disclosure (Burke et al., 2013).

For those who feel excluded by their peers, whether online or face-to-face, the pain is acute. "The social atmosphere in most high schools is poisonously clique-driven and exclusionary," observed social psychologist Elliot Aronson (2001).

"First, I did things for my parents' approval, then I did things for my parents' disapproval, and now I don't know why I do things."

THINKING CRITICALLY ABOUT

How Much Credit or Blame Do Parents Deserve?

In procreation, a woman and a man shuffle their gene decks and deal a life-forming hand to their child-to-be, who is then subjected to countless influences beyond their control. Parents, nonetheless, feel enormous satisfaction in their children's successes or guilt and shame over their failures. They beam over the child who wins trophies and titles. They wonder where they went wrong with the child who is repeatedly in trouble. Freudian psychiatry and psychology encouraged such ideas by blaming problems from asthma to schizophrenia on "bad mothering," and society has reinforced parent blaming. Believing that parents shape their offspring as a potter molds clay, people readily praise parents for their children's virtues and blame them for their children's vices. Popular culture endlessly proclaims the psychological harm toxic parents inflict on their fragile children. No wonder having and raising children can seem so risky.

But do parents really produce future adults with an inner wounded child by being (take your pick from the toxic-parenting lists) overbearing—or uninvolved? Pushy—or indecisive? Overprotective—or distant? Are children really so easily wounded? If so, should we then blame our parents for our failings, and ourselves for

"So I blame you for everything—whose fault is that?"

our children's failings? Or does talk of wounding fragile children through normal parental mistakes trivialize the brutality of real abuse?

Parents do matter. But parenting wields its largest effects at the extremes: the abused children who become abusive, the neglected who become neglectful, the loved but firmly handled who become self-confident and socially competent. The power of the family environment also appears in the remarkable academic and vocational successes of children of people who fled from Vietnam and Cambodia—successes attributed to close-knit, supportive, even demanding families (Caplan et al.,

1992). Asian-Americans and European-Americans tend to differ in their expectations for mothering. An Asian-American mother may push her children to do well, but usually not in a way that strains their relationship (Fu & Markus, 2014). Having a supportive "Tiger Mother"—one who pushes her children and works alongside them—tends to motivate children to work harder. European-Americans tend to view that kind of parenting as "smothering-mothering," believing that it undermines children's motivation (Deal, 2011).

Yet in personality measures, shared environmental influences from the womb onward typically account for less than 10 percent of children's differences. In the words of behavior geneticists Robert Plomin and Denise Daniels (1987; Plomin, 2011), "Two children in the same family are [apart from their shared genes] as different from one another as are pairs of children selected randomly from the population." To developmental psychologist Sandra Scarr (1993), this implied that "parents should be given less credit for kids who turn out great and blamed less for kids who don't." Knowing children's personalities are not easily sculpted by parental nurture, perhaps parents can relax a bit more and love their children for who they are.

emerging adulthood a period from about age 18 to the mid-twenties, when many in Western cultures are no longer adolescents but have not yet achieved full independence as adults.

Most excluded "students suffer in silence. . . . A small number act out in violent ways against their classmates." Those who withdraw are vulnerable to loneliness, low self-esteem, and depression (Steinberg & Morris, 2001). Peer approval matters.

Parent approval may matter in other ways. Teens have seen their parents as influential in shaping their religious faith and in thinking about college and career choices (Emerging Trends, 1997). A Gallup Youth Survey revealed that most shared their parents' political views (Lyons, 2005).

Howard Gardner (1998) has concluded that parents and peers are complementary:

> Parents are more important when it comes to education, discipline, responsibility, order-liness, charitableness, and ways of interacting with authority figures. Peers are more important for learning cooperation, for finding the road to popularity, for inventing styles of interaction among people of the same age. Youngsters may find their peers more interesting, but they will look to their parents when contemplating their own futures. Moreover, parents [often] choose the neighborhoods and schools that supply the peers.

This power to select a child's neighborhood and schools gives parents an ability to influence the culture that shapes the child's peer group. And because neighborhood influences matter, parents may want to become involved in intervention programs that aim at a whole school or neighborhood. If the vapors of a toxic climate are seeping into a child's life, that climate—not just the child—needs reforming.

RETRIEVE IT [✖]

• What is the *selection effect,* and how might it affect a teen's decision to join sports teams at school?

ANSWER: Adolescents tend to *select* similar others and to sort themselves into like-minded groups. For an athletic teen, this could lead to finding other athletic teens and joining school teams together.

Emerging Adulthood

12-5 What is emerging adulthood?

In the Western world, adolescence now roughly corresponds to the teen years. At earlier times, and in other parts of the world today, this slice of life has been much smaller (Baumeister & Tice, 1986). Shortly after sexual maturity, young people would assume adult responsibilities and status. The event might be celebrated with an elaborate initiation—a public rite of passage. The new adult would then work, marry, and have children.

When schooling became compulsory in many Western countries, independence was put on hold until after graduation. Adolescents are now taking more time to establish themselves as adults. In the United States, for example, the average age at first marriage has increased more than 5 years since 1960 (to 29 for men, 27 for women). In 1960, three in four women and two in three men had, by age 30, finished school, left home, become financially independent, married, and had a child. Today, fewer than half of 30-year-old women and one-third of men have met these five milestones (Henig, 2010).

Together, later independence and earlier sexual maturity have widened the once-brief interlude between biological maturity and social independence (**FIGURE 12.2**). In prosperous communities, the time from 18 to the mid-twenties is an increasingly not-yet-settled phase of life, now often called **emerging adulthood** (Arnett, 2006, 2007; Reitzle, 2006). No longer adolescents, these emerging adults, having not yet assumed full adult responsibilities and

---

⌄ FIGURE 12.2

The transition to adulthood is being stretched from both ends In the 1890s, the average interval between a woman's first menstrual period and marriage, which typically marked a transition to adulthood, was about 7 years; a century later in industrialized countries it was about 14 years (Finer & Philbin, 2014; Guttmacher, 1994). Although many adults are unmarried, later marriage combines with prolonged education and earlier menarche to help stretch out the transition to adulthood.

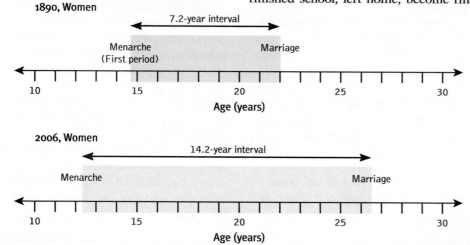

1890, Women

7.2-year interval

Menarche (First period)   Marriage

10   15   20   25   30
Age (years)

2006, Women

14.2-year interval

Menarche   Marriage

10   15   20   25   30
Age (years)

independence, feel "in between." After high school, those who enter the job market or go to college may be managing their own time and priorities more than ever before. Yet they may be doing so from their parents' home—unable to afford their own place and perhaps still emotionally dependent as well. Recognizing today's more gradually emerging adulthood, the U.S. government now allows dependent children up to age 26 to remain on their parents' health insurance (Cohen, 2010).

"I just don't know what to do with myself in that long stretch after college but before social security."

RETRIEVE IT [✱]

• Match the psychosocial development stage below (1–8) with the issue that Erikson believed we wrestle with at that stage (a–h).

1. Infancy	4. Elementary school	7. Middle adulthood
2. Toddlerhood	5. Adolescence	8. Late adulthood
3. Preschool	6. Young adulthood	

a. Generativity vs. stagnation	e. Identity vs. role confusion
b. Integrity vs. despair	f. Competence vs. inferiority
c. Initiative vs. guilt	g. Trust vs. mistrust
d. Intimacy vs. isolation	h. Autonomy vs. shame and doubt

ANSWERS: 1. g, 2. h, 3. c, 4. f, 5. e, 6. d, 7. a, 8. b

MODULE
12 REVIEW Adolescence

◯ Learning Objectives

Test Yourself by taking a moment to answer each of these Learning Objective Questions (repeated here from within the module). Then turn to Appendix D, Complete Module Reviews, to check your answers. Research suggests that trying to answer these questions on your own will improve your long-term memory of the concepts (McDaniel et al., 2009).

12-1 How is adolescence defined, and how do physical changes affect developing teens?

12-2 How did Piaget, Kohlberg, and later researchers describe adolescent cognitive and moral development?

12-3 What are the social tasks and challenges of adolescence?

12-4 How do parents and peers influence adolescents?

12-5 What is emerging adulthood?

■·⊡ Terms and Concepts to Remember

Test yourself on these terms by trying to write down the definition in your own words before flipping back to the referenced page to check your answers.

adolescence, p. 147
puberty, p. 147
identity, p. 153

social identity, p. 153
intimacy, p. 153
emerging adulthood, p. 156

[✱] Experience the Testing Effect

Test yourself repeatedly throughout your studies. This will not only help you figure out what you know and don't know; the testing itself will help you learn and remember the information more effectively thanks to the *testing effect*.

1. Adolescence is marked by the onset of
   a. an identity crisis.   c. separation anxiety.
   b. puberty.   d. parent-child conflict.

2. According to Piaget, a person who can think logically about abstractions is in the _____ _____ stage.

3. In Erikson's stages, the primary task during adolescence is
   a. attaining formal operations.
   b. forging an identity.
   c. developing a sense of intimacy with another person.
   d. living independent of parents.

4. Some developmental psychologists now refer to the period that occurs in some Western cultures from age 18 to the mid-twenties and beyond (up to the time of full adult independence) as _____ _____.

Find answers to these questions in Appendix E, in the back of the book.

Use 🌀 LearningCurve to create your personalized study plan, which will direct you to the resources that will help you most in 🌀 LaunchPad.

menopause the time of natural cessation of menstruation; also refers to the biological changes a woman experiences as her ability to reproduce declines.

How old does a person have to be before you think of him or her as old? Depends on who you ask. For 18- to 29-year-olds, 67 was old. For those 60 and over, old was 76 (Yankelovich, 1995).

"I am still learning."

Michelangelo, 1560, at age 85

Adult abilities vary widely In 2012, George Blair maintained his place in the record books as the world's oldest barefoot water skier. He is shown here in 2002 when he first set the record, at age 87. (He died in 2013 at age 98.)

Rick Doyle/CORBIS

MODULE 13 Adulthood

The unfolding of our lives continues across the life span. It is, however, more difficult to generalize about adulthood stages than about life's early years. If you know that James is a 1-year-old and Jamal is a 10-year-old, you could say a great deal about each child. Not so with adults who differ by a similar number of years. The boss may be 30 or 60; the marathon runner may be 20 or 50; the 19-year-old may be a parent who supports a child or a child who receives an allowance. Yet our life courses are in some ways similar. Physically, cognitively, and especially socially, we differ at age 50 from our 25-year-old selves. In the discussion that follows, we recognize these differences and use three terms: *early adulthood* (roughly twenties and thirties), *middle adulthood* (to age 65), and *late adulthood* (the years after 65). Within each of these stages, people will vary widely in physical, psychological, and social development.

Physical Development

13-1 What physical changes occur during middle and late adulthood?

Like the declining daylight after the summer solstice, our physical abilities—muscular strength, reaction time, sensory keenness, and cardiac output—all begin an almost imperceptible decline in our mid-twenties. Athletes are often the first to notice. World-class sprinters and swimmers peak by their early twenties. Baseball players peak at about age 27—with 60 percent of Most Valuable Player awardees since 1985 coming ±2 years of that (Silver, 2012). Women—who mature earlier than men—peak earlier. But most of us—especially those of us whose daily lives do not require top physical performance—hardly perceive the early signs of decline.

Physical Changes in Middle Adulthood

Athletes over age 40 know all too well that physical decline gradually accelerates. During early and middle adulthood, physical vigor has less to do with age than with a person's health and exercise habits. Many of today's physically fit 50-year-olds run 4 miles with ease, while sedentary 25-year-olds find themselves huffing and puffing up two flights of stairs.

Aging also brings a gradual decline in fertility, especially for women. For a 35- to 39-year-old woman, the chances of getting pregnant after a single act of intercourse are only half those of a woman 19 to 26 (Dunson et al., 2002). Men experience a gradual decline in sperm count, testosterone level, and speed of erection and ejaculation. Women experience **menopause,** as menstrual cycles end, usually within a few years of age 50. Expectations and attitudes influence the emotional impact of this event. Is it a sign of lost femininity and growing old, or liberation from menstrual periods and fears of pregnancy? For men, too, expectations can influence perceptions. Some experience distress related to a perception of declining virility and physical capacities, but most age without such problems.

With age, sexual activity lessens. Nevertheless, most men and women remain capable of satisfying sexual activity, and most express satisfaction with their sex life. This was true of 70 percent of Canadians surveyed (ages 40 to 64) and 75 percent of Finns (ages 65 to 74) (Kontula & Haavio-Mannila, 2009; Wright, 2006). In another survey, 75 percent of respondents reported being sexually active into their eighties (Schick et al., 2010). And in an American Association of Retired Persons sexuality survey, it was not until age 75 or older that most women and nearly half of men reported little sexual desire (DeLamater, 2012; DeLamater & Sill, 2005). As Alex Comfort (1992, p. 240) jested, "The things that stop you having sex with age are exactly the same as those that stop you riding a bicycle (bad health, thinking it looks silly, no bicycle)."

Physical Changes in Late Adulthood

Is old age "more to be feared than death" (Juvenal, *The Satires*)? Or is life "most delightful when it is on the downward slope" (Seneca, *Epistulae ad Lucilium*)? What is it like to grow old?

SENSORY ABILITIES, STRENGTH, AND STAMINA Although physical decline begins in early adulthood, we are not usually acutely aware of it until later in life, when the stairs get steeper, the print gets smaller, and other people seem to mumble more. Muscle strength, reaction time, and stamina diminish in late adulthood. As a lifelong basketball player, I [DM] find myself increasingly not racing for that loose ball. But even diminished vigor is sufficient for normal activities.

With age, visual sharpness diminishes, as does distance perception and adaptation to light-level changes. The eye's pupil shrinks and its lens becomes less transparent, reducing the amount of light reaching the retina: A 65-year-old retina receives only about one-third as much light as its 20-year-old counterpart (Kline & Schieber, 1985). Thus, to see as well as a 20-year-old when reading or driving, a 65-year-old needs three times as much light—a reason for buying cars with untinted windshields. This also explains why older people sometimes ask younger people, "Don't you need better light for reading?"

The senses of smell and hearing also diminish. In Wales, teens' loitering around a convenience store has been discouraged by a device that emits an aversive high-pitched sound almost no one over 30 can hear (Lyall, 2005).

HEALTH As people age, they care less about what their bodies look like and more about how their bodies function. For those growing older, there is both bad and good news about health. The bad news: The body's disease-fighting immune system weakens, making older adults more susceptible to life-threatening ailments such as cancer and pneumonia. The good news: Thanks partly to a lifetime's accumulation of antibodies, people over 65 suffer fewer short-term ailments, such as common flu and cold viruses. One study found they were half as likely as 20-year-olds and one-fifth as likely as preschoolers to suffer upper respiratory flu each year (National Center for Health Statistics, 1990).

THE AGING BRAIN Up to the teen years, we process information with greater and greater speed (Fry & Hale, 1996; Kail, 1991). But compared with teens and young adults, older people take a bit more time to react, to solve perceptual puzzles, even to remember names (Bashore et al., 1997; Verhaeghen & Salthouse, 1997). The neural processing lag is greatest on complex tasks (Cerella, 1985; Poon, 1987). At video games, most 70-year-olds are no match for a 20-year-old.

Slower neural processing combined with diminished sensory abilities can increase accident risks. As **FIGURE 13.1** indicates, fatal accident rates per mile driven increase sharply after age 75. By age 85, they exceed the 16-year-old level. Older drivers appear to focus well on the road ahead, but attend less to vehicles approaching from the side (Pollatsek et al., 2012). Nevertheless, because older people drive less, they account for fewer than 10 percent of crashes (Coughlin et al., 2004).

Brain regions important to memory begin to atrophy during aging (Fraser et al., 2015; Schacter, 1996). The blood-brain barrier also breaks down beginning in the hippocampus, which furthers cognitive decline (Montagne et al., 2015). No wonder adults, after taking a memory test, feel older. "[It's like] aging 5 years in 5 minutes," jested

"Happy fortieth. I'll take the muscle tone in your upper arms, the girlish timbre of your voice, your amazing tolerance for caffeine, and your ability to digest french fries. The rest of you can stay."

"For some reason, possibly to save ink, the restaurants had started printing their menus in letters the height of bacteria."

Dave Barry,
Dave Barry Turns Fifty, *1998*

Most stairway falls taken by older people occur on the top step, precisely where the person typically descends from a window-lit hallway into the darker stairwell (Fozard & Popkin, 1978). Our knowledge of aging could be used to design environments that would reduce such accidents (National Research Council, 1990).

⌄ FIGURE 13.1

Age and driver fatalities Slowing reactions contribute to increased accident risks among those 75 and older, and their greater fragility increases their risk of death when accidents happen (NHTSA, 2000). Would you favor driver exams based on performance, not age, to screen out those whose slow reactions or sensory impairments indicate accident risk?

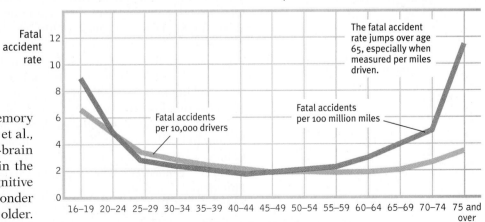

The fatal accident rate jumps over age 65, especially when measured per miles driven.

Fatal accidents per 10,000 drivers

Fatal accidents per 100 million miles

Fatal accident rate

Age (years)

one research report (Hughes et al., 2013). In early adulthood, a small, gradual net loss of brain cells begins, contributing by age 80 to a brain-weight reduction of 5 percent or so. Earlier, we noted that late-maturing frontal lobes help account for teen impulsivity. Late in life, some of that impulsiveness seems to return as inhibition-controlling frontal lobes begin to atrophy (von Hippel, 2007). This helps explain older people's occasional blunt questions and comments ("Have you put on weight?"). But good news: The aging brain is plastic, and partly compensates for what it loses by recruiting and reorganizing neural networks (Park & McDonough, 2013). During memory tasks, for example, the left frontal lobes are especially active in young adult brains, while older adult brains use both left and right frontal lobes.

EXERCISE AND AGING Exercise helps counteract some effects of aging. Physical exercise not only enhances muscles, bones, and energy and helps to prevent obesity and heart disease, it also stimulates brain cell development and neural connections, thanks perhaps to increased oxygen and nutrient flow (Erickson et al., 2013; Fleischman et al., 2015; Pereira et al., 2007). Exercise aids memory by stimulating the development of neural connections and by promoting neurogenesis, the birth of new hippocampus nerve cells. And it increases the cellular mitochondria that help power both muscles and brain cells (Steiner et al., 2011).

Sedentary older adults randomly assigned to aerobic exercise programs exhibit enhanced memory, sharpened judgment, and reduced risk of significant cognitive decline (DeFina et al., 2013; Liang et al., 2010; Nagamatsu et al., 2013). Exercise also helps maintain the *telomeres* (Leslie, 2011). These tips of chromosomes wear down with age, much as the end of a shoelace frays. Telomere wear and tear is accelerated by smoking, obesity, and stress. Children who suffer frequent abuse or bullying exhibit shortened telomeres as biological scars (Shalev et al., 2013). As telomeres shorten, aging cells may die without being replaced by perfect genetic replicas (Epel, 2009).

The message is clear: We are more likely to rust from disuse than to wear out from overuse. Fit bodies support fit minds.

Cognitive Development
Aging and Memory

 13-2 How does memory change with age?

Among the most intriguing developmental psychology questions is whether adult cognitive abilities, such as memory, intelligence, and creativity, parallel the gradually accelerating decline of physical abilities.

As we age, we remember some things well. Looking back in later life, adults asked to recall the one or two most important events over the last half-century tend to name events from their teens or twenties (Conway et al., 2005; Rubin et al., 1998). They also display this "reminiscence bump" when asked to name their all-time favorite music, movies, and athletes (Janssen et al., 2011). Whatever people experience around this time of life—the Vietnam War, the 9/11 terrorist attacks, the election of the first Black U.S. president—becomes pivotal (Pillemer, 1998; Schuman & Scott, 1989). Our teens and twenties hold so many memorable "firsts"—first kiss, first job, first day at college or university, first meeting in-laws.

Early adulthood is indeed a peak time for some types of learning and remembering. In one test of recall, people watched video clips as 14 strangers said their names, using a common format: "Hi, I'm Larry" (Crook & West, 1990). Then those strangers reappeared and gave additional details. For example, they said, "I'm from Philadelphia," providing more visual *and* voice cues for remembering the person's name. As **FIGURE 13.2** shows, after a second and third replay of the introductions, everyone remembered more names, but younger adults consistently surpassed older adults. How well older people remember depends in part on the task. In another

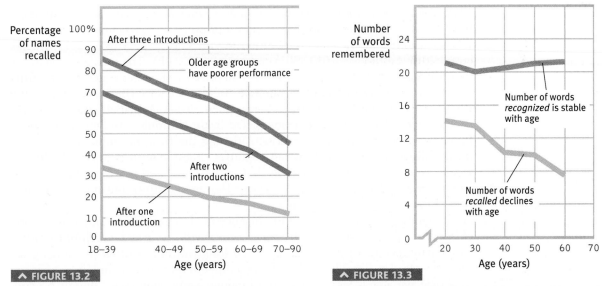

^ FIGURE 13.2

Tests of recall Recalling new names introduced once, twice, or three times is easier for younger adults than for older ones. (Data from Crook & West, 1990.)

^ FIGURE 13.3

Recall and recognition in adulthood In this experiment, the ability to *recall* new information declined during early and middle adulthood, but the ability to *recognize* new information did not. (Data from Schonfield & Robertson, 1966.)

experiment, when asked to *recognize* 24 words they had earlier tried to memorize, people showed only a minimal decline in memory. When asked to *recall* that information without clues, however, the decline was greater (**FIGURE 13.3**).

In our capacity to learn and remember, as in other areas of development, we show individual differences. Younger adults vary in their abilities to learn and remember, but 70-year-olds vary much more. "Differences between the most and least able 70-year-olds become much greater than between the most and least able 50-year-olds," reports Oxford researcher Patrick Rabbitt (2006). Some 70-year-olds perform below nearly all 20-year-olds; other 70-year-olds match or outdo the average 20-year-old.

No matter how quick or slow we are, remembering seems also to depend on the type of information we are trying to retrieve. If the information is meaningless— nonsense syllables or unimportant events—then the older we are, the more errors we are likely to make. If the information is *meaningful*, older people's rich web of existing knowledge will help them to hold it. But they may take longer than younger adults to *produce* the words and things they know. Older adults also more often experience tip-of-the-tongue memories (Ossher et al., 2012). Quick-thinking game show winners are usually young or middle-aged adults (Burke & Shafto, 2004).

Sustaining Mental Abilities

Psychologists who study the aging mind debate whether "brain fitness" computer training programs can build mental muscles and stave off cognitive decline. Our brains remain plastic throughout life (Gutchess, 2014). So, can exercising our brains on a "cognitive treadmill"—with memory, visual tracking, and problem-solving exercises—avert losing our minds? "At every point in life, the brain's natural plasticity gives us the ability to improve . . . function," said one neuroscientist-entrepreneur (Merzenich, 2007). One 5-year study of nearly 3000 people found that 10 one-hour cognitive training sessions, with follow-up booster sessions, led to improved cognitive scores on tests related to their training (Boron et al., 2007; Willis et al., 2006). Other studies with children and adults also found that brain-training exercises can sharpen the mind (Anguera et al., 2013; Jonides et al., 2012; Karr et al., 2014).

Based on such findings, some computer game makers are marketing daily brain-exercise programs for older adults. But other researchers, after reviewing all the available studies, advise caution (Melby-Lervåg & Hulme, 2013; Redick et al., 2013; Salthouse, 2010; Shipstead et al., 2012a,b). The available evidence, they argue, suggests that brain training can produce short-term gains, but mostly on the trained tasks and not for cognitive ability in general (Berkman et al., 2014; Harrison et al., 2013; Karbach & Verhaeghen, 2014). A British study of 11,430 people, who for 6 weeks either completed brain training activities or a control task, confirmed the limited benefits. Although the training improved the practiced skills, it did not boost overall cognitive fitness (Owen et al., 2010). "Play a video game and you'll get better at that video game, and maybe at very similar video games," observes researcher David Hambrick (2014), but not at driving a car or filling out your tax return.

The Thinking, Language, and Intelligence modules explore another dimension of cognitive development: intelligence. As we will see, **cross-sectional studies** (comparing people of different ages) and **longitudinal studies** (restudying the same people over time) have identified mental abilities that do and do not change as people age. Age is less a predictor of memory and intelligence than is proximity to death. Tell us whether someone is 8 months or 8 years from a natural death and, regardless of age, you've given us a clue to that person's mental ability. In the last three or four years of life and especially as death approaches, cognitive decline typically accelerates, and negative feelings increase (Vogel et al., 2013; Wilson et al., 2007). Researchers call this near-death drop *terminal decline* (Backman & MacDonald, 2006). As death approaches, our goals also shift. We're driven less to learn and more to connect socially (Carstensen, 2011).

Social Development

13-3 What themes and influences mark our social journey from early adulthood to death?

Many differences between younger and older adults are created by significant life events. A new job means new relationships, new expectations, and new demands. Marriage brings the joy of intimacy and the stress of merging two lives. The three years surrounding the birth of a child bring increased life satisfaction for most parents (Dyrdal & Lucas, 2011). The death of a loved one creates an irreplaceable loss. Do these adult life events shape a sequence of life changes?

Adulthood's Ages and Stages

As people enter their forties, they undergo a transition to middle adulthood, a time when they realize that life will soon be mostly behind instead of ahead of them. Some psychologists have argued that for many the *midlife transition* is a crisis, a time of great struggle, regret, or even feeling struck down by life. The popular image of the midlife crisis is an early-forties man who forsakes his family for a younger girlfriend and a hot sports car. But the fact—reported by large samples of people—is that unhappiness, job dissatisfaction, marital dissatisfaction, divorce, anxiety, and suicide do *not* surge during the early forties (Hunter & Sundel, 1989; Mroczek & Kolarz, 1998). Divorce, for example, is most common among those in their twenties, suicide among those in their seventies and eighties. One study of emotional instability in nearly 10,000 men and women found "not the slightest evidence" that distress peaks anywhere in the midlife age range (McCrae & Costa, 1990).

For the 1 in 4 adults who report experiencing a life crisis, the trigger is not age but a major event, such as illness, divorce, or job loss (Lachman, 2004). Some middle-aged adults describe themselves as a "sandwich generation,"

LaunchPad See LaunchPad's *Video: Longitudinal and Cross-Sectional Studies* for a helpful tutorial animation.

"The sudden knowledge of the fragility of his life narrowed his focus and altered his desires. . . . It made him visit with his grandchildren more often, put in an extra trip to see his family in India, and tamp down new ventures."

Atul Gawande, Being Mortal: Medicine and What Matters in the End, *2014, describing his father's terminal condition and the way it changed his perspective*

cross-sectional study a study in which people of different ages are compared with one another.

longitudinal study research in which the same people are restudied and retested over a long period.

social clock the culturally preferred timing of social events such as marriage, parenthood, and retirement.

simultaneously supporting their aging parents and their emerging adult children or grandchildren (Riley & Bowen, 2005).

Life events trigger transitions to new life stages at varying ages. The **social clock**—the definition of "the right time" to leave home, get a job, marry, have children, or retire—varies from era to era and culture to culture. The once-rigid sequence has loosened; the social clock still ticks, but people feel freer about being out of sync with it.

Even *chance events* can have lasting significance, by deflecting us down one road rather than another. Albert Bandura (1982, 2005) recalls the ironic true story of a book editor who came to one of Bandura's lectures on the "Psychology of Chance Encounters and Life Paths"—and ended up marrying the woman who happened to sit next to him. The sequence that led to my [DM] authoring this book (which was not my idea) began with my being seated near, and getting to know, a distinguished colleague at an international conference. The road to my [ND] co-authoring this book began in a similar, unplanned manner. DM stumbled on an article about my professional life (which was also not my idea) and invited me to visit his college. We began a conversation that resulted in our collaboration. Chance events can change our lives.

"The important events of a person's life are the products of chains of highly improbable occurrences."

Joseph Traub, "Traub's Law," 2003

Adulthood's Commitments

Two basic aspects of our lives dominate adulthood. Erik Erikson called them *intimacy* (forming close relationships) and *generativity* (being productive and supporting future generations). Sigmund Freud (1935/1960) put this more simply: The healthy adult, he said, is one who can *love* and *work*.

LOVE We typically flirt, fall in love, and commit— one person at a time. "Pair-bonding is a trademark of the human animal," observed anthropologist Helen Fisher (1993). From an evolutionary perspective, relatively monogamous pairing makes sense: Parents who cooperated to nurture their children to maturity were more likely to have their genes passed along to posterity than were parents who didn't.

Adult bonds of love are most satisfying and enduring when marked by a similarity of interests and values, a sharing of emotional and material support, and intimate self-disclosure. There also appears to be "vow power." Straight and gay romantic relationships sealed with commitment—via marriage or civil union vows— more often endure (Balsam et al., 2008; Rosenfeld, 2014). Such bonds are especially likely to last when couples marry after age 20 and are well educated. Compared with their counterparts of 30 years ago, people in Western countries *are* better educated and marrying later. These trends may help explain why the American divorce rate, which surged from 1960 to 1980, has since leveled off and even slightly declined in some areas (Schoen & Canudas-Romo, 2006). If anything, our standards have risen over the years, though. We now hope not only for an enduring bond, but also for a mate who is a wage earner, caregiver, intimate friend, and warm and responsive lover (Finkel et al., 2015).

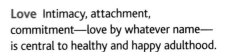

Love Intimacy, attachment, commitment—love by whatever name— is central to healthy and happy adulthood.

Historically, couples have met at school, on the job, through family, or, especially, through friends. Since the advent of the Internet, such matchmaking has been supplemented by a striking rise in couples who meet online—as have nearly a quarter of heterosexual couples and some two-thirds of same-sex couples in one recent national survey (**FIGURE 13.4**).

Might test-driving life together minimize divorce risk? In Europe, Canada, and the United States, those who live together before marriage (and especially before engagement) have had *higher* rates of divorce and marital dysfunction than those who did not (Goodwin et al., 2010; Jose et al., 2010; Manning & Cohen, 2012; Stanley et al., 2010). Two factors contribute. First, those who live together tend to be initially less committed to the ideal of enduring marriage. Second, they tend to become even less marriage-supporting while living together.

Although there is more variety in relationships today, the institution of marriage endures. Ninety-five percent of Americans have either married or want to (Newport & Wilke, 2013). In Western countries, people marry for love. What counts as a "very important" reason to marry? Among Americans, 31 percent say financial stability, and 93 percent say love (Cohn, 2013). And marriage is a predictor of happiness, sexual satisfaction, income, and physical and mental health (Scott et al., 2010). National Opinion Research Center surveys of more than 50,000 Americans since 1972 reveal that 40 percent of married adults, and only 23 percent of unmarried adults, have reported being "very happy." Lesbian couples, too, report greater well-being than those who are single (Peplau & Fingerhut, 2007; Wayment & Peplau, 1995). Moreover, neighborhoods with high marriage rates typically have low rates of social pathologies such as crime, delinquency, and emotional disorders among children (Myers & Scanzoni, 2005).

Relationships that last are not always devoid of conflict. Some couples fight but also shower each other with affection. Other couples never raise their voices yet also seldom praise each other or nuzzle. Both styles can last. After observing the interactions of 2000 couples, John Gottman (1994) reported one indicator of marital success: at least a five-to-one ratio of positive to negative interactions. Stable marriages provide five times more instances of smiling, touching, complimenting, and laughing than of sarcasm, criticism, and insults. So, if you want to predict which couples will stay together, don't pay attention to how passionately they are in love. The pairs who make it are more often those who refrain from putting down their partners. To prevent a cancerous negativity, successful couples learn to fight fair (to state feelings without insulting) and to steer conflict away from chaos with comments like "I know it's not your fault" or "I'll just be quiet for a moment and listen."

What do you think? Does marriage correlate with happiness because marital support and intimacy breed happiness, because happy people more often marry and stay married, or both?

> FIGURE 13.4

The changing way Americans meet their partners A national survey of 2452 straight couples and 462 gay and lesbian couples reveals the increasing role of the Internet. (Data from Rosenfeld, 2013; Rosenfeld & Thomas, 2012.)

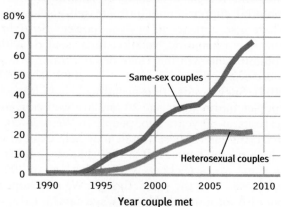

Often, love bears children. For most people, this most enduring of life changes is a happy event—one that adds meaning, joy, and occasional stress (Nelson et al., 2013; Witters, 2014). "I feel an overwhelming love for my children unlike anything I feel for anyone else," said 93 percent of American mothers in a national survey (Erickson & Aird, 2005). Many fathers feel the same. A few weeks after the birth of my first child I [DM] was suddenly struck by a realization: "So *this* is how my parents felt about me!"

When children begin to absorb time, money, and emotional energy, satisfaction with the marriage itself may decline (Doss et al., 2009). This is especially likely among employed women who, more than they expected, may carry the traditional burden of doing the chores at home. Putting effort into creating an equitable relationship can thus pay double dividends: greater satisfaction, which breeds better parent-child relations (Erel & Burman, 1995).

Although love bears children, children eventually leave home. This departure is a significant and sometimes difficult event. For most people, however, an empty nest is a happy place (Adelmann et al., 1989; Gorchoff et al., 2008). Many parents experience a "postlaunch honeymoon," especially if they maintain close relationships with their children (White & Edwards, 1990). As Daniel Gilbert (2006) has said, "The only known symptom of 'empty nest syndrome' is increased smiling."

WORK For many adults, the answer to "Who are you?" depends a great deal on the answer to "What do you do?" For women and men, choosing a career path is difficult, especially during bad economic times. Even in the best of times, few students in their first two years of college or university can predict their later careers.

"Our love for children is so unlike any other human emotion. I fell in love with my babies so quickly and profoundly, almost completely independently of their particular qualities. And yet 20 years later I was (more or less) happy to see them go—I had to be happy to see them go. We are totally devoted to them when they are little and yet the most we can expect in return when they grow up is that they regard us with bemused and tolerant affection."

Developmental psychologist Alison Gopnik, "The Supreme Infant," 2010

"To understand your parents' love, bear your own children."

Chinese proverb

To explore the connection between parenting and happiness, visit LaunchPad's *How Would You Know If Having Children Relates to Being Happier?*

Job satisfaction and life satisfaction Work can provide us with a sense of identity and competence, and opportunities for accomplishment. Perhaps this is why challenging and interesting occupations enhance people's happiness.

In the end, happiness is about having work that fits your interests and provides you with a sense of competence and accomplishment. It is having a close, supportive companion who cheers your accomplishments (Gable et al., 2006). And for some, it includes having children who love you and whom you love and feel proud of.

For more on work, including discovering your own strengths, see Appendix B: Psychology at Work.

RETRIEVE IT [x]

• Freud defined the healthy adult as one who is able to _____ and to _____.

ANSWERS: love; work

Well-Being Across the Life Span

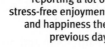 **13-4** How does our well-being change across the life span?

To live is to grow older. This moment marks the oldest you have ever been and the youngest you will henceforth be. That means we all can look back with satisfaction or regret, and forward with hope or dread. When asked what they would have done differently if they could relive their lives, people's most common answer has been "taken my education more seriously and worked harder at it" (Kinnier & Metha, 1989; Roese & Summerville, 2005). Other regrets—"I should have told my father I loved him," "I regret that I never went to Europe"—have also focused less on mistakes made than on the things one *failed* to do (Gilovich & Medvec, 1995).

From the teens to midlife, people typically experience a strengthening sense of identity, confidence, and self-esteem (Huang, 2010; Robins & Trzesniewski, 2005). In later life, challenges arise: Income shrinks. Work is often taken away. The body deteriorates. Recall fades. Energy wanes. Family members and friends die or move away. The great enemy, death, looms ever closer. And for those in the terminal decline phase, life satisfaction does decline as death approaches (Gerstorf et al., 2008).

Prior to the very end, however, Gallup researchers have discovered that the over-65 years are not notably unhappy. Self-esteem remains stable (Wagner et al., 2013). Emotional experiences become more complex, allowing older people to experience various emotions that benefit their mental health (Demiralp et al., 2012; Schneider & Stone, 2015). Positive feelings, supported by enhanced emotional control, tend to grow after midlife, and negative feelings subside (Stone et al., 2010; Urry & Gross, 2010). Older adults increasingly use words that convey positive emotions (Pennebaker & Stone, 2003), and they attend less and less to negative information. Compared with younger Chinese and American adults, for example, older adults are more attentive to positive news (Isaacowitz, 2012; Wang et al., 2015).

Compared with teens and young adults, older adults tend to have a smaller social network, with fewer friendships (Wrzus et al., 2012). Like people of all ages, older adults are, however, happiest when not alone (**FIGURE 13.5**). Older adults experience fewer problems in their relationships—less attachment anxiety, stress, and anger (Chopik et al., 2013; Fingerman & Charles, 2010; Stone et al., 2010). With age, we become more stable and more accepting (Carstensen et al., 2011; Shallcross et al., 2013).

"When you were born, you cried and the world rejoiced. Live your life in a manner so that when you die the world cries and you rejoice."

Native American proverb

"Still married after all these years?
No mystery.
We are each other's habit,
And each other's history."

Judith Viorst,
"The Secret of Staying Married," 2007

> FIGURE 13.5

Humans are social creatures
Both younger and older adults report greater happiness when spending time with others. (Note this correlation could also reflect happier people being more social.) (Gallup survey data reported by Crabtree, 2011.)

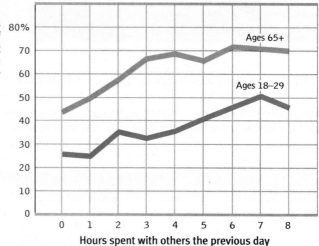

The aging brain may help nurture these positive feelings. Brain scans of older adults show that the amygdala, a neural processing center for emotions, responds less actively to negative events (but not to positive events) (Mather et al., 2004). Brain-wave reactions to negative images also diminish with age (Kisley et al., 2007).

Moreover, at all ages, the bad feelings we associate with negative events fade faster than do the good feelings we associate with positive events (Walker et al., 2003). This leaves most older people with the comforting feeling that life, on balance, has been mostly good. Thanks to biological, psychological, and social-cultural influences, more and more people flourish into later life (**FIGURE 13.6**).

> "At 20 we worry about what others think of us. At 40 we don't care what others think of us. At 60 we discover they haven't been thinking about us at all."
>
> *Anonymous*

> "The best thing about being 100 is *no peer pressure.*"
>
> *Lewis W. Kuester, 2005, on turning 100*

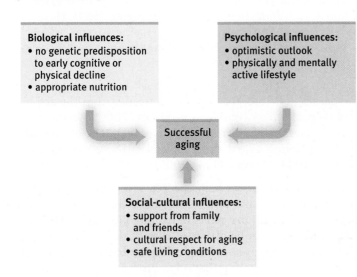

❮ FIGURE 13.6

Biopsychosocial influences on successful aging

 RETRIEVE IT

• What are some of the most significant challenges and rewards of growing old?

ANSWERS: Challenges: decline of muscular strength, reaction times, stamina, sensory keenness, cardiac output, and immune system functioning. Risk of cognitive decline increases. Rewards: positive feelings tend to grow; negative emotions are less intense; and worry, stress, anger, and social-relationship problems decrease.

Death and Dying

13-5 A loved one's death triggers what range of reactions?

Warning: If you begin reading the next paragraph, you will die.

But of course, if you hadn't read this, you would still die in due time. "Time is a great teacher," noted the nineteenth-century composer Hector Berlioz, "but unfortunately it kills all its pupils." Death is our inevitable end. We enter the world with a wail, and usually leave it in silence.

Most of us will also suffer and cope with the deaths of relatives and friends. For most people, the most difficult separation they will experience is the death of a spouse—a loss suffered by four times more women than men. But for some people, grief is especially severe, because a loved one's death comes suddenly and before its expected time on the social clock. The sudden illness or accident claiming a 45-year-old life partner or a child may trigger a year or more of memory-laden mourning that eventually subsides to a mild depression (Lehman et al., 1987).

For some, however, the loss is unbearable. One Danish long-term study of more than 1 million people found that about 17,000 of them had suffered the death of a child under 18. In the 5 years following that death, 3 percent of them

> "Love—why, I'll tell you what love is: It's you at 75 and her at 71, each of you listening for the other's step in the next room, each afraid that a sudden silence, a sudden cry, could mean a lifetime's talk is over."
>
> *Brian Moore, The Luck of Ginger Coffey, 1960*

had a first psychiatric hospitalization, a 67 percent higher rate than among other parents (Li et al., 2005).

Even so, reactions to a loved one's death range more widely than most suppose. Some cultures encourage public weeping and wailing; others hide grief. Within any culture, individuals differ. Given similar losses, some people grieve hard and long, others less so (Ott et al., 2007). Contrary to popular misconceptions, however:

- terminally ill and bereaved people do not go through identical predictable stages, such as denial before anger (Friedman & James, 2008; Nolen-Hoeksema & Larson, 1999).

- those who express the strongest grief immediately do not purge their grief more quickly (Bonanno & Kaltman, 1999; Wortman & Silver, 1989). However, grieving parents who try to protect their partner by "staying strong" and not discussing their child's death may actually prolong the grieving (Stroebe et al., 2013).

- bereavement therapy and self-help groups offer support, but there is similar healing power in the passing of time, the support of friends, and the act of giving support and help to others (Baddeley & Singer, 2009; Brown et al., 2008; Neimeyer & Currier, 2009). Grieving spouses who talk often with others or receive grief counseling adjust about as well as those who grieve more privately (Bonanno, 2004; Stroebe et al., 2005).

Facing death with dignity and openness helps people complete the life cycle with a sense of life's meaningfulness and unity—the sense that their existence has been good and that life and death are parts of an ongoing cycle. Although death may be unwelcome, life itself can be affirmed even at death. This is especially so for people who review their lives not with despair but with what Erik Erikson called a sense of *integrity*—a feeling that one's life has been meaningful and worthwhile.

"Consider, friend, as you pass by, as you are now, so once was I. As I am now, you too shall be. Prepare, therefore, to follow me."

Scottish tombstone epitaph

MODULE 13 REVIEW   Adulthood

👁 Learning Objectives

Test Yourself by taking a moment to answer each of these Learning Objective Questions (repeated here from within the module). Then turn to Appendix D, Complete Module Reviews, to check your answers. Research suggests that trying to answer these questions on your own will improve your long-term memory of the concepts (McDaniel et al., 2009).

13-1 What physical changes occur during middle and late adulthood?

13-2 How does memory change with age?

13-3 What themes and influences mark our social journey from early adulthood to death?

13-4 How does our well-being change across the life span?

13-5 A loved one's death triggers what range of reactions?

💬 Terms and Concepts to Remember

Test yourself on these terms by trying to write down the definition in your own words before flipping back to the referenced page to check your answers.

menopause, p. 158

cross-sectional study, p. 162

longitudinal study, p. 162

social clock, p. 163

[✱] Experience the Testing Effect

Test yourself repeatedly throughout your studies. This will not only help you figure out what you know and don't know; the testing itself will help you learn and remember the information more effectively thanks to the *testing effect*.

1. By age 65, a person would be most likely to experience a cognitive decline in the ability to
   a. recall and list all the important terms and concepts in a module.
   b. select the correct definition in a multiple-choice question.
   c. recall their own birth date.
   d. practice a well-learned skill, such as knitting.

2. How do cross-sectional and longitudinal studies differ?

3. Freud defined the healthy adult as one who is able to love and work. Erikson agreed, observing that the adult struggles to attain intimacy and _____.

4. Contrary to what many people assume,
   a. older people are much less happy than adolescents are.
   b. we become less happy as we move from teen years into midlife.
   c. positive feelings tend to grow after midlife.
   d. those whose children have recently left home—the empty nesters—have the lowest level of happiness of all groups.

Find answers to these questions in Appendix E, in the back of the book.

Use 🅜 LearningCurve to create your personalized study plan, which will direct you to the resources that will help you most in 🅜 LaunchPad.

SEX
(biologically male or female)

If biological SEX is *female*

GENDER identity is usually *girl*.

GENDER identity is sometimes *boy*.

Biological influences (genetics, prenatal and adolescent hormones)

Cultural expectations

Learning and experiences

GENDER IDENTITY
(sense of being male, female, or some combination)

TRANSGENDER
(gender identity differs from birth sex)

PHYSIOLOGY of SEX

Sex hormones

puberty ↓
activate sexual behavior throughout life

Prenatal hormones

direct development as males or females

Sexual response cycle
excitement
resolution   plateau
climax

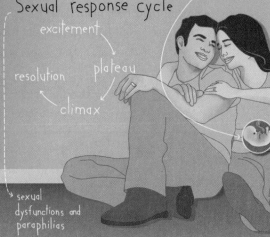

sexual dysfunctions and paraphilias

SEXUAL ORIENTATION

Roughly consistent across time and place

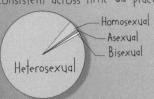

Homosexual
Asexual
Bisexual

Heterosexual

No known environmental influences

Same-sex behaviors observed in other species

Genetic influences

Prenatal influences

Gay-straight brain differences

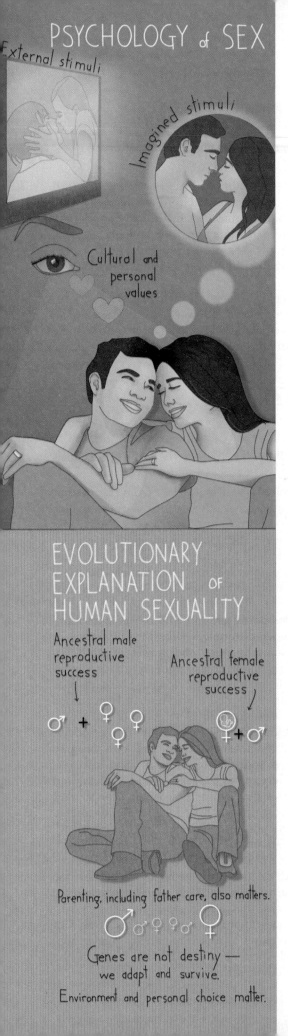

Sex, Gender, and Sexuality

CULTURES change, and their ideas about gender change also. Several decades apart, this text's two authors had similar experiences with different outcomes.

In 1972, as the young chair of our psychology department, I [DM] was proud to make the announcement: We had concluded our search for a new colleague. We had found just who we were looking for—a bright, warm, enthusiastic woman about to receive her Ph.D. in developmental psychology. The vote was unanimous. Alas, our elderly chancellor rejected our recommendation. "As a mother of a preschooler," he said, "she should be home with her child, *not* working full time." No amount of pleading or arguing (for example, that it might be possible to parent a child while employed) could change his mind. So, with a heavy heart, I drove to her city to explain, face to face, my embarrassment in being able to offer her only a temporary position.

This case ended well. She accepted the temporary position and quickly became a beloved, tenured colleague who went on to found our college's women's studies program. Today, she and I marvel at the swift transformation in our culture's thinking about gender.

In 2011, I [ND] experienced something quite different. We, too, were concluding our search for a new colleague. Our department faculty had assessed several candidates, and the top two vote-getters were a man and a woman. Our faculty hiring committee would make the final choice. Before they announced their decision, a senior committee member spoke out. "Look around the table. We're all men. We need to consider that." The accomplished woman was offered the position.

Our ideas about the "proper" behavior for women and men have undergone an extreme makeover. More and more women work in formerly male-dominated professions, and more and more men work in formerly female-dominated professions (England, 2010). Yet women still earn less than men. Women continue to struggle to reach the top of the ladder. In 2015, only 5 percent of the chief executives of Fortune 500 companies were women. And expectant parents in many cultures still hope for a son. Nevertheless, our views of women and men continue to evolve.

In Module 14, we'll look at some of the ways nature and nurture interact to form our unique gender identities. We'll see what researchers tell us about how alike we are as males and females, and how and why we differ. In Module 15, we'll gain insight from psychological science about the psychology and biology of sexual attraction and sexual intimacy. As part of the journey, we'll see how evolutionary psychologists explain our sexuality. ■

MODULE 14 Gender Development

14-1 How does the meaning of *gender* differ from the meaning of *sex?*

We humans share an irresistible urge to organize our worlds into simple categories. Among the ways we classify people—as tall or short, dull or smart, cheerful or churlish—one stands out. Immediately after your birth (or even before), everyone wanted to know, "Boy or girl?" Your parents may have offered clues with pink or blue clothing. The simple answer described your **sex,** your biological status, defined by your chromosomes and anatomy. For most people, those biological traits help define their assigned **gender,** their culture's expectations about what it means to be male or female.

Our gender is the product of the interplay among our biological dispositions, our developmental experiences, and our current situations (Eagly & Wood, 2013). Before we consider that interplay in more detail, let's take a closer look at some ways that males and females are both similar and different.

How Are We Alike? How Do We Differ?

14-2 What are some ways in which males and females tend to be alike and to differ?

Whether male or female, each of us receives 23 chromosomes from our mother and 23 from our father. Of those 46 chromosomes, 45 are unisex—the same for males and females. Both men and women needed to survive, reproduce, and avoid predators, and so today we are in most ways alike. Identify yourself as male or female and you give no clues to your vocabulary, happiness, or ability to see, hear, learn, and remember. Women and men, on average, have comparable creativity and intelligence and feel the same emotions and longings. Our "opposite" sex is, in reality, our very similar sex.

But in some areas, males and females do differ, and differences command attention. Some much-talked-about gender differences (like the difference in self-esteem shown in **FIGURE 14.1**) are actually quite modest (Zell et al., 2015). Others are more striking. The average woman enters puberty about a year earlier than the average man, and her life span is 5 years longer. She expresses emotions more freely, smiling and crying more, and more frequently mentions (in Facebook updates) "love" and being "sooo excited!!!" (Fischer & LaFrance, 2015; Schwartz et al., 2013). She can detect fainter odors, receives offers of help more often, and can become sexually re-aroused sooner after orgasm. She also has twice the risk of developing depression and anxiety, and 10 times the risk of developing an eating disorder. Yet the average man is 4 times more likely to die by suicide or to develop an alcohol use disorder. His "more likely" list also includes autism spectrum disorder (ASD), color-deficient vision, and attention-deficit/hyperactivity disorder (ADHD). And as an adult, he is more at risk for antisocial personality disorder. Male or female, each has its own share of risks.

Gender differences appear throughout this book, but for now let's take a closer look at three areas—aggression, social power, and social connectedness—in which the average male and female differ.

Pink and blue baby outfits illustrate how cultural norms vary and change. "The generally accepted rule is pink for the boy and blue for the girl," declared the *Earnshaw's Infants' Department* in June of 1918 (Frassanito & Pettorini, 2008). "The reason is that pink being a more decided and stronger color is more suitable for the boy, while blue, which is more delicate and dainty, is prettier for the girls."

✓ FIGURE 14.1

Much ado about a small difference in self-esteem These two normal distributions differ by the approximate magnitude (0.21 standard deviation) of the sex difference in self-esteem, averaged over all available samples (Hyde, 2005). Moreover, such comparisons illustrate differences between the *average* female and male. The variation among individual females greatly exceeds this difference, as it also does among individual males.

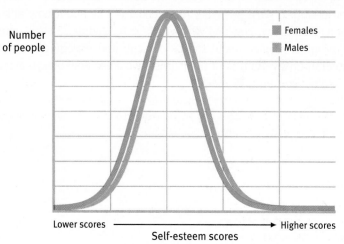

Number of people

Females
Males

Lower scores ⟶ Higher scores
Self-esteem scores

Aggression

To a psychologist, **aggression** is any physical or verbal behavior intended to hurt someone physically or emotionally. Think of some aggressive people you have heard about. Are most of them men? Men generally admit to more aggression. They also commit more extreme physical violence (Bushman & Huesmann, 2010). In romantic relationships between men and women, minor acts of physical aggression, such as slaps, are roughly equal—but especially violent acts are mostly committed by men (Archer, 2000; Johnson, 2008).

Laboratory experiments have demonstrated gender differences in aggression. Men have been more willing to blast people with what they believed was intense and prolonged noise (Bushman et al., 2007). And outside the laboratory, men—worldwide—commit more violent crime (Antonaccio et al., 2011; Caddick & Porter, 2012; Frisell et al., 2012). They also take the lead in hunting, fighting, warring, and supporting war (Liddle et al., 2012; Wood & Eagly, 2002, 2007).

Here's another question: Think of examples of people harming others by passing along hurtful gossip, or by shutting someone out of a social group or situation. Were most of those people men? Perhaps not. Those behaviors are acts of **relational aggression,** and women are slightly more likely than men to commit them (Archer, 2004, 2007, 2009).

Deadly relational aggression
Sladjana Vidovic was a high school student who committed suicide after suffering constant relational aggression by bullies.

Social Power

Imagine you've walked into a job interview and are taking your first look at the two interviewers. The unsmiling person on the left oozes self-confidence and independence, maintaining steady eye contact. The person on the right gives you a warm, welcoming smile but makes less eye contact and seems to expect the other interviewer to take the lead.

Which interviewer is male?

If you said the person on the left, you're not alone. Around the world, from Nigeria to New Zealand, people have perceived gender differences in power (Williams & Best, 1990). Indeed, in most societies men *do* place more importance on power and achievement and *are* socially dominant (Schwartz & Rubel-Lifschitz, 2009):

- When groups form, whether as juries or companies, leadership tends to go to males (Colarelli et al., 2006). And when salaries are paid, those in traditionally male occupations receive more.

- When people run for election, women who appear hungry for political power experience less success than their equally power-hungry male counterparts (Okimoto & Brescoll, 2010). And when elected, political leaders usually are men, who held 78 percent of the seats in the world's governing parliaments in 2015 (IPU, 2015).

Men and women also lead differently. Men tend to be more *directive,* telling people what they want and how to achieve it. Women tend to be more *democratic,* more welcoming of others' input in decision making (Eagly & Carli, 2007; van Engen & Willemsen, 2004). When interacting, men have been more likely to offer opinions, women to express support (Aries, 1987; Wood, 1987). In everyday behavior, men tend to act as powerful people often do: talking assertively, interrupting, initiating touches, and staring. And they smile and apologize less (Leaper & Ayres, 2007; Major et al., 1990; Schumann & Ross, 2010). Such behaviors help sustain men's greater social power.

sex in psychology, the biologically influenced characteristics by which people define *males* and *females*.

gender in psychology, the socially influenced characteristics by which people define *men* and *women*.

aggression any physical or verbal behavior intended to harm someone physically or emotionally.

relational aggression an act of aggression (physical or verbal) intended to harm a person's relationship or social standing.

Women's 2015 representation in national parliaments ranged from 13 percent in the Pacific region to 41 percent in Scandinavia (IPU, 2015).

Social Connectedness

Whether male or female, we all have a need to belong, though we may satisfy this need in different ways (Baumeister, 2010). Males tend to be *independent.* Even as children, males typically form large play groups. Boys' games brim with

Every man for himself, or tend and befriend? Sex differences in the way we interact with others begin to appear at a very young age.

"In the long years liker must they grow;
The man be more of woman, she of man."

Alfred Lord Tennyson,
The Princess, *1847*

activity and competition, with little intimate discussion (Rose & Rudolph, 2006). As adults, men enjoy doing activities side by side, and they tend to use conversation to communicate solutions (Tannen, 1990; Wright, 1989).

Females tend to be more *interdependent.* In childhood, girls usually play in small groups, often with one friend. They compete less and imitate social relationships more (Maccoby, 1990; Roberts, 1991). Teen girls spend more time with friends and less time alone (Wong & Csikszentmihalyi, 1991). In late adolescence, they spend more time on social networking sites (Pryor et al., 2007, 2011), and teen girls average twice as many text messages per day as boys (Lenhart, 2012). As adults, women take more pleasure in talking face to face, and they tend to use conversation more to explore relationships. Brain scans suggest that women's brains are better wired to improve social relationships, and men's brains to connect perception with action (Ingalhalikar et al., 2013).

A gender difference in communication style was apparent in one New Zealand study of student e-mails, when two-thirds of the time people correctly guessed whether the author was male or female (Thomson & Murachver, 2001). In France, women have been found to make 63 percent of phone calls and, when talking to a woman, to stay connected longer (7.2 minutes) than men when talking to other men (4.6 minutes) (Smoreda & Licoppe, 2000).

More than a half-million people's responses to various interest inventories reveal that "men prefer working with things and women prefer working with people" (Su et al., 2009). In one analysis of over 700 million words collected from Facebook messages, women used more family-related words, whereas men used more work-related words (Schwartz et al., 2013). On entering American colleges, men are seven times more likely than women to express interest in computer science (Pryor et al., 2011).

In the workplace, women are less often driven by money and status, and more often opt for reduced work hours (Pinker, 2008). For many, family obligations loom large, with mothers, compared to fathers, spending twice as many hours doing child care (Parker & Wang, 2013). Both men and women have reported their friendships with women as more intimate, enjoyable, and nurturing (Kuttler et al., 1999; Rubin, 1985; Sapadin, 1988). When searching for understanding from someone who will share their worries and hurts, people usually turn to women. How do they cope with their own stress? Compared with men, women are more likely to turn to others for support. They are said to *tend and befriend* (Tamres et al., 2002; Taylor, 2002).

The gender gap in both social connectedness and power peaks in late adolescence and early adulthood—the prime years for dating and mating. Teenage girls become less assertive and more flirtatious, and boys appear more dominant and less expressive. Gender differences in attitudes and behavior often peak after the birth of a first child. Mothers especially may become more traditional (Ferriman et al., 2009; Katz-Wise et al., 2010). By age 50, most parent-related gender differences subside. Men become less domineering and more empathic, and women—especially those with paid employment—become more assertive and self-confident (Kasen et al., 2006; Maccoby, 1998).

So, although women and men are more alike than different, there are some behavior differences between the average woman and man. Are such differences dictated by our biology? Shaped by our cultures and other experiences? Do we vary in the extent to which we are male or female? Read on.

RETRIEVE IT [✗]

• _____ (Men/Women) are more likely to commit relational aggression, and _____ (men/women) are more likely to commit physical aggression.

ANSWERS: Women; men

• _____ (Men/Women) have tended to express more personal and professional interest in people and less interest in things.

ANSWER: Women

The Nature of Gender: Our Biological Sex

14-3 How do sex hormones influence prenatal and adolescent sexual development, and what is a *disorder of sexual development?*

In many physical ways—regulating heat with sweat, preferring energy-rich foods, growing calluses where the skin meets friction—men and women are similar. When looking for a mate, men and women also prize many of the same traits. They prefer having a mate who is kind, honest, and intelligent. But, say evolutionary psychologists, in mating-related domains, guys act like guys whether they're chimpanzees or elephants, rural peasants or corporate presidents (Geary, 2010).

Biology does not *dictate* gender. But in two ways, biology influences gender:

- *Genetically*—males and females have differing *sex chromosomes*.
- *Physiologically*—males and females have differing concentrations of *sex hormones,* which trigger other anatomical differences.

These two influences began to form you long before you were born.

Prenatal Sexual Development

Six weeks after you were conceived, you and someone of the other sex looked much the same. Then, as your genes kicked in, your biological sex—determined by your twenty-third pair of chromosomes (the two sex chromosomes)—became more apparent. Whether you are male or female, your mother's contribution to that chromosome pair was an **X chromosome.** From your father, you received the one chromosome out of 46 that is not unisex—either another X chromosome, making you female, or a **Y chromosome,** making you male.

About seven weeks after conception, a single gene on the Y chromosome throws a master switch, which triggers the testes to develop and to produce **testosterone,** the principal male hormone that promotes development of male sex organs. (Females also have testosterone, but less of it.)

Later, during the fourth and fifth prenatal months, sex hormones bathe the fetal brain and influence its wiring. Different patterns for males and females develop under the influence of the male's greater testosterone and the female's ovarian hormones (Hines, 2004; Udry, 2000).

Adolescent Sexual Development

A flood of hormones triggers another period of dramatic physical change during adolescence, when boys and girls enter **puberty.** In this two-year period of rapid sexual maturation, pronounced male-female differences emerge. A variety of changes begin at about age 11 in girls and at about age 12 in boys, though the subtle beginnings of puberty, such as enlarging testes, appear earlier (Herman-Giddens et al., 2012). A year or two before the physical changes are visible, boys and girls often feel the first stirrings of sexual attraction (McClintock & Herdt, 1996).

Girls' slightly earlier entry into puberty can at first propel them to greater height than boys of the same age (**FIGURE 14.2** on the next page). But boys catch up when they begin puberty, and by age 14, they are usually taller than girls. During these growth spurts, the **primary sex characteristics**—the reproductive organs and external genitalia—develop dramatically. So do **secondary sex characteristics.** Girls develop breasts and larger hips. Boys' facial hair begins growing and their voices deepen. Pubic and underarm hair emerges in both girls and boys (**FIGURE 14.3** on the next page).

For boys, puberty's landmark is the first ejaculation, which often occurs first during sleep (as a "wet dream"). This event, called **spermarche,** usually happens by about age 14.

X chromosome the sex chromosome found in both men and women. Females have two X chromosomes; males have one. An X chromosome from each parent produces a female child.

Y chromosome the sex chromosome found only in males. When paired with an X chromosome from the mother, it produces a male child.

testosterone the most important of the male sex hormones. Both males and females have it, but the additional testosterone in males stimulates the growth of the male sex organs during the fetal period, and the development of the male sex characteristics during puberty.

puberty the period of sexual maturation, when a person becomes capable of reproducing.

primary sex characteristics the body structures (ovaries, testes, and external genitalia) that make sexual reproduction possible.

secondary sex characteristics nonreproductive sexual traits, such as female breasts and hips, male voice quality, and body hair.

spermarche [sper-MAR-key] first ejaculation.

Pubertal boys may not at first like their sparse beard. (But then it grows on them.)

Nick Downes

> **FIGURE 14.2**

Height differences Throughout childhood, boys and girls are similar in height. At puberty, girls surge ahead briefly, but then boys typically overtake them at about age 14. (Data from Tanner, 1978.) Studies suggest that sexual development and growth spurts are now beginning somewhat earlier than was the case a half-century ago (Herman-Giddens et al., 2001).

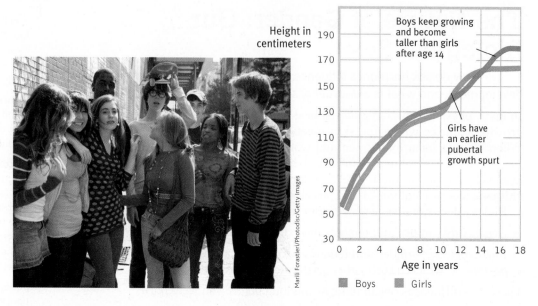

Height in centimeters

Boys keep growing and become taller than girls after age 14

Girls have an earlier pubertal growth spurt

Age in years

■ Boys   ■ Girls

Marili Forastieri/Photodisc/Getty Images

---

menarche [meh-NAR-key] the first menstrual period.

LaunchPad For a 7-minute discussion of our sexual development, visit LaunchPad's *Video: Gender Development*.

In girls, the landmark is the first menstrual period, **menarche,** usually within a year of age 12½ (Anderson et al., 2003). Genes play a major role in predicting when girls experience menarche (Perry et al., 2014). But environment matters, too. Early menarche is more likely following stresses related to father absence, sexual abuse, insecure attachments, or a history of a mother's smoking during pregnancy (DelPriore & Hill, 2013; Rickard et al., 2014; Shrestha et al., 2011). In various countries, girls are developing breasts earlier (sometimes before age 10) and reaching puberty earlier than in the past. Suspected triggers include increased body fat, diets filled with hormone-mimicking chemicals, and possibly greater stress due to family disruption (Biro et al., 2010, 2012; Herman-Giddens, 2012).

Girls prepared for menarche usually experience it positively (Chang et al., 2009). Most women recall their first menstrual period with mixed emotions—pride, excitement, embarrassment, and apprehension (Greif & Ulman, 1982; Woods et al., 1983). Men report mostly positive emotional reactions to spermarche (Fuller & Downs, 1990).

> **FIGURE 14.3**

Body changes at puberty At about age 11 in girls and age 12 in boys, a surge of hormones triggers a variety of visible physical changes.

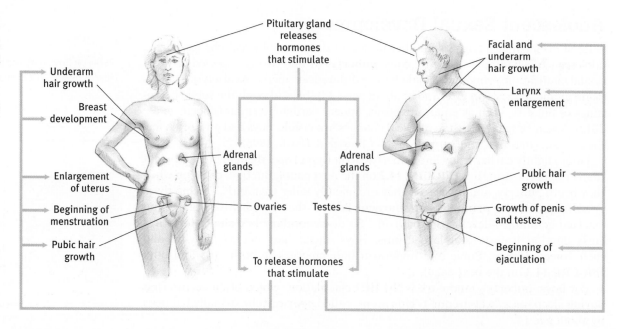

Pituitary gland releases hormones that stimulate

Underarm hair growth

Breast development

Enlargement of uterus

Beginning of menstruation

Pubic hair growth

Adrenal glands

Ovaries

Facial and underarm hair growth

Larynx enlargement

Adrenal glands

Testes

Pubic hair growth

Growth of penis and testes

Beginning of ejaculation

To release hormones that stimulate

• Prenatal sexual development begins about _____ weeks after conception.
  Adolescence is marked by the onset of _____.

ANSWERS: seven; puberty

disorder of sexual development a condition present at birth that involves unusual development of sex chromosomes and anatomy.

role a set of expectations (norms) about a social position, defining how those in the position ought to behave.

gender role a set of expected behaviors, attitudes, and traits for males or for females.

Sexual Development Variations

Sometimes nature blurs the biological line between males and females. When a fetus is exposed to unusual levels of sex hormones, or is especially sensitive to those hormones, the individual may develop a **disorder of sexual development,** with chromosomes or anatomy not typically male or female. For example, a genetic male may be born with normal male hormones and testes but no penis or a very small one.

In the past, medical professionals often recommended *sex-reassignment surgery* to create an unambiguous identity for some children with this condition. One study reviewed 14 cases of boys who had undergone early surgery and had been raised as girls. Of those cases, 6 had later declared themselves male, 5 were living as females, and 3 reported an unclear male or female identity (Reiner & Gearhart, 2004).

Sex-reassignment surgery can create distress among those *not* born with a disorder of sexual development. In one famous case, a little boy lost his penis during a botched circumcision. His parents followed a psychiatrist's advice to raise him as a girl rather than as a damaged boy. Alas, "Brenda" Reimer was not like most other girls. "She" didn't like dolls. She tore her dresses with rough-and-tumble play. At puberty she wanted no part of kissing boys. Finally, Brenda's parents explained what had happened, whereupon "Brenda" immediately rejected the assigned female identity. He cut his hair and chose a male name, David. He eventually married a woman and became a stepfather. And, sadly, he later committed suicide (Colapinto, 2000).

The bottom line: "Sex matters," concluded the National Academy of Sciences (2001). Sex-related genes and physiology "result in behavioral and cognitive differences between males and females." Yet environmental factors matter too, as we will see next. Nature and nurture work together.

"I am who I am."
Dramatic improvements in South African track star Caster Semenya's race times prompted the International Association of Athletics Federations to undertake sex testing in 2009. Semenya was reported to have a disorder of sexual development, with physical characteristics not typically male or female. She was officially cleared to continue competing as a woman. Semenya declared, "God made me the way I am and I accept myself. I am who I am" (YOU, 2009).

Michael Dalder/Reuters

The Nurture of Gender: Our Culture and Experiences

14-4 How do gender roles and gender identity differ?

For many people, biological sex and gender coexist in harmony. Biology draws the outline, and culture paints the details. The physical traits that define us as biological males or females are the same worldwide. But the gender traits that define how men (or boys) and women (or girls) *should* act, interact, or feel about themselves may differ from one place to another (APA, 2009).

Gender Roles

Cultures shape our behaviors by defining how we ought to behave in a particular social position, or **role.** We can see this shaping power in **gender roles**—the social expectations that guide our behavior as men or women. Gender roles shift over

"Sex brought us together, but gender drove us apart."

New Yorker Collection, 2001, Barbara Smaller from cartoonbank.com.

The gendered tsunami In Sri Lanka, Indonesia, and India, the gendered division of labor helps explain the excess of female deaths from the 2004 tsunami. In some villages, 80 percent of those killed were women, who were mostly at home while the men were more likely to be at sea fishing or doing out-of-the-home chores (Oxfam, 2005).

time. A century ago, American women could not vote in national elections, serve in the military, or divorce a husband without cause. And if a woman worked for pay, she would more likely have been a midwife or a seamstress than a surgeon or a shopkeeper.

Gender roles can change dramatically in a thin slice of history. At the beginning of the twentieth century, only one country in the world—New Zealand—granted women the right to vote (Briscoe, 1997). Today, worldwide, only Saudi Arabia denies women the right to vote. More U.S. women than men now graduate from college, and nearly half the workforce is female (DOL, 2015). The college gender role landscape will likely continue to change. Men comprise most faculty positions in science, technology, engineering, and mathematics (STEM) fields (Ceci et al., 2014; Sheltzer & Smith, 2014). Yet, in one recent study that invited U.S. professors to evaluate faculty candidates for STEM positions, most preferred hiring a highly talented woman over a highly talented man (Williams & Ceci, 2015). The modern economy has produced jobs that rely not on brute strength but on social intelligence, open communication, and the ability to sit still and focus (Rosin, 2010).

Gender roles also vary from one place to another. Nomadic societies of food-gathering people have had little division of labor by sex. Boys and girls receive much the same upbringing. In agricultural societies, where women typically work in the nearby fields and men roam while herding livestock, cultures have shaped children to assume more distinct gender roles (Segall et al., 1990; Van Leeuwen, 1978).

Take a minute to check your own gender expectations. Would you agree that "When jobs are scarce, men should have more rights to a job?" In the United States, Britain, and Spain, barely over 12 percent of adults agree. In Nigeria, Pakistan, and India, about 80 percent of adults agree (Pew, 2010). We're all human, but my how our views differ. The Scandinavian countries offer the greatest gender equity, Middle Eastern and North African countries the least (World Economic Forum, 2014).

How Do We Learn Gender?

A *gender role* describes how others expect us to think, feel, and act. Our **gender identity** is our personal sense of being male, female, or, occasionally, some combination of the two. How do we develop that personal viewpoint?

Social learning theory assumes that we acquire our identity in childhood, by observing and imitating others' gender-linked behaviors and by being rewarded or punished for acting in certain ways. ("Tatiana, you're such a good mommy to your dolls"; "Big boys don't cry, Armand.") Some critics think there's more to gender identity than imitating parents and being repeatedly rewarded for certain responses. They point out that **gender typing**—taking on a traditional male or female role—varies from child to child (Tobin et al., 2010). No matter how much parents encourage or discourage traditional gender behavior, children may drift toward what feels right to them. Some organize themselves into "boy worlds" and "girl worlds," each guided by assumed rules. Others conform to these rules more flexibly. Still others seem to prefer **androgyny:** a blend of male and female roles feels right to them. Androgyny has benefits. Androgynous people are more adaptable. They show greater flexibility in behavior and career choices (Bem, 1993). They tend to be more resilient and self-accepting, and they experience less depression (Lam & McBride-Chang, 2007; Mosher & Danoff-Burg, 2008; Ward, 2000).

The social learning of gender Children observe and imitate parental models.

How we feel matters, but so does how we think. Early in life we form *schemas*, or concepts that help us make sense of our world. Our *gender schemas* organize our experiences of male-female characteristics and help us think about our gender identity, about who we are (Bem, 1987, 1993; Martin et al., 2002). Our parents help to transmit their culture's views on gender. In one analysis of 43 studies, parents with traditional gender schemas were more likely to have gender-typed children who shared their culture's expectations about how males and females should act (Tenenbaum & Leaper, 2002).

As a young child, you (like other children) were a "gender detective" (Martin & Ruble, 2004). Before your first birthday, you knew the difference between a male and female voice or face (Martin et al., 2002). After you turned 2, language forced you to label the world in terms of gender. If you are an English speaker, you learned to classify people as *he* and *she*. If you are a French speaker, you learned to classify objects as masculine ("*le train*") or feminine ("*la table*").

Once children grasp that two sorts of people exist—and that they are of one sort—they search for clues about gender. In every culture, people communicate their gender in many ways. Their *gender expression* drops hints not only in their language but also in their clothing, interests, and possessions. Having divided the human world in half, 3-year-olds will then like their own kind better and seek them out for play. "Girls," they may decide, are the ones who watch *My Little Pony* and have long hair. "Boys" watch *Transformers* battles and don't wear dresses. Armed with their newly collected "proof," they then adjust their behaviors to fit their concept of gender. These rigid stereotypes peak at about age 5 or 6. If the new neighbor is a boy, a 6-year-old girl may assume she cannot share his interests. For young children, gender looms large.

For a **transgender** person, gender identity differs from the behaviors or traits considered typical for that person's assigned birth sex (APA, 2010; Bockting, 2014). Even as 5- to 12-year-olds, transgender children typically view themselves in terms of their expressed gender rather than their biological sex (Olson et al., 2015). A person may feel like a man in a woman's body, or like a woman in a man's body. Some transgender people are also *transsexual:* They prefer to live as members of the other birth sex. Some transsexual people (about three times as many men as women) seek medical treatment (including sex-reassignment surgery) to achieve their preferred gender identity (Van Kesteren et al., 1997).

Note that *gender identity* is distinct from *sexual orientation* (the direction of one's sexual attraction). Transgender people may be sexually attracted to people of the other birth sex *(heterosexual)*, the same birth sex *(homosexual)*, both sexes *(bisexual)*, or to no one at all *(asexual)*.

Transgender people sometimes express their gender identity by dressing as a person of the other biological sex typically would. Most who dress this way are biological males who are attracted to women (APA, 2010).

gender identity our sense of being male, female, or some combination of the two.

social learning theory the theory that we learn social behavior by observing and imitating and by being rewarded or punished.

gender typing the acquisition of a traditional masculine or feminine role.

androgyny displaying both traditional masculine and feminine psychological characteristics.

transgender an umbrella term describing people whose gender identity or expression differs from that associated with their birth sex.

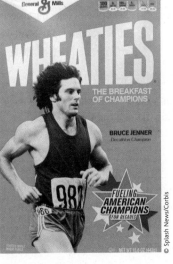

Transgender Olympic decathlon champion and reality TV star, Bruce Jenner, became the world's most famous transgender person and an Internet sensation after transitioning to Caitlyn Jenner.

"The more I was treated as a woman, the more woman I became."

Writer Jan Morris, male-to-female transsexual

LaunchPad For a 6.5-minute exploration of one pioneering transgender person's journey, see LaunchPad's *Video: Renee Richards—A Long Journey.*

RETRIEVE IT [✕]

• What are gender roles, and what do their variations tell us about our human capacity for learning and adaptation?

ANSWER: *Gender roles* are social rules or norms for accepted and expected behavior for females and males. The norms associated with various roles, including gender roles, vary widely in different cultural contexts, which is proof that we are very capable of learning and adapting to the social demands of different environments.

MODULE 14 REVIEW Gender Development

👁 Learning Objectives

Test Yourself by taking a moment to answer each of these Learning Objective Questions (repeated here from within the module). Then turn to Appendix D, Complete Module Reviews, to check your answers. Research suggests that trying to answer these questions on your own will improve your long-term memory of the concepts (McDaniel et al., 2009).

14-1 How does the meaning of *gender* differ from the meaning of *sex*?

14-2 What are some ways in which males and females tend to be alike and to differ?

14-3 How do sex hormones influence prenatal and adolescent sexual development, and what is a *disorder of sexual development*?

14-4 How do gender roles and gender identity differ?

🔲 Terms and Concepts to Remember

Test yourself on these terms by trying to write down the definition in your own words before flipping back to the referenced page to check your answers.

sex, p. 172
gender, p. 172
aggression, p. 173
relational aggression, p. 173

X chromosome, p. 175
Y chromosome, p. 175
testosterone, p. 175
puberty, p. 175
primary sex characteristics, p. 175
secondary sex characteristics, p. 175
spermarche [sper-MAR-key], p. 175
menarche [meh-NAR-key], p. 176

disorder of sexual development, p. 177
role, p. 177
gender role, p. 177
gender identity, p. 178
social learning theory, p. 178
gender typing, p. 178
androgyny, p. 178
transgender, p. 179

[×] Experience the Testing Effect

Test yourself repeatedly throughout your studies. This will not only help you figure out what you know and don't know; the testing itself will help you learn and remember the information more effectively thanks to the *testing effect*.

1. Psychologists define _____ as the biologically influenced characteristics by which people define males and females. The socially influenced characteristics by which people define men and women is _____.

2. Females and males are very similar to each other. But one way they differ is that
   a. females are more physically aggressive than males.
   b. males are more democratic than females in their leadership roles.
   c. girls tend to play in small groups, while boys tend to play in large groups.
   d. females are more likely to commit suicide.

3. A fertilized egg will develop into a boy if it receives a/n _____ chromosome from its father.

4. Primary sex characteristics relate to _____; secondary sex characteristics refer to _____.
   a. ejaculation; menarche
   b. breasts and facial hair; ovaries and testes

c. emotional maturity; hormone surges
d. reproductive organs; nonreproductive traits

5. On average, girls begin puberty at about the age of _____, boys at about the age of _____.

6. An individual who is born with sexual anatomy that differs from typical male or female anatomy has a _____ _____ _____.

7. *Gender role* refers to our
   a. personal sense of being male or female.
   b. culture's expectations about the "right" way for males and females to behave.
   c. birth sex—our chromosomes and anatomy.
   d. unisex characteristics.

8. When children have developed a _____ _____, they have a sense of being male, female, or some combination of the two.

Find answers to these questions in Appendix E, in the back of the book.

Use 🅒 LearningCurve to create your personalized study plan, which will direct you to the resources that will help you most in 🅒 LaunchPad.

MODULE 15 Human Sexuality

As you've probably noticed, we can hardly talk about gender without talking about our sexuality. For all but the tiny fraction of us considered **asexual,** dating and mating become a high priority from puberty on. Our emerging sexual feelings and behaviors reflect both physiological and psychological influences.

The Physiology of Sex

Sex is not like hunger, because it is not an actual *need*. (Without it, we may feel like dying, but we will not.) Yet sex is a part of life. Had this not been so for all your ancestors, you would not be reading this book. Sexual motivation is nature's clever way of making people procreate, thus enabling our species' survival. When we feel an attraction, we hardly stop to think of ourselves as guided by ancestral genes. We may crave our partner's presence, with a brain response similar to when someone struggles with an alcohol craving (Acevedo et al., 2012). As the pleasure we take in eating is nature's method of getting our body nourishment, so the desires and pleasures of sex are our genes' way of preserving and spreading themselves. Life is sexually transmitted.

> "It is a near-universal experience, the invisible clause on one's birth certificate stipulating that one will, upon reaching maturity, feel the urge to engage in activities often associated with the issuance of more birth certificates."
>
> *Science writer Natalie Angier, 2007*

Hormones and Sexual Behavior

15-1 How do hormones influence human sexual motivation?

Among the forces driving sexual behavior are the *sex hormones*. The main male sex hormone is **testosterone.** The main female sex hormones are the **estrogens,** such as *estradiol*. Sex hormones influence us at many points in the life span:

- During the prenatal period, they direct our development as males or females.
- During puberty, a sex hormone surge ushers us into adolescence.
- After puberty and well into the late adult years, sex hormones activate sexual behavior.

In most mammals, nature neatly synchronizes sex with fertility. Females become sexually receptive (in nonhumans, "in heat") when their estrogens peak at ovulation. In experiments, researchers can cause female animals to become receptive by injecting them with estrogens. Male hormone levels are more constant, and hormone injection does not so readily affect the sexual behavior of male animals (Feder, 1984). Nevertheless, male rats that have had their testosterone-making testes surgically removed will gradually lose much of their interest in receptive females. They slowly regain it if injected with testosterone.

Hormones do influence human sexual behavior, but in a looser way. Researchers are exploring and debating whether women's mate preferences change across the menstrual cycle (Gildersleeve et al., 2014; Wood et al., 2014). Some evidence suggests that, among women with mates, sexual desire rises slightly at ovulation, when there is a surge of estrogens and a smaller surge of testosterone—a change that men can sometimes detect in women's behaviors and voices (Haselton & Gildersleeve, 2011).

Women have much less testosterone than men do. And more than other mammalian females, women are responsive to their testosterone level (van Anders, 2012). If a woman's natural testosterone level drops, as happens with removal of the ovaries or adrenal glands, her sexual interest may wane. But as experiments with hundreds of surgically or naturally menopausal women have demonstrated, testosterone-replacement therapy can often restore diminished sexual activity, arousal, and desire (Braunstein et al., 2005; Buster et al., 2005; Petersen & Hyde, 2011).

In human males with abnormally low testosterone levels, testosterone-replacement therapy often increases sexual desire and also energy and vitality (Yates, 2000). But

asexual having no sexual attraction to others.

testosterone the most important of the male sex hormones. Both males and females have it, but the additional testosterone in males stimulates the growth of the male sex organs during the fetal period, and the development of the male sex characteristics during puberty.

estrogens sex hormones, such as estradiol, secreted in greater amounts by females than by males and contributing to female sex characteristics. In nonhuman female mammals, estrogen levels peak during ovulation, promoting sexual receptivity.

normal fluctuations in testosterone levels, from man to man and hour to hour, have little effect on sexual drive (Byrne, 1982). Indeed, male hormones sometimes vary in *response* to sexual stimulation (Escasa et al., 2011). In one study, Australian skateboarders' testosterone surged in the presence of an attractive female, contributing to riskier moves and more crash landings (Ronay & von Hippel, 2010). Thus, sexual arousal can be a *cause* as well as a consequence of increased testosterone levels. At the other end of the mating spectrum, international studies have found that married fathers tend to have lower testosterone levels than do bachelors and married men without children (Edelstein et al., 2015; Gettler et al., 2013; Gray et al., 2006).

Large hormonal surges or declines affect men and women's desire in shifts that tend to occur at two predictable points in the life span, and sometimes at an unpredictable third point:

1. *The pubertal surge in sex hormones triggers the development of sex characteristics and sexual interest.* If the hormonal surge is precluded—as it was during the 1600s and 1700s for prepubertal boys who were castrated to preserve their soprano voices for Italian opera—sex characteristics and sexual desire do not develop normally (Peschel & Peschel, 1987).

2. *In later life, hormone levels fall.* Women experience menopause, males a more gradual change. As sex hormone levels decline, sex remains a part of life, but the frequency of sexual fantasies and intercourse subsides (Leitenberg & Henning, 1995).

3. *For some, surgery or drugs may cause hormonal shifts.* When adult men were castrated, sex drive typically fell as testosterone levels declined sharply (Hucker & Bain, 1990). Male sex offenders who take Depo-Provera, a drug that reduces testosterone levels to that of a prepubertal boy, have similarly lost much of their sexual urge (Bilefsky, 2009; Money et al., 1983).

To summarize: We might compare human sex hormones, especially testosterone, to the fuel in a car. Without fuel, a car will not run. But if the fuel level is minimally adequate, adding more fuel to the gas tank won't change how the car runs. The analogy is imperfect, because hormones and sexual motivation interact. However, it correctly suggests that biology is a necessary but not sufficient explanation of human sexual behavior. The hormonal fuel is essential, but so are the psychological stimuli that turn on the engine, keep it running, and shift it into high gear.

RETRIEVE IT [✱]

• The primary male sex hormone is _____. The primary female sex hormones are the _____.

ANSWERS: testosterone; estrogens

The Sexual Response Cycle

◁▷ 15-2 What is the human sexual response cycle, and how do sexual dysfunctions and paraphilias differ?

The scientific process often begins with careful observations of complex behaviors. When gynecologist-obstetrician William Masters and his collaborator Virginia Johnson (1966) applied this process to human sexual intercourse in the 1960s, they made headlines. They recorded the physiological responses of volunteers who came to their lab to masturbate or have intercourse. With the help of 382 female and 312 male volunteers—a somewhat atypical sample, consisting only of people able and willing to display arousal and orgasm while scientists observed—Masters and Johnson reported observing more than 10,000 sexual "cycles." Their description of the **sexual response cycle** identified four stages:

1. *Excitement* The genital areas become engorged with blood, causing a woman's clitoris and a man's penis to swell. A woman's vagina expands and secretes lubricant; her breasts and nipples may enlarge.

sexual response cycle the four stages of sexual responding described by Masters and Johnson—excitement, plateau, orgasm, and resolution.

2. *Plateau* Excitement peaks as breathing, pulse, and blood pressure rates continue to increase. A man's penis becomes fully engorged—to an average length of 5.6 inches among 1661 men who measured themselves for condom fitting (Herbenick et al., 2014). Some fluid—frequently containing enough live sperm to enable conception—may appear at its tip. A woman's vaginal secretion continues to increase, and her clitoris retracts. Orgasm feels imminent.

3. *Orgasm* Muscle contractions appear all over the body and are accompanied by further increases in breathing, pulse, and blood pressure rates. A woman's arousal and orgasm facilitate conception: They help draw semen from the penis, position the uterus to receive sperm, and carry the sperm further inward, increasing retention (Furlow & Thornhill, 1996). The pleasurable feeling of sexual release is much the same for both sexes. One panel of experts could not reliably distinguish between descriptions of orgasm written by men and those written by women (Vance & Wagner, 1976). In another study, PET scans showed that the same subcortical brain regions were active in men and women during orgasm (Holstege et al., 2003a,b).

4. *Resolution* The body gradually returns to its unaroused state as the genital blood vessels release their accumulated blood. This happens relatively quickly if orgasm has occurred, relatively slowly otherwise. (It's like the nasal tickle that goes away rapidly if you have sneezed, slowly otherwise.) Men then enter a **refractory period** that lasts from a few minutes to a day or more, during which they are incapable of another orgasm. A woman's much shorter refractory period may enable her, if restimulated during or soon after resolution, to have more orgasms.

Sexual Dysfunctions and Paraphilias

Masters and Johnson sought not only to describe the human sexual response cycle but also to understand and treat the inability to complete it. **Sexual dysfunctions** are problems that consistently impair sexual arousal or functioning. Some involve sexual motivation, especially lack of sexual energy and arousability. For men, others include **erectile disorder** (inability to have or maintain an erection) and *premature ejaculation*. For women, the problem may be pain or **female orgasmic disorder** (distress over infrequently or never experiencing orgasm). In separate surveys of some 3000 Boston women and 32,000 other American women, about 4 in 10 reported a sexual problem, such as orgasmic disorder or low desire, but only about 1 in 8 reported that this caused personal distress (Lutfey et al., 2009; Shifren et al., 2008). Most women who have experienced sexual distress have related it to their emotional relationship with their partner during sex (Bancroft et al., 2003).

Therapy can help men and women with sexual dysfunctions (Frühauf et al., 2013). In behaviorally oriented therapy, for example, men learn ways to control their urge to ejaculate, and women are trained to bring themselves to orgasm. Starting with the introduction of Viagra in 1998, erectile disorder has been routinely treated by taking a pill. Some more modestly effective drug treatments for *female sexual interest/arousal disorder* are also available.

Sexual dysfunction involves problems with arousal or sexual functioning. People with **paraphilias** do experience sexual desire, but they direct it in unusual ways. The American Psychiatric Association (2013) only classifies such behavior as disordered if

- a person experiences distress from an unusual sexual interest *or*

- it entails harm or risk of harm to others.

The serial killer Jeffrey Dahmer had *necrophilia,* a sexual attraction to corpses. Those with *exhibitionism* derive pleasure from exposing themselves sexually to

A nonsmoking 50-year-old male has about a 1-in-a-million chance of a heart attack during any hour. This increases to merely 2-in-a-million in the two hours during and following sex (with no increase for those who exercise regularly). Compared with risks associated with heavy exertion or anger, this risk seems not worth losing sleep (or sex) over (Jackson, 2009; Muller et al., 1996).

refractory period a resting period after orgasm, during which a man cannot achieve another orgasm.

sexual dysfunction a problem that consistently impairs sexual arousal or functioning.

erectile disorder inability to develop or maintain an erection due to insufficient bloodflow to the penis.

female orgasmic disorder distress due to infrequently or never experiencing orgasm.

paraphilias sexual arousal from fantasies, behaviors, or urges involving nonhuman objects, the suffering of self or others, and/or nonconsenting persons.

others, without consent. People with the paraphilic disorder *pedophilia* experience sexual arousal toward children who haven't entered puberty.

Sexually Transmitted Infections

 15-3 How can sexually transmitted infections be prevented?

Every day, more than 1 million people worldwide acquire a *sexually transmitted infection (STI;* also called *STD* for *sexually transmitted disease)* (WHO, 2013). Teenage girls, because of their not yet fully mature biological development and lower levels of protective antibodies, are especially vulnerable (Dehne & Riedner, 2005; Guttmacher, 1994). A Centers for Disease Control study of sexually experienced 14- to 19-year-old U.S. females found 39.5 percent had STIs (Forhan et al., 2008).

To comprehend the mathematics of infection transmission, imagine this scenario. Over the course of a year, Pat has sex with 9 people, each of whom, by that point in time, has had sex with the same number of partners as has Pat. How many partners—including "phantom" sexual partners (past partners of partners)—will Pat have? The actual number—511—is more than five times the estimate given by the average student (Brannon & Brock, 1993).

Condoms offer only limited protection against certain skin-to-skin STIs, such as herpes, but they do reduce other risks (Medical Institute for Sexual Health, 1994; NIH, 2001). The effects were clear when Thailand promoted 100 percent condom use by commercial sex workers. Over a four-year period, as condom use soared from 14 to 94 percent, the annual number of bacterial STIs plummeted from 410,406 to 27,362 (WHO, 2000).

Across the available studies, condoms also have been 80 percent effective in preventing transmission of *HIV (human immunodeficiency virus*—the virus that causes **AIDS**) from an infected partner (Weller & Davis-Beaty, 2002; WHO, 2003). Although AIDS can be transmitted by other means, such as needle sharing during drug use, its sexual transmission is most common. Half of all humans with HIV are women, and their proportion is increasing, partly because the virus is passed from man to woman much more often than from woman to man. A man's semen can carry more of the virus than can a woman's vaginal and cervical secretions. The HIV-infected semen can also linger in a woman's vagina and cervix, increasing the time of exposure (Allen & Setlow, 1991; WHO, 2015).

Most Americans with AIDS have been in midlife and younger—ages 25 to 44 (CDC, 2011). Given AIDS' long incubation period, this means that many of these young people were infected as teens. In 2012, the death of 1.6 million people with AIDS worldwide left behind countless grief-stricken partners and millions of orphaned children (UNAIDS, 2013). Sub-Saharan Africa is home to two-thirds of those infected with HIV, and medical treatment that extends life and care for the dying is sapping the region's social resources.

Many people assume that oral sex falls in the category of "safe sex," but recent studies show a significant link between oral sex and transmission of STIs, such as the *human papillomavirus (HPV)*. Risks rise with the number of sexual partners (Gillison et al., 2012). Most HPV infections can now be prevented with a vaccination administered before sexual contact.

AIDS (acquired immune deficiency syndrome) a life-threatening, sexually transmitted infection caused by the *human immunodeficiency virus* (HIV). AIDS depletes the immune system, leaving the person vulnerable to infections.

RETRIEVE IT [✻]

• The inability to complete the sexual response cycle may be considered a _____ _____. Exhibitionism would be considered a _____.

ANSWERS: sexual dysfunction; paraphilia

• From a biological perspective, AIDS is passed more readily from women to men than from men to women. True or false?

ANSWER: False. AIDS is transmitted more easily and more often from men to women.

The Psychology of Sex

◀◉▶ **15-4** How do external and imagined stimuli contribute to sexual arousal?

Biological factors powerfully influence our sexual motivation and behavior. Yet the wide variations over time, across place, and among individuals document the great influence of psychological factors as well (**FIGURE 15.1**). Thus, despite the shared biology that underlies sexual motivation, 281 expressed reasons for having sex ranged widely—from "to get closer to God" to "to get my boyfriend to shut up" (Buss, 2008; Meston & Buss, 2007).

External Stimuli

Men and women become aroused when they see, hear, or read erotic material (Heiman, 1975; Stockton & Murnen, 1992). In 132 experiments, men's feelings of sexual arousal have much more closely mirrored their (more obvious) genital response than have women's (Chivers et al., 2010).

People may find sexual arousal either pleasing or disturbing. (Those who wish to control their arousal often limit their exposure to such materials, just as those wishing to avoid overeating limit their exposure to tempting cues.) With repeated exposure, the emotional response to any erotic stimulus often lessens, or *habituates*. During the 1920s, when Western women's rising hemlines first reached the knee, an exposed leg was a mildly erotic stimulus.

Can exposure to sexually explicit material have adverse effects? Research has indicated that it can:

- *Rape acceptance* Depictions of women being sexually coerced—and liking it—have increased viewers' belief in the false idea that women enjoy rape, and have increased male viewers' willingness to hurt women (Malamuth & Check, 1981; Zillmann, 1989).

- *Devaluing partner* Viewing images of sexually attractive women and men may also lead people to devalue their own partners and relationships. After male college students viewed TV or magazine depictions of sexually attractive women, they often found an average woman, or their own girlfriend or wife, less attractive (Kenrick & Gutierres, 1980; Kenrick et al., 1989; Weaver et al., 1984).

- *Diminished satisfaction* Viewing X-rated sex films has similarly tended to reduce people's satisfaction with their own sexual partner (Zillmann, 1989). Perhaps reading or watching erotica's unlikely scenarios may create expectations that few men and women can fulfill.

Biological influences:
- sexual maturity
- sex hormones, especially testosterone

Psychological influences:
- exposure to stimulating conditions
- sexual fantasies

Sexual motivation

Social-cultural influences:
- family and society values
- religious and personal values
- cultural expectations
- media

Imagined Stimuli

The brain, it has been said, is our most significant sex organ. The stimuli inside our heads—our imagination—can influence sexual arousal and desire. Lacking genital sensation because of a spinal-cord injury, people can still feel sexual desire (Willmuth, 1987).

Wide-awake people become sexually aroused not only by memories of prior sexual activities but also by fantasies, which in a few women can produce orgasms (Komisaruk & Whipple, 2011). About 95 percent of both men and women have said they have sexual fantasies. Men (whether gay or straight) fantasize about sex more often, more physically, and less romantically (Schmitt et al., 2012). They also prefer less personal and faster-paced sexual content in books and videos (Leitenberg & Henning, 1995). Fantasizing about sex does *not* indicate a sexual problem or dissatisfaction. If anything, sexually active people have more sexual fantasies.

△ **FIGURE 15.1**

Levels of analysis for sexual motivation Our sexual motivation is influenced by biological factors, but psychological and social-cultural factors play an even bigger role.

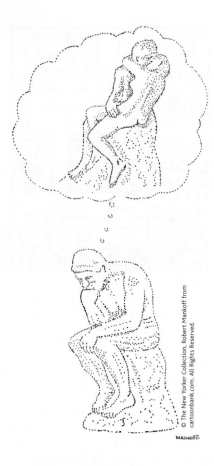

MANKOFF.

"Condoms should be used on every conceivable occasion."

Anonymous

social script culturally modeled guide for how to act in various situations.

• What factors influence our sexual motivation and behavior?

ANSWER: Influences include biological factors such as sexual maturity and sex hormones, psychological factors such as environmental stimuli and fantasies, and social-cultural factors such as the values and expectations absorbed from family and the surrounding culture.

Teen Pregnancy

15-5 What factors influence teenagers' sexual behaviors and use of contraceptives?

Compared with European teens, American teens have a higher rate of STIs and also of teen pregnancy (Call et al., 2002; Sullivan/Anderson, 2009). What environmental factors contribute to teen pregnancy?

Minimal communication about birth control Many teenagers are uncomfortable discussing contraception with their parents, partners, and peers. Teens who talk freely with parents, and who are in an exclusive relationship with a partner with whom they communicate openly, are more likely to use contraceptives (Aspy et al., 2007; Milan & Kilmann, 1987).

Guilt related to sexual activity Among sexually active 12- to 17-year-old American girls, 72 percent said they regretted having had sex (Reuters, 2000). Sexual inhibitions or ambivalence can restrain sexual activity, but also reduce planning for birth control (Gerrard & Luus, 1995; MacDonald & Hynie, 2008).

Alcohol use Most sexual hookups (casual encounters outside of a relationship) occur among people who are intoxicated, with an impaired ability to give and comprehend consent (Fielder et al., 2013; Garcia et al., 2013). Those who use alcohol prior to sex are less likely to use condoms (Kotchick et al., 2001). By depressing the brain centers that control judgment, inhibition, and self-awareness, alcohol disarms normal restraints—a phenomenon well known to sexually coercive males.

Mass media norms of unprotected promiscuity Perceived peer norms influence teens' sexual behavior (van de Bongardt et al., 2015). Teens attend to other teens, who, in turn, are influenced by popular media. Media help write the **social scripts** that affect our perceptions and actions. So what sexual scripts do today's media write on our minds? Sexual content appears in approximately 85 percent of movies, 82 percent of television programs, 59 percent of music videos, and 37 percent of music lyrics (Ward et al., 2014). Twenty percent of middle school students, and 44 percent of 18- to 24-year-olds, report having received a "sext"—a sexually explicit text (Lenhart & Duggan, 2014; Rice et al., 2014). And sexual partners on TV shows have rarely communicated any concern for birth control or STIs (Brown et al., 2002; Kunkel, 2001; Sapolsky & Tabarlet, 1991). The more sexual content adolescents and young adults view or read (even when controlling for other predictors of early sexual activity), the more likely they are to perceive their peers as sexually active, to develop sexually permissive attitudes, and to experience early intercourse (Escobar-Chaves et al., 2005; Kim & Ward, 2012; Parkes et al., 2013).

Media influences can either increase or decrease sexual risk taking. One study asked more than a thousand 12- to 14-year-olds what movies they had seen, and then after age 18 asked them about their teen sexual experiences (O'Hara et al., 2012). After controlling for various adolescent and family characteristics, the more the adolescents viewed movies with high sexual content, the greater was their sexual risk taking—with earlier debut, more partners, and inconsistent condom use. Another study analyzed the effect of MTV's series *16 and Pregnant*, which portrayed the consequences of unprotected sex and the challenges of having a child. By analyzing viewership and pregnancy rates over time in specific areas, the researchers concluded that the program led to a 6 percent reduction in the national teen pregnancy rate (Kearney & Levine, 2014).

Later sex may pay emotional dividends. One national study followed participants to about age 30. Even after controlling for several other factors, those who had later first sex reported greater relationship satisfaction in their marriages and partnerships (Harden, 2012). Several other factors also predict sexual restraint:

- *High intelligence* Teens with high rather than average intelligence test scores more often delayed sex, partly because they considered possible negative consequences and were more focused on future achievement than on here-and-now pleasures (Halpern et al., 2000).

- *Religious engagement* Actively religious teens have more often reserved sexual activity for adulthood (Hull et al., 2011; Lucero et al., 2008).

- *Father presence* In studies that followed hundreds of New Zealand and U.S. girls from age 5 to 18, a father's absence was linked to sexual activity before age 16 and to teen pregnancy (Ellis et al., 2003). These associations held even after adjusting for other adverse influences, such as poverty. Close family attachments—families that eat together and where parents know their teens' activities and friends—also predicted later sexual initiation (Coley et al., 2008).

- *Participation in service learning programs* Several experiments have found that teens volunteering as tutors or teachers' aides, or participating in community projects, had lower pregnancy rates than were found among comparable teens randomly assigned to control conditions (Kirby, 2002; O'Donnell et al., 2002). Researchers are unsure why. Does service learning promote a sense of personal competence, control, and responsibility? Does it encourage more future-oriented thinking? Or does it simply reduce opportunities for unprotected sex?

Keeping abreast of hypersexuality
An analysis of the 60 top-selling video games found 489 characters, 86 percent of whom were males (like most of the game players). The female characters were much more likely than the male characters to be "hypersexualized"—partially nude or revealingly clothed, with large breasts and tiny waists (Downs & Smith, 2010). Such depictions can lead to unrealistic expectations about sexuality and contribute to the early sexualization of girls. The American Psychological Association suggests countering this by teaching girls to "value themselves for who they are rather than how they look" (APA, 2007).

RETRIEVE IT [✖]

- Which THREE of the following five factors contribute to unplanned teen pregnancies?

  a. Alcohol use

  b. Higher intelligence level

  c. Unprotected sex

  d. Mass media models

  e. Increased communication about options

ANSWERS: a, c, d

Sexual Orientation

15-6 What has research taught us about sexual orientation?

We express the *direction* of our sexual interest in our **sexual orientation**—our enduring sexual attraction toward members of our own sex *(homosexual orientation)*, the other sex *(heterosexual orientation)*, or both sexes *(bisexual orientation)*. Cultures vary in their attitudes toward same-sex attractions. "Should society accept homosexuality?" *Yes*, say 88 percent of Spaniards, 80 percent of Canadians, and 1 percent of Nigerians, with women everywhere being more accepting than men (Pew, 2013). Yet whether a culture condemns or accepts same-sex unions, heterosexuality prevails and homosexuality exists. In African countries, in most of which same-sex relationships are illegal, the prevalence of people who are lesbian, gay, or bisexual "is no different from other countries in the rest of the world," reports the Academy of Science of South Africa (2015).

Sexual Orientation: The Numbers

How many people are exclusively homosexual? About 10 percent, as the popular press has often assumed? Or 20 percent, as the average American estimated in a 2013 survey (Jones et al., 2014)? According to more than a dozen national surveys in Europe and the United States, a better estimate is about 3 or 4 percent of men and

In one British survey, of the 18,876 people contacted, 1 percent were asexual, having "never felt sexually attracted to anyone at all" (Bogaert, 2004, 2006b; 2012). People identifying as asexual are, however, nearly as likely as others to report masturbating, noting that it feels good, reduces anxiety, or "cleans out the plumbing."

sexual orientation an enduring sexual attraction toward members of one's own sex (homosexual orientation), the other sex (heterosexual orientation), or both sexes (bisexual orientation).

2 percent of women (Chandra et al., 2011; Herbenick et al., 2010; Savin-Williams et al., 2012). When Gallup asked 121,290 Americans about their sexual identity—"Do you, personally, identify as lesbian, gay, bisexual, or transgender?"—3.4 percent answered *Yes* (Gates & Newport, 2012). When the National Center for Health Statistics asked 34,557 Americans about their sexual identity, they found essentially the same result: All but 3.4 percent answered "straight," with 1.6 percent answering "gay" or "lesbian" and 0.7 percent saying "bisexual" (Ward et al., 2014).

Survey methods that absolutely guarantee people's anonymity reveal another percent or two of nonheterosexual people (Coffman et al., 2013). Moreover, people in less tolerant places are more likely to hide their sexual orientation. About 3 percent of California men express a same-sex preference on Facebook, for example, as do only about 1 percent in Mississippi. Yet about 5 percent of Google pornography searches in both states are for gay porn. And Craigslist ads for males seeking "casual encounters" with other men tend to be at least as common in less tolerant states, where there are also more Google searches for "gay sex" and "Is my husband gay?" (MacInnis & Hodson, 2015; Stephens-Davidowitz, 2013).

Fewer than 1 percent of people—for example, only 12 people out of 7076 Dutch adults in one survey (Sandfort et al., 2001)—reported being actively bisexual. A larger number of adults—13 percent of women and 5 percent of men in a U.S. National Center for Health Statistics survey—report some same-sex sexual contact during their lives (Chandra et al., 2011). And still more have had an occasional homosexual fantasy. In laboratory assessments, some self-identified bisexual men show a homosexual arousal pattern by responding with genital arousal mostly to male erotic images. Others exhibit increased viewing time and genital arousal to both male and female images (Cerny & Janssen, 2011; Lippa, 2013; Rieger et al., 2013; Rosenthal et al., 2012).

What does it feel like to have same-sex attractions in a heterosexual culture? If you are heterosexual, one way to understand is to imagine how you would feel if you were socially isolated for openly admitting or displaying your feelings toward someone of the other sex. How would you react if you overheard people making crude jokes about heterosexual people, or if most movies, TV shows, and advertisements portrayed (or implied) homosexuality? And how would you answer if your family members were pleading with you to change your heterosexual "lifestyle" and to enter into a homosexual marriage?

Facing such reactions, some individuals struggle with their sexual attractions, especially during adolescence and if feeling rejected by parents or harassed by peers. If lacking social support, nonheterosexual teens may experience lower self-esteem and higher anxiety and depression (Becker et al., 2014; Kwon, 2013), as well as an increased risk of contemplating suicide (Plöderl et al., 2013; Ryan et al., 2009; Wang et al., 2012). They may at first try to ignore or deny their desires, hoping they will go away. But they don't. Then they may try to change, through psychotherapy, willpower, or prayer. But the feelings typically persist, as do those of heterosexual people—who are similarly incapable of change (Haldeman, 1994, 2002; Myers & Scanzoni, 2005).

Today's psychologists therefore view sexual orientation as neither willfully chosen nor willfully changed. "Efforts to change sexual orientation are unlikely to be successful and involve some risk of harm," declared a 2009 American Psychological Association report. Sexual orientation in some ways is like handedness: Most people are one way, some the other. A very few are truly ambidextrous. Regardless, the way one is endures.

This conclusion is most strongly established for men. Women's sexual orientation tends to be less strongly felt and potentially more fluid and changing (Chivers, 2005; Diamond, 2008; Dickson et al., 2013). In general, men are sexually simpler. Their lesser sexual variability is apparent in many ways (Baumeister, 2000). Compared with men, women's sexual drive and interests are more flexible and varying. Women, for example, more often prefer to alternate periods of

In tribal cultures in which homosexual behavior is expected of all boys before marriage, heterosexuality nevertheless persists (Hammack, 2005; Money, 1987). As this illustrates, homosexual *behavior* does not always indicate a homosexual *orientation*.

high sexual activity with periods of almost none (Mosher et al., 2005). In their pupil dilation and genital responses to erotic videos, and in their implicit attitudes, heterosexual women exhibit more bisexual attraction than do men (Rieger & Savin-Williams, 2012; Snowden & Gray, 2013). Baumeister calls women's more varying sexuality a difference in *erotic plasticity.*

Origins of Sexual Orientation

So, our sexual orientation is something we do not choose and (especially for males) cannot change. Where, then, do these preferences come from? See if you can anticipate the conclusions that have emerged from hundreds of research studies by responding *Yes* or *No* to the following questions:

1. Is homosexuality linked with problems in a child's relationships with parents, such as with a domineering mother and an ineffectual father, or a possessive mother and a hostile father?

2. Does homosexuality involve a fear or hatred of people of the other sex, leading individuals to direct their desires toward members of their own sex?

3. Is sexual orientation linked with levels of sex hormones currently in the blood?

4. As children, were most homosexuals molested, seduced, or otherwise sexually victimized by an adult homosexual?

The answer to all these questions has been *No* (Storms, 1983). In a search for possible environmental influences on sexual orientation, Kinsey Institute investigators interviewed nearly 1000 homosexuals and 500 heterosexuals. They assessed nearly every imaginable psychological cause of homosexuality—parental relationships, childhood sexual experiences, peer relationships, dating experiences (Bell et al., 1981; Hammersmith, 1982). Their findings: Homosexuals are no more likely than heterosexuals to have been smothered by maternal love or neglected by their father. In one national survey of nearly 35,000 adults, those with a same-sex attraction were somewhat more likely to report having experienced child sexual abuse. But 86 percent of the men and 75 percent of the women with same-sex attraction reported no such abuse (Roberts et al., 2013).

And consider this: If "distant fathers" were more likely to produce homosexual sons, then shouldn't boys growing up in father-absent homes more often be gay? (They are not.) And shouldn't the rising number of such homes have led to a noticeable increase in the gay population? (It has not.) Most children raised by gay or lesbian parents grow up straight (Gartrell & Bos, 2010).

The bottom line from a half-century's theory and research: If there are environmental factors that influence sexual orientation, we do not yet know what they are. The lack of evidence for environmental causes of homosexuality has motivated researchers to explore possible biological influences. They have considered these possibilities:

- Same-sex behaviors in other species
- Gay-straight brain differences
- Genetic influences
- Prenatal influences

SAME-SEX ATTRACTION IN OTHER SPECIES In Boston's Public Gardens, caretakers solved the mystery of why a much-loved swan couple's eggs never hatched. Both swans were female. In New York City's Central Park Zoo, penguins Silo and Roy spent several years as devoted same-sex partners. Same-sex sexual behaviors have also been observed in several hundred other species, including grizzlies, gorillas, monkeys, flamingos, and owls (Bagemihl, 1999). Among rams, for

Driven to suicide In 2010, Rutgers University student Tyler Clementi jumped off this bridge after his intimate encounter with another man reportedly became known. Reports then surfaced of other gay teens who had reacted in a similarly tragic fashion after being taunted. Since 2010, Americans—especially those under 30—have been increasingly supportive of those with same-sex orientations.

Note that the scientific question is not "What causes homosexuality?" (or "What causes heterosexuality?") but "What causes differing sexual orientations?" In pursuit of answers, psychological science compares the backgrounds and physiology of people whose sexual orientations *differ.*

LaunchPad See LaunchPad's *Video: Naturalistic Observation* for a helpful tutorial animation.

Juliet and Juliet Boston's beloved swan couple, "Romeo and Juliet," were discovered actually to be, as are many other animal partners, a same-sex pair.

"Gay men simply don't have the brain cells to be attracted to women."

Simon LeVay, The Sexual Brain, *1993*

example, some 7 to 10 percent display same-sex attraction by shunning ewes and seeking to mount other males (Perkins & Fitzgerald, 1997). Homosexual behavior seems a natural part of the animal world.

GAY-STRAIGHT BRAIN DIFFERENCES Researcher Simon LeVay (1991) studied sections of the hypothalamus (a brain structure linked to emotion) taken from deceased heterosexual and homosexual people. As a gay scientist, LeVay wanted to do "something connected with my gay identity." To avoid biasing the results, he did a *blind study,* not knowing which donors were gay. For nine months he peered through his microscope at a cell cluster he thought might be important. Then, one morning, he broke the code: One cell cluster was reliably larger in heterosexual men than in women and homosexual men. "I was almost in a state of shock," LeVay said (1994). "I took a walk by myself on the cliffs over the ocean. I sat for half an hour just thinking what this might mean."

It should not surprise us that brains differ with sexual orientation. Remember, *everything psychological is simultaneously biological.* But when did the brain difference begin? At conception? During childhood or adolescence? Did experience produce the difference? Or was it genes or prenatal hormones (or genes via prenatal hormones)?

LeVay does not view this cell cluster as an "on-off button" for sexual orientation. Rather, he believes it is an important part of a brain pathway that is active during sexual behavior. He agrees that sexual behavior patterns could influence the brain's anatomy. (Neural pathways in our brain do grow stronger with use.) In fish, birds, rats, and humans, brain structures vary with experience—including sexual experience (Breedlove, 1997). But LeVay believes it more likely that brain anatomy influences sexual orientation. His hunch seems confirmed by the discovery of a similar difference found between the male sheep that do and don't display same-sex attraction (Larkin et al., 2002; Roselli et al., 2002, 2004). Moreover, such differences seem to develop soon after birth, perhaps even before birth (Rahman & Wilson, 2003).

Since LeVay's discovery, other researchers have reported additional gay-straight brain activity differences. One is an area of the hypothalamus that governs sexual arousal (Savic et al., 2005). When straight women were given a whiff of a scent derived from men's sweat (which contains traces of male hormones), this area became active. Gay men's brains responded similarly to the men's scent. Straight men's brains did not. They showed the arousal response only to a female hormone sample. In a similar study, lesbians' responses differed from those of straight women (Kranz & Ishai, 2006; Martins et al., 2005).

GENETIC INFLUENCES Evidence indicates a genetic influence on sexual orientation. "Homosexuality does appear to run in families," noted Brian Mustanski and Michael Bailey (2003). Researchers have speculated about possible reasons why "gay genes" might exist in the human gene pool, given that same-sex couples cannot naturally reproduce. One possible answer is kin selection. Evolutionary psychologists remind us that many of our genes also reside in our biological relatives. Perhaps, then, gay people's genes live on through their supporting the survival and reproductive success of their nieces, nephews, and other relatives. Gay men make generous uncles, suggests one study of Samoans (Vasey & VanderLaan, 2010).

A *fertile females theory* suggests that maternal genetics may also be at work (Bocklandt et al., 2006). Homosexual men tend to have more homosexual relatives on their mother's side than on their father's (Camperio-Ciani et al., 2004, 2009, 2012; VanderLaan et al., 2011, 2012). And the relatives on the mother's side also produce more offspring than do the maternal relatives of heterosexual men. Perhaps the genes that dispose some women to conceive more children with men also dispose some men to be attracted to men (LeVay, 2011). Thus, the decreased reproduction by gay men appears offset by the increased reproduction by their maternal extended family.

Studies of twins also indicate that genes influence sexual orientation. Identical twins (who have identical genes) are somewhat more likely than fraternal twins (whose genes are not identical) to share a homosexual orientation (Alanko et al., 2010; Lángström et al., 2010). However, because sexual orientation differs in many identical twin pairs (especially female twins), other factors must also play a role.

In genetic studies of fruit flies, researchers have altered a single gene and changed the flies' sexual orientation and behavior (Dickson, 2005). During courtship, females acted like males (pursuing other females) and males acted like females (Demir & Dickson, 2005). With humans, it's likely that multiple genes, possibly in interaction with other influences, shape sexual orientation. A genome-wide study of 409 pairs of gay brothers identified sexual orientation links with areas of two chromosomes, one maternally transmitted (Sanders et al., 2015).

PRENATAL INFLUENCES Twins share not only genes, but also a prenatal environment. Two sets of findings indicate that the prenatal environment matters.

First, in humans, a critical period for fetal brain development seems to be the second trimester (Ellis & Ames, 1987; Garcia-Falgueras & Swaab, 2010; Meyer-Bahlburg, 1995). Exposure to the hormone levels typically experienced by female fetuses during this period may predispose a person (female or male) to be attracted to males in later life. When pregnant sheep were injected with testosterone during a similar critical period, their female offspring later showed homosexual behavior (Money, 1987).

Second, the mother's immune system may play a role in the development of sexual orientation. Men who have older brothers are somewhat more likely to be gay—about one-third more likely for each additional older brother (Blanchard, 2004, 2008a,b, 2014; Bogaert, 2003). If the odds of homosexuality are roughly 2 percent among first sons, they would rise to nearly 3 percent among second sons, 4 percent for third sons, and so on for each additional older brother (see **FIGURE 15.2**). The reason for this curious effect—called the *older-brother* or *fraternal birth-order effect*—is unclear. But the explanation does seem biological. The effect does not occur among adopted brothers (Bogaert, 2006a). Researchers suspect the mother's immune system may have a defensive response to substances produced by male fetuses. After each pregnancy with a male fetus, the maternal antibodies may become stronger and may prevent the fetal brain from developing in a typical male pattern.

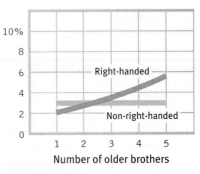

▲ **FIGURE 15.2**

The fraternal birth-order effect Researcher Ray Blanchard (2008a) offers these approximate curves depicting a man's likelihood of homosexuality as a function of his number of older brothers. This correlation has been found in several studies, but only among right-handed men (as about 9 in 10 men are).

"Modern scientific research indicates that sexual orientation is . . . partly determined by genetics, but more specifically by hormonal activity in the womb."

Glenn Wilson and Qazi Rahman,
Born Gay: The Psychobiology of
Sex Orientation, *2005*

Gay-Straight Trait Differences

On several traits, gays and lesbians appear to fall midway between straight females and males (**TABLE 15.1** on the next page; see also LeVay, 2011; Rahman & Koerting, 2008). Gay men tend to be shorter and lighter than straight men—a difference that appears even at birth. Women in same-sex marriages were mostly heavier than average at birth (Bogaert, 2010; Frisch & Zdravkovic, 2010).

Gay-straight spatial abilities also differ. On mental rotation tasks such as the one illustrated in **FIGURE 15.3** on the next page, straight men tend to outscore straight women but the scores of gays and lesbians fall between those of straight men and women (Rahman et al., 2004, 2008). But straight women and gays have both outperformed straight men at remembering objects' spatial locations in tasks like those found in memory games (Hassan & Rahman, 2007).

* * *

Taken together, the brain, genetic, and prenatal findings offer strong support for a biological explanation of sexual orientation (LeVay, 2011; Rahman & Koerting, 2008). Although "much remains to be discovered," concludes Simon LeVay (2011, p. xvii), "the same processes that are involved in the biological development of our bodies and brains as male or female are also involved in the development of sexual orientation."

LaunchPad For an 8-minute overview of the biology of sexual orientation, see LaunchPad's *Video: Homosexuality and the Nature-Nurture Debate.*

"There is no sound scientific evidence that sexual orientation can be changed."

UK Royal College of Psychiatrists, 2009

▾ FIGURE 15.3

Spatial abilities and sexual orientation Which of the four figures can be rotated to match the target figure at the top? Straight males tend to find this an easier task than do straight females, with gays and lesbians intermediate. (From Rahman et al., 2003, with 60 people tested in each group.)

Republished with permission of *Perceptual and Motor Skills*, from "Mental Rotations, A Group Test of Three-Dimensional Spatial Visualization," by Steven G. Vandenberg and Allan R. Kuse, in Volume 47, Issue 2, October 1978: pp. 599–604 (doi:10.2466/pms.1978.47.2.599); permission conveyed through Copyright Clearance Center, Inc.

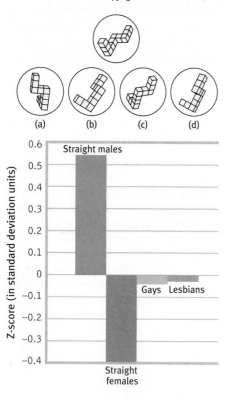

▾ TABLE 15.1

Biological Correlates of Sexual Orientation

Gay-straight trait differences

Sexual orientation is part of a package of traits. Studies—some in need of replication—indicate that homosexuals and heterosexuals differ in the following biological and behavioral traits:

- spatial abilities
- fingerprint ridge counts
- auditory system development
- handedness
- occupational preferences
- relative finger lengths
- gender nonconformity
- age of onset of puberty in males
- male body size
- sleep length
- physical aggression
- walking style

On average (the evidence is strongest for males), results for gays and lesbians fall between those of straight men and straight women. Three biological influences—brain, genetic, and prenatal—may contribute to these differences.

Brain differences

- One hypothalamic cell cluster is smaller in women and gay men than in straight men.
- Anterior commissure is larger in gay men than in straight men.
- Gay men's hypothalamus reacts as do straight women's to the smell of sex-related hormones.

Genetic influences

- Shared sexual orientation is higher among identical twins than among fraternal twins.
- Sexual attraction in fruit flies can be genetically manipulated.
- Male homosexuality often appears to be transmitted from the mother's side of the family.

Prenatal influences

- Altered prenatal hormone exposure may lead to homosexuality in humans and other animals.
- Men with several older biological brothers are more likely to be gay, possibly due to a maternal immune-system reaction.

RETRIEVE IT   [❋]

- Which THREE of the following five factors have researchers found to have an effect on sexual orientation?

  a. A domineering mother

  b. The size of certain cell clusters in the hypothalamus

  c. Prenatal hormone exposure

  d. A distant or ineffectual father

  e. For men, having multiple older biological brothers

ANSWERS: b, c, e

An Evolutionary Explanation of Human Sexuality

15-7 How might an evolutionary psychologist explain male-female differences in sexuality and mating preferences?

Having faced many similar challenges throughout history, males and females have adapted in similar ways: We eat the same foods, avoid the same predators, and perceive, learn, and remember similarly. It is only in those domains where we have faced differing adaptive challenges—most obviously in behaviors related to reproduction—that we differ, say evolutionary psychologists.

Male-Female Differences in Sexuality

And differ we do. Consider sex drives. Both men and women are sexually motivated, some women more so than many men. Yet, on average, who thinks more about

"Not tonight, hon, I have a concussion."

⌄ TABLE 15.2

Predict the Responses Researchers asked samples of U.S. adults whether they agreed or disagreed with the following statements. For each item below, give your best guess about the percentage who agreed with the statement.

Statement	Percentage of males who agreed	Percentage of females who agreed
1. If two people really like each other, it's all right for them to have sex even if they've known each other for a very short time.	_____	_____
2. I can imagine myself being comfortable and enjoying "casual" sex with different partners.	_____	_____
3. Affection was the reason I first had intercourse.	_____	_____
4. I think about sex every day, or several times a day.	_____	_____

ANSWERS: (1) males, 58 percent; females, 34 percent; (2) males, 48 percent; females, 12 percent; (3) males, 25 percent; females, 48 percent; (4) males, 54 percent; females, 19 percent.

Sources: (1) Pryor et al., 2005; (2) Bailey et al., 2000; (3 and 4) Research from Laumann et al., 1994.

sex? Masturbates more often? Initiates more sex? Views more pornography? The answers worldwide—*Men, men, men,* and *men* (Baumeister et al., 2001; Lippa, 2009; Petersen & Hyde, 2010). No surprise, then, that in one BBC survey of more than 200,000 people in 53 nations, men everywhere more strongly agreed that "I have a strong sex drive" and "It doesn't take much to get me sexually excited" (Lippa, 2008).

And there are other sexuality differences between males and females (Hyde, 2005; Petersen & Hyde, 2010; Regan & Atkins, 2007). To see if you can predict some of these differences, take the quiz in **TABLE 15.2**.

Compared with lesbians, gay men (like straight men) report more responsiveness to visual sexual stimuli, and more concern with their partner's physical attractiveness (Bailey et al., 1994; Doyle, 2005; Schmitt, 2007; Sprecher et al., 2013). Gay male couples also report having sex more often than do lesbian couples (Peplau & Fingerhut, 2007). And they report more interest in uncommitted sex. Although men are roughly two-thirds of the U.S. gay population, they are only 36 percent of same-sex legal partners via marriage, civil union, or domestic partnership (Badgett & Mallory, 2014).

Natural Selection and Mating Preferences

Natural selection is nature selecting traits and appetites that contribute to survival and reproduction. Evolutionary psychologists use this principle to explain how men and women differ more in the bedroom than in the boardroom. Our natural yearnings, they say, are our genes' way of reproducing themselves. "Humans are living fossils—collections of mechanisms produced by prior selection pressures" (Buss, 1995).

Why do women tend to be choosier than men when selecting sexual partners? Women have more at stake. To send her genes into the future, a woman must—at a minimum—conceive and protect a fetus growing inside her body for up to nine months. No surprise then, that heterosexual women prefer partners who will offer their joint offspring support and protection. They prefer stick-around dads over likely cads. Heterosexual women are attracted to tall men with slim waists and broad shoulders—all signs of reproductive success (Mautz et al., 2013). And they prefer men who seem mature, dominant, bold, and affluent (Asendorpf et al., 2011; Gangestad & Simpson, 2000; Singh, 1995). One study of hundreds of Welsh pedestrians asked people to rate a driver pictured at the wheel of a humble Ford Fiesta or a swanky Bentley. Men said a female driver was equally attractive in both cars. Women, however, found a male driver more attractive if he was in the luxury car (Dunn & Searle, 2010). When put in a mating mindset, men buy more showy items, express more aggressive intentions, and take more risks (Baker & Maner, 2009; Griskevicius et al., 2009; Shan et al., 2012; Sundie et al., 2011).

⊙ LaunchPad To listen to experts discuss evolutionary psychology and sex differences, visit LaunchPad's *Video: Evolutionary Psychology and Sex Differences.*

"It's not that gay men are oversexed; they are simply men whose male desires bounce off other male desires rather than off female desires."

Steven Pinker, How the Mind Works, *1997*

The mating game Evolutionary psychologists are not surprised that older men, and not just Johnny Depp (pictured with his wife, Amber Heard, who is 23 years younger), often prefer younger women whose features suggest fertility.

The data are in, say evolutionists: Men pair widely; women pair wisely. And what traits do straight men find desirable? Some, such as a woman's smooth skin and youthful shape, cross place and time, and they convey health and fertility (Buss, 1994). Mating with such women might increase a man's chances of sending his genes into the future. And sure enough, men feel most attracted to women whose waists (thanks to their genes or their surgeons) are roughly a third narrower than their hips—a sign of future fertility (Perilloux et al., 2010). Even blind men show this preference for women with a low waist-to-hip ratio (Karremans et al., 2010). Men are most attracted to women whose ages in the ancestral past (when ovulation began later than today) would be associated with peak fertility (Kenrick et al., 2009). Thus, teen boys are most excited by a woman several years older than themselves, mid-twenties men prefer women around their own age, and older men prefer younger women. This pattern consistently appears across European singles ads, Indian marital ads, and marriage records from North and South America, Africa, and the Philippines (Singh, 1993; Singh & Randall, 2007).

There is a principle at work here, say evolutionary psychologists: Nature selects behaviors that increase the likelihood of sending one's genes into the future. As mobile gene machines, we are designed to prefer whatever worked for our ancestors in their environments. They were genetically predisposed to act in ways that would leave grandchildren. Had they not been, we wouldn't be here. As carriers of their genetic legacy, we are similarly predisposed.

Critiquing the Evolutionary Perspective

15-8 What are the key criticisms of evolutionary explanations of human sexuality, and how do evolutionary psychologists respond?

Most psychologists agree that natural selection prepares us for survival and reproduction. But critics say there is a weakness in evolutionary psychology's explanation of our mating preferences. Let's consider how an evolutionary psychologist might explain the findings in a startling study (Clark & Hatfield, 1989), and how a critic might object.

Participants were approached by a "stranger" of the other sex (someone working for the experimenter). The stranger remarked, "I have been noticing you around campus. I find you to be very attractive," and then sometimes asked, "Would you go to bed with me tonight?" What percentage of men and women do you think agreed to this offer? The evolutionary explanation of sexuality predicts that women will be choosier than men in selecting their sexual partners and will be less willing to hop in bed with a complete stranger. In fact, not a single woman agreed—but 70 percent of the men did. A repeat of this study produced a similar result in France (Guéguen, 2011). The research seemed to support an evolutionary explanation.

Or did it? Critics note that evolutionary psychologists start with an effect—in this case, the survey result showing that men were more likely to accept casual sex offers—and work backward to explain what happened. What if research showed the opposite effect? If men refused an offer for casual sex, might we not reason that men who partner with one woman for life make better fathers, whose children more often survive?

Other critics ask why we should try to explain today's behavior based on decisions our distant ancestors made thousands of years ago. Don't cultural expectations also bend the genders? Alice Eagly and Wendy Wood (1999; Eagly, 2009) point to the smaller behavioral differences between men and women in cultures with greater gender equality, for example. Such critics believe *social learning theory* offers a better, more immediate explanation for these results. Women learn *social scripts*—their culture's guide to how

people should act in certain situations. By watching and imitating others in their culture, they may learn that sexual encounters with strangers can be dangerous, and that casual sex may not offer much sexual pleasure (Conley, 2011). This alternative explanation of the study's effects proposes that women react to sexual encounters in ways that their modern culture teaches them. Similarly, men are influenced by social scripts teaching the lesson that "real men" take advantage of every opportunity to have sex.

A third criticism focuses on the social consequences of accepting an evolutionary explanation. Are heterosexual men truly hard-wired to have sex with any woman who approaches them? If so, does it mean that men have no moral responsibility to remain faithful to their partners? Does this explanation excuse men's sexual aggression—"boys will be boys"—because of our evolutionary history?

Evolutionary psychologists agree that much of who we are is *not* hard-wired. "Evolution forcefully rejects a genetic determinism," insisted one research team (Confer et al., 2010). Genes are not destiny. And evolutionary psychologists remind us that men and women, having faced similar adaptive problems, are far more alike than different. Natural selection has prepared us to be flexible. We humans have a great capacity for learning and social progress. We adjust and respond to varied environments. We adapt and survive, whether we live in the Arctic or the desert.

Evolutionary psychologists also agree with their critics that some traits and behaviors, such as suicide, are hard to explain in terms of natural selection (Barash, 2012; Confer et al., 2010). But they ask us to remember evolutionary psychology's scientific goal: to explain behaviors and mental traits by offering testable predictions using principles of natural selection. We can, for example, scientifically test hypotheses such as this: Do we tend to favor others to the extent that they share our genes or can later return our favors? (The answer is *Yes.*) They also remind us that studying how we *came to be* need not dictate how we *ought to be*. Understanding our tendencies can help us overcome them.

> **LaunchPad** To experience a demonstration and explanation of evolutionary psychology and mating preferences, visit LaunchPad's *PsychSim 6: Dating and Mating.*

RETRIEVE IT [×]

• How do evolutionary psychologists explain sex differences in sexuality?

ANSWER: Evolutionary psychologists theorize that females have inherited their ancestors' tendencies to be more cautious, sexually, because of the challenges associated with incubating and nurturing offspring. Males have inherited an inclination to be more casual about sex, because their act of fathering requires a smaller investment.

• What are the three main criticisms of the evolutionary explanation of human sexuality?

ANSWER: (1) It starts with an effect and works backward to propose an explanation. (2) This explanation may overlook the effects of cultural expectations and socialization. (3) Unethical and immoral men could use such explanations to rationalize their behavior toward women.

Social Influences on Human Sexuality

15-9 What role do social factors play in our sexuality, and how do nature, nurture, and our own choices influence gender roles and sexuality?

Human sexuality research does not aim to define the personal meaning of sex in our own lives. We could know every available fact about sex—that the initial spasms of male and female orgasm come at 0.8-second intervals, that female nipples expand 10 millimeters at the peak of sexual arousal, that systolic blood pressure rises some 60 points and respiration rate to 40 breaths per minute—but fail to understand the human significance of sexual intimacy.

Surely one significance of such intimacy is its expression of our profoundly social nature. One study asked 2035 married people when they started having sex (while controlling for education, religious engagement, and relationship length). Those whose relationship first developed to a deep commitment, and then included

Sharing love For most adults, a sexual relationship fulfills not only a biological motive but also a social need for intimacy.

Culture matters As this exhibit at San Diego's Museum of Man illustrates, children learn their culture. A baby's foot can step into any culture.

sex, not only reported greater relationship satisfaction and stability but also better sex than those who had sex very early in their relationship (Busby et al., 2010; Galinsky & Sonenstein, 2013). For both men and women, but especially for women, orgasm occurs more often (and with less morning-after regret) when sex happens in a committed relationship rather than a sexual hookup (Garcia et al., 2012, 2013). Partners who share regular meals are more likely than one-night dinner guests to have educated one another about what seasoning touches suit their food tastes; so likewise with the touches of loyal partners who share a bed.

Sex is a socially significant act. Men and women can achieve orgasm alone, yet most people find greater satisfaction—and experience a much greater surge in the *prolactin* hormone associated with sexual satisfaction and satiety—after intercourse and orgasm with their loved one (Brody & Tillmann, 2006). Thanks to their overlapping brain reward areas, sexual desire and love feed each other (Cacioppo et al., 2012). Sex at its human best is life uniting and love renewing.

Reflections on the Nature and Nurture of Sex, Gender, and Sexuality

Our ancestral history helped form us as a species. Where there is variation, natural selection, and heredity, there will be evolution. Our genes form us. This is a great truth about human nature.

But our culture and experiences also form us. If their genes and hormones predispose males to be more physically aggressive than females, culture can amplify this gender difference through norms that shower benefits on macho men and gentle women. If men are encouraged toward roles that demand physical power, and women toward more nurturing roles, each may act accordingly. By exhibiting the actions expected of those who fill such roles, men and women shape their own traits. Presidents in time become more presidential, servants more servile. Gender roles similarly shape us.

In many modern cultures, gender roles are merging. Brute strength is becoming increasingly less important for power and status (think Mark Zuckerberg and Hillary Clinton). From 1965 to 2013, women soared from 9 to 47 percent of U.S. medical students (AAMC, 2014). In 1965, U.S. married women devoted eight times as many hours to housework as did their husbands; by 2011 this gap had shrunk to less than twice as many (Parker & Wang, 2013). Such swift changes signal that biology does not fix gender roles.

If nature and nurture jointly form us, are we "nothing but" the product of nature and nurture? Are we rigidly determined?

We *are* the product of nature and nurture, but we are also an open system. Genes are all-pervasive but not all-powerful. People may reject their evolutionary role as transmitters of genes and choose not to reproduce. Culture, too, is all-pervasive but not all-powerful. People may defy peer pressures and do the opposite of the expected.

We can't excuse our failings by blaming them solely on bad genes or bad influences. In reality, we are both the creatures and the creators of our worlds. So many things about us—including our gender identities and our mating behaviors—are the products of our genes and environments. Yet the future-shaping stream of causation runs through our present choices. Our decisions today design our environments tomorrow. The human environment is not like the weather—something that just happens. We are its architects. Our hopes, goals, and expectations influence our future. And that is what enables cultures to vary and to change. Mind matters.

15 REVIEW Human Sexuality

◐ Learning Objectives

Test Yourself by taking a moment to answer each of these Learning Objective Questions (repeated here from within the module). Then turn to Appendix D, Complete Module Reviews, to check your answers. Research suggests that trying to answer these questions on your own will improve your long-term memory of the concepts (McDaniel et al., 2009).

15-1 How do hormones influence human sexual motivation?

15-2 What is the human sexual response cycle, and how do sexual dysfunctions and paraphilias differ?

15-3 How can sexually transmitted infections be prevented?

15-4 How do external and imagined stimuli contribute to sexual arousal?

15-5 What factors influence teenagers' sexual behaviors and use of contraceptives?

15-6 What has research taught us about sexual orientation?

15-7 How might an evolutionary psychologist explain male-female differences in sexuality and mating preferences?

15-8 What are the key criticisms of evolutionary explanations of human sexuality, and how do evolutionary psychologists respond?

15-9 What role do social factors play in our sexuality, and how do nature, nurture, and our own choices influence gender roles and sexuality?

▪·[·] Terms and Concepts to Remember

Test yourself on these terms by trying to write down the definition in your own words before flipping back to the referenced page to check your answers.

asexual, p. 181

testosterone, p. 181

estrogens, p. 181

sexual response cycle, p. 182

refractory period, p. 183

sexual dysfunction, p. 183

erectile disorder, p. 183

female orgasmic disorder, p. 183

paraphilias, p. 183

AIDS (acquired immune deficiency syndrome), p. 184

social script, p. 186

sexual orientation, p. 187

[×] Experience the Testing Effect

Test yourself repeatedly throughout your studies. This will not only help you figure out what you know and don't know; the testing itself will help you learn and remember the information more effectively thanks to the *testing effect*.

1. A striking effect of hormonal changes on human sexual behavior is the
   a. end of sexual desire in men over 60.
   b. sharp rise in sexual interest at puberty.
   c. decrease in women's sexual desire at the time of ovulation.
   d. increase in testosterone levels in castrated males.

2. In describing the sexual response cycle, Masters and Johnson noted that
   a. a plateau phase follows orgasm.
   b. men experience a refractory period during which they cannot experience orgasm.
   c. the feeling that accompanies orgasm is stronger in men than in women.
   d. testosterone is released equally in women and men.

3. What is the difference between sexual dysfunctions and paraphilias?

4. The use of condoms during sex _____ (does/doesn't) reduce the risk of getting HIV and _____ (does/doesn't) fully protect against skin-to-skin STIs.

5. An example of an external stimulus that might influence sexual behavior is
   a. blood level of testosterone.
   b. the onset of puberty.
   c. a sexually explicit film.
   d. an erotic fantasy or dream.

6. Which factors have researchers thus far found to be *unrelated* to the development of our sexual orientation?

Find answers to these questions in Appendix E, in the back of the book.

Use 🔁 LearningCurve to create your personalized study plan, which will direct you to the resources that will help you most in 🔁 LaunchPad.

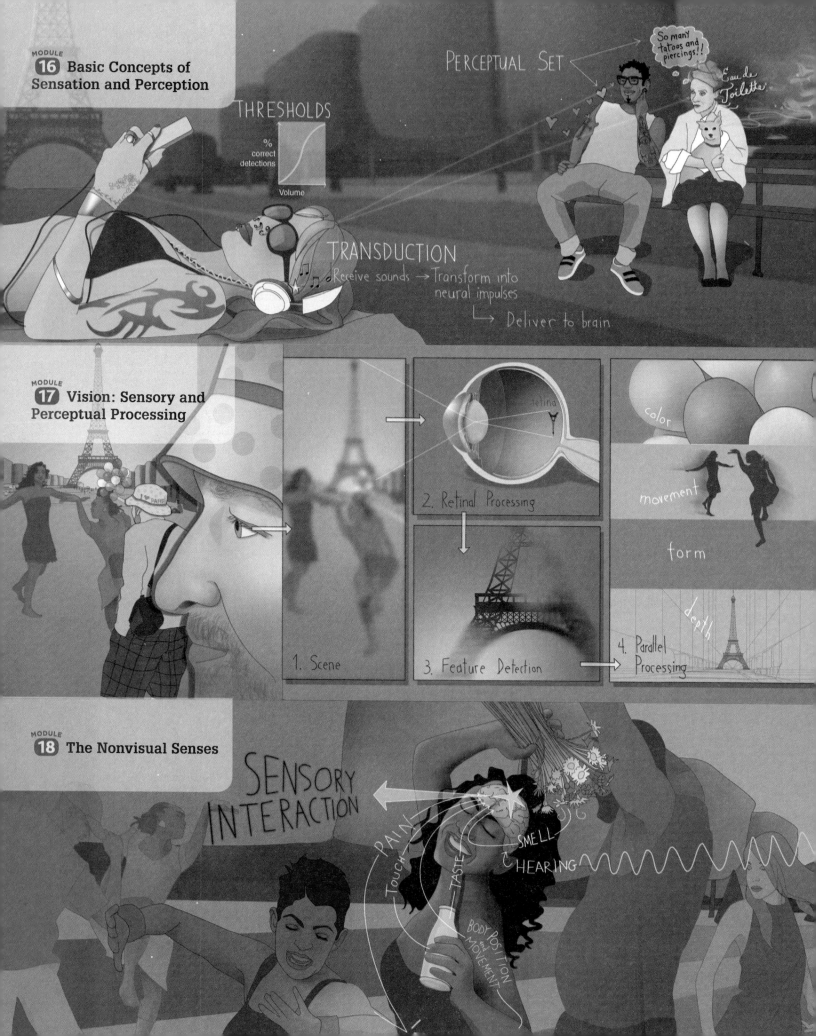

Sensation and Perception

I have perfect vision," explains writer-teacher Heather Sellers. Her vision may be fine, but there is a problem with her perception. In her memoir, *You Don't Look Like Anyone I Know,* Sellers (2010) tells of awkward moments resulting from her lifelong *prosopagnosia*—face blindness.

> In college, on a date at the Spaghetti Station, I returned from the bathroom and plunked myself down in the wrong booth, facing the wrong man. I remained unaware he was not my date even as my date (a stranger to me) accosted Wrong Booth Guy, and then stormed out of the Station. . . . I do not recognize myself in photos or videos. I can't recognize my stepsons in the soccer pick-up line; I failed to determine which husband was mine at a party, in the mall, at the market.

To avoid being perceived as snobby or aloof, Sellers sometimes fakes recognition. She often smiles at people she passes, in case she knows them. Or she pretends to know the person with whom she is talking. (Similarly, those of us with hearing loss may fake hearing or shy away from busy social situations.) But, Sellers points out, there is an upside: When encountering someone who previously irritated her, she typically feels no ill will, because she doesn't recognize the person.

Unlike Sellers, most of us have a functioning area on the underside of our brain's right hemisphere that helps us recognize a familiar human face as soon as we detect it—in only one-seventh of a second (Jacques & Rossion, 2006; Rossion & Boermanse, 2011). This remarkable ability illustrates a broader principle. *Nature's sensory gifts enable each animal to obtain essential information.* Some examples:

- Frogs, which feed on flying insects, have cells in their eyes that fire only in response to small, dark, moving objects. A frog could starve to death knee-deep in motionless flies. But let one zoom by and the frog's "bug detector" cells snap awake. (As Kermit the Frog said, "Time's fun when you're having flies.")

- Male silkworm moths' odor receptors can detect one-billionth of an ounce of sex attractant released by a female one mile away (Sagan, 1977). That is why there continue to be silkworms.

- Human ears are most sensitive to sound frequencies that include human voices, especially a baby's cry.

In these modules, we'll look more closely at what psychologists have learned about how we sense and perceive our world. Module 16 begins by considering some basic principles that apply to all our senses. In Module 17, we take a close look at sensory and perceptual processes in vision. Finally, Module 18 reviews our nonvisual senses. ■

sensation the process by which our sensory receptors and nervous system receive and represent stimulus energies from our environment.

perception the process of organizing and interpreting sensory information, enabling us to recognize meaningful objects and events.

bottom-up processing analysis that begins with the sensory receptors and works up to the brain's integration of sensory information.

top-down processing information processing guided by higher-level mental processes, as when we construct perceptions drawing on our experience and expectations.

transduction conversion of one form of energy into another. In sensation, the transforming of stimulus energies, such as sights, sounds, and smells, into neural impulses our brain can interpret.

MODULE 16 Basic Concepts of Sensation and Perception

How do we create meaning from the blizzard of sensory stimuli that bombards our body 24 hours a day? Meanwhile, in a silent, cushioned, inner world, our brain floats in utter darkness. By itself, it sees nothing. It hears nothing. It feels nothing. *So, how does the world out there get in?* To phrase the question scientifically: How do we construct our representations of the external world? How do a campfire's flicker, crackle, and smoky scent activate neural connections? And how, from this living neurochemistry, do we create our conscious experience of the fire's motion and temperature, its aroma and beauty? In search of answers, let's examine the basics of sensation and perception, and look at some processes that cut across all our sensory systems.

Processing Sensation and Perception

16-1 What are *sensation* and *perception*? What do we mean by *bottom-up processing* and *top-down processing*?

Heather Sellers' curious mix of "perfect vision" and face blindness illustrates the distinction between *sensation* and *perception*. When she looks at a friend, her **sensation** is normal: Her sensory receptors detect the same information yours would, and her nervous system transmits that information to her brain. Her **perception**—the processes by which her brain organizes and interprets sensory input—is *almost* normal. Thus, she may recognize people from their hair, gait, voice, or particular physique, just not their face. Her experience is much like the struggle any person would have trying to recognize a specific penguin.

In our everyday experiences, sensation and perception blend into one continuous process.

- Our **bottom-up processing** starts at the sensory receptors, which receive sensory input, and works up to higher levels of processing.
- Our **top-down processing** creates meaning from this sensory input by drawing on our experience and expectations.

As our brain absorbs the information in **FIGURE 16.1**, bottom-up processing enables our sensory systems to detect the lines, angles, and colors that form the flower and leaves. Sensation is the world's gateway to the brain. Using top-down processing we then interpret what our senses detect.

Transduction

16-2 What three steps are basic to all our sensory systems?

Every second of every day, our sensory systems perform an amazing feat: They convert one form of energy into another. Vision processes light energy. Hearing processes sound waves. All our senses

- *receive* sensory stimulation, often using specialized receptor cells.
- *transform* that stimulation into neural impulses.
- *deliver* the neural information to our brain.

The process of converting one form of energy into another that our brain can use is called **transduction.** How do we see? Hear? Feel pain? Taste? Smell? Keep our balance? In each case, one of our sensory systems receives, transforms, and delivers the information to our brain.

Let's explore some strengths and weaknesses in our ability to detect and interpret stimuli in the vast sea of energy around us.

∨ FIGURE 16.1

What's going on here? Our sensory and perceptual processes work together to help us sort out complex images, including the hidden couple in Sandro Del-Prete's drawing, *The Flowering of Love.*

LA VIE EN ROSE

© Sandro Del-Prete/www.sandrodelprete.com

RETRIEVE IT [✗]

• What is the rough distinction between sensation and perception?

ANSWER: *Sensation* is the bottom-up process by which our sensory receptors and our nervous system receive and represent stimuli. *Perception* is the top-down process in which our brain creates meaning by organizing and interpreting what our senses detect.

Thresholds

16-3 How do *absolute thresholds* and *difference thresholds* differ, and what effect, if any, do stimuli below the absolute threshold have on us?

At this moment, we are being struck by X-rays and radio waves, ultraviolet and infrared light, and sound waves of very high and very low frequencies. To all of these we are blind and deaf. Other animals with differing needs detect a world that lies beyond our experience. Migrating birds stay on course aided by an internal magnetic compass. Bats and dolphins locate prey using sonar, bouncing echoing sound off objects. Bees navigate on cloudy days by detecting invisible (to us) polarized light.

The shades on our own senses are open just a crack, allowing us a restricted awareness of this vast sea of energy. But for our needs, this is enough.

Absolute Thresholds

To some kinds of stimuli we are exquisitely sensitive. Standing atop a mountain on an utterly dark, clear night, most of us could see a candle flame atop another mountain 30 miles away. We could smell a single drop of perfume in a three-room apartment. We could feel the wing of a bee falling on our cheek (Galanter, 1962).

German scientist and philosopher Gustav Fechner (1801–1887) studied our awareness of these faint stimuli and called them our **absolute thresholds**—the minimum stimulation necessary to detect a particular light, sound, pressure, taste, or odor 50 percent of the time. To test your absolute threshold for sounds, a hearing specialist would expose each of your ears to varying sound levels (**FIGURE 16.2**). For each tone, the test would define where half the time you could detect the sound and half the time you could not. That 50-50 point would define your absolute threshold.

Detecting a weak stimulus, or signal (such as a hearing-test tone), depends not only on its strength but also on our psychological state—our experience, expectations, motivation, and alertness. **Signal detection theory** predicts when we will detect weak signals (measured as our ratio of "hits" to "false alarms"). Lonely people at speed-dating events often respond to potential dates unselectively—with a low threshold (McClure et al., 2010). Signal detection theorists seek to understand why people respond differently to the same stimuli, and why the same person's reactions vary as circumstances change.

Stimuli you cannot consciously detect 50 percent of the time are **subliminal**—below your absolute threshold (see Figure 16.2). Under certain conditions, you can still be affected by stimuli so weak that you don't consciously notice them. An unnoticed image or word can reach your visual cortex and briefly **prime** your response to a later question. In a typical experiment, the image or word is quickly flashed, then replaced by a *masking stimulus* that interrupts the brain's processing before conscious perception

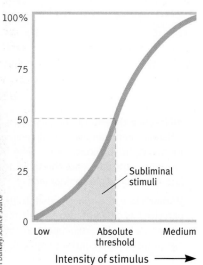

absolute threshold the minimum stimulus energy needed to detect a particular stimulus 50 percent of the time.

signal detection theory a theory predicting how and when we detect the presence of a faint stimulus (*signal*) amid background stimulation (*noise*). Assumes there is no single absolute threshold and that detection depends partly on a person's experience, expectations, motivation, and alertness.

subliminal below one's absolute threshold for conscious awareness.

priming the activation, often unconsciously, of certain associations, thus predisposing one's perception, memory, or response.

∨ FIGURE 16.2

Absolute threshold Can I detect this sound? An *absolute threshold* is the intensity at which a person can detect a stimulus half the time. Hearing tests locate these thresholds for various frequencies.

Percentage of correct detections

100%

75

50

25

0

Subliminal stimuli

Low   Absolute threshold   Medium

Intensity of stimulus ⟶

LaunchPad See LaunchPad's *Video: Experiments* for a helpful tutorial animation about this type of research method.

> **FIGURE 16.3**

The hidden mind After an image of a nude man or woman was flashed to one side or another, then masked before being perceived, people's attention was unconsciously drawn to images in a way that reflected their sexual orientation (Jiang et al., 2006).

From: Y. Jiang et al., "A Gender- and Sexual Orientation-Dependent Spatial Attention Effect of Invisible Images," PNAS, 103, 17048-17052 © 2006 by The National Academy of Sciences, USA

"The heart has its reasons which reason does not know."

Pascal, Pensées, 1670

difference threshold the minimum difference between two stimuli required for detection 50 percent of the time. We experience the difference threshold as a *just noticeable difference* (or *jnd*).

Weber's law the principle that, to be perceived as different, two stimuli must differ by a constant minimum percentage (rather than a constant amount).

(Herring et al., 2013; Van den Bussche et al., 2009). In one such experiment, researchers monitored brain activity as they primed people with either unperceived action words (such as *go* and *start*) or inaction words (such as *still* and *stop*). Without any conscious awareness, the inaction words automatically evoked brain activity associated with inhibiting behavior (Hepler & Albarracin, 2013).

Another priming experiment illustrated the deep reality of sexual orientation. As people gazed at the center of a screen, a photo of a nude person was flashed on one side and a scrambled version of the photo on the other side (Jiang et al., 2006). Because the nude images were immediately masked by a colored checkerboard, viewers consciously perceived nothing but flashes of color and so were unable to state on which side the nude had appeared. To test whether this unseen image had unconsciously attracted their attention, the experimenters then flashed a geometric figure to one side or the other. This, too, was quickly followed by a masking stimulus. When asked to give the figure's angle, straight men guessed more accurately when it appeared where a nude *woman* had been a moment earlier (**FIGURE 16.3**). Gay men (and straight women) guessed more accurately when the geometric figure replaced a nude *man*. As other experiments confirm, we can evaluate a stimulus even when we are not consciously aware of it—and even when we are unaware of our evaluation (Ferguson & Zayas, 2009).

How can we feel or respond to what we do not know and cannot describe? An imperceptibly brief stimulus often triggers a weak response that *can* be detected by brain scanning (Blankenburg et al., 2003; Haynes & Rees, 2005, 2006). The stimulus may reach consciousness only when it triggers synchronized activity in multiple brain areas (Dehaene, 2009, 2014). Such experiments reveal the dual-track mind at work: *Much of our information processing occurs automatically, out of sight, off the radar screen of our conscious mind.* Our conscious minds are top-level executives who delegate routine tasks to lower-level mental assistants.

So can we be controlled by subliminal messages? For more on that question, see Thinking Critically About: Subliminal Persuasion.

Difference Thresholds

To function effectively, we need absolute thresholds low enough to allow us to detect important sights, sounds, textures, tastes, and smells. We also need to detect small differences among stimuli. A musician must detect minute discrepancies when tuning an instrument. Parents must detect the sound of their own child's voice amid other children's voices. I [DM] noticed while living two years in Scotland that sheep *baa*s all sound alike to my ears. But not to those of ewes, who, after shearing, will streak directly to the *baa* of *their* lamb amid the chorus of other distressed lambs.

The **difference threshold** (or the *just noticeable difference [jnd]*) is the minimum difference a person can detect between any two stimuli half the time. That difference threshold increases with the size of the stimulus. If we listen to our music at 40 decibels, we might detect an added 5 decibels. But if we increase the volume to 110 decibels, we probably won't detect a 5-decibel change. In the late 1800s,

Eric Isselée/
Shutterstock

Subliminal Persuasion

16-4 Does subliminal sensation enable subliminal persuasion?

Hoping to penetrate our unconscious, entrepreneurs offer audio and video programs to help us lose weight, stop smoking, or improve our memories. Soothing ocean sounds may mask messages we cannot consciously hear: "I am thin"; "Smoke tastes bad"; or "I do well on tests—I have total recall of information." Such claims make two assumptions: (1) We can unconsciously sense subliminal (literally, "below threshold") stimuli. (2) Without our awareness, these stimuli have extraordinary suggestive powers. Can we? Do they?

As we have seen, subliminal *sensation* is a fact. Remember that an "absolute" threshold is merely the point at which we can consciously detect a stimulus *half the time*. At or slightly below this threshold, we will still consciously detect the stimulus some of the time.

But does this mean that claims of subliminal *persuasion* are also facts? The near-consensus among researchers is *No*. The laboratory research reveals a *subtle, fleeting* effect. Priming parched people with the subliminal word *thirst* might therefore, for a moment, make a thirst-quenching beverage ad more persuasive (Strahan et al., 2002). Likewise, priming thirsty people with Lipton Ice Tea may increase their choosing the primed brand (Karremans et al., 2006; Veltkamp et al., 2011; Verwijmeren et al.,

Babs Reingold

Subliminal persuasion? Although subliminally presented stimuli *can* subtly influence people, experiments discount attempts at subliminal advertising and self-improvement. (The playful message here is not actually subliminal—because you can easily perceive it.)

2011a,b). But the subliminal-message hucksters claim something different: a *powerful, enduring* effect on behavior.

To test whether subliminal recordings have this enduring effect, Anthony Greenwald and his colleagues (1991, 1992) randomly assigned university students to listen daily for five weeks to commercial subliminal messages claiming to improve either self-esteem or memory. But the researchers played a practical joke and switched half the labels. Some students who thought they were receiving affirmations of self-esteem were actually hearing the memory-enhancement message. Others got the self-esteem message but thought their memory was being recharged.

Were the recordings effective? Students' test scores for self-esteem and memory, taken before and after the five weeks, revealed no changes. Yet the students *perceived* themselves receiving the benefits they *expected*. Those who *thought* they had heard a memory recording *believed* their memories had improved. Those who *thought* they had heard a self-esteem recording *believed* their self-esteem had grown. (Reading this research, one hears echoes of the customer testimonies that ooze from ads for such products. Some customers, having purchased supposed messages they are not supposed to hear [and having indeed not heard them!] offer testimonials: "I really know that your recordings were invaluable in reprogramming my mind.")

Over a decade, Greenwald conducted 16 double-blind experiments with uniform results: No recording helped more than a placebo, which works only because of our belief in it (Greenwald, 1992).

Ernst Weber described this with a principle so simple and so widely applicable that we still refer to it as **Weber's law.** This law states that for an average person to perceive a difference, two stimuli must differ by a constant minimum *percentage* (not a constant *amount*). The exact percentage varies, depending on the stimulus. Two lights, for example, must differ in intensity by 8 percent. Two objects must differ in weight by 2 percent. And two tones must differ in frequency by only 0.3 percent (Teghtsoonian, 1971).

The LORD is my shepherd;
    I shall not want.
He maketh me to lie down
        in green pastures:
    he leadeth me
        beside the still waters.
He restoreth my soul:
    he leadeth me
        in the paths of righteousness
        for his name's sake.
Yea, though I walk through the valley
        of the shadow of death,
    I will fear no evil:
for thou art with me;
    thy rod and thy staff
    they comfort me.
Thou preparest a table before me
    in the presence of mine enemies:
    thou anointest my head with oil,
        my cup runneth over.
Surely goodness and mercy
    shall follow me
    all the days of my life:
    and I will dwell
        in the house of the LORD
        for ever.

The difference threshold In this computer-generated copy of the Twenty-third Psalm, each line of the typeface increases slightly. How many lines are required for you to experience a just noticeable difference?

sensory adaptation diminished sensitivity as a consequence of constant stimulation.

perceptual set a mental predisposition to perceive one thing and not another.

Sensory Adaptation

16-5 What is the function of sensory adaptation?

Entering your neighbors' living room, you smell a musty odor. You wonder how they endure it, but within minutes you no longer notice it. **Sensory adaptation** has come to your rescue. When we are constantly exposed to an unchanging stimulus, we typically become less aware of it because our nerve cells fire less frequently. (To experience sensory adaptation, move your watch up your wrist an inch. You will feel it—but only for a few moments.)

Why, then, if we stare at an object without flinching, does it *not* vanish from sight? Because, unnoticed by us, our eyes are always moving (**FIGURE 16.4**). This continual flitting from one spot to another ensures that stimulation on the eyes' receptors continually changes.

What if we actually could stop our eyes from moving? Would sights seem to vanish, as odors do? To find out, psychologists have devised ingenious instruments that maintain a constant image on the eye's inner surface. Imagine that we have fitted a volunteer, Mary, with one of these instruments—a miniature projector mounted on a contact lens (**FIGURE 16.5a**). When Mary's eye moves, the image from the projector moves as well. So everywhere that Mary looks, the scene is sure to go.

If we project images through this instrument, what will Mary see? At first, she will see the complete image. But within a few seconds, as her sensory system begins to fatigue, things get weird. Bit by bit, the image vanishes, only to reappear and then disappear—often in fragments (Figure 16.5b).

Although sensory adaptation reduces our sensitivity to constant stimulation, it offers an important benefit: freedom to focus on *informative* changes in our environment without being distracted by background chatter. Stinky or heavily perfumed people don't notice their odor because, like you and me, they adapt to what's constant and detect only change. Our sensory receptors are alert to novelty; bore them with repetition and they free our attention for more important things. The point to remember: *We perceive the world not exactly as it is, but as it is useful for us to perceive it.*

Our sensitivity to changing stimulation helps explain television's attention-grabbing power. Cuts, edits, zooms, pans, sudden noises—all demand attention. The phenomenon is irresistible even to TV researchers. One noted that during conversations, "I cannot for the life of me stop from periodically glancing over to the screen" (Tannenbaum, 2002).

Sensory adaptation even influences how we perceive emotions. By creating a 50-50 morphed blend of an angry face and a scared face,

"We need above all to know about changes; no one wants or needs to be reminded 16 hours a day that his shoes are on."

Neuroscientist David Hubel (1979)

∨ FIGURE 16.4

The jumpy eye Our gaze jumps from one spot to another every third of a second or so, as eye-tracking equipment illustrated while a person looked at this photograph of Edinburgh's Princes Street Gardens (Henderson, 2007). The circles represent visual fixations, and the numbers indicate the time of fixation in milliseconds (300 milliseconds = three-tenths of a second).

© John M. Henderson

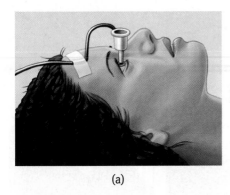

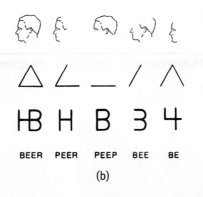

(a)   (b)

researchers showed that our visual system adapts to a static facial expression by becoming less responsive to it (Butler et al., 2008; **FIGURE 16.6**). The effect is created by our brain, not our retinas. We know this because the illusion also works when we view either side image with one eye, and the center image with the other eye.

Sensory adaptation and sensory thresholds are important ingredients in our perceptions of the world around us. Much of what we perceive comes not just from what's "out there," but also from what's behind our eyes and between our ears.

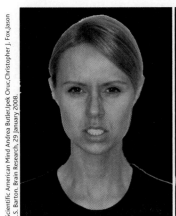

< FIGURE 16.6

Emotion adaptation Gaze at the angry face on the left for 20 to 30 seconds, then look at the center face (looks scared, yes?). Then gaze at the scared face on the right for 20 to 30 seconds, before returning to the center face (now looks angry, yes?). (From Butler et al., 2008.)

RETRIEVE IT [✖]

• Why is it that after wearing shoes for a while, you cease to notice them (until questions like this draw your attention back to them)?

ANSWER: The shoes provide constant stimulation. *Sensory adaptation* allows us to focus on changing stimuli.

Perceptual Set

16-6 How do our expectations, contexts, motivation, and emotions influence our perceptions?

To see is to believe. As we less fully appreciate, to believe is to see. Through experience, we come to expect certain results. Those expectations may give us a **perceptual set**—a set of mental tendencies and assumptions that affects, top-down, what we hear, taste, feel, and see.

Consider: Is the center image in **FIGURE 16.7** on the next page an old or young woman? What we see in such a drawing can be influenced by first looking at either of the two unambiguous versions (Boring, 1930).

W.E. Hill, 1915

> FIGURE 16.7

Perceptual set Show a friend either the left or right image. Then show the center image and ask, "What do you see?" Whether your friend reports seeing an old woman's face or young woman's profile may depend on which of the other two drawings was viewed first. In each of those images, the meaning is clear, and it will establish perceptual expectations.

There
Are Two
Errors in The
The Title Of
This Book—

Book by Robert M. Martin, 2011

In the note above, did you perceive what you expected in this title—and miss the errors? If you are still puzzled, see explanation upside down below.

The title's first error is its repeated "the." Its ironic second error is its misstatement that there are two errors, when there is only one.

"We hear and apprehend only what we already half know."

Henry David Thoreau, Journal, 1860

Everyday examples of perceptual set abound. In 1972, a British newspaper published unretouched photographs of a "monster" in Scotland's Loch Ness—"the most amazing pictures ever taken," stated the paper. If this information creates in you the same expectations it did in most of the paper's readers, you, too, will see the monster in a similar photo in **FIGURE 16.8**. But when a skeptical researcher approached the original photos with different expectations, he saw a curved tree limb—as had others the day that photo was shot (Campbell, 1986). What a difference a new perceptual set makes.

Perceptual set can also affect what we hear. Consider the kindly airline pilot who, on a takeoff run, looked over at his sad co-pilot and said, "Cheer up." Expecting to hear the usual "Gear up," the co-pilot promptly raised the wheels—before they left the ground (Reason & Mycielska, 1982).

Perceptual set similarly affects taste. One experiment invited bar patrons to sample free beer (Lee et al., 2006). The tasters preferred the brand-name beer, even when researchers secretly added a few drops of vinegar to it—unless they had been told they were drinking vinegar-laced beer. Then they expected, and usually experienced, a worse taste. In another experiment, preschool children, by a 6-to-1 margin, thought french fries tasted better when served in a McDonald's bag rather than a plain white bag (Robinson et al., 2007).

What determines our perceptual set? Through experience we form concepts, or *schemas,* that organize and interpret unfamiliar information. Our preexisting schemas for monsters and tree branches influence how we apply top-down processing to interpret ambiguous sensations.

In everyday life, stereotypes about gender (another instance of perceptual set) can color perception. Without the obvious cues of pink or blue, people will struggle over whether to call the new baby "he" or "she." But told an infant is "David," people (especially children) have perceived "him" as bigger and stronger than if the same infant was called "Diana" (Stern & Karraker, 1989). Some differences, it seems, exist merely in the eyes of their beholders.

> FIGURE 16.8

Believing is seeing What do you perceive? Is this Nessie, the Loch Ness monster, or a log?

Keystone/Hulton Archive/Getty Images

Context Effects

A given stimulus may trigger radically different perceptions, partly because of our differing perceptual set (**FIGURE 16.9**), but also because of the immediate context. Some examples:

- When holding a gun, people become more likely to perceive another person as gun-toting—a phenomenon that has led to the shooting of some unarmed people who were actually holding their phone or wallet (Witt & Brockmole, 2012).

- Imagine hearing a noise interrupted by the words "eel is on the wagon." Likely, you would actually perceive the first word as *wheel*. Given "eel is on the orange," you would more likely hear *peel*. This curious phenomenon suggests that the brain can work backward in time to allow a later stimulus to determine how we perceive an earlier one. The context creates an expectation that, top-down, influences our perception (Grossberg, 1995).

- How is the woman in **FIGURE 16.10** feeling?

FIGURE 16.9

Culture and context effects What is above the woman's head? In one classic study, nearly all the rural East Africans questioned said the woman was balancing a metal box or can on her head and that the family was sitting under a tree. Westerners, for whom corners and boxlike architecture were more common, were more likely to perceive the family as being indoors, with the woman sitting under a window (Gregory & Gombrich, 1973).

RETRIEVE IT [✱]

- Does *perceptual set* involve bottom-up or top-down processing? Why?

ANSWER: It involves top-down processing. Our perceptual set influences our interpretation of stimuli based on our experiences, assumptions, and expectations.

Motivation and Emotion

Perceptions are also influenced, top-down, by our motivation and emotions.

Hearing sad rather than happy music can predispose people to perceive a sad meaning in spoken homophonic words—*mourning* rather than *morning, die* rather than *dye, pain* rather than *pane* (Halberstadt et al., 1995). After listening to irritating (and anger-cuing) music, people perceive a harmful action such as robbery as more serious (Seidel & Prinz, 2013). Dennis Proffitt (2006a,b; Schnall et al., 2008) and others have demonstrated the power of emotions with other clever experiments showing that

- walking destinations look farther away to those fatigued by prior exercise.

- a hill looks steeper to those who are wearing a heavy backpack or have just been exposed to sad, heavy classical music rather than light, bouncy music. As with so many of life's challenges, a hill also seems less steep to those who feel others understand them (Oishi et al., 2013).

- a target seems farther away to those throwing a heavy rather than a light object at it.

- a softball appears bigger when you are hitting well. Jessica Witt and Proffitt (2005) observed this after asking players to choose a circle the size of the ball they had just hit well or poorly. (There's also a reciprocal phenomenon: Seeing a target as bigger—as happens when athletes focus directly on a target—improves performance [Witt et al., 2012].)

Motives also matter. Desired objects, such as a water bottle when thirsty, seem closer (Balcetis & Dunning, 2010). This perceptual bias energizes our going for it. Our motives also direct our perception of ambiguous stimuli.

Emotions and motives color our *social* perceptions, too. People more often perceive solitary confinement, sleep deprivation, and cold temperatures as "torture" when experiencing a small dose of such themselves (Nordgren et al., 2011).

FIGURE 16.10

What emotion is this? (See Figure 16.11 on the next page.)

Craig Klomparens

> FIGURE 16.11

Context makes clearer The Hope College volleyball team celebrates its national championship winning moment.

Craig Klomparens

"When you're hitting the ball, it comes at you looking like a grapefruit. When you're not, it looks like a black-eyed pea."

Former major league baseball player
George Scott

Spouses who feel loved and appreciated perceive less threat in stressful marital events—"He's just having a bad day" (Murray et al., 2003). The moral of these stories: To believe is, indeed, to see.

MODULE 16 REVIEW   Basic Concepts of Sensation and Perception

👁 Learning Objectives

Test Yourself by taking a moment to answer each of these Learning Objective Questions (repeated here from within the module). Then turn to Appendix D, Complete Module Reviews, to check your answers. Research suggests that trying to answer these questions on your own will improve your long-term memory of the concepts (McDaniel et al., 2009).

16-1 What are *sensation* and *perception?* What do we mean by *bottom-up processing* and *top-down processing?*

16-2 What three steps are basic to all our sensory systems?

16-3 How do *absolute thresholds* and *difference thresholds* differ, and what effect, if any, do stimuli below the absolute threshold have on us?

16-4 Does subliminal sensation enable subliminal persuasion?

16-5 What is the function of sensory adaptation?

16-6 How do our expectations, contexts, motivation, and emotions influence our perceptions?

▣ Terms and Concepts to Remember

Test yourself on these terms by trying to write down the definition in your own words before flipping back to the referenced page to check your answers.

sensation, p. 200

perception, p. 200

bottom-up processing, p. 200

top-down processing, p. 200

transduction, p. 200

absolute threshold, p. 201

signal detection theory, p. 201

subliminal, p. 201

priming, p. 201

difference threshold, p. 202

Weber's law, p. 203

sensory adaptation, p. 204

perceptual set, p. 205

[✻] Experience the Testing Effect

Test yourself repeatedly throughout your studies. This will not only help you figure out what you know and don't know; the testing itself will help you learn and remember the information more effectively thanks to the *testing effect.*

1. Sensation is to _____ as perception is to _____.

a. absolute threshold; difference threshold

b. bottom-up processing; top-down processing

c. interpretation; detection

d. grouping; priming

2. The process by which we organize and interpret sensory information is called _____.

3. Subliminal stimuli are
   a. too weak to be processed by the brain.
   b. consciously perceived more than 50 percent of the time.
   c. strong enough to affect our behavior at least 50 percent of the time.
   d. below our absolute threshold for conscious awareness.

4. Another term for difference threshold is the
   _____.

5. Weber's law states that for a difference to be perceived, two stimuli must differ by
   a. a fixed or constant energy amount.
   b. a constant minimum percentage.

   c. a constantly changing amount.
   d. more than 7 percent.

6. Sensory adaptation helps us focus on
   a. visual stimuli.
   b. auditory stimuli.
   c. constant features of the environment.
   d. informative changes in the environment.

7. Our perceptual set influences what we perceive. This mental tendency reflects our
   a. experiences, assumptions, and expectations.
   b. sensory adaptation.
   c. priming ability.
   d. difference thresholds.

Find answers to these questions in Appendix E, in the back of the book.

Use 🔵 LearningCurve to create your personalized study plan, which will direct you to the resources that will help you most in 🔵 LaunchPad.

MODULE 17 Vision: Sensory and Perceptual Processing

Light Energy and Eye Structures

◖◗ 17-1 What are the characteristics of the energy that we see as visible light? What structures in the eye help focus that energy?

Our eyes receive light energy and *transduce* (transform) it into neural messages that our brain then processes into what we consciously see. How does such a taken-for-granted yet extraordinary thing happen?

The Stimulus Input: Light Energy

When you look at a bright red tulip, the stimuli striking your eyes are not particles of the color red but pulses of electromagnetic energy that your visual system *perceives* as red. What we see as visible light is but a thin slice of the whole spectrum of electromagnetic energy, ranging from imperceptibly short gamma waves to the long waves of radio transmission (**FIGURE 17.1** on the next page). Other organisms are sensitive to differing portions of the spectrum. Bees, for instance, cannot see what we perceive as red but can see ultraviolet light.

Two physical characteristics of light help determine our experience. Light's **wavelength**—the distance from one wave peak to the next (**FIGURE 17.2a** on the next page)—determines its **hue** (the color we experience, such as a tulip's red petals or green leaves). **Intensity**—the amount of energy in light waves (determined by a wave's *amplitude*, or height)—influences brightness (Figure 17.2b). To understand *how* we transform physical energy into color and meaning, consider the eye.

The Eye

Light enters the eye through the *cornea*, which bends light to help provide focus (**FIGURE 17.3** on the next page). The light then passes through the *pupil*, a small adjustable opening surrounded by the *iris*, a colored muscle that controls the size

wavelength the distance from the peak of one light wave or sound wave to the peak of the next. Electromagnetic wavelengths vary from the short blips of cosmic rays to the long pulses of radio transmission.

hue the dimension of color that is determined by the wavelength of light; what we know as the color names *blue*, *green*, and so forth.

intensity the amount of energy in a light wave or sound wave, which influences what we perceive as brightness or loudness. Intensity is determined by the wave's amplitude (height).

> FIGURE 17.1

The wavelengths we see What we see as light is only a tiny slice of a wide spectrum of electromagnetic energy, which ranges from gamma rays as short as the diameter of an atom to radio waves over a mile long. The wavelengths visible to the human eye (shown enlarged) extend from the shorter waves of blue-violet light to the longer waves of red light.

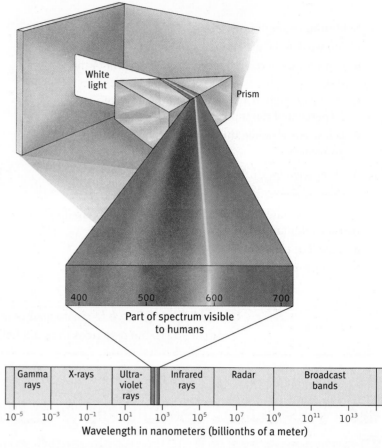

Part of spectrum visible to humans

| Gamma rays | X-rays | Ultra-violet rays | | Infrared rays | Radar | Broadcast bands | |

10^{-5} 10^{-3} 10^{-1} 10^{1} 10^{3} 10^{5} 10^{7} 10^{9} 10^{11} 10^{13}

Wavelength in nanometers (billionths of a meter)

> FIGURE 17.2

The physical properties of waves (a) Waves vary in *wavelength* (the distance between successive peaks). *Frequency*, the number of complete wavelengths that can pass a point in a given time, depends on the wavelength. The shorter the wavelength, the higher the frequency. Wavelength determines the *perceived color* of light. (b) Waves also vary in *amplitude* (the height from peak to trough). Wave amplitude influences the perceived *brightness* of colors.

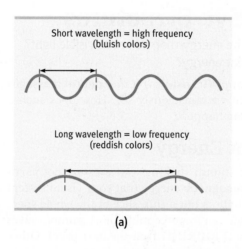

Short wavelength = high frequency (bluish colors)

Long wavelength = low frequency (reddish colors)

(a)

Great amplitude (bright colors)

Small amplitude (dull colors)

(b)

> FIGURE 17.3

The eye Light rays reflected from a candle pass through the cornea, pupil, and lens. The curvature and thickness of the lens change to bring nearby or distant objects into focus on the retina. Rays from the top of the candle strike the bottom of the retina, and those from the left side of the candle strike the right side of the retina. The candle's image on the retina thus appears upside down and reversed.

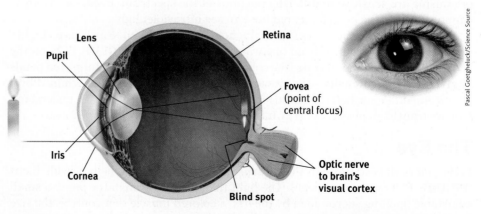
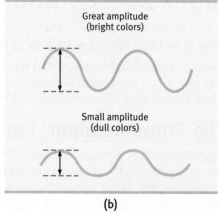

Lens

Pupil

Iris

Cornea

Retina

Fovea (point of central focus)

Optic nerve to brain's visual cortex

Blind spot

Pascal Goetgheluck/Science Source

of the pupil by dilating or constricting in response to light intensity—or even to imagining a sunny sky or a dark room (Laeng & Sulutvedt, 2014). The iris also responds to our cognitive and emotional states. When you feel disgust or you are about to answer *No* to a question, your pupils constrict (de Gee et al., 2014; Goldinger & Papesh, 2012). When you're feeling amorous, your telltale dilated pupils and resulting dark eyes subtly signal your interest. Each iris is so distinctive that an iris-scanning machine can confirm your identity.

Behind the pupil is a transparent *lens* that focuses incoming light rays into an image on the **retina,** a multilayered tissue on the eyeball's sensitive inner surface. The lens focuses the rays by changing its curvature and thickness, in a process called **accommodation.**

For centuries, scientists knew that when an image of a candle passes through a small opening, it casts an inverted mirror image on a dark wall behind. If the image passing through the pupil casts this sort of upside-down image on the retina, as in Figure 17.3, how can we see the world right side up? Eventually, the answer became clear: The retina doesn't "see" a whole image. Rather, its millions of receptor cells convert particles of light energy into neural impulses and forward those to the brain. *There,* the impulses are reassembled into a perceived, upright-seeming image. And along the way, visual information processing percolates through progressively more abstract levels, all at astonishing speed.

Information Processing in the Eye and Brain

Retinal Processing

17-2 How do the rods and cones process information, and what is the path information travels from the eye to the brain?

Imagine that you could follow behind a single light-energy particle after it entered your eye. First, you would thread your way through the retina's sparse outer layer of cells. Then, reaching the back of the eye, you would encounter its buried receptor cells, the **rods** and **cones** (**FIGURE 17.4**). There, you would see the light energy trigger chemical changes. That chemical reaction would spark neural signals, activating nearby *bipolar cells*. The bipolar cells in turn would activate the neighboring *ganglion cells*, whose axons twine together like the strands of a rope to form the **optic nerve.** The optic nerve is an information highway to your brain, where your thalamus stands ready to distribute the information it receives. This nerve can send nearly 1 million messages at once through its nearly 1 million ganglion fibers. (The auditory nerve, which enables hearing, carries much less information through its mere 30,000 fibers.)

We pay a small price for this eye-to-brain highway. Where the optic nerve leaves the eye, there are no receptor cells—creating a **blind spot** (**FIGURE 17.5** on the next page). Without seeking your approval, your brain fills in the hole.

retina the light-sensitive inner surface of the eye, containing the receptor rods and cones plus layers of neurons that begin the processing of visual information.

accommodation the process by which the eye's lens changes shape to focus near or far objects on the retina.

rods retinal receptors that detect black, white, and gray, and are sensitive to movement; necessary for peripheral and twilight vision, when cones don't respond.

cones retinal receptors that are concentrated near the center of the retina and that function in daylight or in well-lit conditions. Cones detect fine detail and give rise to color sensations.

optic nerve the nerve that carries neural impulses from the eye to the brain.

blind spot the point at which the optic nerve leaves the eye, creating a "blind" spot because no receptor cells are located there.

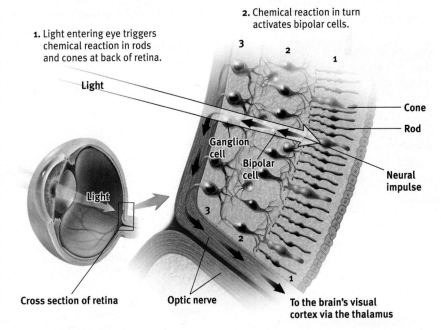

1. Light entering eye triggers chemical reaction in rods and cones at back of retina.

2. Chemical reaction in turn activates bipolar cells.

Light

Cone

Rod

Ganglion cell

Bipolar cell

Neural impulse

Light

Cross section of retina

Optic nerve

To the brain's visual cortex via the thalamus

3. Bipolar cells then activate the ganglion cells, whose combined axons form the optic nerve. This nerve transmits information (via the thalamus) to the brain.

⌃ FIGURE 17.4

The retina's reaction to light

> FIGURE 17.5

The blind spot To demonstrate your blind spot, first close your left eye, look at the spot at right, and move your face away to a distance at which one of the cars disappears (which one do you predict it will be?). Repeat with your right eye closed—and note that now the other car disappears. Can you explain why?

ANSWER: Your blind spot is on the nose side of each retina, which means that objects to your right may fall onto the right eye's blind spot. Objects to your left may fall on the left eye's blind spot. The blind spot does not normally impair your vision, because your eyes are moving and because one eye catches what the other misses.

TABLE 17.1

Receptors in the Human Eye: Rod-Shaped Rods and Cone-Shaped Cones

	Cones	Rods
Number	6 million	120 million
Location in retina	Center	Periphery
Sensitivity in dim light	Low	High
Color sensitivity	High	Low
Detail sensitivity	High	Low

Omikron/Science Source

Rods and cones differ in where they're found and what they do (**TABLE 17.1**). *Cones* cluster in and around the **fovea,** the retina's area of central focus (see Figure 17.3). Many cones have their own hotline to the brain, which devotes a large area to input from the fovea. These direct connections preserve the cones' precise information, making them better able to detect fine detail.

Rods don't have dedicated hotlines. Rods share bipolar cells, which send combined messages. To experience this rod-cone difference in sensitivity to details, pick a word in this sentence and stare directly at it, focusing its image on the cones in your fovea. Notice that words a few inches off to the side appear blurred? Their image strikes the outer regions of your retina, where rods predominate. Thus, when driving or biking, rods help you detect a car in your peripheral vision well before you perceive its details.

Cones also enable you to perceive color. In dim light they become ineffectual, so you see no colors. Rods, which enable black-and-white vision, remain sensitive in dim light. Several rods will funnel their faint energy output onto a single bipolar cell. Thus, cones and rods each provide a special sensitivity—cones to detail and color, and rods to faint light and peripheral motion.

When you enter a darkened theater or turn off the light at night, your eyes adapt. Your pupils dilate to allow more light to reach your retina, but it typically takes 20 minutes or more before your eyes fully adapt. You can demonstrate dark adaptation by closing or covering one eye for 20 minutes. Then make the light in the room not quite bright enough to read this book with your open eye. Now open the dark-adapted eye and read (easily). This period of dark adaptation matches the average natural twilight transition between the Sun's setting and darkness. How wonderfully made we are.

At the entry level, the retina's neural layers don't just pass along electrical impulses; they also help to encode and analyze sensory information. (The third neural layer in a frog's eye, for example, contains the "bug detector" cells that fire only in response to moving fly-like stimuli.) In human eyes, any given retinal area relays its information to a corresponding location in the visual cortex, in the occipital lobe at the back of your brain (**FIGURE 17.6**).

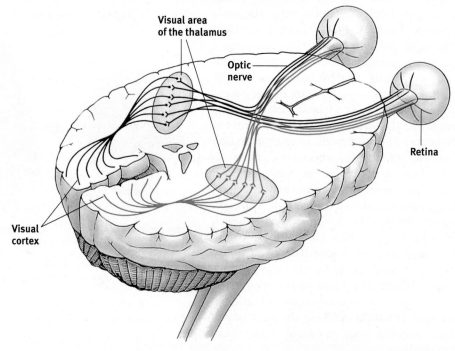

Visual area of the thalamus

Optic nerve

Retina

Visual cortex

> FIGURE 17.6

Pathway from the eyes to the visual cortex Ganglion axons forming the optic nerve run to the thalamus, where they synapse with neurons that run to the visual cortex.

The same sensitivity that enables retinal cells to fire messages can lead them to misfire, as you can demonstrate. Turn your eyes to the left, close them, and then gently rub the right side of your right eyelid with your fingertip. Note the patch of light to the left, moving as your finger moves.

Why do you see light? Why at the left? This happens because your retinal cells are so responsive that even pressure triggers them. But your brain interprets their firing as light. Moreover, it interprets the light as coming from the left—the normal direction of light that activates the right side of the retina.

RETRIEVE IT [✕]

- Some nocturnal animals, such as toads, mice, rats, and bats, have impressive night vision thanks to having many more _____ (rods/cones) than _____ (rods/cones) in their retinas. These creatures probably have very poor _____ (color/black-and-white) vision.

ANSWERS: rods; cones; color

Kruglov_Orda/ Shutterstock

- Cats are able to open their _____ much wider than we can, which allows more light into their eyes so they can see better at night.

ANSWER: pupils

Color Processing

17-3 How do we perceive color in the world around us?

One of vision's most basic and intriguing mysteries is how we see the world in color. In everyday conversation, we talk as though objects possess color: "A tomato is red." Recall the old question, "If a tree falls in the forest and no one hears it, does it make a sound?" We can ask the same of color: If no one sees the tomato, is it red?

The answer is *No*. First, the tomato is everything *but* red, because it *rejects* (reflects) the long wavelengths of red. Second, the tomato's color is our mental construction. As Isaac Newton (1704, p. 125) noted, "The [light] rays are not colored." Like all aspects of vision, our perception of color resides not in the object but in the theater of our brains, as evidenced by our dreaming in color.

How, from the light energy striking the retina, does our brain construct our experience of color—and of such a multitude of colors? Our difference threshold for colors is so low that we can discriminate more than 1 million different color variations (Neitz et al., 2001). At least most of us can. For about 1 person in 50, vision is color deficient—and that person is usually male, because the defect is genetically sex linked.

Modern detective work on the mystery of color vision began in the nineteenth century, when Hermann von Helmholtz built on the insights of an English physicist, Thomas Young. Any color can be created by combinations of different amounts of light waves of three primary colors—red, green, and blue. Knowing that, Young and von Helmholtz formed a hypothesis: The **Young-Helmholtz trichromatic (three-color) theory** thus implies that the eye's receptors do their color magic in teams of three. The eye must have three corresponding types of color receptors. Years later, researchers measured the response of various cones to different color stimuli and confirmed that the retina does have three types of color receptors, each especially sensitive to one of three colors. And those colors are, in fact, red, green, and blue. When we stimulate combinations of these cones, we see other colors. We see yellow when light stimulates both red-sensitive and green-sensitive cones.

Most people with color-deficient vision are not actually "colorblind." They simply lack functioning red- or green-sensitive cones, or sometimes both. Their vision—perhaps unknown to them, because their lifelong vision *seems* normal—is mono-chromatic (one-color) or dichromatic (two-color) instead of trichromatic, making

"Only mind has sight and hearing; all things else are deaf and blind."

Epicharmus, Fragments, 550 *B.C.E.*

fovea the central focal point in the retina, around which the eye's cones cluster.

Young-Helmholtz trichromatic (three-color) theory the theory that the retina contains three different types of color receptors—one most sensitive to red, one to green, one to blue—which, when stimulated in combination, can produce the perception of any color.

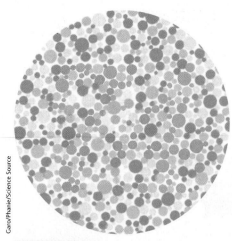

Garo/Phanie/Science Source

∧ FIGURE 17.7

Color-deficient vision People who suffer red-green deficiency have trouble perceiving the number within this design.

❯ FIGURE 17.8

Afterimage effect Stare at the center of the flag for a minute and then shift your eyes to the dot in the white space beside it. What do you see? (After tiring your neural response to black, green, and yellow, you should see their opponent colors.) Stare at a white wall and note how the size of the flag grows with the projection distance.

🅛 **LaunchPad** For an interactive review and demonstration of these color vision principles, visit LaunchPad's *PsychSim 6: Colorful World.*

---

opponent-process theory the theory that opposing retinal processes (red-green, yellow-blue, white-black) enable color vision. For example, some cells are stimulated by green and inhibited by red; others are stimulated by red and inhibited by green.

feature detectors nerve cells in the brain that respond to specific features of the stimulus, such as shape, angle, or movement.

---

it impossible to distinguish the red and green in **FIGURE 17.7.** Dogs, too, lack receptors for the wavelengths of red, giving them only limited, dichromatic color vision (Neitz et al., 1989).

But why do people blind to red and green often still see yellow? And why does yellow appear to be a pure color and not a mixture of red and green, the way purple is of red and blue? As Ewald Hering soon noted, trichromatic theory leaves some parts of the color vision mystery unsolved.

Hering, a physiologist, had found a clue in *afterimages.* Stare at a green square for a while and then look at a white sheet of paper, and you will see red, green's *opponent color.* Stare at a yellow square and its opponent color, blue, will appear on the white paper. (To experience this, try the flag demonstration in **FIGURE 17.8.**) Hering formed another hypothesis: There must be two *additional* color processes, one responsible for red-versus-green perception, and one for blue-versus-yellow.

Indeed, a century later, researchers also confirmed Hering's **opponent-process theory.** Three sets of opponent retinal processes—*red-green, yellow-blue,* and *white-black*—enable color vision. Recall that the thalamus relays visual information from the retina to the visual cortex. In both the retina and the thalamus, some neurons are "turned on" by red but "turned off" by green. Others are turned on by green but off by red (DeValois & DeValois, 1975). Like red and green marbles sent down a narrow tube, "red" and "green" messages cannot both travel at once. Red and green are thus opponents, so we do not experience a reddish green. But red and blue travel in separate channels, so we *can* see a reddish-blue magenta.

How then do we explain afterimages, such as in the flag demonstration? By staring at green, we tire our green response. When we then stare at white (which contains all colors, including red), only the red part of the green-red pairing will fire normally.

The present solution to the mystery of color vision is therefore roughly this: Color processing occurs in two stages. The retina's red, green, and blue cones respond in varying degrees to different color stimuli, as the Young-Helmholtz trichromatic theory suggested. Their responses are then processed by opponent-process cells, as Hering's theory proposed.

RETRIEVE IT [✖]

• What are two key theories of color vision? Are they contradictory or complementary? Explain.

ANSWER: The *Young-Helmholtz trichromatic theory* shows that the retina contains color receptors for red, green, and blue. The *opponent-process theory* shows that we have opponent-process cells in the retina and thalamus for red-green, yellow-blue, and white-black. These theories are complementary and outline the two stages of color vision: (1) The retina's receptors for red, green, and blue respond to different color stimuli. (2) The receptors' signals are then processed by the opponent-process cells on their way to the visual cortex in the brain.

Feature Detection

👁 **17-4** Where are feature detectors located, and what do they do?

Scientists once likened the brain to a movie screen, on which the eye projected images. But then along came David Hubel and Torsten Wiesel (1979), who

showed that our brain's computing system deconstructs visual images and then reassembles them. Hubel and Wiesel received a Nobel Prize for their work on **feature detectors,** nerve cells in the brain that respond to a scene's specific visual features—to particular edges, lines, angles, and movements.

Using microelectrodes, they had discovered that some neurons fired actively when cats were shown lines at one angle, while other neurons responded to lines at a different angle. They surmised that these specialized neurons in the occipital lobe's visual cortex, now known as feature detectors, receive information from individual ganglion cells in the retina. Feature detectors pass this specific information to other cortical areas, where teams of cells *(supercell clusters)* respond to more complex patterns.

For biologically important objects and events, monkey brains (and surely ours as well) have a "vast visual encyclopedia" distributed as specialized cells (Perrett et al., 1990, 1992, 1994). These cells respond to one type of stimulus, such as a specific gaze, head angle, posture, or body movement. Other supercell clusters integrate this information and fire only when the cues collectively indicate the direction of someone's attention and approach. This instant analysis, which aided our ancestors' survival, also helps a soccer player anticipate where to strike the ball, and a driver anticipate a pedestrian's next movement. One temporal lobe area by your right ear (**FIGURE 17.9**) enables you to perceive faces and, thanks to a specialized neural network, to recognize them from varied viewpoints (Connor, 2010). If stimulated in this area, you might spontaneously see faces. If this region were damaged, you might recognize other forms and objects, but not familiar faces.

Researchers can temporarily disrupt the brain's face-processing areas with magnetic pulses. When this happens, people cannot recognize faces, but they can recognize houses, because the brain's face perception occurs separately from its object perception (McKone et al., 2007; Pitcher et al., 2007). Thus, functional MRI (fMRI) scans have shown different brain areas activating when people viewed varied objects (Downing et al., 2001). Brain activity is so specific (**FIGURE 17.10**) that, with the help of brain scans, "we can tell if a person is looking at a shoe, a chair, or a face, based on the pattern of their brain activity," noted one researcher (Haxby, 2001).

v FIGURE 17.9

Face recognition processing In social animals such as humans, a large right temporal lobe area (shown here in a right-facing brain) is dedicated to the crucial task of face recognition.

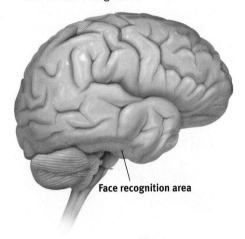

Face recognition area

- ■ Faces
- ■ Houses
- ■ Chairs
- ■ Houses and Chairs

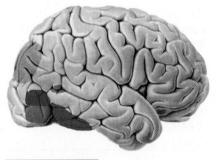

^ FIGURE 17.10

The telltale brain Looking at faces, houses, and chairs activates different brain areas in this right-facing brain.

Alex Livesey/FIFA/Getty Images

Well-developed supercells In this 2011 World Cup match, USA's Abby Wambach instantly processed visual information about the positions and movements of Brazil's defenders and goalkeeper and somehow managed to get the ball around them all and into the net.

▼ FIGURE 17.11

Parallel processing Studies of patients with brain damage suggest that the brain delegates the work of processing motion, form, depth, and color to different areas. After taking a scene apart, the brain integrates these subdimensions into the perceived image. How does the brain do this? The answer to this question is the Holy Grail of vision research.

Parallel Processing

17-5 How does the brain use parallel processing to construct visual perceptions?

Our brain achieves these and other remarkable feats by **parallel processing:** doing many things at once. To analyze a visual scene, the brain divides it into subdimensions—motion, form, depth, color—and works on each aspect simultaneously (Livingstone & Hubel, 1988). We then construct our perceptions by integrating the separate but parallel work of these different visual teams (**FIGURE 17.11**).

To recognize a face, your brain integrates information projected by your retinas to several visual cortex areas, compares it with stored information, and enables you to recognize the face: *Grandmother!* Scientists have debated whether this stored information is contained in a single cell or distributed over a vast network of cells. Some supercells—*grandmother cells*—do appear to respond very selectively to 1 or 2 faces in 100 (Bowers, 2009). The whole face recognition process requires tremendous brain power—30 percent of the cortex (10 times the brain area devoted to hearing).

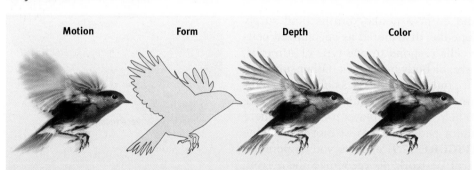

| Motion | Form | Depth | Color |

parallel processing the processing of many aspects of a problem simultaneously; the brain's natural mode of information processing for many functions, including vision.

Destroy or disable a neural workstation for a visual subtask, and something peculiar results, as happened to "Mrs. M." (Hoffman, 1998). After a stroke damaged areas near the rear of both sides of her brain, she found herself unable to perceive movement. People in a room seemed "suddenly here or there but I [did not see] them moving." Pouring tea into a cup became a challenge because the fluid appeared frozen—she could not perceive it rising in the cup.

After stroke or surgery has damaged the brain's visual cortex, others have experienced *blindsight*. Shown a series of sticks, they report seeing nothing. Yet when asked to guess whether the sticks are vertical or horizontal, their visual intuition typically offers the correct response. When told, "You got them all right," they are astounded. There is, it seems, a second "mind"—a parallel processing system—operating unseen. These separate visual systems for perceiving and for acting illustrate once again the astonishing dual processing of our two-track mind.

🅜 LaunchPad For a 4-minute depiction of a blindsight patient, visit the LaunchPad *Video—Blindsight: Seeing Without Awareness.*

* * *

Think about the wonders of visual processing. As you read this page, the letters are transmitted by reflected light rays onto your retina, which triggers a process that sends formless nerve impulses to several areas of your brain, which integrates the information and decodes meaning, thus completing the transfer of information across time and space from our minds to your mind (**FIGURE 17.12**). That all of this happens instantly, effortlessly, and continuously is indeed awesome. As Roger Sperry (1985) observed, the "insights of science give added, not lessened, reasons for awe, respect, and reverence."

"I am . . . wonderfully made."

King David, Psalm 139:14

▼ FIGURE 17.12

A simplified summary of visual information processing

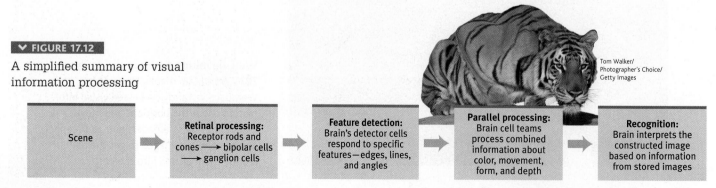

Tom Walker/
Photographer's Choice/
Getty Images

| Scene | → | **Retinal processing:** Receptor rods and cones → bipolar cells → ganglion cells | → | **Feature detection:** Brain's detector cells respond to specific features—edges, lines, and angles | → | **Parallel processing:** Brain cell teams process combined information about color, movement, form, and depth | → | **Recognition:** Brain interprets the constructed image based on information from stored images |

• What is the rapid sequence of events that occurs when you see and recognize a friend?

ANSWER: Light waves reflect off the person and travel into your eye, where the receptor cells in your retina convert the light waves' energy into neural impulses sent to your brain. Your brain processes the subdimensions of this visual input—including depth, movement, form, and color—separately but simultaneously. It interprets this information based on previously stored information and your expectations, and forms a conscious perception of your friend.

Perceptual Organization

17-6 How did the Gestalt psychologists understand perceptual organization, and how do figure-ground and grouping principles contribute to our perceptions?

It's one thing to understand how we see colors and shapes. But how do we organize and interpret those sights so that they become *meaningful* perceptions—a rose in bloom, a familiar face, a sunset?

Early in the twentieth century, a group of German psychologists noticed that when given a cluster of sensations, people tend to organize them into a **gestalt,** a German word meaning a "form" or a "whole." As we look straight ahead, we cannot separate the perceived scene into our left and right fields of view. It is, at every moment, one whole, seamless scene. Our conscious perception is an integrated whole.

Consider **FIGURE 17.13.** Note that the individual elements of this figure, called a *Necker cube,* are really nothing but eight blue circles, each containing three converging white lines. When we view these elements all together, however, we see a cube that sometimes reverses direction. This phenomenon nicely illustrates a favorite saying of Gestalt psychologists: In perception, the whole may exceed the sum of its parts.

Over the years, the Gestalt psychologists demonstrated many principles we use to organize our sensations into perceptions (Wagemans et al., 2012a,b). Underlying all of them is a fundamental truth: *Our brain does more than register information about the world.* Perception is not just opening a shutter and letting a picture print itself on the brain. We filter incoming information and construct perceptions. Mind matters.

Form Perception

Imagine designing a video-computer system that, like your eye-brain system, can recognize faces at a glance. What abilities would it need?

FIGURE AND GROUND To start with, the system would need to separate faces from their backgrounds. Likewise, in our eye-brain system, our first perceptual task is to perceive any object (the *figure*) as distinct from its surroundings (the *ground*). As you hear voices at a party, the one you attend to becomes the figure; all others are part of the ground. As you read, the words are the figure; the white space is the ground. Sometimes the same stimulus can trigger more than one perception. In **FIGURE 17.14,** the **figure-ground** relationship continually reverses—but we always organize the stimulus into a figure seen against a ground.

GROUPING Having discriminated figure from ground, we (and our video-computer system) must also organize the figure into a *meaningful* form. We process some basic features of a scene—such as color, movement, and light-dark contrast—instantly and automatically (Treisman, 1987). Our minds bring order and form to stimuli by following certain rules for **grouping,** also identified by the Gestalt psychologists. These rules, which we apply even as infants and even in our touch perceptions, illustrate how the perceived whole differs from the sum of its parts

∧ FIGURE 17.13

A Necker cube What do you see: circles with white lines, or a cube? If you stare at the cube, you may notice that it reverses location, moving the tiny X in the center from the front edge to the back. At times, the cube may seem to float forward, with circles behind it. At other times, the circles may become holes through which the cube appears, as though it were floating behind them. There is far more to perception than meets the eye. (From Bradley et al., 1976.)

gestalt an organized whole. Gestalt psychologists emphasized our tendency to integrate pieces of information into meaningful wholes.

figure-ground the organization of the visual field into objects (the *figures*) that stand out from their surroundings (the *ground*).

grouping the perceptual tendency to organize stimuli into coherent groups.

∨ FIGURE 17.14

Reversible figure and ground

^ FIGURE 17.15

Grouping principles What's the secret to this impossible doghouse? You probably perceive this doghouse as a gestalt—a whole (though impossible) structure. Actually, your brain imposes this sense of wholeness on the picture. As Figure 17.19 on page 221 shows, Gestalt grouping principles such as closure and continuity are at work here.

(Gallace & Spence, 2011; Quinn et al., 2002; Rock & Palmer, 1990). Three examples:

Proximity We group nearby figures together. We see not six separate lines, but three sets of two lines.

Continuity We perceive smooth, continuous patterns rather than discontinuous ones. This pattern could be a series of alternating semicircles, but we perceive it as two continuous lines—one wavy, one straight.

Closure We fill in gaps to create a complete, whole object. Thus we assume that the circles on the left are complete but partially blocked by the (illusory) triangle. Add nothing more than little line segments to close off the circles and your brain stops constructing a triangle.

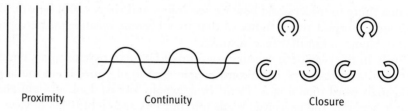

Proximity   Continuity   Closure

Such principles usually help us construct reality. Sometimes, however, they lead us astray, as when we look at the doghouse in **FIGURE 17.15.**

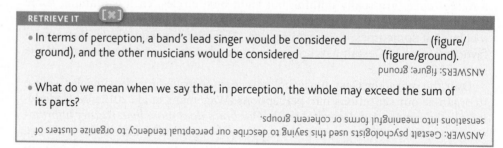

RETRIEVE IT [✖]

• In terms of perception, a band's lead singer would be considered _____ (figure/ground), and the other musicians would be considered _____ (figure/ground).

ANSWERS: figure; ground

• What do we mean when we say that, in perception, the whole may exceed the sum of its parts?

ANSWER: Gestalt psychologists used this saying to describe our perceptual tendency to organize clusters of sensations into meaningful forms or coherent groups.

Depth Perception

👁 **17-7** How do we use binocular and monocular cues to perceive the world in three dimensions?

From the two-dimensional images falling on our retinas, we somehow organize three-dimensional perceptions. **Depth perception** enables us to estimate an object's distance from us. At a glance, we can estimate the distance of an oncoming car or the height of a house. Depth perception is partly innate, as Eleanor Gibson and Richard Walk (1960) discovered using a model of a cliff with a drop-off area (which was covered by sturdy glass). Gibson's inspiration for these **visual cliff** experiments occurred while she was picnicking on the rim of the Grand Canyon. She wondered: Would a toddler peering over the rim perceive the dangerous drop-off and draw back?

Back in their Cornell University laboratory, Gibson and Walk placed 6- to 14-month-old infants on the edge of a safe canyon and had the infants' mothers coax them to crawl out onto the glass (**FIGURE 17.16**). Most infants refused to do so, indicating that they could perceive depth.

Had they *learned* to perceive depth? Mobile, newborn animals, such as kittens, come prepared to see depth—and will not venture across the visual cliff. Learning seems also to be part of the human story, because crawling, no matter when it begins, seems to increase infants' wariness of heights (Adolph et al., 2014; Campos et al., 1992).

depth perception the ability to see objects in three dimensions although the images that strike the retina are two-dimensional; allows us to judge distance.

visual cliff a laboratory device for testing depth perception in infants and young animals.

binocular cues depth cues, such as retinal disparity, that depend on the use of two eyes.

retinal disparity a binocular cue for perceiving depth: By comparing images from the retinas in the two eyes, the brain computes distance—the greater the disparity (difference) between the two images, the closer the object.

monocular cues depth cues, such as interposition and linear perspective, available to either eye alone.

How do we do it? *How* do we transform two differing two-dimensional retinal images into a single three-dimensional perception?

BINOCULAR CUES Try this: With both eyes open, hold two pens or pencils in front of you and touch their tips together. Now do so with one eye closed. With one eye, the task becomes noticeably more difficult, demonstrating the importance of **binocular cues** in judging the distance of nearby objects. Two eyes are better than one.

Because your eyes are about 2½ inches apart, your retinas receive slightly different images of the world. By comparing these two images, your brain can judge how close an object is to you. The greater the **retinal disparity,** or difference between the two images, the closer the object. Try it. Hold your two index fingers, with the tips about half an inch apart, directly in front of your nose, and your retinas will receive quite different views. If you close one eye and then the other, you can see the difference. (Bring your fingers close and you can create a finger sausage, as in **FIGURE 17.17.**) At a greater distance—say, when you hold your fingers at arm's length—the disparity is smaller.

Visual cliff Eleanor Gibson and Richard Walk devised this miniature cliff with a glass-covered drop-off to determine whether crawling infants and newborn animals can perceive depth. Even when coaxed, infants are reluctant to venture onto the glass over the cliff.

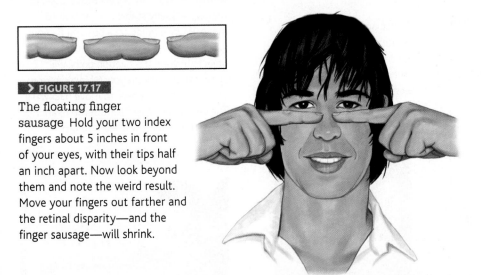

> FIGURE 17.17

The floating finger sausage Hold your two index fingers about 5 inches in front of your eyes, with their tips half an inch apart. Now look beyond them and note the weird result. Move your fingers out farther and the retinal disparity—and the finger sausage—will shrink.

We could easily build this feature into our video-computer system. Movie-makers can simulate or exaggerate retinal disparity by filming a scene with two cameras placed a few inches apart. Viewers then wear glasses that allow the left eye to see only the image from the left camera, and the right eye to see only the image from the right camera. The resulting effect, as 3-D movie fans know, mimics or exaggerates normal retinal disparity. Similarly, twin cameras in airplanes can take photos of terrain for integration into 3-D maps.

MONOCULAR CUES How do we judge whether a person is 10 or 100 meters away? Retinal disparity won't help us here, because there won't be much difference between the images cast on our right and left retinas. At such distances, we depend on **monocular cues** (depth cues available to each eye separately). See **FIGURE 17.18** on the next page for some examples.

LaunchPad For animated demonstrations and explanations of these cues, visit LaunchPad's *Concept Practice: Depth Cues.*

"I can't go on living with such lousy depth perception."

Tom Cheney/New Yorker Cartoon/Cartoon Bank

Relative height We perceive objects higher in our field of vision as farther away. Because we assume the lower part of a figure-ground illustration is closer, we perceive it as figure (Vecera et al., 2002). Invert this illustration and the black will become ground, like a night sky.

Relative size If we assume two objects are similar in size, *most* people perceive the one that casts the smaller retinal image as farther away.

Interposition If one object partially blocks our view of another, we perceive it as closer.

Linear perspective Parallel lines appear to meet in the distance. The sharper the angle of convergence, the greater the perceived distance.

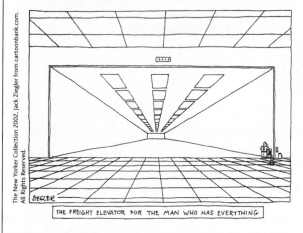

THE FREIGHT ELEVATOR FOR THE MAN WHO HAS EVERYTHING

Light and shadow Shading produces a sense of depth consistent with our assumption that light comes from above. If you invert this illustration, the hollow will become a hill.

Relative motion As we move, objects that are actually stable may appear to move. If while riding on a bus you fix your gaze on some point—say, a house—the objects beyond the fixation point will appear to move with you. Objects in front of the point will appear to move backward. The farther an object is from the fixation point, the faster it will seem to move.

Fixation point

Direction of passenger's motion ⟶

▲ **FIGURE 17.18**

Monocular depth cues

RETRIEVE IT [✗]

• How do we normally perceive depth?

ANSWER: We are normally able to perceive depth thanks to (1) binocular cues (which are based on our retinal disparity), and (2) monocular cues (which include relative height, relative size, interposition, linear perspective, light and shadow, and relative motion).

Perceptual Constancy

17-8 How do perceptual constancies help us construct meaningful perceptions?

So far, we have noted that our video-computer system must perceive objects as we do—as having a distinct form and location. Its next task is to recognize objects without being deceived by changes in their color, brightness, shape, or size—a *top-down* process called **perceptual constancy.** Regardless of the viewing angle, distance, and illumination, we can identify people and things in less time than it takes to draw a breath, a feat that challenges even advanced computers and has intrigued researchers for decades. This would be a monumental challenge for a video-computer system.

COLOR AND BRIGHTNESS CONSTANCIES Our experience of color depends on an object's *context.* This would be clear if you viewed an isolated tomato through a paper tube over the course of a day. The tomato's color would seem to change as the light—and thus the wavelengths reflected from its surface—changed. But if you viewed that tomato as one item in a salad bowl, its color would remain roughly constant as the lighting shifted. This perception of consistent color is known as **color constancy.**

Though we take color constancy for granted, this ability is truly remarkable. A blue poker chip under indoor lighting reflects wavelengths that match those reflected by a sunlit gold chip (Jameson, 1985). Yet bring a goldfinch indoors and it won't look like a bluebird. The color is not in the bird's feathers. We see color thanks to our brain's computations of the light reflected by an object *relative to the objects surrounding it.* **FIGURE 17.20** dramatically illustrates the ability of a blue object to appear very different in three different contexts. Yet we have no trouble seeing these disks as blue. Nor does knowing the truth—that these disks are identically colored—diminish our perception that they are quite different. Because we construct our perceptions, we can simultaneously accept alternative objective and subjective realities.

Brightness constancy (also called *lightness constancy*) similarly depends on context. We perceive an object as having a constant brightness even as its illumination varies. This perception of constancy depends on *relative luminance*—the amount of light an object reflects *relative to its surroundings* (**FIGURE 17.21** on the next page). White paper reflects 90 percent of the light falling on it; black paper, only

^ FIGURE 17.19

The solution Another view of the impossible doghouse in Figure 17.15 reveals the secrets of this illusion. From the photo angle in Figure 17.15, the grouping principle of closure leads us to perceive the boards as continuous.

"From there to here, from here to there, funny things are everywhere."

Dr. Seuss, One Fish, Two Fish, Red Fish, Blue Fish, *1960*

perceptual constancy perceiving objects as unchanging (having consistent color, brightness, shape, and size) even as illumination and retinal images change.

color constancy perceiving familiar objects as having consistent color, even if changing illumination alters the wavelengths reflected by the objects.

(a)

(b)

< FIGURE 17.20

Color depends on context (a) Believe it or not, these three blue disks are identical in color. (b) Remove the surrounding context and see what results.

10 percent. Although a black paper viewed in sunlight may reflect 100 times more light than does a white paper viewed indoors, it will still look black (McBurney & Collings, 1984). But if you view sunlit black paper through a narrow tube so nothing else is visible, it may look gray, because in bright sunshine it reflects a fair amount of light. View it without the tube and it is again black, because it reflects much less light than the objects around it.

This principle—that we perceive objects not in isolation but in their environmental context—matters to artists, interior decorators, and clothing designers. Our perception of the color and brightness of a wall or of a streak of paint on a canvas is determined not just by the paint in the can but by the surrounding colors. The take-home lesson: *Comparisons control our perceptions.*

SHAPE AND SIZE CONSTANCIES Sometimes an object whose actual shape cannot change *seems* to change shape with the angle of our view (**FIGURE 17.22**). More often, thanks to *shape constancy*, we perceive the form of familiar objects, such as the door in **FIGURE 17.23,** as constant even while our retinas receive changing images of them. Our brain manages this feat thanks to visual cortex neurons that rapidly learn to associate different views of an object (Li & DiCarlo, 2008).

Thanks to *size constancy*, we perceive objects as having a constant size, even while our distance from them varies. We assume a car is large enough to carry people, even when we see its tiny image from two blocks away. This assumption also illustrates the close connection between perceived *distance* and perceived *size*. Perceiving an object's distance gives us cues to its size. Likewise, knowing its general size—that the object is a car—provides us with cues to its distance.

Even in size-distance judgments, however, we consider an object's context. This interplay between perceived size and perceived distance helps explain several well-known illusions, including the *Moon illusion:* The Moon looks up to 50 percent larger when near the horizon than when high in the sky. Can you imagine why?

For at least 22 centuries, scholars have wondered (Hershenson, 1989). One reason is that monocular cues to objects' distances make the horizon Moon appear farther away. If it's farther away, our brain assumes, it must be larger than the Moon high in the night sky (Kaufman & Kaufman, 2000). Take away the distance cue, by looking at the horizon Moon through a paper tube, and the object will immediately shrink.

Perceptual illusions reinforce a fundamental lesson: Perception is not merely a projection of the world onto our brain. Rather, our sensations are disassembled into information bits that our brain then reassembles into its own functional model of the external world. During this reassembly process, our assumptions—such as the usual relationship between distance and size—can lead us astray. *Our brain constructs our perceptions.*

* * *

Form perception, depth perception, and perceptual constancies illuminate how we organize our visual experiences. Perceptual organization applies to our other senses, too. Listening to an unfamiliar language, we have trouble hearing where one word stops and the next one begins. Listening to our own language, we automatically hear distinct words. This, too, reflects perceptual organization. But it is more, for we even organize a string of letters—THEDOGATEMEAT—into words that make an intelligible phrase, more likely "The dog ate meat" than "The do gate me at" (McBurney & Collings, 1984). This process involves not only the organization we've been discussing, but also interpretation—discerning meaning in what we perceive.

▲ FIGURE 17.21

Relative luminance Because of its surrounding context, we perceive Square A as lighter than Square B. But believe it or not, they are identical. To channel comedian Richard Pryor, "Who you gonna believe: me, or your lying eyes?" If you believe your lying eyes—actually, your lying brain—you can photocopy (or screen-capture and print) the illustration, then cut out the squares and compare them.

▲ FIGURE 17.22

Perceiving shape Do the tops of these tables have different dimensions? They appear to. But they are identical. (Measure and see.) With both tables, we adjust our perceptions relative to our viewing angle.

❯ FIGURE 17.23

Shape constancy A door casts an increasingly trapezoidal image on our retinas as it opens. Yet we still perceive it as rectangular.

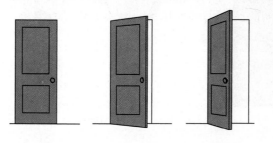

Perceptual Interpretation

Philosophers have debated whether our perceptual abilities should be credited to our nature or our nurture. To what extent do we *learn* to perceive? German philosopher Immanuel Kant (1724–1804) maintained that knowledge comes from our *inborn* ways of organizing sensory experiences. Indeed, we come equipped to process sensory information. But British philosopher John Locke (1632–1704) argued that through our experiences we also *learn* to perceive the world. Indeed, we learn to link an object's distance with its size. So, just how important is experience? How radically does it shape our perceptual interpretations?

Experience and Visual Perception

👁 **17-9** What does research on restored vision, sensory restriction, and perceptual adaptation reveal about the effects of experience on perception?

RESTORED VISION AND SENSORY RESTRICTION Writing to John Locke, William Molyneux wondered whether "a man *born* blind, and now adult, taught by his *touch* to distinguish between a cube and a sphere" could, if made to see, visually distinguish the two. Locke's answer was *No*, because the man would never have *learned* to see the difference.

Molyneux's hypothetical case has since been put to the test with a few dozen adults who, though blind from birth, later gained sight (Gregory, 1978; Huber et al., 2015; von Senden, 1932). Most were born with cataracts—clouded lenses that allowed them to see only diffused light, rather as you might see a foggy image through a Ping-Pong ball sliced in half. After cataract surgery, the patients could distinguish figure from ground and could sense colors—suggesting that these aspects of perception are innate. But much as Locke supposed, they often could not visually recognize objects that were familiar by touch.

Seeking to gain more control than is provided by clinical cases, researchers have outfitted infant kittens and monkeys with goggles through which they could see only diffuse, unpatterned light (Wiesel, 1982). After infancy, when the goggles were removed, these animals exhibited perceptual limitations much like those of humans born with cataracts. They could distinguish color and brightness, but not the form of a circle from that of a square. Their eyes had not degenerated; their retinas still relayed signals to their visual cortex. But lacking stimulation, the cortical cells had not developed normal connections. Thus, the animals remained functionally blind to shape. Experience guides, sustains, and maintains the brain's neural organization that enables our perceptions.

In both humans and animals, similar sensory restrictions later in life do no permanent harm. When researchers cover the eye of an adult animal for several months, its vision will be unaffected after the eye patch is removed. When surgeons remove cataracts that develop during late adulthood, most people are thrilled at the return to normal vision.

The effect of sensory restriction on infant cats, monkeys, and humans suggests that for normal sensory and perceptual development there is a *critical period—an optimal period when exposure to certain stimuli or experiences is required*. Surgery on blind children in India reveals that children blind from birth can benefit from removal of cataracts. The younger they are, the more they will benefit, but their visual acuity (sharpness) may never be normal (Sinha, 2013). Early nurture sculpts what nature has endowed. In less dramatic ways, it continues to do so throughout our lives. Our visual experience matters.

PERCEPTUAL ADAPTATION Given a new pair of glasses, we may feel slightly disoriented, even dizzy. Within a day or two, we adjust. Our **perceptual adaptation** to changed visual input makes the world seem normal again. But imagine a far more

🅜 **LaunchPad** To experience more visual illusions, and to understand what they reveal about how you perceive the world, visit LaunchPad's *PsychSim 6: Visual Illusions.*

"Let us then suppose the mind to be, as we say, white paper void of all characters, without any ideas: How comes it to be furnished? . . . To this I answer, in one word, from EXPERIENCE."

John Locke, An Essay Concerning Human Understanding, *1690*

Learning to see At age 3, Mike May lost his vision in an explosion. Decades later, after a new cornea restored vision to his right eye, he got his first look at his wife and children. Alas, although signals were now reaching his visual cortex, it lacked the experience to interpret them. May could not perceive in 3-D, or recognize expressions or faces, apart from features such as hair. Yet he can see an object in motion and has learned to navigate his world and to marvel at such things as dust floating in sunlight (Abrams, 2002; Huber et al., 2015).

Marcio Jose Sanchez/AP Photo

perceptual adaptation the ability to adjust to changed sensory input, including an artificially displaced or even inverted visual field.

Perceptual adaptation "Oops, missed," thought researcher Hubert Dolezal as he attempted a handshake while viewing the world through inverting goggles. Yet, believe it or not, kittens, monkeys, and humans can adapt to an inverted world.

Courtesy of Hubert Dolezal

dramatic new pair of glasses—one that shifts the apparent location of objects 40 degrees to the left. When you first put them on and toss a ball to a friend, it sails off to the left. Walking forward to shake hands with someone, you veer to the left.

Could you adapt to this distorted world? Not if you were a baby chicken. When fitted with such lenses, baby chicks continue to peck where food grains *seem* to be (Hess, 1956; Rossi, 1968). But we humans adapt to distorting lenses quickly. Within a few minutes your throws would again be accurate, your stride on target. Remove the lenses and you would experience an aftereffect: At first your throws would err in the *opposite* direction, sailing off to the right; but again, within minutes you would readapt.

Indeed, given an even more radical pair of glasses—one that literally turns the world upside down—you could still adapt. Psychologist George Stratton (1896) experienced this. He invented, and for eight days wore, optical headgear that flipped left to right *and* up to down, making him the first person to experience a right-side-up retinal image while standing upright. The ground was up, the sky was down.

At first, when Stratton wanted to walk, he found himself searching for his feet, which were now "up." Eating was nearly impossible. He became nauseated and depressed. But he persisted, and by the eighth day he could comfortably reach for an object in the right direction and walk without bumping into things. When Stratton finally removed the headgear, he readapted quickly.

In later experiments, people wearing the optical gear have even been able to ride a motorcycle, ski the Alps, and fly an airplane (Dolezal, 1982; Kohler, 1962). The world around them still seemed above their heads or on the wrong side. But by actively moving about in these topsy-turvy worlds, they adapted to the context and learned to coordinate their movements.

MODULE 17 REVIEW Vision: Sensory and Perceptual Processing

Learning Objectives

Test Yourself by taking a moment to answer each of these Learning Objective Questions (repeated here from within the module). Then turn to Appendix D, Complete Module Reviews, to check your answers. Research suggests that trying to answer these questions on your own will improve your long-term memory of the concepts (McDaniel et al., 2009).

17-1 What are the characteristics of the energy that we see as visible light? What structures in the eye help focus that energy?

17-2 How do the rods and cones process information, and what is the path information travels from the eye to the brain?

17-3 How do we perceive color in the world around us?

17-4 Where are feature detectors located, and what do they do?

17-5 How does the brain use parallel processing to construct visual perceptions?

17-6 How did the Gestalt psychologists understand perceptual organization, and how do figure-ground and grouping principles contribute to our perceptions?

17-7 How do we use binocular and monocular cues to perceive the world in three dimensions?

17-8 How do perceptual constancies help us construct meaningful perceptions?

17-9 What does research on restored vision, sensory restriction, and perceptual adaptation reveal about the effects of experience on perception?

Terms and Concepts to Remember

Test yourself on these terms by trying to write down the definition in your own words before flipping back to the referenced page to check your answers.

wavelength, p. 209
hue, p. 209
intensity, p. 209

retina, p. 211
accommodation, p. 211
rods, p. 211
cones, p. 211
optic nerve, p. 211
blind spot, p. 211
fovea, p. 212

Young-Helmholtz trichromatic (three-color) theory, p. 213
opponent-process theory, p. 214
feature detectors, p. 215
parallel processing, p. 216
gestalt, p. 217
figure-ground, p. 217

[✻] Experience the Testing Effect

Test yourself repeatedly throughout your studies. This will not only help you figure out what you know and don't know; the testing itself will help you learn and remember the information more effectively thanks to the *testing effect*.

1. The characteristic of light that determines the color we experience, such as blue or green, is _____.

2. The amplitude of a light wave determines our perception of
   a. brightness.
   b. color.
   c. meaning.
   d. distance.

3. The blind spot in your retina is located where
   a. there are rods but no cones.
   b. there are cones but no rods.
   c. the optic nerve leaves the eye.
   d. the bipolar cells meet the ganglion cells.

4. Cones are the eye's receptor cells that are especially sensitive to _____ light and are responsible for our _____ vision.
   a. bright; black-and-white
   b. dim; color
   c. bright; color
   d. dim; black-and-white

5. Two theories together account for color vision. The Young-Helmholtz trichromatic theory shows that the eye contains _____, and the opponent-process theory accounts for the nervous system's having _____.
   a. opposing retinal processes; three pairs of color receptors
   b. opponent-process cells; three types of color receptors
   c. three pairs of color receptors; opposing retinal processes
   d. three types of color receptors; opponent-process cells

6. What mental processes allow you to perceive a lemon as yellow?

7. The cells in the visual cortex that respond to certain lines, edges, and angles are called _____ _____.

8. The brain's ability to process many aspects of an object or a problem simultaneously is called _____ _____.

9. Our tendencies to fill in the gaps and to perceive a pattern as continuous are two different examples of the organizing principle called
   a. interposition.
   b. depth perception.
   c. shape constancy.
   d. grouping.

10. In listening to a concert, you attend to the solo instrument and perceive the orchestra as accompaniment. This illustrates the organizing principle of
    a. figure-ground.
    b. shape constancy.
    c. grouping.
    d. depth perception.

11. The visual cliff experiments suggest that
    a. infants have not yet developed depth perception.
    b. crawling human infants and very young animals perceive depth.
    c. we have no way of knowing whether infants can perceive depth.
    d. unlike other species, humans are able to perceive depth in infancy.

12. Depth perception underlies our ability to
    a. group similar items in a gestalt.
    b. perceive objects as having a constant shape or form.
    c. judge distances.
    d. fill in the gaps in a figure.

13. Two examples of _____ depth cues are interposition and linear perspective.

14. Perceiving a tomato as consistently red, despite lighting shifts, is an example of
    a. shape constancy.
    b. perceptual constancy.
    c. a binocular cue.
    d. continuity.

15. After surgery to restore vision, patients who had been blind from birth had difficulty
    a. recognizing objects by touch.
    b. recognizing objects by sight.
    c. distinguishing figure from ground.
    d. distinguishing between bright and dim light.

16. In experiments, people have worn glasses that turned their visual fields upside down. After a period of adjustment, they learned to function quite well. This ability is called _____ _____.

Find answers to these questions in Appendix E, in the back of the book.

Use 🌀 LearningCurve to create your personalized study plan, which will direct you to the resources that will help you most in 🌀 LaunchPad.

audition the sense or act of hearing.

frequency the number of complete wavelengths that pass a point in a given time (for example, per second).

pitch a tone's experienced highness or lowness; depends on frequency.

middle ear the chamber between the eardrum and cochlea containing three tiny bones (hammer, anvil, and stirrup) that concentrate the vibrations of the eardrum on the cochlea's oval window.

MODULE 18 The Nonvisual Senses

Hearing

Like our other senses, our **audition,** or hearing, helps us adapt and survive. Hearing people share information invisibly—by shooting unseen air waves across space. Hearing loss is therefore an invisible disability. To not catch someone's name, to not grasp what someone is asking, and to miss the hilarious joke is to be deprived of what others know, and sometimes to feel excluded. (As a person with hearing loss, I [DM] know the feeling.)

Most of us, however, can hear a wide range of sounds, and the ones we hear best are those in the range of the human voice. With normal hearing, we are remarkably sensitive to faint sounds, such as a child's whimper. (If our ears were only slightly more sensitive, we would hear a constant hiss from the movement of air molecules.) We are also remarkably attuned to sound variations. Among thousands of possible human voices, we easily recognize an unseen friend's, from the moment she says "Hi." Moreover, hearing is fast. "It might take you a full second to notice something out of the corner of your eye, turn your head toward it, recognize it, and respond to it," notes auditory neuroscientist Seth Horowitz (2012). "The same reaction to a new or sudden sound happens at least 10 times as fast." A fraction of a second after such events stimulate the ear's receptors, millions of neurons have simultaneously coordinated in extracting the essential features, comparing them with past experience, and identifying the stimulus (Freeman, 1991). For hearing as for our other senses, we wonder: How do we do it?

The Stimulus Input: Sound Waves

18-1 What are the characteristics of air pressure waves that we hear as sound?

Draw a bow across a violin, and you will unleash the energy of sound waves. Jostling molecules of air, each bumping into the next, create waves of compressed and expanded air, like the ripples on a pond circling out from a tossed stone. As we swim in our ocean of moving air molecules, our ears detect these brief air pressure changes.

Like light waves, sound waves vary in shape (**FIGURE 18.1**). The height, or *amplitude,* of sound waves determines their *loudness.* Their length, or **frequency,** determines the **pitch** we experience. Long waves have low frequency—and low pitch. Short waves have high frequency—and high pitch. Sound waves produced by a violin are much shorter and faster than those produced by a cello or a bass guitar.

The sounds of music A violin's short, fast waves create a high pitch. The longer, slower waves of a cello or bass create a lower pitch. Differences in the waves' height, or amplitude, also create differing degrees of loudness.

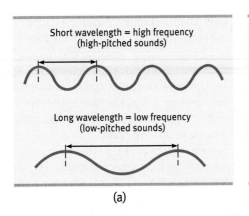

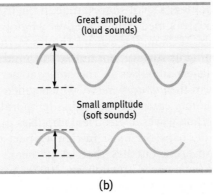

(a)   (b)

The physical properties of waves (a) Waves vary in *wavelength* (the distance between successive peaks). *Frequency,* the number of complete wavelengths that can pass a point in a given time, depends on the wavelength. The shorter the wavelength, the higher the frequency. Wavelength determines the *pitch* of sound. (b) Waves also vary in *amplitude* (the height from peak to trough). Wave amplitude influences sound *intensity.*

We measure sounds in *decibels,* with zero decibels representing the absolute threshold for hearing. Every 10 decibels correspond to a tenfold increase in sound intensity. Thus, normal conversation (60 decibels) is 10,000 times more intense than a 20-decibel whisper. And a temporarily tolerable 100-decibel passing subway train is 10 billion times more intense than the faintest detectable sound.

The Ear

18-2 How does the ear transform sound energy into neural messages?

The intricate process that transforms vibrating air into nerve impulses, which our brain decodes as sounds, begins when sound waves enter the *outer ear.* An elaborate mechanical chain reaction begins as the visible outer ear channels the waves through the *auditory canal* to the *eardrum,* a tight membrane, causing it to vibrate (**FIGURE 18.2**). In the **middle ear,** a piston made of three tiny bones (the *hammer, anvil,* and *stirrup*) picks up the vibrations and transmits them to the

Hear here: How we transform sound waves into nerve impulses that our brain interprets (a) The outer ear funnels sound waves to the eardrum. The bones of the middle ear (hammer, anvil, and stirrup) amplify and relay the eardrum's vibrations through the oval window into the fluid-filled cochlea. (b) As shown in this detail of the middle and inner ear, the resulting pressure changes in the cochlear fluid cause the basilar membrane to ripple, bending the hair cells on its surface. Hair cell movements trigger impulses at the base of the nerve cells, whose fibers converge to form the auditory nerve. That nerve sends neural messages to the thalamus and on to the auditory cortex.

(a)   OUTER EAR   MIDDLE EAR   INNER EAR

Semicircular canals

Bones of the
middle ear

Bone

Auditory nerve

Sound
waves

Cochlea

Eardrum

Oval window
(where stirrup attaches)

Auditory
canal

Auditory cortex
of temporal lobe

(b)

Enlargement of middle ear
and inner ear, showing
cochlea partially uncoiled
for clarity

Cochlea,
partially uncoiled

Sound
waves

Auditory nerve

Nerve fibers to auditory nerve

Protruding hair cells

Basilar membrane

Hammer   Anvil

Eardrum   Stirrup   Oval window   Motion of fluid in the cochlea

cochlea [KOHK-lee-uh] a coiled, bony, fluid-filled tube in the inner ear; sound waves traveling through the cochlear fluid trigger nerve impulses.

inner ear the innermost part of the ear, containing the cochlea, semicircular canals, and vestibular sacs.

sensorineural hearing loss the most common form of hearing loss, also called *nerve deafness;* caused by damage to the cochlea's receptor cells or to the auditory nerves.

conduction hearing loss less common form of hearing loss, caused by damage to the mechanical system that conducts sound waves to the cochlea.

cochlea, a snail-shaped tube in the **inner ear.** The incoming vibrations cause the cochlea's membrane (the *oval window*) to vibrate, jostling the fluid that fills the tube. This motion causes ripples in the *basilar membrane,* bending the *hair cells* lining its surface, not unlike the wind bending a wheat field. Hair cell movement triggers impulses in the adjacent nerve cells. Axons of those cells converge to form the *auditory nerve,* which sends neural messages (via the thalamus) to the *auditory cortex* in the brain's temporal lobe. From vibrating air to moving piston to fluid waves to electrical impulses to the brain: Voila! We hear.

Perhaps the most intriguing part of the hearing process is the hair cells— "quivering bundles that let us hear" thanks to their "extreme sensitivity and extreme speed" (Goldberg, 2007). A cochlea has 16,000 of them, which sounds like a lot until we compare that with an eye's 130 million or so photoreceptors. But consider their responsiveness. Deflect the tiny bundles of *cilia* on the tip of a hair cell by the width of an atom—the equivalent of displacing the top of the Eiffel Tower by half an inch—and the alert hair cell, thanks to a special protein at its tip, triggers a neural response (Corey et al., 2004).

Across the world, 360 million people are challenged by hearing loss (WHO, 2012). Damage to the cochlea's hair cell receptors or their associated nerves can cause **sensorineural hearing loss** (or nerve deafness). Occasionally, disease damages these receptors, but more often the culprits are biological changes linked with heredity, aging, and prolonged exposure to ear-splitting noise or music. Sensorineural hearing loss is more common than **conduction hearing loss,** which is caused by damage to the mechanical system that conducts sound waves to the cochlea.

The cochlea's hair cells have been likened to carpet fibers. Walk around on them and they will spring back. But leave a heavy piece of furniture on them and they may never rebound. As a general rule, if we cannot talk over a noise, it is potentially harmful, especially if prolonged and repeated (Roesser, 1998). Such experiences are common when sound exceeds 100 decibels, as might occur when in a frenzied sports arena, playing loud music through headphones, or listening to bagpipes (**FIGURE 18.3**). Ringing of the ears after exposure to loud sounds indicates that we have been bad to our unhappy hair cells. One study of teen rock concert attendees found that after three hours of sound averaging 99 decibels, 54 percent reported not hearing as well, and 1 in 4 had ringing in their ears. As pain alerts us to possible bodily harm, ringing of the ears alerts us to possible hearing damage. It is hearing's equivalent of bleeding.

The rate of teen hearing loss, now 1 in 5, has risen by a third since the early 1990s (Shargorodsky et al., 2010). Teen boys more than teen girls or adults blast themselves with loud volumes for long periods (Zogby, 2006). Males' greater noise exposure may help explain why men's hearing tends to be less acute than women's. But regardless of gender, those who spend many hours in a loud nightclub, behind a power mower, or above a jackhammer should wear earplugs. "Condoms or, safer yet, abstinence," say sex educators. "Earplugs or walk away," say hearing educators.

∧ FIGURE 18.3

The intensity of some common sounds One study of 3 million Germans found professional musicians having almost four times the average rate of noise-induced hearing loss (Schink et al., 2014).

For now, the only way to restore hearing for people with nerve deafness is a sort of bionic ear—a **cochlear implant,** which 50,000 people a year, including some 30,000 children, now receive (Hochmair, 2013). This electronic device translates sounds into electrical signals that, wired into the cochlea's nerves, convey information about sound to the brain (**FIGURE 18.4**). Cochlear implants in deaf kittens and human infants have seemed to trigger an "awakening" of the pertinent brain area (Klinke et al., 1999; Sireteanu, 1999). These devices can help children become proficient in oral communication (especially if they receive them as preschoolers or even before age 1) (Dettman et al., 2007; Schorr et al., 2005). Cochlear implants also help restore hearing for most adults, but only if their brain learned to process sound during childhood.

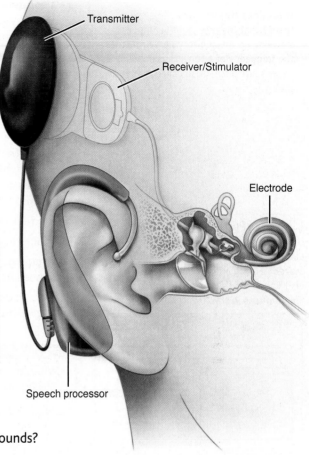

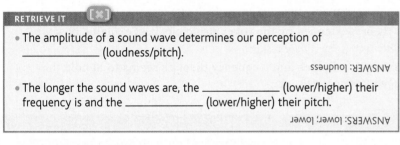

RETRIEVE IT [✖]

• The amplitude of a sound wave determines our perception of _____ (loudness/pitch).

ANSWER: loudness

• The longer the sound waves are, the _____ (lower/higher) their frequency is and the _____ (lower/higher) their pitch.

ANSWERS: lower; lower

Perceiving Loudness, Pitch, and Location

18-3 How do we detect loudness, discriminate pitch, and locate sounds?

RESPONDING TO LOUD AND SOFT SOUNDS How do we detect loudness? If you guessed that it's related to the intensity of a hair cell's response, you'd be wrong. Rather, a soft, pure tone activates only the few hair cells attuned to its frequency. Given louder sounds, neighboring hair cells also respond. Thus, your brain interprets loudness from the *number* of activated hair cells.

If a hair cell loses sensitivity to soft sounds, it may still respond to loud sounds. This helps explain another surprise: Really loud sounds may seem loud to people with or without normal hearing. As a person with hearing loss, I [DM] used to wonder what really loud music must sound like to people with normal hearing. Now I realize it sounds much the same; where we differ is in our perception of soft sounds.

HEARING DIFFERENT PITCHES How do we know whether a sound is the high-frequency, high-pitched chirp of a bird or the low-frequency, low-pitched roar of a truck? Current thinking on how we discriminate pitch combines two theories.

• Hermann von Helmholtz's **place theory** presumes that we hear different pitches because different sound waves trigger activity at different places along the cochlea's basilar membrane. Thus, the brain determines a sound's pitch by recognizing the specific place (on the membrane) that is generating the neural signal. When Nobel laureate-to-be Georg von Békésy (1957) cut holes in the cochleas of guinea pigs and human cadavers and looked inside with a microscope, he discovered that the cochlea vibrated, rather like a shaken bedsheet, in response to sound. High frequencies produced large vibrations near the beginning of the cochlea's membrane. Low frequencies vibrated more of the membrane and were not so neatly localized. So, the problem remains: Place theory can explain how we hear high-pitched sounds, but not low-pitched sounds.

⌃ FIGURE 18.4

Hardware for hearing Cochlear implants work by translating sounds into electrical signals that are transmitted to the cochlea and, via the auditory nerve, on to the brain.

cochlear implant a device for converting sounds into electrical signals and stimulating the auditory nerve through electrodes threaded into the cochlea.

place theory in hearing, the theory that links the pitch we hear with the place where the cochlea's membrane is stimulated.

frequency theory in hearing, the theory that the rate of nerve impulses traveling up the auditory nerve matches the frequency of a tone, thus enabling us to sense its pitch. (Also called *temporal theory*.)

LaunchPad For an interactive review of how we perceive sound, visit LaunchPad's *PsychSim 6: The Auditory System*. For an animated explanation, visit LaunchPad's *Concept Practice: The Auditory Pathway*.

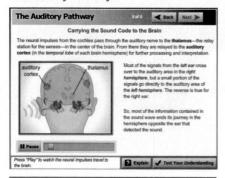

▾ FIGURE 18.5

How we locate sounds Sound waves strike one ear sooner and more intensely than the other. From this information, our nimble brain can compute the sound's location. As you might therefore expect, people who lose all hearing in one ear often have difficulty locating sounds.

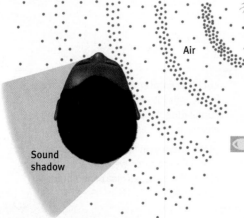

Air

Sound shadow

- **Frequency theory** (also called *temporal theory*) suggests an alternative: The brain reads pitch by monitoring the frequency of neural impulses traveling up the auditory nerve. The whole basilar membrane vibrates with the incoming sound wave, triggering neural impulses to the brain at the same rate as the sound wave. If the sound wave has a frequency of 100 waves per second, then 100 pulses per second travel up the auditory nerve. But again, a problem remains: An individual neuron cannot fire faster than 1000 times per second. How, then, can we sense sounds with frequencies above 1000 waves per second (roughly the upper third of a piano keyboard)?

- Enter the *volley principle:* Like soldiers who alternate firing so that some can shoot while others reload, neural cells can alternate firing. By firing in rapid succession, they can achieve a *combined frequency* above 1000 waves per second.

So, here is our current thinking on how we discriminate pitch:

1. Place theory best explains how we sense *high pitches.*

2. Frequency theory, extended by the volley principle, best explains how we sense *low pitches.*

3. Some combination of place and frequency theories seems to handle the *pitches in the intermediate range.*

RETRIEVE IT [✱]

- Which theory of pitch perception would best explain a symphony audience's enjoyment of a high-pitched piccolo? How about a low-pitched cello?

ANSWERS: place theory; frequency theory

LOCATING SOUNDS Why don't we have one big ear—perhaps above our one nose? "The better to hear you with," the wolf said to Red Riding Hood. Thanks to the placement of our two ears, we enjoy stereophonic ("three-dimensional") hearing. Two ears are better than one for at least two reasons. If a car to your right honks, your right ear will receive a more *intense* sound, and it will receive the sound slightly *sooner* than your left ear (**FIGURE 18.5**). Because sound travels 761 miles per hour and our ears are but 6 inches apart, the intensity difference and the time lag are extremely small. A just noticeable difference in the direction of two sound sources corresponds to a time difference of just 0.000027 second! Lucky for us, our supersensitive auditory system can detect such minute differences (Brown & Deffenbacher, 1979; Middlebrooks & Green, 1991).

The Other Senses

Sharks and dogs rely on their outstanding sense of smell, aided by large brain areas devoted to this system. Our human brain gives seeing and hearing priority in the allocation of cortical tissue. But extraordinary happenings also occur within our other senses. Without our senses of touch, taste, smell, and body position and movement, we humans would be seriously handicapped, and our capacities for enjoying the world would be greatly diminished.

Touch

◁▷ 18-4 How do we sense touch?

Touch is vital. Right from the start, touch aids our development. Infant rats deprived of their mother's grooming produce less growth hormone and have a lower metabolic rate—a good way to keep alive until the mother returns, but a reaction that

stunts growth if prolonged. Infant monkeys allowed to see, hear, and smell—but not touch—their mother become desperately unhappy; those separated by a screen with holes that allow touching are much less miserable. Premature human babies gain weight faster and go home sooner if they are stimulated by hand massage (Field et al., 2006). As adults, we still yearn to touch—to kiss, to stroke, to snuggle. This sort of touch soothes and protects. In one experiment, women felt less threatened by physical pain when holding their husband's hand (Coan et al., 2006). Touch also helps communicate. In experiments, strangers separated by a curtain, using their hands to touch only the other's forearms, have been able to communicate anger, fear, disgust, love, gratitude, and sympathy at levels well above chance (Hertenstein et al., 2006).

Humorist Dave Barry was perhaps right to jest that your skin "keeps people from seeing the inside of your body, which is repulsive, and it prevents your organs from falling onto the ground." But skin does much more. Touching various spots on the skin with a soft hair, a warm or cool wire, and the point of a pin reveals that some spots are especially sensitive to *pressure*, others to *warmth*, others to *cold*, still others to *pain*. Our "sense of touch" is actually a mix of these four basic and distinct skin senses, and our other skin sensations are variations of pressure, warmth, cold, and pain. Some examples:

The precious sense of touch
As William James wrote in his *Principles of Psychology* (1890), "Touch is both the alpha and omega of affection."

- Stroking adjacent pressure spots creates a tickle.
- Repeated gentle stroking of a pain spot creates an itching sensation.
- Touching adjacent cold and pressure spots triggers a sense of wetness, which you can experience by touching dry, cold metal.

Touch sensations involve more than tactile stimulation, however. A self-administered tickle produces less somatosensory cortex activation than does the same tickle from something or someone else (Blakemore et al., 1998). Likewise, a sensual leg caress evokes a different somatosensory cortex response when a heterosexual man believes it comes from an attractive woman rather than a man (Gazzola et al., 2012). Our responses to tickles and caresses reveal how quickly cognition influences our brain's sensory response.

Pain

18-5 What biological, psychological, and social-cultural influences affect our experience of pain? How do placebos, distraction, and hypnosis help control pain?

Be thankful for occasional pain. Pain is your body's way of telling you something has gone wrong. By drawing your attention to a burn, a break, or a sprain, pain orders you to change your behavior—"Stay off that turned ankle!" The rare people born without the ability to feel pain may experience severe injury or even death before early adulthood. Without the discomfort that makes us occasionally shift position, their joints fail from excess strain. Without the warnings of pain, the effects of unchecked infections and injuries accumulate (Neese, 1991).

More numerous are those who live with chronic pain, which is rather like an alarm that won't shut off. The suffering of those with persistent or recurring backaches, arthritis, headaches, and cancer-related pain, prompts two questions: What is pain? How might we control it?

UNDERSTANDING PAIN Our pain experiences vary widely. Women are more sensitive to pain than men are (their senses of hearing and smell also tend to be more sensitive) (Ruau et al., 2012; Wickelgren, 2009). Our individual pain sensitivity varies, too, depending on genes, physiology, experience, attention, and surrounding culture (Gatchel et al., 2007; Reimann et al., 2010). Thus, our experience of pain reflects both *bottom-up* sensations and *top-down* cognition.

The pain circuit Sensory receptors (*nociceptors*) respond to potentially damaging stimuli by sending an impulse to the spinal cord, which passes the message to the brain, which interprets the signal as pain.

Projection to brain

Pain impulse

Cross-section of the spinal cord

Cell body of nociceptor

Nerve cell

Tissue injury

"Pain is a gift." So said a doctor studying Ashlyn Blocker, who has a rare genetic mutation that prevents her from feeling pain. At birth, she didn't cry. As a child, she ran around for two days on a broken ankle. She has put her hands on a hot machine and burned the flesh off. And she has reached into boiling water to retrieve a dropped spoon. "Everyone in my class asks me about it, and I say, 'I can feel pressure, but I can't feel pain.' *Pain!* I cannot feel it!"

Jeff Riedel/Contour/Getty Images

BIOLOGICAL INFLUENCES There is no one type of stimulus that triggers pain (as light triggers vision). Instead, there are different *nociceptors*—sensory receptors in our skin, muscles, and organs that detect harmful temperatures, pressure, or chemicals and send pain signals (**FIGURE 18.6**).

Although no theory of pain explains all available findings, psychologist Ronald Melzack and biologist Patrick Wall's (1965, 1983; Melzack & Katz, 2013) classic **gate-control theory** provides a useful model. The spinal cord contains small nerve fibers that conduct most pain signals, and larger fibers that conduct most other sensory signals. Melzack and Wall theorized that the spinal cord contains a neurological "gate." When tissue is injured, the small fibers activate and open the gate, and you feel pain. Large-fiber activity closes the gate, blocking pain signals and preventing them from reaching the brain. Thus, one way to treat chronic pain is to stimulate (by massage, electric stimulation, or acupuncture) "gate-closing" activity in the large neural fibers (Wall, 2000).

But pain is not merely a physical phenomenon of injured nerves sending impulses to a definable brain area—like pulling on a rope to ring a bell. The brain also creates pain, as it does in people's experiences of *phantom limb sensations* after a limb has been amputated. Their brain may misinterpret the spontaneous central nervous system (CNS) activity that occurs in the absence of normal sensory input: As the dreamer may see with eyes closed, so 7 in 10 such people may feel pain or movement in nonexistent limbs (Melzack, 1992, 2005). (Some may also try to step off a bed onto a phantom leg or to lift a cup with a phantom hand.) Even those born without a limb sometimes perceive sensations from the absent arm or leg. The brain, Melzack (1998) has surmised, comes prepared to anticipate "that it will be getting information from a body that has limbs."

Phantoms may haunt other senses too, as the brain, responding to the absence of sensory signals, amplifies irrelevant neural activity. People with hearing loss often experience the sound of silence: *tinnitus,* the phantom sound of ringing in the ears. Those who lose vision to glaucoma, cataracts, diabetes, or macular degeneration may experience phantom sights—nonthreatening hallucinations (Ramachandran & Blakeslee, 1998). Others who have nerve damage in the systems for tasting and smelling have experienced phantom tastes or smells, such as ice water that seems sickeningly sweet, or fresh air that reeks of rotten food (Goode, 1999). The point to remember: *We feel, see, hear, taste, and smell with our brain, which can sense even without functioning senses.*

PSYCHOLOGICAL INFLUENCES One powerful influence on our perception of pain is the attention we focus on it. Athletes, focused on winning, may play through the pain. Halfway through his lap of the 2012 Olympics 1600-meter relay, Manteo Mitchell broke one of his leg bones—and kept running.

We also seem to edit our *memories* of pain, which often differ from the pain we actually experienced. In experiments, and after medical procedures, people overlook a pain's duration. Their memory snapshots instead record two factors: their pain's *peak* moment (which can lead them to recall variable pain, with peaks, as worse [Stone et al., 2005]), and how much pain they felt at the *end.* In one experiment, researchers asked people to immerse one hand in painfully cold water for

60 seconds, and then the other hand in the same painfully cold water for 60 seconds followed by a slightly less painful 30 seconds more (Kahneman et al., 1993). Which experience would you expect to recall as most painful?

Curiously, when asked which trial they would prefer to repeat, most preferred the 90-second trial, with more net pain—but less pain at the end. Physicians have used this principle with patients undergoing colon exams—lengthening the discomfort by a minute, but lessening its intensity (Kahneman, 1999). Although the extended milder discomfort added to their net pain experience, patients experiencing this taper-down treatment later recalled the exam as less painful than did those whose pain ended abruptly. Likewise, after childbirth, women recall the total amount of pain in terms of the average of the peak and end pain, rather than the duration (Chajut et al., 2014). (Imagine that, at the end of a painful root canal, the oral surgeon asks if you'd like to go home or to have a few more minutes of milder discomfort. If you want to remember less pain, there's a case to be made for prolonging your hurt.)

The end of an experience can color our memory of pleasures, too. In one simple experiment, some people, on receiving a fifth and last piece of chocolate, were told it was their "next" one. Others, told it was their "last" piece, liked it better and also rated the whole experiment as being more enjoyable (O'Brien & Ellsworth, 2012). Endings matter.

SOCIAL-CULTURAL INFLUENCES Our perception of pain varies with our social situation and our cultural traditions. We tend to perceive more pain when others seem to be experiencing pain (Symbaluk et al., 1997). This may help explain other apparent social aspects of pain, as when pockets of Australian keyboard operators during the mid-1980s suffered outbreaks of severe pain while typing or performing other repetitive work—without any discernible physical abnormalities (Gawande, 1998). Sometimes the pain in sprain is mainly in the brain—literally. When people felt empathy for another's pain, their own brain activity partly mirrored the activity of the actual brain in pain (Singer et al., 2004).

Thus, our perception of pain is a biopsychosocial phenomenon (Hadjistavropoulos et al., 2011). Viewing pain from many perspectives can help us better understand how to cope with it and treat it (**FIGURE 18.7**).

Reinhold Matay/AP Photo

Distracted from the pain
After a tackle in the first half of a competitive game, BK Häcken soccer player Mohammed Ali Khan (in white) said he "had a bit of pain" but thought it was "just a bruise." With his attention focused on the game, he played on. In the second half he was surprised to learn from an attending doctor that his leg was broken.

gate-control theory the theory that the spinal cord contains a neurological "gate" that blocks pain signals or allows them to pass on to the brain. The "gate" is opened by the activity of pain signals traveling up small nerve fibers and is closed by activity in larger fibers or by information coming from the brain.

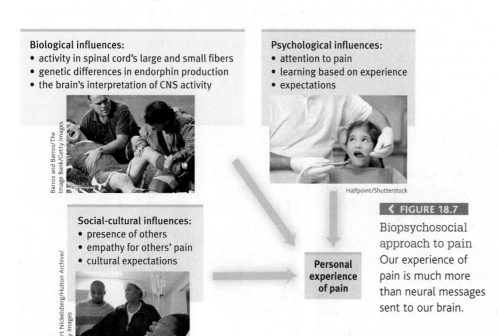

Biological influences:
• activity in spinal cord's large and small fibers
• genetic differences in endorphin production
• the brain's interpretation of CNS activity

Barros and Barros/The Image Bank/Getty Images

Psychological influences:
• attention to pain
• learning based on experience
• expectations

Halfpoint/Shutterstock

Social-cultural influences:
• presence of others
• empathy for others' pain
• cultural expectations

Robert Nickelsberg/Hulton Archive/Getty Images

Personal experience of pain

< **FIGURE 18.7**

Biopsychosocial approach to pain Our experience of pain is much more than neural messages sent to our brain.

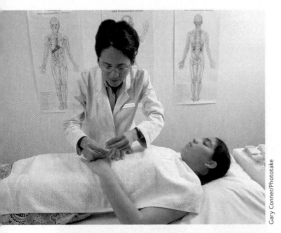

Acupuncture: A jab well done
This acupuncturist is attempting to help this woman gain relief from back pain by using needles on points of the patient's hand.

"Pain is increased by attending to it."
Charles Darwin, The Expression of the Emotions in Man and Animals, *1872*

CONTROLLING PAIN If pain is where body meets mind—if it is both a physical and a psychological phenomenon—then it should be treatable both physically and psychologically. Depending on the patient's symptoms, pain control clinics select one or more therapies from a list that includes drugs, surgery, acupuncture, electrical stimulation, massage, exercise, hypnosis, relaxation training, and thought distraction.

These options reflect some striking influences on pain. When we are distracted from pain (a psychological influence) and soothed by the release of our naturally painkilling *endorphins* (a biological influence), our experience of pain diminishes. Sports injuries may go unnoticed until the after-game shower. People who carry a gene that boosts the availability of endorphins are less bothered by pain, and their brain is less responsive to pain (Zubieta et al., 2003). Others, who carry a mutated gene that disrupts pain circuit neurotransmission, may be unable to experience pain (Cox et al., 2006). Such discoveries could point the way toward new pain medications that mimic these genetic effects.

PLACEBOS Even an inert placebo can help, by dampening the central nervous system's attention and responses to painful experiences—mimicking painkilling drugs (Eippert et al., 2009; Wager & Atlas, 2013). After being injected in the jaw with a stinging saltwater solution, men in one experiment received a placebo said to relieve pain, and they immediately felt better. Sometimes "nothing works." Being given fake painkilling chemicals caused the brain to dispense real ones, as indicated by activity in an area that releases natural painkilling opiates (Scott et al., 2007; Zubieta et al., 2005). "Believing becomes reality," noted one commentator (Thernstrom, 2006), as "the mind unites with the body."

DISTRACTION Distracting people with pleasant images *("Think of a warm, comfortable environment")* or drawing their attention away from painful stimulation *("Count backward by 3's")* is an effective way to activate pain-inhibiting circuits and to increase pain tolerance (Edwards et al., 2009). A well-trained nurse may chat with needle-shy patients and ask them to look away when inserting the needle. Burn victims receiving excruciating wound care can benefit from an even more effective distraction: immersion in a computer-generated 3-D world, like the snow scene in **FIGURE 18.8**. Functional MRI (fMRI) scans have revealed that playing in the virtual reality reduces the brain's pain-related activity (Hoffman, 2004). Because pain is in the brain, diverting the brain's attention may bring relief. Better yet, research suggests, maximize pain relief by combining a placebo with distraction (Buhle et al., 2012), and amplify their effects with hypnosis. Hypnosis can also divert attention (see Thinking Critically About: Hypnosis and Pain Relief).

❯ **FIGURE 18.8**

Virtual-reality pain control For burn victims undergoing painful skin repair, an escape into virtual reality can powerfully distract attention, thus reducing pain and the brain's response to painful stimulation. fMRI scans have illustrated a lowered pain response when the patient is distracted.

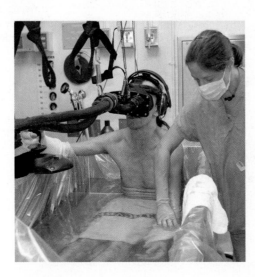

Hypnosis and Pain Relief

Imagine you are about to be hypnotized. The hypnotist invites you to sit back, fix your gaze on a spot high on the wall, and relax. In a quiet, low voice the hypnotist suggests, "Your eyes are growing tired. . . . Your eyelids are becoming heavy . . . now heavier and heavier. . . . They are beginning to close. . . . You are becoming more deeply relaxed. . . . Your breathing is now deep and regular. . . . Your muscles are becoming more and more relaxed. . . . Your whole body is beginning to feel like lead."

After a few minutes of this *hypnotic induction,* you may experience **hypnosis.** Hypnotists have no magical mind-control power; they merely focus people on certain images or behaviors. To some extent, we are all open to suggestion. But highly hypnotizable people—such as the 20 percent who can carry out a suggestion not to smell or react to an open bottle of ammonia held under their nose—are especially suggestible and imaginative (Barnier & McConkey, 2004; Silva & Kirsch, 1992).

Can hypnosis relieve pain? *Yes.* When unhypnotized people put their arms in an ice bath, they felt intense pain within 25 seconds (Elkins et al., 2012; Jensen, 2008). When hypnotized people did the same after being given suggestions to feel no pain, they indeed reported feeling little pain. As some dentists know, light hypnosis can reduce fear, thus reducing hypersensitivity to pain. Hypnosis also lessens some forms of chronic pain (Adachi et al., 2014).

Hypnosis inhibits pain-related brain activity. In surgical experiments, hypnotized patients have required less medication, recovered sooner, and left the hospital earlier than unhypnotized control patients (Askay & Patterson, 2007; Hammond, 2008; Spiegel, 2007). Nearly 10 percent of us can become so deeply hypnotized that even major surgery can be performed without anesthesia. Half of us can gain at least some pain relief from hypnosis. The surgical use of hypnosis has flourished in Europe, where one Belgian medical team has performed more than 5000 surgeries with a combination of hypnosis, local anesthesia, and a mild sedative (Song, 2006).

Psychologists have proposed two explanations for how hypnosis works. One theory proposes that hypnosis is a form of normal *social influence* (Lynn et al., 1990, 2015; Spanos & Coe, 1992). In this view, hypnosis is a by-product of normal social and mental processes. Like actors caught up in their roles, people begin to feel and behave in ways appropriate for "good hypnotic subjects." They may allow the hypnotist to direct their attention and fantasies away from pain.

Another theory views hypnosis as a special dual-processing state of **dissociation**—a split between different levels of consciousness. Dissociation theory offers an explanation for why people hypnotized for pain relief may show brain activity in areas that receive sensory information, but not in areas that normally process pain-related information. It also seeks to explain why, when no one is watching, hypnotized people may carry out **posthypnotic suggestions** (which are made during hypnosis but carried out after the person is no longer hypnotized) (Perugini et al., 1998).

Another form of dual processing—*selective attention*—may also play a role in hypnotic pain relief. Brain scans show that hypnosis increases activity in frontal lobe attention systems (Oakley & Halligan, 2013). And it reduces brain activity in a region that processes painful stimuli, but not in the somatosensory cortex, which receives the raw sensory input (Rainville et al., 1997). So, hypnosis does not block sensory input, but it may block our attention to those stimuli. This helps explain why an injured athlete, caught up in the competition, may feel little or no pain until the game ends.

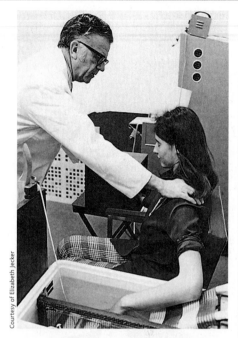

Courtesy of Elizabeth Jecker

Dissociation or social influence? This hypnotized woman being tested by famous researcher Ernest Hilgard showed no pain when her arm was placed in an ice bath. But asked to press a key if some part of her felt the pain, she did so. To Hilgard (1986, 1992), this was evidence of dissociation, or divided consciousness. The social influence perspective, however, maintains that people responding this way are caught up in playing the role of "good subject."

hypnosis a social interaction in which one person (the hypnotist) suggests to another (the subject) that certain perceptions, feelings, thoughts, or behaviors will spontaneously occur.

dissociation a split in consciousness, which allows some thoughts and behaviors to occur simultaneously with others.

posthypnotic suggestion a suggestion, made during a hypnosis session, to be carried out after the subject is no longer hypnotized; used by some clinicians to help control undesired symptoms and behaviors.

RETRIEVE IT

• Which of the following has NOT been proven to reduce pain?

    a. Distraction   b. Placebos   c. Phantom limb sensations   d. Endorphins

ANSWER: c.

Taste

👁 **18-6** In what ways are our senses of taste and smell similar, and how do they differ?

Like touch, our sense of taste involves several basic sensations. Taste's sensations were once thought to be sweet, sour, salty, and bitter, with all others stemming from mixtures of these four (McBurney & Gent, 1979). Then, as investigators searched for specialized nerve fibers for the four taste sensations, they encountered a receptor for what we now know is a fifth—the savory meaty taste of *umami,* best experienced as the flavor enhancer monosodium glutamate (MSG).

Tastes exist for more than our pleasure (see **TABLE 18.1**). Pleasureful tastes attracted our ancestors to energy- or protein-rich foods that enabled their survival. Aversive tastes deterred them from new foods that might be toxic. We see the inheritance of this biological wisdom in today's 2- to 6-year-olds, who are typically fussy eaters, especially when offered new meats or bitter-tasting vegetables, such as spinach and brussels sprouts (Cooke et al., 2003). Meat and plant toxins were both potentially dangerous sources of food poisoning for our ancestors, especially for children. Given repeated small tastes of disliked new foods, however, children begin to accept them (Wardle et al., 2003). We come to like what we eat. Compared with breast-fed babies, German babies bottle-fed vanilla-flavored milk grew up to be adults with a striking preference for vanilla flavoring (Haller et al., 1999).

Taste is a chemical sense. Inside each little bump on the top and sides of your tongue are 200 or more taste buds, each containing a pore that catches food chemicals. Into each taste bud pore, 50 to 100 taste receptor cells project antenna-like hairs that sense food molecules. Some receptors respond mostly to sweet-tasting molecules, others to salty-, sour-, umami-, or bitter-tasting ones, and each has a matching partner cell in the brain (Barretto et al., 2015). It doesn't take much to trigger a response that alerts your brain's temporal lobe. If a stream of water is pumped across your tongue, the addition of a concentrated salty or sweet taste for but one-tenth of a second will get your attention (Kelling & Halpern, 1983). When a friend asks for "just a taste" of your soft drink, you can squeeze off the straw after a mere instant.

Taste receptors reproduce themselves every week or two, so if you burn your tongue with hot food it hardly matters. However, as you grow older, the number of taste buds decreases, as does taste sensitivity (Cowart, 1981). (No wonder adults enjoy strong-tasting foods that children resist.) Smoking and alcohol use accelerate these declines. Those who have lost their sense of taste have reported that food tastes like "straw" and is hard to swallow (Cowart, 2005).

Essential as taste buds are, there's more to taste than meets the tongue. Expectations can influence taste. When told a sausage roll was "vegetarian," people in one experiment found it decidedly inferior to its identical partner labeled "meat" (Allen et al., 2008). In another experiment, being told that a wine cost $90 rather than its real $10 price made it taste better and triggered more activity in a brain area that responds to pleasant experiences (Plassmann et al., 2008).

Smell

Life begins with an inhale and ends with an exhale. Between birth and death, we will, on average, inhale and exhale 500 million breaths of life-sustaining air, bathing our nostrils in a stream of scent-laden molecules. The resulting experiences of smell *(olfaction)* are strikingly intimate: You inhale something of whatever or whoever it is you smell.

Like taste, smell is a chemical sense. We smell something when molecules of a substance carried in the air reach a tiny cluster of 20 million receptor cells at the top of each nasal cavity (**FIGURE 18.9**). These olfactory receptor cells, waving

---

⌄ **TABLE 18.1**

The Survival Functions of Basic Tastes

Taste	Indicates
Sweet	Energy source
Salty	Sodium essential to physiological processes
Sour	Potentially toxic acid
Bitter	Potential poisons
Umami	Proteins to grow and repair tissue

Lauren Burke/Digital Vision/Getty Images

"Life is not measured by the number of breaths we take, but by the moments that take our breath away."

Author unknown

Impress your friends with your new word for the day: People unable to see are said to experience blindness. People unable to hear experience deafness. People unable to smell experience *anosmia*. The 1 in 7500 people born with anosmia not only have trouble cooking and eating, but also are somewhat more prone to depression, accidents, and relationship insecurity (Croy et al., 2012, 2013).

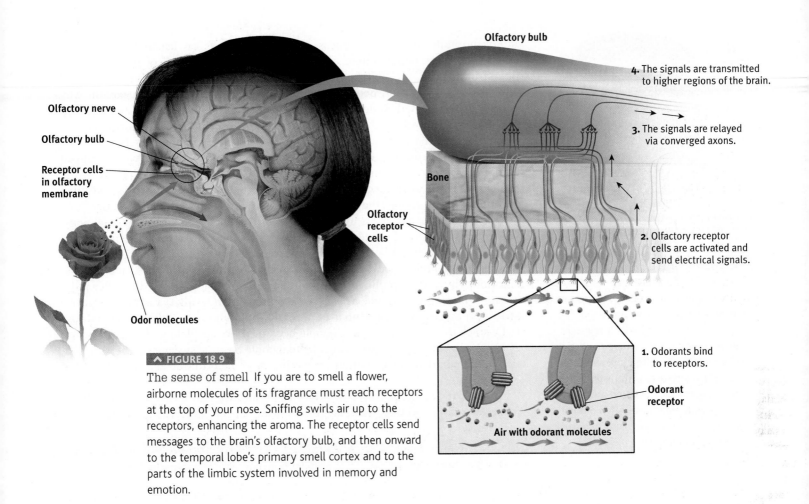

Olfactory bulb

4. The signals are transmitted to higher regions of the brain.

3. The signals are relayed via converged axons.

Olfactory nerve

Olfactory bulb

Receptor cells in olfactory membrane

Bone

Olfactory receptor cells

2. Olfactory receptor cells are activated and send electrical signals.

Odor molecules

1. Odorants bind to receptors.

Odorant receptor

Air with odorant molecules

^ FIGURE 18.9

The sense of smell If you are to smell a flower, airborne molecules of its fragrance must reach receptors at the top of your nose. Sniffing swirls air up to the receptors, enhancing the aroma. The receptor cells send messages to the brain's olfactory bulb, and then onward to the temporal lobe's primary smell cortex and to the parts of the limbic system involved in memory and emotion.

like sea anemones on a reef, respond selectively—to the aroma of a cake baking, to a wisp of smoke, to a friend's fragrance. Instantly, they alert the brain through their axon fibers. Being part of an old, primitive sense, olfactory neurons bypass the brain's sensory control center, the thalamus.

Even nursing infants and their mothers have a literal chemistry to their relationship. They quickly learn to recognize each other's scents (McCarthy, 1986). Aided by smell, a mother fur seal returning to a beach crowded with pups will find her own. Our human sense of smell is less acute than our senses of seeing and hearing. Looking out across a garden, we see its forms and colors in exquisite detail and hear a variety of birds singing, yet we smell little of it without sticking our nose into the blossoms.

Odor molecules come in many shapes and sizes—so many, in fact, that it takes many different receptors to detect them. A large family of genes designs the 350 or so receptor proteins that recognize particular odor molecules (Miller, 2004). Linda Buck and Richard Axel (1991) discovered (in work for which they received a 2004 Nobel Prize) that these receptor proteins are embedded on the surface of nasal cavity neurons. As a key slips into a lock, so odor molecules slip into these receptors. Yet we don't seem to have a distinct receptor for each detectable odor. Odors trigger combinations of receptors, in patterns that are interpreted by the olfactory cortex. As the English alphabet's 26 letters can combine to form many words, so odor molecules bind to different receptor arrays, producing at least 1 trillion odors that we could potentially discriminate (Bushdid et al., 2014). It is the combinations of olfactory receptors, which activate different neuron patterns, that allow us to distinguish between the aromas of fresh-brewed and hours-old coffee (Zou et al., 2005).

LaunchPad For an animated explanation of how we smell, visit LaunchPad's *Concept Practice: Sense of Smell.*

The nose knows Humans have some 20 million olfactory receptors. A bloodhound has 220 million (Herz, 2007).

Layne Bailey/The Charlotte Observer/AP Photo

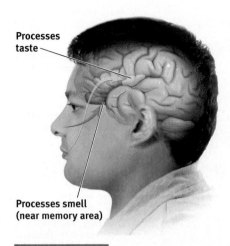

Processes
taste

Processes smell
(near memory area)

∧ FIGURE 18.10

Taste, smell, and memory Information from the taste buds (yellow arrow) travels to an area between the frontal and temporal lobes of the brain. It registers in an area not far from where the brain receives information from our sense of smell, which interacts with taste. The brain's circuitry for smell (red area) also connects with areas involved in memory storage, which helps explain why a smell can trigger a memory.

For humans, the attractiveness of smells depends on learned associations (Herz, 2001). As babies nurse, their preference for the smell of their mother's breast builds. So, too, with other associations. As good experiences are linked with a particular scent, people come to like that scent. This helps explain why people in the United States tend to like the smell of wintergreen (which they associate with candy and gum) more than do those in Great Britain (where it often is associated with medicine). In another example of odors evoking unpleasant emotions, researchers frustrated Brown University students with a rigged computer game in a scented room (Herz et al., 2004). Later, if exposed to the same odor while working on a verbal task, the students' frustration was rekindled and they gave up sooner than others exposed to a different odor or no odor.

Our sensory experiences also interact with other aspects of our psychology. Our brain's circuitry helps explain an odor's power to evoke feelings and memories (**FIGURE 18.10**). A hotline runs between the brain area receiving information from the nose and the brain's ancient limbic centers associated with memory and emotion. Thus, when put in a foul-smelling room, people expressed harsher judgments of immoral acts (such as lying or keeping a found wallet) and more negative attitudes toward gay men (Inbar et al., 2011; Schnall et al., 2008). Exposed to a fishy smell during a trust game, people became more suspicious (Lee & Schwarz, 2012). And when exposed to a sweet taste, people became sweeter on their romantic partners and sweeter to others by acting more helpful (Meier et al., 2012; Ren et al., 2015).

Though it's difficult to recall odors by name, we can easily recognize long-forgotten odors and their associated memories (Engen, 1987; Schab, 1991).

RETRIEVE IT

• How does our system for sensing smell differ from our sensory systems for touch and taste?

ANSWER: We have four basic touch senses and five basic taste sensations. But we have no specific smell receptors. Instead, different combinations of odor receptors send messages to the brain, enabling us to recognize some 1 trillion different smells.

Body Position and Movement

 18-7 How do we sense our body's position and movement?

Important sensors in your joints, tendons, and muscles enable your **kinesthesia**—your sense of the position and movement of your body parts. By closing your eyes or plugging your ears you can momentarily imagine being without sight or sound. But what would it be like to live without touch or kinesthesia—without, therefore, being able to sense the positions of your limbs when you wake during the night? Ian Waterman of Hampshire, England, knows. In 1972, at age 19, Waterman contracted a rare viral infection that destroyed the nerves enabling his sense of light touch and of body position and movement. People with this condition report feeling disembodied, as though their body is dead, not real, not theirs (Sacks, 1985). With prolonged practice, Waterman learned to walk and eat—by visually focusing on his limbs and directing them accordingly. But if the lights go out, he crumples to the floor (Azar, 1998). Even for the rest of us, vision interacts with kinesthesia. Stand with your right heel in front of your left toes. Easy. Now close your eyes and you will probably wobble.

A companion **vestibular sense** monitors your head's (and thus your body's) position and movement. The biological gyroscopes for this sense of equilibrium are two structures in your inner ear. The first, your fluid-filled *semicircular canals,* look like a three-dimensional pretzel (Figure 18.2a). The second, connecting those canals with the cochlea, is the pair of *vestibular sacs,* which also contain fluid that moves when your head rotates or tilts. When this movement stimulates

kinesthesia [kin-ehs-THEE-zhuh] the system for sensing the position and movement of individual body parts.

vestibular sense the sense of body movement and position, including the sense of balance.

sensory interaction the principle that one sense may influence another, as when the smell of food influences its taste.

hair-like receptors, sending messages to the cerebellum at the back of your brain, you sense your body position and maintain your balance.

If you twirl around and then come to an abrupt halt, neither the fluid in your semicircular canals nor your kinesthetic receptors will immediately return to their neutral state. The dizzy aftereffect fools your brain with the sensation that you're still spinning. This illustrates a principle that underlies perceptual illusions: *Mechanisms that normally give us an accurate experience of the world can, under certain conditions, fool us.* Understanding how we get fooled provides clues to how our perceptual system works.

RETRIEVE IT [✖]

• Where are kinesthetic receptors and vestibular sense receptors located?

ANSWER: Kinesthetic receptors are located in our joints, tendons, and muscles. Vestibular sense receptors are located in our inner ear.

Bodies in space These high school competitive cheer team members can thank their inner ears for the information that enables their brains to monitor their bodies' position so expertly.

Sensory Interaction

18-8 How does *sensory interaction* influence our perceptions, and what is *embodied cognition?*

Our senses—seeing, hearing, touching, tasting, smelling—eavesdrop on one another (Rosenblum, 2013). In interpreting the world, our brain blends their inputs. Consider what happens to your sense of taste if you hold your nose, close your eyes, and have someone feed you various foods. A slice of apple may be indistinguishable from a chunk of raw potato. A piece of steak may taste like cardboard. Without their smells, a cup of cold coffee may be hard to distinguish from a glass of red wine. Our sense of smell sticks its nose into the business of taste.

Thus, to savor a taste, we normally breathe the aroma through our nose—which is why eating is not much fun when you have a bad cold. Smell can also change our perception of taste: A drink's strawberry odor enhances our perception of its sweetness. Even touch can influence taste. Depending on its texture, a potato chip "tastes" fresh or stale (Smith, 2011). This is **sensory interaction** at work—the principle that one sense may influence another. Smell + texture + taste = flavor.

Vision and hearing may similarly interact. A weak flicker of light is more easily visible when accompanied by a short burst of sound (Kayser, 2007). And a sound may be easier to hear with a visual cue. If I [DM], as a person with hearing loss, watch a video with simultaneous captioning, I have no trouble hearing the words I am seeing. I may therefore think I don't need the captioning, but if I then turn off the captioning, I suddenly realize I do need it. The eyes guide the ears (**FIGURE 18.11**).

But what do you suppose happens if the eyes and the ears disagree? What if we *see* a speaker saying one syllable while we *hear* another? Surprise: We may perceive a third syllable that blends both inputs. Seeing the mouth movements for *ga* while hearing *ba* we may perceive *da*. This phenomenon is known as the *McGurk effect,* after its discoverers, Scottish psychologist Harry McGurk and his assistant John MacDonald (1976). For all of us, lip reading is part of hearing.

Touch also interacts with our other senses. In detecting events, the brain can combine simultaneous touch and visual signals, thanks to neurons projecting from the somatosensory cortex back to the visual cortex (Macaluso et al., 2000). Touch even interacts with hearing. In one experiment, researchers blew a puff of air (such as our mouths produce when saying *pa* and *ta*) on the neck or hands as people heard either these sounds or the more airless sounds *ba* or *da*. The result? People more often misheard *ba* or *da* as *pa* or *ta* when played with the faint puff (Gick & Derrick, 2009). Thanks to sensory interaction, they heard with their skin.

❯ FIGURE 18.11

"FaceTime" phone improvement Seeing an animated face forming the words being spoken at the other end of a phone line, which Apple's FaceTime function provides, makes those words easier to understand for hard-of-hearing listeners (Knight, 2004).

embodied cognition the influence of bodily sensations, gestures, and other states on cognitive preferences and judgments.

IMMERSIVE LEARNING Are you wondering how researchers test these kinds of questions? Try LaunchPad's *How Would You Know If a Cup of Coffee Can Warm Up Relationships?*

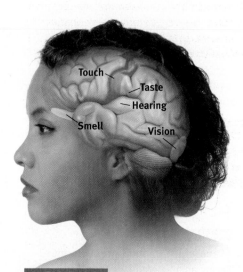

Our sensory experiences also interact with other aspects of our psychology. Our brain even blends our tactile and social judgments, as demonstrated in these playful experiments:

- After holding a warm drink rather than a cold one, people were more likely to rate someone more warmly, feel closer to them, and behave more generously (IJzerman & Semin, 2009; Williams & Bargh, 2008). Physical warmth promotes social warmth.

- After being given the cold shoulder by others in an experiment, people judge the room as colder than do those treated warmly (Zhong & Leonardelli, 2008). Social exclusion literally feels cold.

- Sitting at a wobbly desk and chair makes others' relationships seem less stable (Kille et al., 2013).

- When leaning to the left—by sitting in a left- rather than right-leaning chair, or squeezing a hand-grip with their left hand, or using a mouse with their left hand—people lean more left in their expressed political attitudes (Oppenheimer & Trail, 2010). When holding a soft ball, American students become more likely to categorize a face as a Democrat rather than a Republican, and vice versa when holding a hard ball (Slepian et al., 2012).

These examples of **embodied cognition** illustrate how brain circuits processing bodily sensations connect with brain circuits responsible for cognition. We think from within a body.

So, the senses interact: As we attempt to decipher our world, our brain blends inputs from multiple channels. For many people, an odor, perhaps of mint or chocolate, can evoke a sensation of taste (Stevenson & Tomiczek, 2007). But in a few select individuals, the senses become joined in a phenomenon called *synesthesia*, where one sort of sensation (such as hearing sound) involuntarily produces another (such as seeing color). Thus, hearing music may activate color-sensitive cortex regions and trigger a sensation of color (Brang et al., 2008; Hubbard et al., 2005). Seeing the number 3 may evoke a taste sensation (Ward, 2003).

* * *

For a summary of our sensory systems, see **TABLE 18.2**. The river of perception is fed by streams of sensation, cognition, and emotion.

If perception is the product of these three sources, what can we say about extrasensory perception, which claims that perception can occur apart from sensory input? For more on that question, see Thinking Critically About: ESP—Perception Without Sensation?

❯ TABLE 18.2

Summarizing the Senses

Sensory System	Source	Receptors	Key Brain Areas
Vision	Light waves striking the eye	Rods and cones in the retina	Occipital lobes
Hearing	Sound waves striking the outer ear	Cochlear hair cells in the inner ear	Temporal lobes
Touch	Pressure, warmth, cold	Receptors, most in the skin, detect pressure, warmth, cold, and pain	Somatosensory cortex
Taste	Chemical molecules in the mouth	Basic tongue receptors for sweet, sour, salty, bitter, and umami	Frontal temporal lobe border
Smell	Chemical molecules breathed in through the nose	Millions of receptors at top of nasal cavity	Olfactory bulb
Body position—kinesthesia	Any change in position of a body part, interacting with vision	Kinesthetic sensors in joints, tendons, and muscles	Cerebellum
Body movement—vestibular sense	Movement of fluids in the inner ear caused by head/body movement	Hair-like receptors in the ears' semicircular canals and vestibular sacs	Cerebellum

ESP—Perception Without Sensation?

18-9 What are the claims of ESP, and what have most research psychologists concluded after putting these claims to the test?

Without sensory input, are we capable of **extrasensory perception (ESP)?** Are there indeed people—any people—who can read minds, see through walls, or foretell the future? Nearly half of Americans have agreed there are (AP, 2007; Moore, 2005).

The most testable and, for this discussion, most relevant ESP claims are

• *telepathy:* mind-to-mind communication.

• *clairvoyance:* perceiving remote events, such as a house on fire in another state.

• *precognition:* perceiving future events, such as an unexpected death in the next month.

Closely linked is *psychokinesis,* or "mind movement," such as levitating a table or influencing the roll of a die. (The claim is illustrated by the wry request, "Will all those who believe in psychokinesis please raise my hand?")

If ESP is real, we would need to overturn the scientific understanding that we are creatures whose minds are tied to our physical brains and whose perceptual experiences are built of sensations. Sometimes new evidence does overturn our scientific preconceptions.

Most research psychologists and scientists have been skeptical that paranormal phenomena exist. But in several reputable universities, **parapsychology** researchers perform scientific experiments searching for possible ESP (Storm, 2010a,b; Turpin, 2005). Before seeing how they do so, let's consider some popular beliefs.

Premonitions or Pretensions?

Can psychics see into the future? Although one might wish for a psychic stock forecaster, the tallied forecasts of "leading psychics" reveal meager accuracy. During the 1990s, the tabloid psychics were all wrong in predicting surprising events. (Madonna did not become a gospel singer, the Statue of Liberty did not lose both its arms in a terrorist blast, Queen Elizabeth did not abdicate her throne to enter a convent.) And the psychics have missed big-news events. Why, despite a $50 million reward, could none of them help locate Osama bin Laden after 9/11? Where were the psychics on 9/10 when we needed them? In 2010, when a mine collapse trapped 33 miners, the Chilean government reportedly consulted four psychics. Their verdict? "They're all dead" (Kraul, 2010). But 69 days later, all 33 were rescued. After Amanda Berry went missing in Cleveland in 2003, her distraught and desperate mother turned to a famed psychic on a national television show for answers. "She's not alive, honey," the psychic told the devastated mom, who died without living to see her daughter's brave escape in 2013 (Radford, 2013). According to one analysis, this result brought that psychic's record on 116 missing person and death cases to 83 unknown outcomes, 33 incorrect, and zero mostly correct. To researcher Ryan Shaffer (2013), that's the record of a "psychic defective."

The psychic visions offered to police departments have been no more accurate than guesses made by others (Nickell, 1994, 2005; Radford, 2010; Reiser, 1982). Their sheer volume does, however, increase the odds of an occasional correct guess, which psychics can then report to the media. Police departments are wise to all this. When researchers asked the police departments of America's 50 largest cities whether they ever had used psychics, 65 percent said *No* (Sweat & Durm, 1993). Of those that had, not one had found them helpful.

Psychics' vague predictions sometimes sound correct when later retrofitted to match events. Nostradamus, a sixteenth-century French psychic, explained in an unguarded moment that his ambiguous prophecies "could not possibly be understood till they were interpreted after the event and by it."

Are the spontaneous "visions" of everyday people any more accurate? Do dreams, for example, foretell the future, as people from both Eastern and Western cultures tend to believe—making some people more reluctant to fly after dreaming of a plane crash (Morewedge & Norton, 2009)? Or do they only seem to do so when we recall or reconstruct them in light of what has already happened? Two Harvard psychologists tested the prophetic power of dreams after superhero aviator Charles Lindbergh's baby son was kidnapped and murdered in 1932 (Murray & Wheeler, 1937). Before the body was discovered, they invited people to report their dreams about the child, and 1300 visionaries submitted dream reports. How many accurately envisioned the child dead? Five percent. And how many individuals also correctly anticipated the body's location—buried among trees? Only 4 of the 1300. Although this number was surely no better than chance, to those four dreamers the accuracy of their apparent precognitions must have seemed uncanny.

Given the billions of events in the world each day, and given enough days, some stunning coincidences are sure to occur. By one careful estimate, chance alone would predict that more than a thousand times a day someone on Earth will think of another person and then, within the next five minutes, learn of that person's death (Charpak & Broch, 2004). Thus, when explaining an astonishing event, we should "give chance a chance" (Lilienfeld, 2009). With enough time and people, the improbable becomes inevitable.

extrasensory perception (ESP) the controversial claim that perception can occur apart from sensory input; includes telepathy, clairvoyance, and precognition.

parapsychology the study of paranormal phenomena, including ESP and psychokinesis.

Continued on next page

Will you marry me, live happily for 3 years, become bored, pretend to be taking a pottery class but actually be having an affair, then agree to go to marriage counseling to stay together for the sake of our hyperactive son, Derrick?

WHEN PSYCHICS PROPOSE

BIZARRO © 2014 Dan Piraro, Dist. By King Features

Putting ESP to Experimental Test

When faced with claims of mind reading or out-of-body travel or communication with the dead, how can we separate bizarre ideas from those that sound strange but are true? At the heart of science is a simple answer: *Test them to see if they work.* If they do, so much the better for the ideas. If they don't, so much the better for our skepticism.

This scientific attitude has led both believers and skeptics to agree that what parapsychology needs is a reproducible phenomenon and a theory to explain it. Parapsychologist Rhea White (1998) spoke for many in saying "The image of parapsychology that comes to my mind, based on nearly 44 years in the field, is that of a small airplane [that] has been perpetually taxiing down the runway of the Empirical Science Airport since 1882 . . . its movement punctuated occasionally by lifting a few feet off the ground only to bump back down on the tarmac once again. It has never taken off for any sustained flight."

"To be sure of hitting the target, shoot first and call whatever you hit the target."
Writer-artist Ashleigh Brilliant

"A person who talks a lot is sometimes right."
Spanish proverb

How might we test ESP claims in a controlled, reproducible experiment? An experiment differs from a staged demonstration. In the laboratory, the experimenter controls what the "psychic" sees and hears; on stage, the psychic controls what the audience sees and hears.

Daryl Bem, a respected social psychologist, has been a skeptic of stage psychics; he once quipped that "a psychic is an actor playing the role of a psychic" (1984). Yet he reignited hopes for replicable evidence with nine experiments that seemed to show people anticipating future events (2011). In one, when an erotic scene was about to be displayed in one of two randomly selected

Courtesy of Claire Cole

screen placements, Cornell University participants guessed the right placement 53.1 percent of the time (beating 50 percent by a small but statistically significant margin).

Despite Bem's published research having survived critical reviews by a top-tier journal, other critics found the methods "badly flawed" (Alcock, 2011) or the statistical analyses "biased" (Wagenmakers et al., 2011). "A result—especially one of this importance—must recur several times in tests by independent and skeptical researchers to gain scientific credibility," observed astronomer David Helfand (2011). "I have little doubt that Professor Bem's experiments will fail this test."

Anticipating such skepticism, Bem has made his computer materials available to anyone who wishes to replicate his studies. Multiple attempts have since been made, with minimal success and continuing controversy (Bem et al., 2014; Galak et al., 2012; Ritchie et al., 2012; Wagenmakers, 2014).

"At the heart of science is an essential tension between two seemingly contradictory attitudes—an openness to new ideas, no matter how bizarre or counterintuitive they may be, and the most ruthless skeptical scrutiny of all ideas, old and new."
Carl Sagan (1987)

Testing psychic powers in the British population

Psychologists created a "mind machine" to see if people could influence or predict a coin toss (Wiseman & Greening, 2002). Using a touch-sensitive screen, visitors to British festivals were given four attempts to call heads or tails, playing against a computer that kept score. By the time the experiment ended, nearly 28,000 people had predicted 110,959 tosses—with 49.8 percent correct.

Regardless, science is doing its work. It has been open to a finding that challenges its own assumptions. And then, through follow-up research, it has assessed its validity. And that is how science sifts crazy-sounding ideas, leaving most on the historical waste heap while occasionally surprising us.

One skeptic, magician James Randi, has had a long-standing offer of $1 million to be given "to anyone who proves a genuine psychic power under proper observing conditions" (Randi, 1999; Thompson, 2010). French, Australian, and Indian groups have made similar offers of up to 200,000 euros (CFI, 2003). Large as these sums are, the scientific seal of approval would be worth far more. To refute those who say there is no ESP, one need only produce a single person who can demonstrate a single, reproducible ESP event. (To refute those who say pigs can't talk would take but one talking pig.) So far, no such person has emerged.

RETRIEVE IT [✖]

• If an ESP event occurred under controlled conditions, what would be the next best step to confirm that ESP really exists?

ANSWER: The ESP event would need to be reproduced in other scientific studies.

---

* * *

To feel awe, mystery, and a deep reverence for life, we need look no further than our own perceptual system and its capacity for organizing formless nerve impulses into colorful sights, vivid sounds, and evocative smells. As Shakespeare's Hamlet recognized, "There are more things in Heaven and Earth, Horatio, than are dreamt of in your philosophy." Within our ordinary sensory and perceptual experiences lies much that is truly extraordinary—surely much more than has so far been dreamt of in our psychology.

Learning Objectives

Test Yourself by taking a moment to answer each of these Learning Objective Questions (repeated here from within the module). Then turn to Appendix D, Complete Module Reviews, to check your answers. Research suggests that trying to answer these questions on your own will improve your long-term memory of the concepts (McDaniel et al., 2009).

18-1 What are the characteristics of air pressure waves that we hear as sound?

18-2 How does the ear transform sound energy into neural messages?

18-3 How do we detect loudness, discriminate pitch, and locate sounds?

18-4 How do we sense touch?

18-5 What biological, psychological, and social-cultural influences affect our experience of pain? How do placebos, distraction, and hypnosis help control pain?

18-6 In what ways are our senses of taste and smell similar, and how do they differ?

18-7 How do we sense our body's position and movement?

18-8 How does *sensory interaction* influence our perceptions, and what is *embodied cognition*?

18-9 What are the claims of ESP, and what have most research psychologists concluded after putting these claims to the test?

Terms and Concepts to Remember

Test yourself on these terms by trying to write down the definition in your own words before flipping back to the referenced page to check your answers.

audition, p. 226
frequency, p. 226
pitch, p. 226
middle ear, p. 227
cochlea [KOHK-lee-uh], p. 228

inner ear, p. 228
sensorineural hearing loss, p. 228
conduction hearing loss, p. 228
cochlear implant, p. 229
place theory, p. 229
frequency theory, p. 230
gate-control theory, p. 232
hypnosis, p. 235

dissociation, p. 235
posthypnotic suggestion, p. 235
kinesthesia, p. 238
vestibular sense, p. 238
sensory interaction, p. 239
embodied cognition, p. 240
extrasensory perception (ESP), p. 241
parapsychology, p. 241

Experience the Testing Effect

Test yourself repeatedly throughout your studies. This will not only help you figure out what you know and don't know; the testing itself will help you learn and remember the information more effectively thanks to the *testing effect*.

1. The snail-shaped tube in the inner ear, where sound waves are converted into neural activity, is called the _____.

2. What are the basic steps in transforming sound waves into perceived sound?

3. _____ theory explains how we hear high-pitched sounds, and _____ theory explains how we hear low-pitched sounds.

4. The gate-control theory of pain proposes that
   a. special pain receptors send signals directly to the brain.
   b. pain is a property of the senses, not of the brain.
   c. small spinal cord nerve fibers conduct most pain signals, but large-fiber activity can close access to those pain signals.
   d. pain can often be controlled and managed effectively through the use of relaxation techniques.

5. How does the biopsychosocial approach explain our experience of pain? Provide examples.

6. We have specialized nerve receptors for detecting which five tastes? How did this ability aid our ancestors?

7. _____ is your sense of body position and movement. Your _____ specifically monitors your head's movement, with sensors in the inner ear.

8. Why do you feel a little dizzy immediately after a roller-coaster ride?

9. A food's aroma can greatly enhance its taste. This is an example of
   a. sensory adaptation.   c. kinesthesia.
   b. chemical sensation.   d. sensory interaction.

10. Which of the following ESP phenomena is supported by solid, replicable scientific evidence?
   a. Telepathy   c. Precognition
   b. Clairvoyance   d. None of these answers

Find answers to these questions in Appendix E, in the back of the book.

Use ⓜ LearningCurve to create your personalized study plan, which will direct you to the resources that will help you most in ⓜ LaunchPad.

BASIC CONCEPTS

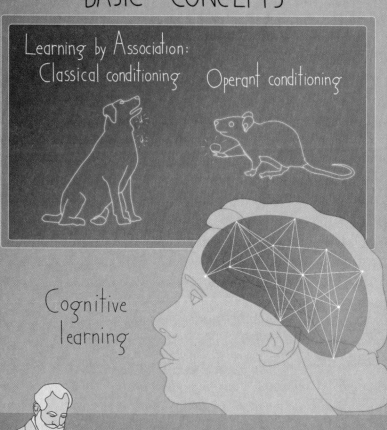

Learning by Association:
Classical conditioning   Operant conditioning

Cognitive learning

CLASSICAL CONDITIONING

Pavlov's dogs *associated* food + what happened just before it appeared; drooled in anticipation.

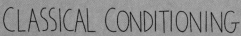

OUR behaviors may be classically conditioned.

Skinner's rats *associated* their action (bar pressing)

with consequences (rewards).

OUR behaviors may be operantly conditioned.

Achieving personal goals —

If I complete my study goals this week, I will go out with friends on Saturday night!

Sunday	Monday	Tuesday	Wednesday	Thursday	Friday	Saturday
PSYCH	English paper	English paper	read for ECON		PSYCH	★

BIOLOGY affects learning:
We drift to what's adaptive.

Eating chocolate
↓
tasty; happy
feeling

Ate whole
bar and felt sick
last week. Trying to
control weight.
Will eat only
small piece.

COGNITION affects learning:
Predictability of reward, *latent
learning*, and *intrinsic motivation*.

We learn by OBSERVING
prosocial and *antisocial*
models.

Learning

IN the early 1940s, University of Minnesota graduate students Marian Breland and Keller Breland witnessed the power of a new learning technology. Their mentor, B. F. Skinner, would become famous for *shaping* rat and pigeon behaviors by delivering well-timed rewards as the animals inched closer and closer to a desired behavior. Impressed by Skinner's results, the Brelands began shaping the behavior of cats, chickens, parakeets, turkeys, pigs, ducks, and hamsters (Bailey & Gillaspy, 2005). The rest is history. They eventually formed Animal Behavior Enterprises and spent the next half-century training more than 15,000 animals from 140 species for movies, traveling shows, amusement parks, corporations, and the government. The Brelands also trained trainers, including Sea World's first training director.

While writing about animal trainers, journalist Amy Sutherland wondered if shaping had uses closer to home (2006a,b). If baboons could be trained to skateboard and elephants to paint, might "the same techniques . . . work on that stubborn but lovable species, the American husband"? Step by step, she "began thanking Scott if he threw one dirty shirt into the hamper. If he threw in two, I'd kiss him [and] as he basked in my appreciation, the piles became smaller." After two years of "thinking of my husband as an exotic animal species," she reports, "my marriage is far smoother, my husband much easier to love."

Like husbands and other animals, much of what we do we learn from experience. Indeed, nature's most important gift may be our *adaptability*—our capacity to learn new behaviors that help us cope with our changing world. We can learn how to build grass huts or snow shelters, submarines or space stations, and thereby adapt to almost any environment.

Learning breeds hope. What is learnable we can potentially teach—a fact that encourages parents, educators, coaches, and animal trainers. What has been learned we can potentially change by new learning—an assumption that underlies counseling, psychotherapy, and rehabilitation programs. No matter how unhappy, unsuccessful, or unloving we are, that need not be the end of our story.

No topic is closer to the heart of psychology than *learning*. Psychologists study infants' learning, and the learning of visual perceptions, a drug's expected effect, and gender roles. They also consider how learning shapes our thoughts and language, our motivations and emotions, our personalities and attitudes. In other modules, we see how the brain stores and retrieves learning. Here, in Modules 19–21, we examine classical conditioning, operant conditioning, the effects of biology and cognition on learning, and learning by observation. ■

learning the process of acquiring through experience new and relatively enduring information or behaviors.

associative learning learning that certain events occur together. The events may be two stimuli (as in classical conditioning) or a response and its consequences (as in operant conditioning).

stimulus any event or situation that evokes a response.

respondent behavior behavior that occurs as an automatic response to some stimulus.

operant behavior behavior that operates on the environment, producing consequences.

cognitive learning the acquisition of mental information, whether by observing events, by watching others, or through language.

MODULE 19 Basic Learning Concepts and Classical Conditioning

How Do We Learn?

19-1 What is *learning*, and what are some basic forms of learning?

Psychologists define **learning** as the process of acquiring new and relatively enduring information or behaviors. By learning, we humans are able to adapt to our environments. We learn to expect and prepare for significant events such as food or pain *(classical conditioning)*. We typically learn to repeat acts that bring rewards and to avoid acts that bring unwanted results *(operant conditioning)*. We learn new behaviors by observing events and by watching others, and through language, we learn things we have neither experienced nor observed *(cognitive learning)*. But *how* do we learn?

One way we learn is by *association*. Our mind naturally connects events that occur in sequence. Suppose you see and smell freshly baked bread, eat some, and find it satisfying. The next time you see and smell fresh bread, you will expect that eating it will again be satisfying. So, too, with sounds. If you associate a sound with a frightening consequence, hearing the sound alone may trigger your fear. As one 4-year-old exclaimed after watching a TV character get mugged, "If I had heard that music, I wouldn't have gone around the corner!" (Wells, 1981).

Learned associations feed our habitual behaviors (Wood et al., 2014). As we repeat behaviors in a given context—sleeping in a certain posture in bed, walking certain routes on campus, eating popcorn in a movie theater—the behaviors become associated with the contexts. Our next experience of the context then evokes our habitual response. Especially in times when our willpower is depleted, such as when we're mentally fatigued, we tend to fall back on our habits (Neal et al., 2013). That's true of both good habits (eating fruit) and bad (overindulging in alcohol) (Graybiel & Smith, 2014).

How long does it take to form such habits? To find out, one British research team asked 96 university students to choose some healthy behavior (such as running before dinner or eating fruit with lunch), to do it daily for 84 days, and to record whether the behavior felt automatic (something they did without thinking and would find it hard not to do). On average, behaviors became habitual after about 66 days (Lally et al., 2010). (Is there something you'd like to make a routine part of your life? Just do it every day for two months, or a bit longer for exercise, and you likely will find yourself with a new habit.)

Other animals also learn by association. Disturbed by a squirt of water, the sea slug *Aplysia* protectively withdraws its gill. If the squirts continue, as happens naturally in choppy water, the withdrawal response diminishes. But if the sea slug repeatedly receives an electric shock just after being squirted, its response to the squirt instead grows stronger. The animal has associated the squirt with the impending shock.

Complex animals can learn to associate their own behavior with its outcomes. An aquarium seal will repeat behaviors, such as slapping and barking, that prompt people to toss it a herring.

By linking two events that occur close together, both animals are exhibiting **associative learning.** The sea slug associates the squirt with an impending shock; the seal associates slapping and barking with a herring treat. Each animal has learned something important to its survival: anticipating the immediate future.

Most of us would be unable to name the order of the songs on our favorite album or playlist. Yet, hearing the end of one piece cues (by association) an anticipation of the next. Likewise, when singing your national anthem, you associate the end of each line with the beginning of the next. (Pick a line out of the middle and notice how much harder it is to recall the *previous* line.)

Two related events:

Stimulus 1:
Lightning

+

Stimulus 2:
Thunder

BOOM!

Response:
Startled
reaction;
wincing

< FIGURE 19.1

Classical conditioning

Result after repetition:

Stimulus:
Lightning

Response:
Anticipation
of booming
thunder;
wincing

This process of learning associations is *conditioning*. It takes two main forms:

- In *classical conditioning,* we learn to associate two stimuli and thus to antici-pate events. (A **stimulus** is any event or situation that evokes a response.) We learn that a flash of lightning signals an impending crack of thunder; when lightning flashes nearby, we start to brace ourselves (**FIGURE 19.1**). We asso-ciate stimuli that we do not control, and we automatically respond (exhibiting **respondent behavior**).

- In *operant conditioning,* we learn to associate a response (our behavior) and its consequence. Thus we (and other animals) learn to repeat acts followed by good results (**FIGURE 19.2**) and avoid acts followed by bad results. These associations produce **operant behaviors.**

To simplify, we will explore these two types of asso-ciative learning separately. Often, though, they occur together, as on one Japanese cattle ranch, where the clever rancher outfits his herd with electronic pagers, which he calls from his cell phone. After a week of training, the animals learn to associate two stimuli— the beep on their pager and the arrival of food (clas-sical conditioning). But they also learn to associate their hustling to the food trough with the pleasure of eating (operant conditioning), which simplifies the rancher's work.

(a) Response: Being polite   (b) Consequence: Getting a treat   (c) Behavior strengthened

∧ FIGURE 19.2

Operant conditioning

Conditioning is not the only form of learning. Through **cognitive learning** we acquire mental information that guides our behavior. *Observational learn-ing,* one form of cognitive learning, lets us learn from others' experiences. Chimpanzees, for example, sometimes learn behaviors merely by watching others perform them. If one animal sees another solve a puzzle and gain a food reward, the observer may perform the trick more quickly. So, too, in humans: We look and we learn.

RETRIEVE IT   [✗]

- Why are habits, such as having something sweet with that cup of coffee, so hard to break?

ANSWER: Habits form when we repeat behaviors in a given context and, as a result, learn associations—often without our awareness. For example, we may have eaten a sweet pastry with a cup of coffee often enough to associate the flavor of the coffee with the treat, so that the cup of coffee alone just doesn't seem right anymore!

classical conditioning a type of learning in which one learns to link two or more stimuli and anticipate events.

behaviorism the view that psychology (1) should be an objective science that (2) studies behavior without reference to mental processes. Most research psychologists today agree with (1) but not with (2).

neutral stimulus (NS) in classical conditioning, a stimulus that elicits no response before conditioning.

Ivan Pavlov "Experimental investigation... should lay a solid foundation for a future true science of psychology" (1927).

▼ FIGURE 19.3

Pavlov's device for recording salivation A tube in the dog's cheek collects saliva, which is measured in a cylinder outside the chamber.

Classical Conditioning

19-2 What was behaviorism's view of learning?

For many people, the name Ivan Pavlov (1849–1936) rings a bell. His early twentieth-century experiments—now psychology's most famous research—are classics, and the phenomenon he explored we justly call **classical conditioning.**

Pavlov's work laid the foundation for many of psychologist John B. Watson's ideas. In searching for laws underlying learning, Watson (1913) urged his colleagues to discard reference to inner thoughts, feelings, and motives. The science of psychology should instead study how organisms respond to stimuli in their environments, said Watson: "Its theoretical goal is the prediction and control of behavior. Introspection forms no essential part of its methods." Simply said, psychology should be an objective science based on observable behavior.

This view, which Watson called **behaviorism,** influenced North American psychology during the first half of the twentieth century. Pavlov and Watson shared both a disdain for "mentalistic" concepts (such as consciousness) and a belief that the basic laws of learning were the same for all animals—whether dogs or humans. Few researchers today propose that psychology should ignore mental processes, but most now agree that classical conditioning is a basic form of learning by which all organisms adapt to their environment.

Pavlov's Experiments

19-3 Who was Pavlov, and what are the basic components of classical conditioning?

Pavlov was driven by a lifelong passion for research. After setting aside his initial plan to follow his father into the Russian Orthodox priesthood, Pavlov received a medical degree at age 33 and spent the next two decades studying the digestive system. This work earned him, in 1904, Russia's first Nobel Prize. But his novel experiments on learning, which consumed the last three decades of his life, earned this feisty scientist his place in history.

Pavlov's new direction came when his creative mind seized on an incidental observation: Without fail, putting food in a dog's mouth caused the animal to salivate. Moreover, the dog began salivating not only at the taste of the food, but also at the mere sight of the food, or the food dish, or the person delivering the food, or even at the sound of that person's approaching footsteps. At first, Pavlov considered these "psychic secretions" an annoyance—until he realized they pointed to a simple but fundamental form of learning.

Pavlov and his assistants tried to imagine what the dog was thinking and feeling as it drooled in anticipation of the food. This only led them into fruitless debates. So, to explore the phenomenon more objectively, they experimented.

To eliminate other possible influences, they isolated the dog in a small room, secured it in a harness, and attached a device to divert its saliva to a measuring instrument (**FIGURE 19.3**). From the next room, they presented food—first by sliding in a food bowl, later by blowing meat powder into the dog's mouth at a precise moment. They then paired various **neutral stimuli (NS)**—events the dog could see or hear but didn't associate with food—with food in the dog's mouth. If a sight or sound regularly signaled the arrival of food, would the dog learn the link? If so, would it begin salivating in anticipation of the food?

The answers proved to be *Yes* and *Yes*. Just before placing food in the dog's mouth to produce salivation, Pavlov sounded a tone. After several pairings of tone and food, the dog, now anticipating the meat powder, began salivating to the tone alone. In later experiments, a buzzer,[1] a light, a touch on the leg, even the sight of a circle set off the drooling. (This procedure works with people, too. When hungry young Londoners viewed abstract figures before smelling peanut butter or vanilla, their brain soon responded in anticipation to the abstract images alone [Gottfried et al., 2003].)

A dog does not learn to salivate in response to food in its mouth. Rather, food in the mouth automatically, *unconditionally*, triggers a dog's salivary reflex (**FIGURE 19.4**). Thus, Pavlov called the drooling an **unconditioned response (UR).** And he called the food an **unconditioned stimulus (US).**

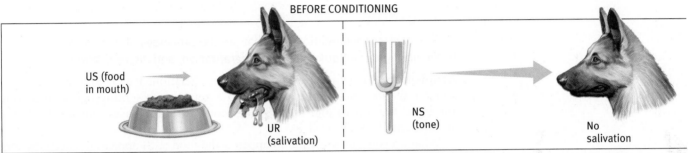

BEFORE CONDITIONING

US (food in mouth) → UR (salivation)

An unconditioned stimulus (US) produces an unconditioned response (UR).

NS (tone) → No salivation

A neutral stimulus (NS) produces no salivation response.

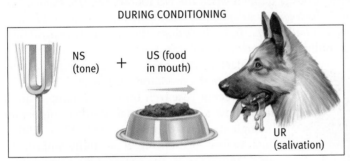

DURING CONDITIONING

NS (tone) + US (food in mouth) → UR (salivation)

The US is repeatedly presented just after the NS.
The US continues to produce a UR.

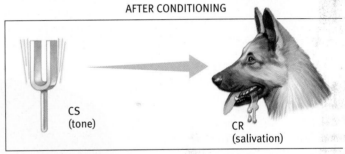

AFTER CONDITIONING

CS (tone) → CR (salivation)

The previously neutral stimulus alone now produces a conditioned response (CR), thereby becoming a conditioned stimulus (CS).

▼ FIGURE 19.4

Pavlov's classic experiment Pavlov presented a neutral stimulus (a tone) just before an unconditioned stimulus (food in mouth). The neutral stimulus then became a conditioned stimulus, producing a conditioned response.

Salivation in response to the tone, however, is learned. It is *conditional* upon the dog's associating the tone with the food. Thus, we call this response the **conditioned response (CR).** The stimulus that used to be neutral (in this case, a previously meaningless tone that now triggers salivation) is the **conditioned stimulus (CS).** Distinguishing these two kinds of stimuli and responses is easy: Conditioned = learned; *un*conditioned = *un*learned.

1. The "buzzer" (English translation) was perhaps Pavlov's supposed bell—a small electric bell (Tully, 2003).

unconditioned response (UR) in classical conditioning, an unlearned, naturally occurring response (such as salivation) to an unconditioned stimulus (US) (such as food in the mouth).

unconditioned stimulus (US) in classical conditioning, a stimulus that unconditionally—naturally and automatically—triggers an unconditioned response (UR).

conditioned response (CR) in classical conditioning, a learned response to a previously neutral (but now conditioned) stimulus (CS).

conditioned stimulus (CS) in classical conditioning, an originally irrelevant stimulus that, after association with an unconditioned stimulus (US), comes to trigger a conditioned response (CR).

PEANUTS

THE EARS HEAR THE CAN OPENER..

RIGHT AWAY THE STOMACH KNOWS THAT SUPPER IS COMING..

HOW DO THE EARS TELL THE STOMACH?

I'VE NEVER BEEN ABLE TO FIGURE THAT OUT..

If Pavlov's demonstration of associative learning was so simple, what did he do for the next three decades? What discoveries did his research factory publish in his 532 papers on salivary conditioning (Windholz, 1997)? He and his associates explored five major conditioning processes: *acquisition, extinction, spontaneous recovery, generalization,* and *discrimination.*

ACQUISITION

 19-4 In classical conditioning, what are the processes of *acquisition, extinction, spontaneous recovery, generalization,* and *discrimination?*

Acquisition is the initial learning of an association. Pavlov and his associates wondered: How much time should elapse between presenting the NS (the tone, the light, the touch) and the US (the food)? In most cases, not much—half a second usually works well.

What do you suppose would happen if the food (US) appeared before the tone (NS) rather than after? Would conditioning occur? Not likely. With but a few exceptions, conditioning doesn't happen when the NS follows the US. *Remember, classical conditioning is biologically adaptive because it helps humans and other animals prepare for good or bad events.* To Pavlov's dogs, the originally neutral tone became a CS after signaling an important biological event—the arrival of food (US). To deer in the forest, the snapping of a twig (CS) may signal a predator's approach (US).

More recent research on male Japanese quail shows how a CS can signal another important biological event (Domjan, 1992, 1994, 2005). Just before presenting a sexually approachable female quail, the researchers turned on a red light. Over time, as the red light continued to herald the female's arrival, the light caused the male quail to become excited. They developed a preference for their cage's red light district, and when a female appeared, they mated with her more quickly and released more semen and sperm (Matthews et al., 2007). This capacity for classical conditioning gives the quail a reproductive edge.

In humans, too, objects, smells, and sights associated with sexual pleasure—even a geometric figure in one experiment—can become conditioned stimuli for sexual arousal (Byrne, 1982; Hoffman, 2012). Onion breath does not usually produce sexual arousal. But when repeatedly paired with a passionate kiss, it can become a CS and do just that (**FIGURE 19.5**). The larger lesson: *Conditioning helps an animal survive and reproduce—by responding to cues that help it gain food, avoid dangers, locate mates, and produce offspring* (Hollis, 1997). Learning makes for yearning.

Eric Isselée/Shutterstock

❯ FIGURE 19.5

An unexpected CS Psychologist Michael Tirrell (1990) recalled: "My first girlfriend loved onions, so I came to associate onion breath with kissing. Before long, onion breath sent tingles up and down my spine. Oh what a feeling!"

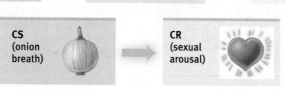

RETRIEVE IT [✖]

• If the aroma of a baking cake sets your mouth to watering, what is the US? The CS? The CR?

ANSWERS: The cake (and its taste) are the US. The associated aroma is the CS. Salivation to the aroma is the CR.

EXTINCTION AND SPONTANEOUS RECOVERY What would happen, Pavlov wondered, if after conditioning, the CS occurred repeatedly without the US? If the tone sounded again and again, but no food appeared, would the tone still trigger salivation? The answer was mixed. The dogs salivated less and less, a reaction known as **extinction,** which is the diminished responding that occurs when the CS (tone) no longer signals an impending US (food). But a different picture emerged when Pavlov allowed several hours to elapse before sounding the tone again. After the delay, the dogs would again begin salivating to the tone (**FIGURE 19.6**). This **spontaneous recovery**—the reappearance of a (weakened) CR after a pause—suggested to Pavlov that extinction was suppressing the CR rather than eliminating it.

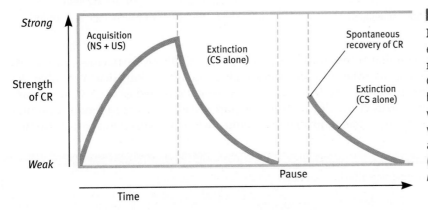

< FIGURE 19.6

Idealized curve of acquisition, extinction, and spontaneous recovery The rising curve shows the CR rapidly growing stronger as the NS becomes a CS due to repeated pairing with the US *(acquisition)*. The CR then weakens rapidly as the CS is presented alone *(extinction)*. After a pause, the (weakened) CR reappears *(spontaneous recovery)*.

RETRIEVE IT [✖]

• The first step of classical conditioning, when an NS becomes a CS, is called _____. When a US no longer follows the CS, and the CR becomes weakened, this is called _____.

ANSWERS: acquisition; extinction

GENERALIZATION Pavlov and his students noticed that a dog conditioned to the sound of one tone also responded somewhat to the sound of a new and different tone. Likewise, a dog conditioned to salivate when rubbed would also drool a bit when scratched (Windholz, 1989) or when touched on a different body part (**FIGURE 19.7** on the next page). This tendency to respond to stimuli similar to the CS is called **generalization.**

Generalization can be adaptive, as when toddlers taught to fear moving cars also become afraid of moving trucks and motorcycles. And generalized fears can linger. One Argentine writer who underwent torture recounted recoiling with fear years later at the sight of black shoes—his first glimpse of his torturers as they approached his cell. Generalized anxiety reactions have been demonstrated in laboratory studies comparing abused with nonabused children (**FIGURE 19.8** on the next page). When an angry face appeared on a computer screen, abused children's brain-wave responses were dramatically stronger and longer lasting (Pollak et al., 1998). And when a face that we've been conditioned to like (or dislike) is morphed into another face, we also have some tendency to like (or dislike) the vaguely similar morphed face (Gawronski & Quinn, 2013).

acquisition in classical conditioning, the initial stage, when one links a neutral stimulus and an unconditioned stimulus so that the neutral stimulus begins triggering the conditioned response. In operant conditioning, the strengthening of a reinforced response.

extinction the diminishing of a conditioned response; occurs in classical conditioning when an unconditioned stimulus (US) does not follow a conditioned stimulus (CS); occurs in operant conditioning when a response is no longer reinforced.

spontaneous recovery the reappearance, after a pause, of an extinguished conditioned response.

generalization the tendency, once a response has been conditioned, for stimuli similar to the conditioned stimulus to elicit similar responses.

> **FIGURE 19.7**

Generalization Pavlov demonstrated generalization by attaching miniature vibrators to various parts of a dog's body. After conditioning salivation to stimulation of the thigh, he stimulated other areas. The closer a stimulated spot was to the dog's thigh, the stronger the conditioned response. (Data from Pavlov, 1927.)

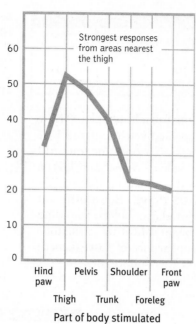

Drops of saliva

Strongest responses from areas nearest the thigh

Part of body stimulated

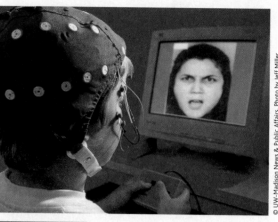

^ **FIGURE 19.8**

Child abuse leaves tracks in the brain Abused children's sensitized brains react more strongly to angry faces (Pollak et al., 1998). This generalized anxiety response may help explain their greater risk of psychological disorder.

Stimuli similar to naturally disgusting objects will, by association, also evoke some disgust, as otherwise desirable fudge did when shaped to resemble dog feces (Rozin et al., 1986). Ditto when sewage gets recycled as utterly pure drinking water (Rozin et al., 2015). Toilet → tap = yuck. In these human examples, people's emotional reactions to one stimulus have generalized to similar stimuli.

RETRIEVE IT [✖]

• What conditioning principle is influencing the snail's affections?

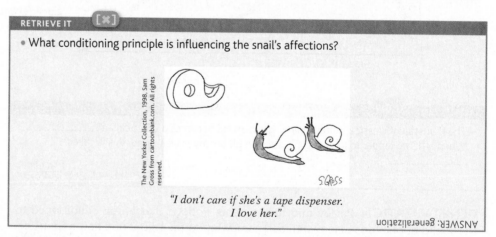

"I don't care if she's a tape dispenser. I love her."

ANSWER: generalization

DISCRIMINATION Pavlov's dogs also learned to respond to the sound of a particular tone and *not* to other tones. This learned ability to *distinguish* between a conditioned stimulus (which predicts the US) and other irrelevant stimuli is called **discrimination**. Being able to recognize differences is adaptive. Slightly different stimuli can be followed by vastly different consequences. Facing a guard dog, your heart may race; facing a guide dog, it probably will not.

Pavlov's Legacy

◁◊▷ **19-5** Why does Pavlov's work remain so important?

What remains today of Pavlov's ideas? A great deal. Most psychologists now agree that classical conditioning is a basic form of learning. Judged with today's knowledge of the interplay of our biology, psychology, and social-cultural environment, Pavlov's ideas were incomplete. But if we see further than Pavlov did, it is because we stand on his shoulders.

discrimination in classical conditioning, the learned ability to distinguish between a conditioned stimulus and stimuli that do not signal an unconditioned stimulus.

Why does Pavlov's work remain so important? If he had merely taught us that old dogs can learn new tricks, his experiments would long ago have been forgotten. Why should we care that dogs can be conditioned to salivate at the sound of a tone? The importance lies first in this finding: *Many other responses to many other stimuli can be classically conditioned in many other organisms—* in fact, in every species tested, from earthworms to fish to dogs to monkeys to people (Schwartz, 1984). Thus, classical conditioning is one way that virtually all organisms learn to adapt to their environment.

Second, *Pavlov showed us how a process such as learning can be studied objectively.* He was proud that his methods involved virtually no subjective judgments or guesses about what went on in a dog's mind. The salivary response is a behavior measurable in cubic centimeters of saliva. Pavlov's success therefore suggested a scientific model for how the young discipline of psychology might proceed—by isolating the basic building blocks of complex behaviors and studying them with objective laboratory procedures.

Video material is provided by BBC Worldwide Learning and CBS New Archives, and produced by Princeton Academic Resources.

LaunchPad To review Pavlov's classic work and to play the role of experimenter in classical conditioning research, visit LaunchPad's *PsychSim 6: Classical Conditioning*. See also a 3-minute re-creation of Pavlov's lab in the *Video: Pavlov's Discovery of Classical Conditioning.*

RETRIEVE IT [✖]

- In slasher movies, sexually arousing images of women are sometimes paired with violence against women. Based on classical conditioning principles, what might be an effect of this pairing?

ANSWER: If viewing an attractive nude or seminude woman (a US) elicits sexual arousal (a UR) in some viewers, then pairing the US with a new stimulus (violence) could turn the violence into a conditioned stimulus (CS) that also becomes sexually arousing, a conditioned response (CR).

APPLICATIONS OF CLASSICAL CONDITIONING

19-6 What have been some applications of Pavlov's work to human health and well-being? How did Watson apply Pavlov's principles to learned fears?

In many areas of psychology, including consciousness, motivation, emotion, health, psychological disorders, and therapy, Pavlov's principles are used to influence human health and well-being. Two examples:

- Former drug users often feel a craving when they are again in the drug-using context—with people or in places they associate with previous highs. Thus, drug counselors advise their clients to steer clear of people and settings that may trigger these cravings (Siegel, 2005).

- Classical conditioning even works on the body's disease-fighting immune system. When a particular taste accompanies a drug that influences immune responses, the taste by itself may come to produce an immune response (Ader & Cohen, 1985).

Pavlov's work also provided a basis for Watson's (1913) idea that human emotions and behaviors, though biologically influenced, are mainly a bundle of conditioned responses. Working with an 11-month-old, Watson and his graduate student Rosalie Rayner (1920; Harris, 1979) showed how specific fears might be conditioned. Like most infants, "Little Albert" feared loud noises but not white rats. Watson and Rayner presented a white rat and, as Little Albert reached to touch it, struck a hammer against a steel bar just behind his head. After seven repeats of seeing the rat and hearing the frightening noise, Albert burst into tears at the mere sight of the rat. Five days later, he had generalized this startled fear reaction to the sight of a rabbit, a dog, and a sealskin coat, but not to dissimilar objects.

For years, people wondered what became of Little Albert. Sleuthing by Russell Powell and his colleagues (2014) found a well-matched child of one of the hospital's wet nurses. The child, William Albert Barger, went by Albert B.—precisely the name used by Watson and Rayner. This Albert lived to 2007. He was an easy-going person, though, perhaps coincidentally, he had an aversion to dogs. Albert died without ever knowing of his early life in a hospital residence or his role in psychology's history.

John B. Watson Watson (1924) admitted to "going beyond my facts" when offering his famous boast: "Give me a dozen healthy infants, well-formed, and my own specified world to bring them up in and I'll guarantee to take any one at random and train him to become any type of specialist I might select—doctor, lawyer, artist, merchant-chief, and, yes, even beggar-man and thief, regardless of his talents, penchants, tendencies, abilities, vocations, and race of his ancestors."

LaunchPad See LaunchPad's *Video: Research Ethics* for a helpful tutorial animation.

People also wondered what became of Watson. After losing his Johns Hopkins professorship over an affair with Rayner (whom he later married), he joined an advertising agency as the company's resident psychologist. There, he used his knowledge of associative learning to conceive many successful advertising campaigns, including one for Maxwell House that helped make the "coffee break" an American custom (Hunt, 1993).

The treatment of Little Albert would be unacceptable by today's ethical standards. Also, some psychologists had difficulty repeating Watson and Rayner's findings with other children. Nevertheless, Little Albert's learned fears led many psychologists to wonder whether each of us might be a walking warehouse of conditioned emotions. If so, might extinction procedures or even new conditioning help us change our unwanted responses to emotion-arousing stimuli?

One patient, who for 30 years had feared entering an elevator alone, did just that. Following his therapist's advice, he forced himself to enter 20 elevators a day. Within 10 days, his fear had nearly vanished (Ellis & Becker, 1982). Other modules offer more examples of how psychologists use behavioral techniques to treat emotional disorders and promote personal growth.

RETRIEVE IT [✖]

- In Watson and Rayner's experiments, "Little Albert" learned to fear a white rat after repeatedly experiencing a loud noise as the rat was presented. In these experiments, what was the US? The UR? The NS? The CS? The CR?

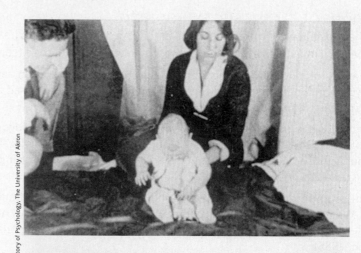

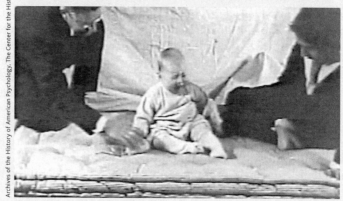

Archives of the History of American Psychology, The Center for the History of Psychology, The University of Akron

ANSWERS: The US was the loud noise; the UR was the fear response to the noise; the NS was the rat before it was paired with the noise; the CS was the rat after pairing; the CR was fear of the rat.

MODULE
19 REVIEW Basic Learning Concepts and Classical Conditioning

◐ Learning Objectives

Test Yourself by taking a moment to answer each of these Learning Objective Questions (repeated here from within the module). Then turn to Appendix D, Complete Module Reviews, to check your answers. Research suggests that trying to answer these questions on your own will improve your long-term memory of the concepts (McDaniel et al., 2009).

19-1 What is *learning*, and what are some basic forms of learning?

19-2 What was behaviorism's view of learning?

19-3 Who was Pavlov, and what are the basic components of classical conditioning?

19-4 In classical conditioning, what are the processes of acquisition, extinction, spontaneous recovery, generalization, and discrimination?

19-5 Why does Pavlov's work remain so important?

19-6 What have been some applications of Pavlov's work to human health and well-being? How did Watson apply Pavlov's principles to learned fears?

▣ Terms and Concepts to Remember

Test yourself on these terms by trying to write down the definition in your own words before flipping back to the referenced page to check your answers.

learning, p. 246
associative learning, p. 246
stimulus, p. 247
respondent behavior, p. 247

operant behavior, p. 247
cognitive learning, p. 247
classical conditioning, p. 248
behaviorism, p. 248
neutral stimulus (NS), p. 248
unconditioned response (UR), p. 249
unconditioned stimulus (US), p. 249

conditioned response (CR), p. 249
conditioned stimulus (CS), p. 249
acquisition, p. 250
extinction, p. 251
spontaneous recovery, p. 251
generalization, p. 251
discrimination, p. 252

▣ Experience the Testing Effect

Test yourself repeatedly throughout your studies. This will not only help you figure out what you know and don't know; the testing itself will help you learn and remember the information more effectively thanks to the *testing effect*.

1. Learning is defined as "the process of acquiring through experience new and relatively enduring _____ or _____."

2. Two forms of associative learning are classical conditioning, in which the organism associates _____, and operant conditioning, in which the organism associates _____.

   a. two or more responses; a response and consequence
   b. two or more stimuli; two or more responses
   c. two or more stimuli; a response and consequence
   d. two or more responses; two or more stimuli

3. In Pavlov's experiments, the tone started as a neutral stimulus, and then became a(n) _____ stimulus.

4. Dogs have been taught to salivate to a circle but not to a square. This process is an example of _____.

5. After Watson and Rayner classically conditioned Little Albert to fear a white rat, the child later showed fear in response to a rabbit, a dog, and a sealskin coat. This illustrates

   a. extinction.
   b. generalization.
   c. spontaneous recovery.
   d. discrimination between two stimuli.

6. "Sex sells!" is a common saying in advertising. Using classical conditioning terms, explain how sexual images in advertisements can condition your response to a product.

Find answers to these questions in Appendix E, in the back of the book.

Use ✿ LearningCurve to create your personalized study plan, which will direct you to the resources that will help you most in ✿ LaunchPad .

learning the process of acquiring through experience new information or behaviors.

associative learning learning that certain events occur together. The events may be two stimuli (as in classical conditioning) or a response and its consequence (as in operant conditioning).

stimulus any event or situation that evokes a response.

respondent behavior behavior that occurs as an automatic response to some stimulus.

operant conditioning a type of learning in which behavior is strengthened if followed by a reinforcer or diminished if followed by a punisher.

operant behavior behavior that operates on the environment, producing consequences.

law of effect Thorndike's principle that behaviors followed by favorable consequences become more likely, and that behaviors followed by unfavorable consequences become less likely.

operant chamber in operant conditioning research, a chamber (also known as a *Skinner box*) containing a bar or key that an animal can manipulate to obtain a food or water reinforcer; attached devices record the animal's rate of bar pressing or key pecking.

MODULE 20 Operant Conditioning

20-1 What is operant conditioning?

It's one thing to classically condition a dog to salivate at the sound of a tone, or a child to fear moving cars. To teach an elephant to **learn** to walk on its hind legs or a child to say *please*, we turn to operant conditioning.

Classical conditioning and operant conditioning are both forms of **associative learning**, yet their differences are straightforward:

- *Classical conditioning* forms associations between **stimuli** (a *conditioned stimulus*, or CS and the *unconditioned stimulus*, or US it signals). It also involves **respondent behavior**—automatic responses to a stimulus (such as salivating in response to meat powder, and later in response to a tone).

- In **operant conditioning**, organisms associate their own actions with consequences. Actions followed by reinforcers increase; those followed by punishers often decrease. Behavior that *operates* on the environment to *produce* rewarding or punishing stimuli is called **operant behavior**.

RETRIEVE IT [✖]

- With classical conditioning, we learn associations between events we _____ (do/do not) control. With operant conditioning, we learn associations between our behavior and _____ (resulting/random) events.

ANSWERS: do not; resulting

Skinner's Experiments

20-2 Who was Skinner, and how is operant behavior reinforced and shaped?

B. F. Skinner (1904–1990) was a college English major and aspiring writer who, seeking a new direction, studied psychology in graduate school. He went on to become modern behaviorism's most influential and controversial figure. Skinner's work elaborated on what psychologist Edward L. Thorndike (1874–1949) called the **law of effect:** Rewarded behavior tends to recur (**FIGURE 20.1**). Using Thorndike's law of effect as a starting point, Skinner developed a behavioral technology that revealed principles of *behavior control*. By shaping pigeons' natural walking and pecking behaviors, for example, Skinner was able to teach pigeons such unpigeon-like behaviors as walking in a figure 8, playing Ping-Pong, and keeping a missile on course by pecking at a screen target.

❤ FIGURE 20.1

Cat in a puzzle box Thorndike used a fish reward to entice cats to find their way out of a puzzle box (left) through a series of maneuvers. The cats' performance tended to improve with successive trials (right), illustrating Thorndike's *law of effect*. (Data from Thorndike, 1898.)

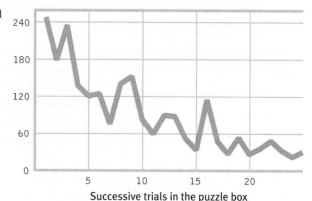

Time required to escape (seconds)

Successive trials in the puzzle box

For his pioneering studies, Skinner designed an **operant chamber,** popularly known as a *Skinner box* (**FIGURE 20.2**). The box has a bar (a lever) that an animal presses (or a key [a disc] the animal pecks) to release a reward of food or water. It also has a device that records these responses. This design creates a stage on which rats and other animals act out Skinner's concept of **reinforcement:** any event that strengthens (increases the frequency of) a preceding response. What is reinforcing depends on the animal and the conditions. For people, it may be praise, attention, or a paycheck. For hungry and thirsty rats, food and water work well. Skinner's experiments have done far more than teach us how to pull habits out of a rat. They have explored the precise conditions that foster efficient and enduring learning.

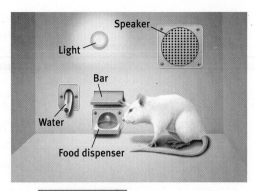

▲ **FIGURE 20.2**

A Skinner box Inside the box, the rat presses a bar for a food reward. Outside, measuring devices (not shown here) record the animal's accumulated responses.

Shaping Behavior

Imagine that you wanted to condition a hungry rat to press a bar. Like Skinner, you could tease out this action with **shaping,** gradually guiding the rat's actions toward the desired behavior. First, you would watch how the animal naturally behaves, so that you could build on its existing behaviors. You might give the rat a bit of food each time it approaches the bar. Once the rat is approaching regularly, you would give the food only when it moves close to the bar, then closer still. Finally, you would require it to touch the bar to get food. With this method of *successive approximations,* you reward responses that are ever-closer to the final desired behavior, and you ignore all other responses. By making rewards contingent on desired behaviors, researchers and animal trainers gradually shape complex behaviors.

Shaping can also help us understand what nonverbal organisms perceive. Can a dog distinguish red and green? Can a baby hear the difference between lower- and higher-pitched tones? If we can shape them to respond to one stimulus and not to another, then we know they can perceive the difference. Such experiments have even shown that some animals can form concepts. When experimenters reinforced pigeons for pecking after seeing a human face, but not after seeing other images, the pigeons' behavior showed that they could recognize human faces (Herrnstein & Loveland, 1964). In this experiment, the human face was a *discriminative stimulus.* Like a green traffic light, discriminative stimuli signal that a response will be reinforced. After being trained to discriminate among classes of events or objects—flowers, people, cars, chairs—pigeons were usually able to identify the category in which a new pictured object belonged (Bhatt et al., 1988; Wasserman, 1993). They have even been trained to discriminate between the music of Bach and Stravinsky (Porter & Neuringer, 1984).

Skinner noted that we continually reinforce and shape others' everyday behaviors, though we may not mean to do so. Isaac's whining annoys his father, for example, but look how he typically responds:

Isaac: *Could you take me to the mall?*

Father: *(Continues reading paper.)*

Isaac: *Dad, I need to go to the mall.*

Father: *Uh, yeah, just a minute.*

Isaac: *DAAAAD! The mall!*

Father: *Show me some manners! Okay, where are my keys . . .*

Isaac's whining is reinforced, because he gets something desirable—his dad's attention. Dad's response is reinforced because it gets rid of something aversive—Isaac's whining.

Or consider a teacher who sticks gold stars on a wall chart beside the names of children scoring 100 percent on spelling tests. As everyone can then see, some children consistently do perfect work. The others, who may have worked harder

Reinforcers vary with circumstances What is reinforcing (a heat lamp) to one animal (a cold meerkat) may not be to another (an overheated child). What is reinforcing in one situation (a cold snap at the Taronga Zoo in Sydney) may not be in another (a sweltering summer day).

reinforcement in operant conditioning, any event that *strengthens* the behavior it follows.

shaping an operant conditioning procedure in which reinforcers guide behavior toward closer and closer approximations of the desired behavior.

than the academic all-stars, get no rewards. The teacher would be better advised to apply the principles of operant conditioning—to reinforce all spellers for gradual improvements (successive approximations toward perfect spelling of words they find challenging).

Types of Reinforcers

20-3 How do positive and negative reinforcement differ, and what are the basic types of reinforcers?

Up to now, we've mainly been discussing **positive reinforcement,** which strengthens a response by *presenting* a typically pleasurable stimulus after a response. But, as we saw in the whining Isaac story, there are *two* basic kinds of reinforcement (**TABLE 20.1**). **Negative reinforcement** strengthens a response by *reducing or removing* something negative. Isaac's whining was *positively* reinforced, because Isaac got something desirable—his father's attention. His dad's response to the whining (doing what Isaac wanted) was *negatively* reinforced, because it ended an aversive event—Isaac's whining. Similarly, taking aspirin may relieve your headache, and hitting *snooze* will silence your annoying alarm. These welcome results provide negative reinforcement and increase the odds that you will repeat these behaviors. For those with drug addiction, the negative reinforcement of ending withdrawal pangs can be a compelling reason to resume using (Baker et al., 2004). Note that *negative reinforcement is not punishment.* (Some friendly advice: Repeat the italicized words in your mind.) Rather, negative reinforcement—psychology's most misunderstood concept—*removes* a punishing (aversive) event. Think of negative reinforcement as something that provides relief—from that whining teen, bad headache, or annoying alarm.

Sometimes negative and positive reinforcement coincide. Imagine a worried student who, after goofing off and getting a bad exam grade, studies harder for the next exam. This increased effort may be *negatively* reinforced by reduced anxiety, and *positively* reinforced by a better grade. We reap the rewards of escaping the aversive stimulus, which increases the chances that we will repeat our behavior. *The point to remember:* Whether it works by reducing something aversive, or by providing something desirable, *reinforcement is any consequence that strengthens behavior.*

▼ TABLE 20.1

Ways to Increase Behavior

Operant Conditioning Term	Description	Examples
Positive reinforcement	Add a desirable stimulus	Pet a dog that comes when you call it; pay the person who paints your house.
Negative reinforcement	Remove an aversive stimulus	Take painkillers to end pain; fasten seat belt to end loud beeping.

positive reinforcement increasing behaviors by presenting positive reinforcers. A positive reinforcer is any stimulus that, when *presented* after a response, strengthens the response.

negative reinforcement increasing behaviors by stopping or reducing negative stimuli. A negative reinforcer is any stimulus that, when *removed* after a response, strengthens the response. (*Note:* Negative reinforcement is not punishment.)

RETRIEVE IT [✖]

• How is operant conditioning at work in this cartoon?

HI & LOIS

ANSWER: The baby negatively reinforces her parents' behavior when she stops crying once they grant her wish. Her parents positively reinforce her cries by letting her sleep with them.

PRIMARY AND CONDITIONED REINFORCERS Getting food when hungry or having a painful headache go away is innately satisfying. These **primary reinforcers** are unlearned. **Conditioned reinforcers,** also called *secondary reinforcers,* get their power through learned association with primary reinforcers. If a rat in a Skinner box learns that a light reliably signals a food delivery, the rat will work to turn on the light. The light has become a conditioned reinforcer. Our lives are filled with conditioned reinforcers—money, good grades, a pleasant tone of voice—each of which has been linked with more basic rewards.

IMMEDIATE AND DELAYED REINFORCERS Let's return to the imaginary shaping experiment in which you were conditioning a rat to press a bar. Before performing this "wanted" behavior, the hungry rat will engage in a sequence of "unwanted" behaviors—scratching, sniffing, and moving around. If you present food immediately after any one of these behaviors, the rat will likely repeat that rewarded behavior. But what if the rat presses the bar while you are distracted, and you delay giving the reinforcer? If the delay lasts longer than about 30 seconds, the rat will not learn to press the bar. It will have moved on to other incidental behaviors, such as scratching, sniffing, and moving, and one of these behaviors will instead get reinforced.

Unlike rats, humans *do* respond to delayed reinforcers: the paycheck at the end of the week, the good grade at the end of the semester, the trophy at the end of the season. Indeed, to function effectively we must learn to delay gratification. In one of psychology's most famous studies, some 4-year-olds showed this ability. In choosing a candy or marshmallow, they preferred having a big one tomorrow to munching on a small one right away. Learning to control our impulses in order to achieve more valued rewards is a big step toward maturity (Logue, 1998a,b). No wonder children who delay gratification have tended to become socially competent and high-achieving adults (Mischel, 2014).

To our detriment, small but immediate pleasures (the enjoyment of watching late-night TV, for example) are sometimes more alluring than big but delayed rewards (resting, then feeling alert tomorrow). For many teens, the immediate gratification of risky, unprotected sex in passionate moments prevails over the delayed gratifications of safe sex or saved sex. And for many people, the immediate rewards of today's gas-guzzling vehicles, air travel, and air conditioning prevail over the bigger future consequences of global climate change, rising seas, and extreme weather.

Reinforcement Schedules

20-4 How do different reinforcement schedules affect behavior?

In most of our examples, the desired response has been reinforced every time it occurs. But **reinforcement schedules** vary. With **continuous reinforcement,** learning occurs rapidly, which makes it the best choice for mastering a behavior. But extinction also occurs rapidly. When reinforcement stops—when we stop delivering food after the rat presses the bar—the behavior soon stops. It extinguishes. If a normally dependable candy machine fails to deliver a chocolate bar twice in a row, we stop putting money into it (although a week later we may exhibit spontaneous recovery by trying again).

Real life rarely provides continuous reinforcement. Salespeople do not make a sale with every pitch. But they persist because their efforts are occasionally rewarded. This persistence is typical with **partial (intermittent) reinforcement schedules,** in which responses are sometimes reinforced, sometimes not. Learning is slower to appear, but *resistance to extinction* is greater than with continuous reinforcement. Imagine a pigeon that has learned to peck a key to obtain food. If you gradually phase out the food delivery until it occurs only rarely, in no predictable pattern, the pigeon may peck 150,000 times without a reward (Skinner, 1953). Slot machines reward gamblers in much the same way—occasionally and unpredictably. And like

primary reinforcer an innately reinforcing stimulus, such as one that satisfies a biological need.

conditioned reinforcer a stimulus that gains its reinforcing power through its association with a primary reinforcer; also known as a *secondary reinforcer.*

reinforcement schedule a pattern that defines how often a desired response will be reinforced.

continuous reinforcement schedule reinforcing the desired response every time it occurs.

partial (intermittent) reinforcement schedule reinforcing a response only part of the time; results in slower acquisition of a response but much greater resistance to extinction than does continuous reinforcement.

"Oh, not bad. The light comes on, I press the bar, they write me a check. How about you?"

pigeons, slot players keep trying, time and time again. With intermittent reinforcement, hope springs eternal.

Lesson for parents: Partial reinforcement also works with children. *Occasionally* giving in to children's tantrums for the sake of peace and quiet intermittently reinforces the tantrums. This is the very best procedure for making a behavior persist.

Skinner (1961) and his collaborators compared four schedules of partial reinforcement. Some are rigidly fixed, some unpredictably variable.

Fixed-ratio schedules reinforce behavior after a set number of responses. Coffee shops may reward us with a free drink after every 10 purchased. Once conditioned, rats may be reinforced on a fixed ratio of, say, one food pellet for every 30 responses. Once conditioned, animals will pause only briefly after a reinforcer before returning to a high rate of responding (**FIGURE 20.3**).

Variable-ratio schedules provide reinforcers after a seemingly unpredictable number of responses. This unpredictable reinforcement is what slot-machine players and fly fishers experience, and it's what makes gambling and fly fishing so hard to extinguish even when they don't produce the desired results. Because reinforcers increase as the number of responses increases, variable-ratio schedules produce high rates of responding.

Fixed-interval schedules reinforce the first response after a fixed time period. Animals on this type of schedule tend to respond more frequently as the anticipated time for reward draws near. People check more frequently for the mail as delivery time approaches. A hungry child jiggles the Jell-O more often to see if it has set. Pigeons peck keys more rapidly as the time for reinforcement draws nearer (see Figure 20.3).

Variable-interval schedules reinforce the first response after *varying* time periods. Like the longed-for message that finally rewards persistence in rechecking e-mail or Facebook, variable-interval schedules tend to produce slow, steady responding. This makes sense, because there is no knowing when the waiting will be over (**TABLE 20.2**).

In general, response rates are higher when reinforcement is linked to the number of responses (a ratio schedule) rather than to time (an interval schedule). But responding is more consistent when reinforcement is unpredictable (a variable schedule) than when it is predictable (a fixed schedule). Animal behaviors differ, yet Skinner (1956) contended that the reinforcement principles of operant conditioning are universal. It matters little, he said, what response, what reinforcer, or what species you use. The effect of a given reinforcement schedule is pretty much the same: "Pigeon, rat, monkey, which is which? It doesn't matter. . . . Behavior shows astonishingly similar properties."

"The charm of fishing is that it is the pursuit of what is elusive but attainable, a perpetual series of occasions for hope."

Scottish author John Buchan (1875–1940)

Vitaly Titov & Maria Sidelnikova/Shutterstock

> FIGURE 20.3

Intermittent reinforcement schedules Skinner's (1961) laboratory pigeons produced these response patterns to each of four reinforcement schedules. (Reinforcers are indicated by diagonal marks.) For people, as for pigeons, reinforcement linked to number of responses (a *ratio schedule*) produces a higher response rate than reinforcement linked to amount of time elapsed (an *interval schedule*). But the predictability of the reward also matters. An unpredictable (*variable*) schedule produces more consistent responding than does a predictable (*fixed*) schedule.

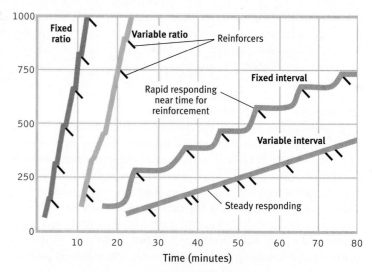

▼ TABLE 20.2
Schedules of Partial Reinforcement

	Fixed	Variable
Ratio	*Every so many:* reinforcement after every *nth* behavior, such as buy 10 coffees, get 1 free, or pay workers per product unit produced	*After an unpredictable number:* reinforcement after a random number of behaviors, as when playing slot machines or fly fishing
Interval	*Every so often:* reinforcement for behavior after a fixed time, such as Tuesday discount prices	*Unpredictably often:* reinforcement for behavior after a random amount of time, as when checking for a Facebook response

---

RETRIEVE IT [✖]

- People who send spam are reinforced by which schedule? Home bakers checking the oven to see if the cookies are done are on which schedule? Airline frequent-flyer programs that offer a free flight after a certain number of miles of travel are using which reinforcement schedule?

ANSWERS: Spammers are reinforced on a variable-ratio schedule (after a varying number of messages). Cookie checkers are reinforced on a fixed-interval schedule. Frequent-flyer programs use a fixed-ratio schedule.

Punishment

◁◦▷ **20-5** How does punishment differ from negative reinforcement, and how does punishment affect behavior?

Reinforcement increases a behavior; **punishment** does the opposite. A *punisher* is any consequence that *decreases* the frequency of a preceding behavior (**TABLE 20.3**). Swift and sure punishers can powerfully restrain unwanted behavior. The rat that is shocked after touching a forbidden object and the child who is burned by touching a hot stove will learn not to repeat those behaviors.

Criminal behavior, much of it impulsive, is also influenced more by swift and sure punishers than by the threat of severe sentences (Darley & Alter, 2013). Thus, when Arizona introduced an exceptionally harsh sentence for first-time drunk drivers, the drunk-driving rate changed very little. But when Kansas City police started patrolling a high crime area to increase the swiftness and sureness of punishment, that city's crime rate dropped dramatically.

How should we interpret the punishment studies in relation to parenting practices? Many psychologists and supporters of nonviolent parenting have noted four major drawbacks of physical punishment (Gershoff, 2002; Marshall, 2002):

1. *Punished behavior is suppressed, not forgotten. This temporary state may (negatively) reinforce parents' punishing behavior.* The child swears, the parent swats, the parent hears no more swearing and feels the punishment successfully stopped the behavior. No wonder spanking has been a hit with so many parents—with 70 percent of American adults agreeing that sometimes children need a "good, hard spanking" (Child Trends, 2013).

fixed-ratio schedule in operant conditioning, a reinforcement schedule that reinforces a response only after a specified number of responses.

variable-ratio schedule in operant conditioning, a reinforcement schedule that reinforces a response after an unpredictable number of responses.

fixed-interval schedule in operant conditioning, a reinforcement schedule that reinforces a response only after a specified time has elapsed.

variable-interval schedule in operant conditioning, a reinforcement schedule that reinforces a response at unpredictable time intervals.

punishment an event that tends to *decrease* the behavior that it follows.

▼ TABLE 20.3
Ways to Decrease Behavior

Type of Punisher	Description	Examples
Positive punishment	Administer an aversive stimulus.	Spray water on a barking dog; give a traffic ticket for speeding.
Negative punishment	Withdraw a rewarding stimulus.	Take away a misbehaving teen's driving privileges; revoke a library card for nonpayment of fines.

2. *Punishment teaches discrimination among situations.* In operant conditioning, *discrimination* occurs when an organism learns that certain responses, but not others, will be reinforced. Did the punishment effectively end the child's swearing? Or did the child simply learn that while it's not okay to swear around the house, it's okay elsewhere?

3. *Punishment can teach fear.* In operant conditioning, *generalization* occurs when an organism's response to similar stimuli is also reinforced. A punished child may associate fear not only with the undesirable behavior but also with the person who delivered the punishment or the place it occurred. Thus, children may learn to fear a punishing teacher and try to avoid school, or may become more anxious (Gershoff et al., 2010). For such reasons, most European countries and most U.S. states now ban hitting children in schools and child-care institutions (www.endcorporalpunishment.org). As of 2015, 47 countries further outlaw hitting by parents, providing children the same legal protection given to adults.

4. *Physical punishment may increase aggression by modeling violence as a way to cope with problems.* Studies find that spanked children are at increased risk for aggression (MacKenzie et al., 2013). We know, for example, that many aggressive delinquents and abusive parents come from abusive families (Straus & Gelles, 1980; Straus et al., 1997).

Some researchers have noted a problem with this logic. Well, yes, they've said, physically punished children may be more aggressive, for the same reason that people who have undergone psychotherapy are more likely to suffer depression—because they had preexisting problems that triggered the treatments (Ferguson, 2013; Larzelere, 2000, Larzelere et al., 2004). Which is the chicken and which is the egg? Correlations don't hand us an answer.

If one adjusts for preexisting antisocial behavior, then an occasional single swat or two to misbehaving 2- to 6-year-olds looks more effective (Baumrind et al., 2002; Larzelere & Kuhn, 2005). That is especially so if two other conditions are met:

1. The swat is used only as a backup when milder disciplinary tactics fail. (Children's compliance often increases after a reprimand and a "time-out" punishment [Owen et al., 2012].)

2. The swat is combined with a generous dose of reasoning and reinforcing.

Other researchers remain unconvinced. After controlling for prior misbehavior, they report that more frequent spankings of young children predict future aggressiveness (Grogan-Kaylor, 2004; Taylor et al., 2010).

Parents of delinquent youths are often unaware of how to achieve desirable behaviors without screaming, hitting, or threatening their children with punishment (Patterson et al., 1982). Training programs can help transform dire threats ("You clean up your room this minute or no dinner!") into positive incentives ("You're welcome at the dinner table after you get your room cleaned up"). Stop and think about it. Aren't many threats of punishment just as forceful, and perhaps more effective, when rephrased positively? Thus, "If you don't get your homework done, there'll be no car" would better be phrased as . . . .

In classrooms, too, teachers can give feedback on papers by saying, "No, but try this . . ." and "Yes, that's it!" Such responses reduce unwanted behavior while reinforcing more desirable alternatives. Remember: Punishment tells you what not to do; reinforcement tells you what to do. Thus, punishment trains a particular sort of morality—one focused on prohibition (what *not* to do) rather than positive obligations (Sheikh & Janoff-Bultman, 2013).

What punishment often teaches, said Skinner, is how to avoid it. Most psychologists now favor an emphasis on reinforcement: Notice people doing something right and affirm them for it.

LaunchPad See LaunchPad's *Video: Correlational Studies* for a helpful tutorial animation.

Skinner's Legacy

20-6 Why did Skinner's ideas provoke controversy, and how might his operant conditioning principles be applied at school, in sports, at work, and at home?

B. F. Skinner stirred a hornet's nest with his outspoken beliefs. He repeatedly insisted that external influences, not internal thoughts and feelings, shape behavior. And he urged people to use operant principles to influence others' behavior at school, work, and home. Knowing that behavior is shaped by its results, he argued that we should use rewards to evoke more desirable behavior.

Skinner's critics objected, saying that he dehumanized people by neglecting their personal freedom and by seeking to control their actions. Skinner's reply: External consequences already haphazardly control people's behavior. Why not administer those consequences toward human betterment? Wouldn't reinforcers be more humane than the punishments used in homes, schools, and prisons? And if it is humbling to think that our history has shaped us, doesn't this very idea also give us hope that we can shape our future?

Applications of Operant Conditioning

Psychologists apply operant conditioning principles to help people with a variety of challenges, from moderating high blood pressure to gaining social skills. Reinforcement technologies are also at work in schools, sports, workplaces, and homes, and these principles can support our self-improvement as well (Flora, 2004).

AT SCHOOL More than 50 years ago, Skinner and others worked toward a day when "machines and textbooks" would shape learning in small steps, by immediately reinforcing correct responses. Such machines and texts, they said, would revolutionize education and free teachers to focus on each student's special needs. "Good instruction demands two things," said Skinner (1989). "Students must be told immediately whether what they do is right or wrong and, when right, they must be directed to the step to be taken next."

Skinner might be pleased to know that many of his ideals for education are now possible. Teachers used to find it difficult to pace material to each student's rate of

B. F. Skinner "I am sometimes asked, 'Do you think of yourself as you think of the organisms you study?' The answer is yes. So far as I know, my behavior at any given moment has been nothing more than the product of my genetic endowment, my personal history, and the current setting" (1983).

 LaunchPad To review and experience simulations of operant conditioning, visit LaunchPad's *PsychSim 6: Operant Conditioning* and also *PsychSim 6: Shaping.*

Computer-assisted learning Electronic technologies have helped realize Skinner's goal of individually paced instruction with immediate feedback.

Christopher Halloran/Shutterstock

learning, and to provide prompt feedback. Online adaptive quizzing, such as the LearningCurve system available with this text, does both. Students move through quizzes at their own pace, according to their own level of understanding. And they get immediate feedback on their efforts, including personalized study plans.

IN SPORTS The key to shaping behavior in athletic performance, as elsewhere, is first reinforcing small successes and then gradually increasing the challenge. Golf students can learn putting by starting with very short putts, and eventually, as they build mastery, stepping back farther and farther. Novice batters can begin with half swings at an oversized ball pitched from 10 feet away, giving them the immediate pleasure of smacking the ball. As the hitters' confidence builds with their success and they achieve mastery at each level, the pitcher gradually moves back and eventually introduces a standard baseball and pitching distance. Compared with children taught by conventional methods, those trained by this behavioral method have shown faster skill improvement (Simek & O'Brien, 1981, 1988).

AT WORK Knowing that reinforcers influence productivity, many organizations have invited employees to share the risks and rewards of company ownership. Others have focused on reinforcing a job well done. Rewards are most likely to increase productivity if the desired performance is well-defined and achievable. The message for managers? *Reward specific, achievable behaviors, not vaguely defined "merit."*

Operant conditioning also reminds us that reinforcement should be *immediate.* IBM legend Thomas Watson understood. When he observed an achievement, he wrote the employee a check on the spot (Peters & Waterman, 1982). But rewards need not be material, or lavish. An effective manager may simply walk the floor and sincerely affirm people for good work, or write notes of appreciation for a completed project. As Skinner said, "How much richer would the whole world be if the reinforcers in daily life were more effectively contingent on productive work?"

AT HOME Parent-training researchers have pointed out how much parents can learn from operant conditioning practices. By saying, "Get ready for bed" and then caving in to protests or defiance, parents reinforce such whining and arguing (Wierson & Forehand, 1994). Exasperated, they may then yell or gesture menacingly. When the child, now frightened, obeys, that reinforces the parents' angry behavior. Over time, a destructive parent-child relationship develops.

To disrupt this cycle, parents should remember that basic rule of shaping: *Notice people doing something right and affirm them for it.* Give children attention and other reinforcers when they are behaving *well.* Target a specific behavior, reward it, and watch it increase. When children misbehave or are defiant, don't yell at them or hit them. Simply explain the misbehavior and give them a time-out.

Finally, we can use operant conditioning in our own lives. To reinforce your own desired behaviors (perhaps to improve your study habits) and extinguish the undesired ones (to stop smoking, for example), psychologists suggest taking these steps:

"I wrote another five hundred words. Can I have another cookie?"

1. *State a realistic goal in measurable terms.* You might, for example, aim to boost your study time by an hour a day.

2. *Decide how, when, and where you will work toward your goal.* Take time to plan. Those who specify how they will implement goals more often fulfill them (Gollwitzer & Oettingen, 2012).

3. *Monitor how often you engage in your desired behavior.* You might log your current study time, noting under what conditions you do and don't study.

4. *Reinforce the desired behavior.* To increase your study time, give yourself a reward (a snack or some activity you enjoy) only after you finish your extra hour of study. Agree with your friends that you will join them for weekend activities only if you have met your realistic weekly studying goal.

5. *Reduce the rewards gradually.* As your new behaviors become more habitual, give yourself a mental pat on the back instead of a cookie.

RETRIEVE IT

- Ethan constantly misbehaves at preschool even though his teacher scolds him repeatedly. Why does Ethan's misbehavior continue, and what can his teacher do to stop it?

ANSWER: If Ethan is seeking attention, the teacher's scolding may be reinforcing rather than punishing. To change Ethan's behavior, his teacher could offer reinforcement (such as praise) each time he behaves well. The teacher might encourage Ethan toward increasingly appropriate behavior through shaping, or by rephrasing rules as rewards instead of punishments. ("You can have a snack if you play nicely with the other children" [reward] rather than "You will not get a snack if you misbehave!" [punishment].)

IMMERSIVE LEARNING

Conditioning principles may also be applied in clinical settings. Explore some of these applications in LaunchPad's *How Would You Know If People Can Learn to Reduce Anxiety?*

Contrasting Classical and Operant Conditioning

20-7 How does operant conditioning differ from classical conditioning?

Both classical and operant conditioning are forms of *associative learning.* Both involve *acquisition, extinction, spontaneous recovery, generalization,* and *discrimination.* But these two forms of learning also differ. Through classical (Pavlovian) conditioning, we associate different stimuli we do not control, and we respond automatically *(respondent behaviors)* (**TABLE 20.4**). Through operant conditioning, we associate our own behaviors—which act on our environment to produce rewarding or punishing stimuli *(operant behaviors)*—with their consequences.

"O! This learning, what a thing it is."
William Shakespeare,
The Taming of the Shrew, *1597*

∨ TABLE 20.4

Comparison of Classical and Operant Conditioning

	Classical Conditioning	Operant Conditioning
Basic idea	Organism associates events	Organism associates behavior and resulting events
Response	Involuntary, automatic	Voluntary, operates on environment
Acquisition	Associating events; NS is paired with US and becomes CS	Associating response with a consequence (reinforcer or punisher)
Extinction	CR decreases when CS is repeatedly presented alone	Responding decreases when reinforcement stops
Spontaneous recovery	The reappearance, after a rest period, of an extinguished CR	The reappearance, after a rest period, of an extinguished response
Generalization	The tendency to respond to stimuli similar to the CS	Organism's response to similar stimuli is also reinforced
Discrimination	The learned ability to distinguish between a CS and other stimuli that do not signal a US	Organism learns that certain responses, but not others, will be reinforced

---

RETRIEVE IT

- Salivating in response to a tone paired with food is a(n) _____ behavior; pressing a bar to obtain food is a(n) _____ behavior.

ANSWERS: respondent; operant

MODULE 20 REVIEW   Operant Conditioning

🔵 Learning Objectives

Test Yourself by taking a moment to answer each of these Learning Objective Questions (repeated here from within the module). Then turn to Appendix D, Complete Module Reviews, to check your answers. Research suggests that trying to answer these questions on your own will improve your long-term memory of the concepts (McDaniel et al., 2009).

20-1 What is operant conditioning?

20-2 Who was Skinner, and how is operant behavior reinforced and shaped?

20-3 How do positive and negative reinforcement differ, and what are the basic types of reinforcers?

20-4 How do different reinforcement schedules affect behavior?

20-5 How does punishment differ from negative reinforcement, and how does punishment affect behavior?

20-6 Why did Skinner's ideas provoke controversy, and how might his operant conditioning principles be applied at school, in sports, at work, and at home?

20-7 How does operant conditioning differ from classical conditioning?

■·[:] Terms and Concepts to Remember

Test yourself on these terms by trying to write down the definition in your own words before flipping back to the referenced page to check your answers.

operant conditioning, p. 256

law of effect, p. 256

operant chamber, p. 257

reinforcement, p. 257

shaping, p. 257

positive reinforcement, p. 258

negative reinforcement, p. 258

primary reinforcer, p. 259

conditioned reinforcer, p. 259

reinforcement schedule, p. 259

continuous reinforcement schedule, p. 259

partial (intermittent) reinforcement schedule, p. 259

fixed-ratio schedule, p. 260

variable-ratio schedule, p. 260

fixed-interval schedule, p. 260

variable-interval schedule, p. 260

punishment, p. 261

[✻] Experience the Testing Effect

Test yourself repeatedly throughout your studies. This will not only help you figure out what you know and don't know; the testing itself will help you learn and remember the information more effectively thanks to the *testing effect*.

1. Thorndike's law of effect was the basis for _____ work on operant conditioning and behavior control.

2. One way to change behavior is to reward natural behaviors in small steps, as the organism gets closer and closer to a desired behavior. This process is called _____.

3. Your dog is barking so loudly that it's making your ears ring. You clap your hands, the dog stops barking, your ears stop ringing, and you think to yourself, "I'll have to do that when he barks again." The end of the barking was for you a
   a. positive reinforcer.
   b. negative reinforcer.
   c. positive punishment.
   d. negative punishment.

4. How could your psychology instructor use negative reinforcement to encourage your attentive behavior during class?

5. Reinforcing a desired response only some of the times it occurs is called _____ reinforcement.

6. A restaurant is running a special deal. After you buy four meals at full price, your fifth meal will be free. This is an example of a _____ schedule of reinforcement.
   a. fixed-ratio
   b. variable-ratio
   c. fixed-interval
   d. variable-interval

7. The partial reinforcement schedule that reinforces a response after unpredictable time periods is a _____-_____ schedule.

8. A medieval proverb notes that "a burnt child dreads the fire." In operant conditioning, the burning would be an example of a
   a. primary reinforcer.
   b. negative reinforcer.
   c. punisher.
   d. positive reinforcer.

Find answers to these questions in Appendix E, in the back of the book.

Use 🌀 LearningCurve to create your personalized study plan, which will direct you to the resources that will help you most in 🌀 LaunchPad .

MODULE 21 Biology, Cognition, and Learning

Biological influences:
- genetic predispositions
- unconditioned responses
- adaptive responses
- neural mirroring

Psychological influences:
- previous experiences
- predictability of associations
- generalization
- discrimination
- expectations

From drooling dogs, running rats, and pecking pigeons we have learned much about the basic processes of **learning** through *classical* and *operant conditioning.* But conditioning principles don't tell us the whole story. Today's learning theorists recognize that learning is the product of the interaction of biological, psychological, and social-cultural influences (**FIGURE 21.1**).

Learning

Social-cultural influences:
- culturally learned preferences
- motivation, affected by presence of others
- modeling

Biological Constraints on Conditioning

▲ FIGURE 21.1

Biopsychosocial influences on learning Our learning results not only from environmental experiences, but also from cognitive and biological influences.

21-1 How do biological constraints affect classical and operant conditioning?

Ever since Charles Darwin, scientists have assumed that all animals share a common evolutionary history and thus share commonalities in their makeup and functioning. Pavlov and Watson, for example, believed the basic laws of learning were essentially similar in all animals. So it should make little difference whether one studied pigeons or people. Moreover, it seemed that any natural response could be conditioned to any *neutral stimulus.*

Limits on Classical Conditioning

In 1956, learning researcher Gregory Kimble proclaimed, "Just about any activity of which the organism is capable can be conditioned and . . . these responses can be conditioned to any stimulus that the organism can perceive" (p. 195). Twenty-five years later, he humbly acknowledged that "half a thousand" scientific reports had proven him wrong (Kimble, 1981). More than the early behaviorists realized, an animal's capacity for conditioning is limited by **biological constraints.** Each species' predispositions prepare it to learn the associations that enhance its survival. Environments are not the whole story.

John Garcia was among those who challenged the prevailing idea that all associations can be learned equally well. While researching the effects of radiation on laboratory animals, Garcia and Robert Koelling (1966) noticed that rats began to avoid drinking water from the plastic bottles in radiation chambers. Could classical conditioning be the culprit? Might the rats have linked the plastic-tasting water (a *conditioned stimulus,* or CS) to the sickness (*unconditioned response,* or UR) triggered by the radiation (*unconditioned stimulus,* or US)?

To test their hunch, Garcia and Koelling exposed the rats to a particular taste, sight, or sound (CS) and later also to radiation or drugs (US) that led to nausea and vomiting (UR). Two startling findings emerged: First, even if sickened as late as several hours after tasting a particular novel flavor, the rats thereafter avoided that flavor. This appeared to violate the widely held belief that for conditioning to occur, the US must immediately follow the CS.

Second, the sickened rats developed aversions to tastes but not to sights or sounds. This contradicted the behaviorists' idea that any perceivable stimulus could serve as a CS. But it made adaptive sense. For rats, the easiest way to identify tainted food is to taste it; if sickened after sampling a new food, they thereafter avoid it. This response, called *taste aversion,* makes it difficult to eradicate a population of "bait-shy" rats by poisoning.

Humans, too, seem biologically prepared to learn some associations rather than others. If you become violently ill four hours after eating contaminated oysters, you will probably develop an aversion to the taste of oysters but usually not to the sight of the associated restaurant, its plates, the people you were with, or the music you

John Garcia As the laboring son of California farmworkers, Garcia attended school only in the off-season during his early childhood years. After entering junior college in his late twenties, and earning his Ph.D. in his late forties, he received the American Psychological Association's Distinguished Scientific Contribution Award "for his highly original, pioneering research in conditioning and learning." He was also elected to the National Academy of Sciences.

learning the process of acquiring through experience new information or behaviors.

biological constraints evolved biological tendencies that predispose animals' behavior and learning. Thus, certain behaviors are more easily learned than others.

Taste aversion If you became violently ill after eating oysters, you would probably have a hard time eating them again. Their smell and taste would have become a CS for nausea. This learning occurs readily because our biology prepares us to learn taste aversions to toxic foods.

heard there. (In contrast, birds, which hunt by sight, appear biologically primed to develop aversions to the *sight* of tainted food [Nicolaus et al., 1983].)

Garcia and Koelling's taste-aversion research is but one instance in which psychological experiments that began with the discomfort of some laboratory animals ended by enhancing the welfare of many others. In one conditioned taste-aversion study, coyotes and wolves were tempted into eating sheep carcasses laced with a sickening poison. Thereafter, they developed an aversion to sheep meat; two wolves later penned with a live sheep seemed actually to fear it (Gustavson et al., 1974, 1976). These studies not only saved the sheep from their predators, but also saved the sheep-shunning coyotes and wolves from angry ranchers and farmers who had wanted to destroy them. Similar applications have prevented baboons from raiding African gardens, raccoons from attacking chickens, ravens and crows from feeding on crane eggs. In all these cases, research helped preserve both the prey and their predators, all of which occupy an important ecological niche (Dingfelder, 2010; Garcia & Gustavson, 1997).

Such research supports Darwin's principle that natural selection favors traits that aid survival. Our ancestors who readily learned taste aversions were unlikely to eat the same toxic food again and were more likely to survive and leave descendants. Nausea, like anxiety, pain, and other bad feelings, serves a good purpose. Like a car's low-oil warning light, each alerts the body to a threat (Neese, 1991).

The tendency to learn behaviors favored by natural selection may help explain why we humans seem naturally disposed to learn associations between the color red and sexuality. Female primates display red when nearing ovulation. In human females, enhanced bloodflow produces the red blush of flirtation and sexual excitation. Does the frequent pairing of red and sex—with Valentine's hearts, red-light districts, and red lipstick—naturally enhance heterosexual men's attraction to women? Experiments (**FIGURE 21.2**) have suggested that, without the men's awareness, it does (Elliot & Niesta, 2008).

Animal taste aversion As an alternative to killing wolves and coyotes that prey on sheep, some ranchers have sickened the animals with lamb laced with a drug.

A genetic predisposition to associate a CS with a US that follows predictably and immediately is adaptive. Causes often do immediately precede effects. But as we saw in the taste-aversion findings, our predisposition to associate an effect with a preceding event can trick us. When chemotherapy triggers nausea and vomiting more than an hour following treatment, cancer patients may over time develop classically conditioned nausea (and sometimes anxiety) to the sights, sounds, and smells associated with the clinic (**FIGURE 21.3**) (Hall, 1997). Merely returning to the clinic's waiting room or seeing the nurses can provoke these conditioned feelings (Burish & Carey, 1986; Davey, 1992). Under normal circumstances, such revulsion to sickening stimuli would be adaptive.

> **FIGURE 21.2**

Romantic red In a series of experiments that controlled for other factors (such as the brightness of the image), heterosexual men found women more attractive and sexually desirable when framed in red (Elliot & Niesta, 2008). The phenomenon has been found not only in North America and Europe, but also in the West African nation of Burkina Faso (Elliot et al., 2013).

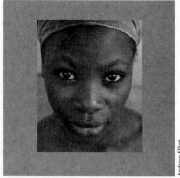

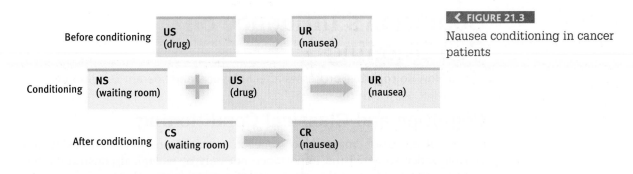

Nausea conditioning in cancer patients

RETRIEVE IT [✖]

- How did Garcia and Koelling's taste-aversion studies help disprove Gregory Kimble's early claim that "just about any activity of which the organism is capable can be conditioned . . . to any stimulus that the organism can perceive"?

ANSWER: Garcia and Koelling demonstrated that rats may learn an aversion to tastes, on which their survival depends, but not to sights or sounds.

Limits on Operant Conditioning

As with classical conditioning, nature sets limits on each species' capacity for operant conditioning. Science fiction writer Robert Heinlein (1907–1988) said it well: "Never try to teach a pig to sing; it wastes your time and annoys the pig."

We most easily learn and retain behaviors that reflect our biological predispositions. Thus, using food as a reinforcer, you could easily condition a hamster to dig or to rear up, because these are among the animal's natural food-searching behaviors. But you won't be so successful if you use food as a reinforcer to shape face washing and other hamster behaviors that aren't normally associated with food or hunger (Shettleworth, 1973). Similarly, you could easily teach pigeons to flap their wings to avoid being shocked, and to peck to obtain food: Fleeing with their wings and eating with their beaks are natural pigeon behaviors. However, pigeons would have a hard time learning to peck to avoid a shock, or to flap their wings to obtain food (Foree & LoLordo, 1973). The principle: *Biological constraints predispose organisms to learn associations that are naturally adaptive.*

In the early years of their work, animal trainers Marian Breland and Keller Breland presumed that operant principles would work on almost any response an animal could make. But they, too, learned about biological constraints. In one act, pigs trained to pick up large wooden "dollars" and deposit them in a piggy bank began to drift back to their natural ways. They dropped the coin, pushed it with their snouts as pigs are prone to do, picked it up again, and then repeated the sequence—delaying their food reinforcer. This *instinctive drift* occurred as the animals reverted to their biologically predisposed patterns.

"Once bitten, twice shy."

G. F. Northall,
Folk-Phrases, 1894

Natural athletes Animals can most easily learn and retain behaviors that draw on their biological predispositions, such as horses' inborn ability to move around obstacles with speed and agility.

Jeffery Jones/The Gallup Independent/AP Photo

Cognition's Influence on Conditioning

21-2 How do cognitive processes affect classical and operant conditioning?

Cognition and Classical Conditioning

In their dismissal of "mentalistic" concepts such as consciousness, Pavlov and Watson underestimated the importance not only of biological constraints, but also the effects of cognitive processes (thoughts, perceptions, expectations). The early behaviorists believed that rats' and dogs' learned behaviors could be reduced to mindless mechanisms, so there was no need to consider cognition. But Robert Rescorla and Allan Wagner (1972) showed that an animal can learn the *predictability* of an event. If a shock always is preceded by a tone, and then may also be preceded by a light that accompanies the tone, a rat will react with fear to the tone but not to the light. Although the light is always followed by the shock, it adds no new information; the tone is a better predictor. The more predictable the association, the stronger the conditioned response. It's as if the animal learns an *expectancy,* an awareness of how likely it is that the US will occur.

Classical conditioning treatments that ignore cognition often have limited success. For example, people receiving therapy for alcohol use disorder may be given alcohol spiked with a nauseating drug. Will they then associate alcohol with sickness? If classical conditioning were merely a matter of "stamping in" stimulus associations, we might hope so, and to some extent this does occur. However, one's awareness that the nausea is induced by the drug, not the alcohol, often weakens the association between drinking alcohol and feeling sick. So, even in classical conditioning, it is—especially with humans—not simply the CS-US association but also the thought that counts.

Cognition and Operant Conditioning

B. F. Skinner acknowledged the biological underpinnings of behavior and the existence of private thought processes. Nevertheless, many psychologists criticized him for discounting cognition's importance.

A mere eight days before dying of leukemia in 1990, Skinner stood before the American Psychological Association convention. In this final address, he again resisted the growing belief that cognitive processes have a necessary place in the science of psychology and even in our understanding of conditioning. He viewed "cognitive science" as a throwback to early twentieth-century introspectionism. For Skinner, thoughts and emotions were behaviors that follow the same laws as other behaviors.

Nevertheless, the evidence of cognitive processes cannot be ignored. For example, animals on a fixed-interval reinforcement schedule respond more and more frequently as the time approaches when a response will produce a reinforcer. Although a strict behaviorist would object to talk of "expectations," the animals behave as if they expected that repeating the response would soon produce the reward.

Evidence of cognitive processes has also come from studying rats in mazes. Rats exploring a maze, given no obvious rewards, seem to develop a **cognitive map,** a mental representation of the maze. When an experimenter then places food in the maze's goal box, these rats run the maze as quickly and efficiently as other rats that were previously reinforced with food for this result. Like people sightseeing in a new town, the exploring rats seemingly experienced **latent learning** during their earlier tours. That learning became apparent only when there was some incentive to demonstrate it. Children, too, may learn from watching a parent

For more information on animal behavior, see books by (we are not making this up) Robin Fox and Lionel Tiger.

"All brains are, in essence, anticipation machines."

Daniel C. Dennett,
Consciousness Explained, 1991

"Bathroom? Sure, it's just down the hall to the left, jog right, left, another left, straight past two more lefts, then right, and it's at the end of the third corridor on your right."

cognitive map a mental representation of the layout of one's environment. For example, after exploring a maze, rats act as if they have learned a cognitive map of it.

latent learning learning that occurs but is not apparent until there is an incentive to demonstrate it.

but demonstrate the learning only much later, as needed. The point to remember: *There is more to learning than associating a response with a consequence; there is also cognition.* In other modules, we will encounter more striking evidence of animals' cognitive abilities in solving problems and in using aspects of language.

The cognitive perspective has also shown us the limits of rewards: Promising people a reward for a task they already enjoy can backfire. Excessive rewards can destroy **intrinsic motivation**—the desire to perform a behavior effectively for its own sake. In experiments, children have been promised a payoff for playing with an interesting puzzle or toy. Later, they played with the toy *less* than did unpaid children (Deci et al., 1999; Tang & Hall, 1995). Likewise, rewarding children with toys or candy for reading diminishes the time they spend reading (Marinak & Gambrell, 2008). It is as if they think, "If I have to be bribed into doing this, it must not be worth doing for its own sake."

Latent learning
Animals, like people, can learn from experience, with or without reinforcement. In a classic experiment, rats in one group repeatedly explored a maze, always with a food reward at the end. Rats in another group explored the maze with no food reward. But once given a food reward at the end, rats in the second group thereafter ran the maze as quickly as (and even faster than) the always-rewarded rats (Tolman & Honzik, 1930).

To sense the difference between intrinsic motivation and **extrinsic motivation** (behaving in certain ways to gain external rewards or avoid threatened punishment), think about your experience in this course. Are you feeling pressured to finish this reading before a deadline? Worried about your grade? Eager for the credits that will count toward graduation? If *Yes,* then you are extrinsically motivated (as, to some extent, almost all students must be). Are you also finding the material interesting? Does learning it make you feel more competent? If there were no grade at stake, might you be curious enough to want to learn the material for its own sake? If *Yes,* intrinsic motivation also fuels your efforts.

Youth sports coaches who aim to promote enduring interest in an activity, not just to pressure players into winning, should focus on the intrinsic joy of playing and of reaching one's potential (Deci & Ryan, 1985, 2009). Doing so may also ultimately lead to greater rewards. Students who focus on learning (intrinsic reward) often get good grades and graduate (extrinsic rewards). Doctors who focus on healing (intrinsic) may make a good living (extrinsic). Indeed, research suggests that people who focus on their work's meaning and significance not only do better work but ultimately enjoy more extrinsic rewards (Wrzesniewski et al., 2014).

Nevertheless, extrinsic rewards used to signal a job well done (rather than to bribe or control someone) can be effective (Boggiano et al., 1985). "Most improved player" awards, for example, can boost feelings of competence and increase enjoyment of a sport. Rightly administered, rewards can improve performance and spark creativity (Eisenberger & Aselage, 2009; Henderlong & Lepper, 2002). And the rewards that often follow academic achievement, such as scholarships and jobs, are here to stay.

TABLE 21.1 compares the biological and cognitive influences on classical and operant conditioning.

intrinsic motivation a desire to perform a behavior effectively for its own sake.

extrinsic motivation a desire to perform a behavior to receive promised rewards or avoid threatened punishment.

∨ **TABLE 21.1**

Biological and Cognitive Influences on Conditioning

	Classical Conditioning	Operant Conditioning
Biological predispositions	Natural predispositions constrain what stimuli and responses can easily be associated.	Organisms most easily learn behaviors similar to their natural behaviors; unnatural behaviors instinctively drift back toward natural ones.
Cognitive processes	Organisms develop expectation that CS signals the arrival of US.	Organisms develop expectation that a response will be reinforced or punished; they also exhibit latent learning, without reinforcement.

Albert Bandura "The Bobo doll follows me wherever I go. The photographs are published in every introductory psychology text and virtually every undergraduate takes introductory psychology. I recently checked into a Washington hotel. The clerk at the desk asked, 'Aren't you the psychologist who did the Bobo doll experiment?' I answered, 'I am afraid that will be my legacy.' He replied, 'That deserves an upgrade. I will put you in a suite in the quiet part of the hotel'" (2005). A recent analysis of citations, awards, and textbook coverage identified Bandura as the world's most eminent psychologist (Diener et al., 2014).

Learning by Observation

21-3 How does observational learning differ from associative learning? How may observational learning be enabled by neural mirroring?

Cognition supports **observational learning,** in which higher animals, especially humans, learn without direct experience, by watching and imitating others. A child who sees his sister burn her fingers on a hot stove learns not to touch it. We learn our native languages and various other specific behaviors by observing and imitating others, a process called **modeling.**

Picture this scene from an experiment by Albert Bandura, the pioneering researcher of observational learning (Bandura et al., 1961): A preschool child is working on a drawing, while an adult in another part of the room builds with Tinkertoys. As the child watches, the adult gets up and for nearly 10 minutes pounds, kicks, and throws around the room a large inflated Bobo doll, yelling, "Sock him in the nose. . . . Hit him down. . . . Kick him."

The child is then taken to another room filled with appealing toys. Soon the experimenter returns and tells the child she has decided to save these good toys "for the other children." She takes the now-frustrated child to a third room containing a few toys, including a Bobo doll. Left alone, what does the child do?

Compared with children not exposed to the adult model, those who viewed the model's actions were more likely to lash out at the doll. Observing the aggressive outburst apparently lowered their inhibitions. But *something more* was also at work, for the children imitated the very acts they had observed and used the very words they had heard (**FIGURE 21.4**).

LaunchPad For three minutes of classic footage, see LaunchPad's *Video: Bandura's Bobo Doll Experiment.*

That "something more," Bandura suggested, was this: By watching models, we experience *vicarious reinforcement* or *vicarious punishment,* and we learn to anticipate a behavior's consequences in situations like those we are observing. We are especially likely to learn from people we perceive as similar to ourselves, or as

❤ FIGURE 21.4

The famous Bobo doll experiment Notice how the children's actions directly imitate the adult's.

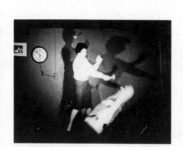

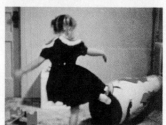

Courtesy of Albert Bandura, Stanford University

successful, or as admirable. fMRI scans show that when people observe someone winning a reward (and especially when it's someone likable and similar to themselves), their own brain reward systems activate, much as if they themselves had won the reward (Mobbs et al., 2009). When we identify with someone, we experience their outcomes vicariously. Even our learned fears may extinguish as we observe another safely navigating the feared situation (Golkar et al., 2013). Lord Chesterfield (1694–1773) had the idea: "We are, in truth, more than half what we are by imitation."

Mirrors and Imitation in the Brain

On a 1991 hot summer day in Parma, Italy, a lab monkey awaited its researchers' return from lunch. The researchers had implanted wires next to its motor cortex, in a frontal lobe brain region that enabled the monkey to plan and enact movements. The monitoring device would alert the researchers to activity in that region of the monkey's brain. When the monkey moved a peanut into its mouth, for example, the device would buzz. That day, as one of the researchers reentered the lab, ice cream cone in hand, the monkey stared at him. As the researcher raised the cone to lick it, the monkey's monitor buzzed—as if the motionless monkey had itself moved (Blakeslee, 2006; Iacoboni, 2008, 2009).

The same buzzing had been heard earlier, when the monkey watched humans or other monkeys move peanuts to their mouths. The flabbergasted researchers had, they believed, stumbled onto a previously unknown type of neuron (Rizzolatti et al., 2002, 2006). These presumed **mirror neurons,** they argued, provide a neural basis for everyday imitation and observational learning. When a monkey grasps, holds, or tears something, these neurons fire. And they likewise fire when the monkey observes another doing so. When one monkey sees, its neurons mirror what another monkey does. (For a debate regarding the importance of mirror neurons, which are sometimes overblown in the popular press, see Gallese et al., 2011; Hickok, 2014.)

Imitation is widespread in other species. Chimpanzees observe and imitate all sorts of novel foraging and tool use behaviors, which are then transmitted from generation to generation within their local culture (Hopper et al., 2008; Whiten et al., 2007). So, too, with monkeys. Researchers trained groups of vervet monkeys to prefer either blue or pink corn by soaking one color in a disgusting-tasting solution (van de Waal et al., 2013). Four to six months later, after a new generation of monkeys was born, the adults stuck with whatever color they had learned to prefer—and, on observing them, so did all but one of 27 infant monkeys. Moreover, when blue- (or pink-) preferring males migrated to the other group, they switched preferences and began eating as the other group did. Monkey see, monkey do.

Mirror neurons at work?

"Your back is killing me!"

Animal social learning Whacking the water to boost feeding has spread among humpback whales through social learning (Allen et al., 2013). Likewise, monkeys learn to prefer whatever color corn they observe other monkeys eating.

Meltzoff, A. N., Kuhl, P. K., Movellan, J. & Sejnowski, T. J. (2009). Foundations for a new science of learning. *Science, 325,* 284–288.

Imitation This 12-month-old infant sees an adult look left, and immediately follows her gaze (Meltzoff et al., 2009).

"Children need models more than they need critics."

Joseph Joubert,
Pensées, *1842*

prosocial behavior positive, constructive, helpful behavior. The opposite of antisocial behavior.

In humans, imitation is pervasive. Our catchphrases, fashions, ceremonies, foods, traditions, morals, and fads all spread by one person copying another. Children and even infants are natural imitators (Marshall & Meltzoff, 2014). Shortly after birth, babies may imitate adults who stick out their tongue. By 8 to 16 months, infants imitate various novel gestures (Jones, 2007). By 12 months (**FIGURE 21.5**), they look where an adult is looking (Meltzoff et al., 2009). And by 14 months, children imitate acts modeled on TV (Meltzoff, 1988; Meltzoff & Moore, 1989, 1997). Even as 2½-year-olds, when many of their mental abilities are near those of adult chimpanzees, young humans surpass chimps at social tasks such as imitating another's solution to a problem (Herrmann et al., 2007). Children see, children do.

So strong is the human predisposition to learn from watching adults that 2- to 5-year-old children *overimitate*. Whether living in urban Australia or rural Africa, they copy even irrelevant adult actions. Before reaching for a toy in a plastic jar, they will first stroke the jar with a feather if that's what they have observed (Lyons et al., 2007). Or, imitating an adult, they will wave a stick over a box and then use the stick to push on a knob that opens the box—when all they needed to do to open the box was to push on the knob (Nielsen & Tomaselli, 2010).

Humans, like monkeys, have brains that support empathy and imitation. Researchers cannot insert experimental electrodes in human brains, but they can use fMRI scans to see brain activity associated with performing and with observing actions. So, is the human capacity to simulate another's action and to share in another's experience due to specialized mirror neurons? Or is it due to distributed brain networks? That issue is currently being debated (Gallese et al., 2011; Iacoboni, 2008, 2009; Mukamel et al., 2010; Spaulding, 2013). Regardless, children's brains do enable their empathy and their ability to infer another's mental state, an ability known as *theory of mind.*

The brain's response to observing others makes emotions contagious. Through its neurological echo, our brain simulates and vicariously experiences what we observe. So real are these mental instant replays that we may misremember an action we have observed as an action we have performed (Lindner et al., 2010). But through these reenactments, we grasp others' states of mind. Observing others' postures, faces, voices, and writing styles, we unconsciously synchronize our own to theirs—which helps us feel what they are feeling (Bernieri et al., 1994; Ireland & Pennebaker, 2010). We find ourselves yawning when they yawn, laughing when they laugh.

Seeing a loved one's pain, our faces mirror the other's emotion. But as **FIGURE 21.6** shows, so do our brains. In this fMRI scan, the pain imagined by an empathic romantic partner triggered some of the same brain activity experienced by the loved one who actually had the pain (Singer et al., 2004). Even fiction reading may trigger such activity, as we mentally simulate (and vicariously experience) the feelings and actions described (Mar & Oatley, 2008; Speer et al., 2009). In one experiment, university students read (and vicariously experienced) a fictional fellow student's description of overcoming obstacles to vote.

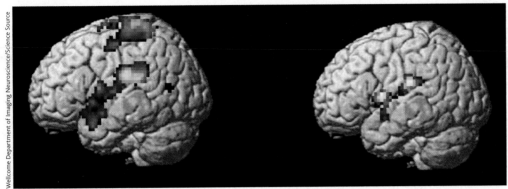

Wellcome Department of Imaging Neuroscience/Science Source

❮ FIGURE 21.6

Experienced and imagined pain in the brain Brain activity related to actual pain (left) is mirrored in the brain of an observing loved one (right). Empathy in the brain shows up in emotional brain areas, but not in the somatosensory cortex, which receives the physical pain input.

A week later, those who read the first-person account were more likely to vote in a presidential primary election (Kaufman & Libby, 2012). In experiments with elementary, high school, and college students, reading *Harry Potter* has reduced prejudice against immigrants, refugees, and gay people (Vezzali et al., 2015). The prejudice reduction is greatest for readers who identify with Harry and his acceptance of stigmatized people such as the "Mudbloods."

Applications of Observational Learning

21-4 What is the impact of prosocial modeling and of antisocial modeling?

So the big news from Bandura's studies and the mirror-neuron research is that we look, we mentally imitate, and we learn. Models—in our family, our neighborhood, or the media we consume—may have effects, good and bad.

PROSOCIAL EFFECTS The good news is that **prosocial** (positive, helpful) models can have prosocial effects. Many business organizations effectively use *behavior modeling* to help new employees learn communication, sales, and customer service skills (Taylor et al., 2005). Trainees gain these skills faster when they are able to observe the skills being modeled effectively by experienced workers (or actors simulating them).

People who exemplify nonviolent, helpful behavior can also prompt similar behavior in others. India's Mahatma Gandhi and America's Martin Luther King, Jr., both drew on the power of modeling, making nonviolent action a powerful force for social change in both countries. The media offer models. For example, one research team found that across seven countries, viewing prosocial TV, movies, and video games boosted later helping behavior (Prot et al., 2014).

Zumapress/Newscom

A model caregiver This girl is learning orphan-nursing skills, as well as compassion, by observing her mentor in this Humane Society program. As the sixteenth-century proverb states, "Example is better than precept."

Parents are also powerful models. European Christians who risked their lives to rescue Jews from the Nazis usually had a close relationship with at least one parent who modeled a strong moral or humanitarian concern; this was also true for U.S. civil rights activists in the 1960s (London, 1970; Oliner & Oliner, 1988). The observational learning of morality begins early. Socially responsive toddlers who readily imitated their parents tended to become preschoolers with a strong internalized conscience (Forman et al., 2004).

Models are most effective when their actions and words are consistent. Sometimes, however, models say one thing and do another. To encourage children to read, read to them and surround them with books and people who read. To increase the odds that your children will practice your religion, worship and attend religious activities with them. Many parents seem to operate according to the principle "Do as I *say,* not as I do." Experiments suggest that children learn to do both (Rice & Grusec, 1975; Rushton, 1975). Exposed to a hypocrite, they tend to imitate the hypocrisy—by doing what the model did and saying what the model said.

Children see, children do?
Children who often experience physical punishment tend to display more aggression.

David Strickler/The Image Works

ANTISOCIAL EFFECTS The bad news is that observational learning may also have *antisocial effects.* This helps us understand why abusive parents might have aggressive children, and why many men who beat their wives had wife-battering fathers (Stith et al., 2000). Critics note that aggressiveness could be genetic. But with monkeys, we know it can be environmental. In study after study, young monkeys separated from their mothers and subjected to high levels of aggression grew up to be aggressive themselves (Chamove, 1980). The lessons we learn as children are not easily replaced as adults, and they are sometimes visited on future generations.

TV shows, movies, and online videos are sources of observational learning. While watching, children may learn that bullying is an effective way to control others, that free and easy sex brings pleasure without later misery or disease, or that men should be tough and women gentle. And they have ample time to learn such lessons. During their first 18 years, most children in developed countries spend more time watching TV than they spend in school. The average teen averages, across 365 days a year, more than 4 hours a day; the average adult, 3 hours (Robinson & Martin, 2009; Strasburger et al., 2010).

"The problem with television is that the people must sit and keep their eyes glued to a screen: The average American family hasn't time for it. Therefore the showmen are convinced that . . . television will never be a serious competitor of [radio] broadcasting."

New York Times, *1939*

Screen time's greatest effect may stem from what it displaces. Children and adults who spend several hours a day in front of a screen spend that many fewer hours in other pursuits—talking, studying, playing, reading, or socializing face-to-face with friends. What would you have done with your extra time if you had spent even half as many hours in front of a screen? How might you be different as a result?

Viewers are learning about life from a rather peculiar storyteller, one that reflects the culture's mythology but not its reality. Between 1998 and 2006, prime-time violence on TV reportedly increased 75 percent (PTC, 2007). The violence numbers escalate with the addition of cable programming and home movie-viewing. An analysis of more than 3000 network and cable programs aired during one closely studied year revealed that nearly 6 in 10 featured violence, that 74 percent of the violence went unpunished, that 58 percent did not show the victims' pain, that nearly half the incidents involved "justified" violence, and that nearly half involved an attractive perpetrator. These conditions define the recipe for the *violence-viewing effect* described in many studies (Donnerstein, 1998, 2011). To read more about this effect, see Thinking Critically About: Does Viewing Media Violence Trigger Violent Behavior?

Does Viewing Media Violence Trigger Violent Behavior?

Was the judge who in 1993 tried two British 10-year-olds for the murder of a 2-year-old right to suspect that the pair had been influenced by "violent video films"? Were the American media right to wonder if Adam Lanza, the 2012 mass killer of young children and their teachers at Connecticut's Sandy Hook Elementary School, was influenced by the violent video games found stockpiled in his home? To understand whether violence viewing leads to violent behavior, researchers have done both correlational and experimental studies (Bushman et al., 2015; Groves et al., 2015).

Correlational studies do support this link:

- In the United States and Canada, homicide rates doubled between 1957 and 1974, just when TV was introduced and spreading. Moreover, census regions with later dates for TV service also had homicide rates that jumped later (Centerwall, 1989).

- White South Africans were first introduced to TV in 1975. A similar near-doubling of the homicide rate began after 1975 (Centerwall, 1989).

- Elementary schoolchildren heavily exposed to media violence (via TV, videos, and video games) tend to get into more fights (**FIGURE 21.7**). As teens, they are at greater risk for violent behavior (Boxer et al., 2009).

But remember, correlation need not mean causation. So correlational studies like these do not, as critics remind us, prove that viewing violence *causes* aggression (Ferguson, 2009; Freedman, 1988; McGuire, 1986).

Maybe aggressive children prefer violent programs. Maybe abused or neglected children are both more aggressive and more often left in front of the TV, video-game console, or computer. Maybe violent programs reflect, rather than affect, violent trends.

To pin down causation, psychologists have experimented. They randomly assigned some viewers to observe violence and others to watch entertaining nonviolence. Does viewing cruelty prepare people, when irritated, to react more cruelly? To some extent, it does. This is especially so when an attractive person commits seemingly justified, realistic violence that goes unpunished and causes no visible pain or harm (Donnerstein, 1998, 2011).

The violence-viewing effect seems to stem from at least two factors. One is *imitation*. More than 100 studies confirm that people sometimes imitate what they've viewed. Watching risk-glorifying behaviors (dangerous driving, extreme sports, unprotected sex) increases viewers' real-life risk taking (Fischer et al., 2011; Geen & Thomas, 1986). In one experiment, violent play increased sevenfold immediately after children viewed *Power Rangers* episodes (Boyatzis et al., 1995). As happened in the Bobo doll experiment, children often precisely imitated the models' violent acts—in this case, flying karate kicks. Another large experiment randomly assigned some preschoolers to a media diet. With their exposure to violence-laden programs limited, and their exposure to educational programs increased, their aggressive behavior diminished (Christakis et al., 2013).

Prolonged exposure to violence also *desensitizes* viewers. They become more indifferent to it when later viewing a brawl, whether on TV or in real life (Fanti et al., 2009; Rule & Ferguson, 1986). Adult males who spent three evenings watching sexually violent movies became progressively less bothered by the rapes and slashings shown. Compared with those in a control group, the film watchers later expressed less sympathy for domestic violence victims, and they rated the victims' injuries as less severe (Mullin & Linz, 1995). Likewise, moviegoers were less likely to help an injured woman pick up her crutches if they had just watched a violent rather than a nonviolent movie (Bushman & Anderson, 2009).

Drawing on such findings, the International Society for Research on Aggression's Media Violence Commission (2012) concluded that violent media are not the primary cause of school shootings, but that "exposure to media violence is one risk factor for increased aggression." And the American Academy of Pediatrics (2009) has advised pediatricians that "media violence can contribute to aggressive behavior, desensitization to violence, nightmares, and fear of being harmed." Indeed, an evil psychologist could hardly imagine a better way to make people indifferent to brutality than to expose them to a graded series of scenes, from fights to killings to the mutilations in slasher movies (Donnerstein et al., 1987). Watching cruelty fosters indifference.

"Thirty seconds worth of glorification of a soap bar sells soap. Twenty-five minutes worth of glorification of violence sells violence."

U.S. Senator Paul Simon,
Remarks to the Communitarian
Network, 1993

❮ FIGURE 21.7

Heavy exposure to media violence predicts future aggressive behavior Researchers studied more than 400 third- to fifth-graders. After controlling for existing differences in hostility and aggression, the researchers reported increased aggression in those heavily exposed to violent TV, videos, and video games (Gentile et al., 2011; Gentile & Bushman, 2012).

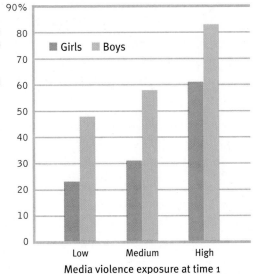

Percentage of students involved in fights at time 2 / Media violence exposure at time 1 (Girls, Boys; Low, Medium, High)

Stanislav Solntsev/Digital Vision/Getty Images

• Jason's parents and older friends all smoke, but they advise him not to. Juan's parents and friends don't smoke, but they say nothing to deter him from doing so. Will Jason or Juan be more likely to start smoking?

ANSWER: Jason may be more likely to smoke, because observational learning studies suggest that children tend to do as others do and say what they say.

* * *

Bandura's work—like that of Ivan Pavlov, John Watson, B. F. Skinner, and thousands of others who advanced our knowledge of learning principles—illustrates the impact that can result from single-minded devotion to a few well-defined problems and ideas. These researchers defined the issues and impressed on us the importance of learning. As their legacy demonstrates, intellectual history is often made by people who risk going to extremes in pushing ideas to their limits (Simonton, 2000).

• Match the examples (1–5) to the appropriate underlying learning principle (a–e):

   a. Classical conditioning   c. Latent learning   e. Biological predispositions

   b. Operant conditioning   d. Observational learning

   1. Knowing the way from your bed to the bathroom in the dark

   2. Your little brother getting in a fight after watching a violent action movie

   3. Salivating when you smell brownies in the oven

   4. Disliking the taste of chili after becoming violently sick a few hours after eating chili

   5. Your dog racing to greet you on your arrival home

ANSWERS: 1. c, 2. d, 3. a, 4. e, 5. b

21 REVIEW Biology, Cognition, and Learning

👁 Learning Objectives

Test Yourself by taking a moment to answer each of these Learning Objective Questions (repeated here from within the module). Then turn to Appendix D, Complete Module Reviews, to check your answers. Research suggests that trying to answer these questions on your own will improve your long-term memory of the concepts (McDaniel et al., 2009).

21-1 How do biological constraints affect classical and operant conditioning?

21-2 How do cognitive processes affect classical and operant conditioning?

21-3 How does observational learning differ from associative learning? How may observational learning be enabled by neural mirroring?

21-4 What is the impact of prosocial modeling and of antisocial modeling?

▣ Terms and Concepts to Remember

Test yourself on these terms by trying to write down the definition in your own words before flipping back to the referenced page to check your answers.

biological constraints, p. 267

cognitive map, p. 270
latent learning, p. 270
intrinsic motivation, p. 271
extrinsic motivation, p. 271

observational learning, p. 272
modeling, p. 272
mirror neurons, p. 273
prosocial behavior, p. 275

▣ Experience the Testing Effect

Test yourself repeatedly throughout your studies. This will not only help you figure out what you know and don't know; the testing itself will help you learn and remember the information more effectively thanks to the *testing effect*.

1. Garcia and Koelling's _____-_____ studies showed that conditioning can occur even when the unconditioned stimulus (US) does not immediately follow the neutral stimulus (NS).

2. Taste-aversion research has shown that some animals develop aversions to certain tastes but not to sights or sounds. What evolutionary psychology finding does this support?

3. Evidence that cognitive processes play an important role in learning comes in part from studies in which rats running a maze develop _____ _____.

4. Rats that explored a maze without any reward were later able to run the maze as well as other rats that had received food rewards for running the maze. The rats that had learned without reinforcement demonstrated _____ _____.

5. Children learn many social behaviors by imitating parents and other models. This type of learning is called _____ _____.

6. According to Bandura, we learn by watching models because we experience _____ reinforcement or _____ punishment.

7. Parents are most effective in getting their children to imitate them if
   a. their words and actions are consistent.
   b. they have outgoing personalities.
   c. one parent works and the other stays home to care for the children.
   d. they carefully explain why a behavior is acceptable in adults but not in children.

8. Some scientists believe that the brain has _____ neurons that enable empathy and imitation.

9. Most experts agree that repeated viewing of media violence
   a. makes all viewers significantly more aggressive.
   b. has little effect on viewers.
   c. dulls viewers' sensitivity to violence.
   d. makes viewers angry and frustrated.

Find answers to these questions in Appendix E, in the back of the book.

Use 🅰 LearningCurve to create your personalized study plan, which will direct you to the resources that will help you most in 🅰 LaunchPad.

MODULE
22 Studying and Encoding Memories

STUDYING
MEMORY

Sensory memory

STUDYING MEMORY

Short-term/Working memory
Happy memories are being associated with their first-dance song.

Long-term memory
In old age, "their song" may retrieve a memory of the start of their relationship.

Recall

Relearning

MAY

Memory is the persistence of *learning* over time

Recognition

Three measures of retention are recall, recognition, and _____
a. hierarchies.
b. chunking.
c. relearning.
d. priming.

FINALS
WEEK

13   14   15 →

MODULE
23 Storing and Retrieving Memories

KEY MEMORY
STRUCTURES

Explicit memory

Implicit memory

Emotional memory

Family wedding in the same context primes flood of memories of their own wedding.

MODULE
24 Forgetting, Memory Construction, and Improving Memory

We may fail to encode, store, or retrieve information.

Brain damage can cause specific memory loss.

We may construct false memories that feel SO real.

ENCODING MEMORIES

Automatic (implicit)
vs
effortful (explicit) processing

Read on for ways
to improve YOUR memory.

Memory[1]

BE thankful for memory. We take it for granted, except when it malfunctions. But it is our memory that accounts for time and defines our life. It is our memory that enables us to recognize family, speak our language, find our way home, and locate food and water. It is our memory that enables us to enjoy an experience and then mentally replay and enjoy it again. It is our memory that enables us to build histories with those we love, and it is our memory that occasionally pits us against those whose offenses we cannot forget.

In large part, we are what we remember. Without memory—our storehouse of accumulated learning—there would be no savoring of past joys, no guilt or anger over painful recollections. We would instead live in an enduring present, each moment fresh. Each person would be a stranger, every language foreign, every task—dressing, cooking, biking—a new challenge. You would even be a stranger to yourself, lacking that continuous sense of self that extends from your distant past to your momentary present.

Researchers study memory from many perspectives. Module 22 introduces the measuring, modeling, and encoding of memories. Module 23 examines how memories are stored and retrieved. Module 24 explores what happens when our memories fail us, and offers some tips for improving memory. ■

---

1. The Memory modules benefit from our collaboration with Janie Wilson, Georgia Southern University, in the previous edition.

MODULE 22 Studying and Encoding Memories

Studying Memory

👁 **22-1** What is *memory*, and how is it measured?

Memory is learning that persists over time; it is information that has been acquired and stored and can be retrieved. Research on memory's extremes has helped us understand how memory works. At age 92, my [DM's] father suffered a small stroke that had but one peculiar effect. He was as mobile as before. His genial personality was intact. He knew us and enjoyed poring over family photo albums and reminiscing about his past. But he had lost most of his ability to lay down new memories of conversations and everyday episodes. He could not tell me what day of the week it was, or what he'd had for lunch. Told repeatedly of his brother-in-law's recent death, he was surprised and saddened each time he heard the news.

At the other extreme are people who would be gold medal winners in a memory Olympics. Russian journalist Solomon Shereshevskii, or S, had merely to listen while other reporters scribbled notes (Luria, 1968). We could parrot back a string of about 7—maybe even 9—digits. S could repeat up to 70, if they were read about 3 seconds apart in an otherwise silent room. Moreover, he could recall digits or words backward as easily as forward. His accuracy was unerring, even when recalling a list 15 years later. "Yes, yes," he might recall. "This was a series you gave me once when we were in your apartment. . . . You were sitting at the table and I in the rocking chair. . . . You were wearing a gray suit. . . ."

Amazing? Yes, but consider your own impressive memory. You remember countless faces, places, and happenings; tastes, smells, and textures; voices, sounds, and songs. In one study, students listened to snippets—a mere four-tenths of a second—from popular songs. How often did they recognize the artist and song? More than 25 percent of the time (Krumhansl, 2010). We often recognize songs as quickly as we recognize a familiar voice.

So, too, with faces and places. Imagine viewing more than 2500 slides of faces and places for 10 seconds each. Later, you see 280 of these slides, paired with others you've never seen. Actual participants in this experiment recognized 90 percent of the slides they had viewed in the first round (Haber, 1970). In a follow-up experiment, people exposed to 2800 images for only 3 seconds each spotted the repeats with 82 percent accuracy (Konkle et al., 2010). Some "super-recognizers" display an extraordinary ability to recognize faces. Eighteen months after viewing a video of an armed robbery, one such police officer spotted and arrested the robber walking on a busy street (Davis et al., 2013).

And it's not just humans who have shown remarkable memory for faces (**FIGURE 22.1**).

How do we accomplish such memory feats? How does our brain pluck information from the world around us and tuck that information away for later use? How can we remember things we have not thought about for years, yet forget the name of someone we met a minute ago? How are memories stored in our brain? Why will you be likely, later in this module, to misrecall this sentence: *"The angry rioter threw the rock at the window"*? Here and in the other Memory modules, we'll consider these fascinating questions and more, including tips on how we can improve our own memories.

The New Yorker Collection, 1987. From cartoonbank.com

MR. TOTAL RECALL

⌄ FIGURE 22.1

Other animals also display face smarts After repeatedly experiencing food rewards associated with some sheep faces, but not with others, sheep remember those faces for two years (Kendrick & Feng, 2011).

Reprinted by permission by Macmillan Publishers Ltd: Nature, "Sheep Don't Forget a Face," Keith M. Kendrick, Ana P. da Costa, Andrea E. Leigh, Michael R. Hinton & Jon W. Pierce Vol. 414, November, 2001, p. 165.

Measuring Retention

To a psychologist, evidence that learning persists includes these three *measures of retention:*

- **recall**—*retrieving* information that is not currently in your conscious awareness but that was learned at an earlier time. A fill-in-the-blank question tests your recall.

- **recognition**—*identifying* items previously learned. A multiple-choice question tests your recognition.

- **relearning**—*learning something more quickly* when you learn it a second or later time. When you study for a final exam or engage a language used in early childhood, you will relearn the material more easily than you did initially.

Long after you cannot recall most of the people in your high school graduating class, you may still be able to recognize their yearbook pictures from a photographic lineup and pick their names from a list. In one experiment, people who had graduated 25 years earlier could not recall many of their old classmates. But they could *recognize* 90 percent of their pictures and names (Bahrick et al., 1975). If you are like most students, you, too, could probably recognize more names of Snow White's seven dwarfs than you could recall (Miserandino, 1991).

memory the persistence of learning over time through the encoding, storage, and retrieval of information.

recall a measure of memory in which the person must retrieve information learned earlier, as on a fill-in-the-blank test.

recognition a measure of memory in which the person identifies items previously learned, as on a multiple-choice test.

relearning a measure of memory that assesses the amount of time saved when learning material again.

National News/ZUMAPRESS.com/Newscom

Remembering things past Even if Taylor Swift and Leonardo DiCaprio had not become famous, their high school classmates would most likely still recognize them in these photos.

Our recognition memory is impressively quick and vast. "Is your friend wearing a new or old outfit?" "Old." "Is this five-second movie clip from a film you've ever seen?" "Yes." "Have you ever seen this person before?" "No." Before the mouth can form our answer to any of millions of such questions, the mind knows, and knows that it knows.

Our response speed when recalling or recognizing information indicates memory strength, as does our speed at *relearning.* Pioneering memory researcher Hermann Ebbinghaus (1850–1909) showed this over a century ago, using nonsense syllables. He randomly selected a sample of syllables, practiced them, and tested himself. To get a feel for his experiments, rapidly read aloud, eight times over, the following list (from Baddeley, 1982), then look away and try to recall the items:

JIH, BAZ, FUB, YOX, SUJ, XIR, DAX, LEQ, VUM, PID, KEL, WAV, TUV, ZOF, GEK, HIW.

The day after learning such a list, Ebbinghaus could recall few of the syllables. But they weren't entirely forgotten. As **FIGURE 22.2** portrays, the more frequently he repeated the list aloud on Day 1, the less time he required to *relearn* the list on Day 2. Additional rehearsal *(overlearning)* of verbal information increases retention, especially when practice is distributed over time. For students, this means that it helps to rehearse course material even after you know it.

The point to remember: Tests of recognition and of time spent relearning demonstrate that we *remember more than we can recall.*

▼ FIGURE 22.2

Ebbinghaus' retention curve Ebbinghaus found that the more times he practiced a list of nonsense syllables on Day 1, the less time he required to relearn it on Day 2. Speed of relearning is one measure of memory retention. (Data from Baddeley, 1982.)

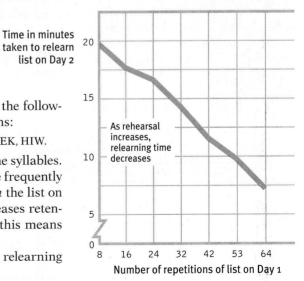

encoding the processing of information into the memory system—for example, by extracting meaning.

storage the process of retaining encoded information over time.

retrieval the process of getting information out of memory storage.

parallel processing the processing of many aspects of a problem simultaneously; the brain's natural mode of information processing for many functions.

sensory memory the immediate, very brief recording of sensory information in the memory system.

short-term memory activated memory that holds a few items briefly, such as the seven digits of a phone number while calling, before the information is stored or forgotten.

long-term memory the relatively permanent and limitless storehouse of the memory system. Includes knowledge, skills, and experiences.

RETRIEVE IT [✱]

• Multiple-choice questions test our _____. Fill-in-the-blank questions test our
_____.

ANSWERS: recognition; recall

• If you want to be sure to remember what you're learning for an upcoming test, would it be better to use *recall* or *recognition* to check your memory? Why?

ANSWER: It would be better to test your memory with *recall* (such as with short-answer or fill-in-the-blank self-test questions) rather than *recognition* (such as with multiple-choice questions). Recalling information is harder than recognizing it. So if you can recall it, that means your retention of the material is better than if you could only recognize it. Your chances of test success are therefore greater.

Memory Models

👁 **22-2** How do psychologists describe the human memory system?

Architects make miniature house models to help clients imagine their future homes. Similarly, psychologists create memory models to help us think about how our brain forms and retrieves memories. An *information-processing model* likens human memory to computer operations. Thus, to remember any event, we must

• *get information into our brain,* a process called **encoding.**

• *retain that information,* a process called **storage.**

• later *get the information back out,* a process called **retrieval.**

Like all analogies, computer models have their limits. Our memories are less literal and more fragile than a computer's. Moreover, most computers process information sequentially, even while alternating between tasks. Our agile brain processes many things simultaneously (some of them unconsciously) by means of **parallel processing.**

To focus on multitrack processing, one information-processing model, *connectionism,* views memories as products of interconnected neural networks. Specific memories arise from particular activation patterns within these networks. Every time you learn something new, your brain's neural connections change, forming and strengthening pathways that allow you to interact with and learn from your constantly changing environment.

To explain our memory-forming process, Richard Atkinson and Richard Shiffrin (1968) earlier proposed another model, with three stages:

1. We first record to-be-remembered information as a fleeting **sensory memory.**

2. From there, we process information into **short-term memory,** where we encode it through *rehearsal.*

3. Finally, information moves into **long-term memory** for later retrieval.

Other psychologists have updated this model (**FIGURE 22.3**) with important newer concepts, including *working memory* and *automatic processing.*

❤ **FIGURE 22.3**

A modified three-stage processing model of memory Atkinson and Shiffrin's classic three-step model helps us to think about how memories are processed, but today's researchers recognize other ways long-term memories form. For example, some information slips into long-term memory via a "back door," without our consciously attending to it *(automatic processing)*. And so much active processing occurs in the short-term memory stage that many now prefer the term *working memory*.

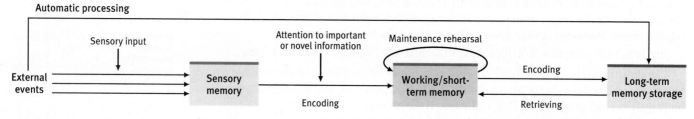

WORKING MEMORY Alan Baddeley and others (Baddeley, 2001, 2002; Barrouillet et al., 2011; Engle, 2002) extended Atkinson and Shiffrin's view of short-term memory as a small, brief storage space for recent thoughts and experiences. This stage is not just a temporary shelf for holding incoming information. It's an active

desktop where your brain processes information by making sense of new input and linking it with long-term memories. It also works in the opposite direction, by actively processing already stored information. Whether we hear *eye-screem* as "ice cream" or "I scream" will depend on how the context and our experience guide our interpreting and encoding the sounds. To emphasize the active processing that takes place in this middle stage, psychologists use the term **working memory.** Right now, you are using your working memory to link the information you're reading with your previously stored information (Cowan, 2010; Kail & Hall, 2001).

For most of you, what you are reading enters working memory through vision. You might also repeat the information using auditory rehearsal. As you integrate these memory inputs with your existing long-term memory, your attention is focused. In Baddeley's (2002) model, a *central executive* handles this focused processing (**FIGURE 22.4**).

Without focused attention, information often fades. If you think you can look something up later, you attend to it less and forget it more quickly. In one experiment, people read and typed new bits of trivia they would later need, such as "An ostrich's eye is bigger than its brain." If they knew the information would be available online, they invested less energy and remembered it less well (Sparrow et al., 2011; Wegner & Ward, 2013). Sometimes Google replaces rehearsal.

⌃ FIGURE 22.4

Working memory Alan Baddeley's (2002) model of working memory, simplified here, includes *visual* and *auditory rehearsal* of new information. A hypothetical *central executive* (manager) focuses attention and pulls information from long-term memory to help make sense of new information.

RETRIEVE IT [✻]

• How does the *working memory* concept update the classic Atkinson-Shiffrin three-stage information-processing model?

ANSWER: The newer idea of a *working memory* emphasizes the active processing that we now know takes place in Atkinson-Shiffrin's short-term memory stage. While the Atkinson-Shiffrin model viewed short-term memory as a temporary holding space, *working memory* plays a key role in processing new information and connecting it to previously stored information.

• What are two basic functions of *working memory*?

ANSWER: (1) Active processing of incoming visual-spatial and auditory information, and (2) focusing our spotlight of attention.

Encoding Memories

Dual-Track Memory: Effortful Versus Automatic Processing

◐ **22-3** How do explicit and implicit memories differ?

Atkinson and Shiffrin's model focused on how we process our **explicit memories**—the facts and experiences we can consciously know and declare (thus, also called *declarative memories*). We encode explicit memories through conscious **effortful processing.** But behind the scenes, other information skips the conscious encoding track and barges directly into storage. This **automatic processing,** which happens without our awareness, produces **implicit memories** (also called *nondeclarative memories*).

Automatic Processing and Implicit Memories

◐ **22-4** What information do we process automatically?

Our implicit memories include *procedural* memory for automatic skills (such as how to ride a bike) and classically conditioned *associations* among stimuli. If attacked by a dog in childhood, years later you may, without recalling the conditioned association, automatically tense up as a dog approaches.

working memory a newer understanding of short-term memory that adds conscious, active processing of incoming auditory and visual-spatial information, and of information retrieved from long-term memory.

explicit memory memory of facts and experiences that one can consciously know and "declare." (Also called *declarative memory.*)

effortful processing encoding that requires attention and conscious effort.

automatic processing unconscious encoding of incidental information, such as space, time, and frequency, and of well-learned information, such as word meanings.

implicit memory retention of learned skills or classically conditioned associations independent of conscious recollection. (Also called *nondeclarative memory.*)

🅐 **LaunchPad** For a 14-minute explanation and demonstration of our memory systems, visit LaunchPad's *Video: Models of Memory.*

iconic memory a momentary sensory memory of visual stimuli; a photographic or picture-image memory lasting no more than a few tenths of a second.

echoic memory a momentary sensory memory of auditory stimuli; if attention is elsewhere, sounds and words can still be recalled within 3 or 4 seconds.

chunking organizing items into familiar, manageable units; often occurs automatically.

Without conscious effort you also automatically process information about

- *space.* While studying, you often encode the place on a page where certain material appears; later, when you want to retrieve the information, you may visualize its location on the page.

- *time.* While going about your day, you unintentionally note the sequence of its events. Later, realizing you've left your coat somewhere, the event sequence your brain automatically encoded will enable you to retrace your steps.

- *frequency.* You effortlessly keep track of how many times things happen, as when you realize, *This is the third time I've run into her today.*

Our two-track mind engages in impressively efficient information processing. As one track automatically tucks away routine details, the other track is free to focus on conscious, effortful processing. Mental feats such as vision, thinking, and memory may seem to be single abilities, but they are not. Rather, we split information into different components for separate and simultaneous processing.

Effortful Processing and Explicit Memories

Automatic processing happens effortlessly. When you see words in your native language, perhaps on the side of a delivery truck, you can't help but read them and register their meaning. *Learning* to read wasn't automatic. You may recall working hard to pick out letters and connect them to certain sounds. But with experience and practice, your reading became automatic. Imagine now learning to read sentences in reverse:

.citamotua emoceb nac gnissecorp luftroffE

At first, this requires effort, but after enough practice, you would also perform this task much more automatically. We develop many skills in this way: driving, texting, and speaking a new language.

SENSORY MEMORY

22-5 How does sensory memory work?

Sensory memory (recall Figure 22.3) feeds our active working memory, recording momentary images of scenes or echoes of sounds. How much of this page could you sense and recall with less exposure than a lightning flash? In one experiment, people viewed three rows of three letters each, for only one-twentieth of a second (**FIGURE 22.5**). After the nine letters disappeared, they could recall only about half of them.

Was it because they had insufficient time to glimpse them? *No.* The researcher, George Sperling, cleverly demonstrated that people actually *could* see and recall all the letters, but only momentarily. Rather than ask them to recall all nine letters at once, he sounded a high, medium, or low tone immediately *after* flashing the nine letters. This tone directed participants to report only the letters of the top, middle, or bottom row, respectively. Now they rarely missed a letter, showing that all nine letters were momentarily available for recall.

Sperling's experiment demonstrated **iconic memory,** a fleeting sensory memory of visual stimuli. For a few tenths of a second, our eyes register a photographic (picture-image) memory of a scene, and we can recall any part of it in amazing detail. But if Sperling delayed the tone signal by more than half a second, the image faded and participants again recalled only about half the letters. Our visual screen clears quickly, as new images replace old ones.

We also have an impeccable, though fleeting, memory for auditory stimuli, called **echoic memory** (Cowan, 1988; Lu et al., 1992). Picture yourself becoming distracted by a text message while in conversation with a friend. If your mildly irked companion tests you by asking, "What did I just say?" you can recover the last few words from your mind's echo chamber. Auditory echoes tend to linger for 3 or 4 seconds.

❯ FIGURE 22.5

Total recall—briefly When George Sperling (1960) flashed a group of letters similar to this for one-twentieth of a second, people could recall only about half the letters. But when signaled to recall a particular row immediately after the letters had disappeared, they could do so with near-perfect accuracy.

K	Z	R
Q	B	T
S	G	N

SHORT-TERM MEMORY CAPACITY

 22-6 What is our short-term memory capacity?

Recall that short-term memory refers to what we can briefly retain, and that the related idea of working memory also includes our active processing, as our brains make sense of incoming information and link it with stored memories. What are the limits of what we can hold in this middle stage?

George Miller (1956) proposed that we can store about seven pieces of information (give or take two) in short-term memory. Miller's magical number seven is psychology's contribution to the list of magical sevens—the seven wonders of the world, the seven seas, the seven deadly sins, the seven primary colors, the seven musical scale notes, the seven days of the week—seven magical sevens. Other researchers have confirmed that we can, if nothing distracts us, recall about seven digits, or about six letters or five words (Baddeley et al., 1975). How quickly do our short-term memories disappear? To find out, Lloyd Peterson and Margaret Peterson (1959) asked people to remember three-consonant groups, such as *CHJ*. To prevent rehearsal, the researchers asked them, for example, to start at 100 and count aloud backward by threes. After 3 seconds, people recalled the letters only about half the time; after 12 seconds, they seldom recalled them at all (**FIGURE 22.6**). Without the active processing that we now understand to be a part of our working memory, short-term memories have a limited life.

Working-memory capacity varies, depending on age and other factors. Compared with children and older adults, young adults have more working-memory capacity, so they can use their mental workspace more efficiently. This means their ability to multitask is relatively greater. But whatever our age, we do better and more efficient work when focused, without distractions, on one task at a time. *The bottom line:* It's probably a bad idea to try to watch TV, text your friends, and write a psychology paper all at the same time (Willingham, 2010)! Those with a large working memory capacity—whose minds can juggle multiple items while processing information—tend also to retain more information after sleep and to be creative problem solvers (De Dreu et al., 2012; Fenn & Hambrick, 2012; Wiley & Jarosz, 2012).

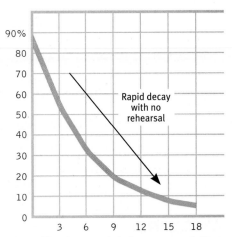

Percentage who recalled consonants

Time in seconds between presentation of consonants and recall request (no rehearsal allowed)

Rapid decay with no rehearsal

⌃ FIGURE 22.6

Short-term memory decay Unless rehearsed, verbal information may be quickly forgotten. (Data from Peterson & Peterson, 1959; see also Brown, 1958.)

After Miller's 2012 death, his daughter recalled his best moment of golf: "He made the one and only hole-in-one of his life at the age of 77, on the seventh green . . . with a seven iron. He loved that" (quoted by Vitello, 2012).

LaunchPad For a review of memory stages and a test of your own short-term memory capacity, visit LaunchPad's *PsychSim 6: Short-Term Memory*.

RETRIEVE IT [✖]

• What is the difference between *automatic* and *effortful* processing, and what are some examples of each?

ANSWER: *Automatic* processing occurs unconsciously (automatically) for such things as the sequence and frequency of a day's events, and reading and comprehending words in our native language(s). *Effortful* processing requires attention and awareness and happens, for example, when we work hard to learn new material in class, or new lines for a play.

• At which of Atkinson-Shiffrin's three memory stages would *iconic* and *echoic* memory occur?

ANSWER: sensory memory

EFFORTFUL PROCESSING STRATEGIES

 22-7 What are some effortful processing strategies that can help us remember new information?

Several effortful processing strategies can boost our ability to form new memories. Later, when we try to retrieve a memory, these strategies can make the difference between success and failure.

CHUNKING Glance for a few seconds at the first set of letters in **FIGURE 22.7** on the next page, then look away and try to reproduce what you saw. Impossible, yes? But you can easily reproduce set 2, which is no less complex. Similarly, you will probably remember sets 4 and 6 more easily than the same elements in sets 3 and 5. As this demonstrates, **chunking** information—organizing items into familiar, manageable units—enables us to recall it more easily. Try remembering 43 individual

1. ꟽ ꓯ ꙅ ꓤ ꟽ ꓕ
2. W G V S R M T

3. VRESLI UEGBN GSORNW CDOUL LWLE NTOD WTO
4. SILVER BEGUN WRONGS CLOUD WELL DONT TWO

5. SILVER BEGUN WRONGS CLOUD DONT TWO
   HALF MAKE WELL HAS A
   EVERY IS RIGHT A DONE LINING

6. WELL BEGUN IS HALF DONE
   EVERY CLOUD HAS A SILVER LINING
   TWO WRONGS DONT MAKE A RIGHT

∧ FIGURE 22.7

Effects of chunking on memory When Doug Hintzman (1978) showed people information similar to this, they recalled it more easily when it was organized into meaningful units, such as letters, words, and phrases.

> FIGURE 22.8

An example of chunking—for those who read Chinese After looking at these characters, can you reproduce them exactly? If so, you are literate in Chinese.

mnemonics [nih-MON-iks] memory aids, especially those techniques that use vivid imagery and organizational devices.

spacing effect the tendency for distributed study or practice to yield better long-term retention than is achieved through massed study or practice.

testing effect enhanced memory after retrieving, rather than simply rereading, information. Also sometimes referred to as a *retrieval practice effect* or *test-enhanced learning*.

shallow processing encoding on a basic level based on the structure or appearance of words.

deep processing encoding semantically, based on the meaning of the words; tends to yield the best retention.

numbers and letters. It would be impossible, unless chunked into, say, seven meaningful chunks, such as "Try remembering 43 individual numbers and letters." ☺

Chunking usually occurs so naturally that we take it for granted. If you are a native English speaker, you can reproduce perfectly the 150 or so line segments that make up the words in the three phrases of set 6 in Figure 22.7. It would astonish someone unfamiliar with the language. I am similarly awed by a Chinese reader's ability to glance at **FIGURE 22.8** and reproduce all the strokes, or a varsity basketball player's recall of players' positions after a 4-second glance at a basketball play (Allard & Burnett, 1985). We all remember information best when we can organize it into personally meaningful arrangements.

MNEMONICS To help them encode lengthy passages and speeches, ancient Greek scholars and orators developed **mnemonics.** Many of these memory aids use vivid imagery, because we are particularly good at remembering mental pictures. We more easily remember concrete, visualizable words than we do abstract words. (When we quiz you later, which three of these words—*bicycle, void, cigarette, inherent, fire, process*—will you most likely recall?) If you still recall the rock-throwing rioter sentence, it is probably not only because of the meaning you encoded but also because the sentence painted a mental image.

The *peg-word system* harnesses our superior visual-imagery skill. This mnemonic requires you to memorize a jingle: *"One is a bun; two is a shoe; three is a tree; four is a door; five is a hive; six is sticks; seven is heaven; eight is a gate; nine is swine; ten is a hen."* Without much effort, you will soon be able to count by peg words instead of numbers—*bun, shoe, tree*—and then to visually associate the peg words with to-be-remembered items. Now you are ready to challenge anyone to give you a grocery list to remember. Carrots? Stick them into the imaginary bun. Milk? Fill the shoe with it. Paper towels? Drape them over the tree branch. Think *bun, shoe, tree* and you see their associated images: carrots, milk, paper towels. With few errors, you will be able to recall the items in any order and to name any given item (Bugelski et al., 1968). Memory whizzes understand the power of such systems. A study of star performers in the World Memory Championships showed them not to have exceptional intelligence, but rather to be superior at using mnemonic strategies (Maguire et al., 2003).

When combined, chunking and mnemonic techniques can be great memory aids for unfamiliar material. Want to remember the colors of the rainbow in order of wavelength? Think of the mnemonic ROY G. BIV (*r*ed, *o*range, *y*ellow, *g*reen, *b*lue, *i*ndigo, *v*iolet). Need to recall the names of North America's five Great Lakes? Just remember HOMES (*H*uron, *O*ntario, *M*ichigan, *E*rie, *S*uperior). In each case, we chunk information into a more familiar form by creating a word (called an *acronym*) from the first letters of the to-be-remembered items.

HIERARCHIES When people develop expertise in an area, they process information not only in chunks but also in *hierarchies* composed of a few broad concepts divided and subdivided into narrower concepts and facts. (Figure 23.4 ahead provides a hierarchy of our automatic and effortful memory processing systems.)

Organizing knowledge in hierarchies helps us retrieve information efficiently, as Gordon Bower and his colleagues (1969) demonstrated by presenting words either randomly or grouped into categories. When the words were organized into categories, recall was two to three times better. Such results show the benefits of organizing what you study—of giving special attention to the visual outlines at the beginning of each group of modules, module headings, numbered Learning Objective Questions, and Retrieve It and Testing Effect questions. Taking lecture and textbook notes in outline format—a type of hierarchical organization—may also prove helpful.

DISTRIBUTED PRACTICE We retain information better when our encoding is distributed over time. More than 300 experiments over the past century have consistently revealed the benefits of this **spacing effect** (Cepeda et al., 2006). *Massed practice* (cramming) can produce speedy short-term learning and a feeling of confidence. But to paraphrase memory researcher Hermann Ebbinghaus (1885/1964), those who learn quickly also forget quickly. *Distributed practice* produces better long-term recall. After you've studied long enough to master the material, further study at that time becomes inefficient. Better to spend that extra reviewing time later—a day later if you need to remember something 10 days hence, or a month later if you need to remember something 6 months hence (Cepeda et al., 2008). The spacing effect is one of psychology's most reliable findings, and it extends to motor skills and online game performance, too (Stafford & Dewar, 2014). Memory researcher Henry Roediger (2013) sums it up: "Hundreds of studies have shown that distributed practice leads to more durable learning."

One effective way to distribute practice is *repeated* self-testing, a phenomenon that Roediger and Jeffrey Karpicke (2006) have called the **testing effect.** Testing does more than assess learning: It improves it (Brown et al., 2014). In this text, for example, the Retrieve It and Testing Effect questions offer such an opportunity. Better to practice retrieval (as any exam will demand) than merely to reread material (which may lull you into a false sense of mastery). Roediger (2013) explains, "Two techniques that students frequently report using for studying—highlighting (or underlining) text and rereading text—[have been found] ineffective." Happily, "retrieval practice (or testing) is [a] powerful and general strategy for learning." As another memory expert explained, "What we recall becomes more recallable" (Bjork, 2011). No wonder daily online quizzing improves introductory psychology students' course performance (Pennebaker et al., 2013).

The point to remember: Spaced study and self-assessment beat cramming and rereading. Practice may not make perfect, but smart practice—occasional rehearsal with self-testing—makes for lasting memories.

"The mind is slow in unlearning what it has been long in learning."

Roman philosopher Seneca (4 B.C.E.–65 C.E.)

LEVELS OF PROCESSING

22-8 What are the levels of processing, and how do they affect encoding?

Memory researchers have discovered that we process verbal information at different levels, and that depth of processing affects our long-term retention. **Shallow processing** encodes on an elementary level, such as a word's letters or, at a more intermediate level, a word's sound. **Deep processing** encodes *semantically*, based on the meaning of the words. The deeper (more meaningful) the processing, the better our retention.

In one classic experiment, researchers Fergus Craik and Endel Tulving (1975) flashed words at viewers. Then they asked questions that would elicit different levels of processing. To experience the task yourself, rapidly answer the following sample questions:

Making things memorable

For suggestions on how to apply the testing effect to your own learning, watch this 5-minute animation: tinyurl.com/HowToRemember.

Sample Questions to Elicit Different Levels of Processing	Word Flashed	Yes	No
Most shallow: Is the word in capital letters?	CHAIR	_____	_____
Shallow: Does the word rhyme with train?	brain	_____	_____
Deep: Would the word fit in this sentence? The girl put the _____ on the table.	doll	_____	_____

Which type of processing would best prepare you to recognize the words at a later time? In Craik and Tulving's experiment, the deeper, *semantic* processing triggered by the third question yielded a much better memory than did the shallower processing elicited by the second question or the very shallow processing elicited by the first question (which was especially ineffective).

MAKING MATERIAL PERSONALLY MEANINGFUL If new information is not meaningful or related to our experience, we have trouble processing it. Put yourself in the place of the students who were asked to remember the following recorded passage:

> The procedure is actually quite simple. First you arrange things into different groups. Of course, one pile may be sufficient depending on how much there is to do. . . . After the procedure is completed, one arranges the materials into different groups again. Then they can be put into their appropriate places. Eventually they will be used once more and the whole cycle will then have to be repeated. However, that is part of life.

When the students heard the paragraph you have just read, without a meaningful context, they remembered little of it (Bransford & Johnson, 1972). When told the paragraph described washing clothes (something meaningful), they remembered much more of it—as you probably could now after rereading it.

Can you repeat the sentence about the rioter that we gave you at this module's beginning ("The angry rioter threw . . .")?

Perhaps, like those in an experiment by William Brewer (1977), you recalled the sentence by the meaning you encoded when you read it (for example, "The angry rioter threw the rock *through* the window") and not as it was written ("The angry rioter threw the rock *at* the window"). Referring to such mental mismatches, some researchers have likened our minds to theater directors who, given a raw script, imagine the finished stage production (Bower & Morrow, 1990). Asked later what we heard or read, we recall not the literal text but what we encoded. Thus, studying for an exam, you may remember your lecture notes rather than the lecture itself.

We can avoid some of these mismatches by rephrasing information into meaningful terms. From his experiments on himself, Ebbinghaus estimated that, compared with learning nonsense material, learning meaningful material required one-tenth the effort. As memory researcher Wayne Wickelgren (1977, p. 346) noted, "The time you spend thinking about material you are reading and relating it to previously stored material is about the most useful thing you can do in learning any new subject matter."

Psychologist-actor team Helga Noice and Tony Noice (2006) have described how actors inject meaning into the daunting task of learning "all those lines." They do it by first coming to understand the flow of meaning: "One actor divided a half-page of dialogue into three [intentions]: 'to flatter,' 'to draw him out,' and 'to allay his fears.'" With this meaningful sequence in mind, the actor more easily remembered the lines.

We have especially good recall for information we can meaningfully relate to ourselves. Asked how well certain adjectives describe someone else, we often forget them; asked how well the adjectives describe us, we remember the words well. This tendency, called the *self-reference effect*, is especially strong in members of individualist Western cultures (Symons & Johnson, 1997; Wagar & Cohen, 2003). Information deemed "relevant to me" is processed more deeply and remains more accessible. Knowing this, you can profit from taking time to find personal meaning in what you are studying.

The point to remember: The amount remembered depends both on the time spent learning and on your making it meaningful for deep processing.

In the discussion of mnemonics, we gave you six words and told you we would quiz you about them later. How many of these words can you now recall? Of these, how many are high-imagery words? How many are low-imagery? (You can check your list against the six inverted words below.)

Bicycle, void, cigarette, inherent, fire, process

RETRIEVE IT [✖]

• Which strategies are better for long-term retention: cramming and rereading material, or spreading out learning over time and repeatedly testing yourself?

ANSWER: Although cramming and rereading may lead to short-term gains in knowledge, distributed practice and repeated self-testing will result in the greatest long-term retention.

• If you try to make the material you are learning personally meaningful, are you processing at a shallow or a deep level? Which level leads to greater retention?

ANSWER: Making material personally meaningful involves processing at a deep level, because you are processing *semantically*—based on the meaning of the words. Deep processing leads to greater retention.

22 REVIEW   Studying and Encoding Memories

◁▷ Learning Objectives

Test Yourself by taking a moment to answer each of these Learning Objective Questions (repeated here from within the module). Then turn to Appendix D, Complete Module Reviews, to check your answers. Research suggests that trying to answer these questions on your own will improve your long-term memory of the concepts (McDaniel et al., 2009).

22-1 What is *memory*, and how is it measured?

22-2 How do psychologists describe the human memory system?

22-3 How do explicit and implicit memories differ?

22-4 What information do we process automatically?

22-5 How does sensory memory work?

22-6 What is our short-term memory capacity?

22-7 What are some effortful processing strategies that can help us remember new information?

22-8 What are the levels of processing, and how do they affect encoding?

Terms and Concepts to Remember

Test yourself on these terms by trying to write down the definition in your own words before flipping back to the referenced page to check your answers.

memory, p. 282

recall, p. 283

recognition, p. 283

relearning, p. 283

encoding, p. 284

storage, p. 284

retrieval, p. 284

parallel processing, p. 284

sensory memory, p. 284

short-term memory, p. 284

long-term memory, p. 284

working memory, p. 285

explicit memory, p. 285

effortful processing, p. 285

automatic processing, p. 285

implicit memory, p. 285

iconic memory, p. 286

echoic memory, p. 286

chunking, p. 287

mnemonics [nih-MON-iks], p. 288

spacing effect, p. 289

testing effect, p. 289

shallow processing, p. 289

deep processing, p. 289

[✲] Experience the Testing Effect

Test yourself repeatedly throughout your studies. This will not only help you figure out what you know and don't know; the testing itself will help you learn and remember the information more effectively thanks to the *testing effect*.

1. A psychologist who asks you to write down as many objects as you can remember having seen a few minutes earlier is testing your _____.

2. The psychological terms for taking in information, retaining it, and later getting it back out are _____, _____, and _____.

3. The concept of working memory
   a. clarifies the idea of short-term memory by focusing on the active processing that occurs in this stage.
   b. splits short-term memory into two substages—sensory memory and working memory.
   c. splits short-term memory into two areas—working (retrievable) memory and inaccessible memory.
   d. clarifies the idea of short-term memory by focusing on space, time, and frequency.

4. Sensory memory may be visual (_____ memory) or auditory (_____ memory).

5. Our short-term memory for new information is limited to about _____ items.

6. Memory aids that use visual imagery (such as peg words) or other organizational devices (such as acronyms) are called _____.

Find answers to these questions in Appendix E, in the back of the book.

Use 🌀 LearningCurve to create your personalized study plan, which will direct you to the resources that will help you most in 🌀 LaunchPad .

MODULE 23 Storing and Retrieving Memories

Memory Storage

23-1 What is the capacity of long-term memory? Are our long-term memories processed and stored in specific locations?

In Arthur Conan Doyle's *A Study in Scarlet,* Sherlock Holmes offers a popular theory of memory capacity:

> I consider that a man's brain originally is like a little empty attic, and you have to stock it with such furniture as you choose. . . . It is a mistake to think that that little room has elastic walls and can distend to any extent. Depend upon it, there comes a time when for every addition of knowledge you forget something that you knew before.

Contrary to Holmes' "memory model," our brains are *not* like attics, which once filled can store more items only if we discard old ones. Our capacity for storing long-term memories is essentially limitless.

Retaining Information in the Brain

I [DM] marveled at my aging mother-in-law, a retired pianist and organist. At age 88, her blind eyes could no longer read music. But let her sit at a keyboard and she would flawlessly play any of hundreds of hymns, including ones she had not thought of for 20 years. Where did her brain store those thousands of sequenced notes?

For a time, some surgeons and memory researchers marveled at patients' apparently vivid memories triggered by brain stimulation during surgery. Did this prove that our whole past, not just well-practiced music, is "in there," in complete detail, just waiting to be relived? On closer analysis, the seeming flashbacks appeared to have been invented, not a vivid reliving of long-forgotten experiences (Loftus & Loftus, 1980). In a further demonstration that memories do not reside in single, specific spots, psychologist Karl Lashley (1950) trained rats to find their way out of a maze, then surgically removed pieces of their brain's cortex and retested their memory. No matter which small brain section he removed, the rats retained at least a partial memory of how to navigate the maze. Memories *are* brain-based, but the brain distributes the components of a memory across a network of locations. These specific locations include some of the circuitry involved in the original experience: Some brain cells that fire when we experience something fire again when we recall it (G. Miller, 2012b; J. F. Miller et al., 2013).

The point to remember: Despite the brain's vast storage capacity, we do not store information as libraries store their books, in single, precise locations. Instead, brain networks encode, store, and retrieve the information that forms our complex memories.

EXPLICIT MEMORY SYSTEM: THE FRONTAL LOBES AND HIPPOCAMPUS

23-2 What are the roles of the frontal lobes and hippocampus in memory processing?

Explicit, conscious memories are either **semantic** (facts and general knowledge) or **episodic** (experienced events). The network that processes and stores your explicit memories for these facts and episodes includes your frontal lobes and hippocampus. When you summon up a mental encore of a past experience, many brain regions send input to your frontal lobes for working memory processing (Fink et al., 1996; Gabrieli et al., 1996; Markowitsch, 1995). The left and right frontal lobes process different types of memories. Recalling a password and holding it in working memory, for example, would activate the left frontal lobe. Calling up a visual party scene would more likely activate the right frontal lobe.

"Our memories are flexible and superimposable, a panoramic blackboard with an endless supply of chalk and erasers."

Elizabeth Loftus and Katherine Ketcham, The Myth of Repressed Memory, 1994

Cognitive neuroscientists have found that the **hippocampus,** a temporal-lobe neural center located in the limbic system, can be likened to a "save" button for explicit memories (**FIGURE 23.1**). The hippocampus and nearby brain networks are active as people form explicit memories of names, images, and events (Squire & Wixted, 2011).

Damage to this structure therefore disrupts recall of explicit memories. Chickadees and other birds can store food in hundreds of places and return to these unmarked caches months later—but not if their hippocampus has been removed (Kamil & Cheng, 2001; Sherry & Vaccarino, 1989). With left-hippocampus damage, people have trouble remembering verbal information, but they have no trouble recalling visual designs and locations. With right-hippocampus damage, the problem is reversed (Schacter, 1996).

Subregions of the hippocampus also serve different functions. One part is active as people learn to associate names with faces (Zeineh et al., 2003). Another part is active as memory champions engage in spatial mnemonics (Maguire et al., 2003). The rear area, which processes spatial memory, grows bigger as London cabbies learn to navigate the city's complicated maze of streets (Woolett & Maguire, 2011).

Memories are not permanently stored in the hippocampus. Instead, this structure seems to act as a loading dock where the brain registers and temporarily holds the elements of a remembered or retrieved episode—its smell, feel, sound, and location. Then, like older files shifted to a basement storeroom, memories migrate for storage elsewhere. This storage process is called **memory consolidation.**

Sleep supports memory consolidation. During deep sleep, the hippocampus processes memories for later retrieval. After a training experience, the greater the hippocampus activity during sleep, the better the next day's memory will be (Peigneux et al., 2004). Researchers have watched the hippocampus and brain cortex displaying simultaneous activity rhythms during sleep, as if they were having a dialogue (Euston et al., 2007; Mehta, 2007). They suspect that the brain is replaying the day's experiences as it transfers them to the cortex for long-term storage. Cortex areas surrounding the hippocampus support the processing and storing of explicit memories (Squire & Zola-Morgan, 1991).

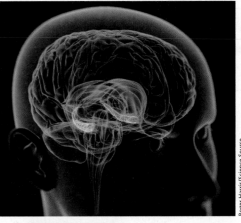

Roger Harris/Science Source

⌃ FIGURE 23.1

The hippocampus Explicit memories for facts and episodes are processed in the hippocampus (orange structures) and fed to other brain regions for storage.

Hippocampus hero
Among animals, one contender for champion memorist would be a mere birdbrain—the Clark's Nutcracker—which during winter and spring can locate up to 6000 caches of pine seed it had previously buried (Shettleworth, 1993).

Tim Zurowski/All Canada Photos/Corbis

IMPLICIT MEMORY SYSTEM: THE CEREBELLUM AND BASAL GANGLIA

◁◇▷ 23-3 What are the roles of the cerebellum and basal ganglia in memory processing?

Your hippocampus and frontal lobes are processing sites for your *explicit* memories. But you could lose those areas and still, thanks to automatic processing, lay down *implicit* memories for skills and newly conditioned associations. Joseph LeDoux (1996) recounted the story of a brain-damaged patient whose amnesia left her unable to recognize her physician as, each day, he shook her hand and introduced himself. One day, she yanked her hand back, for the physician had pricked her with a tack in his palm. The next time he returned to introduce himself she refused to shake his hand but couldn't explain why. Having been classically conditioned, she just wouldn't do it. Intuitively (implicitly) she felt what she could not explain.

The *cerebellum* plays a key role in forming and storing the implicit memories created by classical conditioning. With a damaged cerebellum, people cannot develop certain conditioned reflexes, such as associating a tone with an impending puff of air—and thus do not blink in anticipation of the puff (Daum & Schugens, 1996; Green & Woodruff-Pak, 2000). Implicit memory formation needs the cerebellum.

semantic memory explicit memory of facts and general knowledge; one of our two conscious memory systems (the other is *episodic memory*).

episodic memory explicit memory of personally experienced events; one of our two conscious memory systems (the other is *semantic memory*).

hippocampus a neural center located in the limbic system; helps process explicit memories for storage.

memory consolidation the neural storage of a long-term memory.

off the mark.com   by Mark Parisi

THE BAD NEWS IS WE LEFT A CLAMP IN YOUR TEMPORAL LOBE... THE GOOD NEWS IS THAT YOU WON'T REMEMBER WHAT I JUST SAID...

The *basal ganglia*, deep brain structures involved in motor movement, facilitate formation of our procedural memories for skills (Mishkin, 1982; Mishkin et al., 1997). The basal ganglia receive input from the cortex but do not return the favor of sending information back to the cortex for conscious awareness of procedural learning. If you have learned how to ride a bike, thank your basal ganglia.

Our implicit memory system, enabled partly by these more ancient brain areas, helps explain why the reactions and skills we learned during infancy reach far into our future. Yet as adults, our *conscious* memory of our first three years is blank, an experience called *infantile amnesia*. In one study, events children experienced and discussed with their mothers at age 3 were 60 percent remembered at age 7 but only 34 percent remembered at age 9 (Bauer et al., 2007). Two influences contribute to infantile amnesia: First, we index much of our explicit memory using words that nonspeaking children have not learned. Second, the hippocampus is one of the last brain structures to mature, and as it does, more gets retained (Akers et al., 2014).

RETRIEVE IT   [✱]

• Which parts of the brain are important for *implicit* memory processing, and which parts play a key role in *explicit* memory processing?

ANSWER: The cerebellum and basal ganglia are important for *implicit* memory processing, and the frontal lobes and hippocampus are key to *explicit* memory formation.

• Your friend has experienced brain damage in an accident. He can remember how to tie his shoes but has a hard time remembering anything you tell him during a conversation. What's going on here?

ANSWER: Our *explicit* conscious memories of facts and episodes differ from our *implicit* memories of skills (such as shoe tying) and classically conditioned responses. The parts of the brain involved in explicit memory processing (the frontal lobes and hippocampus) may have sustained damage in the accident, while the parts involved in implicit memory processing (the cerebellum and basal ganglia) appear to have escaped unharmed.

THE AMYGDALA, EMOTIONS, AND MEMORY

◉ **23-4** How do emotions affect our memory processing?

Our emotions trigger stress hormones that influence memory formation. When we are excited or stressed, these hormones make more glucose energy available to fuel brain activity, signaling the brain that something important has happened. Moreover, stress hormones focus memory. Stress provokes the *amygdala* (two limbic system, emotion-processing clusters) to initiate a memory trace that boosts activity in the brain's memory-forming areas (Buchanan, 2007; Kensinger, 2007) (**FIGURE 23.2**). It's as if the amygdala says, "Brain, encode this moment for future reference!" The result? Emotional arousal can sear certain events into the brain, while disrupting memory for irrelevant events that occur around the same time (Birnbaum et al., 2004; Brewin et al., 2007).

Significantly stressful events can form almost indelible memories. After traumatic experiences—a school shooting, a house fire, a rape—vivid recollections of the horrific event may intrude again and again. It is as if they were burned in: "Stronger emotional experiences make for stronger, more reliable memories," noted James McGaugh (1994, 2003). Such experiences even strengthen recall for relevant, immediately preceding events (Dunsmoor et al., 2015). This makes adaptive sense: If we can remember what happened right before, we may recognize potential dangers. Emotional events produce tunnel vision memory. They focus our attention and recall on high-priority information, and reduce our recall of irrelevant details (Mather & Sutherland, 2012). Whatever rivets our attention gets well recalled, at the expense of the surrounding context.

Emotion-triggered hormonal changes help explain why we long remember exciting or shocking events, such as our first kiss or our whereabouts when learning of a loved one's death. In a 2006 Pew survey, 95 percent of

---

⌄ FIGURE 23.2

Review key memory structures in the brain.
Frontal lobes and *hippocampus:* explicit memory formation
Cerebellum and *basal ganglia:* implicit memory formation
Amygdala: emotion-related memory formation

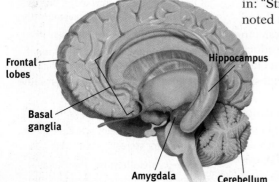

Frontal lobes

Hippocampus

Basal ganglia

Amygdala   Cerebellum

American adults said they could recall exactly where they were or what they were doing when they first heard the news of the 9/11 attacks. This perceived clarity of memories of surprising, significant events leads some psychologists to call them **flashbulb memories.** It's as if the brain commands, "Capture this!"

The people who experienced a 1989 San Francisco earthquake did just that. A year and a half later, they had perfect recall of where they had been and what they were doing (verified by their recorded thoughts within a day or two of the quake). Others' memories for the circumstances under which they merely *heard* about the quake were more prone to errors (Neisser et al., 1991; Palmer et al., 1991).

Our flashbulb memories are noteworthy for their vividness and our confidence in them. But as we relive, rehearse, and discuss them, these memories may come to err. With time, some errors crept into people's 9/11 recollections (compared with their earlier reports taken right after 9/11). Mostly, however, people's memories of 9/11 remained consistent over the next two to three years (Conway et al., 2009; Hirst et al., 2009; Kvavilashvili et al., 2009).

Dramatic experiences remain bright and clear in our memory in part because we rehearse them. We think about them and describe them to others. Memories of our best experiences, which we enjoy recalling and recounting, also endure (Storm & Jobe, 2012; Talarico & Moore, 2012). One study invited 1563 Boston Red Sox and New York Yankees fans to recall the baseball championship games between their two teams in 2003 (Yankees won) and 2004 (Red Sox won). Fans recalled much better the game their team won (Breslin & Safer, 2011).

Synaptic Changes

23-5 How do changes at the synapse level affect our memory processing?

As you read this module and think and learn about memory, your brain is changing. Given increased activity in particular pathways, neural interconnections are forming and strengthening.

The quest to understand the physical basis of memory—how information becomes embedded in brain matter—has sparked study of the synaptic meeting places where neurons communicate with one another via their neurotransmitter messengers. Eric Kandel and James Schwartz (1982) observed synaptic changes during learning in the neurons of the California sea slug, *Aplysia*, a simple animal with a mere 20,000 or so unusually large and accessible nerve cells. A sea slug can be *classically conditioned* (with electric shock) to reflexively withdraw its gills when squirted with water, much as a soldier traumatized by combat jumps at the sound of fireworks. When learning occurs, Kandel and Schwartz discovered, the slug releases more of the neurotransmitter *serotonin* into certain neurons. These synapses then become more efficient at transmitting signals. Experience and learning can increase—even double—the number of synapses, even in slugs (Kandel, 2012).

In experiments with people, rapidly stimulating certain memory-circuit connections has increased their sensitivity for hours or even weeks to come. The sending neuron now needs less prompting to release its neurotransmitter, and more connections exist between neurons. This increased efficiency of potential neural firing, called **long-term potentiation (LTP),** provides a neural basis for learning and remembering associations (Lynch, 2002; Whitlock et al., 2006) (**FIGURE 23.3** on the next page). Several lines of evidence confirm that LTP is a physical basis for memory:

- Drugs that block LTP interfere with learning (Lynch & Staubli, 1991).

- Mutant mice engineered to lack an enzyme needed for LTP couldn't learn their way out of a maze (Silva et al., 1992).

- Rats given a drug that enhanced LTP learned a maze with half the usual number of mistakes (Service, 1994).

Which is more important—your experiences or your memories of them?

flashbulb memory a clear memory of an emotionally significant moment or event.

long-term potentiation (LTP) an increase in a cell's firing potential after brief, rapid stimulation. Believed to be a neural basis for learning and memory.

Aplysia The California sea slug, which neuroscientist Eric Kandel studied for 45 years, has increased our understanding of the neural basis of learning and memory.

From N. Toni et al., Nature, 402, Nov. 25, 1999.
Dominique Muller

> FIGURE 23.3

Doubled receptor sites An electron microscope image (a) shows just one receptor site (gray) reaching toward a sending neuron before long-term potentiation. Image (b) shows that, after LTP, the receptor sites have doubled. This means the receiving neuron has increased sensitivity for detecting the presence of the neurotransmitter molecules that may be released by the sending neuron. (From Toni et al., 1999.)

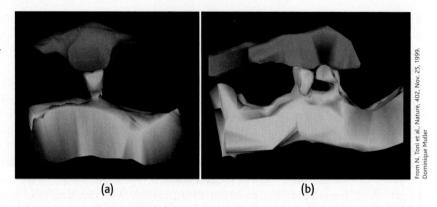

(a)   (b)

After long-term potentiation has occurred, passing an electric current through the brain won't disrupt old memories. But the current will wipe out very recent memories. Such is the experience both of laboratory animals and of severely depressed people given electroconvulsive therapy. A blow to the head can do the same. Football players and boxers momentarily knocked unconscious typically have no memory of events just before the knockout (Yarnell & Lynch, 1970). Their working memory had no time to consolidate the information into long-term memory before the lights went out.

Recently, I [DM] did a little test of memory consolidation. While on an operating table for a basketball-related tendon repair, I was given a face mask and soon could smell the anesthesia gas. "So how much longer will I be with you?" I asked the anesthesiologist. My last moment of memory was her answer: "About 10 seconds." My brain spent that 10 seconds consolidating a memory for her words, but could not tuck any further memory away before I was out cold.

Some memory-biology explorers have helped found companies that are competing to develop memory-altering drugs. The target market for memory-boosting drugs includes millions of people with memory-destroying Alzheimer's disease, millions more with *mild cognitive impairment* that often becomes Alzheimer's, and countless millions who would love to turn back the clock on age-related memory decline. Meanwhile, one safe and free memory enhancer is already available on your college campus: effective study techniques followed by adequate *sleep!*

Some of us may wish instead for memory-*blocking* drugs that, when taken after a traumatic experience, might blunt intrusive memories (Adler, 2012; Kearns et al., 2012). In one experiment, victims of car accidents, rapes, and other traumas received, for 10 days following their horrific event, either one such drug, propranolol, or a placebo. When tested three months later, half the placebo group but none of the drug-treated group showed signs of stress disorder (Pitman et al., 2002, 2005).

FIGURE 23.4 summarizes the brain's two-track memory processing and storage system for implicit (automatic) and explicit (effortful) memories. *The bottom line:* Learn something and you change your brain a little.

⌄ FIGURE 23.4

Our two memory systems

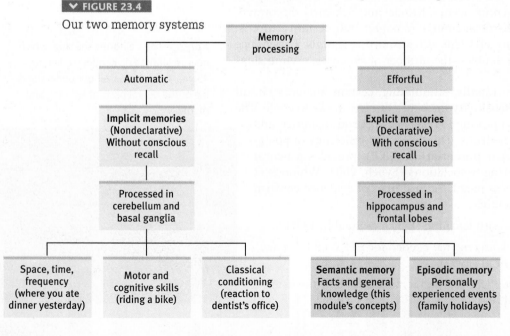

Memory processing

Automatic — Effortful

Implicit memories (Nondeclarative) Without conscious recall

Explicit memories (Declarative) With conscious recall

Processed in cerebellum and basal ganglia

Processed in hippocampus and frontal lobes

Space, time, frequency (where you ate dinner yesterday)

Motor and cognitive skills (riding a bike)

Classical conditioning (reaction to dentist's office)

Semantic memory Facts and general knowledge (this module's concepts)

Episodic memory Personally experienced events (family holidays)

RETRIEVE IT [✱]

- Which brain area responds to stress hormones by helping to create stronger memories?

ANSWER: the amygdala

- The neural basis for learning and memory, found at the synapses in the brain's memory-circuit connections, results from brief, rapid stimulation. It is called _____ -_____ _____.

ANSWER: long-term potentiation

Memory Retrieval

After the magic of brain encoding and storage, we still have the daunting task of retrieving the information. What triggers retrieval?

Retrieval Cues

23-6 How do external cues, internal emotions, and order of appearance influence memory retrieval?

Imagine a spider suspended in the middle of her web, held up by the many strands extending outward from her in all directions to different points. If you were to trace a pathway to the spider, you would first need to create a path from one of these anchor points and then follow the strand down into the web.

The process of retrieving a memory follows a similar principle, because memories are held in storage by a web of associations, each piece of information interconnected with others. When you encode into memory a target piece of information, such as the name of the person sitting next to you in class, you associate with it other bits of information about your surroundings, mood, seating position, and so on. These bits can serve as *retrieval cues* that you can later use to access the information. The more retrieval cues you have, the better your chances of finding a route to the suspended memory.

The best retrieval cues come from associations we form at the time we encode a memory—smells, tastes, and sights that can evoke our memory of the associated person or event. To call up visual cues when trying to recall something, we may mentally place ourselves in the original context. After losing his sight, British scholar John Hull (1990, p. 174) described his difficulty recalling such details:

> I knew I had been somewhere, and had done particular things with certain people, but where? I could not put the conversations . . . into a context. There was no background, no features against which to identify the place. Normally, the memories of people you have spoken to during the day are stored in frames which include the background.

PRIMING Often our associations are activated without our awareness. Philosopher-psychologist William James referred to this process, which we call **priming,** as the "wakening of associations." After seeing or hearing *rabbit*, we are later more likely to spell the spoken word "hair/hare" as *h-a-r-e*, even if we don't recall seeing or hearing *rabbit* (**FIGURE 23.5**).

"Memory is not like a container that gradually fills up; it is more like a tree growing hooks onto which memories are hung."

Peter Russell, The Brain Book, *1979*

⏯ **LaunchPad** For an 8-minute synopsis of how we access what's stored in our brain, visit LaunchPad's *Video: Memory Retrieval.*

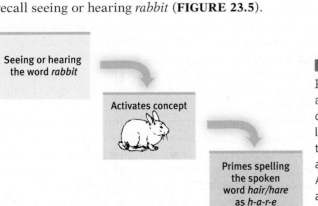

Seeing or hearing the word *rabbit*

Activates concept

Primes spelling the spoken word *hair/hare* as *h-a-r-e*

❮ FIGURE 23.5

Priming—awakening associations After seeing or hearing *rabbit*, we are later more likely to spell the spoken word "hair/hare" as *h-a-r-e* (Bower, 1986). Associations unconsciously activate related associations. This process is called priming.

priming the activation, often unconsciously, of particular associations in memory.

Priming is often "memoryless memory"—invisible memory, without your conscious awareness. If, walking down a hallway, you see a poster of a missing child, you may then unconsciously be primed to interpret an ambiguous adult-child interaction as a possible kidnapping (James, 1986). Although you no longer have the poster in mind, it predisposes your interpretation.

Priming can influence behaviors as well (Herring et al., 2013). In one study, participants primed with money-related words were less likely to help another person when asked (Vohs et al., 2006). In another, people primed with money words or images expressed more support for free-market capitalism and social inequality (Caruso et al., 2013). In such cases, money may prime our materialism and self-interest rather than the social norms that encourage us to help (Ariely, 2009).

CONTEXT-DEPENDENT MEMORY Have you noticed? Putting yourself back in the context where you experienced something, such as in a childhood home or neighborhood, can prime your memory retrieval. When scuba divers listened to a word list in two different settings (either 10 feet underwater or sitting on the beach), they recalled more words if tested in the same place (Godden & Baddeley, 1975).

By contrast, experiencing something outside the usual setting can be confusing. Have you ever run into your doctor in an unusual place, such as at the store or park? You knew the person but struggled to figure out who it was and how you were acquainted? Our memories depend on *context*, and on the cues we have associated with that context.

In several experiments, Carolyn Rovee-Collier (1993) found that a familiar context could activate memories even in 3-month-olds. After infants learned that kicking would make a crib mobile move (via a connecting ribbon from the ankle), the infants kicked more when tested again in the same crib than when in a different context.

STATE-DEPENDENT MEMORY Closely related to context-dependent memory is *state-dependent memory*. What we learn in one state—be it drunk or sober—may be more easily recalled when we are again in that state. What people learn when drunk they don't recall well in *any* state (alcohol disrupts storage). But they recall it slightly better when again drunk. Someone who hides money when drunk may forget the location until drunk again.

Our mood states provide an example of memory's state dependence. Emotions that accompany good or bad events become retrieval cues (Gaddy & Ingram, 2014). Thus, our memories are somewhat **mood congruent.** If you've had a bad evening—your date never showed, your Toledo Mud Hens hat disappeared, your TV went out 10 minutes before the end of a show—your gloomy mood may facilitate recalling other bad times. Being depressed sours memories by priming negative associations, which we then use to explain our current mood. In many experiments, people put in a buoyant mood—whether under hypnosis or just by the day's events (a World Cup soccer victory for German participants in one study)—have recalled the world through rose-colored glasses (DeSteno et al., 2000; Forgas et al., 1984; Schwarz et al., 1987). They recall their behaviors as competent and effective, other people benevolent, happy events more frequent.

Knowing this mood-memory connection, we should not be surprised that in some studies, *currently* depressed people have recalled their parents as rejecting, punitive, and guilt promoting, whereas *formerly* depressed people's recollections more closely resembled the more positive descriptions given by those who never suffered

Ask a friend two rapid-fire questions: (a) How do you pronounce the word spelled by the letters *s-h-o-p*? (b) What do you do when you come to a green light? If your friend answers "stop" to the second question, you have demonstrated priming.

"I can't remember what we're arguing about, either. Let's keep yelling, and maybe it will come back to us."

depression (Lewinsohn & Rosenbaum, 1987; Lewis, 1992). Similarly, adolescents' ratings of parental warmth in one week gave little clue to how they would rate their parents six weeks later (Bornstein et al., 1991). When teens were down, their parents seemed inhuman; as their mood brightened, their parents morphed from devils into angels. We may nod our heads knowingly. Yet, in a good or bad mood, we persist in attributing to reality our own changing judgments, memories, and interpretations. In a bad mood, we may read someone's look as a glare and feel even worse. In a good mood, we may encode the same look as interest and feel even better. Passions exaggerate.

Mood effects on retrieval help explain why our moods persist. When happy, we recall happy events and therefore see the world as a happy place, which helps prolong our good mood. When depressed, we recall sad events, which darkens our interpretations of current events. For those of us with a predisposition to depression, this process can help maintain a vicious, dark cycle. Moods magnify.

> "When a feeling was there, they felt as if it would never go; when it was gone, they felt as if it had never been; when it returned, they felt as if it had never gone."
> *George MacDonald,* What's Mine's Mine, *1886*

SERIAL POSITION EFFECT Another memory-retrieval quirk, the **serial position effect,** explains why we may have large holes in our memory of a list of recent events. Imagine it's your first day in a new job, and your manager is introducing co-workers. As you meet each person, you silently repeat everyone's name, starting from the beginning. As the last person smiles and turns away, you feel confident you'll be able to greet your new co-workers by name the next day.

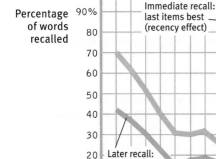
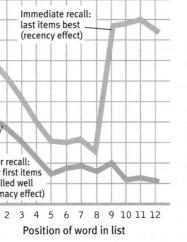

Percentage of words recalled

Immediate recall: last items best (recency effect)

Later recall: only first items recalled well (primacy effect)

Position of word in list

Vincenzo Pinto/AFP/Getty Images

❮ FIGURE 23.6

The serial position effect Immediately after Pope Francis made his way through this receiving line of special guests, he would probably have recalled the names of the last few people best (*recency effect*). But later he may have been able to recall the first few people best (*primacy effect*).

Don't count on it. Because you have spent more time rehearsing the earlier names than the later ones, those are the names you'll probably recall more easily the next day. In experiments, when people viewed a list of items (words, names, dates, even odors) and immediately tried to recall them in any order, they fell prey to the serial position effect (Reed, 2000). They briefly recalled the last items especially quickly and well (a *recency effect*), perhaps because those last items were still in working memory. But after a delay, when their attention was elsewhere, their recall was best for the first items (a *primacy effect;* see **FIGURE 23.6**).

RETRIEVE IT [✗]

• What is priming?

ANSWER: *Priming* is the activation (often without our awareness) of associations. Seeing a gun, for example, might temporarily predispose someone to interpret an ambiguous face as threatening or to recall a boss as nasty.

• When we are tested immediately after viewing a list of words, we tend to recall the first and last items best, which is known as the _____ _____ effect.

ANSWER: serial position

mood-congruent memory the tendency to recall experiences that are consistent with one's current good or bad mood.

serial position effect our tendency to recall best the last (*recency effect*) and first (*primacy effect*) items in a list.

MODULE 23 REVIEW Storing and Retrieving Memories

◯ Learning Objectives

Test Yourself by taking a moment to answer each of these Learning Objective Questions (repeated here from within the module). Then turn to Appendix D, Complete Module Reviews, to check your answers. Research suggests that trying to answer these questions on your own will improve your long-term memory of the concepts (McDaniel et al., 2009).

23-1 What is the capacity of long-term memory? Are our long-term memories processed and stored in specific locations?

23-2 What are the roles of the frontal lobes and hippocampus in memory processing?

23-3 What are the roles of the cerebellum and basal ganglia in memory processing?

23-4 How do emotions affect our memory processing?

23-5 How do changes at the synapse level affect our memory processing?

23-6 How do external cues, internal emotions, and order of appearance influence memory retrieval?

▣⋯ Terms and Concepts to Remember

Test yourself on these terms by trying to write down the definition in your own words before flipping back to the referenced page to check your answers.

semantic memory, p. 292

episodic memory, p. 292
hippocampus, p. 293
memory consolidation, p. 293
flashbulb memory, p. 295

long-term potentiation (LTP), p. 295
priming, p. 297
mood-congruent memory, p. 298
serial position effect, p. 299

[✗] Experience the Testing Effect

Test yourself repeatedly throughout your studies. This will not only help you figure out what you know and don't know; the testing itself will help you learn and remember the information more effectively thanks to the *testing effect*.

1. The hippocampus seems to function as a
   a. temporary processing site for explicit memories.
   b. temporary processing site for implicit memories.
   c. permanent storage area for emotion-based memories.
   d. permanent storage area for iconic and echoic memories.

2. Hippocampus damage typically leaves people unable to learn new facts or recall recent events. However, they may be able to learn new skills, such as riding a bicycle, which is an _____ (explicit/implicit) memory.

3. Long-term potentiation (LTP) refers to
   a. emotion-triggered hormonal changes.
   b. the role of the hippocampus in processing explicit memories.

   c. an increase in a cell's firing potential after brief, rapid stimulation.
   d. aging people's potential for learning.

4. Specific odors, visual images, emotions, or other associations that help us access a memory are examples of _____ _____.

5. When you feel sad, why might it help to look at pictures that reawaken some of your best memories?

6. When tested immediately after viewing a list of words, people tend to recall the first and last items more readily than those in the middle. When retested after a delay, they are most likely to recall
   a. the first items on the list.
   b. the first and last items on the list.
   c. a few items at random.
   d. the last items on the list.

Find answers to these questions in Appendix E, in the back of the book.

Use ◉ LearningCurve to create your personalized study plan, which will direct you to the resources that will help you most in ◉ LaunchPad.

MODULE
24 Forgetting, Memory Construction, and Improving Memory

Forgetting

24-1 Why do we forget?

"Oh, is that today?"

Amid all the applause for memory—all the efforts to understand it, all the books on how to improve it—have any voices been heard in praise of forgetting? William James (1890, p. 680) was such a voice: "If we remembered everything, we should on most occasions be as ill off as if we remembered nothing." To discard the clutter of useless or out-of-date information—where we parked the car yesterday, our old phone number, restaurant orders already cooked and served—is surely a blessing. The Russian memory whiz Solomon Shereshevskii (or S, as he was known) was haunted by his junk heap of memories. They dominated his consciousness. He had difficulty thinking abstractly—generalizing, organizing, evaluating. After reading a story, he could recite it but would struggle to summarize its gist.

A more recent *case study* of a life overtaken by memory is Jill Price, whose experience has been studied and verified by a University of California at Irvine research team, along with several dozen other "highly superior autobiographical memory" cases (McGaugh & LePort, 2014; Parker et al., 2006). Price compares her memory to "a running movie that never stops. It's like a split screen. I'll be talking to someone and seeing something else. . . . Whenever I see a date flash on the television (or anywhere for that matter) I automatically go back to that day and remember where I was, what I was doing, what day it fell on, and on and on and on and on. It is nonstop, uncontrollable, and totally exhausting." A good memory is helpful, but so is the ability to forget. If a memory-enhancing pill becomes available, it had better not be *too* effective.

More often, however, our unpredictable memory dismays and frustrates us. Memories are quirky. My [DM's] own memory can easily call up such episodes as that wonderful first kiss with the woman I love, or trivial facts like the air mileage from London to Detroit. Then it abandons me when I discover I have failed to encode, store, or retrieve a student's name, or where I left my sunglasses. See how you do with remembering this sentence when we ask you about it later: *The fish attacked the swimmer.*

"Amnesia seeps into the crevices of our brains, and amnesia heals."

Joyce Carol Oates, "Words Fail, Memory Blurs, Life Wins," 2001

The woman who can't forget
Jill Price, with writer Bart Davis, told her story in a 2008 published memoir. Price remembers every day of her life since age 14 with detailed clarity, including both the joys and the hurts. Researchers have identified enlarged brain areas in such "super memory" people (Ally et al., 2013; LePort et al., 2012).

Forgetting and the Two-Track Mind

For some, memory loss is severe and permanent. Consider Henry Molaison (1926–2008). Surgeons removed much of his hippocampus in order to stop severe seizures. This resulted "in severe disconnection of the remaining hippocampus" from the rest of the brain (Annese et al., 2014). For 55 years after the procedure, Molaison was unable to form new conscious memories. He was, as before his surgery, intelligent and did daily crossword puzzles. Yet1, reported neuroscientist Suzanne Corkin (2005, 2013), "I've known H. M. since 1962, and he still doesn't know who I am." For about 20 seconds during a conversation he could keep something in mind. When

LaunchPad See LaunchPad's *Video: Case Studies* for a helpful tutorial animation about this type of research method.

distracted, he would lose what was just said or what had just occurred. Without the neural tissue for turning new information into long-term memories, he never could name the current president of the United States (Ogden, 2012).

Molaison suffered from **anterograde amnesia**—he could recall his past, but he could not form new memories. (Those who cannot recall their past—the old information stored in long-term memory—suffer from **retrograde amnesia.**)

Neurologist Oliver Sacks (1985, pp. 26–27) described another patient, Jimmie, who had anterograde amnesia resulting from brain damage. Jimmie had no memories—thus, no sense of elapsed time—beyond his injury in 1945.

When Jimmie gave his age as 19, Sacks set a mirror before him: "Look in the mirror and tell me what you see. Is that a 19-year-old looking out from the mirror?"

Jimmie turned ashen, gripped the chair, cursed, then became frantic: "What's going on? What's happened to me? Is this a nightmare? Am I crazy? Is this a joke?" When his attention was diverted to some children playing baseball, his panic ended, the dreadful mirror forgotten.

Sacks showed Jimmie a photo from *National Geographic*. "What is this?" he asked.

"It's the Moon," Jimmie replied.

"No, it's not," Sacks answered. "It's a picture of the Earth taken from the Moon."

"Doc, you're kidding! Someone would've had to get a camera up there!"

"Naturally."

"Hell! You're joking—how the hell would you do that?" Jimmie's wonder was that of a bright young man from 40 years earlier reacting with amazement to his travel back to the future.

Careful testing of these unique people reveals something even stranger: Although incapable of recalling new facts or anything they have done recently, Molaison, Jimmie, and others with similar conditions can learn nonverbal tasks. Shown hard-to-find figures in pictures (in the *Where's Waldo?* series), they can quickly spot them again later. They can find their way to the bathroom, though without being able to tell you where it is. They can learn to read mirror-image writing or do a jigsaw puzzle, and they have even learned complicated job skills (Schacter, 1992, 1996; Xu & Corkin, 2001). They can be classically conditioned. However, *they do all these things with no awareness of having learned them*. "Well, this is strange," Molaison said, after demonstrating his nondeclarative memory of skillful mirror tracing. "I thought that would be difficult. But it seems as though I've done it quite well" (Shapin, 2013).

Molaison and Jimmie lost their ability to form new explicit memories, but their automatic processing ability remained intact. Like Alzheimer's patients, whose *explicit* memories for new people and events are lost, they could form new *implicit* memories (Lustig & Buckner, 2004). These patients can learn *how* to do something, but they will have no conscious recall of learning their new skill. Such sad cases confirm that we have two distinct memory systems, controlled by different parts of the brain.

For most of us, forgetting is a less drastic process. Let's consider some of the reasons we forget.

Encoding Failure

Much of what we sense we never notice, and what we fail to encode, we will never remember (**FIGURE 24.1**). English novelist and critic C. S. Lewis (1967, p. 107) described the enormity of what we never encode:

> [We are] bombarded every second by sensations, emotions, thoughts . . . nine-tenths of which [we] must simply ignore. The past [is] a roaring cataract of billions upon billions of such moments: Any one of them too complex to grasp in its entirety, and the aggregate beyond all imagination. . . . At every tick of the clock, in every inhabited part of the world, an unimaginable richness and variety of 'history' falls off the world into total oblivion.

"Waiter, I'd like to order, unless I've eaten, in which case bring me the check."

LaunchPad For a 6-minute example of another dramatic case—of an accomplished musician who has lost the ability to form new memories—visit LaunchPad's *Video—Clive Wearing: Living Without Memory*.

anterograde amnesia an inability to form new memories.

retrograde amnesia an inability to retrieve information from one's past.

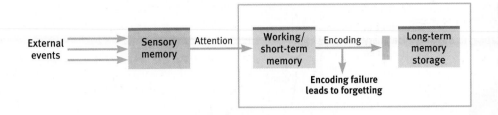

< FIGURE 24.1

Forgetting as encoding failure
We cannot remember what we have not
encoded.

Age can affect encoding efficiency. The brain areas that jump into action when young adults encode new information are less responsive in older adults. This slower encoding helps explain age-related memory decline (Grady et al., 1995).

But no matter how young we are, we selectively attend to few of the myriad sights and sounds continually bombarding us. Consider: You have surely seen the Apple computer logo thousands of times. Can you draw it? In one study, only 1 of 85 UCLA students (including 52 Apple users) could do so accurately (Blake et al., 2015). Without encoding effort, many potential memories never form.

Storage Decay

Even after encoding something well, we sometimes later forget it. To study the durability of stored memories, Ebbinghaus (1885/1964) learned more lists of nonsense syllables and measured how much he retained when relearning each list, from 20 minutes to 30 days later. The result, confirmed by later experiments, was his famous forgetting curve: *The course of forgetting is initially rapid, then levels off with time* (**FIGURE 24.2**; Wixted & Ebbesen, 1991). Harry Bahrick (1984) found a similar forgetting curve for Spanish vocabulary learned in school. Compared with those just completing a high school or college Spanish course, people 3 years out of school had forgotten much of what they had learned (**FIGURE 24.3** on the next page). However, what people remembered then, they still remembered 25 and more years later. Their forgetting had leveled off.

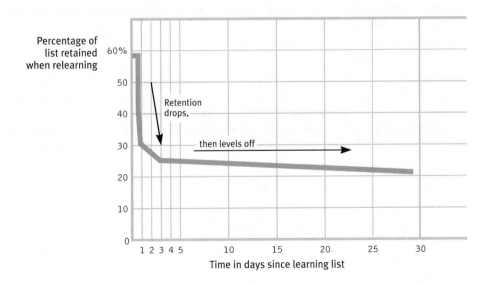

< FIGURE 24.2

Ebbinghaus' forgetting curve After learning lists of nonsense syllables, such as YOX and JIH, Ebbinghaus studied how much he retained up to 30 days later. He found that memory for novel information fades quickly, then levels out. (Data from Ebbinghaus, 1885/1964.)

One explanation for these forgetting curves is a gradual fading of the physical memory trace. Cognitive neuroscientists are getting closer to solving the mystery of the physical storage of memory and are increasing our understanding of how memory storage could decay. Like books you can't find in your campus library, memories may be inaccessible for many reasons. Some were never acquired (not encoded). Others were discarded (stored memories decay). And others are out of reach because we can't retrieve them.

> **FIGURE 24.3**

The forgetting curve for Spanish learned in school Compared with people just completing a Spanish course, those 3 years out of the course remembered much less (on a vocabulary recognition test). Compared with the 3-year group, however, those who studied Spanish even longer ago did not forget much more. (Data from Bahrick, 1984.)

Deaf persons fluent in sign language experience a parallel "tip of the fingers" phenomenon (Thompson et al., 2005).

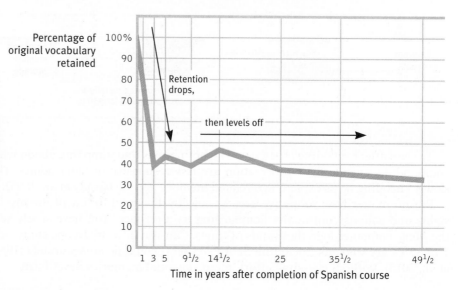

Percentage of original vocabulary retained

Retention drops, then levels off

Time in years after completion of Spanish course

Retrieval Failure

Often, forgetting is not memories faded, but memories unretrieved. We store in long-term memory what's important to us or what we've rehearsed. But sometimes important events defy our attempts to access them (**FIGURE 24.4**). How frustrating when a name lies poised on the tip of our tongue, just beyond reach. Given retrieval cues *("It begins with an M")*, we may easily retrieve the elusive memory. Retrieval problems contribute to the occasional memory failures of older adults, who more frequently are frustrated by tip-of-the-tongue forgetting (Abrams, 2008; Salthouse & Mandell, 2013).

Do you recall the gist of the second sentence we asked you to remember? If not, does the word *shark* serve as a retrieval cue? Experiments show that *shark* (likely what you visualized) more readily retrieves the image you stored than does the sentence's actual word, *fish* (Anderson et al., 1976). (The sentence was *"The fish attacked the swimmer."*)

But retrieval problems occasionally stem from interference and, perhaps, from motivated forgetting.

INTERFERENCE As you collect more and more information, your mental attic never fills, but it surely gets cluttered. Sometimes the clutter wins, and new and old learning collide. **Proactive** *(forward-acting)* **interference** occurs when prior learning disrupts your recall of new information. If you buy a new combination lock, your well-rehearsed old combination may interfere with your retrieval of the new one.

Retroactive *(backward-acting)* **interference** occurs when new learning disrupts recall of old information. If someone sings new lyrics to the tune of an old song, you may have trouble remembering the original words. It is rather like a second stone tossed in a pond, disrupting the waves rippling out from the first.

> **FIGURE 24.4**

Retrieval failure Sometimes even stored information cannot be accessed, which leads to forgetting.

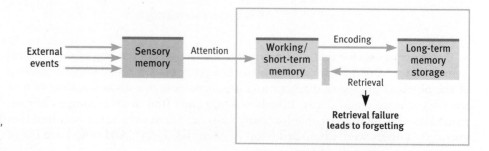

Information presented in the hour before sleep suffers less retroactive interference because the opportunity for interfering events is minimized (Diekelmann & Born, 2010; Nesca & Koulack, 1994). Researchers John Jenkins and Karl Dallenbach (1924) first discovered this in a now-classic experiment. Day after day, two people each learned some nonsense syllables, then tried to recall them after up to eight hours of being awake or asleep at night. As **FIGURE 24.5** shows, forgetting occurred more rapidly after being awake and involved with other activities. The investigators surmised that "forgetting is not so much a matter of the decay of old impressions and associations as it is a matter of interference, inhibition, or obliteration of the old by the new" (1924, p. 612).

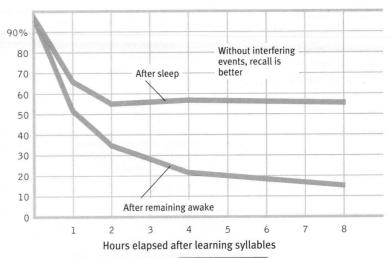

▲ FIGURE 24.5

Retroactive interference More forgetting occurred when a person stayed awake and experienced other new material. (Data from Jenkins & Dallenbach, 1924.)

The hour before sleep is a good time to commit information to memory (Scullin & McDaniel, 2010), though information presented in the *seconds* just before sleep is seldom remembered (Wyatt & Bootzin, 1994). If you're considering learning *while* sleeping, forget it. We have little memory for information played aloud in the room during sleep, although the ears do register it (Wood et al., 1992).

Old and new learning do not always compete with each other, of course. Previously learned information (Latin) often facilitates our learning of new information (French). This phenomenon is called *positive transfer.*

MOTIVATED FORGETTING To remember our past is often to revise it. Years ago, the huge cookie jar in my [DM's] kitchen was jammed with freshly baked chocolate chip cookies. Still more were cooling across racks on the counter. Twenty-four hours later, not a crumb was left. Who had taken them? During that time, my wife, three children, and I were the only people in the house. So while memories were still fresh, I conducted a little memory test. Andy admitted wolfing down as many as 20. Peter thought he had eaten 15. Laura guessed she had stuffed her then-6-year-old body with 15 cookies. My wife, Carol, recalled eating 6, and I remembered consuming 15 and taking 18 more to the office. We sheepishly accepted responsibility for 89 cookies. Still, we had not come close; there had been 160.

Why do our memories fail us? This happens in part because memory is an "unreliable, self-serving historian" (Tavris & Aronson, 2007, p. 6). Consider one study, in which researchers told some participants about the benefits of frequent toothbrushing. Those individuals then recalled (more than others did) having frequently brushed their teeth in the preceding two weeks (Ross et al., 1981).

Peter Johansky/Photolibrary/Getty Images

FIGURE 24.6 on the next page reminds us that as we process information, we filter, alter, or lose much of it. So why were my family and I so far off in our estimates of the cookies we had eaten? Was it an *encoding* problem? (Did we just not notice what we had eaten?) Was it a storage problem? (Might our memories of cookies, like Ebbinghaus' memory of nonsense syllables, have melted away almost as fast as the cookies themselves?) Or was the information still intact but not *retrievable* because it would be embarrassing to remember?[2]

LaunchPad To experience a demonstration and explanation of interference effects on memory, visit LaunchPad's *PsychSim 6: Forgetting.*

proactive interference the forward-acting disruptive effect of prior learning on the recall of new information.

retroactive interference the backward-acting disruptive effect of new learning on the recall of old information.

2. One of my cookie-scarfing sons, on reading this in his father's textbook years later, confessed he had fibbed "a little."

> FIGURE 24.6

When do we forget?
Forgetting can occur at any
memory stage. As we process
information, we filter, alter, or
lose much of it.

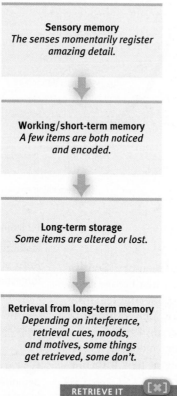

Information bits

Sensory memory
*The senses momentarily register
amazing detail.*

Working/short-term memory
*A few items are both noticed
and encoded.*

Long-term storage
Some items are altered or lost.

Retrieval from long-term memory
*Depending on interference,
retrieval cues, moods,
and motives, some things
get retrieved, some don't.*

Sigmund Freud might have argued that our memory systems self-censored this information. He proposed that we **repress** painful or unacceptable memories to protect our self-concept and to minimize anxiety. But the repressed memory lingers, he believed, and can be retrieved by some later cue or during therapy. Repression was central to Freud's psychoanalytic theory of personality and was a popular idea in mid-twentieth-century psychology and beyond. While an American study revealed that 81 percent of university students, and 60 to 90 percent of therapists (depending on their perspective), believe "traumatic memories are often repressed" (Patihis et al., 2014a,b), increasing numbers of memory researchers think repression rarely, if ever, occurs. People succeed in forgetting unwanted neutral information (yesterday's parking place), but it's harder to forget emotional events (Payne & Corrigan, 2007). Thus, we may have intrusive memories of the very same traumatic experiences we would most like to forget.

RETRIEVE IT [✖]

• What are three ways we forget, and how does each of these happen?

ANSWER: (1) *Encoding failure:* Unattended information never entered our memory system. (2) *Storage decay:* Information fades from our memory. (3) *Retrieval failure:* We cannot access stored information accurately, sometimes due to interference or motivated forgetting.

---

repression in psychoanalytic theory,
the basic defense mechanism that
banishes from consciousness anxiety-
arousing thoughts, feelings, and
memories.

reconsolidation a process in which
previously stored memories, when
retrieved, are potentially altered before
being stored again.

misinformation effect when misleading information has corrupted one's
memory of an event.

Memory Construction Errors

👁 **24-2** How do misinformation, imagination, and source amnesia influence our memory construction? How do we decide whether a memory is real or false?

Memory is not precise. Like scientists who infer a dinosaur's appearance from its remains, we infer our past from stored information plus what we later imagined, expected, saw, and heard. We don't just retrieve memories, we reweave them. Like Wikipedia pages, memories can be continuously revised. When we "replay" a memory, we often replace the original with a slightly modified version (Hardt et al., 2010). (Memory researchers call this **reconsolidation.**) So, in a sense, said Joseph LeDoux (2009), "your memory is only as good as your last memory. The fewer times you use it, the more pristine it is." This means that, to some degree, "all memory is false" (Bernstein & Loftus, 2009b).

Despite knowing all this, I [DM] recently rewrote my own past. It happened at an international conference, where memory researcher Elizabeth Loftus (2012) was demonstrating how memory works. Loftus showed us a handful of individual faces that we were later to identify, as if in a police lineup. Then, she showed us some pairs of faces, one face we had seen earlier and one we had not, and asked us to identify the one we had seen. But one pair she had slipped in included *two* new faces, one of which was rather *like* a face we had seen earlier. Most of us understandably but wrongly identified this face as one we had previously seen. To climax the demonstration, when she showed us the originally seen face and the previously chosen wrong face, most of us picked the wrong face! As a result of our memory reconsolidation, we—an audience of psychologists who should have known better—had replaced the original memory with a false memory.

This is one of those beautiful summer days when I'm flooded with memories of things that never happened to me.

David Sipress

SIPRESS

Clinical researchers have experimented with people's memory reconsolidation. They had people recall a traumatic or negative experience, then disrupt the reconsolidation of that memory with a drug or brief, painless electroconvulsive shock (Kroes et al., 2014; Lonergan, 2013). If, indeed, it becomes possible to erase your memory for a specific traumatic experience—by reactivating your memory and then disrupting its storage—would you wish for this? If brutally assaulted, would you welcome having your memory of the attack and its associated fears deleted?

Misinformation and Imagination Effects

In more than 200 experiments involving more than 20,000 people, Loftus has shown how eyewitnesses reconstruct their memories after a crime or an accident. In one experiment, two groups of people watched a film clip of a traffic accident and then answered questions about what they had seen (Loftus & Palmer, 1974). Those asked, "About how fast were the cars going when they *smashed* into each other?" gave higher speed estimates than those asked, "About how fast were the cars going when they *hit* each other?" A week later, when asked whether they recalled seeing any broken glass, people who had heard *smashed* were more than twice as likely to report seeing glass fragments (**FIGURE 24.7**). In fact, the film showed no broken glass.

In many follow-up experiments around the world, others have witnessed an event, received or not received misleading information about it, and then taken a memory test. The repeated result is a **misinformation effect:** When exposed to misleading information, despite feeling confident, we tend to misremember. A yield sign becomes a stop sign, hammers become screwdrivers, Coke cans become peanut cans, breakfast cereal becomes eggs, and a clean-shaven man morphs into a man with a mustache (Loftus et al., 1992).

So powerful is the misinformation effect that it can influence later attitudes and behaviors (Bernstein & Loftus, 2009a). One experiment falsely suggested to some Dutch university students that, as children, they became ill after eating spoiled egg salad (Geraerts et al., 2008). After absorbing that suggestion, they were less likely to eat egg-salad sandwiches, both immediately and four months later. Even repeatedly *imagining* nonexistent actions and events can create false memories. In one recent experiment, people were prompted to recall two events from their past—one a false event that involved committing a crime. Later, 70 percent reported a detailed false memory of having committed the crime (Shaw & Porter, 2015).

Digitally altered photos have also produced this *imagination inflation*. In experiments, researchers have altered photos from a family album to show some family members taking a hot-air balloon ride. After viewing these photos (rather than photos showing just the balloon), children reported more false memories and indicated high confidence in those memories. When interviewed several

✔ FIGURE 24.7

Memory construction In this experiment, people viewed a film clip of a car accident (*left*). Those who later were asked a leading question recalled a more serious accident than they had witnessed (Loftus & Palmer, 1974).

Leading question:
"About how fast were the cars going when they smashed into each other?"

Image of actual accident

Memory construction

"Memory is insubstantial. Things keep replacing it. Your batch of snapshots will both fix and ruin your memory. . . . You can't remember anything from your trip except the wretched collection of snapshots."

*Annie Dillard,
"To Fashion a Text," 1988*

False memories More than 5000 *Slate* magazine readers were asked whether they remembered various world events—three real, and one of five randomly selected false events (Frenda et al., 2013). For example, when asked if they recalled U.S. President Barack Obama's shaking hands with Iran's former president, Mahmoud Ahmadinejad, 26 percent recalled the event—despite it never having happened. (Ahmadinejad's head was put into another photo.)

days later, they reported even richer details of their false memories (Strange et al., 2008; Wade et al., 2002).

In British and Canadian university surveys, nearly one-fourth of students have reported autobiographical memories that they later realized were not accurate (Mazzoni et al., 2010). I [DM] empathize. For decades, my cherished earliest memory was of my parents getting off the bus and walking to our house, bringing my baby brother home from the hospital. When, in middle age, I shared that memory with my father, he assured me they did *not* bring their newborn home on the Seattle Transit System. The human mind, it seems, comes with built-in Photoshopping software.

© D. Hurst/Alamy

> "It isn't so astonishing, the number of things I can remember, as the number of things I can remember that aren't so."
>
> *Author Mark Twain (1835–1910)*

Source Amnesia

Among the frailest parts of a memory is its source. We may recognize someone but have no idea where we have seen the person. We may dream an event and later be unsure whether it really happened. We may misrecall how we learned about something (Henkel et al., 2000). Psychologists are not immune to this process. Famed child psychologist Jean Piaget was startled as an adult to learn that a vivid, detailed memory from his childhood—a nursemaid's thwarting his kidnapping—was utterly false. He apparently constructed the memory from repeatedly hearing the story (which his nursemaid, after undergoing a religious conversion, later confessed had never happened). In attributing his "memory" to his own experiences, rather than to his nursemaid's stories, Piaget exhibited **source amnesia** (also called *source misattribution*). Misattribution is at the heart of many false memories. Authors and songwriters sometimes suffer from it. They think an idea came from their own creative imagination, when in fact they are unintentionally plagiarizing something they earlier read or heard.

Debra Poole and Stephen Lindsay (1995, 2001, 2002) demonstrated source amnesia among preschoolers. They had the children interact with "Mr. Science," who engaged them in activities such as blowing up a balloon with baking soda and vinegar. Three months later, on three successive days, their parents read them a story describing some things the children had experienced with Mr. Science and some they had not. When a new interviewer asked what Mr. Science had done with them—"Did Mr. Science have a machine with ropes to pull?"—4 in 10 children spontaneously recalled him doing things that had happened only in the story.

Because the misinformation effect and source amnesia happen outside our awareness, it is nearly impossible to sift suggested ideas out of the larger pool of real memories (Schooler et al., 1986). Perhaps you can recall describing a childhood experience to a friend and filling in memory gaps with reasonable guesses and assumptions. We all do it, and after more retellings, those guessed details—now absorbed into our memories—may feel as real as if we had actually experienced them (Roediger et al., 1993). False memories, like fake diamonds, seem real.

Source amnesia also helps explain **déjà vu** (French for "already seen"). Two-thirds of us have experienced this fleeting, eerie sense that "I've been in this exact situation before." It happens most commonly to well-educated, imaginative young adults, especially when tired or stressed (Brown, 2003, 2004; McAneny, 1996). Some wonder, "How could I recognize a situation I'm experiencing for the first time?" Others may think of reincarnation ("I must have experienced this in a previous life") or precognition ("I viewed this scene in my mind before experiencing it").

source amnesia attributing to the wrong source an event we have experienced, heard about, read about, or imagined. (Also called *source misattribution*.) Source amnesia, along with the misinformation effect, is at the heart of many false memories.

déjà vu that eerie sense that "I've experienced this before." Cues from the current situation may unconsciously trigger retrieval of an earlier experience.

The key to déjà vu seems to be familiarity with a stimulus without a clear idea of where we encountered it before (Cleary, 2008). Normally, we experience a feeling of *familiarity* (thanks to temporal lobe processing) before we consciously remember details (thanks to hippocampus and frontal lobe processing). When these functions (and brain regions) are out of sync, we may experience a feeling of familiarity without conscious recall. Our amazing brains try to make sense of such an improbable situation, and we get an eerie feeling that we're reliving some earlier part of our life. Our source amnesia forces us to do our best to make sense of an odd moment.

Discerning True and False Memories

Because memory is reconstruction as well as reproduction, we can't be sure whether a memory is real by how real it feels. Much as perceptual illusions may seem like real perceptions, unreal memories *feel* like real memories.

False memories can be persistent. Imagine that we were to read aloud a list of words such as *candy, sugar, honey,* and *taste.* Later, we ask you to recognize the presented words from a larger list. If you are at all like the people tested by Henry Roediger and Kathleen McDermott (1995), you would err three out of four times—by falsely remembering a nonpresented similar word, such as *sweet.* We more easily remember the gist than the words themselves.

Memory construction helps explain why about 75 percent of 301 convicts exonerated by later DNA testing had been misjudged based on faulty eyewitness identification (Lilienfeld & Byron, 2013). It explains why "hypnotically refreshed" memories of crimes so easily incorporate errors, some of which originate with the hypnotist's leading questions *("Did you hear loud noises?").* It explains why dating partners who fell in love have *over*estimated their first impressions of one another *("It was love at first sight"),* while those who broke up *under*estimated their earlier liking *("We never really clicked")* (McFarland & Ross, 1987). And it explains why people asked how they felt 10 years ago about marijuana or gender issues recalled attitudes closer to their current views than to the views they had actually reported a decade earlier (Markus, 1986). People tend to recall having always felt as they feel today (Mazzoni & Vannucci, 2007). As George Vaillant (1977, p. 197) noted after following adult lives through time, "It is all too common for caterpillars to become butterflies and then to maintain that in their youth they had been little butterflies. Maturation makes liars of us all."

Children's Eyewitness Recall

◀◖▶ 24-3 How reliable are young children's eyewitness descriptions?

If memories can be sincere, yet sincerely wrong, might children's recollections of sexual abuse be prone to error? "It would be truly awful to ever lose sight of the enormity of child abuse," observed Stephen Ceci (1993). Yet Ceci and Maggie Bruck's (1993, 1995) studies of children's memories have made them aware of how easily children's memories can be molded. For example, they asked 3-year-olds to show on anatomically correct dolls where a pediatrician had touched them. Of the children who had not received genital examinations, 55 percent pointed to either genital or anal areas.

In other experiments, the researchers studied the effect of suggestive interviewing techniques (Bruck & Ceci, 1999, 2004). In one study, children chose a card from a deck of possible happenings, and an adult then read the card to them. For example, "Think real hard, and tell me if this ever happened to you. Can you remember going to the hospital with a mousetrap on your finger?" In interviews, the same adult repeatedly asked children to think about several real and fictitious events. After 10 weeks of this, a new adult asked the same

"Do you ever get that strange feeling of vujà dé? Not déjà vu; vujà dé. It's the distinct sense that, somehow, something just happened that has never happened before. Nothing seems familiar. And then suddenly the feeling is gone. Vujà dé."

Comedian George Carlin (1937–2008), in Funny Times, *December 2001*

🖥 LaunchPad To participate in a simulated experiment on false memory formation, and to review related research, visit LaunchPad's *PsychSim 6: Can You Trust Your Memory?* For a 5-minute demonstration and explanation of a false memory experiment, visit LaunchPad's *Video— Creating False Memories: A Laboratory Study.*

© Darren Matthews/Alamy

question. The stunning result: 58 percent of preschoolers produced false (often vivid) stories regarding one or more events they had never experienced (Ceci et al., 1994). Here's one:

> My brother Colin was trying to get Blowtorch [an action figure] from me, and I wouldn't let him take it from me, so he pushed me into the wood pile where the mousetrap was. And then my finger got caught in it. And then we went to the hospital, and my mommy, daddy, and Colin drove me there, to the hospital in our van, because it was far away. And the doctor put a bandage on this finger.

Given such detailed stories, professional psychologists who specialize in interviewing children could not reliably separate the real memories from the false ones. Nor could the children themselves. The above child, reminded that his parents had told him several times that the mousetrap incident never happened—that he had imagined it—protested, "But it really did happen. I remember it!" In another experiment, preschoolers merely overheard an erroneous remark that a magician's missing rabbit had gotten loose in their classroom. Later, when the children were suggestively questioned, 78 percent of them recalled actually seeing the rabbit (Principe et al., 2006). "[The] research leads me to worry about the possibility of false allegations. It is not a tribute to one's scientific integrity to walk down the middle of the road if the data are more to one side," said Ceci (1993). (See Thinking Critically About: Repressed or Constructed Memories of Abuse?)

Children can, however, be accurate eyewitnesses. When questioned about their experiences in neutral words they understood, children often accurately recalled what happened and who did it (Goodman, 2006; Howe, 1997; Pipe, 1996). And when interviewers used less suggestive, more effective techniques, even 4- to 5-year-old children produced more accurate recall (Holliday & Albon, 2004; Pipe et al., 2004). Children were especially accurate when they had not talked with involved adults prior to the interview and when their disclosure was made in a first interview with a neutral person who asked nonleading questions.

IMMERSIVE LEARNING Consider how researchers have studied these issues with LaunchPad's *How Would You Know If People's Memories Are Accurate?*

Like children (whose frontal lobes have not fully matured), older adults—especially those whose frontal lobe functioning has declined—are more susceptible than young adults to false memories. This makes older adults more vulnerable to scams, as when a repair person overcharges by falsely claiming, "I told you it would cost x, and you agreed to pay" (Jacoby et al., 2005; Jacoby & Rhodes, 2006; Roediger & Geraci, 2007; Roediger & McDaniel, 2007).

Improving Memory

◁◁ **24-5** How can you use memory research findings to do better in this and other courses?

Biology's findings benefit medicine. Botany's findings benefit agriculture. So, too, can psychology's research on memory benefit education. Here, for easy reference, is a summary of some research-based suggestions that can help you remember information when you need it. The SQ3R—Survey, Question, *Read, Retrieve, Review*—study technique used in this book incorporates several of these strategies:

Rehearse repeatedly. To master material, use distributed (spaced) practice. To learn a concept, give yourself many separate study sessions. Take advantage of life's little intervals—riding a bus, walking across campus, waiting for class to start. New memories are weak; exercise them and they will strengthen. To memorize specific facts or figures, Thomas Landauer (2001) has advised, "rehearse the name or number you are trying to memorize, wait a few seconds, rehearse again, wait a little longer, rehearse again, then wait longer still and rehearse yet again. The waits should be as long as possible without losing the information." Reading complex material with minimal rehearsal yields little retention. Rehearsal and critical reflection help more. As the testing effect has shown, it pays to study actively. Taking lecture notes in longhand, which requires summarizing material in your own words, leads to better retention than does verbatim laptop note taking. "The pen is mightier than the keyboard," note researchers Pam Mueller and Daniel Oppenheimer (2014).

Repressed or Constructed Memories of Abuse?

24-4 Why are reports of repressed and recovered memories so hotly debated?

The research on source amnesia and the misinformation effect raises concerns about therapist-guided "recovered" memories. There are two tragedies related to adult recollections of child abuse. One happens when people don't believe abuse survivors who tell their secret. The other happens when innocent people are falsely accused.

Some well-intentioned therapists have reasoned with patients that "people who've been abused often have your symptoms, so you probably were abused. Let's see if, aided by hypnosis or drugs, or helped to dig back and visualize your trauma, you can recover it." Patients exposed to such techniques may then form an image of a threatening person. With further visualization, the image grows more vivid. The patient ends up stunned, angry, and ready to confront or sue the remembered abuser. The accused person (often a parent or relative) is equally stunned and devastated, and vigorously denies the accusation.

Critics are not questioning most therapists' professionalism. Nor are they questioning the accusers' sincerity; even if false, their memories are heartfelt. Critics' charges are specifically directed against clinicians who have used "memory work" techniques, such as "guided imagery," hypnosis, and dream analysis. In his discussion of the "false memory wars" of the 1980s and 1990s, science writer Martin Gardner (2006) argued that "thousands of families were cruelly ripped apart," with "previously loving adult daughters" suddenly accusing fathers. Irate clinicians countered that those who discredit recovered memories of abuse are adding to abused people's trauma and playing into the hands of child molesters.

Is there a sensible common ground that might resolve psychology's "memory war," which exposed researcher and expert witness Elizabeth Loftus (2011) to "relentless vitriol and harassment"? Professional organizations (the American Medical, American Psychological, and American Psychiatric Associations; the Australian Psychological Society; the British Psychological Society; and the Canadian Psychiatric Association) have convened study panels and issued public statements, and greater agreement is emerging (Patihis et al., 2014a). Those committed to protecting abused children and those committed to protecting wrongly accused adults have agreed on the following:

- **Sex abuse happens.** And it happens more often than we once supposed. Although sexual abuse can leave its victims at risk for problems ranging from sexual dysfunction to depression (Freyd et al., 2007), there is no characteristic "survivor syndrome"—no group of symptoms that lets us spot victims of sexual abuse (Kendall-Tackett et al., 1993).

- **Injustice happens.** Some innocent people have been falsely convicted. And some guilty people have evaded responsibility by casting doubt on their truth-telling accusers.

- **Forgetting happens.** Many of those actually abused were either very young when abused or may not have understood the meaning of their experience—circumstances under which forgetting is common. Forgetting isolated past events, both negative and positive, is an ordinary part of everyday life.

- **Recovered memories are commonplace.** Cued by a remark or an experience, we all recover memories of long-forgotten events, both pleasant and unpleasant. What psychologists debate is twofold: Does the unconscious mind sometimes *forcibly repress* painful experiences? If so, can these experiences be retrieved by certain therapist-aided techniques? (Memories that surface naturally are more likely to be verified [Geraerts et al., 2007].)

- **Memories of events before age 3 are unreliable.** We cannot reliably recall happenings from our first three years. This *infantile amnesia* happens because our brain pathways have not yet developed enough to form the kinds of memories we will form later in life. Most psychologists—including most clinical and counseling psychologists—therefore doubt "recovered" memories of abuse during infancy (Gore-Felton et al., 2000; Knapp & VandeCreek, 2000). The older a child was when suffering sexual abuse, and the more severe the abuse, the more likely it is to be remembered (Goodman et al., 2003).

- **Memories "recovered" under hypnosis or the influence of drugs are especially unreliable.** Under hypnosis, people will incorporate all kinds of suggestions into their memories, even memories of "past lives."

- **Memories, whether real or false, can be emotionally upsetting.** Both the accuser and the accused may suffer when what was born of mere suggestion becomes, like an actual trauma, a stinging memory that drives bodily stress (McNally, 2003, 2007). Some people knocked unconscious in unremembered accidents know this all too well. They have later developed stress disorders after being haunted by memories they constructed from photos, news reports, and friends' accounts (Bryant, 2001).

So, does repression of threatening memories ever occur? Or is this concept—the cornerstone of Freud's theory and of so much popular psychology—misleading? Other modules discuss this hotly debated issue. But this much appears certain: The most common response to a traumatic experience (witnessing a loved one's murder, being terrorized by a hijacker or a rapist, losing everything in a natural disaster) is not banishment of the experience into the unconscious. Rather, such experiences are typically etched on the mind as vivid, persistent, haunting memories (Porter & Peace, 2007). As Robert Kraft (2002) said of the experience of those trapped in the Nazi death camps, "Horror sears memory, leaving . . . the consuming memories of atrocity."

"When memories are 'recovered' after long periods of amnesia, particularly when extraordinary means were used to secure the recovery of memory, there is a high probability that the memories are false."

Royal College of Psychiatrists Working Group on Reported Recovered Memories of Child Sexual Abuse (Brandon et al., 1998)

RETRIEVE IT

- Imagine being a jury member in a trial for a parent accused of sexual abuse based on a recovered memory. What insights from memory research should you offer the jury?

ANSWER: It will be important to remember the key points agreed upon by most researchers and professional associations: sexual abuse, injustice, forgetting, and memory construction all happen; recovered memories are common; memories from before age 3 are unreliable; memories claimed to be recovered through hypnosis or drug influence are especially unreliable; and memories, whether real or false, can be emotionally upsetting.

Thinking and memory Actively think-ing as we read, by rehearsing and relating ideas, and by making the material person-ally meaningful, yields the best retention.

Make the material meaningful. You can build a network of retrieval cues by taking textbook and class notes in your own words. Apply the concepts to your own life. Form images. Understand and organize information. Relate the material to what you already know or have experienced. As William James (1890) suggested, "Knit each new thing on to some acquisition already there." Restate concepts in your own words. Mindlessly repeating someone else's words won't supply many retrieval cues. On an exam, you may find yourself stuck when a question uses phrasing different from the words you memorized.

Activate retrieval cues. Mentally re-create the situation and the mood in which your original learning occurred. Jog your memory by allowing one thought to cue the next.

Use mnemonic devices. Associate items with peg words. Make up a story that incorporates vivid images of the items. Chunk information into acro-nyms. Create rhythmic rhymes ("i *before* e, *except after* c").

Minimize interference. Study before sleep. Do not schedule back-to-back study times for topics that are likely to interfere with each other, such as Spanish and French.

Sleep more. During sleep, the brain reorganizes and consolidates informa-tion for long-term memory. Sleep deprivation disrupts this process. Even 10 minutes of waking rest enhances memory of what we have read (Dewar et al., 2012). So, after a period of hard study, perhaps just sit or lie down for a few minutes before tackling the next subject.

Test your own knowledge, both to rehearse it and to find out what you don't yet know. Don't be lulled into overconfidence by your ability to recog-nize information. Test your recall using the periodic Retrieve It items and the numbered Learning Objective and Testing Effect questions in the Review sections. Outline sections using a blank page. Define the terms and concepts listed at each section's end before turning back to their definitions. Take practice tests; the online resources that accompany many textbooks, includ-ing this one, are a good source for such tests.

RETRIEVE IT

• Which memory strategies can help you study smarter and retain more information?

ANSWER: Rehearse repeatedly to boost long-term recall. Schedule spaced (not crammed) study times. Spend more time rehearsing or actively thinking about the material. Make the material personally meaningful, with well-organized and vivid associations. Refresh your memory by returning to contexts and moods to activate retrieval cues. Use mnemonic devices. Minimize interference. Plan for a complete night's sleep. Test yourself repeatedly—retrieval practice is a proven retention strategy.

MODULE 24 REVIEW   Forgetting, Memory Construction, and Improving Memory

◐ Learning Objectives

Test Yourself by taking a moment to answer each of these Learning Objective Questions (repeated here from within the module). Then turn to Appendix D, Complete Module Reviews, to check your answers. Research suggests that trying to answer these questions on your own will improve your long-term memory of the concepts (McDaniel et al., 2009).

24-1 Why do we forget?

24-2 How do misinformation, imagination, and source amnesia influence our memory construction? How do we decide whether a memory is real or false?

24-3 How reliable are young children's eyewitness descriptions?

24-4 Why are reports of repressed and recovered memories so hotly debated?

24-5 How can you use memory research findings to do better in this and other courses?

▣·▢ Terms and Concepts to Remember

Test yourself on these terms by trying to write down the definition in your own words before flipping back to the referenced page to check your answers.

anterograde amnesia, p. 302

retrograde amnesia, p. 302
proactive interference, p. 304
retroactive interference, p. 304
repression, p. 306

reconsolidation, p. 306
misinformation effect, p. 307
source amnesia, p. 308
déjà vu, p. 308

▣✲▢ Experience the Testing Effect

Test yourself repeatedly throughout your studies. This will not only help you figure out what you know and don't know; the testing itself will help you learn and remember the information more effectively thanks to the *testing effect*.

1. When forgetting is due to encoding failure, information has not been transferred from
   a. the environment into sensory memory.
   b. sensory memory into long-term memory.
   c. long-term memory into short-term memory.
   d. short-term memory into long-term memory.

2. Ebbinghaus' "forgetting curve" shows that after an initial decline, memory for novel information tends to
   a. increase slightly.
   b. decrease noticeably.
   c. decrease greatly.
   d. level out.

3. The hour before sleep is a good time to memorize information, because going to sleep after learning new material minimizes _____ interference.

4. Freud proposed that painful or unacceptable memories are blocked from consciousness through a mechanism called _____.

5. One reason false memories form is our tendency to fill in memory gaps with our reasonable guesses and assumptions, sometimes based on misleading information. This tendency is an example of
   a. proactive interference.
   b. the misinformation effect.
   c. retroactive interference
   d. the forgetting curve.

6. Eliza's family loves to tell the story of how she "stole the show" as a 2-year-old, dancing at her aunt's wedding reception. Even though she was so young, Eliza says she can recall the event clearly. How is this possible?

7. We may recognize a face at a social gathering but be unable to remember how we know that person. This is an example of _____ _____.

8. When a situation triggers the feeling that "I've been here before," you are experiencing _____ _____.

9. Children can be accurate eyewitnesses if
   a. interviewers give the children hints about what really happened.
   b. a neutral person asks nonleading questions soon after the event.
   c. the children have a chance to talk with involved adults before the interview.
   d. interviewers use precise technical and medical terms.

10. Psychologists involved in the study of memories of abuse tend to *disagree* with each other about which of the following statements?
    a. Memories of events that happened before age 3 are not reliable.
    b. We tend to repress extremely upsetting memories.
    c. Memories can be emotionally upsetting.
    d. Sexual abuse happens.

Find answers to these questions in Appendix E, in the back of the book.

Use ⦿ LearningCurve to create your personalized study plan, which will direct you to the resources that will help you most in ⦿ LaunchPad.

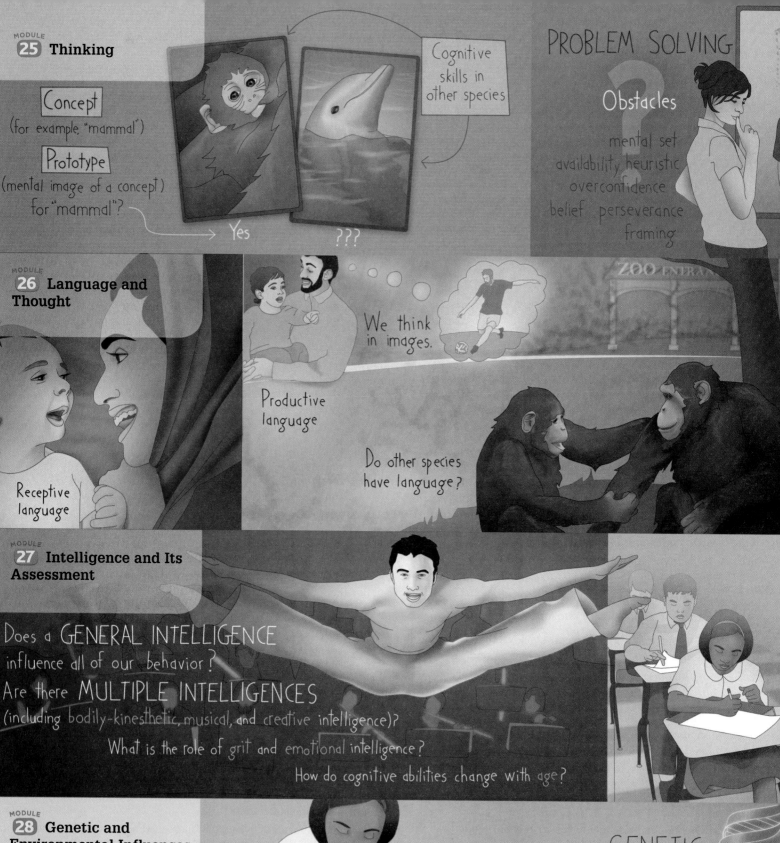

MODULE 25 Thinking

Concept
(for example, "mammal")

Prototype
(mental image of a concept)
for "mammal"?

→ Yes

???

Cognitive skills in other species

PROBLEM SOLVING

Obstacles

mental set
availability heuristic
overconfidence
belief perseverance
framing

MODULE 26 Language and Thought

Receptive language

Productive language

We think in images.

Do other species have language?

ZOO ENTRANCE

MODULE 27 Intelligence and Its Assessment

Does a GENERAL INTELLIGENCE
influence all of our behavior?
Are there MULTIPLE INTELLIGENCES
(including bodily-kinesthetic, musical, and creative intelligence)?
What is the role of grit and emotional intelligence?
How do cognitive abilities change with age?

MODULE 28 Genetic and Environmental Influences on Intelligence

Social expectations influence gender and racial/ethnic
GROUP DIFFERENCES.

Tests may be BIASED.

GENETIC INFLUENCES

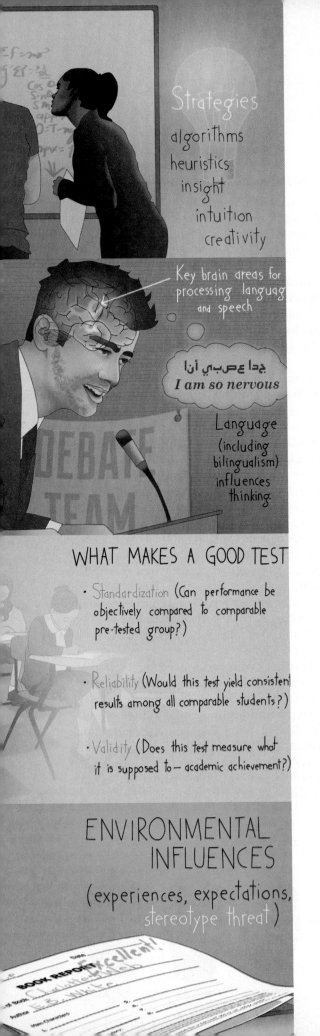

Thinking, Language, and Intelligence

THROUGHOUT history, we humans have both celebrated our wisdom and bemoaned our foolishness. The poet T. S. Eliot was struck by "the hollow men . . . Headpiece filled with straw." But Shakespeare's Hamlet extolled the human species as "noble in reason! . . . infinite in faculties! . . . in apprehension how like a god!" Throughout this text, we likewise marvel at both our abilities and our errors.

We study the human brain—three pounds of wet tissue the size of a small cabbage, yet containing staggeringly complex circuitry. We appreciate the amazing abilities of newborns. We marvel at our visual system, which converts light waves into nerve impulses, distributes them for parallel processing, and reassembles them into colorful perceptions. We ponder our memory's enormous capacity, and the ease with which our two-track mind processes information, with and without our awareness. Little wonder that our species has had the collective genius to invent the camera, the car, and the computer; to unlock the atom and crack the genetic code; to travel out to space and into our brain's depths.

Yet we also see that in other ways, we are less than noble in reason. Our species is kin to the other animals, influenced by the same principles that produce learning in rats and pigeons. We note that we not-so-wise humans are easily deceived by perceptual illusions, pseudopsychic claims, and false memories.

In Modules 25 through 28, we encounter further instances of these two aspects of the human condition—the rational and the irrational. We will consider how we use and misuse the information we receive, perceive, store, and retrieve. We will look at our gift for language and intelligence. And we will reflect on how deserving we are of our species name, *Homo sapiens*—wise human. ■

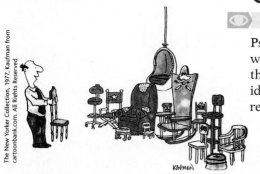

"Attention, everyone! I'd like to introduce the newest member of our family."

∧ FIGURE 25.1

Tasty fungus? Botanically, a mushroom is a fungus. But it doesn't fit most people's *fungus* prototype.

∨ FIGURE 25.2

Categorizing faces influences recollection Shown a face that was 70 percent Caucasian, people tended to classify the person as Caucasian and to recollect the face as more Caucasian than it was. (Recreation of experiment courtesy of Olivier Corneille.)

MODULE 25 Thinking

Concepts

> **25-1** What is cognition, and what are the functions of concepts?

Psychologists who study **cognition** focus on the mental activities associated with thinking, knowing, remembering, and communicating information. One of these activities is forming **concepts**—mental groupings of similar objects, events, ideas, and people. The concept *chair* includes many items—a baby's high chair, a reclining chair, a dentist's chair.

Concepts simplify our thinking. Imagine life without them. We would need a different name for every event, object, and idea. We could not ask a child to "throw the ball" because there would be no concept of *throw* or *ball*. Instead of saying, "They were angry," we would have to describe expressions, intensities, and words. Concepts such as *ball* and *anger* give us much information with little cognitive effort.

We often form our concepts by developing a **prototype**—a mental image or best example of a category (Rosch, 1978). People more quickly agree that "a robin is a bird" than that "a penguin is a bird." For most of us, the robin is the birdier bird; it more closely resembles our *bird* prototype. For people in multiethnic Germany, Caucasian Germans are more prototypically German (Kessler et al., 2010). And the more closely something matches our prototype of a concept—such as *bird* or *German*—the more readily we recognize it as an example of the concept (**FIGURE 25.1**).

Once we place an item in a category, our memory of it later shifts toward the category prototype, as it did for Belgian students who viewed ethnically blended faces. When viewing a blended face in which 70 percent of the features were Caucasian and 30 percent were Asian, the students categorized the face as Caucasian (**FIGURE 25.2**). Later, as their memory shifted toward the Caucasian prototype, they were more likely to remember an 80 percent Caucasian face than the 70 percent Caucasian face they had actually seen (Corneille et al., 2004). Likewise, if shown a 70 percent Asian face, they later remembered a more prototypically Asian face. So, too, with gender: People who viewed 70 percent male faces categorized them as male (no surprise there) and then later misremembered them as even more prototypically male (Huart et al., 2005).

Move away from our prototypes, and category boundaries may blur. Is a tomato a fruit? Is a 17-year-old female a girl or a woman? Is a whale a fish or a mammal? Because a whale fails to match our *mammal* prototype, we are slower to recognize it as a mammal. Similarly, when symptoms don't fit one of our disease prototypes, we are slow to perceive an illness (Bishop, 1991). People whose heart attack symptoms (shortness of breath, exhaustion, a dull weight in the chest) don't match their *heart attack* prototype (sharp chest pain) may not seek help. And when behaviors don't fit our *discrimination* prototypes—of White against Black, male against female, young against old—we often fail to notice prejudice. People more easily detect male prejudice against females than female against males or female against females (Inman & Baron, 1996; Marti et al., 2000). Although concepts speed and guide our thinking, they don't always make us wise.

90% CA   80% CA   70% CA   60% CA   50%/50%   60% AS   70% AS   80% AS   90% AS

Problem Solving: Strategies and Obstacles

25-2 What cognitive strategies assist our problem solving, and what obstacles hinder it?

One tribute to our rationality is our problem-solving skill. What's the best route around this traffic jam? How shall we handle a friend's criticism? How can we get in the house without our keys?

Some problems we solve through *trial and error*. Thomas Edison tried thousands of light bulb filaments before stumbling upon one that worked. For other problems, we use **algorithms,** step-by-step procedures that guarantee a solution. But step-by-step algorithms can be laborious and exasperating. To find a word using the 10 letters in *SPLOYOCHYG*, for example, you could try each letter in each of the 10 positions—907,200 permutations in all. Rather than give you a computing brain the size of a beach ball, nature resorts to **heuristics,** simpler thinking strategies. Thus, you might reduce the number of options in the *SPLOYOCHYG* example by grouping letters that often appear together (*CH* and *GY*) and excluding rare letter combinations (such as two Y's together). By using heuristics and then applying trial and error, you may hit on the answer. Have you guessed it?[1]

Sometimes we puzzle over a problem and the pieces suddenly fall together in a flash of **insight**—an abrupt, true-seeming, and often satisfying solution (Topolinski & Reber, 2010). Ten-year-old Johnny Appleton's insight solved a problem that had stumped construction workers: how to rescue a young robin from a narrow 30-inch-deep hole in a cement-block wall. Johnny's solution: Slowly pour in sand, giving the bird enough time to keep its feet on top of the constantly rising pile (Ruchlis, 1990).

Teams of researchers have identified brain activity associated with sudden flashes of insight (Kounios & Beeman, 2009; Sandkühler & Bhattacharya, 2008). They gave people a problem: Think of a word that will form a compound word or phrase with each of three other words in a set (such as *pine, crab,* and *sauce*), and press a button to sound a bell when you know the answer. (If you need a hint: The word is a fruit.[2]) EEGs or fMRIs (functional MRIs) revealed the problem solvers' brain activity. In the first experiment, about half the solutions arrived through a sudden Aha! insight. Before the Aha! moment, the problem solvers' frontal lobes (which are involved in focusing attention) were active. At the instant of discovery, there was a burst of activity in the right temporal lobe, just above the ear (**FIGURE 25.3** on the next page).

Insight strikes suddenly, with no prior sense of "getting warmer" or feeling close to a solution (Knoblich & Oellinger, 2006; Metcalfe, 1986). When the answer pops into mind *(apple!),* we feel a happy sense of satisfaction. The joy of a joke may similarly lie in our sudden comprehension of an unexpected ending or a double meaning: "You don't need a parachute to skydive. You only need a parachute to skydive twice." Groucho Marx was a master at this: "I once shot an elephant in my pajamas. How he got in my pajamas I'll never know."

Insightful as we are, other cognitive tendencies may lead us astray. For example, we more eagerly seek out and favor evidence that supports our ideas than evidence that refutes them (Klayman & Ha, 1987; Skov & Sherman, 1986). In a classic experiment, Peter Wason (1960) demonstrated this tendency, known as **confirmation bias,** by

---

1. Answer to SPLOYOCHYG anagram: PSYCHOLOGY.

2. The word is *apple*: pineapple, crabapple, applesauce.

cognition all the mental activities associated with thinking, knowing, remembering, and communicating.

concept a mental grouping of similar objects, events, ideas, or people.

prototype a mental image or best example of a category. Matching new items to a prototype provides a quick and easy method for sorting items into categories (as when comparing feathered creatures to a prototypical bird, such as a robin).

algorithm a methodical, logical rule or procedure that guarantees solving a particular problem. Contrasts with the usually speedier—but also more error-prone—use of *heuristics.*

heuristic a simple thinking strategy that often allows us to make judgments and solve problems efficiently; usually speedier but also more error-prone than *algorithms.*

insight a sudden realization of a problem's solution; contrasts with strategy-based solutions.

confirmation bias a tendency to search for information that supports our preconceptions and to ignore or distort contradictory evidence.

Heuristic searching To find guava juice, you could search every supermarket aisle (an algorithm), or check the bottled beverage, natural foods, and produce sections (heuristics). The heuristics approach is often speedier, but an algorithmic search guarantees you will find it eventually.

Jon Feingersh/Blend Images/Getty Images

> FIGURE 25.3

The Aha! moment A burst of right temporal lobe activity accompanied insight solutions to word problems (Jung-Beeman et al., 2004). The red dots designate EEG electrodes. The light gray lines show the distribution of high-frequency activity accompanying insight. The insight-related activity is centered in the right temporal lobe (yellow area).

"The human understanding, when any proposition has been once laid down . . . forces everything else to add fresh support and confirmation."

Francis Bacon,
Novum Organum, 1620

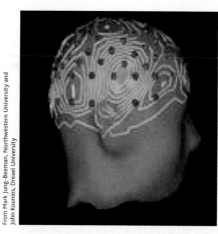

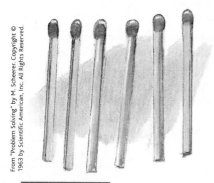

∧ FIGURE 25.4

The matchstick problem How would you arrange six matches to form four equilateral triangles?

"The problem is I can't tell the difference between a deeply wise, intuitive nudge from the Universe and one of my own bone-headed ideas!"

giving British university students the three-number sequence *2-4-6* and asking them to guess the rule he had used to devise the series. (The rule was simple: any three ascending numbers.) Before submitting answers, students generated their own three-number sets and Wason told them whether their sets conformed to his rule. Once *certain* they had the rule, they could announce it. The result? Seldom right but never in doubt. Most students formed a wrong idea *("Maybe it's counting by twos")* and then searched only for confirming evidence (by testing *6-8-10, 100-102-104,* and so forth).

"Ordinary people," said Wason (1981), "evade facts, become inconsistent, or systematically defend themselves against the threat of new information relevant to the issue." Thus, once people form a belief—that vaccines cause (or do not cause) autism spectrum disorder, that people can (or cannot) change their sexual orientation, that gun control does (or does not) save lives—they prefer belief-confirming information.

Once we incorrectly represent a problem, it's hard to restructure how we approach it. If the solution to the matchstick problem in **FIGURE 25.4** eludes you, you may be experiencing *fixation*—an inability to see a problem from a fresh perspective. (For the solution, turn the page to see **FIGURE 25.7**.)

A prime example of fixation is **mental set,** our tendency to approach a problem with the mind-set of what has worked for us previously. Indeed, solutions that worked in the past often do work on new problems. Consider:

Given the sequence *O-T-T-F-?-?-?,* what are the final three letters?

Most people have difficulty recognizing that the three final letters are *F*(ive), *S*(ix), and *S*(even). But solving this problem may make the next one easier:

Given the sequence *J-F-M-A-?-?-?,* what are the final three letters? (If you don't get this one, ask yourself what month it is.)

As a *perceptual set* predisposes what we perceive, a mental set predisposes how we think; sometimes this can be an obstacle to problem solving, as when our mental set from our past experiences with matchsticks predisposes us to arrange them in two dimensions. To suppress these impediments to our natural creativity, researchers have used electrical stimulation to decrease left hemisphere activity and to increase right hemisphere activity (associated with novel thinking). The result was improved insight, less restrained by the assumptions created by past experience (Chi & Snyder, 2011).

Forming Good and Bad Decisions and Judgments

25-3 What is intuition, and how can the availability heuristic, overconfidence, belief perseverance, and framing influence our decisions and judgments?

When making each day's hundreds of judgments and decisions *(Should I take a jacket? Can I trust this person? Should I shoot the basketball or pass to the player who's hot?),* we seldom take the time and effort to reason systematically. We just follow our **intuition**—our fast, automatic, unreasoned feelings and thoughts. After interviewing policy makers in government, business, and education, social psychologist Irving Janis (1986) concluded that they "often do not use a reflective problem-solving approach. How do they usually arrive at their decisions? If you ask, they are likely to tell you . . . they do it mostly *by the seat of their pants.*"

The Availability Heuristic

When we need to act quickly, the mental shortcuts we call *heuristics* enable snap judgments. Thanks to our mind's automatic information processing, intuitive judgments are instantaneous. They also are usually effective (Gigerenzer & Sturm, 2012). However, research by cognitive psychologists Amos Tversky and Daniel Kahneman (1974) showed how these generally helpful shortcuts can lead even the smartest people into dumb decisions.[3] The **availability heuristic** operates when we estimate the likelihood of events based on how mentally available they are—how easily they come to mind. Casinos entice us to gamble by signaling even small wins with bells and lights—making them mentally vivid—while keeping big losses invisible.

The availability heuristic colors our judgments of other people, too. Anything that makes information pop into mind—its vividness, recentness, or distinctiveness—can make it seem commonplace. While this generally helps us to evaluate people and situations quickly, it can also distort our perceptions. If someone from a particular ethnic or religious group commits a terrorist act, as happened on September 11, 2001, our readily available memory of the dramatic event may shape our impression of the whole group.

Even during that horrific year, terrorist acts claimed comparatively few lives. Yet when the statistical reality of greater dangers (see **FIGURE 25.5**) was pitted against the 9/11 terror, the memorable case won: Emotion-laden images of terror exacerbated our fears (Sunstein, 2007).

Although our fears often protect us, we sometimes fear the wrong things. (See Thinking Critically About: The Fear Factor on the next page.) We fear flying because we visualize air disasters. We fear letting our sons and daughters walk to school because we see mental snapshots of abducted and brutalized children. We fear swimming in ocean waters because we replay *Jaws* with ourselves as victims. Even passing by a person who

"Kahneman and his colleagues and students have changed the way we think about the way people think."

American Psychological Association President Sharon Brehm, 2007

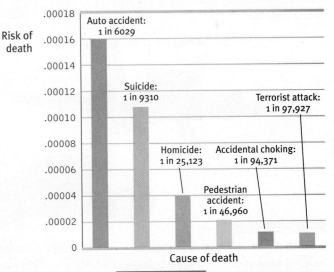

^ FIGURE 25.5

Risk of death from various causes in the United States, 2001 (Data assembled from various government sources by Randall Marshall et al., 2007.)

3. Tversky and Kahneman's joint work on decision making received a 2002 Nobel Prize; sadly, only Kahneman was alive to receive the honor.

"In creating these problems, we didn't set out to fool people. All our problems fooled us, too."
Amos Tversky (1985)

"Intuitive thinking [is] fine most of the time. . . . But sometimes that habit of mind gets us in trouble."
Daniel Kahneman (2005)

mental set a tendency to approach a problem in one particular way, often a way that has been successful in the past.

intuition an effortless, immediate, automatic feeling or thought, as contrasted with explicit, conscious reasoning.

availability heuristic estimating the likelihood of events based on their availability in memory; if instances come readily to mind (perhaps because of their vividness), we presume such events are common.

The Fear Factor—Why We Fear the Wrong Things

25-4 What factors contribute to our fear of unlikely events?

After the 9/11 attacks, many people feared flying more than driving. In a 2006 Gallup survey, only 40 percent of Americans reported being "not afraid at all" to fly. Yet from 2009 to 2011, Americans were—mile for mile—170 times more likely to die in a vehicle accident than on a scheduled flight (National Safety Council, 2014). In 2011, 21,221 people died in U.S. car or light truck accidents, while zero (as in 2010) died on scheduled airline flights. When flying, the most dangerous part of the trip is the drive to the airport.

In a late 2001 essay, I [DM] calculated that if—because of 9/11—we flew 20 percent less and instead drove half those unflown miles, about 800 more people would die in the year after the 9/11 attacks (Myers, 2001). German psychologist Gerd Gigerenzer (2004, 2006; Gaissmater & Gigerenzer, 2012) later checked my estimate against actual accident data. (Why didn't I think to do that?) U.S. traffic deaths did indeed increase significantly in the last three months of 2001 (**FIGURE 25.6**). By the end of 2002, Gigerenzer estimated, 1600 Americans had "lost their lives on the road by trying to avoid the risk of flying."

Why do we in so many ways fear the wrong things? Why do so many American parents fear school shootings, when their child is more likely to be killed by lightning (Ripley, 2013)? Why, in 2014, were so many Americans more frightened of Ebola (which killed no one who contracted it in the United States) than of influenza, which kills some 24,000 Americans annually? Psychologists have identified four influences that feed fear and cause us to ignore higher risks:

1. *We fear what our ancestral history has prepared us to fear.* Human emotions were road tested in the Stone Age. Our old brain prepares us to fear yesterday's

Lars Christensen/Shutterstock

© Transtock/Corbis

> **FIGURE 25.6**

Scared onto deadly highways Images of 9/11 etched a sharper image in American minds than did the millions of fatality-free flights on U.S. airlines during 2002 and after. Dramatic events are readily available to memory, and they shape our perceptions of risk. In the three months after 9/11, those faulty perceptions led more Americans to travel, and some to die, by car. (Data from Gigerenzer, 2004.)

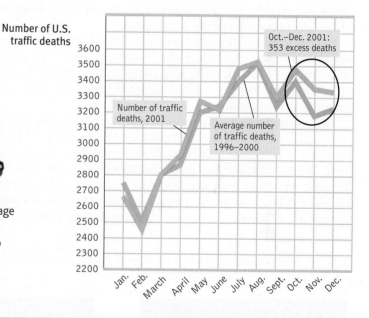

sneezes and coughs can heighten our perceptions of various health risks (Lee et al., 2010). And so, thanks to such readily available images, we come to fear extremely rare events.

Meanwhile, the lack of available images of future climate change disasters—which some scientists regard as "Armageddon in slow motion"—has left most people little concerned (Pew, 2014). What's more cognitively available than slow climate change is our recently experienced local weather, which tells us nothing about long-term planetary trends (Egan & Mullin, 2012; Zaval et al., 2014). Unusually hot local weather increases people's worry about global climate warming, while a recent cold day reduces their concern and overwhelms less memorable scientific data (Li et al., 2011). After Hurricane Sandy devastated New Jersey, its residents' vivid experience of extreme weather increased their environmentalism (Rudman et al., 2013).

Dramatic outcomes make us gasp; probabilities we hardly grasp. As of 2013, some 40 nations have sought to harness the positive power of vivid, memorable images by putting eye-catching warnings and graphic photos on cigarette packages (Riordan, 2013). This campaign has worked (Huang et al., 2013). As

"Don't believe everything you think."

Bumper sticker

"Global warming isn't real because it was cold today! Also great news: World hunger is over because I just ate."

Stephen Colbert tweet, November 18, 2014

overconfidence the tendency to be more confident than correct—to overestimate the accuracy of our beliefs and judgments.

risks: snakes, lizards, and spiders (which combined now kill a tiny fraction of the number killed by modern-day threats, such as cars and cigarettes). Yesterday's risks also prepare us to fear confinement and heights, and therefore flying.

2. *We fear what we cannot control.* Driving we control; flying we do not.

3. *We fear what is immediate.* The dangers of flying are mostly telescoped into the moments of takeoff and landing. The dangers of driving are diffused across many moments, each trivially dangerous.

4. *Thanks to the availability heuristic, we fear what is most readily available in memory.* Vivid images, like that of a horrific air crash, feed our judgments of risk. Shark attacks kill about one American per year, while heart disease kills 800,000—but it's much easier to visualize a shark bite, and thus many people fear sharks more than cigarettes or the effects of an unhealthy diet (Daley, 2011). Similarly, we remember (and fear) widespread disasters (hurricanes, tornadoes, earthquakes) that kill people dramatically, in bunches. But we fear too little the less dramatic threats that claim lives quietly, one by one, continuing into the distant future. Horrified citizens and commentators renewed calls for U.S. gun control in 2015, after nine African-Americans at a Bible study were slain by a racist

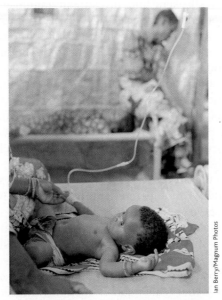

Ian Berry/Magnum Photos

Dramatic deaths in bunches breed concern and fear The memorable 2010 Haitian earthquake that killed some 250,000 people stirred an outpouring of justified concern. Meanwhile, according to the World Health Organization, a silent earthquake of poverty-related malaria was killing about that many people, mostly in Africa, *every four months.*

guest—although guns kill about 30 Americans every day, one by one, in a less dramatic fashion. Philanthropist Bill Gates has noted that each year, a half-million children worldwide die from rotavirus. This is the equivalent of four

747s full of children every day, and we hear nothing of it (Glass, 2004). Media outlets often draw readers and viewers by reporting on the immediate and the dramatic. "If it bleeds, it leads."

The news, and our own memorable experiences, can make us disproportionately fearful of infinitesimal risks—and to spend an estimated $500 million per U.S. terrorist death but only $10,000 per cancer death (Eagan, 2015). As one risk analyst explained, "If it's in the news, don't worry about it. The very definition of *news* is 'something that hardly ever happens'" (Schneier, 2007).

RETRIEVE IT [✕]

• Why can news be described as "something that hardly ever happens"? How does knowing this help us assess our fears?

ANSWER: If a tragic event such as a plane crash makes the news, it grabs our attention more than the much more common bad events, such as traffic accidents. Knowing this, we can worry less about unlikely events and think more about improving the safety of our everyday activities. (For example, we can wear a seat belt when in a vehicle and use the crosswalk when walking.)

"Fearful people are more dependent, more easily manipulated and controlled, more susceptible to deceptively simple, strong, tough measures and hard-line postures."

Media researcher George Gerbner to U.S. Congressional Subcommittee on Communications, 1981

psychologist Paul Slovic (2007) points out, we reason emotionally and neglect probabilities. We overfeel and underthink. In one experiment, donations to a starving 7-year-old were greater when her image was *not* accompanied by statistical information about the millions of needy African children like her (Small et al., 2007). "The more who die, the less we care," noted Slovic (2010).

Overconfidence

Sometimes our judgments and decisions go awry simply because we are more confident than correct. Across various tasks, people overestimate their performance (Metcalfe, 1998). If 60 percent of people correctly answer a factual question, such as "Is absinthe a liqueur or a precious stone?," they will typically average 75 percent confidence (Fischhoff et al., 1977). (It's a licorice-flavored liqueur.) This tendency to overestimate the accuracy of our knowledge and judgments is **overconfidence.**

It was an overconfident BP that, before its exploded drilling platform spewed oil into the Gulf of Mexico, downplayed safety concerns, and then downplayed the

From "Problem Solving" by M. Scheerer. Copyright © 1963 by Scientific American, Inc. All Rights Reserved.

▲ FIGURE 25.7

Solution to the matchstick problem To solve this problem, you must view it from a new perspective, breaking the fixation of limiting solutions to two dimensions.

Predict your own behavior When will you finish reading this module?

Hofstadter's Law: It always takes longer than you expect, even when you take into account Hofstadter's Law.

Douglas Hofstadter, Gödel, Escher, Bach: The Eternal Golden Braid, *1979*

"When you know a thing, to hold that you know it; and when you do not know a thing, to allow that you do not know it; this is knowledge."

Confucius (551–479 B.C.E.), Analects

"I'm happy to say that my final judgment of a case is almost always consistent with my prejudgment of the case."

spill's magnitude (Mohr et al., 2010; Urbina, 2010). It is overconfidence that drives stockbrokers and investment managers to market their ability to outperform stock market averages (Malkiel, 2012). A purchase of stock X, recommended by a broker who judges this to be the time to buy, is usually balanced by a sale made by someone who judges this to be the time to sell. Despite their confidence, buyer and seller cannot both be right.

Overconfidence can also feed extreme political views. People with a superficial understanding of proposals for cap-and-trade carbon emissions or a national flat tax often express strong pro or con views. Asking them to explain the details of these policies exposes them to their own ignorance, which in turn leads them to express more moderate views (Fernbach et al., 2013). Sometimes the less people know, the more immoderate they are.

Classrooms are full of overconfident students who expect to finish assignments and write papers ahead of schedule (Buehler et al., 1994, 2002). In fact, these projects generally take about twice the number of days predicted. This "planning fallacy" (underestimating the time and cost of a project) routinely occurs with construction projects, which often finish late and over budget.

Overconfidence can have adaptive value. People who err on the side of over-confidence live more happily. Their seeming competence can help them gain influence (Anderson et al., 2012). Moreover, given prompt and clear feedback, as weather forecasters receive after each day's predictions, we can learn to be more realistic about the accuracy of our judgments (Fischhoff, 1982). The wisdom to know when we know a thing and when we do not is born of experience.

Belief Perseverance

Our overconfidence is startling. Equally so is our **belief perseverance**—our tendency to cling to our beliefs in the face of contrary evidence. One study of belief perseverance engaged people with opposing views of capital punishment (Lord et al., 1979). After studying two supposedly new research findings, one support-ing and the other refuting the claim that the death penalty deters crime, each side was more impressed by the study supporting its own beliefs. And each read-ily disputed the other study. Thus, showing the pro- and anti-capital-punishment groups the *same* mixed evidence actually *increased* their disagreement.

To rein in belief perseverance, a simple remedy exists: *Consider the opposite.* When the same researchers repeated the capital-punishment study, they asked some participants to be "as *objective* and *unbiased* as possible" (Lord et al., 1984). The plea did nothing to reduce biased evaluations of evidence. They asked a different group to consider "whether you would have made the same high or low evaluations had exactly the same study produced results on the *other* side of the issue." Having imag-ined and pondered *opposite* findings, these people became much less biased.

The more we come to appreciate why our beliefs might be true, the more tightly we cling to them. Once beliefs form and get justified, it takes more compelling evidence to change them than it did to create them. Prejudice persists. Beliefs often persevere.

The Effects of Framing

Framing—the way we present an issue—sways our decisions and judgments. Imagine two surgeons explaining a surgery risk. One tells patients that 10 percent of people die during this surgery. The other tells patients that 90 percent survive. Although the information is the same, the effect is not. Both patients and physi-cians perceive greater risk when they hear that 10 percent *die* (Marteau, 1989; McNeil et al., 1988; Rothman & Salovey, 1997).

Framing can be a powerful persuasion tool. Carefully posed options can nudge people toward decisions that could benefit them or society as a whole (Benartzi & Thaler, 2013; Thaler & Sunstein, 2008):

- *Encouraging citizens to be organ donors.* In many European countries as well as the United States, those renewing their driver's license can decide whether they want to be organ donors. In some countries, the default option is *Yes*, but people can opt out. Nearly 100 percent of the people in opt-out countries have agreed to be donors. In the United States, Britain, and Germany, the default option is *No*, but people can opt in. In these countries, less than half have agreed to be donors (Hajhosseini et al., 2013; Johnson & Goldstein, 2003).

- *Nudging employees to save for their retirement.* A 2006 U.S. pension law recognized the framing effect. Before that law, employees who wanted to contribute to a retirement plan typically had to choose a lower take-home pay, which few people will do. Companies can now automatically enroll their employees in the plan but allow them to opt out. Under the new voluntary opt-out arrangement, enrollments in one analysis of 3.4 million workers soared from 59 to 86 percent (Rosenberg, 2010).

- *Boosting student morale: When 70 percent on an exam feels better than 72 percent.* One economist's students were upset by a "hard" exam, on which they averaged 72 out of 100. So on the next exam, he made the highest possible score 137 points. Although the class average score of 96 was only 70 percent correct, "the students were delighted" (a numerical 96 felt so much better than 72). So he continued the reframed exam results thereafter (Thaler, 2015).

The point to remember: Those who understand the power of framing can use it (for good or ill) to nudge our decisions.

The Perils and Powers of Intuition

25-5 How do smart thinkers use intuition?

The perils of intuition—irrational fears, cloudy judgments, illogical reasoning—feed gut fears and prejudices. Irrational thinking can persist even when people are offered extra pay for thinking smart, even when they are asked to justify their answers, and even when they are expert physicians or clinicians (Shafir & LeBoeuf, 2002). Highly intelligent people (including U.S. federal intelligence agents, in one study) are similarly vulnerable to intuition's distortions of reality (Reyna et al., 2014; Stanovich et al., 2013). Even very smart people can make not-so-smart judgments. So, are our heads indeed "filled with straw," as T. S. Eliot suggested?

Throughout this book you will see examples of smart intuition. In brief,

- *Intuition is analysis "frozen into habit"* (Simon, 2001). It is implicit knowledge—what we've learned and recorded in our brains but can't fully explain (Chassy & Gobet, 2011; Gore & Sadler-Smith, 2011). Chess masters display this tacit expertise in "blitz chess," where, after barely a glance, they intuitively know the right move (Burns, 2004). We see this expertise in the smart and quick judgments of experienced nurses, firefighters, art critics, car mechanics, and musicians. Skilled athletes can react *without thinking.* Indeed, conscious thinking may disrupt well-practiced movements such as batting or shooting free throws. For all of us who have developed some special skill, what feels like instant intuition is actually an acquired ability to perceive and react in an eyeblink.

- *Intuition is usually adaptive, enabling quick reactions.* Our fast and frugal heuristics let us intuitively assume that fuzzy looking objects are far away—which they usually are, except on foggy mornings. Seeing a stranger who looks like someone who has harmed or threatened us in the past, we may automatically react warily. Newlyweds' automatic associations—their gut reactions—to their new spouses likewise predict their future marital happiness (McNulty et al., 2013). Our learned associations surface as gut feelings.

belief perseverance clinging to one's initial conceptions after the basis on which they were formed has been discredited.

framing the way an issue is posed; how an issue is framed can significantly affect decisions and judgments.

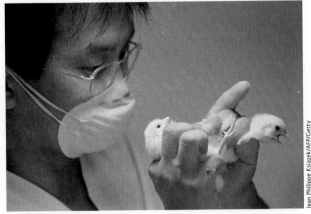

Hmm . . . male or female? When acquired expertise becomes an automatic habit, as it is for experienced chicken sexers, it feels like intuition. At a glance, they just know, yet cannot easily tell you how they know.

Jean Phillipe Ksiazek/AFP/Getty

• *Intuition flows from unconscious processing.* Today's cognitive science offers many examples of unconscious automatic influences on our judgments (Custers & Aarts, 2010). Consider: Most people guess that the more complex the choice, the smarter it is to make decisions rationally rather than intuitively (Inbar et al., 2010). Actually, Dutch psychologists have shown that in making complex decisions, we benefit by letting our brain work on a problem without consciously thinking about it (Strick et al., 2010, 2011). In one series of experiments, three groups of people read complex information (for example, about apartments or soccer matches). The first group's participants stated their preference immediately after reading information about four possible options. The second group, given several minutes to analyze the information, made slightly smarter decisions. But wisest of all, in several studies, was the third group, whose attention was distracted for a time, enabling their minds to engage in automatic, unconscious processing of the complex information. The practical lesson: Letting a problem "incubate" while we attend to other things can pay dividends (Sio & Ormerod, 2009). Facing a difficult decision involving lots of facts, we're wise to gather all the information we can, and then say, "Give me some time *not* to think about this." By taking time to sleep on it, we let our unconscious mental machinery work. Thanks to our active brain, nonconscious thinking (reasoning, problem solving, decision making, planning) is surprisingly astute (Creswell et al., 2013; Hassin, 2013; Lin & Murray, 2015).

Critics note that some studies have not found the supposed power of unconscious thought and remind us that deliberate, conscious thought also furthers smart thinking (Lassiter et al., 2009; Newell, 2015; Nieuwenstein et al., 2015; Payne et al., 2008). In challenging situations, superior decision makers, including chess players, take time to think (Moxley et al., 2012). And with many sorts of problems, deliberative thinkers are aware of the intuitive option, but know when to override it (Mata et al., 2013). Consider:

A bat and a ball together cost 110 cents.
The bat costs 100 cents more than the ball.
How much does the ball cost?

Most people's intuitive response—10 cents—is wrong, and a few moments of deliberate thinking reveals why.[4]

The bottom line: Our two-track mind makes sweet harmony as smart, critical thinking listens to the creative whispers of our vast unseen mind and then evaluates evidence, tests conclusions, and plans for the future.

Thinking Creatively

 25-6 What is creativity, and what fosters it?

Creativity is the ability to produce ideas that are both novel and valuable (Hennessey & Amabile, 2010). Consider Princeton mathematician Andrew Wiles' incredible, creative moment in 1994. Pierre de Fermat, a seventeenth-century mischievous genius, had challenged mathematicians of his day to match his solutions to various number theory problems. His most famous challenge—*Fermat's last theorem*—baffled the greatest mathematical minds, even after a $2 million prize (in today's dollars) was offered in 1908 to whoever first created a proof.

Wiles had pondered Fermat's theorem for more than 30 years and had come to the brink of a solution. One morning, out of the blue, the final "incredible revelation" struck him. "It was so indescribably beautiful; it was so simple and so elegant. I couldn't understand how I'd missed it. . . . It was the most important moment of my working life" (Singh, 1997, p. 25).

creativity the ability to produce new and valuable ideas.

convergent thinking narrowing the available problem solutions to determine the single best solution.

divergent thinking expanding the number of possible problem solutions; creative thinking that diverges in different directions.

4. The answer is 5 cents. The bat would then cost $1.05, for a $1.10 total.

Creativity like Wiles' is supported by a certain level of *aptitude* (ability to learn). Those who score exceptionally high in quantitative (math) aptitude as 13-year-olds, for example, are more likely to obtain graduate science and math degrees and create published or patented work (Park et al., 2008; Robertson et al., 2010). Greater intelligence and working memory also boost creativity (Arneson et al., 2011; Hambrick & Meinz, 2011). But creativity is more than school smarts, and it requires a different kind of thinking: Aptitude tests such as the SAT, which demand a single correct answer, require **convergent thinking.** Creativity tests *(How many uses can you think of for a brick?)* require expansive, **divergent thinking.**

Robert Sternberg and his colleagues believe creativity has five components (Sternberg, 1988, 2003; Sternberg & Lubart, 1991, 1992):

1. *Expertise*—well-developed knowledge—furnishes the ideas, images, and phrases we use as mental building blocks. "Chance favors only the prepared mind," observed Louis Pasteur. The more blocks we have, the more chances we have to combine them in novel ways. Wiles' well-developed knowledge put the needed theorems and methods at his disposal.

2. *Imaginative thinking skills* provide the ability to see things in novel ways, to recognize patterns, and to make connections. Having mastered a problem's basic elements, we redefine or explore it in a new way. Wiles' imaginative solution combined two partial solutions.

3. *A venturesome personality* seeks new experiences, tolerates ambiguity and risk, and perseveres in overcoming obstacles. Wiles said he labored in near-isolation from the mathematics community partly to stay focused and avoid distraction. Such determination is an enduring trait.

4. *Intrinsic motivation* is the quality of being driven more by interest, satisfaction, and challenge than by external pressures (Amabile & Hennessey, 1992). Creative people focus less on extrinsic motivators—meeting deadlines, impressing people, or making money—than on the pleasure and stimulation of the work itself. As Wiles noted, "I was so obsessed by this problem that . . . I was thinking about it all the time—[from] when I woke up in the morning to when I went to sleep at night" (Singh & Riber, 1997).

5. *A creative environment* sparks, supports, and refines creative ideas. Wiles stood on the shoulders of others and collaborated with a former student. After studying the careers of 2026 prominent scientists and inventors, Dean Keith Simonton (1992) noted that the most eminent were mentored, challenged, and supported by their colleagues. Creativity-fostering environments support innovation, team building, and communication (Hülsheger et al., 2009). They also minimize anxiety and foster contemplation (Byron & Khazanchi, 2011). After Jonas Salk solved a problem that led to the polio vaccine while visiting a monastery, he designed the Salk Institute to provide contemplative spaces where scientists could work without interruption (Sternberg, 2006).

For those seeking to boost the creative process, research offers some ideas:

- *Develop your expertise.* Ask yourself what you care about and most enjoy. Follow your passion and become an expert at something.

- *Allow time for incubation.* With enough available knowledge—the mental building blocks we need to create novel connections—a period of inattention to a problem ("sleeping on it") allows for automatic processing to form associations (Zhong et al., 2008). So think hard on a problem, then set it aside and come back to it later.

- *Set aside time for the mind to roam freely.* Take time away from attention-absorbing distractions. Creativity springs from "defocused attention" (Simonton, 2012a,b). So jog, go for a long walk, or meditate. Serenity seeds spontaneity.

Industrious creativity Researcher Sally Reis (2001) found that notably creative women were typically "intelligent, hard working, imaginative, and strong willed" as girls, noting examples such as Nobel Prize–winning geneticist Barbara McClintock. In her acceptance speech for the 2013 Nobel Prize for Literature, author Alice Munro, shown here, also spoke about creativity as hard work. "Stories are so important in the world. . . . [The part that's hardest is] when you go over the story and realize how bad it is. You know, the first part, excitement, the second, pretty good, but then you pick it up one morning and you think, 'what nonsense,' and that is when you really have to get to work on it. And for me, it always seemed the right thing to do."

A creative environment

*"For the love of God, is there a doctor
in the house?"*

Imaginative thinking Cartoonists
often display creativity as they see things
in new ways or make unusual connections.

- *Experience other cultures and ways of thinking.* Living abroad sets the creative juices flowing. Even after controlling for other variables, students who have spent time abroad and embraced their host culture are more adept at working out creative solutions to problems (Lee et al., 2012; Tadmor et al., 2012). Multicultural experiences expose us to multiple perspectives and facilitate flexible thinking, and may also trigger another stimulus for creativity—a sense of difference from others (Kim et al., 2013; Ritter et al., 2012).

RETRIEVE IT [✖]

- Match the process or strategy listed below (1–10) with the description (a–j).

1. Algorithm	5. Fixation	8. Creativity
2. Intuition	6. Confirmation bias	9. Framing
3. Insight	7. Overconfidence	10. Belief perseverance
4. Heuristics		

a. Inability to view problems from a new angle; focuses thinking but hinders creative problem solving.

b. Methodological rule or procedure that guarantees a solution but requires time and effort.

c. Fast, automatic, effortless feelings and thoughts based on our experience; adaptive but can lead us to overfeel and underthink.

d. Simple thinking shortcuts that allow us to act quickly and efficiently, but put us at risk for errors.

e. Sudden Aha! reaction that provides instant realization of the solution.

f. Tendency to search for support for our own views and ignore contradictory evidence.

g. Ignoring evidence that proves our beliefs are wrong; closes our mind to new ideas.

h. Overestimating the accuracy of our beliefs and judgments; allows us to be happy and to make decisions easily, but puts us at risk for errors.

i. Wording a question or statement so that it evokes a desired response; can influence others' decisions and produce a misleading result.

j. The ability to produce novel and valuable ideas.

ANSWERS: 1. b, 2. c, 3. e, 4. d, 5. a, 6. f, 7. h, 8. j, 9. i, 10. g

Do Other Species Share Our Cognitive Skills?

 25-7 What do we know about thinking in other animals?

Other animals are smarter than we often realize. In her 1908 book, *The Animal Mind,* pioneering psychologist Margaret Floy Washburn explained that animals' consciousness and intelligence can be inferred from their behavior. In 2012, neuroscientists convening at the University of Cambridge added that animal consciousness can also be inferred from animals' brains: "Nonhuman animals, including all mammals and birds," possess the neural networks "that generate consciousness" (Low et al., 2012). Consider, then, what animal brains can do.

Using Concepts and Numbers

Even pigeons—mere birdbrains—can sort objects (pictures of cars, cats, chairs, flowers) into categories, or concepts. Shown a picture of a never-before-seen chair, pigeons have reliably pecked a key that represents *chairs* (Wasserman, 1995). By touching screens in quest of a food reward, black bears have learned to sort pictures into animal and nonanimal categories (Vonk et al., 2012). The great apes

also form concepts, such as *cat* and *dog*. After monkeys learned these concepts, certain frontal lobe neurons in their brain fired in response to new "catlike" images, others to new "doglike" images (Freedman et al., 2001).

Displaying Insight

Psychologist Wolfgang Köhler (1925/1957) showed that we are not the only creatures to display insight. He placed a piece of fruit and a long stick outside the cage of a chimpanzee named Sultan, beyond his reach. Inside the cage,

Mike Lovett

he placed a short stick, which Sultan grabbed, using it to try to reach the fruit. After several failed attempts, he dropped the stick and seemed to survey the situation. Then suddenly (as if thinking "Aha!"), Sultan jumped up and seized the short stick again. This time, he used it to pull in the longer stick—which he then used to reach the fruit. Apes have even exhibited foresight by storing a tool they could use to retrieve food the next day (Mulcahy & Call, 2006). Birds, too, have displayed insight. One experiment, by (yes) Christopher Bird and Nathan Emery (2009), has brought to life an Aesop fable in which a thirsty crow was unable to reach the water in a partly filled pitcher. See its solution in **FIGURE 25.8a**.

Using Tools and Transmitting Culture

Like humans, many other species invent behaviors and transmit cultural patterns to their observing peers and offspring (Boesch-Achermann & Boesch, 1993). Forest-dwelling chimpanzees select different tools for different purposes—a heavy stick for making holes, or a light, flexible stick for fishing for termites (Sanz et al., 2004). Researchers have found at least 39 local customs

Chris Bird & Nathan Emery
(a)

Ben Cranke/The Image Bank/Getty Images
(b)

Neurology/PA/AP Photo
(c)

Copyright Amanda K. Coakes
(d)

‹ FIGURE 25.8

Animal talents (a) Crows studied by Christopher Bird and Nathan Emery (2009) quickly learned to raise the water level in a tube and nab a floating worm by dropping in stones. Other crows have used twigs to probe for insects, and bent strips of metal to reach food. (b) Capuchin monkeys have learned not only to use heavy rocks to crack open palm nuts, but also to test stone hammers and select a sturdier, less crumbly one (Visalberghi et al., 2009). (c) One male chimpanzee in Sweden's Furuvik Zoo was observed every morning collecting stones into a neat little pile, which later in the day he used as ammunition to pelt visitors (Osvath & Karvonen, 2012). (d) Dolphins form coalitions, cooperatively hunt, and learn tool use from one another (Bearzi & Stanford, 2010). This bottlenose dolphin in Shark Bay, Western Australia, belongs to a small group that uses marine sponges as protective nose guards when probing the sea floor for fish (Krützen et al., 2005).

Johan Swanepoel/Alamy

related to chimpanzee tool use, grooming, and courtship (Claidière & Whiten, 2012; Whiten & Boesch, 2001). One group may slurp termites directly from a stick, another group may pluck them off individually. One group may break nuts with a stone hammer, their neighbors with a wooden hammer. These group differences, along with differing communication and hunting styles, are the chimpanzee version of cultural diversity.

Other animals have also shown surprising cognitive talents. In tests, elephants have demonstrated self-awareness and displayed their abilities to learn, remember, discriminate smells, empathize, cooperate, teach, and spontaneously use tools (Byrne et al., 2009). As social creatures, chimpanzees have shown altruism, cooperation, and group aggression. Like humans, they will purposefully kill their neighbor to gain land, and they grieve over dead relatives (Anderson et al., 2010; Biro et al., 2010; Mitani et al., 2010).

There is no question that other species display many remarkable cognitive skills. But one big question remains: Do they, like humans, exhibit language? First, let's consider what language is, and how it develops.

* * *

What time is it now? When we asked you (in the section on overconfidence) to estimate how quickly you would finish this module, did you underestimate or overestimate?

Returning to our debate about how deserving we humans are of our name *Homo sapiens*, let's pause to issue an interim report card. On decision making and risk assessment, our error-prone species might rate a C+. On problem solving and creativity, where humans are inventive yet vulnerable to fixation, we would probably receive a better mark, perhaps a B. And when it comes to cognitive efficiency, our fallible but quick heuristics and divergent thinking would surely earn us an A.

MODULE 25 REVIEW Thinking

◉ Learning Objectives

Test Yourself by taking a moment to answer each of these Learning Objective Questions (repeated here from within the module). Then turn to Appendix D, Complete Module Reviews, to check your answers. Research suggests that trying to answer these questions on your own will improve your long-term memory of the concepts (McDaniel et al., 2009).

25-1 What is cognition, and what are the functions of concepts?

25-2 What cognitive strategies assist our problem solving, and what obstacles hinder it?

25-3 What is intuition, and how can the availability heuristic, overconfidence, belief perseverance, and framing influence our decisions and judgments?

25-4 What factors contribute to our fear of unlikely events?

25-5 How do smart thinkers use intuition?

25-6 What is creativity, and what fosters it?

25-7 What do we know about thinking in other animals?

⊡ Terms and Concepts to Remember

Test yourself on these terms by trying to write down the definition in your own words before flipping back to the referenced page to check your answers.

cognition, p. 316

concept, p. 316

prototype, p. 316

algorithm, p. 317

heuristic, p. 317

insight, p. 317

confirmation bias, p. 317

mental set, p. 318

intuition, p. 318

availability heuristic, p. 319

overconfidence, p. 321

belief perseverance, p. 322

framing, p. 322

creativity, p. 324

convergent thinking, p. 325

divergent thinking, p. 325

[✖] Experience the Testing Effect

Test yourself repeatedly throughout your studies. This will not only help you figure out what you know and don't know; the testing itself will help you learn and remember the information more effectively thanks to the *testing effect*.

1. A mental grouping of similar things is called a
   _____.

2. The most systematic procedure for solving a problem is
   a(n) _____.

3. Oscar describes his political beliefs as "strongly liberal," but he has decided to explore opposing viewpoints. How might he be affected by *confirmation bias* and *belief perseverance* in this effort?

4. A major obstacle to problem solving is fixation, which is a(n)
   a. tendency to base our judgments on vivid memories.
   b. tendency to wait for insight to occur.
   c. inability to view a problem from a new perspective.
   d. rule of thumb for judging the likelihood of an event based on its mental availability.

5. Widely reported terrorist attacks, such as on 9/11 in the United States, led some observers to initially assume in 2014 that the missing Malaysian Airlines Flight 370 was probably also the work of terrorists. This assumption illustrates the _____ heuristic.

6. When consumers respond more positively to ground beef described as "75 percent lean" than to the same product labeled "25 percent fat," they have been influenced by _____.

7. Which of the following is NOT a characteristic of a creative person?
   a. Expertise
   b. Extrinsic motivation
   c. A venturesome personality
   d. Imaginative thinking skills

Find answers to these questions in Appendix E, in the back of the book.

Use 🅰 LearningCurve to create your personalized study plan, which will direct you to the resources that will help you most in 🅰 LaunchPad.

MODULE 26 Language and Thought

Imagine an alien species that could pass thoughts from one head to another merely by pulsating air molecules in the space between them. Perhaps these weird creatures could inhabit a future science fiction movie?

Actually, we are those creatures. When we speak, our brain and voice apparatus conjure up air-pressure waves that we send banging against another's eardrum—enabling us to transfer thoughts from our brain into theirs. As cognitive scientist Steven Pinker (1998) has noted, we sometimes sit for hours "listening to other people make noise as they exhale, because those hisses and squeaks contain *information*." And thanks to all those funny sounds created in our heads from the air pressure waves, we get people's attention. We convince them to do things. We maintain relationships (Guerin, 2003). Depending on how you vibrate the air after opening your mouth, you may get a scowl or a kiss.

But **language** is more than vibrating air. As I [DM] create this paragraph, my fingers on a keyboard generate electronic binary numbers that are translated into the squiggles in front of you. When transmitted by reflected light rays into your retina, those squiggles trigger formless nerve impulses that project to several areas of your brain, which integrate the information, compare it to stored information, and decode meaning. Thanks to language, information is moving from my mind to yours. Monkeys mostly know what they see. Thanks to language (spoken, written, or signed), we comprehend much that we've never seen and that our distant ancestors never knew.

language our spoken, written, or signed words and the ways we combine them to communicate meaning.

"Eye dew."

Creating a language Brought together as if on a desert island (actually a school), Nicaragua's young deaf children over time drew upon sign gestures from home to create their own Nicaraguan Sign Language, complete with words and intricate grammar. Our biological predisposition for language does not create language in a vacuum. But activated by a social context, nature and nurture work creatively together (Osborne, 1999; Sandler et al., 2005; Senghas & Coppola, 2001).

If you were able to retain only one cognitive ability, make it language, suggests researcher Lera Boroditsky (2009). Without sight or hearing, you could still have friends, family, and a job. But without language, could you have these things? "Language is so fundamental to our experience, so deeply a part of being human, that it's hard to imagine life without it."

Language Structure

26-1 What are the structural components of a language?

Consider how we might go about inventing a language. For a spoken language, we would need three building blocks:

- **Phonemes** are the smallest distinctive sound units in a language. To say *bat*, English speakers utter the phonemes *b*, *a*, and *t*. (Phonemes aren't the same as letters. *That* also has three phonemes—*th*, *a*, and *t*.) English uses about 40; other languages use anywhere from half to more than twice that many. As a general rule, consonant phonemes carry more information than do vowel phonemes. *The treth ef thes stetement shed be evedent frem thes bref demenstretien.*

- **Morphemes** are the smallest language units that carry meaning. Most morphemes combine two or more phonemes. Some are words, while others are parts of words. The word "readers," for example, contains three morphemes: "read," "er" (signaling that we mean "one who reads"), and "s" (signaling that we mean not one, but multiple readers). Every word in a language contains one or more morphemes.

- **Grammar** is the system of rules that enables us to communicate—by deriving meaning from sounds *(semantics)* and ordering words into sentences *(syntax)*.

Like life constructed from the genetic code's simple alphabet, language is complexity built of simplicity. In English, for example, 40 or so phonemes can be combined to form more than 100,000 morphemes, which alone or in combination produce the 616,500 word forms in the *Oxford English Dictionary*. Using those words, we can then create an infinite number of sentences, most of which (like this one) are original.

Linguist Noam Chomsky has argued that all languages share some basic elements, which he calls *universal grammar*. All human languages, for example, have nouns, verbs, and adjectives as grammatical building blocks. From infancy onward, humans, no matter their language, prefer some syllables, such as *blif*, over others, such as *lbif* (Gómez et al., 2014). Nevertheless, the world's 6000+ languages are structurally very diverse (Evans & Levinson, 2009)—much more diverse than the universal grammar idea implies (Bergen, 2014; Ibbotson, 2012). Behaviorist B. F. Skinner (1957) believed we can explain this diversity with familiar learning principles, such as *association* (of the sights of things with the sounds of words); *imitation* (of the words and syntax modeled by others); and *reinforcement* (with smiles and hugs when the child says something right).

Chomsky also argued that humans are born with a built-in predisposition to learn grammar rules, which helps explain why preschoolers pick up language so readily and use grammar so well. It happens so naturally—as naturally as birds learn to fly—that training hardly helps. We are not born, however, with a built-in *specific* language. Europeans and Native Australia–New Zealand populations, though geographically separated for 50,000 years, can readily learn each other's very different languages (Chater et al., 2009). And whatever language we experience as children, whether spoken or signed, we all readily learn its specific grammar and vocabulary (Bavelier et al., 2003). Yet no matter what language we learn, we start speaking it mostly in nouns *(kitty, da-da)* rather than in verbs and adjectives (Bornstein et al., 2004). Biology and experience work together.

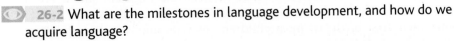
Language Development

26-2 What are the milestones in language development, and how do we acquire language?

Make a quick guess: How many words of your native language(s) did you learn between your first birthday and your high school graduation? Although you use only 150 words for about half of what you say, you probably learned about 60,000 words (Bloom, 2000; McMurray, 2007). That averages (after age 2) to nearly 3500 words each year, or nearly 10 each day! How you did it—how those 3500 words could so far outnumber the roughly 200 words your schoolteachers consciously taught you each year—is one of the great human wonders.

Could you even state the rules of syntax (the correct way to string words together to form sentences) in the language(s) you speak fluently? Most of us cannot. Yet before you were able to add 2 + 2, you were creating your own original and grammatically appropriate sentences. As a preschooler, you comprehended and spoke with a facility that puts to shame college students struggling to learn a new language.

We humans have an astonishing facility for language. With remarkable efficiency, we sample tens of thousands of words in our memory, effortlessly assemble them with near-perfect syntax, and spew them out, three words a second (Vigliocco & Hartsuiker, 2002). Seldom do we form sentences in our minds before speaking them; we organize them on the fly as we speak. And while doing all this, we also adapt our utterances to our social and cultural context. Given how many ways we can mess up, it's amazing that we master this social dance. When and how does it happen?

When and How Do We Learn Language?

RECEPTIVE LANGUAGE Children's language development moves from simplicity to complexity. Infants start without language (*in fantis* means "not speaking"). Yet by 4 months of age, babies can recognize differences in speech sounds (Stager & Werker, 1997). They can also read lips: They prefer to look at a face that matches a sound, so we know they can recognize that *ah* comes from wide open lips and *ee* from a mouth with corners pulled back (Kuhl & Meltzoff, 1982). This marks the beginning of the development of babies' *receptive language*, their ability to understand what is said to and about them. Infants' language comprehension greatly outpaces their language production. Even at six months, long before speaking, many infants recognize object names (Bergelson & Swingley, 2012, 2013). At 7 months and beyond, babies grow in their power to do what adults find difficult when listening to an unfamiliar language: to segment spoken sounds into individual words.

PRODUCTIVE LANGUAGE Long after the beginnings of receptive language, babies' *productive language*, their ability to produce words, matures. Before nurture molds their speech, nature enables a wide range of possible sounds in the **babbling stage,** beginning around 4 months. Many of these spontaneously uttered sounds are consonant-vowel pairs formed by simply bunching the tongue in the front of the mouth (*da-da, na-na, ta-ta*) or by opening and closing the lips (*ma-ma*), both of which babies do naturally for feeding (MacNeilage & Davis, 2000). Babbling does not imitate the adult speech babies hear—it includes sounds from various languages. From this early babbling, a listener could not identify an infant as being, say, French, Korean, or Ethiopian. Deaf infants who observe their deaf parents signing begin to babble more with their hands (Petitto & Marentette, 1991).

phoneme in a language, the smallest distinctive sound unit.

morpheme in a language, the smallest unit that carries meaning; may be a word or a part of a word (such as a prefix).

grammar in a language, a system of rules that enables us to communicate with and understand others. In a given language, *semantics* is the set of rules for deriving meaning from sounds, and *syntax* is the set of rules for combining words into grammatically sensible sentences.

babbling stage beginning at about 4 months, the stage of speech development in which the infant spontaneously utters various sounds at first unrelated to the household language.

Jaimie Duplass/Shutterstock

one-word stage the stage in speech development, from about age 1 to 2, during which a child speaks mostly in single words.

two-word stage beginning about age 2, the stage in speech development during which a child speaks mostly in two-word sentences.

telegraphic speech early speech stage in which a child speaks like a telegram—"go car"—using mostly nouns and verbs.

∨ TABLE 26.1

Summary of Language Development

Month (approximate)	Stage
4	Babbles many speech sounds ("ah-goo").
10	Babbling resembles household language ("ma-ma").
12	One-word stage ("Kitty!").
24	Two-word speech ("Get ball.").
24+	Rapid development into complete sentences.

"Got idea. Talk better. Combine words. Make sentences."

Sidney Harris/Science Cartoons Plus

By about 10 months old, infants' babbling has changed so that a trained ear can identify the household language (de Boysson-Bardies et al., 1989). Without exposure to other languages, babies lose their ability to discriminate and produce sounds and tones found outside their native language (Meltzoff et al., 2009; Pallier et al., 2001). Thus, by adulthood, those who speak only English cannot discriminate certain sounds in Japanese speech. Nor can Japanese adults with no training in English hear the difference between the English *r* and *l*. For a Japanese-speaking adult, *la-la-ra-ra* may sound like the same syllable repeated.

Around their first birthday, most children enter the **one-word stage.** They have already learned that sounds carry meanings, and if repeatedly trained to associate, say, *fish* with a picture of a fish, 1-year-olds will look at a fish when a researcher says, "Fish, fish! Look at the fish!" (Schafer, 2005). They now begin to use sounds—usually only one barely recognizable syllable, such as *ma* or *da*—to communicate meaning. But family members learn to understand, and gradually the infant's language conforms more to the family's language. Across the world, baby's first words are often nouns that label objects or people (Tardif et al., 2008). At this one-word stage, a single inflected word *("Doggy!")* may communicate a sentence *("Look at the dog out there!").*

At about 18 months, children's word learning explodes from about a word per week to a word per day. By their second birthday, most have entered the **two-word stage** (**TABLE 26.1**). They start uttering two-word sentences in **telegraphic speech.** Like today's texts or yesterday's telegrams that charged by the word (TERMS ACCEPTED. SEND MONEY), a 2-year-old's speech contains mostly nouns and verbs *("Want juice").* (Children recognize noun-verb differences—as shown by their responses to a misplaced noun or verb—earlier than they utter sentences with nouns and verbs [Bernal et al., 2010].) Also like telegrams, 2-year-olds' speech follows the rules of syntax specific to their language. English-speaking children typically place adjectives before nouns—*white house* rather than *house white.* Spanish-speaking children reverse this order, as in *casa blanca.*

Moving out of the two-word stage, children quickly begin uttering longer phrases (Fromkin & Rodman, 1983). If they get a late start on learning a particular language, such as after receiving a cochlear implant or being adopted by a family in another country, their language development still proceeds through the same sequence, although usually at a faster pace (Ertmer et al., 2007; Snedeker et al., 2007). By early elementary school, children understand complex sentences and begin to enjoy the humor conveyed by double meanings: "You never starve in the desert because of all the sand-which-is there."

RETRIEVE IT [✖]

• What is the difference between *receptive* and *productive* language, and when do children normally hit these milestones in language development?

ANSWER: Infants normally start developing *receptive* language skills (ability to understand what is said to and about them) around 4 months of age. Then, starting with babbling at 4 months and beyond, infants normally start building *productive* language skills (ability to produce sounds and eventually words).

CRITICAL PERIODS Childhood seems to represent a *critical* (or "sensitive") *period* for mastering certain aspects of language before the language-learning window closes (Hernandez & Li, 2007). People who learn a second language as adults usually speak it with the accent of their native language, and they also have difficulty mastering the new grammar. In one experiment, Korean and Chinese immigrants considered 276 English sentences *("Yesterday the hunter shoots a deer")* and decided whether they were grammatically correct or incorrect

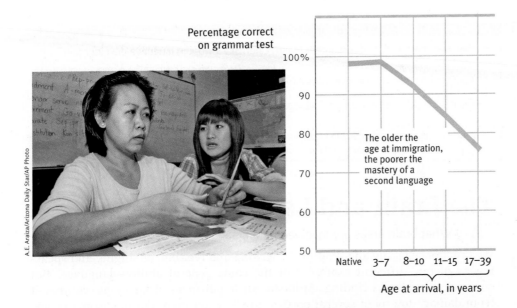

Percentage correct on grammar test

The older the age at immigration, the poorer the mastery of a second language

Native   3–7   8–10   11–15   17–39

Age at arrival, in years

A.E. Araiza/Arizona Daily Star/AP Photo

◀ FIGURE 26.1

Our ability to learn a new language diminishes with age Ten years after coming to the United States, Asian immigrants took an English grammar test. Although there is no sharply defined critical period for second language learning, those who arrived before age 8 understood American English grammar as well as native speakers did. Those who arrived later did not. (Data from Johnson & Newport, 1991.)

(Johnson & Newport, 1991). All had been in the United States for approximately 10 years: Some had arrived in early childhood, others as adults. As **FIGURE 26.1** reveals, those who learned their second language early learned it best. The older one is when moving to a new country, the harder it will be to learn its language and to absorb its culture (Cheung et al., 2011; Hakuta et al., 2003).

The window on language learning closes gradually in early childhood. Later-than-usual exposure to language (at age 2 or 3) unleashes the idle language capacity of a child's brain, producing a rush of language. But by about age 7, those who have not been exposed to either a spoken or a signed language gradually lose their ability to master *any* language.

George Ancona

Don't means *Don't*—no matter how you say it! Deaf children of deaf-signing parents and hearing children of hearing parents have much in common. They develop language skills at about the same rate, and they are equally effective at opposing parental wishes and demanding their way.

"Children can learn multiple languages without an accent and with good grammar, if they are exposed to the language before puberty. But after puberty, it's very difficult to learn a second language so well. Similarly, when I first went to Japan, I was told not even to bother trying to bow, that there were something like a dozen different bows and I was always going to 'bow with an accent.'"

Psychologist Stephen M. Kosslyn, "The World in the Brain," 2008

Deafness and Language Development

The impact of early experiences is evident in language learning in prelingually (before learning language) deaf children born to hearing-nonsigning parents. These children typically do not experience language during their early years. Natively deaf children who learn sign language after age 9 never learn it as well as those who lose their hearing at age 9 after learning a spoken language such as English. They also never learn English as well as other natively deaf children who learned sign in infancy (Mayberry et al., 2002). Those who learn to sign as teens or adults are like immigrants who learn English after childhood: They can master basic words and learn to order them, but they never become as fluent as native signers in producing and comprehending subtle grammatical differences (Newport, 1990). As a flower's growth will be stunted without nourishment, so, too, children will typically become linguistically stunted if isolated from language during the critical period for its acquisition.

Andy Richter/Aurora Photos/Corbis

Hearing improved A boy in Malawi experiences new hearing aids.

aphasia impairment of language, usually caused by left hemisphere damage either to Broca's area (impairing speaking) or to Wernicke's area (impairing understanding).

Broca's area controls language expression—an area of the frontal lobe, usually in the left hemisphere, that directs the muscle movements involved in speech.

Wernicke's area controls language reception—a brain area involved in language comprehension and expression; usually in the left temporal lobe.

LaunchPad To review research on left and right hemisphere language processing—and to test your own speed in processing words presented to your left and right hemispheres—visit LaunchPad's *PsychSim 6: Dueling Hemispheres.*

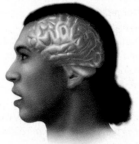 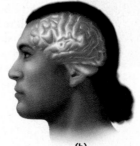

(a)
**Speaking words
(Broca's area and
the motor cortex)**

(b)
**Hearing words
(auditory cortex and
Wernicke's area)**

▲ FIGURE 26.2

Brain activity when speaking and hearing words

"It is the way systems interact and have a dynamic interdependence that is—unless one has lost all sense of wonder—quite awe-inspiring."

*Simon Conway Morris,
"The Boyle Lecture," 2005*

The Brain and Language

⬤ 26-3 What brain areas are involved in language processing and speech?

We think of speaking and reading, or writing and reading, or singing and speaking as merely different examples of the same general ability—language. But consider this curious finding: **Aphasia,** an impairment of language, can result from damage to any of several cortical areas. Even more curious, some people with aphasia can speak fluently but cannot read (despite good vision), while others can comprehend what they read but cannot speak. Still others can write but not read, read but not write, read numbers but not letters, or sing but not speak. Indeed, in 1865, French physician Paul Broca reported that after damage to an area of the left frontal lobe (later called **Broca's area**), a person would struggle to *speak* words while still being able to sing familiar songs and comprehend speech. These cases suggest that language is complex, and that different brain areas serve different language functions.

In 1874, German investigator Carl Wernicke discovered that after damage to an area of the left temporal lobe (**Wernicke's area**), people could speak only meaningless sentences. Asked to describe a picture that showed two boys stealing cookies behind a woman's back, one patient responded: "Mother is away her working her work to get her better, but when she's looking the two boys looking the other part. She's working another time" (Geschwind, 1979). Damage to Wernicke's area also disrupts understanding.

Today's neuroscience has confirmed brain activity in Broca's and Wernicke's areas during language processing (**FIGURE 26.2**). But language functions are distributed across other brain areas as well. Functional MRI scans show that what you experience as a continuous, indivisible stream of experience—language—is actually but the visible tip of an information-processing iceberg. Different neural networks are activated by nouns and verbs (or objects and actions); by different vowels; and by reading stories of visual versus motor experiences (Shapiro et al., 2006; Speer et al., 2009). If you are bilingual, the neural networks that enable your native language differ from those that enable your second language (Perani & Abutalebi, 2005).

The big point to remember: In processing language, as in other forms of information processing, the brain operates by dividing its mental functions—speaking, perceiving, thinking, remembering—into subfunctions. Your conscious experience of reading this page *seems* indivisible, but you are engaging many different neural networks in your brain to compute each word's form, sound, and meaning (Posner & Carr, 1992). Different brain areas also process information about who spoke and what was said (Perrachione et al., 2011). We can also see this distributed processing in vision, as the brain engages in specialized visual subtasks (discerning color, depth, movement, and form). *E pluribus unum:* Out of many, one.

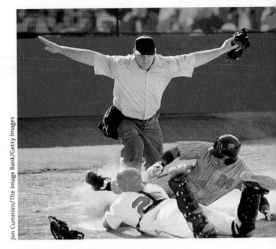

Do Other Species Have Language?

👁 **26-4** What do we know about other animals' capacity for language?

Humans have long and proudly proclaimed that language sets us above all other animals. "When we study human language," asserted Chomsky (1972), "we are approaching what some might call the 'human essence,' the qualities of mind that are, so far as we know, unique [to humans]." Is it true that humans, alone, have language?

Animals display impressive comprehension and communication. Vervet monkeys sound different alarm cries for different predators: a barking call for a leopard, a cough for an eagle, and a chuttering for a snake. Hearing the leopard alarm, other vervets climb the nearest tree. Hearing the eagle alarm, they rush into the bushes. Hearing the snake chutter, they stand up and scan the ground (Byrne, 1991). To indicate threats, monkeys can also combine 6 different calls into a 25-call sequence (Balter, 2010). But is this language? This question launched many studies with chimpanzees.

In the late 1960s, psychologists Allen Gardner and Beatrix Gardner (1969) built on chimpanzees' natural tendencies for gestured communication by teaching sign language to a chimpanzee named Washoe. After four years, Washoe could use 132 signs; by her life's end in 2007, she was using more than 245 signs (Metzler, 2011; Sanz et al., 1998). One *New York Times* reporter, having learned sign language from his deaf parents, visited Washoe and exclaimed, "Suddenly I realized I was conversing with a member of another species in my native tongue." Some chimpanzees strung signs together to form sentences. Washoe, for example, signed "You me go out, please." Some word combinations seemed creative—saying *water bird* for "swan" or *apple-which-is-orange* for "orange" (Patterson, 1978; Rumbaugh, 1977). But some psychologists grew skeptical. Were the chimps language champs or were the researchers chumps? Consider, said the skeptics:

- Ape vocabularies and sentences are simple, rather like those of a 2-year-old child. And unlike speaking or signing children, apes gain their limited vocabularies only with great difficulty (Wynne, 2004, 2008).

- Chimpanzees can make signs or push buttons in sequence to get a reward. But pigeons, too, can peck a sequence of keys to get grain (Straub et al., 1979). The apes' signing might be nothing more than aping their trainers' signs and learning that certain arm movements produce rewards (Terrace, 1979).

- Studies of *perceptual set* show that when information is unclear, we tend to see what we want or expect to see. Interpreting chimpanzee signs as language may be little more than the trainers' wishful thinking (Terrace, 1979). When Washoe signed *water bird*, she may have been separately naming *water* and *bird*.

- "Give orange me give eat orange me eat orange . . ." is a far cry from the exquisite syntax of a 3-year-old (Anderson, 2004; Pinker, 1995).

Controversy can stimulate progress, and in this case, it triggered more evidence of chimpanzees' abilities to think and communicate. Kanzi, a bonobo with a reported 384-word vocabulary, could understand syntax in spoken English (Savage-Rumbaugh et al., 1993, 2009). Kanzi has responded appropriately when

Talking hands Human language appears to have evolved from gestured communications (Corballis, 2002, 2003; Pollick & de Waal, 2007). Even today, gestures are naturally associated with spontaneous speech, especially speech that has spatial content. Both gesture and speech communicate, and when they convey the same rather than different information (as they do in baseball's sign language), we humans understand faster and more accurately (Hostetter, 2011; Kelly et al., 2010). Outfielder William Hoy, the first deaf player to join the major leagues (1892), reportedly helped invent hand signals for "Strike!" "Safe!" (shown here) and "Yerr out!" (Pollard, 1992). Referees in all sports now use invented signs, and fans are fluent in sports sign language.

But is this language? Chimpanzees' ability to express themselves in American Sign Language (ASL) raises questions about the very nature of language. Here, the trainer is asking, "What is this?" The sign in response is "Baby." Does the response constitute language?

Comprehending canine Border collie Rico had a vocabulary of 200 human words. If asked to retrieve a toy with a name he had never heard, Rico would pick out a new toy from a group of familiar items (Kaminski et al., 2004). Hearing that name for the second time four weeks later, Rico more often than not would retrieve the same toy. Another border collie, Chaser, has set an animal record by learning 1022 object names (Pilley & Reid, 2011). Like a 3-year-old child, she can also categorize them by function and shape. She can "fetch a ball" or "fetch a doll."

Susanne Baus/AFP/Getty Images/Newscom

LaunchPad For examples of intelligent communication and problem solving among orangutans, elephants, and killer whales, watch LaunchPad's 6-minute *Video: How Intelligent Are Animals?* See also *Video: Case Studies* for a helpful tutorial animation on this type of research method.

asked, "Can you show me the light?" and "Can you bring me the [flash]light?" and "Can you turn the light on?" Given stuffed animals and asked—for the first time—to "make the dog bite the snake," he put the snake to the dog's mouth.

So, how should we interpret these *case studies*? Are humans the only language-using species? If by *language* we mean verbal or signed expression of complex grammar, most psychologists would now agree that humans alone possess language. Humans, alone, also have a version of a gene *(FOXP2)* that facilitates speech and language development. If we mean, more simply, an ability to communicate through a meaningful sequence of symbols, then apes are indeed capable of language. And other species do exhibit insight, show family loyalty, communicate with one another, care for one another, and transmit cultural patterns across generations. Working out what this means for the moral rights of other animals is an unfinished task.

RETRIEVE IT [✗]

• If your dog barks at a stranger at the front door, does this qualify as language? What if the dog yips in a telltale way to let you know she needs to go out?

ANSWER: These are definitely communications. But if language consists of words and the grammatical rules we use to combine them to communicate meaning, few scientists would label a dog's barking and yipping as language.

Thinking and Language

26-5 What is the relationship between thinking and language, and what is the value of thinking in images?

Thinking and language intricately intertwine. Asking which comes first is one of psychology's chicken-and-egg questions. Do our ideas come first and then the words to name them? Or are our thoughts conceived in words and therefore unthinkable without them?

Language Influences Thinking

Linguist Benjamin Lee Whorf (1956) contended that "language itself shapes a [person's] basic ideas." The Hopi, who have no past tense for their verbs, could not readily *think* about the past, said Whorf.

Whorf's **linguistic determinism** hypothesis is too extreme. We all think about things for which we have no words. (Can you think of a shade of blue you cannot name?) And we routinely have *unsymbolized* (wordless, imageless) thoughts, as when someone, watching two men carry a load of bricks, wondered whether the men would drop them (Heavey & Hurlburt, 2008; Hurlburt et al., 2013).

Nevertheless, to those who speak two dissimilar languages, such as English and Japanese, it seems obvious that a person may think differently in different languages (Brown, 1986). Unlike English, which has a rich vocabulary for self-focused emotions such as anger, Japanese has more words for interpersonal emotions such as sympathy (Markus & Kitayama, 1991). Many bilingual individuals report having different senses of self, depending on which language they are using (Matsumoto, 1994). In one series of studies with bilingual Israeli Arabs (who spoke both Arabic and Hebrew), participants thought

differently about their social world, with differing automatic associations with Arabs and Jews, depending on which language the testing session used (Danziger & Ward, 2010).

Depending on which emotion they want to express, bilingual people will often switch languages. "When my mom gets angry at me, she'll speak in Mandarin," explained one Chinese-American student. "If she's really mad, she'll switch to Cantonese" (Chen et al., 2012). Bilingual individuals may even reveal different personality profiles when taking the same test in two languages, with their differing cultural associations (Chen & Bond, 2010; Dinges & Hull, 1992), as happened when China-born, bilingual University of Waterloo students were asked to describe themselves in English or Chinese (Ross et al., 2002). The students' English-language self-descriptions fit typical Canadian profiles, expressing mostly positive self-statements and moods. Responding in Chinese, the same students gave typically Chinese self-descriptions, reporting more agreement with Chinese values and roughly equal positive and negative self-statements and moods. Similar personality changes have been shown when bicultural, bilingual Americans and Mexicans shifted between the cultural frames associated with English and Spanish (Ramírez-Esparza et al., 2006). When responding in their second language, bilingual people's moral judgments reflect less emotion—they respond with more "head" than "heart" (Costa et al., 2014). "Learn a new language and get a new soul," says a Czech proverb.

Our words may not *determine* what we think, but they do *influence* our thinking (Boroditsky, 2011). We use our language in forming categories. In Brazil, the isolated Piraha people have words for the numbers 1 and 2, but numbers above that are simply "many." Thus, if shown 7 nuts in a row, they struggle to lay out the same number from their own pile (Gordon, 2004).

Words also influence our thinking about colors. Whether we live in New Mexico, New South Wales, or New Guinea, we *see* colors much the same, but we use our native language to *classify* and *remember* them (Davidoff, 2004; Roberson et al., 2004, 2005). Imagine viewing three colors and calling two of them "yellow" and one of them "blue." Later you would likely recall the yellows as being more similar. But if you speak the language of Papua New Guinea's Berinmo tribe, which has words for two different shades of yellow, you would more speedily perceive and better recall the variations between the two yellows. And if your language is Russian, which has distinct names for various shades of blue, such as *goluboy* and *siniy,* you might recall the yellows as more similar and remember the blue better. Words matter.

Perceived differences grow as we assign different names. On the color spectrum, blue blends into green—until we draw a dividing line between the portions we call "blue" and "green." Although equally different on the color spectrum, two different items that share the same color name (as the two "blues" do in **FIGURE 26.3**, contrast B) are harder to distinguish than two items with different names ("blue" and "green," as in Figure 26.3, contrast A) (Özgen, 2004). Likewise, two places seem closer and more vulnerable to the same natural disaster if labeled as in the same state rather than at an equal distance in adjacent states (Burris & Branscombe, 2005; Mishra & Mishra, 2010). Tornadoes don't know about state lines, but people do.

linguistic determinism Whorf's hypothesis that language determines the way we think.

Culture and color In Papua New Guinea, Berinmo children have words for different shades of "yellow," which might enable them to spot and recall yellow variations more quickly. Here and everywhere, "the languages we speak profoundly shape the way we think, the way we see the world, the way we live our lives," notes psychologist Lera Boroditsky (2009).

Prisma Bildagentur AG/Alamy

‹ **FIGURE 26.3**

Language and perception When people view blocks of equally different colors, they perceive those with different names as more different. Thus the "green" and "blue" in contrast A may appear to differ more than the two equally different blues in contrast B (Özgen, 2004).

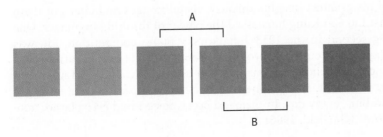

A

B

Given words' subtle influence on thinking, we do well to choose our words carefully. Is "A child learns language as *he* interacts with *his* caregivers" any different from "Children learn language as *they* interact with *their* caregivers"? Many studies have found that it is. When hearing the generic *he* (as in "the artist and his work") people are more likely to picture a male (Henley, 1989; Ng, 1990). If *he* and *his* were truly gender free, we shouldn't skip a beat when hearing that "man, like other mammals, nurses his young."

To expand language is to expand the ability to think. Young children's thinking develops hand in hand with their language (Gopnik & Meltzoff, 1986). Indeed, it is very difficult to think about or conceptualize certain abstract ideas (*commitment*, *freedom*, or *rhyming*) without language! And what is true for preschoolers is true for everyone: *It pays to increase your word power.* That's why most textbooks, including this one, introduce new words—to teach new ideas and new ways of thinking.

Increased word power helps explain what McGill University researcher Wallace Lambert (1992; Lambert et al., 1993) has called the *bilingual advantage.* In published studies—though perhaps less so in unpublished studies (Bialystok et al., 2015; de Bruin et al., 2015a,b)—bilingual people have exhibited skill at inhibiting one language while using the other. And thanks to their well-practiced "executive control" over language, they have also been better at inhibiting their attention to irrelevant information (Kroll & Bialystock, 2013).

Lambert helped devise a Canadian program that has, since 1981, immersed millions of English-speaking children in French (Statistics Canada, 2013). Not surprisingly, the children attain a natural French fluency unrivaled by other methods of language teaching. Moreover, compared with similarly capable children in control groups, they do so without detriment to their English fluency, and with increased aptitude scores, creativity, and appreciation for French-Canadian culture (Genesee & Gándara, 1999; Lazaruk, 2007).

Whether we are in the linguistic minority or majority, language links us to one another. Language also connects us to the past and the future. "To destroy a people, destroy their language," observed poet Joy Harjo.

> "All words are pegs to hang ideas on."
>
> *Henry Ward Beecher,*
> Proverbs from Plymouth Pulpit,
> *1887*

IMMERSIVE LEARNING
To consider how researchers have learned about the benefits of speaking more than one language, visit LaunchPad's *How Would You Know If There Is a Bilingual Advantage?*

RETRIEVE IT [✖]

• Benjamin Lee Whorf's controversial hypothesis, called _____ _____, suggested that we cannot think about things unless we have words for those concepts or ideas.

ANSWER: linguistic determinism

Thinking in Images

When you are alone, do you talk to yourself? Is "thinking" simply conversing with yourself? Words do convey ideas. But sometimes ideas precede words. To turn on the cold water in your bathroom, in which direction do you turn the handle? To answer, you probably thought not in words but with *implicit* (nondeclarative, procedural) memory—a mental picture of how you do it.

Indeed, we often think in images. Artists think in images. So do composers, poets, mathematicians, athletes, and scientists. Albert Einstein reported that he achieved some of his greatest insights through visual images and later put them into words. Pianist Liu Chi Kung harnessed the power of thinking in images. One year after placing second in the 1958 Tchaikovsky piano competition, Liu was imprisoned during China's cultural revolution. Soon after his release, after seven years without touching a piano, he was back on tour. Critics judged Liu's musicianship as better than ever. How did he continue to develop without practice? "I did practice," said Liu, "every day. I rehearsed every piece I had ever played, note by note, in my mind" (Garfield, 1986).

> "When we see a person walking down the street talking to himself, we generally assume that he is mentally ill. But we all talk to ourselves continuously—we just have the good sense of keeping our mouths shut. . . . It's as though we are having a conversation with an imaginary friend possessed of infinite patience. Who are we talking to?"
>
> *Sam Harris,*
> *"We Are Lost in Thought," 2011*

For someone who has learned a skill, such as ballet dancing, even *watching* the activity will activate the brain's internal simulation of it, reported one British research team after people underwent fMRIs while watching videos (Calvo-Merino et al., 2004). So, too, will *imagining* a physical experience, which activates some of the same neural networks that are active during the actual experience (Grèzes & Decety, 2001). Small wonder, then, that mental practice has become a standard part of training for Olympic athletes (Suinn, 1997; Ungerleider, 2005).

One experiment on mental practice and basketball free-throw shooting tracked the University of Tennessee women's team over 35 games (Savoy & Beitel, 1996). During that time, the team's free-throw accuracy increased from approximately 52 percent in games following standard physical practice to some 65 percent after mental practice. Players had repeatedly imagined making free throws under various conditions, including being "trash-talked" by their opposition. In a dramatic conclusion, Tennessee won the national championship game in overtime, thanks in part to their free-throw shooting.

Mental rehearsal can also help you achieve an academic goal, as researchers demonstrated with two groups of introductory psychology students facing a midterm exam one week later (Taylor et al., 1998). (Scores of other students, not engaging in any mental simulation, formed a control group.) The first group spent five minutes each day visualizing themselves scanning the posted grade list, seeing their A, beaming with joy, and feeling proud. This *outcome simulation* had little effect, adding only 2 points to their exam-score average. Another group spent five minutes each day visualizing themselves effectively studying—reading the textbook, going over notes, eliminating distractions, declining an offer to go out. This *process simulation* paid off: This second group began studying sooner, spent more time at it, and beat the others' average by 8 points.

The point to remember: It's better to spend your fantasy time planning *how* to get somewhere than to dwell on the imagined destination.

Blend Images/Jupiterimages

LaunchPad To experience your own thinking as (a) manipulating words and (b) manipulating images, visit LaunchPad's *PsychSim 6: My Head Is Spinning!*

* * *

What, then, should we say about the relationship between thinking and language? As we have seen, language influences our thinking. But if thinking did not also affect language, there would never be any new words. And new words and new combinations of old words express new ideas. The basketball term *slam dunk* was coined after the act itself had become fairly common. So, let us say that *thinking affects our language, which then affects our thought* (**FIGURE 26.4**).

Psychological research on thinking and language suggests that the human mind is simultaneously capable of striking intellectual failures and striking intellectual power.

Jupiterimages

< FIGURE 26.4

The interplay of thought and language The traffic runs both ways between thinking and language. Thinking affects our language, which affects our thought.

Misjudgments are common and can have disastrous consequences. So we do well to appreciate our capacity for error. Yet our efficient heuristics often serve us well. Moreover, our ingenuity at problem solving and our extraordinary power of language mark humankind as almost "infinite in faculties."

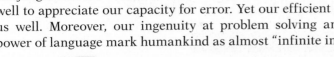

RETRIEVE IT [✱]

• What is mental practice, and how can it help you to prepare for an upcoming event?

ANSWER: Mental practice uses visual imagery to mentally rehearse future behaviors, activating some of the same brain areas used during the actual behaviors. Visualizing the details of the process is more effective than visualizing only your end goal.

MODULE 26 REVIEW   Language and Thought

◉ Learning Objectives

Test Yourself by taking a moment to answer each of these Learning Objective Questions (repeated here from within the module). Then turn to Appendix D, Complete Module Reviews, to check your answers. Research suggests that trying to answer these questions on your own will improve your long-term memory of the concepts (McDaniel et al., 2009).

26-1 What are the structural components of a language?

26-2 What are the milestones in language development, and how do we acquire language?

26-3 What brain areas are involved in language processing and speech?

26-4 What do we know about other animals' capacity for language?

26-5 What is the relationship between thinking and language, and what is the value of thinking in images?

▣ Terms and Concepts to Remember

Test yourself on these terms by trying to write down the definition in your own words before flipping back to the referenced page to check your answers.

language, p. 329

phoneme, p. 330

morpheme, p. 330

grammar, p. 330

babbling stage, p. 331

one-word stage, p. 332

two-word stage, p. 332

telegraphic speech, p. 332

aphasia, p. 334

Broca's area, p. 334

Wernicke's area, p. 334

linguistic determinism, p. 336

[✻] Experience the Testing Effect

Test yourself repeatedly throughout your studies. This will not only help you figure out what you know and don't know; the testing itself will help you learn and remember the information more effectively thanks to the *testing effect*.

1. Children reach the one-word stage of speech development at about
   a. 4 months.
   b. 6 months.
   c. 1 year.
   d. 2 years.

2. The three basic building blocks of language are _____, _____, and _____.

3. When young children speak in short phrases using mostly verbs and nouns, this is referred to as _____ _____.

4. According to Chomsky, all languages share a(n) _____ _____.

5. Most researchers agree that apes can
   a. communicate through symbols.
   b. reproduce most human speech sounds.
   c. master language in adulthood.
   d. surpass a human 3-year-old in language skills.

Find answers to these questions in Appendix E, in the back of the book.

Use ◉ LearningCurve to create your personalized study plan, which will direct you to the resources that will help you most in ◉ LaunchPad.

---

intelligence the mental potential to learn from experience, solve problems, and use knowledge to adapt to new situations.

general intelligence (g) a general intelligence factor that, according to Spearman and others, underlies specific mental abilities and is therefore measured by every task on an intelligence test.

MODULE 27 Intelligence and Its Assessment

So far, we have considered how our species thinks and communicates. But we differ from one another in these abilities. School boards, courts, and scientists debate the use and fairness of tests that assess people's mental abilities and assign them a score. In psychology, no controversy has been more heated than the question of whether there exists in each person a general intellectual capacity that can be measured and quantified as a number.

In this module, we consider some findings from a century of research, as psychologists have searched for answers to these questions and more:

- What is intelligence?
- Is intelligence one general ability or many different abilities?
- How can we best assess intelligence?

What Is Intelligence?

27-1 How do psychologists define *intelligence*, and what are the arguments for *g*?

In many studies, *intelligence* has been defined as whatever *intelligence tests* measure, which has tended to be school smarts. But intelligence is not a quality like height or weight, which has the same meaning to everyone worldwide. People assign the term *intelligence* to the qualities that enable success in their own time and culture (Sternberg & Kaufman, 1998). In Cameroon's equatorial forest, *intelligence* may reflect understanding the medicinal qualities of local plants. In a North American high school, it may reflect mastering difficult concepts in tough courses. In both places, **intelligence** is the mental potential to learn from experience, solve problems, and use knowledge to adapt to new situations.

You probably know some people with talents in science, others who excel in the humanities, and still others gifted in athletics, art, music, or dance. You may also know a talented artist who is stumped by the simplest math problem, or a brilliant math student who struggles when discussing literature. Are all these people intelligent? Could you rate their intelligence on a single scale? Or would you need several different scales? Simply put, is intelligence a single overall ability or several specific abilities?

Spearman's General Intelligence Factor

Charles Spearman (1863–1945) believed we have one **general intelligence** (often shortened to *g*) that is at the heart of all of our intelligent behavior, from navigating the sea to excelling in school. He granted that people often have special, outstanding abilities. But he noted that those who score high in one area, such as verbal intelligence, typically score higher than average in other areas, such as spatial or reasoning ability.

Spearman's belief stemmed in part from his work with *factor analysis*, a statistical procedure that identifies clusters of related items. In this view, mental abilities are much like physical abilities: The ability to run fast is distinct from the eye-hand coordination required to throw a ball on target. Yet there remains some tendency for good things to come packaged together—for running speed and throwing accuracy to correlate. In both athleticism and intelligence, several distinct abilities tend to cluster together and to correlate enough to define a general underlying factor. Distinct brain networks enable distinct abilities, with *g* explained by their coordinated activity (Hampshire et al., 2012).

Theories of Multiple Intelligences

27-2 How do Gardner's and Sternberg's theories of multiple intelligences differ, and what criticisms have they faced?

Other psychologists, particularly since the mid-1980s, have sought to extend the definition of *intelligence* beyond the idea of academic smarts.

GARDNER'S MULTIPLE INTELLIGENCES Howard Gardner has identified eight *relatively independent intelligences*, including the verbal and mathematical aptitudes assessed by standardized tests (**FIGURE 27.1** on the next page). Thus, the computer programmer, the poet, the street-smart adolescent, and the basketball

Hands-on healing The socially constructed concept of intelligence varies from culture to culture. This natural healer in Cameroon displays intelligence in his knowledge about medicinal plants and his understanding of the needs of the people he is helping.

Heiner Heine/© imagebroker/Alamy

"*g* is one of the most reliable and valid measures in the behavioral domain . . . and it predicts important social outcomes such as educational and occupational levels far better than any other trait."

Behavior geneticist Robert Plomin (1999)

Jonathan Larsen/Diadem Images/Alamy

^ FIGURE 27.1

Gardner's eight intelligences
Gardner has also proposed a ninth
possible intelligence—existential
intelligence—the ability to ponder deep
questions about life.

> **savant syndrome** a condition in which
> a person otherwise limited in mental
> ability has an exceptional specific skill,
> such as in computation or drawing.

team's play-making point guard exhibit different kinds of intelligence (Gardner,
1998). Gardner (1999) has also proposed a ninth possible intelligence—*existential*
intelligence—the ability "to ponder large questions about life, death, existence."

Gardner (1983, 2006, 2011; Davis et al., 2011) views these intelligence domains
as multiple abilities that come in different packages. Brain damage, for example,
may destroy one ability but leave others intact. And consider people with
savant syndrome. Despite their island of brilliance, these people often score
low on intelligence tests and may have limited or no language ability (Treffert &
Wallace, 2002). Some can compute complicated calculations quickly and accurately, or identify almost instantly the day of the week corresponding to any historical date, or render incredible works of art or musical performance (Miller, 1999).

Islands of genius: Savant syndrome
After a brief helicopter ride over Singapore
followed by five days of drawing, British
savant artist Stephen Wiltshire accurately
reproduced an aerial view of the city from
memory.

About four in five people with savant syndrome are males. Many also have *autism spectrum disorder (ASD)*, a developmental disorder. The late memory whiz Kim Peek (who did not have ASD) inspired the movie *Rain Man*. In 8 to 10 seconds, he could read and remember a page. During his lifetime, he memorized 9000 books, including Shakespeare's works and the Bible. He could provide GPS-like travel directions within any major U.S. city. Yet he could not button his clothes, and he had little capacity for abstract concepts. Asked by his father at a restaurant to lower his voice, he slid down in his chair to lower his voice box. Asked for Lincoln's Gettysburg Address, he responded, "227 North West Front Street. But he only stayed there one night—he gave the speech the next day" (Treffert & Christensen, 2005).

"You're wise, but you lack tree smarts."

STERNBERG'S THREE INTELLIGENCES Robert Sternberg (1985, 2011) agrees with Gardner that there is more to success than traditional intelligence and that we have multiple intelligences. But his *triarchic theory* proposes three, not eight or nine, intelligences:

- *Analytical intelligence* (school smarts; traditional academic problem solving)
- *Creative intelligence* (the ability to react adaptively to new situations and generate novel ideas)
- *Practical intelligence* (street smarts; skill at handling everyday tasks, which may be ill defined, with multiple solutions)

Gardner and Sternberg differ in some areas, but they agree on two important points: Multiple abilities can contribute to life success, and varieties of giftedness bring spice to life and challenges for education. As a result of this research, many teachers have been trained to appreciate such variety and to apply multiple intelligence theories in their classrooms.

CRITICISMS OF MULTIPLE INTELLIGENCE THEORIES Wouldn't it be wonderful if the world were so just that a weakness in one area would be compensated by genius in another? Alas, say critics, the world is not just (Ferguson, 2009; Scarr, 1989). Research using factor analysis has confirmed that there *is* a general intelligence factor (Johnson et al., 2008): *g* matters. It predicts performance on various complex tasks and in various jobs (Gottfredson, 2002a,b, 2003a,b; see also **FIGURE 27.2**). Much as jumping ability is not a predictor of jumping performance when the bar is set a foot off the ground—but becomes a predictor when the bar is set higher—so extremely high cognitive ability scores predict exceptional attainments, such as doctoral degrees and publications (Kuncel & Hezlett, 2010).

"You have to be careful, if you're good at something, to make sure you don't think you're good at other things that you aren't necessarily so good at. . . . Because I've been very successful at [software development] people come in and expect that I have wisdom about topics that I don't."

Philanthropist Bill Gates (1998)

Street smarts This child selling candy on the streets of Manaus, Brazil, is developing practical intelligence at a very young age.

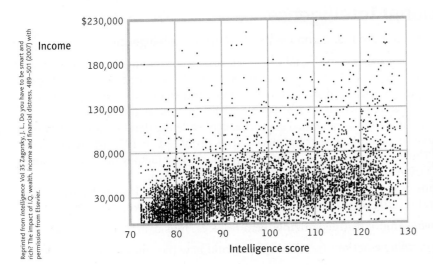

◀ FIGURE 27.2

Smart and rich? Jay Zagorsky (2007) tracked 7403 participants in the U.S. National Longitudinal Survey of Youth across 25 years. As shown in this scatterplot, their intelligence scores correlated +.30, a moderate positive correlation, with their later income. Each dot indicates a given youth's intelligence score and later adult income.

Reprinted from *Intelligence* Vol 35 Zagorsky, J. L., Do you have to be smart and rich? The impact of I.Q. wealth, income and financial distress, 489–501 (2007) with permission from Elsevier.

Spatial intelligence genius In 1998, World Checkers Champion Ron "Suki" King of Barbados set a new record by simultaneously playing 385 players in 3 hours and 44 minutes. Thus, while his opponents often had hours to plot their game moves, King could only devote about 35 seconds to each game. Yet he still managed to win all 385 games!

Bees, birds, chimpanzees, and other species also require time and experience to acquire peak expertise in skills such as foraging (Helton, 2008). As with humans, performance tends to peak near midlife.

See the Motivation and Emotion modules for more on how self-disciplined grit feeds achievement.

Even so, "success" is not a one-ingredient recipe. High intelligence may help you get into a profession (via the schools and training programs that take you there), but it won't make you successful once there. Success is a combination of talent and *grit:* Those who become highly successful tend also to be conscientious, well connected, and doggedly energetic. Researchers report a *10-year rule:* A common ingredient of expert performance in chess, dancing, sports, computer programming, music, and medicine is "about 10 years of intense, daily practice" (Ericsson, 2002, 2007; Simon & Chase, 1973). Becoming a professional musician, for example, requires native ability. But it also requires practice—about 11,000 hours on average, and a *minimum* of 3000 hours (Campitelli & Gobet, 2011). The recipe for success is a gift of nature plus a whole lot of nurture.

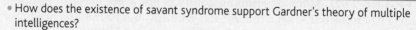

RETRIEVE IT

• How does the existence of savant syndrome support Gardner's theory of multiple intelligences?

ANSWER: People with savant syndrome have limited mental ability overall but possess one or more exceptional skills. According to Howard Gardner, this suggests that our abilities come in separate packages rather than being fully expressed by one general intelligence that encompasses all of our talents.

Emotional Intelligence

 27-3 What are the four components of emotional intelligence?

Is being in tune with yourself and others also a sign of intelligence, distinct from academic intelligence? Some researchers say *Yes.* They define *social intelligence* as the know-how involved in social situations and managing yourself successfully (Cantor & Kihlstrom, 1987). People with high social intelligence can read social situations the way a skilled soccer player reads the defense or a meteorologist reads the weather. The concept was first proposed in 1920 by psychologist Edward Thorndike, who noted, "The best mechanic in a factory may fail as a foreman for lack of social intelligence" (Goleman, 2006, p. 83).

One line of research has explored a specific aspect of social intelligence called **emotional intelligence,** consisting of four abilities (Mayer et al., 2002, 2011, 2012):

• *Perceiving* emotions (recognizing them in faces, music, and stories)

• *Understanding* emotions (predicting them and how they may change and blend)

emotional intelligence the ability to perceive, understand, manage, and use emotions.

intelligence test a method for assessing an individual's mental aptitudes and comparing them with those of others, using numerical scores.

- *Managing* emotions (knowing how to express them in varied situations)
- *Using* emotions to enable adaptive or creative thinking

Emotionally intelligent people are both socially aware and self-aware. Those who score high on managing emotions enjoy higher-quality interactions with friends (Lopes et al., 2004). They avoid being hijacked by overwhelming depression, anxiety, or anger. They can read others' emotional cues and know what to say to soothe a grieving friend, encourage a workmate, and manage a conflict. They can delay gratification in pursuit of long-range rewards, rather than being overtaken by immediate impulses. They often succeed in career, marriage, and parenting situations where academically smarter (but emotionally less intelligent) people might fail (Cherniss, 2001a,b; Ciarrochi et al., 2006). Emotionally intelligent people also perform modestly better on the job (O'Boyle et al., 2011).

Some scholars, however, are concerned that emotional intelligence stretches the intelligence concept too far (Visser et al., 2006). Howard Gardner (1999) includes interpersonal and intrapersonal intelligences as two of his multiple intelligences. But let us instead, he offers, respect emotional sensitivity, creativity, and motivation as important but different. Stretch *intelligence* to include everything we prize and the word will lose its meaning.

The procrastinator's motto: "Hard work pays off later; laziness pays off now."

* * *

For a summary of these theories of intelligence, see **TABLE 27.1**.

∨ TABLE 27.1

Comparing Theories of Intelligence

Theory	Summary	Strengths	Other Considerations
Spearman's general intelligence (*g*)	A basic intelligence predicts our abilities in varied academic areas.	Different abilities, such as verbal and spatial, do have some tendency to correlate.	Human abilities are too diverse to be encapsulated by a single general intelligence factor.
Gardner's multiple intelligences	Our abilities are best classified into eight or nine independent intelligences, which include a broad range of skills beyond traditional school smarts.	Intelligence is more than just verbal and mathematical skills. Other abilities are equally important to our human adaptability.	Should all of our abilities be considered intelligences? Shouldn't some be called less vital talents?
Sternberg's triarchic theory	Our intelligence is best classified into three areas that predict real-world success: analytical, creative, and practical.	These three domains can be reliably measured.	1. These three domains may be less independent than Sternberg thought and may actually share an underlying *g* factor. 2. Additional testing is needed to determine whether these domains can reliably predict success.
Emotional intelligence	Social intelligence is an important indicator of life success. Emotional intelligence is a key aspect, consisting of perceiving, understanding, managing, and using emotions.	The four components that predict social success.	Does this stretch the concept of intelligence too far?

Assessing Intelligence

27-4 What is an intelligence test, and what is the difference between achievement and aptitude tests?

An **intelligence test** assesses people's mental abilities and compares them with others, using numerical scores. Psychologists classify such tests as either **aptitude tests,** intended to predict your ability to learn a new skill, or **achievement tests,** intended to reflect what you have already learned. How do we design such tests, and what makes them credible? Consider why psychologists created tests of mental abilities and how they have used them.

aptitude test a test designed to predict a person's future performance; *aptitude* is the capacity to learn.

achievement test a test designed to assess what a person has learned.

Alfred Binet (1857–1911) "Some recent philosophers have given their moral approval to the deplorable verdict that an individual's intelligence is a fixed quantity, one which cannot be augmented. We must protest and act against this brutal pessimism" (Binet, 1909, p. 141).

"The IQ test was invented to predict academic performance, nothing else. If we wanted something that would predict life success, we'd have to invent another test completely."

Social psychologist Robert Zajonc (1984b)

What Do Intelligence Tests Test?

27-5 When and why were intelligence tests created, and how do today's tests differ from early intelligence tests?

Barely a century ago, psychologists began designing tests to assess people's abilities. Some measured aptitude (ability to learn). Others assessed achievement (what people have already learned).

ALFRED BINET: PREDICTING SCHOOL ACHIEVEMENT Modern intelligence testing traces its birth to early-twentieth-century France, where a new law required all children to attend school. French officials knew that some children, including many newcomers to Paris, would struggle and need special classes. But how could the schools make fair judgments about children's learning potential? Teachers might assess children who had little prior education as slow learners. Or they might sort children into classes on the basis of their social backgrounds. To minimize such bias, France's minister of public education gave Alfred Binet (1857–1911) the task of solving this problem.

In 1905, Binet and his student, Théodore Simon, first presented their work under the archaic title, "New Methods for Diagnosing the Idiot, the Imbecile, and the Moron" (Nicolas & Levine, 2012). They began by assuming that all children follow the same course of intellectual development, but that some develop more rapidly. A "dull" child should score much like a typical younger child, and a "bright" child like a typical older child. Binet and Simon now had a clear goal: They would measure each child's **mental age,** the level of performance typically associated with a certain chronological age. The average 8-year-old, for example, has a mental age of 8. An 8-year-old with a below-average mental age (perhaps performing at the level of a typical 6-year-old) would struggle with schoolwork considered normal for 8-year-olds.

Binet and Simon tested a variety of reasoning and problem-solving questions on Binet's two daughters, and then on "bright" and "backward" Parisian schoolchildren. Items that the successful students more often answered correctly could then be used to predict how well other French children would handle their schoolwork. Binet hoped his test would be used to improve children's education, but he also feared it would be used to label children and limit their opportunities (Gould, 1981).

RETRIEVE IT [✗]

• What did Binet hope to achieve by establishing a child's *mental age*?

ANSWER: Binet hoped that determining *mental age* (the age that typically corresponds to a child's level of performance) would help identify appropriate school placements for children.

---

mental age a measure of intelligence test performance devised by Binet; the chronological age that most typically corresponds to a given level of performance. Thus, a child who does as well as an average 8-year-old is said to have a mental age of 8.

Stanford-Binet the widely used American revision (by Terman at Stanford University) of Binet's original intelligence test.

intelligence quotient (IQ) defined originally as the ratio of mental age (*ma*) to chronological age (*ca*) multiplied by 100 (thus, IQ = *ma/ca* × 100). On contemporary intelligence tests, the average performance for a given age is assigned a score of 100.

LEWIS TERMAN: THE INNATE IQ Binet's fears were realized soon after his death in 1911, when others adapted his tests for use as a numerical measure of inherited intelligence. Stanford University professor Lewis Terman (1877–1956) found that the Paris-developed questions and age norms worked poorly with California schoolchildren. He adapted some items, added others, and established new standards for various ages. He also extended the upper end of the test's range from teenagers to "superior adults" and gave his revision the name it retains today—the **Stanford-Binet.** Terman assumed that certain ethnic groups were naturally more intelligent, and he supported the controversial *eugenics* movement, which aimed to protect and improve human genetic quality through selective sterilization and breeding.

From such tests, German psychologist William Stern derived the famous **intelligence quotient,** or **IQ.** The IQ was simply a person's mental age divided by chronological age and multiplied by 100 to get rid of the decimal point. Thus, an average child, whose mental age (8) and chronological age (8) are the same, has an IQ of 100. But an 8-year-old who answers questions at the level of a typical 10-year-old has an IQ of 125:

$$IQ = \frac{\text{mental age of 10}}{\text{chronological age of 8}} \times 100 = 125$$

The original IQ formula worked fairly well for children but not for adults. (Should a 40-year-old who does as well on the test as an average 20-year-old be assigned an IQ of only 50?) Most current intelligence tests, including the Stanford-Binet, no longer compute an IQ in this manner (though the term *IQ* still lingers in everyday vocabulary as shorthand for "intelligence test score"). Instead, they represent the test-taker's performance *relative to the average performance of others the same age.* This average performance is arbitrarily assigned a score of 100, and about two-thirds of all test-takers fall between 85 and 115.

Mrs. Randolph takes mother's pride too far.

RETRIEVE IT [✗]

• What is the IQ of a 4-year-old with a mental age of 5?

ANSWER: 125 (5 ÷ 4 × 100 = 125)

DAVID WECHSLER: SEPARATE SCORES FOR SEPARATE SKILLS Psychologist David Wechsler created what is now the most widely used individual intelligence test, the **Wechsler Adult Intelligence Scale (WAIS).** There is a version for school-age children (the *Wechsler Intelligence Scale for Children [WISC]*), and another for preschool children (Evers et al., 2012). The WAIS (2008) edition consists of 15 subtests, including:

- *Similarities*—Considering the commonality of two objects or concepts ("In what way are wool and cotton alike?")

- *Vocabulary*—Naming pictured objects, or defining words ("What is a guitar?")

- *Block Design*—Visual abstract processing ("Using the four blocks, make one just like this.")

- *Letter-Number Sequencing*—On hearing a series of numbers and letters, repeat the numbers in ascending order, and then the letters in alphabetical order ("R-2-C-1-M-3.")

The WAIS yields both an overall intelligence score and individual scores for verbal comprehension, perceptual organization, working memory, and processing speed. Striking differences among these individual scores can provide clues to cognitive strengths or weaknesses. For example, a low verbal comprehension score combined with high scores on other subtests could indicate a reading or language disability. Other comparisons can help a therapist establish a rehabilitation plan for a stroke patient. In such ways, these tests help realize Binet's aim: to identify opportunities for improvement and strengths that teachers and others can build upon.

Matching patterns Block design puzzles test visual abstract processing ability. Wechsler's individually administered intelligence test comes in forms suited for adults and children.

RETRIEVE IT [✗]

• An employer with a pool of applicants for a single available position is interested in testing each applicant's potential. To help her decide whom she should hire, she should use an _____ (achievement/aptitude) test. That same employer wishing to test the effectiveness of a new, on-the-job training program would be wise to use an _____ (achievement/aptitude) test.

ANSWERS: aptitude; achievement

Three Tests of a "Good" Test

27-6 What is a normal curve, and what does it mean to say that a test has been standardized and is reliable and valid?

To be widely accepted, a psychological test must be *standardized, reliable,* and *valid.* The Stanford-Binet and Wechsler tests meet these requirements.

┌ **Wechsler Adult Intelligence Scale (WAIS)** the WAIS and its companion versions for children are the most widely used intelligence tests; contain verbal and performance (nonverbal) subtests. ┘

standardization defining uniform testing procedures and meaningful scores by comparison with the performance of a pretested group.

normal curve the bell-shaped curve that describes the distribution of many physical and psychological attributes. Most scores fall near the average, and fewer and fewer scores lie near the extremes.

reliability the extent to which a test yields consistent results, as assessed by the consistency of scores on two halves of the test, on alternative forms of the test, or on retesting.

validity the extent to which a test measures or predicts what it is supposed to. (See also *content validity* and *predictive validity*.)

content validity the extent to which a test samples the behavior that is of interest.

predictive validity the success with which a test predicts the behavior it is designed to predict; it is assessed by computing the correlation between test scores and the criterion behavior. (Also called *criterion-related validity*.)

 LaunchPad See LaunchPad's *Video: Correlational Studies* for a helpful tutorial animation.

WAS THE TEST STANDARDIZED? The number of questions you answer correctly on an intelligence test would reveal almost nothing. To know how well you performed, you would need some basis for comparison. That's why test-makers give new tests to a representative sample of people. The scores from this pretested group become the basis for future comparisons. If you later take the test following the same procedures, your score will be meaningful when compared with others. This process is called **standardization.**

If we construct a graph of test-takers' scores, the scores typically form a bell-shaped pattern called the **normal curve.** No matter what attributes we measure—height, weight, or mental aptitude—people's scores tend to form a *bell curve.* The highest point is the midpoint, or the average score. On an intelligence test, we give this average score a value of 100 (**FIGURE 27.3**). Moving out from the average, toward either extreme, we find fewer and fewer people. For the Stanford-Binet and Wechsler tests, a person's score indicates whether that person's performance fell above or below the average. A performance higher than all but 2 percent of all scores earns an intelligence score of 130. A performance lower than 98 percent of all scores earns an intelligence score of 70.

IS THE TEST RELIABLE? Knowing your score in comparison to the standardization group still won't tell you much unless the test has **reliability.** A reliable test gives consistent scores, no matter who takes the test or when they take it. To check a test's reliability, researchers test people many times. They may retest people using the same test, or they may split the test in half and see whether odd-question scores and even-question scores agree. If the two sets of scores generally agree, or *correlate,* the test is reliable. The higher the correlation, the higher the test's reliability. The tests we have considered so far—the Stanford-Binet, the WAIS, and the WISC—are, after early childhood, very reliable (about +.9). When retested, people's scores generally match their first score closely.

IS THE TEST VALID? High reliability does not ensure a test's **validity**—the extent to which the test actually measures or predicts what it promises. Imagine using a miscalibrated tape measure to measure people's heights. Your results would be very reliable. No matter how many times you measured, people's heights would be the same. But your results would not be valid, because you would not be giving the information you promised: real height.

Tests that tap the pertinent behavior, or *criterion,* have **content validity.** The road test for a driver's license has content validity because it samples the tasks a driver routinely faces. Course exams have content validity if they assess your mastery of course material. But we expect intelligence tests to have **predictive validity:** They should predict future performance, and to some extent they do.

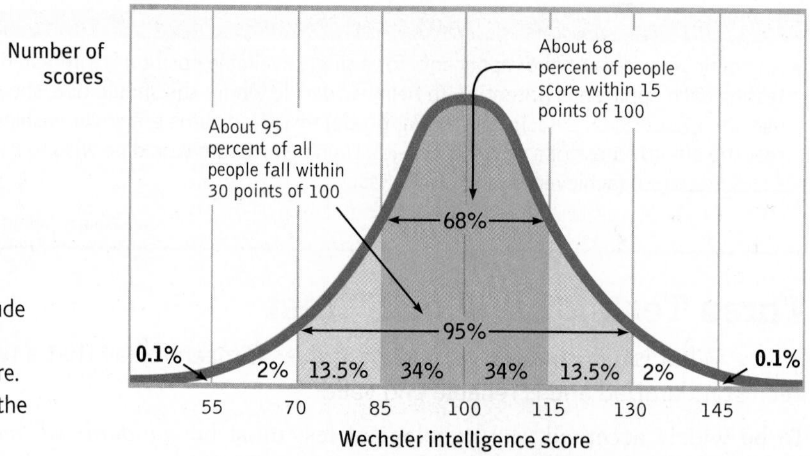

> FIGURE 27.3

The normal curve Scores on aptitude tests tend to form a normal, or bell-shaped, curve around an average score. For the Wechsler scale, for example, the average score is 100.

Number of scores

About 95 percent of all people fall within 30 points of 100

About 68 percent of people score within 15 points of 100

68%

95%

0.1%   2%   13.5%   34%   34%   13.5%   2%   0.1%
     55   70   85   100   115   130   145
                Wechsler intelligence score

The predictive power of aptitude tests is fairly strong in the early school years, but later it weakens. Past grades, which reflect both aptitude and motivation, are better predictors of future achievements.

RETRIEVE IT [✖]

• What are the three criteria that a psychological test must meet in order to be widely accepted? Explain.

ANSWER: A psychological test must be *standardized* (pretested on a representative sample of people), *reliable* (yielding consistent results), and *valid* (measuring what it is supposed to measure).

• Correlation coefficients were used in this module. Here's a quick review: Correlations do not indicate cause-effect, but they do tell us whether two things are associated in some way. A correlation of –1.0 represents perfect _____ (agreement/disagreement) between two sets of scores: As one score goes up, the other score goes _____ (up/down). A correlation of _____ represents no association. The highest correlation, +1.0, represents perfect _____ (agreement/disagreement): As the first score goes up, the other score goes _____ (up/down).

ANSWERS: disagreement; down; zero; agreement; up

The Dynamics of Intelligence

Aging and Intelligence

◉ **27-7** How does aging affect crystallized and fluid intelligence?

Does intelligence increase, decrease, or remain constant as we age? The answer depends on the type of intellectual performance we measure:

• **Crystallized intelligence**—our accumulated knowledge as reflected in vocabulary and analogies tests—*increases* up to old age.

• **Fluid intelligence**—our ability to reason speedily and abstractly, as when solving novel logic problems—*decreases* beginning in the twenties and thirties, slowly up to age 75 or so, then more rapidly, especially after age 85 (Cattell, 1963; Horn, 1982; Salthouse, 2009; 2013).

How do we know? Developmental psychologists use **longitudinal studies** (restudying the same group at different times across their life span) and **cross-sectional studies** (comparing members of different age groups at the same time) to study the way intelligence and other traits change with age. (See Appendix A for more information.) With age we lose and we win. We lose recall memory and processing speed, but we gain vocabulary and knowledge (**FIGURE 27.4** on the next page). Fluid intelligence may decline, but older adults' social reasoning skills increase, as shown by an ability to take multiple perspectives, to appreciate knowledge limits, and to offer helpful wisdom in times of social conflict (Grossman et al., 2010). Decisions also become less distorted by negative emotions such as anxiety, depression, and anger (Blanchard-Fields, 2007; Carstensen & Mikels, 2005).

Age-related cognitive differences help explain why older adults are less likely to embrace new technologies (Charness & Boot, 2009; Lenhart, 2015). These cognitive differences also help explain why mathematicians and scientists produce much of their most creative work during their late twenties or early thirties, when fluid intelligence is at its peak (Jones et al., 2014). In contrast, authors, historians, and philosophers tend to produce their best work in their forties, fifties, and beyond—after accumulating more knowledge (Simonton, 1988, 1990). Poets, for example, who depend on fluid intelligence, reach their peak output earlier than prose authors, who need the deeper knowledge reservoir that accumulates with age. This finding holds in every major literary tradition, for both living and dead languages.

---

crystallized intelligence our accumulated knowledge and verbal skills; tends to increase with age.

fluid intelligence our ability to reason speedily and abstractly; tends to decrease with age, especially during late adulthood.

longitudinal study research in which the same people are restudied and retested over a long period.

cross-sectional study a study in which people of different ages are compared with one another.

📶 **LaunchPad** See LaunchPad's *Video: Longitudinal and Cross-Sectional Studies* for a helpful tutorial animation.

"Knowledge is knowing a tomato is a fruit; wisdom is not putting it in a fruit salad."
Anonymous

"In youth we learn, in age we understand."
Marie Von Ebner-Eschenbach,
Aphorisms, *1883*

With age, we lose and we win.
Studies reveal that word power grows
with age, while fluid intelligence
dimensions decline. (Data from
Salthouse, 2010.)

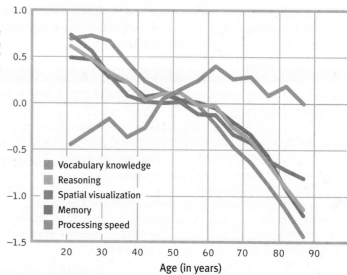

Relative performance
above or below the
mean (in "z-score"
standard deviations)

Age (in years)

Vocabulary knowledge
Reasoning
Spatial visualization
Memory
Processing speed

RETRIEVE IT

- Researcher A is well funded to learn about how intelligence changes over the life span. Researcher B wants to study the intelligence of people who are now at various life stages. Which researcher should use the cross-sectional method, and which should use the longitudinal method?

ANSWER: Researcher A should develop a *longitudinal study* to examine how intelligence changes in the same people over the life span. Researcher B should develop a *cross-sectional study* to examine the intelligence of people now at various life stages.

Stability Over the Life Span

27-8 How stable are intelligence test scores over the life span?

What about the stability of early-life intelligence scores? For most children, casual observation and intelligence tests before age 3 only modestly predict their future aptitudes (Humphreys & Davey, 1988; Tasbihsazan et al., 2003). Even Albert Einstein was once thought "slow"—as he was in learning to talk (Quasha, 1980).

By age 4, however, children's performance on intelligence tests begins to predict their adolescent and adult scores. The consistency of scores over time increases with the age of the child. By age 11, the stability becomes impressive, as Ian Deary and his colleagues (2004, 2009, 2013) discovered. Their amazing longitudinal studies have been enabled by their country, Scotland, which did something that no nation has done before or since. On June 1, 1932, essentially every child in the country born in 1921—87,498 children around age 11—took an intelligence test. The aim was to identify working-class children who would benefit from further education. Sixty-five years later to the day, Patricia Whalley, the wife of Deary's co-worker, Lawrence Whalley, discovered the test results on dusty storeroom shelves at the Scottish Council for Research in Education, not far from Deary's Edinburgh University office. "This will change our lives," Deary replied when Whalley told him the news.

And so it has, with dozens of studies of the stability and the predictive capacity of these early test results. For example, when the intelligence test administered to 11-year-old Scots in 1932 was readministered to 542 survivors as turn-of-the-millennium 80-year-olds, the correlation between the two sets of scores—after nearly 70 years of varied life experiences—was striking (**FIGURE 27.5**). Ditto when 106 survivors were retested at age 90 (Deary et al., 2013). Another study that followed Scots born in 1936 from ages 11 to 70 confirmed the remarkable stability of intelligence, independent of life circumstance (Johnson et al., 2010).

"Whether you live to collect your old-age pension depends in part on your IQ at age 11."

Ian Deary,
"Intelligence, Health, and Death," 2005

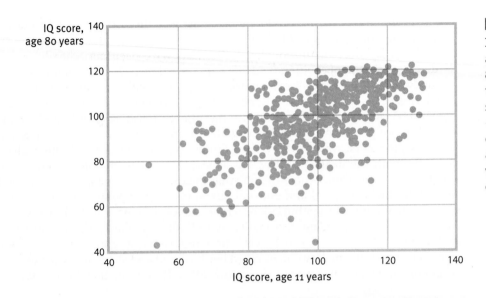

< FIGURE 27.5

Intelligence endures When Ian Deary and his colleagues (2004) retested 80-year-old Scots, using an intelligence test they had taken as 11-year-olds, their scores across seven decades correlated +.66, as shown here. (Data from Deary et al., 2004.) When 106 survivors were again retested at age 90, the correlation with their age 11 scores was +.54 (Deary et al., 2013).

Children and adults who are more intelligent also tend to live healthier and longer lives. Why might this be the case? Deary (2008) proposes four possible explanations:

1. Intelligence facilitates more education, better jobs, and a healthier environment.

2. Intelligence encourages healthy living: less smoking, better diet, more exercise.

3. Prenatal events or early childhood illnesses might have influenced both intelligence and health.

4. A "well-wired body," as evidenced by fast reaction speeds, perhaps fosters both intelligence and longevity.

Extremes of Intelligence

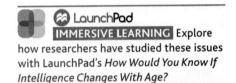 **27-9** What are the traits of those at the low and high intelligence extremes?

One way to glimpse the validity and significance of any test is to compare people who score at the two extremes of the normal curve. The two groups should differ noticeably, and with intelligence testing, they do.

THE LOW EXTREME At one extreme of the intelligence test normal curve are those with unusually low scores. The American Association on Intellectual and Developmental Disabilities guidelines list two criteria for a diagnosis of **intellectual disability** (formerly referred to as *mental retardation*):

1. A test score indicating performance below 98 percent of test-takers (Schalock et al., 2010). For an intelligence test with a midpoint of 100, that is a score of approximately 70 or below.

2. Difficulty adapting to the normal demands of independent living, as expressed in three areas:

   • *conceptual skills* (such as language, literacy, and concepts of money, time, and number).

   • *social skills* (such as interpersonal skills, social responsibility, following basic rules and laws, and avoiding being victimized).

   • *practical skills* (such as daily personal care, occupational skill, travel, and health care).

Intellectual disability is a developmental condition that is apparent before age 18, sometimes with a known physical cause. **Down syndrome,** for example, is a disorder of varying intellectual and physical severity caused by an extra copy of chromosome 21.

LaunchPad

IMMERSIVE LEARNING Explore how researchers have studied these issues with LaunchPad's *How Would You Know If Intelligence Changes With Age?*

intellectual disability a condition of limited mental ability, indicated by an intelligence test score of 70 or below and difficulty adapting to the demands of life. (Formerly referred to as *mental retardation.*)

Down syndrome a condition of mild to severe intellectual disability and associated physical disorders caused by an extra copy of chromosome 21.

People diagnosed with a mild intellectual disability—those just below the 70 score—might be better able to live independently today than many decades ago, when they were institutionalized. The tests have been periodically restandardized. As that happened, individuals who scored near 70 on earlier tests have suddenly lost about 6 test-score points. Two people with the same ability level could thus be classified differently, depending on when they were tested (Kanaya et al., 2003; Reynolds et al., 2010). As the intellectual-disability boundary has shifted, more people have become eligible for special education and for Social Security payments. And in the United States (one of only a few industrialized countries with the death penalty), fewer people are now eligible for execution: The U.S. Supreme Court ruled in 2002 that the execution of people with an intellectual disability is "cruel and unusual punishment." For people near that cutoff score of 70, intelligence testing can be a high-stakes competition. And so it was for Teresa Lewis, a "dependent personality" with limited intellect, who was executed by the state of Virginia in 2010. Lewis, whose reported test score was 72, allegedly agreed to a plot in which two men killed her husband and stepson in exchange for a split of a life insurance payout (Eckholm, 2010). If only she had scored 69.

RETRIEVE IT [✖]

• Why do psychologists NOT diagnose an intellectual disability based solely on a person's intelligence test score?

ANSWER: IQ score is only one measure of a person's ability to function. Other important factors to consider in an overall assessment include conceptual skills, social skills, and practical skills.

THE HIGH EXTREME In one famous project begun in 1921, Lewis Terman studied more than 1500 California schoolchildren with IQ scores over 135. Terman's high-scoring children (the "Termites") were healthy, well adjusted, and unusually successful academically (Friedman & Martin, 2012; Koenen et al., 2009; Lubinski, 2009a). When restudied over the next seven decades, most had attained high levels of education (Austin et al., 2002; Holahan & Sears, 1995). Many were doctors, lawyers, professors, scientists, and writers, though no Nobel Prize winners. (The two future physics Nobel laureates Terman tested failed to score above his gifted-sample cutoff [Hulbert, 2005].)

Recent studies have followed the lives of precocious youths who had aced the math SAT at age 13—by scoring in the top quarter of 1 percent of their age group. By their fifties, these 1650 math whizzes had secured 681 patents (Lubinski et al., 2014). Compared with the math aces, 13-year-olds scoring high on verbal aptitude were, by age 38, more likely to have become humanities professors or written a novel (Kell et al., 2013). About 1 percent of Americans earn doctorates. But among those scoring in the top 1 in 10,000 on the SAT at age 12 or 13, 63 percent had done so.

One of psychology's whiz kids was Jean Piaget, who by age 15 was publishing scientific articles on mollusks and who went on to become the twentieth century's most famous developmental psychologist (Hunt, 1993). Children with extraordinary academic gifts are sometimes more isolated, shy, and in their own worlds (Winner, 2000). But most thrive.

The extremes of intelligence Moshe Kai Cavalin completed his third college degree at age 14, graduating with a UCLA math degree. According to his mother, he started reading at age 2.

Joe Klamar/AFP/Getty Images

MODULE
27 REVIEW Intelligence and Its Assessment

◉ Learning Objectives

Test Yourself by taking a moment to answer each of these Learning Objective Questions (repeated here from within the module). Then turn to Appendix D, Complete Module Reviews, to check your answers. Research suggests that trying to answer these questions on your own will improve your long-term memory of the concepts (McDaniel et al., 2009).

27-1 How do psychologists define *intelligence,* and what are the arguments for *g*?

27-2 How do Gardner's and Sternberg's theories of multiple intelligences differ, and what criticisms have they faced?

27-3 What are the four components of emotional intelligence?

27-4 What is an intelligence test, and what is the difference between achievement and aptitude tests?

27-5 When and why were intelligence tests created, and how do today's tests differ from early intelligence tests?

27-6 What is a normal curve, and what does it mean to say that a test has been standardized and is reliable and valid?

27-7 How does aging affect crystallized and fluid intelligence?

27-8 How stable are intelligence test scores over the life span?

27-9 What are the traits of those at the low and high intelligence extremes?

Terms and Concepts to Remember

Test yourself on these terms by trying to write down the definition in your own words before flipping back to the referenced page to check your answers.

intelligence, p. 341
general intelligence (*g*), p. 341
savant syndrome, p. 342
emotional intelligence, p. 344
intelligence test, p. 345
aptitude test, p. 345

achievement test, p. 345
mental age, p. 346
Stanford-Binet, p. 346
intelligence quotient (IQ), p. 346
Wechsler Adult Intelligence Scale (WAIS), p. 347
standardization, p. 348
normal curve, p. 348
reliability, p. 348

validity, p. 348
content validity, p. 348
predictive validity, p. 348
crystallized intelligence, p. 349
fluid intelligence, p. 349
longitudinal study, p. 349
cross-sectional study, p. 349
intellectual disability, p. 351
Down syndrome, p. 351

Experience the Testing Effect

Test yourself repeatedly throughout your studies. This will not only help you figure out what you know and don't know; the testing itself will help you learn and remember the information more effectively thanks to the *testing effect*.

1. Charles Spearman suggested we have one _____ _____ underlying success across a variety of intellectual abilities.

2. The existence of savant syndrome seems to support
   a. Sternberg's distinction among three types of intelligence.
   b. criticism of multiple intelligence theories.
   c. Gardner's theory of multiple intelligences.
   d. Thorndike's view of social intelligence.

3. Sternberg's three types of intelligence are _____, _____, and _____.

4. Emotionally intelligent people tend to
   a. seek immediate gratification.
   b. understand their own emotions but not those of others.
   c. understand others' emotions but not their own.
   d. succeed in their careers.

5. The IQ of a 6-year-old with a measured mental age of 9 would be
   a. 67.   c. 86.
   b. 133.   d. 150.

6. The Wechsler Adult Intelligence Scale (WAIS) is best able to tell us

   a. what part of an individual's intelligence is determined by genetic inheritance.
   b. whether the test-taker will succeed in a job.
   c. how the test-taker compares with other adults in vocabulary and arithmetic reasoning.
   d. whether the test-taker has specific skills for music and the performing arts.

7. The Stanford-Binet, the Wechsler Adult Intelligence Scale, and the Wechsler Intelligence Scale for Children yield consistent results—on retesting, for example. In other words, these tests have high _____.

8. Use the concepts of crystallized and fluid intelligence to explain why writers tend to produce their most creative work later in life, and scientists may hit their peak much earlier.

9. Which of the following is NOT a possible explanation for the fact that more intelligent people tend to live longer, healthier lives?
   a. Intelligence facilitates more education, better jobs, and a healthier environment.
   b. Intelligence encourages a more health-promoting lifestyle.
   c. Intelligent people have slower reaction times, making it less likely that they will put themselves at risk.
   d. A "well-wired body," as evidenced by fast reaction speeds, may foster both intelligence and longevity.

Find answers to these questions in Appendix E, in the back of the book.

Use LearningCurve to create your personalized study plan, which will direct you to the resources that will help you most in LaunchPad.

heritability the proportion of variation among individuals that we can attribute to genes. The heritability of a trait may vary, depending on the range of populations and environments studied.

"I told my parents that if grades were so important they should have paid for a smarter egg donor."

📱 **LaunchPad** See LaunchPad's *Video: Twin Studies* for a helpful tutorial animation.

⌄ FIGURE 28.1

Intelligence: Nature and nurture The most genetically similar people have the most similar intelligence scores. Remember: 1.0 indicates a perfect correlation; zero indicates no correlation at all. (Data from McGue et al., 1993.)

The New Yorker Collection, 1999, Donald Reilly from cartoonbank.com

MODULE 28 Genetic and Environmental Influences on Intelligence

Intelligence runs in families. But why? Are our intellectual abilities mostly inherited? Or are they molded by our environment? Few issues in psychology arouse so much passion. Let's examine some of the evidence.

Twin and Adoption Studies

👁 **28-1** What evidence points to a genetic influence on intelligence, and what is heritability?

Do people who share the same genes also share mental abilities? As you can see from **FIGURE 28.1**, which summarizes many studies, the answer is clearly *Yes*.

Identical twins who grow up together have intelligence test scores nearly as similar as those of the same person taking the same test twice (Haworth et al., 2009; Lykken, 1999). (Fraternal twins, who typically share only half their genes, differ more.) Even when identical twins are adopted by two different families, their scores are very similar. Estimates of the **heritability** of intelligence—the extent to which intelligence test score variation can be attributed to genetic variation—range from 50 to 80 percent (Calvin et al., 2012; Johnson et al., 2009; Neisser et al., 1996). Identical twins also exhibit substantial similarity (and heritability) in specific talents, such as music, math, and sports. Heredity accounts for more than half the variation in the national math and science exam scores of British 16-year-olds (Shakeshaft et al., 2013; Vinkhuyzen et al., 2009).

Scans of identical twins' brains reveal that gray- and white-matter volume is similar, and areas associated with verbal and spatial intelligence are virtually the same (Deary et al., 2009; Thompson et al., 2001). Their brains also show similar activity while doing mental tasks (Koten et al., 2009).

Although genes matter, there is no known "genius" gene. One worldwide team of more than 200 researchers pooled their data on the DNA and schooling of 126,559 people (Rietveld et al., 2013). No single DNA segment was more than a minuscule predictor of years of schooling. Together, all the genetic variations they examined accounted for only about 2 percent of the schooling differences. The gene sleuthing continues, but this much seems clear: Intelligence is *polygenetic,* involving many

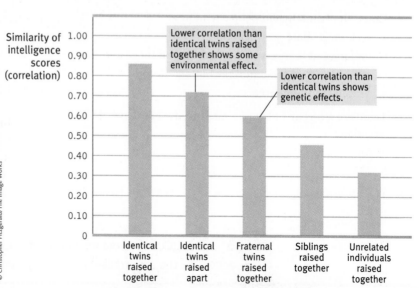

Similarity of intelligence scores (correlation)

Lower correlation than identical twins raised together shows some environmental effect.

Lower correlation than identical twins shows genetic effects.

| | 1.00 |
| 0.90 |
| 0.80 |
| 0.70 |
| 0.60 |
| 0.50 |
| 0.40 |
| 0.30 |
| 0.20 |
| 0.10 |
| 0 |

Identical twins raised together · Identical twins raised apart · Fraternal twins raised together · Siblings raised together · Unrelated individuals raised together

© Christopher Fitzgerald/The Image Works

genes (Bouchard, 2014). Wendy Johnson (2010) likens it to height: 54 specific gene variations together have accounted for 5 percent of our individual differences in height, leaving the rest yet to be explained.

Where environments vary widely, as they do among children of less-educated parents, environmental differences are more predictive of intelligence scores (Rowe et al., 1999; Tucker-Drob et al., 2011; Turkheimer et al., 2003). To see why, consider humorist Mark Twain's fantasy of raising boys in barrels until age 12, feeding them through a hole. Let's take his joke a step further and say we'll give all those boys an intelligence test at age 12. Since their environments were all equal, any difference in their test scores could only be due to heredity—thus, heritability would be 100 percent. But what if a mad scientist cloned 100 boys and raised them in drastically different environments (some in barrels and others in mansions)? In this case, heredity would be equal, so any test-score differences could only be due to environment. The environmental effect would be 100 percent, and heritability would be zero.

Adoption studies help us assess the influence of environment. Consider:

- Adoption of mistreated or neglected children enhances their intelligence scores (van IJzendoorn & Juffer, 2005, 2006). So does adoption from poverty into middle-class homes (Nisbett et al., 2012). In one large Swedish study, children adopted into families with higher socioeconomic status and more educated parents had IQ scores averaging 4.4 points higher than their not-adopted biological siblings (Kendler et al., 2015).

- The intelligence scores of "virtual twins"—same-age, unrelated siblings adopted as infants and raised together—correlate +.28 (Segal et al., 2012). This suggests a modest influence of their shared environment.

Seeking to untangle genes and environment, researchers have also compared the intelligence test scores of adopted children with those of their family members. These include (a) their *biological parents* (the providers of their genes) and (b) their *adoptive parents* (the providers of their home environment). What do you think happens as the years go by and adopted children settle in with their adoptive families? Would you expect the family-environment effect to grow stronger and the genetic-legacy effect to shrink?

If you said *Yes*, behavior geneticists have a stunning surprise for you. Mental similarities between adopted children and their adoptive families *lessen* with age, dropping to roughly zero by adulthood (McGue et al., 1993). Genetic influences—not environmental ones—become more apparent as we accumulate life experience. Identical twins' similarities, for example, continue or increase into their eighties (Deary et al., 2009). In one massive study of 11,000 twin pairs in four countries, the heritability of g increased from 41 percent in middle childhood, to 55 percent in adolescence, to 66 percent in young adulthood (Haworth et al., 2010). Similarly, adopted children's verbal ability scores over time become more like those of their biological parents (**FIGURE 28.2**). Who would have guessed?

"Selective breeding has given me an aptitude for the law, but I still love fetching a dead duck out of freezing water."

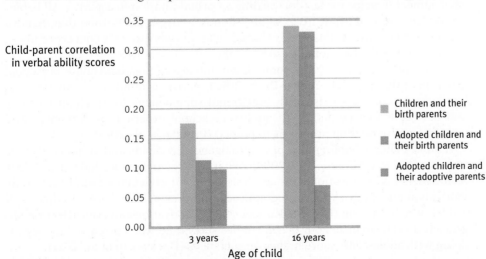

Child-parent correlation in verbal ability scores

- Children and their birth parents
- Adopted children and their birth parents
- Adopted children and their adoptive parents

Age of child

< FIGURE 28.2

In verbal ability, whom do adopted children resemble? As the years went by in their adoptive families, children's verbal ability scores became more like their *biological* parents' scores. (Data from Plomin & DeFries, 1998.)

Environmental Influences

28-2 What does evidence reveal about environmental influences on intelligence?

We have seen that biology and experience intertwine. Nowhere is this more apparent than in the most hopeless human environments. Severe deprivation leaves footprints on the brain, as J. McVicker Hunt (1982) observed in a destitute Iranian orphanage. The typical child Hunt observed there could not sit up unassisted at age 2 or walk at age 4. The little care the infants received was not in response to their crying, cooing, or other behaviors, so the children developed little sense of personal control over their environment. They were instead becoming passive "glum lumps." Extreme deprivation was crushing native intelligence—a finding confirmed by other studies of children raised in poorly run orphanages in Romania and elsewhere (Nelson et al., 2009, 2013; van IJzendoorn et al., 2008).

Devastating neglect Some Romanian orphans, such as this child in the Leaganul Pentru Copii orphanage in 1990, had minimal interaction with caregivers, and suffered delayed development.

Mindful of the effect of early experiences and early intervention, Hunt began a training program for Iranian caregivers, teaching them to play language-fostering games with 11 infants. They learned to imitate the babies' babbling. They engaged them in vocal follow-the-leader. And, finally, they taught the infants sounds from the Persian language. The results were dramatic. By 22 months of age, the infants could name more than 50 objects and body parts. They so charmed visitors that most were adopted—an unprecedented success for the orphanage.

So, extreme conditions—malnutrition, sensory deprivation, and social isolation—can retard normal brain development. Is the reverse also true? Will an "enriched" environment give children a superior intellect? Most experts are doubtful (Bruer, 1999; DeLoache et al., 2010; Reichert et al., 2010). There is no environmental recipe for fast-forwarding a normal infant into a genius. All babies should have normal exposure to sights, sounds, and speech. Beyond that, Sandra Scarr's (1984) verdict still is widely shared: "Parents who are very concerned about providing special educational lessons for their babies are wasting their time."

More encouraging results come from intensive, post-babyhood preschool programs (Mervis, 2011; Tucker-Drob, 2012). Across a number of experiments, intelligence scores also rise with nutritional supplements to pregnant mothers and newborns (3.5 points), with quality preschool experiences (4 points), and with interactive reading programs (6 points) (Protzko et al., 2013).

A child's later schooling also pays intelligence dividends and enhances future income (Ceci & Williams, 1997, 2009). What we accomplish depends also on our own beliefs and motivation. One analysis of 72,431 collegians found that study motivation and study skills rivaled aptitude and previous grades as predictors of academic achievement (Credé & Kuncel, 2008). Motivation can even affect intelligence test performance. Four dozen studies show that, when promised money for doing well, adolescents score higher on such tests (Duckworth et al., 2011).

"A high IQ and a subway token will only get you into town."

Psychologist Richard Nisbett (quoted by Michael Balter), 2011

"It is our choices . . . that show what we truly are, far more than our abilities."

Professor Dumbledore to Harry Potter in J. K. Rowling's Harry Potter and the Chamber of Secrets, *1999*

Group Differences in Intelligence Test Scores

If there were no group differences in aptitude scores, psychologists could politely debate hereditary and environmental influences in their ivory towers. But there are group differences. What are they? And what shall we make of them?

Gender Similarities and Differences

<> **28-3** How and why do the genders differ in mental ability scores?

In science, as in everyday life, differences, not similarities, excite interest. Compared with the anatomical and physiological similarities between men and women, our intelligence differences are minor. In the 1932 study that tested Scottish 11-year-olds, for example, the girls' average intelligence score was 100.6 and the boys' was 100.5 (Deary et al., 2003). So far as *g* is concerned, boys and girls, men and women, are the same species.

Yet, most people find differences more newsworthy. Girls outpace boys in spelling, verbal fluency, locating objects, detecting emotions, and sensitivity to touch, taste, and color (Halpern et al., 2007). Boys outperform girls in tests of spatial ability and complex math problems, though in math computation and overall math performance, boys and girls hardly differ (Else-Quest et al., 2010; Hyde & Mertz, 2009; Lindberg et al., 2010). Males' mental ability scores also vary more than females'. Thus, boys worldwide outnumber girls at both the low extreme and the high extreme (Brunner et al., 2013). Boys, for example, are more often found in special education classes, but also among those scoring very high on the SAT math test.

The most reliable male edge appears in spatial ability tests like the one shown in **FIGURE 28.3** (Maeda & Yoon, 2013; Wei et al., 2012). The solution requires speedily rotating three-dimensional objects in one's mind. Today, such skills help when fitting suitcases into a car trunk, playing chess, or doing certain types of geometry problems. From an evolutionary perspective, those same skills would have helped our ancestral fathers track prey and make their way home (Geary, 1995, 1996; Halpern et al., 2007). The survival of our ancestral mothers may have benefited more from a keen memory for the location of edible plants—a legacy that lives today in women's superior memory for objects and their location.

But social expectations and opportunities also matter. In Asia and Russia, teenage girls have outperformed boys in an international science exam; in North America and Britain, boys have scored higher (Fairfield, 2012). More gender-equal cultures, such as Sweden and Iceland, exhibit little of the gender math gap found in gender-unequal cultures, such as Turkey and Korea (Guiso et al., 2008; Kane & Mertz, 2012).

"The human computer" Indian math wizard Shakuntala Devi made it into the 1982 *Guinness Book of World Records* when she multiplied two randomly selected 13-digit numbers (7,686,369,774,870 × 2,465,099,745,779) to give, within seconds, the 26-digit solution: 18,947,668,177,995,426,462,773,730 (Pandya, 2013).

Barton Silverman/The New York Times/Redux

Which two circles contain a configuration of blocks identical to the one in the circle at the left?

Standard

Responses

< FIGURE 28.3

The mental rotation test This is a test of spatial abilities. See inverted answer below.

ANSWER: The first and fourth alternatives.

Perceptual and Motor Skills, A Group Test of Three-Dimensional Spatial Visualization , Steven G. Vandenberg and Allan R. Ruse, Volume 47, Issue 2, October 1978: pp 599–604(doi: 10.2466/pms.1978.47.2.599).

Racial and Ethnic Similarities and Differences

28-4 How and why do racial and ethnic groups differ in mental ability scores?

Fueling the group-differences debate are two other disturbing but agreed-upon facts:

- Racial and ethnic groups differ in their average intelligence test scores.
- High-scoring people (and groups) are more likely to attain high levels of education and income.

There are many group differences in average intelligence test scores. New Zealanders of European descent outscore native Maori New Zealanders. Israeli Jews outscore Israeli Arabs. Most Japanese outscore most Burakumin, a stigmatized Japanese minority. Those who can hear have outscored those born deaf (Braden, 1994; Steele, 1990; Zeidner, 1990). And White Americans have outscored Black Americans. This Black-White difference has diminished somewhat in recent years, especially among children (Dickens & Flynn, 2006; Nisbett et al., 2012). Such *group* differences provide little basis for judging individuals. Worldwide, women outlive men by four years, but knowing only that you are male or female won't tell us how long you will live.

We have seen that heredity contributes to *individual* differences in intelligence. But group differences in a heritable trait may be entirely environmental. Consider one of nature's experiments: Allow some children to grow up hearing their culture's dominant language, while others, born deaf, do not. Then give both groups an intelligence test rooted in the dominant language, and (no surprise) those with expertise in that language will score highest. Although individual performance differences may be substantially genetic, the group difference is not (**FIGURE 28.4**).

Might the racial gap be similarly environmental? Consider:

Genetics research reveals that under the skin, the races are remarkably alike. The average genetic difference between two Icelandic villagers or between two Kenyans greatly exceeds the group difference between Icelanders and Kenyans (Cavalli-Sforza et al., 1994; Rosenberg et al., 2002). Moreover, looks can deceive. Light-skinned Europeans and dark-skinned Africans are genetically closer than are dark-skinned Africans and dark-skinned Aboriginal Australians.

Race is not a neatly defined biological category. Many social scientists see race primarily as a social construction without well-defined physical boundaries, as each race blends seamlessly into the race of its geographical neighbors (Helms et al., 2005; Smedley & Smedley, 2005). Moreover, with increasingly mixed ancestries, more and more people defy neat racial categorization and self-identify as multiracial (Pauker et al., 2009).

The intelligence test performance of today's better-fed, better-educated, and more test-prepared population exceeds that of the 1930s population—by a greater margin

© Larry Williams/Corbis

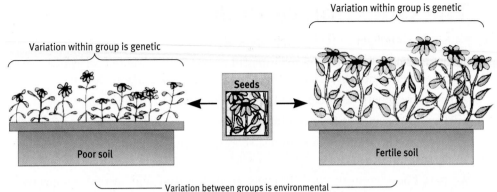

Group differences and environmental impact Even if the variation between members within a group reflects genetic differences, the average difference between groups may be wholly due to environment. Imagine that seeds from the same mixture are sown in different soils. Although height differences *within* each window box of flowers will be genetic, the height difference *between* the two groups will be environmental. (Inspired by Lewontin, 1976.)

than the intelligence test score of the average White today exceeds that of the average Black. One research review noted that the average intelligence test performance of today's sub-Saharan Africans is the same as British adults in 1948, with the possibility of more gains to come, given improved nutrition, economic development, and education (Wicherts et al., 2010).

When Blacks and Whites have or receive the same pertinent knowledge, they exhibit similar information-processing skill. "The data support the view that cultural differences in the provision of information may account for racial differences in [intelligence test performance]," reported researchers Joseph Fagan and Cynthia Holland (2007).

Schools and culture matter. Countries whose economies create a large wealth gap between rich and poor tend also to have a large rich-versus-poor intelligence test score gap (Nisbett, 2009). Moreover, educational policies such as kindergarten attendance, school discipline, and instructional time per year predict national differences in intelligence and knowledge tests (Rindermann & Ceci, 2009). Math achievement, aptitude test differences, and especially grades may reflect conscientiousness more than competence (Poropat, 2014). Asian students, who have outperformed North American students on such tests, have also spent 30 percent more time in school and much more time in and out of school studying math (Geary et al., 1996; Larson & Verma, 1999; Stevenson, 1992).

In different eras, different ethnic groups have experienced golden ages—periods of remarkable achievement. Twenty-five hundred years ago, it was the Greeks and the Egyptians, then the Romans. In the eighth and ninth centuries, genius seemed to reside in the Arab world. Five hundred years ago, the Aztec Indians and the peoples of Northern Europe were the superachievers. Today, people notice Asian technological genius and Jewish cultural success. Cultures rise and fall over centuries; genes do not. That fact makes it difficult to attribute a natural superiority to any race.

Nature's own morphing Nature draws no sharp boundaries between races, which blend gradually one into the next around Earth. But the human urge to classify causes people to socially define themselves in racial categories, which become catchall labels for physical features, social identity, and nationality.

© David Turnley/Corbis; © Rob Howard/Corbis; © Barbara Bannister/Gallo Images/Corbis; © Dave Bartruff/Corbis; © Haruyoshi Yamaguchi/Corbis; © Richard T. Nowitz/Corbis; © Owen Franken/Corbis; © Sean De Burca/Corbis

"Do not obtain your slaves from Britain, because they are so stupid and so utterly incapable of being taught."

Cicero, 106–43 B.C.E.

The Question of Bias

 28-5 Are intelligence tests inappropriately biased?

If one assumes that *race* is a meaningful concept, the debate over racial differences in intelligence divides into three camps (Hunt & Carlson, 2007):

• There are genetically disposed racial differences in intelligence.

• There are socially influenced racial differences in intelligence.

• There are racial differences in test scores, but the tests are inappropriate or biased.

We have considered group differences from the first and second perspectives. Let's turn now to the third: Are intelligence tests biased? The answer depends on the definition of *bias* we use.

Two Meanings of Bias

The *scientific* meaning of *bias* hinges on a test's validity—on whether it predicts future behavior only for some groups of test-takers. For example, if the SAT accurately predicted the college achievement of women but not that of men, then the test would be biased. In this statistical meaning of the term, the near-consensus among psychologists (as summarized by the U.S. National Research Council's Committee on Ability Testing and the American Psychological Association's Task Force on Intelligence) has been that the major U.S. aptitude tests are *not* biased (Hunt & Carlson, 2007; Neisser et al., 1996; Wigdor & Garner, 1982). The tests' predictive validity is roughly the same for women and men, for various races, and for rich and poor. If an intelligence test score of 95 predicts slightly below-average grades, that rough prediction usually applies equally to all.

But we can also consider a test biased if it detects not only innate differences in intelligence but also performance differences caused by cultural experiences. This in fact happened to Eastern European immigrants in the early 1900s. Lacking the experience to answer questions about their new culture, many were classified as "feeble-minded." In this popular sense, intelligence tests are biased. They measure your developed abilities, which reflect, in part, your education and experiences.

You may have read examples of intelligence test items that make assumptions (for example, that a cup goes with a saucer). Such items bias the test (in this case, against those who do not use saucers). Could such questions explain cultural differences in test performance? In such cases, tests can be a vehicle for discrimination, consigning potentially capable children (some of whom may have a different native language) to unchallenging classes and dead-end jobs. For such reasons, some intelligence researchers recommend creating culture-neutral questions—such as assessing people's ability to learn novel words, sayings, and analogies—to enable culture-fair aptitude tests (Fagan & Holland, 2007, 2009).

So, test-makers' expectations can introduce bias in an intelligence test. This is consistent with an observation you have seen throughout this text: Our expectations and attitudes can influence our perceptions and behaviors. This is also true for the person taking the test.

RETRIEVE IT

• What is the difference between a test that is biased culturally and a test that is biased in terms of its validity?

ANSWER: A test may be *culturally* biased if higher scores are achieved by those with certain cultural experiences. That same test may not be biased in terms of *validity* if it predicts what it is supposed to predict. For example, the SAT may be culturally biased in favor of those with experience in the U.S. school system, but it does still accurately predict U.S. college success.

Stereotype Threat

If, when taking an intelligence test or an exam, you are worried that your group or "type" often doesn't do well, your self-doubts and self-monitoring may hijack your working memory and impair your performance (Schmader, 2010). This self-confirming concern that you will be evaluated based on a negative viewpoint is called **stereotype threat,** and it may impair your attention, performance, and learning (Inzlicht & Kang, 2010; Rydell, 2010).

When Steven Spencer and his colleagues (1997) gave a difficult math test to equally capable men and women, women did not do as well—except when they had been led to expect that women usually do as well as men on the test. Otherwise, stereotype threat affected their performance. And with Claude Steele and Joshua Aronson, Spencer (2002) again observed stereotype threat when Black students were reminded of their race just before taking verbal aptitude tests and performed worse. Follow-up experiments have confirmed that negatively stereotyped minorities and women may have unrealized academic potential (Nguyen & Ryan, 2008; Walton & Spencer, 2009).

Critics argue that stereotype threat does not fully account for Black-White aptitude score differences or the gender gap in high-level math achievements (Sackett et al., 2004, 2008; Stoet & Geary, 2012). But it does help explain why Blacks have scored higher when tested by Blacks than when tested by Whites (Danso & Esses, 2001; Inzlicht & Ben-Zeev, 2000). It gives us insight into why women have scored higher on math tests with no male test-takers present, and why women's online chess performance drops sharply when they *think* they are playing a male opponent (Maass et al., 2008). It also explains "the Obama effect"—the finding that African-American adults performed better if they took a verbal aptitude test immediately after watching then-candidate Barack Obama's stereotype-defying nomination acceptance speech, or just after his 2008 presidential victory (Marx et al., 2009).

Steele (1995, 2010) concludes that telling students they probably won't succeed (as is sometimes implied by remedial "minority support" programs) functions as a stereotype that can erode performance. Minority students in university programs that have challenged them to believe in their potential, to increase their sense of belonging, or to focus on the idea that intelligence is malleable and not fixed, have produced markedly higher grades and have had lower dropout rates (Walton & Cohen, 2011; Wilson, 2006).

These observations would not surprise psychologist Carol Dweck (2012a,b, 2015). She reports that believing intelligence is changeable fosters a *growth mind-set,*

stereotype threat a self-confirming concern that one will be evaluated based on a negative stereotype.

"Math class is tough!"

"Teen talk" talking Barbie doll (introduced July 1992, recalled October 1992)

Roy Mehta/Iconica/Getty Images

Stereotype threat Academic success can be hampered by self-doubt and self-monitoring during exams, which may impair attention, memory, and performance.

Alex Wong/Getty Images

U.S. spelling champs Vanya Shivashankar, 13, and Gokul Venkatachalam, 14, celebrate their co-winning the 2015 Scripps National Spelling Bee. Vanya correctly spelled "scherenschnitte" and Gokul "nunatak."

"Almost all the joyful things of life are outside the measure of IQ tests."

Madeleine L'Engle,
A Circle of Quiet, 1972

"[Einstein] showed that genius equals brains plus tenacity squared."

Walter Isaacson,
"Einstein's Final Quest," 2009

which focuses on learning and growing. To foster this mind-set, Dweck teaches early teens that the brain is like a muscle that grows stronger with use as neuron connections grow. Praising children's *effort* rather than their ability also encourages their growth mind-set and their attributing success to hard work (Gunderson et al., 2013). Fostering a growth mind-set makes teens more resilient when others frustrate them (Paunesku et al., 2015; Yeager et al., 2013, 2014). Indeed, superior achievements in fields from sports to science to music arise from the combination of ability, opportunity, and disciplined effort (Ericsson et al., 2007).

Real world studies confirm that ability + opportunity + motivation = success. High school students' math proficiency and college students' grades reflect their aptitude but also their self-discipline, their belief in the power of effort, and a curious "hungry mind" (Murayama et al., 2013; Richardson et al., 2012; von Stumm et al., 2011). Indian-Americans won all seven national spelling bee contests between 2008 and 2014, an achievement likely influenced by a cultural belief that strong effort will meet with success (Rattan et al., 2012). Believing in our ability to learn, and applying ourselves with sustained effort, we are likely to fulfill our potential.

* * *

Perhaps, then, our goals for tests of mental abilities should be threefold.

- We should realize the benefits that intelligence testing pioneer Alfred Binet foresaw—to enable schools to recognize who might profit most from early intervention.

- We must remain alert to Binet's fear that intelligence test scores may be misinterpreted as literal measures of a person's worth and potential.

- We must remember that the competence that general intelligence tests sample is important; without such tests, those who decide on jobs and admissions would rely more on other considerations, such as personal opinion. But these tests reflect only one aspect of personal competence (Stanovich et al., 2013, 2014). Our practical intelligence and emotional intelligence matter, too, as do other forms of creativity, talent, and character.

The point to remember: There are many ways of being successful: Our differences are variations of human adaptability. Life's great achievements result not only from "can do" abilities (and fair opportunity) but also from "will do" motivation. Competence + Diligence ⟶ Accomplishment.

RETRIEVE IT

- What psychological principle helps explain why women tend to perform more poorly when they believe their online chess opponent is male?

ANSWER: stereotype threat

28 REVIEW Genetic and Environmental Influences on Intelligence

Learning Objectives

Test Yourself by taking a moment to answer each of these Learning Objective Questions (repeated here from within the module). Then turn to Appendix D, Complete Module Reviews, to check your answers. Research suggests that trying to answer these questions on your own will improve your long-term memory of the concepts (McDaniel et al., 2009).

28-1 What evidence points to a genetic influence on intelligence, and what is heritability?

28-2 What does evidence reveal about environmental influences on intelligence?

28-3 How and why do the genders differ in mental ability scores?

28-4 How and why do racial and ethnic groups differ in mental ability scores?

28-5 Are intelligence tests inappropriately biased?

Terms and Concepts to Remember

Test yourself on these terms by trying to write down the definition in your own words before flipping back to the referenced page to check your answers.

heritability, p. 354

stereotype threat, p. 361

Experience the Testing Effect

Test yourself repeatedly throughout your studies. This will not only help you figure out what you know and don't know; the testing itself will help you learn and remember the information more effectively thanks to the *testing effect*.

1. The strongest support for heredity's influence on intelligence is the finding that
   a. identical twins, but not other siblings, have nearly identical intelligence test scores.
   b. the correlation between intelligence test scores of fraternal twins is not higher than that for other siblings.
   c. mental similarities between adopted siblings increase with age.
   d. children in impoverished families have similar intelligence scores.

2. To say that the heritability of intelligence is about 50 percent means that 50 percent of
   a. an individual's intelligence is due to genetic factors.
   b. the similarities between two groups of people are attributable to genes.

   c. the variation in intelligence within a group of people is attributable to genetic factors.
   d. an individual's intelligence is due half to each parent's genes.

3. The environmental influence that has the clearest, most profound effect on intellectual development is
   a. exposing normal infants to enrichment programs before age 1.
   b. growing up in an economically disadvantaged home or neighborhood.
   c. being raised in conditions of extreme deprivation.
   d. being an identical twin.

4. _____ _____ can lead to poor performance on tests by undermining test-takers' belief that they can do well on the test.

Find answers to these questions in Appendix E, in the back of the book.

Use **LearningCurve** to create your personalized study plan, which will direct you to the resources that will help you most in **LaunchPad**.

MODULE 29 Basic Motivational Concepts, Affiliation, and Achievement

Instinct theory / evolutionary psychology: ← Sex sells

Need to belong

Maslow's hierarchy: striving to meet survival, then social, esteem, meaning needs

Arousal theory: avoiding boredom

Drive reduction theory: thirst → drinking water

Need to achieve

MODULE 30 Hunger

Psychology of hunger: biological and learned preferences + situational factors

MODULE 31 Theories and Physiology of Emotion

Arousal, Behavior, Cognition

Theorists ask, "Which comes first?"
Arousal (feelings of excitement)
Emotion (joy)
Label (I feel so happy!)
Cognitive interpretation (We won! We won! We won!)

MODULE 32 Expressing and Experiencing Emotion

Gender and Culture affect emotional expression and experience.

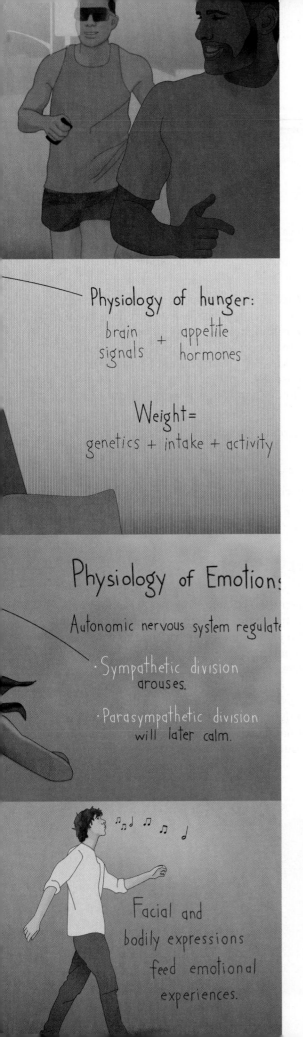

Physiology of hunger:

brain + appetite
signals + hormones

Weight=
genetics + intake + activity

Physiology of Emotions

Autonomic nervous system regulate

· Sympathetic division
arouses.

· Parasympathetic division
will later calm.

Facial and
bodily expressions
feed emotional
experiences.

Motivation and Emotion

HOW WELL I [DM] remember the response to my first discussion question in a new introductory psychology class. Several hands rose, along with one left foot. The foot belonged to Chris Klein, who was the unlikeliest person to have made it to that class. At birth, Chris suffered oxygen deprivation that required 40 minutes of CPR. "One doctor wanted to let him go," recalls his mother.

The result was severe cerebral palsy. With damage to the brain area that controls muscle movement, Chris is unable to control his constantly moving hands (on which he wears protective padded gloves). He cannot feed, dress, or care for himself. And he cannot speak. But what Chris does have is a keen mind and a mobile left foot. With that blessed foot, he controls the joystick on his motorized wheelchair. Using his left big toe, he can type sentences, which his communication system can store, e-mail, or speak. And Chris has motivation, lots of motivation.

When Chris was a high school student in suburban Chicago, three teachers doubted he would be able to leave home for college. Yet he persisted, and, with much support, ventured out to my college called Hope. Five years later, as his left foot drove him across the stage to receive his diploma, his admiring classmates honored his achievement with a spontaneous standing ovation.

Today, Chris is an inspirational speaker for schools, churches, and community events, giving "a voice to those that have none, and a helping hand to those with disabilities." He is past-president of the United States Society of Augmentative Alternative Communication. He is writing a book, *Lessons from the Big Toe*. And he has found love and married.

Although few of us face Chris Klein's challenges, we all seek to direct our energy in ways that will produce satisfaction and success. We are moved by our feelings along the way, and we inspire them in others. We are pushed by social motives, such as affiliation and achievement (Module 29), and biological ones, such as hunger (Module 30). We feel hope and happiness, sadness and pain, tenderness and triumph. Chris Klein's strong will to live, learn, and love highlights the close ties between our own *motivations* and *emotions* (Modules 31 and 32), which energize, direct, and enrich our lives. ■

motivation a need or desire that energizes and directs behavior.

instinct a complex behavior that is rigidly patterned throughout a species and is unlearned.

MODULE 29 Basic Motivational Concepts, Affiliation, and Achievement

Motivational Concepts

👁 **29-1** How do psychologists define *motivation?* From what perspectives do they view motivated behavior?

Psychologists define **motivation** as a need or desire that energizes and directs behavior. Our motivations arise from the interplay between nature (the bodily "push") and nurture (the "pulls" from our thought processes and culture).

If our motivations get hijacked, our lives go awry. Those with *substance use disorder,* for example, may find their cravings for an addictive substance override their longings for sustenance, safety, and social support.

In their attempts to understand ordinary motivated behavior, psychologists have viewed it from four perspectives:

* *Instinct theory* (now replaced by the *evolutionary perspective*) focuses on genetically predisposed behaviors.
* *Drive-reduction theory* focuses on how we respond to our inner pushes.
* *Arousal theory* focuses on finding the right level of stimulation.
* Abraham Maslow's *hierarchy of needs* focuses on the priority of some needs over others.

Instincts and Evolutionary Psychology

To qualify as an **instinct**, a complex behavior must have a fixed pattern throughout a species and be unlearned (Tinbergen, 1951). Such behaviors are common in other species and include imprinting in birds and the return of salmon to their birthplace. A few human behaviors, such as infants' innate reflexes to root for a nipple and suck, exhibit unlearned fixed patterns, but many more are directed by both physiological needs and psychological wants.

Although *instincts* cannot explain most human motives, the underlying assumption continues in *evolutionary psychology:* Genes do predispose some species-typical behavior. Psychologists might apply this perspective, for example, to explain our human similarities, animals' biological predispositions, and the influence of evolution on our phobias, our helping behaviors, and our romantic attractions.

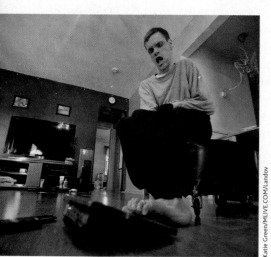

A motivated man: Chris Klein To see and hear Chris presenting his story, visit www.tinyurl.com/ChrisPsychStudent.

Katie Green/MLIVE.COM/Landov

Same motive, different wiring
The more complex the nervous system, the more adaptable the organism. Both humans and weaverbirds satisfy their need for shelter in ways that reflect their inherited capacities. Human behavior is flexible; we can learn whatever skills we need to build a house. The bird's behavior pattern is fixed; it can build only this kind of nest.

Annika Erickson/Blend Images/Getty Images

James Warwick/Science Source

Drives and Incentives

In addition to our predispositions, we have *drives*. Physiological needs (such as for food or water) create an aroused, motivated state—a drive (such as hunger or thirst)—that pushes us to reduce the need. **Drive-reduction theory** explains that, with few exceptions, when a physiological need increases, so does our psychological drive to reduce it.

Drive reduction is one way our bodies strive for **homeostasis (**literally "staying the same")—the maintenance of a steady internal state. For example, our body regulates its temperature in a way similar to a room's thermostat. Both systems operate through feedback loops: Sensors feed room temperature to a control device. If the room's temperature cools, the control device switches on the furnace. Likewise, if our body's temperature cools, our blood vessels constrict (to conserve warmth) and we feel driven to put on more clothes or seek a warmer environment (**FIGURE 29.1**).

Not only are we *pushed* by our need to reduce drives, we also are *pulled* by **incentives**—positive or negative environmental stimuli that lure or repel us. This is one way our individual learning histories influence our motives. Depending on our learning, the aroma of good food, whether fresh roasted peanuts or toasted ants, can motivate our behavior. So can the sight of those we find attractive or threatening.

When there is both a need and an incentive, we feel strongly driven. The food-deprived person who smells pizza baking may feel a strong hunger drive, and the baking pizza may become a compelling incentive. For each motive, we can therefore ask, "How is it pushed by our inborn physiological needs and pulled by learned incentives in the environment?"

drive-reduction theory the idea that a physiological need creates an aroused tension state (a drive) that motivates an organism to satisfy the need.

homeostasis a tendency to maintain a balanced or constant internal state; the regulation of any aspect of body chemistry, such as blood glucose, around a particular level.

incentive a positive or negative environmental stimulus that motivates behavior.

Need (food, water)	→	Drive (hunger, thirst)	→	Drive-reducing behaviors (eating, drinking)

∧ FIGURE 29.1

Drive-reduction theory Drive-reduction motivation arises from *homeostasis*—an organism's natural tendency to maintain a steady internal state. Thus, if we are water deprived, our thirst drives us to drink and to restore the body's normal state.

Optimum Arousal

We are much more than homeostatic systems, however. Some motivated behaviors actually *increase* rather than decrease arousal. Well-fed animals will leave their shelter to explore and gain information, seemingly in the absence of any need-based drive. Curiosity drives monkeys to monkey around trying to figure out how to unlock a latch that opens nothing, or how to open a window that allows them to see outside their room (Butler, 1954). It drives the 9-month-old infant to investigate every accessible corner of the house. It drives the scientists whose work this text discusses. And it drives explorers and adventurers such as mountaineer George Mallory. Asked why he wanted to climb Mount Everest, the *New York Times* reported that Mallory answered, "Because it is there." Sometimes uncertainty brings excitement, which amplifies motivation (Shen et al., 2015). Those who, like Mallory, enjoy high arousal are most likely to seek out intense music, novel foods, and risky behaviors and careers (Roberti et al., 2004; Zuckerman, 1979, 2009).

Driven by curiosity Young monkeys and children are fascinated by the unfamiliar. Their drive to explore maintains an optimum level of arousal and is one of several motives that do not fill any immediate physiological need.

Although they have been called *sensation-seekers*, risk takers may also be motivated by a drive to master their emotions and actions (Barlow et al., 2013).

So, human motivation aims not to eliminate arousal but to seek optimum levels of arousal. Having all our biological needs satisfied, we feel driven to experience stimulation and we hunger for information. Lacking stimulation, we feel bored and look for a way to increase

Harlow Primate Laboratory, University of Wisconsin

Glenn Swier

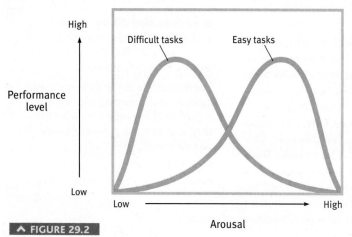

▲ FIGURE 29.2

Optimal arousal varies with difficulty of the task being performed

arousal to some optimum level. If left alone by themselves, most people prefer to do something—even (when given no other option) to self-administer mild electric shocks (Wilson et al., 2014). However, with too much stimulation comes stress, and we then look for a way to decrease arousal. In one experiment, people felt less stress when they cut back checking e-mail to three times a day rather than being continually accessible (Kushlev & Dunn, 2015).

Two early twentieth-century psychologists studied the relationship of arousal to performance and identified the **Yerkes-Dodson law,** suggesting that moderate arousal would lead to optimal performance (Yerkes & Dodson, 1908). When taking an exam, for example, it pays to be moderately aroused—alert but not trembling with nervousness. (If anxious, it's better not to become further aroused with a caffeinated drink.) Between depressed low arousal and anxious hyperarousal lies a flourishing life. But optimal arousal levels depend upon the task as well, with more difficult tasks requiring lower arousal for best performance (Hembree, 1988) (**FIGURE 29.2**).

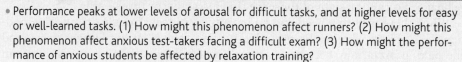

RETRIEVE IT

• Performance peaks at lower levels of arousal for difficult tasks, and at higher levels for easy or well-learned tasks. (1) How might this phenomenon affect runners? (2) How might this phenomenon affect anxious test-takers facing a difficult exam? (3) How might the performance of anxious students be affected by relaxation training?

ANSWER: (1) Runners, who are executing a well-learned task, tend to excel when aroused by competition. (2) High anxiety in test-takers, who are completing a difficult task, may disrupt their performance. (3) Teaching anxious students how to relax before an exam can enable them to perform better (Hembree, 1988).

A Hierarchy of Motives

Some needs take priority over others. At this moment, with your needs for air and water hopefully satisfied, other motives—such as your desire to achieve—are energizing and directing your behavior. Let your need for water go unsatisfied and your thirst will preoccupy you. Deprived of air, your thirst would disappear.

Abraham Maslow (1970) described these priorities as a **hierarchy of needs** (**FIGURE 29.3**). At the base of this pyramid are our physiological needs, such as those for food and water. Only if these needs are met are we prompted to meet our need for safety, and then to satisfy our human needs to give and receive love and to enjoy self-esteem. Beyond this, said Maslow (1971), lies the need for *self-actualization*—to realize our full potential.

Near the end of his life, Maslow proposed that some of us also reach a level of *self-transcendence*. At the self-actualization level, we seek to realize our own potential. At the self-transcendence level, we strive for meaning, purpose, and communion in a way that is transpersonal—beyond the self (Koltko-Rivera, 2006).

The order of Maslow's hierarchy is not universally fixed: People have starved themselves to make a political statement. Culture also influences our priorities: Self-esteem matters most in individualist nations, whose citizens tend to focus more on personal achievements than on family and community identity (Oishi et al., 1999). And, while agreeing with Maslow's basic levels of need, today's evolutionary psychologists add that gaining and retaining mates and parenting offspring are also universal human motives (Kenrick et al., 2010).

Nevertheless, the simple idea that some motives are more compelling than others provides a framework for thinking about motivation. Worldwide

---

"Hunger is the most urgent form of poverty."
Alliance to End Hunger, 2002

LaunchPad To test your understanding of the hierarchy of needs, visit LaunchPad's *Concept Practice: Building Maslow's Hierarchy.*

Yerkes-Dodson law the principle that performance increases with arousal only up to a point, beyond which performance decreases.

hierarchy of needs Maslow's pyramid of human needs, beginning at the base with physiological needs that must first be satisfied before higher-level safety needs and then psychological needs become active.

affiliation need the need to build relationships and to feel part of a group.

life-satisfaction surveys support this basic idea (Oishi et al., 1999; Tay & Diener, 2011). In poorer nations that lack easy access to money and the food and shelter it buys, financial satisfaction more strongly predicts feelings of well-being. In wealthy nations, where most are able to meet basic needs, social connections (such as home-life satisfaction) better predict well-being.

With these classic motivation theories in mind (see **TABLE 29.1**), let's now take a closer look at two specific, higher-level motives: the *need to belong* and the *need to achieve*. As you read about these motives, watch for ways that incentives (the psychological "pull") interact with physiological needs (the biological "push").

Self-transcendence needs
Need to find meaning and identity beyond the self

Self-actualization needs
Need to live up to our fullest and unique potential

Esteem needs
Need for self-esteem, achievement, competence, and independence; need for recognition and respect from others

Belongingness and love needs
Need to love and be loved, to belong and be accepted; need to avoid loneliness and separation

Safety needs
Need to feel that the world is organized and predictable; need to feel safe, secure, and stable

Physiological needs
Need to satisfy hunger and thirst

◄ FIGURE 29.3

Maslow's hierarchy of needs Reduced to near-starvation by their rulers, inhabitants of Suzanne Collins' fictional nation, Panem, hunger for food and survival. *Hunger Games* heroine Katniss Everdeen expresses higher-level needs for actualization and transcendence, and in the process inspires the nation.

⌄ TABLE 29.1

Classic Motivation Theories

Theory	Its Big Idea
Instinct theory/evolutionary psychology	There is a genetic basis for unlearned, species-typical behavior (such as birds building nests or infants rooting for a nipple).
Drive-reduction theory	Physiological needs (such as hunger and thirst) create an aroused state that drives us to reduce the need (for example, by eating or drinking).
Arousal theory	Our need to maintain an optimal level of arousal motivates behaviors that meet no physiological need (such as our yearning for stimulation and our hunger for information).
Maslow's hierarchy of needs	We prioritize survival-based needs and then social needs more than the needs for esteem and meaning.

RETRIEVE IT

• After hours of driving alone in an unfamiliar city, you finally see a diner. Although it looks deserted and a little creepy, you stop because you are *really* hungry and thirsty. How would Maslow's hierarchy of needs explain your behavior?

ANSWER: According to Maslow, our drive to meet the physiological needs of hunger and thirst take priority over safety needs, prompting us to take risks at times.

The Need to Belong

29-2 What evidence points to our human affiliation need—our need to belong?

We are what Greek philosopher Aristotle called *the social animal*. Cut off from friends or family—alone in prison or at a new school or in a foreign land—most people feel keenly their lost connections with important others. This deep *need to belong*—our **affiliation need**—seems to be a central human motivation (Baumeister & Leary, 1995). Although people vary in their wish for privacy and solitude, most of us seek to affiliate—to become strongly attached to certain others in enduring, close relationships. Human beings, contended personality theorist Alfred Adler, have an "urge to community" (Ferguson, 1989, 2001, 2010). Our psychological needs drive our adaptive behaviors and, when satisfied, enhance our psychological well-being (Sheldon, 2011).

The Benefits of Belonging

Social bonds boosted our early ancestors' chances of survival. Adults who formed attachments were more likely to reproduce and to co-nurture their offspring to maturity. Attachment bonds motivated caregivers to keep children close, calming them and protecting them from threats (Esposito et al., 2013). Indeed, to be "wretched" literally means, in its Middle English origin *(wrecched)*, to be without kin nearby.

Cooperation also enhanced survival. In solo combat, our ancestors were not the toughest predators. But as hunters, they learned that six hands were better than two. As food gatherers, they gained protection from two-footed and four-footed enemies by traveling in groups. Those who felt a need to belong survived and reproduced most successfully, and their genes now predominate. Our innate need to belong drives us to befriend people who cooperate and to avoid those who exploit (Feinberg et al., 2014). People in every society on Earth belong to groups and prefer and favor "us" over "them."

Do you have close friends—people with whom you freely disclose your ups and downs? Having someone who rejoices with us over good news helps us feel even better about both the news and the friendship (Reis et al., 2010). A stranger's casual thank-you can warm our heart (Williams & Bartlett, 2015). And close friends can literally make us feel warm, as if we are holding a soothing cup of warm tea (Inagaki & Eisenberger, 2014). The need to belong runs deeper, it seems, than any need to be rich. One study found that *very* happy university students were distinguished not by their money but by their "rich and satisfying close relationships" (Diener & Seligman, 2002).

The need to belong colors our thoughts and emotions. We spend a great deal of time thinking about actual and hoped-for relationships. Asked, "What is necessary for your happiness?" or "What is it that makes your life meaningful?" most people have mentioned—before anything else—close, satisfying relationships with family, friends, or romantic partners (Berscheid, 1985). Happiness hits close to home.

Consider: What was your most satisfying moment in the past week? Researchers asked that question of American and South Korean collegians, then asked them to rate how much that moment had satisfied various needs (Sheldon et al., 2001). In both countries, the peak moment had contributed most to satisfaction of self-esteem and relatedness-belonging needs. When our need for relatedness is satisfied in balance with two other basic psychological needs—*autonomy* (a sense of personal control) and *competence*—we experience a deep sense of well-being, and our self-esteem rides high (Deci & Ryan, 2002, 2009; Milyavskaya et al., 2009). Indeed, *self-esteem* is a gauge of how valued and accepted we feel (Leary, 2012).

Is it surprising, then, that so much of our social behavior aims to increase our feelings of belonging? To gain acceptance, we generally conform to group standards. We monitor our behavior, hoping to make a good impression. We spend billions on clothes, cosmetics, and diet and fitness aids—all motivated by our search for love and acceptance.

Thrown together in groups at school, at work, on a hiking trip, we behave like magnets, moving closer, forming bonds. Parting, we feel distress. We promise to call, to write, to return for reunions. By drawing a sharp circle around "us," the need to belong feeds both deep attachments and menacing threats. Out of our need to define a "we" come loving families, faithful friendships, and team spirit, but also teen gangs, ethnic rivalries, and fanatic nationalism.

Feelings of love activate brain reward and safety systems. In one experiment involving exposure to heat, deeply-in-love university students felt markedly less pain when looking at their beloved's picture (rather than viewing someone else's photo or being distracted by a word task) (Younger et al., 2010). Pictures of our loved ones also activate a brain region associated with safety—the prefrontal cortex—that dampens feelings of physical pain (Eisenberger et al., 2011). Love is a natural painkiller.

"We must love one another or die."

W. H. Auden, "September 1, 1939"

ostracism deliberate social exclusion of individuals or groups.

Even when bad relationships break, people suffer. In one 16-nation survey, and in repeated U.S. surveys, separated and divorced people have been half as likely as married people to say they were "very happy" (Inglehart, 1990; NORC, 2014). Is that simply because happy people more often marry and stay married? A national study following British lives through time revealed that, even after controlling for premarital life satisfaction, "the married are still more satisfied, suggesting a causal effect" of marriage (Grover & Helliwell, 2014). Divorce also predicts earlier mortality. Studies that have followed 6.5 million people in 11 countries reveal that, compared with married people, separated and divorced people are at greater risk for early death (Sbarra et al., 2011).

Children who move through a series of foster homes or through repeated family relocations know the fear of being alone. After repeated disruption of budding attachments, they may have difficulty forming deep attachments (Oishi & Schimmack, 2010). The evidence is clearest at the extremes: Children who grow up in institutions without a sense of belonging to anyone, or who are locked away at home and severely neglected often become withdrawn, frightened, speechless.

No matter how secure our early years were, we all experience anxiety, loneliness, jealousy, or guilt when something threatens or dissolves our social ties. Much as life's best moments occur when close relationships begin—making a new friend, falling in love, having a baby—life's worst moments happen when close relationships end (Jaremka et al., 2011). Bereaved, we may feel life is empty, pointless. Even the first weeks living on a college campus can be distressing. But our need to belong pushes most of us to form a new web of social connections (Oishi et al., 2013).

For immigrants and refugees moving alone to new places, the stress and loneliness can be depressing. After years of placing individual families in isolated communities, U.S. immigration policies began to encourage *chain migration* (Pipher, 2002). The second refugee Sudanese family settling in a town generally has an easier adjustment than the first.

Social isolation can put us at risk for mental decline and ill health (Cacioppo & Hawkley, 2009). Lonely older adults make more doctor visits (Gerst-Emerson & Jayawardhana, 2015). But if feelings of acceptance and connection increase sufficiently, so will self-esteem, positive feelings, and physical health (Blackhart et al., 2009; Holt-Lunstad et al., 2010; Smart Richman & Leary, 2009). A socially connected life is often a happy and healthy life.

The Pain of Being Shut Out

Can you recall feeling excluded or ignored or shunned? Perhaps you received the silent treatment. Perhaps people avoided you or averted their eyes in your presence or even mocked you behind your back. If you are like others, even being in a group speaking a different language may have left you feeling excluded, a linguistic outsider (Dotan-Eliaz, 2009). In one mock-interview study, women felt more excluded if interviewers used gender-exclusive language *(he, his, him)* rather than inclusive *(his or her)* or neutral *(their)* language (Stout & Dasgupta, 2011).

All these experiences are instances of **ostracism**—of social exclusion (Williams, 2007, 2009). Worldwide, humans use many forms of ostracism—exile, imprisonment, solitary confinement—to punish, and therefore control, social behavior. For children, even a brief time-out in isolation can be punishing. Asked to describe personal episodes that made them feel especially *bad* about themselves, people will—about four times in five—describe a relationship difficulty (Pillemer et al., 2007).

The need to connect Six days a week, women from the Philippines work as "domestic helpers" in 154,000 Hong Kong households. On Sundays, they throng to the central business district to picnic, dance, sing, talk, and laugh. "Humanity could stage no greater display of happiness," reported one observer (*Economist*, 2001).

Enduring the pain of ostracism White cadets at the United States Military Academy at West Point ostracized Henry Flipper for years, hoping he would drop out. He somehow resisted their cruelty and in 1877 became the first African-American West Point graduate.

Social acceptance and rejection
Successful participants on the reality TV show *Survivor* form alliances and gain acceptance among their peers. The rest receive the ultimate social punishment as they are "voted off the island."

"Do we really think it makes sense to lock so many people alone in tiny cells for 23 hours a day, sometimes for months or even years at a time? . . . And if those individuals are ultimately released, how are they ever going to adapt?"

U.S. President Barack Obama, July 14, 2015, expressing bipartisan concerns about the solitary confinement of some 75,000 American prisoners

"If no one turned around when we entered, answered when we spoke, or minded that we did, but if every person we met 'cut us dead,' and acted as if we were non-existing things, a kind of rage and impotent despair would ere long well up in us."

William James,
Principles of Psychology, 1890

Being shunned—given the cold shoulder or the silent treatment, with others' eyes avoiding yours—threatens one's need to belong (Wirth et al., 2010). "It's the meanest thing you can do to someone, especially if you know they can't fight back. I never should have been born," said Lea, a lifelong victim of the silent treatment by her mother and grandmother. Like Lea, people often respond to ostracism with initial efforts to restore their acceptance, with depressed moods, and then finally with withdrawal. Prisoner William Blake (2013) has spent more than a quarter-century in solitary confinement. "I cannot fathom how dying any death could be harder and more terrible than living through all that I have been forced to endure," he observed. To many, social exclusion is a sentence worse than death.

To experience ostracism is to experience real pain, as social psychologists Kipling Williams and his colleagues were surprised to discover in their studies of exclusion on social media (Gonsalkorale & Williams, 2006). (Perhaps you can recall the feeling of being unfriended, ignored, or having few followers on a social networking site, or of having a text message or e-mail go unanswered.) Such ostracism, they discovered, takes a toll: It elicits increased activity in brain areas, such as the *anterior cingulate cortex,* that also activate in response to physical pain (Eisenberger, 2015; Rotge et al., 2015). When viewing pictures of romantic partners who caused our hearts to break, our brains and bodies begin to ache (Wager et al., 2013). That helps explain another surprising finding: The pain reliever acetaminophen (as in Tylenol) lessens *social* as well as physical pain (DeWall et al., 2010). Across cultures, people use the same words (for example, *hurt, crushed*) for social pain and physical pain (MacDonald & Leary, 2005). Psychologically, we seem to experience social pain with the same emotional unpleasantness that marks physical pain.

Pain, whatever its source, focuses our attention and motivates corrective action. Rejected and unable to remedy the situation, people may relieve stress by seeking new friends, eating calorie-laden comfort foods, or strengthening their religious faith (Aydin et al., 2010; Maner et al., 2007; Sproesser et al., 2014). Or they may turn nasty. In a series of experiments, researchers told some students (who had taken a personality test) that they were "the type likely to end up alone later in life," or that people they had met didn't want them in a group that was forming (Baumeister et al., 2002; Gaertner et al., 2008; Twenge et al., 2001, 2002, 2007).[1] They told other students that they would have "rewarding relationships throughout life," or that "everyone chose you as someone they'd like to work with." Those who were excluded became much more likely to engage in self-defeating behaviors and to underperform on aptitude tests. The rejection also interfered with their empathy for others and made them more likely to act in disparaging or aggressive ways against those who had excluded them (blasting them with noise, for example). "If intelligent, well-adjusted, successful . . . students can turn aggressive in response to a small laboratory experience of social exclusion," noted the research team, "it is disturbing to imagine the aggressive tendencies that might arise from . . . chronic exclusion from desired groups in actual social life." Indeed, as Williams (2007) has observed, ostracism "weaves through case after case of school violence."

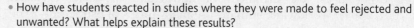

RETRIEVE IT [✖]

● How have students reacted in studies where they were made to feel rejected and unwanted? What helps explain these results?

ANSWER: They engaged in more self-defeating behaviors, underperformed on aptitude tests, and displayed less empathy and more aggression. These students' basic need to belong seems to have been disrupted.

1. Note: The researchers later *debriefed* and reassured the participants.

Connecting and Social Networking

29-3 How does social networking influence us?

As social creatures, we live for connection. Researcher George Vaillant (2013) was asked what he had learned from studying 238 Harvard University men from the 1930s to the end of their lives. He replied, "Happiness is love." South Africans have a word for the human bonds that define us all: *Ubuntu* [oo-BOON-too]. A South African Zulu saying captures the idea: *Umuntu ngumuntu ngabantu*—"a person is a person through other persons."

MOBILE NETWORKS AND SOCIAL MEDIA Look around and see humans connecting: talking, tweeting, texting, posting, chatting, social gaming, e-mailing. Walking across campus, you may see students with noses in their smart phones, making little eye contact with passersby. The changes in how we connect have been fast and vast:

Image Source/SuperStock

> "Facebook . . . was built to accomplish a social mission—to make the world more open and connected."
>
> *Facebook CEO, Mark Zuckerberg, 2012*

- At the end of 2014, the world had 7.3 billion people and 6.9 billion mobile cell-phone subscriptions (ITU, 2015). But phone talking accounts for less than half of U.S. mobile network traffic (Wortham, 2010). In Canada and elsewhere, e-mailing is being displaced by texting, social media sites, and other messaging technology (Ipsos, 2010). Speedy texting is not really writing, said one observer (McWhorter, 2012), but rather a new form of conversation—"fingered speech."

- Three in four U.S. teens text. Half (mostly females) send 60 or more texts daily (Lenhart, 2012). For many, it's as though friends, for better and worse, are always present.

- How many of us are using social networking sites, such as Facebook, Twitter, or Snapchat? Among 2014's entering American college students, 94 percent were (Eagan et al., 2014). With so many of your friends on a social network, its lure becomes hard to resist. Such is our need to belong. Check in or miss out.

THE NET RESULT: SOCIAL EFFECTS OF SOCIAL NETWORKING By connecting like-minded people, the Internet serves as a social amplifier. In times of social crisis or personal stress, it provides information and supportive connections. For better or for worse, it enables people to compare their lives with others (Verduyn et al., 2015). The Internet also functions as a matchmaker. (I [ND] can attest to this. I met my wife online.) As electronic communication has become an integral part of life, researchers have explored how it has affected our relationships.

HAVE SOCIAL NETWORKING SITES MADE US MORE, OR LESS, SOCIALLY ISOLATED? Lonely people tend to spend greater-than-average time online, while social butterflies gravitate toward face-to-face interactions (Bonetti et al., 2010; Pea et al., 2012; Stepanikova et al., 2010). But the Internet also offers opportunities for new social networks. (My [DM's] connections to other hearing-technology advocates across the world continue to grow.) Social networking is also mostly strengthening our connections with the variety of people we already know (DiSalvo, 2010; Ugander et al., 2012; Valkenburg & Peter, 2009). If your social networking helps you connect with friends, stay in touch with extended family, or find support when facing challenges, then you are not alone (Rainie et al., 2011). Social networks connect us. But they can also, as you've surely noticed, become gigantic time- and attention-sucking distractions that interfere with sleep, exercise, and face-to-face relationships. The net result may be an imbalance between face-to-face and online social connection.

DOES ELECTRONIC COMMUNICATION STIMULATE HEALTHY SELF-DISCLOSURE? *Self-disclosure* is sharing ourselves—our joys, worries, and weaknesses—with others. Confiding can be a healthy way of coping with day-to-day challenges. When communicating electronically rather than face-to-face, we often are less focused on others' reactions. We are less self-conscious, and thus less inhibited. Sometimes this is taken to an extreme, as when teens send photos of themselves they later regret, or bullies hound a victim, or hate groups post messages promoting bigotry or crimes. More often, however, the increased self-disclosure serves to deepen friendships (Valkenburg & Peter, 2009).

DO SOCIAL NETWORKS REFLECT PEOPLE'S ACTUAL PERSONALITIES? We've all heard stories of online predators hiding behind false personalities, values, and motives. Generally, however, social network profiles and posts reveal a person's real personality. In one study, participants completed a personality test twice. In one test, they described their "actual personality"; in the other, they described their "ideal self." Other volunteers then used the participants' Facebook profiles to create an independent set of personality ratings. The Facebook profile ratings were much closer to the participants' actual personalities than to their ideal personalities (Back et al., 2010). In another study, people who seemed most likable on their Facebook page also seemed most likable in face-to-face meetings (Weisbuch et al., 2009). Twitter posts similarly reveal people's actual friendliness (Qiu et al., 2012). Your online self may indeed reflect the real you!

DOES SOCIAL NETWORKING PROMOTE NARCISSISM? Narcissistic people are self-important, self-focused, and self-promoting. Personality tests may assess narcissism with items such as "I like to be the center of attention." **Narcissism** is self-esteem gone wild. People with high narcissism scores are especially active on social networking sites. They collect more superficial "friends." They offer more staged, glamorous photos. They retaliate more when people post negative comments. And, not surprisingly, they *seem* more narcissistic to strangers (Buffardi & Campbell, 2008; Carpenter, 2012).

For narcissists, social networking sites are more than a gathering place; they are a feeding trough. In one study, college students were *randomly assigned* either to edit and explain their online profiles for 15 minutes, or to use that time to study and explain a Google Maps routing (Freeman & Twenge, 2010). After completing their tasks, all were tested. Who then scored higher on a narcissism measure? Those who had spent the time focused on themselves.

MAINTAINING BALANCE AND FOCUS It will come as no surprise that excessive online socializing and gaming have been associated with lower grades (Chen & Fu, 2008; Rideout et al., 2010; Walsh et al., 2013). In one U.S. survey, 47 percent of the heaviest users of the Internet and other media were receiving mostly C grades or lower, as were just 23 percent of the lightest users (Kaiser Family Foundation, 2010).

In today's world, each of us is challenged to maintain a healthy balance between our real-world and online time. Experts offer some practical suggestions:

- *Monitor your time.* Keep a log of how you use your time. Then ask yourself, "Does my time use reflect my priorities? Am I spending more or less time online than I intended? Is my time online interfering with school or work performance?"

- *Monitor your feelings.* Ask yourself, "Am I emotionally distracted by my online interests? When I disconnect and move to another activity, how do I feel? Have family or friends commented on this?"

- *Hide from your more distracting online friends when necessary.* And in your own postings, practice the golden rule. Ask yourself, "Is this something I'd care about if someone else posted it?"

"The women on these dating sites don't seem to believe I'm a prince."

LaunchPad See LaunchPad's *Video: Random Assignment* for a helpful tutorial animation.

narcissism excessive self-love and self-absorption.

achievement motivation a desire for significant accomplishment; for mastery of skills or ideas; for control; and for attaining a high standard.

- *When studying, get in the practice of checking your phone only once per hour.* Selective attention—the flashlight of your mind—can be in only one place at a time. When we try to do two things at once, we don't do either one of them very well (Willingham, 2010). If you want to study or work productively, resist the temptation to be always available. Turn your phone face down and turn off all sound and vibration so that you choose when to attend to it. On your laptop, disable sound alerts and pop-ups. (To avoid distraction, I [DM] am proofing and editing this module in a coffee shop without Wi-Fi.)

- *Try a social networking fast* (give it up for an hour, a day, or a week) *or a time-controlled social media diet* (check in only after homework is done, or only during a lunch break). Take notes on what you're losing and gaining on your new "diet."

- *Refocus by taking a nature walk.* People learn better after a peaceful walk in the woods or a park, which—unlike a walk on a busy street—refreshes our capacity for focused attention (Berman et al., 2008). Connecting with nature boosts our spirits and sharpens our minds (Zelenski & Nisbet, 2014).

"It keeps me from looking at my phone every two seconds."

As psychologist Steven Pinker (2010) said, "The solution is not to bemoan technology but to develop strategies of self-control, as we do with every other temptation in life."

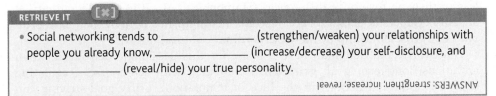

RETRIEVE IT [✱]

- Social networking tends to _____ (strengthen/weaken) your relationships with people you already know, _____ (increase/decrease) your self-disclosure, and _____ (reveal/hide) your true personality.

ANSWERS: strengthen; increase; reveal

Achievement Motivation

 29-4 What is achievement motivation?

Some motives seem to have little obvious survival value. Billionaires may be motivated to make ever more money, reality TV stars to attract ever more social media followers, politicians to achieve ever more power, daredevils to seek ever greater thrills. Such motives seem not to diminish when they are fed. The more we achieve, the more we may need to achieve. Psychologist Henry Murray (1938) defined **achievement motivation** as a desire for significant accomplishment, for mastering skills or ideas, for control, and for attaining a high standard.

Thanks to their persistence and eagerness for challenge, people with high achievement motivation do achieve more. One study followed the lives of 1528 California children whose intelligence test scores were in the top 1 percent. Forty years later, when researchers compared those who were most and least successful professionally, they found a motivational difference. Those most successful were more ambitious, energetic, and persistent. As children, they had more active hobbies. As adults, they participated in more groups and sports (Goleman, 1980). Gifted children are able learners. Accomplished adults are tenacious doers. Most of us are energetic doers when starting and when finishing a project. It's easiest—have you noticed?—to get stuck in the middle. That's when high achievers keep going (Bonezzi et al., 2011).

In other studies of both secondary school and university students, self-discipline has surpassed intelligence test scores to better predict school performance, attendance, and graduation honors. When combined with positive enthusiasm, sustained effort predicts success for teachers, too—with their students making good academic progress (Duckworth et al., 2009). For school performance, "discipline outdoes talent," concluded researchers Angela Duckworth and Martin Seligman (2005, 2006).

"Genius is 1% inspiration and 99% perspiration."

Thomas Edison (1847–1931)

Calum's road: What grit can accomplish Having spent his life on the Scottish island of Raasay, farming a small patch of land, tending its lighthouse, and fishing, Malcolm ("Calum") MacLeod (1911–1988) felt anguished. His local government repeatedly refused to build a road that would enable vehicles to reach his north end of the island. With the once-flourishing population there having dwindled to two—MacLeod and his wife—he responded with heroic determination. One spring morning in 1964, MacLeod, then in his fifties, gathered an ax, a chopper, a shovel, and a wheelbarrow. By hand, he began to transform the existing footpath into a 1.75-mile road (Miers, 2009).

"With a road," a former neighbor explained, "he hoped new generations of people would return to the north end of Raasay," restoring its culture (Hutchinson, 2006). Day after day he worked through rough hillsides, along hazardous cliff faces, and over peat bogs. Finally, 10 years later, he completed his supreme achievement. The road, which the government has since surfaced, remains a visible example of what vision plus determined grit can accomplish. It bids us each to ponder: What "roads"—what achievements— might we, with sustained effort, build in the years before us?

From Calum's Road by Roger Hutchinson, reproduced courtesy of Birlinn Ltd.

Discipline also refines talent. By their early twenties, top violinists have accumulated thousands of lifetime practice hours—in fact, double the practice time of other violin students aiming to be teachers (Ericsson 2001, 2006, 2007). A study of outstanding scholars, athletes, and artists found that all were highly motivated and self-disciplined, willing to dedicate hours every day to the pursuit of their goals (Bloom, 1985). As child prodigies illustrate (think young Mozart composing at age 8), native talent matters, too (Hambrick & Meinz, 2011; Ruthsatz & Urbach, 2012). In sports, music, and chess, for example, people's practice-time differences, while significant, account for a third or less of their performance differences (Hambrick et al., 2014a,b; Macnamara et al., 2014). Superstar achievers are, it seems, distinguished both by their extraordinary daily discipline and by their extraordinary natural talent.

Duckworth and Seligman have a name for this passionate dedication to an ambitious, long-term goal: **grit**. When combined with self-control (regulating one's attention and actions in the face of temptation), gritty goal-striving can produce great achievements. "If you want to look good in front of thousands," the saying goes, "you have to outwork thousands in front of nobody."

Although intelligence is distributed like a bell curve, achievements are not. That tells us that achievement involves much more than raw ability. That is why organizational psychologists seek ways to engage and motivate ordinary people doing ordinary jobs (see Appendix B: Psychology at Work). And that is why training students in *hardiness*—resilience under stress—leads to better grades (Maddi et al., 2009).

---

grit in psychology, passion and perseverance in the pursuit of long-term goals.

RETRIEVE IT [✱]

• What have researchers found to be an even better predictor of school performance than intelligence test scores?

ANSWER: self-discipline (*grit*)

👁 Learning Objectives

Test Yourself by taking a moment to answer each of these Learning Objective Questions (repeated here from within the module). Then turn to Appendix D, Complete Module Reviews, to check your answers. Research suggests that trying to answer these questions on your own will improve your long-term memory of the concepts (McDaniel et al., 2009).

29-1 How do psychologists define *motivation?* From what perspectives do they view motivated behavior?

29-2 What evidence points to our human affiliation need—our need to belong?

29-3 How does social networking influence us?

29-4 What is achievement motivation?

Terms and Concepts to Remember

Test yourself on these terms by trying to write down the definition in your own words before flipping back to the referenced page to check your answers.

motivation, p. 366

instinct, p. 366

drive-reduction theory, p. 367

homeostasis, p. 367

incentive, p. 367

Yerkes-Dodson law, p. 368

hierarchy of needs, p. 368

affiliation need, p. 369

ostracism, p. 371

narcissism, p. 374

achievement motivation, p. 375

grit, p. 376

Experience the Testing Effect

Test yourself repeatedly throughout your studies. This will not only help you figure out what you know and don't know; the testing itself will help you learn and remember the information more effectively thanks to the *testing effect*.

1. Today's evolutionary psychology shares an idea that was an underlying assumption of instinct theory. That idea is that
   a. physiological needs arouse psychological states.
   b. genes predispose species-typical behavior.
   c. physiological needs increase arousal.
   d. external needs energize and direct behavior.

2. An example of a physiological need is _____.
   An example of a psychological drive is _____.
   a. hunger; a "push" to find food
   b. a "push" to find food; hunger
   c. curiosity; a "push" to reduce arousal
   d. a "push" to reduce arousal; curiosity

3. Jan walks into a friend's kitchen, smells cookies baking, and begins to feel very hungry. The smell of baking cookies is a(n) _____ (incentive/drive).

4. _____ theory attempts to explain behaviors that do NOT reduce physiological needs.

5. With a challenging task, such as taking a difficult exam, performance is likely to peak when arousal is
   a. very high.
   b. moderate.
   c. very low.
   d. absent.

6. According to Maslow's hierarchy of needs, our most basic needs are physiological, including the need for food and water; just above these are _____ needs.
   a. safety
   b. self-esteem
   c. belongingness
   d. self-transcendence

7. Which of the following is NOT part of the evidence presented to support the view that humans are strongly motivated by a need to belong?
   a. Students who rated themselves as "very happy" also tended to have satisfying close relationships.
   b. Social exclusion—such as exile or solitary confinement—is considered a severe form of punishment.
   c. As adults, adopted children tend to resemble their biological parents and to yearn for an affiliation with them.
   d. Children who are extremely neglected become withdrawn, frightened, and speechless.

8. What are some ways to manage our social networking time successfully?

Find answers to these questions in Appendix E, in the back of the book.

Use LearningCurve to create your personalized study plan, which will direct you to the resources that will help you most in LaunchPad.

MODULE 30 Hunger

Anyone who has tried to restrict their eating knows that physiological influences are powerful. Their strength was vividly demonstrated when Ancel Keys and his research team (1950) studied semistarvation among wartime conscientious objectors. After three months of normal eating, they cut in half the food intake of 36 men selected from 200 volunteers. The semistarved men became listless and apathetic as their bodies conserved energy. Eventually, their body weights stabilized at about 25 percent below their starting weights.

Hunger hijacks the mind World War II survivor Louis Zamperini (protagonist of the book and movie *Unbroken,* shown here) went down with his plane over the Pacific Ocean. He and two other crew members drifted for 47 days, subsisting on an occasional bird or a fish. To help pass time, the hunger-driven men recited food recipes or recalled their mothers' home cooking.

Consistent with Abraham Maslow's idea of a needs hierarchy, the men became food obsessed. They talked food. They daydreamed food. They collected recipes, read cookbooks, and feasted their eyes on delectable forbidden food. Preoccupied with their unmet basic need, they lost interest in sex and social activities. As one man reported, "If we see a show, the most interesting part of it is contained in scenes where people are eating. I couldn't laugh at the funniest picture in the world, and love scenes are completely dull."

The semistarved men's preoccupations illustrate how powerful motives can hijack our consciousness. When we're hungry, thirsty, fatigued, or sexually aroused, little else seems to matter. When we're not, food, water, sleep, or sex just don't seem like such big things in life, now or ever.

> "Nobody wants to kiss when they are hungry."
>
> *Journalist Dorothy Dix (1861–1951)*

> "Nature often equips life's essentials—sex, eating, nursing—with built-in gratification."
>
> *Frans de Waal, "Morals Without God?" 2010*

In studies, people in a motivational "hot" state (from fatigue, hunger, or sexual arousal) have easily recalled such feelings in their own past and have perceived them as driving forces in others' behavior (Nordgren et al., 2006, 2007). (Interestingly, there is a parallel effect of our current good or bad mood on our memories.) People in another experiment were given $4 cash they could keep or draw from to bid for foods. Hungry people overbid for a snack they would eat later when sated, and sated people underbid for a snack they would eat later when hungry (Fisher & Rangel, 2014). Grocery shop with an empty stomach and you are more likely to see those jelly-filled doughnuts as just what you've always loved and will be wanting tomorrow. *Motives matter mightily.*

> "The full person does not understand the needs of the hungry."
>
> *Irish proverb*

The Physiology of Hunger

👁 **30-1** What physiological factors produce hunger?

Deprived of a normal food supply, Keys' semistarved volunteers were clearly hungry. But what precisely triggers hunger? Is it the pangs of an empty stomach? So it seemed to A. L. Washburn. Working with Walter Cannon (Cannon & Washburn, 1912), Washburn agreed to swallow a balloon attached to a recording device (**FIGURE 30.1**). When inflated to fill his stomach, the balloon transmitted his stomach contractions. Washburn supplied information about his *feelings* of hunger by pressing a key each time he felt a hunger pang. The discovery: Washburn was indeed having stomach contractions whenever he felt hungry.

glucose the form of sugar that circulates in the blood and provides the major source of energy for body tissues. When its level is low, we feel hunger.

set point the point at which your "weight thermostat" is supposedly set. When your body falls below this weight, increased hunger and a lowered metabolic rate may combine to restore the lost weight.

Can hunger exist without stomach pangs? To answer that question, researchers removed some rats' stomachs and created a direct path to their small intestines (Tsang, 1938). Did the rats continue to eat? Indeed they did. Some hunger similarly persists in humans whose ulcerated or cancerous stomachs have been removed. So the pangs of an empty stomach are not the *only* source of hunger. What else might trigger hunger?

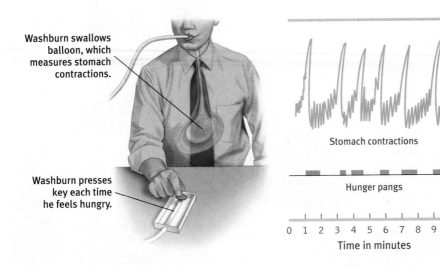

Washburn swallows balloon, which measures stomach contractions.

Washburn presses key each time he feels hungry.

Stomach contractions

Hunger pangs

Time in minutes

❮ FIGURE 30.1

Monitoring stomach contractions Using this procedure, Washburn showed that stomach contractions (transmitted by the stomach balloon) accompany our feelings of hunger (indicated by a key press). (From Cannon, 1929.)

Body Chemistry and the Brain

Somehow, somewhere, your body is keeping tabs on the energy it takes in and the energy it uses. If this weren't true, you would be unable to maintain a stable body weight. A major source of energy in your body is the blood sugar **glucose.** If your blood glucose level drops, you won't consciously feel the lower blood sugar, but your stomach, intestines, and liver will signal your brain to motivate eating. Your brain, which is automatically monitoring your blood chemistry and your body's internal state, will then trigger hunger.

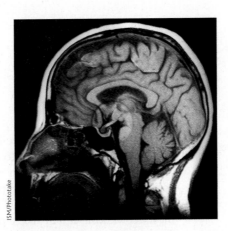

ISM/Phototake

❮ FIGURE 30.2

The hypothalamus The hypothalamus (colored orange) performs various body maintenance functions, including control of hunger. Blood vessels supply the hypothalamus, enabling it to respond to our current blood chemistry as well as to incoming neural information about the body's state.

How does the brain integrate these messages and sound the alarm? The work is done by several neural areas, some housed deep in the brain within the hypothalamus, a neural traffic intersection (**FIGURE 30.2**). For example, one neural arc (called the *arcuate nucleus*) has a center that secretes appetite-stimulating hormones. When stimulated electrically, well-fed animals begin to eat. If the area is destroyed, even starving animals have no interest in food. Another neural center secretes appetite-suppressing hormones. When electrically stimulated, animals will stop eating. Destroy this area and animals can't stop eating and will become obese (Duggan & Booth, 1986; Hoebel & Teitelbaum, 1966).

Blood vessels connect the hypothalamus to the rest of the body, so it can respond to our current blood chemistry and other incoming information. One of its tasks is monitoring levels of appetite hormones, such as *ghrelin*, a hunger-arousing hormone secreted by an empty stomach. During bypass surgery for severe obesity, surgeons seal off or remove part of the stomach. The remaining stomach then produces much less ghrelin, and the person's appetite lessens (Ammori, 2013; Lemonick, 2002). Other appetite hormones include *insulin, leptin, orexin,* and *PYY;* **FIGURE 30.3** on the next page describes how they influence your feelings of hunger.

The interaction of appetite hormones and brain activity suggests that the body has some sort of "weight thermostat." When semistarved rats fall below their normal weight, this system signals the body to restore the lost weight. Fat cells cry out (so to speak) "Feed me!" and grab glucose from the bloodstream (Ludwig & Friedman, 2014). Hunger increases and energy output decreases. In this way, rats (and humans) tend to hover around a stable weight, or **set point,** influenced in part by heredity (Keesey & Corbett, 1984).

Evidence for the brain's control of eating The fat mouse on the left has nonfunctioning receptors in the appetite-suppressing part of the hypothalamus.

Voisin/Phanie/Science Source

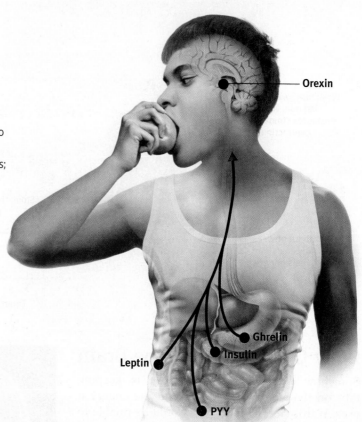

> **FIGURE 30.3**

The appetite hormones
- *Ghrelin:* Hormone secreted by empty stomach; sends "I'm hungry" signals to the brain.
- *Insulin:* Hormone secreted by pancreas; controls blood glucose.
- *Leptin:* Protein hormone secreted by fat cells; when abundant, causes brain to increase metabolism and decrease hunger.
- *Orexin:* Hunger-triggering hormone secreted by hypothalamus.
- *PYY:* Digestive tract hormone; sends "I'm not hungry" signals to the brain.

LaunchPad For an interactive and visual tutorial on the brain and eating, visit LaunchPad's *PsychSim 6: Hunger and the Fat Rat.*

GREGORY

"Never get a tattoo when you're drunk and hungry."

We humans (and other species, too) vary in our **basal metabolic rate,** a measure of how much energy we use to maintain basic body functions when our body is at rest. But we share a common response to decreased food intake: Our basal metabolic rate drops, as it did for participants in Keys' experiment. After 24 weeks of semistarvation, they stabilized at three-quarters of their normal weight, although they were taking in *half* their previous calories. How did their bodies achieve this dieter's nightmare? They reduced their energy expenditure, partly because they were less active, but partly because their basal metabolic rate dropped by 29 percent.

Some researchers have suggested that the idea of a biologically *fixed* set point is too rigid to explain some things. One thing it doesn't address is that slow, sustained changes in body weight can alter a person's set point (Assanand et al., 1998). Another is that when we have unlimited access to a wide variety of tasty foods, we tend to overeat and gain weight (Raynor & Epstein, 2001). And set points don't explain why psychological factors influence hunger. For all these reasons, some prefer the looser term *settling point* to indicate the level at which a person's weight settles in response to caloric intake and energy use. As we will see next, these factors are influenced by environment as well as biology.

RETRIEVE IT [✷]

- Hunger occurs in response to _____ (low/high) blood glucose and _____ (low/high) levels of ghrelin.

ANSWERS: low; high

The Psychology of Hunger

30-2 What cultural and situational factors influence hunger?

Our internal hunger games are pushed by our body chemistry and brain activity. Yet there is more to hunger than meets the stomach. This was strikingly apparent when trickster researchers tested two patients who had no memory for events occurring more than a minute ago (Rozin et al., 1998). If offered a second lunch 20 minutes after eating a normal lunch, both patients readily consumed it . . .

basal metabolic rate the body's resting rate of energy expenditure.

and usually a third meal offered 20 minutes after they finished the second. This suggests that one part of our decision to eat is our memory of the time of our last meal. As time passes, we think about eating again, and those thoughts trigger feelings of hunger.

Taste Preferences: Biology and Culture

Body cues and environmental factors together influence not only the *when* of hunger, but also the *what*—our taste preferences. When feeling tense or depressed, do you tend to take solace in high-calorie foods, as has been found in ardent football fans after a big loss (Cornil & Chandon, 2013)? The carbohydrates in pizza, chips, and sweets help boost levels of the neurotransmitter serotonin, which has calming effects. When stressed, both rats and many humans find it extra rewarding to scarf Oreos (Artiga et al., 2007; Sproesser et al., 2014).

Our preferences for sweet and salty tastes are genetic and universal, but conditioning can intensify or alter those preferences. People given highly salted foods may develop a liking for excess salt (Beauchamp, 1987). People sickened by a food may develop an aversion to it. (The frequency of children's illnesses provides many chances for them to learn to avoid certain foods.)

Our culture teaches us that some foods are acceptable but others are not. Many Japanese people enjoy nattó, a fermented soybean dish that "smells like the marriage of ammonia and a tire fire," reports smell expert Rachel Herz (2012). Although many Westerners find this disgusting, Asians, she adds, are often repulsed by what Westerners love—"the rotted bodily fluid of an ungulate" (a.k.a. cheese, some varieties of which have the same bacteria and odor as stinky feet).

An acquired taste People everywhere learn to enjoy the fatty, bitter, or spicy foods common in their culture. For these Alaska Natives (above), but not for most other North Americans, whale blubber is a tasty treat. For Peruvians (left), roasted guinea pig is similarly delicious.

But there is biological wisdom to many of our taste preferences. For example, in hot climates (where foods spoil more quickly) recipes often include spices that inhibit bacteria growth (**FIGURE 30.4**). Pregnancy-related food dislikes—and the nausea associated with them—peak about the tenth week, when the developing embryo is most vulnerable to toxins.

Rats tend to avoid unfamiliar foods (Sclafani, 1995). So do we, especially those that are animal-based. This *neophobia* (dislike of unfamiliar things) surely was adaptive for our ancestors by protecting them from potentially toxic substances. Disgust works. In time, though, most people who repeatedly sample an initially novel fruit drink or unfamiliar food come to appreciate the new taste (Pliner, 1982, Pliner et al., 1993).

Situational Influences on Eating

To a surprising extent, situations also control our eating—a phenomenon psychologists have called the *ecology of eating*. Here are five situational influences you may have noticed but underestimated:

- *Arousing appetite* In one experiment, watching an intense action movie (rather than a nonarousing interview) doubled snacking (Tal et al., 2014).

- *Friends and food* Do you eat more when eating with others? Most of us do (Herman et al., 2003; Hetherington et al., 2006). After a party, you may realize you've overeaten. This happens because the presence of others tends to amplify our natural behavior tendencies. (We explore this *social facilitation* in the Social Psychology modules.)

- *Serving size is significant* "Unit bias" occurs with similar mindlessness. Investigators studied the effects of portion size by offering people varieties of

❯ FIGURE 30.4

Hot cultures like hot spices Countries with hot climates, in which food historically spoiled more quickly, feature recipes with more bacteria-inhibiting spices (Sherman & Flaxman, 2001). India averages nearly 10 spices per meat recipe; Finland, 2 spices.

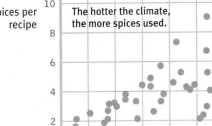

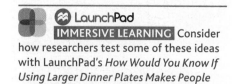

IMMERSIVE LEARNING Consider how researchers test some of these ideas with LaunchPad's *How Would You Know If Using Larger Dinner Plates Makes People Gain Weight?*

free snacks. In an apartment lobby, they laid out full or half pretzels, big or little Tootsie Rolls, or a small or large serving scoop with a bowl of M&M's. Their consistent result: Offered a supersized portion, people put away more calories. In another study, people ate more pasta when given a bigger plate (Van Ittersum & Wansink, 2012). Children also eat more when using adult-sized (rather than child-sized) dishware (DiSantis et al., 2013). Even nutrition experts helped themselves to 31 percent more ice cream when given a big bowl rather than a small one (Wansink, 2014; Wansink et al., 2006). Portion size matters.

- *Selections stimulate* Food variety also stimulates eating. Offered a dessert buffet, we eat more than we do when choosing a portion from one favorite dessert. For our early ancestors, variety was healthy. When foods were abundant and varied, eating more provided a wide range of vitamins and minerals and produced protective fat for winter cold or famine. When a bounty of varied foods was unavailable, eating less extended the food supply until winter or famine ended (Polivy et al., 2008; Remick et al., 2009).

- *Nudging nutrition* One research team quadrupled carrots taken by offering schoolchildren carrots before they picked up other foods in a lunch line (Redden et al., 2015). A planned new school lunch tray will put fruits and veggies up front, and spread the entrée out in a shallow compartment to make it look bigger (Wansink, 2014).

RETRIEVE IT

- After an eight-hour hike without food, your long-awaited favorite dish is placed in front of you, and your mouth waters in anticipation. Why?

ANSWER: You have learned to respond to the sight and aroma that signal the food about to enter your mouth. Both *physiological* cues (low blood sugar) and *psychological* cues (anticipation of the tasty meal) heighten your experienced hunger.

Obesity and Weight Control

 30-3 What factors predispose some people to become and remain obese?

Obesity can be socially toxic, by affecting both how you are treated and how you feel about yourself. Obesity has been associated with lower psychological well-being, especially among women, and increased depression (de Wit et al., 2010; Luppino et al., 2010; Riffkin, 2014). Obese 6- to 9-year-olds are 60 percent more likely to suffer bullying (Lumeng et al., 2010). And obesity has physical health risks as well. Yet few overweight people win the battle of the bulge. Why? And why do some people gain weight while others eat the same amount and don't?

The Physiology of Obesity

Our bodies store fat for good reason. Fat is an ideal form of stored energy—a high-calorie fuel reserve to carry the body through periods when food is scarce—a common occurrence in our prehistoric ancestors' world. No wonder people in impoverished places have often found heavier bodies attractive. Where food is scarce, plumpness may signal affluence and status (Swami, 2015; Swami et al., 2011).

In parts of the world where food and sweets are now abundantly available, the rule that once served our hungry distant ancestors—*When you find energy-rich fat or sugar, eat it!*—has become dysfunctional. Pretty much everywhere this book is being read, people have a growing problem. A worldwide study of 188 countries (Ng et al., 2014) revealed that

- between 1980 and 2013, the proportion of overweight adults increased from 29 to 37 percent among the world's men, and from 30 to 38 percent among women.

- over the last 33 years, *no* country has reduced its obesity rate. Not one.

- national variations are huge, with the percentage overweight ranging from 85 percent in Tonga to 3 percent in Timor-Leste.

According to the World Health Organization (WHO), an overweight person has a *body mass index* (BMI) of 25 or more; someone obese has a BMI of 30 or more. In the United States, the adult obesity rate has more than doubled in the last 40 years, reaching 36 percent, and child-teen obesity has quadrupled (Flegal et al., 2010, 2012). In 1990, no U.S. state had an obesity rate greater than 15 percent. By 2010, no state had an obesity rate of *less* than 20 percent (CDC, 2012).

In one digest of 97 studies of 2.9 million people, being simply overweight was not a health risk, while being obese was (Flegal et al., 2013). Fitness matters more than being a little overweight. But significant obesity increases the risk of diabetes, high blood pressure, heart disease, gallstones, arthritis, and certain types of cancer, thus increasing health care costs and shortening life expectancy (de Gonzales et al., 2010; Jarrett et al., 2010; Sun et al., 2009). Research also has linked women's obesity to their risk of late-life cognitive decline, including Alzheimer's disease and brain tissue loss (Bruce-Keller et al., 2009; Whitmer et al., 2008). One experiment found improved memory performance 12 weeks after severely obese people had weight-loss surgery and lost significant weight. Those not having the surgery showed some further cognitive decline (Gunstad et al., 2011).

SET POINT AND METABOLISM Research on the physiology of obesity challenges the stereotype of severely overweight people being weak-willed gluttons. Once we become fat, we require less food to maintain our weight than we did to attain it. Fat has a lower metabolic rate than does muscle—it takes less food energy to maintain. When an overweight person's body drops below its previous set (or settling) point, the brain triggers increased hunger and decreased metabolism. The body adapts to what it perceives as starvation by burning off fewer calories and seeking to restore lost weight. Blame your brain for weight regain (Cornier, 2011).

Lean people also seem naturally disposed to move about. They burn more calories than do energy-conserving overweight people, who tend to sit still longer (Levine et al., 2005). Individual differences in resting metabolism help explain why two people of the same height, age, and activity level can maintain the same weight, even if one of them eats much less than does the other.

THE GENETIC FACTOR Do our genes predispose us to eat more or less? To burn more calories by fidgeting or fewer by sitting still? Studies confirm a genetic influence on body weight. Consider two examples:

- Despite shared family meals, adoptive siblings' body weights are uncorrelated with one another or with those of their adoptive parents. Rather, people's weights resemble those of their biological parents (Grilo & Pogue-Geile, 1991).

- Identical twins have closely similar weights, even when raised apart (Hjelmborg et al., 2008; Plomin et al., 1997). Across studies, their weight correlates +.74. The much lower +.32 correlation among fraternal twins suggests that genes explain two-thirds of our varying body mass (Maes et al., 1997).

As with other behavior traits (such as intelligence, sexual orientation, and personality) there is no one "weight gene." Rather, many genes—including nearly 100 genes identified from a recent DNA analysis of 340,000 people—each contribute small effects (Locke et al., 2015).

THE FOOD AND ACTIVITY FACTORS Genes tell an important part of the obesity story. But environmental factors are mighty important, too.

Studies in Europe, Japan, and the United States show that children and adults who suffer from *sleep loss* are more vulnerable to obesity (Keith et al., 2006;

See www.tinyurl.com/GiveMyBMI to calculate your BMI and to see where you are in relation to others in your country and in the world.

"Remember when we used to have to fatten the kids up first?"

"American men, on average, say they weigh 196 pounds and women say they weigh 160 pounds. Both figures are nearly 20 pounds heavier than in 1990."

Elizabeth Mendes,
www.gallup.com, 2011

LaunchPad See LaunchPad's *Videos: Twin Studies* and *Correlational Studies* for helpful tutorial animations.

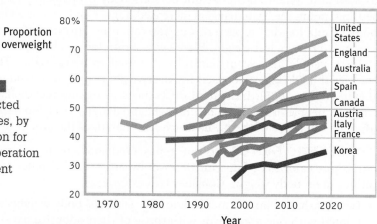

PhotoObjects.net/Jupiterimages

Nedeltcheva et al., 2010; Taheri, 2004; Taheri et al., 2004). With sleep deprivation, the levels of leptin (which reports body fat to the brain) fall, and ghrelin (the appetite-stimulating stomach hormone) rise.

Social influence is another factor. One 32-year study of 12,067 people found them most likely to become obese when a friend became obese (Christakis & Fowler, 2007). If the obese friend was a close one, the odds of likewise becoming obese almost tripled. Moreover, the correlation among friends' weights was not simply a matter of seeking out similar people as friends. Friends matter.

The strongest evidence that environment influences weight comes from our fattening world (**FIGURE 30.5**). What explains this growing problem? Changing food consumption and decreased work-related physical activity. We are eating more and moving less, with lifestyles sometimes approaching those of animal feedlots (where farmers fatten inactive animals). Worldwide, 31 percent of adults (including 43 percent of Americans and 25 percent of Europeans) are now sedentary, which means they average less than 20 minutes per day of moderate activity such as walking (Hallal et al., 2012).

> **FIGURE 30.5**

Past and projected overweight rates, by the Organization for Economic Cooperation and Development

The "bottom" line: New stadiums, theaters, and subway cars—but not airplanes—are widening seats to accommodate the girth growth (Hampson, 2000; Kim & Tong, 2010). Washington State Ferries abandoned a 50-year-old standard: "Eighteen-inch butts are a thing of the past" (Shepherd, 1999). New York City, facing a large problem with Big Apple bottoms, has mostly replaced 17.5-inch bucket-style subway seats with bucketless seats (Hampson, 2000). In the end, today's people need more room.

These results reinforce an important finding from psychology's study of intelligence: There can be high levels of heritability (genetic influence on individual differences) without heredity explaining group differences. Genes mostly determine why one person today is heavier than another. Environment mostly determines why people today are heavier than their counterparts 50 years ago. Our eating behavior also demonstrates the now-familiar interaction among biological, psychological, and social-cultural factors. For tips on shedding unwanted weight, see **TABLE 30.1.**

"We put fast food on every corner, we put junk food in our schools, we got rid of [physical education classes], we put candy and soda at the checkout stand of every retail outlet you can think of. The results are in. It worked."

Harold Goldstein, Executive Director of the California Center for Public Health Advocacy, 2009, when imagining a vast U.S. national experiment to encourage weight gain

▼ TABLE 30.1

Waist Management

People struggling with obesity are well advised to seek medical evaluation and guidance. For others who wish to lose weight, researchers have offered these tips:

- *Begin only if you feel motivated and self-disciplined.* Permanent weight loss requires a lifelong change in eating habits combined with increased exercise.

- *Exercise and get enough sleep.* Especially when supported by 7 to 8 hours of sleep a night, exercise empties fat cells, builds muscle, speeds up metabolism, helps lower your set point, and reduces stress and stress-induced craving for carbohydrate-rich comfort foods (Bennett, 1995; Kolata, 1987; Thompson et al., 1982).

- *Minimize exposure to tempting food cues.* Food shop on a full stomach. Keep tempting foods out of the house, and tuck away special-occasion foods.

- *Limit variety and eat healthy foods.* Given more variety, people consume more. So eat simple meals with vegetables, fruits, and whole grains. Water- and vitamin-rich veggies can fill the stomach with few calories. Healthy fats, such as those found in olive oil and fish, help regulate appetite (Taubes, 2001, 2002). Better crispy greens than Krispy Kremes.

- *Reduce portion sizes.* Serve food with smaller bowls, plates, and utensils.

- *Don't starve all day and eat one big meal at night.* This common eating pattern slows metabolism. Moreover, those who eat a balanced breakfast are, by late morning, more alert and less fatigued (Spring et al., 1992).

- *Beware of the binge.* Drinking alcohol or feeling anxious or depressed can unleash the urge to eat (Herman & Polivy, 1980). And men especially should note that eating slowly can lead to eating less (Martin et al., 2007).

- *Before eating with others, decide how much you want to eat.* Eating with friends can distract us from monitoring our own eating (Ward & Mann, 2000).

- *Remember, most people occasionally lapse.* A lapse need not become a full collapse.

- *Connect to a support group.* Join with others, either face-to-face or online, with whom you can share your goals and progress (Freedman, 2011).

American idle: Couch potatoes beware—TV watching correlates with obesity Over time, lifestyles have become more sedentary and TV watching and other screen time has increased, and so has the percentage of overweight people in Britain, Canada, and the United States (Pagani et al., 2010). As televisions have become flatter, people have become fatter.

RETRIEVE IT

- Why can two people of the same height, age, and activity level maintain the same weight, even if one of them eats much less than the other does?

ANSWER: Individuals have very different set points and genetically influenced metabolism levels, causing them to burn calories differently.

MODULE
30 REVIEW Hunger

◉ Learning Objectives

Test Yourself by taking a moment to answer each of these Learning Objective Questions (repeated here from within the module). Then turn to Appendix D, Complete Module Reviews, to check your answers. Research suggests that trying to answer these questions on your own will improve your long-term memory of the concepts (McDaniel et al., 2009).

30-1 What physiological factors produce hunger?

30-2 What cultural and situational factors influence hunger?

30-3 What factors predispose some people to become and remain obese?

▣ Terms and Concepts to Remember

Test yourself on these terms by trying to write down the definition in your own words before flipping back to the referenced page to check your answers.

glucose, p. 379

set point, p. 379

basal metabolic rate, p. 380

[×] Experience the Testing Effect

Test yourself repeatedly throughout your studies. This will not only help you figure out what you know and don't know; the testing itself will help you learn and remember the information more effectively thanks to the *testing effect*.

1. Journalist Dorothy Dix once remarked, "Nobody wants to kiss when they are hungry." How does Maslow's hierarchy of needs support her statement?

2. According to the concept of _____ _____, our body maintains itself at a particular weight level.

3. Which of the following is a genetically predisposed response to food?
   a. An aversion to eating cats and dogs
   b. An interest in novel foods
   c. A preference for sweet and salty foods
   d. An aversion to carbohydrates

4. The blood sugar _____ provides the body with energy. When it is _____ (low/high), we feel hungry.

5. The rate at which your body expends energy while at rest is referred to as the _____ _____ rate.

6. Obese people find it very difficult to lose weight permanently. This is due to several factors, including the fact that
   a. dieting triggers neophobia.
   b. the set point of obese people is lower than average.
   c. with dieting, metabolism increases.
   d. there is a genetic influence on body weight.

7. Sanjay recently adopted the typical college diet, increasing his intake of processed fat and sugar. He knows he may gain weight, but he figures it's no big deal because he can lose the extra weight in the future. How would you evaluate Sanjay's plan?

Find answers to these questions in Appendix E, in the back of the book.

Use 🔄 LearningCurve to create your personalized study plan, which will direct you to the resources that will help you most in 🔄 LaunchPad.

MODULE
31 Theories and Physiology of Emotion

Emotion: Arousal, Behavior, and Cognition

31-1 How do arousal, expressive behavior, and cognition interact in emotion?

Not only emotion, but most psychological phenomena (vision, sleep, memory, sex, and so forth) can be approached these three ways—physiologically, behaviorally, and cognitively.

emotion a response of the whole organism, involving (1) physiological arousal, (2) expressive behaviors, and (3) conscious experience.

James-Lange theory the theory that our experience of emotion is our awareness of our physiological responses to an emotion-arousing stimulus.

Motivated behavior is often connected to powerful emotions. My [DM's] own need to belong was unforgettably disrupted one day. I went to a huge store and brought along Peter, my toddler first-born child. As I set Peter down on his feet for a moment so I could do some paperwork, a passerby warned, "You'd better be careful or you'll lose that boy!" Not more than a few breaths later, I turned and found no Peter beside me.

With mild anxiety, I peered around one end of the customer service counter. No Peter in sight. With slightly more anxiety, I peered around the other end. No Peter there, either. Now, with my heart accelerating, I circled the neighboring counters. Still no Peter anywhere. As anxiety turned to panic, I began racing up and down the store aisles. He was nowhere to be found. The alerted store manager used the public-address system to ask customers to assist in looking for a missing child. Soon after, I passed the customer who had warned me. "I told you that you were going to lose him!" he now scorned. With visions of kidnapping (strangers routinely adored that beautiful child), I braced for the unthinkable possibility

that my negligence had caused me to lose what I loved above all else, and that I might have to return home and face my wife without our only child.

But then, as I passed the customer service counter yet again, there he was, having been found and returned by some obliging customer. In an instant, the arousal of terror spilled into ecstasy. Clutching my son, with tears suddenly flowing, I found myself unable to speak my thanks and stumbled out of the store awash in grateful joy.

Emotions are subjective. But they are real, says researcher Lisa Feldman Barrett (2012, 2013): "My experience of anger is not an illusion. When I'm angry, I feel angry. That's real." Where do our emotions come from? Why do we have them? What are they made of?

Emotions are our body's adaptive response. They support our survival. When we face challenges, emotions focus our attention and energize our actions (Cyders & Smith, 2008). Our heart races. Our pace quickens. All our senses go on high alert. Receiving unexpected good news, we may find our eyes tearing up. We raise our hands triumphantly. We feel exuberance and a newfound confidence. Yet negative and prolonged emotions can harm our health.

As my panicked search for Peter illustrates, **emotions** are a mix of:

- *bodily arousal* (heart pounding).
- *expressive behaviors* (quickened pace).
- *conscious experience,* including thoughts *("Is this a kidnapping?")* and feelings (panic, fear, joy).

The puzzle for psychologists is figuring out how these three pieces fit together. To do that, the first researchers of emotion considered two big questions:

1. A chicken-and-egg debate: Does your bodily arousal come *before* or *after* your emotional feelings? (Did I first notice my racing heart and faster step, and then feel terror about losing Peter? Or did my sense of fear come first, stirring my heart and legs to respond?)

2. How do *thinking* (cognition) and *feeling* interact? Does cognition always come before emotion? (Did I think about a kidnapping threat before I reacted emotionally?)

Historical emotion theories, as well as current research, have sought to answer these questions.

Historical Emotion Theories

The psychological study of emotion began with the first question: How do bodily responses relate to emotions? Two historical theories provided different answers.

JAMES-LANGE THEORY: AROUSAL COMES BEFORE EMOTION Common sense tells most of us that we cry because we are sad, lash out because we are angry, tremble because we are afraid. First comes conscious awareness, then the feeling. But to pioneering psychologist William James, this commonsense view of emotion had things backward. Rather, "We feel sorry because we cry, angry because we strike, afraid because we tremble" (1890, p. 1066). To James, emotions result from attention to our bodily activity. James' idea was also proposed by Danish physiologist Carl Lange, and so is called the **James-Lange theory.** James and Lange would have guessed that I noticed my racing heart and then, shaking with fright, felt the whoosh of emotion—that my feeling of fear *followed* my body's response.

CANNON-BARD THEORY: AROUSAL AND EMOTION OCCUR SIMULTANEOUSLY Physiologist Walter Cannon (1871–1945) disagreed with the James-Lange theory. Does a racing heart signal fear or anger or love? The body's responses—heart rate, perspiration, and body temperature—are too similar, and they change too slowly, to *cause* the different emotions, said Cannon.

Courtesy of David Myers

Joy expressed According to the James-Lange theory, we don't just smile because we share our teammates' joy. We also share the joy because we are smiling with them.

Matt Sullivan/Reuters/Landov

He, and later another physiologist, Philip Bard, concluded that our bodily responses and experienced emotions occur separately but simultaneously. So, according to the **Cannon-Bard theory,** my heart began pounding *as* I experienced fear. The emotion-triggering stimulus traveled to my sympathetic nervous system, causing my body's arousal. *At the same time,* it traveled to my brain's cortex, causing my awareness of my emotion. My pounding heart did not cause my feeling of fear, nor did my feeling of fear cause my pounding heart.

If our bodily responses and emotional experiences occur simultaneously and independently, as the Cannon-Bard theory suggested, then people who suffer spinal cord injuries should *not* notice a difference in their experience of emotion after the injury. But there *are* differences, according to one study of 25 World War II soldiers (Hohmann, 1966). Those with *lower-spine injuries,* who had lost sensation only in their legs, reported little change in their emotions' intensity. Those with *high spinal cord injury,* who could feel nothing below the neck, did report changes. Some reactions were much less intense than before the injuries. Anger, one man with a high spinal cord injury confessed, "just doesn't have the heat to it that it used to. It's a mental kind of anger." Other emotions, those expressed mostly in body areas above the neck, were felt *more* intensely. These men reported increases in weeping, lumps in the throat, and getting choked up when saying good-bye, worshiping, or watching a touching movie. Such evidence has led some researchers to view feelings as "mostly shadows" of our bodily responses and behaviors (Damasio, 2003). Brain activity underlies our emotions and our emotion-fed actions (Davidson & Begley, 2012).

But our emotions also involve cognition (Averill, 1993; Barrett, 2006). Here we arrive at psychology's second big emotion question: How do thinking and feeling interact? Whether we fear the man behind us on the dark street depends entirely on whether we interpret his actions as threatening or friendly.

RETRIEVE IT [✳]

• According to the Cannon-Bard theory, (a) our *physiological response* to a stimulus (for example, a pounding heart), and (b) the *emotion* we experience (for example, fear) occur _____ (simultaneously/sequentially). According to the James-Lange theory, (a) and (b) occur _____ (simultaneously/sequentially).

ANSWERS: simultaneously; sequentially (first the physiological response, and then the experienced emotion)

Schachter-Singer's Two Factors: Arousal + Label = Emotion

◁◁▷ **31-2** To experience emotions, must we consciously interpret and label them?

Stanley Schachter and Jerome Singer (1962) demonstrated that how we appraise our experiences matters greatly. Our physical reactions and our thoughts (perceptions, memories, and interpretations) together create emotion. In their **two-factor theory,** emotions have two ingredients: physical arousal and cognitive appraisal. An emotional experience, they argued, requires a conscious interpretation of arousal.

Consider how arousal spills over from one event to the next. Imagine arriving home after an invigorating run and finding a message that you got a longed-for job. With arousal lingering from the run, would you feel more elated than if you received this news after staying awake all night studying?

To explore this *spillover effect,* Schachter and Singer injected college men with the hormone epinephrine, which triggers feelings of arousal. Picture yourself as a participant: After receiving the injection, you go to a waiting room, where you find yourself with another person (actually an accomplice of the experimenters) who is acting either euphoric or irritated. As you observe this person, you begin to

---

Cannon-Bard theory the theory that an emotion-arousing stimulus simultaneously triggers (1) physiological responses and (2) the subjective experience of emotion.

two-factor theory the Schachter-Singer theory that to experience emotion one must (1) be physically aroused and (2) cognitively label the arousal.

feel your heart race, your body flush, and your breathing become more rapid. If you had been told to expect these effects from the injection, what would you feel? The actual volunteers felt little emotion—because they attributed their arousal to the drug. But if you had been told the injection would produce no effects, what would you feel? Perhaps you would react as another group of participants did. They "caught" the apparent emotion of the other person in the waiting room. They became happy if the accomplice was acting euphoric, and testy if the accomplice was acting irritated.

This discovery—that a stirred-up state can be experienced as one emotion or another, depending on how we interpret and label it—has been replicated in dozens of experiments (Reisenzein, 1983; Sinclair et al., 1994; Zillmann, 1986). As Daniel Gilbert (2006) noted, "Feelings that one interprets as fear in the presence of a sheer drop may be interpreted as lust in the presence of a sheer blouse."

The point to remember: Arousal fuels emotion; cognition channels it.

The spillover effect Arousal from a soccer match can fuel anger, which can descend into rioting or other violent confrontations.

RETRIEVE IT

- According to Schachter and Singer, two factors lead to our experience of an emotion: (1) physiological arousal and (2) _____ appraisal.

ANSWER: cognitive

🎬 **LaunchPad** For a 4-minute demonstration of the relationship between arousal and cognition, visit LaunchPad's *Video: Emotion = Arousal Plus Interpretation.*

Zajonc, LeDoux, and Lazarus: Does Cognition Always Precede Emotion?

But is the heart always subject to the mind? Must we *always* interpret our arousal before we can experience an emotion? Robert Zajonc (1923–2008) [ZI-yence] didn't think so. Zajonc (1980, 1984) contended that we actually have many emotional reactions apart from, or even before, our conscious interpretation of a situation. Perhaps you can recall liking something or someone immediately, without knowing why.

For example, when people repeatedly view stimuli flashed too briefly for them to interpret, they come to prefer those stimuli. Unaware of having previously seen them, they nevertheless like them. We have an acutely sensitive automatic radar for emotionally significant information; even a subliminally flashed stimulus can prime us to feel better or worse about a follow-up stimulus (Murphy et al., 1995; Zeelenberg et al., 2006).

Neuroscientists are charting the neural pathways of emotions (Ochsner et al., 2009). Our emotional responses can follow two different brain pathways. Some emotions (especially more complex feelings like hatred and love) travel a "high road." A stimulus following this path would travel (by way of the thalamus) to the brain's cortex (**FIGURE 31.1a** on the next page). There, it would be analyzed and labeled before the response command is sent out, via the amygdala (an emotion-control center).

But sometimes our emotions (especially simple likes, dislikes, and fears) take what Joseph LeDoux (2002) has called the "low road," a neural shortcut that bypasses the cortex. Following the low road, a fear-provoking stimulus would travel from the eye or ear (again via the thalamus) directly to the amygdala (Figure 31.1b). This shortcut enables our greased-lightning emotional response before our intellect intervenes. Like speedy reflexes (that also operate apart from the brain's thinking cortex), the amygdala reactions are so fast that we may be unaware of what's transpired (Dimberg et al., 2000).

> FIGURE 31.1

The brain's pathways for emotions In the two-track brain, sensory input may be routed (a) to the cortex (via the thalamus) for analysis and then transmission to the amygdala; or (b) directly to the amygdala (via the thalamus) for an instant emotional reaction.

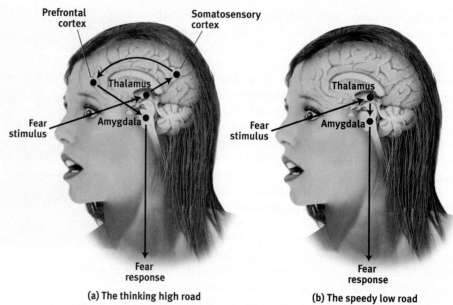

(a) The thinking high road　　　(b) The speedy low road

✓ FIGURE 31.2

Two pathways for emotions Zajonc and LeDoux emphasized that some emotional responses are immediate, before any conscious appraisal. Lazarus, Schachter, and Singer emphasized that our appraisal and labeling of events also determine our emotional responses.

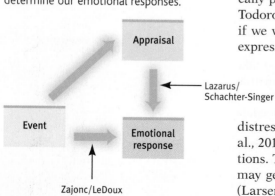

The amygdala sends more neural projections up to the cortex than it receives back, which makes it easier for our feelings to hijack our thinking than for our thinking to rule our feelings (LeDoux & Armony, 1999). Thus, in the forest, we can jump at the sound of rustling bushes nearby, leaving it to our cortex to decide later whether the sound was made by a snake or by the wind. Such experiences support Zajonc's belief that *some* of our emotional reactions involve no deliberate thinking.

Emotion researcher Richard Lazarus (1991, 1998) conceded that our brain processes vast amounts of information without our conscious awareness, and that some emotional responses do not require *conscious* thinking. Much of our emotional life operates via the automatic, speedy low road. But, he asked, how would we *know* what we are reacting to if we did not in some way appraise the situation? The appraisal may be effortless and we may not be conscious of it, but it is still a mental function. To know whether a stimulus is good or bad, the brain must have some idea of what it is (Storbeck et al., 2006). Thus, said Lazarus, emotions arise when we *appraise* an event as harmless or dangerous, whether we truly *know* it is or not. We appraise the sound of the rustling bushes as the presence of a threat. Later, we realize that it was "just the wind."

So, as Zajonc and LeDoux have demonstrated, some emotional responses—especially simple likes, dislikes, and fears—involve no conscious thinking (**FIGURE 31.2**). When I [ND] view a big spider trapped behind glass, I experience fear even though I "know" the spider can't hurt me. Such responses are difficult to alter by changing our thinking. Within a fraction of a second, we may automatically perceive one person as more likeable or trustworthy than another (Willis & Todorov, 2006). This instant appeal can even influence our political decisions if we vote (as many people do) for a candidate we *like* over the candidate who expresses positions closer to our own (Westen, 2007).

But our feelings about politics are also subject to our conscious and unconscious information processing—to our memories, expectations, and interpretations. When we feel emotionally overwhelmed, we can change our interpretations (Gross, 2013). Such *reappraisal* often reduces distress and the corresponding amygdala response (Buhle et al., 2014; Denny et al., 2015). Highly emotional people are intense partly because of their interpretations. They may personalize events as being somehow directed at them, and they may generalize their experiences by blowing single incidents out of proportion (Larsen & Diener, 1987). Thus, learning to *think* more positively can help people

∨ TABLE 31.1

Summary of Emotion Theories

Theory	Explanation of Emotions	Example
James-Lange	Emotions arise from our awareness of our specific bodily responses to emotion-arousing stimuli.	We observe our heart racing after a threat and then feel afraid.
Cannon-Bard	Emotion-arousing stimuli trigger our bodily responses and simultaneous subjective experience.	Our heart races at the same time that we feel afraid.
Schachter-Singer	Our experience of emotion depends on two factors: general arousal and a conscious cognitive label.	We may interpret our arousal as fear or excitement, depending on the context.
Zajonc; LeDoux	Some embodied responses happen instantly, without conscious appraisal.	We automatically feel startled by a sound in the forest before labeling it as a threat.
Lazarus	Cognitive appraisal ("Is it dangerous or not?")—sometimes without our awareness—defines emotion.	The sound is "just the wind."

feel better. Although the emotional low road functions automatically, the thinking high road allows us to retake some control over our emotional life. Together, automatic emotion and conscious thinking weave the fabric of our emotional lives. (**TABLE 31.1** summarizes these emotion theories.)

RETRIEVE IT [✻]

- Emotion researchers have disagreed about whether emotional responses occur in the absence of cognitive processing. How would you characterize the approach of each of the following researchers: Zajonc, LeDoux, Lazarus, Schachter, and Singer?

ANSWERS: Zajonc and LeDoux suggested that we experience some emotions without any conscious, cognitive appraisal. Lazarus, Schachter, and Singer emphasized the importance of appraisal and cognitive labeling in our experience of emotion.

Embodied Emotion

Whether you are falling in love or grieving a death, you need little convincing that emotions involve the body. Feeling without a body is like breathing without lungs. Some physical responses are easy to notice. Other emotional responses we experience without awareness. Before examining our physical responses to specific emotions, consider another big question: How many distinct emotions are there?

The Basic Emotions

 31-3 What are some of the basic emotions?

Carroll Izard (1977) isolated 10 basic emotions (joy, interest-excitement, surprise, sadness, anger, disgust, contempt, fear, shame, and guilt), most present in infancy (**FIGURE 31.3** on the next page). Others believe that pride is also a distinct emotion, signaled by a small smile, head slightly tilted back, and an open posture (Tracy & Robins, 2004). Love, too, may be a basic emotion (Shaver et al., 1996). Izard has argued that other emotions are combinations of these 10, with love, for example, being a mixture of joy and interest-excitement. But are these emotions biologically distinct? Does our body know the difference between fear and anger?

> **FIGURE 31.3**

Some naturally occurring infant emotions To identify the emotions generally present in infancy, Carroll Izard analyzed the facial expressions of infants.

(a) Joy (mouth forming smile, cheeks lifted, twinkle in eye)

(b) Anger (brows drawn together and downward, eyes fixed, mouth squarish)

(c) Interest (brows raised or knitted, mouth softly rounded, lips may be pursed)

(d) Disgust (nose wrinkled, upper lip raised, tongue pushed outward)

(e) Surprise (brows raised, eyes widened, mouth rounded in oval shape)

(f) Sadness (brow's inner corners raised, mouth corners drawn down)

(g) Fear (brows level, drawn in and up, eyelids lifted, mouth corners retracted)

Emotions and the Autonomic Nervous System

👁 **31-4** What is the link between emotional arousal and the autonomic nervous system?

In a crisis, the *sympathetic division* of your *autonomic nervous system (ANS)* mobilizes your body for *fight or flight* (**FIGURE 31.4**). It triggers your adrenal glands to release the stress hormones epinephrine (adrenaline) and norepinephrine (noradrenaline). To provide energy, your liver pours extra sugar into your bloodstream. To help burn the sugar, your respiration increases to supply needed oxygen.

⌄ **FIGURE 31.4**

Emotional arousal Like a crisis control center, the autonomic nervous system arouses the body in a crisis and calms it when danger passes.

Autonomic Nervous System Controls Physiological Arousal

Sympathetic division (arousing)		Parasympathetic division (calming)
Pupils dilate	EYES	Pupils contract
Decreases	SALIVATION	Increases
Perspires	SKIN	Dries
Increases	RESPIRATION	Decreases
Accelerates	HEART	Slows
Inhibits	DIGESTION	Activates
Secrete stress hormones	ADRENAL GLANDS	Decrease secretion of stress hormones
Reduced	IMMUNE SYSTEM FUNCTIONING	Enhanced

Your heart rate and blood pressure increase. Your digestion slows, diverting blood from your internal organs to your muscles. With blood sugar driven into the large muscles, running becomes easier. Your pupils dilate, letting in more light. To cool your stirred-up body, you perspire. If wounded, your blood would clot more quickly.

When the crisis passes, the *parasympathetic division* of your ANS gradually calms your body, as stress hormones slowly leave your bloodstream. After your next crisis, think of this: Without any conscious effort, your body's response to danger is wonderfully coordinated and adaptive—preparing you to fight or flee. So, do the different emotions have distinct arousal fingerprints?

"Fear lends wings to his feet."
Virgil, Aeneid, 19 B.C.E.

The Physiology of Emotions

31-5 Do different emotions activate different physiological and brain-pattern responses?

Imagine conducting an experiment measuring the physiological responses of emotion. In each of four rooms, you have someone watching a movie: In the first, the person is viewing a horror show; in the second, an anger-provoking film; in the third, a sexually arousing film; in the fourth, a boring film. From the control center, you monitor each person's perspiration, breathing, and heart rate. Could you tell who is frightened? Who is angry? Who is sexually aroused? Who is bored?

With training, you could probably pick out the bored viewer. But discerning physiological differences among fear, anger, and sexual arousal is much more difficult (Barrett, 2006). Different emotions can share common biological signatures.

A single brain region can also serve as the seat of seemingly different emotions. Consider the broad emotional portfolio of the *insula*, a neural center deep inside the brain. The insula is activated when we experience various negative social emotions, such as disgust. In brain scans, it becomes active when people bite into some disgusting food, smell disgusting food, think about biting into a disgusting cockroach, or feel moral disgust over a sleazy business exploiting a saintly widow (Sapolsky, 2010). Similar multitasking regions are found in other brains areas.

Scary thrills Elated excitement and panicky fear involve similar physiological arousal. That allows us to flip rapidly between the two emotions.

Yet our emotions—such as fear, anger, sexual arousal, and disgust—*feel* different to us, and they often *look* different to others. We may appear "paralyzed with fear" or "ready to explode." Fear and joy prompt similar increased heart rate, but they stimulate different facial muscles. During fear, your brow muscles tense. During joy, muscles in your cheeks and under your eyes pull into a smile (Witvliet & Vrana, 1995).

Some of our emotions also differ in their brain circuits (Panksepp, 2007). Observers watching fearful faces showed more amygdala activity than did other observers who watched angry faces (Whalen et al., 2001). Brain scans and EEG recordings show that emotions also activate different areas of the brain's cortex. When you experience negative emotions such as disgust, your right prefrontal cortex tends to be more active than the left. Depression-prone people, and those with generally negative personalities, have also shown more right frontal lobe activity (Harmon-Jones et al., 2002).

Positive moods tend to trigger more left frontal lobe activity. People with positive personalities—exuberant infants and alert, enthusiastic, energized, and

"No one ever told me that grief felt so much like fear. I am not afraid, but the sensation is like being afraid. The same fluttering in the stomach, the same restlessness, the yawning. I keep on swallowing."
C. S. Lewis, A Grief Observed, 1961

THINKING CRITICALLY ABOUT

Lie Detection

31-6 How effective are polygraphs in using body states to detect lies?

Can *a lie detector*—a **polygraph**—reveal lies? Polygraphs don't literally detect lies. Instead, they measure emotion-linked changes in breathing, cardiovascular activity, and perspiration. If you were taking this test, an examiner would monitor these responses as you answered questions. She might ask, "In the last 20 years, have you ever taken something that didn't belong to you?" This is a control question, aimed at making everyone a little nervous. If you lied and said *"No!"* (as many people do) the polygraph would detect arousal. This response will establish a baseline, a useful comparison for your responses to *critical questions* ("Did you ever steal anything from your previous employer?"). If your responses to critical questions are weaker than to control questions, the examiner will infer you are telling the truth.

Critics point out two problems: First, our physiological arousal is much the same from one emotion to another. Anxiety, irritation, and guilt all prompt similar physiological reactivity. Second, many innocent people do respond with heightened tension to the accusations implied by the critical questions (**FIGURE 31.5**). Many rape victims, for example, have "failed" these tests when reacting emotionally but truthfully (Lykken, 1991).

▶ FIGURE 31.5

How often do lie detection tests lie? In one study, polygraph experts interpreted the polygraph data of 100 people who had been suspects in theft crimes (Kleinmuntz & Szucko, 1984). Half the suspects were guilty and had confessed; the other half turned out to be not guilty. Had the polygraph experts been the judges, more than one-third of the innocent would have been declared guilty, and one-fourth of the guilty would have been declared not guilty.

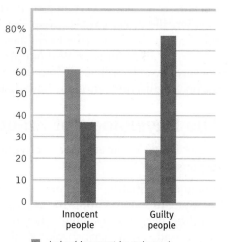

Percentage

- ▮ Judged innocent by polygraph
- ▮ Judged guilty by polygraph

A 2002 U.S. National Academy of Sciences report noted that "no spy has ever been caught [by] using the polygraph." It is not for lack of trying. The FBI, CIA, and U.S. Departments of Defense and Energy have tested tens of thousands of employees, and polygraph use in Europe has also increased (Meijer & Verschuere, 2010). Yet Aldrich Ames, a Russian spy within the CIA, went undetected. Ames took many "polygraph tests and passed them all," noted Robert Park (1999). "Nobody thought to investigate the source of his sudden wealth—after all, he was passing the lie detector tests."

A more effective lie detection approach uses a *guilty knowledge test,* which assesses a suspect's physiological responses to crime-scene details known only to the police and the guilty person (Ben-Shakhar & Elaad, 2003). If a camera and computer had been stolen, for example, only a guilty person should react strongly to the brand names of the stolen items. Given enough such specific probes, an innocent person will seldom be wrongly accused.

polygraph a machine, commonly used in attempts to detect lies, that measures several of the physiological responses (such as perspiration and cardiovascular and breathing changes) accompanying emotion.

persistently goal-directed adults—have also shown more activity in the left frontal lobe than in the right (Davidson, 2000, 2003; Urry et al., 2004).

To sum up, we can't easily see differences in emotions from tracking heart rate, breathing, and perspiration. But facial expressions and brain activity can vary from one emotion to another. So, do we, like Pinocchio, give off telltale signs when we lie? For more on that question, see Thinking Critically About: Lie Detection.

RETRIEVE IT [✖]

- How do the two divisions of the autonomic nervous system affect our emotional responses?

ANSWER: The *sympathetic division* of the ANS arouses us for more intense experiences of emotion, pumping out the stress hormones epinephrine and norepinephrine to prepare our body for fight or flight. The *parasympathetic division* of the ANS takes over when a crisis passes, restoring our body to a calm physiological and emotional state.

MODULE 31 REVIEW Theories and Physiology of Emotion

◉ Learning Objectives

Test Yourself by taking a moment to answer each of these Learning Objective Questions (repeated here from within the module). Then turn to Appendix D, Complete Module Reviews, to check your answers. Research suggests that trying to answer these questions on your own will improve your long-term memory of the concepts (McDaniel et al., 2009).

31-1 How do arousal, expressive behavior, and cognition interact in emotion?

31-2 To experience emotions, must we consciously interpret and label them?

31-3 What are some of the basic emotions?

31-4 What is the link between emotional arousal and the autonomic nervous system?

31-5 Do different emotions activate different physiological and brain-pattern responses?

31-6 How effective are polygraphs in using body states to detect lies?

▣·⟨·⟩ Terms and Concepts to Remember

Test yourself on these terms by trying to write down the definition in your own words before flipping back to the referenced page to check your answers.

emotion, p. 387

James-Lange theory, p. 387

Cannon-Bard theory, p. 388

two-factor theory, p. 388

polygraph, p. 394

[✴] Experience the Testing Effect

Test yourself repeatedly throughout your studies. This will not only help you figure out what you know and don't know; the testing itself will help you learn and remember the information more effectively thanks to the *testing effect*.

1. The _____-_____ theory of emotion maintains that a physiological response happens BEFORE we know what we are feeling.

2. Assume that after spending an hour on a treadmill, you receive a letter saying that your scholarship request has been approved. The two-factor theory of emotion would predict that your physical arousal will
   a. weaken your happiness.
   b. intensify your happiness.
   c. transform your happiness into relief.
   d. have no particular effect on your happiness.

3. Zajonc and LeDoux maintain that some emotional reactions occur before we have had the chance to consciously label or interpret them. Lazarus noted the importance of how we appraise events. These psychologists differ in the emphasis they place on _____ in emotional responses.
   a. physical arousal
   b. the hormone epinephrine
   c. cognitive processing
   d. learning

4. What does a polygraph measure and why are its results questionable?

   Find answers to these questions in Appendix E, in the back of the book.

Use ⓜ LearningCurve to create your personalized study plan, which will direct you to the resources that will help you most in ⓜ LaunchPad.

MODULE 32 Expressing and Experiencing Emotion

Expressive behavior implies emotion. Dolphins, with smiles seemingly plastered on their faces, appear happy. To decipher people's emotions we read their bodies, listen to their voice tones, and study their faces. Does nonverbal language vary with culture—or is it universal? And do our expressions influence our experienced emotions?

"Your face, my thane, is a book where men may read strange matters."

Lady Macbeth to her husband, in William Shakespeare's Macbeth

> **> FIGURE 32.3**
>
> Male or female? Researchers manipulated a gender-neutral face. People were more likely to see it as a male when it wore an angry expression, and as a female when it wore a smile (Becker et al., 2007).

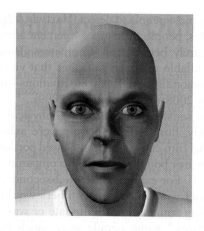 

perceived it as male. If the face was smiling, they were more likely to perceive it as female (**FIGURE 32.3**). Anger strikes most people as a more masculine emotion.

The perception of women's emotionality also feeds—and is fed by—people's attributing women's emotionality to their disposition and men's to their circumstances: "She's emotional. He's having a bad day" (Barrett & Bliss-Moreau, 2009). Many factors influence our attributions, including cultural norms (Mason & Morris, 2010). Nevertheless, there are some gender differences in descriptions of emotional experiences. When surveyed, women are far more likely than men to describe themselves as empathic. If you have *empathy*, you identify with others and imagine what it must be like to walk in their shoes. You rejoice with those who rejoice and weep with those who weep. Fiction readers, who immerse themselves in the lives of their favorite characters, report higher empathy levels and indeed are more often women (Mar et al., 2009; Tepper, 2000). Physiological measures, such as heart rate while seeing another's distress, confirm the empathic gender gap, though a smaller one than indicated in survey self-reports (Eisenberg & Lennon, 1983; Rueckert et al., 2010).

Females are also more likely to *express* empathy—to cry and to report distress when observing someone in distress. As **FIGURE 32.4** shows, this gender difference was clear in videotapes of male and female students watching film clips that were sad (children with a dying parent), happy (slapstick comedy), or frightening (a man nearly falling off the ledge of a tall building) (Kring & Gordon, 1998). Women also tend to experience emotional events, such as viewing pictures of mutilation, more deeply and with more brain activation in areas sensitive to emotion. And they remember the scenes better three weeks later (Canli et al., 2002).

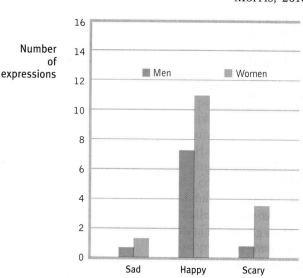

∧ FIGURE 32.4

Gender and expressiveness Male and female film viewers did not differ dramatically in self-reported emotions or physiological responses. But the women's faces *showed* much more emotion. (Data from Kring & Gordon, 1998.)

RETRIEVE IT [✖]

● _____ (Women/Men) report experiencing emotions more deeply, and they tend to be more adept at reading nonverbal behavior.

ANSWER: Women

Culture and Emotion

◉ **32-3** Do gestures and facial expressions mean the same thing in all cultures?

The meaning of *gestures* varies from culture to culture. U.S. President Richard Nixon learned this after making the North American "A-OK" sign before a welcoming crowd of Brazilians, not realizing it was a crude insult in that country.

and truth tellers are too minute for most people to detect (Hartwig & Bond, 2011). In one digest of many studies, people were just 54 percent accurate in discerning truth from lies—barely better than a coin toss (Bond & DePaulo, 2006). Moreover, the available research indicates that virtually no one—save perhaps police professionals in high-stakes situations—beats chance by much (Bond & DePaulo, 2008; O'Sullivan et al., 2009).

Some of us are, however, more sensitive than others to physical cues to various emotions. In one study, hundreds of people were asked to name the emotion displayed in brief film clips. The clips showed portions of a person's emotionally expressive face or body, sometimes accompanied by a garbled voice (Rosenthal et al., 1979). For example, after a 2-second scene revealing only the face of an upset woman, the researchers would ask whether the woman was criticizing someone for being late or was talking about her divorce. Given such "thin slices," some people were much better emotion detectors than others. Introverts tend to excel at reading others' emotions, while extraverts are generally easier to read (Ambady et al., 1995).

Gestures, facial expressions, and voice tones, which are absent in written communication, convey important information. The difference was clear in one study. In one group, participants heard 30-second recordings of people describing their marital separations. In the other group, participants read a script of the recording. Those who heard the recording were better able to predict people's current and future adjustment (Mason et al., 2010).

The absence of expressive emotion can make for ambiguous emotion in electronic communications. To partly remedy that, we sometimes embed cues to emotion (LOL!) in our messages. Without the vocal nuances that signal whether our statement is serious, kidding, or sarcastic, we are in danger of what developmental psychologist Jean Piaget called *egocentrism*, by failing to perceive how others interpret our "just kidding" message (Kruger et al., 2005).

⌃ FIGURE 32.2

Which of researcher Paul Ekman's smiles is feigned, which natural? The smile on the right engages the facial muscles of a natural smile.

Gender and Emotion

32-2 Do the genders differ in their ability to communicate nonverbally?

Do women have greater sensitivity than men to nonverbal cues, as so many believe? After analyzing 125 studies, Judith Hall (1984, 1987) concluded that women generally do surpass men at reading people's emotional cues when given thin slices of behavior. The female advantage emerges early in development. Female infants, children, and adolescents have outperformed males in many studies (McClure, 2000).

Women's nonverbal sensitivity helps explain their greater emotional literacy. When invited to describe how they would feel in certain situations, men described simpler emotional reactions (Barrett et al., 2000). You might like to try this yourself: Ask some people how they might feel when saying good-bye to friends after graduation. Research suggests men are more likely to say, simply, "I'll feel bad," and women to express more complex emotions: "It will be bittersweet; I'll feel both happy and sad."

Women's skill at decoding others' emotions may also contribute to their greater emotional responsiveness and expressiveness (Fischer & LaFrance, 2015; Vigil, 2009). In studies of 23,000 people from 26 cultures, women more than men reported themselves open to feelings (Costa et al., 2001). Children show the same gender difference: Girls express stronger emotions than boys do (Chaplin & Aldao, 2013). That helps explain the extremely strong perception that emotionality is "more true of women"—a perception expressed by nearly 100 percent of 18- to 29-year-old Americans (Newport, 2001).

One exception: Quickly—imagine an angry face. What gender is the person? If you're like 3 in 4 Arizona State University students, you imagined a male (Becker et al., 2007). And when a gender-neutral face was made to look angry, most people

"Now, that wasn't so hard, was it?"

> FIGURE 32.3

Male or female? Researchers manipulated a gender-neutral face. People were more likely to see it as a male when it wore an angry expression, and as a female when it wore a smile (Becker et al., 2007).

©APA/Vaughn Becker

perceived it as male. If the face was smiling, they were more likely to perceive it as female (**FIGURE 32.3**). Anger strikes most people as a more masculine emotion.

The perception of women's emotionality also feeds—and is fed by—people's attributing women's emotionality to their disposition and men's to their circumstances: "She's emotional. He's having a bad day" (Barrett & Bliss-Moreau, 2009). Many factors influence our attributions, including cultural norms (Mason & Morris, 2010). Nevertheless, there are some gender differences in descriptions of emotional experiences. When surveyed, women are far more likely than men to describe themselves as empathic. If you have *empathy*, you identify with others and imagine what it must be like to walk in their shoes. You rejoice with those who rejoice and weep with those who weep. Fiction readers, who immerse themselves in the lives of their favorite characters, report higher empathy levels and indeed are more often women (Mar et al., 2009; Tepper, 2000). Physiological measures, such as heart rate while seeing another's distress, confirm the empathic gender gap, though a smaller one than indicated in survey self-reports (Eisenberg & Lennon, 1983; Rueckert et al., 2010).

Females are also more likely to *express* empathy—to cry and to report distress when observing someone in distress. As **FIGURE 32.4** shows, this gender difference was clear in videotapes of male and female students watching film clips that were sad (children with a dying parent), happy (slapstick comedy), or frightening (a man nearly falling off the ledge of a tall building) (Kring & Gordon, 1998). Women also tend to experience emotional events, such as viewing pictures of mutilation, more deeply and with more brain activation in areas sensitive to emotion. And they remember the scenes better three weeks later (Canli et al., 2002).

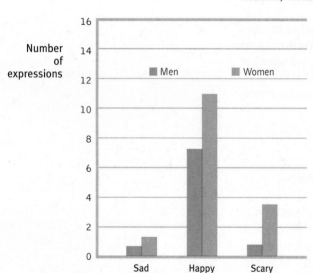

∧ FIGURE 32.4

Gender and expressiveness Male and female film viewers did not differ dramatically in self-reported emotions or physiological responses. But the women's faces *showed* much more emotion. (Data from Kring & Gordon, 1998.)

RETRIEVE IT   [✱]

• _____ (Women/Men) report experiencing emotions more deeply, and they tend to be more adept at reading nonverbal behavior.

ANSWER: Women

Culture and Emotion

👁 **32-3** Do gestures and facial expressions mean the same thing in all cultures?

The meaning of *gestures* varies from culture to culture. U.S. President Richard Nixon learned this after making the North American "A-OK" sign before a welcoming crowd of Brazilians, not realizing it was a crude insult in that country.

MODULE 31 REVIEW   Theories and Physiology of Emotion

Learning Objectives

Test Yourself by taking a moment to answer each of these Learning Objective Questions (repeated here from within the module). Then turn to Appendix D, Complete Module Reviews, to check your answers. Research suggests that trying to answer these questions on your own will improve your long-term memory of the concepts (McDaniel et al., 2009).

31-1 How do arousal, expressive behavior, and cognition interact in emotion?

31-2 To experience emotions, must we consciously interpret and label them?

31-3 What are some of the basic emotions?

31-4 What is the link between emotional arousal and the autonomic nervous system?

31-5 Do different emotions activate different physiological and brain-pattern responses?

31-6 How effective are polygraphs in using body states to detect lies?

Terms and Concepts to Remember

Test yourself on these terms by trying to write down the definition in your own words before flipping back to the referenced page to check your answers.

emotion, p. 387

James-Lange theory, p. 387

Cannon-Bard theory, p. 388

two-factor theory, p. 388

polygraph, p. 394

Experience the Testing Effect

Test yourself repeatedly throughout your studies. This will not only help you figure out what you know and don't know; the testing itself will help you learn and remember the information more effectively thanks to the *testing effect*.

1. The _____-_____ theory of emotion maintains that a physiological response happens BEFORE we know what we are feeling.

2. Assume that after spending an hour on a treadmill, you receive a letter saying that your scholarship request has been approved. The two-factor theory of emotion would predict that your physical arousal will
   a. weaken your happiness.
   b. intensify your happiness.
   c. transform your happiness into relief.
   d. have no particular effect on your happiness.

3. Zajonc and LeDoux maintain that some emotional reactions occur before we have had the chance to consciously label or interpret them. Lazarus noted the importance of how we appraise events. These psychologists differ in the emphasis they place on _____ in emotional responses.
   a. physical arousal
   b. the hormone epinephrine
   c. cognitive processing
   d. learning

4. What does a polygraph measure and why are its results questionable?

Find answers to these questions in Appendix E, in the back of the book.

Use 🐨 LearningCurve to create your personalized study plan, which will direct you to the resources that will help you most in 🐨 LaunchPad.

MODULE 32 Expressing and Experiencing Emotion

Expressive behavior implies emotion. Dolphins, with smiles seemingly plastered on their faces, appear happy. To decipher people's emotions we read their bodies, listen to their voice tones, and study their faces. Does nonverbal language vary with culture—or is it universal? And do our expressions influence our experienced emotions?

> "Your face, my thane, is a book where men may read strange matters."
>
> *Lady Macbeth to her husband,*
> *in William Shakespeare's* Macbeth

Detecting Emotion in Others

◀◉▶ **32-1** How do we communicate nonverbally?

A silent language of emotion Hindu classic dance uses the face and body to effectively convey 10 different emotions (Hejmadi et al., 2000).

To Westerners, a firm handshake conveys an outgoing, expressive personality (Chaplin et al., 2000). A gaze communicates intimacy, while darting eyes signal anxiety (Kleinke, 1986; Perkins et al., 2012). When two people are passionately in love, they typically spend time—quite a bit of time—gazing into each other's eyes (Bolmont et al., 2014; Rubin, 1970). Would such gazes stir these feelings between strangers? To find out, researchers have asked unacquainted (and presumed heterosexual) male-female pairs to gaze intently for 2 minutes either at each other's hands or into each other's eyes. After separating, the eye gazers reported feeling a tingle of attraction and affection (Kellerman et al., 1989).

Most of us read nonverbal cues well. Shown 10 seconds of video from the end of a speed-dating interaction, people can often detect whether one person is attracted to the other (Place et al., 2009). We are adept at detecting a subtle smile (Maher et al., 2014). We also excel at detecting nonverbal threat. We readily sense subliminally presented negative words, such as *snake* or *bomb* (Dijksterhuis & Aarts, 2003). In a crowd, angry faces will "pop out" (Hansen & Hansen, 1988; Pinkham et al., 2010). Signs of status are also easy to spot. When shown someone with arms raised, chest expanded, and a slight smile, people—from Canadian undergraduates to Fijian villagers—perceive that person as experiencing pride and having high status (Tracy et al., 2013).

Experience can sensitize us to particular emotions, as shown by experiments using a series of faces (like those in **FIGURE 32.1**) that morph from anger to fear (or sadness). Viewing such faces, physically abused children are much quicker than other children to spot the signals of anger. Shown a face that is 50 percent fear and 50 percent anger, those with a history of being abused are more likely to perceive anger than fear. Their perceptions become sensitively attuned to glimmers of danger that nonabused children miss.

Hard-to-control facial muscles may reveal signs of emotions, even ones you are trying to conceal. Lifting just the inner part of your eyebrows, which few people do consciously, reveals distress or worry. Eyebrows raised and pulled together signal fear. Activated muscles under the eyes and raised cheeks suggest a natural smile. A feigned smile, such as one we make for a photographer, is often frozen in place for several seconds, then suddenly switched off (**FIGURE 32.2**). Genuine happy smiles tend to be briefer and to fade less abruptly (Bugental, 1986).

Our brain is an amazing detector of subtle expressions. When researchers filmed teachers talking to unseen schoolchildren, a mere 10-second clip of the teacher's voice or face provided enough clues for both young and old viewers to determine whether the teacher liked and admired a child (Babad et al., 1991). In other experiments, even glimpsing a face for one-tenth of a second enabled viewers to judge people's attractiveness or trustworthiness or to rate politicians' competence and predict their voter support (Willis & Todorov, 2006). "First impressions . . . occur with astonishing speed," note Christopher Olivola and Alexander Todorov (2010).

Despite our brain's emotion-detecting skill, we find it difficult to detect deceiving expressions (Porter & ten Brinke, 2008). The behavioral differences between liars

▾ **FIGURE 32.1**

Experience influences how we perceive emotions Viewing the morphed middle face, evenly mixing anger with fear, physically abused children were more likely than nonabused children to perceive the face as angry (Pollak & Kistler, 2002; Pollak & Tolley-Schell, 2003).

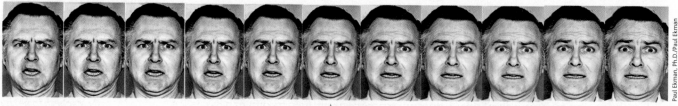

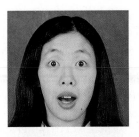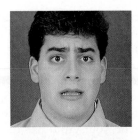
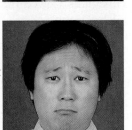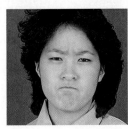

Ekman & Matsumoto, Japanese and Caucasian Facial Expressions of Emotions

< FIGURE 32.5

Culture-specific or culturally universal expressions? As people of differing cultures and races, do our faces speak differing languages? Which face expresses disgust? Anger? Fear? Happiness? Sadness? Surprise? (From Matsumoto & Ekman, 1989.) See inverted answers below.

From left to right, top to bottom: happiness, surprise, fear, sadness, anger, disgust.

The importance of cultural definitions of gestures was again demonstrated in 1968, when North Korea publicized photos of supposedly happy officers from a captured U.S. Navy spy ship. In the photo, three men had raised their middle finger, telling their captors it was a "Hawaiian good luck sign" (Fleming & Scott, 1991).

Do *facial expressions* also have different meanings in different cultures? To find out, two investigative teams showed photographs of various facial expressions to people in different parts of the world and asked them to guess the emotion (Ekman et al., 1975, 1987, 1994; Izard, 1977, 1994). You can try this matching task yourself by pairing the six emotions with the six faces in **FIGURE 32.5**.

Regardless of your cultural background, you probably did pretty well. A smile's a smile the world around. Ditto for sadness, and to a lesser extent the other basic expressions (Jack et al., 2012). There is no culture where people frown when they are happy.

Facial expressions do convey some nonverbal accents that provide clues to one's culture (Marsh et al., 2003). Thus, data from 182 studies have shown slightly enhanced accuracy when people judged emotions from their own culture (Elfenbein & Ambady, 2002, 2003a,b). Still, the telltale signs of emotion generally cross cultures. The world over, children cry when distressed, shake their heads when defiant, and smile when they are happy. So, too, with blind children who have never seen a face (Eibl-Eibesfeldt, 1971). People blind from birth spontaneously exhibit the common facial expressions associated with such emotions as joy, sadness, fear, and anger (Galati et al., 1997).

Universal emotions No matter where on Earth you live, you have no trouble knowing which photo depicts English soccer player Michael Owen and his fans feeling distraught (after missing a goal) and triumphant (after scoring it).

Phil Noble/AP Photo

Tom Purslow/Manchester United/Getty Images

Musical expressions of emotion also cross cultures. Happy and sad music feel happy and sad around the world. Whether you live in an African village or a European city, fast-paced music seems happy, and slow-paced music seems sad (Fritz et al., 2009).

Do these shared emotional categories reflect shared *cultural* experiences, such as movies and TV broadcasts seen around the world? Apparently not. Paul Ekman and his team asked isolated people in New Guinea to respond to such statements as, "Pretend your child has died." When North American collegians viewed the recorded responses, they easily read the New Guineans' facial reactions.

So we can say that facial muscles speak a universal language. This discovery would not have surprised Charles Darwin (1809–1882), who argued that in prehistoric times, before our ancestors communicated in words, they communicated threats, greetings, and submission with facial expressions. Their shared expressions helped them survive (Hess & Thibault, 2009). In confrontations, for example, a human sneer retains elements of an animal baring its teeth in a snarl. Emotional expressions may enhance our survival in other ways, too. Surprise raises the eyebrows and widens the eyes, enabling us to take in more information. Disgust wrinkles the nose, closing it from foul odors.

Smiles are social as well as emotional events. Euphoric Olympic gold-medal winners typically don't smile when they are awaiting their ceremony. But they wear broad grins when interacting with officials and facing the crowd and cameras (Fernández-Dols & Ruiz-Belda, 1995).

Although we share a universal facial language, it has been adaptive for us to interpret faces in particular contexts (**FIGURE 32.6**). People judge an angry face set in a frightening situation as afraid. They judge a fearful face set in a painful situation as pained (Carroll & Russell, 1996). Movie directors harness this phenomenon by creating scenes and soundtracks that amplify our perceptions of particular emotions.

Although cultures share a universal facial language for some basic emotions, they differ in how *much* emotion they express. Those that encourage individuality,

"For news of the heart, ask the face."

Guinean proverb

LaunchPad For a 4-minute demonstration of our universal facial language, visit LaunchPad's *Video: Emotions and Facial Expression.*

While weightless, astronauts' internal bodily fluids move toward their upper body and their faces become puffy. This makes nonverbal communication more difficult, especially among multinational crews (Gelman, 1989).

> FIGURE 32.6

We read faces in context Whether we perceive the man in the top row as disgusted or angry depends on which body his face appears on (Aviezer et al., 2008). In the second row, tears on a face make its expression seem sadder (Provine et al., 2009).

Paul Ekman, Ph.D./Paul Ekman Group, LLC.

R.R. Provine. Emotional tears and NGF: A biographical appreciation and research beginning. Archives Italiennes de Biologie, 149, 271–276.

as in Western Europe, Australia, New Zealand, and North America, display mostly visible emotions (van Hemert et al., 2007). Those that encourage people to adjust to others, as in China, tend to have less visible displays of personal emotions (Matsumoto et al., 2009; Tsai et al., 2007). In Japan, people infer emotion more from the surrounding context. Moreover, the mouth, which is so expressive in North Americans, conveys less emotion than do the telltale eyes (Masuda et al., 2008; Yuki et al., 2007).

Cultural differences also exist *within* nations. The Irish and their Irish-American descendants have tended to be more expressive than the Scandinavians and their Scandinavian-American descendants (Tsai & Chentsova-Dutton, 2003). And that reminds us of a familiar lesson: Like most psychological events, emotion is best understood not only as a biological and cognitive phenomenon, but also as a social-cultural phenomenon.

RETRIEVE IT [✖]

- Are people more likely to differ culturally in their interpretations of facial expressions or of gestures?

ANSWER: gestures

The Effects of Facial Expressions

◀▶ **32-4** How do our facial expressions influence our feelings?

As William James (1890) struggled with feelings of depression and grief, he came to believe that we can control emotions by going "through the outward movements" of any emotion we want to experience. "To feel cheerful," he advised, "sit up cheerfully, look around cheerfully, and act as if cheerfulness were already there."

Studies of emotional effects of facial expressions reveal precisely what James might have predicted. Expressions not only communicate emotion, they also amplify and regulate it. In *The Expression of the Emotions in Man and Animals*, Charles Darwin (1872) contended that "the free expression by outward signs of an emotion intensifies it. . . . He who gives way to violent gestures will increase his rage."

Want to test Darwin's hypothesis? Try this: Fake a big grin. Now scowl. Can you feel the "smile therapy" difference? Participants in dozens of experiments have felt a difference. James Laird and his colleagues (1974, 1984, 1989, 2014) subtly induced students to make a frowning expression by asking them to "contract these muscles" and "pull your brows together" (supposedly to help the researchers attach facial electrodes). The results? The students reported feeling a little angry, as do people who are facing the Sun (squinting activates the frowning muscles) (Marzoli et al., 2013). So, too, for other basic emotions. For example, people reported feeling more fear than anger, disgust, or sadness when made to construct a fearful expression: "Raise your eyebrows. And open your eyes wide. Move your whole head back, so that your chin is tucked in a little bit, and let your mouth relax and hang open a little" (Duclos et al., 1989).

This **facial feedback effect** has been found many times, in many places, for many basic emotions (**FIGURE 32.7** on the next page). Just activating one of the smiling muscles by holding a pen in the teeth (rather than gently in the mouth, which produces a neutral expression) makes stressful situations less upsetting (Kraft & Pressman, 2012). A heartier smile—made not just with the mouth but with raised cheeks that crinkle the eyes—enhances positive feelings even more when you are reacting to something pleasant or funny (Soussignan, 2001). Smile warmly on the outside and you feel better on the inside. We smile when we are happy, and we become happier when we smile. Scowl and the whole world seems to scowl back.

"Whenever I feel afraid
I hold my head erect
And whistle a happy tune."

*Richard Rodgers and
Oscar Hammerstein,*
The King and I, *1958*

facial feedback effect the tendency of facial muscle states to trigger corresponding feelings such as fear, anger, or happiness.

A request from your authors: Smile often as you read this book.

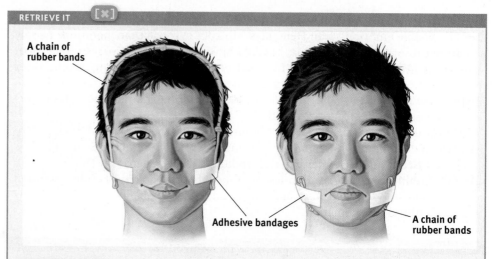

RETRIEVE IT [×]

A chain of rubber bands

Adhesive bandages

A chain of rubber bands

⌃ FIGURE 32.7

How to make people smile without telling them to smile Do as Kazuo Mori and Hideko Mori (2009) did with students in Japan: Attach rubber bands to the sides of the face with adhesive bandages, and then run them either over the head or under the chin. (1) Based on the *facial feedback effect,* how might students report feeling when the rubber bands raise their cheeks as though in a smile? (2) How might students report feeling when the rubber bands pull their cheeks downward?

ANSWERS: (1) Most students report feeling more happy than sad when their cheeks are raised upward. (2) Most students report feeling more sad than happy when their cheeks are pulled downward.

So your face is more than a billboard that displays your feelings; it also feeds your feelings. No wonder some depressed patients reportedly felt better after Botox injections paralyzed their frowning muscles (Wollmer et al., 2012). Four months after treatment, they continued to report lower depression levels. Follow-up studies have found that Botox paralysis of the frowning muscles slowed people's reading of sadness- or anger-related sentences, and it slowed activity in emotion-related brain circuits (Havas et al., 2010; Hennenlotter et al., 2008).

With studies of bodily posture and vocal expressions, researchers have observed a broader **behavior feedback effect** (Flack, 2006; Snodgrass et al., 1986). You can duplicate the participants' experience: Walk for a few minutes with short, shuffling steps, keeping your eyes downcast. Now walk around taking long strides, with your arms swinging and your eyes looking straight ahead. Can you feel your mood shift? Going through the motions awakens the emotions.

Likewise, people perceive ambiguous behaviors differently depending on which finger they move up and down while reading a story. (This was said to be a study of the effect of using finger muscles "located near the reading muscles on the motor cortex.") If participants read the story while moving an extended middle finger, the story behaviors seemed more hostile. If read with a thumb up, they seemed more positive. Hostile gestures prime hostile perceptions (Chandler & Schwarz, 2009; Goldin-Meadow & Beilock, 2010).

You can use your understanding of feedback effects to become more empathic: Let your own face mimic another person's expression. Acting as another acts helps us feel what another feels (Vaughn & Lanzetta, 1981). Losing this ability to mimic others can leave us struggling to make emotional connections, as one social worker with Moebius syndrome, a rare facial paralysis disorder, discovered while working with Hurricane Katrina refugees: When people made a sad expression, "I wasn't able to return it. I tried to do so with words and tone of voice, but it was no use. Stripped of the facial expression, the emotion just dies there, unshared" (Carey, 2010).

behavior feedback effect the tendency of behavior to influence our own and others' thoughts, feelings, and actions.

Our natural mimicry of others' emotions helps explain why emotions are contagious (Dimberg et al., 2000; Neumann & Strack, 2000). Positive, upbeat Facebook posts create a ripple effect, leading Facebook friends to also express more positive emotions (Kramer, 2012).

* * *

We have seen how our motivated behaviors, triggered by the forces of nature and nurture, frequently go hand in hand with significant emotional responses. Our often-adaptive psychological emotions likewise come equipped with physical reactions. Nervous about an important encounter, we feel stomach butterflies. Anxious over public speaking, we frequent the bathroom. Smoldering over a family conflict, we get a splitting headache. As this text's discussion of stress and health next shows, negative emotions and the prolonged high arousal that may accompany them can tax the body and harm our health.

MODULE 32 REVIEW   Expressing and Experiencing Emotion

👁 Learning Objectives

Test Yourself by taking a moment to answer each of these Learning Objective Questions (repeated here from within the module). Then turn to Appendix D, Complete Module Reviews, to check your answers. Research suggests that trying to answer these questions on your own will improve your long-term memory of the concepts (McDaniel et al., 2009).

32-1 How do we communicate nonverbally?

32-2 Do the genders differ in their ability to communicate nonverbally?

32-3 Do gestures and facial expressions mean the same thing in all cultures?

32-4 How do our facial expressions influence our feelings?

▣·▣ Terms and Concepts to Remember

Test yourself on these terms by trying to write down the definition in your own words before flipping back to the referenced page to check your answers.

facial feedback effect, p. 401

behavior feedback effect, p. 402

[×] Experience the Testing Effect

Test yourself repeatedly throughout your studies. This will not only help you figure out what you know and don't know; the testing itself will help you learn and remember the information more effectively thanks to the *testing effect*.

1. When people are induced to assume fearful expressions, they often report feeling a little fear. This result is known as the _____ - _____ effect.

2. Aiden has a bad cold and finds himself shuffling to class with his head down. How might his posture, as well as his cold, affect his emotional well-being?

Find answers to these questions in Appendix E, in the back of the book.

Use 🔄 LearningCurve to create your personalized study plan, which will direct you to the resources that will help you most in 🔄 LaunchPad .

Michigan State Police/AP Photo

Extreme stress From the audio recording of a 911 caller reporting Ben Carpenter's distress: "You are not going to believe this. There is a semitruck pushing a guy in a wheelchair on Red Arrow highway!"

"Too many parents make life hard for their children by trying, too zealously, to make it easy for them."

German author
Johann Wolfgang von Goethe
(1749–1832)

MODULE 33 Stress and Illness

Sometimes we put ourselves in stressful situations. At other times, stress strikes without warning. Imagine being 21-year-old Ben Carpenter, who experienced the world's wildest and fastest wheelchair ride. As he crossed a street, the light changed and a semitruck started moving into the intersection. When they bumped, Ben's wheelchair handles got stuck in the truck's grille. The driver, who hadn't seen Ben and couldn't hear his cries for help, took off down the highway, pushing the wheelchair at 50 miles per hour until reaching his destination two miles away. "It was very scary," said Ben, who has muscular dystrophy.

This module starts by taking a close look at stress and how it affects our health and well-being. Let's begin with some basic terms.

Stress: Some Basic Concepts

33-1 What events provoke stress responses, and how do we respond and adapt to stress?

Psychologists define **stress** as the process of appraising and responding to a threatening or challenging event (**FIGURE 33.1**). But stress is a slippery concept. We sometimes use the word informally to describe threats or challenges ("Ben was under a lot of stress"), and at other times our responses ("Ben experienced acute stress"). To a psychologist, the dangerous truck ride was a *stressor*. Ben's physical and emotional responses were a *stress reaction*. And the process by which he related to the threat was *stress*.

Stress arises less from events themselves than from how we appraise them (Lazarus, 1998). One person, alone in a house, ignores its creaking sounds and experiences no stress; someone else suspects an intruder and becomes alarmed. One person regards a new job as a welcome challenge; someone else appraises it as risking failure. When short-lived, or when perceived as challenges, stressors can have positive effects. A momentary stress can mobilize the immune system for fending off infections and healing wounds (Segerstrom, 2007). Stress also arouses and motivates us to conquer problems. Championship athletes, successful entertainers, and great teachers and leaders all thrive and excel when aroused by a challenge (Blascovich & Mendes, 2010). Having conquered cancer or rebounded from a lost job, some people emerge with stronger self-esteem and a deepened spirituality and sense of purpose. Indeed, experiencing some stress early in life builds resilience (Landauer & Whiting, 1979). Adversity can beget growth.

But extreme or prolonged stress can harm us. Demanding jobs that mentally exhaust workers also can damage their physical health (Huang et al., 2010). Pregnant women with overactive stress systems tend to have shorter pregnancies, which pose health risks for their infants (Entringer et al., 2011).

> **FIGURE 33.1**

Stress appraisal The events of our lives flow through a psychological filter. How we appraise an event influences how much stress we experience and how effectively we respond.

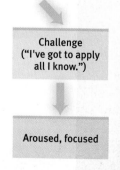

Stressful event
(tough math test)

Appraisal

Threat
("Yikes! This is beyond me!")

Challenge
("I've got to apply all I know.")

Response

Stressed to distraction

Aroused, focused

Fuse/Getty Images

Our natural mimicry of others' emotions helps explain why emotions are contagious (Dimberg et al., 2000; Neumann & Strack, 2000). Positive, upbeat Facebook posts create a ripple effect, leading Facebook friends to also express more positive emotions (Kramer, 2012).

* * *

We have seen how our motivated behaviors, triggered by the forces of nature and nurture, frequently go hand in hand with significant emotional responses. Our often-adaptive psychological emotions likewise come equipped with physical reactions. Nervous about an important encounter, we feel stomach butterflies. Anxious over public speaking, we frequent the bathroom. Smoldering over a family conflict, we get a splitting headache. As this text's discussion of stress and health next shows, negative emotions and the prolonged high arousal that may accompany them can tax the body and harm our health.

MODULE 32 REVIEW — Expressing and Experiencing Emotion

Learning Objectives

Test Yourself by taking a moment to answer each of these Learning Objective Questions (repeated here from within the module). Then turn to Appendix D, Complete Module Reviews, to check your answers. Research suggests that trying to answer these questions on your own will improve your long-term memory of the concepts (McDaniel et al., 2009).

32-1 How do we communicate nonverbally?

32-2 Do the genders differ in their ability to communicate nonverbally?

32-3 Do gestures and facial expressions mean the same thing in all cultures?

32-4 How do our facial expressions influence our feelings?

Terms and Concepts to Remember

Test yourself on these terms by trying to write down the definition in your own words before flipping back to the referenced page to check your answers.

facial feedback effect, p. 401
behavior feedback effect, p. 402

Experience the Testing Effect

Test yourself repeatedly throughout your studies. This will not only help you figure out what you know and don't know; the testing itself will help you learn and remember the information more effectively thanks to the *testing effect*.

1. When people are induced to assume fearful expressions, they often report feeling a little fear. This result is known as the _____ - _____ effect.

2. Aiden has a bad cold and finds himself shuffling to class with his head down. How might his posture, as well as his cold, affect his emotional well-being?

Find answers to these questions in Appendix E, in the back of the book.

Use LearningCurve to create your personalized study plan, which will direct you to the resources that will help you most in LaunchPad.

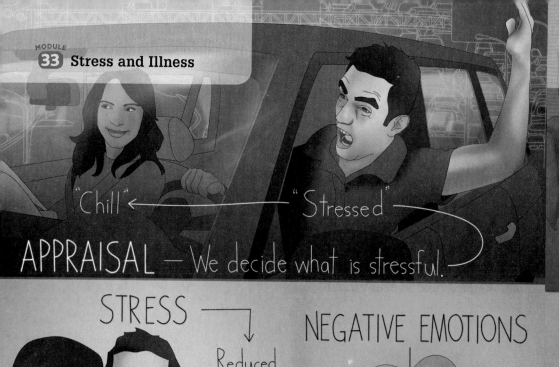

"Chill" ← "Stressed"

APPRAISAL — We decide what is stressful.

STRESS → Reduced immune functioning → More illness

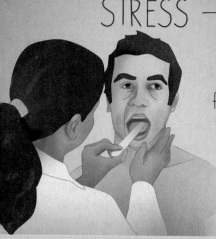

NEGATIVE EMOTIONS

More *heart disease*

REDUCE STRESS with:

exercise,

relaxation,

participation in faith community,

mindfulness meditation.

REDUCING STRESS can help those with *AIDS* or *cancer*.

PSYCHONEUROIMMUNOLOGY

Health Psychologists study interaction of:

Thoughts / feelings

IMMUNE SYSTEM FUNCTIONING

Brain response

Endocrine system response / hormone release

PERSONAL CONTROL/ CHOICE

improves health/ well-being

INCREASE HAPPINESS by:

acting happy,

seeking *flow* activities,

managing your time,

buying shared *experiences* (not things). $$

exercising, sleeping,

nurturing relationships,

focusing beyond self.

Stress, Health, and Human Flourishing

SIR RANULPH FIENNES, called "the world's greatest living explorer" by Guinness World Records, has experienced significant stress—much of it self-imposed. He has persevered through what should have been impossible Arctic expeditions and grueling long-distance athletic endeavors. Yet he has thrived.

Just before his birth, Fiennes' father died in WWII, which was a particularly difficult time to grow up fatherless. As an adult adventurer, Fiennes tried to walk solo to the North Pole, but his sleds fell through the ice. He pulled them out by hand and later sawed off his own frostbitten fingertips. Years later, as he was preparing to run seven marathons on seven continents in seven days, he experienced a heart attack and had double bypass surgery. Then his beloved wife of 33 years died of cancer. And when he tried to become the oldest Briton to climb Mount Everest, he had to quit near the summit when having another heart attack.

Fiennes did not perceive these events as stressful setbacks, but rather chose to press on with his relentless, can-do spirit. With his upbeat nature, Fiennes' presence could light up a room. He did finally achieve his goal of running seven marathons on seven continents in seven days, and of becoming the oldest Briton to summit Mount Everest. He remarried and has enjoyed parenting his daughter. And in 2015, at age 71, he finished a 6-day, 156-mile running race across the Sahara desert. After the race, he described his exhausting ordeal as "more hellish than hell" (Silverman, 2015). And yet Fiennes is already planning for his next big challenge.

How often do you experience *stress* in your daily life? Do you feel differently about stressors that seem imposed on you (deadlines, assignments, tragic events) than about the "stress" you impose on yourself (adventures, challenges, happy changes)? As we will see, our definition of events affects our experience of those events and whether we even consider them "stressful."

Fiennes' life, and yours, embodies what Modules 33 and 34 explore: the difficulty of unwanted stress, the important ways we are affected by our interpretation of events, how we cope with stress and setbacks, and the possibilities for a happy, flourishing life. ■

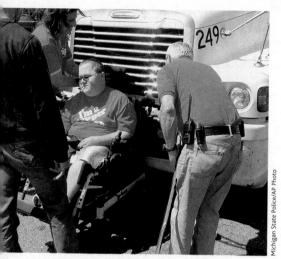

Michigan State Police/AP Photo

Extreme stress From the audio recording of a 911 caller reporting Ben Carpenter's distress: "You are not going to believe this. There is a semitruck pushing a guy in a wheelchair on Red Arrow highway!"

"Too many parents make life hard for their children by trying, too zealously, to make it easy for them."

German author
Johann Wolfgang von Goethe
(1749–1832)

MODULE 33 Stress and Illness

Sometimes we put ourselves in stressful situations. At other times, stress strikes without warning. Imagine being 21-year-old Ben Carpenter, who experienced the world's wildest and fastest wheelchair ride. As he crossed a street, the light changed and a semitruck started moving into the intersection. When they bumped, Ben's wheelchair handles got stuck in the truck's grille. The driver, who hadn't seen Ben and couldn't hear his cries for help, took off down the highway, pushing the wheelchair at 50 miles per hour until reaching his destination two miles away. "It was very scary," said Ben, who has muscular dystrophy.

This module starts by taking a close look at stress and how it affects our health and well-being. Let's begin with some basic terms.

Stress: Some Basic Concepts

33-1 What events provoke stress responses, and how do we respond and adapt to stress?

Psychologists define **stress** as the process of appraising and responding to a threatening or challenging event (**FIGURE 33.1**). But stress is a slippery concept. We sometimes use the word informally to describe threats or challenges ("Ben was under a lot of stress"), and at other times our responses ("Ben experienced acute stress"). To a psychologist, the dangerous truck ride was a *stressor*. Ben's physical and emotional responses were a *stress reaction*. And the process by which he related to the threat was *stress*.

Stress arises less from events themselves than from how we appraise them (Lazarus, 1998). One person, alone in a house, ignores its creaking sounds and experiences no stress; someone else suspects an intruder and becomes alarmed. One person regards a new job as a welcome challenge; someone else appraises it as risking failure. When short-lived, or when perceived as challenges, stressors can have positive effects. A momentary stress can mobilize the immune system for fending off infections and healing wounds (Segerstrom, 2007). Stress also arouses and motivates us to conquer problems. Championship athletes, successful entertainers, and great teachers and leaders all thrive and excel when aroused by a challenge (Blascovich & Mendes, 2010). Having conquered cancer or rebounded from a lost job, some people emerge with stronger self-esteem and a deepened spirituality and sense of purpose. Indeed, experiencing some stress early in life builds resilience (Landauer & Whiting, 1979). Adversity can beget growth.

But extreme or prolonged stress can harm us. Demanding jobs that mentally exhaust workers also can damage their physical health (Huang et al., 2010). Pregnant women with overactive stress systems tend to have shorter pregnancies, which pose health risks for their infants (Entringer et al., 2011).

⟩ **FIGURE 33.1**

Stress appraisal The events of our lives flow through a psychological filter. How we appraise an event influences how much stress we experience and how effectively we respond.

Stressful event
(tough math test)

Appraisal

Threat
("Yikes! This is beyond me!")

Challenge
("I've got to apply all I know.")

Response

Stressed to distraction

Aroused, focused

Fuse/Getty Images

So there is an interplay between our head and our health. Psychological states are physiological events that influence other parts of our physiological system. Just pausing to *think* about biting into an orange wedge—the sweet, tangy juice from the pulpy fruit flooding across your tongue—can trigger salivation. We'll explore that interplay shortly, but first, let's look more closely at stressors and stress reactions.

stress the process by which we perceive and respond to certain events, called *stressors*, that we appraise as threatening or challenging.

Stressors—Things That Push Our Buttons

Stressors fall into three main types: catastrophes, significant life changes, and daily hassles. All can be toxic.

CATASTROPHES Catastrophes are unpredictable large-scale events, such as earthquakes, floods, wildfires, and storms. After such events, damage to emotional and physical health can be significant. In the four months after Hurricane Katrina, New Orleans' suicide rate reportedly tripled (Saulny, 2006). And in surveys taken in the three weeks after the 9/11 terrorist attacks, 58 percent of Americans said they were experiencing greater-than-average arousal and anxiety (Silver et al., 2002). In the New York City area, people were especially likely to report such symptoms, and sleeping pill prescriptions rose by a reported 28 percent (HMHL, 2002; NSF, 2001). Extensively watching 9/11 television footage predicted worse health outcomes two to three years later (Silver et al., 2013).

For those who respond to catastrophes by relocating to another country, the stress may be twofold. The trauma of uprooting and family separation may combine with the challenges of adjusting to a new culture's language, ethnicity, climate, and social norms (Pipher, 2002; Williams & Berry, 1991). In the first half-year, before their morale begins to rebound, newcomers often experience culture shock and deteriorating well-being (Markovizky & Samid, 2008). This *acculturative stress* declines over time, especially when people engage in meaningful activities and connect socially (Kim et al., 2012). In years to come, such relocations may become increasingly common due to climate change.

SIGNIFICANT LIFE CHANGES Life transitions—leaving home, becoming divorced, losing a job, having a loved one die—are often keenly felt. Even happy events, such as getting married or graduating from college, can be stressful life transitions. We might worry that our relationship will end or that we will not find a desirable job. Many of these changes happen during young adulthood. One survey, in which 15,000 Canadian adults were asked whether they were "trying to take on too many things at once," found the highest stress levels among young adults (Statistics Canada, 1999). This stress effect appeared again when 650,000 Americans were asked if they had experienced a lot of stress "yesterday." Younger adults reported higher daily stress (Newport & Pelham, 2009).

Some psychologists study the health effects of life changes by following people over time. Others compare the life changes recalled by those who have or have not suffered a specific health problem, such as a heart attack. In such studies, those recently widowed, fired, or divorced have been more vulnerable to disease (Dohrenwend et al., 1982; Strully, 2009). One Finnish study of 96,000 widowed people found that the survivor's risk of death doubled in the week following a partner's death (Kaprio et al., 1987). A cluster of crises—losing a job, home, and partner—puts one even more at risk.

DAILY HASSLES AND SOCIAL STRESS Events don't have to remake our lives to cause stress. Stress also comes from *daily hassles*—spotty phone connections, aggravating housemates, long lines, too many things to do, e-mail and text spam, and loud talkers behind us in line (Lazarus, 1990; Pascoe & Richman, 2009; Ruffin, 1993). We might have to give a public speech or do difficult math problems (Balodis et al., 2010; Dickerson & Kemeny, 2004) (**FIGURE 33.2** on the next page).

© Julien Tack

Seismic stress Unpredictable large-scale events, such as the severe earthquake that devastated Haiti in 2010, trigger significant levels of stress-related ills. When an earthquake struck Los Angeles in 1994, sudden-death heart attacks increased fivefold. Most occurred in the first two hours after the quake and near its center and were unrelated to physical exertion (Muller & Verrier, 1996).

Participants chew gum so that collecting saliva is easy.

Researcher takes a saliva sample from each participant at the beginning of the experiment to measure levels of the stress hormone, cortisol.

Participant gives simulated job interview speech to a critical panel.

What is 1223 minus 17?

Next, the participant is asked to complete difficult math problems out loud.

Cortisol (stress hormone) levels

High

Medium

Low

Beginning of experiment   After social stress

(Balodis et al., 2010; Dickerson & Kemeny, 2004.)

Measuring cortisol in participants' saliva before and after tells us that although they enter the lab experiencing some stress, that level goes up 40 percent after they experience social stress.

THANK YOU!

Research team thanks and *debriefs* the participant—explaining the purpose of the experiment and the role she played.

> **FIGURE 33.2**

Studying stress Most people experience stress when giving a public speech. To study stress, researchers re-create this type of situation. At the end, they *debrief* and reassure each participant.

Some people shrug off such hassles. For others, the everyday annoyances add up and take a toll on health and well-being (DeLongis et al., 1982, 1988; Piazza et al., 2013; Sin et al., 2015).

Many people face more significant daily hassles. As the Great Recession of 2008–2009 bottomed out, Americans' most oft-cited stressors related to money (76 percent), work (70 percent), and the economy (65 percent) (APA, 2010). In impoverished areas—where many people routinely face inadequate income, unemployment, solo parenting, and overcrowding—such stressors are part of daily life.

Daily economic pressures may be compounded by prejudice against our gender identity, sexual orientation, or race, which—like other stressors—can have both psychological and physical consequences (Lick et al., 2013; Pascoe & Richman, 2009; Schetter et al., 2013). Thinking that some of the people you encounter each day will dislike you, distrust you, or doubt your abilities makes daily life stressful. When prolonged, such stress takes a toll on our health, especially our cardiovascular system. For many African-Americans, for example, stress helps drive up blood pressure levels (Mays et al., 2007; Ong et al., 2009).

The Stress Response System

Medical interest in stress dates back to Hippocrates (460–377 B.C.E.). In the 1920s, Walter Cannon (1929) confirmed that the stress response is part of a unified mind-body system. He observed that extreme cold, lack of oxygen, and emotion-arousing events all trigger an outpouring of the stress hormones epinephrine and norepinephrine from the core of the adrenal glands. When alerted by any of a number of brain pathways, the sympathetic nervous system arouses us, preparing the body for the wonderfully adaptive response that Cannon called *fight or flight*. It increases heart rate and respiration, diverts blood from digestion to the skeletal muscles, dulls feelings of pain, and releases sugar and fat from the body's stores. By fighting or fleeing, we increase our chances of surviving and reproducing.

Canadian scientist Hans Selye's (1936, 1976) 40 years of research on stress extended Cannon's findings. His studies of animals' reactions to various stressors, such as electric shock and surgery, helped make stress a major concept in both psychology and medicine. Selye proposed that the body's adaptive response to stress is so general that, like a single burglar alarm, it sounds, no matter what intrudes. He named this response the **general adaptation syndrome (GAS),** and he saw it as a three-phase process (**FIGURE 33.3**). Let's say you suffer a physical or an emotional trauma:

- In *Phase 1,* you have an *alarm reaction,* as your sympathetic nervous system is suddenly activated. Your heart rate zooms. Blood is diverted to your skeletal muscles. You feel the faintness of shock. With your resources mobilized, you are now ready to fight back.

- During *Phase 2, resistance,* your temperature, blood pressure, and respiration remain high. Your adrenal glands pump hormones into your bloodstream. You are fully engaged, summoning all your resources to meet the challenge. As time passes, with no relief from stress, your body's reserves dwindle.

- You have reached *Phase 3, exhaustion.* With exhaustion, you become more vulnerable to illness or even, in extreme cases, collapse and death.

Selye's basic point: Although the human body copes well with temporary stress, prolonged stress can damage it. Severe childhood stress, such as from abuse, gets under the skin, leading to greater stress responses and disease risk (Hanson et al., 2015; Miller et al., 2011).

general adaptation syndrome (GAS) Selye's concept of the body's adaptive response to stress in three phases—alarm, resistance, exhaustion.

❯ FIGURE 33.3

Selye's general adaptation syndrome When a gold and copper mine in Chile collapsed in 2010, family and friends rushed to the scene, fearing the worst. Many of those holding vigil outside the mine were nearly exhausted with the stress of waiting and worrying when, after 18 days, they received news that all 33 of the miners inside were alive and well.

Luis Hidalgo/AP Photo

Chile's Presidency/AP Photo

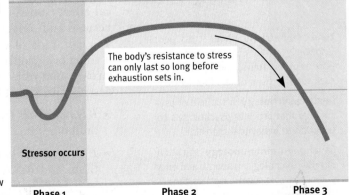

The body's resistance to stress can only last so long before exhaustion sets in.

High

Stress resistance

Low

Stressor occurs

Phase 1
Alarm reaction
(mobilize resources)

Phase 2
Resistance
(cope with stressor)

Phase 3
Exhaustion
(reserves depleted)

"You may be suffering from what's known as full-nest syndrome."

"You've got to know when to hold 'em; know when to fold 'em. Know when to walk away, and know when to run."

Kenny Rogers, "The Gambler," 1978

tend and befriend under stress, people (especially women) often provide support to others (tend) and bond with and seek support from others (befriend).

health psychology a subfield of psychology that provides psychology's contribution to behavioral medicine.

psychoneuroimmunology the study of how psychological, neural, and endocrine processes together affect the immune system and resulting health.

Even fearful, stressed rats have been found to die sooner, after about 600 days, than their more confident siblings, which average 700-day life spans (Cavigelli & McClintock, 2003).

There are other ways to deal with stress. One option is a common response to a loved one's death: Withdraw. Pull back. Conserve energy. Faced with an extreme disaster, such as a ship sinking, some people become paralyzed by fear. Another option (often found among women) is to give and seek support—what's called the **tend-and-befriend** stress response (Taylor et al., 2000, 2006).

Facing stress, men more often than women tend to withdraw socially, turn to alcohol, or become aggressive. Women more often respond to stress by nurturing and banding together. This may in part be due to *oxytocin,* a stress-moderating hormone associated with pair bonding in animals and released by cuddling, massage, and breast feeding in humans (Campbell, 2010; Taylor, 2006).

It often pays to spend our resources in fighting or fleeing an external threat. But we do so at a cost. When stress is momentary, the cost is small. When stress persists, the cost may be much higher, in the form of lowered resistance to infections and other threats to mental and physical well-being.

RETRIEVE IT   [✱]

• The stress response system: When alerted to a negative, uncontrollable event, our _____ nervous system arouses us. Heart rate and respiration _____ (increase/decrease). Blood is diverted from digestion to the skeletal _____. The body releases sugar and fat. All this prepares the body for the _____-_____-_____ response.

ANSWERS: sympathetic; increase; muscles; fight-or-flight

Stress and Vulnerability to Disease

33-2 How does stress make us more vulnerable to disease?

To study how stress and healthy and unhealthy behaviors influence health and illness, psychologists and physicians have created the interdisciplinary field of *behavioral medicine,* integrating behavioral and medical knowledge. One subfield, **health psychology,** provides psychology's contribution to behavioral medicine. A branch of health psychology called **psychoneuroimmunology** focuses on mind-body interactions (Kiecolt-Glaser, 2009). This awkward name makes sense when said slowly: Your thoughts and feelings (*psycho*) influence your brain (*neuro*), which influences the endocrine hormones that affect your disease-fighting *immune* system. And this subfield is the study of (*ology*) those interactions.

If you've ever had a stress headache, or felt your blood pressure rise with anger, you don't need to be convinced that our psychological states have physiological effects. Stress can even leave you less able to fight off disease because your nervous and endocrine systems influence your immune system (Sternberg, 2009). You can think of your immune system as a complex surveillance system. When it functions properly, it keeps you healthy by isolating and destroying bacteria, viruses, and other invaders. Four types of cells are active in these search-and-destroy missions (**FIGURE 33.4**):

• *B lymphocytes* (white blood cells) mature in the *b*one marrow and release antibodies that fight bacterial infections.

• *T lymphocytes* (white blood cells) mature in the *t*hymus and other lymphatic tissue and attack cancer cells, viruses, and foreign substances.

• *Macrophages* ("big eaters") identify, pursue, and ingest harmful invaders and worn-out cells.

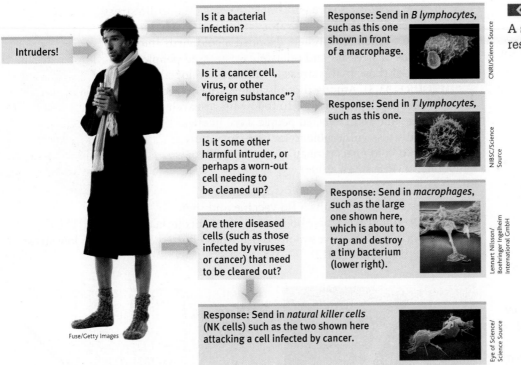

< FIGURE 33.4

A simplified view of immune responses

- *Natural killer cells* (NK cells) pursue diseased cells (such as those infected by viruses or cancer).

Your age, nutrition, genetics, body temperature, and stress all influence your immune system's activity. If it doesn't function properly, your immune system can err in two directions:

1. Responding too strongly, the immune system may attack the body's own tissues, causing an allergic reaction or a self-attacking disease such as lupus, multiple sclerosis, or some forms of arthritis. Women, who are immunologically stronger than men, are more susceptible to self-attacking diseases (Nussinovitch & Schoenfeld, 2012; Schwartzman-Morris & Putterman, 2012).

2. Underreacting, the immune system may allow a bacterial infection to flare, a dormant virus to erupt, or cancer cells to multiply. To protect transplanted organs, which the recipient's immune system would view as a foreign body, surgeons may deliberately suppress the patient's immune system.

Stress can also trigger immune suppression by reducing the release of disease-fighting lymphocytes. This has been observed when animals were stressed by physical restraints, unavoidable electric shocks, noise, crowding, cold water, social defeat, or separation from their mothers (Maier et al., 1994). One study monitored immune responses in 43 monkeys over six months (Cohen et al., 1992). Half were left in stable groups. The rest were stressed by being housed with new roommates—3 or 4 new monkeys each month. By the end of the experiment, the socially disrupted monkeys had weaker immune systems.

Human immune systems react similarly. Some examples:

- *Surgical wounds heal more slowly in stressed people.* In one experiment, dental students received punch wounds (precise small holes punched in the skin). Compared with wounds placed during summer vacation, those placed three days before a major exam healed 40 percent more slowly (Kiecolt-Glaser et al., 1998). In other studies, marriage conflict has also slowed punch-wound healing (Kiecolt-Glaser et al., 2005).

- *Stressed people are more vulnerable to colds.* Major life stress increases the risk of a respiratory infection (Pedersen et al., 2010). When researchers dropped a cold virus into the noses of stressed and relatively unstressed people, 47 percent of those living stress-filled lives developed colds (**FIGURE 33.5**). Among those living relatively free of stress, only 27 percent did. In follow-up research, the happiest and most relaxed people were likewise markedly less vulnerable to an experimentally delivered cold virus (Cohen et al., 2003, 2006; Cohen & Pressman, 2006).

- *Vaccine effectiveness declines with stress.* Nurses gave older adults a flu vaccine and then measured how well their bodies fought off bacteria and viruses. The vaccine was most effective among those who reported experiencing low stress (Segerstrom et al., 2012).

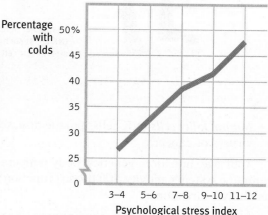

> **FIGURE 33.5**

Stress and colds In an experiment by Sheldon Cohen and colleagues (1991), people with the highest life stress scores were also most vulnerable when exposed to an experimentally delivered cold virus.

The stress effect on immunity makes physiological sense. It takes energy to track down invaders, produce swelling, and maintain fevers. Thus, when diseased, your body reduces its muscular energy output by decreasing activity and increasing sleep. Stress does the opposite. It creates a competing energy need. During an aroused fight-or-flight reaction, your stress responses divert energy from your disease-fighting immune system and send it to your muscles and brain. This increases your vulnerability to illness. *The point to remember:* Stress does not make us sick, but it does alter our immune functioning, which leaves us less able to resist infection.

RETRIEVE IT [✖]

- The field of _____ studies mind-body interactions, including the effects of psychological, neural, and endocrine functioning on the immune system and overall health.

ANSWER: psychoneuroimmunology

- What general effect does stress have on our overall health?

ANSWER: Stress tends to reduce our immune system's ability to function properly, so that higher stress generally leads to greater incidence of physical illness.

Stress and AIDS

We know that stress suppresses immune system functioning. What does this mean for people with *AIDS (acquired immune deficiency syndrome)*? As its name tells us, AIDS is an immune disorder, caused by the *human immunodeficiency virus (HIV)*. Although AIDS-related deaths have decreased 35 percent since 2005, AIDS remains the world's sixth leading cause of death and Africa's number one

killer (UNAIDS, 2015; WHO, 2013). Worldwide, some 2.1 million people—slightly more than half of them women—became infected with HIV in 2013, often without their awareness (UNAIDS, 2014). Years after the initial infection, when AIDS appears, people have difficulty fighting off other diseases, such as pneumonia.

Stress cannot give people AIDS. But could stress and negative emotions speed the transition from HIV infection to AIDS? And might stress predict a faster decline in those with AIDS? An analysis of 33,252 participants from around the world suggests the answer to both questions is *Yes* (Chida & Vedhara, 2009). The greater the stress that HIV-infected people experience, the faster their disease progresses.

Would efforts to reduce stress help control the disease? Again, the answer appears to be *Yes*. Educational initiatives, bereavement support groups, cognitive therapy, relaxation training, and exercise programs that reduce distress have all had positive consequences for HIV-positive people (Baum & Posluszny, 1999; McCain et al., 2008; Schneiderman, 1999). But compared with available drug treatments, the benefits have been small. Although AIDS is now more treatable than ever before, preventing HIV infection is a far better option. In addition to efforts to influence sexual norms and behaviors, today's *combination prevention* programs also include medical strategies (such as drugs that reduce HIV transmission) and efforts to reduce social inequalities that increase HIV risk (UNAIDS, 2010).

Stress and Cancer

Stress does not create cancer cells. But in a healthy, functioning immune system, lymphocytes, macrophages, and NK cells search out and destroy cancer cells and cancer-damaged cells. If stress weakens the immune system, might this weaken a person's ability to fight off cancer? To explore a possible connection between stress and cancer, experimenters have implanted tumor cells in rodents or given them *carcinogens* (cancer-producing substances). They then exposed some rodents to uncontrollable stress, such as inescapable shocks, that weakened their immune systems (Sklar & Anisman, 1981). Stressed rodents, compared with their unstressed counterparts, developed cancer more often, experienced tumor growth sooner, and grew larger tumors.

Does this stress-cancer link also hold with humans? The results are generally the same (Lutgendorf & Andersen, 2015). Some studies find that people are at increased risk for cancer within a year after experiencing depression, helplessness, or bereavement (Chida et al., 2008; Steptoe et al., 2010). In one large Swedish study, the risk of colon cancer was 5.5 times greater among people with a history of workplace stress than among those who reported no such problems. This difference was not due to group differences in age, smoking, drinking, or physical characteristics (Courtney et al., 1993). Not all studies, however, have found a link between stress and human cancer (Coyne et al., 2010; Petticrew et al., 1999, 2002). Concentration camp survivors and former prisoners of war, for example, do not have elevated cancer rates.

One danger in hyping reports on emotions and cancer is that some patients may then blame themselves for their illness: "If only I had been more expressive, relaxed, and hopeful." A corollary danger is a "wellness macho" among the healthy, who take credit for their "healthy character" and lay a guilt trip on the ill: "She has cancer? That's what you get for holding your feelings in and being so nice." Dying thus becomes the ultimate failure.

It's important enough to repeat: *Stress does not create cancer cells*. At worst, it may affect their growth by weakening the body's natural defenses against multiplying malignant cells (Lutgendorf et al., 2008; Nausheen et al., 2010; Sood et al., 2010). Although a relaxed, hopeful state may enhance these defenses, we should be aware of the thin line that divides science from wishful thinking. The powerful biological processes at work in advanced cancer or AIDS are not likely to be completely derailed by avoiding stress or maintaining a relaxed but determined spirit (Anderson, 2002; Kessler et al., 1991). And that explains why research consistently indicates that psychotherapy does not extend cancer patients' survival (Coyne et al., 2007, 2009; Coyne & Tennen, 2010).

"I didn't give myself cancer."
*Mayor Barbara Boggs Sigmund
(1939–1990), Princeton, New Jersey*

When organic causes of illness are unknown, it is tempting to invent psychological explanations. Before the germ that causes tuberculosis was discovered, personality explanations of TB were popular (Sontag, 1978).

LaunchPad For a 7-minute demonstration of the links between stress, cancer, and the immune system, visit LaunchPad's *Video: Fighting Cancer— Mobilizing the Immune System.*

coronary heart disease the clogging of the vessels that nourish the heart muscle; the leading cause of death in many developed countries.

Type A Friedman and Rosenman's term for competitive, hard-driving, impatient, verbally aggressive, and anger-prone people.

Type B Friedman and Rosenman's term for easygoing, relaxed people.

LaunchPad See LaunchPad's *Video: Longitudinal and Cross-Sectional Studies* for a helpful tutorial animation about these types of research studies.

In both India and America, Type A bus drivers are literally hard-driving: They brake, pass, and honk their horns more often than their more easygoing Type B colleagues (Evans et al., 1987).

Stress and Heart Disease

33-3 Why are some of us more prone than others to coronary heart disease?

Depart from reality for a moment. In this new world, you wake up each day, eat your breakfast, and check the news. Four 747 jumbo jet airplanes crashed yesterday and all 1642 passengers died. You finish your breakfast, grab your things, and head to class. It's just an average day.

Replace airline crashes with **coronary heart disease,** the United States' leading cause of death, and you have reentered reality. About 610,000 Americans die annually from heart disease (CDC, 2015). High blood pressure and a family history of the disease increase the risk. So do smoking, obesity, physical inactivity, and a high cholesterol level.

Stress and personality also play a big role in heart disease. The more psychological trauma people experience, the more their bodies generate *inflammation,* which is associated with heart and other health problems (O'Donovan et al., 2012). Plucking a hair and measuring its level of cortisol (a stress hormone) can help predict whether a child has experienced prolonged stress or an adult will have a future heart attack (Karlén et al., 2015; Pereg et al., 2011).

TYPE A PERSONALITY In a classic study, Meyer Friedman, Ray Rosenman, and their colleagues tested the idea that stress increases heart disease risk by measuring the blood cholesterol level and clotting speed of 40 U.S. male tax accountants at different times of year (Friedman & Ulmer, 1984). From January through March, the test results were completely normal. Then, as the accountants began scrambling to finish their clients' tax returns before the April 15 filing deadline, their cholesterol and clotting measures rose to dangerous levels. In May and June, with the deadline past, the measures returned to normal. For these men, stress predicted heart attack risk. Blood pressure also rises as students approach stressful exams (Conley & Lehman, 2012).

So, are some of us at high risk of stress-related coronary heart disease? To answer this question, the researchers who studied the tax accountants launched a nine-year *longitudinal study* of more than 3000 healthy men, aged 35 to 59. The researchers first interviewed each man for 15 minutes, noting his work and eating habits, manner of talking, and other behavior patterns. Those who seemed the most reactive, competitive, hard-driving, impatient, time-conscious, super-motivated, verbally aggressive, and easily angered they called **Type A.** The roughly equal number who were more easygoing they called **Type B.** Which group do you suppose turned out to be the most prone to coronary heart disease?

Nine years later, 257 men had suffered heart attacks, and 69 percent of them were Type A. Moreover, not one of the "pure" Type Bs—the most mellow and laid-back of their group—had suffered a heart attack.

As often happens in science, this exciting discovery provoked enormous public interest. After that initial honeymoon period, researchers wanted to know more. Was the finding reliable? If so, what was the toxic component of the Type A profile: Time-consciousness? Competitiveness? Anger?

More than 700 studies have now explored possible psychological correlates or predictors of cardiovascular health (Chida & Hamer, 2008; Chida & Steptoe, 2009). These reveal that Type A's toxic core is negative emotions—especially the anger associated with an aggressively reactive temperament. When we are harassed or challenged, our active sympathetic nervous system redistributes bloodflow to our muscles, pulling it away from our internal organs. One of those organs, the liver, which normally removes cholesterol and fat from the blood, can't do its job. Type A individuals are more often "combat ready." Thus, excess cholesterol and fat may continue to circulate in their blood and later get deposited around the heart. Further stress—sometimes conflicts brought on by their own abrasiveness—may trigger altered heart rhythms. In people with weakened hearts, this altered pattern

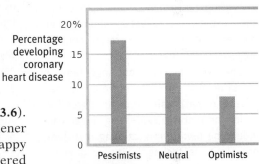

can cause sudden death (Kamarck & Jennings, 1991). Hostility also correlates with other risk factors, such as smoking, drinking, and obesity (Bunde & Suls, 2006). In important ways, people's minds and hearts interact.

Hundreds of other studies of young and middle-aged men and women have confirmed the finding that people who react with anger over little things are most prone to heart disease. As researchers have noted, rage "seems to lash back and strike us in the heart muscle" (Spielberger & London, 1982). (See Thinking Critically About: Anger Management on the next page.)

TYPE D PERSONALITY In recent years, another personality type has interested stress and heart disease researchers. Type A individuals direct their negative emotion toward dominating others. People with another personality type—Type D—suppress their negative emotion to avoid social disapproval. The negative emotion these Type D individuals experience during social interactions is mainly *distress* (Denollet, 2005; Denollet et al., 1996). In one analysis of 12 studies, having a Type D personality significantly increased risk for mortality and nonfatal heart attack (Grande et al., 2012).

EFFECTS OF PESSIMISM AND DEPRESSION Pessimism seems to be similarly toxic. Laura Kubzansky and her colleagues (2001) studied 1306 initially healthy men who a decade earlier had scored as optimists, pessimists, or neither. Even after other risk factors such as smoking had been ruled out, pessimists were more than twice as likely as optimists to develop coronary heart disease (**FIGURE 33.6**). Happy people tend to be healthier and to outlive their unhappy peers (Diener & Chan, 2011; Siahpush et al., 2008). Even a big, happy smile predicts longevity, as researchers discovered when they examined the photographs of 150 Major League Baseball players who had appeared in the 1952 *Baseball Register* and had died by 2009 (Abel & Kruger, 2010). On average, the nonsmilers had died at 73, compared with an average 80 years for those with a broad, genuine smile. People with broad smiles tend to have extensive social networks, which predict longer life (Hertenstein, 2009).

Depression, too, can be lethal. The accumulated evidence suggests that "depression substantially increases the risk of death, especially death by unnatural causes and cardiovascular disease" (Wulsin et al., 1999). In one study, nearly 4000 English adults (ages 52 to 79) provided mood reports from a single day. Compared with those in a good mood on that day, those in a blue mood were twice as likely to be dead five years later (Steptoe & Wardle, 2011). After following 63,469 women over a dozen years, researchers found more than a doubled rate of heart attack death among those who initially scored as depressed (Whang et al., 2009). In the years following a heart attack, people with high depression scores were four times more likely than their low-scoring counterparts to develop further heart problems (Frasure-Smith & Lesperance, 2005). Depression is disheartening.

> "The fire you kindle for your enemy often burns you more than him."
>
> *Chinese proverb*

FIGURE 33.6

Pessimism and heart disease
A Harvard School of Public Health team found pessimistic men at doubled risk of developing heart disease over a 10-year period. (Data from Kubzansky et al., 2001.)

> "A cheerful heart is a good medicine, but a downcast spirit dries up the bones."
>
> *Proverbs 17:22*

IMMERSIVE LEARNING To consider how researchers have studied these issues, visit LaunchPad's *How Would You Know If Stress Increases Risk of Disease?*

Anger Management

33-4 How do strategies for handling anger compare in their effectiveness?

When we face a threat or challenge, fear triggers flight but anger triggers fight— each at times an adaptive behavior. Yet chronic hostility, as in the Type A personality, is linked to heart disease. How, then, can we manage our anger?

Individualist cultures encourage people to vent their rage. Such advice is seldom heard in cultures where people's identity is centered more on the group. People who keenly sense their *inter*dependence see anger as a threat to group harmony (Markus & Kitayama, 1991). In Tahiti, for instance, people learn to be considerate and gentle. In Japan, from infancy on, angry expressions are less common than in Western cultures, where in recent politics, anger seems all the rage.

The Western vent-your-anger advice presumes that we can achieve emotional release, or **catharsis,** through aggressive action or fantasy. Expressing anger can indeed be *temporarily* calming if it does not leave us feeling guilty or anxious

(Geen & Quanty, 1977; Hokanson & Edelman, 1966).

However, catharsis usually fails to cleanse our rage. More often, expressing anger breeds more anger. For one thing, it may provoke further retaliation, causing a minor conflict to escalate into a major confrontation. For another, expressing anger can magnify anger. As *behavior feedback* research indicates, *acting* angry can make us *feel* angrier (Flack, 2006; Snodgrass et al., 1986). In one study, people who had been provoked were asked to wallop a punching bag while ruminating about the person who had angered them. Later, when given a chance for revenge, they became even more aggressive (Bushman, 2002).

Angry outbursts that temporarily calm us may also become reinforcing and therefore habit forming. If stressed managers find they can drain off some of their tension by berating an employee, then the next time they feel irritated and tense they may be more likely to explode again.

What are some better ways to manage anger? Experts offer three suggestions:

- *Wait.* You can reduce the level of physiological arousal of anger by waiting. "It is

true of the body as of arrows," noted Carol Tavris (1982), "what goes up must come down. Any emotional arousal will simmer down if you just wait long enough."

- *Find a healthy distraction or support.* Calm yourself by exercising, playing an instrument, or talking it through with a friend. Brain scans show that ruminating inwardly about why you are angry serves only to increase amygdala bloodflow (Fabiansson et al., 2012).

- *Distance yourself.* Try to move away from the situation mentally, as if you are watching it unfold from a distance. Self-distancing reduces rumination, anger, and aggression (Kross & Ayduk, 2011; Mischkowski et al., 2012; White et al., 2015).

Anger is not always wrong. Used wisely, it can communicate strength and competence (Tiedens, 2001). Anger also motivates people to take action and achieve goals (Aarts & Custers, 2012). Controlled expressions of anger are more adaptive than either hostile outbursts or pent-up angry feelings. Civility means not only keeping silent about trivial irritations but also

STRESS AND INFLAMMATION Depressed people tend to smoke more and exercise less (Whooley et al., 2008), but stress itself is also disheartening:

- When following 17,415 middle-aged American women, researchers found an 88 percent increased risk of heart attacks among those facing significant work stress (Slopen et al., 2010).

- In Denmark, a study of 12,116 female nurses found that those reporting "much too high" work pressures had a 40 percent increased risk of heart disease (Allesøe et al., 2010).

- In the United States, a 10-year study of middle-aged workers found that involuntary job loss more than doubled their risk of a heart attack (Gallo et al., 2006).

Both heart disease and depression may result when stress triggers blood vessel inflammation (Matthews, 2005; Miller & Blackwell, 2006). As the body focuses its energies on fleeing or fighting a threat, stress hormones boost the production of proteins that contribute to inflammation. Persistent inflammation can lead to asthma or clogged arteries and can worsen depression.

We can view the stress effect on our disease resistance as a price we pay for the benefits of stress (**FIGURE 33.7**). Stress invigorates our lives by arousing and motivating us. An unstressed life would hardly be challenging or productive.

communicating important ones clearly and assertively. A nonaccusing statement of feeling—perhaps letting one's housemate know that "I get irritated when you leave dirty dishes for me to clean up"—can help resolve the conflicts that cause anger. Anger can benefit a relationship when it expresses a grievance in ways that promote reconciliation rather than retaliation.

What if someone's behavior really hurts you, and you cannot resolve the conflict? Research commends the age-old response of forgiveness. Without letting the offender off the hook or inviting further harm, forgiveness releases anger and calms the body.

catharsis in psychology, the idea that "releasing" aggressive energy (through action or fantasy) relieves aggressive urges.

To explore the neural effects of forgiveness, German students had their brain scanned while someone blocked their opportunity to earn money (Strang et al., 2014). Next, the students were asked whether they forgave the wrongdoer. Forgiveness increased bloodflow to brain regions that help people understand their own emotions and make socially appropriate decisions.

"Venting to reduce anger is like using gasoline to put out a fire."
Researcher Brad Bushman (2002)

"Anger will never disappear so long as thoughts of resentment are cherished in the mind."
The Buddha, 500 B.C.E.

Mike Hutchings/Reuters/Landov

Blowing off steam Fans seem to experience a *temporary* catharsis while cheering at World Cup soccer matches, such as this one in South Africa. My [DM's] daughter, a resident, noted, "Every time I got angry at Uruguay, blowing that vuvuzela and joining the chorus of dissent released something in me."

RETRIEVE IT

• Which one of the following is an effective strategy for reducing angry feelings?
  a. Retaliate verbally or physically
  b. Wait or "simmer down"
  c. Express anger in action or fantasy
  d. Review the grievance silently

ANSWER: b

Ko Sasaki/The New York Times/Redux

Persistent stressors and negative emotions → Release of stress hormones → Immune suppression

Autonomic nervous system effects (headaches, high blood pressure, inflammation)

Unhealthy behaviors (smoking, drinking, poor nutrition and sleep)

Heart disease

⟨ FIGURE 33.7

Stress can have a variety of health-related consequences This is especially so when stress is experienced by angry, depressed, or anxious people. Job and income loss caused by economic recessions creates stress for many people, such as this jobless Japanese man living in a Tokyo "capsule hotel."

* * *

Traditionally, people have thought about their health only when something goes wrong—visiting a physician for diagnosis and treatment. That, say health psychologists, is like ignoring a car's maintenance and going to a mechanic only when the car breaks down. Health maintenance begins with implementing strategies that prevent illness by alleviating stress and enhancing well-being.

RETRIEVE IT [✱]

• Which component of the Type A personality has been linked most closely to coronary heart disease?

ANSWER: Feeling angry and negative much of the time.

• How does Type D personality differ from Type A?

ANSWER: Type D individuals experience distress rather than anger, and they tend to suppress their negative emotions to avoid social disapproval.

MODULE 33 REVIEW   Stress and Illness

👁 Learning Objectives

Test Yourself by taking a moment to answer each of these Learning Objective Questions (repeated here from within the module). Then turn to Appendix D, Complete Module Reviews, to check your answers. Research suggests that trying to answer these questions on your own will improve your long-term memory of the concepts (McDaniel et al., 2009).

33-1 What events provoke stress responses, and how do we respond and adapt to stress?

33-2 How does stress make us more vulnerable to disease?

33-3 Why are some of us more prone than others to coronary heart disease?

33-4 How do strategies for handling anger compare in their effectiveness?

Terms and Concepts to Remember

Test yourself on these terms by trying to write down the definition in your own words before flipping back to the referenced page to check your answers.

stress, p. 406

general adaptation syndrome (GAS), p. 409

tend-and-befriend, p. 410

health psychology, p. 410

psychoneuroimmunology, p. 410

coronary heart disease, p. 414

Type A, p. 414

Type B, p. 414

catharsis, p. 416

[✱] Experience the Testing Effect

Test yourself repeatedly throughout your studies. This will not only help you figure out what you know and don't know; the testing itself will help you learn and remember the information more effectively thanks to the *testing effect*.

1. Selye's general adaptation syndrome (GAS) consists of an alarm reaction followed by _____, then _____.

2. When faced with stress, women are more likely than men to experience the_____-and-_____ response.

3. The number of short-term illnesses and stress-related psychological disorders was higher than usual in the months following an earthquake. Such findings suggest that

   a. daily hassles have adverse health consequences.

   b. experiencing a very stressful event increases a person's vulnerability to illness.

   c. the amount of stress a person feels is directly related to the number of stressors experienced.

   d. small, bad events don't cause stress, but large ones can be toxic.

4. Which of the following is NOT one of the three main types of stressors?

   a. Catastrophes

   b. Significant life changes

   c. Daily hassles

   d. Distant threats that we hear about

5. Stress can suppress the immune system by prompting a decrease in the release of _____, the immune cells that ordinarily attack bacteria, viruses, cancer cells, and other foreign substances.

6. Research has shown that people are at increased risk for cancer a year or so after experiencing depression, helplessness, or bereavement. In describing this link, researchers are quick to point out that

   a. accumulated stress causes cancer.

   b. anger is the negative emotion most closely linked to cancer.

   c. stress does not create cancer cells, but it weakens the body's natural defenses against them.

   d. feeling optimistic about chances of survival ensures that a cancer patient will get well.

7. A Chinese proverb warns, "The fire you kindle for your enemy often burns you more than him." How is this true of Type A individuals?

Find answers to these questions in Appendix E, in the back of the book.

Use 🅐 LearningCurve to create your personalized study plan, which will direct you to the resources that will help you most in 🅐 LaunchPad.

Health and Happiness

Coping With Stress

34-1 In what two ways do people try to alleviate stress?

Stressors are unavoidable. This fact, coupled with the fact that persistent stress correlates with heart disease, depression, and lowered immunity, gives us a clear message: We need to learn to **cope** with the stress in our lives, alleviating it with emotional, cognitive, or behavioral methods.

Some stressors we address directly, with **problem-focused coping.** If our impatience leads to a family fight, we may go directly to that family member to work things out. We tend to use problem-focused strategies when we feel a sense of control over a situation and think we can change the circumstances, or at least change ourselves to deal with the circumstances more capably. We turn to **emotion-focused coping** when we believe we cannot change a situation. If, despite our best efforts, we cannot get along with that family member, we may relieve stress by reaching out to friends for support and comfort.

When challenged, some of us tend to respond with problem-focused coping, others with emotion-focused coping (Connor-Smith & Flachsbart, 2007). Our feelings of personal control, our explanatory style, and our supportive connections all influence our ability to cope successfully.

Personal Control

34-2 How does a perceived lack of control affect health?

Picture the scene: Two rats receive simultaneous shocks. One can turn a wheel to stop the shocks. The helpless rat, but not the wheel turner, becomes more susceptible to ulcers and lowered immunity to disease (Laudenslager & Reite, 1984). In humans, too, uncontrollable threats trigger the strongest stress responses (Dickerson & Kemeny, 2004).

At times, we all feel helpless, hopeless, and depressed after experiencing a series of bad events beyond our control. Martin Seligman and his colleagues have shown that for some animals and people, a series of uncontrollable events creates a state of **learned helplessness,** with feelings of passive resignation (**FIGURE 34.1** on the next page). In one series of experiments, dogs were strapped in a

coping alleviating stress using emotional, cognitive, or behavioral methods.

problem-focused coping attempting to alleviate stress directly—by changing the stressor or the way we interact with that stressor.

emotion-focused coping attempting to alleviate stress by avoiding or ignoring a stressor and attending to emotional needs related to our stress reaction.

learned helplessness the hopelessness and passive resignation an animal or person learns when unable to avoid repeated aversive events.

PRNewsFoto/Home Interiors & Gifts; Habitat for Humanity Women Build/AP Photo

> **FIGURE 34.1**

Learned helplessness When animals and people experience no control over repeated bad events, they often learn helplessness.

| Uncontrollable bad events | ➡ | Perceived lack of control | ➡ | Generalized helpless behavior |

harness and given repeated shocks, with no opportunity to avoid them (Seligman & Maier, 1967). Later, when placed in another situation where they *could* escape the punishment by simply leaping a hurdle, the dogs cowered as if without hope. Other dogs that had been able to escape the first shocks reacted differently. They had learned they were in control and easily escaped the shocks in the new situation (Seligman & Maier, 1967). In other experiments, people have shown similar patterns of learned helplessness (Abramson et al., 1978, 1989; Seligman, 1975).

Perceiving a loss of control, we become more vulnerable to ill health. A famous study of elderly nursing home residents with little perceived control over their activities found that they declined faster and died sooner than those given more control (Rodin, 1986). Workers able to adjust office furnishings and control interruptions and distractions in their work environment have experienced less stress (O'Neill, 1993). Such findings may help explain why British executives have tended to outlive those in clerical or laboring positions, and why Finnish workers with low job stress have been less than half as likely to die of stroke or heart disease as those with a demanding job and little control. The more control workers have, the longer they live (Bosma et al., 1997, 1998; Kivimaki et al., 2002; Marmot et al., 1997).

Increasing control—allowing prisoners to move chairs and to control room lights and the TV; having workers participate in decision making; allowing people to personalize their work space—has noticeably improved health and morale (Humphrey et al., 2007; Wang et al., 2010). In the case of the nursing home residents, 93 percent of those encouraged to exert more control became more alert, active, and happy (Rodin, 1986). As researcher Ellen Langer concluded, "Perceived control is basic to human functioning" (1983, p. 291).

Control also helps explain a link between economic status and longevity (Jokela et al., 2009). In one study of 843 grave markers in an old cemetery in Glasgow, Scotland, those with the costliest, highest pillars (indicating the most affluence) tended to have lived the longest (Carroll et al., 1994). Likewise, American presidents, who are generally wealthy and well-educated, have had above-average life spans (Olshansky, 2011). Across cultures, high economic status predicts a lower risk of heart and respiratory diseases (Sapolsky, 2005). Wealthy parents tend to have healthy children, too (Chen, 2004). With higher economic status come reduced risks of low birth weight, infant mortality, smoking, and violence. Even among other primates, individuals at the bottom of the social pecking order have been more likely than their higher-status companions to become sick when exposed to a cold-like virus (Cohen et al., 1997).

Happy to have control This family is finally experiencing the joy of having their own new home, after working on the building, together with Habitat for Humanity volunteers, for several months.

Why does perceived loss of control predict health problems? Because losing control provokes an outpouring of stress hormones. When rats cannot control shock or when humans or other primates feel unable to control their environment, stress hormone levels rise, blood pressure increases, and immune responses drop (Rodin, 1986; Sapolsky, 2005). Captive animals experience more stress and are more vulnerable to disease than their wild counterparts (Roberts, 1988). Human studies confirm that stress increases when we lack control. The greater nurses' workload, the higher their cortisol level and blood pressure—but only among nurses who reported little control over their environment (Fox et al., 1993). The crowding in high-density neighborhoods, prisons, and college and university dorms is another source of diminished feelings of control—and of elevated levels of stress hormones and blood pressure (Fleming et al., 1987; Ostfeld et al., 1987). By boosting feelings of control, people often lead happier and healthier lives (Ng et al., 2012).

INTERNAL VERSUS EXTERNAL LOCUS OF CONTROL If experiencing a loss of control can be stressful and unhealthy, do people who generally *perceive* they have control of their lives enjoy better health? Consider your own perceptions of control. Do you believe that your life is beyond your control? That getting a good job depends mainly on being in the right place at the right time? Or do you more strongly believe that you control your own fate? That being a success is a matter of hard work? Did your parents influence your feelings of control? Did your culture?

Hundreds of studies have compared people who differ in their perceptions of control. On one side are those who have what psychologist Julian Rotter called an **external locus of control**—the perception that chance or outside forces control their fate. On the other side are those who perceive an **internal locus of control,** who believe they control their own destiny. In study after study, the "internals" have achieved more in school and work, acted more independently, enjoyed better health, and felt less depressed than did the "externals" (Lefcourt, 1982; Ng et al., 2006). In one long-term study of more than 7500 people, those who had expressed a more internal locus of control at age 10 exhibited less obesity, lower blood pressure, and less distress at age 30 (Gale et al., 2008). Compared with nonleaders, military and business leaders have lower-than-average levels of stress hormones and report less anxiety, thanks to their greater sense of control (Sherman et al., 2012).

Another way to say that we believe we are in control of our own life is to say we have *free will*, or that we control our own willpower. Studies show that people who believe in their freedom learn better, perform better at work, behave more helpfully, and have a stronger desire to punish rule breakers (Clark et al., 2014; Job et al., 2010; Stillman et al., 2010).

Compared with their parents' generation, more young Americans now express an external locus of control (Twenge et al., 2004). This shift may help explain an associated increase in rates of depression and other psychological disorders in young people (Twenge et al., 2010).

> **external locus of control** the perception that chance or outside forces beyond our personal control determine our fate.
>
> **internal locus of control** the perception that we control our own fate.
>
> **self-control** the ability to control impulses and delay short-term gratification for greater long-term rewards.

RETRIEVE IT [✖]

- To cope with stress when we feel in control of our world, we tend to use _____-focused (emotion/problem) strategies. To cope with stress when we believe we cannot change a situation, we tend to use _____-focused (emotion/problem) strategies.

ANSWERS: problem; emotion

DEPLETING AND STRENGTHENING SELF-CONTROL

34-3 How can our self-control be depleted, and why is it important to build this strength?

Self-control is the ability to control impulses and delay short-term gratification for longer-term rewards. Self-control predicts good health, higher income, and better grades (Kuhnle et al., 2012; Moffitt et al., 2011). In one year-long study of eighth-graders' academic success, self-control had double the predictive power of intelligence score (Duckworth & Seligman, 2005).

Self-control constantly changes—from day to day, hour to hour, and even minute to minute. Like a muscle, self-control weakens after use, recovers after rest, and grows stronger with exercise (Baumeister & Tierney, 2012; Hagger et al., 2010; Vohs & Baumeister, 2011). Exercising willpower temporarily depletes the mental energy needed for self-control on other tasks (Grillon et al., 2015; Vohs et al., 2012). In one experiment, hungry people who had resisted the temptation to eat chocolate chip cookies abandoned a tedious task sooner than those who had not resisted the cookies (Baumeister et al., 1998). And after expending willpower on laboratory tasks, such as stifling prejudice or ignoring flashing words on a computer screen, people were less restrained in their aggressive responses to provocation and in their sexual behavior (Finkel et al., 2012; Gaillot & Baumeister, 2007). Similar

Marty Lederhandler/AP Photo

Extreme self-control Our ability to exert self-control increases with practice, and some of us have practiced more than others! Magician David Blaine (left) endured standing in a block of ice (in which a small space had been carved out for him) for nearly 62 hours for a stunt in New York's Times Square. A number of performing artists make their living as very convincing human statues, as does this actress (right) performing on The Royal Mile in Edinburgh, Scotland.

LatitudeStock/Brian Fairbrother/Getty Images

self-control weakening happens when people flex their self-control muscle outside the laboratory, such as when trying to control alcohol use (Hofmann et al., 2012).

Exercising willpower decreases neural activation in brain regions associated with mental control (Wagner et al., 2013). Might sugar provide a sweet solution to self-control fatigue? Sugar not only makes us feel good, it also increases neural activation in mental control regions (Chambers et al., 2009). In one study, giving sugar (in a naturally rather than an artificially sweetened lemonade) had a sweet effect: It reduced people's financial impulsiveness (Wang & Dvorak, 2010). Even dogs can experience self-control depletion and rejuvenation with sugar (Miller et al., 2010).

Researchers do not encourage candy bar diets to improve self-control. Even rinsing your mouth with sugary liquid can activate the brain's self-control centers (Hagger & Chatzisarantis, 2013; Sanders et al., 2012). You will get the boost in self-control without the bulge in your waistline.

The decreased mental energy after exercising self-control is short-lived. But the long-term effect of exercising self-control is strengthened self-control, much as a hard physical workout leaves you temporarily tired out, but stronger in the long term. Strengthened self-control improves people's performance on laboratory tasks and improves their self-management of eating, drinking, anger, and household chores (Denson et al., 2011; Oaten & Cheng, 2006a,b).

The point to remember: Develop self-discipline in one area of your life, and your strengthened self-control may spill over into other areas as well, making for a healthier, happier, and more successful life (Tuk et al., 2015).

Explanatory Style: Optimism Versus Pessimism

34-4 How does an optimistic outlook affect health and longevity?

In *The How of Happiness*, social psychologist Sonja Lyubomirsky (2008) tells the true story of Randy, who has lived a hard life. His dad and best friend both died by suicide. Growing up, his mother's boyfriend treated him poorly. Randy's first wife was unfaithful, and they divorced. Despite these misfortunes, Randy has a sunny disposition. He remarried and enjoys being the stepfather to three boys. His work is rewarding. Randy says he survived his life challenges by seeing the "silver lining in the cloud."

Randy's story illustrates how our outlook—what we expect from the world—influences how we cope with stress. *Pessimists* expect things to go badly (Aspinwall & Tedeschi, 2010; Carver et al., 2010; Rasmussen et al., 2009). When bad things happen, pessimists knew it all along. They attribute their poor performance to a basic lack of ability ("I can't do this") or to situations enduringly beyond their control ("There is nothing I can do about it"). *Optimists,* such as Randy, expect to have more control, to cope better with stressful events, and to enjoy better health (Aspinwall & Tedeschi, 2010; Boehm & Kubzansky, 2012; Carver et al., 2010; Hernandez et al., 2015). During a semester's last month, students previously identified as optimistic reported less fatigue and fewer coughs, aches, and pains. And during the stressful first few weeks of law school, those who were optimistic ("It's unlikely that I will fail") enjoyed better moods and stronger immune systems

(Segerstrom et al., 1998). Optimists also respond to stress with smaller increases in blood pressure, and they recover more quickly from heart bypass surgery.

Optimistic students have also tended to get better grades because they often respond to setbacks with the hopeful attitude that effort, good study habits, and self-discipline make a difference (Noel et al., 1987; Peterson & Barrett, 1987). When dating couples wrestle with conflicts, optimists and their partners see each other as engaging constructively, and they then tend to feel more supported and satisfied with the resolution and with their relationship (Srivastava et al., 2006). Optimism relates to well-being and success in many places, including China and Japan (Qin & Piao, 2011). Realistic positive expectations fuel motivation and success (Oettingen & Mayer, 2002).

Consider the consistency and startling magnitude of the optimism and positive emotions factor in several other studies:

- When Finnish researchers followed 2428 men for up to a decade, the number of deaths among those with a bleak, hopeless outlook was more than double that found among their optimistic counterparts (Everson et al., 1996). American researchers found the same when following 4256 Vietnam-era veterans (Phillips et al., 2009).

- A now-famous study followed up on 180 Catholic nuns who had written brief autobiographies at about 22 years of age and had thereafter lived similar lifestyles. Those who had expressed happiness, love, and other positive feelings in their autobiographies lived an average 7 years longer than their more dour counterparts (Danner et al., 2001). By age 80, some 54 percent of those expressing few positive emotions had died, as had only 24 percent of the most positive spirited.

- Optimists not only live long lives, but they maintain a positive view as they approach the end of their lives. One study followed more than 68,000 American women, ages 50 to 79 years, for nearly two decades (Zaslavsky et al., 2015). As death grew nearer, the optimistic women tended to feel more life satisfaction than did the pessimistic women.

Optimism runs in families, so some people truly are born with a sunny, hopeful outlook. With identical twins, if one is optimistic, the other often will be as well (Bates, 2015; Mosing et al., 2009). One genetic marker of optimism is a gene that enhances the social-bonding hormone *oxytocin* (Saphire-Bernstein et al., 2011).

The good news is that all of us, even the most pessimistic, can learn to become more optimistic. Compared with a control group of pessimists who simply kept diaries of their daily activities, pessimists in a skill-building group, who learned ways of seeing the bright side of difficult situations and how to view their goals as achievable, reported lower levels of depression (Sergeant & Mongrain, 2014). Optimism is the light bulb that can brighten anyone's mood.

Social Support

34-5 How does social support promote good health?

Social support—feeling liked and encouraged by intimate friends and family—promotes both happiness and health. People in different cultures vary in how much they seek social support. Those from collectivist cultures tend to keep their struggles to themselves, in part because they do not want to show signs of weakness that may reflect poorly on their group (Kim et al., 2008). In individualist cultures, distressed people feel more comfortable turning to friends and family (Mortenson, 2006). Despite these cultural differences, social support is universally related to greater happiness (Brannan et al., 2013; Chu et al., 2010; Gable et al., 2012; Ren et al., 2010).

Close relationships have also predicted health. People are less likely to die early if supported by close relationships (Shor et al., 2013; Uchino, 2009). When

Positive expectations often motivate eventual success.

"We just haven't been flapping them hard enough."

"The optimist proclaims we live in the best of all possible worlds; and the pessimist fears this is true."

James Branch Cabell,
The Silver Stallion, *1926*

Laughter among friends is good medicine
Laughter arouses us, massages muscles, and then leaves us feeling relaxed (Robinson, 1983). Humor (though not hostile sarcasm) may defuse stress, ease pain, and strengthen immune activity (Ayan, 2009; Berk et al., 2001; Dunbar et al., 2011; Kimata, 2001). People who laugh a lot have also tended to have lower rates of heart disease (Clark et al., 2001).

Mark Andersen/Rubberball/Getty Images

Brigham Young University researchers combined data from 70 studies of 3.4 million people worldwide, they confirmed a striking effect of social support (Holt-Lunstad et al., 2015). Compared with those with ample social connections, those with few connections had a 30 percent greater death rate during the average 7-year study period. Social isolation's association with risk of death is equivalent to smoking (Holt-Lunstad et al., 2010).

To combat social isolation, we need to do more than collect lots of acquaintances. We need people who genuinely care about us (Cacioppo et al., 2014; Hawkley et al., 2008). Some fill this need by connecting with friends, family, co-workers, members of a faith community, or other support groups. Others connect in positive, happy, supportive marriages. One seven-decade-long study found that at age 50, healthy aging was better predicted by a good marriage than by a low cholesterol level (Vaillant, 2002). On the flip side, divorce predicts poor health. In one analysis of 32 studies involving more than 6.5 million people, divorced people were 23 percent more likely to die early (Sbarra et al., 2011). But it's less marital status than marital *quality* that predicts health—to about the same extent that healthy behaviors, such as a healthy diet and physical activity predict health (Robles, 2015; Robles et al., 2014).

What explains the link between social support and health? Are middle-aged and older adults who live with little social engagement more likely to smoke, be obese, and have high cholesterol—and therefore to have a doubled risk of heart attacks (Nielsen et al., 2006)? Or are healthy people simply more sociable? Research suggests that social support itself creates health benefits.

Social support calms us and reduces blood pressure and stress hormones. Numerous studies support this finding (Hostinar et al., 2014; Uchino et al., 1996, 1999). To see if social support might calm people's response to threats, one research team subjected happily married women, while lying in an fMRI machine, to the threat of electric shock to an ankle (Coan et al., 2006). During the experiment, some women held their husband's hand. Others held the hand of an unknown person or no hand at all. While awaiting the occasional shocks, women holding their husband's hand showed less activity in threat-responsive areas. This soothing benefit was greatest for those reporting the highest-quality marriages. People with supportive marriages also have lower-than-average stress hormone levels 10 years later (Slatcher et al., 2015). Even animal support helps buffer stress. After stressful events, Medicare patients with a dog or other companionable pet have been less likely to visit their doctor (Siegel, 1990).

Social support fosters stronger immune functioning. Volunteers in studies of resistance to cold viruses showed this benefit (Cohen et al., 1997, 2004). Healthy volunteers inhaled nasal drops laden with a cold virus and were quarantined and observed for five days. (In these experiments, more than 600 volunteers received

$800 each to endure this experience.) Age, race, sex, and health habits being equal, those with the most social ties were least likely to catch a cold. If they did catch one, they produced less mucus. People whose daily life included frequent hugs likewise experienced fewer cold symptoms and less symptom severity (Cohen et al., 2015). More sociability meant less susceptibility. The cold fact is that the effect of social ties is nothing to sneeze at!

Close relationships give us an opportunity for "open heart therapy," *a chance to confide painful feelings* (Frattaroli, 2006). Talking about a stressful event can temporarily arouse us, but in the long run it calms us, by calming limbic system activity (Lieberman et al., 2007; Mendolia & Kleck, 1993). In one study, 33 Holocaust survivors spent two hours recalling their experiences, many in intimate detail never before disclosed (Pennebaker et al., 1989). In the weeks following, most watched a video of their recollections and showed it to family and friends. Those who were most self-disclosing had the most improved health 14 months later. Confiding is good for the body and the soul. In another study, of surviving spouses of people who had committed suicide or died in car accidents, those who bore their grief alone had more health problems than those who could share it with others (Pennebaker & O'Heeron, 1984).

Suppressing emotions can be detrimental to physical health. When psychologist James Pennebaker (1985) surveyed more than 700 undergraduate women, some of them reported a traumatic childhood sexual experience. The sexually abused women—especially those who had kept their secret to themselves—reported more headaches and stomach ailments than did other women who had experienced nonsexual traumas, such as parental death or divorce. Another study, of 437 Australian ambulance drivers, confirmed the ill effects of suppressing one's emotions after witnessing traumas (Wastell, 2002).

Even writing about personal traumas in a diary can help (Burton & King, 2008; Hemenover, 2003; Lyubomirsky et al., 2006). In an analysis of 633 trauma victims, writing therapy was as effective as psychotherapy in reducing psychological trauma (van Emmerik et al., 2013). In another experiment, volunteers who wrote trauma diaries had fewer health problems during the ensuing four to six months (Pennebaker, 1990). As one participant explained, "Although I have not talked with anyone about what I wrote, I was finally able to deal with it, work through the pain instead of trying to block it out. Now it doesn't hurt to think about it."

If we are aiming to exercise more, drink less, quit smoking, or attain a healthy weight, our social ties can tug us away from or toward our goal. If you are trying to achieve some goal, think about whether your social network can help or hinder you. That social net covers not only the people you know but friends of your friends, and friends of their friends. That's three degrees of separation between you and the most remote people. Within that network, others can influence your thoughts, feelings, and actions without your awareness (Christakis & Fowler, 2009).

Reducing Stress

Having a sense of control, developing more optimistic thinking, and building social support can help us *experience* less stress and thus improve our health. Moreover, these factors interrelate: People who are upbeat about themselves and their future have tended also to enjoy health-promoting social ties (Stinson et al., 2008). But sometimes we cannot alleviate stress and simply need to *manage* our stress. Aerobic exercise, relaxation, meditation, and active spiritual engagement may help us gather inner strength and lessen stress effects.

Pets are friends, too Pets can provide social support, which increases the odds of survival after a heart attack, relieves depression among AIDS patients, and lowers the levels of blood pressure and blood lipids that contribute to cardiovascular risk (Allen, 2003; McConnell et al., 2011; Wells, 2009). To lower blood pressure, pets are no substitute for effective drugs and exercise. But for people who enjoy animals, and especially for those who live alone, pets are a healthy pleasure (Allen, 2003).

Photos.com/Getty Images

"Woe to one who is alone and falls and does not have another to help."

Ecclesiastes 4:10

aerobic exercise sustained exercise that increases heart and lung fitness; may also alleviate depression and anxiety.

Aerobic Exercise

34-6 How effective is aerobic exercise as a way to manage stress and improve well-being?

Aerobic exercise is sustained, oxygen-consuming exercise—such as jogging, swimming, or biking—that increases heart and lung fitness. It's hard to find bad things to say about exercise. Estimates vary, but moderate exercise adds quantity of life—two additional years, on average—and also quality of life, with more energy, better mood, and stronger relationships (Hogan et al., 2015; Seligman, 1994; Wang et al., 2011).

Exercise helps fight heart disease by strengthening the heart, increasing bloodflow, keeping blood vessels open, and lowering both blood pressure and the blood pressure reaction to stress (Ford, 2002; Manson, 2002). Inactivity can be toxic. People who exercise suffer half as many heart attacks as do others who are inactive (Powell et al., 1987; Visich & Fletcher, 2009). Exercise makes your muscles hungry for the fats that, if not used by muscles, can contribute to clogged arteries (Barinaga, 1997). In one study of over 650,000 American adults, walking 150 minutes per week predicted living seven more years (Moore et al., 2012). Regular exercise in later life also predicts better cognitive functioning and reduced risk of neurocognitive disorder and Alzheimer's disease (Kramer & Erickson, 2007).

Does exercise also boost the spirit? Many studies reveal that aerobic exercise can reduce stress, depression, and anxiety. Americans, Canadians, and Britons who have at least three weekly aerobic exercise sessions manage stress better, exhibit more self-confidence, and feel more vigor and less depression and fatigue than do their inactive peers (Ekkekakis, 2015; Smits et al., 2011). Going from active exerciser to couch potato can increase the likelihood of depression—by 51 percent in two years for the women in one study (Wang et al., 2011). And in a 21-country survey of university students, physical exercise was a strong and consistent predictor of life satisfaction (Grant et al., 2009).

But we could state this observation another way: Stressed and depressed people exercise less. These findings are correlations, and cause and effect are unclear. To sort out cause and effect, researchers experiment. They *randomly assign* stressed, depressed, or anxious people either to an aerobic exercise group or to a control group. Next, they measure whether aerobic exercise (compared with a control activity that doesn't involve exercise) produces a change in stress, depression, anxiety, or some other health-related outcome. One classic experiment randomly assigned mildly depressed female college students to three groups. One-third participated in a program of aerobic exercise. Another third took part in a program of relaxation exercises. The remaining third (the control group) formed a no-treatment group (McCann & Holmes, 1984). As **FIGURE 34.2** shows, 10 weeks later, the women in the aerobic exercise program reported the greatest decrease in depression. Many had, quite literally, run away from their troubles.

Dozens of other experiments and longitudinal studies confirm that exercise prevents or reduces depression and anxiety (Conn, 2010; Pinto Pereira et al., 2014; Windle et al., 2010). When experimenters randomly assigned depressed people

∨ FIGURE 34.2

Aerobic exercise and depression Mildly depressed college women who participated in an aerobic exercise program showed markedly reduced depression, compared with those who did relaxation exercises or received no treatment. (Data from McCann & Holmes, 1984.)

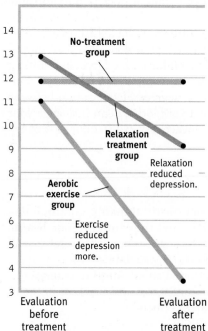

Depression score

No-treatment group

Relaxation treatment group

Relaxation reduced depression.

Aerobic exercise group

Exercise reduced depression more.

Evaluation before treatment

Evaluation after treatment

to an exercise group, an antidepressant group, or a placebo pill group, exercise diminished depression as effectively as antidepressants—and with longer-lasting effects (Hoffman et al., 2011).

Vigorous exercise provides a substantial and immediate mood boost (Watson, 2000). Even a 10-minute walk stimulates 2 hours of increased well-being by raising energy levels and lowering tension (Thayer, 1987, 1993). Exercise works its magic in several ways. It increases arousal, thus counteracting depression's low arousal state. It produces toned muscles, which filter a depression-causing toxin (Agudelo et al., 2014). It enables muscle relaxation and sounder sleep. Like an antidepressant drug, it orders up mood-boosting chemicals from our body's internal pharmacy—neurotransmitters such as norepinephrine, serotonin, and the endorphins (Jacobs, 1994; Salmon, 2001). Exercise also fosters *neurogenesis*. In mice, exercise causes the brain to produce a molecule that stimulates the production of new, stress-resistant neurons (Hunsberger et al., 2007; Reynolds, 2009; van Praag, 2009).

On a simpler level, the sense of accomplishment and improved physique and body image that often accompany a successful exercise routine may enhance one's self-image, leading to a better emotional state. Exercising at least a half-hour on 5 or more days each week is like taking a drug that prevents and treats disease, increases energy, calms anxiety, and boosts mood—a drug we would all take, if available. Yet few people (only 1 in 4 in the United States) take advantage of it (Mendes, 2010). Over the past 20 years, the number of Americans who report no physical activity has doubled (Ladabaum et al., 2014). To help reverse this trend, U.S. First Lady Michelle Obama started the *Let's Move!* initiative to motivate children to embrace a healthy, active lifestyle.

Relaxation and Meditation

👁 **34-7** In what ways might relaxation and meditation influence stress and health?

Knowing the damaging effects of stress, could we learn to counteract our stress responses by altering our thinking and lifestyle? In the late 1960s, some respected psychologists began experimenting with *biofeedback*, a system of recording, amplifying, and feeding back information about subtle physiological responses, many controlled by the autonomic nervous system. Biofeedback instruments mirror the results of a person's own efforts, enabling the person to learn which techniques do (or do not) control a particular physiological response. After a decade of study, however, the initial claims for biofeedback seemed overblown and oversold (Miller, 1985). In 1995, a National Institutes of Health panel declared that biofeedback works best on tension headaches.

Simple methods of relaxation, which require no expensive equipment, produce many of the results biofeedback once promised. Figure 34.2 pointed out that aerobic exercise reduces depression. But did you notice in that figure that depression also decreased among women in the relaxation treatment group? More than 60 studies have found that relaxation procedures can also help alleviate headaches, hypertension, anxiety, and insomnia (Nestoriuc et al., 2008; Stetter & Kupper, 2002).

Such findings would not surprise Meyer Friedman, Ray Rosenman, and their colleagues. They tested relaxation in a program designed to help *Type A* heart attack survivors (who are more prone to heart attacks than their *Type B* peers) reduce their risk of future attacks. They randomly assigned hundreds of middle-aged men to

🅜 **LaunchPad** See LaunchPad's *Video: Random Assignment* for a helpful tutorial animation about this important part of effective research design.

The mood boost When energy or spirits are sagging, few things reboot the day better than exercising, as I [DM] can confirm from my noontime basketball, and as I [ND] can confirm from my running.

Furry friends for finals week Some schools bring cuddly critters on campus for finals week as a way to help students relax and bring disruptive stress levels down. This student at Emory University is relaxing with dogs and puppies. Other schools offer petting zoos or encourage instructors to bring in their own pets that week.

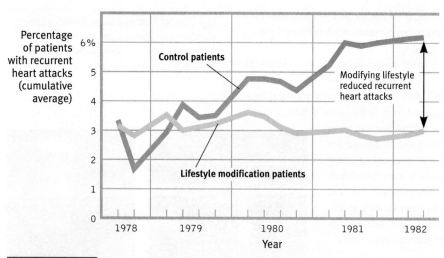

Percentage of patients with recurrent heart attacks (cumulative average)

Control patients

Modifying lifestyle reduced recurrent heart attacks

Lifestyle modification patients

Year

⌃ FIGURE 34.3

Recurrent heart attacks and lifestyle modification The San Francisco Recurrent Coronary Prevention Project offered counseling from a cardiologist to survivors of heart attacks. Those who were also guided in modifying their Type A lifestyle suffered fewer repeat heart attacks. (Data from Friedman & Ulmer, 1984.)

"Sit down alone and in silence. Lower your head, shut your eyes, breathe out gently, and imagine yourself looking into your own heart. . . . As you breathe out, say 'Lord Jesus Christ, have mercy on me.' . . . Try to put all other thoughts aside. Be calm, be patient, and repeat the process very frequently."

Gregory of Sinai, died 1346

one of two groups. The first group received standard advice from cardiologists about medications, diet, and exercise habits. The second group received similar advice, but they also were taught ways of modifying their lifestyles. They learned to slow down and relax by walking, talking, and eating more slowly. They learned to smile at others and laugh at themselves. They learned to admit their mistakes, to take time to enjoy life, and to renew their religious faith. The training paid off (**FIGURE 34.3**). During the next three years, the lifestyle modification group had half as many repeat heart attacks as did the first group. This, wrote the exuberant Friedman, was an unprecedented, spectacular reduction in heart attack recurrence. A smaller-scale British study similarly divided heart-attack-prone people into control and lifestyle modification groups (Eysenck & Grossarth-Maticek, 1991). During the next 13 years, people trained to alter their thinking and lifestyle showed a 50 percent reduction in death rate. After suffering a heart attack at age 55, Friedman started taking his own behavioral medicine—and lived to age 90 (Wargo, 2007).

Time may heal all wounds, but relaxation can help speed that process. In one study, surgery patients were randomly assigned to two groups. Both groups received standard treatment, but the second group also experienced a 45-minute relaxation exercise and received relaxation recordings to use before and after surgery. A week after surgery, patients in the relaxation group reported lower stress and showed better wound healing (Broadbent et al., 2012).

Meditation is a modern practice with a long history. In many of the world's great religions, meditation has been used to reduce suffering and improve awareness, insight, and compassion. Numerous studies have confirmed the psychological benefits of meditation (Goyal et al., 2014; Sedlmeier et al., 2012). Today, it has found a new home in stress management programs, such as **mindfulness meditation.** If you were taught this practice, you would relax and silently attend to your inner state, without judging it (Kabat-Zinn, 2001). You would sit down, close your eyes, and mentally scan your body from head to toe. Zooming your focus on certain body parts and responses, you would remain aware and accepting. You would also pay attention to your breathing, attending to each breath as if it were a material object.

Practicing mindfulness may improve many health measures. In one study of 1140 people, some received mindfulness-based therapy for several weeks. Others did not. Levels of anxiety and depression were lower among those who received the therapy (Hofmann et al., 2010). In another study, mindfulness training improved immune system functioning and coping in a group of women newly diagnosed with early-stage breast cancer (Witek-Janusek et al., 2008). Mindfulness practices have also been linked with reductions in sleep problems, cigarette use, binge eating, and alcohol and other substance use disorders (Bowen et al., 2006; Brewer et al., 2011; Cincotta et al., 2011; de Dios et al., 2012; Kristeller et al., 2006). Just 15 minutes of daily mindfulness meditation is enough to improve decision-making performance (Hafenbrack et al., 2014).

So what's going on in the brain as we practice mindfulness? Correlational and experimental studies offer three explanations. Mindfulness

- *strengthens connections among regions in our brain.* The affected regions are those associated with focusing our attention, processing what we see and hear, and being reflective and aware (Berkovich-Ohana et al., 2014; Ives-Deliperi et al., 2011; Kilpatrick et al., 2011).

- *activates brain regions associated with more reflective awareness* (Davidson et al., 2003; Way et al., 2010). When labeling emotions, "mindful people" show less activation in the amygdala, a brain region associated with fear, and more activation in the prefrontal cortex, which aids emotion regulation (Creswell et al., 2007).

- *calms brain activation in emotional situations.* This lower activation was clear in one study in which participants watched two movies—one sad, one neutral. Those in the control group, who were not trained in mindfulness, showed strong differences in brain activation when watching the two movies. Those who had received mindfulness training showed little change in brain response to the two movies (Farb et al., 2010). Emotionally unpleasant images also trigger weaker electrical brain responses in mindful people than in their less mindful counterparts (Brown et al., 2013). A mindful brain is strong, reflective, and calm.

Dean Mitchell/Shutterstock

> **mindfulness meditation** a reflective practice in which people attend to current experiences in a nonjudgmental and accepting manner.

Exercise and meditation are not the only routes to healthy relaxation. Massage helps relax premature infants and those suffering pain. An analysis of 17 experiments revealed another benefit: Massage therapy relaxes muscles and helps reduce depression (Hou et al., 2010).

And then there are the mystics who seek to use the mind's power to enable novocaine-free cavity repair. Their aim: transcend dental medication.

Faith Communities and Health

34-8 What is the faith factor, and what are some possible explanations for the link between faith and health?

A wealth of studies—some 1800 of them in the twenty-first century's first decade alone—has revealed another curious correlation: the *faith factor* (Koenig et al., 2012). Religiously active people tend to live longer than those who are not religiously active. One such study compared the death rates for 3900 people living in two Israeli communities. The first community contained 11 religiously orthodox collective settlements; the second contained 11 matched, nonreligious collective settlements (Kark et al., 1996). Over a 16-year period, "belonging to a religious collective was associated with a strong protective effect" not explained by age or economic differences. In every age group, religious community members were about half as likely to have died as were their nonreligious counterparts. This difference is roughly comparable to the gender difference in mortality.

How should we interpret such findings? Correlations are not cause-effect statements, and they leave many factors uncontrolled (Sloan et al., 1999, 2000, 2002, 2005). Here is another possible interpretation: Women are more religiously active

© MaRoDee Photography/Alamy

Fuse/Jupiterimages

Sura Nualpradid/Shutterstock

casejustin/Shutterstock

©Georgios Kollidas/Alamy

Georgios Kollidas/Shutterstock

ppart/Shutterstock

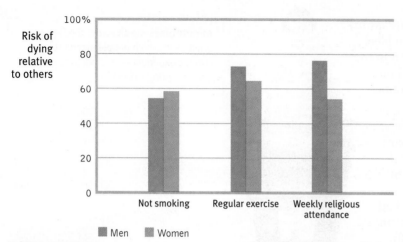

Risk of dying relative to others

100%

80

60

40

20

0

Not smoking   Regular exercise   Weekly religious attendance

■ Men   ■ Women

∧ FIGURE 34.4

Predictors of longer life: Not smoking, frequent exercise, and regular religious attendance Epidemiologist William Strawbridge and his co-workers (1997, 1999; Oman et al., 2002) followed 5286 Alameda, California, adults over 28 years. After adjusting for age and education, the researchers found that not smoking, regular exercise, and religious attendance all predicted a lowered risk of death in any given year. Women attending weekly religious services, for example, were only 54 percent as likely to die in a typical study year as were nonattenders.

than men, and women outlive men. Might religious involvement merely reflect this gender-longevity link? Apparently not. One 8-year National Institutes of Health study followed 92,395 women (ages 50 to 79). After controlling for many factors, researchers found that women attending religious services weekly (or more) experienced an approximately 20 percent reduced risk of death during the study period (Schnall et al., 2010). Moreover, the association between religious involvement and life expectancy is also found among men (Benjamins et al., 2010; McCullough et al., 2000, 2005, 2009). A 28-year study that followed 5286 Californians found that, after controlling for age, gender, ethnicity, and education, frequent religious attenders were 36 percent less likely to have died in any year (**FIGURE 34.4**). In another 8-year controlled study of more than 20,000 people (Hummer et al., 1999), this effect translated into a life expectancy at age 20 of 83 years for frequent attenders at religious services and 75 years for nonattenders.

These correlational findings do not indicate that people who have not been religiously active can suddenly add 8 years of life if they start attending services and change nothing else. Nevertheless, the findings do indicate that religious involvement, like nonsmoking and exercise, is a *predictor* of health and longevity. Research points to three possible explanations for the religiosity-longevity correlation (**FIGURE 34.5**):

- *Healthy behaviors* Religion promotes self-control (DeWall et al., 2014; McCullough & Willoughby, 2009). And that helps explain why religiously active people tend to smoke and drink much less and to have healthier lifestyles (Islam & Johnson, 2003; Koenig & Vaillant, 2009; Masters & Hooker, 2013; Park, 2007). In one Gallup survey of 550,000 Americans, 15 percent of the very religious were smokers, as were 28 percent of those nonreligious (Newport et al., 2010). But such lifestyle differences are not great enough to explain the dramatically reduced mortality in the Israeli religious settlements. In American studies, too, about 75 percent of the longevity difference remained when researchers controlled for unhealthy behaviors, such as inactivity and smoking (Musick et al., 1999).

- *Social support* Could social support explain the faith factor (Ai et al., 2007; George et al., 2002; Kim-Yeary et al., 2012)? Faith is often a communal experience. To belong to one of these faith communities is to have access to a support network. Religiously active people are there for one another when misfortune strikes. Moreover, religion encourages marriage, another predictor of health and longevity. In the Israeli religious settlements, for example, divorce has been almost nonexistent.

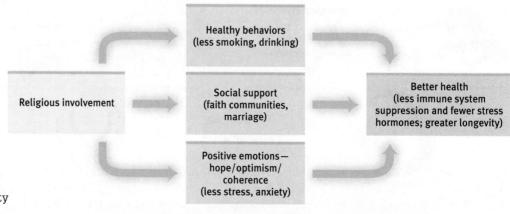

> FIGURE 34.5

Possible explanations for the correlation between religious involvement and health/longevity

Religious involvement → Healthy behaviors (less smoking, drinking) → Better health (less immune system suppression and fewer stress hormones; greater longevity)

Social support (faith communities, marriage)

Positive emotions— hope/optimism/ coherence (less stress, anxiety)

• *Positive emotions* Even after controlling for gender, unhealthy behaviors, preexisting health problems, and social support, the mortality studies have found that religiously engaged people tend to live longer (Chida et al., 2009). Researchers speculate that religiously active people may benefit from a stable, coherent worldview, a sense of hope for the long-term future, feelings of ultimate acceptance, and the relaxed meditation of prayer or other religious observances. These intervening variables may also help to explain why the religiously active seem to have healthier immune functioning, fewer hospital admissions, and, for AIDS patients, fewer stress hormones and longer survival (Ironson et al., 2002; Koenig & Larson, 1998; Lutgendorf et al., 2004).

RETRIEVE IT

• What are some of the tactics we can use to manage successfully the stress we cannot avoid?

ANSWER: aerobic exercise, relaxation procedures, mindfulness meditation, and religious engagement

Happiness

 34-9 What is the *feel-good, do-good phenomenon,* and what is the focus of positive psychology research?

People aspire to, and wish one another, health and happiness. And for good reason. Our state of happiness or unhappiness colors everything. Happy people perceive the world as safer and feel more confident. They are more decisive and cooperate more easily. They rate job applicants more favorably, savor their positive past experiences without dwelling on the negative, and are more socially connected. They live healthier and more energized and satisfied lives (Boehm et al., 2015; De Neve et al., 2013; Mauss et al., 2011; Stellar et al., 2015).

Moods matter. When your mood is gloomy, life as a whole seems depressing and meaningless—and you think more skeptically and attend more critically to your surroundings. Let your mood brighten, and your thinking broadens and becomes more playful and creative (Baas et al., 2008; Forgas, 2008; Fredrickson, 2013). Relationships, self-image, and hopes for the future also seem more promising. One study showed that the happiest 20-year-olds were later more likely to marry and less likely to divorce (Stutzer & Frey, 2006). In another study, which surveyed thousands of U.S. college students in 1976 and restudied them at age 37, happy students had gone on to earn significantly more money than their less-happy-than-average peers (Diener et al., 2002).

Moreover—and this is one of psychology's most consistent findings—happiness doesn't just feel good, it *does* good. In study after study, a mood-boosting experience such as recalling a happy event has made people more likely to give money, pick up someone's dropped papers, volunteer time, and do other good deeds. Psychologists call it the **feel-good, do-good phenomenon** (Salovey, 1990).

The reverse is also true: Doing good also promotes good feeling. One survey of more than 200,000 people in 136 countries found that, nearly everywhere, people report feeling happier after spending money on others rather than on themselves (Aknin et al., 2013; Dunn et al., 2014). Feeling good even increases people's willingness to donate kidneys. And kidney donation leaves donors feeling good (Brethel-Haurwitz & Marsh, 2014). Young children also show more positive emotion when they give, rather than receive, gifts (Aknin et al., 2015). Some happiness coaches harness the *do-good, feel-good phenomenon* as they assign people to perform a daily "random act of kindness" and keep records of the results.

Positive Psychology

William James was writing about the importance of happiness ("the secret motive for all [we] do") as early as 1902. By the 1960s, the *humanistic psychologists* were interested in advancing human fulfillment. In the twenty-first century, under

feel-good, do-good phenomenon people's tendency to be helpful when already in a good mood.

positive psychology the scientific study of human flourishing, with the goals of discovering and promoting strengths and virtues that help individuals and communities to thrive.

subjective well-being self-perceived happiness or satisfaction with life. Used along with measures of objective well-being (for example, physical and economic indicators) to evaluate people's quality of life.

LaunchPad To test your own well-being and learn about ways to nurture improved well-being, try LaunchPad's *self-assessment activity—Assess Your Strengths: Satisfaction With Life Scale.*

Martin E. P. Seligman "The main purpose of a positive psychology is to measure, understand, and then build the human strengths and the civic virtues."

Courtesy of Martin Seligman

LaunchPad See LaunchPad's *Video: Naturalistic Observation* for a helpful tutorial animation about this type of research design.

"No happiness lasts for long."
Seneca, Agamemnon, C.E. 60

the leadership of American Psychological Association past-president Martin Seligman, **positive psychology** is using scientific methods to study human flourishing. This young subfield includes studies of **subjective well-being**—our feelings of happiness (sometimes defined as a high ratio of positive to negative feelings) or sense of satisfaction with life.

Taken together, satisfaction with the past, happiness with the present, and optimism about the future define the positive psychology movement's first pillar: *positive well-being.* Seligman views happiness as a by-product of a pleasant, engaged, and meaningful life.

Positive psychology is about building not just a pleasant life, says Seligman, but also a good life that engages one's skills, and a meaningful life that points beyond oneself. Thus, the second pillar, *positive character,* focuses on exploring and enhancing creativity, courage, compassion, integrity, self-control, leadership, wisdom, and spirituality.

The third pillar, *positive groups, communities,* and *cultures,* seeks to foster a positive social ecology. This includes healthy families, communal neighborhoods, effective schools, socially responsible media, and civil dialogue.

"Positive psychology," Seligman and colleagues have said (2005), "is an umbrella term for the study of positive emotions, positive character traits, and enabling institutions." Its focus differs from psychology's traditional interests during its first century, when attention was directed toward understanding and alleviating negative states—abuse and anxiety, depression and disease, prejudice and poverty. Indeed, articles on selected negative emotions since 1887 have outnumbered those on positive emotions by 17 to 1.

In ages past, times of relative peace and prosperity have enabled cultures to turn their attention from repairing weakness and damage to promoting what Seligman (2002) has called "the highest qualities of life." Prosperous fifth-century Athens nurtured philosophy and democracy. Flourishing fifteenth-century Florence nurtured great art. Victorian England, flush with the bounty of the British Empire, nurtured honor, discipline, and duty. In this millennium, Seligman believes, thriving Western cultures have a parallel opportunity to create, as a "humane, scientific monument," a more positive psychology, concerned not only with weakness and damage but also with strength and virtue. Thanks to his leadership, the movement has gained strength, with supporters in 77 countries from Croatia to China (IPPA, 2009, 2010; Seligman, 2004, 2011).

What Affects Our Well-Being?

34-10 How do time, wealth, adaptation, and comparison affect our happiness levels?

THE SHORT LIFE OF EMOTIONAL UPS AND DOWNS Are some days of the week happier than others? In what is likely psychology's biggest-ever data sample, social psychologist Adam Kramer (at my [DM's] request and in cooperation with Facebook) did a *naturalistic observation* of emotion words in "billions" of status updates. After eliminating exceptional days, such as holidays, he tracked the frequency of positive and negative emotion words by day of the week. The most positive moods days? Friday and Saturday (**FIGURE 34.6**). A similar analysis of emotion-related words in 59 million Twitter messages found Friday to Sunday the week's happiest days (Golder & Macy, 2011). For you, too?

Over the long run, our emotional ups and downs tend to balance out. This is true even over the course of the day. Positive emotion rises over the early to middle part of most days and then drops off (Kahneman et al., 2004; Watson, 2000). A stressful event—an argument, a sick child, a car problem—can trigger a bad mood. No surprise there. But by the next day, the gloom nearly always lifts (Affleck et al., 1994; Bolger et al., 1989; Stone & Neale, 1984). Our overall judgments of our lives often show lingering effects of good or bad events, but our

daily moods typically rebound (Luhmann et al., 2012). If anything, people tend to bounce back from a bad day to a *better*-than-usual good mood the following day.

Even when negative events drag us down for longer periods, our bad mood usually ends. A romantic breakup feels devastating, but eventually the wound heals. In one study, faculty members up for tenure expected their lives would be deflated by a negative decision. Actually, 5 to 10 years later, their happiness level was about the same as for those who received tenure (Gilbert et al., 1998).

Grief over the loss of a loved one or anxiety after a severe trauma (such as child abuse, rape, or the terrors of war) can linger. But usually, even tragedy is not permanently depressing. People who become blind or paralyzed may not completely recover their previous well-being, but those with an agreeable personality usually recover near-normal levels of day-to-day happiness (Boyce & Wood, 2011). So do those who must go on kidney dialysis or have permanent colostomies (Riis et al., 2005; Smith et al., 2009). Even if you lose the use of all four limbs, explained Daniel Kahneman (2005), "you will gradually start thinking of other things, and the more time you spend thinking of other things the less miserable you are going to be." Contrary to what many people believe, even most patients "locked in" a motionless body do not indicate they want to die (Bruno et al., 2008, 2011; Nizzi et al., 2012; Smith & Delargy, 2005).

The surprising reality: *We overestimate the duration of our emotions and underestimate our resiliency.*

WEALTH AND WELL-BEING "Do you think you would be happier if you made more money?" *Yes,* replied 73 percent of Americans in a 2006 Gallup poll. How important is "being very well off financially"? *Very important,* say 82 percent of entering U.S. collegians (**FIGURE 34.7**).

Money does buy happiness, up to a point. Having enough money to buy your way out of hunger and to have a sense of control over your life predicts greater happiness (Fischer & Boer, 2011). As Australian data confirm, the power of more money to increase happiness is strongest at low incomes (Cummins, 2006). A $1000 annual wage increase does a lot more for the average person in Malawi than for the average person in Switzerland. Raising low incomes will increase happiness more than will raising high incomes.

Once we have enough money for comfort and security, piling up more and more matters less and less. Experiencing luxury diminishes our savoring of life's simpler pleasures (Cooney et al., 2014; Quoidbach et al., 2010). If you ski the Alps once, your neighborhood sledding hill pales. If you ski the Alps every winter, it becomes an ordinary part of life rather than an experience to treasure (Quoidbach et al., 2015).

And consider this: During the last half-century, the average U.S. citizen's buying power almost tripled. Did this greater ability to purchase material

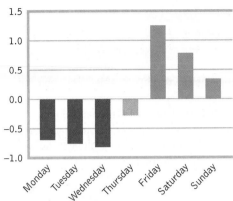

⌃ FIGURE 34.6

Using web science to track happy days Adam Kramer (personal correspondence, 2010) tracked positive and negative emotion words in many "billions" (the exact number is proprietary information) of status updates of U.S. users of Facebook between September 7, 2007, and November 17, 2010.

"Weeping may tarry for the night, but joy comes with the morning."

Psalm 30:5

"But on the positive side, money can't buy happiness—so who cares?"

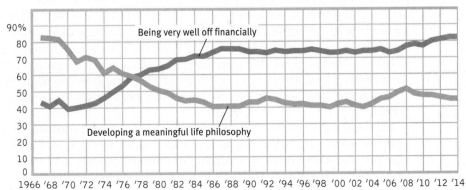

⟨ FIGURE 34.7

The changing materialism of entering collegians Surveys of more than 200,000 entering U.S. collegians per year have revealed an increasing desire for wealth after 1970. (Data from *The American Freshman* surveys, UCLA, 1966 to 2014.)

Does money buy happiness? It surely helps us to avoid certain types of pain. Yet, though average buying power has almost tripled since the 1950s, Americans' reported happiness has remained almost unchanged. (Happiness data from National Opinion Research Center surveys; income data from Historical Statistics of the United States and Economic Indicators.)

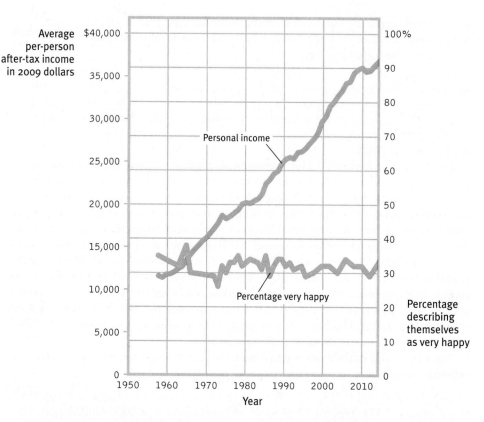

goods—enabling larger homes and twice as many cars per person, not to mention iPads and smart phones—also buy more happiness? As **FIGURE 34.8** shows, Americans have become no happier. In 1957, some 35 percent said they were "very happy," as did slightly fewer—33 percent—in 2012. Much the same has been true of Europe, Australia, and Japan, where increasing real incomes have *not* produced increasing happiness (Australian Unity, 2008; Diener & Biswas-Diener, 2002, 2008; Di Tella & MacCulloch, 2010). Ditto China, where living standards have risen but life satisfaction has not (Davey & Rato, 2012; Easterlin et al., 2012). These findings lob a bombshell at modern materialism: *Economic growth in affluent countries has provided no apparent boost to morale or social well-being.*

HAPPINESS IS RELATIVE: ADAPTATION AND COMPARISON Two psychological principles explain why, for those who are not poor, more money buys little more than a temporary surge of happiness and why our emotions seem attached to elastic bands that pull us back from highs or lows. In its own way, each principle suggests that happiness is relative.

HAPPINESS IS RELATIVE TO OUR OWN EXPERIENCE The **adaptation-level phenomenon** describes our tendency to judge various stimuli in comparison with our past experiences. As psychologist Harry Helson (1898–1977) explained, we adjust our *neutral* levels—the points at which sounds seem neither loud nor soft, temperatures neither hot nor cold, events neither pleasant nor unpleasant—based on our experience. We then notice and react to variations up or down from these levels. Thus, after an initial surge of pleasure, improvements become our "new normal," and we then require something even better to give us a happiness boost.

So, could we ever create a permanent social paradise? Probably not (Campbell, 1975; Di Tella et al., 2010). People who have experienced a recent windfall—from a lottery, an inheritance, or a surging economy—typically feel elated (Diener & Oishi, 2000; Gardner & Oswald, 2007). So would you, if you woke up tomorrow to your utopia—perhaps a world with no bills, no ills, and perfect scores.

adaptation-level phenomenon our tendency to form judgments (of sounds, of lights, of income) relative to a neutral level defined by our prior experience.

relative deprivation the perception that one is worse off relative to those with whom one compares oneself.

But after a time, your utopia would become your new normal. Before long, you would again sometimes feel gratified (when events exceed your expectations) and sometimes feel deprived (when they fall below), and sometimes feel neutral. *The point to remember:* Feelings of satisfaction and dissatisfaction, success and failure are judgments we make based partly on our prior experience (Rutledge et al., 2014). Satisfaction, as Richard Ryan (1999) said, "has a short half-life." Ditto disappointment, which means that you may bounce back from a setback sooner than you expect.

HAPPINESS IS RELATIVE TO OTHERS' SUCCESS We are always comparing ourselves with others. And whether we feel good or bad depends on who those others are (Lyubomirsky, 2001). We are slow-witted or clumsy only when others are smarter or more agile. When we sense that we are worse off than others with whom we compare ourselves, we experience **relative deprivation.**

When expectations soar above attainments, we feel disappointed. Thus, the middle- and upper-income people in a given country, who can compare themselves with the relatively poor, tend to have greater life satisfaction than their less-fortunate compatriots. Nevertheless, once people reach a moderate income level, further increases buy little more happiness. Why? Because as people climb the ladder of success they mostly compare themselves with local peers who are at or above their current level (Gruder, 1977; Suls & Tesch, 1978; Zell & Alicke, 2010). "Beggars do not envy millionaires, though of course they will envy other beggars who are more successful," noted British philosopher Bertrand Russell (1930/1985, p. 90). Thus, "Napoleon envied Caesar, Caesar envied Alexander, and Alexander, I daresay, envied Hercules, who never existed. You cannot, therefore, get away from envy by means of success alone, for there will always be in history or legend some person even more successful than you are" (1930, pp. 68–69).

Over the last half-century, inequality in Western countries has increased. Consider the ratio of pay of an average American CEO listed in Standard & Poor's stock market index (the S&P 500) to the average employee. In 1965, the ratio was 20 to 1. By 2012, the ratio had swelled to 354 to 1 (Kiatpongsan & Norton, 2014). The rising economic tide shown in Figure 34.8 has lifted the yachts higher than the rowboats. Does it matter? *Yes.* Places with great inequality have higher crime rates, obesity, anxiety, and drug use, and lower life expectancy (Kawachi et al., 1999; Ratcliff, 2013; Wilkinson & Pickett, 2009). Times and places with great income inequality also tend to be less happy—a result that people's social comparisons help explain (Cheung & Lucas, 2015; Hagerty, 2000; Helliwell et al., 2013; Oishi et al., 2011).

Just as comparing ourselves with those who are better off creates envy, so counting our blessings as we compare ourselves with those worse off boosts our contentment. In one study, university women considered others' deprivation and suffering (Dermer et al., 1979). They viewed vivid depictions of how grim city life could be in 1900. They imagined and then wrote about various personal tragedies, such as being burned and disfigured. Later, the women expressed greater satisfaction with their own lives. Similarly, when mildly depressed people have read about someone who was even more depressed, they felt somewhat better (Gibbons, 1986). "I cried because I had no shoes," states a Persian saying, "until I met a man who had no feet."

What Predicts Our Happiness Levels?

⟨ ⟩ **34-11** What are some predictors of happiness, and how can we be happier?

Happy people share many characteristics (**TABLE 34.1** on the next page). But why are some people normally so joyful and others so somber? Here, as in so many other areas, the answer is found in the interplay between nature and nurture.

> "I have a 'fortune cookie maxim' that I'm very proud of: Nothing in life is quite as important as you think it is while you are thinking about it. So, nothing will ever make you as happy as you think it will."
>
> *Nobel laureate psychologist Daniel Kahneman, Gallup interview, "What Were They Thinking?" 2005*

"Researchers say I'm not happier for being richer, but do you know how much researchers make?"

The effect of comparison with others helps explain why students of a given level of academic ability tended to have a higher academic self-concept if they attended a school where most other students were not exceptionally able (Marsh & Parker, 1984). If you were near the top of your graduating class, you might feel inferior upon entering a college or university where all students were near the top of their class.

> "Comparison is the thief of joy."
>
> *Attributed to Theodore Roosevelt*

🅼 **LaunchPad** For a 6.5-minute examination of historical and modern views of happiness, visit LaunchPad's *Video: The Search for Happiness.*

∨ TABLE 34.1

Happiness Is . . .

Researchers Have Found That Happy People Tend to	However, Happiness Seems Not Much Related to Other Factors, Such as
Have high self-esteem (in individualist countries).	Age.
Be optimistic, outgoing, and agreeable.	Gender (women are more often depressed, but also more often joyful).
Have close friendships or a satisfying marriage.	Physical attractiveness.
Have work and leisure that engage their skills.	
Have an active religious faith (especially in more religious cultures).	
Sleep well and exercise.	

Sources: DeNeve & Cooper, 1998; Diener et al., 2003, 2011; Headey et al., 2010; Lucas et al., 2004; Myers, 1993, 2000; Myers & Diener, 1995, 1996; Steel et al., 2008. Veenhoven (2014) offers a database of 13,000+ correlates of happiness at www.worlddatabaseofhappiness.eur.nl.

"I could cry when I think of the years I wasted accumulating money, only to learn that my cheerful disposition is genetic."

The New Yorker Collection, 1996. From cartoonbank.com

Genes matter. In one study of hundreds of identical and fraternal twins, about 50 percent of the difference among people's happiness ratings was heritable—attributable to genes (Gigantesco et al., 2011; Lykken & Tellegen, 1996). Other twin studies report similar or slightly less heritability (Bartels & Boomsma, 2009; Lucas, 2008; Nes et al., 2010). Identical twins raised apart are often similarly happy. Moreover, researchers are now drilling down to identify how specific genes influence our happiness (De Neve et al., 2012; Fredrickson et al., 2013).

But our personal history and our culture matter, too. On the personal level, as we have seen, our emotions tend to balance around a level defined by our experience. On the cultural level, groups vary in the traits they value. Self-esteem and achievement matter more to individualist Westerners. Social acceptance and harmony matter more to those in collectivist cultures such as Japan, which stress family and community (Diener et al., 2003; Fulmer et al., 2010; Uchida & Kitayama, 2009).

Depending on our genes, our outlook, and our recent experiences, our happiness seems to fluctuate around our "happiness set point," which disposes some people to be ever upbeat and others more negative. Even so, after following thousands of lives over two decades, researchers have determined that our satisfaction with life can change (Lucas & Donnellan, 2007). Happiness rises and falls, and it can be influenced by factors that are under our control. A striking example: In a long-term German study, married partners were as similarly satisfied with their lives as were identical twins (Schimmack & Lucas, 2007). Relationship quality matters.

If we can enhance our happiness on an *individual* level, could we use happiness research to refocus our *national* priorities more on the pursuit of happiness? Many psychologists believe we could. Ed Diener (2006, 2009, 2013), supported by 52 colleagues, has proposed ways in which nations might measure national well-being. Happiness research offers new ways to assess the impacts of various public policies, argue Diener and his colleagues (Diener et al., 2015). Happy societies are not only prosperous but are also places where people trust one another, feel free, and enjoy close relationships (Helliwell et al., 2013; Oishi & Schimmack, 2010). Thus, in debates about the minimum wage, economic inequality, tax rates, divorce laws, and health care, people's psychological well-being should be a prime consideration—a point now affirmed by 43 nations that have added well-being measures to their national agendas (Diener et al., 2015). Britain's Annual Population Survey, for example, asks its citizens how satisfied they are with their lives, how worthwhile they judge their lives, and how happy and how anxious they felt yesterday (ONS, 2015). Such measures may help guide nations toward policies that decrease stress and foster human flourishing.

Evidence-Based Suggestions for a Happier Life[1]

Your happiness, like your cholesterol level, is genetically influenced. Yet as cholesterol is also influenced by diet and exercise, so happiness is partly under your control (Layous & Lyubomirsky, 2014; Nes, 2010). Here are 11 research-based suggestions for improving your mood and increasing your satisfaction with life.

1. ***Realize that enduring happiness may not come from financial success.*** We adapt to change by adjusting our expectations. Neither wealth, nor any other circumstance we long for, will guarantee happiness.

2. ***Take control of your time.*** Happy people feel in control of their lives. To master your use of time, set goals and divide them into daily aims. We all tend to overestimate how much we will accomplish in any given day. The good news is that we generally *underestimate* how much we can accomplish in a year, given just a little daily progress.

3. ***Act happy.*** Research shows that people who are manipulated into a smiling expression feel better. So put on a happy face. Talk *as if* you feel positive self-esteem, are optimistic, and are outgoing. We can often act our way into a happier state of mind.

4. ***Seek work and leisure that engage your skills.*** Happy people often are in a zone called *flow*—absorbed in tasks that challenge but don't overwhelm them. Passive forms of leisure (watching TV) often provide less flow experience than active forms, such as exercising, socializing, or expressing your musical interests.

5. ***Buy shared experiences rather than things.*** Compared with money spent on stuff, money buys more happiness when spent on experiences that you look forward to, enjoy, remember, and talk about (Carter & Gilovich, 2010; Kumar & Gilovich, 2013). This is especially so for socially shared experiences (Caprariello & Reis, 2012). The shared experience of a college education may cost a lot, but, as pundit Art Buchwald said, "The best things in life aren't things."

RubberBall Selects/Alamy

6. ***Join the "movement" movement.*** Aerobic exercise can relieve mild depression and anxiety as it promotes health and energy. Sound minds reside in sound bodies.

7. ***Give your body the sleep it wants.*** Happy people live active lives yet reserve time for renewing sleep and solitude. Many people suffer from sleep debt, with resulting fatigue, diminished alertness, and gloomy moods.

8. ***Give priority to close relationships.*** Intimate friendships can help you weather difficult times. Confiding is good for soul and body. Compared with unhappy people, happy people engage in less superficial small talk and more meaningful conversations (Mehl et al., 2010). So resolve to nurture your closest relationships by *not* taking your loved ones for granted. This means displaying to them the sort of kindness you display to others, affirming them, playing together, and sharing together.

9. ***Focus beyond self.*** Reach out to those in need. Perform acts of kindness. Happiness increases helpfulness (those who feel good do good). But doing good also makes us feel good.

---

1. Digested from David G. Myers, *The Pursuit of Happiness* (Harper).

10. ***Count your blessings and record your gratitude.*** Keeping a gratitude journal heightens well-being (Emmons, 2007; Seligman et al., 2005). When something good happens, take time to appreciate and savor the experience (Sheldon & Lyubomirsky, 2012). Record positive events and why they occurred. Express your gratitude to others.

11. ***Nurture your spiritual self.*** For many people, faith provides a support community, a reason to focus beyond self, and a sense of purpose and hope. That helps explain why people active in faith communities report greater-than-average happiness and often cope well with crises.

RETRIEVE IT [✻]

• Which of the following factors do NOT predict self-reported happiness? Which factors are better predictors?

a. Age   d. Gender

b. Personality traits   e. Sleep and exercise

c. Close relationships   f. Active religious faith

ANSWERS: Age and gender (a. and d.) do NOT effectively predict happiness levels. Better predictors are personality traits, close relationships, sleep and exercise, and religious faith (b., c., e., and f.).

◔ Learning Objectives

Test Yourself by taking a moment to answer each of these Learning Objective Questions (repeated here from within the module). Then turn to Appendix D, Complete Module Reviews, to check your answers. Research suggests that trying to answer these questions on your own will improve your long-term memory of the concepts (McDaniel et al., 2009).

34-1 In what two ways do people try to alleviate stress?

34-2 How does a perceived lack of control affect health?

34-3 How can our self-control be depleted, and why is it important to build this strength?

34-4 How does an optimistic outlook affect health and longevity?

34-5 How does social support promote good health?

34-6 How effective is aerobic exercise as a way to manage stress and improve well-being?

34-7 In what ways might relaxation and meditation influence stress and health?

34-8 What is the faith factor, and what are some possible explanations for the link between faith and health?

34-9 What is the *feel-good, do-good phenomenon,* and what is the focus of positive psychology research?

34-10 How do time, wealth, adaptation, and comparison affect our happiness levels?

34-11 What are some predictors of happiness, and how can we be happier?

▣⁛ Terms and Concepts to Remember

Test yourself on these terms by trying to write down the definition in your own words before flipping back to the referenced page to check your answers.

coping, p. 419

problem-focused coping, p. 419

emotion-focused coping, p. 419

learned helplessness, p. 419

external locus of control, p. 421

internal locus of control, p. 421

self-control, p. 421

aerobic exercise, p. 426

mindfulness meditation, p. 428

feel-good, do-good phenomenon, p. 431

positive psychology, p. 432

subjective well-being, p. 432

adaptation-level phenomenon, p. 434

relative deprivation, p. 435

[✱] Experience the Testing Effect

Test yourself repeatedly throughout your studies. This will not only help you figure out what you know and don't know; the testing itself will help you learn and remember the information more effectively thanks to the *testing effect*.

1. When faced with a situation over which you feel you have no sense of control, it is most effective to use _____ (emotion/problem)-focused coping.

2. Seligman's research showed that a dog will respond with learned helplessness if it has received repeated shocks and has had
   a. the opportunity to escape.
   b. no control over the shocks.
   c. pain or discomfort.
   d. no food or water prior to the shocks.

3. When elderly patients take an active part in managing their own care and surroundings, their morale and health tend to improve. Such findings indicate that people do better when they experience an _____ (internal/external) locus of control.

4. People who have close relationships are less likely to die prematurely than those who do not, supporting the idea that
   a. social ties can be a source of stress.
   b. gender influences longevity.
   c. Type A behavior is responsible for many premature deaths.
   d. social support has a beneficial effect on health.

5. Because it triggers the release of mood-boosting neurotransmitters such as norepinephrine, serotonin, and the endorphins, _____ exercise raises energy levels and helps alleviate depression and anxiety.

6. Research on the faith factor has found that
   a. pessimists tend to be healthier than optimists.
   b. our expectations influence our feelings of stress.
   c. religiously active people tend to outlive those who are not religiously active.
   d. religious engagement promotes isolation, repression, and ill health.

7. One of the most consistent findings of psychological research is that happy people are also
   a. more likely to express anger.
   b. generally luckier than others.
   c. concentrated in the wealthier nations.
   d. more likely to help others.

8. _____ psychology is a scientific field of study focused on how humans thrive and flourish.

9. After moving to a new apartment, you find the street noise irritatingly loud, but after a while, it no longer bothers you. This reaction illustrates the
   a. relative deprivation principle.
   b. adaptation-level phenomenon.
   c. feel-good, do-good phenomenon.
   d. importance of mindfulness meditation.

10. A philosopher observed that we cannot escape envy, because there will always be someone more successful, more accomplished, or richer with whom to compare ourselves. In psychology, this observation is embodied in the _____ _____ principle.

Find answers to these questions in Appendix E, in the back of the book.

Use 🅜 LearningCurve to create your personalized study plan, which will direct you to the resources that will help you most in 🅜 LaunchPad.

MODULE 35 Social Thinking and Social Influence

SOCIAL INFLUENCE
—Conformity and Group Behavior

Advertisers employ **SOCIAL THINKING** principles

Cool Clothes Inc.

① "learner" at a distance.

MODULE 36 Antisocial Relations

Explicit or *implicit* prejudice demonstrate social inequalities.

PREJUDICE =
stereotypes
(Teenagers are lazy!)
+
emotions (dislike)
+
discrimination
(I'm not hiring him.)

Job Interview

AGGRESSION

- Biological factors: *genetic*, ♂, *neural*, and *biochemical* (testosterone and alcohol)
- Psychological factors: *environment* (hot, crowded, insulting) and *learning* (aggressive behavior models)
- Social/cultural factors: violent *social scripts* from media, music lyrics

MODULE 37 Prosocial Relations

ROMANTIC LOVE = proximity + attractivenes + similarity

- Liking others who reward us
- Passionate love → Companionate love over time
- Best relationships = equity
  +
  mutual self-disclosure
  +
  positive support

ALTRUISM

When do we help, and why?

Are you okay?

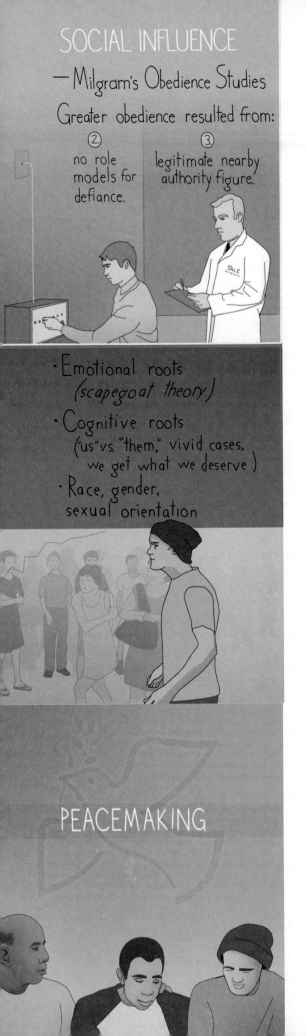

Social Psychology

DIRK Willems faced a moment of decision in 1569. Threatened with torture and death as a member of a persecuted religious minority, he escaped from his Asperen, Holland, prison and fled across an ice-covered pond. His stronger and heavier jailer pursued him but fell through the ice and, unable to climb out, pled for help.

With his freedom in front of him, Willems acted with ultimate selflessness. He turned back and rescued his pursuer, who, under orders, took him back to captivity. A few weeks later Willems was condemned to be "executed with fire, until death ensues." For his martyrdom, present-day Asperen has named a street in honor of its folk hero (Toews, 2004).

What drives people to feel contempt for minority-group members, such as Dirk Willems, and to act so spitefully? And what motivated the selflessness of Willems' response, and of so many who have died trying to save others? Indeed, what motivates any of us when we volunteer kindness and generosity toward others?

As such examples demonstrate, we are social animals. We may assume the best or the worst in others. We may approach them with closed fists or open arms. As the novelist Herman Melville remarked, "We cannot live for ourselves alone. Our lives are connected by a thousand invisible threads." *Social psychologists* explore these connections by scientifically studying how we *think about* and *influence* others (Module 35), and also how we *relate to* one another (Modules 36 and 37). ■

35 Social Thinking and Social Influence

35-1 What do social psychologists study? How do we tend to explain others' behavior and our own?

Unlike sociology, which studies societies and social groupings, social psychologists focus more on how *individuals* view and affect one another.

An etching of Dirk Willems by Dutch artist Jan Luyken (from *Martyrs Mirror, 1685*)

Mennonite Library and Archives/Bethel College

Social Thinking

Personality psychologists focus on the person. They study the personal traits and dynamics that explain why *different people* may act differently in a given *situation,* such as the one Willems faced. (Would you have helped the jailer out of the icy water?) **Social psychologists** focus on the situation. They study the social influences that explain why *the same person* will act differently in *different situations*. Might the jailer have acted differently—opting not to march Willems back to jail—under differing circumstances?

The Fundamental Attribution Error

Our social behavior arises from our social thinking. Especially when the unexpected occurs, we want to understand and explain why people act as they do. After studying how people explain others' behavior, Fritz Heider (1958) proposed an **attribution theory:** We can attribute the behavior to the person's stable, enduring traits (a *dispositional attribution*), or we can attribute it to the situation (a *situational attribution*).

For example, in class, we notice that Juliette seldom talks. Over coffee, Jack talks nonstop. That must be the sort of people they are, we decide. Juliette must be shy and Jack outgoing. Such attributions—to their dispositions—can be valid, because people do have enduring personality traits. But sometimes we fall prey to the **fundamental attribution error** (Ross, 1977): We overestimate the influence of personality and underestimate the influence of situations. In class, Jack may be as quiet as Juliette. Catch Juliette at a party and you may hardly recognize your quiet classmate.

David Napolitan and George Goethals (1979) demonstrated the fundamental attribution error in an experiment with Williams College students. They had students talk, one at a time, with a young woman who acted either cold and critical or warm and friendly. Before the conversations, the researchers told half the students that the woman's behavior would be spontaneous. They told the other half the truth—that they had instructed her to *act* friendly (or unfriendly).

Did hearing the truth affect students' impressions of the woman? Not at all! If the woman acted friendly, both groups decided she really was a warm person. If she acted unfriendly, both decided she really was a cold person. They attributed her behavior to her personal disposition *even when told that her behavior was situational*—that she was merely acting that way for the purposes of the experiment.

WHAT FACTORS AFFECT OUR ATTRIBUTIONS? The fundamental attribution error appears more often in some cultures than in others. Individualist Westerners more often attribute behavior to people's personal traits. People in East Asian cultures are somewhat more sensitive to the power of the situation (Heine & Ruby, 2010; Kitayama et al., 2009). This difference has appeared in experiments that asked people to view scenes, such as a big fish swimming. Americans focused more on the individual fish, and Japanese people more on the whole scene (Chua et al., 2005; Nisbett, 2003).

---

social psychology the scientific study of how we think about, influence, and relate to one another.

attribution theory the theory that we explain someone's behavior by crediting either the situation or the person's disposition.

fundamental attribution error the tendency for observers, when analyzing others' behavior, to underestimate the impact of the situation and to overestimate the impact of personal disposition.

We all commit the fundamental attribution error. Most of us have had the experience of meeting someone we know from a particular situation—a teacher, a boss, a family doctor—in a different context. Often, we may find ourselves surprised by the difference: A teacher who is authoritative and assertive in class seems lower key. The doctor, a revered authority in the office, seems like an ordinary person. Outside their assigned roles, professors seem less professorial, presidents less presidential, managers less managerial.

When we explain *our own* behavior, we are sensitive to how behavior changes with the situation (Idson & Mischel, 2001). (An important exception: We more often attribute our deliberate and admirable actions not to situations but to our own good reasons [Malle, 2006; Malle et al., 2007].) We also are sensitive to the power of the situation when we explain the behavior of people we know well and have seen in different contexts. We more often commit the fundamental attribution error when a stranger acts badly. Having only seen that red-faced fan screaming at the referee in the heat of competition, we may assume he is a bad person. But outside the stadium, he may be a good neighbor and a great parent.

As we act, our eyes look outward; we see others' faces, not our own. If we could take the observer's point of view, would we become more aware of our own personal style? To test this idea, researchers have filmed two people interacting with a camera behind each person. Then they showed each person a replay of their interaction—filmed from the other person's perspective. Seeing their behavior from the other person's perspective, participants better appreciated the power of the situation (Lassiter & Irvine, 1986; Storms, 1973).

WHAT ARE THE CONSEQUENCES OF OUR ATTRIBUTIONS? The way we explain others' actions, attributing them to the person or the situation, can have important real-life effects (Fincham & Bradbury, 1993; Fletcher et al., 1990). A person must decide whether to attribute another's friendliness to romantic interest or social obligation. A partner must decide whether a loved one's tart-tongued remark reflects a mean disposition or a bad day. A jury must decide whether a shooting was malicious or in self-defense. In one study, 181 state judges gave lighter sentences to a violent offender who a scientist testified had a gene that altered brain areas related to aggressiveness (Aspinwall et al., 2012).

Consider the social and economic effects of attribution. How do we explain poverty or unemployment? In Britain, India, Australia, and the United States (Furnham, 1982; Pandey et al., 1982; Wagstaff, 1982; Zucker & Weiner, 1993), political conservatives have tended to attribute responsibility to the personal dispositions of the poor and unemployed: "People generally get what they deserve. Those who take initiative can choose to get ahead." After inviting people to reflect on the power of choice—by having them recall their own choices or take note of another's choices—people become more likely to think that people get what they deserve (Savani & Rattan, 2012). Political liberals, and those not primed to consider the power of choice, are more likely to blame past and present situations: "If you or I had to live with the same poor education, lack of opportunity, and discrimination, would we be any better off? Better to drain the swamps than swat the mosquitoes."

The point to remember: Our attributions—to a person's disposition or to the situation—have real consequences.

🅐 LaunchPad For a quick interactive tutorial, visit LaunchPad's *Concept Practice: Making Attributions.*

Some 7 in 10 college women report having experienced a man misattributing her friendliness as a sexual come-on (Jacques-Tiura et al., 2007).

Dispositional versus situational attributions Should the 2015 slaughter of nine African-Americans attending a church Bible study in Charleston be attributed to the shooter's disposition ("There is one person to blame here. A person filled with hate," said South Carolina governor Nikki Haley)? To America's gun culture ("At some point, we as a country will have to reckon with the fact that this type of mass violence does not happen in other advanced countries . . . with this kind of frequency," said President Obama)? Or to both?

© Richard Ellis/Alamy

Attitudes and Actions

 35-2 How do attitudes and actions interact?

Attitudes are feelings, often influenced by our beliefs, that predispose our reactions to objects, people, and events. If we *believe* someone is threatening us, we may *feel* fear and anger toward the person and *act* defensively. The traffic between our attitudes and our actions is two-way. Our attitudes affect our actions. And our actions affect our attitudes.

ATTITUDES AFFECT ACTIONS Consider the climate change debate. On one side are climate change activists and the Intergovernmental Panel on Climate Change (2014), who warn of accumulating greenhouse gases, melting glaciers, shrinking Arctic ice, rising seas, dying coral reefs, migrating species and vegetation, and extreme and warming weather. On the other side are climate change skeptics, who include many in the general public. The 31 percent who in 1998 thought "the seriousness of global warming is generally exaggerated" had increased to 42 percent by 2014 (Dugan, 2014).

Knowing that public attitudes affect public policies, people on both sides aim to persuade. Persuasion efforts generally take two forms:

- **Peripheral route persuasion** doesn't engage systematic thinking, but does produce fast results as people respond to uninformative cues (such as celebrity endorsements) and make snap judgments. A trusted politician may declare climate change a hoax. A perfume ad may lure us with images of beautiful or famous people in love.

- **Central route persuasion** offers evidence and arguments that aim to trigger favorable thoughts. It occurs mostly when people are naturally analytical or involved in the issue. Climate scientists marshal evidence of climate warming. An automotive ad may itemize a car's great features.

Persuaders try to influence our behavior by changing our attitudes. But other factors, including the situation, also influence our behavior. Strong social pressures, for example, can weaken the attitude-behavior connection (Wallace et al., 2005). In roll-call votes, politicians will sometimes vote what their supporters demand, despite privately disagreeing with those demands (Nagourney, 2002). In such cases, external pressure overrides the attitude-behavior link.

Attitudes are especially likely to affect behavior when external influences are minimal, and when the attitude is stable, specific to the behavior, and easily recalled (Glasman & Albarracín, 2006). One experiment used vivid, easily recalled information to persuade people that sustained tanning put them at risk for future skin cancer. One month later, 72 percent of the participants, and only 16 percent of those in a waitlist control group, had lighter skin (McClendon & Prentice-Dunn, 2001). Persuasion changed attitudes (concerning skin cancer risk), which changed behavior (less tanning).

ACTIONS AFFECT ATTITUDES Now consider a more surprising principle: Not only will people stand up for what they believe, they also will more strongly believe in what they have stood up for. Many streams of evidence confirm that *attitudes follow behavior* (**FIGURE 35.1**).

THE FOOT-IN-THE-DOOR PHENOMENON How do you think you would react if someone induced you to act against your beliefs? In many cases, people adjust their attitudes. During the Korean war, many U.S. prisoners of war were held in war camps run by Chinese communists. Without using brutality, the captors secured the prisoners' collaboration in various activities. Some prisoners merely ran errands or did simple tasks to gain privileges. Others made radio appeals and false confessions. Still others informed

✓ FIGURE 35.1

Attitudes follow behavior Cooperative actions, such as those performed by people on sports teams (including Germany, shown here celebrating their World Cup 2014 victory), feed mutual liking. Such attitudes, in turn, promote positive behavior.

Actions

Attitudes

Jeff J. Mitchell/Getty Images

on fellow prisoners and divulged military information. When the war ended, 21 prisoners chose to stay with the communists. Some of the others returned home "brainwashed"—convinced that communism was a good thing for Asia.

How did the Chinese captors achieve these amazing results? A key ingredient was their effective use of the **foot-in-the-door phenomenon:** They knew that people who agreed to a small request would find it easier to comply later with a larger one. The Chinese began with harmless requests, such as copying a trivial statement, but gradually escalated their demands (Schein, 1956). The next statement to be copied might list flaws of capitalism. Then, to gain privileges, the prisoners participated in group discussions, wrote self-criticisms, or uttered public confessions. After doing so, they often adjusted their beliefs to be more consistent with their public acts. The point is simple: To get people to agree to something big, start small and build (Cialdini, 1993). A trivial act makes the next act easier. Telling a small lie paves the way to telling a bigger lie. Succumb to a temptation and the next temptation becomes harder to resist.

In dozens of experiments, researchers have coaxed people into acting against their attitudes or violating their moral standards, with the same result: Doing becomes believing. After giving in to a request to harm an innocent victim—by making nasty comments or delivering presumed electric shocks—people begin to look down on their victim. After speaking or writing on behalf of a position they have qualms about, they begin to believe their own words.

Fortunately, the attitudes-follow-behavior principle works with good deeds as well. The foot-in-the-door tactic has helped boost charitable contributions and blood donations. In one classic experiment, researchers posing as safe-driving volunteers asked Californians to permit the installation of a large, poorly lettered "Drive Carefully" sign in their front yards. Only 17 percent consented. They approached other homeowners with a small request first: Would they display a 3-inch-high "Be a Safe Driver" sign? Nearly all readily agreed. When reapproached two weeks later to allow the large, ugly sign in their front yards, 76 percent consented (Freedman & Fraser, 1966). To secure a big commitment, it often pays to put your foot in the door.

Racial attitudes likewise follow behavior. In the years immediately following the introduction of school desegregation in the United States and the passage of the Civil Rights Act of 1964, White Americans expressed diminishing racial prejudice. And as Americans in different regions came to act more alike—thanks to more uniform national standards against discrimination—they began to think more alike. Experiments confirm the observation: Moral action strengthens moral convictions.

ROLE PLAYING AFFECTS ATTITUDES When you adopt a new **role**—when you become a college student, marry, or begin a new job—you strive to follow the social prescriptions. At first, your behaviors may feel phony, because you are *acting* a role. Soldiers may at first feel they are playing war games. Newlyweds may feel they are "playing house." Before long, however, what began as playacting in the theater of life becomes *you*. Researchers have confirmed this effect by assessing people's attitudes before and after they adopt a new role—sometimes in laboratory situations and sometimes in everyday situations, such as before and after taking a job.

Role playing morphed into real life in one famous and controversial study in which male college students volunteered to spend time in a simulated prison. Stanford psychologist Philip Zimbardo (1972) randomly assigned some volunteers to be guards. He gave them uniforms, clubs, and whistles and instructed them to enforce certain rules. Others became prisoners, locked in barren cells and forced to wear humiliating outfits. For a day or two, the volunteers self-consciously "played" their roles. Then the simulation became real—too real. Some guards

---

attitude feelings, often influenced by our beliefs, that predispose us to respond in a particular way to objects, people, and events.

peripheral route persuasion occurs when people are influenced by incidental cues, such as a speaker's attractiveness.

central route persuasion occurs when interested people focus on the arguments and respond with favorable thoughts.

foot-in-the-door phenomenon the tendency for people who have first agreed to a small request to comply later with a larger request.

role a set of expectations (norms) about a social position, defining how those in the position ought to behave.

"If the King destroys a man, that's proof to the King it must have been a bad man."
Thomas Cromwell, in Robert Bolt's A Man for All Seasons, 1960

"Fake it until you make it."
Alcoholics Anonymous saying

Video material is provided by BBC Worldwide Learning and CBS New Archives, and produced by Princeton Academic Resources.

LaunchPad To view Philip Zimbardo's 14-minute illustration and explanation of his famous prison simulation, visit the LaunchPad *Video—The Stanford Prison Study: The Power of the Situation.*

developed disparaging attitudes, and devised cruel and degrading routines. One by one, the prisoners broke down, rebelled, or became passively resigned. After only six days, Zimbardo called off the study.

Critics question the reliability of Zimbardo's results (Griggs, 2014). But this much seems true: Role playing can train torturers (Staub, 1989). In the early 1970s, the Greek military government eased men into their roles. First, a trainee stood guard outside an interrogation cell. After this "foot in the door" step, he stood guard inside. Only then was he ready to become actively involved in the questioning and torture. What we do, we gradually become. In one study of German males, military training toughened their personalities, leaving them less agreeable even five years later, after leaving the military (Jackson et al., 2012). And it's true of us all: Every time we act like the people around us, we slightly change ourselves to be more like them, and less like who we used to be.

Yet people differ. In Zimbardo's Stanford Prison simulation and in other atrocity-producing situations, some people have succumbed to the situation and others have not (Carnahan & McFarland, 2007; Haslam & Reicher, 2007, 2012; Mastroianni & Reed, 2006; Zimbardo, 2007). Person and situation interact. Much as water dissolves salt but not sand, so rotten situations turn some people into bad apples while others resist (Johnson, 2007).

The power of the situation
In his 1972 Stanford Prison simulation, Philip Zimbardo created a toxic situation (left). Those assigned to the guard role soon degraded the prisoners. In real life in 2004, some U.S. military guards tormented Iraqi prisoners at the U.S.-run Abu Ghraib prison (right). To Zimbardo (2004, 2007), it was a bad barrel rather than a few bad apples that led to the Abu Ghraib atrocities: "When ordinary people are put in a novel, evil place, such as most prisons, Situations Win, People Lose."

Philip G. Zimbardo, Inc.

AP Photo

COGNITIVE DISSONANCE: RELIEF FROM TENSION So far, we have seen that actions can affect attitudes, sometimes turning prisoners of war into collaborators, doubters into believers, and compliant guards into abusers. But why? One explanation is that when we become aware that our attitudes and actions don't coincide, we experience tension, or *cognitive dissonance*. Indeed, the brain regions that become active when people experience cognitive conflict and negative arousal also become active when people experience cognitive dissonance (Kitayama et al., 2013). To relieve this tension, according to Leon Festinger's (1957) **cognitive dissonance theory,** we often bring our attitudes into line with our actions.

Dozens of experiments have explored this cognitive dissonance phenomenon. Many have made people feel responsible for behavior that clashed with their attitudes and had foreseeable consequences. In one of these experiments, you might agree for a measly $2 to help a researcher by writing an essay that supports something you don't believe in (perhaps a tuition increase). Feeling responsible for the statements (which are inconsistent with your attitudes), you would probably feel dissonance, especially if you thought your essay might influence an administrator. To reduce the uncomfortable tension, you might start believing your phony words. At such times, it's as if we rationalize, "If I chose to do it (or say it), I must believe in it." The less coerced and more responsible we feel for a troubling act—

cognitive dissonance theory the theory that we act to reduce the discomfort (dissonance) we feel when two of our thoughts (cognitions) are inconsistent. For example, when we become aware that our attitudes and our actions clash, we can reduce the resulting dissonance by changing our attitudes.

as after writing that essay for only $2 and not $100—the more dissonance we feel. The more dissonance we feel, the more motivated we are to find consistency, such as changing our attitudes to help justify the act.

The attitudes-follow-behavior principle has a heartening implication: We cannot directly control all our feelings, but we can influence them by altering our behavior. If we are down in the dumps, we can do as cognitive-behavioral therapists advise and talk in more positive, self-accepting ways with fewer self–put-downs. If we are unloving, we can become more loving by behaving as if we were so—by doing thoughtful things, expressing affection, giving affirmation. That helps explain why teens' doing volunteer work promotes a compassionate identity. "Assume a virtue, if you have it not," says Hamlet to his mother. "For use can almost change the stamp of nature." Pretense can become reality. Conduct sculpts character. What we do we become.

The point to remember: Cruel acts shape the self. But so do acts of good will. Act as though you like someone, and you soon may. Changing our behavior can change how we think about others and how we feel about ourselves.

LaunchPad To check your understanding of cognitive dissonance, visit LaunchPad's *Concept Practice: Cognitive Dissonance.*

"Sit all day in a moping posture, sigh, and reply to everything with a dismal voice, and your melancholy lingers. . . . If we wish to conquer undesirable emotional tendencies in ourselves, we must . . . go through the outward movements of those contrary dispositions which we prefer to cultivate."

William James,
Principles of Psychology, *1890*

RETRIEVE IT [✖]

• Driving to school one snowy day, Marco narrowly misses a car that slides through a red light. "Slow down! What a terrible driver," he thinks to himself. Moments later, Marco himself slips through an intersection and yelps, "Wow! These roads are awful. The city plows need to get out here." What social psychology principle has Marco just demonstrated? Explain.

ANSWER: By attributing the other person's behavior to the person ("he's a terrible driver") and his own to the situation ("these roads are awful!"), Marco has exhibited the *fundamental attribution error*.

• How do our attitudes and our actions affect each other?

ANSWER: Our attitudes often influence our actions as we behave in ways consistent with our beliefs. However, our actions also influence our attitudes; we come to believe in what we have done.

• When people act in a way that is not in keeping with their attitudes, and then change their attitudes to match those actions, _____ _____ theory attempts to explain why.

ANSWER: cognitive dissonance

Social Influence

Social psychology's great lesson is the enormous power of social influence. This influence can be seen in our conformity, our obedience to authority, and our group behavior. Suicides, bomb threats, airplane hijackings, and UFO sightings all have a curious tendency to come in clusters. On campus, jeans are the dress code; on New York's Wall Street or London's Bond Street, dress suits are the norm. When we know how to act, how to groom, how to talk, life functions smoothly. Armed with social influence principles, advertisers, fundraisers, and campaign workers aim to sway our decisions to buy, to donate, to vote. Isolated with others who share their grievances, dissenters may gradually become rebels, and rebels may become terrorists. We'll start by considering the nature of our cultural influences. Then we will examine the pull of our social strings. How strong are they? How do they operate? When do we break them?

"Have you ever noticed how one example—good or bad—can prompt others to follow? How one illegally parked car can give permission for others to do likewise? How one racial joke can fuel another?"

Marian Wright Edelman,
The Measure of Our Success, *1992*

Cultural Influences

 35-3 How does culture affect our behavior?

Compared with the narrow path taken by flies, fish, and foxes, the road along which environment drives us is wider. The mark of our species—nature's great gift to us—is our ability to learn and adapt. We come equipped with a huge cerebral hard drive ready to receive cultural software.

Culture is the behaviors, ideas, attitudes, values, and traditions shared by a group of people and transmitted from one generation to the next (Brislin, 1988; Cohen, 2009). Human nature, noted Roy Baumeister (2005), seems designed for culture. We are social animals, but more. Wolves are social animals; they live and hunt in packs. Ants are incessantly social, never alone. But "culture is a better way of being social," observed Baumeister. Wolves function pretty much as they did 10,000 years ago. We enjoy things that were unknown to most of our century-ago ancestors, including electricity, indoor plumbing, antibiotics, and the Internet.

We can thank our culture's mastery of language for this *preservation of innovation.* The *division of labor* also helps. Although two lucky people get their names on the cover of this book (which transmits accumulated cultural wisdom), the product actually results from the coordination and commitment of a gifted team of people, no one of whom could produce it alone.

Across cultures, we differ in our language, our monetary systems, our sports, even which side of the road we drive on. But beneath these differences is our great similarity—our capacity for culture. Culture works. It transmits the customs and beliefs that enable us to communicate, to exchange money for things, to play, to eat, and to drive with agreed-upon rules and without crashing into one another.

VARIATION ACROSS CULTURES We see our adaptability in cultural variations among our beliefs and our values, in how we nurture our children and bury our dead, and in what we wear (or whether we wear anything at all). We are ever mindful that the readers of this book are culturally diverse. You and your ancestors reach from Australia to Africa and from Singapore to Sweden.

Riding along with a unified culture is like running with the wind: As it carries us along, we hardly notice it. When we try running *against* the wind we feel its force. Face to face with a different culture, we become aware of the cultural winds. Stationed in Iraq, Afghanistan, and Kuwait, American and European soldiers were reminded how liberal their home cultures were. Each cultural group evolves its own **norms**—rules for accepted and expected behavior. The British have a norm for orderly waiting in line. Many South Asians use only the right hand's fingers for eating. Sometimes social expectations seem oppressive: "Why should it matter what I wear?" Yet, norms grease the social machinery and can free us from self-preoccupation.

When cultures collide, their differing norms often befuddle. Should we greet people by shaking hands, bowing, or kissing one or both cheeks? Knowing what sorts of gestures and compliments are culturally appropriate helps us avoid accidental insults and embarrassment.

VARIATION OVER TIME Like biological creatures, cultures vary and compete for resources, and thus evolve over time (Mesoudi, 2009). Consider how rapidly cultures may change. English poet Geoffrey Chaucer (1342–1400) is separated from a modern Briton by only 20 generations, but the two would have difficulty communicating. In the thin slice of history since 1960, most Western cultures have changed with remarkable speed. Minority groups enjoy expanded human rights. Middle-class people today fly to places they once only read about. They enjoy the convenience of air-conditioned housing, online shopping, anywhere-anytime electronic communication, and—enriched by doubled per-person real income— eating out more than twice as often as did their grandparents.

But some changes seem not so wonderfully positive. Had you fallen asleep in the United States in 1960 and awakened today, you would open your eyes to a culture with more divorce and depression. You would also find North Americans—like their counterparts in Britain, Australia, and New Zealand—spending more hours at work, fewer hours with friends and family, and fewer hours asleep (BLS, 2011; Putnam, 2000).

Whether we love or loathe these changes, we cannot fail to be impressed by their breathtaking speed. And we cannot explain them by changes in the human gene pool, which evolves far too slowly to account for high-speed cultural transformations. Cultures vary. Cultures change. And cultures shape our lives.

culture the enduring behaviors, ideas, attitudes, values, and traditions shared by a group of people and transmitted from one generation to the next.

norm an understood rule for accepted and expected behavior. Norms prescribe "proper" behavior.

• What is *culture*, and how does its transmission distinguish us from other social animals?

ANSWER: Culture represents our shared behaviors, ideas, attitudes, values, and traditions, which we transmit across generations by way of our language ability. Culture, with its language and efficient division of labor, allows us to preserve innovation.

Conformity: Complying With Social Pressures

35-4 What is automatic mimicry, and how do conformity experiments reveal the power of social influence?

AUTOMATIC MIMICRY Fish swim in schools. Birds fly in flocks. And humans, too, tend to go with their group, to think what it thinks and do what it does. Behavior is contagious. Chimpanzees are more likely to yawn after observing another chimpanzee yawn (Anderson et al., 2004). Ditto for humans. If one of us yawns, laughs, coughs, scratches an itch, stares at the sky, or checks a cell phone, others in our group will often do the same (Holle et al., 2012). Yawn mimicry can also occur across species: Dogs more often yawn after observing their owners' yawn (Silva et al., 2012). Even just reading about yawning increases people's yawning (Provine, 2012), as perhaps you have noticed?

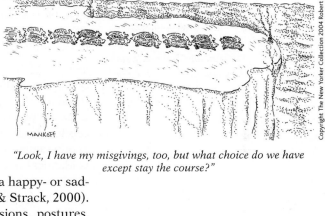

"Look, I have my misgivings, too, but what choice do we have except stay the course?"

Like the chameleon lizards that take on the color of their surroundings, we humans take on the emotional tones of those around us. Just hearing someone reading a neutral text in either a happy- or sad-sounding voice creates "mood contagion" in listeners (Neumann & Strack, 2000). We are natural mimics, unconsciously imitating others' expressions, postures, and voice tones.

Tanya Chartrand and John Bargh captured this automatic mimicry, which they call the *chameleon effect* (Chartrand & Bargh, 1999). They had students work in a room alongside another person, who was actually a "confederate" working for the experimenters. Sometimes the confederates rubbed their own face. Sometimes they shook their foot. Sure enough, the students tended to rub their face with the face-rubbing person and shake their foot with the foot-shaking person.

Automatic mimicry helps us to *empathize*—to feel what others are feeling. This helps explain why we feel happier around happy people than around depressed people. It also helps explain why studies of groups of British workers have revealed *mood linkage*—or the sharing of moods (Totterdell et al., 1998). Empathic people yawn more after seeing others yawn (Morrison, 2007). And empathic mimicking fosters fondness (van Baaren et al., 2003, 2004). Rejected people, who crave social acceptance, often try to mimic their way into new relationships (Lakin et al., 2008). Perhaps you've noticed that when someone nods their head as you do and echoes your words, you feel a certain rapport and liking?

Suggestibility and mimicry sometimes lead to tragedy. In the eight days following the 1999 shooting rampage at Colorado's Columbine High School, every U.S. state except Vermont experienced threats of copycat violence. Pennsylvania alone recorded 60 such threats (Cooper, 1999). Sociologist David Phillips and his colleagues (1985, 1989) found that suicides, too, sometimes increase following a highly publicized suicide. In the wake of screen idol Marilyn Monroe's suicide on August 5, 1962, for example, the number of suicides in the United States exceeded the usual August count by 200.

Conforming to nonconformity Are these students asserting their individuality or identifying themselves with others of the same microculture?

conformity adjusting our behavior or thinking to coincide with a group standard.

normative social influence influence resulting from a person's desire to gain approval or avoid disapproval.

informational social influence influence resulting from one's willingness to accept others' opinions about reality.

NON SEQUITUR   by WILEY

"When I see synchrony and mimicry—whether it concerns yawning, laughing, dancing, or aping—I see social connection and bonding."

Primatologist Frans de Waal
"The Empathy Instinct," 2009

What causes behavior clusters? Do people act similarly because of their influence on one another? Or because they are simultaneously exposed to the same events and conditions? Seeking answers to such questions, social psychologists have conducted experiments on group pressure and conformity.

CONFORMITY AND SOCIAL NORMS Suggestibility and mimicry are subtle types of **conformity**—adjusting our behavior or thinking toward some group standard. To study conformity, Solomon Asch (1955) devised a simple test. Imagine yourself as a participant in what you believe is a study of visual perception. You arrive in time to take a seat at a table with five other people. The experimenter asks the group to state, one by one, which of three comparison lines is identical to a standard line. You see clearly that the answer is Line 2, and you await your turn to say so. Your boredom begins to show when the next set of lines proves equally easy.

Now comes the third trial, and the correct answer seems just as clear-cut (**FIGURE 35.2**). But the first person gives what strikes you as a wrong answer: "Line 3." When the second person and then the third and fourth give the same wrong answer, you sit up straight and squint. When the fifth person agrees with the first four, you feel your heart begin to pound. The experimenter then looks to you for your answer. Torn between the unanimity voiced by the five others and the evidence of your own eyes, you feel tense and suddenly unsure. You hesitate before answering, wondering whether you should suffer the discomfort of being the oddball. What answer do you give?

In Asch's experiments, college students, answering questions alone, erred less than 1 percent of the time. But what about when several others—confederates working for the experimenter—answered incorrectly? Although most people told the truth even when others did not, Asch was disturbed by his result: More than one-third of the time, these "intelligent and well-meaning" college students were "willing to call white black" by going along with the group.

▼ FIGURE 35.2

Asch's conformity experiments Which of the three comparison lines is equal to the standard line? What do you suppose most people would say after hearing five others say, "Line 3"? In this photo from one of Asch's experiments, the student in the center shows the severe discomfort that comes from disagreeing with the responses of other group members (in this case, accomplices of the experimenter).

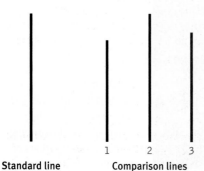

Standard line   Comparison lines

Later investigations have not always found as much conformity as Asch found, but they have revealed that we are more likely to conform when we

- are made to feel incompetent or insecure.

- are in a group with at least three people.

- are in a group in which everyone else agrees. (If just one other person disagrees, the odds of our disagreeing greatly increase.)

- admire the group's status and attractiveness.

- have not made a prior commitment to any response.

- know that others in the group will observe our behavior.

- are from a culture that strongly encourages respect for social standards.

Tattoos: Yesterday's nonconformity, today's conformity? As tattoos become perceived as fashion conformity, their popularity may wane.

Why do we so often think what others think and do what they do? Why, in college residence halls, do students' attitudes become more similar to those living near them (Cullum & Harton, 2007)? Why, when asked controversial questions, are students' answers more diverse when using anonymous electronic clickers than when publicly raising hands (Stowell et al., 2010)? Why do we clap when others clap, eat as others eat, believe what others believe, say what others say, even see what others see?

Frequently, we conform to avoid rejection or to gain social approval (Williams & Sommer, 1997). In such cases, we are responding to **normative social influence.** We are sensitive to social norms—understood rules for accepted and expected behavior—because the price we pay for being different can be severe. We need to belong.

At other times, we conform because we want to be accurate. Groups provide information, and only an uncommonly stubborn person will never listen to others. "Those who never retract their opinions love themselves more than they love truth," observed Joseph Joubert, an eighteenth-century French essayist. When we accept others' opinions about reality, we are responding to **informational social influence.** As Rebecca Denton demonstrated in 2004, sometimes it pays to assume others are right and to follow their lead. Denton set a record for the longest distance driven on the wrong side of a British divided highway—30 miles, with only one minor sideswipe, before the motorway ran out and police were able to puncture her tires. Denton, who was intoxicated, later explained that she thought the hundreds of other drivers coming at her were all on the wrong side of the road (Woolcock, 2004).

"I love the little ways you're identical to everyone else."

Is conformity good or bad? The answer depends partly on our culturally influenced values. Western Europeans and people in most English-speaking countries tend to prize *individualism* (cultural focus on an independent self). People in many Asian, African, and Latin American countries place a higher value on *collectivism* (honoring group standards). In social influence experiments across 17 countries, conformity rates have been lower in individualist cultures (Bond & Smith, 1996).

Like humans, migrating and herding animals conform for both informational and normative reasons (Claidière & Whiten, 2012). Following others is informative: Compared with solo geese, a flock of geese migrate more accurately. (There is wisdom in the crowd.) But staying with the herd also sustains group membership.

LaunchPad To review the classic conformity studies and experience a simulated experiment, visit LaunchPad's *PsychSim 6: Everybody's Doing It!*

RETRIEVE IT

- Which of the following strengthens conformity to a group?

 a. Finding the group attractive

 b. Feeling secure

 c. Coming from an individualist culture

 d. Having made a prior commitment

ANSWER: a

Obedience: Following Orders

35-5 What did Milgram's obedience experiments teach us about the power of social influence?

Social psychologist Stanley Milgram (1963, 1974), a high school classmate of Philip Zimbardo and later a student of Solomon Asch, knew that people often give in to social pressures. But how would they respond to outright commands? To find out, he undertook what became social psychology's most famous and controversial experiments (Benjamin & Simpson, 2009).

Imagine yourself as one of the nearly 1000 people who took part in Milgram's 20 experiments. You respond to an advertisement for participants in a Yale University psychology study of the effect of punishment on learning. Professor Milgram's assistant asks you and another person to draw slips from a hat to see who will be the "teacher" and who will be the "learner." Because (unknown to you) both slips say "teacher," you draw a "teacher" slip and are asked to sit down in front of a machine, which has a series of labeled switches. The supposed learner, a mild and submissive-seeming man, is led to an adjoining room and strapped into a chair. From the chair, wires run through the wall to your machine. You are given your task: Teach and then test the learner on a list of word pairs. If the learner gives a wrong answer, you are to flip a switch to deliver a brief electric shock. For the first wrong answer, you will flip the switch labeled "15 Volts—Slight Shock." With each succeeding error, you will move to the next higher voltage. With each flip of a switch, lights flash and electronic switches buzz.

The experiment begins, and you deliver the shocks after the first and second wrong answers. If you continue, you hear the learner grunt when you flick the third, fourth, and fifth switches. After you activate the eighth switch ("120 Volts—Moderate Shock"), the learner cries out that the shocks are painful. After the tenth switch ("150 Volts—Strong Shock"), he begins shouting. "Get me out of here! I won't be in the experiment anymore! I refuse to go on!" You draw back, but the stern experimenter prods you: "Please continue—the experiment requires that you continue." You resist, but the experimenter insists, "It is absolutely essential that you continue," or "You have no other choice, you *must* go on."

If you obey, you hear the learner shriek in apparent agony as you continue to raise the shock level after each new error. After the 330-volt level, the learner refuses to answer and falls silent. Still, the experimenter pushes you toward the final, 450-volt switch. "Ask the question," he says. "And if no correct answer is given, administer the next shock level."

Would you follow the experimenter's commands to shock someone? At what level would you refuse to obey? Before undertaking the experiments, Milgram asked nonparticipating people what they would do. Most people were sure they would stop soon after the learner first indicated pain, certainly before he shrieked in agony. Forty psychiatrists agreed with that prediction when Milgram asked them. Were the predictions accurate? Not even close. When Milgram conducted the experiment with other men aged 20 to 50, he was astonished. More than 60 percent complied fully—right up to the last switch. When he ran a new study, with 40 new "teachers" and a learner who complained of a "slight heart condition," the results were similar. A full 65 percent of the new teachers obeyed the experimenter right up to 450 volts (**FIGURE 35.3**). In 10 later studies, women obeyed at rates similar to men's (Blass, 1999).

Cultures change over time. Researchers wondered if Milgram's results could be explained by the 1960s American mind-set. To find out, Jerry Burger (2009) replicated Milgram's basic experiment. Seventy percent of the participants obeyed up to the 150-volt point, only a slight reduction from Milgram's 83 percent. And in a French reality TV show replication, 81 percent of people, egged on by a cheering audience, obeyed and tortured a screaming victim (Beauvois et al., 2012).

LaunchPad See LaunchPad's *Video: Research Ethics* for a helpful tutorial animation.

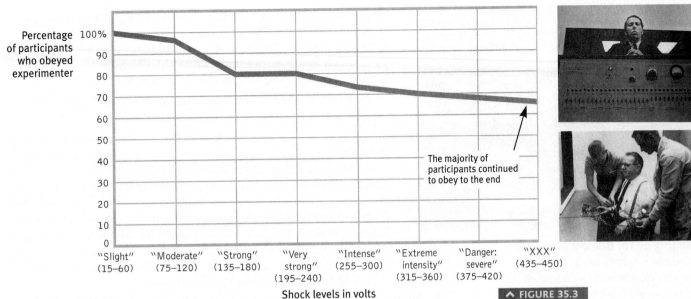

Percentage of participants who obeyed experimenter

The majority of participants continued to obey to the end

"Slight" (15–60)   "Moderate" (75–120)   "Strong" (135–180)   "Very strong" (195–240)   "Intense" (255–300)   "Extreme intensity" (315–360)   "Danger: severe" (375–420)   "XXX" (435–450)

Shock levels in volts

Stanley Milgram, from the film "Obedience." Rights Courtesy of Alexandra Milgram

∧ FIGURE 35.3

Milgram's follow-up obedience experiment In a repeat of the earlier experiment, 65 percent of the adult male "teachers" fully obeyed the experimenter's commands to continue. They did so despite the "learner's" earlier mention of a heart condition, and despite hearing cries of protest after they administered what they thought were 150 volts and agonized protests after 330 volts. (Data from Milgram, 1974.)

Did the teachers figure out the hoax—that no real shock was being delivered and the learner was in fact a confederate who was pretending to feel pain? Did they realize the experiment was really testing their willingness to comply with commands to inflict punishment? *No.* The teachers typically displayed genuine distress: They perspired, trembled, laughed nervously, and bit their lips.

Milgram's use of deception and stress triggered a debate over his research ethics. In his own defense, Milgram pointed out that, after the participants learned of the deception and actual research purposes, virtually none regretted taking part (though perhaps by then the participants had reduced their cognitive dissonance—the discomfort they felt when their actions conflicted with their attitudes). When 40 of the teachers who had agonized most were later interviewed by a psychiatrist, none appeared to be suffering emotional aftereffects. All in all, said Milgram, the experiments provoked less enduring stress than university students experience when facing and failing big exams (Blass, 1996). Other scholars, however, after delving into Milgram's archives, report that his debriefing was less extensive and his participants' distress greater than what he had suggested (Nicholson, 2011; Perry, 2013).

In later experiments, Milgram discovered some conditions that influence people's behavior. When he varied the situation, full obedience ranged from 0 to 93 percent. Obedience was highest when

- *the person giving the orders was close at hand and was perceived to be a legitimate authority figure.* Such was the case in 2005 when Temple University's basketball coach sent a 250-pound bench player, Nehemiah Ingram, into a game with instructions to commit "hard fouls." Following orders, Ingram fouled out in four minutes after breaking an opposing player's right arm.

- *the authority figure was supported by a powerful or prestigious institution.* Compliance was somewhat lower when Milgram dissociated his experiments from Yale University. People have wondered: Why, during the 1994 Rwandan genocide, did so many Hutu citizens slaughter their Tutsi neighbors? It was partly because they were part of "a culture in which orders from above, even if evil," were understood as having the force of law (Kamatali, 2014).

- *the victim was depersonalized or at a distance, even in another room.* Similarly, many soldiers in combat either have not fired their rifles at an enemy they can see, or have not aimed them properly. Such refusals to kill have been

Jeff Widener/AP Photo

Standing up for democracy Some individuals—roughly one in three in Milgram's experiments—resist social coercion, as did this unarmed man in Beijing, by single-handedly challenging an advancing line of tanks the day after the 1989 Tiananmen Square student uprising was suppressed.

rare among soldiers who were operating long-distance artillery or aircraft weapons (Padgett, 1989). Those who killed from a distance—by operating remotely piloted drones—also have suffered much less posttraumatic stress than have on-the-ground Afghanistan and Iraq War veterans (Miller, 2012a).

- *there were no role models for defiance.* "Teachers" did not see any other participant disobey the experimenter.

The power of legitimate, close-at-hand authorities was apparent among those who followed orders to carry out the Nazis' Holocaust atrocities. Obedience alone does not explain the Holocaust—anti-Semitic ideology also contributed (Mastroianni, 2002). But obedience was a factor. In the summer of 1942, nearly 500 middle-aged German reserve police officers were dispatched to German-occupied Jozefow, Poland. On July 13, the group's visibly upset commander informed his recruits, mostly family men, of their orders. They were to round up the village's Jews, who were said to be aiding the enemy. Able-bodied men would be sent to work camps, and the rest would be shot on the spot.

The commander gave the recruits a chance to refuse to participate in the executions. Only about a dozen immediately refused. Within 17 hours, the remaining 485 officers killed 1500 helpless women, children, and elderly, shooting them in the back of the head as they lay face down. Hearing the victims' pleas, and seeing the gruesome results, some 20 percent of the officers did eventually dissent, managing either to miss their victims or to wander away and hide until the slaughter was over (Browning, 1992). In real life, as in Milgram's experiments, those who resisted were the minority.

A different story played out in the French village of Le Chambon. There, villagers openly defied orders to cooperate with the "New Order": they sheltered French Jews, who were destined for deportation to Germany, and sometimes helped them escape across the Swiss border. The villagers' Protestant ancestors had themselves been persecuted, and their pastors taught them to "resist whenever our adversaries will demand of us obedience contrary to the orders of the Gospel" (Rochat, 1993). Ordered by police to give a list of sheltered Jews, the head pastor modeled defiance: "I don't know of Jews, I only know of human beings." At great personal risk, the resisters made an initial commitment to resist. Throughout the long, terrible war, they suffered poverty and were punished for their disobedience. Still, supported by their beliefs, their role models, their interactions with one another, and their own initial acts, they remained defiant to the war's end.

LESSONS FROM THE OBEDIENCE STUDIES What do the Milgram experiments teach us about ourselves? How does flicking a shock switch relate to everyday social behavior? Psychological experiments aim not to re-create the literal behaviors of everyday life but to capture and explore the underlying processes that shape those behaviors. Participants in Milgram's experiments confronted a dilemma we all face frequently: Do I adhere to my own standards, even when they conflict with expectations?

In Milgram's experiments and their modern replications, participants were torn. Should they respond to the pleas of the victim or the orders of the experimenter? Their moral sense warned them not to harm another, yet it also prompted them to obey the experimenter and to be a good research participant. With kindness and obedience on a collision course, obedience usually won.

These experiments demonstrated that strong social influences can make people conform to falsehoods or capitulate to cruelty. Milgram saw this as the fundamental lesson of this work: "Ordinary people, simply doing their jobs, and without any particular hostility on their part, can become agents in a terrible destructive process" (1974, p. 6).

"I was only following orders."

Adolf Eichmann,
director of Nazi deportation of Jews
to concentration camps

Focusing on the end point—450 volts, or someone's real-life violence—we can hardly comprehend the inhumanity. But we ignore how they get there, in tiny increments. Milgram did not entrap his teachers by asking them first to zap learners with enough electricity to make their hair stand on end. Rather, he exploited the foot-in-the-door effect, beginning with a little tickle of electricity and escalating step by step. In the minds of those throwing the switches, the small action became justified, making the next act tolerable. In Le Chambon, as in Milgram's experiments, those who resisted usually did so early. After the first acts of compliance or resistance, attitudes began to follow and justify behavior.

So it happens when people succumb, gradually, to evil. In any society, great evils often grow out of people's compliance with lesser evils. The Nazi leaders suspected that most German civil servants would resist shooting or gassing Jews directly, but they found them surprisingly willing to handle the paperwork of the Holocaust (Silver & Geller, 1978). Milgram found a similar reaction in his experiments. When he asked 40 men to administer the learning test while someone else did the shocking, 93 percent complied. Cruelty does not require devilish villains. All it takes is ordinary people corrupted by an evil situation. Ordinary students may follow orders to haze initiates into their group. Ordinary employees may follow orders to produce and market harmful products. Ordinary soldiers may follow orders to punish and torture prisoners (Lankford, 2009).

> "All evil begins with 15 volts."
>
> *Philip Zimbardo,*
> *Stanford lecture, 2010*

RETRIEVE IT [✕]

- Psychology's most famous obedience experiments, in which most participants obeyed an authority figure's demands to inflict presumed painful, dangerous shocks on an innocent participant, were conducted by social psychologist _____ _____.

  ANSWER: Stanley Milgram

- What situations have researchers found to be most likely to encourage obedience in participants?

  ANSWER: The Milgram studies showed that people were most likely to follow orders when the experimenter was nearby and was a legitimate authority figure, the victim was not nearby, and there were no models for defiance.

Group Behavior

 35-6 How is our behavior affected by the presence of others?

Imagine standing in a room, holding a fishing pole. Your task is to wind the reel as fast as you can. On some occasions you wind in the presence of another participant, who is also winding as fast as possible. Will the other's presence affect your own performance?

In one of social psychology's first experiments, Norman Triplett (1898) reported that adolescents would wind a fishing reel faster in the presence of someone doing the same thing. Although a modern reanalysis revealed that the difference was modest (Stroebe, 2012), Triplett inspired later social psychologists to study how others' presence affects our behavior. Group influences operate both in simple groups—one person in the presence of another—and in more complex groups.

SOCIAL FACILITATION Triplett's claim—of strengthened performance in others' presence—is called **social facilitation.** But on tougher tasks (learning nonsense syllables or solving complex multiplication problems), people perform worse when observers or others working on the same task are present. Further studies revealed that the presence of others sometimes helps and sometimes hinders performance (Guerin, 1986; Zajonc, 1965). Why? Because when others observe us, we become aroused, and this arousal amplifies our reactions. It strengthens our most *likely* response—the correct one on an easy task, an incorrect one on a difficult task. Thus, expert pool players who made 71 percent of their shots when alone made 80 percent when four people came to watch them

> **social facilitation** improved performance on simple or well-learned tasks in the presence of others.

Hope College

Social facilitation Skilled athletes often find they are "on" before an audience. What they do well, they do even better when people are watching.

(Michaels et al., 1982). Poor shooters, who made 36 percent of their shots when alone, made only 25 percent when watched.

The energizing effect of an enthusiastic audience probably contributes to the home advantage that has shown up in studies of more than a quarter-million college and professional athletic events in various countries (Allen & Jones, 2014; Jamieson, 2010). Home teams win about 6 in 10 games—see **TABLE 35.1**. For most sports, home cooking is best.

Social facilitation also helps explain a funny effect of crowding. Comedians and actors know that a "good house" is a full one. Crowding triggers arousal. Comedy routines that are mildly amusing to people in an uncrowded room seem funnier in a densely packed room (Aiello et al., 1983; Freedman & Perlick, 1979). In experiments, participants, when seated close to one another, like a friendly person even more and an unfriendly person even less (Schiffenbauer & Schiavo, 1976; Storms & Thomas, 1977). So, to ensure an energetic class or event, choose a room or set up seating that will just barely accommodate everyone.

The point to remember: What you do well, you are likely to do even better in front of an audience, especially a friendly audience. What you normally find difficult may seem all but impossible when you are being watched.

∨ TABLE 35.1

Home Advantage in Team Sports

Sport	Years	Home games won
Nippon League Baseball	1998–2009	53.6%
Major League Baseball	1903–2009	53.9%
National Hockey League	1917–2009	55.7%
International Rugby	1871–2009	56.9%
National Football League	1966–2009	57.3%
International Cricket	1877–2009	57.4%
National Basketball Association	1946–2009	60.5%
Women's National Basketball Association	2003–2009	61.7%
English Premier League Soccer	1993–2009	63.0%
NCAA Men's Basketball	1947–2009	68.8%
Major League Soccer	2002–2009	69.1%

Source: Data from Moskowitz & Wertheim, 2011.

SOCIAL LOAFING Social facilitation experiments test the effect of others' presence on performance of an individual task, such as shooting pool. But what happens when people perform as a group? In a team tug-of-war, would you exert more, less, or the same effort as you would exert in a one-on-one tug-of-war?

To find out, a University of Massachusetts research team asked blindfolded students "to pull as hard as you can" on a rope. When they fooled the students into believing three others were also pulling behind them, students exerted only 82 percent as much effort as when they knew they were pulling alone (Ingham et al., 1974). And consider what happened when blindfolded people seated in a group clapped or shouted as loudly as they could while hearing (through headphones) other people clapping or shouting loudly (Latané, 1981). When they thought they were part of a group effort, the participants produced about one-third less noise than when clapping or shouting "alone."

Bibb Latané and his colleagues (1981; Jackson & Williams, 1988) described this diminished effort as **social loafing.** Experiments in the United States, India,

Thailand, Japan, China, and Taiwan have found social loafing on various tasks, though it was especially common among men in individualist cultures (Karau & Williams, 1993). What causes social loafing? Three things:

- People acting as part of a group feel *less accountable,* and therefore worry less about what others think.

- Group members may view their individual contributions as *dispensable* (Harkins & Szymanski, 1989; Kerr & Bruun, 1983).

- When group members share equally in the benefits, regardless of how much they contribute, some may slack off (as you perhaps have observed on group assignments). Unless highly motivated and strongly identified with the group, people may *free ride* on others' efforts.

DEINDIVIDUATION We've seen that the presence of others can arouse people (social facilitation), or it can diminish their feelings of responsibility (social loafing). But sometimes the presence of others does both. The uninhibited behavior that results can range from a food fight to vandalism or rioting. This process of losing self-awareness and self-restraint, called **deindividuation,** often occurs when group participation makes people both *aroused* and *anonymous.* In one experiment, New York University women dressed in depersonalizing Ku Klux Klan–style hoods. Compared with identifiable women in a control group, the hooded women delivered twice as much electric shock to a victim (Zimbardo, 1970). (As in all such experiments, the "victim" did not actually receive the shocks.)

Deindividuation During England's 2011 riots and looting, rioters were disinhibited by social arousal and by the anonymity provided by darkness and their hoods and masks. Later, some of those arrested expressed bewilderment over their own behavior.

Deindividuation thrives, for better or for worse, in many settings. Tribal warriors who depersonalize themselves with face paints or masks are more likely than those with exposed faces to kill, torture, or mutilate captured enemies (Watson, 1973). On discussion boards, Internet bullies, who would never say "You're so fake" to someone's face, may hide behind anonymity. When we shed self-awareness and self-restraint—whether in a mob, at a rock concert, at a ballgame, or at worship—we become more responsive to the group experience, whether bad or good. For a comparison of social facilitation, social loafing, and deindividuation, see **TABLE 35.2.**

∨ TABLE 35.2

Behavior in the Presence of Others: Three Phenomena

Phenomenon	Social context	Psychological effect of others' presence	Behavioral effect
Social facilitation	Individual being observed	Increased arousal	Amplified dominant behavior, such as doing better what one does well (or doing worse what is difficult)
Social loafing	Group projects	Diminished feelings of responsibility when not individually accountable	Decreased effort
Deindividuation	Group setting that fosters arousal and anonymity	Reduced self-awareness	Lowered self-restraint

* * *

We have examined the conditions under which the *presence* of others can motivate people to exert themselves or tempt them to free ride on the efforts of others, make easy tasks easier or difficult tasks harder, and enhance humor or fuel mob violence. Research also shows that *interacting* with others can similarly have both bad and good effects.

social loafing the tendency for people in a group to exert less effort when pooling their efforts toward attaining a common goal than when individually accountable.

deindividuation the loss of self-awareness and self-restraint occurring in group situations that foster arousal and anonymity.

Group Polarization

◁▷ **35-7** What are *group polarization* and *groupthink,* and how much power do we have as individuals?

Over time, initial differences between groups of college and university students tend to grow. If the first-year students at College X tend to have interests in the arts, and those at College Y tend to be business-oriented, those differences will probably be even greater by the time they graduate. Similarly, gender differences tend to widen over time, as Eleanor Maccoby (2002) noted from her decades of observing gender development. Girls talk more intimately than boys do and play and fantasize less aggressively; these differences will be amplified as boys and girls interact mostly with their own gender.

In each case, the beliefs and attitudes we bring to a group grow stronger as we discuss them with like-minded others. This process, called **group polarization,** can have beneficial results, as when it amplifies a sought-after spiritual awareness, reinforces the resolve of those in a self-help group, or motivates activists working for a cause. But it can also have dire consequences. George Bishop and I [DM] discovered that when high-prejudice students discussed racial issues, they became *more* prejudiced (**FIGURE 35.4**). Low-prejudice students, alternatively, became even more accepting.

Group polarization can feed extremism and even suicide terrorism. Analyses of terrorist organizations around the world reveal that the terrorist mentality does not erupt suddenly, on a whim (McCauley, 2002; McCauley & Segal, 1987; Merari, 2002). It usually begins slowly, among people who share a grievance. As they interact in isolation (sometimes with other "brothers" and "sisters" in camps) their views grow more and more extreme. Increasingly, they categorize the world as "us" against "them" (Moghaddam, 2005; Qirko, 2004). Given that the self-segregation of the like-minded polarizes people, a 2006 U.S. National Intelligence estimate speculated "that the operational threat from self-radicalized cells will grow."

When I [DM] got my start in social psychology with experiments on group polarization, I never imagined the potential dangers, or the creative possibilities, of polarization in *virtual* groups. Electronic communication and social networking have created virtual town halls where people can isolate themselves from those with different perspectives. By attuning our bookmarks and social media feeds to sites that trash the views we despise, we can retreat into partisan tribes and revel in foregone conclusions. Facebook prioritizes News Feed posts that it anticipates we will like. But we ourselves have a bigger effect as we click to content we agree with and unfollow irksome friends, thus blocking those with opposing political views (Bakshy et al., 2015). People read blogs that reinforce their views, and those blogs link to kindred blogs (**FIGURE 35.5**). Over time, the resulting political polarization—"loathing across party lines," say some political scientists (Iyengar & Westwood, 2014)—has become much more intense than racial polarization.

As the Internet connects the like-minded and pools their ideas, climate change skeptics, UFO abductees, and conspiracy theorists find support for their shared ideas and suspicions. White supremacists may become more racist. And militia members may become more terror prone. The longer participants spend in closed "Dark Web" forums, the more violent their messages become (Chen, 2012). Boston Marathon bombers Dzhokhar and Tamerlan Tsarnaev reportedly were "self-radicalized" through their Internet participation (Wilson et al., 2013). In the echo chambers of virtual worlds, as in the real world, separation + conversation = polarization.

But the Internet-as-social-amplifier can also work for good. Social networking sites connect friends and family members sharing common interests or coping

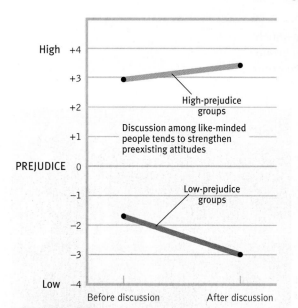

⌃ FIGURE 35.4

Group polarization If a group is like-minded, discussion strengthens its prevailing opinions. Talking over racial issues increased prejudice in a high-prejudice group of high school students and decreased it in a low-prejudice group. (Data from Myers & Bishop, 1970.)

"What explains the rise of fascism in the 1930s? The emergence of student radicalism in the 1960s? The growth of Islamic terrorism in the 1990s?... The unifying theme is simple: *When people find themselves in groups of like-minded types, they are especially likely to move to extremes.* [This] is the phenomenon of *group polarization.*"

Cass Sunstein,
Going to Extremes, 2009

group polarization the enhancement of a group's prevailing inclinations through discussion within the group.

groupthink the mode of thinking that occurs when the desire for harmony in a decision-making group overrides a realistic appraisal of alternatives.

Lada Adamic and Natalie Glance.

Like minds network in the blogosphere Blue liberal blogs link mostly to one another, as do red conservative blogs. (The intervening colors display links across the liberal-conservative boundary.) Each dot represents a blog, and each dot's size reflects the number of other blogs linking to that blog. (From Lazer et al., 2009.)

with similar challenges. Peacemakers, cancer survivors, and bereaved parents can find strength and solace from kindred spirits. By amplifying shared concerns and ideas, Internet-enhanced communication can also foster social ventures. (I [DM] know this personally from social networking with others with hearing loss in an effort to transform American assistive listening technology.)

The point to remember: By connecting and magnifying the inclinations of like-minded people, the Internet can be very, very bad, but also very, very good.

GROUPTHINK So, group interaction can influence our personal decisions. Does it ever distort important national decisions? Consider the "Bay of Pigs fiasco." In 1961, President John F. Kennedy and his advisers decided to invade Cuba with 1400 CIA-trained Cuban exiles. When the invaders were easily captured and soon linked to the U.S. government, Kennedy wondered aloud, "How could we have been so stupid?"

Social psychologist Irving Janis (1982) studied the decision-making process leading to the ill-fated invasion. He discovered that the soaring morale of the recently elected president and his advisers fostered undue confidence. To preserve the good feeling, group members suppressed or self-censored their dissenting views, especially after President Kennedy voiced his enthusiasm for the scheme. Since no one spoke strongly against the idea, everyone assumed the support was unanimous. To describe this harmonious but unrealistic group thinking, Janis coined the term **groupthink.**

Later studies showed that groupthink—fed by overconfidence, conformity, self-justification, and group polarization—contributed to other fiascos as well. Among them were the failure to anticipate the 1941 Japanese attack on Pearl Harbor; the escalation of the Vietnam war; the U.S. Watergate cover-up; the Chernobyl nuclear reactor accident (Reason, 1987); the U.S. space shuttle *Challenger* explosion (Esser & Lindoerfer, 1989); and the Iraq war, launched on the false idea that Iraq had weapons of mass destruction (U.S. Senate Intelligence Committee, 2004).

Despite the dangers of groupthink, two heads are often better than one. Knowing this, Janis also studied instances in which U.S. presidents and their advisers collectively made good decisions, such as when the Truman administration formulated the Marshall Plan, which offered assistance to Europe after World War II, and when the Kennedy administration successfully prevented the Soviets from installing missiles in Cuba. In such instances—and in the business world, too, Janis believed—groupthink is prevented when a leader welcomes various opinions, invites experts' critiques of developing plans, and assigns people to identify possible problems. Just as the suppression of dissent bends a group toward bad decisions, open debate often shapes good ones. This is especially the case with diverse groups, whose varied perspectives often enable creative or superior outcomes (Nemeth & Ormiston, 2007; Page, 2007). None of us is as smart as all of us.

Frank Cotham/The New Yorker Collection/Condé Nast

"I wonder if we might benefit from socializing more with those who don't harbor anti-government views."

"One of the dangers in the White House, based on my reading of history, is that you get wrapped up in groupthink and everybody agrees with everything, and there's no discussion and there are no dissenting views."

Barack Obama, December 1, 2008, press conference

"Truth springs from argument among friends."

Philosopher David Hume, 1711–1776

"If you have an apple and I have an apple and we exchange apples then you and I will still each have one apple. But if you have an idea and I have an idea and we exchange these ideas, then each of us will have two ideas."

Attributed to dramatist George Bernard Shaw, 1856–1950

Gandhi As the life of Hindu nationalist and spiritual leader Mahatma Gandhi powerfully testifies, a consistent and persistent minority voice can sometimes sway the majority. Gandhi's nonviolent appeals and fasts were instrumental in winning India's independence from Britain in 1947.

THE POWER OF INDIVIDUALS In affirming the power of social influence, we must not overlook the power of individuals. *Social control* (the power of the situation) and *personal control* (the power of the individual) interact. People aren't billiard balls. When feeling coerced, we may react by doing the opposite of what is expected, thereby reasserting our sense of freedom (Brehm & Brehm, 1981).

Committed individuals can sway the majority and make social history. Were this not so, communism would have remained an obscure theory, Christianity would be a small Middle Eastern sect, and Rosa Parks' refusal to sit at the back of the bus would not have ignited the U.S. civil rights movement. Technological history, too, is often made by innovative minorities who overcome the majority's resistance to change. To many, the railroad was a nonsensical idea; some farmers even feared that train noise would prevent hens from laying eggs. People derided Robert Fulton's steamboat as "Fulton's Folly." As Fulton later said, "Never did a single encouraging remark, a bright hope, a warm wish, cross my path." Much the same reaction greeted the printing press, the telegraph, the incandescent lamp, and the typewriter (Cantril & Bumstead, 1960).

The power of one or two individuals to sway majorities is *minority influence* (Moscovici, 1985). In studies of groups in which one or two individuals consistently express a controversial attitude or an unusual perceptual judgment, one finding repeatedly stands out: When you are the minority, you are far more likely to sway the majority if you hold firmly to your position and don't waffle. This tactic won't make you popular, but it may make you influential, especially if your self-confidence stimulates others to consider *why* you react as you do. Even when a minority's influence is not yet visible, people may privately develop sympathy for the minority position and rethink their views (Wood et al., 1994).

The bottom line: The powers of social influence are enormous, but so are the powers of the committed individual. For classical music, Mozart mattered. For drama, Shakespeare mattered. For world history, Hitler and Mao—and Gandhi and Mandela—mattered. Social forces matter. But individuals matter, too.

RETRIEVE IT [✷]

• What is social facilitation, and why is it more likely to occur with a well-learned task?

ANSWER: This improved performance in the presence of others is most likely to occur with a well-learned task, because the added arousal caused by an audience tends to strengthen the most likely response. This also predicts poorer performance on a difficult task in others' presence.

• People tend to exert less effort when working with a group than they would alone, which is called _____ _____.

ANSWER: social loafing

• You are organizing a meeting of fiercely competitive political candidates and their supporters. To add to the fun, friends have suggested handing out masks of the candidates' faces for supporters to wear. What phenomenon might these masks engage?

ANSWER: The anonymity provided by the masks, combined with the arousal of the contentious setting, might create *deindividuation* (lessened self-awareness and self-restraint).

• When like-minded groups discuss a topic, and the result is the strengthening of the prevailing opinion, this is called _____ _____.

ANSWER: group polarization

• When a group's desire for harmony overrides its realistic analysis of other options, _____ has occurred.

ANSWER: groupthink

◑ Learning Objectives

Test Yourself by taking a moment to answer each of these Learning Objective Questions (repeated here from within the module). Then turn to Appendix D, Complete Module Reviews, to check your answers. Research suggests that trying to answer these questions on your own will improve your long-term memory of the concepts (McDaniel et al., 2009).

35-1 What do social psychologists study? How do we tend to explain others' behavior and our own?

35-2 How do attitudes and actions interact?

35-3 How does culture affect our behavior?

35-4 What is automatic mimicry, and how do conformity experiments reveal the power of social influence?

35-5 What did Milgram's obedience experiments teach us about the power of social influence?

35-6 How is our behavior affected by the presence of others?

35-7 What are *group polarization* and *groupthink*, and how much power do we have as individuals?

▣·[:] Terms and Concepts to Remember

Test yourself on these terms by trying to write down the definition in your own words before flipping back to the referenced page to check your answers.

social psychology, p. 442

attribution theory, p. 442

fundamental attribution error, p. 442

attitude, p. 444

peripheral route persuasion, p. 444

central route persuasion, p. 444

foot-in-the-door phenomenon, p. 445

role, p. 445

cognitive dissonance theory, p. 446

culture, p. 448

norms, p. 448

conformity, p. 450

normative social influence, p. 451

informational social influence, p. 451

social facilitation, p. 455

social loafing, p. 456

deindividuation, p. 457

group polarization, p. 458

groupthink, p. 459

[×] Experience the Testing Effect

Test yourself repeatedly throughout your studies. This will not only help you figure out what you know and don't know; the testing itself will help you learn and remember the information more effectively thanks to the *testing effect*.

1. If we encounter a person who appears to be high on drugs, and we make the fundamental attribution error, we will probably attribute the person's behavior to
   a. moral weakness or an addictive personality.
   b. peer pressure.
   c. the easy availability of drugs on city streets.
   d. society's acceptance of drug use.

2. Celebrity endorsements in advertising often lead consumers to purchase products through _____ (central/peripheral) route persuasion.

3. We tend to agree to a larger request more readily if we have already agreed to a small request. This tendency is called the _____-_____-_____-_____ phenomenon.

4. Jamal's therapist has suggested that Jamal should "act as if" he is confident, even though he feels insecure and shy. Which social psychological theory would best support this suggestion, and what might the therapist be hoping to achieve?

5. Researchers have found that a person is most likely to conform to a group if
   a. the group members have diverse opinions.
   b. the person feels competent and secure.
   c. the person admires the group's status.
   d. no one else will observe the person's behavior.

6. In Milgram's experiments, the rate of compliance was highest when
   a. the "learner" was at a distance from the "teacher."
   b. the "learner" was close at hand.
   c. other "teachers" refused to go along with the experimenter.
   d. the "teacher" disliked the "learner."

7. Dr. Huang, a popular music professor, delivers fascinating lectures on music history but gets nervous and makes mistakes when describing exam statistics in front of the class. Why does his performance vary by task?

8. In a group situation that fosters arousal and anonymity, a person sometimes loses self-consciousness and self-control. This phenomenon is called _____.

9. Sharing our opinions with like-minded others tends to strengthen our views, a phenomenon referred to as _____ _____.

Find answers to these questions in Appendix E, in the back of the book.

Use ⊚ LearningCurve to create your personalized study plan, which will direct you to the resources that will help you most in ⊚ LaunchPad.

MODULE 36 Antisocial Relations

Social psychology studies how we think about and influence one another, and also how we *relate* to one another. What are the roots of prejudice? What causes us to harm, or to help, or to fall in love? How can we move a destructive conflict toward a just peace? In this section we ponder insights into *antisocial* relations gleaned by researchers who have studied prejudice and aggression.

Prejudice

36-1 What is *prejudice?* What are its social and emotional roots?

Prejudice means "prejudgment." It is an unjustifiable and usually negative attitude toward a group—often a different cultural, ethnic, or gender group. Like all attitudes, prejudice is a three-part mixture of

- *beliefs* (in this case, called **stereotypes**).
- *emotions* (for example, hostility or fear).
- predispositions to *action* (to discriminate).

Home-grown terrorism Despite America's fears of attacks from foreign terrorists, most lethal terrorist events since 2001 have come from within—as when a neo-Nazi slaughtered six people in a shooting at a Wisconsin Sikh temple.

Some stereotypes may be at least partly accurate. If you presume that young men tend to drive faster than elderly women, you may be right. People perceive Australians as having a rougher culture than the British, and in one analysis of millions of Facebook status updates, Australians did use more profanity (Kramer & Chung, 2011). But stereotypes can exaggerate—as when liberals and conservatives overestimate the extremity of the other's views (Graham et al., 2012). In the 14 years after the terror of September 11, 2001, many Americans feared attacks in the United States by the Muslim radical fringe, yet were nearly twice as likely to be killed by home-grown White supremacists and other non-Muslim extremists (Shane, 2015).

Stereotypes can also bias behavior. To *believe* that obese people are gluttonous, and to *feel* dislike for an obese person, is to be *prejudiced;* prejudice is a negative *attitude*. To pass over all the obese people on a dating site, or to reject an obese person as a potential job candidate, is to discriminate; **discrimination** is a negative *behavior.*

How Prejudiced Are People?

Prejudice comes as both explicit (overt) and implicit (automatic) attitudes toward people of a particular ethnic group, gender, sexual orientation, or viewpoint. Some examples:

EXPLICIT ETHNIC PREJUDICE Americans' expressed racial attitudes have changed dramatically in the last half-century. "It's all right for Blacks and Whites to date each other," agreed 48 percent of Americans in 1987 and 86 percent in 2012 (Pew, 2012). "Marriage between Blacks and Whites" was approved by 4 percent of Americans in 1958 and 87 percent in 2013 (Newport, 2013).

Yet as *overt* prejudice wanes, *subtle* prejudice lingers. Despite increased verbal support for interracial marriage, many people admit that in socially intimate settings (dating, dancing, marrying), they, personally, would feel uncomfortable with someone of another race. And many people who *say* they would feel upset with someone making racist slurs actually, when hearing such racism, respond

indifferently (Kawakami et al., 2009). Subtle prejudice may also take the form of "microaggressions," such as race-related traffic stops or people's reluctance to choose a train seat next to someone of a different race (Wang et al., 2011). A slew of recent experiments illustrates that prejudice can be not only subtle but also automatic and unconscious.

IMPLICIT ETHNIC PREJUDICE As we have seen throughout this book, the human mind processes thoughts, memories, and attitudes on two different tracks. Sometimes that processing is *explicit*—on the radar screen of our awareness. To a much greater extent, it is *implicit*—below the radar, leaving us unaware of how our attitudes are influencing our behavior. Modern studies indicate that prejudice is often implicit, an automatic attitude—an unthinking knee-jerk response. Consider these findings:

IMPLICIT RACIAL ASSOCIATIONS Using Implicit Association Tests, researchers have demonstrated that even people who deny harboring racial prejudice may carry negative associations (Banaji & Greenwald, 2013). For example, 9 in 10 White respondents took longer to identify pleasant words (such as *peace* and *paradise*) as "good" when presented with Black-sounding names (such as *Latisha* and *Darnell*) rather than with White-sounding names (such as *Katie* and *Ian*). Moreover, people who more quickly associated good things with White names or faces also were the quickest to perceive anger and apparent threat in Black faces (Hugenberg & Bodenhausen, 2003). (By 2014, about 16 million people had taken an Implicit Association Test, as you can at www.implicit.harvard.edu.)

Although the test is useful for studying automatic prejudice, critics caution against using it to assess or label individuals (Oswald et al., 2013, 2015). Defenders counter that implicit biases predict behaviors ranging from simple acts of friendliness to the evaluation of work quality (Greenwald et al., 2015). In the 2008 U.S. presidential election, those demonstrating explicit *or* implicit prejudice were less likely to vote for candidate Barack Obama. His election in turn served to reduce implicit prejudice (Bernstein et al., 2010; Payne et al., 2010; Stephens-Davidowitz, 2014).

UNCONSCIOUS PATRONIZATION In one experiment, White university women assessed flawed student essays. When assessing essays supposedly written by White students, the women gave low evaluations, often with harsh comments, but not so when the same essays were said to have been written by Black students (Harber, 1998). Did the evaluators calibrate their evaluations to their racial stereotypes, leading to less exacting standards and a patronizing attitude? In real-world evaluations, such low expectations and the resulting "inflated praise and insufficient criticism" could hinder minority student achievement, the researcher noted. (To preclude such bias, many teachers read essays while "blind" to their authors.)

RACE-INFLUENCED PERCEPTIONS Our expectations influence our perceptions. In 1999, Amadou Diallo was accosted as he approached his apartment house doorway by police officers looking for a rapist. When he pulled out his wallet, the officers, perceiving a gun, riddled his body with 19 bullets from 41 shots. Curious about this tragic killing of an unarmed, innocent man, two research teams simulated the situation (Correll et al., 2002, 2007; Greenwald et al., 2003; Sadler et al., 2012). They asked viewers to press buttons quickly to "shoot" or not shoot men who suddenly appeared on screen. Some of the on-screen men held a gun. Others held a harmless object, such as a flashlight or bottle. People (both Blacks and Whites, in one study) more often shot Black men than White men who were holding the harmless objects. Priming people with a flashed Black face rather than White face also made them more likely to misperceive a flashed tool as a gun (**FIGURE 36.1**). Fatigue, which diminishes one's conscious control and increases automatic reactions, amplifies racial bias in decisions to shoot (Ma et al., 2013).

prejudice an unjustifiable (and usually negative) attitude toward a group and its members. Prejudice generally involves stereotyped beliefs, negative feelings, and a predisposition to discriminatory action.

stereotype a generalized (sometimes accurate but often overgeneralized) belief about a group of people.

discrimination unjustifiable negative behavior toward a group and its members.

∨ FIGURE 36.1

Race primes perceptions In experiments by Keith Payne (2006), people viewed (1) a White or Black face, immediately followed by (2) a gun or hand tool, which was then followed by (3) a visual mask. Participants were more likely to misperceive a tool as a gun when it was preceded by a Black rather than White face.

1.   2.   3.

Race-related perceptions Does automatic racial bias research help us understand the 2013 death of Trayvon Martin (shown here 7 months before he was killed)? As he walked alone to his father's fiancé's house in a gated Florida neighborhood, a suspicious resident started following him. A confrontation led to the unarmed Martin being shot. Commentators wondered: Had Martin been an unarmed White teen, would he have been perceived and treated the same way?

just-world phenomenon the tendency for people to believe the world is just and that people therefore get what they deserve and deserve what they get.

ingroup "us"—people with whom we share a common identity.

outgroup "them"—those perceived as different or apart from our ingroup.

ingroup bias the tendency to favor our own group.

In 2015, the U.S. Supreme Court, in upholding the Fair Housing Act, affirmed implicit bias research when noting that "unconscious prejudices" can cause discrimination even without conscious discriminatory intent. If your own gut-check reveals you sometimes have feelings you would rather not have about other people, remember this: It is what we *do* with our feelings that matters. By monitoring our feelings and actions, and by replacing old habits with new ones based on new friendships, we can work to free ourselves from prejudice.

GENDER PREJUDICE Overt gender prejudice has also declined sharply. The one-third of Americans who in 1937 told Gallup pollsters that they would vote for a qualified woman whom their party nominated for president soared to 95 percent in 2012 (Gallup Brain, 2008; Jones, 2012). Nearly everyone now agrees that women and men should receive the same pay for the same job.

But gender prejudice and discrimination persist. Despite equality between the sexes in intelligence scores, people have tended to perceive their fathers as more intelligent than their mothers (Furnham & Wu, 2008). We pay more to those (usually men) who care for our streets than to those (usually women) who care for our children. Worldwide, women are more likely to live in poverty (UN, 2010); they represent nearly two-thirds of illiterate adults (UNESCO, 2013); and 30 percent have experienced intimate partner violence (Devries et al., 2013).

Unwanted female infants are no longer left out on a hillside to die of exposure, as was the practice in ancient Greece. Yet natural female mortality and the normal male-to-female newborn ratio (105-to-100) hardly explain the world's estimated 163 million (say that number slowly) "missing women" (Hvistendahl, 2011). In many places, sons are valued more than daughters. In India, there are 3.5 times more Google searches asking how to conceive a boy than how to conceive a girl (Stephens-Davidowitz, 2014). With scientific testing that enables sex-selective abortions, several Asian countries have experienced a shortfall in female births. Although China has declared that sex-selective abortions—gender genocide—are now a criminal offense, the country's newborn sex ratio has been 111 boys for every 100 girls, similar to India's 112 to 100 ratio (CIA, 2014). Some 95 percent of the children in Chinese orphanages have been girls (Webley, 2009). With under-age-20 males exceeding females by 32 million, many Chinese bachelors will be unable to find mates (Zhu et al., 2009). A shortage of women also contributes to increased crime, violence, prostitution, and trafficking of women (Brooks, 2012).

SEXUAL ORIENTATION PREJUDICE In most of the world, gay and lesbian people cannot openly and comfortably disclose who they are and whom they love (Katz-Wise & Hyde, 2012; United Nations, 2011). Dozens of countries have laws criminalizing same-sex relationships. But cultural variation is enormous—ranging from the 6 percent in Spain who say that "homosexuality is morally unacceptable" to 98 percent in Ghana (Pew, 2014). Anti-gay prejudice, though rapidly subsiding in Western countries, persists. In national surveys, 39 percent of LGBT Americans reported having "been rejected by a friend or family member" because of their sexual orientation or gender identity. And 58 percent reported being "subject to slurs or jokes" (Pew, 2013). Worldwide, anti-gay attitudes are most common among men, older adults, and those less educated (Jäckle & Wenzelburger, 2014).

Do attitudes and practices that label, disparage, and discriminate against gay and lesbian people increase their risk of psychological disorder and ill health? In U.S. states without protections against LGBT hate crimes and discrimination, gay and lesbian people experience substantially higher rates for depression and related disorders, even after controlling for income and education differences. In communities where anti-gay prejudice is high, so are gay and lesbian suicide and cardiovascular deaths. In 16 states that banned same-sex marriage between 2001 and 2005, gays and lesbians (but not heterosexuals) experienced a 37 percent increase in depressive disorder rates, a 42 percent increase in alcohol use disorder, and a 248 percent increase in general anxiety disorder. Meanwhile, gays and lesbians in other states did not experience increased psychiatric disorders (Hatzenbuehler, 2014).

Social Roots of Prejudice

Why does prejudice arise? Social inequalities and divisions are partly responsible.

SOCIAL INEQUALITIES When some people have money, power, and prestige and others do not, the "haves" usually develop attitudes that justify things as they are. The **just-world phenomenon** reflects an idea we commonly teach our children—that good is rewarded and evil is punished. From this it is but a short leap to assume that those who succeed must be good and those who suffer must be bad. Such reasoning enables the rich to see both their own wealth and the poor's misfortune as justly deserved. When slavery existed in the United States, slaveholders perceived slaves as innately lazy, ignorant, and irresponsible—as having the very traits that justified enslaving them. Stereotypes rationalize inequalities.

Victims of discrimination may react in ways that feed prejudice through the classic *blame-the-victim* dynamic (Allport, 1954). Do the circumstances of poverty breed a higher crime rate? If so, that higher crime rate can be used to justify discrimination against those who live in poverty.

US AND THEM: INGROUP AND OUTGROUP We have inherited our Stone Age ancestors' need to belong, to live and love in groups. There was safety in solidarity (those who didn't band together left fewer descendants). Whether hunting, defending, or attacking, 10 hands were better than 2. Dividing the world into "us" and "them" entails prejudice and war, but it also provides the benefits of communal solidarity. Thus, we cheer for our groups, kill for them, die for them. Indeed, we define who we are partly in terms of our groups. Through our *social identities* we associate ourselves with certain groups and contrast ourselves with others (Dunham et al., 2013; Hogg, 1996, 2006; Turner, 1987, 2007). When Ian identifies himself as a man, an Aussie, a University of Sydney student, a Catholic, and a MacGregor, he knows who he is, and so do we.

Evolution prepared us, when encountering strangers, to make instant judgments: friend or foe? Those from our group, those who look like us, and also those who *sound* like us—with accents like our own—we instantly tend to like, from childhood onward (Gluszek & Dovidio, 2010; Kinzler et al., 2009). Mentally drawing a circle defines "us," the **ingroup.** But the social definition of who you are also states who you are not. People outside that circle are "them," the **outgroup.** An **ingroup bias**—a favoring of our own group—soon follows. Even arbitrarily creating us-them groups by tossing a coin creates this bias. In experiments, people have favored their own group when dividing any rewards (Tajfel, 1982; Wilder, 1981). Much discrimination involves not outgroup hostility but ingroup networking and mutual support, such as hiring a friend's child at the expense of other job candidates (Greenwald & Pettigrew, 2014).

The ingroup Scotland's famed "Tartan Army" soccer fans, shown here during a match against archrival England, share a social identity that defines "us" (the Scottish ingroup) and "them" (the English outgroup).

The urge to distinguish enemies from friends predisposes prejudice against strangers (Whitley, 1999). To Greeks of the classical era, all non-Greeks were "barbarians." In our own era, most children believe their school is better than all other schools in town. Many high school students form cliques—theater people, athletes (sorted by sport), gangsters, preps, nerds—and disparage those outside their own group. Even chimpanzees have been seen to wipe clean the spot where they were touched by a chimpanzee from another group (Goodall, 1986). They also display ingroup empathy by yawning more after seeing ingroup (rather than outgroup) members yawn (Campbell & de Waal, 2011).

Ingroup bias explains the cognitive power of political partisanship (Cooper, 2010; Douthat, 2010). In the United States in the late 1980s, most Democrats believed inflation had risen under Republican president Ronald Reagan (it had dropped). In 2010, most Republicans believed that taxes had increased under Democratic president Barack Obama (for most, they had decreased).

> ## RETRIEVE IT
>
> ● Why do sports fans tend to feel a sense of satisfaction when their archrival team loses? Why do such feelings, in other settings, make conflict resolution more challenging?
>
> ANSWER: Sports fans may feel a part of an *ingroup* that sets itself apart from an *outgroup* (fans of the archrival team). Ingroup bias tends to develop, leading to prejudice and the view that the outgroup "deserves" misfortune. So, the archrival team's loss may seem justified. In conflicts, this kind of thinking is problematic, especially when each side in the conflict develops *mirror-image perceptions* of the other (distorted, negative images that are ironically similar).

Emotional Roots of Prejudice

Prejudice springs not only from the divisions of society but also from the passions of the heart. **Scapegoat theory** notes that when things go wrong, finding someone to blame can provide a target for anger. Following the 9/11 attacks, some outraged people lashed out at innocent Arab-Americans. Others called for eliminating Saddam Hussein, the Iraqi leader whom Americans had been grudgingly tolerating. "Fear and anger create aggression, and aggression against citizens of different ethnicity or race creates racism and, in turn, new forms of terrorism," noted Philip Zimbardo (2001). A decade after 9/11, anti-Muslim animosities still flared in the United States, with mosque burnings and efforts to block construction of an Islamic community center near Ground Zero in New York City.

Evidence for the scapegoat theory of prejudice comes from high prejudice among economically frustrated people. And it comes from experiments in which a temporary frustration intensifies prejudice. Students who experienced failure or were made to feel insecure often restored their self-esteem by disparaging a rival school or another person (Cialdini & Richardson, 1980; Crocker et al., 1987). To boost their own sense of status, people may denigrate others. That explains why a rival's misfortune sometimes provides a twinge of pleasure. (The German language has a word—*Schadenfreude*—for this secret joy that we sometimes take in another's failure [Hoogland et al., 2015].) By contrast, those made to feel loved and supported become more open to and accepting of others who differ (Mikulincer & Shaver, 2001).

Negative emotions feed prejudice. When facing death, fearing threats, or experiencing frustration, people cling more tightly to their ingroup and their friends. Fears of terrorism both heighten patriotism and produce loathing and aggression toward "them"—those who threaten our world (Pyszczynski et al., 2002, 2008). The few individuals who lack fear and its associated activity in the emotion-processing amygdala—such as children with the genetic disorder Williams syndrome—also display a notable lack of racial stereotypes and prejudice (Santos et al., 2010).

"For if [people were] to choose out of all the customs in the world [they would] end by preferring their own."

Greek historian Herodotus, 440 B.C.E.

"If the Tiber reaches the walls, if the Nile does not rise to the fields, if the sky doesn't move or the Earth does, if there is famine, if there is plague, the cry is at once: 'The Christians to the lion!'"

Tertullian, Apologeticus, *197 C.E.*

"The misfortunes of others are the taste of honey."

Japanese saying

Cognitive Roots of Prejudice

36-2 What are the cognitive roots of prejudice?

Prejudice springs from a culture's divisions, the heart's passions, and also from the mind's natural workings. Stereotyped beliefs are a by-product of how we cognitively simplify the world.

FORMING CATEGORIES One way we simplify our world is to categorize. A chemist categorizes molecules as organic and inorganic. Therapists categorize psychological disorders. All of us categorize people by race, with mixed-race people often assigned to their minority identity. Despite his mixed-race background and being raised by a White mother and White grandparents, President Barack Obama has been perceived by White Americans (and American culture) as Black. Researchers believe this happens because people's attention is drawn to the distinctive features of the less-familiar minority. Jamin Halberstadt and his colleagues (2011) illustrated this learned-association effect by showing New Zealanders blended Chinese-Caucasian faces. Compared with participants of Chinese descent, European-descent New Zealanders more readily classified ambiguous faces as Chinese (see **FIGURE 36.2**).

scapegoat theory the theory that prejudice offers an outlet for anger by providing someone to blame.

other-race effect the tendency to recall faces of one's own race more accurately than faces of other races. Also called the *cross-race effect* and the *own-race bias*.

| 100% Chinese | 80% Chinese 20% Caucasian | 60% Chinese 40% Caucasian | 40% Chinese 60% Caucasian | 20% Chinese 80% Caucasian | 100% Caucasian |

When categorizing people into groups, we often stereotype. We recognize how greatly *we* differ from other individuals in *our* groups. But we overestimate the homogeneity of other groups (we perceive *outgroup homogeneity*). "They"—the members of some other group—seem to look and act alike, while "we" are more diverse (Bothwell et al., 1989). To those in one ethnic group, members of another often seem more alike than they really are in attitudes, personality, and appearance. Our greater recognition for individual own-race faces—called the **other-race effect** (also called the *cross-race* effect or *own-race bias*)—emerges during infancy, between 3 and 9 months of age (Anzures et al., 2013; Telzer et al., 2013).

With effort and with experience, people get better at recognizing individual faces from another group (Hugenberg et al., 2010; Young et al., 2012). People of European descent, for example, more accurately identify individual African faces if they have watched a great deal of basketball on television, exposing them to many African-heritage faces (Li et al., 1996). And the longer Chinese people have resided in a Western country, the less they exhibit the other-race effect (Hancock & Rhodes, 2008).

REMEMBERING VIVID CASES We often judge the frequency of events by instances that readily come to mind. In a classic experiment, researchers showed two groups of University of Oregon students lists containing information about 50 men (Rothbart et al., 1978). The first group's list included 10 men arrested for *non-violent* crimes, such as forgery. The second group's list

∧ FIGURE 36.2

Categorizing mixed-race people When New Zealanders quickly classified 104 photos by race, those of European descent more often than those of Chinese descent classified the ambiguous middle two as Chinese (Halberstadt et al., 2011).

Gilbert Laurie/Getty Images

> FIGURE 36.3

Vivid cases feed stereotypes
The 9/11 Muslim terrorists created,
in many minds, an exaggerated
stereotype of Muslims as
terrorism-prone. Actually, reported
a U.S. National Research Council panel
on terrorism, when offering this inexact
illustration, most terrorists are not Muslim
and "the vast majority of Islamic people have
no connection with and do not sympathize
with terrorism" (Smelser & Mitchell, 2002).

LaunchPad To review attribution
research and experience a simulation
of how stereotypes form, visit Launch-
Pad's *PsychSim 6: Not My Type*. And for
a 6.5-minute synopsis of the cognitive
and social psychology of prejudice, visit
LaunchPad's *Video: Prejudice*.

**Do guns in the home save or take
more lives?** In the last 40 years in
the United States, well over 1 million
people—more than all deaths in all
wars in American history—have been
killed by firearms in nonwar settings.
Compared with people of the same
sex, race, age, and neighborhood, those
who keep a gun in the home (ironically,
often for protection) have been twice as
likely to be murdered and three times
as likely to commit suicide (Anglemyer
et al., 2014; Stroebe, 2013). States and
countries with high gun ownership rates
also tend to have high gun death rates
(VPC, 2013).

included 10 men arrested for *violent* crimes, such
as assault. Later, both groups were asked
how many men on their list had committed *any* sort of crime. The second group
overestimated the number. Vivid—in
this case violent—cases are more readily
available to our memory and feed our stereotypes (**FIGURE 36.3**).

BELIEVING THE WORLD IS JUST As we noted earlier, people often justify their
prejudices by blaming victims. If the world is just, they assume, people must get
what they deserve. As one German civilian is said to have remarked when visiting
the Bergen-Belsen concentration camp shortly after World War II, "What terrible
criminals these prisoners must have been to receive such treatment."

Hindsight bias is also at work here (Carli & Leonard, 1989). Have you ever
heard people say that rape victims, abused spouses, or people with AIDS got
what they deserved? In some countries, such as Pakistan, rape victims have been
sentenced to severe punishment for violating adultery prohibitions (Mydans,
2002). In one experiment illustrating the blame-the-victim phenomenon, people
were given a detailed account of a date that ended with the woman being raped
(Janoff-Bulman et al., 1985). They perceived the woman's behavior as at least
partly to blame, and in hindsight, they thought, "She should have known better."
Others, given the same account with the rape ending deleted, did not perceive the
woman's behavior as inviting rape. Hindsight bias promoted a blame-the-victim
mentality among members of the first group. Blaming the victim also serves to
reassure people that it couldn't happen to them.

People also have a basic tendency to justify their culture's social systems
(Jost et al., 2009; Kay et al., 2009). We're inclined to see the way things are as
the way things ought to be. This natural conservatism makes it difficult to legis-
late major social changes, such as health care or climate change policies. Once
such policies are in place, however, our "system justification" tends to preserve
them as well.

RETRIEVE IT [✶]

• When prejudiced judgment causes us to blame an undeserving person for a problem, that
person is called a _____.

ANSWER: scapegoat

Aggression

36-3 How does psychology's definition of *aggression* differ from everyday
usage? What biological factors make us more prone to hurt one another?

Prejudice hurts, but aggression sometimes hurts more. In psychology, **aggression**
is any physical or verbal behavior intended to harm someone, whether done out
of hostility or as a calculated means to an end. The assertive, persistent
salesperson is not aggressive. Nor is the dentist who makes you wince
with pain. But the person who passes along a vicious rumor about you,
someone who bullies you in person or online, and the attacker who
mugs you for your money are aggressive.

Aggressive behavior emerges from the interaction of biology and
experience. For a gun to fire, the trigger must be pulled; with some
people, as with hair-trigger guns, it doesn't take much to trip an explosion. Let's look first at some biological factors that influence our
thresholds for aggressive behavior, then at the psychological factors
that pull the trigger.

The Biology of Aggression

Aggression varies too widely from culture to culture, era to era, and person to person to be considered an unlearned instinct. But biology does *influence* aggression. We can look for biological influences at three levels—genetic, neural, and biochemical.

GENETIC INFLUENCES Genes influence aggression. Animals have been bred for aggressiveness—sometimes for sport, sometimes for research. The effect of genes also appears in human *twin studies* (Miles & Carey, 1997; Rowe et al., 1999). If one identical twin admits to "having a violent temper," the other twin will often independently admit the same. Fraternal twins are much less likely to respond similarly.

Researchers continue to search for genetic markers in those who commit violent acts. One is already well known and is carried by half the human race: the Y chromosome. Another such marker is the *monoamine oxidase A (MAOA) gene*, which helps break down neurotransmitters such as dopamine and serotonin. Sometimes called the "warrior gene," people who have low *MAOA* gene expression tend to behave aggressively when provoked. In one experiment, low (compared with high) *MAOA* gene carriers gave more unpleasant hot sauce to someone who provoked them (McDermott et al., 2009).

NEURAL INFLUENCES There is no one spot in the brain that controls aggression. Aggression is a complex behavior, and it occurs in particular contexts. But animal and human brains have neural systems that, given provocation, will either inhibit or facilitate aggression (Denson, 2011; Moyer, 1983; Wilkowski et al., 2011). Consider:

- Researchers implanted a radio-controlled electrode in the brain of the domineering leader of a caged monkey colony. The electrode was in an area that, when stimulated, inhibits aggression. When researchers placed the control button for the electrode in the colony's cage, one small monkey learned to push it every time the boss became threatening.

- A neurosurgeon, seeking to diagnose a disorder, implanted an electrode in the amygdala of a mild-mannered woman. Because the brain has no sensory receptors, she was unable to feel the stimulation. But at the flick of a switch she snarled, "Take my blood pressure. Take it now," then stood up and began to strike the doctor.

- Studies of violent criminals have revealed diminished activity in the frontal lobes, which play an important role in controlling impulses. If the frontal lobes are damaged, inactive, disconnected, or not yet fully mature, aggression may be more likely (Amen et al., 1996; Davidson et al., 2000; Raine, 2013).

BIOCHEMICAL INFLUENCES Our genes engineer our individual nervous systems, which operate electrochemically. The hormone testosterone, for example, circulates in the bloodstream and influences the neural systems that control aggression. A raging bull becomes a gentle giant when castration reduces its testosterone level. Conversely, when injected with testosterone, gentle, castrated mice once again become aggressive.

Humans are less sensitive to hormonal changes. But as men age, their testosterone levels—and their aggressiveness—diminish. Hormonally charged, aggressive 17-year-olds mature into hormonally quieter and gentler 70-year-olds. Drugs that sharply reduce testosterone levels also subdue men's aggressive tendencies.

Another drug that sometimes circulates in the bloodstream—alcohol— *unleashes* aggressive responses to frustration. Across police data, prison surveys, and experiments, aggression-prone people are more likely to drink, and to become violent when intoxicated (White et al., 1993). National crime data indicate that

aggression any physical or verbal behavior intended to harm someone physically or emotionally.

LaunchPad See LaunchPad's *Video: Twin Studies* for a helpful tutorial animation.

"It's a guy thing."

The New Yorker Collection, 1995, D. Reilly from cartoonbank.com

"We could avoid two-thirds of all crime simply by putting all able-bodied young men in cryogenic sleep from the age of 12 through 28."

David T. Lykken,
The Antisocial Personalities, *1995*

A lean, mean fighting machine— the testosterone-laden female hyena The hyena's unusual embryology pumps testosterone into female fetuses. The result is revved-up young female hyenas who seem born to fight.

Karl Ammann/Getty Images

❯ **FIGURE 36.4**

Temperature and retaliation Richard Larrick and his colleagues (2011) looked for occurrences of batters hit by pitches during 4,566,468 pitcher-batter matchups across 57,293 Major League Baseball games since 1952. The probability of a hit batter increased if one or more of the pitcher's teammates had been hit, and also with temperature.

Brita Meng Outzen/AP Photo

73 percent of Russian homicides and 57 percent of U.S. homicides are alcohol-influenced (Landberg & Norström, 2011). Alcohol affects aggression both biologically and psychologically (Bushman, 1993; Ito et al., 1996; Taylor & Chermack, 1993). Just *thinking* you've imbibed alcohol can increase aggression (Bègue et al., 2009). Alcohol also inclines people to interpret ambiguous acts (such as a bump in a crowd) as provocations (Bègue et al., 2010).

Psychological and Social-Cultural Factors in Aggression

36-4 What psychological and social-cultural factors may trigger aggressive behavior?

Biological factors influence how easily aggression is triggered. But what psychological and social-cultural factors pull the trigger?

AVERSIVE EVENTS Suffering sometimes builds character. In laboratory experiments, however, those made miserable have often made others miserable (Berkowitz, 1983, 1989). This phenomenon is called the **frustration-aggression principle:** Frustration creates anger, which can spark aggression. One analysis of 27,667 hit-by-pitch Major League Baseball incidents between 1960 and 2004 revealed this link (Timmerman, 2007). Pitchers were most likely to hit batters when

- they had been frustrated by the previous batter hitting a home run.
- the current batter had hit a home run the last time at bat.
- a teammate of the pitcher had been hit by a pitch in the previous half inning.

Other aversive stimuli—hot temperatures, physical pain, personal insults, foul odors, cigarette smoke, crowding, and a host of others—can also evoke hostility. In laboratory experiments, when people get overheated, they think, feel, and act more aggressively. When provoked, simply thinking about words related to hot temperatures is enough to increase hostile behavior (Fay & Maner, 2014). In baseball games, the number of hit batters rises with the temperature (Reifman et al., 1991; see **FIGURE 36.4**). In the wider world, violent crime and spousal abuse rates have been higher during hotter years, seasons, months, and days (Anderson et al., 1997). Studies from other social science fields converge in finding that throughout history, higher temperatures have predicted increased individual violence, wars, and revolutions (Hsiang et al., 2013). Craig Anderson and his colleagues (2000, 2011) have projected that, other things

Probability of hit batter

.012

Number of teammates hit:
3 or More
2
1
0

.011

.010

.009

.008

.007

.006

59 and Below   60–69   70–79   80–89   90 and Above

Temperature (°F)

being equal, global warming of 4 degrees Fahrenheit (about 2 degrees Celsius) could induce tens of thousands of additional assaults and murders—and that's before the added violence inducement from climate-change–related drought, poverty, food insecurity, and migration.

REINFORCEMENT, MODELING, AND SELF-CONTROL Aggression may naturally follow aversive events, but learning can alter natural reactions. We learn when our behavior is reinforced, and we learn by watching others.

In situations where experience has taught us that aggression pays, we are likely to act aggressively again. Children whose aggression has successfully intimidated other children may become bullies. Animals that have successfully fought to get food or mates become increasingly ferocious. To foster a kinder, gentler world we had best model and reward sensitivity and cooperation from an early age, perhaps by training parents to discipline without modeling violence. Parent-training programs often advise parents to avoid modeling violence by avoiding screaming and hitting. Instead, parents should reinforce desirable behaviors and frame statements positively. ("When you finish loading the dishwasher you can go play," rather than "If you don't load the dishwasher, there'll be no playing.").

Different cultures model, reinforce, and evoke different tendencies toward violence. For example, crime rates have also been higher and average happiness has been lower in times and places marked by a great disparity between rich and poor (Messias et al., 2011; Oishi et al., 2011; Wilkinson & Pickett, 2009). In the United States, cultures and families in which fathers are minimally involved also have had high violence rates (Triandis, 1994). Even after controlling for parental education, race, income, and teen motherhood, American male youths from father-absent homes are incarcerated at twice the rate of their peers (Harper & McLanahan, 2004).

Violence can vary by culture within a country. Richard Nisbett and Dov Cohen (1996) analyzed violence among White Americans in southern towns settled by Scots-Irish herders whose tradition emphasized "manly honor," the use of arms to protect one's flock, and a history of coercive slavery. Compared with their White counterparts in New England towns settled by the more traditionally peaceful Puritan, Quaker, and Dutch farmer-artisans, the cultural descendants of those herders have had triple the homicide rates and were more supportive of physically punishing children, of warfare initiatives, and of uncontrolled gun ownership. "Culture-of-honor" states also have higher rates of students bringing weapons to school and of school shootings (Brown et al., 2009).

MEDIA MODELS FOR VIOLENCE Parents are hardly the only aggression models. In the United States and elsewhere, TV, films, video games, and the Internet offer supersized portions of violence. Repeatedly viewing on-screen violence tends to make us less sensitive to cruelty (Montag et al., 2012). It also primes us to respond aggressively when provoked. And it teaches us **social scripts**—culturally provided mental files for how to act. When we find ourselves in new situations, uncertain how to behave, we rely on social scripts. After watching so many action films, adolescent boys may acquire a script that plays in their head when they face real-life conflicts. Challenged, they may "act like a man" by intimidating or eliminating the threat. More than 100 studies together confirm that people sometimes imitate what they've viewed. Watching risk-glorifying behaviors (dangerous driving, extreme sports, unprotected sex) increases viewers' real-life risk taking (Fischer et al., 2011).

Music lyrics also write social scripts. In experiments, German university men who listened to woman-hating song lyrics administered hotter chili sauce to a woman. Man-hating song lyrics likewise increase aggression in women (Fischer & Greitemeyer, 2006).

Sexual scripts depicted in pornographic films can also be toxic. Repeatedly watching pornographic films, even nonviolent films, makes sexual aggression seem less serious (Harris, 1994). In one experiment, undergraduates viewed six brief, sexually explicit films each week for six weeks (Zillmann & Bryant, 1984).

IMMERSIVE LEARNING How have researchers studied these concepts? Learn more at LaunchPad's *How Would You Know If Hot Temperatures Cause Aggression?*

frustration-aggression principle the principle that frustration—the blocking of an attempt to achieve some goal—creates anger, which can generate aggression.

social script culturally modeled guide for how to act in various situations.

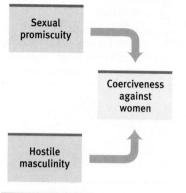

▲ FIGURE 36.5

Men who sexually coerce women The recipe for coercion against women combines an impersonal approach to sex with a hostile masculinity. (Adapted from Malamuth, 1996.)

Coincidence or cause? In 2011, Norwegian Anders Behring Breivik bombed government buildings in Oslo, and then went to a youth camp where he shot and killed 69 people, mostly teens. As a player of first-person shooter games, Breivik stirred debate when he commented that "I see MW2 *[Modern Warfare 2]* more as a part of my training-simulation than anything else." Did his violent game playing—and that of the 2012 mass murderer of Newtown, Connecticut's first-grade children—contribute to the violence, or was it a merely coincidental association? To explore such questions, psychologists experiment.

Andrew Berwick via www.freak.no/Reuters/Landov

A control group viewed films with no sexual content during the same six-week period. Three weeks later, both groups read a newspaper report about a man convicted of raping a hitchhiker and were asked to suggest an appropriate prison term. Sentences recommended by those viewing the sexually explicit films were only half as long as the sentences recommended by the control group.

While nonviolent sexual content affects aggression-related sexual attitudes, violent sexual content can increase men's readiness to actually behave aggressively toward women. A statement by 21 social scientists, including many of the researchers who conducted these experiments, noted, "Pornography that portrays sexual aggression as pleasurable for the victim increases the acceptance of the use of coercion in sexual relations" (Surgeon General, 1986). Contrary to much popular opinion, viewing such depictions does not provide an outlet for bottled-up impulses. Rather, "in laboratory studies measuring short-term effects, exposure to violent pornography increases punitive behavior toward women."

To a lesser extent, nonviolent pornography can also influence aggression. One set of studies explored pornography's effects on aggression toward relationship partners. The result: pornography consumption predicted both self-reported aggression and participants' willingness to administer laboratory noise blasts to their partner (Lambert et al., 2011). Abstaining from one's customary pornography consumption decreased aggression. Abstaining from a favorite food did not (**FIGURE 36.5**).

DO VIOLENT VIDEO GAMES TEACH SOCIAL SCRIPTS FOR VIOLENCE?

Experiments in North America, Western Europe, Singapore, and Japan indicate that playing positive games produces positive effects (Greitemeyer & Osswald, 2010, 2011; Prot et al., 2014). For example, playing *Lemmings,* where a goal is to help others, increases real-life helping. So, might a parallel effect occur after playing games that enact violence? Violent video games became an issue for public debate after teenagers in more than a dozen places seemed to mimic the carnage in the shooter games they had so often played (Anderson, 2004, 2013).

In 2002, three young men in Michigan spent part of a night drinking beer and playing *Grand Theft Auto III.* Using simulated cars, they ran down pedestrians, then beat them with fists, leaving a bloody body behind (Kolker, 2002). These same young men then went out for a real drive. Spotting a 38-year-old man on a bicycle, they ran him down with their car, got out, stomped and punched him, and returned home to play the game some more. (The victim, a father of three, died six days later.)

Such violent mimicry causes some to wonder: What are the effects of actively role-playing aggression? Does it cause young people to become less sensitive to violence and more open to violent acts? Nearly 400 studies of 130,000 people offer an answer (Anderson et al., 2010). Video games can prime aggressive thoughts, decrease empathy, and increase aggression. University men who spent the most hours playing violent video games have also tended to be the most physically aggressive (Anderson & Dill, 2000). (For example, they more often acknowledged having hit or attacked someone else.) And people randomly assigned to play a game involving bloody murders with groaning victims (rather than to play nonviolent *Myst*) became more hostile. On a follow-up task, they were more likely to blast intense noise at a fellow student. Studies of young adolescents reveal that those who play a lot of violent video games become more aggressive and see the world as more hostile (Gentile, 2009; Hassin et al., 2013). Compared with nongaming kids, they get into more arguments and fights and earn poorer grades.

Ah, but is this merely because naturally hostile kids are drawn to such games? Apparently not. Comparisons of gamers and nongamers who scored low on hostility measures revealed a difference in the number of fights reported. Almost 4 in 10 violent-game players had been in fights, compared with only 4 in 100 of the

nongaming kids (Anderson, 2004). Some researchers believe that, due partly to the more active participation and rewarded violence of game play, violent video games have even greater effects on aggressive behavior and cognition than do violent TV shows and movies (Anderson & Warburton, 2012).

Other researchers are unimpressed by such findings (Ferguson, 2013, 2014). They note that from 1996 to 2006, youth violence declined while video game sales increased, and argue that other factors—depression, family violence, peer influence—better predict aggression. Also, game playing keeps people off the streets and out of trouble (Cunningham et al., 2011). The focused fun of game playing can also satisfy basic needs for a sense of competence, control, and social connection (Granic et al., 2014).

* * *

To sum up, research reveals biological, psychological, and social-cultural influences on aggressive behavior. Complex behaviors, including violence, have many causes, making any single explanation an oversimplification. Asking what causes violence is therefore like asking what causes cancer. Those who study the effects of asbestos exposure on cancer rates may remind us that asbestos is indeed a cancer cause, but it is only one among many. Like so much else, aggression is a biopsychosocial phenomenon (**FIGURE 36.6**).

A happy concluding note: Historical trends suggest that the world is becoming less violent over time (Pinker, 2011). That people vary across time and place reminds us that environments differ. Yesterday's plundering Vikings have become today's peace-promoting Scandinavians. Like all behavior, aggression arises from the interaction of persons and situations.

"What sense does it make to forbid selling to a 13-year-old a magazine with an image of a nude woman, while protecting the sale to that 13-year-old of an interactive video game in which he actively, but virtually, binds and gags the woman, then tortures and kills her?"

U.S. Supreme Court Justice Stephen Breyer, dissenting opinion, 2011

Biological influences:
- genetic influences
- biochemical influences, such as testosterone and alcohol
- neural influences, such as a severe head injury

Psychological influences:
- dominating behavior (which boosts testosterone levels in the blood)
- believing that alcohol has been ingested (whether it has or not)
- frustration
- aggressive role models
- rewards for aggressive behavior
- low self-control

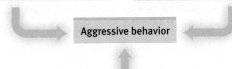

Aggressive behavior

Social-cultural influences:
- *deindividuation*, or a loss of self-awareness and self-restraint
- challenging environmental factors, such as crowding, heat, and direct provocations
- parental models of aggression
- minimal father involvement
- exposure to violent media

< FIGURE 36.6

Biopsychosocial understanding of aggression Because many factors contribute to aggressive behavior, there are many ways to change such behavior, including learning anger management and communication skills, and avoiding violent media and video games.

RETRIEVE IT [✱]

- What biological, psychological, and social-cultural influences interact to produce aggressive behaviors?

ANSWER: Our biology (our genes, neural systems, and biochemistry—including testosterone and alcohol levels) influences our aggressive tendencies. Psychological factors (such as frustration, previous rewards for aggressive acts, and observation of others' aggression) can trigger any aggressive tendencies we may have. Social influences, such as exposure to violent media and cultural influences, such as whether we've grown up in a "culture of honor," or a father-absent home, can also affect our aggressive responses.

Learning Objectives

Test Yourself by taking a moment to answer each of these Learning Objective Questions (repeated here from within the module). Then turn to Appendix D, Complete Module Reviews, to check your answers. Research suggests that trying to answer these questions on your own will improve your long-term memory of the concepts (McDaniel et al., 2009).

36-1 What is *prejudice*? What are its social and emotional roots?

36-2 What are the cognitive roots of prejudice?

36-3 How does psychology's definition of *aggression* differ from everyday usage? What biological factors make us more prone to hurt one another?

36-4 What psychological and social-cultural factors may trigger aggressive behavior?

Terms and Concepts to Remember

Test yourself on these terms by trying to write down the definition in your own words before flipping back to the referenced page to check your answers.

prejudice, p. 462

stereotype, p. 462

discrimination, p. 462

just-world phenomenon, p. 465

ingroup, p. 465

outgroup, p. 465

ingroup bias, p. 465

scapegoat theory, p. 466

other-race effect, p. 467

aggression, p. 468

frustration-aggression principle, p. 470

social script, p. 471

Experience the Testing Effect

Test yourself repeatedly throughout your studies. This will not only help you figure out what you know and don't know; the testing itself will help you learn and remember the information more effectively thanks to the *testing effect*.

1. Prejudice toward a group involves negative feelings, a tendency to discriminate, and overly generalized beliefs referred to as _____.

2. If several well-publicized murders are committed by members of a particular group, we may tend to react with fear and suspicion toward all members of that group. What psychological principle can help explain this reaction?

3. The other-race effect occurs when we assume that other groups are _____ (more/less) homogeneous than our own group.

4. Evidence of a biochemical influence on aggression is the finding that
   a. aggressive behavior varies widely from culture to culture.
   b. animals can be bred for aggressiveness.
   c. stimulation of an area of the brain's limbic system produces aggressive behavior.

   d. a higher-than-average level of the hormone testosterone is associated with violent behavior in males.

5. When those who feel frustrated become angry and aggressive, this is referred to as the _____-_____ _____.

6. Studies show that parents of delinquent young people tend to use beatings to enforce discipline. This suggests that aggression can be
   a. learned through direct rewards.
   b. triggered by exposure to violent media.
   c. learned through observation of aggressive models.
   d. caused by hormone changes at puberty.

7. Social scientists studying the effects of pornography have mostly agreed that violent pornography
   a. has little effect on most viewers.
   b. is the primary cause of reported and unreported rapes.
   c. leads viewers to be more accepting of coercion in sexual relations.
   d. has no effect, other than short-term arousal and entertainment.

Find answers to these questions in Appendix E, in the back of the book.

Use 🎓 LearningCurve to create your personalized study plan, which will direct you to the resources that will help you most in 🎓 LaunchPad.

MODULE 37 Prosocial Relations

Social psychologists focus not only on the dark side of social relationships, but also on the bright side, by studying *prosocial* behavior—behavior that intends to help or benefit someone. Our positive behaviors toward others are evident from explorations of attraction, altruism, and peacemaking.

Attraction

Pause a moment and think about your relationships with two people—a close friend and someone who has stirred your feelings of romantic love. What psychological chemistry binds us together in these special attachments? Social psychology suggests some answers.

The Psychology of Attraction

37-1 Why do we befriend or fall in love with some people but not others?

We endlessly wonder how we can win others' affection and what makes our own affections flourish or fade. Does familiarity breed contempt, or does it intensify affection? Do birds of a feather flock together, or do opposites attract? Is it what's inside that counts, or does physical attractiveness matter greatly? To explore these questions, let's consider three ingredients of our liking for one another: proximity, attractiveness, and similarity.

PROXIMITY Before friendships become close, they must begin. *Proximity*—geographic nearness—is friendship's most powerful predictor. Proximity provides opportunities for aggression, but much more often it breeds liking. Study after study reveals that people are most inclined to like, and even to marry, those who live in the same neighborhood, who sit nearby in class, who work in the same office, who share the same parking lot, who eat in the same dining hall. Look around. Mating starts with meeting.

Proximity breeds liking partly because of the **mere exposure effect.** Repeated exposure to novel stimuli increases our liking for them. By age three months, infants prefer photos of the race they most often see—usually their own race (Kelly et al., 2007). Mere exposure increases our liking not only for familiar faces, but also for nonsense syllables, musical selections, geometric figures, Chinese characters, and the letters of our own name (Moreland & Zajonc, 1982; Nuttin, 1987; Zajonc, 2001). We are even somewhat more likely to marry someone whose first or last name resembles our own (Jones et al., 2004).

So, within certain limits, familiarity feeds fondness (Bornstein, 1989, 1999). Researchers demonstrated this by having four equally attractive women silently attend a 200-student class for zero, 5, 10, or 15 class sessions (Moreland & Beach, 1992). At the end of the course, students viewed slides of each woman and rated her attractiveness. The most attractive? The ones they'd seen most often. This phenomenon would come as no surprise to the young Taiwanese man who wrote more than 700 letters to his girlfriend, urging her to marry him. She did marry—the mail carrier (Steinberg, 1993).

No face is more familiar than your own. And that helps explain an interesting finding by Lisa DeBruine (2004): We like other people when their faces incorporate some morphed features of our own. When DeBruine (2002) had McMaster University

> **mere exposure effect** the phenomenon that repeated exposure to novel stimuli increases liking of them.

The mere exposure effect The mere exposure effect applies even to ourselves. Because the human face is not perfectly symmetrical, the face we see in the mirror is not the same face our friends see. Most of us prefer the familiar mirror image, while our friends like the reverse (Mita et al., 1977). The person German Chancellor Angela Merkel sees in the mirror each morning is shown at right, and that's the photo she would probably prefer. We might feel more comfortable with the reverse image (left), the one we see.

Dan Kitwood/Getty Images

In the eye of the beholder
Conceptions of attractiveness vary by culture. Yet some adult physical features, such as a healthy appearance and symmetrical face, seem attractive everywhere.

Percentage of Men and Women Who "Constantly Think About Their Looks"

	Men	Women
Canada	18%	20%
United States	17	27
Mexico	40	45
Venezuela	47	65

From Roper Starch survey, reported by McCool (1999).

Women have 91 percent of cosmetic procedures (ASPS, 2010). Women also recall others' appearances better than do men (Mast & Hall, 2006).

a slim one, applied chemicals hoping to rid themselves of unwanted hair or to regrow wanted hair, strapped on leather garments to make their breasts seem smaller or surgically filled their breasts with silicone and worn push-up bras to make them look bigger. Cultural ideals change over time. For women in North America, the ultrathin ideal of the Roaring Twenties gave way to the soft, voluptuous Marilyn Monroe ideal of the 1950s, only to be replaced by today's lean yet busty ideal.

Some aspects of heterosexual attractiveness, however, do cross place and time (Cunningham et al., 2005; Langlois et al., 2000). By providing reproductive clues, bodies influence sexual attraction. As evolutionary psychologists explain, men in many cultures, from Australia to Zambia, judge women as more attractive if they have a youthful, fertile appearance, suggested by a low waist-to-hip ratio (Karremans et al., 2010; Perilloux et al., 2010; Platek & Singh, 2010). (I [DM] always thought my wife looked cute in her genes.) Women feel attracted to healthy-looking men, but especially—and more so when ovulating—to those who seem mature, dominant, masculine, and affluent (Gallup & Frederick, 2010; Gangestad et al., 2010). But faces matter, too. When people rate opposite-sex faces and bodies separately, the face tends to be the better predictor of overall physical attractiveness (Currie & Little, 2009; Peters et al., 2007).

Our feelings also influence our attractiveness judgments. Imagine two people. The first is honest, humorous, and polite. The second is rude, unfair, and abusive. Which one is more attractive? Most people perceive the person with the appealing traits as more physically attractive (Lewandowski et al., 2007). Those we like we find attractive. In a Rodgers and Hammerstein musical, Prince Charming asks Cinderella, "Do I love you because you're beautiful, or are you beautiful because I love you?" Chances are it's both. As we see our loved ones again and again, their physical imperfections grow less noticeable and their attractiveness grows more apparent (Beaman & Klentz, 1983; Gross & Crofton, 1977). Shakespeare said it in *A Midsummer Night's Dream:* "Love looks not with the eyes, but with the mind." Come to love someone and watch beauty grow.

SIMILARITY So proximity has brought you into contact with someone, and your appearance has made an acceptable first impression. What influences whether you will become friends? As you get to know each other, will the chemistry be better if you are opposites or if you are alike?

It makes a good story—extremely different types liking or loving each other: Frog and Toad in Arnold Lobel's books, Edward and Bella in the *Twilight* series.

Extreme makeover In affluent, beauty-conscious cultures, increasing numbers of people, such as this woman from the former American TV show *Extreme Makeover,* have turned to cosmetic surgery to improve their looks.

For many participants, 4 minutes is enough time to form a feeling about a conversational partner and to register whether the partner likes them (Eastwick & Finkel, 2008a,b).

For researchers, speed dating offers a unique opportunity for studying influences on our first impressions of potential romantic partners. Among recent findings are these:

- People who fear rejection often elicit it. After a 3-minute speed date, those who most feared rejection were least often selected for a follow-up date (McClure & Lydon, 2014).

- Given more options, people's choices become more superficial. Meeting lots of potential partners leads people to focus on more easily assessed characteristics, such as height and weight (Lenton & Francesconi, 2010). This was true even when researchers controlled for time spent with each partner.

- Men wish for future contact with more of their speed dates; women tend to be choosier. But this difference disappears if the conventional roles are reversed, so that men stay seated while women circulate (Finkel & Eastwick, 2009).

PHYSICAL ATTRACTIVENESS Once proximity affords us contact, what most affects our first impressions? The person's sincerity? Intelligence? Personality? Hundreds of experiments (all in a heterosexual context) reveal that it is something far more superficial: physical appearance. This finding is unnerving for those of us taught that "beauty is only skin deep" and "appearances can be deceiving."

In one early study, researchers randomly matched new University of Minnesota students for a Welcome Week dance (Walster et al., 1966). Before the dance, the researchers gave each student a battery of personality and aptitude tests, and they rated each student's physical attractiveness. During the blind date, the couples danced and talked for more than two hours and then took a brief intermission to rate their dates. What determined whether they liked each other? Only one thing seemed to matter: appearance. Both the men and the women liked good-looking dates best. Women are more likely than men to say that another's looks don't affect them (Lippa, 2007). But studies show that a man's looks do affect women's behavior (Eastwick et al., 2014a,b). Speed-dating experiments confirm that attractiveness influences first impressions for both sexes (Belot & Francesconi, 2006; Finkel & Eastwick, 2008).

Physical attractiveness also predicts how often people date and how popular they feel. And it affects initial impressions of people's personalities. We don't assume that attractive people are more compassionate, but research participants perceive them as healthier, happier, more sensitive, more successful, and more socially skilled (Eagly et al., 1991; Feingold, 1992; Hatfield & Sprecher, 1986). Attractive, well-dressed people have been more likely to make a favorable impression on potential employers, and they have tended to be more successful in their jobs (Cash & Janda, 1984; Langlois et al., 2000; Solomon, 1987). Income analyses show a penalty for plainness or obesity and a premium for beauty (Engemann & Owyang, 2005).

For those who find the importance of looks unfair and unenlightened, two findings may be reassuring. First, people's attractiveness is surprisingly unrelated to their self-esteem and happiness (Diener et al., 1995; Major et al., 1984). Unless we have just compared ourselves with superattractive people, few of us (thanks, perhaps, to the mere exposure effect) view ourselves as unattractive (Thornton & Moore, 1993). Second, strikingly attractive people are sometimes suspicious that praise for their work may simply be a reaction to their looks. Less attractive people have been more likely to accept praise as sincere (Berscheid, 1981).

Beauty is also in the eye of the culture. Hoping to look attractive, people across the globe have pierced and tattooed their bodies, lengthened their necks, bound their feet, dyed their hair, and artificially lightened or darkened their skin. They have gorged themselves to achieve a full figure or liposuctioned fat to achieve

"I'd like to meet the algorithm that thought we'd be a good match."

When Neanderthals fall in love.

"Personal beauty is a greater recommendation than any letter of introduction."

Aristotle, Apothegms, *330 B.C.E.*

In the eye of the beholder
Conceptions of attractiveness vary by culture. Yet some adult physical features, such as a healthy appearance and symmetrical face, seem attractive everywhere.

Percentage of Men and Women Who
"Constantly Think About Their Looks"

	Men	Women
Canada	18%	20%
United States	17	27
Mexico	40	45
Venezuela	47	65

From Roper Starch survey, reported by McCool (1999).

Women have 91 percent of cosmetic procedures (ASPS, 2010). Women also recall others' appearances better than do men (Mast & Hall, 2006).

a slim one, applied chemicals hoping to rid themselves of unwanted hair or to regrow wanted hair, strapped on leather garments to make their breasts seem smaller or surgically filled their breasts with silicone and worn push-up bras to make them look bigger. Cultural ideals change over time. For women in North America, the ultrathin ideal of the Roaring Twenties gave way to the soft, voluptuous Marilyn Monroe ideal of the 1950s, only to be replaced by today's lean yet busty ideal.

Some aspects of heterosexual attractiveness, however, do cross place and time (Cunningham et al., 2005; Langlois et al., 2000). By providing reproductive clues, bodies influence sexual attraction. As evolutionary psychologists explain, men in many cultures, from Australia to Zambia, judge women as more attractive if they have a youthful, fertile appearance, suggested by a low waist-to-hip ratio (Karremans et al., 2010; Perilloux et al., 2010; Platek & Singh, 2010). (I [DM] always thought my wife looked cute in her genes.) Women feel attracted to healthy-looking men, but especially—and more so when ovulating—to those who seem mature, dominant, masculine, and affluent (Gallup & Frederick, 2010; Gangestad et al., 2010). But faces matter, too. When people rate opposite-sex faces and bodies separately, the face tends to be the better predictor of overall physical attractiveness (Currie & Little, 2009; Peters et al., 2007).

Our feelings also influence our attractiveness judgments. Imagine two people. The first is honest, humorous, and polite. The second is rude, unfair, and abusive. Which one is more attractive? Most people perceive the person with the appealing traits as more physically attractive (Lewandowski et al., 2007). Those we like we find attractive. In a Rodgers and Hammerstein musical, Prince Charming asks Cinderella, "Do I love you because you're beautiful, or are you beautiful because I love you?" Chances are it's both. As we see our loved ones again and again, their physical imperfections grow less noticeable and their attractiveness grows more apparent (Beaman & Klentz, 1983; Gross & Crofton, 1977). Shakespeare said it in *A Midsummer Night's Dream:* "Love looks not with the eyes, but with the mind." Come to love someone and watch beauty grow.

SIMILARITY So proximity has brought you into contact with someone, and your appearance has made an acceptable first impression. What influences whether you will become friends? As you get to know each other, will the chemistry be better if you are opposites or if you are alike?

It makes a good story—extremely different types liking or loving each other: Frog and Toad in Arnold Lobel's books, Edward and Bella in the *Twilight* series.

Extreme makeover In affluent, beauty-conscious cultures, increasing numbers of people, such as this woman from the former American TV show *Extreme Makeover,* have turned to cosmetic surgery to improve their looks.

MODULE
37 **Prosocial Relations**

Social psychologists focus not only on the dark side of social relationships, but also on the bright side, by studying *prosocial* behavior—behavior that intends to help or benefit someone. Our positive behaviors toward others are evident from explorations of attraction, altruism, and peacemaking.

> **mere exposure effect** the phenomenon that repeated exposure to novel stimuli increases liking of them.

Attraction

Pause a moment and think about your relationships with two people—a close friend and someone who has stirred your feelings of romantic love. What psychological chemistry binds us together in these special attachments? Social psychology suggests some answers.

The Psychology of Attraction

37-1 Why do we befriend or fall in love with some people but not others?

We endlessly wonder how we can win others' affection and what makes our own affections flourish or fade. Does familiarity breed contempt, or does it intensify affection? Do birds of a feather flock together, or do opposites attract? Is it what's inside that counts, or does physical attractiveness matter greatly? To explore these questions, let's consider three ingredients of our liking for one another: proximity, attractiveness, and similarity.

PROXIMITY Before friendships become close, they must begin. *Proximity*—geographic nearness—is friendship's most powerful predictor. Proximity provides opportunities for aggression, but much more often it breeds liking. Study after study reveals that people are most inclined to like, and even to marry, those who live in the same neighborhood, who sit nearby in class, who work in the same office, who share the same parking lot, who eat in the same dining hall. Look around. Mating starts with meeting.

Proximity breeds liking partly because of the **mere exposure effect.** Repeated exposure to novel stimuli increases our liking for them. By age three months, infants prefer photos of the race they most often see—usually their own race (Kelly et al., 2007). Mere exposure increases our liking not only for familiar faces, but also for nonsense syllables, musical selections, geometric figures, Chinese characters, and the letters of our own name (Moreland & Zajonc, 1982; Nuttin, 1987; Zajonc, 2001). We are even somewhat more likely to marry someone whose first or last name resembles our own (Jones et al., 2004).

So, within certain limits, familiarity feeds fondness (Bornstein, 1989, 1999). Researchers demonstrated this by having four equally attractive women silently attend a 200-student class for zero, 5, 10, or 15 class sessions (Moreland & Beach, 1992). At the end of the course, students viewed slides of each woman and rated her attractiveness. The most attractive? The ones they'd seen most often. This phenomenon would come as no surprise to the young Taiwanese man who wrote more than 700 letters to his girlfriend, urging her to marry him. She did marry—the mail carrier (Steinberg, 1993).

No face is more familiar than your own. And that helps explain an interesting finding by Lisa DeBruine (2004): We like other people when their faces incorporate some morphed features of our own. When DeBruine (2002) had McMaster University

The mere exposure effect The mere exposure effect applies even to ourselves. Because the human face is not perfectly symmetrical, the face we see in the mirror is not the same face our friends see. Most of us prefer the familiar mirror image, while our friends like the reverse (Mita et al., 1977). The person German Chancellor Angela Merkel sees in the mirror each morning is shown at right, and that's the photo she would probably prefer. We might feel more comfortable with the reverse image (left), the one we see.

Dan Kitwood/Getty Images

> FIGURE 37.1

I like the candidate who looks a bit like dear old me Jeremy Bailenson and his colleagues (2005) incorporated morphed features of voters' faces into the faces of 2004 U.S. presidential candidates George Bush and John Kerry. Without conscious awareness of their own incorporated features, the participants became more likely to favor the candidate whose face incorporated some of their own features.

Voter

George Bush

60:40 Blend

© Jeremy Bailenson and Nick Yee

students (both men and women) play a game with a supposed other player whose face they viewed on a monitor, they were more trusting and cooperative when the other person's image had some of their own facial features morphed into it. In me I trust. (See also **FIGURE 37.1.**)

MODERN MATCHMAKING Those who have not found a romantic partner in their immediate proximity may cast a wider net by joining an online dating service. Some people, including occasional predators, dishonestly represent their age, attractiveness, occupation, or other details, and thus are not who they seem to be. Nevertheless, Katelyn McKenna and John Bargh and their colleagues have offered a reassuring finding: Compared with relationships formed in person, Internet-formed friendships and romantic relationships are, on average, slightly more likely to last and be satisfying (Bargh et al., 2002, 2004; Cacioppo et al., 2013; McKenna et al., 2002). In one of their studies, people disclosed more, with less posturing, to those they met online. When conversing online with someone for 20 minutes, they felt more liking for that person than they did for someone they had met and talked with face to face. This was true even when (unknown to them) it was the same person!

Internet friendships often feel as real and important as in-person relationships. Small wonder that the historic ways couples have met—at school, on the job, through family, or, especially, through friends—have been supplemented by a striking rise in couples who meet online. In a national survey of straight and gay/lesbian couples, nearly a quarter of heterosexual couples and some two-thirds of same-sex couples met online (Rosenfeld & Thomas, 2012; see **FIGURE 37.2**).

Speed dating pushes the search for romance into high gear. In a process pioneered by a matchmaking Jewish rabbi, people meet a succession of prospective partners, either in person or via webcam (Bower, 2009). After a 3- to 8-minute conversation, people move on to the next prospect. (In an in-person heterosexual meeting, one group—usually the women—remains seated while the other group circulates.) Those who want to meet again can arrange for future contact.

Dave Coverly/Speed Bump

> FIGURE 37.2

Percentage of same-sex and heterosexual couples who met online (Data from Rosenfeld & Thomas, 2012.)

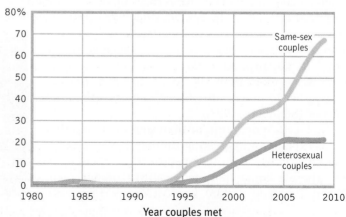

These stories delight us by expressing what we seldom experience. In real life, opposites retract (Rosenbaum, 1986; Montoya & Horton, 2013). Compared with randomly paired people, friends and couples have been far more likely to share common attitudes, beliefs, and interests (and, for that matter, age, religion, race, education, intelligence, smoking behavior, and economic status).

Moreover, the more alike people are, the more their liking endures (Byrne, 1971). Journalist Walter Lippmann was right to suppose that love lasts "when the lovers love many things together, and not merely each other." Similarity breeds content. One app therefore matches people with potential dates based on their proximity, and on the similarity of their Facebook profiles.

Proximity, attractiveness, and similarity are not the only determinants of attraction. We also like those who like us. This is especially true when our self-image is low. When we believe someone likes us, we feel good and respond to them warmly, which leads them to like us even more (Curtis & Miller, 1986). To be liked is powerfully rewarding.

Indeed, all the findings we have considered so far can be explained by a simple *reward theory of attraction:* We will like those whose behavior is rewarding to us, including those who are both able and willing to help us achieve our goals (Montoya & Horton, 2014). When people live or work in close proximity to us, it requires less time and effort to develop the friendship and enjoy its benefits. When people are attractive, they are aesthetically pleasing, and associating with them can be socially rewarding. When people share our views, they reward us by validating our beliefs.

Beauty grows with mere exposure Herman Miller, Inc.'s famed Aeron chair initially received high comfort ratings but abysmal beauty ratings. To some it looked like "lawn furniture" or "a giant prehistoric insect" (Gladwell, 2005). But then, with design awards, media visibility, and imitators, the ugly duckling became the company's best-selling chair ever and came to be seen as beautiful. With people, too, beauty lies partly in the beholder's eye and can grow with exposure.

> **RETRIEVE IT** [✖]
>
> • People tend to marry someone who lives or works nearby. This is an example of the
> _____ _____ _____ in action.
>
> ANSWER: mere exposure effect
>
> • How does being physically attractive influence others' perceptions?
>
> ANSWER: Being physically attractive tends to elicit positive first impressions. People tend to assume that attractive people are healthier, happier, and more socially skilled than others are.

Romantic Love

37-2 How does romantic love typically change as time passes?

Sometimes people move quickly from initial impressions, to friendship, to the more intense, complex, and mysterious state of romantic love. If love endures, temporary *passionate love* will mellow into a lingering *companionate love* (Hatfield, 1988).

PASSIONATE LOVE A key ingredient of **passionate love** is arousal. Stanley Schachter and Jerome Singer's *two-factor theory of emotion* can help us understand this intense positive absorption in another (Hatfield, 1988). That theory assumes that:

• emotions have two ingredients—*physical arousal* plus *cognitive appraisal.*

• arousal from any source can enhance one emotion or another, depending on how we interpret and label the arousal.

In one famous experiment, researchers studied people crossing two bridges above British Columbia's rocky Capilano River (Dutton & Aron, 1974, 1989). One, a swaying footbridge, was 230 feet above the rocks; the other was low and solid. The researchers had an attractive young woman intercept men coming off each bridge, and ask their help in filling out a short questionnaire. She then offered her phone number in case they wanted to hear more about her project. Far more of those who had just crossed the high bridge—which left their hearts pounding—accepted the number and later called the woman. To be revved up and to associate some of that arousal with a desirable person is to feel the pull of passion. Adrenaline makes the heart grow fonder. And when sexual desire is supplemented by a growing attachment, the result is the passion of romantic love (Berscheid, 2010).

Snapshots at jasonlove.com

Bill looked at Susan, Susan at Bill. Suddenly death didn't seem like an option. This was love at first sight.

passionate love an aroused state of intense positive absorption in another, usually present at the beginning of a love relationship.

companionate love the deep affectionate attachment we feel for those with whom our lives are intertwined.

equity a condition in which people receive from a relationship in proportion to what they give to it.

self-disclosure the act of revealing intimate aspects of oneself to others.

altruism unselfish regard for the welfare of others.

"When two people are under the influence of the most violent, most insane, most delusive, and most transient of passions, they are required to swear that they will remain in that excited, abnormal, and exhausting condition continuously until death do them part."

George Bernard Shaw,
"Getting Married," 1908

COMPANIONATE LOVE Although the desire and attachment of romantic love often endure, the intense absorption in the other, the thrill of the romance, the giddy "floating on a cloud" feelings typically fade. Does this mean the French are correct in saying that "love makes the time pass and time makes love pass"? Or can friendship and commitment keep a relationship going after the passion cools?

As love matures, it typically becomes a steadier **companionate love**—a deep, affectionate attachment (Hatfield, 1988). The flood of passion-facilitating hormones (testosterone, dopamine, adrenaline) subsides and another hormone, *oxytocin*, supports feelings of trust, calmness, and bonding with the mate. In the most satisfying of marriages, attraction and sexual desire endure, minus the obsession of early stage romance (Acevedo & Aron, 2009).

There may be adaptive wisdom in the shift from passion to attachment (Reis & Aron, 2008). Passionate love often produces children, whose survival is aided by the parents' waning obsession with each another. Failure to appreciate passionate love's limited half-life can doom a relationship (Berscheid et al., 1984). Indeed, recognizing the short duration of obsessive passionate love, some societies deem such feelings to be an irrational reason for marrying. Better, they say, to choose (or have someone choose for you) a partner with a compatible background and interests. Non-Western cultures, where people rate love less important for marriage, do have lower divorce rates (Levine et al., 1995).

One key to a gratifying and enduring relationship is **equity.** When equity exists—when both partners receive in proportion to what they give—their chances for sustained and satisfying companionate love have been good (Gray-Little & Burks, 1983; Van Yperen & Buunk, 1990). In one national survey, "sharing household chores" ranked third, after "faithfulness" and a "happy sexual relationship," on a list of nine things people associated with successful marriages. "I like hugs. I like kisses. But what I really love is help with the dishes," summarized the Pew Research Center (2007).

Equity's importance extends beyond marriage. Mutually sharing one's self and possessions, making decisions together, giving and getting emotional support, promoting and caring about each other's welfare—all of these acts are at the core of every type of loving relationship (Sternberg & Grajek, 1984). It's true for lovers, for parent and child, and for close friends.

Another vital ingredient of loving relationships is **self-disclosure,** the revealing of intimate details about ourselves—our likes and dislikes, our dreams and worries, our proud and shameful moments. "When I am with my friend," noted the Roman statesman Seneca, "me thinks I am alone, and as much at liberty to speak anything as to think it." Self-disclosure breeds liking, and liking breeds self-disclosure (Collins & Miller, 1994). As one person reveals a little, the other reciprocates, the first then reveals more, and on and on, as friends or lovers move to deeper intimacy (Baumeister & Bratslavsky, 1999).

One experiment marched student pairs through 45 minutes of increasingly self-disclosing conversation—from "When did you last sing to yourself?" to "When did you last cry in front of another person? By yourself?" Others spent the time with small-talk questions, such as "What was your high school like?" (Aron et al., 1997). By the experiment's end, those experiencing the escalating intimacy felt much closer to their conversation partner than did the small-talkers.

In addition to equity and self-disclosure, a third key to enduring love is *positive support.* While relationship conflicts are inevitable, we can ask ourselves whether our communications more often express sarcasm or support, scorn or sympathy, sneers or smiles. For unhappy couples,

HI & LOIS

disagreements, criticisms, and put-downs are routine. For happy couples in enduring relationships, positive interactions (compliments, touches, laughing) outnumber negative interactions (sarcasm, disapproval, insults) by at least 5 to 1 (Gottman, 2007; see also Sullivan et al., 2010).

In the mathematics of love, self-disclosing intimacy + mutually supportive equity = enduring companionate love.

RETRIEVE IT [**✗**]

- How does the two-factor theory of emotion help explain *passionate love*?

ANSWER: Emotions consist of (1) physical arousal and (2) our interpretation of that arousal. Researchers have found that any source of arousal (running, fear, laughter) may be interpreted as passion in the presence of a desirable person.

- Two vital components for maintaining *companionate love* are _____ and _____-_____.

ANSWERS: equity; self-disclosure

Love is an ancient thing In 2007, a 5000- to 6000-year-old "Romeo and Juliet" young couple was unearthed locked in embrace, near Rome.

Altruism

◀◉▶ **37-3** When are people most—and least—likely to help?

Altruism is an unselfish concern for the welfare of others. In rescuing his jailer, Dirk Willems exemplified altruism. So also did Carl Wilkens and Paul Rusesabagina in Kigali, Rwanda. Wilkens, a Seventh-day Adventist missionary, was living there in 1994 with his family when militia from the Hutu ethnic group began to slaughter members of a minority ethnic group, the Tutsis. The U.S. government, church leaders, and friends all implored Wilkens to leave. He refused. After evacuating his family, and even after every other American had left Kigali, he alone stayed and contested the 800,000-person genocide. When the militia came to kill him and his Tutsi servants, Wilkens' Hutu neighbors deterred them. Despite repeated death threats, he spent his days running roadblocks to take food and water to orphanages and to negotiate, plead, and bully his way through the bloodshed, saving lives time and again. "It just seemed the right thing to do," he later explained (Kristof, 2004).

Elsewhere in Kigali, Rusesabagina, a Hutu married to a Tutsi and the acting manager of a luxury hotel, was sheltering more than 1200 terrified Tutsis and moderate Hutus. When international peacekeepers abandoned the city and hostile militia threatened his guests in the "Hotel Rwanda" (as it came to be called in a 2004 movie), the courageous Rusesabagina began cashing in past favors. He bribed the militia and telephoned influential people abroad to exert pressure on local authorities, thereby sparing the lives of the hotel's occupants despite the surrounding chaos. Both Wilkens and Rusesabagina were displaying altruism, an unselfish regard for the welfare of others.

Altruism became a major concern of social psychologists after an especially vile act. On March 13, 1964, a stalker repeatedly stabbed Kitty Genovese, then raped her as she lay dying outside her Queens, New York, apartment at 3:30 A.M. "Oh, my God, he stabbed me!" Genovese screamed into the early morning stillness. "Please help me!" Windows opened and lights went on as some neighbors heard her screams. Her attacker fled and then returned to stab and rape her again. Not until he had fled for good did anyone so much as call the police, at 3:50 A.M.

Why do genocides occur? An estimated 800,000 people died during the Rwandan Genocide of 1994, when Hutu groups carried out mass killings of Tutsis. Social psychology research helps us understand some of the factors motivating genocides. We tend to categorize our world into us and them, and, when threatened, to feel greater animosity toward outside groups.

Bystander Intervention

Reflecting on initial reports of the Genovese murder and other such tragedies, most commentators were outraged by the bystanders' apparent "apathy" and "indifference." Rather than blaming the onlookers, social

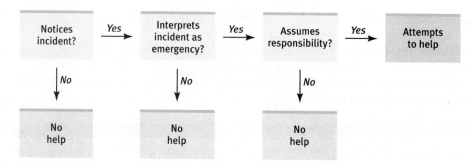

^ FIGURE 37.3

The decision-making process for bystander intervention Before helping, one must first notice an emergency, then correctly interpret it, and then feel responsible. (Adapted from Darley & Latané, 1968b.)

LaunchPad For a review of research on emergency helping, visit LaunchPad's *Concept Practice: When Will People Help Others?*

---

bystander effect the tendency for any given bystander to be less likely to give aid if other bystanders are present.

social exchange theory the theory that our social behavior is an exchange process, the aim of which is to maximize benefits and minimize costs.

reciprocity norm an expectation that people will help, not hurt, those who have helped them.

---

psychologists John Darley and Bibb Latané (1968b) attributed their inaction to an important situational factor—the presence of others. Given certain circumstances, they suspected, most of us might behave similarly. To paraphrase the French writer Voltaire, we all are guilty of the good we did not do.

After staging emergencies under various conditions, Darley and Latané assembled their findings into a decision scheme: We will help only if the situation enables us first to *notice* the incident, then to *interpret* it as an emergency, and finally to *assume responsibility* for helping (**FIGURE 37.3**). At each step, the presence of others can turn us away from the path that leads to helping.

Darley and Latané reached their conclusions after interpreting the results of a series of experiments. For example, as students in different laboratory rooms talked over an intercom, the experimenters simulated an emergency. Each student was in a separate cubicle, and only the person whose microphone was switched on could be heard. When his turn came, one student (an accomplice of the experimenters) made sounds as though he were having an epileptic seizure, and he called for help (Darley & Latané, 1968a).

How did the others react? As **FIGURE 37.4** shows, those who believed only they could hear the victim—and therefore thought they alone were responsible for helping him—usually went to his aid. Students who thought others could also hear the victim's cries were more likely to do nothing. When more people shared responsibility for helping—when there was a *diffusion of responsibility*—any single listener was less likely to help.

Hundreds of additional experiments have confirmed this **bystander effect.** For example, researchers and their assistants took 1497 elevator rides in three cities and "accidentally" dropped coins or pencils in front of 4813 fellow passengers (Latané & Dabbs, 1975). When alone with the person in need, 40 percent helped; in the presence of 5 other bystanders, only 20 percent helped.

Observations of behavior in thousands of these situations—relaying an emergency phone call, aiding a stranded motorist, donating blood, picking up dropped books, contributing money, giving time—show that the *best* odds of our helping someone occur when

- the person appears to need and deserve help.
- the person is in some way similar to us.
- the person is a woman.
- we have just observed someone else being helpful.
- we are not in a hurry.
- we are in a small town or rural area.
- we are feeling guilty.
- we are focused on others and not preoccupied.
- we are in a good mood.

This last result, that happy people are helpful people, is one of the most consistent findings in all of psychology. As poet Robert Browning (1867) observed, "Oh,

make us happy and you make us good!" It doesn't matter how we are cheered. Whether by being made to feel successful and intelligent, by thinking happy thoughts, by finding money, or even by receiving a posthypnotic suggestion, we become more generous and more eager to help (Carlson et al., 1988).

So happiness breeds helpfulness. But it's also true that helpfulness breeds happiness. Making charitable donations activates brain areas associated with reward (Harbaugh et al., 2007). That helps explain a curious finding: People who give money away are happier than those who spend it almost entirely on themselves. In a survey of more than 200,000 people worldwide, people in both rich and poor countries were happier with their lives if they had donated to a charity in the last month (Aknin et al., 2013). Just reflecting on a time when one spent money on others provides most people with a mood boost. And in one experiment, researchers gave people an envelope with cash and instructions: Some were to spend the money on themselves, while others were told to spend it on others (Dunn et al., 2008, 2013). Which group was happiest at the day's end? It was, indeed, those assigned to the spend-it-on-others condition.

Percentage attempting to help

Number of others presumed available to help

Fewer people help if others seem available

◀ **FIGURE 37.4**

Responses to a simulated emergency When people thought they alone heard the calls for help from a person they believed to be having an epileptic seizure, they usually helped. But when they thought four others were also hearing the calls, fewer than one third responded. (Data from Darley & Latané, 1968a.)

 RETRIEVE IT **[✱]**

- Why didn't anybody help Kitty Genovese? What social psychology principle did this incident illustrate?

ANSWER: In the presence of others, an individual is less likely to notice a situation, correctly interpret it as an emergency, and take responsibility for offering help. The Kitty Genovese case demonstrated this *bystander effect*, as each witness assumed many others were also aware of the event.

The Norms for Helping

 37-4 How do social exchange theory and social norms explain helping behavior?

Why do we help? One widely held view is that self-interest underlies all human interactions, that our constant goal is to maximize rewards and minimize costs. Accountants call it *cost-benefit analysis*. Philosophers call it *utilitarianism*. Social psychologists call it **social exchange theory.** If you are pondering whether to donate blood, you may weigh the costs of doing so (time, discomfort, and anxiety) against the benefits (reduced guilt, social approval, and good feelings). If the rewards exceed the costs, you will help.

Others believe that we help because we have been socialized to do so, through norms that prescribe how we *ought* to behave. Through socialization, we learn the **reciprocity norm:** the expectation that we should return help, not harm, to those who have helped us. In our relations with others of similar status, the reciprocity norm compels us to give (in favors, gifts, or social invitations) about as much as we receive. In one experiment, people who were generously treated also became more likely to be generous to a stranger—to "pay it forward" (Tsvetkova & Macy, 2014).

The reciprocity norm kicked in after Dave Tally, a Tempe, Arizona, homeless man, found $3300 in a backpack that an Arizona State University student had misplaced on his way to buy a used car (Lacey, 2010). Instead of using the cash for much-needed bike repairs, food, and shelter, Tally turned the backpack in to the social service agency where he volunteered. To reciprocate Tally's help, the student thanked him with a monetary reward. Hearing about Tally's self-giving deeds, dozens of others also sent him money and job offers.

We also learn a **social-responsibility norm:** that we should help those who need our help, such as young children and others who cannot give as much as they receive, even if the costs outweigh the benefits. People who attend weekly religious services often are admonished to practice the social-responsibility norm, and sometimes they do. In American surveys, they have reported twice as many volunteer hours spent helping the poor and infirm, compared with those who rarely or never attend religious services (Hodgkinson & Weitzman, 1992; Independent Sector, 2002). Between 2006 and 2008, Gallup polls sampled more than 300,000 people across 140 countries, comparing the "highly religious" (who said religion was important to them and who had attended a religious service in the prior week) to the less religious. The highly religious, despite being poorer, were about 50 percent more likely to report having "donated money to a charity in the last month" and to have volunteered time to an organization (Pelham & Crabtree, 2008).

Peacemaking

With astonishing speed, recent democratic movements have swept away totalitarian rule in Eastern European and Arab countries. Yet *every day,* the world continues to spend almost $5 billion for arms and armies—money that could have been used for housing, nutrition, education, and health care. Knowing that wars begin in human minds, psychologists have wondered: What in the human mind causes destructive conflict? How might the perceived threats of social diversity be replaced by a spirit of cooperation?

Elements of Conflict

👁 **37-5** How do social traps and mirror-image perceptions fuel social conflict?

To a social psychologist, a **conflict** is a perceived incompatibility of actions, goals, or ideas. The elements of conflict are much the same, whether we are speaking of nations at war, cultural groups feuding within a society, or partners sparring in a relationship. In each situation, people become enmeshed in potentially destructive processes that can produce unwanted results. Among these processes are social traps and distorted perceptions.

SOCIAL TRAPS In some situations, we support our collective well-being by pursuing our personal interests. As capitalist Adam Smith wrote in *The Wealth of Nations* (1776), "It is not from the benevolence of the butcher, the brewer, or the baker that we expect our dinner, but from their regard to their own interest." In other situations, we harm our collective well-being by pursuing our personal interests. Such situations are **social traps.**

Researchers have created mini social traps in laboratory games that require two participants to choose between pursuing their immediate self-interest (in

Not in my ocean! Many people support alternative energy sources, including wind turbines. But proposals to construct wind farms in real-world places elicit less support. Potential wind turbines in the Highlands and off the coast of Scotland produced heated debate over the benefits of clean energy versus the costs of altering treasured views.

Jeff J. Mitchell/Getty Images

hopes of a big gain, at risk of loss if both do the same) versus cooperating to their mutual benefit. Many real-life situations similarly pit our individual interests against our communal well-being. Individual car owners reason, "Hybrid and electric cars are more expensive and not as cool as the model I'd like to buy. Besides, the fuel that I burn in my one car doesn't noticeably add to the greenhouse gases." When enough people reason similarly, the collective result risks disaster—climate change with rising seas and more extreme weather.

Social traps challenge us to reconcile our right to pursue our personal well-being with our responsibility for the well-being of all. Psychologists have therefore explored ways to convince people to cooperate for their mutual betterment—through agreed-upon *regulations*, through better *communication*, and through promoting *awareness* of our responsibilities toward community, nation, and the whole of humanity (Dawes, 1980; Linder, 1982; Sato, 1987). Given effective regulations, communication, and awareness, people more often cooperate, whether playing a laboratory game or the real game of life.

ENEMY PERCEPTIONS Psychologists have noted that those in conflict have a curious tendency to form diabolical images of one another. These distorted images are, ironically, so similar that we call them **mirror-image perceptions:** As we see "them"—as untrustworthy, with evil intentions—so "they" see us. Each demonizes the other.

Mirror-image perceptions can often feed a vicious cycle of hostility. If Juan believes Maria is annoyed with him, he may snub her, causing her to act in ways that justify his perception. As with individuals, so with countries. Perceptions can become **self-fulfilling prophecies.** They may confirm themselves by influencing the other country to react in ways that seem to justify them.

Individuals and nations alike tend to see their own actions as responses to provocation, not as the causes of what happens next. Perceiving themselves as returning tit for tat, they often hit back harder, as University College London volunteers did in one experiment (Shergill et al., 2003). After feeling pressure on their own finger, they were to use a mechanical device to press on another volunteer's finger. Although told to reciprocate with the same amount of pressure, they typically responded with about 40 percent more force than they had just experienced. Despite seeking only to respond in kind, their touches soon escalated to hard presses, much as when each child after a fight claims that "I just poked him, but he hit me harder."

Mirror-image perceptions feed similar cycles of hostility on the world stage. To most people, torture seems more justified when done by "us" rather than "them" (Tarrant et al., 2012). In American media reports, Muslims who kill have been portrayed as fanatical, hateful terrorists, while an American who allegedly killed 16 Afghans was portrayed as struggling financially and stressed out from marriage problems, four tours of duty, and a friend's having had his leg blown off (Greenwald, 2012).

The point is not that truth must lie midway between two such views; one may be more accurate. The point is that enemy perceptions often form mirror images. Moreover, as enemies change, so do perceptions. In American minds and media, the "bloodthirsty, cruel, treacherous" Japanese of World War II later became our "intelligent, hardworking, self-disciplined, resourceful allies" (Gallup, 1972).

Promoting Peace

37-6 How can we transform feelings of prejudice, aggression, and conflict into attitudes that promote peace?

How can we make peace? Can contact, cooperation, communication, and conciliation transform the antagonisms fed by prejudice and conflict into attitudes that promote peace? Research indicates that, in some cases, they can.

---

social-responsibility norm an expectation that people will help those needing their help.

conflict a perceived incompatibility of actions, goals, or ideas.

social trap a situation in which the conflicting parties, by each pursuing their self-interest rather than the good of the group, become caught in mutually destructive behavior.

mirror-image perceptions mutual views often held by conflicting people, as when each side sees itself as ethical and peaceful and views the other side as evil and aggressive.

self-fulfilling prophecy a belief that leads to its own fulfillment.

CONTACT Does it help to put two conflicting parties into close contact? It depends. Negative contact increases *dis*liking (Barlow et al., 2012). But positive contact—especially noncompetitive contact between parties of equal status, such as fellow store clerks—typically helps. Initially prejudiced co-workers of different races have, in such circumstances, usually come to accept one another. This finding is confirmed by a statistical digest of more than 500 studies of face-to-face contact between majority people and outgroups (such as ethnic minorities, the elderly, and those with disabilities). Among the quarter-million people studied across 38 nations, contact has been correlated with, or in experimental studies has led to, more positive attitudes (Al Ramiah & Hewstone, 2013; Pettigrew & Tropp, 2011). Some examples:

- With cross-racial contact, South Africans' interracial attitudes have moved "into closer alignment" (Dixon et al., 2007; Finchilescu & Tredoux, 2010).

- Heterosexuals' attitudes toward gay people are influenced not only by *what* they know but also by *whom* they know (Collier et al., 2012; Smith et al., 2009). In surveys, the reason people most often give for becoming more supportive of same-sex marriage is "having friends, family, or acquaintances who are gay or lesbian" (Pew, 2013).

- Even indirect contact with an outgroup member (via reading a story or through a friend who has an outgroup friend) has reduced prejudice (Cameron & Rutland, 2006; Pettigrew et al., 2007).

However, contact is not always enough. In many schools, ethnic groups segregate themselves in lunchrooms, in classrooms, and elsewhere on school grounds (Alexander & Tredoux, 2010; Clack et al., 2005; Schofield, 1986). People in each group often think that they would welcome more contact with the other group, but they assume the other group does not reciprocate the wish (Richeson & Shelton, 2007). "I don't reach out to them, because I don't want to be rebuffed; they don't reach out to me, because they're just not interested." When such mirror-image misperceptions are corrected, friendships may form and prejudices melt.

COOPERATION To see if enemies could overcome their differences, researcher Muzafer Sherif (1966) set a conflict in motion at a boys' summer camp. He separated 22 Oklahoma City boys into two separate camp areas. Then he had the two groups compete for prizes in a series of activities. Before long, each group became intensely proud of itself and hostile to the other group's "sneaky," "smart-alecky stinkers." Food wars broke out. Cabins were ransacked. Fistfights had to be broken up by camp counselors. Brought together, the two groups avoided each other, except to taunt and threaten. Little did they know that within a few days, they would be friends.

"You cannot shake hands with a clenched fist."

Indira Gandhi, 1971

Sherif accomplished this by giving them **superordinate goals**—shared goals that could be achieved only through cooperation. When he arranged for the camp water supply to "fail," all 22 boys had to work together to restore the water. To rent a movie in those pre-Netflix days, they all had to pool their resources. To move a stalled truck, the boys needed to combine their strength, pulling and pushing together. Having used isolation and competition to make strangers into enemies, Sherif used shared predicaments and goals to turn enemies into friends. What reduced conflict was not mere contact, but *cooperative* contact.

A shared predicament likewise had a powerfully unifying effect in the weeks after the 9/11 attacks. Patriotism soared as Americans felt "we" were under attack. Gallup-surveyed approval of "our President" shot up from 51 percent the week before the attack to a highest-ever 90 percent level 10 days after (Newport, 2002). In chat groups and everyday speech, even the word *we* (relative to *I*) surged in the immediate aftermath (Pennebaker, 2002). Children and youth exposed to war, and minority group members facing rejection or discrimination, likewise develop strong ingroup identification (Bauer et al., 2014; Ramos et al., 2012).

superordinate goals shared goals that override differences among people and require their cooperation.

At such times, cooperation can lead people to define a new, inclusive group that dissolves their former subgroups (Dovidio & Gaertner, 1999). To accomplish this, you might seat members of two groups not on opposite sides, but alternately around a table. Give them a new, shared name. Have them work together. Then watch "us" and "them" become "we." After 9/11, one 18-year-old New Jersey man described this shift in his own social identity: "I just thought of myself as Black. But now I feel like I'm an American, more than ever" (Sengupta, 2001). In a real experiment, White Americans who read a newspaper article about a terrorist threat against all Americans subsequently expressed reduced prejudice against Black Americans (Dovidio et al., 2004).

Kofi Annan: "Most of us have overlapping identities which unite us with very different groups. We *can* love what we are, without hating what— and who—we are *not*. We can thrive in our own tradition, even as we learn from others" (Nobel lecture, 2001).

If cooperative contact between rival group members encourages positive attitudes, might this principle bring people together in multicultural schools? Could interracial friendships replace competitive classroom situations with cooperative ones? Could cooperative learning maintain or even enhance student achievement? Experiments with adolescents from 11 countries confirm that, in each case, the answer is *Yes* (Roseth et al., 2008). In the classroom as in the sports arena, members of interracial groups who work together on projects typically come to feel friendly toward one another. Knowing this, thousands of teachers have made interracial cooperative learning part of their classroom experience.

The power of cooperative activity to make friends of former enemies has led psychologists to urge increased international exchange and cooperation. Some experiments have found that just imagining the shared threat of global climate change reduces international hostilities (Pyszczynski et al., 2012). From adjacent Brazilian tribes to European countries, formerly conflicting groups have managed to build interconnections, interdependence, and a shared social identity as they seek common goals (Fry, 2012). As we engage in mutually beneficial trade, as we work to protect our common destiny on this fragile planet, and as we become more aware that our hopes and fears are shared, we can transform misperceptions that feed conflict into feelings of solidarity based on common interests.

Superordinate goals override differences Cooperative efforts to achieve shared goals are an effective way to break down social barriers.

COMMUNICATION When real-life conflicts become intense, a third-party mediator—a marriage counselor, labor mediator, diplomat, community volunteer—may facilitate much-needed communication (Rubin et al., 1994). Mediators help each party to voice its viewpoint and to understand the other's needs and goals. If successful, mediators can replace a competitive *win-lose* orientation with a cooperative *win-win* orientation that leads to a mutually beneficial resolution. A classic example: Two friends, after quarreling over an orange, agreed to split it. One squeezed his half for juice. The other used the peel from her half to flavor a cake. If only the two had communicated their motives to one another, they could have hit on the win-win solution of one having all the juice, the other all the peel.

CONCILIATION Understanding and cooperative resolution are most needed, yet least likely, in times of anger or crisis (Bodenhausen et al., 1994; Tetlock, 1988). When conflicts intensify, images become more stereotyped, judgments more rigid, and communication more difficult, or even impossible. Each party is likely to threaten, coerce, or retaliate. In the weeks before the 1990 Gulf War, the first

GRIT Graduated and Reciprocated Initiatives in Tension-Reduction—a strategy designed to decrease international tensions.

President George Bush threatened, in the full glare of publicity, to "kick Saddam's ass." Saddam Hussein communicated in kind, threatening to make Americans "swim in their own blood."

Under such conditions, is there an alternative to war or surrender? Social psychologist Charles Osgood (1962, 1980) advocated a strategy of *Graduated and Reciprocated Initiatives in Tension-Reduction*, nicknamed **GRIT.** In applying GRIT, one side first announces its recognition of mutual interests and its intent to reduce tensions. It then initiates one or more small, conciliatory acts. Without weakening one's retaliatory capability, this modest beginning opens the door for reciprocity by the other party. Should the enemy respond with hostility, one reciprocates in kind. But so, too, with any conciliatory response.

In laboratory experiments, small conciliatory gestures—a smile, a touch, a word of apology—have allowed both parties to begin edging down the tension ladder to a safer rung where communication and mutual understanding can begin (Lindskold et al., 1978, 1988). In a real-world international conflict, U.S. President John F. Kennedy's gesture of stopping atmospheric nuclear tests began a series of reciprocated conciliatory acts that culminated in the 1963 atmospheric test-ban treaty.

As working toward shared goals reminds us, we are more alike than different. Civilization advances not by conflict and cultural isolation, but by tapping the knowledge, the skills, and the arts that are each culture's legacy to the whole human race. Thanks to cultural sharing, every modern society is enriched by a cultural mix (Sowell, 1991). We have China to thank for paper and printing and for the magnetic compass that enabled the great explorations. We have Egypt to thank for trigonometry. We have the Islamic world and India's Hindus to thank for our Arabic numerals. While celebrating and claiming these diverse cultural legacies, we can also welcome the enrichment of today's social diversity. We can view ourselves as instruments in a human orchestra. And we—including this book's worldwide readers—can therefore affirm our own culture's heritage while building bridges of communication, understanding, and cooperation across our cultural traditions.

RETRIEVE IT

• What are some ways to reconcile conflicts and promote peace?

ANSWER: Peacemakers should encourage equal-status contact, cooperation to achieve *superordinate goals* (shared goals that override differences), understanding through communication, and reciprocated conciliatory gestures (each side gives a little).

MODULE 37 REVIEW Prosocial Relations

◯ Learning Objectives

Test Yourself by taking a moment to answer each of these Learning Objective Questions (repeated here from within the module). Then turn to Appendix D, Complete Module Reviews, to check your answers. Research suggests that trying to answer these questions on your own will improve your long-term memory of the concepts (McDaniel et al., 2009).

37-1 Why do we befriend or fall in love with some people but not others?

37-2 How does romantic love typically change as time passes?

37-3 When are people most—and least—likely to help?

37-4 How do social exchange theory and social norms explain helping behavior?

37-5 How do social traps and mirror-image perceptions fuel social conflict?

37-6 How can we transform feelings of prejudice, aggression, and conflict into attitudes that promote peace?

▣ Terms and Concepts to Remember

Test yourself on these terms by trying to write down the definition in your own words before flipping back to the referenced page to check your answers.

mere exposure effect, p. 475

passionate love, p. 479

companionate love, p. 480

equity, p. 480

self-disclosure, p. 480

altruism, p. 481

bystander effect, p. 482

social exchange theory, p. 483

reciprocity norm, p. 483

social-responsibility norm, p. 484

conflict, p. 484

social trap, p. 484

mirror-image perceptions, p. 485

self-fulfilling prophecy, p. 485

superordinate goals, p. 486

GRIT, p. 488

[✶] Experience the Testing Effect

Test yourself repeatedly throughout your studies. This will not only help you figure out what you know and don't know; the testing itself will help you learn and remember the information more effectively thanks to the *testing effect*.

1. The more familiar a stimulus becomes, the more we tend to like it. This exemplifies the _____ _____ effect.

2. A happy couple celebrating their 50th wedding anniversary is likely to experience deep _____ love, even though their _____ love has probably decreased over the years.

3. After vigorous exercise, you meet an attractive person, and you are suddenly seized by romantic feelings for that person. This response supports the two-factor theory of emotion, which assumes that emotions, such as passionate love, consist of physical arousal plus

   a. a reward.
   b. proximity.
   c. companionate love.
   d. our interpretation of that arousal.

4. The bystander effect states that a particular bystander is less likely to give aid if

   a. the victim is similar to the bystander in appearance.
   b. no one else is present.
   c. other people are present.
   d. the incident occurs in a deserted or rural area.

5. Our enemies often have many of the same negative impressions of us as we have of them. This exemplifies the concept of _____-_____ perceptions.

6. One way of resolving conflicts and fostering cooperation is by giving rival groups shared goals that help them override their differences. These are called _____ goals.

Find answers to these questions in Appendix E, in the back of the book.

Use ⊛ LearningCurve to create your personalized study plan, which will direct you to the resources that will help you most in ⊛ LaunchPad.

- How did *humanistic psychology* provide a fresh perspective?

ANSWER: This movement sought to turn psychology's attention away from drives and conflicts and toward our growth potential. This focus on the way healthy people strive for self-determination and self-realization was in contrast to Freudian theory and strict behaviorism.

- What does it mean to be *empathic?* How about *self-actualized?* Which humanistic psychologists used these terms?

ANSWER: To be *empathic* is to share and mirror another person's feelings. Carl Rogers believed that people nurture growth in others by being empathic. Abraham Maslow proposed that *self-actualization* is the motivation to fulfill one's potential, and one of the ultimate psychological needs (the other is self-transcendence).

MODULE 38 REVIEW   Classic Perspectives on Personality

◯ Learning Objectives

Test Yourself by taking a moment to answer each of these Learning Objective Questions (repeated here from within the module). Then turn to Appendix D, Complete Module Reviews, to check your answers. Research suggests that trying to answer these questions on your own will improve your long-term memory of the concepts (McDaniel et al., 2009).

38-1 What theories inform our understanding of personality?

38-2 How did Sigmund Freud's treatment of psychological disorders lead to his view of the unconscious mind?

38-3 What was Freud's view of personality?

38-4 What developmental stages did Freud propose?

38-5 How did Freud think people defended themselves against anxiety?

38-6 Which of Freud's ideas did his followers accept or reject?

38-7 What are projective tests, how are they used, and what are some criticisms of them?

38-8 How do contemporary psychologists view Freud's psychoanalysis?

38-9 How has modern research developed our understanding of the unconscious?

38-10 How did humanistic psychologists view personality, and what was their goal in studying personality?

38-11 How did humanistic psychologists assess a person's sense of self?

38-12 How have humanistic theories influenced psychology? What criticisms have they faced?

▣ Terms and Concepts to Remember

Test yourself on these terms by trying to write down the definition in your own words before flipping back to the referenced page to check your answers.

personality, p. 492
psychodynamic theories, p. 492
psychoanalysis, p. 492
unconscious, p. 493
free association, p. 493

id, p. 493
ego, p. 493
superego, p. 494
psychosexual stages, p. 494
Oedipus [ED-uh-puss] complex, p. 494
identification, p. 494
fixation, p. 494
defense mechanisms, p. 495
repression, p. 495

collective unconscious, p. 496
projective test, p. 497
Thematic Apperception Test (TAT), p. 497
Rorschach inkblot test, p. 498
humanistic theories, p. 501
self-actualization, p. 501
unconditional positive regard, p. 502
self-concept, p. 502

[✴] Experience the Testing Effect

Test yourself repeatedly throughout your studies. This will not only help you figure out what you know and don't know; the testing itself will help you learn and remember the information more effectively thanks to the *testing effect*.

1. Freud believed that we may block painful or unacceptable thoughts, wishes, feelings, or memories from consciousness through an unconscious process called _____.

2. According to Freud's view of personality structure, the "executive" system, the _____, seeks to gratify the impulses of the _____ in more acceptable ways.

   a. id; ego
   b. ego; superego
   c. ego; id
   d. id; superego

3. Freud proposed that the development of the "voice of conscience" is related to the _____, which internalizes ideals and provides standards for judgments.

Some humanistic psychologists believed that any standardized assessment of personality, even a questionnaire, is depersonalizing. Rather than forcing the person to respond to narrow categories, these humanistic psychologists presumed that interviews and intimate conversation would provide a better understanding of each person's unique experiences. Some modern personality researchers believe our identity may be helpfully revealed using the *life story approach*—collecting a rich narrative detailing each person's unique life history (McAdams & Guo, 2015).

unconditional positive regard according to Rogers, an attitude of total acceptance toward another person.

self-concept all our thoughts and feelings about ourselves, in answer to the question, "Who am I?"

Evaluating Humanistic Theories

38-12 How have humanistic theories influenced psychology? What criticisms have they faced?

One thing said of Freud can also be said of the humanistic psychologists: Their impact has been pervasive. Maslow's and Rogers' ideas have influenced counseling, education, child raising, and management. And they laid the groundwork for today's scientific *positive psychology* subfield.

They have also influenced—sometimes in unintended ways—much of today's popular psychology. Is a positive self-concept the key to happiness and success? Do acceptance and empathy nurture positive feelings about ourselves? Are people basically good and capable of self-improvement? Many people answer *Yes, Yes,* and *Yes.* In 2006, U.S. high school students reported notably higher self-esteem and greater expectations of future career success than did students living in 1975 (Twenge & Campbell, 2008). Given a choice, today's North American college students mostly say they'd rather get a self-esteem boost, such as a compliment or good grade on a paper, than enjoy a favorite food or sexual activity (Bushman et al., 2011). Humanistic psychology's message has been heard.

The prominence of the humanistic perspective set off a backlash of criticism. First, said the critics, its concepts are vague and *subjective.* Consider Maslow's description of self-actualizing people as open, spontaneous, loving, self-accepting, and productive. Is this a scientific description? Or is it merely a description of the theorist's own values and ideals? Maslow, noted M. Brewster Smith (1978), offered impressions of his own personal heroes. Imagine another theorist who began with a different set of heroes—perhaps Napoleon, John D. Rockefeller, Sr., and Donald Trump. This theorist would likely describe self-actualizing people as "undeterred by others' needs and opinions," "motivated to achieve," and "comfortable with power."

Critics also objected to the idea that, as Rogers put it, "The only question which matters is, 'Am I living in a way which is deeply satisfying to me, and which truly expresses me?'" (quoted by Wallach & Wallach, 1985). This emphasis on *individualism*—trusting and acting on one's feelings, being true to oneself, fulfilling oneself—could lead to self-indulgence, selfishness, and an erosion of moral restraint (Campbell & Specht, 1985; Wallach & Wallach, 1983). Imagine working on a group project with people who refuse to complete any task that is not deeply satisfying or does not truly express their identity.

Humanistic psychologists have replied that a secure, nondefensive self-acceptance is actually the first step toward loving others. Indeed, people who feel intrinsically liked and accepted—for who they are, not just for their achievements—exhibit less defensive attitudes (Schimel et al., 2001). Those feeling liked and accepted by a romantic partner report being happier in their relationships and acting more kindly toward their partner (Gordon & Chen, 2010).

A final critique has been that humanistic psychology is *naive,* that it fails to appreciate the reality of our human capacity for evil (May, 1982). Faced with climate change, overpopulation, terrorism, and the spread of nuclear weapons, we may become apathetic from either of two rationalizations. One is a starry-eyed optimism that denies the threat ("People are basically good; everything will work out"). The other is a dark despair ("It's hopeless; why try?"). Action requires enough realism to fuel concern and enough optimism to provide hope.

"We do pretty well when you stop to think that people are basically good."

RETRIEVE IT   [✱]

- How did *humanistic psychology* provide a fresh perspective?

ANSWER: This movement sought to turn psychology's attention away from drives and conflicts and toward our growth potential. This focus on the way healthy people strive for self-determination and self-realization was in contrast to Freudian theory and strict behaviorism.

- What does it mean to be *empathic*? How about *self-actualized*? Which humanistic psychologists used these terms?

ANSWER: To be *empathic* is to share and mirror another person's feelings. Carl Rogers believed that people nurture growth in others by being empathic. Abraham Maslow proposed that *self-actualization* is the motivation to fulfill one's potential, and one of the ultimate psychological needs (the other is self-transcendence).

MODULE 38 REVIEW   Classic Perspectives on Personality

◉ Learning Objectives

Test Yourself by taking a moment to answer each of these Learning Objective Questions (repeated here from within the module). Then turn to Appendix D, Complete Module Reviews, to check your answers. Research suggests that trying to answer these questions on your own will improve your long-term memory of the concepts (McDaniel et al., 2009).

38-1 What theories inform our understanding of personality?

38-2 How did Sigmund Freud's treatment of psychological disorders lead to his view of the unconscious mind?

38-3 What was Freud's view of personality?

38-4 What developmental stages did Freud propose?

38-5 How did Freud think people defended themselves against anxiety?

38-6 Which of Freud's ideas did his followers accept or reject?

38-7 What are projective tests, how are they used, and what are some criticisms of them?

38-8 How do contemporary psychologists view Freud's psychoanalysis?

38-9 How has modern research developed our understanding of the unconscious?

38-10 How did humanistic psychologists view personality, and what was their goal in studying personality?

38-11 How did humanistic psychologists assess a person's sense of self?

38-12 How have humanistic theories influenced psychology? What criticisms have they faced?

▣ Terms and Concepts to Remember

Test yourself on these terms by trying to write down the definition in your own words before flipping back to the referenced page to check your answers.

personality, p. 492

psychodynamic theories, p. 492

psychoanalysis, p. 492

unconscious, p. 493

free association, p. 493

id, p. 493

ego, p. 493

superego, p. 494

psychosexual stages, p. 494

Oedipus [ED-uh-puss] complex, p. 494

identification, p. 494

fixation, p. 494

defense mechanisms, p. 495

repression, p. 495

collective unconscious, p. 496

projective test, p. 497

Thematic Apperception Test (TAT), p. 497

Rorschach inkblot test, p. 498

humanistic theories, p. 501

self-actualization, p. 501

unconditional positive regard, p. 502

self-concept, p. 502

[✱] Experience the Testing Effect

Test yourself repeatedly throughout your studies. This will not only help you figure out what you know and don't know; the testing itself will help you learn and remember the information more effectively thanks to the *testing effect*.

1. Freud believed that we may block painful or unacceptable thoughts, wishes, feelings, or memories from consciousness through an unconscious process called _____.

2. According to Freud's view of personality structure, the "executive" system, the _____, seeks to gratify the impulses of the _____ in more acceptable ways.

   a. id; ego   c. ego; id

   b. ego; superego   d. id; superego

3. Freud proposed that the development of the "voice of conscience" is related to the _____, which internalizes ideals and provides standards for judgments.

A father *not* offering unconditional positive regard:

"Just remember, son, it doesn't matter whether you win or lose—unless you want Daddy's love."

Carl Rogers' Person-Centered Perspective

Fellow humanistic psychologist Carl Rogers agreed with much of Maslow's thinking. Rogers' *person-centered perspective* held that people are basically good and are, as Maslow said, endowed with self-actualizing tendencies. Unless thwarted by a growth-inhibiting environment, each of us is like an acorn, primed for growth and fulfillment. Rogers (1980) believed that a growth-promoting climate required three conditions.

- *Genuineness:* When people are *genuine,* they are open with their own feelings, drop their facades, and are transparent and self-disclosing.

- *Acceptance:* When people are *accepting,* they offer **unconditional positive regard,** an attitude of grace that values us even knowing our failings. It is a profound relief to drop our pretenses, confess our worst feelings, and discover that we are still accepted. In a good marriage, a close family, or an intimate friendship, we are free to be spontaneous without fearing the loss of others' esteem.

- *Empathy:* When people are *empathic,* they share and mirror other's feelings and reflect their meanings. "Rarely do we listen with real understanding, true empathy," said Rogers. "Yet listening, of this very special kind, is one of the most potent forces for change that I know."

Genuineness, acceptance, and empathy are, Rogers believed, the water, sun, and nutrients that enable people to grow like vigorous oak trees. For "as persons are accepted and prized, they tend to develop a more caring attitude toward themselves" (Rogers, 1980, p. 116). As persons are empathically heard, "it becomes possible for them to listen more accurately to the flow of inner experiencings."

Writer Calvin Trillin (2006) recalled an example of parental genuineness and acceptance at a camp for children with severe disorders, where his wife, Alice, worked. L., a "magical child," had genetic diseases that meant she had to be tube-fed and could walk only with difficulty. Alice recalled,

> One day, when we were playing duck-duck-goose, I was sitting behind her and she asked me to hold her mail for her while she took her turn to be chased around the circle. It took her a while to make the circuit, and I had time to see that on top of the pile [of mail] was a note from her mom. Then I did something truly awful. . . . I simply had to know what this child's parents could have done to make her so spectacular, to make her the most optimistic, most enthusiastic, most hopeful human being I had ever encountered. I snuck a quick look at the note, and my eyes fell on this sentence: "If God had given us all of the children in the world to choose from, L., we would only have chosen you." Before L. got back to her place in the circle, I showed the note to Bud, who was sitting next to me. "Quick. Read this," I whispered. "It's the secret of life."

Maslow and Rogers would have smiled knowingly. For them, a central feature of personality is one's **self-concept**—all the thoughts and feelings we have in response to the question, "Who am I?" If our self-concept is positive, we tend to act and perceive the world positively. If it is negative—if in our own eyes we fall far short of our *ideal self*—said Rogers, we feel dissatisfied and unhappy. A worthwhile goal for therapists, parents, teachers, and friends is therefore, he said, to help others know, accept, and be true to themselves.

The picture of empathy Being open and sharing confidences is easier when the listener shows real understanding. Within such relationships we can relax and fully express our true selves. Consider a conversation when you knew someone was waiting for their turn to speak instead of listening to you. Now consider the last time someone heard you with empathy. How did those two experiences differ?

Assessing the Self

⟨ ⟩ 38-11 How did humanistic psychologists assess a person's sense of self?

Humanistic psychologists sometimes assessed personality by asking people to fill out questionnaires that would evaluate their self-concept. One questionnaire, inspired by Carl Rogers, asked people to describe themselves both as they would *ideally* like to be and as they *actually* are. When the ideal and the actual self are nearly alike, said Rogers, the self-concept is positive. Assessing his clients' personal growth during therapy, he looked for successively closer ratings of actual and ideal selves.

Humanistic Theories

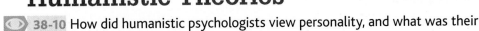 **38-10** How did humanistic psychologists view personality, and what was their goal in studying personality?

By the 1960s, some personality psychologists had become discontented with the sometimes bleak focus on drives and conflicts in *psychodynamic theory,* and the mechanistic psychology of B. F. Skinner's *behaviorism.* In contrast to Freud's emphasis on disorders born out of dark conflicts, these **humanistic theorists** focused on the ways people strive for self-determination and self-realization. In contrast to behaviorism's scientific objectivity, they studied people through their own self-reported experiences and feelings.

Two pioneering theorists—Abraham Maslow (1908–1970) and Carl Rogers (1902–1987)—offered a *third-force perspective* that emphasized human potential.

Abraham Maslow's Self-Actualizing Person

Maslow proposed that we are motivated by a *hierarchy of needs.* If our physiological needs are met, we become concerned with personal safety; if we achieve a sense of security, we then seek to love, to be loved, and to love ourselves; with our love needs satisfied, we seek self-esteem. Having achieved self-esteem, we ultimately seek **self-actualization** (the process of fulfilling our potential) and *self-transcendence* (meaning, purpose, and communion beyond the self).

Maslow (1970) developed his ideas by studying healthy, creative people rather than troubled clinical cases. He based his description of self-actualization on a study of those, such as Abraham Lincoln, who seemed notable for their rich and productive lives. Maslow reported that such people shared certain characteristics: They were self-aware and self-accepting, open and spontaneous, loving and caring, and not paralyzed by others' opinions. Secure in their sense of who they were, their interests were problem-centered rather than self-centered. They focused their energies on a particular task, one they often regarded as their mission in life. Most enjoyed a few deep relationships rather than many superficial ones. Many had been moved by spiritual or personal *peak experiences* that surpassed ordinary consciousness.

These, said Maslow, are mature adult qualities found in those who have learned enough about life to be compassionate, to have outgrown their mixed feelings toward their parents, to have found their calling, to have "acquired enough courage to be unpopular, to be unashamed about being openly virtuous." Maslow's work with college students led him to speculate that those likely to become self-actualizing adults were likable, caring, "privately affectionate to those of their elders who deserve it," and "secretly uneasy about the cruelty, meanness, and mob spirit so often found in young people."

Abraham Maslow "Any theory of motivation that is worthy of attention must deal with the highest capacities of the healthy and strong person as well as with the defensive maneuvers of crippled spirits" (*Motivation and Personality*, 1970, p. 33).

humanistic theories view personality with a focus on the potential for healthy personal growth.

self-actualization according to Maslow, one of the ultimate psychological needs that arises after basic physical and psychological needs are met and self-esteem is achieved; the motivation to fulfill one's potential.

(Schacter, 1996). But the far more common reality is that high stress and associated stress hormones *enhance* memory. Indeed, rape, torture, and other traumatic events haunt survivors, who experience unwanted flashbacks. They are seared onto the soul. "You see the babies," said Holocaust survivor Sally H. (1979). "You see the screaming mothers. You see hanging people. You sit and you see that face there. It's something you don't forget."

THE MODERN UNCONSCIOUS MIND

38-9 How has modern research developed our understanding of the unconscious?

Freud was right about a big idea that underlies today's psychodynamic thinking: We indeed have limited access to all that goes on in our minds (Erdelyi, 1985, 1988, 2006; Norman, 2010). Our two-track mind has a vast out-of-sight realm. Some researchers even argue that "most of a person's everyday life is determined by unconscious thought processes" (Bargh & Chartrand, 1999).

Yet many research psychologists now think of the unconscious not as seething passions and repressive censoring but as cooler information processing that occurs without our awareness. To these researchers, the unconscious also involves

- the *schemas* that automatically control our perceptions and interpretations.

- the *priming* by stimuli to which we have not consciously attended.

- the right-hemisphere activity that enables the *split-brain* patient's left hand to carry out an instruction the patient cannot verbalize.

- the *implicit memories* that operate without conscious recall, even among those with amnesia.

- the *emotions* that activate instantly, before conscious analysis.

- the *stereotypes* that automatically and unconsciously influence how we process information about others.

More than we realize, we fly on autopilot. Our lives are guided by off-screen, out-of-sight, unconscious information processing. The unconscious mind is huge. However, our current understanding of unconscious information processing is more like the pre-Freudian view of an underground, unattended stream of thought from which spontaneous behavior and creative ideas surface (Bargh & Morsella, 2008).

Research also supports two of Freud's defense mechanisms. One study demonstrated *reaction formation* (trading unacceptable impulses for their opposite) in men who reported strong anti-gay attitudes. Compared with those who did not report such attitudes, these men experienced greater measured erections when watching videos of homosexual men having sex, even though they said the films did not make them sexually aroused (Adams et al., 1996). Likewise, preliminary evidence suggests that people who unconsciously identify as homosexual—but who consciously identify as straight—report more negative attitudes toward gays and less support for pro-gay policies (Weinstein et al., 2012).

Freud's *projection* (attributing our own threatening impulses to others) has also been confirmed. People do tend to see their traits, attitudes, and goals in others (Baumeister et al., 1998; Maner et al., 2005). Today's researchers call this the *false consensus effect*—the tendency to overestimate the extent to which others share our beliefs and behaviors. People who binge-drink or break speed limits tend to think many others do the same. However, defense mechanisms seem motivated less by the sexual and aggressive undercurrents that Freud imagined than by our need to protect our self-image.

disguise sexual and aggressive impulses (though our cognitive gymnastics do indeed work to protect our self-esteem). History also has failed to support another of Freud's ideas—that suppressed sexuality causes psychological disorders. From Freud's time to ours, sexual inhibition has diminished; psychological disorders have not.

Psychologists also criticize Freud's theory for its scientific shortcomings. It's important to remember that good scientific theories explain observations and offer testable hypotheses. Freud's theory rests on few objective observations, and parts of it offer few testable hypotheses. For Freud, his own recollections and interpretations of patients' free associations, dreams, and slips were evidence enough.

What is the most serious problem with Freud's theory? It offers after-the-fact explanations of any characteristic (of one person's smoking, another's fear of horses, another's sexual orientation) yet fails to *predict* such behaviors and traits. If you feel angry at your mother's death, you illustrate his theory because "your unresolved childhood dependency needs are threatened." If you do not feel angry, you again illustrate his theory because "you are repressing your anger." That "is like betting on a horse after the race has been run" (Hall & Lindzey, 1978, p. 68). A good theory makes testable predictions.

So, should psychology post an "Allow Natural Death" order on this old theory? Freud's supporters object. To criticize Freudian theory for not making testable predictions is, they say, like criticizing baseball for not being an aerobic exercise, something it was never intended to be. Freud never claimed that psychoanalysis was predictive science. He merely claimed that, looking back, psychoanalysts could find meaning in our state of mind (Rieff, 1979).

Freud's supporters also note that some of his ideas *are* enduring. It was Freud who drew our attention to the unconscious and the irrational, at a time when such ideas were not popular. Today many researchers study our irrationality (Ariely, 2010). Psychologist Daniel Kahneman won the 2002 Nobel Prize in Economics for his studies of our faulty decision making. Freud also drew our attention to the importance of human sexuality, and to the tension between our biological impulses and our social well-being. It was Freud who challenged our self-righteousness, exposed our self-protective defenses, and reminded us of our potential for evil.

MODERN RESEARCH CHALLENGES THE IDEA OF REPRESSION

Psychoanalytic theory presumes that we often *repress* offending wishes, banishing them into the unconscious until they resurface, like long-lost books in a dusty attic. Recover and resolve childhood's conflicted wishes, and emotional healing should follow. Repression became a widely accepted concept, used to explain hypnotic phenomena and psychological disorders. Some psychodynamic followers extended repression to explain apparently lost and recovered memories of childhood traumas (Boag, 2006; Cheit, 1998; Erdelyi, 2006). In one survey, 88 percent of university students believed that painful experiences commonly get pushed out of awareness and into the unconscious (Garry et al., 1994).

Today's researchers agree that we sometimes spare our egos by neglecting threatening information (Green et al., 2008). Yet many contend that repression, if it ever occurs, is a rare mental response to terrible trauma. Even those who witnessed a parent's murder or survived Nazi death camps have retained their unrepressed memories of the horror (Helmreich, 1992, 1994; Malmquist, 1986; Pennebaker, 1990). "Dozens of formal studies have yielded not a single convincing case of repression in the entire literature on trauma," concluded personality researcher John Kihlstrom (2006).

Some researchers do believe that extreme, prolonged stress, such as the stress some severely abused children experience, might disrupt memory by damaging the hippocampus, which is important for processing conscious memories

"We are arguing like a man who should say, 'If there were an invisible cat in that chair, the chair would look empty; but the chair does look empty; therefore there is an invisible cat in it'."

C. S. Lewis, Four Loves, *1958*

"Although [Freud] clearly made a number of mistakes in the formulation of his ideas, his understanding of unconscious mental processes was pretty much on target. In fact, it is very consistent with modern neuroscientists' belief that most mental processes are unconscious."

Nobel Prize–winning neuroscientist Eric Kandel (2012)

"The overall findings . . . seriously challenge the classical psychoanalytic notion of repression."

Psychologist Yacov Rofé, "Does Repression Exist?" 2008

The Rorschach test In this projective test, people tell what they see in a series of symmetrical inkblots. Some who use this test are confident that the interpretation of ambiguous stimuli will reveal unconscious aspects of the test-taker's personality.

Spencer Grant/Science Source

"We don't see things as they are; we see things as we are."

The Talmud

"The Rorschach [Inkblot Test] has the dubious distinction of being, simultaneously, the most cherished and the most reviled of all psychological assessment tools."

John Hunsley and J. Michael Bailey, 1999

"Many aspects of Freudian theory are indeed out of date, and they should be: Freud died in 1939, and he has been slow to undertake further revisions."

Psychologist Drew Westen (1998)

Rorschach inkblot test the most widely used projective test, a set of 10 inkblots, designed by Hermann Rorschach; seeks to identify people's inner feelings by analyzing their interpretations of the blots.

The most widely used projective test left some blots on the name of Swiss psychiatrist Hermann Rorschach [ROAR-shock; 1884–1922]. He based his famous **Rorschach inkblot test,** in which people describe what they see in a series of inkblots (**FIGURE 38.2**), on a childhood game. He and his friends would drip ink on a paper, fold it, and then say what they saw in the resulting blot (Sdorow, 2005). Do you see predatory animals or weapons? Perhaps you have aggressive tendencies. But is this a reasonable assumption? The answer varies.

Some clinicians cherish the Rorschach, even offering Rorschach-based assessments of criminals' violence potential. Others view the test as a source of suggestive leads, an icebreaker, or a revealing interview technique.

Critics of the Rorschach insist the test is no emotional MRI. They argue that only a few of the many Rorschach-derived scores, such as those for cognitive impairment and thought disorder, have demonstrated reliability and validity (Mihura et al., 2013, 2015; Wood et al., 2015). And inkblot assessments have inaccurately diagnosed many normal adults as pathological (Wood et al., 2003, 2006, 2010).

Evaluating Freud's Psychoanalytic Perspective and Modern Views of the Unconscious

👁 38-8 How do contemporary psychologists view Freud's psychoanalysis?

MODERN RESEARCH CONTRADICTS MANY OF FREUD'S IDEAS We critique Freud from a twenty-first-century perspective, a perspective that itself will be subject to revision. Freud did not have access to neurotransmitter or DNA studies, or to all that we have since learned about human development, thinking, and emotion. To criticize his theory by comparing it with today's thinking, some say, is like criticizing Henry Ford's Model T by comparing it with today's hybrid cars. How tempting it always is to judge people in the past from our perspective in the present.

But both Freud's devotees and detractors agree that recent research contradicts many of his specific ideas. Today's developmental psychologists see our development as lifelong, not fixed in childhood. They doubt that infants' neural networks are mature enough to sustain as much emotional trauma as Freud assumed. Some think Freud overestimated parental influence and underestimated peer influence. They also doubt that conscience and gender identity form as the child resolves the Oedipus complex at age 5 or 6. We gain our gender identity earlier, and those who become strongly masculine or feminine do so even without a same-sex parent present. And they note that Freud's ideas about childhood sexuality arose from stories of childhood sexual abuse told by his female patients—stories that some scholars believe Freud expressed skepticism about, and attributed to his patients' own childhood sexual wishes and conflicts (Esterson, 2001; Powell & Boer, 1994). Today, we understand how Freud's questioning might have created false memories of abuse, and we also know that childhood sexual abuse does happen.

Modern dream research disputes Freud's belief that dreams disguise and fulfill wishes. And slips of the tongue can be explained as competition between similar verbal choices in our memory network. Someone who says "I don't want to do that—it's a lot of brothel" may simply be blending *bother* and *trouble* (Foss & Hakes, 1978). Researchers find little support for Freud's idea that defense mechanisms

Alfred Adler "The individual feels at home in life and feels his existence to be worthwhile just so far as he is useful to others and is overcoming feelings of inferiority" (*Problems of Neurosis*, 1964).

Karen Horney "The view that women are infantile and emotional creatures, and as such, incapable of responsibility and independence is the work of the masculine tendency to lower women's self-respect" (*Feminine Psychology*, 1932).

Carl Jung "From the living fountain of instinct flows everything that is creative; hence the unconscious is the very source of the creative impulse" (*The Structure and Dynamics of the Psyche*, 1960).

[psychodynamic] theorists and therapists are not wedded to the idea that sex is the basis of personality," noted Drew Westen (1996). They "do not talk about ids and egos, and do not go around classifying their patients as oral, anal, or phallic characters." What they do assume, with Freud and with much support from today's psychological science, is that much of our mental life is unconscious. With Freud, they also assume that we often struggle with inner conflicts among our wishes, fears, and values, and that childhood shapes our personality and ways of becoming attached to others.

> **Ⓛ LaunchPad** For a helpful, 9-minute overview, visit LaunchPad's *Video: Psychodynamic Theories of Personality*.

Assessing Unconscious Processes

◀◉▶ **38-7** What are projective tests, how are they used, and what are some criticisms of them?

Personality tests reflect the basic ideas of particular personality theories. So, what might be the assessment tool of choice for someone working in the Freudian tradition?

Such a test would need to provide some sort of road into the unconscious—to unearth the residue of early childhood experiences, move beneath surface pretensions, and reveal hidden conflicts and impulses. Objective assessment tools, such as agree-disagree or true-false questionnaires, would be inadequate because they would merely tap the conscious surface.

Projective tests aim to provide this "psychological X-ray" by asking test-takers to describe an ambiguous stimulus or tell a story about it. The clinician may presume that any hopes, desires, and fears that people see in the ambiguous image are projections of their own inner feelings or conflicts.

Henry Murray (1933) demonstrated a possible basis for such a test at a party hosted by his 11-year-old daughter. Murray engaged the children in a frightening game called "Murder." When shown some photographs after the game, the children perceived the photos as more malicious than they had before the game. These children, it seemed to Murray, had *projected* their inner feelings into the pictures.

A few years later, Murray introduced the **Thematic Apperception Test (TAT)**—a test in which people view ambiguous pictures then make up stories about them. One use of such storytelling has been to assess achievement motivation (Schultheiss et al., 2014). Shown a daydreaming boy, those who imagine he is fantasizing about an achievement are presumed to be projecting their own goals. "As a rule," said Murray, "the subject leaves the test happily unaware that he has presented the psychologist with what amounts to an X-ray of his inner self" (quoted by Talbot, 1999).

"The forward thrust of the antlers shows a determined personality, yet the small sun indicates a lack of self-confidence. . . ."

projective test a personality test, such as the Rorschach, that provides ambiguous stimuli designed to trigger projection of one's inner dynamics.

Thematic Apperception Test (TAT) a projective test in which people express their inner feelings and interests through the stories they make up about ambiguous scenes.

"I remember your name perfectly but I just can't think of your face."

Oxford professor W. A. Spooner (1844–1930) famous for his linguistic flip-flops (spoonerisms). Spooner rebuked one student for "fighting a liar in the quadrangle" and another who "hissed my mystery lecture," adding "You have tasted two worms."

- According to Freud's ideas about the three-part personality structure, the _____ operates on the *reality principle* and tries to balance demands in a way that produces long-term pleasure rather than pain; the _____ operates on the *pleasure principle* and seeks immediate gratification; and the _____ represents the voice of our internalized ideals (our *conscience*).

  ANSWERS: ego; id; superego

- In the psychoanalytic view, conflicts unresolved during one of the psychosexual stages may lead to _____ at that stage.

  ANSWER: fixation

- Freud believed that our defense mechanisms operate _____ (consciously/unconsciously) and defend us against _____.

  ANSWERS: unconsciously; anxiety

Regression Faced with a mild stressor, children and young orangutans seek protection and comfort from their caregivers. Freud might have interpreted these behaviors as regression, a retreat to an earlier developmental stage.

---

collective unconscious Carl Jung's concept of a shared, inherited reservoir of memory traces from our species' history.

The Neo-Freudian and Later Psychodynamic Theorists

38-6 Which of Freud's ideas did his followers accept or reject?

In a historical period when people never talked about sex, and certainly not conscious desires for sex with one's parent, Freud's writings prompted debate. "In the Middle Ages, they would have burned me," observed Freud to a friend. "Now they are content with burning my books" (Jones, 1957). Despite the controversy, Freud attracted followers. Several young, ambitious physicians formed an inner circle around their strong-minded leader. These pioneering psychoanalysts, whom we often call *neo-Freudians*, adopted Freud's interviewing technique and accepted his basic ideas: the personality structures of id, ego, and superego; the importance of the unconscious; the childhood roots of personality; and the dynamics of anxiety and the defense mechanisms. But they broke away from Freud in two important ways. First, they placed more emphasis on the conscious mind's role in interpreting experience and in coping with the environment. And second, they doubted that sex and aggression were all-consuming motivations. Instead, they tended to emphasize loftier motives and social interactions.

Alfred Adler and Karen Horney [HORN-eye], for example, agreed with Freud that childhood is important. But they believed that childhood *social*, not sexual, tensions are crucial for personality formation (Ferguson, 2003). Adler (responsible for the still popular idea of the *inferiority complex*) had struggled to overcome childhood illnesses and accidents. He believed that much of our behavior is driven by efforts to conquer childhood inferiority feelings that trigger our strivings for superiority and power. Horney said childhood anxiety triggers our desire for love and security. She also countered Freud's assumptions, rooted in his conservative culture, that women have weak superegos and suffer "penis envy," and she attempted to balance his masculine bias.

Carl Jung [Yoong] started out a strong follower of Freud, but then veered off on his own. Jung placed less emphasis on social factors and agreed with Freud that the unconscious exerts a powerful influence. But to Jung, the unconscious contains more than our repressed thoughts and feelings. He believed we also have a **collective unconscious,** a common reservoir of images, or *archetypes*, derived from our species' universal experiences. Jung said that the collective unconscious explains why, for many people, spiritual concerns are deeply rooted and why people in different cultures share certain myths and images. Most of today's psychologists discount the idea of inherited experiences. But they do believe that our shared evolutionary history shaped some universal dispositions and that experience can leave *epigenetic* marks.

Freud died in 1939. Since then, some of his ideas have been incorporated into the diversity of perspectives that make up psychodynamic theory. "Most contemporary

an exaggerated denial of this dependence (by acting tough or uttering biting sarcasm). Or the person might continue to seek oral gratification by smoking or excessive eating. In such ways, Freud suggested, the twig of personality is bent at an early age.

Freud's ideas of sexuality were controversial in his own time. "Freud was called a dirty-minded pansexualist and Viennese libertine," noted Morton Hunt, historian of psychology (2007, p. 211). Today, Freud's ideas of Oedipal conflict and castration anxiety are disputed even by psychodynamic theorists and therapists (Shedler, 2010). Yet they are still considered an important part of the history of Western ideas.

"Good morning, beheaded—uh, I mean beloved."

DEFENSE MECHANISMS

38-5 How did Freud think people defended themselves against anxiety?

Anxiety, said Freud, is the price we pay for civilization. As members of social groups, we must control our sexual and aggressive impulses, not act them out. But sometimes the ego fears losing control of this inner id-superego war. The presumed result is a dark cloud of unfocused anxiety that leaves us feeling unsettled but unsure why.

Freud proposed that the ego protects itself with **defense mechanisms**—tactics that reduce or redirect anxiety by distorting reality. For Freud, *all defense mechanisms function indirectly and unconsciously*. Just as the body unconsciously defends itself against disease, so also does the ego unconsciously defend itself against anxiety. For example, **repression** banishes anxiety-arousing wishes and feelings from consciousness. According to Freud, *repression underlies all the other defense mechanisms*. However, because repression is often incomplete, repressed urges may appear as symbols in dreams or as slips of the tongue in casual conversation.

Freud believed he could glimpse the unconscious seeping through when a financially stressed patient, not wanting any large pills, said, "Please do not give me any bills, because I cannot swallow them." Freud also viewed jokes as expressions of repressed sexual and aggressive tendencies, and dreams as the "royal road to the unconscious." The remembered content of dreams (their *manifest content*) he believed to be a censored expression of the dreamer's unconscious wishes (the dream's *latent content*). In his dream analyses, Freud searched for patients' inner conflicts.

TABLE 38.2 describes a sampling of six other well-known defense mechanisms.

psychosexual stages the childhood stages of development (oral, anal, phallic, latency, genital) during which, according to Freud, the id's pleasure-seeking energies focus on distinct erogenous zones.

Oedipus [ED-uh-puss] **complex** according to Freud, a boy's sexual desires toward his mother and feelings of jealousy and hatred for the rival father.

identification the process by which, according to Freud, children incorporate their parents' values into their developing superegos.

fixation according to Freud, a lingering focus of pleasure-seeking energies at an earlier psychosexual stage, in which conflicts were unresolved.

defense mechanisms in psychoanalytic theory, the ego's protective methods of reducing anxiety by unconsciously distorting reality.

repression in psychoanalytic theory, the basic defense mechanism that banishes from consciousness anxiety-arousing thoughts, feelings, and memories.

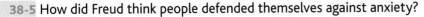

> **✕ TABLE 38.2**

Six Defense Mechanisms Freud believed that *repression*, the basic mechanism that banishes anxiety-arousing impulses, enables other defense mechanisms, six of which are listed here.

Defense Mechanism	Unconscious Process Employed to Avoid Anxiety-Arousing Thoughts or Feelings	Example
Regression	Retreating to a more infantile psychosexual stage, where some psychic energy remains fixated.	A little boy reverts to the oral comfort of thumb sucking in the car on the way to his first day of school.
Reaction formation	Switching unacceptable impulses into their opposites.	Repressing angry feelings, a person displays exaggerated friendliness.
Projection	Disguising one's own threatening impulses by attributing them to others.	"The thief thinks everyone else is a thief" (an El Salvadoran saying).
Rationalization	Offering self-justifying explanations in place of the real, more threatening unconscious reasons for one's actions.	A habitual drinker says she drinks with her friends "just to be sociable."
Displacement	Shifting sexual or aggressive impulses toward a more acceptable or less threatening object or person.	A little girl kicks the family dog after her mother sends her to her room.
Denial	Refusing to believe or even perceive painful realities.	A partner denies evidence of his loved one's affair.

"Fifty is plenty."   "Hundred and fifty."

The ego struggles to reconcile the demands of superego and id, said Freud.

"I heard that as soon as we become aware of our sexual impulses, whatever they are, we'll have to hide them."

"Oh, for goodness' sake! Smoke!"

superego the part of personality that, according to Freud, represents internalized ideals and provides standards for judgment (the conscience) and for future aspirations.

Around age 4 or 5, Freud theorized, a child's ego recognizes the demands of the newly emerging **superego,** the voice of our moral compass (conscience) that forces the ego to consider not only the real but the *ideal*. The superego focuses on how we *ought* to behave. It strives for perfection, judging actions and producing positive feelings of pride or negative feelings of guilt. Someone with an exceptionally strong superego may be virtuous yet guilt ridden; another with a weak superego may be outrageously self-indulgent and remorseless.

Because the superego's demands often oppose the id's, the ego struggles to reconcile the two. The ego is the personality "executive," mediating among the impulsive demands of the id, the restraining demands of the superego, and the real-life demands of the external world. If chaste Conner feels sexually attracted to Tatiana, he may satisfy both id and superego by joining a volunteer organization that Tatiana attends regularly.

PERSONALITY DEVELOPMENT

38-4 What developmental stages did Freud propose?

Analysis of his patients' histories convinced Freud that personality forms during life's first few years. He concluded that children pass through a series of **psychosexual stages,** during which the id's pleasure-seeking energies focus on distinct pleasure-sensitive areas of the body called *erogenous zones* (**TABLE 38.1**). Each stage offers its own challenges, which Freud saw as conflicting tendencies.

Freud believed that during the *phallic stage*, for example, boys develop both unconscious sexual desires for their mother and jealousy and hatred for their father, whom they consider a rival. Given these feelings, he thought, boys also experience guilt and a lurking fear of punishment, perhaps by castration, from their father. Freud called this collection of feelings the **Oedipus complex** after the Greek legend of Oedipus, who unknowingly killed his father and married his mother. Some psychoanalysts in Freud's era believed that girls experienced a parallel *Electra complex*.

Children eventually cope with the threatening feelings, said Freud, by repressing them and by trying to become like the rival parent. It's as though something inside the child decides, "If you can't beat 'em [the same-sex parent], join 'em." Through this **identification** process, children's superegos gain strength as they incorporate many of their parents' values. Freud believed that identification with the same-sex parent provides what psychologists now call our *gender identity*—our sense of being male, female, or a combination of the two. Freud presumed that our early childhood relations—especially with our parents and other caregivers—influence our developing identity, personality, and frailties.

In Freud's view, conflicts unresolved during earlier psychosexual stages could surface as maladaptive behavior in the adult years. At any point in the oral, anal, or phallic stages, strong conflict could lock, or **fixate,** the person's pleasure-seeking energies in that stage. A person who had been either orally overindulged or deprived (perhaps by abrupt, early weaning) might fixate at the oral stage. This orally fixated adult could exhibit either passive dependence (like that of a nursing infant) or

▾ TABLE 38.1

Freud's Psychosexual Stages

Stage	Focus
Oral (0–18 months)	Pleasure centers on the mouth—sucking, biting, chewing
Anal (18–36 months)	Pleasure focuses on bowel and bladder elimination; coping with demands for control
Phallic (3–6 years)	Pleasure zone is the genitals; coping with incestuous sexual feelings
Latency (6 to puberty)	A phase of dormant sexual feelings
Genital (puberty on)	Maturation of sexual interests

A patient might have lost all feeling in a hand—yet there is no sensory nerve that, if damaged, would numb the entire hand and nothing else. Freud's search for a cause for such disorders set his mind running in a direction destined to change human self-understanding.

Might some neurological disorders have psychological causes? Observing patients led Freud to his "discovery" of the **unconscious**. He speculated that lost feeling in one's hand might be caused by a fear of touching one's genitals; that unexplained blindness or deafness might be caused by not wanting to see or hear something that aroused intense anxiety. How might such disorders be treated? After some early unsuccessful trials with hypnosis, Freud turned to **free association,** in which he told the patient to relax and say whatever came to mind, no matter how embarrassing or trivial. He assumed that a line of mental dominoes had fallen from his patients' distant past to their troubled present, and that the chain of thought revealed by free association would allow him to retrace that line into a patient's unconscious. There, painful memories, often from childhood, could then be retrieved from the unconscious and brought into conscious awareness.

Basic to Freud's theory was his belief that the mind is mostly hidden (**FIGURE 38.1**). Our *conscious* awareness is like the part of an iceberg that floats above the surface. Beneath our awareness is the larger *unconscious* mind, with its thoughts, wishes, feelings, and memories. Some of these thoughts we store temporarily in a *preconscious* area, from which we can retrieve them into conscious awareness. Of greater interest to Freud was the mass of unacceptable passions and thoughts that he believed we *repress*, or forcibly block from our consciousness because they would be too unsettling to acknowledge. Freud believed that without our awareness, these troublesome feelings and ideas powerfully influence us. Such feelings, he said, sometimes surface in disguised forms—the work we choose, the beliefs we hold, our daily habits, our troubling symptoms.

PERSONALITY STRUCTURE

38-3 What was Freud's view of personality?

In Freud's view, human personality—including its emotions and strivings—arises from a conflict between impulse and restraint—between our aggressive, pleasure-seeking biological urges and our internalized social controls over these urges. Freud believed personality arises from our efforts to resolve this basic conflict—to express these impulses in ways that bring satisfaction without also bringing guilt or punishment. To understand the mind's dynamics during this conflict, Freud proposed three interacting systems: the *id, ego,* and *superego* (Figure 38.1).

The **id's** unconscious psychic energy constantly strives to satisfy basic drives to survive, reproduce, and aggress. The id operates on the *pleasure principle:* It seeks immediate gratification. To envision an id-dominated person, think of a newborn infant crying out for satisfaction, caring nothing for the outside world's conditions and demands. Or think of people with a present rather than future time perspective—those who heavily use tobacco, alcohol, and other drugs, and would sooner party now than sacrifice today's pleasure for future success and happiness (Fernie et al., 2013; Friedel et al., 2014; Keough et al., 1999).

As the **ego** develops, the young child responds to the real world. The ego, operating on the *reality principle*, seeks to gratify the id's impulses in realistic ways that will bring long-term pleasure. (Imagine what would happen if, lacking an ego, we expressed all our unrestrained sexual or aggressive impulses.) The ego contains our partly conscious perceptions, thoughts, judgments, and memories.

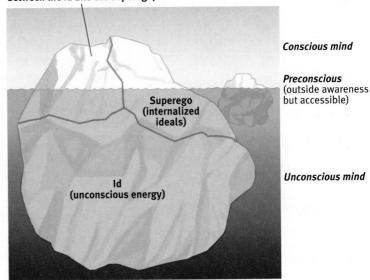

Ego (mostly conscious; makes peace between the id and the superego)

Conscious mind

Preconscious (outside awareness but accessible)

Superego (internalized ideals)

Unconscious mind

Id (unconscious energy)

⌃ FIGURE 38.1

Freud's idea of the mind's structure Psychologists have used an iceberg image to illustrate Freud's idea that the mind is mostly hidden beneath the conscious surface. Note that the id is totally unconscious, but ego and superego operate both consciously and unconsciously. Unlike the parts of a frozen iceberg, however, the id, ego, and superego interact.

unconscious according to Freud, a reservoir of mostly unacceptable thoughts, wishes, feelings, and memories. According to contemporary psychologists, information processing of which we are unaware.

free association in psychoanalysis, a method of exploring the unconscious in which the person relaxes and says whatever comes to mind, no matter how trivial or embarrassing.

id a reservoir of unconscious psychic energy that, according to Freud, strives to satisfy basic sexual and aggressive drives. The id operates on the *pleasure principle*, demanding immediate gratification.

ego the largely conscious, "executive" part of personality that, according to Freud, mediates among the demands of the id, superego, and reality. The ego operates on the *reality principle*, satisfying the id's desires in ways that will realistically bring pleasure rather than pain.

personality an individual's characteristic pattern of thinking, feeling, and acting.

psychodynamic theories view personality with a focus on the unconscious and the importance of childhood experiences.

psychoanalysis Freud's theory of personality that attributes thoughts and actions to unconscious motives and conflicts; the techniques used in treating psychological disorders by seeking to expose and interpret unconscious tensions.

Sigmund Freud (1856–1939) "I was the only worker in a new field."

"The female . . . acknowledges the fact of her castration, and with it, too, the superiority of the male and her own inferiority; but she rebels against this unwelcome state of affairs."

Sigmund Freud,
Female Sexuality, *1931*

MODULE 38 Classic Perspectives on Personality

What Is Personality?

38-1 What theories inform our understanding of personality?

Our **personality** is our characteristic pattern of thinking, feeling, and acting. Two historically significant personality theories have become part of our cultural legacy. Sigmund Freud's *psychoanalytic theory* proposed that childhood sexuality and unconscious motivations influence personality. (Freud's ideas inspired today's *psychodynamic theorists.*) The *humanistic theories* focused on our inner capacities for growth and self-fulfillment. Later theorists built upon these two broad perspectives. *Trait theories,* for example, examine characteristic patterns of behavior (traits). *Social-cognitive theories* explore the interaction between people's traits (including their thinking) and their social context. Let's begin with psychodynamic theories.

The Psychodynamic Theories

Psychodynamic theories of personality view human behavior as a dynamic interaction between the conscious mind and the unconscious mind, including associated motives and conflicts. These theories are descended from Freud's **psychoanalysis**—his theory of personality and the associated treatment techniques. Freud was the first to focus clinical attention on our unconscious mind.

Freud's Psychoanalytic Perspective: Exploring the Unconscious

38-2 How did Sigmund Freud's treatment of psychological disorders lead to his view of the unconscious mind?

Ask 100 people on the street to name a notable deceased psychologist, suggested Keith Stanovich (1996, p. 1), and "Freud would be the winner hands down." In the popular mind, he is to psychology what Elvis Presley is to rock music. Freud's influence not only lingers in psychiatry and clinical psychology, but also in literary and film interpretation. Almost 9 in 10 American college courses that reference psychoanalysis have been outside of psychology departments (Cohen, 2007). Today's psychological science is, as we will see, skeptical about many of Freud's ideas and methods. Yet his early twentieth-century concepts penetrate our twenty-first-century language. Without realizing their source, we may speak of *ego, repression, projection, sibling rivalry, Freudian slips,* and *fixation.* So, who was Freud, and what did he teach?

Like all of us, Sigmund Freud was a product of his times. His Victorian era was a time of tremendous discovery and scientific advancement, but it is also known today as a time of sexual repression and male dominance. Men's and women's roles were clearly defined, with male superiority assumed and only male sexuality generally acknowledged (discreetly).

Long before entering the University of Vienna in 1873, young Freud showed signs of independence and brilliance. He so loved reading plays, poetry, and philosophy that he once ran up a bookstore debt beyond his means. As a teen he often took his evening meal in his tiny bedroom in order to lose no time from his studies. After medical school he set up a private practice specializing in nervous disorders. Before long, however, he faced patients whose disorders made no neurological sense.

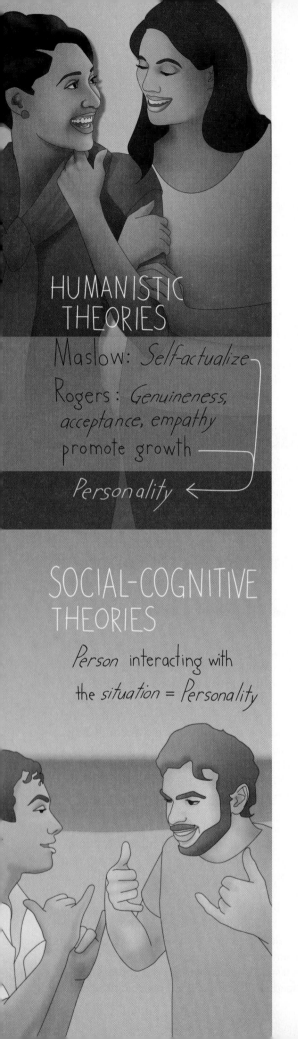

HUMANISTIC
THEORIES

Maslow: *Self-actualize*

Rogers: *Genuineness, acceptance, empathy promote growth*

Personality

SOCIAL-COGNITIVE
THEORIES

Person interacting with the *situation* = *Personality*

Personality

LADY GAGA dazzles millions with her unique musical arrangements, tantalizing outfits, and provocative performance theatrics. In shows around the world, Lady Gaga's most predictable feature is her unpredictability. She has worn a meat dress to an awards show, sported 16-inch heels to meet with U.S. President Barack Obama (who later described the interaction as "a little intimidating"), and wowed Oscar viewers with her *Sound of Music* tribute to Julie Andrews.

Yet even Lady Gaga exhibits distinctive and enduring ways of thinking, feeling, and behaving, including an openness to new experiences, a spotlight-fueled energy, and a painstaking dedication to her performances. "I'm very detailed—every minute of the show has got to be perfect," she says. This conscientiousness continues from her high school self, which she describes as "very dedicated, very studious, and very disciplined." Modules 38 and 39 focus on the ways we all demonstrate unique and persisting patterns of thinking and behaving—our *personality*.

Much of this book deals with personality. Other modules consider biological influences on personality; personality development across the life span; how personality relates to learning, motivation, emotion, and health; social influences on personality; and disorders of personality. These modules focus on personality itself—what it is and how researchers study it.

We begin with two historically important theories of personality: Sigmund Freud's *psychoanalytic theory* and the *humanistic* approach (Module 38). These sweeping perspectives on human nature laid the foundation for later personality theorists and for what Module 39 presents: newer scientific explorations of personality. Today's personality researchers study the basic dimensions of personality, and the interaction of persons and environments. They also study self-esteem, self-serving bias, and cultural influences on our concept of self—that sense of "Who I am." And they study the unconscious mind—with findings that probably would have surprised even Freud. ■

37 REVIEW Prosocial Relations

👁 Learning Objectives

Test Yourself by taking a moment to answer each of these Learning Objective Questions (repeated here from within the module). Then turn to Appendix D, Complete Module Reviews, to check your answers. Research suggests that trying to answer these questions on your own will improve your long-term memory of the concepts (McDaniel et al., 2009).

37-1 Why do we befriend or fall in love with some people but not others?

37-2 How does romantic love typically change as time passes?

37-3 When are people most—and least—likely to help?

37-4 How do social exchange theory and social norms explain helping behavior?

37-5 How do social traps and mirror-image perceptions fuel social conflict?

37-6 How can we transform feelings of prejudice, aggression, and conflict into attitudes that promote peace?

Terms and Concepts to Remember

Test yourself on these terms by trying to write down the definition in your own words before flipping back to the referenced page to check your answers.

mere exposure effect, p. 475

passionate love, p. 479

companionate love, p. 480

equity, p. 480

self-disclosure, p. 480

altruism, p. 481

bystander effect, p. 482

social exchange theory, p. 483

reciprocity norm, p. 483

social-responsibility norm, p. 484

conflict, p. 484

social trap, p. 484

mirror-image perceptions, p. 485

self-fulfilling prophecy, p. 485

superordinate goals, p. 486

GRIT, p. 488

Experience the Testing Effect

Test yourself repeatedly throughout your studies. This will not only help you figure out what you know and don't know; the testing itself will help you learn and remember the information more effectively thanks to the *testing effect*.

1. The more familiar a stimulus becomes, the more we tend to like it. This exemplifies the _____ _____ effect.

2. A happy couple celebrating their 50th wedding anniversary is likely to experience deep _____ love, even though their _____ love has probably decreased over the years.

3. After vigorous exercise, you meet an attractive person, and you are suddenly seized by romantic feelings for that person. This response supports the two-factor theory of emotion, which assumes that emotions, such as passionate love, consist of physical arousal plus

   a. a reward.
   b. proximity.
   c. companionate love.
   d. our interpretation of that arousal.

4. The bystander effect states that a particular bystander is less likely to give aid if

   a. the victim is similar to the bystander in appearance.
   b. no one else is present.
   c. other people are present.
   d. the incident occurs in a deserted or rural area.

5. Our enemies often have many of the same negative impressions of us as we have of them. This exemplifies the concept of _____-_____ perceptions.

6. One way of resolving conflicts and fostering cooperation is by giving rival groups shared goals that help them override their differences. These are called _____ goals.

Find answers to these questions in Appendix E, in the back of the book.

Use 🅐 LearningCurve to create your personalized study plan, which will direct you to the resources that will help you most in 🅐 LaunchPad.

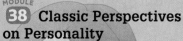

Personality our characteristic pattern of thinking, feeling, and acting

FREUD'S PSYCHOANALYTIC THEORY

Fixation at childhood *psychosexual development stages*

↪ *Unconscious* motives and conflicts ⟶ *Personality*

Id
("Give me that donut!")

Superego
("Donuts are unhealthy.")

Ego
("One small taste is enough.")

PSYCHODYNAMIC THEORIES

~~psychosexual development stages~~

Childhood experiences ⟶ Interaction of *unconscious* and *conscious* mind ⟶ *Personality*

TRAIT THEORIES

Where do you rate on the *Big Five* basic personality traits?

Conscientiousness
Agreeableness
Neuroticism (emotional stability/instability)
Openness
Extraversion

EXPLORING THE SELF

Personality psychologists study:

· *Self-esteem* (benefits, and dangers of too much)
· Pervasive *self-serving bias*, and *narcissism*
· Cultural influences (*individualism* vs *collectivism*)

4. According to the psychoanalytic view of development, we all pass through a series of psychosexual stages, including the oral, anal, and phallic stages. Conflicts unresolved at any of these stages may lead to

   a. dormant sexual feelings.

   b. fixation at that stage.

   c. preconscious blocking of impulses.

   d. a distorted gender identity.

5. Freud believed that defense mechanisms are unconscious attempts to distort or disguise reality, all in an effort to reduce our _____.

6. _____ tests ask test-takers to respond to an ambiguous stimulus, for example, by describing it or telling a story about it.

7. In general, neo-Freudians such as Adler and Horney accepted many of Freud's views but placed more emphasis than he did on

   a. development throughout the life span.

   b. the collective unconscious.

   c. the role of the id.

   d. social interactions.

8. Modern-day psychodynamic theorists and therapists agree with Freud about

   a. the existence of unconscious mental processes.

   b. the Oedipus complex.

   c. the predictive value of Freudian theory.

   d. the superego's role as the executive part of personality.

9. Which of the following is NOT part of the contemporary view of the unconscious?

   a. Repressed memories of anxiety-provoking events

   b. Schemas that influence our perceptions and interpretations

   c. Stereotypes that affect our information processing

   d. Instantly activated emotions and implicit memories of learned skills

10. Maslow's hierarchy of needs proposes that we must satisfy basic physiological and safety needs before we seek ultimate psychological needs, such as self-actualization. Maslow based his ideas on

    a. Freudian theory.

    b. his experiences with patients.

    c. a series of laboratory experiments.

    d. his study of healthy, creative people.

11. How might Rogers explain how environment influences the development of a criminal?

12. The total acceptance Rogers advocated as part of a growth-promoting environment is called

    _____ _____ _____.

Find answers to these questions in Appendix E, in the back of the book.

Use 🅰 LearningCurve to create your personalized study plan, which will direct you to the resources that will help you most in 🅰 LaunchPad.

Contemporary Perspectives on Personality

Trait Theories

⟨◦⟩ 39-1 How do psychologists use traits to describe personality?

Rather than focusing on unconscious forces and thwarted growth opportunities, some researchers attempt to define personality in terms of stable and enduring behavior patterns, such as Lady Gaga's openness to new experiences and her self-discipline. This perspective can be traced in part to a remarkable meeting in 1919, when Gordon Allport, a curious 22-year-old psychology student, interviewed Sigmund Freud in Vienna. Allport soon discovered just how preoccupied the founder of psychoanalysis was with finding hidden motives, even in Allport's own behavior during the interview. That experience ultimately led Allport to do what Freud did not do—to describe personality in terms of fundamental **traits**—people's characteristic behaviors and conscious motives (such as the curiosity that actually motivated

> **trait** a characteristic pattern of behavior or a disposition to feel and act, as assessed by self-report inventories and peer reports.

"Russ is the sort of person who never wants to be alone with his thoughts."

Allport to see Freud). Meeting Freud, said Allport, "taught me that [psychoanalysis], for all its merits, may plunge too deep, and that psychologists would do well to give full recognition to manifest motives before probing the unconscious." Allport came to define personality in terms of identifiable behavior patterns. He was concerned less with *explaining* individual traits than with *describing* them.

Exploring Traits

Classifying people as one or another distinct personality type fails to capture their full individuality. We are each a unique complex of multiple traits. So how else could we describe our personalities? We might describe an apple by placing it along several trait dimensions—relatively large or small, red or green, sweet or sour. By placing people on several trait dimensions simultaneously, psychologists can describe countless individual personality variations, just as researchers can describe thousands of colors in terms of their variations on just three color dimensions—*hue, saturation,* and *brightness.*

What trait dimensions describe personality? If you had an upcoming blind date, what personality traits might give you an accurate sense of the person? Allport and his associate H. S. Odbert (1936) counted all the words in an unabridged dictionary with which one could describe people. There were almost 18,000! How, then, could psychologists condense the list to a manageable number of basic traits?

FACTOR ANALYSIS One technique is *factor analysis,* a statistical procedure that has been used to identify clusters (factors) of test items that tap basic components of a trait, such as intelligence (spatial ability or verbal skill). Imagine that people who describe themselves as outgoing also tend to say that they like excitement and practical jokes and dislike quiet reading. Such a statistically correlated cluster of behaviors reflects a basic factor, or trait—in this case, *extraversion.*

British psychologists Hans Eysenck and Sybil Eysenck [EYE-zink] believed that we can reduce many of our normal individual variations to two or three dimensions, including *extraversion–introversion* and *emotional stability–instability* (**FIGURE 39.1**). People in 35 countries around the world, from China to Uganda to Russia, have taken the *Eysenck Personality Questionnaire.* When their answers were analyzed, the extraversion and emotionality factors inevitably emerged as basic personality dimensions (Eysenck, 1990, 1992). The Eysencks believed, and research confirms, that these factors are genetically influenced.

BIOLOGY AND PERSONALITY Brain-activity scans of extraverts add to the growing list of traits and mental states now being explored with brain-imaging procedures. Such studies indicate that extraverts seek stimulation because their

∨ FIGURE 39.1

Two personality dimensions Mapmakers can tell us a lot by using two axes (north–south and east–west). Two primary personality factors (extraversion–introversion and stability–instability) are similarly useful as axes for describing personality variation. Varying combinations define other, more specific traits (from Eysenck & Eysenck, 1963). Those who are naturally introverted, such as primatologist Jane Goodall, may be particularly gifted in field studies. Successful politicians, including former U.S. President Bill Clinton, are often natural extraverts.

UNSTABLE

Moody   Touchy
Anxious   Restless
Rigid   Aggressive
Sober   Excitable
Pessimistic   Changeable
Reserved   Impulsive
Unsociable   Optimistic
Quiet   Active
INTROVERTED ———————— EXTRAVERTED
Passive   Sociable
Careful   Outgoing
Thoughtful   Talkative
Peaceful   Responsive
Controlled   Easygoing
Reliable   Lively
Even-tempered   Carefree
Calm   Leadership

STABLE

normal *brain arousal* is relatively low. For example, PET scans have shown that a frontal lobe area involved in behavior inhibition is less active in extraverts than in introverts (Johnson et al., 1999). Dopamine and dopamine-related neural activity tend to be higher in extraverts (Kim et al., 2008; Wacker et al., 2006).

Our biology influences our personality in other ways as well. As we know from twin and adoption studies, our genes have much to say about the *temperament* and behavioral style that help define our personality. Children's shyness and inhibition may differ as an aspect of autonomic nervous system reactivity: Those with a reactive autonomic nervous system respond to stress with greater anxiety and inhibition (Kagan, 2010) (see Thinking Critically About: The Stigma of Introversion). The fearless, curious child may become the rock-climbing or fast-driving adult.

Personality differences among dogs (in energy, affection, reactivity, and curious intelligence) are as evident, and as consistently judged, as personality differences among humans (Gosling et al., 2003; Jones & Gosling, 2005). Monkeys,

Erik Lam/Shutterstock

The Stigma of Introversion

39-2 What are some common misunderstandings about introversion? Does extraversion lead to greater success than introversion?

Psychologists describe and measure personality, but they don't advise which traits people should have. Society does this. Western cultures, for example, prize extraversion. In one study, 87 percent of people wanted to be more extraverted (Hudson & Roberts, 2014). Being introverted seems to imply that you don't have the "right stuff" (Cain, 2012).

Just look at our superheroes. Extraverted Superman is bold and energetic. His introverted alter ego, Clark Kent, is mild-mannered and bumbling. Take-charge Elastigirl saves the day in *The Incredibles*. The message is clear: It's the extraverts who are the superheroes.

TV shows also portray heartthrobs and examples of success as extraverts. Many consider Don Draper, the highly successful, attractive advertising executive in the show *Mad Men* to be a classic extravert. He is dominant and charismatic. Women clamor for his attention. His quiet secretary, Peggy Olson, gains respect and career advancement as the series progresses and she becomes more outspoken. Here again, extraversion equals success.

Why do we celebrate extraversion and belittle introversion? Many people may not understand what introversion really is. Introversion is not shyness. Introverted people seek low levels of stimulation from

AMC/The Kobal Collection/Art Resource

their environment because they're sensitive. One classic study suggested that introverted people even have greater taste sensitivity. When given lemon juice, introverted people salivated more than extraverted people (Corcoran, 1964). Shy people, in contrast, remain quiet because they fear others will evaluate them negatively.

We also tend to believe that introversion acts as a barrier to success, yet introversion actually has many benefits. As supervisors, introverts show greater receptiveness when their employees voice their ideas, challenge existing norms, and take charge. Under these circumstances, introverted leaders outperform extraverted ones (Grant et al.,

2011). One striking analysis of 35 studies showed no correlation between extraversion and sales performance (Barrick et al., 2001). Many introverts prosper. Consider the American presidency, which may offer the best example of the misperception that introversion hinders career success. The top-rated U.S. president of all time was introverted. His name was Abraham Lincoln.

So, introversion should not be considered a sign of weakness. Those who need a quiet break from a loud party are not social rejects nor are they incapable of great things. They simply need a less stimulating environment in order to thrive. It's important for extraverts to understand that not everyone feels driven by high levels of stimulation. It's not a crime to unwind.

John Parrot/Stocktrek Images/Getty Images

chimpanzees, orangutans, and even birds also have stable personalities (Weiss et al., 2006). Among the Great Tit (a European relative of the American chickadee), bold birds more quickly inspect new objects and explore trees (Groothuis & Carere, 2005; Verbeek et al., 1994). By selective breeding, researchers can produce bold or shy birds. Both have their place in natural history: In lean years, bold birds are more likely to find food; in abundant years, shy birds feed with less risk.

RETRIEVE IT [✱]

- Which two primary dimensions did Hans Eysenck and Sybil Eysenck propose for describing personality variation?

ANSWER: introversion–extraversion and emotional stability–instability

---

Assessing Traits

39-3 What are personality inventories, and what are their strengths and weaknesses as trait-assessment tools?

If stable and enduring traits guide our actions, can we devise valid and reliable tests of them? Several trait-assessment techniques exist—some more valid than others. Some provide quick assessments of a single trait, such as extraversion, anxiety, or self-esteem. **Personality inventories**—longer questionnaires covering a wide range of feelings and behaviors—assess several traits at once.

The classic personality inventory is the **Minnesota Multiphasic Personality Inventory (MMPI).** Although the MMPI was originally developed to identify emotional disorders, it also assesses people's personality traits. One of its creators, Starke Hathaway (1960), compared his effort with that of Alfred Binet. Binet, the founder of modern intelligence testing, developed the first intelligence test by selecting items that identified children who would probably have trouble progressing normally in French schools. Like Binet's items, the MMPI items were **empirically derived:** From a large pool of items, Hathaway and his colleagues selected those on which particular diagnostic groups differed. "Nothing in the newspaper interests me except the comics" may seem senseless, but it just so happened that depressed people were more likely to answer *True*. The researchers grouped the questions into 10 clinical scales, including scales that assess depressive tendencies, masculinity–femininity, and introversion–extraversion. Today's MMPI-2 has additional scales that assess work attitudes, family problems, and anger.

Whereas most projective tests are scored subjectively, personality inventories are scored objectively. (Software can administer and score these tests, and can also provide descriptions of people who previously responded similarly.) Objectivity does not, however, guarantee validity. Individuals taking the MMPI for employment purposes can give socially desirable answers to create a good impression. But in so doing they may also score high on a *lie scale* that assesses faking (as when people respond *False* to a universally true statement, such as "I get angry sometimes"). The objectivity of the MMPI has contributed to its popularity and to its translation into more than 100 languages.

The Big Five Factors

39-4 Which traits seem to provide the most useful information about personality variation?

Today's trait researchers believe that simple trait factors, such as the Eysencks' introversion–extraversion and stability–instability dimensions, are important, but they do not tell the whole story. A slightly expanded set of factors—dubbed the *Big Five*—does a better job (Costa & McCrae, 2011). If a test specifies where you are on the five dimensions (conscientiousness, agreeableness, neuroticism, openness, and extraversion; see **TABLE 39.1**), it has said much of what there is to say

---

LaunchPad

IMMERSIVE LEARNING Might astrology hold the secret to our personality traits? To consider this question, visit LaunchPad's *How Would You Know If Astrologers Can Describe People's Personality?*

People have had fun spoofing the MMPI with their own mock items: "Weeping brings tears to my eyes," "Frantic screams make me nervous," and "I stay in the bathtub until I look like a raisin" (Frankel et al., 1983).

---

personality inventory a questionnaire (often with *true-false* or *agree-disagree* items) on which people respond to items designed to gauge a wide range of feelings and behaviors; used to assess selected personality traits.

Minnesota Multiphasic Personality Inventory (MMPI) the most widely researched and clinically used of all personality tests. Originally developed to identify emotional disorders (still considered its most appropriate use), this test is now used for many other screening purposes.

empirically derived test a test (such as the MMPI) developed by testing a pool of items and then selecting those that discriminate between groups.

TABLE 39.1

The "Big Five" Personality Factors Researchers use self-report inventories and peer reports to assess and score the Big Five personality factors.

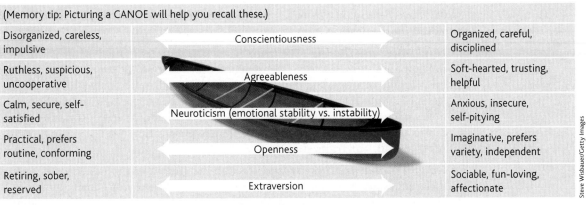

(Memory tip: Picturing a CANOE will help you recall these.)		
Disorganized, careless, impulsive	Conscientiousness	Organized, careful, disciplined
Ruthless, suspicious, uncooperative	Agreeableness	Soft-hearted, trusting, helpful
Calm, secure, self-satisfied	Neuroticism (emotional stability vs. instability)	Anxious, insecure, self-pitying
Practical, prefers routine, conforming	Openness	Imaginative, prefers variety, independent
Retiring, sober, reserved	Extraversion	Sociable, fun-loving, affectionate

Steve Wisbauer/Getty Images

Source: Information from McCrae & Costa (1986, 2008).

about your personality. Around the world—across 56 nations and 29 languages in one study (Schmitt et al., 2007)—people describe others in terms roughly consistent with this list. The Big Five may not be the last word. Some researchers report that basic personality dimensions can be described by only one or two or three factors (such as conscientiousness, agreeableness, and extraversion) (Block, 2010; De Raad et al., 2010). But for now, at least, five is the winning number in the personality lottery (Heine & Buchtel, 2009; McCrae, 2009). To find out how your personality measures up, try the brief self-assessment in **FIGURE 39.2**.

The Big Five is currently our best approximation of the basic trait dimensions. This "common currency for personality psychology" (Funder, 2001) has been the

---

How Accurately Can You Describe Yourself?

Describe yourself as you generally are now, not as you wish to be in the future. Describe yourself as you honestly see yourself, in relation to other people you know of the same sex and roughly the same age. Use the scale below to enter a number for each statement. Then, use the scoring guide at the bottom to see where you fall on the spectrum for each of the Big Five traits.

1	2	3	4	5
Very Inaccurate	Moderately Inaccurate	Neither Accurate Nor Inaccurate	Moderately Accurate	Very Accurate

1. ___Am the life of the party

2. ___Sympathize with others' feelings

3. ___Get stressed out easily

4. ___Am always prepared

5. ___Am full of ideas

6. ___Start conversations

7. ___Take time out for others

8. ___Follow a schedule

9. ___Worry about things

10. ___Have a vivid imagination

SCORING GUIDE SORTED BY BIG FIVE PERSONALITY TRAITS

Conscientiousness: statements 4, 8

Agreeableness: statements 2, 7

Neuroticism: statements 3, 9

Openness: statements 5, 10

Extraversion: statements 1, 6

How to score:
Separate your responses by each Big Five personality trait, as noted at left, and divide by two to obtain your score for each trait. So, for example, for the "Agreeableness" trait let's say you scored 3 for statement 2 ("Sympathize with others' feelings") and 4 for statement 7 ("Take time out for others"). That means on a scale from 1 to 5, your overall score for the "Agreeableness" trait is 3 + 4 = 7 ÷ 2 = **3.5**.

FIGURE 39.2

The Big Five self-assessment

Scale data from Goldberg, L. R. (1992). The development of markers for the Big-Five factor structure. *Psychological Assessment*, 4, 26-42.

most active personality research topic since the early 1990s, as researchers have explored these questions and more:

- **How stable are the Big Five traits?** One research team analyzed 1.25 million participants ages 10 to 65. They learned that personality continues to develop and change through late childhood and adolescence. Up to age 40, we show signs of a *maturity principle:* We become more conscientious and agreeable and less neurotic (emotionally unstable) (Bleidorn, 2015; Roberts et al., 2008). Great apes show similar personality maturation (Weiss & King, 2015). After age 40, our traits stabilize.

- **How heritable are these traits?** Heritability (the extent to which individual differences are attributable to genes) generally runs about 40 percent for each dimension (Vukasović & Bratko, 2015). Many genes, each having small effects, combine to influence our traits (McCrae et al., 2010).

- **How do these traits reflect differing brain structure?** The size of different brain regions correlates with several Big Five traits (DeYoung et al., 2010; Grodin & White, 2015). For example, those who score high on conscientiousness tend to have a larger frontal lobe area that aids in planning and controlling behavior. Brain connections also influence the Big Five traits (Adelstein et al., 2011). People high in openness have brains that are wired to experience intense imagination, curiosity, and fantasy.

- **Have levels of these traits changed over time?** Cultures change over time, which can influence shifts in personality. Within the United States and the Netherlands, extraversion and conscientiousness have increased (Mroczek & Spiro, 2003; Smits et al., 2011; Twenge, 2001).

- **How well do these traits apply to various cultures?** The Big Five dimensions describe personality in various cultures reasonably well (Schmitt et al., 2007; Vazsonyi et al., 2015; Yamagata et al., 2006). "Features of personality traits are common to all human groups," concluded Robert McCrae and 79 co-researchers (2005) from their 50-culture study.

- **Do the Big Five traits predict our actual behaviors?** *Yes.* If people report being outgoing, conscientious, and agreeable, "they probably are telling the truth," reports McCrae (2011). For example, our traits appear in our language patterns. In text messaging, extraversion predicts use of personal pronouns. Agreeableness predicts positive-emotion words. Neuroticism (emotional instability) predicts negative-emotion words (Holtgraves, 2011). (In the next section, we will see that situations matter, too.)

By exploring such questions, Big Five research has sustained trait psychology and renewed appreciation for the importance of personality. Traits matter.

LaunchPad For an 8-minute demonstration of trait research, visit LaunchPad's *Video: Trait Theories of Personality.*

RETRIEVE IT

- What are the Big Five personality factors, and why are they scientifically useful?

ANSWER: The Big Five personality factors are conscientiousness, agreeableness, neuroticism (emotional stability vs. instability), openness, and extraversion (CANOE). These factors may be objectively measured, they are relatively stable over the life span, and they apply to all cultures in which they have been studied.

Evaluating Trait Theories

39-5 Does research support the consistency of personality traits over time and across situations?

Are our personality traits stable and enduring? Or does our behavior depend on where and with whom we find ourselves? In some ways, our personality seems stable. Cheerful, friendly children tend to become cheerful, friendly adults. At a recent college reunion, I [DM] was amazed to find that my jovial former classmates were still jovial, the shy ones still shy, the happy-seeming people still smiling

and laughing—50 years later. But it's also true that a fun-loving jokester can suddenly turn serious and respectful at a job interview. And the personality traits we express can change from one situation to another. Major life events, such as becoming unemployed, can shift our personality from agreeable to slightly rude (Boyce et al., 2015).

THE PERSON-SITUATION CONTROVERSY Our behavior is influenced by the interaction of our inner disposition with our environment. Still, the question lingers: Which is more important? When we explore this *person-situation contro-versy,* we look for genuine personality traits that persist over time *and* across situations. Are some people dependably conscientious and others unreliable? Some cheerful and others dour? Some friendly and outgoing and others shy? If we are to consider friendliness a trait, friendly people must act friendly at different times and places. Do they?

In considering research that has followed lives through time, some scholars (especially those who study infants) are impressed with personality change; others are struck by personality stability during adulthood. As **FIGURE 39.3** illustrates, data from 152 long-term studies reveal that personality trait scores are positively correlated with scores obtained seven years later, and that as people grow older their personality stabilizes. Interests may change—the avid tropical-fish collec-tor may become an avid gardener. Careers may change—the determined sales-person may become a determined social worker. Relationships may change—the hostile spouse may start over with a new partner. But most people recognize their traits as their own, as Robert McCrae and Paul Costa noted (1994), "and it is well that they do. A person's recognition of the inevitability of his or her one and only personality is . . . the culminating wisdom of a lifetime."

So most people—including most psychologists—would probably presume the stability of personality traits. Moreover, our traits are socially significant. They influence our health, our thinking, and our job choices and performance (Deary & Matthews, 1993; Hogan, 1998; Jackson et al., 2012; Sutin et al., 2011). Studies that follow lives through time show that personality traits rival socioeconomic status and cognitive ability as predictors of mortality, divorce, and occupational attainment (Roberts et al., 2007).

Any of these tendencies, taken to an extreme, become maladaptive. Agreeableness ranges from cynical combativeness at its low extreme to gullible subservience at its high extreme. Conscientiousness ranges from irresponsible negligence to workaholic perfectionism (Widiger & Costa, 2012).

Although our personality *traits* may be both stable and potent, the consistency of our specific *behaviors* from one situation to the next is another matter. As Walter Mischel (1968, 2009) has pointed out, people do not act with predictable consistency. Mischel's studies of college students' conscientiousness revealed only a modest relation-ship between a student's being conscientious on one occasion (say, showing up for class on time) and being similarly conscientious on another occasion (say,

"There is as much difference between us and ourselves, as between us and others."
Michel de Montaigne, Essays, *1588*

Roughly speaking, the temporary, external influences on behavior are the focus of social psychology, and the enduring, inner influences are the focus of personality psychology. In actuality, behavior always depends on the interaction of persons with situations.

Change and consistency can co-exist. If all people were to become somewhat less shy with age, there would be personality change, but also relative stability and predictability.

It's not just personality that stabilizes with age:

my hair over time

childhood

teens and twenties - experimentation

thirties and up

mitra farmand

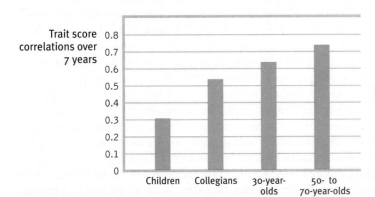

< FIGURE 39.3

Personality stability With age, personality traits become more stable, as reflected in the stronger correlation of trait scores with follow-up scores 7 years later. (Data from Roberts & DelVecchio, 2000.)

*"I'm going to France—I'm a different
person in France."*

turning in assignments on time). If you've noticed how outgoing you are in some situations and how reserved you are in others, perhaps you're not surprised.

This inconsistency in behaviors also makes personality test scores weak predictors of behaviors. People's scores on an extraversion test, for example, do not neatly predict how sociable they actually will be on any given occasion. If we remember this, says Mischel, we will be more cautious about labeling and pigeonholing individuals. Years in advance, science can tell us the phase of the Moon for any given date. A day in advance, meteorologists can often predict the weather. But we are much further from being able to predict how *you* will feel and act tomorrow.

However, people's *average* outgoingness, happiness, or carelessness over many situations is predictable (Epstein, 1983a,b). People who know someone well, therefore, generally agree when rating that person's shyness or agreeableness (Jackson et al., 2015; Kenrick & Funder, 1988). The predictability of average behavior across many situations was again confirmed when researchers collected snippets of people's daily experience via body-worn recording devices: Extraverts really do talk more (Mehl et al., 2006). (I [DM] have repeatedly vowed to cut back on my jabbering and joking during my noontime pickup basketball games with friends. Alas, moments later, the irrepressible chatterbox inevitably reoccupies my body. And I [ND] have a similar experience each time I try to stay quiet in taxis. Somehow, I always end up chatting with the driver!) As our best friends can verify, we do have genetically influenced personality traits. And those traits even lurk, report Samuel Gosling and his colleagues in a series of studies, in our

- *music preferences.* Your playlist says a lot about your personality. Classical, jazz, blues, and folk music lovers tend to be open to experience and verbally intelligent. Extraverts tend to prefer upbeat and energetic music. Country, pop, and religious music lovers tend to be cheerful, outgoing, and conscientious (Langmeyer et al., 2012; Rentfrow & Gosling, 2003, 2006).

- *online spaces.* Is a personal website, social media profile, online avatar, or instant messaging account also a canvas for self-expression? Or is it an opportunity for people to present themselves in false or misleading ways? It's more the former (Back et al., 2010; Fong & Mar, 2015; Gosling et al., 2007). Viewers quickly gain important clues to the creator's extraversion, conscientiousness, and openness to experience.

Room with a cue Even at "zero acquaintance," people can catch a glimpse of others' personality from looking at their website, bedroom, or office. So, what's your read on this person's office?

- *written communications.* If you have ever felt you could detect others' personality from their writing voice, you are right!! (What a cool, exciting finding!!! . . . if you know what we're saying.) People's ratings of others' personality based solely on their e-mails, blogs, and Facebook posts correlate with actual personality scores on measures such as extraversion and neuroticism (Park et al., 2015; Pennebaker, 2011; Yarkoni, 2010). Extraverts, for example, use more adjectives.

In unfamiliar, formal situations—perhaps as a guest in the home of a person from another culture—our traits remain hidden as we carefully attend to social cues. In familiar, informal situations—just hanging out with friends—we feel less constrained, allowing our traits to emerge (Buss, 1989). In these informal situations, our expressive styles—our animation, manner of speaking, and gestures—are impressively consistent. Viewing "thin slices" of someone's behavior—such as seeing a photo for a mere fraction of a second or seeing three, 2-second clips of a teacher in action—can tell us a lot about the person's basic personality traits (Ambady, 2010; Rule et al., 2009).

To sum up, we can say that at any moment the immediate situation powerfully influences a person's behavior. Social psychologists have learned that this is especially so when a "strong situation" makes clear demands (Cooper & Withey, 2009). We can better predict drivers' behavior at traffic lights from knowing the color of the lights than from knowing the drivers' personalities. Averaging our behavior across many occasions does, however, reveal distinct personality traits. Traits exist. We differ. And our differences matter.

RETRIEVE IT [✱]

• How well do personality test scores predict our behavior? Explain.

ANSWER: Our scores on personality tests predict our *average* behavior across many situations much better than they predict our specific behavior in any given situation.

social-cognitive perspective views behavior as influenced by the interaction between people's traits (including their thinking) and their social context.

reciprocal determinism the interacting influences of behavior, internal cognition, and environment.

Social-Cognitive Theories

39-6 How do social-cognitive theorists view personality development, and how do they explore behavior?

The **social-cognitive perspective** on personality, proposed by Albert Bandura (1986, 2006, 2008), emphasizes the interaction of our traits with our situations. Much as nature and nurture always work together, so do individuals and their situations.

Social-cognitive theorists believe we learn many of our behaviors either through conditioning or by observing and imitating others. (That's the "social" part.) They also emphasize the importance of mental processes: What we *think* about a situation affects our behavior in that situation. (That's the "cognitive" part.) Instead of focusing solely on how our environment *controls* us (behaviorism), social-cognitive theorists focus on how we and our environment *interact:* How do we interpret and respond to external events? How do our schemas, our memories, and our expectations influence our behavior patterns?

Reciprocal Influences

Bandura (1986, 2006) views the person-environment interaction as **reciprocal determinism.** "Behavior, internal personal factors, and environmental influences," he said, "all operate as interlocking determinants of each other" (**FIGURE 39.4**). We can see this interaction in people's relationships. For example, Rosa's romantic history (past behavior) influences her attitudes toward new relationships (internal factor), which affects how she now responds to Ryan (environmental factor).

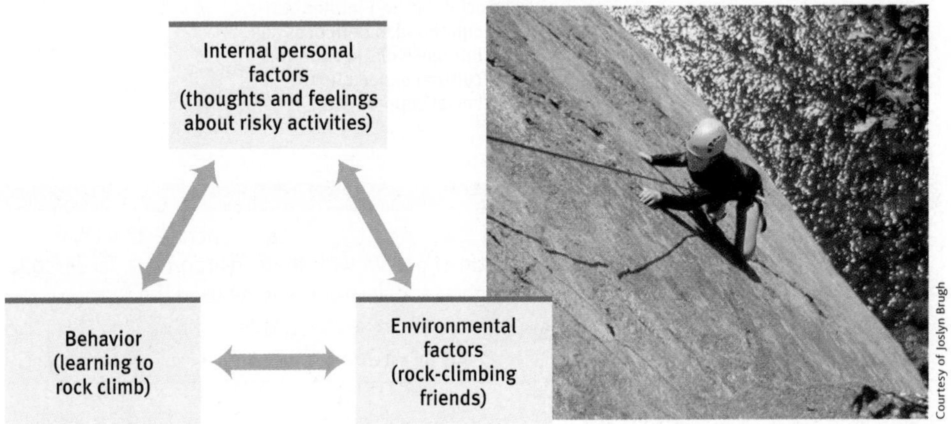

Internal personal factors (thoughts and feelings about risky activities)

Behavior (learning to rock climb)

Environmental factors (rock-climbing friends)

Courtesy of Joslyn Brugh

< FIGURE 39.4

Reciprocal determinism

Consider three specific ways in which individuals and environments interact:

1. *Different people choose different environments.* The schools we attend, the reading we do, the movies we watch, the music we listen to, the friends we associate with—all are part of an environment we have chosen, based partly on our dispositions (Funder, 2009; Ickes et al., 1997). We choose our environment and it then shapes us.

2. *Our personalities shape how we interpret and react to events.* Anxious people tend to attend and react strongly to relationship threats (Campbell & Marshall, 2011). If we perceive the world as threatening, we will watch for threats and be prepared to defend ourselves.

3. ***Our personalities help create situations to which we react.*** How we view and treat people influences how they then treat us. If we expect that others will not like us, our desperate attempts to seek their approval might cause them to reject us. Depressed people often engage in this excessive reassurance seeking, which may confirm their negative self-views (Coyne, 1976a,b).

In addition to the interaction of internal personal factors, the environment, and our behaviors, we also experience *gene-environment interaction.* Our genetically influenced traits evoke certain responses from others, which may nudge us in one direction or another. In one classic study, those with the interacting factors of (1) having a specific gene associated with aggression and (2) being raised in a difficult environment were most likely to demonstrate adult antisocial behavior (Caspi et al., 2002).

In such ways, we are both the products and the architects of our environments: *Behavior emerges from the interplay of external and internal influences.* Boiling water turns an egg hard and a potato soft. A threatening environment turns one person into a hero, another into a scoundrel. Extraverts enjoy greater well-being in an extraverted culture than in an introverted one (Fulmer et al., 2010). *At every moment,* our behavior is influenced by our biology, our social and cultural experiences, and our cognition and dispositions (**FIGURE 39.5**).

> **FIGURE 39.5**

The biopsychosocial approach to the study of personality As with other psychological phenomena, personality is fruitfully studied at multiple levels.

Biological influences:
• genetically determined temperament
• autonomic nervous system reactivity
• brain activity

Psychological influences:
• learned responses
• unconscious thought processes
• expectations and interpretations

Personality

Social-cultural influences:
• childhood experiences
• influence of the situation
• cultural expectations
• social support

Gustavo Caballero/Getty Images

If you can't stand the heat. . . On the Food Network's *Chopped*, contestants are pitted against one another in stressful situations. The entertaining episodes illustrate a valid point: A chef's behavior in such job-relevant situations is a valid assessment of that person's ability and can help predict job performance.

RETRIEVE IT [✖]

• Albert Bandura proposed the _____ - _____ perspective on personality, which emphasizes the interaction of people with their environment. To describe the interacting influences of behavior, thoughts, and environment, he used the term _____ _____ .

ANSWERS: social-cognitive; reciprocal determinism

Assessing Behavior in Situations

To predict behavior, social-cognitive psychologists often observe behavior in realistic situations. One ambitious example was the U.S. Army's World War II strategy for assessing candidates for spy missions. Rather than using paper-and-pencil tests, Army psychologists subjected the candidates to simulated undercover conditions. They tested their ability to handle stress, solve problems, maintain leadership, and withstand intense interrogation without blowing their cover. Although time-consuming and expensive, this assessment of behavior in a realistic situation helped predict later success on actual spy missions (OSS Assessment Staff, 1948).

Military and educational organizations and many Fortune 500 companies have adopted assessment center strategies (Bray et al., 1991, 1997; Eurich et al.,

2009). AT&T has observed prospective managers doing simulated managerial work. Many colleges assess students' potential via internships and student teaching, and assess potential faculty members' teaching abilities by observing them teach. Most American cities with populations of 50,000 or more have used assessment centers in evaluating police officers and firefighters (Lowry, 1997).

Assessment center exercises have some limitations. They are more revealing of visible dimensions, such as communication ability, than of others, such as inner achievement drive (Bowler & Woehr, 2006). Nevertheless, these procedures exploit a valid principle: The best means of predicting future behavior is neither a personality test nor an interviewer's intuition; rather, it is *the person's past behavior patterns in similar situations* (Lyons et al., 2011; Mischel, 1981; Schmidt & Hunter, 1998). As long as the situation and the person remain much the same, the best predictor of future job performance is past job performance; the best predictor of future grades is past grades; the best predictor of future aggressiveness is past aggressiveness. If you can't check the person's past behavior, the next best thing is to create an assessment situation that simulates the task so you can see how the person handles it (Lievens et al., 2009; Meriac et al., 2008).

"What's past is prologue."

William Shakespeare,
The Tempest, *1611*

Evaluating Social-Cognitive Theories

39-7 What criticisms have social-cognitive theorists faced?

Social-cognitive theories of personality sensitize researchers to how situations affect, and are affected by, individuals. More than other personality theories (see **TABLE 39.2**), they build from psychological research on learning and cognition.

⌄ TABLE 39.2

Comparing the Major Personality Theories

Personality Theory	Key Proponents	Assumptions	View of Personality	Personality Assessment Methods
Psychoanalytic	Freud	Emotional disorders spring from unconscious dynamics, such as unresolved sexual and other childhood conflicts, and fixation at various developmental stages. Defense mechanisms fend off anxiety.	Personality consists of pleasure-seeking impulses (the id), a reality-oriented executive (the ego), and an internalized set of ideals (the superego).	Free association, projective tests, dream analysis
Psychodynamic	Adler, Horney, Jung	The unconscious and conscious minds interact. Childhood experiences and defense mechanisms are important.	The dynamic interplay of conscious and unconscious motives and conflicts shape our personality.	Projective tests, therapy sessions
Humanistic	Rogers, Maslow	Rather than examining the struggles of sick people, it's better to focus on the ways healthy people strive for self-realization.	If our basic human needs are met, people will strive toward self-actualization. In a climate of unconditional positive regard, we can develop self-awareness and a more realistic and positive self-concept.	Questionnaires, therapy sessions
Trait	Allport, Eysenck, McCrae, Costa	We have certain stable and enduring characteristics, influenced by genetic predispositions.	Scientific study of traits has isolated important dimensions of personality, such as the Big Five traits (conscientiousness, agreeableness, neuroticism, openness, and extraversion).	Personality inventories
Social-Cognitive	Bandura	Our traits and the social context interact to produce our behaviors.	Conditioning and observational learning interact with cognition to create behavior patterns.	Our behavior in one situation is best predicted by considering our past behavior in similar situations.

Critics charge that social-cognitive theories focus so much on the situation that they fail to appreciate the person's inner traits. Where is the person in this view of personality, ask the dissenters, and where are human emotions? True, the situation does guide our behavior. But, say the critics, in many instances our unconscious motives, our emotions, and our pervasive traits shine through. Personality traits have been shown to predict behavior at work, love, and play. Our biologically influenced traits really do matter. Consider Percy Ray Pridgen and Charles Gill. Each faced the same situation: They had jointly won a $90 million lottery jackpot (Harriston, 1993). When Pridgen learned of the winning numbers, he began trembling uncontrollably, huddled with a friend behind a bathroom door while confirming the win, then sobbed. When Gill heard the news, he told his wife and then went to sleep.

RETRIEVE IT [✗]

- What is the best way to predict a person's future behavior?

ANSWER: examine the person's past behavior patterns in similar situations

---

Exploring the Self

39-8 Why has psychology generated so much research on the self? How important is self-esteem to our well-being?

Psychology's concern with people's sense of self dates back at least to William James, who devoted more than 100 pages of his 1890 *Principles of Psychology* to the topic. By 1943, Gordon Allport lamented that the self had become "lost to view." Although humanistic psychology's later emphasis on the self did not instigate much scientific research, it did help renew the concept of self and keep it alive. Now, more than a century after James, the self is one of Western psychology's most vigorously researched topics. Every year, new studies galore appear on self-esteem, self-disclosure, self-awareness, self-schemas, self-monitoring, and more. Even neuroscientists have searched for the self, by identifying a central frontal lobe region that activates when people respond to self-reflective questions about their traits and dispositions (Damasio, 2010; Mitchell, 2009; Pauly et al., 2013). Underlying all this research is an assumption that the **self,** as organizer of our thoughts, feelings, and actions, is the center of personality.

One example of thinking about self is the concept of *possible selves* (Cross & Markus, 1991; Markus & Nurius, 1986). Your possible selves include your visions of the self you dream of becoming—the rich self, the successful self, the loved and admired self. Your possible selves also include the self you fear becoming—the unemployed self, the academically failed self, the lonely and unpopular self. Possible selves motivate us to lay out specific goals that direct our energy effectively and efficiently (Landau et al, 2014). High school students enrolled in a gifted program for math and science were more likely to become scientists if they had a clear vision of themselves as successful scientists (Buday et al., 2012). Dreams do often give birth to achievements.

"The first step to better times is to imagine them."

Chinese fortune cookie

Our self-focused perspective may motivate us, but it can also lead us to presume too readily that others are noticing and evaluating us. Most of them aren't. Thomas Gilovich has demonstrated this **spotlight effect.** He and his colleagues found that fewer people than we presume actually notice our dorky clothes, bad hair, nervousness, or irritation (Gilovich & Savitsky, 1999). Others are also less aware than we suppose of the variability—the ups and downs—of our appearance and performance (Gilovich et al., 2002). Even after a blunder (setting off a library alarm, showing up in the wrong clothes), we stick out like a sore thumb less than we imagine (Savitsky et al., 2001). To turn down the brightness of the spotlight, we can use two strategies. The first is simply knowing about the spotlight effect.

Public speakers perform better if they understand that their natural nervousness is not obvious (Savitsky & Gilovich, 2003). The second is to take the audience's perspective. When we imagine audience members empathizing with our situation, we tend to expect we will not be judged as harshly (Epley et al., 2002).

The Benefits of Self-Esteem

Self-esteem—our feelings of high or low self-worth—is important. So also is **self-efficacy,** our sense of competence on a task. A person with high self-esteem will strongly agree with self-affirming questionnaire statements such as, "I am fun to be with," or "I have good ideas." A person with low self-esteem responds to these statements with qualifying adjectives, such as *somewhat* or *sometimes.*

High self-esteem pays dividends. People who feel good about themselves have fewer sleepless nights. They are less likely to give in to pressures to conform. They make more positive Facebook posts, causing others to like them more (Forest & Wood, 2012). They are more persistent at difficult tasks, and they are less shy, anxious, and lonely. They try harder to shake their bad moods because they think they deserve better (Wood et al., 2009). And they are more successful and just plain happier (Greenberg, 2008; Orth & Robins, 2014).

But is high self-esteem the horse or the cart? Is it really "the armor that protects kids" from life's problems (McKay, 2000)? Some psychologists have had their doubts (Baumeister, 2006, 2015; Dawes, 1994; Leary, 1999; Seligman, 1994, 2002). Children's academic self-efficacy—their confidence that they can do well in a subject—predicts school achievement, but their general self-image does not (Marsh & Craven, 2006; Swann et al., 2007; Trautwein et al., 2006). Maybe self-esteem simply reflects reality. Maybe it's a side effect of meeting challenges and surmounting difficulties. Maybe self-esteem is a gauge that reads out the state of our relationships with others. If so, isn't pushing the gauge artificially higher with empty compliments much like forcing a car's low fuel gauge to display "full"?

If feeling good *follows* doing well, then giving praise in the absence of good performance may actually harm people. After receiving weekly self-esteem-boosting messages, struggling students earned *lower*-than-expected grades (Forsyth et al., 2007). Other research showed that giving people random rewards hurt their productivity. Martin Seligman (2012) reported that "when good things occurred that weren't earned, like nickels coming out of slot machines, it did not increase people's well-being. It produced helplessness. People gave up and became passive."

Experiments have revealed an *effect* of low self-esteem. When researchers temporarily deflated participants' self-image (by telling them they did poorly on an aptitude test or by disparaging their personality), those participants became more likely to disparage others or to express heightened racial prejudice (vanDellen et al., 2011; van Dijk et al., 2011; Ybarra, 1999). Self-image threat even increases unconscious racial bias (Allen & Sherman, 2011). In other studies, people who were negative about themselves also tended to be oversensitive and judgmental (Baumgardner et al., 1989; Pelham, 1993). Self-esteem threats also lead people to spend more time with their online profiles—safe havens in which to rebuild their self-worth (Toma & Hancock, 2013). Such findings are consistent with humanistic psychology's presumption that a healthy self-image is essential. Accept yourself and you'll find it easier to accept others. Disparage yourself and you will be prone to the floccinaucinihilipilification[1] of others. Said more simply, people who are down on themselves tend to be down on others. Some people "love their neighbors as themselves"; others loathe their neighbors as themselves.

self in contemporary psychology, assumed to be the center of personality, the organizer of our thoughts, feelings, and actions.

spotlight effect overestimating others' noticing and evaluating our appearance, performance, and blunders (as if we presume a spotlight shines on us).

self-esteem one's feelings of high or low self-worth.

self-efficacy one's sense of competence and effectiveness.

"When kids increase in self-control, their grades go up later. But when kids increase their self-esteem, there is no effect on their grades."

Angela Duckworth,
In Character *interview, 2009*

LOW SELF-ESTEEM

---

1. We couldn't resist throwing that in. But don't worry, you won't be tested on floccinaucinihilipilification, which is the act of estimating something as worthless (and was the longest nontechnical word in the first edition of the *Oxford English Dictionary*).

Self-Serving Bias

39-9 What evidence reveals self-serving bias, and how do defensive and secure self-esteem differ?

self-serving bias a readiness to perceive oneself favorably.

Imagine dashing to class, hoping not to miss the first few minutes. But you arrive five minutes late, huffing and puffing. As you sink into your seat, what sorts of thoughts go through your mind? Do you go through a negative door, with thoughts such as, "I hate myself" and "I'm a loser"? Or do you go through a positive door, saying to yourself, "At least I made it to class" and "I really tried to get here on time"?

Personality psychologists have found that most people choose the second door, which leads to positive self-thoughts. We have a good reputation with ourselves. We show a **self-serving bias**—a readiness to perceive ourselves favorably (Myers, 2010). Consider:

People accept more responsibility for good deeds than for bad, and for successes than for failures. Athletes often privately credit their victories to their own prowess, and their losses to bad breaks, lousy officiating, or the other team's exceptional performance. Most students who receive poor grades on an exam criticize the test, not themselves. Drivers filling out insurance forms explain their accidents in such words as "As I reached an intersection, a hedge sprang up, obscuring my vision, and I did not see the other car" and "A pedestrian hit me and went under my car." The question "What have I done to deserve this?" is one we usually ask of our troubles, not our successes. Although a self-serving bias can lead us to avoid uncomfortable truths, it can also motivate us to approach difficult tasks with confidence instead of despair (Tomaka et al., 1992; von Hippel & Trivers, 2011).

Most people see themselves as better than average. Compared with most other people, how nice are you? How appealing are you as a friend or romantic partner? Where would you rank yourself from the 1st to the 99th percentile? Most people put themselves well above the 50th percentile. This better-than-average effect appears for nearly any subjectively assessed and socially desirable behavior. Some examples:

- In national surveys, most business executives say they are more ethical than their average counterpart. In several studies, 90 percent of business managers and more than 90 percent of college professors also rated their performance as superior to that of their average peer.

- In Australia, 86 percent of people rate their job performance as above average, and only 1 percent as below average.

Blindness to one's own incompetence Ironically, people often are most overconfident when most incompetent. That, say Justin Kruger and David Dunning (1999), is because it often takes competence to recognize competence. Our ignorance of what we don't know sustains our self-confidence, leading us to make the same mistakes (Williams et al., 2013).

- In the National Survey of Families and Households, 49 percent of men said they provided half or more of the child care, though only 31 percent of their wives or partners saw things that way (Galinsky et al., 2008).

- Brain scans reveal that the more people judge themselves as better-than-average, the less brain activation they show in regions that aid careful self-reflection (Beer & Hughes, 2010). It seems our brain's default setting is to think we are better than others.

The self-serving bias reflects an overestimation of ourselves as well as a desire to maintain a positive self-view (Brown, 2012; Epley & Dunning, 2000). This phenomenon is less striking in Asia, where people value modesty (Falk et al., 2009; Heine & Hamamura, 2007). Yet self-serving biases have been observed worldwide: In every one of 53 countries surveyed, people expressed self-esteem above the midpoint of the most widely used scale (Schmitt & Allik, 2005).

Ironically, people even see themselves as more immune than others to self-serving bias (Pronin, 2007). That's right, people believe they are above average at not believing they are above average. (Isn't psychology fun?) The world, it seems, is Garrison Keillor's Lake Wobegon writ large—a place where "all the women are strong, all the men are good-looking, and all the children are above average."

PEANUTS

Finding their self-esteem threatened, people with large egos may react violently. Researchers Brad Bushman and Roy Baumeister (1998; Bushman et al., 2009) had undergraduate volunteers write a brief essay, in response to which another supposed student gave them either praise ("Great essay!") or stinging criticism ("One of the worst essays I have read!"). Then the essay writers played a reaction-time game against the other student. After wins, they could assault their opponent with noise of any intensity for any duration.

Can you anticipate the result? After criticism, those with inflated self-esteem were "exceptionally aggressive." They delivered three times the auditory torture of those with normal self-esteem. "Encouraging people to feel good about themselves when they haven't earned it" poses problems, Baumeister (2001) concluded. "Conceited, self-important individuals turn nasty toward those who puncture their bubbles of self-love."

Are self-serving perceptions on the rise in North America? Some researchers believe they are. From 1980 to 2007, popular song lyrics became more self-focused (DeWall et al., 2011). An analysis of 766,513 American books published between 1960 and 2008 showed a similar result: Self-focused words increased (Twenge et al., 2013). Surveys of over 9 million high school seniors and entering college students between 1966 and 2009 also found increasing interest in gaining money, fame, and prestige, and decreasing concern for others (Twenge et al., 2012).

Psychologist Jean Twenge has reported that **narcissism**—excessive self-love and self-absorption—has also been rising (2006; Twenge & Foster, 2010). After tracking self-importance across the last several decades, Twenge found that what she calls *Generation Me* (born in the 1980s and 1990s) is expressing more narcissism by agreeing more often with statements such as, "If I ruled the world, it would be a better place," or "I think I am a special person." What gives birth to narcissism? One ingredient is parents who tell their kids they are superior to others (Brummelman et al., 2015). Why does a rise in narcissism matter? Narcissists (more often men [Grijalva et al. 2015]) tend to be materialistic, desire fame, have inflated expectations, hook up more often without commitment, and gamble and cheat more—all of which have been increasing as narcissism has increased.

"If you are like most people, then like most people, you don't know you're like most people. Science has given us a lot of facts about the average person, and one of the most reliable of these facts is the average person doesn't see herself as average."

Daniel Gilbert,
Stumbling on Happiness, *2006*

narcissism excessive self-love and self-absorption.

Shannon Wheeler

"The [self-]portraits that we actually believe, when we are given freedom to voice them, are dramatically more positive than reality can sustain."

Shelley Taylor,
Positive Illusions, *1989*

"The enthusiastic claims of the self-esteem movement mostly range from fantasy to hogwash. The effects of self-esteem are small, limited, and not all good."

Roy Baumeister (1996)

"If you compare yourself with others, you may become vain and bitter; for always there will be greater and lesser persons than yourself."

Max Ehrmann, "Desiderata," 1927

Some critics of the concept of self-serving bias claim that it overlooks those who feel worthless and unlovable: If self-serving bias prevails, why do so many people disparage themselves? For four reasons: (1) Self-directed put-downs can be *subtly strategic*—they elicit reassuring strokes. Saying "No one likes me" may at least elicit "But not everyone has met you!" (2) Before an important event, such as a game or an exam, self-disparaging comments *prepare us for possible failure.* The coach who extols the superior strength of the upcoming opponent makes a loss understandable, a victory noteworthy. (3) A self-disparaging "How could I have been so stupid!" can help us *learn from our mistakes.* (4) Self-disparagement frequently *pertains to one's old self.* Asked to remember their really bad behaviors, people recall things from long ago; good behaviors more easily come to mind from their recent past (Escobedo & Adolphs, 2010). People are much more critical of their distant past selves than of their current selves—even when they have not changed (Wilson & Ross, 2001). "At 18, I was a jerk; today I'm more sensitive." In their own eyes, chumps yesterday, champs today.

Even so, it's true: All of us some of the time, and some of us much of the time, do feel inferior—especially when we compare ourselves with those who are a step or two higher on the ladder of status, looks, income, or ability. For example, Olympians who win silver medals, barely missing gold, show greater sadness on the awards podium compared with the bronze medal winners (Medvec et al., 1995). The deeper and more frequently we have such feelings, the more unhappy, even depressed, we are. But for most people, thinking has a naturally positive bias.

While recognizing the dark side of self-serving bias and self-esteem, some researchers prefer isolating the effects of two types of self-esteem—defensive and secure (Kernis, 2003; Lambird & Mann, 2006; Ryan & Deci, 2004). *Defensive self-esteem* is fragile. It focuses on sustaining itself, which makes failure and criticism feel threatening. Perceived threats feed anger and feelings of vulnerability (Crocker & Park, 2004).

Secure self-esteem is less fragile, because it is less contingent on external evaluations. Feeling accepted for who we are, and not for our looks, wealth, or acclaim, relieves pressures to succeed and enables us to focus beyond ourselves. By losing ourselves in relationships and purposes larger than self, we may achieve a more secure self-esteem, satisfying relationships, and greater quality of life (Crocker & Park, 2004). Authentic pride, rooted in actual achievement, supports self-confidence and leadership (Tracy et al., 2009; Weidman et al., in press; Williams & DeSteno, 2009).

RETRIEVE IT   [×]

• What are the positive and negative effects of high self-esteem?

ANSWER: People who feel confident in their abilities are often happier, have greater motivation, and are less susceptible to depression. Inflated self-esteem can lead to self-serving bias, greater aggression, and narcissism.

• The tendency to accept responsibility for success and blame circumstances or bad luck for failure is called _____-_____ _____.

ANSWER: self-serving bias

• _____ (Secure/Defensive) self-esteem correlates with more anger and greater feelings of vulnerability. _____ (Secure/Defensive) self-esteem is a healthier self-image that allows us to focus beyond ourselves and enjoy a higher quality of life.

ANSWERS: Defensive; Secure

Culture and the Self

39-10 How do individualist and collectivist cultures differ in their values and goals?

Our consideration of personality—of people's characteristic ways of thinking, feeling, and acting—concludes with a look at cultural variations. Imagine that someone ripped away your social connections, making you a solitary refugee in a foreign land. How much of your identity would remain intact?

If you are an **individualist,** a great deal of your identity would survive. You would have an independent sense of "me," and an awareness of your unique personal convictions and values. Individualists give higher priority to personal goals. They define their identity mostly in terms of personal traits. They strive for personal control and individual achievement.

Although people within cultures vary, different cultures emphasize either individualism or *collectivism* (Markus & Kitayama, 1991). Individualism is valued in most areas of North America, Western Europe, Australia, and New Zealand. The United States is mostly an individualist culture. Founded by settlers who wanted to differentiate themselves from others, Americans have cherished the "pioneer" spirit (Kitayama et al., 2010). Some 85 percent of Americans say it is possible to "pretty much be who you want to be" (Sampson, 2000).

Individualists share the human need to belong. They join groups. But they are less focused on group harmony and doing their duty to the group (Brewer & Chen, 2007). Being more self-contained, individualists move in and out of social groups more easily. They feel relatively free to switch places of worship, change jobs, or even leave their extended families and migrate to a new place. Marriage is often for as long as they both shall love.

Individualists even prefer unusual names, as Jean Twenge noticed while seeking a name for her first child. Over time, the most common American names listed by year on the U.S. Social Security baby names website were becoming less desirable. An analysis of the first names of 325 million American babies born between 1880 and 2007 confirmed this trend (Twenge et al., 2010). As **FIGURE 39.6** illustrates, the percentage of boys and girls given one of the 10 most common names for their birth year has plunged, especially in recent years. Even within the United States, parents from more recently settled states (for example, Utah and Arizona) give their children more distinct names compared with parents who live in more established states (for example, New York and Massachusetts) (Varnum & Kitayama, 2011).

If set adrift in a foreign land as a **collectivist,** you might experience a greater loss of identity. Cut off from family, groups, and loyal friends, you would lose the

individualism giving priority to one's own goals over group goals and defining one's identity in terms of personal attributes rather than group identifications.

collectivism giving priority to the goals of one's group (often one's extended family or work group) and defining one's identity accordingly.

The New Yorker Collection, 2000. From cartoonbank.com

❮ FIGURE 39.6

A child like no other Americans' individualist tendencies are reflected in their choice of names for their babies. In recent years, the percentage of American babies receiving one of that year's 10 most common names has plunged. (Data from Twenge et al., 2010.)

Considerate collectivists Japan's collectivist values, including duty to others and social harmony, were on display after the devastating 2011 earthquake and tsunami. Virtually no looting was reported, and residents remained calm and orderly, as shown here while waiting for drinking water.

Kyodo/Reuters/Landov

connections that have defined who you are. *Group identifications* provide a sense of belonging, a set of values, and an assurance of security in collectivist cultures. In return, collectivists have deeper, more stable attachments to their groups—their family, clan, or company. Elders receive great respect. In some collectivist cultures, disrespecting family elders violates the law. *The Law of the People's Republic of China on Protection of the Rights and Interests of the Elderly* states that parents aged 60 or above can sue their sons and daughters if they fail to provide "for the elderly, taking care of them and comforting them, and cater[ing] to their special needs."

Collectivists are like athletes who take more pleasure in their team's victory than in their own performance. They find satisfaction in advancing their groups' interests, even at the expense of personal needs. Preserving group spirit and avoiding social embarrassment are important goals. Collectivists therefore avoid direct confrontation, blunt honesty, and uncomfortable topics. They value humility, not self-importance (Bond et al., 2012). Instead of dominating conversations, collectivists hold back and display shyness when meeting strangers (Cheek & Melchoir, 1990). When the priority is "we," not "me," that individualized latte—"decaf, single shot, skinny, extra hot"—that feels so good to a North American might sound selfishly demanding in Seoul (Kim & Markus, 1999).

"One needs to cultivate the spirit of sacrificing the little me to achieve the benefits of the big me."

Chinese saying

Within many countries, there are also distinct subcultures related to one's religion, economic status, and region (Cohen, 2009). In China, greater collectivist

Collectivist culture Although the United States is largely individualist, many cultural subgroups remain collectivist. This is true for Alaska Natives, who demonstrate respect for tribal elders, and whose identity springs largely from their group affiliations.

Sam Harrel/ZUMApress/Newscom

thinking occurs in provinces that produce large amounts of rice, a difficult-to-grow crop that often involves cooperation between groups of people (Talhelm et al., 2014). In collectivist Japan, a spirit of individualism marks the "northern frontier" island of Hokkaido (Kitayama et al., 2006). And even in the most individualist countries, some people have collectivist values. But in general, people (especially men) in competitive, individualist cultures have more personal freedom, are less geographically bound to their families, enjoy more privacy, and take more pride in personal achievements (**TABLE 39.3**).

∨ TABLE 39.3

Value Contrasts Between Individualism and Collectivism

Concept	Individualism	Collectivism
Self	Independent (identity from individual traits)	Interdependent (identity from belonging)
Life task	Discover and express one's uniqueness	Maintain connections, fit in, perform role
What matters	Me—personal achievement and fulfillment; rights and liberties; self-esteem	Us—group goals and solidarity; social responsibilities and relationships; family duty
Coping method	Change reality	Accommodate to reality
Morality	Defined by individuals (self-based)	Defined by social networks (duty-based)
Relationships	Many, often temporary or casual; confrontation acceptable	Few, close and enduring; harmony valued
Attributing behavior	Behavior reflects one's personality and attitudes	Behavior reflects social norms and roles

Sources: Information from Thomas Schoeneman (1994) and Harry Triandis (1994).

Individualism's benefits may come at a cost. There has been more loneliness, divorce, homicide, and stress-related disease in individualist cultures (Popenoe, 1993; Triandis et al., 1988). Demands for more romance and personal fulfillment in marriage can subject relationships to more pressure (Dion & Dion, 1993). In one survey, "keeping romance alive" was rated as important to a good marriage by 78 percent of U.S. women but only 29 percent of Japanese women (*American Enterprise*, 1992). In China, love songs have often expressed enduring commitment and friendship (Rothbaum & Tsang, 1998): "We will be together from now on . . . I will never change from now to forever."

What predicts change in one culture over time, or between differing cultures? Social history matters. In Western cultures, individualism and independence have been fostered by voluntary emigration, a capitalist economy, and a sparsely populated, challenging environment (Kitayama et al., 2009, 2010; Varnum et al., 2010). Might biology also play a role? In search of biological underpinnings to such cultural differences, a new subfield, *cultural neuroscience,* is studying how neurobiology and cultural traits influence each other (Chiao et al., 2013). One study compared collectivists' and individualists' brain activity when viewing other people in distress. The brain scans suggested that collectivists experienced greater emotional pain when exposed to others' distress (Cheon et al., 2011). As we have seen in personality and beyond, we are biopsychosocial creatures.

RETRIEVE IT [✻]

• How do individualist and collectivist cultures differ?

ANSWER: Individualists give priority to personal goals over group goals and tend to define their identity in terms of their own personal attributes. Collectivists give priority to group goals over individual goals and tend to define their identity in terms of group identifications.

MODULE
39 REVIEW   Contemporary Perspectives on Personality

◉ Learning Objectives

Test Yourself by taking a moment to answer each of these Learning Objective Questions (repeated here from within the module). Then turn to Appendix D, Complete Module Reviews, to check your answers. Research suggests that trying to answer these questions on your own will improve your long-term memory of the concepts (McDaniel et al., 2009).

39-1 How do psychologists use traits to describe personality?

39-2 What are some common misunderstandings about introversion? Does extraversion lead to greater success than introversion?

39-3 What are personality inventories, and what are their strengths and weaknesses as trait-assessment tools?

39-4 Which traits seem to provide the most useful information about personality variation?

39-5 Does research support the consistency of personality traits over time and across situations?

39-6 How do social-cognitive theorists view personality development, and how do they explore behavior?

39-7 What criticisms have social-cognitive theorists faced?

39-8 Why has psychology generated so much research on the self? How important is self-esteem to our well-being?

39-9 What evidence reveals self-serving bias, and how do defensive and secure self-esteem differ?

39-10 How do individualist and collectivist cultures differ in their values and goals?

▣ Terms and Concepts to Remember

Test yourself on these terms by trying to write down the definition in your own words before flipping back to the referenced page to check your answers.

trait, p. 505

personality inventory, p. 508

Minnesota Multiphasic Personality Inventory (MMPI), p. 508

empirically derived test, p. 508

social-cognitive perspective, p. 513

reciprocal determinism, p. 513

self, p. 516

spotlight effect, p. 516

self-esteem, p. 517

self-efficacy, p. 517

self-serving bias, p. 518

narcissism, p. 519

individualism, p. 521

collectivism, p. 521

✖ Experience the Testing Effect

Test yourself repeatedly throughout your studies. This will not only help you figure out what you know and don't know; the testing itself will help you learn and remember the information more effectively thanks to the *testing effect*.

1. _____ theories of personality focus on describing characteristic behavior patterns, such as agreeableness or extraversion.

2. One famous personality inventory is the
   a. Extraversion–Introversion Scale.
   b. Person–Situation Inventory.
   c. MMPI.
   d. Rorschach.

3. Which of the following is NOT one of the Big Five personality factors?
   a. Conscientiousness
   b. Anxiety
   c. Extraversion
   d. Agreeableness

4. Our scores on personality tests best predict
   a. our behavior on a specific occasion.
   b. our average behavior across many situations.
   c. behavior involving a single trait, such as conscientiousness.
   d. behavior that depends on the situation or context.

5. The social-cognitive perspective proposes our personality is shaped by a process called reciprocal determinism, as personal factors, environmental factors, and behaviors interact. An example of an environmental factor is
   a. the presence of books in a home.
   b. a preference for outdoor play.
   c. the ability to read at a fourth-grade level.
   d. the fear of violent action on television.

6. Critics say that _____-_____ personality theory is very sensitive to an individual's interactions with particular situations, but that it gives too little attention to the person's enduring traits.

7. Researchers have found that low self-esteem tends to be linked with life problems. How should this link be interpreted?

   a. Life problems cause low self-esteem.

   b. The answer isn't clear because the link is correlational and does not indicate cause and effect.

   c. Low self-esteem leads to life problems.

   d. Because of the self-serving bias, we must assume that external factors cause low self-esteem.

8. A fortune cookie advises, "Love yourself and happiness will follow." Is this good advice?

9. The tendency to overestimate others' attention to and evaluation of our appearance, performance, and blunders is called the _____ _____.

10. Individualist cultures tend to value _____; collectivist cultures tend to value _____.

    a. interdependence; independence

    b. independence; interdependence

    c. solidarity; uniqueness

    d. duty; fulfillment

Find answers to these questions in Appendix E, in the back of the book.

Use 🅜 LearningCurve to create your personalized study plan, which will direct you to the resources that will help you most in 🅜 LaunchPad.

9.5% Depressive disorders or bipolar disorder

6.8% Social anxiety disorder

3.5% Posttraumatic stress disorder

1.1% Schizophrenia

Anxiety and obsessive-compulsive disorder

Major depressive disorder

Bipolar disorder

Possible causes:
- Heredity
- Maternal flu
- Stress

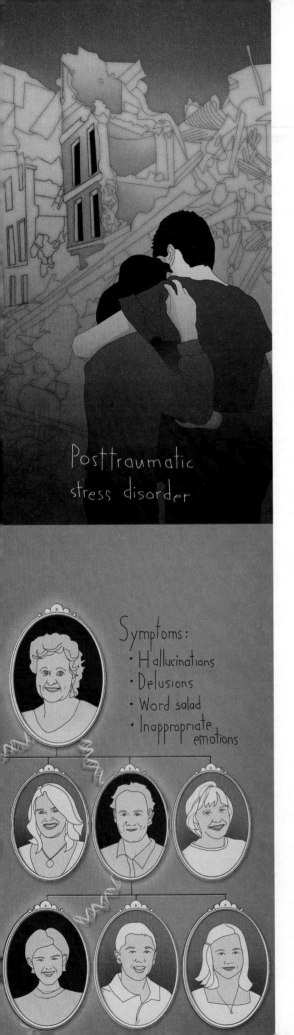

Posttraumatic stress disorder

Symptoms:
• Hallucinations
• Delusions
• Word salad
• Inappropriate emotions

Psychological Disorders

I felt the need to clean my room . . . and would spend four to five hours at it. I would take every book out of the bookcase, dust and put it back . . . I couldn't stop.

Marc, diagnosed with obsessive-compulsive disorder (from Summers, 1996)

Whenever I get depressed it's because I've lost a sense of self. I can't find reasons to like myself. I think I'm ugly. I think no one likes me.

Greta, diagnosed with depression (from Thorne, 1993, p. 21)

Voices, like the roar of a crowd, came. I felt like Jesus; I was being crucified.

Stuart, diagnosed with schizophrenia (from Emmons et al., 1997)

NOW and then, all of us feel, think, or act in ways that may resemble a psychological disorder. We feel anxious, depressed, withdrawn, or suspicious. So it's no wonder that we sometimes see ourselves in the psychological disorders we study.

Personally or through friends or family, many of us will know the confusion and pain of unexplained physical symptoms, irrational fears, or a feeling that life is not worth living. On American college campuses, 32 percent of students report an apparent mental health problem (Eisenberg et al., 2011).

Worldwide, some 450 million people live with mental or behavioral disorders (WHO, 2010). Modules 40 through 43 examine these disorders. The Therapy modules consider their *treatment*. ■

psychological disorder a syndrome marked by a clinically significant disturbance in an individual's cognition, emotion regulation, or behavior.

medical model the concept that diseases, in this case psychological disorders, have physical causes that can be *diagnosed, treated,* and, in most cases, *cured,* often through treatment in a *hospital.*

"Who in the rainbow can draw the line where the violet tint ends and the orange tint begins? Distinctly we see the difference of the colors, but where exactly does the one first blendingly enter into the other? So with sanity and insanity."

Herman Melville,
Billy Budd, Sailor, *1924*

MODULE 40 Basic Concepts of Psychological Disorders

40-1 How should we draw the line between normality and disorder?

Most of us would agree that a family member who is depressed and isolated for three months has a psychological disorder. But what should we say about a grieving father who can't resume his usual social activities three months after his child has died? Where do we draw the line between clinical depression and understandable grief? Between bizarre irrationality and zany creativity? Between abnormality and normality? In their search for answers, theorists and clinicians ask:

- How should we *define* psychological disorders?

- How should we *understand* disorders? How do underlying biological factors contribute to disorder? How do troubling environments influence our well-being? And how do these effects of nature and nurture interact?

- How should we *classify* psychological disorders? And can we do so in a way that allows us to help people without stigmatizing or labeling them?

- What do we know about *rates* of psychological disorders? How many people have them? Who is vulnerable, and when?

A **psychological disorder** is a syndrome (a symptom collection) marked by a "clinically significant disturbance in an individual's cognition, emotion regulation, or behavior" (American Psychiatric Association, 2013). Such thoughts, emotions, or behaviors are *dysfunctional* or *maladaptive*—they interfere with normal day-to-day life. Believing your home must be thoroughly cleaned every weekend is not a disorder. But if cleaning rituals interfere with work and leisure, as Marc's rituals (noted earlier) did, they may be signs of a disorder. And occasional sad moods that persist and become disabling may likewise signal a psychological disorder.

Distress often accompanies dysfunctional behaviors. Marc, Greta, and Stuart were all distressed by their behaviors or emotions.

Over time, definitions of what makes for a "significant disturbance" have varied. In 1973, the American Psychiatric Association dropped homosexuality as a disorder after mental health workers came to consider same-sex attraction as not inherently dysfunctional or distressing. In the 1970s, high-energy children were typically viewed as normal youngsters running a bit wild. Today, more of them are seen as dysfunctional and diagnosed with *attention-deficit/hyperactivity disorder (ADHD).*

Carol Beckwith

© Image Source/Corbis

Culture and normality Young men of the West African Wodaabe tribe put on elaborate makeup and costumes to attract women. Young American men may buy flashy cars with loud stereos to do the same. Each culture may view the other's behavior as abnormal.

Understanding Psychological Disorders

40-2 How do the medical model and the biopsychosocial approach influence our understanding of psychological disorders?

The way we view a problem influences how we try to solve it. In earlier times, people often thought that strange behaviors were evidence that strange forces—the movements of the stars, godlike powers, or evil spirits—were at work. Had you lived during the Middle Ages, you might have said "The devil made him do it." To drive out demons, people considered "mad" were sometimes caged or given "therapies" such as genital mutilation, beatings, removal of teeth or lengths of intestines, or transfusions of animal blood (Farina, 1982).

Reformers, such as Philippe Pinel (1745–1826) in France, opposed such brutal treatments. Madness is not demon possession, he insisted, but a sickness of the mind caused by severe stress and inhumane conditions. Curing the sickness, he said, requires "moral treatment," including boosting patients' morale by unchaining them and talking with them. He and others worked to replace brutality with gentleness, isolation with activity, and filth with clean air and sunshine.

Barbaric treatments for mental illness linger even today. In some places, people are chained to a bed, confined to their rooms, or even locked in a space with wild hyenas, in the belief that the animals will see and attack evil spirits (Hooper, 2013). Noting the physical and emotional damage of such restraint, the World Health Organization launched a "chain-free initiative" that aims to reform hospitals "into patient-friendly and humane places with minimum restraints" (WHO, 2014).

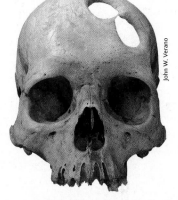

John W. Verano

Yesterday's "therapy" Through the ages, psychologically disordered people have received brutal treatments, including the trephination evident in this Stone Age skull. Drilling skull holes like these may have been an attempt to release evil spirits and cure those with mental disorders. Did this patient survive the "cure"?

The Medical Model

By the 1800s, a medical breakthrough prompted further reform. Researchers discovered that syphilis, a sexually transmitted infection, invades the brain and distorts the mind. This discovery triggered an excited search for physical causes of mental disorders and for treatments that would cure them. Hospitals replaced asylums, and the **medical model** of mental disorders was born. This model is reflected in words we still use today. We speak of the mental *health* movement. A mental *illness* (also called a psycho*pathology*) needs to be *diagnosed* on the basis of its *symptoms*. It needs to be *treated* through *therapy*, which may include treatment in a psychiatric *hospital*. Recent discoveries that genetically influenced abnormalities in brain structure and biochemistry contribute to many disorders have energized the medical perspective.

∨ FIGURE 40.1

The biopsychosocial approach to psychological disorders Today's psychology studies how biological, psychological, and social-cultural factors interact to produce specific psychological disorders.

Biological influences:
• evolution
• individual genes
• brain structure and chemistry

Psychological influences:
• stress
• trauma
• learned helplessness
• mood-related perceptions and memories

Psychological disorder

Social-cultural influences:
• roles
• expectations
• definitions of *normality* and *disorder*

Wavebreakmedia Ltd./ Getty Images

The Biopsychosocial Approach

To call psychological disorders "sicknesses" tilts research heavily toward the influence of biology and away from the influence of our personal histories and social and cultural surroundings. But as we have seen throughout this text, biological, psychological, and social-cultural influences together weave the fabric of our thoughts, feelings, and behaviors (**FIGURE 40.1**). As individuals, we differ in the amount of stress we experience and in the ways we cope with stressors. Cultures

epigenetics the study of environmental influences on gene expression that occur without a DNA change.

DSM-5 the American Psychiatric Association's *Diagnostic and Statistical Manual of Mental Disorders,* Fifth Edition; a widely used system for classifying psychological disorders.

also differ in the sources of stress they produce and in the traditional ways of coping they provide. We are physically embodied and socially embedded.

The environment's influence on disorders can be seen in culture-related symptoms (Beardsley, 1994; Castillo, 1997). Anxiety, for example, may be manifested in different ways in different cultures. In Latin American cultures, people may display symptoms of *susto,* a condition marked by severe anxiety, restlessness, and a fear of black magic. In Japanese culture, people may experience *taijin-kyofusho*—social anxiety about their appearance, combined with a readiness to blush and a fear of eye contact. The eating disorders *anorexia nervosa* and *bulimia nervosa* occur mostly in food-abundant North American and other Western cultures. Increasingly, however, such North American disorders have, along with McDonald's and MTV, spread across the globe (Watters, 2010). Even disordered aggression may be explained differently in other cultures. In Malaysia, a sudden outburst of violent behavior, called *amok* (as in the English phrase "run amok"), was traditionally attributed to an evil spirit.

Two other disorders—depression and schizophrenia—occur worldwide. From Asia to Africa and across the Americas, people with schizophrenia often act irrationally and speak in disorganized ways; people with depression experience long-term hopelessness and lethargy, have trouble concentrating, and lose interest in activities that once brought them pleasure.

Disorders reflect genetic predispositions and physiological states, psychological dynamics, and social and cultural circumstances. The biopsychosocial approach emphasizes that mind and body are inseparable (see Figure 40.1). Negative emotions contribute to physical illness, and physical abnormalities contribute to negative emotions. As research on **epigenetics** shows, our environment can also affect whether a gene is *expressed,* thus affecting the development of psychological disorders.

RETRIEVE IT [✻]

• Are psychological disorders universal, or are they culture-specific? Explain with examples.

ANSWER: Some psychological disorders are culture-specific. For example, anorexia nervosa occurs mostly in North American cultures, and *taijin-kyofusho* appears largely in Japan. Other disorders, such as schizophrenia, are universal—occurring in all cultures.

• What is the biopsychosocial approach, and why is it important in our understanding of psychological disorders?

ANSWER: Biological, psychological, and social-cultural influences combine to produce psychological disorders. This broad perspective helps us understand that our well-being is affected by our genes, brain functioning, inner thoughts and feelings, and the influences of our social and cultural environment.

Classifying Disorders—and Labeling People

⬤ **40-3** How and why do clinicians classify psychological disorders, and why do some psychologists criticize the use of diagnostic labels?

In biology, classification creates order. To classify an animal as a "mammal" says a great deal—that it is warm-blooded, has hair or fur, and produces milk to feed its young. In psychiatry and psychology, too, classification orders and describes symptoms. To classify a person's disorder as "schizophrenia" suggests that the person talks incoherently, has bizarre beliefs, shows either little emotion or inappropriate emotion, or is socially withdrawn. "Schizophrenia" is a quick way of describing a complex disorder.

But diagnostic classification gives more than a thumbnail sketch of a person's disordered behavior, thoughts, or feelings. In psychiatry and psychology, classification also attempts to

• *predict* a disorder's future course.
• *suggest* appropriate treatment.
• *prompt research* into a disorder's causes.

"*I'm always like this, and my family was wondering if you could prescribe a mild depressant.*"

The most common tool for describing disorders and estimating how often they occur is the American Psychiatric Association's 2013 *Diagnostic and Statistical Manual of Mental Disorders,* now in its fifth edition **(DSM-5).** Physicians and mental health workers use the DSM-5 to guide medical diagnoses and treatment. For example, a person may be diagnosed with and treated for "insomnia disorder" if he or she meets *all* of the criteria in **TABLE 40.1.**

In the new DSM-5, some diagnostic labels changed. The conditions formerly called "autism" and "Asperger's syndrome" were combined under the label *autism spectrum disorder.* "Mental retardation" became *intellectual disability.* New categories, such as *hoarding disorder* and *binge-eating disorder,* were added.

Real-world tests *(field trials)* have assessed the reliability of the new DSM-5 categories (Freedman et al., 2013). Some diagnoses—such as *adult posttraumatic stress disorder* and *childhood autism spectrum disorder*—fared well, with clinician agreement near 70 percent (meaning that if one psychiatrist or psychologist diagnosed someone with one of these disorders, there was a 70 percent chance that another mental health worker would independently give the same diagnosis). Others, such as *antisocial personality disorder* and *generalized anxiety disorder,* have fared poorly, with about 20 percent agreement.

Critics have long faulted the DSM for casting too wide a net, and for bringing "almost any kind of behavior within the compass of psychiatry" (Eysenck et al., 1983). Some now worry that the DSM-5's even wider net will extend the pathologizing of everyday life—for example, by turning bereavement grief into a depressive disorder and childish rambunctiousness into ADHD (Frances, 2013). (See *Thinking Critically About: ADHD—Normal High Energy or Disordered Behavior?* on the next page.) Others respond that enduring hyperactivity and grief-related depression are genuine disorders (Kendler, 2011; Kupfer, 2012).

Other critics register a more basic complaint—that these labels are at best subjective and at worst value judgments masquerading as science. Once we label a person, we view that person differently (Bathje & Pryor, 2011; Farina, 1982; Sadler et al., 2012). Labels can change reality by putting us on alert for evidence that confirms our view. When teachers were told certain students were "gifted," they acted in ways that brought out the creative behaviors they expected (Snyder, 1984). If we hear that a new co-worker is a difficult person, we may treat this person suspiciously. He or she may in turn react to us as a difficult person would. Labels can be self-fulfilling.

The biasing power of labels was clear in a classic study. David Rosenhan (1973) and seven others went to hospital admissions offices, complaining (falsely) of "hearing voices" saying *empty, hollow,* and *thud.* Apart from this complaint and giving false names and occupations, they answered questions truthfully. All eight healthy people were misdiagnosed with disorders.

Should we be surprised? Surely not. As one psychiatrist noted, if someone swallowed blood, went to an emergency room, and spat it up, would we blame a doctor for diagnosing a bleeding ulcer? But what followed the Rosenhan study diagnoses was startling. Until being released an average of 19 days later, these eight "patients" showed no other symptoms. Yet after analyzing their (quite normal) life histories, clinicians were able to "discover" the causes of their disorders, such as having mixed emotions about a parent. Even the patients' routine note-taking behavior was misinterpreted as a symptom.

✔ TABLE 40.1

Insomnia Disorder (American Psychiatric Association, 2013)

- Feeling unsatisfied with amount or quality of sleep (trouble falling asleep, staying asleep, or returning to sleep)
- Sleep disruption causes distress or diminished everyday functioning
- Happens three or more nights each week
- Occurs during at least three consecutive months
- Happens even with sufficient sleep opportunities
- Independent from other sleep disorders (such as narcolepsy)
- Independent from substance use or abuse
- Independent from other mental disorders or medical conditions

Struggles and recovery During his campaign, Boston Mayor Martin Walsh spoke openly about his past struggles with alcohol. In the process, he moved beyond potentially biasing labels, and won a close election.

Gretchen Ertl/The New York Times/Redux

ADHD—Normal High Energy or Disordered Behavior?

40-4 Why is there controversy over attention-deficit/hyperactivity disorder?

Eight-year-old Todd has always been energetic. At home, he chatters away and darts from one activity to the next, rarely settling down to read a book or focus on a game. At play, he is reckless and overreacts when playmates bump into him or take one of his toys. At school, Todd fidgets, and his exasperated teacher complains that he doesn't listen, follow instructions, or stay in his seat to do his lessons. As Todd matures to adulthood, his hyperactivity likely will subside, but his inattentiveness may persist (Kessler et al., 2010).

If taken for a psychological evaluation, Todd may be diagnosed with **attention-deficit/ hyperactivity disorder (ADHD).** Some 11 percent of American 4- to 17-year-old children receive the diagnosis after displaying its key symptoms (extreme inattention, hyperactivity, and impulsivity) (Schwarz & Cohen, 2013). Studies also find 2.5 percent of adults—though the number diminishes with age—exhibiting ADHD symptoms (Simon et al., 2009). The looser criteria for adult ADHD in the DSM-5 has led critics to fear increased diagnosis and overuse of prescription drugs (Frances, 2012, 2014).

To skeptics, being distractible, fidgety, and impulsive sounds like a "disorder" caused by a single genetic variation: a Y chromosome (the male sex chromosome). And sure enough, ADHD is diagnosed three times more often in boys than in girls. Does energetic child + boring school = ADHD overdiagnosis? Is the label being applied to healthy schoolchildren who, in more natural outdoor environments, would seem perfectly normal? Is ADHD a disease that is

marketed by companies offering drugs that treat it (Thomas, 2015)?

Skeptics think so. In the decade after 1987, they note, the proportion of American children being treated for ADHD nearly quadrupled (Olfson et al., 2003). Minority youth less often receive an ADHD diagnosis than do White youth, but this difference has shrunk as minority ADHD diagnoses have increased (Getahun at al., 2013). How commonplace the diagnosis is depends in part on teacher referrals. Some teachers refer lots of kids for ADHD assessment, others none. ADHD rates have varied by a factor of 10 in different counties of New York State (Carlson, 2000). Depending on where they live, children who are "a persistent pain in the neck in school" are often diagnosed with ADHD and given powerful prescription drugs, notes Peter Gray (2010). But the problem may reside less in the child than in today's abnormal environment, which forces children to do what evolution has not prepared them to do—to sit for long hours in chairs. In more natural outdoor environments, these children might seem perfectly healthy. When given cognitive tests, children with ADHD concentrate better when allowed to fidget (Hartanto et al., 2015).

Not everyone agrees that ADHD is being overdiagnosed. Some argue that today's more frequent diagnoses of ADHD reflect increased awareness of the disorder, especially in those areas where rates are highest. They acknowledge that diagnoses can be inconsistent—ADHD is not as clearly defined as a broken arm. Nevertheless, declared the World Federation for Mental Health (2005), "there is strong agreement among the international scientific

community that ADHD is a real neurobiological disorder whose existence should no longer be debated." A consensus statement by 75 neuroimaging researchers noted that abnormal brain activity often accompanies ADHD (Barkley et al., 2002).

What, then, is known about ADHD's causes? It is not caused by too much sugar or poor schools. ADHD often coexists with a learning disorder or with defiant and temper-prone behavior. ADHD is *heritable,* and research teams are sleuthing the culprit genes and abnormal neural pathways (Lionel et al., 2013; Poelmans et al., 2011; Volkow et al., 2009; Williams et al., 2010). It is treatable with medications such as Ritalin and Adderall, which are considered stimulants but help calm hyperactivity and increase one's ability to sit and focus on a task—and to progress normally in school (Barbaresi et al., 2007). Psychological therapies, such as those focused on shaping classroom and at-home behaviors, also help to address the distress of ADHD (Fabiano et al., 2008).

The bottom line: Extreme inattention, hyperactivity, and impulsivity can derail social, academic, and vocational achievements, and these symptoms can be treated with medication and other therapies (Hinshaw & Scheffler, 2014). But the debate continues over whether normal high energy is too often diagnosed as a psychiatric disorder, and whether there is a cost to the long-term use of stimulant drugs in treating ADHD.

---

attention-deficit/hyperactivity disorder (ADHD) a psychological disorder marked by extreme inattention and/or hyperactivity and impulsivity.

In another study, people watched videotaped interviews. If told the interviewees were job applicants, the viewers perceived them as normal (Langer & Abelson, 1974; Langer & Imber, 1980). Other viewers who were told they were watching psychiatric or cancer patients perceived the same interviewees as "different from most people." Therapists who thought they were watching an interview of a psychiatric patient perceived him as "frightened of his own aggressive impulses," a "passive, dependent type," and so forth. As Rosenhan discovered, a label can have "a life and an influence of its own." Labels matter.

Are People With Psychological Disorders Dangerous?

40-5 Do psychological disorders predict violent behavior?

September 16, 2013, started like any other Monday at Washington, DC's, Navy Yard, with people arriving early to begin work. Then government contractor Aaron Alexis parked his car, entered the building, and began shooting people. An hour later, 13 people were dead, including Alexis. Reports later confirmed that Alexis had a history of mental illness. Before the shooting, he had stated that an "ultra low frequency attack is what I've been subject to for the last three months. And to be perfectly honest, that is what has driven me to this." After a horrifying mass shooting in a Connecticut elementary school in 2012, New York's governor declared, "People who have mental issues should not have guns" (Kaplan & Hakim, 2013). These devastating mass shootings, like many others since then, reinforced public perceptions that people with psychological disorders pose a threat (Barry et al., 2013; Jorm et al., 2012). So did an incident in March of 2015, when Germanwings co-pilot Andreas Lubitz, who had a history of mental illness, killed 150 people by locking his pilot out of the cockpit and intentionally crashing a commercial jet into the French Alps.

Does scientific evidence support the governor's statement? If disorders actually increase the risk of violence, then denying people with psychological disorders the right to bear arms might reduce violent crimes. But real life tells a different story. Most people with mental disorders commit no violent crimes, and the vast majority of violent crimes are committed by people with no diagnosed disorder (Fazel & Grann, 2006; Skeem et al., 2015; Walkup & Rubin, 2013).

People with disorders are more likely to be *victims* than perpetrators of violence (Marley & Bulia, 2001). According to the

Adrees Latif/Reuters/Landov

U.S. Surgeon General's Office (1999, p. 7), "There is very little risk of violence or harm to a stranger from casual contact with an individual who has a mental disorder." *The bottom line:* Psychological disorders only rarely lead to violent acts, and focusing gun restrictions only on mentally ill people will likely not reduce gun violence (Friedman, 2012).

If mental illness is not a good predictor of violence, what is? Better predictors are a history of violence, use of alcohol or drugs, and access to a gun. The mass-killing shooters have one more thing in common: They tend to be young males. "We could avoid two-thirds of all crime simply by putting all able-bodied young men in cryogenic sleep from the age of 12 through 28," said one psychologist (Lykken, 1995).

Mental disorders seldom lead to violence, and clinical prediction of violence is unreliable. What, then, are the triggers for the few people with psychological disorders who do commit violent acts? For some, the trigger is substance abuse. For others, like the Navy Yard shooter, it's threatening delusions and hallucinated voices that command them to act (Douglas et al., 2009; Elbogen

How to prevent mass shootings? Following the Newtown, Connecticut, slaughter of 20 young children and 6 adults, people wondered: Could those at risk for violence be identified in advance by mental health workers and reported to police? Would laws that require such reporting discourage disturbed gun owners from seeking mental health treatment?

& Johnson, 2009; Fazel et al., 2009, 2010). Whether people with mental disorders who turn violent should be held responsible for their behavior remains controversial. U.S. President Ronald Reagan's near-assassin, John Hinckley, was sent to a hospital rather than to prison. The public was outraged. "Hinckley insane. Public mad," declared one headline. They were outraged again in 2011, when Jared Lee Loughner killed six people and injured several others, including U.S. Representative Gabrielle Giffords. Loughner was diagnosed with schizophrenia and twice found incompetent to stand trial. He was later judged competent to stand trial, pled guilty to 19 charges of murder and attempted murder, and was sentenced to life in prison without parole.

Which decision was correct? The first two, which blamed Loughner's "madness" for clouding his judgment? Or the final one, which decided that he should be held responsible for the acts he committed? As we come to better understand the biological and environmental bases for all human behavior, from generosity to vandalism, when should we—and should we not—hold people accountable for their actions?

Labels also have power outside the laboratory. Getting a job or finding a place to rent can be a challenge for people recently released from a mental hospital. Label someone as "mentally ill" and people may fear them as potentially violent (see Thinking Critically About: Are People With Psychological Disorders Dangerous?). Such negative reactions may fade as people better understand that many

Better portrayals Old stereotypes are slowly being replaced in media portrayals of psychological disorders. Recent films offer fairly realistic depictions. *Iron Man 3* (2013) portrayed a main character, shown here, with posttraumatic stress disorder. *Black Swan* (2010) dramatized a lead character suffering a delusional disorder. *A Single Man* (2009) depicted depression.

"What's the use of their having names," the Gnat said, "if they won't answer to them?"
"No use to *them*," said Alice; "but it's useful to the people that name them, I suppose."

Lewis Carroll,
Through the Looking-Glass, *1871*

📱 LaunchPad To test your ability to form diagnoses, visit LaunchPad's *PsychSim 6: Classifying Disorders.*

Paramount Pictures/Photofest

psychological disorders involve diseases of the brain, not failures of character (Solomon, 1996). Public figures have helped foster this understanding by speaking openly about their own struggles with disorders such as depression and substance abuse. The more contact we have with people with disorders, the more accepting our attitudes become (Kolodziej & Johnson, 1996).

Despite their risks, diagnostic labels have benefits. They help mental health professionals communicate about their cases and study the causes and treatments of disorder. Clients are often relieved to learn that the nature of their suffering has a name, and that they are not alone in experiencing their symptoms.

RETRIEVE IT [✗]

• What is the value, and what are the dangers, of labeling individuals with disorders?

ANSWER: Therapists and others apply disorder labels to communicate with one another using a common language, and to share concepts during research. Clients may benefit from knowing that they are not the only ones with these symptoms. The dangers of labeling people are that (1) people may begin to act as they have been labeled, and (2) the labels can trigger assumptions that will change people's behavior toward those labelled.

Rates of Psychological Disorders

👁 **40-6** How many people have, or have had, a psychological disorder? Is poverty a risk factor?

Who is most vulnerable to psychological disorders? At what times of life? To answer such questions, various countries have conducted lengthy, structured interviews with representative samples of thousands of their citizens. After asking hundreds of questions that probe for symptoms—"Has there ever been a period of two weeks or more when you felt like you wanted to die?"—the researchers have estimated the current, prior-year, and lifetime prevalence of various disorders.

How many people have, or have had, a psychological disorder? More than most of us suppose:

• The U.S. National Institute of Mental Health (2008, based on Kessler et al., 2005) has estimated that just over 1 in 4 adult Americans "suffer from a diagnosable mental disorder in a given year" (**TABLE 40.2**).

• A World Health Organization (2004) study—based on 90-minute interviews of 60,463 people—estimated the number of prior-year mental disorders in 20 countries. As **FIGURE 40.2** illustrates, the lowest rate of reported mental disorders was in China (Shanghai), the highest rate in the United States. Moreover, people immigrating to the United States from Mexico, Africa, and Asia averaged better mental health than their U.S. counterparts with the same ethnic heritage (Breslau et al., 2007; Maldonado-Molina et al., 2011). For example, compared with people who have recently immigrated from Mexico, Mexican-Americans born in the United States are at greater risk of mental disorder—a phenomenon known as the *immigrant paradox* (Schwartz et al., 2010).

What increases vulnerability to mental disorders? As we have seen, the answer varies with the disorder (**TABLE 40.3**). One predictor of mental disorders—poverty—crosses ethnic and gender lines. The incidence of serious psychological disorders has been doubly high among those below the poverty line (Centers for

▼ TABLE 40.2

Percentage of Americans Reporting Selected Psychological Disorders in the Past Year

Psychological Disorder	Percentage
Generalized anxiety disorder	3.1
Social anxiety disorder	6.8
Phobia of specific object or situation	8.7
Depressive disorders or bipolar disorder	9.5
Obsessive-compulsive disorder (OCD)	1.0
Schizophrenia	1.1
Posttraumatic stress disorder (PTSD)	3.5
Attention-deficit/ hyperactivity disorder (ADHD)	4.1

Data from: National Institute of Mental Health, 2008.

Disease Control, 1992). This *correlation*, like so many others, raises further questions: Does poverty cause disorders? Or do disorders cause poverty? It is both, though the answer varies with the disorder. Schizophrenia understandably leads to poverty. Yet the stresses and demoralization of poverty can also breed disorders, especially depression in women and substance abuse in men (Dohrenwend et al., 1992). In one natural experiment investigating the poverty-pathology link, researchers tracked rates of behavior problems in North Carolina Native American children as economic development enabled a dramatic reduction in their community's poverty rate. As the study began, children of poverty exhibited more deviant and aggressive behaviors. After four years, children whose families had moved above the poverty line exhibited a 40 percent decrease in behavior problems. Those who maintained their previous positions below or above the poverty line exhibited no change (Costello et al., 2003).

At what times of life do disorders strike? Usually by early adulthood. "Over 75 percent of our sample with any disorder had experienced [their] first symptoms by age 24," reported Lee Robins and Darrel Regier (1991, p. 331). Among the earliest to appear are the symptoms of antisocial personality disorder (median age 8) and of phobias (median age 10). Alcohol use disorder, obsessive-compulsive disorder, bipolar disorder, and schizophrenia symptoms appear at a median age near 20. Major depressive disorder often hits somewhat later, at a median age of 25.

LaunchPad See LaunchPad's *Video: Correlational Studies* for a helpful tutorial animation about this research design.

▼ FIGURE 40.2

Prior-year prevalence of disorders in selected areas From World Health Organization interviews in 20 countries (WHO, 2004a).

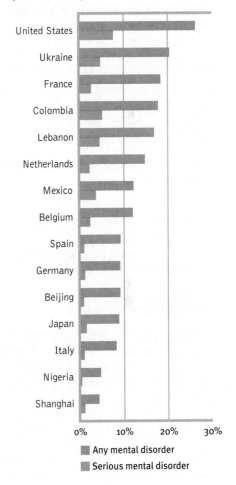

■ Any mental disorder
■ Serious mental disorder

▼ TABLE 40.3

Risk and Protective Factors for Mental Disorders

Risk Factors	Protective Factors
Academic failure	Aerobic exercise
Birth complications	Community offering empowerment, opportunity, and security
Caring for those who are chronically ill or who have a neurocognitive disorder	Economic independence
Child abuse and neglect	Effective parenting
Chronic insomnia	Feelings of mastery and control
Chronic pain	Feelings of security
Family disorganization or conflict	Literacy
Low birth weight	Positive attachment and early bonding
Low socioeconomic status	Positive parent-child relationships
Medical illness	Problem-solving skills
Neurochemical imbalance	Resilient coping with stress and adversity
Parental mental illness	Self-esteem
Parental substance abuse	Social and work skills
Personal loss and bereavement	Social support from family and friends
Poor work skills and habits	
Reading disabilities	
Sensory disabilities	
Social incompetence	
Stressful life events	
Substance abuse	
Trauma experiences	

Research from: World Health Organization (WHO, 2004b,c).

RETRIEVE IT [✖]

• What is the relationship between poverty and psychological disorders?

ANSWER: Poverty-related stresses can help trigger disorders, but disabling disorders can also contribute to poverty. Thus, poverty and disorder are often a chicken-and-egg situation: It's hard to know which came first.

Learning Objectives

Test Yourself by taking a moment to answer each of these Learning Objective Questions (repeated here from within the module). Then turn to Appendix D, Complete Module Reviews, to check your answers. Research suggests that trying to answer these questions on your own will improve your long-term memory of the concepts (McDaniel et al., 2009).

40-1 How should we draw the line between normality and disorder?

40-2 How do the medical model and the biopsychosocial approach influence our understanding of psychological disorders?

40-3 How and why do clinicians classify psychological disorders, and why do some psychologists criticize the use of diagnostic labels?

40-4 Why is there controversy over attention-deficit/hyperactivity disorder?

40-5 Do psychological disorders predict violent behavior?

40-6 How many people have, or have had, a psychological disorder? Is poverty a risk factor?

Terms and Concepts to Remember

Test yourself on these terms by trying to write down the definition in your own words before flipping back to the referenced page to check your answers.

psychological disorder, p. 528

medical model, p. 529

epigenetics, p. 530

DSM-5, p. 531

attention-deficit/hyperactivity disorder (ADHD), p. 532

Experience the Testing Effect

Test yourself repeatedly throughout your studies. This will not only help you figure out what you know and don't know; the testing itself will help you learn and remember the information more effectively thanks to the *testing effect*.

1. Two major disorders that are found worldwide are schizophrenia and _____.

2. Anna is embarrassed that it takes her several minutes to parallel park her car. She usually gets out of the car once or twice to inspect her distance both from the curb and from the nearby cars. Should she worry about having a psychological disorder?

3. What is *susto*, and is this a culture-specific or universal psychological disorder?

4. A therapist says that psychological disorders are sicknesses and people with these disorders should be treated as patients in a hospital. This therapist believes in the _____ model.

5. Many psychologists reject the "disorders-as-illness" view and instead contend that other factors may also be involved—for example, the person's bad habits and poor social skills. This view represents the _____ approach.

   a. medical
   b. culture-specific
   c. biopsychosocial
   d. diagnostic

6. Why is the DSM, and the DSM-5 in particular, considered controversial?

7. One predictor of psychiatric disorders that crosses ethnic and gender lines is _____.

8. The symptoms of _____ appear around age 10; _____ tend[s] to appear later, around age 25.

   a. schizophrenia; bipolar disorder
   b. bipolar disorder; schizophrenia
   c. major depressive disorder; phobias
   d. phobias; major depressive disorder

Find answers to these questions in Appendix E, in the back of the book.

Use **LearningCurve** to create your personalized study plan, which will direct you to the resources that will help you most in **LaunchPad**.

MODULE 41 Anxiety Disorders, OCD, and PTSD

Anxiety is part of life. Speaking in front of a class, peering down from a ladder, or waiting to play in a big game might make any one of us feel nervous. Anxiety may even cause us to avoid talking or making eye contact—"shyness," we call it. Fortunately for most of us, our uneasiness is not intense and persistent. Some of us, however, are more prone to notice and remember information perceived

as threatening (Mitte, 2008). When the brain's danger-detection system becomes hyperactive, we are at greater risk for an *anxiety disorder,* or for two other disorders that involve anxiety: *obsessive-compulsive disorder (OCD)* and *posttraumatic stress disorder (PTSD).*[1]

Anxiety Disorders

41-1 How do generalized anxiety disorder, panic disorder, and phobias differ?

The **anxiety disorders** are marked by distressing, persistent anxiety and often dysfunctional anxiety-reducing behaviors. These include:

- *Generalized anxiety disorder,* in which a person is unexplainably and continually tense and uneasy.
- *Panic disorder,* in which a person experiences *panic attacks*—sudden episodes of intense dread—and fears the next episode's unpredictable onset.
- *Phobias,* in which a person is intensely and irrationally afraid of a specific object, activity, or situation.

Generalized Anxiety Disorder

Tom was a 27-year-old electrician. For two years, he had been bothered by dizziness, sweating palms, and irregular heartbeat. He felt on edge and sometimes found himself shaking. Tom had been reasonably successful in hiding his symptoms from his family and co-workers, but occasionally he had to leave work. He allowed himself few other social contacts. Neither his family doctor nor a neurologist had been able to find any physical problem.

Tom's unfocused, out-of-control, agitated feelings suggest a **generalized anxiety disorder.** The symptoms of this disorder are commonplace; their persistence, for six months or more, is not. People with this condition (two-thirds women) worry continually, and they are often jittery, on edge, and sleep deprived (McLean & Anderson, 2009). Concentration is difficult as attention switches from worry to worry. Their tension and apprehension may leak out through furrowed brows, twitching eyelids, trembling, perspiration, or fidgeting from autonomic nervous system arousal.

People may not be able to identify the cause of their anxiety, and therefore cannot relieve or avoid it. To use Sigmund Freud's term, the anxiety is *free-floating* (not linked to a specific stressor or threat). Generalized anxiety disorder and depression often go hand in hand, but even without depression, this disorder tends to be disabling (Hunt et al., 2004; Moffitt et al., 2007). Moreover, it may lead to physical problems, such as high blood pressure.

Panic Disorder

For the 1 person in 75 with **panic disorder,** anxiety suddenly escalates into a terrifying panic attack—a minutes-long episode of intense fear that something horrible is about to happen. Physical symptoms, such as irregular heartbeat, chest pains, shortness of breath, choking, trembling, or dizziness may accompany the panic. One woman recalled suddenly feeling

> hot and as though I couldn't breathe. My heart was racing and I started to sweat and tremble and I was sure I was going to faint. Then my fingers started to feel numb and tingly and things seemed unreal. It was so bad I wondered if I was dying and asked my husband to take me to the emergency room. By the time we got there (about 10 minutes) the worst of the attack was over and I just felt washed out (Greist et al., 1986).

These anxiety tornados strike suddenly, wreak havoc, and disappear, but they are not forgotten. Ironically, worries about anxiety—perhaps fearing another

anxiety disorders psychological disorders characterized by distressing, persistent anxiety or maladaptive behaviors that reduce anxiety.

generalized anxiety disorder an anxiety disorder in which a person is continually tense, apprehensive, and in a state of autonomic nervous system arousal.

panic disorder an anxiety disorder marked by unpredictable, minutes-long episodes of intense dread in which a person experiences terror and accompanying chest pain, choking, or other frightening sensations. Often followed by worry over a possible next attack.

---

1. OCD and PTSD were formerly classified as anxiety disorders, but the DSM-5 now classifies them separately.

Panic on the course Golfer Charlie Beljan experienced what he later learned were panic attacks during an important tournament. His thumping heartbeat and shortness of breath led him to think he was having a heart attack. But hospital tests revealed that his symptoms, though serious, were not related to a physical illness. He recovered, went on to win $846,000, and has become an inspiration to others.

panic attack, or fearing anxiety-related symptoms in public—can amplify anxiety symptoms (Olatunji & Wolitzky-Taylor, 2009). After several panic attacks, people may come to fear the fear itself. This may trigger *agoraphobia*—fear or avoidance of public situations from which escape might be difficult. People with agoraphobia may avoid being outside the home, in a crowd, on a bus, or in an elevator.

Charles Darwin began suffering from panic disorder at age 28, after spending five years sailing the world. As a result, he moved to the country, avoided social gatherings, and traveled only in his wife's company. But the relative seclusion did free him to develop his evolutionary theory. "Even ill health," he reflected, "has saved me from the distraction of society and its amusements" (quoted in Ma, 1997).

Smokers have at least a doubled risk of panic disorder (Zvolensky & Bernstein, 2005). They also show greater panic symptoms in situations that often produce panic attacks (Knuts et al., 2010). Because nicotine is a stimulant, lighting up doesn't help us lighten up.

Phobias

We all live with some fears. But people with **phobias** are consumed by a persistent, irrational fear and avoidance of some object, activity, or situation. *Specific phobias* may focus on particular animals, insects, heights, blood, or closed spaces (**FIGURE 41.1**). Many people avoid the triggers, such as high places, that arouse their fear. Marilyn[2], an otherwise healthy and happy 28-year-old, so feared thunderstorms that she felt anxious as soon as a weather forecaster mentioned possible storms later in the week. If her husband was away and a storm was forecast, she would often stay with a close relative. During a storm, she hid from windows and buried her head to avoid seeing the lightning.

2. A book of case illustrations accompanying the previous edition of the *Diagnostic and Statistical Manual of Mental Disorders* provided this example and several others you will see in these Psychological Disorders modules.

Martin Harvey/
Digital Vision/Getty Images

> FIGURE 41.1

Some common and uncommon specific fears Researchers surveyed Dutch people to identify the most common events or objects they feared. A strong fear becomes a phobia if it provokes a compelling but irrational desire to avoid the dreaded object or situation. (Data from Depla et al., 2008.)

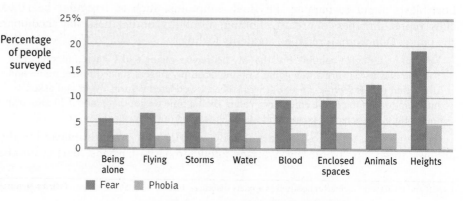

Not all phobias are so specific. *Social anxiety disorder* (formerly called "social phobia") is shyness taken to an extreme. People with this disorder have an intense fear of other people's negative judgments. They may avoid social situations, such as speaking up in a group, eating out, or going to parties. Finding themselves in such a situation, they may experience symptoms of their anxiety, such as sweating or trembling.

> **phobia** an anxiety disorder marked by a persistent, irrational fear and avoidance of a specific object, activity, or situation.
>
> **obsessive-compulsive disorder (OCD)** a disorder characterized by unwanted repetitive thoughts (obsessions), actions (compulsions), or both.

RETRIEVE IT

- Unfocused tension, apprehension, and arousal are symptoms of _____ _____ disorder.

  ANSWER: generalized anxiety

- Those who experience unpredictable periods of terror and intense dread, accompanied by frightening physical sensations, may be diagnosed with a _____ disorder.

  ANSWER: panic

- If a person is focusing anxiety on specific feared objects or situations, that person may have a _____.

  ANSWER: phobia

Obsessive-Compulsive Disorder

41-2 What is *OCD*?

As with the anxiety disorders, we can see aspects of our own behavior in **obsessive-compulsive disorder (OCD)**. *Obsessive thoughts* are unwanted and so repetitive it may seem they will never end. *Compulsive behaviors* are responses to those thoughts.

We all are at times obsessed with thoughts that will not go away, and we all at times behave compulsively. Anxious about how your place will appear to others, you may catch yourself compulsively cleaning before guests arrive. Concerned that you may not make the grade on your final, you may find yourself lining up books and pencils "just so" before studying. On a small scale, obsessive thoughts and compulsive behaviors are a part of everyday life. They cross the fine line between normality and disorder when they *persistently interfere* with everyday life and cause us distress. Checking to see that you locked the door is normal; checking 10 times is not. Washing your hands is normal; washing so often that your skin becomes raw is not. (**TABLE 41.1** offers more examples.) At some time during their lives, often during their late teens or twenties, some 2 percent of people cross that line from normal preoccupations and fussy behaviors to debilitating disorder (Kessler et al., 2012). Twin studies reveal that OCD has a strong genetic basis (Taylor, 2011). Although the person knows the anxiety-fueled obsessive thoughts

Making everything perfect Soccer star David Beckham has openly discussed his obsessive-compulsive tendencies, which have driven him to line up objects in pairs or to spend hours straightening furniture (Adams, 2011).

Stephen Dunn/Getty Images

⌄ TABLE 41.1

Common Obsessions and Compulsions Among Children and Adolescents With Obsessive-Compulsive Disorder

Thought or Behavior	Percentage Reporting Symptom
Obsessions (repetitive *thoughts*)	
Concern with dirt, germs, or toxins	40
Something terrible happening (fire, death, illness)	24
Symmetry, order, or exactness	17
Compulsions (repetitive *behaviors*)	
Excessive hand washing, bathing, toothbrushing, or grooming	85
Repeating rituals (in/out of a door, up/down from a chair)	51
Checking doors, locks, appliances, car brakes, homework	46

Data from: Rapoport, 1989.

LaunchPad For a 7-minute video illustrating struggles associated with compulsive rituals, visit LaunchPad's *Video: Obsessive-Compulsive Disorder: A Young Mother's Struggle.*

are irrational, these thoughts can become so haunting, and the compulsive rituals so senselessly time consuming, that effective functioning becomes impossible.

OCD is more common among teens and young adults than among older people (Nestadt & Samuels, 1997). A 40-year follow-up study of 144 Swedish people diagnosed with the disorder found that, for most, the obsessions and compulsions had gradually lessened, though only 1 in 5 had completely recovered (Skoog & Skoog, 1999).

Posttraumatic Stress Disorder

41-3 What is *PTSD?*

While serving his country in war, one soldier, Jesse, observed the killing "of children and women. It was just horrible for anyone to experience." After calling in a helicopter strike on one house where he had seen ammunition crates carried in, he heard the screams of children from within. "I didn't know there were kids there," he recalled. Back home, he suffered "real bad flashbacks" (Welch, 2005).

Jesse is not alone. In one study of 103,788 veterans returning from Iraq and Afghanistan, 25 percent were diagnosed with a psychological disorder (Seal et al., 2007). Some had *traumatic brain injuries (TBI),* but the most frequent diagnosis was **posttraumatic stress disorder (PTSD).** Typical symptoms include recurring haunting memories and nightmares, a numb feeling of social withdrawal, jumpy anxiety, and trouble sleeping (Germain, 2013; Hoge et al., 2004, 2006, 2007; Kessler, 2000). Survivors of accidents, disasters, and violent and sexual assaults (including an estimated two-thirds of prostitutes) have also experienced PTSD symptoms (Brewin et al., 1999; Farley et al., 1998; Taylor et al., 1998). Reliving traumas such as 9/11 or the Boston Marathon bombing—by being glued to television replays, for example—sustains the stress response (Holman et al., 2014).

The greater one's emotional distress during a trauma, the higher the risk for posttraumatic symptoms (Ozer et al., 2003). Among American military personnel in Afghanistan, 7.6 percent of combatants and 1.4 percent of noncombatants developed PTSD (McNally, 2012). Among New Yorkers who witnessed or responded to the 9/11 terrorist attacks, most did not experience PTSD (Neria et al., 2011). PTSD diagnoses among survivors who had been inside the World Trade Center during the attack were, however, double the rates found among those who were outside (Bonanno et al., 2006).

About half of us will experience at least one traumatic event in our lifetime. Why do some 5 to 10 percent of people develop PTSD after a traumatic event, but others don't (Bonanno et al., 2011)? Some people may have a more sensitive emotion-processing limbic system that floods their bodies with stress hormones (Kosslyn, 2005; Ozer & Weiss, 2004). The odds of getting this disorder after a traumatic event are higher for women (about 1 in 10) than for men (1 in 20) (Olff et al., 2007; Ozer & Weiss, 2004).

Some psychologists believe that PTSD has been overdiagnosed (Dobbs, 2009; McNally, 2003). Too often, say critics, PTSD gets stretched to include normal stress-related bad memories and dreams. And "debriefing" people, by having them relive a trauma soon after, may actually worsen normal stress reactions (Bonanno et al., 2010; Wakefield & Spitzer, 2002).

Most people, male and female, display an impressive *survivor resiliency,* or ability to recover after severe stress (Bonanno et al., 2010). Struggling with crises may also lead to *posttraumatic growth.*

Bringing the war home Nearly a quarter-million Iraq and Afghanistan war veterans have been diagnosed with PTSD or traumatic brain injury (TBI). Many vets participate in an intensive recovery program using deep breathing, massage, and group and individual discussion techniques to treat their PTSD or TBI.

© Lynn Johnson/National Geographic Society/Corbis

RETRIEVE IT [✗]

- Those who express anxiety through unwanted repetitive thoughts or actions may have a(n) _____-_____ disorder.

ANSWER: obsessive-compulsive

- Those with symptoms of recurring memories and nightmares, social withdrawal, jumpy anxiety, numbness of feeling, and/or insomnia for weeks after a traumatic event may be diagnosed with _____ _____ disorder.

ANSWER: posttraumatic stress

Understanding Anxiety Disorders, OCD, and PTSD

41-4 How do conditioning, cognition, and biology contribute to the feelings and thoughts that mark anxiety disorders, OCD, and PTSD?

Anxiety is both a feeling and a cognition—a doubt-laden appraisal of one's safety or social skill. How do these anxious feelings and cognitions arise? Sigmund Freud's psychoanalytic theory proposed that, beginning in childhood, people *repress* intolerable impulses, ideas, and feelings. This submerged mental energy sometimes, he thought, leaks out in odd symptoms, such as anxious hand washing. Few of today's psychologists interpret anxiety this way. Most believe that three modern perspectives—conditioning, cognition, and biology—are more helpful.

Conditioning

Some bad events come with a warning. You're running late and might miss the bus. But when bad events happen unpredictably and uncontrollably, anxiety or other disorders often develop (Field, 2006; Mineka & Oehlberg, 2008). In a classic experiment, infant "Little Albert" learned to fear furry objects that were paired with loud noises. In other experiments, researchers have created anxious animals by giving rats unpredictable electric shocks (Schwartz, 1984). The rats, like assault victims who report feeling anxious when returning to the scene of the crime, learn to become uneasy in their lab environment. The lab had become a cue for fear.

Such research helps explain how panic-prone people learn to associate anxiety with certain cues, and why anxious people are hyperattentive to possible threats (Bar-Haim et al., 2007; Duits et al., 2015). In one survey, 58 percent of those with social anxiety disorder said their disorder began after a traumatic event (Ost & Hugdahl, 1981).

How might learning magnify a single painful and frightening event into a full-blown phobia? The answer lies in part in two conditioning processes: *stimulus generalization* and *reinforcement*.

Stimulus generalization occurs when a person experiences a fearful event and later develops a fear of similar events. My [DM's] car was once struck by another whose driver missed a stop sign. For months afterward, I felt a twinge of unease when any car approached from a side street. Likewise, I [ND] was watching a terrifying movie about spiders, *Arachnophobia*, when a severe thunderstorm struck and the theater lost power. For months, I experienced anxiety at the sight of spiders or cobwebs. Those fears eventually disappeared, but sometimes fears linger and grow. Marilyn's thunderstorm phobia may have similarly generalized after a terrifying or painful experience during a thunderstorm.

Once fears and anxieties are learned, *reinforcement* helps maintain them. Anything that helps us avoid or escape the feared situation reduces anxiety.

posttraumatic stress disorder (PTSD) a disorder characterized by haunting memories, nightmares, social withdrawal, jumpy anxiety, numbness of feeling, and/or insomnia that lingers for four weeks or more after a traumatic experience.

This feeling of relief can reinforce phobic behaviors. Fearing a panic attack, we may decide not to leave the house. Reinforced by feeling calmer, we are likely to repeat that maladaptive behavior in the future (Antony et al., 1992). So, too, with compulsive behaviors. If washing our hands relieves our feelings of anxiety, we may wash our hands again when those feelings return.

Cognition

Conditioning influences our feelings of anxiety, but so does cognition—our thoughts, memories, interpretations, and expectations. We learn some fears by observing others. Nearly all monkeys raised in the wild fear snakes, yet lab-raised monkeys do not. Surely, most wild monkeys do not actually suffer snake bites. Do they learn their fear through observation? To find out, Susan Mineka (1985, 2002) experimented with six monkeys raised in the wild (all strongly fearful of snakes) and their lab-raised offspring (virtually none of which feared snakes). After repeatedly observing their parents or peers refusing to reach for food in the presence of a snake, the younger monkeys developed a similar strong fear of snakes. When the monkeys were retested three months later, their learned fear persisted. We humans learn many of our own fears by observing others (Helsen et al., 2011; Olsson et al., 2007).

Hemera Technologies/PhotoObjects.net/ 360/Getty Images

Our interpretations and expectations also shape our reactions. Whether we interpret the creaky sound in the old house simply as the wind or as a possible knife-wielding intruder determines whether we panic. People with anxiety disorders tend to be *hypervigilant*. They *attend* more to threatening stimuli. They more often *interpret* ambiguous stimuli as threatening: a pounding heart signals a heart attack, a lone spider near the bed indicates an infestation, and an everyday disagreement with a friend or a boss spells doom for the relationship. And they more readily *remember* threatening events (Van Bockstaele et al., 2014). Anxiety is especially common when people cannot switch off such intrusive thoughts and perceive a loss of control and a sense of helplessness (Franklin & Foa, 2011).

Biology

Some aspects of anxiety disorders, OCD, and PTSD are not easily understandable in terms of conditioning and cognitive processes alone. Why do some of us develop lasting phobias after suffering traumas, but others do not? Why do we all learn some fears more readily? Our biology also plays a role.

GENES Among monkeys, fearfulness runs in families. A monkey reacts more strongly to stress if its close biological relatives have sensitive, high-strung temperaments (Suomi, 1986). So, too, with people. Some of us are predisposed to anxiety. If one identical twin has an anxiety disorder, the other is likewise at risk (Hettema et al., 2001; Kendler et al., 2002a,b; Van Houtem et al., 2013). Even when raised separately, identical twins may develop similar phobias (Carey, 1990; Eckert et al., 1981). One pair of separated identical twins independently became so afraid of water that, at age 35, they would wade into the ocean backward and only up to their knees.

Given the genetic contribution to anxiety disorders, researchers are now sleuthing the culprit genes. Among their findings are 17 gene variations associated with typical anxiety disorder symptoms (Hovatta et al., 2005), and others that are associated specifically with OCD (Taylor, 2013).

Some genes influence anxiety disorders by regulating brain levels of neurotransmitters. These include *serotonin*, which influences sleep, mood, and attending to threat (Canli, 2008; Pergamin-Hight et al., 2012), and *glutamate*, which heightens activity in the brain's alarm centers (Lafleur et al., 2006; Welch et al., 2007).

So genes matter. Some of us have genes that make us like orchids—fragile, yet capable of beauty under favorable circumstances. Others of us are like dandelions—hardy, and able to thrive in varied circumstances (Ellis & Boyce, 2008; Pluess & Belsky, 2013).

But experience affects gene expression. Among PTSD patients, a history of child abuse leaves long-term *epigenetic marks*, which are often organic molecules. These molecular tags attach to our chromosomes and turn certain genes on or off. Thus, experiences such as abuse can increase the likelihood that a genetic vulnerability to a disorder will be expressed (Mehta et al., 2013). Suicide victims show a similar epigenetic effect (McGowan et al., 2009).

THE BRAIN Our experiences change our brain, paving new pathways. Traumatic fear-learning experiences can leave tracks in the brain, creating fear circuits within the amygdala (Etkin & Wager, 2007; Herringa et al., 2013; Kolassa & Elbert, 2007). These fear pathways create easy inroads for more fear experiences (Armony et al., 1998). Some antidepressant drugs dampen this fear-circuit activity and associated obsessive-compulsive behaviors.

Anxiety-related disorders all involve biological events. Brain scans of people with PTSD show higher-than-normal activity in the amygdala when they view traumatic images (Nutt & Malizia, 2004). When the disordered brain of an OCD patient detects that something is amiss, it generates a mental hiccup of repeating thoughts (obsessions) or actions (compulsions) (Gehring et al., 2000). Brain scans reveal elevated activity in specific brain areas during behaviors such as compulsive hand washing, checking, ordering, or hoarding (Insel, 2010; Mataix-Cols et al., 2004, 2005). As **FIGURE 41.2** shows, the *anterior cingulate cortex*, a brain region that monitors our actions and checks for errors, seems especially likely to be hyperactive (Maltby et al., 2005).

NATURAL SELECTION We seem biologically prepared to fear the threats our ancestors faced—spiders and snakes, enclosed spaces and heights, storms and darkness. (In the distant past, those who did not fear these threats were less likely to survive and leave descendants.) Thus, in Britain, which has only one poisonous snake species, people often fear snakes. Even 9-month-olds attend less to modern danger sounds than to sounds signaling ancient threats—hisses, thunder, angry voices (Erlich et al., 2013). Our Stone Age fears are easy to condition and hard to extinguish (Coelho & Purkis, 2009; Davey, 1995; Öhman, 2009). Some of our modern fears may also have an evolutionary explanation. A fear of flying may be rooted in our biological predisposition to fear confinement and heights.

Compare our easily conditioned fears to what we *do not* easily learn to fear. World War II air raids, for example, produced remarkably few lasting phobias. As the air strikes continued, the British, Japanese, and German populations did not

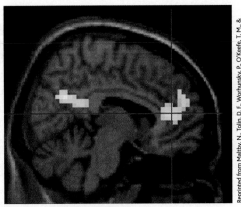

Reprinted from Maltby, N., Tolin, D. F., Worhunsky, P., O'Keefe, T. M., & Kiehl, K. A, Dysfunctional action monitoring hyperactivates frontal-striatal circuits in obsessive-compulsive disorder: An event-related fMRI study, *NeuroImage, 24* (2005): 495–503, with permission from Elsevier.

∧ FIGURE 41.2

An obsessive-compulsive brain Neuroscientists Nicholas Maltby, David Tolin, and their colleagues (2005) used functional MRI scans to compare the brains of those with and without OCD as they engaged in a challenging cognitive task. The scans of those with OCD showed elevated activity in the anterior cingulate cortex in the brain's frontal area (indicated by the yellow area on the far right).

Red Bull Stratos/AP Photo

Fearless The biological perspective helps us understand why most of us have more fear of heights than does Felix Baumgartner, shown here skydiving from 24 miles above the Earth in 2012.

become more and more panicked. Rather, they grew increasingly indifferent to planes outside their immediate neighborhoods (Mineka & Zinbarg, 1996). Evolution has not prepared us to fear bombs dropping from the sky.

Our phobias focus on dangers our ancestors faced. Our compulsive acts typically exaggerate behaviors that helped them survive. Grooming had survival value; it detected insects and infections. Gone wild, it becomes compulsive hair pulling. Washing up helped people stay healthy. Out of control, it becomes ritual hand washing. Checking territorial boundaries helped ward off enemies. In OCD, it becomes checking and rechecking an already locked door (Rapoport, 1989).

RETRIEVE IT [✖]

- Researchers believe that conditioning and cognitive processes contribute to anxiety disorders, OCD, and PTSD. What *biological* factors also contribute to these disorders?

ANSWER: Biological factors include inherited temperament differences and other gene variations; learned fears that have altered brain pathways; and outdated, inherited responses that had survival value for our distant ancestors.

MODULE

41 REVIEW   Anxiety Disorders, OCD, and PTSD

◁▷ Learning Objectives

Test Yourself by taking a moment to answer each of these Learning Objective Questions (repeated here from within the module). Then turn to Appendix D, Complete Module Reviews, to check your answers. Research suggests that trying to answer these questions on your own will improve your long-term memory of the concepts (McDaniel et al., 2009).

41-1 How do generalized anxiety disorder, panic disorder, and phobias differ?

41-2 What is *OCD?*

41-3 What is *PTSD?*

41-4 How do conditioning, cognition, and biology contribute to the feelings and thoughts that mark anxiety disorders, OCD, and PTSD?

■·[·] Terms and Concepts to Remember

Test yourself on these terms by trying to write down the definition in your own words before flipping back to the referenced page to check your answers.

anxiety disorders, p. 537

generalized anxiety disorder, p. 537

panic disorder, p. 537

phobia, p. 538

obsessive-compulsive disorder (OCD), p. 539

posttraumatic stress disorder (PTSD), p. 540

[✖] Experience the Testing Effect

Test yourself repeatedly throughout your studies. This will not only help you figure out what you know and don't know; the testing itself will help you learn and remember the information more effectively thanks to the *testing effect*.

1. Anxiety that takes the form of an irrational and maladaptive fear of a specific object, activity, or situation is called a _____.

2. An episode of intense dread, accompanied by trembling, dizziness, chest pains, or choking sensations and by feelings of terror, is called
   a. a specific phobia.
   b. a compulsion.
   c. a panic attack.
   d. an obsessive fear.

3. Marina became consumed with the need to clean the entire house and refused to participate in any other activities. Her family consulted a therapist, who diagnosed her as having _____-_____ disorder.

4. When a person with an anxiety disorder eases anxiety by avoiding or escaping a situation that inspires fear, this is called
   a. conditioning.
   b. reinforcement.
   c. an epigenetic mark.
   d. hypervigilance.

Find answers to these questions in Appendix E, in the back of the book.

Use 🌐 **LearningCurve** to create your personalized study plan, which will direct you to the resources that will help you most in 🌐 **LaunchPad**.

MODULE 42 Major Depressive Disorder and Bipolar Disorder

Brad Wenner/Moment Select/Getty Images

42-1 How do major depressive disorder and bipolar disorder differ?

Most of us will have some direct or indirect experience with depression. *Major depressive disorder* is a prolonged state of hopeless depression. *Bipolar disorder* (formerly called *manic-depressive disorder*) alternates between depression and overexcited hyperactivity.

Anxiety is a response to the threat of future loss. Depression is often a response to past and current loss. To feel bad in reaction to profoundly sad events (such as the death of a loved one) is to be in touch with reality. In such times, depression is like a car's low-fuel light—a signal that warns us to stop and take appropriate measures.

In the past year, have you, like one in three American collegians, at some time "felt so depressed that it was difficult to function" (ACHA, 2009)? Perhaps you're weary from juggling school, work, and family responsibilities. Perhaps social stresses, such as loneliness, feeling you are the target of prejudice, or experiencing a romantic breakup, have plunged you into despair. And perhaps low self-esteem increases your brooding, worsening your self-torment (Sowislo & Orth, 2012; Steiger et al., 2014). Dwelling on these thoughts may leave you feeling deeply discouraged about your life or your future. You may lack the energy to get things done or even to force yourself out of bed. You may be unable to concentrate, eat, or sleep normally. Occasionally you may even wonder if you would be better off dead.

For some people suffering major depressive disorder or bipolar disorder, symptoms may have a *seasonal pattern*. Depression may regularly return each fall or winter, and a reprieve from depression—or possibly, *mania*—may dependably arrive with spring. For many others, winter darkness simply means more blue moods. When asked "Have you cried today?" Americans answer *Yes* doubly often in the winter (**TABLE 42.1**).

Biologically speaking, life's purpose is survival and reproduction, not happiness. Coughing, vomiting, and various sorts of pain protect our body from dangerous toxins and stimuli. Depression similarly protects us, sending us into a sort of psychic hibernation. It slows us down, defuses aggression, helps us let go of unattainable goals, and restrains risk taking (Andrews & Thomson, 2009a, b; Wrosch & Miller, 2009). When we grind temporarily to a halt and reassess our life, as depressed people do, we can redirect our energy in more promising ways (Watkins, 2008). Even mild sadness can improve people's recall, make them more discerning, and help them make complex decisions (Forgas, 2009, 2013). It can also help them process and recall faces more accurately (Hills et al., 2011). There is sense to suffering. But sometimes depression becomes seriously maladaptive. How do we recognize the fine line between a blue mood and disabling depression?

Major Depressive Disorder

Joy, contentment, sadness, and despair exist at different points on a continuum, points at which any of us may find ourselves at any given moment. The difference between a blue mood after bad news and **major depressive disorder** is like the difference between gasping for breath after a hard run and having chronic asthma. Major depressive disorder occurs when at least five signs of depression

"My life had come to a sudden stop. I was able to breathe, to eat, to drink, to sleep. I could not, indeed, help doing so; but there was no real life in me."

Leo Tolstoy, My Confession, 1887

▼ TABLE 42.1

Percentage Answering *Yes* When Asked "Have You Cried Today?"

	Men	Women
In August	4%	7%
In December	8%	21%

Data from: Time/CNN survey, 1994.

"If someone offered you a pill that would make you permanently happy, you would be well advised to run fast and run far. Emotion is a compass that tells us what to do, and a compass that is perpetually stuck on NORTH is worthless."

Daniel Gilbert, "The Science of Happiness," 2006

major depressive disorder a disorder in which a person experiences, in the absence of drugs or another medical condition, two or more weeks with five or more symptoms, at least one of which must be either (1) depressed mood or (2) loss of interest or pleasure.

▼ TABLE 42.2

Diagnosing Major Depressive Disorder The DSM-5 classifies major depressive disorder as the presence of at least five of the following symptoms over a two-week period of time (minimally including depressed mood or reduced interest) (American Psychiatric Association, 2013).

- Depressed mood most of the time
- Dramatically reduced interest or enjoyment in most activities most of the time
- Significant challenges regulating appetite and weight
- Significant challenges regulating sleep
- Physical agitation or lethargy
- Feeling listless or with much less energy
- Feeling worthless, or feeling unwarranted guilt
- Problems in thinking, concentrating, or making decisions
- Thinking repetitively of death and suicide

last two or more weeks (**TABLE 42.2**). To sense what major depressive disorder feels like, suggest some clinicians, imagine combining the anguish of grief with the exhaustion you feel after pulling an all-nighter.

Although phobias are more common, depression is the number-one reason people seek mental health services. In the United States, 7.6 percent of people interviewed by the Centers for Disease Control and Prevention (2014) reported they were experiencing moderate or severe depression. Worldwide, depression trails only low back pain as the leading cause of disability (Global, 2015). In any given year, 3.9 percent of men and 7.2 percent of women worldwide will have a depressive episode (Ferrari et al., 2013).

Bipolar Disorder

Our genes dispose some of us, more than others, to respond emotionally to good and bad events (Whisman et al., 2014). In **bipolar disorder,** people bounce from one emotional extreme to the other. When a depressive episode ends, a hyperactive, overly talkative, wildly optimistic state called **mania** follows. But before long, the elated mood either returns to normal or plunges again into depression.

If depression is living in slow motion, mania is fast forward. During mania, people typically have little need for sleep. They show fewer sexual inhibitions. Their positive emotions persist abnormally (Gruber, 2011; Gruber et al., 2013). Their speech is loud, flighty, and hard to interrupt. Feeling extreme optimism and self-esteem, they find advice irritating. Yet they need protection from their poor judgment, which may lead to reckless spending or unsafe sex. Thinking fast feels good, but it also increases risk taking (Chandler & Pronin, 2012; Pronin, 2013).

In milder forms, mania's energy and flood of ideas fuel creativity. Clusters of genes that predict creativity also increase the likelihood of having bipolar disorder (Power et al., 2015). George Frideric Handel (1685–1759), who many believe suffered from a mild form of bipolar disorder, composed his nearly four-hour-long *Messiah* during three weeks of intense, creative energy in 1742 (Keynes, 1980). Bipolar disorder strikes more often among those who rely on emotional expression and vivid imagery, such as poets and artists, and less often among those who rely on precision and logic, such

Bipolar disorder Artist Abigail Southworth illustrated her experience of bipolar disorder.

Actor Russell Brand

Writer Virginia Woolf

Humorist Samuel Clemens (Mark Twain)

Creativity and bipolar disorder
There have been many creative artists, composers, writers, and musical performers with bipolar disorder.

as architects, designers, and journalists (Jamison, 1993, 1995; Kaufman & Baer, 2002; Ludwig, 1995). Indeed, one analysis of over a million individuals showed that the only psychiatric condition linked to working in a creative profession was bipolar disorder (Kyaga et al., 2013).

Bipolar disorder is much less common than major depressive disorder, but it is often more dysfunctional. It afflicts as many men as women. The diagnosis has been on the rise among adolescents, whose mood swings, sometimes prolonged, vary from raging to bubbly. The trend was clear in U.S. National Center for Health Statistics annual physician surveys. Between 1994 and 2003, bipolar diagnoses in under-20 people showed an astonishing 40-fold increase—from an estimated 20,000 to 800,000 (Carey, 2007; Flora & Bobby, 2008; Moreno et al., 2007). Americans are twice as likely as people elsewhere to have had a bipolar disorder diagnosis (Merikangas et al., 2011). Under the DSM-5 classifications, the number of child and adolescent bipolar diagnoses (two-thirds boys) will likely decline: Some individuals with emotional volatility will now be diagnosed with *disruptive mood dysregulation disorder*, a new DSM-5 diagnosis for children "who exhibit persistent irritability and frequent episodes of behavior outbursts three or more times a week for more than a year" (Miller, 2010).

Understanding Major Depressive Disorder and Bipolar Disorder

42-2 How can the biological and social-cognitive perspectives help us understand major depressive disorder and bipolar disorder?

From thousands of studies of the causes, treatment, and prevention of major depressive disorder and bipolar disorder, researchers have pulled out some common threads. Here, we focus primarily on major depressive disorder. Any theory of depression must explain at least the following (Lewinsohn et al., 1985, 1998, 2003):

BEHAVIORS AND THOUGHTS CHANGE WITH DEPRESSION. People trapped in a depressed mood become inactive and feel alone, empty, and without a meaningful future (Bullock & Murray, 2014; Smith & Rhodes, 2014). They attend more selectively to negative aspects of their environments and situations (Peckham et al., 2010). They recall negative information. And they expect negative outcomes (my team will lose, my grades will fall, my love will fail). When the depression lifts, these behaviors and thoughts disappear. Nearly half the time, people with depression also have symptoms of another disorder, such as anxiety or substance abuse.

DEPRESSION IS WIDESPREAD. Worldwide, 300 million people suffer major depressive or bipolar disorder (Global, 2015). Depression is found worldwide. This suggests that depression's causes must also be common.

WOMEN'S RISK OF MAJOR DEPRESSIVE DISORDER IS NEARLY DOUBLE MEN'S. In 2009, when Gallup pollsters asked more than a quarter-million Americans if they had ever been diagnosed with depression, 13 percent of men and 22 percent of women said *Yes* (Pelham, 2009). When Gallup asked Americans if they had

Life after depression J. K. Rowling, author of the Harry Potter books, reported suffering acute depression—a "dark time," with suicidal thoughts—between ages 25 and 28. It was a "terrible place," she said, but it formed a foundation that allowed her "to come back stronger" (McLaughlin, 2010).

bipolar disorder a disorder in which a person alternates between the hopelessness and lethargy of depression and the overexcited state of mania. (Formerly called *manic-depressive disorder*.)

mania a hyperactive, wildly optimistic state in which dangerously poor judgment is common.

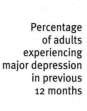

> FIGURE 42.1

Gender and major depressive disorder Interviews with 89,037 adults in 18 countries (10 of which are shown here) confirm what many smaller studies have found: Women's risk of major depression is nearly double that of men's. (Data from Bromet et al., 2011.)

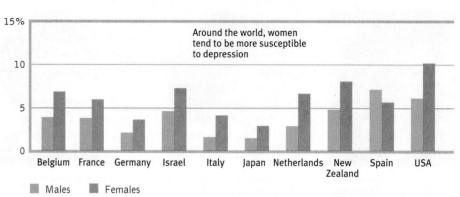

Percentage of adults experiencing major depression in previous 12 months

Around the world, women tend to be more susceptible to depression

Belgium France Germany Israel Italy Japan Netherlands New Zealand Spain USA

▮ Males   ▮ Females

experienced sadness "during a lot of the day yesterday," 17 percent of men and 28 percent of women answered *Yes* (Mendes & McGeeney, 2012). This depression gender gap—with U.S. women experiencing depression 1.7 times more often than men (CDC, 2014)—has been found worldwide (**FIGURE 42.1**). The trend begins in adolescence; preadolescent girls are not more depression-prone than boys are (Hyde et al., 2008).

The depression gender gap fits a bigger pattern: Women are generally more vulnerable to disorders involving internalized states, such as depression, anxiety, and inhibited sexual desire. Women experience more situations that may increase their risk for depression, such as receiving less pay for equal work, juggling multiple roles, and caring for children and elderly family members (Freeman & Freeman, 2013). Men's disorders tend to be more external—alcohol use disorder, antisocial conduct, lack of impulse control. When women get sad, they often get sadder than men do. When men get mad, they often get madder than women do.

MOST MAJOR DEPRESSIVE EPISODES END ON THEIR OWN. Therapy often helps and tends to speed recovery. But even without professional help, most people recover from major depression and return to normal. The black cloud of depression comes and, a few weeks or months later, it often goes. For about half of those people, it eventually returns (Burcusa & Iacono, 2007; Curry et al., 2011; Hardeveld et al., 2010). The condition will be chronic for about 20 percent (Klein, 2010).

On average, a person with major depressive disorder today will spend about three-fourths of the next decade in a normal, nondepressed state (Furukawa et al., 2009). An enduring recovery is more likely if the first episode strikes later in life, there were few previous episodes, the person experiences minimal stress, and there is ample social support (Belsher & Costello, 1988; Fergusson & Woodward, 2002; Kendler et al., 2001).

STRESSFUL EVENTS OFTEN PRECEDE DEPRESSION. About one person in four diagnosed with depression has been brought down by a significant loss or trauma, such as a loved one's death, a ruptured marriage, a physical assault, or a lost job (Kendler et al., 2008; Monroe & Reid, 2009; Orth et al., 2009; Wakefield et al., 2007). Moving to a new culture can also increase depression, especially among younger people who have not yet formed their identities (Zhang et al., 2013). One long-term study tracked rates of depression in 2000 people (Kendler, 1998). Among those who had experienced no stressful life event in the preceding month, the risk of depression was less than 1 percent. Among those who had experienced three such events in that month, the risk was 24 percent. For some, grappling with life's minor daily stressors can also negatively affect mental health. People who overreacted to minor stressors, such as a broken appliance, were more often depressed 10 years later (Charles et al., 2013).

WITH EACH NEW GENERATION, DEPRESSION STRIKES EARLIER (NOW OFTEN IN THE LATE TEENS) AND AFFECTS MORE PEOPLE, WITH THE HIGHEST RATES AMONG YOUNG ADULTS IN DEVELOPED COUNTRIES. This trend has been reported in Canada, England, France, Germany, Italy, Lebanon, New Zealand, Puerto Rico, Taiwan, and the United States (Collishaw et al., 2007; Cross-National Collaborative Group, 1992; Kessler et al., 2010; Twenge et al.,

2008). In one study of Australian adolescents, 12 percent reported symptoms of depression (Sawyer et al., 2000). Most hid it from their parents, almost 90 percent of whom perceived their depressed teen as not suffering depression. In North America, young adults are three times more likely than their grandparents to report having recently—or ever—suffered depression.

The increased risk among young adults appears partly real, but it may also reflect cultural differences between generations. Today's young people are more willing to talk openly about their depression. We also tend to forget many negative experiences over time, so older generations may overlook depressed feelings they had in earlier years.

The Biological Perspective

Depression is a whole-body disorder. It involves genetic predispositions and biochemical imbalances, as well as negative thoughts and a gloomy mood.

GENES AND DEPRESSION Major depressive disorder and bipolar disorder run in families. The risk of major depressive disorder and bipolar disorder increases if you have a parent or sibling with the disorder (Sullivan et al., 2000). If one identical twin is diagnosed with major depressive disorder, the chances are about 1 in 2 that at some time the other twin will be, too. This effect is even stronger for bipolar disorder: If one identical twin has it, the chances are 7 in 10 that the other twin will at some point be diagnosed similarly—even if the twins were raised apart (DiLalla et al., 1996). Among fraternal twins, the corresponding odds are just under 2 in 10 (Tsuang & Faraone, 1990). Summarizing the major twin studies (see **FIGURE 42.2**), one research team estimated the heritability of major depressive disorder (the extent to which individual differences are attributable to genes) at 37 percent (Bienvenu et al., 2011).

Emotions are "postcards from our genes" (Plotkin, 1994). To tease out the genes that put people at risk for depression, researchers may use *linkage analysis*. First, geneticists find families in which the disorder appears across several generations. Next, the researchers look for differences in DNA from affected and unaffected family members. Linkage analysis points them to a chromosome neighborhood; "A house-to-house search is then needed to find the culprit gene" (Plomin & McGuffin, 2003). Such studies reinforce the view that depression is a complex condition. Many genes work together, producing a mosaic of small effects that interact with other factors to put some people at greater risk. If the culprit gene variations can be identified, they may open the door to more effective drug therapy.

THE DEPRESSED BRAIN Scanning devices open a window on the brain's activity during depressed and manic states. During depression, brain activity slows; during mania, it increases (**FIGURE 42.3** on the next page). The left frontal lobe and an adjacent brain reward center become more active during positive emotions (Davidson et al., 2002; Heller et al., 2009; Robinson et al., 2012).

At least two neurotransmitter systems are at work during the periods of brain inactivity and hyperactivity that accompany major depressive disorder and bipolar disorder. *Norepinephrine*, which increases arousal and boosts mood, is scarce during depression. Norepinephrine is overabundant during mania. Drugs that decrease mania reduce norepinephrine.

Serotonin is also scarce or inactive during depression (Carver et al., 2008). Drugs that relieve depression tend to increase serotonin or norepinephrine supplies by blocking either their reuptake (as Prozac, Zoloft, and Paxil do with

> "I see depression as the plague of the modern era."
>
> *Lewis Judd, former chief, National Institute of Mental Health, 2000*

LaunchPad For a 9-minute video demonstrating one young man's struggle with depression, visit LaunchPad's *Video: Depression.*

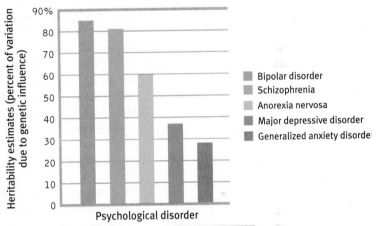

⌃ FIGURE 42.2

The heritability of various psychological disorders Researchers Joseph Bienvenu, Dimitry Davydow, and Kenneth Kendler (2011) aggregated data from studies of identical and fraternal twins to estimate the heritability of bipolar disorder, schizophrenia, anorexia nervosa, major depressive disorder, and generalized anxiety disorder. (Heritability was calculated by a formula that compares the extent of similarity among identical versus fraternal twins.)

Digestive system microbes also produce "neuroactive" chemicals that appear to influence human emotions and social interactions (Dinan et al., 2015).

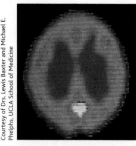
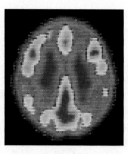
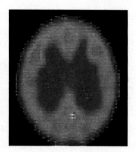

Depressed state
(May 17)

Manic state
(May 18)

Depressed state
(May 27)

The ups and downs of bipolar disorder These top-facing PET scans show that brain energy consumption rises and falls with the patient's emotional switches. Red areas are where the brain rapidly consumes glucose.

serotonin) or their chemical breakdown. Repetitive physical exercise, such as jogging, reduces depression by increasing serotonin (Airan et al., 2007; Ilardi et al., 2009; Jacobs, 1994). In one study, running for two hours increased brain activation in regions associated with euphoria (Boecker et al., 2008). To run away from a bad mood, you can use your own two feet.

NUTRITIONAL EFFECTS What's good for the heart is also good for the brain and mind. People who eat a heart-healthy "Mediterranean diet" (heavy on vegetables, fish, and olive oil) have a comparatively low risk of developing heart disease, stroke, late-life cognitive decline, and depression—all of which are associated with inflammation (Dowlati et al., 2010; Psaltopoulou et al., 2013; Sánchez-Villegas et al., 2009; Tangney et al., 2011). Excessive alcohol use also correlates with depression, partly because depression can increase alcohol use mostly because alcohol misuse *leads to* depression (Fergusson et al., 2009).

The Social-Cognitive Perspective

Biological influences contribute to depression, but in the nature–nurture dance, our actions also play a part. Diet, drugs, stress, and other life experiences lay down *epigenetic marks*, molecular genetic tags that can turn certain genes on or off. Animal studies suggested that epigenetic influences may play a long-lasting role in depression (Nestler, 2011).

Thinking matters, too. The *social-cognitive perspective* explores how people's assumptions and expectations influence what they perceive. Many depressed people see life through the dark glasses of low self-esteem (Kuster et al., 2012; Sowislo & Orth, 2012). They have intensely negative views of themselves, their situation, and their future. Listen to Norman, a Canadian college professor, recalling his depression:

> I [despaired] of ever being human again. I honestly felt subhuman, lower than the lowest vermin. Furthermore, I . . . could not understand why anyone would want to associate with me, let alone love me. . . . I was positive that I was a fraud and a phony and that I didn't deserve my Ph.D. I didn't deserve to have tenure; I didn't deserve to be a Full Professor. . . . I didn't deserve the research grants I had been awarded; I couldn't understand how I had written books and journal articles. . . . I must have conned a lot of people. (Endler, 1982, pp. 45–49)

Expecting the worst, depressed people magnify bad experiences and minimize good ones (Wenze et al., 2012). Their *self-defeating beliefs* and *negative explanatory style* feed depression's vicious cycle.

NEGATIVE THOUGHTS AND NEGATIVE MOODS INTERACT Self-defeating beliefs may arise from *learned helplessness*, the hopelessness and passive resignation animals and humans learn when they experience uncontrollable painful events. Learned helplessness has been found more often in women, who may respond more strongly to stress (Hankin & Abramson, 2001; Mazure et al., 2002; Nolen-Hoeksema, 2001, 2003). Do you agree or disagree that you "at least occasionally feel overwhelmed by all I have to do"? In a survey of women and men, 38 percent of women, but only 17 percent of men, agreed (Pryor et al., 2006).

Why are women nearly twice as vulnerable to depression? Susan Nolen-Hoeksema (2003) related women's higher risk of depression to what she described as their tendency to ruminate or *overthink*. **Rumination** can be adaptive when it helps us focus intently on a problem, thanks to the continuous firing of an attention-sustaining frontal lobe area (Altamirano et al., 2010; Andrews & Thomson, 2009a,b). But relentless, self-focused rumination can divert us from

rumination compulsive fretting; *overthinking* about our problems and their causes.

thinking about other life tasks and can increase negative moods (Kuppens et al., 2010; Kuster et al., 2012).

Even so, why do life's unavoidable failures lead only some people to become depressed? The answer lies partly in their *explanatory style*—who or what they blame for their failures. Think of how you might feel if you failed a test. If you can blame someone else ("What an unfair test!"), you are more likely to feel angry. If you blame yourself, you probably will feel stupid and depressed.

When bad events happen, depression-prone people tend to blame themselves (Mor & Winquist, 2002; Pyszczynski et al., 1991; Wood et al., 1990a,b). As **FIGURE 42.4** illustrates, they explain bad events in terms that are *stable* ("I'll never get over this"), *global* ("I can't do anything right"), and *internal* ("It's all my fault"). Their explanations are pessimistic, overgeneralized, self-focused, and self-blaming. When they describe themselves, their brains show extra activity in a region that processes self-relevant information (Sarsam et al., 2013). The result may be a depressing sense of hopelessness (Abramson et al., 1989; Panzarella et al., 2006). As Martin Seligman has noted, "A recipe for severe depression is preexisting pessimism encountering failure" (1991, p. 78).

What then might we expect of new college students who are not depressed, but do exhibit a pessimistic explanatory style? Lauren Alloy and her colleagues (1999) monitored 349 students every 6 weeks for 2.5 years. Among those identified as having a pessimistic thinking style, 17 percent had a first episode of major depression, as did only 1 percent of those who began college with an optimistic thinking style.

Critics note a chicken-and-egg problem nesting in the social-cognitive explanation of depression. Which comes first? The pessimistic explanatory style, or the depressed mood? The negative explanations *coincide* with a depressed mood, and they are *indicators* of depression. (Before or after being depressed, people's thoughts are less negative.) But do negative thoughts *cause* depression, any more than a speedometer's reading 70 mph *causes* a car's speed? Perhaps a depressed mood triggers negative thoughts. If you temporarily put people in a bad or sad mood, their memories, judgments, and expectations suddenly become more pessimistic—a phenomenon that memory researchers call *state-dependent memory*.

Susan Nolen-Hoeksema (1959–2013) "This epidemic of morbid meditation is a disease that women suffer much more than men. Women can ruminate about anything and everything—our appearance, our families, our career, our health." (*Women Who Think Too Much: How to Break Free of Overthinking and Reclaim Your Life*, 2003)

"You should never engage in unsupervised introspection."

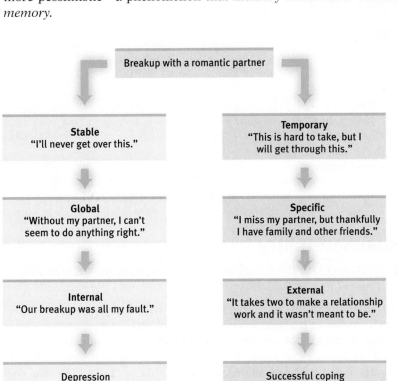

Breakup with a romantic partner

Stable "I'll never get over this."	Temporary "This is hard to take, but I will get through this."
Global "Without my partner, I can't seem to do anything right."	Specific "I miss my partner, but thankfully I have family and other friends."
Internal "Our breakup was all my fault."	External "It takes two to make a relationship work and it wasn't meant to be."
Depression	Successful coping

< FIGURE 42.4

Explanatory style and depression After a negative experience, a depression-prone person may respond with a negative explanatory style.

Cultural forces may also nudge people toward or away from depression. Why is depression so common among young Westerners? Seligman (1991, 1995) has pointed to the rise of individualism and the decline of commitment to religion and family, which forces young people to take responsibility for failure or rejection. In non-Western cultures, where close-knit relationships and cooperation are the norm, major depressive disorder is less common and less tied to self-blame over personal failure (Ferrari et al., 2013; WHO, 2004). In Japan, for example, depressed people instead tend to report feeling shame over letting others down (Draguns, 1990b).

DEPRESSION'S VICIOUS CYCLE No matter which comes first, rejection and depression feed each other. Depression is both a cause and an effect of stressful experiences that disrupt our sense of who we are and why we are worthy. Such disruptions can lead to brooding, which is rich soil for growing negative feelings. And that negativity—being withdrawn, self-focused, and complaining—can by itself cause others to reject us (Furr & Funder, 1998; Gotlib & Hammen, 1992). Indeed, people deep in depression are at high risk for divorce, job loss, and other stressful life events. Weary of the person's fatigue, hopeless attitude, and negativity, a spouse may threaten to leave, or a boss may begin to question the person's competence. New losses and stress then plunge the already-depressed person into even deeper misery. Misery may love another's company, but company does not love another's misery.

We can now assemble pieces of the depression puzzle (**FIGURE 42.5**): (1) Stressful events interpreted through (2) a brooding, negative explanatory style create (3) a hopeless, depressed state that (4) hampers the way the person thinks and acts. These thoughts and actions, in turn, fuel (1) stressful experiences such as rejection. Depression is a snake that bites its own tail.

It is a cycle we can all recognize. When we feel down, we think negatively and remember bad experiences. Britain's Prime Minister Winston Churchill called depression a "black dog" that periodically hounded him. Abraham Lincoln was so withdrawn and brooding as a young man that his friends feared he might take his own life (Kline, 1974). As their lives remind us, people can and do struggle through depression. Most regain their capacity to love, to work, and even to succeed at the highest levels.

> **"Man never reasons so much and becomes so introspective as when he suffers, since he is anxious to get at the cause of his sufferings."**
>
> *Luigi Pirandello,*
> Six Characters in Search of an Author, *1922*

> **"Some cause happiness wherever they go; others, whenever they go."**
>
> *Irish writer Oscar Wilde (1854–1900)*

> **FIGURE 42.5**

The vicious cycle of depressed thinking Therapists recognize this cycle, and they work to help depressed people break out of it, by changing their negative thinking, turning their attention outward, and engaging them in more pleasant and competent behavior.

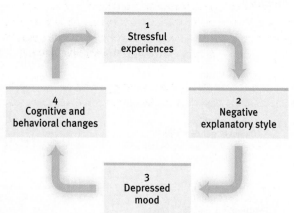

Suicide and Self-Injury

42-3 What factors increase the risk of suicide, and what do we know about nonsuicidal self-injury?

Each year over 800,000 despairing people worldwide will elect a permanent solution to what might have been a temporary problem (WHO, 2014). For those who have been depressed, the risk of suicide is at least five times greater than for the general population (Bostwick & Pankratz, 2000). People seldom commit suicide while in the depths of depression, when energy and initiative are lacking. The risk increases when they begin to rebound and become capable of following through.

> **"But life, being weary of these worldly bars, Never lacks power to dismiss itself."**
>
> *William Shakespeare,*
> Julius Caesar, *1599*

Comparing the suicide rates of different groups, researchers have found

- *national differences:* Britain's, Italy's, and Spain's suicide rates are little more than half those of Canada, Australia, and the United States. Austria's and Finland's are about double (WHO, 2011). Within Europe, people in the most suicide-prone country (Belarus) have been 16 times more likely to kill themselves than those in the least (Georgia).

- *racial differences:* Within the United States, Whites and Native Americans kill themselves twice as often as Blacks, Hispanics, and Asians (CDC, 2012).

- *gender differences:* Women are much more likely than men to attempt suicide (WHO, 2011). But men are two to four times more likely (depending on the country) to actually end their lives. Men use more lethal methods, such as firing a bullet into the head, the method of choice in 6 of 10 U.S. suicides.

- *age differences and trends:* In late adulthood, rates increase, with the highest rate among 45- to 64-year-olds and the second-highest among those 85 and older (AFSP, 2013). In the last half of the twentieth century, the global rate of annual suicide deaths nearly doubled (WHO, 2008a).

- *other group differences:* Suicide rates have been much higher among the rich, the nonreligious, and those who were single, widowed, or divorced (Hoyer & Lund, 1993; Okada & Samreth, 2013; Stack, 1992; Stengel, 1981). Witnessing physical pain and trauma can increase the risk of suicide, which may help explain physicians' elevated suicide rates (Bender et al., 2012; Cornette et al., 2009). Gay and lesbian youth facing an unsupportive environment, including family or peer rejection, are also at increased risk of attempting suicide (Goldfried, 2001; Haas et al., 2011; Hatzenbuehler, 2011). Among people with alcohol use disorder, 3 percent die by suicide. This rate is roughly 100 times greater than the rate for people without alcohol use disorder (Murphy & Wetzel, 1990; Sher, 2006).

- *day of the week differences:* Negative emotion tends to go up midweek, which can have tragic consequences (Watson, 2000). A surprising 25 percent of U.S. suicides occur on Wednesdays (Kposowa & D'Auria, 2009).

Social suggestion may trigger suicide. Following highly publicized suicides and TV programs featuring suicide, known suicides increase. So do fatal auto and private airplane "accidents." One six-year study tracked suicide cases among all 1.2 million people who lived in metropolitan Stockholm at any time during the 1990s (Hedström et al., 2008). Men exposed to a family suicide were 8 times more likely to commit suicide than were nonexposed men. That phenomenon may be partly attributable to family genes. But shared genetic predispositions cannot explain why men exposed to a co-worker's suicide were 3.5 times more likely to commit suicide, compared with nonexposed men.

Because suicide is so often an impulsive act, environmental barriers (such as jump barriers on high bridges and the unavailability of loaded guns) can save lives (Anderson, 2008). Common sense may suggest that a determined person will simply find another way to complete the act, but such restrictions give time for self-destructive impulses to subside.

Suicide is not necessarily an act of hostility or revenge. People—especially older adults—may choose death as an alternative to current or future suffering, a way to switch off unendurable pain and relieve a perceived burden on family members. Suicidal urges typically arise when people feel disconnected from others and a burden to them, or when they feel defeated and trapped by an inescapable situation (Joiner, 2010; Taylor et al., 2011). Thus, suicide rates increase with unemployment during economic recessions (DeFina & Hannon, 2015; Reeves et al., 2014). Suicidal thoughts also may increase when people are driven to reach a goal or standard—to become thin or straight or rich—and find it unattainable (Chatard & Selimbegović, 2011).

In hindsight, families and friends may recall signs they believe should have fore-warned them—verbal hints, giving possessions away, or withdrawal and preoc-cupation with death. To judge from surveys of 84,850 people across 17 nations, about 9 percent of people at some point in their lives have thought seriously of suicide. About 3 in 10 of those who think about it will actually attempt suicide (Nock et al., 2008). Only about 1 in 25 Americans die in that attempt (AAS, 2009). Of those who die, one-third had tried to kill themselves previously. For young adults who have previously attempted suicide, the risk of suicide increases seven-fold, with the greatest risk in the ensuing three years (Al-Sayegh et al., 2015). Most will have discussed it beforehand.

How to be helpful to someone who is talking suicide. How should we respond to someone who says, for example, "I wish I could just end it all" or "I hate my life; I can't go on"?

If people write such things online, you can contact the safety teams at vari-ous social media websites. Facebook, Twitter, Instagram, YouTube, and Tumblr all allow you to anonymously report someone's suicidal expressions. In response, the site's safety team will, if it concurs, send the writer an e-mail with a link to a counselor at the U.S. National Suicide Prevention Lifeline (1-800-273-TALK) or its counterpart in other countries.

If a friend or family member talks suicide, you can:

- *listen.* Better to empathize ("It must be awful to feel that way") than to antag-onize ("But you have so much to live for").

- *connect.* Although you are not a mental health professional, you can attempt to link people with the Lifeline or campus health services.

- *protect.* If someone appears at immediate risk for suicide, the National Institute of Mental Health advises seeking "immediate help from a doctor or the nearest hospital emergency room, or call[ing] 911. Remove access to firearms or other potential tools for suicide, including medications." Better to violate a confidence than to attend a funeral.

NONSUICIDAL SELF-INJURY Suicide is not the only way to send a message or deal with distress. Some people, especially adolescents and young adults, may engage in *nonsuicidal self-injury (NSSI)* (**FIGURE 42.6**). These people hurt themselves in various ways. They may cut or burn their skin, hit themselves, insert objects under their nails or skin, or tattoo themselves (Fikke et al., 2011). Though painful, these self-injuries are not fatal. People who engage in NSSI tend to be less able to tolerate emotional distress. They are extremely self-critical and often have poor communication and problem-solving skills (Nock, 2010).

❯ FIGURE 42.6

Rates of nonfatal self-injury in the U.S. Self-injury rates peak higher for females than for males. (Data from CDC, 2009.)

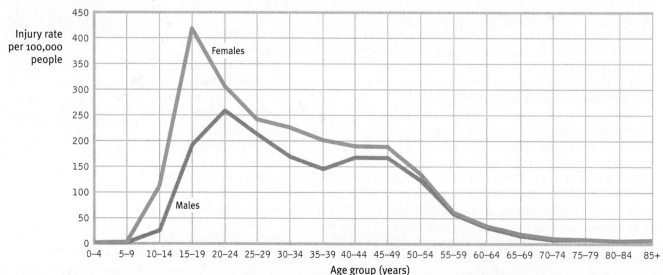

Why do they hurt themselves? Reinforcement processes are at work (Bentley et al., 2014). Through NSSI they may

- find relief from intense negative thoughts through the distraction of pain.
- attract attention and possibly get help.
- relieve guilt by inflicting self-punishment.
- get others to change their negative behavior (bullying, criticism).
- fit in with a peer group.

Does NSSI lead to suicide? Usually not. Those who engage in NSSI are typically suicide gesturers, not suicide attempters (Nock & Kessler, 2006). Suicide gesturers engage in NSSI as a desperate but non-life-threatening form of communication or when they are feeling overwhelmed. Nevertheless, NSSI is considered a risk factor for suicidal thoughts and future suicide attempts (Dickstein et al., 2015; Wilkinson & Goodyer, 2011). If people do not find help, their nonsuicidal behavior may escalate to suicidal thoughts and, finally, to suicide attempts.

"People desire death when two fundamental needs are frustrated to the point of extinction: The need to belong with or connect to others, and the need to feel effective with or to influence others."

Thomas Joiner (2006, p. 47)

RETRIEVE IT   [✕]

- What does it mean to say that "depression is a whole-body disorder"?

ANSWER: Many factors contribute to depression, including the biological influences of genetics and brain function. Social-cognitive factors also matter, including the interaction of explanatory style, mood, our responses to stressful experiences, and changes in our patterns of thinking and behaving. The whole body is involved.

MODULE 42 REVIEW   Major Depressive Disorder and Bipolar Disorder

Learning Objectives

Test Yourself by taking a moment to answer each of these Learning Objective Questions (repeated here from within the module). Then turn to Appendix D, Complete Module Reviews, to check your answers. Research suggests that trying to answer these questions on your own will improve your long-term memory of the concepts (McDaniel et al., 2009).

42-1 How do major depressive disorder and bipolar disorder differ?

42-2 How can the biological and social-cognitive perspectives help us understand major depressive disorder and bipolar disorder?

42-3 What factors increase the risk of suicide, and what do we know about nonsuicidal self-injury?

▪▪▪ Terms and Concepts to Remember

Test yourself on these terms by trying to write down the definition in your own words before flipping back to the referenced page to check your answers.

major depressive disorder, p. 545

bipolar disorder, p. 546

mania, p. 546

rumination, p. 550

[✕] Experience the Testing Effect

Test yourself repeatedly throughout your studies. This will not only help you figure out what you know and don't know; the testing itself will help you learn and remember the information more effectively thanks to the *testing effect*.

1. The "gender gap" in depression refers to the finding that _____ (men's/women's) risk of depression is nearly double that of _____ (men's/women's).

2. Rates of bipolar disorder have risen dramatically in the twenty-first century, especially among
   a. middle-aged women.
   b. middle-aged men.
   c. people 20 and over.
   d. people 19 and under.

3. Treatment for depression often includes drugs that increase supplies of the neurotransmitters _____ and _____.

4. Psychologists who emphasize the importance of negative perceptions, beliefs, and thoughts in depression are working within the _____-_____ perspective.

Find answers to these questions in Appendix E, in the back of the book.

Use 🔵 LearningCurve to create your personalized study plan, which will direct you to the resources that will help you most in 🔵 LaunchPad.

MODULE 43 Schizophrenia and Other Disorders

"When someone asks me to explain schizophrenia I tell them, you know how sometimes in your dreams you are in them yourself and some of them feel like real nightmares? My schizophrenia was like I was walking through a dream. But everything around me was real. At times, today's world seems so boring and I wonder if I would like to step back into the schizophrenic dream, but then I remember all the scary and horrifying experiences."

Stuart Emmons, with Craig Geiser, Kalman J. Kaplan, and Martin Harrow, Living With Schizophrenia, 1997

Schizophrenia

During their most severe periods, people with **schizophrenia** live in a private inner world, preoccupied with the strange ideas and images that haunt them. The word itself means "split" *(schizo)* "mind" *(phrenia)*. It refers *not* to a multiple-personality split but rather to the mind's split from reality, as shown in disturbed perceptions, disorganized thinking and speech, and diminished, inappropriate emotions. Schizophrenia is the chief example of a **psychotic disorder.** This group of disorders is marked by irrationality, distorted perceptions, and lost contact with reality.

As you can imagine, these characteristics profoundly disrupt relationships and work. Given a supportive environment and medication, over 40 percent of people with schizophrenia will have periods of a year or more of normal life experience (Jobe & Harrow, 2010). But only 1 in 7 experience a full and enduring recovery (Jääskeläinen et al., 2013).

Symptoms of Schizophrenia

43-1 What patterns of perceiving, thinking, and feeling characterize schizophrenia?

Schizophrenia comes in varied forms. Schizophrenia patients with *positive symptoms*—the *presence* of *inappropriate* behaviors—may experience hallucinations, talk in disorganized and deluded ways, and exhibit inappropriate laughter, tears, or rage. Those with *negative symptoms*—the *absence* of *appropriate* behaviors—may have toneless voices, expressionless faces, or mute and rigid bodies.

DISTURBED PERCEPTIONS People with schizophrenia sometimes have *hallucinations*—they see, feel, taste, or smell things that exist only in their minds. Usually, the hallucinations are sounds, often voices making insulting remarks or giving orders. The voices may tell the person that she is bad or that she must burn herself with a cigarette lighter. Imagine your own reaction if a dream broke into your waking consciousness, making it hard to separate your experience from your imagination. When the unreal seems real, the resulting perceptions are at best bizarre, at worst terrifying.

Art by someone diagnosed with schizophrenia Commenting on the kind of artwork shown here (from Craig Geiser's 2010 art exhibit in Michigan), poet and art critic John Ashbery wrote: "The lure of the work is strong, but so is the terror of the unanswerable riddles it proposes."

DISORGANIZED THINKING AND SPEECH Hallucinations are false *perceptions*. People with schizophrenia also have disorganized, fragmented thinking, which is often distorted by false *beliefs* called **delusions.** If they have *paranoid* tendencies, they may believe they are being threatened or pursued.

Maxine, a young woman with schizophrenia, believed she was Mary Poppins. Communicating with Maxine was difficult because her thoughts spilled out in no logical order. Her biographer, Susan Sheehan (1982, p. 25), observed her saying aloud to no one in particular, "This morning, when I was at Hillside [Hospital], I was making a movie. I was surrounded by movie stars. . . . I'm Mary Poppins. Is this room painted blue to get me upset? My grandmother died four weeks after my eighteenth birthday."

Jumbled ideas may make no sense even within sentences, forming what is known as *word salad*. One young man begged for "a little more allegro in the treatment," and suggested that "liberationary movement with a view to the widening of the horizon" will "ergo extort some wit in lectures."

One cause of disorganized thinking may be a breakdown in *selective attention*. Normally, we have a remarkable capacity for giving our undivided attention to one set of sensory stimuli while filtering out others. People with schizophrenia

2006

cannot do this. Thus, tiny, irrelevant stimuli, such as the grooves on a brick or the inflections of a voice, may distract their attention from a bigger event or a speaker's meaning. As one former patient recalled, "What had happened to me . . . was a breakdown in the filter, and a hodge-podge of unrelated stimuli were distracting me from things which should have had my undivided attention" (MacDonald, 1960, p. 218). This selective-attention difficulty is but one of dozens of cognitive differences associated with schizophrenia (Reichenberg & Harvey, 2007).

DIMINISHED AND INAPPROPRIATE EMOTIONS The expressed emotions of schizophrenia are often utterly inappropriate, split off from reality (Kring & Caponigro, 2010). Maxine laughed after recalling her grandmother's death. On other occasions, she cried when others laughed, or became angry for no apparent reason. Others with schizophrenia lapse into an emotionless *flat affect* state of no apparent feeling. Most also have an *impaired theory of mind*—they have difficulty reading other people's facial emotions and state of mind (Green & Horan, 2010; Kohler et al., 2010). These emotional deficiencies occur early in the illness and have a genetic basis (Bora & Pantelis, 2013).

Motor behavior may also be inappropriate and disruptive. Those with schizophrenia may experience *catatonia*, characterized by motor behaviors ranging from a physical stupor—motionless for hours—to senseless, compulsive actions, such as continually rocking or rubbing an arm, to severe and dangerous agitation.

Onset and Development of Schizophrenia

43-2 How do *chronic* and *acute schizophrenia* differ?

Nearly 1 in 100 people (about 60 percent of them men) will experience schizophrenia this year, joining an estimated 24 million people worldwide (Global, 2015). It typically strikes as young people are maturing into adulthood. It knows no national boundaries. Men tend to be struck earlier, more severely, and slightly more often (Aleman et al., 2003; Eranti et al., 2013; Picchioni & Murray, 2007).

When schizophrenia is a slow-developing process, called **chronic schizophrenia,** recovery is doubtful (WHO, 1979). This was the case with Maxine's schizophrenia, which took a slow course, emerging from a long history of social inadequacy and poor school performance (MacCabe et al., 2008). Those with chronic schizophrenia often exhibit the persistent and incapacitating negative symptom of social withdrawal (Kirkpatrick et al., 2006). Men, whose schizophrenia develops on average four years earlier than women's, more often exhibit negative symptoms and chronic schizophrenia (Räsänen et al., 2000).

When previously well-adjusted people develop schizophrenia rapidly following particular life stresses, this is called **acute schizophrenia,** and recovery is much more likely. People with acute schizophrenia often have positive symptoms that respond to drug therapy (Fenton & McGlashan, 1991, 1994; Fowles, 1992).

Understanding Schizophrenia

Schizophrenia is a dreaded psychological disorder. It is also one of the most heavily researched. Most studies now link it with abnormal brain tissue and genetic predispositions. Schizophrenia is a disease of the brain manifested in symptoms of the mind.

BRAIN ABNORMALITIES

43-3 What brain abnormalities are associated with schizophrenia?

Might chemical imbalances in the brain explain schizophrenia? Scientists have long known that strange behavior can have strange chemical causes. Have you ever heard the saying "mad as a hatter"? That phrase dates back to the behavior of British hatmakers whose brains were slowly poisoned as they used their tongue and lips to moisten the brims of mercury-laden felt hats (Smith, 1983). Could schizophrenia symptoms have a similar biochemical key? Scientists continue to track the mechanisms by which chemicals produce hallucinations and other symptoms.

schizophrenia a psychological disorder characterized by delusions, hallucinations, disorganized speech, and/or diminished, inappropriate emotional expression.

psychotic disorders a group of psychological disorders marked by irrational ideas, distorted perceptions, and a loss of contact with reality.

delusion a false belief, often of persecution or grandeur, that may accompany psychotic disorders.

chronic schizophrenia (also called *process schizophrenia*) a form of schizophrenia in which symptoms usually appear by late adolescence or early adulthood. As people age, psychotic episodes last longer and recovery periods shorten.

acute schizophrenia (also called *reactive schizophrenia*) a form of schizophrenia that can begin at any age, frequently occurs in response to an emotionally traumatic event, and has extended recovery periods.

DOPAMINE OVERACTIVITY One possible answer emerged when researchers examined schizophrenia patients' brains after death. They found an excess number of *dopamine* receptors, including a sixfold excess for the dopamine receptor D4 (Seeman et al., 1993; Wong et al., 1986). The resulting hyper-responsive dopamine system could intensify brain signals, creating positive symptoms such as hallucinations and paranoia (Grace, 2010). Drugs that block dopamine receptors often lessen these symptoms. Drugs that increase dopamine levels, such as amphetamines and cocaine, sometimes intensify them (Seeman, 2007; Swerdlow & Koob, 1987).

ABNORMAL BRAIN ACTIVITY AND ANATOMY Abnormal brain activity accompanies schizophrenia. Some people diagnosed with schizophrenia have abnormally low brain activity in the brain's frontal lobes, which help us reason, plan, and solve problems (Morey et al., 2005; Pettegrew et al., 1993; Resnick, 1992). The brain waves that reflect synchronized neural firing in the frontal lobes decline noticeably (Spencer et al., 2004; Symond et al., 2005).

One study took PET scans of brain activity while people were hallucinating (Silbersweig et al., 1995). When participants heard a voice or saw something, their brain became vigorously active in several core regions. One was the thalamus, the structure that filters incoming sensory signals and transmits them to the brain's cortex. Another PET scan study of people with paranoia found increased activity in the amygdala, a fear-processing center (Epstein et al., 1998).

Many studies of people with schizophrenia have found enlarged, fluid-filled areas and a corresponding shrinkage and thinning of cerebral tissue (Goldman et al., 2009; Wright et al., 2000). People often inherit these brain differences. If one affected identical twin shows brain abnormalities, the odds are at least 1 in 2 that the other twin will have them (van Haren et al., 2012). Even people who will *later* develop the disorder may show these symptoms (Karlsgodt et al., 2010). The greater the brain shrinkage, the more severe the thought disorder (Collinson et al., 2003; Nelson et al., 1998; Shenton, 1992).

Two smaller-than-normal areas are the cortex, and the corpus callosum that connects the brain's two hemispheres (Arnone et al., 2008). Another is the thalamus, which may explain why filtering sensory input and focusing attention can be difficult for people with schizophrenia (Andreasen et al., 1994; Ellison-Wright et al., 2008). *The bottom line:* Schizophrenia involves not one isolated brain abnormality but problems with several brain regions and their interconnections (Andreasen, 1997, 2001).

PRENATAL ENVIRONMENT AND RISK

43-4 What prenatal events are associated with increased risk of developing schizophrenia?

What causes brain abnormalities in people with schizophrenia? Some scientists point to mishaps during prenatal development or delivery (Fatemi & Folsom, 2009; Walker et al., 2010). Risk factors for schizophrenia include low birth weight, maternal diabetes, older paternal age, and oxygen deprivation during delivery (King et al., 2010). Famine may also increase risks. People conceived during the peak of World War II's Dutch famine later developed schizophrenia at twice the normal rate. Those conceived during the famine of 1959 to 1961 in eastern China also displayed this doubled rate (St. Clair et al., 2005; Susser et al., 1996).

Let's consider another possible culprit. Might a midpregnancy viral infection impair fetal brain development (Brown & Patterson, 2011)? To test this fetal-virus idea, scientists have asked these questions:

- *Are people at increased risk of schizophrenia if, during the middle of their fetal development, their country experienced a flu epidemic?* The repeated answer has been *Yes* (Mednick et al., 1994; Murray et al., 1992; Wright et al., 1995).

- *Are people born in densely populated areas, where viral diseases spread more readily, at greater risk for schizophrenia?* The answer, confirmed in a study of 1.75 million Danes, has again been *Yes* (Jablensky, 1999; Mortensen, 1999).

Most people with schizophrenia smoke, often heavily. Nicotine apparently stimulates certain brain receptors, which helps focus attention (Diaz et al., 2008; Javitt & Coyle, 2004).

- *Are people born during the winter and spring months—those who were in utero during the fall-winter flu season—also at increased risk?* The answer is again *Yes,* and the risk increases from 5 to 8 percent (Fox, 2010; Schwartz, 2011; Torrey et al., 1997, 2002).

- *In the Southern Hemisphere, where the seasons are the reverse of the Northern Hemisphere, are the months of above-average pre-schizophrenia births similarly reversed?* Again, the answer has been *Yes.* In Australia, people born between August and October are at greater risk. But there is an exception: For people born in the Northern Hemisphere who later moved to Australia, the risk is greater if they were born between January and March (McGrath et al., 1995, 1999).

- *Are mothers who report being sick with influenza during pregnancy more likely to bear children who develop schizophrenia?* In one study of nearly 8000 women, the answer was *Yes.* The schizophrenia risk increased from the customary 1 percent to about 2 percent—but only when infections occurred during the second trimester (Brown et al., 2000). Maternal influenza infection during pregnancy affects brain development in monkeys as well (Short et al., 2010).

- *Does blood drawn from pregnant women whose offspring develop schizophrenia show higher-than-normal levels of antibodies that suggest a viral infection?* In several studies, the answer has been *Yes* (Brown et al., 2004; Buka et al., 2001; Canetta et al., 2014).

These converging lines of evidence suggest that fetal-virus infections contribute to the development of schizophrenia. This finding strengthens the U.S. government recommendation that "pregnant women need a flu shot" (CDC, 2014).

Why might a second-trimester maternal flu bout put fetuses at risk? Is the virus itself the culprit? The mother's immune response to it? Medications taken (Wyatt et al., 2001)? Does the infection weaken the fetal brain's supportive glial cells, leading to reduced synaptic connections (Moises et al., 2002)? In time, answers may become available.

GENETIC INFLUENCES

43-5 How do genes influence schizophrenia?

Fetal-virus infections may increase the odds that a child will develop schizophrenia. But many women get the flu during their second trimester of pregnancy, and only 2 percent of them bear children who develop schizophrenia. Why does prenatal exposure to the flu virus put some children at risk but not others? Might some people be more vulnerable because of an inherited predisposition? The evidence indicates that, *Yes,* some may inherit a predisposition to schizophrenia. For most people, the odds of being diagnosed with schizophrenia are only 1 in 100. For those who have a sibling or parent with the disorder, the odds increase to about 1 in 10. And if the affected sibling is an identical twin, the odds increase to nearly 1 in 2 (**FIGURE 43.1**). Those odds are unchanged even when the twins are reared apart (Plomin et al., 1997). (Only about a dozen such cases are on record.)

 LaunchPad See LaunchPad's *Video: Twin Studies* for a helpful tutorial animation about this type of research design.

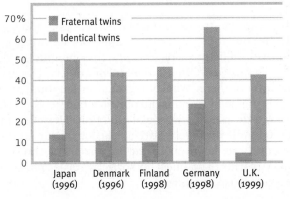

< FIGURE 43.1

Risk of developing schizophrenia The lifetime risk of developing schizophrenia varies with one's genetic relatedness to someone having this disorder. Across countries, barely more than 1 in 10 fraternal twins, but some 5 in 10 identical twins, share a schizophrenia diagnosis. (Data from Gottesman, 2001.)

Remember, though, that identical twins share more than their genes. They also share a prenatal environment. About two-thirds also share a placenta and the blood it supplies; the other one-third have separate placentas. Shared placentas matter. If the co-twin of an identical twin with schizophrenia shared the placenta, the chances of developing the disorder are 6 in 10. If the identical twins had separate placentas, the co-twin's chances of developing schizophrenia drop to 1 in 10 (Davis & Phelps, 1995; Davis et al., 1995; Phelps et al., 1997). Twins who share a placenta are more likely to share the same prenatal viruses. So perhaps shared germs as well as shared genes produce identical twin similarities.

Adoption studies help untangle genetic and environmental influences. Children adopted by someone who develops schizophrenia do not "catch" the disorder. Rather, adopted children have a higher risk if a *biological* parent has schizophrenia (Gottesman, 1991). Genes matter.

The search is on for specific genes that, in some combination, predispose schizophrenia-inducing brain abnormalities (**FIGURE 43.2**). (It is not our genes but our brains that directly control our behavior.) In the biggest-ever study of the genetics of psychiatric disorder, scientists from 35 countries pooled data from the genomes of 37,000 people with schizophrenia and 113,000 people without (Schizophrenia Working Group, 2014). They found 103 genome locations linked with the disorder. Some of these genes influence the activity of dopamine and other brain neurotransmitters. Others affect the production of *myelin*, a fatty substance that coats the axons of nerve cells and lets impulses travel at high speed through neural networks.

> **FIGURE 43.2**

Schizophrenia in identical twins When twins differ, only the one afflicted with schizophrenia typically has enlarged, fluid-filled cranial cavities (right) (Suddath et al., 1990). The difference between the twins implies some nongenetic factor, such as a virus, is also at work.

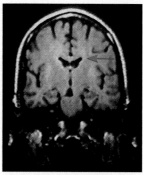
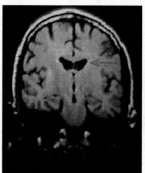

No schizophrenia   **Schizophrenia**

From Daniel Weinberger, M.D., CBDB, NIMH

Although genes matter, the genetic formula is not as straightforward as the inheritance of eye color. The new result confirms other genome studies which show that schizophrenia is a group of disorders that are influenced by many genes, each with very small effects (Arnedo et al., 2015; International Schizophrenia Consortium, 2009).

As we have seen in so many different contexts, nature and nurture interact. Recall that *epigenetic* (literally "in addition to genetic") factors influence whether or not genes will be expressed. Like hot water activating a tea bag, environmental factors such as viral infections, nutritional deprivation, and maternal stress can "turn on" the genes that put some of us at higher risk for this disorder. Identical twins' differing histories in the womb and beyond explain why they may show differing gene expressions (Dempster et al., 2013; Walker et al., 2010). Our heredity and our life experiences work together. Neither hand claps alone.

Thanks to our expanding understanding of genetic and brain influences on maladies such as schizophrenia, the general public increasingly attributes psychiatric disorders to biological factors (Pescosolido et al., 2010).

LaunchPad

IMMERSIVE LEARNING Consider how researchers have studied these issues with LaunchPad's *How Would You Know If Schizophrenia Is Inherited?*

* * *

Few of us can relate to the strange thoughts, perceptions, and behaviors of schizophrenia. Sometimes our thoughts jump around, but we rarely talk nonsensically. Occasionally we feel unjustly suspicious of someone, but we do not believe the world is plotting against us. Often our perceptions err, but rarely do we see or hear things that are not there. We feel regret after laughing at someone's misfortune, but we rarely giggle in response to our own bad news. At times we just want to be alone, but we do not live in social isolation. However, millions of people around the world do talk strangely, suffer delusions, hear nonexistent voices, see things that are not there, laugh or cry at inappropriate times, or withdraw into private imaginary worlds. The quest to solve the cruel puzzle of schizophrenia continues, more vigorously than ever.

RETRIEVE IT [✖]

- A person with schizophrenia who has _____ (positive/negative) symptoms may have an expressionless face and toneless voice. These symptoms are most common with _____ (chronic/acute) schizophrenia and are not likely to respond to drug therapy. Those with _____ (positive/negative) symptoms are likely to experience delusions and to be diagnosed with _____ (chronic/acute) schizophrenia, which is much more likely to respond to drug therapy.

ANSWERS: negative; chronic; positive; acute

- What factors contribute to the onset and development of schizophrenia?

ANSWER: Biological factors include abnormalities in brain structure and function, prenatal exposure to a maternal virus, and a genetic predisposition to the disorder. However, a high-risk environment, with many environmental triggers, can increase the odds of developing schizophrenia.

LaunchPad For an 8-minute description of how clinicians define and treat schizophrenia, visit LaunchPad's *Video— Schizophrenia: New Definitions, New Therapies*.

Other Disorders
Dissociative Disorders

◆❯ **43-6** What are dissociative disorders, and why are they controversial?

Among the most bewildering disorders are the rare **dissociative disorders,** in which a person's conscious awareness *dissociates* (separates) from painful memories, thoughts, and feelings. The result may be a *fugue state,* a sudden loss of memory or change in identity, often in response to an overwhelmingly stressful situation. Such was the case for one Vietnam veteran who was haunted by his comrades' deaths, and who had left his World Trade Center office shortly before the 9/11 attack. Later, he disappeared. Six months later, when he was discovered in a Chicago homeless shelter, he reported no memory of his identity or family (Stone, 2006).

Dissociation itself is not so rare. Any one of us may have a fleeting sense of being unreal, of being separated from our body, of watching ourselves as if in a movie. A massive dissociation of self from ordinary consciousness occurs in **dissociative identity disorder (DID),** in which two or more distinct identities— each with its own voice and mannerisms—seem to control the person's behavior. Thus, the person may be prim and proper one moment, loud and flirtatious the next. Typically, the original personality denies any awareness of the other(s).

People diagnosed with DID (formerly called *multiple personality disorder*) are rarely violent. But cases have been reported of dissociations into a "good" and a "bad" (or aggressive) personality—a modest version of the Dr. Jekyll-Mr. Hyde split immortalized in Robert Louis Stevenson's story. One unusual case involved Kenneth Bianchi, accused in the "Hillside Strangler" rapes and murders of 10 California women. During a hypnosis session, Bianchi's psychologist "called forth" a hidden personality: "I've talked a bit to Ken, but I think that perhaps there might be another part of Ken that . . . maybe feels somewhat differently from the part that I've talked to. . . . Would you talk with me, Part, by saying, 'I'm here'?" Bianchi answered "Yes" and then claimed to be "Steve" (Watkins, 1984).

Speaking as Steve, Bianchi stated that he hated Ken because Ken was nice and that he (Steve), aided by a cousin, had murdered women. He also claimed Ken knew nothing about Steve's existence and was innocent of the murders. Was Bianchi's second personality a trick, simply a way of disavowing responsibility for his actions? Indeed, Bianchi—a practiced liar who had read about multiple personality in psychology books—was later convicted.

UNDERSTANDING DISSOCIATIVE IDENTITY DISORDER Skeptics have raised serious concerns about DID. First, they find it *suspicious that the disorder has such a short and localized history.* Between 1930 and 1960, the number of North American DID diagnoses averaged 2 per decade. By the 1980s, when the

dissociative disorders controversial, rare disorders in which conscious awareness becomes separated (dissociated) from previous memories, thoughts, and feelings.

dissociative identity disorder (DID) a rare dissociative disorder in which a person exhibits two or more distinct and alternating personalities. Formerly called *multiple personality disorder.*

Multiple personalities Chris Sizemore's story, told in the book and movie, *The Three Faces of Eve,* gave early visibility to what is now called *dissociative identity disorder.*

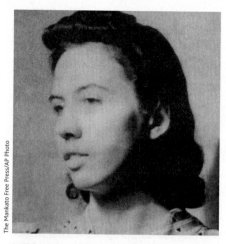

Widespread dissociation Shirley Mason was a psychiatric patient diagnosed with dissociative identity disorder. Her life formed the basis of the bestselling book, *Sybil* (Schreiber, 1973), and of two movies. Some argue that the book and movies' popularity fueled the dramatic rise in diagnoses of DID. Skeptics wonder whether she actually had DID (Nathan, 2011).

"Pretense may become reality."

Chinese proverb

"Though this be madness, yet there is method in 't."

William Shakespeare, Hamlet, *1600*

"Would it be possible to speak with the personality that pays the bills?"

American Psychiatric Association's *Diagnostic and Statistical Manual of Mental Disorders* (DSM) contained the first formal code for this disorder, the number exploded to more than 20,000 (McHugh, 1995b). The average number of displayed personalities also mushroomed—from 3 to 12 per patient (Goff & Simms, 1993).

Second, note the skeptics, DID *varies by culture.* It is much less prevalent outside North America. In Britain, DID—which some have considered "a wacky American fad" (Cohen, 1995)—is rare. In India and Japan, it is essentially nonexistent (or at least unreported). Such findings, skeptics have noted, point to a disorder of suggestible, fantasy-prone people created by therapists in a particular social context (Giesbrecht et al., 2008, 2010; Lynn et al., 2014; Merskey, 1992).

Third, skeptics have asked, could DID be *an extension of our normal capacity for personality shifts?* Nicholas Spanos (1986, 1994, 1996) asked college students to pretend they were accused murderers being examined by a psychiatrist. Given the same hypnotic treatment Bianchi received, most spontaneously expressed a second personality. This discovery made Spanos wonder: Are dissociative identities simply a more extreme version of the varied "selves" we normally present—as when we display a goofy, loud self while hanging out with friends, and a subdued, respectful self around grandparents? If so, say the critics, clinicians who discover multiple personalities may merely have triggered role playing by fantasy-prone people. After all, clients do not enter therapy saying "Allow me to introduce myselves." Rather, charge the critics, some therapists go fishing for multiple personalities: *"Have you ever felt like another part of you does things you can't control? Does this part of you have a name? Can I talk to the angry part of you?"* Once patients permit a therapist to talk, by name, "to the part of you that says those angry things," they begin acting out the fantasy. Like actors who lose themselves in their roles, vulnerable patients may "become" the parts they are acting out. The result may be the experience of another self.

Other researchers and clinicians believe DID is a real disorder. They find support for this view in the distinct body and brain states associated with differing personalities (Putnam, 1991). People with DID exhibit heightened activity in brain areas linked with the control and inhibition of traumatic memories (Elzinga et al., 2007). Abnormal brain anatomy can also accompany DID. Brain scans show shrinkage in areas that aid memory and detection of threat (Vermetten et al., 2006).

Both the psychodynamic and learning perspectives have interpreted DID symptoms as ways of coping with anxiety. Some psychodynamic theorists see them as defenses against the anxiety caused by unacceptable impulses. In this view, a second personality could allow the discharge of forbidden impulses. Learning theorists see dissociative disorders as behaviors reinforced by anxiety reduction.

Some clinicians include dissociative disorders under the umbrella of post-traumatic stress disorder. In this view, DID is a natural, protective response to traumatic experiences during childhood (Putnam, 1995; Spiegel, 2008). Many DID patients recall being physically, sexually, or emotionally abused as children (Gleaves, 1996; Lilienfeld et al., 1999). In one study of 12 murderers diagnosed with DID, 11 had suffered severe abuse, even torture, in childhood (Lewis et al., 1997). One had been set afire by his parents. Another had been used in child pornography and was scarred from being made to sit on a stove burner. Some critics wonder, however, whether vivid imagination or therapist suggestion contributed to such recollections (Kihlstrom, 2005).

So the debate continues. On one side are those who believe multiple personalities are the desperate efforts of people trying to detach from a horrific existence. On the other are skeptics who think DID is constructed out of the therapist-patient interaction and acted out by fantasy-prone, emotionally vulnerable people. If the skeptics' view wins, predicted psychiatrist Paul McHugh (1995a), "this epidemic will end in the way that the witch craze ended in Salem. The [multiple personality phenomenon] will be seen as manufactured."

Personality Disorders

 43-7 What are the three clusters of personality disorders? What behaviors and brain activity characterize the antisocial personality?

The disruptive, inflexible, and enduring behavior patterns of **personality disorders** interfere with social functioning. These disorders tend to form three clusters, characterized by

- anxiety, such as a fearful sensitivity to rejection that predisposes the withdrawn *avoidant personality disorder*.
- eccentric or odd behaviors, such as the emotionless disengagement of *schizotypal personality disorder*.
- dramatic or impulsive behaviors, such as the attention-getting *borderline personality disorder*, the self-focused and self-inflating *narcissistic personality disorder*, and—what we next discuss as an in-depth example—the callous, and sometimes dangerous, *antisocial personality disorder*.

ANTISOCIAL PERSONALITY DISORDER
A person with **antisocial personality disorder** is typically a male whose lack of conscience becomes plain before age 15, as he begins to lie, steal, fight, or display unrestrained sexual behavior (Cale & Lilienfeld, 2002). About half of such children become antisocial adults—unable to keep a job, irresponsible as a spouse and parent, and violent or otherwise criminal (Farrington, 1991). (These people are sometimes called *sociopaths* or *psychopaths*.) They may show lower *emotional intelligence*—the ability to understand, manage, and perceive emotions (Ermer et al., 2012). Despite their remorseless and sometimes criminal behavior, criminality is not an essential component of antisocial behavior (Skeem & Cooke, 2010). Moreover, many criminals do not fit the description of antisocial personality disorder. Why? Because they show responsible concern for their friends and family members.

Antisocial personalities behave impulsively, and then feel and fear little (Fowles & Dindo, 2009). Their impulsivity can have violent, horrifying consequences (Camp et al., 2013). Consider the case of Henry Lee Lucas. He killed his first victim when he was 13. He felt little regret then or later. He confessed that, during his 32 years of crime, he had brutally beaten, suffocated, stabbed, shot, or mutilated some 360 women, men, and children. For the last six years of his reign of terror, Lucas teamed with Ottis Elwood Toole, who reportedly slaughtered about 50 people he "didn't think was worth living anyhow" (Darrach & Norris, 1984).

UNDERSTANDING ANTISOCIAL PERSONALITY DISORDER
Antisocial personality disorder is woven of both biological and psychological strands. Twin and adoption studies reveal that biological relatives of people with antisocial and unemotional tendencies are at increased risk for antisocial behavior (Frisell et al., 2012; Tuvblad et al., 2011). No single gene codes for a complex behavior such as crime. Molecular geneticists have, however, identified some specific genes that are more common in those with antisocial personality disorder (Gunter et al., 2010). There may be a genetic predisposition toward a fearless and uninhibited life. The genes that put people at risk for antisocial behavior also increase the risk for substance use disorder, which helps explain why these disorders often appear in combination (Dick, 2007).

No remorse Dennis Rader, known as the "BTK killer" in Kansas, was convicted in 2005 of killing 10 people over a 30-year span. Rader exhibited the extreme lack of conscience that marks antisocial personality disorder.

"Thursday is out. I have jury duty."

Many criminals, like this one, exhibit a sense of conscience and responsibility in other areas of their life, and thus do not exhibit antisocial personality disorder.

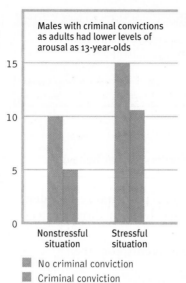

Adrenaline
excretion (ng/min.)

Males with criminal convictions
as adults had lower levels of
arousal as 13-year-olds

> FIGURE 43.3

Cold-blooded arousability and risk
of crime Levels of the stress hormone
adrenaline were measured in two groups
of 13-year-old Swedish boys. In both
stressful and nonstressful situations,
those who would later be convicted of
a crime as 18- to 26-year-olds showed
relatively low arousal. (Data from
Magnusson, 1990.)

Does a full Moon trigger "madness" in some
people? James Rotton and I. W. Kelly (1985)
examined data from 37 studies that related
lunar phase to crime, homicides, crisis
calls, and mental hospital admissions. Their
conclusion: There is virtually no evidence
of "Moon madness." Nor does lunar phase
correlate with suicides, assaults, emergency
room visits, or traffic disasters (Martin et
al., 1992; Raison et al., 1999).

✓ FIGURE 43.4

Murderous minds Researchers have
found reduced activation in a murderer's
frontal lobes. This brain area (shown in a
left-facing brain) helps brake impulsive,
aggressive behavior (Raine, 1999).

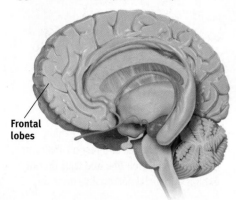

Frontal
lobes

Genetic influences, often in combination with
negative environmental factors such as childhood
abuse, family instability, or poverty, help wire
the brain (Dodge, 2009). In people with antisocial criminal tendencies, the emotion-controlling
amygdala is smaller (Pardini et al., 2014). The
genetic vulnerability of people with antisocial and
unemotional tendencies appears as low arousal.
Awaiting events that most people would find
unnerving, such as electric shocks or loud noises,
they show little autonomic nervous system arousal
(Hare, 1975; van Goozen et al., 2007). Long-term
studies show that their stress hormone levels are
lower than average in their early teens, before
they have committed any crime (**FIGURE 43.3**).
And children who are slow to develop conditioned
fears at age 3 are in later years more likely to
commit a crime (Gao et al., 2010). Other studies
have found that preschool boys who later became aggressive or antisocial adolescents tended to be impulsive, uninhibited, unconcerned with social rewards, and
low in anxiety (Caspi et al., 1996; Tremblay et al., 1994).

Traits such as fearlessness and dominance can be adaptive. If channeled in
more productive directions, fearlessness may lead to athletic stardom, adventur-
ism, or courageous heroism (Poulton & Milne, 2002; Smith et al., 2013). One analysis of 42 American presidents showed that they scored higher than the general
population on such traits as fearlessness and dominance (Lilienfeld et al., 2012).
Lacking a sense of social responsibility, the same disposition may produce a cool
con artist or killer (Lykken, 1995).

With antisocial behavior, as with so much else, nature and nurture interact
and the biopsychosocial perspective helps us understand the whole story. To
explore the neural basis of antisocial personality disorder, scientists are trying
to identify brain activity differences in antisocial criminals. Shown emotionally
evocative photographs, such as a man holding a knife to a woman's throat, criminals with antisocial personality disorder display blunted heart rate and perspiration responses, and less activity in brain areas that typically respond to emotional
stimuli (Harenski et al., 2010; Kiehl & Buckholtz, 2010). They also have a larger
and hyper-reactive dopamine reward system, which predisposes their impulsive drive to do something rewarding despite the consequences (Buckholtz et al.,
2010; Glenn et al., 2010). One study compared PET scans of 41 murderers' brains
with those from people of similar age and sex. The murderers' frontal lobes, an
area that helps control impulses, displayed reduced activity (Raine, 1999, 2005;
FIGURE 43.4). The reduced activation was especially apparent in those who
murdered impulsively. In a follow-up study, researchers found that violent repeat
offenders had 11 percent less frontal lobe tissue than normal (Raine et al., 2000).
This helps explain another finding: People with antisocial personality disorder
fall far below normal in aspects of thinking such as planning, organization, and
inhibition, which are all frontal lobe functions (Morgan & Lilienfeld, 2000). Such
data remind us: Everything psychological is also biological.

RETRIEVE IT   [✱]

• How do biological and psychological factors contribute to antisocial personality disorder?

Eating Disorders

43-8 What are the three main eating disorders, and how do biological, psychological, and social-cultural influences make people more vulnerable to them?

Our bodies are naturally disposed to maintain a steady weight, including stored energy reserves for times when food becomes unavailable. But sometimes psychological influences overwhelm biological wisdom. This becomes painfully clear in three eating disorders:

- **Anorexia nervosa** typically begins as a weight-loss diet. People with anorexia—usually adolescents and 9 out of 10 times females—drop significantly below normal weight. Yet they feel fat, fear being fat, diet obsessively, and sometimes exercise excessively. About half of those with anorexia display a binge-purge-depression cycle.

- **Bulimia nervosa,** unlike anorexia, is marked by weight fluctuations within or above normal ranges. This makes the condition easy to hide. Bulimia may also be triggered by a weight-loss diet, broken by gorging on forbidden foods. In a cycle of repeating episodes, people with this disorder—mostly women in their late teens or early twenties—alternate binge eating and purging (through vomiting or laxative use) (Wonderlich et al., 2007). Fasting or excessive exercise may follow. Preoccupied with food (craving sweets and high-fat foods), and fearful of becoming overweight, binge-purge eaters experience bouts of depression, guilt, and anxiety during and following binges (Hinz & Williamson, 1987; Johnson et al., 2002).

© Nick Holt Photography

anorexia nervosa an eating disorder in which a person (usually an adolescent female) maintains a starvation diet despite being significantly underweight; sometimes accompanied by excessive exercise.

bulimia nervosa an eating disorder in which a person alternates binge eating (usually of high-calorie foods) with purging (by vomiting or laxative use) or fasting.

binge-eating disorder significant binge-eating episodes, followed by distress, disgust, or guilt, but without the compensatory purging or fasting that marks bulimia nervosa.

Sibling rivalry gone awry Twins Maria and Katy Campbell have anorexia nervosa. As children they competed to see who could be thinner. Now, says Maria, her anorexia nervosa is "like a ball and chain around my ankle that I can't throw off" (Foster, 2011).

- Those with **binge-eating disorder** engage in significant bouts of overeating, followed by remorse. But they do not purge, fast, or exercise excessively, and thus may be overweight.

A U.S. National Institute of Mental Health-funded study reported that, at some point during their lifetime, 0.6 percent of Americans met the criteria for anorexia, 1 percent for bulimia, and 2.8 percent for binge-eating disorder (Hudson et al., 2007). So, how can we explain these disorders?

UNDERSTANDING EATING DISORDERS Eating disorders are *not* (as some have speculated) a telltale sign of childhood sexual abuse (Smolak & Murnen, 2002; Stice, 2002). The family environment may influence eating disorders in other ways, however. For example, anorexia patients' families tend to be competitive, high achieving, and protective (Berg et al., 2014; Pate et al., 1992; Yates, 1989, 1990). Those with eating disorders often have low self-evaluations, set perfectionist standards, fret about falling short of expectations, and are intensely concerned with how others perceive them (Brauhardt et al., 2014; Pieters et al., 2007; Yiend et al., 2014). Some of these factors also predict teen boys' pursuit of unrealistic muscularity (Ricciardelli & McCabe, 2004).

Heredity also matters. Identical twins share these disorders more often than fraternal twins do (Culbert et al., 2009; Klump et al., 2009; Root et al., 2010). Scientists are now searching for culprit genes, which may influence the body's available serotonin and estrogen (Klump & Culbert, 2007). Data from 15 studies

A distorted body image underlies anorexia.

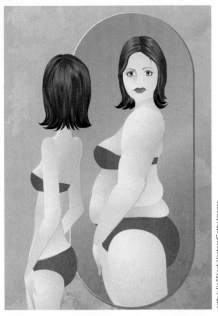

artbyjulie/iStock Vectors/Getty Images

"Thanks, but we don't eat."

"Why do women have such low self-esteem? There are many complex psychological and societal reasons, by which I mean Barbie."

Dave Barry, 1999

Too thin? Many worry that such superthin models make self-starvation seem fashionable.

indicate that having a gene that reduces available serotonin adds 30 percent to a person's risk of anorexia or bulimia (Calati et al., 2011).

But eating disorders also have cultural and gender components. Ideal shapes vary across culture and time. In impoverished countries—where plumpness means prosperity and thinness can signal poverty or illness—bigger often seems better (Knickmeyer, 2001; Swami et al., 2010). Bigger does not seem better in Western cultures, where, according to 222 studies of 141,000 people, the rise in eating disorders in the last half of the twentieth century coincided with a dramatic increase in women having a poor body image (Feingold & Mazzella, 1998).

Those most vulnerable to eating disorders are also those (usually women or gay men) who most idealize thinness and have the greatest body dissatisfaction (Feldman & Meyer, 2010; Kane, 2010; Stice et al., 2010). Should it surprise us, then, that when women view real and doctored images of unnaturally thin models and celebrities, they often feel ashamed, depressed, and dissatisfied with their own bodies—the very attitudes that predispose eating disorders (Grabe et al., 2008; Myers & Crowther, 2009; Tiggeman & Miller, 2010)? Eric Stice and his colleagues (2001) tested this modeling idea by giving some adolescent girls (but not others) a 15-month subscription to an American teen-fashion magazine. Compared with those who had not received the magazine, vulnerable girls—defined as those who were already dissatisfied, idealizing thinness, and lacking social support—exhibited increased body dissatisfaction and eating disorder tendencies. Even ultra-thin models do not reflect the impossible standard of the classic Barbie doll, who had, when adjusted to a height of 5 feet 7 inches, a 32–16–29 figure (in centimeters, 82–41–73) (Norton et al., 1996).

There is, however, more to body dissatisfaction and anorexia than media effects (Ferguson et al., 2011). Peer influences, such as teasing, also matter. Nevertheless, the sickness of today's eating disorders stems in part from today's weight-obsessed culture—a culture that says "Fat is bad" in countless ways, that motivates millions of women to diet constantly, and that invites eating binges by pressuring women to live in a constant state of semistarvation. One former model recalled walking into a meeting with her agent, starving and with her organs failing as a result of anorexia (Caroll, 2013). Her agent's greeting: "Whatever you are doing, keep doing it."

If cultural learning contributes to eating behavior, then might prevention programs increase acceptance of one's body? Reviews of prevention studies answer *Yes*. They seem especially effective if the programs are interactive and focused on girls over age 15 (Beintner et al., 2012; Stice et al., 2007; Vocks et al., 2010).

* * *

The bewilderment, fear, and sorrow caused by psychological disorders are real. But as this text's discussion of therapy shows, hope, too, is real.

RETRIEVE IT   [✷]

• People with _____ (anorexia nervosa/bulimia nervosa) continue to want to lose weight even when they are underweight. Those with _____ (anorexia nervosa/bulimia nervosa) tend to have weight that fluctuates within or above normal ranges.

ANSWERS: anorexia nervosa; bulimia nervosa

Learning Objectives

Test Yourself by taking a moment to answer each of these Learning Objective Questions (repeated here from within the module). Then turn to Appendix D, Complete Module Reviews, to check your answers. Research suggests that trying to answer these questions on your own will improve your long-term memory of the concepts (McDaniel et al., 2009).

43-1 What patterns of perceiving, thinking, and feeling characterize schizophrenia?

43-2 How do *chronic* and *acute schizophrenia* differ?

43-3 What brain abnormalities are associated with schizophrenia?

43-4 What prenatal events are associated with increased risk of developing schizophrenia?

43-5 How do genes influence schizophrenia?

43-6 What are dissociative disorders, and why are they controversial?

43-7 What are the three clusters of personality disorders? What behaviors and brain activity characterize the antisocial personality?

43-8 What are the three main eating disorders, and how do biological, psychological, and social-cultural influences make people more vulnerable to them?

Terms and Concepts to Remember

Test yourself on these terms by trying to write down the definition in your own words before flipping back to the referenced page to check your answers.

schizophrenia, p. 556

psychotic disorder, p. 556

delusion, p. 556

chronic schizophrenia, p. 557

acute schizophrenia, p. 557

dissociative disorders, p. 561

dissociative identity disorder (DID), p. 561

personality disorders, p. 563

antisocial personality disorder, p. 563

anorexia nervosa, p. 565

bulimia nervosa, p. 565

binge-eating disorder, p. 565

Experience the Testing Effect

Test yourself repeatedly throughout your studies. This will not only help you figure out what you know and don't know; the testing itself will help you learn and remember the information more effectively thanks to the *testing effect*.

1. Victor exclaimed, "The weather has been so schizophrenic lately: It's hot one day and freezing the next!" Is this an accurate comparison? Why or why not?

2. A person with positive symptoms of schizophrenia is most likely to experience
   a. catatonia.
   b. delusions.
   c. withdrawal.
   d. flat emotion.

3. People with schizophrenia may hear voices urging self-destruction, an example of a(n) _____.

4. Chances for recovery from schizophrenia are best when
   a. onset is sudden, in response to stress.
   b. deterioration occurs gradually, during childhood.
   c. no environmental causes can be identified.
   d. there is a detectable brain abnormality.

5. Dissociative identity disorder is controversial because
   a. dissociation is quite rare.
   b. it was reported frequently in the 1920s but rarely today.
   c. it is almost never reported outside North America.
   d. its symptoms are nearly identical to those of obsessive-compulsive disorder.

6. A personality disorder, such as antisocial personality, is characterized by
   a. depression.
   b. hallucinations.
   c. inflexible and enduring behavior patterns that impair social functioning.
   d. an elevated level of autonomic nervous system arousal.

7. PET scans of murderers' brains have revealed
   a. higher-than-normal activation in the frontal lobes.
   b. lower-than-normal activation in the frontal lobes.
   c. more frontal lobe tissue than normal.
   d. no differences in brain structures or activity.

8. Which of the following statements is true of bulimia nervosa?
   a. People with bulimia continue to want to lose weight even when they are underweight.
   b. Bulimia is marked by weight fluctuations within or above normal ranges.
   c. Bulimia patients often come from middle-class families that are competitive, high-achieving, and protective.
   d. If one twin is diagnosed with bulimia, the chances of the other twin's sharing the disorder are greater if they are fraternal rather than identical twins.

Find answers to these questions in Appendix E, in the back of the book.

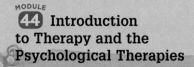

MODULE 44 Introduction to Therapy and the Psychological Therapies

Psychological therapies are talk therapies.

Biomedical therapies offer medications or other biological treatments.

Freud's PSYCHOANALYSIS

free association

Modern-day PSYCHODYNAMIC THERAPY

face-to-face

HUMANISTIC THERAPY

Focus on present/future, not past.

BEHAVIOR THERAPIES

Modify behavior —sometimes through exposure

All effective therapies provide: hope; new perspective; empathic, trusting, caring relationship.

MODULE 45 The Biomedical Therapies and Preventing Psychological Disorders

DRUG THERAPIES

including *antipsychotics*, *antianxiety drugs*, *antidepressants*, and *mood-stabilizing medications*

BRAIN STIMULATION

including *electroconvulsive therapy* and other *neurostimulation techniques*

Psychosurgery has become very rare.

Prevention efforts include addressing community effects, and building *resilience*.

COGNITIVE THERAPIES

Modify thinking

GROUP AND FAMILY THERAPIES

Treat person in family/group context

LIFESTYLE MODIFICATION

including aerobic exercise, improved sleep, light exposure, social connection, anti-rumination, and improved nutrition

Therapy

KAY Redfield Jamison, an award-winning clinical psychologist and world expert on the emotional extremes of bipolar disorder, knows her subject firsthand. "For as long as I can remember," she recalled in her memoir *An Unquiet Mind,* "I was frighteningly, although often wonderfully, beholden to moods. Intensely emotional as a child, mercurial as a young girl, first severely depressed as an adolescent, and then unrelentingly caught up in the cycles of manic-depressive illness *[bipolar disorder]* by the time I began my professional life, I became, both by necessity and intellectual inclination, a student of moods" (1995, pp. 4–5). Her life was blessed with times of intense sensitivity and passionate energy. But like her father's, it was also at times plagued by reckless spending, racing conversation, and sleeplessness, alternating with swings into "the blackest caves of the mind."

Then, "in the midst of utter confusion," she made a sane and profoundly helpful decision. Risking professional embarrassment, she made an appointment with a therapist, a psychiatrist she would visit weekly for years to come:

> He kept me alive a thousand times over. He saw me through madness, despair, wonderful and terrible love affairs, disillusionments and triumphs, recurrences of illness, an almost fatal suicide attempt, the death of a man I greatly loved, and the enormous pleasures and aggravations of my professional life. . . . He was very tough, as well as very kind, and even though he understood more than anyone how much I felt I was losing—in energy, vivacity, and originality—by taking medication, he never was seduced into losing sight of the overall perspective of how costly, damaging, and life threatening my illness was. . . . Although I went to him to be treated for an illness, he taught me . . . the total beholdenness of brain to mind and mind to brain (pp. 87–88).

"Psychotherapy heals," Jamison concluded. "It makes some sense of the confusion, reins in the terrifying thoughts and feelings, returns some control and hope and possibility from it all."

In these modules, we consider some of the healing options available to therapists and the people who seek their help. We will begin with *psychotherapies* (Module 44), and then focus on *biomedical therapies* and preventing disorders (Module 45). ◼

Dorothea Dix "I . . . call your attention to the state of the Insane Persons confined within this Commonwealth, in cages."

MODULE 44 Introduction to Therapy and the Psychological Therapies

The long history of efforts to treat psychological disorders has included a bewildering mix of methods, harsh and gentle. Well-meaning individuals have cut holes in people's heads and restrained, bled, or "beat the devil" out of them. But they also have given warm baths and massages and placed people in sunny, serene environments. They have administered drugs. And they have talked with their patients about childhood experiences, current feelings, and maladaptive thoughts and behaviors.

Reformers Philippe Pinel (1745–1826) and Dorothea Dix (1802–1887) pushed for gentler, more humane treatments and for constructing mental hospitals. Since the 1950s, drug therapies and community-based treatment programs have replaced most of those hospitals.

Treating Psychological Disorders

44-1 How do *psychotherapy* and the *biomedical therapies* differ?

Modern Western therapies can be classified into two main categories.

- In **psychotherapy,** a trained therapist uses psychological techniques to assist someone seeking to overcome difficulties or achieve personal growth. The therapist may explore a client's early relationships, encourage the client to adopt new ways of thinking, or coach the client in replacing old behaviors with new ones.

- **Biomedical therapy** offers medication or other biological treatments. For example, a person with severe depression may receive antidepressants, electroconvulsive shock therapy (ECT), or deep brain stimulation.

The care provider's training and expertise, as well as the disorder itself, influence the choice of treatment. Psychotherapy and medication are often combined. Kay Redfield Jamison received psychotherapy in her meetings with her psychiatrist, and she took medications to control her wild mood swings.

Let's look first at the psychotherapy options for those treated with "talk therapies." Each is built on one or more of psychology's major theories: psychodynamic, humanistic, behavioral, and cognitive. Most of these techniques can be used one-on-one or in groups. Some therapists combine techniques in an integrative, **eclectic approach.** And like Jamison, many patients receive psychotherapy combined with medication.

Psychoanalysis and Psychodynamic Therapies

44-2 What are the goals and techniques of psychoanalysis, and how have they been adapted in psychodynamic therapy?

The first major psychological therapy was Sigmund Freud's **psychoanalysis.** Although few clinicians today practice therapy as Freud did, his work deserves discussion. It helped form the foundation for treating psychological disorders, and it continues to influence modern therapists working from the *psychodynamic* perspective.

The history of treatment Visitors to eighteenth-century mental hospitals paid to gawk at patients, as though they were viewing zoo animals. William Hogarth's (1697–1764) painting captured one of these visits to London's St. Mary of Bethlehem hospital (commonly called Bedlam).

The Goals of Psychoanalysis

Freud believed that in therapy, people could achieve healthier, less anxious living by releasing the energy they had previously devoted to *id-ego-superego* conflicts. Freud assumed that we do not fully know ourselves. There are threatening things that we seem not to want to know—that we disavow or deny. Psychoanalysis was Freud's method of helping people to face such unwelcome facts.

Freud's therapy aimed to bring patients' repressed or disowned feelings into conscious awareness. By helping them reclaim their unconscious thoughts and feelings, and by giving them *insight* into the origins of their disorders, he aimed to help them reduce growth-impeding inner conflicts.

The Techniques of Psychoanalysis

Psychoanalysis is historical reconstruction. Psychoanalytic theory emphasizes the power of childhood experiences to mold the adult. Thus, it aims to unearth the past in the hope of loosening its bonds on the present. After discarding hypnosis as an unreliable excavator, Freud turned to *free association*.

Imagine yourself as a patient using free association. You begin by relaxing, perhaps by lying on a couch. As the psychoanalyst sits out of your line of vision, you say aloud whatever comes to mind. At one moment, you're relating a child-hood memory. At another, you're describing a dream or recent experience. It sounds easy, but soon you may notice how often you edit your thoughts as you speak. You pause for a second before uttering an embarrassing thought. You omit what seems trivial, irrelevant, or shameful. Sometimes your mind goes blank or you clutch up, unable to remember important details. You may joke or change the subject to something less threatening.

To the analyst, these mental blocks indicate **resistance.** They hint that anxiety lurks and you are defending against sensitive material. The analyst will note your resistances and then provide insight into their meaning. If offered at the right moment, this **interpretation—**of, say, your not wanting to talk about your mother—may illuminate the underlying wishes, feelings, and conflicts you are avoiding. The analyst may also offer an explanation of how this resistance fits with other pieces of your psychological puzzle, including those based on analysis of your dream content.

Over many such sessions, your relationship patterns surface in your interactions with your therapist. You may find yourself experiencing strong positive or negative feelings for your analyst. The analyst may suggest you are **transferring** feelings, such as feelings of dependency or mingled love and anger, that you experienced in earlier relationships with family members or other important people. By exposing such feelings, you may gain insight into your current relationships.

Relatively few North American therapists now offer traditional psycho-analysis. Much of its underlying theory is not supported by scientific research. Analysts' interpretations do not follow the scientific method—they cannot be proven or disproven. And psychoanalysis takes considerable time and money, often years of several expensive sessions each week. Some of these problems have been addressed in the modern *psychodynamic perspective* that has evolved from psychoanalysis.

---

psychotherapy treatment involving psychological techniques; consists of interactions between a trained therapist and someone seeking to overcome psychological difficulties or achieve personal growth.

biomedical therapy prescribed medications or procedures that act directly on the person's physiology.

eclectic approach an approach to psychotherapy that uses techniques from various forms of therapy.

psychoanalysis Sigmund Freud's therapeutic technique. Freud believed the patient's free associations, resistances, dreams, and transferences—and the therapist's interpretations of them—released previously repressed feelings, allowing the patient to gain self-insight.

resistance in psychoanalysis, the blocking from consciousness of anxiety-laden material.

interpretation in psychoanalysis, the analyst's noting supposed dream meanings, resistances, and other significant behaviors and events in order to promote insight.

transference in psychoanalysis, the patient's transfer to the analyst of emotions linked with other relationships (such as love or hatred for a parent).

"I'm more interested in hearing about the eggs you're hiding from yourself."

"I haven't seen my analyst in 200 years. He was a strict Freudian. If I'd been going all this time, I'd probably almost be cured by now."

Woody Allen, after awakening from suspended animation in the movie Sleeper

---

RETRIEVE IT [✗]

• In psychoanalysis, when patients experience strong feelings for their therapist, this is called _____. Patients are said to demonstrate anxiety when they put up mental blocks around sensitive memories, indicating _____. The therapist will attempt to provide insight into the underlying anxiety by offering a(n) _____ of the mental blocks.

ANSWERS: transference; resistance; interpretation

Face-to-face therapy In this type of therapy session, the couch has disappeared. But the influence of psychoanalytic theory may not have, especially if the therapist seeks information about the patient's childhood and helps the patient reclaim unconscious feelings.

Psychodynamic Therapy

Although influenced by Freud's ideas, **psychodynamic therapists** don't talk much about id, ego, and superego. Instead, they try to help people understand their current symptoms by focusing on themes across important relationships, including childhood experiences and the therapist relationship. "We can have loving feelings and hateful feelings toward the same person," notes psychodynamic therapist Jonathan Shedler (2009), and "we can desire something and also fear it." Client-therapist meetings take place once or twice a week (rather than several times per week), and often for only a few weeks or months. Rather than lying on a couch, out of the therapist's line of vision, patients meet with their therapist face-to-face and gain perspective by exploring defended-against thoughts and feelings.

Therapist David Shapiro (1999, p. 8) illustrates this method with the case of a young man who had told women that he loved them, when he knew that he didn't. His explanation: They expected it, so he said it. But with his wife, who wished he would say that he loved her, he found he *couldn't* do that—"I don't know why, but I can't."

Therapist: *Do you mean, then, that if you could, you would like to?*

Patient: *Well, I don't know. . . . Maybe I can't say it because I'm not sure it's true. Maybe I don't love her.*

Further interactions revealed that he could not express real love because it would feel "mushy" and "soft" and therefore unmanly. Shapiro noted that this young man was "in conflict with himself, and he [was] cut off from the nature of that conflict." With such patients, who are estranged from themselves, therapists using psychodynamic techniques "are in a position to introduce them to themselves. We can restore their awareness of their own wishes and feelings, and their awareness, as well, of their reactions against those wishes and feelings."

Exploring past relationship troubles may help clients understand the origin of their current difficulties. Jonathan Shedler (2010) recalled his patient "Jeffrey's" complaints of difficulty getting along with his colleagues and wife, who saw him as hypercritical. Jeffrey then "began responding to me as if I were an unpredictable, angry adversary." Shedler seized this opportunity to help Jeffrey recognize the relationship pattern, and its roots in the attacks and humiliation he experienced from his alcohol-abusing father. He was then able to work through and let go of this defensive style of responding to people. Without embracing all aspects of Freud's theory, psychodynamic therapists aim to help people gain beneficial insight into their childhood experiences and unconscious dynamics.

Humanistic Therapies

44-3 What are the basic themes of humanistic therapy? What are the specific goals and techniques of Rogers' client-centered approach?

The *humanistic* perspective emphasizes people's inherent potential for self-fulfillment. Not surprisingly, humanistic therapies attempt to reduce the inner conflicts that interfere with natural development and growth. To achieve this goal, humanistic therapists try to give clients new insights. Indeed, because they share this goal, the psychodynamic and humanistic therapies are often referred to as **insight therapies.** But humanistic therapies differ from psychodynamic therapies in many other ways:

- *Humanistic therapists aim to boost people's self-fulfillment by helping them grow in self-awareness and self-acceptance.*

- *Promoting this growth, not curing illness, is the therapy focus.* Thus, those in therapy became "clients" or just "persons" rather than "patients" (a change many other therapists have adopted).

- *The path to growth is taking immediate responsibility for one's feelings and actions, rather than uncovering hidden causes.*

- *Conscious thoughts are more important than the unconscious.*

- *The present and future are more important than the past.* Therapy thus focuses on exploring feelings as they occur, rather than achieving insight into the childhood origins of those feelings.

All these themes are present in the widely used humanistic technique that Carl Rogers (1902–1987) developed and called **client-centered therapy.** In this *nondirective therapy*, the therapist listens, without judging or interpreting, and refrains from directing the client toward certain insights.

Believing that most people possess the resources for growth, Rogers (1961, 1980) encouraged therapists to foster that growth by exhibiting *genuineness, acceptance,* and *empathy.* By being *genuine*, therapists hope to encourage clients to likewise express their true feelings. By being *accepting*, therapists may help clients feel freer and more open to change. By showing *empathy*—by sensing and reflecting their clients' feelings—therapists can help clients experience a deeper self-understanding and self-acceptance (Hill & Nakayama, 2000). As Rogers (1980, p. 10) explained:

> Hearing has consequences. When I truly hear a person and the meanings that are important to him at that moment, hearing not simply his words, but him, and when I let him know that I have heard his own private personal meanings, many things happen. There is first of all a grateful look. He feels released. He wants to tell me more about his world. He surges forth in a new sense of freedom. He becomes more open to the process of change.
>
> I have often noticed that the more deeply I hear the meanings of the person, the more there is that happens. Almost always, when a person realizes he has been deeply heard, his eyes moisten. I think in some real sense he is weeping for joy. It is as though he were saying, "Thank God, somebody heard me. Someone knows what it's like to be me."

To Rogers, "hearing" was **active listening.** The therapist echoes, restates, and clarifies what the client has expressed verbally or nonverbally. The therapist also acknowledges those expressed feelings. Active listening is now an accepted part of counseling practices in many schools, colleges, and clinics. Counselors listen attentively. They interrupt only to restate and confirm feelings, to accept what was said, or to check their understanding of something. In the following brief excerpt, note how Rogers tried to provide a psychological mirror that would help the client see himself more clearly:

Rogers: *Feeling that now, hm? That you're just no good to yourself, no good to anybody. Never will be any good to anybody. Just that you're completely worthless, huh?—Those really are lousy feelings. Just feel that you're no good at all, hm?*

Client: Yeah. (Muttering in low, discouraged voice) *That's what this guy I went to town with just the other day told me.*

Rogers: *This guy that you went to town with really told you that you were no good? Is that what you're saying? Did I get that right?*

Client: *M-hm.*

Rogers: *I guess the meaning of that if I get it right is that here's somebody that meant something to you and what does he think of you? Why, he's told you that he thinks you're no good at all. And that just really knocks the props out from under you.* (Client weeps quietly.) *It just brings the tears.* (Silence of 20 seconds)

Client: (Rather defiantly) *I don't care though.*

Rogers: *You tell yourself you don't care at all, but somehow I guess some part of you cares because some part of you weeps over it.*

(Meador & Rogers, 1984, p. 167)

psychodynamic therapy therapy deriving from the psychoanalytic tradition; views individuals as responding to unconscious forces and childhood experiences, and seeks to enhance self-insight.

insight therapies a variety of therapies that aim to improve psychological functioning by increasing a person's awareness of underlying motives and defenses.

client-centered therapy a humanistic therapy, developed by Carl Rogers, in which the therapist uses techniques such as active listening within a genuine, accepting, empathic environment to facilitate clients' growth. (Also called *person-centered therapy.*)

active listening empathic listening in which the listener echoes, restates, and clarifies. A feature of Rogers' client-centered therapy.

"We have two ears and one mouth that we may listen the more and talk the less."
Zeno, 335–263 B.C.E., Diogenes Laertius

Michael Rougier/The LIFE Picture Collection/Getty Images

Active listening Carl Rogers (right) empathized with a client during this group therapy session.

Can a therapist be a perfect mirror, critics have asked, without selecting and interpreting what is reflected? Rogers conceded that no one can be *totally* nondirective. Nevertheless, he said, the therapist's most important contribution is to accept and understand the client. Given a nonjudgmental, grace-filled environment that provides **unconditional positive regard,** people may accept even their worst traits and feel valued and whole.

How can we improve communication in our own relationships by listening more actively? Three Rogers-inspired hints may help:

1. *Paraphrase.* Rather than saying "I know how you feel," check your understandings by summarizing the person's words in your own words.

2. *Invite clarification.* "What might be an example of that?" may encourage the person to say more.

3. *Reflect feelings.* "It sounds frustrating" might mirror what you're sensing from the person's body language and intensity.

Behavior Therapies

44-4 How does the basic assumption of behavior therapy differ from the assumptions of psychodynamic and humanistic therapies? What techniques are used in exposure therapies and aversive conditioning?

The insight therapies assume that self-awareness and psychological well-being go hand in hand. Psychodynamic therapists expect people's problems to diminish as they gain insight into their unresolved and unconscious tensions. Humanistic therapists expect people's problems to diminish as they get in touch with their feelings. **Behavior therapists,** however, doubt the healing power of self-awareness. (You can become aware of why you are highly anxious during exams and still be anxious.) Rather than delving deeply below the surface looking for inner causes, behavior therapists assume that problem behaviors *are* the problems, and they view learning principles as useful tools for eliminating those behaviors. If phobias or sexual dysfunctions are learned behaviors, they reason, why not replace them with new, constructive behaviors learned through classical or operant conditioning?

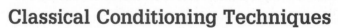

ScienceCartoonsPlus.com

Classical Conditioning Techniques

One cluster of behavior therapies derives from principles developed in Ivan Pavlov's conditioning experiments. As Pavlov and others showed, we learn various behaviors and emotions through *classical conditioning*. If we're attacked by a dog, we may thereafter have a conditioned fear response when other dogs approach: Our fear generalizes and all dogs become conditioned stimuli.

Could maladaptive symptoms be examples of conditioned responses? If so, might reconditioning be a solution? Learning theorist O. H. Mowrer thought so. He developed a successful conditioning therapy for chronic bed-wetters, using a liquid-sensitive pad connected to an alarm. If the sleeping child wets the bed pad, moisture triggers the alarm, waking the child. With sufficient repetition, this association of bladder relaxation with waking stops the bed-wetting. The treatment has been effective in three out of four cases and the success provides a boost to the child's self-image (Christophersen & Edwards, 1992; Houts et al., 1994).

Can we unlearn fear responses through new conditioning? Many people have. One example: The fear of riding in an elevator is often a learned fear response to being in a confined space. **Counterconditioning** pairs the trigger stimulus (in this case, the enclosed space of the elevator) with a new response (relaxation) that is incompatible with fear. Two specific counterconditioning techniques—*exposure therapies* and *aversive conditioning*—have successfully counterconditioned many people with such fears.

RETRIEVE IT [✱]

• What might a psychodynamic therapist say about Mowrer's therapy for bed-wetting? How about a humanistic therapist? How might a behavior therapist reply?

ANSWER: Psychodynamic therapists might be more interested in helping the child develop insight about the underlying problems that have caused the bed-wetting response. Humanistic therapists may prefer to encourage the child toward self-fulfillment and personal growth as a means of combating the problem behavior. Behavior therapists would be more likely to agree with Mowrer that the bed-wetting symptom *is* the problem, and that counterconditioning the unwanted behavior would indeed bring emotional relief.

EXPOSURE THERAPIES Picture this scene: Behavioral psychologist Mary Cover Jones is working with 3-year-old Peter, who is petrified of rabbits and other furry objects. To rid Peter of his fear, Jones plans to associate the fear-evoking rabbit with the pleasurable, relaxed response associated with eating. As Peter begins his midafternoon snack, she introduces a caged rabbit on the other side of the huge room. Peter, eagerly munching away on his crackers and drinking his milk, hardly notices. On succeeding days, she gradually moves the rabbit closer and closer. Within two months, Peter is holding the rabbit in his lap, even stroking it while he eats. Moreover, his fear of other furry objects has also gone away, having been *countered,* or replaced, by a relaxed state that cannot coexist with fear (Fisher, 1984; Jones, 1924).

Unfortunately for many who might have been helped by Jones' procedures, her story of Peter and the rabbit did not enter psychology's lore when it was reported in 1924. It was more than 30 years before psychiatrist Joseph Wolpe (1958; Wolpe & Plaud, 1997) refined Jones' counterconditioning technique into the **exposure therapies** used today. These therapies, in a variety of ways, try to change people's reactions by repeatedly exposing them to stimuli that trigger unwanted reactions. With repeated exposure to what they normally avoid or escape, people adapt. We all experience this process in everyday life. A person moving to a new apartment may be annoyed by nearby loud traffic noise, but only for a while. With repeated exposure, the person adapts. So, too, with people who have fear reactions to specific events. Exposed repeatedly to the situation that once petrified them, they can learn to react less anxiously (Barrera et al., 2013; Foa et al., 2013).

One form of exposure therapy widely used to treat phobias is **systematic desensitization.** You cannot simultaneously be anxious and relaxed. Therefore, if you can repeatedly relax when facing anxiety-provoking stimuli, you can gradually eliminate your anxiety. The trick is to proceed gradually. If you fear public speaking, a behavior therapist might first ask you to make a list of anxiety-triggering speaking situations. Your list would range from situations that cause you to feel mildly anxious (perhaps speaking up in a small group of friends) to those that provoke panic (having to address a large audience).

In the next step, the therapist would train you in *progressive relaxation.* You would learn to relax one muscle group after another, until you achieved a comfortable, complete relaxation. The therapist might then ask you to imagine, with your eyes closed, a mildly anxiety-arousing situation: You are having coffee with a group of friends and are trying to decide whether to speak up. If you feel any anxiety while imagining the scene, you will signal by raising your finger. Seeing the signal, the therapist will instruct you to switch off the mental image and go back to deep relaxation. This imagined scene is repeatedly paired with relaxation until you feel no trace of anxiety.

---

unconditional positive regard a caring, accepting, nonjudgmental attitude, which Carl Rogers believed would help clients develop self-awareness and self-acceptance.

behavior therapy therapy that applies learning principles to the elimination of unwanted behaviors.

counterconditioning behavior therapy procedures that use classical conditioning to evoke new responses to stimuli that are triggering unwanted behaviors; include *exposure therapies* and *aversive conditioning.*

exposure therapies behavioral techniques, such as *systematic desensitization* and *virtual reality exposure therapy,* that treat anxieties by exposing people (in imagination or actual situations) to the things they fear and avoid.

systematic desensitization a type of exposure therapy that associates a pleasant, relaxed state with gradually increasing anxiety-triggering stimuli. Commonly used to treat phobias.

Kim Reinick/Shutterstock
Creativ Studio Heinemann/
Getty Images

The therapist will then move to the next item on your list, again using relaxation techniques to desensitize you to each imagined situation. After several sessions, you will move to actual situations and practice what you had only imagined before. You will begin with relatively easy tasks and gradually move to more anxiety-filled ones. Conquering your anxiety in an actual situation, not just in your imagination, will increase your self-confidence (Foa & Kozak, 1986; Williams, 1987). Eventually, you may even become a confident public speaker. Often people fear not just a situation (such as public speaking), but also being incapacitated by their own fear response (for example, standing in front of an audience and being unable to speak). As their fear subsides, so also does their fear of the fear.

"The only thing we have to fear is fear itself."

U.S. President Franklin D. Roosevelt, First Inaugural Address, 1933

If an anxiety-arousing situation is too expensive, difficult, or embarrassing to re-create, the therapist may recommend **virtual reality exposure therapy.** You would don a head-mounted display unit that projects a three-dimensional virtual world in front of your eyes. The lifelike scenes, which shift as your head turns, would be tailored to your particular fear. Experimentally treated fears include flying, heights, particular animals, and public speaking (Parsons & Rizzo, 2008). If you fear flying, you could peer out a virtual window of a simulated plane. You would feel the engine's vibrations and hear it roar as the plane taxis down the runway and takes off. In controlled studies, people participating in virtual reality exposure therapy have experienced significant relief from real-life fear (Turner & Casey, 2014).

Virtual reality exposure therapy Within the confines of a room, virtual reality technology exposes people to vivid simulations of feared stimuli, such as walking across a rickety bridge high off the ground.

AVERSIVE CONDITIONING Exposure therapies enable a more relaxed, positive response to an upsetting *harmless* stimulus. **Aversive conditioning** creates a negative (aversive) response to a *harmful* stimulus (such as alcohol). Exposure therapies help you accept what you *should* do. Aversive conditioning helps you to learn what you *should not* do.

The aversive conditioning procedure is simple: It associates the unwanted behavior with unpleasant feelings. To treat nail biting, one can paint the fingernails with a nasty-tasting nail polish (Baskind, 1997). To treat alcohol use disorder, an aversion therapist offers the client appealing drinks laced with a drug that produces severe nausea. By linking alcohol with violent nausea (many *taste-aversion* experiments were first done with rats and coyotes), the therapist seeks to transform the person's reaction to alcohol from positive to negative (**FIGURE 44.1**).

Does aversive conditioning work? In the short run it may. In one classic study, 685 hospital patients with alcohol use disorder completed an aversion therapy

program (Wiens & Menustik, 1983). Over the next year, they returned for several booster treatments in which alcohol was paired with sickness. At the end of that year, 63 percent were still successfully abstaining. But after three years, only 33 percent had remained abstinent.

The problem is that in therapy (as in research), cognition influences conditioning. People know that outside the therapist's office they can drink without fear of nausea. Their ability to discriminate between the aversive conditioning situation and all other situations can limit the treatment's effectiveness. Thus, therapists often use aversive conditioning in combination with other treatments.

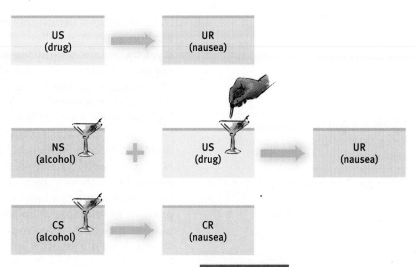

▲ FIGURE 44.1

Aversion therapy for alcohol use disorder After repeatedly imbibing an alcoholic drink mixed with a drug that produces severe nausea, some people with a history of alcohol use disorder develop at least a temporary conditioned aversion to alcohol. (Remember: US is unconditioned stimulus, UR is unconditioned response, NS is neutral stimulus, CS is conditioned stimulus, and CR is conditioned response.)

Operant Conditioning

44-5 What is the main premise of therapy based on operant conditioning principles, and what are the views of its proponents and critics?

The work of B. F. Skinner and others teaches us a basic principle of operant conditioning: Voluntary behaviors are strongly influenced by their consequences. Knowing this, some behavior therapists practice *behavior modification*. They reinforce behaviors they consider desirable. And they fail to reinforce—or sometimes punish—behaviors they consider undesirable.

Using operant conditioning to solve specific behavior problems has raised hopes for some seemingly hopeless cases. Children with intellectual disabilities have been taught to care for themselves. Socially withdrawn children with autism spectrum disorder (ASD) have learned to interact. People with schizophrenia have been helped to behave more rationally in their hospital ward. In such cases, therapists used positive reinforcers to *shape* behavior. In a step-by-step manner, they rewarded behaviors that came closer and closer to the desired behavior.

In extreme cases, treatment must be intensive. One study worked with 19 withdrawn, uncommunicative 3-year-olds with ASD. For two years, 40 hours each week, the children's parents attempted to shape their behavior (Lovaas, 1987). They positively reinforced desired behaviors and ignored or punished aggressive and self-abusive behaviors. The combination worked wonders for some children. By first grade, 9 of the 19 were functioning successfully in school and exhibiting normal intelligence. In a group of 40 comparable children not undergoing this treatment, only one showed similar improvement. Later studies focused on positive reinforcement—the effective aspect of this "Early Intensive Behavioral Intervention" (Reichow, 2012).

The rewards used to modify behavior vary because people differ in what they find reinforcing. For some, the reinforcing power of attention or praise is enough. Others require concrete rewards, such as food. In institutional settings, therapists may create a **token economy.** When people display desired behavior, such as getting out of bed, washing, dressing, eating, talking meaningfully, cleaning their rooms, or playing cooperatively, they receive a token or plastic coin. Later, they can exchange a number of these tokens for rewards, such as candy, TV time, day trips, or better living quarters. Token economies have been used successfully in various settings (homes, classrooms, hospitals, institutions for juvenile offenders) and among members of various populations (including disturbed children and people with schizophrenia and other mental disabilities).

Behavior modification critics express two concerns. The first is practical: *How durable are the behaviors?* Will people become so dependent on extrinsic rewards

virtual reality exposure therapy an anxiety treatment that progressively exposes people to electronic simulations of their greatest fears, such as airplane flying, spiders, or public speaking.

aversive conditioning a type of counterconditioning that associates an unpleasant state (such as nausea) with an unwanted behavior (such as drinking alcohol).

token economy an operant conditioning procedure in which people earn a token of some sort for exhibiting a desired behavior and can later exchange their tokens for various privileges or treats.

that the desired behaviors will stop when the reinforcers stop? Behavior modification advocates believe the behaviors will endure if therapists wean people from the tokens by shifting them toward other, real-life rewards, such as social approval. Further, they point out that the desired behaviors themselves can be rewarding. As people become more socially competent, the intrinsic satisfactions of social interaction may help them maintain the desired behaviors.

The second concern is ethical: *Is it right for one human to control another's behavior?* Those who set up token economies deprive people of something they desire and decide which behaviors to reinforce. To critics, this whole process has an authoritarian taint. Advocates reply that control already exists; people's destructive behavior patterns are already being maintained and perpetuated by natural reinforcers and punishers in their environments. Isn't using positive rewards to reinforce adaptive behavior more humane than institutionalizing or punishing people? Advocates also argue that the right to effective treatment and an improved life justifies temporary deprivation.

LaunchPad See LaunchPad's *Video: Research Ethics* for a helpful tutorial animation.

RETRIEVE IT [✷]

• What are the *insight therapies,* and how do they differ from behavior therapies?

ANSWER: The *insight therapies*—psychodynamic and humanistic therapies—seek to relieve problems by providing an understanding of their origins. Behavior therapies assume the problem behavior *is* the problem and treat it directly, paying less attention to its origins.

• Some maladaptive behaviors are learned. What hope does this fact provide?

ANSWER: If a behavior can be learned, it can be *unlearned* and replaced by other, more adaptive responses.

• Exposure therapies and aversive conditioning are applications of _____ conditioning. Token economies are an application of _____ conditioning.

ANSWERS: classical; operant

Cognitive Therapies

44-6 What are the goals and techniques of cognitive therapy and of cognitive-behavioral therapy?

People with specific fears and problem behaviors may respond to behavior therapy. But how would you modify the wide assortment of behaviors that accompany depressive disorders? And how would you treat generalized anxiety disorders, where unfocused anxiety doesn't lend itself to a neat list of anxiety-triggering situations? The *cognitive revolution* that has influenced other areas of psychology during the last half-century has influenced therapy as well.

The **cognitive therapies** assume that our thinking colors our feelings (**FIGURE 44.2**). Between an event and our response lies the mind. Self-blaming and overgeneralized explanations of bad events feed depression. Anxiety arises from an "attention bias to threat" (MacLeod & Clarke, 2015). If depressed, we may interpret a suggestion as criticism, disagreement as dislike, praise as flattery, friendliness as pity. Dwelling on such thoughts sustains negative thinking. Cognitive therapies aim to help people change their minds with new, more constructive ways of perceiving and interpreting events (Kazdin, 2015).

"Life does not consist mainly, or even largely, of facts and happenings. It consists mainly of the storm of thoughts that are forever blowing through one's mind."

Mark Twain, 1835–1910

> **FIGURE 44.2**

A cognitive perspective on psychological disorders The person's emotional reactions are produced not directly by the event, but by the person's thoughts in response to the event.

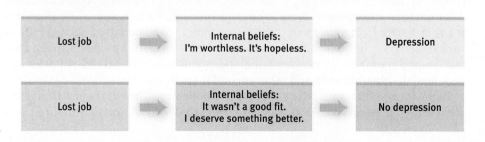

Beck's Therapy for Depression

Cognitive therapist Aaron Beck believes that changing people's thinking can change their functioning. Depressed people, he found, often reported dreams with negative themes of loss, rejection, and abandonment. These thoughts extended into their waking thoughts, and even into therapy, as clients recalled and rehearsed their failings and worst impulses (Kelly, 2000). With cognitive therapy, Beck and his colleagues (1979) sought to reverse clients' negativity about themselves, their situations, and their futures. With this technique, gentle questioning seeks to reveal irrational thinking, and then to persuade people to remove the dark glasses through which they view life (Beck et al., 1979, pp. 145–146):

Lara Jo Regan

Cognitive therapy for eating disorders aided by journaling
Cognitive therapists guide people toward new ways of explaining their good and bad experiences. By recording positive events and how she has enabled them, this woman may become more mindful of her self-control and more optimistic.

Client: *I agree with the descriptions of me but I guess I don't agree that the way I think makes me depressed.*

Beck: *How do you understand it?*

Client: *I get depressed when things go wrong. Like when I fail a test.*

Beck: *How can failing a test make you depressed?*

Client: *Well, if I fail I'll never get into law school.*

Beck: *So failing the test means a lot to you. But if failing a test could drive people into clinical depression, wouldn't you expect everyone who failed the test to have a depression? . . . Did everyone who failed get depressed enough to require treatment?*

Client: *No, but it depends on how important the test was to the person.*

Beck: *Right, and who decides the importance?*

Client: *I do.*

Beck: *And so, what we have to examine is your way of viewing the test (or the way that you think about the test) and how it affects your chances of getting into law school. Do you agree?*

Client: *Right.*

Beck: *Do you agree that the way you interpret the results of the test will affect you? You might feel depressed, you might have trouble sleeping, not feel like eating, and you might even wonder if you should drop out of the course.*

Client: *I have been thinking that I wasn't going to make it. Yes, I agree.*

Beck: *Now what did failing mean?*

Client: (tearful) *That I couldn't get into law school.*

Beck: *And what does that mean to you?*

Client: *That I'm just not smart enough.*

Beck: *Anything else?*

Client: *That I can never be happy.*

Beck: *And how do these thoughts make you feel?*

Client: *Very unhappy.*

Beck: *So it is the meaning of failing a test that makes you very unhappy. In fact, believing that you can never be happy is a powerful factor in producing unhappiness. So, you get yourself into a trap—by definition, failure to get into law school equals "I can never be happy."*

cognitive therapy therapy that teaches people new, more adaptive ways of thinking; based on the assumption that thoughts intervene between events and our emotional reactions.

PEANUTS

We often think in words. Therefore, getting people to change what they say to themselves is an effective way to change their thinking. Perhaps you can identify with the anxious students who, before an exam, make matters worse with self-defeating thoughts: "This exam's probably going to be impossible. All these other students seem so relaxed and confident. I wish I were better prepared. I'm so nervous I'll forget everything." Psychologists call this sort of relentless, overgeneralized, self-blaming behavior *catastrophizing.*

To change such negative self-talk, therapists teach people to restructure their thinking in stressful situations (Meichenbaum, 1977, 1985). Sometimes it may be enough simply to say more positive things to yourself: "Relax. The exam may be hard, but it will be hard for everyone else, too. I studied harder than most people. Besides, I don't need a perfect score to get a good grade." After learning to "talk back" to negative thoughts, depression-prone children, teens, and college students have shown a greatly reduced rate of future depression (Reivich et al., 2013; Seligman et al., 2009). To a large extent, it *is* the thought that counts. **TABLE 44.1** provides a sampling of techniques commonly used in cognitive therapy.

It's not just depressed people who can benefit from positive self-talk. We all talk to ourselves (thinking "I wish I hadn't said that" can protect us from repeating the blunder). The findings of nearly three dozen sport psychology studies show that self-talk interventions can enhance the learning of athletic skills (Hatzigeorgiadis et al., 2011). For example, novice basketball players may be trained to think "focus" and "follow through," swimmers to think "high elbow," and tennis players to think "look at the ball."

⌄ TABLE 44.1

Selected Cognitive Therapy Techniques

Aim of Technique	Technique	Therapists' Directives
Reveal beliefs	Question your interpretations	Explore your beliefs, revealing faulty assumptions such as "I must be liked by everyone."
	Rank thoughts and emotions	Gain perspective by ranking your thoughts and emotions from mildly to extremely upsetting.
Test beliefs	Examine consequences	Explore difficult situations, assessing possible consequences and challenging faulty reasoning.
	Decatastrophize thinking	Work through the actual worst-case consequences of the situation you face (it is often not as bad as imagined). Then determine how to cope with the real situation you face.
Change beliefs	Take appropriate responsibility	Challenge total self-blame and negative thinking, noting aspects for which you may be truly responsible, as well as aspects that aren't your responsibility.
	Resist extremes	Develop new ways of thinking and feeling to replace maladaptive habits. For example, change from thinking "I am a total failure" to "I got a failing grade on that paper, and I can make these changes to succeed next time."

Cognitive-Behavioral Therapy

"The trouble with most therapy," said therapist Albert Ellis (1913–2007), "is that it helps you to feel better. But you don't get better. You have to back it up with action, action, action." **Cognitive-behavioral therapy (CBT),** today's most widely practiced psychotherapy, aims not only to alter the way people *think* but also to alter the way they *act*. Like other cognitive therapies, this *integrative* therapy seeks to make people aware of their irrational negative thinking and to replace it with new ways of thinking. Like other behavior therapies, it trains people to *practice* the more positive approach in everyday settings.

Anxiety, depressive disorders, and bipolar disorder share a common problem: emotion regulation (Aldao & Nolen-Hoeksema, 2010). An effective CBT program for these emotional disorders trains people both to replace their catastrophizing thinking with more realistic appraisals and, as homework, to practice behaviors that are incompatible with their problem (Kazantzis & Dattilio, 2010; Kazantzis et al., 2010; Moses & Barlow, 2006). A person might, for example, keep a log of daily situations associated with negative and positive emotions and attempt to engage more in activities that lead to feeling good. Those who fear social situations might learn to restrain the negative thoughts surrounding their social anxiety and practice approaching people.

CBT may also be useful with obsessive-compulsive disorder. In one study, people learned to prevent their compulsive behaviors by relabeling their obsessive thoughts (Schwartz et al., 1996). Feeling the urge to wash their hands again, they would tell themselves, "I'm having a compulsive urge." They would explain to themselves that the hand-washing urge was a result of their brain's abnormal activity, which they had previously viewed in PET scans. Then, instead of giving in, they would spend 15 minutes in an enjoyable, alternative behavior, such as practicing an instrument, taking a walk, or gardening. This helped "unstick" the brain by shifting attention and engaging other brain areas. For two or three months, the weekly therapy sessions continued, with relabeling and refocusing practice at home. By the study's end, most participants' symptoms had diminished, and their PET scans revealed normalized brain activity. Many other studies confirm CBT's effectiveness for treating anxiety, depression, and eating disorders (Covin et al., 2008; Milrod et al., 2015; Zalta, 2011).

A newer CBT variation, *dialectical behavior therapy (DBT)*, helps change harmful and even suicidal behavior patterns (Linehan et al., 2015; Valentine et al., 2015). DBT combines cognitive tactics for tolerating distress and regulating emotions with social skills training and mindfulness meditation. Individual therapy aims to teach both acceptance *and* change—the dialectical, or opposing, forces from which this therapy derives its name. Patients may also participate in a training group that teaches skills, provides a social context for skills practice, and assigns further practice as homework.

> **cognitive-behavioral therapy (CBT)** a popular integrative therapy that combines cognitive therapy (changing self-defeating thinking) with behavior therapy (changing behavior).

RETRIEVE IT [✖]

• How do the humanistic and cognitive therapies differ?

ANSWER: By reflecting clients' feelings in a nondirective setting, the *humanistic therapies* attempt to foster personal growth by helping clients become more self-aware and self-accepting. By making clients aware of self-defeating patterns of thinking, *cognitive therapies* guide people toward more adaptive ways of thinking about themselves and their world.

• An influential cognitive therapy for depression was developed by _____ _____.

ANSWER: Aaron Beck

• What is cognitive-behavioral therapy, and what sorts of problems does this therapy best address?

ANSWER: This integrative therapy helps people change self-defeating thinking and behavior. It has been shown to be effective for those with anxiety disorders, obsessive-compulsive disorder, depressive disorders, bipolar disorder, and eating disorders.

group therapy therapy conducted with groups rather than individuals, permitting therapeutic benefits from group interaction.

family therapy therapy that treats the family as a system. Views an individual's unwanted behaviors as influenced by, or directed at, other family members.

Group and Family Therapies

👁 **44-7** What are the aims and benefits of group and family therapies?

Group Therapy

Except for traditional psychoanalysis, most therapies may also occur in small groups. **Group therapy** does not provide the same degree of therapist involvement with each client. However, it offers many benefits:

- *It saves therapists' time and clients' money,* often with no less effectiveness than individual therapy (Fuhriman & Burlingame, 1994).

- *It offers a social laboratory for exploring social behaviors and developing social skills.* Therapists frequently suggest group therapy for people experiencing frequent conflicts or whose behavior distresses others. For up to 90 minutes weekly, the therapist guides people's interactions as they discuss issues and try out new behaviors.

- *It enables people to see that others share their problems.* It can be a relief to discover that you are not alone—to learn that others, despite their composure, experience some of the same troublesome feelings and behaviors.

- *It provides feedback as clients try out new ways of behaving.* Hearing that you look poised, even though you feel anxious and self-conscious, can be reassuring.

Family Therapy

One special type of group interaction, **family therapy,** assumes that no person is an island. We live and grow in relation to others, especially our families, yet we also work to find an identity outside of our family. These two opposing tendencies can create stress for both the individual and the family.

Unlike most psychotherapy, which focuses on what happens inside the person's own skin, family therapists work with multiple family members to heal relationships and to mobilize family resources. They tend to view the family as a system in which each person's actions trigger reactions from others, and they help family members discover their role within their family's social system. A child's rebellion, for example, affects and is affected by other family tensions. Therapists also attempt—usually with some success, research suggests—to open up communication within the family or to help family members discover new ways of preventing or resolving conflicts (Hazelrigg et al., 1987; Shadish et al., 1993).

Family therapy This type of therapy often acts as a preventive mental health strategy and may include marriage therapy, as shown here at a retreat for military families. The therapist helps family members understand how their ways of relating to one another create problems. The treatment's emphasis is not on changing the individuals, but on changing their relationships and interactions.

Self-Help Groups

More than 100 million Americans belong to small religious, interest, or support groups that meet regularly—and 9 in 10 report that group members "support each other emotionally" (Gallup, 1994). One analysis of online support groups and more than 14,000 other self-help groups reported that most such groups focus on stigmatized or hard-to-discuss illnesses (Davison et al., 2000). AIDS patients were 250 times more likely than hypertension patients to be in support groups. People with anorexia and alcohol use disorder often join groups; those with migraines and ulcers usually do not.

The grandparent of support groups, Alcoholics Anonymous (AA), reports having 2.1 million members in 115,000 groups worldwide. Its famous 12-step program, emulated by many other self-help groups, asks members to admit their powerlessness, to seek help from a higher power and from one another, and (the twelfth step) to take the message to others in need of it. Studies of 12-step programs such as AA

have found that they help reduce alcohol use disorder at rates comparable with other treatment interventions (Ferri et al., 2006; Moos & Moos, 2005). In one eight-year, $27 million investigation, AA participants reduced their drinking sharply, as did those assigned to cognitive-behavioral therapy or an alternative therapy (Project MATCH, 1997). In one study of 2300 veterans who sought treatment for alcohol use disorder, a high level of AA involvement was followed by diminished alcohol problems (McKellar et al., 2003). The more meetings members attend, the greater their alcohol abstinence (Moos & Moos, 2006). Those whose personal stories include a "redemptive narrative"—who see something good as having come from their experience—more often sustain sobriety (Dunlop & Tracy, 2013).

In an individualist age, with more and more people living alone or feeling isolated, the popularity of support groups—for the addicted, the bereaved, the divorced, or simply those seeking fellowship and growth—may reflect a longing for community and connectedness.

* * *

For a synopsis of these modern psychotherapies, see **TABLE 44.2**.

With more than 2 million members worldwide, AA is said to be "the largest organization on Earth that nobody wanted to join" (Finlay, 2000).

LaunchPad To review the aims and techniques of different psychotherapies, and assess your ability to recognize excerpts from each, visit LaunchPad's *PsychSim 6: Mystery Therapist.*

∨ TABLE 44.2

Comparing Modern Psychotherapies

Therapy	Presumed Problem	Therapy Aim	Therapy Technique
Psychodynamic	Unconscious conflicts from childhood experiences	Reduce anxiety through self-insight.	Interpret patients' memories and feelings.
Client-centered	Barriers to self-understanding and self-acceptance	Enable growth via unconditional positive regard, genuineness, acceptance, and empathy.	Listen actively and reflect clients' feelings.
Behavior	Dysfunctional behaviors	Learn adaptive behaviors; extinguish problem ones.	Use classical conditioning (via exposure or aversion therapy) or operant conditioning (as in token economies).
Cognitive	Negative, self-defeating thinking	Promote healthier thinking and self-talk.	Train people to dispute negative thoughts and attributions.
Cognitive-behavioral	Self-harmful thoughts and behaviors	Promote healthier thinking and adaptive behaviors.	Train people to counter self-harmful thoughts and to act out their new ways of thinking.
Group and family	Stressful relationships	Heal relationships.	Develop an understanding of family and other social systems, explore roles, and improve communication.

RETRIEVE IT

• Which therapeutic technique focuses more on the present and future than the past, and involves unconditional positive regard and active listening?

ANSWER: humanistic therapy—specifically Carl Rogers' client-centered therapy

• Which of the following is NOT a benefit of group therapy?

  a. more focused attention from the therapist   c. social feedback

  b. less expensive   d. reassurance that others share troubles

ANSWER: a

Evaluating Psychotherapies

Many Americans have great confidence in psychotherapy's effectiveness. "Seek counseling" or "Ask your mate to find a therapist," advice columnists often advise. Before 1950, psychiatrists were the primary providers of mental health care.

Today's providers include clinical and counseling psychologists; clinical social workers; pastoral, marital, abuse, and school counselors; and psychiatric nurses. With such an enormous outlay of time as well as money and effort, it is important to ask: Are the millions of people worldwide justified in placing their hopes in psychotherapy?

Is Psychotherapy Effective?

44-8 Does psychotherapy work? How can we know?

Asking whether psychotherapy has worked is not as simple as asking whether antibiotics have worked to treat an infection. So how can we assess psychotherapy's effectiveness? By how we feel about our progress? By how our therapist feels about it? By how our friends and family feel about it? By how our behavior has changed?

CLIENTS' PERCEPTIONS If clients' testimonials were the only measuring stick, we could strongly assert psychotherapy's effectiveness. Consider the 2900 *Consumer Reports* readers who reported on their experiences with mental health professionals (1995; Kotkin et al., 1996; Seligman, 1995). How many were at least "fairly well satisfied"? Almost 90 percent. Among those who recalled feeling *fair* or *very poor* when beginning therapy, 9 in 10 now were feeling *very good, good,* or at least *so-so.* We have their word for it—and who should know better?

But client testimonials don't persuade everyone. Critics note reasons for skepticism:

- *People often enter therapy in crisis.* When, with the normal ebb and flow of events, the crisis passes, people may assume their improvement was a result of the therapy. Depressed people often get better no matter what they do.

- *Clients believe that treatment will be effective.* The *placebo effect* is the healing power of positive expectations.

- *Clients generally speak kindly of their therapists.* Even if the problems remain, clients "work hard to find something positive to say. The therapist had been very understanding, the client had gained a new perspective, he learned to communicate better, his mind was eased, anything at all so as not to have to say treatment was a failure" (Zilbergeld, 1983, p. 117).

- *Clients want to believe the therapy was worth the effort.* People may feel the need to justify their investment of money, time, and hope.

CLINICIANS' PERCEPTIONS If clinicians' perceptions were proof of therapy's effectiveness, we would have even more reason to celebrate. Case studies of successful treatment abound. Furthermore, therapists are like the rest of us. They treasure compliments from clients saying good-bye or later expressing their gratitude. The problem is that clients justify entering psychotherapy by emphasizing their unhappiness. They justify leaving by emphasizing their well-being. And they stay in touch only if they are satisfied. Thus, therapists are most aware of the failures of *other* therapists—those whose clients, having experienced only temporary relief, are now seeking a new therapist for their recurring problems. The same person, with the same recurring anxieties, depression, or marital difficulty, may be a "success" story in several therapists' files. Moreover, therapists, like the rest of us, are vulnerable to cognitive errors, such as *confirmation bias* and *illusory correlation* (Lilienfeld et al., 2014).

OUTCOME RESEARCH How, then, can we objectively assess psychotherapy's effectiveness? What *outcomes* can we expect—what types of people and problems are helped, and by what type of psychotherapy?

Trauma These women were mourning the tragic loss of lives and homes in the 2010 earthquake in China. Those who suffer through such trauma may benefit from counseling, though many people recover on their own or with the help of supportive relationships with family and friends. "Life itself still remains a very effective therapist," noted psychodynamic therapist Karen Horney (*Our Inner Conflicts*, 1945).

Feng Li/Getty Images

In search of answers, psychologists have turned to controlled research. This is a well-traveled path. In the 1800s, skeptical medical doctors began to realize that many patients got better on their own and that many fashionable treatments (bleeding, purging) might be doing no good. Sorting fact from superstition required following patients and recording outcomes with and without a particular treatment. Typhoid fever patients, for example, often improved after being bled, convincing most physicians that the treatment worked. Then came the shock. A control group was given mere bed rest, and after five weeks of fever, 70 percent improved, showing that the bleeding was worthless (Thomas, 1992).

In the twentieth century, psychology, with its many different therapy options, faced a similar challenge. British psychologist Hans Eysenck (1952) launched a spirited debate when he summarized 24 studies of psychotherapy outcomes. He found that two-thirds of those receiving psychotherapy for disorders not involving hallucinations or delusions improved markedly. To this day, no one disputes that optimistic estimate.

Why, then, are we still debating psychotherapy's effectiveness? Because Eysenck also reported similar improvement among *untreated* persons, such as those who were on waiting lists for treatment. With or without psychotherapy, he said, roughly two-thirds improved noticeably. Time was a great healer.

An avalanche of criticism greeted Eysenck's conclusions. Some pointed out errors in his analyses. Others noted that he based his ideas on only 24 studies. Now, more than a half-century later, there are hundreds of studies. The best of these are *randomized clinical trials:* Researchers randomly assign people on a waiting list to therapy or to no therapy. Later, they evaluate everyone and compare the outcomes, with assessments by others who don't know whether therapy was given. Statistical digests of the results of many studies, or *meta-analyses,* give us the bottom-line result.

Therapists welcomed the first meta-analysis of some 475 psychotherapy outcome studies (Smith et al., 1980). It showed that the average therapy client ends up better off than 80 percent of the untreated individuals on waiting lists (**FIGURE 44.3**). The claim is modest—by definition, about 50 percent of untreated people also are better off than the average untreated person.

Dozens of subsequent summaries have now examined psychotherapy's effectiveness. Their verdict echoes the results of the earlier outcome studies: *Those not undergoing therapy often improve, but those undergoing therapy are more likely to improve, and to improve more quickly and with less risk of relapse.* Moreover, between the treatment sessions for depression and anxiety, many people experience sudden symptom reductions. Those "sudden gains" bode well for long-term improvement (Aderka et al., 2012).

LaunchPad To test your own therapeutic listening skills, visit LaunchPad's *Assess Your Strengths self-assessment quiz, Are You a Skilled "Opener"?*

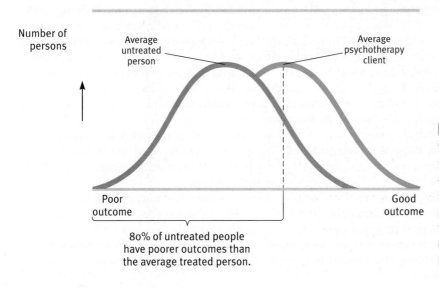

< FIGURE 44.3

Treatment versus no treatment These two normal distribution curves based on data from 475 studies show the improvement of untreated people and psychotherapy clients. The outcome for the average therapy client surpassed the outcome for 80 percent of the untreated people. (Data from Smith et al., 1980.)

Is psychotherapy also cost-effective? Again, the answer is *Yes*. Studies show that when people seek psychological treatment, their search for other medical treatment drops—by 16 percent in one digest of 91 studies (Chiles et al., 1999). Given the staggering annual cost of psychological disorders and substance abuse—including crime, accidents, lost work, and treatment—psychotherapy is a good investment, much like money spent on prenatal and well-baby care. Both *reduce* long-term costs. Boosting employees' psychological well-being can lower medical costs, improve work efficiency, and diminish absenteeism.

But note that the claim—that psychotherapy, *on average*, is somewhat effective—refers to no one therapy in particular. It is like reassuring lung-cancer patients that medical treatment of health problems is, "on average," somewhat effective. What people want to know is whether a *particular* treatment is effective for their specific problem.

RETRIEVE IT

• How might the *placebo effect* bias clients' and clinicians' appraisals of the effectiveness of psychotherapies?

ANSWER: The *placebo effect* is the healing power of *belief* in a treatment. Patients and therapists who expect a treatment to be effective may believe it was.

Which Psychotherapies Work Best?

 44-9 Are some psychotherapies more effective than others for specific disorders?

The early statistical summaries and surveys did not find that any one type of psychotherapy is generally better than others (Smith et al., 1977, 1980). Later studies have similarly found little connection between clients' outcomes and their clinicians' experience, training, supervision, and licensing (Luborsky et al., 2002; Wampold, 2007). A *Consumer Reports* survey illustrated this point by asking: Were clients treated by a psychiatrist, psychologist, or social worker? Were they seen in a group or individual context? Did the therapist have extensive or relatively limited training and experience? It didn't matter. Clients seemed equally satisfied (Seligman, 1995).

So, was the dodo bird in *Alice in Wonderland* right: "Everyone has won and all must have prizes"? Not quite. Some forms of therapy get prizes for effectively treating *particular* problems. Behavioral conditioning therapies have had especially good results with specific behavior problems, such as bed-wetting, phobias, compulsions, marital problems, and sexual dysfunctions (Baker et al., 2008; Hunsley & DiGiulio, 2002; Shadish & Baldwin, 2005). Psychodynamic therapy has helped treat depression and anxiety (Driessen et al., 2010; Leichsenring & Rabung, 2008; Shedler, 2010). With mild to moderate depression, nondirective (client-centered) counseling often helps (Cuijpers et al., 2013). And many studies confirm cognitive and cognitive-behavioral therapy's effectiveness (some say superiority) in coping with anxiety, posttraumatic stress disorder, and depression (Baker et al., 2008; De Los Reyes & Kazdin, 2009; Stewart & Chambliss, 2009; Tolin, 2010).

Moreover, we can say that therapy is most effective when the problem is clear-cut (Singer, 1981; Westen & Morrison, 2001). Those who experience phobias or panic, who are unassertive, or who are frustrated by sexual performance problems can hope for improvement. Those with less-focused problems, such as depression and anxiety, usually benefit in the short term but often relapse later. The more specific the problem, the greater the hope.

But no prizes—and little or no scientific support—go to certain other therapies (Arkowitz & Lilienfeld, 2006). We would all therefore be wise to avoid energy therapies that propose to manipulate people's invisible energy fields, recovered-memory therapies that aim to unearth "repressed memories" of early child abuse, and rebirthing therapies that engage people in reenacting the supposed trauma of their birth.

"Whatever differences in treatment efficacy exist, they appear to be extremely small, at best."

Bruce Wampold et al. (1997)

"Different sores have different salves."

English proverb

As with some medical treatments, it's possible for psychological treatments to be not only ineffective but also harmful—by making people worse or preventing their getting better (Barlow, 2010; Castonguay et al., 2010; Dimidjian & Hollon, 2010). The National Science and Technology Council cites the Scared Straight program (seeking to deter children and youth from crime) as an example of well-intentioned programs that have proved ineffective or even harmful.

The evaluation question—which therapies get prizes and which do not?—lies at the heart of what some call psychology's civil war. To what extent should science guide both clinical practice and the willingness of health care providers and insurers to pay for psychotherapy? On one side are research psychologists using scientific methods to extend the list of well-defined and validated therapies for various disorders. They decry clinicians who "give more weight to their personal experiences" (Baker et al., 2008). On the other side are nonscientist therapists who view their practice as more art than science, something that cannot be described in a manual or tested in an experiment. People are too complex and psychotherapy is too intuitive for such an approach, many therapists say.

Between these two factions stand the science-oriented clinicians calling for **evidence-based practice,** which has been endorsed by the American Psychological Association and others (2006; Lilienfeld et al., 2013). Therapists using this approach integrate the best available research with clinical expertise and with patient preferences and characteristics (**FIGURE 44.4**). After rigorous evaluation, clinicians apply therapies suited to their own skills and their patients' unique situations. Increasingly, insurer and government support for mental health services requires evidence-based practice.

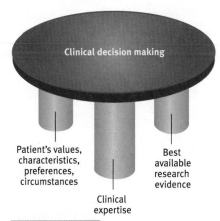

∧ FIGURE 44.4

Evidence-based clinical decision making Ideal clinical decision making can be visualized as a three-legged stool, upheld by research evidence, clinical expertise, and knowledge of the patient.

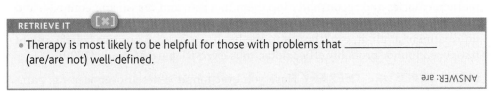

RETRIEVE IT [✖]

• Therapy is most likely to be helpful for those with problems that _____ (are/are not) well-defined.

ANSWER: are

Evaluating Alternative Therapies

44-10 How do alternative therapies fare under scientific scrutiny?

The tendency of many abnormal states of mind to return to normal, combined with the placebo effect (the healing power of mere belief in a treatment), creates fertile soil for pseudotherapies. Bolstered by anecdotes, boosted by the media, and broadcast on the Internet, alternative therapies—newer, nontraditional therapies, which often claim healing powers for various ailments—can spread like wildfire. In one national survey, 57 percent of those with a history of anxiety attacks and 54 percent of those with a history of depression had used alternative treatments, such as herbal medicine, massage, and spiritual healing (Kessler et al., 2001).

Proponents of alternative therapies often feel that their personal testimonials are evidence enough. But how well do these therapies stand up to scientific scrutiny? There is little evidence for or against most of them. Some, however, have been the subject of controlled research. Let's consider two. As we do, remember that sifting sense from nonsense requires the scientific attitude: being skeptical but not cynical, open to surprises but not gullible.

EYE MOVEMENT DESENSITIZATION AND REPROCESSING *EMDR (eye movement desensitization and reprocessing)* is a therapy adored by thousands and dismissed by thousands more as a sham—"an excellent vehicle for illustrating the differences between scientific and pseudoscientific therapy techniques," suggested James Herbert and six others (2000).

Psychologist Francine Shapiro (1989, 2007, 2012) developed EMDR while walking in a park and observing that anxious thoughts vanished as her eyes spontaneously darted about. Back in the clinic, she had people imagine traumatic scenes

evidence-based practice clinical decision making that integrates the best available research with clinical expertise and patient characteristics and preferences.

while she triggered eye movements by waving her finger in front of their eyes, supposedly enabling them to unlock and reprocess previously frozen memories. Tens of thousands of mental health professionals from more than 75 countries have since undergone training (EMDR, 2011). No new therapy has attracted so many devotees so quickly since Franz Anton Mesmer introduced hypnosis (then called *animal magnetism*) more than two centuries ago (also after feeling inspired by an outdoor experience).

Does EMDR work? Shapiro believes it does, and she cites four studies in which it worked for 84 to 100 percent of single-trauma victims (Shapiro, 1999, 2002). Moreover, the treatment need take no more than three 90-minute sessions. The Society of Clinical Psychology task force on empirically validated treatments has acknowledged that EMDR is "probably efficacious" for the treatment of nonmilitary posttraumatic stress disorder (Chambless et al., 1997; see also Bisson & Andrew, 2007; Rodenburg et al., 2009; Seidler & Wagner, 2006).

Why, wonder the skeptics, would rapidly moving one's eyes while recalling traumas be therapeutic? Some argue that the eye movements relax or distract patients, thus allowing memory-associated emotions to extinguish (Gunter & Bodner, 2008). Others believe the eye movements in themselves are *not* the therapeutic ingredient (nor is watching high-speed Ping-Pong therapeutic). Trials in which people imagined traumatic scenes and tapped a finger, or just stared straight ahead while the therapist's finger wagged, have also produced therapeutic results (Devilly, 2003). EMDR does work better than doing nothing, acknowledge the skeptics (Lilienfeld & Arkowitz, 2006/2007). But skeptics suspect that what is therapeutic is the combination of exposure therapy—repeatedly calling up traumatic memories and reconsolidating them in a safe and reassuring context—and perhaps some placebo effect. Had Mesmer's pseudotherapy been compared with no treatment at all, it, too (thanks to the healing power of positive belief), might have been found "probably efficacious," observed Richard McNally (1999).

"Studies indicate that EMDR is just as effective with fixed eyes. If that conclusion is right, what's useful in the therapy (chiefly behavioral desensitization) is not new, and what's new is superfluous."

Harvard Mental Health Letter, *2002*

LIGHT EXPOSURE THERAPY Have you ever found yourself oversleeping, gaining weight, and feeling lethargic during the dark mornings and overcast days of winter? Slowing down and conserving energy during the cold, barren winters likely gave our distant ancestors a survival advantage. For people today, however—especially for women and those living far from the equator—the wintertime blahs may constitute a seasonal pattern for major depressive disorder. To counteract these dark feelings, National Institute of Mental Health researchers in the early 1980s had an idea: Give people a timed daily dose of intense light. Sure enough, people reported feeling better.

Was light exposure a bright idea, or another dim-witted example of the placebo effect? Research illuminates the issue. One study exposed some people with a seasonal pattern in their depression symptoms to 90 minutes of bright light and others to a sham placebo treatment—a hissing "negative ion generator" about which the staff expressed similar enthusiasm (but which was generating nothing). After four weeks, 61 percent of those exposed to morning light had greatly improved, as had 50 percent of those exposed to evening light and 32 percent of those exposed to the placebo (Eastman et al., 1998). Other studies have found that 30 minutes of exposure to 10,000-lux white fluorescent light produced relief for more than half the people receiving morning light therapy (Flory et al., 2010; Terman et al.,

Light therapy To counteract winter depression, some people spend time each morning exposed to intense light that mimics natural outdoor light. Light boxes are available from health supply and lighting stores.

1998, 2001). From 20 carefully controlled trials we have a verdict (Golden et al., 2005; Wirz-Justice, 2009): Morning bright light *does* dim depression symptoms for many of those suffering in a seasonal pattern. Moreover, it does so as effectively as taking antidepressant drugs or undergoing cognitive-behavioral therapy (Lam et al., 2006; Rohan et al., 2007). The effects are clear in brain scans; light therapy sparks activity in a brain region that influences the body's arousal and hormones (Ishida et al., 2005).

RETRIEVE IT

• What is evidence-based clinical decision making?

ANSWER: Using this approach, therapists make decisions about treatment based on research evidence, clinical expertise, and knowledge of the client.

• Which of the following alternative therapies HAS shown promise as an effective treatment?

a. light therapy

b. rebirthing therapies

c. recovered-memory therapies

d. energy therapies

ANSWER: a

How Do Psychotherapies Help People?

 44-11 What three elements are shared by all forms of psychotherapy?

How can it be that therapists' training and experience do not seem to influence clients' outcomes? The answer seems to be that all psychotherapies offer three basic benefits (Frank, 1982; Goldfried & Padawer, 1982; Strupp, 1986; Wampold 2001, 2007).

HOPE FOR DEMORALIZED PEOPLE People seeking therapy typically feel anxious, depressed, self-disapproving, and incapable of turning things around. What any psychotherapy offers is the expectation that, with commitment from the therapy seeker, things can and will get better. This belief, apart from any therapy technique, may improve morale, create feelings of self-efficacy, and reduce symptoms (Corrigan, 2014; Prioleau et al., 1983).

A NEW PERSPECTIVE LEADING TO NEW BEHAVIORS Every psychotherapy offers people an explanation of their symptoms. Therapy is a new experience that can help people change their behaviors and their views of themselves. Armed with a believable fresh perspective, they may approach life with new energy.

AN EMPATHIC, TRUSTING, CARING RELATIONSHIP No matter what technique they use, effective psychotherapists are empathic. They seek to understand people's experience. They communicate care and concern. And they earn trust through respectful listening, reassurance, and guidance. These qualities were clear in recorded therapy sessions from 36 recognized master therapists (Goldfried et al., 1998). Some took a cognitive-behavioral approach. Others used psychodynamic principles. Regardless, they were strikingly similar during the most significant parts of their sessions. At key moments, the empathic therapists of both types would help clients evaluate themselves, link one aspect of their life with another, and gain insight into their interactions with others. The emotional bond between psychotherapist and client—the **therapeutic alliance**—helps explain why some therapists are more effective than others (Klein et al., 2003; Wampold, 2001). One U.S. National Institute of Mental Health depression-treatment study confirmed that the most effective therapists were those who were perceived as most empathic and caring and who established the closest therapeutic bonds with their clients (Blatt et al., 1996).

That all psychotherapies offer hope through a fresh perspective provided by a caring person is what also enables paraprofessionals (briefly trained caregivers) to assist so many troubled people so effectively (Christensen & Jacobson, 1994).

LaunchPad To test your own levels of hopefulness, visit LaunchPad's *Assess Your Strengths self-assessment quiz, Hope Scale.*

therapeutic alliance a bond of trust and mutual understanding between a therapist and client, who work together constructively to overcome the client's problem.

A caring relationship Effective counselors, such as this chaplain working aboard a ship, form a bond of trust with the people they are serving.

Steve Szydlowski/KRT/Newscom

These three common elements are also part of what the growing numbers of self-help support groups offer their members. And they are part of what traditional healers have offered (Jackson, 1992). Healers everywhere—special people to whom others disclose their suffering, whether psychiatrists, witch doctors, or shamans—have listened in order to understand and to empathize, reassure, advise, console, interpret, or explain (Torrey, 1986). Such qualities may explain why people who feel supported by close relationships—who enjoy the fellowship and friendship of caring people—have been less likely to need or seek therapy (Frank, 1982; O'Connor & Brown, 1984).

* * *

To recap, people who seek help usually improve. So do many of those who do not undergo psychotherapy, and that is a tribute to our human resourcefulness and our capacity to care for one another. Nevertheless, though the therapist's orientation and experience appear not to matter much, people who receive some psychotherapy usually improve more than those who do not. People with clear-cut, specific problems tend to improve the most.

RETRIEVE IT [x]

- Those who undergo psychotherapy are _____ (more/less) likely to show improvement than those who do not undergo psychotherapy.

ANSWER: more

Culture and Values in Psychotherapy

◁ ▷ 44-12 How do culture and values influence the therapist-client relationship?

All psychotherapies offer hope. Nearly all psychotherapists attempt to enhance their clients' sensitivity, openness, personal responsibility, and sense of purpose (Jensen & Bergin, 1988). But therapists also differ from one another and may differ from their clients (Delaney et al., 2007; Kelly, 1990).

These differences can create a mismatch when a therapist from one culture interacts with a client from another. In North America, Europe, and Australia, for example, many therapists reflect the majority culture's *individualism,* which often gives priority to personal desires and identity. Clients with a *collectivist* perspective, as with many from Asian cultures, may assume people will be more mindful of others' expectations. These clients may have trouble relating to therapies that require them to think only of their own well-being.

Such differences help explain minority populations' reluctance to use mental health services, and their tendency to prematurely terminate therapy (Chen et al.,

2009; Sue, 2006). In one experiment, Asian-American clients matched with counselors who shared their cultural values (rather than mismatched with those who did not) perceived more counselor empathy and felt a stronger alliance with the counselor (Kim et al., 2005). Recognizing that therapists and clients may differ in their values, communication styles, and language, all American Psychological Association–accredited therapy-training programs provide training in cultural sensitivity and welcome members of underrepresented cultural groups.

Therapist and client may also have differing religious perspectives. Highly religious people may prefer and benefit from religiously similar therapists (Masters, 2010; Smith et al., 2007; Wade et al., 2006). They may have trouble establishing an emotional bond with a therapist who does not share their values. People living in "cultures of honor"—which prize being strong and tough—tend to be more reluctant to seek mental health care, as it may be viewed as an admission of weakness (Brown et al., 2014).

Finding a Mental Health Professional

44-13 What should a person look for when selecting a therapist?

Life for everyone is marked by a mix of serenity and stress, blessing and bereavement, good moods and bad. So, when should we seek a mental health professional's help? The American Psychological Association offers these common trouble signals:

- Feelings of hopelessness
- Deep and lasting depression
- Self-destructive behavior, such as substance abuse
- Disruptive fears
- Sudden mood shifts
- Thoughts of suicide
- Compulsive rituals, such as hand washing
- Sexual difficulties
- Hearing voices or seeing things that others don't experience

In looking for a therapist, you may want to have a preliminary consultation with two or three. College health centers are generally good starting points, and may offer some free services. You can describe your problem and learn each therapist's treatment approach. You can ask questions about the therapist's values, credentials (**TABLE 44.3**), and fees. And you can assess your own feelings about each of them. The emotional bond between therapist and client is perhaps the most important factor in effective therapy.

∨ TABLE 44.3

Therapists and Their Training

Type	Description
Clinical psychologists	Most are psychologists with a Ph.D. (includes research training) or Psy.D. (focuses on therapy) supplemented by a supervised internship and, often, postdoctoral training. About half work in agencies and institutions, half in private practice.
Psychiatrists	Psychiatrists are physicians who specialize in the treatment of psychological disorders. Not all psychiatrists have had extensive training in psychotherapy, but as M.D.s or D.O.s they can prescribe medications. Thus, they tend to see those with the most serious problems. Many have their own private practice.
Clinical or psychiatric social workers	A two-year master of social work graduate program plus postgraduate supervision prepares some social workers to offer psychotherapy, mostly to people with everyday personal and family problems. About half have earned the National Association of Social Workers' designation of clinical social worker.
Counselors	Marriage and family counselors specialize in problems arising from family relations. Clergy provide counseling to countless people. Abuse counselors work with substance abusers and with spouse and child abusers and their victims. Mental health and other counselors may be required to have a two-year master's degree.

MODULE 44 REVIEW   Introduction to Therapy and the Psychological Therapies

◉ Learning Objectives

Test Yourself by taking a moment to answer each of these Learning Objective Questions (repeated here from within the module). Then turn to Appendix D, Complete Module Reviews, to check your answers. Research suggests that trying to answer these questions on your own will improve your long-term memory of the concepts (McDaniel et al., 2009).

44-1 How do *psychotherapy* and the *biomedical therapies* differ?

44-2 What are the goals and techniques of psychoanalysis, and how have they been adapted in psychodynamic therapy?

44-3 What are the basic themes of humanistic therapy? What are the specific goals and techniques of Rogers' client-centered approach?

44-4 How does the basic assumption of behavior therapy differ from the assumptions of psychodynamic and humanistic therapies? What techniques are used in exposure therapies and aversive conditioning?

44-5 What is the main premise of therapy based on operant conditioning principles, and what are the views of its proponents and critics?

44-6 What are the goals and techniques of cognitive therapy and of cognitive-behavioral therapy?

44-7 What are the aims and benefits of group and family therapies?

44-8 Does psychotherapy work? How can we know?

44-9 Are some psychotherapies more effective than others for specific disorders?

44-10 How do alternative therapies fare under scientific scrutiny?

44-11 What three elements are shared by all forms of psychotherapy?

44-12 How do culture and values influence the therapist-client relationship?

44-13 What should a person look for when selecting a therapist?

▣ Terms and Concepts to Remember

Test yourself on these terms by trying to write down the definition in your own words before flipping back to the referenced page to check your answers.

psychotherapy, p. 570

biomedical therapy, p. 570

eclectic approach, p. 570

psychoanalysis, p. 570

resistance, p. 571

interpretation, p. 571

transference, p. 571

psychodynamic therapy, p. 572

insight therapies, p. 572

client-centered therapy, p. 573

active listening, p. 573

unconditional positive regard, p. 574

behavior therapy, p. 574

counterconditioning, p. 575

exposure therapies, p. 575

systematic desensitization, p. 575

virtual reality exposure therapy, p. 576

aversive conditioning, p. 576

token economy, p. 577

cognitive therapy, p. 578

cognitive-behavioral therapy (CBT), p. 581

group therapy, p. 582

family therapy, p. 582

evidence-based practice, p. 587

therapeutic alliance, p. 589

[✱] Experience the Testing Effect

Test yourself repeatedly throughout your studies. This will not only help you figure out what you know and don't know; the testing itself will help you learn and remember the information more effectively thanks to the *testing effect*.

1. A therapist who helps patients search for the unconscious roots of their problem and offers interpretations of their behaviors, feelings, and dreams is drawing from
   a. psychoanalysis.
   b. humanistic therapies.
   c. client-centered therapy.
   d. behavior therapy.

2. _____ therapies are designed to help individuals discover the thoughts and feelings that guide their motivation and behavior.

3. Compared with psychoanalysts, humanistic therapists are more likely to emphasize
   a. hidden or repressed feelings.
   b. childhood experiences.
   c. psychological disorders.
   d. self-fulfillment and growth.

4. A therapist who restates and clarifies the client's statements is practicing _____ _____.

5. The goal of behavior therapy is to
   a. identify and treat the underlying causes of the problem.
   b. improve learning and insight.
   c. eliminate the unwanted behavior.
   d. improve communication and social sensitivity.

6. Behavior therapies often use _____ techniques, such as systematic desensitization and aversive conditioning, to encourage clients to produce new responses to old stimuli.

7. The technique of _____ _____ teaches people to relax in the presence of progressively more anxiety-provoking stimuli.

8. After a near-fatal car accident, Rico developed such an intense fear of driving on the freeway that he takes lengthy alternative routes to work each day. Which psychological therapy might best help Rico overcome his phobia, and why?

9. At a treatment center, people who display a desired behavior receive coins that they can later exchange for other rewards. This is an example of a(n) _____ _____.

10. Cognitive therapy has been especially effective in treating
    a. nail biting.
    b. phobias.
    c. alcohol use disorder.
    d. depression.

11. _____-_____ therapy helps people to change their self-defeating ways of thinking and to act out those changes in their daily behavior.

12. In family therapy, the therapist assumes that
    a. only one family member needs to change.
    b. each person's actions trigger reactions from other family members.
    c. dysfunctional family behaviors are based largely on genetic factors.
    d. therapy is most effective when clients are treated apart from the family unit.

13. The most enthusiastic or optimistic view of the effectiveness of psychotherapy comes from
    a. outcome research.
    b. randomized clinical trials.
    c. reports of clinicians and clients.
    d. a government study of treatment for depression.

14. Studies show that _____ therapy is the most effective treatment for most psychological disorders.
    a. behavior
    b. humanistic
    c. psychodynamic
    d. no one type of

15. What are the three components of evidence-based practice?

16. How does the placebo effect bias patients' attitudes about the effectiveness of various therapies?

Find answers to these questions in Appendix E, in the back of the book.

Use 🅐 LearningCurve to create your personalized study plan, which will direct you to the resources that will help you most in 🅐 LaunchPad.

The Biomedical Therapies and Preventing Psychological Disorders

Psychotherapy is one way to treat psychological disorders. The other is **biomedical therapy**—physically changing the brain's functioning by altering its chemistry with drugs; affecting its circuitry with electrical stimulation, magnetic impulses, or psychosurgery; or influencing its responses with lifestyle changes. By far the most widely used biomedical treatments today are the drug therapies. Primary care providers prescribe most drugs for anxiety and depression, followed by psychiatrists and, in some states, psychologists.

Drug Therapies

👁 45-1 What are the drug therapies? How do double-blind studies help researchers evaluate a drug's effectiveness?

Since the 1950s, discoveries in **psychopharmacology** (the study of drug effects on mind and behavior) have revolutionized the treatment of people with severe disorders. Thanks to drug therapy and support from community mental health

> **biomedical therapy** prescribed medications or procedures that act directly on the person's physiology.
>
> **psychopharmacology** the study of the effects of drugs on mind and behavior.

"Our psychopharmacologist is a genius."

Perhaps you can guess an occasional side effect of L-dopa, a drug that raises dopamine levels for Parkinson's patients: hallucinations.

programs, today's resident population of U.S. state and county mental hospitals has dropped to a small fraction of what it was a half-century ago. For some who are unable to care for themselves, however, release from hospitals has meant homelessness.

Many new treatments are greeted by an initial wave of enthusiasm as many people apparently improve. But that enthusiasm often diminishes after researchers subtract the rates of (1) normal recovery among untreated persons and (2) recovery due to the placebo effect, which arises from the positive expectations of patients and mental health workers alike. Even mere exposure to advertising about a drug's supposed effectiveness can increase its effect (Kamenica et al., 2013). To control for these influences when testing a new drug, researchers give half the patients the drug, and the other half a similar-appearing placebo. Because neither the staff nor the patients know who gets which, this is called a *double-blind procedure*. The good news: In double-blind studies, several types of drugs lessen psychological disorders.

Antipsychotic Drugs

An accidental discovery launched a treatment revolution for people with *psychosis*. The discovery was that some drugs used for other medical purposes calmed the hallucinations or delusions that are part of these patients' split from reality. First-generation **antipsychotic drugs,** such as chlorpromazine (sold as Thorazine), reduce patients' overreactions to irrelevant stimuli. Thus, they provide the most help to people experiencing positive symptoms of schizophrenia, such as auditory hallucinations and paranoia (Lehman et al., 1998; Lenzenweger et al., 1989).

The molecules of most conventional antipsychotic drugs are similar enough to molecules of the neurotransmitter dopamine to occupy its receptor sites and block its activity. This finding reinforces the idea that an overactive dopamine system contributes to schizophrenia.

Antipsychotics also have powerful side effects. Some produce sluggishness, tremors, and twitches similar to those of Parkinson's disease (Kaplan & Saddock, 1989). Long-term use of antipsychotics can produce *tardive dyskinesia,* with involuntary movements of the facial muscles (such as grimacing), tongue, and limbs. Although not more effective in controlling schizophrenia symptoms, many of the newer-generation antipsychotics, such as risperidone (Risperdal) and olanzapine (Zyprexa), work best for those with severe symptoms and have fewer side effects (Furukawa et al., 2015). These drugs may, however, increase the risk of obesity and diabetes (Buchanan et al., 2010; Tiihonen et al., 2009).

Despite their drawbacks, antipsychotics, combined with life-skills programs and family support, have given new hope to many people with schizophrenia (Guo, 2010). Hundreds of thousands of patients have left the wards of mental hospitals and returned to work and to near-normal lives (Leucht et al., 2003).

Antianxiety Drugs

Like alcohol, **antianxiety drugs,** such as Xanax or Ativan, depress central nervous system activity (and so should not be used in combination with alcohol). Antianxiety drugs are often successfully used in combination with psychological therapy. Experiments indicate that a drug can enhance exposure therapy's extinction of learned fears and help relieve the symptoms of posttraumatic stress disorder and obsessive-compulsive disorder (Davis, 2005; Kushner et al., 2007).

One criticism made of antianxiety drugs is that they may reduce symptoms without resolving underlying problems, especially if used as an ongoing treatment. "Popping a Xanax" at the first sign of tension can create a learned response; the immediate relief reinforces a person's tendency to take drugs when anxious. Anxiety drugs can also be addictive. Regular users who stop taking antianxiety drugs may experience increased anxiety, insomnia, and other withdrawal symptoms.

antipsychotic drugs drugs used to treat schizophrenia and other forms of severe thought disorder.

antianxiety drugs drugs used to control anxiety and agitation.

antidepressant drugs drugs used to treat depression, anxiety disorders, obsessive-compulsive disorder, and post-traumatic stress disorder. (Several widely used antidepressant drugs are *selective serotonin reuptake inhibitors—SSRIs.*)

Over the dozen years at the end of the twentieth century, the rate of outpatient treatment for anxiety disorders, obsessive-compulsive disorder, and posttraumatic stress disorder nearly doubled. The proportion of psychiatric patients receiving medication during that time increased from 52 to 70 percent (Olfson et al., 2004). And the new standard drug treatment for anxiety disorders? Antidepressants.

Antidepressant Drugs

The **antidepressant drugs** were named for their ability to lift people up from a state of depression. Until recently, this was their main use. These drugs are now increasingly used to treat anxiety disorders, obsessive-compulsive disorder, and posttraumatic stress disorder (Wetherell et al., 2013). Many of these drugs work by increasing the availability of neurotransmitters, such as norepinephrine or serotonin, which elevate arousal and mood and are scarce when a person experiences feelings of depression or anxiety.

© John Greim/Age fotostoc

The most commonly prescribed drugs in this group, including Prozac and its cousins Zoloft and Paxil, work by blocking the normal reuptake of excess serotonin from synapses (**FIGURE 45.1**). Given their use in treating disorders other than depression, from anxiety to strokes, these drugs are most often called *SSRIs—selective serotonin reuptake inhibitors* (rather than antidepressants) (Kramer, 2011).

Some of the older antidepressant drugs work by blocking the reabsorption or breakdown of both norepinephrine and serotonin. Though effective, these dual-action drugs have more potential side effects, such as dry mouth, weight gain, hypertension, or dizzy spells (Anderson, 2000; Mulrow, 1999). Administering them by means of a patch, which bypasses the intestines and liver, helps reduce such side effects (Bodkin & Amsterdam, 2002).

Be advised: Patients with depression who begin taking antidepressants do not wake up the next morning singing "It's a beautiful day!" Although the drugs begin to influence neurotransmission within hours, their full psychological effect often requires four weeks (and may involve a side effect of diminished sexual desire). One possible reason for the delay is that increased serotonin promotes new synapses plus *neurogenesis*—the birth of new brain cells, reversing stress-induced neuron loss (Launay et al., 2011). Researchers are also exploring the possibility of quicker-acting antidepressants. One, ketamine, blocks hyperactive receptors for glutamate, a neurotransmitter, and causes a burst of new synapses—but with

∨ FIGURE 45.1

Biology of antidepressants Shown here is the action of Prozac, which partially blocks the reuptake of serotonin.

Prozac partially blocks normal reuptake of the neurotransmitter serotonin; excess serotonin in synapse enhances its mood-lifting effect.

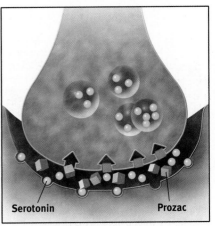

Message is sent across synaptic gap.

Message is received; excess serotonin molecules are reabsorbed by sending neuron.

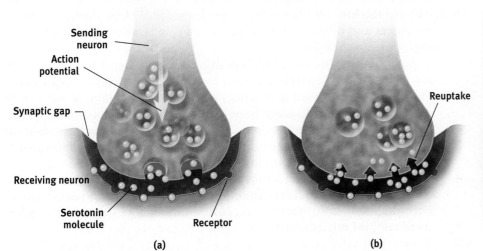

(a)   (b)   (c)

"If this doesn't help you don't worry, it's a placebo."

"No twisted thought without a twisted molecule."

Attributed to psychologist Ralph Gerard

IMMERSIVE LEARNING To better understand how clinical researchers have evaluated drug therapies, complete LaunchPad's *How Would You Know How Well Antidepressants Work?*

"First of all I think you should know that last quarter's sales figures are interfering with my mood-stabilizing drugs."

possible side effects such as hallucinations (Grimm & Scheidegger, 2013; McGirr et al., 2015; Naughton et al., 2014).

Antidepressant drugs are not the only way to give the body a lift. Aerobic exercise, which calms people who feel anxious and energizes those who feel depressed, does about as much good as antidepressant drugs for most people with mild to moderate depression, and has additional positive side effects.

Cognitive therapy, which helps people reverse their habits of thinking negatively, can boost the drug-aided relief from depression and reduce posttreatment relapses (Hollon et al., 2002; Keller et al., 2000; Vittengl et al., 2007). Antidepressant drugs work from the bottom up to affect the emotion-forming limbic system. Cognitive-behavioral therapy works from the top down to alter frontal lobe activity and change thought processes. Together, they can attack depression (and anxiety) from both directions (Cuijpers et al., 2010; Hollon et al., 2014; Kennard et al., 2014; Walkup et al., 2008).

Researchers generally agree that people with depression often improve after a month on antidepressant drugs. But after allowing for natural recovery and the placebo effect, how big is the drug effect? Not big, report some researchers (Kirsch et al., 1998, 2002, 2010, 2014). In double-blind clinical trials, placebos produced improvement comparable with about 75 percent of the active drug's effect. In a follow-up review that included unpublished clinical trials, the antidepressant drug effect was again modest (Kirsch et al., 2008). The placebo effect was less for those with severe depression, which made the added benefit of the drug somewhat greater for them. "Given these results, there seems little reason to prescribe antidepressant medication to any but the most severely depressed patients, unless alternative treatments have failed," Irving Kirsch concluded (BBC, 2008). A newer analysis confirms that the antidepressant benefit compared to placebos is "minimal or nonexistent, on average, in patients with mild or moderate symptoms." For those folks, aerobic exercise or psychotherapy is often effective. But among patients with "very severe" depression, the medication advantage becomes "substantial" (Fournier et al., 2010).

Mood-Stabilizing Medications

In addition to antipsychotic, antianxiety, and antidepressant drugs, psychiatrists have *mood-stabilizing drugs* in their arsenal. One of them, Depakote, was originally used to treat epilepsy. It was also found effective in controlling the manic episodes associated with bipolar disorder. Another, the simple salt *lithium*, effectively levels the emotional highs and lows of this disorder. Kay Redfield Jamison (1995, pp. 88–89) described the effect: "Lithium prevents my seductive but disastrous highs, diminishes my depressions, clears out the wool and webbing from my disordered thinking, slows me down, gentles me out, keeps me from ruining my career and relationships, keeps me out of a hospital, alive, and makes psychotherapy possible."

Australian physician John Cade discovered the benefits of lithium in the 1940s when he administered it to a patient with severe mania and the patient became well in less than a week (Snyder, 1986). About 7 in 10 people with bipolar disorder benefit from a long-term daily dose of this cheap salt (Solomon et al., 1995). Their risk of suicide is but one-sixth that of people with bipolar disorder who are not taking lithium (Oquendo et al., 2011). Naturally occurring lithium in drinking water has correlated with lower suicide rates (across 18 Japanese cities and towns) and lower crime rates (across 27 Texas counties) (Ohgami et al., 2009; Schrauzer & Shrestha, 1990, 2010; Terao et al., 2010). Although we do not fully understand why, lithium works.

• How do researchers evaluate the effectiveness of particular drug therapies?

ANSWER: Researchers assign people to treatment and no-treatment conditions to see if those who receive the drug therapy improve more than those who don't. *Double-blind* controlled studies are most effective. If neither the therapist nor the client knows which participants have received the drug treatment, then any difference between the treated and untreated groups will reflect the drug treatment's actual effect.

• The drugs given most often to treat depression are called _____. Schizophrenia is often treated with _____ drugs.

ANSWERS: antidepressants; antipsychotic

electroconvulsive therapy (ECT) a biomedical therapy for severely depressed patients in which a brief electric current is sent through the brain of an anesthetized patient.

Brain Stimulation

45-2 How are brain stimulation and psychosurgery used in treating specific disorders?

Electroconvulsive Therapy

Another biomedical treatment, **electroconvulsive therapy (ECT),** manipulates the brain by shocking it. When ECT was first introduced in 1938, the wide-awake patient was strapped to a table and jolted with roughly 100 volts of electricity to the brain. The procedure, which produced racking convulsions and brief unconsciousness, gained a barbaric image. Although that image lingers, today's ECT is much kinder and gentler. The patient receives a general anesthetic and a muscle relaxant to prevent convulsions. A psychiatrist then delivers to the patient's brain 30 to 60 seconds of electric current in briefer pulses, sometimes only to the brain's right side (**FIGURE 45.2**). Within 30 minutes, the patient awakens and remembers nothing of the treatment or of the preceding hours.

The medical use of electricity is an ancient practice. Physicians treated the Roman Emperor Claudius (10 B.C.E.–54 C.E.) for headaches by pressing electric eels to his temples.

Stimulating electrodes
Recording EEG
ECT device
Ground
Recording
ECG (heart rate)
Blood pressure cuff
Intravenous line (sedative, muscle relaxant)
Oximeter (blood-oxygen monitor)
Blood pressure cuff
EMG (records electrical activity from the muscles)

❮ FIGURE 45.2

Electroconvulsive therapy Although controversial, ECT is often an effective treatment for depression that does not respond to drug therapy. ("Electroconvulsive" is no longer accurate, because patients are now given a drug that prevents bodily convulsions.)

Study after study confirms that ECT can effectively treat severe depression in "treatment-resistant" patients who have not responded to drug therapy (Bailine et al., 2010; Fink, 2009; Lima et al., 2013). After three such sessions each week for two to four weeks, 80 percent or more of those receiving ECT improve markedly. They show some memory loss for the treatment period but no apparent brain damage. Modern ECT causes less memory disruption than earlier versions did (HMHL, 2007). ECT also reduces suicidal thoughts and has been credited with saving many from suicide (Kellner et al., 2005). A *Journal of the American Medical Association* editorial concluded that "the results of ECT in treating severe depression are among the most positive treatment effects in all of medicine" (Glass, 2001).

How does ECT relieve severe depression? After more than 70 years, no one knows for sure. One patient likened ECT to the smallpox vaccine, which was saving lives before we knew how it worked. Perhaps the brief electric current calms neural centers where overactivity produces depression. Some research indicates that ECT works by weakening connections in a "hyperconnected" neural hub in the left frontal lobe (Perrin et al., 2012).

No matter how impressive the results, the idea of electrically shocking people still strikes many as barbaric, especially given our ignorance about why ECT works. Moreover, about 4 in 10 people treated with ECT relapse into depression within six months (Kellner et al., 2006). Nevertheless, in the minds of many psychiatrists and patients, ECT is a lesser evil than severe depression's misery, anguish, and risk of suicide. As research psychologist Norman Endler (1982) reported after ECT alleviated his deep depression, "A miracle had happened in two weeks."

Alternative Neurostimulation Therapies

Two other neural stimulation techniques—magnetic stimulation and deep brain stimulation—also treat the depressed brain.

MAGNETIC STIMULATION Depressed moods sometimes improve when repeated pulses surge through a magnetic coil held close to a person's skull (**FIGURE 45.3**). The painless procedure—called **repetitive transcranial magnetic stimulation (rTMS)**—is performed on wide-awake patients over several weeks. Unlike ECT, the rTMS procedure produces no brain seizures, memory loss, or other serious side effects aside from possible headaches.

> "I used to . . . be unable to shake the dread even when I was feeling good, because I knew the bad feelings would return. ECT has wiped away that foreboding. It has given me a sense of control, of hope."
>
> *Kitty Dukakis (2006)*

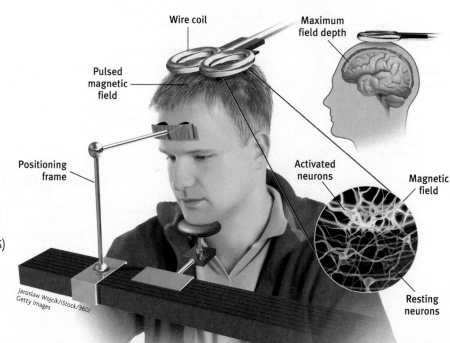

> FIGURE 45.3

Magnets for the mind Repetitive transcranial magnetic stimulation (rTMS) sends a painless magnetic field through the skull to the surface of the cortex. Pulses can be used to alter activity in various cortical areas.

Jaroslaw Wojcik/iStock/360/ Getty Images

Initial studies have found a small antidepressant benefit of rTMS (Lepping et al., 2014). How it works is unclear. One possible explanation is that the stimulation energizes the brain's left frontal lobe (Helmuth, 2001). Repeated stimulation may cause nerve cells to form new functioning circuits through the process of long-term potentiation.

DEEP BRAIN STIMULATION Other patients whose depression has resisted both drugs that flood the body and ECT that jolts at least half the brain have benefited from an experimental treatment pinpointing a brain depression center. Neuroscientist Helen Mayberg and her colleagues (2005, 2006, 2007, 2009) have been focusing on a neural hub that bridges the thinking frontal lobes to the limbic system. This area, which is overactive in the brain of a depressed or temporarily sad person, calms when treated by ECT or antidepressants. To experimentally excite neurons that inhibit this negative emotion-feeding activity, Mayberg drew upon the deep brain stimulation technology sometimes used to treat Parkinson's tremors. Since 2003, she and others have treated some 200 depressed patients with deep brain stimulation via implanted electrodes in the neural "sadness center" (Lozano & Mayberg, 2015). About one-third reportedly have responded "extremely well" and another 30 percent have modestly improved (Underwood, 2013). Some felt suddenly more aware and became more talkative and engaged; others improved only slightly, if at all. Future research will explore whether Mayberg has discovered a switch that can lift depression. Other researchers are following up on reports that deep brain stimulation can offer relief to people with obsessive-compulsive disorder and with drug and alcohol addictions (Corse et al., 2013; Kisely et al., 2014; Luigjes et al., 2012).

A meta-analysis of 17 clinical experiments found that one other stimulation procedure alleviates depression: massage therapy (Hou et al., 2010).

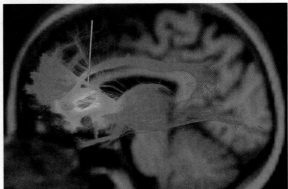

A depression switch? By comparing the brains of patients with and without depression, researcher Helen Mayberg identified a brain area (highlighted in red) that appears active in people who are depressed or sad, and whose activity may be calmed by deep brain stimulation.

RETRIEVE IT [✖]

- Severe depression that has not responded to other therapy may be treated with _____ _____, which can cause brain seizures and memory loss. More moderate neural stimulation techniques designed to help alleviate depression include _____ _____ magnetic stimulation and _____ _____ stimulation.

ANSWERS: electroconvulsive therapy (ECT); repetitive transcranial; deep brain

---

Psychosurgery

Because its effects are irreversible, **psychosurgery**—surgery that removes or destroys brain tissue—is the most drastic and least-used biomedical intervention for changing thoughts and behavior. In the 1930s, Portuguese physician Egas Moniz developed what would become the best-known psychosurgical operation: the **lobotomy.** Moniz cut nerves connecting the frontal lobes with the emotion-controlling centers of the inner brain. His crude but easy and inexpensive procedure took only about 10 minutes. After shocking the patient into a coma, he (and later, other neurosurgeons) would hammer an instrument shaped like an ice pick through the top of each eye socket, driving it into the brain. He then wiggled the instrument to sever connections running up to the frontal lobes. Tens of thousands of severely disturbed people were given lobotomies between 1936 and 1954 (Valenstein, 1986).

Although the intention was simply to disconnect emotion from thought, the effect was often more drastic. A lobotomy usually decreased the person's misery or tension. But it also produced a permanently listless, immature, uncreative personality. During the 1950s, after some 35,000 people had been lobotomized in the

repetitive transcranial magnetic stimulation (rTMS) the application of repeated pulses of magnetic energy to the brain; used to stimulate or suppress brain activity.

psychosurgery surgery that removes or destroys brain tissue in an effort to change behavior.

lobotomy a psychosurgical procedure once used to calm uncontrollably emotional or violent patients. The procedure cut the nerves connecting the frontal lobes to the emotion-controlling centers of the inner brain.

Failed lobotomy This 1940 photo shows Rosemary Kennedy (center) at age 22, with brother (and future U.S. president) John and sister Jean. A year later her father, on medical advice, approved a lobotomy that was promised to control her reportedly violent mood swings. The procedure left her confined to a hospital with an infantile mentality until her death in 2005 at age 86.

New York Times Co./Getty Images

United States alone, calming drugs became available and psychosurgery became scorned—as in the saying sometimes attributed to W. C. Fields that "I'd rather have a bottle in front of me than a frontal lobotomy."

Today, lobotomies are history. More precise, microscale psychosurgery is sometimes used in extreme cases. For example, if a patient has uncontrollable seizures, surgeons can destroy the specific nerve clusters that cause or transmit the convulsions. MRI-guided precision surgery is also occasionally done to cut the circuits involved in severe obsessive-compulsive disorder (Carey, 2009, 2011; Sachdev & Sachdev, 1997). Because these procedures are irreversible, neurosurgeons perform them only as a last resort.

Forest bathing In several small studies, Japanese researchers have found that walks in the woods—a practice called *shinrin-yoku,* or forest bathing—help lower stress hormone and blood pressure levels (Phillips, 2011).

©Randy Faris/Corbis

Therapeutic Lifestyle Change

45-3 How, by taking care of themselves with a healthy lifestyle, might people find some relief from depression? How does this reinforce the idea that we are biopsychosocial systems?

The effectiveness of the biomedical therapies reminds us of a fundamental lesson: We find it convenient to talk of separate psychological and biological influences, but everything psychological is also biological. Every thought and feeling depends on the functioning brain. Every creative idea, every moment of joy or anger, every period of depression emerges from the electrochemical activity of the living brain. The influence is two-way: When psychotherapy relieves obsessive-compulsive behavior, PET scans reveal a calmer brain (Schwartz et al., 1996).

For years, we have trusted our bodies to physicians and our minds to psychiatrists and psychologists. That neat separation no longer seems valid. Stress affects body chemistry and health. Anxiety disorders, obsessive-compulsive disorder, posttraumatic stress disorder, major depressive disorder, bipolar disorder, and schizophrenia are all biological events. As we have seen over and again, *a human being is an integrated biopsychosocial system.* Thus, our lifestyle—our exercise, nutrition, relationships, recreation, relaxation, and religious or spiritual engagement—affects our mental health (Walsh, 2011).

That lesson has been applied by Stephen Ilardi (2009) in training seminars promoting *therapeutic lifestyle change.* Human brains and bodies were designed for physical activity and social engagement, he notes. Our ancestors hunted, gathered, and built in groups. Indeed, those whose way of life entails strenuous physical activity, strong community ties, sunlight exposure, and plenty of sleep (think of foraging bands in Papua New Guinea, or Amish farming communities in North America) rarely experience depression. For both children and adults, outdoor activity in natural environments—perhaps a walk in the woods—reduces stress and promotes health (MacKerron & Mourato, 2013; NEEF, n.d., Phillips, 2011). "We were never designed for the sedentary, indoor, sleep-deprived, socially-isolated, fast-food-laden, frenetic pace of modern life," says Ilardi (2014).

Ilardi was also impressed by research showing that regular aerobic exercise rivals the healing power of antidepressant drugs, and that a complete night's sleep boosts mood and energy. So he invited small groups of people with depression to undergo a 12-week training program with the following goals:

- *Aerobic exercise,* 30 minutes a day, at least three times weekly (increases fitness and vitality, stimulates endorphins)

- *Adequate sleep,* with a goal of 7 to 8 hours a night (increases energy and alertness, boosts immunity)

- *Light exposure,* 15 to 30 minutes each morning with a light box (amplifies arousal, influences hormones)

- *Social connection,* with less alone time and at least two meaningful social engagements weekly (helps satisfy the human need to belong)

- *Anti-rumination,* by identifying and redirecting negative thoughts (enhances positive thinking)

- *Nutritional supplements,* including a daily fish oil supplement with omega-3 fatty acids (supports healthy brain functioning)

In one study of 74 people, 77 percent of those who completed the program experienced relief from depressive symptoms, compared with 19 percent in those assigned to a treatment-as-usual control condition. Future research will seek to replicate this striking result of lifestyle change. Researchers will also try to identify which parts of the treatment produce the therapeutic effect. There is wisdom in the Latin adage *Mens sana in corpore sano:* "A healthy mind in a healthy body." **(FIGURE 45.4)**

TABLE 45.1 summarizes selected biomedical therapies.

Nicole Hill/Rubberball/ Getty Images

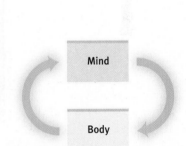

▲ FIGURE 45.4

Mind-body interaction The biomedical therapies assume that mind and body are a unit: Affect one and you will affect the other.

∨ TABLE 45.1

Comparing Biomedical Therapies

Therapy	Presumed Problem	Therapy Aim	Therapy Technique
Drug therapies	Neurotransmitter malfunction	Control symptoms of psychological disorders.	Alter brain chemistry through drugs.
Brain stimulation	Severe, treatment-resistant depression	Alleviate depression that is unresponsive to drug therapy.	Stimulate brain through electroconvulsive shock, magnetic impulses, or deep brain stimulation.
Psychosurgery	Brain malfunction	Relieve severe disorders.	Remove or destroy brain tissue.
Therapeutic lifestyle change	Stress and unhealthy lifestyle	Restore healthy biological state.	Alter lifestyle through adequate exercise, sleep, and other changes.

Preventing Psychological Disorders and Building Resilience

45-4 What is the rationale for preventive mental health programs, and why is it important to develop resilience?

Psychotherapies and biomedical therapies tend to locate the cause of psychological disorders within the person. We infer that people who act cruelly must be cruel and that people who act "crazy" must be "sick." We attach labels to such people, thereby distinguishing them from "normal" folks. It follows, then, that we try to treat "abnormal" people by giving them insight into their problems, by changing their thinking, by helping them gain control with drugs.

There is an alternative viewpoint: We could interpret many psychological disorders as understandable responses to a disturbing and stressful society. According to this view, it is not just the person who needs treatment, but also the person's social context. Better to prevent a problem by reforming a sick situation and by developing people's coping competencies than to wait for and treat problems.

Preventive Mental Health

A story about the rescue of a drowning person from a rushing river illustrates this viewpoint: Having successfully administered first aid to the first victim, the rescuer spots another struggling person and pulls her out, too. After a half-dozen repetitions, the rescuer suddenly turns and starts running away while the river sweeps yet another floundering person into view. "Aren't you going to rescue that fellow?" asks a bystander. "Heck no," the rescuer replies. "I'm going upstream to find out what's pushing all these people in."

Preventive mental health is upstream work. It seeks to prevent psychological casualties by identifying and alleviating the conditions that cause them. As George Albee (1986; also Yoshikawa et al., 2012) pointed out, there is abundant evidence that poverty, meaningless work, constant criticism, unemployment, racism, and sexism undermine people's sense of competence, personal control, and self-esteem. Such stresses increase their risk of depression, alcohol use disorder, and suicide.

We who care about preventing psychological casualties should, Albee contended, support programs that alleviate these demoralizing situations. We eliminated smallpox not by treating the afflicted but by inoculating the unafflicted. We conquered yellow fever by controlling mosquitoes. Preventing psychological problems means empowering those who have learned an attitude of helplessness and changing environments that breed loneliness. It means renewing fragile family ties and boosting parents' and teachers' skills at nurturing children's competence and belief in their ability to grow. In short, "Everything aimed at improving the human condition, at making life more fulfilling and meaningful, may be considered part of primary prevention of mental or emotional disturbance" (Kessler & Albee, 1975, p. 557). Prevention can sometimes provide a double payoff. People

"It is better to prevent than to cure."
Peruvian folk wisdom

"Mental disorders arise from physical ones, and likewise physical disorders arise from mental ones."
The Mahabharata, *200 B.C.E.*

with a strong sense of life's meaning are more engaging socially (Stillman et al., 2011). If we can strengthen people's sense of meaning in life, we may also lessen their loneliness as they grow into more engaging companions.

Among the upstream prevention workers are *community psychologists.* Mindful of how people interact with their environment, they focus on creating environments that support psychological health. Through their research and social action, community psychologists aim to empower people and to enhance their competence, health, and well-being.

Building Resilience

We have seen that lifestyle change can lessen psychological disorders. Might such change also prevent some disorders by building individuals' **resilience**—the ability to cope with stress and recover from adversity? Faced with unforeseen trauma, most adults exhibit resilience. This was true of New Yorkers in the aftermath of the September 11 terror attacks, especially those who enjoyed supportive close relationships and who had not recently experienced other stressful events (Bonanno et al., 2007). More than 9 in 10 New Yorkers, although stunned and grief-stricken by 9/11, did *not* have a dysfunctional stress reaction. By the following January, the stress symptoms of those who did were mostly gone (Person et al., 2006). Even most combat-stressed veterans, most political rebels who have survived torture, and most people with spinal cord injuries do not later exhibit posttraumatic stress disorder (Bonanno et al., 2012; Mineka & Zinbarg, 1996).

Struggling with challenging crises can even lead to **posttraumatic growth.** Many cancer survivors have reported a greater appreciation for life, more meaningful relationships, increased personal strength, changed priorities, and a richer spiritual life (Tedeschi & Calhoun, 2004). Out of even our worst experiences, some good can come, especially when we can envision new possibilities (Roepke & Seligman, 2015). Through preventive efforts, such as community building and personal growth, fewer of us will fall into the rushing river of psychological disorders.

> **resilience** the personal strength that helps most people cope with stress and recover from adversity and even trauma.
>
> **posttraumatic growth** positive psychological changes as a result of struggling with extremely challenging circumstances and life crises.

RETRIEVE IT [✱]

- What is the difference between preventive mental health and psychological or biomedical therapy?

ANSWER: Psychological and biomedical therapies attempt to relieve people's suffering from psychological disorders. Preventive mental health attempts to prevent suffering by identifying and eliminating the conditions that cause disorders.

---

* * *

If you just finished reading this book, your introduction to psychological science is completed. Our tour of psychological science has taught us much—and you, too?—about our moods and memories, about the reach of our unconscious, about how we flourish and struggle, about how we perceive our physical and social worlds, and about how our biology and culture shape us. Our hope, as your guides on this tour, is that you have shared some of our fascination, grown in your understanding and compassion, and sharpened your critical thinking. And we hope you enjoyed the ride.

With every good wish in your future endeavors,

David G. Myers
www.DavidMyers.org

Nathan DeWall
www.NathanDeWall.com

MODULE 45 REVIEW The Biomedical Therapies and Preventing Psychological Disorders

👁 Learning Objectives

Test Yourself by taking a moment to answer each of these Learning Objective Questions (repeated here from within the module). Then turn to Appendix D, Complete Module Reviews, to check your answers. Research suggests that trying to answer these questions on your own will improve your long-term memory of the concepts (McDaniel et al., 2009).

45-1 What are the drug therapies? How do double-blind studies help researchers evaluate a drug's effectiveness?

45-2 How are brain stimulation and psychosurgery used in treating specific disorders?

45-3 How, by taking care of themselves with a healthy lifestyle, might people find some relief from depression? How does this reinforce the idea that we are biopsychosocial systems?

45-4 What is the rationale for preventive mental health programs, and why is it important to develop resilience?

▣▣ Terms and Concepts to Remember

Test yourself on these terms by trying to write down the definition in your own words before flipping back to the referenced page to check your answers.

biomedical therapy, p. 593

psychopharmacology, p. 593

antipsychotic drugs, p. 594

antianxiety drugs, p. 594

antidepressant drugs, p. 595

electroconvulsive therapy (ECT), p. 597

repetitive transcranial magnetic stimulation (rTMS), p. 598

psychosurgery, p. 599

lobotomy, p. 599

resilience, p. 603

posttraumatic growth, p. 603

▣ Experience the Testing Effect

Test yourself repeatedly throughout your studies. This will not only help you figure out what you know and don't know; the testing itself will help you learn and remember the information more effectively thanks to the *testing effect*.

1. Some antipsychotic drugs, used to calm people with schizophrenia, can have unpleasant side effects, most notably

   a. hyperactivity.

   b. convulsions and momentary memory loss.

   c. sluggishness, tremors, and twitches.

   d. paranoia.

2. Drugs such as Xanax and Ativan, which depress central nervous system activity, can become addictive when used as ongoing treatment. These drugs are referred to as _____ drugs.

3. A simple salt that often brings relief to patients suffering the highs and lows of bipolar disorder is _____.

4. When drug therapies have not been effective, electroconvulsive therapy (ECT) may be used as treatment, largely for people with

   a. severe obsessive-compulsive disorder.

   b. severe depression.

   c. schizophrenia.

   d. anxiety disorders.

5. An approach that seeks to identify and alleviate conditions that put people at high risk for developing psychological disorders is called

   a. deep brain stimulation.

   b. the mood-stabilizing perspective.

   c. spontaneous recovery.

   d. preventive mental health.

   Find answers to these questions in Appendix E, in the back of the book.

Use 🌀 LearningCurve to create your personalized study plan, which will direct you to the resources that will help you most in 🌀 LaunchPad.

Statistical Reasoning in Everyday Life

Statistics are important tools in psychological research. But statistics also benefit us all, by helping us see what the unaided eye might miss. To be an educated person today is to be able to apply simple statistical principles to everyday reasoning. We needn't memorize complicated formulas to think more clearly and critically about data.

Off-the-top-of-the-head estimates often misread reality and then mislead the public. Someone throws out a big, round number. Others echo it, and before long the big, round number becomes public misinformation. Here are a few examples:

- *Ten percent of people are homosexual.* Or is it 2 to 4 percent, as suggested by various national surveys (Module 15)?

- *We ordinarily use only 10 percent of our brain.* Or is it closer to 100 percent (Module 5)?

- *The human brain has 100 billion nerve cells.* Or is it more like 86 billion, as suggested by one analysis (Module 3)?

The point to remember: Doubt big, round, undocumented numbers. That's actually a lesson we intuitively appreciate, by finding precise numbers more credible (Oppenheimer et al., 2014). When U.S. Secretary of State John Kerry sought to rally American support in 2013 for a military response to Syria's apparent use of chemical weapons, his argument gained credibility from its precision: "The United States government now knows that at least 1429 Syrians were killed in this attack, including at least 426 children."

Statistical illiteracy also feeds needless health scares (Gigerenzer et al., 2008, 2009, 2010). In the 1990s, the British press reported a study showing that women taking a particular contraceptive pill had a 100 percent increased risk of blood clots that could produce strokes. This caused thousands of women to stop taking the pill, leading to a wave of unwanted pregnancies and an estimated 13,000 additional abortions (which also are associated with increased blood clot risk). And what did the study actually find? A 100 percent increased risk, indeed—but only from 1 in 7000 to 2 in 7000. Such false alarms underscore the need to teach statistical reasoning and to present statistical information more transparently.

When setting goals, we love big round numbers. We're far more likely to want to lose 20 pounds than 19 or 21 pounds. We're far more likely to retake the SAT if our verbal plus math score is just short of a big round number, such as 1200. By modifying their behavior, batters are nearly four times more likely to finish the season with a .300 average than with a .299 average (Pope & Simonsohn, 2011).

Describing Data

A-1 How do we describe data using three measures of central tendency, and what is the relative usefulness of the two measures of variation?

Once researchers have gathered their data, they may use *descriptive statistics* to organize that data meaningfully. One way to do this is to show the data in a simple *bar graph,* as in **FIGURE A.1** (on the next page), which displays a distribution of different brands of trucks still on the road after a decade. When reading

"Figures can be misleading—so I've written a song which I think expresses the real story of the firm's performance this quarter."

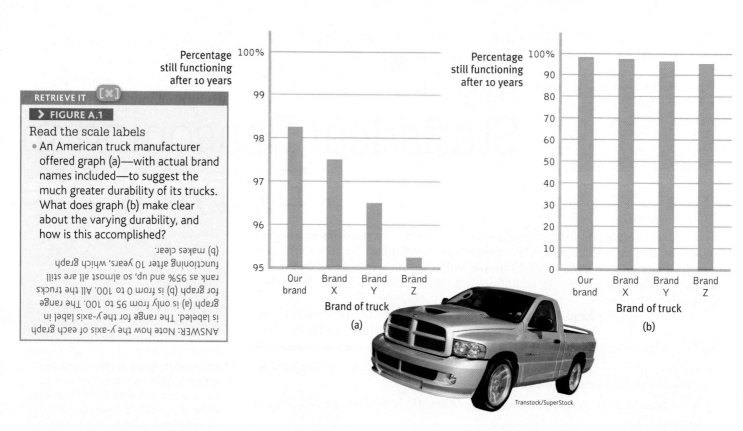

RETRIEVE IT [✗]

> FIGURE A.1

Read the scale labels

• An American truck manufacturer offered graph (a)—with actual brand names included—to suggest the much greater durability of its trucks. What does graph (b) make clear about the varying durability, and how is this accomplished?

ANSWER: Note how the y-axis of each graph is labeled. The range for the y-axis label in graph (a) is only from 95 to 100. The range for graph (b) is from 0 to 100. All the trucks rank as 95% and up, so almost all are still functioning after 10 years, which graph (b) makes clear.

statistical graphs such as this one, take care. It's easy to design a graph to make a difference look big (Figure A.1a) or small (Figure A.1b). The secret lies in how you label the vertical scale (the *y*-axis).

The point to remember: Think smart. When viewing graphs, read the scale labels and note their range.

The average person has one ovary and one testicle.

Measures of Central Tendency

The next step is to summarize the data using some *measure of central tendency,* a single score that represents a whole set of scores. The simplest measure is the **mode,** the most frequently occurring score or scores. The most familiar is the **mean,** or arithmetic average—the total sum of all the scores divided by the number of scores. The midpoint—the 50th percentile—is the **median.** On a divided highway, the median is the middle. So, too, with data: If you arrange all the scores in order from the highest to the lowest, half will be above the median and half will be below it.

Measures of central tendency neatly summarize data. But consider what happens to the mean when a distribution is lopsided, when it's *skewed* by a few way-out scores. With income data, for example, the mode, median, and mean often tell very different stories (**FIGURE A.2**). This happens because the mean is biased

∨ FIGURE A.2

A skewed distribution This graphic representation of the distribution of a village's incomes illustrates the three measures of central tendency—mode, median, and mean. Note how just a few high incomes make the mean—the fulcrum point that balances the incomes above and below—deceptively high.

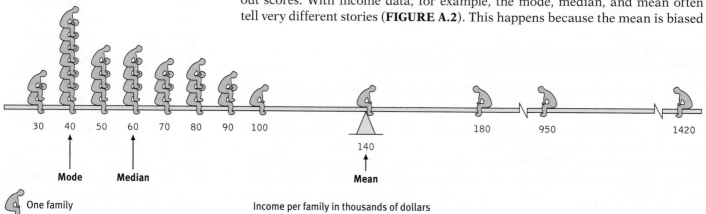

Income per family in thousands of dollars

by a few extreme scores. When Microsoft co-founder Bill Gates sits down in a small café, its average (mean) customer instantly becomes a billionaire. But the median customer's wealth remains unchanged. Understanding this, you can see why, according to the 2010 U.S. Census, nearly 65 percent of U.S. households have "below average" income. The bottom half of earners receive much less than half the national income cake. So, most Americans make less than the mean. Mean and median tell different true stories.

The point to remember: Always note which measure of central tendency is reported. If it is a mean, consider whether a few atypical scores could be distorting it.

Measures of Variation

Knowing the value of an appropriate measure of central tendency can tell us a great deal. But the single number omits other information. It helps to know something about the amount of *variation* in the data—how similar or diverse the scores are. Averages derived from scores with low variability are more reliable than averages based on scores with high variability. Consider a basketball player who scored between 13 and 17 points in each of the season's first 10 games. Knowing this, we would be more confident that she would score near 15 points in her next game than if her scores had varied from 5 to 25 points.

The **range** of scores—the gap between the lowest and highest—provides only a crude estimate of variation. In an otherwise uniform group, a couple of extreme scores, such as the $950,000 and $1,420,000 incomes in Figure A.2, will create a deceptively large range.

The more useful standard for measuring how much scores deviate from one another is the **standard deviation.** It better gauges whether scores are packed together or dispersed, because it uses information from each score. The computation[1] assembles information about how much individual scores differ from the mean, which can be very telling. Let's say test scores from Class A and Class B both have the same mean (75 percent) but very different standard deviations (5.0 for Class A and 15.0 for Class B). Have you ever had test experiences like that—where two-thirds of your classmates in one course score in the 70 to 80 percent range, with scores in another course more spread out (two-thirds between 60 and 90)? The standard deviation tells us more about how each class is really faring than does the mean score alone. As another example, consider varsity and intramural sports. A school's varsity volleyball players' ability levels will have a relatively small standard deviation compared with the more diverse ability levels found in those playing on intramural volleyball teams.

You can grasp the meaning of the standard deviation if you consider how scores tend naturally to be distributed. Large numbers of data—heights, weights, intelligence scores, grades (though not incomes)—often form a symmetrical, *bell-shaped* distribution. Most cases fall near the mean, and fewer cases fall near either extreme. This *bell-shaped* distribution is so typical that we call the curve it forms the **normal curve.**

As **FIGURE A.3** (on the next page) shows, a useful property of the normal curve is that roughly 68 percent of the cases fall within one standard deviation on either side of the mean. About 95 percent of cases fall within two standard deviations. Thus, about 68 percent of people taking an intelligence test will score within ±15 points of 100. About 95 percent will score within ±30 points.

mode the most frequently occurring score(s) in a distribution.

mean the arithmetic average of a distribution, obtained by adding the scores and then dividing by the number of scores.

median the middle score in a distribution; half the scores are above it and half are below it.

range the difference between the highest and lowest scores in a distribution.

standard deviation a computed measure of how much scores vary around the mean score.

normal curve *(normal distribution)* a symmetrical, bell-shaped curve that describes the distribution of many types of data; most scores fall near the mean (about 68 percent fall within one standard deviation of it) and fewer and fewer near the extremes.

---

1. The actual standard deviation formula is:

$$\sqrt{\frac{\textit{Sum of (deviations from mean)}^2}{\textit{Number of scores} - 1}}$$

> FIGURE A.3

The normal curve Scores on aptitude tests tend to form a normal, or bell-shaped, curve. For example, the most commonly used intelligence test, the Wechsler Adult Intelligence Scale, calls the average score 100.

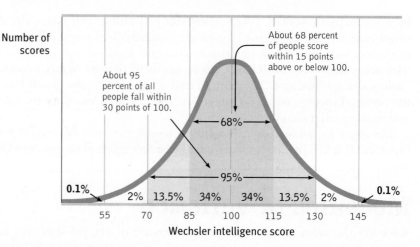

Number of scores

About 95 percent of all people fall within 30 points of 100.

About 68 percent of people score within 15 points above or below 100.

68%

95%

0.1%   2%   13.5%   34%   34%   13.5%   2%   0.1%

55   70   85   100   115   130   145

Wechsler intelligence score

LaunchPad For an interactive tutorial on these statistical concepts, visit Launch-Pad's *PsychSim 6: Descriptive Statistics*.

correlation coefficient a statistical index of the relationship between two things (from −1.00 to +1.00).

scatterplot a graphed cluster of dots, each of which represents the values of two variables. The slope of the points suggests the direction of the relationship between the two variables. The amount of scatter suggests the strength of the correlation (little scatter indicates high correlation).

RETRIEVE IT   [✖]

• The average of a distribution of scores is the _____. The score that shows up most often is the _____. The score right in the middle of a distribution (half the scores above it; half below) is the _____. We determine how much scores vary around the average in a way that includes information about the _____ of scores (difference between highest and lowest) by using the _____ _____ formula.

ANSWERS: mean; mode; median; range; standard deviation

Correlation: A Measure of Relationships

A-2 What does it mean when we say two things are correlated?

Throughout this book, we often ask how strongly two things are related: For example, how closely related are the personality scores of identical twins? How well do intelligence test scores predict career achievement? How closely is stress related to disease?

Describing behavior is a first step toward predicting it. When naturalistic observation and surveys reveal that one trait or behavior accompanies another, we say the two *correlate*. A **correlation coefficient** is a statistical measure of relationship. In such cases, **scatterplots** can be very revealing.

Each dot in a scatterplot represents the values of two variables. The three scatterplots in **FIGURE A.4** illustrate the range of possible correlations from a perfect positive to a perfect negative. (Perfect correlations rarely occur in the real world.) A correlation is positive if two sets of scores, such as height and weight, tend to rise or fall together.

⌄ FIGURE A.4

Scatterplots, showing patterns of correlation Correlations—abbreviated *r*—can range from +1.00 (scores on one measure increase in direct proportion to scores on another), to 0.00 (no relationship), to −1.00 (scores on one measure decrease precisely as scores rise on the other).

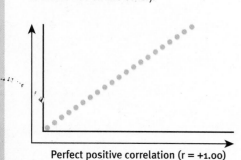

Perfect positive correlation (r = +1.00)

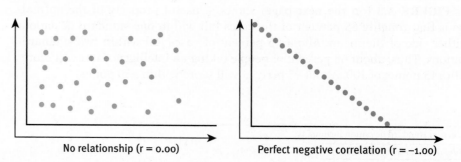

No relationship (r = 0.00)

Perfect negative correlation (r = −1.00)

🅿 LaunchPad For an animated tutorial on correlations, visit LaunchPad's *Concept Practice: Positive and Negative Correlations*. See also LaunchPad's *Video: Correlational Studies* for another helpful tutorial animation.

Saying that a correlation is "negative" says nothing about its strength. A correlation is negative if two sets of scores relate inversely, one set going up as the other goes down.

Statistics can help us see what the naked eye sometimes misses. To demonstrate this for yourself, try an imaginary project. You wonder if tall men are more or less easygoing, so you collect two sets of scores: men's heights and men's anxiety. You measure the heights of 20 men, and you have them take an anxiety test.

With all the relevant data right in front of you **(TABLE A.1)**, can you tell whether the correlation between height and anxiety is positive, negative, or close to zero?

Comparing the columns in Table A.1, most people detect very little relationship between height and anxiety. In fact, the correlation in this imaginary example is positive (r = +0.63), as we can see if we display the data as a scatterplot **(FIGURE A.5)**.

If we fail to see a relationship when data are presented as systematically as in Table A.1, how much less likely are we to notice them in everyday life? To see what is right in front of us, we sometimes need statistical illumination. We can easily see evidence of gender discrimination when given statistically summarized information about job level, seniority, performance, gender, and salary. But we often see no discrimination when the same information dribbles in, case by case (Twiss et al., 1989).

The point to remember: Correlation coefficients tell us nothing about cause and effect, but they can help us see the world more clearly by revealing the extent to which two things relate.

⌄ TABLE A.1		
Height and Anxiety Scores of 20 Men		
Person	Height in Inches	Anxiety Score
1	80	75
2	63	66
3	61	60
4	79	90
5	74	60
6	69	42
7	62	42
8	75	60
9	77	81
10	60	39
11	64	48
12	76	69
13	71	72
14	66	57
15	73	63
16	70	75
17	63	30
18	71	57
19	68	84
20	70	39

Regression Toward the Mean

◉ A-3 What is regression toward the mean?

Correlations not only make visible the relationships we might otherwise miss, they also restrain our "seeing" nonexistent relationships. When we believe there is

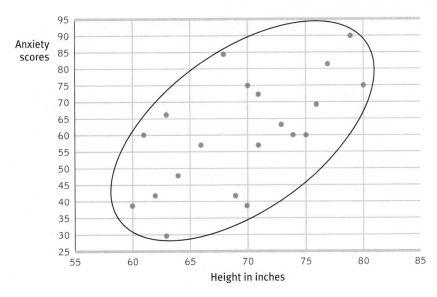

⟨ FIGURE A.5

Scatterplot for height and anxiety This display of data from 20 imagined people (each represented by a data point) reveals an upward slope, indicating a positive correlation. The considerable scatter of the data indicates the correlation is much lower than +1.00.

> **regression toward the mean** the tendency for extreme or unusual scores or events to fall back (regress) toward the average.

a relationship between two things, we are likely to notice and recall instances that confirm our belief. If we believe that dreams are forecasts of actual events, we may notice and recall confirming instances more than disconfirming instances. The result is an *illusory correlation*.

Illusory correlations feed an illusion of control—that chance events are subject to our personal control. Gamblers, remembering their lucky rolls, may come to believe they can influence the roll of the dice by again throwing gently for low numbers and hard for high numbers. The illusion that uncontrollable events correlate with our actions is also fed by a statistical phenomenon called **regression toward the mean.** Average results are more typical than extreme results. Thus, after an unusual event, things tend to return toward their average level; extraordinary happenings tend to be followed by more ordinary ones.

The point may seem obvious, yet we regularly miss it: We sometimes attribute what may be a normal regression (the expected return to normal) to something we have done. Consider two examples:

- Students who score much lower or higher on an exam than they usually do are likely, when retested, to return to their average.
- Unusual ESP subjects who defy chance when first tested nearly always lose their "psychic powers" when retested (a phenomenon parapsychologists have called the *decline effect*).

Failure to recognize regression is the source of many superstitions and of some ineffective practices as well. When day-to-day behavior has a large element of chance fluctuation, we may notice that others' behavior improves (regresses toward average) after we criticize them for very bad performance, and that it worsens (regresses toward average) after we warmly praise them for an exceptionally fine performance. Ironically, then, regression toward the average can mislead us into feeling rewarded for having criticized others and into feeling punished for having praised them (Tversky & Kahneman, 1974).

The point to remember: When a fluctuating behavior returns to normal, there is no need to invent fancy explanations for why it does so. Regression toward the mean is probably at work.

> "Once you become sensitized to it, you see regression everywhere."
> *Psychologist Daniel Kahneman (1985)*

RETRIEVE IT

- You hear the school basketball coach telling her friend that she rescued her team's winning streak by yelling at the players after they played an unusually bad first half. What is another explanation of why the team's performance improved?

ANSWER: The team's poor performance was not their typical behavior. Their return to their normal—their winning streak—may just have been a case of regression toward the mean.

Significant Differences

A-4 How do we know whether an observed difference can be generalized to other populations?

Data are "noisy." The average score in one group could conceivably differ from the average score in another group not because of any real difference but merely because of chance fluctuations in the people sampled. How confidently, then, can we *infer* that an observed difference is not just a fluke—a chance result from the research sample? For guidance, we can ask whether the observed difference between the two groups is reliable and significant. These *inferential statistics* help us determine if results describe a larger population.

When Is an Observed Difference Reliable?

In deciding when it is safe to generalize from a sample, we should keep three principles in mind:

1. **Representative samples are better than biased (unrepresentative) samples.** The best basis for generalizing is from a representative sample of cases, not from the exceptional and memorable cases one finds at the extremes. Research never randomly samples the whole human population. Thus, it pays to keep in mind what population a study has sampled. (To see how an unrepresentative sample can lead you astray, see Thinking Critically About: Cross-Sectional and Longitudinal Studies on the next page.)

2. **Less-variable observations are more reliable than those that are more variable.** As we noted earlier in the example of the basketball player whose game-to-game points were consistent, an average is more reliable when it comes from scores with low variability.

3. **More cases are better than fewer cases.** An eager prospective student visits two university campuses, each for a day. At the first, the student randomly attends two classes and discovers both instructors to be witty and engaging. At the next campus, the two sampled instructors seem dull and uninspiring. Returning home, the student (discounting the small sample size of only two teachers at each institution) tells friends about the "great teachers" at the first school, and the "bores" at the second. Again, we know it but we ignore it: *Averages based on many cases are more reliable* (less variable) than averages based on only a few cases.

The greater variability of small samples explains why small schools often are top producers of high-achieving students—a finding that led several foundations to invest in the creation of smaller schools. Alas, underperforming schools also are disproportionately small, because small populations are more variable (Kahneman, 2011).

The point to remember: Smart thinkers are not overly impressed by a few anecdotes. Generalizations based on a few unrepresentative cases are unreliable.

"The poor are getting poorer, but with the rich getting richer it all averages out in the long run."

When Is an Observed Difference "Significant"?

Perhaps you've compared men's and women's scores on a laboratory test of aggression, and you've found a gender difference. But individuals differ. How likely is it that the difference you observed was just a fluke? Statistical testing can estimate the probability of the result occurring by chance.

Here is the underlying logic: When averages from two samples are each reliable measures of their respective populations (as when each is based on many observations that have small variability), then their *difference* is probably reliable as well. (Example: The less the variability in women's and in men's aggression scores, the more confidence we would have that any observed gender difference is reliable.) And when the difference between the sample averages is *large,* we have even more confidence that the difference between them reflects a real difference in their populations.

In short, when sample averages are reliable, and when the difference between them is relatively large, we say the difference has **statistical significance.** This

> **statistical significance** a statistical statement of how likely it is that an obtained result occurred by chance.

Cross-Sectional and Longitudinal Studies

A-5 What are cross-sectional studies and longitudinal studies, and why is it important to know which method was used?

When interpreting research results, smart thinkers consider how researchers arrived at their conclusions. One way studies vary is in the time period for gathering data.

In **cross-sectional studies**, researchers compare different groups at the same time. When researchers compare intelligence test scores among people in differing age groups, older adults, on average, give fewer correct answers than do younger adults. This could suggest that mental ability declines with age, and indeed, that was the conclusion drawn from many early cross-sectional studies of intelligence.

In **longitudinal studies**, researchers study and restudy the same people at different times in their life span. Around 1920, colleges began giving intelligence tests to entering students, and several psychologists saw their chance to study intelligence longitudinally. What they expected to find was a decrease in intelligence after about age 30 (Schaie & Geiwitz, 1982). What they actually found was a surprise: Until late in life, intelligence remained stable. On some tests, it even increased.

Why did these new results differ from the earlier cross-sectional findings? In retrospect, researchers realized that cross-sectional studies that compared 70-year-olds and 30-year-olds were comparing people not only of two different ages but also of two different eras.

They were comparing

- generally less-educated people (born, say, in the early 1900s) with better-educated people (born after 1950).

- people raised in large families with people raised in smaller families.

- people from less-affluent families with people from more-affluent families.

Others have since pointed out that longitudinal studies have their own pitfalls. Participants who survive to the end of longitudinal studies may be the healthiest (and brightest) people. When researchers adjust for the loss of participants, as did one study following more than 2000 people over age 75 in Cambridge, England, they find a steeper intelligence decline, especially as people age after 85 (Brayne et al., 1999).

The point to remember: When interpreting research results, pay attention to the methodology used, such as whether it was a longitudinal or cross-sectional study.

LaunchPad See LaunchPad's *Video: Longitudinal and Cross-Sectional Studies* for a helpful tutorial animation.

---

cross-sectional study research in which people of different ages are compared with one another.

longitudinal study research in which the same people are restudied and retested over a long period of time.

means that the observed difference is probably not due to chance variation between the samples.

In judging statistical significance, psychologists are conservative. They are like juries who must presume innocence until guilt is proven. For most psychologists, proof beyond a reasonable doubt means not making much of a finding unless the odds of its occurring by chance, if no real effect exists, are less than 5 percent.

When reading about research, you should remember that, given large enough or homogeneous enough samples, a difference between them may be "statistically significant" yet have little practical significance. For example, comparisons of intelligence test scores among hundreds of thousands of first-born and later-born individuals indicate a highly significant tendency for first-born individuals to have higher average scores than their later-born siblings (Rohrer et al., 2015; Zajonc & Markus, 1975). But because the scores differ by only one to three points, the difference has little practical importance.

PEANUTS

The point to remember: Statistical significance indicates the *likelihood* that a result will happen by chance. But this does not say anything about the *importance* of the result.

RETRIEVE IT

• Can you solve this puzzle?

The registrar's office at the University of Michigan has found that usually about 100 students in Arts and Sciences have perfect marks at the end of their first term at the University. However, only about 10 to 15 students graduate with perfect marks. What do you think is the most likely explanation for the fact that there are more perfect marks after one term than at graduation (Jepson et al., 1983)?

ANSWER: Averages based on fewer courses are more variable, which guarantees a greater number of extremely low and high marks at the end of the first term.

• _____ statistics summarize data, while _____ statistics determine if data can be generalized to other populations.

ANSWERS: Descriptive; inferential

LaunchPad For a 9.5-minute video synopsis of psychology's scientific research strategies, visit LaunchPad's *Video: Research Methods.*

···> REVIEW Statistical Reasoning in Everyday Life

◉ Learning Objectives

Test Yourself by taking a moment to answer each of these Learning Objective Questions (repeated here from within Appendix A). Then turn to Appendix D, Complete Module Reviews, to check your answers. Research suggests that trying to answer these questions on your own will improve your long-term memory of the concepts (McDaniel et al., 2009).

A-1 How do we describe data using three measures of central tendency, and what is the relative usefulness of the two measures of variation?

A-2 What does it mean when we say two things are correlated?

A-3 What is regression toward the mean?

A-4 How do we know whether an observed difference can be generalized to other populations?

A-5 What are cross-sectional studies and longitudinal studies, and why is it important to know which method was used?

■·[·] Terms and Concepts to Remember

Test yourself on these terms by trying to write down the definition in your own words before flipping back to the referenced page to check your answers.

mode, p. A-2
mean, p. A-2

median, p. A-2
range, p. A-3
standard deviation, p. A-3
normal curve, p. A-3
correlation coefficient, p. A-4

scatterplot, p. A-4
regression toward the mean, p. A-6
statistical significance, p. A-7
cross-sectional study, p. A-8
longitudinal study, p. A-8

[✱] Experience the Testing Effect

Test yourself repeatedly throughout your studies. This will not only help you figure out what you know and don't know; the testing itself will help you learn and remember the information more effectively thanks to the *testing effect.*

1. Which of the three measures of central tendency is most easily distorted by a few very large or very small scores?

   a. The mode
   b. The mean
   c. The median
   d. They are all equally vulnerable to distortion from atypical scores.

2. The standard deviation is the most useful measure of variation in a set of data because it tells us

   a. the difference between the highest and lowest scores in the set.
   b. the extent to which the sample being used deviates from the bigger population it represents.
   c. how much individual scores differ from the mode.
   d. how much individual scores differ from the mean.

3. Another name for a bell-shaped distribution, in which most scores fall near the middle and fewer scores fall at each extreme, is a _____ _____.

4. In a _____ correlation, the scores rise and fall together; in a(n) _____ correlation, one score falls and the other rises.

   a. positive; negative
   b. positive; illusory
   c. negative; inverse
   d. strong; weak

5. If a study revealed that tall people were less intelligent than short people, this would suggest that the correlation between height and intelligence is _____ (positive/negative).

6. A _____ provides a visual representation of the direction and the strength of a relationship between two variables.

7. What is regression toward the mean, and how can it influence our interpretation of events?

8. In _____ - _____ studies, a characteristic is assessed across different age groups at the same time.

9. When sample averages are _____ and the difference between them is _____, we can say the difference has statistical significance.

   a. reliable; large
   b. reliable; small
   c. due to chance; large
   d. due to chance; small

Find answers to these questions in Appendix E.

Use 🅜 LearningCurve to create your personalized study plan, which will direct you to the resources that will help you most in 🅜 LaunchPad .

Psychology at Work

B-1 What is *flow*, and what are the key subfields related to industrial-organizational psychology?

For most people, work is life's biggest single waking activity. To live is to work. Work helps satisfy several levels of need identified in Abraham Maslow's (1970) *hierarchy of needs*. Work supports us. Work connects us. Work defines us. Meeting someone for the first time, and wondering who they are, we may ask, "So, what do you do?"

Individuals across various occupations vary in their attitudes toward their work. Some view their work as a *job*, an unfulfilling but necessary way to make money. Others view their work as a *career*, an opportunity to advance from one position to a better position. The rest—those who view their work as a *calling*, a fulfilling and socially useful activity—report the highest satisfaction with their work and with their lives (Dik & Duffy, 2012; Wrzesniewski et al., 1997, 2001).

This finding would not surprise Mihaly Csikszentmihalyi [chick-SENT-me-hi] (1990, 1999). He observed that people's quality of life increases when they are purposefully engaged. Between the anxiety of being overwhelmed and stressed, and the apathy of being underwhelmed and bored, lies a zone in which people experience **flow.** Can you recall being in a zoned-out flow state while texting or playing a video game? If so, then perhaps you can sympathize with the two Northwest Airlines pilots who in 2009 were so focused on their laptops that they missed Earth-to-pilot messages from their control tower. The pilots flew 150 miles past their Minneapolis destination—and lost their jobs.

Csikszentmihalyi formulated the flow concept after studying artists who spent hour after hour painting or sculpting with focused concentration. Immersed in a project, they worked as if nothing else mattered, and then, when finished, they promptly forgot about it. The artists seemed driven less by external rewards—money, praise, promotion—than by the intrinsic rewards of creating the art. Nearly 200 other studies confirm that intrinsic motivation, as well as extrinsic incentives, predict performance (Cerasoli & Nicklin, 2014).

Csikszentmihalyi's later observations, of people from varied occupations and countries, and of all ages, confirmed an overriding principle: It's exhilarating to flow with an activity that fully engages our skills (Fong et al., 2015). Flow experiences boost our sense of self-esteem, competence, and well-being. Idleness may sound like bliss, but purposeful work enriches our lives. Busy people are happier (Hsee et al., 2010; Robinson & Martin, 2008). One research team interrupted people on about a quarter-million occasions (using a smart phone app), and found people's minds wandering 47 percent of the time. They were, on average, happier when *not* mind-wandering (Killingsworth & Gilbert, 2010).

In many nations, work has changed, from farming to manufacturing to *knowledge work*. More and more work is outsourced to temporary employees and consultants or to workers communicating electronically from off-site workplaces. As work changes,

flow a completely involved, focused state of consciousness, with diminished awareness of self and time, resulting from optimal engagement of one's skills.

Sometimes, Gene Weingarten noted (2002), a humor writer knows "when to just get out of the way." Here are some sample job titles from the U.S. Department of Labor *Dictionary of Occupational Titles:* animal impersonator, human projectile, banana ripening-room supervisor, impregnator, impregnator helper, dope sprayer, finger waver, rug scratcher, egg smeller, bottom buffer, cookie breaker, brain picker, hand pouncer, bosom presser, and mother repairer.

Have you ever noticed that when you are immersed in an activity, time flies? And that when you are watching the clock, it seems to move more slowly? French researchers have confirmed that the more we attend to an event's duration, the longer it seems to last (Couli et al., 2004).

Life disrupted Playing and socializing online are ever-present sources of distraction. It takes energy to resist checking our phones, and time to refocus mental concentration after each disruption. Such regular interruptions disrupt flow, so it's a good idea to instead schedule breaks for checking our handheld devices.

Hope College; Danielle Stevens; Rachel Losh; Kathryn Brownson; Lorie Hailey; Don Probert; Tracey Kuehn; Trish Morgan; Christine Brune.

The modern workforce The editorial team that supports the creation of this book and its teaching package works both in-house and from far-flung places. Starting from the top, from left to right are Nancy Fleming in Massachusetts, Danielle Slevens in Massachusetts, Rachel Losh in New York, Kathryn Brownson in Michigan, Lorie Hailey in Kentucky, Betty Probert in Florida, Tracey Kuehn in New York, Trish Morgan in Alberta, and Christine Brune in Alaska.

have our attitudes toward our work also changed? Has our satisfaction with work increased or decreased? Has the *psychological contract*—the sense of mutual obligations between workers and employers—become more or less trusting and secure? These are among the questions that fascinate psychologists who study work-related behavior.

Industrial-organizational (I/O) psychology applies psychology's principles to the workplace (**TABLE B.1**). Here we consider two of I/O psychology's subfields and a related field:

- **Personnel psychology** applies psychology's methods and principles to selecting and evaluating workers. Personnel psychologists match people with jobs, by identifying and placing well-suited candidates.

- **Organizational psychology** considers how work environments and management styles influence worker motivation, satisfaction, and productivity. Organizational psychologists modify jobs and supervision in ways that boost morale and productivity.

- **Human factors psychology,** now a distinct field allied with I/O psychology, explores how machines and environments can be optimally designed to fit human abilities. Human factors psychologists study people's natural perceptions and inclinations to create user-friendly machines and work settings.

RETRIEVE IT

- What is the value of finding flow in our work?

ANSWER: We become more likely to view our work as fulfilling and socially useful.

---

industrial-organizational (I/O) psychology the application of psychological concepts and methods to optimizing human behavior in workplaces.

personnel psychology an I/O psychology subfield that helps with job seeking, and with employee recruitment, selection, placement, training, appraisal, and development.

organizational psychology an I/O psychology subfield that examines organizational influences on worker satisfaction and productivity and facilitates organizational change.

human factors psychology a field of psychology allied with I/O psychology that explores how people and machines interact and how machines and physical environments can be made safe and easy to use.

∨ TABLE B.1

I/O Psychology at Work As scientists, consultants, and management professionals, industrial-organizational (I/O) psychologists are found working in varied areas:

Personnel Psychology: Maximizing Human Potential	Organizational Psychology: Building Better Organizations
Developing training programs to increase job seekers' success	**Developing organizations**
Selecting and placing employees	• Analyzing organizational structures
• Developing and validating assessment tools for selecting, placing, and promoting workers	• Maximizing worker satisfaction and productivity
• Analyzing job content	• Facilitating organizational change
• Optimizing worker placement	**Enhancing quality of work life**
Training and developing employees	• Expanding individual productivity
• Identifying needs	• Identifying elements of satisfaction
• Designing training programs	• Redesigning jobs
• Evaluating training programs	• Balancing work and nonwork life in an era of social media, smart phones, and other technologies
Appraising performance	**Human Factors (Engineering) Psychology**
• Developing criteria	
• Measuring individual performance	• Designing optimum work environments
• Measuring organizational performance	• Optimizing person-machine interactions
	• Developing systems technologies

Source: Information from the Society of Industrial and Organizational Psychology. For more information about I/O psychology and related job opportunities, visit www.siop.org.

∙∙> Personnel Psychology

B-2 How do personnel psychologists help with job seeking, employee selection, work placement, and performance appraisal?

Psychologists can assist organizations at various stages of selecting and assessing employees. They may help identify needed job skills, decide upon selection methods, recruit and evaluate applicants, introduce and train new employees, and appraise their performance. They can also help job seekers. Across four dozen studies, training programs (which teach job-search skills, improve self-presentation, boost self-confidence, and promote goal setting and enlisting support) have increased job-seekers' success by 2.7 times (Liu et al., 2014).

Matching Interests and Strengths to Work

The best job is one that pays you to do what you love, which may be doing things with your hands, thinking of solutions, expressing yourself creatively, assisting people, being in charge, or working with data. Do what you love and you will love what you do.

A career counseling science aims, first, to assess our differing values, personalities, and, especially, *interests,* which are remarkably stable (Dik & Rottinghaus, 2013). (Your job may change, but your interests today will likely still be your interests in 10 years.) Second, it aims to alert us to well-matched vocations—vocations with a good *person-environment fit.* One study assessed 400,000 high school students' interests and then followed them over time. Researchers found that, "Interests uniquely predict academic and career success over and above cognitive ability and personality" (Rounds & Su, 2014). The power of well-matched interests to predict income, for example, "greatly exceeded the contributions of ability and personality." Sixty other studies confirm the point both for students in school and workers on the job: Interests predict both performance and persistence (Nye et al., 2012).

Discovering Your Interests and Strengths

You can use some of the techniques personnel psychologists have developed to identify your own interests and strengths and pinpoint types of work that will likely prove satisfying and successful. Gallup researchers Marcus Buckingham and Donald Clifton (2001) have suggested asking yourself these questions:

- What activities give me pleasure? Bringing order out of chaos? Playing host? Helping others? Challenging sloppy thinking?
- What activities leave me wondering, "When can I do this again?" rather than, "When will this be over?"
- What sorts of challenges do I relish? And which do I dread?
- What sorts of tasks do I learn easily? And which do I struggle with?

Some people find themselves in flow—their skills engaged and time flying—when teaching or selling or writing or cleaning or consoling or creating or repairing. If an activity feels good, if it comes easily, if you look forward to it, then look deeper and see your strengths at work. For a free (requires registration) assessment of your personal strengths, visit www.authentichappiness.sas.upenn.edu and select the "Brief Strengths Test."

The U.S. Department of Labor also offers a vocational interest questionnaire via its Occupational Information Network (O*NET). At www.mynextmove.org/explore/ip you will need about 10 minutes to respond to 60 items, indicating how

If told certain applicants have been prescreened, interviewers are disposed to judge them more favorably.

- *Interviewers judge people relative to those interviewed just before and after them* (Simonsohn & Gino, 2013). If you are being interviewed for business or medical school, hope for a day when the other interviewees have been weak.

- *Interviewers more often follow the successful careers of those they have hired than the successful careers of those they have rejected.* This missing feedback prevents interviewers from getting a reality check on their hiring ability.

- *Interviews disclose the interviewee's good intentions, which are less revealing than habitual behaviors* (Ouellette & Wood, 1998). Intentions matter. People can change. But the best predictor of the person we will be is the person we have been. Educational attainments predict job performance partly because people who have shown up for school each day and stayed on task also tend to show up for work and stay on task (Ng & Feldman, 2009). Wherever we go, we take ourselves along.

Hoping to improve prediction and selection, personnel psychologists have put people in simulated work situations, sought information on past performance, aggregated evaluations from multiple interviews, administered tests, and developed job-specific interviews.

Structured Interviews

Unlike casual conversation aimed at getting a feel for someone, **structured interviews** offer a disciplined method of collecting information. A personnel psychologist may analyze a job, script questions, and train interviewers. The interviewers then ask all applicants the same questions, in the same order, and rate each applicant on established scales.

In an unstructured interview, someone might ask, "How organized are you?" "How well do you get along with people?" or "How do you handle stress?" Street-smart applicants know how to score high: "Although I sometimes drive myself too hard, I handle stress by prioritizing and delegating, and by making sure I leave time for sleep and exercise."

By contrast, structured interviews pinpoint strengths (attitudes, behaviors, knowledge, and skills) that distinguish high performers in a particular line of work. The process includes outlining job-specific situations and asking candidates to explain how they would handle them, and how they handled similar situations in their prior employment. "Tell me about a time when you were caught between conflicting demands, without time to accomplish both. How did you handle that?"

To reduce memory distortions and bias, the interviewer takes notes and makes ratings as the interview proceeds and avoids irrelevant and follow-up questions. The structured interview therefore feels less warm, but that can be explained to the applicant: "This conversation won't typify how we relate to each other in this organization."

A review of 150 findings revealed that structured interviews had double the predictive accuracy of unstructured interviews (Schmidt & Hunter, 1998; Wiesner & Cronshaw, 1988). Structured interviews also reduce bias, such as against overweight applicants (Kutcher & Bragger, 2004).

If, instead, we let our intuitions bias the hiring process, noted writer Malcolm Gladwell (2000, p. 86), then "all we will have done is replace the old-boy network, where you hired your nephew, with the new-boy network, where you hire whoever impressed you most when you shook his hand. Social progress, unless we're careful, can merely be the means by which we replace the obviously arbitrary with the not so obviously arbitrary."

"Between the idea and reality . . . falls the shadow."

T. S. Eliot, **The Hollow Men,** *1925*

structured interview interview process that asks the same job-relevant questions of all applicants, each of whom is rated on established scales.

study of more than 5000 telecommunications customer-service representatives, those evaluated most favorably by their managers were strong in "harmony" and "responsibility," while those actually rated most effective by customers were strong in energy, assertiveness, and eagerness to learn.

For example, if you were interested in harnessing the strengths needed for success in software development, and you had discovered that your best software developers are analytical, disciplined, and eager to learn, you would focus employment ads less on experience than on the identified strengths. You might ask: "Do you take a logical and systematic approach to problem solving *[analytical]*? Are you a perfectionist who strives for timely completion of your projects *[disciplined]*? Do you want to master Java, C++, and Python *[eager to learn]*?"

Identifying people's strengths and matching those strengths to work is a first step toward workplace effectiveness. To assess applicants' strengths and decide who is best suited to the job, personnel managers use various tools. These include ability tests, personality tests, and behavioral observations in "assessment centers" and work situations that test applicants on tasks that mimic the job they seek (Ryan & Ployhart, 2014; Sackett & Lievens, 2008). Some traits predict success in many types of jobs. If you are both conscientious and agreeable, you will likely flourish in many work settings (Cohen et al., 2014; Sackett & Walmsley, 2014).

Do Interviews Predict Performance?

Many interviewers feel confident of their ability to predict long-term job performance from a get-acquainted interview. However, it is shocking how error-prone interviewers are when predicting job or graduate school success. From their review of 85 years of personnel-selection research, I/O psychologists Frank Schmidt and John Hunter (1998; Schmidt, 2002) determined that for all but less-skilled jobs, general mental ability best predicts on-the-job performance. Subjective overall evaluations from informal interviews are more useful than handwriting analysis (which is worthless). But informal interviews are less informative than aptitude tests, work samples, job knowledge tests, and past job performance. If there's a contest between what our gut tells us about someone and what test scores, work samples, and past performance tell us, we should distrust our gut (Highhouse, 2008).

> "Interviews are a terrible predictor of performance."
>
> *Laszlo Bock, Google's Vice President, People Operations, 2007*

Unstructured Interviews and the Interviewer Illusion

Traditional *unstructured interviews* can provide a sense of someone's personality—their expressiveness, warmth, and verbal ability, for example. But these informal interviews also give interviewees considerable power to control the impression they are making in the interview situation (Barrick et al., 2009). Interviewers' tendency to overrate their ability to predict interviewees' fitness for a job is called the *interviewer illusion* (Dana et al., 2013; Nisbett, 1987). Five factors explain the gap between interviewers' overconfidence and the resulting reality:

- *Interviewers presume that people are what they seem to be in the interview situation.* An unstructured interview may create a false impression of a person's behavior toward others in different situations. But research reveals that how we behave reflects not only our enduring traits, but also the details of the particular situation (such as wanting to impress in a job interview).

- *Interviewers' preconceptions and moods color how they perceive interviewees' responses* (Cable & Gilovich, 1998; Macan & Dipboye, 1994). If interviewers instantly like a person who perhaps is similar to themselves, they may interpret the person's assertiveness as indicating "confidence" rather than "arrogance."

"Between the idea and reality . . . falls the shadow."

T. S. Eliot, **The Hollow Men,** *1925*

If told certain applicants have been prescreened, interviewers are disposed to judge them more favorably.

- *Interviewers judge people relative to those interviewed just before and after them* (Simonsohn & Gino, 2013). If you are being interviewed for business or medical school, hope for a day when the other interviewees have been weak.

- *Interviewers more often follow the successful careers of those they have hired than the successful careers of those they have rejected.* This missing feedback prevents interviewers from getting a reality check on their hiring ability.

- *Interviews disclose the interviewee's good intentions, which are less revealing than habitual behaviors* (Ouellette & Wood, 1998). Intentions matter. People can change. But the best predictor of the person we will be is the person we have been. Educational attainments predict job performance partly because people who have shown up for school each day and stayed on task also tend to show up for work and stay on task (Ng & Feldman, 2009). Wherever we go, we take ourselves along.

Hoping to improve prediction and selection, personnel psychologists have put people in simulated work situations, sought information on past performance, aggregated evaluations from multiple interviews, administered tests, and developed job-specific interviews.

Structured Interviews

Unlike casual conversation aimed at getting a feel for someone, **structured interviews** offer a disciplined method of collecting information. A personnel psychologist may analyze a job, script questions, and train interviewers. The interviewers then ask all applicants the same questions, in the same order, and rate each applicant on established scales.

In an unstructured interview, someone might ask, "How organized are you?" "How well do you get along with people?" or "How do you handle stress?" Street-smart applicants know how to score high: "Although I sometimes drive myself too hard, I handle stress by prioritizing and delegating, and by making sure I leave time for sleep and exercise."

By contrast, structured interviews pinpoint strengths (attitudes, behaviors, knowledge, and skills) that distinguish high performers in a particular line of work. The process includes outlining job-specific situations and asking candidates to explain how they would handle them, and how they handled similar situations in their prior employment. "Tell me about a time when you were caught between conflicting demands, without time to accomplish both. How did you handle that?"

To reduce memory distortions and bias, the interviewer takes notes and makes ratings as the interview proceeds and avoids irrelevant and follow-up questions. The structured interview therefore feels less warm, but that can be explained to the applicant: "This conversation won't typify how we relate to each other in this organization."

A review of 150 findings revealed that structured interviews had double the predictive accuracy of unstructured interviews (Schmidt & Hunter, 1998; Wiesner & Cronshaw, 1988). Structured interviews also reduce bias, such as against overweight applicants (Kutcher & Bragger, 2004).

If, instead, we let our intuitions bias the hiring process, noted writer Malcolm Gladwell (2000, p. 86), then "all we will have done is replace the old-boy network, where you hired your nephew, with the new-boy network, where you hire whoever impressed you most when you shook his hand. Social progress, unless we're careful, can merely be the means by which we replace the obviously arbitrary with the not so obviously arbitrary."

structured interview interview process that asks the same job-relevant questions of all applicants, each of whom is rated on established scales.

···> Personnel Psychology

B-2 How do personnel psychologists help with job seeking, employee selection, work placement, and performance appraisal?

Psychologists can assist organizations at various stages of selecting and assessing employees. They may help identify needed job skills, decide upon selection methods, recruit and evaluate applicants, introduce and train new employees, and appraise their performance. They can also help job seekers. Across four dozen studies, training programs (which teach job-search skills, improve self-presentation, boost self-confidence, and promote goal setting and enlisting support) have increased job-seekers' success by 2.7 times (Liu et al., 2014).

Matching Interests and Strengths to Work

The best job is one that pays you to do what you love, which may be doing things with your hands, thinking of solutions, expressing yourself creatively, assisting people, being in charge, or working with data. Do what you love and you will love what you do.

A career counseling science aims, first, to assess our differing values, personalities, and, especially, *interests*, which are remarkably stable (Dik & Rottinghaus, 2013). (Your job may change, but your interests today will likely still be your interests in 10 years.) Second, it aims to alert us to well-matched vocations—vocations with a good *person-environment fit*. One study assessed 400,000 high school students' interests and then followed them over time. Researchers found that, "Interests uniquely predict academic and career success over and above cognitive ability and personality" (Rounds & Su, 2014). The power of well-matched interests to predict income, for example, "greatly exceeded the contributions of ability and personality." Sixty other studies confirm the point both for students in school and workers on the job: Interests predict both performance and persistence (Nye et al., 2012).

Discovering Your Interests and Strengths

You can use some of the techniques personnel psychologists have developed to identify your own interests and strengths and pinpoint types of work that will likely prove satisfying and successful. Gallup researchers Marcus Buckingham and Donald Clifton (2001) have suggested asking yourself these questions:

- What activities give me pleasure? Bringing order out of chaos? Playing host? Helping others? Challenging sloppy thinking?

- What activities leave me wondering, "When can I do this again?" rather than, "When will this be over?"

- What sorts of challenges do I relish? And which do I dread?

- What sorts of tasks do I learn easily? And which do I struggle with?

Some people find themselves in flow—their skills engaged and time flying—when teaching or selling or writing or cleaning or consoling or creating or repairing. If an activity feels good, if it comes easily, if you look forward to it, then look deeper and see your strengths at work. For a free (requires registration) assessment of your personal strengths, visit www.authentichappiness.sas.upenn.edu and select the "Brief Strengths Test."

The U.S. Department of Labor also offers a vocational interest questionnaire via its Occupational Information Network (O*NET). At www.mynextmove.org/explore/ip you will need about 10 minutes to respond to 60 items, indicating how

much you would like or dislike activities ranging from building kitchen cabinets to playing a musical instrument. You will then receive feedback on how strongly your responses reflect six interest types specified by vocational psychologist John L. Holland (1996):

- *realistic* (hands-on doers),
- *investigative* (thinkers),
- *artistic* (creators),
- *social* (helpers, teachers),
- *enterprising* (persuaders, deciders), and
- *conventional* (organizers).

Finally, depending on how much training you indicate being willing to undertake, you will be shown occupations that fit with your interest pattern (selected from a national database of 900+ occupations). A more comprehensive (and fee-based) online service (called VIP) assesses people's values, interests, and personalities; suggests occupations; and connects people to job listings at www.jobzology.com.

Satisfied and successful people devote far less time to correcting their deficiencies than to accentuating their strengths. Top performers are "rarely well rounded," Buckingham and Clifton found (p. 26). Instead, they have sharpened their existing skills. Given the persistence of our traits and temperaments, we should focus not on our deficiencies, but rather on identifying and employing our talents. There may be limits to the benefits of assertiveness training if you are extremely shy, of public speaking courses if you tend to be nervous and soft-spoken, or of drawing classes if you express your artistic side in stick figures.

Identifying your interests can help you recognize the activities you learn quickly and find absorbing. Knowing your strengths, you can develop them further.

Matching Strengths to Work

As a new AT&T human resources executive, psychologist Mary Tenopyr (1997) was assigned to solve a problem: Customer-service representatives were failing at a high rate. After concluding that many of the hires were ill-matched to the demands of their new job, Tenopyr developed a new selection instrument:

1. She asked new applicants to respond to various test questions (without as yet making any use of their responses).
2. She followed up later to assess which of the applicants excelled on the job.
3. She identified the earlier test questions that best predicted success.

The happy result of her data-driven work was a new test that enabled AT&T to identify likely-to-succeed representatives. Personnel selection techniques such as this one aim to match people's strengths with work that enables them and their organization to flourish. Marry the strengths of people with the tasks of organizations and the result is often prosperity and profit.

Your strengths are any enduring qualities that can be productively applied. Are you naturally curious? Persuasive? Charming? Persistent? Competitive? Analytical? Empathic? Organized? Articulate? Neat? Mechanical? Any such trait, if matched with suitable work, can function as a strength (Buckingham, 2007).

Buckingham and Clifton (2001) have argued that the first step to a stronger organization is instituting a *strengths-based selection system*. Thus, as a manager, you would first identify a group of the most effective people in any role—the ones you would want to hire more of—and compare their strengths with those of a group of the least effective people in that role. In defining these groups, you would try to measure performance as objectively as possible. In one Gallup

Alvin Langdon Coburn/George Eastman House/Getty Images

Artistic strengths At age 21, Henri Matisse was a sickly and often depressed lawyer's clerk. When his mother gave him a box of paints to cheer him up one day, he felt the darkness lift and his energy surge. He began to fill his days with painting and drawing and went on to art school and a life as one of the world's great painters. For Matisse, doing art felt like "a comfortable armchair." That is how exercising our strengths often feels.

To recap, personnel psychologists help job candidates to assess their own interests and strengths, and they assist organizations in matching employee strengths to appropriate jobs. Personnel psychologists also appraise employees' performance (**FIGURE B.1**)—the topic we turn to next.

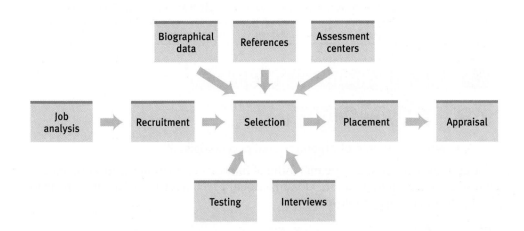

< FIGURE B.1
Personnel psychologists at work When personnel psychologists work with organizations, they consult in human resources activities, from job definition to harnessing employee strengths to employee appraisal.

Appraising Performance

Performance appraisal serves organizational purposes: It helps decide who to retain, how to appropriately reward and pay people, and how to better harness employee strengths, sometimes with job shifts or promotions. Performance appraisal also serves individual purposes: Feedback affirms workers' strengths and helps motivate needed improvement.

Performance appraisal methods include

- *checklists* on which supervisors simply check specific behaviors that describe the worker ("always attends to customers' needs," "takes long breaks").

- *graphic rating scales* on which a supervisor checks, perhaps on a five-point scale, how often a worker is dependable, productive, and so forth.

- *behavior rating scales* on which a supervisor checks scaled behaviors that describe a worker's performance. If rating the extent to which a worker "follows procedures," the supervisor might mark the employee somewhere between "often takes shortcuts" and "always follows established procedures" (Levy, 2003).

In some organizations, performance feedback comes not only from supervisors but also from all organizational levels. If you join an organization that practices *360-degree feedback* (**FIGURE B.2**), you will rate yourself, your manager, and your other colleagues, and you will be rated by your manager, other colleagues, and customers (Green, 2002). The net result is often more open communication and more complete appraisal.

Performance appraisal, like other social judgments, is vulnerable to bias (Murphy & Cleveland, 1995). *Halo errors* occur when one's overall evaluation of an employee, or of a personal trait such as their friendliness, biases ratings of their specific work-related behaviors, such as their reliability. *Leniency* and *severity errors* reflect evaluators' tendencies to be either too easy or too harsh on everyone. *Recency errors* occur when raters focus only on easily remembered recent behavior. By using multiple raters and developing objective, job-relevant performance measures, personnel psychologists seek to support their organizations while also helping employees perceive the appraisal process as fair.

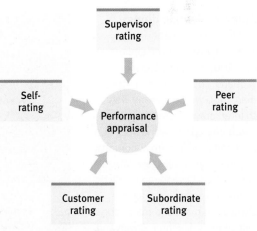

^ FIGURE B.2
360-degree feedback With multisource 360-degree feedback, our knowledge, skills, and behaviors are rated by ourselves and surrounding others. Professors, for example, may be rated by their department chairs, their students, and their colleagues. After receiving all these ratings, professors discuss the 360-degree feedback with their department chair.

Organizational Psychology

👁 **B-3** What is the role of organizational psychologists?

The appraisal of work and the matching of interests and strengths to work matter, but so does overall motivation. Organizational psychologists assist with efforts to motivate and engage employees.

Satisfaction and Engagement

Partly because work is such a big part of life, I/O psychologists study employee satisfaction. Satisfaction with work and with the balance between one's work and nonwork life feeds overall satisfaction with life (Bowling et al., 2010). Moreover, as health psychologists tell us, decreased job stress feeds improved health.

Satisfied employees also contribute to successful organizations. Positive moods at work enhance creativity, persistence, and helpfulness (Ford et al., 2011; Jeffrey et al., 2014; Shockley et al., 2012). Are engaged, happy workers also less often absent? Less likely to quit? Less prone to theft? More punctual? More productive?

> "The only place success comes before work is in the dictionary."
>
> *Former Green Bay Packers football coach Vince Lombardi*

Doing well while doing good—"The Great Experiment" At the end of the 1700s, the New Lanark, Scotland, cotton mill had more than 1000 workers. Many were children drawn from Glasgow's poorhouses. They worked 13-hour days and lived in grim conditions.

On a visit to Glasgow, Welsh-born Robert Owen—an idealistic young cotton-mill manager—chanced to meet and marry the mill owner's daughter. Owen and some partners purchased the mill and on the first day of the 1800s began what he said was "the most important experiment for the happiness of the human race that had yet been instituted at any time in any part of the world" (Owen, 1814). The exploitation of child and adult labor was, he observed, producing unhappy and inefficient workers. So he undertook numerous innovations: a nursery for preschool children, education for older

Courtesy of New Lanark Trust

children (with encouragement rather than corporal punishment), Sundays off, health care, paid sick days, unemployment pay for days when the mill could not operate, and a company store selling goods at reduced prices.

He also innovated a goals- and worker-assessment program that included detailed records of daily productivity and costs but with "no beating, no abusive language."

The ensuing commercial success fueled a humanitarian reform movement. By 1816, with decades of profitability still ahead, Owen believed he had demonstrated "that society may be formed so as to exist without crime, without poverty, with health greatly improved, with little if any misery, and with intelligence and happiness increased a hundredfold." Although his Utopian vision has not been fulfilled, Owen's great experiment laid the groundwork for employment practices that have today become accepted in much of the world.

Darren Breen/The Grand Rapids Press//Landov

An engaged employee Mohamed Mamow, left, was joined by his employer in saying the Pledge of Allegiance as he became a U.S. citizen. Mamow and his wife met in a Somali refugee camp and now are parents of five children, whom he supports by working as a machine operator. Mindful of his responsibility—"I don't like to lose my job. I have a responsibility for my children and my family"—he arrives for work a half hour early and tends to every detail on his shift. "He is an extremely hard-working employee," noted his employer, and "a reminder to all of us that we are really blessed" (Roelofs, 2010).

Statistical digests of prior research have found only a modest positive correlation between individual job satisfaction and performance (Judge et al., 2001; Ng et al., 2009; Parker et al., 2003). In one analysis of 4500 employees at 42 British manufacturing companies, the most productive workers tended to be those in satisfying work environments (Patterson et al., 2004). Happy workers are usually good workers. But does satisfaction *produce* better job performance? The debate continues.

Nevertheless, some organizations do have a knack for cultivating more engaged and productive employees. In the United States, the *Fortune* "100 Best Companies to Work For" have also produced markedly higher-than-average returns for their investors (Fulmer et al., 2003). Other positive data come from the biggest-ever I/O study, an analysis of Gallup data from more than 198,000 employees (**TABLE B.2**) in nearly 8000 business units of 36 large companies (including some 1100 bank branches, 1200 stores, and 4200 teams or departments). James Harter, Frank Schmidt, and Theodore Hayes (2002) explored correlations between various measures of organizational success and *employee engagement*—the extent of workers' involvement, enthusiasm, and identification with their organizations

✔ TABLE B.2

The Gallup Workplace Audit Overall satisfaction—On a 5-point scale, where 5 is extremely satisfied and 1 is extremely dissatisfied, how satisfied are you with (*name of company*) as a place to work? On a scale of 1 to 5, where 1 is strongly disagree and 5 is strongly agree, please indicate your agreement with the following items:

1. I know what is expected from me at work.
2. I have the materials and equipment I need to do my work right.
3. At work, I have the opportunity to do what I do best every day.
4. In the last seven days, I have received recognition or praise for doing good work.
5. My supervisor, or someone at work, seems to care about me as a person.
6. There is someone at work who encourages my development.
7. At work, my opinions seem to count.
8. The mission/purpose of my company makes me feel my job is important.
9. My associates (fellow employees) are committed to doing quality work.
10. I have a best friend at work.
11. In the last six months, someone at work has talked to me about my progress.
12. This last year, I have had opportunities at work to learn and grow.

Note: These statements are proprietary and copyrighted by The Gallup Organization. They may not be printed or reproduced in any manner without the written consent of The Gallup Organization. Reprinted here by permission.

TABLE B.3

Three Types of Employees

Engaged: working with passion and feeling a profound connection to their company or organization.

Not engaged: putting in the time but investing little passion or energy in their work.

Actively disengaged: unhappy workers undermining what their colleagues accomplish.

Source: Information from Gallup via Crabtree, 2005.

(**TABLE B.3**). They found that engaged workers (compared with disengaged workers who were just putting in time) knew what was expected of them, had what they needed to do their work, felt fulfilled in their work, had regular opportunities to do what they do best, perceived that they were part of something significant, and had opportunities to learn and develop. They also found that business units with engaged employees had more loyal customers, lower turnover rates, higher productivity, and greater profits.

But what causal arrows explain this correlation between business success and employee morale and engagement? Does success boost morale, or does high morale boost success? In a follow-up longitudinal study of 142,000 workers, researchers found that, over time, employee attitudes predicted *future* business success (more than the other way around) (Harter et al., 2010). Another analysis compared companies with top-quartile versus below-average employee engagement levels. Over a three-year period, earnings grew 2.6 times faster for the companies with highly engaged workers (Ott, 2007).

Managing Well

◀◎▶   B-4   What are some effective leadership techniques?

Every leader dreams of managing in ways that enhance people's satisfaction, engagement, and productivity and their organization's success. Effective leaders harness job-relevant strengths, set goals, and choose an appropriate leadership style.

Harnessing Job-Relevant Strengths

"The major challenge for CEOs [is] the effective deployment of human assets," observed Marcus Buckingham (2001). That challenge is "about psychology. It's about getting [individuals] to be more productive, more focused, more fulfilled than [they were] yesterday." The first step, he and others have maintained, is selecting the right people, followed by discerning employees' natural interests, adjusting work roles to suit those interests, and developing interests into great strengths (**FIGURE B.3**). Consider the faculty at a given college or university. Should everyone be expected to teach the same course load, advise the same number of students, serve on the same number of committees, and engage in the same amount of research? Or should each job description be tailored to harness a specific person's unique strengths?

Given that our temperament and our traits tend to follow us through our lives, managers would be wise to spend less time trying to instill strengths that are not there and more time developing and drawing out those that are there (Tucker, 2002). Managers who excel

- start by helping people identify and measure their strengths.
- match tasks to strengths and then give people freedom to do what they do best.
- care how their people feel about their work.
- reinforce positive behaviors through recognition and reward.

> FIGURE B.3

On the right path The Gallup Organization offers this path to organizational success. (Information from Fleming, 2001.)

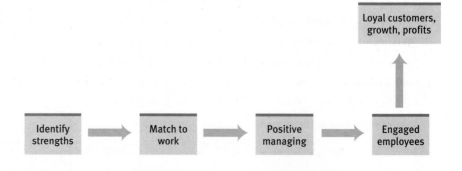

In Gallup surveys, 77 percent of engaged workers, and only 23 percent of not-engaged workers, strongly agreed that "my supervisor focuses on my strengths or positive characteristics" (Krueger & Killham, 2005).

Celebrating engaged and productive employees in every organizational role builds upon a basic principle of *operant conditioning:* To teach a behavior, catch a person doing something right and reinforce it. It sounds simple, but many managers are like parents who, when a child brings home near-perfect grades, focus on the one low grade in a troublesome biology class and ignore the rest. "Sixty-five percent of Americans received NO praise or recognition in the workplace last year," reported the Gallup Organization (2004).

The bottom line: In the workplace, great managers support employees' well-being. By caring about their employees and engaging and affirming their strengths, they support happier, more creative, more productive workers with less absenteeism and turnover (Amabile & Kramer, 2011; De Neve et al., 2013). People tolerate bad companies more than bad managers (Busteed, 2012). Moreover, the same principles affect college students' satisfaction, retention, and future success (Larkin et al., 2013; Ray & Kafka, 2014). Students who feel supported by caring friends and mentors, and engaged in their campus life, tend to persist and ultimately succeed during and after college.

Scott Eklund/AP Photo

The power of positive coaching
Football coach Pete Carroll, who led the University of Southern California to two national championships and the Seattle Seahawks to a Super Bowl championship, combines positive enthusiasm and fun workouts with "a commitment to a nurturing environment that allows people to be themselves while still being accountable to the team" (Trotter, 2014). "It shows you can win with positivity," notes Seahawks star defensive player Richard Sherman.

Setting Specific, Challenging Goals

Specific, challenging goals motivate achievement, especially when combined with progress reports (Johnson et al., 2006; Latham & Locke, 2007). Specific, measurable objectives, such as "finish gathering the history paper information by Friday," serve to direct attention, promote effort, motivate persistence, and stimulate creative strategies.

When people state goals together with *subgoals* and *implementation intentions*—action plans that specify when, where, and how they will march toward achieving those goals—they become more focused in their work, and on-time completion becomes more likely (Burgess et al., 2004; Fishbach et al., 2006; Koestner et al., 2002). Through a task's ups and downs, people best sustain their mood and motivation when they focus on immediate goals (such as daily study) rather than distant goals (such as a course grade). Better to have one's nose to the grindstone than one's eye on the ultimate prize (Houser-Marko & Sheldon, 2008).

Thus, before beginning each new edition of this book, our author-editor team *manages by objectives*—we agree on target dates for the completion and editing of each module draft. If we focus on achieving each of these short-term goals, the prize—an on-time book—takes care of itself. So, to motivate high productivity, effective leaders work with people to define explicit goals, subgoals, and implementation plans, and then provide feedback on progress.

Choosing an Appropriate Leadership Style

Leadership varies from a boss-focused directive style to an empowered-worker democratic style in which people cooperate in setting goals and developing strategies. Which works best depends on the situation and the leader. The best leadership style for leading a discussion may not be the best style for leading troops on a charge (Fiedler, 1981). Moreover, different leaders are suited to different styles. Some excel at **task leadership**—setting standards, organizing work, and focusing attention on goals. Being goal-oriented, task leaders are good at keeping a

task leadership goal-oriented leadership that sets standards, organizes work, and focuses attention on goals.

---

social leadership group-oriented leadership that builds teamwork, mediates conflict, and offers support.

"Good leaders don't ask more than their constituents can give, but they often ask—and get—more than their constituents intended to give or thought it was possible to give."

John W. Gardner, Excellence, *1984*

---

group centered on its mission. Typically, they have a directive style, which can work well if the leader is bright enough to give good orders (Fiedler, 1987).

Other managers, many of whom are women, excel at **social leadership**—explaining decisions, mediating conflicts, and building high-achieving teams (Evans & Dion, 1991; Pfaff et al., 2013). Social leaders often have a democratic style: They delegate authority and welcome team members' participation. Many experiments show that social leadership and team-building increase morale and productivity (Shuffler et al., 2011, 2013). Subordinates usually felt more satisfied and motivated, and performed better, when they participated in decision making (Cawley et al., 1998; Pereira & Osburn, 2007). Moreover, when members are sensitive to one another and participate equally, groups solve problems with greater "collective intelligence" (Woolley et al., 2010).

Effective leaders tend to be neither extremely assertive (impairing social relationships) nor unassertive (limiting task leadership) (Ames, 2008). Effective leaders of laboratory groups, work teams, corporations, and society have also been found to exude a *charisma* that blends a *goal-based vision, clear communication,* and *optimism* that inspires others to follow (Goethals & Allison, 2014; House & Singh, 1987; Shamir et al., 1993).

In one study of 50 Dutch companies, the firms with the highest morale had chief executives who most inspired their colleagues "to transcend their own self-interests for the sake of the collective" (de Hoogh et al., 2004). *Transformational leadership* of this kind motivates others to identify with and commit themselves to the group's mission. Transformational leaders, many of whom are natural extraverts, articulate high standards, inspire people to share their vision, and offer personal attention (Bono & Judge, 2004). The frequent result is more engaged, trusting, and effective workers (Turner et al., 2002). As leaders, women more than men tend to exhibit transformational leadership qualities. Alice Eagly (2007, 2013) believes this helps explain why companies with female top managers have tended to enjoy superior financial results, even after controlling for such variables as company size.

Data compiled from studies in India, Taiwan, and Iran indicate that effective managers—whether in coal mines, banks, or government offices—often exhibit a high degree of *both* task and social leadership (Smith & Tayeb, 1989). As achievement-minded people, effective managers certainly care about how well work is done, yet at the same time they are sensitive to their subordinates' needs. Workers in family-friendly organizations that offer flexible-time hours report feeling greater job satisfaction and loyalty to their employers (Butts et al., 2013; Roehling et al., 2001).

A work environment that satisfies one's need to belong also energizes employees. Employees who enjoy high-quality colleague relationships also engage in their work with more vigor (Carmeli et al., 2009). Gallup researchers have asked

more than 15 million employees worldwide if they have a "best friend at work." The 30 percent who do "are *seven times* as likely to be engaged in their jobs" as those who don't, they report (Rath & Harter, 2010). And, as we noted earlier, positive, engaged employees are a mark of thriving organizations.

Increased employee participation in decision making is part of a management style that has spread from Sweden and Japan to many other locations (Naylor, 1990; Sundstrom et al., 1990). Although managers often think better of work they have directly supervised, studies reveal a *voice effect:* Given a chance to voice their opinion and be part of a decision-making process, people have responded more positively to the decision (van den Bos & Spruijt, 2002). They also feel more empowered and are likely, therefore, to be more creative (Hennessey & Amabile, 2010; Seibert et al., 2011).

The ultimate in employee participation is the employee-owned company. One such company in my [DM's] town, the Fleetwood Group, is a thriving 165-employee manufacturer of educational furniture and wireless electronic clickers. Every employee owns part of the company, and as a group they own 100 percent. Like every corporate president, Doug Ruch works for his stockholders—who also just happen to be his employees. As a company that endorses faith-inspired "servant leadership" and "respect and care for each team member-owner," Fleetwood is free to place people above profits. Thus, when orders lagged during a recession, the employee-owners decided that job security meant more to them than profits. So the company paid otherwise idle workers to do community service, such as answering phones at nonprofit agencies and building Habitat for Humanity houses. Fleetwood employees "act like they own the place," notes Ruch. Employee ownership attracts and retains talented people, "drives dedication," and gives Fleetwood "a sustainable competitive advantage," he contends.

* * *

We have considered *personnel psychology* (the I/O subfield that focuses on employee's job seeking, selection, placement, appraisal, and development). And we have considered *organizational psychology* (the I/O subfield that focuses on worker satisfaction and productivity, and on organizational change). Finally, we turn to *human factors psychology*, which explores the human-machine interface.

RETRIEVE IT [✖]

• What characteristics are important for transformational leaders?

ANSWER: Transformational leaders are able to inspire others to share a vision and commit themselves to a group's mission. They tend to be naturally extraverted and set high standards.

The Human Factor

B-5 How do human factors psychologists work to create user-friendly machines and work settings?

Designs sometimes neglect the human factor. Psychologist Donald Norman bemoaned the complexity of assembling his new HDTV, related components, and seven remotes into a usable home theater system: "I was VP of Advanced Technology at Apple. I can program dozens of computers in dozens of languages. I understand television, really, I do. . . . It doesn't matter: I am overwhelmed."

How much easier life might be if engineers would routinely test their designs and instructions on real people. *Human factors psychologists* work with designers and engineers to tailor appliances, machines, and work settings to our natural perceptions and inclinations. Bank ATM machines are internally more complex than remote controls ever were, yet, thanks to human factors engineering, ATMs are easier to operate. Digital recorders have solved the TV recording problem

> **FIGURE B.4**

Designing products that fit people
Human factors psychologist Donald
Norman offers these and other examples
of effectively designed products. The Ride
On Carry On foldable chair attachment
(left), "designed by a flight attendant
mom," enables a small suitcase to double
as a stroller. The Oxo measuring cup
(right) allows the user to see the quantity
from above.

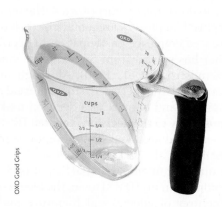

with a simple select-and-click menu system ("record that one"). Apple has similarly engineered easy usability with the iPhone and iPad.

Norman (2001) hosts a website (www.jnd.org) that illustrates good designs that fit people (**FIGURE B.4**). Human factors psychologists also help design efficient environments. An ideal kitchen layout, researchers have found, puts needed items close to their usage point and near eye level. It locates work areas to enable doing tasks in order, such as placing the refrigerator, stove, and sink in a triangle. It creates counters that enable hands to work at or slightly below elbow height (Boehm-Davis, 2005).

Understanding human factors can help prevent accidents. By studying the human factor in driving accidents, psychologists seek to devise ways to reduce the distractions, fatigue, and inattention that contribute to 1.3 million annual worldwide traffic fatalities (Lee, 2008). After beginning commercial flights in the 1960s, the Boeing 727 was involved in several landing accidents caused by pilot error. Psychologist Conrad Kraft (1978) noted a common setting for these accidents: All took place at night, and all involved landing short of the runway after crossing a dark stretch of water or unilluminated ground. Kraft reasoned that, on rising terrain, city lights beyond the runway would project a larger retinal image, making the ground seem farther away than it was. By re-creating these conditions in flight simulations, Kraft discovered that pilots were deceived into thinking they were flying higher than their actual altitudes (**FIGURE B.5**). Aided by Kraft's finding, the airlines began requiring the co-pilot to monitor the altimeter—calling out altitudes during the descent—and the accidents diminished.

Human factors psychologists can also help us to function in other settings. Consider the available *assistive listening* technologies in various theaters, auditoriums, and places of worship. One technology, commonly available in the United States, requires a headset attached to a pocket-sized receiver that detects infrared or FM signals from the room's sound system. The well-meaning people who design, purchase, and install these systems correctly understand that the technology puts sound directly into the user's ears. Alas, few people with hearing loss undergo the hassle and embarrassment of locating, requesting, wearing, and returning a conspicuous headset. Most such units therefore sit in closets. Britain, the Scandinavian countries, and Australia, and now many parts of the United States, have instead installed *loop systems* (see www.hearing-loop.org) that broadcast customized sound directly through a person's own hearing aid. When suitably equipped, a hearing aid can be transformed by a discreet touch of a switch into an in-the-ear loudspeaker. Offered convenient, inconspicuous, personalized sound, many more people elect to use assistive listening.

⌄ **FIGURE B.5**

The human factor in accidents
Lacking distance cues when approaching
a runway from over a dark surface, pilots
simulating a night landing tended to fly
too low. (Data from Kraft, 1978.)

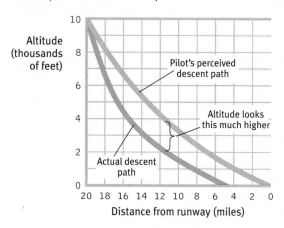

Designs that enable safe, easy, and effective interactions between people and technology often seem obvious after the fact. Why, then, aren't they more common? Technology developers sometimes mistakenly assume that others share their expertise—that what's clear to them will similarly be clear to others (Camerer et al., 1989; Nickerson, 1999). When people rap their knuckles on a table to convey a familiar tune (try this with a friend), they often expect their listener to recognize it. But for the listener, this is a near-impossible task (Newton, 1991). When you know a thing, it's hard to mentally simulate what it's like not to know, and that is called the *curse of knowledge*.

The point to remember: Everyone benefits when designers and engineers tailor machines and environments to fit human abilities and behaviors, when they user-test their inventions before production and distribution, and when they remain mindful of the curse of knowledge.

"The better you know something, the less you remember about how hard it was to learn."

Psychologist Steven Pinker,
The Sense of Style, *2014*

RETRIEVE IT [×]

• Name two main divisions of industrial-organizational psychology, and a related field.

ANSWER: personnel psychology, organizational psychology, human factors psychology

---

Steven Day/AP Photo

The human factor in safe landings Advanced cockpit design and rehearsed emergency procedures aided pilot Chesley "Sully" Sullenberger, a U.S. Air Force Academy graduate who earned a Master's degree in industrial psychology. In January 2009, Sullenberger's instantaneous decisions safely guided his disabled airplane onto New York City's Hudson River, where all 155 of the passengers and crew were safely evacuated.

···> REVIEW Psychology at Work

◉ Learning Objectives

Test Yourself by taking a moment to answer each of these Learning Objective Questions (repeated here from within the Appendix). Then turn to Appendix D, Complete Module Reviews, to check your answers. Research suggests that trying to answer these questions on your own will improve your long-term memory of the concepts (McDaniel et al., 2009).

B-1 What is *flow*, and what are the key subfields related to industrial-organizational psychology?

B-2 How do personnel psychologists help with job seeking, employee selection, work placement, and performance appraisal?

B-3 What is the role of organizational psychologists?

B-4 What are some effective leadership techniques?

B-5 How do human factors psychologists work to create user-friendly machines and work settings?

▪·[·] Terms and Concepts to Remember

Test yourself on these terms by trying to write down the definition in your own words before flipping back to the referenced page to check your answers.

flow, p. B-1

industrial-organizational (I/O) psychology, p. B-2

personnel psychology, p. B-2

organizational psychology, p. B-2

human factors psychology, p. B-2

structured interview, p. B-6

task leadership, p. B-11

social leadership, p. B-12

[×] Experience the Testing Effect

Test yourself repeatedly throughout your studies. This will not only help you figure out what you know and don't know; the testing itself will help you learn and remember the information more effectively thanks to the *testing effect*.

1. People who view their work as a calling often experience _____, a focused state of consciousness, with diminished awareness of themselves and of time.
   a. stress
   b. apathy
   c. flow
   d. facilitation

2. _____ psychologists study the recruitment, selection, placement, training, appraisal, and development of employees; _____ _____ psychologists focus on how people and machines interact, and on optimizing devices and work environments.

3. A personnel psychologist scripted a set of questions to ask all applicants for a job opening. She then trained the firm's interviewers to ask only these questions, to take notes, and to rate applicants' responses. This technique is known as a(n)
   a. structured interview.
   b. unstructured interview.
   c. performance appraisal checklist.
   d. behavior rating scale.

4. In your job, you rate your own performance, your manager's, and your peers'. Your manager, your peers, and your customers also rate your performance. Your organization is using a form of performance appraisal called
   a. flow procedure.
   b. graphic feedback.
   c. structured interviews.
   d. 360-degree feedback.

5. What type of goals will best help you stay focused and motivated to do your best work in this class?

6. Research indicates that women are more likely than men to have a _____ leadership style.

7. Effective managers often exhibit
   a. only task leadership.
   b. only social leadership.
   c. both task and social leadership, depending on the situation and the person.
   d. task leadership for building teams and social leadership for setting standards.

8. To reduce users' frustration and to avoid accidents, human factors psychologists help organizations avoid the curse of knowledge, which is the tendency for
   a. a little bit of knowledge to be dangerous for the user.
   b. users to override machines and resort to familiar habits.
   c. engineers and designers to assume that users are idiots and need overly detailed instructions.
   d. engineers and designers to assume that others will share their knowledge.

Find answers to these questions in Appendix E.

Use 🅐 LearningCurve to create your personalized study plan, which will direct you to the resources that will help you most in 🅐 LaunchPad .

Subfields of Psychology

Jennifer Zwolinski
University of San Diego

What can you do with a degree in psychology? Lots!

As a psychology major, you will graduate with a scientific mind-set and an awareness of basic principles of human behavior (biological mechanisms, development, cognition, psychological disorders, social interaction). This background will prepare you for success in many areas, including business, the helping professions, health services, marketing, law, sales, and teaching. You may even go on to graduate school for specialized training to become a psychology professional. This appendix describes psychology's specialized subfields.[1] I also provide updated information about CAREERS IN PSYCHOLOGY at www.macmillanhighered .com/launchpad/exploring10einmodules, where you can learn more about the many interesting options available to those with bachelor's, master's, and doctoral degrees in psychology.

If you are like most psychology students, you may be unaware of the wide variety of specialties and work settings available in psychology (Terre & Stoddart, 2000). To date, the American Psychological Association (APA) has 56 divisions (**TABLE C.1** on the next page). Use social media to learn more about the divisions by visiting www.tinyurl.com/APA-SocialMedia.

The following paragraphs (arranged alphabetically) describe some careers in the main specialty areas of psychology, most of which require a graduate degree in psychology.

CLINICAL PSYCHOLOGISTS promote psychological health in individuals, groups, and organizations. Some clinical psychologists specialize in specific psychological disorders. Others treat a range of disorders, from adjustment difficulties to severe psychopathology. Clinical psychologists might engage in research, teaching, assessment, and consultation. Some hold workshops and lectures on psychological issues for other professionals or for the public. Clinical psychologists work in a variety of settings, including private practice, mental health service organizations, schools, universities, industries, legal systems, medical systems, counseling centers, government agencies, and military services.

To become a clinical psychologist, you will need to earn a doctorate from a clinical psychology program. The APA sets the standards for clinical psychology graduate programs, offering accreditation (official recognition) to those who meet their standards. In all U.S. states, clinical psychologists working in independent practice must obtain a license to offer services such as therapy and testing.

COGNITIVE PSYCHOLOGISTS study thought processes and focus on such topics as perception, language, attention, problem solving, memory, judgment and decision making, forgetting, and intelligence. Research interests include designing computer-based models of thought processes and identifying biological

---

1. Although this text covers the world of psychology for students in many countries, this appendix draws primarily from available U.S. data. Its descriptions of psychology's subfields are, however, also applicable in many other countries.

∨ **TABLE C.1**

APA Divisions by Number and Name

1. Society for General Psychology	29. Society for the Advancement of Psychotherapy
2. Society for the Teaching of Psychology	30. Society of Psychological Hypnosis
3. Experimental Psychology	31. State, Provincial, and Territorial Psychological Association Affairs
4. There is no Division 4.	32. Society for Humanistic Psychology
5. Division for Quantitative and Qualitative Methods	33. Intellectual and Developmental Disabilities
6. Behavioral Neuroscience and Comparative Psychology	34. Society for Environmental, Population, and Conservation Psychology
7. Developmental Psychology	35. Society for the Psychology of Women
8. Society for Personality and Social Psychology	36. Society for the Psychology of Religion and Spirituality
9. Society for the Psychological Study of Social Issues	37. Society for Child and Family Policy and Practice
10. Society for the Psychology of Aesthetics, Creativity, and the Arts	38. Health Psychology
11. There is no Division 11.	39. Psychoanalysis
12. Society of Clinical Psychology	40. Society for Clinical Neuropsychology
13. Society of Consulting Psychology	41. American Psychology-Law Society
14. Society for Industrial and Organizational Psychology	42. Psychologists in Independent Practice
15. Educational Psychology	43. Society for Family Psychology
16. School Psychology	44. Society for the Psychological Study of Lesbian, Gay, Bisexual, and Transgender Issues
17. Society of Counseling Psychology	45. Society for the Psychological Study of Culture, Ethnicity, and Race
18. Psychologists in Public Service	46. Society for Media Psychology and Technology
19. Society for Military Psychology	47. Exercise and Sport Psychology
20. Adult Development and Aging	48. Society for the Study of Peace, Conflict, and Violence: Peace Psychology Division
21. Applied Experimental and Engineering Psychology	49. Society of Group Psychology and Group Psychotherapy
22. Rehabilitation Psychology	50. Society of Addiction Psychology
23. Society for Consumer Psychology	51. Society for the Psychological Study of Men and Masculinity
24. Society for Theoretical and Philosophical Psychology	52. International Psychology
25. Behavior Analysis	53. Society of Clinical Child and Adolescent Psychology
26. Society for the History of Psychology	54. Society of Pediatric Psychology
27. Society for Community Research and Action: Division of Community Psychology	55. American Society for the Advancement of Pharmacotherapy
28. Psychopharmacology and Substance Abuse	56. Trauma Psychology

Source: American Psychological Association. For a chronological history of the 56 divisions including why Divisions 4 and 11 are vacant, please see Appendix VIII at www.tinyurl.com/APA-DivisionHistory.

correlates of cognition. As a cognitive psychologist, you might work as a professor, industrial consultant, or human factors specialist in an educational or business setting.

COMMUNITY PSYCHOLOGISTS move beyond focusing on specific individuals or families and deal with broad problems of mental health in community settings. These psychologists believe that human behavior is powerfully influenced by the interaction between people and their physical, social, political, and economic environments. They seek to promote psychological health by enhancing environmental settings, focusing on preventive measures and crisis intervention, with special attention to the problems of underserved groups and ethnic minorities. Given the shared emphasis on prevention, some community psychologists

collaborate with professionals in other areas, such as public health. As a community psychologist, your work settings could include federal, state, and local departments of mental health, corrections, and welfare. You might conduct research or help evaluate research in health service settings, serve as an independent consultant for a private or government agency, or teach and consult as a college or university faculty member.

COUNSELING PSYCHOLOGISTS help people adjust to life transitions or make lifestyle changes. Although similar to clinical psychologists, counseling psychologists typically help people with adjustment problems rather than severe psychopathology. Like clinical psychologists, counseling psychologists conduct therapy and provide assessments to individuals and groups. As a counseling psychologist, you would emphasize your clients' strengths, helping them to use their own skills, interests, and abilities to cope during transitions. You might find yourself working in an academic setting as a faculty member or administrator or in a university counseling center, community mental health center, business, or private practice. As with clinical psychology, if you plan to work in independent practice you will need to obtain a state license to provide counseling services to the public.

Cognitive consulting Cognitive psychologists may advise businesses on how to operate more effectively by understanding the human factors involved.

DEVELOPMENTAL PSYCHOLOGISTS conduct research in age-related behavioral changes and apply their scientific knowledge to educational, child-care, policy, and related settings. As a developmental psychologist, you would investigate change across a broad range of topics, including the biological, psychological, cognitive, and social aspects of development. Developmental psychology informs a number of applied fields, including educational psychology, school psychology, child psychopathology, and gerontology. The field also informs public policy in areas such as education and child-care reform, maternal and child health, and attachment and adoption. You would probably specialize in a specific stage of the life span, such as infancy, childhood, adolescence, or middle or late adulthood. Your work setting could be an educational institution, day-care center, youth group program, or senior center.

EDUCATIONAL PSYCHOLOGISTS are interested in the psychological processes involved in learning. They study the relationship between learning and the physical and social environments, and they develop strategies for enhancing the learning process. As an educational psychologist, working in a university psychology department or school of education, you might conduct basic research on topics related to learning, or develop innovative methods of teaching to enhance the learning process. You might design effective tests, including measures of aptitude and achievement. You might be employed by a school or government agency or charged with designing and implementing effective employee-training programs in a business setting.

Community care This community psychologist (left) helped residents work through the emotional challenges that followed the devastating 2010 earthquake in Haiti.

EXPERIMENTAL PSYCHOLOGISTS are a diverse group of scientists who investigate a variety of basic behavioral processes in humans and other animals. Prominent areas of experimental research include comparative methods of science, motivation, learning, thought, attention, memory, perception, and language. Most experimental psychologists identify with a particular subfield, such as cognitive psychology, depending on their interests and training. It is important to note that experimental research methods are not limited to the field of experimental psychology; many other subfields rely on experimental methodology to

Criminal investigation Forensic psychologists may be called on to assist police officers who are investigating a crime scene, as seen here after a shooting in Florida. Most forensic work, however, occurs in the lab and for the judicial system.

conduct studies. As an experimental psychologist, you would most likely work in an academic setting, teaching courses and supervising students' research in addition to conducting your own research. Or you might be employed by a research institution, zoo, business, or government agency.

FORENSIC PSYCHOLOGISTS apply psychological principles to legal issues. They conduct research on the interface of law and psychology, help to create public policies related to mental health, help law-enforcement agencies in criminal investigations, or consult on jury selection and deliberation processes. They also provide assessment to assist the legal community. Although most forensic psychologists are clinical psychologists, they might have expertise in other areas of psychology, such as social or cognitive psychology. Some also hold law degrees. As a forensic psychologist, you might work in a university psychology department, law school, research organization, community mental health agency, law-enforcement agency, court, or correctional setting.

HEALTH PSYCHOLOGISTS are researchers and practitioners concerned with psychology's contribution to promoting health and preventing disease. As applied psychologists or clinicians, they may help individuals lead healthier lives by designing, conducting, and evaluating programs to stop smoking, lose weight, improve sleep, manage pain, prevent the spread of sexually transmitted infections, or treat psychosocial problems associated with chronic and terminal illnesses. As researchers and clinicians, they identify conditions and practices associated with health and illness to help create effective interventions. In public service, health psychologists study and work to improve government policies and health care systems. As a health psychologist, you could be employed in a hospital, medical school, rehabilitation center, public health agency, college or university, or, if you are also a clinical psychologist, in private practice.

INDUSTRIAL-ORGANIZATIONAL (I/O) PSYCHOLOGISTS study the relationship between people and their working environments. They may develop new ways to increase productivity, improve personnel selection, or promote job satisfaction in an organizational setting. Their interests include organizational structure and change, consumer behavior, and personnel selection and training. As an I/O psychologist, you might conduct workplace training or provide organizational analysis and development. You may find yourself working in business, industry, the government, or a college or university. Or you may be self-employed as a consultant or work for a management consulting firm.

NEUROPSYCHOLOGISTS investigate the relationship between neurological processes (structure and function of the brain) and behavior. As a neuropsychologist you might assess, diagnose, or treat central nervous system disorders, such as Alzheimer's disease or stroke. You might also evaluate individuals for evidence of head injuries; learning and developmental disabilities, such as autism; and other psychiatric disorders, such as attention-deficit hyperactivity disorder (ADHD). If you are a *clinical neuropsychologist*, you might work in a hospital's neurology, neurosurgery, or psychiatric unit. Neuropsychologists also work in academic settings, where they conduct research and teach.

PSYCHOMETRIC AND QUANTITATIVE PSYCHOLOGISTS study the methods and techniques used to acquire psychological knowledge. A psychometrician may update existing neurocognitive or personality tests or devise new tests for use in clinical and school settings or in business and industry. These psychologists also administer, score, and interpret such tests. Quantitative psychologists collaborate with researchers to design, analyze, and interpret the results of research

programs. As a psychometric or quantitative psychologist, you will need to be well trained in research methods, statistics, and computer technology. You will most likely be employed by a university or college, testing company, private research firm, or government agency.

REHABILITATION PSYCHOLOGISTS are researchers and practitioners who work with people who have lost optimal functioning after an accident, illness, or other event. As a rehabilitation psychologist, you would probably work in a medical rehabilitation institution or hospital. You might also work in a medical school, university, state or federal vocational rehabilitation agency, or in private practice serving people with physical disabilities.

SCHOOL PSYCHOLOGISTS are involved in the assessment of and intervention for children in educational settings. They diagnose and treat cognitive, social, and emotional problems that may negatively influence children's learning or overall functioning at school. As a school psychologist, you would collaborate with teachers, parents, and administrators, making recommendations to improve student learning. You would work in an academic setting, a federal or state government agency, a child guidance center, or a behavioral research laboratory.

SOCIAL PSYCHOLOGISTS are interested in our interactions with others. Social psychologists study how our beliefs, feelings, and behaviors are affected by and influence other people. They study topics such as attitudes, aggression, prejudice, interpersonal attraction, group behavior, and leadership. As a social psychologist, you would probably be a college or university faculty member. You might also work in organizational consultation, market research, or other applied psychology fields, including social neuroscience. Some social psychologists work for hospitals, federal agencies, or businesses performing applied research.

SPORT PSYCHOLOGISTS study the psychological factors that influence, and are influenced by, participation in sports and other physical activities. Their professional activities include coach education and athlete preparation, as well as research and teaching. Sport psychologists who also have a clinical or counseling degree can apply those skills to working with individuals with psychological problems, such as anxiety or substance abuse, that might interfere with optimal performance. As a sport psychologist, if you were not working in an academic or research setting, you would most likely work as part of a team or an organization or in a private capacity.

* * *

So, the next time someone asks you what you will do with your psychology degree, tell them you have a lot of options. You might use your acquired skills and understanding to get a job and succeed in any number of fields, or you might pursue graduate school and then career opportunities in associated professions. In any case, what you have learned about behavior and mental processes will surely enrich your life (Hammer, 2003).

Class counselor School psychologists, who have their master's degree in psychology, may find themselves working with students individually or in groups, as well as in a consultative role for their school's administrators.

Cricket cures Sport psychologists often work directly with athletes to help them improve their performance. Here a team psychologist consults with Brendon McCullum, a record-breaking athlete who plays international cricket for New Zealand.

Complete Module Reviews

Thinking Critically With Psychological Science

1 The History and Scope of Psychology

1-1 How do the scientific attitude's three main components relate to critical thinking?

The scientific attitude equips us to be curious, skeptical, and humble in scrutinizing competing ideas or our own observations. This attitude carries into everyday life as *critical thinking*, which puts ideas to the test by examining assumptions, appraising the source, discerning hidden biases, evaluating evidence, and assessing conclusions.

1-2 What were some important milestones in psychology's early development?

Wilhelm Wundt established the first psychological laboratory in 1879 in Germany. Two early schools were *structuralism* and *functionalism*.

1-3 How did psychology continue to develop from the 1920s through today?

Early researchers defined *psychology* as "the science of mental life." In the 1920s, under the influence of John B. Watson and the behaviorists, the field's focus changed to the "scientific study of observable behavior." *Behaviorism* became one of psychology's two major forces well into the 1960s. However, the second major force of *Freudian psychology,* along with the influences of *humanistic psychology* and *cognitive psychology,* revived interest in the study of mental processes. Psychology is now defined as the science of behavior and mental processes.

1-4 How has our understanding of biology and experience, culture and gender, and human flourishing shaped contemporary psychology?

Our growing understanding of biology and experience has fed psychology's most enduring debate. The *nature–nurture issue* centers on the relative contributions of genes and experience, and their interaction in specific environments. Charles Darwin's view that *natural selection* shapes behaviors as well as bodies led to *evolutionary psychology's* study of our similarities because of our common biology and evolutionary history, and *behavior genetics'* focus on the relative power and limits of genetic and environmental influences on behavior. Cross-cultural and gender studies have diversified psychology's assumptions while also reminding us of our similarities. Attitudes and behaviors may vary somewhat by gender or across *cultures,* but because of our shared human kinship, the underlying processes and principles are more similar than different. Psychology's traditional focus on understanding and treating troubles has expanded with *positive psychology's* call for more research on human flourishing and its attempt to discover and promote traits that help people to thrive.

1-5 What are psychology's levels of analysis and related perspectives?

The *biopsychosocial approach* integrates information from three differing but complementary *levels of analysis:* biological, psychological, and social-cultural.

This approach offers a more complete understanding than could usually be reached by relying on only one of psychology's current perspectives (neuroscience, evolutionary, behavior genetics, psychodynamic, behavioral, cognitive, and social-cultural).

1-6 What are psychology's main subfields?

Within the science of psychology, researchers may conduct *basic research* to increase the field's knowledge base (often in biological, developmental, cognitive, personality, and social psychology) or *applied research* to solve practical problems (in industrial-organizational psychology and other areas). Those who engage in psychology as a helping profession may assist people as *counseling psychologists,* helping people with problems in living or achieving greater well-being, or as *clinical psychologists,* studying and assessing people with psychological disorders and treating them with psychotherapy. (*Psychiatrists* also study, assess, and treat people with disorders, but as medical doctors, they may prescribe drugs in addition to psychotherapy.) *Community psychologists* work to create healthy social and physical environments (in schools, for example).

MODULE 2 Research Strategies: How Psychologists Ask and Answer Questions

2-1 How does our everyday thinking sometimes lead us to a wrong conclusion?

Our everyday thinking can be perilous because of three phenomena: hindsight bias, overconfidence, and a tendency to perceive order in random events. *Hindsight bias* (also called the "I-knew-it-all-along phenomenon") is the tendency to believe, after learning an outcome, that we would have foreseen it. Overconfidence in our judgments results partly from our bias to seek information that confirms them. These tendencies, plus our eagerness to perceive patterns in random events, lead us to overestimate our *intuition.* Although limited by the testable questions it can address, scientific inquiry can help us overcome our intuition's biases and shortcomings.

2-2 How do theories advance psychological science?

Psychological *theories* are explanations that apply an integrated set of principles to organize observations and generate *hypotheses*—predictions that can be used to check the theory or produce practical applications of it. By testing their hypotheses, researchers can confirm, reject, or revise their theories. To enable other researchers to *replicate* the studies, researchers report them using precise *operational definitions* of their procedures and concepts. If others achieve similar results, confidence in the conclusion will be greater.

2-3 How do psychologists use case studies, naturalistic observations, and surveys to observe and describe behavior, and why is random sampling important?

Descriptive methods, which include *case studies, naturalistic observations,* and *surveys,* show us what can happen, and they may offer ideas for further study. The best basis for generalizing about a *population* is a representative sample; in a *random sample,* every person in the entire population being studied has an equal chance of participating. Descriptive methods cannot show cause and effect because researchers cannot control variables.

2-4 What are positive and negative correlations, and why do they enable prediction but not cause-effect explanation?

In a positive *correlation,* two factors increase or decrease together. In a negative correlation, one item increases as the other decreases. A *correlation coefficient* can describe the strength and direction of a relationship between two variables,

from +1.00 (a perfect positive correlation) through zero (no correlation at all) to –1.00 (a perfect negative correlation). A correlation can indicate the possibility of a cause-effect relationship, but it does not prove the direction of the influence, or whether an underlying third factor may explain the correlation.

2-5 What are the characteristics of experimentation that make it possible to isolate cause and effect?

To discover cause-effect relationships, psychologists conduct *experiments,* manipulating one or more factors of interest and controlling other factors. Using *random assignment,* they can minimize *confounding variables,* such as preexisting differences between the *experimental group* (exposed to the treatment) and the *control group* (given a placebo or different version of the treatment). The *independent variable* is the factor the experimenter manipulates to study its effect; the *dependent variable* is the factor the experimenter measures to discover any changes occurring in response to the manipulations. Studies may use a *double-blind procedure* to avoid the *placebo effect.* Psychological scientists must design studies and choose research methods that will best provide meaningful results. (The Immersive Learning: How Would You Know? activities in LaunchPad show how testable questions are developed and studied.)

2-6 Can laboratory experiments illuminate everyday life?

Researchers intentionally create a controlled, artificial environment in the laboratory in order to test general theoretical principles. These general principles help explain everyday behaviors.

2-7 Why do psychologists study animals, and what ethical guidelines safeguard human and animal research participants? How do human values influence psychology?

Some psychologists are primarily interested in animal behavior; others want to better understand the physiological and psychological processes shared by humans and other species. Government agencies have established standards for animal care and housing. Professional associations and funding agencies also establish guidelines for protecting animals' well-being. The APA ethics code outlines standards for safeguarding human participants' well-being, including obtaining their *informed consent* and *debriefing* them later. Psychologists' values influence their choice of research topics, their theories and observations, their labels for behavior, and their professional advice. Applications of psychology's principles have been used mainly in the service of humanity.

2-8 How can psychological principles help you learn and remember?

The *testing effect* shows that learning and memory are enhanced by actively retrieving, rather than simply rereading, previously studied material. The *SQ3R* study method—survey, question, read, retrieve, and review—applies principles derived from memory research. Four additional tips are (1) distribute your study time; (2) learn to think critically; (3) process class information actively; and (4) overlearn.

The Biology of Behavior

MODULE
3 Neural and Hormonal Systems

3-1 Why are psychologists concerned with human biology?

Psychologists working from a *biological* perspective study the links between biology and behavior. We are biopsychosocial systems, in which biological, psychological, and social-cultural factors interact to influence behavior.

3-2 What are neurons, and how do they transmit information?

Neurons are the basic building blocks of the nervous system, the body's speedy electrochemical information system. A neuron receives signals through its branching *dendrites,* and sends signals through its *axons.* Some axons are encased in a *myelin sheath,* which enables faster transmission. *Glial cells* provide myelin, and they support, nourish, and protect neurons; they may also play a role in learning and thinking. If the combined signals received by a neuron exceed a minimum *threshold* (about negative 55 millivolts), the neuron fires, transmitting an electrical impulse (the *action potential*) down its axon by means of a chemistry-to-electricity process. The neuron's reaction is an *all-or-none process. Absolute or relative refractory periods* are tiny (millisecond) breaks between action potentials.

3-3 How do nerve cells communicate with other nerve cells?

When action potentials reach the end of an axon (the axon terminals), they stimulate the release of *neurotransmitters.* These chemical messengers carry a message from the sending neuron across a *synapse* to receptor sites on a receiving neuron. The sending neuron, in a process called *reuptake,* then normally reabsorbs the excess neurotransmitter molecules in the synaptic gap. If incoming signals are strong enough, the receiving neuron generates its own action potential and relays the message to other cells.

3-4 How do neurotransmitters influence behavior, and how do drugs and other chemicals affect neurotransmission?

Neurotransmitters travel designated pathways in the brain and may influence specific behaviors and emotions. Acetylcholine (ACh) affects muscle action, learning, and memory. *Endorphins* are natural opiates released in response to pain and exercise. Drugs and other chemicals affect brain chemistry at synapses. *Agonists* increase a neurotransmitter's action, and may do so in various ways. *Antagonists* decrease a neurotransmitter's action by blocking production or release.

3-5 What are the functions of the nervous system's main divisions, and what are the three main types of neurons?

The *central nervous system (CNS)*—the brain and the spinal cord—is the *nervous system's* decision maker. The *peripheral nervous system (PNS),* which connects the CNS to the rest of the body by means of *nerves,* gathers information and transmits CNS decisions to the rest of the body. The two main PNS divisions are the *somatic nervous system* (which enables voluntary control of the skeletal muscles) and the *autonomic nervous system* (which controls involuntary muscles and glands by means of its *sympathetic* and *parasympathetic* divisions). Neurons cluster into working networks. There are three types of neurons: (1) *Sensory (afferent) neurons* carry incoming information from sensory receptors to the brain and spinal cord. (2) *Motor (efferent) neurons* carry information from the brain and spinal cord out to the muscles and glands. (3) *Interneurons* communicate within the brain and spinal cord and between sensory and motor neurons.

3-6 How does the endocrine system transmit information and interact with the nervous system?

The *endocrine system* is a set of glands that secrete *hormones* into the bloodstream, where they travel through the body and affect other tissues, including the brain. The endocrine system's master gland, the *pituitary,* influences hormone release by other glands, including the *adrenal glands.* In an intricate feedback system, the brain's hypothalamus influences the pituitary gland, which influences other glands, which release hormones, which in turn influence the brain.

MODULE 4 Tools of Discovery and Older Brain Structures

4-1 How do neuroscientists study the brain's connections to behavior and mind?

Clinical observations and *lesioning* reveal the general effects of brain damage. Electrical, chemical, or magnetic stimulation can also reveal aspects of information processing in the brain. *MRI* scans show anatomy. *EEG, PET,* and *fMRI (functional MRI)* recordings reveal brain function.

4-2 What structures make up the brainstem, and what are the functions of the brainstem, thalamus, reticular formation, and cerebellum?

The *brainstem,* the oldest part of the brain, is responsible for automatic survival functions. Its components are the *medulla* (which controls heartbeat and breathing), the pons (which helps coordinate movements and control sleep), and the *reticular formation* (which affects arousal). The *thalamus,* sitting above the brainstem, acts as the brain's sensory control center. The *cerebellum,* attached to the rear of the brainstem, enables nonverbal learning and skill memory, helps coordinates muscle movement and balance, and also helps process sensory information.

4-3 What are the limbic system's structures and functions?

The *limbic system* is linked to emotions, memory, and drives. Its neural centers include the *amygdala* (involved in responses of aggression and fear); the *hypothalamus* (involved in various bodily maintenance functions, pleasurable rewards, and the control of the endocrine system); and the *hippocampus* (which processes conscious memories). The hypothalamus also controls the pituitary (the "master gland") by stimulating it to trigger the release of hormones.

MODULE 5 The Cerebral Cortex and Our Divided Brain

5-1 What are the functions of the various cerebral cortex regions?

The *cerebral cortex* has two hemispheres, and each hemisphere has four lobes: the *frontal, parietal, occipital,* and *temporal.* Each lobe performs many functions and interacts with other areas of the cortex. The *motor cortex,* at the rear of the frontal lobes, controls voluntary movements. The *somatosensory cortex,* at the front of the parietal lobes, registers and processes body touch and movement sensations. Body parts requiring precise control (in the motor cortex) or those that are especially sensitive (in the somatosensory cortex) occupy the greatest amount of space. Most of the brain's cortex—the major portion of each of the four lobes—is devoted to uncommitted *association areas,* which integrate information involved in learning, remembering, thinking, and other higher-level functions. Our mental experiences arise from coordinated brain activity.

5-2 To what extent can a damaged brain reorganize itself, and what is neurogenesis?

If one hemisphere is damaged early in life, the other will pick up many of its functions by reorganizing or building new pathways. This *plasticity* diminishes later in life. The brain sometimes mends itself by forming new neurons, a process known as *neurogenesis.*

5-3 What do split brains reveal about the functions of our two brain hemispheres?

Split-brain research (experiments on people with a severed *corpus callosum*) has confirmed that in most people, the left hemisphere is the more verbal, and that the right hemisphere excels in visual perception and the recognition of emotion.

Studies of healthy people with intact brains confirm that each hemisphere makes unique contributions to the integrated functioning of the brain.

MODULE 6 Genetics, Evolutionary Psychology, and Behavior

6-1 What are *chromosomes, DNA, genes,* and the human *genome?* How do behavior geneticists explain our individual differences?

Genes are the biochemical units of heredity that make up *chromosomes*, the threadlike coils of *DNA*. When genes are "turned on" (expressed), they provide the code for creating the proteins that form our body's building blocks. Most human traits are influenced by many genes acting together. The *human genome* is the shared genetic profile that distinguishes humans from other species, consisting at an individual level of all the genetic material in an organism's chromosomes. *Behavior geneticists* study the relative power and limits of genetic (our *heredity*) and *environmental* influences on behavior.

6-2 How do twin and adoption studies help us understand the effects and interactions of nature and nurture?

Studies of *identical (monozygotic) twins* versus *fraternal (dizygotic) twins*, separated twins, and biological versus adoptive relatives allow researchers to tease apart the influences of heredity and environment. Research studies on separated identical twins maintain the same genes while testing the effects of different home environments. Studies of adoptive families let researchers maintain the same home environment while studying the effects of genetic differences. Heritable individual differences (in traits such as height and weight) do not necessarily explain gender or ethnic group differences. Shared family environments have little effect on personality, though parenting does influence other factors (such as attitudes).

6-3 How do heredity and environment work together?

Our genetic predispositions and our specific environments *interact*. Environments can trigger or block genetic expression, and genetically influenced traits can evoke responses from others. The field of *epigenetics* studies the influences on gene expression that occur without changes in DNA.

6-4 How do evolutionary psychologists use natural selection to explain behavior tendencies?

Evolutionary psychologists seek to understand how our traits and behavior tendencies are shaped by *natural selection*, as genetic variations increasing the odds of reproducing and surviving in their particular environment are most likely to be passed on to future generations. Some variations arise from *mutations* (random errors in gene replication), others from new gene combinations at conception. Humans share a genetic legacy and are predisposed to behave in ways that promoted our ancestors' surviving and reproducing. Charles Darwin's theory of evolution is an organizing principle in biology. He anticipated today's application of evolutionary principles in psychology.

Consciousness and the Two-Track Mind

MODULE 7 Consciousness: Some Basic Concepts

7-1 What is the place of consciousness in psychology's history?

Since 1960, under the influence of cognitive psychology, neuroscience, and *cognitive neuroscience*, our awareness of ourselves and our environment—our

consciousness—has reclaimed its place as an important area of research. After initially claiming consciousness as its area of study in the nineteenth century, psychologists had abandoned it in the first half of the twentieth century, turning instead to the study of observable behavior because they believed consciousness was too difficult to study scientifically.

7-2 How does selective attention direct our perceptions?

We *selectively attend* to, and process, a very limited portion of incoming information, blocking out much and often shifting the spotlight of our attention from one thing to another. Focused intently on one task, we often display *inattentional blindness* to other events and *change blindness* to changes around us.

7-3 What is the *dual processing* being revealed by today's cognitive neuroscience?

Scientists studying the brain mechanisms underlying consciousness and cognition have discovered that the mind processes information on two separate tracks. One operates at an explicit, conscious level (conscious sequential processing that requires focused attention) and the other at an implicit, unconscious level (unconscious *parallel processing* of routine business). Together, this *dual processing*—conscious and unconscious—affects our perception, memory, attitudes, and other cognitions.

MODULE
8 Sleep and Dreams

8-1 What is sleep?

Sleep is the periodic, natural loss of consciousness—as distinct from unconsciousness resulting from a coma, general anesthesia, or hibernation. (Adapted from Dement, 1999.)

8-2 How do our biological rhythms influence our daily functioning?

Our bodies have an internal biological clock, roughly synchronized with the 24-hour cycle of night and day. This *circadian rhythm* appears in our daily patterns of body temperature, arousal, sleeping, and waking. Age and experiences can alter these patterns, resetting our biological clock.

8-3 What is the biological rhythm of our sleeping and dreaming stages?

Younger adults cycle through four distinct sleep stages about every 90 minutes. (The sleep cycle repeats more frequently for older adults.) Leaving the *alpha waves* of the awake, relaxed stage, we descend into the irregular brain waves of non-REM stage 1 (NREM-1) sleep, often with *hallucinations*, such as the sensation of falling or floating. NREM-2 sleep (in which we spend the most time) follows, lasting about 20 minutes, with its characteristic sleep spindles. We then enter NREM-3 sleep, lasting about 30 minutes, with large, slow *delta waves*. About an hour after falling asleep, we begin periods of *REM (rapid eye movement) sleep*. Most dreaming occurs in this stage (also known as paradoxical sleep) of internal arousal but outward paralysis. During a normal night's sleep, NREM-3 sleep shortens and REM and NREM-2 sleep lengthens.

8-4 How do biology and environment interact in our sleep patterns?

Our biology—our circadian rhythm as well as our age and our body's production of melatonin (influenced by the brain's *suprachiasmatic nucleus*)—interacts with cultural expectations and individual behaviors to determine our sleeping and waking patterns.

8-5 What are sleep's functions?

Sleep may have played a protective role in human evolution by keeping people safe during potentially dangerous periods. Sleep also helps restore and repair

damaged neurons. REM and NREM-2 sleep help strengthen neural connections that build enduring memories. Sleep promotes creative problem solving the next day. Finally, during deep sleep, the pituitary gland secretes a growth hormone necessary for muscle development.

8-6   How does sleep loss affect us, and what are the major sleep disorders?

Sleep deprivation causes fatigue and irritability, and it impairs concentration, productivity, and memory consolidation. It can also lead to depression, obesity, joint pain, a suppressed immune system, and slowed performance (with greater vulnerability to accidents). Sleep disorders include *insomnia* (recurring wakefulness); *narcolepsy* (sudden uncontrollable sleepiness or lapsing into REM sleep); *sleep apnea* (the stopping of breathing while asleep; associated with obesity, especially in men); *night terrors* (high arousal and the appearance of being terrified; NREM-3 disorder found mainly in children); sleepwalking (NREM-3 disorder also found mainly in children); and sleeptalking.

8-7   What do we dream?

We usually *dream* of ordinary events and everyday experiences, most involving some anxiety or misfortune. Fewer than 10 percent of dreams among men (and fewer still among women) have any sexual content. Most dreams occur during REM sleep.

8-8   What functions have theorists proposed for dreams?

There are five major views of the function of dreams. (1) Freud's wish-fulfillment: Dreams provide a psychic "safety valve," with *manifest content* (story line) acting as a censored version of *latent content* (underlying meaning that gratifies our unconscious wishes). (2) Information-processing: Dreams help us sort out the day's events and consolidate them in memory. (3) Physiological function: Regular brain stimulation may help develop and preserve neural pathways in the brain. (4) Neural activation: The brain attempts to make sense of neural static by weaving it into a story line. (5) Cognitive development: Dreams reflect the dreamer's level of development. Most sleep theorists agree that REM sleep and its associated dreams serve an important function, as shown by the *REM rebound* that occurs following REM deprivation in humans and other species.

MODULE
9 Drugs and Consciousness

9-1   What are substance use disorders, and what roles do tolerance, withdrawal, and addiction play in these disorders?

Those with a *substance use disorder* may exhibit impaired control, social disruption, risky behavior, and the physical effects of tolerance and withdrawal. *Psychoactive drugs* are any chemical substances that alter perceptions and moods. They may produce *tolerance*—requiring larger doses to achieve the desired effect—and *withdrawal*—significant discomfort accompanying attempts to quit. Continued use may lead to *addiction*, which is the compulsive craving of drugs or certain behaviors (such as gambling) despite known adverse consequences.

9-2   How has the concept of addiction changed?

Psychologists debate whether the concept of addiction has been stretched too far, and whether addictions are really as irresistible as commonly believed. Addictions can be powerful, and many with addictions do benefit from therapy or group support. But viewing addiction as an uncontrollable disease can undermine people's self-confidence and their belief that they can change. The addiction-as-disease-needing-treatment idea has been extended to a host of excessive, driven behaviors, but labeling a behavior doesn't explain it. The concept of addiction continues to evolve, as psychiatry's manual of disorders now includes behavior

addictions such as "gambling disorder" and proposes "Internet gaming disorder" for further study.

9-3 What are depressants, and what are their effects?

Depressants, such as alcohol, *barbiturates,* and the *opiates,* dampen neural activity and slow body functions. Alcohol tends to disinhibit, increasing the likelihood that we will act on our impulses, whether harmful or helpful. It also impairs judgment, disrupts memory processes by suppressing REM sleep, and reduces self-awareness and self-control. User expectations strongly influence alcohol's behavioral effects, and *alcohol use disorder* is marked by tolerance, withdrawal, and a drive to continue problematic use.

9-4 What are stimulants, and what are their effects?

Stimulants—including caffeine, *nicotine, cocaine,* the *amphetamines, methamphetamine,* and *Ecstasy*—excite neural activity and speed up body functions, triggering energy and mood changes. All are highly addictive. Nicotine's effects make the use of tobacco products a difficult habit to kick, but the percentage of Americans who use them continues to decrease. Cocaine gives users a fast high, followed within an hour by a crash. Its risks include cardiovascular stress and suspiciousness. Use of methamphetamines may permanently reduce dopamine production. Ecstasy (MDMA) is a combined stimulant and mild hallucinogen that produces euphoria and feelings of intimacy. Its users risk immune system suppression, permanent damage to mood and memory, and (if taken during physical activity) dehydration and escalating body temperatures.

9-5 What are hallucinogens, and what are their effects?

Hallucinogens—such as *LSD* and marijuana—distort perceptions and evoke hallucinations—sensory images in the absence of sensory input. The user's mood and expectations influence the effects of LSD, but common experiences are hallucinations and emotions varying from euphoria to panic. Marijuana's main ingredient, *THC,* may trigger feelings of disinhibition, euphoria, relaxation, relief from pain, and intense sensitivity to sensory stimuli. It may also increase feelings of depression or anxiety, impair motor coordination and reaction time, disrupt memory formation, and damage lung tissue (when inhaled).

9-6 Why do some people become regular users of consciousness-altering drugs?

Some people may be biologically vulnerable to particular drugs, such as alcohol. Psychological factors (such as stress, depression, and hopelessness) and social factors (such as peer pressure) combine to lead many people to experiment with—and sometimes become addicted to—drugs. Cultural and ethnic groups have differing rates of drug use. Each type of influence—biological, psychological, and social-cultural—offers a possible path for drug misuse prevention and treatment programs.

Developing Through the Life Span

MODULE
10 Developmental Issues, Prenatal Development, and the Newborn

10-1 What three issues have engaged developmental psychologists?

Developmental psychologists study physical, mental, and social changes throughout the life span. They focus on three issues: nature and nurture (the interaction between our genetic inheritance and our experiences); continuity and stages (whether development is gradual and continuous or a series of relatively

abrupt changes); and stability and change (whether our traits endure or change as we age).

10-2 What is the course of prenatal development, and how do teratogens affect that development?

The life cycle begins at conception, when one sperm cell unites with an egg to form a *zygote*. The zygote's inner cells become the *embryo*, and the outer cells become the placenta. In the next 6 weeks, body organs begin to form and function, and by 9 weeks, the *fetus* is recognizably human. *Teratogens* are potentially harmful agents that can pass through the placental screen and harm the developing embryo or fetus, as happens with *fetal alcohol syndrome*.

10-3 What are some newborn abilities, and how do researchers explore infants' mental abilities?

Babies are born with sensory equipment and reflexes that facilitate their survival and their social interactions with adults. For example, they quickly learn to discriminate their mother's smell and sound. Researchers use techniques that test *habituation,* such as the novelty-preference procedure, to explore infants' abilities.

MODULE 11 Infancy and Childhood

11-1 During infancy and childhood, how do the brain and motor skills develop?

The brain's nerve cells are sculpted by heredity and experience. As a child's brain develops, neural connections grow more numerous and complex. Experiences then trigger a pruning process, in which unused connections weaken and heavily used ones strengthen. This process continues until puberty. Early childhood is an important period for shaping the brain, but our brain modifies itself in response to our learning throughout life. In childhood, complex motor skills—sitting, standing, walking—develop in a predictable sequence, though the timing of that sequence is a function of individual *maturation* and culture. We have no conscious memories of events occurring before about age 3½. This infantile amnesia occurs in part because major brain areas have not yet matured.

11-2 From the perspectives of Piaget, Vygotsky, and today's researchers, how does a child's mind develop?

In his theory of *cognitive* development, Jean Piaget proposed that children actively construct and modify their understanding of the world through the processes of *assimilation* and *accommodation*. They form *schemas* that help them organize their experiences. Progressing from the simplicity of the *sensorimotor stage* of the first two years, in which they develop *object permanence*, children move to more complex ways of thinking. In the *preoperational stage* (about age 2 to about 6 or 7), they develop a *theory of mind*. In the preoperational stage, children are *egocentric* and unable to perform simple logical operations. At about age 7, they enter the *concrete operational stage* and are able to comprehend the principle of *conservation*. By about age 12, children enter the *formal operational stage* and can reason systematically. Research supports the sequence Piaget proposed, but it also shows that young children are more capable, and their development more continuous, than he believed. Lev Vygotsky's studies of child development focused on the ways a child's mind grows by interacting with the social environment. In his view, parents and caretakers provide temporary scaffolds enabling children to step to higher levels of learning.

11-3 What is autism spectrum disorder?

Autism spectrum disorder (ASD) is a disorder marked by social deficiencies and repetitive behaviors. By age 8, 1 in 68 U.S. children now gets diagnosed with ASD, though the reported rates vary by place. The increase in ASD diagnoses has been

offset by a decrease in the number of children with a "cognitive disability" or "learning disability," suggesting a relabeling of children's disorders.

11-4 How do parent-infant attachment bonds form?

At about 8 months, soon after object permanence develops, children separated from their caregivers display *stranger anxiety*. Infants form *attachments* not simply because parents gratify biological needs but, more important, because they are comfortable, familiar, and responsive. Many birds and other animals have a more rigid attachment process, called *imprinting*, that occurs during a *critical period*.

11-5 How have psychologists studied attachment differences, and what have they learned?

Attachment has been studied in strange situation experiments, which show that some children are securely attached and others are insecurely attached. Infants' differing attachment styles reflect both their individual *temperament* and the responsiveness of their parents and child-care providers. Adult relationships seem to reflect the attachment styles of early childhood, lending support to Erik Erikson's idea that *basic trust* is formed in infancy by our experiences with responsive caregivers.

11-6 How does childhood neglect or abuse affect children's attachments?

Children are very resilient, but those who are severely neglected by their parents, or otherwise prevented from forming attachments at an early age, may be at risk for attachment problems.

11-7 What are three parenting styles, and how do children's traits relate to them?

Parenting styles—authoritarian, permissive, and authoritative—reflect varying degrees of control. Children with high self-esteem tend to have authoritative parents and to be self-reliant and socially competent, but the direction of cause and effect in this relationship is not clear. Child-raising practices reflect both individual and cultural values.

MODULE
12 Adolescence

12-1 How is adolescence defined, and how do physical changes affect developing teens?

Adolescence is the transition period from childhood to adulthood, extending from *puberty* to social independence. Boys seem to benefit (though with risks) from "early" maturation, girls from "late" maturation. The brain's frontal lobes mature and myelin growth increases during adolescence and the early twenties, enabling improved judgment, impulse control, and long-term planning.

12-2 How did Piaget, Kohlberg, and later researchers describe adolescent cognitive and moral development?

Piaget theorized that adolescents develop a capacity for formal operations and that this development is the foundation for moral judgment. Lawrence Kohlberg proposed a stage theory of moral reasoning, from a preconventional morality of self-interest, to a conventional morality concerned with upholding laws and social rules, to (in some people) a postconventional morality of universal ethical principles. Other researchers believe that morality lies in moral intuition and moral action as well as thinking. Some critics argue that Kohlberg's postconventional level represents morality from the perspective of individualist, middle-class people.

12-3 What are the social tasks and challenges of adolescence?

Erikson theorized that each life stage has its own psychosocial task, and that a chief task of adolescence is solidifying one's sense of self—one's *identity*. This

often means trying out a number of different roles. *Social identity* is the part of the self-concept that comes from a person's group memberships.

12-4 How do parents and peers influence adolescents?

During adolescence, parental influence diminishes and peer influence increases, in part because of the selection effect—the tendency to choose similar others. But adolescents also do adopt their peers' ways of dressing, acting, and communicating. Parents have more influence in religion, politics, and college and career choices.

12-5 What is emerging adulthood?

The transition from adolescence to adulthood is now taking longer. *Emerging adulthood* is the period from age 18 to the mid-twenties, when many young people are not yet fully independent. But observers note that this stage is found mostly in today's Western cultures.

MODULE
13 Adulthood

13-1 What physical changes occur during middle and late adulthood?

Muscular strength, reaction time, sensory abilities, and cardiac output begin to decline in the late twenties and continue to decline throughout middle adulthood (roughly age 40 to 65) and late adulthood (the years after 65). Women's period of fertility ends with *menopause* around age 50; men have no similar age-related sharp drop in hormone levels or fertility. In late adulthood, the immune system weakens, increasing susceptibility to life-threatening illnesses. Chromosome tips (telomeres) wear down, reducing the chances of normal genetic replication. But for some, longevity-supporting genes, low stress, and good health habits enable better health in later life.

13-2 How does memory change with age?

As the years pass, recall begins to decline, especially for meaningless information, but recognition memory remains strong. Developmental researchers study age-related changes such as in memory with *cross-sectional studies* (comparing people of different ages) and *longitudinal studies* (retesting the same people over a period of years). "Terminal decline" describes the cognitive decline in the final few years of life.

13-3 What themes and influences mark our social journey from early adulthood to death?

Adults do not progress through an orderly sequence of age-related social stages. Chance events can determine life choices. The *social clock* is a culture's preferred timing for social events, such as marriage, parenthood, and retirement. Adulthood's dominant themes are love and work, which Erikson called *intimacy* and *generativity*.

13-4 How does our well-being change across the life span?

Self-confidence tends to strengthen across the life span. Surveys show that life satisfaction is unrelated to age. Positive emotions increase after midlife and negative ones decrease.

13-5 A loved one's death triggers what range of reactions?

People do not grieve in predictable stages, as was once supposed. Strong expressions of emotion do not purge grief, and bereavement therapy is not significantly more effective than grieving without such aid. Erikson viewed the late-adulthood psychosocial task as developing a sense of integrity (versus despair).

Sex, Gender, and Sexuality

MODULE
14 Gender Development

14-1 How does the meaning of *gender* differ from the meaning of *sex?*

In psychology, *gender* is the socially influenced characteristics by which people define men and women. *Sex* refers to the biologically influenced characteristics by which people define males and females. Our gender is thus the product of the interplay among our biological dispositions, our developmental experiences, and our current situation.

14-2 What are some ways in which males and females tend to be alike and to differ?

We are more alike than different, thanks to our similar genetic makeup—we see, hear, learn, and remember similarly. Males and females do differ in body fat, muscle, height, age of onset of puberty, life expectancy, and vulnerability to certain disorders. Men admit to more *aggression* than women do, and they are more likely to be physically aggressive. Women's aggression is more likely to be *relational.* In most societies, men have more social power, and their leadership style tends to be directive, whereas women's is more democratic. Women focus more on social connectedness, and they "tend and befriend."

14-3 How do sex hormones influence prenatal and adolescent sexual development, and what is a *disorder of sexual development?*

Both sex chromosomes and sex hormones influence development. Biological sex is determined by the father's contribution to the twenty-third pair of chromosomes. The mother always contributes an *X chromosome.* The father may also contribute an X chromosome, producing a female, or a *Y chromosome,* producing a male by triggering additional *testosterone* release and the development of male sex organs. During *puberty,* both *primary* and *secondary sex characteristics* develop. Sex-related genes and physiology influence behavioral and cognitive differences between males and females. *Disorders of sexual development* are inherited conditions that involve unusual development of sex chromosomes and anatomy.

14-4 How do gender roles and gender identity differ?

Gender roles, the behaviors a culture expects from its males and females, vary across place and time. *Social learning theory* proposes that we learn *gender identity*—our sense of being male, female, or some combination of the two— as we learn other things: through reinforcement, punishment, and observation. Critics argue that cognition also plays a role because modeling and rewards cannot explain variability in *gender typing.* Some children organize themselves into "boy worlds" and "girl worlds"; others prefer *androgyny. Transgender* people's gender identity or expression differs from their birth sex. Their sexual orientation may be heterosexual, homosexual, bisexual, or asexual.

MODULE
15 Human Sexuality

15-1 How do hormones influence human sexual motivation?

For all but the tiny fraction of us considered *asexual,* dating and mating become a high priority from puberty on. The female *estrogen* and male *testosterone* hormones influence human sexual behavior less directly than they influence sexual behavior in other species. Women's sexuality is more responsive to testosterone level than to estrogen level. Short-term shifts in testosterone level are normal in men, partly in response to stimulation.

15-2 What is the human sexual response cycle, and how do sexual dysfunctions and paraphilias differ?

William Masters and Virginia Johnson described four stages in the human *sexual response cycle:* excitement, plateau, orgasm (which involves similar feelings and brain activity in males and females), and resolution. During the resolution phase, males experience a *refractory period* in which renewed arousal and orgasm are impossible. *Sexual dysfunctions* are problems that consistently impair sexual arousal or functioning. They include *erectile disorder* and *female orgasmic disorder*, and can often be successfully treated by behaviorally oriented therapy or drug therapy. *Paraphilias* are conditions, which may be classified as disorders, in which sexual arousal is related to nonhuman objects, the suffering of self or others, and/or nonconsenting persons.

15-3 How can sexually transmitted infections be prevented?

Safe-sex practices help prevent sexually transmitted infections (STIs). Condoms are especially effective in preventing transmission of HIV, the virus that causes *AIDS.* A vaccination administered before sexual contact can prevent most human papilloma virus infections.

15-4 How do external and imagined stimuli contribute to sexual arousal?

External stimuli can trigger sexual arousal in both men and women. In experiments, depictions of sexual coercion have increased acceptance of rape. Sexually explicit material may lead people to perceive their partners as comparatively less appealing and to devalue their relationships. Imagined stimuli (dreams and fantasies) also influence sexual arousal.

15-5 What factors influence teenagers' sexual behaviors and use of contraceptives?

Rates of teen intercourse vary from culture to culture and era to era. Factors contributing to teen pregnancy include minimal communication about birth control with parents, partners, and peers; guilt related to sexual activity; alcohol use; and mass media norms of unprotected and impulsive sexuality. High intelligence, religious engagement, father presence, and participation in service learning programs have been predictors of teen sexual restraint.

15-6 What has research taught us about sexual orientation?

Sexual orientation is an enduring sexual attraction toward members of one's own sex (homosexual orientation), the other sex (heterosexual orientation), or both sexes (bisexual orientation). About 3 or 4 percent of men and 2 percent of women in Europe and the United States identify as exclusively homosexual, and 3.4 percent of Americans describe themselves as lesbian, gay, bisexual, or transgender. There is no evidence that environmental influences determine sexual orientation. Evidence for biological influences includes the presence of same-sex attraction in many animal species; straight-gay brain differences; higher rates in certain families and in identical twins; exposure to certain hormones during critical periods of prenatal development; and the fraternal birth-order effect.

15-7 How might an evolutionary psychologist explain male-female differences in sexuality and mating preferences?

Evolutionary psychologists use natural selection to explain why women tend to be choosier than men when selecting sexual partners. These psychologists reason that men's attraction to multiple healthy, fertile-appearing partners increases their chances of spreading their genes widely. Because women incubate and nurse babies, they have more at stake. Women increase their own and their children's chances of survival by searching for mates with the potential for long-term investment in their joint offspring.

15-8 What are the key criticisms of evolutionary explanations of human sexuality, and how do evolutionary psychologists respond?

Critics argue that evolutionary psychologists start with an effect and work backward to an explanation. They also charge that evolutionary psychologists try to explain today's behavior based on decisions our distant ancestors made thousands of years ago, noting that a better, more immediate explanation takes learned *social scripts* into account. And, the critics wonder, does this kind of explanation absolve people from taking responsibility for their sexual behavior? Evolutionary psychologists respond that understanding our predispositions can help us overcome them. They recognize the importance of social and cultural influences, but they also cite the value of testable predictions based on evolutionary principles.

15-9 What role do social factors play in our sexuality, and how do nature, nurture, and our own choices influence gender roles and sexuality?

Our ancestral history helped form us as a species. Our genes form us, but our culture and experiences also form us. Sex is a socially significant act, and our gender identities and mating behaviors are the products of both our genes and our environments. We are both the creatures and creators of our worlds, with our own hopes, goals, and expectations directing our future.

Sensation and Perception

MODULE
16 Basic Concepts of Sensation and Perception

16-1 What are *sensation* and *perception?* What do we mean by *bottom-up processing* and *top-down processing?*

Sensation is the process by which our sensory receptors and nervous system receive and represent stimulus energies from our environment. *Perception* is the process of organizing and interpreting this information, enabling recognition of meaningful events. Sensation and perception are actually parts of one continuous process. *Bottom-up processing* is sensory analysis that begins at the entry level, with information flowing from the sensory receptors to the brain. *Top-down processing* is information processing guided by high-level mental processes, as when we construct perceptions by filtering information through our experience and expectations.

16-2 What three steps are basic to all our sensory systems?

Our senses (1) receive sensory stimulation (often using specialized receptor cells); (2) transform that stimulation into neural impulses; and (3) deliver the neural information to the brain. *Transduction* is the process of converting one form of energy into another.

16-3 How do *absolute thresholds* and *difference thresholds* differ, and what effect, if any, do stimuli below the absolute threshold have on us?

Our *absolute threshold* for any stimulus is the minimum stimulation necessary for us to be consciously aware of it 50 percent of the time. *Signal detection theory* predicts how and when we will detect a faint stimulus amid background noise. Individual absolute thresholds vary, depending on the strength of the signal and also on our experience, expectations, motivation, and alertness. Our *difference threshold* (also called *just noticeable difference,* or *jnd*) is the difference we can discern between two stimuli 50 percent of the time. *Weber's law* states that two stimuli must differ by a constant minimum percentage (not a constant amount) to be perceived as different. *Priming* shows that we process some information from stimuli below our absolute threshold for conscious awareness.

16-4 Does subliminal sensation enable subliminal persuasion?

Subliminal stimuli are those that are too weak to detect 50 percent of the time. While subliminal sensation is a fact, such sensations are too fleeting to enable exploitation with subliminal messages: There is no powerful, enduring effect.

16-5 What is the function of sensory adaptation?

Sensory adaptation (our diminished sensitivity to constant or routine odors, sounds, and touches) focuses our attention on informative changes in our environment.

16-6 How do our expectations, contexts, motivation, and emotions influence our perceptions?

Perceptual set is a mental predisposition that functions as a lens through which we perceive the world. Our learned concepts (schemas) prime us to organize and interpret ambiguous stimuli in certain ways. Our physical and emotional context, as well as our motivation, can create expectations and color our interpretation of events and behaviors.

MODULE
17 Vision: Sensory and Perceptual Processing

17-1 What are the characteristics of the energy that we see as visible light? What structures in the eye help focus that energy?

What we see as light is only a thin slice of the broad spectrum of electromagnetic energy. The portion visible to humans extends from the blue-violet to the red light wavelengths. After entering the eye and being focused by a *lens*, light energy particles strike the eye's inner surface, the *retina*. The *hue* we perceive in a light depends on its *wavelength*, and its brightness depends on its *intensity*.

17-2 How do the rods and cones process information, and what is the path information travels from the eye to the brain?

Light entering the eye triggers chemical changes in the light-sensitive *rods* and color-sensitive *cones* at the back of the retina, which convert light energy into neural impulses. After processing by bipolar and ganglion cells, neural impulses travel from the retina through the *optic nerve* to the thalamus, and on to the visual cortex.

17-3 How do we perceive color in the world around us?

According to the *Young-Helmholtz trichromatic (three-color) theory*, the retina contains three types of color receptors. Contemporary research has found three types of cones, each most sensitive to the wavelengths of one of the three primary colors of light (red, green, or blue). Hering's *opponent-process theory* proposed three additional color processes (red-versus-green, blue-versus-yellow, black-versus-white). Research has confirmed that, en route to the brain, neurons in the retina and the thalamus code the color-related information from the cones into pairs of opponent colors. These two theories, and the research supporting them, show that color processing occurs in two stages.

17-4 Where are feature detectors located, and what do they do?

Feature detectors, located in the visual cortex, respond to specific features of the visual stimulus, such as shape, angle, or movement. Supercell clusters in other critical areas respond to more complex patterns.

17-5 How does the brain use parallel processing to construct visual perceptions?

Through *parallel processing,* the brain handles many aspects of vision (color, movement, form, and depth) simultaneously. Other neural teams integrate the results, comparing them with stored information and enabling perceptions.

17-6 How did the Gestalt psychologists understand perceptual organization, and how do figure-ground and grouping principles contribute to our perceptions?

Gestalt psychologists searched for rules by which the brain organizes fragments of sensory data into *gestalts* (from the German word for "whole"), or meaningful forms. In pointing out that the whole may exceed the sum of its parts, they noted that we filter sensory information and construct our perceptions. To recognize an object, we must first perceive it (see it as a *figure*) as distinct from its surroundings (the *ground*). We bring order and form to stimuli by organizing them into meaningful *groups*, following such rules as proximity, continuity, and closure.

17-7 How do we use binocular and monocular cues to perceive the world in three dimensions?

Depth perception is our ability to see objects in three dimensions and judge distance. The *visual cliff* and other research demonstrate that many species perceive the world in three dimensions at, or very soon after, birth. *Binocular cues,* such as *retinal disparity,* are depth cues that rely on information from both eyes. *Monocular cues* (such as relative size, interposition, relative height, relative motion, linear perspective, and light and shadow) let us judge depth using information transmitted by only one eye.

17-8 How do perceptual constancies help us construct meaningful perceptions?

Perceptual constancies enable us to perceive objects as stable despite the changing image they cast on our retinas. *Color constancy* is our ability to perceive consistent color in objects, even though the lighting and wavelengths shift. Brightness (or lightness) constancy is our ability to perceive an object as having a constant lightness even when its illumination—the light cast upon it—changes. Our brain constructs our experience of an object's color or brightness through comparisons with other surrounding objects. Shape constancy is our ability to perceive familiar objects (such as an opening door) as unchanging in shape. Size constancy is perceiving objects as unchanging in size despite their changing retinal images. Knowing an object's size gives us clues to its distance; knowing its distance gives clues about its size, but we sometimes misread monocular distance cues and reach the wrong conclusions, as in the Moon illusion.

17-9 What does research on restored vision, sensory restriction, and perceptual adaptation reveal about the effects of experience on perception?

Experience guides our perceptual interpretations. People blind from birth who gained sight after surgery lack the experience to visually recognize shapes, forms, and complete faces. Sensory restriction research indicates that there is a critical period for some aspects of sensory and perceptual development. Without early stimulation, the brain's neural organization does not develop normally. People given glasses that shift the world slightly to the left or right, or even upside down, experience *perceptual adaptation.* They are initially disoriented, but they manage to adapt to their new context.

MODULE
18 The Nonvisual Senses

18-1 What are the characteristics of air pressure waves that we hear as sound?

Sound waves are bands of compressed and expanded air. Our ears detect these changes in air pressure and transform them into neural impulses, which the brain decodes as sound. Sound waves vary in amplitude, which we perceive as differing loudness, and in *frequency,* which we experience as differing *pitch*.

18-2 How does the ear transform sound energy into neural messages?

The outer ear is the visible portion of the ear. The *middle ear* is the chamber between the eardrum and *cochlea.* The *inner ear* consists of the cochlea,

semicircular canals, and vestibular sacs. Through a mechanical chain of events, sound waves traveling through the auditory canal cause tiny vibrations in the eardrum. The bones of the middle ear amplify the vibrations and relay them to the fluid-filled cochlea. Rippling of the basilar membrane, caused by pressure changes in the cochlear fluid, causes movement of the tiny hair cells, triggering neural messages to be sent (via the thalamus) to the auditory cortex in the brain. *Sensorineural hearing loss* (or nerve deafness) results from damage to the cochlea's hair cells or their associated nerves. *Conduction hearing loss* results from damage to the mechanical system that transmits sound waves to the cochlea. *Cochlear implants* can restore hearing for some people.

18-3 How do we detect loudness, discriminate pitch, and locate sounds?

Loudness is not related to the intensity of a hair cell's response. The brain interprets loudness from the number of activated hair cells. *Place theory* explains how we hear high-pitched sounds, and *frequency theory* explains how we hear low-pitched sounds. (A combination of the two theories explains how we hear pitches in the middle range.) Place theory proposes that our brain interprets a particular pitch by decoding the place where a sound wave stimulates the cochlea's basilar membrane. Frequency theory proposes that the brain deciphers the frequency of the neural impulses traveling up the auditory nerve to the brain. Sound waves strike one ear sooner and more intensely than the other. To locate sounds, the brain analyzes the minute differences in the sounds received by the two ears and computes the sound's source.

18-4 How do we sense touch?

Our sense of touch is actually several senses—pressure, warmth, cold, and pain—that combine to produce other sensations, such as "hot."

18-5 What biological, psychological, and social-cultural influences affect our experience of pain? How do placebos, distraction, and hypnosis help control pain?

Pain reflects bottom-up sensations (such as input from nociceptors, the sensory receptors that detect hurtful temperatures, pressure, or chemicals) and top-down processes (such as experience, attention, and culture). One theory of pain is that a *"gate"* in the spinal cord either opens to permit pain signals traveling up small nerve fibers to reach the brain, or closes to prevent their passage. The biopsychosocial perspective views our perception of pain as the sum of biological, psychological, and social-cultural influences. For example, our experience of pain is influenced by activity in the spinal cord's large and small fibers (a biological influence), attention to pain (a psychological influence), and cultural expectations (a social-cultural influence). Pain treatments often combine physical and psychological elements. Placebos can help by dampening the central nervous system's attention and response to painful experiences. Distractions draw people's attention away from painful stimulation. *Hypnosis,* which increases our response to suggestions, can also help relieve pain. *Posthypnotic suggestion* is used by some clinicians to control undesired symptoms.

18-6 In what ways are our senses of taste and smell similar, and how do they differ?

Taste and smell are both chemical senses. Taste is a composite of five basic sensations—sweet, sour, salty, bitter, and umami—and of the aromas that interact with information from the taste receptor cells of the taste buds. There are no basic sensations for smell. We smell something when molecules of a substance carried in the air reach a tiny cluster of 20 million receptor cells at the top of each nasal cavity. Odor molecules trigger combinations of receptors, in patterns that the olfactory cortex interprets. The receptor cells send messages to the brain's olfactory bulb, then to the temporal lobe, and to parts of the limbic system.

18-7 How do we sense our body's position and movement?

Through *kinesthesia*, we sense the position and movement of our body parts. We monitor our head's (and thus our body's) position and movement, and maintain our balance, with our *vestibular sense*.

18-8 How does *sensory interaction* influence our perceptions, and what is *embodied cognition*?

Our senses can influence one another. This *sensory interaction* occurs, for example, when the smell of a favorite food amplifies its taste. *Embodied cognition* is the influence of bodily sensations, gestures, and other states on cognitive preferences and judgments.

18-9 What are the claims of ESP, and what have most research psychologists concluded after putting these claims to the test?

Parapsychology is the study of paranormal phenomena, including *extrasensory perception (ESP)* and psychokinesis. The three most testable forms of ESP are telepathy (mind-to-mind communication), clairvoyance (perceiving remote events), and precognition (perceiving future events). Skeptics argue that (1) to believe in ESP, you must believe the brain is capable of perceiving without sensory input, and (2) researchers have been unable to replicate ESP phenomena under controlled conditions.

Learning

MODULE
⑲ Basic Learning Concepts and Classical Conditioning

19-1 What is *learning*, and what are some basic forms of learning?

Learning is the process of acquiring through experience new and relatively enduring information or behaviors. In *associative learning*, we learn that certain events occur together. In classical conditioning, we learn to associate two or more stimuli (a *stimulus* is any event or situation that evokes a response). We associate stimuli that we do not control, and we respond automatically. This is called *respondent behavior*. In operant conditioning, we learn to associate a response and its consequences. These associations produce *operant behaviors*. Through *cognitive learning*, we acquire mental information that guides our behavior. For example, in observational learning, we learn new behaviors by observing events and watching others.

19-2 What was behaviorism's view of learning?

Ivan Pavlov's work on classical conditioning laid the foundation for *behaviorism*, the view that psychology should be an objective science that studies behavior without reference to mental processes. The behaviorists believed that the basic laws of learning are the same for all species, including humans.

19-3 Who was Pavlov, and what are the basic components of classical conditioning?

Ivan Pavlov, a Russian physiologist, created novel experiments on learning. His early twentieth-century research over the last three decades of his life demonstrated that classical conditioning is a basic form of learning. *Classical conditioning* is a type of learning in which an organism comes to associate stimuli. In classical conditioning, an *NS* is a stimulus that elicits no response before conditioning. A *UR* is an event that occurs naturally (such as salivation), in response to some stimulus. A *US* is something that naturally and automatically (without learning) triggers the unlearned response (as food in the mouth triggers salivation). A *CS* is a previously neutral stimulus (such as a tone) that, after association with a US (such as food) comes to trigger a CR. A *CR* is the learned response (salivating) to the originally neutral (but now conditioned) stimulus.

19-4 In classical conditioning, what are the processes of acquisition, extinction, spontaneous recovery, generalization, and discrimination?

In classical conditioning, *acquisition* is associating an NS with the US so that the NS begins triggering the CR. Acquisition occurs most readily when the NS is presented just before (ideally, about a half-second before) a US, preparing the organism for the upcoming event. This finding supports the view that classical conditioning is biologically adaptive. *Extinction* is diminished responding when the CS no longer signals an impending US. *Spontaneous recovery* is the appearance of a formerly extinguished response, following a rest period. *Generalization* is the tendency to respond to stimuli that are similar to a CS. *Discrimination* is the learned ability to distinguish between a CS and other irrelevant stimuli.

19-5 Why does Pavlov's work remain so important?

Pavlov taught us that significant psychological phenomena can be studied objectively, and that classical conditioning is a basic form of learning that applies to all species.

19-6 What have been some applications of Pavlov's work to human health and well-being? How did Watson apply Pavlov's principles to learned fears?

Classical conditioning techniques are used to improve human health and well-being in many areas, including behavioral therapy for some types of psychological disorders. The body's immune system may also respond to classical conditioning. Pavlov's work also provided a basis for Watson's idea that human emotions and behaviors, though biologically influenced, are mainly a bundle of conditioned responses. Watson applied classical conditioning principles in his studies of "Little Albert" to demonstrate how specific fears might be conditioned.

MODULE 20 Operant Conditioning

20-1 What is operant conditioning?

In *operant conditioning,* behaviors followed by reinforcers increase; those followed by punishers often decrease.

20-2 Who was Skinner, and how is operant behavior reinforced and shaped?

B. F. Skinner was a college English major and aspiring writer who later entered psychology graduate school. He became modern behaviorism's most influential and controversial figure. Expanding on Edward Thorndike's *law of effect,* Skinner and others found that the behavior of rats or pigeons placed in an *operant chamber* (Skinner box) can be *shaped* by using reinforcers to guide closer and closer approximations of the desired behavior.

20-3 How do positive and negative reinforcement differ, and what are the basic types of reinforcers?

Reinforcement is any consequence that strengthens behavior. *Positive reinforcement* adds a desirable stimulus to increase the frequency of a behavior. *Negative reinforcement* removes an aversive stimulus to increase the frequency of a behavior. *Primary reinforcers* (such as receiving food when hungry or having nausea end during an illness) are innately satisfying—no learning is required. *Conditioned* (or secondary) *reinforcers* (such as cash) are satisfying because we have learned to associate them with more basic rewards (such as the food or medicine we buy with them). Immediate reinforcers (such as a purchased treat) offer immediate payback; delayed reinforcers (such as a weekly paycheck) require the ability to delay gratification.

20-4 How do different reinforcement schedules affect behavior?

A *reinforcement schedule* defines how often a response will be reinforced. In *continuous reinforcement* (reinforcing desired responses every time they occur),

learning is rapid, but so is extinction if rewards cease. In *partial (intermittent) reinforcement* (reinforcing responses only sometimes), initial learning is slower, but the behavior is much more resistant to extinction. *Fixed-ratio schedules* reinforce behaviors after a set number of responses; *variable-ratio schedules,* after an unpredictable number. *Fixed-interval schedules* reinforce behaviors after set time periods; *variable-interval schedules,* after unpredictable time periods.

20-5 How does punishment differ from negative reinforcement, and how does punishment affect behavior?

Punishment administers an undesirable consequence (such as spanking) or withdraws something desirable (such as taking away a favorite toy) in an attempt to decrease the frequency of a behavior (a child's disobedience). Negative reinforcement (taking an aspirin) removes an aversive stimulus (a headache). This desired consequence (freedom from pain) increases the likelihood that the behavior (taking aspirin to end pain) will be repeated. Punishment can have undesirable side effects, such as suppressing rather than changing unwanted behaviors; teaching aggression; creating fear; encouraging discrimination (so that the undesirable behavior appears when the punisher is not present); and fostering depression and feelings of helplessness.

20-6 Why did Skinner's ideas provoke controversy, and how might his operant conditioning principles be applied at school, in sports, at work, and at home?

Critics of Skinner's principles believed the approach dehumanized people by neglecting their personal freedom and seeking to control their actions. Skinner replied that people's actions are already controlled by external consequences, and that reinforcement is more humane than punishment as a means for controlling behavior. At school, teachers can use shaping techniques to guide students' behaviors, and they can use interactive software and websites to provide immediate feedback. (For example, the LearningCurve system available with this text provides such feedback and allows students to direct the pace of their own learning.) In sports, coaches can build players' skills and self-confidence by rewarding small improvements. At work, managers can boost productivity and morale by rewarding well-defined and achievable behaviors. At home, parents can reward desired behaviors but not undesirable ones. We can shape our own behavior by stating a realistic goal, planning how we will achieve it, monitoring the frequency of the desired behavior, reinforcing the desired behavior, and gradually reducing rewards as the behavior becomes habitual.

20-7 How does operant conditioning differ from classical conditioning?

In operant conditioning, an organism learns associations between its own behavior and resulting events; this form of conditioning involves operant behavior (behavior that operates on the environment, producing rewarding or punishing consequences). In classical conditioning, the organism forms associations between stimuli—events it does not control; this form of conditioning involves respondent behavior (automatic responses to some stimulus).

MODULE
21 Biology, Cognition, and Learning

21-1 How do biological constraints affect classical and operant conditioning?

Classical conditioning principles, we now know, are constrained by biological predispositions, so that learning some associations is easier than learning others. Learning is adaptive: Each species learns behaviors that aid its survival. Biological constraints also place limits on operant conditioning. Training that attempts to override biological constraints will probably not endure because animals will revert to predisposed patterns.

21-2 How do cognitive processes affect classical and operant conditioning?

In classical conditioning, animals may learn when to expect a US and may be aware of the link between stimuli and responses. In operant conditioning, *cognitive mapping* and *latent learning* research demonstrate the importance of cognitive processes in learning. Other research shows that excessive rewards (driving *extrinsic motivation*) can undermine *intrinsic motivation.*

21-3 How does observational learning differ from associative learning? How may observational learning be enabled by neural mirroring?

In *observational learning,* as we observe and imitate others we learn to anticipate a behavior's consequences because we experience vicarious reinforcement or vicarious punishment. In associative learning, we merely learn associations between different events. Our brain's frontal lobes have a demonstrated ability to mirror the activity of another's brain. Some psychologists believe *mirror neurons* enable this process. (Others argue it may be more due to the brain's distributed brain networks.) The same areas fire when we perform certain actions (such as responding to pain or moving our mouth to form words) as when we observe someone else performing those actions.

21-4 What is the impact of prosocial modeling and of antisocial modeling?

Children tend to imitate what a model does and says, whether the behavior being *modeled* is *prosocial* (positive, constructive, and helpful) or antisocial. If a model's actions and words are inconsistent, children may imitate the hypocrisy they observe.

Memory

MODULE
22 Studying and Encoding Memories

22-1 What is *memory,* and how is it measured?

Memory is learning that has persisted over time, through the encoding, storage, and retrieval of information. Evidence of memory may be *recalling* information, *recognizing* it, or *relearning* it more easily on a later attempt.

22-2 How do psychologists describe the human memory system?

Psychologists use memory models to think and communicate about memory. Information-processing models involve three processes: *encoding, storage,* and *retrieval.* Our agile brain processes many things simultaneously by means of *parallel processing.* The connectionism information-processing model focuses on this multitrack processing, viewing memories as products of interconnected neural networks. The three processing stages in the Atkinson-Shiffrin model are *sensory memory, short-term memory,* and *long-term memory.* This model has since been updated to include two important concepts: (1) *working memory,* to stress the active processing occurring in the second memory stage; and (2) automatic processing, to address the processing of information outside of conscious awareness.

22-3 How do explicit and implicit memories differ?

The human brain processes information on dual tracks, consciously and unconsciously. *Explicit* (declarative) *memories*—our conscious memories of facts and experiences—form through *effortful processing,* which requires conscious effort and attention. *Implicit* (nondeclarative) *memories*—of skills and classically conditioned associations—happen without our awareness, through *automatic processing.*

22-4 What information do we process automatically?

In addition to skills and classically conditioned associations, we automatically process incidental information about space, time, and frequency.

22-5 How does sensory memory work?

Sensory memory feeds some information into working memory for active processing there. An *iconic memory* is a very brief (a few tenths of a second) sensory memory of visual stimuli; an *echoic memory* is a three- or four-second sensory memory of auditory stimuli.

22-6 What is our short-term memory capacity?

Short-term memory capacity is about seven items, plus or minus two, but this information disappears from memory quickly without rehearsal. Our working memory capacity for active processing varies, depending on age, intelligence level, and other factors.

22-7 What are some effortful processing strategies that can help us remember new information?

Effective effortful processing strategies include *chunking, mnemonics,* hierarchies, and distributed practice sessions. The *testing effect* is enhanced memory after consciously retrieving, rather than simply rereading, information.

22-8 What are the levels of processing, and how do they affect encoding?

Depth of processing affects long-term retention. In *shallow processing,* we encode words based on their structure or appearance. Retention is best when we use *deep processing,* encoding words based on their meaning. We also more easily remember material that is personally meaningful—the self-reference effect.

MODULE
23 Storing and Retrieving Memories

23-1 What is the capacity of long-term memory? Are our long-term memories processed and stored in specific locations?

Our long-term memory capacity is essentially unlimited. Memories are not stored intact in the brain in single spots. Many parts of the brain interact as we encode, store, and retrieve memories.

23-2 What are the roles of the frontal lobes and hippocampus in memory processing?

The frontal lobes and *hippocampus* are parts of the brain network dedicated to explicit memory formation. Many brain regions send information to the frontal lobes for processing. The hippocampus, with the help of surrounding areas of cortex, registers and temporarily holds elements of explicit memories (which are either *semantic* or *episodic*) before moving them to other brain regions for long-term storage. The neural storage of long-term memories is called *memory consolidation.*

23-3 What are the roles of the cerebellum and basal ganglia in memory processing?

The cerebellum and basal ganglia are parts of the brain network dedicated to implicit memory formation. The cerebellum is important for storing classically conditioned memories. The basal ganglia are involved in motor movement and help form procedural memories for skills. Many reactions and skills learned during our first three years continue into our adult lives, but we cannot consciously remember learning these associations and skills, a phenomenon psychologists call infantile amnesia.

23-4 How do emotions affect our memory processing?

Emotional arousal causes an outpouring of stress hormones, which lead to activity in the brain's memory-forming areas. Significantly stressful events can trigger very clear *flashbulb memories.*

23-5 How do changes at the synapse level affect our memory processing?

Long-term potentiation (LTP) appears to be the neural basis of learning. In LTP, neurons become more efficient at releasing and sensing the presence of neurotransmitters, and more connections develop between neurons.

23-6 How do external cues, internal emotions, and order of appearance influence memory retrieval?

External cues activate associations that help us retrieve memories; this process may occur without our awareness, as it does in *priming*. Returning to the same physical context or emotional state *(mood congruency)* in which we formed a memory can help us retrieve it. The *serial position effect* accounts for our tendency to recall best the last items (which may still be in working memory) and the first items (which we've spent more time rehearsing) in a list.

MODULE 24 Forgetting, Memory Construction, and Improving Memory

24-1 Why do we forget?

Anterograde amnesia is an inability to form new memories. *Retrograde amnesia* is an inability to retrieve old memories. Normal forgetting can happen because we have never encoded information (encoding failure); because the physical trace has decayed (storage decay); or because we cannot retrieve what we have encoded and stored (retrieval failure). Retrieval problems may result from *proactive* (forward-acting) *interference*, as prior learning interferes with recall of new information, or from *retroactive* (backward-acting) *interference*, as new learning disrupts recall of old information. Some believe that motivated forgetting occurs, but researchers have found little evidence of *repression*.

24-2 How do misinformation, imagination, and source amnesia influence our memory construction? How do we decide whether a memory is real or false?

Memories can be continually revised when retrieved, a process memory researchers call *reconsolidation*. In experiments demonstrating the *misinformation effect*, people have formed false memories, incorporating misleading details after receiving the wrong information after an event or after repeatedly imagining and rehearsing something that never happened. When we reassemble a memory during retrieval, we may attribute it to the wrong source *(source amnesia)*. Source amnesia may help explain *déjà vu*. False memories feel like real memories and can be persistent but are usually limited to the gist of the event.

24-3 How reliable are young children's eyewitness descriptions?

Children are susceptible to the misinformation effect, but if questioned in neutral words they understand, they can accurately recall events and people involved in them.

24-4 Why are reports of repressed and recovered memories so hotly debated?

The debate (between memory researchers and some well-meaning therapists) focuses on whether most memories of early childhood abuse are repressed and can be recovered during therapy using "memory work" techniques often involving leading questions or hypnosis. Psychologists now agree that (1) sexual abuse happens; (2) injustice happens; (3) forgetting happens; (4) recovered memories are commonplace; (5) memories of things that happened before age 3 are unreliable; (6) memories "recovered" under hypnosis or the influence of drugs are especially unreliable; and (7) memories, whether real or false, can be emotionally upsetting.

24-5 How can you use memory research findings to do better in this and other courses?

Memory research findings suggest the following strategies for improving memory: Study repeatedly, make material meaningful, activate retrieval cues, use mnemonic devices, minimize interference, sleep more, and test yourself to be sure you can retrieve, as well as recognize, material.

Thinking, Language, and Intelligence

MODULE
25 Thinking

25-1 What is cognition, and what are the functions of concepts?

Cognition refers to all the mental activities associated with thinking, knowing, remembering, and communicating. We use *concepts*, mental groupings of similar objects, events, ideas, or people, to simplify and order the world around us. We form most concepts around *prototypes*, or best examples of a category.

25-2 What cognitive strategies assist our problem solving, and what obstacles hinder it?

An *algorithm* is a methodical, logical rule or procedure (such as a step-by-step description for evacuating a building during a fire) that guarantees a solution to a problem. A *heuristic* is a simpler strategy (such as running for an exit if you smell smoke) that is usually speedier than an algorithm but is also more error prone. *Insight* is not a strategy-based solution, but rather a sudden flash of inspiration that solves a problem. Obstacles to problem solving include *confirmation bias*, which predisposes us to verify rather than challenge our hypotheses, and fixation, such as *mental set*, which may prevent us from taking the fresh perspective that would lead to a solution.

25-3 What is intuition, and how can the availability heuristic, overconfidence, belief perseverance, and framing influence our decisions and judgments?

Intuition is the effortless, immediate, automatic feelings or thoughts we often use instead of systematic reasoning. Heuristics enable snap judgments. Using the *availability heuristic*, we judge the likelihood of things based on how readily they come to mind, which often leads us to fear the wrong things. *Overconfidence* can lead us to overestimate the accuracy of our beliefs. When a belief we have formed and explained has been discredited, *belief perseverance* may cause us to cling to that belief. A remedy for belief perseverance is to consider how we might have explained an opposite result. *Framing* is the way a question or statement is worded. Subtle wording differences can dramatically alter our responses.

25-4 What factors contribute to our fear of unlikely events?

We tend to be afraid of what our ancestral history has prepared us to fear (thus, snakes instead of cigarettes); what we cannot control (flying instead of driving); what is immediate (the takeoff and landing of flying instead of countless moments of trivial danger while driving); and what is most readily available (vivid images of air disasters instead of countless safe car trips).

25-5 How do smart thinkers use intuition?

As people gain expertise, they grow adept at making quick, shrewd judgments. Smart thinkers welcome their intuitions (which are usually adaptive), but when making complex decisions they gather as much information as possible and then take time to let their two-track mind process all available information.

25-6 What is creativity, and what fosters it?

Creativity, the ability to produce novel and valuable ideas, correlates somewhat with aptitude, but is more than school smarts. Aptitude tests require *convergent thinking,* but creativity requires *divergent thinking.* Robert Sternberg has proposed that creativity has five components: expertise; imaginative thinking skills; a venturesome personality; intrinsic motivation; and a creative environment that sparks, supports, and refines creative ideas.

25-7 What do we know about thinking in other animals?

Researchers make inferences about other species' consciousness and intelligence based on behavior. Evidence from studies of various species shows that many other animals use concepts, numbers, and tools and that they transmit learning from one generation to the next (cultural transmission). And, like humans, some other species show insight, self-awareness, altruism, cooperation, and grief.

MODULE 26 Language and Thought

26-1 What are the structural components of a language?

Phonemes are a *language's* basic units of sound. *Morphemes* are the elementary units of meaning. *Grammar*—the system of rules that enables us to communicate—includes semantics (rules for deriving meaning) and syntax (rules for ordering words into sentences). Linguist Noam Chomsky has proposed that all human languages share a universal grammar—the basic building blocks of language—and that humans are born with a predisposition to learn language. We acquire a specific language through learning as our biology and experience interact. B. F. Skinner believed we learn language as we learn other things—by association, imitation, and reinforcement.

26-2 What are the milestones in language development, and how do we acquire language?

Language development's timing varies, but all children follow the same sequence. Receptive language (the ability to understand what is said to or about you) develops before productive language (the ability to produce words). At about 4 months of age, infants *babble,* making sounds found in languages from all over the world. By about 10 months, their babbling contains only the sounds found in their household language. Around 12 months of age, children begin to speak in single words. This *one-word stage* evolves into *two-word (telegraphic)* utterances before their second birthday, after which they begin speaking in full sentences. Childhood is a critical period for learning to speak and/or sign fluently. This is an important consideration for parents of deaf children, who might master oral communication if given a cochlear implant during this critical period.

26-3 What brain areas are involved in language processing and speech?

Aphasia is an impairment of language, usually caused by left-hemisphere damage. Two important language- and speech-processing areas are *Broca's area,* a region of the frontal lobe that controls language expression, and *Wernicke's area,* a region in the left temporal lobe that controls language reception. Language processing is spread across other brain areas as well, where different neural networks handle specific linguistic subtasks.

26-4 What do we know about other animals' capacity for language?

A number of chimpanzees and bonobos have (1) learned to communicate with humans by signing or by pushing buttons wired to a computer, (2) developed vocabularies of nearly 400 words, (3) communicated by stringing these words together, (4) taught their skills to younger animals, and (5) demonstrated some

understanding of syntax. But only humans communicate in complex sentences. Nevertheless, other animals' impressive abilities to think and communicate challenge humans to consider what this means about the moral rights of other species.

26-5 What is the relationship between thinking and language, and what is the value of thinking in images?

Although Benjamin Lee Whorf's *linguistic determinism* hypothesis suggested that language determines thought, it is in fact more accurate to say that language influences thought. Different languages embody different ways of thinking, and immersion in bilingual education can enhance thinking. We often think in images when we use implicit (nondeclarative, procedural) memory—our automatic memory system for motor and cognitive skills and classically conditioned associations. Thinking in images can increase our skills when we mentally practice upcoming events.

MODULE
27 Intelligence and Its Assessment

27-1 How do psychologists define *intelligence,* and what are the arguments for *g?*

Intelligence is a mental quality consisting of the potential to learn from experience, solve problems, and use knowledge to adapt to new situations. Charles Spearman proposed that we have one *general intelligence (g)* underlying all other specific mental abilities. He helped develop factor analysis, a statistical procedure that identifies clusters of related abilities.

27-2 How do Gardner's and Sternberg's theories of multiple intelligences differ, and what criticisms have they faced?

Savant syndrome seems to support Howard Gardner's view that we have multiple intelligences. He proposed eight independent intelligences: linguistic, logical-mathematical, musical, spatial, bodily-kinesthetic, intrapersonal, interpersonal, and naturalist. (He has also proposed a ninth possible intelligence—existential intelligence—the ability to ponder deep questions about life.) Robert Sternberg's triarchic theory proposes three intelligence areas that predict real-world skills: analytical (academic problem solving), creative, and practical. Critics note research that has confirmed a general intelligence factor. But highly successful people also tend to be conscientious, well-connected, and doggedly energetic.

27-3 What are the four components of emotional intelligence?

Emotional intelligence, which is an aspect of social intelligence, is the ability to perceive, understand, manage, and use emotions. Emotionally intelligent people achieve greater personal and professional success. Some critics question whether calling these abilities "intelligence" stretches that concept too far.

27-4 What is an intelligence test, and what is the difference between achievement and aptitude tests?

An *intelligence test* is a method for assessing an individual's mental aptitudes and comparing them with others, using numerical scores. *Aptitude tests* measure the ability to learn, while *achievement tests* measure what we have already learned.

27-5 When and why were intelligence tests created, and how do today's tests differ from early intelligence tests?

Alfred Binet started the modern intelligence-testing movement in France in 1904 when he developed questions to help predict children's future progress in the Paris school system. During the early twentieth century, Lewis Terman of Stanford University revised Binet's work for use in the United States. He believed intelligence

was inherited, and he thought his *Stanford-Binet* could help guide people toward appropriate opportunities. Terman's assumption that certain ethnic groups were naturally more intelligent realized Binet's fear that intelligence tests would be used to label children and limit their opportunities. William Stern contributed the concept of the *IQ* (intelligence quotient). The most widely used intelligence tests today are the *Wechsler Adult Intelligence Scale (WAIS)* and Wechsler's tests for children. These tests differ from their predecessors in the way they offer an overall intelligence score as well as scores for various verbal and performance areas.

27-6 What is a normal curve, and what does it mean to say that a test has been standardized and is reliable and valid?

The distribution of test scores often forms a *normal* (bell-shaped) *curve* around the central average score, with fewer and fewer scores at the extremes. *Standardization* establishes a basis for meaningful score comparisons by giving a test to a representative sample of future test-takers. *Reliability* is the extent to which a test yields consistent results (on two halves of the test, on alternative forms of the test, or when people are retested). *Validity* is the extent to which a test measures or predicts what it is supposed to. A test has *content validity* if it samples the pertinent behavior (as a driving test measures driving ability). It has *predictive validity* if it predicts a behavior it was designed to predict. (Aptitude tests have predictive ability if they can predict future achievements; their predictive power is best for the early school years.)

27-7 How does aging affect crystallized and fluid intelligence?

Cross-sectional studies (comparing people of different ages) and longitudinal studies (retesting the same group over a period of years) have shown that *fluid intelligence* declines in older adults, in part because neural processing slows. However, *crystallized intelligence* tends to increase.

27-8 How stable are intelligence test scores over the life span?

The stability of intelligence test scores increases with age. At age 4, scores fluctuate somewhat but begin to predict adolescent and adult scores. By early adolescence, scores are very stable and predictive.

27-9 What are the traits of those at the low and high intelligence extremes?

At the low extreme are those with unusually low scores. An intelligence test score of or below 70 is one diagnostic criterion for the diagnosis of *intellectual disability;* other criteria are limited conceptual, social, and practical skills. One condition included in this category is *Down syndrome,* a developmental disorder caused by an extra copy of chromosome 21. People at the high-intelligence extreme tend to be healthy and well-adjusted, as well as unusually successful academically.

MODULE
28 Genetic and Environmental Influences on Intelligence

28-1 What evidence points to a genetic influence on intelligence, and what is heritability?

Studies of twins, family members, and adoptees indicate a significant hereditary contribution to intelligence scores. Intelligence seems to be polygenetic, and researchers are searching for genes that exert an influence. *Heritability* is the proportion of variation among individuals that can be attributed to genes.

28-2 What does evidence reveal about environmental influences on intelligence?

Studies of twins, family members, and adoptees also provide evidence of environmental influences. Test scores of identical twins raised apart are slightly less similar (though still very highly correlated) than the scores of identical twins raised together. Studies of children raised in extremely impoverished environments with

minimal social interaction indicate that life experiences can significantly influence intelligence test performance. No evidence supports the idea that normal, healthy children can be molded into geniuses by growing up in an exceptionally enriched environment.

28-3 How and why do the genders differ in mental ability scores?

Males and females tend to have the same average intelligence test scores, but they differ in some specific abilities. Girls are better spellers, more verbally fluent, better at locating objects, better at detecting emotions, and more sensitive to touch, taste, and color. Boys outperform girls at spatial ability and related mathematics, though in math computation and overall math performance, boys and girls hardly differ. Boys also outnumber girls at the low and high extremes of mental abilities. Evolutionary and cultural explanations have been proposed for these gender differences.

28-4 How and why do racial and ethnic groups differ in mental ability scores?

Racial and ethnic groups differ in their average intelligence test scores. The evidence suggests that environmental differences are responsible for these group differences.

28-5 Are intelligence tests inappropriately biased?

Aptitude tests aim to predict how well a test-taker will perform in a given situation. So they are necessarily "biased" in the sense that they are sensitive to performance differences caused by cultural experience. By "inappropriately biased," psychologists mean that a test predicts less accurately for one group than for another. In this sense, most experts consider the major aptitude tests unbiased. *Stereotype threat,* a self-confirming concern that one will be evaluated based on a negative stereotype, affects performance on all kinds of tests.

Motivation and Emotion

MODULE
29 Basic Motivational Concepts, Affiliation, and Achievement

29-1 How do psychologists define *motivation?* From what perspectives do they view motivated behavior?

Motivation is a need or desire that energizes and directs behavior. The *instinct/ evolutionary* perspective explores genetic influences on complex behaviors. *Drive-reduction theory* explores how physiological needs create aroused tension states (drives) that direct us to satisfy those needs. Environmental *incentives* can intensify drives. Drive-reduction's goal is *homeostasis,* maintaining a steady internal state. Arousal theory proposes that some behaviors (such as those driven by curiosity) do not reduce physiological needs but rather are prompted by a search for an optimum level of arousal. The *Yerkes-Dodson law* states that performance increases with arousal, but only to a certain point, after which it decreases. Performance peaks at lower levels of arousal for difficult tasks, and at higher levels for easy or well-learned tasks. Abraham Maslow's *hierarchy of needs* proposes a pyramid of human needs, from basic needs such as hunger and thirst up to higher-level needs such as self-actualization and self-transcendence.

29-2 What evidence points to our human affiliation need—our need to belong?

Our *need to affiliate* or belong—to feel connected and identified with others—had survival value for our ancestors, which may explain why humans in every society live in groups. Because of their need to belong, people suffer when socially excluded, and they may engage in self-defeating behaviors (performing below

their ability) or in antisocial behaviors. Feeling loved activates brain regions associated with reward and safety systems. *Ostracism* is the deliberate exclusion of individuals or groups. Social isolation can put us at risk mentally and physically.

29-3 How does social networking influence us?

We connect with others through social networking, strengthening our relationships with those we already know. When networking, people tend toward increased self-disclosure. People with high *narcissism* are especially active on social networking sites. Working out strategies for self-control and disciplined usage can help people maintain a healthy balance between social connections and school and work performance.

29-4 What is achievement motivation?

Achievement motivation is a desire for significant accomplishment, for mastery of skills or ideas, for control, and for attaining a high standard. Achievements are more closely related to *grit* (passionate dedication to a long-term goal) than to raw ability.

MODULE 30 Hunger

30-1 What physiological factors produce hunger?

Hunger pangs correspond to stomach contractions, but hunger also has other causes. Neural areas in the brain, some within the hypothalamus, monitor blood chemistry (including level of *glucose*) and incoming information about the body's state. Appetite hormones include ghrelin (secreted by an empty stomach); insulin (controls blood glucose); leptin (secreted by fat cells); orexin (secreted by the hypothalamus); and PYY (secreted by the digestive tract). *Basal metabolic rate* is the body's resting rate of energy expenditure. The body may have a *set point* (a biologically fixed tendency to maintain an optimum weight) or a looser settling point (also influenced by the environment).

30-2 What cultural and situational factors influence hunger?

Hunger also reflects our memory of when we last ate and our expectation of when we should eat again. Humans as a species prefer certain tastes (such as sweet and salty), but our individual preferences are also influenced by conditioning, culture, and situation. Some taste preferences, such as the avoidance of new foods, or of foods that have made us ill, have survival value.

30-3 What factors predispose some people to become and remain obese?

Genes and environment interact to produce obesity. Obesity correlates with depression, especially among women. Twin and adoption studies indicate that body weight is also genetically influenced. Environmental influences include lack of exercise, an abundance of high-calorie food, and social influence. Those wishing to lose weight are advised to make a lifelong change in habits: Begin only if you feel motivated and self-disciplined; exercise and get enough sleep; minimize exposure to tempting food cues; limit variety and eat healthy foods; reduce portion sizes; space meals throughout the day; beware of the binge; plan eating to help monitor yourself during social events; forgive the occasional lapse; and connect to a support group.

MODULE 31 Theories and Physiology of Emotion

31-1 How do arousal, expressive behavior, and cognition interact in emotion?

Emotions are psychological responses of the whole organism involving an interplay among physiological arousal, expressive behaviors, and conscious experience. Theories of emotion generally address two major questions: (1) Does physiological

arousal come before or after emotional feelings, and (2) how do feeling and cognition interact? The *James-Lange theory* maintains that emotional feelings follow our body's response to emotion-inducing stimuli. The *Cannon-Bard theory* proposes that our physiological response to an emotion-inducing stimulus occurs at the same time as our subjective feeling of the emotion (one does not cause the other).

31-2 To experience emotions, must we consciously interpret and label them?

The Schachter-Singer *two-factor theory* holds that our emotions have two ingredients, physical arousal and a cognitive label, and the cognitive labels we put on our states of arousal are an essential ingredient of emotion. Lazarus agreed that many important emotions arise from our interpretations or inferences. Zajonc and LeDoux, however, have contended that some simple emotional responses occur instantly, not only outside our conscious awareness, but before any cognitive processing occurs. This interplay between emotion and cognition illustrates our dual-track mind.

31-3 What are some of the basic emotions?

Carroll Izard's 10 basic emotions are joy, interest-excitement, surprise, sadness, anger, disgust, contempt, fear, shame, and guilt.

31-4 What is the link between emotional arousal and the autonomic nervous system?

The arousal component of emotion is regulated by the autonomic nervous system's sympathetic (arousing) and parasympathetic (calming) divisions. In a crisis, the fight-or-flight response automatically mobilizes your body for action.

31-5 Do different emotions activate different physiological and brain-pattern responses?

Emotions may be similarly arousing, but some subtle physiological responses, such as facial muscle movements, distinguish them. More meaningful differences have been found in activity in some brain pathways and cortical areas.

31-6 How effective are polygraphs in using body states to detect lies?

Polygraphs, which measure several physiological indicators of emotion, are not accurate enough to justify widespread use in business and law enforcement. The use of guilty knowledge questions and new forms of technology may produce better indications of lying.

MODULE 32 Expressing and Experiencing Emotion

32-1 How do we communicate nonverbally?

Much of our communication is through body movements, facial expressions, and voice tones. Even seconds-long filmed slices of behavior can reveal feelings.

32-2 Do the genders differ in their ability to communicate nonverbally?

Women tend to read emotional cues more easily and to be more empathic. Their faces also express more emotion.

32-3 Do gestures and facial expressions mean the same thing in all cultures?

The meaning of gestures varies with culture, but facial expressions, such as those of happiness and sadness, are common the world over. Cultures also differ in the amount of emotion they express.

32-4 How do our facial expressions influence our feelings?

Research on the *facial feedback effect* shows that our facial expressions can trigger emotional feelings and signal our body to respond accordingly. We also mimic

others' expressions, which helps us empathize. A similar *behavior feedback effect* is the tendency of behavior to influence our own and others' thoughts, feelings, and actions.

Stress, Health, and Human Flourishing

MODULE 33 Stress and Illness

33-1 What events provoke stress responses, and how do we respond and adapt to stress?

Stress is the process by which we appraise and respond to stressors (catastrophic events, significant life changes, and daily hassles) that challenge or threaten us. Walter Cannon viewed the stress response as a "fight-or-flight" system. Hans Selye proposed a general three-phase (alarm-resistance-exhaustion) *general adaptation syndrome (GAS)*. Facing stress, women may have a *tend-and-befriend* response; men may withdraw socially, turn to alcohol, or become aggressive.

33-2 How does stress make us more vulnerable to disease?

As we know from *psychoneuroimmunology* studies, stress diverts energy from the immune system, inhibiting the activities of its B and T lymphocytes, macrophages, and NK cells. Stress does not cause diseases such as AIDS and cancer, but by altering our immune functioning it may make us more vulnerable to them and influence their progression.

33-3 Why are some of us more prone than others to coronary heart disease?

Coronary heart disease, the United States' number one cause of death, has been linked with the reactive, anger-prone *Type A* personality. Compared with relaxed, easygoing *Type B* personalities, Type A people secrete more stress hormones. Chronic stress also contributes to persistent inflammation, which heightens the risk of clogged arteries and depression.

33-4 How do strategies for handling anger compare in their effectiveness?

Chronic hostility is one of the negative emotions linked to heart disease. Emotional *catharsis* may be temporarily calming, but in the long run it does not reduce anger. Expressing anger can make us angrier. Experts suggest reducing the level of physiological arousal of anger by waiting, finding a healthy distraction or support, and trying to move away from the situation mentally. Controlled assertions of feelings may resolve conflicts, and forgiveness may rid us of angry feelings.

MODULE 34 Health and Happiness

34-1 In what two ways do people try to alleviate stress?

We use *problem-focused coping* to change the stressor or the way we interact with it. We use *emotion-focused coping* to avoid or ignore stressors and attend to emotional needs related to stress reactions.

34-2 How does a perceived lack of control affect health?

A perceived lack of control provokes an outpouring of hormones that put people's health at risk. Being unable to avoid repeated aversive events can lead to *learned helplessness.* People who perceive an *internal locus of control* achieve more, enjoy better health, and are happier than those who perceive an *external locus of control.*

34-3 How can our self-control be depleted, and why is it important to build this strength?

Exercising willpower temporarily depletes the mental energy needed for *self-control* on other tasks. Self-control requires attention and energy, but it predicts good health, higher income, and better grades.

34-4 How does an optimistic outlook affect health and longevity?

Studies of people with an optimistic outlook show that their immune system is stronger, their blood pressure does not increase as sharply in response to stress, their recovery from heart bypass surgery is faster, and their life expectancy is longer, compared with their pessimistic counterparts.

34-5 How does social support promote good health?

Social support promotes health by calming us, by reducing blood pressure and stress hormones, and by fostering stronger immune functioning.

34-6 How effective is aerobic exercise as a way to manage stress and improve well-being?

Aerobic exercise is sustained, oxygen-consuming activity that increases heart and lung fitness. It increases arousal, leads to muscle relaxation and sounder sleep, triggers the production of neurotransmitters, and enhances self-image. It can relieve depression and, in later life, is associated with better cognitive functioning and longer life.

34-7 In what ways might relaxation and meditation influence stress and health?

Relaxation and *mindfulness meditation* have been shown to reduce stress by relaxing muscles, lowering blood pressure, improving immune functioning, and lessening anxiety and depression. Massage therapy also relaxes muscles and reduces depression.

34-8 What is the faith factor, and what are some possible explanations for the link between faith and health?

The faith factor is the finding that religiously active people tend to live longer than those who are not religiously active. Possible explanations may include the effect of intervening variables, such as the healthy behaviors, social support, or positive emotions often found among people who regularly attend religious services.

34-9 What is the *feel-good, do-good phenomenon*, and what is the focus of positive psychology research?

A good mood brightens people's perceptions of the world. *Subjective well-being* is your perception of being happy or satisfied with life. Happy people tend to be healthy, energized, and satisfied with life. They also are more willing to help others (the *feel-good, do-good phenomenon*). *Positive psychologists* use scientific methods to study human flourishing, with the goals of discovering and promoting strengths and virtues that help individuals and communities to thrive. The three pillars of positive psychology are positive well-being; positive character; and positive groups, communities, and cultures.

34-10 How do time, wealth, adaptation, and comparison affect our happiness levels?

The moods triggered by good or bad events seldom last beyond that day. Even significant good events, such as sudden wealth, seldom increase happiness for long. Happiness is relative to our own experiences (the *adaptation-level phenomenon*) and to others' success (the *relative deprivation* principle).

34-11 What are some predictors of happiness, and how can we be happier?

Some individuals, because of their genetic predispositions and personal histories, are happier than others. Cultures, which vary in the traits they value and the behaviors they expect and reward, also influence personal levels of happiness. Those who want to be happier can (1) realize that financial success may not lead to enduring happiness; (2) take control of their time; (3) act happy to trigger facial and behavioral feedback; (4) seek skill-engaging work and leisure to foster flow; (5) buy shared experiences rather than things; (6) exercise; (7) get adequate sleep; (8) nurture close relationships; (9) focus beyond themselves; (10) record and express their gratitude; and (11) nurture their spiritual self.

Social Psychology

MODULE
35 **Social Thinking and Social Influence**

35-1 What do social psychologists study? How do we tend to explain others' behavior and our own?

Social psychologists use scientific methods to study how people think about, influence, and relate to one another. They study the social influences that explain why the same person will act differently in different situations. When explaining others' behavior, we may—especially if we come from an individualist Western culture—commit the *fundamental attribution error,* by underestimating the influence of the situation and overestimating the effects of stable, enduring traits. When explaining our own behavior, we more readily attribute it to the influence of the situation.

35-2 How do attitudes and actions interact?

Attitudes are feelings, often influenced by our beliefs, that predispose us to respond in certain ways. *Peripheral route persuasion* uses incidental cues (such as celebrity endorsement) to try to produce fast but relatively thoughtless changes in attitudes. *Central route persuasion* offers evidence and arguments to trigger thoughtful responses. When other influences are minimal, attitudes that are stable, specific, and easily recalled can affect our actions. Actions can modify attitudes, as in the *foot-in-the-door phenomenon* (complying with a large request after having agreed to a small request) and *role* playing (acting a social part by following guidelines for expected behavior). When our attitudes don't fit with our actions, *cognitive dissonance theory* suggests that we will reduce tension by changing our attitudes to match our actions.

35-3 How does culture affect our behavior?

A *culture* is an enduring set of behaviors, ideas, attitudes, values, and traditions shared by a group and transmitted from one generation to the next. Cultural *norms* are understood rules that inform members of a culture about accepted and expected behaviors. Cultures differ across time and space.

35-4 What is automatic mimicry, and how do conformity experiments reveal the power of social influence?

Automatic mimicry (the chameleon effect)—our tendency to unconsciously imitate others' expressions, postures, and voice tones—is a form of *conformity.* Solomon Asch and others have found that we are most likely to adjust our behavior or thinking to coincide with a group standard when (a) we feel incompetent or insecure, (b) our group has at least three people, (c) everyone else agrees, (d) we admire the group's status and attractiveness, (e) we have not already committed to another response, (f) we know we are being observed, and (g) our culture

encourages respect for social standards. We may conform to gain approval *(normative social influence)* or because we are willing to accept others' opinions as new information *(informational social influence)*.

35-5 What did Milgram's obedience experiments teach us about the power of social influence?

Stanley Milgram's experiments—in which people obeyed orders even when they thought they were harming another person—demonstrated that strong social influences can make ordinary people conform to falsehoods or give in to cruelty. Obedience was highest when (a) the person giving orders was nearby and was perceived as a legitimate authority figure; (b) the research was supported by a prestigious institution; (c) the victim was depersonalized or at a distance; and (d) there were no role models for defiance.

35-6 How is our behavior affected by the presence of others?

In *social facilitation,* the mere presence of others arouses us, improving our performance on easy or well-learned tasks but decreasing it on difficult ones. In *social loafing,* participating in a group project makes us feel less responsible, and we may free ride on others' efforts. When the presence of others both arouses us and makes us feel anonymous, we may experience *deindividuation*—loss of self-awareness and self-restraint.

35-7 What are *group polarization* and *groupthink,* and how much power do we have as individuals?

In *group polarization,* group discussions with like-minded others strengthen members' prevailing beliefs and attitudes. Internet communication magnifies this effect, for better and for worse. *Groupthink* is driven by a desire for harmony within a decision-making group, overriding realistic appraisal of alternatives. The power of the individual and the power of the situation interact. A small minority that consistently expresses its views may sway the majority.

MODULE 36 Antisocial Relations

36-1 What is *prejudice?* What are its social and emotional roots?

Prejudice is an unjustifiable, usually negative, attitude toward a group and its members. Prejudice's three components are beliefs (often *stereotypes*), emotions, and predispositions to action *(discrimination)*. Overt prejudice in North America has decreased over time, but implicit prejudice—an automatic, unthinking attitude—continues. The social roots of prejudice include social inequalities and divisions. Higher-status groups often justify their privileged position with the *just-world phenomenon.* We tend to favor our own group *(ingroup bias)* as we divide ourselves into "us" (the *ingroup*) and "them" (the *outgroup*). Prejudice can also be a tool for protecting our emotional well-being, as when we focus our anger by blaming events on a *scapegoat.*

36-2 What are the cognitive roots of prejudice?

The cognitive roots of prejudice grow from our natural ways of processing information: forming categories, remembering vivid cases, and believing that the world is just and that our own and our culture's ways of doing things are the right ways.

36-3 How does psychology's definition of *aggression* differ from everyday usage? What biological factors make us more prone to hurt one another?

In psychology's more specific meaning, *aggression* is any act intended to harm someone physically or emotionally. Biology influences our threshold for

aggressive behaviors at three levels: genetic (inherited traits), neural (activity in key brain areas), and biochemical (such as alcohol or excess testosterone in the bloodstream). Aggression is a complex behavior resulting from the interaction of biology and experience.

36-4 What psychological and social-cultural factors may trigger aggressive behavior?

Frustration *(frustration-aggression principle)*, previous reinforcement for aggressive behavior, observing an aggressive role model, and poor self-control can all contribute to aggression. Media portrayals of violence provide *social scripts* that children learn to follow. Viewing sexual violence contributes to greater aggression toward women. Playing violent video games increases aggressive thoughts, emotions, and behaviors.

MODULE 37 Prosocial Relations

37-1 Why do we befriend or fall in love with some people but not others?

Proximity (geographical nearness) increases liking, in part because of the *mere exposure effect*—exposure to novel stimuli increases liking of those stimuli. Physical attractiveness increases social opportunities and improves the way we are perceived. Similarity of attitudes and interests greatly increases liking, especially as relationships develop. We also like those who like us.

37-2 How does romantic love typically change as time passes?

Intimate love relationships start with *passionate love*—an intensely aroused state. Over time, the strong affection of *companionate love* may develop, especially if enhanced by an *equitable* relationship and by intimate *self-disclosure*.

37-3 When are people most—and least—likely to help?

Altruism is unselfish regard for the well-being of others. We are most likely to help when we (a) notice an incident, (b) interpret it as an emergency, and (c) assume responsibility for helping. Other factors, including our mood and our similarity to the victim, also affect our willingness to help. We are least likely to help if other bystanders are present (the *bystander effect*).

37-4 How do social exchange theory and social norms explain helping behavior?

Social exchange theory is the view that we help others because it is in our own self-interest; in this view, the goal of social behavior is maximizing personal benefits and minimizing costs. Others believe that helping results from socialization, in which we are taught guidelines for expected behaviors in social situations, such as the *reciprocity norm* and the *social-responsibility norm*.

37-5 How do social traps and mirror-image perceptions fuel social conflict?

A *conflict* is a perceived incompatibility of actions, goals, or ideas. *Social traps* are situations in which people in conflict pursue their own individual self-interest, harming the collective well-being. Individuals and cultures in conflict also tend to form *mirror-image perceptions:* Each party views the opponent as untrustworthy and evil-intentioned, and itself as an ethical, peaceful victim. Perceptions can become *self-fulfilling prophecies*.

37-6 How can we transform feelings of prejudice, aggression, and conflict into attitudes that promote peace?

Peace can result when individuals or groups work together to achieve *superordinate* (shared) *goals*. Research indicates that four processes—contact, cooperation, communication, and conciliation—help promote peace.

Personality

MODULE 38 Classic Perspectives on Personality

38-1 What theories inform our understanding of personality?

Personality is an individual's characteristic pattern of thinking, feeling, and acting. *Psychodynamic theories* view personality from the perspective that behavior is a dynamic interaction between the conscious and unconscious mind. These theories trace their origin to Sigmund Freud's theory of *psychoanalysis*. The humanistic approach focused on our inner capacities for growth and self-fulfillment. Trait theories examine characteristic patterns of behavior (traits). Social-cognitive theories explore the interaction between people's traits (including their thinking) and their social context.

38-2 How did Sigmund Freud's treatment of psychological disorders lead to his view of the unconscious mind?

In treating patients whose disorders had no clear physical explanation, Freud concluded that these problems reflected unacceptable thoughts and feelings, hidden away in the *unconscious* mind. To explore this hidden part of a patient's mind, Freud used *free association* and dream analysis.

38-3 What was Freud's view of personality?

Freud believed that personality results from conflict arising from the interaction among the mind's three systems: the *id* (pleasure-seeking impulses), *ego* (reality-oriented executive), and *superego* (internalized set of ideals, or conscience).

38-4 What developmental stages did Freud propose?

He believed children pass through five *psychosexual stages* (oral, anal, phallic, latency, and genital). Unresolved conflicts at any stage can leave a person's pleasure-seeking impulses *fixated* (stalled) at that stage.

38-5 How did Freud think people defended themselves against anxiety?

For Freud, anxiety was the product of tensions between the demands of the id and superego. The ego copes by using unconscious *defense mechanisms*, such as *repression*, which he viewed as the basic mechanism underlying and enabling all the others.

38-6 Which of Freud's ideas did his followers accept or reject?

Freud's early followers, the neo-Freudians, accepted many of his ideas. They differed in placing more emphasis on the conscious mind and in stressing social motives more than sex or aggression. Most contemporary psychodynamic theorists and therapists reject Freud's emphasis on sexual motivation. They stress, with support from modern research findings, the view that much of our mental life is unconscious, and they believe that our childhood experiences influence our adult personality and attachment patterns. Many also believe that our species' shared evolutionary history shaped some universal predispositions.

38-7 What are projective tests, how are they used, and what are some criticisms of them?

Projective tests attempt to assess personality by showing people stimuli that are open to many possible interpretations and treating their answers as revelations of unconscious motives. One such test, the *Thematic Apperception Test (TAT)*, asks people to make up stories about ambiguous pictures. In another, the *Rorschach inkblot test*, people examine a series of inkblots; this test has low reliability and validity except in a few areas, such as cognitive impairment and thought disorder.

38-8 How do contemporary psychologists view Freud's psychoanalysis?

They give Freud credit for drawing attention to the vast unconscious, to the struggle to cope with our sexuality, to the conflict between biological impulses and social restraints, and for some forms of defense mechanisms (false consensus effect/projection; reaction formation). But his concept of repression, and his view of the unconscious as a collection of repressed and unacceptable thoughts, wishes, feelings, and memories, cannot survive scientific scrutiny. Freud offered after-the-fact explanations, which are hard to test scientifically. Research does not support many of Freud's specific ideas, such as the view that development is fixed in childhood. (We now know it is lifelong.)

38-9 How has modern research developed our understanding of the unconscious?

Current research confirms that we do not have full access to all that goes on in our mind, but the current view of the unconscious is that it is a separate and parallel track of information processing that occurs outside our awareness. This processing includes schemas that control our perceptions; priming; implicit memories of learned skills; instantly activated emotions; and stereotypes that filter our information processing of others' traits and characteristics.

38-10 How did humanistic psychologists view personality, and what was their goal in studying personality?

The *humanistic* psychologists' view of personality focused on the potential for healthy personal growth and people's striving for self-determination and self-realization. Abraham Maslow proposed that human motivations form a hierarchy of needs; if basic needs are fulfilled, people will strive toward *self-actualization* and self-transcendence. Carl Rogers believed that the ingredients of a growth-promoting environment are genuineness, acceptance (including *unconditional positive regard*), and empathy. *Self-concept* was a central feature of personality for both Maslow and Rogers.

38-11 How did humanistic psychologists assess a person's sense of self?

Some rejected any standardized assessments and relied on interviews and conversations. Rogers sometimes used questionnaires in which people described their ideal and actual selves, which he later used to judge progress during therapy.

38-12 How have humanistic theories influenced psychology? What criticisms have they faced?

Humanistic psychology helped renew interest in the concept of self. Critics have said that humanistic psychology's concepts were vague and subjective, its values self-centered, and its assumptions naively optimistic.

MODULE 39 Contemporary Perspectives on Personality

39-1 How do psychologists use traits to describe personality?

Trait theorists see personality as a stable and enduring pattern of behavior. They describe our differences rather than trying to explain them. Using factor analysis, they identify clusters of behavior tendencies that occur together. Genetic predispositions influence many traits.

39-2 What are some common misunderstandings about introversion? Does extraversion lead to greater success than introversion?

Introversion is often misunderstood as shyness, but introverted people often simply seek low levels of stimulation from their environment. Introversion is also sometimes thought to be a barrier to success, but in fact introverts often experience great achievement, even in sales.

39-3 What are personality inventories, and what are their strengths and weaknesses as trait-assessment tools?

Personality inventories (such as the *MMPI*) are questionnaires on which people respond to items designed to gauge a wide range of feelings and behaviors. Test items are *empirically derived*, and the tests are objectively scored. But people can fake their answers to create a good impression, and the ease of computerized testing may lead to misuse of the tests.

39-4 Which traits seem to provide the most useful information about personality variation?

The Big Five personality factors—conscientiousness, agreeableness, neuroticism, openness, and extraversion (CANOE)—currently offer the clearest picture of personality. These factors are quite stable and appear to be found in all cultures.

39-5 Does research support the consistency of personality traits over time and across situations?

A person's average traits persist over time and are predictable over many different situations. But traits cannot predict behavior in any one particular situation.

39-6 How do social-cognitive theorists view personality development, and how do they explore behavior?

Albert Bandura first proposed the *social-cognitive perspective*, which emphasizes the interaction of our traits with our situations. Social-cognitive researchers apply principles of learning, cognition, and social behavior to personality. *Reciprocal determinism* is a term describing the interaction and mutual influence of behavior, internal personal factors, and environmental factors.

39-7 What criticisms have social-cognitive theorists faced?

Social-cognitive theorists build on well-established concepts of learning and cognition. They tend to believe that the best way to predict someone's behavior in a given situation is to observe that person's behavior in similar situations. They have been faulted for underemphasizing the importance of unconscious motives, emotions, and biologically influenced traits.

39-8 Why has psychology generated so much research on the self? How important is self-esteem to our well-being?

The *self* is the center of personality, organizing our thoughts, feelings, and actions. Considering possible selves helps motivate us toward positive development, but focusing too intensely on ourselves can lead to the *spotlight effect*. *Self-esteem* is our feeling of self-worth; *self-efficacy* is our sense of competence on a task. High self-esteem correlates with less pressure to conform, with persistence at difficult tasks, and with happiness. But the direction of the correlation is not clear. Psychologists caution against unrealistically promoting children's feelings of self-worth. It's better to reward their achievements, which leads to feelings of competence.

39-9 What evidence reveals self-serving bias, and how do defensive and secure self-esteem differ?

Self-serving bias is our tendency to perceive ourselves favorably, as when viewing ourselves as better than average or when accepting credit for our successes but not blame for our failures. *Narcissism* is excessive self-love and self-absorption. Defensive self-esteem is fragile, focuses on sustaining itself, and views failure or criticism as a threat. Secure self-esteem enables us to feel accepted for who we are.

39-10 How do individualist and collectivist cultures differ in their values and goals?

Within any culture, the degree of individualism or collectivism varies from person to person. Cultures based on self-reliant *individualism*, like those found in North America and Western Europe, tend to value personal independence and individual achievement. They define identity in terms of self-esteem, personal goals and attributes, and personal rights and liberties. Cultures based on socially connected *collectivism*, like those in many parts of Asia and Africa, tend to value interdependence, tradition, and harmony, and they define identity in terms of group goals, commitments, and belonging to one's group.

Psychological Disorders

MODULE

40 Basic Concepts of Psychological Disorders

40-1 How should we draw the line between normality and disorder?

According to psychologists and psychiatrists, *psychological disorders* are marked by a clinically significant disturbance in an individual's cognition, emotion regulation, or behavior.

40-2 How do the medical model and the biopsychosocial approach influence our understanding of psychological disorders?

The *medical model* assumes that psychological disorders are mental illnesses with physical causes that can be diagnosed, treated, and, in most cases, cured through therapy, sometimes in a hospital. The biopsychosocial perspective assumes that three sets of influences—biological (evolution, genetics, brain structure and chemistry), psychological (stress, trauma, learned helplessness, mood-related perceptions and memories), and social and cultural circumstances (roles, expectations, definitions of "normality" and "disorder")—interact to produce specific psychological disorders. *Epigenetics* also informs our understanding of disorders.

40-3 How and why do clinicians classify psychological disorders, and why do some psychologists criticize the use of diagnostic labels?

The American Psychiatric Association's DSM-5 (*Diagnostic and Statistical Manual of Mental Disorders,* Fifth Edition) contains diagnostic labels and descriptions that provide a common language and shared concepts for communication and research. Most U.S. health insurance organizations require a DSM diagnosis before paying for treatment. Some critics believe the DSM editions have become too detailed and extensive. Others view DSM diagnoses as arbitrary labels that create preconceptions, which bias perceptions of the labeled person's past and present behavior.

40-4 Why is there controversy over attention-deficit/hyperactivity disorder?

A child (or, less commonly, an adult) who displays extreme inattention and/or hyperactivity and impulsivity may be diagnosed with *attention-deficit/hyperactivity disorder (ADHD)* and treated with medication and other therapy. The controversy centers on whether the growing number of ADHD cases reflects overdiagnosis or increased awareness of the disorder. Long-term effects of stimulant-drug treatment for ADHD are not yet known.

40-5 Do psychological disorders predict violent behavior?

Mental disorders seldom lead to violence, but when they do, they raise moral and ethical questions about whether society should hold people with disorders responsible for their violent actions. Most people with disorders are nonviolent and are more likely to be victims than attackers.

40-6 How many people have, or have had, a psychological disorder? Is poverty a risk factor?

Psychological disorder rates vary, depending on the time and place of the survey. In one multinational survey, rates for any disorder ranged from less than 5 percent (Shanghai) to more than 25 percent (the United States). Poverty is a risk factor: Conditions and experiences associated with poverty contribute to the development of psychological disorders. But some disorders, such as schizophrenia, can drive people into poverty.

MODULE 41 Anxiety Disorders, OCD, and PTSD

41-1 How do generalized anxiety disorder, panic disorder, and phobias differ?

Anxious feelings and behaviors are classified as an *anxiety disorder* only when they form a pattern of distressing, persistent anxiety or maladaptive behaviors that reduce anxiety. People with *generalized anxiety disorder* feel persistently and uncontrollably tense and apprehensive, for no apparent reason. In the more extreme *panic disorder,* anxiety escalates into periodic episodes of intense dread. Those with a *phobia* may be irrationally afraid of a specific object, activity, or situation. Two other disorders (OCD and PTSD) involve anxiety but are classified separately from the anxiety disorders.

41-2 What is *OCD?*

Persistent and repetitive thoughts (obsessions), actions (compulsions), or both characterize *obsessive-compulsive disorder (OCD).*

41-3 What is *PTSD?*

Symptoms of *posttraumatic stress disorder (PTSD)* include four or more weeks of haunting memories, nightmares, social withdrawal, jumpy anxiety, numbness of feeling, and/or sleep problems following some traumatic experience.

41-4 How do conditioning, cognition, and biology contribute to the feelings and thoughts that mark anxiety disorders, OCD, and PTSD?

The learning perspective views anxiety disorders, OCD, and PTSD as products of fear conditioning, stimulus generalization, fearful-behavior reinforcement, and observational learning of others' fears and cognitions (interpretations, irrational beliefs, and hypervigilance). The biological perspective considers the role that fears of life-threatening animals, objects, or situations played in natural selection and evolution; genetic predispositions for high levels of emotional reactivity and neurotransmitter production; and abnormal responses in the brain's fear circuits.

MODULE 42 Major Depressive Disorder and Bipolar Disorder

42-1 How do major depressive disorder and bipolar disorder differ?

A person with *major depressive disorder* experiences two or more weeks with five or more symptoms, at least one of which must be either (1) depressed mood or (2) loss of interest or pleasure. A person with the less common condition of *bipolar disorder* experiences not only depression but also *mania*—episodes of hyperactive and wildly optimistic, impulsive behavior.

42-2 How can the biological and social-cognitive perspectives help us understand major depressive disorder and bipolar disorder?

The biological perspective on major depressive disorder and bipolar disorder focuses on genetic predispositions and on abnormalities in brain structures and function (including those found in neurotransmitter systems). The

social-cognitive perspective views depression as an ongoing cycle of stressful experiences (interpreted through negative beliefs, attributions, and memories) leading to negative moods and actions and fueling new stressful experiences.

42-3 What factors increase the risk of suicide, and what do we know about nonsuicidal self-injury?

Suicide rates differ by nation, race, gender, age group, income, religious involvement, marital status, and (for gay and lesbian youth, for example) social support structure. Those with depression are more at risk for suicide than others are, but social suggestion, health status, and economic and social frustration are also contributing factors. Environmental barriers (such as jump barriers) are effective in preventing suicides. Forewarnings of suicide may include verbal hints, giving away possessions, withdrawal, preoccupation with death, and discussing one's own suicide. Nonsuicidal self-injury (NSSI) does not usually lead to suicide but may escalate to suicidal thoughts and acts if untreated. People who engage in NSSI do not tolerate stress well and tend to be self-critical, with poor communication and problem-solving skills.

MODULE 43 Schizophrenia and Other Disorders

43-1 What patterns of perceiving, thinking, and feeling characterize schizophrenia?

Symptoms of *schizophrenia* include disturbed perceptions, disorganized thinking and speech, and diminished, inappropriate emotions. *Delusions* are false beliefs; hallucinations are sensory experiences without sensory stimulation. Schizophrenia symptoms may be positive (the presence of inappropriate behaviors) or negative (the absence of appropriate behaviors).

43-2 How do *chronic* and *acute schizophrenia* differ?

Schizophrenia typically strikes during late adolescence, affects men slightly more than women, and seems to occur in all cultures. In *chronic* (or process) schizophrenia, the disorder develops gradually and recovery is doubtful. In *acute* (or reactive) schizophrenia, the onset is sudden, in reaction to stress, and the prospects for recovery are brighter.

43-3 What brain abnormalities are associated with schizophrenia?

People with schizophrenia have increased dopamine receptors, which may intensify brain signals, creating positive symptoms such as hallucinations and paranoia. Brain abnormalities associated with schizophrenia include enlarged, fluid-filled cerebral cavities and corresponding decreases in the cortex. Brain scans reveal abnormal activity in the frontal lobes, thalamus, and amygdala. Interacting malfunctions in multiple brain regions and their connections may produce schizophrenia's symptoms.

43-4 What prenatal events are associated with increased risk of developing schizophrenia?

Possible contributing factors include viral infections or famine conditions during the mother's pregnancy; low weight or oxygen deprivation at birth; and maternal diabetes or older paternal age.

43-5 How do genes influence schizophrenia?

Twin and adoption studies indicate that the predisposition to schizophrenia is inherited. Multiple genes probably interact to produce schizophrenia. No environmental causes invariably produce schizophrenia, but environmental events (such as prenatal viruses or maternal stress) may "turn on" genes for this disorder in those who are predisposed to it.

43-6 What are dissociative disorders, and why are they controversial?

Dissociative disorders are conditions in which conscious awareness seems to become separated from previous memories, thoughts, and feelings. Skeptics note that *dissociative identity disorder*, formerly known as multiple personality disorder, increased dramatically in the late twentieth century; is rarely found outside North America; and may reflect role playing by people who are vulnerable to therapists' suggestions. Others view this disorder as a manifestation of feelings of anxiety, or as a response learned when behaviors are reinforced by anxiety-reduction.

43-7 What are the three clusters of personality disorders? What behaviors and brain activity characterize the antisocial personality?

Personality disorders are disruptive, inflexible, and enduring behavior patterns that impair social functioning. These disorders form three clusters, characterized by (1) anxiety, (2) eccentric or odd behaviors, and (3) dramatic or impulsive behaviors. *Antisocial personality disorder* (one of those in the third cluster) is characterized by a lack of conscience and, sometimes, by aggressive and fearless behavior. Genetic predispositions may interact with the environment to produce the altered brain activity associated with antisocial personality disorder.

43-8 What are the three main eating disorders, and how do biological, psychological, and social-cultural influences make people more vulnerable to them?

In those with eating disorders (most often women or gay men), psychological factors can overwhelm the body's tendency to maintain a normal weight. Despite being significantly underweight, people with *anorexia nervosa* (usually adolescent females) continue to diet and exercise excessively because they view themselves as fat. Those with *bulimia nervosa* (usually females in their teens and twenties) secretly binge and then compensate by purging, fasting, or excessive exercise. Those with *binge-eating disorder* binge but do not follow with purging, fasting, and exercise. Cultural pressures, low self-esteem, and negative emotions interact with stressful life experiences and genetics to produce eating disorders.

Therapy

MODULE
44 Introduction to Therapy and the Psychological Therapies

44-1 How do *psychotherapy* and the *biomedical therapies* differ?

Psychotherapy is treatment involving psychological techniques; it consists of interactions between a trained therapist and someone seeking to overcome psychological difficulties or achieve personal growth. The major psychotherapies derive from psychology's psychodynamic, humanistic, behavioral, and cognitive perspectives. *Biomedical therapy* treats psychological disorders with medications or procedures that act directly on a patient's physiology. An *eclectic approach* combines techniques from various forms of therapy.

44-2 What are the goals and techniques of psychoanalysis, and how have they been adapted in psychodynamic therapy?

Through *psychoanalysis*, Sigmund Freud tried to give people self-insight and relief from their disorders by bringing anxiety-laden feelings and thoughts into conscious awareness. Psychoanalytic techniques included using free association and *interpretation* of instances of *resistance* and *transference*. *Psychodynamic therapy* has been influenced by traditional psychoanalysis but differs from it in many ways, including the lack of belief in id, ego, and superego. This contemporary

therapy is briefer, less expensive, and more focused on helping the client find relief from current symptoms. Psychodynamic therapists help clients understand how past relationships create themes that may be acted out in present relationships.

44-3 What are the basic themes of humanistic therapy? What are the specific goals and techniques of Rogers' client-centered approach?

Both psychoanalytic and humanistic therapists are *insight therapies*—they attempt to improve functioning by increasing clients' awareness of motives and defenses. Humanistic therapy's goals have included helping clients grow in self-awareness and self-acceptance; promoting personal growth rather than curing illness; helping clients take responsibility for their own growth; focusing on conscious thoughts rather than unconscious motivations; and seeing the present and future as more important than the past. Carl Rogers' *client-centered therapy* proposed that therapists' most important contributions are to function as a psychological mirror through *active listening* and to provide a growth-fostering environment of *unconditional positive regard*, characterized by genuineness, acceptance, and empathy.

44-4 How does the basic assumption of behavior therapy differ from the assumptions of psychodynamic and humanistic therapies? What techniques are used in exposure therapies and aversive conditioning?

Behavior therapies are not insight therapies. Their goal is to apply learning principles to modify problem behaviors. Classical conditioning techniques, including *exposure therapies* (such as *systematic desensitization* or *virtual reality exposure therapy*) and *aversive conditioning*, attempt to change behaviors through *counterconditioning*—evoking new responses to old stimuli that trigger unwanted behaviors.

44-5 What is the main premise of therapy based on operant conditioning principles, and what are the views of its proponents and critics?

Operant conditioning operates under the premise that voluntary behaviors are strongly influenced by their consequences. Therapy based on operant conditioning principles uses behavior modification techniques to change unwanted behaviors through positively reinforcing desired behaviors and ignoring or punishing undesirable behaviors. Critics maintain that (1) techniques such as those used in *token economies* may produce behavior changes that disappear when rewards end, and (2) deciding which behaviors should change is authoritarian and unethical. Proponents argue that treatment with positive rewards is more humane than punishing people or institutionalizing them for undesired behaviors.

44-6 What are the goals and techniques of cognitive therapy and of cognitive-behavioral therapy?

The *cognitive therapies*, such as Aaron Beck's cognitive therapy for depression, assume that our thinking influences our feelings, and that the therapist's role is to change clients' self-defeating thinking by training them to view themselves in more positive ways. The widely researched and practiced *cognitive-behavioral therapy (CBT)* combines cognitive therapy and behavior therapy by helping clients regularly act out their new ways of thinking and behaving in their everyday life. A newer CBT variation, dialectical behavior therapy (DBT), combines cognitive tactics for tolerating distress and regulating emotions with social skills training and mindfulness meditation.

44-7 What are the aims and benefits of group and family therapies?

Group therapy sessions can help more people and cost less per person than individual therapy would. Clients may benefit from exploring feelings and developing social skills in a group situation, from learning that others have similar problems, and from getting feedback on new ways of behaving. *Family therapy* views a

family as an interactive system and attempts to help members discover the roles they play and to learn to communicate more openly and directly.

44-8   Does psychotherapy work? How can we know?

Clients' and therapists' positive testimonials cannot prove that psychotherapy is actually effective, and the placebo effect makes it difficult to judge whether improvement occurred because of the treatment. Using meta-analyses to statistically combine the results of hundreds of randomized psychotherapy outcome studies, researchers have found that those not undergoing treatment often improve, but those undergoing psychotherapy are more likely to improve more quickly, and with less chance of relapse.

44-9   Are some psychotherapies more effective than others for specific disorders?

No one type of psychotherapy is generally superior to all others. Therapy is most effective for those with clear-cut, specific problems. Some therapies—such as behavior conditioning for treating phobias and compulsions—are more effective for specific disorders. Psychodynamic therapy has been effective for depression and anxiety, and cognitive and cognitive-behavioral therapies have been effective in coping with anxiety, posttraumatic stress disorder, and depression. *Evidence-based practice* integrates the best available research with clinicians' expertise and patients' characteristics, preferences, and circumstances.

44-10   How do alternative therapies fare under scientific scrutiny?

Abnormal states tend to return to normal on their own, and the placebo effect can create the impression that a treatment has been effective. These two tendencies complicate assessments of alternative therapies (nontraditional therapies that claim to cure certain ailments). Eye movement desensitization and reprocessing (EMDR) has shown some effectiveness—not from the eye movement but rather from the exposure therapy nature of the treatments. Light exposure therapy does seem to relieve depression symptoms for those with a seasonal pattern of major depressive disorder by activating a brain region that influences arousal and hormones.

44-11   What three elements are shared by all forms of psychotherapy?

All psychotherapies offer new hope for demoralized people; a fresh perspective; and (if the therapist is effective) an empathic, trusting, and caring relationship. The emotional bond of trust and understanding between therapist and client—the *therapeutic alliance*—is an important element in effective therapy.

44-12   How do culture and values influence the therapist-client relationship?

Therapists differ in the values that influence their goals in therapy and their views of progress. These differences may create problems if therapists and clients differ in their cultural or religious perspectives.

44-13   What should a person look for when selecting a therapist?

A person seeking therapy may want to ask about the therapist's treatment approach, values, credentials, and fees. An important consideration is whether the therapy seeker feels comfortable and able to establish a bond with the therapist.

MODULE
45 The Biomedical Therapies and Preventing Psychological Disorders

45-1   What are the drug therapies? How do double-blind studies help researchers evaluate a drug's effectiveness?

Psychopharmacology, the study of drug effects on mind and behavior, has helped make drug therapy the most widely used biomedical therapy. *Antipsychotic drugs,*

used in treating schizophrenia, block dopamine activity. Side effects may include tardive dyskinesia (with involuntary movements of facial muscles, tongue, and limbs) or increased risk of obesity and diabetes. *Antianxiety drugs,* which depress central nervous system activity, are used to treat anxiety disorders, obsessive-compulsive disorder, and posttraumatic stress disorder. These drugs can be physically and psychologically addictive. *Antidepressant drugs,* which increase the availability of serotonin and norepinephrine, are used for depression, with modest effectiveness beyond that of placebo drugs. The antidepressants known as selective serotonin reuptake inhibitors (often called SSRI drugs) are now used to treat other disorders, including strokes and anxiety disorders. Lithium and Depakote are mood stabilizers prescribed for those with bipolar disorder. Studies may use a double-blind procedure to avoid the placebo effect and researcher's bias.

45-2 How are brain stimulation and psychosurgery used in treating specific disorders?

Electroconvulsive therapy (ECT), in which a brief electric current is sent through the brain of an anesthetized patient, is an effective, last-resort treatment for severely depressed people who have not responded to other therapy. Newer alternative treatments for depression include *repetitive transcranial magnetic stimulation (rTMS)* and, in preliminary clinical experiments, deep-brain stimulation that calms an overactive brain region linked with negative emotions. *Psychosurgery* removes or destroys brain tissue in hopes of modifying behavior. Radical psychosurgical procedures such as *lobotomy* were once popular, but neurosurgeons now rarely perform brain surgery to change behavior or moods. Brain surgery is a last-resort treatment because its effects are irreversible.

45-3 How, by taking care of themselves with a healthy lifestyle, might people find some relief from depression? How does this reinforce the idea that we are biopsychosocial systems?

Depressed people who undergo a program of aerobic exercise, adequate sleep, light exposure, social engagement, negative-thought reduction, and better nutrition often gain some relief. In our integrated biopsychosocial system, stress affects our body chemistry and health; chemical imbalances can produce depression; and social support and other lifestyle changes can lead to relief of symptoms.

45-4 What is the rationale for preventive mental health programs, and why is it important to develop resilience?

Preventive mental health programs are based on the idea that many psychological disorders could be prevented by changing oppressive, esteem-destroying environments into more benevolent, nurturing environments that foster growth, self-confidence, and *resilience*. Struggling with challenges can lead to *posttraumatic growth*. Community psychologists are often active in preventive mental health programs.

APPENDIX A

Statistical Reasoning in Everyday Life

A-1 How do we describe data using three measures of central tendency, and what is the relative usefulness of the two measures of variation?

Researchers may use descriptive statistics to meaningfully organize data. A measure of central tendency is a single score that represents a whole set of scores. Three such measures that we use to describe data are the *mode* (the most frequently occurring score), the *mean* (the arithmetic average), and the *median* (the middle score in

a group of data). Measures of variation tell us how diverse data are. Two measures of variation are the *range* (which describes the gap between the highest and lowest scores) and the *standard deviation* (which states how much scores vary around the mean, or average, score). Scores often form a *normal* (or bell-shaped) *curve*.

A-2 What does it mean when we say two things are correlated?

When we say two things are correlated, we are saying that they accompany each other in their movements. The strength of their relationship is expressed as a *correlation coefficient*. Their relationship may be displayed in a *scatterplot,* in which each dot represents a value for the two variables. Correlations predict but cannot explain.

A-3 What is regression toward the mean?

Regression toward the mean is the tendency for extreme or unusual scores to fall back toward their average.

A-4 How do we know whether an observed difference can be generalized to other populations?

Researchers use inferential statistics to help determine the reliability and significance of a study finding. To feel confident about generalizing an observed difference to other populations, we would want to know that the sample studied was representative of the larger population being studied; that the observations, on average, had low variability; that the sample consisted of more than a few cases; and that the observed difference was *statistically significant.*

A-5 What are cross-sectional studies and longitudinal studies, and why is it important to know which method was used?

In a *cross-sectional study,* people of different ages are compared. In a *longitudinal study,* a group of people is studied periodically over a long period of time. To draw meaningful conclusions about a study's results, we need to know whether the study used a representative sample to draw its conclusions. Studies of intelligence and aging, for example, have drawn different conclusions depending on whether a cross-sectional or longitudinal study was used.

APPENDIX B
Psychology at Work

B-1 What is *flow,* and what are the key subfields related to industrial-organizational psychology?

Flow is a completely involved, focused state of consciousness with diminished awareness of self and time. It results from fully engaging one's skills. *Personnel psychology* and *organizational psychology* are two key subfields of I/O psychology, and an allied field is *human factors psychology.*

B-2 How do personnel psychologists help with job seeking, employee selection, work placement, and performance appraisal?

Personnel psychologists work to provide training programs for job seekers; devise selection methods for new employees; recruit and evaluate applicants; design and evaluate training programs; identify people's interests and strengths; analyze job content; and appraise individual and organizational performance. Unstructured, subjective interviews foster the interviewer illusion; *structured interviews* pinpoint job-relevant strengths and are better predictors of performance. Checklists, graphic rating scales, and behavior rating scales are useful performance appraisal methods.

B-3 What is the role of organizational psychologists?

Organizational psychologists examine influences on worker satisfaction and productivity and facilitate organizational change. Employee satisfaction and engagement tend to correlate with organizational success.

B-4 What are some effective leadership techniques?

Effective leaders harness job-relevant strengths; set specific, challenging goals; and choose an appropriate leadership style. Leadership style may be goal-oriented (*task leadership*), group-oriented (*social leadership*), or some combination of the two.

B-5 How do human factors psychologists work to create user-friendly machines and work settings?

Human factors psychologists contribute to human safety and improved design by encouraging developers and designers to consider human perceptual abilities, to avoid the curse of knowledge, and to test users to reveal perception-based problems.

Answers to *Experience the Testing Effect* Questions

Thinking Critically With Psychological Science

MODULE 1 The History and Scope of Psychology

1. Wilhelm Wundt

2. a

3. a

4. b

5. The environment (nurture) has an influence on us, but that influence is constrained by our biology (nature). Nature and nurture interact. People predisposed to be very tall (nature), for example, are unlikely to become Olympic gymnasts, no matter how hard they work (nurture).

6. d

7. psychiatrist

8. c

MODULE 2 Research Strategies: How Psychologists Ask and Answer Questions

1. Hindsight bias

2. d

3. Critical thinking examines assumptions, appraises the source, discerns hidden values, evaluates evidence, and assesses conclusions. In evaluating a claim in the media, look for any signs of empirical evidence, preferably from several studies. Ask the following questions in your analysis: Are claims based on scientific findings? Have several studies replicated the findings and confirmed them? Are any experts cited? If so, research their background. Are they affiliated with a credible university, college, or institution? Have they conducted or written about scientific research?

4. hypotheses

5. c

6. representative

7. negative

8. a

9. (a) *Alcohol use is associated with violence. (One interpretation: Drinking triggers or unleashes aggressive behavior.)* Perhaps anger triggers drinking, or perhaps the same genes or child-raising practices are predisposing both drinking and aggression. (Here researchers have learned that drinking does indeed trigger aggressive behavior.)

(b) *Educated people live longer, on average, than less-educated people. (One interpretation: Education lengthens life and enhances health.)* Perhaps richer people can afford more education and better health care. (Research supports this conclusion.)

(c) *Teens engaged in team sports are less likely to use drugs, smoke, have sex, carry weapons, and eat junk food than are teens who do not engage in team sports. (One interpretation: Team sports encourage healthy living.)* Perhaps some third factor explains this correlation—teens who use drugs, smoke, have sex, carry weapons, and eat junk food may be "loners" who do not enjoy playing on any team.

(d) *Adolescents who frequently see smoking in movies are more likely to smoke. (One interpretation: Movie stars' behavior influences impressionable teens.)* Perhaps adolescents who smoke and attend movies frequently have less parental supervision and more access to spending money than other adolescents.

10. experiments

11. placebo

12. c

13. independent variable

14. b

15. d

The Biology of Behavior

MODULE 3 Neural and Hormonal Systems

1. axon

2. c

3. a

4. neurotransmitters

5. b

6. c

7. autonomic

8. central

9. a

10. adrenal glands

MODULE
4 Tools of Discovery and Older Brain Structures

1. b

2. d

3. c

4. cerebellum

5. b

6. amygdala

7. b

8. hypothalamus

MODULE
5 The Cerebral Cortex and Our Divided Brain

1. d

2. The visual cortex is a neural network of sensory neurons connected via interneurons to other neural networks, including auditory networks. This allows you to integrate visual and auditory information to respond when a friend you recognize greets you at a party.

3. c

4. frontal

5. You would hear sounds, but without the temporal lobe association areas you would be unable to make sense of what you were hearing.

6. association areas

7. c

8. ON; HER

9. a

10. b

MODULE
6 Genetics, Evolutionary Psychology, and Behavior

1. chromosomes

2. gene

3. b

4. c

5. Identical

6. b

7. environments

8. differences; commonalities

9. c

Consciousness and the Two-Track Mind

MODULE
7 Consciousness: Some Basic Concepts

1. inattentional blindness

2. unconscious; conscious

3. inattentional

MODULE
8 Sleep and Dreams

1. circadian rhythm

2. b

3. NREM-3

4. It increases in duration.

5. c

6. With narcolepsy, the person periodically falls directly into REM sleep, with no warning; with sleep apnea, the person repeatedly awakens during the night.

7. d

8. The activation-synthesis theory suggests that dreams are the brain's attempt to synthesize random neural activity.

9. The information-processing explanation of dreaming proposes that brain activity during REM sleep enables us to sift through *what one has dwelt on by day.*

10. REM rebound

MODULE
9 Drugs and Consciousness

1. tolerance

2. a

3. Alcohol is a disinhibitor—it makes us more likely to do what we would have done when sober, whether that is being helpful or being aggressive.

4. d

5. hallucinogenic

6. a

7. b

Developing Through the Life Span

MODULE 10 Developmental Issues, Prenatal Development, and the Newborn

1. continuity/stages
2. b
3. temperament
4. c
5. teratogens

MODULE 11 Infancy and Childhood

1. a
2. frontal
3. b
4. We have no conscious memories of events occurring before about age 3½, in part because major brain areas have not yet matured.
5. Infants in Piaget's *sensorimotor stage* tend to be focused only on their own perceptions of the world and may, for example, be unaware that objects continue to exist when unseen. A child in the *preoperational stage* is still egocentric and incapable of appreciating simple logic, such as the reversibility of operations. A preteen in the *concrete operational stage* is beginning to think logically about concrete events but not about abstract concepts.
6. a
7. stranger anxiety
8. Before these studies, many psychologists believed that infants became attached to those who nourished them.

MODULE 12 Adolescence

1. b
2. formal operations
3. b
4. emerging adulthood

MODULE 13 Adulthood

1. a
2. Cross-sectional studies compare people of different ages. Longitudinal studies restudy and retest the same people over a long period of time.
3. generativity
4. c

Sex, Gender, and Sexuality

MODULE 14 Gender Development

1. sex; gender
2. c
3. Y
4. d
5. 11; 12
6. disorder of sexual development
7. b
8. gender identity

MODULE 15 Human Sexuality

1. b
2. b
3. Sexual dysfunctions are problems that men and women may have related to sexual arousal and sexual function. Paraphilias are conditions, which may be classified as psychological disorders, in which sexual arousal is associated with nonhuman objects, the suffering of self or others, and/or nonconsenting persons.
4. does; doesn't
5. c
6. Researchers have found no evidence that any environmental factor (parental relationships, childhood experiences, peer relationships, or dating experiences) influences the development of our sexual orientation.

Sensation and Perception

MODULE 16 Basic Concepts of Sensation and Perception

1. b
2. perception
3. d
4. just noticeable difference
5. b
6. d
7. a

MODULE 17 Vision: Sensory and Perceptual Processing

1. wavelength
2. a
3. c
4. c

5. d

6. Your brain constructs this perception of color in two stages. In the first stage, the lemon reflects light energy into your eyes, where it is transformed into neural messages. Three sets of cones, each sensitive to a different light frequency (red, blue, and green) process color. In this case, the light energy stimulates both red-sensitive and green-sensitive cones. In the second stage, opponent-process cells sensitive to paired opposites of color (red/green, yellow/blue, and black/white) evaluate the incoming neural messages as they pass through your optic nerve to the thalamus and visual cortex. When the yellow-sensitive opponent-process cells are stimulated, you identify the lemon as yellow.

7. feature detectors

8. parallel processing

9. d

10. a

11. b

12. c

13. monocular

14. b

15. b

16. perceptual adaptation

MODULE 18 The Nonvisual Senses

1. cochlea

2. The *outer ear* collects sound waves, which are translated into mechanical waves by the *middle ear* and turned into fluid waves in the *inner ear*. The *auditory nerve* then translates the energy into electrical waves and sends them to the brain, which perceives and interprets the sound.

3. Place; frequency

4. c

5. Our experience of pain is influenced by biological factors (such as sensory receptors that detect pressure), psychological factors (such as our focused attention), and social-cultural factors (such as social expectations about tolerance and expression of pain).

6. We have specialized receptors for detecting sweet, salty, sour, bitter, and umami tastes. Being able to detect pleasurable tastes enabled our ancestors to seek out energy- and protein-rich foods. Detecting aversive tastes deterred them from eating toxic substances, increasing their chances of survival.

7. Kinesthesia; vestibular sense

8. Your vestibular sense regulates balance and body positioning through kinesthetic receptors triggered by fluid in your inner ear. Wobbly legs and a spinning world are signs that these receptors are still responding to the ride's turbulence. As your vestibular sense adjusts to solid ground, your balance will be restored.

9. d

10. d

Learning

MODULE 19 Basic Learning Concepts and Classical Conditioning

1. information; behaviors

2. c

3. conditioned

4. discrimination

5. b

6. A sexual image is a US that triggers a UR of interest or arousal. Before the advertisement pairs a product with a sexual image, the product is an NS. Over time the product can become a CS that triggers the CR of interest or arousal.

MODULE 20 Operant Conditioning

1. Skinner's

2. shaping

3. b

4. Your instructor could reinforce your attentive behavior by taking away something you dislike. For example, your instructor could offer to shorten the length of an assigned paper or replace lecture time with an in-class activity. In both cases, the instructor would remove something aversive in order to negatively reinforce your focused attention.

5. partial

6. a

7. variable-interval

8. c

MODULE 21 Biology, Cognition, and Learning

1. taste-aversion

2. This finding supports Darwin's principle that natural selection favors traits that aid survival.

3. cognitive maps

4. latent learning

5. observational learning

6. vicarious; vicarious

7. a

8. mirror

9. c

Memory

MODULE
22 Studying and Encoding Memories

1. recall

2. encoding; storage; retrieval

3. a

4. iconic; echoic

5. seven

6. mnemonics

MODULE
23 Storing and Retrieving Memories

1. a

2. implicit

3. c

4. retrieval cues

5. Memories are stored within a web of many associations, one of which is mood. When you recall happy moments from your past, you deliberately activate these positive links. You may then experience mood-congruent memory and recall other happy moments, which could improve your mood and brighten your interpretation of current events.

6. a

MODULE
24 Forgetting, Memory Construction, and Improving Memory

1. d

2. d

3. retroactive

4. repression

5. b

6. Eliza's immature hippocampus and lack of verbal skills would have prevented her from encoding an explicit memory of the wedding reception at the age of two. It's more likely that Eliza learned information (from hearing the story repeatedly) that she eventually constructed into a memory that feels very real.

7. source amnesia

8. déjà vu

9. b

10. b

Thinking, Language, and Intelligence

MODULE
25 Thinking

1. concept

2. algorithm

3. Oscar will need to guard against *confirmation bias* (searching for support for his own views and ignoring contradictory evidence) as he seeks out opposing viewpoints. Even if Oscar encounters new information that disproves his beliefs, *belief perseverance* may lead him to cling to these views anyway. It will take more compelling evidence to change his beliefs than it took to create them.

4. c

5. availability

6. framing

7. b

MODULE
26 Language and Thought

1. c

2. phonemes; morphemes; grammar

3. telegraphic speech

4. universal grammar

5. a

MODULE
27 Intelligence and Its Assessment

1. general intelligence (g)

2. c

3. analytical; practical; creative

4. d

5. d

6. c

7. reliability

8. Writers' work relies more on crystallized intelligence, or accumulated knowledge, which increases with age. For top performance, scientists doing research may need more fluid intelligence (speedy and abstract reasoning), which tends to decrease with age.

9. c

MODULE
28 Genetic and Environmental Influences on Intelligence

1. a

2. c

3. c

4. Stereotype threat

Motivation and Emotion

MODULE
29 Basic Motivational Concepts, Affiliation, and Achievement

1. b

2. a

3. incentive

4. Arousal

5. b

6. a

7. c

8. Monitor the time spent online, as well as our feelings about that time. Hide distracting online friends. Turn off or put away distracting devices. Consider a social networking fast, and get outside and away from technology regularly.

MODULE
30 Hunger

1. Maslow's hierarchy of needs supports this statement because it addresses the primacy of some motives over others. Once our basic physiological needs are met, safety concerns are addressed next, followed by belongingness and love needs (such as the desire to kiss).

2. set point

3. c

4. glucose; low

5. basal metabolic

6. d

7. Sanjay's plan is problematic. After he gains weight, the extra fat will require less energy to maintain than it did to gain in the first place. Sanjay may have a hard time getting rid of it later, when his metabolism slows down in an effort to retain his body weight.

MODULE
31 Theories and Physiology of Emotion

1. James-Lange

2. b

3. c

4. A polygraph measures physiological changes, such as heart rate and perspiration, that are associated with emotions. Its use as a lie detector is controversial because the measure cannot distinguish between emotions with similar physiology (such as anxiety and guilt).

MODULE
32 Expressing and Experiencing Emotion

1. facial feedback

2. Aiden's droopy posture could negatively affect his mood thanks to the behavior feedback effect, which tends to make us feel the way we act.

Stress, Health, and Human Flourishing

MODULE
33 Stress and Illness

1. resistance; exhaustion

2. tend; befriend

3. b

4. d

5. lymphocytes

6. c

7. Type A individuals frequently experience negative emotions (anger, depression), during which the sympathetic nervous system diverts blood away from the liver. This leaves fat and cholesterol circulating in the bloodstream for deposit near the heart and other organs, increasing the risk of heart disease and other health problems. Thus, Type A individuals actually harm themselves by directing anger at others.

MODULE
34 Health and Happiness

1. emotion

2. b

3. internal

4. d

5. aerobic

6. c

7. d

8. Positive

9. b

10. relative deprivation

Social Psychology

MODULE
35 Social Thinking and Social Influence

1. a

2. peripheral

3. foot-in-the-door

4. Cognitive dissonance theory best supports this suggestion. If Jamal acts confident, his behavior will contradict his negative self-thoughts, creating cognitive dissonance. To relieve the tension, Jamal may realign his attitudes with his actions by viewing himself as more outgoing and confident.

5. c

6. a

7. The presence of a large audience generates arousal and strengthens Dr. Huang's most likely response: enhanced performance on a task he has mastered (teaching music history) and impaired performance on a task he finds difficult (statistics).

8. deindividuation

9. group polarization

MODULE 36 Antisocial Relations

1. stereotypes

2. This reaction could occur because we tend to overgeneralize from vivid, memorable cases.

3. more

4. d

5. frustration-aggression principle

6. c

7. c

MODULE 37 Prosocial Relations

1. mere exposure

2. companionate; passionate

3. d

4. c

5. mirror-image

6. superordinate

Personality

MODULE 38 Classic Perspectives on Personality

1. repression

2. c

3. superego

4. b

5. anxiety

6. Projective

7. d

8. a

9. a

10. d

11. Rogers might assert that the criminal was raised in an environment lacking genuineness, acceptance (unconditional positive regard), and empathy, which inhibited psychological growth and led to a negative self-concept.

12. unconditional positive regard

MODULE 39 Contemporary Perspectives on Personality

1. Trait

2. c

3. b

4. b

5. a

6. social-cognitive

7. b

8. Yes, if that self-love is of the *secure* type. Secure self-esteem promotes a focus beyond the self and a higher quality of life. Excessive self-love may promote artificially high or defensive self-esteem, which may lead to unhappiness if negative external feedback triggers anger or aggression.

9. spotlight effect

10. b

Psychological Disorders

MODULE 40 Basic Concepts of Psychological Disorders

1. depression

2. No. Anna's behavior is unusual, causes her distress, and may make her a few minutes late on occasion, but it does not appear to significantly disrupt her ability to function. Like most of us, Anna demonstrates some unusual behaviors that are not disabling or dysfunctional, and, thus, do not suggest a psychological disorder.

3. Susto is a condition marked by severe anxiety, restlessness, and fear of black magic. It is culture-specific to Latin America.

4. medical

5. c

6. Critics have expressed concerns about the negative effects of the DSM's labeling. Recent critics suggest the DSM-5 casts too wide a net on disorders, pathologizing normal behavior.

7. poverty

8. d

MODULE 41 Anxiety Disorders, OCD, and PTSD

1. phobia

2. c

3. obsessive-compulsive

4. b

42 Major Depressive Disorder and Bipolar Disorder

1. women's; men's

2. d

3. norepinephrine; serotonin

4. social-cognitive

43 Schizophrenia and Other Disorders

1. No. Schizophrenia involves the altered perceptions, emotions, and behaviors of a mind split from reality. It does not involve the rapid changes in mood or identity suggested by this comparison.

2. b

3. hallucination

4. a

5. c

6. c

7. b

8. b

Therapy

44 Introduction to Therapy and the Psychological Therapies

1. a

2. Insight

3. d

4. active listening

5. c

6. counterconditioning

7. systematic desensitization

8. Behavior therapies are often the best choice for treating phobias. Viewing Rico's fear of the freeway as a learned response, a behavior therapist might help Rico learn to replace his anxious response to freeway driving with a relaxation response.

9. token economy

10. d

11. Cognitive-behavioral

12. b

13. c

14. d

15. research evidence, clinical expertise, and knowledge of the patient

16. The placebo effect is the healing power of belief in a treatment. When patients expect a treatment to be effective, they may believe it was.

45 The Biomedical Therapies and Preventing Psychological Disorders

1. c

2. antianxiety

3. lithium

4. b

5. d

APPENDIX A

Statistical Reasoning in Everyday Life

1. b

2. d

3. normal curve

4. a

5. negative

6. scatterplot

7. Regression toward the mean is a statistical phenomenon describing the tendency of extreme scores or outcomes to return to normal after an unusual event. Without knowing this, we may inaccurately decide the return to normal was a result of our own behavior.

8. cross-sectional

9. a

APPENDIX B

Psychology at Work

1. c

2. Personnel; human factors

3. a

4. d

5. Focusing on specific, short-term goals, such as maintaining a regular study schedule, will be more helpful than focusing on more distant general goals, such as earning a good grade in this class.

6. transformational

7. c

8. d

Glossary

absolute threshold the minimum stimulus energy needed to detect a particular stimulus 50 percent of the time. (p. 201)

accommodation (1) in developmental psychology, adapting our current understandings (schemas) to incorporate new information. (2) in sensation and perception, the process by which the eye's lens changes shape to focus near or far objects on the retina. (pp. 130, 211)

achievement motivation a desire for significant accomplishment; for mastery of skills or ideas; for control; and for attaining a high standard. (p. 375)

achievement test a test designed to assess what a person has learned. (p. 345)

acquisition in classical conditioning, the initial stage, when one links a neutral stimulus and an unconditioned stimulus so that the neutral stimulus begins triggering the conditioned response. In operant conditioning, the strengthening of a reinforced response. (p. 250)

action potential a neural impulse; a brief electrical charge that travels down an axon. (p. 37)

active listening empathic listening in which the listener echoes, restates, and clarifies. A feature of Rogers' client-centered therapy. (p. 573)

acute schizophrenia (also called *reactive schizophrenia*) a form of schizophrenia that can begin at any age, frequently occurs in response to an emotionally traumatic event, and has extended recovery periods. (p. 557)

adaptation-level phenomenon our tendency to form judgments (of sounds, of lights, of income) relative to a neutral level defined by our prior experience. (p. 434)

addiction compulsive craving of drugs or certain behaviors (such as gambling) despite known adverse consequences. (p. 105)

adolescence the transition period from childhood to adulthood, extending from puberty to independence. (p. 147)

adrenal [ah-DREEN-el] **glands** a pair of endocrine glands that sit just above the kidneys and secrete hormones (epinephrine and norepinephrine) that help arouse the body in times of stress. (p. 46)

aerobic exercise sustained exercise that increases heart and lung fitness; may also alleviate depression and anxiety. (p. 426)

affiliation need the need to build relationships and to feel part of a group. (p. 369)

aggression any physical or verbal behavior intended to harm someone physically or emotionally. (pp. 173, 468)

agonist a molecule that increases a neurotransmitter's action. (p. 42)

AIDS (acquired immune deficiency syndrome) a life-threatening, sexually transmitted infection caused by the *human immunodeficiency virus* (HIV). AIDS depletes the immune system, leaving the person vulnerable to infections. (p. 184)

alcohol use disorder (popularly known as *alcoholism*) alcohol use marked by tolerance, withdrawal, and a drive to continue problematic use. (p. 106)

algorithm a methodical, logical rule or procedure that guarantees solving a particular problem. Contrasts with the usually speedier—but also more error-prone—use of *heuristics*. (p. 317)

all-or-none response a neuron's reaction of either firing (with a full-strength response) or not firing. (p. 39)

alpha waves the relatively slow brain waves of a relaxed, awake state. (p. 89)

altruism unselfish regard for the welfare of others. (p. 480)

amphetamines drugs that stimulate neural activity, causing accelerated body functions and associated energy and mood changes. (p. 108)

amygdala [uh-MIG-duh-la] two lima-bean-sized neural clusters in the limbic system; linked to emotion. (p. 52)

androgyny displaying both traditional masculine and feminine psychological characteristics. (p. 178)

anorexia nervosa an eating disorder in which a person (usually an adolescent female) maintains a starvation diet despite being significantly underweight; sometimes accompanied by excessive exercise. (p. 565)

antagonist a molecule that inhibits or blocks a neurotransmitter's action. (p. 42)

anterograde amnesia an inability to form new memories. (p. 302)

antianxiety drugs drugs used to control anxiety and agitation. (p. 594)

antidepressant drugs drugs used to treat depression, anxiety disorders, obsessive-compulsive disorder, and posttraumatic stress disorder. (Several widely used antidepressant drugs are *selective serotonin reuptake inhibitors—SSRIs*) (p. 595)

antipsychotic drugs drugs used to treat schizophrenia and other forms of severe thought disorder. (p. 594)

antisocial personality disorder a personality disorder in which a person (usually a man) exhibits a lack of conscience for wrongdoing, even toward friends and family members; may be aggressive and ruthless or a clever con artist. (p. 563)

anxiety disorders psychological disorders characterized by distressing, persistent anxiety or maladaptive behaviors that reduce anxiety. (p. 537)

aphasia impairment of language, usually caused by left hemisphere damage either to Broca's area (impairing speaking) or to Wernicke's area (impairing understanding). (p. 334)

applied research scientific study that aims to solve practical problems. (p. 12)

aptitude test a test designed to predict a person's future performance; *aptitude* is the capacity to learn. (p. 345)

asexual having no sexual attraction to others. (p. 181)

assimilation interpreting our new experiences in terms of our existing schemas. (p. 130)

association areas areas of the cerebral cortex that are not involved in primary motor or sensory functions; rather, they are involved in higher mental functions such as learning, remembering, thinking, and speaking. (p. 59)

associative learning learning that certain events occur together. The events may be two stimuli (as in classical conditioning) or a response and its consequences (as in operant conditioning). (pp. 246, 256)

attachment an emotional tie with another person; shown in young children by their seeking closeness to the caregiver and showing distress on separation. (p. 138)

attention-deficit/hyperactivity disorder (ADHD) a psychological disorder marked by extreme inattention and/or hyperactivity and impulsivity. (p. 532)

attitude feelings, often influenced by our beliefs, that predispose us to respond in a particular way to objects, people, and events. (p. 444)

attribution theory the theory that we explain someone's behavior by crediting either the situation or the person's disposition. (p. 442)

audition the sense or act of hearing. (p. 226)

autism spectrum disorder (ASD) a disorder that appears in childhood and is marked by significant deficiencies in communication and social interaction, and by rigidly fixated interests and repetitive behaviors. (p. 135)

automatic processing unconscious encoding of incidental information, such as space, time, and frequency, and of well-learned information, such as word meanings. (p. 285)

autonomic [aw-tuh-NAHM-ik] **nervous system (ANS)** the part of the peripheral nervous system that controls the glands and the muscles of the internal organs (such as the heart). Its sympathetic division arouses; its parasympathetic division calms. (p. 43)

availability heuristic estimating the likelihood of events based on their availability in memory; if instances come readily to mind (perhaps because of their vividness), we presume such events are common. (p. 319)

aversive conditioning a type of counterconditioning that associates an unpleasant state (such as nausea) with an unwanted behavior (such as drinking alcohol). (p. 576)

axon the neuron extension that passes messages through its branches to other neurons or to muscles or glands. (p. 36)

babbling stage beginning at about 4 months, the stage of speech development in which the infant spontaneously utters various sounds at first unrelated to the household language. (p. 331)

barbiturates drugs that depress central nervous system activity, reducing anxiety but impairing memory and judgment. (p. 107)

basal metabolic rate the body's resting rate of energy expenditure. (p. 380)

basic research pure science that aims to increase the scientific knowledge base. (p. 12)

basic trust according to Erik Erikson, a sense that the world is predictable and trustworthy; said to be formed during infancy by appropriate experiences with responsive caregivers. (p. 142)

behavior feedback effect the tendency of behavior to influence our own and others' thoughts, feelings, and actions. (p. 402)

behavior genetics the study of the relative power and limits of genetic and environmental influences on behavior. (pp. 8, 66)

behavior therapy therapy that applies learning principles to the elimination of unwanted behaviors. (p. 574)

behaviorism the view that psychology (1) should be an objective science that (2) studies behavior without reference to mental processes. Most psychologists today agree with (1) but not with (2). (pp. 6, 248)

belief perseverance clinging to one's initial conceptions after the basis on which they were formed has been discredited. (p. 322)

binge-eating disorder significant binge-eating episodes, followed by distress, disgust, or guilt, but without the compensatory purging or fasting that marks bulimia nervosa. (p. 565)

binocular cues depth cues, such as retinal disparity, that depend on the use of two eyes. (p. 219)

biological constraints evolved biological tendencies that predispose animals' behavior and learning. Thus, certain behaviors are more easily learned than others. (p. 267)

biological psychology the scientific study of the links between biological (genetic, neural, hormonal) and psychological processes. (Some biological psychologists call themselves *behavioral neuroscientists, neuropsychologists, behavior geneticists, physiological psychologists,* or *biopsychologists*) (p. 36)

biomedical therapy prescribed medications or procedures that act directly on the person's physiology. (p. 570)

biopsychosocial approach an integrated approach that incorporates biological, psychological, and social-cultural levels of analysis. (p. 10)

bipolar disorder a disorder in which a person alternates between the hopelessness and lethargy of depression and the overexcited state of mania. (Formerly called *manic-depressive disorder*) (p. 546)

blind spot the point at which the optic nerve leaves the eye, creating a "blind" spot because no receptor cells are located there. (p. 211)

blindsight a condition in which a person can respond to a visual stimulus without consciously experiencing it. (p. 85)

bottom-up processing analysis that begins with the sensory receptors and works up to the brain's integration of sensory information. (p. 200)

brainstem the oldest part and central core of the brain, beginning where the spinal cord swells as it enters the skull; the brainstem is responsible for automatic survival functions. (p. 50)

Broca's area controls language expression—an area of the frontal lobe, usually in the left hemisphere, that directs the muscle movements involved in speech. (p. 334)

bulimia nervosa an eating disorder in which a person alternates binge eating (usually of high-calorie foods) with purging (by vomiting or laxative use) or fasting. (p. 565)

bystander effect the tendency for any given bystander to be less likely to give aid if other bystanders are present. (p. 482)

Cannon-Bard theory the theory that an emotion-arousing stimulus simultaneously triggers (1) physiological responses and (2) the subjective experience of emotion. (p. 388)

case study a descriptive technique in which one individual or group is studied in depth in the hope of revealing universal principles. (p. 19)

catharsis in psychology, the idea that "releasing" aggressive energy (through action or fantasy) relieves aggressive urges. (p. 416)

central nervous system (CNS) the brain and spinal cord. (p. 42)

central route persuasion occurs when interested people focus on the arguments and respond with favorable thoughts. (p. 444)

cerebellum [sehr-uh-BELL-um] the "little brain" at the rear of the brainstem; functions include processing sensory input, coordinating movement output and balance, and enabling nonverbal learning and memory. (p. 52)

cerebral [seh-REE-bruhl] **cortex** the intricate fabric of interconnected neural cells covering the cerebral hemispheres; the body's ultimate control and information-processing center. (p. 56)

change blindness failing to notice changes in the environment. (p. 83)

chromosomes threadlike structures made of DNA molecules that contain the genes. (p. 66)

chronic schizophrenia (also called *process schizophrenia*) a form of schizophrenia in which symptoms usually appear by late adolescence or early adulthood. As people age, psychotic episodes last longer and recovery periods shorten. (p. 557)

chunking organizing items into familiar, manageable units; often occurs automatically. (p. 287)

circadian [ser-KAY-dee-an] **rhythm** the biological clock; regular bodily rhythms (for example, of temperature and wakefulness) that occur on a 24-hour cycle. (p. 87)

classical conditioning a type of learning in which one learns to link two or more stimuli and anticipate events. (p. 248)

client-centered therapy a humanistic therapy, developed by Carl Rogers, in which the therapist uses techniques such as active listening within a genuine, accepting, empathic environment to facilitate clients' growth. (Also called *person-centered therapy*) (p. 573)

clinical psychology a branch of psychology that studies, assesses, and treats people with psychological disorders. (p. 12)

cocaine a powerful and addictive stimulant derived from the coca plant; produces temporarily increased alertness and euphoria. (p. 110)

cochlea [KOHK-lee-uh] a coiled, bony, fluid-filled tube in the inner ear; sound waves traveling through the cochlear fluid trigger nerve impulses. (p. 228)

cochlear implant a device for converting sounds into electrical signals and stimulating the auditory nerve through electrodes threaded into the cochlea. (p. 229)

cognition all the mental activities associated with thinking, knowing, remembering, and communicating. (pp. 130, 316)

cognitive dissonance theory the theory that we act to reduce the discomfort (dissonance) we feel when two of our thoughts (cognitions) are inconsistent. For example, when we become aware that our attitudes and our actions clash, we can reduce the resulting dissonance by changing our attitudes. (p. 446)

cognitive learning the acquisition of mental information, whether by observing events, by watching others, or through language. (p. 247)

cognitive map a mental representation of the layout of one's environment. For example, after exploring a maze, rats act as if they have learned a cognitive map of it. (p. 270)

cognitive neuroscience the interdisciplinary study of the brain activity linked with cognition (including perception, thinking, memory, and language). (pp. 8, 81)

cognitive therapy therapy that teaches people new, more adaptive ways of thinking; based on the assumption that thoughts intervene between events and our emotional reactions. (p. 578)

cognitive-behavioral therapy (CBT) a popular integrative therapy that combines cognitive therapy (changing self-defeating thinking) with behavior therapy (changing behavior). (p. 581)

collective unconscious Carl Jung's concept of a shared, inherited reservoir of memory traces from our species' history. (p. 496)

collectivism giving priority to the goals of one's group (often one's extended family or work group) and defining one's identity accordingly. (p. 521)

color constancy perceiving familiar objects as having consistent color, even if changing illumination alters the wavelengths reflected by the objects. (p. 221)

community psychology a branch of psychology that studies how people interact with their social environments and how social institutions affect individuals and groups. (p. 12)

companionate love the deep affectionate attachment we feel for those with whom our lives are intertwined. (p. 480)

concept a mental grouping of similar objects, events, ideas, or people. (p. 316)

concrete operational stage in Piaget's theory, the stage of cognitive development (from about 7 to 11 years of age) during which children gain the mental operations that enable them to think logically about concrete events. (p. 133)

conditioned reinforcer a stimulus that gains its reinforcing power through its association with a primary reinforcer; also known as a *secondary reinforcer*. (p. 259)

conditioned response (CR) in classical conditioning, a learned response to a previously neutral (but now conditioned) stimulus (CS). (p. 249)

conditioned stimulus (CS) in classical conditioning, an originally irrelevant stimulus that, after association with an unconditioned stimulus (US), comes to trigger a conditioned response (CR). (p. 249)

conduction hearing loss less common form of hearing loss, caused by damage to the mechanical system that conducts sound waves to the cochlea. (p. 228)

cones retinal receptors that are concentrated near the center of the retina and that function in daylight or in well-lit conditions. Cones detect fine detail and give rise to color sensations. (p. 211)

confirmation bias a tendency to search for information that supports our preconceptions and to ignore or distort contradictory evidence. (p. 317)

conflict a perceived incompatibility of actions, goals, or ideas. (p. 484)

conformity adjusting our behavior or thinking to coincide with a group standard. (p. 450)

confounding variable a factor other than the factor being studied that might produce an effect. (p. 25)

consciousness our awareness of ourselves and our environment. (p. 80)

conservation the principle (which Piaget believed to be a part of concrete operational reasoning) that properties such as mass, volume, and number remain the same despite changes in the forms of objects. (p. 132)

content validity the extent to which a test samples the behavior that is of interest. (p. 348)

continuous reinforcement schedule reinforcing the desired response every time it occurs. (p. 259)

control group in an experiment, the group *not* exposed to the treatment; contrasts with the experimental group and serves as a comparison for evaluating the effect of the treatment. (p. 23)

convergent thinking narrowing the available problem solutions to determine the single best solution. (p. 325)

coping alleviating stress using emotional, cognitive, or behavioral methods. (p. 419)

coronary heart disease the clogging of the vessels that nourish the heart muscle; the leading cause of death in many developed countries. (p. 414)

corpus callosum [KOR-pus kah-LOW-sum] the large band of neural fibers connecting the two brain hemispheres and carrying messages between them. (p. 62)

correlation a measure of the extent to which two factors vary together, and thus of how well either factor predicts the other. (p. 22)

correlation coefficient a statistical index of the relationship between two things (from –1.00 to +1.00). (pp. 22, A-4)

counseling psychology a branch of psychology that assists people with problems in living (often related to school, work, or marriage) and in achieving greater well-being. (p. 12)

counterconditioning behavior therapy procedures that use classical conditioning to evoke new responses to stimuli that are triggering unwanted behaviors; include *exposure therapies* and *aversive conditioning*. (p. 575)

creativity the ability to produce new and valuable ideas. (p. 324)

critical period an optimal period early in the life of an organism when exposure to certain stimuli or experiences produces normal development. (p. 128)

critical thinking thinking that does not blindly accept arguments and conclusions. Rather, it examines assumptions, appraises the source, discerns hidden biases, evaluates evidence, and assesses conclusions. (p. 3)

cross-sectional study a study in which people of different ages are compared with one another. (pp. 162, 349, A-8)

crystallized intelligence our accumulated knowledge and verbal skills; tends to increase with age. (p. 349)

culture the enduring behaviors, ideas, attitudes, values, and traditions shared by a group of people and transmitted from one generation to the next. (pp. 9, 448)

debriefing the postexperimental explanation of a study, including its purpose and any deceptions, to its participants. (p. 29)

deep processing encoding semantically, based on the meaning of the words; tends to yield the best retention. (p. 289)

defense mechanisms in psychoanalytic theory, the ego's protective methods of reducing anxiety by unconsciously distorting reality. (p. 495)

deindividuation the loss of self-awareness and self-restraint occurring in group situations that foster arousal and anonymity. (p. 457)

déjà vu that eerie sense that "I've experienced this before." Cues from the current situation may unconsciously trigger retrieval of an earlier experience. (p. 308)

delta waves the large, slow brain waves associated with deep sleep. (p. 89)

delusion a false belief, often of persecution or grandeur, that may accompany psychotic disorders. (p. 556)

dendrites a neuron's often bushy, branching extensions that receive messages and conduct impulses toward the cell body. (p. 36)

dependent variable in an experiment, the outcome that is measured; the variable that may change when the independent variable is manipulated. (p. 25)

depressants drugs (such as alcohol, barbiturates, and opiates) that reduce neural activity and slow body functions. (p. 106)

depth perception the ability to see objects in three dimensions although the images that strike the retina are two-dimensional; allows us to judge distance. (p. 218)

developmental psychology a branch of psychology that studies physical, cognitive, and social change throughout the life span. (p. 120)

difference threshold the minimum difference between two stimuli required for detection 50 percent of the time. We experience the difference threshold as a *just noticeable difference* (or *jnd*). (p. 202)

discrimination (1) in classical conditioning, the learned ability to distinguish between a conditioned stimulus and stimuli that do not signal an unconditioned stimulus. (2) in social psychology, unjustifiable negative behavior toward a group and its members. (pp. 252, 462)

disorder of sexual development a condition present at birth that involves unusual development of sex chromosomes and anatomy. (p. 177)

dissociation a split in consciousness, which allows some thoughts and behaviors to occur simultaneously with others. (p. 235)

dissociative disorders controversial, rare disorders in which conscious awareness becomes separated (dissociated) from previous memories, thoughts, and feelings. (p. 561)

dissociative identity disorder (DID) a rare dissociative disorder in which a person exhibits two or more distinct and alternating personalities. Formerly called *multiple personality disorder*. (p. 561)

divergent thinking expanding the number of possible problem solutions; creative thinking that diverges in different directions. (p. 325)

DNA (deoxyribonucleic acid) a complex molecule containing the genetic information that makes up the chromosomes. (p. 66)

double-blind procedure an experimental procedure in which both the research participants and the research staff are ignorant (blind) about whether the research participants have received the treatment or a placebo. Commonly used in drug-evaluation studies. (p. 24)

Down syndrome a condition of mild to severe intellectual disability and associated physical disorders caused by an extra copy of chromosome 21. (p. 351)

dream a sequence of images, emotions, and thoughts passing through a sleeping person's mind. (p. 99)

drive-reduction theory the idea that a physiological need creates an aroused tension state (a drive) that motivates an organism to satisfy the need. (p. 367)

DSM-5 the American Psychiatric Association's *Diagnostic and Statistical Manual of Mental Disorders,* Fifth Edition; a widely used system for classifying psychological disorders. (p. 531)

dual processing the principle that information is often simultaneously processed on separate conscious and unconscious tracks. (p. 85)

echoic memory a momentary sensory memory of auditory stimuli; if attention is elsewhere, sounds and words can still be recalled within 3 or 4 seconds. (p. 286)

eclectic approach an approach to psychotherapy that uses techniques from various forms of therapy. (p. 570)

Ecstasy (MDMA) a synthetic stimulant and mild hallucinogen. Produces euphoria and social intimacy, but with short-term health risks and longer-term harm to serotonin-producing neurons and to mood and cognition. (p. 111)

effortful processing encoding that requires attention and conscious effort. (p. 285)

ego the largely conscious, "executive" part of personality that, according to Freud, mediates among the demands of the id, superego, and reality. The ego operates on the *reality principle,* satisfying the id's desires in ways that will realistically bring pleasure rather than pain. (p. 493)

egocentrism in Piaget's theory, the preoperational child's difficulty taking another's point of view. (p. 132)

electroconvulsive therapy (ECT) a biomedical therapy for severely depressed patients in which a brief electric current is sent through the brain of an anesthetized patient. (p. 597)

electroencephalogram (EEG) an amplified recording of the waves of electrical activity sweeping across the brain's surface. These waves are measured by electrodes placed on the scalp. (p. 48)

embodied cognition the influence of bodily sensations, gestures, and other states on cognitive preferences and judgments. (p. 240)

embryo the developing human organism from about 2 weeks after fertilization through the second month. (p. 123)

emerging adulthood a period from about age 18 to the mid-twenties, when many in Western cultures are no longer adolescents but have not yet achieved full independence as adults. (p. 156)

emotion a response of the whole organism, involving (1) physiological arousal, (2) expressive behaviors, and (3) conscious experience. (p. 387)

emotion-focused coping attempting to alleviate stress by avoiding or ignoring a stressor and attending to emotional needs related to our stress reaction. (p. 419)

emotional intelligence the ability to perceive, understand, manage, and use emotions. (p. 344)

empirically derived test a test (such as the MMPI) developed by testing a pool of items and then selecting those that discriminate between groups. (p. 508)

encoding the processing of information into the memory system—for example, by extracting meaning. (p. 284)

endocrine [EN-duh-krin] **system** the body's "slow" chemical communication system; a set of glands that secrete hormones into the bloodstream. (p. 45)

endorphins [en-DOR-fins] "morphine within"—natural, opiate-like neurotransmitters linked to pain control and to pleasure. (p. 41)

environment every nongenetic influence, from prenatal nutrition to the people and things around us. (p. 66)

epigenetics the study of environmental influences on gene expression that occur without a DNA change. (pp. 72, 530)

episodic memory explicit memory of personally experienced events; one of our two conscious memory systems (the other is *semantic memory*). (p. 292)

equity a condition in which people receive from a relationship in proportion to what they give to it. (p. 480)

erectile disorder inability to develop or maintain an erection due to insufficient bloodflow to the penis. (p. 183)

estrogens sex hormones, such as estradiol, secreted in greater amounts by females than by males and contributing to female sex characteristics. In nonhuman female mammals, estrogen levels peak during ovulation, promoting sexual receptivity. (p. 181)

evidence-based practice clinical decision making that integrates the best available research with clinical expertise and patient characteristics and preferences. (p. 587)

evolutionary psychology the study of the evolution of behavior and the mind, using principles of natural selection. (pp. 8, 73)

experiment a research method in which an investigator manipulates one or more factors (independent variables) to observe the effect on some behavior or mental process (the dependent variable). By *random assignment* of participants, the experimenter aims to control other relevant factors. (p. 23)

experimental group in an experiment, the group exposed to the treatment, that is, to one version of the independent variable. (p. 23)

explicit memory memory of facts and experiences that one can consciously know and "declare." (Also called *declarative memory*) (p. 285)

exposure therapies behavioral techniques, such as *systematic desensitization* and *virtual reality exposure therapy,* that treat anxieties by exposing people (in imagination or actual situations) to the things they fear and avoid. (p. 575)

external locus of control the perception that chance or outside forces beyond our personal control determine our fate. (p. 421)

extinction the diminishing of a conditioned response; occurs in classical conditioning when an unconditioned stimulus (US) does not follow a conditioned stimulus (CS); occurs in operant conditioning when a response is no longer reinforced. (p. 251)

extrasensory perception (ESP) the controversial claim that perception can occur apart from sensory input; includes telepathy, clairvoyance, and precognition. (p. 241)

extrinsic motivation a desire to perform a behavior to receive promised rewards or avoid threatened punishment. (p. 271)

facial feedback effect the tendency of facial muscle states to trigger corresponding feelings such as fear, anger, or happiness. (p. 401)

family therapy therapy that treats the family as a system. Views an individual's unwanted behaviors as influenced by, or directed at, other family members. (p. 582)

feature detectors nerve cells in the brain that respond to specific features of the stimulus, such as shape, angle, or movement. (p. 215)

feel-good, do-good phenomenon people's tendency to be helpful when already in a good mood. (p. 431)

female orgasmic disorder distress due to infrequently or never experiencing orgasm. (p. 183)

fetal alcohol syndrome (FAS) physical and cognitive abnormalities in children caused by a pregnant woman's heavy drinking. In severe cases, signs include a small, out-of-proportion head and abnormal facial features. (p. 124)

fetus the developing human organism from 9 weeks after conception to birth. (p. 123)

figure-ground the organization of the visual field into objects (the *figures*) that stand out from their surroundings (the *ground*). (p. 217)

fixation according to Freud, a lingering focus of pleasure-seeking energies at an earlier psychosexual stage, in which conflicts were unresolved. (p. 494)

fixed-interval schedule in operant conditioning, a reinforcement schedule that reinforces a response only after a specified time has elapsed. (p. 260)

fixed-ratio schedule in operant conditioning, a reinforcement schedule that reinforces a response only after a specified number of responses. (p. 260)

flashbulb memory a clear memory of an emotionally significant moment or event. (p. 295)

flow a completely involved, focused state of consciousness, with diminished awareness of self and time, resulting from optimal engagement of one's skills. (p. B-1)

fluid intelligence our ability to reason speedily and abstractly; tends to decrease with age, especially during late adulthood. (p. 349)

fMRI (functional MRI) a technique for revealing bloodflow and, therefore, brain activity by comparing successive MRI scans. fMRI scans show brain function as well as structure. (p. 49)

foot-in-the-door phenomenon the tendency for people who have first agreed to a small request to comply later with a larger request. (p. 445)

formal operational stage in Piaget's theory, the stage of cognitive development (normally beginning about age 12) during which people begin to think logically about abstract concepts. (p. 133)

fovea the central focal point in the retina, around which the eye's cones cluster. (p. 212)

framing the way an issue is posed; how an issue is framed can significantly affect decisions and judgments. (p. 322)

fraternal (dizygotic) twins develop from separate fertilized eggs. They are genetically no closer than ordinary brothers and sisters, but they share a prenatal environment. (p. 68)

free association in psychoanalysis, a method of exploring the unconscious in which the person relaxes and says whatever comes to mind, no matter how trivial or embarrassing. (p. 493)

frequency the number of complete wavelengths that pass a point in a given time (for example, per second). (p. 226)

frequency theory in hearing, the theory that the rate of nerve impulses traveling up the auditory nerve matches the frequency of a tone, thus enabling us to sense its pitch. (Also called *temporal theory*) (p. 230)

frontal lobes portion of the cerebral cortex lying just behind the forehead; involved in speaking and muscle movements and in making plans and judgments. (p. 56)

frustration-aggression principle the principle that frustration—the blocking of an attempt to achieve some goal—creates anger, which can generate aggression. (p. 470)

functionalism early school of thought promoted by James and influenced by Darwin; explored how mental and behavioral processes function—how they enable the organism to adapt, survive, and flourish. (p. 5)

fundamental attribution error the tendency for observers, when analyzing others' behavior, to underestimate the impact of the situation and to overestimate the impact of personal disposition. (p. 442)

gate-control theory the theory that the spinal cord contains a neurological "gate" that blocks pain signals or allows them to pass on to the brain. The "gate" is opened by the activity of pain signals traveling up small nerve fibers and is closed by activity in larger fibers or by information coming from the brain. (p. 232)

gender identity our sense of being male, female, or some combination of the two. (p. 179)

gender in psychology, the socially influenced characteristics by which people define *men* and *women*. (p. 172)

gender role a set of expected behaviors, attitudes, and traits for males or for females. (p. 177)

gender typing the acquisition of a traditional masculine or feminine role. (p. 178)

general adaptation syndrome (GAS) Selye's concept of the body's adaptive response to stress in three phases—alarm, resistance, exhaustion. (p. 409)

general intelligence (g) a general intelligence factor that, according to Spearman and others, underlies specific mental abilities and is therefore measured by every task on an intelligence test. (p. 341)

generalization the tendency, once a response has been conditioned, for stimuli similar to the conditioned stimulus to elicit similar responses. (p. 251)

generalized anxiety disorder an anxiety disorder in which a person is continually tense, apprehensive, and in a state of autonomic nervous system arousal. (p. 537)

genes the biochemical units of heredity that make up the chromosomes; segments of DNA capable of synthesizing proteins. (p. 66)

genome the complete instructions for making an organism, consisting of all the genetic material in that organism's chromosomes. (p. 66)

gestalt an organized whole. Gestalt psychologists emphasized our tendency to integrate pieces of information into meaningful wholes. (p. 217)

glial cells (glia) cells in the nervous system that support, nourish, and protect neurons; they may also play a role in learning, thinking, and memory. (p. 37)

glucose the form of sugar that circulates in the blood and provides the major source of energy for body tissues. When its level is low, we feel hunger. (p. 379)

grammar in a language, a system of rules that enables us to communicate with and understand others. In a given language, *semantics* is the set of rules for deriving meaning from sounds, and *syntax* is the set of rules for combining words into grammatically sensible sentences. (p. 330)

GRIT Graduated and Reciprocated Initiatives in Tension-Reduction—a strategy designed to decrease international tensions. (p. 488)

grit in psychology, passion and perseverance in the pursuit of long-term goals. (p. 376)

group polarization the enhancement of a group's prevailing inclinations through discussion within the group. (p. 458)

group therapy therapy conducted with groups rather than individuals, permitting therapeutic benefits from group interaction. (p. 582)

grouping the perceptual tendency to organize stimuli into coherent groups. (p. 217)

groupthink the mode of thinking that occurs when the desire for harmony in a decision-making group overrides a realistic appraisal of alternatives. (p. 459)

habituation decreasing responsiveness with repeated stimulation. As infants gain familiarity with repeated exposure to a stimulus, their interest wanes and they look away sooner. (p. 125)

hallucinations false sensory experiences, such as seeing something in the absence of an external visual stimulus. (p. 89)

hallucinogens psychedelic ("mind-manifesting") drugs, such as LSD, that distort perceptions and evoke sensory images in the absence of sensory input. (p. 111)

health psychology a subfield of psychology that provides psychology's contribution to behavioral medicine. (p. 410)

heredity the genetic transfer of characteristics from parents to offspring. (p. 66)

heritability the proportion of variation among individuals that we can attribute to genes. The heritability of a trait may vary, depending on the range of populations and environments studied. (p. 354)

heuristic a simple thinking strategy that often allows us to make judgments and solve problems efficiently; usually speedier but also more error-prone than *algorithms*. (p. 317)

hierarchy of needs Maslow's pyramid of human needs, beginning at the base with physiological needs that must first be satisfied before higher-level safety needs and then psychological needs become active. (p. 368)

hindsight bias the tendency to believe, after learning an outcome, that one would have foreseen it. (Also known as the *I-knew-it-all-along phenomenon*) (p. 15)

hippocampus a neural center located in the limbic system; helps process explicit memories for storage. (pp. 54, 293)

homeostasis a tendency to maintain a balanced or constant internal state; the regulation of any aspect of body chemistry, such as blood glucose, around a particular level. (p. 367)

hormones chemical messengers that are manufactured by the endocrine glands, travel through the bloodstream, and affect other tissues. (p. 45)

hue the dimension of color that is determined by the wavelength of light; what we know as the color names *blue, green,* and so forth. (p. 209)

human factors psychology a field of psychology allied with I/O psychology that explores how people and machines interact and how machines and physical environments can be made safe and easy to use. (p. B-2)

humanistic psychology historically significant perspective that emphasized human growth potential. (p. 7)

humanistic theories view personality with a focus on the potential for healthy personal growth. (p. 501)

hypnosis a social interaction in which one person (the hypnotist) suggests to another (the subject) that certain perceptions, feelings, thoughts, or behaviors will spontaneously occur. (p. 235)

hypothalamus [hi-po-THAL-uh-muss] a neural structure lying below *(hypo)* the thalamus; it directs several maintenance activities (eating, drinking, body temperature), helps govern the endocrine system via the pituitary gland, and is linked to emotion and reward. (p. 53)

hypothesis a testable prediction, often implied by a theory. (p. 17)

iconic memory a momentary sensory memory of visual stimuli; a photographic or picture-image memory lasting no more than a few tenths of a second. (p. 286)

id a reservoir of unconscious psychic energy that, according to Freud, strives to satisfy basic sexual and aggressive drives. The id operates on the *pleasure principle*, demanding immediate gratification. (p. 493)

identical (monozygotic) twins develop from a single fertilized egg that splits in two, creating two genetically identical organisms. (p. 67)

identification the process by which, according to Freud, children incorporate their parents' values into their developing superegos. (p. 494)

identity our sense of self; according to Erikson, the adolescent's task is to solidify a sense of self by testing and integrating various roles. (p. 153)

implicit memory retention of learned skills or classically conditioned associations independent of conscious recollection. (Also called *nondeclarative memory*) (p. 285)

imprinting the process by which certain animals form strong attachments during early life. (p. 139)

inattentional blindness failing to see visible objects when our attention is directed elsewhere. (p. 82)

incentive a positive or negative environmental stimulus that motivates behavior. (p. 367)

independent variable in an experiment, the factor that is manipulated; the variable whose effect is being studied. (p. 25)

individualism giving priority to one's own goals over group goals and defining one's identity in terms of personal attributes rather than group identifications. (p. 521)

industrial-organizational (I/O) psychology the application of psychological concepts and methods to optimizing human behavior in workplaces. (p. B-2)

informational social influence influence resulting from one's willingness to accept others' opinions about reality. (p. 451)

informed consent giving potential participants enough information about a study to enable them to choose whether they wish to participate. (p. 29)

ingroup "us"—people with whom we share a common identity. (p. 465)

ingroup bias the tendency to favor our own group. (p. 465)

inner ear the innermost part of the ear, containing the cochlea, semicircular canals, and vestibular sacs. (p. 228)

insight a sudden realization of a problem's solution; contrasts with strategy-based solutions. (p. 317)

insight therapies a variety of therapies that aim to improve psychological functioning by increasing a person's awareness of underlying motives and defenses. (p. 572)

insomnia recurring problems in falling or staying asleep. (p. 96)

instinct a complex behavior that is rigidly patterned throughout a species and is unlearned. (p. 366)

intellectual disability a condition of limited mental ability, indicated by an intelligence test score of 70 or below and difficulty adapting to the demands of life. (Formerly referred to as *mental retardation*) (p. 351)

intelligence quotient (IQ) defined originally as the ratio of mental age (*ma*) to chronological age (*ca*) multiplied by 100 (thus, IQ = *ma/ca* × 100). On contemporary intelligence tests, the average performance for a given age is assigned a score of 100. (p. 346)

intelligence test a method for assessing an individual's mental aptitudes and comparing them with those of others, using numerical scores. (p. 345)

intelligence the mental potential to learn from experience, solve problems, and use knowledge to adapt to new situations. (p. 341)

intensity the amount of energy in a light wave or sound wave, which influences what we perceive as brightness or loudness. Intensity is determined by the wave's amplitude (height). (p. 209)

interaction the interplay that occurs when the effect of one factor (such as environment) depends on another factor (such as heredity). (p. 71)

internal locus of control the perception that we control our own fate. (p. 421)

interneurons neurons within the brain and spinal cord; communicate internally and process information between the sensory inputs and motor outputs. (p. 43)

interpretation in psychoanalysis, the analyst's noting supposed dream meanings, resistances, and other significant behaviors and events in order to promote insight. (p. 571)

intimacy in Erikson's theory, the ability to form close, loving relationships; a primary developmental task in young adulthood. (p. 153)

intrinsic motivation a desire to perform a behavior effectively for its own sake. (p. 271)

intuition an effortless, immediate, automatic feeling or thought, as contrasted with explicit, conscious reasoning. (pp. 15, 319)

James-Lange theory the theory that our experience of emotion is our awareness of our physiological responses to an emotion-arousing stimulus. (p. 387)

just-world phenomenon the tendency for people to believe the world is just and that people therefore get what they deserve and deserve what they get. (p. 465)

kinesthesia [kin-ehs-THEE-zhuh] the system for sensing the position and movement of individual body parts. (p. 238)

language our spoken, written, or signed words and the ways we combine them to communicate meaning. (p. 329)

latent content according to Freud, the underlying meaning of a dream (as distinct from its manifest content). (p. 100)

latent learning learning that occurs but is not apparent until there is an incentive to demonstrate it. (p. 270)

law of effect Thorndike's principle that behaviors followed by favorable consequences become more likely, and that behaviors followed by unfavorable consequences become less likely. (p. 256)

law of effect Thorndike's principle that behaviors followed by favorable consequences become more likely, and that behaviors followed by unfavorable consequences become less likely.(p. 256)

learned helplessness the hopelessness and passive resignation an animal or person learns when unable to avoid repeated aversive events. (p. 419)

learning the process of acquiring through experience new and relatively enduring information or behaviors. (pp. 246, 256)

learning the process of acquiring through experience new information or behaviors. (p. 267)

lesion [LEE-zhuhn] tissue destruction. A brain lesion is a naturally or experimentally caused destruction of brain tissue. (p. 48)

levels of analysis the differing complementary views, from biological to psychological to social-cultural, for analyzing any given phenomenon. (p. 10)

limbic system neural system (including the *amygdala*, *hypothalamus*, and *hippocampus*) located below the cerebral hemispheres; associated with emotions and drives. (p. 52)

linguistic determinism Whorf's hypothesis that language determines the way we think. (p. 336)

lobotomy a psychosurgical procedure once used to calm uncontrollably emotional or violent patients. The procedure cut the nerves connecting the frontal lobes to the emotion-controlling centers of the inner brain. (p. 599)

long-term memory the relatively permanent and limitless storehouse of the memory system. Includes knowledge, skills, and experiences. (p. 284)

long-term potentiation (LTP) an increase in a cell's firing potential after brief, rapid stimulation. Believed to be a neural basis for learning and memory. (p. 295)

longitudinal study research in which the same people are restudied and retested over a long period. (pp. 162, 349, A-8)

LSD a powerful hallucinogenic drug; also known as acid *(lysergic acid diethylamide)*. (p. 112)

major depressive disorder a disorder in which a person experiences, in the absence of drugs or another medical condition, two or more weeks with five or more symptoms, at least one of which must be either (1) depressed mood or (2) loss of interest or pleasure. (p. 545)

mania a hyperactive, wildly optimistic state in which dangerously poor judgment is common. (p. 546)

manifest content according to Freud, the remembered story line of a dream (as distinct from its latent, or hidden, content). (p. 100)

maturation biological growth processes that enable orderly changes in behavior, relatively uninfluenced by experience. (p. 127)

mean the arithmetic average of a distribution, obtained by adding the scores and then dividing by the number of scores. (p. A-2)

median the middle score in a distribution; half the scores are above it and half are below it. (p. A-2)

medical model the concept that diseases, in this case psychological disorders, have physical causes that can be *diagnosed*, *treated*, and, in most cases, *cured*, often through treatment in a *hospital*. (p. 529)

medulla [muh-DUL-uh] the base of the brainstem; controls heartbeat and breathing. (p. 50)

memory consolidation the neural storage of a long-term memory. (p. 293)

memory the persistence of learning over time through the encoding, storage, and retrieval of information. (p. 282)

menarche [meh-NAR-key] the first menstrual period. (p. 176)

menopause the time of natural cessation of menstruation; also refers to the biological changes a woman experiences as her ability to reproduce declines. (p. 158)

mental age a measure of intelligence test performance devised by Binet; the chronological age that most typically corresponds to a given level of performance. Thus, a child who does as well as an average 8-year-old is said to have a mental age of 8. (p. 346)

mental set a tendency to approach a problem in one particular way, often a way that has been successful in the past. (p. 318)

mere exposure effect the phenomenon that repeated exposure to novel stimuli increases liking of them. (p. 475)

methamphetamine a powerfully addictive drug that stimulates the central nervous system, with accelerated body functions and associated energy and mood changes; over time, appears to reduce baseline dopamine levels. (p. 111)

middle ear the chamber between the eardrum and cochlea containing three tiny bones (hammer, anvil, and stirrup) that concentrate the vibrations of the eardrum on the cochlea's oval window. (p. 227)

mindfulness meditation a reflective practice in which people attend to current experiences in a nonjudgmental and accepting manner. (p. 428)

Minnesota Multiphasic Personality Inventory (MMPI) the most widely researched and clinically used of all personality tests. Originally developed to identify emotional disorders (still considered its most appropriate use), this test is now used for many other screening purposes. (p. 508)

mirror neurons frontal lobe neurons that some scientists believe fire when performing certain actions or when observing another doing so. The brain's mirroring of another's action may enable imitation and empathy. (p. 273)

mirror-image perceptions mutual views often held by conflicting people, as when each side sees itself as ethical and peaceful and views the other side as evil and aggressive. (p. 485)

misinformation effect when misleading information has corrupted one's memory of an event. (p. 307)

mnemonics [nih-MON-iks] memory aids, especially those techniques that use vivid imagery and organizational devices. (p. 288)

mode the most frequently occurring score(s) in a distribution. (p. A-2)

modeling the process of observing and imitating a specific behavior. (p. 273)

monocular cues depth cues, such as interposition and linear perspective, available to either eye alone. (p. 219)

mood-congruent memory the tendency to recall experiences that are consistent with one's current good or bad mood. (p. 298)

morpheme in a language, the smallest unit that carries meaning; may be a word or a part of a word (such as a prefix). (p. 330)

motivation a need or desire that energizes and directs behavior. (p. 366)

motor (efferent) neurons neurons that carry outgoing information from the brain and spinal cord to the muscles and glands. (p. 43)

motor cortex an area at the rear of the frontal lobes that controls voluntary movements. (p. 57)

MRI (magnetic resonance imaging) a technique that uses magnetic fields and radio waves to produce computer-generated images of soft tissue. MRI scans show brain anatomy. (p. 49)

mutation a random error in gene replication that leads to a change. (p. 74)

myelin [MY-uh-lin] **sheath** a fatty tissue layer segmentally encasing the axons of some neurons; enables vastly greater transmission speed as neural impulses hop from one node to the next. (p. 37)

narcissism excessive self-love and self-absorption. (pp. 374, 519)

narcolepsy a sleep disorder characterized by uncontrollable sleep attacks. The sufferer may lapse directly into REM sleep, often at inopportune times. (p. 97)

natural selection the principle that those chance inherited traits that better enable an organism to survive and reproduce in a particular environment will most likely be passed on to succeeding generations. (pp. 8, 73)

naturalistic observation a descriptive technique of observing and recording behavior in naturally occurring situations without trying to manipulate and control the situation. (p. 19)

nature–nurture issue the longstanding controversy over the relative contributions that genes and experience make to the development of psychological traits and behaviors. Today's science sees traits and behaviors arising from the interaction of nature and nurture. (p. 8)

near-death experience an altered state of consciousness reported after a close brush with death (such as cardiac arrest); often similar to drug-induced hallucinations. (p. 112)

negative reinforcement increasing behaviors by stopping or reducing negative stimuli. A negative reinforcer is any stimulus that, when *removed* after a response, strengthens the response. (*Note:* Negative reinforcement is not punishment) (p. 258)

nerves bundled axons that form neural cables connecting the central nervous system with muscles, glands, and sense organs. (p. 42)

nervous system the body's speedy, electrochemical communication network, consisting of all the nerve cells of the peripheral and central nervous systems. (p. 42)

neurogenesis the formation of new neurons. (p. 61)

neuron a nerve cell; the basic building block of the nervous system. (p. 36)

neurotransmitters chemical messengers that cross the synaptic gaps between neurons. When released by the sending neuron, neurotransmitters travel across the synapse and bind to receptor sites on the receiving neuron, thereby influencing whether that neuron will generate a neural impulse. (p. 40)

neutral stimulus (NS) in classical conditioning, a stimulus that elicits no response before conditioning. (p. 248)

nicotine a stimulating and highly addictive psychoactive drug in tobacco. (p. 108)

night terrors a sleep disorder characterized by high arousal and an appearance of being terrified; unlike nightmares, night terrors occur during NREM-3 sleep, within two or three hours of falling asleep, and are seldom remembered. (p. 98)

norm an understood rule for accepted and expected behavior. Norms prescribe "proper" behavior. (p. 448)

normal curve (*normal distribution*) a symmetrical, bell-shaped curve that describes the distribution of many types of data; most scores fall near the mean (about 68 percent fall within one standard deviation of it) and fewer and fewer near the extremes. (pp. 348, A-3)

normative social influence influence resulting from a person's desire to gain approval or avoid disapproval. (p. 451)

object permanence the awareness that things continue to exist even when not perceived. (p. 130)

observational learning learning by observing others. (p. 272)

obsessive-compulsive disorder (OCD) a disorder characterized by unwanted repetitive thoughts (obsessions), actions (compulsions), or both. (p. 539)

occipital [ahk-SIP-uh-tuhl] **lobes** portion of the cerebral cortex lying at the back of the head; includes areas that receive information from the visual fields. (p. 56)

Oedipus [ED-uh-puss] **complex** according to Freud, a boy's sexual desires toward his mother and feelings of jealousy and hatred for the rival father. (p. 494)

one-word stage the stage in speech development, from about age 1 to 2, during which a child speaks mostly in single words. (p. 332)

operant behavior behavior that operates on the environment, producing consequences. (p. 247)

operant chamber in operant conditioning research, a chamber (also known as a *Skinner box*) containing a bar or key that an animal can manipulate to obtain a food or water reinforcer; attached devices record the animal's rate of bar pressing or key pecking. (p. 256)

operant chamber in operant conditioning research, a chamber (also known as a *Skinner box*) containing a bar or key that an animal can manipulate to obtain a food or water reinforcer; attached devices record the animal's rate of bar pressing or key pecking. (p. 256)

operant conditioning a type of learning in which behavior is strengthened if followed by a reinforcer or diminished if followed by a punisher. (p. 256)

operational definition a carefully worded statement of the exact procedures (operations) used in a research study. For example, *human intelligence* may be operationally defined as what an intelligence test measures. (p. 17)

opiates opium and its derivatives, such as morphine and heroin; depress neural activity, temporarily lessening pain and anxiety. (p. 107)

opponent-process theory the theory that opposing retinal processes (red-green, yellow-blue, white-black) enable color vision. For example, some cells are stimulated by green and inhibited by red; others are stimulated by red and inhibited by green. (p. 214)

optic nerve the nerve that carries neural impulses from the eye to the brain. (p. 211)

organizational psychology an I/O psychology subfield that examines organizational influences on worker satisfaction and productivity and facilitates organizational change. (p. B-2)

ostracism deliberate social exclusion of individuals or groups. (p. 371)

other-race effect the tendency to recall faces of one's own race more accurately than faces of other races. Also called the *cross-race effect* and the *own-race bias*. (p. 467)

outgroup "them"—those perceived as different or apart from our ingroup. (p. 465)

overconfidence the tendency to be more confident than correct—to overestimate the accuracy of our beliefs and judgments. (p. 321)

panic disorder an anxiety disorder marked by unpredictable, minutes-long episodes of intense dread in which a person experiences terror and accompanying chest pain, choking, or other frightening sensations. Often followed by worry over a possible next attack. (p. 537)

parallel processing the processing of many aspects of a problem simultaneously; the brain's natural mode of information processing for many functions. (pp. 86, 216, 284)

paraphilias sexual arousal from fantasies, behaviors, or urges involving nonhuman objects, the suffering of self or others, and/or nonconsenting persons. (p. 183)

parapsychology the study of paranormal phenomena, including ESP and psychokinesis. (p. 241)

parasympathetic nervous system the division of the autonomic nervous system that calms the body, conserving its energy. (p. 44)

parietal [puh-RYE-uh-tuhl] **lobes** -portion of the cerebral cortex lying at the top of the head and toward the rear; receives sensory input for touch and body position. (p. 56)

partial (intermittent) reinforcement schedule reinforcing a response only part of the time; results in slower acquisition of a response but much greater resistance to extinction than does continuous reinforcement. (p. 259)

passionate love an aroused state of intense positive absorption in another, usually present at the beginning of a love relationship. (p. 479)

perception the process of organizing and interpreting sensory information, enabling us to recognize meaningful objects and events. (p. 200)

perceptual adaptation the ability to adjust to changed sensory input, including an artificially displaced or even inverted visual field. (p. 223)

perceptual constancy perceiving objects as unchanging (having consistent color, brightness, shape, and size) even as illumination and retinal images change. (p. 221)

perceptual set a mental predisposition to perceive one thing and not another. (p. 205)

peripheral nervous system (PNS) the sensory and motor neurons that connect the central nervous system (CNS) to the rest of the body. (p. 42)

peripheral route persuasion occurs when people are influenced by incidental cues, such as a speaker's attractiveness. (p. 444)

personality an individual's characteristic pattern of thinking, feeling, and acting. (p. 492)

personality disorders inflexible and enduring behavior patterns that impair social functioning. (p. 563)

personality inventory a questionnaire (often with *true-false* or *agree-disagree* items) on which people respond to items designed to gauge a wide range of feelings and behaviors; used to assess selected personality traits. (p. 508)

personnel psychology an I/O psychology subfield that helps with job seeking, and with employee recruitment, selection, placement, training, appraisal, and development. (p. B-2)

PET (positron emission tomography) scan a visual display of brain activity that detects where a radioactive form of glucose goes while the brain performs a given task. (p. 48)

phobia an anxiety disorder marked by a persistent, irrational fear and avoidance of a specific object, activity, or situation. (p. 538)

phoneme in a language, the smallest distinctive sound unit. (p. 330)

pitch a tone's experienced highness or lowness; depends on frequency. (p. 226)

pituitary gland the endocrine system's most influential gland. Under the influence of the hypothalamus, the pituitary regulates growth and controls other endocrine glands. (p. 46)

place theory in hearing, the theory that links the pitch we hear with the place where the cochlea's membrane is stimulated. (p. 229)

placebo [pluh-SEE-bo; Latin for "I shall please"] **effect** experimental results caused by expectations alone; any effect on behavior caused by the administration of an inert substance or condition, which the recipient assumes is an active agent. (p. 24)

plasticity the brain's ability to change, especially during childhood, by reorganizing after damage or by building new pathways based on experience. (p. 60)

polygraph a machine, commonly used in attempts to detect lies, that measures several of the physiological responses (such as perspiration and cardiovascular and breathing changes) accompanying emotion. (p. 394)

population all those in a group being studied, from which samples may be drawn. (*Note:* Except for national studies, this does *not* refer to a country's whole population) (p. 21)

positive psychology the scientific study of human flourishing, with the goals of discovering and promoting strengths and virtues that help individuals and communities to thrive. (pp. 10, 432)

positive reinforcement increasing behaviors by presenting positive reinforcers. A positive reinforcer is any stimulus that, when *presented* after a response, strengthens the response. (p. 258)

posthypnotic suggestion a suggestion, made during a hypnosis session, to be carried out after the subject is no longer hypnotized; used by some clinicians to help control undesired symptoms and behaviors. (p. 235)

posttraumatic growth positive psychological changes as a result of struggling with extremely challenging circumstances and life crises. (p. 603)

posttraumatic stress disorder (PTSD) a disorder characterized by haunting memories, nightmares, social withdrawal, jumpy anxiety, numbness of feeling, and/or insomnia that lingers for four weeks or more after a traumatic experience. (p. 540)

predictive validity the success with which a test predicts the behavior it is designed to predict; it is assessed by computing the correlation between test scores and the criterion behavior. (Also called *criterion-related validity*) (p. 348)

prejudice an unjustifiable (and usually negative) attitude toward a group and its members. Prejudice generally involves stereotyped beliefs, negative feelings, and a predisposition to discriminatory action. (p. 462)

preoperational stage in Piaget's theory, the stage (from about 2 to about 6 or 7 years of age) during which a child learns to use language but does not yet comprehend the mental operations of concrete logic. (p. 131)

primary reinforcer an innately reinforcing stimulus, such as one that satisfies a biological need. (p. 259)

primary sex characteristics the body structures (ovaries, testes, and external genitalia) that make sexual reproduction possible. (p. 175)

priming the activation, often unconsciously, of certain associations, thus predisposing one's perception, memory, or response. (pp. 201, 297)

proactive interference the forward-acting disruptive effect of prior learning on the recall of new information. (p. 304)

problem-focused coping attempting to alleviate stress directly—by changing the stressor or the way we interact with that stressor. (p. 419)

projective test a personality test, such as the Rorschach, that provides ambiguous stimuli designed to trigger projection of one's inner dynamics. (p. 497)

prosocial behavior positive, constructive, helpful behavior. The opposite of antisocial behavior. (p. 275)

prototype a mental image or best example of a category. Matching new items to a prototype provides a quick and easy method for sorting items into categories (as when comparing feathered creatures to a prototypical bird, such as a robin). (p. 316)

psychiatry a branch of medicine dealing with psychological disorders; practiced by physicians who sometimes provide medical (for example, drug) treatments as well as psychological therapy. (p. 12)

psychoactive drug a chemical substance that alters perceptions and moods. (p. 104)

psychoanalysis (1) Freud's theory of personality that attributes thoughts and actions to unconscious motives and conflicts. (2) Freud's therapeutic technique used in treating psychological disorders. Freud believed the patient's free associations, resistances, dreams, and transferences—and the therapist's interpretations of them—released previously repressed feelings, allowing the patient to gain self-insight. (pp. 492, 570)

psychodynamic theories view personality with a focus on the unconscious and the importance of childhood experiences. (p. 492)

psychodynamic therapy therapy deriving from the psychoanalytic tradition; views individuals as responding to unconscious forces and childhood experiences, and seeks to enhance self-insight. (p. 572)

psychological disorder a syndrome marked by a clinically significant disturbance in an individual's cognition, emotion regulation, or behavior. (p. 528)

psychology the science of behavior and mental processes. (p. 7)

psychoneuroimmunology the study of how psychological, neural, and endocrine processes together affect the immune system and resulting health. (p. 410)

psychopharmacology the study of the effects of drugs on mind and behavior. (p. 593)

psychosexual stages the childhood stages of development (oral, anal, phallic, latency, genital) during which, according to Freud, the id's pleasure-seeking energies focus on distinct erogenous zones. (p. 494)

psychosurgery surgery that removes or destroys brain tissue in an effort to change behavior. (p. 599)

psychotherapy treatment involving psychological techniques; consists of interactions between a trained therapist and someone seeking to overcome psychological difficulties or achieve personal growth. (p. 570)

psychotic disorders a group of psychological disorders marked by irrational ideas, distorted perceptions, and a loss of contact with reality. (p. 556)

puberty the period of sexual maturation, during which a person becomes capable of reproducing. (pp. 147, 175)

punishment an event that tends to *decrease* the behavior that it follows. (p. 261)

random assignment assigning participants to experimental and control groups by chance, thus minimizing preexisting differences between the different groups. (p. 24)

random sample a sample that fairly represents a population because each member has an equal chance of inclusion. (p. 21)

range the difference between the highest and lowest scores in a distribution. (p. A-3)

recall a measure of memory in which the person must retrieve information learned earlier, as on a fill-in-the-blank test. (p. 283)

reciprocal determinism the interacting influences of behavior, internal cognition, and environment. (p. 513)

reciprocity norm an expectation that people will help, not hurt, those who have helped them. (p. 483)

recognition a measure of memory in which the person identifies items previously learned, as on a multiple-choice test. (p. 283)

reconsolidation a process in which previously stored memories, when retrieved, are potentially altered before being stored again. (p. 306)

reflex a simple, automatic response to a sensory stimulus, such as the knee-jerk response. (p. 44)

refractory period (1) in neuroscience, a brief resting pause that occurs after a neuron has fired; subsequent action potentials cannot occur until the axon returns to its resting state. (2) in human sexuality, a resting period after orgasm, during which a man cannot achieve another orgasm. (pp. 39, 183)

regression toward the mean the tendency for extreme or unusual scores or events to fall back (regress) toward the average. (p. A-6)

reinforcement in operant conditioning, any event that *strengthens* the behavior it follows. (p. 257)

reinforcement schedule a pattern that defines how often a desired response will be reinforced. (p. 259)

relational aggression an act of aggression (physical or verbal) intended to harm a person's relationship or social standing. (p. 173)

relative deprivation the perception that one is worse off relative to those with whom one compares oneself. (p. 435)

relearning a measure of memory that assesses the amount of time saved when learning material again. (p. 283)

reliability the extent to which a test yields consistent results, as assessed by the consistency of scores on two halves of the test, on alternative forms of the test, or on retesting. (p. 348)

REM rebound the tendency for REM sleep to increase following REM sleep deprivation. (p. 102)

REM sleep rapid eye movement sleep; a recurring sleep stage during which vivid dreams commonly occur. Also known as *paradoxical sleep*, because the muscles are relaxed (except for minor twitches) but other body systems are active. (p. 88)

repetitive transcranial magnetic stimulation (rTMS) the application of repeated pulses of magnetic energy to the brain; used to stimulate or suppress brain activity. (p. 598)

replication repeating the essence of a research study, usually with different participants in different situations, to see whether the basic finding can be reproduced. (p. 17)

repression in psychoanalytic theory, the basic defense mechanism that banishes from consciousness anxiety-arousing thoughts, feelings, and memories. (pp. 306, 495)

resilience the personal strength that helps most people cope with stress and recover from adversity and even trauma. (p. 603)

resistance in psychoanalysis, the blocking from consciousness of anxiety-laden material. (p. 571)

respondent behavior behavior that occurs as an automatic response to some stimulus. (p. 247)

reticular formation a nerve network that travels through the brainstem into the thalamus and plays an important role in controlling arousal. (p. 52)

retina the light-sensitive inner surface of the eye, containing the receptor rods and cones plus layers of neurons that begin the processing of visual information. (p. 211)

retinal disparity a binocular cue for perceiving depth: By comparing images from the retinas in the two eyes, the brain computes distance—the greater the disparity (difference) between the two images, the closer the object. (p. 219)

retrieval the process of getting information out of memory storage. (p. 284)

retroactive interference the backward-acting disruptive effect of new learning on the recall of old information. (p. 304)

retrograde amnesia an inability to retrieve information from one's past. (p. 302)

reuptake a neurotransmitter's reabsorption by the sending neuron. (p. 40)

rods retinal receptors that detect black, white, and gray, and are sensitive to movement; necessary for peripheral and twilight vision, when cones don't respond. (p. 211)

role a set of expectations (norms) about a social position, defining how those in the position ought to behave. (pp. 177, 445)

Rorschach inkblot test the most widely used projective test, a set of 10 inkblots, designed by Hermann Rorschach; seeks to identify people's inner feelings by analyzing their interpretations of the blots. (p. 498)

rumination compulsive fretting; *overthinking* about our problems and their causes. (p. 550)

savant syndrome a condition in which a person otherwise limited in mental ability has an exceptional specific skill, such as in computation or drawing. (p. 342)

scapegoat theory the theory that prejudice offers an outlet for anger by providing someone to blame. (p. 466)

scatterplot a graphed cluster of dots, each of which represents the values of two variables. The slope of the points suggests the direction of the relationship between the two variables. The amount of scatter suggests the strength of the correlation (little scatter indicates high correlation). (p. A-4)

schema a concept or framework that organizes and interprets information. (p. 130)

schizophrenia a psychological disorder characterized by delusions, hallucinations, disorganized speech, and/or diminished, inappropriate emotional expression. (p. 556)

secondary sex characteristics nonreproductive sexual traits, such as female breasts and hips, male voice quality, and body hair. (p. 175)

selective attention the focusing of conscious awareness on a particular stimulus. (p. 81)

self in contemporary psychology, assumed to be the center of personality, the organizer of our thoughts, feelings, and actions. (p. 516)

self-actualization according to Maslow, one of the ultimate psychological needs that arises after basic physical and psychological needs are met and self-esteem is achieved; the motivation to fulfill one's potential. (p. 501)

self-concept all our thoughts and feelings about ourselves, in answer to the question, "Who am I?" (p. 502)

self-control the ability to control impulses and delay short-term gratification for greater long-term rewards. (p. 421)

self-disclosure the act of revealing intimate aspects of oneself to others. (p. 480)

self-efficacy one's sense of competence and effectiveness. (p. 517)

self-esteem one's feelings of high or low self-worth. (p. 517)

self-fulfilling prophecy a belief that leads to its own fulfillment. (p. 485)

self-serving bias a readiness to perceive oneself favorably. (p. 518)

semantic memory explicit memory of facts and general knowledge; one of our two conscious memory systems (the other is *episodic memory*). (p. 292)

sensation the process by which our sensory receptors and nervous system receive and represent stimulus energies from our environment. (p. 200)

sensorimotor stage in Piaget's theory, the stage (from birth to nearly 2 years of age) during which infants know the world mostly in terms of their sensory impressions and motor activities. (p. 130)

sensorineural hearing loss the most common form of hearing loss, also called *nerve deafness;* caused by damage to the cochlea's receptor cells or to the auditory nerves. (p. 228)

sensory (afferent) neurons neurons that carry incoming information from the sensory receptors to the brain and spinal cord. (p. 42)

sensory adaptation diminished sensitivity as a consequence of constant stimulation. (p. 204)

sensory interaction the principle that one sense may influence another, as when the smell of food influences its taste. (p. 239)

sensory memory the immediate, very brief recording of sensory information in the memory system. (p. 284)

serial position effect our tendency to recall best the last (*recency effect*) and first (*primacy effect*) items in a list. (p. 299)

set point the point at which your "weight thermostat" is supposedly set. When your body falls below this weight, increased hunger and a lowered metabolic rate may combine to restore the lost weight. (p. 379)

sex in psychology, the biologically influenced characteristics by which people define *males* and *females.* (p. 172)

sexual dysfunction a problem that consistently impairs sexual arousal or functioning. (p. 183)

sexual orientation an enduring sexual attraction toward members of one's own sex (homosexual orientation), the other sex (heterosexual orientation), or both sexes (bisexual orientation). (p. 187)

sexual response cycle the four stages of sexual responding described by Masters and Johnson—excitement, plateau, orgasm, and resolution. (p. 182)

shallow processing encoding on a basic level based on the structure or appearance of words. (p. 289)

shaping an operant conditioning procedure in which reinforcers guide behavior toward closer and closer approximations of the desired behavior. (p. 257)

short-term memory activated memory that holds a few items briefly, such as the seven digits of a phone number while calling, before the information is stored or forgotten. (p. 284)

signal detection theory a theory predicting how and when we detect the presence of a faint stimulus (*signal*) amid background stimulation (*noise*). Assumes there is no single absolute threshold and that detection depends partly on a person's experience, expectations, motivation, and alertness. (p. 201)

sleep apnea a sleep disorder characterized by temporary cessations of breathing during sleep and repeated momentary awakenings. (p. 97)

sleep periodic, natural loss of consciousness—as distinct from unconsciousness resulting from a coma, general anesthesia, or hibernation. (Adapted from Dement, 1999) (p. 87)

social clock the culturally preferred timing of social events such as marriage, parenthood, and retirement. (p. 163)

social exchange theory the theory that our social behavior is an exchange process, the aim of which is to maximize benefits and minimize costs. (p. 483)

social facilitation improved performance on simple or well-learned tasks in the presence of others. (p. 455)

social identity the "we" aspect of our self-concept; the part of our answer to "Who am I?" that comes from our group memberships. (p. 153)

social leadership group-oriented leadership that builds teamwork, mediates conflict, and offers support. (p. B-12)

social learning theory the theory that we learn social behavior by observing and imitating and by being rewarded or punished. (p. 178)

social loafing the tendency for people in a group to exert less effort when pooling their efforts toward attaining a common goal than when individually accountable. (p. 456)

social psychology the scientific study of how we think about, influence, and relate to one another. (p. 442)

social script culturally modeled guide for how to act in various situations. (p. 186, 471)

social trap a situation in which the conflicting parties, by each pursuing their self-interest rather than the good of the group, become caught in mutually destructive behavior. (p. 484)

social-cognitive perspective views behavior as influenced by the interaction between people's traits (including their thinking) and their social context. (p. 513)

social-responsibility norm an expectation that people will help those needing their help. (p. 484)

somatic nervous system the division of the peripheral nervous system that controls the body's skeletal muscles. Also called the *skeletal nervous system.* (p. 43)

somatosensory cortex area at the front of the parietal lobes that registers and processes body touch and movement sensations. (p. 58)

source amnesia attributing to the wrong source an event we have experienced, heard about, read about, or imagined. (Also called *source misattribution*) Source amnesia, along with the misinformation effect, is at the heart of many false memories. (p. 308)

spacing effect the tendency for distributed study or practice to yield better long-term retention than is achieved through massed study or practice. (p. 289)

spermarche [sper-MAR-key] first ejaculation. (p. 175)

split brain a condition resulting from surgery that isolates the brain's two hemispheres by cutting the fibers (mainly those of the corpus callosum) connecting them. (p. 62)

spontaneous recovery the reappearance, after a pause, of an extinguished conditioned response. (p. 251)

spotlight effect overestimating others' noticing and evaluating our appearance, performance, and blunders (as if we presume a spotlight shines on us). (p. 516)

SQ3R a study method incorporating five steps: *S*urvey, *Q*uestion, *R*ead, *R*etrieve, *R*eview. (p. 30)

standard deviation a computed measure of how much scores vary around the mean score. (p. A-3)

standardization defining uniform testing procedures and meaningful scores by comparison with the performance of a pretested group. (p. 348)

Stanford-Binet the widely used American revision (by Terman at Stanford University) of Binet's original intelligence test. (p. 346)

statistical significance a statistical statement of how likely it is that an obtained result occurred by chance. (p. A-8)

stereotype a generalized (sometimes accurate but often overgeneralized) belief about a group of people. (p. 462)

stereotype threat a self-confirming concern that one will be evaluated based on a negative stereotype. (p. 361)

stimulants drugs (such as caffeine, nicotine, and the more powerful amphetamines, cocaine, Ecstasy, and methamphetamine) that excite neural activity and speed up body functions. (p. 108)

stimulus any event or situation that evokes a response. (p. 247)

storage the process of retaining encoded information over time. (p. 284)

stranger anxiety the fear of strangers that infants commonly display, beginning by about 8 months of age. (p. 139)

stress the process by which we perceive and respond to certain events, called *stressors*, that we appraise as threatening or challenging. (p. 406)

structuralism early school of thought promoted by Wundt and Titchener; used introspection to reveal the structure of the human mind. (p. 5)

structured interview interview process that asks the same job-relevant questions of all applicants, each of whom is rated on established scales. (p. B-6)

subjective well-being self-perceived happiness or satisfaction with life. Used along with measures of objective well-being (for example, physical and economic indicators) to evaluate people's quality of life. (p. 432)

subliminal below one's absolute threshold for conscious awareness. (p. 201)

substance use disorder continued substance craving and use despite significant life disruption and/or physical risk. (p. 104)

superego the part of personality that, according to Freud, represents internalized ideals and provides standards for judgment (the conscience) and for future aspirations. (p. 494)

superordinate goals shared goals that override differences among people and require their cooperation. (p. 486)

suprachiasmatic nucleus (SCN) a pair of cell clusters in the hypothalamus that controls circadian rhythm. In response to light, the SCN causes the pineal gland to adjust melatonin production, thus modifying our feelings of sleepiness. (p. 92)

survey a descriptive technique for obtaining the self-reported attitudes or behaviors of a particular group, usually by questioning a representative, *random sample* of the group. (p. 21)

sympathetic nervous system the division of the autonomic nervous system that arouses the body, mobilizing its energy. (p. 43)

synapse [SIN-aps] the junction between the axon tip of the sending neuron and the dendrite or cell body of the receiving neuron. The tiny gap at this junction is called the *synaptic gap* or *synaptic cleft*. (p. 39)

systematic desensitization a type of exposure therapy that associates a pleasant, relaxed state with gradually increasing anxiety-triggering stimuli. Commonly used to treat phobias. (p. 575)

task leadership goal-oriented leadership that sets standards, organizes work, and focuses attention on goals. (p. B-11)

telegraphic speech early speech stage in which a child speaks like a telegram—"go car"—using mostly nouns and verbs. (p. 332)

temperament a person's characteristic emotional reactivity and intensity. (p. 140)

temporal lobes portion of the cerebral cortex lying roughly above the ears; includes the auditory areas, each receiving information primarily from the opposite ear. (p. 56)

tend and befriend under stress, people (especially women) often provide support to others (tend) and bond with and seek support from others (befriend). (p. 410)

teratogens (literally, "monster maker") agents, such as chemicals and viruses, that can reach the embryo or fetus during prenatal development and cause harm. (p. 124)

testing effect enhanced memory after retrieving, rather than simply rereading, information. Also referred to as a *retrieval practice effect* or *test-enhanced learning*. (pp. 30, 289)

testosterone the most important of the male sex hormones. Both males and females have it, but the additional testosterone in males stimulates the growth of the male sex organs during the fetal period, and the development of the male sex characteristics during puberty. (pp. 175, 181)

thalamus [THAL-uh-muss] the brain's sensory control center, located on top of the brainstem; it directs messages to the sensory receiving areas in the cortex and transmits replies to the cerebellum and medulla. (p. 51)

THC the major active ingredient in marijuana; triggers a variety of effects, including mild hallucinations. (p. 112)

Thematic Apperception Test (TAT) a projective test in which people express their inner feelings and interests through the stories they make up about ambiguous scenes. (p. 497)

theory an explanation using an integrated set of principles that organizes observations and predicts behaviors or events. (p. 17)

theory of mind people's ideas about their own and others' mental states—about their feelings, perceptions, and thoughts, and the behaviors these might predict. (p. 133)

therapeutic alliance a bond of trust and mutual understanding between a therapist and client, who work together constructively to overcome the client's problem. (p. 589)

threshold the level of stimulation required to trigger a neural impulse. (p. 38)

token economy an operant conditioning procedure in which people earn a token of some sort for exhibiting a desired behavior and can later exchange their tokens for various privileges or treats. (p. 577)

tolerance the diminishing effect with regular use of the same dose of a drug, requiring the user to take larger and larger doses before experiencing the drug's effect. (p. 105)

top-down processing information processing guided by higher-level mental processes, as when we construct perceptions drawing on our experience and expectations. (p. 200)

trait a characteristic pattern of behavior or a disposition to feel and act, as assessed by self-report inventories and peer reports. (p. 505)

transduction conversion of one form of energy into another. In sensation, the transforming of stimulus energies, such as sights, sounds, and smells, into neural impulses our brain can interpret. (p. 200)

transference in psychoanalysis, the patient's transfer to the analyst of emotions linked with other relationships (such as love or hatred for a parent). (p. 571)

transgender an umbrella term describing people whose gender identity or expression differs from that associated with their birth sex. (p. 179)

two-factor theory the Schachter-Singer theory that to experience emotion one must (1) be physically aroused and (2) cognitively label the arousal. (p. 388)

two-word stage beginning about age 2, the stage in speech development during which a child speaks mostly in two-word sentences. (p. 332)

Type A Friedman and Rosenman's term for competitive, hard-driving, impatient, verbally aggressive, and anger-prone people. (p. 414)

Type B Friedman and Rosenman's term for easygoing, relaxed people. (p. 414)

unconditional positive regard a caring, accepting, nonjudgmental attitude, which Rogers believed would help clients develop self-awareness and self-acceptance. (pp. 503, 574)

unconditioned response (UR) in classical conditioning, an unlearned, naturally occurring response (such as salivation) to an unconditioned stimulus (US) (such as food in the mouth). (p. 249)

unconditioned stimulus (US) in classical conditioning, a stimulus that unconditionally—naturally and automatically—triggers an unconditioned response (UR). (p. 249)

unconscious according to Freud, a reservoir of mostly unacceptable thoughts, wishes, feelings, and memories. According to contemporary psychologists, information processing of which we are unaware. (p. 493)

validity the extent to which a test measures or predicts what it is supposed to. (See also *content validity* and *predictive validity*) (p. 348)

variable-interval schedule in operant conditioning, a reinforcement schedule that reinforces a response at unpredictable time intervals. (p. 260)

variable-ratio schedule in operant conditioning, a reinforcement schedule that reinforces a response after an unpredictable number of responses. (p. 260)

vestibular sense the sense of body movement and position, including the sense of balance. (p. 238)

virtual reality exposure therapy an anxiety treatment that progressively exposes people to electronic simulations of their greatest fears, such as airplane flying, spiders, or public speaking. (p. 576)

visual cliff a laboratory device for testing depth perception in infants and young animals. (p. 218)

wavelength the distance from the peak of one light wave or sound wave to the peak of the next. Electromagnetic wavelengths vary from the short blips of cosmic rays to the long pulses of radio transmission. (p. 209)

Weber's law the principle that, to be perceived as different, two stimuli must differ by a constant minimum percentage (rather than a constant amount). (p. 203)

Wechsler Adult Intelligence Scale (WAIS) the WAIS and its companion versions for children are the most widely used intelligence tests; contain verbal and performance (nonverbal) subtests. (p. 347)

Wernicke's area controls language reception—a brain area involved in language comprehension and expression; usually in the left temporal lobe. (p. 334)

withdrawal the discomfort and distress that follow discontinuing an addictive drug or behavior. (p. 105)

working memory a newer understanding of short-term memory that adds conscious, active processing of incoming auditory and visual-spatial information, and of information retrieved from long-term memory. (p. 285)

X chromosome the sex chromosome found in both men and women. Females have two X chromosomes; males have one. An X chromosome from each parent produces a female child. (p. 175)

Y chromosome the sex chromosome found only in males. When paired with an X chromosome from the mother, it produces a male child. (p. 175)

Yerkes-Dodson law the principle that performance increases with arousal only up to a point, beyond which performance decreases. (p. 368)

Young-Helmholtz trichromatic (three-color) theory the theory that the retina contains three different types of color receptors—one most sensitive to red, one to green, one to blue—which, when stimulated in combination, can produce the perception of any color. (p. 213)

zygote the fertilized egg; it enters a 2-week period of rapid cell division and develops into an embryo. (p. 123)

References

A

AAA. (2015). *Teen driver safety: Environmental factors and driver behaviors in teen driver crashes.* AAA Foundation for Traffic Safety. Retrieved from https://www.aaafoundation.org/sites/default/files/2015TeenCrashCausationFS.pdf (p. 82)

AAMC. (2014). *Medical students, selected years, 1965–2013.* Association of American Medical Colleges. Retrieved from http://www.aamc.org/download/411782/data/2014_table1.pdf (p. 196)

Aarts, H., & Custers, R. (2012). Unconscious goal pursuit: Nonconscious goal regulation and motivation. In R. M. Ryan (Ed.), *The Oxford handbook of human motivation* (pp. 232–247). New York: Oxford University Press. (p. 416)

AAS. (2009, April 25). *U.S.A. suicide 2006: Official final data* (Prepared for the American Association of Suicidology by J. L. McIntosh). Retrieved from http://www.suicidology.org/ (p. 554)

Abel, E. L., & Kruger, M. L. (2010). Smile intensity in photographs predicts longevity. *Psychological Science, 21,* 542–544. (p. 415)

Abrams, D. B., & Wilson, G. T. (1983). Alcohol, sexual arousal, and self-control. *Journal of Personality and Social Psychology, 45,* 188–198. (p. 107)

Abrams, L. (2008). Tip-of-the-tongue states yield language insights. *American Scientist, 96,* 234–239. (p. 304)

Abrams, M. (2002, June). Sight unseen—Restoring a blind man's vision is now a real possibility through stem-cell surgery. But even perfect eyes cannot see unless the brain has been taught to use them. *Discover, 23,* 54–60. (p. 223)

Abramson, L. Y., Metalsky, G. I., & Alloy, L. B. (1989). Hopelessness depression: A theory-based subtype. *Psychological Review, 96,* 358–372. (pp. 420, 551)

Abramson, L. Y., Seligman, M. E. P., & Teasdale, J. D. (1978). Learned helplessness in humans: Critique and reformulation. *Journal of Abnormal Psychology, 87,* 49–74. (p. 420)

Academy of Science of South Africa. (2015). *Diversity in human sexuality: Implications for policy in Africa.* Retrieved from http://www.assaf.co.za/wp-content/uploads/2015/06/8-June-Diversity-in-human-sexuality1.pdf (p. 187)

Acevedo, B. P., & Aron, A. (2009). Does a long-term relationship kill romantic love? *Review of General Psychology, 13,* 59–65. (p. 480)

Acevedo, B. P., Aron, A., Fisher, H. E., & Brown, L. L. (2012). Neural correlates of long-term intense romantic love. *Social Cognitive and Affective Neuroscience, 7,* 145–159. (p. 181)

ACHA. (2009). *American College Health Association National College Health Assessment II: Reference group executive summary fall 2008.* Baltimore: Author. (p. 545)

Ackerman, D. (2004). *An alchemy of mind: The marvel and mystery of the brain.* New York: Scribner's. (p. 39)

ACMD. (2009). *MDMA ('Ecstasy'): A review of its harms and classification under the Misuse of Drugs Act 1971.* London: Home Office & Advisory Council on the Misuse of Drugs. (pp. 110, 111)

Adachi, T., Fujino, H., Nakae, A., Mashimo, T., & Sasaki, J. (2014). A meta-analysis of hypnosis for chronic pain problems: A comparison between hypnosis, standard care, and other psychological interventions. *International Journal of Clinical and Experimental Hypnosis, 62,* 1–28. (p. 235)

Adams, H. E., Wright, L. W., Jr., & Lohr, B. A. (1996). Is homophobia associated with homosexual arousal? *Journal of Abnormal Psychology, 105,* 440–446. (p. 500)

Adams, S. (2011, February 6). OCD: David Beckham has it—as do over a million other Britons. *The Telegraph.* Retrieved from http://www.telegraph.co.uk/news/health/news/8306947/OCD-David-Beckham-has-it-as-do-over-a-million-other-Britons.html (p. 539)

Adelmann, P. K., Antonucci, T. C., Crohan, S. F., & Coleman, L. M. (1989). Empty nest, cohort, and employment in the well-being of midlife women. *Sex Roles, 20,* 173–189. (p. 165)

Adelstein, J. S., Shehzad, Z., Mennes, M., DeYoung, C. G., Zuo, X.-N., Kelly, C., . . . Milham, M. P. (2011). Personality is reflected in the brain's intrinsic functional architecture. *PLOS ONE, 6*(11), e27633. doi:10.1371/journal.pone.0027633 (p. 510)

Ader, R., & Cohen, N. (1985). CNS–immune system interactions: Conditioning phenomena. *Behavioral and Brain Sciences, 8,* 379–394. (p. 253)

Aderka, I. M., Nickerson, A., Bøe, H. J., & Hofmann, S. G. (2012). Sudden gains during psychological treatments of anxiety and depression: A meta-analysis. *Journal of Consulting and Clinical Psychology, 80,* 93–101. (p. 585)

Adler, J. (2012, May). Erasing painful memories. *Scientific American,* pp. 56–61. (p. 296)

Adolph, K. E., Kretch, K. S., & LoBue, V. (2014). Fear of heights in infants? *Current Directions in Psychological Science, 23,* 60–66. (p. 218)

Affleck, G., Tennen, H., Urrows, S., & Higgins, P. (1994). Person and contextual features of daily stress reactivity: Individual differences in relations of undesirable daily events with mood disturbance and chronic pain intensity. *Journal of Personality and Social Psychology, 66,* 329–340. (p. 432)

AFSP. (2015). *Facts and figures.* American Foundation for Suicide Prevention. Retrieved from http://www.afsp.org/understanding-suicide/facts-and-figures (p. 553)

Agrillo, C. (2011). Near-death experience: Out-of-body and out-of-brain? *Review of General Psychology, 15,* 1–10. (p. 112)

Agudelo, L. Z., Femenía, T., Orhan, F., Porsmyr-Palmertz, M., Goiny, M., Martinez-Redondo, V., . . . Ruas, J. L. (2014). Skeletal muscle PGC-1α1 modulates kynurenine metabolism and mediates resilience to stress-induced depression. *Cell, 159,* 33–45. (p. 427)

Ai, A. L., Park, C. L., Huang, B., Rodgers, W., & Tice, T. N. (2007). Psychosocial mediation of religious coping styles: A study of short-term psychological distress following cardiac surgery. *Personality and Social Psychology Bulletin, 33,* 867–882. (p. 430)

Aiello, J. R., Thompson, D. D., & Brodzinsky, D. M. (1983). How funny is crowding anyway? Effects of room size, group size, and the introduction of humor. *Basic and Applied Social Psychology, 4,* 193–207. (p. 456)

Aimone, J. B., Jessberger, S., & Gage, F. H. (2010). Adult neurogenesis. *Scholarpedia, 2*(2), 2100. Retrieved from http://www.scholarpedia.org/article/Adult_neurogenesis (p. 61)

Ainsworth, M. D. S. (1973). The development of infant-mother attachment. In B. Caldwell & H. Ricciuti (Eds.), *Review of child development research* (Vol. 3, pp. 1–94). Chicago: University of Chicago Press. (p. 140)

Ainsworth, M. D. S. (1979). Infant–mother attachment. *American Psychologist, 34,* 932–937. (p. 140)

Ainsworth, M. D. S. (1989). Attachments beyond infancy. *American Psychologist, 44,* 709–716. (p. 140)

Airan, R. D., Meltzer, L. A., Roy, M., Gong, Y., Chen, H., & Deisseroth, K. (2007). High-speed imaging reveals neurophysiological links to behavior in an animal model of depression. *Science, 317,* 819–823. (p. 550)

Akers, K. G., Alonso Martinez-Canabal, A., Restivo, L., Yiu, A. P., De Cristofaro, A., Hsiang, H.-L., . . . Frankland, P. W. (2014). Hippocampal neurogenesis regulates forgetting during adulthood and infancy. *Science, 344,* 598–602. (p. 294)

Akers, K. G., Martinez-Canabal, A., Restivo, L., Yiu, A. P., de Cristofaro, A., Hsiang, H.-L., . . . Frankland, P. W. (2014). Hippocampal neurogenesis regulates forgetting during adulthood and infancy. *Science, 344,* 598–602. (p. 129)

Aknin, L. B., Barrington-Leigh, C., Dunn, E. W., Helliwell, J. F., Burns, J., Biswas-Diener, R., . . . Norton, M. I. (2013). Prosocial spending and well-being: Cross-cultural evidence for a psychological universal. *Journal of Personality and Social Psychology, 104,* 635–652. (pp. 431, 483)

Aknin, L. B., Broesch, T., Kiley Hamlin, J., & Van de Vondervoort, J. W. (2015). Prosocial behavior leads to happiness in a small-scale rural society. *Journal of Experimental Psychology: General, 144,* 788–795. (p. 431)

Alanko, K., Santtila, P., Harlaar, N., Witting, K., Varjonen, M., Jern, P., . . . Sandnabba, N. K. (2010). Common genetic effects of gender atypical behavior in childhood and sexual orientation in adulthood: A study of Finnish twins. *Archives of Sexual Behavior, 39,* 81–92. (p. 191)

Albee, G. W. (1986). Toward a just society: Lessons from observations on the primary prevention of psychopathology. *American Psychologist, 41,* 891–898. (p. 602)

Albert, D., Chein, J., & Steinberg, L. (2013). Peer influences on adolescent decision making. *Current Directions in Psychological Science, 22,* 80–86. (p. 154)

Alcock, J. E. (2011, March/April). Back from the future: Parapsychology and the Bem affair. *Skeptical Inquirer,* pp. 31–39. (p. 242)

Aldao, A., & Nolen-Hoeksema, S. (2010). Emotion-regulation strategies across psychopathology: A meta-analytic review. *Clinical Psychology Review, 30,* 217–237. (p. 581)

Aldrich, M. S. (1989). Automobile accidents in patients with sleep disorders. *Sleep, 12,* 487–494. (p. 97)

Aleman, A., Kahn, R. S., & Selten, J.-P. (2003). Sex differences in the risk of schizophrenia: Evidence from meta-analysis. *Archives of General Psychiatry, 60,* 565–571. (p. 557)

Alexander, L., & Tredoux, C. (2010). The spaces between us: A spatial analysis of informal segregation. *Journal of Social Issues, 66,* 367–386. (p. 486)

Allard, F., & Burnett, N. (1985). Skill in sport. *Canadian Journal of Psychology, 39,* 294–312. (p. 288)

Allen, J., Weinrich, M., Hoppitt, W., & Rendell, L. (2013). Network-based diffusion analysis reveals cultural transmission of lobtail feeding in humpback whales. *Science, 340,* 485–488. (p. 273)

Allen, J. R., & Setlow, V. P. (1991). Heterosexual transmission of HIV: A view of the future. *Journal of the American Medical Association, 266,* 1695–1696. (p. 184)

Allen, K. (2003). Are pets a healthy pleasure? The influence of pets on blood pressure. *Current Directions in Psychological Science, 12,* 236–239. (p. 425)

Allen, M. S., & Jones, M. V. (2014). The "home advantage" in athletic competitions. *Current Directions in Psychological Science, 23,* 48–53. (p. 456)

Allen, M. W., Gupta, R., & Monnier, A. (2008). The interactive effect of cultural symbols and human values on taste evaluation. *Journal of Consumer Research, 35,* 294–308. (p. 236)

Allen, T., & Sherman, J. (2011). Ego threat and intergroup bias: A test of motivated-activation versus self-regulatory accounts. *Psychological Science, 22,* 331–333. (p. 517)

Allesøe, K., Hundrup, V. A., Thomsen, J. F., & Osler, M. (2010). Psychosocial work environment and risk of ischaemic heart disease in women: The Danish Nurse Cohort Study. *Occupational and Environmental Medicine, 67,* 318–322. (p. 416)

Alloy, L. B., Abramson, L. Y., Whitehouse, W. G., Hogan, M. E., Tashman, N. A., Steinberg, D. L., . . . Donovan, P. (1999). Depressogenic cognitive styles: Predictive validity, information processing and personality characteristics, and developmental origins. *Behaviour Research and Therapy, 37,* 503–531. (p. 551)

Allport, G. W. (1954). *The nature of prejudice.* New York: Addison-Wesley. (pp. 19, 465)

Allport, G. W., & Odbert, H. S. (1936). Trait-names: A psycho-lexical study. *Psychological Monographs, 47*(1, Whole No. 211). (p. 506)

Ally, B. A., Hussey, E. P., & Donahue, M. J. (2013). A case of hyperthymesia: Rethinking the role of the amygdala in autobiographical memory. *Neurocase, 19,* 166–181. (p. 301)

Almås, I., Cappelen, A. W., Sørensen, E. Ø., & Tungodden, B. (2010). Fairness and the development of inequality acceptance. *Science, 328,* 1176–1178. (p. 149)

Al Ramiah, A., & Hewstone, M. (2013). Intergroup contact as a tool for reducing, resolving, and preventing intergroup conflict: Evidence, limitations, and potential. *American Psychologist, 68,* 527–542. (p. 486)

Al-Sayegh, H., Lowry, J., Polur, R. N., Hines, R. B., Liu, F., & Zhang, J. (2015). Suicide history and mortality: A follow-up of a national cohort in the United States. *Archives of Suicide Research, 19,* 35–47. (p. 554)

Altamirano, L. J., Miyake, A., & Whitmer, A. J. (2010). When mental inflexibility facilitates executive control: Beneficial side effects of ruminative tendencies on goal maintenance. *Psychological Science, 21,* 1377–1382. (p. 550)

Alving, C. R. (2011, March 2). "I was swimming in a pool of liposomes" [Podcast]. *Science.* Retrieved from http://www.membercentral.aas.org (p. 93)

Alwin, D. F. (1990). Historical changes in parental orientations to children. In N. Mandell (Ed.), *Sociological studies of child development* (Vol. 3, pp. 65–86). Greenwich, CT: JAI Press. (p. 145)

Amabile, T. M., & Hennessey, B. A. (1992). The motivation for creativity in children. In A. K. Boggiano & T. S. Pittman (Eds.), *Achievement and motivation: A social-developmental perspective* (pp. 54–74). New York: Cambridge University Press. (p. 325)

Amabile, T. M., &. Kramer, S. J. (2011). *The progress principle: Using small wins to ignite joy, engagement, and creativity at work.* Cambridge, MA: Harvard Business Review Press. (p. B-11)

Ambady, N. (2010). The perils of pondering: Intuition and thin slice judgments. *Psychological Inquiry, 21,* 271–278. (p. 512)

Ambady, N., Hallahan, M., & Rosenthal, R. (1995). On judging and being judged accurately in zero-acquaintance situations. *Journal of Personality and Social Psychology, 69,* 518–529. (p. 397)

Ambrose, C. T. (2010). The widening gyrus. *American Scientist, 98,* 270–274. (p. 128)

Amedi, A., Merabet, L. B., Bermpohl, F., & Pascual-Leone, A. (2005). The occipital cortex in the blind: Lessons about plasticity and vision. *Current Directions in Psychological Science, 14,* 306–311 (p. 61)

Amen, D. G., Stubblefield, M., Carmichael, B., & Thisted, R. (1996). Brain SPECT findings and aggressiveness. *Annals of Clinical Psychiatry, 8,* 129–137. (p. 469)

American Academy of Pediatrics. (2009). Media violence. *Pediatrics, 124,* 1495–1503. (p. 277)

American Academy of Pediatrics. (2013). *Promoting the well-being of children whose parents are gay or lesbian.* Retrieved from http://pediatrics.aappublications.org/content/early/2013/03/18/peds.2013-0377 (p. 141)

American Academy of Pediatrics. (2014). Policy statement: School start times for adolescents. *Pediatrics, 134,* 642–649. (p. 95)

American Enterprise. (1992, January/February). Women, men, marriages and ministers. *The American Enterprise,* p. 106. (p. 523)

American Psychiatric Association. (2013). *Diagnostic and statistical manual of mental disorders* (5th ed.). Washington, DC: Author. (pp. 104, 105, 183, 528, 531, 546)

American Psychological Association. (2002). *Ethical principles of psychologists and code of conduct.* Washington, DC: Author. (p. 28)

American Psychological Association [APA Presidential Task Force on Evidence-Based Practice]. (2006). Evidence-based practice in psychology. *American Psychologist, 61,* 271–285. (p. 587)

American Sociological Association. (2013, February 28). *Brief of* amicus curiae *American Sociological Association in support of respondent Kristin M. Perry and respondent Edith Schlain Windsor* (In the Supreme Court of the United States, Nos. 12-144, 12-307). Retrieved from http://www.asanet.org/documents/ASA/pdfs/12-144_307_Amicus_%20(C_%20Gottlieb)_ASA_Same-Sex_Marriage.pdf (p. 141)

Ames, D. R. (2008). In search of the right touch: Interpersonal assertiveness in organizational life. *Current Directions in Psychological Science, 17,* 381–385. (p. B-12)

Ammori, B. (2013, January 4). Viewpoint: Benefits of bariatric surgery. *GP Magazine.* Retrieved from http://www.gponline.com/viewpoint-benefits-bariatric-surgery/obesity/bariatric-surgery/article/1164873 (p. 379)

Andersen, R. A., Hwang, E. J., & Mulliken, G. H. (2010). Cognitive neural prosthetics. *Annual Review of Psychology, 61,* 169–190. (p. 58)

Andersen, S. M. (1998, September). *Service learning: A national strategy for youth development.* Washington, DC: Institute for Communitarian Policy Studies, George Washington University. (p. 151)

Anderson, B. L. (2002). Biobehavioral outcomes following psychological interventions for cancer patients. *Journal of Consulting and Clinical Psychology, 70,* 590–610. (p. 413)

Anderson, C. A. (2004). An update on the effects of playing violent video games. *Journal of Adolescence, 27,* 113–122. (pp. 472, 473)

Anderson, C. A. (2013, June). Guns, games, and mass shootings in the U.S. *Bulletin of the International Society for Research on Aggression,* pp. 14–19. (p. 472)

Anderson, C. A., Anderson, K. B., Dorr, N., DeNeve, K. M., & Flanagan, M. (2000). Temperature and aggression. In M. P. Zanna (Ed.), *Advances in experimental social psychology* (Vol. 32, pp. 63–133). San Diego, CA: Academic Press. (p. 470)

Anderson, C. A., Brion, S., Moore, D. A., & Kennedy, J. A. (2012). A status-enhancement account of overconfidence. *Journal of Personality and Social Psychology, 103,* 718–735. (p. 322)

Anderson, C. A., Bushman, B. J., & Groom, R. W. (1997). Hot years and serious and deadly assault: Empirical tests of the heat hypothesis. *Journal of Personality and Social Psychology, 73,* 1213–1223. (p. 470)

Anderson, C. A., & Delisi, M. (2011). Implications of global climate change for violence in developed and developing countries. In J. Forgas, A. Kruglanski., & K. Williams (Eds.), *The psychology of social conflict and aggression* (pp. 249–265). New York: Psychology Press. (p. 470)

Anderson, C. A., & Dill, K. E. (2000). Video games and aggressive thoughts, feelings, and behavior in the laboratory and in life. *Journal of Personality and Social Psychology, 78*, 772–790. (p. 472)

Anderson, C. A., Lindsay, J. J., & Bushman, B. J. (1999). Research in the psychological laboratory: Truth or triviality? *Current Directions in Psychological Science, 8*, 3–9. (p. 27)

Anderson, C. A., Shibuya, A., Ihori, N., Swing, E. L., Bushman, B. J., Sakamoto, A., . . . Saleem, M. (2010). Violent video game effects on aggression, empathy, and prosocial behavior in Eastern and Western countries: A meta-analytic review. *Psychological Bulletin, 136*, 151–173. (pp. 328, 472)

Anderson, C. A., & Warburton, W. A. (2012). The impact of violent video games: An overview. In W. Warburton & D. Braunstein (Eds.), *Growing up fast and furious: Reviewing the impacts of violent and sexualized media on children* (pp. 56–84). Annandale, New South Wales, Australia: Federation Press. (pp. 105, 473)

Anderson, I. M. (2000). Selective serotonin reuptake inhibitors versus tricyclic antidepressants: A meta-analysis of efficacy and tolerability. *Journal of Affective Disorders, 58*, 19–36. (p. 595)

Anderson, J. R., Myowa-Yamakoshi, M., & Matsuzawa, T. (2004). Contagious yawning in chimpanzees. *Biology Letters, 271*, S468–S470. (p. 449)

Anderson, R. C., Pichert, J. W., Goetz, E. T., Schallert, D. L., Stevens, K. V., & Trollip, S. R. (1976). Instantiation of general terms. *Journal of Verbal Learning and Verbal Behavior, 15*, 667–679. (p. 304)

Anderson, S. (2008, July 6). The urge to end it all. *The New York Times Magazine.* http://www.nytimes.com/2008/07/06/magazine/06suicide-t.html?pagewanted=print&_r=0 (p. 553)

Anderson, S. E., Dallal, G. E., & Must, A. (2003). Relative weight and race influence average age at menarche: Results from two nationally representative surveys of U.S. girls studied 25 years apart. *Pediatrics, 111*, 844–850. (p. 176)

Anderson, S. R. (2004). *Doctor Dolittle's delusion: Animals and the uniqueness of human language.* New Haven, CT: Yale University Press. (p. 335)

Andreasen, N. C. (1997). Linking mind and brain in the study of mental illnesses: A project for a scientific psychopathology. *Science, 275*, 1586–1593. (p. 558)

Andreasen, N. C. (2001). *Brave new brain: Conquering mental illness in the era of the genome.* New York: Oxford University Press. (p. 558)

Andreasen, N. C., Arndt, S., Swayze, V., II, Cizadlo, T., & Flaum, M. (1994). Thalamic abnormalities in schizophrenia visualized through magnetic resonance image averaging. *Science, 266*, 294–298. (p. 558)

Andrews, P. W., & Thomson, J. A., Jr. (2009a). The bright side of being blue: Depression as an adaptation for analyzing complex problems. *Psychological Review, 116*, 620–654. (pp. 545, 550)

Andrews, P. W., & Thomson, J. A., Jr. (2009b, January/February). Depression's evolutionary roots. *Scientific American Mind*, pp. 57–61. (pp. 545, 550)

Angelsen, N. K., Vik, T., Jacobsen, G., & Bakketeig, L. S. (2001). Breast feeding and cognitive development at age 1 and 5 years. *Archives of Disease in Childhood, 85*, 183–188. (p. 23)

Anglemyer, A., Horvath, T., & Rutherford, G. (2014). The accessibility of firearms and risk for suicide and homicide victimization among household members. *Annals of Internal Medicine, 160*, 101–112. (p. 468)

Anguera, J. A., Boccanfuso, J., Rintoul, J. L., Al-Hashimi, O., Faraji, F., Janowich, J., . . . Gazzaley, A. (2013). Video game training enhances cognitive control in older adults. *Nature, 501*, 97–101. (p. 161)

Annan, K. A. (2001, December 10). *We can love what we are, without hating who—and what—we are not.* Lecture delivered on receipt of the 2001 Nobel Peace Prize, Oslo, Norway. (p. 487)

Annese, J., Schenker-Ahmed, N. M., Bartsch, H., Maechler, P., Sheh, C., Thomas, N., . . . Corkin, S. (2014). Postmortem examination of patient H. M.'s brain based on histological sectioning and digital 3D reconstruction. *Nature Communications, 5*, Article 3122. doi:10.1038/ncomms4122 (p. 301)

Antonaccio, O., Botchkovar, E. V., & Tittle, C. R. (2011). Attracted to crime: Exploration of criminal motivation among respondents in three European cities. *Criminal Justice and Behavior, 38*, 1200–1221. (p. 173)

Antony, M. M., Brown, T. A., & Barlow, D. H. (1992). Current perspectives on panic and panic disorder. *Current Directions in Psychological Science, 1*, 79–82. (p. 542)

Antrobus, J. (1991). Dreaming: Cognitive processes during cortical activation and high afferent thresholds. *Psychological Review, 98*, 96–121. (p. 100)

Anzures, G., Quinn, P. C., Pascalis, O., Slater, A. M., Tanaka, J. W., & Lee, K. (2013). Developmental origins of the other-race effect. *Current Directions in Psychological Science, 22*, 173–178. (p. 467)

AP. (2007, October 25). *AP/Ipsos poll: One-third in AP poll believe in ghosts and UFOs, half accept ESP.* Associated Press. Retrieved from http://www.ap-ipsos-results.com/ (p. 241)

AP. (2009, May 9). *AP-mtvU AP 2009 Economy, College Stress and Mental Health Poll.* Associated Press. Retrieved from http://www.hosted.ap.org (p. 94)

APA. (2007). *Report of the APA Task Force on the Sexualization of Girls.* Washington, DC: American Psychological Association. (p. 187)

APA. (2009). *Report of the American Psychological Association Task Force on Appropriate Therapeutic Responses to Sexual Orientation.* American Psychological Association. Retrieved from https://www.apa.org/pi/lgbt/resources/therapeutic-response.pdf (pp. 177, 188)

APA. (2010). *Answers to your questions about transgender individuals and gender identity.* American Psychological Association. Retrieved from http://www.apa.org/ (p. 179)

APA. (2010, November 9). *Stress in America findings.* Washington, DC: American Psychological Association. (p. 409)

Archer, J. (2000). Sex differences in aggression between heterosexual partners: A meta-analytic review. *Psychological Bulletin, 126*, 651–680. (p. 173)

Archer, J. (2004). Sex differences in aggression in real-world settings: A meta-analytic review. *Review of General Psychology, 8*, 291–322. (p. 173)

Archer, J. (2007). A cross-cultural perspective on physical aggression between partners. *Issues in Forensic Psychology, 6*, 125–131. (p. 173)

Archer, J. (2009). Does sexual selection explain human sex differences in aggression? *Behavioral and Brain Sciences, 32*, 249–311. (p. 173)

Arendt, H. (1963). *Eichmann in Jerusalem: A report on the banality of evil.* New York: Viking. (p. 151)

Ariely, D. (2009). *Predictably irrational: The hidden forces that shape our decisions.* New York: HarperCollins. (p. 298)

Ariely, D. (2010). *Predictably irrational: The hidden forces that shape our decisions* (Rev., expanded ed.). New York: Harper Perennial. (p. 499)

Aries, E. (1987). Gender and communication. In P. Shaver & C. Henrick (Eds.), *Review of personality and social psychology: Vol. 7. Sex and gender* (pp. 149–176). Beverly Hills, CA: Sage. (p. 173)

Arkowitz, H., & Lilienfeld, S. O. (2006, April/May). Psychotherapy on trial. *Scientific American Mind*, pp. 42–49. (p. 586)

Armony, J. L., Quirk, G. J., & LeDoux, J. E. (1998). Differential effects of amygdala lesions on early and late plastic components of auditory cortex spike trains during fear conditioning. *Journal of Neuroscience, 18*, 2592–2601. (p. 543)

Arnedo, J., Svrakic, D. M., del Val, C., Romero-Zaliz, R., Hernández-Cuervo, H., Fanous, A. H., . . . Zwir, I. (2015). Uncovering the hidden risk architecture of the schizophrenias: Confirmation in three independent genome-wide association studies. *American Journal of Psychiatry, 172*, 139–153. (p. 560)

Arneson, J. J., Sackett, P. R., & Beatty, A. S. (2011). Ability-performance relationships in education and employment settings: Critical tests of the more-is-better and the good-enough hypotheses. *Psychological Science, 22*, 1336–1342. (p. 325)

Arnett, J. J. (1999). Adolescent storm and stress, reconsidered. *American Psychologist, 54*, 317–326. (p. 147)

Arnett, J. J. (2006). Emerging adulthood: Understanding the new way of coming of age. In J. J. Arnett & J. L. Tanner (Eds.), *Emerging adults in America: Coming of age in the 21st century* (pp. 3–19). Washington, DC: American Psychological Association. (p. 156)

Arnett, J. J. (2007). Socialization in emerging adulthood: From the family to the wider world, from socialization to self-socialization. In J. E. Grusec & P. D. Hastings (Eds.), *Handbook of socialization: Theory and research* (pp. 208–230). New York: Guilford Press. (p. 156)

Arnone, D., McIntosh, A. M., Tan, G. M. Y., & Ebmeier, K. P. (2008). Meta-analysis of magnetic resonance imaging studies of the corpus callosum in schizophrenia. *Schizophrenia Research, 101*, 124–132. (p. 558)

Aron, A. P., Melinat, E., Aron, E. N., Vallone, R. D., & Bator, R. J. (1997). The experimental generation of interpersonal closeness: A procedure and some preliminary findings. *Personality and Social Psychology Bulletin, 23*, 363–377. (p. 480)

Aronson, E. (2001, April 13). *Newsworthy violence* [E-mail to Society for Personality and Social Psychology discussion list, drawing from *Nobody left to hate: Teaching compassion after Columbine.* (2000). New York: Freeman]. (p. 155)

Artiga, A. I., Viana, J. B., Maldonado, C. R., Chandler-Laney, P. C., Oswald, K. D., & Boggiano, M. M. (2007). Body composition and endocrine status of long-term stress-induced binge-eating rats. *Physiology and Behavior, 91,* 424–431. (p. 381)

Arzi, A., Shedlesky, L., Ben-Shaul, M., Nasser, K., Oksenberg, A., Hairston I. S., & Sobel, N. (2012). Humans can learn new information during sleep. *Nature Neuroscience, 15,* 1460–1465. (p. 99)

Asch, S. E. (1955). Opinions and social pressure. *Scientific American, 193,* 31–35. (p. 450)

Asendorpf, J. B., Penke, L., & Back, M. D. (2011). From dating to mating and relating: Predictors of initial and long-term outcomes of speed-dating in a community sample. *European Journal of Personality, 25,* 16–30. (p. 193)

Aserinsky, E. (1988, January 17). Personal communication. (p. 88)

Askay, S. W., & Patterson, D. R. (2007). Hypnotic analgesia. *Expert Review of Neurotherapeutics, 7,* 1675–1683. (p. 235)

Aspinwall, L. G., Brown, T. R., & Tabery, J. (2012). The double-edged sword: Does biomechanism increase or decrease judges' sentencing of psychopaths? *Science, 337,* 846–849. (p. 443)

Aspinwall, L. G., & Tedeschi, R. G. (2010). The value of positive psychology for health psychology: Progress and pitfalls in examining the relation of positive phenomena to health. *Annals of Behavioral Medicine, 39,* 4–15. (p. 422)

ASPS. (2010). *2010 report of the 2009 statistics: National Clearinghouse of Plastic Surgery Statistics.* American Society of Plastic Surgeons. Retrieved from http://www.plasticsurgery.org/Documents/news-resources/statistics/2009-statistics/2009-US-cosmeticreconstructiveplasticsurgeryminimally-invasive-statistics.pdf (p. 478)

Aspy, C. B., Vesely, S. K., Oman, R. F., Rodine, S., Marshall, L., & McLeroy, K. (2007). Parental communication and youth sexual behaviour. *Journal of Adolescence, 30,* 449–466. (p. 186)

Assanand, S., Pinel, J. P. J., & Lehman, D. R. (1998). Personal theories of hunger and eating. *Journal of Applied Social Psychology, 28,* 998–1015. (p. 380)

Astin, A. W., Astin, H. S., & Lindholm, J. A. (2004). *Spirituality in higher education: A national study of college students' search for meaning and purpose.* Los Angeles: Higher Education Research Institute, University of California, Los Angeles. (p. 153)

Atkinson, R. C., & Shiffrin, R. M. (1968). Human memory: A proposed system and its control processes. In K. Spence (Ed.), *The psychology of learning and motivation* (Vol. 2, pp. 89–195). New York: Academic Press. (p. 284)

Austin, E. J., Deary, I. J., Whiteman, M. C., Fowkes, F. G. R., Pedersen, N. L., Rabbitt, P., . . . McInnes, L. (2002). Relationships between ability and personality: Does intelligence contribute positively to personal and social adjustment? *Personality and Individual Differences, 32,* 1391–1411. (p. 352)

Australian Unity. (2008). *What makes us happy? The Australian Unity Wellbeing Index.* South Melbourne, Victoria, Australia: Author. (p. 434)

Auyeung, B., Baron-Cohen, S., Ashwin, E., Knickmeyer, R., Taylor, K., Hackett, G., & Hines, M. (2009). Fetal testosterone predicts sexually differentiated childhood behavior in girls and in boys. *Psychological Science, 20,* 144–148. (p. 136)

Averill, J. R. (1993). William James's other theory of emotion. In M. E. Donnelly (Ed.), *Reinterpreting the legacy of William James* (pp. 221–229). Washington, DC: American Psychological Association. (p. 388)

Aviezer, H., Hassin, R. R., Ryan, J., Grady, C., Susskind, J., Anderson, A., . . . Bentin, S. (2008). Angry, disgusted, or afraid? Studies on the malleability of emotion perception. *Psychological Science, 19,* 724–732. (p. 400)

Ayan, S. (2009, April/May). Laughing matters. *Scientific American Mind,* pp. 24–31. (p. 424)

Aydin, N., Fischer, P., & Frey, D. (2010). Turning to God in the face of ostracism: Effects of social exclusion on religiousness. *Personality and Social Psychology Bulletin, 36,* 742–753. (p. 372)

Azar, B. (1998, June). Why can't this man feel whether or not he's standing up? *APA Monitor,* pp. 18, 20. (p. 238)

Azevedo, F. A., Carvalho, L. R., Grinberg, L. T., Farfel, J. M., Ferretti, R. E., Leite, R. E., . . . Herculano-Houzel, S. (2009). Equal numbers of neuronal and nonneuronal cells make the human brain an isometrically scaled-up primate brain. *Journal of Comparative Neurology, 513,* 532–541. (p. 44)

B

Baas, M., De Dreu, C. K. W., & Nijstad, B. A. (2008). A meta-analysis of 25 years of mood–creativity research: Hedonic tone, activation, or regulatory focus? *Psychological Bulletin, 134,* 779–806. (p. 431)

Babad, E., Bernieri, F., & Rosenthal, R. (1991). Students as judges of teachers' verbal and nonverbal behavior. *American Educational Research Journal, 28,* 211–234. (p. 396)

Bachman, J., O'Malley, P. M., Schulenberg, J. E., Johnston, L. D., Freedman-Doan, P., & Messersmith, E. E. (2007). *The education–drug use connection: How successes and failures in school relate to adolescent smoking, drinking, drug use, and delinquency.* Mahwah, NJ: Erlbaum. (p. 115)

Back, M. D., Stopfer, J. M., Vazire, S., Gaddis, S., Schmukle, S. C., Egloff, B., & Gosling, S. D. (2010). Facebook profiles reflect actual personality, not self-idealization. *Psychological Science, 21,* 372–374. (pp. 374, 512)

Backman, L., & MacDonald, S. W. S. (2006). Death and cognition: Synthesis and outlook. *European Psychologist, 11,* 224–235. (p. 162)

Baddeley, A. D. (1982). *Your memory: A user's guide.* New York: Macmillan. (p. 283)

Baddeley, A. D. (2001). Is working memory still working? *American Psychologist, 56,* 849–864. (p. 284)

Baddeley, A. D. (2002, June). Is working memory still working? *European Psychologist, 7,* 85–97. (pp. 284, 285)

Baddeley, A. D., Thomson, N., & Buchanan, M. (1975). Word length and the structure of short-term memory. *Journal of Verbal Learning and Verbal Behavior, 14,* 575–589. (p. 287)

Baddeley, J. L., & Singer J. A. (2009). A social interactional model of bereavement narrative disclosure. *Review of General Psychology, 13,* 202–218. (p. 168)

Badgett, M. V. L., & Mallory, C. (2014, December). *Relationship recognition patterns of same-sex couples by gender.* Retrieved from http://williamsinstitute.law.ucla.edu/wp-content/uploads/Badgett-Mallory-Gender-Dec-2014.pdf (p. 193)

Bagemihl, B. (1999). *Biological exuberance: Animal homosexuality and natural diversity.* New York: St. Martin's Press. (p. 189)

Baglioni, C., Battagliese, G., Feige, B., Spiegelhalder, K., Nissen, C., Voderholzer, U., . . . Riemann, D. (2011). Insomnia as a predictor of depression: A meta-analytic evaluation of longitudinal epidemiological studies. *Journal of Affective Disorders, 135,* 10–19. (p. 96)

Bahrick, H. P. (1984). Semantic memory content in permastore: 50 years of memory for Spanish learned in school. *Journal of Experimental Psychology: General, 111,* 1–29. (pp. 303, 304)

Bahrick, H. P., Bahrick, P. O., & Wittlinger, R. P. (1975). Fifty years of memory for names and faces: A cross-sectional approach. *Journal of Experimental Psychology: General, 104,* 54–75. (p. 283)

Bailenson, J. N., Iyengar, S., & Yee, N. (2005, May). *Facial identity capture and presidential candidate preference.* Paper presented at the 55th Annual Conference of the International Communication Association, New York, NY. (p. 476)

Bailey, J. M., Gaulin, S., Agyei, Y., & Gladue, B. A. (1994). Effects of gender and sexual orientation on evolutionary relevant aspects of human mating psychology. *Journal of Personality and Social Psychology, 66,* 1081–1093. (p. 193)

Bailey, J. M., Kirk, K. M., Zhu, G., Dunne, M. P., & Martin, N. G. (2000). Do individual differences in sociosexuality represent genetic or environmentally contingent strategies? Evidence from the Australian Twin Registry. *Journal of Personality and Social Psychology, 78,* 537–545. (p. 193)

Bailey, R. E., & Gillaspy, J. A., Jr. (2005). Operant psychology goes to the fair: Marian and Keller Breland in the popular press, 1947–1966. *The Behavior Analyst, 28,* 143–159. (p. 245)

Bailine, S., Fink, M., Knapp, R., Petrides, G., Husain, M. M., Rasmussen, K., . . . Kellner, C. H. (2010). Electroconvulsive therapy is equally effective in unipolar and bipolar depression. *Acta Psychiatrica Scandinavica, 121,* 431–436. (p. 598)

Baillargeon, R. (1995). A model of physical reasoning in infancy. In C. Rovee-Collier & L. P. Lipsitt (Eds.), *Advances in infancy research* (Vol. 9, pp. 305–371). Stamford, CT: Ablex. (p. 131)

Baillargeon, R. (2008). Innate ideas revisited: For a principle of persistence in infants' physical reasoning. *Perspectives in Psychological Science, 3,* 2–13. (p. 131)

Baker, M. & Maner, J. (2009). Male risk-taking as a context-sensitive signaling device. *Journal of Experimental Social Psychology, 45,* 1136–1139. (p. 193)

Baker, T. B., McFall, R. M., & Shoham, V. (2008). Current status and future prospects of clinical psychology: Toward a scientifically principled approach to mental and behavioral health care. *Psychological Science in the Public Interest, 9*, 67–103. (pp. 586, 587)

Baker, T. B., Piper, M. E., McCarthy, D. E., Majeskie, M. R., & Fiore, M. C. (2004). Addiction motivation reformulated: An affective processing model of negative reinforcement. *Psychological Review, 111*, 33–51. (p. 258)

Bakermans-Kranenburg, M. J., van IJzendoorn, M. H., & Juffer, F. (2003). Less is more: Meta-analyses of sensitivity and attachment interventions in early childhood. *Psychological Bulletin, 129*, 195–215. (p. 141)

Bakshy, E., Messing, S., & Adamic, L. A. (2015). Exposure to ideologically diverse news and opinion on Facebook. *Science, 348*, 1130–1132. (p. 458)

Balcetis, E., & Dunning, D. (2010). Wishful seeing: More desired objects are seen as closer. *Psychological Science, 21*, 147–152. (p. 207)

Balodis, I. M., & Potenza, M. N. (2015). Anticipatory reward processing in addicted populations: A focus on the monetary incentive delay task. *Biological Psychiatry, 77*, 434–444. (p. 54)

Balodis, I. M., Wynne-Edwards, K. E., & Olmstead, M. C. (2010). The other side of the curve: Examining the relationship between pre-stressor physiological responses and stress reactivity. *Psychoneuroendocrinology, 35*, 1363–1373. (pp. 407, 408)

Balsam, K. F., Beauchaine, T. P., Rothblum, E. S., & Solomon, S. E. (2008). Three-year follow-up of same-sex couples who had civil unions in Vermont, same-sex couples not in civil unions, and heterosexual married couples. *Developmental Psychology, 44*, 102–116. (p. 163)

Balter, M. (2010). Animal communication helps reveal roots of language. *Science, 328*, 969–970. (p. 335)

Bambico, F. R., Nguyen N.-T., Katz, N., & Gobbi, G. (2010). Chronic exposure to cannabinoids during adolescence but not during adulthood impairs emotional behaviour and monoaminergic neurotransmission. *Neurobiology of Disease, 37*, 641–655. (p. 112)

Banaji, M. R., & Greenwald, A. G. (2013). *Blindspot: Hidden biases of good people.* New York: Delacorte Press. (p. 463)

Bancroft, J., Loftus, J., & Long, J. S. (2003). Distress about sex: A national survey of women in heterosexual relationships. *Archives of Sexual Behavior, 32*, 193–208. (p. 183)

Bandura, A. (1982). The psychology of chance encounters and life paths. *American Psychologist, 37*, 747–755. (p. 163)

Bandura, A. (1986). *Social foundations of thought and action: A social cognitive theory.* Englewood Cliffs, NJ: Prentice-Hall. (p. 513)

Bandura, A. (2005). The evolution of social cognitive theory. In K. G. Smith & M. A. Hitt (Eds.), *Great minds in management: The process of theory development* (pp. 9–35). Oxford, England: Oxford University Press. (pp. 163, 272)

Bandura, A. (2006). Toward a psychology of human agency. *Perspectives on Psychological Science, 1*, 164–180. (p. 513)

Bandura, A. (2008). An agentic perspective on positive psychology. In S. J. Lopez (Ed.), *Positive psychology: Exploring the best in people: Vol. 1. Discovering human strengths* (pp. 167–196). Westport, CT: Praeger. (p. 513)

Bandura, A., Ross, D., & Ross, S. A. (1961). Transmission of aggression through imitation of aggressive models. *Journal of Abnormal and Social Psychology, 63*, 575–582. (p. 272)

Banville, J. (2012, April). APA weighs in on the constitutionality of life without parole for juvenile offenders. *Monitor on Psychology*, p. 12. (p. 149)

Barash, D. P. (2006, July 14). I am, therefore I think. *The Chronicle of Higher Education*, pp. B9, B10. (p. 80)

Barash, D. P. (2012). *Homo mysterius: Evolutionary puzzles of human nature.* New York: Oxford University Press. (p. 195)

Barbaresi,, W. J., Katusic, S. K., Colligan, R. C., Weaver, A. L., & Jacobsen, S. J. (2007). Modifiers of long-term school outcomes for children with attention-deficit/hyperactivity disorder: Does treatment with stimulant medication make a difference? Results from a population-based study. *Journal of Developmental and Behavioral Pediatrics, 28*, 274–287. (p. 532)

Bargh, J. A., & Chartrand, T. L. (1999). The unbearable automaticity of being. *American Psychologist, 54*, 462–479. (pp. 85–86, 500)

Bargh, J. A., & McKenna, K. Y. A. (2004). The Internet and social life. *Annual Review of Psychology, 55*, 573–590. (p. 476)

Bargh, J. A., McKenna, K. Y. A., & Fitzsimons, G. M. (2002). Can you see the real me? Activation and expression of the "true self" on the Internet. *Journal of Social Issues, 58*, 33–48. (p. 476)

Bargh, J. A., & Morsella, E. (2008). The unconscious mind. *Perspectives on Psychological Science, 3*, 73–79. (p. 500)

Bar-Haim, Y., Lamy, D., Pergamin, L., Bakermans-Kranenburg, M. J., & van IJzendoorn, M. H. (2007). Threat-related attentional bias in anxious and nonanxious individuals: A meta-analytic study. *Psychological Bulletin, 133*, 1–24. (p. 541)

Barinaga, M. B. (1992). The brain remaps its own contours. *Science, 258*, 216–218. (p. 61)

Barinaga, M. B. (1997). How exercise works its magic. *Science, 276*, 1325. (p. 426)

Barkley, R. A., Cook, E. H., Jr., Diamond, A., Zametkin, A., Thapar, A., Teeter, A., . . . Pelham, W., Jr. (2002). International consensus statement on ADHD: January 2002. *Clinical Child and Family Psychology Review, 5*, 89–111. (p. 532)

Barkley-Levenson, E., & Galván, A. (2014). Neural representation of expected value in the adolescent brain. *Proceedings of the National Academy of Sciences of the United States of America, 111*, 1646–1651. (p. 148)

Barlow, D. H. (2010). Negative effects from psychological treatments: A perspective. *American Psychologist, 65*, 13–20. (p. 587)

Barlow, F. K., Paolini, S., Pedersen, A., Hornsey, M. J., Radke, H. R. M., Harwood, J., . . . Sibley, C. G. (2012). The contact caveat: Negative contact predicts increased prejudice more than positive contact predicts reduced prejudice. *Personality and Social Psychology Bulletin, 38*, 1629–1643. (p. 486)

Barlow, M., Woodman, T., & Hardy, L. (2013). Great expectations: Different high-risk activities satisfy different motives. *Journal of Personality and Social Psychology, 105*, 458–475. (p. 367)

Barnier, A. J., & McConkey, K. M. (2004). Defining and identifying the highly hypnotizable person. In M. Heap, R. J. Brown, & D. A. Oakley (Eds.), *The highly hypnotizable person: Theoretical, experimental and clinical issues* (pp. 30–60). London: Brunner-Routledge. (p. 235)

Baron-Cohen, S. (2008). Autism, hypersystemizing, and truth. *Quarterly Journal of Experimental Psychology, 61*, 64–75. (p. 136)

Baron-Cohen, S. (2009). Autism: The empathizing–systemizing (E-S) theory. *Annals of the New York Academy of Sciences, 1156*, 68–80. (p. 136)

Baron-Cohen, S., Golan, O., Chapman, E., & Granader, Y. (2007). Transported to a world of emotion. *The Psychologist, 20*, 76–77. (p. 137)

Barrera, T. L., Mott, J. M., Hofstein, R. F., & Teng, E. J. (2013). A meta-analytic review of exposure in group cognitive behavioral therapy for posttraumatic stress disorder. *Clinical Psychology Review, 33*, 24–32. (p. 575)

Barrett, D. (2011, November/December). Answers in your dreams. *Scientific American Mind*, 26–33. (p. 93)

Barrett, L. F. (2006). Are emotions natural kinds? *Perspectives on Psychological Science, 1*, 28–58. (pp. 388, 393)

Barrett, L. F. (2012). Emotions are real. *Emotion, 12*, 413–429. (p. 387)

Barrett, L. F. (2013). Quoted in S. Fischer, About face: Emotional and facial expressions may not be directly related. *Boston Magazine*. Retrieved from http://www.bostonmagazine.com/news/article/2013/06/25/emotions-facial-expressions-not-related/ (p. 387)

Barrett, L. F., & Bliss-Moreau, E. (2009). She's emotional. He's having a bad day: Attributional explanations for emotion stereotypes. *Emotion, 9*, 649–658. (p. 398)

Barrett, L. F., Lane, R. D., Sechrest, L., & Schwartz, G. E. (2000). Sex differences in emotional awareness. *Personality and Social Psychology Bulletin, 26*, 1027–1035. (p. 397)

Barretto, R. P., Gillis-Smith, S., Chandrashekar, J., Yarmolinsky, D. A., Schnitzer, M. J., Ryba, N. J., & Zuker, C. S. (2015). The neural representation of taste quality at the periphery. *Nature, 517*, 373–376. (p. 236)

Barrick, M. R., Mount, M. K., & Judge, T. A. (2001). Personality and performance at the beginning of the new millennium: What do we know and where do we go next? *International Journal of Selection and Assessment, 9*, 9–30. (p. 507)

Barrick, M. R., Shaffer, J. A., & DeGrassi, S. W. (2009). What you see may not be what you get: Relationships among self-presentation tactics and ratings of interview and job performance. *Journal of Applied Psychology, 94*, 1304–1411. (p. B-5)

Barrouillet, P., Portrat, S., & Camos, V. (2011). On the law relating processing to storage in working memory. *Psychological Review, 118*, 175–192. (p. 284)

Barry, C. L., McGinty, E. E., Vernick, J. S., & Webster, D. W. (2013). After Newtown—Public opinion on gun policy and mental illness. *New England Journal of Medicine, 368*, 1077–1081. (p. 533)

Barry, D. (1995, September 17). Teen smokers, too, get cool, toxic, waste-blackened lungs. *The Asbury Park Press*, p. D3. (p. 109)

Bartels, M., & Boomsma, D. I. (2009). Born to be happy? The etiology of subjective well-being. *Behavior Genetics, 39*, 605–615. (p. 436)

Bashore, T. R., Ridderinkhof, K. R., & van der Molen, M. W. (1997). The decline of cognitive processing speed in old age. *Current Directions in Psychological Science, 6*, 163–169. (p. 159)

Baskind, D. E. (1997, December 14). Personal communication. (p. 576)

Bates, T. C. (2015). The glass is half full *and* half empty: A population-representative twin study testing if optimism and pessimism are distinct systems. *Journal of Positive Psychology, 10*, 533–542. (p. 423)

Bathje, G. J., & Pryor, J. B. (2011). The relationships of public and self-stigma to seeking mental health services. *Journal of Mental Health Counseling, 33*, 161–177. (p. 531)

Bauer, M., Cassar, A., Chytilová, J., & Henrich, J. (2014). War's enduring effects on the development of egalitarian motivations and in-group biases. *Psychological Science, 25*, 47–57. (p. 486)

Bauer, P. J. (2002). Long-term recall memory: Behavioral and neurodevelopmental changes in the first 2 years of life. *Current Directions in Psychology, 11*, 137–141. (p. 129)

Bauer, P. J. (2007). Recall in infancy: A neurodevelopmental account. *Current Directions in Psychological Science, 16*, 142–146. (p. 129)

Bauer, P. J., Burch, M. M., Scholin, S. E., & Güler, O. E. (2007). Using cue words to investigate the distribution of autobiographical memories in childhood. *Psychological Science, 18*, 910–916. (p. 294)

Bauer, P. J., & Larkina, M. (2014). The onset of childhood amnesia in childhood: A prospective investigation of the course and determinants of forgetting of early-life events. *Memory, 22*, 907–924. (p. 129)

Baum, A., & Posluszny, D. M. (1999). Health psychology: Mapping biobehavioral contributions to health and illness. *Annual Review of Psychology, 50*, 137–163. (p. 413)

Baumeister, R. F. (1996). Should schools try to boost self-esteem? Beware the dark side. *American Educator, 20*(2), 14–19. (p. 520)

Baumeister, R. F. (2000). Gender differences in erotic plasticity: The female sex drive as socially flexible and responsive. *Psychological Bulletin, 126*, 347–374. (p. 188)

Baumeister, R. F. (2001, April). Violent pride: Do people turn violent because of self-hate, or self-love? *Scientific American*, pp. 96–101. (p. 519)

Baumeister, R. F. (2005). *The cultural animal: Human nature, meaning, and social life.* New York: Oxford University Press. (p. 448)

Baumeister, R. F. (2006, August/September). Violent pride. *Scientific American Mind*, pp. 54–59. (p. 517)

Baumeister, R. F. (2010). *Is there anything good about men? How cultures flourish by exploiting men.* New York: Oxford University Press. (p. 173)

Baumeister, R. F. (2015, April). Conquer yourself, conquer the world. *Scientific American*, pp. 61–65. (p. 517)

Baumeister, R. F., & Bratslavsky, E. (1999). Passion, intimacy, and time: Passionate love as a function of change in intimacy. *Personality and Social Psychology Review, 3*, 49–67. (p. 480)

Baumeister, R. F., Bratslavsky, E., Muraven, M., & Tice, D. M. (1998). Ego depletion: Is the active self a limited resource? *Journal of Personality and Social Psychology, 74*, 1252–1265. (p. 421)

Baumeister, R. F., Catanese, K. R., & Vohs, K. D. (2001). Is there a gender difference in strength of sex drive? Theoretical views, conceptual distinctions, and a review of relevant evidence. *Personality and Social Psychology Review, 5*, 242–273. (p. 193)

Baumeister, R. F., Dale, K., & Sommer, K. L. (1998). Freudian defense mechanisms and empirical findings in modern personality and social psychology: Reaction formation, projection, displacement, undoing, isolation, sublimation, and denial. *Journal of Personality, 66*, 1081–1125. (p. 500)

Baumeister, R. F., & Leary, M. R. (1995). The need to belong: Desire for interpersonal attachments as a fundamental human motivation. *Psychological Bulletin, 117*, 497–529. (p. 369)

Baumeister, R. F., & Tice, D. M. (1986). How adolescence became the struggle for self: A historical transformation of psychological development. In J. Suls & A. G. Greenwald (Eds.), *Psychological perspectives on the self* (Vol. 3, pp. 183–201). Hillsdale, NJ: Erlbaum. (p. 156)

Baumeister, R. F., & Tierney, J. (2012). *Willpower: Rediscovering the greatest human strength.* New York: Penguin. (p. 421)

Baumeister, R. F., Twenge, J. M., & Nuss, C. K. (2002). Effects of social exclusion on cognitive processes: Anticipated aloneness reduces intelligent thought. *Journal of Personality and Social Psychology, 83*, 817–827. (p. 372)

Baumgardner, A. H., Kaufman, C. M., & Levy, P. E. (1989). Regulating affect interpersonally: When low esteem leads to greater enhancement. *Journal of Personality and Social Psychology, 56*, 907–921. (p. 517)

Baumrind, D. (1996). The discipline controversy revisited. *Family Relations, 45*, 405–414. (p. 144)

Baumrind, D. (2013). Is a pejorative view of power assertion in the socialization process justified? *Review of General Psychology, 17*, 420–427. (p. 144)

Baumrind, D., Larzelere, R. E., & Cowan, P. A. (2002). Ordinary physical punishment: Is it harmful? Comment on Gershoff (2002). *Psychological Bulletin, 128*, 602–611. (p. 262)

Bavelier, D., Newport, E. L., & Supalla, T. (2003, January). Children need natural languages, signed or spoken. *Cerebrum*, pp. 19–32. (p. 330)

BBC. (2008, February 26). Anti-depressants' "little effect." British Broadcasting Corporation. Retrieved from http://news.bbc.co.uk/2/hi/health/7263494.stm (p. 596)

Beaman, A. L., & Klentz, B. (1983). The supposed physical attractiveness bias against supporters of the women's movement: A meta-analysis. *Personality and Social Psychology Bulletin, 9*, 544–550. (p. 478)

Beardsley, L. M. (1994). Medical diagnosis and treatment across cultures. In W. J. Lonner & R. Malpass (Eds.), *Psychology and culture* (pp. 279–284). Boston: Allyn & Bacon. (p. 530)

Bearzi, M., & Stanford, C. (2010). A bigger, better brain. *American Scientist, 98*, 402–409. (p. 327)

Beauchamp, G. K. (1987). The human preference for excess salt. *American Scientist, 75*, 27–33. (p. 381)

Beauvois, J.-L. Courbet, D., & Oberlé, D. (2012). The prescriptive power of the television host: A transposition of Milgram's obedience paradigm to the context of TV game show. *European Review of Applied Psychology/Revue Européenne de Psychologie Appliquée, 62*, 111–119. (p. 452)

Beck, A. T., Rush, A. J., Shaw, B. F., & Emery, G. (1979). *Cognitive therapy of depression.* New York: Guilford Press. (p. 579)

Becker, D. V., Kenrick, D. T., Neuberg, S. L., Blackwell, K. C., & Smith, D. M. (2007). The confounded nature of angry men and happy women. *Journal of Personality and Social Psychology, 92*, 179–190. (pp. 397, 398)

Becker, M., Cortina, K. S., Tsai, Y., & Eccles, J. S. (2014). Sexual orientation, psychological well-being, and mental health: A longitudinal analysis from adolescence to young adulthood. *Psychology of Sexual Orientation and Gender Diversity, 1*, 132–145. (p. 188)

Becklen, R., & Cervone, D. (1983). Selective looking and the noticing of unexpected events. *Memory and Cognition, 11*, 601–608. (p. 83)

Beeman, M. J., & Chiarello, C. (1998). Complementary right- and left-hemisphere language comprehension. *Current Directions in Psychological Science, 7*, 2–8. (p. 64)

Beer, J. S., & Hughes, B. L. (2010). Neural systems of social comparison and the "above-average" effect. *NeuroImage, 49*, 2671–2679. (p. 519)

Bègue, L., Bushman, B. J., Giancola, P. R., Subra, B., & Rosset, E. (2010). "There is no such thing as an accident," especially when people are drunk. *Personality and Social Psychology Bulletin, 36*, 1301–1304. (p. 470)

Bègue, L., Subra, B., Arvers, P., Muller, D., Bricout, V., & Zorman, M. (2009). A message in a bottle: Extrapharmacological effects of alcohol on aggression. *Journal of Experimental Social Psychology, 45*, 137–142. (p. 470)

Beilin, H. (1992). Piaget's enduring contribution to developmental psychology. *Developmental Psychology, 28*, 191–204. (p. 135)

Beintner, I., Jacobi, C., & Taylor, C. B. (2012). Effects of an Internet-based prevention programme for eating disorders in the USA and Germany: A meta-analytic review. *European Eating Disorders Review, 20*, 1–8. (p. 566)

Bell, A. P., Weinberg, M. S., & Hammersmith, S. K. (1981). *Sexual preference: Its development in men and women.* Bloomington: Indiana University Press. (p. 189)

Belluck, P. (2013, February 5). People with mental illness more likely to be smokers, study finds. *The New York Times.* Retrieved from http://www.nytimes.com/2013/02/06/health/more-smoking-found-by-mentally-ill-people.html?_r=0 (p. 22)

Belot, M., & Francesconi, M. (2006, November). *Can anyone be "the" one? Evidence on mate selection from speed dating.* London: Centre for Economic Policy Research. (p. 477)

Belsher, G., & Costello, C. G. (1988). Relapse after recovery from unipolar depression: A critical review. *Psychological Bulletin, 104,* 84–96. (p. 548)

Bem, D. (1984). Quoted in the *Skeptical Inquirer, 8,* 194. (p. 242)

Bem, D., Tressoldi, P. E., Rabeyron, T., & Duggan, M. (2014, April 11). *Feeling the future: A meta-analysis of 90 experiments on the anomalous anticipation of random future events.* Retrieved from http://papers.ssrn.com/sol3/papers.cfm?abstract_id=2423692 (p. 242)

Bem, S. L. (1987). Masculinity and femininity exist only in the mind of the perceiver. In J. M. Reinisch, L. A. Rosenblum, & S. A. Sanders (Eds.), *Masculinity/femininity: Basic perspectives* (pp. 304–311). New York: Oxford University Press. (p. 179)

Bem, S. L. (1993). *The lenses of gender: Transforming the debate on sexual inequality.* New Haven, CT: Yale University Press. (pp. 178, 179)

Benartzi, S., & Thaler, R. H. (2013). Behavioral economics and the retirement savings crisis. *Science, 339,* 1152–1153. (p. 322)

Bender, T. W., Anestis, M. D., Anestis, J. C., Gordon, K. H., & Joiner, T. E. (2012). Affective and behavioral paths toward the acquired capacity for suicide. *Journal of Social and Clinical Psychology, 31,* 81–100. (p. 553)

Benedict, C., Brooks, S. J., O'Daly, O. G., Almen, M. S., Morell, A., Aberg, K., . . . Schiöth, H. B. (2012). Acute sleep deprivation enhances the brain's response to hedonic food stimuli: An fMRI study. *Journal of Clinical Endocrinology and Metabolism, 97,* 2011–2759. (p. 95)

Benjamin, L. T., Jr., & Simpson, J. A. (2009). The power of the situation: The impact of Milgram's obedience studies on personality and social psychology. *American Psychologist, 64,* 12–19. (p. 452)

Benjamins, M. R., Ellison, C. G., & Rogers, R. G. (2010). Religious involvement and mortality risk among pre-retirement aged U.S. adults. In C. E. Ellison & R. A. Hummer (Eds.), *Religion, families, and health: Population-based research in the United States* (pp. 273–291). New Brunswick, NJ: Rutgers University Press. (p. 430)

Bennett, W. I. (1995). Beyond overeating. *New England Journal of Medicine, 332,* 673–674. (p. 385)

Ben-Shakhar, G., & Elaad, E. (2003). The validity of psychophysiological detection of information with the guilt knowledge test: A meta-analytic review. *Journal of Applied Psychology, 88,* 131–151. (p. 394)

Bentley, K. H., Nock, M. K., & Barlow, D. H. (2014). The four-function model of non-suicidal self-injury: Key directions for future research. *Clinical Psychological Science, 2,* 638–656. (p. 555)

Berg, J. M., Wall, M., Larson, N., Eisenberg, M. E., Loth, K. A., & Neumark-Sztainer, D. (2014). The unique and additive associations of family functioning and parenting practices with disordered eating behaviors in diverse adolescents. *Journal of Behavioral Medicine, 37,* 205–217. (p. 565)

Bergelson, E., & Swingley, D. (2012). At 6–9 months, human infants know the meanings of many common nouns. *Proceedings of the National Academy of Sciences of the United States of America, 109,* 3253–3258. (p. 331)

Bergelson, E., & Swingley, D. (2013). The acquisition of abstract words by young infants. *Cognition, 127,* 391–397. (p. 331)

Bergen, B. K. (2014). *Universal grammar.* Retrieved from https://edge.org/response-detail/25539 (p. 330)

Berk, L. E. (1994, November). Why children talk to themselves. *Scientific American,* pp. 78–83. (p. 134)

Berk, L. S., Felten, D. L., Tan, S. A., Bittman, B. B., & Westengard, J. (2001). Modulation of neuroimmune parameters during the eustress of humor-associated mirthful laughter. *Alternative Therapies, 7,* 62–76. (p. 424)

Berkman, E. T., Kahn, L. E., & Merchant, J. S. (2014). Training-induced changes in inhibitory control network activity. *Journal of Neuroscience, 34,* 149–157. (p. 162)

Berkowitz, L. (1983). Aversively stimulated aggression: Some parallels and differences in research with animals and humans. *American Psychologist, 38,* 1135–1144. (p. 470)

Berkowitz, L. (1989). Frustration–aggression hypothesis: Examination and reformulation. *Psychological Bulletin, 106,* 59–73. (p. 470)

Berman, M. G., Jonides, J., & Kaplan, S. (2008). The cognitive benefits of interacting with nature. *Psychological Science, 19,* 1207–1212. (p. 375)

Berkovich-Ohana, A., Glickson, J., & Goldstein, A. (2014). Studying the default mode and its mindfulness-induced changes using EEF functional connectivity. *Social Cognitive and Affective Neuroscience, 9,* 1616–1624. (p. 428)

Bernal, S., Dehaene-Lambertz, G., Millotte, S., & Christophe, A. (2010). Two-year-olds compute syntactic structure on-line. *Developmental Science, 13,* 69–76. (p. 332)

Bernieri, F., Davis, J., Rosenthal, R., & Knee, C. (1994). Interactional synchrony and rapport: Measuring synchrony in displays devoid of sound and facial affect. *Personality and Social Psychology Bulletin, 20,* 303–311. (p. 274)

Bernstein, D. M., & Loftus, E. F. (2009a). The consequences of false memories for food preferences and choices. *Perspectives on Psychological Science, 4,* 135–139. (p. 307)

Bernstein, D. M., & Loftus, E. F. (2009b). How to tell if a particular memory is true or false. *Perspectives on Psychological Science, 4,* 370–374. (p. 306)

Bernstein, M. J., Young, S. G., & Claypool, H. M. (2010). Is Obama's win a gain for Blacks? Changes in implicit racial prejudice following the 2008 election. *Social Psychology, 41,* 147–151. (p. 463)

Berntson, G. G., Norman, G. J., Bechara, A., Bruss, J., Tranel, D., & Cacioppo, J. T. (2011). The insula and evaluative processes. *Psychological Science, 22,* 80–86. (p. 52)

Berscheid, E. (1981). An overview of the psychological effects of physical attractiveness and some comments upon the psychological effects of knowledge of the effects of physical attractiveness. In G. W. Lucker, K. Ribbens, & J. A. McNamara (Eds.), *Psychological aspects of facial form* (pp. 1–23). Ann Arbor: Center for Human Growth and Development, University of Michigan. (p. 477)

Berscheid, E. (1985). Interpersonal attraction. In G. Lindzey & E. Aronson (Eds.), *The handbook of social psychology* (3rd ed., Vol. 2, pp. 413–484). New York: Random House. (p. 370)

Berscheid, E. (2010). Love in the fourth dimension. *Annual Review of Psychology, 61,* 1–25. (p. 479)

Berscheid, E., Gangestad, S. W., & Kulakowski, D. (1984). Emotion in close relationships: Implications for relationship counseling. In S. D. Brown & R. W. Lent (Eds.), *Handbook of counseling psychology* (pp. 435–476). New York: Wiley. (p. 480)

Berti, A., Cottini, G., Gandola, M., Pia, L., Smania, N., Stracciari, A., . . . Paulesu, E. (2005). Shared cortical anatomy for motor awareness and motor control. *Science, 309,* 488–491. (p. 64)

Bértolo, H. (2005). Visual imagery without visual perception? *Psicológica, 26,* 173–188. (p. 99)

Bhatt, R. S., Wasserman, E. A., Reynolds, W. F., Jr., & Knauss, K. S. (1988). Conceptual behavior in pigeons: Categorization of both familiar and novel examples from four classes of natural and artificial stimuli. *Journal of Experimental Psychology: Animal Behavior Processes, 14,* 219–234. (p. 257)

Bialystok, E., Kroll, J. F., Green, D. W., MacWhinney, B., & Craik, F. I. M. (2015). Publication bias and the validity of evidence: What's the connection? *Psychological Science, 26,* 944–946. (p. 338)

Bianconi, E., Piovesan, A., Facchin, F., Beraudi, A., Casadei, R., Frabetti, F., . . . Canaider, S. (2013). An estimation of the number of cells in the human body. *Annals of Human Biology, 40,* 463–471. (p. 123)

Bick, J., Zhu, T., Stamoulis, C., Fox, N. A., Zeanah, C., & Nelson, C. A. (2015). Effect of early institutionalization and foster care on long-term white matter development: A randomized clinical trial. *JAMA Pediatrics, 169,* 211–219. (p. 143)

Bienvenu, O. J., Davydow, D. S., & Kendler, K. S. (2011). Psychiatric "diseases" versus behavioral disorders and degree of genetic influence. *Psychological Medicine, 41,* 33–40. (p. 549)

Bilefsky, D. (2009, March 10). Europeans debate castration of sex offenders. *The New York Times.* Retrieved from http://www.nytimes.com/2009/03/11/world/europe/11castrate.html?_r=0 (p. 182)

Billock, V. A., & Tsou, B. H. (2012). Elementary visual hallucinations and their relationships to neural pattern-forming mechanisms. *Psychological Bulletin, 138,* 744–774. (p. 112)

Binet, A. (1909). *Les idées modernes sur les enfants* [Modern ideas about children]. Paris: Flammarion. Quoted in A. Clarke & A. Clarke (2006), Born to be bright. *The Psychologist, 19,* 409. (p. 346)

Bird, C. D., & Emery, N. J. (2009). Rooks use stones to raise the water level to reach a floating worm. *Current Biology, 19,* 1410–1414. (p. 327)

Birnbaum, G. E., Reis, H. T., Mikulincer, M., Gillath, O., & Orpaz, A. (2006). When sex is more than just sex: Attachment orientations, sexual experience, and relationship quality. *Journal of Personality and Social Psychology, 91,* 929–943. (p. 142)

Birnbaum, S. G., Yuan, P. X., Wang, M., Vijayraghavan, S., Bloom, A. K., Davis, D. J., . . . Arnsten, A. F. T. (2004). Protein kinase C overactivity impairs prefrontal cortical regulation of working memory. *Science, 306,* 882–884. (p. 294)

Biro, D., Humle, T., Koops, K., Sousa, C., Hayashi, M., & Matsuzawa, T. (2010). Chimpanzee mothers at Bossou, Guinea carry the mummified remains of their dead infants. *Current Biology, 20,* R351–R352. (p. 328)

Biro, F. M., Galvez, M. P., Greenspan, L. C., Succop, P. A., Vangeepuram, N., Pinney, S. M., . . . Wolff, M. S. (2010). Pubertal assessment method and baseline characteristics in a mixed longitudinal study of girls. *Pediatrics, 126,* e583–e590. doi:10.1542/peds.2009-3079 (p. 176)

Biro, F. M., Greenspan, L. C., & Galvez, M. P. (2012). Puberty in girls of the 21st century. *Journal of Pediatric and Adolescent Gynecology, 25,* 289–294. (p. 176)

Bishop, D. I., Weisgram, E. S., Holleque, K. M., Lund, K. E., & Wheeler, J. R. (2005). Identity development and alcohol consumption: Current and retrospective self-reports by college students. *Journal of Adolescence, 28,* 523–533. (pp. 115, 153)

Bishop, G. D. (1991). Understanding the understanding of illness: Lay disease representations. In J. A. Skelton & R. T. Croyle (Eds.), *Mental representation in health and illness* (pp. 32–59). New York: Springer-Verlag. (p. 316)

Bisson, J., & Andrew, M. (2007). Psychological treatment of post-traumatic stress disorder (PTSD). *Cochrane Database of Systematic Reviews,* Issue 3, Article CD003388. doi:10.1002/14651858.CD003388.pub3 (p. 588)

Bjork, E. L., & Bjork, R. (2011). Making things hard on yourself, but in a good way: Creating desirable difficulties to enhance learning. In M. A. Gernsbacher, M. A. Pew, L. M. Hough, & J. R. Pomerantz (Eds.), *Psychology and the real world* (pp. 55–64). New York: Worth. (p. 32)

Bjork, R. (2011, January 20). Quoted in P. Belluck, To really learn, quit studying and take a test. *The New York Times.* Retrieved from http://www.nytimes.com/2011/01/21/science/21memory.html (p. 289)

Bjorklund, D. F., & Green, B. L. (1992). The adaptive nature of cognitive immaturity. *American Psychologist, 47,* 46–54. (p. 135)

Blackhart, G. C., Nelson, B. C., Knowles, M. L., & Baumeister, R. F. (2009). Rejection elicits emotional reactions but neither causes immediate distress nor lowers self-esteem: A meta-analytic review of 192 studies on social exclusion. *Personality and Social Psychology Bulletin, 13,* 269–309. (p. 371)

Blake, A., Nazarian, M., & Castel, A. (2015). The Apple of the mind's eye: Everyday attention, metamemory, and reconstructive memory for the Apple logo. *Quarterly Journal of Experimental Psychology, 68,* 858–865. (p. 303)

Blake, W. (2013, March 11). *Voices from solitary: A sentence worse than death.* Retrieved from http://solitarywatch.com/2013/03/11/voices-from-solitary-a-sentence-worse-than-death/ (p. 372)

Blakemore, S.-J. (2008). Development of the social brain during adolescence. *Quarterly Journal of Experimental Psychology, 61,* 40–49. (p. 148)

Blakemore, S.-J., Wolpert, D. M., & Frith, C. D. (1998). Central cancellation of self-produced tickle sensation. *Nature Neuroscience, 1,* 635–640. (p. 231)

Blakeslee, S. (2006, January 10). Cells that read minds. *The New York Times.* Retrieved from http://www.nytimes.com/2006/01/10/science/10mirr.html?pagewanted=all (p. 273)

Blanchard, R. (2004). Quantitative and theoretical analyses of the relation between older brothers and homosexuality in men. *Journal of Theoretical Biology, 230,* 173–187. (p. 191)

Blanchard, R. (2008a). Review and theory of handedness, birth order, and homosexuality in men. *Laterality, 13,* 51–70. (p. 191)

Blanchard, R. (2008b). Sex ratio of older siblings in heterosexual and homosexual, right-handed and non-right-handed men. *Archives of Sexual Behavior, 37,* 977–981. (p. 191)

Blanchard, R. (2014). Detecting and correcting for family size differences in the study of sexual orientation and fraternal birth order. *Archives of Sexual Behavior, 43,* 845–852. (p. 191)

Blanchard-Fields, F. (2007). Everyday problem solving and emotion: An adult developmental perspective. *Current Directions in Psychological Science, 16,* 26–31. (p. 349)

Blanke, O. (2012). Multisensory brain mechanisms of bodily self-consciousness. *Nature Reviews Neuroscience, 13,* 556–571. (p. 81)

Blankenburg, F., Taskin, B., Ruben, J., Moosmann, M., Ritter, P., Curio, G., & Villringer, A. (2003). Imperceptive stimuli and sensory processing impediment. *Science, 299,* 1864. (p. 202)

Blascovich, J., & Mendes, W. B. (2010). Social psychophysiology and embodiment. In S. T. Fiske, D. T. Gilbert, & G. Lindzey (Eds.), *The handbook of social psychology* (5th ed., pp. 194–227). New York: Wiley. (p. 406)

Blass, T. (1996). Stanley Milgram: A life of inventiveness and controversy. In G. A. Kimble, C. A. Boneau, & M. Wertheimer (Eds.), *Portraits of pioneers in psychology* (Vol. 2, pp. 315–333). Washington, DC, and Mahwah, NJ: American Psychological Association and Erlbaum. (p. 443)

Blass, T. (1999). The Milgram paradigm after 35 years: Some things we now know about obedience to authority. *Journal of Applied Social Psychology, 29,* 955–978. (p. 442)

Blatt, S. J., Sanislow, C. A., III, Zuroff, D. C., & Pilkonis, P. (1996). Characteristics of effective therapists: Further analyses of data from the National Institute of Mental Health Treatment of Depression Collaborative Research Program. *Journal of Consulting and Clinical Psychology, 64,* 1276–1284. (p. 589)

Bleidorn, W. (2015). What accounts for personality maturation in early adulthood? *Current Directions in Psychological Science, 24,* 245–252. (p. 510)

BLF. (2012). *The impact of cannabis on your lungs.* London: British Lung Foundation. (p. 113)

Block, J. (2010). The five-factor framing of personality and beyond: Some ruminations. *Psychological Inquiry, 21,* 2–25. (p. 509)

Bloom, B. C. (Ed.). (1985). *Developing talent in young people.* New York: Ballantine. (p. 376)

Bloom, F. E. (1993, January/February). What's new in neurotransmitters. *BrainWork,* pp. 7–9. (p. 41)

Bloom, P. (2000). *How children learn the meanings of words.* Cambridge, MA: MIT Press. (p. 331)

BLS. (2011, June 22). *American Time Use Survey summary.* Bureau of Labor Statistics. Retrieved from http://www.bls.gov/ (p. 448)

Blum, D. (2002). *Love at Goon Park: Harry Harlow and the science of affection* New York: Perseus. (p. 140)

Blum, K., Cull, J. G., Braverman, E. R., & Comings, D. E. (1996). Reward deficiency syndrome. *American Scientist, 84,* 132–145. (p. 54)

Boag, S. (2006). Freudian repression, the common view, and pathological science. *Review of General Psychology, 10,* 74–86. (p. 499)

Boccardi, M., Frisoni, G. B., Hare, R. D., Cavedo, E., Najt, P., Pievani, M., . . . Tihonen, J. (2011). Cortex and amygdala morphology in psychopathy. *Psychiatry Research: Neuroimaging, 193,* 85–92. (p. 53)

Bocklandt, S., Horvath, S., Vilain, E., & Hamer, D. H. (2006). Extreme skewing of X chromosome inactivation in mothers of homosexual men. *Human Genetics, 118,* 691–694. (p. 190)

Bockting, W. O. (2014). Transgender identity development. In D. L. Tolman & L. M. Diamond (Eds.), *APA handbook of sexuality and psychology: Vol. 1. Person-based approaches* (pp. 739–758). Washington, DC: American Psychological Association. (p. 179)

Bodenhausen, G. V., Sheppard, L. A., & Kramer, G. P. (1994). Negative affect and social judgment: The differential impact of anger and sadness. *European Journal of Social Psychology, 24,* 45–62. (p. 487)

Bodkin, J. A., & Amsterdam, J. D. (2002). Transdermal selegiline in major depression: A double-blind, placebo-controlled, parallel-group study in outpatients. *American Journal of Psychiatry, 159,* 1869–1875. (p. 595)

Boecker, H., Sprenger, T., Spilker, M. E., Henriksen, G., Koppenhoefer, M., Wagner, K. J., . . . Tolle, T. R. (2008). The runner's high: Opioidergic mechanisms in the human brain. *Cerebral Cortex, 18,* 2523–2531. (pp. 41, 550)

Boehm, J. K., & Kubzansky, L. D. (2012). The heart's content: The association between positive psychological well-being and cardiovascular health. *Psychological Bulletin, 138,* 655–691. (p. 422)

Boehm, J. K., Trudel-Fitzgerald, C., Kivimaki, M., & Kubzansky, L. D. (2015). The prospective association between positive psychological well-being and diabetes. *Health Psychology, 34,* 1013–1021. (p. 431)

Boehm-Davis, D. A. (2005). Improving product safety and effectiveness in the home. In R. S. Nickerson (Ed.), *Reviews of human factors and ergonomics* (Vol. 1, pp. 219–253). Santa Monica, CA: Human Factors and Ergonomics Society. (p. B-14)

Boesch-Achermann, H., & Boesch, C. (1993). Tool use in wild chimpanzees: New light from dark forests. *Current Directions in Psychological Science, 2,* 18–21. (p. 327)

Bogaert, A. F. (2003). Number of older brothers and sexual orientation: New texts and the attraction/behavior distinction in two national probability samples. *Journal of Personality and Social Psychology, 84,* 644–652. (p. 191)

Bogaert, A. F. (2004). Asexuality: Prevalence and associated factors in a national probability sample. *Journal of Sex Research, 41,* 279–287. (p. 187)

Bogaert, A. F. (2006). Biological versus nonbiological older brothers and men's sexual orientation. *Proceedings of the National Academy of Sciences of the United States of America, 103,* 10771–10774. (p. 191)

Bogaert, A. F. (2006). Toward a conceptual understanding of asexuality. *Review of General Psychology, 10,* 241–250. (p. 187)

Bogaert, A. F. (2010). Physical development and sexual orientation in men and women: An analysis of NATSAL-2000. *Archives of Sexual Behavior, 39*, 110–116. (p. 191)

Bogaert, A. F. (2012). *Understanding asexuality.* Lanham, MD: Rowman & Littlefield. (p. 187)

Boggiano, A. K., Harackiewicz, J. M., Bessette, M. M., & Main, D. S. (1985). Increasing children's interest through performance-contingent reward. *Social Cognition, 3*, 400–411. (p. 271)

Bohman, M., & Sigvardsson, S. (1990). Outcome in adoption: Lessons from longitudinal studies. In D. Brodzinsky & M. Schechter (Eds.), *The psychology of adoption* (pp. 93–106). New York: Oxford University Press. (p. 71)

Bolger, N., DeLongis, A., Kessler, R. C., & Schilling, E. A. (1989). Effects of daily stress on negative mood. *Journal of Personality and Social Psychology, 57*, 808–818. (p. 432)

Bolmont, M., Cacioppo, J. T., & Cacioppo, S. (2014). Love is in the gaze: An eye-tracking study of love and sexual desire. *Psychological Science, 25*, 1748–1756. (p. 396)

Boly, M., Garrido, M. I., Gosseries, O., Bruno, M.-A., Boveroux, P., Schnakers, C., . . . Friston, K. (2011). Preserved feed-forward but impaired top-down processes in the vegetative state. *Science, 332*, 858–862. (p. 81)

Bonanno, G. A. (2004). Loss, trauma, and human resilience: Have we underestimated the human capacity to thrive after extremely aversive events? *American Psychologist, 59*, 20–28. (p. 168)

Bonanno, G. A., Brewin, C. R., Kaniasty, K., & La Greca, A. M. (2010). Weighing the costs of disaster: Consequences, risks, and resilience in individuals, families, and communities. *Psychological Science in the Public Interest, 11*, 1–49. (p. 540)

Bonanno, G. A., Galea, S., Bucciarelli, A., & Vlahov, D. (2006). Psychological resilience after disaster. *Psychological Science, 17*, 181–186. (p. 540)

Bonanno, G. A., Galea, S., Bucciarelli, A., & Vlahov, D. (2007). What predicts psychological resilience after disaster? The role of demographics, resources, and life stress. *Journal of Consulting and Clinical Psychology, 75*, 671–682. (p. 603)

Bonanno, G. A., & Kaltman, S. (1999). Toward an integrative perspective on bereavement. *Psychological Bulletin, 125*, 760–777. (p. 168)

Bonanno, G. A., Kennedy, P., Galatzer-Levy, I. R., Lude, P., & Elfström, M. L. (2012). Trajectories of resilience, depression, and anxiety following spinal cord injury. *Rehabilitation Psychology, 57*, 236–247. (p. 603)

Bonanno, G. A., Westphal, M., & Mancini, A. D. (2011). Resilience to loss and potential trauma. *Annual Review of Clinical Psychology, 11*, 511–535. (p. 540)

Bond, C. F., Jr., & DePaulo, B. M. (2006). Accuracy of deception judgments. *Personality and Social Psychology Review, 10*, 214–234. (p. 397)

Bond, C. F., Jr., & DePaulo, B. M. (2008). Individual differences in detecting deception: Accuracy and bias. *Psychological Bulletin, 134*, 477–492. (p. 397)

Bond, M. H., Lun, V. M.-C., Chan, J., Chan, W. W.-Y., & Wong, D. (2012). Enacting modesty in Chinese culture: The joint contribution of personal characteristics and contextual features. *Asian Journal of Social Psychology, 15*, 14–25. (p. 522)

Bond, R., & Smith, P. B. (1996). Culture and conformity: A meta-analysis of studies using Asch's (1952b, 1956) line judgment task. *Psychological Bulletin, 119*, 111–137. (p. 451)

Bonetti, L., Campbell, M. A., & Gilmore, L. (2010). The relationship of loneliness and social anxiety with children's and adolescents' online communication. *Cyberpsychology, Behavior, and Social Networking, 13*, 279–285. (p. 373)

Bonezzi, A., Brendl, C. M., & DeAngelis, M. (2011). Stuck in the middle: The psychophysics of goal pursuit. *Psychological Science, 22*, 607–612. (p. 375)

Bonneville-Roussy, A., Rentfrow, P. J., Xu, K. M. & Potter, J. (2013). Music through the ages: Trends in musical attitudes and preferences from adolescence through middle adulthood. *Journal of Personality and Social Psychology, 105*, 703–717. (p. 148)

Bono, J. E., & Judge, T. A. (2004). Personality and transformational and transactional leadership: A meta-analysis. *Journal of Applied Psychology, 89*, 901–910. (p. B-12)

Bora, E., & Pantelis, C. (2013). Theory of mind impairments in first-episode psychosis, individuals at ultra-high risk for psychosis and in first-degree relatives of schizophrenia: Systematic review and meta-analysis. *Schizophrenia Research, 144*, 31–36. (p. 557)

Boring, E. G. (1930). A new ambiguous figure. *American Journal of Psychology, 42*, 444–445. (p. 205)

Bornstein, M. H., Cote, L. R., Maital, S., Painter, K., Park, S.-Y., Pascual, L., . . . Vyt, A. (2004). Cross-linguistic analysis of vocabulary in young children: Spanish, Dutch, French, Hebrew, Italian, Korean, and American English. *Child Development, 75*, 1115–1139. (p. 330)

Bornstein, M. H., Tal, J., Rahn, C., Galperin, C. Z., Pecheux, M.-G., Lamour, M., . . . Tamis-LeMonda, C. S. (1992a). Functional analysis of the contents of maternal speech to infants of 5 and 13 months in four cultures: Argentina, France, Japan, and the United States. *Developmental Psychology, 28*, 593–603. (p. 120)

Bornstein, M. H., Tamis-LeMonda, C. S., Tal, J., Ludemann, P., Toda, S., Rahn, C. W., . . . Vardi, D. (1992b). Maternal responsiveness to infants in three societies: The United States, France, and Japan. *Child Development, 63*, 808–821. (p. 120)

Bornstein, R. F. (1989). Exposure and affect: Overview and meta-analysis of research, 1968–1987. *Psychological Bulletin, 106*, 265–289. (pp. 139, 475)

Bornstein, R. F. (1999). Source amnesia, misattribution, and the power of unconscious perceptions and memories. *Psychoanalytic Psychology, 16*, 155–178. (p. 475)

Bornstein, R. F., Galley, D. J., Leone, D. R., & Kale, A. R. (1991). The temporal stability of ratings of parents: Test–retest reliability and influence of parental contact. *Journal of Social Behavior and Personality, 6*, 641–649. (p. 299)

Boroditsky, L. (2009, June 11). *How does our language shape the way we think?* Retrieved from http://edge.org/conversation/how-does-our-language-shape-the-way-we-think (pp. 330, 337)

Boroditsky, L. (2011, February). How language shapes thought. *Scientific American*, pp. 63–65. (p. 337)

Boron, J. B., Willis, S. L., & Schaie, K. W. (2007). Cognitive training gain as a predictor of mental status. *Journal of Gerontology: Psychological Sciences and Social Sciences, 62B*, 45–52. (p. 161)

Bosma, H., Marmot, M. G., Hemingway, H., Nicolson, A. C., Brunner, E., & Stansfeld, S. A. (1997). Low job control and risk of coronary heart disease in Whitehall II (prospective cohort) study. *British Medical Journal, 314*, 558–565. (p. 420)

Bosma, H., Peter, R., Siegrist, J., & Marmot, M. (1998). Two alternative job stress models and the risk of coronary heart disease. *American Journal of Public Health, 88*, 68–74. (p. 420)

Bossong, M. G., Jansma, J. M., van Hellm, H. H., Jagerm, G., Oudman, E., Saliasi, E., . . . Ramsey, N. F. (2012). Effects of Δ9-tetrahydrocannabinol in human working memory function. *Biological Psychiatry, 71*, 693–699. (p. 112)

Bostwick, J. M., & Pankratz, V. S. (2000). Affective disorders and suicide risk: A reexamination. *American Journal of Psychiatry, 157*, 1925–1932. (p. 552)

Bosworth, R. G., & Dobkins, K. R. (1999). Left-hemisphere dominance for motion processing in deaf signers. *Psychological Science, 10*, 256–262. (p. 61)

Bothwell, R. K., Brigham, J. C., & Malpass, R. S. (1989). Cross-racial identification. *Personality and Social Psychology Bulletin, 15*, 19–25. (p. 467)

Bouchard, T. J., Jr. (2009). Genetic influences on human intelligence (Spearman's g): How much? *Annals of Human Biology, 36*, 527–544. (p. 69)

Bouchard, T. J., Jr. (2014). Genes, evolution and intelligence. *Behavior Genetics, 44*, 549–577. (p. 355)

Boucher, J., Mayes, A., & Bigham, S. (2012). Memory in autistic spectrum disorder. *Psychological Bulletin, 138*, 458–496. (p. 136)

Bowden, E. M., & Beeman, M. J. (1998). Getting the right idea: Semantic activation in the right hemisphere may help solve insight problems. *Psychological Science, 9*, 435–440. (p. 64)

Bowen, L. (2012, November). Certain video games may lead teens to drive recklessly. *Monitor on Psychology, 43*, p. 15. (p. 22)

Bowen, S., Witkiewitz, K., Dillworth, T. M., Chawla, N., Simpson, T. L., Ostafin, B. D., . . . Marlatt, G. A. (2006). Mindfulness meditation and substance use in an incarcerated population. *Psychology of Addictive Behaviors, 20*, 343–347. (p. 428)

Bower, B. (2009, February 14). The dating go round. *Science News*, pp. 22–25. (p. 476)

Bower, G. H., Clark, M. C., Lesgold, A. M., & Winzenz, D. (1969). Hierarchical retrieval schemes in recall of categorized word lists. *Journal of Verbal Learning and Verbal Behavior, 8*, 323–343. (p. 288)

Bower, G. H. (1986). Prime time in cognitive psychology. In P. Eelen & O. Fontaine (Eds.), *Behavior therapy: Beyond the conditioning paradigm* (pp. 22–47). Leuven, Belgium: Leuven University Press. (p. 297)

Bower, G. H., & Morrow, D. G. (1990). Mental models in narrative comprehension. *Science, 247*, 44–48. (p. 290)

Bower, J. M., & Parsons, L. M. (2003, August). Rethinking the "lesser brain." *Scientific American*, pp. 50–57. (p. 52)

Bowers, J. S. (2009). On the biological plausibility of grandmother cells: Implications for neural network theories in psychology and neuroscience. *Psychological Review, 116*, 220–251. (p. 216)

Bowers, J. S., Mattys, S. L., & Gage, S. H. (2009). Preserved implicit knowledge of a forgotten childhood language. *Psychological Science, 20*, 1064–1069. (p. 129)

Bowler, M. C., & Woehr, D. J. (2006). A meta-analytic evaluation of the impact of dimension and exercise factors on assessment center ratings. *Journal of Applied Psychology, 91*, 1114–1124. (p. 515)

Bowling, N. A., Eschleman, K. J., & Wang, Q. (2010). A meta-analytic examination of the relationship between job satisfaction and subjective well-being. *Journal of Occupational and Organizational Psychology, 83*, 915–934. (p. B-8)

Boxer, P., Huesmann, L. R., Bushman, B. J., O'Brien, M., & Moceri, D. (2009). The role of violent media preference in cumulative developmental risk for violence and general aggression. *Journal of Youth and Adolescence, 38*, 417–428. (p. 277)

Boyatzis, C. J. (2012). Spiritual development during childhood and adolescence. In L. J. Miller (Ed.), *The Oxford handbook of psychology and spirituality* (pp. 151–164). New York: Oxford University Press. (p. 149)

Boyatzis, C. J., Matillo, G. M., & Nesbitt, K. M. (1995). Effects of the "Mighty Morphin Power Rangers" on children's aggression with peers. *Child Study Journal, 25*, 45–55. (p. 277)

Boyce, C. J., & Wood, A. M. (2011). Personality prior to disability determines adaptation: Agreeable individuals recover lost life satisfaction faster and more completely. *Psychological Science, 22*, 1397–1402. (p. 433)

Boyce, C. J., Wood, A. M., Daly, M., & Sedikides, C. (2015). Personality change following unemployment. *Journal of Applied Psychology, 100*, 991–1011. (p. 511)

Braden, J. P. (1994). *Deafness, deprivation, and IQ*. New York: Plenum Press. (p. 358)

Bradley, D. R., Dumais, S. T., & Petry, H. M. (1976). Reply to Cavonius. *Nature, 261*, 78. (p. 217)

Bradley, R. B., Binder, E. B., Epstein, M. P., Tang, Y., Nair, H. P., Liu, W., . . . Ressler, K. J. (2008). Influence of child abuse on adult depression: Moderation by the corticotropin-releasing hormone receptor gene. *Archives of General Psychiatry, 65*, 190–200. (p. 144)

Bradshaw, C., Sawyer, A., & O'Brennan, L. (2009). A social disorganization perspective on bullying-related attitudes and behaviors: The influence of school context. *American Journal of Community Psychology, 43*, 204–220. (pp. 12–13)

Braiker, B. (2005, October 18). A quiet revolt against the rules on SIDS. *The New York Times*. Retrieved from http://www.nytimes.com/2005/10/18/health/a-quiet-revolt-against-the-rules-on-sids.html?_r=0 (p. 129)

Brainerd, C. J. (1996). Piaget: A centennial celebration. *Psychological Science, 7*, 191–195. (p. 130)

Brandon, S., Boakes, J., Glaser, & Green, R. (1998). Recovered memories of childhood sexual abuse: Implications for clinical practice. *British Journal of Psychiatry, 172*, 294–307. (p. 311)

Brang, D., Edwards, L., Ramachandran, V. S., & Coulson, S. (2008). Is the sky 2? Contextual priming in grapheme-color synaesthesia. *Psychological Science, 19*, 421–428. (p. 240)

Brannan, D., Biswas-Diener, R., Mohr, C., Mortazavi, S., & Stein, N. (2013). Friends and family: A cross-cultural investigation of social support and subjective well-being among college students. *Journal of Positive Psychology, 8*, 65–75. (p. 423)

Brannon, L. A., & Brock, T. C. (1993). Comment on report of HIV infection in rural Florida: Failure of instructions to correct for gross underestimation of phantom sex partners in perception of AIDS risk. *New England Journal of Medicine, 328*, 1351–1352. (p. 184)

Bransford, J. D., & Johnson, M. K. (1972). Contextual prerequisites for understanding: Some investigations of comprehension and recall. *Journal of Verbal Learning and Verbal Behavior, 11*, 717–726. (p. 290)

Brasel, S. A., & Gips, J. (2011). Media multitasking behavior: Concurrent television and computer usage. *Cyberpsychology, Behavior, and Social Networking, 14*, 527–534. (p. 82)

Brauhardt, A., Rudolph, A., & Hilbert, A. (2014). Implicit cognitive processes in binge-eating disorder and obesity. *Journal of Behavioral Therapy and Experimental Psychiatry, 45*, 285–290. (p. 565)

Braun, S. (1996). New experiments underscore warnings on maternal drinking. *Science, 273*, 738–739. (p. 124)

Braun, S. (2001, April). Seeking insight by prescription. *Cerebrum*, pp. 10–21. (p. 111)

Braunstein, G. D., Sundwall, D. A., Katz, M., Shifren, J. L., Buster, J. E., Simon, J. A., . . . Watts, N. B. (2005). Safety and efficacy of a testosterone patch for the treatment of hypoactive sexual desire disorder in surgically menopausal women: A randomized, placebo-controlled trial. *Archives of Internal Medicine, 165*, 1582–1589. (p. 181)

Bray, D. W., & Byham, W. C. (1991, Winter). Assessment centers and their derivatives. *Journal of Continuing Higher Education*, pp. 8–11. (p. 514)

Bray, D. W., Byham, W. C., & Mayes, B. T. (1997). Insights into the history and future of assessment centers: An interview with Dr. Douglas W. Bray and Dr. William Byham. *Journal of Social Behavior and Personality, 12*, 3–12. (p. 514)

Brayne, C., Spiegelhalter, D. J., Dufouil, C., Chi, L.-Y., Dening, T. R., Paykel, E. S., . . . Huppert, F. A. (1999). Estimating the true extent of cognitive decline in the old old. *Journal of the American Geriatrics Society, 47*, 1283–1288. (p. A-8)

Breedlove, S. M. (1997). Sex on the brain. *Nature, 389*, 801. (p. 190)

Brehm, S., & Brehm, J. W. (1981). *Psychological reactance: A theory of freedom and control*. New York: Academic Press. (p. 460)

Breslau, J., Aguilar-Gaxiola, S., Borges, G., Kendler, K. S., Su, M., & Kessler, R. C. (2007). Risk for psychiatric disorder among immigrants and their US-born descendants. *Journal of Nervous and Mental Disease, 195*, 189–195. (p. 534)

Breslin, C. W. & Safer, M. A. (2011). Effects of event valence on long-term memory for two baseball championship games. *Psychological Science, 22*, 1408–1412. (p. 295)

Brethel-Haurwitz, K. M., & Marsh, A. A. (2014). Geographical differences in subjective well-being predict extraordinary altruism. *Psychological Science, 25*, 762–771. (p. 431)

Brewer, C. L. (1996). Personal communication. (p. 10)

Brewer, J. A., Malik, S., Babuscio, T. A., Nich, C., Johnson, H. E., Deleone, C. M., . . . Rounsaville, B. J. (2011). Mindfulness training for smoking cessation: Results from a randomized controlled trial. *Drug and Alcohol Dependence, 119*, 72–80. (p. 428)

Brewer, M. B., & Chen, Y.-R. (2007). Where (who) are collectives in collectivism? Toward conceptual clarification of individualism and collectivism. *Psychological Review, 114*, 133–151. (p. 521)

Brewer, W. F. (1977). Memory for the pragmatic implications of sentences. *Memory & Cognition, 5*, 673–678. (p. 290)

Brewin, C. R., Andrews, B., Rose, S., & Kirk, M. (1999). Acute stress disorder and posttraumatic stress disorder in victims of violent crime. *American Journal of Psychiatry, 156*, 360–366. (p. 540)

Brewin, C. R., Kleiner, J. S., Vasterling J. J., & Field, A. P. (2007). Memory for emotionally neutral information in posttraumatic stress disorder: A meta-analytic investigation. *Journal of Abnormal Psychology, 116*, 448–463. (p. 294)

Briscoe, D. (1997, February 16). Women lawmakers still not in charge. *The Grand Rapids Press*, p. A23. (p. 178)

Brislin, R. W. (1988). Increasing awareness of class, ethnicity, culture, and race by expanding on students' own experiences. In I. Cohen (Ed.), *The G. Stanley Hall Lecture Series* (Vol. 8, pp. 137–180). Washington, DC: American Psychological Association. (p. 448)

Broadbent, E., Kakokehr, A., Booth, R. J., Thomas, J., Windsor, J. A., Buchanan, C. M., . . . Hill, A. G. (2012). A brief relaxation intervention reduces stress and improves surgical wound healing response: A randomized trial. *Brain, Behavior, and Immunity, 26*, 212–217. (p. 428)

Brody, J. E. (2002, November 26). When the eyelids snap shut at 65 miles an hour. *The New York Times*. Retrieved from http://www.nytimes.com/2002/11/26/science/when-the-eyelids-snap-shut-at-65-miles-an-hour.html (p. 95)

Brody, J. E. (2003, September 30). Addiction: A brain ailment, not a moral lapse. *The New York Times*. Retrieved from http://www.nytimes.com/2003/09/30/health/personal-health-addiction-a-brain-ailment-not-a-moral-lapse.html (p. 104)

Brody, S., & Tillmann, H. C. (2006). The post-orgasmic prolactin increase following intercourse is greater than following masturbation and suggests greater satiety. *Biological Psychology, 71*, 312–315. (p. 196)

Bromet, E., Andrade, L. H., Hwang, I., Sampson, N. A., Alonso, J., de Girolamo, G., . . . Kessler, R. C. (2011). Cross-national epidemiology of DSM-IV major depressive episode. *BMC Medicine, 9*, 90. http://www.biomedcentral.com/1741-7015/9/90 (p. 548)

Brooks, R. (2012). "Asia's missing women" as a problem in applied evolutionary psychology? *Evolutionary Psychology, 12*, 910–925. (p. 464)

Brown, A. S. (2003). A review of the déjà vu experience. *Psychological Bulletin, 129*, 394–413. (p. 308)

Brown, A. S. (2004). Getting to grips with déja vu. *The Psychologist, 17*, 694–696. (p. 308)

Brown, A. S., Begg, M. D., Gravenstein, S., Schaefer, C. A., Wyatt, R. J., Bresnahan, M., . . . Susser, E. S. (2004). Serologic evidence of prenatal influenza in the etiology of schizophrenia. *Archives of General Psychiatry, 61*, 774–780. (p. 559)

Brown, A. S., & Patterson, P. H. (2011). Maternal infection and schizophrenia: Implications for prevention. *Schizophrenia Bulletin, 37*, 284–290. (p. 558)

Brown, A. S., Schaefer, C. A., Wyatt, R. J., Goetz, R., Begg, M. D., Gorman, J. M., & Susser, E. S. (2000). Maternal exposure to respiratory infections and adult schizophrenia spectrum disorders: A prospective birth cohort study. *Schizophrenia Bulletin, 26*, 287–295. (p. 559)

Brown, E. L., & Deffenbacher, K. (1979). *Perception and the senses.* New York: Oxford University Press. (p. 230)

Brown, J. A. (1958). Some tests of the decay theory of immediate memory. *Quarterly Journal of Experimental Psychology, 10*, 12–21. (p. 287)

Brown, J. D. (2012). Understanding the better than average effect: Motives (still) matter. *Personality and Social Psychology Bulletin, 38*, 209–219. (p. 519)

Brown, J. D., Steele, J. R., & Walsh-Childers, K. (2002). *Sexual teens, sexual media: Investigating media's influence on adolescent sexuality.* Mahwah, NJ: Erlbaum. (p. 186)

Brown, K. W., Goodman, R. J., & Inzlicht, M. (2013). Dispositional mindfulness and the attenuation of neural responses to emotional stimuli. *Social Cognitive and Affective Neuroscience, 8*, 93–99. (p. 429)

Brown, P. C., Roediger, III, H. L., & McDaniel, M. A. (2014). *Make it stick: The science of successful learning.* Cambridge, MA: Harvard University Press. (p. 289)

Brown, R. (1986). Linguistic relativity. In S. H. Hulse & B. F. Green Jr. (Eds.), *One hundred years of psychological research in America: G. S. Hall and the Johns Hopkins tradition* (pp. 241–276). Baltimore: Johns Hopkins University Press. (p. 336)

Brown, R. P., Imura, M., & Mayeux, L. (2014). Honor and the stigma of mental healthcare. *Personality and Social Psychology Bulletin, 40*, 1119–1131. (p. 591)

Brown, R. P., Osterman, L. L., & Barnes, C. D. (2009). School violence and the culture of honor. *Psychological Science, 20*, 1400–1405. (p. 471)

Brown, S. L., Brown, R. M., House, J. S., & Smith, D. M. (2008). Coping with spousal loss: Potential buffering effects of self-reported helping behavior. *Personality and Social Psychology Bulletin, 34*, 849–861. (p. 168)

Browning, C. (1992). *Ordinary men: Reserve Police Battalion 101 and the final solution in Poland.* New York: HarperCollins. (p. 454)

Browning, R. (1867). *The ring and the book. IV—Tertium quid.* New York: Thomas Y. Crowell. (p. 482)

Bruce-Keller, A. J., Keller, J. N., & Morrison, C. D. (2009). Obesity and vulnerability of the CNS. *Biochemica et Biophysica Acta, 1792*, 395–400. (p. 383)

Bruck, M., & Ceci, S. J. (1999). The suggestibility of children's memory. *Annual Review of Psychology, 50*, 419–439. (p. 309)

Bruck, M., & Ceci, S. J. (2004). Forensic developmental psychology: Unveiling four common misconceptions. *Current Directions in Psychological Science, 15*, 229–232. (p. 309)

Bruer, J. T. (1999). *The myth of the first three years: A new understanding of early brain development and lifelong learning.* New York: Free Press. (p. 356)

Brummelman, E., Thomaes, S., Nelemans, S. A., Orobio de Castro, B., Overbeek, G., & Bushman, B. J. (2015). Origins of narcissism in children. *Proceedings of the National Academy of Sciences of the United States of America, 112*, 3659–3662. (pp. 145, 519)

Brunner, M., Gogol, K. M., Sonnleitner, P., Keller, U., Krauss, S., & Preckel, F. (2013). Gender differences in the mean level, variability, and profile shape of student achievement: Results from 41 countries. *Intelligence, 41*, 378–395. (p. 357)

Bruno, M.-A., Bernheim, J. L., Ledoux, D., Pellas, F., Demertzi, A., & Laureys, S. (2011). A survey on self-assessed well-being in a cohort of chronic locked-in syndrome patients: Happy majority, miserable minority. *BMJ Open, 1*(1), e000039. Retrieved from http://bmjopen.bmj.com/content/1/1/e000039.full (p. 433)

Bruno, M.-A., Pellas, F., & Laureys, S. (2008). Quality of life in locked-in syndrome survivors. In J. L. Vincent (Ed.), *2008 yearbook of intensive care and emergency medicine* (pp. 881–890). New York: Springer. (p. 433)

Bryant, A. N., & Astin, H. A. (2008). The correlates of spiritual struggle during the college years. *Journal of Higher Education, 79*, 1–27. (p. 153)

Bryant, R. A. (2001). Posttraumatic stress disorder and traumatic brain injury: Can they co-exist? *Clinical Psychology Review, 21*, 931–948. (p. 311)

Buchanan, R. W., Kreyenbuhl, J., Kelly, D. L., Noel, J. M., Boggs, D. L., Fischer, B. A., . . . Keller, W. (2010). The 2009 schizophrenia PORT psychopharmacological treatment recommendations and summary statements. *Schizophrenia Bulletin, 36*, 71–93. (p. 594)

Buchanan, T. W. (2007). Retrieval of emotional memories. *Psychological Bulletin, 133*, 761–779. (p. 294)

Buck, L. B., & Axel, R. (1991). A novel multigene family may encode odorant receptors: A molecular basis for odor recognition. *Cell, 65*, 175–187. (p. 237)

Buckholtz, J. W., Treadway, M. T., Cowan, R. L., Woodward, N. D., Benning, S. D., Li, R., . . . Zald, D. H. (2010). Mesolimbic dopamine reward system hypersensitivity in individuals with psychopathic traits. *Nature Neuroscience, 13*, 419–421. (p. 564)

Buckingham, M. (2001, August). Quoted in P. LaBarre, Marcus Buckingham thinks your boss has an attitude problem. *Fast Company.* Retrieved from http://www.fastcompany.com/43419/marcus-buckingham-thinks-your-boss-has-attitude-problem (p. B-10)

Buckingham, M. (2007). *Go put your strengths to work: 6 powerful steps to achieve outstanding performance.* New York: Free Press. (p. B-4)

Buckingham, M., & Clifton, D. O. (2001). *Now, discover your strengths.* New York: Free Press. (pp. B-3, B-4)

Buday, S. K., Stake, J. E., & Peterson, Z. D. (2012). Gender and the choice of a science career: The impact of social support and possible selves. *Sex Roles, 66*, 197–209. (p. 516)

Buehler, R., Griffin, D., & Ross, M. (1994). Exploring the "planning fallacy": Why people underestimate their task completion times. *Journal of Personality and Social Psychology, 67*, 366–381. (p. 322)

Buehler, R., Griffin, D., & Ross, M. (2002). Inside the planning fallacy: The causes and consequences of optimistic time predictions. In T. Gilovich, D. Griffin, & D. Kahneman (Eds.), *Heuristics and biases: The psychology of intuitive judgment* (pp. 250–270). Cambridge, England: Cambridge University Press. (p. 322)

Buffardi, L. E., & Campbell, W. K. (2008). Narcissism and social networking web sites. *Personality and Social Psychology Bulletin, 34*, 1303–1314. (p. 374)

Bugelski, B. R., Kidd, E., & Segmen, J. (1968). Image as a mediator in one-trial paired-associate learning. *Journal of Experimental Psychology, 76*, 69–73. (p. 288)

Bugental, D. B. (1986). Unmasking the "polite smile": Situational and personal determinants of managed affect in adult-child interaction. *Personality and Social Psychology Bulletin, 12*, 7–16. (p. 396)

Buhle, J. T., Silvers, J. A., Wager, T. D., Lopez, R., Onyemekwu, C., Kober, H., . . . Ochsner, K. N. (2014). Cognitive reappraisal of emotion: A meta-analysis of human neuroimaging studies. *Cerebral Cortex, 24*, 2981–2990. (p. 390)

Buhle, J. T., Stevens, B. L., Friedman, J. J., & Wager, T. D. (2012). Distraction and placebo: Two separate routes to pain control. *Psychological Science, 23*, 246–253. (p. 234)

Buka, S. L., Tsuang, M. T., Torrey, E. F., Klebanoff, M. A., Wagner, R. L., & Yolken, R. H. (2001). Maternal infections and subsequent psychosis among offspring. *Archives of General Psychiatry, 58*, 1032–1037. (p. 559)

Bullock, B., & Murray, G. (2014). Reduced amplitude of the 24 hour activity rhythm: A biomarker of vulnerability to bipolar disorder? *Clinical Psychological Science, 2*, 86–96. (p. 547)

Bunde, J., & Suls, J. (2006). A quantitative analysis of the relationship between the Cook-Medley Hostility Scale and traditional coronary artery disease risk factors. *Health Psychology, 25*, 493–500. (p. 415)

Buquet, R. (1988). Le rêve et les déficients visuels [Dreams and the visually impaired]. *Psychanalyse-a-l'Universite, 13*, 319–327. (p. 99)

Burcusa, S. L., & Iacono, W. G. (2007). Risk for recurrence in depression. *Clinical Psychology Review, 27*, 959–985. (p. 548)

Burger, J. M. (2009). Replicating Milgram: Would people still obey today? *American Psychologist, 64*, 1–11. (p. 452)

Burgess, M., Enzle, M. E., & Schmaltz, R. (2004). Defeating the potentially deleterious effects of externally imposed deadlines: Practitioners' rules-of-thumb. *Personality and Social Psychology Bulletin, 30*, 868–877. (p. B-11)

Buri, J. R., Louiselle, P. A., Misukanis, T. M., & Mueller, R. A. (1988). Effects of parental authoritarianism and authoritativeness on self-esteem. *Personality and Social Psychology Bulletin, 14*, 271–282. (p. 144)

Burish, T. G., & Carey, M. P. (1986). Conditioned aversive responses in cancer chemotherapy patients: Theoretical and developmental analysis. *Journal of Counseling and Clinical Psychology, 54*, 593–600. (p. 268)

Burk, W. J., Denissen, J., Van Doorn, M. D., Branje, S. J. T., & Laursen, B. (2009). The vicissitudes of conflict measurement: Stability and reliability in the frequency of disagreements. *European Psychologist, 14,* 153–159. (p. 154)

Burke, D. M., & Shafto, M. A. (2004). Aging and language production. *Current Directions in Psychological Science, 13,* 21–24. (p. 161)

Burke, M., Adamic, L. A., & Marciniak, K. (2013, July). *Families on Facebook.* Paper presented at the Seventh International AAAI Conference on Weblogs and Social Media, Cambridge, MA. Retrieved from http://www.aaai.org/ocs/index.php/ICWSM/ICWSM13/paper/view/5992 (p. 155)

Burns, B. C. (2004). The effects of speed on skilled chess performance. *Psychological Science, 15,* 442–447. (p. 323)

Burns, J. M., & Swerdlow, R. H. (2003). Right orbitofrontal tumor with pedophilia symptom and constructional apraxia sign. *Archives of Neurology, 60,* 437–440. (p. 35)

Burris, C. T., & Branscombe, N. R. (2005). Distorted distance estimation induced by a self-relevant national boundary. *Journal of Experimental Social Psychology, 41,* 305–312. (p. 337)

Burton, C. M., & King, L. A. (2008). Effects of (very) brief writing on health: The two-minute miracle. *British Journal of Health Psychology, 13,* 9–14. (p. 425)

Busby, D. M., Carroll, J. S., & Willoughby, B. J. (2010). Compatibility or restraint? The effects of sexual timing on marriage relationships. *Journal of Family Psychology, 24,* 766–774. (p. 196)

Bushdid, C., Magnasco, M. O., Vosshall, L. B., & Keller, A. (2014). Humans can discriminate more than 1 trillion olfactory stimuli. *Science, 343,* 1370–1372. (p. 237)

Bushman, B. J. (1993). Human aggression while under the influence of alcohol and other drugs: An integrative research review. *Current Directions in Psychological Science, 2,* 148–152. (p. 470)

Bushman, B. J. (2002). Does venting anger feed or extinguish the flame? Catharsis, rumination, distraction, anger, and aggressive responding. *Personality and Social Psychology Bulletin, 28,* 724–731. (pp. 416, 417)

Bushman, B. J., & Anderson, C. A. (2009). Comfortably numb: Desensitizing effects of violent media on helping others. *Psychological Science, 20,* 273–277. (p. 277)

Bushman, B. J., & Baumeister, R. F. (1998). Threatened egotism, narcissism, self-esteem, and direct and displaced aggression: Does self-love or self-hate lead to violence? *Journal of Personality and Social Psychology, 75,* 219–229. (p. 519)

Bushman, B. J., Baumeister, R. F., Thomaes, S., Ryu, E., Begeer, S., & West, S. G. (2009). Looking again, and harder, for a link between low self-esteem and aggression. *Journal of Personality, 77,* 427–446. (p. 519)

Bushman, B. J., Gollwitzer, M., & Cruz, C. (2015). There is broad consensus: Media researchers agree that violent media increase aggression in children, and pediatricians and parents concur. *Psychology of Popular Media Culture, 4,* 200–214. (p. 277)

Bushman, B. J., & Huesmann, L. R. (2010). Aggression. In S. T. Fiske, D. T. Gilbert, & G. Lindzey (Eds.), *Handbook of social psychology* (5th ed., pp. 833–863). New York: Wiley. (p. 173)

Bushman, B. J., Moeller, S. J., & Crocker, J. (2011). Sweets, sex, or self-esteem? Comparing the value of self-esteem boosts with other pleasant rewards. *Journal of Personality, 79,* 993–1012. (p. 503)

Bushman, B. J., Ridge, R. D., Das, E., Key, C. W., & Busath, G. L. (2007). When God sanctions killing: Effects of scriptural violence on aggression. *Psychological Science, 18,* 204–207. (p. 173)

Busnel, M. C., Granier-Deferre, C., & Lecanuet, J. P. (1992, October). Fetal audition. *Annals of the New York Academy of Sciences, 662,* 118–134. (p. 123)

Buss, A. H. (1989). Personality as traits. *American Psychologist, 44,* 1378–1388. (p. 512)

Buss, D. M. (1994). The strategies of human mating: People worldwide are attracted to the same qualities in the opposite sex. *American Scientist, 82,* 238–249. (p. 194)

Buss, D. M. (1995). Evolutionary psychology: A new paradigm for psychological science. *Psychological Inquiry, 6,* 1–30. (p. 193)

Buss, D. M. (2008). *Female sexual psychology.* Edge.org. Retrieved from http://edge.org/q2008/q08_12.html#buss (p. 185)

Busteed, B. (2012, August 27). College grads need to interview the job. *Huffington Post.* Retrieved from http://www.huffingtonpost.com/brandon-busteed/job-interview-tips_b_1822109.html (p. B-11)

Buster, J. E., Kingsberg, S. A., Aguirre, O., Brown, C., Breaux, J. G., Buch, A., . . . Casson, P. (2005). Testosterone patch for low sexual desire in surgically menopausal women: A randomized trial. *Obstetrics and Gynecology, 105,* 944–952. (p. 181)

Butler, A., Oruc, I., Fox, C. J., & Barton, J. J. S. (2008). Factors contributing to the adaptation aftereffects of facial expression. *Brain Research, 1191,* 116–126. (p. 205)

Butler, R. A. (1954, February). Curiosity in monkeys. *Scientific American,* pp. 70–75. (p. 367)

Butts, M. M., Casper, W. J., & Yang, T. S. (2013). How important are work–family support policies? A meta-analytic investigation of their effects on employee outcomes. *Journal of Applied Psychology, 98,* 1–25. (p. B-12)

Buxton, O. M., Cain, S. W., O'Connor, S. P., Porter, J. H., Duffy, J. F., Wang, W., . . . Shea, S. A. (2012). Adverse metabolic consequences in humans of prolonged sleep restriction combined with circadian disruption. *Science Translational Medicine, 4,* 129–143. (p. 95)

Byck, R., & Van Dyke, C. (1982, March). Cocaine. *Scientific American,* pp. 128–141. (p. 110)

Byers-Heinlein, K., Burns, T. C., & Werker, J. F. (2010). The roots of bilingualism in newborns. *Psychological Science, 21,* 343–348. (p. 124)

Byrne, D. (1971). *The attraction paradigm.* New York: Academic Press. (p. 479)

Byrne, D. (1982). Predicting human sexual behavior. In A. G. Kraut (Ed.), *The G. Stanley Hall Lecture Series* (Vol. 2, pp. 211–254). Washington, DC: American Psychological Association. (pp. 182, 250)

Byrne, R. W. (1991, May/June). Brute intellect. *The Sciences,* pp. 42–47. (p. 335)

Byrne, R. W., Bates, L. A., & Moss, C. J. (2009). Elephant cognition in primate perspective. *Comparative Cognition & Behavior Reviews, 4,* 1–15. (p. 328)

Byrne, R. W., & Whiten, A. (1988). Toward the next generation in data quality: A new survey of primate tactical deception. *Behavioral and Brain Sciences, 11,* 267–273. (p. 20)

Byron, K., & Khazanchi, S. (2011). A meta-analytic investigation of the relationship of state and trait anxiety to performance on figural and verbal creative tasks. *Personality and Social Psychology Bulletin, 37,* 269–283. (p. 325)

C

Cable, D. M., & Gilovich, T. (1998). Looked over or overlooked? Prescreening decisions and postinterview evaluations. *Journal of Personality and Social Psychology, 83,* 501–508. (p. B-5)

Cacioppo, J. T., Cacioppo, S., Gonzaga, G. C., Ogburn, E. L., & VanderWeele, T. J. (2013). Marital satisfaction and break-ups differ across on-line and off-line meeting venues. *Proceedings of the National Academy of Sciences of the United States of America, 110,* 10135–10140. (p. 476)

Cacioppo, J. T., & Hawkley, L. C. (2009). Perceived social isolation and cognition. *Trends in Cognitive Sciences, 13,* 447–454. (p. 371)

Cacioppo, S., Bianchi-Demicheli, F., Frum, C., Pfaus, J. G., & Lewis, J. W. (2012). The common neural bases between sexual desire and love: A multilevel kernel density fMRI analysis. *Journal of Sexual Medicine, 12,* 1048–1054. (p. 196)

Cacioppo, S., Capitanio, J. P., & Cacioppo, J. T. (2014). Toward a neurology of loneliness. *Psychological Bulletin, 140,* 1464–1504. (p. 424)

Caddick, A., & Porter, L. E. (2012). Exploring a model of professionalism in multiple perpetrator violent crime in the UK. *Criminological and Criminal Justice, 12,* 61–82. (p. 173)

Cain, S. (2012). *Quiet: The power of introverts in a world that can't stop talking.* New York: Crown. (p. 507)

Calati, R., De Ronchi, D., Bellini, M., & Serretti, A. (2011). The 5-HTTLPR polymorphism and eating disorders: A meta-analysis. *International Journal of Eating Disorders, 44,* 191–199. (p. 566)

Caldwell, J. A. (2012). Crew schedules, sleep deprivation, and aviation performance. *Current Directions in Psychological Science, 21,* 85–89. (p. 95)

Cale, E. M., & Lilienfeld, S. O. (2002). Sex differences in psychopathy and antisocial personality disorder: A review and integration. *Clinical Psychology Review, 22,* 1179–1207. (p. 563)

Call, K. T., Riedel, A. A., Hein, K., McLoyd, V., Petersen, A., & Kipke, M. (2002). Adolescent health and well-being in the twenty-first century: A global perspective. *Journal of Research on Adolescence, 12,* 69–98. (p. 186)

Callaghan, T., Rochat, P., Lillard, A., Claux, M. L., Odden, H., Itakura, S., . . . Singh, S. (2005). Synchrony in the onset of mental-state reasoning. *Psychological Science, 16,* 378–384. (p. 133)

Callan, M. J., Shead, N. W., & Olson, J. M. (2011). Personal relative deprivation, delay discounting, and gambling. *Journal of Personality and Social Psychology, 101,* 955–973. (p. 152)

Calvin, C. M., Deary, I. J., Webbink, D., Smith, P., Fernandes, C., Lee, S. H., . . . Visscher, P. M. (2012). Multivariate genetic analyses of cognition and academic achievement from two population samples of 174,000 and 166,000 school children. *Behavior Genetics, 42,* 699–710. (p. 354)

Calvo-Merino, B., Glaser, D. E., Grèzes, J., Passingham, R. E., & Haggard, P. (2004). Action observation and acquired motor skills: An fMRI study with expert dancers. *Cerebral Cortex, 15,* 1243–1249. (p. 339)

Camerer, C. F., Loewenstein, G., & Weber, M. (1989). The curse of knowledge in economic settings: An experimental analysis. *Journal of Political Economy, 97,* 1232–1254. (p. B-15)

Cameron, L., & Rutland, A. (2006). Extended contact through story reading in school: Reducing children's prejudice toward the disabled. *Journal of Social Issues, 62,* 469–488. (p. 486)

Camp, J. P., Skeem, J. L., Barchard, K., Lilienfeld, S. O., & Poythress, N. G. (2013). Psychopathic predators? Getting specific about the relation between psychopathy and violence. *Journal of Consulting and Clinical Psychology, 81,* 467–480. (p. 563)

Campbell, A. (2010). Oxytocin and human social behavior. *Personality and Social Psychology Review, 14,* 281–285. (p. 410)

Campbell, D. T. (1975). On the conflicts between biological and social evolution and between psychology and moral tradition. *American Psychologist, 30,* 1103–1126. (p. 434)

Campbell, D. T., & Specht, J. C. (1985). Altruism: Biology, culture, and religion. *Journal of Social and Clinical Psychology, 3,* 33–42. (p. 503)

Campbell, L., & Marshall, T. (2011). Anxious attachment and relationship processes: An interactionist perspective. *Journal of Personality, 79,* 1219–1249. (p. 513)

Campbell, M. W., & de Waal, F. B. M. (2011). Ingroup-outgroup bias in contagious yawning by chimpanzees supports link to empathy. *PLOS ONE, 6*(4), e18283. doi:10.1371/journal.pone.0018283 (p. 466)

Campbell, S. (1986). *The Loch Ness Monster: The evidence.* Wellingborough, England: Aquarian Press. (p. 206)

Camperio-Ciani, A., Corna, F., & Capiluppi, C. (2004). Evidence for maternally inherited factors favouring male homosexuality and promoting female fecundity. *Proceedings of the Royal Society of London: Series B, 271,* 2217–2221. (p. 190)

Camperio-Ciani, A., Lemmola, F., & Blecher, S. R. (2009). Genetic factors increase fecundity in female maternal relatives of bisexual men as in homosexuals. *Journal of Sexual Medicine, 6,* 449–455. (p. 190)

Camperio-Ciani, A., & Pellizzari, E. (2012). Fecundity of paternal and maternal non-parental female relatives of homosexual and heterosexual men. *PLOS ONE, 7*(12), e51088. doi:10.1371/journal.pone.0051088 (p. 190)

Campitelli, G., & Gobet, F. (2011). Deliberate practice: Necessary but not sufficient. *Current Directions in Psychological Science, 20,* 280–285. (p. 344)

Campos, J. J., Bertenthal, B. I., & Kermoian, R. (1992). Early experience and emotional development: The emergence of wariness and heights. *Psychological Science, 3,* 61–64. (p. 218)

Canetta, S., Sourander, A., Surcel, H., Hinkka-Yli-Salomäki, S., Leiviskä, J., Kellendonk, C., . . . Brown, A. S. (2014). Elevated maternal C-reactive protein and increased risk of schizophrenia in a national birth cohort. *American Journal of Psychiatry, 171,* 960–968. (p. 559)

Canli, T. (2008, February/March). The character code. *Scientific American Mind,* pp. 53–57. (p. 542)

Canli, T., Desmond, J. E., Zhao, Z., & Gabrieli, J. D. E. (2002). Sex differences in the neural basis of emotional memories. *Proceedings of the National Academy of Sciences of the United States of America, 99,* 10789–10794. (p. 398)

Cannon, W. B. (1929). *Bodily changes in pain, hunger, fear, and rage.* New York: Branford. (pp. 379, 409)

Cannon, W. B., & Washburn, A. L. (1912). An explanation of hunger. *American Journal of Physiology, 29,* 441–454. (p. 378)

Cantor, N., & Kihlstrom, J. F. (1987). *Personality and social intelligence.* Englewood Cliffs, NJ: Prentice-Hall. (p. 344)

Cantril, H., & Bumstead, C. H. (1960). *Reflections on the human venture.* New York: New York University Press. (p. 460)

Caplan, N., Choy, M. H., & Whitmore, J. K. (1992, February). Indochinese refugee families and academic achievement. *Scientific American,* pp. 36–42. (p. 155)

Caprariello, P. A., & Reis, H. T. (2013). To do, to have, or to share? Valuing experiences over material possessions depends on the involvement of others. *Journal of Personality and Social Psychology, 104,* 199–215. (p. 437)

Carey, B. (2007, September 4). Bipolar illness soars as a diagnosis for the young. *The New York Times.* Retrieved from http://www.nytimes.com/2007/09/04/health/04psych.html?_r=0 (p. 547)

Carey, B. (2009, November 27). Surgery for mental ills offers both hope and risk. *The New York Times.* Retrieved from http://www.nytimes.com/2009/11/27/health/research/27brain.html (p. 600)

Carey, B. (2010, April 56). Seeking emotional clues without facial cues. *The New York Times.* Retrieved from http://www.nytimes.com/2010/04/06/health/06mind.html?pagewanted=all&_r=0 (p. 402)

Carey, B. (2011, February 14). Wariness on surgery of the mind. *The New York Times.* Retrieved from http://www.nytimes.com/2011/02/15/health/15brain.html (p. 600)

Carey, G. (1990). Genes, fears, phobias, and phobic disorders. *Journal of Counseling and Development, 68,* 628–632. (p. 542)

Carli, L. L., & Leonard, J. B. (1989). The effect of hindsight on victim derogation. *Journal of Social and Clinical Psychology, 8,* 331–343. (p. 468)

Carlson, C. L. (2000). ADHD is overdiagnosed. In R. L. Atkinson, R. C. Atkinson, E. E. Smith, D. J. Bem, & S. Nolen-Hoeksema (Eds.), *Hilgard's introduction to psychology* (13th ed.). Fort Worth: Harcourt. (p. 532)

Carlson, M., Charlin, V., & Miller, N. (1988). Positive mood and helping behavior: A test of six hypotheses. *Journal of Personality and Social Psychology, 55,* 211–229. (p. 483)

Carmeli, A., Ben-Hador, B., Waldman, D. A., & Rupp, D. E. (2009). How leaders cultivate social capital and nurture employee vigor: Implications for job performance. *Journal of Applied Psychology, 94,* 1553–1561. (p. B-12)

Carnahan, T., & McFarland, S. (2007). Revisiting the Stanford Prison Experiment: Could participant self-selection have led to the cruelty? *Personality and Social Psychology Bulletin, 33,* 603–614. (p. 446)

Caroll, H. (2013, October). Teen fashion model Georgina got so thin her organs were failing. But fashion designers still queued up to book her. Now she's telling her story to shame the whole industry. *The Daily Mail.* http://www.dailymail.co.uk/femail/article-2442084/Anorexic-model-Georgina-Wilkin-organs-failing-designers-booked-her.html (p. 566)

Carpenter, C. J. (2012). Narcissism on Facebook: Self-promotional and antisocial behavior. *Personality and Individual Differences, 52,* 482–486. (p. 374)

Carpusor, A., & Loges, W. E. (2006). Rental discrimination and ethnicity in names. *Journal of Applied Social Psychology, 36,* 934–952. (p. 25)

Carragan, R. C., & Dweck, C. S. (2014). Rethinking natural altruism: Simple reciprocal interactions trigger children's benevolence. *Proceedings of the National Academy of Sciences of the United States of America, 111,* 17071–17074. (p. 150)

Carroll, D., Davey Smith, G., & Bennett, P. (1994). Health and socio-economic status. *The Psychologist, 7,* 122–125. (p. 420)

Carroll, J. M., & Russell, J. A. (1996). Do facial expressions signal specific emotions? Judging emotion from the face in context. *Journal of Personality and Social Psychology, 70,* 205–218. (p. 400)

Carskadon, M. (2002). Adolescent sleep patterns: Biological, social, and psychological influences. New York: Cambridge University Press. (p. 95)

Carstensen, L. L. (2011). *A long bright future: Happiness, health and financial security in an age of increased longevity.* New York: PublicAffairs. (p. 162)

Carstensen, L. L., & Mikels, J. A. (2005). At the intersection of emotion and cognition: Aging and the positivity effect. *Current Directions in Psychological Science, 14,* 117–121. (p. 349)

Carstensen, L. L., Turan, B., Scheibe, S., Ram, N., Ersner-Hershfield, H., Samanez-Larkin, G. R., . . . Nesselroade, J. R. (2011). Emotional experience improves with age: Evidence based on over 10 years of experience sampling. *Psychology and Aging, 26,* 21–33. (p. 166)

Carter, T. J., & Gilovich, T. (2010). The relative relativity of material and experiential purchases. *Journal of Personality and Social Psychology, 98,* 146–159. (p. 437)

Caruso, E. M., Vohs, K. D., Baxter, B., & Waytz, A. (2013). Mere exposure to money increases endorsement of free-market systems and social inequality. *Journal of Experimental Psychology: General, 142,* 301–306. (p. 298)

Carver, C. S., Johnson, S. L., & Joormann, J. (2008). Serotonergic function, two-mode models of self-regulation, and vulnerability to depression: What depression has in common with impulsive aggression. *Psychological Bulletin, 134,* 912–943. (p. 549)

Carver, C. S., Scheier, M. F., & Segerstrom, S. C. (2010). Optimism. *Clinical Psychology Review, 30,* 879–889. (p. 422)

CASA. (2003). *The formative years: Pathways to substance abuse among girls and young women ages 8–22.* National Center on Addiction and Substance Use at Columbia University. Retrieved from http://www.casacolumbia.org/addiction-research/reports/formative-years-pathways-substance-abuse-among-girls-and-young-women-ages (pp. 106, 115)

Casey, B. J., & Caudle, K. (2013). The teenage brain: Self-control. *Current Directions in Psychological Science, 22,* 82–87. (p. 148)

Casey, B. J., Getz, S., & Galvan, A. (2008). The adolescent brain. *Developmental Review, 28,* 62–77. (p. 148)

Casey, B. J., Somerville, L. H., Gotlib, I. H., Ayduk, O., Franklin, N. T., Askren, M. K., . . . Shoda, Y. (2011). Behavioral and neural correlates of delay of gratification 40 years later. *Proceedings of the National Academy of Sciences of the United States of America, 108,* 14998–15003. (p. 151)

Cash, T., & Janda, L. H. (1984, December). The eye of the beholder. *Psychology Today,* pp. 46–52. (p. 477)

Caspi, A. (2000). The child is father of the man: Personality continuities from childhood to adulthood. *Journal of Personality and Social Psychology, 78,* 158–172. (p. 141)

Caspi, A., McClay, J., Moffitt, T., Mill, J., Martin, J., Craig, I. W., . . . Poulton, R. (2002). Role of genotype in the cycle of violence in maltreated children. *Science, 297,* 851–854. (p. 514)

Caspi, A., Moffitt, T. E., Newman, D. L., & Silva, P. A. (1996). Behavioral observations at age 3 years predict adult psychiatric disorders: Longitudinal evidence from a birth cohort. *Archives of General Psychiatry, 53,* 1033–1039. (p. 564)

Cassidy, J., & Shaver, P. R. (1999). *Handbook of attachment: Theory, research, and clinical applications.* New York: Guilford Press. (p. 139)

Castillo, R. J. (1997). *Culture and mental illness: A client-centered approach.* Pacific Grove, CA: Brooks/Cole. (p. 530)

Castonguay, L. G., Boswell, J. F., Constantino, M. J., Goldfried, M. R., & Hill, C. E. (2010). Training implications of harmful effects of psychological treatments. *American Psychologist, 65,* 34–49. (p. 587)

Cattell, R. B. (1963). Theory of fluid and crystallized intelligence: A critical experiment. *Journal of Educational Psychology, 54,* 1–22. (p. 349)

Cavalli-Sforza, L., Menozzi, P., & Piazza, A. (1994). *The history and geography of human genes.* Princeton, NJ: Princeton University Press. (p. 358)

Cavigelli, S. A., & McClintock, M. K. (2003). Fear of novelty in infant rats predicts adult corticosterone dynamics and an early death. *Proceedings of the National Academy of Sciences of the United States of America, 100,* 16131–16136. (p. 410)

Cawley, B. D., Keeping, L. M., & Levy, P. E. (1998). Participation in the performance appraisal process and employee reactions: A meta-analytic review of field investigations. *Journal of Applied Psychology, 83,* 615–633. (p. B-12)

CDC. (1992, September 16). *Serious mental illness and disability in the adult household population: United States, 1989* (Advance Data No. 218 from Vital and Health Statistics). Centers for Disease Control and Prevention. Retrieved from http://www.cdc.gov/nchs/data/ad/ad218.pdf (pp. 534–535)

CDC. (2009). *Self-harm, all injury causes, nonfatal injuries and rates per 100,000.* Centers for Disease Control and Prevention. Retrieved from http://webappa.cdc.gov/cgi-bin/broker.exe (p. 554)

CDC. (2011, February). *HIV surveillance report: Vol. 21. Diagnoses of HIV infection and AIDS in the United States and dependent areas, 2009.* Centers for Disease Control and Prevention. Retrieved from http://www.cdc.gov/hiv/pdf/statistics_2009_hiv_surveillance_report_vol_21.pdf (p. 184)

CDC. (2011). *Who's at risk? Tobacco use—smoking.* Centers for Disease Control and Prevention. Retrieved from http://cdc.gov/vitalsigns/TobaccoUse/Smoking/Risk.html (p. 116)

CDC. (2012). *Obesity trends among U.S. adults between 1985 and 2010.* Centers for Disease Control and Prevention. Retrieved from http://www.cdc.gov/obesity/downloads/obesity_trends_2010.ppt (p. 383)

CDC. (2012, May 11). *Suicide rates among persons ages 10 years and older, by race/ethnicity and sex, United States, 2005–2009.* Centers for Disease Control and Prevention. Retrieved from http://www.cdc.gov (p. 553)

CDC. (2014, December). *Depression in the U.S. household population, 2009–2012* (NCHS Data Brief No. 172). Centers for Disease Control and Prevention. Retrieved from http://www.cdc.gov/nchs/data/databriefs/db172.htm (pp. 546, 548)

CDC. (2014). *Pregnant women need a flu shot.* Centers for Disease Control and Prevention. Retrieved from www.cdc.gov/flu/pdf/freeresources/pregnant/flushot_pregnant_factsheet.pdf (p. 559)

CDC. (2014, March 28). Prevalence of autism spectrum disorder among children aged 8 years—Autism and Developmental Disabilities Monitoring Network, 11 sites, United States, 2010. *Morbidity and Mortality Weekly Report, 63*(SS02), 1–21. (p. 136)

CDC. (2015, August 10). *Heart disease facts.* Centers for Disease Control and Prevention. Retrieved from http://www.cdc.gov/heartdisease/facts/htm (p. 414)

Ceci, S. J. (1993, August). *Cognitive and social factors in children's testimony.* Master lecture presented at the 101st Annual Convention of the American Psychological Association, Toronto, Ontario, Canada. (pp. 309, 310)

Ceci, S. J., & Bruck, M. (1993). Child witnesses: Translating research into policy. *Social Policy Report, 7*(3), 1–30. (p. 309)

Ceci, S. J., & Bruck, M. (1995). *Jeopardy in the courtroom: A scientific analysis of children's testimony.* Washington, DC: American Psychological Association. (p. 309)

Ceci, S. J., Ginther, D. K., Kahn, S., & Williams, W. M. (2014). Women in academic science: A changing landscape. *Psychological Science in the Public Interest, 15,* 75–141. (p. 178)

Ceci, S. J., Huffman, M. L. C., Smith, E., & Loftus, E. F. (1994). Repeatedly thinking about a non-event: Source misattributions among preschoolers. *Consciousness and Cognition, 3,* 388–407. (p. 310)

Ceci, S. J., & Williams, W. M. (1997). Schooling, intelligence, and income. *American Psychologist, 52,* 1051–1058. (p. 356)

Ceci, S. J., & Williams, W. M. (2009). *The mathematics of sex: How biology and society conspire to limit talented women and girls.* New York: Oxford University Press. (p. 356)

Centerwall, B. S. (1989). Exposure to television as a risk factor for violence. *American Journal of Epidemiology, 129,* 643–652. (p. 277)

Cepeda, N. J., Pashler, H., Vul, E., Wixted, J. T., & Rohrer, D. (2006). Distributed practice in verbal recall tasks: A review and quantitative synthesis. *Psychological Bulletin, 132,* 354–380. (p. 289)

Cepeda, N. J., Vul, E., Rohrer, D., Wixed, J. T., & Pashler, H. (2008). Spacing effects in learning: A temporal ridgeline of optimal retention. *Psychological Science, 19,* 1095–1102. (p. 289)

Cerasoli, C. P., Nicklin, J. M., & Ford, M. T. (2014). Intrinsic motivation and extrinsic incentives jointly predict performance: A 40-year meta-analysis. *Psychological Bulletin, 140,* 980–1008. (p. B-1)

Cerella, J. (1985). Information processing rates in the elderly. *Psychological Bulletin, 98,* 67–83. (p. 159)

Cerny, J. A., & Janssen, E. (2011). Patterns of sexual arousal in homosexual, bisexual, and heterosexual men. *Archives of Sexual Behavior, 40,* 687–697. (p. 188)

CFI. (2003, July). *International developments: Report.* Amherst, NY: Center for Inquiry. (p. 242)

Chabris, C. F., & Simons, D. (2010). *The invisible gorilla: And other ways our intuitions deceive us.* New York: Crown. (p. 84)

Chajut, E., Caspi, A., Chen, R., Hod, M., & Ariely, D. (2014). In pain thou shalt bring forth children: The peak-and-end rule in recall of labor pain. *Psychological Science, 25,* 2266–2271. (p. 233)

Chambers, E. S., Bridge, M. W., & Jones, D. A. (2009). Carbohydrate sensing in the human mouth: Effects on exercise performance and brain activity. *Journal of Physiology, 587,* 1779–1794. (p. 421)

Chambless, D. L., Baker, M. J., Baucom, D. H., Beutler, L. E., Calhoun, K. S., Crits-Christoph, P., . . . Woody, S. R. (1997, Fall). Update on empirically validated therapies, II. *The Clinical Psychologist,* pp. 3–16. (p. 588)

Chamove, A. S. (1980). Nongenetic induction of acquired levels of aggression. *Journal of Abnormal Psychology, 89,* 469–488. (p. 276)

Champagne, F. A. (2010). Early adversity and developmental outcomes: Interaction between genetics, epigenetics, and social experiences across the life span. *Perspectives on Psychological Science, 5,* 564–574. (p. 72)

Champagne, F. A., Francis, D. D., Mar, A., & Meaney, M. J. (2003). Variations in maternal care in the rat as a mediating influence for the effects of environment on development. *Physiology & Behavior, 79,* 359–371. (p. 72)

Champagne, F. A., & Mashoodh, R. (2009). Genes in context: Gene–environment interplay and the origins of individual differences in behavior. *Current Directions in Psychological Science, 18,* 127–131. (p. 72)

Chance News. (1997, November 25). *More on the frequency of letters in texts.* Retrieved from Dart.Chance@Dartmouth.edu (p. 21)

Chandler, J. J., & Pronin, E. (2012). Fast thought speed induces risk taking. *Psychological Science, 23,* 370–374. (p. 546)

Chandler, J., & Schwarz, N. (2009). How extending your middle finger affects your perception of others: Learned movements influence concept accessibility. *Journal of Experimental Social Psychology, 45,* 123–128. (p. 402)

Chandra, A., Mosher, W. D., & Copen, C. (2011, March 3). *Sexual behavior, sexual attraction, and sexual identity in the United States: Data from the 2006–2008 National Survey of Family Growth* (National Health Statistics Report No. 36). Retrieved from http://www.cdc.gov/nchs/data/nhsr/nhsr036.pdf (p. 188)

Chang, Y.-T., Chen, Y.-C., Hayter, M., & Lin, M.-L. (2009). Menstrual and menarche experience among pubescent female students in Taiwan: Implications for health education and promotion service. *Journal of Clinical Nursing, 18,* 2040–2048. (p. 176)

Chaplin, T. M., & Aldao, A. (2013). Gender differences in emotion expression in children: A meta-analytic review. *Psychological Bulletin, 139,* 735–765. (p. 397)

Chaplin, W. F., Phillips, J. B., Brown, J. D., Clanton, N. R., & Stein, J. L. (2000). Handshaking, gender, personality, and first impressions. *Journal of Personality and Social Psychology, 79,* 110–117. (p. 396)

Charles, S. T., Piazza, J. R., Mogle, J., Sliwinski, M. J., & Almeida, D. M. (2013). The wear and tear of daily stressors on mental health. *Psychological Science, 24,* 733–741. (p. 548)

Charness, N., & Boot, W. R. (2009). Aging and information technology use. *Current Directions in Psychological Science, 18,* 253–258. (p. 349)

Charpak, G., & Broch, H. (2004). *Debunked! ESP, telekinesis, and other pseudoscience.* Baltimore: Johns Hopkins University Press. (p. 241)

Chartrand, T. L., & Bargh, J. A. (1999). The chameleon effect: The perception–behavior link and social interaction. *Journal of Personality and Social Psychology, 76,* 893–910. (p. 449)

Chassy, P., & Gobet, F. (2011). A hypothesis about the biological basis of expert intuition. *Review of General Psychology, 15,* 198–212. (p. 323)

Chatard, A., & Selimbegović, L. (2011). When self-destructive thoughts flash through the mind: Failure to meet standards affects the accessibility of suicide-related thoughts. *Journal of Personality and Social Psychology, 100,* 587–605. (p. 553)

Chater, N., Reali, F., & Christiansen, M. H. (2009). Restrictions on biological adaptation in language evolution. *Proceedings of the National Academy of Sciences of the United States of America, 106,* 1015–1020. (p. 330)

Cheek, J. M., & Melchior, L. A. (1990). Shyness, self-esteem, and self-consciousness. In H. Leitenberg (Ed.), *Handbook of social and evaluation anxiety* (pp. 47–82). New York: Plenum Press. (p. 522)

Chein, J., Albert, D., O'Brien, L., Uckert, K., & Steinberg, L. (2011). Peers increase adolescent risk taking by enhancing activity in the brain's reward circuitry. *Developmental Science, 14,* F1–F10. (p. 154)

Chein, J. M., & Schneider, W. (2012). The brain's learning and control architecture. *Current Directions in Psychological Science, 21,* 78–84. (p. 59)

Cheit, R. E. (1998). Consider this, skeptics of recovered memory. *Ethics & Behavior, 8,* 141–160. (p. 499)

Chen, A. W., Kazanjian, A., & Wong, H. (2009). Why do Chinese Canadians not consult mental health services: Health status, language or culture? *Transcultural Psychiatry, 46,* 623–640. (pp. 590–591)

Chen, E. (2004). Why socioeconomic status affects the health of children: A psychosocial perspective. *Current Directions in Psychological Science, 13,* 112–115. (p. 420)

Chen, H. (2012). *Dark web: Exploring and data mining the dark side of the web.* New York: Springer. (p. 458)

Chen, S. H., Kennedy, M., & Zhou, Q. (2012). Parents' expression and discussion of emotion in the multilingual family: Does language matter? *Perspectives on Psychological Science, 7,* 365–383. (p. 337)

Chen, S. X., & Bond, M. H. (2010). Two languages, two personalities? Examining language effects on the expression of personality in a bilingual context. *Personality and Social Psychology Bulletin, 36,* 1514–1528. (p. 337)

Chen, S.-Y., & Fu, Y.-C. (2008). Internet use and academic achievement: Gender differences in early adolescence. *Adolescence, 44,* 797–812. (p. 374)

Cheon, B. K., Im, D.-M., Harada, T., Kim, J.-S., Mathur, V. A., Scimeca, J. M., . . . Chiao, J. Y. (2013). Cultural modulation of the neural correlates of emotional pain perception: The role of other-focusedness. *Neuropsychologia, 51,* 1177–1186. (p. 523)

Cherniss, C. (2010a). Emotional intelligence: New insights and further clarifications. *Industrial and Organizational Psychology, 3,* 183–191. (p. 345)

Cherniss, C. (2010b). Emotional intelligence: Toward clarification of a concept. *Industrial and Organizational Psychology, 3,* 110–126. (p. 345)

Chess, S., & Thomas, A. (1987). *Know your child: An authoritative guide for today's parents.* New York: Basic Books. (p. 140)

Cheung, B. Y., Chudek, M., & Heine, S. J. (2011). Evidence for a sensitive period for acculturation: Younger immigrants report acculturating at a faster rate. *Psychological Science, 22,* 147–152. (p. 333)

Cheung, F., & Lucas, R. E. (2015). Income inequality is associated with stronger social comparison effects: The effect of relative income on life satisfaction. *Journal of Personality and Social Psychology.* Advance online publication. doi:10.1037/pspp0000059 (p. 435)

Chi, R. P., & Snyder, A. W. (2011). Facilitate insight by non-invasive brain stimulation. *PLOS ONE, 6*(2), e16655. doi:10.1371/journal.pone.0016655 (p. 318)

Chiao, J. Y., Cheon, B. K., Pornpattananangkul, N., Mrazek, A. J., & Blizinsky, K. D. (2013). Cultural neuroscience: Progress and promise. *Psychological Inquiry, 24,* 1–19. (p. 523)

Chida, Y., & Hamer, M. (2008). Chronic psychosocial factors and acute physiological responses to laboratory-induced stress in healthy populations: A quantitative review of 30 years of investigations. *Psychological Bulletin, 134,* 829–885. (p. 414)

Chida, Y., Hamer, M., Wardle, J., & Steptoe, A. (2008). Do stress-related psychosocial factors contribute to cancer incidence and survival? *Nature Clinical Practice Oncology, 5,* 466–475. (p. 413)

Chida, Y., & Steptoe, A. (2009). The association of anger and hostility with future coronary heart disease: A meta-analytic review of prospective evidence. *Journal of the American College of Cardiology, 17,* 936–946. (p. 414)

Chida, Y., Steptoe, A., & Powell, L. H. (2009). Religiosity/spirituality and mortality. *Psychotherapy and Psychosomatics, 78,* 81–90. (p. 431)

Chida, Y., & Vedhara, K. (2009). Adverse psychosocial factors predict poorer prognosis in HIV disease: A meta-analytic review of prospective investigations. *Brain, Behavior, and Immunity, 2*(4), 434–445. (p. 413)

Child Trends. (2013). *Attitudes toward spanking.* Child Trends Data Bank. Retrieved from http://www.childtrends.org/?indicators=attitudes-toward-spanking (p. 261)

Chiles, J. A., Lambert, M. J., & Hatch, A. L. (1999). The impact of psychological interventions on medical cost offset: A meta-analytic review. *Clinical Psychology: Science and Practice, 6,* 204–220. (p. 586)

Chivers, M. L. (2005). A brief review and discussion of sex differences in the specificity of sexual arousal. *Sexual and Relationship Therapy, 20,* 377–390. (p. 188)

Chivers, M. L., Seto, M. C., Lalumière, M. L., Laan, E., & Grimbos, T. (2010). Agreement of self-reported and genital measures of sexual arousal in men and women: A meta-analysis. *Archives of Sexual Behavior, 39,* 5–56. (p. 185)

Choi, C. Q. (2008, March). Do you need only half your brain? *Scientific American,* p. 104. (p. 61)

Chomsky, N. (1972). *Language and mind.* New York: Harcourt Brace. (p. 335)

Chopik, W. J., & Edelstein, R. S. (2014). Age differences in romantic attachment around the world. *Social Psychological and Personality Science, 5,* 892–900. (p. 142)

Chopik, W. J., Edelstein, R. S., & Fraley, R. C. (2013). From the cradle to the grave: Age differences in attachment from early adulthood to old age. *Journal of Personality, 81,* 171–183. (p. 166)

Christakis, D. A., Garrison, M. M., Herrenkohl, T., Haggerty, K., Rivara, K. P., Zhou, C., & Liekweg, K. (2013). Modifying media content for preschool children: A randomized control trial. *Pediatrics, 131,* 431–438. (p. 277)

Christakis, N. A., & Fowler, J. H. (2007). The spread of obesity in a large social network over 32 years. *New England Journal of Medicine, 357,* 370–379. (p. 384)

Christakis, N. A., & Fowler, J. H. (2008). The collective dynamics of smoking in a large social network. *New England Journal of Medicine, 358,* 2249–2258. (p. 116)

Christakis, N. A., & Fowler, J. H. (2009). *Connected: The surprising power of social networks and how they shape our lives.* New York: Little, Brown. (p. 425)

Christensen, A., & Jacobson, N. S. (1994). Who (or what) can do psychotherapy: The status and challenge of nonprofessional therapies. *Psychological Science, 5,* 8–14. (p. 589)

Christophersen, E. R., & Edwards, K. J. (1992). Treatment of elimination disorders: State of the art 1991. *Applied and Preventive Psychology, 1,* 15–22. (p. 574)

Chu, P. S., Saucier, D. A., & Hafner, E. (2010). Meta-analysis of the relationships between social support and well-being in children and adolescents. *Journal of Social and Clinical Psychology, 29,* 624–645. (p. 423)

Chua, H. F., Boland, J. E., & Nisbett, R. E. (2005). Cultural variation in eye movements during scene perception. *Proceedings of the National Academy of Sciences of the United States of America, 102*, 12629–12633. (p. 442)

Chugani, H. T., & Phelps, M. E. (1986). Maturational changes in cerebral function in infants determined by 18FDG positron emission tomography. *Science, 231*, 840–843. (p. 127)

Chung, J. M., Robins, R. W., Trzesniewski, K. H., Noftle, E. E., Roberts, B. W., & Widaman, K. F. (2014). Continuity and change in self-esteem during emerging adulthood. *Journal of Personality and Social Psychology, 106*, 469–483. (p. 153)

Churchland, P. S. (2013). *Touching a nerve: The self as brain*. New York: Norton. (p. 112)

CIA. (2014). Sex ratio. In *The world factbook*. Central Intelligence Agency. Retrieved from https://www.cia.gov/ (p. 464)

Cialdini, R. B. (1993). *Influence: Science and practice* (3rd ed.). New York: HarperCollins. (p. 445)

Cialdini, R. B., & Richardson, K. D. (1980). Two indirect tactics of image management: Basking and blasting. *Journal of Personality and Social Psychology, 39*, 406–415. (p. 466)

Ciarrochi, J., Forgas, J. P., & Mayer, J. D. (2006). *Emotional intelligence in everyday life* (2nd ed.). New York: Psychology Press. (p. 345)

Cin, S. D., Gibson, B., Zanna, M. P., Shumate, R., & Fong, G. T. (2007). Smoking in movies, implicit associations of smoking with the self, and intentions to smoke. *Psychological Science, 18*, 559–563. (p. 115)

Cincotta, A. L., Gehrman, P., Gooneratne, N. S., & Baime, M. J. (2011). The effects of a mindfulness-based stress reduction programme on pre-sleep cognitive arousal and insomnia symptoms: A pilot study. *Stress and Health, 27*, e299–e305. (p. 428)

Clack, B., Dixon, J., & Tredoux, C. (2005). Eating together apart: Patterns of segregation in a multi-ethnic cafeteria. *Journal of Community and Applied Social Psychology, 15*, 1–16. (p. 486)

Claidière, N., & Whiten, A. (2012). Integrating the study of conformity and culture in humans and nonhuman animals. *Psychological Bulletin, 138*, 126–145. (pp. 328, 451)

Clancy, S. A. (2005). *Abducted: How people come to believe they were kidnapped by aliens*. Cambridge, MA: Harvard University Press. (p. 89)

Clancy, S. A. (2010). *The trauma myth: The truth about the sexual abuse of children—and its aftermath*. New York: Basic Books. (p. 143)

Clark, A., Seidler, A., & Miller, M. (2001). Inverse association between sense of humor and coronary heart disease. *International Journal of Cardiology, 80*, 87–88. (p. 424)

Clark, C. J., Luguri, J. B., Ditto, P. H., Knobe, J., Shariff, A. F., & Baumeister, R. F. (2014). Free to punish: A motivated account of free will belief. *Journal of Personality and Social Psychology, 106*, 501–513. (p. 421)

Clark, K. B., & Clark, M. P. (1947). Racial identification and preference in Negro children. In T. M. Newcomb & E. L. Hartley (Eds.), *Readings in social psychology* (pp. 169–178). New York: Holt. (p. 30)

Clark, R. D., III, & Hatfield, E. (1989). Gender differences in willingness to engage in casual sex. *Journal of Psychology and Human Sexuality, 2*, 39–55. (p. 194)

Cleary, A. M. (2008). Recognition memory, familiarity, and déjà vu experiences. *Current Directions in Psychological Science, 17*, 353–357. (p. 309)

Coan, J. A., Schaefer, H. S., & Davidson, R. J. (2006). Lending a hand: Social regulation of the neural response to threat. *Psychological Science, 17*, 1032–1039. (pp. 231, 424)

Coelho, C. M., & Purkis, H. (2009). The origins of specific phobias: Influential theories and current perspectives. *Review of General Psychology, 13*, 335–348. (p. 543)

Coffman, K. B., Coffman, L. C., & Ericson, K. M. M. (2013, October). *The size of the LGBT population and the magnitude of anti-gay sentiment are substantially underestimated* (NBER Working Paper No. 19508). Retrieved from http://www.nber.org/papers/w19508 (p. 188)

Cohen, A. B. (2009). Many forms of culture. *American Psychologist, 64*, 194–204. (pp. 448, 522)

Cohen, D. (1995, June 17). Now we are one, or two, or three. *New Scientist*, pp. 14–15. (p. 562)

Cohen, P. (2007, November 15). Freud is widely taught at universities, except in the psychology department. *The New York Times*. Retrieved from http://www.nytimes.com/2007/11/25/weekinreview/25cohen.html?_r=0 (p. 492)

Cohen, P. (2010, June 11). Long road to adulthood is growing even longer. *The New York Times*. Retrieved from http://www.nytimes.com/2010/06/13/us/13generations.html (p. 157)

Cohen, S. (2004). Social relationships and health. *American Psychologist, 59*, 676–684. (p. 424)

Cohen, S., Alper, C. M., Doyle, W. J., Treanor, J. J., & Turner, R. B. (2006). Positive emotional style predicts resistance to illness after experimental exposure to rhinovirus or influenza A virus. *Psychosomatic Medicine, 68*, 809–815. (p. 412)

Cohen, S., Doyle, W. J., Alper, C. M., Janicki-Deverts, D., & Turner, R. B. (2009). Sleep habits and susceptibility to the common cold. *Archives of Internal Medicine, 169*, 62–67. (p. 95)

Cohen, S., Doyle, W. J., Skoner, D. P., Rabin, B. S., & Gwaltney, J. M., Jr. (1997). Social ties and susceptibility to the common cold. *Journal of the American Medical Association, 277*, 1940–1944. (pp. 420, 424)

Cohen, S., Doyle, W. J., Turner, R., Alper, C. M., & Skoner, D. P. (2003). Sociability and susceptibility to the common cold. *Psychological Science, 14*, 389–395. (p. 412)

Cohen, S., Janicki-Deverts, D., Turner, R. B., & Doyle, W. J. (2015). Does hugging provide stress-buffering social support? A study of susceptibility to upper respiratory infection and illness. *Psychological Science, 26*, 135–147. (p. 425)

Cohen, S., Kaplan, J. R., Cunnick, J. E., Manuck, S. B., & Rabin, B. S. (1992). Chronic social stress, affiliation, and cellular immune response in nonhuman primates. *Psychological Science, 3*, 301–304. (p. 411)

Cohen, S., & Pressman, S. D. (2006). Positive affect and health. *Current Directions in Psychological Science, 15*, 122–125. (p. 412)

Cohen, S., Tyrrell, D. A. J., & Smith, A. P. (1991). Psychological stress and susceptibility to the common cold. *New England Journal of Medicine, 325*, 606–612. (p. 412)

Cohen, T. R., Panter, A. T., Turan, N., Morse, L., & Kim, Y. (2014). Moral character in the workplace. *Journal of Personality and Social Psychology, 107*, 943–963. (p. B-5)

Cohn, D. (2013, February 13). *Love and marriage*. Retrieved from http://www.pewsocialtrends.org/2013/02/13/love-and-marriage/ (p. 164)

Colapinto, J. (2000). *As nature made him: The boy who was raised as a girl*. New York: HarperCollins. (p. 177)

Colarelli, S. M., Spranger, J. L., & Hechanova, M. R. (2006). Women, power, and sex composition in small groups: An evolutionary perspective. *Journal of Organizational Behavior, 27*, 163–184. (p. 173)

Cole, K. C. (1998). *The universe and the teacup: The mathematics of truth and beauty*. New York: Harcourt Brace. (p. 108)

Colen, C. G., & Ramey, D. M. (2014). Is breast truly best? Estimating the effects of breastfeeding on long-term child health and well-being in the United States using sibling comparisons. *Social Science & Medicine, 109*, 55–65. (p. 23)

Coley, R. L., Medeiros, B. L., & Schindler, H. (2008). Using sibling differences to estimate effects of parenting on adolescent sexual risk behaviors. *Journal of Adolescent Health, 43*, 133–140. (p. 187)

Collier, K. L., Bos, H. M. W., & Sandfort, T. G. M. (2012). Intergroup contact, attitudes toward homosexuality, and the role of acceptance of gender non-conformity in young adolescents. *Journal of Adolescence, 35*, 899–907. (p. 486)

Collinger, J. L., Wodlinger, B., Downey, J. E., Wang, W., Tyler-Kabara, E. C., Weber, D. J., . . . Schwartz, A. B. (2013). High-performance neuroprosthetic control by an individual with tetraplegia. *The Lancet, 381*, 557–564. (p. 58)

Collins, F. (2006). *The language of God*. New York: Free Press. (p. 75)

Collins, G. (2009, March 4). The rant list. *The New York Times*. Retrieved from http://www.nytimes.com/2009/03/05/opinion/05collins.html (p. 29)

Collins, N. L., & Miller, L. C. (1994). Self-disclosure and liking: A meta-analytic review. *Psychological Bulletin, 116*, 457–475. (p. 480)

Collins, R. L., Elliott, M. N., Berry, S. H., Danouse, D. E., Kunkel, D., Hunter, S. B., & Miu, A. (2004). Watching sex on television predicts adolescent initiation of sexual behavior. *Pediatrics, 114*, 280–289. (p. 22)

Collins, W. A., Welsh, D. P., & Furman, W. (2009). Adolescent romantic relationships. *Annual Review of Psychology, 60*, 631–652. (p. 153)

Collinson, S. L., MacKay, C. E., James, A. C., Quested, D. J., Phillips, T., Roberts, N., & Crow, T. J. (2003). Brain volume, asymmetry and intellectual impairment in relation to sex in early-onset schizophrenia. *British Journal of Psychiatry, 183*, 114–120. (p. 558)

Collishaw, S., Pickles, A., Natarajan, L., & Maughan, B. (2007, June). *20-year trends in depression and anxiety in England*. Paper presented at the 13th Scientific Meeting on the Brain and the Developing Child, London, England. (p. 548)

Colombo, J. (1982). The critical period concept: Research, methodology, and theoretical issues. *Psychological Bulletin, 91,* 260–275. (p. 139)

Comfort, A. (1992). *The new joy of sex.* New York: Pocket Books. (p. 158)

Confer, J. C., Easton, J. A., Fleischman, D. S., Goetz, C. D., Lewis, D. M. G., Perilloux, C., & Buss, D. M. (2010). Evolutionary psychology: Controversies, questions, prospects, and limitations. *American Psychologist, 65,* 110–126. (p. 195)

Conley, C. S., & Rudolph, K. D. (2009). The emerging sex difference in adolescent depression: Interacting contributions of puberty and peer stress. *Development and Psychopathology, 21,* 593–620. (p. 148)

Conley, K. M. & Lehman, B. J. (2012). Test anxiety and cardiovascular responses to daily academic stressors. *Stress and Health, 28,* 41–50. (p. 414)

Conley, T. D. (2011). Perceived proposer personality characteristics and gender differences in acceptance of casual sex offers. *Journal of Personality and Social Psychology, 100,* 309–329. (p. 195)

Conn, V. S. (2010). Depressive symptom outcomes of physical activity interventions: Meta-analysis findings. *Annals of Behavioral Medicine, 39,* 128–138. (p. 426)

Connor, C. E. (2010). A new viewpoint on faces. *Science, 330,* 764–765. (p. 215)

Connor-Smith, J. K., & Flachsbart, C. (2007). Relations between personality and coping: A meta-analysis. *Journal of Personality and Social Psychology, 93,* 1080–1107. (p. 419)

Consumer Reports. (1995, November). Does therapy help? pp. 734–739. (p. 584)

Conway, A. R. A., Skitka, L. J., Hemmerich, J. A., & Kershaw, T. C. (2009). Flashbulb memory for 11 September 2001. *Applied Cognitive Psychology, 23,* 605–623. (p. 295)

Conway, M. A., Wang, Q., Hanyu, K., & Haque, S. (2005). A cross-cultural investigation of autobiographical memory: On the universality and cultural variation of the reminiscence bump. *Journal of Cross-Cultural Psychology, 36,* 739–749. (p. 160)

Cooke, L. J., Wardle, J., & Gibson, E. L. (2003). Relationship between parental report of food neophobia and everyday food consumption in 2–6-year-old children. *Appetite, 41,* 205–206. (p. 236)

Cooney, G., Gilbert, D. T., & Wilson, T. D. (2014). The unforeseen costs of extraordinary experience. *Psychological Science, 25,* 2259–2265. (p. 433)

Cooper, K. J. (1999, May 1). This time, copycat wave is broader. *The Washington Post.* Retrieved from http://www.washingtonpost.com/wp-srv/national/longterm/juvmurders/stories/copycat050199.htm (p. 449)

Cooper, M. (2010, October 18). From Obama, the tax cut nobody heard of. *The New York Times.* Retrieved from http://www.nytimes.com/2010/10/19/us/politics/19taxes.html?_r=0 (p. 466)

Cooper, W. H., & Withey, M. J. (2009). The strong situation hypothesis. *Personality and Social Psychology Review, 13,* 62–72. (p. 512)

Coopersmith, S. (1967). *The antecedents of self-esteem.* San Francisco: Freeman. (p. 144)

Copeland, W., Shanahan, L., Miller, S., Costello, E. J., Angold, A., & Maughan, B. (2010). Outcomes of early pubertal timing in young women: A prospective population-based study. *American Journal of Psychiatry, 167,* 1218–1225. (p. 148)

Corballis, M. C. (2002). *From hand to mouth: The origins of language.* Princeton, NJ: Princeton University Press. (p. 335)

Corballis, M. C. (2003). From mouth to hand: Gesture, speech, and the evolution of right-handedness. *Behavioral and Brain Sciences, 26,* 199–260. (p. 335)

Corcoran, D. W. J. (1964). The relation between introversion and salivation. *American Journal of Psychology, 77,* 298–300. (p. 507)

Coren, S. (1996). *Sleep thieves: An eye-opening exploration into the science and mysteries of sleep.* New York: Free Press. (pp. 94, 96)

Corey, D. P., García-Añoveros, J., Holt, J. R., Kwan, K. Y., Lin, S.-Y., Vollrath, M. A., . . . Zhang, D.-S. (2004). TRPA1 is a candidate for the mechanosensitive transduction channel of vertebrate hair cells. *Nature, 432,* 723–730. (p. 228)

Corina, D. P. (1998). The processing of sign language: Evidence from aphasia. In B. Stemmer & H. A. Whittaker (Eds.), *Handbook of neurolinguistics* (pp. 313–329). San Diego, CA: Academic Press. (p. 64)

Corina, D. P., Vaid, J., & Bellugi, U. (1992). The linguistic basis of left hemisphere specialization. *Science, 255,* 1258–1260. (p. 64)

Corkin, S. (2005, September). Quoted in R. Adelson, Lessons from H. M. *Monitor on Psychology,* p. 59. (p. 301)

Corkin, S. (2013). *Permanent present tense: The unforgettable life of the amnesic patient.* New York: Basic Books. (p. 301)

Corneille, O., Huart, J., Becquart, E., & Brédart, S. (2004). When memory shifts toward more typical category exemplars: Accentuation effects in the recollection of ethnically ambiguous faces. *Journal of Personality and Social Psychology, 86,* 236–250. (p. 316)

Cornette, M. M., deRoon-Cassini, T. A., Fosco, G. M., Holloway, R. L., Clark, D. C., & Joiner, T. E. (2009). Application of an interpersonal-psychological model of suicidal behavior to physicians and medical trainees. *Archives of Suicide Research, 13,* 1–14. (p. 553)

Cornier, M.-A. (2011). Is your brain to blame for weight regain? *Physiology & Behavior, 104,* 608–612. (p. 383)

Cornil, Y., & Chandon, P. (2013). From fan to fat? Vicarious losing increases unhealthy eating, but self-affirmation is an effective remedy. *Psychological Science, 24,* 1936–1946. (p. 381)

Correll, J., Park, B., Judd, C. M., & Wittenbrink, B. (2002). The police officer's dilemma: Using ethnicity to disambiguate potentially threatening individuals. *Journal of Personality and Social Psychology, 83,* 1314–1329. (p. 463)

Correll, J., Park, B., Judd, C. M., Wittenbrink, B., Sadler, M. S., & Keesee, T. (2007). Across the thin blue line: Police officers and racial bias in the decision to shoot. *Journal of Personality and Social Psychology, 92,* 1006–1023. (p. 463)

Corrigan, P. W. (2014). Can there be false hope in recovery? *British Journal of Psychiatry, 205,* 423–424. (p. 589)

Corse, A. K., Chou, T., Arulpragasm, A. R., Kaur, N., Deckersbach, T., & Cusin, C. (2013). Deep brain stimulation for obsessive-compulsive disorder. *Psychiatric Annals, 43,* 351–357. (p. 599)

Costa, A., Foucart, A., Hayakawa, S., Aparici, M., Apesteguia, J., Heafner, J., & Keysar, B. (2014). Your morals depend on language. *PLOS ONE, 9*(4), e94842. doi:10.1371/journal.pone.0094842 (p. 337)

Costa, P. T., Jr., & McCrae, R. R. (2011). The five-factor model, five factor theory, and interpersonal psychology. In L. M. Horowitz & S. Strack (Eds.), *Handbook of interpersonal psychology: Theory, research, assessment, and therapeutic interventions* (pp. 91–104). Hoboken, NJ: Wiley. (p. 508)

Costa, P. T., Jr., Terracciano, A., & McCrae, R. R. (2001). Gender differences in personality traits across cultures: Robust and surprising findings. *Journal of Personality and Social Psychology, 81,* 322–331. (p. 397)

Costello, E. J., Compton, S. N., Keeler, G., & Angold, A. (2003). Relationships between poverty and psychopathology: A natural experiment. *Journal of the American Medical Association, 290,* 2023–2029. (pp. 22, 535)

Coughlin, J. F., Mohyde, M., D'Ambrosio, L. A., & Gilbert, J. (2004). *Who drives older driver decisions?* Cambridge, MA: MIT Age Lab. (p. 159)

Couli, J. T., Vidal, F., Nazarian, B., & Macar, F. (2004). Functional anatomy of the attentional modulation of time estimation. *Science, 303,* 1506–1508. (p. B-1)

Courtney, J. G., Longnecker, M. P., Theorell, T., & de Verdier, M. G. (1993). Stressful life events and the risk of colorectal cancer. *Epidemiology, 4,* 407–414. (p. 413)

Covin, R., Ouimet, A. J., Seeds, P. M., & Dozois, D. J. A. (2008). A meta-analysis of CBT for pathological worry among clients with GAD. *Journal of Anxiety Disorders, 22,* 108–116. (p. 581)

Cowan, N. (1988). Evolving conceptions of memory storage, selective attention, and their mutual constraints within the human information-processing system. *Psychological Bulletin, 104,* 163–191. (p. 286)

Cowan, N. (2010). The magical mystery four: How is working memory capacity limited, and why? *Current Directions in Psychological Science, 19,* 51–57. (p. 285)

Cowart, B. J. (1981). Development of taste perception in humans: Sensitivity and preference throughout the life span. *Psychological Bulletin, 90,* 43–73. (p. 236)

Cowart, B. J. (2005, April). Taste, our body's gustatory gatekeeper. *Cerebrum,* pp. 7–22. (p. 236)

Cox, J. J., Reimann, F., Nicholas, A. K., Thornton, G., Roberts, E., Springell, K., . . . Woods, G. C. (2006). An *SCN9A* channelopathy causes congenital inability to experience pain. *Nature, 444,* 894–898. (p. 234)

Coyne, J. C. (1976a). Depression and the response of others. *Journal of Abnormal Psychology, 85,* 186–193. (p. 514)

Coyne, J. C. (1976b). Toward an interactional description of depression. *Psychiatry, 39,* 28–40. (p. 514)

Coyne, J. C., Ranchor, A. V., & Palmer, S. C. (2010). Meta-analysis of stress-related factors in cancer. *Nature Reviews Clinical Oncology, 7*(5). doi:10.1038/ncponc1134-c1 (p. 413)

Coyne, J. C., Stefanek, M., & Palmer, S. C. (2007). Psychotherapy and survival in cancer: The conflict between hope and evidence. *Psychological Bulletin, 133,* 367–394. (p. 413)

Coyne, J. C., & Tennen, H. (2010). Positive psychology in cancer care: Bad science, exaggerated claims, and unproven medicine. *Annals of Behavioral Medicine, 39,* 16–26. (p. 413)

Coyne, J. C., Thombs, B. C., Stefanek, M., & Palmer, S. C. (2009). Time to let go of the illusion that psychotherapy extends the survival of cancer patients: Reply to Kraemer, Kuchler, and Spiegel (2009). *Psychological Bulletin, 135,* 179–182. (p. 413)

Crabbe, J. C. (2002). Genetic contributions to addiction. *Annual Review of Psychology, 53,* 435–462. (p. 114)

Crabtree, S. (2005, January 13). Engagement keeps the doctor away. *Gallup Management Journal.* Retrieved from http://www.gallup.com/businessjournal/14500/engagement-keeps-doctor-away.aspx (p. B-10)

Crabtree, S. (2011, December 12). *U.S. seniors maintain happiness highs with less social time.* Retrieved from http://www.gallup.com/poll/151457/seniors-maintain-happiness-highs-less-social-time.aspx (p. 166)

Craik, F. I. M., & Tulving, E. (1975). Depth of processing and the retention of words in episodic memory. *Journal of Experimental Psychology: General, 104,* 268–294. (p. 289)

Credé, M., & Kuncel, N. R. (2008). Study habits, skills, and attitudes: The third pillar supporting collegiate academic performance. *Perspectives on Psychological Science, 3,* 425–453. (p. 356)

Creswell, J. D., Bursley, J. K., & Satpute, A. B. (2013). Neural reactivation links unconscious thought to decision making performance. *Social Cognitive and Affective Neuroscience, 8,* 863–869. (p. 324)

Creswell, J. D., Way, B. M., Eisenberger, N. I., & Lieberman, M. D. (2007). Neural correlates of dispositional mindfulness during affect labeling. *Psychosomatic Medicine, 69,* 560–565. (p. 429)

Crews, F. T., He, J., & Hodge, C. (2007). Adolescent cortical development: A critical period of vulnerability for addiction. *Pharmacology Biochemistry and Behavior, 86,* 189–199. (p. 107, 148)

Crews, F. T., Mdzinarishvilli, A., Kim, D., He, J., & Nixon, K. (2006). Neurogenesis in adolescent brain is potently inhibited by ethanol. *Neuroscience, 137,* 437–445. (p. 107)

Crocker, J., & Park, L. E. (2004). The costly pursuit of self-esteem. *Psychological Bulletin, 130,* 392–414. (p. 520)

Crocker, J., Thompson, L. L., McGraw, K. M., & Ingerman, C. (1987). Downward comparison, prejudice, and evaluation of others: Effects of self-esteem and threat. *Journal of Personality and Social Psychology, 52,* 907–916. (p. 466)

Crockett, M. J., Kurth-Nelson, Z., Siegel, J. Z., Dayan, P., & Dolan, R. J. (2014). Harm to others outweighs harm to self in moral decision making. *Proceedings of the National Academy of Sciences of the United States of America, 111,* 17320–17325. (p. 150)

Croft, R. J., Klugman, A., Baldeweg, T., & Gruzelier, J. H. (2001). Electrophysiological evidence of serotonergic impairment in long-term MDMA ("Ecstasy") users. *American Journal of Psychiatry, 158,* 1687–1692. (p. 111)

Crook, T. H., & West, R. L. (1990). Name recall performance across the adult life-span. *British Journal of Psychology, 81,* 335–340. (pp. 160, 161)

Cross, S., & Markus, H. (1991). Possible selves across the life span. *Human Development, 34,* 230–255. (p. 516)

Cross-National Collaborative Group. (1992). The changing rate of major depression. *Journal of the American Medical Association, 268,* 3098–3105. (p. 548)

Crowell, J. A., & Waters, E. (1994). Bowlby's theory grown up: The role of attachment in adult love relationships. *Psychological Inquiry, 5,* 1–22. (p. 139)

Croy, I., Bojanowski, V., & Hummel, T. (2013). Men without a sense of smell exhibit a strongly reduced number of sexual relationships, women exhibit reduced partnership security: A reanalysis of previously published data. *Biological Psychology, 92,* 292–294. (p. 236)

Croy, I., Negoias, S., Novakova, L., Landis, B. N., & Hummel, T. (2012). Learning about the functions of the olfactory system from people without a sense of smell. *PLOS ONE, 7*(3), e33365. doi:10.1371/journal.pone.0033365 (p. 236)

Csikszentmihalyi, M. (1990). *Flow: The psychology of optimal experience.* New York: Harper & Row. (p. B-1)

Csikszentmihalyi, M. (1999). If we are so rich, why aren't we happy? *American Psychologist, 54,* 821–827. (p. B-1)

Csikszentmihalyi, M., & Hunter, J. (2003). Happiness in everyday life: The uses of experience sampling. *Journal of Happiness Studies, 4,* 185–199. (p. 153)

Cuijpers, P., van Straten, A., Schuurmans, J., van Oppen, P., Hollon, S. D., & Andersson, G. (2010). Psychotherapy for chronic major depression and dysthymia: A meta-analysis. *Clinical Psychology Review, 30,* 51–62. (p. 596)

Cuijpers, P., Driessen, E., Hollon, S. D., van Oppen, P., Barth, J., & Andersson, G. (2012). The efficacy of non-directive supportive therapy for adult depression: A meta-analysis. *Clinical Psychology Review, 32,* 280–291. (p. 586)

Culbert, K. M., Burt, S. A., McGue, M., Iacono, W. G., & Klump, K. L. (2009). Puberty and the genetic diathesis of disordered eating attitudes and behaviors. *Journal of Abnormal Psychology, 118,* 788–796. (p. 565)

Cullum, J., & Harton, H. C. (2007). Cultural evolution: Interpersonal influence, issue importance, and the development of shared attitudes in college residence halls. *Personality and Social Psychology Bulletin, 33,* 1327–1339. (p. 451)

Cummins, R. A. (2006, April 4). *Australian Unity Wellbeing Index: Survey 14.1.* Melbourne, Victoria, Australia: Australian Centre on Quality of Life, Deakin University. (p. 433)

Cunningham, A. S., Engelstätter, B. A., & Ward, M. R. (2011). *Understanding the effects of violent video games on violent crime* (Centre for European Economic Research Discussion Paper No. 11-042). Retrieved from http://ftp.zew.de/pub/zew-docs/dp/dp11042.pdf (p. 473)

Cunningham, M. R., Roberts, A. R., Barbee, A. P., Druen, P. B., & Wu, C.-H. (2005). "Their ideas of beauty are, on the whole, the same as ours": Consistency and variability in the cross-cultural perception of female physical attractiveness. *Journal of Personality and Social Psychology, 68,* 261–279. (p. 478)

Currie, T. E., & Little, A. C. (2009). The relative importance of the face and body in judgments of human physical attractiveness. *Evolution and Human Behavior, 30,* 409–416. (p. 478)

Curry, J., Silva, S., Rohde, P., Ginsburg, G., Kratochvil, C., Simons, A., . . . March, J. (2011). Recovery and recurrence following treatment for adolescent major depression. *Archives of General Psychiatry, 68,* 263–269. (p. 548)

Curtis, R. C., & Miller, K. (1986). Believing another likes or dislikes you: Behaviors making the beliefs come true. *Journal of Personality and Social Psychology, 51,* 284–290. (p. 479)

Custers, R., & Aarts, H. (2010). The unconscious will: How the pursuit of goals operates outside of conscious awareness. *Science, 329,* 47–50. (p. 324)

Cyders, M. A., & Smith, G. T. (2008). Emotion-based dispositions to rash action: Positive and negative urgency. *Psychological Bulletin, 134,* 807–828. (p. 387)

Czeisler, C. A., Allan, J. S., Strogatz, S. H., Ronda, J. M., Sanchez, R., Rios, C. D., . . . Kronauer, R. E. (1986). Bright light resets the human circadian pacemaker independent of the timing of the sleep-wake cycle. *Science, 233,* 667–671. (p. 92)

Czeisler, C. A., Duffy, J. F., Shanahan, T. L., Brown, E. N., Mitchell, J. F., Rimmer, . . . Kronauer, R. E. (1999). Stability, precision, and near-24-hour period of the human circadian pacemaker. *Science, 284,* 2177–2181. (p. 92)

Czeisler, C. A., Kronauer, R. E., Allan, J. S., & Duffy, J. F. (1989). Bright light induction of strong (Type O) resetting of the human circadian pacemaker. *Science, 244,* 1328–1333. (p. 92)

D

Daley, J. (2011, July/August). What you don't know can kill you. *Discover.* Retrieved from http://discovermagazine.com/2011/jul-aug/11-what-you-dont-know-can-kill-you (p. 321)

Damasio, A. R. (2003). *Looking for Spinoza: Joy, sorrow, and the feeling brain.* New York: Harcourt. (p. 388)

Damasio, A. R. (2010). *Self comes to mind: Constructing the conscious brain.* New York: Pantheon. (p. 516)

Damon, W., Menon, J., & Bronk, K. (2003). The development of purpose during adolescence. *Applied Developmental Science, 7,* 119–128. (p. 153)

Dana, J., Dawes, R., & Peterson, N. (2013). Belief in the unstructured interview: The persistence of an illusion. *Judgment and Decision Making, 8,* 512–520. (p. B-5)

Danelli, L., Cossu, G., Berlingeri, M., Bottini, G., Sberna, M., & Paulesu, E. (2013). Is a lone right hemisphere enough? Neurolinguistic architecture in a case with a very early left hemispherectomy. *Neurocase, 19,* 209–231. (p. 61)

Danner, D. D., Snowdon, D. A., & Friesen, W. V. (2001). Positive emotions in early life and longevity: Findings from the Nun Study. *Journal of Personality and Social Psychology, 80,* 804–813. (p. 423)

Danso, H., & Esses, V. (2001). Black experimenters and the intellectual test performance of White participants: The tables are turned. *Journal of Experimental Social Psychology, 37,* 158–165. (p. 361)

Danziger, S., & Ward, R. (2010). Language changes implicit associations between ethnic groups and evaluation in bilinguals. *Psychological Science, 21,* 799–800. (p. 337)

Dapretto, M., Davies, M. S., Pfeifer, J. H., Scott, A. A., Sigman, M., Bookheimer, S. Y., & Iacoboni, M. (2006). Understanding emotions in others: Mirror neuron dysfunction in children with autism spectrum disorders. *Nature Neuroscience, 9,* 28–30. (p. 137)

Darley, J. M. (2009). Morality in the law: The psychological foundations of citizens' desires to punish transgressions. *Annual Review of Law and Social Science, 5,* 1–23. (p. 151)

Darley, J. M., & Alter, A. (2013). Behavioral issues of punishment, retribution, and deterrence. In E. Shafir (Ed.), *The behavioral foundations of public policy* (pp. 181–194). Princeton, NJ: Princeton University Press. (p. 261)

Darley, J. M., & Latané, B. (1968a). Bystander intervention in emergencies: Diffusion of responsibility. *Journal of Personality and Social Psychology, 8,* 377–383. (pp. 482, 483)

Darley, J. M., & Latané, B. (1968b, December). When will people help in a crisis? *Psychology Today,* pp. 54–57, 70–71. (p. 482)

Darrach, B., & Norris, J. (1984, August). An American tragedy. *Life,* pp. 58–74. (p. 563)

Darwin, C. (1859). *On the origin of species by means of natural selection.* London: John Murray. (p. 75)

Darwin, C. (1872). *The expression of the emotions in man and animals.* London: John Murray. (pp. 234, 401)

Daum, I., & Schugens, M. M. (1996). On the cerebellum and classical conditioning. *Psychological Science, 5,* 58–61. (p. 293)

Davey, G., & Rato, R. (2012). Subjective well-being in China: A review. *Journal of Happiness Studies, 13,* 333–346. (p. 434)

Davey, G. C. L. (1992). Classical conditioning and the acquisition of human fears and phobias: A review and synthesis of the literature. *Advances in Behavior Research and Therapy, 14,* 29–66. (p. 268)

Davey, G. C. L. (1995). Preparedness and phobias: Specific evolved associations or a generalized expectancy bias? *Behavioral and Brain Sciences, 18,* 289–297. (p. 543)

Davidoff, J. (2004). Coloured thinking. *The Psychologist, 17,* 570–572. (p. 337)

Davidson, R. J. (2000). Affective style, psychopathology, and resilience: Brain mechanisms and plasticity. *American Psychologist, 55,* 1196–1209. (p. 394)

Davidson, R. J. (2003). Affective neuroscience and psychophysiology: Toward a synthesis. *Psychophysiology, 40,* 655–665. (p. 394)

Davidson, R. J., & Begley, S. (2012). *The emotional life of your brain: How its unique patterns affect the way you think, feel, and live—and how you can change them.* New York: Hudson Street Press. (p. 388)

Davidson, R. J., Kabat-Zinn, J., Schumacher, J., Rosenkranz, M., Muller, D., Santorelli, S. F., . . . Sheridan, J. F. (2003). Alterations in brain and immune function produced by mindfulness meditation. *Psychosomatic Medicine, 65,* 564–570. (p. 429)

Davidson, R. J., Pizzagalli, D., Nitschke, J. B., & Putnam, K. (2002). Depression: Perspectives from affective neuroscience. *Annual Review of Psychology, 53,* 545–574. (p. 549)

Davidson, R. J., Putnam, K. M., & Larson, C. L. (2000). Dysfunction in the neural circuitry of emotion regulation—a possible prelude to violence. *Science, 289,* 591–594. (p. 469)

Davies, P. (2007). *Cosmic jackpot: Why our universe is just right for life.* Boston: Houghton Mifflin. (p. 76)

Davis, B. E., Moon, R. Y., Sachs, H. C., & Ottolini, M. C. (1998). Effects of sleep position on infant motor development. *Pediatrics, 102,* 1135–1140. (p. 129)

Davis, J. O., & Phelps, J. A. (1995). Twins with schizophrenia: Genes or germs? *Schizophrenia Bulletin, 21,* 13–18. (p. 560)

Davis, J. O., Phelps, J. A., & Bracha, H. S. (1995). Prenatal development of monozygotic twins and concordance for schizophrenia. *Schizophrenia Bulletin, 21,* 357–366. (p. 560)

Davis, J. P., Lander, K., & Jansari, A. (2013). I never forget a face. *The Psychologist, 26,* 726–729. (p. 282)

Davis, K., Christodoulou, J., Seider, S., & Gardner, H. (2011). The theory of multiple intelligences. In R. J. Sternberg & S. B. Kaufman (Eds.), *The Cambridge handbook of intelligence* (pp. 485–503). New York: Cambridge University Press. (p. 342)

Davis, M. (2005, July). Searching for a drug to extinguish fear. *Cerebrum,* pp. 47–58. (p. 594)

Davison, K. P., Pennebaker, J. W., & Dickerson, S. S. (2000). Who talks? The social psychology of illness support groups. *American Psychologist, 55,* 205–217. (p. 582)

Dawes, R. M. (1980). Social dilemmas. *Annual Review of Psychology, 31,* 169–193. (p. 485)

Dawes, R. M. (1994). *House of cards: Psychology and psychotherapy built on myth.* New York: Free Press. (p. 517)

Dawkins, L., Shahzad, F.-Z., Ahmed, S. S., & Edmonds, C. J. (2011). Expectation of having consumed caffeine can improve performance and moods. *Appetite, 57,* 597–600. (p. 24)

Dawkins, R. (1998). *Unweaving the rainbow: Science, delusion and the appetite for wonder.* Boston: Houghton Mifflin. (p. 75)

Deal, G. (2011, January 14). Chinese parenting: Thanks, I'll pass. *The Wall Street Journal.* Retrieved from http://blogs.wsj.com/wsjam/2011/01/14/chinese-parenting-thanks-ill-pass/ (p. 155)

Deary, I. J. (2008). Why do intelligent people live longer? *Nature, 456,* 175–176. (p. 351)

Deary, I. J., Johnson, W., & Houlihan, L. M. (2009). Genetic foundations of human intelligence. *Human Genetics, 126,* 215–232. (pp. 354, 355)

Deary, I. J., & Matthews, G. (1993). Personality traits are alive and well. *The Psychologist, 6,* 299–311. (p. 511)

Deary, I. J., Pattie, A., & Starr, J. M. (2013). The stability of intelligence from age 11 to age 90 years: The Lothian birth cohort of 1921. *Psychological Science, 24,* 2361–2368. (pp. 350, 351)

Deary, I. J., Thorpe, G., Wilson, V., Starr, J. M., & Whalley, L. J. (2003). Population sex differences in IQ at age 11: The Scottish Mental Survey 1932. *Intelligence, 31,* 533–541. (p. 357)

Deary, I. J., Whalley, L. J., & Starr, J. M. (2009). *A lifetime of intelligence: Follow-up studies of the Scottish Mental Surveys of 1932 and 1947.* Washington, DC: American Psychological Association. (p. 350)

Deary, I. J., Whiteman, M. C., Starr, J. M., Whalley, L. J., & Fox, H. C. (2004). The impact of childhood intelligence on later life: Following up the Scottish Mental Surveys of 1932 and 1947. *Journal of Personality and Social Psychology, 86,* 130–147. (pp. 350, 351)

de Boysson-Bardies, B., Halle, P., Sagart, L., & Durand, C. (1989). A cross linguistic investigation of vowel formats in babbling. *Journal of Child Language, 16,* 1–17. (p. 332)

de Bruin, A., Barbara, T., & Della Sala, S. (2015a). Cognitive advantage in bilingualism: An example of publication bias? *Psychological Science, 26,* 99–107. (p. 338)

de Bruin, A., Treccani, B., & Della Sala, S. (2015b). The connection is in the data: We should consider them all. *Psychological Science, 26,* 947–949. (p. 338)

DeBruine, L. M. (2002). Facial resemblance enhances trust. *Proceedings of the Royal Society of London: Series B, 269,* 1307–1312. (p. 475)

DeBruine, L. M. (2004). Facial resemblance increases the attractiveness of same-sex faces more than other-sex faces. *Proceedings of the Royal Society of London: Series B, 271,* 2085–2090. (p. 475)

DeCasper, A. J., Lecanuet, J.-P., Busnel, M.-C., Granier-Deferre, C., & Maugeais, R. (1994). Fetal reactions to recurrent maternal speech. *Infant Behavior and Development, 17,* 159–164. (p. 123)

DeCasper, A. J., & Prescott, P. A. (1984). Human newborns' perception of male voices: Preference, discrimination and reinforcing value. *Developmental Psychobiology, 17,* 481–491. (p. 123)

DeCasper, A. J., & Spence, M. J. (1986). Prenatal maternal speech influences newborns' perception of speech sounds. *Infant Behavior and Development, 9,* 133–150. (p. 123)

Deci, E. L., Koestner, R., & Ryan, R. M. (1999, November). A meta-analytic review of experiments examining the effects of extrinsic rewards on intrinsic motivation. *Psychological Bulletin, 125,* 627–668. (p. 271)

Deci, E. L., & Ryan, R. M. (1985). *Intrinsic motivation and self-determination in human behavior.* New York: Plenum Press. (p. 271)

Deci, E. L., & Ryan, R. M. (Eds.). (2002). *Handbook of self-determination research.* Rochester, NY: University of Rochester Press. (p. 370)

Deci, E. L., & Ryan, R. M. (2009). Self-determination theory: A consideration of human motivational universals. In P. J. Corr & G. Matthews (Eds.), *The Cambridge handbook of personality psychology* (pp. 441–456). New York: Cambridge University Press. (pp. 271, 370)

Dechesne, M., Pyszczynski, T., Arndt, J., Ransom, S., Sheldon, K. M., van Knippenberg, A., & Janssen, J. (2003). Literal and symbolic immortality: The effect of evidence of literal immortality on self-esteem striving in response to mortality salience. *Journal of Personality and Social Psychology, 84,* 722–737. (p. 26)

de Courten-Myers, G. M. (2005, February 4). Personal communication. (p. 56)

de Dios, M. A., Herman, D. S., Britton, W. B., Hagerty, C. E., Anderson, B. J., & Stein, M. D. (2012). Motivational and mindfulness intervention for young adult female marijuana users. *Journal of Substance Abuse Treatment, 42*, 56–64. (p. 428)

De Dreu, C. K. W., Greer, L. L., Handgraaf, M. J. J., Shalvi, S., Van Kleef, G. A., Baas, M., . . . Feith, S. W. W. (2010). The neuropeptide oxytocin regulated parochial altruism in intergroup conflict among humans. *Science, 328*, 1409–1411. (p. 46)

De Dreu, C. K. W., Nijstad, B. A., Baas, M., Wolsink, I., & Roskes, M. (2012). Working memory benefits creative insight, musical improvisation, and original ideation through maintained task-focused attention. *Personality and Social Psychology Bulletin, 38*, 656–669. (p. 287)

DeFina, R., & Hannon, L. (2015). The changing relationship between unemployment and suicide. *Suicide and Life-Threatening Behavior, 45*, 217–229. (p. 553)

DeFina, L. F., Willis, B. L., Radford, N. B., Gao, A., Leonard, D., Haskell, W. L., . . . Berry, J. D. (2013). The association between midlife cardiorespiratory fitness levels and later-life dementia. *Annals of Internal Medicine, 158*, 162–168. (p. 160)

de Gee, J., Knapen, T., & Donner, T. H. (2014). Decision-related pupil dilation reflects upcoming choice and individual bias. *Proceedings of the National Academy of Sciences of the United States of America, 111*, E618–E625. (p. 211)

de Gelder, B. (2010, May). Uncanny sight in the blind. *Scientific American*, pp. 60–65. (p. 85)

de Gonzales, A. B., Hartge, P., Cerhan, J. R., Flint, A. J., Hannan, L., MacInnis, R. J., . . . Thun, M. J. (2010). Body-mass index and mortality among 1.46 million white adults. *New England Journal of Medicine, 363*, 2211–2219. (p. 383)

Dehaene, S. (2009, November 24). *Signatures of consciousness.* Retrieved from http://edge.org/conversation/signatures-of-consciousness (p. 202)

Dehaene, S. (2014). *Consciousness and the brain: Deciphering how the brain codes our thoughts.* New York: Viking. (p. 202)

Dehne, K. L., & Riedner, G. (2005). *Sexually transmitted infections among adolescents: The need for adequate health services.* Geneva, Switzerland: World Health Organization. (p. 184)

de Hoogh, A. H. B., den Hartog, D. N., Koopman, P. L., Thierry, H., van den Berg, P. T., van der Weide, J. G., & Wilderom, C. P. M. (2004). Charismatic leadership, environmental dynamism, and performance. *European Journal of Work and Organisational Psychology, 13*, 447–471. (p. B-12)

De Koninck, J. (2000). Waking experiences and dreaming. In M. Kryger, T. Roth, & W. Dement (Eds.), *Principles and practice of sleep medicine* (3rd ed., pp. 502–511). Philadelphia: W. B. Saunders. (p. 99)

DeLamater, J. (2012). Sexual expression in later life: A review and synthesis. *Journal of Sex Research, 49*, 125–141. (p. 158)

DeLamater, J. D., & Sill, M. (2005). Sexual desire in later life. *Journal of Sex Research, 42*, 138–149. (p. 158)

Delaney, H. D., Miller, W. R., & Bisonó, A. M. (2007). Religiosity and spirituality among psychologists: A survey of clinician members of the American Psychological Association. *Professional Psychology: Research and Practice, 38*, 538–546. (p. 590)

Delaunay-El Allam, M., Soussignan, R., Patris, B., Marlier, L., & Schaal, B. (2010). Long-lasting memory for an odor acquired at the mother's breast. *Developmental Science, 13*, 849–863. (p. 126)

Delgado, J. M. R. (1969). *Physical control of the mind: Toward a psychocivilized society.* New York: Harper & Row. (p. 57)

DeLoache, J. S. (1987). Rapid change in the symbolic functioning of very young children. *Science, 238*, 1556–1557. (p. 132)

DeLoache, J. S., Chiong, C., Sherman, K., Islam, N., Vanderborght, M., Troseth, G. L., . . . O'Doherty, K. (2010). Do babies learn from baby media? *Psychological Science, 21*, 1570–1574. (p. 356)

DeLongis, A., Coyne, J. C., Dakof, G., Folkman, S., & Lazarus, R. S. (1982). Relationship of daily hassles, uplifts, and major life events to health status. *Health Psychology, 1*, 119–136. (p. 409)

DeLongis, A., Folkman, S., & Lazarus, R. S. (1988). The impact of daily stress on health and mood: Psychological and social resources as mediators. *Journal of Personality and Social Psychology, 54*, 486–495. (p. 409)

De Los Reyes, A., & Kazdin, A. E. (2009). Identifying evidence-based interventions for children and adolescents using the range of possible changes model: A meta-analytic illustration. *Behavior Modification, 33*, 583–617. (p. 586)

DelPriore, D. J., & Hill, S. E. (2013). The effects of paternal disengagement on women's sexual decision making: An experimental approach. *Journal of Personality and Social Psychology, 105*, 234–246. (p. 176)

Dement, W. C. (1978). *Some must watch while some must sleep.* New York: Norton. (pp. 88, 89, 97)

Dement, W. C. (1999). *The promise of sleep.* New York: Delacorte Press. (pp. 89, 92, 94, 95, 97, 98)

Dement, W. C., & Wolpert, E. A. (1958). The relation of eye movements, body mobility, and external stimuli to dream content. *Journal of Experimental Psychology, 55*, 543–553. (p. 99)

Demicheli, V., Rivetti, A., Debalini, M. G., & Di Pietrantonj, C. (2012, February 15). Vaccines for measles, mumps and rubella in children. *Cochrane Database of Systematic Reviews*, Issue 2, Article CD004407. doi:10.1002/14651858.CD004407. pub3 (p. 136)

Demir, E., & Dickson, B. J. (2005). *fruitless* splicing specifies male courtship behavior in *Drosophila. Cell, 121*, 785–794. (p. 191)

Demiralp, E., Thompson, R. J., Mata, J., Barrett, L. F., Ellsworth, P. C., Demiralp, M., . . . Jonides, J. (2012). Feeling blue or turquoise? Emotional differentiation in major depressive disorder. *Psychological Science, 23*, 1410–1416. (p. 166)

Dempster, E., Viana, J., Pidsley, R., & Mill, J. (2013). Epigenetic studies of schizophrenia: Progress, predicaments, and promises for the future. *Schizophrenia Bulletin, 39*, 11–16. (p. 560)

De Neve, J.-E., Christakis, N. A., Fowler, J. H., & Frey, B. S. (2012). Genes, economics, and happiness. *Journal of Neuroscience, Psychology, and Economics, 5*, 193–211. (p. 436)

De Neve, J.-E., Diener, E., Tay, L., & Xuereb, C. (2013). The objective benefits of subjective well-being. In J. F. Helliwell, R. Layard, & J. Sachs (Eds.), *World happiness report 2013* (Vol. 2., pp. 54–79). New York: UN Sustainable Network Development Solutions Network. (pp. 431, B-11)

DeNeve, K. M., & Cooper, H. (1998). The happy personality: A meta-analysis of 137 personality traits and subjective well-being. *Psychological Bulletin, 124*, 197–229. (p. 436)

Dennett, D. C. (1991). *Consciousness explained.* Boston: Little, Brown. (p. 270)

Denny, B. T., Inhoff, M. C., Zerubavel, N., Davachi, L., & Ochsner, K. N. (2015). Getting over it: Long-lasting effects of emotion regulation on amygdala response. *Psychological Science, 26*, 1377–1388. (p. 390)

Denollet, J. (2005). DS14: Standard assessment of negative affectivity, social inhibition, and Type D personality. *Psychosomatic Medicine, 67*, 89–97. (p. 415)

Denollet, J., Sys, S. U., Stroobant, N., Rombouts, H., Gillebert, T. C., & Brutsaert, D. L. (1996). Personality as independent predictor of long-term mortality in patients with coronary heart disease. *The Lancet, 347*, 417–421. (p. 415)

Denson, T. F. (2011). A social neuroscience perspective on the neurobiological bases of aggression. In P. R. Shaver & M. Mikulincer (Eds.), *Human aggression and violence: Causes, manifestations, and consequences* (pp. 105–120). Washington, DC: American Psychological Association. (p. 469)

Denson, T. F., Capper, M. M., Oaten, M., Friese, M., & Schofield, T. P. (2011). Self-control training decreases aggression in response to provocation in aggressive individuals. *Journal of Research in Personality, 45*, 252–256. (p. 422)

Denton, K., & Krebs, D. (1990). From the scene to the crime: The effect of alcohol and social context on moral judgment. *Journal of Personality and Social Psychology, 59*, 242–248. (p. 106)

Depla, M. F. I. A., ten Have, M. L., van Balkom, A. J. L. M., & de Graaf, R. (2008). Specific fears and phobias in the general population: Results from the Netherlands Mental Health Survey and Incidence Study (NEMESIS). *Social Psychiatry and Psychiatric Epidemiology, 43*, 200–208. (p. 538)

De Raad, B., Barelds, D. P. H., Levert, E., Ostendorf, F., Mlačić, B., Di Blas, L., . . . Katigbak, M. S. (2010). Only three factors of personality description are fully replicable across languages: A comparison of 14 trait taxonomies. *Journal of Personality and Social Psychology, 98*, 160–173. (p. 509)

Dermer, M., Cohen, S. J., Jacobsen, E., & Anderson, E. A. (1979). Evaluative judgments of aspects of life as a function of vicarious exposure to hedonic extremes. *Journal of Personality and Social Psychology, 37*, 247–260. (p. 435)

DeStefano, F., Price, C. S., & Weintraub, E. S. (2013). Increasing exposure to antibody-stimulating proteins and polysaccharides in vaccines is not associated with risk of autism. *Journal of Pediatrics, 163*, 561–567. (p. 136)

DeSteno, D., Petty, R. E., Wegener, D. T., & Rucker, D. D. (2000). Beyond valence in the perception of likelihood: The role of emotion specificity. *Journal of Personality and Social Psychology, 78*, 397–416. (p. 298)

Dettman, S. J., Pinder, D., Briggs, R. J. S., Dowell, R. C., & Leigh, J. R. (2007). Communication development in children who receive the cochlear implant younger than 12 months: Risk versus benefits. *Ear and Hearing, 28*(2, Suppl.), 11S–18S. (p. 229)

Deutsch, J. A. (1972, July). Brain reward: ESP and ecstasy. *Psychology Today*, 46–48. (p. 54)

DeValois, R. L., & DeValois, K. K. (1975). Neural coding of color. In E. C. Carterette & M. P. Friedman (Eds.), *Handbook of perception: Vol. 5. Seeing* (pp. 117–166). New York: Academic Press. (p. 214)

Devilly, G. J. (2003). Eye movement desensitization and reprocessing: A chronology of its development and scientific standing. *Scientific Review of Mental Health Practice, 1*, 113–118. (p. 588)

Devries, K. M., Mak, J. Y. T., García-Moreno, C., Petzold, M., Falder, G., Lim, S., . . . Watts, C. H. (2013). The global prevalence of intimate partner violence against women. *Science, 340*, 1527. (p. 464)

Dew, M. A., Hoch, C. C., Buysse, D. J., Monk, T. H., Begley, A. E., Houck, P. R., . . . Reynolds, C. F., III. (2003). Healthy older adults' sleep predicts all-cause mortality at 4 to 19 years of follow-up. *Psychosomatic Medicine, 65*, 63–73. (p. 95)

DeWall, C. N., Lambert, N. M., Slotter, E. B., Pond, R. S., Jr., Deckman, T., Finkel, E. J., . . . Fincham, F. D. (2011). So far away from one's partner, yet so close to romantic alternatives: Avoidant attachment, interest in alternatives, and infidelity. *Journal of Personality and Social Psychology, 101*, 1302–1316. (p. 142)

DeWall, C. N., MacDonald, G., Webster, G. D., Masten, C. L., Baumeister, R. F., Powell, C., . . . Eisenberger, N. I. (2010). Acetaminophen reduces social pain: Behavioral and neural evidence. *Psychological Science, 21*, 931–937. (p. 372)

DeWall, C. N., & Pond, R. S., Jr. (2011). Loneliness and smoking: The costs of the desire to reconnect. *Self and Identity, 10*, 375–385. (p. 115)

DeWall, C. N., Pond, R. S., Jr., Campbell, W. K., & Twenge, J. M. (2011). Tuning in to psychological change: Linguistic markers of psychological traits and emotions over time in popular U.S. song lyrics. *Psychology of Aesthetics, Creativity, and the Arts, 5*, 200–207. (p. 519)

DeWall, C. N., Pond, R. S., Jr., Carter, M. E., Lambert, N. M., Fincham, F. D., & Nezlek, J. B. (2014). Explaining the relationship between religiousness and substance use: Self-control matters. *Journal of Personality and Social Psychology, 107*, 339–351. (p. 430)

Dewar, M., Alber, J., Butler, C., Cowan, N., & Sala, S. D. (2012). Brief wakeful resting boosts new memories over the long term. *Psychological Science, 23*, 955–960. (p. 312)

de Wit, L., Luppino, F., van Straten, A., Penninx, B., Zitman, F., & Cuijpers, P. (2010). Depression and obesity: A meta-analysis of community-based studies. *Psychiatry Research, 178*, 230–235. (p. 382)

De Wolff, M. S., & van Ijzendoorn, M. H. (1997). Sensitivity and attachment: A meta-analysis on parental antecedents of infant attachment. *Child Development, 68*, 571–591. (p. 140)

DeYoung, C. G., Hirsch, J. B., Shane, M. S., Papademetris, X., Rajeevan, N., & Gray, J. R. (2010). Testing predictions from personality neuroscience: Brain structure and the Big Five. *Psychological Science, 21*, 820–828. (p. 510)

Diaconis, P., & Mosteller, F. (1989). Methods for studying coincidences. *Journal of the American Statistical Association, 84*, 853–861. (p. 17)

Diamond, J. (2001, February). A tale of two reputations: Why we revere Darwin and give Freud a hard time. *Natural History*, pp. 20–24. (p. 75)

Diamond, L. (2008). *Sexual fluidity: Understanding women's love and desire*. Cambridge, MA: Harvard University Press. (p. 188)

Diaz, F. J., Velásquex, D. M., Susce, M. T., & de Leon, J. (2008). The association between schizophrenia and smoking: Unexplained by either the illness or the prodromal period. *Schizophrenia Research, 104*, 214–219. (p. 558)

Dick, D. M. (2007). Identification of genes influencing a spectrum of externalizing psychopathology. *Current Directions in Psychological Science, 16*, 331–335. (p. 563)

Dickens, W. T., & Flynn, J. R. (2006). Black Americans reduce the racial IQ gap: Evidence from standardization samples. *Psychological Science, 17*, 913–920. (p. 358)

Dickerson, S. S., & Kemeny, M. E. (2004). Acute stressors and cortisol responses: A theoretical integration and synthesis of laboratory research. *Psychological Bulletin, 130*, 355–391. (pp. 407, 408, 419)

Dickson, B. J. (2005, June 3). Quoted in E. Rosenthal, For fruit flies, gene shift tilts sex orientation. *The New York Times*. Retrieved from http://www.nytimes.com/2005/06/03/science/for-fruit-flies-gene-shift-tilts-sex-orientation.html?_r=0 (p. 191)

Dickson, N., van Roode, T., Cameron, C., & Paul, C. (2013). Stability and change in same-sex attraction, experience, and identity by sex and age in a New Zealand birth cohort. *Archives of Sexual Behavior, 42*, 753–763. (p. 188)

Dickstein, D. P., Puzia, M. E., Cushman, G. K., Weissman, A. B., Wegbreit, E., . . . Spirito, A. (2015). Self-injurious implicit attitudes among adolescent suicide attempters versus those engaged in nonsuicidal self-injury. *Journal of Child Psychology and Psychiatry, 56*, 1127–1136. (p. 555)

Diekelmann, S., & Born, J. (2010). The memory function of sleep. *Nature Neuroscience, 11*, 114–126. (pp. 93, 100, 305)

Diener, E. (2006). Guidelines of national indicators of subjective well-being and ill-being. *Journal of Happiness Studies, 7*, 397–404. (p. 436)

Diener, E. (2013). The remarkable changes in the science of well-being. *Perspectives on Psychological Science, 8*, 663–666. (p. 436)

Diener, E., & Biswas-Diener, R. (2002). Will money increase subjective well-being? A literature review and guide to needed research. *Social Indicators Research, 57*, 119–169. (p. 434)

Diener, E., & Biswas-Diener, R. (2008). *Happiness: Unlocking the mysteries of psychological wealth*. Malden, MA: Blackwell. (p. 434)

Diener, E., & Chan, M. (2011). Happy people live longer: Subjective well-being contributes to health and longevity. *Applied Psychology: Health and Well-Being, 3*, 1–43. (p. 415)

Diener, E., Nickerson, C., Lucas, R. E., & Sandvik, E. (2002). Dispositional affect and job outcomes. *Social Indicators Research, 59*, 229–259. (p. 431)

Diener, E., & Oishi, S. (2000). Money and happiness: Income and subjective well-being across nations. In E. Diener & E. M. Suh (Eds.), *Subjective well-being across cultures* (pp. 185–218). Cambridge, MA: MIT Press. (p. 434)

Diener, E., Oishi, S., & Lucas, R. E. (2003). Personality, culture, and subjective well-being: Emotional and cognitive evaluations of life. *Annual Review of Psychology, 54*, 403–425. (p. 436)

Diener, E., Oishi, S., & Lucas, R. E. (2009). Subjective well-being: The science of happiness and life satisfaction. In S. J. Lopez & C. R. Snyder (Eds.), *The Oxford Handbook of Positive Psychology* (2nd ed., pp. 187–194). New York: Oxford University Press. (p. 436)

Diener, E., Oishi, S., & Lucas, R. E. (2015). National accounts of subjective well-being. *American Psychologist, 70*, 234–242. (p. 436)

Diener, E., Oishi, S., & Park, J. Y. (2014). An incomplete list of eminent psychologists of the modern era. *Archives of Scientific Psychology, 21*, 20–31. (p. 272)

Diener, E., & Seligman, M. E. P. (2002). Very happy people. *Psychological Science, 13*, 81–84. (p. 370)

Diener, E., Tay, L., & Myers, D. G. (2011). The religion paradox: If religion makes people happy, why are so many dropping out? *Journal of Personality and Social Psychology, 101*, 1278–1290. (pp. 21, 436)

Diener, E., Wolsic, B., & Fujita, F. (1995). Physical attractiveness and subjective well-being. *Journal of Personality and Social Psychology, 69*, 120–129. (p. 477)

DiFranza, J. R. (2008, May). Hooked from the first cigarette. *Scientific American*, pp. 82–87. (p. 108)

Dijksterhuis, A., & Aarts, H. (2003). On wildebeests and humans: The preferential detection of negative stimuli. *Psychological Science, 14*, 14–18. (p. 396)

Dik, B. J., & Duffy, R. D. (2012). *Make your job a calling: How the psychology of vocation can change your life at work*. Conshohocken, PA: Templeton Press. (p. B-1)

Dik, B. J., & Rottinghaus, P. J. (2013). Assessments of interests. In K. F. Geisinger, B. A. Bracken, J. F. Carlson, J.-I. C. Hansen, N. R. Kuncel, S. P. Reise, & M. C. Rodriguez (Eds.), *APA handbook of testing and assessment in psychology: Vol. 2. Testing and assessment in clinical and counseling psychology* (pp. 325–348). Washington, DC: American Psychological Association. (p. B-3)

DiLalla, D. L., Carey, G., Gottesman, I. I., & Bouchard, T. J., Jr. (1996). Heritability of MMPI personality indicators of psychopathology in twins reared apart. *Journal of Abnormal Psychology, 105*, 491–499. (p. 549)

Dimidjian, S., & Hollon, S. D. (2010). How would we know if psychotherapy were harmful? *American Psychologist, 65*, 21–33. (p. 587)

Dinan, T. G., Stilling, R. M., Stanton, C., & Cryan, J. F. (2015). Collective unconscious: How gut microbes shape human behavior. *Journal of Psychiatric Research, 63*, 1–9. (p. 549)

Dimberg, U., Thunberg, M., & Elmehed, K. (2000). Unconscious facial reactions to emotional facial expressions. *Psychological Science, 11*, 86–89. (pp. 389, 403)

Dinges, N. G., & Hull, P. (1992). Personality, culture, and international studies. In D. Lieberman & M. Gurtov (Eds.), *Revealing the world: An interdisciplinary reader for international studies* (pp. 133–162). Dubuque, IA: Kendall-Hunt. (p. 337)

Dingfelder, S. F. (2010, November). A second chance for the Mexican wolf. *Monitor on Psychology*, pp. 20–21. (p. 268)

Dion, K. K., & Dion, K. L. (1993). Individualistic and collectivistic perspectives on gender and the cultural context of love and intimacy. *Journal of Social Issues*, *49*, 53–69. (p. 523)

Dirix, C. E. H., Nijhuis, J. G., Jongsma, H. W., & Hornstra, G. (2009). Aspects of fetal learning and memory. *Child Development*, *80*, 1251–1258. (p. 124)

DiSalvo, D. (2010, January/February). Are social networks messing with your head? *Scientific American Mind*, pp. 48–55. (p. 373)

DiSantis, K. I., Birch, L. L., Davey, A., Serrano, E. L., Zhang, J., Bruton, Y., & Fisher, J. O. (2013). Plate size and children's appetite: Effects of larger dishware on self-served portions and intake. *Pediatrics*, *131*, e1451–e1458. doi:10.1542/peds.2012-2330 (p. 382)

Discover. (1996, May). A fistful of risks, pp. 82–83. (p. 108)

Di Tella, R., Haisken-De New, J., & MacCulloch, R. (2010). Happiness adaptation to income and to status in an individual panel. *Journal of Economic Behavior & Organization*, *76*, 834–852. (p. 434)

Di Tella, R., & MacCulloch, R. (2010). Happiness adaptation to income beyond "basic needs." In E. Diener, J. Helliwell, & D. Kahneman (Eds.), *International differences in well-being* (pp. 217–247). New York: Oxford University Press. (p. 434)

Ditre, J. W., Brandon, T. H., Zale, E. L., & Meagher, M. M. (2011). Pain, nicotine, and smoking: Research findings and mechanistic considerations. *Psychological Bulletin*, *137*, 1065–1093. (p. 109)

Dixon, J., Durrheim, K., & Tredoux, C. (2007). Intergroup contact and attitudes toward the principle and practice of racial equality. *Psychological Science*, *18*, 867–872. (p. 486)

Dobbs, D. (2009, April). The post-traumatic stress trap. *Scientific American*, pp. 64–69. (p. 540)

Dodge, K. A. (2009). Mechanisms of gene–environment interaction effects in the development of conduct disorder. *Perspectives on Psychological Science*, *4*, 408–414. (p. 564)

Doherty, E. W., & Doherty, W. J. (1998). Smoke gets in your eyes: Cigarette smoking and divorce in a national sample of American adults. *Families, Systems, and Health*, *16*, 393–400. (p. 109)

Dohrenwend, B. P., Levav, I., Shrout, P. E., Schwartz, S., Naveh, G., Link, B. G., Skodol, A. E., & Stueve, A. (1992). Socioeconomic status and psychiatric disorders: The causation-selection issue. *Science*, *255*, 946–952. (p. 535)

Dohrenwend, B. P., Pearlin, L., Clayton, P., Hamburg, B., Dohrenwend, B. S., Riley, M., & Rose, R. (1982). Report on stress and life events. In G. R. Elliott & C. Eisdorfer (Eds.), *Stress and human health: Analysis and implications of research* (pp. 55–80). New York: Springer. (p. 407)

DOL. (2015). *Women in labor force.* U.S. Department of Labor. Retrieved from http://www.dol.gov/wb/stats/facts_over_time.htm (p. 178)

Dolezal, H. (1982). *Living in a world transformed.* New York: Academic Press. (p. 224)

Dolinoy, D. C., Huang, D., & Jirtle, R. L. (2007). Maternal nutrient supplementation counteracts bisphenol A-induced DNA hypomethylation in early development. *Proceedings of the National Academy of Sciences of the United States of America*, *104*, 13056–13061. (p. 72)

Domhoff, G. W. (1996). *Finding meaning in dreams: A quantitative approach.* New York: Plenum Press. (p. 99)

Domhoff, G. W. (2003). *The scientific study of dreams: Neural networks, cognitive development, and content analysis.* Washington, DC: American Psychological Association. (pp. 100, 101)

Domhoff, G. W. (2007). Realistic simulations and bizarreness in dream content: Past findings and suggestions for future research. In D. Barrett & P. McNamara (Eds.), *The new science of dreaming: Content, recall, and personality characteristics* (Vol. 2, pp. 1–27). Westport, CT: Praeger. (p. 99)

Domhoff, G. W. (2010). *The case for a cognitive theory of dreams.* Retrieved from http://www2.ucsc.edu/dreams/Library/domhoff_2010a.html (p. 101)

Domhoff, G. W. (2011). The neural substrate for dreaming: Is it a subsystem of the default network? *Consciousness and Cognition*, *20*, 1163–1174. (p. 101)

Domjan, M. (1992). Adult learning and mate choice: Possibilities and experimental evidence. *American Zoologist*, *32*, 48–61. (p. 250)

Domjan, M. (1994). Formulation of a behavior system for sexual conditioning. *Psychonomic Bulletin & Review*, *1*, 421–428. (p. 250)

Domjan, M. (2005). Pavlovian conditioning: A functional perspective. *Annual Review of Psychology*, *56*, 179–206. (p. 250)

Donlea, J. M., Ramanan, N., & Shaw, P. J. (2009). Use-dependent plasticity in clock neurons regulates sleep need in *Drosophila*. *Science*, *324*, 105–108. (p. 92)

Donnerstein, E. (1998, January). *Why do we have those new ratings on television?* Address at the 20th Annual National Institute on the Teaching of Psychology, St. Pete Beach, FL. (pp. 276, 277)

Donnerstein, E. (2011). The media and aggression: From TV to the Internet. In J. Forgas, A. Kruglanski, & K. Williams (Eds.), *The psychology of social conflict and aggression* (pp. 267–284). New York: Psychology Press. (pp. 276, 277)

Donnerstein, E., Linz, D., & Penrod, S. (1987). *The question of pornography.* New York: Free Press. (p. 277)

Donvan, J., & Zucker, C. (2010, October). Autism's first child. *The Atlantic.* Retrieved from http://www.theatlantic.com/magazine/archive/2010/10/autisms-first-child/308227/ (p. 136)

Doss, B. D., Rhoades, G. K., Stanley, S. M., & Markman, H. J. (2009). The effect of the transition to parenthood on relationship quality: An 8-year prospective study. *Journal of Personality and Social Psychology*, *96*, 601–619. (p. 165)

Dotan-Eliaz, O., Sommer, K. L., & Rubin, S. (2009). Multilingual groups: Effects of linguistic ostracism on felt rejection and anger, coworker attraction, perceived team potency, and creative performance. *Basic and Applied Social Psychology*, *31*, 363–375. (p. 371)

Douglas, K. S., Guy, L. S., & Hart, S. D. (2009). Psychosis as a risk factor for violence to others: A meta-analysis. *Psychological Bulletin*, *135*, 679–706. (p. 533)

Douthat, R. (2010, November 28). The partisan mind. *The New York Times.* Retrieved from https://www.youtube.com/watch?v=kbJeiWYFrio (p. 466)

Dovidio, J. F., & Gaertner, S. L. (1999). Reducing prejudice: Combating intergroup biases. *Current Directions in Psychological Science*, *8*, 101–105. (p. 487)

Dovidio, J. F., ten Vergert, M., Stewart, T. L., Gaertner, S. L., Johnson, J. D., Esses, V. M., . . . Pearson, A. R. (2004). Perspective and prejudice: Antecedents and mediating mechanisms. *Personality and Social Psychology Bulletin*, *30*, 1537–1549. (p. 487)

Dowlati, Y., Herrmann, N., Swardfager, W., Liu, H., Sham, L., Reim, E. K., & Lanctôt, K. (2010). A meta-analysis of cytokines in major depression. *Biological Psychiatry*, *67*, 466–457. (p. 550)

Downing, P. E., Jiang, Y., & Shuman, M. (2001). A cortical area selective for visual processing of the human body. *Science*, *293*, 2470–2473. (p. 215)

Downs, E., & Smith, S. L. (2010). Keeping abreast of hypersexuality: A video game character content analysis. *Sex Roles*, *62*, 721–733. (p. 187)

Doyle, R. (2005, March). Gay and lesbian census. *Scientific American*, p. 28. (p. 193)

Draguns, J. G. (1990). Normal and abnormal behavior in cross-cultural perspective: Specifying the nature of their relationship. In J. J. Berman (Ed.), *Cross-cultural perspectives: Nebraska Symposium on Motivation, 1989* (Vol. 37, pp. 235–277). Lincoln: University of Nebraska Press. (p. 552)

Drew, T., Võ, M. L.-H., & Wolfe, J. M. (2013). The invisible gorilla strikes again: Sustained inattentional blindness in expert observers. *Psychological Science*, *24*, 1848–1853. (p. 83)

Driessen, E., Cuijpers, P., de Maat, S.C.M., Abbas, A. A., de Jonghe, F., & Dekker, J. J. M. (2010). The efficacy of short-term psychodynamic psychotherapy for depression: A meta-analysis. *Clinical Psychology Review*, *30*, 25–36. (p. 586)

Drummond, S. (2010, February). *Relationship between changes in sleep and memory in older adults.* Paper presented at the annual meeting of the American Association for the Advancement of Science, San Diego, CA. (p. 93)

Duckworth, A. L., Quinn, P. D., Lynam, D. R., Loeber, R., & Stouthamer-Loeber, M. (2011). Role of test motivation in intelligence testing. *Proceedings of the National Academy of Sciences of the United States of America*, *108*, 7716–7720. (p. 356)

Duckworth, A. L., Quinn, P. D., & Seligman, M. E. P. (2009). Positive predictors of teacher effectiveness. *Journal of Positive Psychology*, *4*, 540–547. (p. 375)

Duckworth, A. L., & Seligman, M. E. P. (2005). Discipline outdoes talent: Self-discipline predicts academic performance in adolescents. *Psychological Science*, *12*, 939–944. (pp. 375, 421)

Duckworth, A. L., & Seligman, M. E. P. (2006). Self-discipline gives girls the edge: Gender in self-discipline, grades, and achievement tests. *Journal of Educational Psychology*, *98*, 198–208. (p. 375)

Duckworth, A. L., Tsukayama, E., & Kirby, T. A. (2013). Is it really self-control? Examining the predictive power of the delay of gratification task. *Personality and Social Psychology Bulletin*, *39*, 843–855. (p. 151)

Duclos, S. E., Laird, J. D., Sexter, M., Stern, L., & Van Lighten, O. (1989). Emotion-specific effects of facial expressions and postures on emotional experience. *Journal of Personality and Social Psychology*, *57*, 100–108. (p. 401)

Dugan, A. (2014, March 17). *Americans most likely to say global warming is exaggerated.* Retrieved from http://www.gallup.com/poll/167960/americans-likely-say-global-warming-exaggerated.aspx (p. 444)

Duggan, J. P., & Booth, D. A. (1986). Obesity, overeating, and rapid gastric emptying in rats with ventromedial hypothalamic lesions. *Science, 231,* 609–611. (p. 379)

Duits, P., Cath, D. C., Lissek, S., Hox, J. J., Hamm, A. O., Engelhard, I. M., . . . Baas, J. M. P. (2015). Updated meta-analysis of classical fear conditioning in the anxiety disorders. *Depression and Anxiety, 32,* 239–253. (p. 541)

Dukakis, K. (2006). *Shock: The healing power of electroconvulsive therapy.* New York: Avery Press. (p. 598)

Dumont, K. A., Widom, C. S., & Czaja, S. J. (2007). Predictors of resilience in abused and neglected children grown-up: The role of individual and neighborhood characteristics. *Child Abuse & Neglect, 31,* 255–274. (p. 143)

Dunbar, R. I. M., Baron, R., Frangou, A., Pearce, E., van Leeuwin, E. J. C., Stow, J., . . . van Vugt, M. (2011). Social laughter is correlated with an elevated pain threshold. *Proceedings of the Royal Society: Series B, 279,* 1161–1167. (p. 424)

Dunham, Y., Chen, E. E., & Banaji, M. R. (2013). Two signatures of implicit intergroup attitudes: Developmental invariance and early enculturation. *Psychological Science, 24,* 860–868. (p. 465)

Dunlop, W. L., & Tracy, J. L. (2013). Sobering stories: Narratives of self-redemption predict behavioral change and improved health among recovering alcoholics. *Journal of Personality and Social Psychology, 104,* 576–590. (p. 583)

Dunn, E. W., Aknin, L. B., & Norton, M. I. (2008). Spending money on others promotes happiness. *Science, 319,* 1687–1688. (p. 483)

Dunn, E., & Norton, M. (2013). *Happy money: The science of smarter spending.* New York: Simon & Schuster. (p. 483)

Dunn, E. W., Aknin, L. B., & Norton, M. I. (2014). Prosocial spending and happiness: Using money to benefit others pays off. *Current Directions in Psychological Science, 13,* 347–355. (p. 431)

Dunn, M., & Searle, R. (2010). Effect of manipulated prestige-car ownership on both sex attractiveness ratings. *British Journal of Psychology, 101,* 69–80. (p. 193)

Dunsmoor, J. E., Murty, V. P., Davachi, L., & Phelps, E. A. (2015). Emotional learning selectively and retroactively strengthens memories for related events. *Nature, 520,* 345–348. (p. 294)

Dunson, D. B., Colombo, B., & Baird, D. D. (2002). Changes with age in the level and duration of fertility in the menstrual cycle. *Human Reproduction, 17,* 1399–1403. (p. 158)

Dutton, D. G., & Aron, A. P. (1974). Some evidence for heightened sexual attraction under conditions of high anxiety. *Journal of Personality and Social Psychology, 30,* 510–517. (p. 479)

Dutton, D. G., & Aron, A. P. (1989). Romantic attraction and generalized liking for others who are sources of conflict-based arousal. *Canadian Journal of Behavioural Sciences, 21,* 246–257. (p. 479)

Dweck, C. S. (2012a). Implicit theories. In P. A. M. Van Lange, A. Kruglanski, & E. T. Higgins (Eds.), *Handbook of theories of social psychology* (Vol. 2, pp. 43–61). Thousand Oaks, CA: Sage. (p. 361)

Dweck, C. S. (2012b). Mindsets and human nature: Promoting change in the Middle East, the schoolyard, the racial divide, and willpower. *American Psychologist, 67,* 614–622. (p. 361)

Dweck, C. S. (2015, January 1). The secret to raising smart kids. *Scientific American.* Retrieved from http://www.scientificamerican.com/article/the-secret-to-raising-smart-kids1/ (p. 361)

Dyrdal, G. M., & Lucas, R. E. (2011). *Reaction and adaptation to the birth of a child: A couple-level analysis.* Unpublished manuscript, Michigan State University, East Lansing, MI. (p. 162)

E

Eagan, K., Stolzenberg, E. B., Ramirez, J. J., Aragon, M. C., Suchard, M. R., & Hurtado, S. (2014). *The American freshman: National norms fall 2014.* Los Angeles: UCLA Higher Education Research Institute. (p. 373)

Eagan, T. (2015, June 5). What to be afraid of. *The New York Times.* Retrieved from http://www.nytimes.com/2015/06/05/opinion/what-to-be-afraid-of.html?_r=0 (p. 321)

Eagleman, D. (2011, September). Secret life of the mind. *Discover,* pp. 50–53. (p. 85)

Eagly, A. H. (2007). Female leadership advantage and disadvantage: Resolving the contradictions. *Psychology of Women Quarterly, 31,* 1–12. (p. B-12)

Eagly, A. H. (2009). The his and hers of prosocial behavior: An examination of the social psychology of gender. *American Psychologist, 64,* 644–658. (p. 194)

Eagly, A. H. (2013, March 20). Hybrid style works, and women are best at it. *The New York Times.* Retrieved from http://www.nytimes.com/roomfordebate/2013/03/20/shery-sandberg-says-lean-in-but-is-that-really-the-way-to-lead/why-lean-in-hybrid-style-succeeds-and-women-are-best-at-it (p. B-12)

Eagly, A. H., Ashmore, R. D., Makhijani, M. G., & Kennedy, L. C. (1991). What is beautiful is good, but . . .: A meta-analytic review of research on the physical attractiveness stereotype. *Psychological Bulletin, 110,* 109–128. (p. 477)

Eagly, A. H., & Carli, L. (2007). *Through the labyrinth: The truth about how women become leaders.* Cambridge, MA: Harvard University Press. (p. 173)

Eagly, A. H., & Wood, W. (1999). The origins of sex differences in human behavior: Evolved dispositions versus social roles. *American Psychologist, 54,* 408–423. (p. 194)

Eagly, A. H., & Wood, W. (2013). The nature–nurture debates: 25 years of challenges in understanding the psychology of gender. *Perspectives on Psychological Science, 8,* 340–357. (p. 172)

Easterlin, R. A., Morgan, R., Switek, M., & Wang, F. (2012). China's life satisfaction, 1990–2010. *Proceedings of the National Academy of Sciences of the United States of America, 109,* 9670–9671. (p. 434)

Eastman, C. L., Boulos, Z., Terman, M., Campbell, S. S., Dijk, D.-J., & Lewy, A. J. (1995). Light treatment for sleep disorders: Consensus report. VI. Shift work. *Journal of Biological Rhythms, 10,* 157–164. (p. 92)

Eastman, C. L., Young, M. A., Fogg, L. F., Liu, L., & Meaden, P. M. (1998). Bright light treatment of winter depression: A placebo-controlled trial. *Archives of General Psychiatry, 55,* 883–889. (p. 588)

Eastwick, P. W., & Finkel, E. J. (2008a). Sex differences in mate preferences revisited: Do people know what they initially desire in a romantic partner? *Journal of Personality and Social Psychology, 94,* 245–264. (p. 477)

Eastwick, P. W., & Finkel, E. J. (2008b). Speed-dating as a methodological innovation. *The Psychologist, 21,* 402–403. (p. 477)

Eastwick, P. W., Luchies, L. B., Finkel, E. J., & Hunt, L. L. (2014a). The many voices of Darwin's descendants: Reply to Schmitt (2014). *Psychological Bulletin, 140,* 673–681. (p. 477)

Eastwick, P. W., Luchies, L. B., Finkel, E. J., & Hunt, L. L. (2014b). The predictive validity of ideal partner preferences: A review and meta-analysis. *Psychological Bulletin, 140,* 623–665. (p. 477)

Ebbinghaus, H. (1885/1964). *Memory: A contribution to experimental psychology* (H. A. Ruger & C. E. Bussenius, Trans.). New York: Dover. (Original work published 1885) (pp. 289, 303)

Eckensberger, L. H. (1994). Moral development and its measurement across cultures. In W. J. Lonner & R. Malpass (Eds.), *Psychology and culture* (pp. 71–78). Boston: Allyn & Bacon. (p. 150)

Ecker, C., Suckling, J., Deoni, S. C., Lombardo, M. V., Bullmore, E. T., Baron-Cohen, S., . . . Murphy, D. G. (2012). Brain anatomy and its relationship to behavior in adults with autism spectrum disorder: A multicenter magnetic resonance imaging study. *Archives of General Psychiatry, 69,* 195–209. (p. 137)

Eckert, E. D., Heston, L. L., & Bouchard, T. J., Jr. (1981). MZ twins reared apart: Preliminary findings of psychiatric disturbances and traits. In L. Gedda, P. Paris, & W. D. Nance (Eds.), *Twin research 3: Part B. Intelligence, personality, and development* (pp. 179–188). New York: Alan Liss. (p. 542)

Eckholm, E. (2010, September 21). Woman on death row runs out of appeals. *The New York Times.* Retrieved from http://www.nytimes.com/2010/09/22/us/22execute.html?_r=0 (p. 352)

Ecklund-Flores, L. (1992, August). *The infant as a model for the teaching of introductory psychology.* Paper presented at the 100th Annual Convention of the American Psychological Association, Washington, DC. (p. 123)

Economist. (2001, December 20). *An anthropology of happiness.* Retrieved from http://www.economist.com/node/883909 (p. 371)

Edelstein, R. S., Wardecker, B. M., Chopik, W. J., Moors, A. C., Shipman, E. L., & Lin, N. J. (2015). Prenatal hormones in first-time expectant parents: Longitudinal changes and within-couple correlations. *American Journal of Human Biology, 27,* 317–325. (p. 182)

Edwards, A. C., & Kendler, K. S. (2012). A twin study of depression and nicotine dependence: Shared liability or causal relationship? *Journal of Affective Disorders, 142,* 90–97. (p. 109)

Edwards, R. R., Campbell, C., Jamison, R. N., & Wiech, K. (2009). The neurobiological underpinnings of coping with pain. *Current Directions in Psychological Science, 18,* 237–241. (p. 234)

Egan, P. J., & Mullin, M. (2012). Turning personal experience into political attitudes: The effects of local weather on Americans' perceptions about global warming. *Journal of Politics, 74,* 796–809. (p. 320)

Eibl-Eibesfeldt, I. (1971). *Love and hate: The natural history of behavior patterns.* New York: Holt, Rinehart & Winston. (p. 399)

Eich, E. (1990). Learning during sleep. In R. B. Bootzin, J. F. Kihlstrom, & D. L. Schacter (Eds.), *Sleep and cognition* (pp. 88–108). Washington, DC: American Psychological Association. (p. 99)

Eichstaedt, J. C., Schwartz, H. A., Kern, M. L., Park, G., Labarthe, D. R., Merchant, R. M., . . . Seligman, M. E. P. (2015). Psychological language on Twitter predicts county-level heart disease mortality. *Psychological Science, 26,* 159–169. (p. 20)

Ein-Dor, T., Mikulincer, M., Doron, G., & Shaver, P. R. (2010). The attachment paradox: How can so many of us (the insecure ones) have no adaptive advantages? *Perspectives on Psychological Science, 5,* 123–141. (p. 142)

Eippert, F., Finsterbush, J., Bingel, U., & Büchel, C. (2009). Direct evidence for spinal cord involvement in placebo analgesia. *Science, 326,* 404. (p. 234)

Eisenberg, D., Hunt, J., Speer, N., & Zivin, K. (2011). Mental health service utilization among college students in the United States. *Journal of Nervous and Mental Disease, 199,* 301–308. (p. 527)

Eisenberg, N., & Lennon, R. (1983). Sex differences in empathy and related capacities. *Psychological Bulletin, 94,* 100–131. (p. 398)

Eisenberger, N. I. (2015). Social pain and the brain: Controversies, questions, and where to go from here. *Annual Review of Psychology, 66,* 601–629. (p. 372)

Eisenberger, N. I., Master, S. L., Inagaki, T. K., Taylor, S. E., Shirinyan, D., Lieberman, M. D., & Naliboff, B. D. (2011). Attachment figures activate a safety signal-related neural region and reduce pain experience. *Proceedings of the National Academy of Sciences of the United States of America, 108,* 11721–11726. (p. 370)

Eisenberger, R., & Aselage, J. (2009). Incremental effects of reward on experienced performance pressure: Positive outcomes for intrinsic interest and creativity. *Journal of Organizational Behavior, 30,* 95–117. (p. 271)

Ekkekakis, P. (2015). Honey, I shrunk the pooled SMD! Guide to critical appraisal of systematic reviews and meta-analyses using the Cochrane review on exercise for depression as example. *Mental Health and Physical Activity, 8,* 21–36. (p. 426)

Ekman, P. (1994). Strong evidence for universals in facial expressions: A reply to Russell's mistaken critique. *Psychological Bulletin, 115,* 268–287. (p. 399)

Ekman, P., & Friesen, W. V. (1975). *Unmasking the face.* Englewood Cliffs, NJ: Prentice-Hall. (p. 399)

Ekman, P., Friesen, W. V., O'Sullivan, M., Chan, A., Diacoyanni-Tarlatzis, I., Heider, K., . . . Tzavaras, A. (1987). Universals and cultural differences in the judgments of facial expressions of emotion. *Journal of Personality and Social Psychology, 53,* 712–717. (p. 399)

Elbert, T., Pantev, C., Wienbruch, C., Rockstroh, B., & Taub, E. (1995). Increased cortical representation of the fingers of the left hand in string players. *Science, 270,* 305–307. (p. 127)

Elbogen, E. B., & Johnson, S. C. (2009). The intricate link between violence and mental disorder: Results from the National Epidemiologic Survey on Alcohol and Related Conditions. *Archives of General Psychiatry, 66,* 152–161. (p. 533)

Elfenbein, H. A., & Ambady, N. (2002). On the universality and cultural specificity of emotion recognition: A meta-analysis. *Psychological Bulletin, 128,* 203–235. (p. 399)

Elfenbein, H. A., & Ambady, N. (2003a). Universals and cultural differences in recognizing emotions. *Current Directions in Psychological Science, 12,* 159–164. (p. 399)

Elfenbein, H. A., & Ambady, N. (2003b). When familiarity breeds accuracy: Cultural exposure and facial emotion recognition. *Journal of Personality and Social Psychology, 85,* 276–290. (p. 399)

Elkind, D. (1970). The origins of religion in the child. *Review of Religious Research, 12,* 35–42. (p. 149)

Elkind, D. (1978). *The child's reality: Three developmental themes.* Hillsdale, NJ: Erlbaum. (p. 149)

Elkins, G., Johnson, A., & Fisher, W. (2012). Cognitive hypnotherapy for pain management. *American Journal of Clinical Hypnosis, 54,* 294–310. (p. 235)

Ellenbogen, J. M., Hu, P. T., Payne, J. D., Titone, D., & Walker, M. P. (2007). Human relational memory requires time and sleep. *Proceedings of the National Academy of Sciences of the United States of America, 104,* 7723–7728. (p. 93)

Elliot, A. J., & Niesta, D. (2008). Romantic red: Red enhances men's attraction to women. *Journal of Personality and Social Psychology, 95,* 1150–1164. (p. 268)

Elliot, A. J., Tracy, J. L., Pazda, A. D., & Beall, A. T. (2013). Red enhances women's attractiveness to men: First evidence suggesting universality. *Journal of Experimental Social Psychology, 49,* 165–168. (p. 268)

Ellis, A., & Becker, I. M. (1982). *A guide to personal happiness.* North Hollywood, CA: Wilshire. (p. 254)

Ellis, B. J., Bates, J. E., Dodge, K. A., Fergusson, D. M., John, H. L., Pettit, G. S., & Woodward, L. (2003). Does father absence place daughters at special risk for early sexual activity and teenage pregnancy? *Child Development, 74,* 801–821. (p. 187)

Ellis, B. J., & Boyce, W. T. (2008). Biological sensitivity to context. *Current Directions in Psychological Science, 17,* 183–187. (p. 543)

Ellis, L., & Ames, M. A. (1987). Neurohormonal functioning and sexual orientation: A theory of homosexuality–heterosexuality. *Psychological Bulletin, 101,* 233–258. (p. 191)

Ellison-Wright, I., Glahn, D. C., Laird, A. R., Thelen, S. M., & Bullmore, E. (2008). The anatomy of first-episode and chronic schizophrenia: An anatomical likelihood estimation meta-analysis. *American Journal of Psychiatry, 165,* 1015–1023. (p. 558)

Else-Quest, N. M., Hyde, J. S., & Linn, M. C. (2010). Cross-national patterns of gender differences in mathematics: A meta-analysis. *Psychological Bulletin, 136,* 103–127. (p. 357)

Elzinga, B. M., Ardon, A. M., Heijnis, M. K., De Ruiter, M. B., Van Dyck, R., & Veltman, D. J. (2007). Neural correlates of enhanced working-memory performance in dissociative disorder: A functional MRI study. *Psychological Medicine, 37,* 235–245. (p. 562)

EMDR. (2011, February 18). Personal communication [R. Dunton, EMDR Institute]. (p. 588)

Emerging Trends. (1997, September). *Teens turn more to parents than friends on whether to attend church.* Princeton, NJ: Princeton Religion Research Center. (p. 156)

Emmons, R. A. (2007). *Thanks! How the new science of gratitude can make you happier.* Boston: Houghton Mifflin. (p. 438)

Emmons, S., Geisler, C., Kaplan, K. J., & Harrow, M. (1997). *Living with schizophrenia.* New York: Taylor & Francis. (p. 527)

Empson, J. A. C., & Clarke, P. R. F. (1970). Rapid eye movements and remembering. *Nature, 227,* 287–288. (p. 100)

Endler, N. S. (1982). *Holiday of darkness: A psychologist's personal journey out of his depression.* New York: Wiley. (pp. 550, 598)

Engemann, K. M., & Owyang, M. T. (2005, April). So much for that merit raise: The link between wages and appearance. *Regional Economist.* Retrieved from https://www.stlouisfed.org/Publications/Regional-Economist/April-2005/So-Much-for-That-Merit-Raise-The-Link-between-Wages-and-Appearance (p. 477)

Engen, T. (1987). Remembering odors and their names. *American Scientist, 75,* 497–503. (p. 238)

England, P. (2010). The gender revolution: Uneven and stalled. *Gender & Society, 24,* 149–166. (p. 171)

Engle, R. W. (2002). Working memory capacity as executive attention. *Current Directions in Psychological Science, 11,* 19–23. (p. 284)

Entringer, S., Buss, C., Andersen, J., Chicz-DeMet, A., & Wadhwa, P. D. (2011). Ecological momentary assessment of maternal cortisol profiles over a multiple-day period predicts the length of human gestation. *Psychosomatic Medicine, 73,* 469–474. (p. 406)

Epel, E. S. (2009). Telomeres in a life-span perspective: A new "psychobiomarker"? *Current Directions in Psychological Science, 18,* 6–9. (p. 160)

Epley, N., & Dunning, D. (2000). Feeling "holier than thou": Are self-serving assessments produced by errors in self- or social prediction? *Journal of Personality and Social Psychology, 79,* 861–875. (p. 519)

Epley, N., Savitsky, K., & Gilovich, T. (2002). Empathy neglect: Reconciling the spotlight effect and the correspondence bias. *Journal of Personality and Social Psychology, 83,* 300–312. (p. 517)

Epley, N., Keysar, B., Van Boven, L., & Gilovich, T. (2004). Perspective taking as egocentric anchoring and adjustment. *Journal of Personality and Social Psychology, 87,* 327–339. (p. 132)

Epstein, J., Stern, E., & Silbersweig, D. (1998). Mesolimbic activity associated with psychosis in schizophrenia: Symptom-specific PET studies. *Annals of the New York Academy of Sciences, 877,* 562–574. (p. 558)

Epstein, S. (1983a). Aggregation and beyond: Some basic issues on the prediction of behavior. *Journal of Personality, 51,* 360–392. (p. 512)

Epstein, S. (1983b). The stability of behavior across time and situations. In R. Zucker, J. Aronoff, & A. I. Rabin (Eds.), *Personality and the prediction of behavior* (pp. 209–268). San Diego, CA: Academic Press. (p. 512)

Eranti, S. V., MacCabe, J. H., Bundy, H., & Murray, R. M. (2013). Gender difference in age at onset of schizophrenia: A meta-analysis. *Psychological Medicine, 43,* 155–167. (p. 557)

Erdelyi, M. H. (1985). *Psychoanalysis: Freud's cognitive psychology.* New York: Freeman. (p. 500)

Erdelyi, M. H. (1988). Repression, reconstruction, and defense: History and integration of the psychoanalytic and experimental frameworks. In J. Singer (Ed.), *Repression: Defense mechanism and cognitive style* (pp. 1–31). Chicago: University of Chicago Press. (p. 500)

Erdelyi, M. H. (2006). The unified theory of repression. *Behavioral and Brain Sciences, 29,* 499–551. (pp. 499, 500)

Erel, O., & Burman, B. (1995). Interrelatedness of marital relations and parent–child relations: A meta-analytic review. *Psychological Bulletin, 118,* 108–132. (p. 165)

Erickson, K. I., Banducci, S. E., Weinstein, A. M., MacDonald, A. W., III, Ferrell, R. E., Halder, I., . . . Manuck, S. B. (2013). The brain-derived neurotrophic factor Val-66Met polymorphism moderates an effect of physical activity on working memory performance. *Psychological Science, 24,* 1770–1779. (p. 160)

Erickson, M. F., & Aird, E. G. (2005). *The motherhood study: Fresh insights on mothers' attitudes and concerns.* New York: The Motherhood Project, Institute for American Values. (p. 165)

Ericsson, K. A. (2001). Attaining excellence through deliberate practice: Insights from the study of expert performance. In M. Ferrari (Ed.), *The pursuit of excellence in education* (pp. 21–55). Hillsdale, NJ: Erlbaum. (p. 376)

Ericsson, K. A. (2002). Attaining excellence through deliberate practice: Insights from the study of expert performance. In C. Desforges & R. Fox (Eds.), *Teaching and learning: The essential readings* (pp. 4–37). Malden, MA: Blackwell. (p. 344)

Ericsson, K. A. (2006). The influence of experience and deliberate practice on the development of superior expert performance. In K. A. Ericsson, N. Charness, P. J. Feltovich, & R. R. Hoffman (Eds.), *The Cambridge handbook of expertise and expert performance* (pp. 685–705). Cambridge, England: Cambridge University Press. (p. 376)

Ericsson, K. A. (2007). Deliberate practice and the modifiability of body and mind: Toward a science of the structure and acquisition of expert and elite performance. *International Journal of Sport Psychology, 38,* 4–34. (pp. 344, 376)

Ericsson, K. A., Roring, R. W., & Nandagopal, K. (2007). Giftedness and evidence for reproducibly superior performance: An account based on the expert performance framework. *High Ability Studies, 18,* 3–56. (p. 362)

Erikson, E. H. (1963). *Childhood and society.* New York: Norton. (p. 152)

Erikson, E. H. (1983, June). A conversation with Erikson [by E. Hall]. *Psychology Today,* pp. 22–30. (p. 142)

Erlich, N., Lipp, O. V., & Slaughter, V. (2013). Of hissing snakes and angry voices: Human infants are differentially responsive to evolutionary fear-relevant sounds. *Developmental Science, 16,* 894–904. (p. 543)

Ermer, E., Cope, L. M., Nyalakanti, P. K., Calhoun, V. D., & Kiehl, K. A. (2012). Aberrant paralimbic gray matter in criminal psychopathy. *Journal of Abnormal Psychology, 121,* 649–658. (p. 53)

Ermer, E., Kahn, R. E., Salovey, P., & Kiehl, K. A. (2012). Emotional intelligence in incarcerated men with psychopathic traits. *Journal of Personality and Social Psychology, 103,* 194–204. (p. 563)

Ert, E., Yechiam, E., & Arshavsky, O. (2013). Smokers' decision making: More than mere risk taking. *PLOS ONE, 8*(7), e68064. doi:10.1371/journal.pone.0068064 (p. 152)

Ertmer, D. J., Young, N. M., & Nathani, S. (2007). Profiles of focal development in young cochlear implant recipients. *Journal of Speech, Language, and Hearing Research, 50,* 393–407. (p. 332)

Escasa, M. J., Casey, J. F., & Gray, P. B. (2011). Salivary testosterone levels in men at a U.S. sex club. *Archives of Sexual Behavior, 40,* 921–926. (p. 182)

Escobar-Chaves, S. L., Tortolero, S. R., Markham, C. M., Low, B. J., Eitel, P., & Thickstun, P. (2005). Impact of the media on adolescent sexual attitudes and behaviors. *Pediatrics, 116,* 303–326. (p. 186)

Escobedo, J. R., & Adolphs, R. (2010). Becoming a better person: Temporal remoteness biases autobiographical memories for moral events. *Emotion, 10,* 511–518. (p. 520)

Eskine, K. J., Kacinik, N. A., & Prinz, J. J. (2011). A bad taste in the mouth: Gustatory disgust influences moral judgment. *Psychological Science, 22,* 295–299. (p. 150)

ESPAD. (2003). *Summary of the 2003 findings.* European School Survey Project on Alcohol and Other Drugs. Retrieved from http://www.espad.org (p. 115)

Esposito, G., Yoshida, S., Ohnishi, R., Tsuneoka, Y., del Carmen Rostagno, M., Yokata, S., . . . Kuroda, K. O. (2013). Infant calming responses during maternal carrying in humans and mice. *Current Biology, 23,* 739–745. (p. 370)

Esser, J. K., & Lindoerfer, J. S. (1989). Groupthink and the space shuttle Challenger accident: Toward a quantitative case analysis. *Journal of Behavioral Decision Making, 2,* 167–177. (p. 459)

Esterson, A. (2001). The mythologizing of psychoanalytic history: Deception and self-deception in Freud's accounts of the seduction theory episode. *History of Psychiatry, 12,* 329–352. (p. 498)

Etkin, A., & Wager, T. D. (2007). Functional neuroimaging of anxiety: A meta-analysis of emotional processing in PTSD, social anxiety disorder, and specific phobia. *American Journal of Psychiatry, 164,* 1476–1488. (p. 543)

Eurich, T. L., Krause, D. E., Cigularov, K., & Thornton, G. C., III. (2009). Assessment centers: Current practices in the United States. *Journal of Business Psychology, 24,* 387–407. (pp. 514–515)

Euston, D. R., Tatsuno, M., & McNaughton, B. L. (2007). Fast-forward playback of recent memory sequences in prefrontal cortex during sleep. *Science, 318,* 1147–1150. (p. 293)

Evans, C. R., & Dion, K. L. (1991). Group cohesion and performance: A meta-analysis. *Small Group Research, 22,* 175–186. (p. B-12)

Evans, G. W., Palsane, M. N., & Carrere, S. (1987). Type A behavior and occupational stress: A cross-cultural study of blue-collar workers. *Journal of Personality and Social Psychology, 52,* 1002–1007. (p. 414)

Evans, J. St. B. T., & Stanovich, K. E. (2013). Dual-process theories of higher cognition: Advancing the debate. *Perspectives on Psychological Science, 8,* 223–241. (p. 85)

Evans, N., & Levinson, S. C. (2009). The myth of language universals: Language diversity and its importance for cognitive science. *Behavioral and Brain Sciences, 32,* 429–492. (p. 330)

Evers, A., Muñiz, J., Bartram, D., Boben, D., Egeland, J., & Fernández Hermida, J. R. (2012). Testing practices in the 21st century: Developments and European psychologists' opinions. *European Psychologist, 17,* 300–319. (p. 347)

Everson, S. A., Goldberg, D. E., Kaplan, G. A., Cohen, R. D., Pukkala, E., Tuomilehto, J., & Salonen, J. T. (1996). Hopelessness and risk of mortality and incidence of myocardial infarction and cancer. *Psychosomatic Medicine, 58,* 113–121. (p. 423)

Eysenck, H. J. (1952). The effects of psychotherapy: An evaluation. *Journal of Consulting Psychology, 16,* 319–324. (p. 585)

Eysenck, H. J. (1990, May 28). An improvement on personality inventory. *Current Contents: Social and Behavioral Sciences,* p. 20. (p. 506)

Eysenck, H. J. (1992). Four ways five factors are not basic. *Personality and Individual Differences, 13,* 667–673. (p. 506)

Eysenck, H. J., & Grossarth-Maticek, R. (1991). Creative novation behaviour therapy as a prophylactic treatment for cancer and coronary heart disease: Part II—Effects of treatment. *Behaviour Research and Therapy, 29,* 17–31. (p. 428)

Eysenck, H. J., Wakefield, J. A., Jr., & Friedman, A. F. (1983). Diagnosis and clinical assessment: The DSM-III. *Annual Review of Psychology, 34,* 167–193. (p. 531)

Eysenck, S. B. G., & Eysenck, H. J. (1963). The validity of questionnaire and rating assessments of extraversion and neuroticism, and their factorial stability. *British Journal of Psychology, 54,* 51–62. (p. 506)

F

Fabiano, G. A., Pelham, W. E., Jr., Coles, E. K., Gnagy, E. M., Chronis-Tuscano, A., & O'Connor, B. C. (2008). A meta-analysis of behavioral treatments for attention-deficit/hyperactivity disorder. *Clinical Psychology Review, 29,* 129–140. (p. 532)

Fabiansson, E. C., Denson, T. F., Moulds, M. L., Grisham, J. R., & Schira, M. M. (2012). Don't look back in anger: Neural correlates of reappraisal, analytical rumination, and angry rumination during a recall of an anger-inducing autobiographical memory. *NeuroImage, 59,* 2974–2981. (p. 416)

Fagan, J. F., & Holland, C. R. (2007). Equal opportunity and racial differences in IQ. *Intelligence, 30,* 361–387. (p. 359)

Fagan, J. F., & Holland, C. R. (2007). Racial equality in intelligence: Predictions from a theory of intelligence as processing. *Intelligence, 35,* 319–334. (p. 360)

Fagan, J. F., & Holland, C. R. (2009). Culture-fair prediction of academic achievement. *Intelligence, 37,* 62–67. (p. 360)

Fagundes, C. P., & Way, B. (2014). Early-life stress and adult inflammation. *Current Directions in Psychological Science, 23,* 277–283. (p. 144)

Fairfield, H. (2012, February 4). Girls lead in science exam, but not in the United States. *The New York Times.* Retrieved from http://www.nytimes.com/interactive/2013/02/04/science/girls-lead-in-science-exam-but-not-in-the-united-states.html (p. 357)

Falk, C. F., Heine, S. J., Yuki, M., & Takemura, K. (2009). Why do Westerners self-enhance more than East Asians? *European Journal of Personality, 23,* 183–203. (p. 519)

Falk, R., Falk, R., & Ayton, P. (2009). Subjective patterns of randomness and choice: Some consequences of collective responses. *Journal of Experimental Psychology: Human Perception and Performance, 35,* 203–224. (p. 16)

Fang, Z., Spaeth, A. M., Ma, N., Zhu, S., Hu, S., Goel, N., . . . Rao, H. (2015). Altered salience network connectivity predicts macronutrient intake after sleep deprivation. *Scientific Reports, 5,* Article 8215. doi:10.1038/srep08215 (p. 95)

Fanti, K. A., Vanman, E., Henrich, C. C., & Avraamides, M. N. (2009). Desensitization to media violence over a short period of time. *Aggressive Behavior, 35,* 179–187. (p. 277)

Farah, M. J., Rabinowitz, C., Quinn, G. E., & Liu, G. T. (2000). Early commitment of neural substrates for face recognition. *Cognitive Neuropsychology, 17,* 117–124. (p. 61)

Farb, N. A. S., Anderson, A. K., Mayberg, H., Bean, J., McKeon, D., & Segal, Z. V. (2010). Minding one's emotions: Mindfulness training alters the neural expression of sadness. *Emotion, 10,* 25–33. (p. 429)

Farina, A. (1982). The stigma of mental disorders. In A. G. Miller (Ed.), *In the eye of the beholder* (pp. 305–363). New York: Praeger. (pp. 529, 531)

Farley, M., Baral, I., Kiremire, M., & Sezgin, U. (1998). Prostitution in five countries: Violence and post-traumatic stress disorder. *Feminism and Psychology, 8,* 405–426. (p. 540)

Farrington, D. P. (1991). Antisocial personality from childhood to adulthood. *The Psychologist, 4,* 389–394. (p. 563)

Fatemi, S. H., & Folsom, T. D. (2009). The neurodevelopmental hypothesis of schizophrenia, revisted. *Schizophrenia Bulletin, 35,* 528–548. (p. 558)

Fay, A. J., & Maner, J. K. (2014). When does heat promote hostility? Person by situation interactions shape the psychological effects of haptic sensations. *Journal of Experimental Social Psychology, 50,* 210–216. (p. 470)

Fazel, S., & Grann, M. (2006). The population impact of severe mental illness on violent crime. *American Journal of Psychiatry, 163,* 1397–1403. (p. 533)

Fazel, S., Langstrom, N., Hjern, A., Grann, M., & Lichtenstein, P. (2009). Schizophrenia, substance abuse, and violent crime. *Journal of the American Medical Association, 301,* 2016–2023. (p. 533)

Fazel, S., Lichtenstein, P., Grann, M., Goodwin, G. M., & Långström, N. (2010). Bipolar disorder and violent crime: New evidence from population-based longitudinal studies and systematic review. *Archives of General Psychiatry, 67,* 931–938. (p. 533)

Feder, H. H. (1984). Hormones and sexual behavior. *Annual Review of Psychology, 35,* 165–200. (p. 181)

Feeney, D. M. (1987). Human rights and animal welfare. *American Psychologist, 42,* 593–599. (p. 29)

Feigenson, L., Carey, S., & Spelke, E. (2002). Infants' discrimination of number vs. continuous extent. *Cognitive Psychology, 44,* 33–66. (p. 131)

Feinberg, M., Willer, R., Antonenko, O., & John, O. P. (2012). Liberating reason from the passions: Overriding intuitionist moral judgments through emotion reappraisal. *Psychological Science, 23,* 788–795. (p. 151)

Feinberg, M., Willer, R., & Schultz, M. (2014). Gossip and ostracism promote cooperation in groups. *Psychological Science, 25,* 656–664. (p. 370)

Feingold, A. (1992). Good-looking people are not what we think. *Psychological Bulletin, 111,* 304–341. (p. 477)

Feingold, A., & Mazzella, R. (1998). Gender differences in body image are increasing. *Psychological Science, 9,* 190–195. (p. 566)

Feinstein, J. S., Buzza, C., Hurlemann, R., Follmer, R. L., Dahdaleh, N. S., Coryell, W. H., . . . Wemmie, J. A. (2013). Fear and panic in humans with bilateral amygdala damage. *Nature Neuroscience, 16,* 270–272. (p. 52)

Feldman, M. B., & Meyer, I. H. (2010). Comorbidity and age of onset of eating disorders in gay men, lesbians, and bisexuals. *Psychiatry Research, 180,* 126–131. (p. 566)

Feldman, R., Rosenthal, Z., & Eidelman, A. I. (2014). Maternal-preterm skin-to-skin contact enhances child physiologic organization and cognitive control across the first 10 years of life. *Biological Psychiatry, 75,* 56–64. (p. 128)

Fenn, K. M., & Hambrick, D. Z. (2012). Individual differences in working memory capacity predict sleep-dependent memory consolidation. *Journal of Experimental Psychology: General, 141,* 404–410. (p. 287)

Fenton, W. S., & McGlashan, T. H. (1991). Natural history of schizophrenia subtypes: II. Positive and negative symptoms and long-term course. *Archives of General Psychiatry, 48,* 978–986. (p. 557)

Fenton, W. S., & McGlashan, T. H. (1994). Antecedents, symptom progression, and long-term outcome of the deficit syndrome in schizophrenia. *American Journal of Psychiatry, 151,* 351–356. (p. 557)

Ferguson, C. J. (2009). Media violence effects: Confirmed truth or just another X-file? *Journal of Forensic Psychology Practice, 9,* 103–126. (p. 277)

Ferguson, C. (2009, June 14). Not every child is secretly a genius. *The Chronicle Review.* Retrieved from http://chronicle.com/article/Not-Every-Child-Is-Secretly/48001 (p. 343)

Ferguson, C. J. (2013). Spanking, corporal punishment and negative long-term outcomes: A meta-analytic review of longitudinal studies. *Clinical Psychology Review, 33,* 196–208. (p. 262)

Ferguson, C. J. (2013). Violent video games and the Supreme Court: Lessons for the scientific community in the wake of Brown v. Entertainment Merchants Association. *American Psychologist, 68,* 57–74. (p. 473)

Ferguson, C. J. (2014). Is video game violence bad? *The Psychologist, 27,* 324–327. (p. 473)

Ferguson, C. J., San Miguel, C., Garza, A., & Jerabeck, J. M. (2011). A longitudinal test of video game violence influences on dating and aggression: A 3-year longitudinal study of adolescents. *Journal of Psychiatric Research, 46,* 141–146. (p. 105)

Ferguson, C. J., Winegard, B., & Winegard, B. M. (2011). Who is the fairest one of all? How evolution guides peer and media influences on female body dissatisfaction. *Review of General Psychology, 15,* 11–28. (p. 566)

Ferguson, E. D. (1989). Adler's motivational theory: An historical perspective on belonging and the fundamental human striving. *Individual Psychology, 45,* 354–361. (p. 369)

Ferguson, E. D. (2001). Adler and Dreikurs: Cognitive-social dynamic innovators. *Journal of Individual Psychology, 57,* 324–341. (p. 369)

Ferguson, E. D. (2003). Social processes, personal goals, and their intertwining: Their importance in Adlerian theory and practice. *Journal of Individual Psychology, 59,* 136–144. (p. 496)

Ferguson, E. D. (2010). Editor's notes: Adler's innovative contributions regarding the need to belong. *Journal of Individual Psychology, 66,* 1–7. (p. 369)

Ferguson, M. J., & Zayas, V. (2009). Automatic evaluation. *Current Directions in Psychological Science, 18,* 362–366. (p. 202)

Fergusson, D. M., Boden, J. M., & Horwood, L. J. (2009). Tests of causal links between alcohol abuse or dependence and major depression. *Archives of General Psychiatry, 66,* 260–266. (p. 550)

Fergusson, D. M., & Woodward, L. G. (2002). Mental health, educational, and social role outcomes of adolescents with depression. *Archives of General Psychiatry, 59,* 225–231. (p. 548)

Fernández-Dols, J.-M., & Ruiz-Belda, M.-A. (1995). Are smiles a sign of happiness? Gold medal winners at the Olympic Games. *Journal of Personality and Social Psychology, 69,* 1113–1119. (p. 400)

Fernbach, P. M., Rogers, T., Fox, C. R., & Sloman, S. A. (2013). Political extremism is supported by an illusion of understanding. *Psychological Science, 24,* 939–946. (p. 322)

Fernie, G., Peeters, M., Gullo, M. J., Christianson, P., Cole, J. C., Sumnall, H., & Field, M. (2013). Multiple behavioral impulsivity tasks predict prospective alcohol involvement in adolescents. *Addiction, 108,* 1916–1923. (p. 493)

Fernyhough, C. (2008). Getting Vygotskian about theory of mind: Mediation, dialogue, and the development of social understanding. *Developmental Review, 28,* 225–262. (p. 134)

Ferrari, A. J., Charlson, F. J., Norman, R. E., Patten, S. B., Freedman, G., Murray, C. J. L., ... Whiteford, H. A. (2013). Burden of depressive disorders by country, sex, age, and year: Findings from the Global Burden of Disease Study 2010. *PLOS Medicine, 10*(11), e1001547. doi:10.1371/journal.pmed.1001547 (pp. 546, 552)

Ferri, M., Amato, L., & Davoli, M. (2006). Alcoholics Anonymous and other 12-step programmes for alcohol dependence. *Cochrane Database of Systematic Reviews,* Issue 3, Article CD005032. doi:10.1002/14651858.CD005032.pub2 (p. 583)

Ferriman, K., Lubinski, D., & Benbow, C. P. (2009). Work preferences, life values, and personal views of top math/science graduate students and the profoundly gifted: Developmental changes and gender differences during emerging adulthood and parenthood. *Journal of Personality and Social Psychology, 97,* 517–522. (p. 174)

Ferris, C. F. (1996, March). The rage of innocents. *The Sciences,* pp. 22–26. (p. 144)

Festinger, L. (1957). *A theory of cognitive dissonance.* Stanford, CA: Stanford University Press. (p. 446)

Fiedler, F. E. (1981). Leadership effectiveness. *American Behavioral Scientist, 24,* 619–632. (p. B-11)

Fiedler, F. E. (1987, September). When to lead, when to stand back. *Psychology Today,* pp. 26–27. (p. B-12)

Field, A. P. (2006). Is conditioning a useful framework for understanding the development and treatment of phobias? *Clinical Psychology Review, 26,* 857–875. (p. 541)

Field, T., Diego, M., & Hernandez-Reif, M. (2007). Massage therapy research. *Developmental Review, 27,* 75–89. (p. 127)

Field, T., Hernandez-Reif, M., Feijo, L., & Freedman, J. (2006). Prenatal, perinatal and neonatal stimulation: A survey of neonatal nurseries. *Infant Behavior & Development, 29,* 24–31. (p. 231)

Fielder, R. L., Walsh, J. L., Carey, K. B., & Carey, M. P. (2013). Predictors of sexual hookups: A theory-based, prospective study of first-year college women. *Archives of Sexual Behavior, 42,* 1425–1441. (p. 186)

Fielder, R. L., Walsh, J. L., Carey, K. B., & Carey, M. P. (2014). Sexual hookups and adverse health outcomes: A longitudinal study of first-year college women. *Journal of Sex Research, 51,* 131–144. (p. 23)

Fields, R. D. (2004, April). The other half of the brain. *Scientific American,* pp. 54–61. (p. 37)

Fields, R. D. (2008, March). White matter. *Scientific American,* pp. 54–61. (p. 37)

Fields, R. D. (2011, May/June). The hidden brain. *Scientific American,* pp. 53–59. (p. 37)

Fields, R. D. (2013). Neuroscience: Map the other brain. *Nature, 501,* 25–27. (p. 37)

Fikke, L. T., Melinder, A., & Landrø, N. I. (2011). Executive functions are impaired in adolescents engaging in non-suicidal self-injury. *Psychological Medicine, 41,* 601–610. (p. 554)

Filbey, F. M., Aslan, S., Calhoun, V. D., Spence, J. S., Damaraju, E., Caprihan, A., & Segall, J. (2014). Long-term effects of marijuana use on the brain. *Proceedings of the National Academy of Sciences of the United States of America, 111,* 16913–16918. (p. 112)

Fincham, F. D., & Bradbury, T. N. (1993). Marital satisfaction, depression, and attributions: A longitudinal analysis. *Journal of Personality and Social Psychology, 64,* 442–452. (p. 443)

Finchilescu, G., & Tredoux, C. (Eds.). (2010). Intergroup relations in post apartheid South Africa: Change, and obstacles to change. *Journal of Social Issues, 66,* 223–236. (p. 486)

Fine, C. (2010). From scanner to sound bite: Issues in interpreting and reporting sex differences in the brain. *Current Directions in Psychological Science, 19,* 280–283. (p. 50)

Finer, L. B. & Philbin, J. M. (2014). Trends in ages at key reproductive transitions in the United States, 1951–2010. *Women's Health Issues, 24,* e271–e279. http://dx.doi.org/10.1016/j.whi.2014.02.002 (p. 156)

Fingelkurts, A. A., & Fingelkurts, A. A. (2009). Is our brain hardwired to produce God, or is our brain hardwired to perceive God? A systematic review on the role of the brain in mediating religious experience. *Cognitive Processes, 10,* 293–326. (p. 60)

Fingerman, K. L., & Charles, S. T. (2010). It takes two to tango: Why older people have the best relationships. *Current Directions in Psychological Science, 19,* 172–176. (p. 166)

Fink, G. R., Markowitsch, H. J., Reinkemeier, M., Bruckbauer, T., Kessler, J., & Heiss, W.-D. (1996). Cerebral representation of one's own past: Neural networks involved in autobiographical memory. *Journal of Neuroscience, 16,* 4275–4282. (p. 292)

Fink, M. (2009). *Electroconvulsive therapy: A guide for professionals and their patients.* New York: Oxford University Press. (p. 598)

Finkel, E. J., Cheung, E. O., Emery, L. F., Carswell, K. L., & Larson, G. M. (2015). The suffocation model: Why marriage in America is becoming an all-or-nothing institution. *Current Directions in Psychological Science, 24,* 238–244. (p. 163)

Finkel, E. J., DeWall, C. N., Slotter, E. B., McNulty, J. K., Pond, R. S., Jr., & Atkins, D. C. (2012). Using I³ theory to clarify when dispositional aggressiveness predicts intimate partner violence perpetration. *Journal of Personality and Social Psychology, 102,* 533–549. (p. 421)

Finkel, E. J., & Eastwick, P. W. (2008). Speed-dating. *Current Directions in Psychological Science, 17,* 193–197. (p. 477)

Finkel, E. J., & Eastwick, P. W. (2009). Arbitrary social norms influence sex differences in romantic selectivity. *Psychological Science 20,* 1290–1295. (p. 477)

Finlay, S. W. (2000). Influence of Carl Jung and William James on the origin of alcoholics anonymous. *Review of General Psychology, 4,* 3–12. (p. 583)

Fiore, M. C., Jaén, C. R., Baker, T. B., Bailey, W. C., Benowitz, N. L., Curry, S. J., ... Wewers, M. E. (2008, May). *Treating tobacco use and dependence: 2008 update.* Rockville, MD: U.S. Department of Health and Human Services, Public Health Service. (p. 109)

Fischer, A., & LaFrance, M. (2015). What drives the smile and the tear: Why women are more emotionally expressive than men. *Emotion Review, 7,* 22–29. (pp. 172, 397)

Fischer, P., & Greitemeyer, T. (2006). Music and aggression: The impact of sexual-aggressive song lyrics on aggression-related thoughts, emotions, and behavior toward the same and the opposite sex. *Personality and Social Psychology Bulletin, 32,* 1165–1176. (p. 471)

Fischer, P., Greitemeyer, T., Kastenmúller, A., Vogrincic, C., & Sauer, A. (2011). The effects of risk-glorifying media exposure on risk-positive cognitions, emotions, and behaviors: A meta-analytic review. *Psychological Bulletin, 137,* 367–390. (pp. 277, 471)

Fischer, R., & Boer, D. (2011). What is more important for national well-being: Money or autonomy? A meta-analysis of well-being, burnout, and anxiety across 63 societies. *Journal of Personality and Social Psychology, 101,* 164–184. (p. 433)

Fishbach, A., Dhar, R., & Zhang, Y. (2006). Subgoals as substitutes or complements: The role of goal accessibility. *Journal of Personality and Social Psychology, 91,* 232–242. (p. B-11)

Fisher, G., & Rangel, A. (2014). Symmetry in cold-to-hot and hot-to-cold valuation gaps. *Psychological Science, 25,* 120–127. (p. 378)

Fisher, H. E. (1993, March/April). After all, maybe it's biology. *Psychology Today,* pp. 40–45. (p. 163)

Fisher, H. T. (1984). Little Albert and Little Peter. *Bulletin of the British Psychological Society, 37,* 269. (p. 575)

Fischhoff, B. (1982). Debiasing. In D. Kahneman, P. Slovic, & A. Tversky (Eds.), *Judgment under uncertainty: Heuristics and biases* (pp. 422–444). New York: Cambridge University Press. (p. 322)

Fischhoff, B., Slovic, P., & Lichtenstein, S. (1977). Knowing with certainty: The appropriateness of extreme confidence. *Journal of Experimental Psychology: Human Perception and Performance, 3,* 552–564. (p. 321)

Flack, W. F. (2006). Peripheral feedback effects of facial expressions, bodily postures, and vocal expressions on emotional feelings. *Cognition and Emotion, 20,* 177–195. (pp. 402, 416)

Flaherty, D. K. (2011). The vaccine-autism connection: A public health crisis caused by unethical medical practices and fraudulent science. *Annals of Pharmacotherapy, 45,* 1302–1304. (p. 136)

Flegal, K. M., Carroll, M. D., Kit, B. K., & Ogden, C. L. (2012). Prevalence of obesity and trends in the distribution of body mass index among US adults, 1999–2010. *Journal of the American Medical Association, 307,* 491–497. (p. 383)

Flegal, K. M., Carroll, M. D., Ogden, C. L., & Curtin, L. R. (2010). Prevalence and trends in obesity among US adults, 1999–2008. *Journal of the American Medical Association, 303,* 235–241. (p. 383)

Flegal, K. M., Kit, B. K., Orpana, H., & Graubard, B. I. (2013). Association of all-cause mortality with overweight and obesity using standard body mass index categories: A systematic review and meta-analysis. *Journal of the American Medical Association, 309,* 71–82. (p. 383)

Fleischman, D. A., Yang, J., Arfanakis, K., Avanitakis, Z., Leurgans, S. E., Turner, A. D., . . . Buchman, A. S. (2015). Physical activity, motor function, and white matter hyperintensity burden in healthy older adults. *Neurology, 84,* 1294–1300. (p. 160)

Fleming, I., Baum, A., & Weiss, L. (1987). Social density and perceived control as mediator of crowding stress in high-density residential neighborhoods. *Journal of Personality and Social Psychology, 52,* 899–906. (p. 420)

Fleming, J. H. (2001, Winter/Spring). Introduction to the special issue on linkage analysis. *Gallup Research Journal,* pp. i–vi. (p. B-10)

Fleming, J. H., & Scott, B. A. (1991). The costs of confession: The Persian Gulf War POW tapes in historical and theoretical perspective. *Contemporary Social Psychology, 15,* 127–138. (p. 399)

Fletcher, G. J. O., Fitness, J., & Blampied, N. M. (1990). The link between attributions and happiness in close relationships: The roles of depression and explanatory style. *Journal of Social and Clinical Psychology, 9,* 243–255. (p. 443)

Flora, S. R. (2004). *The power of reinforcement.* Albany: State University of New York Press. (p. 263)

Flora, S. R., & Bobby, S. E. (2008, September/October). The bipolar bamboozle. *Skeptical Inquirer,* pp. 41–45. (p. 547)

Flory, R., Ametepe, J., & Bowers, B. (2010). A randomized, place-controlled trial of bright light and high-density negative air ions for treatment of seasonal affective disorder. *Psychiatry Research, 177,* 101–108. (p. 588)

Flouri, E., & Buchanan, A. (2004). Early father's and mother's involvement and child's later educational outcomes. *British Journal of Educational Psychology, 74,* 141–153. (p. 141)

Foa, E. B., Gillihan, S. J., & Bryant, R. A. (2013). Challenges and successes in dissemination of evidence-based treatments for posttraumatic stress: Lessons learned from prolonged exposure therapy for PTSD. *Psychological Science in the Public Interest, 14,* 65–111. (p. 575)

Foa, E. B., & Kozak, M. J. (1986). Emotional processing of fear: Exposure to corrective information. *Psychological Bulletin, 99,* 20–35. (p. 576)

Fong, C. J., Zaleski, D. J., & Leach, J. K. (2015). The challenge–skill balance and antecedents of flow: A meta-analytic investigation. *Journal of Positive Psychology, 10,* 425–446. (p. B-1)

Fong, K., & Mar, R. A. (2015). What does my avatar say about me? Inferring personality from avatars. *Personality and Social Psychology Bulletin, 41,* 237–249. (p. 512)

Ford, E. S. (2002). Does exercise reduce inflammation? Physical activity and C-reactive protein among U.S. adults. *Epidemiology, 13,* 561–568. (p. 426)

Ford, M. T., Cerasoli, C. P., Higgins, J. A., & Deccesare, A. L. (2011). Relationships between psychological, physical, and behavioural health and work performance: A review and meta-analysis. *Work & Stress, 25,* 185–204. (p. B-8)

Foree, D. D., & LoLordo, V. M. (1973). Attention in the pigeon: Differential effects of food-getting versus shock-avoidance procedures. *Journal of Comparative and Physiological Psychology, 85,* 551–558. (p. 269)

Forest, A. & Wood, J. (2012). When social networking is not working: Individuals with low self-esteem recognize but do not reap the benefits of self-disclosure on Facebook. *Psychological Science, 23,* 295–302. (p. 517)

Forgas, J. P. (2008). Affect and cognition. *Perspectives on Psychological Science, 3,* 94–101. (p. 431)

Forgas, J. P. (2009, November/December). Think negative! *Australian Science,* pp. 14–17. (p. 545)

Forgas, J. P. (2013). Don't worry, be sad! On the cognitive, motivational, and interpersonal benefits of negative mood. *Current Directions in Psychological Science, 22,* 225–232. (p. 545)

Forgas, J. P., Bower, G. H., & Krantz, S. E. (1984). The influence of mood on perceptions of social interactions. *Journal of Experimental Social Psychology, 20,* 497–513. (p. 298)

Forhan, S. E., Gottlieb, S. L., Sternberg, M. R., Xu, F., Datta, D., Berman, S., & Markowitz, L. (2008, March). *Prevalence of sexually transmitted infections and bacterial vaginosis among female adolescents in the United States: Data from the National Health and Nutrition Examination Survey (NHANES) 2003–2004.* Paper presented at the 2008 National STD Prevention Conference, Chicago, IL. (p. 184)

Forman, D. R., Aksan, N., & Kochanska, G. (2004). Toddlers' responsive imitation predicts preschool-age conscience. *Psychological Science, 15,* 699–704. (p. 276)

Forstmann, M., & Burgmer, P. (2015). Adults are intuitive mind–body dualists. *Journal of Experimental Psychology: General, 144,* 222–235. (p. 36)

Forsyth, D. R., Lawrence, N. K., Burnette, J. L., & Baumeister, R. F. (2007). Attempting to improve academic performance of struggling college students by bolstering their self-esteem: An intervention that backfired. *Journal of Social and Clinical Psychology, 26,* 447–459. (p. 517)

Foss, D. J., & Hakes, D. T. (1978). *Psycholinguistics: An introduction to the psychology of language.* Englewood Cliffs, NJ: Prentice-Hall. (p. 498)

Foster, J. (2011, June 16). Our deadly anorexic pact. *The Daily Mail.* Retrieved from http://www.dailymail.co.uk/femail/article-2004003/Anorexia-pact-Identical-twins-compete-disturbing-way.html (p. 565)

Foulkes, D. (1999). *Children's dreaming and the development of consciousness.* Cambridge, MA: Harvard University Press. (p. 101)

Fournier, J. C., DeRubeis, R. J., Hollon, S. D., Dimidjian, S., Amsterdam, J. D., Shelton, R. C., & Fawcett, J. (2010). Antidepressant drug effects and depression severity: A patient-level meta-analysis. *Journal of the American Medical Association, 303,* 47–53. (p. 596)

Fowles, D. C. (1992). Schizophrenia: Diathesis-stress revisited. *Annual Review of Psychology, 43,* 303–336. (p. 557)

Fowles, D. C., & Dindo, L. (2009). Temperament and psychopathy: A dual-pathway model. *Current Directions in Psychological Science, 18,* 179–183. (p. 563)

Fox, D. (2010, June). The insanity virus. *Discover,* pp. 58–64. (p. 559)

Fox, J. L. (1984). The brain's dynamic way of keeping in touch. *Science, 225,* 820–821. (p. 61)

Fox, K. C. R., Nijeboer, S., Solomonova, E., Domhoff, G. W., & Christoff, K. (2013). Dreaming as mind wandering: Evidence from functional neuroimaging and first-person content reports. *Frontiers in Human Neuroscience, 7,* Article 412. http://dx.doi.org/10.3389/fnhum.2013.00412 (p. 102)

Fox, M. L., Dwyer, D. J., & Ganster, D. C. (1993). Effects of stressful job demands and control on physiological and attitudinal outcomes in a hospital setting. *Academy of Management Journal, 36,* 289–318. (p. 420)

Fozard, J. L., & Popkin, S. J. (1978). Optimizing adult development: Ends and means of an applied psychology of aging. *American Psychologist, 33,* 975–989. (p. 159)

Fraley, R. C., Roisman, G. I., Booth-LaForce, C., Owen, M. T., & Holland, A. S. (2013). Interpersonal and genetic origins of adult attachment styles: A longitudinal study from infancy to early adulthood. *Journal of Personality and Social Psychology, 104,* 817–838. (p. 142)

Fraley, R. C., & Tancredy, C. M. (2012). Twin and sibling attachment in a nationally representative sample. *Personality and Social Psychology Bulletin, 38,* 308–316. (p. 141)

Fraley, R. C., Vicary, A. M., Brumbaugh, C. C., & Roisman, G. I. (2011). Patterns of stability in adult attachment: An empirical test of two models of continuity and change. *Journal of Personality and Social Psychology, 101,* 974–992. (p. 142)

Frances, A. J. (2012, December 2). *DSM-5 is guide not bible—Ignore its ten worst changes.* Retrieved from http://www.psychologytoday.com/blog/dsm5-in-distress/201212/dsm-5-is-guide-not-bible-ignore-its-ten-worst-changes (p. 532)

Frances, A. J. (2013). *Saving normal: An insider's revolt against out-of-control psychiatric diagnosis,* DSM-5, *big pharma, and the medicalization of ordinary life.* New York: HarperCollins. (p. 531)

Frances, A. J. (2014, September/October). No child left undiagnosed. *Psychology Today,* pp. 49–50. (p. 532)

Frank, J. D. (1982). Therapeutic components shared by all psychotherapies. In J. H. Harvey & M. M. Parks (Eds.), *The master lecture series: Vol. 1. Psychotherapy research and behavior change* (pp. 9–37). Washington, DC: American Psychological Association. (pp. 589, 590)

Frankel, A., Strange, D. R., & Schoonover, R. (1983). CRAP: Consumer rated assessment procedure. In G. H. Scherr & R. Liebmann-Smith (Eds.), *The best of* The Journal of Irreproducible Results (pp. 55–56). New York: Workman. (p. 508)

Frankenburg, W., Dodds, J., Archer, P., Shapiro, H., & Bresnick, B. (1992). The Denver II: A major revision and restandardization of the Denver Developmental Screening Test. *Pediatrics, 89,* 91–97. (p. 129)

Franklin, M., & Foa, E. B. (2011). Treatment of obsessive compulsive disorder. *Annual Review of Clinical Psychology, 7,* 229–243. (p. 542)

Franz, E. A., Waldie, K. E., & Smith, M. J. (2000). The effect of callosotomy on novel versus familiar bimanual actions: A neural dissociation between controlled and automatic processes? *Psychological Science, 11,* 82–85. (p. 63)

Fraser, M. A., Shaw, M. E., & Cherubin, N. (2015). A systematic review and meta-analysis of longitudinal hippocampal atrophy in healthy human ageing. *NeuroImage, 112,* 364–374. (p. 159)

Frassanito, P., & Pettorini, B. (2008). Pink and blue: The color of gender. *Child's Nervous System, 24,* 881–882. (p. 172)

Frasure-Smith, N., & Lesperance, F. (2005). Depression and coronary heart disease: Complex synergism of mind, body, and environment. *Current Directions in Psychological Science, 14,* 39–43. (p. 415)

Frattaroli, J. (2006). Experimental disclosure and its moderators: A meta-analysis. *Psychological Bulletin, 132,* 823–865. (p. 425)

Fredrickson, B. L. (2013). Updated thinking on positivity ratios. *American Psychologist, 68,* 814–822. (p. 431)

Fredrickson, B. L., Grewen, K. M., Coffey, K. A., Algoe, S. B., Firestine, A. M., Arevalo, J. M. G., . . . Cole, S. W. (2013). A functional genomic perspective on human well-being. *Proceedings of the National Academy of Sciences of the United States of America, 110,* 13684–13689. (p. 436)

Freedman, D. H. (2011, February). How to fix the obesity crisis. *Scientific American,* pp. 40–47. (p. 385)

Freedman, D. J., Riesenhuber, M., Poggio, T., & Miller, E. K. (2001). Categorical representation of visual stimuli in the primate prefrontal cortex. *Science, 291,* 312–316. (p. 327)

Freedman, J. L. (1988). Television violence and aggression: What the evidence shows. In S. Oskamp (Ed.), *Television as a social issue* (pp. 144–162). Newbury Park, CA: Sage. (p. 277)

Freedman, J. L., & Fraser, S. C. (1966). Compliance without pressure: The foot-in-the-door technique. *Journal of Personality and Social Psychology, 4,* 195–202. (p. 445)

Freedman, J. L., & Perlick, D. (1979). Crowding, contagion, and laughter. *Journal of Experimental Social Psychology, 15,* 295–303. (p. 456)

Freedman, R., Lewis, D. A., Michels, R., Pine, D. S., Scultz, S. K., Tamminga, C. A., . . . Yager, J. (2013). The initial field trials of DSM-5: New blooms and old thorns. *American Journal of Psychiatry, 170,* 1–5. (p. 531)

Freeman, D., & Freeman, J. (2013). *The stressed sex: Uncovering the truth about men, women, and mental health.* Oxford, England: Oxford University Press. (p. 548)

Freeman, E. C., & Twenge, J. M. (2010, January). *Using MySpace increases the endorsement of narcissistic personality traits.* Poster session presented at the 12th Annual Convention of the Society for Personality and Social Psychology, Las Vegas, NV. (p. 374)

Freeman, W. J. (1991, February). The physiology of perception. *Scientific American,* pp. 78–85. (p. 226)

Frenda, S. J., Knowles, E. D., Saletan, W., & Loftus, E. F. (2013). False memories of fabricated political events. *Journal of Experimental Social Psychology, 49,* 280–286. (p. 307)

Freud, S. (1960). *A general introduction to psychoanalysis* (J. Riviere, Trans.). New York: Washington Square Press. (Original work published 1935) (p. 163)

Freyd, J. J., DePrince, A. P., & Gleaves, D. H. (2007). The state of betrayal trauma theory: Reply to McNally—Conceptual issues and future directions. *Memory, 15,* 295–311. (p. 311)

Friedel, J. E., DeHart, W. B., Madden, G. J., & Odum, A. L. (2014). Impulsivity and cigarette smoking: Discounting of monetary and consumable outcomes in current and non-smokers. *Psychopharmacology, 231,* 4517–4526. (p. 493)

Friedman, H. S., & Martin, L. R. (2012). *The longevity project: Surprising discoveries for health and long life from the landmark eight-decade study.* New York: Plume. (p. 352)

Friedman, M., & Ulmer, D. (1984). *Treating Type A behavior—and your heart.* New York: Knopf. (pp. 414, 428)

Friedman, R., & James, J. W. (2008). The myth of the sages of dying, death and grief. *Skeptic, 14*(2), 37–41. (p. 168)

Friedman, R. A. (2012, December 17). In gun debate, a misguided focus on mental illness. *The New York Times.* Retrieved from http://www.nytimes.com/2012/12/18/health/a-misguided-focus-on-mental-illness-in-gun-control-debate.html (p. 533)

Friedrich, M., Wilhelm, I., Born, J., & Friederici, A. D. (2015). Generalization of word meanings during infant sleep. *Nature Communications, 6,* Article 6004. doi:10.1038/ncomms7004 (p. 93)

Frisch, M., & Zdravkovic, S. (2010). Body size at birth and same-sex marriage in young adulthood. *Archives of Sexual Behavior, 39,* 117–123. (p. 191)

Frisell, T., Pawitan, Y., Långström, N., & Lichtenstein, P. (2012). Heritability, assortative mating and gender differences in violent crime: Results from a total population sample using twin, adoption, and sibling models. *Behavior Genetics, 42,* 3–18. (pp. 173, 563)

Frith, U., & Frith, C. (2001). The biological basis of social interaction. *Current Directions in Psychological Science, 10,* 151–155. (p. 136)

Fritz, T., Jentschke, S., Gosselin, N., Sammler, D., Peretz, I., Turner, R., . . . Koelsch, S. (2009). Universal recognition of three basic emotions in music. *Current Biology, 19,* 573–576. (p. 400)

Fromkin, V., & Rodman, R. (1983). *An introduction to language* (3rd ed.). New York: Holt, Rinehart & Winston. (p. 332)

Frühauf, S., Gerger, H., Schmidt, H. M., Munder, T., & Barth, J. (2013). Efficacy of psychological interventions for sexual dysfunction: A systematic review and meta-analysis. *Archives of Sexual Behavior, 42,* 915–933. (p. 183)

Fry, A. F., & Hale, S. (1996). Processing speed, working memory, and fluid intelligence: Evidence for a developmental cascade. *Psychological Science, 7,* 237–241. (p. 159)

Fry, D. P. (2012). Life without war. *Science, 336,* 879–884. (p. 487)

Fu, A., & Markus, H. R. (2014). My mother and me: Why tiger mothers motivate Asian Americans but not European Americans. *Personality and Social Psychology Bulletin, 40,* 739–749. (p. 155)

Fuhriman, A., & Burlingame, G. M. (1994). Group psychotherapy: Research and practice. In A. Fuhriman & G. M. Burlingame (Eds.), *Handbook of group psychotherapy: An empirical synthesis* (pp. 3–40). New York: Wiley. (p. 582)

Fuller, M. J., & Downs, A. C. (1990, June). Spermarche is a salient biological marker in men's development. Poster session presented at the Second Annual Convention of the American Psychological Society, Dallas, TX. (p. 176)

Fulmer, C. A., Gelfand, M. J., Kruglanski, A. W., Kim-Prieto, C., Diener, E., Pierro, A., & Higgins, E. T. (2010). On "feeling right" in cultural contexts: How person–culture match affects self-esteem and subjective well-being. *Psychological Science, 21,* 1563–1569. (pp. 436, 514)

Fulmer, I. S., Gerhart, B., & Scott, K. S. (2003). Are the 100 best better? An empirical investigation of the relationship between being a "great place to work" and firm performance. *Personnel Psychology, 56,* 965–993. (p. B-9)

Funder, D. C. (2001). Personality. *Annual Review of Psychology, 52,* 197–221. (p. 509)

Funder, D. C. (2009). Persons, behaviors and situations: An agenda for personality psychology in the postwar era. *Journal of Research in Personality, 43,* 155–162. (p. 513)

Furlow, F. B., & Thornhill, R. (1996, January/February). The orgasm wars. *Psychology Today,* pp. 42–46. (p. 183)

Furnham, A. (1982). Explanations for unemployment in Britain. *European Journal of Social Psychology, 12,* 335–352. (p. 443)

Furnham, A., & Wu, J. (2008). Gender differences in estimates of one's own and parental intelligence in China. *Individual Differences Research, 6,* 1–12. (p. 464)

Furr, R. M., & Funder, D. C. (1998). A multimodal analysis of personal negativity. *Journal of Personality and Social Psychology, 74,* 1580–1591. (p. 552)

Furukawa, T. A., Levine, S. Z., Tanaka, S., Goldberg, Y., Samara, M., Davis, J. M., . . . Leucht, S. (2015). Initial severity of schizophrenia and efficacy of antipsychotics: Participant-level mega-analysis of 6 placebo-controlled studies. *JAMA Psychiatry, 72,* 14–21. (p. 594)

Furukawa, T. A., Yoshimura, R., Harai, H., Imaizumi, T., Takeuchi, H., Kitamua, T., & Takahashi, K. (2009). How many well vs. unwell days can you expect over 10 years, once you become depressed? *Acta Psychiatrica Scandinavica, 119,* 290–297. (p. 548)

G

Gable, S. L., Gonzaga, G. C., & Strachman, A. (2006). Will you be there for me when things go right? Supportive responses to positive event disclosures. *Journal of Personality and Social Psychology, 91,* 904–917. (p. 165)

Gable, S. L., Gosnell, C. L., Maisel, N. C., & Strachman, A. (2012). Safely testing the alarm: Close others' responses to personal positive events. *Journal of Personality and Social Psychology, 103,* 963–981. (p. 423)

Gabrieli, J. D. E., Desmond, J. E., Demb, J. E., Wagner, A. D., Stone, M. V., Vaidya, C. J., & Glover, G. H. (1996). Functional magnetic resonance imaging of semantic memory processes in the frontal lobes. *Psychological Science, 7,* 278–283. (p. 292)

Gaddy, M. A., & Ingram, R. E. (2014). A meta-analytic review of mood-congruent implicit memory in depressed mood. *Clinical Psychology Review, 34*, 402–416. (p. 298)

Gaertner, L., Iuzzini, J., & O'Mara, E. M. (2008). When rejection by one fosters aggression against many: Multiple-victim aggression as a consequence of social rejection and perceived groupness. *Journal of Experimental Social Psychology, 44*, 958–970. (p. 372)

Gaillard, R., Dehaene, S., Adam, C., Clémenceau, S., Hasboun, D., Baulac, M., . . . Naccache, L. (2009). Converging intracranial markers of conscious access. *PLOS Biology, 7*(e): e1000061. (p. 81)

Gaillot, M. T., & Baumeister, R. F. (2007). Self-regulation and sexual restraint: Dispositionally and temporarily poor self-regulatory abilities contribute to failures at restraining sexual behavior. *Personality and Social Psychology Bulletin, 33*, 173–186. (p. 421)

Gaissmaier, W., & Gigerenzer, G. (2012). 9/11, Act II: A fine-grained analysis of regional variations in traffic fatalities in the aftermath of the terrorist attacks. *Psychological Science, 23*, 1449–1454. (p. 320)

Galak, J., Leboeuf, R. A., Nelson, L. D., & Simmons, J. P. (2012). Correcting the past: Failures to replicate psi. *Journal of Personality and Social Psychology, 103*, 933–948. (p. 242)

Galambos, N. L. (1992). Parent–adolescent relations. *Current Directions in Psychological Science, 1*, 146–149. (p. 154)

Galanter, E. (1962). Contemporary psychophysics. In R. Brown, E. Galanter, E. H. Hess, & G. Mandler (Eds.), *New directions in psychology* (pp. 87–156). New York: Holt, Rinehart & Winston. (p. 201)

Galati, D., Scherer, K. R., & Ricci-Bitti, P. E. (1997). Voluntary facial expression of emotion: Comparing congenitally blind with normally sighted encoders. *Journal of Personality and Social Psychology, 73*, 1363–1379. (p. 399)

Gale, C. R., Batty, G. D., & Deary, I. J. (2008). Locus of control at age 10 years and health outcomes and behaviors at age 30 years: The 1970 British Cohort Study. *Psychosomatic Medicine, 70*, 397–403. (p. 421)

Gale, C. R., Booth, T., Möttus, R., Kuh, D., & Deary, I. J. (2013). Neuroticism and extraversion in youth predict mental well-being and life satisfaction 40 years later. *Journal of Research in Personality, 47*, 687–697. (p. 121)

Galinsky, E., Aumann, K., & Bond, J. T. (2008). *Times are changing: Gender and generation at work and at home.* Retrieved from http://www.familiesandwork.org/ (p. 519)

Gallace, A. (2012). Living with touch. *The Psychologist, 25*, 896–899. (p. 83)

Gallace, A., & Spence, C. (2011). To what extent do Gestalt grouping principles influence tactile perception? *Psychological Bulletin, 137*, 538–561. (p. 218)

Gallese, V., Gernsbacher, M. A., Heyes, C., Hickok, G., & Iacoboni, M. (2011). Mirror neuron forum. *Perspectives on Psychological Science, 6*, 369–407. (pp. 137, 273, 274)

Gallo, W. T., Teng, H. M., Falba, T. A., Kasl, S. V., Krumholz, H. M., & Bradley, E. H. (2006). The impact of late career job loss on myocardial infarction and stroke: A 10-year follow up using the health and retirement survey. *Occupational and Environmental Medicine, 63*, 683–687. (p. 416)

Gallup, G. G., Jr., & Frederick, D. A. (2010). The science of sex appeal: An evolutionary perspective. *Review of General Psychology, 14*, 240–250. (p. 478)

Gallup, G. H. (1972). *The Gallup poll: Public opinion 1935–1971* (Vol. 3). New York: Random House. (p. 485)

Gallup, G. H., Jr. (1994, October). Millions finding care and support in small groups. *Emerging Trends*, pp. 2–5. (p. 582)

Gallup Brain. (2008). *Woman for president: Question qn2f, March, 2007 wave.* Retrieved from http://www.gallup.com (p. 464)

Gallup Organization. (2004, August 16). Personal communication [T. Rath: bucketbook@gallup.com]. (p. B-11)

Galinsky, A. M., & Sonenstein, F. L. (2013). Relationship commitment, perceived equity, and sexual enjoyment among young adults in the United States. *Archives of Sexual Behavior, 42*, 93–104. (p. 196)

Gandhi, A. V., Mosser, E. A., Oikonomou, G., & Prober, D. A. (2015). Melatonin is required for the circadian regulation of sleep. *Neuron, 85*, 1193–1199. (p. 92)

Gangestad, S. W., & Simpson, J. A. (2000). The evolution of human mating: Trade-offs and strategic pluralism. *Behavioral and Brain Sciences, 23*, 573–587. (p. 193)

Gangestad, S. W., Thornhill, R., & Garver-Apgar, C. E. (2010). Men's facial masculinity predicts changes in their female partners' sexual interests across the ovulatory cycle, whereas men's intelligence does not. *Evolution and Human Behavior, 31*, 412–424. (p. 478)

Gangwisch, J. E., Babiss, L. A., Malaspina, D., Turner, J. B., Zammit, G. K., & Posner, K. (2010). Earlier parental set bedtimes as a protective factor against depression and suicidal ideation. *Sleep, 33*, 97–106. (p. 94)

Gao, Y., Raine, A., Venables, P. H., Dawson, M. E., & Mednick, S. A. (2010). Association of poor child fear conditioning and adult crime. *American Journal of Psychiatry, 167*, 56–60. (p. 564)

Garcia, J., & Gustavson, A. R. (1997, January). Carl R. Gustavson (1946–1996): Pioneering wildlife psychologist. *APS Observer*, pp. 34–35. (p. 268)

Garcia, J., & Koelling, R. A. (1966). Relation of cue to consequence in avoidance learning. *Psychonomic Science, 4*, 123–124. (p. 267)

Garcia, J. R., Massey, S. G., Merriwether, A. M., & Seibold-Simpson, S. M. (2013, May). *Orgasm experience among emerging adult men and women: Relationship context and attitudes toward uncommitted sex.* Poster session presented at the 25th Annual Convention of the Association for Psychological Science, Washington, DC. (p. 196)

Garcia, J. R., Reiber, C., Massey, S. G., & Merriwether, A. M. (2012). Sexual hookup culture: A review. *Review of General Psychology, 16*, 161–176. (pp. 106, 196)

Garcia, J. R., Reiber, C., Massey, S. G., & Merriwether, A. M. (2013, February). Sexual hook-up culture. *Monitor on Psychology*, pp. 60–66. (p. 186)

Garcia-Falgueras, A., & Swaab, D. F. (2010). Sexual hormones and the brain: An essential alliance for sexual identity and sexual orientation. *Endocrine Development, 17*, 22–35. (p. 191)

Gardner, H. (1983). *Frames of mind: The theory of multiple intelligences.* New York: Basic Books. (p. 342)

Gardner, H. (1998, November 5). Do parents count? *The New York Review of Books.* Retrieved from http://www.nybooks.com/articles/archives/1998/nov/05/do-parents-count/ (p. 156)

Gardner, H. (1998, March 19). An intelligent way to progress. *The Independent*, p. E4. (p. 342)

Gardner, H. (1999). *Multiple views of multiple intelligence.* New York: Basic Books. (pp. 342, 345)

Gardner, H. (2006). *The development and education of the mind: The selected works of Howard Gardner.* New York: Routledge. (p. 342)

Gardner, H. (2011, October 22). *The theory of multiple intelligences: As psychology, as education, as social science.* Address on the receipt of an honorary degree from José Cela University, Madrid, Spain, and the Prince of Asturias Prize for Social Science. (p. 342)

Gardner, J., & Oswald, A. J. (2007). Money and mental well-being: A longitudinal study of medium-sized lottery wins. *Journal of Health Economics, 6*, 49–60. (p. 434)

Gardner, M. (2006, January/February). The memory wars: Part 1. *Skeptical Inquirer*, pp. 28–31. (p. 311)

Gardner, R. A., & Gardner, B. I. (1969). Teaching sign language to a chimpanzee. *Science, 165*, 664–672. (p. 335)

Garfield, C. (1986). *Peak performers: The new heroes of American business.* New York: Morrow. (p. 338)

Garon, N., Bryson, S. E., & Smith, I. M. (2008). Executive function in preschoolers: A review using an integrative framework. *Psychological Bulletin, 134*, 31–60. (p. 127)

Garry, M., Loftus, E. F., & Brown, S. W. (1994). Memory: A river runs through it. *Consciousness and Cognition, 3*, 438–451. (p. 499)

Gartrell, N., & Bos, H. (2010). US National Longitudinal Lesbian Family Study: Psychological adjustment of 17-year-old adolescents. *Pediatrics, 126*, 28–36. (p. 189)

Gaspar, J. G., Street, W. N., Windsor, M. B., Carbonari, R., Kaczmarski, H., Kramer, A. F., & Mathewson, K. E. (2014). Providing view of the driving scene to drivers' conversation partners mitigates cell-phone-related distraction. *Psychological Science, 25*, 2136–2146. (p. 82)

Gatchel, R. J., Peng, Y. B., Peters, M. L., Fuchs, P. N., & Turk, D. C. (2007). The biopsychosocial approach to chronic pain: Scientific advances and future directions. *Psychological Bulletin, 133*, 581–624. (p. 231)

Gates, B. (1998, July 20). The Bill & Warren show [Interview with B. Sclender & W. Buffet]. *Fortune.* Retrieved from http://archive.fortune.com/magazines/fortune/fortune_archive/1998/07/20/245683/index.htm (p. 343)

Gates, G. J., & Newport, F. (2012, October 18). *Special report: 3.4% of U.S. adults identify as LGBT.* Retrieved from http://www.gallup.com/poll/158066/special-report-adults-identify-lgbt.aspx (p. 188)

Gaugler, T., Klei, L., Sanders, S. J., Bodea, C. A., Goldberg, A. P., Lee, A. B., . . . Buxbaum, J. D. (2014). Most genetic risk for autism resides with common variation. *Nature Genetics, 46,* 881–885. (p. 136)

Gavin, K. (2004, November 9). *U-M team reports evidence that smoking affects human brain's natural "feel good" chemical system* [Press release]. Retrieved from http://www.med.umich.edu/ (p. 109)

Gawin, F. H. (1991). Cocaine addiction: Psychology and neurophysiology. *Science, 251,* 1580–1586. (p. 110)

Gawande, A. (1998, September 21). The pain perplex. *The New Yorker,* pp. 86–94. (p. 233)

Gawronski, B., & Quinn, K. (2013). Guilty by mere similarity: Assimilative effects of facial resemblance on automatic evaluation. *Journal of Experimental Social Psychology, 49,* 120–125. (p. 251)

Gazzaniga, M. S. (1967, August). The split brain in man. *Scientific American,* pp. 24–29. (p. 62)

Gazzaniga, M. S. (1983). Right hemisphere language following brain bisection: A 20-year perspective. *American Psychologist, 38,* 525–537. (p. 63)

Gazzaniga, M. S. (1989). Organization of the human brain. *Science, 245,* 947–952. (p. 64)

Gazzola, V., Spezio, M. L., Etzel, J.A., Catelli, F., Adolphs, R., & Keysers, C. (2012). Primary somatosensory cortex discriminates affective significance in social touch. *Proceedings of the National Academy of Sciences of the United States of America, 109,* E1657–E1666. (p. 231)

Ge, X., & Natsuaki, M. N. (2009). In search of explanations for early pubertal timing effects on developmental psychopathology. *Current Directions in Psychological Science, 18,* 327–441. (p. 148)

Geary, D. C. (1995). Sexual selection and sex differences in spatial cognition. *Learning and Individual Differences, 7,* 289–301. (p. 357)

Geary, D. C. (1996). Sexual selection and sex differences in mathematical abilities. *Behavioral and Brain Sciences, 19,* 229–247. (p. 357)

Geary, D. C. (2010). *Male, female: The evolution of human sex differences* (2nd ed.). Washington, DC: American Psychological Association. (p. 175)

Geary, D. C., Salthouse, T. A., Chen, G.-P., & Fan, L. (1996). Are East Asian versus American differences in arithmetical ability a recent phenomenon? *Developmental Psychology, 32,* 254–262. (p. 359)

Geen, R. G., & Quanty, M. B. (1977). The catharsis of aggression: An evaluation of a hypothesis. In L. Berkowitz (Ed.), *Advances in experimental social psychology* (Vol. 10, pp. 1–37). New York: Academic Press. (p. 416)

Geen, R. G., & Thomas, S. L. (1986). The immediate effects of media violence on behavior. *Journal of Social Issues, 42*(3), 7–28. (p. 277)

Gehring, W. J., Wimke, J., & Nisenson, L. G. (2000). Action-monitoring dysfunction in obsessive-compulsive disorder. *Psychological Science, 11,* 1–6. (p. 543)

Gellis, L. A., Arigo, D., & Elliott, J. C. (2013). Cognitive refocusing treatment for insomnia: A randomized controlled trial in university students. *Behavior Therapy, 44,* 100–110. (p. 97)

Gelman, D. (1989, May 15). Voyages to the unknown. *Newsweek,* pp. 66–69. (p. 400)

Genesee, F., & Gándara, P. (1999). Bilingual education programs: A cross-national perspective. *Journal of Social Issues, 55,* 665–685. (p. 338)

Gentile, D. (2009). Pathological video-game use among youth ages 8 to 18: A national study. *Psychological Science, 20,* 594–602. (pp. 105, 472)

Gentile, D. A., & Bushman, B. J. (2012). Reassessing media violence effects using a risk and resilience approach to understanding aggression. *Psychology of Popular Media Culture, 1,* 138–151. (p. 277)

Gentile, D. A., Coyne, S., & Walsh, D. A. (2011). Media violence, physical aggression and relational aggression in school age children: A short-term longitudinal study. *Aggressive Behavior, 37,* 193–206. (p. 277)

George, L. K., Ellison, C. G., & Larson, D. B. (2002). Explaining the relationships between religious involvement and health. *Psychological Inquiry, 13,* 190–200. (p. 430)

Geraerts, E., Bernstein, D. M., Merckelbach, H., Linders, C., Raymaekers, L., & Loftus, E. F. (2008). Lasting false beliefs and their behavioral consequences. *Psychological Science, 19,* 749–753. (p. 307)

Geraerts, E., Schooler, J. W., Merckelbach, H., Jelicic, M., Hauer, B. J. A., & Ambadar, Z. (2007). The reality of recovered memories: Corroborating continuous and discontinuous memories of childhood sexual abuse. *Psychological Science, 18,* 564–568. (p. 311)

Germain, A. (2013). Sleep disturbances as the hallmark of PTSD: Where are we now? *Archives of Journal of Psychiatry, 170,* 372–382. (p. 540)

Gernsbacher, M. A., Dawson, M., & Goldsmith, H. H. (2005). Three reasons not to believe in an autism epidemic. *Current Directions in Psychological Science, 14,* 55–58. (p. 136)

Gerrard, M., & Luus, C. A. E. (1995). Judgments of vulnerability to pregnancy: The role of risk factors and individual differences. *Personality and Social Psychology Bulletin, 21,* 160–171. (p. 186)

Gershoff, E. T. (2002). Parental corporal punishment and associated child behaviors and experiences: A meta-analytic and theoretical review. *Psychological Bulletin, 128,* 539–579. (p. 261)

Gershoff, E. T., Grogan-Kaylor, A., Lansford, J. E., Chang, L., Zelli, A., Deater-Deckard, K., & Dodge, K. A. (2010). Parent discipline practices in an international sample: Associations with child behaviors and moderation by perceived normativeness. *Child Development, 81,* 487–502. (p. 262)

Gerst-Emerson, K., & Jayawardhana, J. (2015). Loneliness as a public health issue: The impact of loneliness on health care utilization among older adults. *American Journal of Public Health, 105,* 1013–1019. (p. 371)

Gerstorf, D., Ram, N., Röcke, C., Lindenberger, U., & Smith, J. (2008). Decline in life satisfaction in old age: Longitudinal evidence for links to distance-to-death. *Psychology and Aging, 23,* 154–168. (p. 166)

Geschwind, N. (1979, September). Specializations of the human brain. *Scientific American,* pp. 180–199. (p. 334)

Getahun, D., Jacobsen, S. J., Fassett, M. J., Chen, W., Demissie, K., & Rhoads, G. G. (2013). Recent trends in childhood attention-deficit/hyperactivity disorder. *JAMA Pediatrics, 167,* 282–288. (p. 532)

Gettler, L. T., McDade, T. W., Agustin, S. S., Feranil, A. B., & Kuzawa, C. W. (2013). Do testosterone declines during the transition to marriage and fatherhood relate to men's sexual behavior? Evidence from the Philippines. *Hormones and Behavior, 64,* 755–763. (p. 182)

Giampietro, M., & Cavallera, G. M. (2007). Morning and evening types and creative thinking. *Personality and Individual Differences, 42,* 453–463. (p. 88)

Giancola, P. R., Josephs, R. A., Parrott, D. J., & Duke, A. A. (2010). Alcohol myopia revisited: Clarifying aggression and other acts of disinhibition through a distorted lens. *Perspectives on Psychological Science, 5,* 265–278. (p. 107)

Gibbons, F. X. (1986). Social comparison and depression: Company's effect on misery. *Journal of Personality and Social Psychology, 51,* 140–148. (p. 435)

Gibbs, W. W. (1996, June). Mind readings. *Scientific American,* pp. 34–36. (p. 58)

Gibson, E. J., & Walk, R. D. (1960, April). The "visual cliff." *Scientific American,* pp. 64–71. (p. 218)

Gick, B., & Derrick, D. (2009). Aero-tactile integration in speech perception. *Nature, 462,* 502–504. (p. 239)

Giedd, J. N. (2015, June). The amazing teen brain. *Scientific American,* pp. 33–37. (p. 148)

Giesbrecht, T., Lynn, S. J., Lilienfeld, S. O., & Merckelbach, H. (2008). Cognitive processes in dissociation: An analysis of core theoretical assumptions. *Psychological Bulletin, 134,* 617–647. (p. 562)

Giesbrecht, T., Lynn, S. J., Lilienfeld, S. O., & Merckelbach, H. (2010). Cognitive processes, trauma, and dissociation—Misconceptions and misrepresentations: Reply to Bremmer (2010). *Psychological Bulletin, 136,* 7–11. (p. 562)

Gigantesco, A., Stazi, M. A., Alessandri, G., Medda, E., Tarolla, E., & Fagnani, C. (2011). Psychological well-being (PWB): A natural life outlook? An Italian twin study of heritability on PWB in young adults. *Psychological Medicine, 41,* 2637–2649. (p. 436)

Gigerenzer, G. (2004). Dread risk, September 11, and fatal traffic accidents. *Psychological Science, 15,* 286–287. (p. 320)

Gigerenzer, G. (2006). Out of the frying pan into the fire: Behavioral reactions to terrorist attacks. *Risk Analysis, 26,* 347–351. (p. 320)

Gigerenzer, G. (2010). *Rationality for mortals: How people cope with uncertainty.* New York: Oxford University Press. (p. A-1)

Gigerenzer, G., Gaissmaier, W., Kurz-Milcke, E., Schwartz, L. M., & Woloshin, S. (2008). Helping doctors and patients make sense of health statistics. *Psychological Science in the Public Interest, 8,* 53–96. (p. A-1)

Gigerenzer, G., Gaissmaier, W., Kurz-Milcke, E., Schwartz, L. M., & Woloshin, S. (2009, April/May). Knowing your chances. *Scientific American Mind,* pp. 44–51. (p. A-1)

Gigerenzer, G., & Sturm, T. (2012). How (far) can rationality be naturalized? *Synthese, 187,* 243–268. (p. 319)

Gilbert, D. T. (2006). *Stumbling on happiness.* New York: Knopf. (pp. 165, 389)

Gilbert, D. T., Pinel, E. C., Wilson, T. D., Blumberg, S. J., & Wheatley, T. P. (1998). Immune neglect: A source of durability bias in affective forecasting. *Journal of Personality and Social Psychology, 75,* 617–638. (p. 433)

Gildersleeve, K., Haselton, M., & Fales, M. R. (2014). Do women's mate preferences change across the menstrual cycle? A meta-analytic review. *Psychological Bulletin, 140,* 1205–1259. (p. 181)

Giles, D. E., Dahl, R. E., & Coble, P. A. (1994). Childbearing, developmental, and familial aspects of sleep. In J. M. Oldham & M. B. Riba (Eds.), *Review of psychiatry* (Vol. 13, pp. 621–649). Washington, DC: American Psychiatric Press. (p. 98)

Gilestro, G. F., Tononi, G., & Cirelli, C. (2009). Widespread changes in synaptic markers as a function of sleep and wakefulness in *Drosophila. Science, 324,* 109–112. (p. 93)

Gillen-O'Neel, C., Huynh, V. W., & Fuligni, A. J. (2013). To study or to sleep? The academic costs of extra studying at the expense of sleep. *Child Development, 84,* 133–142. (p. 100)

Gillison, M. L., Broutian, T., Pickard, R. K. L., Tong, Z.-Y., Xiao, W., Kahle, L., . . . Chaturvedi, A. K. (2012). Prevalence of oral HPV infection in the United States, 2009–2010. *Journal of the American Medical Association, 307,* 693–703. (p. 184)

Gilovich, T. D., Kruger, J., & Medvec, V. H. (2002). The spotlight effect revisited: Overestimating the manifest variability of our actions and appearance. *Journal of Experimental Social Psychology, 38,* 93–99. (p. 516)

Gilovich, T. D., & Medvec, V. H. (1995). The experience of regret: What, when, and why. *Psychological Review, 102,* 379–395. (p. 166)

Gilovich, T. D., & Savitsky, K. (1999). The spotlight effect and the illusion of transparency: Egocentric assessments of how we are seen by others. *Current Directions in Psychological Science, 8,* 165–168. (p. 516)

Gingerich, O. (1999, February 6). *Is there a role for natural theology today?* Retrieved from http://www.origins.org/real/n9501/natural.html (p. 76)

Gladwell, M. (2000, May 9). The new-boy network: What do job interviews really tell us? *The New Yorker,* pp. 68–86. (p. B-6)

Gladwell, M. (2005). *Blink: The power of thinking without thinking.* New York: Little, Brown. (p. 479)

Glasman, L. R., & Albarracín, D. (2006). Forming attitudes that predict future behavior: A meta-analysis of the attitude-behavior relation. *Psychological Bulletin, 132,* 778–822. (p. 444)

Glass, R. I. (2004). Perceived threats and real killers. *Science, 304,* 927. (p. 321)

Glass, R. M. (2001). Electroconvulsive therapy: Time to bring it out of the shadows. *Journal of the American Medical Association, 285,* 1346–1348. (p. 598)

Gleaves, D. H. (1996). The sociocognitive model of dissociative identity disorder: A reexamination of the evidence. *Psychological Bulletin, 120,* 42–59. (p. 562)

Glenn, A. L., Raine, A., Yaralian, P. S., & Yang, Y. (2010). Increased volume of the striatum in psychopathic individuals. *Biological Psychiatry, 67,* 52–58. (p. 564)

Global Burden of Disease Study 2013 Collaborators. (2015). Global, regional, and national incidence, prevalence, and years lived with disability for 301 acute and chronic diseases and injuries in 188 countries, 1990–2013: A systematic analysis for the Global Burden of Disease Study 2013. *The Lancet, 386,* 743–800. (pp. 546, 547, 557)

Gluszek, A., & Dovidio, J. F. (2010). The way they speak: A social psychological perspective on the stigma of nonnative accents in communication. *Personality and Social Psychology Review, 14,* 214–237. (p. 465)

Glynn, L. M., & Sandman, C. A. (2011). Prenatal origins of neurological development: A critical period for fetus and mothers. *Current Directions in Psychological Science, 20,* 384–389. (p. 125)

Godden, D. R., & Baddeley, A. D. (1975). Context-dependent memory in two natural environments: On land and underwater. *British Journal of Psychology, 66,* 325–331. (p. 298)

Goethals, G. R., & Allison, S. T. (2014). Kings and charisma, Lincoln and leadership: An evolutionary perspective. In G. R. Goethals, S. T. Allison, R. M. Kramer, & D. M. Messick (Eds.), *Conceptions of leadership: Enduring ideas and emerging insights* (pp. 111–124). New York: Palgrave Macmillan. (p. B-12)

Goetz, S. M. M., Tang, L., Thomason, M. E., Diamond, M. P., Hariri, A. R., & Carré, J. (2014). Testosterone rapidly increases neural reactivity to threat in healthy men: A novel two-step pharmacological challenge paradigm. *Biological Psychiatry, 76,* 324–331. (p. 46)

Goff, D. C., & Simms, C. A. (1993). Has multiple personality disorder remained consistent over time? *Journal of Nervous and Mental Disease, 181,* 595–600. (p. 562)

Golan, O., Ashwin, E., Granader, Y., McClintock, S., Day, K., Leggett, V., & Baron-Cohen, S. (2010). Enhancing emotion recognition in children with autism spectrum conditions: An intervention using animated vehicles with real emotional faces. *Journal of Autism Development and Disorders, 40,* 269–279. (p. 137)

Gold, M., & Yanof, D. S. (1985). Mothers, daughters, and girlfriends. *Journal of Personality and Social Psychology, 49,* 654–659. (p. 154)

Golden, R. N., Gaynes, B. N., Ekstrom, R. D., Hamer, R. M., Jacobsen, F. M., Suppes, T., . . . Nemeroff, C. B. (2005). The efficacy of light therapy in the treatment of mood disorders: A review and meta-analysis of the evidence. *American Journal of Psychiatry, 162,* 656–662. (p. 589)

Goldberg, J. (2007). *Quivering bundles that let us hear.* Retrieved from http://www.hhmi.org/senses/c120.html (p. 228)

Goldberg, L. R. (1992). The development of markers for the Big-Five factor structure. *Psychological Assessment, 4,* 26–42. (p. 509)

Golder, S. A., & Macy, M. W. (2011). Diurnal and seasonal mood vary with work, sleep, and day-length across diverse cultures. *Science, 333,* 1878–1881. (pp. 20, 432)

Goldfried, M. R. (2001). Integrating gay, lesbian, and bisexual issues into mainstream psychology. *American Psychologist, 56,* 977–988. (p. 553)

Goldfried, M. R., & Padawer, W. (1982). Current status and future directions in psychotherapy. In M. R. Goldfried (Ed.), *Converging themes in psychotherapy: Trends in psychodynamic, humanistic, and behavioral practice* (pp. 3–49). New York: Springer. (p. 589)

Goldfried, M. R., Raue, P. J., & Castonguay, L. G. (1998). The therapeutic focus in significant sessions of master therapists: A comparison of cognitive–behavioral and psychodynamic–interpersonal interventions. *Journal of Consulting and Clinical Psychology, 66,* 803–810. (p. 589)

Goldinger, S. D., & Papesh, M. H. (2012). Pupil dilation reflects the creation and retrieval of memories. *Current Directions in Psychological Science, 21,* 90–95. (p. 211)

Goldin-Meadow, S., & Beilock, S. L. (2010). Action's influence on thought: The case of gesture. *Perspectives on Psychological Science, 5,* 664–674. (p. 402)

Goldman, A. L., Pezawas, L., Mattay, V. S., Fischl, B., Verchinski, B. A., Chen, Q., . . . Meyer-Lindenberg, A. (2009). Widespread reductions of cortical thickness in schizophrenia and spectrum disorders and evidence of heritability. *Archives of General Psychiatry, 66,* 467–477. (p. 558)

Goldstein, I. (2000, August). Male sexual circuitry. *Scientific American,* pp. 70–75. (p. 45)

Goldstein, I., Lue, T. F., Padma-Nathan, H., Rosen, R. C., Steers, W. D., & Wicker, P. A. (1998). Oral sildenafil in the treatment of erectile dysfunction. *New England Journal of Medicine, 338,* 1397–1404. (p. 25)

Goleman, D. (1980, February). 1,528 little geniuses and how they grew. *Psychology Today,* pp. 28–53. (p. 375)

Goleman, D. (2006). *Social intelligence.* New York: Bantam Books. (p. 344)

Golkar, A., Selbing, I., Flygare, O., Öhman, A., & Olsson, A. (2013). Other people as means to a safe end: Vicarious extinction blocks the return of learned fear. *Psychological Science, 24,* 2182–2190. (p. 273)

Gollwitzer, P. M., & Oettingen, G. (2012). Goal pursuit. In P. M. Gollwitzer & G. Oettingen (Eds.), *The Oxford handbook of human motivation* (pp. 208–231). New York: Oxford University Press. (p. 264)

Gómez, D. M., Berent, I., Benavides-Varela, S., Bion, R. A. H., Cattarossi, L., Nespor, M., & Mehler, J. (2014). Language universals at birth. *Proceedings of the National Academy of Sciences of the United States of America, 111,* 5837–5841. (p. 330)

Gonsalkorale, K., & Williams, K. D. (2006). The KKK would not let me play: Ostracism even by a despised out-group hurts. *European Journal of Social Psychology, 36,* 1–11. (p. 372)

Goodale, M. A., & Milner, D. A. (2004). *Sight unseen: An exploration of conscious and unconscious vision.* Oxford, England: Oxford University Press. (p. 85)

Goodall, J. (1986). *The chimpanzees of Gombe: Patterns of behavior.* Cambridge, MA: Harvard University Press. (p. 466)

Goodall, J. (1998). Learning from the chimpanzees: A message humans can understand. *Science, 282,* 2184–2185. (p. 20)

Goode, E. (1999, April 13). If things taste bad, 'phantoms' may be at work. *The New York Times.* Retrieved from http://www.nytimes.com/1999/04/13/science/if-things-taste-bad-phantoms-may-be-at-work.html?pagewanted=all (p. 232)

Goodman, G. S. (2006). Children's eyewitness memory: A modern history and contemporary commentary. *Journal of Social Issues, 62,* 811–832. (p. 310)

Goodman, G. S., Ghetti, S., Quas, J. A., Edelstein, R. S., Alexander, K. W., Redlich, A. D., . . . Jones, D. P. H. (2003). A prospective study of memory for child sexual abuse: New findings relevant to the repressed-memory controversy. *Psychological Science, 14,* 113–118. (p. 311)

Goodwin, P. Y., Mosher, W. D., & Chandra, A. (2010, February). *Marriage and cohabitation in the United States: A statistical portrait based on Cycle 6 (2002) of the National Survey of Family Growth* (Vital Health Statistics Series 23, No. 28). Washington, DC: U.S. Department of Health and Human Services, Centers for Disease Control and Prevention, National Center for Health Statistics. (p. 164)

Gopnik, A., Griffiths, T. L., & Lucas, C. G. (2015). When younger learners can be better (or at least more open-minded) than older ones. *Current Directions in Psychological Science, 24,* 87–92. (p. 131)

Gopnik, A., & Meltzoff, A. N. (1986). Relations between semantic and cognitive development in the one-word stage: The specificity hypothesis. *Child Development, 57,* 1040–1053. (p. 338)

Goranson, R. E. (1978). *The hindsight effect in problem solving.* Unpublished manuscript cited in G. Wood (1984), Research methodology: A decision-making perspective. In A. M. Rogers & C. J. Scheirer (Eds.), *The G. Stanley Hall Lecture Series* (Vol. 4, pp. 193–217). Washington, DC: American Psychological Association. (p. 16)

Gorchoff, S. M., John, O. P., & Helson, R. (2008). Contextualizing change in marital satisfaction during middle age. *Psychological Science, 19,* 1194–1200. (p. 165)

Gordon, A. M., & Chen, S. (2010). When you accept me for me: The relational benefits of intrinsic affirmations from one's relationship partner. *Personality and Social Psychology Bulletin, 36,* 1439–1453. (p. 503)

Gordon, A. M., & Chen, S. (2014). The role of sleep in interpersonal conflict: Do sleepless nights mean worse fights? *Social Psychological and Personality Science, 5,* 168–175. (p. 94)

Gordon, I., Vander Wyk, B. C., Bennett, R. H., Cordeaux, C., Lucas, M. V., Eilbott, J. A., . . . Pelphrey, K. A. (2013). Oxytocin enhances brain function in children with autism. *Proceedings of the National Academy of Sciences of the United States of America, 110,* 20953–20958. (p. 137)

Gordon, P. (2004). Numerical cognition without words: Evidence from Amazonia. *Science, 306,* 496–499. (p. 337)

Gore, J., & Sadler-Smith, E. (2011). Unpacking intuition: A process and outcome framework. *Review of General Psychology, 15,* 304–316. (p. 323)

Gore-Felton, C., Koopman, C., Thoresen, C., Arnow, B., Bridges, E., & Spiegel, D. (2000). Psychologists' beliefs and clinical characteristics: Judging the veracity of childhood sexual abuse memories. *Professional Psychology: Research and Practice, 31,* 372–377. (p. 311)

Gorman, J. (2014, January 6). The brain, in exquisite detail. *The New York Times.* Retrieved from http://www.nytimes.com/2014/01/07/science/the-brain-in-exquisite-detail.html?_r=0 (p. 50)

Gorrese, A., & Ruggieri, R. (2012). Peer attachment: A meta-analytic review of gender and age differences and associations with parent attachment. *Journal of Youth and Adolescence, 41,* 650–672. (p. 142)

Gosling, S. D., Gladdis, S., & Vazire, S. (2007, January). *Personality impressions based on Facebook profiles.* Paper presented at the Eighth Annual Meeting of Society for Personality and Social Psychology, Memphis, TN. (p. 512)

Gosling, S. D., Kwan, V. S. Y., & John, O. P. (2003). A dog's got personality: A cross-species comparative approach to personality judgments in dogs and humans. *Journal of Personality and Social Psychology, 85,* 1161–1169. (p. 507)

Gotlib, I. H., & Hammen, C. L. (1992). *Psychological aspects of depression: Toward a cognitive-interpersonal integration.* New York: Wiley. (p. 552)

Gottesman, I. I. (1991). *Schizophrenia genesis: The origins of madness.* New York: Freeman. (p. 560)

Gottesman, I. I. (2001). Psychopathology through a life span–genetic prism. *American Psychologist, 56,* 867–881. (p. 559)

Gottfredson, L. S. (2002a). *g*: Highly general and highly practical. In R. J. Sternberg & E. L. Grigorenko (Eds.), *The general factor of intelligence: How general is it?* (pp. 331–380). Mahwah, NJ: Erlbaum. (p. 343)

Gottfredson, L. S. (2002b). Where and why *g* matters: Not a mystery. *Human Performance, 15,* 25–46. (p. 343)

Gottfredson, L. S. (2003a). Dissecting practical intelligence theory: Its claims and evidence. *Intelligence, 31,* 343–397. (p. 343)

Gottfredson, L. S. (2003b). On Sternberg's "Reply to Gottfredson." *Intelligence, 31,* 415–424. (p. 343)

Gottfried, J. A., O'Doherty, J., & Dolan, R. J. (2003). Encoding predictive reward value in human amygdala and orbitofrontal cortex. *Science, 301,* 1104–1108. (p. 249)

Gottman, J. (1994). *Why marriages succeed or fail: And how you can make yours last.* New York: Simon & Schuster. (p. 164)

Gottman, J. (2007). *Why marriages succeed or fail—2007 publication.* London: Bloomsbury. (p. 481)

Gould, E. (2007). How widespread is adult neurogenesis in mammals? *Nature Neuroscience, 8,* 481–488. (p. 61)

Gould, S. J. (1981). *The mismeasure of man.* New York: Norton. (p. 346)

Goyal, M., Singh, S., Sibinga, E. S., Gould, N. F., Rowland-Seymour, A., Sharma, R., . . . Haythornthwaite, J. A. (2014). Meditation programs for psychological stress and well-being: A systematic review and meta-analysis. *JAMA Internal Medicine, 174,* 357–368. (p. 428)

Grabe, S., Ward, L. M., & Hyde, J. S. (2008). The role of the media in body image concerns among women: A meta-analysis of experimental and correlational studies. *Psychological Bulletin, 134,* 460–476. (p. 566)

Grace, A. A. (2010). Ventral hippocampus, interneurons, and schizophrenia: A new understanding of the pathophysiology of schizophrenia and its implications for treatment and prevention. *Current Directions in Psychological Science, 19,* 232–237. (p. 558)

Grady, C. L., McIntosh, A. R., Horwitz, B., Maisog, J. M., Ungeleider, L. G., Mentis, M. J., . . . Haxby, J. V. (1995). Age-related reductions in human recognition memory due to impaired encoding. *Science, 269,* 218–221. (p. 303)

Graham, A. M., Fisher, P. A., & Pfeifer, J. H. (2013). What sleeping babies hear: A functional MRI study of interparental conflict and infants' emotion processing. *Psychological Science, 24,* 782–789. (p. 143)

Graham, J., Nosek, B. A., & Haidt, J. (2012). The moral stereotypes of liberals and conservatives: Exaggeration of differences across the political spectrum. *PLOS ONE, 7*(12), e50092. doi:10.1371/journal.pone.0050092 (p. 462)

Grande, G., Romppel, M., & Barth, J. (2012). Association between Type D personality and prognosis in patients with cardiovascular diseases: A systematic review and meta-analysis. *Annals of Behavioral Medicine, 43,* 299–310. (p. 415)

Granic, I., Lobel, A., & Engels, R. C. M. E. (2014). The benefits of playing video games. *American Psychologist, 69,* 66–78. (p. 473)

Granqvist, P., Mikulincer, M., & Shaver, P. R. (2010). Religion as attachment: Normative processes and individual differences. *Personality and Social Psychology Review, 14,* 49–59. (p. 139)

Grant, A. M., Gino, F., & Hofmann, D. A. (2011). Reversing the extraverted leadership advantage: The role of employee proactivity. *Academy of Management Journal, 54,* 528–550. (p. 507)

Grant, N., Wardle, J., & Steptoe, A. (2009). The relationship between life satisfaction and health behavior: A cross-cultural analysis of young adults. *International Journal of Behavioral Medicine, 16,* 259–268. (p. 426)

Gray, P. (2010, July 7). *ADHD & school: Assessing normalcy in an abnormal environment.* Retrieved from https://www.psychologytoday.com/blog/freedom-learn/201007/adhd-school-assessing-normalcy-in-abnormal-environment (p. 532)

Gray, P. B., Yang, C.-F. J., & Pope, H. G., Jr. (2006). Fathers have lower salivary testosterone levels than unmarried men and married non-fathers in Beijing, China. *Proceedings of the Royal Society: Series B, 273,* 333–339. (p. 182)

Graybiel, A. M., & Smith, K. S. (2014, June). Good habits, bad habits. *Scientific American,* pp. 39–43. (p. 246)

Gray-Little, B., & Burks, N. (1983). Power and satisfaction in marriage: A review and critique. *Psychological Bulletin, 93,* 513–538. (p. 480)

Green, B. (2002). Listening to leaders: Feedback on 360-degree feedback one year later. *Organizational Development Journal, 20,* 8–16. (p. B-7)

Green, J. D., Sedikides, C., & Gregg, A. P. (2008). Forgotten but not gone: The recall and recognition of self-threatening memories. *Journal of Experimental Social Psychology, 44,* 547–561. (p. 499)

Green, J. T., & Woodruff-Pak, D. S. (2000). Eyeblink classical conditioning: Hippocampal formation is for neutral stimulus associations as cerebellum is for association–response. *Psychological Bulletin, 126,* 138–158. (p. 293)

Green, M. F., & Horan, W. P. (2010). Social cognition in schizophrenia. *Current Directions in Psychological Science, 19,* 243–248. (p. 557)

Greenberg, J. (2008). Understanding the vital human quest for self-esteem. *Perspectives on Psychological Science, 3,* 48–55. (p. 517)

Greene, J. D. (2010). *A new science of morality, Part 2.* Retrieved from http://edge.org/conversation/a-new-science-of-morality-part-2 (p. 151)

Greene, J. D., Sommerville, R. B., Nystrom, L. E., Darley, J. M., & Cohen, J. D. (2001). An fMRI investigation of emotional engagement in moral judgment. *Science, 293,* 2105–2108. (p. 151)

Greenwald, A. G. (1992, August). *Subliminal semantic activation and subliminal snake oil.* Paper presented at the 100th Annual Convention of the American Psychological Association, Washington, DC. (p. 203)

Greenwald, A. G., Banaji, M. R., & Nosek, B. A. (2015). Statistically small effects of the implicit association test can have societally large effects. *Journal of Personality and Social Psychology, 108,* 553–561. (p. 463)

Greenwald, A. G., Oakes, M. A., & Hoffman, H. (2003). Targets of discrimination: Effects of race on responses to weapons holders. *Journal of Experimental Social Psychology, 39,* 399–405. (p. 463)

Greenwald, A. G., & Pettigrew, T. F. (2014). With malice toward none and charity for some: Ingroup favoritism enables discrimination. *American Psychologist, 69,* 645–655. (p. 465)

Greenwald, A. G., Spangenberg, E. R., Pratkanis, A. R., & Eskenazi, J. (1991). Double-blind tests of subliminal self-help audiotapes. *Psychological Science, 2,* 119–122. (p. 203)

Greenwald, G. (2012, March 19). *Discussing the motives of the Afghan shooter.* Retrieved from http://www.salon.com/2012/03/19/discussing_the_motives_of_the_afghan_shooter/ (p. 485)

Greer, S. G., Goldstein, A. N., & Walker, M. P. (2013). The impact of sleep deprivation on food desire in the human brain. *Nature Communications, 4,* Article 2259. doi:10.1038/ncomms3259 (p. 95)

Gregory, A. M., Rijksdijk, F. V., Lau, J. Y., Dahl, R. E., & Eley, T. C. (2009). The direction of longitudinal associations between sleep problems and depression symptoms: A study of twins aged 8 and 10 years. *Sleep, 32,* 189–199. (pp. 94, 95)

Gregory, R. L. (1978). *Eye and brain: The psychology of seeing* (3rd ed.). New York: McGraw-Hill. (pp. 128, 223)

Gregory, R. L., & Gombrich, E. H. (Eds.). (1973). *Illusion in nature and art.* New York: Scribner's. (p. 207)

Greif, E. B., & Ulman, K. J. (1982). The psychological impact of menarche on early adolescent females: A review of the literature. *Child Development, 53,* 1413–1430. (p. 176)

Greist, J. H., Jefferson, J. W., & Marks, I. M. (1986). *Anxiety and its treatment: Help is available.* Washington, DC: American Psychiatric Press. (p. 537)

Greitemeyer, T., & Osswald, S. (2010). Effects of prosocial video games on prosocial behavior. *Journal of Personality and Social Psychology, 98,* 211–221. (p. 472)

Greitemeyer, T., & Osswald, S. (2011). Playing prosocial video games increases the accessibility of prosocial thoughts. *Journal of Social Psychology, 151,* 121–128. (p. 472)

Greyson, B. (2010). Implications of near-death experiences for a postmaterialist psychology. *Review of Religion and Spirituality, 2,* 37–45. (p. 112)

Grèzes, J., & Decety, J. (2001). Function anatomy of execution, mental simulation, observation, and verb generation of actions: A meta-analysis. *Human Brain Mapping, 12,* 1–19. (p. 339)

Griffiths, M. (2001). Sex on the Internet: Observations and implications for Internet sex addiction. *Journal of Sex Research, 38,* 333–342. (p. 105)

Griggs, R. (2014). Coverage of the Stanford Prison Experiment in introductory psychology textbooks. *Teaching of Psychology, 41,* 195–203. (p. 446)

Grijalva, E., Newman, D. A., Tay, L., Donnellan, M. B., Harms, P. D., Robins, R. W., & Yan, T. (2015). Gender differences in narcissism: A meta-analytic review. *Psychological Bulletin, 141,* 261–310. (p. 519)

Grillon, C., Quispe-Escudero, D., Mathur, A., & Ernst, M. (2015). Mental fatigue impairs emotion regulation. *Emotion, 15,* 383–389. (p. 421)

Grilo, C. M., & Pogue-Geile, M. F. (1991). The nature of environmental influences on weight and obesity: A behavior genetic analysis. *Psychological Bulletin, 110,* 520–537. (p. 383)

Grimm, S., & Scheidegger, M. (2013, May/June). A trip out of depression. *Scientific American Mind,* pp. 67–71. (p. 596)

Grinker, R. R. (2007). *Unstrange minds: Remapping the world of autism.* New York: Basic Books. (p. 136)

Griskevicius, V., Tybur, J. M., Gangestad, S. W., Perea, E. F., Shapiro, J. R., & Kenrick, D. T. (2009). Aggress to impress: Hostility as an evolved context-dependent strategy. *Journal of Personality and Social Psychology, 96,* 980–994. (p. 193)

Grobstein, C. (1979, June). External human fertilization. *Scientific American,* pp. 57–67. (p. 123)

Grodin, E. N., & White, T. L. (2015). The neuroanatomical delineation of agentic and affiliative extraversion. *Cognitive, Affective, and Behavioral Neuroscience, 15,* 321–334. (p. 510)

Grogan-Kaylor, A. (2004). The effect of corporal punishment on antisocial behavior in children. *Social Work Research, 28,* 153–162. (p. 262)

Groothuis, T. G. G., & Carere, C. (2005). Avian personalities: Characterization and epigenesis. *Neuroscience and Biobehavioral Reviews, 29,* 137–150. (p. 508)

Gross, A. E., & Crofton, C. (1977). What is good is beautiful. *Sociometry, 40,* 85–90. (p. 478)

Gross, J. J. (2013). Emotion regulation: Taking stock and moving forward. *Emotion, 13,* 359–365. (p. 390)

Grossberg, S. (1995). The attentive brain. *American Scientist, 83,* 438–449. (p. 207)

Grossmann, I., Na, J., Varnum, M. E. W., Park, D. C., Kitayama, S., & Nisbett, R. E. (2010). Reasoning about social conflicts improves into old age. *Proceedings of the National Academy of Sciences of the United States of America, 107,* 7246–7250. (p. 349)

Grover, S. & Helliwell, J. F. (2014, December). *How's life at home? New evidence on marriage and the set point for happiness* (NBER Working Paper No. 20794). Retrieved from http://www.nber.org/papers/w20794 (p. 371)

Groves, C. L., Prot, S., & Anderson, C. A. (2015). Violent media effects: Theory and evidence. In H. Friedman (Ed.), *Encyclopedia of mental health* (2nd ed.) San Diego, CA: Elsevier. (p. 277)

Gruber, J. (2011). Can feeling too good be bad? Positive emotion persistence (PEP) in bipolar disorder. *Current Directions in Psychological Science, 20,* 217–221. (p. 546)

Gruber, J., Gilbert, K. E., Youngstrom, E., Kogos Youngstrom, J., Feeny, N. C., Findling, R. L. (2013). Reward dysregulation and mood symptoms in an adolescent outpatient sample. *Journal of Abnormal Child Psychology, 41,* 1053–1065. (p. 546)

Gruder, C. L. (1977). Choice of comparison persons in evaluating oneself. In J. M. Suls & R. L. Miller (Eds.), *Social comparison processes* (pp. 21–41). New York: Hemisphere. (p. 435)

Gu, X., Lohrenz, T., Salas, R., Baldwin, P. R., Soltani, A., Kirk, U., . . . Montague, P. R. (2015). Belief about nicotine selectively modulates value and reward prediction error signals in smokers. *Proceedings of the National Academy of Sciences of the United States of America, 112,* 2539–2544. (p. 104)

Guéguen, N. (2011). Effects of solicitor sex and attractiveness on receptivity to sexual offers: A field study. *Archives of Sexual Behavior, 40,* 915–919. (p. 194)

Guerin, B. (1986). Mere presence effects in humans: A review. *Journal of Personality and Social Psychology, 22,* 38–77. (p. 455)

Guerin, B. (2003). Language use as social strategy: A review and an analytic framework for the social sciences. *Review of General Psychology, 7,* 251–298. (p. 329)

Guiso, L., Monte, F., Sapienza, P., & Zingales, L. (2008). Culture, gender, and math. *Science, 320,* 1164–1165. (p. 357)

Gunderson, E. A., Gripshover, S. J., Romero, C., Dweck, C. S., Goldin-Meadow, S., & Levine, S. C. (2013). Parent praise to 1- to 3-year-olds predicts children's motivational frameworks 5 years later. *Child Development, 84,* 1526–1541. (p. 362)

Gunstad, J., Strain, G., Devlin, M. J., Wing, R., Cohen, R. A., Paul, R. H., . . . Mitchell, J. E. (2011). Improved memory function 12 weeks after bariatric surgery. *Surgery for Obesity and Related Diseases, 7,* 465–472. (p. 383)

Gunter, R. W., & Bodner, G. E. (2008). How eye movements affect unpleasant memories: Support for a working-memory account. *Behaviour Research and Therapy, 46,* 913–931. (p. 588)

Gunter, T. D., Vaughn, M. G., & Philibert, R. A. (2010). Behavioral genetics in antisocial spectrum disorders and psychopathy: A review of the recent literature. *Behavioral Sciences and the Law, 28,* 148–173. (p. 563)

Guo, X., Zhai, J., Liu, Z., Fang, M., Wang, B., Wang, C., . . . Zhao, J. (2010). Effect of antipsychotic medication alone vs combined with psychosocial intervention on outcomes of early-stage schizophrenia. *Archives of General Psychiatry, 67,* 895–904. (p. 594)

Gustavson, C. R., Garcia, J., Hankins, W. G., & Rusiniak, K. W. (1974). Coyote predation control by aversive conditioning. *Science, 184,* 581–583. (p. 268)

Gustavson, C. R., Kelly, D. J., & Sweeney, M. (1976). Prey-lithium aversions I: Coyotes and wolves. *Behavioral Biology, 17,* 61–72. (p. 268)

Gutchess, A. (2014). Plasticity in the aging brain: New directions in cognitive neuroscience. *Science, 346,* 579–582. (p. 161)

Guttmacher. (1994). *Sex and America's teenagers.* New York: Alan Guttmacher Institute. (pp. 156, 184)

H

H., Sally. (1979, August). [Videotape recording No. T–3]. New Haven, CT: Fortunoff Video Archive for Holocaust Testimonies, Yale University Library. (p. 500)

Haas, A. P., Eliason, M., Mays, V. M., Mathy, R. M., Cochran, S. D., D'Augelli, A. R., . . . Clayton, P. J. (2011). Suicide and suicide risk in lesbian, gay, bisexual, and transgender populations: Review and recommendations. *Journal of Homosexuality, 58,* 10–51. (p. 553)

Haase, C. M., Tomasik, M. J. H., & Silbereisen, R. K. (2008). Premature behavioral autonomy: Correlates in late adolescence and young adulthood. *European Psychologist, 13,* 255–266. (p. 145)

Haber, R. N. (1970, May). How we remember what we see. *Scientific American,* pp. 104–112. (p. 282)

Hadden, B. W., Smith, C. V., & Webster, G. D. (2014). Relationship duration moderates associations between attachment and relationship quality: Meta-analytic support for the temporal adult romantic attachment model. *Personality and Social Psychology Review, 18,* 42–58. (p. 142)

Hadjistavropoulos, T., Craig, K. D., Duck, S., Cano, A., Goubert, L., Jackson, P. L., . . . Fitzgerald, T. D. (2011). A biopsychosocial formulation of pain communication. *Psychological Bulletin, 137,* 910–939. (p. 233)

Hafenbrack, A. C., Kinias, Z., & Barsade, S. G. (2014). Debiasing the mind through meditation: Mindfulness and the sunk-cost bias. *Psychological Science, 25,* 369–376. (p. 428)

Hagerty, M. R. (2000). Social comparisons of income in one's community: Evidence from national surveys of income and happiness. *Journal of Personality and Social Psychology, 78,* 764–771. (p. 435)

Hagger, M. S., & Chatzisarantis, N. L. D. (2013). The sweet taste of success: The presence of glucose in the oral cavity moderates the depletion of self-control resources. *Personality and Social Psychology Bulletin, 39,* 28–42. (p. 422)

Hagger, M. S., Wood, C., Stiff, C., & Chatzisarantis, N. L. D. (2010). Ego depletion and the strength model of self-control: A meta-analysis. *Psychological Bulletin, 136,* 495–525. (p. 421)

Haidt, J. (2000). The positive emotion of elevation. *Prevention & Treatment, 3*(1). http://dx.doi.org/10.1037/1522-3736.3.1.33c (p. 150)

Haidt, J. (2003). The moral emotions. In R. J. Davidson, K. Scherer, & H. H. Goldsmith (Eds.), *Handbook of affective sciences* (pp. 852–870). New York: Oxford University Press. (p. 150)

Haidt, J. (2012). *The righteous mind: Why good people are divided by politics and religion.* New York: Pantheon. (p. 150)

Hajhosseini, B., Stewart, B., Tan, J. C., Busque, S., & Melcher, M. L. (2013). Evaluating deceased donor registries: Identifying predictive factors of donor designation. *American Surgeon, 79,* 235–241. (p. 323)

Hakuta, K., Bialystok, E., & Wiley, E. (2003). Critical evidence: A test of the critical-period hypothesis for second-language acquisition. *Psychological Science, 14,* 31–38. (p. 333)

Halberstadt, J. B., Niedenthal, P. M., & Kushner, J. (1995). Resolution of lexical ambiguity by emotional state. *Psychological Science, 6,* 278–281. (p. 207)

Halberstadt, J., Sherman, S. J., & Sherman, J. W. (2011). Why Barack Obama is Black. *Psychological Science, 22,* 29–33. (p. 467)

Haldeman, D. C. (1994). The practice and ethics of sexual orientation conversion therapy. *Journal of Consulting and Clinical Psychology, 62,* 221–227. (p. 188)

Haldeman, D. C. (2002). Gay rights, patient rights: The implications of sexual orientation conversion therapy. *Professional Psychology: Research and Practice, 33,* 260–264. (p. 188)

Hall, C. S., Dornhoff, W., Blick, K. A., & Weesner, K. E. (1982). The dreams of college men and women in 1950 and 1980: A comparison of dream contents and sex differences. *Sleep, 5,* 188–194. (p. 99)

Hall, C. S., & Lindzey, G. (1978). *Theories of personality* (2nd ed.). New York: Wiley. (p. 499)

Hall, G. (1997). Context aversion, Pavlovian conditioning, and the psychological side effects of chemotherapy. *European Psychologist, 2,* 118–124. (p. 268)

Hall, G. S. (1904). *Adolescence: Its psychology and its relations to physiology, anthropology, sex, crime, religion and education* (Vol. 1). New York: Appleton-Century-Crofts. (p. 147)

Hall, J. A. (1984). *Nonverbal sex differences: Communication accuracy and expressive style.* Baltimore: Johns Hopkins University Press. (p. 397)

Hall, J. A. (1987). On explaining gender differences: The case of nonverbal communication. In P. Shaver & C. Hendrick (Eds.), *Review of personality and social psychology: Vol. 7. Sex and gender* (pp. 177–200). Beverly Hills, CA: Sage. (p. 397)

Hall, S. S. (2004, May). The good egg. *Discover,* pp. 30–39. (p. 123)

Hallal, P. C., Andersen, L. B., Bull, F. C., Guthold, R., Haskell, W., & Ekelund, U. (2012). Global physical activity levels: Surveillance progress, pitfalls, and prospects. *The Lancet, 380,* 247–257. (p. 384)

Haller, R., Rummel, C., Henneberg, S., Pollmer, U., & Köster, E. P. (1999). The influence of early experience with vanillin on food preference later in life. *Chemical Senses, 24,* 465–467. (p. 236)

Halpern, C. T., Joyner, K., Udry, J. R., & Suchindran, C. (2000). Smart teens don't have sex (or kiss much either). *Journal of Adolescent Health, 26,* 213–215. (p. 187)

Halpern, D. F., Benbow, C. P., Geary, D. C., Gur, R. C., Hyde, J. S., & Gernsbacher, M. A. (2007). The science of sex differences in science and mathematics. *Psychological Science in the Public Interest, 8,* 1–51. (p. 357)

Hambrick, D. Z. (2014, December 2). Brain training doesn't make you smarter. *Scientific American.* Retrieved from http://www.scientificamerican.com/article/brain-training-doesn-t-make-you-smarter/ (p. 162)

Hambrick, D. Z., Altmann, E. M., Oswald, F. L., Meinz, E. J., Gobet, F., & Campitelli, G. (2014a). Accounting for expert performance: The devil is in the details. *Intelligence, 45,* 112–114. (p. 376)

Hambrick, D. Z., & Meinz, E. J. (2011). Limits on the predictive power of domain-specific experience and knowledge in skilled performance. *Current Directions in Psychological Science, 20,* 275–279. (pp. 325, 376)

Hambrick, D. Z., Oswald, F. L., Altmann, E. M., Meinz, E. J., Gobet, F., & Campitelli, G. (2014b). Deliberate practice: Is that all it takes to become an expert? *Intelligence, 45,* 34–45. (p. 376)

Hampshire, A., Highfield, R. R., Parkin, B. L., & Owen, A. M. (2012). Fractionating human intelligence. *Neuron, 76,* 1225–1237. (p. 341)

Hampson, R. (2000, April 10). In the end, people just need more room. *USA Today,* p. 19A. (p. 384)

Harlow, H. F., Harlow, M. K., & Suomi, S. J. (1971). From thought to therapy: Lessons from a primate laboratory. *American Scientist, 59,* 538–549. (p. 138)

Hambrick, D. Z. (2014, December 2). Brain training doesn't make you smarter. *Scientific American.* Retrieved from http://www.scientificamerican.com/article/brain-training-doesn-t-make-you-smarter/ (p. 162)

Hammack, P. L. (2005). The life course development of human sexual orientation: An integrative paradigm. *Human Development, 48,* 267–290. (p. 188)

Hammer, E. (2003, Winter). How lucky you are to be a psychology major. *Eye on Psi Chi,* pp. 4–5. (p. C-5)

Hammersmith, S. K. (1982, August). *Sexual preference: An empirical study from the Alfred C. Kinsey Institute for Sex Research.* Paper presented at the 90th Annual Convention of the American Psychological Association, Washington, DC. (p. 189)

Hammond, D. C. (2008). Hypnosis as sole anesthesia for major surgeries: Historical and contemporary perspectives. *American Journal of Clinical Hypnosis, 51,* 101–121. (p. 235)

Hancock, K. J., & Rhodes, G. (2008). Contact, configural coding and the other-race effect in face recognition. *British Journal of Psychology, 99,* 45–56. (p. 467)

Hankin, B. L., & Abramson, L. Y. (2001). Development of gender differences in depression: An elaborated cognitive vulnerability–transactional stress theory. *Psychological Bulletin, 127,* 773–796. (p. 550)

Hansen, C. H., & Hansen, R. D. (1988). Finding the face-in-the-crowd: An anger superiority effect. *Journal of Personality and Social Psychology, 54,* 917–924. (p. 396)

Hanson, J. L., Nacewicz, B. M., Sutterer, M. J., Cayo, A. A., Schaefer, S. M., Rudolph, K. D., . . . Davidson, R. J. (2015). Behavioral problems after early life stress: Contributions of the hippocampus and amygdala. *Biological Psychiatry, 77,* 314–323. (p. 409)

Harbaugh, W. T., Mayr, U., & Burghart, D. R. (2007). Neural responses to taxation and voluntary giving reveal motives for charitable donations. *Science, 316,* 1622–1625. (p. 483)

Harber, K. D. (1998). Feedback to minorities: Evidence of a positive bias. *Journal of Personality and Social Psychology, 74,* 622–628. (p. 463)

Harden, K. P. (2012). True love waits? A sibling-comparison study of age at first sexual intercourse and romantic relationships in young adulthood. *Psychological Science, 23,* 1324–1336. (p. 187)

Hardeveld, H. S., De Graaf, R., Nolen, W. A., & Beckman, A. T. F. (2010). Prevalence and predictors of recurrence of major depressive disorder in the adult population. *Acta Psychiatrica Scandinavia, 122,* 184–191. (p. 548)

Hardt, O., Einarsson, E. O., & Nader, K. (2010). A bridge over troubled water: Re-consolidation as a link between cognitive and neuroscientific memory research traditions. *Annual Review of Psychology, 61,* 141–167. (p. 306)

Hare, R. D. (1975). Psychophysiological studies of psychopathy. In D. C. Fowles (Ed.), *Clinical applications of psychophysiology* (pp. 77–105). New York: Columbia University Press. (p. 564)

Harenski, C. L., Harenski, K. A., Shane, M. W., & Kiehl, K. A. (2010). Aberrant neural processing of moral violations in criminal psychopaths. *Journal of Abnormal Psychology, 119,* 863–874. (p. 564)

Harkins, S. G., & Szymanski, K. (1989). Social loafing and group evaluation. *Journal of Personality and Social Psychology, 56,* 934–941. (p. 457)

Harmon-Jones, E., Abramson, L. Y., Sigelman, J., Bohlig, A., Hogan, M. E., & Harmon-Jones, C. (2002). Proneness to hypomania/mania symptoms or depression symptoms and asymmetrical frontal cortical responses to an anger-evoking event. *Journal of Personality and Social Psychology, 82,* 610–618. (p. 393)

Harper, C., & McLanahan, S. (2004). Father absence and youth incarceration. *Journal of Research on Adolescence, 14,* 369–397. (p. 471)

Harris, B. (1979). Whatever happened to Little Albert? *American Psychologist, 34,* 151–160. (p. 253)

Harris, J. R. (1998). *The nurture assumption: Why children turn out the way they do.* New York: Free Press. (pp. 141, 154)

Harris, J. R. (2002). Beyond the nurture assumption: Testing hypotheses about the child's environment. In J. G. Borkowski, S. L. Ramey, & M. Bristol-Power (Eds.), *Parenting and the child's world: Influences on academic, intellectual, and social-emotional development* (pp. 3–20). Mahwah, NJ: Erlbaum. (p. 154)

Harris, J. R. (2006). *No two are alike: Human nature and human individuality.* New York: Norton. (p. 69)

Harris, R. J. (1994). The impact of sexually explicit media. In J. Bryant & D. Zillmann (Eds.), *Media effects: Advances in theory and research* (pp. 247–272). Hillsdale, NJ: Erlbaum. (p. 471)

Harrison, T. L., Shipstead, Z., Hicks, K. L., Hambrick, D. Z., Redick, T. S., & Engle, R. W. (2013). Working memory training may increase working memory capacity but not fluid intelligence. *Psychological Science, 24,* 2409–2419. (p. 162)

Harriston, K. A. (1993, December 24). 1 shakes, 1 snoozes: Both win $45 million. *The Tacoma News Tribune,* pp. A1, A2. (p. 516)

Hartanto, T. A., Krafft, C. E., Losif, A. M., & Schweitzer, J. B. (2015). A trial-by-trial analysis reveals more intense physical activity is associated with better cognitive control performance in attention-deficit/hyperactivity disorder. *Child Neuropsychology.* Advance online publication. doi10.1080/09297049.2015.1044511 (p. 532)

Harter, J. K., Schmidt, F. L., Asplund, J. W., Killham, E. A., & Agrawal, S. (2010). Causal impact of employee work perceptions on the bottom line of organizations. *Perspectives on Psychological Science, 5,* 378–389. (p. B-10)

Harter, J. K., Schmidt, F. L., & Hayes, T. L. (2002). Business-unit-level relationship between employee satisfaction, employee engagement, and business outcomes: A meta-analysis. *Journal of Applied Psychology, 87,* 268–279. (p. B-9)

Hartmann, E. (1981, April). The strangest sleep disorder. *Psychology Today,* pp. 14, 16, 18. (p. 88)

Hartwig, M., & Bond, C. F., Jr. (2011). Why do lie-catchers fail? A lens model meta-analysis of human lie judgments. *Psychological Bulletin, 137,* 643–659. (p. 397)

Harvey, A. G., & Tang, N. K. Y. (2012). (Mis)perception of sleep in insomnia: A puzzle and a resolution. *Psychological Bulletin, 138,* 77–101. (p. 97)

Hasan, Y., Bègue, L., Scharkow, M., & Bushman, B. J. (2013). The more you play, the more aggressive you become: A long-term experimental study of cumulative violent video game effects on hostile expectations and aggressive behavior. *Journal of Experimental Social Psychology, 49,* 224–227. (p. 472)

Haselton, M. G., & Gildersleeve, K. (2011). Can men detect ovulation? *Current Directions in Psychological Science, 20,* 87–92. (p. 181)

Haslam, S. A., & Reicher, S. D. (2007). Beyond the banality of evil: Three dynamics of an interactionist social psychology of tyranny. *Personality and Social Psychology Bulletin, 33,* 615–622. (p. 446)

Haslam, S. A., & Reicher, S. D. (2012). Contesting the "nature" of conformity: What Milgram and Zimbardo's studies really show. *PLOS Biology, 10*(11), e1001426. doi:10.1371/journal.pbio.1001426 (p. 446)

Hassan, B., & Rahman, Q. (2007). Selective sexual orientation–related differences in object location memory. *Behavioral Neuroscience, 121,* 625–633. (p. 191)

Hassin, R. R. (2013). Yes it can: On the functional abilities of the human unconscious. *Perspectives on Psychological Science, 8,* 195–207. (p. 324)

Hatfield, E. (1988). Passionate and companionate love. In R. J. Sternberg & M. L. Barnes (Eds.), *The psychology of love* (pp. 191–217). New Haven, CT: Yale University Press. (pp. 479, 480)

Hatfield, E., & Sprecher, S. (1986). *Mirror, mirror: The importance of looks in everyday life.* Albany: State University of New York Press. (p. 477)

Hathaway, S. R. (1960). Foreword. In S. R. Hathaway, W. G. Dahlstrom, & G. S. Welsh, *An MMPI handbook* (Vol. 1, Rev. ed., p. 1972). Minneapolis: University of Minnesota Press. (p. 508)

Hatzenbuehler, M. L. (2011). The social environment and suicide attempts in lesbian, gay, and bisexual youth. *Pediatrics, 127,* 896–903. (p. 553)

Hatzenbuehler, M. L. (2014). Structural stigma and the health of lesbian, gay, and bisexual populations. *Current Directions in Psychological Science, 23,* 127–132. (p. 464)

Hatzigeorgiadis, A., Zourbanos, N., Galanis, E., & Theodorakis, Y. (2011). Self-talk and sports performance: A meta-analysis. *Perspectives on Psychological Science, 6,* 348–356. (p. 580)

Haun, D. B. M., Rekers, Y., & Tomasello, M. (2014). Children conform to the behavior of peers; other great apes stick with what they know. *Psychological Science, 25,* 2160–2167. (p. 150)

Havas, D. A., Glenberg, A. M., Gutowski, K. A., Lucarelli, M. J., & Davidson, R. J. (2010). Cosmetic use of botulinum toxin-A affects processing of emotional language. *Psychological Science, 21,* 895–900. (p. 402)

Hawkley, L. C., Hughes, M. E., Waite, L. J., Masi, C. M., Thisted, R. A., & Cacioppo, J. T. (2008). From social structure factors to perceptions of relationship quality and loneliness: The Chicago Health, Aging, and Social Relations Study. *Journal of Gerontology: Series B, 63,* S375–S384. (p. 424)

Haworth, C. M. A., Wright, M. J., Luciano, M., Martin, N. G., de Geus, E. J., van Beijsterveldt, C. E., . . . Plomin, R. (2010). The heritability of general cognitive ability increases linearly from childhood to young adulthood. *Molecular Psychiatry, 15,* 1112–1120. (p. 355)

Haworth, C. M. A., Wright, M. J., Martin, N. W., Martin, N. G., Boomsma, D. I., Bartels, M., . . . Plomin, R. (2009). A twin study of the genetics of high cognitive ability selected from 11,000 twin pairs in sex studies from four countries. *Behavior Genetics, 39,* 359–370. (p. 354)

Haxby, J. V. (2001, July 7). Quoted in B. Bower, Faces of perception. *Science News,* pp. 10–12. See also J. V. Haxby, M. I. Gobbini, M. L. Furey, A. Ishai, J. L. Schouten & P. Pietrini (2001), Distributed and overlapping representations of faces and objects in ventral temporal cortex. *Science, 293,* 2425–2430. (p. 215)

Haynes, J.-D., & Rees, G. (2005). Predicting the orientation of invisible stimuli from activity in human primary visual cortex. *Nature Neuroscience, 8,* 686–691. (p. 202)

Haynes, J.-D., & Rees, G. (2006). Decoding mental states from brain activity in humans. *Nature Reviews Neuroscience, 7,* 523–534. (p. 202)

Hazan, C., & Shaver, P. R. (1994). Attachment as an organizational framework for research on close relationships. *Psychological Inquiry, 5,* 1–22. (p. 144)

Hazelrigg, M. D., Cooper, H. M., & Borduin, C. M. (1987). Evaluating the effectiveness of family therapies: An integrative review and analysis. *Psychological Bulletin, 101,* 428–442. (p. 582)

He, Y., Jones, C. R., Fujiki, N., Xu, Y., Guo, B., Holder, J. L., Jr., . . . Fu, Y.-H. (2009). The transcriptional repressor DEC2 regulates sleep length in mammals. *Science, 325,* 866–870. (p. 92)

Headey, B., Muffels, R., & Wagner, G. G. (2010). Long-running German panel survey shows that personal and economic choices, not just genes, matter for happiness. *Proceedings of the National Academy of Sciences of the United States of America, 107,* 17922–17926. (p. 436)

Health Canada. (2012). *Major findings from the Canadian Alcohol and Drug Use Monitoring Survey (CADUMS) 2011.* Retrieved from http://www.hc-sc.gc.ca/hc-ps/drugs-drogues/stat/index-eng.php (p. 114)

Heavey, C. L., & Hurlburt, R. T. (2008). The phenomena of inner experience. *Consciousness and Cognition, 17,* 798–810. (p. 336)

Hedström, P., Liu, K.-Y., & Nordvik, M. K. (2008). Interaction domains and suicides: A population-based panel study of suicides in the Stockholm metropolitan area, 1991–1999. *Social Forces, 2,* 713–740. (p. 553)

Heider, F. (1958). *The psychology of interpersonal relations.* New York: Wiley. (p. 442)

Heil, K. M., & Schaaf, C. P. (2013). The genetics of autism spectrum disorders—A guide for clinicians. *Current Psychiatry Reports, 15,* 334. doi:10.1007/s11920-012-0334-3 (p. 136)

Heiman, J. R. (1975, April). The physiology of erotica: Women's sexual arousal. *Psychology Today*, pp. 90–94. (p. 185)

Heine, S. J., & Buchtel, E. E. (2009). Personality: The universal and the culturally specific. *Annual Review of Psychology, 60*, 369–394. (p. 509)

Heine, S. J., & Hamamura, T. (2007). In search of East Asian self-enhancement. *Personality and Social Psychology Review, 11*, 4–27. (p. 519)

Heine, S. J., & Ruby, M. B. (2010). *Cultural psychology. Wiley Interdisciplinary Reviews: Cognitive Science, 1*, 254–266. (p. 442)

Hejmadi, A., Davidson, R. J., & Rozin, P. (2000). Exploring Hindu Indian emotion expressions: Evidence for accurate recognition by Americans and Indians. *Psychological Science, 11*, 183–187. (p. 396)

Helfand, D. (2011, January 7). An assault on rationality. *The New York Times*. Retrieved from http://www.nytimes.com/roomfordebate/2011/01/06/the-esp-study-when-science-goes-psychic/esp-and-the-assault-on-rationality (p. 242)

Helleberg, M., Afzal, S., Kronborg, G., Larsen, C. S., Pedersen, G., Pedersen, C., . . . Obel, N. (2013). Mortality attributable to smoking among HIV-1-infected individuals: A nationwide, population-based cohort study. *Clinical Infectious Diseases, 56*, 727–734. (p. 108)

Heller, A. S., Johnstone, T., Schackman, A. J., Light, S. N., Peterson, M. J., Kolden, G. G., . . . Davidson, R. J. (2009). Reduced capacity to sustain positive emotion in major depression reflects diminished maintenance of fronto-striatal brain activation. *Proceedings of the National Academy of Sciences of the United States of America, 106*, 22445–22450. (p. 549)

Heller, W. (1990, May/June). Of one mind: Second thoughts about the brain's dual nature. *The Sciences*, pp. 38–44. (p. 64)

Helliwell, J., Layard, R., & Sachs, J. (Eds.) (2013). *World happiness report*. New York: Earth Institute, Columbia University. (pp. 435, 436)

Helmreich, W. B. (1992). *Against all odds: Holocaust survivors and the successful lives they made in America*. New York: Simon & Schuster. (pp. 143, 499)

Helmreich, W. B. (1994). Personal communication [Department of Sociology, City University of New York]. (p. 499)

Helms, J. E., Jernigan, M., & Mascher, J. (2005). The meaning of race in psychology and how to change it: A methodological perspective. *American Psychologist, 60*, 27–36. (p. 358)

Helmuth, L. (2001). Boosting brain activity from the outside in. *Science, 292*, 1284–1286. (p. 599)

Helsen, K., Goubert, L., Peters, M. L., & Vlaeyen, J. W. S. (2011). Observational learning and pain-related fear: An experimental study with colored cold pressor tasks. *Journal of Pain, 12*, 1230–1239. (p. 542)

Helton, W. S. (2008). Expertise acquisition as sustained learning in humans and other animals: Commonalities across species. *Animal Cognition, 11*, 99–107. (p. 344)

Hembree, R. (1988). Correlates, causes, effects, and treatment of test anxiety. *Review of Educational Research, 58*, 47–77. (p. 368)

Hemenover, S. H. (2003). The good, the bad, and the healthy: Impacts of emotional disclosure of trauma on resilient self-concept and psychological distress. *Personality and Social Psychology Bulletin, 29*, 1236–1244. (p. 425)

Henderlong, J., & Lepper, M. R. (2002). The effects of praise on children's intrinsic motivation: A review and synthesis. *Psychological Bulletin, 128*, 774–795. (p. 271)

Henderson, J. M. (2007). Regarding scenes. *Current Directions in Psychological Science, 16*, 219–222. (p. 204)

Henig, R. M. (2010, August 18). What is it about 20-somethings? *The New York Times Magazine*. Retrieved from http://www.nytimes.com/2010/08/22/magazine/22Adulthood-t.html?pagewanted=all&_r=0 (p. 156)

Henkel, L. A., Franklin, N., & Johnson, M. K. (2000, March). Cross-modal source monitoring confusions between perceived and imagined events. *Journal of Experimental Psychology: Learning, Memory, and Cognition, 26*, 321–335. (p. 308)

Henley, N. M. (1989). Molehill or mountain? What we know and don't know about sex bias in language. In M. Crawford & M. Gentry (Eds.), *Gender and thought: Psychological perspectives* (pp. 59–78). New York: Springer-Verlag. (p. 338)

Hennenlotter, A., Dresel, C., Castrop, F., Ceballos Baumann, A., Wohlschlager, A., & Haslinger, B. (2008). The link between facial feedback and neural activity within central circuitries of emotion—New insights from botulinum toxin–induced denervation of frown muscles. *Cerebral Cortex, 19*, 537–542. (p. 402)

Hennessey, B. A., & Amabile, T. M. (2010). Creativity. *Annual Review of Psychology, 61*, 569–598. (pp. 324, B-13)

Henrich, J., Heine, S. J., & Norenzayan, A. (2010). The weirdest people in the world? *Behavioral and Brain Sciences, 33*, 61–135. (p. 9)

Hepper, P. (2005). Unravelling our beginnings. *The Psychologist, 18*, 474–477. (p. 123)

Hepler, J., & Albarracin, D. (2013). Complete unconscious control: Using (in)action primes to demonstrate completely unconscious activation of inhibitory control mechanisms. *Cognition, 128*, 271–279. (p. 202)

Herbenick, D., Reece, M., Schick, V., & Sanders, S. A. (2014). Erect penile length and circumference dimensions of 1,661 sexually active men in the United States. *Journal of Sexual Medicine, 11*, 93–101. (p. 183)

Herbenick, D., Reece, M., Schick, V., Sanders, S. A., Dodge, B., & Fortenberry, J. D. (2010). Sexual behavior in the United States: Results from a national probability sample of men and women ages 14–94. *Journal of Sexual Medicine, 7*(Suppl. 5), 255–265. (p. 188)

Herbert, J. D., Lilienfeld, S. O., Lohr, J. M., Montgomery, R. W., O'Donohue, W. T., Rosen, G. M., & Tolin, D. F. (2000). Science and pseudoscience in the development of eye movement desensitization and reprocessing: Implications for clinical psychology. *Clinical Psychology Review, 20*, 945–971. (p. 587)

Herculano-Houzel, S. (2012). The remarkable, yet not extraordinary, human brain as a scaled-up primate brain and its associated cost. *Proceedings of the National Academy of Sciences of the United States of America, 109*(Suppl. 1), 10661–10668. (p. 44)

Herman, C. P., & Polivy, J. (1980). Restrained eating. In A. J. Stunkard (Ed.), *Obesity* (pp. 208–225). Philadelphia: W. B. Saunders. (p. 385)

Herman, C. P., Roth, D. A., & Polivy, J. (2003). Effects of the presence of others on food intake: A normative interpretation. *Psychological Bulletin, 129*, 873–886. (p. 381)

Herman-Giddens, M. E., Steffes, J., Harris, D., Slora, E., Hussey, M., Dowshen, S. A., . . . Reiter, E. O. (2012). Secondary sexual characteristics in boys: Data from the pediatric research in office settings network. *Pediatrics, 130*, 1058–1068. (pp. 175, 176)

Herman-Giddens, M. E., Wang, L., & Koch, G. (2001). Secondary sexual characteristics in boys: Estimates from the National Health and Nutrition Examination Survey III, 1988–1994. *Archives of Pediatrics and Adolescent Medicine, 155*, 1022–1028. (p. 176)

Hernandez, A. E., & Li, P. (2007). Age of acquisition: Its neural and computational mechanisms. *Psychological Bulletin, 133*, 638–650. (p. 332)

Hernandez, R., Kershaw, K. N., Siddique, J., Boehm, J. K., Kubzansky, L. D., Diez-Roux, A., . . . Lloyd-Jones, D. M. (2015). Optimism and cardiovascular health: Multi-Ethnic Study of Atherosclerosis (MESA). *Health Behavior and Policy Review, 2*, 62–73. (p. 422)

Herring, D. R., White, K. R., Jabeen, L. N., Hinojos, M., & Terrazas, G. (2013). On the automatic activation of attitudes: A quarter century of evaluative priming research. *Psychological Bulletin, 132*, 1062–1089. (pp. 202, 298)

Herringa, R. J., Phillips, M. L., Fournier, J. C., Kronhaus, D. M., & Germain, A. (2013). Childhood and adult trauma both correlate with dorsal anterior cingulate activation to threat in combat veterans. *Psychological Medicine, 43*, 1533–1542. (p. 543)

Herrmann, E., Call, J., Hernández-Lloreda, M. V., Hare, B., & Tomasello, M. (2007). Humans have evolved specialized skills of social cognition: The cultural intelligence hypothesis. *Science, 317*, 1360–1365. (p. 274)

Herrnstein, R. J., & Loveland, D. H. (1964). Complex visual concept in the pigeon. *Science, 146*, 549–551. (p. 257)

Hershenson, M. (1989). *The moon illusion*. Hillsdale, NJ: Erlbaum. (p. 222)

Hertenstein, M. (2009). *The tell: The little clues that reveal big truths about who we are*. New York: Basic Books. (p. 415)

Hertenstein, M. J., Hansel, C., Butts, S., Hile, S. (2009). Smile intensity in photographs predicts divorce later in life. *Motivation and Emotion, 33*, 99–105. (p. 122)

Hertenstein, M. J., Keltner, D., App, B., Bulleit, B., & Jaskolka, A. (2006). Touch communicates distinct emotions. *Emotion, 6*, 528–533. (p. 231)

Hertenstein, M. J., Verkamp, J. M., Kerestes, A. M., & Holmes, R. M. (2006). The communicative functions of touch in humans, nonhuman primates, and rats: A review and synthesis of the empirical research. *Genetic, Social, and General Psychology Monographs, 132*, 5–94. (p. 139)

Herz, R. S. (2001, October). Ah, sweet skunk! Why we like or dislike what we smell. *Cerebrum*, pp. 31–47. (p. 238)

Herz, R. (2007). *The scent of desire: Discovering our enigmatic sense of smell*. New York: Morrow. (p. 237)

Herz, R. (2012, January 28). You eat that? *The Wall Street Journal*. Retrieved from http://www.wsj.com/articles/SB10001424052970204661604577186843056 231170 (p. 381)

Herz, R. S., Beland, S. L., & Hellerstein, M. (2004). Changing odor hedonic perception through emotional associations in humans. *International Journal of Comparative Psychology, 17*, 315–339. (p. 238)

Hess, E. H. (1956, July). Space perception in the chick. *Scientific American*, pp. 71–80. (p. 224)

Hess, U., & Thibault, P. (2009). Darwin and emotion expression. *American Psychologist, 64*, 120–128. (p. 400)

Hetherington, M. M., Anderson, A. S., Norton, G. N. M., & Newson, L. (2006). Situational effects on meal intake: A comparison of eating alone and eating with others. *Physiology and Behavior, 88*, 498–505. (p. 381)

Hettema, J. M., Neale, M. C., & Kendler, K. S. (2001). A review and meta-analysis of the genetic epidemiology of anxiety disorders. *American Journal of Psychiatry, 158*, 1568–1578. (p. 542)

Hickok, G. (2014). *The myth of mirror neurons: The real neuroscience of communication and cognition*. New York: Norton. (p. 273)

Hickok, G., Bellugi, U., & Klima, E. S. (2001, June). Sign language in the brain. *Scientific American*, pp. 58–65. (p. 64)

Highhouse, S. (2008). Stubborn reliance on intuition and subjectivity in employee selection. *Industrial and Organizational Psychology: Perspectives on Science and Practice, 1*, 333–342. (p. B-5)

Hilgard, E. R. (1986). *Divided consciousness: Multiple controls in human thought and action*. New York: Wiley. (p. 235)

Hilgard, E. R. (1992). Dissociation and theories of hypnosis. In E. Fromm & M. R. Nash (Eds.), *Contemporary hypnosis research* (pp. 69–101). New York: Guilford Press. (p. 235)

Hill, C. E., & Nakayama, E. Y. (2000). Client-centered therapy: Where has it been and where is it going? A comment on Hathaway. *Journal of Clinical Psychology, 56*, 861–875. (p. 573)

Hills, P. J., Werno, M. A., & Lewis, M. B. (2011). Sad people are more accurate at face recognition than happy people. *Consciousness and Cognition, 20*, 1502–1517. (p. 545)

Hines, M. (2004). *Brain gender*. New York: Oxford University Press. (p. 175)

Hingson, R. W., Heeren, T., & Winter, M. R. (2006). Age at drinking onset and alcohol dependence. *Archives of Pediatrics & Adolescent Medicine, 160*, 739–746. (p. 115)

Hinshaw, S. P., & Scheffler, R. M. (2014). *The ADHD explosion: Myths, medication, money, and today's push for performance*. New York: Oxford University Press. (p. 532)

Hintzman, D. L. (1978). *The psychology of learning and memory*. San Francisco: Freeman. (p. 288)

Hinshaw, S. P., & Scheffler, R. M. (2014). *The ADHD explosion: Myths, medication, money, and today's push for performance*. New York: Oxford University Press. (p. 532)

Hinz, L. D., & Williamson, D. A. (1987). Bulimia and depression: A review of the affective variant hypothesis. *Psychological Bulletin, 102*, 150–158. (p. 565)

Hirsh, J. B., Galinsky, A. D., & Zhong, C.-B. (2011). Drunk, powerful, and in the dark: How general processes of disinhibition produce both prosocial and antisocial behavior. *Perspectives on Psychological Science, 6*, 415–427. (p. 106)

Hirst, W., Phelps, E. A., Buckner, R. L., Budson, A. E., Cuc, A., Gabrieli, J. D. E., . . . Vaidya, C. J. (2009). Long-term memory for the terrorist attack of September 11: Flashbulb memories, event memories, and the factors that influence their retention. *Journal of Experimental Psychology: General, 138*, 161–176. (p. 295)

Hjelmborg, J. v.B., Fagnani, C., Silventoinen, K., McGue, M., Korkeila, M., Christensen, K., . . . Kaprio, J. (2008). Genetic influences on growth traits of BMI: A longitudinal study of adult twins. *Obesity, 16*, 847–852. (p. 383)

HMHL. (2002, January). Disaster and trauma. *Harvard Mental Health Letter*, pp. 1–5. (p. 407)

HMHL. (2007, February). Electroconvulsive therapy. *Harvard Mental Health Letter*, pp. 1–4. (p. 598)

Hobson, J. A. (1995, September). Quoted in G. H. Colt, The power of dreams. *Life*, pp. 36–49. (p. 100)

Hobson, J. A. (2003). *Dreaming: An introduction to the science of sleep*. New York: Oxford University Press. (p. 100)

Hobson, J. A. (2004). *13 dreams Freud never had: The new mind science*. New York: Pi Press. (p. 100)

Hobson, J. A. (2009). REM sleep and dreaming: Towards a theory of protoconsciousness. *Nature Reviews Neuroscience, 10*, 803–814. (p. 100)

Hochberg, L. R., Bacher, D., Jarosiewicz, B., Masse, N. Y., Simeral, J. D., Vogel, J., . . . Donoghue, J. P. (2012). Reach and grasp by people with tetraplegia using a neutrally controlled robotic arm. *Nature, 485*, 375–375. (p. 58)

Hochberg, L. R., Serruya, M. D., Friehs, G. M., Mukand, J. A., Saleh, M., Caplan, A. H., . . . Donoghue, J. P. (2006). Neuronal ensemble control of prosthetic devices by a human with tetraplegia. *Nature, 442*, 164–171. (p. 58)

Hochmair, I. (2013, September). *Cochlear implants: The size of the task concerning children born deaf*. Retrieved from http://www.medel.com/cochlear-implants-facts (p. 229)

Hodgins, S., Larm, P., Ellenbogen, M., Vitaro, F., & Tremblay, R. E. (2013). Teachers' ratings of childhood behaviours predict adolescent and adult crime among 3016 males and females. *Canadian Journal of Psychiatry/Revue Canadienne de Psychiatrie, 58*, 143–150. (p. 121)

Hodgkinson, V. A., & Weitzman, M. S. (1992). *Giving and volunteering in the United States*. Washington, DC: Independent Sector. (p. 484)

Hoebel, B. G., & Teitelbaum, P. (1966). Effects of forcefeeding and starvation on food intake and body weight in a rat with ventromedial hypothalamic lesions. *Journal of Comparative and Physiological Psychology, 61*, 189–193. (p. 379)

Hoeft, F., Watson, C. L., Kesler, S. R., Bettinger, K. E., & Reiss, A. L. (2008). Gender differences in the mesocorticolimbic system during computer game-play. *Journal of Psychiatric Research, 42*, 253–258. (p. 105)

Hoffman, B. M., Babyak, M. A., Craighead, W. E., Sherwood, A., Doraiswamy, P. M., Coons, M. J., & Blumenthal, J. A. (2011). Exercise and pharmacotherapy in patients with major depression: One-year follow-up of the SMILE Study. *Psychosomatic Medicine, 73*, 127–133. (p. 427)

Hoffman, D. D. (1998). *Visual intelligence: How we create what we see*. New York: Norton. (p. 216)

Hoffman, H. (2012). Considering the role of conditioning in sexual orientation. *Archives of Sexual Behavior, 41*, 63–71. (p. 250)

Hoffman, H. G. (2004, August). Virtual-reality therapy. *Scientific American*, pp. 58–65. (p. 234)

Hofmann, S. G., Sawyer, A. T., Witt, A. A., & Oh, D. (2010). The effect of mindfulness-based therapy on anxiety and depression: A meta-analytic review. *Journal of Consulting and Clinical Psychology, 78*, 169–183. (p. 428)

Hofmann, W., Vohs, K. D. & Baumeister, R. F. (2012). What people desire, feel conflicted about, and try to resist in everyday life. *Psychological Science, 23*, 582–588. (p. 422)

Hogan, C. L., Catalino, L. I., Mata, J., & Fredrickson, B. L. (2015). Beyond emotional benefits: Physical activity and sedentary behavior affect psychosocial resources through emotions. *Psychology & Health, 30*, 354–369. (p. 426)

Hogan, R. (1998). Reinventing personality. *Journal of Social and Clinical Psychology, 17*, 1–10. (p. 511)

Hoge, C. W., & Castro, C. A. (2006). Post-traumatic stress disorder in UK and US forces deployed to Iraq. *The Lancet, 368*, 837. (p. 540)

Hoge, C. W., Castro, C. A., Messer, S. C., McGurk, D., Cotting, D. I., & Koffman, R. L. (2004). Combat duty in Iraq and Afghanistan, mental health problems, and barriers to care. *New England Journal of Medicine, 351*, 13–22. (p. 540)

Hoge, C. W., Terhakopian, A., Castro, C. A., Messer, S. C., & Engel, C. C. (2007). Association of posttraumatic stress disorder with somatic symptoms, health care visits, and absenteeism among Iraq War veterans. *American Journal of Psychiatry, 164*, 150–153. (p. 540)

Hogg, M. A. (1996). Intragroup processes, group structure and social identity. In W. P. Robinson (Ed.), *Social groups and identities: Developing the legacy of Henri Tajfel* (pp. 65–93). Oxford, England: Butterworth-Heinemann. (p. 465)

Hogg, M. A. (2006). Social identity theory. In P. J. Burke (Ed.), *Contemporary social psychological theories* (pp. 111–136). Stanford, CA: Stanford University Press. (p. 465)

Hohmann, G. W. (1966). Some effects of spinal cord lesions on experienced emotional feelings. *Psychophysiology, 3*, 143–156. (p. 388)

Hokanson, J. E., & Edelman, R. (1966). Effects of three social responses on vascular processes. *Journal of Personality and Social Psychology, 3*, 442–447. (p. 416)

Holahan, C. K., & Sears, R. R. (1995). *The gifted group in later maturity*. Stanford, CA: Stanford University Press. (p. 352)

Holland, D., Chang, L., Ernst, T. M., Curran, M., Buchthal, S. D., Alicata, D., . . . Dale, A. M. (2014). Structural growth trajectories and rates of change in the first 3 months of infant brain development. *JAMA Neurology, 71*, 1266–1274. (p. 127)

Holland, J. L. (1996). Exploring careers with a typology: What we have learned and some new directions. *American Psychologist, 51*, 397–406. (p. B-4)

Holle, H., Warne, K., Seth, A. K., Critchley, H. D., & Ward, J. (2012). Neural basis of contagious itch and why some people are more prone to it. *Proceedings of the National Academy of Sciences of the United States of America, 109*, 19816–19821. (p. 449)

Holliday, R. E., & Albon, A. J. (2004). Minimizing misinformation effects in young children with cognitive interview mnemonics. *Applied Cognitive Psychology, 18*, 263–281. (p. 310)

Hollis, K. L. (1997). Contemporary research on Pavlovian conditioning: A "new" functional analysis. *American Psychologist, 52*, 956–965. (p. 250)

Hollon, S. D., DeRubeis, R. J., Fawcett, J., Amsterdam, J. D., Shelton, R. C., Zajecka, J., . . . Gallop, R. (2014). Effect of cognitive therapy with antidepressant medications vs. antidepressants alone on the rate of recovery in major depressive disorder. *JAMA Psychiatry, 71*, 1157–1164. (p. 596)

Hollon, S. D., Thase, M. E., & Markowitz, J. C. (2002). Treatment and prevention of depression. *Psychological Science in the Public Interest, 3*, 39–77. (p. 596)

Holman, E. A., Garfin, D. R., & Silver, R. C. (2014). Media's role in broadcasting acute stress following the Boston marathon bombings. *Proceedings of the National Academy of Sciences of the United States of America, 111*, 93–98. (p. 540)

Holstege, G., Georgiadis, J. R., Paans, A. M. J., Meiners, L. C., van der Graaf, F. H. C. E., & Reinders, A. A. T. S. (2003a). Brain activation during male ejaculation. *Journal of Neuroscience, 23*, 9185–9193. (p. 183)

Holstege, G., Reinders, A. A. T., Paans, A. M. J., Meiners, L. C., Pruim, J., & Georgiadis, J. R. (2003b). *Brain activation during female sexual orgasm* (Annual Conference Abstract Viewer/Itinerary Planner Program No. 727.7). Washington, DC: Society for Neuroscience. (p. 183)

Holtgraves, T. (2011). Text messaging, personality, and the social context. *Journal of Research in Personality, 45*, 92–99. (p. 510)

Holt-Lunstad, J., Smith, T. B., Baker, M., Harris, T., & Stephenson, D. (2015). Loneliness and social isolation as risk factors for mortality: A meta-analytic review. *Perspectives on Psychological Science, 10*, 227–237. (p. 424)

Holt-Lunstad, J., Smith, T. B., & Layton, J. B. (2010). Social relationships and mortality risk: A meta-analytic review. *PLOS Medicine, 7*(7), e1000316. doi:10.1371/journal.pmed.1000316 (pp. 371, 424)

Homer, B. D., Solomon, T. M., Moeller, R. W., Mascia, A., DeRaleau, L., & Halkitis, P. N. (2008). Methamphetamine abuse and impairment of social functioning: A review of the underlying neurophysiological causes and behavioral implications. *Psychological Bulletin, 134*, 301–310. (p. 111)

Hoogland, C. E., Schurtz, D. R., Cooper, C. M., Combs, D. J., Brown, E. G., & Smith, R. H. (2014). The joy of pain and the pain of joy: In-group identification predicts schadenfreude and gluckschmerz following rival groups' fortunes. *Motivation and Emotion, 39*, 260–281. (p. 466)

Hooper, J., & Teresi, D. (1986). *The three-pound universe.* New York: Macmillan. (p. 54)

Hooper, R. (2013, October 17). *Where hyenas are used to treat mental illness.* Retrieved from http://www.bbc.com/news/magazine-24539989 (p. 529)

Hopkins, E. D., & Cantalupo, C. (2008). Theoretical speculations on the evolutionary origins of hemispheric specialization. *Current Directions in Psychological Science, 17*, 233–237. (p. 64)

Hopper, L. M., Lambeth, S. P., Schapiro, S. J., & Whiten, A. (2008). Observational learning in chimpanzees and children studied through "ghost" conditions. *Proceedings of the Royal Society: Series B, 275*, 835–840. (p. 273)

Hor, H., & Tafti, M. (2009). How much sleep do we need? *Science, 325*, 825–826. (p. 92)

Horn, J. L. (1982). The aging of human abilities. In B. B. Wolman (Ed.), *Handbook of developmental psychology* (pp. 847–870). Englewood Cliffs, NJ: Prentice-Hall. (p. 349)

Horne, J. (2011). The end of sleep: 'Sleep debt' versus biological adaptation of human sleep to waking needs. *Biological Psychology, 87*, 1–14. (p. 92)

Horowitz, S. S. (2012, November 9). The science and art of listening. *The New York Times.* Retrieved from http://www.nytimes.com/2012/11/11/opinion/sunday/why-listening-is-so-much-more-than-hearing.html?_r=0 (p. 226)

Horwood, L. J., & Fergusson, D. M. (1998). Breastfeeding and later cognitive and academic outcomes. *Pediatrics, 101*(1), e9. Retrieved from http://pediatrics.aappublications.org/content/101/1/e9.full (p. 22)

Hostetter, A. B. (2011). When do gestures communicate? A meta-analysis. *Psychological Bulletin, 137*, 297–315. (p. 335)

Hostinar, C. E., Sullivan, R., & Gunnar, M. R. (2014). Psychobiological mechanisms underlying the social buffering of the hypothalamic–pituitary–adrenocortical axis: A review of animal models and human studies across development. *Psychological Bulletin, 140*, 256–282. (p. 424)

Hou, W.-H., Chiang, P.-T., Hsu, T.-Y., Chiu, S.-Y., & Yen, Y.-C. (2010). Treatment effects of massage therapy in depressed people: A meta-analysis. *Journal of Clinical Psychiatry, 71*, 894–901. (pp. 429, 599)

House, R. J., & Singh, J. V. (1987). Organizational behavior: Some new directions for I/O psychology. *Annual Review of Psychology, 38*, 669–718. (p. B-12)

Houser-Marko, L., & Sheldon, K. M. (2008). Eyes on the prize or nose to the grindstone? The effects of level of goal evaluation on mood and motivation. *Personality and Social Psychology Bulletin, 34*, 1556–1569. (p. B-11)

Houts, A. C., Berman, J. S., & Abramson, H. (1994). Effectiveness of psychological and pharmacological treatments for nocturnal enuresis. *Journal of Consulting and Clinical Psychology, 62*, 737–745. (p. 574)

Houts, R. M., Caspi, A., Pianta, R. C., Arseneault, L., & Moffitt, T. E. (2010). The challenging pupil in the classroom: The effect of the child on the teacher. *Psychological Science, 21*, 1802–1810. (p. 121)

Hovatta, I., Tennant, R. S., Helton, R., Marr, R. A., Singer, O., Redwine, J. M., . . . Barlow, C. (2005). Glyoxalase 1 and glutathione reductase 1 regulate anxiety in mice. *Nature, 438*, 662–666. (p. 542)

Howe, M. L. (1997). Children's memory for traumatic experiences. *Learning and Individual Differences, 9*, 153–174. (p. 310)

Hoyer, G., & Lund, E. (1993). Suicide among women related to number of children in marriage. *Archives of General Psychiatry, 50*, 134–137. (p. 553)

Hsee, C. K., Yang, A. X., & Wang, L. (2010). Idleness aversion and the need for justifiable busyness. *Psychological Science, 21*, 926–930. (p. B-1)

Hsiang, S. M., Burke, M., & Miguel, E. (2013). Quantifying the influence of climate on human conflict. *Science, 341*, 1212. (p. 470)

Huang, C. (2010). Mean-level change in self-esteem from childhood through adulthood meta-analysis of longitudinal studies. *Review of General Psychology, 14*, 251–260. (p. 166)

Huang, J., Chaloupka, F. J., & Fong, G. T. (2013). Cigarette graphic warning labels and smoking prevalence in Canada: A critical examination and reformulation of the FDA regulatory impact analysis. *Tobacco Control.* Advance online publication. doi:10.1136/tobaccocontrol-2013-051170 (p. 320)

Huang, X., Iun, J., Liu, A., & Gong, Y. (2010). Does participative leadership enhance work performance by inducing empowerment or trust? The differential effects on managerial and non-managerial subordinates. *Journal of Organizational Behavior, 31*, 122–143. (p. 406)

Huart, J., Corneille, O., & Becquart, E. (2005). Face-based categorization, context-based categorization, and distortions in the recollection of gender ambiguous faces. *Journal of Experimental Social Psychology, 41*, 598–608. (p. 316)

Hubbard, E. M., Arman, A. C., Ramachandran, V. S., & Boynton, G. M. (2005). Individual differences among grapheme-color synesthetes: Brain-behavior correlations. *Neuron, 45*, 975–985. (p. 240)

Hubel, D. H. (1979, September). The brain. *Scientific American*, pp. 45–53. (p. 204)

Hubel, D. H., & Wiesel, T. N. (1979, September). Brian mechanisms of vision. *Scientific American*, pp. 150–162. (p. 214)

Huber, E., Webster, J. M., Brewer, A. A., MacLeod, D. I. A., Wandell, B. A., Boynton, G. M., . . . Fine, I. (2015). A lack of experience-dependent plasticity after more than a decade of recovered sight. *Psychological Science, 26*, 393–401. (p. 223)

Hublin, C., Kaprio, J., Partinen, M., Heikkila, K., & Koskenvuo, M. (1997). Prevalence and genetics of sleep-walking—A population-based twin study. *Neurology, 48*, 177–181. (p. 98)

Hublin, C., Kaprio, J., Partinen, M., & Koskenvuo, M. (1998). Sleeptalking in twins: Epidemiology and psychiatric comorbidity. *Behavior Genetics, 28*, 289–298. (p. 98)

Hucker, S. J., & Bain, J. (1990). Androgenic hormones and sexual assault. In W. L. Marshall, D. R. Laws, & H. E. Barbaree (Eds.), *Handbook of sexual assault: Issues, theories, and treatment of the offender* (pp. 209–229). New York: Plenum Press. (p. 182)

Hudson, J. I., Hiripi, E., Pope, H. G., & Kessler, R. C. (2007). The prevalence and correlates of eating disorders in the National Comorbidity Survey Replication. *Biological Psychiatry, 61*, 348–358. (p. 565)

Hudson, N. W., & Roberts, B. W. (2014). Goals to change personality traits: Concurrent links between personality traits, daily behavior, and goals to change oneself. *Journal of Research in Personality, 53*, 68–83. (p. 507)

Huey, E. D., Krueger, F., & Grafman, J. (2006). Representations in the human prefrontal cortex. *Current Directions in Psychological Science, 15*, 167–171. (p. 59)

Hugenberg, K., & Bodenhausen, G. V. (2003). Facing prejudice: Implicit prejudice and the perception of facial threat. *Psychological Science, 14*, 640–643. (p. 463)

Hugenberg, K., Young, S. G., Bernstein, M. J., & Sacco, D. F. (2010). The categorization–individuation model: An integrative account of the other-race recognition deficit. *Psychological Review, 117*, 1168–1187. (p. 467)

Hughes, J. R. (2010). Craving among long-abstinent smokers: An Internet survey. *Nicotine & Tobacco Research, 12*, 459–462. (p. 109)

Hughes, M. L., Geraci, L., & De Forrest, R. L. (2013). Aging 5 years in 5 minutes: The effect of taking a memory test on older adults' subjective age. *Psychological Science, 24*, 2481–2488. (p. 160)

Hulbert, A. (2005, November 20). The prodigy puzzle. *The New York Times Magazine.* Retrieved from http://www.nytimes.com/2005/11/20/magazine/the-prodigy-puzzle.html (p. 352)

Hull, H. R., Morrow, M. L., Dinger, M. K., Han, J. L., & Fields, D. A. (2007, November 20). Characterization of body weight and composition changes during the sophomore year of college. *BMC Women's Health, 7*, Article 21. Retrieved from http://www.biomedcentral.com/1472-6874/7/21 (p. 95)

Hull, J. G., & Bond, C. F., Jr. (1986). Social and behavioral consequences of alcohol consumption and expectancy: A meta-analysis. *Psychological Bulletin, 99*, 347–360. (p. 107)

Hull, J. M. (1990). *Touching the rock: An experience of blindness.* New York: Vintage Books. (p. 297)

Hull, S. J., Hennessy, M., Bleakley, A., Fishbein, M., & Jordan, A. (2011). Identifying the causal pathways from religiosity to delayed adolescent sexual behavior. *Journal of Sex Research, 48*, 543–553. (p. 187)

Hülsheger, U. R., Anderson, N., & Salgado, J. F. (2009). Team-level predictors of innovation at work: A comprehensive meta-analysis spanning three decades of research. *Journal of Applied Psychology, 94*, 1128–1145. (p. 325)

Human Connectome Project. (2013). *The Human Connectome Project.* Retrieved from http://www.humanconnectome.org/ (p. 50)

Hummer, R. A., Rogers, R. G., Nam, C. B., & Ellison, C. G. (1999). Religious involvement and U.S. adult mortality. *Demography, 36*, 273–285. (p. 430)

Humphrey, S. E., Nahrgang, J. D., & Morgeson, F. P. (2007). Integrating motivational, social, and contextual work design features: A meta-analytic summary and theoretical extension of the work design literature. *Journal of Applied Psychology, 92*, 1332–1356. (p. 420)

Humphreys, L. G., & Davey, T. C. (1988). Continuity in intellectual growth from 12 months to 9 years. *Intelligence, 12*, 183–197. (p. 350)

Hunsberger, J. G., Newton, S. S., Bennett, A. H., Duman, C. H., Russell, D. S., Salton, S. R., & Duman, R. S. (2007). Antidepressant actions of the exercise-regulated gene VGF. *Nature Medicine, 13*, 1476–1482. (p. 427)

Hunsley, J., & Di Giulio, G. (2002). Dodo bird, phoenix, or urban legend? The question of psychotherapy equivalence. *Scientific Review of Mental Health Practice, 1*, 11–22. (p. 586)

Hunt, C., Slade, T., & Andrews, G. (2004). Generalized anxiety disorder and major depressive disorder comorbidity in the National Survey of Mental Health and Well-Being. *Depression and Anxiety, 20*, 23–31. (p. 537)

Hunt, E., & Carlson, J. (2007). Considerations relating to the study of group differences in intelligence. *Perspectives on Psychological Science, 2*, 194–213. (p. 360)

Hunt, J. M. (1982). Toward equalizing the developmental opportunities of infants and preschool children. *Journal of Social Issues, 38*, 163–191. (p. 356)

Hunt, M. (1990). *The compassionate beast: What science is discovering about the humane side of humankind.* New York: Morrow. (p. 29)

Hunt, M. (1993). *The story of psychology.* New York: Doubleday. (pp. 5, 7, 254, 352)

Hunt, M. (2007). *The story of psychology* (Updated, rev. ed.). New York: Anchor. (p. 495)

Hunter, S., & Sundel, M. (Eds.). (1989). *Midlife myths: Issues, findings, and practice implications.* Newbury Park, CA: Sage. (p. 162)

Hurd, Y. L., Michaelides, M., Miller, M. L., & Jutras-Aswad, D. (2013). Trajectory of adolescent cannabis use on addiction vulnerability. *Neuropharmacology, 76*, 416–424. (p. 112)

Hurlburt, R. T., Heavey, C. L., & Kelsey, J. M. (2013). Toward a phenomenology of inner speaking. *Consciousness and Cognition, 22*, 1477–1494. (p. 336)

Hutchinson, R. (2006). *Calum's road.* Edinburgh, Scotland: Burlinn Limited. (p. 376)

Hvistendahl, M. (2011). China's population growing slowly, changing fast. *Science, 332*, 650–651. (p. 464)

Hyde, J. S. (2005). The gender similarities hypothesis. *American Psychologist, 60*, 581–592. (pp. 172, 193)

Hyde, J. S., & Mertz, J. E. (2009). Gender, culture, and mathematics performance. *Proceedings of the National Academy of Sciences of the United States of America, 106*, 8801–8807. (p. 357)

Hyde, J. S., Mezulis, A. H., & Abramson, L. Y. (2008). The ABCs of depression: Integrating affective, biological, and cognitive models to explain the emergence of the gender difference in depression. *Psychological Review, 115*, 291–313. (p. 548)

Hymowitz, K., Carroll, J. S., Wilcox, W. B., & Kaye, K. (2013). *Knot yet: The benefits and costs of delayed marriage in America.* Charlottesville: National Marriage Project, University of Virginia. (p. 141)

I

Iacoboni, M. (2008). *Mirroring people: The new science of how we connect with others.* New York: Farrar, Straus and Giroux. (pp. 273, 274)

Iacoboni, M. (2009). Imitation, empathy, and mirror neurons. *Annual Review of Psychology, 60*, 653–670. (pp. 273, 274)

Ibbotson, P. (2012). A new kind of language. *The Psychologist, 25*, 122–125. (p. 330)

Ibos, G., & Freedman, D. J. (2014). Dynamic integration of task-relevant visual features in posterior parietal cortex. *Neuron, 83*, 1468–1480. (p. 60)

Ickes, W., Snyder, M., & Garcia, S. (1997). Personality influences on the choice of situations. In R. Hogan, J. Johnson, & S. Briggs (Eds.), *Handbook of personality psychology* (pp. 165–195). San Diego, CA: Academic Press. (p. 513)

Idson, L. C., & Mischel, W. (2001). The personality of familiar and significant people: The lay perceiver as a social–cognitive theorist. *Journal of Personality and Social Psychology, 80*, 585–596. (p. 443)

IJzerman, H., & Semin, G. R. (2009). The thermometer of social relations: Mapping social proximity on temperature. *Psychological Science, 20*, 1214–1220. (p. 240)

Ilardi, S. S. (2009). *The depression cure: The six-step program to beat depression without drugs.* Cambridge, MA: De Capo Lifelong Books. (pp. 550, 600)

Ilardi, S. (2014). *Therapeutic lifestyle change.* Retrieved from http://web.archive.org/web/20140719163123/http://psych.ku.edu/tlc/ (p. 600)

Inagaki, T., & Eisenberg, N. (2014). Shared neural mechanisms underlying social warmth and physical warmth. *Psychological Science, 24*, 2272–2280. (p. 370)

Inbar, Y., Cone, J., & Gilovich, T. (2010). People's intuitions about intuitive insight and intuitive choice. *Journal of Personality and Social Psychology, 99*, 232–247. (p. 324)

Inbar, Y., Pizarro, D., & Bloom, P. (2011). *Disgusting smells cause decreased liking of gay men.* Unpublished manuscript, Tilburg University, Tilburg, the Netherlands. (p. 238)

Independent Sector. (2002). *Faith and philanthropy: The connection between charitable giving behavior and giving to religion.* Washington, DC: Author. (p. 484)

Ingham, A. G., Levinger, G., Graves, J., & Peckham, V. (1974). The Ringelmann effect: Studies of group size and group performance. *Journal of Experimental Social Psychology, 10*, 371–384. (p. 456)

Inglehart, R. (1990). *Culture shift in advanced industrial society.* Princeton, NJ: Princeton University Press. (p. 371)

Inman, M. L., & Baron, R. S. (1996). Influence of prototypes on perceptions of prejudice. *Journal of Personality and Social Psychology, 70*, 727–739. (p. 316)

Insel, T. R. (2010, April). Faulty circuits. *Scientific American*, pp. 44–51. (p. 543)

Intergovernmental Panel on Climate Change. (2014). *Climate change 2014: Mitigation of climate change.* Retrieved from http://mitigation2014.org/ (p. 444)

International Schizophrenia Consortium. (2009). Common polygenic variation contributes to risk of schizophrenia and bipolar disorder. *Nature, 460*, 748–752. (p. 560)

Inzlicht, M., & Ben-Zeev, T. (2000). A threatening intellectual environment: Why females are susceptible to experiencing problem-solving deficits in the presence of males. *Psychological Science, 11*, 365–371. (p. 361)

Inzlicht, M., & Kang, S. K. (2010). Stereotype threat spillover: How coping with threats to social identity affects aggression, eating, decision making, and attention. *Journal of Personality and Social Psychology, 99*, 467–481. (p. 361)

IPPA. (2009, January 22). [Membership letter]. International Positive Psychology Association. (p. 432)

IPPA. (2010, August). International conference on positive psychology and education in China [by S. Choong]. *IPPA Newsletter.* International Positive Psychology Association. (p. 432)

Ipsos. (2010, April 8). *One in five (20%) global citizens believe that alien beings have come down to earth and walk amongst us in our communities disguised as humans.* Retrieved from http://www.ipsos-na.com/news-polls/pressrelease.aspx?id=4742 (p. 21)

Ipsos. (2010, June 29). *Online Canadians report a large 35% decline in the amount of email received.* Retrieved from http://www.ipsos-na.com/news-polls/pressrelease.aspx?id=4844 (p. 373)

Ikonomidou, C., Bittigau, P., Ishimaru, M. J., Wozniak, D. F., Koch, C., Genz, K., . . . Olney, J. W. (2000). Ethanol-induced apoptotic neurodegeneration and fetal alcohol syndrome. *Science, 287,* 1056–1060. (p. 124)

Ingalhalikar, M., Smith, A., Parker, D., Satterthwaite, T. D., Elliott, M. A., Ruparel, K., . . . Verma, R. (2013). Sex differences in the structural connectome of the human brain. *Proceedings of the National Academy of Sciences of the United States of America, 111,* 823–828. (p. 174)

International Society for Research on Aggression (ISRA). (2012). Report of the Media Violence Commission. *Aggressive Behavior, 38,* 335–341. (p. 277)

IPU. (2015, January 1). *Women in national parliaments: Situation as of 1st January 2015.* International Parliamentary Union. Retrieved from http://www.ipu.org/wmn-e/arc/world010115.htm (p. 173)

Ireland, M. E., & Pennebaker, J. W. (2010). Language style matching in writing: Synchrony in essays, correspondence, and poetry. *Journal of Personality and Social Psychology, 99,* 549–571. (p. 274)

Ironson, G., Solomon, G. F., Balbin, E. G., O'Cleirigh, C., George, A., Kumar, M., . . . Woods, T. E. (2002). The Ironson–Woods Spiritual/Religiousness Index is associated with long survival, health behaviors, less distress, and low cortisol in people with HIV/AIDS. *Annals of Behavioral Medicine, 24,* 34–48. (p. 431)

Irwin, M. R., Cole, J. C., & Nicassio, P. M. (2006). Comparative meta-analysis of behavioral interventions for insomnia and their efficacy in middle-aged adults and in older adults 55+ years of age. *Health Psychology, 25,* 3–14. (p. 96)

Isaacowitz, D. M. (2012). Mood regulation in real time: Age differences in the role of looking. *Current Directions in Psychological Science, 21,* 237–242. (p. 166)

Ishida, A., Mutoh, T., Ueyama, T., Brando, H., Masubuchi, S., Nakahara, D., . . . Okamura, H. (2005). Light activates the adrenal gland: Timing of gene expression and glucocorticoid release. *Cell Metabolism, 2,* 297–307. (p. 589)

Islam, S. S., & Johnson, C. (2003). Correlates of smoking behavior among Muslim Arab-American adolescents. *Ethnicity & Health, 8,* 319–337. (p. 430)

Iso, H., Simoda, S., & Matsuyama, T. (2007). Environmental change during postnatal development alters behaviour. *Behavioural Brain Research, 179,* 90–98. (p. 61)

Ito, T. A., Miller, N., & Pollock, V. E. (1996). Alcohol and aggression: A meta-analysis on the moderating effects of inhibitory cues, triggering events, and self-focused attention. *Psychological Bulletin, 120,* 60–82. (p. 470)

ITU. (2015). *Aggregate statistics.* International Telecommunications Union. Retrieved from http://www.itu.int/en/ITU-D/Statistics/Pages/stat/default.aspx (p. 373)

Ives-Deliperi, V. L., Solms, M., & Meintjes, E. M. (2011). The neural substrates of mindfulness: An fMRI investigation. *Social Neuroscience, 6,* 231–242. (p. 428)

Iyengar, S., & Westwood, S. J. (2014). Fear and loathing across party lines: New evidence on group polarization. *American Journal of Political Science, 59,* 690–707. (p. 458)

Izard, C. E. (1977). *Human emotions.* New York: Plenum Press. (pp. 391, 399)

Izard, C. E. (1994). Innate and universal facial expressions: Evidence from developmental and cross-cultural research. *Psychological Bulletin, 114,* 288–299. (p. 399)

J

Jääskeläinen, E., Juola, P., Hirvonen, N., McGrath, J. J., Saha, S., Isohanni, M. , . . . Miettunen, J. (2013). A systematic review and meta-analysis of recovery in schizophrenia. *Schizophrenia Bulletin, 39,* 1296–1306. (p. 556)

Jablensky, A. (1999). Schizophrenia: Epidemiology. *Current Opinion in Psychiatry, 12,* 19–28. (p. 558)

Jack, R. E., Garrod, O. G. B., Yu, H., Caldara, R., & Schyns, P. G. (2012). Facial expressions of emotion are not culturally universal. *Proceedings of the National Academy of Sciences of the United States of America, 109,* 7241–7244. (p. 399)

Jäckle, S., & Wenzelburger, G. (2015). Religion, religiosity, and the attitudes toward homosexuality—A multilevel analysis of 79 countries. *Journal of Homosexuality, 62,* 207–241. (p. 464)

Jackson, G. (2009). Sexual response in cardiovascular disease. *Journal of Sex Research, 46,* 233–236. (p. 183)

Jackson, J. J., Connolly, J. J., Garrison, S. M., Leveille, M. M., & Connolly, S. L. (2015). Your friends know how long you will live: A 75-year study of peer-rated personality traits. *Psychological Science, 26,* 335–340. (p. 512)

Jackson, J. J., Thoemmes, F., Jonkmann, K., Lüdtke, O., & Trautwein, U. (2012). Military training and personality trait development: Does the military make the man, or does the man make the military? *Psychological Science, 23,* 270–277. (pp. 446, 511)

Jackson, J. M., & Williams, K. D. (1988). *Social loafing: A review and theoretical analysis.* Unpublished manuscript, Fordham University, New York, NY. (p. 456)

Jackson, S. W. (1992). The listening healer in the history of psychological healing. *American Journal Psychiatry, 149,* 1623–1632. (p. 590)

Jacobs, B. L. (1994). Serotonin, motor activity, and depression-related disorders. *American Scientist, 82,* 456–463. (pp. 427, 550)

Jacoby, L. L., Bishara, A. J., Hessels, S., & Toth, J. P. (2005). Aging, subjective experience, and cognitive control: Dramatic false remembering by older adults. *Journal of Experimental Psychology: General, 154,* 131–148. (p. 310)

Jacoby, L. L., & Rhodes, M. G. (2006). False remembering in the aged. *Current Directions in Psychological Science, 15,* 49–53. (p. 310)

Jacques, C., & Rossion, B. (2006). The speed of individual face categorization. *Psychological Science, 17,* 485–492. (p. 199)

Jacques-Tiura, A. J., Abbey, A., Parkhill, M. R., & Zawacki, T. (2007). Why do some men misperceive women's sexual intentions more frequently than others do? An application of the confluence model. *Personality and Social Psychology Bulletin, 33,* 1467–1480. (p. 443)

James, K. (1986). Priming and social categorizational factors: Impact on awareness of emergency situations. *Personality and Social Psychology Bulletin, 12,* 462–467. (p. 298)

James, W. (1890). *The principles of psychology* (Vol. 2). New York: Holt. (pp. 231, 301, 312, 372, 387, 401)

Jameson, D. (1985). Opponent-colors theory in light of physiological findings. In D. Ottoson & S. Zeki (Eds.), *Central and peripheral mechanisms of color vision* (pp. 83–102). New York: Macmillan. (p. 221)

Jamieson, J. P. (2010). The home field advantage in athletics: A meta-analysis. *Journal of Applied Social Psychology, 40,* 1819–1848. (p. 456)

Jamison, K. R. (1993). *Touched with fire: Manic-depressive illness and the artistic temperament.* New York: Free Press. (p. 547)

Jamison, K. R. (1995). *An unquiet mind.* New York: Knopf. (pp. 547, 569, 596)

Janis, I. L. (1982). *Groupthink: Psychological studies of policy decisions and fiascoes.* Boston: Houghton Mifflin. (p. 459)

Janis, I. L. (1986). Problems of international crisis management in the nuclear age. *Journal of Social Issues, 42,* 201–220. (p. 318)

Janoff-Bulman, R., Timko, C., & Carli, L. L. (1985). Cognitive biases in blaming the victim. *Journal of Experimental Social Psychology, 21,* 161–177. (p. 468)

Janssen, S. M. J., Rubin, D. C., & Conway, M. A. (2012). The reminiscence bump in the temporal distribution of the best football players of all time: Pelé, Cruijff or Maradona? *Quarterly Journal of Experimental Psychology, 65,* 165–178. (p. 160)

Jarbo, K., & Verstynen, T. D. (2015). Converging structural and functional connectivity of orbitofrontal, dorsolateral prefrontal, and posterior parietal cortex in the human striatum. *Journal of Neuroscience, 35,* 3865–3878. (p. 50)

Jaremka, L. M., Gabriel, S., & Carvallo, M. (2011). What makes us feel the best also makes us feel the worst: The emotional impact of independent and interdependent experiences. *Self and Identity, 10,* 44–63. (p. 371)

Jarrett, B., Bloch, G. J., Bennett, D., Bleazard, B., & Hedges, D. (2010). The influence of body mass index, age and gender on current illness: A cross-sectional study. *International Journal of Obesity, 34,* 429–436. (p. 383)

Jaschik, S. (2013, January 14). Spoiled children. *Inside Higher Education.* Retrieved from https://www.insidehighered.com/news/2013/01/14/study-finds-increased-parental-support-college-results-lower-grades (p. 22)

Javitt, D. C., & Coyle, J. T. (2004, January). Decoding schizophrenia. *Scientific American*, pp. 48–55. (p. 558)

Jayakar, R., King, T. Z., Morris, R., & Na, S. (2015). Hippocampal volume and auditory attention on a verbal memory task with adult survivors of pediatric brain tumor. *Neuropsychology, 29*, 303–319. (p. 54)

Jedrychowski, W., Perera, F., Jankowski, J., Butscher, M., Mroz, E., Flak, E., . . . Sowa, A. (2012). Effect of exclusive breastfeeding on the development of children's cognitive function in the Krakow prospective birth cohort study. *European Journal of Pediatrics, 171*, 151–158. (p. 23)

Jeffrey, K., Mahoney, S., Michaelson, J., & Abdallah, S. (2014). *Well-being at work: A review of the literature*. Retrieved from http://www.neweconomics.org/publications/entry/well-being-at-work (p. B-8)

Jenkins, J. G., & Dallenbach, K. M. (1924). Obliviscence during sleep and waking. *American Journal of Psychology, 35*, 605–612. (p. 305)

Jenkins, J. M., & Astington, J. W. (1996). Cognitive factors and family structure associated with theory of mind development in young children. *Developmental Psychology, 32*, 70–78. (p. 133)

Jensen, J. P., & Bergin, A. E. (1988). Mental health values of professional therapists: A national interdisciplinary survey. *Professional Psychology: Research and Practice, 19*, 290–297. (p. 590)

Jensen, M. P. (2008). The neurophysiology of pain perception and hypnotic analgesia: Implications for clinical practice. *American Journal of Clinical Hypnosis, 51*, 123–147. (p. 235)

Jepson, C., Krantz, D. H., & Nisbett, R. E. (1983). Inductive reasoning: Competence or skill? *Behavioral and Brain Sciences, 3*, 494–501. (p. A-9)

Jessberger, S., Aimone, J. B., & Gage, F. H. (2008). Neurogenesis. In J. H. Byrne (Ed.), *Learning and memory: A comprehensive reference: Vol. 4. Molecular mechanisms of memory* (pp. 839–858). Oxford, England: Elsevier. (p. 61)

Jha, P., Ramasundarahettige, C., Landsman, V., Rostron, B., Thun, M. D., Anderson, R. N., McAfee, T., & Peto, R. (2013). 21st-century hazards of smoking and benefits of cessation in the United States. *New England Journal of Medicine, 368*, 341–350. (p. 108)

Jiang, Y., Costello, P., Fang, F., Huang, M., & He, S. (2006). A gender- and sexual orientation-dependent spatial attentional effect of invisible things. *Proceedings of the National Academy of Sciences of the United States of America, 103*, 17048–17052. (p. 202)

Job, V., Dweck, C. S., & Walton, G. M. (2010). Ego depletion—is it all in your head? Implicit theories about willpower affect self-regulation. *Psychological Science, 21*, 1686–1693. (p. 421)

Jobe, T. H., & Harrow, M. (2010). Schizophrenia course, long-term outcome, recovery, and prognosis. *Current Directions in Psychological Science, 19*, 220–225. (p. 556)

Johnson, D. F. (1997, Winter). Margaret Floy Washburn. *Psychology of Women Newsletter*, pp. 17, 22. (p. 6)

Johnson, D. L., Wiebe, J. S., Gold, S. M., Andreasen, N. C., Hichwa, R. D., Watkins, G. L., & Ponto, L.L.B. (1999). Cerebral blood flow and personality: A positron emission tomography study. *American Journal of Psychiatry, 156*, 252–257. (p. 507)

Johnson, E. J., & Goldstein, D. (2003). Do defaults save lives? *Science, 302*, 1338–1339. (p. 323)

Johnson, J. A. (2007, June 26). *Not so situational* [Commentary on the Society for Personality and Social Psychology Listserv]. Retrieved from spsp-discuss @stolaf.edu (p. 446)

Johnson, J. G., Cohen, P., Kotler, L., Kasen, S., & Brook, J. S. (2002). Psychiatric disorders associated with risk for the development of eating disorders during adolescence and early adulthood. *Journal of Consulting and Clinical Psychology, 70*, 1119–1128. (p. 565)

Johnson, J. S., & Newport, E. L. (1991). Critical period effects on universal properties of language: The status of subjacency in the acquisition of a second language. *Cognition, 39*, 215–258. (p. 333)

Johnson, K. (2008, January 29). For many of USA's inmates, crime runs in the family. *USA Today*, pp. 1A, 2A. (p. 173)

Johnson, M. (2014). *Morality for humans: Ethical understanding from the perspective of cognitive science*. Chicago: University of Chicago Press. (p. 151)

Johnson, M. H. (1992). Imprinting and the development of face recognition: From chick to man. *Current Directions in Psychological Science, 1*, 52–55. (p. 139)

Johnson, M. H., & Morton, J. (1991). *Biology and cognitive development: The case of face recognition*. Oxford, England: Blackwell. (p. 125)

Johnson, R. E., Chang, C.-H., & Lord, R. G. (2006). Moving from cognition to behavior: What the research says. *Psychological Bulletin, 132*, 381–415. (p. B-11)

Johnson, W. (2010). Understanding the genetics of intelligence: Can height help? Can corn oil? *Current Directions in Psychological Science, 19*, 177–182. (p. 355)

Johnson, W., Carothers, A., & Deary, I. J. (2008). Sex differences in variability in general intelligence: A new look at the old question. *Perspectives on Psychological Science, 3*, 518–531. (p. 343)

Johnson, W., Gow, A. J., Corley, J., Starr, J. M., & Deary, I. J. (2010). Location in cognitive and residential space at age 70 reflects a lifelong trait over parental and environmental circumstances: The Lothian birth cohort 1936. *Intelligence, 38*, 403–411. (p. 350)

Johnson, W., Turkheimer, E., Gottesman, I. I., & Bouchard, T. J., Jr. (2009). Beyond heritability: Twin studies in behavioral research. *Current Directions in Psychological Science, 18*, 217–220. (pp. 68, 354)

Johnston, L. D., O'Malley, P. M., Bachman, J. G., & Schulenberg, J. E. (2007, May). *Monitoring the Future national results on adolescent drug use: Overview of key findings, 2006*. Bethesda, MD: National Institute on Drug Abuse. (p. 115)

Johnston, L. D., O'Malley, P. M., Miech, R. A., Bachman, J. G., & Schulenberg, J. E. (2015, February). *Monitoring the Future national results on drug use: 1975–2014: 2014 overview, key findings on adolescent drug use*. Ann Arbor: Institute for Social Research, University of Michigan. (pp. 110, 114)

Joiner, T. E., Jr. (2006). *Why people die by suicide*. Cambridge, MA: Harvard University Press. (p. 555)

Joiner, T. E., Jr. (2010). *Myths about suicide*. Cambridge, MA: Harvard University Press. (p. 553)

Jokela, M., Elovainio, M., Archana, S.-M., & Kivimäki, M. (2009). IQ, socioeconomic status, and early death: The US National Longitudinal Survey of Youth. *Psychosomatic Medicine, 71*, 322–328. (p. 420)

Jones, A. C., & Gosling, S. D. (2005). Temperament and personality in dogs (*Canis familiaris*): A review and evaluation of past research. *Applied Animal Behaviour Science, 95*, 1–53. (p. 507)

Jones, B., Reedy, E. J., & Weinberg, B. A. (2014, January). *Age and scientific genius* (NBER Working Paper No. 19866). Retrieved from http://www.nber.org/papers/w19866 (p. 349)

Jones, E. (1957). *The life and work of Sigmund Freud: Vol. 3. The last phase (1919–1939)* (Pt. 1, chap. 4). New York: Basic Books. (p. 496)

Jones, J. D., Cassidy, J., & Shaver, P. R. (2015). Parents' self-reported attachment styles: A review of links with parenting behaviors, emotions, and cognitions. *Personality and Social Psychology Review, 19*, 44–76. (p. 142)

Jones, J. M. (2012, June 21). *Atheists, Muslims see most bias as presidential candidates*. Retrieved from http://www.gallup.com/poll/155285/atheists-muslims-bias-presidential-candidates.aspx (p. 464)

Jones, J. M. (2013, December 19). *In U.S., 40% get less than recommended amount of sleep*. Retrieved from http://www.gallup.com/poll/166553/less-recommended-amount-sleep.aspx (p. 95)

Jones, J. T., Pelham, B. W., Carvallo, M., & Mirenberg, M. C. (2004). How do I love thee? Let me count the Js: Implicit egotism and interpersonal attraction. *Journal of Personality and Social Psychology, 87*, 665–683. (p. 475)

Jones, M. C. (1924). A laboratory study of fear: The case of Peter. *Journal of Genetic Psychology, 31*, 308–315. (p. 575)

Jones, R. P., Cox, D., & Navarro-Rivera, J. (2014). *A shifting landscape: A decade of change in American attitudes about same-sex marriage and LGBT issues*. Washington, DC: Public Religion Research Institute. (p. 187)

Jones, W., & Klin, A. (2013). Attention to eyes is present but in decline in 2–6-month-old infants later diagnosed with autism. *Nature, 504*, 427–431. (p. 136)

Jones, W. H., Carpenter, B. N., & Quintana, D. (1985). Personality and interpersonal predictors of loneliness in two cultures. *Journal of Personality and Social Psychology, 48*, 1503–1511. (p. 9)

Jonides, J., Jaeggi, S. M., Buschkuehl, M., & Shah, P. (2012, September/October). Building better brains. *Scientific American Mind*, pp. 59–63. (p. 161)

Jorm, A. F., Reavley, N. J., & Ross, A. M. (2012). Belief in the dangerousness of people with mental disorders: A review. *Australian and New Zealand Journal of Psychiatry, 46*, 1029–1045. (p. 533)

Jose, A., O'Leary, D., & Moyer, A. (2010). Does premarital cohabitation predict subsequent marital stability and marital quality? A meta-analysis. *Journal of Marriage and Family, 72*, 105–116. (p. 164)

Joseph, J. (2001). Separated twins and the genetics of personality differences: A critique. *American Journal of Psychology, 114,* 1–30. (p. 69)

Jost, J. T., Kay, A. C., & Thorisdottir, H. (Eds.). (2009). *Social and psychological bases of ideology and system justification.* New York: Oxford University Press. (p. 468)

Jovanovic, T., Blanding, N. Q., Norrholm, S. D., Duncan, E., Bradley, B., & Ressler, K. J. (2009). Childhood abuse is associated with increased startle reactivity in adulthood. *Depression and Anxiety, 26,* 1018–1026. (p. 143)

Judge, T. A., Thoresen, C. J., Bono, J. E., & Patton, G. K. (2001). The job satisfaction/job performance relationship: A qualitative and quantitative review. *Psychological Bulletin, 127,* 376–407. (p. B-9)

Jung-Beeman, M., Bowden, E. M., Haberman, J., Frymiare, J. L., Arambel-Liu, S., Greenblatt, R., . . . Kounios, J. (2004). Neural activity when people solve verbal problems with insight. *PLoS Biology, 2*(4), e97. doi:10.1371/journal.pbio.0020097 (p. 318)

Just, M. A., Keller, T. A., & Cynkar, J. (2008). A decrease in brain activation associated with driving when listening to someone speak. *Brain Research, 1205,* 70–80. (p. 82)

Just, M. A., Keller, T. A., Malave, V. L., Kana, R. K., & Varma, S. (2012). Autism as a neural systems disorder: A theory of frontal-posterior underconnectivity. *Neuroscience and Biobehavioral Reviews, 36,* 1292–1313. (p. 137)

K

Kabat-Zinn, J. (2001). Mindfulness-based interventions in context: Past, present, and future. *Clinical Psychology: Science and Practice, 10,* 144–156. (p. 428)

Kagan, J. (1976). Emergent themes in human development. *American Scientist, 64,* 186–196. (p. 142)

Kagan, J. (1984). *The nature of the child.* New York: Basic Books. (p. 138)

Kagan, J. (1995). On attachment. *Harvard Review of Psychiatry, 3,* 104–106. (p. 140)

Kagan, J. (2010). *The temperamental thread: How genes, culture, time, and luck make us who we are.* Washington, DC: Dana Press. (p. 507)

Kagan, J., & Snidman, N. (2004). *The long shadow of temperament.* Cambridge, MA: Belknap Press. (p. 140)

Kahneman, D. (1985, June). Quoted in K. McKean, Decisions, decisions. *Discover,* pp. 22–31. (p. A-6)

Kahneman, D. (1999). Objective happiness. In D. Kahneman, E. Diener, & N. Schwartz (Eds.), *Well-being: The foundations of hedonic psychology* (pp. 3–25). New York: Russell Sage Foundation. (p. 233)

Kahneman, D. (2005, February 10). Are you happy now? [Interview]. *Gallup Management Journal.* Retrieved from http://www.gallup.com/businessjournal/14872/happy-now.aspx (p. 433)

Kahneman, D. (2005, January 13). What were they thinking? *Gallup Business Journal.* Retrieved from http://www.gallup.com/businessjournal/14503/what-were-they-thinking.aspx (p. 319)

Kahneman, D. (2011). *Thinking, fast and slow.* New York: Farrar, Straus and Giroux. (pp. 85, A-7)

Kahneman, D., Fredrickson, B. L., Schreiber, C. A., & Redelmeier, D. A. (1993). When more pain is preferred to less: Adding a better end. *Psychological Science, 4,* 401–405. (p. 233)

Kahneman, D., Krueger, A. B., Schkade, D. A., Schwarz, N., & Stone, A. A. (2004). A survey method for characterizing daily life experience: The day reconstruction method. *Science, 306,* 1776–1780. (p. 432)

Kail, R. (1991). Developmental change in speed of processing during childhood and adolescence. *Psychological Bulletin, 109,* 490–501. (p. 159)

Kail, R., & Hall, L. K. (2001). Distinguishing short-term memory from working memory. *Memory & Cognition, 29,* 1–9. (p. 285)

Kamarck, T., & Jennings, J. R. (1991). Biobehavioral factors in sudden cardiac death. *Psychological Bulletin, 109,* 42–75. (p. 415)

Kamatali, J.-M. (2014, April 4). Following orders in Rwanda. *The New York Times.* Retrieved from http://www.nytimes.com/2014/04/05/opinion/following-orders-in-rwanda.html?_r=0 (p. 453)

Kamel, N. S., & Gammack, J. K. (2006). Insomnia in the elderly: Cause, approach, and treatment. *American Journal of Medicine, 119,* 463–469. (p. 90)

Kamenica, E., Naclerio, R., & Malani, A. (2013). Advertisements impact the physiological efficacy of a branded drug. *Proceedings of the National Academy of Sciences of the United States of America, 110,* 12931–12935. (p. 594)

Kamil, A. C., & Cheng, K. (2001). Way-finding and landmarks: The multiple-bearings hypothesis. *Journal of Experimental Biology, 204,* 103–113. (p. 293)

Kaminski, J., Cali, J., & Fischer, J. (2004). Word learning in a domestic dog: Evidence for "fast mapping." *Science, 304,* 1682–1683. (p. 336)

Kanaya, T., Scullin, M. H., & Ceci, S. J. (2003). The Flynn effect and U.S. policies: The impact of rising IQ scores on American society via mental retardation diagnoses. *American Psychologist, 58,* 778–790. (p. 352)

Kandel, E. (2008, October/November). Quoted in S. Avan, Speaking of memory. *Scientific American Mind,* pp. 16–17. (p. 86)

Kandel, D. B., & Raveis, V. H. (1989). Cessation of illicit drug use in young adulthood. *Archives of General Psychiatry, 46,* 109–116. (p. 116)

Kandel, E. R. (2012, March 5). In C. Dreifus, A quest to understand how memory works [Interview]. *The New York Times.* Retrieved from http://www.nytimes.com/2012/03/06/science/a-quest-to-understand-how-memory-works.html?_r=0 (pp. 295, 499)

Kandel, E. R., & Schwartz, J. H. (1982). Molecular biology of learning: Modulation of transmitter release. *Science, 218,* 433–443. (p. 295)

Kandler, C., Bleidorn, W., Riemann, R., Angleitner, A., & Spinath, F. M. (2011). The genetic links between the Big Five personality traits and general interest domains. *Personality and Social Psychology Bulletin, 37,* 1633–1643. (p. 68)

Kandler, C., Bleidorn, W., Riemann, R., Angleitner, A., & Spinath, F. M. (2012). Life events as environmental states and genetic traits and the role of personality: A longitudinal twin study. *Behavior Genetics, 42,* 57–72. (p. 72)

Kandler, C., Riemann, R., & Angleitner, A. (2013). Patterns and sources of continuity and change of energetic and temporal aspects of temperament in adulthood: A longitudinal twin study of self- and peer reports. *Developmental Psychology, 49,* 1739–1753. (p. 141)

Kane, G. D. (2010). Revisiting gay men's body image issues: Exposing the fault lines. *Review of General Psychology, 14,* 311–317. (p. 566)

Kane, J. M., & Mertz, J. E. (2012). Debunking myths about gender and mathematics performance. *Notices of the American Mathematical Society, 59,* 10–21. (p. 357)

Kaplan, H. I., & Saddock, B. J. (Eds.). (1989). *Comprehensive textbook of psychiatry, V.* Baltimore: Williams & Wilkins. (p. 594)

Kaplan, T., & Hakim, D. (2013, January 14). New York has gun deal, with focus on mental ills. *The New York Times.* Retrieved from http://www.nytimes.com/2013/01/15/nyregion/new-york-legislators-hope-for-speedy-vote-on-gun-laws.html (p. 533)

Kaprio, J., Koskenvuo, M., & Rita, H. (1987). Mortality after bereavement: A prospective study of 95,647 widowed persons. *American Journal of Public Health, 77,* 283–287. (p. 407)

Karacan, I., Aslan, C., & Hirshkowitz, M. (1983). Erectile mechanisms in man. *Science, 220,* 1080–1082. (p. 90)

Karacan, I., Goodenough, D. R., Shapiro, A., & Starker, S. (1966). Erection cycle during sleep in relation to dream anxiety. *Archives of General Psychiatry, 15,* 183–189. (p. 90)

Karasik, L. B., Adolph, K. E., Tamis-LeMonda, C. S., & Bornstein, M. H. (2010). WEIRD walking: Cross-cultural research on motor development. *Behavioral and Brain Sciences, 33,* 95–96. (p. 129)

Karau, S. J., & Williams, K. D. (1993). Social loafing: A meta-analytic review and theoretical integration. *Journal of Personality and Social Psychology, 65,* 681–706. (p. 457)

Karbach, J., & Verhaeghen, P. (2014). Making working memory work: A meta-analysis of executive-control and working memory training in older adults. *Psychological Science, 25,* 2027–2037. (p. 162)

Kark, J. D., Shemi, G., Friedlander, Y., Martin, O., Manor, O., & Blondheim, S. H. (1996). Does religious observance promote health? Mortality in secular vs. religious kibbutzim in Israel. *American Journal of Public Health, 86,* 341–346. (p. 429)

Karlén, J., Ludvigsson, J., Hedmark, M., Faresjö, Å., Theodorsson, E., & Faresjö, T. (2015). Early psychosocial exposures, hair cortisol levels, and disease risk. *Pediatrics, 135,* e1450–e1457. doi:10.1542/peds.2014-2561 (p. 414)

Karlsgodt, K. H., Sun, D., & Cannon, T. D. (2010). Structural and functional brain abnormalities in schizophrenia. *Current Directions in Psychological Science, 19,* 226–231. (p. 558)

Karni, A., Meyer, G., Rey-Hipolito, C., Jezzard, P., Adams, M. M., Turner, R., & Ungerleider, L. G. (1998). The acquisition of skilled motor performance: Fast and slow experience-driven changes in primary motor cortex. *Proceedings of the National Academy of Sciences of the United States of America, 95,* 861–868. (p. 128)

Karni, A., & Sagi, D. (1994). Dependence on REM sleep for overnight improvement of perceptual skills. *Science, 265,* 679–682. (p. 100)

Karpicke, J. D. (2012). Retrieval-based learning: Active retrieval promotes meaningful learning. *Current Directions in Psychological Science, 21,* 157–163. (p. 31)

Karpicke, J. D., & Roediger, H. L., III. (2008). The critical importance of retrieval for learning. *Science, 319,* 966–968. (p. 30)

Karr, J. E., Areshenkoff, C. N., Rast, P., & Garcia-Barrera, M. (2014). An empirical comparison of the therapeutic benefits of physical exercise and cognitive training on the executive functions of older adults: A meta-analysis of controlled trials. *Neuropsychology, 28,* 829–845. (p. 161)

Karremans, J. C., Frankenhis, W. E., & Arons, S. (2010). Blind men prefer a low waist-to-hip ratio. *Evolution and Human Behavior, 31,* 182–186. (pp. 194, 478)

Karremans, J. C., Stroebe, W., & Claus, J. (2006). Beyond Vicary's fantasies: The impact of subliminal priming and brand choice. *Journal of Experimental Social Psychology, 42,* 792–798. (p. 203)

Kasen, S., Chen, H., Sneed, J., Crawford, T., & Cohen, P. (2006). Social role and birth cohort influences on gender-linked personality traits in women: A 20-year longitudinal analysis. *Journal of Personality and Social Psychology, 91,* 944–958. (p. 174)

Katz-Wise, S. L., & Hyde, J. S. (2012). Victimization experiences of lesbian, gay, and bisexual individuals: A meta-analysis. *Journal of Sex Research, 49,* 142–167. (p. 464)

Katz-Wise, S. L., Priess, H. A., & Hyde, J. S. (2010). Gender-role attitudes and behavior across the transition to parenthood. *Developmental Psychology, 46,* 18–28. (p. 174)

Kaufman, G., & Libby, L. K. (2012). Changing beliefs and behavior through experience-taking. *Journal of Personality and Social Psychology, 103,* 1–19. (p. 275)

Kaufman, J., & Zigler, E. (1987). Do abused children become abusive parents? *American Journal of Orthopsychiatry, 57,* 186–192. (p. 143)

Kaufman, J. C., & Baer, J. (2002). I bask in dreams of suicide: Mental illness, poetry, and women. *Review of General Psychology, 6,* 271–286. (p. 547)

Kaufman, L., & Kaufman, J. H. (2000). Explaining the moon illusion. *Proceedings of the National Academy of Sciences of the United States of America, 97,* 500–505. (p. 222)

Kawachi, I., Kennedy, B. P., & Wilkinson, R. G. (1999). Crime: Social disorganization and relative deprivation. *Social Science and Medicine, 48,* 719–731. (p. 435)

Kawakami, K., Dunn, E., Karmali, F., & Dovidio, J. F. (2009). Mispredicting affective and behavioral responses to racism. *Science, 323,* 276–278. (p. 463)

Kay, A. C., Baucher, D., Peach, J. M., Laurin, K., Friesen, J., Zanna, M. P., & Spencer, S. J. (2009). Inequality, discrimination, and the power of the status quo: Direct evidence for a motivation to see the way things are as the way they should be. *Journal of Personality and Social Psychology, 97,* 421–434. (p. 468)

Kayser, C. (2007, April/May). Listening with your eyes. *Scientific American Mind,* pp. 24–29. (p. 239)

Kazantzis, N., & Dattilio, F. M. (2010). Definitions of homework, types of homework and ratings of the importance of homework among psychologists with cognitive behavior therapy and psychoanalytic theoretical orientations. *Journal of Clinical Psychology, 66,* 758–773. (p. 581)

Kazantzis, N., Whittington, C., & Dattilio, F. M. (2010). Meta-analysis of homework effects in cognitive and behavioral therapy: A replication and extension. *Clinical Psychology: Science and Practice, 17,* 144–156. (p. 581)

Kazdin, A. E. (2015). Editor's introduction to the special series: Targeted training of cognitive processes for behavioral and emotional disorders. *Clinical Psychological Science, 3,* 38. (p. 578)

Kearney, M. S., & Levine, P. B. (2014, January). *Media influences on social outcomes: The impact of MTV's 16 and Pregnant on teen childbearing* (NBER Working Paper No. 19795). Retrieved from http://www.nber.org/papers/w19795 (p. 186)

Kearns, M. C., Ressler, K. J., Zatzick, D., & Rothbaum, B. O. (2012). Early interventions for PTSD: A review. *Depression and Anxiety, 29,* 833–842. (p. 296)

Keesey, R. E., & Corbett, S. W. (1984). Metabolic defense of the body weight setpoint. In A. J. Stunkard & E. Stellar (Eds.), *Eating and its disorders* (pp. 87–96). New York: Raven Press. (p. 379)

Keith, S. W., Redden, D. T., Katzmarzyk, P. T., Boggiano, M. M., Hanlon, E. C., Benca, R. M., . . . Allison, D. B. (2006). Putative contributors to the secular increase in obesity: Exploring the roads less traveled. *International Journal of Obesity, 30,* 1585–1594. (p. 383)

Kell, H. J., Lubinski, D., & Benbow, C. P. (2013). Who rises to the top? Early indicators. *Psychological Science, 24,* 648–659. (p. 352)

Keller, J. (2007, March 9). As football players get bigger, more of them risk a dangerous sleep disorder. *The Chronicle of Higher Education,* pp. A43–A44. (p. 97)

Keller, M. B., McCullough, J. P., Klein, D. N., Arnow, B., Dunner, D. L., Gelenberg, A. J., . . . Zajecka, J. (2000). A comparison of nefazodone, the cognitive behavioral-analysis system of psychotherapy, and their combination for the treatment of chronic depression. *New England Journal of Medicine, 342,* 1462–1470. (p. 596)

Kellerman, J., Lewis, J., & Laird, J. D. (1989). Looking and loving: The effects of mutual gaze on feelings of romantic love. *Journal of Research in Personality, 23,* 145–161. (p. 396)

Kelling, S. T., & Halpern, B. P. (1983). Taste flashes: Reaction times, intensity, and quality. *Science, 219,* 412–414. (p. 236)

Kellner, C. H., Fink, M., Knapp, R., Petrides, G., Husain, M., Rummans, T., . . . Malur, C. (2005). Relief of expressed suicidal intent by ECT: A consortium for research in ECT study. *American Journal of Psychiatry, 162,* 977–982. (p. 598)

Kellner, C. H., Knapp, R. G., Petrides, G., Rummans, T. A., Husain, M. M., Rasmussen, K., . . . Fink, M. (2006). Continuation electroconvulsive therapy vs. pharmacotherapy for relapse prevention in major depression: A multisite study from the Consortium for Research in Electroconvulsive Therapy (CORE). *Archives of General Psychiatry, 63,* 1337–1344. (p. 598)

Kelly, A. E. (2000). Helping construct desirable identities: A self-presentational view of psychotherapy. *Psychological Bulletin, 126,* 475–494. (p. 579)

Kelly, D. J., Quinn, P. C., Slater, A. M., Lee, K., Ge, L., & Pascalis, O. (2007). The other-race effect develops during infancy: Evidence of perceptual narrowing. *Psychological Science, 18,* 1084–1089. (p. 475)

Kelly, S. D., Özyürek, A., & Maris, E. (2010). Two sides of the same coin: Speech and gesture mutually interact to enhance comprehension. *Psychological Science, 21,* 260–267. (p. 335)

Kelly, T. A. (1990). The role of values in psychotherapy: A critical review of process and outcome effects. *Clinical Psychology Review, 10,* 171–186. (p. 590)

Kempe, R. S., & Kempe, C. C. (1978). *Child abuse.* Cambridge, MA: Harvard University Press. (p. 143)

Kendall-Tackett, K. A., Williams, L. M., & Finkelhor, D. (1993). Impact of sexual abuse on children: A review and synthesis of recent empirical studies. *Psychological Bulletin, 113,* 164–180. (p. 311)

Kendler, K. S. (1998, January). Major depression and the environment: A psychiatric genetic perspective. *Pharmacopsychiatry, 31,* 5–9. (p. 548)

Kendler, K. S. (2011). [Statement on the proposal to eliminate the grief exclusion criterion from major depression]. Retrieved from http://www.dsm5.org/about/Documents/grief%20exclusion_Kendler.pdf (p. 531)

Kendler, K. S., Jacobson, K. C., Myers, J., & Prescott, C. A. (2002a). Sex differences in genetic and environmental risk factors for irrational fears and phobias. *Psychological Medicine, 32,* 209–217. (p. 542)

Kendler, K. S., Myers, J., & Prescott, C. A. (2002b). The etiology of phobias: An evaluation of the stress-diathesis model. *Archives of General Psychiatry, 59,* 242–248. (p. 542)

Kendler, K. S., Myers, J., & Zisook, S. (2008). Does bereavement-related major depression differ from major depression associated with other stressful life events? *American Journal of Psychiatry, 165,* 1449–1455. (p. 548)

Kendler, K. S., Neale, M. C., Kessler, R. C., Heath, A. C., & Eaves, L. J. (1994). Parent treatment and the equal environment assumption in twin studies of psychiatric illness. *Psychological Medicine, 24,* 579–590. (p. 68)

Kendler, K. S., Neale, M. C., Thornton, L. M., Aggen, S. H., Gilman, S. E., & Kessler, R. C. (2002). Cannabis use in the last year in a U.S. national sample of twin and sibling pairs. *Psychological Medicine, 32,* 551–554. (p. 114)

Kendler, K. S., Sundquist, K., Ohlsson, H., Palmer, K., Maes, H., Winkleby, M. A., & Sundquist, J. (2012). Genetic and familiar environmental influences on the risk for drug abuse: A Swedish adoption study. *Archives of General Psychiatry, 69,* 690–697. (p. 115)

Kendler, K. S., Thornton, L. M., & Gardner, C. O. (2001). Genetic risk, number of previous depressive episodes, and stressful life events in predicting onset of major depression. *American Journal of Psychiatry, 158,* 582–586. (p. 548)

Kendler, K. S., Turkheimer, E., Ohlsson, H., Sundquist, J., & Sundquist, K. (2015). Family environment and the malleability of cognitive ability: A Swedish national home-reared and adopted-away cosibling control study. *Proceedings of the National Academy of Sciences of the United States of America, 112,* 4612–4617. (pp. 70–71, 355)

Kendrick, K. M., & Feng, J. (2011). Neural encoding principles in face perception revealed using non-primate models. In G. Rhodes, A. Calder, M. Johnson, & J. V. Haxby (Eds.), *The Oxford handbook of face perception* (pp. 675–690). Oxford, England: Oxford University Press. (p. 282)

Kennard, B. D., Emslie, G. J., Mayes, T. L., Nakonezny, P. A., Jones, J. M., Foxwell, A. A., & King, J. (2014). Sequential treatment of fluoextine and relapse-prevention CBT to improve outcomes in pediatric depression. *American Journal of Psychiatry, 171,* 1083–1090. (p. 596)

Kennedy, S., & Over, R. (1990). Psychophysiological assessment of male sexual arousal following spinal cord injury. *Archives of Sexual Behavior, 19,* 15–27. (p. 45)

Kenrick, D. T., & Funder, D. C. (1988). Profiting from controversy: Lessons from the person–situation debate. *American Psychologist, 43,* 23–34. (p. 512)

Kenrick, D. T., Griskevicious, V., Neuberg, S. L., & Schaller, M. (2010). Renovating the pyramid of needs: Contemporary extensions build upon ancient foundations. *Perspectives on Psychological Science, 5,* 292–314. (p. 368)

Kenrick, D. T., & Gutierres, S. E. (1980). Contrast effects and judgments of physical attractiveness: When beauty becomes a social problem. *Journal of Personality and Social Psychology, 38,* 131–140. (p. 185)

Kenrick, D. T., Gutierres, S. E., & Goldberg, L. L. (1989). Influence of popular erotica on judgments of strangers and mates. *Journal of Experimental Social Psychology, 25,* 159–167. (p. 185)

Kenrick, D. T., Nieuweboer, S., & Buunk, A. P. (2009). Universal mechanisms and cultural diversity: Replacing the blank slate with a coloring book. In M. Schaller, A. Norenzayan, S. Heine, A. Norenzayan, T. Yamagishi, & T. Kameda (Eds.), *Evolution, culture, and the human mind* (pp. 257–271). Mahwah, NJ: Erlbaum. (pp. 127, 194)

Kensinger, E. A. (2007). Negative emotion enhances memory accuracy: Behavioral and neuroimaging evidence. *Current Directions in Psychological Science, 16,* 213–218. (p. 294)

Keough, K. A., Zimbardo, P. G., & Boyd, J. N. (1999). Who's smoking, drinking, and using drugs? Time perspective as a predictor of substance use. *Basic and Applied Social Psychology, 2,* 149–164. (p. 493)

Kernis, M. H. (2003). Toward a conceptualization of optimal self-esteem. *Psychological Inquiry, 14,* 1–26. (p. 520)

Kerr, N. L., & Bruun, S. E. (1983). Dispensability of member effort and group motivation losses: Free-rider effects. *Journal of Personality and Social Psychology, 44,* 78–94. (p. 457)

Kessler, M., & Albee, G. (1975). Primary prevention. *Annual Review of Psychology, 26,* 557–591. (p. 602)

Kessler, R. C. (2000). Posttraumatic stress disorder: The burden to the individual and to society. *Journal of Clinical Psychiatry, 61*(Suppl. 5), 4–12. (p. 540)

Kessler, R. C., Berglund, P., Demler, O., Jin, R., Merikangos, K. R., & Walters, E. E. (2005). Lifetime prevalence and age-of-onset distributions of *DSM-IV* disorders in the National Comorbidity Survey replication. *Archives of General Psychiatry, 62,* 593–602. (p. 534)

Kessler, R. C., Birnbaum, H. G., Shahly, V., Bromet, E., Hwang, I., McLaughlin, K. A., . . . Stein, D. J. (2010). Age differences in the prevalence and co-morbidity of DSM-IV major depressive episodes: Results from the WHO World Mental Health Survey Initiative. *Depression and Anxiety, 27,* 351–364. (p. 548)

Kessler, R. C., Foster, C., Joseph, J., Ostrow, D., Wortman, C., Phair, J., & Chmiel, J. (1991). Stressful life events and symptom onset in HIV infection. *American Journal of Psychiatry, 148,* 733–738. (p. 413)

Kessler, R. C., Green, J. G., Adler, L. A., Barkley, R. A., Chatterji, S., Faraone, S. V., . . . Van Brunt, D. L. (2010). Structure and diagnosis of adult attention-deficit/hyperactivity disorder: Analysis of expanded symptom criteria from the adult ADHD Clinical Diagnostic Scale. *Archives of General Psychiatry, 67,* 1168–1178. (p. 532)

Kessler, R. C., Petukhova, M., Sampson, N. A., Zaslavsky, A. M., & Wittchen, H.-A. (2012). Twelve-month and lifetime morbid risk of anxiety and mood disorders in the United States. *International Journal of Methods in Psychiatric Research, 21,* 169–184. (p. 539)

Kessler, R. C., Soukup, J., Davis, R. B., Foster, D. F., Wilkey, S. A., Van Rompay, M. I., & Eisenberg, D. M. (2001). The use of complementary and alternative therapies to treat anxiety and depression in the United States. *American Journal of Psychiatry, 158,* 289–294. (p. 587)

Kessler, T., Mummendey, A., Funke, F., Brown, R̆., Binder, J., Zagefka, H., . . . Maquil, A. (2010). We all live in Germany but . . . ingroup projection, group-based emotions and prejudice against immigrants. *European Journal of Social Psychology, 40,* 985–997. (p. 316)

Keyes, K. M., Maslowsky, J., Hamilton, A., & Schulenberg, J. (2015). The great sleep recession: Changes in sleep duration among U.S. adolescents, 1991–2012. *Pediatrics, 135,* 460–468. (p. 94)

Keynes, M. (1980, December 20/27). Handel's illnesses. *The Lancet, 316,* 1354–1355. (p. 546)

Keys, A., Brozek, J., Henschel, A., Mickelsen, O., & Taylor, H. L. (1950). *The biology of human starvation.* Minneapolis: University of Minnesota Press. (p. 377)

Kiatpongsan, S., & Norton, M. I. (2014). How much (more) should CEOs make? A universal desire for more equal pay. *Perspectives on Psychological Science, 9,* 587–593. (p. 435)

Kiecolt-Glaser, J. K. (2009). Psychoneuroimmunology: Psychology's gateway to the biomedical future. *Perspectives on Psychological Science, 4,* 367–369. (p. 410)

Kiecolt-Glaser, J. K., Loving, T. J., Stowell, J. R., Malarkey, W. B., Lemeshow, S., Dickinson, S. L., & Glaser, R. (2005). Hostile marital interactions, proinflammatory cytokine production, and wound healing. *Archives of General Psychiatry, 62,* 1377–1384. (p. 411)

Kiecolt-Glaser, J. K., Page, G. G., Marucha, P. T., MacCallum, R. C., & Glaser, R. (1998). Psychological influences on surgical recovery: Perspectives from psychoneuroimmunology. *American Psychologist, 53,* 1209–1218. (p. 411)

Kiehl, K. A., & Buckholtz, J. W. (2010, September/October). Inside the mind of a psychopath. *Scientific American Mind,* pp. 22–29. (p. 564)

Kihlstrom, J. F. (2005). Dissociative disorders. *Annual Review of Clinical Psychology, 1,* 227–253. (p. 562)

Kihlstrom, J. F. (2006). Repression: A unified theory of a will-o'-the-wisp. *Behavioral and Brain Sciences, 29,* 523. (p. 499)

Kille, D. R., Forest, A. L., & Wood, J. V. (2013). Tall, dark, and stable: Embodiment motivates mate selection preferences. *Psychological Science, 24,* 112–114. (p. 240)

Killingsworth, M. A., & Gilbert, D. T. (2010). A wandering mind is an unhappy mind. *Science, 330,* 932. (p. B-1)

Kilpatrick, L. A., Suyenobu, B. Y., Smith, S. R., Bueller, J. A., Goodman, T., Creswell, J. D., . . . Naliboff, B. D. (2011). Impact of mindfulness-based stress reduction training on intrinsic brain activity. *NeuroImage, 56,* 290–298. (p. 428)

Kim, B. S. K., Ng, G. F., & Ahn, A. J. (2005). Effects of client expectation for counseling success, client–counselor worldview match, and client adherence to Asian and European American cultural values on counseling process with Asian Americans. *Journal of Counseling Psychology, 52,* 67–76. (p. 591)

Kim, G., & Tong, A. (2010, February 23). Airline passengers have grown, seats haven't. *The Grand Rapids Press,* pp. B1, B3. (p. 384)

Kim, H., & Markus, H. R. (1999). Deviance or uniqueness, harmony or conformity? A cultural analysis. *Journal of Personality and Social Psychology, 77,* 785–800. (p. 522)

Kim, H. S., Sherman, D. K., & Taylor, S. E. (2008). Culture and social support. *American Psychologist, 63,* 518–526. (p. 423).

Kim, J., Suh, W., Kim, S., & Gopalan, H. (2012). Coping strategies to manage acculturative stress: Meaningful activity participation, social support, and positive emotion among Korean immigrant adolescents in the USA. *International Journal of Qualitative Studies on Health and Well-Being, 7,* Article 18870. http://dx.doi.org/10.3402/qhw.v7i0.18870 (p. 407)

Kim, J. L., & Ward, L. M. (2012). Striving for pleasure without fear: Short-term effects of reading a women's magazine on women's sexual attitudes. *Psychology of Women Quarterly, 36,* 326–336. (p. 186)

Kim, S. H., Hwang, J. H., Park, H. S., & Kim, S. E. (2008). Resting brain metabolic correlates of neuroticism and extraversion in young men. *NeuroReport, 19,* 883–886. (p. 423, 507)

Kim, S. H., Vincent, L. C., & Goncalo, J. A. (2013). Outside advantage: Can social rejection fuel creative thought? *Journal of Experimental Psychology: General, 142,* 605–611. (p. 326)

Kim, Y. S., Leventhal, B. L., Koh, Y., Fombonne, E., Laska, E., Lim, E., . . . Grinker, R. R. (2011). Prevalence of autism spectrum disorders in a total population sample. *American Journal of Psychiatry, 168,* 904–912. (p. 136)

Kimata, H. (2001). Effect of humor on allergen-induced wheal reactions. *Journal of the American Medical Association, 285,* 737. (p. 424)

Kimble, G. A. (1956). *Principles of general psychology*. New York: Ronald Press. (p. 267)

Kimble, G. A. (1981). *Biological and cognitive constraints on learning*. Washington, DC: American Psychological Association. (p. 267)

Kim-Yeary, K. H., Ounpraseuth, S., Moore, P., Bursac, Z., & Greene, P. (2012). Religion, social capital, and health. *Review of Religious Research, 54*, 331–347. (p. 430)

King, S., St.-Hilaire, A., & Heidkamp, D. (2010). Prenatal factors in schizophrenia. *Current Directions in Psychological Science, 19*, 209–213. (p. 558)

Kinnier, R. T., & Metha, A. T. (1989). Regrets and priorities at three stages of life. *Counseling and Values, 33*, 182–193. (p. 166)

Kinzler, K. D., Shutts, K., Dejesus, J., & Spelke, E. S. (2009). Accent trumps race in guiding children's social preferences. *Social Cognition, 27*, 623–634. (p. 465)

Kirby, D. (2002). Effective approaches to reducing adolescent unprotected sex, pregnancy, and childbearing. *Journal of Sex Research, 39*, 51–57. (p. 187)

Kirkpatrick, B., Fenton, W. S., Carpenter, W. T., Jr., & Marder, S. R. (2006). The NIMH-MATRICS consensus statement on negative symptoms. *Schizophrenia Bulletin, 32*, 214–219. (p. 557)

Kirkpatrick, L. (1999). Attachment and religious representations and behavior. In J. Cassidy & P. R. Shaver (Eds.), *Handbook of attachment: Theory, research, and clinical applications* (pp. 803–822). New York: Guilford Press. (p. 139)

Kirsch, I. (2010). *The emperor's new drugs: Exploding the antidepressant myth*. New York: Basic Books. (pp. 24, 596)

Kirsch, I., Deacon, B. J., Huedo-Medina, T. B., Scoboria, A., Moore, T. J., & Johnson, B. T. (2008). Initial severity and antidepressant benefits: A meta-analysis of data submitted to the Food and Drug Administration. *PLOS Medicine, 5*(2), e45. doi:10.1371/journal.pmed.0050045 (p. 596)

Kirsch, I., Kong, J., Sadler, P., Spaeth, R., Cook, A., Kaptchuk, T. J., & Gollub, R. (2014). Expectancy and conditioning in placebo analgesia: Separate or connected processes? *Psychology of Consciousness: Theory, Research, and Practice, 1*, 51–59. (p. 596)

Kirsch, I., Moore, T. J., Scoboria, A., & Nicholls, S. S. (2002). The emperor's new drugs: An analysis of antidepressant medication data submitted to the U.S. Food and Drug Administration. *Prevention & Treatment, 5*(1). http://dx.doi.org/10.1037/1522-3736.5.1.523a (p. 596)

Kirsch, I., & Sapirstein, G. (1998). Listening to Prozac but hearing placebo: A meta-analysis of antidepressant medication. *Prevention & Treatment, 1*(2). http://dx.doi.org/10.1037/1522-3736.1.1.12a (p. 596)

Kisley, M. A., Wood, S., & Burrows, C. L. (2007). Looking at the sunny side of life: Age-related change in an event-related potential measure of the negativity bias. *Psychological Science, 18*, 838–843. (p. 167)

Kisely, S., Hall, K., Siskind, D., Frater, J., Olson, S., & Crompton, D. (2014). Deep brain stimulation for obsessive-compulsive disorder: A systematic review and meta-analysis. *Psychological Medicine, 44*, 3533–3542. (p. 599)

Kitayama, S., Chua, H. F., Tompson, S., & Han, S. (2013). Neural mechanisms of dissonance: An fMRI investigation of choice justification. *NeuroImage, 69*, 206–212. (p. 446)

Kitayama, S., Conway, L. G., III, Pietromonaci, P. R., Park, H., & Plaut, V. C. (2010). Ethos of independence across regions in the United States: The production–adoption model of cultural change. *American Psychologist, 65*, 559–574. (pp. 521, 523)

Kitayama, S., Ishii, K., Imada, T., Takemura, K., & Ramaswamy, J. (2006). Voluntary settlement and the spirit of independence: Evidence from Japan's "northern frontier." *Journal of Personality and Social Psychology, 91*, 369–384. (p. 523)

Kitayama, S., Park, H., Sevincer, A. T., Karasawa, M., & Uskul, A. K. (2009). A cultural task analysis of implicit independence: Comparing North America, Western Europe, and East Asia. *Journal of Personality and Social Psychology, 97*, 236–255. (pp. 442, 523)

Kivimaki, M., Leino-Arjas, P., Luukkonen, R., Rihimaki, H., & Kirjonen, J. (2002). Work stress and risk of cardiovascular mortality: Prospective cohort study of industrial employees. *British Medical Journal, 325*, 857. http://dx.doi.org/10.1136/bmj.325.7369.857 (p. 420)

Klauer, S. G., Feng, G., Simons-Morton, B. G., Ouimet, M. C., Lee, S. E., & Dingus, T. A. (2014). Distracted driving and risk of road crashes among novice and experienced drivers. *New England Journal of Medicine, 370*, 54–59. (p. 82)

Klayman, J., & Ha, Y.-W. (1987). Confirmation, disconfirmation, and information in hypothesis testing. *Psychological Review, 94*, 211–228. (p. 317)

Klein, D. N. (2010). Chronic depression: Diagnosis and classification. *Current Directions in Psychological Science, 19*, 96–100. (p. 548)

Klein, D. N., Schwartz, J. E., Santiago, N. J., Vivian, D., Vocisano, C., Castonguay, L. G., . . . Keller, M. B. (2003). Therapeutic alliance in depression treatment: Controlling for prior change and patient characteristics. *Journal of Consulting and Clinical Psychology, 71*, 997–1006. (p. 589)

Klein, R. A., Ratliff, K. A., Vianello, M., Adams, R. B., Jr., Bahník, Š., Bernstein, M. J., . . . Nosek, B. A. (2014). Investigating variation in replicability: A "many labs" replication project. *Social Psychology, 45*, 142–152. (p. 18)

Kleinke, C. L. (1986). Gaze and eye contact: A research review. *Psychological Bulletin, 100*, 78–100. (p. 396)

Kleinmuntz, B., & Szucko, J. J. (1984). A field study of the fallibility of polygraph lie detection. *Nature, 308*, 449–450. (p. 394)

Kleitman, N. (1960, November). Patterns of dreaming. *Scientific American*, pp. 82–88. (p. 88)

Klemm, W. R. (1990). Historical and introductory perspectives on brainstem-mediated behaviors. In W. R. Klemm & R. P. Vertes (Eds.), *Brainstem mechanisms of behavior* (pp. 3–32). New York: Wiley. (p. 51)

Klimstra, T. A., Hale, W. W., III, Raaijmakers, Q. A. W., Branje, S. J. T., & Meeus, W. H. J. (2009). Maturation of personality in adolescence. *Journal of Personality and Social Psychology, 96*, 898–912. (p. 153)

Klimstra, T. A., Kuppens, P., Luyckx, K., Branje, S., Hale, W. W., Oosterwegel, A., . . . Meeus, W. H. J. (2015). Daily dynamics of adolescent mood and identity. *Journal of Research on Adolescence*. Advance online publication. doi:10.1111/jora.12205 (p. 153)

Kline, D., & Schieber, F. (1985). Vision and aging. In J. E. Birren & K. W. Schaie (Eds.), *Handbook of the psychology of aging* (2nd ed., pp. 296–331). New York: Van Nostrand Reinhold. (p. 159)

Kline, N. S. (1974). *From sad to glad*. New York: Ballantine Books. (p. 552)

Klinke, R., Kral, A., Heid, S., Tillein, J., & Hartmann, R. (1999). Recruitment of the auditory cortex in congenitally deaf cats by long-term cochlear electrostimulation. *Science, 285*, 1729–1733. (p. 229)

Klump, K. L., & Culbert, K. M. (2007). Molecular genetic studies of eating disorders: Current status and future directions. *Current Directions in Psychological Science, 16*, 37–41. (p. 565)

Klump, K. L., Suisman, J. L., Burt, S. A., McGue, M., & Iacono, W. G. (2009). Genetic and environmental influences on disordered eating: An adoption study. *Journal of Abnormal Psychology, 118*, 797–805. (p. 565)

Knapp, S., & VandeCreek, L. (2000). Recovered memories of childhood abuse: Is there an underlying professional consensus? *Professional Psychology: Research and Practice, 31*, 365–371. (p. 311)

Knickmeyer, E. (2001, August 7). In Africa, big is definitely better. *The Seattle Times*, p. A7. (p. 566)

Knight, R. T. (2007). Neural networks debunk phrenology. *Science, 316*, 1578–1579. (p. 60)

Knight, W. (2004, August 2). Animated face helps deaf with phone chat. *New Scientist*. Retrieved from https://www.newscientist.com/article/dn6228-animated-face-helps-deaf-with-phone-chat/ (p. 239)

Knoblich, G., & Oellinger, M. (2006, October/November). The eureka moment. *Scientific American Mind*, pp. 38–43. (p. 317)

Knuts, I. J. E., Cosci, F., Esquivel, G., Goossens, L., van Duinen, M., Bareman, M., . . . Schruers, K. R. J. (2010). Cigarette smoking and 35% CO_2 induced panic in panic disorder patients. *Journal of Affective Disorders, 124*, 215–218. (p. 538)

Ko, C.-K., Yen, J.-Y., Chen, C.-C., Chen, S.-H., & Yen, C.-F. (2005). Proposed diagnostic criteria of Internet addiction for adolescents. *Journal of Nervous and Mental Disease, 193*, 728–733. (p. 105)

Koch, C., & Greenfield, S. (2007, October). How does consciousness happen? *Scientific American*, pp. 76–83. (p. 81)

Koenen, K. C., Moffitt, T. E., Roberts, A. L., Martin, L. T., Kubzansky, L., Harrington, H., . . . Caspi, A. (2009). Childhood IQ and adult mental disorders: A test of the cognitive reserve hypothesis. *American Journal of Psychiatry, 166*, 50–57. (p. 352)

Koenig, H. G., King, D. E., & Carson, V. B. (2012). *Handbook of religion and health* (2nd ed.). New York: Oxford University Press. (p. 429)

Koenig, H. G., & Larson, D. B. (1998). Use of hospital services, religious attendance, and religious affiliation. *Southern Medical Journal, 91*, 925–932. (p. 431)

Koenig, L. B., & Vaillant, G. E. (2009). A prospective study of church attendance and health over the lifespan. *Health Psychology, 28*, 117–124. (p. 430)

Koenig, L. B., McGue, M., Krueger, R. F., & Bouchard, T. J., Jr. (2005). Genetic and environmental influences on religiousness: Findings for retrospective and current religiousness ratings. *Journal of Personality, 73*, 471–488. (p. 70)

Koenigs, M., Young, L., Adolphs, R., Tranel, D., Cushman, F., Hauser, M., & Damasio, A. (2007). Damage to the prefrontal cortex increases utilitarian moral judgements. *Nature, 446*, 908–911. (p. 60)

Koestner, R., Lekes, N., Powers, T. A., & Chicoine, E. (2002). Attaining personal goals: Self-concordance plus implementation intentions equals success. *Journal of Personality and Social Psychology, 83*, 231–244. (p. B-11)

Kohlberg, L. (1981). *The philosophy of moral development: Essays on moral development* (Vol. 1). San Francisco: Harper & Row. (p. 150)

Kohlberg, L. (1984). *The psychology of moral development: Essays on moral development* (Vol. 2). San Francisco: Harper & Row. (p. 150)

Kohler, C. G., Walker, J. B., Martin, E. A., Healey, K. M., & Moberg, P. J. (2010). Facial emotion perception in schizophrenia: A meta-analytic review. *Schizophrenia Bulletin, 36*, 1009–1019. (p. 557)

Kohler, I. (1962, May). Experiments with goggles. *Scientific American*, pp. 62–72. (p. 224)

Köhler, W. (1925/1957). *The mentality of apes* (E. Winter, Trans.). London: Pelican. (Original work published 1925) (p. 327)

Kolassa, I.-T., & Elbert, T. (2007). Structural and functional neuroplasticity in relation to traumatic stress. *Current Directions in Psychological Science, 16*, 321–325. (p. 543)

Kolata, G. (1987). Metabolic catch-22 of exercise regimens. *Science, 236*, 146–147. (p. 385)

Kolb, B. (1989). Brain development, plasticity, and behavior. *American Psychologist, 44*, 1203–1212. (p. 61)

Kolb, B., & Whishaw, I. Q. (1998). Brain plasticity and behavior. *Annual Review of Psychology, 49*, 43–64. (p. 127)

Kolker, K. (2002, December 8). Video violence disturbs some: Others scoff at influence. *The Grand Rapids Press*, pp. A1, A12. (p. 472)

Kolodziej, M. E., & Johnson, B. T. (1996). Interpersonal contact and acceptance of persons with psychiatric disorders: A research synthesis. *Journal of Consulting and Clinical Psychology, 64*, 1387–1396. (p. 534)

Kotkin, M., Daviet, C., & Gurin, J. (1996). The *Consumer Reports* mental health survey. *American Psychologist, 51*, 1080–1082. (p. 584)

Koltko-Rivera, M. E. (2006). Rediscovering the later version of Maslow's hierarchy of needs: Self-transcendence and opportunities for theory, research, and unification. *Review of General Psychology, 10*, 302–317. (p. 368)

Komisaruk, B. R., & Whipple, B. (2011). Non-genital orgasms. *Sexual and Relationship Therapy, 26*, 356–372. (p. 185)

Konkle, T., Brady, T. F., Alvarez, G. A., & Oliva, A. (2010). Conceptual distinctiveness supports detailed visual long-term memory for real-world objects. *Journal of Experimental Psychology: General, 139*, 558–578. (p. 282)

Kontula, O., & Haavio-Mannila, E. (2009). The impact of aging on human sexual activity and sexual desire. *Journal of Sex Research, 46*, 46–56. (p. 158)

Kornell, N., & Bjork, R. A. (2008). Learning concepts and categories: Is spacing the "enemy of induction?" *Psychological Science, 19*, 585–592. (p. 31)

Kosfeld, M., Heinrichs, M., Zak, P. J., Fischbacher, U., & Fehr, E. (2005). Oxytocin increases trust in humans. *Nature, 435*, 673–676. (p. 46)

Kosslyn, S. M. (2005). Reflective thinking and mental imagery: A perspective on the development of posttraumatic stress disorder. *Development and Psychopathology, 17*, 851–863. (p. 540)

Kosslyn, S. M., & Koenig, O. (1992). *Wet mind: The new cognitive neuroscience.* New York: Free Press. (p. 44)

Kotchick, B. A., Shaffer, A., & Forehand, R. (2001). Adolescent sexual risk behavior: A multi-system perspective. *Clinical Psychology Review, 21*, 493–519. (p. 186)

Koten, J. W., Jr., Wood, G., Hagoort, P., Goebel, R., Propping, P., Willmes, K., & Boomsma, D. I. (2009). Genetic contribution to variation in cognitive function: An fMRI study in twins. *Science, 323*, 1737–1740. (p. 354)

Kounios, J., & Beeman, M. (2009). The *aha!* moment: The cognitive neuroscience of insight. *Current Directions in Psychological Science, 18*, 210–215. (p. 317)

Kposowa, A. J., & D'Auria, S. (2009). Association of temporal factors and suicides in the United States, 2000–2004. *Social Psychiatry and Psychiatric Epidemiology, 45*, 433–445. (p. 553)

Kraft, C. (1978). A psychophysical approach to air safety: Simulator studies of visual illusions in night approaches. In H. L. Pick, H. W. Leibowitz, J. E. Singer, A. Steinschneider, & H. W. Stevenson (Eds.), *Psychology: From research to practice* (pp. 363–385). New York: Plenum Press. (p. B-14)

Kraft, R. N. (2002). *Memory perceived: Recalling the Holocaust.* Westport, CT: Praeger. (p. 311)

Kraft, T., & Pressman, S. (2012). Grin and bear it: The influence of the manipulated facial expression on the stress response. *Psychological Science, 23*, 1372–1378. (p. 401)

Kramer, A. (2010). Personal communication. (p. 433)

Kramer, A. D. I. (2012). The spread of emotion via Facebook. In *Proceedings of the SIGCHI Conference on Human Factors in Computing Systems* (pp. 767–770). New York: Association for Computing Machinery. (p. 403)

Kramer, A. D. I., & Chung, C. K. (2011). Dimensions of self-expression in Facebook status updates. In *Proceedings of the Fifth International AAAI Conference on Weblogs and Social Media.* Retrieved from http://www.aaai.org/Library/ICWSM/icwsm11contents.php (p. 462)

Kramer, A. F., & Erickson, K. I. (2007). Capitalizing on cortical plasticity: Influence of physical activity on cognition and brain function. *Trends in Cognitive Sciences, 11*, 342–348. (p. 426)

Kramer, M. S., Aboud, F., Mironova, E., Vanilovich, I., Platt, R. W., Matush, L., . . . Promotion of Breastfeeding Intervention Trial (PROBIT) Study Group. (2008). Breastfeeding and child cognitive development: New evidence from a large randomized trial. *Archives of General Psychiatry, 65*, 578–584. (p. 24)

Kramer, P. D. (2011, July 9). In defense of antidepressants. *The New York Times.* Retrieved from http://www.nytimes.com/2011/07/10/opinion/sunday/10antidepressants.html?_r=0 (p. 595)

Kranz, F., & Ishai, A. (2006). Face perception is modulated by sexual preference. *Current Biology, 16*, 63–68. (p. 190)

Kraul, C. (2010, October 12). Chief engineer knew it would take a miracle. *The Los Angeles Times.* Retrieved from http://articles.latimes.com/2010/oct/12/world/la-fg-chile-miners-rescuer-20101013 (p. 241)

Kring, A. M., & Caponigro, J. M. (2010). Emotion in schizophrenia: Where feeling meets thinking. *Current Directions in Psychological Science, 19*, 255–259. (p. 557)

Kring, A. M., & Gordon, A. H. (1998). Sex differences in emotion: Expression, experience, and physiology. *Journal of Personality and Social Psychology, 74*, 686–703. (p. 398)

Kringelbach, M. L., & Berridge, K. C. (2012, August). The joyful mind. *Scientific American*, pp. 40–45. (p. 54)

Kristeller, J. L., Baer, R. A., & Quillian-Wolever, R. (2006). Mindfulness-based approaches to eating disorders. In R. A. Baer (Ed.), *Mindfulness-based treatment approaches: A clinician's guide to evidence base and applications* (pp. 75–91). San Diego, CA: Academic Press. (p. 428)

Kristensen, P., & Bjerkedal, T. (2007). Explaining the relation between birth order and intelligence. *Science, 316*, 1717. (p. A-8)

Kristof, N. D. (2004, July 21). Saying no to killers. *The New York Times.* http://www.nytimes.com/2004/07/21/opinion/saying-no-to-killers.html (p. 481)

Kroes, M. C. W., Tendolkar, I., van Wingen, G. A., van Waarde, J. A., Strange, B. A., & Fernández, G. (2014). An electroconvulsive therapy procedure impairs reconsolidation of episodic memories in humans. *Nature Neuroscience, 17*, 204–206. (p. 307)

Kroll, J. F., & Bialystok, E. (2013). Understanding the consequences of bilingualism for language processing and cognition. *Journal of Cognitive Psychology, 25*, 497–514. (p. 338)

Kross, E., & Ayduk, O. (2011). Making meaning out of negative experiences by self-distancing. *Current Directions in Psychological Science, 20*, 187–191. (p. 416)

Kross, E., Bruehlman-Senecal, E., Park, J., Burson, A., Dougherty, A., Shablack, H., . . . Ayduk, O. (2014). Self-talk as a regulatory mechanism: How you do it matters. *Journal of Personality and Social Psychology, 106*, 304–324. (p. 134)

Krueger, J., & Killham, E. (2005, December 8). At work, feeling good matters. *Gallup Management Journal.* Retrieved from http://www.gallup.com/businessjournal/20311/work-feeling-good-matters.aspx (p. B-11)

Kruger, J., & Dunning, D. (1999). Unskilled and unaware of it: How difficulties in recognizing one's own incompetence lead to inflated self-assessments. *Journal of Personality and Social Psychology, 77*, 1121–1134. (p. 518)

Kruger, J., Epley, N., Parker, J., & Ng, Z.-W. (2005). Egocentrism over e-mail: Can we communicate as well as we think? *Journal of Personality and Social Psychology, 89*, 925–936. (pp. 133, 397)

Krumhansl, C. L. (2010). Plink: "Thin slices" of music. *Music Perception, 27*, 337–354. (p. 282)

Krützen, M., Mann, J., Heithaus, M. R., Connor, R. C., Bejder, L., & Sherwin, W. B. (2005). Cultural transmission of tool use in bottlenose dolphins. *Proceedings of the National Academy of Sciences of the United States of America, 102*, 8939–8943. (p. 326)

Kubzansky, L. D., Sparrow, D., Vokanas, P., & Kawachi, I. (2001). Is the glass half empty or half full? A prospective study of optimism and coronary heart disease in the normative aging study. *Psychosomatic Medicine, 63*, 910–916. (p. 415)

Kuhl, P. K., & Meltzoff, A. N. (1982). The bimodal perception of speech in infancy. *Science, 218*, 1138–1141. (p. 331)

Kuhn, D. (2006). Do cognitive changes accompany developments in the adolescent brain? *Perspectives on Psychological Science, 1*, 59–67. (p. 148)

Kuhnle, C., Hofer, M., & Kilian, B. (2012). Self-control as predictor of school grades, life balance, and flow in adolescents. *British Journal of Educational Psychology, 82*, 533–548. (p. 421)

Kumar, A. & Gilovich, T. (2013). *Talking about what you did and what you have: The differential story utility of experiential and material purchases.* Manuscript submitted for publication. (p. 437)

Kuncel, N. R., & Hezlett, S. A. (2010). Fact and fiction in cognitive ability testing for admissions and hiring decisions. *Current Directions in Psychological Science, 19*, 339–345. (p. 343)

Kunkel, D. (2001). *Sex on TV: A biennial report to the Henry J. Kaiser Family Foundation.* Menlo Park, CA: Henry J. Kaiser Family Foundation. (p. 186)

Kupfer, D. J. (2012, June 1). *Dr. Kupfer defends DSM-5.* Retrieved from http://www.medscape.com/viewarticle/764735 (p. 531)

Kuppens, P., Allen, N. B., & Sheeber, L. B. (2010). Emotional inertia and psychological maladjustment. *Psychological Science, 21*, 984–991. (p. 551)

Kurdziel, L., Duclos, K., & Spencer, R. M. C. (2013). Sleep spindles in midday naps enhance learning in preschool children. *Proceedings of the National Academy of Sciences of the United States of America, 110*, 17267–17272. (p. 93)

Kushlev, K., & Dunn, E. W. (2015). Checking email less frequently reduces stress. *Computers in Human Behavior, 43*, 220–228. (p. 368)

Kushner, M. G., Kim, S. W., Conahue, C., Thuras, P., Adson, D., Kotlyar, M., . . . Foa, E. B. (2007). D-cycloserine augmented exposure therapy for obsessive-compulsive disorder. *Biological Psychiatry, 62*, 835–838. (p. 594)

Kuster, F., Orth, U., & Meier, L. L. (2012). Rumination mediates the prospective effect of low self-esteem on depression: A five-wave longitudinal study. *Personality and Social Psychology Bulletin, 38*, 747–759. (pp. 550, 551)

Kutas, M. (1990). Event-related brain potential (ERP) studies of cognition during sleep: Is it more than a dream? In R. R. Bootzin, J. F. Kihlstrom, & D. Schacter (Eds.), *Sleep and cognition* (pp. 43–57). Washington, DC: American Psychological Association. (p. 87)

Kutcher, E. J., & Bragger, J. D. (2004). Selection interviews of overweight job applicants: Can structure reduce the bias? *Journal of Applied Social Psychology, 34*, 1993–2022. (p. B-6)

Kuttler, A. F., La Greca, A. M., & Prinstein, M. J. (1999). Friendship qualities and social–emotional functioning of adolescents with close, cross-sex friendships. *Journal of Research on Adolescence, 9*, 339–366. (p. 174)

Kuzawa, C. W., Chugani, H. T., Grossman, L. I., Lipovich, L., Muzik, O., Hof, P. R., . . . Lange, N. (2014). Metabolic costs and evolutionary implications of human brain development. *Proceedings of the National Academy of Sciences of the United States of America, 111*, 13010–13015. (p. 127)

Kvavilashvili, L., Mirani, J., Schlagman, S., Foley, K., & Kornbrot, D. E. (2009). Consistency of flashbulb memories of September 11 over long delays: Implications for consolidation and wrong time slice hypotheses. *Journal of Memory and Language, 61*, 556–572. (p. 295)

Kwon, P. (2013). Resilience in lesbian, gay, and bisexual individuals. *Personality and Social Psychology Review, 17*, 371–383. (p. 188)

Kyaga, S., Landén, M., Boman, M., Hultman, C. M., Lǻngström, N., & Lichtenstein, P. (2013). Mental illness, suicide, and creativity: 40-year prospective total population study. *Journal of Psychiatric Research, 47*, 83–90. (p. 547)

L

Laceulle, O. M., Ormel, J., Aggen, S. H., Neale, N. C., & Kendler, K. S. (2011). Genetic and environmental influences on the longitudinal structure of neuroticism: A trait-state approach. *Psychological Science, 24*, 1780–1790. (p. 68)

Lacey, M. (2010, December 11). He found bag of cash, but did the unexpected. *The New York Times.* Retrieved from http://www.nytimes.com/2010/12/12/us/12backpack.html?_r=0 (p. 484)

Lachman, M. E. (2004). Development in midlife. *Annual Review of Psychology, 55*, 305–331. (p. 162)

Ladabaum, U., Mannalithara, A., Myer, P. A., & Singh, G. (2014). Obesity, abdominal obesity, physical activity, and caloric intake in US adults: 1988 to 2010. *American Journal of Medicine, 127*, 717–727. (p. 427)

Ladd, G. T. (1887). *Elements of physiological psychology.* New York: Scribner's. (p. 80)

Laeng, B., & Sulutvedt, U. (2014). The eye pupil adjusts to imaginary light. *Psychological Science, 25*, 188–197. (p. 211)

Lafleur, D. L., Pittenger, C., Kelmendi, B., Gardner, T., Wasylink, S., Malison, R. T., . . . Coric, V. (2006). *N*-acetylcysteine augmentation in serotonin reuptake inhibitor refractory obsessive-compulsive disorder. *Psychopharmacology, 184*, 254–256. (p. 542)

Laird, J. D. (1974). Self-attribution of emotion: The effects of expressive behavior on the quality of emotional experience. *Journal of Personality and Social Psychology, 29*, 475–486. (p. 401)

Laird, J. D. (1984). The real role of facial response in the experience of emotion: A reply to Tourangeau and Ellsworth, and others. *Journal of Personality and Social Psychology, 47*, 909–917. (p. 401)

Laird, J. D., Cuniff, M., Sheehan, K., Shulman, D., & Strum, G. (1989). Emotion specific effects of facial expressions on memory for life events. *Journal of Social Behavior and Personality, 4*, 87–98. (p. 401)

Laird, J. D., & Lacasse, K. (2014). Bodily influences on emotional feelings: Accumulating evidence and extensions of William James's theory of emotion. *Emotion Review, 6*, 27–34. (p. 401)

Lakin, J. L., Chartrand, T. L., & Arkin, R. M. (2008). I am too just like you: Nonconscious mimicry as an automatic behavioral response to social exclusion. *Psychological Science, 19*, 816–822. (p. 449)

Lally, P., Van Jaarsveld, C. H. M., Potts, H. W. W., & Wardle, J. (2010). How are habits formed: Modelling habit formation in the real world. *European Journal of Social Psychology, 40*, 998–1009. (p. 246)

Lam, C. B., & McBride-Chang, C. A. (2007). Resilience in young adulthood: The moderating influences of gender-related personality traits and coping flexibility. *Sex Roles, 56*, 159–172. (p. 178)

Lam, R. W., Levitt, A. J., Levitan, R. D., Enns, M. W., Morehouse, R., Michalak, E. E., & Tam, E. M. (2006). The Can-SAD Study: A randomized controlled trial of the effectiveness of light therapy and fluoxetine in patients with winter seasonal affective disorder. *American Journal of Psychiatry, 163*, 805–812. (p. 589)

Lambird, K. H., & Mann, T. (2006). When do ego threats lead to self-regulation failure? Negative consequences of defensive high self-esteem. *Personality and Social Psychology Bulletin, 32*, 1177–1187. (p. 520)

Lambert, N. M., DeWall, C. N., Bushman, B. J., Tillman, T. F., Fincham, F. D., Pond, R. S., Jr., & Gwinn, A. M. (2011, January). *Lashing out in lust: Effect of pornography on nonsexual, physical aggression against relationship partners.* Paper presented at the 12th Annual Convention of the Society for Personality and Social Psychology, San Antonio, TX. (p. 472)

Lambert, W. E. (1992). Challenging established views on social issues: The power and limitations of research. *American Psychologist, 47*, 533–542. (p. 338)

Lambert, W. E., Genesee, F., Holobow, N., & Chartrand, L. (1993). Bilingual education for majority English-speaking children. *European Journal of Psychology of Education, 8*, 3–22. (p. 338)

Landau, M. J., Oyserman, D., Keefer, L. A., & Smith, G. C. (2014). The college journey and academic engagement: How metaphor use enhances identity-based motivation. *Journal of Personality and Social Psychology, 106*, 679–698. (p. 516)

Landauer, T. (2001, September). Quoted in R. Herbert, You must remember this. *APS Observer*, p. 11. (p. 310)

Landauer, T. K., & Whiting, J. W. M. (1979). Correlates and consequences of stress in infancy. In R. Munroe, B. Munroe, & B. Whiting (Eds.), *Handbook of cross-cultural human development* (pp. 355–375). New York: Garland. (p. 406)

Landberg, J., & Norström, T. (2011). Alcohol and homicide in Russia and the United States: A comparative analysis. *Journal of Studies on Alcohol and Drugs, 72*, 723–730. (p. 470)

Landry, M. J. (2002). MDMA: A review of epidemiologic data. *Journal of Psychoactive Drugs, 34*, 163–169. (p. 111)

Lange, N., & McDougle, C. J. (2013, October). Help for the child with autism. *Scientific American*, pp. 72–77. (p. 137)

Langer, E. J. (1983). *The psychology of control*. Beverly Hills, CA: Sage. (p. 420)

Langer, E. J., & Abelson, R. P. (1974). A patient by any other name . . .: Clinician group differences in labeling bias. *Journal of Consulting and Clinical Psychology, 42*, 4–9. (p. 532)

Langer, E. J., & Imber, L. (1980). The role of mindlessness in the perception of deviance. *Journal of Personality and Social Psychology, 39*, 360–367. (p. 532)

Langlois, J. H., Kalakanis, L., Rubenstein, A. J., Larson, A., Hallam, M., & Smoot, M. (2000). Maxims or myths of beauty? A meta-analytic and theoretical review. *Psychological Bulletin, 126*, 390–423. (pp. 477, 478)

Langmeyer, A., Guglhör-Rudan, A., & Tarnai, C. (2012). What do music preferences reveal about personality? A cross-cultural replication using self-ratings and ratings of music samples. *Journal of Individual Differences, 33*, 119–130. (p. 512)

Långström, N. H., Rahman, Q., Carlström, E., & Lichtenstein, P. (2010). Genetic and environmental effects on same-sex sexual behavior: A population study of twins in Sweden. *Archives of Sexual Behavior, 39*, 75–80. (p. 191)

Lankford, A. (2009). Promoting aggression and violence at Abu Ghraib: The U.S. military's transformation of ordinary people into torturers. *Aggression and Violent Behavior, 14*, 388–395. (p. 455)

Larkin, J. E., Brasel, A. M., & Pines, H. A. (2013). Cross-disciplinary applications of I/O psychology concepts: Predicting student retention and employee turnover. *Review of General Psychology, 17*, 82–92. (p. B-11)

Larkin, K., Resko, J. A., Stormshak, F., Stellflug, J. N., & Roselli, C. E. (2002, November). Neuroanatomical correlates of sex and sexual partner preference in sheep. Paper presented at the annual meeting of the Society for Neuroscience, Orlando, FL. (p. 190)

Larrick, R. P., Timmerman, T. A., Carton, A. M., & Abrevaya, J. (2011). Temper, temperature, and temptation: Heat-related retaliation in baseball. *Psychological Science, 22*, 423–428. (p. 470)

Larsen, R. J., & Diener, E. (1987). Affect intensity as an individual difference characteristic: A review. *Journal of Research in Personality, 21*, 1–39. (pp. 141, 390)

Larson, R. W., & Verma, S. (1999). How children and adolescents spend time across the world: Work, play, and developmental opportunities. *Psychological Bulletin, 125*, 701–736. (p. 359)

Larzelere, R. E. (2000). Child outcomes of non-abusive and customary physical punishment by parents: An updated literature review. *Clinical Child and Family Psychology Review, 3*, 199–221. (p. 262)

Larzelere, R. E., & Kuhn, B. R. (2005). Comparing child outcomes of physical punishment and alternative disciplinary tactics: A meta-analysis. *Clinical Child and Family Psychology Review, 8*, 1–37. (p. 262)

Larzelere, R. E., Kuhn, B. R., & Johnson, B. (2004). The intervention selection bias: An underrecognized confound in intervention research. *Psychological Bulletin, 130*, 289–303. (p. 262)

Lashley, K. S. (1950). In search of the engram. In J. F. Danielli & R. Brown (Eds.), *Symposia of the Society for Experimental Biology: Vol. 4. Physiological mechanisms in animal behaviour* (pp. 454–482). New York: Cambridge University Press. (p. 292)

Lassiter, G. D., & Irvine, A. A. (1986). Video-taped confessions: The impact of camera point of view on judgments of coercion. *Journal of Applied Social Psychology, 16*, 268–276. (p. 443)

Lassiter, G. D., Lindberg, M. J., Gonzáles-Vallejo, C., Bellezza, F. S., & Phillips, N. D. (2009). The deliberation-without-attention effect: Evidence for an artifactual interpretation. *Psychological Science, 20*, 671–675. (p. 324)

Latané, B. (1981). The psychology of social impact. *American Psychologist, 36*, 343–356. (p. 456)

Latané, B., & Dabbs, J. M., Jr. (1975). Sex, group size and helping in three cities. *Sociometry, 38*, 180–194. (p. 482)

Latané, B., & Nida, S. (1981). Ten years of research on group size and helping. *Psychological Bulletin, 89*, 308–324. (p. 456)

Latham, G. P., & Locke, E. A. (2007). New developments in and directions for goal-setting research. *European Psychologist, 12*, 290–300. (p. B-11)

Laudenslager, M. L., & Reite, M. L. (1984). Losses and separations: Immunological consequences and health implications. *Review of Personality and Social Psychology, 5*, 285–312. (p. 419)

Laumann, E. O., Gagnon, J. H., Michael, R. T., & Michaels, S. (1994). *The social organization of sexuality: Sexual practices in the United States.* Chicago: University of Chicago Press. (p. 193)

Launay, J. M., Mouillet-Richard, S., Baudry, A., Pietri, M., & Kellermann, O. (2011). Raphe-mediated signals control the hippocampal response to SRI antidepressants via miR-16. *Translational Psychiatry, 1*(11), e56. doi:10.1038/tp.2011.54 (p. 595)

Laws, K. R., & Kokkalis, J. (2007). Ecstasy (MDMA) and memory function: A meta-analytic update. *Human Psychopharmacology: Clinical and Experimental, 22*, 381–388. (p. 111)

Layous, K., & Lyubomirsky, S. (2014). The how, who, what, when, and why of happiness: Mechanisms underlying the success of positive activity interventions. In J. Gruber & J. T. Moskowitz (Eds.), *Positive emotions: Integrating the light and dark sides* (pp. 473–495). New York: Oxford University Press. (p. 437)

Lazaruk, W. (2007). Linguistic, academic, and cognitive benefits of French immersion. *Canadian Modern Language Review, 63*, 605–628. (p. 338)

Lazarus, R. S. (1990). Theory-based stress measurement. *Psychological Inquiry, 1*, 3–13. (p. 407)

Lazarus, R. S. (1991). Progress on a cognitive-motivational-relational theory of emotion. *American Psychologist, 46*, 352–367. (p. 390)

Lazarus, R. S. (1998). *Fifty years of the research and theory of R. S. Lazarus: An analysis of historical and perennial issues.* Mahwah, NJ: Erlbaum. (pp. 390, 406)

Lazer, D., Pentland, A., Adamic, L., Aral, S., Barabási, A.-L., Brewer, D., . . . Van Alstyne, M. (2009). Computational social science. *Science, 323*, 721–723. (p. 459)

Lea, S. E. G. (2000). Towards an ethical use of animals. *The Psychologist, 13*, 556–557. (p. 28)

Leaper, C., & Ayres, M. M. (2007). A meta-analytic review of gender variations in adults' language use: Talkativeness, affiliative speech, and assertive speech. *Personality and Social Psychology Review, 11*, 328–363. (p. 173)

Leary, M. R. (1999). The social and psychological importance of self-esteem. In R. M. Kowalski & M. R. Leary (Eds.), *The social psychology of emotional and behavioral problems: Interfaces of social and clinical psychology* (pp. 197–221). Washington, DC: American Psychological Association. (p. 517)

Leary, M. R. (2012). Sociometer theory. In P. A. M. Van Lange, A. W. Kruglanski, & E. T. Higgins (Eds.), *Handbook of theories of social psychology* (Vol. 2, pp. 141–159). Thousand Oaks, CA: Sage. (p. 370)

LeDoux, J. (1996). *The emotional brain: The mysterious underpinnings of emotional life.* New York: Simon & Schuster. (p. 293)

LeDoux, J. (2002). *The synaptic self.* London: Macmillan. (p. 389)

LeDoux, J. (2009, July/August). Quoted in K. McGowan, Out of the past. *Discover*, pp. 28–37. (p. 306)

LeDoux, J. E., & Armony, J. (1999). Can neurobiology tell us anything about human feelings? In D. Kahneman, E. Diener, & N. Schwartz (Eds.), *Well-being: The foundations of hedonic psychology* (pp. 489–499). New York: Russell Sage Foundation. (p. 390)

Lee, C. S., Therriault, D. J., & Linderholm, T. (2012). On the cognitive benefits of cultural experience: Exploring the relationship between studying abroad and creative thinking. *Applied Cognitive Psychology, 26*, 768–778. (p. 326)

Lee, J. D. (2008). Fifty years of driving safety research. *Human Factors, 50*, 521–528. (p. B-14)

Lee, L., Frederick, S., & Ariely, D. (2006). Try it, you'll like it: The influence of expectation, consumption, and revelation on preferences for beer. *Psychological Science, 17*, 1054–1058. (p. 206)

Lee, S. W. S., & Schwarz, N. (2012). Bidirectionality, mediation, and moderation of metaphorical effects: The embodiment of social suspicions and fishy smells. *Journal of Personality and Social Psychology, 103*, 737–749. (p. 238)

Lee, S. W. S., Schwarz, N., Taubman, D., & Hou, M. (2010). Sneezing in times of a flu pandemic: Public sneezing increases perception of unrelated risks and shifts preferences for federal spending. *Psychological Science, 21*, 375–377. (p. 320)

Lefcourt, H. M. (1982). *Locus of control: Current trends in theory and research.* Hillsdale, NJ: Erlbaum. (p. 421)

Lehman, A. F., Steinwachs, D. M., Dixon, L. B., Goldman, H. H., Osher, F., Postrado, L., . . . Zito, J. (1998). Translating research into practice: The schizophrenic patient outcomes research team (PORT) treatment recommendations. *Schizophrenia Bulletin, 24,* 1–10. (p. 594)

Lehman, D. R., Wortman, C. B., & Williams, A. F. (1987). Long-term effects of losing a spouse or child in a motor vehicle crash. *Journal of Personality and Social Psychology, 52,* 218–231. (p. 167)

Leichsenring, F., & Rabung, S. (2008). Effectiveness of long-term psychodynamic psychotherapy: A meta-analysis. *Journal of the American Medical Association, 300,* 1551–1565. (p. 586)

Leitenberg, H., & Henning, K. (1995). Sexual fantasy. *Psychological Bulletin, 117,* 469–496. (pp. 182, 185)

Lemonick, M. D. (2002, June 3). Lean and hungrier. *Time,* p. 54. (p. 379)

L'Engle, M. (1973). *A wind in the door.* New York: Farrar, Straus and Giroux. (p. 15)

Lenhart, A. (2012, March 19). *Teens, smartphones & texting.* Retrieved from http://www.pewinternet.org/2012/03/19/teens-smartphones-texting/ (pp. 174, 373)

Lenhart, A. (2015, April 9). *Teens, social media & technology overview 2015.* Retrieved from http://www.pewinternet.org/2015/04/09/teens-social-media-technology-2015/ (p. 155)

Lenhart, A., & Duggan, M. (2014, February 11). *Couples, the Internet, and social media: How American couples use digital technology to manage life, logistics, and emotional intimacy within their relationships.* Retrieved from http://www.pewinternet.org/2014/02/11/couples-the-internet-and-social-media/ (p. 186)

Lennox, B. R., Bert, S., Park, G., Jones, P. B., & Morris, P. G. (1999). Spatial and temporal mapping of neural activity associated with auditory hallucinations. *The Lancet, 353,* 644. (p. 58)

Lenton, A. P., & Francesconi, M. (2010). How humans cognitively manage an abundance of mate options. *Psychological Science, 21,* 528–533. (p. 477)

Lenzenweger, M. F., Dworkin, R. H., & Wethington, E. (1989). Models of positive and negative symptoms in schizophrenia: An empirical evaluation of latent structures. *Journal of Abnormal Psychology, 98,* 62–70. (p. 594)

Leonhard, C., & Randler, C. (2009). In sync with the family: Children and partners influence the sleep-wake circadian rhythm and social habits of women. *Chronobiology International, 26,* 510–525. (p. 88)

LePort, A. K. R., Mattfeld, A. T., Dickinson-Anson, H., Fallon, J. H., Stark, C. E. L., Kruggel, F., . . . McGaugh, J. L. (2012). Behavioral and neuroanatomical investigation of highly superior autobiographical memory (HSAM). *Neurobiology of Learning and Memory, 98,* 78–92. (p. 301)

Lepping, P., Schönfeldt-Lecuona, C., Sambhi, R. S., Lanka, S. V. N., Lane, S., Whittington, R., . . . Poole, R. (2014). A systematic review of the clinical relevance of repetitive transcranial magnetic stimulation. *Acta Psychiatrica Scandinavica, 130,* 326–341. (p. 599)

Lereya, S. T., Copeland, W. E., Costello, E. J., & Wolke, D. (2015). Adult mental health consequences of peer bullying and maltreatment in childhood: Two cohorts in two countries. *Lancet Psychiatry, 2,* 524–531. (p. 144)

Leslie, M. (2011). Are telomere tests ready for prime time? *Science, 322,* 414–415. (p. 160)

Leucht, S., Barnes, T. R. E., Kissling, W., Engel, R. R., Correll, C., & Kane, J. M. (2003). Relapse prevention in schizophrenia with new-generation antipsychotics: A systematic review and exploratory meta-analysis of randomized, controlled trials. *American Journal of Psychiatry, 160,* 1209–1222. (p. 594)

LeVay, S. (1991). A difference in hypothalamic structure between heterosexual and homosexual men. *Science, 253,* 1034–1037. (p. 190)

LeVay, S. (1994, March). Quoted in D. Nimmons, Sex and the brain. *Discover,* pp. 64–71. (p. 190)

LeVay, S. (2011). *Gay, straight, and the reason why: The science of sexual orientation.* New York: Oxford University Press. (pp. 190, 191)

Levin, R., & Nielsen, T. A. (2007). Disturbed dreaming, posttraumatic stress disorder, and affect distress: A review and neurocognitive model. *Psychological Bulletin, 133,* 482–528. (p. 99)

Levin, R., & Nielsen, T. A. (2009). Nightmares, bad dreams, and emotion dysregulation. *Current Directions in Psychological Science, 18,* 84–87. (p. 99)

Levine, D. (2012, October 18). Treating sleep improves psychiatric symptoms. *Scientific American Mind.* Retrieved from http://www.scientificamerican.com/article/treating-sleep-improves-psychiatric-symptoms/ (p. 98)

Levine, J. A., Lanningham-Foster, L. M., McCrady, S. K., Krizan, A. C., Olson, L. R., Kane, P. H., . . . Clark, M. M. (2005). Interindividual variation in posture allocation: Possible role in human obesity. *Science, 307,* 584–586. (p. 383)

Levine, R. V., & Norenzayan, A. (1999). The pace of life in 31 countries. *Journal of Cross-Cultural Psychology, 30,* 178–205. (p. 20)

Levine, R., Sato, S., Hashimoto, T., & Verma, J. (1995). Love and marriage in eleven cultures. *Journal of Cross-Cultural Psychology, 26,* 554–571. (p. 480)

Levy, P. E. (2003). *Industrial/organizational psychology: Understanding the workplace.* Boston: Houghton Mifflin. (p. B-7)

Lewandowski, G. W., Jr., Aron, A., & Gee, J. (2007). Personality goes a long way: The malleability of opposite-sex physical attractiveness. *Personality Relationships, 14,* 571–585. (p. 478)

Lewinsohn, P. M., Hoberman, H., Teri, L., & Hautziner, M. (1985). An integrative theory of depression. In S. Reiss & R. Bootzin (Eds.), *Theoretical issues in behavior therapy* (pp. 331–359). Orlando, FL: Academic Press. (p. 547)

Lewinsohn, P. M., Petit, J., Joiner, T. E., Jr., & Seeley, J. R. (2003). The symptomatic expression of major depressive disorder in adolescents and young adults. *Journal of Abnormal Psychology, 112,* 244–252. (p. 547)

Lewinsohn, P. M., Rohde, P., & Seeley, J. R. (1998). Major depressive disorder in older adolescents: Prevalence, risk factors, and clinical implications. *Clinical Psychology Review, 18,* 765–794. (p. 547)

Lewinsohn, P. M., & Rosenbaum, M. (1987). Recall of parental behavior by acute depressives, remitted depressives, and nondepressives. *Journal of Personality and Social Psychology, 52,* 611–619. (p. 299)

Lewis, C. S. (1960). *Mere Christianity.* New York: Macmillan. (p. 6)

Lewis, C. S. (1967). *Christian reflections.* Grand Rapids, MI: Eerdmans. (p. 302)

Lewis, D. O., Pincus, J. H., Bard, B., Richardson, E., Prichep, L. S., Feldman, M., & Yeager, C. (1988). Neuropsychiatric, psychoeducational, and family characteristics of 14 juveniles condemned to death in the United States. *American Journal of Psychiatry, 145,* 584–589. (p. 143)

Lewis, D. O., Yeager, C. A., Swica, Y., Pincus, J. H., & Lewis, M. (1997). Objective documentation of child abuse and dissociation in 12 murderers with dissociative identity disorder. *American Journal of Psychiatry, 154,* 1703–1710. (p. 562)

Lewis, M. (1992). Commentary. *Human Development, 35,* 44–51. (p. 299)

Lewontin, R. (1976). Race and intelligence. In N. J. Block & G. Dworkin (Eds.), *The IQ controversy: Critical readings* (pp. 78–92). New York: Pantheon. (p. 359)

Li, J., Laursen, T. M., Precht, D. H., Olsen, J., & Mortensen, P. B. (2005). Hospitalization for mental illness among parents after the death of a child. *New England Journal of Medicine, 352,* 1190–1196. (p. 168)

Li, J. C., Dunning, D., & Malpass, R. L. (1996). *Cross-racial identification among European-Americans basketball fandom and the contact hypothesis.* Unpublished manuscript, Cornell University, Ithaca, NY. (p. 467)

Li, N., & DiCarlo, J. J. (2008). Unsupervised natural experience rapidly alters invariant object representation in visual cortex. *Science, 321,* 1502–1506. (p. 222)

Li, T., & Chan, D. K.-S. (2012). How anxious and avoidant attachment affect romantic relationship quality differently: A meta-analytic review. *European Journal of Social Psychology, 42,* 406–419. (p. 142)

Li, Y., Johnson, E. J., & Zaval, L. (2011). Local warming: Daily temperature change influences belief in global warming. *Psychological Science, 22,* 454–459. (p. 320)

Li, Z. H., Jiang, D., Pepler, D., & Craig, W. (2010). Adolescent romantic relationships in China and Canada: A cross-national comparison. *Internal Journal of Behavioral Development, 34,* 113–120. (p. 153)

Liang, K. Y., Mintun, M. A., Fagan, A. M., Goate, A. M., Bugg, J. M., Holtzman, D. M., . . . Head, D. (2010). Exercise and Alzheimer's disease biomarkers in cognitively normal older adults. *Annals of Neurology, 68,* 311–318. (p. 160)

Libertus, M. E., & Brannon, E. M. (2009). Behavioral and neural basis of number sense in infancy. *Current Directions in Psychological Science, 18,* 346–351. (p. 131)

Licata, A., Taylor, S., Berman, M., & Cranston, J. (1993). Effects of cocaine on human aggression. *Pharmacology Biochemistry and Behavior, 45,* 549–552. (p. 110)

Lichtenstein, P., Calström, E., Råstam, M., Gillberg, C., & Anckarsäter, H. (2010). The genetics of autism spectrum disorders and related neuropsychiatric disorders in childhood. *American Journal of Psychiatry, 167,* 1357–1363. (pp. 109, 136)

Lick, D. J., Durso, L. E., & Johnson, K. L. (2013). Minority stress and physical health among sexual minorities. *Perspectives on Psychological Science, 8,* 521–548. (p. 409)

Liddle, J. R., Shackelford, T. K., & Weekes-Shackelford, V. W. (2012). Why can't we all just get along? Evolutionary perspectives on violence, homicide, and war. *Review of General Psychology, 16,* 24–36. (p. 173)

Lieberman, M. D., Eisenberger, N. L., Crockett, M. J., Tom, S. M., Pfeifer, J. H., & Way, B. M. (2007). Putting feelings into words: Affect labeling disrupts amygdala activity in response to affective stimuli. *Psychological Science, 18*, 421–428. (p. 425)

Lievens, F., Dilchert, S., & Ones, D. S. (2009). The importance of exercise and dimension factors in assessment centers: Simultaneous examinations of construct-related and criterion-related validity. *Human Performance, 22*, 375–390. (p. 515)

Lilienfeld, S. O. (2009, Winter). Tips for spotting psychological pseudoscience: A student-friendly guide. *Eye on Psi Chi*, pp. 23–26. (p. 241)

Lilienfeld, S. O., & Arkowitz, H. (2006, December/2007, January). Taking a closer look: Can moving your eyes back and forth help to ease anxiety? *Scientific American Mind*, pp. 80–81. (p. 588)

Lilienfeld, S. O., & Byron, R. (2013, January). Your brain on trial. *Scientific American Mind*, pp. 44–53. (p. 309)

Lilienfeld, S. O., Lynn, S. J., Kirsch, I., Chaves, J. F., Sarbin, T. R., Ganaway, G. K., & Powell, R. A. (1999). Dissociative identity disorder and the sociocognitive model: Recalling the lessons of the past. *Psychological Bulletin, 125*, 507–523. (p. 562)

Lilienfeld, S. O., Marshall, J., Todd, J. T., & Shane, H. C. (2014). The persistence of fad interventions in the face of negative scientific evidence: Facilitated communication for autism as a case example. *Evidence-Based Communication and Assessment, 8*, 62–101. (p. 136)

Lilienfeld, S. O., Ritschel, L. A., Lynn, S. J., Cautin, R. L., & Latzman, R. D. (2013). Why many clinical psychologists are resistant to evidence-based practice: Root causes and constructive remedies. *Clinical Psychology Review, 33*, 883–900. (p. 587)

Lilienfeld, S. O., Ritschel, L. A., Lynn, S. J., Cautin, R. L., & Latzman, R. D. (2014). Why ineffective psychotherapies appear to work: A taxonomy of causes of spurious therapeutic effectiveness. *Perspectives on Psychological Science, 9*, 355–387. (p. 584)

Lilienfeld, S. O., Waldman, I. D., Landfield, K., Watts, A. L., Rubenzer, S., & Fashing-bauer, T. R. (2012). Fearless dominance and the U.S. presidency: Implications of psychopathic personality traits for successful and unsuccessful political leadership. *Journal of Personality and Social Psychology, 103*, 489–505. (p. 564)

Lim, J., & Dinges, D. F. (2010). A meta-analysis of the impact of short-term sleep deprivation on cognitive variables. *Psychological Bulletin, 136*, 375–389. (p. 95)

Lima, N., Nascimento, V., Peixoto, J. A. C., Moreira, M. M., Neto, M. L. R., Almeida, J. C., . . . Reis, A. O. A. (2013). Electroconvulsive therapy use in adolescents: A systematic review. *Annals of General Psychiatry, 12*, 17. http://www.annals-general-psychiatry.com/content/12/1/17 (p. 598)

Lin, Z., & Murray, S. O. (2015). More power to the unconscious: Conscious, but not unconscious, exogenous attention requires location variation. *Psychological Science, 26*, 221–230. (p. 324)

Lindberg, S. M., Hyde, J. S., Linn, M. C., & Petersen, J. L. (2010). New trends in gender and mathematics performance: A meta-analysis. *Psychological Bulletin, 136*, 1125–1135. (p. 357)

Linder, D. (1982). Social trap analogs: The tragedy of the commons in the laboratory. In V. J. Derlega & J. Grzelak (Eds.), *Cooperative and helping behavior: Theories and research* (pp. 183–205). New York: Academic Press. (p. 485)

Lindner, I., Echterhoff, G., Davidson, P. S. R., & Brand, M. (2010). Observation inflation: Your actions become mine. *Psychological Science, 21*, 1291–1299. (p. 274)

Lindskold, S. (1978). Trust development, the GRIT proposal, and the effects of conciliatory acts on conflict and cooperation. *Psychological Bulletin, 85*, 772–793. (p. 488)

Lindskold, S., & Han, G. (1988). GRIT as a foundation for integrative bargaining. *Personality and Social Psychology Bulletin, 14*, 335–345. (p. 488)

Lindson, N., Aveyard, P., & Hughes, J. R. (2010). Reduction versus abrupt cessation in smokers who want to quit. *Cochrane Database of Systematic Reviews 2010*, Issue 3, Article CD008033. doi:10.1002/14651858.CD008033.pub2 (p. 109)

Linehan, M. M., Korslund, K. E., Harned, M. S., Gallop, R. J., Lungu, A., Neacsiu, A. D., . . . Murray-Gregory, A. M. (2015). Dialectical behavior therapy for high suicide risk in individuals with borderline personality disorder: A randomized clinical trial and component analysis. *JAMA Psychiatry, 72*, 475–482. (p. 581)

Lionel, A. C., Tammimies, K., Vaags, A. K., Rosenfeld, J. A., Ahn, J. W., Merico, D., . . . Scherer, S. W. (2014). Disruption of the *ASTN2/TRIM32* locus at 9q33.1 is a risk factor in males for autism spectrum disorders, ADHD and other neurodevelopmental phenotypes. *Human Molecular Genetics, 23*, 2752–2768. (p. 532)

Lippa, R. A. (2007). The relation between sex drive and sexual attraction to men and women: A cross-national study of heterosexual, bisexual, and homosexual men and women. *Archives of Sexual Behavior, 36*, 209–222. (p. 477)

Lippa, R. A. (2008). Sex differences and sexual orientation differences in personality: Findings from the BBC Internet survey. *Archives of Sexual Behavior, 37*, 173–187. (p. 193)

Lippa, R. A. (2009). Sex differences in sex drive, sociosexuality, and height across 53 nations: Testing evolutionary and social structural theories. *Archives of Sexual Behavior, 38*, 631–651. (p. 193)

Lippa, R. A. (2013). Men and women with bisexual identities show bisexual patterns of sexual attraction to male and female "swimsuit models." *Archives of Sexual Behavior, 42*, 187–196. (p. 188)

Lipsitt, L. P. (2003). Crib death: A biobehavioral phenomenon? *Current Directions in Psychological Science, 12*, 164–170. (p. 129)

Liu, S., Huang, J. L., & Wang, M. (2014). Effectiveness of job search interventions: A meta-analytic review. *Psychological Bulletin, 140*, 1009–1041. (p. B-3)

Liu, Y., Balaraman, Y., Wang, G., Nephew, K. P., & Zhou, F. C. (2009). Alcohol exposure alters DNA methylation profiles in mouse embryos at early neurulation. *Epigenetics, 4*, 500–511. (p. 124)

Livingston, G., & Parker, K. (2011, June 15). *A tale of two fathers: More are active, but more are absent*. Retrieved from http://www.pewsocialtrends.org/2011/06/15/a-tale-of-two-fathers/ (p. 141)

Livingstone, M., & Hubel, D. (1988). Segregation of form, color, movement, and depth: Anatomy, physiology, and perception. *Science, 240*, 740–749. (p. 216)

Locke, A. E., Kahali, B., Berndt, S. I., Justice, A. E., Pers, T. H., Day, F. R., . . . Speliotes, E. K. (2015). Genetic studies of body mass index yield new insights for obesity biology. *Nature, 518*, 195–206. (p. 383)

Loehlin, J. C. (2012). The differential heritability of personality item clusters. *Behavior Genetics, 42*, 500–507. (p. 68)

Loehlin, J. C., Horn, J. M., & Ernst, J. L. (2007). Genetic and environmental influences on adult life outcomes: Evidence from the Texas Adoption Project. *Behavior Genetics, 37*, 463–476. (p. 70)

Loehlin, J. C., & Nichols, R. C. (1976). *Heredity, environment, and personality*. Austin: University of Texas Press. (p. 68)

Loftus, E. (2011, May/June). We live in perilous times for science. *Skeptical Inquirer*, p. 13. (p. 311)

Loftus, E. F. (2012, July). *Manufacturing memories*. Address at the 27th International Congress of Psychology, Cape Town, South Africa. (p. 306)

Loftus, E. F., & Ketcham, K. (1994). *The myth of repressed memory: False memories and allegations of sexual abuse*. New York: St. Martin's Press. (p. 292)

Loftus, E. F., Levidow, B., & Duensing, S. (1992). Who remembers best? Individual differences in memory for events that occurred in a science museum. *Applied Cognitive Psychology, 6*, 93–107. (p. 307)

Loftus, E. F., & Loftus, G. R. (1980). On the permanence of stored information in the human brain. *American Psychologist, 35*, 409–420. (p. 292)

Loftus, E. F., & Palmer, J. C. (1974). Reconstruction of automobile destruction: An example of the interaction between language and memory. *Journal of Verbal Learning and Verbal Behavior, 13*, 585–589. (p. 307)

Logan, T. K., Walker, R., Cole, J., & Leukefeld, C. (2002). Victimization and substance abuse among women: Contributing factors, interventions, and implications. *Review of General Psychology, 6*, 325–397. (p. 115)

Logue, A. W. (1998a). Laboratory research on self-control: Applications to administration. *Review of General Psychology, 2*, 221–238. (p. 259)

Logue, A. W. (1998b). Self-control. In W. T. O'Donohue (Ed.), *Learning and behavior therapy* (pp. 252–273). Boston: Allyn & Bacon. (p. 259)

London, P. (1970). The rescuers: Motivational hypotheses about Christians who saved Jews from the Nazis. In J. Macaulay & L. Berkowitz (Eds.), *Altruism and helping behavior* (pp. 241–250). New York: Academic Press. (p. 276)

Lonergan, M. H., Olivera-Figueroa, L., Pitman, R. K., & Brunet, A. (2013). Propranolol's effects on the consolidation and reconsolidation of long-term emotional memory in healthy participants: A meta-analysis. *Journal of Psychiatry & Neuroscience, 38*, 222–231. (p. 307)

Lopes, P. N., Brackett, M. A., Nezlek, J. B., Schutz, A., Sellin, I. I., & Salovey, P. (2004). Emotional intelligence and social interaction. *Personality and Social Psychology Bulletin, 30*, 1018–1034. (p. 345)

Lord, C. G., Lepper, M. R., & Preston, E. (1984). Considering the opposite: A corrective strategy for social judgment. *Journal of Personality and Social Psychology, 47*, 1231–1247. (p. 322)

Lord, C. G., Ross, L., & Lepper, M. (1979). Biased assimilation and attitude polarization: The effects of prior theories on subsequently considered evidence. *Journal of Personality and Social Psychology, 37*, 2098–2109. (p. 322)

Lorenz, K. (1937). The companion in the bird's world. *Auk, 54*, 245–273. (p. 139)

Louie, K., & Wilson, M. A. (2001). Temporally structured replay of awake hippocampal ensemble activity during rapid eye movement sleep. *Neuron, 29,* 145–156. (p. 100)

Lourenco, O., & Machado, A. (1996). In defense of Piaget's theory: A reply to 10 common criticisms. *Psychological Review, 103,* 143–164. (p. 135)

Lovaas, O. I. (1987). Behavioral treatment and normal educational and intellectual functioning in young autistic children. *Journal of Consulting and Clinical Psychology, 55,* 3–9. (p. 577)

Low, P. (2012, July 7). *The Cambridge Declaration on Consciousness.* Publicly proclaimed at the Francis Crick Memorial Conference on Consciousness in Human and non-Human Animals, Churchill College, University of Cambridge, Cambridge, England, and currently available at http://www.all-creatures.org/articles/ar-conscious.pdf (p. 326)

Lowry, P. E. (1997). The assessment center process: New directions. *Journal of Social Behavior and Personality, 12,* 53–62. (p. 515)

Lozano, A. M., & Mayberg, H. S. (2015, February). Treating depression at the source. *Scientific American,* pp. 68–73. (p. 599)

Lu, Z.-L., Williamson, S. J., & Kaufman, L. (1992). Behavioral lifetime of human auditory sensory memory predicted by physiological measures. *Science, 258,* 1668–1670. (p. 286)

Lubinski, D. (2009). Cognitive epidemiology: With emphasis on untangling cognitive ability and socioeconomic status. *Intelligence, 37,* 625–633. (p. 352)

Lubinski, D., Benbow, C. P., & Kell, H. J. (2014). Life paths and accomplishments of mathematically precocious males and females four decades later. *Psychological Science, 25,* 2217–2232. (p. 352)

Luborsky, L., Rosenthal, R., Diguer, L., Andrusyna, T. P., Berman, J. S., Levitt, J. T., . . . Krause, E. D. (2002). The dodo bird verdict is alive and well—mostly. *Clinical Psychology: Science and Practice, 9,* 2–34. (p. 586)

Lucas, A., Morley, R., Cole, T. J., Lister, G., & Leeson-Payne, C. (1992). Breast milk and subsequent intelligence quotient in children born preterm. *The Lancet, 339,* 261–264. (p. 24)

Lucas, R. E. (2008). Personality and subjective well-being. In M. Eid & R. Larsen (Eds.), *The science of subjective well-being* (pp. 171–194). New York: Guilford Press. (p. 436)

Lucas, R. E., Clark, A. E., Georgellis, Y., & Diener, E. (2004). Unemployment alters the set point for life satisfaction. *Psychological Science, 15,* 8–13. (p. 436)

Lucas, R. E., & Donnellan, M. B. (2007). How stable is happiness? Using the STARTS model to estimate the stability of life satisfaction. *Journal of Research in Personality, 41,* 1091–1098. (p. 436)

Lucas, R. E., & Donnellan, M. B. (2009). Age differences in personality: Evidence from a nationally representative Australian sample. *Developmental Psychology, 45,* 1353–1363. (p. 122)

Lucas, R. E., & Donnellan, M. B. (2011). Personality development across the life span: Longitudinal analyses with a national sample from Germany. *Journal of Personality and Social Psychology, 101,* 847–861. (p. 122)

Lucero, S. M., Kusner, K. G., & Speace, E. A. (2008, May). *Religiousness and adolescent sexual behavior: A meta-analytic review.* Paper presented at the 20th Annual Convention of the Association for Psychological Science, Chicago, IL. (p. 187)

Ludwig, A. M. (1995). *The price of greatness: Resolving the creativity and madness controversy.* New York: Guilford Press. (p. 547)

Ludwig, D. S., & Friedman, M. I. (2014). Increasing adiposity: Consequence or cause of overeating? *Journal of the American Medical Association, 311,* 2167–2168. (p. 379)

Luhmann, M., Hofmann, W., Eid, M., & Lucas, R. E. (2012). Subjective well-being and adaptation to life events: A meta-analysis. *Journal of Personality and Social Psychology, 102,* 592–615. (p. 433)

Luigjes, J., van den Brin, W., Feenstra, M., van den Munckhof, P., Schuurman, P. R., Schippers, R., . . . Denys, D. (2012). Deep brain stimulation in addiction: A review of potential brain targets. *Molecular Psychiatry, 17,* 572–583. (p. 599)

Lumeng, J. C., Forrest, P., Appugliese, D. P., Kaciroti, N., Corwyn, R. F., & Bradley, R. H. (2010). Weight status as a predictor of being bullied in third through sixth grades. *Pediatrics, 125,* e1301–e1307. doi:10.1542/peds.2009-0774 (p. 382)

Lund, T. J., & Dearing, E. (2012). Is growing up affluent risky for adolescents or is the problem growing up in an affluent neighborhood? *Journal of Research on Adolescence, 23,* 274–282. (p. 143)

Luppino, F. S., de Wit, L. M., Bouvy, P. F., Stijnen, T., Cuijpers, P., Penninx, W. J. H., & Zitman, F. G. (2010). Overweight, obesity, and depression. *Archives of General Psychiatry, 67,* 220–229. (p. 382)

Luria, A. R. (1968). *The mind of a mnemonist* (L. Solotaroff, Trans.). New York: Basic Books. (p. 282)

Lustig, C., & Buckner, R. L. (2004). Preserved neural correlates of priming in old age and dementia. *Neuron, 42,* 865–875. (p. 302)

Lutfey, K. E., Link, C. L., Rosen, R. C., Wiegel, M., & McKinlay, J. B. (2009). Prevalence and correlates of sexual activity and function in women: Results from the Boston Area Community Health (BACH) Survey. *Archives of Sexual Behavior, 38,* 514–527. (p. 183)

Lutgendorf, S. K., & Andersen, B. L. (2015). Biobehavioral approaches to cancer progression and survival. *American Psychologist, 70,* 186–197. (p. 413)

Lutgendorf, S. K., Lamkin, D. M., Jennings, N. B., Arevalo, J. M. G., Penedo, F., DeGeest, K., . . . Sood, A. K. (2008). Biobehavioral influences on matrix metalloproteinase expression in ovarian carcinoma. *Clinical Cancer Research, 14,* 6839–6846. (p. 413)

Lutgendorf, S. K., Russell, D., Ullrich, P., Harris, T. B., & Wallace, R. (2004). Religious participation, interleukin-6, and mortality in older adults. *Health Psychology, 23,* 465–475. (p. 431)

Luthar, S. S., Barkin, S. H., & Crossman, E. J. (2013). "I can, therefore I must": Fragility in the upper-middle classes. *Development and Psychopathology, 25,* 1529–1549. (p. 143)

Lyall, S. (2005, November 29). What's the buzz? Rowdy teenagers don't want to hear it. *The New York Times.* Retrieved from http://www.nytimes.com/2005/11/29/world/europe/whats-the-buzz-rowdy-teenagers-dont-want-to-hear-it.html (p. 159)

Lykes, V. A., & Kemmelmeier, M. (2014). What predicts loneliness? Cultural difference between individualistic and collectivistic societies in Europe. *Journal of Cross-Cultural Psychology, 45,* 468–490. (p. 9)

Lykken, D. T. (1991, August). *Science, lies, and controversy: An epitaph for the polygraph.* Invited address at the 99th Annual Convention of the American Psychological Association, San Francisco, CA. (p. 394)

Lykken, D. T. (1995). *The antisocial personalities.* Hillsdale, NJ: Erlbaum. (pp. 533, 564)

Lykken, D. T. (1999). *Happiness: The nature and nurture of joy and contentment.* New York: Golden Books. (p. 354)

Lykken, D. T., & Tellegen, A. (1996). Happiness is a stochastic phenomenon. *Psychological Science, 7,* 186–189. (p. 436)

Lynch, G. (2002). Memory enhancement: The search for mechanism-based drugs. *Nature Neuroscience, 5*(Suppl.), 1035–1038. (p. 295)

Lynch, G., & Staubli, U. (1991). Possible contributions of long-term potentiation to the encoding and organization of memory. *Brain Research Reviews, 16,* 204–206. (p. 295)

Lynn, M. (1988). The effects of alcohol consumption on restaurant tipping. *Personality and Social Psychology Bulletin, 14,* 87–91. (p. 106)

Lynn, S. J., Laurence, J., & Kirsch, I. (2015). Hypnosis, suggestion, and suggestibility: An integrative model. *American Journal of Clinical Hypnosis, 57,* 314–329. (p. 235)

Lynn, S. J., Lilienfeld, S. O., Merckelbach, H., Giesbrecht, T., McNally, R. J., Loftus, E. F., . . . Malaktaris, A. (2014). The trauma model of dissociation: Inconvenient truths and stubborn fictions. Comment on Dalenberg et al. (2012). *Psychological Bulletin, 140,* 896–910. (p. 562)

Lynn, S. J., Rhue, J. W., & Weekes, J. R. (1990). Hypnotic involuntariness: A social cognitive analysis. *Psychological Review, 97,* 169–184. (p. 235)

Lynne, S. D., Graber, J. A., Nichols, T. R., Brooks-Gunn, J., & Botvin, G. J. (2007). Links between pubertal timing, peer influences, and externalizing behaviors among urban students followed through middle school. *Journal of Adolescent Health, 40,* 181.e7–181.e13. http://dx.doi.org/10.1016/j.jadohealth.2006.09.008 (p. 148)

Lyons, B. D., Hoffman, B. J., Michel, J. W., & Williams, K. J. (2011). On the predictive efficiency of past performance and physical ability: The case of the National Football League. *Human Performance, 24,* 158–172. (p. 515)

Lyons, D. E., Young, A. G., & Keil, F. C. (2007). The hidden structure of overimitation. *Proceedings of the National Academy of Sciences of the United States of America, 104,* 19751–19756. (p. 274)

Lyons, L. (2004, February 3). *Growing up lonely: Examining teen alienation.* Retrieved from http://www.gallup.com/poll/10465/growing-lonely-examining-teen-alienation.aspx (p. 153)

Lyons, L. (2005, January 4). *Teens stay true to parents' political perspectives.* Retrieved from http://www.gallup.com/poll/14515/teens-stay-true-parents-political-perspectives.aspx (p. 156)

Lyubomirsky, S. (2001). Why are some people happier than others? The role of cognitive and motivational processes in well-being. *American Psychologist, 56,* 239–249. (p. 435)

Lyubomirsky, S. (2008). The how of happiness: A scientific approach to getting the life you want. New York: Penguin. (p. 422)

Lyubomirsky, S., Sousa, L., & Dickerhoof, R. (2006). The costs and benefits of writing, talking, and thinking about life's triumphs and defeats. *Journal of Personality and Social Psychology, 90,* 690–708. (p. 425)

M

Ma, D. S., Correll, J., Wittenbrink, B., Bar-Anan, Y., Sriram, N., & Nosek, B. A. (2013). When fatigue turns deadly: The association between fatigue and racial bias in the decision to shoot. *Basic and Applied Social Psychology, 35,* 515–524. (p. 463)

Ma, L. (1997, September). On the origin of Darwin's ills. *Discover,* p. 27. (p. 538)

Maas, J. B. (1999). *Power sleep: The revolutionary program that prepares your mind and body for peak performance.* New York: HarperCollins. (p. 95)

Maas, J. B., & Robbins, R. S. (2010). *Sleep for success: Everything you must know about sleep but are too tired to ask.* Bloomington, IN: Author House. (p. 93)

Maass, A., D'Ettole, C., & Cadinu, M. (2008). Checkmate? The role of gender stereotypes in the ultimate intellectual sport. *European Journal of Social Psychology, 38,* 231–245. (p. 361)

Macaluso, E., Frith, C. D., & Driver, J. (2000). Modulation of human visual cortex by crossmodal spatial attention. *Science, 289,* 1206–1208. (p. 239)

Macan, T. H., & Dipboye, R. L. (1994). The effects of the application on processing of information from the employment interview. *Journal of Applied Social Psychology, 24,* 1291–1314. (p. B-5)

MacCabe, J. H., Lambe, M. P., Cnattingius, S., Torrång, A., Björk, C., Sham, P. C., . . . Hultman, C. M. (2008). Scholastic achievement at age 16 and risk of schizophrenia and other psychoses: A national cohort study. *Psychological Medicine, 38,* 1133–1140. (p. 557)

Maccoby, E. E. (1990). Gender and relationships: A developmental account. *American Psychologist, 45,* 513–520. (p. 174)

Maccoby, E. E. (1998). *The two sexes: Growing up apart, coming together.* Cambridge, MA: Belknap Press. (p. 174)

Maccoby, E. E. (2002). Gender and group process: A developmental perspective. *Current Directions in Psychological Science, 11,* 54–58. (p. 458)

MacDonald, G., & Leary, M. R. (2005). Why does social exclusion hurt? The relationship between social and physical pain. *Psychological Bulletin, 131,* 202–223. (p. 372)

MacDonald, N. (1960). Living with schizophrenia. *Canadian Medical Association Journal, 82,* 218–221. (p. 557)

MacDonald, T. K., & Hynie, M. (2008). Ambivalence and unprotected sex: Failure to predict sexual activity and decreased condom use. *Journal of Applied Social Psychology, 38,* 1092–1107. (p. 186)

MacDonald, T. K., Zanna, M. P., & Fong, G. T. (1995). Decision making in altered states: Effects of alcohol on attitudes toward drinking and driving. *Journal of Personality and Social Psychology, 68,* 973–985. (p. 106)

MacFarlane, A. (1978, February). What a baby knows. *Human Nature,* pp. 74–81. (p. 125)

Macfarlane, J. W. (1964). Perspectives on personality consistency and change from the guidance study. *Vita Humana, 7,* 115–126. (p. 147)

MacInnis, C. C., & Hodson, G. (2015). Do American states with more religious or conservative populations search more for sexual content on Google? *Archives of Sexual Behavior, 44,* 137–147. (p. 188)

Mack, A., & Rock, I. (2000). *Inattentional blindness.* Cambridge, MA: MIT Press. (p. 83)

MacKenzie, M. J., Nicklas, E., Waldfogel, J., & Brooks-Gunn, J. (2013). Spanking and child development across the first decade of life. *Pediatrics, 132,* e1118–e1125. doi:10.1542/peds.2013-1227 (p. 262)

MacKerron, G., & Mourato, S. (2013). Happiness is greater in natural environments. *Global Environmental Change, 23,* 992–1000. (p. 600)

MacLeod, C., & Clarke, P. J. F. (2015). The attentional bias modification approach to anxiety intervention. *Clinical Psychological Science, 3,* 58–78. (p. 578)

Macmillan, M., & Lena, M. L. (2010). Rehabilitating Phineas Gage. *Neuropsychological Rehabilitation, 17,* 1–18. (p. 60)

Macnamara, B. N., Hambrick, D. Z., & Oswald, F. L. (2014). Deliberate practice and performance in music, games, sports, education, and professions: A meta-analysis. *Psychological Science, 25,* 1608–1618. (p. 376)

MacNeilage, P. F., & Davis, B. L. (2000). On the origin of internal structure of word forms. *Science, 288,* 527–531. (p. 331)

MacNeilage, P. F., Rogers, L. J., & Vallortigara, G. (2009, July). Origins of the left and right brain. *Scientific American,* pp. 60–67. (p. 64)

Maddi, S. R., Harvey, R. H., Khoshaba, D. M., Fazel, M., & Resurreccion, N. (2009). Hardiness training facilitates performance in college. *Journal of Positive Psychology, 4,* 566–577. (p. 376)

Maeda, Y., & Yoon, S. Y. (2013). A meta-analysis on gender differences in mental rotation ability measured by the Purdue Spatial Visualization Tests: Visualization of Rotations (PSVT:R). *Educational Psychology Review, 25,* 69–94. (p. 357)

Maes, H. H. M., Neale, M. C., & Eaves, L. J. (1997). Genetic and environmental factors in relative body weight and human adiposity. *Behavior Genetics, 27,* 325–351. (p. 383)

Maestripieri, D. (2003). Similarities in affiliation and aggression between crossfostered rhesus macaque females and their biological mothers. *Developmental Psychobiology, 43,* 321–327. (p. 70)

Maestripieri, D. (2005). Early experience affects the intergenerational transmission of infant abuse in rhesus monkeys. *Proceedings of the National Academy of Sciences of the United States of America, 102,* 9726–9729. (p. 143)

Magnusson, D. (1990). Personality research—Challenges for the future. *European Journal of Personality, 4,* 1–17. (p. 564)

Maguire, E. A., Gadian, D. G., Johnsrude, I. S., Good, C. D., Ashburner, J., Frackowiak, R. S. J., & Frith, C. D. (2000). Navigation-related structural change in the hippocampi of taxi drivers. *Proceedings of the National Academy of Sciences of the United States of America, 97,* 4398–4403. (p. 128)

Maguire, E. A., Spiers, H. J., Good, C. D., Hartley, T., Frackowiak, R. S. J., & Burgess, N. (2003). Navigation expertise and the human hippocampus: A structural brain imaging analysis. *Hippocampus, 13,* 250–259. (p. 293)

Maguire, E. A., Valentine, E. R., Wilding, J. M., & Kapur, N. (2003). Routes to remembering: The brains behind superior memory. *Nature Neuroscience, 6,* 90–95. (p. 288)

Maher, S., Ekstrom, T., & Chen, Y. (2014). Greater perceptual sensitivity to happy facial expression. *Perception, 43,* 1353–1364. (p. 396)

Mahowald, M. W., & Ettinger, M. G. (1990). Things that go bump in the night: The parasomnias revisited. *Journal of Clinical Neurophysiology, 7,* 119–143. (p. 98)

Maier, S. F., Watkins, L. R., & Fleshner, M. (1994). Psychoneuroimmunology: The interface between behavior, brain, and immunity. *American Psychologist, 49,* 1004–1017. (p. 411)

Major, B., Carrington, P. I., & Carnevale, P. J. D. (1984). Physical attractiveness and self-esteem: Attribution for praise from an other-sex evaluator. *Personality and Social Psychology Bulletin, 10,* 43–50. (p. 477)

Major, B., Schmidlin, A. M., & Williams, L. (1990). Gender patterns in social touch: The impact of setting and age. *Journal of Personality and Social Psychology, 58,* 634–643. (p. 173)

Malamuth, N. M. (1996). Sexually explicit media, gender differences, and evolutionary theory. *Journal of Communication, 46,* 8–31. (p. 472)

Malamuth, N. M., & Check, J. V. P. (1981). The effects of media exposure on acceptance of violence against women: A field experiment. *Journal of Research in Personality, 15,* 436–446. (p. 185)

Maldonado-Molina, M. M., Reingle, J. M., Jennings, W. G., & Prado, G. (2011). Drinking and driving among immigrant and US-born Hispanic young adults: Results from a longitudinal and nationally representative study. *Addictive Behaviors, 36,* 381–388. (p. 534)

Malkiel, B. G. (2012). *A random walk down Wall Street: The time-tested strategy for successful investing* (10th ed.). New York: Norton. (p. 322)

Malle, B. F. (2006). The actor–observer asymmetry in attribution: A (surprising) meta-analysis. *Psychological Bulletin, 132,* 895–919. (p. 443)

Malle, B. F., Knobe, J. M., & Nelson, S. E. (2007). Actor–observer asymmetries in explanations of behavior: New answers to an old question. *Journal of Personality and Social Psychology, 93,* 491–514. (p. 443)

Malmquist, C. P. (1986). Children who witness parental murder: Post-traumatic aspects. *Journal of the American Academy of Child Psychiatry, 25,* 320–325. (p. 499)

Maltby, N., Tolin, D. F., Worhunsky, P., O'Keefe, T. M., & Kiehl, K. A. (2005). Dysfunctional action monitoring hyperactivates frontal-striatal circuits in obsessive-compulsive disorder: An event-related fMRI study. *NeuroImage, 24,* 495–503. (p. 543)

Mampe, B., Friederici, A. D., Christophe, A., & Wermke, K. (2009). Newborns' cry melody is shaped by their native language. *Current Biology, 19,* 1–4. (p. 124)

Maner, J. K., DeWall, C. N, Baumeister, R. F., & Schaller, M. (2007). Does social exclusion motivate interpersonal reconnection? Resolving the "porcupine problem." *Journal of Personality and Social Psychology, 92*, 42–55. (p. 372)

Maner, J. K., Kenrick, D. T., Neuberg, S. L., Becker, D. V., Robertson, T., Hofer, B., . . . Schaller, M. (2005). Functional projection: How fundamental social motives can bias interpersonal perception. *Journal of Personality and Social Psychology, 88*, 63–78. (p. 500)

Manning, W., & Cohen, J. A. (2012). Premarital cohabitation and marital dissolution: An examination of recent marriages. *Journal of Marriage and Family 74*, 377–387. (p. 164)

Manson, J. E. (2002). Walking compared with vigorous exercise for the prevention of cardiovascular events in women. *New England Journal of Medicine, 347*, 716–725. (p. 426)

Maquet, P. (2001). The role of sleep in learning and memory. *Science, 294*, 1048–1052. (p. 100)

Maquet, P., Peters, J.-M., Aerts, J., Delfiore, G., Degueldre, C., Luxen, A., & Franck, G. (1996). Functional neuroanatomy of human rapid-eye-movement sleep and dreaming. *Nature, 383*, 163–166. (p. 101)

Mar, R. A., & Oatley, K. (2008). The function of fiction is the abstraction and simulation of social experience. *Perspectives on Psychological Science, 3*, 173–192. (p. 274)

Mar, R. A., Oatley, K., & Peterson, J. B. (2009). Exploring the link between reading fiction and empathy: Ruling out individual differences and examining outcomes. *Communications, 34*, 407–428. (p. 398)

Margolis, M. L. (2000). Brahms' lullaby revisited: Did the composer have obstructive sleep apnea? *Chest, 118*, 210–213. (p. 97)

Marinak, B. A., & Gambrell, L. B. (2008). Intrinsic motivation and rewards: What sustains young children's engagement with text? *Literacy Research and Instruction, 47*, 9–26. (p. 271)

Marjonen, H., Sierra, A., Nyman, A., Rogojin, V., Gröhn, Ol, Linden, A.-M., . . . Kaminen-Ahola, N. (2015). Early maternal alcohol consumption alters hippocampal DNA methylation, gene expression and volume in a mouse model. *PLOS ONE, 10*(5), e0124931. doi:10.1371/journal.pone.0124931 (p. 124)

Markovizky, G., & Samid, Y. (2008). The process of immigrant adjustment: The role of time in determining psychological adjustment. *Journal of Cross-Cultural Psychology, 39*, 782–798. (p. 407)

Markowitsch, H. J. (1995). Which brain regions are critically involved in the retrieval of old episodic memory? *Brain Research Reviews, 21*, 117–127. (p. 292)

Markus, G. B. (1986). Stability and change in political attitudes: Observe, recall, and "explain." *Political Behavior, 8*, 21–44. (p. 309)

Markus, H. R., & Kitayama, S. (1991). Culture and the self: Implications for cognition, emotion, and motivation. *Psychological Review, 98*, 224–253. (pp. 336, 416, 521)

Markus, H. R., & Nurius, P. (1986). Possible selves. *American Psychologist, 41*, 954–969. (p. 516)

Marley, J., & Bulia, S. (2001). Crimes against people with mental illness: Types, perpetrators and influencing factors. *Social Work, 46*, 115–124. (p. 533)

Marmot, M. G., Bosma, H., Hemingway, H., Brunner, E., & Stansfeld, S. (1997). Contribution to job control and other risk factors to social variations in coronary heart disease incidents. *The Lancet, 350*, 235–239. (p. 420)

Marsh, A. A., Elfenbein, H. A., & Ambady, N. (2003). Nonverbal "accents": Cultural differences in facial expressions of emotion. *Psychological Science, 14*, 373–376. (p. 399)

Marsh, H. W., & Craven, R. G. (2006). Reciprocal effects of self-concept and performance from a multidimensional perspective: Beyond seductive pleasure and unidimensional perspectives. *Perspectives on Psychological Science, 1*, 133–163. (p. 517)

Marsh, H. W., & Parker, J. W. (1984). Determinants of student self-concept: Is it better to be a relatively large fish in a small pond even if you don't learn to swim as well? *Journal of Personality and Social Psychology, 47*, 213–231. (p. 435)

Marshall, M. J. (2002). *Why spanking doesn't work.* Springville, UT: Bonneville Books. (p. 261)

Marshall, P. J., & Meltzoff, A. N. (2014). Neural mirroring mechanisms and imitation in human infants. *Philosophical Transactions of the Royal Society: Series B, 369*(1644). doi:10.1098/rstb.2013.0620 (p. 274)

Marshall, R. D., Bryant, R. A., Amsel, L., Suh, E. J., Cook, J. M., & Neria, Y. (2007). The psychology of ongoing threat: Relative risk appraisal, the September 11 attacks, and terrorism-related fears. *American Psychologist, 62*, 304–316. (p. 319)

Marteau, T. M. (1989). Framing of information: Its influences upon decisions of doctors and patients. *British Journal of Social Psychology, 28*, 89–94. (p. 322)

Marti, M. W., Robier, D. M., & Baron, R. S. (2000). Right before our eyes: The failure to recognize non-prototypical forms of prejudice. *Group Processes & Intergroup Relations, 3*, 403–418. (p. 316)

Martin, C. K., Anton, S. D., Walden, H., Arnett, C., Greenway, F. L., & Williamson, D. A. (2007). Slower eating rate reduces the food intake of men, but not women: Implications for behavioural weight control. *Behaviour Research and Therapy, 45*, 2349–2359. (p. 385)

Martin, C. L., & Ruble, D. (2004). Children's search for gender cues. *Current Directions in Psychological Science, 13*, 67–70. (p. 179)

Martin, C. L., Ruble, D. N., & Szkrybalo, J. (2002). Cognitive theories of early gender development. *Psychological Bulletin, 128*, 903–933. (p. 179)

Martin, S. J., Kelly, I. W., & Saklofske, D. H. (1992). Suicide and lunar cycles: A critical review over 28 years. *Psychological Reports, 71*, 787–795. (p. 564)

Martins, Y., Preti, G., Crabtree, C. R., & Wysocki, C. J. (2005). Preference for human body odors is influenced by gender and sexual orientation. *Psychological Science, 16*, 694–701. (p. 190)

Marx, D. M., Ko, S. J., & Friedman, R. A. (2009). The "Obama effect": How a salient role model reduces race-based performance differences. *Journal of Experimental Social Psychology, 45*, 953–956. (p. 361)

Marzoli, D., Custodero, M., Pagliara, A., & Tommasi, L. (2013). Sun-induced frowning fosters aggressive feelings. *Cognition and Emotion, 27*, 1513–1521. (p. 401)

Masicampo, E. J., & Baumeister, R. F. (2008). Toward a physiology of dual-process reasoning and judgment: Lemonade, willpower, and the expensive rule-based analysis. *Psychological Science, 19*, 255–260. (p. 422)

Maslow, A. H. (1970). *Motivation and personality* (2nd ed.). New York: Harper & Row. (pp. 368, 501, B-1)

Maslow, A. H. (1971). *The farther reaches of human nature.* New York: Viking. (p. 368)

Mason, A. E., Sbarra, D. A., & Mehl, M. R. (2010). Thin-slicing divorce: Thirty seconds of information predict changes in psychological adjustment over 90 days. *Psychological Science, 21*, 1420–1422. (p. 397)

Mason, C., & Kandel, E. R. (1991). Central visual pathways. In E. R. Kandel, J. H. Schwartz, & T. M. Jessell (Eds.), *Principles of neural science* (3rd ed., pp. 421–439). New York: Elsevier. (p. 42)

Mason, H. (2003, March 25). *Wake up, sleepy teen.* Retrieved from http://www.gallup.com/poll/8059/wake-up-sleepy-teen.aspx (p. 95)

Mason, H. (2005, January 25). *Who dreams, perchance to sleep?* Retrieved from http://www.gallup.com/poll/14716/who-dreams-perchance-sleep.aspx (pp. 94, 95)

Mason, M. F., & Morris, M. W. (2010). Culture, attribution and automaticity: A social cognitive neuroscience view. *Social Cognitive and Affective Neuroscience, 5*, 292–306. (p. 398)

Mason, M. F., Norton, M. I., Van Horn, J. D., Wegner, D. M., Grafton, S. T., & Macrae, C. N. (2007). Wandering minds: The default network and stimulus-independent thought. *Science, 315*, 393–395. (p. 49)

Mason, R. A., & Just, M. A. (2004). How the brain processes causal inferences in text. *Psychological Science, 15*, 1–7. (p. 64)

Masse, L. C., & Tremblay, R. E. (1997). Behavior of boys in kindergarten and the onset of substance use during adolescence. *Archives of General Psychiatry, 54*, 62–68. (p. 114)

Massimini, M., Ferrarelli, F., Huber, R., Esser, S. K., Singh, H., & Tononi, G. (2005). Breakdown of cortical effective connectivity during sleep. *Science, 309*, 2228–2232. (p. 88)

Mast, M. S., & Hall, J. A. (2006). Women's advantage at remembering others' appearance: A systematic look at the why and when of a gender difference. *Personality and Social Psychology Bulletin, 32*, 353–364. (p. 478)

Masten, A. S. (2001). Ordinary magic: Resilience processes in development. *American Psychologist, 56*, 227–238. (p. 143)

Masters, K. S. (2010). The role of religion in therapy: Time for psychologists to have a little faith? *Cognitive and Behavioral Practice, 17*, 393–400. (p. 591)

Masters, K. S., & Hooker, S. A. (2013). Religiousness/spirituality, cardiovascular disease, and cancer: Cultural integration for health research and intervention. *Journal of Consulting and Clinical Psychology, 81,* 206–216. (p. 430)

Masters, W. H., & Johnson, V. E. (1966). *Human sexual response.* Boston: Little, Brown. (p. 182)

Mastroianni, G. R. (2002). Milgram and the Holocaust: A reexamination. *Journal of Theoretical and Philosophical Psychology, 22,* 158–173. (p. 454)

Mastroianni, G. R., & Reed, G. (2006). Apples, barrels, and Abu Ghraib. *Sociological Focus, 39,* 239–250. (p. 446)

Masuda, T., Ellsworth, P. C., Mesquita, B., Leu, J., Tanida, S., & Van de Veerdonk, E. (2008). Placing the face in context: Cultural differences in the perception of facial emotion. *Journal of Personality and Social Psychology, 94,* 365–381. (p. 401)

Mata, A., Ferreira, M. B., & Sherman, S. J. (2013). The metacognitive advantage of deliberative thinkers: A dual-process perspective on overconfidence. *Journal of Personality and Social Psychology, 105,* 353–373. (p. 324)

Mataix-Cols, D., Rosario-Campos, M. C., & Leckman, J. F. (2005). A multidimensional model of obsessive-compulsive disorder. *American Journal of Psychiatry, 162,* 228–238. (p. 543)

Mataix-Cols, D., Wooderson, S., Lawrence, N., Brammer, M. J., Speckens, A., & Phillips, M. L. (2004). Distinct neural correlates of washing, checking, and hoarding symptom dimensions in obsessive-compulsive disorder. *Archives of General Psychiatry, 61,* 564–576. (p. 543)

Mather, M., Cacioppo, J. T., & Kanwisher, N. (2013). How fMRI can inform cognitive theories. *Perspectives on Psychological Science, 8,* 108–113. (p. 50)

Mather, M., Canli, T., English, T., Whitfield, S., Wais, P., Ochsner, K., . . . Carstensen, L. L. (2004). Amygdala responses to emotionally valenced stimuli in older and younger adults. *Psychological Science, 15,* 259–263. (p. 167)

Mather, M., & Sutherland, M. (2012, February). *The selective effects of emotional arousal on memory.* Retrieved from http://www.apa.org/science/about/psa/2012/02/emotional-arousal.aspx (p. 294)

Matsumoto, D. (1994). *People: Psychology from a cultural perspective.* Pacific Grove, CA: Brooks/Cole. (p. 336)

Matsumoto, D., & Ekman, P. (1989). American-Japanese cultural differences in intensity ratings of facial expressions of emotion. *Motivation and Emotion, 13,* 143–157. (p. 399)

Matsumoto, D., Willingham, B., & Olide, A. (2009). Sequential dynamics of culturally moderated facial expressions of emotion. *Psychological Science, 20,* 1269–1275. (p. 401)

Mattanah, J. F., Lopez, F. G., & Govern, J. M. (2011). The contributions of parental attachment bonds to college student development and adjustment: A meta-analytic review. *Journal of Counseling Psychology, 58,* 565–596. (p. 142)

Matthews, K. A. (2005). Psychological perspectives on the development of coronary heart disease. *American Psychologist, 60,* 783–796. (p. 416)

Matthews, R. N., Domjan, M., Ramsey, M., & Crews, D. (2007). Learning effects on sperm competition and reproductive fitness. *Psychological Science, 18,* 758–762. (p. 250)

Maurer, D., & Maurer, C. (1988). *The world of the newborn.* New York: Basic Books. (p. 125)

Mauss, I. B., Shallcross, A. J., Troy, A. S., John, O. P., Ferrer, E., Wilhelm, F. H., & Gross, J. J. (2011). Don't hide your happiness! Positive emotion dissociation, social connectedness, and psychological functioning. *Journal of Personality and Social Psychology, 100,* 738–748. (p. 431)

Mautz, B., Wong, B., Peters, R., & Jennions, M. (2013). Penis size interacts with body shape and height to influence male attractiveness. *Proceedings of the National Academy of Sciences of the United States of America, 110,* 6925–6930. (p. 193)

May, C., & Hasher, L. (1998). Synchrony effects in inhibitory control over thought and action. *Journal of Experimental Psychology: Human Perception and Performance, 24,* 363–380. (p. 87)

May, P. A., Baete, J., Russo, A. J., Elliott, J., Blankenship, J., Kalberg, W. O., . . . Hoyme, H. E. (2014). Prevalence and characteristics of fetal alcohol spectrum disorders. *Pediatrics, 134,* 855–866. (p. 124)

May, R. (1982). The problem of evil: An open letter to Carl Rogers. *Journal of Humanistic Psychology, 22,* 10–21. (p. 503)

Mayberg, H. S. (2006). Defining neurocircuits in depression: Strategies toward treatment selection based on neuroimaging phenotypes. *Psychiatric Annals, 36,* 259–268. (p. 599)

Mayberg, H. S. (2007). Defining the neural circuitry of depression: Toward a new nosology with therapeutic implications. *Biological Psychiatry, 61,* 729–730. (p. 599)

Mayberg, H. S. (2009). Targeted modulation of neural circuits: A new treatment strategy for depression. *Journal of Clinical Investigation, 119,* 717–725. (p. 599)

Mayberg, H. S., Lozano, A. M., Voon, V., McNeely, H. E., Seminowicz, D., Hamani, C., . . . Kennedy, S. H. (2005). Deep brain stimulation for treatment-resistant depression. *Neuron, 45,* 651–660. (p. 599)

Mayberry, R. I., Lock, E., & Kazmi, H. (2002). Linguistic ability and early language exposure. *Nature, 417,* 38. (p. 333)

Mayer, J. D., Salovey, P., & Caruso, D. R. (2002). *The Mayer-Salovey-Caruso Emotional Intelligence Test (MSCEIT).* Toronto, Ontario, Canada: Multi-Health Systems. (p. 344)

Mayer, J. D., Salovey, P., & Caruso, D. R. (2012). The validity of the MSCEIT: Additional analyses and evidence. *Emotion Review, 4,* 403–408. (p. 344)

Mayer, J. D., Salovey, P., Caruso, D. R., & Cherkasskiy, L. (2011). Emotional intelligence. In R. J. Sternberg & S. B. Kaufman (Eds.), *The Cambridge handbook of intelligence* (pp. 528–549). New York: Cambridge University Press. (p. 344)

Mays, V. M., Cochran, S. D., & Barnes, N. W. (2007). Race, race-based discrimination, and health outcomes among African Americans. *Annual Review of Psychology, 58,* 201–225. (p. 409)

Mazure, C., Keita, G., & Blehar, M. (2002, April). *Summit on women and depression: Proceedings and recommendations.* Retrieved from https://www.apa.org/pi/women/programs/depression/summit-2002.pdf (p. 550)

Mazzoni, G., Scoboria, A., & Harvey, L. (2010). Nonbelieved memories. *Psychological Science, 21,* 1334–1340. (p. 308)

Mazzoni, G., & Vannucci, M. (2007). Hindsight bias, the misinformation effect, and false autobiographical memories. *Social Cognition, 25,* 203–220. (p. 309)

McAdams, D. P., & Guo, J. (2015). Narrating the generative life. *Psychological Science, 26,* 475–483. (p. 503)

McAneny, L. (1996, September). Large majority think government conceals information about UFO's. *Gallup Poll Monthly,* pp. 23–26. (p. 308)

McBurney, D. H. (1996). *How to think like a psychologist: Critical thinking in psychology.* Upper Saddle River, NJ: Prentice-Hall. (p. 59)

McBurney, D. H., & Collings, V. B. (1984). *Introduction to sensation and perception* (2nd ed.). Englewood Cliffs, NJ: Prentice-Hall. (p. 222)

McBurney, D. H., & Gent, J. F. (1979). On the nature of taste qualities. *Psychological Bulletin, 86,* 151–167. (p. 236)

McCain, N. L., Gray, D. P., Elswick, R. K., Jr., Robins, J. W., Tuck, I., Walter, J. M., . . . Ketchum, J. M. (2008). A randomized clinical trial of alternative stress management interventions in persons with HIV infection. *Journal of Consulting and Clinical Psychology, 76,* 431–441. (p. 413)

McCann, I. L., & Holmes, D. S. (1984). Influence of aerobic exercise on depression. *Journal of Personality and Social Psychology, 46,* 1142–1147. (p. 426)

McCann, U. D., Eligulashvili, V., & Ricaurte, G. A. (2000). (±)3,4-Methylenedioxymethamphetamine ('Ecstasy')-induced serotonin neurotoxicity: Clinical studies. *Neuropsychobiology, 42,* 11–16. (p. 111)

McCarthy, P. (1986, July). Scent: The tie that binds? *Psychology Today,* pp. 6, 10. (p. 237)

McCauley, C. R. (2002). Psychological issues in understanding terrorism and the response to terrorism. In C. E. Stout (Ed.), *The psychology of terrorism: Vol. 3. Theoretical understandings and perspectives* (pp. 3–30). Westport, CT: Praeger. (p. 458)

McCauley, C. R., & Segal, M. E. (1987). Social psychology of terrorist groups. In C. Hendrick (Ed.), *Review of personality and social psychology: Vol. 9. Group processes and intergroup relations* (pp. 231–256). Beverly Hills, CA: Sage. (p. 458)

McClendon, B. T., & Prentice-Dunn, S. (2001). Reducing skin cancer risk: An intervention based on protection motivation theory. *Journal of Health Psychology, 6,* 321–328. (p. 444)

McClintock, M. K., & Herdt, G. (1996). Rethinking puberty: The development of sexual attraction. *Current Directions in Psychological Science, 5,* 178–183. (p. 175)

McClung, M., & Collins, D. (2007). "Because I know it will!": Placebo effects of an ergogenic aid on athletic performance. *Journal of Sport & Exercise Psychology, 29,* 382–394. (p. 24)

McClure, E. B. (2000). A meta-analytic review of sex differences in facial expression processing and their development in infants, children, and adolescents. *Psychological Bulletin, 126,* 424–453. (p. 397)

McClure, M. J., & Lydon, J. E. (2014). Anxiety doesn't become you: How attachment compromises relational opportunities. *Journal of Personality and Social Psychology, 106,* 89–111. (p. 477)

McClure, M. J., Lydon, J. E., Baccus, J. R., & Baldwin, M. W. (2010). A signal detection analysis of chronic attachment anxiety at speed dating: Being unpopular is only the first part of the problem. *Personality and Social Psychology Bulletin, 36,* 1024–1036. (p. 201)

McConnell, A. R., Brown, C. M., Shoda, T. M., Stayton, L. E., & Martin, C. E. (2011). Friends with benefits: On the positive consequences of pet ownership. *Journal of Personality and Social Psychology, 101,* 1239–1252. (p. 425)

McCool, G. (1999, October 26). Mirror-gazing Venezuelans top of vanity stakes. *The Toronto Star.* Retrieved from web.lexis-nexis.com (p. 478)

McCrae, R. R. (2009). The five-factor model of personality traits: Consensus and controversy. In P. J. Corr & G. Matthews (Eds.), *The Cambridge handbook of personality psychology* (pp. 148–161). New York: Cambridge University Press. (p. 509)

McCrae, R. R. (2011). Personality theories for the 21st century. *Teaching of Psychology, 38,* 209–214. (p. 510)

McCrae, R. R., & Costa, P. T., Jr. (1986). Clinical assessment can benefit from recent advances in personality psychology. *American Psychologist, 41,* 1001–1003. (p. 509)

McCrae, R. R., & Costa, P. T., Jr. (1990). *Personality in adulthood.* New York: Guilford Press. (p. 162)

McCrae, R. R., & Costa, P. T., Jr. (1994). The stability of personality: Observations and evaluations. *Current Directions in Psychological Science, 3,* 173–175. (p. 511)

McCrae, R. R., & Costa, P. T., Jr. (2008). The five-factor theory of personality. In O. P. John, R. W., Robins, & L. A. Pervin (Eds.), *Handbook of personality: Theory and research* (3rd ed., pp. 159–181) New York: Guilford Press. (p. 509)

McCrae, R. R., Scally, M., Terracciano, A., Abecasis, G. R., & Costa, P. T., Jr. (2010). An alternative to the search for single polymorphisms: Toward molecular personality scales for the five-factor model. *Journal of Personality and Social Psychology, 99,* 1014–1024. (p. 510)

McCrae, R. R., Terracciano, A., & 78 Members of the Personality Profiles of Cultures Project. (2005). Universal features of personality traits from the observer's perspective: Data from 50 cultures. *Journal of Personality and Social Psychology, 88,* 547–561. (p. 510)

McCrink, K., & Wynn, K. (2004). Large-number addition and subtraction by 9-month-old infants. *Psychological Science, 15,* 776–781. (p. 131)

McCrory, E. J., De Brito, S. A., Sebastian, C. L., Mechelli, A., Bird, G., Kelly, P. A., & Viding, E. (2011). Heightened neural reactivity to threat in child victims of family violence. *Current Biology, 21,* R947–R948. (p. 143)

McCullough, M. E., Hoyt, W. T., Larson, D. B., Koenig, H. G., & Thoresen, C. (2000). Religious involvement and mortality: A meta-analytic review. *Health Psychology, 19,* 211–222. (p. 430)

McCullough, M. E., & Laurenceau, J.-P. (2005). Religiousness and the trajectory of self-rated health across adulthood. *Personality and Social Psychology Bulletin, 31,* 560–573. (p. 430)

McCullough, M. E., & Willoughby, B. L. B. (2009). Religion, self-regulation, and self-control: Associations, explanations, and implications. *Psychological Bulletin, 135,* 69–93. (p. 430)

McDaniel, M. A., Howard, D. C., & Einstein, G. O. (2009). The read-recite-review study strategy: Effective and portable. *Psychological Science, 20,* 516–522. (pp. 13, 30, 32, 47, 55, 65, 77, 86, 103, 117, 126, 146, 157, 168, 180, 197, 208, 224, 243, 255, 266, 279, 291, 300, 313, 328, 340, 352, 363, 376, 385, 395, 403, 418, 438, 461, 474, 489, 504, 524, 536, 544, 555, 567, 592, 604, A-9, B-15)

McDermott, R., Tingley, D., Cowden, J., Frazzetto, G., & Johnson, D. D. P. (2009). Monoamine oxidase A gene (MAOA) predicts behavioral aggression following provocation. *Proceedings of the National Academy of Sciences of the United States of America, 106,* 2118–2123. (p. 469)

McEvoy, S. P., Stevenson, M. R., McCartt, A. T., Woodward, M., Hawroth, C., Palamara, P., & Ceracelli, R. (2005). Role of mobile phones in motor vehicle crashes resulting in hospital attendance: A case-crossover study. *British Medical Journal, 331,* 428. http://dx.doi.org/10.1136/bmj.38537.397512.55 (p. 82)

McEvoy, S. P., Stevenson, M. R., & Woodward, M. (2007). The contribution of passengers versus mobile phone use to motor vehicle crashes resulting in hospital attendance by the driver. *Accident Analysis and Prevention, 39,* 1170–1176. (p. 82)

McFarland, C., & Ross, M. (1987). The relation between current impressions and memories of self and dating partners. *Psychological Bulletin, 13,* 228–238. (p. 309)

McGaugh, J. L. (1994, October 22). Quoted in B. Bower, Stress hormones hike emotional memories. *Science News, 146*(17), 262. (p. 294)

McGaugh, J. L. (2003). *Memory and emotion: The making of lasting memories.* New York: Columbia University Press. (p. 294)

McGaugh, J. L., & LePort, A. (2014, February). Remembrance of all things past. *Scientific American,* pp. 41–45. (p. 301)

McGhee, P. E. (June, 1976). Children's appreciation of humor: A test of the cognitive congruency principle. *Child Development, 47,* 420–426. (p. 133)

McGirr, A., Berlim, M. T., Bond, D. J., Fleck, M. P., Yatham, L. N., & Lam, R. W. (2015). A systematic review and meta-analysis of randomized, double-blind, placebo-controlled trials of ketamine in the rapid treatment of major depressive episodes. *Psychological Medicine, 45,* 693–704. (p. 596)

McGowan, P. O., Sasaki, A., D'Alessio, A. C., Dymov, S., Labonté, B., Szyl, M., . . . Meaney, M. J. (2009). Epigenetic regulation of the glucocorticoid receptor in human brain associates with childhood abuse. *Nature Neuroscience, 12,* 342–348. (pp. 144, 543)

McGrath, J. J., & Welham, J. L. (1999). Season of birth and schizophrenia: A systematic review and meta-analysis of data from the Southern Hemisphere. *Schizophrenia Research, 35,* 237–242. (p. 559)

McGrath, J. J., Welham, J., & Pemberton, M. (1995). Month of birth, hemisphere of birth and schizophrenia. *British Journal of Psychiatry, 167,* 783–785. (p. 559)

McGue, M. (2010). The end of behavioral genetics? *Behavioral Genetics, 40,* 284–296. (p. 73)

McGue, M., & Bouchard, T. J., Jr. (1998). Genetic and environmental influences on human behavioral differences. *Annual Review of Neuroscience, 21,* 1–24. (p. 70)

McGue, M., Bouchard, T. J., Jr., Iacono, W. G., & Lykken, D. T. (1993). Behavioral genetics of cognitive ability: A life-span perspective. In R. Plomin & G. E. McClearn (Eds.), *Nature, nurture, and psychology* (pp. 59–76). Washington, DC: American Psychological Association. (pp. 354, 355)

McGuire, W. J. (1986). The myth of massive media impact: Savings and salvagings. In G. Comstock (Ed.), *Public communication and behavior* (pp. 173–257). Orlando, FL: Academic Press. (p. 277)

McGurk, H., & MacDonald, J. (1976). Hearing lips and seeing voices. *Nature, 264,* 746–748. (p. 239)

McHugh, P. R. (1995a). Resolved: Multiple personality disorder is an individually and socially created artifact. *Journal of the American Academy of Child and Adolescent Psychiatry, 34,* 957–959. (p. 562)

McHugh, P. R. (1995b). Witches, multiple personalities, and other psychiatric artifacts. *Nature Medicine, 1,* 110–114. (p. 562)

McKay, J. (2000). Building self-esteem in children. In M. McKay & P. Fanning, *Self-esteem* (pp. 327–373). New York: New Harbinger. (p. 517)

McKellar, J., Stewart, E., & Humphreys, K. (2003). Alcoholics Anonymous involvement and positive alcohol-related outcomes: Cause, consequence, or just a correlate? A prospective 2-year study of 2,319 alcohol-dependent men. *Journal of Consulting and Clinical Psychology, 71,* 302–308. (p. 583)

McKenna, K. Y. A., Green, A. S., & Gleason, M. E. J. (2002). What's the big attraction? Relationship formation on the Internet. *Journal of Social Issues, 58,* 9–31. (p. 476)

McKone, E., Kanwisher, N., & Duchaine, B. C. (2007). Can generic expertise explain special processing for faces? *Trends in Cognitive Sciences, 11,* 8–15. (p. 215)

McLaughlin, K. A., Sheridan, M. A., Tibu, F., Fox, N. A., Zeanah, C. H., & Nelson, C. A. (2015). Causal effects of the early caregiving environment on development of stress response systems in children. *Proceedings of the National Academy of Sciences of the United States of America, 112,* 5637–5642. (p. 143)

McLaughlin, M. (2010, October 2). JK Rowling: Depression, the "terrible place that allowed me to come back stronger." *The Scotsman.* Retrieved from http://www.scotsman.com/news/jk-rowling-depression-the-terrible-place-that-allowed-me-to-come-back-stronger-1-823425 (p. 547)

McLean, C. P., & Anderson, E. R. (2009). Brave men and timid women? A review of the gender differences in fear and anxiety. *Clinical Psychology Review, 29,* 496–505. (p. 537)

McMurray, B. (2007). Defusing the childhood vocabulary explosion. *Science, 317,* 631. (p. 331)

McMurray, C. (2004, January 13). *U.S., Canada, Britain: Who's getting in shape?* Retrieved from http://www.gallup.com/poll/10312/us-canada-britain-whos-getting-shape.aspx (p. 426)

McNally, R. J. (1999). EMDR and Mesmerism: A comparative historical analysis. *Journal of Anxiety Disorders, 13,* 225–236. (p. 588)

McNally, R. J. (2003). *Remembering trauma.* Cambridge, MA: Harvard University Press. (pp. 311, 540)

McNally, R. J. (2007). Betrayal trauma theory: A critical appraisal. *Memory, 15,* 280–294. (p. 311)

McNally, R. J. (2012). Are we winning the war against posttraumatic stress disorder? *Science, 336,* 872–874. (pp. 89, 540)

McNeil, B. J., Pauker, S. G., & Tversky, A. (1988). On the framing of medical decisions. In D. E. Bell, H. Raiffa, & A. Tversky (Eds.), *Decision making: Descriptive, normative, and prescriptive interactions* (pp. 562–568). New York: Cambridge University Press. (p. 322)

McNulty, J. K., Olson, M. A., Meltzer, A. L., & Shaffer, M. J. (2013). Though they may be unaware, newlyweds implicitly know whether their marriage will be satisfying. *Science, 342,* 1119–1120. (p. 323)

McWhorter, J. (2012, April 23). Talking with your fingers. *The New York Times.* Retrieved from http://opinionator.blogs.nytimes.com/2012/04/23/talking-with-your-fingers/ (p. 373)

Mead, G. E., Morley, W., Campbell, P., Greig, C. A., McMurdo, M., & Lawlor, D. A. (2009). Exercise for depression. *Cochrane Database of Systematic Reviews,* Issue 3, Article CD004366. doi:10.1002/14651858.CD004366.pub4 (p. 426)

Meador, B. D., & Rogers, C. R. (1984). Person-centered therapy. In R. J. Corsini (Ed.), *Current psychotherapies* (3rd ed., pp. 142–195). Itasca, IL: F. E. Peacock. (p. 573)

Medical Institute for Sexual Health. (1994, April). Condoms ineffective against human papilloma virus. *Sexual Health Update,* p. 2. (p. 184)

Mednick, S. A., Huttunen, M. O., & Machon, R. A. (1994). Prenatal influenza infections and adult schizophrenia. *Schizophrenia Bulletin, 20,* 263–267. (p. 558)

Medvec, V. H., Madey, S. F., & Gilovich, T. (1995). When less is more: Counterfactual thinking and satisfaction among Olympic medalists. *Journal of Personality and Social Psychology, 69,* 603–610. (p. 520)

Mehl, M., Gosling, S. D., & Pennebaker, J. W. (2006). Personality in its natural habitat: Manifestations and implicit folk theories of personality in daily life. *Journal of Personality and Social Psychology, 90,* 862–877. (p. 512)

Mehl, M. R., & Pennebaker, J. W. (2003). The sounds of social life: A psychometric analysis of students' daily social environments and natural conversations. *Journal of Personality and Social Psychology, 84,* 857–870. (p. 20)

Mehl, M. R., Vazire, S., Holleran, S. E., & Clark, C. S. (2010). Eavesdropping on happiness: Well-being is related to having less small talk and more substantive conversations. *Psychological Science, 21,* 539–541. (p. 437)

Mehta, D., Klengel, T., Conneely, K. N., Smith, A. K., Altmann, A., Pace, T. W., . . . Binder, E. B. (2013). Childhood maltreatment is associated with distinct genomic and epigenetic profiles in posttraumatic stress disorder. *Proceedings of the National Academy of Sciences of the United States of America, 110,* 8302–8307. (p. 543)

Mehta, M. R. (2007). Cortico-hippocampal interaction during up-down states and memory consolidation. *Nature Neuroscience, 10,* 13–15. (p. 293)

Meichenbaum, D. (1977). *Cognitive-behavior modification: An integrative approach.* New York: Plenum Press. (p. 580)

Meichenbaum, D. (1985). *Stress inoculation training.* New York: Pergamon Press. (p. 580)

Meier, B. P., Moeller, S. K., Riemer-Peltz, M., & Robinson, M. D. (2012). Sweet taste preferences and experiences predict prosocial inferences, personalities, and behaviors. *Journal of Personality and Social Psychology, 102,* 163–174. (p. 238)

Meier, M. H., Caspi, A., Ambler, A., Harrington, H., Houts, R., Keefe, R. S., . . . Moffitt, T. E. (2012). Persistent cannabis users show neuropsychological decline from childhood to midlife. *Proceedings of the National Academy of Sciences of the United States of America, 109,* E2657–2664. (p. 112)

Meijer, E. H., & Verschuere, B. (2010). The polygraph and the detection of deception. *Journal of Forensic Psychology Practice, 10,* 525–538. (p. 394)

Melby-Lervåg, M., & Hulme, C. (2013). Is working memory training effective? A meta-analytic review. *Developmental Psychology, 49,* 270–291. (p. 162)

Meltzoff, A. N. (1988). Infant imitation after a 1-week delay: Long-term memory for novel acts and multiple stimuli. *Developmental Psychology, 24,* 470–476. (p. 274)

Meltzoff, A. N., Kuhl, P. K., Movellan, J., & Sejnowski, T. J. (2009). Foundations for a new science of learning. *Science, 325,* 284–288. (pp. 274, 332)

Meltzoff, A. N., & Moore, M. K. (1989). Imitation in newborn infants: Exploring the range of gestures imitated and the underlying mechanisms. *Developmental Psychology, 25,* 954–962. (p. 274)

Meltzoff, A. N., & Moore, M. K. (1997). Explaining facial imitation: A theoretical model. *Early Development and Parenting, 6,* 179–192. (p. 274)

Melzack, R. (1998, February). Quoted in Phantom limbs. *Discover,* pp. 120–126. (p. 232)

Melzack, R. (2005). Evolution of the neuromatrix theory of pain. *Pain Practice, 5,* 85–94. (p. 232)

Melzack, R., & Katz, J. (2013). Pain. *Wiley Interdisciplinary Reviews: Cognitive Science, 4,* 1–15. (p. 232)

Melzack, R., & Wall, P. D. (1965). Pain mechanisms: A new theory. *Science, 150,* 971–979. (p. 232)

Melzack, R., & Wall, P. D. (1983). *The challenge of pain.* New York: Basic Books. (p. 232)

Mendes, E. (2010, June 2). *U.S. exercise levels up, but demographic differences remain.* Retrieved from http://www.gallup.com/poll/139340/exercise-levels-demographic-differences-remain.aspx (p. 427)

Mendes, E., & McGeeney, K. (2012, July 9). *Women's health trails men's most in former Soviet Union.* Retrieved from http://www.gallup.com/poll/155558/women-health-trails-men-former-soviet-union.aspx (p. 548)

Mendle, J., Turkheimer, E., & Emery, R. E. (2007). Detrimental psychological outcomes associated with early pubertal timing in adolescent girls. *Developmental Review, 27,* 151–171. (p. 148)

Mendolia, M., & Kleck, R. E. (1993). Effects of talking about a stressful event on arousal: Does what we talk about make a difference? *Journal of Personality and Social Psychology, 64,* 283–292. (p. 425)

Merari, A. (2002, August). *Explaining suicidal terrorism: Theories versus empirical evidence.* Invited address at the 110th Annual Convention of the American Psychological Association, Chicago, IL. (p. 458)

Meriac, J. P., Hoffman, B. J., Woehr, D. J., & Fleisher, M. S. (2008). Further evidence for the validity of assessment center dimensions: A meta-analysis of the incremental criterion-related validity of dimension ratings. *Journal of Applied Psychology, 93,* 1042–1052. (p. 515)

Merikangas, K. R., Jin, R., He, J. P., Kessler, R. C., Lee, S., Sampson, N. A., . . . Zarkov, Z. (2011). Prevalence and correlates of bipolar spectrum disorder in the world mental health survey initiative. *Archives of General Psychiatry, 68,* 241–251. (p. 547)

Merskey, H. (1992). The manufacture of personalities: The production of multiple personality disorder. *British Journal of Psychiatry, 160,* 327–340. (p. 562)

Mervis, J. (2011). Giving children a Head Start is possible—but it's not easy. *Science, 333,* 956–957. (p. 356)

Merzenich, M. (2007). Quoted in the Posit Science Brain Fitness Program. Retrieved from http://www.positscience.com/ (p. 161)

Mesoudi, A. (2009). How cultural evolutionary theory can inform social psychology and vice versa. *Psychological Review, 116,* 929–952. (p. 448)

Messias, E., Eaton, W. W., Grooms, A. N. (2011). Economic grand rounds: Income inequality and depression prevalence across the United States: An ecological study. *Psychiatric Services, 62,* 710–712. (p. 471)

Messinis, L., Kyprianidou, A., Malefaki, S., & Papathanasopoulos, P. (2006). Neuropsychological deficits in long-term frequent cannabis users. *Neurology, 66,* 737–739. (p. 112)

Mestel, R. (1997, April 26). Get real, Siggi. *New Scientist.* Retrieved from http://www.newscientist.com/ns/970426/siggi.html (p. 99)

Meston, C. M., & Buss, D. M. (2007). Why humans have sex. *Archives of Sexual Behavior, 36,* 477–507. (p. 185)

Metcalfe, J. (1986). Premonitions of insight predict impending error. *Journal of Experimental Psychology: Learning, Memory, and Cognition, 12,* 623–634. (p. 317)

Metcalfe, J. (1998). Cognitive optimism: Self-deception or memory-based processing heuristics. *Personality and Social Psychology Review, 2,* 100–110. (p. 321)

Metzler, D. (2011, Spring). Vocabulary growth in adult cross-fostered chimpanzees. *Friends of Washoe, 32*(3), 11–13. (p. 335)

Meyer-Bahlburg, H. F. L. (1995). Psychoneuroendocrinology and sexual pleasure: The aspect of sexual orientation. In P. R. Abramson & S. D. Pinkerton (Eds.), *Sexual nature/sexual culture* (pp. 135–153). Chicago: University of Chicago Press. (p. 191)

Michael, R. B., Garry, M., & Kirsch, I. (2012). Suggestion, cognition, and behavior. *Current Directions in Psychological Science, 21,* 151–156. (p. 24)

Michaels, J. W., Bloomel, J. M., Brocato, R. M., Linkous, R. A., & Rowe, J. S. (1982). Social facilitation and inhibition in a natural setting. *Replications in Social Psychology, 2,* 21–24. (p. 456)

Middlebrooks, J. C., & Green, D. M. (1991). Sound localization by human listeners. *Annual Review of Psychology, 42,* 135–159. (p. 230)

Miers, R. (2009, Spring). Calum's road. *Scottish Life,* pp. 36–39, 75. (p. 376)

Mihura, J. L., Meyer, G. J., Bombel, G., & Dumitrascu, N. (2015). Standards, accuracy, and questions of bias in Rorschach meta-analyses: Reply to Wood, Garb, Nezworski, Lilienfeld, and Duke (2015). *Psychological Bulletin, 141,* 250–260. (p. 498)

Mihura, J. L., Meyer, G. J., Dumitrascu, N., & Bombel, G. (2013). The validity of individual Rorschach variables: Systematic reviews and meta-analyses of the comprehensive system. *Psychological Bulletin, 139,* 548–605. (p. 498)

Mikolajczak, M., Pinon, N., Lane, A., de Timary, P., & Luminet, O. (2010). Oxytocin not only increases trust when money is at stake, but also when confidential information is in the balance. *Biological Psychology, 85,* 182–184. (p. 46)

Mikulincer, M., & Shaver, P. R. (2001). Attachment theory and intergroup bias: Evidence that priming the secure base schema attenuates negative reactions to out-groups. *Journal of Personality and Social Psychology, 81,* 97–115. (p. 466)

Milan, R. J., Jr., & Kilmann, P. R. (1987). Interpersonal factors in premarital contraception. *Journal of Sex Research, 23,* 289–321. (p. 186)

Miles, D. R., & Carey, G. (1997). Genetic and environmental architecture of human aggression. *Journal of Personality and Social Psychology, 72,* 207–217. (p. 469)

Milgram, S. (1963). Behavioral study of obedience. *Journal of Abnormal and Social Psychology, 67,* 371–378. (p. 452)

Milgram, S. (1974). *Obedience to authority.* New York: Harper & Row. (pp. 452, 453, 454)

Miller, G. (2004). Axel, Buck share award for deciphering how the nose knows. *Science, 306,* 207. (p. 237)

Miller, G. (2005). The dark side of glia. *Science, 308,* 778–781. (p. 37)

Miller, G. (2008). Tackling alcoholism with drugs. *Science, 320,* 168–170. (p. 114)

Miller, G. (2010). Anything but child's play. *Science, 327,* 1192–1193. (p. 547)

Miller, G. (2012a). Drone wars: Are remotely piloted aircraft changing the nature of war? *Science, 336,* 842–843. (p. 454)

Miller, G. (2012b). How are memories retrieved? *Science, 338,* 30–31. (p. 292)

Miller, G. A. (1956). The magical number seven, plus or minus two: Some limits on our capacity for processing information. *Psychological Review, 63,* 81–97. (p. 287)

Miller, G. E., & Blackwell, E. (2006). Turning up the heat: Inflammation as a mechanism linking chronic stress, depression, and heart disease. *Current Directions in Psychological Science, 15,* 269–272. (p. 416)

Miller, G. E., Chen, E., & Parker, K. (2011). Psychological stress in childhood and susceptibility to the chronic diseases of aging: Moving toward a model of behavioral and biological mechanisms. *Psychological Bulletin, 137,* 959–997. (p. 409)

Miller, H. C., Pattison, K. F., DeWall, C. N., Rayburn-Reeves, R., & Zentall, T. R. (2010). Self-control without a "self"? Common self-control processes in humans and dogs. *Psychological Science, 21,* 534–538. (p. 422)

Miller, J. F., Neufang, M., Solway, A., Brandt, A., Trippel, M., Mader, I., . . . Schulze-Bonhage, A. (2013). Neural activity in human hippocampal formation reveals the spatial context of retrieved memories. *Science, 342,* 1111–1114. (p. 292)

Miller, J. G., & Bersoff, D. M. (1995). Development in the context of everyday family relationships: Culture, interpersonal morality and adaptation. In M. Killen & D. Hart (Eds.), *Morality in everyday life: A developmental perspective* (pp. 259–282). New York: Cambridge University Press. (p. 150)

Miller, L. K. (1999). The savant syndrome: Intellectual impairment and exceptional skill. *Psychological Bulletin, 125,* 31–46. (p. 342)

Miller, N. E. (1985, February). Rx: Biofeedback. *Psychology Today,* pp. 54–59. (p. 427)

Miller, P. (2012, January). A thing or two about twins. *National Geographic,* pp. 38–65. (p. 69)

Miller, P. J. O., Aoki, K., Rendell, L. E., & Amano, M. (2008). Stereotypical resting behavior of the sperm whale. *Current Biology, 18,* R21–R23. (p. 89)

Milner, A. D., & Goodale, M. A. (2008). Two visual systems reviewed. *Neuropsychologia, 46,* 774–785. (p. 85)

Milrod, B., Chambless, D. L., Gallop, R., Busch, F. N., Schwalberg, M., McCarthy, K. S., . . . Barber, J. P. (2015). Psychotherapies for panic disorder: A tale of two sites. *Journal of Clinical Psychiatry.* Advance online publication. (p. 581)

Milyavskaya, M., Gingras, I., Mageau, G. A., Koestner, R., Gagnon, H., Fang, J., & Bolché, J. (2009). Balance across contexts: Importance of balanced need satisfaction across various life domains. *Personality and Social Psychology Bulletin, 35,* 1031–1045. (p. 370)

Mineka, S. (1985). The frightful complexity of the origins of fears. In F. R. Brush & J. B. Overmier (Eds.), *Affect, conditioning, and cognition: Essays on the determinants of behavior* (pp. 55–73). Hillsdale, NJ: Erlbaum. (p. 542)

Mineka, S. (2002). Animal models of clinical psychology. In N. Smelser & P. Baltes (Eds.), *International encyclopedia of the social and behavioral sciences.* Oxford, England: Elsevier Science. (p. 542)

Mineka, S., & Oehlberg, K. (2008). The relevance of recent developments in classical conditioning to understanding the etiology and maintenance of anxiety disorders. *Acta Psychologica, 127,* 567–580. (p. 541)

Mineka, S., & Zinbarg, R. (1996). Conditioning and ethological models of anxiety disorders: Stress-in-dynamic-context anxiety models. In D. Hope (Ed.), *Perspectives on anxiety, panic, and fear: 43rd Annual Nebraska Symposium on Motivation* (pp. 135–211). Lincoln: University of Nebraska Press. (pp. 544, 603)

Minsky, M. (1986). *The society of mind.* New York: Simon & Schuster. (p. 80)

Mischel, W. (1968). *Personality and assessment.* New York: Wiley. (p. 511)

Mischel, W. (1981). Current issues and challenges in personality. In L. T. Benjamin Jr. (Ed.), *The G. Stanley Hall Lecture Series* (Vol. 1, pp. 85–99). Washington, DC: American Psychological Association. (p. 515)

Mischel, W. (2009). From *Personality and Assessment* (1968) to personality science. *Journal of Research in Personality, 43,* 282–290. (p. 511)

Mischel, W. (2014). *The marshmallow test: Mastering self-control.* Boston: Little, Brown. (pp. 151, 259)

Mischel, W., Shoda, Y., & Peake, P. K. (1988). The nature of adolescent competencies predicted by preschool delay of gratification. *Journal of Personality and Social Psychology, 54,* 687–696. (p. 151)

Mischel, W., Shoda, Y., & Rodriguez, M. L. (1989). Delay of gratification in children. *Science, 244,* 933–938. (p. 151)

Mischkowski, D., Kross, E., & Bushman, B. (2012). Flies on the wall are less aggressive: Self-distancing "in the heat of the moment" reduces aggressive thoughts, angry feelings and aggressive behavior. *Journal of Experimental Social Psychology, 48,* 1187–1191. (p. 416)

Miserandino, M. (1991). Memory and the seven dwarfs. *Teaching of Psychology, 18,* 169–171. (p. 283)

Mishkin, M. (1982). A memory system in the monkey. *Philosophical Transactions of the Royal Society of London: Series B, 298,* 83–95. (p. 294)

Mishkin, M., Suzuki, W. A., Gadian, D. G., & Vargha-Khadem, F. (1997). Hierarchical organization of cognitive memory. *Philosophical Transactions of the Royal Society of London: Series B, 352,* 1461–1467. (p. 294)

Mishra, A., & Mishra, H. (2010). Border bias: The belief that state borders can protect against disasters. *Psychological Science, 21,* 1582–1586. (p. 337)

Mita, T. H., Dermer, M., & Knight, J. (1977). Reversed facial images and the mere-exposure hypothesis. *Journal of Personality and Social Psychology, 35,* 597–601. (p. 475)

Mitani, J. C., Watts, D. P., & Amsler, S. J. (2010). Lethal intergroup aggression leads to territorial expansion in wild chimpanzees. *Current Biology, 20,* R507–R509. (p. 328)

Mitchell, J. P. (2009). Social psychology as a natural kind. *Cell, 13,* 246–251. (p. 516)

Mitte, K. (2008). Memory bias for threatening information in anxiety and anxiety disorders: A meta-analytic review. *Psychological Bulletin, 134,* 886–911. (p. 537)

Mobbs, D., Yu, R., Meyer, M., Passamonti, L., Seymour, B., Calder, A. J., . . . Dalgleish, T. (2009). A key role for similarity in vicarious reward. *Science, 324,* 900. (p. 273)

Moffitt, T. E., Arsenault, L., Belsky, D., Dickson, N., Hancox, R. J., Harrington, H., . . . Caspi, A. (2011). A gradient of childhood self-control predicts health, wealth, and public safety. *Proceedings of the National Academy of Sciences of the United States of America, 108,* 2693–2698. (p. 421)

Moffitt, T. E., Caspi, A., Harrington, H., & Milne, B. J. (2002). Males on the life-course-persistent and adolescence-limited antisocial pathways: Follow-up at age 26 years. *Development and Psychopathology, 14,* 179–207. (p. 122)

Moffitt, T. E., Harrington, H., Caspi, A., Kim-Cohen, J., Goldberg, D., Gregory, A. M., & Poulton, R. (2007). Depression and generalized anxiety disorder: Cumulative and sequential comorbidity in a birth cohort followed prospectively to age 32 years. *Archives of General Psychiatry, 64,* 651–660. (p. 537)

Moffitt, T. E., Poulton, R., & Caspi, A. (2013). Lifelong impact of early self-control. *American Scientist, 101,* 352–359. (p. 121)

Moghaddam, F. M. (2005). The staircase to terrorism: A psychological exploration. *American Psychologist, 60,* 161–169. (p. 458)

Mohr, H., Pritchard, J., & Lush, T. (2010, May 29). *BP has been good at downplaying disaster.* Retrieved from http://www.nbcnews.com/id/37414728/ns/disaster_in_the_gulf/t/bp-has-been-good-downplaying-disaster/#.Vgi7DiLD85s (p. 322)

Moises, H. W., Zoega, T., & Gottesman, I. I. (2002, July 3). The glial growth factors deficiency and synaptic destabilization hypothesis of schizophrenia. *BMC Psychiatry, 2*(8). Retrieved from http://www.biomedcentral.com/1471-244X/2/8 (p. 559)

Molenberghs, P., Ogilivie, C., Louis, W. R., Decety, J., Bagnall, & Bain, P. G. (2015). The neural correlates of justified and unjustified killing: An fMRI study. *Social Cognitive and Affective Neuroscience, 10,* 1397–1404. (p. 60)

Möller-Levet, C. S., Archer, S. N., Bucca, G., Laing, E. E., Slak, A., Kabiljo, R., . . . Dijk, D.-J. (2013). Effects of insufficient sleep on circadian rhythmicity and expression amplitude of the human blood transcriptome. *Proceedings of the National Academy of Sciences of the United States of America, 110,* E1132–E1141. (p. 95)

Mondloch, C. J., Lewis, T. L., Budreau, D. R., Maurer, D., Dannemiller, J. L., Stephens, B. R., & Kleiner-Gathercoal, K. A. (1999). Face perception during early infancy. *Psychological Science, 10,* 419–422. (p. 125)

Money, J. (1987). Sin, sickness, or status? Homosexual gender identity and psychoneuroendocrinology. *American Psychologist, 42,* 384–399. (pp. 188, 191)

Money, J., Berlin, F. S., Falck, A., & Stein, M. (1983). *Antiandrogenic and counseling treatment of sex offenders.* Baltimore: Johns Hopkins University School of Medicine, Department of Psychiatry and Behavioral Sciences. (p. 182)

Monroe, S. M., & Reid, M. W. (2009). Life stress and major depression. *Current Directions in Psychological Science, 18,* 68–72. (p. 548)

Montag, C., Weber, B., Trautner, P., Newport, B., Markett, S., Walter, N. T., . . . Reuter, M. (2012). Does excessive play of violent first-person-shooter-video-games dampen brain activity in response to emotional stimuli? *Biological Psychology, 89,* 107–111. (p. 471)

Montagne, A., Barnes, S. R., Sweeney, M. D., Halliday, M. R., Sagare, A. P., Zhao, Z., . . . Zlokovic, B. V. (2015). Blood-brain barrier breakdown in the aging human hippocampus. *Neuron, 85,* 296–302. (p. 159)

Montoya, R. M., & Horton, R. S. (2013). A meta-analytic investigation of the processes underlying the similarity-attraction effect. *Journal of Social and Personal Relationships, 30,* 64–94. (p. 479)

Montoya, R. M., & Horton, R. S. (2014). A two-dimensional model for the study of interpersonal attraction. *Personality and Social Psychology Review, 18,* 59–86. (p. 479)

Mooallem, J. (2009, February 19). Rescue flight. *The New York Times Magazine.* Retrieved from http://www.nytimes.com/2009/02/22/magazine/22cranes-t.html?_r=0 (p. 139)

Mook, D. G. (1983). In defense of external invalidity. *American Psychologist, 38,* 379–387. (p. 27)

Moon, C., Lagercrantz, H., & Kuhl, P. K. (2013). Language experienced in utero affects vowel perception after birth: A two-country study. *Acta Paediatrica, 102,* 156–160. (p. 124)

Moorcroft, W. H. (2003). *Understanding sleep and dreaming.* New York: Kluwer Academic/Plenum Press. (pp. 88, 101)

Moore, D. W. (2004, December 17). *Sweet dreams go with a good night's sleep.* Retrieved from http://www.gallup.com/poll/14380/sweet-dreams-good-nights-sleep.aspx (p. 91)

Moore, D. W. (2005, June 16). *Three in four Americans believe in paranormal.* Retrieved from http://www.gallup.com/poll/16915/three-four-americans-believe-paranormal.aspx (p. 241)

Moore, S. C., Patel, A. V., Matthews, C. E., Berrington de Gonzalez, A., Park, Y., Katki, H. A., . . . Lee, I.-M. (2012). Leisure time physical activity of moderate to vigorous intensity and mortality: A large pooled cohort analysis. *PLOS Medicine, 9*(11), e1001335. doi:10.1371/journal.pmed.1001335 (p. 426)

Moos, R. H., & Moos, B. S. (2005). Sixteen-year changes and stable remission among treated and untreated individuals with alcohol use disorders. *Drug and Alcohol Dependence, 80,* 337–347. (p. 583)

Moos, R. H., & Moos, B. S. (2006). Participation in treatment and Alcoholics Anonymous: A 16-year follow-up of initially untreated individuals. *Journal of Clinical Psychology, 62,* 735–750. (p. 583)

Mor, N., & Winquist, J. (2002). Self-focused attention and negative affect: A meta-analysis. *Psychological Bulletin, 128,* 638–662. (p. 551)

More, H. L., Hutchinson, J. R., Collins, D. F., Weber, D. J., Aung, S. K. H., & Donelan, J. M. (2010). Scaling of sensorimotor control in terrestrial mammals. *Proceedings of the Royal Society: Series B, 277,* 3563–3568. (p. 37)

Moreira, M. T., Smith, L. A., & Foxcroft, D. (2009). Social norms interventions to reduce alcohol misuse in university or college students. *Cochrane Database of Systematic Reviews 2009,* Issue 3, Article CD006748. doi:10.1002/14651858.CD006748.pub2 (p. 116)

Moreland, R. L., & Beach, S. R. (1992). Exposure effects in the classroom: The development of affinity among students. *Journal of Experimental Social Psychology, 28,* 255–276. (p. 475)

Moreland, R. L., & Zajonc, R. B. (1982). Exposure effects in person perception: Familiarity, similarity, and attraction. *Journal of Experimental Social Psychology, 18,* 395–415. (p. 475)

Morelli, G. A., Rogoff, B., Oppenheim, D., & Goldsmith, D. (1992). Cultural variation in infants' sleeping arrangements: Questions of independence. *Developmental Psychology, 26,* 604–613. (p. 145)

Moreno, C., Laje, G., Blanco, C., Jiang, H., Schmidt, A. B., & Olfson, M. (2007). National trends in the outpatient diagnosis and treatment of bipolar disorder in youth. *Archives of General Psychiatry, 64,* 1032–1039. (p. 547)

Morewedge, C. K., & Norton, M. I. (2009). When dreaming is believing: The (motivated) interpretation of dreams. *Journal of Personality and Social Psychology, 96,* 249–264. (p. 241)

Morey, R. A., Inan, S., Mitchell, T. V., Perkins, D. O., Lieberman, J. A., & Belger, A. (2005). Imaging frontostriatal function in ultra-high-risk, early, and chronic schizophrenia during executive processing. *Archives of General Psychiatry, 62,* 254–262. (p. 558)

Mori, K., & Mori, H. (2009). Another test of the passive facial feedback hypothesis: When your face smiles, you feel happy. *Perceptual and Motor Skills, 109,* 76–78. (p. 402)

Morris, G., Baker-Ward, L., & Bauer, P. J. (2010). What remains of that day: The survival of children's autobiographical memories across time. *Applied Cognitive Psychology, 24,* 527–544. (p. 129)

Morrison, A. R. (2003, July). The brain on night shift. *Cerebrum,* pp. 23–36. (p. 90)

Morrison, C. (2007). *What does contagious yawning tell us about the mind?* Unpublished manuscript, University of Leeds, Leeds, England. (p. 449)

Morgan, A. B., & Lilienfeld, S. O. (2000). A meta-analytic review of the relation between antisocial behavior and neuropsychological measures of executive function. *Clinical Psychology Review, 20,* 113–136. (p. 564)

Mortensen, E. L., Michaelsen, K. F., Sanders, S. A., & Reinisch, J. M. (2002). The association between duration of breastfeeding and adult intelligence. *Journal of the American Medical Association, 287,* 2365–2371. (p. 23)

Mortensen, P. B. (1999). Effects of family history and place and season of birth on the risk of schizophrenia. *New England Journal of Medicine, 340,* 603–608. (p. 558)

Mortenson, S. T. (2006). Cultural differences and similarities in seeking social support as a response to academic failure: A comparison of American and Chinese college students. *Communication Education, 55,* 127–146. (p. 423)

Moscovici, S. (1985). Social influence and conformity. In G. Lindzey & E. Aronson (Eds.), *The handbook of social psychology* (3rd ed., Vol. 2, pp. 347–412). Hillsdale, NJ: Erlbaum. (p. 460)

Moses, E. B., & Barlow, D. H. (2006). A new unified treatment approach for emotional disorders based on emotion science. *Current Directions in Psychological Science, 15,* 146–150. (p. 581)

Mosher, C. E., & Danoff-Burg, S. (2008). Agentic and communal personality traits: Relations to disordered eating behavior, body shape concern, and depressive symptoms. *Eating Behaviors, 9,* 497–500. (p. 178)

Mosher, W. D., Chandra, A., & Jones, J. (2005, September 15). *Sexual behavior and selected health measures: Men and women 15–44 years of age, United States, 2002* (Advance Data from Vital and Health Statistics No. 362). Hyattsville, MD: National Center for Health Statistics. (p. 189)

Mosing, M. A., Zietsch, B. P., Shekar, S. N., Wright, M. J., & Martin, N. G. (2009). Genetic and environmental influences on optimism and its relationship to mental and self-rated health: A study of aging twins. *Behavior Genetics, 39,* 597–604. (p. 423)

Moskowitz, T. J., & Wertheim, L. J. (2011). *Scorecasting: The hidden influences behind how sports are played and games are won.* New York: Crown Archetype. (p. 456)

Moss, A. C., & Albery, I. P. (2009). A dual-process model of the alcohol–behavior link for social drinking. *Psychological Bulletin, 135,* 516–530. (p. 107)

Moss, A. J., Allen, K. F., Giovino, G. A., & Mills, S. L. (1992, December 2). *Recent trends in adolescent smoking, smoking-update correlates, and expectations about the future* (Advance Data from Vital and Health Statistics No. 221). Hyattsville, MD: National Center for Health Statistics. (p. 115)

Moss, H. A., & Susman, E. J. (1980). Longitudinal study of personality development. In O. G. Brim Jr., & J. Kagan (Eds.), *Constancy and change in human development* (pp. 530–595). Cambridge, MA: Harvard University Press. (p. 122)

Motivala, S. J., & Irwin, M. R. (2007). Sleep and immunity: Cytokine pathways linking sleep and health outcomes. *Current Directions in Psychological Science, 16,* 21–25. (p. 95)

Moxley, J. H., Ericsson, K. A., Charness, N., & Krampe, R. T. (2012). The role of intuition and deliberative thinking in experts' superior tactical decision-making. *Cognition, 124,* 72–78. (p. 324)

Moyer, K. E. (1983). The physiology of motivation: Aggression as a model. In C. J. Scheier & A. M. Rogers (Eds.), *The G. Stanley Hall Lecture Series* (Vol. 3, pp. 123–139). Washington, DC: American Psychological Association. (p. 469)

Mroczek, D. K., & Kolarz, D. M. (1998). The effect of age on positive and negative affect: A developmental perspective on happiness. *Journal of Personality and Social Psychology, 75,* 1333–1349. (p. 162)

Mroczek, D. K., & Spiro, A., III. (2003). Modeling intraindividual change in personality traits: Findings from the Normative Aging Study. *Journals of Gerontology: Series B, 58,* P153–P165. (p. 510)

Mueller, P. A., & Oppenheimer, D. M. (2014). The pen is mightier than the keyboard: Advantages of longhand over laptop note-taking. *Psychological Science, 25,* 1159–1168. (p. 310)

Muhlnickel, W. (1998). Reorganization of auditory cortex in tinnitus. *Proceedings of the National Academy of Sciences of the United States of America, 95,* 10340–10343. (p. 58)

Mukamel, R., Ekstrom, A. D., Kaplan, J., Iacoboni, M., & Fried, I. (2010). Single-neuron responses in humans during execution and observation of actions. *Current Biology, 20,* 750–756. (p. 274)

Mulcahy, N. J., & Call, J. (2006). Apes save tools for future use. *Science, 312,* 1038–1040. (p. 327)

Muller, J. E., Mittleman, M. A., Maclure, M., Sherwood, J. B., & Tofler, G. H. (1996). Triggering myocardial infarction by sexual activity. *Journal of the American Medical Association, 275,* 1405–1409. (p. 183)

Muller, J. E., & Verrier, R. L. (1996). Triggering of sudden death—Lessons from an earthquake. *New England Journal of Medicine, 334,* 461. (p. 407)

Mullin, C. R., & Linz, D. (1995). Desensitization and resensitization to violence against women: Effects of exposure to sexually violent films on judgments of domestic violence victims. *Journal of Personality and Social Psychology, 69,* 449–459. (p. 277)

Mulrow, C. D. (1999, March). *Treatment of depression—newer pharmacotherapies, summary* (Evidence Report/Technology Assessment No. 7). Rockville, MD: Agency for Health Care Policy and Research. (p. 595)

Munsey, C. (2010, June). Medicine or menace? Psychologists' research can inform the growing debate over legalizing marijuana. *Monitor on Psychology,* pp. 50–55. (p. 113)

Murayama, K., Pekrun, R., Lichtenfeld, S., & vom Hofe, R. (2013). Predicting long-term growth in students' mathematics achievement: The unique contributions of motivation and cognitive strategies. *Child Development, 84,* 1475–1490. (p. 362)

Murdik, L., Breska, A., Lamy, D., & Deouell, L. Y. (2011). Integration without awareness: Expanding the limits of unconscious processing. *Psychological Science, 22,* 764–770. (p. 80)

Murphy, G. E., & Wetzel, R. D. (1990). The lifetime risk of suicide in alcoholism. *Archives of General Psychiatry, 47,* 383–392. (p. 553)

Murphy, K. R., & Cleveland, J. N. (1995). *Understanding performance appraisal: Social, organizational, and goal-based perspectives.* Thousand Oaks, CA: Sage. (p. B-7)

Murphy, S. T., Monahan, J. L., & Zajonc, R. B. (1995). Additivity of nonconscious affect: Combined effects of priming and exposure. *Journal of Personality and Social Psychology, 69,* 589–602. (p. 389)

Murray, H. A. (1933). The effect of fear upon estimates of the maliciousness of other personalities. *Journal of Social Psychology, 4,* 310–329. (p. 497)

Murray, H. A. (1938). *Explorations in personality.* New York: Oxford University Press. (p. 375)

Murray, H. A., & Wheeler, D. R. (1937). A note on the possible clairvoyance of dreams. *Journal of Psychology, 3,* 309–313. (pp. 19, 241)

Murray, R., Jones, P., O'Callaghan, E., Takei, N., & Sham, P. (1992). Genes, viruses, and neurodevelopmental schizophrenia. *Journal of Psychiatric Research, 26,* 225–235. (p. 558)

Murray, R. M., Morrison, P. D., Henquet, C., & Di Forti, M. (2007). Cannabis, the mind and society: The hash realities. *Nature Reviews Neuroscience, 8,* 885–895. (p. 112)

Murray, S. L., Bellavia, G. M., Rose, P., & Griffin, D. W. (2003). Once hurt, twice hurtful: How perceived regard regulates daily marital interactions. *Journal of Personality and Social Psychology, 84,* 126–147. (p. 208)

Musick, M. A., Herzog, A. R., & House, J. S. (1999). Volunteering and mortality among older adults: Findings from a national sample. *Journal of Gerontology, 54B,* S173–S180. (p. 430)

Mustanski, B. S., & Bailey, J. M. (2003). A therapist's guide to the genetics of human sexual orientation. *Sexual and Relationship Therapy, 18,* 1468–1479. (p. 190)

Mydans, S. (2002, May 17). In Pakistan, rape victims are the "criminals." *The New York Times.* Retrieved from http://www.nytimes.com/2002/05/17/world/in-pakistan-rape-victims-are-the-criminals.html (p. 468)

Myers, D. G. (1993). *The pursuit of happiness.* New York: Harper. (p. 436)

Myers, D. G. (2000). *The American paradox: Spiritual hunger in an age of plenty.* New Haven, CT: Yale University Press. (p. 436)

Myers, D. G. (2001, December). Do we fear the right things? *APS Observer,* p. 3. (p. 320)

Myers, D. G. (2010). *Social psychology* (10th ed.). New York: McGraw-Hill. (p. 518)

Myers, D. G., & Bishop, G. D. (1970). Discussion effects on racial attitudes. *Science, 169,* 778–779. (p. 458)

Myers, D. G., & Diener, E. (1995). Who is happy? *Psychological Science, 6,* 10–19. (p. 436)

Myers, D. G., & Diener, E. (1996, May). The pursuit of happiness. *Scientific American.* Retrieved from http://www.scientificamerican.com/ (p. 436)

Myers, D. G., & Scanzoni, L. D. (2005). *What God has joined together?* San Francisco: Harper. (pp. 164, 188)

Myers, T. A., & Crowther, J. H. (2009). Social comparison as a predictor of body dissatisfaction: A meta-analytic review. *Journal of Abnormal Psychology, 118,* 683–698. (p. 566)

N

Nagamatsu, L. S., Chan, A., Davis, J. C., Beattie, B. L., Graf, P., Voss, M. W., . . . Liu-Ambrose, T. (2013). Physical activity improves verbal and spatial memory in older adults with probable mild cognitive impairment: A 6-month randomized controlled trial. *Journal of Aging Research, 2013,* Article 861893. doi:10.1155/2013/861893 (p. 160)

Nagourney, A. (2002, September 25). For remarks on Iraq, Gore gets praise and scorn. *The New York Times.* Retrieved from http://www.nytimes.com/2002/09/25/politics/25GORE.html (p. 444)

Nanni, V., Uher, R., & Danese, A. (2012). Childhood maltreatment predicts unfavorable course of illness and treatment outcome in depression: A meta-analysis. *American Journal of Psychiatry, 169,* 141–151. (p. 144)

Napolitan, D. A., & Goethals, G. R. (1979). The attribution of friendliness. *Journal of Experimental Social Psychology, 15,* 105–113. (p. 442)

Narvaez, D. (2010). Moral complexity: The fatal attraction of truthiness and the importance of mature moral functioning. *Perspectives on Psychological Science, 5,* 163–181. (p. 151)

NAS. (2011). *Statistics: How many people have autism spectrum disorders.* National Autistic Society. Retrieved from http://www.autism.org.uk/ (p. 136)

Nathan, D. (2011). *Sybil exposed: The extraordinary story behind the famous multiple personality case.* New York: Simon & Schuster. (p. 562)

National Academy of Sciences. (2001). *Exploring the biological contributions to human health: Does sex matter?* Washington, DC: National Academy Press. (p. 177)

National Academy of Sciences. (2002). *The polygraph and lie detection.* Washington, DC: National Academies Press. (p. 394)

National Center for Health Statistics. (1990). *Health, United States, 1989.* Washington, DC: U.S. Department of Health and Human Services. (p. 159)

National Institute of Mental Health. (2008). *The numbers count: Mental disorders in America.* Retrieved from http://www.nimh.nih.gov (p. 534)

National Research Council. (1990). *Human factors research needs for an aging population.* Washington, DC: National Academy Press. (p. 159)

National Safety Council. (2010). Transportation mode comparisons. In *Injury facts 2010 edition.* Retrieved from http://www.nsc.org/ (p. 82)

National Safety Council. (2014). Transportation mode comparisons. In *Injury facts 2014 edition.* Retrieved from http://www.nsc.org/ (p. 320)

National Sleep Foundation. (2006, August 16). *The ABCs of back-to-school sleep schedules: The consequences of insufficient sleep* [Press release]. Retrieved from http://www.sleepfoundation.org (p. 94)

National Sleep Foundation. (2013). *2013 International Bedroom Poll: Summary of findings.* Retrieved from http://sleepfoundation.org/sleep-polls-data/other-polls/2013-international-bedroom-poll (p. 92)

Naughton, M., Clarke, G., O'Leary, O. F, Cryan, J. F., & Dinan, T. G. (2014). A review of ketamine in affective disorders: Current evidence of clinical efficacy, limitations of use and pre-clinical evidence on proposed mechanisms of action. *Journal of Affective Disorders, 156,* 24–35. (p. 596)

Nausheen, B., Carr, N. J., Peveler, R. C., Moss-Morris, R., Verrill, C., Robbins, E., . . . Gidron, Y. (2010). Relationship between loneliness and proangiogenic cytokines in newly diagnosed tumors of colon and rectum. *Psychosomatic Medicine, 72,* 912–916. (p. 413)

Nave, C. S., Sherman, R. A., Funder, D.C., Hampson, S. E., & Goldberg, L. R. (2010). On the contextual independence of personality: Teachers' assessments predict directly observed behavior after four decades. *Social Psychological and Personality Science, 3,* 1–9. (p. 122)

Naylor, T. H. (1990). Redefining corporate motivation, Swedish style. *Christian Century, 107,* 566–570. (p. B-13)

NCASA. (2007). *Wasting the best and the brightest: Substance abuse at America's colleges and universities.* New York: National Center on Addiction and Drug Abuse, Columbia University. (p. 116)

Neal, D. T., Wood, W., & Drolet, A. (2013). How do people adhere to goals when willpower is low? The profits (and pitfalls) of strong habits. *Journal of Personality and Social Psychology, 104,* 959–975. (p. 246)

Nedeltcheva, A. V., Kilkus, J. M., Imperial, J., Schoeller, D. A., & Penev, P. D. (2010). Insufficient sleep undermines dietary efforts to reduce adiposity. *Annals of Internal Medicine, 153,* 435–441. (p. 384)

NEEF. (n.d.). *Fact sheet: Children's health and nature.* National Environmental Education Foundation. Retrieved from http://www.neefusa.org/assets/files/NIFactSheet.pdf (p. 600)

Neese, R. M. (1991, November/December). What good is feeling bad? The evolutionary benefits of psychic pain. *The Sciences,* pp. 30–37. (pp. 231, 268)

Neimeyer, R. A., & Currier, J. M. (2009). Grief therapy: Evidence of efficacy and emerging directions. *Current Directions in Psychological Science, 18,* 352–356. (p. 168)

Neisser, U. (1979). The control of information pickup in selective looking. In A. D. Pick (Ed.), *Perception and its development: A tribute to Eleanor J. Gibson* (pp. 209–219). Hillsdale, NJ: Erlbaum. (p. 83)

Neisser, U., Boodoo, G., Bouchard, T. J., Jr., Boykin, A. W., Brody, N., Ceci, S. J., . . . Urbina, S. (1996). Intelligence: Knowns and unknowns. *American Psychologist, 51,* 77–101. (pp. 354, 360)

Neisser, U., Winograd, E., & Weldon, M. S. (1991, November). *Remembering the earthquake: "What I experienced" vs. "how I heard the news."* Paper presented at the 32nd Annual Meeting of the Psychonomic Society, San Francisco, CA. (p. 295)

Neitz, J., Carroll, J., & Neitz, M. (2001). Color vision: Almost reason enough for having eyes. *Optics & Photonics News, 12,* 26–33. (p. 213)

Neitz, J., Geist, T., & Jacobs, G. H. (1989). Color vision in the dog. *Visual Neuroscience, 3,* 119–125. (p. 214)

Nelson, C. A., III, Fox, N. A., & Zeanah, C. H., Jr. (2014). *Romania's abandoned children.* Cambridge, MA: Harvard University Press. (pp. 143, 356)

Nelson, C. A., III, Furtado, E. Z., Fox, N. A., & Zeanah, C. H., Jr. (2009). The deprived human brain. *American Scientist, 97,* 222–229. (pp. 143, 356)

Nelson, M. D., Saykin, A. J., Flashman, L. A., & Riordan, H. J. (1998). Hippocampal volume reduction in schizophrenia as assessed by magnetic resonance imaging. *Archives of General Psychiatry, 55,* 433–440. (p. 558)

Nelson, S. K., Kushlev, K., English, T., Dunn, E. W., & Lyubomirsky, S. (2013). In defense of parenthood: Children are associated with more joy than misery. *Psychological Science, 24,* 3–10. (p. 165)

Nemeth, C. J., & Ormiston, M. (2007). Creative idea generation: Harmony versus stimulation. *European Journal of Social Psychology, 37,* 524–535. (p. 459)

Neria, Y., DiGrande, L., & Adams, B. G. (2011). Posttraumatic stress disorder following the September 11, 2001, terrorist attacks: A review of the literature among highly exposed populations. *American Psychologist, 66,* 429–446. (p. 540)

Nes, R. B. (2010). Happiness in behaviour genetics: Findings and implications. *Journal of Happiness Studies, 11,* 369–381. (p. 437)

Nes, R. B., Czajkowski, N., & Tambs, K. (2010). Family matters: Happiness in nuclear families and twins. *Behavior Genetics, 40,* 577–590. (p. 436)

Nesca, M., & Koulack, D. (1994). Recognition memory, sleep and circadian rhythms. *Canadian Journal of Experimental Psychology, 48,* 359–379. (p. 305)

Nestadt, G., & Samuels, J. (1997). Epidemiology and genetics of obsessive-compulsive disorder. *International Review of Psychiatry, 9,* 61–71. (p. 540)

Nestler, E. J. (2011, December). Hidden switches in the mind. *Scientific American,* pp. 77–83. (p. 550)

Nestoriuc, Y., Rief, W., & Martin, A. (2008). Meta-analysis of biofeedback for tension-type headache: Efficacy, specificity, and treatment moderators. *Journal of Consulting and Clinical Psychology, 76,* 379–396. (p. 427)

Neubauer, D. N. (1999). Sleep problems in the elderly. *American Family Physician, 59,* 2551–2558. (p. 90)

Neumann, R., & Strack, F. (2000). "Mood contagion": The automatic transfer of mood between persons. *Journal of Personality and Social Psychology, 79,* 211–223. (pp. 403, 449)

Newcomb, M. D., & Harlow, L. L. (1986). Life events and substance use among adolescents: Mediating effects of perceived loss of control and meaninglessness in life. *Journal of Personality and Social Psychology, 51,* 564–577. (p. 115)

Newell, B. R. (2015). "Wait! Just let me not think about that for a minute": What role do implicit processes play in higher-level cognition? *Current Directions in Psychological Science, 24,* 65–70. (p. 324)

Newport, E. L. (1990). Maturational constraints on language learning. *Cognitive Science, 14,* 11–28. (p. 333)

Newport, F. (2001, February). Americans see women as emotional and affectionate, men as more aggressive. *The Gallup Poll Monthly,* pp. 34–38. (p. 397)

Newport, F. (2002, July 29). *Bush job approval update.* Retrieved from http://www.gallup.com/poll/6478/bush-job-approval-update.aspx (p. 486)

Newport, F. (2013, July 25). *In U.S. 87% approve of Black-White marriage, vs. 4% in 1958.* Retrieved from http://www.gallup.com/poll/163697/approve-marriage-blacks-whites.aspxGallup Poll (p. 462)

Newport, F. (2013, July 31). *Most U.S. smokers want to quit, have tried multiple times: Former smokers say best way to quit is just to stop "cold turkey."* Retrieved from http://www.gallup.com/poll/163763/smokers-quit-tried-multiple-times.aspx (pp. 105, 109)

Newport, F. (2014, June 2). *In U.S., 42% believe creationist view of human origins.* Retrieved from http://www.gallup.com/poll/170822/believe-creationist-view-human-origins.aspx (p. 75)

Newport, F., & Wilke, J. (2013, August 2). *Most in U.S. want marriage, but its importance has dropped.* Retrieved from http://www.gallup.com/poll/163802/marriage-importance-dropped.aspx (p. 164)

Newport, F., Argrawal, S., & Witters, D. (2010, December 23). *Very religious Americans lead healthier lives.* Retrieved from http://www.gallup.com/poll/145379/religious-americans-lead-healthier-lives.aspx (p. 430)

Newport, F., & Pelham, B. (2009, December 14). *Don't worry, be 80: Worry and stress decline with age.* Retrieved from http://www.gallup.com/poll/124655/dont-worry-be-80-worry-stress-decline-age.aspx (p. 407)

Newton, E. L. (1991). The rocky road from actions to intentions. *Dissertation Abstracts International, 51*(08–B), 4105. (p. B-15)

Newton, I. (1704). *Opticks: Or, a treatise of the reflexions, refractions, inflexions and colours of light.* London: Royal Society. (p. 213)

Ng, J. Y. Y., Ntoumanis, N., Thøgersen-Ntoumani, C., Deci, E. L., Ryan, R. M., Duda, J. L., & Williams, G. C. (2012). Self-determination theory applied to health contexts: A meta-analysis. *Perspectives on Psychological Science, 7,* 325–340. (p. 420)

Ng, M., Fleming, T., Robinson, M., Thomson, B., Graetz, N., Margono, C., . . . Gakidou, E. (2014). Global, regional, and national prevalence of overweight and obesity in children and adults during 1980–2013: A systematic analysis for the Global Burden of Disease Study 2013. *The Lancet, 384,* 766–781. (p. 382)

Ng, S. H. (1990). Androcentric coding of *man* and *his* in memory by language users. *Journal of Experimental Social Psychology, 26,* 455–464. (p. 338)

Ng, T. W. H., & Feldman, D. C. (2009). How broadly does education contribute to job performance. *Personnel Psychology, 62,* 89–134. (p. B-6)

Ng, T. W. H., Sorensen, K. L., & Yim, F. H. K. (2009). Does the job satisfaction–job performance relationship vary across cultures? *Journal of Cross-Cultural Psychology, 40,* 761–796. (p. B-9)

Ng, W. W. H., Sorensen, K. L., & Eby, L. T. (2006). Locus of control at work: A meta-analysis. *Journal of Organizational Behavior, 27,* 1057–1087. (p. 421)

Nguyen, H.-H. D., & Ryan, A. M. (2008). Does stereotype threat affect test performance of minorities and women? A meta-analysis of experimental evidence. *Journal of Applied Psychology, 93,* 1314–1334. (p. 361)

NHTSA. (2000). *Traffic safety facts 1999: Older population.* National Highway Traffic Safety Administration. Retrieved from http://www.ntl.bts.gov/ (p. 159)

Nicholson, I. (2011). "Torture at Yale": Experimental subjects, laboratory torment and the "rehabilitation" of Milgram's "Obedience to Authority." *Theory and Psychology, 21,* 737–761. (p. 453)

Nickell, J. (Ed.). (1994). *Psychic sleuths: ESP and sensational cases.* Buffalo, NY: Prometheus Books. (p. 241)

Nickell, J. (2005, July/August). The case of the psychic detectives. *Skeptical Inquirer,* pp. 16–19. (p. 241)

Nickerson, R. S. (1999). How we know—and sometimes misjudge—what others know: Imputing one's own knowledge to others. *Psychological Bulletin, 125,* 737–759. (p. B-15)

Nickerson, R. S. (2002). The production and perception of randomness. *Psychological Review, 109,* 330–357. (p. 16)

Nickerson, R. S. (2005). Bertrand's chord, Buffon's needles, and the concept of randomness. *Thinking & Reasoning, 11,* 67–96. (p. 16)

Nicolas, S., & Levine, Z. (2012). Beyond intelligence testing: Remembering Alfred Binet after a century. *European Psychologist, 17,* 320–325. (p. 346)

Nicolaus, L. K., Cassel, J. F., Carlson, R. B., & Gustavson, C. R. (1983). Taste-aversion conditioning of crows to control predation on eggs. *Science, 220,* 212–214. (p. 268)

NIDA. (2002). *NIDA Research Report Series: Methamphetamine abuse and addiction* (NIH Publication No. 02-4210). Bethesda, MD: National Institute on Drug Abuse. (p. 111)

NIDA. (2005, May). *DrugFacts: Methamphetamine.* Bethesda, MD: National Institute on Drug Abuse. (p. 111)

Nielsen, K. M., Faergeman, O., Larsen, M. L., & Foldspang, A. (2006). Danish singles have a twofold risk of acute coronary syndrome: Data from a cohort of 138,290 persons. *Journal of Epidemiology and Community Health, 60,* 721–728. (p. 424)

Nielsen, M., & Tomaselli, K. (2010). Overimitation in Kalahari Bushman children and the origins of human cultural cognition. *Psychological Science, 21,* 729–736. (p. 274)

Nieuwenstein, M. R., Wierenga, T., Morey, R. D., Wicherts, J. M., Blom, T. N., Wagenmakers, E., & van Rijn, H. (2015). On making the right choice: A meta-analysis and large-scale replication attempt of the unconscious thought advantage. *Judgment and Decision Making, 10,* 1–17. (p. 324)

NIH. (2001, July 20). *Workshop summary: Scientific evidence on condom effectiveness for sexually transmitted disease (STD) prevention.* Bethesda, MD: National Institute of Allergy and Infectious Diseases, National Institutes of Health. (p. 184)

NIH. (2010). *Teacher's guide: Information about sleep.* National Institutes of Health. Retrieved from http://www.science.education.nih.gov/ (p. 93)

NIH. (2013, January 24). *Prenatal inflammation linked to autism risk.* National Institutes of Health. Retrieved from http://www.nih.gov/news/health/jan2013/niehs-24.htm (p. 136)

Nir, Y., & Tononi, G. (2010). Dreaming and the brain: From phenomenology to neurophysiology. *Trends in Cognitive Sciences, 14,* 88–100. (p. 102)

Nisbett, R. E. (1987). Lay personality theory: Its nature, origin, and utility. In N. E. Grunberg, R. E. Nisbett, J. Rodin, & J. E. Singer (Eds.), *A distinctive approach to psychological research: The influence of Stanley Schachter* (pp. 87–117). Hillsdale, NJ: Erlbaum. (p. B-5)

Nisbett, R. E. (2003). *The geography of thought: How Asians and Westerners think differently . . . and why.* New York: Free Press. (p. 442)

Nisbett, R. E. (2009). *Intelligence and how to get it: Why schools and culture count.* New York: Norton. (p. 359)

Nisbett, R. E., Aronson, J., Blair, C., Dickens, W., Flynn, J., Halpern, D. F., & Turkheimer, E. (2012). Intelligence: New findings and theoretical developments. *American Psychologist, 67,* 130–159. (pp. 355, 358)

Nisbett, R. E., & Cohen, D. (1996). *Culture of honor: The psychology of violence in the South.* Boulder, CO: Westview Press. (p. 471)

Nixon, G. M., Thompson, J. M. D., Han, D. Y., Becroft, D. M., Clark, P. M., Robinson, E., . . . Mitchell, E. A. (2008). Short sleep duration in middle childhood: Risk factors and consequences. *Sleep, 31,* 71–78. (p. 95)

Nizzi, M. C., Demertzi, A., Gosseries, O., Bruno, M.-A., Jouen, F., & Laureys, S. (2012). From armchair to wheelchair: How patients with a locked-in syndrome integrate bodily changes in experienced identity. *Consciousness and Cognition, 21,* 431–437. (p. 433)

Nock, M. K. (2010). Self-injury. *Annual Review of Clinical Psychology, 6,* 339–363. (p. 554)

Nock, M. K., Borges, G., Bromet, E. J., Alonso, J., Angermeyer, M., Beautrais, A., . . . Williams, D. (2008). Cross-national prevalence and risk factors for suicidal ideation, plans, and attempts. *British Journal of Psychiatry, 192,* 98–105. (p. 554)

Nock, M. K., & Kessler, R. C. (2006). Prevalence of and risk factors for suicide attempts versus suicide gestures: Analysis of the National Comorbidity Survey. *Journal of Abnormal Psychology, 115,* 616–623. (p. 555)

Noel, J. G., Forsyth, D. R., & Kelley, K. N. (1987). Improving the performance of failing students by overcoming their self-serving attributional biases. *Basic and Applied Social Psychology, 8,* 151–162. (p. 423)

Noice, H., & Noice, T. (2006). What studies of actors and acting can tell us about memory and cognitive functioning. *Current Directions in Psychological Science, 15,* 14–18. (p. 290)

Nolen-Hoeksema, S. (2001). Gender differences in depression. *Current Directions in Psychological Science, 10,* 173–176. (p. 550)

Nolen-Hoeksema, S. (2003). *Women who think too much: How to break free of overthinking and reclaim your life.* New York: Holt. (p. 550)

Nolen-Hoeksema, S., & Larson, J. (1999). *Coping with loss.* Mahwah, NJ: Erlbaum. (p. 168)

NORC. (2014). *General social survey data, 1972–2012.* National Opinion Research Center, University of Chicago. Retrieved via http://sda.berkeley.edu/ (p. 371)

Nordgren, L. F., McDonnell, M.-H. M., & Loewenstein, G. (2011). What constitutes torture? Psychological impediments to an objective evaluation of enhanced interrogation tactics. *Psychological Science, 22,* 689–694. (p. 207)

Nordgren, L. F., van der Pligt, J., & van Harreveld, F. (2006). Visceral drives in retrospect: Explanations about the inaccessible past. *Psychological Science, 17,* 635–640. (p. 378)

Nordgren, L. F., van der Pligt, J., & van Harreveld, F. (2007). Evaluating Eve: Visceral states influence the evaluation of impulsive behavior. *Journal of Personality and Social Psychology, 93,* 75–84. (p. 378)

Norman, D. A. (2001). *The perils of home theater.* Retrieved from http://www.jnd.org/dn.mss/the_perils_of_home_t.html (p. B-14)

Norman, E. (2010). "The unconscious" in current psychology. *European Psychologist, 15,* 193–201. (p. 500)

Norton, K. L., Olds, T. S., Olive, S., & Dank, S. (1996). Ken and Barbie at life size. *Sex Roles, 34,* 287–294. (p. 566)

NSF. (2001, October 24). *Public bounces back after Sept. 11 attacks, national study shows.* National Science Foundation. Retrieved from http://www.nsf.gov/od/lpa/news/press/ol/pr0185.htm (p. 407)

Nurmikko, A. V., Donoghue, J. P., Hochberg, L. R., Patterson, W. R., Song, Y.-K., Bull, C. W., . . . Aceros, J. (2010). Listening to brain microcircuits for interfacing with external world—Progress in wireless implantable microelectronic neuroengineering devices. *Proceedings of the IEEE, 98,* 375–388. (p. 58)

Nussinovitch, U., & Shoenfeld, Y. (2012). The role of gender and organ specific autoimmunity. *Autoimmunity Reviews, 11,* A377–A385. (p. 411)

Nutt, D. J., & Malizia, A. L. (2004). Structural and functional brain changes in posttraumatic stress disorder. *Journal of Clinical Psychology, 65,* 11–17. (p. 543)

Nuttin, J. M., Jr. (1987). Affective consequences of mere ownership: The name letter effect in twelve European languages. *European Journal of Social Psychology, 17,* 381–402. (p. 475)

Nye, C. D., Su, R., Rounds, J., & Drasgow, F. (2012). Vocational interests and performance: A quantitative summary of over 60 years of research. *Perspectives on Psychological Science, 7,* 384–403. (p. B-3)

O

Oakley, D. A., & Halligan, P. W. (2013). Hypnotic suggestion: Opportunities for cognitive neuroscience. *Nature Reviews Neuroscience, 14,* 565–576. (p. 235)

Oaten, M., & Cheng, K. (2006a). Improved self-control: The benefits of a regular program of academic study. *Basic and Applied Social Psychology, 28,* 1–16. (p. 422)

Oaten, M., & Cheng, K. (2006b). Longitudinal gains in self-regulation from regular physical exercise. *British Journal of Health Psychology, 11,* 717–733. (p. 422)

Oberman, L. M., & Ramachandran, V. S. (2007). The simulating social mind: The role of the mirror neuron system and simulation in the social and communicative deficits of autism spectrum disorders. *Psychological Bulletin, 133,* 310–327. (p. 137)

O'Boyle, E. H., Jr., Humphrey, R. H., Pollack, J. M., Hawver, T. H., & Story, P. A. (2011). The relation between emotional intelligence and job performance: A meta-analysis. *Journal of Organizational Behavior, 32,* 788–818. (p. 345)

O'Brien, E., & Ellsworth, P. C. (2012). Saving the last for best: A positivity bias for end experiences. *Psychological Science, 23,* 163–165. (p. 233)

O'Brien, L., Albert, D., Chein, J., & Steinberg, L. (2011). Adolescents prefer more immediate rewards when in the presence of their peers. *Journal of Research on Adolescence, 21,* 747–753. (p. 155)

Ochsner, K. N., Ray, R. R., Hughes, B., McRae, K., Cooper, J. C., Weber, J., . . . Gross, J. J. (2009). Bottom-up and top-down processes in emotion generation: Common and distinct neural mechanisms. *Psychological Science, 20,* 1322–1331. (p. 389)

O'Connor, P., & Brown, G. W. (1984). Supportive relationships: Fact or fancy? *Journal of Social and Personal Relationships, 1,* 159–175. (p. 590)

Odgers, C. L., Caspi, A., Nagin, D. S., Piquero, A. R., Slutske, W. S., Milne, B. J., . . . Moffitt, T. E. (2008). Is it important to prevent early exposure to drugs and alcohol among adolescents? *Psychological Science, 19,* 1037–1044. (p. 115)

O'Donnell, L., Stueve, A., O'Donnell, C., Duran, R., San Doval, A., Wilson, R. F., . . . Pleck, J. H. (2002). Long-term reduction in sexual initiation and sexual activity among urban middle schoolers in the reach for health service learning program. *Journal of Adolescent Health, 31,* 93–100. (p. 187)

O'Donovan, A., Neylan, T. C., Metzler, T., & Cohen, B. E. (2012). Lifetime exposure to traumatic psychological stress is associated with elevated inflammation in the heart and soul study. *Brain, Behavior, and Immunity, 26,* 642–649. (p. 414)

Oettingen, G., & Mayer, D. (2002). The motivating function of thinking about the future: Expectations versus fantasies. *Journal of Personality and Social Psychology, 83,* 1198–1212. (p. 423)

Offer, D., Ostrov, E., Howard, K. I., & Atkinson, R. (1988). *The teenage world: Adolescents' self-image in ten countries.* New York: Plenum Press. (p. 154)

Ogden, J. (2012, January 16). HM, the man with no memory. *Psychology Today.* Retrieved from https://www.psychologytoday.com/blog/trouble-in-mind/201201/hm-the-man-no-memory (p. 302)

O'Hara, R. E., Gibbons, F. X., Gerrard, M., Li, Z., & Sargent, J. D. (2012). Greater exposure to sexual content in popular movies predicts earlier sexual debut and increased sexual risk taking. *Psychological Science, 23,* 984–993. (p. 186)

Ohgami, H., Terao, T., Shiotsuki, I., Ishii, N., & Iwata, N. (2009). Lithium levels in drinking water and risk of suicide. *British Journal of Psychiatry, 194,* 464–465. (p. 596)

Öhman, A. (2009). Of snakes and fears: An evolutionary perspective on the psychology of fear. *Scandinavian Journal of Psychology, 50,* 543–552. (p. 543)

Oishi, S., Diener, E. F., Lucas, R. E., & Suh, E. M. (1999). Cross-cultural variations in predictors of life satisfaction: Perspectives from needs and values. *Personality and Social Psychology Bulletin, 25,* 980–990. (pp. 368, 369)

Oishi, S., Kesebir, S., & Diener, E. (2011). Income inequality and happiness. *Psychological Science, 22,* 1095–1100. (pp. 435, 471)

Oishi, S., Kesebir, S., Miao, F., Talhelm, T., Endo, Y., Uchida, Y., . . . Norasakkunkit, Y. (2013). Residential mobility increases motivation to expand social network. But why? *Journal of Experimental Social Psychology, 49,* 217–223. (p. 371)

Oishi, S., Schiller, J., & Blair, E. G. (2013). Felt understanding and misunderstanding affect the perception of pain, slant, and distance. *Social Psychological and Personality Science, 4,* 259–266. (p. 207)

Oishi, S., & Schimmack, U. (2010). Culture and well-being: A new inquiry into the psychological wealth of nations. *Perspectives in Psychological Science, 5,* 463–471. (p. 435)

Oishi, S., & Schimmack, U. (2010). Residential mobility, well-being, and mortality. *Journal of Personality and Social Psychology, 98,* 980–994. (p. 371)

Okada, K., & Samreth, S. (2013). A study on the socio-economic determinants of suicide: Evidence from 13 European OECD countries. *Journal of Behavioral Economics, 45,* 78–85. (p. 553)

Okimoto, T. G., & Brescoll, V. L. (2010). The price of power: Power seeking and backlash against female politicians. *Personality and Social Psychology Bulletin, 36,* 923–936. (p. 173)

Olatunji, B. O., & Puncochar, B. D. (2014). Delineating the influence of emotion and reason on morality and punishment. *Review of General Psychology, 18,* 186–207. (p. 150)

Olatunji, B. O., & Wolitzky-Taylor, K. B. (2009). Anxiety sensitivity and the anxiety disorders: A meta-analytic review and synthesis. *Psychological Bulletin, 135,* 974–999. (p. 538)

Olds, J. (1958). Self-stimulation of the brain. *Science, 127,* 315–324. (p. 53)

Olds, J. (1975). Mapping the mind onto the brain. In F. G. Worden, J. P. Swazey, & G. Adelman (Eds.), *The neurosciences: Paths of discovery* (pp. 375–400). Cambridge, MA: MIT Press. (p. 53)

Olds, J., & Milner, P. (1954). Positive reinforcement produced by electrical stimulation of the septal area and other regions of rat brain. *Journal of Comparative and Physiological Psychology, 47,* 419–427. (p. 53)

Olff, M., Langeland, W., Draijer, N., & Gersons, B. P. R. (2007). Gender differences in posttraumatic stress disorder. *Psychological Bulletin, 135,* 183–204. (p. 540)

Olfson, M., Gameroff, M. J., Marcus, S. C., & Jensen, P. S. (2003). National trends in the treatment of attention deficit hyperactivity disorder. *American Journal of Psychiatry, 160,* 1071–1077. (p. 532)

Olfson, M., Marcus, S. C., Wan, G. J., & Geissler, E. C. (2004). National trends in the outpatient treatment of anxiety disorders. *Journal of Clinical Psychiatry, 65,* 1166–1173. (p. 595)

Oliner, S. P., & Oliner, P. M. (1988). *The altruistic personality: Rescuers of Jews in Nazi Europe.* New York: Free Press. (p. 276)

Olivé, I., Templemann, C., Berthoz, A., & Heinze, H.-J. (2015). Increased functional connectivity between superior colliculus and brain regions implicated in bodily self-consciousness during the rubber band illusion. *Human Brain Mapping, 36,* 717–730. (p. 81)

Olivola, C. Y., & Todorov, A. (2010). Elected in 100 milliseconds: Appearance-based trait inferences and voting. *Journal of Nonverbal Behavior, 54,* 83–110. (p. 396)

Olshansky, S. J. (2011). Aging of US Presidents. *Journal of the American Medical Association, 306,* 2328–2329. (p. 420)

Olson, K. R., Key, A. C., & Eaton, N. R. (2015). Gender cognition in transgender children. *Psychological Science, 26,* 467–474. (p. 179)

Olson, R. L., Hanowski, R. J., Hickman, J. S., & Bocanegra, J. (2009, September). *Driver distraction in commercial vehicle operations.* Washington, DC: U.S. Department of Transportation, Federal Motor Carrier Safety Administration. (p. 82)

Olsson, A., Nearing, K. I., & Phelps, E. A. (2007). Learning fears by observing others: The neural systems of social fear transmission. *Social Cognitive and Affective Neuroscience, 2,* 3–11. (p. 542)

Oman, D., Kurata, J. H., Strawbridge, W. J., & Cohen, R. D. (2002). Religious attendance and cause of death over 31 years. *International Journal of Psychiatry in Medicine, 32,* 69–89. (p. 430)

O'Neill, M. J. (1993, October). *The relationship between privacy, control, and stress responses in office workers.* Paper presented at the annual meeting of the Human Factors and Ergonomics Society. (p. 420)

Ong, A. D., Fuller-Rowell, T., & Burrow, A. L. (2009). Racial discrimination and the stress process. *Journal of Personality and Social Psychology, 96*, 1259–1271. (p. 409)

ONS. (2015, September 23). *Personal well-being in the UK, 2014/2015.* Office for National Statistics. Retrieved from http://www.ons.gov.uk/ (p. 436)

Oppenheimer, D., Jerez-Fernandez, A., & Angulo, A. N. (2014). Show me the numbers. *Psychological Science, 25*, 633–635. (p. A-1)

Oppenheimer, D. M., & Trail, T. E. (2010). Why leaning to the left makes you lean to the left: Effects of spatial orientation on political attitudes. *Social Cognition, 28*, 651–661. (p. 240)

Oquendo, M. A., Galfalvy, H. C., Currier, D., Grunebaum, M. F., Sher, L., Sullivan, G. M., . . . Mann, J. J. (2011). Treatment of suicide attempters with bipolar disorder: A randomized clinical trial comparing lithium and valproate in the prevention of suicidal behavior. *American Journal of Psychiatry, 168*, 1050–1056. (p. 596)

Oren, D. A., & Terman, M. (1998). Tweaking the human circadian clock with light. *Science, 279*, 333–334. (p. 92)

Orth, U., Maes, J., & Schmitt, M. (2015). Self-esteem development across the life span: A longitudinal study with a large sample from Germany. *Developmental Psychology, 51*, 248–259. (pp. 122, 153)

Orth, U., & Robins, R. W. (2014). The development of self-esteem. *Current Directions in Psychological Science, 23*, 381–387. (p. 517)

Orth, U., Robins, R. W., Trzesniewski, K. H., Maes, J., & Schmitt, M. (2009). Low self-esteem is a risk factor for depressive symptoms from young adulthood to old age. *Journal of Abnormal Psychology, 118*, 472–478. (p. 548)

Orth, U., Robins, R. W., & Widaman, K. F. (2012). Life-span development of self-esteem and its effects on important life outcomes. *Journal of Personality and Social Psychology, 102*, 1271–1288. (p. 122)

Osborne, L. (1999, October 24). A linguistic big bang. *The New York Times Magazine.* Retrieved from http://www.nytimes.com/library/magazine/home/19991024mag-sign-language.html (p. 330)

Osgood, C. E. (1962). *An alternative to war or surrender.* Urbana: University of Illinois Press. (p. 488)

Osgood, C. E. (1980). *GRIT: A strategy for survival in mankind's nuclear age?* Paper presented at the Pugwash Conference on New Directions in Disarmament, Racine, WI. (p. 488)

Oskarsson, A. T., Van Voven, L., McClelland, G. H., & Hastie, R. (2009). What's next? Judging sequences of binary events. *Psychological Bulletin, 135*, 262–285. (p. 16)

OSS Assessment Staff. (1948). *The assessment of men.* New York: Rinehart. (p. 514)

Ossher, L., Flegal, K. E., & Lustig, C. (2012). Everyday memory errors in older adults. *Aging, Neuropsychology, and Cognition, 20*, 220–242. (p. 161)

Ost, L. G., & Hugdahl, K. (1981). Acquisition of phobias and anxiety response patterns in clinical patients. *Behaviour Research and Therapy, 16*, 439–447. (p. 541)

Ostfeld, A. M., Kasl, S. V., D'Atri, D. A., & Fitzgerald, E. F. (1987). *Stress, crowding, and blood pressure in prison.* Hillsdale, NJ: Erlbaum. (p. 420)

O'Sullivan, M., Frank, M. G., Hurley, C. M., & Tiwana, J. (2009). Police lie detection accuracy: The effect of lie scenario. *Law and Human Behavior, 33*, 530–538. (p. 397)

Osvath, M., & Karvonen, E. (2012). Spontaneous innovation for future deception in a male chimpanzee. *PLOS ONE, 7*(5), e36782. doi:10.1371/journal.pone.0036782 (p. 327)

Oswald, F. L., Mitchell, G., Blanton, H., Jaccard, J., & Tetlock, P. E. (2013). Predicting ethnic and racial discrimination: A meta-analysis of IAT criterion studies. *Journal of Personality and Social Psychology, 105*, 171–192. (p. 463)

Oswald, F. L., Mitchell, G., Blanton, H., Jaccard, J., & Tetlock, P. E. (2015). Using the IAT to predict ethnic and racial discrimination: Small effect sizes of unknown societal significance. *Journal of Personality and Social Psychology, 108*, 562–571. (p. 463)

Ott, B. (2007, June 14). Investors, take note: Engagement boosts earnings. *Gallup Management Journal.* Retrieved from http://www.gallup.com/business journal/27799/investors-take-note-engagement-boosts-earnings.aspx (p. B-10)

Ott, C. H., Lueger, R. J., Kelber, S. T., & Prigerson, H. G. (2007). Spousal bereavement in older adults: Common, resilient, and chronic grief with defining characteristics. *Journal of Nervous and Mental Disease, 195*, 332–341. (p. 168)

Ouellette, J. A., & Wood, W. (1998). Habit and intention in everyday life: The multiple processes by which past behavior predicts future behavior. *Psychological Bulletin, 124*, 54–74. (p. B-6)

Owen, A. M. (2014). Disorders of consciousness: Diagnostic accuracy of brain imaging in the vegetative state. *Nature Reviews Neurology, 10*, 370–371. (p. 81)

Owen, A. M., Coleman, M. R., Boly, M., Davis, M. H., Laureys, S., & Pickard, J. D. (2006). Detecting awareness in the vegetative state. *Science, 313*, 1402. (p. 81)

Owen, A. M., Hampshire, A., Grahn, J. A., Stenton, R., Dajani, S., Burns, A. S., . . . Ballard, C. G. (2010). Putting brain training to the test. *Nature, 465*, 775–778. (p. 162)

Owen, D. J., Slep, A. M. S., & Heyman, R. E. (2012). The effect of praise, positive nonverbal response, reprimand, and negative nonverbal response on child compliance: A systematic review. *Clinical Child and Family Psychology Review, 15*, 364–385. (p. 262)

Owen, R. (1814). First essay. In *A new view of society, or, essays on the principle of the formation of the human character, and the application of the principle to practice.* Quoted in New Lanark Trust, *The story of New Lanark* (1993). New Lanark Mills, Lanark, Scotland: Author. (p. B-8)

Owens, J. A., Belon, K., & Moss, P. (2010). Impact of delaying school start time on adolescent sleep, mood, and behavior. *Archives of Pediatric Adolescent Medicine, 164*, 608–614. (p. 95)

Oxfam. (2005, March 29). *Three months on: New figures show tsunami impacted more heavily on women* [Press release]. Retrieved from http://www.oxfam.org.nz/news/three-months-on-new-figures-show-tsunami-impacted-more-heavily-on-women (p. 178)

Ozer, E. J., Best, S. R., Lipsey, T. L., & Weiss, D. S. (2003). Predictors of posttraumatic stress disorder and symptoms in adults: A meta-analysis. *Psychological Bulletin, 129*, 52–73. (p. 540)

Ozer, E. J., & Weiss, D. S. (2004). Who develops posttraumatic stress disorder? *Current Directions in Psychological Science, 13*, 169–172. (p. 540)

Özgen, E. (2004). Language, learning, and color perception. *Current Directions in Psychological Science, 13*, 95–98. (p. 337)

P

Padgett, V. R. (1989, August). *Predicting organizational violence: An application of 11 powerful principles of obedience.* Paper presented at the 97th Annual Convention of the American Psychological Association, New Orleans, LA. (p. 454)

Pagani, L. S., Fitzpatrick, C., Barnett, T. A., & Dubow, E. (2010). Prospective associations between early childhood television exposure and academic, psychosocial, and physical well-being by middle childhood. *Archive of Pediatric and Adolescent Medicine, 164*, 425–431. (p. 385)

Page, S. E. (2007). *The difference: How the power of diversity creates better groups, firms, schools, and societies.* Princeton, NJ: Princeton University Press. (p. 459)

Palladino, J. J., & Carducci, B. J. (1983). *"Things that go bump in the night": Students' knowledge of sleep and dreams.* Paper presented at the meeting of the Southeastern Psychological Association. (p. 87)

Paller, K. A., & Suzuki, S. (2014). The source of consciousness. *Trends in Cognitive Sciences, 18*, 387–389. (p. 80)

Pallier, C., Colomé, A., & Sebastián-Gallés, N. (2001). The influence of native-language phonology on lexical access: Exemplar-based versus abstract lexical entries. *Psychological Science, 12*, 445–448. (p. 332)

Palmer, S., Schreiber, C., & Box, C. (1991, November). *Remembering the earthquake: "Flashbulb" memory for experienced vs. reported events.* Paper presented at the 32nd Annual Meeting of the Psychonomic Society, San Francisco, CA. (p. 295)

Pandey, J., Sinha, Y., Prakash, A., & Tripathi, R. C. (1982). Right–left political ideologies and attribution of the causes of poverty. *European Journal of Social Psychology, 12*, 327–331. (p. 443)

Pandya, H. (2013, April 23). Shakuntala Devi, "human computer" who bested the machines, dies at 83. *The New York Times.* Retrieved from http://www.nytimes.com/2013/04/24/world/asia/shakuntala-devi-human-computer-dies-in-india-at-83.html?_r=0 (p. 357)

Panksepp, J. (2007). Neurologizing the psychology of affects: How appraisal-based constructivism and basic emotion theory can coexist. *Perspectives on Psychological Science, 2*, 281–295. (p. 393)

Panzarella, C., Alloy, L. B., & Whitehouse, W. G. (2006). Expanded hopelessness theory of depression: On the mechanisms by which social support protects against depression. *Cognitive Theory and Research, 30*, 307–333. (p. 551)

Pardini, D. A., Raine, A., Erickson, K., & Loeber, R. (2014). Lower amygdala volume in men is associated with childhood aggression, early psychopathic traits, and future violence. *Biological Psychiatry, 75,* 73–80. (p. 564)

Park, C. L. (2007). Religiousness/spirituality and health: A meaning systems perspective. *Journal of Behavioral Medicine, 30,* 319–328. (p. 430)

Park, D. C., & McDonough, I. M. (2013). The dynamic aging mind: Revelations from functional neuroimaging research. *Perspectives on Psychological Science, 8,* 62–67. (p. 160)

Park, G., Lubinski, D., & Benbow, C. P. (2008). Ability differences among people who have commensurate degrees matter for scientific creativity. *Psychological Science, 19,* 957–961. (p. 325)

Park, G., Schwartz, H. A., Eichstaedt, J. C., Kern, M. L., Kosinski, M., Stillwell, D. J., . . . Seligman, M. E. P. (2015). Automatic personality assessment through social media language. *Journal of Personality and Social Psychology, 108,* 934–952. (p. 512)

Park, R. L. (1999, July 12). Liars never break a sweat. *The New York Times,* p. A15. (p. 394)

Parker, C. P., Baltes, B. B., Young, S. A., Huff, J. W., Altmann, R. A., LaCost, H. A., & Roberts, J. E. (2003). Relationships between psychological climate perceptions and work outcomes: A meta-analytic review. *Journal of Organizational Behavior, 24,* 389–416. (p. B-9)

Parker, E. S., Cahill, L., & McGaugh, J. L. (2006). A case of unusual autobiographical remembering. *Neurocase, 12,* 35–49. (p. 301)

Parker, K., & Wang, W. (2013. March 14). *Modern parenthood: Roles of moms and dads converge as they balance work and family.* Retrieved from http://www.pewsocialtrends.org/2013/03/14/modern-parenthood-roles-of-moms-and-dads-converge-as-they-balance-work-and-family/ (pp. 174, 196)

Parkes, A., Wight, D., Hunt, K., Henderson, M., & Sargent, J. (2013). Are sexual media exposure, parental restrictions on media use and co-viewing TV and DVDs with parents and friends associated with teenagers' early sexual behaviour? *Journal of Adolescence, 36,* 1121–1133. (p. 186)

Parkinson, C., & Wheatley, T. (2015). The repurposed social brain. *Trends in Cognitive Sciences, 19,* 133–141. (p. 75)

Parnia, S., Fenwick, P., Spearpoint K., & Devos, G. (2014). AWAreness during REsuscitation (AWARE). *Circulation, 128,* A236. (p. 112)

Parsons, T. D., & Rizzo, A. A. (2008). Affective outcomes of virtual reality exposure therapy for anxiety and specific phobias: A meta-analysis. *Journal of Behavior Therapy and Experimental Psychiatry, 39,* 250–261. (p. 576)

Partanen, E., Kujala, T., Näätänen, R., Liitola, A., Sambeth, A., & Huotilainen, M. (2013). Learning-induced neural plasticity of speech processing before birth. *Proceedings of the National Academy of Sciences of the United States of America, 110,* 15145–15150. (p. 124)

Parthasarathy, S., Vasquez, M. M., Halonen, M., Bootzin, R., Quan, S. F., Martinez, F. D., & Guerra, S. (2015). Persistent insomnia is associated with mortality risk. *American Journal of Medicine, 128,* 268–275. (p. 95)

Pascoe, E. A., & Richman, L. S. (2009). Perceived discrimination and health: A meta-analytic review. *Psychological Bulletin, 135,* 531–554. (pp. 407, 409)

Passell, P. (1993, March 9). Like a new drug, social programs are put to the test. *The New York Times,* pp. C1, C10. (p. 25)

Pate, J. E., Pumariega, A. J., Hester, C., & Garner, D. M. (1992). Cross-cultural patterns in eating disorders: A review. *Journal of the American Academy of Child and Adolescent Psychiatry, 31,* 802–809. (p. 565)

Patel, S. R., Malhotra, A., White, D. P., Gottlieb, D. J., & Hu, F. B. (2006). Association between reduced sleep and weight gain in women. *American Journal of Epidemiology, 164,* 947–954. (p. 95)

Patihis, L., Ho, L. Y., Tingen, I. W., Lilienfeld, S. O., & Loftus, E. F. (2014a). Are the "memory wars" over? A scientist–practitioner gap in beliefs about repressed memory. *Psychological Science, 25,* 519–530. (pp. 306, 311)

Patihis, L., Lilienfeld, S. O., Ho, L. Y., & Loftus, E. F. (2014b). Unconscious repressed memory is scientifically questionable. *Psychological Science, 25,* 1967–1968. (p. 306)

Patterson, F. (1978, October). Conversations with a gorilla. *National Geographic,* pp. 438–465. (p. 335)

Patterson, G. R., Chamberlain, P., & Reid, J. B. (1982). A comparative evaluation of parent training procedures. *Behavior Therapy, 13,* 638–650. (p. 262)

Patterson, M., Warr, P., & West, M. (2004). Organizational climate and company productivity: The role of employee affect and employee level. *Journal of Occupational and Organizational Psychology, 77,* 193–216. (p. B-9)

Pauker, K., Weisbuch, M., Ambady, N., Sommers, S. R., Adams, R. B., Jr., & Ivcevic, Z. (2009). Not so Black and White: Memory for ambiguous group members. *Journal of Personality and Social Psychology, 96,* 795–810. (p. 358)

Paulesu, E., Demonet, J.-F., Fazio, F., McCrory, E., Chanoine, V., Brunswick, N., . . . Frith, U. (2001). Dyslexia: Cultural diversity and biological unity. *Science, 291,* 2165–2167. (p. 9)

Pauly, K., Finkelmeyer, A., Schneider, F., & Habel, U. (2013). The neural correlates of positive self-evaluation and self-related memory. *Social Cognitive and Affective Neuroscience, 8,* 878–886. (p. 516)

Paunesku, D., Walton, G. M., Romero, C., Smith, E. N., Yeager, D. S., & Dweck, C. S. (2015). Mind-set interventions are a scalable treatment for academic underachievement. *Psychological Science, 26,* 784–793. (p. 362)

Paus, T., Zijdenbos, A., Worsley, K., Collins, D. L., Blumenthal, J., Giedd, J. N., . . . Evans, A. C. (1999). Structural maturation of neural pathways in children and adolescents: In vivo study. *Science, 283,* 1908–1911. (p. 127)

Pavlov, I. (1927). *Conditioned reflexes: An investigation of the physiological activity of the cerebral cortex* (G. V. Anrep, Trans.). Oxford, England: Oxford University Press. (pp. 248, 252)

Payne, B. K. (2006). Weapon bias: Split-second decisions and unintended stereotyping. *Current Directions in Psychological Science, 15,* 287–291. (p. 463)

Payne, B. K., & Corrigan, E. (2007). Emotional constraints on intentional forgetting. *Journal of Experimental Social Psychology, 43,* 780–786. (p. 306)

Payne, B. K., Krosnick, J. A., Pasek, J., Lelkes, Y., Akhtar, O., & Tompson, T. (2010). Implicit and explicit prejudice in the 2008 American presidential election. *Journal of Experimental Social Psychology, 46,* 367–374. (p. 463)

Payne, J. W., Samper, A., Bettman, J. R., & Luce, M. F. (2008). Boundary conditions on unconscious thought in complex decision making. *Psychological Science, 19,* 1118–1123. (p. 324)

Pea, R., Nass, C., Meheula, L., Rance, M., Kumar, A., Bamford, H., . . . Zhou, M. (2012). Media use, face-to-face communication, media multitasking, and social wellbeing among 8- to 12-year-old girls. *Developmental Psychology, 48,* 327–336. (p. 373)

Peckham, A. D., McHugh, R. K., & Otto, M. W. (2010). A meta-analysis of the magnitude of biased attention in depression. *Depression and Anxiety, 27,* 1135–1142. (p. 547)

Pedersen, A., Zachariae, R., & Bovbjerg, D. H. (2010). Influence of psychological stress on upper respiratory infection—A meta-analysis of prospective studies. *Psychosomatic Medicine, 72,* 823–832. (p. 412)

Pedersen, N. L., Plomin, R., McClearn, G. E., & Friberg, L. (1988). Neuroticism, extraversion, and related traits in adult twins reared apart and reared together. *Journal of Personality and Social Psychology, 55,* 950–957. (p. 69)

Peigneux, P., Laureys, S., Fuchs, S., Collette, F., Perrin, F., Reggers, J., . . . Maquet, P. (2004). Are spatial memories strengthened in the human hippocampus during slow wave sleep? *Neuron, 44,* 535–545. (p. 293)

Pelham, B. W. (1993). On the highly positive thoughts of the highly depressed. In R. F. Baumeister (Ed.), *Self-esteem: The puzzle of low self-regard* (pp. 183–199). New York: Plenum Press. (p. 517)

Pelham, B. W. (2009, October 22). *About one in six Americans report history of depression.* Retrieved from http://www.gallup.com/poll/123821/one-six-americans-report-history-depression.aspx (p. 547)

Pelham, B., & Crabtree, S. (2008, October 8). *Worldwide, highly religious more likely to help others.* Retrieved from http://www.gallup.com/poll/111013/worldwide-highly-religious-more-likely-to-help-others.aspx (p. 484)

Pennebaker, J. W. (1985). Traumatic experience and psychosomatic disease: Exploring the roles of behavioral inhibition, obsession, and confiding. *Canadian Psychology, 26,* 82–95. (p. 425)

Pennebaker, J. W. (1990). *Opening up: The healing power of confiding in others.* New York: Morrow. (pp. 425, 499)

Pennebaker, J. W. (2002, January 28). Personal communication. (p. 486)

Pennebaker, J. W. (2011). *The secret life of pronouns: What our words say about us.* New York: Bloomsbury Press. (p. 512)

Pennebaker, J. W., Barger, S. D., & Tiebout, J. (1989). Disclosure of traumas and health among Holocaust survivors. *Psychosomatic Medicine, 51,* 577–589. (p. 425)

Pennebaker, J. W., Gosling, S. D., & Ferrell, J. D. (2013). Daily online testing in large classes: Boosting college performance while reducing achievement gaps. *PLOS ONE, 8*(11), e79774. (pp. 30, 289)

Pennebaker, J. W., & O'Heeron, R. C. (1984). Confiding in others and illness rate among spouses of suicide and accidental death victims. *Journal of Abnormal Psychology, 93*, 473–476. (p. 425)

Pennebaker, J. W., & Stone, L. D. (2003). Words of wisdom: Language use over the life span. *Journal of Personality and Social Psychology, 85*, 291–301. (p. 166)

Peplau, L. A., & Fingerhut, A. W. (2007). The close relationships of lesbians and gay men. *Annual Review of Psychology, 58*, 405–424. (pp. 164, 193)

Peppard, P. E., Szklo-Coxe, M., Hia, K. M., & Young, T. (2006). Longitudinal association of sleep-related breathing disorder and depression. *Archives of Internal Medicine, 166*, 1709–1715. (p. 97)

Pepperberg, I. M. (2009). *Alex & me: How a scientist and a parrot discovered a hidden world of animal intelligence—and formed a deep bond in the process.* New York: Harper. (p. 327)

Pepperberg, I. M. (2012). Further evidence for addition and numerical competence by a grey parrot (*Psittacus erithacus*). *Animal Cognition, 15*, 711–717. (p. 327)

Pepperberg, I. M. (2013). Abstract concepts: Data from a grey parrot. *Behavioural Processes, 93*, 82–90. (p. 327)

Perani, D., & Abutalebi, J. (2005). The neural basis of first and second language processing. *Current Opinion in Neurobiology, 15*, 202–206. (p. 334)

Pereg, D., Gow, R., Mosseri, M., Lishner, M., Rieder, M., Van Uum, S., & Koren, G. (2011). Hair cortisol and the risk for acute myocardial infarction in adult men. *Stress, 14*, 73–81. (p. 414)

Pereira, A. C., Huddleston, D. E., Brickman, A. M., Sosunov, A. A., Hen, R., McKhann, G. M., . . . Small, S. A. (2007). An *in vivo* correlate of exercise-induced neurogenesis in the adult dentate gyrus. *Proceedings of the National Academy of Sciences of the United States of America, 104*, 5638–5643. (pp. 61, 160)

Pereira, G. M., & Osburn, H. G. (2007). Effects of participation in decision making on performance and employee attitudes: A quality circles meta-analysis. *Journal of Business Psychology, 22*, 145–153. (p. B-12)

Pergamin-Hight, L., Bakermans-Kranenburg, M. J., van IJzendoorn, M. H., & Bar-Haim, Y. (2012). Variations in the promoter region of the serotonin transporter gene and biased attention for emotional information: A meta-analysis. *Biological Psychiatry, 71*, 373–379. (p. 542)

Perilloux, H. K., Webster, G. D., & Gaulin, S. J. (2010). Signals of genetic quality and maternal investment capacity: The dynamic effects of fluctuating asymmetry and waist-to-hip ratio on men's ratings of women's attractiveness. *Social Psychology and Personality Science, 1*, 34–42. (pp. 194, 478)

Perkins, A., & Fitzgerald, J. A. (1997). Sexual orientation in domestic rams: Some biological and social correlates. In L. Ellis & L. Ebertz (Eds.), *Sexual orientation: Toward biological understanding* (p. 107–128). Westport, CT: Praeger. (p. 190)

Perkins, A. M., Inchley-Mort, S. L., Pickering, A. D., Corr, P. J., & Burgess, A. P. (2012). A facial expression for anxiety. *Journal of Personality and Social Psychology, 102*, 910–924. (p. 396)

Perkinson-Gloor, N., Lemola, S., & Grob, A. (2013). Sleep duration, positive attitude toward life, and academic achievement: The role of daytime tiredness, behavioral persistence, and school start times. *Journal of Adolescence, 36*, 311–318. (p. 95)

Perra, O., Williams, J. H. G., Whiten, A., Fraser, L., Benzie, H., & Perrett, D. I. (2008). Imitation and "theory of mind" competencies in discrimination of autism from other neurodevelopmental disorders. *Research in Autism Disorders, 2*, 456–468. (p. 137)

Perrachione, T. K., Del Tufo, S. N., & Gabrieli, J. D. E. (2011). Human voice recognition depends on language ability. *Science, 333*, 595. (p. 334)

Perrett, D. I., Harries, M., Mistlin, A. J., & Chitty, A. J. (1990). Three stages in the classification of body movements by visual neurons. In H. Barlow, C. Blakemore, & M. Weston-Smith (Eds.), *Images and understanding* (pp. 94–108). Cambridge, England: Cambridge University Press. (p. 215)

Perrett, D. I., Hietanen, J. K., Oram, M. W., & Benson, P. J. (1992). Organization and functions of cells responsive to faces in the temporal cortex. *Philosophical Transactions of the Royal Society of London: Series B, 335*, 23–30. (p. 215)

Perrett, D. I., May, K. A., & Yoshikawa, S. (1994). Facial shape and judgments of female attractiveness. *Nature, 368*, 239–242. (p. 215)

Perrin, J. S., Merz, S., Bennett, D. M., Currie, J., Steele, D. J., Reid, I. C., & Schwarzbauer, C. (2012). Electroconvulsive therapy reduced frontal cortical connectivity in severe depressive disorder. *Proceedings of the National Academy of Sciences of the United States of America, 109*, 5464–5468. (p. 598)

Perry, G. (2013). *Behind the shock machine: The untold story of the notorious Milgram psychology experiments.* New York: New Press. (p. 453)

Perry, J. R. B., Day, F., Elks, C. E., Sulem, P., Thompson, D. J., Ferreira, T., . . . Ong, K. K. (2014). Parent-of-origin-specific allelic associations among 106 genomic loci for age at menarche. *Nature, 514*, 92–97. (p. 176)

Person, C., Tracy, M., & Galea, S. (2006). Risk factors for depression after a disaster. *Journal of Nervous and Mental Disease, 194*, 659–666. (p. 603)

Pert, C. B. (1986). Quoted in J. Hooper & D. Teresi, *The three-pound universe.* New York: Macmillan. (p. 54)

Pert, C. B., & Snyder, S. H. (1973). Opiate receptor: Demonstration in nervous tissue. *Science, 179*, 1011–1014. (p. 41)

Perugini, E. M., Kirsch, I., Allen, S. T., Coldwell, E., Meredith, J., Montgomery, G. H., & Sheehan, J. (1998). Surreptitious observation of responses to hypnotically suggested hallucinations: A test of the compliance hypothesis. *International Journal of Clinical and Experimental Hypnosis, 46*, 191–203. (p. 235)

Peschel, E. R., & Peschel, R. E. (1987). Medical insights into the castrati in opera. *American Scientist, 75*, 578–583. (p. 182)

Pescosolido, B. A., Martin, J. K., Long, J. S., Medina, T. R., Phelan, J. C., & Link, B. G. (2010). "A disease like any other"? A decade of change in public reactions to schizophrenia, depression, and alcohol dependence. *American Journal of Psychiatry, 167*, 1321–1330. (p. 560)

Pesko, M. F. (2014). Stress and smoking: Associations with terrorism and causal impact. *Contemporary Economic Policy, 32*, 351–371. (p. 109)

Peters, M., Rhodes, G., & Simmons, L. W. (2007). Contributions of the face and body to overall attractiveness. *Animal Behaviour, 73*, 937–942. (p. 478)

Peters, T. J., & Waterman, R. H., Jr. (1982). *In search of excellence: Lessons from America's best-run companies.* New York: Harper & Row. (p. 264)

Petersen, J. L., & Hyde, J. S. (2010). A meta-analytic review of research on gender differences in sexuality, 1993–2007. *Psychological Bulletin, 136*, 21–38. (p. 193)

Petersen, J. L., & Hyde, J. S. (2011). Gender differences in sexual attitudes and behaviors: A review of meta-analytic results and large datasets. *Journal of Sex Research, 48*, 149–165. (pp. 181, 193)

Peterson, C., & Barrett, L. C. (1987). Explanatory style and academic performance among university freshmen. *Journal of Personality and Social Psychology, 53*, 603–607. (p. 423)

Peterson, C., Peterson, J., & Skevington, S. (1986). Heated argument and adolescent development. *Journal of Social and Personal Relationships, 3*, 229–240. (p. 149)

Peterson, L. R., & Peterson, M. J. (1959). Short-term retention of individual verbal items. *Journal of Experimental Psychology, 58*, 193–198. (p. 287)

Petitto, L. A., & Marentette, P. F. (1991). Babbling in the manual mode: Evidence for the ontogeny of language. *Science, 251*, 1493–1496. (p. 331)

Pettegrew, J. W., Keshavan, M. S., & Minshew, N. J. (1993). 31P nuclear magnetic resonance spectroscopy: Neurodevelopment and schizophrenia. *Schizophrenia Bulletin, 19*, 35–53. (p. 558)

Petticrew, M., Bell, R., & Hunter, D. (2002). Influence of psychological coping on survival and recurrence in people with cancer: Systematic review. *British Medical Journal, 325*, 1066. http://dx.doi.org/10.1136/bmj.325.7372.1066 (p. 413)

Petticrew, M., Fraser, J. M., & Regan, M. F. (1999). Adverse life events and risk of breast cancer: A meta-analysis. *British Journal of Health Psychology, 4*, 1–17. (p. 413)

Pettigrew, T. F., Christ, O., Wagner, U., & Stellmacher, J. (2007). Direct and indirect intergroup contact effects on prejudice: A normative interpretation. *International Journal of Intercultural Relations, 31*, 411–425. (p. 486)

Pettigrew, T. F., & Tropp, L. R. (2011). *When groups meet: The dynamics of intergroup contact.* New York: Psychology Press. (p. 486)

Pew. (2007, July 18). *Modern marriage: "I like hugs. I like kisses. But what I really love is help with the dishes."* Pew Research Center. Retrieved from http://www.pewsocialtrends.org/2007/07/18/modern-marriage/ (p. 480)

Pew. (2010, July 1). *Gender equality universally embraced, but inequalities acknowledged: Men's lives often seen as better.* Pew Research Center. Retrieved from http://www.pewglobal.org/2010/07/01/gender-equality/ (p. 178)

Pew. (2011, December 15). *17% and 61%—Texting, talking on the phone and driving.* Pew Research Center. Retrieved from http://www.pewresearch.org/ (p. 82)

Pew. (2012, June 4). Section 8: *Values about immigration and race.* Pew Research Center. Retrieved from http://www.people-press.org/2012/06/04/section-8-values-about-immigration-and-race/ (p. 462)

Pew. (2013, June 11). *Gay marriage: Key data points from Pew research.* Pew Research Center. Retrieved from http://www.pewresearch.org (p. 486)

Pew. (2013, June 4). *The global divide on homosexuality: Greater acceptance in more secular and affluent countries.* Pew Research Center. Retrieved from http://www.pewglobal.org/files/2013/06/Pew-Global-Attitudes-Homosexuality-Report-FINAL-JUNE-4-2013.pdf (p. 187)

Pew. (2013, June 13). *A survey of LGBT Americans: Attitudes, experiences and values in changing times.* Pew Research Center. http://www.pewsocialtrends.org/2013/06/13/a-survey-of-lgbt-americans/ (p. 464)

Pew. (2014, January 27). *Climate change: Key data points from Pew research.* Pew Research Center. Retrieved from http://www.pewresearch.org/ (p. 320)

Pew. (2014). *Global views on morality.* Pew Research Center. Retrieved from http://www.pewglobal.org/ (p. 464)

Pew. (2015). *Broadband technology fact sheet.* Pew Research Center. Retrieved from http://www.pewinternet.org/fact-sheets/broadband-technology-fact-sheet/ (p. 349)

Pfaff, L. A., Boatwright, K. J., Potthoff, A. L., Finan, C., Ulrey, L. A., & Huber, D. M. (2013). Perceptions of women and men leaders following 360-degree feedback evaluations. *Performance Improvement Quarterly, 26,* 35–56. (p. B-12)

Phelps, J. A., Davis J. O., & Schartz, K. M. (1997). Nature, nurture, and twin research strategies. *Current Directions in Psychological Science, 6,* 117–120. (p. 560)

Philip Morris. (2003). Philip Morris USA youth smoking prevention: Teenage attitudes and behavior study, 2002. *Raising Kids Who Don't Smoke, 1*(2). (p. 115)

Phillips, A. C., Batty, G. D., Gale, C. R., Deary, I. J., Osborn, D., MacIntyre, K., & Carroll, D. (2009). Generalized anxiety disorder, major depressive disorder, and their comorbidity as predictors of all-cause and cardiovascular mortality: The Vietnam Experience Study. *Psychosomatic Medicine, 71,* 395–403. (p. 423)

Phillips, A. L. (2011). A walk in the woods. *American Scientist, 69,* 301–302. (p. 600)

Phillips, D. P. (1985). Natural experiments on the effects of mass media violence on fatal aggression: Strengths and weaknesses of a new approach. In L. Berkowitz (Ed.), *Advances in experimental social psychology* (Vol. 19, pp. 207–250). Orlando, FL: Academic Press. (p. 449)

Phillips, D. P., Carstensen, L. L., & Paight, D. J. (1989). Effects of mass media news stories on suicide, with new evidence on the role of story content. In C. R. Pfeffer (Ed.), *Suicide among youth: Perspectives on risk and prevention* (pp. 101–116). Washington, DC: American Psychiatric Press. (p. 449)

Phillips, J. L. (1969). *Origins of intellect: Piaget's theory.* San Francisco: Freeman. (p. 132)

Piaget, J. (1930). *The child's conception of physical causality* (M. Gabain, Trans.). London: Routledge & Kegan Paul. (p. 130)

Piaget, J. (1932). *The moral judgment of the child* (M. Gabain, Trans.). New York: Harcourt, Brace & World. (p. 150)

Piazza, J. R., Charles, S. T., Silwinski, M. J., Mogle, J., & Almeida, D. M. (2013). Affective reactivity to daily stressors and long-term risk of reporting a chronic health condition. *Annals of Behavioral Medicine, 45,* 110–120. (p. 409)

Picardi, A., Fagnani, C., Nisticò, L., & Stazi, M. A. (2011). A twin study of attachment style in young adults. *Journal of Personality, 79,* 965–992. (p. 140)

Picchioni, M. M., & Murray, R. M. (2007). Schizophrenia. *British Medical Journal, 335,* 91–95. (p. 557)

Pieters, G. L. M., de Bruijn, E. R. A., Maas, Y., Hultijn, W., Vandereycken, W., Peuskens, J., & Sabbe, B. G. (2007). Action monitoring and perfectionism in anorexia nervosa. *Brain and Cognition, 63,* 42–50. (p. 565)

Piliavin, J. A. (2003). Doing well by doing good: Benefits for the benefactor. In C. L. M. Keyes & J. Haidt (Eds.), *Flourishing: Positive psychology and the life well-lived* (pp. 227–247). Washington, DC: American Psychological Association. (p. 151)

Pillemer, D. B. (1998). *Momentous events, vivid memories.* Cambridge, MA: Harvard University Press. (p. 160)

Pillemer, D. B., Ivcevic, Z., Gooze, R. A., & Collins, K. A. (2007). Self-esteem memories: Feeling good about achievement success, feeling bad about relationship distress. *Personality and Social Psychology Bulletin, 33,* 1292–1305. (p. 371)

Pilley, J. W., & Reid, A. K. (2011). Border collie comprehends object names as verbal referents. *Behavioural Processes, 86,* 184–195. (p. 336)

Pinker, S. (1995). The language instinct. *The General Psychologist, 31,* 63–65. (p. 335)

Pinker, S. (1998). Words and rules. *Lingua, 106,* 219–242. (p. 329)

Pinker, S. (2008). *The sexual paradox: Men, women, and the real gender gap.* New York: Scribner's. (p. 174)

Pinker, S. (2010, June 10). Mind over mass media. *The New York Times,* p. A31. (p. 375)

Pinker, S. (2011, September 27). *A history of violence.* Retrieved from http://edge.org/conversation/steven_pinker-a-history-of-violence-edge-master-class-2011 (p. 473)

Pinkham, A. E., Griffin, M., Baron, R., Sasson, N. J., & Gur, R. C. (2010). The face in the crowd effect: Anger superiority when using real faces and multiple identities. *Emotion, 10,* 141–146. (p. 396)

Pinto Pereira, S. M., Geoffroy, M., & Power, C. (2014). Depressive symptoms and physical activity during 3 decades in adult life: Bidirectional associations in a prospective cohort study. *JAMA Psychiatry, 71,* 1373–1380. (p. 426)

Pipe, M.-E. (1996). Children's eyewitness memory. *New Zealand Journal of Psychology, 25,* 36–43. (p. 310)

Pipe, M.-E., Lamb, M. E., Orbach, Y., & Esplin, P. W. (2004). Recent research on children's testimony about experienced and witnessed events. *Developmental Review, 24,* 440–468. (p. 310)

Pipher, M. (2002). *The middle of everywhere: The world's refugees come to our town.* New York: Harcourt. (pp. 371, 407)

Pitcher, D., Walsh, V., Yovel, G., & Duchaine, B. (2007). TMS evidence for the involvement of the right occipital face area in early face processing. *Current Biology, 17,* 1568–1573. (p. 215)

Pitman, R. K., & Delahanty, D. L. (2005). Conceptually driven pharmacologic approaches to acute trauma. *CNS Spectrums, 10*(2), 99–106. (p. 296)

Pitman, R. K., Sanders, K. M., Zusman, R. M., Healy, A. R., Cheema, F., Lasko, N. B., . . . Orr, S. P. (2002). Pilot study of secondary prevention of posttraumatic stress disorder with propranolol. *Biological Psychiatry, 51,* 189–192. (p. 296)

Place, S. S., Todd, P. M., Penke, L., & Asendorph, J. B. (2009). The ability to judge the romantic interest of others. *Psychological Science, 20,* 22–26. (p. 396)

Plassmann, H., O'Doherty, J., Shiv, B., & Rangel, A. (2008). Marketing actions can modulate neural representations of experienced pleasantness. *Proceedings of the National Academy of Sciences of the United States of America, 105,* 1050–1054. (p. 236)

Platek, S. M., & Singh, D. (2010) Optimal waist-to-hip ratios in women activate neural reward centers in men. *PLOS ONE, 5*(2), e9042. doi:10.1371/journal.pone.0009042 (p. 477)

Pliner, P. (1982). The effects of mere exposure on liking for edible substances. *Appetite, 3,* 283–290. (p. 381)

Pliner, P., Pelchat, M., & Grabski, M. (1993). Reduction of neophobia in humans by exposure to novel foods. *Appetite, 20,* 111–123. (p. 381)

Plöderl, M., Wagenmakers, E., Tremblay, P., Ramsay, R., Kralovec, K., Fartacek, C., & Fartacek, R. (2013). Suicide risk and sexual orientation: A critical review. *Archives of Sexual Behavior, 42,* 715–727. (p. 188)

Plomin, R. (1999). Genetics and general cognitive ability. *Nature, 402*(Suppl.), C25–C29. (p. 341)

Plomin, R. (2011). Why are children in the same family so different? Nonshared environment three decades later. *International Journal of Epidemiology, 40,* 582–592. (pp. 70, 155)

Plomin, R., & Bergeman, C. S. (1991). The nature of nurture: Genetic influence on "environmental" measures. *Behavioral and Brain Sciences, 14,* 373–427. (p. 72)

Plomin, R., & Daniels, D. (1987). Why are children in the same family so different from one another? *Behavioral and Brain Sciences, 10,* 1–60. (p. 155)

Plomin, R., & DeFries, J. C. (1998, May). The genetics of cognitive abilities and disabilities. *Scientific American,* pp. 62–69. (p. 355)

Plomin, R., DeFries, J. C., McClearn, G. E., & Rutter, M. (1997). *Behavioral genetics.* New York: Freeman. (pp. 74, 383, 559)

Plomin, R., McClearn, G. E., Pedersen, N. L., Nesselroade, J. R., & Bergeman, C. S. (1988). Genetic influence on childhood family environment perceived retrospectively from the last half of the life span. *Developmental Psychology, 24,* 37–45. (p. 72)

Plomin, R., & McGuffin, P. (2003). Psychopathology in the postgenomic era. *Annual Review of Psychology, 54,* 205–228. (p. 549)

Plomin, R., Reiss, D., Hetherington, E. M., & Howe, G. W. (January, 1994). Nature and nurture: Genetic contributions to measures of the family environment. *Developmental Psychology, 30,* 32–43. (p. 72)

Plotkin, H. (1994). *Darwin machines and the nature of knowledge.* Cambridge, MA: Harvard University Press. (p. 549)

Plous, S., & Herzog, H. A. (2000). Poll shows researchers favor lab animal protection. *Science, 290,* 711. (p. 28)

Pluess, M., & Belsky, J. (2013). Vantage sensitivity: Individual differences in response to positive experiences. *Psychological Bulletin, 139,* 901–916. (p. 543)

Poelmans, G., Pauls, D. L., Buitelaar, J. K., & Franke, B. (2011). Integrated genome-wide association study findings: Identification of a neurodevelopmental network for attention deficit hyperactivity disorder. *American Journal of Psychiatry, 168,* 365–377. (p. 532)

Polanin, J. R., Espelage, D. L., & Pigott, T. D. (2012). A meta-analysis of school-based bully prevention programs' effects on bystander intervention behavior. *School Psychology Review, 41,* 47–65. (p. 13)

Poldrack, R. A., Halchenko, Y. O., & Hanson, S. J. (2009). Decoding the large-scale structure of brain function by classifying mental states across individuals. *Psychological Science, 20,* 1364–1372. (p. 49)

Polivy, J., Herman, C. P., & Coelho, J. S. (2008). Caloric restriction in the presence of attractive food cues: External cues, eating, and weight. *Physiology and Behavior, 94,* 729–733. (p. 382)

Pollak, S., Cicchetti, D., & Klorman, R. (1998). Stress, memory, and emotion: Developmental considerations from the study of child maltreatment. *Developmental Psychopathology, 10,* 811–828. (pp. 251, 252)

Pollak, S. D., & Kistler, D. J. (2002). Early experience is associated with the development of categorical representations for facial expressions of emotion. *Proceedings of the National Academy of Sciences of the United States of America, 99,* 9072–9076. (p. 396)

Pollak, S. D., & Tolley-Schell, S. A. (2003). Selective attention to facial emotion in physically abused children. *Journal of Abnormal Psychology, 112,* 323–328. (p. 396)

Pollard, R. (1992). *100 years in psychology and deafness: A centennial retrospective.* Invited address at the 100th Annual Convention of the American Psychological Association, Washington, DC. (p. 335)

Pollatsek, A., Romoser, M. R. E., & Fisher, D. L. (2012). Identifying and remediating failures of selective attention in older drivers. *Current Directions in Psychological Science, 21,* 3–7. (p. 159)

Pollick, A. S., & de Waal, F. B. M. (2007). Ape gestures and language evolution. *Proceedings of the National Academy of Sciences of the United States of America, 104,* 8184–8189. (p. 335)

Poole, D. A., & Lindsay, D. S. (1995). Interviewing preschoolers: Effects of nonsuggestive techniques, parental coaching and leading questions on reports of nonexperienced events. *Journal of Experimental Child Psychology, 60,* 129–154. (p. 308)

Poole, D. A., & Lindsay, D. S. (2001). Children's eyewitness reports after exposure to misinformation from parents. *Journal of Experimental Psychology: Applied, 7,* 27–50. (p. 308)

Poole, D. A., & Lindsay, D. S. (2002). Reducing child witnesses' false reports of misinformation from parents. *Journal of Experimental Child Psychology, 81,* 117–140. (p. 308)

Poon, L. W. (1987). *Myths and truisms: Beyond extant analyses of speed of behavior and age.* Address at the annual meeting of the Eastern Psychological Association, Arlington, VA. (p. 159)

Pope, D., & Simonsohn, U. (2011). Round numbers as goals: Evidence from baseball, SAT takers, and the lab. *Psychological Science, 22,* 71–79. (p. A-1)

Popenoe, D. (1993, October). *The evolution of marriage and the problem of stepfamilies: A biosocial perspective.* Paper presented at the First Annual Symposium on Stepfamilies, State College, PA. (p. 523)

Poropat, A. E. (2014). Other-rated personality and academic performance: Evidence and implications. *Learning and Individual Differences, 34,* 24–32. (p. 359)

Porter, D., & Neuringer, A. (1984). Music discriminations by pigeons. *Journal of Experimental Psychology: Animal Behavior Processes, 10,* 138–148. (p. 257)

Porter, S., & Peace, K. A. (2007). The scars of memory: A prospective, longitudinal investigation of the consistency of traumatic and positive emotional memories in adulthood. *Psychological Science, 18,* 435–441. (p. 311)

Porter, S., & ten Brinke, L. (2008). Reading between the lies: Identifying concealed and falsified emotions in universal facial expressions. *Psychological Science, 19,* 508–514. (p. 396)

Posner, M. I., & Carr, T. H. (1992). Lexical access and the brain: Anatomical constraints on cognitive models of word recognition. *American Journal of Psychology, 105,* 1–26. (p. 334)

Poulton, R., & Milne, B. J. (2002). Low fear in childhood is associated with sporting prowess in adolescence and young adulthood. *Behaviour Research and Therapy, 40,* 1191–1197. (p. 564)

Powell, K. E., Thompson, P. D., Caspersen, C. J., & Kendrick, J. S. (1987). Physical activity and the incidence of coronary heart disease. *Annual Review of Public Health, 8,* 253–287. (p. 426)

Powell, R. A., & Boer, D. P. (1994). Did Freud mislead patients to confabulate memories of abuse? *Psychological Reports, 74,* 1283–1298. (p. 498)

Powell, R. A., Digdon, N. A., Harris, B., & Smithson, C. (2014). Correcting the record on Watson, Rayner, and Little Albert: Albert Barger as "psychology's lost boy." *American Psychologist, 69,* 600–611. (p. 253)

Power, R. A., Steinberg, S., Bjornsdottir, G., Rietveld, C. A., Abdellaoui, A., Nivard, M. M., . . . Stefansson, K. (2015). Polygenic risk scores for schizophrenia and bipolar disorder predict creativity. *Nature Neuroscience, 18,* 953–955. (p. 546)

Preckel, F., Lipnevich, A., Boehme, K., Branderner, L., Georgi, K., Könen, T., . . . Roberts, R. (2013). Morningness–eveningness and educational outcomes: The lark has an advantage over the owl at high school. *British Journal of Educational Psychology, 83,* 114–134. (p. 88)

Premack, D. G., & Woodruff, G. (1978). Does the chimpanzee have a theory of mind? *Behavioral and Brain Sciences, 1,* 515–526. (p. 133)

Prentice, D. A., & Miller, D. T. (1993). Pluralistic ignorance and alcohol use on campus: Some consequences of misperceiving the social norm. *Journal of Personality and Social Psychology, 64,* 243–256. (p. 116)

Prince Charles. (2000). *A royal view . . .* [BBC Reith Lecture]. Retrieved from http://news.bbc.co.uk/hi/english/static/events/reith_2000/lecture6.stm (p. 15)

Principe, G. F., Kanaya, T., Ceci, S. J., & Singh, M. (2006). Believing is seeing: How rumors can engender false memories in preschoolers. *Psychological Science, 17,* 243–248. (p. 310)

Prioleau, L., Murdock, M., & Brody, N. (1983). An analysis of psychotherapy versus placebo studies. *Behavioral and Brain Sciences, 6,* 275–310. (p. 589)

Prior, M., Smart, D., Sanson, A., & Oberklaid, F. (2000). Does shy-inhibited temperament in childhood lead to anxiety problems in adolescence? *Journal of American Academy of Child and Adolescent Psychiatry, 39,* 461–468. (p. 140)

Pritchard, R. M. (1961, June). Stabilized images on the retina. *Scientific American,* pp. 72–78. (p. 205)

Profet, M. (1992). Pregnancy sickness as adaptation: A deterrent to maternal ingestion of teratogens. In J. H. Barkow, L. Cosmides, & J. Tooby (Eds.), *The adapted mind: Evolutionary psychology and the generation of culture* (pp. 327–366). New York: Oxford University Press. (p. 74)

Proffitt, D. R. (2006a). Distance perception. *Current Directions in Psychological Research, 15,* 131–135. (p. 207)

Proffitt, D. R. (2006b). Embodied perception and the economy of action. *Perspectives on Psychological Science, 1,* 110–122. (p. 207)

Project MATCH Research Group. (1997). Matching alcoholism treatments to client heterogeneity: Project MATCH posttreatment drinking outcomes. *Journal of Studies on Alcohol, 58,* 7–29. (p. 583)

Pronin, E. (2007). Perception and misperception of bias in human judgment. *Trends in Cognitive Sciences, 11,* 37–43. (p. 519)

Pronin, E. (2013). When the mind races: Effects of thought speed on feeling and action. *Current Directions in Psychological Science, 22,* 283–288. (p. 546)

Propper, R. E., Stickgold, R., Keeley, R., & Christman, S. D. (2007). Is television traumatic? Dreams, stress, and media exposure in the aftermath of September 11, 2001. *Psychological Science, 18,* 334–340. (p. 99)

Prot, S., Gentile, D., Anderson, C. A., Suzuli, K., Swing, E., Lim, K. M., . . . Lam, B. C. P. (2014). Long-term relations among prosocial-media use, empathy, and prosocial behavior. *Psychological Science, 25,* 358–368. (pp. 275, 472)

Protzko, J., Aronson, J., & Blair, C. (2013). How to make a young child smarter: Evidence from the database of raising intelligence. *Perspectives on Psychological Science, 8,* 25–40. (p. 356)

Provine, R. R. (2001). *Laughter: A scientific investigation.* New York: Penguin. (p. 20)

Provine, R. R. (2012). *Curious behavior: Yawning, laughing, hiccuping, and beyond.* Cambridge, MA: Harvard University Press. (pp. 19, 449)

Provine, R. R., Krosnowski, K. A., & Brocato, N. W. (2009). Tearing: Breakthrough in human emotional signaling. *Evolutionary Psychology, 7,* 52–56. (p. 400)

Pryor, J. H., Hurtado, S., DeAngelo, L., Blake, L. P., & Tran, S. (2011). *The American freshman: National norms fall 2010.* Los Angeles: UCLA Higher Education Research Institute. (p. 174)

Pryor, J. H., Hurtado, S., Saenz, V. B., Korn, J. S., Santos, J. L., & Korn, W. S. (2006). *The American freshman: National norms for fall 2006.* Los Angeles: UCLA Higher Education Research Institute. (p. 550)

Pryor, J. H., Hurtado, S., Saenz, V. B., Lindholm, J. A., Korn, W. S., & Mahoney, K. M. (2005). *The American freshman: National norms for fall 2005.* Los Angeles: UCLA Higher Education Research Institute. (p. 193)

Pryor, J. H., Hurtado, S., Sharkness, J., & Korn, W. S. (2007). *The American freshman: National norms for fall 2007.* Los Angeles: UCLA Higher Education Research Institute. (p. 174)

Psaltopoulou, T., Sergentanis, T. N., Panagiotakos, D. B., Sergentanis, I. N., Kosti, R., & Scarmeas, N. (2013). Mediterranean diet, stroke, cognitive impairment, and depression: A meta-analysis. *Annals of Neurology, 74,* 580–591. (p. 550)

Psychologist. (2003). Who's the greatest? *The Psychologist, 16,* 170–175. (p. 135)

PTC. (2007, January 10). *Dying to entertain: Violence on prime time broadcast TV, 1998 to 2006.* Parents Television Council. Retrieved from http://www.parentstv.org/PTC/publications/reports/violencestudy/DyingtoEntertain.pdf (p. 276)

Puetz, T. W., O'Connor, P. J., & Dishman, R. K. (2006). Effects of chronic exercise on feelings of energy and fatigue: A quantitative synthesis. *Psychological Bulletin, 132,* 866–876. (p. 426)

Putnam, F. W. (1991). Recent research on multiple personality disorder. *Psychiatric Clinics of North America, 14,* 489–502. (p. 562)

Putnam, F. W. (1995). Rebuttal of Paul McHugh. *Journal of the American Academy of Child and Adolescent Psychiatry, 34,* 963. (p. 562)

Putnam, R. D. (2000). *Bowling alone: The collapse and revival of American community.* New York: Simon & Schuster. (p. 448)

Pyszczynski, T. A., Hamilton, J. C., Greenberg, J., & Becker, S. E. (1991). Self-awareness and psychological dysfunction. In C. R. Snyder & D. O. Forsyth (Eds.), *Handbook of social and clinical psychology: The health perspective* (pp. 138–157). New York: Pergamon Press. (p. 551)

Pyszczynski, T. A., Motyl, M., Vail, K. E., III, Hirschberger, G., Arndt, J., & Kesebir, P. (2012). Drawing attention to global climate change decreases support for war. *Peace and Conflict: Journal of Peace Psychology, 18,* 354–368. (p. 487)

Pyszczynski, T. A., Rothschild, Z., & Abdollahi, A. (2008). Terrorism, violence, and hope for peace: A terror management perspective. *Current Directions in Psychological Science 17,* 318–322. (p. 466)

Pyszczynski, T. A., Solomon, S., & Greenberg, J. (2002). *In the wake of 9/11: The psychology of terror.* Washington, DC: American Psychological Association. (p. 466)

Q

Qin, H.-F., & Piao, T.-J. (2011). Dispositional optimism and life satisfaction of Chinese and Japanese college students: Examining the mediating effects of affects and coping efficacy. *Chinese Journal of Clinical Psychology, 19,* 259–261. (p. 423)

Qirko, H. N. (2004). "Fictive kin" and suicide terrorism. *Science, 304,* 49–50. (p. 458)

Qiu, L., Lin, H., Ramsay, J., & Yang, F. (2012). You are what you tweet: Personality expression and perception on Twitter. *Journal of Research in Personality, 46,* 710–718. (p. 374)

Quasha, S. (1980). *Albert Einstein: An intimate portrait.* New York: Forest. (p. 350)

Quinn, P. C., Bhatt, R. S., Brush, D., Grimes, A., & Sharpnack, H. (2002). Development of form similarity as a Gestalt grouping principle in infancy. *Psychological Science, 13,* 320–328. (p. 218)

Quinn, P. J., Williams, G. M., Najman, J. M., Andersen, M. J., & Bor, W. (2001). The effect of breastfeeding on child development at 5 years: A cohort study. *Journal of Pediatrics & Child Health, 3,* 465–469. (p. 23)

Quoidbach, J., Dunn, E. W., Hansenne, M., & Bustin, G. (2015). The price of abundance: How a wealth of experiences impoverishes savoring. *Personality and Social Psychology Bulletin, 41,* 393–404. (p. 433)

Quoidbach, J., Dunn, E. W., Petrides, K. V., & Mikolajczak, M. (2010). Money giveth, money taketh away: The dual effect of wealth on happiness. *Psychological Science, 21,* 759–763. (p. 433)

Quoidbach, J., Gilbert, D. T., & Wilson, T. D. (2013). The end of history illusion. *Science, 339,* 96–98. (p. 122)

R

Rabbitt, P. (2006). Tales of the unexpected: 25 years of cognitive gerontology. *The Psychologist, 19,* 674–676. (p. 161)

Raby, K. L., Cicchetti, D., Carlson, E. A., Cutuli, J. J., Englund, M. M., & Egeland, B. (2012). Genetic and care-giving-based contributions to infant attachment: Unique associations with distress reactivity and attachment security. *Psychological Science, 23,* 1016–1023. (p. 140)

Raby, K. L., Roisman, G. I., Fraley, R. C., & Simpson, J. A. (2014). The enduring predictive significance of early maternal sensitivity: Social and academic competence through age 32 years. *Child Development, 86,* 695–708. (p. 142)

Racsmány, M., Conway, M. A., & Demeter, G. (2010). Consolidation of episodic memories during sleep: Long-term effects of retrieval practice. *Psychological Science, 21,* 80–85. (p. 93)

Radford, B. (2010, February 18). *Tiger Woods and sex addiction: Real disease or easy excuse?* Retrieved from http://www.livescience.com/9813-tiger-woods-sex-addiction-real-disease-easy-excuse.html (pp. 105, 241)

Radford, B. (2013, May 8). *Psychic claimed Amanda Berry was dead.* Retrieved from http://news.discovery.com/human/psychic-claimed-amanda-berry-dead-130508.htm (p. 241)

Rahman, Q., & Koerting, J. (2008). Sexual orientation-related differences in allocentric spatial memory tasks. *Hippocampus, 18,* 55–63. (p. 191)

Rahman, Q., & Wilson, G. D. (2003). Born gay? The psychobiology of human sexual orientation. *Personality and Individual Differences, 34,* 1337–1382. (p. 190)

Rahman, Q., Wilson, G. D., & Abrahams, S. (2004). Biosocial factors, sexual orientation and neurocognitive functioning. *Psychoneuroendocrinology, 29,* 867–881. (p. 191)

Raichle, M. (2010, March). The brain's dark energy. *Scientific American,* pp. 44–49. (p. 86)

Raine, A. (1999, April). Murderous minds: Can we see the mark of Cain? *Cerebrum,* pp. 15–29. (p. 564)

Raine, A. (2005). The interaction of biological and social measures in the explanation of antisocial and violent behavior. In D. M. Stoff & E. J. Susman (Eds.) *Developmental psychobiology of aggression* (pp. 13–42). New York: Cambridge University Press. (p. 564)

Raine, A. (2013). *The anatomy of violence: The biological roots of crime.* New York: Pantheon. (p. 469)

Raine, A., Lencz, T., Bihrle, S., LaCasse, L., & Colletti, P. (2000). Reduced prefrontal gray matter volume and reduced autonomic activity in antisocial personality disorder. *Archives of General Psychiatry, 57,* 119–127. (p. 564)

Rainie, L., Purcell, K., Goulet, L. S., & Hampton, K. H. (2011, June 16). *Social networking sites and our lives.* Retrieved from http://www.pewinternet.org/2011/06/16/social-networking-sites-and-our-lives/ (p. 373)

Rainville, P., Duncan, G. H., Price, D. D., Carrier, B., & Bushnell, M. C. (1997). Pain affect encoded in human anterior cingulate but not somatosensory cortex. *Science, 277,* 968–971. (p. 235)

Raison, C. L., Klein, H. M., & Steckler, M. (1999). The mood and madness reconsidered. *Journal of Affective Disorders, 53,* 99–106. (p. 564)

Rajendran, G., & Mitchell, P. (2007). Cognitive theories of autism. *Developmental Review, 27,* 224–260. (p. 136)

Ramachandran, V. S., & Blakeslee, S. (1998). *Phantoms in the brain: Probing the mysteries of the human mind.* New York: Morrow. (pp. 61, 232)

Ramírez-Esparza, N., Gosling, S. D., Benet-Martínez, V., Potter, J. P., & Pennebaker, J. W. (2006). Do bilinguals have two personalities? A special case of cultural frame switching. *Journal of Research in Personality, 40,* 99–120. (p. 337)

Ramos, M. R., Cassidy, C., Reicher, S., & Haslam, S. A. (2012). A longitudinal investigation of the rejection-identification hypothesis. *British Journal of Social Psychology, 51,* 642–660. (p. 486)

Randall, D. K. (2012, September 22). Rethinking sleep. *The New York Times.* Retrieved from http://www.nytimes.com/2012/09/23/opinion/sunday/rethinking-sleep.html?_r=0 (p. 92)

Randi, J. (1999, February 4). [2000 club mailing list e-mail letter]. (p. 242)

Randler, C. (2008). Morningness–eveningness and satisfaction with life. *Social Indicators Research, 86,* 297–302. (p. 88)

Randler, C. (2009). Proactive people are morning people. *Journal of Applied Social Psychology, 39,* 2787–2797. (p. 88)

Randler, C., & Bausback, V. (2010). Morningness-eveningness in women around the transition through menopause and its relationship with climacteric complaints. *Biological Rhythm Research, 41,* 415–431. (p. 88)

Rapoport, J. L. (1989, March). The biology of obsessions and compulsions. *Scientific American,* pp. 83–89. (pp. 539, 544)

Räsänen, S., Pakaslahti, A., Syvalahti, E., Jones, P. B., & Isohanni, M. (2000). Sex differences in schizophrenia: A review. *Nordic Journal of Psychiatry, 54,* 37–45. (p. 557)

Rasmussen, H. N., Scheier, M. F., & Greenhouse, J. B. (2009). Optimism and physical health: A meta-analytic review. *Annals of Behavioral Medicine, 37,* 239–256. (p. 422)

Ratcliff, K. S. (2013). The power of poverty: Individual agency and structural constraints. In K. M. Fitzpatrick (Ed.), *Poverty and health: A crisis among America's most vulnerable* (Vol. 1, pp. 5–30). Santa Barbara, CA: Praeger. (p. 435)

Rath, T., & Harter, J. K. (2010, August 19). Your friends and your social wellbeing. *Gallup Management Journal.* (p. B-13)

Rattan, A., Savani, K., Naidu, N. V. R., & Dweck, C. S. (2012). Can everyone become highly intelligent? Cultural differences in and societal consequences of beliefs about the universal potential for intelligence. *Journal of Personality and Social Psychology, 103,* 787–803. (p. 362)

Ray, J., & Kafka, S. (2014, May 6). *Life in college matters for life after college.* Retrieved from http://www.gallup.com/poll/168848/life-college-matters-life-college.aspx (p. B-11)

Ray, O., & Ksir, C. (1990). *Drugs, society, and human behavior* (5th ed.). St. Louis, MO: Times Mirror/Mosby. (p. 110)

Raynor, H. A., & Epstein, L. H. (2001). Dietary variety, energy regulation, and obesity. *Psychological Bulletin, 127,* 325–341. (p. 380)

Reason, J. (1987). The Chernobyl errors. *Bulletin of the British Psychological Society, 40,* 201–206. (p. 459)

Reason, J., & Mycielska, K. (1982). *Absent-minded? The psychology of mental lapses and everyday errors.* Englewood Cliffs, NJ: Prentice-Hall. (p. 206)

Redden, J. P., Mann, T., Vickers, Z., Mykerezi, E., Reicks, M., & Elsbernd, E. (2015). Serving first in isolation increases vegetable intake among elementary schoolchildren. *PLOS ONE, 10*(4), e0121283. doi:10.1371/journal.pone.0121283 (p. 382)

Redick, T. S., Shipstead, Z., Harrison, T. L., Hicks, K. L., Fried, D.E., Hambrick, D. Z., . . . Engle, R. W. (2013). No evidence of intelligence improvement after working memory training: A randomized, placebo-controlled study. *Journal of Experimental Psychology: General, 142,* 359–379. (p. 162)

Reed, D. (2011, January). Quoted in P. Miller, A thing or two about twins. *National Geographic,* pp. 39–65. (p. 72)

Reed, P. (2000). Serial position effects in recognition memory for odors. *Journal of Experimental Psychology: Learning, Memory, and Cognition, 26,* 411–422. (p. 299)

Rees, M. (1999). *Just six numbers: The deep forces that shape the universe.* New York: Basic Books. (p. 76)

Reeves, A., McKee, M., & Stuckler, D. (2014). Economic suicides in the Great Recession in Europe and North America. *British Journal of Psychiatry, 205,* 246–247. (p. 553)

Regan, P. C., & Atkins, L. (2007). Sex differences and similarities in frequency and intensity of sexual desire. *Social Behavior and Personality, 34,* 95–102. (p. 191)

Rehm, J., Shield, K. D., Joharchi, M., & Shuper, P. A. (2012). Alcohol consumption and the intention to engage in unprotected sex: Systematic review and meta-analysis of experimental studies. *Addiction, 107,* 51–59. (p. 106)

Reichenberg, A., Gross, R., Weiser, M., Bresnahan, M., Silverman, J., Harlap, S., . . . Susser, E. (2007). Advancing paternal age and autism. *Archives of General Psychiatry, 63,* 1026–1032. (p. 136)

Reichenberg, A., & Harvey, P. D. (2007). Neuropsychological impairments in schizophrenia: Integration of performance-based and brain imaging findings. *Psychological Bulletin, 133,* 833–858. (p. 557)

Reichert, R. A., Robb, M. B., Fender, J. G., & Wartella, E. (2010). Word learning from baby videos. *Archives of Pediatrics & Adolescent Medicine, 164,* 432–437. (p. 356)

Reichow, B. (2012). Overview of meta-analyses on early intensive behavioral intervention for young children with autism spectrum disorders. *Journal of Autism and Developmental Disorders, 42,* 512–520. (p. 577)

Reifman, A., & Cleveland, H. H. (2007). *Shared environment: A quantitative review.* Paper presented to the Society for Research in Child Development, Boston, MA. (p. 70)

Reifman, A. S., Larrick, R. P., & Fein, S. (1991). Temper and temperature on the diamond: The heat-aggression relationship in major league baseball. *Personality and Social Psychology Bulletin, 17,* 580–585. (p. 470)

Reimann, F., Cox, J. J., Belfer, I., Diatchenko, L., Zaykin, D. V., McHale, D. P., . . . Woods, C. G. (2010). Pain perception is altered by a nucleotide polymorphism in SCN9A. *Proceedings of the National Academy of Sciences of the United States of America, 107,* 5148–5153. (p. 231)

Reiner, W. G., & Gearhart, J. P. (2004). Discordant sexual identity in some genetic males with cloacal exstrophy assigned to female sex at birth. *New England Journal of Medicine, 350,* 333–341. (p. 177)

Reis, H. T., & Aron, A. (2008). Love: What is it, why does it matter, and how does it operate? *Perspectives on Psychological Science, 3,* 80–86. (p. 480)

Reis, H. T., Smith, S. M., Carmichael, C. L., Caprariello, P. A., Tsa, F.-F., Rodrigues, A., & Maniaci, M. R. (2010). Are you happy for me? How sharing positive events with others provides personal and interpersonal benefits. *Journal of Personality and Social Psychology, 99,* 311–329. (p. 370)

Reis, S. M. (2001). Toward a theory of creativity in diverse creative women. In M. Bloom & T. Gullotta (Eds.), *Promoting creativity across the life span* (pp. 231–275). Washington, DC: CWLA Press. (p. 325)

Reisenzein, R. (1983). The Schachter theory of emotion: Two decades later. *Psychological Bulletin, 94,* 239–264. (p. 389)

Reiser, M. (1982). *Police psychology: Collected papers.* Los Angeles: LEHI. (p. 241)

Reitzle, M. (2006). The connections between adulthood transitions and the self-perception of being adult in the changing contexts of East and West Germany. *European Psychologist, 11,* 25–38. (p. 156)

Reivich, K., Gillham, J. E., Chaplin, T. M., & Seligman, M. E. P. (2013). From helplessness to optimism: The role of resilience in treating and preventing depression in youth. In S. Goldstein & R. B. Brooks (Eds.), *Handbook of resilience in children* (pp. 201–214). New York: Springer Science+Business Media. (p. 580)

Remick, A. K., Polivy, J., & Pliner, P. (2009). Internal and external moderators of the effect of variety on food intake. *Psychological Bulletin, 135,* 434–451. (p. 382)

Remington, A., Swettenham, J., Campbell, R., & Coleman, M. (2009). Selective attention and perceptual load in autism spectrum disorder. *Psychological Science, 20,* 1388–1393. (p. 136)

Remley, A. (1988, October). From obedience to independence. *Psychology Today,* pp. 56–59. (p. 145)

Ren, D., Tan, K., Arriaga, X. B., & Chan, K. Q. (2015). Sweet love: The effects of sweet taste experience on romantic perceptions. *Journal of Social and Personal Relationships.* Advance online publication. doi:10.1177/0265407514554512 (p. 238)

Ren, J., Jin, Z.-C., & Yang, Q.-J. (2010). A meta-analysis of factors affecting subjective well-being of the elderly in China. *Chinese Journal of Clinical Psychology, 18,* 119–121. (p. 423)

Renner, M. J., & Renner, C. H. (1993). Expert and novice intuitive judgments about animal behavior. *Bulletin of the Psychonomic Society, 31,* 551–552. (p. 127)

Renninger, K. A., & Granott, N. (2005). The process of scaffolding in learning and development. *New Ideas in Psychology, 23,* 111–114. (p. 134)

Rentfrow, P. J., & Gosling, S. D. (2003). The do re mi's of everyday life: The structure and personality correlates of music preferences. *Journal of Personality and Social Psychology, 84,* 1236–1256. (p. 512)

Rentfrow, P. J., & Gosling, S. D. (2006). Message in a ballad: The role of music preferences in interpersonal perception. *Psychological Science, 17,* 236–242. (p. 512)

Rescorla, R. A., & Wagner, A. R. (1972). A theory of Pavlovian conditioning: Variations in the effectiveness of reinforcement and nonreinforcement. In A. H. Black & W. F. Perokasy (Eds.), *Classical conditioning II: Current theory* (pp. 64–99). New York: Appleton-Century-Crofts. (p. 270)

Resnick, M. D., Bearman, P. S., Blum, R. W., Bauman, K. E., Harris, K. M., Jones, J., . . . Udry, J. R. (1997). Protecting adolescents from harm: Findings from the National Longitudinal Study on Adolescent Health. *Journal of the American Medical Association, 278,* 823–832. (pp. 23, 84, 154)

Resnick, S. M. (1992). Positron emission tomography in psychiatric illness. *Current Directions in Psychological Science, 1,* 92–98. (p. 558)

Reuters. (2000, July 5). *Many teens regret decision to have sex (National Campaign to Prevent Teen Pregnancy survey).* Retrieved from http://www.washingtonpost.com (p. 186)

Reyna, V. F., Chick, C. F., Corbin, J. C., & Hsia, A. N. (2014). Developmental reversals in risky decision making: Intelligence agents show larger decision biases than college students. *Psychological Science, 25,* 76–84. (p. 323)

Reyna, V. F., & Farley, F. (2006). Risk and rationality in adolescent decision making: Implications for theory, practice, and public policy. *Psychological Science in the Public Interest, 7,* 1–44. (p. 148)

Reynolds, C. R., Niland, J., Wright, J. E., & Rosenn, M. (2010). Failure to apply the Flynn correction in death penalty litigation: Standard practice of today maybe, but certainly malpractice of tomorrow. *Journal of Psychoeducational Assessment, 28*, 477–481. (p. 352)

Reynolds, G. (2009, November 18). Phys ed: Why exercise makes you less anxious. *The New York Times.* Retrieved from http://well.blogs.nytimes.com/2009/11/18/phys-ed-why-exercise-makes-you-less-anxious/?_r=0 (p. 427)

Ricciardelli, L. A., & McCabe, M. P. (2004). A biopsychosocial model of disordered eating and the pursuit of muscularity in adolescent boys. *Psychological Bulletin, 130*, 179–205. (p. 565)

Rice, E., Gibbs, J., Winetrobe, H., Rhoades, H., Plant, A., Montoya, J., & Kordic, T. (2014). Sexting and sexual behavior among middle school students. *Pediatrics, 134*, e21–e28. doi:10.1542/peds.2013-2991 (p. 186)

Rice, M. E., & Grusec, J. E. (1975). Saying and doing: Effects on observer performance. *Journal of Personality and Social Psychology, 32*, 584–593. (p. 276)

Richardson, M., Abraham, C., & Bond, R. (2012). Psychological correlates of university students' academic performance: A systematic review and meta-analysis. *Psychological Bulletin, 138*, 353–387. (p. 362)

Richeson, J. A., & Shelton, J. N. (2007). Negotiating interracial interactions. *Current Directions in Psychological Science, 16*, 316–320. (p. 486)

Rickard, I. J., Frankenhuis, W. E., & Nettle, D. (2014). Why are childhood family factors associated with timing of maturation? A role for internal prediction. *Perspectives on Psychological Science, 9*, 3–15. (p. 176)

Rideout, V. J., Foehr, U. G., & Roberts, D. F. (2010, January). *Generation M2: Media in the lives of 8- to 18-year-olds.* Menlo Park, CA: Henry J. Kaiser Family Foundation. (pp. 22, 374)

Rieff, P. (1979). *Freud: The mind of a moralist* (3rd ed.). Chicago: University of Chicago Press. (p. 499)

Rieger, G., Rosenthal, A. M., Cash, B. M., Linsenmeier, J. A. W., Bailey, J. M., & Savin-Williams, R. (2013). Male bisexual arousal: A matter of curiosity? *Biological Psychology, 94*, 479–489. (p. 188)

Rieger, G., & Savin-Williams, R. (2012). The eyes have it: Sex and sexual orientation differences in pupil dilation patterns. *PLOS ONE, 7*(8), e40256. doi:10.1371/journal.pone.0040256 (p. 189)

Rietveld, C. A., Medland, S. E., Derringer, J., Yang, J., Esko, T., Martin, N. W., . . . Koellinger, P. D. (2013). GWAS of 126,559 individuals identifies genetic variants associated with educational attainment. *Science, 340*, 1467–1471. (p. 354)

Riffkin, R. (2014, July 9). *Obesity linked to lower social well-being: Americans with high social well-being exercise more frequently.* Retrieved from http://www.gallup.com/poll/172253/obesity-linked-lower-social.aspx (p. 382)

Riis, J., Loewenstein, G., Baron, J., Jepson, C., Fagerlin, A., & Ubel, P. A. (2005). Ignorance of hedonic adaptation to hemodialysis: A study using ecological momentary assessment. *Journal of Experimental Psychology: General, 134*, 3–9. (p. 433)

Riley, L. D., & Bowen, C. (2005). The sandwich generation: Challenges and coping strategies of multigenerational families. *The Family Journal, 13*, 52–58. (p. 163)

Rindermann, H., & Ceci, S. J. (2009). Educational policy and country outcomes in international cognitive competence studies. *Perspectives on Psychological Science, 4*, 551–577. (p. 359)

Riordan, M. (2013, March 19). *Tobacco warning labels: Evidence of effectiveness.* Retrieved from http://www.tobaccofreekids.org/research/factsheets/pdf/0325.pdf (p. 320)

Ripley, A. (2013, January 28). Your brain under fire. *Time*, pp. 34ff. (p. 320)

Ritchie, S. J., Wiseman, R., & French, C. C. (2012). Failing the future: Three unsuccessful attempts to replicate Bem's "retroactive facilitation of recall" effect. *PLOS ONE, 7*(3), e33r23. doi:10.1371/journal.pone.0033423 (p. 242)

Ritter, S. M., Damian, R. I., Simonton, D. K., van Baaren, R. B., Strick, M., Derks, J., & Dijksterhuis, A. (2012). Diversifying experiences enhance cognitive flexibility. *Journal of Experimental Social Psychology, 48*, 961–964. (p. 326)

Rizzolatti, G., Fadiga, L., Fogassi, L., & Gallese, V. (2002). From mirror neurons to imitation: Facts and speculations. In A. N. Meltzoff & W. Prinz (Eds.), *The imitative mind: Development, evolution, and brain bases* (pp. 247–265). Cambridge, England: Cambridge University Press. (p. 273)

Rizzolatti, G., Fogassi, L., & Gallese, V. (2006, November). Mirrors in the mind. *Scientific American*, pp. 54–61. (p. 273)

Roberson, D., Davidoff, J., Davies, I. R. L., & Shapiro, L. R. (2004). The development of color categories in two languages: A longitudinal study. *Journal of Experimental Psychology: General, 133*, 554–571. (p. 337)

Roberson, D., Davies, I. R. L., Corbett, G. G., & Vandervyver, M. (2005). Free-sorting of colors across cultures: Are there universal grounds for grouping? *Journal of Cognition and Culture, 5*, 349–386. (p. 337)

Roberti, J. W., Storch, E. A., & Bravata, E. A. (2004). Sensation seeking, exposure to psychosocial stressors, and body modifications in a college population. *Personality and Individual Differences, 37*, 1167–1177. (p. 367)

Roberts, A. L., Glymour, M. M., & Koenen, K. C. (2013). Does maltreatment in childhood affect sexual orientation in adulthood? *Archives of Sexual Behavior, 42*, 161–171. (p. 189)

Roberts, B. W., & DelVecchio, W. F. (2000). The rank-order consistency of personality traits from childhood to old age: A quantitative review of longitudinal studies. *Psychological Bulletin, 126*, 3–25. (p. 511)

Roberts, B. W., Donnellan, M. B., & Hill, P. L. (2013). Personality trait development in adulthood. In I. B. Weiner (Ed.-in-Chief) & H. Tennen & J. Suls (Vol. Eds.), *Handbook of psychology: Vol. 5. Personality and social psychology* (2nd ed., pp. 183–196). Hoboken, NJ: Wiley. (p. 122)

Roberts, B. W., Kuncel, N. R., Shiner, R., Caspi, A., & Goldberg, L. R. (2007). The power of personality: The comparative validity of personality traits, socioeconomic status, and cognitive ability for predicting important life outcomes. *Perspectives on Psychological Science, 2*, 313–345. (p. 511)

Roberts, B. W., & Mroczek, D. K. (2008). Personality trait change in adulthood. *Current Directions in Psychological Science, 17*, 31–35. (p. 122)

Roberts, B. W., Wood, D., & Caspi, A. (2008). The development of personality traits in adulthood. In O. P. John (Ed.), *Handbook of personality: Theory and research* (3rd ed., pp. 375–398). New York: Guilford Press. (p. 510)

Roberts, L. (1988). Beyond Noah's ark: What do we need to know? *Science, 242*, 1247. (p. 420)

Roberts, T.-A. (1991). Determinants of gender differences in responsiveness to others' evaluations. *Dissertation Abstracts International, 51*(08–B). (p. 174)

Robertson, K. F., Smeets, S., Lubinski, D., & Benbow, C. P. (2010). Beyond the threshold hypothesis: Even among the gifted and top math/science graduate students, cognitive abilities, vocational interests, and lifestyle preferences matter for career choice, performance, and persistence. *Current Directions in Psychological Science, 19*, 346–351. (p. 325)

Robins, L., & Regier, D. (Eds.). (1991). *Psychiatric disorders in America.* New York: Free Press. (p. 535)

Robins, L. N., Davis, D. H., & Goodwin, D. W. (1974). Drug use by U.S. Army enlisted men in Vietnam: A follow-up on their return home. *American Journal of Epidemiology, 99*, 235–249. (p. 116)

Robins, R. W., & Trzesniewski, K. H. (2005). Self-esteem development across the lifespan. *Current Directions in Psychological Science, 14*, 158–162. (p. 166)

Robinson, F. P. (1970). *Effective study.* New York: Harper & Row. (p. 30)

Robinson, J. P., & Martin, S. (2008). What do happy people do? *Social Indicators Research, 89*, 565–571. (p. B-1)

Robinson, J. P., & Martin, S. (2009). Changes in American daily life: 1965–2005. *Social Indicators Research, 93*, 47–56. (p. 276)

Robinson, O. J., Cools, R., Carlisi, C. O., & Drevets, W. C. (2012). Ventral striatum response during reward and punishment reversal learning in unmedicated major depressive disorder. *American Journal of Psychiatry, 169*, 152–159. (p. 549)

Robinson, T. E., & Berridge, K. C. (2003). Addiction. *Annual Review of Psychology, 54*, 25–53. (p. 105)

Robinson, T. N., Borzekowski, D. L. G., Matheson, D. M., & Kraemer, H. C. (2007). Effects of fast food branding on young children's taste preferences. *Archives of Pediatric and Adolescent Medicine, 161*, 792–797. (p. 206)

Robinson, V. M. (1983). Humor and health. In P. E. McGhee & J. H. Goldstein (Eds.), *Handbook of humor research: Vol. 2. Applied studies* (pp. 109–128). New York: Springer-Verlag. (p. 424)

Robles, T. F. (2015). Marital quality and health: Implications for marriage in the 21st century. *Current Directions in Psychological Science, 23*, 427–432. (p. 424)

Robles, T. F., Slatcher, R. B., Trombello, J. M., & McGinn, M. M. (2014). Marital quality and health: A meta-analytic review. *Psychological Bulletin, 140*, 140–187. (p. 424)

Rochat, F. (1993, August). *How did they resist authority? Protecting refugees in Le Chambon during World War II.* Paper presented at the 101st Annual Convention of the American Psychological Association, Toronto, Ontario, Canada. (p. 454)

Rock, I., & Palmer, S. (1990, December). The legacy of Gestalt psychology. *Scientific American,* pp. 84–90. (p. 218)

Rodenburg, R., Benjamin, A., de Roos, C., Meijer, A. M., & Stams, G. J. (2009). Efficacy of EMDR in children: A meta-analysis. *Clinical Psychology Review, 29,* 599–606. (p. 588)

Rodin, J. (1986). Aging and health: Effects of the sense of control. *Science, 233,* 1271–1276. (p. 420)

Roediger, H. L., III. (2013). Applying cognitive psychology to education: Translational educational science. *Psychological Science in the Public Interest, 14,* 1–3. (p. 289)

Roediger, H. L., & Finn, B. (2009, October 20). Getting it wrong: Surprising tips on how to learn. *Scientific American Mind.* Retrieved from http://www.scientific american.com/article/getting-it-wrong/ (p. 31)

Roediger, H. L., III, & Geraci, L. (2007). Aging and the misinformation effect: A neuropsychological analysis. *Journal of Experimental Psychology, 33,* 321–334. (p. 310)

Roediger, H. L., III, & Karpicke, J. D. (2006). Test-enhanced learning: Taking memory tests improves long-term retention. *Psychological Science, 17,* 249–255. (pp. 30, 289)

Roediger, H. L., III, & McDaniel, M. A. (2007). Illusory recollection in older adults: Testing Mark Twain's conjecture. In M. Garry & H. Hayne (Eds.), *Do justice and let the sky fall: Elizabeth F. Loftus and her contributions to science, law, and academic freedom* (pp. 105–136). Mahwah, NJ: Erlbaum. (p. 310)

Roediger, H. L., III, & McDermott, K. B. (1995). Creating false memories: Remembering words not presented in lists. *Journal of Experimental Psychology: Learning, Memory, and Cognition, 21,* 803–814. (p. 309)

Roediger, H. L., III, Wheeler, M. A., & Rajaram, S. (1993). Remembering, knowing, and reconstructing the past. In D. L. Medin (Ed.), *The psychology of learning and motivation: Advances in research and theory* (Vol. 30, pp. 97–134). Orlando, FL: Academic Press. (p. 308)

Roehling, P. V., Roehling, M. V., & Moen, P. (2001). The relationship between work-life policies and practices and employee loyalty: A life course perspective. *Journal of Family and Economic Issues, 22,* 141–170. (p. B-12)

Roelofs, T. (2010, September 22). Somali refugee takes oath of U.S. citizenship year after his brother. *The Grand Rapids Press.* Retrieved from http://www.mlive. com/news/grand-rapids/index.ssf/2010/09/somali_refugee_takes_oath_of_u.html (p. B-9)

Roenneberg, T., Kuehnle, T., Pramstaller, P. P., Ricken, J., Havel, M., Guth, A., Merrow, M. (2004). A marker for the end of adolescence. *Current Biology, 14,* R1038–R1039. (p. 88)

Roepke, A. M., & Seligman, M. E. P. (2015). Doors opening: A mechanism for growth after adversity. *Journal of Positive Psychology, 10,* 107–115. (p. 603)

Roese, N. J., & Summerville, A. (2005). What we regret most . . . and why. *Personality and Social Psychology Bulletin, 31,* 1273–1285. (p. 166)

Roese, N. J., & Vohs, K. D. (2012). Hindsight bias. *Perspectives on Psychological Science, 7,* 411–426. (p. 15)

Roesser, R. (1998). *What you should know about hearing conservation.* Retrieved from http://www.betterhearing.org/ (p. 228)

Rogeberg, O. (2013). Correlations between cannabis use and IQ change in the Dunedin cohort are consistent with confounding from socioeconomic status. *Proceedings of the National Academy of Sciences of the United States of America, 110,* 4251–4254. (p. 112)

Rogers, C. R. (1961). *On becoming a person: A therapist's view of psychotherapy.* Boston: Houghton Mifflin. (p. 573)

Rogers, C. R. (1980). *A way of being.* Boston: Houghton Mifflin. (pp. 502, 573)

Rohan, K. J., Roecklein, K. A., Lindsey, K. T., Johnson, L. G., Lippy, R. D., Lacy, T. J., & Barton, F. B. (2007). A randomized controlled trial of cognitive–behavioral therapy, light therapy, and their combination for seasonal affective disorder. *Journal of Consulting and Clinical Psychology, 75,* 489–500. (p. 589)

Rohner, R. P. (1986). *The warmth dimension: Foundations of parental acceptance-rejection theory.* Newbury Park, CA: Sage. (p. 120)

Rohner, R. P., & Veneziano, R. A. (2001). The importance of father love: History and contemporary evidence. *Review of General Psychology, 5,* 382–405. (pp. 141, 145)

Rohrer, J. M., Egloff, B., & Schmukle, S. C. (2015). Examining the effects of birth order on personality. *Proceedings of the National Academy of Sciences of the United States of America.* Advance online publication. doi: 10.1073/pnas.1506451112 (p. A-8)

Roiser, J. P., Cook, L. J., Cooper, J. D., Rubinsztein, D. C., & Sahakian, B. J. (2005). Association of a functional polymorphism in the serotonin transporter gene with abnormal emotional processing in Ecstasy users. *American Journal of Psychiatry, 162,* 609–612. (p. 111)

Rokach, A., Orzeck, T., Moya, M., & Expósito, F. (2002). Causes of loneliness in North America and Spain. *European Psychologist, 7,* 70–79. (p. 9)

Romens, S. E., McDonald, J., Svaren, J., & Pollak, S. D. (2015). Associations between early life stress and gene methylation in children. *Child Development, 86,* 303–309. (p. 144)

Ronald, A., & Hoekstra, R. A. (2011). Autism spectrum disorders and autistic traits: A decade of new twin studies. *American Journal of Medical Genetics Part B: Neuropsychiatric Genetics, 156,* 255–274. (p. 68)

Ronay, R., & von Hippel, W. (2010). The presence of an attractive woman elevates testosterone and physical risk taking in young men. *Social Psychology and Personality Science, 1,* 57–64. (p. 182)

Root, T. L., Thornton, L. M., Lindroos, A. K., Stunkard, A. J., Lichtenstein, P., Pedersen, N. L., . . . Bulik, C. M. (2010). Shared and unique genetic and environmental influences on binge eating and night eating: A Swedish twin study. *Eating Behaviors, 11,* 92–98. (p. 565)

Roque, L., Verissimo, M., Oliveira, T. F., & Oliveira, R. F. (2012). Attachment security and HPA axis reactivity to positive and challenging emotional situations in child–mother dyads in naturalistic settings. *Developmental Psychobiology, 54,* 401–411. (p. 140)

Rosch, E. (1978). Principles of categorization. In E. Rosch & B. L. Lloyd (Eds.), *Cognition and categorization* (pp. 27–48). Hillsdale, NJ: Erlbaum. (p. 316)

Rose, A. J., & Rudolph, K. D. (2006). A review of sex differences in peer relationship processes: Potential trade-offs for the emotional and behavioral development of girls and boys. *Psychological Bulletin, 132,* 98–131. (p. 174)

Rose, J. S., Chassin, L., Presson, C. C., & Sherman, S. J. (1999). Peer influences on adolescent cigarette smoking: A prospective sibling analysis. *Merrill-Palmer Quarterly, 45,* 62–84. (pp. 115, 154)

Rose, R. J., Viken, R. J., Dick, D. M., Bates, J. E., Pulkkinen, L., & Kaprio, J. (2003). It *does* take a village: Nonfamiliar environments and children's behavior. *Psychological Science, 14,* 273–277. (p. 154)

Roselli, C. E., Larkin, K., Schrunk, J. M., & Stormshak, F. (2004). Sexual partner preference, hypothalamic morphology and aromatase in rams. *Physiology and Behavior, 83,* 233–245. (p. 190)

Roselli, C. E., Resko, J. A., & Stormshak, F. (2002). Hormonal influences on sexual partner preference in rams. *Archives of Sexual Behavior, 31,* 43–49. (p. 190)

Rosenbaum, M. (1986). The repulsion hypothesis: On the nondevelopment of relationships. *Journal of Personality and Social Psychology, 51,* 1156–1166. (p. 479)

Rosenberg, N. A., Pritchard, J. K., Weber, J. L., Cann, H. M., Kidd, K. K., Zhivotosky, L. A., & Feldman, M. W. (2002). Genetic structure of human populations. *Science, 298,* 2381–2385. (p. 358)

Rosenberg, T. (2010, November 1). The opt-out solution. *The New York Times.* Retrieved from http://opinionator.blogs.nytimes.com/2010/11/01/the-opt-out-solution/ (p. 323)

Rosenblum, L. D. (2013, January). A confederacy of senses. *Scientific American,* pp. 73–78. (p. 239)

Rosenfeld, M. J. (2013, August 26). Personal communication. (p. 164)

Rosenfeld, M. J. (2014). Couple longevity in the era of same-sex marriage in the United States. *Journal of Marriage and Family, 76,* 905–911. (p. 163)

Rosenfeld, M. J., & Thomas, R. J. (2012). Searching for a mate: The rise of the Internet as a social intermediary. *American Sociological Review, 77,* 523–547. (pp. 164, 476)

Rosenhan, D. L. (1973). On being sane in insane places. *Science, 179,* 250–258. (p. 531)

Rosenthal, A. M., Sylva, D., Safron, A., & Bailey, J. M. (2012). The male bisexuality debate revisited: Some bisexual men have bisexual arousal patterns. *Archives of Sexual Behavior, 41,* 135–147. (p. 188)

Rosenthal, E. (2005, June 3). For fruit flies, gene shift tilts sex orientation. *The New York Times.* Retrieved from http://www.nytimes.com/2005/06/03/science/for-fruit-flies-gene-shift-tilts-sex-orientation.html?_r=0 (p. 191)

Rosenthal, R., Hall, J. A., Archer, D., DiMatteo, M. R., & Rogers, P. L. (1979). The PONS test: Measuring sensitivity to nonverbal cues. In S. Weitz (Ed.), *Nonverbal communication* (2nd ed., pp. 357–370). New York: Oxford University Press. (p. 396)

Rosenzweig, M. R., Krech, D., Bennett, E. L., & Diamond, M. C. (1962). Effects of environmental complexity and training on brain chemistry and anatomy: A replication and extension. *Journal of Comparative and Physiological Psychology, 55,* 429–437. (pp. 127, 128)

Roseth, C. J., Johnson, D. W., & Johnson, R. T. (2008). Promoting early adolescents' achievement and peer relationships: The effects of cooperative, competitive, and individualistic goal structures. *Psychological Bulletin, 134,* 223–246. (p. 487)

Rosin, H. (2010, July/August). The end of men. *The Atlantic.* Retrieved from http://www.theatlantic.com/magazine/archive/2010/07/the-end-of-men/308135/ (p. 178)

Ross, J. (2006). Sleep on a problem . . . it works like a dream. *The Psychologist, 19,* 738–740. (p. 93)

Ross, L. (1977). The intuitive psychologist and his shortcomings: Distortions in the attribution process. In L. Berkowitz (Ed.) *Advances in experimental social psychology* (Vol. 10, pp. 173–220). New York: Academic Press. (p. 442)

Ross, M., McFarland, C., & Fletcher, G.J.O. (1981). The effect of attitude on the recall of personal histories. *Journal of Personality and Social Psychology, 40,* 627–634. (p. 305)

Ross, M., Xun, W. Q. E., & Wilson, A. E. (2002). Language and the bicultural self. *Personality and Social Psychology Bulletin, 28,* 1040–1050. (p. 337)

Rossi, P. J. (1968). Adaptation and negative aftereffect to lateral optical displacement in newly hatched chicks. *Science, 160,* 430–432. (p. 224)

Rossion, B., & Boremanse, A. (2011). Robust sensitivity to facial identity in the right human occipito-temporal cortex as revealed by steady-state visual-evoked potentials. *Journal of Vision, 11*(2), Article 16. doi:10.1167/11.2.16 (p. 199)

Rotge, J.-Y., Lemogne, C., Hinfray, S., Huguet, P., Grynszpan, O., Tartour, E., . . . Fossati, P. (2015). A meta-analysis of the anterior cingulate contribution to social pain. *Social Cognitive and Affective Neuroscience, 10,* 19–27. (p. 372)

Roth, T., Roehrs, T., Zwyghuizen-Doorenbos, A., Stpeanski, E., & Witting, R. (1988). Sleep and memory. In I. Hindmarch & H. Ott (Eds.), *Benzodiazepine receptor ligands, memory and information processing* (pp. 140–145). Berlin, Germany: Springer-Verlag. (p. 99)

Rothbart, M., Fulero, S., Jensen, C., Howard, J., & Birrell, P. (1978). From individual to group impressions: Availability heuristics in stereotype formation. *Journal of Experimental Social Psychology, 14,* 237–255. (p. 467)

Rothbaum, F., & Tsang, B. Y.-P. (1998). Lovesongs in the United States and China: On the nature of romantic love. *Journal of Cross-Cultural Psychology, 29,* 306–319. (p. 523)

Rothman, A. J., & Salovey, P. (1997). Shaping perceptions to motivate healthy behavior: The role of message framing. *Psychological Bulletin, 121,* 3–19. (p. 322)

Rotton, J., & Kelly, I. W. (1985). Much ado about the full moon: A meta-analysis of lunar-lunacy research. *Psychological Bulletin, 97,* 286–306. (p. 564)

Rounds, J., & Su, R. (2014). The nature and power of interests. *Current Directions in Psychological Science, 23,* 98–103. (p. B-3)

Rovee-Collier, C. (1989). The joy of kicking: Memories, motives, and mobiles. In P. R. Solomon, G. R. Goethals, C. M. Kelley, & B. R. Stephens (Eds.), *Memory: Interdisciplinary approaches* (pp. 151–179). New York: Springer-Verlag. (p. 129)

Rovee-Collier, C. (1993). The capacity for long-term memory in infancy. *Current Directions in Psychological Science, 2,* 130–135. (p. 298)

Rovee-Collier, C. (1997). Dissociations in infant memory: Rethinking the development of implicit and explicit memory. *Psychological Review, 104,* 467–498. (p. 129)

Rovee-Collier, C. (1999). The development of infant memory. *Current Directions in Psychological Science, 8,* 80–85. (p. 129)

Rowe, D. C. (1990). As the twig is bent? The myth of child-rearing influences on personality development. *Journal of Counseling and Development, 68,* 606–611. (p. 70)

Rowe, D. C., Almeida, D. M., & Jacobson, K. C. (1999). School context and genetic influences on aggression in adolescence. *Psychological Science, 10,* 277–280. (p. 469)

Rowe, D. C., Jacobson, K. C., & Van den Oord, E.J.C.G. (1999). Genetic and environmental influences on vocabulary IQ: Parental education level as moderator. *Child Development, 70,* 1151–1162. (p. 355)

Rowland, C. A. (2014). The effect of testing versus restudy on retention: A meta-analytic review of the testing effect. *Psychological Bulletin, 140,* 1432–1463. (p. 30)

Rozin, P., Dow, S., Mosovitch, M., & Rajaram, S. (1998). What causes humans to begin and end a meal? A role for memory for what has been eaten, as evidenced by a study of multiple meal eating in amnesic patients. *Psychological Science, 9,* 392–396. (p. 380)

Rozin, P., Haddad, B., Nemeroff, C., & Slovic, P. (2015). Psychological aspects of the rejection of recycled water: Contamination, purification and disgust. *Judgment and Decision Making, 10,* 50–63. (p. 252)

Rozin, P., Millman, L., & Nemeroff, C. (1986). Operation of the laws of sympathetic magic in disgust and other domains. *Journal of Personality and Social Psychology, 50,* 703–712. (p. 252)

Ruau, D., Liu, L. Y., Clark, J. D., Angst, M. S., & Butte, A. J. (2012). Sex differences in reported pain across 11,000 patients captured in electronic medical records. *Journal of Pain, 13,* 228–234. (p. 231)

Rubenstein, J. S., Meyer, D. E., & Evans, J. E. (2001). Executive control of cognitive processes in task switching. *Journal of Experimental Psychology: Human Perception and Performance, 27,* 763–797. (p. 82)

Rubin, D. C., Rahhal, T. A., & Poon, L. W. (1998). Things learned in early adulthood are remembered best. *Memory and Cognition, 26,* 3–19. (p. 160)

Rubin, J. Z., Pruitt, D. G., & Kim, S. H. (1994). *Social conflict: Escalation, stalemate, and settlement.* New York: McGraw-Hill. (p. 487)

Rubin, L. B. (1985). *Just friends: The role of friendship in our lives.* New York: Harper & Row. (p. 174)

Rubin, Z. (1970). Measurement of romantic love. *Journal of Personality and Social Psychology, 16,* 265–273. (p. 396)

Rubio-Fernández, P., & Geurts, B. (2013). How to pass the false-belief task before your fourth birthday. *Psychological Science, 24,* 27–33. (p. 133)

Ruchlis, H. (1990). *Clear thinking: A practical introduction.* Buffalo, NY: Prometheus Books. (p. 317)

Rudman, L. A., McLean, M. C., & Bunzl, M. (2013). When truth is personally inconvenient, attitudes change: The impact of extreme weather on implicit support for green politicians and explicit climate-change beliefs. *Psychological Science, 14,* 2290–2296. (p. 320)

Rueckert, L., Doan, T., & Branch, B. (2010, May). *Emotion and relationship effects on gender differences in empathy.* Paper presented at the 22nd Annual Convention of the Association for Psychological Science, Boston, MA. (p. 398)

Ruffin, C. L. (1993). Stress and health—little hassles vs. major life events. *Australian Psychologist, 28,* 201–208. (p. 407)

Rule, B. G., & Ferguson, T. J. (1986). The effects of media violence on attitudes, emotions, and cognitions. *Journal of Social Issues, 42*(3), 29–50. (p. 277)

Rule, N. O., Ambady, N., & Hallett, K. C. (2009). Female sexual orientation is perceived accurately, rapidly, and automatically from the face and its features. *Journal of Experimental Social Psychology, 45,* 1245–1251. (p. 512)

Rumbaugh, D. M. (1977). *Language learning by a chimpanzee: The Lana project.* New York: Academic Press. (p. 335)

Rushton, J. P. (1975). Generosity in children: Immediate and long-term effects of modeling, preaching, and moral judgment. *Journal of Personality and Social Psychology, 31,* 459–466. (p. 276)

Russell, B. (1985). *The conquest of happiness.* London: Unwin. (Original work published 1930) (p. 435)

Ruthsatz, J., & Urbach, J. B. (2012). Child prodigy: A novel cognitive profile places elevated general intelligence, exceptional working memory and attention to detail at the root of prodigiousness. *Intelligence, 40,* 419–426. (p. 376)

Rutledge, R. B., Skandali, N., Dayan, P., & Dolan, R. J. (2014). A computational and neural model of momentary subjective well-being. *Proceedings of the National Academy of Sciences of the United States of America, 111,* 12252–12257. (p. 435)

Ryan, A. M., & Ployhart, R. E. (2014). A century of selection. *Annual Review of Psychology, 65,* 693–717. (p. B-5)

Ryan, C., Huebner, D., Diaz, R. M., & Sanchez, J. (2009). Family rejection as a predictor of negative health outcomes in White and Latino lesbian, gay, and bisexual young adults. *Pediatrics, 123,* 346–352. (p. 188)

Ryan, R. (1999, February 2). Quoted in A. Kohn, In pursuit of affluence, at a high price. *The New York Times.* Retrieved from http://www.alfiekohn.org/article/pursuit-affluence-high-price/ (p. 435)

Ryan, R. M., & Deci, E. L. (2004). Avoiding death or engaging life as accounts of meaning and culture: Comment on Pyszczynski et al. (2004). *Psychological Bulletin, 130,* 473–477. (p. 520)

Rydell, R. J., Rydell, M. T., & Boucher, K. L. (2010). The effect of negative performance stereotypes on learning. *Journal of Personality and Social Psychology, 99,* 883–896. (p. 361)

S

Saad, L. (2002, November 21). *Most smokers wish they could quit.* Retrieved from http://www.gallup.com/poll/7270/most-smokers-wish-they-could-quit.aspx (p. 109)

Sabbagh, M. A., Xu, F., Carlson, S. M., Moses, L. J., & Lee, K. (2006). The development of executive functioning and theory of mind: A comparison of Chinese and U.S. preschoolers. *Psychological Science, 17,* 74–81. (p. 133)

Sachdev, P., & Sachdev, J. (1997). Sixty years of psychosurgery: Its present status and its future. *Australian and New Zealand Journal of Psychiatry, 31,* 457–464. (p. 600)

Sackett, P. R., Borneman, M. J., & Connelly, B. S. (2008). High-stakes testing in higher education and employment: Appraising the evidence for validity and fairness. *American Psychologist, 63,* 215–227. (p. 361)

Sackett, P. R., Hardison, C. M., & Cullen, M. J. (2004). On interpreting stereotype threat as accounting for African American–White differences on cognitive tests. *American Psychologist, 59,* 7–13. (p. 361)

Sackett, P. R., & Lievens, F. (2008). Personnel selection. *Annual Review of Psychology, 59,* 419–450. (p. B-5)

Sackett, P. R., & Walmsley, P. T. (2014). Which personality attributes are most important in the workplace? *Perspectives on Psychological Science, 9,* 538–551. (p. B-5)

Sacks, O. (1985). *The man who mistook his wife for a hat.* New York: Summit Books. (pp. 238, 302)

Sadato, N., Pascual-Leone, A., Grafman, J., Ibanez, V., Deiber, M.-P., Dold, G., & Hallett, M. (1996). Activation of the primary visual cortex by Braille reading in blind subjects. *Nature, 380,* 526–528. (p. 61)

Sadler, M. S., Correll, J., Park, B., & Judd, C. M. (2012). The world is not Black and White: Racial bias in the decision to shoot in a multiethnic context. *Journal of Social Issues, 68,* 286–313. (p. 463)

Sadler, M. S., Meagor, E. L., & Kaye, M. E. (2012). Stereotypes of mental disorders differ in competence and warmth. *Social Science and Medicine, 74,* 915–922. (p. 531)

Sagan, C. (1977). *The dragons of Eden: Speculations on the evolution of human intelligence.* New York: Ballantine. (p. 199)

Sagan, C. (1979). *Broca's brain: Reflections on the romance of science.* New York: Random House. (p. 5)

Sagan, C. (1987, February 1). The fine art of baloney detection. *Parade.* (p. 242)

Salas-Wright, C. P., Vaughn, M. G., Hodge, D. R., & Perron, B. E. (2012). Religiosity profiles of American youth in relation to substance use, violence, and delinquency. *Journal of Youth and Adolescence, 41,* 1560–1575. (p. 115)

Salmon, P. (2001). Effects of physical exercise on anxiety, depression, and sensitivity to stress: A unifying theory. *Clinical Psychology Review, 21,* 33–61. (p. 427)

Salovey, P. (1990). Interview. *American Scientist, 78,* 25–29. (p. 431)

Salthouse, T. A. (2009). When does age-related cognitive decline begin? *Neurobiology of Aging, 30,* 507–514. (p. 349)

Salthouse, T. A. (2010). Selective review of cognitive aging. *Journal of the International Neuropsychological Society, 16,* 754–760. (pp. 162, 350)

Salthouse, T. A. (2013). Within-cohort age-related differences in cognitive functioning. *Psychological Science, 24,* 123–130. (p. 349)

Salthouse, T. A., & Mandell, A. R. (2013). Do age-related increases in tip-of-the-tongue experiences signify episodic memory impairments? *Psychological Science, 24,* 2489–2497. (p. 304)

Sampson, E. E. (2000). Reinterpreting individualism and collectivism: Their religious roots and monologic versus dialogic person–other relationship. *American Psychologist, 55,* 1425–1432. (p. 521)

Sánchez-Villegas, A., Delgado-Rodríguez, M., Alonson, A., Schlatter, J., Lahortiga, F., Majem, L. S., & Martínez-González, M. A. (2009). Association of the Mediterranean dietary pattern with the incidence of depression. *Archives of General Psychiatry, 66,* 1090–1098. (p. 550)

Sanders, A. R., Martin, E. R., Beecham, G. W., Guo, S., Dawood, K., Rieger, G., . . . Bailey, J. M. (2015). Genome-wide scan demonstrates significant linkage for male sexual orientation. *Psychological Medicine, 45,* 1379–1388. (p. 191)

Sanders, M. A., Shirk, S. D., Burgin, C. J., & Martin, L. L. (2012). The gargle effect: Rinsing the mouth with glucose enhances self-control. *Psychological Science, 23,* 1470–1472. (p. 422)

Sandfort, T. G. M., de Graaf, R., Bijl, R., & Schnabel, P. (2001). Same-sex sexual behavior and psychiatric disorders. *Archives of General Psychiatry, 58,* 85–91. (p. 188)

Sandkühler, S., & Bhattacharya, J. (2008). Deconstructing insight: EEG correlates of insightful problem solving. *PLOS ONE, 3*(1), e1459. doi:10.1371/journal.pone.0001459 (p. 317)

Sandler, W., Meir, I., Padden, C., & Aronoff, M. (2005). The emergence of grammar: Systematic structure in a new language. *Proceedings of the National Academy of Sciences of the United States of America, 102,* 2261–2265. (p. 330)

Santos, A., Meyer-Lindenberg, A., & Deruelle, C. (2010). Absence of racial, but not gender, stereotyping in Williams syndrome children. *Current Biology, 20,* R307–R308. (p. 466)

Sanz, C., Blicher, A., Dalke, K., Gratton-Fabri, L., McClure-Richards, T., & Fouts, R. (1998, Winter/Spring). Enrichment object use: Five chimpanzees' use of temporary and semi-permanent enrichment objects. *Friends of Washoe, 19*(1–2), 9–14. (p. 335)

Sanz, C., Morgan, D., & Gulick, S. (2004). New insights into chimpanzees, tools, and termites from the Congo Basin. *American Naturalist, 164,* 567–581. (p. 327)

Sapadin, L. A. (1988). Friendship and gender: Perspectives of professional men and women. *Journal of Social and Personal Relationships, 5,* 387–403. (p. 174)

Saphire-Bernstein, S., Way, B. M., Kim, H. S, Sherman, D. K., & Taylor, S. E. (2011). Oxytocin receptor gene (*OXTR*) is related to psychological resources. *Proceedings of the National Academy of Sciences of the United States of America, 108,* 15118–15122. (p. 423)

Sapolsky, B. S., & Tabarlet, J. O. (1991). Sex in primetime television: 1979 versus 1989. *Journal of Broadcasting and Electronic Media, 35,* 505–516. (p. 186)

Sapolsky, R. (2005). The influence of social hierarchy on primate health. *Science, 308,* 648–652. (p. 420)

Sapolsky, R. (2010, November 14). This is your brain on metaphors. *The New York Times.* Retrieved from http://opinionator.blogs.nytimes.com/2010/11/14/this-is-your-brain-on-metaphors/?_r=0 (p. 393)

Sarro, E. C., Wilson, D. A., & Sullivan, R. M. (2014). Maternal regulation of infant brain state. *Current Biology, 24,* 1664–1669. (pp. 127–128)

Sarsam, M., Parkes, L. M., Roberts, N., Reid, G. S., & Kinderman, P. (2013). The queen and I: Neural correlates of altered self-related cognitions in major depressive episode. *PLOS ONE, 8*(10), e78844. doi:10.1371/journal.pone.0078844 (p. 551)

Satel, S., & Lilienfeld, S. G. (2013). *Brainwashed: The seductive appeal of mindless neuroscience.* New York: Basic Books. (p. 50)

Sato, K. (1987). Distribution of the cost of maintaining common resources. *Journal of Experimental Social Psychology, 23,* 19–31. (p. 485)

Saulny, S. (2006, June 21). A legacy of the storm: Depression and suicide. *The New York Times.* Retrieved from http://www.nytimes.com/2006/06/21/us/21depress.html?pagewanted=all&_r=0 (p. 407)

Saurat, M., Agbakou, M., Attigui, P., Golmard, J., & Arnulf, I. (2011). Walking dreams in congenital and acquired paraplegia. *Consciousness and Cognition, 20,* 1425–1432. (p. 99)

Savage-Rumbaugh, E. S., Murphy, J., Sevcik, R. A., Brakke, K. E., Williams, S. L., Rumbaugh, D. M., & Bates, E. (1993). Language comprehension in ape and child. *Monographs of the Society for Research in Child Development, 58*(3–4, Serial No. 233). (p. 335)

Savage-Rumbaugh, E. S., Rumbaugh, D., & Fields, W. M. (2009). Empirical Kanzi: The ape language controversy revisited. *Skeptic, 15*(1), 25–33. (p. 335)

Savani, K., & Rattan, A. (2012). A choice mind-set increases the acceptance and maintenance of wealth inequality. *Psychological Science, 23,* 796–804. (p. 443)

Savic, I., Berglund, H., & Lindstrom, P. (2005). Brain response to putative pheromones in homosexual men. *Proceedings of the National Academy of Sciences of the United States of America, 102,* 7356–7361. (p. 190)

Savin-Williams, R., Joyner, K., & Rieger, G. (2012). Prevalence and stability of self-reported sexual orientation identity during young adulthood. *Archives of Sexual Behavior, 41,* 103–110. (p. 188)

Savitsky, K., Epley, N., & Gilovich, T. D. (2001). Do others judge us as harshly as we think? Overestimating the impact of our failures, shortcomings, and mishaps. *Journal of Personality and Social Psychology, 81,* 44–56. (p. 516)

Savitsky, K., & Gilovich, T. D. (2003). The illusion of transparency and the alleviation of speech anxiety. *Journal of Experimental Social Psychology, 39*, 618–625. (p. 517)

Savoy, C., & Beitel, P. (1996). Mental imagery for basketball. *International Journal of Sport Psychology, 27*, 454–462. (p. 339)

Sawyer, M. G., Arney, F. M., Baghurst, P. A., Clark, J. J., Graetz, B. W., Kosky, R. J., . . . Zubrick, S. R. (2000). *The mental health of young people in Australia.* Canberra, Australian Capital Territory, Australia: Mental Health and Special Programs Branch, Commonwealth Department of Health and Aged Care. (p. 549)

Sayal, K., Heron, J., Golding, J., Alati, R., Smith, G. D., Gray, R., & Emond, A. (2009). Binge pattern of alcohol consumption during pregnancy and childhood mental health outcomes: Longitudinal population-based study. *Pediatrics, 123*, e289–e296. doi:10.1542/peds.2008-1861 (p. 124)

Sayette, M. A., Creswell, K. G., Kimoff, J. D., Fairbairn, C. E., Cohn, J. F., Heckman, B. W., . . . Moreland, R. L. (2012). Alcohol and group formation: A multimodal investigation of the effects of alcohol on emotion and social bonding. *Psychological Science, 23*, 869–878. (p. 106)

Sayette, M. A., Loewenstein, G., Griffin, K. M., & Black, J. J. (2008). Exploring the cold-to-hot empathy gap in smokers. *Psychological Science, 19*, 926–932. (p. 109)

Sayette, M. A., Reichle, E. D., & Schooler, J. W. (2009). Lost in the sauce: The effects of alcohol on mind wandering. *Psychological Science, 20*, 747–752. (p. 107)

Sayette, M. A., Schooler, J. W., & Reichle, E. D. (2010). Out for a smoke: The impact of cigarette craving on zoning out during reading. *Psychological Science, 21*, 26–30. (p. 109)

Sbarra, D. A., Law, R. W., & Portley, R. M. (2011). Divorce and death: A meta-analysis and research agenda for clinical, social, and health psychology. *Perspectives on Psychological Science, 6*, 454–474. (pp. 371, 424)

Scarborough, E., & Furumoto, L. (1987). *Untold lives: The first generation of American women psychologists.* New York: Columbia University Press. (p. 5)

Scarr, S. (1984, May). What's a parent to do? A conversation with E. Hall. *Psychology Today*, pp. 58–63. (p. 356)

Scarr, S. (1989). Protecting general intelligence: Constructs and consequences for interventions. In R. J. Linn (Ed.), *Intelligence: Measurement, theory, and public policy* (pp. 74–115). Champaign: University of Illinois Press. (p. 343)

Scarr, S. (1990). [Back cover comments on J. Dunn & R. Plomin, *Separate lives: Why siblings are so different.* New York: Basic Books]. (p. 72)

Scarr, S. (1993, May/June). Quoted in Nature's thumbprint: So long, superparents. *Psychology Today*, p. 16. (p. 155)

Schab, F. R. (1991). Odor memory: Taking stock. *Psychological Bulletin, 109*, 242–251. (p. 238)

Schachter, S., & Singer, J. E. (1962). Cognitive, social and physiological determinants of emotional state. *Psychological Review, 69*, 379–399. (p. 388)

Schacter, D. L. (1992). Understanding implicit memory: A cognitive neuroscience approach. *American Psychologist, 47*, 559–569. (p. 302)

Schacter, D. L. (1996). *Searching for memory: The brain, the mind, and the past.* New York: Basic Books. (pp. 159, 293, 302, 500)

Schafer, G. (2005). Infants can learn decontextualized words before their first birthday. *Child Development, 76*, 87–96. (p. 332)

Schafer, S. M., Colloca, L., & Wager, T. D. (2015). Conditioned placebo analgesia persists when subjects know they are receiving a placebo. *Journal of Pain, 16*, 412–420. (p. 25)

Schaie, K. W., & Geiwitz, J. (1982). *Adult development and aging.* Boston: Little, Brown. (p. A-8)

Schalock, R. L., Borthwick-Duffy, S., Bradley, V. J., Buntinx, W. H. E., Coulter, D. L., Craig, E. M., . . . Yeager, M. H. (2010). *Intellectual disability: Definition, classification, and systems of supports* (11th ed.). Washington, DC: American Association on Intellectual and Developmental Disabilities. (p. 351)

Schein, E. H. (1956). The Chinese indoctrination program for prisoners of war: A study of attempted brainwashing. *Psychiatry, 19*, 149–172. (p. 445)

Schetter, C. D., Schafer, P., Lanzi, R. G., Clark-Kauffman, E., Raju., T. N. K., & Hillemeier, M. M. (2013). Shedding light on the mechanisms underlying health disparities through community participatory methods: The stress pathway. *Perspectives on Psychological Science, 8*, 613–633. (p. 409)

Schiavi, R. C., & Schreiner-Engel, P. (1988). Nocturnal penile tumescence in healthy aging men. *Journal of Gerontology: Medical Sciences, 43*, M146–M150. (p. 90)

Schick, V., Herbenick, D., Reece, M., Sanders, S. A., Dodge, B., Middlestadt, S. E., & Fortenberry, J. D. (2010). Sexual behaviors, condom use, and sexual health of Americans over 50: Implications for sexual health promotion for older adults. *Journal of Sexual Medicine, 7*(Suppl. 5), 315–329. (p. 158)

Schiffenbauer, A., & Schiavo, R. S. (1976). Physical distance and attraction: An intensification effect. *Journal of Experimental Social Psychology, 12*, 274–282. (p. 456)

Schilt, T., de Win, M. M. L, Koeter, M., Jager, G., Korf, D. J., van den Brink, W., & Schmand, B. (2007). Cognition in novice Ecstasy users with minimal exposure to other drugs. *Archives of General Psychiatry, 64*, 728–736. (p. 111)

Schimel, J., Arndt, J., Pyszczynski, T., & Greenberg, J. (2001). Being accepted for who we are: Evidence that social validation of the intrinsic self reduces general defensiveness. *Journal of Personality and Social Psychology, 80*, 35–52. (p. 503)

Schimmack, U., & Lucas, R. (2007). Marriage matters: Spousal similarity in life satisfaction. *Schmollers Jahrbuch, 127*, 1–7. (p. 436)

Schink, T., Kreutz, G., Busch V., Pigeot, I., & Ahrens, W. (2014). Incidence and relative risk of hearing disorders in professional musicians. *Occupational and Environmental Medicine, 71*, 472–476. (p. 228)

Schizophrenia Working Group of the Psychiatric Genomics Consortium. (2014). Biological insights from 108 schizophrenia-associated genetic loci. *Nature, 511*, 421–427. (p. 560)

Schlaug, G., Jancke, L., Huang, Y., & Steinmetz, H. (1995). In vivo evidence of structural brain asymmetry in musicians. *Science, 267*, 699–701. (p. 49)

Schlomer, G. L., Del Giudice, M., & Ellis, B. J. (2011). Parent–offspring conflict theory: An evolutionary framework for understanding conflict within human families. *Psychological Review, 118*, 496–521. (p. 154)

Schmader, T. (2010). Stereotype threat deconstructed. *Current Directions in Psychological Science, 19*, 14–18. (p. 361)

Schmidt, F. L. (2002). The role of general cognitive ability and job performance: Why there cannot be a debate. *Human Performance, 15*, 187–210. (p. B-5)

Schmidt, F. L., & Hunter, J. E. (1998). The validity and utility of selection methods in personnel psychology: Practical and theoretical implications of 85 years of research findings. *Psychological Bulletin, 124*, 262–274. (pp. 515, B-5, B-6)

Schmidt, M. F. H., & Tomasello, M. (2012). Young children enforce social norms. *Current Directions in Psychological Science, 21*, 232–236. (p. 150)

Schmitt, D. P. (2007). Sexual strategies across sexual orientations: How personality traits and culture relate to sociosexuality among gays, lesbians, bisexuals, and heterosexuals. *Journal of Psychology and Human Sexuality, 18*, 183–214. (p. 193)

Schmitt, D. P., & Allik, J. (2005). Simultaneous administration of the Rosenberg Self-Esteem Scale in 53 nations: Exploring the universal and culture-specific features of global self-esteem. *Journal of Personality and Social Psychology, 89*, 623–642. (p. 519)

Schmitt, D. P., Allik, J., McCrae, R. R., & Benet-Martínez, V. (2007). The geographic distribution of Big Five personality traits: Patterns and profiles of human self-description across 56 nations. *Journal of Cross-Cultural Psychology, 38*, 173–212. (pp. 509, 510)

Schmitt, D. P., Jonason, P. K., Byerley, G. J., Flores, S. D., Illbeck, B. E., O'Leary, K. N., & Qudrat, A. (2012). A reexamination of sex differences in sexuality: New studies reveal old truths. *Current Directions in Psychological Science, 21*, 135–139. (p. 185)

Schmitt, D. P., & Pilcher, J. J. (2004). Evaluating evidence of psychological adaptation: How do we know one when we see one? *Psychological Science, 15*, 643–649. (p. 74)

Schnall, E., Wassertheil-Smoller, S., Swencionis, C., Zemon, V., Tinker, L., O'Sullivan. M. J., . . . Goodwin, M. (2010). The relationship between religion and cardiovascular outcomes and all-cause mortality in the women's health initiative observational study. *Psychology and Health, 25*, 249–263. (p. 430)

Schnall, S., Haidt, J., Clore, G. L., & Jordan, A. (2008). Disgust as embodied moral judgment. *Personality and Social Psychology Bulletin, 34*, 1096–1109. (pp. 207, 238)

Schneider, S., & Stone, A. A. (2015). Mixed emotions across the adult life span in the United States. *Psychology and Aging, 30*, 369–382. (p. 166)

Schneier, B. (2007, May 17). Virginia Tech lesson: Rare risks breed irrational responses. *Wired.* Retrieved from http://archive.wired.com/politics/security/commentary/securitymatters/2007/05/securitymatters_0517 (p. 321)

Schneiderman, N. (1999). Behavioral medicine and the management of HIV/AIDS. *International Journal of Behavioral Medicine, 6*, 3–12. (p. 413)

Schoen, R., & Canudas-Romo, V. (2006). Timing effects on divorce: 20th century experience in the United States. *Journal of Marriage and Family, 68,* 749–758. (p. 163)

Schoeneman, T. J. (1994). Individualism. In V. S. Ramachandran (Ed.), *Encyclopedia of human behavior* (Vol. 2, pp. 631–643). San Diego, CA: Academic Press. (p. 523)

Schofield, J. W. (1986). Black-White contact in desegregated schools. In M. Hewstone & R. Brown (Eds.), *Contact and conflict in intergroup encounters* (pp. 79–92). Oxford, England: Basil Blackwell. (p. 486)

Schonfield, D., & Robertson, B. A. (1966). Memory storage and aging. *Canadian Journal of Psychology, 20,* 228–236. (p. 161)

Schooler, J. W., Gerhard, D., & Loftus, E. F. (1986). Qualities of the unreal. *Journal of Experimental Psychology: Learning, Memory, and Cognition, 12,* 171–181. (p. 308)

Schorr, E. A., Fox, N. A., van Wassenhove, V., & Knudsen, E. I. (2005). Auditory–visual fusion in speech perception in children with cochlear implants. *Proceedings of the National Academy of Sciences of the United States of America, 102,* 18748–18750. (p. 229)

Schrauzer, G. N., & Shrestha, K. P. (1990). Lithium in drinking water and the incidences of crimes, suicides, and arrests related to drug addictions. *Biological Trace Element Research, 25,* 105–113. (p. 596)

Schrauzer, G. N., & Shrestha, K. P. (2010). Lithium in drinking water. *British Journal of Psychiatry, 196,* 159. (p. 596)

Schreiber, F. R. (1973). *Sybil.* Chicago: Regnery. (p. 562)

Schultheiss, O., Wiemers, U. & Wolf, O. (2014). Implicit need for achievement predicts attenuated cortisol responses to difficult tasks. *Journal of Research in Personality, 48,* 84–92. (p. 497)

Schuman, H., & Scott, J. (1989). Generations and collective memories. *American Sociological Review, 54,* 359–381. (p. 160)

Schumann, K., & Ross, M. (2010). Why women apologize more than men: Gender differences in thresholds for perceiving offensive behavior. *Psychological Science, 21,* 1649–1655. (p. 173)

Schurger, A., Pereira, F., Treisman, A., & Cohen, J. D. (2010). Reproducibility distinguishes conscious from nonconscious neural representations. *Science, 327,* 97–99. (p. 81)

Schwartz, B. (1984). *Psychology of learning and behavior* (2nd ed.). New York: Norton. (pp. 253, 541)

Schwartz, H. A., Eichstaedt, J. C., Kern, M. L., Dziurzynski, L., Ramones, S. M., Agrawal, M., . . . Ungar, L. H. (2013). Personality, gender, and age in the language of social media: The open-vocabulary approach. *PLOS ONE, 8*(9), e73791. doi:10.1371/journal.pone.0073791 (pp. 172, 174)

Schwartz, J. M., Stoessel, P. W., Baxter, L. R., Jr., Martin, K. M., & Phelps, M. E. (1996). Systematic changes in cerebral glucose metabolic rate after successful behavior modification treatment of obsessive-compulsive disorder. *Archives of General Psychiatry, 53,* 109–113. (pp. 581, 600)

Schwartz, P. J. (2011). Season of birth in schizophrenia: A maternal–fetal chronobiological hypothesis. *Medical Hypotheses, 76,* 785–793. (p. 559)

Schwartz, S. (2012). Dreams, emotions and brain plasticity. In *Aquém e além do cérebro* [Behind and beyond the brain]. Bial: Fundação Bial Institution of Public Utility. (p. 101)

Schwartz, S. H., & Rubel-Lifschitz, T. (2009). Cross-national variation in the size of sex differences in values: Effects of gender equality. *Journal of Personality and Social Psychology, 97,* 171–185. (p. 173)

Schwartz, S. J., Unger, J. B., Zamboanga, B. L., & Szapocznik, J. (2010). Rethinking the concept of acculturation: Implications for theory and research. *American Psychologist, 65,* 237–251. (p. 534)

Schwartzman-Morris, J., & Putterman, C. (2012). Gender differences in the pathogenesis and outcome of lupus and of lupus nephritis. *Clinical and Developmental Immunology, 2012,* Article 604892. doi:10.1155/2012/604892 (p. 411)

Schwarz, A., & Cohen, S. (2013, March 31). A.D.H.D. seen in 11% of U.S. children as diagnoses rise. *The New York Times.* Retrieved from http://www.nytimes.com/2013/04/01/health/more-diagnoses-of-hyperactivity-causing-concern.html?_r=0 (p. 532)

Schwarz, N., Strack, F., Kommer, D., & Wagner, D. (1987). Soccer, rooms, and the quality of your life: Mood effects on judgments of satisfaction with life in general and with specific domains. *European Journal of Social Psychology, 17,* 69–79. (p. 298)

Sclafani, A. (1995). How food preferences are learned: Laboratory animal models. *Proceedings of the Nutrition Society, 54,* 419–427. (p. 381)

Scott, D. J., Stohler, C. S., Egnatuk, C. M., Wang, H., Koeppe, R. A., & Zubieta, J.-K. (2007). Individual differences in reward responding explain placebo-induced expectations and effects. *Neuron, 55,* 325–336. (p. 234)

Scott, K. M., Wells, J. E., Angermeyer, M., Brugha, T. S., Bromet, E., Demyttenaere, K., . . . Kessler, R. C. (2010). Gender and the relationship between marital status and first onset of mood, anxiety and substance use disorders. *Psychological Medicine, 40,* 1495–1505. (p. 164)

Scott, W. A., Scott, R., & McCabe, M. (1991). Family relationships and children's personality: A cross-cultural, cross-source comparison. *British Journal of Social Psychology, 30,* 1–20. (p. 120)

Scott-Sheldon, L. A. J., Carey, K. B., Elliott, J. C., Garey, L., & Carey, M. P. (2014). Efficacy of alcohol interventions for first-year college students: A meta-analytic review of randomized controlled trials. *Journal of Consulting and Clinical Psychology, 82,* 177–188. (p. 107)

Scullin, M. K., & McDaniel, M. A. (2010). Remembering to execute a goal: Sleep on it! *Psychological Science, 21,* 1028–1035. (p. 305)

Sdorow, L. M. (2005). The people behind psychology: Enliven your lectures with biographical vignettes. In B. Perlman, L. McCann, & W. Buskist (Eds.), *Voices of experience: Memorable talks from the National Institute on the Teaching of Psychology* (pp. 1–16). Washington, DC: American Psychological Society. (p. 498)

Seal, K. H., Bertenthal, D., Miner, C. R., Sen, S., & Marmar, C. (2007). Bringing the war back home: Mental health disorders among 103,788 U.S. veterans returning from Iraq and Afghanistan seen at Department of Veterans Affairs facilities. *Archives of Internal Medicine, 167,* 467–482. (p. 540)

Sebat, J., Lakshmi, B., Malhotra, D., Troge, J., Lese-Martin, C., Walsh, T., . . . Wigler, M. (2007). Strong association of de novo copy number mutations with autism. *Science, 316,* 445–449. (p. 136)

Sedlmeier, P., Eberth, J., Schwarz, M., Zimmermann, D., Haarig, F., Jaeger, S., & Kunze, S. (2012). The psychological effects of meditation: A meta-analysis. *Psychological Bulletin, 138,* 1139–1171. (p. 428)

Seeman, P. (2007). Dopamine and schizophrenia. *Scholarpedia, 2*(10), 3634. Retrieved from http://www.scholarpedia.org/article/Dopamine_and_schizophrenia (p. 558)

Seeman, P., Guan, H.-C., & Van Tol, H. H. M. (1993). Dopamine D4 receptors elevated in schizophrenia. *Nature, 365,* 441–445. (p. 558)

Seery, M. D. (2011). Resilience: A silver lining to experiencing adverse life events. *Current Directions in Psychological Science, 20,* 390–394. (p. 143)

Segal, N. L. (2013). Personality similarity in unrelated look-alike pairs: Addressing a twin study challenge. *Personality and Individual Differences, 54,* 23–28. (p. 68)

Segal, N. L., McGuire, S. A., & Stohs, J. H. (2012). What virtual twins reveal about general intelligence and other behaviors. *Personality and Individual Differences, 53,* 405–410. (p. 355)

Segall, M. H., Dasen, P. R., Berry, J. W., & Poortinga, Y. H. (1990). *Human behavior in global perspective: An introduction to cross-cultural psychology.* New York: Pergamon Press. (pp. 135, 178)

Segerstrom, S. C. (2007). Stress, energy, and immunity. *Current Directions in Psychological Science, 16,* 326–330. (p. 406)

Segerstrom, S. C., Hardy, J. K., Evans, D. R., & Greenberg, R. N. (2012). Vulnerability, distress, and immune response to vaccination in older adults. *Brain, Behavior, and Immunity, 26,* 747–753. (p. 412)

Segerstrom, S. C., Taylor, S. E., Kemeny, M. E., & Fahey, J. L. (1998). Optimism is associated with mood, coping, and immune change in response to stress. *Journal of Personality and Social Psychology, 74,* 1646–1655. (p. 423)

Seibert, S. E., Wang, G., & Courtright, S. H. (2011). Antecedents and consequences of psychological and team empowerment in organizations: A meta-analytic review. *Journal of Applied Psychology, 96,* 981–1003. (p. B-13)

Seidel, A., & Prinz, J. (2013). Sound morality: Irritating and icky noises amplify judgments in divergent moral domains. *Cognition, 127,* 1–5. (p. 207)

Seidler, G. H., & Wagner, F. E. (2006). Comparing the efficacy of EMDR and trauma-focused cognitive-behavioral therapy in the treatment of PTSD: A meta-analytic study. *Psychological Medicine, 36,* 1515–1522. (p. 588)

Self, C. E. (1994). *Moral culture and victimization in residence halls.* Unpublished master's thesis, Bowling Green State University, Bowling Green, OH. (p. 116)

Seligman, M. E. P. (1975). *Helplessness: On depression, development and death.* San Francisco: Freeman. (p. 420)

Seligman, M. E. P. (1991). *Learned optimism: How to change your mind and your life.* New York: Knopf. (pp. 80, 551, 552)

Seligman, M. E. P. (1994). *What you can change and what you can't.* New York: Knopf. (pp. 426, 517)

Seligman, M. E. P. (1995). The effectiveness of psychotherapy: The *Consumer Reports* study. *American Psychologist, 50,* 965–974. (pp. 552, 584, 586)

Seligman, M. E. P. (2002). *Authentic happiness: Using the new positive psychology to realize your potential for lasting fulfillment.* New York: Free Press. (pp. 10, 432, 517)

Seligman, M. E. P. (2004). *Eudaemonia, the good life: A talk with Martin Seligman.* Retrieved from http://edge.org/3rd_culture/seligman04/seligman_index.html (p. 432)

Seligman, M. E. P. (2011). *Flourish: A visionary new understanding of happiness and well-being.* New York: Free Press. (pp. 10, 432)

Seligman, M. E. P. (2012, May 8). Quoted in A. C. Brooks, America and the value of "earned success." *The Wall Street Journal.* Retrieved from http://www.wsj.com/articles/SB10001424052702304749904577385650652966894 (p. 517)

Seligman, M. E. P., Ernst, R. M., Gillham, J., Reivich, K., & Linkins, M. (2009). Positive education: Positive psychology and classroom interventions. *Oxford Review of Education, 35,* 293–311. (p. 580)

Seligman, M. E. P., & Maier, S. F. (1967). Failure to escape traumatic shock. *Journal of Experimental Psychology, 74,* 1–9. (p. 420)

Seligman, M. E. P., Steen, T. A., Park, N., & Peterson, C. (2005). Positive psychology progress: Empirical validation of interventions. *American Psychologist, 60,* 410–421. (pp. 10, 432, 438)

Seligman, M. E. P., & Yellen, A. (1987). What is a dream? *Behavior Research and Therapy, 25,* 1–24. (p. 88)

Sellers, H. (2010). *You don't look like anyone I know.* New York: Riverhead Books. (p. 199)

Selye, H. (1936). A syndrome produced by diverse nocuous agents. *Nature, 138,* 32. (p. 409)

Selye, H. (1976). *The stress of life.* New York: McGraw-Hill. (p. 409)

Senghas, A., & Coppola, M. (2001). Children creating language: How Nicaraguan Sign Language acquired a spatial grammar. *Psychological Science, 12,* 323–328. (p. 330)

Sengupta, S. (2001, October 10). Sept. 11 attack narrows the racial divide. *The New York Times.* Retrieved from http://www.nytimes.com/2001/10/10/nyregion/a-nation-challenged-relations-sept-11-attack-narrows-the-racial-divide.html?pagewanted=all (p. 487)

Senju, A., Maeda, M., Kikuchi, Y., Hasegawa, T., Tojo, Y., & Osanai, H. (2007). Absence of contagious yawning in children with autism spectrum disorder. *Biology Letters, 3,* 706–708. (p. 137)

Senju, A., Southgate, V., White, S., & Frith, U. (2009). Mindblind eyes: An absence of spontaneous theory of mind in Asperger syndrome. *Science, 325,* 883–885. (p. 136)

Sergeant, S., & Mongrain, M. (2014). An online optimism intervention reduces depression in pessimistic individuals. *Journal of Consulting and Clinical Psychology, 82,* 263–274. (p. 423)

Service, R. F. (1994). Will a new type of drug make memory-making easier? *Science, 266,* 218–219. (p. 295)

Shadish, W. R., & Baldwin, S. A. (2005). Effects of behavioral marital therapy: A meta-analysis of randomized controlled trials. *Journal of Consulting and Clinical Psychology, 73,* 6–14. (p. 586)

Shadish, W. R., Montgomery, L. M., Wilson, P., Wilson, M. R., Bright, I., & Okwumabua, T. (1993). Effects of family and marital psychotherapies: A meta-analysis. *Journal of Consulting and Clinical Psychology, 61,* 992–1002. (p. 582)

Shaffer, R. (2013, September/October). The psychic: Years later, Sylvia Browne's accuracy remains dismal. *Skeptical Inquirer,* pp. 30–35. (p. 241)

Shafir, E. (Ed.). (2013). *The behavioral foundations of public policy.* Princeton, NJ: Princeton University Press. (p. 4)

Shafir, E., & LeBoeuf, R. A. (2002). Rationality. *Annual Review of Psychology, 53,* 491–517. (p. 323)

Shakeshaft, N. G., Trzaskowski, M., McMillan, A., Rimfeld, K., Krapohl, E., Haworth, C. M. A., . . . Plomin, R. (2013). Strong genetic influence on a UK nationwide test of educational achievement at the end of compulsory education at age 16. *PLOS ONE, 8*(12), e80341. doi:10.1371/journal.pone.0080341 (p. 354)

Shaki, S. (2013). What's in a kiss? Spatial experience shapes directional bias during kissing. *Journal of Nonverbal Behavior, 37,* 43–50. (p. 9)

Shalev, I., Moffitt, T. E., Sugden, K., Williams, B., Houts, R. M., Danese, A., . . . Caspi, A. (2013). Exposure to violence during childhood is associated with telomere erosion from 5 to 10 years of age: A longitudinal study. *Molecular Psychiatry, 18,* 576–581. (p. 160)

Shallcross, A. J., Ford, B. Q., Floerke, V. A., & Mauss, I. B. (2013). Getting better with age: The relationship between age, acceptance, and negative affect. *Journal of Personality and Social Psychology, 104,* 734–749. (p. 166)

Shamir, B., House, R. J., & Arthur, M. B. (1993). The motivational effects of charismatic leadership: A self-concept based theory. *Organizational Science, 4,* 577–594. (p. B-12)

Shan, W., Shengua, J., Davis, H., Hunter, M., Peng, K., Shao, X., . . . Wang, Y. (2012). Mating strategies in Chinese culture: Female risk-avoiding vs. male risk-taking. *Evolution and Human Behavior, 33,* 182–192. (p. 193)

Shanahan, L., McHale, S. M., Osgood, D. W., & Crouter, A. C. (2007). Conflict frequency with mothers and fathers from middle childhood to late adolescence: Within- and between-families comparisons. *Developmental Psychology, 43,* 539–550. (p. 154)

Shane, S. (2015, June 24). Homegrown extremists tied to deadlier toll than jihadis in U.S. since 9/11. *The New York Times.* Retrieved from http://www.nytimes.com/2015/06/25/us/tally-of-attacks-in-us-challenges-perceptions-of-top-terror-threat.html (p. 462)

Shannon, B. J., Raichle, M. E., Snyder, A. Z., Fair, D. A., Mills, K. L., Zhanga, D., . . . Kiehl, K. A. (2011). Premotor functional connectivity predicts impulsivity in juvenile offenders. *Proceedings of the National Academy of Sciences of the United States of America, 108,* 11241–11245. (p. 149)

Shapin, S. (2013, October 15). The man who forgot everything. *The New Yorker.* Retrieved from http://www.newyorker.com/books/page-turner/the-man-who-forgot-everything (p. 302)

Shapiro, D. (1999). *Psychotherapy of neurotic character.* New York: Basic Books. (p. 572)

Shapiro, F. (1989). Efficacy of the eye movement desensitization procedure in the treatment of traumatic memories. *Journal of Traumatic Stress, 2,* 199–223. (p. 587)

Shapiro, F. (1999). Eye movement desensitization and reprocessing (EMDR) and the anxiety disorders: Clinical and research implications of an integrated psychotherapy treatment. *Journal of Anxiety Disorders, 13,* 35–67. (p. 588)

Shapiro, F. (Ed.). (2002). *EMDR as an integrative psychotherapy approach: Experts of diverse orientations explore the paradigm prism.* Washington, DC: American Psychological Association. (p. 588)

Shapiro, F. (2007). EMDR and case conceptualization from an adaptive information processing perspective. In F. Shapiro, F. W. Kaslow, & L. Maxfield (Eds.), *Handbook of EMDR and family therapy processes* (pp. 3–36). Hoboken, NJ: Wiley. (p. 587)

Shapiro, F. (2012, March 2). The evidence on E.M.D.R. *The New York Times.* Retrieved from http://consults.blogs.nytimes.com/2012/03/02/the-evidence-on-e-m-d-r/?_r=00 (p. 587)

Shapiro, K. A., Moo, L. R., & Caramazza, A. (2006). Cortical signatures of noun and verb production. *Proceedings of the National Academy of Sciences of the United States of America, 103,* 1644–1649. (p. 334)

Shargorodsky, J., Curhan, S. G., Curhan, G. C., & Eavey, R. (2010). Changes of prevalence of hearing loss in US adolescents. *Journal of the American Medical Association, 304,* 772–778. (p. 228)

Shariff, A. F., Greene, J. D., Karremans, J. C., Luguri, J. B., Clark, C. J., Schooler, J. W., . . . Vohs, K. D. (2014). Free will and punishment: A mechanistic view of human nature reduces retribution. *Psychological Science, 25,* 1563–1570. (p. 26)

Sharma, A. R., McGue, M. K., & Benson, P. L. (1998). The psychological adjustment of United States adopted adolescents and their nonadopted siblings. *Child Development, 69,* 791–802. (p. 70)

Shattuck, P. T. (2006). The contribution of diagnostic substitution to the growing administrative prevalence of autism in US special education. *Pediatrics, 117,* 1028–1037. (p. 136)

Shaver, P. R., Morgan, H. J., & Wu, S. (1996). Is love a basic emotion? *Personal Relationships, 3,* 81–96. (p. 391)

Shaw, B. A., Liang, J., & Krause, N. (2010). Age and race differences in the trajectories of self-esteem. *Psychology and Aging, 25,* 84–94. (p. 122)

Shaw, J., & Porter, S. (2015). Constructing rich false memories of committing crime. *Psychological Science, 26,* 291–301. (p. 307)

Shedler, J. (2009, March 23). *That was then, this is now: Psychoanalytic psychotherapy for the rest of us.* Unpublished manuscript, Department of Psychiatry, University of Colorado Health Sciences Center, Aurora, CO. (p. 572)

Shedler, J. (2010). The efficacy of psychodynamic psychotherapy. *American Psychologist, 65,* 98–109. (pp. 495, 586)

Shedler, J. (2010, November/December). Getting to know me. *Scientific American Mind,* pp. 53–57. (p. 572)

Sheehan, S. (1982). *Is there no place on earth for me?* Boston: Houghton Mifflin. (p. 556)

Sheikh, S., & Janoff-Bulman, R. (2013). Paradoxical consequences of prohibitions. *Journal of Personality and Social Psychology, 105,* 301–315. (p. 262)

Sheldon, K. M. (2011). Integrating behavioral-motive and experiential-requirement perspectives on psychological needs: A two process model. *Psychological Review, 118,* 552–569. (p. 369)

Sheldon, K. M., Elliot, A. J., Kim, Y., & Kasser, T. (2001). What is satisfying about satisfying events? Testing 10 candidate psychological needs. *Journal of Personality and Social Psychology, 80,* 325–339. (p. 370)

Sheldon, K. M., & Lyubomirsky, S. (2012). The challenge of staying happier: Testing the hedonic adaptation prevention model. *Personality and Social Psychology Bulletin, 38,* 670–680. (p. 438)

Sheltzer, J. M., & Smith, J. C. (2014). Elite male faculty in the life sciences employ fewer females. *Proceedings of the National Academy of Sciences of the United States of America, 111,* 10107–10112. (p. 178)

Shen, L., Fishbach, A., & Hsee, C. K. (2015). The motivating-uncertainty effect: Uncertainty increases resource investment in the process of reward pursuit. *Journal of Consumer Research.* Advance online publication. http://dx.doi.org/10.1086/679418 (p. 367)

Shenton, M. E. (1992). Abnormalities of the left temporal lobe and thought disorder in schizophrenia: A quantitative magnetic resonance imaging study. *New England Journal of Medicine, 327,* 604–612. (p. 558)

Shepard, R. N. (1990). *Mind sights: Original visual illusions, ambiguities, and other anomalies.* New York: Freeman. (p. 29)

Shepherd, C. (1997, April). News of the weird. *Funny Times,* p. 15. (p. 68)

Shepherd, C. (1999, June). News of the weird. *Funny Times,* p. 21. (p. 384)

Sher, L. (2006). Alcohol consumption and suicide. *QJM: An International Journal of Medicine, 99,* 57–61. (p. 553)

Shergill, S. S., Bays, P. M., Frith, C. D., & Wolpert, D. M. (2003). Two eyes for an eye: The neuroscience of force escalation. *Science, 301,* 187. (p. 485)

Sherif, M. (1966). *In common predicament: Social psychology of intergroup conflict and cooperation.* Boston: Houghton Mifflin. (p. 486)

Sherman, G. D., Lee, J. J., Cuddy, A. J. C., Renshon, J., Oveis, C., Gross, J. J., & Lerner, J. S. (2012). Leadership is associated with lower levels of stress. *Proceedings of the National Academy of Sciences of the United States of America, 109,* 17903–17907. (p. 421)

Sherman, P. W., & Flaxman, S. M. (2001). Protecting ourselves from food. *American Scientist, 89,* 142–151. (p. 381)

Sherry, D., & Vaccarino, A. L. (1989). Hippocampus and memory for food caches in black-capped chickadees. *Behavioral Neuroscience, 103,* 308–318. (p. 293)

Shettleworth, S. J. (1973). Food reinforcement and the organization of behavior in golden hamsters. In R. A. Hinde & J. Stevenson-Hinde (Eds.), *Constraints on learning* (pp. 243–264). London: Academic Press. (p. 269)

Shettleworth, S. J. (1993). Where is the comparison in comparative cognition? Alternative research programs. *Psychological Science, 4,* 179–184. (p. 293)

Shiell, M. M., Champoux, F., & Zatorre, R. (2014). Enhancement of visual motion detection thresholds in early deaf people. *PLOS ONE, 9*(2), e90498. doi:10.1371/journal.pone.0090498 (p. 61)

Shifren, J. L., Monz, B. U., Russo, P. A., Segreti, A., Johannes, C. B. (2008). Sexual problems and distress in United States women: Prevalence and correlates. *Obstetrics & Gynecology, 112,* 970–978. (p. 183)

Shilsky, J. D., Hartman, T. J., Kris-Etherton, P. M., Rogers, C. J., Sharkey, N. A., & Nickols-Richardson, S. M. (2012). Partial sleep deprivation and energy balance in adults: An emerging issue for consideration by dietetics practitioners. *Journal of the Academy of Nutrition and Dietetics, 112,* 1785–1797. (p. 95)

Shipstead, Z., Hicks, K. L., & Engle, R. W. (2012a). Cogmed working memory training: Does the evidence support the claims? *Journal of Applied Research in Memory and Cognition, 1,* 185–193. (p. 162)

Shipstead, Z., Redick, T. S., & Engle, R. W. (2012b). Is working memory training effective? *Psychological Bulletin, 138,* 628–654. (p. 162)

Shiromani, P. J., Horvath, T., Redline, S., & Van Cauter E. (Eds.) (2012). *Sleep loss and obesity: Intersecting epidemics.* New York: Springer Science. (p. 95)

Shockley, K. M., Ispas, D., Rossi, M. E., & Levine, E. L. (2012). A meta-analytic investigation of the relationship between state affect, discrete emotions, and job performance. *Human Performance, 25,* 377–411. (p. B-8)

Shor, E., Roelfs, D. J., & Yogev, T. (2013). The strength of family ties: A meta-analysis and meta-regression of self-reported social support and mortality. *Social Networks, 35,* 626–638. (p. 423)

Shors, T. J. (2014). The adult brain makes new neurons, and effortful learning keeps them alive. *Current Directions in Psychological Science, 23,* 311–318. (p. 36)

Short, S. J., Lubach, G. R., Karasin, A. I., Olsen, C. W., Styner, M., Knickmeyer, R. C., . . . Coe, C. L. (2010). Maternal influenza infection during pregnancy impacts postnatal brain development in the rhesus monkey. *Biological Psychiatry, 67,* 965–973. (p. 559)

Shrestha, A., Nohr, E. A., Bech, B. H., Ramlau-Hansen, C. H., & Olsen, J. (2011). Smoking and alcohol during pregnancy and age of menarche in daughters. *Human Reproduction, 26,* 259–265. (p. 176)

Shuffler, M. L., Burke, C. S., Kramer, W. S., & Salas, E. (2013). Leading teams: Past, present, and future perspectives. In M. G. Rumsey (Ed.), *The Oxford handbook of leadership* (pp. 144–166). New York: Oxford University Press. (p. B-12)

Shuffler, M. L., DiazGranados, D., & Salas, E. (2011). There's a science for that: Team development interventions in organizations. *Current Directions in Psychological Science, 20,* 365–372. (p. B-12)

Shute, N. (2010, October). Desperate for an autism cure. *Scientific American,* pp. 80–85. (p. 136)

Shuwairi, S. M., & Johnson, S. P. (2013). Oculomotor exploration of impossible figures in early infancy. *Infancy, 18,* 221–232. (p. 131)

Siahpush, M., Spittal, M., & Singh, G. K. (2008). Happiness and life satisfaction prospectively predict self-rated health, physical health and the presence of limiting long-term health conditions. *American Journal of Health Promotion, 23,* 18–26. (p. 415)

Siegel, J. M. (1982, October). Quoted in J. Hooper, Mind tripping. *Omni,* pp. 72–82, 159–160. (p. 111)

Siegel, J. M. (1990). Stressful life events and use of physician services among the elderly: The moderating role of pet ownership. *Journal of Personality and Social Psychology, 58,* 1081–1086. (p. 424)

Siegel, J. M. (2009). Sleep viewed as a state of adaptive inactivity. *Nature Reviews Neuroscience, 10,* 747–753. (p. 93)

Siegel, J. M. (2012). Suppression of sleep for mating. *Science, 337,* 1610–1611. (p. 93)

Siegel, R. K. (1977, October). Hallucinations. *Scientific American,* pp. 132–140. (p. 112)

Siegel, R. K. (1980). The psychology of life after death. *American Psychologist, 35,* 911–931. (p. 112)

Siegel, R. K. (1984, March 15). Personal communication. (p. 112)

Siegel, R. K. (1990). *Intoxication: Life in pursuit of artificial paradise.* New York: Pocket Books. (p. 112)

Siegel, S. (2005). Drug tolerance, drug addiction, and drug anticipation. *Current Directions in Psychological Science, 14,* 296–300. (p. 253)

Silber, M. H., Ancoli-Israel, S., Bonnet, M. H., Chokroverty, S., Grigg-Damberger, M. M., Hirshkowitz, M., . . . Iber, C. (2008). The visual scoring of sleep in adults. *Journal of Clinical Sleep Medicine, 3,* 121–131. (p. 89)

Silbersweig, D. A., Stern, E., Frith, C., Cahill, C., Holmes, A., Grootoonk, S., Seaward, J., . . . Frackowiak, R. S. J. (1995). A functional neuroanatomy of hallucinations in schizophrenia. *Nature, 378,* 176–179. (p. 558)

Silva, A. J., Stevens, C. F., Tonegawa, S., & Wang, Y. (1992). Deficient hippocampal long-term potentiation in alpha-calcium-calmodulin kinase II mutant mice. *Science, 257,* 201–206. (p. 295)

Silva, C. E., & Kirsch, I. (1992). Interpretive sets, expectancy, fantasy proneness, and dissociation as predictors of hypnotic response. *Journal of Personality and Social Psychology, 63,* 847–856. (p. 235)

Silva, K., Bessa, J., & de Sousa, L. (2012). Auditory contagious yawning in domestic dogs (*Canis familiaris*): First evidence for social modulation. *Animal Cognition, 15,* 721–724. (p. 449)

Silver, M., & Geller, D. (1978). On the irrelevance of evil: The organization and individual action. *Journal of Social Issues, 34,* 125–136. (p. 455)

Silver, N. (2012). *The signal and the noise: Why so many predictions fail—but some don't.* New York: Penguin. (p. 158)

Silver, R. C., Holman, E. A., Anderson, J. P., Poulin, M., McIntosh, D. N., & Gil-Rivas, V. (2013). Mental- and physical-health effects of acute exposure to media images of the September 11, 2001 attacks and Iraq War. *Psychological Science, 24,* 1623–1634. (p. 407)

Silver, R. C., Holman, E. A., McIntosh, D. N., Poulin, M., & Gil-Rivas, V. (2002). Nationwide longitudinal study of psychological responses to September 11. *Journal of the American Medical Association, 288,* 1235–1244. (p. 407)

Silveri, M. M., Rohan, M. L., Pimental, P. J., Gruber, S. A., Rosso, I. M., & Yurgelun-Todd, D. A. (2006). Sex differences in the relationship between white matter microstructure and impulsivity in adolescents. *Magnetic Resonance Imaging, 24,* 833–841. (p. 148)

Silverman, K., Evans, S. M., Strain, E. C., & Griffiths, R. R. (1992). Withdrawal syndrome after the double-blind cessation of caffeine consumption. *New England Journal of Medicine, 327,* 1109–1114. (p. 108)

Silverman, L. (2015, April 12). Ranulph Fiennes: Marathon des Sables was hell on Earth. *The Telegraph.* Retrieved from http://www.telegraph.co.uk/good-life/11529641/Ranulph-Fiennes-Marathon-des-Sables-was-hell-on-Earth.html (p. 405)

Simek, T. C., & O'Brien, R. M. (1981). *Total golf: A behavioral approach to lowering your score and getting more out of your game.* Huntington, NY: B-MOD Associates. (p. 264)

Simek, T. C., & O'Brien, R. M. (1988). A chaining-mastery, discrimination training program to teach Little Leaguers to hit a baseball. *Human Performance, 1,* 73–84. (p. 264)

Simon, H. (2001, February). Quoted in A. M. Hayashi, When to trust your gut. *Harvard Business Review,* pp. 59–65. (p. 323)

Simon, H. A., & Chase, W. G. (1973). Skill in chess. *American Scientist, 61,* 394–403. (p. 344)

Simon, V., Czobor, P., Bálint, S., Mésáros, A., & Bitter, I. (2009). Prevalence and correlates of adult attention-deficit hyperactivity disorder: Meta-analysis. *British Journal of Psychiatry, 194,* 204–211. (p. 532)

Simons, D. J., & Chabris, C. F. (1999). Gorillas in our midst: Sustained inattentional blindness for dynamic events. *Perception, 28,* 1059–1074. (p. 83)

Simons, D. J., & Levin, D. T. (1998). Failure to detect changes to people during a real-world interaction. *Psychonomic Bulletin & Review, 5,* 644–649. (p. 84)

Simonsohn, U., & Gino, F. (2013). Daily horizons: Evidence of narrow bracketing in judgment from 10 years of M.B.A. admissions interviews. *Psychological Science, 24,* 219–224. (p. B-6)

Simonton, D. K. (1988). Age and outstanding achievement: What do we know after a century of research? *Psychological Bulletin, 104,* 251–267. (p. 349)

Simonton, D. K. (1990). Creativity in the later years: Optimistic prospects for achievement. *The Gerontologist, 30,* 626–631. (p. 349)

Simonton, D. K. (1992). The social context of career success and course for 2,026 scientists and inventors. *Personality and Social Psychology Bulletin, 18,* 452–463. (p. 325)

Simonton, D. K. (2000). Methodological and theoretical orientation and the long-term disciplinary impact of 54 eminent psychologists. *Review of General Psychology, 4,* 13–24. (p. 278)

Simonton, D. K. (2012a, November/December). The science of genius. *Scientific American Mind,* pp. 35–41. (p. 325)

Simonton, D. K. (2012b). Teaching creativity: Current findings, trends, and controversies in the psychology of creativity. *Teaching of Psychology, 39,* 217–222. (p. 325)

Sin, N. L., Graham-Engeland, J. E., Ong, A. D., & Almeida, D. M. (2015). Affective reactivity to daily stressors is associated with elevated inflammation. *Health Psychology.* Advance online publication. http://dx.doi.org/10.1037/hea0000240 (p. 409)

Sinclair, R. C., Hoffman, C., Mark, M. M., Martin, L. L., & Pickering, T. L. (1994). Construct accessibility and the misattribution of arousal: Schachter and Singer revisited. *Psychological Science, 5,* 15–18. (p. 389)

Singer, J. L. (1981). Clinical intervention: New developments in methods and evaluation. In L. T. Benjamin, Jr. (Ed.), *The G. Stanley Hall Lecture Series* (Vol. 1, pp. 105–128). Washington, DC: American Psychological Association. (p. 586)

Singer, T., Seymour, B., O'Doherty, J., Kaube, H., Dolan, R. J., & Frith, C. (2004). Empathy for pain involves the affective but not sensory components of pain. *Science, 303,* 1157–1162. (pp. 233, 274)

Singh, D. (1993). Adaptive significance of female physical attractiveness: Role of waist-to-hip ratio. *Journal of Personality and Social Psychology, 65,* 293–307. (p. 194)

Singh, D. (1995). Female health, attractiveness, and desirability for relationships: Role of breast asymmetry and waist-to-hip ratio. *Ethology and Sociobiology, 16,* 465–481. (p. 193)

Singh, D., & Randall, P. K. (2007). Beauty is in the eye of the plastic surgeon: Waist-hip ration (WHR) and women's attractiveness. *Personality and Individual Differences, 43,* 329–340. (p. 194)

Singh, S. (1997). *Fermat's enigma: The epic quest to solve the world's greatest mathematical problem.* New York: Bantam Books. (p. 324)

Singh, S., & Riber, K. A. (1997, November). Fermat's last stand. *Scientific American,* pp. 68–73. (p. 325)

Sio, U. N., Monahan, P., & Ormerod, T. (2013). Sleep on it, but only if it is difficult: Effects of sleep on problem solving. *Memory and Cognition, 41,* 159–166. (p. 93)

Sio, U. N., & Ormerod, T. C. (2009). Does incubation enhance problem solving? A meta-analtic review. *Psychological Bulletin, 135,* 94–120. (p. 324)

Sipski, M. L., & Alexander, C. J. (1999). Sexual response in women with spinal cord injuries: Implications for our understanding of the able bodied. *Journal of Sex and Marital Therapy, 25,* 11–22. (p. 45)

Sireteanu, R. (1999). Switching on the infant brain. *Science, 286,* 59–61. (p. 229)

Skeem, J. L., & Cooke, D. J. (2010). Is criminal behavior a central component of psychopathy? Conceptual directions for resolving the debate. *Psychological Assessment, 22,* 433–445. (p. 563)

Skeem, J., Kennealy, P., Monahan, J., Peterson, J., & Appelbaum, P. (2015). Psychosis uncommonly and inconsistently precedes violence among high-risk individuals. *Clinical Psychological Science.* Advance online publication. doi:10.1177/2167702615575879 (p. 533)

Skinner, B. F. (1953). *Science and human behavior.* New York: Macmillan. (p. 259)

Skinner, B. F. (1956). A case history in scientific method. *American Psychologist, 11,* 221–233. (p. 260)

Skinner, B. F. (1957). *Verbal behavior.* Englewood Cliffs, NJ: Prentice-Hall. (p. 330)

Skinner, B. F. (1961, November). Teaching machines. *Scientific American,* pp. 91–102. (p. 260)

Skinner, B. F. (1983, September). Origins of a behaviorist. *Psychology Today,* pp. 22–33. (p. 263)

Skinner, B. F. (1989). Teaching machines. *Science, 243,* 1535. (p. 263)

Sklar, L. S., & Anisman, H. (1981). Stress and cancer. *Psychological Bulletin, 89,* 369–406. (p. 413)

Skoog, G., & Skoog, I. (1999). A 40-year follow-up of patients with obsessive-compulsive disorder. *Archives of General Psychiatry, 56,* 121–127. (p. 540)

Skov, R. B., & Sherman, S. J. (1986). Information-gathering processes: Diagnosticity, hypothesis-confirmatory strategies, and perceived hypothesis confirmation. *Journal of Experimental Social Psychology, 22,* 93–121. (p. 317)

Slatcher, R. B., Selcuk, E., & Ong, A. (2015). Perceived partner responsiveness predicts diurnal cortisol profiles 10 years later. *Psychological Science, 26,* 972–982. (p. 424)

Slaughter, V., Imuta, K., Peterson, C. C., & Henry, J. D. (2015). Meta-analysis of theory of mind and peer popularity in the preschool and early school years. *Child Development, 86,* 1159–1174. (p. 133)

Slepian, M. L., Rule, N. O., & Ambady, N. (2012). Proprioception and person perception: Politicians and professors. *Personality and Social Psychology Bulletin, 38,* 1621–1628. (p. 240)

Sloan, R. P. (2005). *Field analysis of the literature on religion, spirituality, and health.* Retrieved from http://metanexus.net/archive/templetonadvanced researchprogram/pdf/TARP-Sloan.pdf (p. 429)

Sloan, R. P., & Bagiella, E. (2002). Claims about religious involvement and health outcomes. *Annals of Behavioral Medicine, 24,* 14–21. (p. 429)

Sloan, R. P., Bagiella, E., & Powell, T. (1999). Religion, spirituality, and medicine. *The Lancet, 353,* 664–667. (p. 429)

Sloan, R. P., Bagiella, E., VandeCreek, L., & Poulos, P. (2000). Should physicians prescribe religious activities? *New England Journal of Medicine, 342,* 1913–1917. (p. 429)

Slopen, N., Glynn, R. J., Buring, J., & Albert, M. A. (2010, November 23). Job strain, job insecurity, and incident cardiovascular disease in the Women's Health Study. *Circulation, 122*(21, Suppl.), Abstract A18520. (p. 416)

Slovic, P. (2007). "If I look at the mass I will never act": Psychic numbing and genocide. *Judgment and Decision Making, 2,* 79–95. (p. 321)

Slovic, P. (2010, Winter). The more who die, the less we care: Confronting psychic numbing. *Trauma Psychology*, pp. 4–8. (p. 321)

Slovic, P., Finucane, M., Peters, E., & MacGregor, D. G. (2002). The affect heuristic. In T. Gilovich, D. Griffin, & D. Kahneman (Eds.), *Intuitive judgment: Heuristics and biases* (pp. 397–420). New York: Cambridge University Press. (p. 109)

Slutske, W. S., Moffitt, T. E., Poulton, R., & Caspi A. (2012). Undercontrolled temperament at age 3 predicts disordered gambling at age 32: A longitudinal study of a complete birth cohort. *Psychological Science, 23,* 510–516. (p. 121)

Small, D. A., Loewenstein, G., & Slovic, P. (2007). Sympathy and callousness: The impact of deliberative thought on donations to identifiable and statistical victims. *Organizational Behavior and Human Decision Processes, 102,* 143–153. (p. 321)

Small, M. F. (1997). Making connections. *American Scientist, 85,* 502–504. (p. 145)

Smart Richman, L., & Leary, M. (2009). Reactions to discrimination, stigmatization, ostracism, and other forms of interpersonal rejection: A multimotive model. *Psychological Review, 116,* 365–383. (p. 371)

Smedley, A., & Smedley, B. D. (2005). Race as biology is fiction, racism as a social problem is real: Anthropological and historical perspectives on the social construction of race. *American Psychologist, 60,* 16–26. (p. 358)

Smelser, N. J., & Mitchell, F. (Eds.). (2002). *Terrorism: Perspectives from the behavioral and social sciences.* Washington, DC: National Academies Press. (p. 468)

Smith, A. (1983). Personal communication. (p. 557)

Smith, B. C. (2011, January 16). *The senses and the multi-sensory.* Retrieved from https://edge.org/response-detail/11677 (p. 239)

Smith, C. (2006, January 7). Nearly 100, LSD's father ponders his "problem child." *The New York Times.* Retrieved from http://www.nytimes.com/2006/01/07/international/europe/07hoffman.html?pagewanted=all&_r=0 (p. 112)

Smith, D. M., Loewenstein, G., Jankovic, A., & Ubel, P. A. (2009). Happily hopeless: Adaptation to a permanent, but not to a temporary, disability. *Health Psychology, 28,* 787–791. (p. 433)

Smith, E., & Delargy, M. (2005). Locked-in syndrome. *British Medical Journal, 330,* 406–409. (p. 433)

Smith, M. B. (1978). Psychology and values. *Journal of Social Issues, 34,* 181–199. (p. 503)

Smith, M. L., & Glass, G. V. (1977). Meta-analysis of psychotherapy outcome studies. *American Psychologist, 32,* 752–760. (p. 586)

Smith, M. L., Glass, G. V., & Miller, R. L. (1980). *The benefits of psychotherapy.* Baltimore: Johns Hopkins University Press. (pp. 585, 586)

Smith, P. B., & Tayeb, M. (1989). Organizational structure and processes. In M. Bond (Ed.), *The cross-cultural challenge to social psychology* (pp. 116–127). Newbury Park, CA: Sage. (p. B-12)

Smith, S. J., Axelton, A. M., & Saucier, D. A. (2009). The effects of contact on sexual prejudice: A meta-analysis. *Sex Roles, 61,* 178–191. (p. 486)

Smith, T. B., Bartz, J., & Richards, P. S. (2007). Outcomes of religious and spiritual adaptations to psychotherapy: A meta-analytic review. *Psychotherapy Research, 17,* 643–655. (p. 591)

Smith, J. A., & Rhodes, J. E. (2014). Being depleted and being shaken: An interpretative phenomenological analysis of the experiential features of a first episode of depression. *Psychology and Psychotherapy: Theory, Research and Practice, 88,* 197–209. (p. 547)

Smith, S. F., Lilienfeld, S. O., Coffey, K., & Dabbs, J. M. (2013). Are psychopaths and heroes twigs off the same branch? Evidence from college, community, and presidential samples. *Journal of Research in Personality, 47,* 634–646. (p. 564)

Smits, I.A.M., Dolan, C. V., Vorst, H.C.M., Wicherts, J. M., & Timmerman, M. E. (2011). Cohort differences in Big Five personality traits over a period of 25 years. *Journal of Personality and Social Psychology, 100,* 1124–1138. (pp. 426, 510)

Smolak, L., & Murnen, S. K. (2002). A meta-analytic examination of the relationship between child sexual abuse and eating disorders. *International Journal of Eating Disorders, 31,* 136–150. (p. 565)

Smoreda, Z., & Licoppe, C. (2000). Gender-specific use of the domestic telephone. *Social Psychology Quarterly, 63,* 238–252. (p. 174)

Snedeker, J., Geren, J., & Shafto, C. L. (2007). Starting over: International adoption as a natural experiment in language development. *Psychological Science, 18,* 79–86. (p. 332)

Snodgrass, S. E., Higgins, J. G., & Todisco, L. (1986, August). *The effects of walking behavior on mood.* Paper presented at the 94th Annual Convention of the American Psychological Association, Washington, DC. (pp. 402, 416)

Snowden, R. J., & Gray, N. S. (2013). Implicit sexual associations in heterosexual and homosexual women and men. *Archives of Sexual Behavior, 42,* 475–485. (p. 189)

Snyder, F., & Scott, J. (1972). The psychophysiology of sleep. In N. S. Greenfield & R. A. Sterbach (Eds.), *Handbook of psychophysiology* (pp. 645–708). New York: Holt, Rinehart & Winston. (p. 101)

Snyder, S. H. (1984). Neurosciences: An integrative discipline. *Science, 225,* 1255–1257. (pp. 39, 531)

Snyder, S. H. (1986). *Drugs and the brain.* New York: Scientific American Library. (p. 596)

Solomon, D. A., Keitner, G. I., Miller, I. W., Shea, M. T., & Keller, M. B. (1995). Course of illness and maintenance treatments for patients with bipolar disorder. *Journal of Clinical Psychiatry, 56,* 5–13. (p. 596)

Solomon, J. (1996, May 20). Breaking the silence. *Newsweek,* pp. 20–22. (p. 534)

Solomon, M. (1987, December). Standard issue. *Psychology Today,* pp. 30–31. (p. 477)

Somerville, L. H., Jones, R. M., Ruberry, E. J., Dyke, J. P., Glover, G., & Casey, B. J. (2013). The medial prefrontal cortex and the emergence of self-conscious emotion in adolescence. *Psychological Science, 24,* 1554–1562. (p. 148)

Song, S. (2006, March 27). Mind over medicine. *Time,* p. 47. (p. 235)

Sontag, S. (1978). *Illness as metaphor.* New York: Farrar, Straus and Giroux. (p. 413)

Sood, A. K., Armaiz-Pena, G. N., Halder, J., Nick, A. M., Stone, R. L., Hu, W., . . . Lutgendorf, S. K. (2010). Adrenergic modulation of focal adhesion kinase protects human ovarian cancer cells from anoikis. *Journal of Clinical Investigation, 120,* 1515–1523. (p. 413)

Sorkhabi, N. (2005). Applicability of Baumrind's parent typology to collective cultures: Analysis of cultural explanations of parent socialization effects. *International Journal of Behavioral Development, 29,* 552–563. (p. 145)

Soussignan, R. (2001). Duchenne smile, emotional experience, and autonomic reactivity: A test of the facial feedback hypothesis. *Emotion, 2,* 52–74. (p. 401)

Sowell, T. (1991, May/June). Cultural diversity: A world view. *The American Enterprise,* pp. 44–55. (p. 488)

Sowislo, J. F., & Orth, U. (2012). Does low self-esteem predict depression and anxiety? A meta-analysis of longitudinal studies. *Psychological Bulletin, 139,* 213–240. (pp. 545, 550)

Spanos, N. P. (1986). Hypnosis, nonvolitional responding, and multiple personality: A social psychological perspective. *Progress in Experimental Personality Research, 14,* 1–62. (p. 562)

Spanos, N. P. (1994). Multiple identity enactments and multiple personality disorder: A sociocognitive perspective. *Psychological Bulletin, 116,* 143–165. (p. 562)

Spanos, N. P. (1996). *Multiple identities and false memories: A sociocognitive perspective.* Washington, DC: American Psychological Association. (p. 562)

Spanos, N. P., & Coe, W. C. (1992). A social-psychological approach to hypnosis. In E. Fromm & M. R. Nash (Eds.), *Contemporary hypnosis research* (pp. 102–130). New York: Guilford Press. (p. 235)

Sparrow, B., Liu, J., & Wegner, D. M. (2011). Google effects on memory: Cognitive consequences of having in-formation at our fingertips. *Science, 333,* 776–778. (p. 285)

Spaulding, S. (2013). Mirror neurons and social cognition. *Mind and Language, 28,* 233–257. (p. 274)

Specht, J., Egloff, B., & Schmukle, S. C. (2011). Stability and change of personality across the life course: The impact of age and major life events on mean-level and rank-order stability of the Big Five. *Journal of Personality and Social Psychology, 101,* 862–882. (p. 122)

Spector, T. (2012). *Identically different: Why you can change your genes.* London: Weidenfeld & Nicolson. (p. 72)

Speer, N. K., Reynolds, J. R., Swallow, K. M., & Zacks, J. M. (2009). Reading stories activates neural representations of visual and motor experiences. *Psychological Science, 20,* 989–999. (pp. 274, 334)

Spelke, E. S., Bernier, E. P., & Skerry, A. E. (2013). Core social cognition. In M. R. Banaji & S. A. Gelman (Eds.), *Navigating the social world: What infants, children, and other species can teach us* (pp. 11–16). New York: Oxford University Press. (p. 131)

Spencer, K. M., Nestor, P. G., Perlmutter, R., Niznikiewicz, M. A., Klump, M. C., Frumin, M., . . . McCarley, R. W. (2004). Neural synchrony indexes disordered perception and cognition in schizophrenia. *Proceedings of the National Academy of Sciences of the United States of America, 101,* 17288–17293. (p. 558)

Spencer, S. J., Steele, C. M., & Quinn, D. M. (1997). *Stereotype threat and women's math performance.* Unpublished manuscript, Hope College, Holland, MI. (p. 361)

Sperling, G. (1960). The information available in brief visual presentations. *Psychological Monographs, 74*(Whole No. 498). (p. 286)

Sperry, R. W. (1964). *Problems outstanding in the evolution of brain function.* The James Arthur Lecture, delivered at the American Museum of Natural History, New York, NY. Cited in R. Ornstein (1977), *The psychology of consciousness* (2nd ed.). New York: Harcourt Brace Jovanovich. (p. 63)

Sperry, R. W. (1985). Changed concepts of brain and consciousness: Some value implications. *Zygon, 20,* 41–57. (p. 216)

Spiegel, D. (2007). The mind prepared: Hypnosis in surgery. *Journal of the National Cancer Institute, 99,* 1280–1281. (p. 235)

Spiegel, D. (2008, January 31). *Coming apart: Trauma and the fragmentation of the self.* Retrieved from http://www.dana.org/Cerebrum/2008/Coming_Apart__Trauma_and_the_Fragmentation_of_the_Self/ (p. 562)

Spiegel, K., Leproult, R., L'Hermite-Balériaux, M., Copinschi, G., Penev, P. D., & Van Cauter, E. (2004). Leptin levels are dependent on sleep duration: Relationships with sympathovagal balance, carbohydrate regulation, cortisol, and thyrotropin. *Journal of Clinical Endocrinology and Metabolism, 89,* 5762–5771. (p. 95)

Spielberger, C., & London, P. (1982). Rage boomerangs. *American Health, 1,* 52–56. (p. 415)

Sprecher, S., Treger, S., & Sakaluk, J. K. (2013). Premarital sexual standards and sociosexuality: Gender, ethnicity, and cohort differences. *Archives of Sexual Behavior, 42,* 1395–1405. (p. 193)

Spring, B., Pingitore, R., Bourgeois, M., Kessler, K. H., & Bruckner, E. (1992, August). *The effects and non-effects of skipping breakfast: Results of three studies.* Paper presented at the 100th Annual Convention of the American Psychological Association, Washington, DC. (p. 385)

Sproesser, G., Schupp, H. T., & Renner, B. (2014). The bright side of stress-induced eating: Eating more when stressed but less when pleased. *Psychological Science, 25,* 58–65. (pp. 372, 381)

Squire, L. R., & Wixted, J. T. (2011). The cognitive neuroscience of human memory since H.M. *Annual Review of Neuroscience, 34,* 259–288. (p. 293)

Squire, L. R., & Zola-Morgan, S. (1991). The medial temporal lobe memory system. *Science, 253,* 1380–1386. (p. 293)

Srivastava, S., McGonigal, K. M., Richards, J. M., Butler, E. A., & Gross, J. J. (2006). Optimism in close relationships: How seeing things in a positive light makes them so. *Journal of Personality and Social Psychology, 91,* 143–153. (p. 423)

Stacey, D., Bilbao, A., Maroteaux, M., Jia, T., Easton, A. E., Longueville, S., . . . the IMAGEN Consortium. (2012). *RASGRF2* regulates alcohol-induced reinforcement by influencing mesolimbic dopamine neuron activity and dopamine release. *Proceedings of the National Academy of Sciences of the United States of America, 109,* 21128–21133. (p. 114)

Stack, S. (1992). Marriage, family, religion, and suicide. In R. Maris, A. Berman, J. Maltsberger, & R. Yufit (Eds.), *Assessment and prediction of suicide* (pp. 540–552). New York: Guilford Press. (p. 553)

Stafford, T., & Dewar, M. (2014). Tracing the trajectory of skill learning with a very large sample of online game players. *Psychological Science, 25,* 511–518. (p. 289)

Stager, C. L., & Werker, J. F. (1997). Infants listen for more phonetic detail in speech perception than in word-learning tasks. *Nature, 388,* 381–382. (p. 331)

Stahl, A. E., & Feigenson, L. (2015). Observing the unexpected enhances infants' learning and exploration. *Science, 348,* 91–94. (p. 131)

Stanford University Center for Narcolepsy. (2002). *Narcolepsy is a serious medical disorder and a key to understanding other sleep disorders.* Retrieved from http://www.med.stanford.edu/school/Psychiatry/narcolepsy (p. 97)

Stanley, S. M., Rhoades, G. K., Amato, P. R., Markman, H. J., & Johnson, C. A. (2010). The timing of cohabitation and engagement: Impact on first and second marriages. *Journal of Marriage and Family, 72,* 906–918. (p. 164)

Stanovich, K. E. (1996). *How to think straight about psychology.* New York: HarperCollins. (p. 492)

Stanovich, K. E., & West, R. F. (2014). What intelligence tests miss. *The Psychologist, 27,* 80–83. (p. 362)

Stanovich, K. E., West, R. F., & Toplak, M. E. (2013). My side bias, rational thinking, and intelligence. *Current Directions in Psychological Science, 22,* 259–264. (pp. 323, 362)

Stark, R. (2003a, October/November). False conflict: Christianity is not only compatible with science—it created it. *The American Enterprise, 27–33.* (p. 3)

Stark, R. (2003b). *For the glory of God: How monotheism led to reformations, science, witch-hunts, and the end of slavery.* Princeton, NJ: Princeton University Press. (p. 3)

State, M. W., & Šestan, N. (2012). The emerging biology of autism spectrum disorders. *Science, 337,* 1301–1304. (p. 136)

Statistics Canada. (1999, September). *Statistical report on the health of Canadians.* Prepared by the Federal, Provincial and Territorial Advisory Committee on Population Health for the Meeting of Ministers of Health, Charlottetown, P.E.I. (p. 407)

Statistics Canada. (2013). *Table A.5.1: Second language immersion program enrolments in public elementary and secondary schools, Canada, provinces and territories, 2005/2006 to 2009/2010.* Retrieved from http://www.statcan.gc.ca/pub/81-595-m/2011095/tbl/tbla.5.1-eng.htm (p. 338)

Staub, E. (1989). *The roots of evil: The psychological and cultural sources of genocide.* New York: Cambridge University Press. (p. 446)

St. Clair, D., Xu, M., Wang, P., Yu, Y., Fang, Y., Zhang, F., . . . & He, L. (2005). Rates of adult schizophrenia following prenatal exposure to the Chinese famine of 1959–1961. *Journal of the American Medical Association, 294,* 557–562. (p. 558)

Steel, P., Schmidt, J., & Schultz, J. (2008). Refining the relationship between personality and subject well-being. *Psychological Bulletin, 134,* 138–161. (p. 436)

Steele, C. M. (1990, May). A conversation with Claude Steele. *APS Observer,* pp. 11–17. (p. 358)

Steele, C. M. (1995, August 31). Black students live down to expectations. *The New York Times.* (p. 361)

Steele, C. M. (2010). *Whistling Vivaldi: And other clues to how stereotypes affect us.* New York: Norton. (p. 361)

Steele, C. M., & Josephs, R. A. (1990). Alcohol myopia: Its prized and dangerous effects. *American Psychologist, 45,* 921–933. (p. 107)

Steele, C. M., Spencer, S. J., & Aronson, J. (2002). Contending with group image: The psychology of stereotype and social identity threat. *Advances in Experimental Social Psychology, 34,* 379–440. (p. 361)

Steger, M. F., Hicks, B. M., Krueger, R. F., & Bouchard, T. J. (2011). Genetic and environmental influences and covariance among meaning in life, religiousness, and spirituality. *Journal of Positive Psychology, 6,* 181–191. (p. 70)

Steiger, A. E., Allemand, M., Robins, R. W., & Fend, H. A. (2014). Low and decreasing self-esteem during adolescence predict adult depression two decades later. *Journal of Personality and Social Psychology, 106,* 325–338. (p. 545)

Steinberg, L. (1987, September). Bound to bicker. *Psychology Today,* pp. 36–39. (p. 154)

Steinberg, L. (2007). Risk taking in adolescence: New perspectives from brain and behavioral science. *Current Directions in Psychological Science, 16,* 55–59. (p. 148)

Steinberg, L. (2010, March). Analyzing adolescence [Interview by Sara Martin]. *Monitor on Psychology,* pp. 26–29. (p. 148)

Steinberg, L. (2012, Spring). Should the science of adolescent brain development inform public policy? *Issues in Science and Technology,* pp. 67–78. (p. 148)

Steinberg, L. (2013). The influence of neuroscience on U.S. Supreme Court decisions involving adolescents' criminal culpability. *Nature Reviews Neuroscience, 14,* 513–518. (pp. 148, 149)

Steinberg, L., Cauffman, E., Woolard, J., Graham, S., & Banich, M. (2009). Are adolescents less mature than adults? Minors' access to abortion, the juvenile death penalty, and the alleged APA "flip-flop." *American Psychologist, 64,* 583–594. (p. 149)

Steinberg, L., & Morris, A. S. (2001). Adolescent development. *Annual Review of Psychology, 52,* 83–110. (pp. 145, 154, 156)

Steinberg, L., & Scott, E. S. (2003). Less guilty by reason of adolescence: Developmental immaturity, diminished responsibility, and the juvenile death penalty. *American Psychologist, 58,* 1009–1018. (p. 149)

Steinberg, N. (1993, February). Astonishing love stories [From an earlier United Press International report]. *Games,* p. 47. (p. 475)

Steiner, J. L., Murphy, E. A., McClellan, J. L., Carmichael, M. D., & Davis, J. M. (2011). Exercise training increases mitochondrial biogenesis in the brain. *Journal of Applied Physiology, 111,* 1066–1071. (p. 160)

Stellar, J. E., John-Henderson, N., Anderson, C. L., Gordon, A. M., McNeil, G. D., & Keltner, D. (2015). Positive affect and markers of inflammation: Discrete positive emotions predict lower levels of inflammatory cytokines. *Emotion, 15,* 129–133. (p. 431)

Stender, J., Gosseries, O., Bruno, M.-A., Charland-Vervilee, V., Vanhaudenhuyse, A., Demertzi, A., . . . Laureys, S. (2014). Diagnostic precision of PET imaging and functional MRI in disorders of consciousness: A clinical validation study. *The Lancet, 384,* 514–522. (p. 81)

Stengel, E. (1981). Suicide. In *The new Encyclopaedia Britannica, macropaedia* (Vol. 17, pp. 777–782). Chicago: Encyclopaedia Britannica. (p. 553)

Stepanikova, I., Nie, N. H., & He, X. (2010). Time on the Internet at home, loneliness, and life satisfaction: Evidence from panel time-diary data. *Computers in Human Behavior, 26,* 329–338. (p. 373)

Stephens-Davidowitz, S. (2013, December 7). How many American men are gay? *The New York Times.* Retrieved from http://www.nytimes.com/2013/12/08/opinion/sunday/how-many-american-men-are-gay.html (p. 188)

Stephens-Davidowitz, S. (2014). The effects of racial animus on a Black candidate: Evidence using Google search data. *Journal of Public Economics, 118,* 26–40. (pp. 463, 464)

Steptoe, A., Chida, Y., Hamer, M., & Wardle, J. (2010). Author reply: Meta-analysis of stress-related factors in cancer. *Nature Reviews Clinical Oncology, 7*(5). doi:10.1038/ncponc1134-c2 (p. 413)

Steptoe, A., & Wardle, J. (2011). Positive affect measured using ecological momentary assessment and survival in older men and woman. *Proceedings of the National Academy of Sciences of the United States of America, 108,* 18244–18248. (p. 415)

Stern, M., & Karraker, K. H. (1989). Sex stereotyping of infants: A review of gender labeling studies. *Sex Roles, 20,* 501–522. (p. 206)

Sternberg, E. M. (2009). *Healing spaces: The science of place and well-being.* Cambridge, MA: Harvard University Press. (p. 410)

Sternberg, R. J. (1985). *Beyond IQ: A triarchic theory of human intelligence.* New York: Cambridge University Press. (p. 343)

Sternberg, R. J. (1988). Applying cognitive theory to the testing and teaching of intelligence. *Applied Cognitive Psychology, 2,* 231–255. (p. 325)

Sternberg, R. J. (2003). Our research program validating the triarchic theory of successful intelligence: Reply to Gottfredson. *Intelligence, 31,* 399–413. (p. 325)

Sternberg, R. J. (2006). The Rainbow Project: Enhance the SAT through assessments of analytical, practical, and creative skills. *Intelligence, 34,* 321–350. (p. 325)

Sternberg, R. J. (2011). The theory of successful intelligence. In R. J. Sternberg & S. B. Kaufman (Eds.), *The Cambridge handbook of intelligence* (pp. 504–527). New York: Cambridge University Press. (p. 343)

Sternberg, R. J., & Grajek, S. (1984). The nature of love. *Journal of Personality and Social Psychology, 47,* 312–329. (p. 480)

Sternberg, R. J., & Kaufman, J. C. (1998). Human abilities. *Annual Review of Psychology, 49,* 479–502. (p. 341)

Sternberg, R. J., & Lubart, T. I. (1991). An investment theory of creativity and its development. *Human Development, 34,* 1–31. (p. 325)

Sternberg, R. J., & Lubart, T. I. (1992). Buy low and sell high: An investment approach to creativity. *Psychological Science, 1,* 1–5. (p. 325)

Sterzing, P. R., Shattuck, P. T., Narendorf, S. C., Wagner, M., & Cooper, B. P. (2012). Bullying involvement and autism spectrum disorders: Prevalence and correlates of bullying involvement among adolescents with an autism spectrum disorder. *Archives of Pediatric and Adolescent Medicine, 166,* 1058–1064. (p. 136)

Stetter, F., & Kupper, S. (2002). Autogenic training: A meta-analysis of clinical outcome studies. *Applied Psychophysiology and Biofeedback, 27,* 45–98. (p. 427)

Stevenson, H. W. (1992, December). Learning from Asian schools. *Scientific American,* pp. 70–76. (p. 359)

Stevenson, R. J., & Tomiczek, C. (2007). Olfactory-induced synesthesias: A review and model. *Psychological Bulletin, 133,* 294–309. (p. 240)

Stewart, R. E., & Chambless, D. L. (2009). Cognitive–behavioral therapy for adult anxiety disorders in clinical practice: A meta-analysis of effectiveness studies. *Journal of Consulting and Clinical Psychology, 77,* 595–606. (p. 586)

Stice, E. (2002). Risk and maintenance factors for eating pathology: A meta-analytic review. *Psychological Bulletin, 128,* 825–848. (p. 565)

Stice, E., Ng, J., & Shaw, H. (2010). Risk factors and prodromal eating pathology. *Journal of Child Psychology and Psychiatry, 51,* 518–525. (p. 566)

Stice, E., Shaw, H., & Marti, C. N. (2007). A meta-analytic review of eating disorder prevention programs: Encouraging findings. *Annual Review of Clinical Psychology, 3,* 233–257. (p. 566)

Stice, E., Spangler, D., & Agras, W. S. (2001). Exposure to media-portrayed thin-ideal images adversely affects vulnerable girls: A longitudinal experiment. *Journal of Social and Clinical Psychology, 20,* 270–288. (p. 566)

Stickgold, R. (2000, March 7). Quoted in S. Blakeslee, For better learning, researchers endorse "sleep on it" adage. *The New York Times,* p. F2. (p. 100)

Stickgold, R. (2012). Sleep, memory and dreams: Putting it all together. In *Aquém e além do cérebro* [Behind and beyond the brain]. Bial: Fundação Bial Institution of Public Utility. (p. 100)

Stickgold, R., & Ellenbogen, J. M. (2008, August/September). Quiet! Sleeping brain at work. *Scientific American Mind,* pp. 23–29. (p. 93)

Stillman, T. F., Baumeister, R. F., Vohs, K. D., Lambert, N. M., Fincham, F. D., & Brewer, L. E. (2010). Personal philosophy and personnel achievement: Belief in free will predicts better job performance. *Social Psychological and Personality Science, 1,* 43–50. (p. 421)

Stillman, T. F., Lambet, N. M., Fincham, F. D., & Baumeister, R. F. (2011). Meaning as magnetic force: Evidence that meaning in life promotes interpersonal appeal. *Social Psychological and Personality Science, 2,* 13–20. (p. 603)

Stinson, D. A., Logel, C., Zanna, M. P., Holmes, J. G., Cameron, J. J., Wood, J. V., & Spencer, S. J. (2008). The cost of lower self-esteem: Testing a self- and social-bonds model of health. *Journal of Personality and Social Psychology, 94,* 412–428. (p. 425)

Stith, S. M., Rosen, K. H., Middleton, K. A., Busch, A. L., Lunderberg, K., & Carlton, R. P. (2000). The intergenerational transmission of spouse abuse: A meta-analysis. *Journal of Marriage and the Family, 62,* 640–654. (p. 276)

Stockton, M. C., & Murnen, S. K. (1992, June). *Gender and sexual arousal in response to sexual stimuli: A meta-analytic review.* Paper presented at the Fourth Annual Convention of the American Psychological Society, San Diego, CA. (p. 185)

Stoet, G., & Geary, D. C. (2012). Can stereotype threat explain the gender gap in mathematics performance and achievement? *Review of General Psychology, 16,* 93–102. (p. 361)

Stone, A. A., & Neale, J. M. (1984). Effects of severe daily events on mood. *Journal of Personality and Social Psychology, 46,* 137–144. (p. 432)

Stone, A. A., Schneider, S., & Harter, J. K. (2012). Day-of-week mood patterns in the United States: On the existence of "Blue Monday," "Thank God it's Friday" and weekend effects. *Journal of Positive Psychology, 7,* 306–314. (p. 21)

Stone, A. A., Schwartz, J. E., Broderick, J. E., & Deaton, A. (2010). A snapshot of the age distribution of psychological well-being in the United States. *Proceedings of the National Academy of Sciences of the United States of America, 107,* 9985–9990. (p. 166)

Stone, A. A., Schwartz, J. E., Broderick, J. E., & Shiffman, S. S. (2005). Variability of momentary pain predicts recall of weekly pain: A consequences of the peak (or salience) memory heuristic. *Personality and Social Psychology Bulletin, 31,* 1340–1346. (p. 232)

Stone, G. (2006, February 17). *Homeless man discovered to be lawyer with amnesia.* Retrieved from http://abcnews.go.com/US/story?id=1629645 (p. 561)

St-Onge, M.-P., McReynolds, A., Trivedi, Z. B., Roberts, A. L., Sy, M., & Hirsch, J. (2012). Sleep restriction leads to increased activation of brain regions sensitive to food stimuli. *American Journal of Clinical Nutrition, 95,* 818–824. (p. 95)

Storbeck, J., Robinson, M. D., & McCourt, M. E. (2006). Semantic processing precedes affect retrieval: The neurological case for cognitive primary in visual processing. *Review of General Psychology, 10,* 41–55. (p. 390)

Storm, B. C., & Jobe, T. A. (2012). Retrieval-induced forgetting predicts failure to recall negative autobiographical memories. *Psychological Science, 23,* 1356–1363. (p. 295)

Storm, L., Tressoldi, P. E., & Di Risio, L. (2010a). A meta-analysis with nothing to hide: Reply to Hyman (2010). *Psychological Bulletin, 136,* 491–494. (p. 241)

Storm, L., Tressoldi, P. E., & Di Risio, L. (2010b). Meta-analysis of free-response studies, 1992–2008: Assessing the noise reduction model in parapsychology. *Psychological Bulletin, 136*, 471–485. (p. 241)

Storms, M. D. (1973). Videotape and the attribution process: Reversing actors' and observers' points of view. *Journal of Personality and Social Psychology, 27*, 165–175. (p. 443)

Storms, M. D. (1983). *Development of sexual orientation.* Washington, DC: Office of Social and Ethical Responsibility, American Psychological Association. (p. 189)

Storms, M. D., & Thomas, G. C. (1977). Reactions to physical closeness. *Journal of Personality and Social Psychology, 35*, 412–418. (p. 456)

Stout, J. A., & Dasgupta, N. (2011). When he doesn't mean you: Gender-exclusive language as ostracism. *Personality and Social Psychology Bulletin, 37*, 757–769. (p. 371)

Stowell, J. R., Oldham, T., & Bennett, D. (2010). Using student response systems ("clickers") to combat conformity and shyness. *Teaching of Psychology, 37*, 135–140. (p. 451)

Strahan, E. J., Spencer, S. J., & Zanna, M. P. (2002). Subliminal priming and persuasion: Striking while the iron is hot. *Journal of Experimental Social Psychology, 38*, 556–568. (p. 203)

Stranahan, A. M., Khalil, D., & Gould, E. (2006). Social isolation delays the positive effects of running on adult neurogenesis. *Nature Neuroscience, 9*, 526–533. (p. 61)

Strang, S., Utikal, V., Fischbacher, U., Weber, B., & Falk, A. (2014). Neural correlates of receiving an apology and active forgiveness: An fMRI study. *PLOS ONE, 9*(2), e87654. doi:10.1371/journal.pone.0087654 (p. 417)

Strange, D., Hayne, H., & Garry, M. (2008). A photo, a suggestion, a false memory. *Applied Cognitive Psychology, 22*, 587–603. (p. 308)

Strasburger, V. C., Jordan, A. B., & Donnerstein, E. (2010). Health effects of media on children and adolescents. *Pediatrics, 125*, 756–767. (p. 276)

Stratton, G. M. (1896). Some preliminary experiments on vision without inversion of the retinal image. *Psychological Review, 3*, 611–617. (p. 224)

Straub, R. O., Seidenberg, M. S., Bever, T. G., & Terrace, H. S. (1979). Serial learning in the pigeon. *Journal of the Experimental Analysis of Behavior, 32*, 137–148. (p. 335)

Straus, M. A., & Gelles, R. J. (1980). *Behind closed doors: Violence in the American family.* New York: Anchor/Doubleday. (p. 262)

Straus, M. A., Sugarman, D. B., & Giles-Sims, J. (1997). Spanking by parents and subsequent antisocial behavior of children. *Archives of Pediatric Adolescent Medicine, 151*, 761–767. (p. 262)

Strawbridge, W. J. (1999). *Mortality and religious involvement: A review and critique of the results, the methods, and the measures.* Paper presented at Harvard University conference on religion and health sponsored by the National Institute for Health Research and the John Templeton Foundation. (p. 430)

Strawbridge, W. J., Cohen, R. D., & Shema, S. J. (1997). Frequent attendance at religious services and mortality over 28 years. *American Journal of Public Health, 87*, 957–961. (p. 430)

Strayer, D. L., & Drews, F. A. (2007). Cell-phone-induced driver distraction. *Current Directions in Psychological Science, 16*, 128–131. (p. 82)

Strayer, D. L., & Watson, J. M. (2012, March/April). Supertaskers and the multitasking brain. *Scientific American Mind*, pp. 22–29. (p. 82)

Strick, M., Dijksterhuis, A., Bos, M. W., Sjoerdsma, A., & van Baaren, R. B. (2011). A meta-analysis on unconscious thought effects. *Social Cognition, 29*, 738–762. (p. 324)

Strick, M., Dijksterhuis, A., & van Baaren, R. B. (2010). Unconscious-thought effects take place off-line, not on-line. *Psychological Science, 21*, 484–488. (p. 324)

Stroebe, M., Finenauer, C., Wijngaards-de Meij, L., Schut, H., van den Bout, J., & Stroebe, W. (2013). Partner-oriented self-regulation among bereaved parents: The costs of holding in grief for the partner's sake. *Psychological Science, 24*, 395–402. (p. 168)

Stroebe, W. (2012). The truth about Triplett (1898), but nobody seems to care. *Perspectives on Psychological Science, 7*, 54–57. (p. 455)

Stroebe, W. (2013). Firearm possession and violent death: A critical review. *Aggression and Violent Behavior, 18*, 709–721. (p. 468)

Stroebe, W., Schut, H., & Stroebe, M. S. (2005). Grief work, disclosure and counseling: Do they help the bereaved? *Clinical Psychology Review, 25*, 395–414. (p. 168)

Stroud, L. R., Panadonatos, G. D., Rodriguez, D., McCallum, M., Salisbury, A. L., Phipps, M. G., . . . Marsit, C. J. (2014). Maternal smoking during pregnancy and infant stress response: Test of a prenatal programming hypothesis. *Psychoneuroendocrinology, 48*, 29–40. (p. 124)

Strully, K. W. (2009). Job loss and health in the U.S. labor market. *Demography, 46*, 221–246. (p. 407)

Strupp, H. H. (1986). Psychotherapy: Research, practice, and public policy (how to avoid dead ends). *American Psychologist, 41*, 120–130. (p. 589)

Stutzer, A., & Frey, B. S. (2006). Does marriage make people happy, or do happy people get married? *Journal of Socio-Economics, 35*, 326–347. (p. 431)

Su, R., Rounds, J., & Armstrong, P. I. (2009). Men and things, women and people: A meta-analysis of sex differences in interests. *Psychological Bulletin, 135*, 859–884. (p. 174)

Subrahmanyam, K., & Greenfield, P. (2008). Online communication and adolescent relationships. *The Future of Children, 18*, 119–146. (p. 155)

Suddath, R. L., Christison, G. W., Torrey, E. F., Casanova, M. F., & Weinberger, D. R. (1990). Anatomical abnormalities in the brains of monozygotic twins discordant for schizophrenia. *New England Journal of Medicine, 322*, 789–794. (p. 560)

Sue, S. (2006). Research to address racial and ethnic disparities in mental health: Some lessons learned. In S. I. Donaldson, D. E. Berger, & K. Pezdek (Eds.), *Applied psychology: New frontiers and rewarding careers* (pp. 119–134). Mahwah, NJ: Erlbaum. (p. 591)

Suedfeld, P., & Mocellin, J. S. P. (1987). The "sensed presence" in unusual environments. *Environment and Behavior, 19*, 33–52. (p. 112)

Sugaya, L., Hasin, D. S., Olfson, M., Lin, K.-H., Grant, B. F., & Blanco, C. (2012). Child physical abuse and adult mental health: A national study. *Journal of Traumatic Stress, 25*, 384–392. (p. 144)

Suinn, R. M. (1997). Mental practice in sports psychology: Where have we been, Where do we go? *Clinical Psychology: Science and Practice, 4*, 189–207. (p. 345)

Sullivan, K. T., Pasch, L. A., Johnson, M. D., & Bradbury, T. N. (2010). Social support, problem solving, and the longitudinal course of newlywed marriage. *Journal of Personality and Social Psychology, 98*, 631–644. (p. 481)

Sullivan, P. F., Neale, M. C., & Kendler, K. S. (2000). Genetic epidemiology of major depression: Review and meta-analysis. *American Journal of Psychiatry, 157*, 1552–1562. (p. 549)

Sullivan/Anderson, A. (2009, March 19). How to bring an end to the war over sex ed. *Time*, pp. 40–43. (p. 186)

Suls, J. M., & Tesch, F. (1978). Students' preferences for information about their test performance: A social comparison study. *Journal of Experimental Social Psychology, 8*, 189–197. (p. 435)

Summers, M. (1996, December 9). Mister clean. *People Weekly*, pp. 139–142. (p. 527)

Sun, Q. I., Townsend, M. K., Okereke, O., Franco, O. H., Hu, F. B., & Grodstein, F. (2009). Adiposity and weight change in mid-life in relation to healthy survival after age 70 in women: Prospective cohort study. *British Medical Journal, 339*, b3796. http://dx.doi.org/10.1136/bmj.b3796 (p. 383)

Sundie, J. M., Kenrick, D. T., Griskevicius, V., Tybur, J. M., Vohs, K. D., & Beal, D. J. (2011). Peacocks, Porsches, and Thorsten Veblen: Conspicuous consumption as a sexual signaling system. *Journal of Personality and Social Psychology, 100*, 664–680. (p. 193)

Sundstrom, E., De Meuse, K. P., & Futrell, D. (1990). Work teams: Applications and effectiveness. *American Psychologist, 45*, 120–133. (p. B-13)

Sunstein, C. R. (2007). On the divergent American reactions to terrorism and climate change. *Columbia Law Review, 107*, 503–557. (p. 319)

Suomi, S. J. (1986). Anxiety-like disorders in young nonhuman primates. In R. Gettleman (Ed.), *Anxiety disorders of childhood* (pp. 1–23). New York: Guilford Press. (p. 542)

Suppes, P. (1982). Quoted in R. H. Ennis, Children's ability to handle Piaget's propositional logic: A conceptual critique. In S. Modgil & C. Modgil (Eds.), *Jean Piaget: Consensus and controversy* (pp. 101–130). New York: Praeger. (p. 133)

Surgeon General. (1986, August 4). *Report of the Surgeon General's Workshop on Pornography and Public Health, June 22–24.* Retrieved from http://profiles.nlm.nih.gov/ps/access/NNBCKH.pdf (p. 472)

Surgeon General. (2012). *Preventing tobacco use among youth and young adults: A report of the Surgeon General.* Rockville, MD: Department of Health and Human Services, Office of the Surgeon General. (p. 115)

Surgeon General's Office. (1999). *Mental health: A report of the surgeon general.* Rockville, MD: U.S. Department of Health and Human Services. (p. 533)

Susser, E. S., Neugenbauer, R., Hoek, H. W., Brown, A. S., Lin, S., Labovitz, D., & Gorman, J. M. (1996). Schizophrenia after prenatal famine. *Archives of General Psychiatry, 53,* 25–31. (p. 558)

Sutcliffe, J. S. (2008). Insights into the pathogenesis of autism. *Science, 321,* 208–209. (p. 136)

Sutherland, A. (2006a). *Bitten and scratched: Life and lessons at the premier school for exotic animal trainers.* New York: Viking. (p. 245)

Sutherland, A. (2006b, June 25). What Shamu taught me about a happy marriage. *The New York Times.* Retrieved from http://www.nytimes.com/2006/06/25/fashion/25love.html?pagewanted=all&_r=0 (p. 245)

Sutin, A. R., Ferrucci, L., Zonderman, A. B., & Terracciano, A. (2011). Personality and obesity across the adult life span. *Journal of Personality and Social Psychology, 101,* 579–592. (p. 511)

Swami, V. (2015). Cultural influences on body size ideals: Unpacking the impact of Westernization and modernization. *European Psychologist, 20,* 44–51. (p. 382)

Swami, V., Frederick, D. A., Aavik, T., Alcalay, L., Allik, J., Anderson, D., . . . Zivcic-Becirevic, I. (2010). The attractive female body weight and female body dissatisfaction in 26 countries across 10 world regions: Results of the International Body Project I. *Personality and Social Psychology Bulletin, 36,* 309–325. (p. 566)

Swami, V., Henderson, G., Custance, D., & Tovée, M. J. (2011). A cross-cultural investigation of men's judgments of female body weight in Britain and Indonesia. *Journal of Cross-Cultural Psychology, 42,* 140–145. (p. 382)

Swann, W. B., Jr., Chang-Schneider, C., & McClarty, K. L. (2007). Do people's self-views matter: Self-concept and self-esteem in everyday life. *American Psychologist, 62,* 84–94. (p. 517)

Sweat, J. A., & Durm, M. W. (1993). Psychics: Do police departments really use them? *Skeptical Inquirer, 17,* 148–158. (p. 241)

Swerdlow, N. R., & Koob, G. F. (1987). Dopamine, schizophrenia, mania, and depression: Toward a unified hypothesis of cortico-stiatopallido-thalamic function (with commentary). *Behavioral and Brain Sciences, 10,* 197–246. (p. 558)

Symbaluk, D. G., Heth, C. D., Cameron, J., & Pierce, W. D. (1997). Social modeling, monetary incentives, and pain endurance: The role of self-efficacy and pain perception. *Personality and Social Psychology Bulletin, 23,* 258–269. (p. 233)

Symond, M. B., Harris, A. W. F., Gordon, E., & Williams, L. M. (2005). "Gamma synchrony" in first-episode schizophrenia: A disorder of temporal connectivity? *American Journal of Psychiatry, 162,* 459–465. (p. 558)

Symons, C. S., & Johnson, B. T. (1997). The self-reference effect in memory: A meta-analysis. *Psychological Bulletin, 121,* 371–394. (p. 290)

T

Tadmor, C. T., Galinsky, A. D., & Maddux, W. W. (2012). Getting the most out of living abroad: Biculturalism and integrative complexity as key drivers of creative and professional success. *Journal of Personality and Social Psychology, 103,* 520–542. (p. 326)

Taha, F. A. (1972). A comparative study of how sighted and blind perceive the manifest content of dreams. *National Review of Social Sciences, 9*(3), 28. (p. 99)

Taheri, S. (2004, 20 December). *Does the lack of sleep make you fat?* Retrieved from http://www.bristol.ac.uk/news/2004/1113989409.html (p. 384)

Taheri, S., Lin, L., Austin, D., Young, T., & Mignot, E. (2004). Short sleep duration is associated with reduced leptin, elevated ghrelin, and increased body mass index. *PLoS Medicine, 1*(3), e62. doi:10.1371/journal.pmed.0010062 (p. 384)

Tajfel, H. (Ed.). (1982). *Social identity and intergroup relations.* New York: Cambridge University Press. (p. 465)

Tal, A., Zuckerman, S., & Wansink, B. (2014). Watch what you eat: Action-related television content increases food intake. *JAMA Internal Medicine, 174,* 1842–1843. (p. 381)

Talarico, J. M., & Moore, K. M. (2012). Memories of "The Rivalry": Differences in how fans of the winning and losing teams remember the same game. *Applied Cognitive Psychology, 26,* 746–756. (p. 295)

Talbot, M. (1999, October 17). The Rorschach chronicles. *The New York Times.* Retrieved from http://www.nytimes.com/1999/10/17/magazine/the-rorschach-chronicles.html?pagewanted=all (p. 497)

Talhelm, T., Zhang, X., Oishi, S., Shimin, C., Duan, D., Lan, X., & Kitayama, S. (2014). Large-scale psychological differences within China explained by rice versus wheat agriculture. *Science, 344,* 603–608. (p. 523)

Tamres, L. K., Janicki, D., & Helgeson, V. S. (2002). Sex differences in coping behavior: A meta-analytic review and an examination of relative coping. *Personality and Social Psychology Review, 6,* 2–30. (p. 174)

Tang, S.-H., & Hall, V. C. (1995). The overjustification effect: A meta-analysis. *Applied Cognitive Psychology, 9,* 365–404. (p. 271)

Tangney, C. C., Kwasny, M. J., Li, H., Wilson, R. S., Evans, D. A., & Morris, M. C. (2011). Adherence to a Mediterranean-type dietary pattern and cognitive decline in a community population. *American Journal of Clinical Nutrition, 93,* 601–607. (p. 550)

Tannen, D. (1990). *You just don't understand: Women and men in conversation.* New York: HarperCollins. (pp. 9, 174)

Tannenbaum, P. (2002, February). Quoted in R. Kubey & M. Csikszentmihalyi, Television addiction is no mere metaphor. *Scientific American,* pp. 74–80. (p. 204)

Tanner, J. M. (1978). *Fetus into man: Physical growth from conception to maturity.* Cambridge, MA: Harvard University Press. (p. 176)

Tardif, T., Fletcher, P., Liang, W., Zhang, Z., Kaciroti, N., & Marchman, V. A. (2008). Baby's first 10 words. *Developmental Psychology, 44,* 929–938. (p. 332)

Tarrant, M., Branscombe, N. R., Warner, R. H., & Weston, D. (2012). Social identity and perceptions of torture: It's moral when we do it. *Journal of Experimental Social Psychology, 48,* 513–518. (p. 485)

Tasbihsazan, R., Nettelbeck, T., & Kirby, N. (2003). Predictive validity of the Fagan Test of Infant Intelligence. *British Journal of Developmental Psychology, 21,* 585–597. (p. 350)

Taubes, G. (2001). The soft science of dietary fat. *Science, 291,* 2536–2545. (p. 385)

Taubes, G. (2002, July 7). What if it's all been a big fat lie? *The New York Times.* Retrieved from http://www.nytimes.com/2002/07/07/magazine/what-if-it-s-all-been-a-big-fat-lie.html (p. 385)

Tavernier, R., & Willoughby, T. (2014). Bidirectional associations between sleep (quality and duration) and psychosocial functioning across the university years. *Developmental Psychology, 50,* 674–682. (p. 94)

Tavris, C. (1982, November). Anger defused. *Psychology Today,* pp. 25–35. (p. 416)

Tavris, C., & Aronson, E. (2007). *Mistakes were made (but not by me).* Orlando, FL: Harcourt. (p. 305)

Tay, L., & Diener, E. (2011). Needs and subjective well-being around the world. *Journal of Personality and Social Psychology, 101,* 354–365. (p. 369)

Taylor, C. A., Manganello, J. A., Lee, S. J., & Rice, J. C. (2010). Mothers' spanking of 3-year-old children and subsequent risk of children's aggressive behavior. *Pediatrics, 125,* 1057–1065. (p. 262)

Taylor, K., & Rohrer, D. (2010). The effects of interleaved practice. *Applied Cognitive Psychology, 24,* 837–848. (p. 31)

Taylor, P. (2014). *The next America: Boomers, millennials, and the looming generational showdown.* New York: Public Affairs. (p. 141)

Taylor, P. J., Gooding, P., Wood, A. M., & Tarrier, N. (2011). The role of defeat and entrapment in depression, anxiety, and suicide. *Psychological Bulletin, 137,* 391–420. (p. 553)

Taylor, P. J., Russ-Eft, D. F., & Chan, D. W. L. (2005). A meta-analytic review of behavior modeling training. *Journal of Applied Psychology, 90,* 692–709. (p. 275)

Taylor, S. (2011). Etiology of obsessions and compulsions: A meta-analysis and narrative review of twin studies. *Clinical Psychology Review, 31,* 1361–1372. (p. 539)

Taylor, S. (2013). Molecular genetics of obsessive–compulsive disorder: A comprehensive meta-analysis of genetic association studies. *Molecular Psychiatry, 18,* 799–805. (p. 542)

Taylor, S., Kuch, K., Koch, W. J., Crockett, D. J., & Passey, G. (1998). The structure of posttraumatic stress symptoms. *Journal of Abnormal Psychology, 107,* 154–160. (p. 540)

Taylor, S. E. (2002). *The tending instinct: How nurturing is essential to who we are and how we live.* New York: Times Books. (p. 174)

Taylor, S. E. (2006). Tend and befriend: Biobehavioral bases of affiliation under stress. *Current Directions in Psychological Science, 15,* 273–277. (p. 410)

Taylor, S. E., Cousino, L. K., Lewis, B. P., Gruenewald, T. L., Gurung, R. A. R., & Updegraff, J. A. (2000). Biobehavioral responses to stress in females: Tend-and-befriend, not fight-or-flight. *Psychological Review, 107,* 411–430. (p. 410)

Taylor, S. E., Pham, L. B., Rivkin, I. D., & Armor, D. A. (1998). Harnessing the imagination: Mental simulation, self-regulation, and coping. *American Psychologist*, *53*, 429–439. (p. 339)

Taylor, S. P., & Chermack, S. T. (1993). Alcohol, drugs and human physical aggression. *Journal of Studies on Alcohol, Supplement 11*, 78–88. (p. 470)

Tedeschi, R. G., & Calhoun, L. G. (2004). Posttraumatic growth: Conceptual foundations and empirical evidence. *Psychological Inquiry*, *15*, 1–18. (p. 603)

Teghtsoonian, R. (1971). On the exponents in Stevens' law and the constant in Ekman's law. *Psychological Review*, *78*, 71–80. (p. 203)

Teicher, M. H. (2002, March). The neurobiology of child abuse. *Scientific American*, pp. 68–75. (p. 144)

Teller. (2009, April 20). Quoted in J. Lehrer, Magic and the brain: Teller reveals the neuroscience of illusion. *Wired Magazine*. Retrieved from http://archive.wired.com/science/discoveries/magazine/17-05/ff_neuroscienceofmagic?currentPage=all (p. 83)

Telzer, E. H., Flannery, J., Shapiro, M., Humphreys, K. L., Goff, B., Gabard-Durman, L., . . . Tottenham, N. (2013). Early experience shapes amygdala sensitivity to race: An international adoption design. *Journal of Neuroscience*, *33*, 13484–13488. (p. 467)

Tenenbaum, H. R., & Leaper, C. (2002). Are parents' gender schemas related to their children's gender-related cognitions? A meta-analysis. *Developmental Psychology*, *38*, 615–630. (p. 179)

Tenopyr, M. L. (1997). Improving the workplace: Industrial/organizational psychology as a career. In R. J. Sternberg (Ed.), *Career paths in psychology: Where your degree can take you* (pp. 185–196). Washington, DC: American Psychological Association. (p. B-4)

Tepper, S. J. (2000). Fiction reading in America: Explaining the gender gap. *Poetics*, *27*, 255–275. (p. 398)

Terao, T., Ohgami, H., Shlotsuki, I., Ishil, N., & Iwata, N. (2010). Authors' reply. *British Journal of Psychiatry*, *196*, 160. (p. 596)

Terman, J. S., Terman, M., Lo, E.-S., & Cooper, T. B. (2001). Circadian time of morning light administration and therapeutic response in winter depression. *Archives of General Psychiatry*, *58*, 69–73. (pp. 588–589)

Terman, M., Terman, J. S., & Ross, D. C. (1998). A controlled trial of timed bright light and negative air ionization for treatment of winter depression. *Archives of General Psychiatry*, *55*, 875–882. (pp. 588–589)

Terrace, H. S. (1979, November). How Nim Chimpsky changed my mind. *Psychology Today*, pp. 65–76. (p. 335)

Terre, L., & Stoddart, R. (2000, Fall). Cutting edge specialties for graduate study in psychology. *Eye on Psi Chi*, pp. 23–26. (p. C-1)

Tesser, A., Forehand, R., Brody, G., & Long, N. (1989). Conflict: The role of calm and angry parent-child discussion in adolescent development. *Journal of Social and Clinical Psychology*, *8*, 317–330. (p. 154)

Tetlock, P. E. (1988). Monitoring the integrative complexity of American and Soviet policy rhetoric: What can be learned? *Journal of Social Issues*, *44*, 101–131. (p. 487)

Tetlock, P. E. (1998). Close-call counterfactuals and belief-system defenses: I was not almost wrong but I was almost right. *Journal of Personality and Social Psychology*, *75*, 639–652. (p. 16)

Tetlock, P. E. (2005). *Expert political judgement: How good is it? How can we know?* Princeton, NJ: Princeton University Press. (p. 16)

Thaler, R. H. (2015, May 8). Unless you are Spock, irrelevant things matter in economic behavior. *The New York Times*. Retrieved from http://www.nytimes.com/2015/05/10/upshot/unless-you-are-spock-irrelevant-things-matter-in-economic-behavior.html?_r=0 (p. 323)

Thaler, R. H., & Sunstein, C. R. (2008). *Nudge: Improving decisions about health, wealth, and happiness*. New Haven, CT: Yale University Press. (p. 322)

Thatcher, R. W., Walker, R. A., & Giudice, S. (1987). Human cerebral hemispheres develop at different rates and ages. *Science*, *236*, 1110–1113. (pp. 121, 127)

Thayer, R. E. (1987). Energy, tiredness, and tension effects of a sugar snack versus moderate exercise. *Journal of Personality and Social Psychology*, *52*, 119–125. (p. 427)

Thayer, R. E. (1993). Mood and behavior (smoking and sugar snacking) following moderate exercise: A partial test of self-regulation theory. *Personality and Individual Differences*, *14*, 97–104. (p. 427)

Théoret, H., Halligan, H., Kobayashi, M., Fregni, F., Tager-Flusberg, H., & Pascual-Leone, A. (2005). Impaired motor facilitation during action observation in individuals with autism spectrum disorder. *Current Biology*, *15*, R84–R85. (p. 137)

Thernstrom, M. (2006, May 14). My pain, my brain. *The New York Times*. Retrieved from http://www.nytimes.com/2006/05/14/magazine/14pain.html?pagewanted=all&_r=0 (p. 234)

Thiel, A., Hadedank, B., Herholz, K., Kessler, J., Winhuisen, L., Haupt, W. F., & Heiss, W.-D. (2006). From the left to the right: How the brain compensates progressive loss of language function. *Brain and Language*, *98*, 57–65. (p. 61)

Thomas, A., & Chess, S. (1986). The New York Longitudinal Study: From infancy to early adult life. In R. Plomin & J. Dunn (Eds.), *The study of temperament: Changes, continuities, and challenges* (pp. 39–52). Hillsdale, NJ: Erlbaum. (p. 122)

Thomas, K. (2015, February 24). Shire, maker of binge-eating drug Vyvanse, first marketed the disease. *The New York Times*. Retrieved from http://www.nytimes.com/2015/02/25/business/shire-maker-of-binge-eating-drug-vyvanse-first-marketed-the-disease.html (p. 532)

Thomas, L. (1992). *The fragile species*. New York: Scribner's. (pp. 76, 585)

Thompson, G. (2010). The $1 million dollar challenge. *Skeptic*, *15*(4), 8–9. (p. 242)

Thompson, J. K., Jarvie, G. J., Lahey, B. B., & Cureton, K. J. (1982). Exercise and obesity: Etiology, physiology, and intervention. *Psychological Bulletin*, *91*, 55–79. (p. 385)

Thompson, P. M., Cannon, T. D., Narr, K. L., van Erp, T., Poutanen, V.-P., Huttunen, M., . . . Toga, A. W. (2001). Genetic influences on brain structure. *Nature Neuroscience*, *4*, 1253–1258. (p. 354)

Thompson, P. M., Giedd, J. N., Woods, R. P., MacDonald, D., Evans, A. C., & Toga, A. W. (2000). Growth patterns in the developing brain detected by using continuum mechanical tensor maps. *Nature*, *404*, 190–193. (p. 127)

Thompson, R., Emmorey, K., & Gollan, T. H. (2005). "Tip of the fingers" experiences by deaf signers. *Psychological Science*, *16*, 856–860. (p. 304)

Thompson-Schill, S. L., Ramscar, M., & Chrysikou, E. G. (2009). Cognition without control: When a little frontal lobe goes a long way. *Current Directions in Psychological Science*, *18*, 259–263. (p. 127)

Thomson, R., & Murachver, T. (2001). Predicting gender from electronic discourse. *British Journal of Social Psychology*, *40*, 193–208 [and personal communication, T. Murachver, May 23, 2002]. (p. 174)

Thorndike, E. L. (1898). Animal intelligence: An experimental study of the associative processes in animals. *Psychological Review: Monograph Supplements*, *2*(4), i–109. (p. 256)

Thorne, J. (1993). *You are not alone: Words of experience and hope for the journey through depression* (With L. Rothstein). New York: HarperPerennial. (p. 527)

Thornton, B., & Moore, S. (1993). Physical attractiveness contrast effect: Implications for self-esteem and evaluations of the social self. *Personality and Social Psychology Bulletin*, *19*, 474–480. (p. 477)

Tickle, J. J., Hull, J. G., Sargent, J. D., Dalton, M. A., & Heatherton, T. F. (2006). A structural equation model of social influences and exposure to media smoking on adolescent smoking. *Basic and Applied Social Psychology*, *28*, 117–129. (p. 115)

Tiedens, L. Z. (2001). Anger and advancement versus sadness and subjugation: The effect of negative emotion expressions on social status conferral. *Journal of Personality and Social Psychology*, *80*, 86–94. (p. 416)

Tiggemann, M., & Miller, J. (2010). The Internet and adolescent girls' weight satisfaction and drive for thinness. *Sex Roles*, *63*, 79–90. (p. 566)

Tiihonen, J., Lönnqvist, J., Wahlbeck, K., Klaukka, T., Niskanen, L., Tanskanen, A., Haukka, J. (2009). 11-year follow-up of mortality in patients with schizophrenia: A population-based cohort study (FIN11 study). *The Lancet*, *374*, 260–267. (p. 594)

Time/CNN Survey. (1994, December 19). Vox pop: Happy holidays. *Time*. Retrieved from http://time.com/ (p. 545)

Timmerman, T. A. (2007). "It was a thought pitch": Personal, situational, and target influences on hit-by-pitch events across time. *Journal of Applied Psychology*, *92*, 876–884. (p. 470)

Tinbergen, N. (1951). *The study of instinct*. Oxford, England: Clarendon Press. (p. 366)

Tirrell, M. E. (1990). Personal communication. (p. 250)

Tobin, D. D., Menon, M., Menon, M., Spatta, B. C., Hodges, E. V. E., & Perry, D. G. (2010). The intrapsychics of gender: A model of self-socialization. *Psychological Review*, *117*, 601–622. (p. 178)

Toews, P. (2004, December 30). *Dirk Willems: A heart undivided*. Retrieved from http://www.mbhistory.org/profiles/dirk.en.html (p. 441)

Tolin, D. F. (2010). Is cognitive–behavioral therapy more effective than other therapies? A meta-analytic review. *Clinical Psychology Review, 30,* 710–720. (p. 586)

Tolman, E. C., & Honzik, C. H. (1930). Introduction and removal of reward, and maze performance in rats. *University of California Publications in Psychology, 4,* 257–275. (p. 271)

Tolstóy, L. (1904). My confession. In L. Wiener (Trans. & Ed.), *The complete works of Count Tolstóy* (Vol. 13, pp. 3–90). Boston: Dana Estes. (p. 29)

Toma, C., & Hancock, J. (2013). Self-affirmation underlies Facebook use. *Personality and Social Psychology Bulletin, 369,* 321–331. (p. 517)

Tomaka, J., Blascovich, J., & Kelsey, R. M. (1992). Effects of self-deception, social desirability, and repressive coping on psychophysiological reactivity to stress. *Personality and Social Psychology Bulletin, 18,* 616–624. (p. 518)

Toni, N., Buchs, P.-A., Nikonenko, I., Bron, C. R., & Muller, D. (1999). LTP promotes formation of multiple spine synapses between a single axon terminal and a dendrite. *Nature, 402,* 421–442. (p. 296)

Tononi, G., & Cirelli, C. (2013, August). Perchance to prune. *Scientific American,* pp. 34–39. (p. 93)

Topolinski, S., & Reber, R. (2010). Gaining insight into the "aha" experience. *Current Directions in Psychological Science, 19,* 401–405. (p. 317)

Torrey, E. F. (1986). *Witchdoctors and psychiatrists.* New York: Harper & Row. (p. 590)

Torrey, E. F., & Miller, J. (2002). *The invisible plague: The rise of mental illness from 1750 to the present.* New Brunswick, NJ: Rutgers University Press. (p. 559)

Torrey, E. F., Miller, J., Rawlings, R., & Yolken, R. H. (1997). Seasonality of births in schizophrenia and bipolar disorder: A review of the literature. *Schizophrenia Research, 28,* 1–38. (p. 559)

Totterdell, P., Kellett, S., Briner, R. B., & Teuchmann, K. (1998). Evidence of mood linkage in work groups. *Journal of Personality and Social Psychology, 74,* 1504–1515. (p. 449)

Tracy, J. L., Cheng, J. T., Robins, R. W., & Trzesniewski, K. H. (2009). Authentic and hubristic pride: The affective core of self-esteem and narcissism. *Self and Identity, 8,* 196–213. (p. 520)

Tracy, J. L., & Robins, R. W. (2004). Show your pride: Evidence for a discrete emotion expression. *Psychological Science, 15,* 194–197. (p. 391)

Tracy, J. L., Shariff, A. F., Zhao, W., & Henrich, J. (2013). Cross-cultural evidence that the nonverbal expression of pride is an automatic status signal. *Journal of Experimental Psychology: General, 142,* 163–180. (p. 396)

Trautwein, U., Lüdtke, O., Köller, O., & Baumert, J. (2006). Self-esteem, academic self-concept, and achievement: How the learning environment moderates the dynamics of self-concept. *Journal of Personality and Social Psychology, 90,* 334–349. (p. 517)

Treffert, D. A., & Christensen, D. D. (2005, December). Inside the mind of a savant. *Scientific American,* pp. 108–113. (p. 343)

Treffert, D. A., & Wallace, G. L. (2002, June). Islands of genius. *Scientific American,* pp. 76–86. (p. 342)

Treisman, A. (1987). Properties, parts, and objects. In K. R. Boff, L. Kaufman, & J. P. Thomas (Eds.), *Handbook of perception and human performance* (pp. 159–198). New York: Wiley. (p. 217)

Tremblay, R. E., Pihl, R. O., Vitaro, F., & Dobkin, P. L. (1994). Predicting early onset of male antisocial behavior from preschool behavior. *Archives of General Psychiatry, 51,* 732–739. (p. 564)

Triandis, H. C. (1994). *Culture and social behavior.* New York: McGraw-Hill. (pp. 471, 523)

Triandis, H. C., Bontempo, R., Villareal, M. J., Asai, M., & Lucca, N. (1988). Individualism and collectivism: Cross-cultural perspectives on self–ingroup relationships. *Journal of Personality and Social Psychology, 54,* 323–338. (p. 523)

Trickett, E. (2009). Community psychology: Individuals and interventions in community context. *Annual Review of Psychology, 60,* 395–419. (p. 13)

Trickett, P. K., Noll, J. G., & Putnam, F. W. (2011). The impact of sexual abuse on female development: Lessons from a multigenerational, longitudinal research study. *Development and Psychopathology, 23,* 453–476. (p. 144)

Trillin, C. (2006, March 27). Alice off the page. *The New Yorker,* p. 44. (p. 502)

Triplett, N. (1898). The dynamogenic factors in pacemaking and competition. *American Journal of Psychology, 9,* 507–533. (p. 455)

Trotter, J. (2014, January 23). The power of positive coaching. *Sports Illustrated.* Retrieved from http://mmqb.si.com/2014/01/23/pete-carroll-seattle-seahawks-super-bowl-48 (p. B-11)

Trut, L. N. (1999). Early canid domestication: The farm-fox experiment. *American Scientist, 87,* 160–169. (p. 73)

Tsai, J. L., & Chentsova-Dutton, Y. (2003). Variation among European Americans in emotional facial expression. *Journal of Cross-Cultural Psychology, 34,* 650–657. (p. 401)

Tsai, J. L., Miao, F. F., Seppala, E., Fung, H. H., & Yeung, D. Y. (2007). Influence and adjustment goals: Sources of cultural differences in ideal affect. *Journal of Personality and Social Psychology, 92,* 1102–1117. (p. 401)

Tsang, Y. C. (1938). Hunger motivation in gastrectomized rats. *Journal of Comparative Psychology, 26,* 1–17. (p. 378)

Tsuang, M. T., & Faraone, S. V. (1990). *The genetics of mood disorders.* Baltimore: Johns Hopkins University Press. (p. 549)

Tsvetkova, M., & Macy, M. W. (2014). The social contagion of generosity. *PLOS ONE, 9*(2), e87275. doi:10.1371/journal.pone.0087275 (p. 483)

Tuber, D. S., Miller, D. D., Caris, K. A., Halter, R., Linden, F., & Hennessy, M. B. (1999). Dogs in animal shelters: Problems, suggestions, and needed expertise. *Psychological Science, 10,* 379–386. (p. 28)

Tucker, K. A. (2002, May 20). I believe you can fly. *Gallup Management Journal.* Retrieved from http://www.gallup.com/businessjournal/373/believe-can-fly.aspx (p. B A-10)

Tucker-Drob, E. (2012). Preschools reduce early academic-achievement gaps: A longitudinal twin approach. *Psychological Science, 23,* 310–319. (p. 356)

Tucker-Drob, E. M., Rhemtulla, M., Harden, K. P., Turkheimer, E., & Fask, D. (2011). Emergence of a Gene × Socioeconomic Status interaction on infant mental ability between 10 months and 2 years. *Psychological Science, 22,* 125–133. (p. 355)

Tuk, M. A., Zhang, K., & Sweldens, S. (2015). The propagation of self-control: Self-control in one domain simultaneously improves self-control in other domains. *Journal of Experimental Psychology: General, 144,* 639–654. (p. 422)

Tully, T. (2003). Reply: The myth of a myth. *Current Biology, 13,* R426. (p. 249)

Turkheimer, E., Haley, A., Waldron, M., D'Onofrio, B., & Gottesman, I. I. (2003). Socioeconomic status modifies heritability of IQ in young children. *Psychological Science, 14,* 623–628. (p. 355)

Turner, J. C. (1987). *Rediscovering the social group: A self-categorization theory.* New York: Basil Blackwell. (p. 465)

Turner, J. C. (2007) Self-categorization theory. In R. Baumeister & K. Vohs (Eds.), *Encyclopedia of social psychology* (pp. 793–795). Thousand Oaks, CA: Sage. (p. 465)

Turner, N., Barling, J., & Zacharatos, A. (2002). Positive psychology at work. In C. R. Snyder & S. J. Lopez (Eds.), *The handbook of positive psychology* (pp. 715–728). New York: Oxford University Press. (p. B-12)

Turner, W. A., & Casey, L. M. (2014). Outcomes associated with virtual reality in psychological interventions: Where are we now? *Clinical Psychology Review, 34,* 634–644. (p. 576)

Turpin, A. (2005, April 3). The science of psi. *FT Weekend,* pp. W1, W2. (p. 241)

Tuvblad, C., Narusyte, J., Grann, M., Sarnecki, J., & Lichtenstein, P. (2011). The genetic and environmental etiology of antisocial behavior from childhood to emerging adulthood. *Behavior Genetics, 41,* 629–640. (p. 563)

Tversky, A. (1985, June). Quoted in K. McKean, Decisions, decisions. *Discover,* pp. 22–31. (p. 319)

Tversky, A., & Kahneman, D. (1974). Judgment under uncertainty: Heuristics and biases. *Science, 185,* 1124–1131. (pp. 319, A-6)

Twenge, J. M. (2001). Birth cohort changes in extraversion: A cross-temporal meta-analysis, 1966–1993. *Personality and Individual Differences, 30,* 735–748. (p. 510)

Twenge, J. M. (2006). *Generation me.* New York: Free Press. (p. 519)

Twenge, J. M., Abebe, E. M., & Campbell, W. K. (2010). Fitting in or standing out: Trends in American parents' choices for children's names, 1880–2007. *Social Psychology and Personality Science, 1,* 19–25. (p. 521)

Twenge, J. M., Baumeister, R. F., DeWall, C. N., Ciarocco, N. J., & Bartels, J. M. (2007). Social exclusion decreases prosocial behavior. *Journal of Personality and Social Psychology, 92,* 56–66. (p. 372)

Twenge, J. M., Baumeister, R. F., Tice, D. M., & Stucke, T. S. (2001). If you can't join them, beat them: Effects of social exclusion on aggressive behavior. *Journal of Personality and Social Psychology, 81,* 1058–1069. (p. 372)

Twenge, J. M., & Campbell, W. K. (2008). Increases in positive self-views among high school students: Birth-cohort changes in anticipated performance, self-satisfaction, self-liking, and self-competence. *Psychological Science, 19,* 1082–1086. (p. 503)

Twenge, J. M., Campbell, W. K., & Freeman, E. C. (2012). Generational differences in young adults' life goals, concern for others, and civic orientation, 1966–2009. *Journal of Personality and Social Psychology, 102*, 1045–1062. (p. 519)

Twenge, J. M., Campbell, W. K., & Gentile, B. (2013). Changes in pronoun use in American books and the rise of individualism, 1960–2008. *Journal of Cross-Cultural Psychology, 44*, 406–415. (p. 519)

Twenge, J. M., Catanese, K. R., & Baumeister, R. F. (2002). Social exclusion causes self-defeating behavior. *Journal of Personality and Social Psychology, 83*, 606–615. (p. 372)

Twenge, J. M., Gentile, B., DeWall, C. D., Ma, D., & Lacefield, K. (2008). *A growing disturbance: Increasing psychopathology in young people 1938–2007 in a meta-analysis of the MMPI.* Unpublished manuscript, San Diego State University, San Diego, CA. (pp. 548–549)

Twenge, J. M., Gentile, B., DeWall, C. N., Ma, D., Lacefield, K., & Schurtz, D. R. (2010). Birth cohort increases in psychopathology among young Americans, 1938–2007: A cross-temporal meta-analysis of the MMPI. *Clinical Psychology Review, 30*, 145–154. (p. 421)

Twenge, J. M., & Foster, J. D. (2010). Birth cohort increases in narcissistic personality traits among American college students, 1982–2009. *Social Psychological and Personality Science, 1*, 99–106. (p. 519)

Twenge, J. M., Zhang, L., & Im, C. (2004). It's beyond my control: A cross-temporal meta-analysis of increasing externality in locus of control, 1960–2002. *Personality and Social Psychology Review, 8*, 308–319. (p. 421)

U

Uchida, Y., & Kitayama, S. (2009). Happiness and unhappiness in East and West: Themes and variations. *Emotion, 9*, 441–456. (p. 436)

Uchino, B. N. (2009). Understanding the links between social support and physical health. *Perspectives on Psychological Science, 4*, 236–255. (p. 423)

Uchino, B. N., Cacioppo, J. T., & Kiecolt-Glaser, J. K. (1996). The relationship between social support and physiological processes: A review with emphasis on underlying mechanisms and implications for health. *Psychological Bulletin, 119*, 488–531. (p. 424)

Uchino, B. N., Uno, D., & Holt-Lunstad, J. (1999). Social support, physiological processes, and health. *Current Directions in Psychological Science, 8*, 145–148. (p. 424)

Udry, J. R. (2000). Biological limits of gender construction. *American Sociological Review, 65*, 443–457. (p. 175)

Uga, V., Lemut, M. C., Zampi, C., Zilli, I., & Salzarulo, P. (2006). Music in dreams. *Consciousness and Cognition, 15*, 351–357. (p. 99)

Ugander, J., Backstrom, L., Marlow, C., & Kleinberg, J. (2012). Structural diversity in social contagion. *Proceedings of the National Academy of Sciences of the United States of America, 109*, 5962–5966. (p. 373)

UN. (2010). *The world's women 2010: Trends and statistics.* New York: United Nations. (p. 464)

UN. (2011, November 17). *Discriminatory laws and practices and acts of violence against individuals based on their sexual orientation and gender identity: Report of the United Nations High Commissioner for Human Rights.* United Nations. Retrieved from http://www.ohchr.org/Documents/Issues/Discrimination/A.HRC.19.41_English.pdf (p. 464)

UNAIDS. (2010). *UNAIDS report on the global AIDS epidemic 2010.* Joint United Nations Programme on HIV/AIDS. Retrieved from http://www.unaids.org/globalreport/Global_report.htm (p. 413)

UNAIDS. (2013). *Global report: UNAIDS report on the global AIDS epidemic 2013.* Joint United Nations Programme on HIV/AIDS. Retrieved from http://www.unaids.org/sites/default/files/media_asset/UNAIDS_Global_Report_2013_en_1.pdf (p. 184)

UNAIDS. (2015, June 10). *World AIDS Day 2014 report.* Joint United Nations Programme on HIV/AIDS. Retrieved from http://www.unaids.org/en/resources/campaigns/World-AIDS-Day-Report-2014/factsheet (p. 413)

Underwood, E. (2013). Short-circuiting depression. *Science, 342*, 548–551. (p. 599)

UNESCO. (2013, September). *Adult and youth literacy* (UIS Fact Sheet No. 26). United Nations Education, Scientific and Cultural Organization. Retrieved from http://www.uis.unesco.org/literacy/Documents/fs26-2013-literacy-en.pdf (p. 464)

Ungerleider, S. (2005). *Mental training for peak performance, revised and updated edition.* New York: Rodale. (p. 345) Urbina, I. (2010, May 29). Documents show early worries about safety of rig. *The New York Times.* Retrieved from http://www.nytimes.com/2010/05/30/us/30rig.html (p. 322)

Urry, H. L., & Gross, J. J. (2010). Emotion regulation in older age. *Current Directions in Psychological Science, 19*, 352–357. (p. 166)

Urry, H. L., Nitschke, J. B., Dolski, I., Jackson, D. C., Dalton, K. M., Mueller, C. J., . . . Davidson, R. J. (2004). Making a life worth living: Neural correlates of well-being. *Psychological Science, 15*, 367–372. (p. 394)

U.S. Senate Intelligence Committee. (2004, July 9). *Report of the Select Committee on Intelligence on the U.S. intelligence community's prewar intelligence assessments on Iraq.* Washington, DC: Author. (p. 459)

V

Vaillant, G. E. (1977). *Adaptation to life.* New York: Little, Brown. (p. 309)

Vaillant, G. E. (2002). *Aging well: Surprising guideposts to a happier life from the landmark Harvard Study of Adult Development.* Boston: Little, Brown. (p. 424)

Vaillant, G. (2013, May). Quoted in S. Stossel, What makes us happy, revisited. *The Atlantic.* Retrieved from http://www.theatlantic.com/magazine/archive/2013/05/thanks-mom/309287/ (p. 373)

Valenstein, E. S. (1986). *Great and desperate cures: The rise and decline of psychosurgery.* New York: Basic Books. (p. 599)

Valentine, S. E., Bankoff, S. M., Poulin, R. M., Reidler, E. B., & Pantalone, D. W. (2015). The use of dialectical behavior therapy skills training as stand-alone treatment: A systematic review of the treatment outcome literature. *Journal of Clinical Psychology, 71*, 1–20. (p. 581)

Valkenburg, P. M., & Peter, J. (2009). Social consequences of the Internet for adolescents: A decade of research. *Current Directions in Psychological Science, 18*, 1–5. (pp. 155, 373, 374)

van Anders, S. M. (2012). Testosterone and sexual desire in healthy women and men. *Archives of Sexual Behavior, 41*, 1471–1484. (p. 181)

van Baaren, R. B., Holland, R. W., Kawakami, K., & van Knippenberg, A. (2004). Mimicry and prosocial behavior. *Psychological Science, 15*, 71–74. (p. 449)

van Baaren, R. B., Holland, R. W., Steenaert, B., & van Knippenberg, A. (2003). Mimicry for money: Behavioral consequences of imitation. *Journal of Experimental Social Psychology, 39*, 393–398. (p. 449)

Van Bockstaele, B., Verschuere, B., Tibboel, H., De Houwer, J., Crombez, G., & Koster, E. H. W. (2014). A review of current evidence for the causal impact of attentional bias on fear and anxiety. *Psychological Bulletin, 140*, 682–721. (p. 542)

Van Cauter, E., Holmback, U., Knutson, K., Leproult, R., Miller, A., Nedeltcheva, A., . . . Spiegel, K. (2007). Impact of sleep and sleep loss on neuroendocrine and metabolic function. *Hormone Research, 67*(1, Suppl. 1), 2–9. (p. 95)

Vance, E. B., & Wagner, N. N. (1976). Written descriptions of orgasm: A study of sex differences. *Archives of Sexual Behavior, 5*, 87–98. (p. 183)

van de Bongardt, D., Reitz, E., Sandfort, T., & Deković, M. (2015). A meta-analysis of the relations between three types of peer norms and adolescent sexual behavior. *Personality and Social Psychology Review, 19*, 203–234. (p. 186)

vanDellen, M. R., Campbell, W. K., Hoyle, R. H., & Bradfield, E. K. (2011). Compensating, resisting, and breaking: A meta-analytic examination of reactions to self-esteem threat. *Personality and Social Psychological Review, 15*, 51–74. (p. 517)

Vandenberg, S. G., & Kuse, A. R. (1978). Mental rotations: A group test of three-dimensional spatial visualization. *Perceptual and Motor Skills, 47*, 599–604. (pp. 192, 357)

van den Bos, K., & Spruijt, N. (2002). Appropriateness of decisions as a moderator of the psychology of voice. *European Journal of Social Psychology, 32*, 57–72. (p. B-13)

Van den Bussche, E., Van Den Noortgate, W., & Reynvoet, B. (2009). Mechanisms of masked priming: A meta-analysis. *Psychological Bulletin, 135*, 452–477. (p. 202)

VanderLaan, D. P., Forrester, D. L., Petterson, L. J., & Vasey, P. L. (2012). Offspring production among the extended relatives of Samoan men and fa'afafine. *PLOS ONE, 7*(4), e36088. doi:10.1371/journal.pone.0036088 (p. 190)

VanderLaan, D. P., & Vasey, P. L. (2011). Male sexual orientation in Independent Samoa: Evidence for fraternal birth order and maternal fecundity effects. *Archives of Sexual Behavior, 40*, 495–503. (p. 190)

van de Waal, E., Borgeaud, C., & Whiten, A. (2013). Potent social learning and conformity shape a wild primate's foraging decisions. *Science, 340*, 483–485. (p. 273)

van Dijk, W. W., van Koningsbruggen, G. M., Ouwerkerk, J. W., & Wesseling, Y. M. (2011). Self-esteem, self-affirmation, and schadenfreude. *Emotion, 11,* 1445–1449. (p. 517)

van Emmerik, A. A. P., Reijntjes, A., & Kamphuis, J. H. (2013). Writing therapy for posttraumatic stress: A meta-analysis. *Psychotherapy and Psychosomatics, 82,* 82–88. (p. 425)

van Engen, M. L., & Willemsen, T. M. (2004). Sex and leadership styles: A meta-analysis of research published in the 1990s. *Psychological Reports, 94,* 3–18. (p. 173)

van Gelder, J., Hershfield, H. E., & Nordgren, L. F. (2013). Vividness of the future self predicts delinquency. *Psychological Science, 24,* 974–980. (p. 152)

van Goozen, S. H. M., Fairchild, G., Snoek, H., & Harold, G. T. (2007). The evidence for a neurobiological model of childhood antisocial behavior. *Psychological Bulletin, 133,* 149–182. (p. 564)

van Haren, N. M., Rijsdijk, F., Schnack, H. G., Picchioni, M. M., Toulopoulou, T., Weisbrod, M., . . . Kahn, R. S. (2012). The genetic and environmental determinants of the association between brain abnormalities and schizophrenia: The Schizophrenia Twins and Relatives Consortium. *Biological Psychiatry, 71,* 915–921. (p. 558)

van Hemert, D. A., Poortinga, Y. H., & van de Vijver, F. J. R. (2007). Emotion and culture: A meta-analysis. *Cognition and Emotion, 21,* 913–943. (p. 401)

van Honk, J., Schutter, D. J., Bos, P. A., Kruijt, A.-W., Lentje, E. G. & Baron-Cohen, S. (2011). Testosterone administration impairs cognitive empathy in women depending on second-to-fourth digit ratio. *Proceedings of the National Academy of Sciences of the United States of America, 108,* 3448–3452. (p. 136)

Van Horn, J., Irimia, A., Torgerson, C., Chambers, M., Kikinis, R., & Toga, A. (2012). Mapping connectivity damage in the case of Phineas Gage. *PLOS ONE, 7*(5), e37454. doi:10.1371/journal.pone.0037454 (pp. 59, 60)

Van Houtem, C. M. H. H., Lain, M. L., Boomsma, D. I., Ligthart, L., van Wijk, A. J., & De Jongh, A. (2013). A review and meta-analysis of the heritability of specific phobia subtypes and corresponding fears. *Journal of Anxiety Disorders, 27,* 379–388. (p. 542)

van IJzendoorn, M. H., & Juffer, F. (2005). Adoption is a successful natural intervention enhancing adopted children's IQ and school performance. *Current Directions in Psychological Science, 14,* 326–330. (p. 355)

van IJzendoorn, M. H., & Juffer, F. (2006). The Emanual Miller Memorial Lecture 2006: Adoption as intervention. Meta-analytic evidence for massive catch-up and plasticity in physical, socio-emotional, and cognitive development. *Journal of Child Psychology and Psychiatry, 47,* 1228–1245. (pp. 70, 355)

van IJzendoorn, M. H., Juffer, F., & Poelhuis, C. W. K. (2005). Adoption and cognitive development: A meta-analytic comparison of adopted and nonadopted children's IQ and school performance. *Psychological Bulletin, 131,* 301–316. (p. 71)

van IJzendoorn, M. H., & Kroonenberg, P. M. (1988). Cross-cultural patterns of attachment: A meta-analysis of the strange situation. *Child Development, 59,* 147–156. (p. 140)

van IJzendoorn, M. H., Luijk, M. P. C. M., & Juffer, F. (2008). IQ of children growing up in children's homes: A meta-analysis on IQ delays in orphanages. *Merrill-Palmer Quarterly, 54,* 341–366. (pp. 143, 356)

Van Ittersum, K., & Wansink, B. (2012). Plate size and color suggestibility: The Delboeuf illusion's bias on serving and eating behavior. *Journal of Consumer Research, 39,* 215–228. (p. 382)

Van Kesteren, P. J. M., Asscheman, H., Megens, J. A. J., & Gooren, L. J. G. (1997). Mortality and morbidity in transsexual subjects treated with cross-sex hormones. *Clinical Endocrinology, 47,* 337–342. (p. 179)

Van Leeuwen, M. S. (1978). A cross-cultural examination of psychological differentiation in males and females. *International Journal of Psychology, 13,* 87–122. (p. 178)

van Praag, H. (2009). Exercise and the brain: Something to chew on. *Trends in Neuroscience, 32,* 283–290. (p. 427)

Van Yperen, N. W., & Buunk, B. P. (1990). A longitudinal study of equity and satisfaction in intimate relationships. *European Journal of Social Psychology, 20,* 287–309. (p. 480)

Van Zeijl, J., Mesman, J., van IJzendoorn, M. H., Bakermans-Kranenburg, M. J., Juffer, F., Stolk, M. N., . . . Alink, L. R. A. (2006). Attachment-based intervention for enhancing sensitive discipline in mothers of 1- to 3-year-old children at risk for externalizing behavior problems: A randomized controlled trial. *Journal of Consulting and Clinical Psychology, 74,* 994–1005. (p. 141)

van Zuiden, M., Geuze, E., Willemen, H. L., Vermetten, E., Maas, M., Amarouchi, K., . . . Heijnen, C. J. (2012). Glucocorticoid receptor pathway components predict posttraumatic stress disorder symptom development: A prospective study. *Biological Psychiatry, 71,* 309–316. (p. 144)

Varnum, M. E. W., Grossmann, I., Kitayama, S., & Nisbett, R. E. (2010). The origin of cultural differences in cognition: The social orientation hypothesis. *Current Directions in Psychological Science, 19,* 9–13. (p. 523)

Varnum, M. E. W., & Kitayama, S. (2011). What's in a name? Popular names are less common on frontiers. *Psychological Science, 22,* 176–183. (p. 521)

Vasey, P. L., & VanderLaan, D. P. (2010). An adaptive cognitive dissociation between willingness to help kin and nonkin in Samoan *fa'afafine. Psychological Science, 21,* 292–297. (p. 190)

Vaughn, E. L., de Dios, M. A., Steinfeldt, J. A., & Kratz, L. M. (2011). Religiosity, alcohol use attitudes, and alcohol use in a national sample of adolescents. *Psychology of Addictive Behaviors, 25,* 547–553. (p. 115)

Vaughn, K. B., & Lanzetta, J. T. (1981). The effect of modification of expressive displays on vicarious emotional arousal. *Journal of Experimental Social Psychology, 17,* 16–30. (p. 402)

Vazsonyi, A., Ksinan, A., Mikuška, J., & Jiskrova, G. (2015). The Big Five and adolescent adjustment: An empirical test across six cultures. *Personality and Individual Differences, 83,* 234–244. (p. 510)

Vecera, S. P., Vogel, E. K., & Woodman, G. F. (2002). Lower region: A new cue for figure–ground assignment. *Journal of Experimental Psychology: General, 13,* 194–205. (p. 220)

Veenhoven, R. (2014). *World database of happiness.* Retrieved from http://www. worlddatabaseofhappiness.eur.nl/ (p. 436)

Vekassy, L. (1977). Dreams of the blind. *Magyar Pszichologiai Szemle, 34,* 478–491. (p. 99)

Veltkamp, M., Custers, R., & Aarts, H. (2011). Motivating consumer behavior by subliminal conditioning in the absence of basic needs: Striking even while the iron is cold. *Journal of Consumer Psychology, 21,* 49–56. (p. 203)

Verbeek, M. E. M., Drent, P. J., & Wiepkema, P. R. (1994). Consistent individual differences in early exploratory behaviour of male great tits. *Animal Behaviour, 48,* 1113–1121. (p. 508)

Verduyn, P., Lee, D. S., Park, J., Shablack, H., Orvell, A., Bayer, J., . . . Kross, E. (2015). Passive Facebook usage undermines affective well-being: Experimental and longitudinal evidence. *Journal of Experimental Psychology: General, 144,* 480–488. (p. 373)

Verhaeghen, P., & Salthouse, T. A. (1997). Meta-analyses of age–cognition relations in adulthood: Estimates of linear and nonlinear age effects and structural models. *Psychological Bulletin, 122,* 231–249. (p. 159)

Vermetten, E., Schmahl, C., Lindner, S., Loewenstein, R. J., & Bremner, J. D. (2006). Hippocampal and amygdalar volumes in dissociative identity disorder. *American Journal of Psychiatry, 163,* 630–636. (p. 562)

Verwijmeren, T., Karremans, J. C., Stroebe, W., & Wigboldus, D. H. J. (2011a). The workings and limits of subliminal advertising: The role of habits. *Journal of Consumer Psychology, 21,* 206–213. (p. 203)

Verwijmeren, T., Karremans, J. C., Stroebe, W., Wigboldus, D. H. J., & Ooigen, I. (2011b). *Vicary's victory: Subliminal ads in movies work!* Poster session presented at the 12th Annual Convention of the Society for Personality and Social Psychology, San Antonio, TX. (p. 203)

Vezzali, L., Stathi, S., Giovannini, D., Capozza, D., & Trifiletti, E. (2015). The greatest magic of Harry Potter: Reducing prejudice. *Journal of Applied Social Psychology, 45,* 105–121. (p. 275)

Vigil, J. M. (2009). A socio-relational framework of sex differences in the expression of emotion. *Behavioral and Brain Sciences, 32,* 375–428. (p. 397)

Vigliocco, G., & Hartsuiker, R. J. (2002). The interplay of meaning, sound, and syntax in sentence production. *Psychological Bulletin, 128,* 442–472. (p. 331)

Vining, E. P. G., Freeman, J. M., Pillas, D. J., Uematsu, S., Carson, B. S., Brandt, J., . . . Zukerberg, A. (1997). Why would you remove half a brain? The outcome of 58 children after hemispherectomy—The Johns Hopkins experience: 1968 to 1996. *Pediatrics, 100,* 163–171. (p. 61)

Vinkhuyzen, A. A. E., van der Sluis, S., Posthuma, D., & Boomsma, D. I. (2009). The heritability of aptitude and exceptional talent across different domains in adolescents and young adults. *Behavior Genetics, 39,* 380–392. (p. 354)

Visalberghi, E. Addessi, E., Truppa, V., Spagnoletti, N., Ottoni, E., Izar, P., & Fragaszy, D. (2009). Selection of effective stone tools by wild bearded capuchin monkeys. *Current Biology, 19,* 213–217. (p. 327)

Visich, P. S., & Fletcher, E. (2009). Myocardial infarction. In J. K. Ehrman, P. M. Gordon, P. S. Visich, & S. J. Keleyian (Eds.), *Clinical exercise physiology* (2nd ed.). Champaign, IL: Human Kinetics. (p. 426)

Visser, B. A., Ashton, M. C., & Vernon, P. A. (2006). Beyond *g:* Putting multiple intelligences theory to the test. *Intelligence, 34,* 487–502. (p. 345)

Vita, A. J., Terry, R. B., Hubert, H. B., & Fries, J. F. (1998). Aging, health risks, and cumulative disability. *New England Journal of Medicine, 338,* 1035–1041. (p. 109)

Vitello, P. (2012, August 1). George A. Miller, a pioneer in cognitive psychology, is dead at 92. *The New York Times.* Retrieved from http://www.nytimes.com/2012/08/02/us/george-a-miller-cognitive-psychology-pioneer-dies-at-92.html?_r=0 (p. 287)

Vitiello, M. V. (2009). Recent advances in understanding sleep and sleep disturbances in older adults: Growing older does not mean sleeping poorly. *Current Directions in Psychological Science, 18,* 316–320. (p. 97)

Vitória, P. D., Salgueiro, M. F., Silva, S. A., & De Vries, H. (2009). The impact of social influence on adolescent intention to smoke: Combining types and referents of influence. *British Journal of Health Psychology, 14,* 681–699. (p. 116)

Vittengl, J. R., Clark, L. A., Dunn, T. W., & Jarrett, R. B. (2007). Reducing relapse and recurrence in unipolar depression: A comparative meta-analysis of cognitive–behavioral therapy's effects. *Journal of Consulting and Clinical Psychology, 75,* 475–488. (p. 596)

Vocks, S., Tuschen-Caffier, B., Pietrowsky, R., Rustenbach, S. J., Kersting, A., & Herpertz, S. (2010). Meta-analysis of the effectiveness of psychological and pharmacological treatments for binge eating disorder. *International Journal of Eating Disorders, 43,* 205–217. (p. 566)

Vogel, N., Schilling, Wahl, H.-W., Beekman, A.T.F., & Penninx, B. W. J. H. (2013). Time-to-death-related change in positive and negative affect among older adults approaching the end of life. *Psychology and Aging, 28,* 128–141. (p. 162)

Vohs, K. D., & Baumeister, R. F. (Eds.) (2011). *Handbook of self-regulation* (2nd ed.). New York: Guilford Press. (p. 421)

Vohs, K. D., Baumeister, R. F., & Schmeichel, B. J. (2012). Motivation, personal beliefs, and limited resources all contribute to self-control. *Journal of Experimental Social Psychology, 48,* 943–947. (p. 421)

Vohs, K. D., Mead, N. L., & Goode, M. R. (2006). The psychological consequences of money. *Science, 314,* 1154–1156. (p. 298)

Volkow, N. D., Wang, G. J., Kollins, S. H., Wigal, T. L., Newcorn, J. H., Telang, F., . . . Swanson, J. M. (2009). Evaluating dopamine reward pathway in ADHD: Clinical implications. *Journal of the American Medical Association, 302,* 1084–1091. (p. 532)

von Békésy, G. (1957, August). The ear. *Scientific American,* pp. 66–78. (p. 229)

von Hippel, W. (2007). Aging, executive functioning, and social control. *Current Directions in Psychological Science, 16,* 240–244. (p. 160)

von Hippel, W. & Trivers, R. (2011). The evolution and psychology of self-deception. *Behavioral and Brain Sciences, 34,* 1–56. (p. 518)

Vonk, J., Jett, S. E., & Mosteller, K. W. (2012). Concept formation in American black bears, *Ursus americanus. Animal Behaviour, 84,* 953–964. (p. 326)

von Senden, M. (1932). *The perception of space and shape in the congenitally blind before and after operation.* Glencoe, IL: Free Press. (p. 223)

von Stumm, S., Hell, B., & Chamorro-Premuzic, T. (2011). The hungry mind: Intellectual curiosity is the third pillar of academic performance. *Perspectives on Psychological Science, 6,* 574–588. (p. 362)

Vorona, R. D., Szklo-Coxe, M., Wu, A., Dubik, M., Zhao, Y., & Ware, J. C. (2011). Dissimilar teen crash rates in two neighboring Southeastern Virginia cities with different high school start times. *Journal of Clinical Sleep Medicine, 7,* 145–151. (p. 95)

Voss, U., Tuin, I., Schermelleh-Engel, K., & Hobson, A. (2011). Waking and dreaming: Related but structurally independent. Dream reports of congenitally paraplegic and deaf-mute persons. *Consciousness and Cognition, 20,* 673–687. (p. 99)

VPC. (2013, February 7). *States with higher gun ownership and weak gun laws lead nation in gun death.* Violence Policy Center. Retrieved from http://www.vpc.org/press/press-release-archive/states-with-higher-gun-ownership-and-weak-gun-laws-lead-nation-in-gun-death/ (p. 468)

Vukasović, T., & Bratko, D. (2015). Heritablity of personality: A meta-analysis of behavior genetic studies. *Psychological Bulletin, 141,* 769–785. (p. 510)

Vul, E., Harris, C., Winkielman, P., & Pashler, H. (2009a). Puzzlingly high correlations in fMRI studies of emotion, personality, and social cognition. *Perspectives on Psychological Science, 4,* 274–290. (p. 50)

Vul, E., Harris, C., Winkielman, P., & Pashler, H. (2009b). Reply to comments on "Puzzlingly High Correlations in fMRI Studies of Emotion, Personality, and Social Cognition." *Perspectives on Psychological Science, 4,* 319–324. (p. 50)

W

Waber, R. L., Shiv, B., Carmon, & Ariely, D. (2008). Commercial features of placebo and therapeutic efficacy. *Journal of the American Medical Association, 299,* 1016–1017. (p. 25)

Wacker, J., Chavanon, M.-L., & Stemmler, G. (2006). Investigating the dopaminergic basis of extraversion in humans: A multilevel approach. *Journal of Personality and Social Psychology, 91,* 177–187. (p. 507)

Wade, K. A., Garry, M., Read, J. D., & Lindsay, D. S. (2002). A picture is worth a thousand lies: Using false photographs to create false childhood memories. *Psychonomic Bulletin & Review, 9,* 597–603. (p. 308)

Wade, N. G., Worthington, E. L., Jr., & Vogel, D. L. (2006). Effectiveness of religiously tailored interventions in Christian therapy. *Psychotherapy Research, 17,* 91–105. (p. 591)

Wagar, B. M., & Cohen, D. (2003). Culture, memory, and the self: An analysis of the personal and collective self in long-term memory. *Journal of Experimental Social Psychology, 39,* 458–475. (p. 290)

Wagemans, J., Elder, J. H., Kubovy, M., Palmer, S. E., Peterson, M. A., Singh, M., & von der Heydt, R. (2012a). A century of Gestalt psychology in visual perception: I. Perceptual grouping and figure–ground organization. *Psychological Bulletin, 138,* 1172–1217. (p. 217)

Wagemans, J., Feldman, J., Gepshtein, S., Kimchi, R., Pomerantz, J. R, van der Helm, P., & van Leeuwen C. (2012b). A century of Gestalt psychology in visual perception: II. Conceptual and theoretical foundations. *Psychological Bulletin, 138,* 1218–1252. (p. 217)

Wagenmakers, E. J. (2014, June 25). *Bem is back: A skeptic's review of a meta-analysis on psi.* Retrieved from http://www.centerforopenscience.github.io/osc/2014/06/25/a-skeptics-review (p. 242)

Wagenmakers, E.-J., Wetzels, R., Borsboom, D., & van der Maas, H. (2011). Why psychologists must change the way they analyze their data: The case of psi. *Journal of Personality and Social Psychology, 100,* 1–12. (p. 242)

Wager, R. D., & Atlas, L. Y. (2013). How is pain influenced by cognition? Neuroimaging weighs in. *Perspectives on Psychological Science, 8,* 91–97. (p. 234)

Wager, T., Atlas, L. Y., Lindquist, M. A., Roy, M., Woo, C. W. & Kross, E. (2013). An fMRI-based neurologic signature of physical pain. *New England Journal of Medicine, 368,* 1388–1397. (p. 372)

Wagner, D., Becker, B., Koester, P., Gouzoulis-Mayfrank, E., & Daumann, J. (2012). A prospective study of learning, memory, and executive function in new MDMA users. *Addiction, 108,* 136–145. (p. 111)

Wagner, D. D., Altman, M., Boswell, R. G., Kelley, W. M., & Heatherton, T. F. (2013). Self-regulatory depletion enhances neural responses to rewards and impairs top-down control. *Psychological Science, 24,* 2262–2271. (p. 421)

Wagner, J., Gerstorf, D., Hoppmann, C., & Luszcz, M. A. (2013). The nature and correlates of self-esteem trajectories in late life. *Journal of Personality and Social Psychology, 105,* 139–153. (pp. 153, 166)

Wagstaff, G. (1982). Attitudes to rape: The "just world" strikes again? *Bulletin of the British Psychological Society, 13,* 275–283. (p. 443)

Wakefield, J. C., Schmitz, M. F., First, M. B., & Horwitz, A. V. (2007). Extending the bereavement exclusion for major depression to other losses: Evidence from the National Comorbidity Survey. *Archives of General Psychiatry, 64,* 433–440. (p. 548)

Wakefield, J. C., & Spitzer, R. L. (2002). Lowered estimates—but of what? *Archives of General Psychiatry, 59,* 129–130. (p. 540)

Walker, E., Shapiro, D., Esterberg, M., & Trotman, H. (2010). Neurodevelopment and schizophrenia: Broadening the focus. *Current Directions in Psychological Science, 19,* 204–208. (pp. 558, 560)

Walker, M. P., & van der Helm, E. (2009). Overnight therapy? The role of sleep in emotional brain processing. *Psychological Bulletin, 135,* 731–748. (p. 94)

Walker, W. R., Skowronski, J. J., & Thompson, C. P. (2003). Life is pleasant—and memory helps to keep it that way! *Review of General Psychology, 7,* 203–210. (p. 167)

Walkup, J. T., Albano, A. M., Piacentini, J., Birmaher, B., Compton, S. N., Sherrill, J. T., . . . Kendall, P. C. (2008). Cognitive behavioral therapy, sertraline, or a combination in childhood anxiety. *New England Journal of Medicine, 359,* 2753–2766. (p. 596)

Walkup, J. T., & Rubin, D. H. (2013). Social withdrawal and violence. Newtown, Connecticut. *New England Journal of Medicine, 368,* 399–401. (p. 533)

Wall, P. D. (2000). *Pain: The science of suffering.* New York: Columbia University Press. (p. 232)

Wallace, D. S., Paulson, R. M., Lord, C. G., & Bond, C. F., Jr. (2005). Which behaviors do attitudes predict? Meta-analyzing the effects of social pressure and perceived difficulty. *Review of General Psychology, 9,* 214–227. (p. 444)

Wallach, M. A., & Wallach, L. (1983). *Psychology's sanction for selfishness: The error of egoism in theory and therapy.* New York: Freeman. (p. 503)

Wallach, M. A., & Wallach, L. (1985, February). How psychology sanctions the cult of the self. *Washington Monthly,* pp. 46–56. (p. 503)

Walsh, J. L., Fielder, R. L., Carey, K. B., & Carey, M. P. (2013). Female college students' media use and academic outcomes: Results from a longitudinal cohort study. *Emerging Adulthood, 1,* 219–232. (p. 374)

Walsh, R. (2011). Lifestyle and mental health. *American Psychologist, 66,* 579–592. (p. 600)

Walster, E., Aronson, V., Abrahams, D., & Rottman, L. (1966). Importance of physical attractiveness in dating behavior. *Journal of Personality and Social Psychology, 4,* 508–516. (p. 477)

Walton, G. M., & Cohen, G. L. (2011). A brief social-belonging intervention improves academic and health outcomes of minority students. *Science, 331,* 1447–1451. (p. 361)

Walton, G. M., & Spencer S. J. (2009). Latent ability: Grades and test scores systematically underestimate the intellectual ability of negatively stereotyped students. *Psychological Science, 20,* 1132–1139. (p. 361)

Wampold, B. E. (2001). *The great psychotherapy debate: Models, methods, and findings.* Mahwah, NJ: Erlbaum. (p. 589)

Wampold, B. E. (2007). Psychotherapy: The humanistic (and effective) treatment. *American Psychologist, 62,* 857–873. (pp. 586, 589)

Wampold, B. E., Mondin, G. W., Moody, M., & Ahn, H. (1997). The flat earth as a metaphor for the evidence for uniform efficacy of bona fide psychotherapies: Reply to Crits-Christoph (1997) and Howard et al. (1997). *Psychological Bulletin, 122,* 226–230. (p. 586)

Wang, F., DesMeules, M., Luo, W., Dai, S., Lagace, C. & Morrison, H. (2011). Leisure-time physical activity and marital status in relation to depression between men and women: A prospective study. *Health Psychology, 30,* 204–211. (p. 426)

Wang, J., Häusermann, M., Wydler, H., Mohler-Kuo, M., & Weiss, M. G. (2012). Suicidality and sexual orientation among men in Switzerland: Findings from 3 probability surveys. *Journal of Psychiatric Research, 46,* 980–986. (p. 188)

Wang, J., He, L., Liping, J., Tian, J., & Benson, V. (2015). The "positive effect" is present in older Chinese adults: Evidence from an eye tracking study. *PLOS ONE, 10*(4), e0121372. doi:10.1371/journal.pone.0121372 (p. 166)

Wang, J., Leu, J., & Shoda, Y. (2011). When the seemingly innocuous "stings": Racial microaggressions and their emotional consequences. *Personality and Social Psychology Bulletin, 37,* 1666–1678. (p. 463)

Wang, Q., Bowling, N. A., & Eschleman, K. J. (2010). A meta-analytic examination of work and general locus of control. *Journal of Applied Psychology, 95,* 761–768. (p. 420)

Wang, S. (2014, March 29). How to think about the risk of autism. *The New York Times.* Retrieved from http://www.nytimes.com/2014/03/30/opinion/sunday/how-to-think-about-the-risk-of-autism.html (p. 136)

Wang, S.-H., Baillargeon, R., & Brueckner, L. (2004). Young infants' reasoning about hidden objects: Evidence from violation-of-expectation tasks with test trials only. *Cognition, 93,* 167–198. (p. 131)

Wang, X. T., & Dvorak, R. D. (2010). Sweet future: Fluctuating blood glucose levels affect future discounting. *Psychological Science, 21,* 183–188. (p. 422)

Wansink, B. (2014). *Slim by design: Mindless eating solutions for everyday life.* New York: Morrow. (p. 382)

Wansink, B., van Ittersum, K., & Painter, J. E. (2006). Ice cream illusions: Bowls, spoons, and self-served portion sizes. *American Journal of Preventive Medicine, 31,* 240–243. (p. 382)

Ward, A., & Mann, T. (2000). Don't mind if I do: Disinhibited eating under cognitive load. *Journal of Personality and Social Psychology, 78,* 753–763. (p. 385)

Ward, B. W., Dahlhamer, J. M., Galinsky, A. M., & Joestl, S. S. (2014, July 15). *Sexual orientation and health among U.S. adults: National Health Interview Survey, 2013* (National Health Statistics Reports No. 77). Retrieved from http://www.cdc.gov/nchs/data/nhsr/nhsr077.pdf (pp. 186, 188)

Ward, C. (1994). Culture and altered states of consciousness. In W. J. Lonner & R. Malpass (Eds.), *Psychology and culture* (pp. 59–64). Boston: Allyn & Bacon. (p. 104)

Ward, C. A. (2000). Models and measurements of psychological androgyny: A cross-cultural extension of theory and research. *Sex Roles, 43,* 529–552. (p. 178)

Ward, J. (2003). State of the art synaesthesia. *The Psychologist, 16,* 196–199. (p. 240)

Ward, K. D., Klesges, R. C., & Halpern, M. T. (1997). Predictors of smoking cessation and state-of-the-art smoking interventions. *Journal of Social Issues, 53,* 129–145. (p. 109)

Wardle, J., Cooke, L. J., Gibson, L., Sapochnik, M., Sheiham, A., & Lawson, M. (2003). Increasing children's acceptance of vegetables: A randomized trial of parent-led exposure. *Appetite, 40,* 155–162. (p. 236)

Wargo, E. (2007, December). Understanding the have-knots. *APS Observer,* pp. 18–21. (p. 428)

Wason, P. C. (1960). On the failure to eliminate hypotheses in a conceptual task. *Quarterly Journal of Experimental Psychology, 12,* 129–140. (p. 317)

Wason, P. C. (1981). The importance of cognitive illusions. *Behavioral and Brain Sciences, 4,* 356. (p. 318)

Wasserman, E. A. (1993). Comparative cognition: Toward a general understanding of cognition in behavior. *Psychological Science, 4,* 156–161. (p. 257)

Wasserman, E. A. (1995). The conceptual abilities of pigeons. *American Scientist, 83,* 246–255. (p. 326)

Wastell, C. A. (2002). Exposure to trauma: The long-term effects of suppressing emotional reactions. *Journal of Nervous and Mental Disorders, 190,* 839–845. (p. 425)

Waterman, A. S. (1988). Identity status theory and Erikson's theory: Commonalities and differences. *Developmental Review, 8,* 185–208. (p. 153)

Watkins, E. R. (2008). Constructive and unconstructive repetitive thought. *Psychological Bulletin, 134,* 163–206. (p. 545)

Watkins, J. G. (1984). The Bianchi (L.A. Hillside Strangler) case: Sociopath or multiple personality? *International Journal of Clinical and Experimental Hypnosis, 32,* 67–101. (p. 561)

Watson, D. (2000). *Mood and temperament.* New York: Guilford Press. (pp. 427, 432, 553)

Watson, J. B. (1913). Psychology as the behaviorist views it. *Psychological Review, 20,* 158–177. (pp. 80, 248)

Watson, J. B. (1924). The unverbalized in human behavior. *Psychological Review, 31,* 339–347. (p. 253)

Watson, J. B., & Rayner, R. (1920). Conditioned emotional reactions. *Journal of Experimental Psychology, 3,* 1–14. (p. 253)

Watson, R. I., Jr. (1973). Investigation into deindividuation using a cross-cultural survey technique. *Journal of Personality and Social Psychology, 25,* 342–345. (p. 457)

Watson, S. J., Benson, J. A., Jr., & Joy, J. E. (2000). Marijuana and medicine: Assessing the science base: A summary of the 1999 Institute of Medicine report. *Archives of General Psychiatry, 57,* 547–553. (p. 113)

Watters, E. (2010). *Crazy like us: The globalization of the American psyche.* New York: Free Press. (p. 530)

Way, B. M., Creswell, J. D., Eisenberger, N. I., & Lieberman, M. D. (2010). Dispositional mindfulness and depressive symptomatology: Correlations with limbic and self-referential neural activity during rest. *Emotion, 10,* 12–24. (p. 429)

Wayment, H. A., & Peplau, L. A. (1995). Social support and well-being among lesbian and heterosexual women: A structural modeling approach. *Personality and Social Psychology Bulletin, 21,* 1189–1199. (p. 164)

Weaver, J. B., Masland, J. L., & Zillmann, D. (1984). Effect of erotica on young men's aesthetic perception of their female sexual partners. *Perceptual and Motor Skills, 58,* 929–930. (p. 185)

Webb, W. B. (1992). *Sleep: The gentle tyrant* (2nd ed.). Bolton, MA: Anker. (p. 97)

Webley, K. (2009, June 15). Behind the drop in Chinese adoptions. *Time,* p. 55. (p. 464)

Webster, G. D., DeWall, C. N., Pond, R. S., Jr., Deckman, T., Jonason, P. K., Le, B. M., . . . Bator, R. J. (2014). The Brief Aggression Questionnaire: Psychometric and behavioral evidence for an efficient measure of trait aggression. *Aggressive Behavior, 40,* 120–139. (p. 26)

Wegner, D. M., & Ward, A. F. (2013, December). How Google is changing your brain. *Scientific American,* pp. 58–61. (p. 285)

Wei, Q., Fentress, H. M., Hoversten, M. T., Zhang, L., Hebda-Bauer, E. K., Watson, S. J., . . . Akil, H. (2012). Early-life forebrain glucocorticoid receptor overexpression increases anxiety behavior and cocaine sensitization. *Biological Psychiatry, 71,* 224–231. (p. 144)

Wei, W., Lu, H., Zhao, H., Chen, C., Dong, Q., & Zhou, X. (2012). Gender differences in children's arithmetic performance are accounted for by gender differences in language abilities. *Psychological Science, 23,* 320–330. (p. 357)

Weidman, A. C., Tracy, J. L., & Elliot, A. J. (in press). The benefits of following your pride: Authentic pride promotes achievement. *Journal of Personality.* (p. 520)

Weiland, B. J., Thayer, R. E., Depue, B. E., Sabbineni, A., Bryan, A. D., & Hutchison, K. E. (2015). Daily marijuana use is not associated with brain morphometric measures in adolescents or adults. *Journal of Neuroscience, 35,* 1505–1512. (p. 112)

Weingarden, H., & Renshaw, K. D. (2012). Early and late perceived pubertal timing as risk factors for anxiety disorders in adult women. *Journal of Psychiatric Research, 46,* 1524–1529. (p. 148)

Weingarten, G. (2002, March 10). Below the beltway. *The Washington Post,* p. WO3. (p. B-1)

Weinstein, N. D., Ryan, W. S., DeHaan, C. R., Przbylski, A. K., Legate, N., & Ryan, R. M. (2012). Parental autonomy support and discrepancies between implicit and explicit sexual identities: Dynamics of self-acceptance and defense. *Journal of Personality and Social Psychology, 102,* 815–832. (p. 500)

Weir, K. (2013, May). Captive audience. *Monitor on Psychology, 44,* 44–49. (p. 28)

Weisbuch, M., Ivcevic, Z., & Ambady, N. (2009). On being liked on the web and in the "real world": Consistency in first impressions across personal webpages and spontaneous behavior. *Journal of Experimental Social Psychology, 45,* 573–576. (p. 374)

Weiskrantz, L. (2009). *Blindsight: A case study spanning 35 years and new developments.* Oxford, England: Oxford University Press. (p. 85)

Weiskrantz, L. (2010). Looking back: Blindsight in hindsight. *The Psychologist, 23,* 356–358. (p. 85)

Weiss, A., & King, J. E. (2015). Great ape origins of personality maturation and sex differences: A study of orangutans and chimpanzees. *Journal of Personality and Social Psychology, 108,* 648–664. (p. 510)

Weiss, A., King, J. E., & Perkins, L. (2006). Personality and subjective well-being in orangutans (*Pongo pygmaeus* and *Pongo abelii*). *Journal of Personality and Social Psychology, 90,* 501–511. (p. 508)

Welch, J. M., Lu, J., Rodriquiz, R. M., Trotta, N. C., Peca, J., Ding, J.-D., . . . Feng, G. (2007). Cortico-striatal synaptic defects and OCD-like behaviours in *Sapap3*-mutant mice. *Nature, 448,* 894–900. (p. 542)

Welch, W. W. (2005, February 28). Trauma of Iraq war haunting thousands returning home. *USA Today.* Retrieved from http://usatoday30.usatoday.com/news/world/iraq/2005-02-28-cover-iraq-injuries_x.htm (p. 540)

Weller, S. C., & Davis-Beaty, K. (2002). Condom effectiveness in reducing heterosexual HIV transmission. *Cochrane Database of Systematic Reviews,* Issue 1, Article CD003255. doi:10.1002/14651858.CD003255 (p. 184)

Wells, D. L. (2009). The effects of animals on human health and well-being. *Journal of Social Issues, 65,* 523–543. (p. 425)

Wells, G. L. (1981). Lay analyses of causal forces on behavior. In J. Harvey (Ed.), *Cognition, social behavior and the environment* (pp. 309–324). Hillsdale, NJ: Erlbaum. (p. 246)

Wenze, S. J., Gunthert, K. C., & German, R. E. (2012). Biases in affective forecasting and recall in individuals with depression and anxiety symptoms. *Personality and Social Psychology Bulletin, 38,* 895–906. (p. 550)

Werner, L., Geisler, J., & Randler, C. (2015). Morningness as a personality predictor of punctuality. *Current Psychology, 34,* 130–139. (p. 88)

Westen, D. (1996, January). *Is Freud really dead? Teaching psychodynamic theory to introductory psychology.* Presentation at the 18th Annual National Institute on the Teaching of Psychology, St. Petersburg Beach, FL. (p. 497)

Westen, D. (1998). The scientific legacy of Sigmund Freud: Toward a psychodynamically informed psychological science. *Psychological Bulletin, 124,* 333–371. (p. 498)

Westen, D. (2007). *The political brain: The role of emotion in deciding the fate of the nation.* New York: PublicAffairs. (p. 390)

Westen, D., & Morrison, K. (2001). A multidimensional meta-analysis of treatments for depression, panic, and generalized anxiety disorder: An empirical examination of the status of empirically supported therapies. *Journal of Consulting and Clinical Psychology, 69,* 875–899. (p. 586)

Wetherell, J. L., Petkus, A. J., White, K. S., Nguyen, H., Kornblith, S., Andreescu, C., . . . Lenze, E. J. (2013). Antidepressant medication augmented with cognitive-behavioral therapy for generalized anxiety disorder in older adults. *American Journal of Psychiatry, 170,* 782–789. (p. 595)

Whalen, P. J., Shin, L. M., McInerney, S. C., Fisher, H., Wright, C. I., & Rauch, S. L. (2001). A functional MRI study of human amygdala responses to facial expressions of fear versus anger. *Emotion, 1,* 70–83. (p. 393)

Whang, W., Kubzansky, L, D., Kawachi, I., Rexrode, K. M., Kroenke, C. H., Glynn, R. J., . . . Albert, C. M. (2009). Depression and risk of sudden cardiac death and coronary heart disease in women. *Journal of the American College of Cardiology, 53,* 950–958. (p. 415)

Wheaton, A. G., Perry, G. S., Chapman, D. P., & Croft, J. B. (2012). Sleep disordered breathing and depression among U.S. adults: National Health and Nutrition Examination Survey, 2005–2008. *Sleep, 35,* 461–467. (p. 98)

Whelan, R., Conrod, P. J., Poline, J.-B., Lourdusamy, A., Banaschewski, T., Barker, G. J., . . . Garavan, H. (2012). Adolescent impulsivity phenotypes characterized by distinct brain networks. *Nature Neuroscience, 15,* 920–925. (p. 149)

Whisman, M. A., Johnson, D. P., & Rhee, S. H. (2014). A behavior genetic analysis of pleasant events, depressive symptoms, and their covariation. *Clinical Psychological Science, 2,* 535–544. (p. 546)

White, H. R., Brick, J., & Hansell, S. (1993). A longitudinal investigation of alcohol use and aggression in adolescence. *Journal of Studies on Alcohol, Supplement 11,* 62–77. (p. 469)

White, L., & Edwards, J. (1990). Emptying the nest and parental well-being: An analysis of national panel data. *American Sociological Review, 55,* 235–242. (p. 165)

White, R. A. (1998). Intuition, heart knowledge, and parapsychology. *Journal of the American Society for Psychical Research, 92,* 158–171. (p. 242)

White, R. E., Kross, E., & Duckworth, A. L. (2015). Spontaneous self-distancing and adaptive self-reflection across adolescence. *Child Development, 86,* 1272–1281. (p. 416)

Whitelock, C. F., Lamb, M. E., & Rentfrow, P. J. (2013). Overcoming trauma: Psychological and demographic characteristics of child sexual abuse survivors in adulthood. *Clinical Psychological Science, 1,* 351–362. (p. 144)

Whiten, A., & Boesch, C. (2001, January). Cultures of chimpanzees. *Scientific American,* pp. 60–67. (p. 328)

Whiten, A., & Byrne, R. W. (1988). Tactical deception in primates. *Behavioral and Brain Sciences, 11,* 233–244. (p. 20)

Whiten, A., Spiteri, A., Horner, V., Bonnie, K. E., Lambeth, S. P., Schapiro, S. J., & de Waal, F.B.M. (2007). Transmission of multiple traditions within and between chimpanzee groups. *Current Biology, 17,* 1038–1043. (p. 273)

Whiting, B. B., & Edwards, C. P. (1988). *Children of different worlds: The formation of social behavior.* Cambridge, MA: Harvard University Press. (p. 145)

Whitlock, J. R., Heynen, A. L., Shuler, M. G., & Bear, M. F. (2006). Learning induces long-term potentiation in the hippocampus. *Science, 313,* 1093–1097. (p. 295)

Whitley, B. E., Jr. (1999). Right-wing authoritarianism, social dominance orientation, and prejudice. *Journal of Personality and Social Psychology, 77,* 126–134. (p. 466)

Whitmer, R. A., Gustafson, D. R., Barrett-Connor, E. B., Haan, M. N., Gunderson, E. P., & Yaffe, K. (2008). Central obesity and increased risk of dementia more than three decades later. *Neurology, 71,* 1057–1064. (p. 383)

WHO. (1979). *Schizophrenia: An international followup study.* Chicester, England: Wiley. (p. 557)

WHO. (2000). *Effectiveness of male latex condoms in protecting against pregnancy and sexually transmitted infections.* World Health Organization. Retrieved from http://www.who.int/ (p. 184)

WHO. (2003). *The male latex condom: Specification and guidelines for condom procurement.* Department of Reproductive Health and Research, Family and Community Health, World Health Organization. Retrieved from http://apps.who.int/iris/bitstream/10665/42873/1/9241591277.pdf (p. 184)

WHO. (2004a). Prevalence, severity, and unmet need for treatment of mental disorders in the World Health Organization World Mental Health Surveys. *Journal of the American Medical Association, 291,* 2581–2590. (pp. 534, 535, 552)

WHO. (2004b). *Prevention of mental disorders: Effective interventions and policy options: Summary report.* Geneva, Switzerland: World Health Organization, Department of Mental Health and Substance Abuse. (p. 535)

WHO. (2004c). *Promoting mental health: Concepts, emerging evidence, practice: Summary report.* Geneva, Switzerland: World Health Organization, Department of Mental Health and Substance Abuse. (p. 535)

WHO. (2008a). *Mental health (nearly 1 million annual suicide deaths).* World Health Organization. Retrieved from http://www.who.int/mental_health/en (p. 553)

WHO. (2008b). *The numbers count: Mental disorders in America.* World Health Organization. Retrieved from http://www.nimh.nih.gov (p. 105)

WHO. (2010, September). *Mental health: Strengthening our response* (Fact Sheet No. 220). World Health Organization. Retrieved from http://www.who.int/mediacentre/factsheets/fs220/en/ (p. 527)

WHO. (2011). *Country reports and charts available.* World Health Organization. Retrieved from http://www.who.int/mental_health/prevention/suicide/country_reports/en/index.html (p. 553)

WHO. (2012, May). *Tobacco* (Fact Sheet No. 339). World Health Organization. Retrieved from http://www.who.int/mediacentre/factsheets/fs339/en/ (p. 108)

WHO. (2012). *WHO global estimates on prevalence of hearing loss: Mortality and burden of diseases and prevention of blindness and deafness.* World Health Organization. Retrieved from http://www.who.int/pbd/deafness/WHO_GE_HL.pdf (p. 228)

WHO. (2013, November). *Sexually transmitted infections (STIs)* (Fact Sheet No. 110). World Health Organization. Retrieved from http://www.who.int/mediacentre/factsheets/fs110/en/ (pp. 184, 413)

WHO. (2014). *Chain-free initiative.* World Health Organization. Retrieved from http://www.emro.who.int/mental-health/chain-free-initiative (p. 529)

WHO. (2014, October). *Mental disorders.* World Health Organization. Retrieved from http://www.who.int/mediacentre/factsheets/fs396/en/ (p. 552)

WHO. (2015). *Gender inequalities and HIV.* World Health Organization. Retrieved from http://www.who.int/gender/hiv_aids/en (p. 184)

Whooley, M. A., de Jonge, P., Vittinghoff, E., Otte, C., Moos, R., Carney, R. M., . . . Browner, W. S. (2008). Depressive symptoms, health behaviors, and risk of cardiovascular events in patients with coronary heart disease. *Journal of the American Medical Association, 300,* 2379–2388. (p. 416)

Whorf, B. L. (1956). Science and linguistics. In J. B. Carroll (Ed.), *Language, thought, and reality: Selected writings of Benjamin Lee Whorf* (pp. 207–219). Cambridge, MA: MIT Press. (p. 336)

Wicherts, J. M., Dolan, C. V., Carlson, J. S., & van der Maas, H. L. J. (2010). Raven's test performance of sub-Saharan Africans: Mean level, psychometric properties, and the Flynn effect. *Learning and Individual Differences, 20,* 135–151. (p. 359)

Wickelgren, I. (2009, September/October). I do not feel your pain. *Scientific American Mind,* pp. 51–57. (p. 231)

Wickelgren, W. A. (1977). *Learning and memory.* Englewood Cliffs, NJ: Prentice-Hall. (p. 290)

Widiger, T. A., & Costa, P. T., Jr. (2012). Integrating normal and abnormal personality structure: The five-factor model. *Journal of Personality, 80,* 1471–1505. (p. 511)

Wiens, A. N., & Menustik, C. E. (1983). Treatment outcome and patient characteristics in an aversion therapy program for alcoholism. *American Psychologist, 38,* 1089–1096. (p. 577)

Wierson, M., & Forehand, R. (1994). Parent behavioral training for child noncompliance: Rationale, concepts, and effectiveness. *Current Directions in Psychological Science, 3,* 146–149. (p. 264)

Wierzbicki, M. (1993). Psychological adjustment of adoptees: A meta-analysis. *Journal of Clinical Child Psychology, 22,* 447–454. (p. 70)

Wiesel, T. N. (1982). Postnatal development of the visual cortex and the influence of environment. *Nature, 299,* 583–591. (pp. 128, 223)

Wiesner, W. H., & Cronshow, S. P. (1988). A meta-analytic investigation of the impact of interview format and degree of structure on the validity of the employment interview. *Journal of Occupational Psychology, 61,* 275–290. (p. B-6)

Wigdor, A. K., & Garner, W. R. (1982). *Ability testing: Uses, consequences, and controversies.* Washington, DC: National Academy Press. (p. 366)

Wilcox, W. B., & Marquardt, E. (2011, December). *When baby makes three: How parenthood makes life meaningful and how marriage makes parenthood bearable.* Charlottesville: National Marriage Project, University of Virginia. (p. 141)

Wilder, D. A. (1981). Perceiving persons as a group: Categorization and intergroup relations. In D. L. Hamilton (Ed.), *Cognitive processes in stereotyping and intergroup behavior* (pp. 213–258). Hillsdale, NJ: Erlbaum. (p. 465)

Wiley, J., & Jarosz, A. F. (2012). Working memory capacity, attentional focus, and problem solving. *Current Directions in Psychological Science, 21,* 258–262. (p. 287)

Wilford, J. N. (1999, February 9). New findings help balance the cosmological books. *The New York Times.* Retrieved from http://www.nytimes.com/1999/02/09/science/new-findings-help-balance-the-cosmological-books.html (p. 76)

Wilkinson, P., & Goodyer, I. (2011). Non-suicidal self-injury. *European Child & Adolescent Psychiatry, 20,* 103–108. (p. 555)

Wilkinson, R., & Pickett, K. (2009). *The spirit level: Why greater equality makes societies stronger.* London: Bloomsbury Press. (pp. 435, 471)

Wilkowski, B. M., Robinson, M. D., & Troop-Gordon, W. (2011). How does cognitive control reduce anger and aggression? The role of conflict monitoring and forgiveness processes. *Journal of Personality and Social Psychology, 98,* 830–840. (p. 469)

Williams, C. L., & Berry, J. W. (1991). Primary prevention of acculturative stress among refugees. *American Psychologist, 46,* 632–641. (p. 407)

Williams, E. F., Dunning, D., & Kruger, J. (2013). The hobgoblin of consistency: Algorithmic judgment strategies underlie inflated self-assessments of performance. *Journal of Personality and Social Psychology, 104,* 976–994. (p. 518)

Williams, J. E., & Best, D. L. (1990). *Measuring sex stereotypes: A multination study.* Newbury Park, CA: Sage. (p. 173)

Williams, K. D. (2007). Ostracism. *Annual Review of Psychology, 58,* 425–452. (pp. 371, 372)

Williams, K. D. (2009). Ostracism: A temporal need-threat model. *Advances in Experimental Social Psychology, 41,* 275–313. (p. 371)

Williams, K. D., & Sommer, K. L. (1997). Social ostracism by coworkers: Does rejection lead to loafing or compensation? *Personality and Social Psychology Bulletin, 23,* 693–706. (p. 451)

Williams, L. A., & Bartlett, M. Y. (2015). Warm thanks: Gratitude expression facilitates social affiliation in new relationships via perceived warmth. *Emotion, 15,* 1–5. (p. 370)

Williams, L. A., & DeSteno, D. (2009). Adaptive social emotion or seventh sin? *Psychological Science, 20,* 284–288. (p. 520)

Williams, L. E., & Bargh, J. A. (2008). Experiencing physical warmth promotes interpersonal warmth. *Science, 322,* 606–607. (p. 240)

Williams, N. M., Zaharieva, I., Martin, A., Langley, K., Mantripragada, K., Fossdal, R., . . . Thapar, A. (2010). Rare chromosomal deletions and duplications in attention-deficit hyperactivity disorder: A genome-wide analysis. *The Lancet, 376,* 1401–1408. (p. 532)

Williams, S. L. (1987, August). *Self-efficacy and mastery-oriented treatment for severe phobias.* Paper presented at the 95th Annual Convention of the American Psychological Association, New York, NY. (p. 576)

Williams, T. (2015, March 17). Missouri executes killer who had brain injury. *The New York Times.* Retrieved from http://www.nytimes.com/2015/03/18/us/missouri-executes-killer-who-had-brain-injury.html (p. 60)

Williams, W. W., & Ceci, S. J. (2015). National hiring experiments reveal 2:1 faculty preference for women on STEM tenure track. *Proceedings of the National Academy of Sciences of the United States of America, 112,* 5360–5365. (p. 178)

Willingham, D. T. (2010, Summer). Have technology and multitasking rewired how students learn? *American Educator,* pp. 23–28, 42. (pp. 287, 375)

Willis, J., & Todorov, A. (2006). First impressions: Making up your mind after a 100-ms. exposure to a face. *Psychological Science, 17,* 592–598. (pp. 390, 396)

Willis, S. L., Tennstedt, S. L., Marsiske, M., Ball, K., Elias, J., Koepke, K. M., . . . Wright, E. (2006). Long-term effects of cognitive training on everyday functional outcomes in older adults. *Journal of the American Medical Association, 296,* 2805–2814. (p. 161)

Willmuth, M. E. (1987). Sexuality after spinal cord injury: A critical review. *Clinical Psychology Review, 7,* 389–412. (p. 185)

Willoughby, B. J., Carroll, J. S., & Busby, D. M. (2014). Differing relationship outcomes when sex happens before, on, or after first dates. *Journal of Sex Research, 51*, 52–61. (p. 23)

Wilson, A. E., & Ross, M. (2001). From chump to champ: People's appraisals of their earlier and present selves. *Journal of Personality and Social Psychology, 80*, 572–584. (p. 520)

Wilson, G. D., & Rahman, Q. (2005). *Born gay: The biology of sex orientation.* London: Peter Owen. (p. 191)

Wilson, R. S. (1979). Analysis of longitudinal twin data: Basic model and applications to physical growth measures. *Acta Geneticae Medicae et Gemellologiae, 28*, 93–105. (p. 129)

Wilson, R. S., Arnold, S. E., Schneider, J. A., Tang, Y., & Bennett, D. A. (2007). The relationship between cerebral Alzheimer's disease pathology and odour identification in old age. *Journal of Neurology, Neurosurgery, and Psychiatry, 78*, 30–35. (p. 162)

Wilson, R. S., & Matheny, A. P., Jr. (1986). Behavior genetics research in infant temperament: The Louisville Twin Study. In R. Plomin & J. Dunn (Eds.), *The study of temperament: Changes, continuities, and challenges* (pp. 81–97). Hillsdale, NJ: Erlbaum. (p. 140)

Wilson, S., Miller, G., & Horwitz, S. (2013, April 23). Boston bombing suspect cites U.S. wars as motivation, officials say. *The Washington Post.* Retrieved from https://www.washingtonpost.com/national/boston-bombing-suspect-cites-us-wars-as-motivation-officials-say/2013/04/23/324b9cea-ac29-11e2-b6fd-ba6f5f26d70e_story.html (p. 458)

Wilson, T. D. (2002). *Strangers to ourselves: Discovering the adaptive unconscious.* Cambridge, MA: Harvard University Press. (p. 81)

Wilson, T. D. (2006). The power of social psychological interventions. *Science, 313*, 1251–1252. (p. 361)

Wilson, T. D., Reinhard, D. A., Westgate, E. C., Gilbert, D. T., Ellerbeck, N., Hahn, C., . . . Shaked, A. (2014). Just think: The challenges of the disengaged mind. *Science, 345*, 75–77. (p. 368)

Wilson, W. A., & Kuhn, C. M. (2005, April). How addiction hijacks our reward system. *Cerebrum*, pp. 53–66. (p. 114)

Windholz, G. (1989). The discovery of the principles of reinforcement, extinction, generalization, and differentiation of conditional reflexes in Pavlov's laboratories. *Pavlovian Journal of Biological Science, 26*(2), 64–74. (p. 251)

Windholz, G. (1997). Ivan P. Pavlov: An overview of his life and psychological work. *American Psychologist, 52*, 941–946. (p. 250)

Windle, G., Hughes, D., Linck, P., Russell, I., & Woods, B. (2010). Is exercise effective in promoting mental well-being in older age? A systematic review. *Aging and Mental Health, 14*, 652–669. (p. 426)

Winkler, A., Dörsing, B., Rief, W., Shen, Y., & Glombiewski, J. A. (2013). Treatment of Internet addiction: A meta-analysis. *Clinical Psychology Review, 33*, 317–329. (p. 105)

Winner, E. (2000). The origins and ends of giftedness. *American Psychologist, 55*, 159–169. (p. 352)

Winter, W. C., Hammond, W. R., Green, N. H., Zhang, Z., & Bilwise, D. L. (2009). Measuring circadian advantage in Major League Baseball: A 10-year retrospective study. *International Journal of Sports Physiology and Performance, 4*, 394–401. (p. 92)

Wirth, J. H., Sacco, D. F., Hugenberg, K., & Williams, K. D. (2010). Eye gaze as relational evaluation: Averted eye gaze leads to feelings of ostracism and relational devaluation. *Personality and Social Psychology Bulletin, 36*, 869–882. (p. 372)

Wirz-Justice, A. (2009). From the basic neuroscience of circadian clock function to light therapy for depression: On the emergence of chronotherapeutics. *Journal of Affective Disorders, 116*, 159–160. (p. 589)

Wiseman, R., & Greening, E. (2002). The mind machine: A mass participation experiment into the possible existence of extra-sensory perception. *British Journal of Psychology, 93*, 487–499. (p. 242)

Witek-Janusek, L., Albuquerque, K., Chroniak, K. R., Chroniak, C., Durazo, R., & Mathews, H. L. (2008). Effect of mindfulness based stress reduction on immune function, quality of life and coping in women newly diagnosed with early stage breast cancer. *Brain, Behavior, and Immunity, 22*, 969–981. (p. 428)

Witelson, S. F., Kigar, D. L., & Harvey, T. (1999). The exceptional brain of Albert Einstein. *The Lancet, 353*, 2149–2153. (p. 60)

Witt, J. K., & Brockmole, J. R. (2012). Action alters object identification: Wielding a gun increases the bias to see guns. *Journal of Experimental Psychology: Human Perception and Performance, 38*, 1159–1167. (p. 207)

Witt, J. K., Linkenauger, S. A., & Proffitt, D. R. (2012). Get me out of this slump! Visual illusions improve sports performance. *Psychological Science, 23*, 397–399. (p. 207)

Witt, J. K., & Proffitt, D. R. (2005). See the ball, hit the ball: Apparent ball size is correlated with batting average. *Psychological Science, 16*, 937–938. (p. 207)

Witters, D. (2014, October 20). *U.S. adults with children at home have greater joy, stress.* Retrieved from http://www.gallup.com/poll/178631/adults-children-home-greater-joy-stress.aspx (pp. 145–146, 165)

Wittgenstein, L. (1922). *Tractatus logico-philosophicus* (C. K. Ogden, Trans.). New York: Harcourt, Brace. (p. 76)

Witvliet, C. V. O., & Vrana, S. R. (1995). Psychophysiological responses as indices of affective dimensions. *Psychophysiology, 32*, 436–443. (p. 393)

Wixted, J. T., & Ebbesen, E. B. (1991). On the form of forgetting. *Psychological Science, 2*, 409–415. (p. 303)

Wolff, J. J., Gu, H., Gerig, G., Elison, J. T., Styner, M., Gouttard, S., . . . Piven, J. (2012). Differences in white matter fiber tract development present from 6 to 24 months in infants with autism. *American Journal of Psychiatry, 169*, 589–600. (p. 137)

Wolfson, A. R., & Carskadon, M. A. (1998). Sleep schedules and daytime functioning in adolescents. *Child Development, 69*, 875–887. (p. 100)

Wolke, D., Copeland, W. E., Angold, A., & Costello, E. J. (2013). Impact of bullying in childhood on adult health, wealth, crime, and social outcomes. *Psychological Science, 24*, 1958–1970. (p. 144)

Wollmer, M. A., de Boer , C., Kalak, N., Beck, J., Götz, T., Schmidt, T., . . . Kruger, T. H. C. (2012). Facing depression with botulinum toxin: A randomized controlled trial. *Journal of Psychiatric Research, 46*, 574–581. (p. 402)

Wolpe, J. (1958). *Psychotherapy by reciprocal inhibition.* Stanford, CA: Stanford University Press. (p. 575)

Wolpe, J., & Plaud, J. J. (1997). Pavlov's contributions to behavior therapy: The obvious and the not so obvious. *American Psychologist, 52*, 966–972. (p. 575)

Wonderlich, S. A., Joiner, T. E., Jr., Keel, P. K., Williamson, D. A., & Crosby, R. D. (2007). Eating disorder diagnoses: Empirical approaches to classification. *American Psychologist, 62*, 167–180. (p. 565)

Wong, D. F., Wagner, H. N., Tune, L. E., Dannals, R. F., Pearlson, G. D., Links, J. M., . . . Gjedde, A. (1986). Positron emission tomography reveals elevated D2 dopamine receptors in drug-naive schizophrenics. *Science, 234*, 1588–1593. (p. 558)

Wong, M. M., & Csikszentmihalyi, M. (1991). Affiliation motivation and daily experience: Some issues on gender differences. *Journal of Personality and Social Psychology, 60*, 154–164. (p. 174)

Wood, J. M. (2003, May 19). Quoted in R. Mestel, Rorschach tested: Blot out the famous method? Some experts say it has no place in psychiatry. *The Los Angeles Times.* Retrieved from http://articles.latimes.com/2003/may/19/health/he-rorschach19 (p. 498)

Wood, J. M. (2006, Spring). *The controversy over Exner's comprehensive system for the Rorschach: The critics speak.* Retrieved from http://works.bepress.com/james_wood/7/ (p. 498)

Wood, J. M., Bootzin, R. R., Kihlstrom, J. F., & Schacter, D. L. (1992). Implicit and explicit memory for verbal information presented during sleep. *Psychological Science, 3*, 236–239. (p. 305)

Wood, J. M., Garb, H. N., Nezworski, M. T., Lilienfeld, S. O., & Duke, M. C. (2015). A second look at the validity of widely used Rorschach indices: Comment on Mihura, Meyer, Dumitrascu, and Bombel (2013). *Psychological Bulletin, 141*, 236–249. (p. 498)

Wood, J. M., Lilienfeld, S. O., Nezworski, M. T., Garb, H. N., Allen, K. H., & Wildermuth, J. L. (2010). Validity of Rorschach inkblot scores for discriminating psychopaths from nonpsychopaths in forensic populations: A meta-analysis. *Psychological Assessment, 22*, 336–349. (p. 498)

Wood, J. V., Heimpel, S. A., Manwell, L. A., & Whittington, E. J. (2009). This mood is familiar and I don't deserve to feel better anyway: Mechanisms underlying self-esteem differences in motivation to repair sad moods. *Journal of Personality and Social Psychology, 96*, 363–380. (p. 517)

Wood, J. V., Saltzberg, J. A., & Goldsamt, L. A. (1990a). Does affect induce self-focused attention? *Journal of Personality and Social Psychology, 58*, 899–908. (p. 551)

Wood, J. V., Saltzberg, J. A., Neale, J. M., Stone, A. A., & Rachmiel, T. B. (1990b). Self-focused attention, coping responses, and distressed mood in everyday life. *Journal of Personality and Social Psychology, 58*, 1027–1036. (p. 551)

Wood, W. (1987). Meta-analytic review of sex differences in group performance. *Psychological Bulletin, 102*, 53–71. (p. 173)

Wood, W., & Eagly, A. H. (2002). A cross-cultural analysis of the behavior of women and men: Implications for the origins of sex differences. *Psychological Bulletin, 128*, 699–727. (p. 173)

Wood, W., & Eagly, A. H. (2007). Social structural origins of sex differences in human mating. In S. W. Gagestad & J. A. Simpson (Eds.), *The evolution of mind: Fundamental questions and controversies* (pp. 383–390). New York: Guilford Press. (p. 173)

Wood, W., Kressel, L., Joshi, P. D., & Louie, B. (2014). Meta-analysis of menstrual cycle effects on women's mate preferences. *Emotion Review, 6*, 229–249. (p. 181)

Wood, W., Labrecque, J. S., Lin, P.-T., & Rúnger, D. (2014). Habits in dual process models. In J. Sherman, B. Gawronski, & Y. Trope (Eds.), *Dual process theories of the social mind* (pp. 371–385). New York: Guilford Press. (p. 246)

Wood, W., Lundgren, S., Ouellette, J. A., Busceme, S., & Blackstone, T. (1994). Minority influence: A meta-analytic review of social influence processes. *Psychological Bulletin, 115*, 323–345. (p. 460)

Woods, N. F., Dery, G. K., & Most, A. (1983). Recollections of menarche, current menstrual attitudes, and premenstrual symptoms. In S. Golub (Ed.), *Menarche: The transition from girl to woman* (pp. 87–97). Lexington, MA: Lexington Books. (p. 176)

Woolcock, N. (2004, September 3). Driver thought everyone else was on wrong side. *The Times*, p. 22. (p. 451)

Woolett, K., & Maguire, E. A. (2011). Acquiring "the knowledge" of London's layout drives structural brain changes. *Current Biology, 21*, 2109–2114. (p. 293)

Woolley, A. W., Chabris, C. F., Pentland, A., Hasmi, N., & Malone, T. W. (2010). Evidence for a collective intelligence factor in the performance of human groups. *Science, 330*, 686–688. (p. B-12)

World Economic Forum. (2014). *The global gender gap report 2014*. Retrieved from http://www3.weforum.org/docs/GGGR14/GGGR_CompleteReport_2014.pdf (p. 178)

World Federation for Mental Health. (2005). *ADHD: The hope behind the hype*. Retrieved from http://www.wfmh.org (p. 532)

Worldwatch Institute. (2013). *Meat production continues to rise* (Product No. VST116). Retrieved from http://www.worldwatch.org/node/5443#notes (p. 28)

Worobey, J., & Blajda, V. M. (1989). Temperament ratings at 2 weeks, 2 months, and 1 year: Differential stability of activity and emotionality. *Developmental Psychology, 25*, 257–263. (p. 140)

Wortham, J. (2010, May 13). Cellphones now used more for data than for calls. *The New York Times*. Retrieved from http://www.nytimes.com/2010/05/14/technology/personaltech/14talk.html?_r=0 (p. 373)

Wortman, C. B., & Silver, R. C. (1989). The myths of coping with loss. *Journal of Consulting and Clinical Psychology, 57*, 349–357. (p. 168)

Wren, C. S. (1999, April 8). Drug survey of children finds middle school a pivotal time. *The New York Times*. Retrieved from http://www.nytimes.com (p. 116)

Wright, I. C., Rabe-Hesketh, S., Woodruff, P. W. R., David, A. S., Murray, R. M., & Bullmore, E. T. (2000). Meta-analysis of regional brain volumes in schizophrenia. *American Journal of Psychiatry, 157*, 16–25. (p. 558)

Wright, J. (2006, March 16). *Boomers in the bedroom: Sexual attitudes and behaviours in the boomer generation*. Retrieved from http://www.ipsos-na.com/news-polls/pressrelease.aspx?id=3011 (p. 158)

Wright, P., Takei, N., Rifkin, L., & Murray, R. M. (1995). Maternal influenza, obstetric complications, and schizophrenia. *American Journal of Psychiatry, 152*, 1714–1720. (p. 558)

Wright, P. H. (1989). Gender differences in adults' same- and cross-gender friendships. In R. G. Adams & R. Blieszner (Eds.), *Older adult friendships: Structure and process* (pp. 197–221). Newbury Park, CA: Sage. (p. 174)

Wrosch, C., & Miller, G. E. (2009). Depressive symptoms can be useful: Self-regulatory and emotional benefits of dysphoric mood in adolescence. *Journal of Personality and Social Psychology, 96*, 1181–1190. (p. 545)

Wrzesniewski, A., & Dutton, J. E. (2001). Crafting a job: Revisioning employees as active crafters of their work. *Academy of Management Review, 26*, 179–201. (p. B-1)

Wrzesniewski, A., McCauley, C. R., Rozin, P., & Schwartz, B. (1997). Jobs, careers, and callings: People's relations to their work. *Journal of Research in Personality, 31*, 21–33. (p. B-1)

Wrzesniewski, A., Schwartz, B., Cong, X., Kane, M., Omar, A., & Kolditz, T. (2014). Multiple types of motives don't multiply the motivation of West Point cadets. *Proceedings of the National Academy of Sciences of the United States of America, 111*, 10990–10995. (p. 271)

Wrzus, C., Hänel, M., Wagner, J., & Neyer, F. J. (2012). Social network changes and life events across the life span: A meta-analysis. *Psychological Bulletin, 139*, 53–80. (p. 166)

Wulsin, L. R., Vaillant, G. E., & Wells, V. E. (1999). A systematic review of the mortality of depression. *Psychosomatic Medicine, 61*, 6–17. (p. 415)

Wyatt, J. K., & Bootzin, R. R. (1994). Cognitive processing and sleep: Implications for enhancing job performance. *Human Performance, 7*, 119–139. (pp. 99, 305)

Wyatt, R. J., Henter, I., & Sherman-Elvy, E. (2001, October). Tantalizing clues to preventing schizophrenia. *Cerebrum*, pp. 15–30. (p. 559)

Wynn, K. (1992). Addition and subtraction by human infants. *Nature, 358*, 749–759. (p. 131)

Wynn, K. (2000). Findings of addition and subtraction in infants are robust and consistent: Reply to Wakeley, Rivera, and Langer. *Child Development, 71*, 1535–1536. (p. 131)

Wynn, K. (2008). Some innate foundations of social and moral cognition. In K. Wynn (Ed.), *The innate mind: Vol. 3. Foundations and the future* (pp. 330–347). New York: Oxford University Press. (p. 131)

Wynne, C. D. L. (2004). *Do animals think?* Princeton, NJ: Princeton University Press. (p. 335)

Wynne, C. (2008). Aping language: A skeptical analysis of the evidence for non-human primate language. *Skeptic, 13*(4), 10–13. (p. 335)

X

Xie, L., Kang, H., Xu, Q., Chen, M. J., Liao, Y., Thiyagarajan, M., . . . Nedergaard, M. (2013). Sleep drives metabolite clearance from the adult brain. *Science, 342*, 373–377. (p. 93)

Xu, Y., & Corkin, S. (2001). H.M. revisits the Tower of Hanoi Puzzle. *Neuropsychology, 15*, 69–79. (p. 302)

Y

Yamagata, S., Suzuki, A., Ando, J., Ono, Y., Kijima, N., Yoshimura. K., . . . Jang, K. L. (2006). Is the genetic structure of human personality universal? A cross-cultural twin study from North America, Europe, and Asia. *Journal of Personality and Social Psychology, 90*, 987–998. (p. 510)

Yang, G., Lai, G. S. W., Cichon, J., Ma, L., Li, W., & Gan, W.-B. (2014). Sleep promotes branch-specific formation of dendritic spines after learning. *Science, 344*, 1173–1178. (p. 93)

Yang, Y., & Raine, A. (2009). Prefrontal structural and functional brain imaging findings in antisocial, violent, and psychopathic individuals: A meta-analysis. *Psychiatry Research: Neuroimaging, 174*, 81–88. (p. 60)

Yankelovich. (1995, May/June). Growing old. *The American Enterprise*, p. 108. (p. 158)

Yarkoni, T. (2010). Personality in 100,000 words: A large-scale analysis of personality and word use among bloggers. *Journal of Research in Personality, 44*, 363–373. (p. 512)

Yarnell, P. R., & Lynch, S. (1970). Retrograde memory immediately after concussion. *The Lancet, 295*, 863–865. (p. 296)

Yates, A. (1989). Current perspectives on the eating disorders: I. History, psychological and biological aspects. *Journal of the American Academy of Child and Adolescent Psychiatry, 28*, 813–828. (p. 565)

Yates, A. (1990). Current perspectives on the eating disorders: II. Treatment, outcome, and research directions. *Journal of the American Academy of Child and Adolescent Psychiatry, 29*, 1–9. (p. 565)

Yates, W. R. (2000). Testosterone in psychiatry. *Archives of General Psychiatry, 57*, 155–156. (p. 181)

Ybarra, O. (1999). Misanthropic person memory when the need to self-enhance is absent. *Personality and Social Psychology Bulletin, 25*, 261–269. (p. 517)

Yeager, D. S., Johnson, R., Spitzer, B. J., Trzesniewski, K. H., Powers, J., & Dweck, C. S. (2014). The far-reaching effects of believing people can change: Implicit theories of personality shape stress, health, and achievement during adolescence. *Journal of Personality and Social Psychology, 106*, 867–884. (p. 362)

Yeager, D. S., Miu, A. S., Powers, J., & Dweck, C. S. (2013). Implicit theories of personality and attributions of hostile intent: A meta-analysis, an experiment, and a longitudinal intervention. *Child Development, 84*, 1651–1667. (p. 362)

Yerkes, R. M., & Dodson, J. D. (1908). The relation of strength of stimulus to rapidity of habit-formation. *Journal of Comparative Neurology and Psychology, 18,* 459–482. (p. 368)

Yeung, J. W. K., Chan, Y, & Lee, B. L. K. (2009). Youth religiosity and substance use: A meta-analysis from 1995 to 2007. *Psychological Reports, 105,* 255–266. (p. 115)

Yiend, J., Parnes, C., Shepherd, K., Roche, M.-K., & Cooper, M. J. (2014). Negative self-beliefs in eating disorders: A cognitive-bias-modification study. *Clinical Psychological Science, 2,* 756–766. (p. 565)

Yoshikawa, H., Aber, J. L., & Beardslee, W. R. (2012). The effects of poverty on the mental, emotional, and behavioral health of children and youth: Implications for prevention. *American Psychologist, 67,* 272–284. (p. 602)

YOU Magazine. (2009, September 10). Wow, look at Caster now! Quoted in *The Telegraph,* September 8, 2009. (p. 177)

Young, C. B., Wu, S. S., & Menon, V. (2012). The neurodevelopmental basis of math anxiety. *Psychological Science, 23,* 492–501. (p. 53)

Young, S. G., Hugenberg, K., Bernstein, M. J., & Sacco, D. F. (2012). Perception and motivation in face recognition: A critical review of theories of the cross-race effect. *Personality and Social Psychology Review, 16,* 116–142. (p. 467)

Youngentob, S. L., & Glendinning, J. I. (2009). Fetal ethanol exposure increases ethanol intake by making it smell and taste better. *Proceedings of the National Academy of Sciences of the United States of America, 106,* 5359. (p. 124)

Youngentob, S. L., Kent, P. F., Scheehe, P. R., Molina, J. C., Spear, N. E., & Youngentob, L. M. (2007). Experience-induced fetal plasticity: The effect of gestational ethanol exposure on the behavioral and neurophysiologic olfactory response to ethanol odor in early postnatal and adult rats. *Behavioral Neuroscience, 121,* 1293–1305. (p. 124)

Younger, J., Aron, A., Parke, S., Chatterjee, N., & Mackey, S. (2010) Viewing pictures of a romantic partner reduces experimental pain: Involvement of neural reward systems. *PLOS ONE, 5*(10), e13309. doi:10.1371/journal.pone.0013309 (p. 370)

Yücel, M., Solowij, N., Respondek, C., Whittle, S., Fornito, A., Pantelis, C., & Lubman, D. I. (2008). Regional brain abnormalities associated with long-term cannabis use. *Archives of General Psychiatry, 65,* 694–701. (p. 112)

Yuki, M., Maddux, W. W., & Masuda. T. (2007). Are the windows to the soul the same in the East and West? Cultural differences in using the eyes and mouth as cues to recognize emotions in Japan and the United States. *Journal of Experimental Social Psychology, 43,* 303–311. (p. 401)

Z

Zagorsky, J. L. (2007). Do you have to be smart to be rich? The impact of IQ on wealth, income and financial distress. *Intelligence, 35,* 489–501. (p. 343)

Zajonc, R. B. (1965). Social facilitation. *Science, 149,* 269–274. (p. 455)

Zajonc, R. B. (1980). Feeling and thinking: Preferences need no inferences. *American Psychologist, 35,* 151–175. (p. 389)

Zajonc, R. B. (1984). On the primacy of affect. *American Psychologist, 39,* 117–123. (p. 389)

Zajonc, R. B. (1984, July 22). Quoted in D. Goleman, Rethinking IQ tests and their value. *The New York Times,* p. D22. (p. 346)

Zajonc, R. B. (2001). Mere exposure: A gateway to the subliminal. *Current Directions in Psychological Science, 10,* 224–228. (p. 475)

Zajonc, R. B., & Markus, G. B. (1975). Birth order and intellectual development. *Psychological Review, 82,* 74–88. (p. A-8)

Zak, P. J. (2012). *The moral molecule: The source of love and prosperity.* New York: Dutton. (p. 46)

Zalta, A. K. (2011). A meta-analysis of anxiety symptom prevention with cognitive-behavioral interventions. *Journal of Anxiety Disorders, 25,* 749–760. (p. 581)

Zaslavsky, O., Palgi, Y., Rillamas-Sun, E., LaCroix, A. Z., Schnall, E., Woods, N. F., . . . Shrira, A. (2015). Dispositional optimism and terminal decline in global quality of life. *Developmental Psychology, 51,* 856–863. (p. 423)

Zaval, L., Keenan, E. A., Johnson, E. J., & Weber, E. U. (2014). How warm days increase belief in global warming. *Nature Climate Change, 4,* 143–147. (p. 320)

Zeelenberg, R., Wagenmakers, E.-J., & Rotteveel, M. (2006). The impact of emotion on perception. *Psychological Science, 17,* 287–291. (p. 389)

Zeidner, M. (1990). Perceptions of ethnic group modal intelligence: Reflections of cultural stereotypes or intelligence test scores? *Journal of Cross-Cultural Psychology, 21,* 214–231. (p. 358)

Zeineh, M. M., Engel, S. A., Thompson, P. M., & Bookheimer, S. Y. (2003). Dynamics of the hippocampus during encoding and retrieval of face-name pairs. *Science, 299,* 577–580. (p. 293)

Zelenski, J. M., & Nisbet, E. K. (2014). Happiness and feeling connected: The distinct role of nature relatedness. *Environmental Behavior, 46,* 3–23. (p. 375)

Zell, E., & Alicke, M. D. (2010). The local dominance effect in self-evaluation: Evidence and explanations. *Personality and Social Psychology Review, 14,* 368–384. (p. 435)

Zell, E., Krizan, Z., & Teeter, S. R. (2015). Evaluating gender similarities and differences using metasynthesis. *American Psychologist, 70,* 10–20. (p. 172)

Zhang, J., Fang, L., Yow-Wu, B. W., & Wieczorek, W. F. (2013). Depression, anxiety, and suicidal ideation among Chinese Americans: A study of immigration-related factors. *Journal of Nervous and Mental Disease, 201,* 17–22. (p. 548)

Zhong, C.-B., Dijksterhuis, A., & Galinsky, A. D. (2008). The merits of unconscious thought in creativity. *Psychological Science, 19,* 912–918. (p. 325)

Zhong, C.-B., & Leonardelli, G. J. (2008). Cold and lonely: Does social exclusion literally feel cold? *Psychological Science, 19,* 838–842. (p. 240)

Zhu, W. X., Lu, L., & Hesketh, T. (2009). China's excess males, sex selective abortion, and one child policy: Analysis of data from 2005 national intercensus survey. *British Medical Journal, 338,* b1211. http://dx.doi.org/10.1136/bmj.b1211 (p. 464)

Zilbergeld, B. (1983). *The shrinking of America: Myths of psychological change.* Boston: Little, Brown. (p. 584)

Zillmann, D. (1986). *Effects of prolonged consumption of pornography* [Background paper for the Surgeon General's Workshop on Pornography and Public Health, June 22–24, 1986]. Retrieved from http://130.14.81.99/ps/access/NNBCKV.pdf (p. 389)

Zillmann, D. (1989). Effects of prolonged consumption of pornography. In D. Zillmann & J. Bryant (Eds.), *Pornography: Research advances and policy considerations* (pp. 127–157). Hillsdale, NJ: Erlbaum. (p. 185)

Zillmann, D., & Bryant, J. (1984). Effects of massive exposure to pornography. In N. Malamuth & E. Donnerstein (Eds.), *Pornography and sexual aggression* (pp. 115–141). Orlando, FL: Academic Press. (p. 471)

Zimbardo, P. G. (1970). The human choice: Individuation, reason, and order versus deindividuation, impulse, and chaos. In W. J. Arnold & D. Levine (Eds.), *Nebraska Symposium on Motivation, 1969* (pp. 237–307). Lincoln: University of Nebraska Press. (p. 457)

Zimbardo, P. G. (1972, April). Pathology of imprisonment. *Transaction/Society,* pp. 4–8. (p. 445)

Zimbardo, P. G. (2001, September 16). *Fighting terrorism by understanding man's capacity for evil.* Retrieved from spsp-discuss@stolaf.edu (p. 466)

Zimbardo, P. G. (2004, May 25). Journalist interview re: Abu Ghraib prison abuses: Eleven answers to eleven questions. Unpublished manuscript, Stanford University, Stanford, CA. (p. 446)

Zimbardo, P. G. (2007, September). Person × Situation × System Dynamics. *APS Observer,* p. 43. (p. 446)

Zogby, J. (2006, March). *Survey of teens and adults about the use of personal electronic devices and head phones.* Utica, NY: Zogby International. (p. 228)

Zou, Z., Li, F., & Buck, L. B. (2005). From the cover: Odor maps in the olfactory cortex. *Proceedings of the National Academy of Sciences of the United States of America, 102,* 7724–7729. (p. 237)

Zubieta, J.-K., Bueller, J. A., Jackson, L. R., Scott, D. J., Xu, Y., Koeppe, R. A., . . . Stohler, C. S. (2005). Placebo effects mediated by endogenous opioid activity on μ-opioid receptors. *Journal of Neuroscience, 25,* 7754–7762. (p. 234)

Zubieta, J.-K., Heitzeg, M. M., Smith, Y. R., Bueller, J. A., Xu, K., Xu, Y., . . . Goldman, D. (2003). COMT *val158met* genotype affects μ-opioid neurotransmitter responses to a pain stressor. *Science, 299,* 1240–1243. (p. 234)

Zucker, G. S., & Weiner, B. (1993). Conservatism and perceptions of poverty: An attributional analysis. *Journal of Applied Social Psychology, 23,* 925–943. (p. 443)

Zuckerman, M. (1979). *Sensation seeking: Beyond the optimal level of arousal.* Hillsdale, NJ: Erlbaum. (p. 367)

Zuckerman, M. (2009). Sensation seeking. In M. R. Leary & R. H. Hoyle (Eds.), *Handbook of individual differences in social behavior* (pp. 455–465). New York: Guilford Press. (p. 367)

Zvolensky, M. J., & Bernstein, A. (2005). Cigarette smoking and panic psychopathology. *Current Directions in Psychological Science, 14,* 301–305. (p. 538)

Name Index

Subject Index

1869 — Francis Galton, Charles Darwin's cousin, publishes *Hereditary Genius*, in which he claims that intelligence is inherited. In **1876** he coins the expression "nature and nurture" to correspond with "heredity and environment."

1874 — Carl Wernicke, a German neurologist and psychiatrist, shows that damage to a specific area in the left temporal lobe (now called Wernicke's area) disrupts ability to comprehend or produce spoken or written language.

1878 — G. Stanley Hall receives from Harvard University's Department of Philosophy the first U.S. Ph.D. degree based on psychological research.

1879 — Wilhelm Wundt establishes at the University of Leipzig, Germany, the first psychology laboratory, which becomes a mecca for psychology students from all over the world.

1883 — G. Stanley Hall, student of Wilhelm Wundt, establishes the first formal U.S. psychology laboratory at Johns Hopkins University.

1885 — Hermann Ebbinghaus publishes *On Memory*, summarizing his extensive research on learning and memory, including the "forgetting curve."

1886 — Joseph Jastrow receives from Johns Hopkins University the first Ph.D. degree in psychology awarded by a Department of Psychology in the United States.

1889 — Alfred Binet and Henri Beaunis establish the first psychology laboratory in France at the Sorbonne, and the first International Congress of Psychology meets in Paris.

1890 — William James, Harvard University philosopher and psychologist, publishes *The Principles of Psychology*, describing psychology as "the science of mental life."

1891 — James Mark Baldwin establishes the first psychology laboratory in the British Commonwealth at the University of Toronto.

1892 — G. Stanley Hall spearheads the founding of the American Psychological Association (APA) and becomes its first president.

1893 — Mary Whiton Calkins and Christine Ladd-Franklin are the first women elected to membership in the APA.

1894 — Margaret Floy Washburn is the first woman to receive a Ph.D. degree in psychology (Cornell University).

1896 — Harvard University denies Mary Whiton Calkins admission to doctoral candidacy because of her gender, despite Hugo Münsterberg's claim that she was the best student he had ever had there.

John Dewey publishes "The Reflex Arc Concept in Psychology," helping to formalize the school of psychology called functionalism.

1898 — In *Animal Intelligence*, Edward L. Thorndike, Columbia University, describes his learning experiments with cats in "puzzle boxes." In **1905**, he proposes the "law of effect."

1900 — Sigmund Freud publishes *The Interpretation of Dreams*, his major theoretical work on psychoanalysis.

1933 — Inez Beverly Prosser becomes the first African-American woman to receive a doctoral degree in psychology from a U.S. institution (Ph.D., University of Cincinnati).

1935 — Christiana Morgan and Henry Murray introduce the Thematic Apperception Test to elicit fantasies from people undergoing psychoanalysis.

1936 — Egas Moniz, a Portuguese physician, publishes work on the first frontal lobotomies performed on humans.

1938 — B. F. Skinner publishes *The Behavior of Organisms*, which describes operant conditioning of animals.

In *Primary Mental Abilities*, Louis L. Thurstone proposes seven such abilities.

Ugo Cerletti and Lucio Bini use electroshock treatment with a human patient.

1939 — David Wechsler publishes the Wechsler–Bellevue intelligence test, forerunner of the Wechsler Intelligence Scale for Children (WISC) and the Wechsler Adult Intelligence Scale (WAIS).

Mamie Phipps Clark receives a master's degree from Howard University. In collaboration with Kenneth B. Clark, she later extends her thesis, "The Development of Consciousness of Self in Negro Preschool Children," providing joint research cited in the U.S. Supreme Court's **1954** decision to end racial segregation in public schools.

Edward Alexander Bott helps found the Canadian Psychological Association. He becomes its first president in **1940**.

World War II provides many opportunities for psychologists to enhance the popularity and influence of psychology, especially in applied areas.

1943 — Psychologist Starke Hathaway and physician J. Charnley McKinley publish the Minnesota Multiphasic Personality Inventory (MMPI).

1945 — Karen Horney, who criticized Freud's theory of female sexual development, publishes *Our Inner Conflicts*.

1946 — Benjamin Spock's first edition of *The Commonsense Book of Baby and Child Care* appears; the book will influence child raising in North America for several decades.

1948 — Alfred Kinsey and his colleagues publish *Sexual Behavior in the Human Male*, and they publish *Sexual Behavior in the Human Female* in **1953**.

B. F. Skinner's novel, *Walden Two*, describes a Utopian community based on positive reinforcement, which becomes a clarion c for applying psychological principles in everyday living, especi communal living.

Ernest R. Hilgard publishes *Theories of Learning*, which was required reading for several generations of psychology student North America.

1949 — Raymond B. Cattell publishes the Sixteen Personality Factor Questionnaire (16PF),

Continued on inside back co

The Story of Psychology: A Timeline (continued from inside front cover)

1949 — In *The Organization of Behavior: A Neuropsychological Theory*, Canadian psychologist Donald O. Hebb outlines a new and influential conceptualization of how the nervous system functions.

1950 — Solomon Asch publishes studies of effects of conformity on judgments of line length.

1951 — In *Childhood and Society*, Erik Erikson outlines his stages of psychosocial development.

1952 — Carl Rogers publishes *Client-Centered Therapy*.

The American Psychiatric Association publishes the *Diagnostic and Statistical Manual of Mental Disorders*, an influential book that will be updated periodically.

1953 — Eugene Aserinski and Nathaniel Kleitman describe rapid eye movements (REM) that occur during sleep.

Janet Taylor's Manifest Anxiety Scale appears in the *Journal of Abnormal Psychology*.

1954 — In *Motivation and Personality*, Abraham Maslow proposes a hierarchy of motives ranging from physiological needs to self-actualization. (Maslow later updates the hierarchy to include self-transcendence needs.)

James Olds and Peter Milner, McGill University neuropsychologists, describe rewarding effects of electrical stimulation of the hypothalamus in rats.

Gordon Allport publishes *The Nature of Prejudice*.

1956 — In his *Psychological Review* article titled "The Magical Number Seven, Plus or Minus Two: Some Limits on Our Capacity for Processing Information," George Miller coins the term *chunk* for memory researchers.

1957 — Robert Sears, Eleanor Maccoby, and Harry Levin publish *Patterns of Child Rearing*.

Charles Ferster and B. F. Skinner publish *Schedules of Reinforcement*.

1958 — Harry Harlow outlines "The Nature of Love," his work on attachment in monkeys.

1959 — Noam Chomsky's critical review of B. F. Skinner's *Verbal Behavior* appears in the journal *Language*.

Eleanor Gibson and Richard Walk report their research on infants' depth perception in "The Visual Cliff."

Lloyd Peterson and Margaret Peterson in the *Journal of Experimental Psychology* article, "Short-Term Retention of Individual Verbal Items," highlight the importance of rehearsal in memory.

John Thibaut and Harold Kelley publish *The Social Psychology of Groups*.

1969 — In his APA presidential address, "Psychology as a Means of Promoting Human Welfare," George Miller emphasizes the importance of "giving psychology away."

1971 — Kenneth B. Clark becomes the first African-American president of the American Psychological Association.

Albert Bandura publishes *Social Learning Theory*.

Allan Paivio publishes *Imagery and Verbal Processes*.

B. F. Skinner publishes *Beyond Freedom and Dignity*.

1972 — Elliot Aronson publishes *The Social Animal*.

Fergus Craik and Robert Lockhart's "Levels of Processing: A Framework for Memory Research" appears in the *Journal of Verbal Learning and Verbal Behavior*.

Robert Rescorla and Allan Wagner publish their associative model of Pavlovian conditioning.

1973 — Ethologists Karl von Frisch, Konrad Lorenz, and Nikolaas Tinbergen receive the Nobel Prize for their research on animal behavior.

Under the leadership of Derald Sue and Stanley Sue, the Asian American Psychological Association is founded.

1974 — APA's Division 2 first publishes its journal, *Teaching of Psychology*, with Robert S. Daniel as editor.

1975 — Eleanor Maccoby and Carol Jacklin publish *The Psychology of Sex Differences*.

Biologist Edward O. Wilson's *Sociobiology* appears; it will be a controversial precursor to evolutionary psychology.

1976 — Sandra Wood Scarr and Richard A. Weinberg publish "IQ Test Performance of Black Children Adopted by White Families" in *American Psychologist*.

1978 — Psychologist Herbert A. Simon, Carnegie-Mellon University, wins a Nobel Prize for pioneering research on computer simulations of human thinking and problem solving.

1979 — James J. Gibson publishes *The Ecological Approach to Visual Perception*.

Elizabeth Loftus publishes *Eyewitness Testimony*.

1981 — David Hubel and Torsten Wiesel receive a Nobel Prize for research on single-cell recordings that identified feature detector cells in the visual cortex.

Roger Sperry receives a Nobel Prize for research on split-brain patients.

Paleontologist Stephen Jay Gould publishes *The Mismeasure of Man*, highlighting the debate concerning biological determination of intelligence.